THE BANTAM NEW COLLEGE GERMAN & ENGLISH DICTIONARY

The Best Low-Priced Dictionary You Can Own

With more entries than any other compact paperbound dictionary—including thousands of new words—*The Bantam New College German & English Dictionary* is the most complete budget dictionary available today.

Whether you need it at home, the office, school, or in the library, this one indispensable, authoritative volume will prove its value over and over again, every time you use it.

THE BANTAM NEW COLLEGE DICTIONARY SERIES

John C. Traupman, Author

JOHN C. TRAUPMAN received his B.A. in German and in Latin at Moravian College and his M.A. and Ph.D. in Classics at Princeton University. He is chairman of the Department of Classical Languages at St. Joseph's University (Philadelphia). He served as president of the Philadelphia Classical Society, of the Pennsylvania Classical Association, and of the Classical and Modern Language League. He has published widely in learned journals and is the author of *The New College Latin & English Dictionary* (Bantam Books, 1966) and an associate editor of *The Scribner-Bantam English Dictionary* (Scribner's, 1977; Bantam Books, 1979).

Edwin B. Williams, General Editor

EDWIN B. WILLIAMS (1891–1975), A.B., A.M., Ph.D., Doct. d'Univ., LL.D., L.H.D., was chairman of the Department of Romance Languages, dean of the Graduate School, and provost of the University of Pennsylvania. He was a member of the American Philosophical Society and the Hispanic Society of America. Among his many lexicographical works are *The Williams Spanish and English Dictionary* (Scribner's, formerly Holt) and *The Bantam New College Spanish and English Dictionary*. He created and coordinated the Bantam series of original dictionaries—English, French, German, Italian, Latin, and Spanish.

THE BANTAM NEW COLLEGE
GERMAN & ENGLISH
DICTIONARY

JOHN C. TRAUPMAN, Ph.D.
St. Joseph's University, Philadelphia

THE BANTAM NEW COLLEGE
GERMAN & ENGLISH DICTIONARY
A Bantam Book / February 1981

ISBN 0-553-14155-4

Published simultaneously in the United States and Canada

Bantam Books are published by Bantam Books, Inc. Its trade-
mark, consisting of the words "Bantam Books" and the por-
trayal of a bantam, is Registered in U.S. Patent and Trademark
Office and in other countries. Marca Registrada. Bantam
Books, Inc., 666 Fifth Avenue, New York, New York 10103.

PRINTED IN THE UNITED STATES OF AMERICA

0 9 8 7 6 5 4 3 2 1

CONTENTS

I wish to express my appreciation to the many persons on whose help I relied in researching and compiling this Dictionary. I am particularly indebted to Edwin B. Williams, Walter D. Glanze, Donald Reis, Rudolf Pillwein, and Helmut Kreitz.

J. C. T.

HOW TO USE
THIS DICTIONARY

HINWEISE FÜR
DEN BENUTZER

All entry words are treated in a fixed order according to the parts of speech and the functions of verbs. On the German-English side: past participle, adjective, adverb, pronoun, preposition, conjunction, interjection, transitive verb, reflexive verb, reciprocal verb, intransitive verb, impersonal verb, auxiliary verb, substantive; on the English-German side: adjective, substantive, pronoun, adverb, preposition, conjunction, transitive verb, intransitive verb, auxiliary verb, impersonal verb, interjection.

Alle Stichwörter werden in einheitlicher Reihenfolge gemäß der Wortart und der Verbfunktion behandelt. Im deutsch-englischen Teil: Partizip Perfekt, Adjektiv, Adverb, Pronomen, Präposition, Konjunktion, Interjektion, transitives Verb, reflexives Verb, reziprokes Verb, intransitives Verb, unpersönliches Verb, Hilfsverb, Substantiv; im englisch-deutschen Teil: Adjektiv, Substantiv, Pronomen, Adverb, Präposition, Konjunktion, transitives Verb, intransitives Verb, Hilfsverb, unpersönliches Verb, Interjektion.

The order of meanings within an entry is as follows: first, the more general meanings; second, the meanings with usage labels; third, the meanings with subject labels in alphabetical order; fourth, illustrative phrases in alphabetical order.

Die verschiedenen Bedeutungen sind innerhalb eines Stichwortartikels in folgender Anordnung gegeben: zuerst die allgemeinen Bedeutungen; dann die Bedeutungen mit Bezeichnung der Sprachgebrauchsebene; dann die Bedeutungen mit Bezeichnung des Sachgebietes, in alphabetischer Reihenfolge; zuletzt die Anwendungsbeispiele, in alphabetischer Reihenfolge.

Subject and usage labels (printed in roman and in parentheses) refer to the preceding entry word or illustrative phrase in the source language (printed in boldface), e.g.,

Die Bezeichnungen der Sprachgebrauchsebene und des Sachgebiets (in Antiqua und in Klammern) beziehen sich auf das vorangehende Stichwort oder Anwendungsbeispiel in der Ausgangssprache (halbfett gedruckt), z.B.

mund′tot *adj*—**j–n m. machen** (fig) silence s.o.
Pinke [′pɪŋkə] *f* (–;) (coll) dough

Words in parentheses and in roman coming after a meaning serve to clarify that meaning, e.g.,

Kursiv gedruckte Wörter in Klammern, die nach einer Bedeutung stehen, sollen diese Bedeutung illustrieren, z.B.

überschau′en *tr* look over, survey; overlook (*a scene*)

Words in parenthese and in roman type coming after or before a meaning are optional additions to the word in the target language, e.g.,

In Antiqua gedruckte Wörter in Klammern, die nach oder vor einer Bedeutung stehen, sind wahlfreie Erweiterungen des Wortes der Zielsprache, z.B.

Tanne ['tanə] *f* (–;–n) fir (tree)
Pap'rikaschote *f* (green) pepper

Meaning discriminations are given in the source language and are in italics, e.g.,

Bedeutungsdifferenzierungen sind in der Ausgangssprache angegeben und kursiv gedruckt, z.B.

überrei'zen *tr* overexcite; (*Augen, Nerven*) strain
earn [ʌrn] *tr* (*money*) verdienen; (*interest*) einbringen

Since vocabulary entries are not determined on the basis of etymology, homographs are listed as a single entry.

Da die Etymologie bei der Anführung der Stichwörter unberücksichtigt bleibt, sind gleichgeschriebene Wörter als ein und dasselbe Stichwort verzeichnet.

The entry word is represented within the entry by its initial letter followed by a period (if the entry word contains more than three letters), provided the form is identical. The same applies to a word that follows the parallels. The entry word is not abbreviated within the entry when associated with suspension points, e.g.,

Innerhalb eines Stichwortartikels wird das Stichwort (wenn es mehr als drei Buchstaben enthält) durch seinen Anfangsbuchstaben und einen Punkt angegeben, vorausgesetzt, daß die betreffende Form mit dem Stichwort identisch ist. Das Gleiche gilt für ein Wort, das nach den Vertikalstrichen steht. Wenn ein Stichwort innerhalb eines Stichwortartikels in Verbindung mit Auslassungspunkten angegeben ist, wird es nicht abgekürzt, z.B.

weder ... noch

Parallels are used (a) to separate parts of speech, (b) to separate transitive, reflexive, reciprocal, intransitive, impersonal, and auxiliary verbs, (c) to separate verbs taking HABEN from those taking SEIN, (d) to indicate a change in pronunciation of the entry word, depending on the meaning, e.g.,

Es ist der Zweck der Vertikalstriche, (a) Wortarten voneinander zu trennen, (b) transitive, reflexive, reziproke, intransitive, unpersönliche Verben und Hilfsverben zu trennen, (c) Verben mit dem Hilfsverb HABEN von Verben mit dem Hilfsverb SEIN zu trennen, (d) verschiedene Aussprachen des Stichwortes je nach Bedeutung anzuzeigen, z.B.

bow [baʊ] *s* Verbeugung *f*; (naut) Bug *m* ...
 ‖ [bo] *s* (*weapon*) Bogen *m*; ...

(e) to show change from a strong verb to a weak verb and vice versa, (f) to show a change in the case governed by

(e) den Wechsel von einem starken zu einem schwachen Verb und umgekehrt anzuzeigen, (f) den Wechsel in einem

a preposition where the entry word is a preposition, (g) to show a shift of accent, e.g.,

von einer Präposition regierten Fall anzuzeigen, wo das Stichwort selbst eine Präposition ist, (g) unterschiedliche Stellungen des Akzents anzuzeigen, z.B.

ü′bergleßen *tr* . . . ‖ **übergie′ßen** *tr* . . .

The centered period in the English word on the German-English side marks the point at which the following letters are dropped before irregular plural endings are added. The centered period in the entry word on the English-German side marks the point at which the following letters are dropped before irregular plural endings are added to nouns and inflections are added to verbs. The centered period in the phonetic spelling indicates diaeresis, e.g.,

Der auf Mitte stehende Punkt im Stichwort des deutsch-englischen Teils zeigt die Stelle an, wo die nachfolgenden Buchstaben abzutrennen sind, bevor unregelmäßige Pluralendungen angefügt werden können. Der auf Mitte stehende Punkt im Stichwort des englisch-deutschen Teils zeigt die Stelle an, wo die nachfolgenden Buchstaben abzutrennen sind, bevor unregelmäßige Pluralendungen an Hauptwörter and Flexionen an Verben angefügt werden können. Der auf Mitte stehende Punkt in der Lautschrift zeigt Diärese an, z.B.

befähigt [bə′fe·ıçt]

On the German-English and the English-German side, in the case of a transitive verb, the meaning discrimination in parentheses before the target word is always the object of the verb. On the German-English side, in the case of an intransitive verb, the meaning discrimination in parentheses before the target word is always the subject of the verb. On the English-German side, the suggested subject of a verb is prefaced by the words "said of".

Im deutsch-englischen und im englisch-deutschen Teil ist die bei transitiven Verben in Klammern vor dem Wort in der Zielsprache angegebene Bedeutungsdifferenzierung immer das Objekt des Verbs. Im deutsch-englischen Teil ist bei intransitiven Verben die vor dem Wort in der Zielsprache angegebene Bedeutungsdifferenzierung immer das Subjekt des Verbs. Im englisch-deutschen Teil stehen vor dem beabsichtigten Subjekt eines Verbs die Worte "said of."

Inflections are generally not shown for compound entry words, since the inflections have been shown where the components are entry words. However, when the last component of a compound noun on the German-English side has various inflections depending on meaning, the inflection is shown for the compound, e.g.,

Bei zusammengesetzten Stichwörtern ist die Flexion im Allgemeinen nicht angegeben, da sie unter den als Stichwörter angeführten Teilen des Kompositums angegeben ist. Falls jedoch der letzte Teil eines deutschen Kompositums je nach der Bedeutung verschieden flektiert wird, ist die Flexion für das Kompositum angegeben, z.B.

Ton′band *n* (–[e]s;⸚er) . . .

German verbs are regarded as reflexive regardless of whether the reflexive pronoun is the direct or indirect object of the verb.

Deutsche Verben gelten als reflexiv ohne Rücksicht darauf, ob das Reflexivpronomen das direkte oder indirekte Objekt des Verbs ist.

On the English-German side, when the pronunciation of an entry word is not given, stress in the entry word is shown as follows: a high-set primary stress mark ′ follows the syllable that receives the primary stress, and a high-set secondary stress mark ′ follows the syllable that receives the secondary stress. When the pronunciation of an entry word *is* provided [given in brackets], a high-set primary stress mark ‵ *precedes* the syllable that receives the primary stress, and a *low*-set secondary stress mark , *precedes* the syllable that receives the secondary stress.

On the German-English side, when the pronunciation of an entry word is not given, a high-set primary stress mark ′ follows the syllable of the entry word that receives the primary stress. When the pronunciation of the entry *is* provided [given in brackets], a high-set primary stress mark ‵ *precedes* the syllable that receives the primary stress. (Because opinions on the system of secondary stress in German differ widely, secondary stress marks are not employed in this Dictionary.)

Wo die Aussprache des Stichwortes im englisch-deutschen Teil nicht angegeben ist, wird die Betonung des Stichwortes folgendermaßen angedeutet: Das stärkere, obere graphische Zeichen ′ steht nach der Silbe mit dem Haupttonakzent, und das schwächere, obere Zeichen ′ steht nach der Silbe mit dem Nebentonakzent. Wo hingegen die Aussprache des Stichwortes im englisch-deutschen Teil [in eckigen Klammern] angegeben ist, steht das stärkere, obere Zeichen ‵ *vor* der Silbe mit dem Haupttonakzent und das schwächere, *untere* Zeichen , *vor* der Silbe mit dem Nebentonakzent.

Wo die Aussprache das Stichwortes im deutsch-englischen Teil nicht angegeben ist, steht das starke Zeichen ′ nach der Stichwortsilbe mit dem Haupttonakzent. Wo hingegen die Aussprache des Stichwortes im deutsch-englischen Teil [in eckigen Klammern] angegeben ist, steht das starke Zeichen ‵ *vor* der Silbe mit dem Haupttonakzent. (Wegen der widersprüchlichen Theorien, die die Frage des Nebentonakzents im Deutschen umgeben, wendet dieses Wörterbuch keine Nebentonakzente für die deutschen Wörter an.)

Proper nouns and general abbreviations are listed in their alphabetical position in the main body of the Dictionary.

Eigennamen und allgemeine Abkürzungen sind in den beiden Hauptteilen des Wörterbuches in alphabetischer Reihenfolge angegeben.

This Dictionary contains approximately 75,000 "entries." As entries are counted (a) nonindented boldface headwords and (b) elements that could have been set nonindented as separate headwords, too, but that for reasons of style and typography are grouped under the nonindented headwords, namely, separate parts of speech and boldface idioms and phrases.

Dieses Wörterbuch enthält ungefähr 75.000 "Stichwörter." Die folgenden Elemente gelten als Stichwörter: (a) die nicht eingerückten fettgedruckten Wörter am Anfang eines Stichwortartikels und (b) Elemente, die man auf dieselbe Weise hatte drucken können, die aber aus Stil– und Typographiegründen eingerückt wurden, nämlich die unterschiedlichen Wortarten und die fettgedruckten Redewendungen.

PART ONE

German-English

A

A, a [α] *invar n* A, a; (mus) A; **das A und O** the beginning and the end; (*das Wichtigste*) the most important thing

Aal [αl] *m* (-[e]s;-e) eel; (nav) torpedo

aal′glatt′ *adj* (fig) sly as a fox

Aas [αs] *n* (-es;-e) carrion; (sl) louse

ab [ap] *adv* off; away; down; on, e.g., **von heute ab** from today on; (theat) exit, exeunt, e.g., **Hamlet ab** exit Hamlet; **ab und zu** now and then || *prep* (*dat*) from, e.g., **ab Frankfurt** from Frankfurt; minus, e.g., **ab Skonto** minus discount

ab′ändern *tr* alter; (*völlig*) change; (*mildern*) modify; (parl) amend

Ab′änderung *f* (-;-en) alteration; change; modification; (parl) amendment

Ab′änderungsantrag *m* (parl) (proposed) amendment

ab′arbeiten *tr* work off || *ref* work hard

Ab′art *f* variety, type

ab′arten *intr* (SEIN) deviate from type

Ab′bau *m* (-[e]s) demolition; reduction; cutback; layoff; (chem) decomposition; (min) exploitation

ab′bauen *tr* demolish; (*Maschinen, Fabriken*) dismantle; (*Steuern, Preise, Truppen*) reduce; (*Zelt*) take down; (*Lager*) break; (*Angestellte*) lay off; (chem) decompose; (min) work, exploit

ab′beißen §53 *tr* bite off || *intr* take a bite

ab′bekommen §99 *tr* (*seinen Teil*) get; (*Schmutz*) get out; (*Deckel*) get off; **du wirst was a.!** you're going to get it!

ab′berufen §122 *tr* (dipl) recall

ab′bestellen *tr* cancel

ab′betteln *tr*—**die ganze Straße a.** beg up and down the street; **j-m etw a.** chisel s.th. from s.o.

ab′biegen §57 *tr* bend, twist off; (*Gefahr*) avert; (*Plan*) thwart; **das Gespräch a.** change the subject || *intr* (SEIN) branch off; (fig) get off the track; **in e-e Seitenstraße a.** turn down a side street; **nach links a.** turn left; **von e-r Straße a.** turn off a road

Ab′bild *n* picture, image

ab′bilden *tr* represent

Ab′bildung *f* (-;-en) illustration, figure

ab′binden §59 *tr* untie; (*Kalb*) wean; (*Arm*) apply a tourniquet to; (surg) tie off || *intr* (*Zement*) set

Ab′bitte *f* apology; **A. tun wegen** apologize for

ab′bitten §60 *tr* apologize for || *intr* apologize

ab′blasen §61 *tr* blow off; (fig) call off || *intr* (mil) sound the retreat

ab′blättern *intr* (SEIN) shed leaves; (*Farben, Haut*) flake, peel

ab′blenden *tr* dim; (cin) fade out; (phot) stop down || *intr* (aut) dim the lights; (nav) darken ship; (phot) stop down the lens

Ab′blendlicht *n* (aut) low-beam lights

ab′blitzen *intr* (SEIN) be unsuccessful; **j-n a. lassen** snub s.o.

ab′blühen *intr* stop blooming || *intr* (SEIN) fade

ab′böschen *tr* slope; (*Mauer*) batter

ab′brausen *tr* hose down || *ref* shower off || *intr* (SEIN) (coll) roar off

ab′brechen §64 *tr* break off; (*Belagerung*) raise; (*Gebäude*) demolish; (*Zelt*) take down; (sport) call; **das Lager a.** break camp || *intr* (SEIN) (& fig) break off

ab′bremsen *tr* slow down; (*Streik*) prevent; (*Motoren*) (aer) rev || *intr* put on the brakes; (aer) fishtail

ab′brennen §97 *tr* burn off; (*Feuerwerk*) set off; (*Geschütz*) fire; (chem) distil out; (metal) refine; (naut) bream; **ich bin vollkommen abgebrannt** (coll) I'm dead broke || *intr* (SEIN) burn down

ab′bringen §65 *tr* (*Fleck*) remove; (*gestrandetes Schiff*) refloat; **davon a. zu** (*inf*) dissuade from (ger); **vom rechten Weg a.** lead astray; **vom Thema a.** throw off; **von der Spur a.** throw off the scent; **von e-r Gewohnheit a.** break of the habit

ab′bröckeln *intr* crumble; (*Farbe*) peel (off); (*Preis, Aktie*) go slowly down; (*Mitglieder*) fall off

Ab′bruch *m* (e-s Zweiges, der Beziehungen) breaking off; (e-s Gebäudes) demolition; (*Schaden*) damage; **A. des Spiels** (sport) calling of the game; **A. tun** (*dat*) harm, spoil; **auf A. verkaufen** sell at demolition value; (*Maschinen*) sell for junk

ab′brühen *tr* (culin) scald

ab′brummen *tr* (*Strafe*) (coll) serve, do || *intr* (SEIN) (coll) clear out

ab′buchen *tr* (*abschreiben*) write off; (acct) debit

ab′bürsten *tr* brush off

ab′büßen *tr* atone for; **e-e Strafe a.** serve time; **er hat es schwer a. müssen** (coll) he had to pay for it dearly

Abc [αbe′tse] *n* (-;-) ABC's

Abc′-Schütze *m* (-n;-n) pupil

ab′danken *tr* dismiss; (*pensionieren*)

retire || *intr* resign; (*Herrscher*) abdicate; (mil) get a discharge

ab'decken *tr* uncover; (*Tisch*) clear; (*Bett*) turn down; (*Vieh*) skin; (*e-e Schuld*) pay back; (mil) camouflage; (phot) mask

ab'dichten *tr* seal (off); (*Loch*) plug up; (*mit weichem Material*) pack; (naut) caulk

ab'dienen *tr* (*Schuld*) work off; (mil) serve (*one's term*)

ab'drehen *tr* twist off; (*Gas, Licht, Wasser*) turn off || *intr* turn away

ab'dreschen §67 *tr* thrash

Ab'druck *m* (*-s;-e*) reprint; offprint; copy; (*Abguß*) casting; (phot, typ) proof || *m* (*-s;⁻e*) impression, imprint

ab'drucken *tr* print

ab'drücken *tr* (*abformen*) mold; (*Gewehr*) fire; (*Pfeil*) shoot; (*umarmen*) hug; **den Hahn a.** pull the trigger || *ref* leave an impression || *intr* pull the trigger

ab'duschen *ref* shower off

Abend ['abənt] *m* (*-s;-e*) evening; **am A.** in the evening; **bunter A.** social; (telv) variety show; **des Abends in the evening(s)**; **zu A. essen** eat dinner

A'bendblatt *n* evening paper

A'bendbrot *n* supper, dinner

A'benddämmerung *f* twilight, dusk

A'bendessen *n* supper, dinner

abend'füllend ['abəntfYlənt] *adj* full-length (*movie*)

A'bendgesellschaft *f* party (*in the evening*)

A'bendland *n* West, Occident

abendländisch ['abəntlɛndɪʃ] *adj* occidental

a'bendlich *adj* evening || *adv* evenings

A'bendmahl *n* supper; **das Heilige A.** Holy Communion

abends ['abənts] *adv* in the evening

Abenteuer ['abəntɔɪ-ər] *s* (*-s;-*) adventure; **galantes A.** (love) affair

a'benteuerlich *adj* adventurous; (*Unternehmen*) risky

aber ['abər] *adv* yet, however; (before adjectives and adverbs) really, indeed; **a. und abermals** over and over again; **hundert und a. hundert** hundreds and hundreds of || *conj* but || *interj*—**aber, aber!** now, now! || **Aber** *n* (*-s;-s*) but; **hier gibt es kein A.!** no ifs and buts

A'berglaube *m* superstition

abergläubisch ['abərglɔɪbɪʃ] *adj* superstitious

ab'erkennen §97 *tr*—**j-m etw a.** deny s.o. s.th.; (jur) dispossess s.o. of s.th.

Ab'erkennung *f* (*-;-en*) denial; (jur) dispossession

abermalig ['abərmalɪç] *adj* repeated

abermals ['abərmals] *adv* once more

ab'ernten *tr* reap, harvest

ab'fahren §71 *tr* cart away; (*Strecke*) cover; (*Straße*) wear out; (*Reifen*) wear down || *intr* (SEIN) depart; drive off

Ab'fahrt *f* departure

Ab'fall *m* (*der Blätter*) falling; (*Bö-*

schung) steep slope; (*von e-m Glauben*) falling away; (*von e-r Partei*) defection; (*Sinken*) drop, decrease; **Abfälle** garbage, trash; chips, shavings

ab'fallen §72 *intr* (SEIN) fall off; (*von e-r Partei*) defect; (*vom Glauben*) fall away; (*abnehmen*) decrease, fail; (*Kunden*) stay away; (sport) fall behind; **a. gegen** compare badly with; **es wird etw für dich a.** there'll be s.th. in it for you; **körperlich a.** lose weight; **steil a.** drop away

abfällig ['apfɛlɪç] *adj* disparaging

Ab'fallprodukt *n* by-product

ab'fangen §73 *tr* catch; (*Angriff*) foil; (*Brief*) intercept; (aer) pull out of a dive; (*U-Boot*) navy trim; (sport) catch (up with); **j-m die Kunden a.** steal s.o.'s customers

ab'färben *intr* (*Farben*) run; (*Stoff*) fade; **a. auf** (acc) stain; (fig) rub off on

ab'fassen *tr* compose, draft; (*erwischen*) catch

Ab'fassung *f* (*-;-en*) wording; composition

ab'faulen *intr* (SEIN) rot away

ab'fegen *tr* sweep off, whisk off

abfertigen ['apfɛrtɪgən] *tr* get ready for sending off; (*Gepäck*) check; (*Zollgüter*) clear; (*Kunden*) wait on; (*abweisen*) snub; (*verwaltungsmäßig*) process; (adm) process

Ab'fertigung *f* (*-;-en*) dispatch; snub; **zollamtliche A.** clearance

ab'feuern *tr* fire; (rok) launch

ab'finden §59 *tr* (*Gläubiger*) satisfy; (*Partner*) buy off; (*entschädigen*) (*für*) compensate (for) || *ref*—**sich a. lassen** settle for a lump-sum payment; **sich a. mit** put up with; come to terms with

Ab'findung *f* (*-;-en*) satisfaction; lump-sum settlement

Ab'findungsvertrag *m* lump-sum settlement

abflachen ['apflaxən] *tr* level; (*abschrägen*) bevel || *ref* flatten out

abflauen ['apflau-ən] *intr* (SEIN) slack off; (*Interesse*) flag; (*Preis*) go down; (st. exch.) ease off

ab'fliegen §57 *intr* (SEIN) take off

ab'fließen §76 *intr* (SEIN) flow off, drain off

Ab'flug *m* takeoff, departure

Ab'fluß *m* discharge; drain, gutter, gully; **See ohne A.** lake without outlet

Ab'flußrinne *f* drainage ditch

Ab'flußrohr *n* drainpipe; soil pipe; (*vom Dach*) downspout

ab'fordern *tr*—**j-m etw a.** demand s.th. from s.o.

ab'fragen *tr*—**j-n etw a.** question s.o. about s.th.; quiz s.o. on s.th.

ab'fressen §70 *tr* eat up; crop, chew off; (*Metall*) corrode

ab'frieren §77 *intr* (SEIN) be nipped by the frost; **abgefroren** frostbitten

Abfuhr ['apfur] *f* (*-;-en*) removal; (*Abweisung*) (coll) cold shoulder, snub

ab'führen *tr* lead away; (*festnehmen*) arrest; (*fencing*) defeat ‖ *intr* cause the bowels to move

Abführmittel ['apfʏrmɪtəl] *n* laxative

ab'füllen *tr* (*Wein, Bier*) bottle

Ab'gabe *f* (*Auslieferung*) delivery; (*Verkauf*) sale; (*Steuer*) tax; (*Zoll*) duty; (*der Wahlstimme*) casting; (*e-s Urteils*) pronouncing; (*e-r Meinung*) expressing; (fb) pass; **Abgaben** taxes, fees

ab'gabenfrei *adj* tax-free, duty-free

abgabenpflichtig ['apgabənpflɪçtɪç] *adj* taxable, subject to duty

Ab'gang *m* departure; (*von e–m Amt*) retirement; (*von der Schule*) dropping out; (*Verlust*) loss; (*Abnahme*) decrease; (*gym*) finish; (*pathol*) discharge; (*pathol*) miscarriage; (*theat*) exit; **guten A. haben** sell well

abgängig ['apgɛnɪç] *adj* lost, missing; (*com*) marketable

Ab'gangsprüfung *f* final examination

Ab'gangspunkt *m* point of departure

Ab'gas *n* (aut) exhaust; (*indust*) waste gas

ab'geben §80 *tr* (*Paß*) hand over; (*Gepäck*) check; (*abliefern*) deliver; (*Schulheft*) hand in; (*Urteil*) pass; (*Meinung*) express; (*Gutachten*) give; (*Amt*) lay down; (*gute Ernte*) yield; (*Schuß*) fire; (*Wahlstimme*) cast; (*Waren*) sell, let go; (*sich eignen als*) act as, serve as; be cut out to be; (elec) deliver; (fb) pass; (phys) give off; **e–e Offerte a.** (jur) make an offer; **e–n Narren a.** play the fool; **er würde e–n guten Vater a.** he would make a good father; **|–m eins a.** (coll) let s.o. have it; **|–m von etw a.** share s.th. with s.o. ‖ *ref*—**sich a. mit** bother with; associate with; spend time on

abgebrannt ['apgəbrant] *adj* (coll) broke

abgebrüht ['apgəbryt] *adj* (fig) hardened

abgedroschen ['apgədrɔʃən] *adj* trite, hackneyed; (*Witz*) stale

abgefeimt ['apgəfaɪmt] *adj* cunning, out-and-out

abgegriffen ['apgəgrɪfən] *adj* well-thumbed

abgehackt ['apgəhakt] *adj* jerky

abgehärmt ['apgəhɛrmt] *adj* careworn, drawn

ab'gehen §82 *intr* (SEIN) leave, depart; (*Brief*) go off; (*Knopf*) come off; (*Schuß*) go off; (*Farbe*) fade; (*Seitenweg*) branch off; (*vom Gesprächsgegenstand*) digress, go off; (*vom rechten Wege*) stray; (*aus e–m Amt*) resign, retire; (*von der Bühne*) retire; (*von der Schule*) drop out; graduate; (com) sell; (theat) exit; **bei Barzahlung gehen fünf Prozent ab** you get a five-percent reduction for paying cash; **davon kann ich nicht a.** I must insist on it; **er geht mir sehr ab** I miss him a lot; **nicht a. von** stick to; **reißend a.** sell like hotcakes; ‖ *ref*—**sich [dat] nichts a.**

lassen deny oneself nothing ‖ *impers* —**es geht ihm nichts ab** he lacks for nothing; **es gehen mir zehn Dollar ab** I am ten dollars short; **es ist alles glatt abgegangen** everything went well

ab'gehend *adj* (*Post, Beamte*) outgoing; (*Zug*) departing

abgekämpft ['apgəkɛmpft] *adj* exhausted

abgekartet ['apgəkartət] *adj* (*Spiel*) fixed; **abgekartete Sache** put-up job

abgeklappert ['apgəklapərt] *adj* hackneyed

abgeklärt ['apgəklɛrt] *adj* mellow, wise

abgelebt ['apgəlept] *adj* decrepit

abgelegen ['apgəlegən] *adj* out-of-the-way, outlying

ab'gelten §83 *tr* meet, satisfy

abgemacht ['apgəmaxt] *adj* settled ‖ *interj* agreed!

abgemagert ['apgəmagərt] *adj* emaciated

abgemessen ['apgəmesən] *adj* measured; (*genau*) exact; (*Rede*) deliberate; (*Person*) stiff, formal

abgeneigt ['apgənaɪt] *adj* reluctant; (dat) averse to; **ich bin durchaus nicht a.** (coll) I don't mind if I do

Ab'geneigtheit *f* (–;) aversion

abgenutzt ['apgənutst] *adj* worn out

Abgeordnete ['apgə-ɔrdnətə] §5 *mf* delegate; (pol) representative; deputy (*member of the Bundestag*); (Brit) Member of Parliament

Ab'geordnetenhaus *n* House of Representatives; (Brit) House of Commons

abgerissen ['apgərɪsən] *adj* torn; (*zerlumpt*) ragged; (*ohne Zusammenhang*) incoherent, disconnected

Abgesandte ['apgəzantə] §5 *mf* envoy

abgeschieden ['apgəʃidən] *adj* secluded; (*verstorben*) deceased, late

Ab'geschiedenheit *f* (–;) seclusion

abgeschliffen ['apgəʃlɪfən] *adj* polished

abgeschlossen ['apgəʃlɔsən] *adj* isolated; (*Leben*) secluded; (*Ausbildung*) completed

abgeschmackt ['apgəʃmakt] *adj* tactless, tasteless; (fig) insipid

abgesehen ['apgəze-ən] *adj*—**a. davon, daß** not to mention that; **a. von** aside from, except for

abgespannt ['apgəʃpant] *adj* tired out

abgestanden ['apgəʃtandən] *adj* stale

abgestorben ['apgəʃtɔrbən] *adj* (*Pflanze, Gewebe*) dead; (*Glied*) numb

abgestumpft ['apgəʃtumpft] *adj* blunt; (*Kegel*) truncated; (fig) dull; (*gegen*) indifferent (to)

abgetakelt ['apgətakəlt] *adj* (*Person*) seedy; (*Schiff*) unrigged

abgetan ['apgətan] *adj* settled

abgetragen ['apgətragən] *adj* threadbare

abgetreten ['apgətretən] *adj* worn-down

ab'gewinnen §52 *tr* win; **e–r Sache Geschmack a.** acquire a taste for s.th.; **e–r Sache Vergnügen a.** derive pleasure from s.th.; **j–m e–n Vorteil a.** gain an advantage over s.o.

abgewirtschaftet [ˈapgəvɪrt/aftət] *adj* run-down

ab'gewöhnen *tr*—**ich kann es mir nicht a.** I can't get it out of my system; **j–m etw a.** break s.o. of s.th.

abgezehrt [ˈapgətsert] *adj* emaciated

ab'gießen §76 *tr* pour off; (*Statue*) cast; (chem) decant; (culin) strain off

Ab'glanz *m* reflection

ab'gleiten §86 *intr* (SEIN) slip off; (an *dat*) glance off (*s.th.*); (aer, aut) skid; (st. exch.) decline

Ab'gott *m* idol

Abgötterei [apgœtəˈraɪ] *f* (–;–en) idolatry; **A. treiben** worship idols; **mit j–m A. treiben** idolize s.o.

abgöttisch [ˈapgœtɪ/] *adj* idolatrous || *adv*—**a. lieben** idolize

Ab'gottschlange *f* boa constrictor

ab'graben §87 *tr* (*Bach*) divert; (*Feld*) drain; (*Hügel*) level

ab'grämen *ref* eat one's heart out

ab'grasen *tr* (*Wiese*) graze on; (fig) scour, search

ab'greifen §88 *tr* wear out (*by constant handling*); (*Buch*) thumb

ab'grenzen *tr* mark off, demarcate; delimit; (fig) differentiate

Ab'grund *m* abyss; precipice

abgründig [ˈapgrʏndɪç] *adj* precipitous; (fig) deep, unfathomable

ab'gucken *tr* (coll) copy, crib; (coll) pick up a habit from || *intr* (coll) copy, crib

Ab'guß *m* (sculp) cast; **A. in Gips** plaster cast

ab'hacken *tr* chop off; (*Baum*) chop down

ab'haken *tr* unhook, undo; (in e–r *Liste*) check off; (telp) take off (*the receiver*)

ab'halftern *tr* unharness; (fig) sack

ab'halten §90 *tr* hold off; (*Vorlesung*) give; (*Regen*) keep out; (*Versammlung, Parade*) hold; (**von**) keep (from)

Ab'haltung *f* (–;–en) hindrance; (e–r *Versammlung*) holding; (e–s *Festes*) celebration

ab'handeln *tr* (*Thema*) treat; (erörtern) discuss; **er läßt sich nichts a.** he won't come down (in *price*); **etw vom Preise a.** get s.th. off the price (*by bargaining*)

abhanden [apˈhandən] *adv*—**a. kommen** get lost; **a. sein** be missing

Ab'handlung *f* (–;–en) essay; (*Vortrag in e–m gelehrten Verein*) paper; (*Doktorarbeit*) thesis, dissertation; (*mündlich*) discourse, discussion

Ab'hang *m* slope

ab'hängen *tr* (*vom Haken*) take off; (e–n *Verfolger*) shake off; (rr) uncouple || *intr* (telp) hang up; **a. von** depend on; be subject to (*s.o.'s approval*)

abhängig [ˈaphɛnɪç] *adj* (*Stellung*) subordinate; (*Satz*) dependent; (*Rede*) indirect; (*Kasus*) oblique; (**von**) dependent (on), contingent (upon)

Ab'hängigkeit *f* (–;–en) dependence; (gram) subordination; **gegenseitige A.** interdependence

ab'härmen *ref* pine away; **sich a. wegen** (or **über** *acc*) fret about

ab'härten *tr* harden; (**gegen**) inure (to) || *ref* (**gegen**) become hardened (to)

ab'hauen §93 *tr* cut off; chop off || §109 *intr* (SEIN) (coll) scram, get lost

ab'häuten *tr* skin, flay

ab'heben §94 *tr* lift off; (*Rahm*) skim; (*Geld*) withdraw; (*Dividende*) collect; (*Haut*) (surg) strip off || *ref* become airborne; (**von**) contrast (with)

Ab'hebung *f* (–;–en) lifting; (*vom Bankkonto*) withdrawal; (cards) cutting

Ab'hebungsformular *n* withdrawal slip

ab'heften *tr* (*Briefe*) file; (sew) tack

ab'heilen *intr* (HABEN & SEIN) heal

ab'helfen §96 *intr* (*dat*) (e–m *Unrecht*) redress; (e–r *Schwierigkeit*) remove; (e–m *Mangel*) relieve; **dem ist nicht abzuhelfen** that can't be helped

ab'hetzen *tr* drive hard, work to death; (hunt) hunt down || *ref* rush; tire oneself out

Ab'hilfe *f* remedy, redress; **A. schaffen** take remedial measures; **A. schaffen für** remedy, redress

ab'hobeln *tr* plane (down)

abhold [ˈaphɔlt] *adj* (*dat*) ill-disposed (towards), averse (to)

Abholdienst [ˈapholdɪnst] *m* pickup service

ab'holen *tr* fetch, call for, pick up

ab'holzen *tr* clear (of trees), deforest

Abhörapparat [ˈaphørapɑraɪ] *m* (mil, nav) listening device

ab'horchen *tr* overhear; (med) sound; (rad, telp) monitor

ab'hören *tr* overhear, eavesdrop on; (*Studenten*) quiz; (*Schallplatte, Tonband*) listen to; (mil) intercept; (telp) monitor

Ab'hörgerät *n* bugging device

Ab'hörraum *m* (rad, telv) control room

Ab'irrung *f* (–;–en) deviation; (opt) aberration

Abitur [abiˈtur] *n* (–s;–e) final examination (*at end of junior college*); **das A. bestehen** graduate

Abiturient –in [abituriˈɛnt(ɪn)] §7 *mf* graduate (*of a junior college*)

Abitur'zeugnis *n* diploma (*from senior high school or junior college*)

ab'jagen *tr* drive hard; **j–m etw a.** recover s.th. from s.o. || *ref* run one's head off

abkanzeln [ˈapkantsəln] *tr* (coll) give (*s.o.*) a good talking to

ab'kauen *tr* chew off || *ref*—**sich** [*dat*] **die Nägel a.** bite one's nails

ab'kaufen *tr*—**j–m etw a.** buy s.th. from s.o.

Abkehr [ˈapker] *f* (–;) turning away; estrangement; (*Verzicht*) renunciation

ab'kehren *tr* turn away, avert; (*mit dem Besen*) sweep off || *ref* turn away; become estranged

ab'klappern *tr* (coll) scour, search

ab′klatschen *tr* imitate slavishly; make an exact copy of; (*beim Tanzen*) cut in on; (typ) pull (*a proof*)

ab′klingen §142 *intr* (SEIN) (*Farbe*) fade; (*Töne*) die away; (*Schmerz*) ease off

ab′klopfen *tr* beat off, knock off; (*Teppich*) beat; (med) tap, percuss || *intr* stop the music (*with the rap of the baton*)

ab′knabbern *tr* (coll) nibble off

ab′knallen *tr* fire off; (sl) bump off

ab′knicken *tr* snap off || *intr* (SEIN) snap off

ab′knipsen *tr* pinch off, snip off; (*Film*) use up

ab′knöpfen *tr* unbutton; **j-m Geld a.** squeeze money out of s.o.

ab′knutschen *tr* (coll) pet

ab′kochen *tr* boil; (*Obst*) stew; (*Milch*) scald || *intr* cook out

ab′kommandieren *tr* detach, detail

ab′kommen §99 *intr* (SEIN) (von) get away (from); (*Mode*) go out of style; (naut) become afloat (again); **auf zwei Tage a.** get away for two days; **gut** (or **schlecht**) **a.** (sport) get off to a good (or bad) start; **hoch** (or **tief**) **a.** aim too high (or low); **vom Kurs a.** go off course; **vom Boden a.** become airborne; **vom Thema a.** get off the subject; **vom Wege a.** lose one's way, stray; **von der Wahrheit a.** deviate from the truth; **von e-r Ansicht a.** change one's views || **Abkommen** *n* (-s;-) (com, pol) agreement; (jur) settlement

abkömmlich ['apkœmlɪç] *adj*—**a. sein** be able to get away

Abkömmling ['apkœmlɪŋ] *m* (-s;-e) descendant, scion

ab′koppeln *tr* uncouple

ab′kratzen *tr* scratch off; (*Schuhe*) scuff up || *intr* (*sterben*) (sl) croak; (*abhauen*) (sl) beat it; **kratz ab!** drop dead!

ab′kriegen *tr* (coll) get off or out

ab′kühlen *tr*, *ref & intr* cool off

Abkunft ['apkʊnft] *f* (-;) lineage

ab′kürzen *tr* shorten; (*Inhalt*) abridge; (*Wort*) abbreviate; (math) reduce

Ab′kürzung *f* (-;-en) shortening; abridgement; abbreviation; (*kürzerer Weg*) shortcut

ab′küssen *tr* smother with kisses

ab′laden §103 *tr* unload; (*Schutt*) dump

Ab′ladeplatz *m* dump; (mil) unloading point

Ab′lage *f* (*für Kleider*) cloakroom; (*Lagerhaus*) depot, warehouse; (*abgelegte Akten*) files; (mil) dump

ab′lagern *tr* (*Wein, usw.*) age; (geol) deposit || *ref* (geol) be deposited || *intr*—**a. lassen** age, season

Ab′laß *m* (-lasses;-lässe) outlet, drain; (com) deduction; (eccl) indulgence

ab′lassen §104 *tr* leave off; (*Bier*) tap; (*Dampf*) let off; (*Teich, Faß*) drain; (*Waren*) sell; **etw vom Preise a.** knock s.th. off the price; **j-m etw billig a.** (com) let s.o. have s.th. cheaply || *intr* desist, stop; **a. von** let go of, give up

Ablativ ['ablatif] *m* (-s;-e) ablative

Ab′lauf *m* overflow; (*e-r Frist, e-s Vertrags*) expiration; (*der Ereignisse*) course; (sport) start

ab′laufen §105 *tr* (*Strecke*) run; (*Stadt*) scour; (*Schuhe*) wear out; **j-m den Rang a.** get the better of s.o.; outrun s.o. || *intr* (SEIN) run away; (*Zeit*) expire; (*ausfallen*) turn out; (com) fall due; (sport) start

Ab′laut *m* ablaut

Ab′leben *n* demise, decease

ab′lecken *tr* lick (off)

ab′legen *tr* (*Last, Waffen*) lay down; (*ausziehen*) take off; (*Schwert*) lay aside; (*die alte Haut*) slough; (*Karten*) discard; (*Akten, Dokumente*) file; (*Briefe*) sort; (*Namen*) drop, stop using; (*Sorgen, Kummer*) put away; (*Prüfung, Gelübde, Eid*) take; (*Predigt*) deliver; (*Gewohnheit*) give up; (*Rechenschaft*) render, give; **Bekenntnis a.** make a confession; **die Maske a.** (fig) throw off all disguise; **die Trauer a.** come out of mourning; **ein volles Geständnis a.** come clean; **Probe a.** furnish proof; **seine Fehler a.** mend one's ways; **Zeugnis a.** (für or gegen) testify (for or against) || *intr* take off one's coat or hat and coat); **bitte, legen Sie ab!** please take your things off

Ab′leger *m* (-s;-) (bot) shoot; (com) subsidiary; (hort) slip, cutting

ab′lehnen *tr* refuse, turn down; (*Antrag*) reject; (*Zeugen*) challenge; (*Erbschaft*) renounce; **durch Abstimmung a.** vote down

ab′lehnend *adj* negative

Ab′lehnung *f* (-;-en) refusal

ab′leiern *tr* recite mechanically

ab′leisten *tr* (*Eid*) take; **den Militärdienst a.** (mil) serve one's time

ab′leiten *tr* lead away; (*Herkunft*) trace back; (*Fluß, Blitz*) divert; (*Wasser*) drain off; (*Wärme*) conduct; (chem) derive; (elec) shunt; (gram, math) derive; **abgeleitetes Wort** derivative || *ref* (aus, von) be derived (from)

Ab′leitung *f* (-;-en) (*e-s Flusses*) diversion; (*des Wassers*) drainage; (elec, phys) conduction; (gram, math) derivation; (phys) convection

ab′lenken *tr* turn away, divert; (*Gefahr, Verdacht*) ward off; (fencing) parry; (opt, phys) deflect

Ab′lenkung *f* (-;-en) diversion; distraction; (opt) refraction

ab′lernen *tr*—**j-m etw a.** learn s.th. from s.o.

ab′lesen §107 *tr* read off; (*Zähler*) read; (*Obst*) pick; **es j-m vom Gesicht a.,** daß tell by looking at s.o. that

ab′leugnen *tr* deny, disown; (*Glauben*) renounce

Ab′leugnung *f* (-;-en) denial, disavowal

ab′liefern *tr* deliver, hand over, surrender

Ab′lieferung *f* (-;-en) delivery; (*der Schußwaffen*) surrender

ab'liegen §108 *intr* (*Wein*) mature; (*Obst*) ripen || *intr* (SEIN) be remote
ab'löschen *tr* extinguish; (*Stahl*) temper; (*Tinte*) blot; (*Kalk*) slake
ab'lösen *tr* loosen, detach; (*Posten*) relieve; (*Schuld*) discharge; (*Pfand*) redeem; (*Haut*) peel off || *ref* (bei) –take turns (at)
Ab'lösung *f* (–;-en) loosening; relief; discharge
ab'machen *tr* undo, untie; (*erledigen*) settle, arrange; (*Vertrag*) conclude; (*Rechnung*) close
Ab'machung *f* (–;-en) settlement
abmagern ['apmagərn] *intr* (SEIN) grow thin, thin down
Ab'magerung *f* (–;) emaciation
ab'mähen *tr* mow
ab'malen *tr* portray; (fig) depict
Ab'marsch *m* departure
ab'marschieren *intr* (SEIN) march off
Ab'mattung *f* (–;) fatigue
ab'melden *tr* (*Besuch*) (coll) call off; **der ist bei mir abgemeldet** (coll) I've had it with him; **j–n bei der Polizei a.** give notice to the police that s.o. is leaving town || *ref* (mil) report off duty
ab'messen §70 *tr* measure (off); (*Worte*) weigh; (*Land*) survey
ab'montieren *tr* dismantle; (*Geschütz*) disassemble; (*Reifen*) take off || *ref* (aer) (coll) disintegrate in the air
ab'mühen *ref* exert oneself, slave
ab'murksen *tr* (sl) do in
ab'nagen *tr* gnaw (off); (*Knochen*) pick
Ab'nahme *f* (–;-n) (*Verminderung*) (an *dat*) reduction (in), drop (in); (*des Gewichts*) loss; (*des Mondes*) waning; (*des Tages*) shortening; (*e-s Eides*) administering; (*e-r Rechnung*) auditing; (indust) final inspection; (surg) amputation; **A. der Geschäfte** decline in business; **A. e-r Parade** reviewing of the troops; **A. finden** be sold; **in A. geraten** decline, wane
ab'nehmen §116 *tr* take off, remove; (*Wäsche*) take down; (*Schnurrbart*) shave off; (*wegnehmen*) take away; (*Hörer*) lift, unhook; (*Strom*) use; (*Obst*) pick; (*Eid*) administer; (*Waren*) purchase; (*Rechnung*) audit; (*prüfen*) inspect and pass; (*Verband*) remove; (phot) take; (surg) amputate; **aus Berichten a.** gather from reports; **das kann ich dir nicht a.** I can't accept what you are saying; **die Parade a.** inspect the troops; **j–m die Arbeit a.** take the work off s.o.'s shoulders; **j–m die Beichte a.** hear s.o.'s confession; **j–m die Maske a.** unmask s.o., expose s.o.; **j–m die Verantwortung a.** relieve s.o. of responsibility; **j–m ein Versprechen a.** make s.o. make a promise; **j–m zuviel a.** charge s.o. too much || *intr* diminish; (*Preise*) drop; (*Wasser*) recede; (*Kräfte*) fail; (*Mond*) be on the wane; **an Dicke a.** taper; **an Gewicht a.** lose weight; **an Kräften a.** lose strength || **Abnehmen**

n (–s;) decrease; **im A. sein** be on the decrease
Ab'nehmer –in §6 *mf* buyer, consumer; (*Kunde*) customer; (*Hehler*) fence
Ab'neigung *f* (–;-en) (gegen, vor *dat*) aversion (to, for), dislike (of)
abnorm [ap'nɔrm] *adj* abnormal
Abnormität [apnɔrmi'tɛt] *f* (–;-en) abnormity, monstrosity
ab'nötigen *tr* (*dat*) extort (from)
ab'nutzen, ab'nützen *tr* wear out || *ref* wear out, become worn out
Ab'nutzung *f* (–;-en) wear and tear; (*Abrieb*) abrasion; (mil) attrition
Ab'öl *n* (–s;-e) used oil
Abonnement [abɔn(ə)'mã] *n* (–s;-s) (auf *acc*) subscription (to)
Abonnements'karte *f* commutation ticket
Abonnent –in [abɔ'nɛnt(ɪn)] §7 *mf* subscriber
abonnieren [abɔ'nirən] *tr* subscribe to; **abonniert sein auf** (*acc*) have a subscription to || *intr* (auf *acc*) subscribe (to)
ab'ordnen *tr* delegate, deputize
Ab'ordnung *f* (–;-en) delegation
Abort ['abɔrt] *m* (–;-e) toilet || [a'bɔrt] *m* (–s;-e) abortion
ab'passen *tr* measure, fit; (*abwarten*) watch for; (*auflauern*) waylay
ab'pfeifen §88 *tr* (sport) stop
ab'pflücken *tr* pluck (off)
ab'placken, ab'plagen *ref* work oneself to death, slave
ab'platzen *intr* (SEIN) come loose
Abprall ['apral] *m* rebound; (*Geschoß*) richochet
ab'prallen *intr* (SEIN) rebound; ricochet
ab'pressen *tr* extort
ab'putzen *tr* clean (off); (*polieren*) polish; (*Mauer*) roughcast, plaster
ab'raten §63 *intr*–j–m von etw a. advise s.o. against s.th.
Ab'raum *m* (–es;) rubble; (min) overburden
ab'räumen *tr* clear away; (*Tisch*) clear
ab'reagieren *tr* (*Spannung, Erregung*) work off || *ref* (coll) calm down
ab'rechnen *tr* subtract; (*Spesen*) account for; (com) deduct || *intr* settle accounts
Ab'rechnung *f* (–;-en) (*von Konten*) settlement; (*Abzug*) deduction; **A. halten** balance accounts
Ab'rede *f* agreement, arrangement; **in A. stellen** deny
ab'reden *intr*–j–m von etw a. dissuade s.o. from s.th.
ab'reiben *tr* rub off; (*Körper*) rub down
Ab'reise *f* departure
ab'reisen *intr* (SEIN) (nach) depart (for)
ab'reißen §53 *tr* tear off; (*Haus*) tear down; (*Kleid*) wear out || *intr* (SEIN) tear off
ab'richten *tr* (*Tier*) train; (*Pferd*) break in; (*Brett*) dress
Ab'richter –in §6 *mf* trainer
ab'riegeln *tr* (*Tür*) bolt; (mil) seal off

ab'ringen §142 *tr*—**j—m etw a.** wrest s.th. from s.o.

ab'rinnen §121 *intr* (SEIN) run off, run down

Ab'riß *m* summary, outline; (*Skizze*) sketch

ab'rollen *tr & ref* unroll, unwind || *intr* (SEIN) unroll, unwind

ab'rücken *tr* push away, move back || *intr* (SEIN) clear out; (fig) dissociate oneself; (mil) march off

Ab'ruf *m* recall; **auf A.** on call

ab'rufen §122 *tr* call away; (*Zug*) call out, announce

ab'runden *tr* round off

ab'rupfen *tr* pluck (off)

ab'rüsten *tr & intr* disarm

Ab'rüstung *f* (–s) disarmament

ab'rutschen *intr* (SEIN) slip (off)

absacken ['apzakən] *intr* (SEIN) sink; (*Flugzeug*) pancake

Ab'sage *f* cancellation; (*Ablehnung*) refusal

ab'sagen *tr* cancel || *intr* decline; (*dat*) renounce, repudiate

ab'sägen *tr* saw off

ab'sahnen *tr* (& fig) skim (off)

Ab'satz *m* stop, pause, break; (*Zeileneinrückung*) indentation; (*Abschnitt*) paragraph; (*des Schuhes*) heel; (*der Treppen*) landing; (*Vertrieb*) market, sale(s); **ohne A.** without a break

ab'satzfähig *adj* marketable

Ab'satzgebiet *n* territory (*of a salesman*)

Ab'satzmarkt *m* (com) outlet

Ab'satzstockung *f* slump in sales

ab'saugen *tr* suck off; (*Teppich*) vacuum

Ab'saugventilator *m* exhaust fan

ab'schaben *tr* scrape off

ab'schaffen *tr* abolish, do away with; (*Mißbrauch*) redress; (*Diener*) dismiss

ab'schälen *tr* peel

ab'schalten *tr* switch off

ab'schätzen *tr* (*Wert*) estimate; (*für die Steuer*) assess, appraise

abschätzig ['apʃetsɪç] *adj* disparaging

Ab'schaum *m* (–[e]s; & fig) scum

ab'scheiden §112 *tr* part, sever; (physiol) excrete; (physiol) secrete || *intr* (SEIN) pass away, pass on

Ab'scheu *m* (–[e]s;) (*vor dat, gegen*) abhorrence (of), disgust (at)

ab'scheuern *tr* scrub off, scour; (*Haut*) scrape; (*abnutzen*) wear out

abscheu'lich *adj* atrocious

ab'schicken *tr* send away; (*Post*) mail

ab'schieben §130 *tr* shove off; deport

Abschied ['apʃit] *m* (–[e]s;–e) (*Weggang*) departure; (*Entlassung*) dismissal; (mil) discharge; **A. nehmen von** take leave of; (*e–m Amt*) resign, retire from

Ab'schiedsfeier *f* farewell party

Ab'schiedsrede *f* valediction

Ab'schiedsschmaus *m* farewell dinner

ab'schießen §76 *tr* (*Gewehr*) fire, shoot; (*Flugzeug*) shoot down; (*Panzer*) knock out; (rok) launch; **j–n a.** bring about s.o.'s downfall

ab'schinden §167 *tr* skin || *ref* slave

ab'schirmen *tr* screen (off); (gegen) guard (against)

ab'schlachten *tr* butcher; (fig) massacre

Ab'schlag *m* discount; (golf) tee shot; **auf A.** in part payment, on account

ab'schlagen §132 *tr* knock off; (*Baum*) fell; (*Angriff*) repel; (*Bitte*) refuse; **das Wasser a.** pass water || *intr* (golf) tee off

abschlägig ['apʃlɛɪç] *adj* negative; **a. bescheiden** turn down

Ab'schlagszahlung *f* installment

ab'schleifen §88 *tr* grind off; (fig) refine, polish || *ref* become refined

ab'schleppen *tr* drag away, tow away

Ab'schleppwagen *m* tow truck

ab'schleudern *tr* fling off, catapult

ab'schließen §76 *tr* lock (up); (*Straße*) close off; (*Rechnung*) close, settle; (*Bücher*) balance; (*Vertrag*) conclude; (*Rede*) wind up; (*Wette*) wager || *ref* seclude oneself, shut oneself off || *intr* conclude

ab'schließend *adj* definitive; (*Worte*) concluding || *adv* definitively; (*schließlich*) in conclusion

Ab'schluß *m* completion; (*e–s Vertrags*) conclusion; (*Geschäft*) transaction, deal; (*Verkauf*) sale; (*Rechnungs-, Konto-, Buch-*) closing; (mach) seal

ab'schmeicheln *tr*—**j—m etw a.** coax s.th. out of s.o.

ab'schmelzen §133 *tr* (*Erz*) smelt; (*Schnee*) melt || *intr* (SEIN) melt

ab'schmieren *tr* copy carelessly; (coll) beat up; (aut) lubricate || *intr* (SEIN) (aer) (coll) crash

ab'schnallen *tr* unbuckle, unstrap

ab'schnappen *intr* (SEIN) (coll) stop dead; (coll) die

ab'schneiden §106 *tr* cut (off); (*Hecke*) trim; **den Weg. a.** take a shortcut; **j–m das Wort a.** cut s.o. short; **j–n die Ehre a.** steal s.o.'s good name || *intr*—gut a. do well

Ab'schnitt *m* cut, cutting; (*Teilstück*) part, section; (*im Scheckbuch*) stub; (*Kapitel*) section, paragraph; (math) segment; (mil) sector

ab'schnüren *tr* untie; (surg) ligature; **j–m den Atem a.** choke s.o.

ab'schöpfen *tr* skim off

ab'schrägen *tr & ref* slant, slope

ab'schrauben *tr* unscrew

ab'schrecken §134 *tr* scare off; (*abbringen*) deter

ab'schreiben §62 *tr* copy; (*Schularbeit*) crib; (*uneinbringliche Forderung*) write off; (*Literaturwerk*) plagiarize; (*Wert*) depreciate || *intr* send a refusal

Ab'schreiber **–in** §6 *mf* plagiarist

Ab'schreibung *f* (–;–en) write-off

ab'schreiten §86 *tr* pace off; (mil) review; **die Front a.** review the troops

Ab'schrift *f* copy, transcript; (com, jur) duplicate

ab'schriftlich *adj & adv* in duplicate

ab'schuften *ref* work oneself to death

ab'schürfen *ref*—**sich** [*dat*] **die Haut a.** skin oneself

Ab'schürfung *f* (-;-en) abrasion

Ab'schuß *m* (e-r *Waffe*) firing; (e-r *Rakete*) launching; (e-s *Panzers*) knocking out; (e-s *Flugzeugs*) downing, kill; (hunt) kill

abschüssig [ˈapʃʏsɪç] *adj* sloping; (*steil*) steep

Ab'schußrampe *f* launch pad

ab'schütteln *tr* shake off

ab'schwächen *tr* weaken; (*vermindern*) diminish, reduce; (*Farben*) tone down || *ref* (*Preis*) decline

ab'schweifen *intr* (SEIN) stray, digress

Ab'schweifung *f* (-;-en) digression

ab'schwellen §119 *intr* (SEIN) go down; (*Lärm, Gesang*) die down

ab'schwenken *intr* (SEIN) swerve

ab'schwören *intr* (*dat*) (*dem Glauben*) deny; (*dem Trunk*) swear off

ab'segeln *intr* (SEIN) set sail

absehbar [ˈapzeːbaːr] *adj* foreseeable

ab'sehen §138 *tr* foresee; **es abgesehen haben auf** (*acc*) be out to get || *intr*—**a. von** disregard; refrain from

ab'seifen *tr* soap down

abseits [ˈapzaɪts] *adv* aside; (sport) offside || *prep* (*genit*) off

ab'senden §140 *tr* send (off), dispatch; (*Post*) mail; (*befördern*) forward

Ab'sender –in §6 *mf* sender, dispatcher

Ab'sendung *f* (-;-en) sending, dispatching; mailing, shipping

ab'sengen *tr* singe off

Absentismus [apzenˈtɪsmʊs] *m* (-;) absenteeism

ab'setzen *tr* (*Betrag*) deduct; (*Last*) set down; (*entwöhnen*) wean; (*Beamten*) remove; (*König*) depose; (*Fallschirmtruppen, Passagiere*) drop; (com) sell; (typ) set up || *ref* settle, set; (mil) disengage || *intr* stop, pause

Absetzung *f* (-;-en) dismissal

Ab'sicht *f* intention, purpose; **in der A.** with the intention; **mit A.** on purpose; **ohne A.** unintentionally

ab'sichtlich *adj* intentional || *adv* on purpose, intentionally

ab'sitzen §144 *tr* (*Strafzeit*) serve, do || *intr* (SEIN) (*vom Pferde*) dismount; **a. lassen** (chem) let settle

absolut [apzoˈluːt] *adj*

absolvieren [apzɔlˈviːrən] *tr* absolve; (*Studien*) finish; (*Hochschule*) graduate from; (*Prüfung*) pass

abson'derlich *adj* peculiar, strange

ab'sondern *tr* separate, segregate; (*Kranken*) isolate; (physiol) secrete || *ref* keep aloof

absorbieren [apzɔrˈbiːrən] *tr* absorb

ab'speisen *tr* feed; **j-n mit schönen Worten a.** put s.o. off with polite words

abspenstig [ˈapʃpɛnstɪç] *adj*—**a. machen** lure away; **j-m a. werden** desert s.o.

ab'sperren *tr* shut off, block off; (*Tür*) lock; (*Strom*) cut off; (*Gas*) turn off

ab'spielen *tr* play through to the end; (*Schallplatte, Tonband*) play; (*Tonbandaufnahme*) play back || *ref* take place

ab'sprechen §64 *tr* dispute, deny; (*ab-* machen) arrange; **j-m das Recht a. zu** (*inf*) dispute s.o.'s right to (*inf*)

ab'sprechend *adj* (*Urteil*) unfavorable; (*Kritik*) adverse; (*tadelnd*) disparaging

ab'springen §142 *intr* (SEIN) jump down, jump off; (*Ball*) rebound; (*Glasur*) chip; (*abschweifen*) digress; (aer) bail out, jump; **a. von** quit, desert

Ab'sprung *m* jump; (ins *Wasser*) dive; (des *Balles*) rebound

ab'spulen *tr* unwind, unreel

ab'spülen *tr* rinse (off)

ab'stammen *intr* (SEIN) (**von**) be descended (from); (**von**) be derived (from)

Abstammung *f* (-;-en) descent, extraction; (gram) derivation

Ab'stand *m* distance; (*räumlich und zeitlich*) interval; **A. nehmen von** refrain from; **A. zahlen** pay compensation

abstatten [ˈapʃtatən] *tr* (*Besuch*) pay; (*Bericht*) file; (*Dank*) give, return

ab'stauben *tr* dust off; (sl) swipe

ab'stechen §64 *tr* (*töten*) stab; (*Rasen*) cut; (*Hochofen*) tap; (*Karten*) trump || *intr*—**gegen** (or **von**) **etwa a.** contrast with s.th.

Ab'stecher *m* (-s;-) side trip; (*Umweg*) detour; (fig) digression

ab'stecken *tr* (*Haar*) unpin, let down; (*Kleid*) pin, fit; (surv) mark off

ab'stehen §146 *intr* (*entfernt sein*) (**von**) be, stand away (from); (*Ohren, usw.*) stick out || *intr* (HABEN & SEIN) (**von**) refrain (from)

ab'steigen §148 *intr* (SEIN) get down, descend; **in e-m Gasthof a.** stay at a hotel

ab'stellen *tr* (*Last*) put down; (*Radio, Gas, usw.*) turn off; (*Motor*) switch off; (*Auto*) park; (*Mißstand*) redress; (mil) detach, assign; **a. auf** (*acc*) gear to

Ab'stellraum *m* storage room

ab'stempeln *tr* stamp

ab'sterben §149 *intr* (SEIN) die off; (*Pflanzen*) wither; (*Glieder*) get numb

Abstieg [ˈapʃtiːk] *m* (-[e]s;) descent

ab'stimmen *tr* tune; (com) balance; **a. auf** (*acc*) (fig) atune (to) || *intr* (*über acc*) vote (on)

Abstinenzler –in [apstiˈnɛntslər(ɪn)] §6 *mf* teetotaler

ab'stoppen *tr* stop; (sport) clock

ab'stoßen §150 *tr* push off; (*Waren*) get rid of, sell; (*Schulden*) pay off; (*Geweih*) shed; (fig) disgust, sicken; (phys) repel || *ref*—**sich** (*dat*) **die Hörner a.** (fig) sow one's wild oats || *intr* (SEIN) shove off

ab'stoßend *adj* repulsive

abstrakt [apˈstrakt] *adj* abstract

ab'streichen *tr* (*abwischen*) wipe off; (*Rasiermesser*) strop; (*abhaken*) check off; (bact) swab; (com) deduct

ab'streifen *tr* (*Handschuh, usw.*) take off; (*Haut*) slough off; (*Gewohnheit*) break || *intr* (SEIN) deviate, stray

ab'streiten §86 *tr* contest, dispute

Ab'strich *m* (*beim Schreiben*) down-stroke; (*Abzug*) cut; (bact) swab

ab'stufen *tr* (*Gelände*) terrace; (*Farben*) shade off

abstumpfen ['apstumpfən] *tr* blunt

Ab'sturz *m* fall; (*Abhang*) precipice; (aer) crash

abstürzen *intr* (SEIN) fall down; (aer) crash

ab'suchen *tr* (*Gebiet*) scour, comb

Ab-szeß [ap'stses] *m* (**-szesses;** **-szesse**) abscess

Abt [apt] *m* (**-[e]s;—e**) abbot

ab'takeln *tr* unrig; (coll) sack, fire

ab'tasten *tr* probe; (rad) scan

Abtei [ap'taɪ] *f* (**-;-en**) abbey

Ab'teil *m* compartment

ab'teilen *tr* divide, partition

Ab'teilung *f* (**-;-en**) department, division; (*im Krankenhaus*) ward; (arti) battery; (mil) detachment, unit

Ab'teilungsleiter **-in** §6 *mf* department head, section head

Ab'teilungszeichen *n* hyphen

Äbtissin [ep'tɪsɪn] *f* (**-;-nen**) abbess

ab'tönen *tr* tone down, shade off

ab'töten *tr* (*Bakterien*) kill; (*das Fleisch*) mortify

Abtrag ['aptrak] *m* (**-[e]s;—e**)—j-m A. leisten compensate s.o.; j-m A. tun hurt s.o.

ab'tragen §132 *tr* carry away; (*Gebäude*) raze; (*Kleid*) wear out; (*Schuld*) pay

abträglich ['aptreklɪç] *adj* detrimental

ab'treiben §62 *tr* drive away; (*Leibesfrucht*) abort ‖ *intr* (SEIN) drift away; vom Kurs a. drift off course

Ab'treibung *f* (**-;-en**) abortion

ab'trennen *tr* separate, detach; (*Glied*) sever; (*Genähtes*) unstitch

ab'treten §152 *tr* wear out (*by walking*); (*aufgeben*) cede, turn over ‖ *intr* (SEIN) retire, resign; (theat) exit

Ab'treter *m* (**-s;-**) doormat

Ab'tretung *f* (**-;-en**) (*von Grundeigentum*) transfer; (pol) cession

ab'trocknen *tr* dry ‖ *intr* (SEIN) dry

ab'tropfen *intr* (SEIN) trickle, drip

ab'trudeln *intr* (SEIN) go into a tailspin; (coll) toddle off, saunter off

abtrünnig ['aptrynɪç] *adj* unfaithful; (eccl) apostate; **a. werden** defect

Ab'trünnigkeit *f* (**-;**) desertion, defection; (eccl) apostasy

ab'tun §154 *tr* (*ablegen*) take off; (*beiseite schieben*) get rid of; (*töten*) kill; (*erledigen*) settle; **a. als** dismiss as; **kurz a.** make short work of; **mit e-m Achselzucken a.** shrug off

ab'urteilen *tr* pass final judgment on

ab'verlangen *tr*—j-m etw **a.** demand s.th. of s.o.

ab'wägen §156 *tr* weigh

ab'wälzen *tr* roll away; (*Schuld*) shift

ab'wandeln *tr* (*Thema*) vary; (*Hauptwort*) (gram) decline; (*Zeitwort*) (gram) conjugate

ab'wandern *intr* (SEIN) wander off; (*Bevölkerung*) migrate; (*Arbeitskräfte*) drift away

Ab'wanderung *f* (**-;-en**) exodus, migration

Ab'wandlung *f* (**-;-en**) variation; (*e-s Hauptwortes*) declension; (*e-s Zeitwortes*) conjugation

ab'warten *tr* wait for; (*Anweisung*) await; **das bleibt abzuwarten!** that remains to be seen! **s-e Zeit a.** bide one's time ‖ *intr* wait and see

abwärts ['apverts] *adv* down, downwards; **mit ihm geht es a.** (coll) he's going downhill

ab'waschen §158 *tr* wash (off)

ab'wechseln *tr & intr* alternate

ab'wechselnd *adj* alternate

Ab'wechs(e)lung *f* (**-;-en**) variation; (*Mannigfaltigkeit*) variety; (*Zerstreuung*) diversion, entertainment

Ab'weg *m* wrong way; **auf Abwege führen** mislead; **auf Abwege geraten** go wrong

Ab'wehr *f* (**-;**) defense; (*e-s Stoßes, usw.*) warding off; (mil) counter-espionage service

ab'wehren *tr* ward off, avert

ab'weichen §85 *intr* (SEIN) deviate, diverge; (*verschieden sein*) differ

Ab'weichung *f* (**-;-en**) deviation; difference; (math) divergence

ab'weiden *tr* graze on

ab'weisen §118 *tr* refuse, turn down; (*Angriff*) repel; (*Berufung*) deny

ab'weisend *adj* (gegen) unfriendly (to)

Ab'weisung *f* (**-;-en**) refusal; (jur) denial; (mil) repulse

ab'wenden *tr* turn away, turn aside; (*Augen*) avert; (*Aufmerksamkeit*) divert; (*Krieg, Gefahr*) prevent ‖ §140 & 120 *ref* (von) turn away (from)

ab'werfen §160 *tr* throw off; (*Bomben*) drop; (*Blätter, Geweih*) shed; (*Gewinn*) bring in, yield; (*Zinsen*) bear; (*Karten*) discard; (*Joch*) shake off

ab'werten *tr* devaluate

Ab'wertung *f* (**-;-en**) devaluation

abwesend ['apvezənt] *adj* absent, missing; (fig) absent-minded

Ab'wesenheit *f* (**-;**) absence; (fig) absent-mindedness

ab'wickeln *tr* unwind, unroll; (*Geschäfte*) transact; (*Schulden*) settle; (*Aktiengesellschaft*) liquidate ‖ *ref* unwind; (fig) develop **sich gut a.** (com) turn out well

ab'wiegen §57 *tr* weigh

ab'wischen *tr* wipe off, wipe clean

Abwurf ['apvurf] *m* drop(ping); (*Bomben*) release; (*Ertrag*) yield

ab'würgen *tr* wring the neck of; (aut) stall

ab'zahlen *tr* pay off

ab'zählen *tr* count off

Ab'zahlung *f* (**-;-en**) payment in installments; (*Rate*) installment; **auf A.** on terms

Ab'zahlungsgeschäft *n* deferred-payment system

ab'zapfen *tr* (*Bier*) tap; (*Blut*) draw

Ab'zehrung *f* emaciation; consumption

Ab'zeichen *n* distinguishing mark; badge; (mil) decoration

ab'zeichnen *tr* copy, draw, sketch;

(Dokument) initial || *ref* become apparent; **(gegen)** stand out (against)

Ab'ziehbild *n* decal

ab'ziehen §163 *tr* pull off; *(Kunden)* lure away; *(Reifen)* take off; *(Bett)* strip; *(vom Preise)* deduct, knock off; *(vervielfältigen)* run off; *(Abziehbild)* transfer; *(Schlüssel vom Loch)* take out; *(Rasiermesser)* strop; *(Wein)* draw; *(Truppen)* withdraw; *(Aufmerksamkeit)* divert; (arith) deduct; (phot) print; (typ) pull || *intr* (SEIN) depart; *(abmarschieren)* march off; *(Rauch)* disperse

Ab'zug *m* *(e–r Summe)* deduction; *(Rabatt)* rebate, allowance; *(Skonto)* discount; *(am Gewehr)* trigger; *(Weggang)* departure; *(für Wasser)* outlet; *(für Rauch)* escape; (mil) withdrawal; (phot) print; (typ) proof sheet

abzüglich ['aptsyklıç] *prep* (genit or acc) less, minus

Ab'zugsbogen *m* proof sheet

Ab'zugspapier *n* duplicating paper; (phot) printing paper

Ab'zugsrohr *n* drainpipe

ab'zweigen *tr* divert || *intr* (SEIN) branch off

ach [ax] *interj* oh!; ah!; **ach so!** oh, I see!; **ach was!** nonsense!; **ach wo!** of course not!

Achse ['aksə] *f* (–;–n) axis; *(am Wagen)* axle; (mach) shaft; **auf der A.** on the move; **per A.** by truck; by rail

Achsel ['aksəl] *f* (–;–n) shoulder; **auf die leichte A. nehmen** make light of; **mit den Achseln zucken** shrug one's shoulders; **über die Achseln ansehen** look down on

Ach'selbein *n* shoulder blade

Ach'selgrube *f*, **Ach'selhöhle** *f* armpit

Ach'selträger **–in** §6 *mf* opportunist

acht [axt] *adj* eight; **alle a. Tage** once a week; **in a. Tagen** within a week; **über a. Tage** a week from today || **Acht** *f* (–;–en) eight || *f* (–;) *(Bann)* outlawry; *(Obacht)* care, attention; **in die A. erklären** outlaw; (fig) ostracize; **sich in a. nehmen vor** *(dat)* watch out for

achtbar ['axtbar] *adj* respectable

achte ['axtə] §9 *adj & pron* eight

achteckig ['axtekıç] *adj* octagonal

Achtel ['axtəl] *n* (–s;–) eighth *(part)*

achten ['axtən] *tr (beachten)* respect; *(schätzen)* esteem; *(erachten)* consider || *intr*—a. **auf** (acc) pay attention to; **a. darauf, daß** see to it that

ächten ['eçtən] *tr* outlaw, proscribe; *(gesellschaftlich)* ostracize

ach'tenswert *adj* respectable

achter(n) ['axtər(n)] *adv* aft, astern

acht'geben §80 *intr* **(auf** acc) pay attention (to); **gib acht!** watch out!

acht'los *adj* careless

Acht'losigkeit *f* (–;) carelessness

acht'sam *adj* **(axtzam]** cautious; **(auf** acc) attentive (to); **(auf** acc) careful (of)

Acht'samkeit *f* (–;) carefulness

achttägig ['axttegıç] *adj* eight-day; eight-day old; one-week

Ach'tung *f* (–;) attention; **(vor** dat) respect (for); **A.!** watch out!; (mil) attention!

ach'tungsvoll *adj* respectful; *(als Briefschluß)* Yours truly

acht'zehn *adj & pron* eighteen || **Acht-zehn** *f* (–;–en) eighteen

acht'zehnte §9 *adj & pron* eighteenth

achtzig ['axtsıç] *adj* eighty

achtziger ['axtsıgər] *invar adj* of the eighties; **die a. Jahre** the eighties || **Achtziger** **–in** §6 *mf* octogenarian

achtzigste ['axtsıçstə] §9 *adj* eightieth

ächzen ['eçtsən] *intr* groan, moan

Acker ['akər] *m* (–s;⸚) soil, (arable) land, field; *(Maß)* acre

Ackerbau (Ak'kerbau) *m* farming

ackerbautreibend ['akərbautraıbənt] *adj* agricultural

Ackerbestellung (Ak'kerbestellung) *f* cultivation, tilling

Ackerland (Ak'kerland) *n* arable land

ackern ['akərn] *tr & intr* plow

addieren [a'dirən] *tr & intr* add

Addiermaschine [a'dirma/inə] *f* adding machine

Addition [adı'tsjon] *f* (–;–en) addition

ade [a'de] *interj* farewell!; bye-bye!

Adel ['adəl] *m* (–s;) nobility, noble birth; *(edle Gesinnung)* noblemindedness

ad(e)lig ['ad(ə)lıç] *adj* noble, titled; nobleman's || **Ad(e)lige** §5 *m* nobleman || §5 *f* noblewoman

A'delsstand *m* nobility

Ader ['adər] *f* (–;–n) vein

adieu [a'djø] *interj* adieu!

Adjektiv ['atjektif] *n* (–s;–e) adjective

Adjutant **–in** [atju'tant(ın)] §7 *mf* adjutant; *(e-s Generals)* aide-(de-camp)

Adler ['adlər] *m* (–s;–) eagle

Ad'lernase *f* aquiline nose

Admiral [atmı'ral] *m* (–[e]s;–e) admiral

Admiralität [atmıralı'tet] *f* (–;) admiralty

adoptieren [adop'tirən] *tr* adopt

Adoption [adop'tsjon] *f* (–;–en) adoption

Adoptiv– [adop'tif] *comb. fm.* adoptive

Adressat **–in** [adre'sat(ın)] §7 *mf* addressee; *(e-r Warensendung)* consignee

Adresse [a'dresə] *f* (–;–n) address; **an die falsche A. kommen** (fig) bark up the wrong tree; **per A.** care of

adressieren [adre'sirən] *tr* address; *(Waren)* consign

adrett [a'dret] *adj* smart, neat

Advent [at'vent] *m* (–s;–e) Advent

Adverb [at'verp] *n* (–[e]s;–ien [-ı.ən]) adverb

Advokat **–in** [atvo'kat(ın)] §7 *mf* lawyer

Affäre [a'ferə] *f* (–;–n) affair

Affe ['afə] *m* (–n;–n) ape, monkey; **e-n Affen haben** (sl) be drunk

Affekt [a'fekt] *m* (–[e]s;–e) emotion; *(Leidenschaft)* passion

affektiert [afek'tirt] *adj* affected

Affektiert'heit f (-;-en) affectation
äffen ['ɛfən] tr ape, mimic
Af'fenliebe f doting
Af'fenpossen pl monkeyshines
Af'fenschande f crying shame
Af'fentheater n farce, joke
affig ['afɪç] adj affected; (geckenhaft) foppish
Äffin ['ɛfɪn] f (-;-nen) female ape, female monkey
Afrika ['afrɪka] n (-s) Africa
afrikanisch [afrɪ'kanɪʃ] adj African
After ['aftər] m (-s;-) anus
AG, A.G., A.-G. abbr (Aktiengesellschaft) stock company
ägäisch [ɛ'gɛ.ɪʃ] adj Aegean
Agende [a'gendə] f (-;-n) memo pad
Agent –in [a'gent(ɪn)] §7 mf agent, representative; (Geheim-) secret agent
Agentur [agen'tur] f (-;-en) agency
aggressiv [agrɛ'sif] adj aggressive
Ägide [ɛ'gidə] f (-;-n) aegis
Agio ['aʒɪ.o] n (-s;-s) premium
Agitation [agita'tsjon] f (-;-en) agitation, rabble-rousing
Agi-tator [agi'tatər] m (-s;-tatoren [ta'torən] (& mach) agitator
agitatorisch [agita'torɪʃ] adj inflammatory
agitieren [agi'tirən] intr agitate
Agraffe [a'grafə] f (-;-n) clasp
agrarisch [a'grarɪʃ] adj agrarian
Ägypten [ɛ'gyptən] n (-s) Egypt
Ägypter –in [ɛ'gyptər(ɪn)] §6 mf Egyptian
ägyptisch [ɛ'gyptɪʃ] adj Egyptian
ah [a] interj aha!
Ahle ['alə] f (-;-n) awl, punch
Ahn [an] m (-(e)s & -en;-en) ancestor
ahnden ['andən] tr (strafen) punish; (rächen) avenge
Ahn'dung f (-;) revenge
ähneln ['ɛnəln] intr (dat) resemble
ahnen ['anən] tr have a premonition of, suspect; (erfassen) divine
Ah'nentafel f family tree
ähnlich ['ɛnlɪç] adj alike; (dat) similar (to), analogous (to): das sieht ihm ä. that's just like him; j–m ä sehen look like s.o.
Ähn'lichkeit f (-;-en) (mit) resemblance (to)
Ah'nung ['anʊŋ] f (-;-en) (Vorgefühl) presentiment, hunch; (böse) misgiving; (Argwohn) suspicion; keine A. haben have no idea
ah'nungslos adj unsuspecting
ah'nungsvoll adj full of misgivings
Ahorn ['ahɔrn] m (-[e]s;-e) maple
Ähre ['ɛrə] f (-;-n) (Korn) ear; (e–r Blume) spike; Ähren lesen glean
Ais ['a.ɪs] n (-;-) (mus) A sharp
Akade-mie [akadə'mi] f (-;-mien ['mi.ən]) academy; university
Akademiker –in [aka'demɪkər(ɪn)] §6 mf university graduate
akademisch [aka'demɪʃ] adj academic; university
Akazie [a'katsjə] f (-;-n) acacia
akklimatisieren [aklimatɪ'zirən] tr acclimate ‖ ref become acclimated
Akkord [a'kɔrt] m (-[e]s;-e) chord;

(Vereinbarung) accord; (com) settlement; im A. arbeiten do piecework
Akkord'arbeit f piecework
Akkordeon [a'kɔrde.ɔn] n (-s;-s) accordion
akkreditieren [akredɪ'tirən] tr accredit; open an account for
Akkreditiv [akredɪ'tif] n (-[e]s;-e) (Beglaubigungsschreiben) credentials; (com) letter of credit
Akkumula-tor [akumu'latɔr] m (-s; -toren [torən]) storage battery
akkurat [aku'rat] adj accurate
Akkusativ ['akuzatif] m (-[e]s;-e) accusative (case)
Akrobat [akro'bat] §7 m acrobat
Akrobatik [akro'batɪk] f (-;) acrobatics
Akrobatin [akro'batɪn] §7 f acrobat
Akt [akt] m (-[e]s;-e) act, action; (paint) nude; (theat) act
Akte ['aktə] f (-;-n) document; record, file; (jur) instrument; zu den Akten legen file; (fig) shelve
Ak'tendeckel m file folder
Ak'tenklammer f paper clip
Ak'tenmappe f brief case, portfolio
ak'tenmäßig adj documentary
Ak'tenschrank m file cabinet
Ak'tentasche f brief case
Ak'tenzeichen n file number
Aktie ['aktsjə] f (-;-n) stock
Ak'tienbesitzer –in §6 mf stockholder
Ak'tienbörse f stock exchange
Ak'tiengesellschaft f corporation
Ak'tieninhaber –in §6 mf stockholder
Ak'tienmakler –in §6 mf stockbroker
Ak'tienmarkt m stock market
Ak'tienschein m stock certificate
Aktion [ak'tsjon] f (-;-en) action; (Unternehmung) campaign, drive; (polizeiliche) raid; (mil) operation; **Aktionen** activity
Aktionär –in [aktsjɔ'ner(ɪn)] §8 mf stockholder
aktiv [ak'tif] adj active; (Bilanz) favorable; (chem) activated; (gram) active; a. werden become a member (of a student club) ‖ **Aktiv** n (-s;) (gram) active voice
Aktiva [ak'tiva] pl assets; A. und Passiva assets and liabilities
Aktiv'posten m asset
aktuell [aktu'ɛl] adj current, topical ‖ **Aktuelle** pl (journ) newsbriefs
Akustik [a'kʊstɪk] f (-;) acoustics
akustisch [a'kʊstɪç] adj acoustic(al)
akut [a'kut] adj acute
Akzent [ak'tsent] m (-[e]s;-e) accent (mark); (Nachdruck) emphasis; (phonet) stress
akzentuieren [aktsentu'irən] tr accent; (fig) stress, accentuate
akzeptieren [aktsep'tirən] tr accept
Alabaster [ala'bastər] m (-s;) alabaster
Alarm [a'larm] m (-[e]s;-e) alarm; A. blasen (or schlagen) (mil & fig) sound the alarm; blinder A. false alarm
Alarm'anlage f alarm system; warning system (in civil defense)
alarm'bereit adj on the alert

Alarm'bereitschaft f (state of) readiness; **in A.** on the alert

alarmieren [alar'miːrən] tr alert; alarm

Alaun [a'laun] m (-s;-e) alum

Alaun'stift m steptic pencil

Albanien [al'baːnjən] n (-s;) Albania

albanisch [al'baniʃ] adj Albanian

albern ['albərn] adj silly

Al·bum ['album] n (-s;-ben [bən]) album

Alchimist [alçı'mɪst] §7 m alchemist

Alge ['algə] f (-;-n) alga; seaweed

Algebra ['algebra] f (-;) algebra

algebraisch [alge'braːɪʃ] adj algebraic

Algerien [al'geːrjən] n (-s;) Algeria

algerisch [al'geːrɪʃ] adj Algerian

Algier ['alʒir] n (-s;) Algiers

Alibi ['aliːbi] n (-s;-s) alibi

Alimente [ali'mentə] pl child support

alimentieren [aliːmen'tiːrən] tr pay alimony to; (Kind) support

Alkohol ['alkohol] m (-s;-e) alcohol

al'koholfrei adj non-alcoholic

Alkoholiker –in [alkə'holikər(ɪn)] §8 mf alcoholic

alkoholisch [alkə'holɪʃ] adj alcoholic

all [al] adj all; (jeder) every; (jeder beliebige) any; **alle beide** both (of them); **alles Gute!** take care!; (im Brief) best wishes; **alle zehn Minuten** every ten minutes; **alle zwei Tage** every other day; **auf alle Fälle** in any case || indef pron each, each one; everyone, everything; all; **aller und jeder** each and every one; **in allem** all told; **vor allem** above all, first of all

alle ['alə] adv all gone; **a. machen** finish off; **a. sein** be all gone; **a. werden** run low

Allee [a'le] f (-;-n) (tree-lined) avenue; (tree-lined) walk

Allego·rie [alego'ri] f (-;-rien ['riːən]) allegory

allegorisch [ale'goriʃ] adj allegoric(al)

allein [a'laɪn] adj alone || adv alone; only; however; no fewer than, no less than; **schon a. der Gedanke** the mere thought

Allein'berechtigung f exclusive right

Allein'flug m solo flight

Allein'handel m monopoly

Allein'herrschaft f autocracy

Allein'herrscher –in §6 mf autocrat

allei'nig adj (ausschließlich) sole, exclusive; (einzig) only

allein'stehend adj alone in the world; (unverheiratet) single; (Gebäude) detached

Allein'verkauf m, **Allein'vertrieb** m franchise

al'lemal adv every time; **ein für a.** once and for all

al'lenfalls adv if need be; (vielleicht) possibly; (höchstens) at most

allenthalben ['alənt'halbən] adv everywhere

al'lerart invar adj all kinds of

al'lerbe'ste §9 adj very best; **aufs a.** in the best possible manner

al'lerdings' adv (gewiß) certainly (strong affirmative answer); (zugestehend) admittedly, I must admit

al'lerer'ste §9 adj very first, first ... of all

Aller·gie [aler'gi] (-;-gien ['giːən]) allergy

allergisch [a'lergɪʃ] adj allergic

al'lerhand' invar adj all kinds of; (viel) a lot of || indef pron —das ist a.! that's great!; **das ist doch a.!** the nerve!

Allerhei'ligen invar n All Saints' Day

allerlei ['alər'laɪ] invar adj all kinds of || **Allerlei** n (-s;-s) hotchpotch; (mus) medley

al'lerlet'zte §9 adj very last, last of all; latest

allerliebste ['alər'liːpstə] §9 adj dearest ... of all; (Kind) sweet

al'lermei'ste §9 adj most; **am allermeisten** most of all; chiefly

al'lernäch'ste §9 adj very next

al'lerneu'este §9 adj latest, newest

Allersee'len invar n All Souls' Day

allesamt [alə'zamt] adv all together

al'lezeit adv always

Allge'genwart f omnipresence

all'gemein adj general, universal

All'gemeinheit f universality; (Öffentlichkeit) public

Allheil'mittel n cure-all

Allianz [ali'ants] f (-;-en) alliance

alliieren [ali'iːrən] ref—**sich a. mit** ally oneself with

alliiert [ali'iːrt] adj allied || **Alliierte** §5 mf ally

alljähr'lich adj annual, yearly

All'macht f omnipotence

allmäch'tig adj omnipotent, almighty

allmählich [al'meːlıç] adj gradual

allnächt'lich adj nightly

allseitig ['alzaıtıç] adj all-round || adv from all sides, on all sides

All'tag m daily routine

alltäg'lich adj daily; (fig) everyday

all'tags adv daily; (wochentags) weekdays

All'tags– comb.fm. everyday; (fig) commonplace

All'tagsmensch m common man

All'tagswort n (-[e]s;¨er) household word

allwissend [al'vɪsənt] adj omniscient

allwö'chentlich adj & adv weekly

allzu– comb.fm. all too

all'zumal adv one and all, all together

all'zusammen adv all together

Alm [alm] f (-;-en) Alpine meadow

Almanach ['almanax] m (-[e]s;-e) almanac

Almosen ['almozen] n (-s;-) alms

Alp [alp] m (-[e]s;-e) elf, goblin; (Alptraum) nightmare

Alp'druck m (-[e]s;), **Alp'drücken** n (-s;) nightmare

Alpen ['alpən] pl Alps

Alphabet [alfa'bet] n (-[e]s;-e) alphabet

alphabetisch [alfa'betıʃ] adj alphabetical

alpin [al'pin] adj alpine

als [als] adv as, like || conj than; when, as; but, except; **als ob** as if

alsbald' adv presently, immediately

alsdann' adv then, thereupon

also ['alzo] *adv* so, thus; therefore, consequently; **na a.!** well then!

alt [alt] *adj* (**älter** ['eltər], **älteste** ['eltəstə] §9) *adj* old; (*bejahrt*) aged; (*gebraucht*) second-hand; (*abgestanden*) stale; (*antik*) antique; (*Sprache*) ancient || **Alt** *m* (-[e]s;-e) contralto || **Alte** §5 *m* (coll) old man; **die Alten** the ancients; **mein Alter** (coll) my husband || **Alte** §5 *f* (coll) old woman; **meine Alte** (coll) my wife

Altan [al'tɑn] *m* (-[e]s;-e), **Altane** [al'tɑnə] *f* (-;-n) balcony, gallery

Altar [al'tɑr] *m* (-[e]s;-̈e) altar

alt'bewährt *adj* long-standing

Alt'eisen *n* scrap iron

Alt'eisenhändler *m* junk dealer

Alter ['altər] *n* (-s;-) age; (*Greisen-*) old age; (*Zeit-*) epoch; (*Dienst-*) seniority; **er ist in meinem A.** he is my age; **im A. von** at the age of; **mittleren Alters** middle-aged

altern ['altərn] *intr* (SEIN) age

Alternative [alterna'tivə] *f* (-;-n) alternative

Al'tersgrenze *f* age limit; (*für Beamte*) retirement age

Al'tersheim *n* home for the aged

Al'tersrente *f* old-age pension

al'tersschwach *adj* decrepit; senile

Al'tersschwäche *f* (feebleness of) old age

Al'tersversorgungskasse *f* old-age pension fund

Altertum ['altərtum] *n* (-s) antiquity

altertümlich ['altərtymlıç] *adj* ancient; (*Möbel*) antique; (*veraltet*) archaic

Al'tertumsforscher -in §6 *mf* archaeologist; (*Antiquar*) antiquarian

Al'tertumskunde *f*, **Al'tertumswissenschaft** *f* study of antiquity; classical studies

althergebracht ['alt'hergəbraxt] *adj* long-standing, traditional

alther'kömmlich *adj* ancient, traditional

Altist [al'tıst] §7 *m* alto (*singer*)

Altistin [al'tıstın] §7 *f* contralto (*female singer*)

alt'klug *adj* precocious

ältlich ['eltlıç] *adj* elderly

Alt'meister *m* past master; (sport) ex-champion

alt'modisch *adj* old-fashioned

Alt'stadt *f* old (part of the) city

Alt'stadtsanierung *f* urban renewal

Alt'stimme *f* alto; contralto (*female voice*)

altväterlich ['altfetərlıç], **altväterisch** ['altfetərıʃ] *adj* old-fashioned; old-time

Alt'warenhändler -in §6 *mf* second-hand dealer

Altweibersommer [alt'vaibərzomər] *m* Indian summer; (*Spinnweb*) gossamer

Aluminium [alu'minjum] *n* (-s;) aluminum

am [am] *contr* **an dem**

amalgamieren [amalga'mirən] *tr* amalgamate

Amateur [ama'tør] *m* (-s;-e) amateur

Amazone [ama'tsonə] *f* (-;-n) Amazon

Am·boß ['ambɔs] *m* (-bosses;-bosse) anvil

ambulant [ambu'lant] *adj* ambulatory || *adv*—**a. Behandelte** out-patient

Ambulanz [ambu'lants] *f* (-;-en) out-patient clinic; (*Krankenwagen*) ambulance

Ameise ['amaizə] *f* (-;-n) ant

Amerika [a'merika] *n* (-s;) America

Amerikaner -in [ameri'kanər(ın)] §6 *mf* American

amerikanisch [ameri'kanıʃ] *adj* American

Ami ['ami] *m* (-s;-s) (sl) Yank || *f* (-;-s) American cigarette

Amme ['amə] *f* (-;-n) nurse, wet-nurse

Amnestie [amnes'ti] *f* (-;-tien ['ti-ən]) amnesty

amnestieren [amnes'tirən] *tr* pardon

A·mor ['amɔr] *m* (-s;-moren ['morən]) (myth) Cupid

Amortisation [amɔrtiza'tsjon] *f* (-;-en) amortization

Amortisations'kasse *f* sinking fund

amortisieren [amɔrti'zirən] *tr* amortize

Ampel ['ampəl] *f* (-;-n) hanging lamp; (*Verkehrs-*) traffic light

Ampere [am'per] *n* (-s;-) ampere

Amphibie [am'fibjə] *f* (-;-n) amphibian

Amphi'bienpanzerwagen *m* amphibious tank

Amphitheater [am'fite-ɑtər] *n* (-s;-) amphitheater

Ampulle [am'pulə] *f* (-;-n) phial

Amputation [amputa'tsjon] *f* (-;-en) amputation

amputieren [ampu'tirən] *tr* amputate

Amputierte [ampu'tirtə] §5 *mf* amputee

Amsel ['amzəl] *f* (-;-n) blackbird

Amt [amt] *n* (-[e]s;-̈er) office; (*Pflicht*) duty, function; (dipl) post; (eccl) divine service; (telp) exchange

amtieren [am'tirən] *intr* be in office, hold office; (eccl) officiate

amt'lich *adj* official

Amts- *comb.fm.* official, of (an) office

Amts'antritt *m* inauguration

Amts'befugnis *f* competence

Amts'bereich *m* jurisdiction

Amts'bewerber -in §6 *mf* office seeker

Amts'bezirk *m* jurisdiction

Amts'blatt *n* official bulletin

Amts'eid *m* oath of office

Amts'enthebung *f* dismissal

Amts'führung *f* administration

amts'gemäß *adj* official || *adv* officially

Amts'gericht *n* district court

Amts'gerichtsrat *m* (official rank of) district-court judge

Amts'geschäfte *pl* official duties

Amts'gewalt *f* (official) authority

Amts'handlung *f* official act

Amts'niederlegung *f* resignation

Amts'schimmel *m* bureaucracy; (coll) red tape

Amts'siegel *n* seal of office

Amts'sprache *f* official language; (coll) officialese, gobbledygook

Amts'tracht *f* robes

Amts'träger –in §6 *mf* officeholder

Amts'verletzung *f* misconduct in office

Amts'weg *m*—auf dem Amtswege through official channels

Amts'zeichen *n* (telp) dial tone

Amulett [amʊ'let] *n* (–[e]s;–e) amulet

amüsant [amy'zant] *adj* amusing

amüsieren [amy'zirən] *tr* amuse, entertain || *ref* amuse oneself; (*sich gut unterhalten*) enjoy oneself

an [an] *adv* on; onward || *prep* (*dat*) at, against, on, upon, by, to; (*Grad, Maß*) in; an sich per se; an und für sich properly speaking; es ist an dir zu (*inf*) it's up to you to (*inf*) || *prep* (*acc*) at, on, upon, against, to

analog [ana'lok] *adj* analogous

Analo·gie [analɔ'gi] *f* (–;–gien ['gi·ən]) analogy

Analphabet –in [analfa'bet(ɪn) §7 *mf* illiterate

Analphabetentum [analfa'betəntum] *n* (–s;), **Analphabetismus** [analfabe'tɪsmʊs] *m* (–;) illiteracy

analphabetisch [analfa'betɪʃ] *adj* illiterate

Analyse [ana'lyzə] *f* (–;–n) analysis; (gram) parsing; durch A. analytically

analysieren [analy'zirən] *tr* analyze; (gram) parse

Analy·sis [a'nalyzɪs] *f* (–;–sen [ana-'lyzən]) (math) analysis

Analytiker –in [ana'lytikər(ɪn)] §6 *mf* analyst

analytisch [ana'lytɪʃ] *adj* analytic(al)

Anämie [anɛ'mi] *f* (–;) anemia

anämisch [an'ɛmi] *adj* anemic

Ananas ['ananas] *f* (–;–se) pineapple

Anarchie [anar'çi] *f* (–;) anarchy

anästhesieren [anɛste'zirən] *tr* anesthetize

Anästheti·kum [anɛs'tetikʊm] *n* (–s; –ka [ka]) anesthetic

an'atmen *tr* breathe on

Anato·mie [anatɔ'mi] *f* (–;–mien ['mi·ən]) anatomy

anatomisch [ana'tomɪʃ] *adj* anatomical

an'backen §50 *tr* bake gently || *intr* (HABEN & SEIN) cake on

an'bahnen *tr* pave the way for

anbandeln ['anbandəln] *intr*—a. mit flirt with

An'bau *m* (–[e]s;) cultivation || *m* (–[e]s;–bauten) annex, new wing

an'bauen *tr* cultivate; (*Gebäudeteil*) add on

An'baufläche *f* (arable) acreage

An'baumöbel *pl* sectional furniture

An'beginn *m* outset

an'behalten §90 *tr* keep (*garment*) on

anbei [an'baɪ] *adv* enclosed (herewith)

an'beißen §53 *tr* bite into, take the first bite of || *intr* nibble at the bait; (fig) bite

an'belangen *tr*—was mich anbelangt as far as I am concerned, as for me

an'bellen *tr* bark at

anberaumen ['anbəraumən] *tr* schedule

an'beten *tr* (& fig) worship

An'betracht *m*—in A. (*genit*) in consideration of, in view of

an'betteln *tr* bum, chisel

An'betung *f* (–;) worship

an'betungswürdig *adj* adorable

an'bieten §58 *tr* offer || *ref* offer one's services

an'binden §59 *tr* tie (up) || *intr*—mit j–m a. pick a quarrel with s.o.

an'blasen §61 *tr* blow at, blow on

An'blick *m* look, view, sight

an'blicken *tr* look at; (*besehen*) view; (*mustern*) eye

an'blinzeln *tr* wink at

an'brechen §64 *tr* (*Vorräte*) break into; (*Flasche, Kiste*) open || *intr* (SEIN) (*Tag*) dawn; (*Nacht*) come on

an'brennen §97 *tr* light || *intr* (SEIN) catch fire; (*Speise*) burn

an'bringen §65 *tr* bring, fetch; (*befestigen*) (an *acc*) attach (to): (*Bitte*) make; (*Klage*) lodge; (*Geld*) invest; (*Tochter*) marry off; (*Waren*) sell, get rid of; (*Bemerkung*) insert; (*Licht, Lampe*) install; (*Geld*) (coll) blow

An'bruch *m* break; bei A. der Nacht at nightfall; bei A. des Tages at daybreak

an'brüllen *tr* roar at

Andacht ['andaxt] *f* (–;–en) devotion; (*Gottesdienst*) devotions

andächtig ['andeçtɪç] *adj* devout

an'dauern *intr* continue, last; (*hartnäckig sein*) persist

An'denken *n* (–s;–) remembrance; souvenir; zum A. an (*acc*) in remembrance of

andere ['andərə] §9 *adj* & *pron* other; (*folgend*) next; ein anderer another; another one; kein anderer no one else

ändern ['endərn] *tr* change; (*Wortlaut*) modify || *ref* change

andernfalls ['andərn'fals] *adv* (or) else

anders ['andərs] *adj* else; (als) different (from); a. werden change || *adv* otherwise differently

an'dersartig *adj* of a different kind

anderseits ['andər'zaɪts] *adv* on the other hand

an'derswo *adv* somewhere else

anderthalb ['andərt'halp] *invar adj* one and a half

Än'derung *f* (–;–en) change, variation; modification

Än'derungsantrag *m* amendment

anderwärts ['andər'verts] *adv* elsewhere

anderweitig ['andər'vaɪtɪç] *adj* other, further || *adv* otherwise; elsewhere

an'deuten *tr* indicate, suggest; (*anspielen*) hint at, allude to; (*zu verstehen geben*) imply, intimate

an'deutungsweise *adv* by way of suggestion

an'dichten *tr*—j–m etw a. impute s.th. to s.o.

An'drang *m* rush; crowd; heavy traffic; (*von Arbeit*) pressure

an'drehen *tr* turn on; j–m etw a. palm s.th. off on s.o.

an'drohen *tr*—j—m etw a. threaten s.o. with s.th.

an'drücken *tr*—etw a. an (*acc*) press s.th. against

an'eignen *ref*—sich [*dat*] a. appropriate; (*Gewohnheit*) acquire; (*Meinungen*) adopt; (*Sprache*) master; (*widerrechtlich*) appropriate, usurp

aneinan'der *adv* together

aneinan'dergeraten §63 *intr* (SEIN) come to blows

Anekdote [anɛk'doːtə] *f* (-;-n) anecdote

an'ekeln *tr* disgust, nauseate

an'empfehlen §147 *tr* recommend

An'erbieten *n* (-s;-) offer, proposal

an'erkennbar *adj* recognizable

an'erkennen §97 *tr* (als) recognize (as); (als) acknowledge (as); (*Schuld*) admit; (*billigen*) approve; (*lobend*) appreciate; (*Anspruch*) allow; nicht a. repudiate, disown; (sport) disallow

An'erkennung *f* (-;-en) acknowledgement; recognition; appreciation; admission; lobende A. honorable mention

anfachen ['anfaxən] *tr* (*Feuer*) fan; (*Gefühle*) inflame; (*Haß*) stir up

an'fahren §71 *tr* (*herbeibringen*) carry, convey; (*anstoßen*) run into; (fig) snap at; (naut) run afoul of ‖ *intr* (SEIN) drive up; (*losfahren*) start off

An'fall *m* attack

an'fallen §72 *tr* attack, assail ‖ *intr* (SEIN) accumulate, accrue

anfällig ['anfɛlɪç] *adj* (für) susceptible (to)

An'fang *m* beginning, start; von A. an from the very beginning

an'fangen §73 *tr & intr* begin, start

Anfänger -in ['anfɛŋər(ɪn)] §6 *mf* beginner; (*Neuling*) novice

anfänglich ['anfɛŋlɪç] *adj* initial

an'fangs *adv* at the start, initially

An'fangsbuchstabe *m* initial (letter)

An'fangsgründe *pl* rudiments, elements

an'fassen *tr* take hold of; (*behandeln*) handle, touch ‖ *intr* lend a hand

an'faulen *intr* (SEIN) begin to rot

anfechtbar ['anfɛçtbar] *adj* debatable, questionable; (jur) contestable

an'fechten §74 *tr* (*Richtigkeit*) contest; (*beunruhigen*) trouble; (jur) challenge

An'fechtung *f* (-;-en) (eccl) temptation; (jur) challenge

an'fertigen *tr* make, manufacture

an'feuchten *tr* moisten, wet

an'feuern *tr* inflame; (sport) cheer

an'flehen *tr* implore

an'fliegen §57 *tr* (aer) approach

An'flug *m* (*Anzeichen*) suggestion, trace; (*oberflächliche Kenntnis*) smattering; (*dünner Überzug*) film; A. von Bart down; leichter A. von slight case of

an'fordern *tr* call for, demand; (mil) requisition

an'fragen *intr* (über *acc*, wegen, nach) ask (about s.th.); (bei) inquire (of s.o.)

an'fressen §70 *tr* gnaw; (*Metall*) corrode

anfreunden ['anfrɔɪndən] *ref* (mit) make friends (with)

an'frieren §77 *intr* (SEIN) begin to freeze; a. an (*acc*) freeze onto

an'fügen *tr* (an *acc*) join (to)

an'fühlen *tr & ref* feel

Anfuhr ['anfuːr] *f* (-;-en) delivery

an'führen *tr* lead; (*Worte*) quote; (*Grund*) adduce; (*täuschen*) take in, fool; (mil) lead, command

An'führer -in §6 *mf* leader; (mil) commander; (pol) boss

An'führung *f* quotation

An'führungszeichen *n* quotation mark

an'füllen *tr & ref* fill up

An'gabe *f* (*Erklärung*) statement; (beim Zollamt) declaration; (coll) showing off; Angaben data; directions; nähere Angaben machen give particulars; wer hat die A.? whose serve is it?

an'geben §80 *tr* (*mitteilen*) state; (*bestimmen*) appoint; (*anzeigen*) inform against; (*vorgeben*) pretend; (*Preis*) quote ‖ *intr* (coll) show off; (cards) deal first; (tennis) serve

An'geber -in §6 *mf* informer; (*Prahler*) show-off

angeblich ['angeplɪç] *adj* alleged

an'geboren *adj* innate, natural

An'gebot *n* offer; (bei Auktionen) bid; A. und Nachfrage supply and demand

angebracht ['angəbraxt] *adj* advisable; es für a. halten zu (*inf*) see fit to (*inf*); gut a. appropriate; schlecht a. ill-timed

angegossen ['angəgɔsən] *adj*—wie a. sitzen fit like a glove

angeheiratet ['angəhairatət] *adj* related by marriage

angeheitert ['angəhaitərt] *adj* tipsy

an'gehen §82 *tr* charge, attack; (*Problem*) tackle; das geht dich gar nichts an that's none of your business; j—n um etw a. approach s.o. for s.th. ‖ *intr* (SEIN) begin; (*zulässig sein*) be allowable; (*leidlich sein*) be tolerable; das geht nicht an that won't do

an'gehend *adj* future, prospective

an'gehören *intr* (*dat*) be a member (of)

Angehörige ['angəhøːrɪgə] §5 *mf* member; nächste Angehörigen next of kin; seine Angehörigen his relatives

Angeklagte ['angəklaːktə] §5 *mf* defendant; (*wenn verhaftet*) suspect

Angel ['aŋəl] *f* (-;-n) fishing tackle; (e-r Tür) hinge; aus den Angeln heben (& fig) unhinge

an'gelangen *intr* (SEIN) (an *dat*, bei) arrive (at)

an'gelegen *adj*—sich [*dat*] etw a. sein lassen make s.th. one's business

An'gelegenheit *f* (-;-en) affair, business

angelehnt ['angəleːnt] *adj* ajar

An'gelgerät *n* fishing tackle

An'gelhaken *m* fish(ing) hook

angeln ['aŋəln] *intr* (nach) fish (for)

An'gelpunkt *m* pivot, central point

An'gelrute *f* fishing rod

angelsächsisch ['aŋəlzeksɪʃ] *adj* Anglo-Saxon

An'gelschnur *f* fishing line

angemessen ['aŋəmesən] *adj* suitable (*ausreichend*) adequate; (*annehmbar*) reasonable; (*Benehmen*) proper; (*dat*) in keeping (with); **für a. halten** think fit

angenehm ['aŋənem] *adj* pleasant; **sehr a! pleased to meet you!**

angeregt ['aŋərekt] *adj* lively

angeschlagen ['aŋəʃlagən] *adj* chipped; (*Boxer*) groggy; (*mil*) hard-hit

angesehen ['aŋəzeˑən] *adj* respected; (*ausgezeichnet*) distinguished

An'gesicht *n* countenance, face; **von A. by sight**

an'gesichts *prep* (*genit*) in the presence of; (fig) in view of

angestammt ['aŋəʃtamt] *adj* hereditary

Angestellte ['aŋəʃteltə] §5 *mf* employee; **die Angestellten** the staff

angetan ['aŋətan] (**mit**) clad (in); **a. sein von** have a liking for; **ganz danach a. zu** (*inf*) very likely to (*inf*)

angetrunken ['aŋətruŋkən] *adj* tipsy

angewandt ['aŋəvant] *adj* applied

angewiesen ['aŋəvizən] *adj*—**a. sein auf** (*acc*) have to rely on

an'gewöhnen *tr*—**j—m etw a.** accustom s.o. to s.th.

An'gewohnheit *f* (—;-en) habit

an'gleichen §85 *tr* adapt, adjust

Angler —**in** ['aŋlər(ɪn)] §6 *mf* fisher

an'gliedern *tr* link, attach; (*Gesellschaft*) affiliate

an'greifen §88 *tr* (*anfassen*) handle; (*Vorräte*) draw on, dip into; (*Körper*) affect; (mil) attack

an'greifend *adj* aggressive, offensive

An'greifer —**in** §6 *mf* aggressor

an'grenzen *intr* (**an** *acc*) be adjacent (to), border (on)

An'griff *m* attack

An'griffskrieg *m* war of aggression

an'griffslustig *adj* aggressive

Angst [aŋst] *f* (—;-̈e) fear, anxiety

ängstigen ['ɛŋstigən] *tr* alarm || *ref* (**vor**) be afraid (of); (**um**) be alarmed (about)

ängstlich ['ɛŋstlɪç] *adj* uneasy, jittery; (*besorgt*) anxious; (*sorgfältig*) scrupulous; (*schüchtern*) timid

Angst'zustände *pl* jitters

an'haben §89 *tr* have on; **j—m etw a. have s.th. on s.o.; j—m etw a. können** be able to harm s.o.

an'haften *intr* (*dat*) stick (to)

an'haken *tr* check off; (**an** *acc*) hook (onto)

an'halten §90 *tr* stop; (*Atem, Ton*) hold; || *intr* stop; (*andauern*) continue, last

an'haltend *adj* continuous

An'halter *m*—**per A. fahren** hitch-hike

An'haltspunkt *m* clue, lead

An'hang *m* (—[e]s;-̈e) appendix; (*Gefolgschaft*) following; (jur) codicil

an'hängen §92 & §109 *tr* (*Hörer*) hang up; (*hinzufügen*) add on; **j—m e-e Krankheit a.** infect s.o. with a disease; **j—m e-n Prozeß a. bring suit**

---

against s.o.; j—m etw a. pin s.th. on s.o. || §92 *intr* (**an** *dat*) adhere (to)

An'hänger —**in** §6 *mf* follower || *m* (*Schmuck*) pendant; (aut) trailer

anhänglich ['anhɛŋlɪç] *adj* (**an** *acc*) attached (to), devoted (to)

Anhängsel ['anhɛŋzəl] *m* (—s;-) appendage, adjunct

an'hauchen *tr* breathe on

An'häufen *tr & ref* pile up

An'häufung *f* (—;-en) accumulation

an'heben §94 *tr* lift (up); (*Lied*) strike up; (aut) jack up

an'heften *tr* fasten; (*annähen*) stitch

an'heilen *tr & intr* heal up

anheim'fallen §72 *intr* (SEIN) (*dat*) devolve (upon)

anheim'stellen *tr* (*dat*) leave (to)

An'höhe *f* rise, hill

an'hören *tr* listen to, hear || *ref* —**sich gut a.** sound good

Anilin [anɪˈlin] *n* (—s;) aniline

Animier'dame *f* B-girl

animieren [anɪˈmirən] *tr* encourage

Anis [aˈnis] *m* (—es;-e) anise

an'kämpfen *intr* (**gegen**) struggle (against)

An'kauf *m* purchase

an'kaufen *tr* purchase

Anker ['aŋkər] *m* (—s;-) anchor; (elec) armature; **vor A. gehen** drop anchor

ankern ['aŋkərn] *intr* anchor

an'ketten *tr* (**an** *acc*) chain (to)

An'klage *f* accusation, charge; (jur) indictment; **A. erheben** prefer charges; **die A. vertreten** be counsel for the prosecution; **unter A. stellen** indict

an'klagen *tr* (**wegen**) accuse (of), charge (with), indict (for)

An'kläger —**in** §6 *mf* accuser; (jur) prosecutor

An'klageschrift *f* (bill of) indictment

an'klammern *tr* (**an** *acc*) clip (to) || *ref* (**an** *acc*) cling (to)

An'klang *m* (**an** *acc*) reminiscence (of), trace (of); **A. finden** be well received, catch on

an'kleben *tr* (**an** *acc*) paste (on), stick (on) || *intr* (HABEN & SEIN) stick

an'kleiden *tr & ref* dress

an'klingeln *tr* ring, call up || *intr*—**bei j—m a.** ring s.o.'s doorbell

an'klopfen *intr* (**an** *acc*) knock (on)

an'knipsen *tr* switch on

an'knüpfen *tr* tie, attach; (*Gespräch*) start || *intr* (**an** *acc*) link up (with)

an'kommen §99 *intr* (SEIN) (**in** *dat*) arrive (at); (**bei**) be well received (by); (**bei**) get a job (with); **es darauf a. lassen** take one's chances; **es kommt ganz darauf an, ob** it (all) depends on whether

Ankömmling ['ankœmlɪŋ] *m* (—s;-e) newcomer, arrival

an'kündigen *tr* announce, proclaim; **j—m etw a.** notify s.o. of s.th.

An'kündigung *f* (—;-en) announcement

Ankunft ['ankʊnft] *f* (—;-̈e) arrival

an'kurbeln *tr* crank up; **die Wirtschaft a.** prime the economy

an'lachen *tr* laugh at

An'lage *f* (*Anordnung*) plan, layout;

(*Bau*) construction; (*Errichtung*) installation; (*Fabrik*) plant, works; (*Garten*) park, grounds; (*Fähigkeit*) ability, aptitude (*im Brief*) enclosure; **in der A.** enclosed

An'lagekapital n invested capital; permanent assets

an'langen tr—was mich anlangt as far as I'm concerned ‖ intr (SEIN) arrive

An-laß ['anlas] m (-lasses;-lässe) occasion; (*Grund*) reason, motive; **A. geben zu** give rise to; **ohne allen A.** without any reason

an'lassen §104 tr (*Kleid*) keep on; (*Motor*) start (up); (*Wasser*) turn on; (*Pumpe*) prime; (*Stahl*) temper; **j-n hart a.** rebuke s.o. sharply ‖ ref **sich gut a.** shape up

Anlasser ['anlasər] m (-s;-) starter

anläßlich ['anleslıç] prep (genit) on the occasion of

An'lauf m run, start

an'laufen §105 tr run at; (*Hafen*) put into ‖ intr (SEIN) (*Motor*) start up; (*Brille*) fog up; (*Metall*) tarnish; (*anwachsen*) accumulate; (*Schulden*) mount up; (*Film*) start, come on; **angelaufen kommen** come running up; **ins Rollen a.** (fig) get rolling; **rot a.** blush

an'legen tr (an acc) put (on), lay (on); (*Garten*; *Geld*) lay out; (*Kapital*) invest; (*Leitung*) install; (*Verband*) apply; (*Kolonie*) found ‖ ref—**sich a. mit** have a run-in with ‖ intr put ashore; moor

An'legeplatz m pier

an'lehnen tr (an acc) lean (against); (*Tür*) leave ajar ‖ ref (an acc) lean (against); (fig) be based (on), rely (on)

Anleihe ['anlaɪ-ə] f (-;-n) loan

an'leiten tr (zu) guide (to); **a. in** (dat) instruct in

An'leitung f (-;-en) guidance; (*Lehre*) instruction

an'lernen tr train, break in

an'liegen §108 intr (*passen*) fit; (an dat) lie near, be adjacent (to); **eng a.** fit tight; **j-m a.** pester s.o. ‖ **Anliegen** n (-s;-) request; **ein A. an j-n haben** have a request to make of s.o.

an'liegend adj adjacent; (*Kleid*) tight-fitting; (*im Brief*) enclosed

an'locken tr lure (on)

an'machen tr (*Licht*) switch on; (*Feuer*) light; (*zubereiten*) prepare; (an acc) attach (to)

an'malen tr paint

an'marschieren intr (SEIN) approach

anmaßen ['anmasən] ref—**sich** [dat] **etw a.** usurp s.th.; **sich** [dat] **a., etw zu sein** pretend to be s.th.

an'maßend adj arrogant

An'meldeformular n registration form

an'melden tr announce; report; (*Anspruch*, *Berufung*) file; (*Konkurs*) declare; (*Patent*) apply for; (educ) register; (sport) enter ‖ ref (bei) make an appointment (with); (zu) enroll (in); (mil) report in

an'merken tr note down; **j-m etw a.** notice s.th. in s.o.

an'messen §70 tr—j-m etw a. measure s.o. for s.th.

An'mut f (-;) charm, attractiveness

an'mutig adj charming

an'nageln tr (an acc) nail (to)

an'nähen tr (an acc) sew on (to)

annähernd ['anne-ərnt] adj approximate

An'näherung f (-;-en) approach

An'näherungsversuch m (romantic) pass; attempt at reconciliation

an'näherungsweise adv approximately

An'nahme f (-;-n) acceptance; (*Vermutung*) assumption

annehmbar ['annembar] adj acceptable

an'nehmen §116 tr accept, take; (*vermuten*) assume, suppose, guess; (*Glauben*) embrace; (*Gewohnheit*) acquire; (*Gesetz*) pass; (*Kind*) adopt; (*Arbeiter*) hire; (*Farbe*, *Gestalt*) take on; (*Titel*) assume; **etw als erwiesen a.** take s.th. for granted ‖ ref (genit) take care of

annektieren [anek'tirən] tr annex

Annexion [ane'ksjon] f (-;-en) annexation

Annonce [a'nõsə] f (-;-n) advertisement

annoncieren [anõ'sirən] tr advertise

anöden [a'nødən] tr bore to death

anonym [ano'nym] adj anonymous

an'ordnen tr arrange; (*befehlen*) order

an'packen tr grab hold of, seize; (*Problem*) tackle

an'passen tr fit; (*Worte*) adapt; ‖ ref (dat or an acc) adapt oneself (to)

an'passungsfähig adj adaptable

an'pflanzen tr plant, cultivate

an'pflaumen tr (coll) kid

anpöbeln ['anpøbəln] tr mob

an'pochen tr (an acc) knock (on)

An'prall m impact; (e-s Angriffs) brunt

an'prallen intr (SEIN) (gegen, an acc) collide (with), run (into)

an'preisen tr praise; **j-m etw a.** recommend s.th. to s.o.

An'probe f fitting, trying on

an'probieren tr try on

an'pumpen tr—j-n a. um hit s.o. for

an'quatschen tr talk the ears off

an'raten §63 tr advise, recommend

an'rechnen tr charge; **hoch a.** appreciate; **j-m etw a.** charge s.o. for s.th.

An'recht n (auf acc) right (to)

An'rede f address

an'reden tr address, speak to

an'regen tr stimulate; suggest

An'reiz m incentive

an'reizen tr stimulate; spur on

an'rennen §97 intr (SEIN) (gegen) run (into); **angerannt kommen** come running

an'richten tr (*Schaden*) cause, do; (culin) prepare

anrüchig ['anrʏçıç] adj disreputable

an'rücken intr (SEIN) approach

An'ruf m (telephone) call

an'rufen §122 tr call; (*Gott*) invoke; (*Schiff*) hail; (jur) appeal to; (mil) challenge; (telp) call up

an'rühren tr touch; (*Thema*) touch on; (*mischen*) stir

An'sage f announcement

an'sagen *tr* announce; (*Trumpf*) declare

An'sager –in §6 *mf* announcer

an'sammeln *tr* gather; (*anhäufen*) amass; (*Truppen*) concentrate || *ref* gather; (*Zinsen*) accumulate

ansässig ['anzɛsɪç] *adj* residing; a. werden (or sich a. machen) settle || Ansässige §5 *mf* resident

An'satz *m* start; (*Mundstück*) mouthpiece; (*Spur*) trace; (*in e-r Rechnung*) charge; (*Schätzung*) estimate; (geol) deposit; (mach) attachment; (math) statement

an'saugen §125 *tr* suck in; (*Pumpe*) prime

an'schaffen *tr* procure; (*kaufen*) get, purchase; Kinder a. (coll) have kids

an'schalten *tr* switch on

an'schauen *tr* look at

an'schaulich *adj* graphic

An'schauung *f* outlook, opinion; (*Vorstellung*) perception; (*Auffassung*) conception; (*Erkenntnis*) intuition; (*Betrachtung*) contemplation

An'schauungsbild *n* mental image

An'schauungsmaterial *n* visual aids

An'schein *m* appearance

an'scheinend *adj* apparent, seeming

an'scheinlich *adv* apparently

an'schicken *ref* get ready

an'schießen §130 *tr* give (*s.th.*) a push

anschirren ['anʃɪrən] *tr* harness

An'schlag *m* (an *acc*, gegen) striking (against); (*Anprall*) impact; (*Attentat*) attempt; (*Bekanntmachung*) notice; (*e-r Uhr*) stroke; (*e-r Taste*) hitting; (*Berechnung*) calculation; (*e-s Gewehrs*) firing position; (*Komplott*) plot; (mach) stop (*for arresting motion*); (mus) touch; (tennis) serve; A. spielen play tag

An'schlagbrett *n* bulletin board

an'schlagen §132 *tr* (an *acc*) fasten (to); (*Plakat*) post; (*Gewehr*) level; (*Tasse, usw.*) chip; (*Taste*) hit; (*einschätzen*) estimate; (*Gegner*) (box) have in trouble; e–n anderen Ton a. (fig) change one's tune || *ref* bump oneself || *intr* (*Wellen*) (an *acc*) beat against; (*Hund*) let out a bark; (*Arznei*) work

An'schlagzettel *m* notice; poster

an'schließen §76 *tr* padlock; (*anketten*) chain; (*verbinden*) connect; (*anfügen*) join; (com) affiliate; (elec) plug in || *ref* (*dat*, an *acc*) join, side with ||*intr* (*Kleid*) be tight

an'schließend *adj* (an *acc*) subsequent (to); adjacent (to) || *adv* next, then

An'schluß *m* connection; (pol) annexation, union; sie sucht A. (coll) she is looking for a man

An'schlußbahn *f* (rr) branch line

An'schlußdose *f* (elec) receptacle

An'schlußschnur *f* (elec) cord

An'schlußzug *m* connection, connecting train

an'schmachten *tr* make eyes at

an'schmiegen *ref* (an *acc*) nestle up (to); (*Kleid*) (an *acc*) cling (to)

anschmiegsam ['anʃmikzam] *adj* accommodating; cuddly

an'schmieren *tr* smear; (coll) bamboozle

an'schnallen *tr* buckle || *ref* fasten one's seat belt

an'schnauzen *tr* snap at, bawl out

an'schneiden §106 *tr* cut into; (*Thema*) take up

An'schnitt *m* first cut

an'schrauben *tr* (an *acc*) screw on (to)

an'schreiben §62 *tr* write down; (*Spielstand*) mark; (*dat*) charge (to): (com) write to; etw a. lassen buy s.th. on credit

An'schreiber –in §6 *mf* scorekeeper

An'schreibetafel *f* scoreboard

an'schreien §135 *tr* yell at

An'schrift *f* address

An'schriftenmaschine *f* addressograph

an'schwärzen *tr* blacken, disparage

an'schwellen *tr* cause to swell; (*Unkosten, usw.*) swell || §119 *intr* (SEIN) swell up, puff up; increase

an'schwemmen *tr* wash (*s.th.*) ashore; (geol) deposit

an'sehen §138 *tr* look at; (fig) regard || Ansehen *n* (–s;-) appearance; (*Achtung*) reputation; (*Geltung*) prestige, authority; von A. by sight; of high repute

ansehnlich ['anze:nlɪç] *adj* good-looking; (*beträchtlich*) considerable; (*eindrucksvoll*) imposing

An'sehung *f* (–;)–in A. (*genit*) in consideration of

anseilen ['anzaɪlən] *tr* rope together

an'setzen *tr* (an *acc*) put (on), apply (to): (*zum Kochen*) put on; (*Frist, Preis*) set; (*abschätzen*) rate; (*berechnen*) charge; (*Knospen*) put forth || *intr* begin; (*fett werden*) get fat

An'sicht *f* view; (*Meinung*) opinion; zur A. on approval

an'sichtig *adj*—a. werden (*genit*) catch sight of

An'sichtspostkarte *f* picture postcard

An'sichtssache *f* matter of opinion

An'sichtsseite *f* frontal view, façade

An'sichtssendung *f* article(s) sent on approval

ansiedeln *tr* & *ref* settle

An'siedler –in §6 *mf* settler

An'siedlung *f* (–;-en) settlement

An'sinnen *n* (–s;-) unreasonable demand

an'spannen *tr* stretch; (*Pferd*) hitch up; (fig) exert, strain

An'spannung *f* (–;-en) exertion, strain

an'speien §135 *tr* spit on

an'spielen *tr* (cards) lead with || *intr* (auf *acc*) allude (to); (mus) start playing; (sport) kick off, serve, break

An'spielung *f* (–;-en) allusion, hint

an'spitzen *tr* sharpen (*to a point*)

An'sporn *m* spur, stimulus

an'spornen *tr* spur

An'sprache *f* (an *acc*) address (to); e–e A. halten deliver an address

an'sprechen §64 *tr* speak to, address; (*Ziel, Punkt*) make out; a. als regard as; j–n a. um ask s.o. for || *intr* (*dat*) appeal to, interest; (auf *acc*) respond (to)

an'sprechend *adj* appealing

an'springen §142 *tr* leap at ‖ *intr* (SEIN) (*Motor*) start (up); **angesprungen kommen** come skipping along

an'spritzen *tr* sprinkle, squirt

An'spruch *m* claim; **A. haben auf** (*acc*) be entitled to; **A. machen** (or **erheben**) **auf** (*acc*), **in A. nehmen** demand, require, claim; **große Ansprüche stellen** ask too much

an'spruchslos *adj* unpretentious

an'spruchsvoll *adj* pretentious; (*wählerisch*) choosey, hard to please

an'spucken *tr* spit on

an'spülen *tr* wash ashore; (geol) deposit

an'stacheln *tr* goad on

Anstalt ['anʃtalt] *f* (-;-en) institution, establishment; **Anstalten treffen zu** make preparations for

An'stand *m* (*Schicklichkeit*) decency; (*Bedenken*) hesitation; (*Einwendung*) objection; (hunt) blind

anständig ['anʃtendɪç] *adj* decent

An'standsbesuch *m* formal call

An'standsdame *f* chaperone

An'standsgefühl *n* tact

an'standshalber *adv* out of politeness, out of human decency

an'standslos *adv* without fuss

an'starren *tr* stare at, gaze at

anstatt [an'ʃtat] *prep* (genit) instead of

an'stauen *tr* dam up ‖ *ref* pile up

an'staunen *tr* gaze at in astonishment

an'stecken *tr* stick on; (*Ring*) put on; (*anzünden*) set on fire; (*Zigarette, Feuer*) light; (pathol) infect ‖ *ref* become infected

an'steckend *adj* infectious; (*durch Berührung*) contagious

An'steckung *f* (-;-en) infection; (*durch Berührung*) contagion

an'stehen §146 *intr* (nach) line up (for); (*zögern*) hesitate; **j–m gut a.** fit s.o. well, become s.o.

an'steigen §148 *intr* (SEIN) rise, ascend; (*zunehmen*) increase, mount up

an'stellen *tr* (an *acc*) place (against); (*beschäftigen*) hire; (*Versuch, usw.*) (*Vergleich*) draw; (*Heizung, Radio*) turn on ‖ *ref* (nach) line up (for); **sich a., als ob** act as if; **stell dich nicht so dumm an!** don't play dumb!

anstellig ['anʃtelɪç] *adj* skilful

An'stellung *f* (-;-en) hiring; job

an'steuern *tr* steer for

Anstieg ['anʃtik] *m* (-[e]s;-e) rise; (*e–s Weges*) grade

an'stieren *tr* stare at, glower at

an'stiften *tr* instigate

An'stifter –in §6 *mf* instigator

an'stimmen *tr* (*Lied*) strike up; (*Geheul*) let out

An'stoß *m* impact; (*Antrieb*) impulse; (*Ärgernis*) offense; (sport) kickoff; **den A. geben zu** start

an'stoßen §150 *tr* bump against; (*Ball*) kick off; (*Wagen*) give a push; (*mit dem Ellbogen*) nudge, poke ‖ *intr* clink glasses; **a. an** (*acc*) adjoin; **bei j–m a.** shock s.o.; **mit den Gläsern a.** clink glasses; **mit der Zunge a.** lisp ‖

intr (SEIN)—**mit dem Kopf a. an** (*acc*) bump one's head against

an'stoßend *adj* adjoining

anstößig ['anʃtøsɪç] *adj* shocking

an'strahlen *tr* beam on; (fig) beam at; (*mit Scheinwerfern*) floodlight

an'streben *tr* strive for

an'streichen §85 *tr* paint; (*Fehler*) underline; (*anhaken*) check off

An'streicher *m* house painter

an'streifen *tr* brush against, graze

an'strengen *tr* exert; (*Geist*) tax; **e–n Prozeß a.** file suit ‖ *intr* be a strain

an'strengend *adj* strenuous, trying

An'strengung *f* (-;-en) exertion, effort

An'strich *m* (*Farbe*) paint; (*Überzug*) coat (*of paint*); (fig) tinge

An'sturm *m* assault, charge

antarktisch [ant'arktɪʃ] *adj* antarctic

an'tasten *tr* touch, finger

An'teil *m* share, portion; (*Quote*) quota; (st. exch.) share; **A. nehmen an** (*dat*) take part in; (fig) sympathize with

an'teilmäßig *adj* proportional

An'teilnahme *f* (-;) (an *dat*) participation (in); (*Mitleid*) sympathy

Antenne [an'tenə] *f* (-;-n) antenna, aerial; (ent) antenna, feeler

Antibioti·kum [antıbı'otıkum] *n* (-s; -ka [ka]) antibiotic

antik [an'tik] *adj* ancient; classical ‖ **Antike** *f* (-;-n) (classical) antiquity; (*Kunstwerk*) antique

Anti'kenhändler –in §6 *mf* antique dealer

Antilope [antı'lopə] *f* (-;-n) antelope

Antipa·thie [antıpa'ti] *f* (-;-thien ['ti·ən]) antipathy

an'tippen *tr & intr* tap

Antiqua [an'tikva] *f* (-;) roman (type)

Antiquar –in [antı'kvar(-ın)] §8 *mf* antique dealer; second-hand bookdealer

Antiquariat [antıkva'rjat] *n* (-[e]s;-e) second-hand bookstore

antiquarisch [antı'kvarıʃ] *adj* second-hand

Antiquität [antıkvı'tet] *f* (-;-en) antique

Antlitz ['antlıts] *m* (-es;-e) (Bib, poet) countenance

Antrag ['antrak] *m* (-[e]s;⁻e) (*Angebot*) offer; (*Vorschlag*) proposal; (*Gesuch*) application; (pol) motion

an'tragen §132 *tr* offer; (*vorschlagen*) propose ‖ *intr*—**a. auf** (*acc*) make a motion for; propose, suggest

An'tragsformular *n* application form

Antragsteller –in ['antrak/telər(-ın)] §6 *mf* applicant; (parl) mover

an'treffen §151 *tr* meet; find at home

an'treiben §62 *tr* drive on, urge on; (*Schiff*) propel; (*anreizen*) egg on ‖ *intr* (SEIN) wash ashore

an'treten §152 *tr* (*Amt, Erbschaft*) enter (upon); (*Reise*) set out on; (*Motorrad*) start up ‖ *intr* (SEIN) take one's place; (mil) fall in; (sport) enter

An'trieb *m* (-s;-e) (*Beweggrund*) motive; (*Anreiz*) incentive; (mech) drive, impetus; **aus eigenem A.** on

one's own initiative; **neuen A. verleihen** (dat) give fresh impetus to

An'tritt m (-[e]s;-e) beginning, start;
(e-s Amtes) entrance upon

an'tun §154 tr (Kleid) put on; **j—m
etw a.** do s.th. to s.o.

Antwort ['antvɔrt] f (-;-en) answer

antworten ['antvɔrtən] intr (auf acc)
reply (to), answer; **j—m a.** answer s.o.

an'vertrauen tr entrust; (mitteilen)
tell, confide

an'verwandt adj related ‖ **Anver-
wandte** §5 mf relative

an'wachsen §155 intr (SEIN) begin to
grow; grow together; (Wurzel schlagen) take root; (zunehmen) increase

Anwalt ['anvalt] m (-[e]s;-e) attorney

An'waltschaft f legal profession, bar

an'wandeln tr—**mich wandelte die Lust
an zu** (inf) I got a yen to (inf); **was
wandelte dich an?** what got into
you?

An'wandlung f (-;-en) impulse, sudden feeling; (von Zorn) fit

An'wärter –in §6 mf candidate; (mil)
cadet, officer candidate

Anwartschaft ['anvart/aft] f (-;) expectancy; (Aussicht) prospect

an'wehen tr blow on ‖ intr (SEIN)
drift

an'weisen §118 tr (beauftragen) instruct; (zuteilen) assign; (Geld) remit

An'weisung f (-;-en) instruction; assignment; (fin) money order

anwendbar ['anventbar] adj (auf acc)
applicable (to); (für, zu) that can be
used (for)

an'wenden §140 tr (auf acc) apply
(to); (für, zu) use (for)

An'wendung f (-;-en) application;
use

an'werben §149 tr recruit

an'werfen §160 tr (Motor) start up

An'wesen n estate, property; presence

anwesend ['anvezənt] adj present ‖
Anwesende §5 mf person present;
verehrte Anwesende! ladies and
gentlemen!

An'wesenheit f (-;) presence

an'wurzeln ref & intr (SEIN) take root;
wie angewurzelt rooted to the spot

An'zahl f (-;) number, quantity

an'zahlen tr pay down ‖ intr make a
down payment

an'zapfen tr tap

An'zeichen n indication, sign; (Vorbe-
deutung) omen; (pathol) symptom

Anzeige ['antsaɪgə] f (-;-n) (Ankündigung) announcement, notice; (Reklame) ad; (med) advice; **kleine
Anzeigen** classified ads

an'zeigen tr announce; notify; (Symp-
tome, Fieber) show, indicate; (bei
der Polizei) report, inform against;
(inserieren) advertise

An'zeigenvermittlung f advertising
agency

an'zetteln tr (Verschwörung) hatch

an'ziehen §163 tr pull; (& fig) attract;
(Kleid) put on; (e-e Person) dress;
(Riemen, Schraube) tighten; (Bremse)
apply; (Beispiele, Quellen) quote ‖

intr pull, start pulling; (Preis) go up;
(chess) go first

An'ziehung f (-;-en) attraction; (Zitat)
quotation

An'ziehungskraft f appeal; (& phys)
attraction; (astr) gravitation

An'zug m suit; (mil) uniform; **in A.
sein** (Armee) be approaching;
(Sturm) be gathering; (Gefahr) be
imminent

anzüglich ['antsylɪç] adj offensive; **a.
werden** become personal

an'zünden tr set on fire; (Feuer) light

an'zweifeln tr doubt, question

apart [a'part] adj charming; (coll)
cute

Apathie [apa'ti] f (-;) apathy

apathisch [a'patɪʃ] adj apathetic

Apfel ['apfəl] m (-s;-) apple

Ap'felkompott n stewed apples

Ap'felmus n applesauce

Ap'felsaft m apple juice

Apfelsine [apfəl'zinə] f (-;-n) orange

Ap'feltorte f apple tart; **gedeckte A.**
apple pie

Ap'felwein m cider

Apostel [a'pɔstəl] m (-s;-) apostle

Apostroph [apo'strof] m (-[e]s;-e)
apostrophe

Apotheke [apo'tekə] f (-;-n) pharmacy

Apotheker –in [apo'tekər(ɪn)] §6 mf
druggist

Apothe'kerwaren pl drugs

Apparat [apa'rat] m (-[e]s;-e) apparatus, device; (phot) camera; (rad,
telv) set; (telp) telephone; **am A.!**
speaking

Appell [a'pɛl] m (-[e]s;-e) appeal;
(mil) roll call; (mil) inspection

appellieren [apɛ'lirən] intr (& jur)
(an acc) appeal (to)

Appetit [ape'tit] m (-[e]s;-e) appetite

Appetit'brötchen n canapé

appetit'lich adj appetizing; (Mädchen)
attractive

applaudieren [aplau'dirən] tr & intr
applaud

Applaus [a'plaus] m (-es;-e) applause

Appretur [apre'tur] f (-;-en) (tex)
finish

Aprikose [apri'kozə] f (-;-n) apricot

April [a'prɪl] m (-[s];-e) April

Aquarell [akva'rɛl] n (-[e]s;-e) watercolor; watercolor painting

Aqua·rium [a'kvarjum] n (-s;-rien
[rɪ-ən]) aquarium

Äqua·tor [ɛ'kvator] m (-s;-toren
['torən]) equator

Ära ['ɛra] f (-;Ären ['ɛrən]) era

Araber –in ['arabər(ɪn)] §6 mf Arab

Arabien [a'rabjən] n (-s;) Arabia

arabisch [a'rabɪʃ] adj Arabian; (Ziffer) Arabic

Arbeit ['arbaɪt] f (-;-en) work

arbeiten ['arbaɪtən] tr & intr work

Arbeiter –in ['arbaɪtər(ɪn)] §6 mf worker;
A. und Unternehmer pl labor and
management

Ar'beiterausstand m walkout, strike

Ar'beitergewerkschaft f labor union

Arbeiterin ['arbaɪtərɪn] f (-;-nen)
working woman, working girl

Ar′beiterschaft f (−;) working class
Arbeitertum [′arbaɪtərtum] n (−s;) working class, workers
Ar′beitgeber −in §6 mf employer
Ar′beitnehmer −in §6 mf employee
arbeitsam [′arbaɪtzəm] adj industrious
Ar′beitsanzug m overalls; (mil) fatigue clothes, fatigues
Ar′beitseinkommen n earned income
Ar′beitseinstellung f work stoppage
ar′beitsfähig adj fit for work
Ar′beitsgang m process; operation (single step of a process)
Ar′beitsgemeinschaft f team; (educ) workshop
Ar′beitsgerät n equipment, tools
Ar′beitskommando n (mil) work detail
Ar′beitskraft f labor force; **Arbeitskräfte** personnel
Ar′beitslager n work camp
Ar′beitsleistung f (work) quota; (e-r Maschine, Fabrik) output
Ar′beitslohn m wages, pay
ar′beitslos adj unemployed
Ar′beitslosenunterstützung f unemployment compensation
Ar′beitslosigkeit f unemployment
Ar′beitsmarkt m labor market
Ar′beitsminister m secretary of labor
Ar′beitsministerium n department of labor
Ar′beitsnachweis m, **Ar′beitsnachweisstelle** f employment agency
Ar′beitsniederlegung f walkout, strike
ar′beitsparend adj labor-saving
Ar′beitspause f break, rest period
Arbeitspferd n (& fig) workhorse
Ar′beitsplatz m job, place of employment
Ar′beitsrecht n labor law
ar′beitsscheu adj work-shy, lazy
Ar′beitsschicht f shift
Ar′beitsstätte f place of employment; workshop; yard
Ar′beitsstelle f job, position
Ar′beitstag m workday
Ar′beitsvermittlung f employment agency
Ar′beitsversäumnis n absenteeism
Ar′beitszeug n tools
Ar′beitszimmer n study; workroom
archaisch [ar′çaɪʃ] adj archaic
Archäologe [arçe·ɔ′logə] m (−n;−n) archaeologist
Archäologie [arçe·ɔlɔ′gi] f (−;) archaeology
Archäologin [arçe·ɔ′login] f (−;−nen) archaeologist
archäologisch [arçe·ɔ′logiʃ] adj archaeological
Architekt −in [arçi′tekt(ɪn)] §7 mf architect
Architektur [arçitek′tur] f (−;−en) architecture
Ar·chiv [ar′çif] n (−[e]s;−chive [′çivə]) archives; (für Zeitungen) morgue
Areal [are′al] n (−s;−e) area
Are·na [a′rena] f (−;−nen [nən]) arena
arg [ark] adj (ärger [′ergər]; ärgste [′erkstə] §9) bad, evil, wicked; (coll) awful; (schlimm) grave; (Raucher)

heavy ‖ **Arg** n (−s;) malice, cunning ‖ **Arge** §5 m Evil One ‖ §5 n evil
Argentinien [argen′tinjən] n (−s;) Argentina
Argentinier −in [argen′tinjər(ɪn)] §6 mf Argentinean
Ärger [′ergər] m (−s;) irritation; mit j−m Ä. haben have trouble with s.o.
är′gerlich adj (auf acc or über acc) annoyed (at); irritating, annoying
ärgern [′ergərn] tr annoy ‖ ref (über acc) be annoyed (at)
Ärgernis [′ergərnɪs] n (−ses;−se) scandal, offense; (Mißstand) nuisance
Arg′list f craft, cunning
arg′listig adj crafty, cunning
arg′los adj guileless; (nichtsahnend) unsuspecting
Argwohn [′arkvon] m (−s;) suspicion
argwöhnen [′arkvønən] tr suspect
argwöhnisch [′arkvønɪʃ] adj suspicious
Arie [′arjə] f (−;−n) aria
Arier −in [′arjər(ɪn)] §6 Aryan
arisch [′arɪʃ] adj Aryan
Aristokrat [arɪstə′krat] m (−en;−en) aristocrat
Aristokra·tie [arɪstəkra′ti] f (−;−tien [′ti·ən]) aristocracy
Aristokratin [arɪstə′kratɪn] f (−;−nen) aristocrat
Arithmetik [arɪt′metɪk] f (−;) arithmetic
Arktis [′arktɪs] f (−;) Arctic
arktisch [′arktɪʃ] adj arctic
arm [arm] adj (ärmer [′ermər], ärmste [′ermstə] §9 (an dat) poor in) ‖ **Arm** m (−[e]s;−e) arm; (e-s Flusses) branch
Armatur [arma′tur] f (−;−en) armature; **Armaturen** fittings, mountings
Armatu′renbrett n instrument panel; (aut) dashboard
Arm′band n (−[e]s;=er) bracelet; watchband; (Armabzeichen) brassard
Arm′banduhr f wrist watch
Arm′binde f brassard; (med) sling
Ar·mee [ar′me] f (−;−meen [′me·ən]) army
Ärmel [′erməl] m (−s;−) sleeve
Är′melaufschlag m cuff
Är′melkanal m English Channel
är′mellos adj sleeveless
Armen− [armən] comb.fm. for the poor
Ar′menhaus n poorhouse
Armenien [ar′menjən] n (−s;) Armenia
armenisch [ar′meniç] adj Armenian
Ar′menpflege f public assistance
Ar′menunterstützung f public assistance, welfare
Ar′menviertel n slums
Armesün′dermiene f hangdog look
Arm′lehne f arm, armrest
Arm′leuchter m candelabrum
ärmlich [′ermlɪç] adj poor, humble
arm′selig adj poor, wretched; (kläglich) paltry
Armut [′armut] f (−s;) poverty
Arm′zeichen n semaphore
Aro·ma [a′roma] n (−s;−men [mən], −mata [mata]) aroma
aromatisch [arə′matɪʃ] adj aromatic
Arrest [a′rest] m (−[e]s;−e) arrest;

(*in der Schule*) detention; (jur) impounding, seizure

Arsch [arʃ] *m* (-es;⸚e) (sl) ass

Arsch'backe *f* (sl) buttock

Arsch'kriecher *m* (sl) brown-noser

Arsch'lecker *m* (sl) brown-noser

Arsen [ar'zen] *n* (-s;) arsenic

Arsenal [arze'nɑl] *n* (-s;-e) arsenal

Art [art] *f* (-;en) sort, kind; nature; (*Rasse*) race, breed; species; (*Weise*) manner; (*Verfahren*) procedure; (*Muster*) model; **das ist keine Art!** that's no way to behave!

art'eigen *adj* true to type

arten ['artən] *intr* (SEIN)—**a. nach** take after

Arterie [ar'terjə] *f* (-;-n) artery

artig ['urtɪç] *adj* (brav) good, well-behaved; (höflich) polite

Artikel [ar'tikəl] *m* (-s;-) (com, gram, journ) article

Artillerie [artɪlə'ri] *f* (-;) artillery

Artillerie'aufklärer *m* artillery spotter

Artischocke [artɪ'ʃɔkə] *f* (-;-n) artichoke

Artist –in [ar'tɪst(ɪn)] §7 *mf* artist; (*beim Zirkus*) performer

Arznei [arts'nai] *f* (-;-en) medicine, medication, drug

Arznei'kraut *n* herb, medicinal plant

Arznei'kunde *f*, **Arznei'kunst** *f* pharmaceutics; pharmacology

Arznei'mittel *n* medication

Arzt [artst] *m* (-[e]s;⸚e) doctor

Ärztin ['ertstɪn] *f* (-;-nen) doctor

ärztlich ['ertstlɪç] *adj* medical

As [as] *n* (Asses; Asse) ace ‖ *n* (-;-) (mus) A flat

Asbest [as'best] *m* (-[e]s;-e) asbestos

asch'bleich *adj* ashen, pale

Asche ['aʃə] *f* (-;-n) ash(es), cinders

Aschen– comb.fm. ash; cinder; funerary

A'schenbahn *f* cinder track

A'schenbecher *m* ashtray

Aschenbrödel ['aʃənbrødəl] *n* (-s;-) Cinderella; drudge

Aschermittwoch [aʃər'mɪtvɔx] *m* (-s; -e) Ash Wednesday

asch'fahl *adj* ashen, pale

äsen ['ezən] *intr* graze, feed

asiatisch [azi'ati] *adj* Asiatic

Asien ['azjən] *n* (-s;) Asia

Asket [as'ket] *m* (-en;-en) ascetic

asketisch [as'ketɪʃ] *adj* ascetic

Asphalt [as'falt] *m* (-[e]s;-e) asphalt

asphaltieren [asfal'tirən] *tr* asphalt

Asphalt'pappe *f* tar paper

aß [as] *pret of* essen

Assistent –in [asɪs'tent(ɪn)] §7 *mf* assistant

Assistenz [asɪs'tents] *f* (-;-en) assistance

Assistenz'arzt *m*, **Assistenz'ärztin** *f* intern

Ast [ast] *m* (-es;⸚e) bough, branch; (*im Holz*) knot, knob

ästhetisch [es'tetɪʃ] *adj* esthetic(al)

Asthma ['astma] *n* (-s;) asthma

ast'rein *adj* free of knots; **nicht ganz a.** (coll) not quite kosher

Astrologe [astro'logə] *m* (-n;-n) astrologer

Astrologie [astrolo'gi] *f* (-;) astrology

Astronaut [astro'naut] *m* (-en;-en) astronaut

Astronom [astro'nom] *m* (-en;-en) astronomer

Astronomie [astrono'mi] (-;) astronomy

astronomisch [astro'nomɪʃ] *adj* astronomic(al)

Astrophysik [astrofy'zik] *f* (-;) astrophysics

Asyl [a'zyl] *n* (-[e]s;-e) asylum, sanctuary; (*Obdach*) shelter; **ohne A.** homeless

Atelier [ate'lje] *n* (-s;-s) studio

Atem ['atəm] *m* (-s;) breath

A'tembeklemmung *f* shortness of breath

A'temholen *n* (-s;) respiration

a'temlos *adj* breathless

A'temnot *f* breathing difficulty

A'tempause *f* breathing spell

a'temraubend *adj* breath-taking

A'temzug *m* breath

Atheismus (ate'ismus] *m* (-;) atheism

Atheist –in [ate'ist(ɪn)] §7 *mf* atheist

Äther ['etər] *m* (-s;) ether

Athlet [at'let] *m* (-en;-en) athlete

Athletik [at'letɪk] *f* (-;) athletics

Athletin [at'letɪn] *f* (-;-nen) athlete

athletisch [at'letɪʃ] *adj* athletic

Atlantik [at'lantɪk] *m* (-s;) Atlantic

At·las ['atlas] *m* (-;) (myth) Atlas ‖ *m* (-lasses; -lanten ['lantən] & -lasse) atlas ‖ *m* (- & -lasses;-lasse) satin

atmen ['atmən] *tr & intr* breathe

Atmosphäre [atmo'sferə] *f* (-;-n) (& fig) atmosphere

atmosphärisch [atmo'sferɪʃ] *adj* atmospheric; **atmosphärische Störungen** (rad) static

At'mung *f* (-;) breathing

Atom [a'tom] *n* (-s;-e) atom

Atom– comb. fm. atom, atomic

Atom'abfall *m* fallout; atomic waste

atomar [ato'mar] *adj* atomic

Atom'bau *m* atomic structure

atom'betrieben *adj* atomic-powered

Atom'bombe *f* atomic bomb

Atom'bombenversuch *m* atomic test

Atom'-Epoche *f* atomic age

Atom'kern *m* atomic nucleus

Atom'müll *m* atomic waste

Atom'regen *m* fallout

Atom'schutt *m* atomic waste

ätsch [etʃ] *interj* (to express gloating) serves you right!, good for you!

Attentat [aten'tat] *n* (-s;-e) attempt (*on s.o.'s life*); assassination

Attentäter –in [aten'tetər(ɪn)] §6 *mf* assailant, would-be assassin; assassin

Attest [a'test] *n* (-es;-e) certificate

attestieren [ates'tirən] *tr* attest (to)

Attrappe [a'trapə] *f* (-;-n) dummy

Attribut [atri'but] *n* (-[e]s;-e) attribute; (gram) attributive

atzen ['atsən] *tr* feed

ätzen ['etsən] *tr* corrode; (med) cauterize; (typ) etch

ät'zend *adj* corrosive; caustic

Au [au] *f* (-;-en) (poet) mead, meadow

au *interj* owl, ouch!; oh!

Aubergine [ɔbɛr'ʒin(ə)] *f* (-;-n) eggplant

auch [aux] *adv* also, too; *(selbst)* even

Audienz [au'djɛnts] *f* (-;-en) audience; *(jur)* hearing

auf [auf] *adv* up; **auf und ab** up and down; **von Kind auf** from childhood on ‖ *prep (dat)* on, upon; **auf der ganzen Welt** in the whole world; **auf der Universität** at the university ‖ *prep (acc)* on; up; to; **auf den Bahnhof gehen** go to the station; **auf deutsch** in German; **drei aufs Dutzend** three to a dozen; **es geht auf vier Uhr** zu it's going on four; **Monat auf Monat** verging month after month passed ‖ *interj* get up! ‖ **Auf** *n*—**das Auf und Nieder** the ups and downs

auf'arbeiten *tr (Rückstände)* catch up on; *(verbrauchen)* use up; *(erneuern)* renovate; *(mach)* recondition ‖ *ref* work one's way up

auf'atmen *intr* breathe a sigh of relief

aufbahren ['aufbɑrən] *tr* lay out

Auf'bau *m* (-[e]s;) construction; structure; organization; *(Anlage)* arrangement, setup; *(chem)* synthesis ‖ *m* (-[e]s;-ten) structure; *(aer)* framework; *(aut)* body; *(naut)* superstructure

auf'bauen *tr* erect; *(Organization)* establish; *(chem)* synthesize; *(mach)* assemble ‖ *ref*—**er baute sich vor mir auf** he planted himself in front of me; **sich** [*dat*] **e-e Existenz a.** make a life for oneself

auf'bäumen *ref* rear; *(fig)* rebel

auf'bauschen *tr* puff up; *(fig)* exaggerate

auf'begehren *intr* flare up; *(gegen)* protest (against), rebel (against)

auf'behalten §90 *tr* keep on; keep open

auf'bekommen §99 *tr (Tür)* get open; *(Knoten)* loosen; *(Hausaufgabe)* be assigned

auf'bereiten *tr* prepare, process

auf'bessern *tr (Gehalt)* improve, raise

auf'bewahren *tr* keep, store; **das Gepäck a. lassen** check one's baggage

auf'bieten §58 *tr* summon; *(Brautpaar)* announce the banns of; *(mil)* call up

auf'binden §58 *tr* tie up; *(lösen)* untie; **j-m etw a.** put s.th. over on s.o.

auf'blähen *tr* inflate, distend

auf'blasen §61 *tr* inflate ‖ *ref* get puffed up

auf'bleiben §62 *intr* (SEIN) *(Tür)* stay open; *(wachen)* stay up

auf'blenden *intr* turn on the high beam

auf'blicken *intr* glance up

auf'blitzen *intr* (HABEN & SEIN) flash

auf'blühen *intr* (SEIN) begin to bloom

auf'bocken *tr* (aut) jack up

auf'brauchen *tr* use up

auf'brausen *intr* (HABEN & SEIN) bubble, seethe; *(Wind)* roar; *(fig)* flare up

auf'brausend *adj* effervescent; irascible

auf'brechen §64 *tr* break up; break open; *(hunt)* eviscerate ‖ *intr* (SEIN)

burst open; *(fortgehen)* (nach) set out (for)

auf'bringen §65 *tr* bring up; *(Geld, Truppen)* raise; *(Schiff)* capture; *(Kraft)* gather; *(Mut)* get up; *(erzürnen)* infuriate

Auf'bruch *m* departure

auf'brühen *tr* bring to a boil

auf'bügeln *tr* iron, press; refresh *(one's knowledge of s.th.)*

aufbürden ['aufbyrdən] *tr*—**j-m etw a.** saddle s.o. with s.th.

auf'decken *tr* uncover; *(Bett)* turn down; *(Tischtuch)* spread

auf'drängen *tr* force open; **j-m etw a.** force s.th. on s.o.

auf'drehen *tr* turn up; *(Uhr)* wind; *(Hahn)* turn on; *(Schraube)* unscrew; *(Strick)* untwist ‖ *intr (Wagen)* increase speed; *(coll)* step on it, get a move on

auf'dringlich *adj* pushy; *(Farben)* gaudy

Auf'druck *m* print, imprint

auf'drücken *tr* impress, imprint, affix; *(öffnen)* squeeze open

aufeinan'der *adv* one after the other

Aufeinan'derfolge *f* succession; series

aufeinan'derfolgen *intr* (SEIN) follow one another

aufeinan'derfolgend *adj* successive

Aufenthalt ['aufɛnthalt] *m* (-[e]s;-e) holdup, delay; **ohne A.** nonstop

Auf'enthaltsgenehmigung *f* residence permit

Auf'enthaltsort *m (Wohnsitz)* residence; *(Verbleib)* whereabouts

Auf'enthaltsraum *m* lounge

auf'erlegen *tr* impose ‖ *ref*—**sich** [*dat*] **die Pflicht a. zu** (*inf*) make it one's duty to (*inf*); **sich** [*dat*] **Zwang a.** müssen have to restrain oneself

auf'erstehen §146 *intr* (SEIN) rise (from the dead)

Auf'erstehung *f* (-;) resurrection

auf'erwecken *tr* raise from the dead

auf'erziehen §163 *tr* bring up, raise

auf'essen §70 *tr* eat up

auf'fädeln *tr (Perlen)* string

auf'fahren §71 *tr (Fahrzeuge)* park; *(Geschütze)* bring up; *(Wein, Speisen)* serve up ‖ *intr* (SEIN) rise, mount; *(im Auto)* pull up; *(in Erregung)* jump (up); *(arti)* move into position; **a. auf** *(acc)* run into

Auf'fahrt *f* ascent; *(Zufahrt)* driveway

auf'fallen §72 *intr* (SEIN) be conspicuous; **j-m a.** strike s.o.

auf'fallend, auf'fällig *adj* striking; noticeable; *(Farben)* loud, gaudy

auf'fangen §73 *tr (Ball, Worte)* catch; *(Briefe, Nachrichten)* intercept

auf'fassen *tr* comprehend; *(deuten)* interpret; *(Perlen)* string

Auf'fassung *f* (-;-en) understanding, interpretation; *(Meinung)* view

auf'finden §59 *tr* find *(after searching)*

auf'fliegen §57 *intr* (SEIN) fly up; *(Tür)* fly open; *(scheitern)* fail; **a. lassen** break up *(e.g., a gang)*

auf'fordern *tr* call upon, ask

Auf'forderung *f* (-;-en) invitation; *(jur)* summons

auf'frischen *tr* freshen up, touch up

auf'führen *tr* (*Bau*) erect; (*Schauspiel*) present; (*eintragen*) enter; (*Zeugen*) produce; (*anführen*) cite; (*mil*) post; **einzeln a.** itemize || *ref* behave, act

Auf'führung *f* (–;–en) erection; performance; entry; specification; behavior

auf'füllen *tr* fill up

Auf'gabe *f* task, job; (*e-s Briefes*) mailing; (*des Gepäcks*) checking; (*e-r Bestellung*) placing; (*e-s Amtes, e-s Geschäfts*) giving up; (*educ*) homework; (*jur*) waiver; (*math*) problem; (*mil*) assignment

auf'gabeln *tr* (& coll) pick up

Auf'gang *m* ascent; (*Treppe*) stairs; (*astr*) rising

auf'geben §80 *tr* give up; (*Amt*) resign; (*Post*) mail; (*Gepäck*) check in; (*Anzeige*) place; (*Preis*) quote; (*Arbeit*) assign; (*Telegramm*) send

auf'geblasen *adj* (fig) uppity

Auf'gebot *n* public notice; (eccl) banns; (mil) call-up

auf'gebracht *adj* angry, irate

auf'gedonnert *adj* (coll) dolled up

auf'gehen §82 *intr* (SEIN) rise; (*Tür*) open; (*Pflanzen*) come up; (arith) go into; **genau a.** come out exactly

auf'geklärt *adj* enlightened

auf'geknöpft *adj* (coll) chatty

auf'gekratzt *adj* (coll) chipper

Auf'geld *n* surcharge; premium

auf'gelegt *adj* (zu) disposed (to)

auf'geräumt *adj* (fig) good-humored

auf'geschlossen *adj* open-minded; (für) receptive (to)

auf'geschmissen *adj* (coll) stuck

auf'gestaut *adj* pent-up

auf'geweckt *adj* smart, bright

auf'geworfen *adj* (*Lippen*) pouting; (*Nase*) turned-up

auf'gießen §76 *tr* (auf acc) pour (on); (*Tee, Kaffee*) make, brew

auf'graben §87 *tr* dig up

auf'greifen §88 *tr* pick up; (*Dieb*) catch; (fig) take up

auf'haben §98 *tr* (*Hut*) have on; (*Tür, Mund*) have open; (*Aufgabe*) have to do

auf'hacken *tr* hoe up

auf'haken *tr* unhook

auf'halten §90 *tr* hold up; (*Tür*) hold open; (*anhalten*) stop, delay || *ref* stay; (*wohnen*) live; **sich über etw a.** find fault with s.th.

Auf'hängeleine *f* clothesline

auf'hängen §92 *tr* hang up; **j-m etw a.** push s.th. on s.o.; (*Wertloses*) palm s.th. off on s.o.

auf'häufen *tr* & *ref* pile up

auf'heben §94 *tr* lift up, pick up; (*bewahren*) preserve; (*ungültig machen*) cancel; (*Gesetz*) repeal; (*ausgleichen*) cancel out, offset; (*Strafe, Belagerung*) lift; **gut aufgehoben sein** be in good hands

auf'heitern *tr* cheer up || *ref* cheer up; (*Gesicht*) brighten; (*Wetter*) clear up

auf'hellen *ref* & *intr* brighten

auf'hetzen *tr* incite, egg on

auf'holen *tr* hoist; (*Verspätung*) make up for || *intr* catch up

auf'horchen *intr* prick up one's ears

auf'hören *intr* stop, quit

auf'jauchzen *intr* shout for joy

auf'kaufen *tr* buy up; (*Markt*) corner

auf'klären *tr* clear up; enlighten; (mil) reconnoitre || *ref* clear up; (*Gesicht*) light up, brighten

Auf'klärer *m* (–s;–) (aer) reconnaissance plane; (mil) scout

Auf'klärung *f* (–;–en) explanation; enlightenment; (mil) reconnaissance

Auf'klärungsbuch *n* sex-education book

Auf'klärungsspähtrupp *m* reconnaissance patrol

auf'kleben *tr* (auf acc) paste (onto)

auf'klinken *tr* unlatch

auf'knacken *tr* crack open

auf'knöpfen *tr* unbutton

auf'knüpfen *tr* (lösen) untie; (hängen) (coll) string up

auf'kochen *tr* & *intr* boil

auf'kommen §99 *intr* (SEIN) come up, rise; (*Gedanke*) occur; (*Mode*) come into fashion; (*Schiff*) appear on the horizon; **a. für** answer for; (*Kosten*) defray; **a. gegen** stand up against, cope with; **a. von** recover from ||

Aufkommen *n* (–s;) rise; recovery

auf'krempeln *tr* roll up

auf'kreuzen *intr* (coll) show up

auf'kriegen *tr* see aufbekommen

auf'lachen *intr* burst out laughing

auf'laden §103 *tr* load up; (*Batterie*) charge || *ref–sich* [*dat*] **etw a.** saddle oneself with s.th.

Auf'lage *f* edition, printing; (*e-r Zeitung*) circulation; (*Steuer*) tax; (*Stütze*) rest, support

auf'lassen §104 *tr* leave open; (*Fabrik, Bergwerk*) abandon

auf'lauern *intr* (dat) lie in wait (for)

Auf'lauf *m* gathering, crowd; (*Tumult*) riot; (com) accumulation; (culin) soufflé

auf'laufen §105 *intr* (SEIN) rise; (*anwachsen*) accrue; (*Schiff*) get stranded; (*Panzer*) get stuck

auf'leben *intr* (SEIN) revive

auf'lecken *tr* lick up

auf'legen *tr* (auf acc) put (on); (*Steuer*) impose; (*Hörer*) hang up; (*Buch*) publish; (*Karten*) lay on the table; (*Liste*) make available for inspection; (*Anleihe*) float; (*Faß Bier*) put on || *intr* (telp) hang up

auf'lehnen *tr* (auf acc) lean (on) || *ref* (auf acc) lean (on); (gegen) rebel (against)

Auf'lehnung *f* (–;–en) rebellion; resistance

auf'lesen §107 *tr* pick up, gather

auf'liegen §108 *intr* (auf dat) lie (on); (zur Ansicht) be displayed

auf'lockern *tr* loosen; (*Eintönigkeit, Vortrag*) break (up)

auf'lösbar *adj* soluble; solvable

auf'lösen *tr* untie; (öffnen) loosen; (entwirren) disentangle; (*Versammlung*) break up; (*Heer*) disband; (*Ehe*) dissolve; (*Verbindung*) sever; (*Firma*) liquidate; (*Rätsel*) solve;

(*zerlegen*) break down; dissolve; (*entziffern*) decode; **ganz aufgelöst** all out of breath

Auf'lösung *f* (-;-en) solution; disentanglement; (*e-r Versammlung, Ehe*) breakup; (*Zerfall*) disintegration; (*von Beziehungen*) severance; (com) liquidation

auf'machen *tr* open (up); (*Geschäft*) open; (*Dampf*) get up; (coll) do up (*e.g., big, tastefully*) || *ref* (*Wind*) rise; (*nach*) set out (for)

Auf'machung *f* (-;-en) layout, format; (*Kleidung*) outfit

Auf'marsch *m* parade; (mil) concentration; (*zum Gefecht*) (mil) deployment

auf'marschieren *intr* (SEIN) parade; (*strategisch*) assemble; (*taktisch*) deploy

auf'merken *tr* (auf *acc*) pay attention (to)

aufmerksam ['aufmerkzam] *adj* (auf *acc*) attentive (to)

Auf'merksamkeit *f* (-;) attention

auf'möbeln *tr* (coll) dress up; (*anherrschen*) (sl) chew out; (*aufmuntern*) (coll) pep up || *ref* (coll) doll up

auf'muntern *tr* cheer up

Auf'nahme *f* (-;-n) taking up; (*Empfang*) reception (*Zulassung*) admission; (*von Beziehungen*) establishment; (*Inventur*) stock-taking; (electron) recording; (phot) photograph

Auf'nahmeapparat *m* camera; recorder

Auf'nahmegerät *n* camera; recorder

Auf'nahmeprüfung *f* entrance exam

auf'nehmen §116 *tr* take up; (*erfassen*) grasp; (*Diktat*) take down; (*Gast*) receive; (*Inventar*) take; (*Geld*) borrow; (*Anleihe*) float; (*Spur*) pick up; (*Beziehungen*) establish; (*eintragen*) enter; (*durch* Tonband, Schallplatte) record; (geog) map out; (phot) take

auf'opfern *tr* offer up, sacrifice

auf'päpeln *tr* spoon-feed

auf'passen *intr* pay attention; look out; **paß auf!** watch out!

auf'pflanzen *tr* set up; (*Seitengewehr*) fix

auf'platzen *intr* (SEIN) burst (open)

auf'polieren *tr* polish up

auf'prägen *tr* (auf *acc*) (& fig) impress (on)

auf'prallen *intr* (auf *acc*) crash (into)

auf'pumpen *tr* pump up

auf'putschen *tr* incite; (coll) pep up

auf'putzen *tr* dress up; clean up || *ref* dress up

auf'raffen *tr* pick up || *ref* stand up; (fig) pull oneself together

auf'ragen *intr* tower, stand high

auf'räumen *tr* (*Zimmer*) straighten up; (*wegräumen*) clear away || *intra*—**a. mit** do away with, get rid of

Auf'räumungsarbeiten *pl* clearance

auf'rechnen *tr* add up; (acct) balance

auf'recht *adj* upright, erect

auf'rechterhalten §90 *tr* maintain

auf'regen *tr* excite, stir up; (*unruhig machen*) disturb, upset

Auf'regung *f* (-;-en) excitement

auf'reiben §62 *tr* rub off; (*wundreiben*) rub sore; (*vertilgen*) destroy; (*Heer*) grind up; (*Kräfte*) sap; (*Nerven*) fray || *ref* worry onself to death

auf'reibend *adj* wearing, exhausting

auf'reihen *tr* string, thread

auf'reißen §53 *tr* tear open; (*Straße*) tear up; (*Tür*) fling open; (*Augen*) open wide; (*zeichnen*) sketch || *intr* (SEIN) split open, crack

auf'reizen *tr* provoke, incite; (*stark erregen*) excite

auf'reizend *adj* provoking, annoying; (*Rede*) inflammatory; (*Anblick*) sexy

auf'richten *tr* erect, set up; (*trösten*) comfort || *ref* sit up

auf'richtig *adj* upright, sincere

Auf'richtigkeit *f* sincerity

auf'riegeln *tr* unbolt

Auf'riß *m* front view

auf'rollen *tr* roll up; (*entfalten*) unroll

auf'rücken *intr* (SEIN) advance; (zu) be promoted (to)

Auf'ruf *m* (*Aufschrei*) outcry; (*Aufforderung*) call; (mil) call-up

auf'rufen §122 *tr* call on; (*appellieren an*) appeal to; (*Banknoten*) call in

Auf'ruhr *m* uproar; (*Tumult*) riot

auf'rühren *tr* stir up

aufrührerisch ['aufryrərɪʃ] *adj* inflammatory, rebellious; (mil) mutinous

auf'runden *tr* round out

auf'rüsten *tr* & *intr* arm; rearm

Auf'rüstung *f* (-;-en) rearmament

auf'rütteln *tr* wake up (by shaking)

auf'sagen *tr* recite; (*ein Ende machen mit*) terminate

auf'sammeln *tr* gather up

aufsässig ['aufzɛsɪç] *adj* hostile; (*widerspenstig*) rebellious

Auf'satz *m* superstructure; (*auf dem Tische*) centerpiece; (*Schularbeit*) essay, composition; (*in der Zeitung*) article; (golf) tee; (mil) gun sight

auf'saugen §125 *tr* suck up; absorb

auf'schauen *intr* look up

auf'scheuchen *tr* scare up

auf'scheuern *tr* scrape

auf'schichten *tr* stack (up), pile (up)

auf'schieben §130 *tr* push up; (*Tür*) push open; (*verschieben*) postpone

auf'schießen §76 *intr* (SEIN) shoot up

Auf'schlag *m* (auf *acc*) striking (up), impact (on); (*an Kleidung*) cuff, lapel; (*Steuer–*) surtax; (*Preis–*) price hike; (tennis) service, serve

auf'schlagen §132 *tr* (*öffnen*) open; (*Ei*) crack; (*Karte, Ärmel*) turn up; (*Zelt*) pitch; (*Wohnung*) take up; (*Preis*) raise; (*Knie, usw.*) bruise; (*Ball*) serve || *intr* (SEIN) (*Tür*) fly open; (*Flugzeug*) crash; (*Ball*) bounce; (tennis) serve

auf'schließen §76 *tr* unlock, open || *ref* (*dat*) pour out one's heart (to) || *intr* (mil) close ranks

auf'schlitzen *tr* slit open

Auf'schluß *m* information; (chem) decomposition

auf'schlußreich *adj* informative

auf'schnallen *tr* buckle; unbuckle

auf'schnappen *tr* snap up; (*Nachricht*) pick up

Auf′schneidemaschine *f* meat slicer
auf′schneiden §106 *tr* cut open; *(Fleisch)* slice ‖ *intr* (coll) talk big
Auf′schneider *m* boaster
Auf′schnitt *m—kalter A.* cold cuts
auf′schnüren *tr* untie, undo
auf′schrauben *tr* unscrew; (auf *acc*) screw (on)
auf′schrecken §134 *tr* startle; *(Wild)* scare up ‖ *intr* (SEIN) be startled
Auf′schrei *m* scream, yell; (fig) outcry
auf′schreiben §62 *tr* write down
auf′schreien §135 *intr* scream, yell
Auf′schrift *f* inscription; *(Anschrift)* address; *(e-r Flasche)* label
Auf′schub *m* deferment, postponement; *(Verzögerung)* delay; (jur) stay
auf′schürfen *tr* scrape; *(Bein)* skin
auf′schwellen §119 *intr* (SEIN) swell up; *(Fluß)* rise
auf′schwemmen *tr* bloat
auf′schwingen §142 *ref* (& fig) soar; **sich a.,** etw zu tun bring oneself to do s.th.
Auf′schwung *m* (& fig) upswing
auf′sehen §138 *intr* look up ‖ **Aufsehen** *n* (–s;) sensation, stir
auf′sehenerregend *adj* sensational
Auf′seher –in *m* §6 *mf* supervisor; *(im Museum)* guard; *(im Geschäft)* floorwalker
auf′sein §139 *intr* (SEIN) be up; *(Tür)* be open
auf′setzen *tr* put on; *(aufrichten)* set up; *(schriftlich)* compose, draft ‖ *ref* sit up ‖ *intr* (aer) touch down; (rok) splash down
Auf′sicht *f* inspection, supervision
Auf′sichtsbeamte *m,* **Auf′sichtsbeamtin** *f* inspector, supervisor
Auf′sichtsbehörde *f* control board
Auf′sichtsdame *f* floorwalker
Auf′sichtsherr *m* floorwalker
Auf′sichtsrat *m* board of trustees; *(Mitglied)* trustee
auf′sitzen §144 *intr* (SEIN) sit up; (auf *dat*) sit (on), rest (on); **j—m a.** be taken in by s.o.; **j—n a.** lassen stand s.o. up
auf′spannen *tr* stretch, spread; *(Regenschirm)* open
auf′sparen *tr* save (up)
auf′speichern *tr* store (up)
auf′sperren *tr* unlock; *(Augen, Tür)* open wide
auf′spielen *tr* strike up ‖ *ref* (mit) show off (with) ‖ *intr* play dance music
auf′spießen *tr* spear, pierce
auf′sprengen *tr* force open; *(mit Sprengstoff)* blow up
auf′springen §142 *intr* (SEIN) jump up; *(Tür)* fly open; *(Ball)* bounce; *(Haut)* chap, crack
auf′spritzen *tr (Farbe)* spray on; (sl) shoot up ‖ *intr* (SEIN) squirt up
auf′sprudeln *intr* (SEIN) bubble (up)
auf′spulen *tr* wind up
auf′spüren *tr* track down, ferret out
auf′stacheln *tr* goad; (fig) stir up
auf′stampfen *intr—mit dem Fuß a.* stamp one's foot
Auf′stand *m* insurrection, uprising

aufständisch ['ɑʊf/tɛndɪʃ] *adj* insurgent ‖ **Aufständischen** *pl* insurgents
auf′stapeln *tr* stack up, pile up
auf′stechen §64 *tr* puncture; (surg) lance
auf′stecken *tr (Flagge)* plant; *(Haar)* pin up; (coll) give up; **j—m ein Licht a.** enlighten s.o.
auf′stehen §146 *intr* (HABEN) stand open ‖ *intr* (SEIN) stand up, get up; *(gegen)* revolt (against)
auf′steigen §148 *intr* (SEIN) climb; *(Reiter)* mount; *(Rauch)* rise; *(Gewitter)* come up; *(Tränen)* well up; **a. auf** (*acc*) get on
auf′stellen *tr* set up, put up; *(Beispiel)* set; *(Behauptung)* make; *(Wachposten)* post; *(Bauten)* erect; *(Leiter)* raise; *(Waren)* display; *(Maschine)* assemble; *(als Kandidaten)* nominate; *(Regel, Problem)* state; *(Lehre)* propound; *(Rekord)* set; *(Liste)* make out; *(Rechnung)* draw up, make out; *(Stühle)* arrange; *(Falle)* set; *(Bedingungen, Grundsätze)* lay down; *(Beweis)* furnish ‖ *ref* station oneself
Auf′stellung *f* (–;–en) erection; assertion; list, schedule; (mil) formation; (pol) nomination; (sport) lineup
auf′stemmen *tr* pry open ‖ *ref* prop oneself up
Auf′stieg *m* climb; *(Steigung)* slope; (fig) advancement
auf′stöbern *tr* ferret out; (fig) unearth
auf′stoßen §150 *tr* push open ‖ *ref—* **sich** *[dat]* **das Knie a.** skin one's knee ‖ *intr* (HABEN) belch ‖ *intr* (HABEN & SEIN) bump, touch; *(Schiff)* touch bottom ‖ *intr* (SEIN)—**j—m a.** strike s.o., cross s.o.'s mind
auf′streichen §85 *tr (Butter)* spread
auf′streuen *tr* (auf *acc*) sprinkle (on)
Auf′strich *m* upstroke; *(auf Brot)* spread
auf′stützen *tr* prop up
auf′suchen *tr* search for; *(nachschlagen)* look up; *(Ort)* visit; *(aufsammeln)* pick up; *(Arzt)* go to see
Auf′takt *m* upbeat; (fig) prelude
auf′tauchen *intr* (SEIN) turn up, appear; *(Frage)* crop up; *(U-Boot)* surface; *(Gerücht)* arise
auf′tauen *tr & intr* (SEIN) thaw
auf′teilen *tr* divide up
Auf′trag *m* (–[e]s;̈e) *(Anweisung)* orders, instructions; *(Bestellung)* order, commission; *(Sendung)* mission; **in A. von** on behalf of
auf′tragen §132 *tr* instruct, order; *(Speise)* serve; *(Farben, Butter)* put on; *(Kleidungsstück)* wear out; (surv) plot; **j—m etw a.** impose s.th. on s.o. ‖ *intr—dick* (or stark) a. (sl) put it on thick
Auf′traggeber –in *m* §6 *mf* employer; *(Besteller)* client, customer
Auf′tragsformular *n* order blank
auf′tragsgemäß, auf′trag(s)mäßig *adv* as ordered, according to instructions
auf′treffen §151 *intr* (SEIN) strike
Auf′treffpunkt *m* point of impact
auf′treiben §62 *tr (Staub; Geld)* raise;

(*Wild*) flush; (*aufblähen*) distend; (*Teig*) cause to rise

auf'trennen *tr* rip, undo, unstitch

auf'treten §152 *tr* (*Tür*) kick open || *intr* (SEIN) step, tread; (*erscheinen*) appear; (*handeln*) act, behave; (*eintreten*) occur, crop up; (*pathol*) break out; (*theat*) enter || **Auftreten** *n* (-s;) appearance; occurrence; behavior; **sicheres A.** poise

Auf'trieb *m* drive; buoyancy; (aer & fig) lift; (agr) cattle drive; **j-m A. geben** encourage s.o.

Auf'tritt *m* (*Streit*) scene, row; (theat) entrance (*of an actor*); (theat) scene

auf'trumpfen *intr* play a higher trump; **gegen j-n a.** go to s.o. better

auf'tun §154 *tr* & *ref* open

auf'türmen *tr* & *intr* pile up

auf'wachen *intr* (SEIN) awaken, wake up

auf'wachsen §155 *intr* (SEIN) grow up

auf'wallen *intr* (SEIN) boil, seethe; (fig) surge, rise up

Auf'wallung *f* (-;-en) (fig) outburst

Aufwand ['aufvant] *m* (-[e]s;) (an *dat*) expenditure (of); (*Prunk*) show

auf'wärmen *tr* warm up; (fig) drag up

Auf'wartefrau *f* cleaning woman

auf'warten *intr* (*dat*) wait on; **a. mit** oblige with, offer

Auf'wärter –in §6 *mf* attendant || *f* cleaning woman

aufwärts ['aufverts] *adv* upward(s)

Auf'wärtshaken *m* (box) uppercut

Auf'wartung *f* (-;) attendance; (*bei Tisch*) service; (*Besuch*) call; **j-m seine A. machen** pay one's respects to s.o.

Aufwasch ['aufva/] *m* (-es;) washing; dirty dishes

auf'waschen §158 *tr* & *intr* wash up

auf'wecken *tr* wake (up)

auf'weichen *tr* soften; soak || *intr* (SEIN) become soft; become sodden

auf'weisen §118 *tr* produce, show

auf'wenden §140 *tr* spend, expend; **Mühe a.** take pains

auf'werfen §160 *tr* throw up; (*Tür*) fling open; (*Graben*) dig; (*Frage*) raise || *ref*—**sich a. zu** set oneself up as

auf'wickeln *tr* wind up; (*Haar*) curl; (*loswickeln*) unwind

auf'wiegeln ['aufvigəln] *tr* instigate

Aufwiegler –in ['aufviglər(in)] §6 *mf* instigator

aufwieglerisch ['aufvigləri/] *adj* inflammatory

Auf'wind *m* updraft

auf'winden §59 *tr* wind up; (*Anker*) weigh || *ref* coil up

auf'wirbeln *tr* (*Staub*) raise; **viel Staub a.** (coll) make quite a stir

auf'wischen *tr* wipe up

auf'wühlen *tr* dig up; (*Wasser*) churn up; (fig) stir up

auf'zählen *tr* enumerate, itemize

auf'zäumen *tr* bridle

auf'zehren *tr* consume

auf'zeichnen *tr* make a sketch of; (*notieren*) write down, record

aufzeigen *tr* point out

auf'ziehen §163 *tr* pull up; (*öffnen*) pull open; (*Uhr*) wind; (*Saite*) put on; (*Perlen*) string; (*Kind*) bring up; (*Tier*) breed; (*Pflanzen*) grow; (*Flagge, Segel*) hoist (*Anker*) weigh; (*Veranstaltung*) arrange, organize; (coll) kid || *intr* (SEIN) approach, pull up

Auf'zucht *f* breeding, raising

Auf'zug *m* elevator; (*-r Uhr*) winder; (*Aufmarsch*) parade , procession; (gym) chin-up; (theat) act

auf'zwingen §142 *tr*—**j-m etw a.** force s.th. on s.o.; **j-m seinen Willen a.** impose one's will on s.o.

Augapfel ['aukapfəl] *m* eyeball; (fig) apple of the eye

Auge ['augə] *n* (-s;-n) eye; (*auf Würfeln*) dot; (*hort*) bud; (*typ*) face

äugeln ['ɔɪgəln] *intr*—**ä. mit** wink at

Augen— [augən] *comb.fm.* eye, of the eye(s), in the eye(s); visual; (anat) ocular, optic(al)

Au'genblick *m* moment, instant

au'genblicklich *adj* momentary; (*sofortig*) immediate, instantaneous

Au'genblicksmensch *m* hedonist; impulsive person

Au'genbraue *f* eyebrow

Au'genbrauenstift *m* eyebrow pencil

au'genfällig *adj* conspicuous, obvious

Au'genhöhle *f* eye socket

Au'genlicht *n* eyesight

Au'genlid *n* eyelid

Au'genmaß *n* sense of proportion; **ein gutes A. haben** have a keen eye; **nach dem A.** by eye

Au'genmerk *n* attention

Au'gennerv *m* optic nerve

Au'genschein *m* inspection; (*Anschein*) appearances; **in A. nehmen** inspect

au'genscheinlich *adj* obvious

Au'genstern *m* pupil; iris

Au'gentäuschung *f* optical illusion

Au'gentrost *m* sight for sore eyes

Au'genwasser *n* eyewash

Au'genweide *f* sight for sore eyes

Au'genwimper *f* eyelash

Au'genwinkel *m* corner of the eye

Au'genzeuge *m*, **Au'genzeugin** *f* eyewitness

-äugig [ɔɪgɪç] *comb.fm.* -eyed

August [au'gust] *m* (-[e]s & -;-e) August

Auktion [auk'tsjon] *f* (-;-en) auction

Auktio-nator [auktsjo'natɔr] *m* (-s; -natoren [na'torən]) auctioneeer

auktionieren [auktsjo'nirən] *tr* auction off, put up for auction

Au-la ['aula] *f* (-;-s & -len [lən]) auditorium

aus [aus] *adv* out; **von ... aus** from, e.g., **vom Fenster aus** from the window || *prep* (*dat*) out of, from; **because of**

aus'arbeiten *tr* elaborate; finish || *ref* work out, take physical exercise

Aus'arbeitung *f* (-;-en) elaboration; (*schriftlich*) composition; (*körperlich*) workout; (tech) finish

aus'arten *intr* (SEIN) get out of hand; (**in** *acc*) degenerate (into)

aus'atmen *tr* exhale

aus'baden *tr* (coll) take the rap for
aus'baggern *tr* dredge
Aus'bau *m* (–[e]s;) completion; expansion, development
aus'bauen *tr* complete; (*erweitern*) expand, develop
aus'bedingen *tr* stipulate
aus'bessern *tr* repair; (*Kleid*) mend; (*Bild*) retouch
aus'beulen *tr* take the dents out of
Aus'beute *f* (*Ertrag*) output; (*Gewinn*) profit, gain
ausbeuten ['ausbɔɪtən] *tr* exploit
aus'biegen §57 *tr* bend out || *intr* (SEIN) curve; (*dat*, **vor** *dat*) make way (for)
aus'bilden *tr* develop; (*lehren*) train, educate; (mil) drill || *ref* train
Aus'bilder *m* (mil) drill instructor
aus'bitten §60 *ref*—**sich** [*dat*] **etw a.** ask for s.th.; insist on s.th.
aus'bleiben §62 *intr* (SEIN) stay out; stay away; be missing
aus'bleichen §85 *tr & intr* (SEIN) bleach; fade
aus'blenden *tr* (cin, rad) fade-out
Aus'blick *m* (**auf** *acc*) view (of); (fig) outlook
aus'bohren *tr* bore (out), drill (out)
aus'borgen *ref*—**sich** [*dat*] **etw a. von** borrow s.th. from
aus'brechen §64 *tr* break off || *intr* (SEIN) (**aus**) break out (of)
aus'breiten *tr & ref* spread; extend
aus'brennen §97 *tr* burn out, gut; (*Sonne*) parch; (med) cauterize || *intr* (SEIN) burn out; (*Haus*) be gutted
Aus'bruch *m* outbreak; (*e–s Vulkans*) eruption; (*e–s Gefangenen*) breakout; (*des Gelächters*) outburst
aus'brüten *tr* incubate; hatch
Ausbuchtung ['ausbuxtuŋ] *f* (–;–en) bulge
ausbuddeln ['ausbudəln] *tr* (coll) dig out
aus'bügeln *tr* iron out
Aus'bund *m* (**von**) very embodiment (of)
ausbürgern ['ausbʏrgərn] *tr* expatriate
aus'bürsten *tr* brush out
Aus'dauer *f* perseverance
aus'dauern *intr* persevere, persist
aus'dauernd *adj* persevering; (bot) perennial
aus'dehnen *tr & ref* stretch, expand; (*Organ*) dilate
aus'denken §66 *tr* think out; think up; **nicht auszudenken** inconceivable
aus'deuten *tr* interpret, explain
aus'dienen *intr* serve one's time
aus'dorren *intr* (SEIN) dry up; wither
aus'dörren *tr* dry up, parch
aus'drehen *tr* turn out; turn off
Aus'druck *m* expression
aus'drücken *tr* squeeze out; (fig) express
ausdrücklich ['ausdrʏklɪç] *adj* express, explicit
aus'druckslos *adj* expressionless
aus'drucksvoll *adj* expressive
Aus'drucksweise *f* way of speaking
aus'dünsten *tr* exhale, give off || *intr* evaporate; (*schwitzen*) sweat

auseinan'der *adv* apart; separately
auseinan'derfallen §72 *intr* (SEIN) fall apart
auseinan'dergehen §82 *intr* (SEIN) part; (*Versammlung*) break up; (*Meinungen*) differ; (*Wege*) branch off; (*auseinanderfallen*) come apart
auseinan'derhalten §90 *tr* keep apart
auseinan'derlaufen §105 *intr* (SEIN) (*Menge*) disperse; (*Wege*) diverge
auseinan'dernehmen §116 *tr* take apart
auseinan'dersetzen *tr* explain || *ref*—**sich mit etw a.** come to grips with s.th.; **sich mit j–m a.** have it out with s.o.; (*gütlich*) come to an understanding with s.o.
Auseinan'dersetzung *f* explanation; (*Erörterung*) discussion, controversy; (*Übereinkommen*) arrangement
aus'erkoren *adj* chosen; predestined
aus'erlesen *adj* choice || §107 *tr* choose, select
aus'ersehen §138 *tr* destine
aus'erwählen *tr* pick out, choose
aus'fahren §71 *tr* (*Straße, Gleis*) wear out; (aer) let down; **den Motor a.** (coll) open it up; **die Kurve a.** not cut the corner || *intr* (SEIN) drive out; (naut) put to sea; (rr) pull out
Aus'fahrt *f* departure; exit; (*Spazierfahrt*) ride, drive; (*Torweg*) gateway
Aus'fall *m* falling out; (*Ergebnis*) result; (*Verlust*) loss; (fencing) lunge; (mach) breakdown; (mil) sally
aus'fallen §72 *intr* (SEIN) fall out; (*nicht stattfinden*) fail to take place; (*ausgelassen werden*) be omitted; (*versagen*) go out of commission; (*Ergebnis*) turn out; (mil) sortie
aus'fallend *adj* aggressive, insulting
aus'fechten §74 *tr* (*Kampf*) fight; (*Streit*) settle (by fighting)
aus'fegen *tr* sweep (out)
aus'fertigen *tr* finish; (*Paß*) issue; (*Scheck*) write out; (*Schriftstück*) draw up, draft; **doppelt a.** draw up in duplicate
aus'findig *adj*—**a. machen** find out; (*aufspüren*) trace
aus'fliegen §57 *intr* (SEIN) fly out; (*wegfliegen*) fly away; (*von Hause wegziehen*) leave home; go on a trip
aus'fließen §76 *intr* (SEIN) flow out
Aus'flucht *f* evasion; **Ausflüchte machen** dodge, beat around the bush
aus'fluchten *tr* align
Aus'flug *m* trip, outing
Ausflügler ['ausflyglər] *m* (–;–) tourist, vacationer
Aus'fluß *m* outflow; (*Eiter*) discharge; (*Ergebnis*) outcome; (*Mündung*) outlet
aus'folgen *tr* hand over
aus'forschen *tr* investigate; sound out
aus'fragen *tr* interrogate, quiz
aus'fressen §70 *tr* empty (by eating); (chem) corrode; (geol) erode; **was hast du denn ausgefressen?** (coll) what were you up to?
Ausfuhr ['ausfur] *f* (–;–en) export
Aus'fuhrabgabe *f* export duty
ausführbar ['ausfyrbar] *adj* feasible

aus'führen tr carry out; export, ship; (Auftrag) fill; (darlegen) explain

Aus'fuhrhändler –in §6 mf exporter

ausführlich ['ausfyrlıç] adj detailed || adv in detail, in full

Aus'führung f (-;-en) carrying out, performance; (Qualität) workmanship; (Darlegung) explanation; (e–s Gesetzes, Befehls) implementation; (Fertigstellung) completion; (e–s Verbrechens) perpetrations; (typ) type, model; copy

Aus'fuhrwaren pl exports

aus'füllen tr fill out; (Zeit) occupy; (Lücke; Stellung) fill

Aus'gabe f (Verteilung) distribution; (von Geldern) expenditure; (von Briefen) delivery; (e–s Buches) edition; (von Aktien) issue

Aus'gang m exit; (Auslaß) outlet; (Ergebnis) result; (Ende) close, end; (aer) gate

Aus'gangspunkt m starting point

Aus'gangssprache f source language

aus'geben §80 tr give out, distribute; (Aktien; Befehl) issue; (Geld) spend; (Briefe) deliver; (Karten) deal || ref—**sich a. für** pass oneself off as

ausgebeult ['ausgəbɔılt] adj baggy

Aus'geburt f figment

aus'gedehnt adj extensive

aus'gedient adj retired; (educ) emeritus

aus'gefallen adj (fig) eccentric, odd

aus'gefeilt adj (fig) flawless

aus'geglichen adj (Person) well-balanced; (Styl) balanced

aus'gehen §82 intr (SEIN) go out; (Vorräte, Geld, Geduld) run out; (Haar) fall out; (Farbe) fade; **a. auf** (acc) aim at, be bent on; **a. von** proceed from; **die Sache ging von ihm aus** it was his idea; **frei a.** get off scot-free; **gut a.** turn out well; **leer a.** come away empty-handed; **wenn wir davon a., daß** going on the assumption that

Aus'gehverbot n curfew

aus'gekocht adj (Lügner) out-and-out; (Verbrecher) hardened

aus'gelassen adj boisterous

aus'geleiert adj trite; worn-out; (Gewinde) stripped

aus'gemacht adj settled; downright

ausgenommen prep (acc) except; **niemand a.** bar none

aus'gepicht adj inveterate

aus'gerechnet adv just, of all ...; **a. Sie!** you of all people!

aus'geschlossen adj out of the question, impossible

Ausgesiedelte ['ausgəzidəltə] §5 mf evacuee, displaced person

aus'gestalten tr make arrangements for

aus'gesucht adj choice

aus'gezeichnet adj excellent

ausgiebig ['ausgibıç] adj abundant; (ergiebig) productive

aus'gießen §76 tr pour out, pour away

Aus'gleich m (-s;-e) (Ersatz) compensation; (Vergleich) compromise; (acct) settlement; (tennis) deuce

aus'gleichen §85 tr level, smooth out; (Konten) balance; (Verlust) compensate for || ref cancel one another out

Ausgleichs– comb.fm. balancing, compensating

Aus'gleichung f (-;-en) equalization; settlement; compensation

aus'gleiten §86 intr (SEIN) slip

aus'graben §87 tr dig out, dig up; (Leiche) exhume; (archeol) excavate

aus'greifen §88 intr reach out; **weit ausgreifend** far-reaching

Ausguck ['ausguk] m (-s;-e) lookout

aus'gucken intr (nach) be on the lookout (for)

Aus'guß m sink; (Tülle) spout, nozzle

aus'haken tr unhook

aus'halten §90 tr endure, stand || intr persevere, stick it out

aus'handeln tr get by bargaining

aushändigen ['aushendıgən] tr hand over, surrender

Aus'hang m notice, shingle

Aus'hängeschild n (-[e]s;-er) sign board, shingle; (fig) front, cover

aus'harren intr hold out, last

aus'hauchen tr breathe out, exhale

aus'heben §94 tr lift out; (Tür) lift off its hinges; (Truppen) recruit

aushecken ['aushekən] tr (fig) hatch

aus'heilen tr heal completely || intr (SEIN) heal up

aus'helfen §96 intr (dat) help out

Aus'hilfe f (temporary) help; (temporary) helper; makeshift

Aushilfs– comb.fm. temporary, emergency

Aus'hilfsarbeit f part-time work

Aus'hilfslehrer –in §6 mf substitute teacher

aus'hilfsweise adv temporarily

aus'höhlen tr hollow out

aus'holen tr (ausfragen) sound out || intr (beim Schwimmen) stroke; **mit dem Arm a.** raise the arm (before striking); **weit a.** start from the beginning

aus'horchen tr sound out, pump

aus'hülsen tr (Bohnen, usw.) shell

aus'hungern tr starve (out)

aus'husten tr cough up

aus'kehlen tr groove

Aus'kehlung f (-;-en) groove

aus'kehren tr sweep (out)

aus'kennen §97 ref know one's way; (in e–m Fach) be well versed

Aus'klang m end, close

aus'klappen tr pull out (a fold-away bed)

aus'kleiden tr line, panel; (ausziehen) undress || ref undress

aus'klopfen tr beat the dust out of

ausklügeln ['ausklygəln] tr figure out (ingeniously)

aus'kneifen §88 intr (SEIN) beat it

aus'knipsen tr (coll) switch off

ausknobeln ['ausknobəln] tr figure out

aus'kochen tr boil out; boil clean

aus'kommen §99 intr (SEIN) come out, get out; (ausreichen) manage || **Auskommen** n (-s;) livelihood

auskömmlich ['auskœmlıç] adj adequate

aus'kosten tr relish

aus'kramen ['auskramən] tr (aus Schubladen) drag out; (fig) show off

aus'kratzen *tr* scratch out; (surg) curette

aus'kriechen §102 *intr* (SEIN) be hatched

aus'kugeln *ref*—**sich** [*dat*] **den Arm a.** dislocate the shoulder

aus'kundschaften *tr* explore; (mil) scout

Auskunft ['ɑʊskʊnft] *f* (–;-̈e) information, piece of information

Auskunftei [ɑʊskʊnf'taɪ] *f* (–;-en) private detective agency

Aus'kunftschalter *m* information desk

aus'kuppeln *tr* uncouple; (*die Kupplung*) release || *intr* disengage the clutch

aus'lachen *tr* laugh at || *ref* have a good laugh

aus'laden §103 *tr* unload; (*Gast*) put off || *intr* project, jut out || **Ausladen** *n* (–s;) unloading; projection

Aus'lage *f* (*von Geld*) outlay; (*Unkosten*) expenses; (*von Waren*) display; (*Schaufenster*) display window

Aus'land *n* foreign country, foreign countries; **im A. leben** live abroad; **ins A. gehen** go abroad

Ausländer –in ['ɑʊslɛndər(ɪn)] §6 *mf* foreigner, alien

aus'ländisch *adj* foreign, alien

Auslands– *comb.fm.* foreign

Aus'laß ['ɑʊslas] *m* (–lasses;-lässe) outlet

aus'lassen §104 *tr* let out; (*weglassen*) omit; (*Wut*) (*an dat*) vent (on) || *ref* express one's opinion

Aus'lassung *f* omission; (*Bemerkung*) remark

Aus'lassungszeichen *n* (gram) apostrophe; (typ) caret

Aus'lauf *m* sailing; room to run

aus'laufen §105 *intr* (SEIN) run out; (*Schiff*) put out to sea; (*Farbe*) run; **a. in** (*acc*) end in; (*Straße*) run into

Aus'läufer *m* (geol) spur; (hort) runner

aus'leben *tr* live out || *ref* make the most of one's life || *intr* die

aus'lecken *tr* lick clean

aus'leeren *tr* empty || *ref* have a bowel movement

aus'legen *tr* lay out; (*Waren*) display; (*erklären*) construe; (*Geld*) advance; (*Fußboden*) cover (*with carpeting*); (*Minen*) lay; (*Schlinge*) set; **falsch a.** misconstrue, misinterpret

Aus'leger –in §6 *mf* interpreter || *m* outrigger; (*e-s Krans*) boom

aus'leihen §81 *tr* lend (out) || *ref*—**sich** [*dat*] **etw a.** borrow s.th.

aus'lernen *intr* finish one's apprenticeship; **man lernt nie aus** one never stops learning

Aus'lese *f* pick, choice

aus'lesen §107 *tr* pick out; (*Buch*) finish reading

aus'liefern *tr* deliver, turn over; (*verteilen*) distribute; (*Verbrecher*) extradite; **j–m ausgeliefert sein** be at s.o.'s mercy

aus'liegen §108 *intr* (SEIN) be on display

aus'löffeln *tr* spoon out; **etw a. zu haben** have to face the consequences of s.th.

aus'löschen *tr* (*Feuer*) extinguish; (*Licht*) put out; (*Schreiben*) erase

aus'losen *tr* draw lots for

aus'lösen *tr* loosen, release; (*Gefangegen*) ransom; (*Pfand*) redeem

Aus'löser *m* (–s;-) release

aus'loten *tr* (naut & fig) plumb

aus'lüften *tr* air, ventilate

aus'machen *tr* (*Feuer*) put out; (*sichten*) make out; (*betragen*) amount to; (*Fleck*) remove; (*Licht*) turn out; (*bilden*) constitute; (*vereinbaren*) agree upon; **es macht nichts aus** it doesn't matter

aus'malen *tr* paint || *ref*—**sich** [*dat*] **etw a.** picture s.th.

aus'marschieren *intr* (SEIN) march out

Aus'maß *n* measurement; dimensions; **in großem A.** on a large scale; (fig) to a great extent

ausmergeln ['ɑʊsmɛrgərln] *tr* exhaust

ausmerzen ['ɑʊsmɛrtsən] *tr* reject; (*ausrotten*) eradicate

aus'messen §70 *tr* measure; survey

aus'misten *tr* (*Stall*) clean; (fig) clean up

aus'mustern *tr* discard; (mil) discharge

Aus'nahme *f* (–;-n) exception

Aus'nahmezustand *m* state of emergency

aus'nahmslos *adj* & *adv* without exception

aus'nahmsweise *adv* by way of exception

aus'nehmen §116 *tr* take out; (*Fisch, Huhn*) clean; (*ausschließen*) exclude; (sl) clean out (of money) || *ref*—**sich gut a.** look good

aus'nutzen, aus'nützen *tr* utilize; (*Gelegenheit*) take advantage of

aus'packen *tr* unpack; (*Geheimnis*) disclose || *intr* (coll) unburden oneself, open up

aus'pfeifen §88 *tr* hiss (off the stage)

aus'plappern *tr* blurt out, blab out

aus'plaudern *tr* blab out

aus'plündern *tr* ransack; (coll) clean out (of money)

aus'polstern *tr* stuff, pad

aus'posaunen *tr* (coll) broadcast

aus'probieren *tr* try out, test

Aus'puff *m* (–[e]s;-e) exhaust

Aus'puffleitung *f* (aut) manifold

Aus'puffrohr *n* exhaust pipe

Aus'pufftopf *m* (aut) muffler

aus'pumpen *tr* pump out; **ausgepumpt** (coll) exhausted

aus'putzen *tr* (*reinigen*) clean out; (*schmücken*) adorn || *ref* dress up

aus'quartieren *tr* put out (*of s.o.'s room*)

aus'radieren *tr* erase

aus'rangieren *tr* (coll) scrap

aus'rauben *tr* rob, ransack

aus'räumen *tr* (*Schrank*) clear out; (*Möbel*) remove; (med) clean out

aus'rechnen *tr* figure out

aus'recken *tr* stretch || *ref*—**sich** [*dat*] **den Hals a.** crane one's neck

Aus'rede *f* evasion, excuse

aus'reden *tr*—**j–m etw a.** talk s.o. out

of s.th. || *ref* make excuses || *intr* finish speaking

aus'reiben §62 *tr* rub out; (mach) ream

aus'reichen *tr* suffice, be enough

aus'reichend *adj* sufficient

Aus'reise *f* departure; way out

aus'reißen §53 *tr* tear out || *ref*—**er reißt sich** [*dat*] **dabei kein Bein aus** he's not exactly killing himself || *intr* (SEIN) run away

Aus'reißer *m* runaway

aus'renken *tr* dislocate

aus'richten *tr* straighten; (in e-e Linie bringen) align; (vollbringen) accomplish; (Botschaft, Gruß) convey

aus'rollen *tr* root out; (Wald) clear

aus'rollen *tr* roll out || *intr* (SEIN) (aer) taxi to a standstill

ausrotten ['ausrotən] *tr* root out; (Volk, Tierrasse) exterminate; (Übel) eradicate

aus'rücken *tr* (Kupplung) disengage || *intr* (SEIN) march off; run away

Aus'ruf *m* outcry; (öffentlich) proclamation; (gram) interjection

aus'rufen §122 *tr* call out; exclaim; **a. als** (or **zum**) proclaim

Aus'rufungszeichen *n* exclamation point

aus'ruhen *ref* & *intr* rest

aus'rupfen *tr* pluck

aus'rüsten *tr* equip, fit out; arm

aus'rutschen *intr* (SEIN) slip (out)

Aus'saat *f* sowing; (& fig) seed(s)

aus'säen *tr* sow; (fig) disseminate

Aus'sage *f* statement; (gram) predicate; (jur) affidavit

aus'sagen *tr* state || *intr* give evidence, make a statement

Aus'sagesatz *m* declarative sentence

Aus'sageweise *f* (gram) mood

Aus'satz *m* leprosy

Aussätzige ['auszetsigə] §5 *mf* leper

aus'saugen §125 *tr* suck dry; (fig) bleed white

Aus'sauger –**in** §6 *mf* (coll) bloodsucker

aus'schalten *tr* (Licht, Radio, Fernseher) turn off; (fig) shut out

Aus'schalter *m* circuit breaker

Aus'schank *m* sale of alcoholic drinks; (Kneipe) bar, taproom

aus'scharren *tr* dig up

Aus'schau *f*—**A. halten nach** be on the lookout for

aus'schauen *intr*—**a. nach** look out for; look like; **gut schaust du aus!** what a mess you are!

aus'scheiden §112 *tr* eliminate; (physiol) excrete, secrete || *intr* (SEIN) retire, resign; (sport) drop out; **das scheidet aus!** that's out!

Aus'scheidung *f* (–;–en) elimination; retirement; (physiol) excretion, secretion

Aus'scheidungskampf *m* elimination bout

aus'schelten §83 *tr* scold, berate

aus'schenken *tr* pour (drinks)

aus'scheren *intr* (aus) veer away (from)

aus'schiffen *tr* disembark; (Ladung) unload || *ref* disembark

aus'schimpfen *tr* scold, take to task

aus'schirren *tr* unharness

aus'schlachten *tr* cut up; (Flugzeuge, usw.) cannibalize; (ausnutzen) make the most of

aus'schlafen §131 *tr* sleep off || *ref* & *intr* get enough sleep

Aus'schlag *m* rash; (e–s Zeigers) deflection; **den A. geben** turn the scales

aus'schlagen §132 *tr* knock out; (Feuer) beat out; (Metall) hammer out; (Innenraum) line; (Angebot) refuse || *intr* bud; sprout; (Pferd) kick; (Pendel) swing; (Zeiger) move || *intr* (SEIN) turn out

aus'schlaggebend *adj* decisive

aus'schließen §76 *tr* lock out; (von der Schule) expel; (ausscheiden) exclude; (sport) disqualify

aus'schließlich *adj* exclusive, sole || *adv* exclusively, only || *prep* (genit) exclusive of

aus'schlürfen *tr* sip

aus'schmieren *tr* grease; (mit) smear (with); (fig) pull a fast one on; (mas) point

aus'schmücken *tr* adorn, decorate; (Geschichte) embellish

aus'schnaufen *intr* get one's wind

aus'schneiden §106 *tr* cut out; **tief ausgeschnitten** low-cut, low-necked

Aus'schnitt *m* cut; (Zeitungs-) clipping; (Kleid-) neckline; (literarisch) extract; (geom) sector

aus'schreiben §62 *tr* write out (in full); finish writing; (ankündigen) announce; (Formular) fill out; (Rezept) make out

aus'schreiten §86 *tr* pace off || *intr* (SEIN) walk briskly

Aus'schreitung *f* (–;–en) excess

Aus'schuß *m* waste, scrap; (Komitee) committee

Aus'schußware *f* (indust) reject

aus'schütten *tr* pour out, spill; (Dividende) pay || *ref*—**sich vor Lachen a.** split one's sides laughing

aus'schwärmen *intr* (SEIN) swarm out; (Truppen) deploy

aus'schwatzen *tr* blab out, blurt out

aus'schweifend *adj* (Phantasie) wild; (liederlich) wild, dissolute

Aus'schweifung *f* (–;–en) excess; curve; digression

aus'schwemmen *tr* rinse out; wash out

aus'schwenken *tr* rinse

aus'schwitzen *tr* sweat out; exude

aus'sehen §138 *intr* look; **nach j–m a.** look out for s.o.; **nach Regen a.** look like rain; **wie sieht er aus?** what does he look like? || **Aussehen** *n* (–s;) look(s); appearance(s)

außen ['ausən] *adv* outside; **nach a.** out(wards)

außen-, Außen- *comb.fm.* external; outer; exterior; outdoor; foreign

Au'ßenaufnahme *f* (phot) outdoor shot

Au'ßenbahn *f* (sport) outside lane

aus'senden §140 *tr* send out

Au'ßenfläche *f* outer surface

Au'ßenminister *m* Secretary of State; (Brit) Foreign Secretary

Au'ßenpolitik *f* foreign policy

Au'ßenseite *f* outside

Außenseiter ['ausənzaɪtər] m (-s;-) dark horse, long shot; (Einzelgänger) loner; (Nichtfachmann) layman

Außenstände ['ausən/tendə] pl accounts receivable

Au'ßenstelle f branch office

außer ['ausər] prep (genit)—a. Landes abroad ‖ prep (dat) outside, out of; except, but; besides, in addition to; a. Hause not at home; a. sich sein be beside oneself

au'ßeramtlich adj unofficial, private

außerdem ['ausərdem] adv also, besides; moreover, furthermore

au'ßerdienstlich adj unofficial, private; (mil) off duty

äußere ['ɔɪsərə] §9 adj outer, exterior, external ‖ Äußere §5 n exterior

au'ßerehelich adj extra-marital; (Kind) illegitimate

au'ßergewöhnlich adj extraordinary

außerhalb ['ausərhalp] prep (genit) outside, out of

äußerlich ['ɔɪsərlɪç] adj external, outward; (oberflächlich) superficial

Äu'ßerlichkeit f superficiality; (Formalität) formality; Äußerlichkeiten externals; formalities

äußern ['ɔɪsərn] tr express ‖ ref (über acc) express one's mind (about); (in dat) be manifested (in)

au'ßerordentlich adj extraordinary; außerordentlicher Professor associate professor

äußerst ['ɔɪsərst] adj outermost; (fig) extreme, utmost ‖ adv extremely, highly ‖ Äußerste §5 n extremity, extreme(s); aufs Ä. to the utmost; bis zum Äußersten to extremes; to the bitter end

außerstande ['ausər/andə] adj unable

Äu'ßerung f (-;-en) (Ausdruck) expression; (Bemerkung) remark

aus'setzen tr set out, put out; (an der Küste) maroon; (Kind; dem Wetter) expose; (Boot) lower; (Wachen) post; (Belohnung) hold out, promise; (Tätigkeit) discontinue; auszusetzen haben an (dat) find fault with ‖ intr stop, halt

Aus'sicht f (auf acc) view (of); (fig) (auf acc) hope (of); in A. nehmen consider, plan

aus'sichtslos adj hopeless

Aus'sichtspunkt m vantage point

aus'sichtsreich adj promising

Aus'sichtsturm m lookout tower

aussichtsvoll adj promising

aus'sieben tr sift out; (fig) screen

aus'siedeln tr evacuate by force

Aus'siedlung f (-;-en) forced evacuation

aus'sinnen §121 tr think up, devise

aussöhnen ['auszøːnən] tr reconcile

aus'sondern tr (trennen) separate; (auswählen) single out; (physiol) excrete

aus'spähen tr spy out ‖ intr (nach) keep a lookout (for), reconnoiter

aus'spannen tr stretch; extend; (Zugtiere) unhitch ‖ intr relax

Aus'spannung f (-;) relaxation

aus'speien §135 tr spit out

aus'sperren tr lock out, shut out

aus'spielen tr (Karten) lead with; (Preis) play for ‖ intr lead off

aus'spionieren tr spy out

Aus'sprache f pronunciation; (Erörterung) discussion, talk

aus'sprechen §64 tr pronounce; (deutlich) articulate; (ausdrücken) express ‖ ref (über acc) speak one's mind (about); (für; gegen) declare oneself (for; against); sich mit j-m über etw a. talk s.th. over with s.o. ‖ intr finish speaking

Aus'spruch m statement

aus'spülen tr rinse

aus'spüren tr trace (down)

aus'staffieren tr fit out, furnish

aus'stampfen tr stamp out

Aus'stand m walkout

aus'ständig adj on strike, striking; (fin) in arrears, outstanding

ausstatten ['aus/tatən] tr furnish, equip; (Tochter) give a dowry to

Aus'stattung f (-;-en) furnishings; equipment; trousseau

aus'stechen §64 tr cut out; (Auge) poke out; (fig) outdo

aus'stehen §146 tr endure, stand ‖ intr still be expected, be overdue

aus'steigen §148 intr (SEIN) get out, get off

aus'stellen tr exhibit; (Wache) post; (Quittung, Scheck) make out; (Paß) issue

Aus'stellung f (-;-en) exhibit; issuance; criticism

Aus'stelungsdatum n date of issue

aus'sterben §149 intr (SEIN) die out

Aus'steuer f hope chest, dowry

aus'stopfen tr stuff, pad

Aus'stoß m (indust) output

aus'stoßen §150 tr knock out; (vertreiben) eject; (Seufzer, Schrei, Fluch) utter; (Torpedo) launch; (math) eliminate; (phonet) elide; (phys) emit

Aus'stoßrohr n torpedo tube

Aus'stoßung f (-;-en) ejection; utterance; (gram) elision

Aus'stoßzahlen pl (indust) production figures

aus'strahlen tr & intr radiate

aus'strecken tr & ref stretch out

aus'streichen §85 tr cross out; (glätten) smooth out; (Bratpfanne) grease

aus'streuen tr strew, scatter, spread

aus'strömen tr & intr (SEIN) pour out

aus'studieren tr study thoroughly

aus'suchen tr pick out

Aus'tausch m exchange

aus'tauschbar adj exchangeable; interchangeable

aus'tauschen tr exchange; interchange

Aus'tauschstoff m substitute

Aus'tauschstück n spare part

aus'teilen tr distribute, deal out

Auster ['austər] f (-;-n) oyster

aus'tilgen tr exterminate, wipe out

aus'toben tr give vent to ‖ (Person) let one's hair down; (Kinder) raise a rumpus; (Gewitter) stop raging

aus'tollen ref make a racket

Austrag ['austrak] m (-[e]s;)—bis zum A. der Sache until the matter is decided; zum A. bringen bring to a head; (jur) settle; **zum A. kommen** come up for a decision

aus'tragen §132 *tr* carry out; (*Briefe*) deliver; (*Kleider*) wear out; (*Meisterschaft*) decide; (*Klatschereien*) spread; (acct) cancel

Aus'träger *m* deliveryman

Australien [aus'traljən] *n* (**-s;**) Australia

Australier –in [aus'traljər(ɪn)] §6 *mf* Australian

aus'treiben §62 *tr* drive out; exorcise

aus'treten §152 *tr* (*Feuer*) tread out; (*Schuhe, Treppen*) wear out ‖ *intr* (SEIN) step out; (*Blut*) come out; (coll) go to the bathroom; **a. aus** leave (*school, a company, club*)

aus'trinken §143 *tr* drink up, drain

Aus'tritt *m* withdrawal

aus'trocknen *tr & intr* (SEIN) dry up

aus'tüfteln *tr* puzzle out

aus'üben *tr* (*Aufsicht, Macht*) exercise; (*Beruf*) practice; (*Pflicht*) carry out; (*Einfluß, Druck*) exert; (*Verbrechen*) commit; **ausübende Gewalt** executive power

Aus'verkauf *m* clearance sale

aus'verkaufen *tr* sell out; close out

aus'wachsen §155 *tr* outgrow

Aus'wahl *f* choice, selection

aus'wählen *tr* select, pick out

Aus'wanderer –in §6 *mf* emigrant

aus'wandern *intr* (SEIN) emigrate

auswärtig ['ausvɛrtɪç] *adj* out-of-town; (*ausländisch*) foreign

auswärts ['ausvɛrts] *adv* outward(s); out, away from home; (*außer der Stadt*) out of town; (*im Ausland*) abroad

Aus'wärtsspiel *n* away game

aus'wechselbar *adj* interchangeable

aus'wechseln *tr* exchange, interchange; (*ersetzen*) replace

Aus'weg *m* way out; escape

Ausweich– *comb.fm.* evasive; alternate; substitute; emergency; reserve

aus'weichen §85 *intr* (SEIN) (*dat*) make way (for), get out of the way (of); (*dat*) evade; **a. auf** (*acc*) switch to

aus'weichend *adj* evasive

Aus'weichklausel *f* escape clause

Aus'weichlager *n* emergency store

Aus'weichstelle *f* passing zone

Aus'weichstraße *f* bypass

Aus'weichziel *n* secondary target

aus'weinen *ref* have a good cry ‖ *intr* stop crying

Ausweis ['ausvais] *m* (**-es;-e**) identification (card); (com) statement

aus'weisen §118 *tr* expel; (*aus Besitz*) evict; (*verbannen*) banish, deport; (*zeigen*) show ‖ *ref* prove one's identity

Aus'weispapiere *pl* identification papers

Aus'weisung *f* (**-;-en**) expulsion; eviction; deportation

aus'weiten *tr & ref* widen, expand

auswendig ['ausvɛndɪç] *adj* outer ‖ *adv* outside; outwardly; by heart

aus'werfen §160 *tr* throw out; (*Graben*) dig; (*Summe*) allocate; (*Lava*) eject; (*Blut, Schleim*) spit up; (angl) cast

aus'werten *tr* evaluate; (*ausnützen*) utilize; (*Statistik*) interpret

aus'wickeln *tr* unwrap

aus'wiegen §57 *tr* weigh out

aus'wirken *tr* knead ‖ *ref* take effect; **sich a. auf** (*acc*) affect; **sich** [*dat*] **etw bei j–m a.** obtain s.th. from s.o.

Aus'wirkung *f* (**-;-en**) effect

aus'wischen *tr* wipe out; wipe clean; **j–m eins a.** play a dirty joke on s.o.

aus'wittern *tr* season ‖ *intr* weather

aus'wringen §142 *tr* wring out

Aus'wuchs *m* outgrowth; (pathol) tumor

Aus'wurf *m* throwing out; (fig) scum; (mach) ejection

aus'zacken *tr* indent; (*wellenförmig*) scallop

aus'zahlen *tr* pay out; pay off ‖ *ref*— **es zahlt sich nicht aus** it doesn't pay

aus'zählen *tr* count out

aus'zanken *tr* scold

aus'zehren *tr* consume, waste

Aus'zehrung *f* (**-;**) consumption

aus'zeichnen *tr* mark, tag; (*ehren*) honor; (fig) distinguish

Aus'zeichnung *f* (**-;-en**) labeling; decoration, honor; distinction

aus'ziehen §163 *tr* pull out; (*Kleid*) take off; (*Stelle*) excerpt; (*Zeichnung*) ink in; (chem) extract ‖ *ref* undress ‖ *intr* (SEIN) set out; (*aus e–r Wohnung*) move out

aus'zischen *tr* hiss off the stage

Aus'zug *m* departure; moving; excerpt; (*Abriß*) summary; (Bib) Exodus; (chem) extract; (com) statement

aus'zugsweise *adv* in summary form

aus'zupfen *tr* pluck out

authentisch [au'tɛntɪʃ] *adj* authentic

Auto ['auto] *n* (**-s;-s**) auto(mobile)

Au'tobahn *f* superhighway

Au'tobus *m* bus

Autodidakt [autodɪ'dakt] *m* (**-en;-en**) self-educated person

Au'todroschke *f* taxi

Au'tofahrer –in §6 *mf* motorist

Au'tofahrschule *f* driving school

Au'tofahrt *f* car ride, drive

Au'tofalle *f* speed trap

Autogramm [auto'gram] *n* (**-[e]s;-e**) autograph

Autogramm'jäger –in §6 *mf* autograph hound

Au'tokino *n* drive-in movie

Au'tokolonne *f* motorcade

Autokrat [auto'krat] *m* (**-en;-en**) autocrat

autokratisch [auto'kratɪʃ] *adj* autocratic

Automat [auto'mat] *m* (**-en;-en**) vending machine; (*Musik–*) jukebox; (*Spiel–*) slot machine

Automa'tenrestaurant *n* automat

automatisch [auto'matɪʃ] *adj* automatic

Automobil [automo'bil] *n* (**-[e]s;-e**) automobile

autonom [auto'nom] *adj* autonomous

Autonomie [autono'mi] *f* (**-;**) autonomy

Au·tor ['autor] *m* (**-s;-toren** ['torən]) author

Autoreparatur′werkstatt f auto repair shop, garage
Autorin [au′torɪn] f (-;-nen) authoress
autorisieren [autorɪ′zirən] tr authorize
autoritär [autorɪ′ter] adj authoritarian
Autorität [autorɪ′tet] f (-;-en) authority
Au′toschlosser m automobile mechanic
Au′toschuppen m carport

Au′tounfall m automobile accident
avancieren [avã′sirən] intr (SEIN) advance; (zu) be promoted (to)
avisieren [avɪ′zirən] tr advise, notify
Axt [akst] f (-;⁻e) ax
Azalee [atsa′le·ə] f (-;-n) azalea
Azetat [atse′tat] n (-[e]s;-e) acetate
Azeton [atse′ton] n (-s;) acetone
Azetylen [atsety′len] n (-s;) acetylene
azurn [a′tsurn] adj azure, sky-blue

B

B, b [be] invar n B, b; (mus) B flat
babbeln [′babəln] intr babble
Baby [′bebi] n (-s;-s) baby
Babysitter [′bebɪzɪtər] m (-s;-) babysitter
Bach [bax] m (-[e]s;⁻e) brook, creek
Backe [′bakə] f (-;-n) cheek; jaw (of a vise); (mach) die
backen [′bakən] §50 (& pret **backte**) tr bake; (in der Pfanne) fry || (pret **backte**; pp **gebacken**) intr bake || §109 intr (HABEN & SEIN) cake; stick
Backenbart (Bak′kenbart) m side whiskers
Backenstreich (Bak′kenstreich) m slap
Backenzahn (Bak′kenzahn) m molar; kleiner (or vorderer) B. bicuspid
Bäcker [′bekər] m (-s;-) baker
Bäckerei [bekə′raɪ] f (-;-en) bakery
Back′fett n shortening
Back′fisch m fried fish; (fig) teenager
Back′fischalter n teens (of girls)
Back′form f cake pan
Back′hähnchen n fried chicken
Back′hendel n (Aust) fried chicken
Back′huhn n fried chicken
Back′obst n dried fruit
Back′ofen m baking oven
Back′pfeife f slap in the face, smack
Back′pflaume f prune
Back′pulver n baking powder
Back′stein m brick
Back′trog m kneading trough
Back′waren pl baked goods
Back′werk n pastries
Bad [bat] n (-[e]s;⁻er) bath; bathroom; (Badeort) spa
Ba′deanstalt f public baths; public pool
Ba′deanzug m swim suit
Ba′dehaube f bathing cap
Ba′dehose f bathing trunks
Ba′dekappe f bathing cap
Ba′demantel m bathrobe
baden [′badən] tr & ref bathe || intr take a bath; b. gehen go swimming
Ba′deort m bathing resort; spa
Ba′destrand m bathing beach
Ba′detuch n bath towel
Ba′dewanne f bathtub
Badende [′badəndə] §5 mf bather
Ba′dewärter –in §6 mf lifeguard; bathhouse attendant
Ba′dezimmer n bathroom
baff [baf] adj dumbfounded

Bagage [ba′gaʒə] f (-;) (fig) rabble; (mil) baggage
Bagatelle [baga′telə] f (-;-n) trifle
Bagatel′lesache f petty offense
bagatellisieren [bagatelɪ′zirən] tr minimize, make light of
Bagger [′bagər] m (-s;-) dredge
baggern [′bagərn] tr & intr dredge
bähen [′be·ən] intr bleat
Bahn [ban] f (-;-en) way, path; (aer) runway; (astr) orbit; (aut) lane; (rr) railroad; (sport) course, track; (Eis–) (sport) rink; **auf die schiefe B. geraten** go astray; **B. brechen** (dat) pave the way (for); **mit der B. fahren** travel by train
bahn′brechend adj pioneering, epoch-making
Bahn′brecher –in §6 mf pioneer
Bahn′damm m railroad embankment
bahnen [′banən] tr—e–n Weg. b. clear a path, open up a path
Bahn′fahrt f train trip
bahn′frei adj free on board, f.o.b.
Bahn′hof m railroad station
Bahn′hofshalle f concourse
Bahn′hofsvorsteher m stationmaster
Bahn′linie f railroad line
Bahn′schranke f (rr) barrier
Bahn′steig m (rr) platform
Bahn′strecke f (rr) line, track
Bahn′übergang m railroad crossing
Bahn′wärter m (rr) signalman
Bahre [′barə] f (-;-n) stretcher; bier
Bahr′tuch n pall
Bai [baɪ] f (-;-en) bay
Baiser [be′ze] m & n (-s;-s) meringue cookie
Baisse [′besə] f (-;-n) (com) slump
Bais′sestimmung f downward trend
Baissier [bes′je] m (-s;-s) (st.exch.) bear
Bajonett [bajo′net] n (-[e]s;-e) bayonet
Bake [′bakə] f (-;-n) beacon
Bakterie [bak′terjə] f (-;-n) bacterium
Bakte′rienforscher –in §6 mf bacteriologist
Bakte′rienkunde f bacteriology
Balance [ba′lãsə] f (-;-n) balance
balancieren [balã′sirən] tr & intr balance
bald [balt] adv (eher [′e·ər]; eheste [′e·əstə] §9 soon; (beinahe) nearly
baldig [′baldɪç] adj speedy; (Antwort) early

baldigst [ˈbaldɪçst] *adv* very soon; at the earliest possible moment

Balg [balk] *m* (-[e]s;⁼e) skin, pelt; (*Hülse*) shell, husk; **Bälge** bellows; **j-m den B. abziehen** fleece s.o. ‖ *m & n* (-[e]s;⁼er) (coll) brat

balgen [ˈbalgən] *ref* roll around, romp; (*raufen*) scuffle ‖ **Balgen** *m* (-s;-) (phot) bellows

Balgerei [balgəˈraɪ] *f* (-;-en) scuffle

Balken [ˈbalkən] *m* (-s;-) beam, rafter

Bal′kenwerk *n* framework

Balkon [balˈkon] *m* (-s;-e) balcony

Ball [bal] *m* (-[e]s;⁼e) ball; (*Tanz*) ball

Ballade [baˈladə] *f* (-;-n) ballad

Ballast [ˈbalast] *m* (-[e]s;-e) ballast; (fig) drag; (coll) padding

ballen [ˈbalən] *tr*—**die Faust b.** clench one's fist ‖ *ref* form a cluster ‖ **Ballen** *m* (-s;-) (anat) ball; (com) bale; (pathol) bunion

ballern [ˈbalərn] *intr* (coll) bang away

Ballett [baˈlet] *n* (-[e]s;-e) ballet

Ballistik [baˈlɪstɪk] *f* (-;) ballistics

Ballon [baˈlon] *m* (-s;-s) balloon

Ball′saal *m* ballroom

Ball′schläger *m* (sport) bat

Ball′spiel *n* ball game

Bal′lung *f* (-;-en) (mil) massing (of troops)

Balsam [ˈbalzam] *m* (-s;-e) balm, balsam; (fig) balm

balsamieren [balzaˈmirən] *tr* embalm

balzen [ˈbaltsən] *intr* perform a mating dance

Bambus [ˈbambus] *m* (-; & -ses;-se) bamboo

Bam′busrohr *n* bamboo, bamboo cane

banal [baˈnal] *adj* banal

Banane [baˈnanə] *f* (-;-n) banana

Banause [baˈnauzə] *f* (-n;-n) philistine

banausisch [baˈnauzɪʃ] *adj* narrow-minded

Band [bant] *m* (-[e]s;⁼e) volume; (*Einband*) binding ‖ *n* (-[e]s;⁼e) bond, tie; **Bande** chains, shackles ‖ *n* [-[e]s;⁼er] (*e-s Hutes, usw.*) band; (*Bindfaden*) string; (*zum Schmuck*) ribbon; tape; (anat) ligament; (electron) recording tape; (rad) band; **am laufenden B.** continuously

Bandage [banˈdaʒə] *f* (-;-n) bandage

bandagieren [bandaˈʒirən] *tr* bandage

Bande [ˈbandə] *f* (-;-n) band, gang, crew; (billiards) cushion

Ban′denkrieg *m* guerilla war(fare)

Ban′denmitglied *n* gangster; (mil) guerilla

Ban′denunwesen *n* gangsterism; partisan activities

bändigen [ˈbendɪgən] *tr* tame; (fig) subdue, overcome, master

Bandit [banˈdit] *m* (-en;-en) bandit

Band′maß *n* tape measure

Band′säge *f* band saw

Band′scheibe *f* (anat) disk

Band′scheibenquetschung *f* slipped disk

Band′wurm *m* tapeworm

bang(e) [ˈbaŋ(ə)] *adj* scared, anxious; (*Gefühl*) disquieting; **j-m b. machen** scare s.o. ‖ **Bange** *f* (-;) fear

Bangigkeit [ˈbaŋɪçkaɪt] *f* (-;) fear

Bank [baŋk] *f* (-;⁼e) bench; pew; (geol) layer, bed ‖ *f* (-;-en) bank

Bank′anweisung *f* check

Bank′ausweis *m* bank statement

Bank′einlage *f* bank deposit

Bankett [baŋˈket] *n* (-s;-e) banquet

bank′fähig *adj* negotiable

Bank′guthaben *n* bank balance

Bank′halter **-in** §6 *mf* banker (*in games*)

Bankier [baŋˈkje] *m* (-s;-s) banker

Bank′konto *n* bank account

bank′mäßig *adj* by check

bankrott [baŋˈrɔt] *adj* bankrupt ‖ *m* (-[e]s;-e) bankruptcy

Bank′verkehr *m* banking (*activity*)

Bank′wesen *n* banking

Bann [ban] *m* (-[e]s;-e) ban; (*Zauber*) spell; (eccl) excommunication

bannen [ˈbanən] *tr* banish; (*Geister*) exorcize; (eccl) excommunicate

Banner [ˈbanər] *n* (-s;-) banner; standard

Ban′nerträger *m* standard-bearer

Bann′fluch *m* anathema

Bann′kreis *m* spell; **in j-s B. geraten** come under s.o.'s spell

Bann′meile *f* (fig) city limits

Bann′ware *f* contraband

bar [bar] *adj* bare; (*rein*) pure, sheer; (fin) cash ‖ *adv* cash ‖ *prep* (genit) devoid of, lacking ‖ **Bar** *f* (-;-s) bar, taproom

Bär [ber] *m* (-en;-en) bear; (astr) Dipper; **j-m e-n B. aufbinden** tell s.o. a fish story

Bar- *comb.fm.* cash

Baracke [baˈrakə] *f* (-;-n) barrack; (wooden) hut

Barbar **-in** [barˈbar(ɪn)] §7 *mf* barbarian

Barbarei [barbaˈraɪ] *f* (-;-en) barbarism; (*Grausamkeit*) barbarity

barbarisch [barˈbarɪʃ] *adj* barbarous; barbaric, primitive

bärbeißig [ˈberbaɪsɪç] *adj* surly

Bar′bestand *m* cash on hand

Bar′betrag *m* amount in cash

Barbier [barˈbir] *m* (-s;-e) barber

barbieren [barˈbirən] *tr* shave; (fig) fleece

Barett [baˈret] *n* (-[e]s;-e) beret

barfuß [ˈbarfus] *adv* barefoot

barfüßig [ˈbarfysɪç] *adj* barefooted

barg [bark] *pret* of **bergen**

Bar′geld *n* cash

barhäuptig [ˈbarhɔɪptɪç] *adj* bareheaded

Bar′hocker *m* bar stool

Bariton [ˈbarɪton] *m* (-s;-e) baritone

Barkasse [barˈkasə] *f* (-;-n) launch

Bärme [ˈbermə] *f* (-;) yeast, leaven

barmherzig [barmˈhertsɪç] *adj* merciful

Bar′mittel *pl* cash

barock [baˈrɔk] *adj* baroque ‖ **Barock** *m & n* (-[s];) baroque; baroque period

Barometer [baroˈmetər] *n* (-s;-) barometer

Baron [baˈron] *m* (-s;-e) baron

Baronin [baˈronɪn] *f* (-;-nen) baroness

Barre ['barə] f (-;-n) bar
Barren ['barən] m (-s;-) bar; ingot; (gym) parallel bars
Barriere [bar'jerə] f (-;-n) barrier
barsch [barʃ] adj gruff, rude ‖ **Barsch** m (-es;-e) (ichth) perch
Barschaft ['barʃaft] f (-;) cash
barst [barst] pret of **bersten**
Bart [bart] m (-[e]s;ӟе) beard; (e-r Katze) whiskers; (e-s Fisches) barb; **der B. ist ab!** the jig is up!; **sich** [dat] **e-n B. wachsen lassen** grow a beard
bärtig ['bertɪç] adj bearded
bart'los adj beardless
Bar'verlust m straight loss
Basalt [ba'zalt] m (-[e]s;-e) basalt
Basar [ba'zar] m (-s;-e) bazaar
Ba·sis ['bazɪs] f (-;-sen [zən]) basis; (archit, math, mil) base
Baß [bas] m (Basses;Bässe) (mus) bass
Baß'geige f bass viol, contrabass
Bassin [ba'sɛ̃] n (-s;-s) reservoir; swimming pool; (naut) dock, basin
Baß'schlüssel m bass clef
Baß'stimme f bass (voice), basso
basta ['basta] interj—**und damit b.!** and that's that!
Bastard ['bastart] m (-[e]s;-e) bastard; (bot) hybrid
Bastei [bas'taɪ] f (-;-en) bastion
basteln ['bastəln] intr tinker
Bast'ler –in §6 mf hobbyist
bat [bat] pret of **bitten**
Bataillon [batal'jon] n (-s;-e) battalion
Batte·rie [batə'ri] f (-;-rien ['ri·ən] battery
Bau [baʊ] m (-[e]s; erection, construction, building; (Bauart) structure, design; (Körper-) build; **er ist beim Bau** he is in the building trade; **er ist vom Bau** (coll) he's in the racket; **im Bau** under construction ‖ m (-[e]s;-ten) building; **auf dem Bau** at the construction site ‖ m (-[e]s;-e) burrow, hole; (min) mine
–bau m comb.fm. –construction, –building; –culture; –mining
Bau'abnahme f building inspection
Bau'arbeiter m construction worker
Bau'art f build; structure; type, model
Bauch [baʊx] m (-[e]s;ӟе) belly, stomach; (Leib) bowels; (coll) pot-belly
Bauch– comb.fm. abdominal
bauchig ['baʊxɪç] adj bulging; convex
Bauch'klatscher m belly flop
Bauch'laden m vendor's tray
Bauch'landung f belly-landing
Bauch'redner –in §6 mf ventriloquist
Bauch'speicheldrüse f pancreas
Bauch'weh n stomach ache, bellyache
bauen ['baʊ·ən] tr build; erect; make, manufacture; (ackern) till; (anbauen) grow ‖ intr build; (an dat) work (at); (auf acc) depend (on), trust
Bauer ['baʊ·ər] m (-s & -n;-n) farmer; (cards) jack; (chess) pawn ‖ m (-s;-) builder ‖ m & n (-s;-) bird-cage
Bäuerchen ['bɔɪ·ərçən] n (-s;-) small farmer; (baby's) burp

Bäuerin ['bɔɪ·ərɪn] f (-;-nen) farmer's wife
bäuerisch ['bɔɪ·ərɪʃ] adj boorish
Bau'erlaubnis f building permit
bäuerlich ['bɔɪ·ərlɪç] adj rural
Bau'ernbursche m country lad
Bau'erndirne f country girl
Bauernfänger ['baʊ·ərnfɛŋər] m (-s;-) confidence man
Bau'erngut n, **Bau'ernhof** m farm
Bau'fach n architecture
bau'fällig adj dilapidated
Bau'genehmigung f building permit
Bau'gerüst n scaffold(ing)
Bau'gewerbe n building trade
Bau'gewerkschule f school of architecture and civil engineering
Bau'grundstück n building site
Bau'holz n lumber
Bau'kasten m building set
Bau'kunst f architecture
bau'lich adj architectural; structural; **in gutem baulichen Zustand** in good repair
Baum [baʊm] m (-[e]s;ӟе) tree; (mach) shaft, axle; (naut) boom
Bau'meister m building contractor, builder; architect
baumeln ['baʊməln] intr dangle
bäumen ['bɔɪmən] ref rear
Baum'garten m orchard
Baum'grenze f timber line
Baum'krone f treetop
Baum'schere f pruning shears
Baum'schule f nursery (of saplings)
Baum'stamm m tree trunk
baum'stark' adj strong as an ox
Bau'muster n model (number)
Baum'wolle f cotton
Baum'wollkapsel f cotton boll
Baum'wollsamt m velveteen
Bau'plan m ground plan
Bau'platz m building lot
Bau'rat m (-[e]s;ӟе) building inspector
Bausch [baʊʃ] m (-[e]s;-e) pad, wad; (e-s Segels) bulge, belly; **in B. und Bogen** wholesale
bauschen ['baʊʃən] tr, ref & intr bulge, swell
bauschig ['baʊʃɪç] adj puffy; baggy
Bau'schule f school of architecture and civil engineering
Bau'sparkasse f building and loan association
Bau'stahl m structural steel
Bau'stein m building stone; brick
Bau'stelle f building site; road construction
Bau'stoff m building material
Bau'techniker m construction engineer
Bau'unternehmer m contractor
Bau'unternehmung f building firm, building contractors
Bau'werk n building, edifice
Bau'wesen n building industry
Bau'zaun m hoarding
Bau'zeichnung f blueprint
Bayer –in ['baɪ·ər(ɪn)] §6 mf Bavarian
bayerisch ['baɪ·ərɪʃ] adj Bavarian
Bayern ['baɪ·ərn] n (-s;) Bavaria
Bazillenträger [ba'tsɪləntregər] m germ carrier

Bazil·lus [ba'tsɪlʊs] *m* (-;-len [lən]) bacillus

be– [bə] *insep pref*

beabsichtigen [bə'apzɪçtɪgən] *tr* intend; (mit) mean (by)

beach'ten *tr* pay attention to; (*merken*) note, notice; (*befolgen*) observe; (*berücksichtigen*) consider

beach'tenswert *adj* noteworthy

Beach'tung *f* (-;) attention; notice; observance; consideration

Beamte [bə'amtə] *m* (-n;-n) official

Beam'tenherrschaft *f* bureaucracy

Beam'tenlaufbahn *f* civil service career

Beamtentum [bə'amtəntum] *n* (-[e]s;) officialdom, bureaucracy

Beamtin [bə'amtɪn] *f* (-;-nen) official

beäng'stigen *tr* make anxious, alarm

beanspruchen [bə'an/pruxən] *tr* claim; (*Zeit, Raum*) require; **zu stark beansprucht werden be** worked too hard

beanstanden [bə'an/tandən] *tr* object to, find fault with; (*Waren*) reject; (*Wahl*) contest; (*Recht*) challenge

Bean'standung *f* (-;-en) objection; complaint

bean'tragen *tr* propose; (**bei**) apply for (to)

beant'worten *tr* answer

Beant'wortung *f* (-;-en) answer

bear'beiten *tr* work; (*Land*) cultivate; (*Buch, Text*) revise; (*Wörterbuch*) compile; (*für die Bühne*) adapt; (*ein Manuskript*) prepare; (*Thema; Kunden*) work on; (*Person*) try to influence; (chem) treat; (*Auftrag*) (com) handle; (*Fall*) (jur) handle; (metal) machine, tool; (mus) arrange

bearg'wöhnen *tr* be suspicious of

beaufsichtigen [bə'aufzɪçtɪgən] *tr* supervise; (*Arbeiten*) superintend; (*Kinder*) look after; (educ) proctor; **streng b.** keep a sharp eye on

beauf'tragen *tr* commission, appoint; (**mit**) entrust (with)

Beauftragte [bə'auftraktə] §5 *mf* representative; (com) agent

bebau'en *tr* cultivate; (*Gelände*) build up

beben ['bebən] *intr* (**vor**) tremble (with), shake (with); (*Erde*) quake

bebrillt [bə'brɪlt] *adj* bespectacled

Becher ['bɛçər] *m* (-s;-) cup, mug

bechern ['bɛçərn] *intr* (coll) booze

Becken ['bɛkən] *n* (-s;-) basin, bowl; (anat) pelvis; (mus) cymbal

bedacht [bə'daxt] *adj* (**auf** *acc*) intent (on); **auf alles b. sein** think of everything; **darauf b. sein zu** (*inf*) be anxious to (*inf*) || **Bedacht** *m*—**B. nehmen auf** (*acc*) take into consideration; **mit B.** deliberately; with caution

bedächtig [bə'dɛçtɪç], **bedachtsam** [bə'daxtzam] *adj* cautious, deliberate

bedan'ken *ref*—**ich würde mich bestens b., wenn** (iron) I would be most indignant if; **sich b. bei j–m für** thank s.o. for

Bedarf [bə'darf] *m* (-[e]s;) demand; requirement; (**an** *dat*) need (of); **bei B.** if required; **den B. decken** meet the demand; **nach B.** as required;

seinen B. decken an (*dat*) get one's supply of

Bedarfs'artikel *pl* needs, supplies

Bedarfs'fall *m*—**im B.** in case of need

Bedarfs'güter *pl* consumer goods

Bedarfs'haltestelle *f* optional bus or trolley stop

Bedarfs'träger *m* consumer

bedauerlich [bə'dau·ərlɪç] *adj* regrettable

bedau'erlicherweise *adv* unfortunately

bedauern [bə'dau·ərn] *tr* pity, feel sorry for; regret, deplore || **Bedauern** *n* (-s;) (**über** *acc*) regret (over); (*Mitleid*) (mit) pity (for)

bedau'ernswert *adj* pitiful, pitiable

bedecken (bedek'ken) *tr* cover; **bedeckt** overcast

Bedeckung (Bedek'kung) *f* (-;-en) cover; escort; (mil) escort; (nav) convoy

beden'ken §66 *tr* consider; (*beachten*) bear in mind; (*im Testament*) provide for || *ref* deliberate, think a matter over; **sich e–s anderen b.** change one's mind || **Bedenken** *n* (-s;-) (*Erwägung*) consideration, reflection; (*Einwand*) objection; (*Zweifel*) doubt, scruple

bedenk'lich *adj* (*ernst*) serious, critical; (*gefährlich*) risky; (*heikel*) ticklish; (*Charakter*) questionable

bedeu'ten *tr* mean; **das hat nichts zu b.** that doesn't matter; **j–m b., daß** make it clear to s.o. that

bedeu'tend *adj* important; (*beträchtlich*) considerable

bedeutsam [bə'dɔɪtzam] *adj* significant; (*Blick*) meaningful

Bedeu'tung *f* (-;-en) meaning; (*Wichtigkeit*) importance

bedeu'tungsvoll *adj* significant

bedie'nen *tr* wait on, serve; (*Maschine*) operate || *ref* (*genit*) make use of; **bedienen Sie sich** help yourself || *intr* wait on people; (cards) follow suit

Bedie'nung *f* (-;) service; servants; waitresses

Bedienungs– *comb.fm.* control

Bedie'nungsanweisung *f* instructions

Bedie'nungsmannshaft *f* gun crew

bedingen [bə'dɪŋən] *tr* condition, stipulate; (*in sich schließen*) imply; **bedingt** conditioned, conditional

bedin'gungsweise *adv* conditionally

bedrän'gen *tr* press hard; (*beunruhigen*) pester; **bedrängte Lage** state of distress; **bedrängte Verhältnisse** financial difficulties

Bedrängnis [bə'drɛŋnɪs] *f* (-;-se) distress; **in ärgster B.** in dire straits

bedro'hen *tr* threaten, menace

bedroh'lich *adj* threatening

bedrucken (bedruk'ken) *tr* print on; (*Stoff*) print

bedrücken (bedrük'ken) *tr* oppress

bedür'fen §69 *intr* (*genit*) require

Bedürfnis [bə'dyrfnɪs] *n* (-ses;-se) need, requirement; (*Wunsch*) desire; **Bedürfnisse** necessities; **das dringende B. haben zu** (*inf*) have the urge to (*inf*)

Bedürf'nisanstalt *f* comfort station
bedürf'nislos *adj* having few needs
bedürftig [bə'dyrftɪç] *adj* needy; **b. sein** (*genit*) be in need of
Beefsteak ['bifstek] *n* (*-s;-s*) steak; **Deutsches B.** hamburger
beehren [bə'erən] *tr* honor || *ref—sich b. zu* (*inf*) have the honor of (*ger*)
beei'len *ref* hurry (up)
beein'drucken *tr* impress
beeinflussen [bə'aɪnflusən] *tr* influence
Beein'flussung *f* (*-;*) (*genit*) influence (on), effect (on); (*pol*) lobbying
beeinträchtigen [bə'aɪntrɛçtɪgən] *tr* (*Ruf*) damage; (*Wert*) detract from; (*Rechte*) encroach upon; (*Aussichten*) hurt, spoil
been'den, been'digen *tr* end, conclude; (*Arbeit*) complete
beengen [bə'ɛŋən] *tr* confine, cramp; **sich beengt fühlen** feel cramped; (fig) feel restricted
beer'ben *tr—j—n b.* inherit s.o.'s estate
beerdigen [bə'erdɪgən] *tr* bury, inter
Beer'digung *f* (*-;-en*) burial
Beere ['berə] *f* (*-;-n*) berry
Beet [bet] *n* (*-[e]s;-e*) (agr) bed
befähigen [bə'fɛ·ɪgən] *tr* enable, qualify
befähigt [bə'fɛ·ɪçt] *adj* able, capable
Befä'higung *f* (*-;-en*) qualification; (*Fähigkeit*) ability
befahl [bə'fal] *pret* of **befehlen**
befahrbar [bə'farbar] *adj* (*Weg*) passable; (*Wasser*) navigable
befah'ren §71 *tr* travel; (*Meer*) sail; (*Fluß*) navigate; (*Küste*) sail along; (*Schacht*) go down
befal'len §72 *tr* strike, attack; infest
befan'gen *adj* embarrassed; (*schüchtern*) shy; (*voreingenommen*) prejudiced; (*parteiisch*) partial
befas'sen *tr* touch, handle || *ref—sich b. mit* concern oneself with
befehden [bə'fedən] *tr* make war on
Befehl [bə'fel] *m* (*-s;-e*) order, command; **auf B.** (*genit*) by order of
befeh'len §51 *tr* order, command; **was b. Sie?** what is your pleasure?
befehligen [bə'felɪgən] *tr* command, be in command of
Befehls'form *f* imperative mood
Befehlshaber [bə'felshabər] *m* (*-s;-*) (mil) commanding officer; (nav) commander in chief; **oberster B.** supreme commander
befehlshaberisch [bə'felshabərɪʃ] *adj* imperious
Befehls'stelle *f* command post
befe'stigen *tr* (an *dat*) fasten (to), attach (to); (mil) fortify
Befe'stigung *f* (*-;-en*) fortification
befeuchten [bə'fɔɪçtən] *tr* moisten, wet
befeu'ern *tr* (aer, naut) mark with lights; (mil) fire on, shoot at
befin'den §59 *tr* deem || *ref* be, feel || **Befinden** *n* (*-s;*) judgment, view; (state of) health; **je nach B.** according to taste
befindlich [bə'fɪntlɪç] *adj* present, to

be found; **all die im Hafen befindlichen Schiffe** the ships (present) in the harbor; **b. sein** happen to be
beflecken (beflek'ken) *tr* stain, taint
beflissen [bə'flɪsən] *adj* (*genit*) keen (on), interested (in) || **Beflissene** §5 *mf* (*genit*) student (of)
befohlen [bə'folən] *pp* of **befehlen**
befol'gen *tr* obey, comply with
Befol'gung *f* (*-;*) observance
beför'dern *tr* ship; (*spedieren*) forward; (*im Rang*) promote; (*fördern*) further
Beför'derungsmittel *n* means of transportation
befra'gen *tr* question, interrogate; poll; (*um Rat*) consult
befrakt [bə'frakt] *adj* in tails
befrei'en *tr* free; liberate; (*vom Militärdienst*) exempt; (*von e-r Aufgabe*) excuse; (*von Sorgen, e-r Last*) relieve
Befrei'ung *f* (*-;-en*) freeing; liberation; exemption; rescue
befremden [bə'fremdən] *tr* surprise, astonish; strike as odd || **Befremden** *n* (*-s;*) surprise, astonishment
befreunden [bə'frɔɪndən] *ref—sich mit etw b.* reconcile oneself to s.th.; **sich mit j—m b.** make friends with s.o.
befrieden [bə'fridən] *tr* pacify
befriedigen [bə'fridɪgən] *tr* satisfy
befrie'digend *adj* satisfactory
befristen [bə'frɪstən] *tr* set a time limit on
Befri'stung *f* (*-;-en*) time limit
befruchten [bə'fruxtən] *tr* (*Land*) make fertile; (*schwängern*) impregnate; (*Ei*) fertilize; **künstlich b.** inseminate; (bot) pollinate
befugt [bə'fukt] *adj* authorized
befüh'len *tr* feel, touch
Befund' *m* (*-[e]s;-e*) findings, facts
befürch'ten *tr* fear, be afraid of
Befürch'tung *f* (*-;-en*) apprehension
befürworten [bə'fyrvɔrtən] *tr* support; (*anraten*) recommend
begabt [bə'gapt] *adj* gifted, talented
Bega'bung *f* (*-;-en*) aptitude; (natural) gift, talent
Bega'bungsprüfung *f* intelligence test
begann [bə'gan] *pret* of **beginnen**
begatten [bə'gatən] *tr* mate with || *ref* copulate, mate
bege'ben §80 *tr* (*Anleihen*) float, place; (*Wertpapiere*) sell || *ref* go; occur; **es begab sich** (Bib) it came to pass; **sich an die Arbeit b.** set to work; **sich auf die Flucht b.** take to flight; **sich auf die Reise b.** set out on a trip; **sich b.** (*genit*) renounce; **sich in Gefahr b.** expose oneself to danger
Bege'benheit *f* (*-;-en*) event, incident
begegnen [bə'gegnən] *intr* (SEIN) (*dat*) meet, come upon; (*Schwierigkeiten, Feind*) encounter; (*Gefahr*) face
bege'hen §82 *tr* walk on; walk along; (*Verbrechen, Irrtum*) commit; (*Fest*) celebrate
Begehr [bə'ger] *m & n* (*-s;*) desire; request; (econ) demand
begehren [bə'gerən] *tr* wish for; crave;

(Bib) covet; etw von j–m b. ask s.o. for s.th. || *intr* (nach) yearn (for)

begeh′renswert *adj* desirable

begehr′lich *adj* covetous

begehrt [bə'gert] *adj* in demand

begeistert [bə'gaɪstərt] *adj* enthusiastic

Begei′sterung *f* (–;) enthusiasm

Begier [bə'gir] *f* (–;) var of **Begierde**

Begierde [bə'girdə] *f* (–;–n) desire; (fleshly) appetite; eagerness; craving

begierig [bə'giriç] *adj* eager; (*Augen*) hungry; (nach, auf *acc*) desirous (of); b. zu (*inf*) eager to (*inf*)

begie′ßen §76 *tr* water; (culin) baste; das wollen wir b. we want to celebrate it (*by drinking*)

Beginn [bə'gɪn] *m* (–[e]s;) beginning; (*Ursprung*) origin

beginnen [bə'gɪnən] §52 *tr & intr* begin

beglaubigen [bə'glaubɪgən] *tr* certify, authenticate; (*Gesandten*) accredit

Beglau′bigung *f* (–;) authentication; accreditation

Beglau′bigungsschreiben *n* (dipl) credentials

beglei′chen §85 *tr* balance; (*Rechnung*) pay in full; (*Streit*) settle

begleiten [bə'glaɪtən] *tr* accompany, escort; see (*e.g., off, home*); hinaus b. see to the door

Beglei′ter –in §6 *mf* companion

Beglei′terscheinung *f* concomitant

Beglei′tmusik *f* background music

Beglei′tschreiben *s* covering letter

Beglei′tung *f* (–;–en) company; escort; (*Gefolge*) retinue; (mus) accompaniment

beglück′wünschen *tr* (zu) congratulate (on)

Beglück′wünschung *f* (–;–en) congratulation

begnadet [bə'gnadət] *adj* highly gifted

begnadigen [bə'gnadɪgən] *tr* pardon; (pol) grant amnesty to

Begna′digung *f* (–;–en) pardon; amnesty

begnügen [bə'gnygən] *ref* (mit) content oneself (with), be satisfied (with)

begonnen [bə'gɔnən] *pp* of **beginnen**

begra′ben §87 *tr* bury

Begräbnis [bə'grepnɪs] *n* (–ses;–se) burial; funeral

Begräb′nisfeier *f* funeral

Begräb′nisstätte *f* burial place

begradigen [bə'gradɪgən] *tr* straighten; (tech) align

begrei′fen §88 *tr* touch, handle; (*verstehen*) grasp; (*enthalten*) comprise

begreif′lich *adj* understandable

begreif′licherweise *adv* understandably

begren′zen *tr* bound; limit, restrict

Begren′zung *f* (–;–en) limitation

Begriff [bə'grɪf] *m* (–[e]s;–e) idea, notion; (*Ausdruck*) term; (philos) concept; im B. sein zu (*inf*) be on the point of (*ger*)

begriffen [bə'grɪfən] *adj*—b. sein in (*dat*) be in the process of

begrün′den *tr* found, establish; (*Behauptung*) substantiate, prove

Begrün′der –in §6 *mf* founder

Begrün′dung *f* (–;–en) establishment; proof; (*Grund*) ground, reason

begrüßen *tr* greet; welcome

begünstigen [bə'gynstɪgən] *tr* favor; (*fördern*) promote, support; (jur) aid and abet

Begün′stiger *m* (–s;–) accessory after the fact

Begün′stigte [bə'gynstɪçtə] §5 *mf* (ins) beneficiary

Begün′stigung *f* (–;–en) promotion, encouragement; support, backing; (jur) aiding and abetting

begut′achten *tr* give an expert opinion on; b. lassen obtain expert opinion on

begütert [bə'gytərt] *adj* well-to-do

begütigen [bə'gytɪgən] *tr* appease

behaart [bə'hart] *adj* hairy

behäbig [bə'hebɪç] *adj* comfort-loving; (*beleibt*) portly

behaftet [bə'haftət] *adj* afflicted

behagen [bə'hagən] *intr* (dat) please, suit || **Behagen** *n* (–s;) pleasure

behaglich [bə'haklɪç] *adj* pleasant; (*traulich*) snug, cozy

behal′ten §90 *tr* keep, retain; **Recht b.** turn out to be right

Behälter [bə'heltər] *m* (–s;–) container; box; (*für Öl, usw.*) tank

behan′deln *tr* treat; deal with; handle

behän′gen §92 *tr* hang; deck out

beharren [bə'harən] *intr* remain (unchanged); (in *dat*) persevere (in); (auf *dat*) persist (in), stick (to)

beharrlich [bə'harlɪç] *adj* steadfast

behau′en §93 *tr* hew

behaupten [bə'hauptən] *tr* declare, assert; (*festhalten*) maintain, retain; allege || *ref* stand one's ground; (*Preise*) remain steady

behausen [bə'hauzən] *tr* lodge, house

Behau′sung *f* (–;–en) dwelling

behe′ben §94 *tr* (*Schwierigkeiten*) remove; (*Zweifel*) dispel; (*Schaden*) repair; (*Lage*) remedy; (*Geld*) withdraw; (*Schmerzen*) eliminate

beheimatet [bə'haɪmatət] *adj*—b. sein in (*dat*) reside in; come from

Behelf [bə'helf] *m* (–[e]s;–e) expedient; makeshift

behel′fen §96 *ref* (mit) make do (with)

Behelfs– *comb.fm.* temporary

behelfs′mäßig *adj* temporary, makeshift

behelligen [bə'helɪgən] *tr* bother

Behel′ligung *f* (–;–en) bother, trouble

behende [bə'hendə] *adj* agile, quick; (*gewandt*) handy; (geistig) smart

beherbergen [bə'herbergən] *tr* take in, put up (*as guest*)

beherr′schen *tr* (*Land*) rule; (*Sprache*) master; (*Gefühle*) control; (*überragen*) tower over; den Luftraum b. (mil) have air supremacy

Beherr′scher –in §6 *mf* ruler || *m* master || *f* mistress

beherzigen [bə'hertsɪgən] *tr* take to heart, remember

beherzt [bə'hertst] *adj* courageous

behe′xen *tr* bewitch; (fig) captivate

behilflich [bə'hɪlflɪç] *adj* helpful

behin′dern *tr* hinder; hamper; block

behor′chen *tr* overhear

Behörde [bə'hørdə] *f* (-;-n) authority, board; *die Behörden* the authorities

behördlich [bə'hørtlıç] *adj* official

behü'ten *tr* (**vor** *dat*) protect (against); **Gott behüte!** God forbid!

behutsam [bə'hutzam] *adj* wary

bei [baɪ] *prep* (*dat*) (*Ort*) by, beside, at, with, in; (*in Anschriften*) in care of, c/o; (*Zeit, Umstände*) at, by, during, on; (*Zustände, Eigenschaften*) at, while, in; **bei mir haben** have on me; **bei meiner Ehre** upon my honor; **bei Schiller** in the works of Schiller; **bei uns** at our house; **bei weitem** by far

bei'behalten §90 *tr* retain, keep

Bei'blatt *n* supplement

bei'bringen §65 *tr* obtain, procure; (*Beweise, Zeugen*) produce; (*Arznei, Gift*) administer; (*Wunde, Niederlage, Schlag, Verluste*) inflict; **j-m die Nachricht schonend b.** break the news gently to s.o.; **j-m etw b.** teach s.o. s.th., make s.th. clear to s.o.

Beichte ['baɪçtə] *f* (-;-n) confession

beichten ['baɪçtən] *tr* (*eccl*) confess

Beicht'kind *n* (*eccl*) penitent

Beicht'stuhl *m* (*eccl*) confessional

beide ['baɪdə] *adj* both; two || *pron* both; two; **keiner von beiden** neither of them

beiderlei ['baɪdər'laɪ] *invar adj* both kinds of

beiderseitig ['baɪdər'zaɪtɪç] *adj* bilateral; (*gemeinsam*) mutual

beiderseits ['baɪdər'zaɪts] *adv* on both sides; mutually, reciprocally || *prep* (*genit*) on both sides of

beieinan'der *adv* together; **gut b. sein** (coll) be in good shape

Bei'fahrer –in §6 *mf* relief driver; passenger (*next to the driver*)

Bei'fall *m* approval; applause

bei'fällig *adj* approving; (*Bericht*) favorable || *adv* approvingly

Bei'fallklatschen *n* clapping, applause

Bei'fallsgeschrei *n* loud cheering

Bei'fallsruf *m* cheer

Bei'film *m* (cin) second feature

bei'folgend *adj* enclosed

bei'fügen *tr* add; (*e-m Brief*) enclose

bei'fügid *adj* (gram) attributive

Bei'fügung *f* (-;-en) addition; enclosure; (gram) attributive

Bei'gabe *f* extra; funerary gift

bei'geben §80 *tr* add; assign || *intr* give in; **klein b.** knuckle under

Bei'geschmack *m* taste, flavor; tinge

Bei'hilfe *f* aid; (*Stipendium*) grant; (*Unterstützung*) subsidy; allowance; (jur) aiding and abetting

bei'kommen § 99 *intr* (SEIN) (*dat*) get the better of; (*dat*) reach; *e-r Schwierigkeit* overcome

Beil [baɪl] *n* (-[e]s;-e) hatchet

Bei'lage *f* (*im Brief*) enclosure; (*e-r Zeitung*) supplement; **Fleisch mit B.** meat and vegetables

beiläufig ['baɪlɔɪfɪç] *adj* incidental; casual || *adv* by the way, incidentally; **b. erwähnen** mention in passing

bei'legen *tr* add; (*Titel*) confer; (*Wichtigkeit*) attach; (*Streit*) settle; **etw**

e-m Brief b. enclose s.th. in a letter || *intr* heave to

Bei'leid *n* (-s;) condolence(s)

bei'liegen §108 *intr*—**e-m Brief b.** be enclosed in a letter; **j-m b.** lie with s.o

beim *abbr* **bei dem**

bei'messen §70 *tr* attribute, impute

bei'mischen *tr* mix in

Bein [baɪn] *n* (-[e]s;-e) leg; (*Knochen*) bone; (fig) foot; **j-m ein B. stellen** trip s.o.

beinahe ['baɪna·ə], [baɪ'na·e] *adv* almost, nearly

Bei'name *m* appellation; (*Spitzname*) nickname

Bein'bruch *m* fracture, broken leg

Bein'schiene *f* (surg) splint; (sport) shin guard

Bein'schützer *m* (sport) shin guard

bei'ordnen *tr* assign, appoint (*s.o.*) as assistant; (*dat*) place (*s.th.*) on a level (with)

beipflichten ['baɪpflıçtən] *intr* (*dat*) agree with (*s.o.*), agree to (*s.th.*)

Bei'programm *n* (cin) second feature

Bei'rat *m* (-s;-̈e) adviser, counselor; (*Körperschaft*) advisory board

beir'ren *tr* mislead

beisammen [baɪ'zamən] *adv* together

Beisam'mensein *n* (-s;) being together; gathering, reunion; **geselliges B.** social; informal reception

Bei'satz *m* addition; (*bei Legierung*) alloy; (gram) appositive

Bei'schlaf *m* sexual intercourse

bei'schließen §76 *tr* enclose

Bei'schluß *m*—**unter B. von allen Dokumenten** with all documents attached

bei'schreiben §62 *tr* write in the margin; add as a postscript

Bei'schrift *f* postscript

Bei'sein *n* (-s;) presence

beisei'te *adv* aside; **b. schaffen** remove; (coll) do (*s.o.*) in

bei'setzen *tr* bury, inter

Bei'sitzer *m* associate judge

Bei'spiel *n* example; **zum B.** for example

bei'spielhaft *adj* exemplary

bei'spiellos *adj* unparalleled

bei'spielsweise *adv* by way of example

bei'springen §142 *intr* (*dat*) come to the aid of

beißen ['baɪsən] §53 *tr & intr* bite

bei'ßend *adj* biting; stinging, pungent, acrid; sarcastic; (*Reue*) bitter

Beiß'korb *m* muzzle

Beiß'zahn *m* (anat) incisor

Beiß'zange *f* pincers, nippers

Bei'stand *m* aid, support; (*Person*) assistant

bei'stehen §146 *intr* (*dat*) stand by, back, support

Bei'steuer *f* contribution

bei'steuern *tr* contribute

bei'stimmen *intr* (*dat*) agree with

Bei'stimmung *f* (-;) approval

Bei'strich *m* comma

Beitrag ['baɪtrak] *m* (-[e]s;-̈e) contribution; (*e-s Mitglieds*) dues

bei'tragen §132 *tr & intr* contribute
bei'treiben §62 *tr* collect; (*Abgaben*) exact; (mil) commandeer, requisition
bei'treten §152 *intr* (SEIN) (*dat*) join; (*j-s Meinung*) concur in
Bei'tritt *m* joining; concurrence
Bei'wagen *m* (aut) sidecar
Bei'werk *n* (-[e]s;) accessories
bei'wohnen *intr* (*dat*) attend; (*e-m Ereignis*) be witness to; (*j-m*) have intercourse with (s.o.)
Bei'wort *n* (-[e]s;╧er) epithet; (gram) adjective
Beize ['baɪtsə] *f* (-;-n) corrosive; (wood) stain; (*Falken-*) falconry; (culin) marinade
beizeiten [baɪ'tsaɪtən] *adv* on time; (*frühzeitig*) early
beizen ['baɪtsən] *tr* (*ätzen*) corrode; (*Holz*) stain; (*Wunde*) cauterize; (hunt) go hawking
bejahen [bə'jɑ·ən] *tr* say 'yes' to
beja'hend *adj* affirmative
bejahrt [bə'jɑrt] *adj* aged
bekämp'fen *tr* fight, oppose
bekannt [bə'kant] *adj* known; familiar; (*berühmt*) well-known || **Bekannte** §5 *mf* acquaintance
Bekannt'gabe *f* announcement
bekannt'geben §80 *tr* announce
bekannt'lich *adv* as is well known
bekannt'machen *tr* announce; (*Gesetz*) promulgate
Bekannt'machung *f* (-;-en) publication, announcement; (*Plakat*) poster
Bekannt'schaft *f* (-;) acquaintance; (coll) acquaintances
bekeh'ren *tr* convert || *ref* (zu) become a convert (to)
Bekehrte [bə'kertə] §5 *mf* convert
beken'nen §97 *tr* (*Sünde*) confess; (*zugestehen*) admit; **Farbe b.** follow suit; (fig) put one's cards on the table || *ref—sich* **schuldig b.** plead guilty; **sich zu e-r Religion b.** profess a religion; **sich zu e-r Tat b.** own up to a deed; **sich zu j-m b.** stand by s.o., believe in s.o.
Bekennt'nis *n* (eccl) confession; (*Konfession*) denomination
bekla'gen *tr* deplore; (*Tod*) mourn || *ref* (über *acc*) complain (about), find fault (with)
bekla'genswert *adj* deplorable
Beklagte [bə'klɑktə] §5 *mf* defendant
beklat'schen *tr* applaud
bekle'ben *tr* paste; (*mit Etiketten*) label; **e-e Mauer mit Plakaten b.** paste posters on a wall
beklei'den *tr* clothe, dress; (*Mauer*) face, cover; (*Amt*) hold
beklem'men *tr* stifle, oppress
Beklem'mung *f* (-;-en) worry, anxiety; **Beklemmungen** claustrophobia
beklommen [bə'kləmən] *adj* uneasy
bekom'men §99 *tr* get; obtain; receive; (*Schnupfen*) catch; (*Risse*) develop || *intr* (*dat*) do good; **j-m schlecht b.** do s.o. harm; **wohl bekomm's!** to your health!
bekömmlich [bə'kœmlɪç] *adj* digestible; (*gesund*) healthful; (*zuträglich*) wholesome

beköstigen [bə'kœstɪgən] *tr* board, feed || *ref—sich selbst* **b.** do one's own cooking
bekräf'tigen *tr* (*Vorschlag*) support; (*bestätigen*) substantiate; **mit e-m Eid b.** seal with an oath
bekrän'zen *tr* wreath, crown
bekreu'zen, bekreu'zigen *ref* cross oneself, make the sign of the cross
bekrie'gen *tr* make war on
bekrit'teln *tr* criticize, pick at
bekrit'zeln *tr* scribble on, doodle on
beküm'mern *tr* worry, trouble || *ref* (um) concern oneself (with), bother (about)
beküm'mert *adj* (über *acc*) worried (about)
bekunden [bə'kundən] *tr* manifest, show; (*öffentlich*) state publicly
bela'den §103 *tr* load; (fig) burden
Belag [bə'lɑk] *m* (-[e]s;╧) covering; coat(ing); flooring; layer; surface
bela'gern *tr* besiege, beleaguer
Bela'gerung *f* (-;-en) siege
Belang [bə'laŋ] *m* (-[e]s;e) importance, consequence; **Belange** interests
belan'gen *tr* (jur) sue; **was mich belangt** as far as I am concerned
belang'los *adj* unimportant
bela'sten *tr* load (down); (*Grundstück*) encumber; (fig) burden; (acct) charge; (jur) incriminate
belästigen [bə'lestɪgən] *tr* annoy, bother; (*mit Fragen*) pester; (*unabsichtlich*) inconvenience
Bela'stung *f* (-;-en) load; encumbrance; (fig) burden; (acct) debit; **die Zeiten größter B.** the peak hours
Bela'stungsprobe *f* (fig) acid test
Bela'stungszeuge *m* witness for the prosecution
belau'fen §105 *ref—sich* **b. auf** (*acc*) amount to, come to
belau'schen *tr* overhear
bele'ben *tr* animate; (*Getränk*) spike; **wieder b.** revive
belebt [bə'lept] *adj* animated, lively
Bele'bungsmittel *n* stimulant
Beleg [bə'lek] *m* (-s;-e) (*Beweisstück*) evidence; (*Unterlage*) voucher; (*Beispiel*) example; (jur) exhibit
bele'gen *tr* cover; (*Platz*) take, occupy; (*bemannen*) man; (*beweisen*) verify; (*Vorlesung*) register for; **ein Brötchen mit Schinken b.** make a ham sandwich; **mit Beispielen b.** exemplify; **mit Fliesen b.** tile; **mit Steuern b.** tax; **mit Teppichen b.** carpet || *ref* become coated
Beleg'schaft *f* (-;-en) crew; personnel; shift
Beleg'schein *m* voucher; receipt
Beleg'stelle *f* reference
belegt [bə'lekt] *adj* (*Platz*) reserved; (*Zunge*) coated; (*Stimme*) husky; (telp) busy; **belegtes Brot** sandwich
beleh'ren *tr* instruct || *ref—sich* **b. lassen** listen to reason
beleh'rend *adj* instructive
Beleh'rung *f* (-;-en) instruction; (*Lehre*) lesson; (*Rat*) advice; **zu Ihrer B.** for your information

beleibt [bə'laɪpt] *adj* stout
beleidigen [bə'laɪdɪgən] *tr* offend
belei′digend *adj* offensive
bele′sen *adj* well-read
beleuch′ten *tr* light (up), illuminate; (fig) throw light on
Beleuch′ter *m* (aer) pathfinder; (theat) juicer
Beleuch′tung *f* (–;-en) lighting, illumination; (fig) elucidation
Beleuch′tungskörper *m* lighting fixture
Belgien ['bɛlgjən] *n* (–;s) Belgium
Belgier –in ['bɛlgjər(ɪn)] §6 *mf* Belgian
belgisch ['bɛlgɪʃ] *adj* Belgian
belichten [bə'lɪçtən] *tr* (phot) expose
Belich′tung *f* (–;-en) exposure
belie′ben *intr* please ‖ *impers* (*dat*)—wenn es Ihnen beliebt if you please ‖ **Belieben** *n* (–;s) liking; es steht in Ihrem B. it's up to you; nach B. as you like
beliebig [bə'libɪç] *adj* any (you please) ‖ *adv* as . . . as you please
beliebt [bə'lipt] *adj* favorite; (bei) popular (with)
Beliebt′heit *f* (–;) popularity
belie′fern *tr* supply, furnish
bellen ['bɛlən] *intr* bark
belob(ig)en [bə'lob(ɪg)ən] *tr* praise; commend; (mil) cite
beloh′nen *tr* reward
belü′gen §111 *tr* lie to, deceive
belustigen [bə'lʊstɪgən] *tr* amuse
bemächtigen [bə'mɛçtɪgən] *intr* (*genit*) seize, get hold of; (mil) seize
bemä′keln *tr* criticize, carp at
bema′len *tr* paint; decorate
bemängeln [bə'mɛŋəln] *tr* criticize
bemannen [bə'manən] *tr* man
Beman′nung *f* (–;-en) (nav) crew
bemänteln [bə'mɛntəln] *tr* gloss over; (*Fehler, Fehltritt*) cover up
bemei′stern *tr* master ‖ *ref* control oneself; (*genit*) get hold of
bemerk′bar *adj* perceptible
bemer′ken *tr* notice; (*äußern*) remark
bemer′kenswert *adj* remarkable
Bemer′kung *f* (–;-en) note; remark
bemes′sen §70 *tr* measure; proportion
bemit′leiden *tr* pity, feel sorry for
bemittelt [bə'mɪtəlt] *adj* well-to-do
bemogeln [bə'mogəln] *tr* cheat
bemü′hen *tr* trouble, bother; **bemüht sein zu** (*inf*) take pains to (*inf*) ‖ *ref* bother, exert oneself; **sich für j-n b.** intervene for s.o.; **sich um etw b.** make an effort to obtain s.th.; **sich um j-n b.** attend to s.o.; **sich zu j-m b.** go to s.o.
Bemü′hung *f* (–;-en) bother; effort
bemüßigt [bə'mysɪçt] *adj*—**sich b. fühlen zu** (*inf*) feel obliged to (*inf*)
bemu′stern *tr*—**ein Angebot b.** (com) send samples of an offer
bemuttern [bə'mʊtərn] *tr* mother
benachbart [bə'naxbart] *adj* neighboring; (*Fachgebiet*) related, allied
benachrichtigen [bə'naxrɪçtɪgən] *tr* notify; put on notice
Benach′richtigung *f* (–;-en) notification; notice
benachteiligen [bə'naxtaɪlɪgən] *tr* place at a disadvantage, handicap; discriminate against

benebelt [bə'nebəlt] *adj* covered in mist; (fig) groggy
benedeien [bene'daɪ-ən] *tr* bless
beneh′men §116 *tr*—**j-m etw b.** take s.th. away from s.o. ‖ *ref* behave ‖ **Benehmen** *n* (–;s) behavior
beneiden [bə'naɪdən] *tr*—**j-n um etw b.** begrudge s.o. s.th.
benei′denswert *adj* enviable
benen′nen §97 *tr* name, term
Bengel ['bɛŋəl] *m* (–;s) rascal
benommen [bə'nɔmən] *adj* dazed
benö′tigen *tr* need
benutz′bar *adj* usable
benut′zen, benüt′zen *tr* use, make use of
Benut′zerkarte *f* library card
Benzin [bɛnt'sin] *n* (–;s;-e) gasoline
Benzin′behälter *m* gas tank
beobachten [bə'obaxtən] *tr* observe; (*polizeilich*) keep under surveillance; (med) keep under observation
Beob′achtung *f* (–;-en) observation; (*e-s Gesetzes*) observance
beor′dern *tr* order (*to go to a place*)
bepacken (bepak′ken) *tr* load (down)
bepflan′zen *tr* plant
bequem [bə'kvem] *adj* comfortable; cozy; (*Stellung*) soft; (*Raten, Lösung*) easy; (*faul*) lazy; **b. zur Hand haben** have handy
berappen [bə'rapən] *tr* (coll) shell out
bera′ten §63 *tr* (über *acc*) advise (on); discuss ‖ *ref & intr* (über *acc*) confer (about), deliberate (on)
bera′tend *adj* advisory, consulting
beratschlagen [bə'ratʃlagən] *intr* (über *acc*) consult (on); **mit j-m b.** consult s.o., confer with s.o.
berat′schlagend *adj* advisory
Bera′tung *f* (–;-en) advice; (jur, med) consultation; **in B. sein** be under consideration
Bera′tungsstelle *f* counseling center
berau′ben *tr* (*genit*) rob (of); (*genit*) dispossess (of); (*genit*) deprive (of); (*genit*) bereave (of)
berech′nen *tr* calculate, figure out; (*schätzen*) estimate; (com) charge
berech′nend *adj* calculating
Berech′nung *f* (–;-en) calculation
berechtigen [bə'rɛçtɪgən] *tr* authorize; justify, warrant; (zu) entitle (to)
Berech′tigung *f* (–;-en) right, authorization; justification; (zu) title (to)
bereden [bə'redən] *tr* talk over, discuss; **j-n zu etw b.** talk s.o. into s.th. ‖ *ref*—**sich mit j-m über etw b.** confer with s.o. on s.th.
beredsam [bə'retzam] *adj* eloquent
beredt [bə'ret] *adj* eloquent
Bereich *m & n* (–[e]s;-e) region; range; (fig) field, sphere; **es fällt nicht in meinen B.** it's not within my province
bereichern [bə'raɪçərn] *tr* enrich
berei′fen *tr* cover with frost; (aut) put tires on
berei′nigen *tr* (*Streit, Konto*) setttle; (*Mißverständnis*) clear up
berei′sen *tr* tour

bereit [bə'raɪt] *adj* ready

bereiten [bə'raɪtən] *tr* prepare; (*Kaffee*) make; (*Freude*) give

Bereit'schaft *f* (–;) readiness; team, squad; (mil) alert

bereit'stellen *tr* make available

Berei'tung *f* (–;-en) preparation; (*Herstellung*) manufacture

bereit'willig *adj* ready, willing

bereu'en *tr* rue, regret

Berg [berk] *m* (–[e]s;-e) mountain; (*Hügel*) hill; **über alle Berge sein** be off and away; **zu Berge stehen** stand on end

bergab' *adv* downhill, down the mountain

bergauf' *adv* uphill; up the mountain

Berg'bahn *f* mountain railroad

Berg'bau *m* (–[e]s;) mining

Berg'bewohner –in §6 *mf* mountaineer

bergen ['bergən] §54 *tr* rescue; (*enthalten*) hold; (*Gefahr*) involve; (*Segel*) take in; (naut) salvage; (poet) conceal; (rok) recover ‖ *ref*—**in sich b.** involve

bergig ['bergɪç] *adj* mountainous

Berg'kessel *m* gorge

Berg'kette *f* mountain range

Berg'kluft *f* ravine, gully

Berg'kristall *m* rock crystal, quartz

Berg'land *n* hill country

Berg'mann *m* (–[e]s;-leute) miner

Berg'predigt *f* Sermon on the Mount

Berg'recht *n* mining law

Berg'rücken *m* ridge

Berg'rutsch *m* landslide

Berg'schlucht *f* gorge, ravine

Berg'spitze *f* mountain peak

Berg'steiger –in §6 *mf* mountain climber

Berg'steigerei *f* mountain climbing

Berg'sturz *m* landslide

Ber'gung *f* (–;-en) rescue; (naut) salvage; (rok) recovery

Ber'gungsarbeiten *pl* salvage operations

Ber'gungsschiff *n* salvage vessel; (rok) recovery ship

Berg'wacht *f* mountain rescue service

Berg'werk *n* mine

Berg'wesen *n* mining

Bericht [bə'rɪçt] *m* (–[e]s;-e) report

berichten [bə'rɪçtən] *tr & intr* report

Berichterstatter –in [bə'rɪçtɐʃtatɐ] (ɪn)] §6 *mf* reporter; correspondent; (rad) commentator

Bericht'erstattung *f* (–;) reporting

berichtigen [bə'rɪçtɪgən] *tr* rectify; (*Text*) emend; (*Schuld*) pay off

berie'chen §102 *tr* sniff at; (fig) size up ‖ *recip* (coll) sound each other out

Berlin [ber'lin] *n* (–s;) Berlin

Bernstein ['bern/ʃtaɪn] *m* amber

bersten ['berstən] §55 *intr* (SEIN) (vor *dat*) burst (with)

berüchtigt [bə'rʏçtɪçt] *adj* notorious

berücken (berük'ken) *tr* captivate

berücksichtigen [bə'rʏkzɪçtɪgən] *tr* (*erwägen*) consider; (*in Betracht ziehen*) make allowance for

Berück'sichtigung *f* (–;-en) consideration

Beruf' *m* (–[e]s;-e) vocation; profession; (*Gewerbe*) trade; (*Tätigkeit*) occupation; (*Laufbahn*) career

beru'fen *adj* called; authorized ‖ §122 *tr* call; (*ernennen*) appoint; (*Geister*) conjure up ‖ *ref*—**sich auf ein Gesetz b.** quote a law (*in support*); **sich auf j-n b.** use s.o.'s name as a reference

beruf'lich *adj* professional; vocational

Berufs- *comb.fm.* professional; vocational

Berufs'diplomat *m* career diplomat

Berufs'genossenschaft *f* professional association; trade association

Berufs'heer *n* regular army

Berufs'schule *f* vocational school

Berufs'sportler –in §6 *mf* professional

berufs'tätig *adj* working

Beru'fung *f* (–;-en) call; vocation; appointment; (jur) appeal; **B. einlegen** (jur) appeal; **unter B. auf** (*acc*) referring to

Beru'fungsgericht *n* appellate court

beru'hen *intr* (auf *dat*) be based (on); (auf *dat*) be due (to); **e-e Sache auf sich b. lassen** let a matter rest

beruhigen [bə'ru·ɪgən] *tr* calm; appease

beru'higend *adj* soothing; reassuring

Beru'higung *f* (–;) calming; appeasement, pacification; reassurance; (*der Lage*) stabilization; **zu meiner großen B.** much to my relief

Beru'higungsmittel *n* sedative

berühmt [bə'rymt] *adj* (**wegen**) famous (for)

Berühmt'heit *f* (–;-en) renown; (*berühmte Persönlichkeit*) celebrity

berüh'ren *tr* touch; (*erwähnen*) touch on; (*wirken auf*) affect; (*Zug*) pass through ‖ *ref* come in contact, meet

Berüh'rung *f* (–;-en) touch; contact

besä'en *tr* sow; (*bestreuen*) strew; **mit Sternen besät** star-spangled

besa'gen *tr* say; (*bedeuten*) mean

besagt [bə'zakt] *adj* aforesaid

besänftigen [bə'zenftɪgən] *tr* calm; appease ‖ *ref* calm down

Besatz' *m* trimming

Besat'zung *f* (–;-en) garrison; occupation; army of occupation; (aer, nav) crew

Besat'zungsarmee *f* army of occupation

Besat'zungsbehörde *f* military government

besau'fen §124 *ref* (coll) get drunk

beschä'digen *tr* damage ‖ *ref* injure oneself

beschaf'fen *adj*—**ich bin eben so b.** that's the way I am; **übel b. sein** be in bad shape ‖ *tr* get, procure; (*Geld*) raise

Beschaf'fenheit *f* (–;-en) quality, property; (*Zustand*) state; (*Art*) nature; (*Anlage*) design

Beschaf'fung *f* (–;-en) procuring; (*Erwerb*) acquisition

beschäftigen [bə'ʃeftɪgən] *tr* occupy; keep busy; (*anstellen*) employ; **beschäftigt sein bei** work for (*a company*); **beschäftigt sein mit** be busy with

beschä′men tr shame, make ashamed; **beschämt sein** be ashamed
Beschau′ f inspection
beschau′en tr look at; inspect
beschau′lich adj contemplative
Bescheid [bə′ʃaɪt] m (-[e]s;-e) answer; (Anweisung) instructions, directions; (Auskunft) information; (jur) decision; **B. hinterlassen bei** leave word with; **B. wissen** be well-informed; **j-m B. geben** (or **sagen**) give s.o. information or directions
beschei′den adj modest; (Preise) moderate; (Auswahl) limited; (einfach) simple, plain ‖ §112 tr inform; (beordern) order, direct; (vorladen) summon; (zuteilen) allot; **abschlägig b.** turn down; **es ist mir beschieden** it fell to my lot ‖ ref be satisfied
Beschei′denheit f (-;) modesty
bescheinigen [bə′ʃaɪnɪgən] tr (Empfang) acknowledge; (bezeugen) certify
Beschei′nigung f (-;-en) acknowledgement; certification; (Schein) certificate; (im Brief) to whom it may concern
beschei′ßen §53 tr (sl) cheat
beschen′ken tr—**j-n b. mit** present s.o. with
bescheren [bə′ʃerən] tr give gifts to
Besche′rung f (-;-en) distribution of gifts (especially at Christmas); **e-e schöne B.** (coll) a nice mess
beschicken (**beschik′ken**) tr (mit Waren) supply; (Messe) exhibit at, send exhibits to; (Kongreß) send delegates to; (Hochofen) feed, charge
beschie′ßen §76 tr shoot up; (mil, phys) bombard
beschimp′fen tr insult, call (s.o.) names
beschir′men tr shield, protect
beschla′fen tr (e-e Frau) sleep with; (e-e Sache) sleep on
Beschlag m (-s;⸗e) hardware; (Huf-) horse shoes; (auf Fensterscheiben) steam, vapor; (Überzug) thin coating; **in B. nehmen** confiscate; (Schiff) seize; (Gehalt) attach
beschla′gen adj—**b. in** (dat) well-versed in ‖ §132 tr cover, coat; (Metallverzierungen) fit, mount; (Pferd) shoe ‖ ref & intr steam up; (Mauer) sweat; (Metall) oxidize
beschlagnahmen [bə′ʃlaknamən] tr confiscate; (Schuldnervermögen) attach; (mil) requisition; (naut) seize
beschlei′chen §85 tr stalk, creep up on
beschleunigen [bə′ʃlɔɪnɪgən] tr accelerate, speed up
Beschleu′niger m (-s;-) accelerator
beschlie′ßen §76 tr end, wind up; (sich entschließen) decide
Beschluß′ m conclusion; decision; resolution; (jur) order; **unter B.** under lock and key; **zum B.** in conclusion
beschluß′fähig adj—**b. sein** have a quorum; **beschlußfähige Anzahl** quorum
beschmie′ren tr smear, coat; grease
beschmut′zen tr soil, dirty

beschnei′den §106 tr clip, trim; (fig) curtail; (surg) circumcise
beschneit [bə′ʃnaɪt] adj snow-covered
beschönigen [bə′ʃønɪgən] tr (Fehler) whitewash, cover up, gloss over
beschrän′ken tr limit
beschränkt′ adj limited; (Verhältnisse) straitened; (geistig) dense
beschrei′ben §62 tr describe; use up (in writing)
Beschrei′bung f (-;-en) description
beschrei′ten §86 tr walk on; **den Rechtsweg b.** take legal action
beschriften [bə′ʃrɪftən] tr inscribe; (Kisten) mark; (mit Etikett) label
Beschrif′tung f (-;-en) inscription; lettering; (erläuternde) caption
beschuldigen [bə′ʃuldɪgən] tr (genit) accuse (of), charge (with)
beschummeln [bə′ʃuməln] tr (coll) (um) cheat (out of)
Beschuß′ m test firing
beschüt′zen tr protect, defend
beschwat′zen tr gossip about; **j-n dazu b. zu** (inf) talk s.o. into (ger)
Beschwerde [bə′ʃverdə] f (-;-n) trouble; (Klage, Krankheit) complaint
beschweren [bə′ʃverən] tr burden ‖ ref (über acc) complain (about)
beschwer′lich adj troublesome
beschwichtigen [bə′ʃvɪçtɪgən] tr appease; (Hunger) satisfy; (Gewissen) soothe
beschwin′deln tr (um) swindle (out of)
beschwingt [bə′ʃvɪŋt] adj lively
beschwipst [bə′ʃvɪpst] adj tipsy, high
beschwö′ren tr swear to; (Geister) conjure up; (bitten) implore, entreat
Beschwö′rungsformel f incantation
beseelen [bə′zelən] tr inspire, animate
beseelt′ adj animated; (von Hoffnungen) filled; (Spiel) inspired
bese′hen §138 tr look at; inspect
beseitigen [bə′zaɪtɪgən] tr eliminate, remove, clear away; (Übel, Fehler) redress; (Schwierigkeit) overcome; (töten) do away with; (pol) purge
Besen [′bezən] m (-s;-) broom
Be′senstiel m broomstick
besessen [bə′zesən] adj (von) obsessed (by); (vom Teufel) possessed
Beses′senheit f (-;-en) obsession; (vom Teufel) possession
beset′zen tr occupy; (mit Juwelen) set off; (Amt, Rolle) fill; (Hut) trim
besetzt′ adj (Platz, Abort) occupied; (Stelle) filled; (Kleid) trimmed, set off; (telp) busy
Besetzt′zeichen n (telp) busy signal
Beset′zung f (-;-en) decoration; (e-r Stelle) filling; (mil) occupation; (theat) cast
besichtigen [bə′zɪçtɪgən] tr view; tour; inspect; (mil) inspect, review
Besich′tigung f (-;-en) sightseeing; inspection; (mil) inspection, review
besie′deln tr colonize; populate
besie′geln tr seal
besie′gen tr defeat; (Widerstand) overcome; (Gefühle) master
besin′nen §121 ref consider; (auf acc) think (of); **sich anders b.** change

one's mind; **sich e-s Besseren b.** think better of it

besinn'lich adj reflective

Besin'nung f (-;) consciousness; reflection; **j-n zur B. bringen** bring s.o. to his senses

besin'nungslos adj unconscious; (*unüberlegt*) senseless

Besitz' m (-es;-e) possession; **in B. nehmen** take possession of

besitz'anzeigend adj possessive

besit'zen §144 tr own, possess

Besit'zer -in §6 mf possessor, owner

Besitz'ergreifung f (-;-en) occupancy; seizure

Besitz'stand m ownership; (fin) assets

Besitztum [bə'zɪtstum] n (-s;-̈er) possession

Besit'zung f (-;-en) possession, property; (*Landgut*) estate

besoffen [bə'zɔfən] adj (coll) soused

besohlen [bə'zolən] tr sole

besolden [bə'zɔldən] tr pay

Besol'dung f (-;-en) pay, salary

beson'dere §9 adj particular, special

Beson'derheit f (-;-en) peculiarity; (com) specialty

beson'ders adv especially; separately

besonnen [bə'zɔnən] adj prudent; (*bedacht*) considerate; level-headed

besor'gen tr take care of; (*beschaffen*) procure, get; (*befürchten*) fear

Besorgnis [bə'zɔrknɪs] f (-;-se) concern; (*Furcht*) fear

besorg'niserregend adj alarming

besorgt [bə'zɔrkt] adj (um) worried (about), anxious (for)

Besor'gung f (-;-en) care; procurement; (*Auftrag*) errand; **Besorgungen machen** run errands

bespre'chen §64 tr discuss; (*Buch*) review; **e-e Schallplatte b.** make a recording ‖ ref confer

Bespre'cher -in §6 mf reviewer, critic

besprengen tr sprinkle

besprit'zen tr splash; spray

besser ['bɛsər] adj & adv better

bessern ['bɛsərn] tr better, improve ‖ ref improve

Bes'serung f (-;-en) improvement; **baldige B.** speedy recovery

Bes'serungsanstalt f reform school

Bestand' m (-[e]s;-̈e) existence; (*Vorrat*) stock, inventory; (*Kassen-*) cash on hand; (*Baum-*) stand; **B. an** (dat) number of; **B. an kampffähigen Truppen** effective strength; **B. haben, von B. sein** have endurance, be lasting

bestän'dig adj constant, steady

Bestands'aufnahme f inventory

Bestand'teil m component; ingredient

bestär'ken tr strengthen, fortify

bestätigen [bə'ʃtɛtɪgən] tr confirm; (*Zeugnis*) corroborate; (*Empfang*) acknowledge; (*Vertrag*) ratify ‖ ref prove true, come true

bestatten [bə'ʃtatən] tr bury, inter

Bestat'tungsinstitut n funeral home

bestau'ben, bestäuben (bə'ʃtɔrbən) tr cover with dust; sprinkle; (bot) pollinate

beste ['bɛstə] §9 adj best; **am besten**

best (of all); **auf dem besten Weg sein zu** be well on the way to; **aufs b.** in the best way; **der erste b.** anybody

beste'chen §64 tr bribe; (fig) impress

beste'chend adj fascinating, charming

bestech'lich adj open to bribery

Beste'chung f (-;) bribery

Beste'chungsgeld n bribe

Besteck [bə'ʃtek] n (-[e]s;-e) kit; (*Tisch-*) single service; (aer, naut) reckoning, position; (med) set of instruments

bestecken (bestek'ken) tr stick; (culin) garnish

beste'hen §146 tr undergo; (*Prüfung*) pass ‖ intr exist, be; (**gegen**) hold one's own (against); (im e-r Prüfung) pass; **b. auf** (dat) insist on; **b. aus** consist of; **b. in** (dat) consist in

beste'hend adj existing, extant; present

besteh'len §147 tr (um) rob (of)

bestei'gen §148 tr climb; (*Schiff*) board; (*Pferd*) mount; (*Thron*) ascend

bestel'len tr order; (*Zimmer*) reserve; (*Zeitung*) subscribe to; (*ernennen*) appoint; (*Briefe*) deliver; (*Feld*) till; (*kommen lassen*) send for

Bestell'buch n order book

Bestell'zettel m order slip

be'stenfalls adv at best

besteu'ern tr tax

bestialisch [bɛst'jalɪʃ] adj beastly

Bestie ['bɛstjə] f (-;-n) beast

bestim'men tr determine; (*Zeit, Preis*) set; (*ernennen*) appoint; (*Begriff*) define; (gram) modify; (math) find; **j-n b. zu** (or **für**) destine s.o. for; talk s.o. into ‖ intr decree; **b. in** (dat) have a say in; **b. über** (acc) dispose of

bestimmt' adj determined; definite; particular ‖ adv definitely

Bestim'mung f (-;-en) determination; (*e-r Zeit, e-s Preises*) setting; destination; mission, goal; (*e-s Begriffs*) definition; (*Schicksal*) fate; (*Vorschrift*) regulation; (*e-s Vertrags*) provision; (gram) modifier; **mit B. nach** (naut) heading for; **seiner B. übergeben** dedicate, open

bestrah'fen tr punish

bestrah'len tr irradiate; (med) give radiation treatment to

bestre'ben ref strive, endeavor ‖ **Bestreben** n (-s;) tendency

Bestre'bung f (-;-en) effort

bestrei'chen §85 tr spread; (mit Feuer) rake; **mit Butter b.** butter

bestrei'ken tr strike

bestrei'ten §86 tr contest; fight; (*Ausgaben*) defray; (*Recht*) challenge; (*leugnen*) deny; **e-e Unterhaltung allein b.** do all the talking

bestreu'en tr (mit) strew (with)

bestricken (bestrik'ken) tr (fig) charm

bestücken [bə'ʃtykən] tr arm, equip

bestür'men tr storm; (fig) bombard

Bestür'mung f (-;-en) storming

bestür'zen tr dismay

Besuch [bə'zux] m (-[e]s;-e) visit; (*Besucher*) visitor(s), company;

(*genit*) visit (to); **auf B. gehen** pay a visit

besu'chen *tr* visit; (*Gasthaus, usw.*) frequent; (*Schule, Versammlung*) attend; (*Kino*) go to

Besu'cher –in §6 *mf* visitor, caller

Besuchs'zeit *f* visiting hours

besudeln *tr* soil, stain

betagt [bə'takt] *adj* advanced in years

beta'sten *tr* finger, touch, handle

betätigen [bə'tɛtɪgən] *tr* set in operation; (*Maschine*) operate; (*Bremse*) apply || *ref*—**sich nützlich b.** make oneself useful; **sich politisch b.** be active in politics

betäuben [bə'tɔɪbən] *tr* deafen; stun; (*Schmerz*) deaden; (*durch Rauschgift*) drug, dope; (*med*) anesthetize

Betäu'bungsmittel *n* drug; painkiller; (*med*) anesthetic

Bete ['betə] *f* (–;–n) beet

beteiligen [bə'taɪlɪgən] *tr* (**an** *dat*, **bei**) give (*s.o.*) a share (in) || *ref* (**an** *dat*) participate (in)

Betei'ligung *f* (–;–en) participation; (*Teilhaberschaft*) partnership; (*Teilnehmerzahl*) attendance

beten ['betən] *tr & intr* pray

beteuern [bə'tɔɪ⋅ərn] *tr* affirm

betiteln [bə'titəln] *tr* entitle

Beton [be'ton] *m* (–s;) concrete

betonen [bə'tonən] *tr* (*Silbe*) stress, accent; (*nachdrücklich*) emphasize

betonieren [bəto'nirən] *tr* cement

Betonmisch'maschine *f* cement mixer

betören [bə'tørən] *tr* infatuate

Betracht' *m* (–[e]s;) consideration; **außer B. lassen** rule out; **es kommt nicht in B.** it is out of the question; **in B. ziehen** take into account, consider

betrachten [bə'traxtən] *tr* look at; consider

beträchtlich [bə'trɛçtlɪç] *adj* considerable

Betrach'tung *f* (–;–en) observation; consideration; meditation; **Betrachtungen anstellen über** (*acc*) reflect on

Betrag [bə'trak] *m* (–[e]s;⸚e) amount; **über den B. von** in the amount of

betra'gen §132 *tr* amount to || *ref* behave || **Betragen** *n* (–s;) behavior

betrau'en *tr* entrust

betrau'ern *tr* mourn for

Betreff' [bə'trɛf] *m* (–[e]s;) (*am Briefanfang*) re; **in B.** (*genit*) in regard to

betref'fen §151 *tr* befall; (*berühren*) affect, hit; (*angehen*) concern; **betrifft** (*acc*) re; **was das betrifft** as far as that is concerned; **was mich betrifft** I for one

betreffs [bə'trɛfs] *prep* (*genit*) concerning

betrei'ben §62 *tr* carry on; (*leiten*) manage; (*Beruf*) practice; (*Studien*) pursue; (*Maschine*) operate

betre'ten *adj* embarrassed || §152 *tr* step on; set foot on or in; (*Raum*) enter; (*unbefugt*) trespass on

betreuen [bə'trɔɪ⋅ən] *tr* look after

Betrieb [bə'trip] *m* (–s;⸚e) operation,

running; (*Unternehmen*) business; (*Anlage*) plant; (*Werkstatt*) workshop; (fig) rush, bustle; **aus dem B. ziehen** take out of service; **außer B.** out of order; **großer B.** hustle and bustle; **in vollem B.** in full swing

betriebsam [bə'tripzam] *adj* enterprising, active

Betrieb'samkeit *f* (–;) hustle

betriebs'fähig *adj* in working order

betriebs'fertig *adj* ready for use

Betriebs'ingenieur *m* production engineer

Betriebs'kosten *pl* operating costs

Betriebs'leiter *m* superintendent

Betriebs'material *n* (rr) rolling stock

Betriebs'prüfer –in §6 *mf* auditor

Betriebs'ruhe *f*—**heute B.** (public sign) closed today

Betriebs'stoff *m* fuel

Betriebs'störung *f* breakdown

Betriebs'wirtschaft *f* industrial management

betrin'ken §143 *ref* get drunk

betroffen [bə'trofən] *adj* shocked, stunned; (*heimgesucht*) afflicted

betrü'ben *tr* sadden, distress

betrüb'lich *adj* sad, distressing

betrübt [bə'trypt] *adj* sad, sorrowful

Betrug [bə'truk] *m* (–[e]s;) fraud, swindle; **frommer B.** white lie

betrü'gen §111 *tr* cheat, swindle

Betrügerei [bətryɡə'raɪ] *f* (–;–en) deceit, cheating

betrü'gerisch *adj* deceitful; fraudulent

betrunken [bə'truŋkən] *adj* drunk

Bett [bet] *n* (–[e]s;–en) bed

Bett'decke *f* bedspread

Bettelei [betə'laɪ] *f* (–;) begging

betteln ['betəln] *intr* (**um**) beg (for)

betten ['betən] *tr* put to bed || *ref* **make onself a bed; bed down**

Bett'genosse *m* bedfellow

Bett'gestell *n* bedstead

Bett'himmel *m* canopy (*over a bed*)

bettlägerig ['betlɛɡərɪç] *adj* bedridden

Bett'laken *n* bed sheet

Bettler –in ['betlər(ɪn)] §6 *mf* beggar

Bett'stelle *f* bedstead

Bettuch (**Bett'tuch**) *n* sheet

Bet'tung *f* (–s) bedding; (mil) emplacement; (rr) bed

Bett'vorleger *m* bedside rug

Bett'wäsche *f* bed linen

Bett'zeug *n* bedding

betupfen [bə'tupfən] *tr* dab (at); (surg) swab

beugen ['bɔɪgən] *tr* bend; (fig) humble; (gram) inflect || *ref* bend; bow

Beu'gung *f* (–;–en) bending; bowing; (gram) inflection

Beule ['bɔɪlə] *f* (–;–n) lump; (*Geschwür*) boil; (*kleiner Blechschaden*) dent

beunruhigen [bə'unru⋅ɪgən] *tr* make uneasy, worry, disturb

Beun'ruhigung *f* (–;–en) anxiety, uneasiness; disturbance

beurkunden [bə'urkundən] *tr* authenticate

beurlauben [bə'urlaubən] *tr* grant leave of absence to; (*vom Amt*) suspend; (mil) furlough; **sich b. lassen**

ask for time off || *ref* (**bei**) take one's leave (of)

beur′teilen *tr* evaluate; (**nach**) judge (by); falsch b. misjudge

Beute [ˈbɔɪtə] *f* (—;) booty, loot; zur B. fallen (*dat*) fall prey to

Beutel [ˈbɔɪtəl] *m* (—s;—) bag, pouch; purse; (billiards) pocket

beu′telig *adj* baggy

Beu′tezug *m* raid

bevölkern [beˈfœlkərn] *tr* populate

Bevöl′kerung *f* (—;-en) population

bevollmächtigen [beˈfɔlmɛçtɪgən] *tr* authorize; (jur) give (*s.o.*) power of attorney

Bevoll′mächtigte §5 *mf* authorized agent; proxy; (pol) plenipotentiary

bevor [beˈfor] *conj* before; **bevor . . . nicht** until

bevormunden [beˈformʊndən] *tr* treat in a patronizing manner

bevor′raten *tr* stock; stockpile

bevorrechtet [bəˈforreçtət] *adj* privileged

bevor′stehen §146 *intr* be imminent, be on hand; **bevorstehend** forthcoming; **j—m b.** be in store for s.o.

bevorzugen [beˈfortsugən] *tr* prefer

bevor′zugt *adj* preferential; high-priority; privileged; favorite

bewa′chen *tr* guard, watch over

bewach′sen §155 *tr* overgrow, cover

Bewa′chung *f* (—;-en) guard, custody

bewaff′nen *tr* arm

Bewaff′nung *f* (—;) armament, arms

Bewahr′anstalt *f* detention home

bewah′ren *tr* keep, preserve; (**vor** *dat*) save (from), protect (against)

bewäh′ren *tr* prove || *ref* prove one's worth; **sich nicht b.** prove a failure

Bewah′rer —in §6 *mf* keeper

bewahrheiten [bəˈvarhaɪtən] *tr* verify || *ref* come true

bewährt [bəˈvert] *adj* tried, trustworthy

Bewah′rung *f* (—;) preservation

Bewäh′rung *f* (—;-en) testing, trial; (jur) probation

Bewäh′rungsfrist *f* (jur) probation; **j—m B.** zubilligen put s.o. on probation

Bewäh′rungsprobe *f* test

bewaldet [bəˈvaldət] *adj* woody

bewältigen [bəˈvɛltɪgən] *tr* (*Hindernis*) overcome; (*Lehrstoff*) master

bewandert [bəˈvandərt] *adj* experienced

Bewandtnis [bəˈvantnɪs] *f* (—;) circumstances, situation

bewäs′sern *tr* water, irrigate

bewegen [bəˈvegən] *tr* move, stir || *ref* move, stir; (**von der Stelle**) budge; (*Temperatur*) vary; (*exerzieren*) take exercise; (astr) revolve || §56 *tr* prompt, induce

Beweg′grund *m* motive; incentive

beweg′lich *adj* movable; (*behend*) agile; (*Geist*) versatile; (*Zunge*) glib

Beweg′lichkeit *f* (—;) mobility; agility; versatility

bewegt [bəˈvekt] *adj* agitated; (*ergreifend*) stirring; (*Stimme*) trembling; (*Unterhaltung*) lively; (*Leben*) eventful; (*unruhig*) turbulent

Bewe′gung *f* (—;-en) movement; mo-

tion; move; (*Gebärde*) gesture; (fig) emotion; **in B.** setzen set in motion

Bewe′gungsfreiheit *f* room to move; (fig) leeway, freedom of action

bewe′gungslos *adj* motionless

beweh′ren *tr* arm; (*Beton*) reinforce

beweihräuchern [bəˈvaɪrɔɪçərn] *tr* (fig) flatter; (eccl) incense

bewei′nen *tr* mourn, shed tears over

Beweis [bəˈvaɪs] *m* (—es;-e) (**für**) proof (of), evidence (of)

beweisen [bəˈvaɪzən] §118 *tr* prove, demonstrate; (*bestätigen*) substantiate

Beweis′führung *f* argumentation

Beweis′grund *m* argument

Beweis′kraft *f* cogency, force

beweis′kräftig *adj* convincing

Beweis′last *f* burden of proof

Beweis′stück *n* exhibit

bewen′den *intr*—es dabei b. lassen leave it at that || **Bewenden** *n*—damit hat es sein B.** there the matter rests

bewer′ben §149 *ref*—**sich b. um** apply for; (*kandidieren*) run for; (*Vertrag*) bid for; (*Preis*) compete for; (*Frau*) court

Bewer′ber —in §6 *mf* applicant; candidate; bidder; competitor || *m* suitor

Bewer′bungsformular *n* application form

Bewer′bungsschreiben *n* written application

bewer′fen §160 *tr* pelt; (*Mauer*) plaster

bewerkstelligen [bəˈverkˌstelɪgən] *tr* manage, bring off

bewer′ten *tr* (auf *acc*) value (at), appraise (at); **b. mit fünf Punkten** give five points to (*e.g., a performance*); **zu hoch b.** overrate

Bewer′tung *f* (—;-en) valuation

bewilligen [bəˈvɪlɪgən] *tr* approve, grant

Bewil′ligung *f* (—;-en) approval; permit

bewillkommnen [bəˈvɪlkɔmnən] *tr* welcome

bewir′ken *tr* cause, occasion, effect

bewir′ten *tr* entertain

bewirt′schaften *tr* (*Acker*) cultivate; (*Betrieb*) manage; (*Mangelware*) ration

Bewir′tung *f* (—;) hospitality

bewitzeln [bəˈvɪtsəln] *tr* poke fun at

bewog [bəˈvok] *pret* of bewegen

bewogen [bəˈvogən] *pp* of bewegen

bewoh′nen *tr* inhabit, occupy

Bewoh′ner —in §6 *mf* (*e-s Landes*) inhabitant; (*e-s Hauses*) occupant

bewölken [bəˈvœlkən] *tr* cloud || *ref* cloud over, get cloudy

bewölkt′ *adj* cloudy, overcast

Bewöl′kung *f* (—;) clouds

bewun′dern *tr* admire

bewun′dernswert, bewun′dernswürdig *adj* admirable

bewußt [bəˈvʊst] *adj* conscious; **die bewußte Sache** the matter in question

bewußt′los *adj* unconscious

Bewußt′sein *n* consciousness; **bei B.** sein be conscious

Bewußt′seinsspaltung *f* schizophrenia

bezah′len *tr* pay; (*Gekauftes*) pay for

Bezah'lung *f* (-;-en) payment; (*Lohn*) pay

bezäh'men *tr* tame; (fig) control

bezau'bern *tr* bewitch; (fig) fascinate

bezeich'nen *tr* (*zeichnen*) mark; (*bedeuten*) signify; (*benennen*) designate; (*kennzeichnen*) characterize; (*zeigen*) point out

bezeich'nend *adj* characteristic

Bezeich'nung *f* (-;-en) marking, mark; (*Name*) name; (*Ausdruck*) term

bezei'gen *tr* show, manifest, express

bezeu'gen *tr* attest; (jur) testify to

bezichtigen [bə'tsɪçtɪgən] *tr* accuse

bezieh'bar *adj* (*Ware*) obtainable; (*Wohnung*) ready for occupancy; (*auf acc*) referable (to)

bezie'hen §163 *tr* (*Polstermöbel*) cover; (*Wohnung*) move into; (*Universität*) go to; (*geliefert bekommen*) get; (*Gehalt*) draw; (*auf acc*) relate (to), refer (to); **das Bett frisch b.** change the bed linens; **die Stellung b.** (mil) occupy the position; **die Wache b.** (mil) go on guard duty || *ref* become overcast; **sich auf j-n b.** use s.o.'s name as a reference

Bezie'hung *f* (-;-en) relation, connection, respect; **in B. auf** (*acc*) in respect to; **in guten Beziehungen stehen zu** be on good terms with

bezie'hungslos *adj* unrelated; irrelevant

Bezie'hungssatz *m* relative clause

bezie'hungsweise *adv* respectively

Bezie'hungswort *n* (-[e]s; -̈er) (gram) antecedent

beziffern [bə'tsɪfərn] *tr* (*auf acc*) estimate (at) || *ref*—**sich b. auf** (*acc*) amount to, number

Bezirk [bə'tsɪrk] *m* (-s;-e) district, ward, precinct; (*Bereich*) sphere

Bezug *m* (-[e]s; -̈e) cover, case; (*von Waren*) purchase; (*von Zeitungen*) subscription; (*Auftrag*) order; **Bezüge** earnings; **B. nehmen auf** (*acc*) refer to; **in B. auf** (*acc*) in reference to

bezüglich [bə'tsyklɪç] *adj* (*auf acc*) relative (to); **bezügliches Fürwort** relative pronoun || *prep* (*genit*) concerning, as to, with regard to

Bezugnahme [bə'tsuknamə] *f*—**unter B. auf** (*acc*) with reference to

Bezugs'anweisung *f* delivery order

bezugs'berechtigt *adj* entitled to receive || **Bezugsberechtigte** §5 *mf* (ins) beneficiary

bezwecken [bə'tsvekən] *tr* aim at, have in mind; (mit) intend (by)

bezwei'feln *tr* doubt, question

bezwin'gen §142 *tr* conquer; (fig) control, master

Bibel ['bibəl] *f* (-;-n) Bible

Bi'belforscher **-in** §6 *mf* Jehovah's Witness

Biber ['bibər] *m* (-s;-) beaver

Bibliothek [bɪblɪ·o'tek] *f* (-;-en) library

Bibliothekar **-in** [bɪblɪ·ote'kar(ɪn)] §8 *mf* librarian

biblisch ['biblɪʃ] *adj* biblical

bieder ['bidər] *adj* honest; (*leichtgläubig*) gullible

Bie'dermann *m* (-[e]s; -̈er) honest man

biegen ['bigən] §57 *tr* bend; (gram) inflect || *rej*—**sich vor Lachen b.** double up with laughter || *intr* (SEIN) bend; **um die Ecke b.** go around the corner

biegsam ['bikzam] *adj* flexible

Bie'gung *f* (-;-en) bend, bending; (gram) inflection

Biene ['binə] *f* (-;-n) bee

Bie'nenfleiß *m*—**mit B. arbeiten** work like a bee

Bie'nenhaus *n* beehive

Bie'nenkorb *m* beehive

Bie'nenstich *m* bee sting; (culin) almond pastry

Bie'nenstock *m* beehive

Bie'nenzucht *f* beekeeping

Bier [bir] *n* (-[e]s;-e) beer

bie'ten ['bitən] §58 *tr* offer; **b. auf** (*acc*) bid for || *ref* present itself; **das läßt er sich nicht b.** he won't stand for it

Bigamie [bɪga'mi] *f* (-;) bigamy

bigott [bɪ'gɔt] *adj* bigoted

Bigotterie [bɪgɔtə'ri] *f* (-;) bigotry

Bilanz [bɪ'lants] *f* (*acct*) balance; (acct) balance sheet

Bilanz'abteilung *f* auditing department

bilanzieren [bɪlan'tsirən] *intr* balance

Bild [bɪlt] *n* (-[e]s;-er) picture; image; (*Bildnis*) portrait; (*in e-m Buch*) illustration; (*Vorstellung*) idea; (rhet) metaphor, figure of speech; **im Bilde sein** be in the know

Bild'band *m* (-[e]s; -̈e) picture book || *n* (-[e]s; -̈e) (telv) video tape

Bild'bandgerät *n* video tape recorder

Bild'betrachter *m* slide viewer

Bildchen ['bɪltçən] *n* (-s;-) small picture; (cin) frame

Bild'einstellung *f* (-;-en) focusing

bilden ['bɪldən] *tr* form, fashion, create; (*entwerfen*) design; (*gründen*) establish; (*Geist*) educate, develop; (*Gruppe*) constitute || *ref* form, be produced; develop; educate oneself

bil'dend *adj* instructive; **bildende Künste** fine arts, plastic arts

bil'derreich *adj* (*Buch*) richly illustrated; (*Sprache*) picturesque, ornate

Bil'derschrift *f* picture writing

Bil'dersprache *f* imagery

Bil'derstürmer *m* iconoclast

Bild'frequenz *f* camera speed

Bild'funk *m* television

bild'haft *adj* pictorial; graphic

Bildhauer ['bɪlthau·ər] *m* (-s;-) sculptor

Bildhauerei ['bɪlthau·əraɪ] *f* (-;) sculpture

Bildhauerin ['bɪlthau·ərɪn] *f* (-;-nen) sculptress

bild'hübsch *adj* pretty as a picture

Bild'karte *f* photographic map; (cards) face card

bild'lich *adj* pictorial; figurative

Bildner **-in** ['bɪldnər(ɪn)] §6 *mf* sculptor || *m* (fig) molder || *f* sculptress

Bildnis ['bɪltnɪs] *n* (-ses;-se) portrait

Bild'röhre *f* picture tube, TV tube

bildsam ['bɪltzam] *adj* plastic; (fig) pliant

Bild'säule f statue
Bild'schirm m television screen
bild'schön adj very beautiful
Bild'schriftzeichen n hieroglyph
Bild'seite f head, obverse
Bild'signal n video signal
Bild'stock m wayside shrine
Bild'streifen m filmstrip; (journ) comic strip
Bild'sucher m (phot) viewfinder
Bild'teppich m tapestry
Bild'ton'kamera f sound-film camera
Bil'dung f (-;-en) formation; shape; education, culture
Bil'dungsanstalt f educational institution
Bild'werfer m projector
Bild'werk n sculpture; imagery
Billard ['bɪljart] n (-s;) billiards
Bil'lardkugel f billiard ball
Bil'lardloch n pocket
Bil'lardstab, Bil'lardstock m cue
Billett [bɪl'jet] n (-s;-e) ticket
Billett'ausgabe f, **Billett'schalter** m ticket office; (theat) box office
billig ['bɪlɪç] adj cheap; (Preis) low; (Ausrede, Trost) poor
billigen ['bɪlɪgən] tr approve
Bil'ligung f (-;) approval
Billion [bɪl'jon] f (-;-en) trillion; (Brit) billion
bimbam ['bɪm'bam] interj ding-dong || **Bimbam** m—**heiliger B.!** holy smokes!
bimmeln ['bɪməln] intr (coll) jingle; (telp) ring
Bimsstein ['bɪms/taɪn] m (-s;-e) pumice stone
Binde ['bɪndə] f (-;-n) band; (Krawatte) tie; (Armschlinge) sling; (für Frauen) sanitary napkin; (med) bandage
Bin'deglied n link; (fig) bond, tie
binden ['bɪndən] §59 tr bind, tie
Bin'destrich m hyphen; **mit B. schreiben** hyphenate
Bin'dewort n (-[e]s;-̈er) conjunction
Bind'faden m string, twine; **es regnet Bindfäden** it's raining cats and dogs
Bin'dung f (-;-en) binding; tie, bond, obligation; (mus) ligature
binnen ['bɪnən] prep (genit & dat) within; **b. kurzem** before long
Binnen- comb.fm. inner; internal; inland; domestic, home
Bin'nengewässer n inland water
Bin'nenhandel m domestic trade
Bin'nenland n inland; interior; **im B.** inland
Binse ['bɪnzə] f (-;-n) rush, reed; **in die Binsen gehen** (coll) go to pot
Bin'senwahrheit f truism
Biochemie [bɪ·oçe'mi] f (-;) biochemistry
Biogra·phie [bɪ·ogra'fi] (-;-phien [·'fi·ən]) biography
biographisch [bɪ·o'grafɪ/] adj biographic(al)
Biologie [bɪ·olo'gi] f (-;) biology
biologisch [bɪ·o'logɪ/] adj biological
Biophysik [bɪ·ofy'zik] f (-;) biophysics
Birke ['bɪrkə] f (-;-n) birch
Birma ['bɪrma] n (-s;) Burma

Birne ['bɪrnə] f (-;-n) pear; (elec) bulb; (Kopf) (sl) bean
bis [bɪs] prep (acc) (zeitlich) till, until; (örtlich) up to, to; **bis an** (acc) up to; **bis auf** (acc) except for; **bis nach** as far as || conj until, till
Bisamratte ['bizamratə] f (-;-n) muskrat
Bischof ['bɪ/əf] m (-;-̈e) bishop
bischöflich ['bɪ/øflɪç] adj episcopal
Bi'schofsamt n episcopate
Bi'schofsmütze f miter
Bi'schofssitz m episcopal see
Bi'schofsstab m crosier
bisher [bɪs'her] adv till now
bisherig [bɪs'herɪç] adj former, previous; (Präsident) outgoing
Biskuit [bɪs'kvit] m & n (-[e]s;-e) biscuit
bislang adv till now
biß [bɪs] pret of **beißen** || **Biß** m (Bisses; Bisse) bite; sting
bißchen ['bɪsçən] n (also used as invar adj & adv) bit, little bit
Bissen ['bɪsən] m (-s;-) bit, morsel
bissig ['bɪsɪç] adj biting, snappish
Bistum ['bɪstum] n (-s;-̈er) bishopric
bisweilen [bɪs'vaɪlən] adv sometimes
Bitte ['bɪtə] f (-;-n) request; **e-e B. einlegen bei** intercede with
bitten ['bɪtən] §60 tr ask || intr **b. für** intercede for; **b. um** ask for; **wie bitte?** I beg your pardon? || interj please!; you are welcome!
bitter ['bɪtər] adj bitter
bit'terböse adj (coll) furious
Bit'terkeit f (-;) bitterness
bit'terlich adv bitterly; deeply
Bit'tersalz n Epsom salts
Bittgang ['bɪtgaŋ] m (-[e]s;-̈e) (eccl) procession
Bittsteller ['bɪt/telər] m (-s;-) petitioner, suppliant
Biwak ['bivak] n (-s;-s) bivouac
biwakieren [biva'kiran] intr bivouac
bizarr [bɪ'tsar] adj bizarre
blähen ['ble·ən] tr inflate, distend || ref swell || intr cause gas
blaken ['blakən] intr smolder
Blamage [bla'maʒə] f (-;-n) disgrace
blamieren [bla'miran] tr embarrass || ref make a fool of oneself
blank [blaŋk] adj bright; (Schuh) shiny; (bloß) bare; (Schwert) drawn; (sl) broke; **blanke Waffe** side arms; **b. ziehen** draw one's sword
Blankett [blaŋ'ket] n (-s;-e) blank
blanko ['blaŋko] adv—**b. lassen** leave blank; **b. verkaufen** sell short
Blan'koscheck m blank check
Blan'kovollmacht f blanket authority
Blank'vers m blank verse
Bläschen ['blesçən] n (-s;-) small blister; small bubble
Blase ['blazə] f (-;-n) blister; bubble; (coll) gang; (anat) bladder; **Blasen werfen** (Farbe) blister; **Blasen ziehen** (Haut) blister
Bla'sebalg m pair of bellows
blasen ['blazən] tr blow; (Instrument) play || intr blow
Bla'senleiden n bladder trouble
Bläser ['blezər] m (-s;-) blower

blasiert [bla'zirt] *adj* blasé

blasig ['blɑːzɪç] *adj* blistery; bubbly

Blas'instrument *n* wind instrument

Blasphe•mie [blasfe'mi] *f* (-;-mien ['miːən]) blasphemy

blasphemieren [blasfe'mirən] *intr* blaspheme

Blas'rohr *n* blowpipe; peashooter

blaß [blas] *adj* pale; **keine blasse Ahnung** not the foggiest notion

Blässe ['blesə] *f* (-;) paleness, pallor

Blatt [blat] *n* (-s;ⸯer) leaf; (*Papier-*) sheet; (*Gras-*) blade

Blatter ['blatər] *f* (-;-n) pustule; **die Blattern** smallpox

blätterig ['bletərɪç] *adj* leafy; scaly

blättern ['bletərn] *intr*—**in e-m Buch b.** page through a book

Blat'ternarbe *f* pockmark

Blät'terwerk *n* foliage

Blatt'gold *n* gold leaf, gold foil

Blatt'laus *f* aphid

Blatt'pflanze *f* house plant

blättrig ['bletrɪç] *adj var of* **blätterig**

Blatt'zinn *n* tin foil

blau [blau] *adj* (& *fig*) blue; (*coll*) drunk; **blaues Auge** black eye; **keinen blauen Dunst haben** (coll) not have the foggiest notion; **mit e-m blauen Auge davonkommen** (coll) get off easy ‖ **Blau** *n* (-s;-s) blue; blueness

blau'äugig *adj* blue-eyed

Blau'beere *f* blueberry

Bläue ['blɔɪ•ə] *f* (-;) blue; blueness

bläuen ['blɔɪ•ən] *tr* dye blue

bläulich ['blɔɪlɪç] *adj* bluish

blau'machen *intr* (coll) take off from work

Blech [bleç] *n* (-[e]s;-e) sheet metal; (sl) baloney; (mus) brass

Blech'büchse *f* tin can

blechen ['bleçən] *tr* (coll) pay out ‖ *intr* (coll) cough up the dough

Blech'instrument *n* brass instrument

blecken ['blekən] *tr*—**die Zähnen b.** bare one's teeth

Blei [blaɪ] *n* (-[e]s;-e) lead

Bleibe ['blaɪbə] *f* (-;-n) place to stay

bleiben ['blaɪbən] §62 *intr* (SEIN) remain, stay; **am Leben b.** survive; **bei etw b.** stick to s.th.; **dabei bleibt es!** that's final!; **für sich b.** keep to oneself; **sich** [dat] **gleich b.** never change; **und wo bleibe ich?** (coll) and where do I come in?

blei'bend *adj* lasting, permanent

bleich [blaɪç] *adj* pale ‖ **Bleiche** *f* (-;) bleaching; paleness

blei'chen *tr* bleach; make pale ‖ *intr* (SEIN) bleach; (*verblassen*) fade

Bleich'gesicht *n* paleface

Bleich'mittel *n* bleach

bleiern ['blaɪ•ərn] *adj* leaden

Blei'soldat *m* tin soldier

Blei'stift *m* pencil

Bleistiftspitzer ['blaɪstɪft/pɪtsər] *m* (-s;-) pencil sharpener

Blende ['blendə] *f* (-;-n) window blind; shutter; (phot) diaphragm

blen'den *tr* blind; (*bezaubern*) dazzle

blen'dend *adj* fabulous

Blen'der *m* (-s;-) (coll) fourflusher

Blendling ['blentlɪŋ] *m* (-s;-e) (*Mischling*) mongrel; (bot) hybrid

Blick [blɪk] *m* (-[e]s;-e) glance, look; (**auf** *acc*) view (of)

blicken (blik'ken) *intr* (**auf** *acc*, **nach**) glance (at), look (at); **sich b. lassen** show one's face

Blick'fang *m* (coll) eye catcher

blieb [blip] *pret of* **bleiben**

blies [blis] *pret of* **blasen**

blind [blɪnt] *adj* (**für, gegen**) blind (to); (*Spiegel*) clouded; (*trübe*) dull; (*Alarm*) false; (*Patrone*) blank; **blinder Passagier** stowaway

Blind'band *m* (-[e]s;ⸯe) (typ) dummy

Blind'boden *m* subfloor

Blind'darm *m* appendix

Blind'darmentzündung *f* appendicitis

Blind'darmoperation *f* appendectomy

Blin'denheim *n* home for the blind

Blin'denhund *m* Seeing-Eye dog

Blin'denschrift *f* braille

Blind'flug *m* blind flying

Blind'gänger *m* (mil) dud

Blind'landung *f* instrument landing

blindlings ['blɪntlɪŋs] *adv* blindly

Blind'schreiben *n* touch typing

blinken ['blɪŋkən] *intr* blink, twinkle; (*Sonne*) shine; (mil) signal

Blin'ker *m*, **Blink'licht** *n* (aut) blinker

blinzeln ['blɪntsəln] *intr* blink, wink

Blitz [blɪts] *m* (-es;-e) lightning; (fig & phot) flash

Blitz'ableiter *m* lightning rod

blitz'blank' *adj* shining; spick and span

Blitz'krieg *m* blitzkrieg

Blitz'licht *n* (phot) flash

Blitz'lichtaufnahme *f* (phot) flash shot

Blitz'lichtbirne *f* (phot) flash bulb

Blitz'lichtgerät *n* flash gun

Blitz'lichtröhre *f* (phot) electronic flash, flash tube

Blitz'schlag *m* stroke of lightning

blitz'schnell' *adj* quick as lightning

Blitz'strahl *m* flash of lightning

Block [blɔk] *m* (-s;ⸯe) block, log; (*Stück Seife*) cake; (*von Schokolade*) bar; (*von Löschpapier*) pad; (geol) boulder; (metal) ingot; (pol) bloc

Blockade [blɔ'kadə] *f* (-;-n) blockade

Blocka'debrecher *m* blockade runner

blocken (blok'ken) *tr* (sport) block

Block'haus *n* log cabin

blockieren [blɔ'kirən] *tr* block up; (mil) blockade

Block'kalender *m* tear-off calendar

Block'schrift *f* block letters

blöd(e) ['blød(ə)] *adj* stupid, idiotic; feeble-minded; (*schüchtern*) shy

Blöd'heit *f* (-;) stupidity, idiocy

Blö'digkeit *f* (-;) shyness

Blöd'sinn *m* idiocy; nonsense

blöd'sinnig *adj* idiotic ‖ *adv* idiotically; (*sehr*) (coll) awfully

blöken ['bløkən] *intr* bleat; (*Kuh*) moo

blond [blɔnt] *adj* blond, fair ‖ **Blonde** §5 *m* blond ‖ *f* blonde

blondieren [blɔn'dirən] *tr* bleach

Blondine [blɔn'dinə] *f* (-;-n) blonde

bloß [blos] *adj* bare; (*nichts als*) mere *adv* only; barely

Blöße ['bløsə] *f* bareness; nakedness; (fig) weak point

bloß'legen tr lay bare
bloß'stellen tr expose
blühen ['bly·ən] intr blossom, bloom; (Backen) be rosy; (fig) flourish
Blume ['blumə] f (-;-n) flower; (des Weins) bouquet; (des Biers) head
Blu'menbeet n flower bed
Blu'menblatt n petal
Blu'mengewinde n garland, festoon
Blu'menhändler –in §6 mf florist
Blu'menkelch m calyx
Blu'menkohl m cauliflower
Blu'menstaub m pollen
Blu'mentopf m flowerpot
Bluse ['bluzə] f (-;-n) blouse
Blut [blut] n (-[e]s); blood; **bis aufs B.** almost to death; **B. lecken** taste blood; **heißes B.** hot temper
blut'arm adj anemic
Blut'armut f anemia
Blut'bahn f bloodstream
Blut'bild n blood count
blut'dürstig adj bloodthirsty
Blüte ['blytə] f (-;-n) blossom, flower, bloom; (fig) prime
Blut'egel m leech
bluten ['blutən] intr bleed
Blü'tenblatt n petal
Blü'tenstaub m pollen
Blu'terguß m bruise
Blu'terkrankheit f hemophilia
Blü'tezeit f blooming period; (fig) heyday
Blut'farbstoff m hemoglobin
Blut'gerinnsel n blood clot
Blut'hund m bloodhound
blutig ['blutıç] adj bloody
blut'jung adj very young, green
Blut'körperchen n corpuscle
Blut'kreislauf m blood circulation
blut'leer, blut'los adj bloodless
Blut'pfropfen m blood clot
Blut'probe f blood test
Blut'rache f blood feud
Blut'rausch m mania to kill
blutrünstig ['blutrʏnstıç] adj gory
Blut'sauger m bloodsucker, leech
Blut'schande f incest
blutschänderisch ['blutʃɛndərıʃ] adj incestuous
Blut'spender –in §6 mf blood donor
blut'stillend adj coagulant
Blut'sturz m hemorrhage
Bluts'verwandte §5 mf blood relation
Blut'übertragung f blood transfusion
blut'unterlaufen adj bloodshot
Blut'vergießen n (-s;) bloodshed
blut'voll adj lively, vivid
Blut'wasser n lymph
Blut'zeuge m, **Blut'zeugin** f martyr
Bö [bø] f (-;-en) gust, squall
Bob [bɔb] m (-s;-s) bobsled
Bock [bɔk] m (-[e]s; ⸗e) buck; ram; he-goat; (Kutsch-) driver's seat; (tech) horse; **B. springen** play leapfrog; **e–n B. schießen** pull a boner
bockbeinig ['bɔkbaınıç] adj stubborn
bocken ['bɔkən] intr buck; (sich aufbäumen) rear; (ausschlagen) kick; (brunsten) be in heat; (aut) hesitate
bockig ['bɔkıç] adj thickheaded
Bock'sprung m caper; leapfrog

Boden ['bodən] m (-s;⸗) (Erd-) ground, soil; (Meeres-) bottom; (Fuß-) floor; (Dach-) attic; (Trocken-) loft; **B. fassen** get a firm footing; **zu B. drücken** crush
Bo'denertrag m (agr) yield
Bo'denfenster n dormer window
Bo'denfläche f floor space; (agr) acreage
Bo'denfliese f floor tile
Bodenfräse ['bodənfrɛzə] f (-;-n) Rototiller
Bo'denhaftung f roadability
Bo'denkammer f attic
bo'denlos adj bottomless; (fig) unmitigated
Bo'denmannschaft f (aer) ground crew
Bo'denreform f agrarian reform
Bo'densatz m grounds, sediment
Bodenschätze ['bodənʃɛtsə] pl mineral resources
Bo'densee m (-s;) Lake Constance
bo'denständig adj native, indigenous
bog [bok] pret of **biegen**
Bogen ['bogən] m (-s;⸗) bow; (Kurve) curve; (Papier-) sheet; (beim Schilaufen) turn; (beim Eislaufen) circle; (archit) arch; (math) arc; **den B. raushaben** have the hang of it; **den B. überspannen** (fig) go too far; **e–n großen B. um j–n machen** give s.o. wide berth
Bo'genfenster n bow window
bo'genförmig adj arched
Bo'gengang m arcade; archway
Bo'genschießen n (-s;) archery
Bo'genschütze m archer
Bo'gensehne f bowstring
Bohle ['bolə] f (-;-n) plank
Böhme ['bømə] m (-n;-n) Bohemian
Böhmen ['bømən] n (-s;) Bohemia
Bohne ['bonə] f (-;-n) bean; **blaue Bohnen** bullets; **grüne Bohnen** string beans
Boh'nermasse f polish; floor polish
bohnern ['bonərn] tr wax, polish
Boh'nerwachs n floor wax
Bohr- [bor] comb.fm. drill, drilling, bore, boring
bohren ['borən] tr drill, bore
Bohrer m (-s;-) drill; (ent) borer
Bohr'insel f offshore drilling platform
Bohr'presse f drill press
Bohr'turm m derrick
böig ['bø·ıç] adj gusty; (aer) bumpy
Boje ['bojə] f (-;-n) buoy
Böller ['bœlər] m (-s;-) mortar
böllern ['bœlərn] intr fire a mortar
Bollwerk ['bɔlvɛrk] n (-s;-e) bulwark
Bolzen ['bɔltsən] m (-s;-) bolt; dowel
Bombardement [bɔmbardə'mã] n (-s; -s) bombardment
bombardieren [bɔmbar'dirən] tr bombard
Bombe ['bɔmbə] f (-;-n) bomb, bombshell; (coll) smash hit
Bomben- comb.fm. bomb, bombing; huge
Bom'benabwurf m bombing; **gezielter B.** precision bombing
Bom'benerfolg m (theat) smash hit
bom'benfest adj bombproof
Bom'benflugzeug m bomber

Bom'bengeschäft n (coll) gold mine

Bom'benpunktzielwurf m precision bombing

Bom'benreihenwurf m stick bombing

Bom'bensache f (coll) humdinger

Bom'benschütze m bombardier

Bom'benschacht m bomb bay

Bom'bentrichter m bomb crater

Bom'benzielanflug m bombing run

Bom'benzielgerät n bombsight

Bon [bõ] m (-s;-s) sales slip; (Gutschein) credit note

Bonbon [bõ'bõ] m & n (-s;-s) piece of candy; Bonbons candy

Bonbonniere [bõbɔnɪ'erə] f (-;-n) box of candy

Bonze ['bɔntsə] m (-;-n) (coll) big shot, bigwig; (pol) boss

Boot [bot] n (-[e]s;-e) boat

Boots'mann m (-es;-leute) boatswain; (nav) petty officer

Bord [bɔrt] m (-es;e) edge; bookshelf; (naut) board, side; an B. aboard, on board; von B. gehen leave the ship

Bordell [bɔr'del] n (-s;-e) brothel

Bord'karte f boarding pass

Bord'schütze m aerial gunner

Bord'schwelle f curb

Bord'stein m curb

Bord'waffen pl (aer, mil) armament

Bord'wand f ship's side

Borg [bɔrk] m (-s;) borrowing; auf B. on credit; on loan

borgen ['bɔrgən] tr (von, bei) borrow (from); loan out, lend

Borke ['bɔrkə] f (-;-n) bark

Born [bɔrn] m (-es; -e) (poet) fountain

borniert [bɔr'nirt] adj narrow-minded

Borsäure ['bɔrzɔɪrə] f (-;) boric acid

Börse ['bœrzə] f (-;-n) purse; stock exchange

Bör'senkurs m market price; quotation

Bör'senmakler -in §6 mf stockbroker

Bör'senmarkt m stockmarket

Bör'sennotierung f (st.exch.) quotation

Bör'senpapiere pl stocks, shares, securities

Borste ['bɔrstə] f (-;-n) bristle

bortstig ['bɔrstɪç] adj birstly; (fig) crusty

Borte ['bɔrtə] f (-;-n) trim; braid; (Saum) hem

bös [bøs] var of böse

bös'artig adj nasty; (Tier) vicious; (pathol) malignant

Böschung ['bœʃʊŋ] f (-;-en) slope; (e-s Flusses) bank; (rr) embankment

böse ['bøzə] adj bad, evil, nasty; angry || Böse §5 mf wicked person || m devil || n evil; harm

Bösewicht ['bøzəvɪçt] m (-s;-e) villain

boshaft ['boshaft] adj malicious; wicked; (tückisch) spiteful

bossieren [bɔ'sirən] tr emboss

bös'willig adj malicious, willful

bot [bot] pret of bieten

Botanik [bo'tanɪk] f (-;) botany

Botaniker -in §6 mf botanist

botanisch [bo'tanɪʃ] adj botanic(al)

Bote ['botə] m (-n;-n) messenger

Bo'tengang m errand

Botin ['botɪn] f (-;-nen) messenger

Bot'schaft f (-;-en) message, news; (Amt) embassy; (Auftrag) mission

Botschafter -in ['bot/aftər(ɪn)] §6 ambassador

Bottich ['bɔtɪç] m (-s;-e) tub; vat

Bouillon (bul'jõ] f (-;-s) bouillon

Bowle ['bolə] f (-;-n) punch

boxen ['bɔksən] tr & intr box

Bo'xer m (-s;-) boxer

Box'kampf m boxing match

Boykott [bɔɪ'kɔt] m (-s;-e) boycott

boykottieren [bɔɪko'tirən] tr boycott

brach [brax] pret of brechen || adj fallow

brachte ['braxtə] pret of bringen

brackig ['brakɪç] adj brackish

Branche ['brã/ə] f (-;-n) line of business; (com) branch

Brand [brant] m (-[e]s;-e) burning; fire; (coll) thirst; (agr) blight; (pathol) gangrene in B. geraten catch fire; in B. setzen (or stecken) set on fire

Brand'blase f blister

Brand'bombe f incendiary bomb

Brand'brief m urgent letter

Brand'direktor m fire chief

branden ['brandən] intr surge, break

Brand'fackel f firebrand

brandig ['brandɪç] adj (agr) blighted; (pathol) gangrenous

Brand'mal n brand; (fig) moral stigma

brand'marken tr stigmatize

Brand'mauer f fire wall

brandschatzen ['brant/atsən] tr sack

Brand'stifter -in §6 mf arsonist

Bran'dung f (-;) breakers

Bran'dungswelle f breaker

Brand'wunde f burn

Brand'zeichen n brand

brannte ['brantə] pret of brennen

Branntwein ['brantvaɪn] m brandy

Brasilien [bra'ziljən] n (-s;) Brazil

Bratapfel ['bratapfəl] m baked apple

braten ['bratən] §63 tr & intr roast; (im Ofen) bake; (auf dem Rost) broil, grill; (in der Pfanne) fry || Braten m (-s;-) roast

Bra'tensoße f gravy

Brat'fisch m fried fish

Brat'huhn n broiler

Brat'kartoffeln pl fried potatoes

Brat'pfanne f frying pan, skillet

Bratsche ['brat/ə] f (-;-n) viola

Bräu [brɔɪ] m & n (-[e]s;-e) brew

Brauch [braux] m (-[e]s;-e) custom

brauchbar ['brauxbar] adj useful

brauchen ['brauxən] tr need; (Zeit) take; (gebrauchen) use

Brauchtum ['brauxtum] n (-s;) tradition

Braue ['brau-ə] f (-;-n) eyebrow

brauen ['brau-ən] tr brew

Brau'er m (-s;-) brewer

Brauerei [brau-ə'raɪ] f (-;-en), Brau'haus n brewery

braun [braun] adj brown; (Pferd) bay

Bräune ['brɔɪnə] f (-;) brown; sun tan; (pathol) diphtheria

bräunen ['brɔɪnən] tr tan; (culin) brown || ref & intr tan

bräunlich ['brɔɪnlɪç] adj brownish

Braus [braus] m (-es;) noise; revelry

Brause ['brauzə] f (-;-n) soda, soft drink; (*Duschbad*) shower; (*an Gieß-kannen*) nozzle

Brau/sebad n shower

Brau/sekopf m hothead

Brau/selimonade f soda, soft drink

brau/sen tr spray, water ‖ intr bubble; (*toben*) roar ‖ intr (SEIN) rush

Braut [braut] f (-;:e) fiancée; bride

Braut/ausstattung f trousseau

Braut/führer m usher

Bräutigam ['brɔɪtɪgam] m (-s;-e) fiancé; bridegroom

Braut/jungfer f (-;-n) bridesmaid; er-ste B. maid of honor

Braut/kleid n bridal gown

Braut/leute pl engaged couple

bräutlich ['brɔɪtlɪç] adj bridal; nuptial

Braut/schatz m dowry

Braut/werber -in §6 mf matchmaker

Braut/werbung f courting

Braut/zeit f period of engagement

Braut/zeuge m best man

brav [braf] adj well-mannered, good, honest

Brav/heit f good behavior

Bravour [bra'vur] f (-;) bravado

Brech/eisen n crowbar, jimmy

brechen ['brɛçən] §64 tr break; (*Papier*) fold; (*Steine*) quarry; (*Blumen*) pick; (coll) vomit; (opt) refract; **die Ehe b.** commit adultery ‖ ref break; (opt) be refracted ‖ intr (SEIN) break; (coll) vomit

Brech/reiz m nausea

Brech/stange f crowbar

Bre/chung f (-;-en) (opt) refraction

Brei [braɪ] m (-s;-e) paste; pap, gruel; **zu B. schlagen** beat to a pulp

breit [braɪt] adj broad, wide

breitbeinig ['braɪtbaɪnɪç] adv with legs outspread

breit/drücken tr flatten (out)

Brei/te f (-;-n) width; latitude

Brei/tengrad m degree of latitude

breit/machen ref take up (too much) room; (fig) throw one's weight around

breit/schlagen §132 tr (coll) persuade

breitschulterig ['braɪtʃultərɪç] adj broad-shouldered

breitspurig ['braɪtʃpurɪç] adj (coll) pompous; (rr) broad-gauge

breit/treten §152 tr belabor

Breit/wand f (cin) wide screen

Bremsbelag ['bremsbəlak] m brake lining

Bremse ['bremzə] f (-;-n) brake; (ent) horsefly

bremsen ['bremzən] tr brake; (fig) curb; (atom phys) slow down ‖ intr brake

Brem/ser m (-s;-) brakeman

Brems/flüssigkeit f brake fluid

Brems/fußhebel m brake pedal

Brems/klotz m wheel chock

Bremsleuchte ['bremslɔɪçtə] f, **Brems/-licht** n (aut) brake light

Brems/rakete f (rok) retrorocket

Brems/schuh m brake shoe

brems/sicher adj skidproof

Brems/spur f skid mark

Brems/wagen m (rr) caboose

Brems/weg m braking distance

Brennapparat ['brenaparat] m still

brennbar ['brenbar] adj inflammable, combustible

brennen §97 tr burn; (*Branntwein*) dis-til; (*Kaffee*) roast; (*Haar*) curl; (*Ziegel*) fire ‖ intr burn; smart

Bren/ner m (-s;-) burner; distiller

Brennerei [brenə'raɪ] f (-;-en) distil-lery

Brenn/holz n firewood

Brenn/material n fuel

Brenn/ofen m kiln

Brenn/punkt m focus; **im B. stehen** be the focal point

Brenn/schere f curler

Brenn/schluß m (rok) burnout

Brenn/spiegel m concave mirror

Brenn/stoff m fuel

brenzlig ['brentslɪç] adj (*Geruch*) burnt; (*Situation*) precarious

Bresche ['breʃə] f (-;-n) breach; **e-e B. schlagen** make a breach

Brett [bret] n (-[e]s;-er) board; plank; (*für Bücher, Geschirr*) shelf; **Bretter** (coll) skis; (theat) stage; **Schwarzes B.** bulletin board

Bret/terbude f shack

Bret/terverschlag m wooden partition

Brett/säge f ripsaw

Brezel ['bretsəl] f (-;-n) pretzel

Brief [brif] m (-[e]s;-e) letter; **Briefe wechseln** correspond

Brief/ausgabe f mail delivery

Briefbeschwerer ['brifbəverər] m (-s;-) paperweight

Brief/bestellung f mail delivery

Brief/beutel m mail bag

Brief/bogen m piece of notepaper

Brief/bote m mailman, postman

Briefchen ['brifçən] n (-s;-) note; **B. Streichhölzer** book of matches

Brief/einwurf m slot in a mailbox; let-terdrop; mailbox

Brief/fach n pigeonhole; post-office box

Brief/freund -in §8 mf pen pal

Brief/hülle f envelope

Brief/kasten m mailbox

Brief/klammer f paper clip

Brief/kopf m letterhead

Brief/kurs m (st.exch.) selling price

brief/lich adj written; (*brieflicher Ver-kehr*) correspondence ‖ adv by letter

Brief/mappe f folder

Brief/marke f postage stamp

Brief/markenautomat m stamp ma-chine

Brief/ordner m ring binder

Brief/papier n stationery; note paper

Brief/porto n postage

Brief/post f first-class mail

Brief/schaften pl correspondence

Brief/stempel m postmark

Brief/tasche f billfold, wallet

Brief/taube f carrier pigeon

Brief/träger m mailman, postman

Brief/umschlag m envelope

Brief/verkehr m correspondence

Brief/waage f postage scales

Brief/wahl f absentee ballot

Brief/wechsel m correspondence

briet [brit] pret of braten

Brigade [brɪ'gɑːdə] *f* (-;-n) brigade
Briga'degeneral *m* brigadier general; (*Brit*) brigadier
Brikett [brɪ'ket] *n* (-[e]s;-s) briquette
brillant [brɪl'jant] *adj* brilliant || **Brillant** *m* (-en;-en) precious stone (esp. diamond)
Brille ['brɪlə] *f* (-;-n) eyeglasses; (*für Pferde*) blinkers; (*Toilettenring*) toilet seat; **B. mit doppeltem Brennpunkt** bifocals
Bril'lenbügel *m* sidepiece (*of glasses*)
Bril'lenfassung *f* eyeglass frame
Bril'lenschlange *f* cobra
bringen ['brɪŋən] §65 *tr* bring, take; **an sich b.** acquire; **es mit sich b., daß** bring it about that; **es zu etw b.** achieve s.th.; **etw hinter sich b.** get s.th. over and done with; **etw über sich (or übers Herz) b.** be able to bear s.th.; **j-n auf etw b.** put s.o. on to s.th.; **j-n außer sich b.** enrage s.o.; **j-n dazu b. zu** (*inf*) get s.o. to (*inf*); **j-m um etw b.** deprive s.o. of s.th.; **j-n zum Lachen b.** make s.o. laugh; **unter die Leute b.** circulate
brisant [brɪ'zant] *adj* high-explosive
Brise ['briːzə] *f* (-;-n) breeze
Britannien [brɪ'tanjən] *n* (-s;) Britain
Brite ['brɪtə] *m* (-n;-n) Briton, Britisher; **die Briten** the British
Britin ['brɪtɪn] *f* (-;-nen) Briton, British woman
britisch ['brɪtɪʃ] *adj* British
Broché [brɔ'ʃe] *n* (-s;) broché; brocaded fabric
Bröckchen ['brœkçən] *n* (-s;-) bit; morsel, crumb; fragment
bröck(e)lig ['brœk(ə)lɪç] *adj* crumbly
bröckeln ['brœkəln] *tr & intr* crumble
brocken ['brɔkən] *tr*—**Brot in die Suppe b.** break bread into the soup || **Brocken** *m* (-s;-) piece, bit; lump; **Brocken** *pl* scraps, bits and pieces; **harter B.** (coll) tough job
brockenweise (**brok'kenweise**) *adv* bit by bit
brodeln ['broːdəln] *intr* bubble, simmer
Brokat [brɔ'kɑːt] *m* (-s;-e) brocade
Brombeere ['brɔmbeːrə] *f* (-;-n) blackberry
Bromid [brɔ'miːt] *n* (-[e]s;-e) bromide
Bronchitis [brɔn'çiːtɪs] *f* (-;) bronchitis
Bronze ['brɔ̃sə] *f* (-;-n) bronze
Brosche ['brɔʃə] *f* (-s;-n) brooch
broschieren [brɔ'ʃiːrən] *tr* stitch; brocade; **broschiert** with stapled binding
Broschüre [brɔ'ʃyːrə] *f* (-;-n) brochure
Brösel ['brøːzəl] *m* (-s;-) crumb
Brot [broːt] *n* (-[e]s;-e) bread; loaf; **geröstetes B.** toast
Brot'aufstrich *m* spread
Brötchen ['brøːtçən] *n* (-s;-) roll
Brot'erwerb *m* livelihood, living
Brot'geber *m*, **Brot'herr** *m* employer
Brot'kasten *m* breadbox
brot'los *adj* unemployed; unprofitable
Brot'neid *m* professional jealousy
Brot'röster *m* toaster
Brot'schnitte *f* slice of bread
Brot'studium *n* bread-and-butter courses
Brot'zeit *f* breakfast

Bruch [brʊx] *m* (-[e]s;˵e) breaking; break, crack; breakage; (aer) crash; (geol) fault; (math) fraction; (min) quarry; (pathol) hernia; (surg) fracture; **B. machen** crash-land; **in die Brüche gehen** go to pot; **zu B. gehen** break || [brʊx] *m & n* (-s;˵e) bog
Bruch'band *n* (-s;˵er) (surg) truss
Bruch'bude *f* shanty
brüchig ['brʏçɪç] *adj* fragile, brittle
Bruch'landung *f* crash landing
Bruch'rechnung *f* fractions
Bruch'stück *n* fragment, chip; **Bruchstücke** (fig) scraps, snatches
bruch'stückhaft *adj* fragmentary
Bruch'teil *m* fraction; **im B. e-r Sekunde** in a split second
Bruch'zahl *f* fractional number
Brücke ['brʏkə] *f* (-;-n) bridge; (*Teppich*) small (narrow) rug; (gym) backbend
Brückenkopf (**Brük'kenkopf**) *m* bridgehead
Brückenpfeiler (**Brük'kenpfeiler**) *m* pier of a bridge
Brückenwaage (**Brük'kenwaage**) *f* platform scale
Brückenzoll (**Brük'kenzoll**) *m* bridge toll
Bruder ['bruːdər] *m* (-s;˵) brother; (*Genosse*) companion; (eccl) lay brother
brüderlich ['brydərlɪç] *adj* brotherly
Brüderschaft ['brydərʃaft] *f* (-;-en) brotherhood; fraternity
Brühe ['bryːə] *f* (-;-n) broth; (*Fleisch-*) gravy; **in der B. stecken** be in a jam
brühen ['bryːən] *tr* boil; scald
brüh'heiß *adj* piping hot
Brüh'kartoffeln *pl* potatoes boiled in broth
Brüh'würfel *m* bouillon cube
brüllen ['brylən] *tr & intr* roar, bellow; (*Sturm*) howl; (*Ochse*) low; **b. vor Lachen** roar with laughter
Brummbär ['brumbeːr] *m* (-en;-en) grouch
brummen ['brumən] *tr* mumble; grumble; growl || *intr* mumble; grumble; growl; (*summen*) buzz, hum; (*Orgel*) boom; (*im Gefängnis*) do time, do a stretch
brummig ['brumɪç] *adj* grouchy
brünett [bry'net] *adj* brunet(te) || **Brünette** §5 brunette
Brunft [brunft] *f* (-;) rut
Brunft'zeit *f* rutting season
Brunnen ['brunən] *m* (-s;-) well; (*Spring-*) spring
Brunnenkresse ['brunənkresə] *f* (-;-n) watercress
Brunst [brunst] *f* (-;) rut, heat; (fig) ardor, passion
brunsten ['brunstən] *intr* be in heat
brünstig ['brynstɪç] *adj* in heat; (fig) passionate
brüsk [brusk] *adj* brusque
brüskieren [brus'kiːrən] *tr* snub
Brust [brust] *f* (-;˵e) breast, chest
Brust'bein *n* breastbone, sternum
Brust'bild *n* portrait; (sculp) bust
brüsten ['brystən] *ref* show off

Brust'fellentzündung f pleurisy
Brust'kasten m, **Brust'korb** m thorax
Brust'schwimmen n breast stroke
Brust'stück n (culin) brisket
Brust'ton m —**im B. der Überzeugung** with utter conviction
Brust'umfang m chest measurement; (**bei Frauen**) bust measurement
Brü'stung f (-;-en) balustrade
Brust'warze f nipple
Brust'wehr f breastwork
Brut [brut] f (-;-en) brood; (pej) scum
brutal [bru'tɑl] adj brutal
Brut'apparat m, **Brut'ofen** m incubator
brüten ['brytən] tr hatch; (fig) plan || intr incubate; **b. auf** (dat) (fig) sit on; **b. über** (dat) brood over; pore over
brutto ['bruto] adj (com) gross
Brut'tosozialprodukt n gross national product
Bube ['bubə] m (-n;-n) boy; (Schurke) rascal; (cards) jack
Bu'benstreich m, **Bu'benstück** n prank; dirty trick
bübisch ['bybɪʃ] adj rascally
Buch [bux] n (-[e]s;̈er) book; (cards) straight
Buch'besprechung f book review
Buchbinderei ['buxbɪndərɑɪ] f (-;-en) bookbindery; (Gewerbe) bookbinding
Buch'binderleinwand f buckram
Buch'deckel m book cover
Buch'drama n closet drama
Buch'druck m printing, typography
Buch'drucker m printer
Buch'druckerei f print shop; (Gewerbe) printing
Buche ['buxə] f (-;-n) beech
Buchecker ['buxekər] f (-;-n) beechnut
buchen ['buxən] tr book, reserve; (com) enter
Bücher— [byçər] comb.fm. book
Bü'cherabschluß m balancing of books
Bücherausgabe f circulation desk
Bü'cherbrett n bookshelf
Bücherei [byçə'rɑɪ] f (-;-en) library
Bü'cherfreund m bibliophile
Bü'chergestell n bookrack, bookcase
Bü'cherregal n bookshelf; bookcase
Bü'cherrevision f audit
Bü'cherrevisor m auditor; accountant
Bü'cherschrank m bookcase
Bü'cherstütze f book end
Buch'führung f bookkeeping, accounting
Buch'halter –**in** §6 mf bookkeeper
Buch'haltung f bookkeeping; accounting department
Buch'händler –**in** §6 mf book dealer
Buch'handlung f bookstore
Büchlein ['byçlaɪn] n (-s;-) booklet
Buch'macher m bookmaker
Buch'prüfer –**in** §6 mf auditor
Buchsbaum ['buksbaum] m boxwood
Buchse ['buksə] f (-;-n) (mach) bushing
Büchse ['byksə] f (-;-n) box, case; (Dose) can; (Gewhr) rifle
Büch'senfleisch n canned meat

Büch'senöffner m can opener
Buchstabe ['bux/tabə] m (-n;-n) letter
buchstabieren [bux/ta'birən] tr & intr spell
buchstäblich ['bux/teplɪç] adj literal
Bucht [buxt] f (-;-en) bay
Buch'umschlag m book jacket
Bu'chung f (-;-en) booking; (acct) entry
Buckel ['bʊkəl] m (-s;-) hump; (coll) back; **B. haben** be hunchback; **e-n B. machen** arch its back
buck(e)lig ['bʊk(ə)lɪç] adj hunchbacked || .**Buck(e)lige** §5 mf hunchback
bücken ['bykən] tr & ref bow (down)
Bückling ['byklɪŋ] m (-s;-e) bow
Bude ['budə] f (-;-n) booth, stall; (coll) shanty; (coll) hole in the wall
Budget [by'dʒe] n (-s;-s) budget
Büfett [by'fe], [by'fet] n (-s;-s) buffet, sideboard; counter; (Schanktisch) bar; **kaltes B.** cold buffet
Büffel ['byfəl] m (-s;-) buffalo
Büffelei [byfə'laɪ] f (-;-en) cramming
büffeln ['byfəln] intr (für) cram (for)
Bug [buk] m (-[e]s;-e) (aer) nose; (naut) bow; (zool) shoulder, withers
Bügel ['bygəl] m (-s;-) handle; (Kleider-) coat hanger; (Steig-) stirrup; (e-r Säge) frame
Bü'gelbrett n ironing board
Bü'geleisen n iron, flatiron
Bü'gelfalte f crease
bü'gelfrei adj drip-dry
bügeln ['bygəln] tr iron, press
Bü'gelsäge f hacksaw
bugsieren [buk'sirən] tr tow
Buhldirne ['buldɪrnə] f (-;-n) bawd
buhlen ['bulən] intr have an affair; **um j–s Gunst b.** curry favor with s.o.
Bühne ['bynə] f (-;-n) stage; platform
Büh'nenanweisung f stage direction
Büh'nenaussprache f standard pronunciation
Büh'nenausstattung f, **Büh'nenbild** n set
Büh'nenbildner –**in** §6 mf stage designer
Büh'nendeutsch n standard German
Büh'nendichter –**in** §6 mf playwright
Büh'nendichtung f drama, play
Büh'nenkünstler m actor
Büh'nenkünstlerin f actress
Büh'nenleiter –**in** §6 mf stage manager
Büh'nenstück n play, stage play
buk [buk] pret of **backen**
Bukarest ['bukarest] n (-s;) Bucharest
Bulette [bu'letə] f (-;-n) meatball
Bulgarien [bul'qɑrjən] n (-s;) Bulgaria
Bullauge ['bulaugə] n (-s;-en) porthole
Bulldogge ['buldɔgə] f (-;-n) bulldog
Bulle ['bulə] m (-n;-n) bull; brawny fellow; (sl) cop || f (-;-n) (eccl) bull
bullern ['bulərn] intr bubble, boil; (Feuer) roar; (Sturm) rage
Bummel ['buməl] m (-s;) stroll
Bummelei [bumə'laɪ] f (-;-en) dawdling; loafing; sloppiness
bummelig ['bumulɪç] adj slow; sloppy
bummeln ['buməln] intr loaf; dawdle; (Autos) crawl || intr (SEIN) stroll

Bum'melstreik *m* slowdown
Bum'melzug *m* (coll) slow train, local
Bummler ['bʊmlər] *m* (-s;-) loafer, bum; slowpoke; gadabout
Bums [bʊms] *m* (-es;-e) thud, thump, bang || *interj* boom!; bang!
bumsen ['bʊmsən] *intr* thud, thump, bump; (sl) have intercourse
Bums'lokal *n* (coll) dive, joint
Bund [bʊnt] *m* (-[e]s;-e) union, federation; (*Schlüssel*-) ring; (*Rand an Hose*) waistband; (*Ehe*-) bond; (mach) flange; (mus) fret; (pol) federal government; **im Bunde mit** with the cooperation of || *n* (-[e]s;- & -e) bunch, bundle
Bündel ['bʏndəl] *n* (-s;-) bunch, bundle; (phys) beam
Bundes– *comb.fm.*
Bun'desgenosse *m* ally, confederate
Bun'desgerichtshof *m* federal supreme court
Bun'deslade *f* ark of the covenant
bun'desstaatlich *adj* state; federal
Bun'destag *m* lower house
bündig ['bʏndɪç] *adj* binding; (*überzeugend*) convincing; (*treffend*) succint; **b. liegen** be flush
Bündnis ['bʏntnɪs] *n* (-ses;-se) agreement, pact, alliance
Bunker ['bʊŋkər] *m* (-s;-) bin; (agr) silo; (aer) air-raid shelter; (mil) bunker; (nav) submarine pen
bunt [bʊnt] *adj* colored; (*mehrfarbig*) multicolored; (*gefleckt*) dappled; (*gemischt*) varied, motley; (*Farbe*) bright, gay; (*Wiese*) gay with flowers; **bunter Abend** variety show; **buntes Durcheinander** complete muddle
Bunt'metall *n* nonferrous metal
Bunt'stift *m* colored pencil, crayon
Bürde ['bʏrdə] *f* (-;-n) burden
Burg [bʊrk] *f* (-;-en) fortress, stronghold; citadel; castle
Bürge ['bʏrgə] *m* (-;-n) bondsman, guarantor, surety; **B. sein für** (or **als B. haften für**) stand surety for (*s.o.*); vouch for (*s.th.*)
bürgen ['bʏrgən] *intr*—**b. für** put up bail for (*s.o.*); vouch for (*s.th.*)
Bürger –in ['bʏrgər(ɪn)] §6 *mf* citizen; member of the middle class; commoner
Bür'gerkrieg *m* civil war
bür'gerlich *adj* civic; civil; middle-class; (*nicht überfeinert*) plain
Bür'germeister *m* mayor
Bür'gerrecht *n* civil rights
Bür'gerschaft *f* (-;) citizens

Bür'gersteig *m* sidewalk
Bürgschaft ['bʏrkʃaft] *f* (-;-en) security, guarantee; (jur) bail; **gegen B. freilassen** release on bail
Büro [bʏ'ro] *n* (-s;-s) office
Büro'angestellte §5 *mf* clerk
Büro'bedarf *m* office supplies
Büro'klammer *f* paper clip
Büro'kraft *f* office worker; **Bürokräfte** office personnel
Bürokrat [bʏro'krat] *m* (-en;-en) bureaucrat
Bürokra•tie [bʏrokra'ti] *f* (-;-tien ['ti-ən]) bureaucracy; (fig) red tape
bürokratisch [bʏro'kratɪ] *adj* bureaucratic
Bursch(e) ['bʊrʃ(ə)] *m* (-[e]n;-[e]n) boy, fellow; (mil) orderly; **ein übler B.** a bad egg
burschikos [bʊrʃɪ'kos] *adj* tomboyish; devil-may-care
Bürste ['bʏrstə] *f* (-;-n) brush; (coll) crewcut
bürsten ['bʏrstən] *tr* brush
Bürzel ['bʏrtsəl] *m* (-s;-) rump (*of bird*)
Bus [bʊs] *m* (-ses;-se) bus
Busch [bʊʃ] *m* (-es;-e) bush; forest
Büschel ['bʏʃəl] *m & n* clump, bunch, cluster; (*Haar*-) tuft; (elec) brush
Busch'holz *n* brushwood
buschig ['bʊʃɪç] *adj* bushy; shaggy
Busch'klepper *m* bushwacker
Busch'messer *n* machete
Busch'werk *n* bushes, brush
Busen ['buzən] *m* (-s;-) bosom, breast; (*Bucht*) bay, gulf; (fig) bosom
Bussard ['bʊsart] *m* (-s;-e) buzzard
Buße ['busə] *f* (-n;-n) penance; (*Sühne*) atonement; (*Strafgeld*) fine
büßen ['bysən] *tr* atone for, pay for
Büßer –in ['bysər(ɪn)] §6 *mf* penitent
Busserl ['bʊsərl] *n* (-s;-n) kiss
buß'fertig *adj* repentant
Bussole [bʊ'solə] *f* (-;-n) compass
Büste ['bʏstə] *f* (-;-n) bust
Bü'stenhalter *m* brassière, bra
Bütte ['bʏtə] *f* (-;-n) tub; vat
Butter ['bʊtər] *f* (-;) butter
But'terbrot *n* bread and butter
But'terdose *f* butter dish
But'termilch *f* buttermilk
buttern ['bʊtərn] butter || *intr* make butter
byzantinisch [bytsan'tinɪʃ] *adj* Byzantine
Byzanz [by'tsants] *n* (-';) Byzantium
bzw. *abbr* (**beziehungsweise**) respectively

C

C, c [tze] *invar n* C, c; (meteor) centigrade; (mus) C
Café [ka'fe] *n* (-s;-s) café; coffee shop
Camping ['kempɪŋ] *n* (-s;-s) camping
Canaille [ka'naljə] *f* (-;-n) scoundrel
Cäsar ['tsezar] *m* (-s;) Caesar
Cellist –in [tʃɛ'lɪst(ɪn)] §7 *mf* cellist

Cello ['tʃɛlo] *n* (-s;-s) cello
Cellophan [tsɛlo'fan] *n* (-s;) cellophane
Celsius ['tsɛlzjʊs] centigrade
Cembalo ['tʃembalo] *n* (-s;-s) harpsichord
Ces [tsɛs] *n* (-;-) (mus) C flat

Champagner [ʃamˈpanjər] *m* (-s;-) champagne

Champignon [ˈʃampɪnjõ] *m* (-s;-s) mushroom

Chance [ˈʃãsə] *f* (-;-n) chance

Chaos [ˈkaːɔs] *n* (-;) chaos

chaotisch [kaˈoːtɪʃ] *adj* chaotic

Charak•ter [kaˈraktər] *m* (-s;-tere [ˈteːrə]) character; (mil) honorary rank

Charak'terbild *n* character sketch

Charak'tereigenschaft *f* trait

charak'terfest *adj* of a strong character

charakterisieren [karaktɛrˈziːrən] *tr* characterize

Charakteristik [karakteˈrɪstɪk] *f* (-; -en) characterization

Charakteristi-kum [karakteˈrɪstɪkum] *n* (-s;-ka [ka]) characteristic

charakteristisch [karakteˈrɪstɪʃ] *adj* (für) characteristic (of)

charak'terlich *adj* of character || *adv* in character

charak'terlos *adj* wishy-washy

Charak'terzug *m* characteristic, trait

Charge [ˈʃarʒə] *f* (-;-n) (metal) charge; (mil) rank; **Chargen** (mil) non-coms

charmant [ʃarˈmant] *adj* charming

Charme [ʃarm] *m* (-s;) charm, grace

Chas•sis [ʃaˈsi] *n* -sis [ˈsi[s]]; -sis [ˈsis]) chassis

Chaus•see [ʃoˈse] *f* (-;-seen [ˈseˑən]) highway

Chef [ʃef] *m* (-s;-s) chief, head; (com) boss; (culin) chef; **C. des Generalstabs** chief of staff; **C. des Heeresjustizwesens** judge advocate general

Chemie [çeˈmi] *f* (-;) chemistry; **technische C.** chemical engineering

Chemie'faser *f* synthetic fiber

Chemikalien [çemɪˈkaljən] *pl* chemicals

Chemiker –in [ˈçemɪkər(ɪn)] §6 *mf* chemist; student of chemistry

chemisch [ˈçemɪʃ] *adj* chemical; **chemische Reinigung** dry cleaning

Chemotechniker –in [çemoˈtɛçnɪkər(ɪn)] §6 *mf* chemical engineer

Chiffre [ˈʃifər] *f* (-;-n) cipher; code; *(in Anzeigen)* box number

Chif'freschrift *f* code

chiffrieren [ʃiˈfriːrən] *tr* code

China [ˈçina] *n* (-s;) China

Chinese [çiˈneːzə] *m* (-n;-n;), **Chinesin** [çiˈneːzɪn] *f* (-;-nen) Chinese

chinesisch [çiˈneːzɪʃ] *adj* Chinese

Chinin [çiˈnin] *n* (-s;) quinine

Chirurg [çiˈrurg] *m* (-en;-en) surgeon

Chirurgie [çirurˈgi] *f* (-;) surgery

chirurgisch [çiˈrurgɪʃ] *adj* surgical

Chlor [klor] *n* (-s;) chlorine

chloren [ˈkloːrən] *tr* chlorinate

Chlorid [kloˈrit] *n* (-[e]s;-e) chloride

Chloroform [kloːrəˈfɔrm] *n* (-s;) chloroform

chloroformieren [kloːrəfɔrˈmiːrən] *tr* chloroform

Cholera [ˈkolera] *f* (-;) cholera

cholerisch [koˈleːrɪʃ] *adj* choleric

Chor [kor] *m* (-s;⁻e) choir; chorus

Choral [koˈral] *m* (-s;⁻e) Gregorian chant; (Prot) hymn

Chor'altar *m* high altar

Chor'anlage *f* (archit) choir

Chor'bühne *f* choir loft

Choreograph –in [kɔreˑoˈgraf(ɪn)] §7 *mf* choreographer

Chor'hemd *n* surplice

Chor'stuhl *m* choir stall

Christ [krist] *m* (-s;) Christ || *m* (-en; -en) Christian

Christ'abend *m* Christmas Eve

Christ'baum *m* Christmas tree

Chri'stenheit *f* (-;) Christendom

Christentum [ˈkristəntum] *n* (-s;) Christianity

Christin [ˈkristɪn] *f* (-;-nen) Christian

Christ'kind *n* Christ child

christ'lich *adj* Christian

Christ'nacht *f* Holy Night

Chri•stus [ˈkristus] *m* (-sti [sti];) Christ; **nach Christi Geburt** A.D.; **vor Christus** B.C.

Chri'stusbild *n* crucifix; picture of Christ

Chrom [krom] *n* (-s;) chromium, chrome

chromatisch [kroˈmatɪʃ] *adj* chromatic

Chromosom [kroməˈzom] *n* (-s;-en) chromosome

Chronik [ˈkronɪk] *f* (-;-en) chronicle

chronisch [ˈkronɪʃ] *adj* chronic

Chronist –in [kroˈnist(ɪn)] §7 *mf* chronicler

Chronolo•gie [kronoləˈgi] *f* (-;-gien [ˈgiˑən]) chronology

chronologisch [kronoˈlogɪʃ] *adj* chronological

circa [ˈtsirka] *adv* approximately

Cis [tsɪs] *n* (-;-) (mus) C sharp

Clique [ˈklɪkə] *f* (-;-n) clique

Cocktail [ˈkɔktel] *m* (-s;-s) cocktail

Conferencier [kõferãˈsje] *m* (-s;-s) master of ceremony

Couch [kautʃ] *f* (-;-es) couch

Countdown [ˈkauntdaun] *m* (-s;-s) (rok) countdown

Couplet [kuˈple] *n* (-s;-s) song *(in a musical)*

Coupon [kuˈpõ] *m* (-s;-s) coupon

Courage [kuˈraʒə] *f* (-;) courage

Courtage [kurˈtaʒə] *f* (-;-n) brokerage

Cousin [kuˈzɛ̃] *m* (-s;-s) cousin

Cousine [kuˈzina] *f* (-;-n) cousin

Cowboy [ˈkaubɔi] *m* (-s;-s) cowboy

creme [krem] *adj* cream-colored || **Creme** [ˈkrem(ə)] *f* (-s;) cream; custard

Crew [kru] *f* (-s;) crew; (nav) cadets *(of the same year)*

Cut [kœt] *m* (-s;-s) cutaway

D

D, d [de] *invar n* D, d; (mus) D
da [dɑ] *adv* there; then; in that case,
  da und da at such and such a place;
  wieder da back again ‖ *conj* since,
  because; when
dabei [da'baɪ] *adv* nearby; besides,
  moreover; at that; at the same time;
  (*trotzdem*) yet; **d. bleiben** stick to
  one's point; **d. sein** be present, take
  part; **bis zu** (*inf*) be on the point
  of (*ger*); **es ist nichts d.** there's nothing to it
da capo [da'kɑpo] *interj* encore!
Dach [dax] *n* (**–[e]s;⁼er**) roof; (fig)
  shelter; **unter D. und Fach** under
  cover
Dach′boden *m* attic
Dach′decker *m* roofer
Dach′fenster *n* dormer window; sky-
  light
Dach′first *m* ridge of a roof
Dach′geschoß *n* top floor
Dach′gesellschaft *f* holding company
Dach′kammer *f* attic room
Dach′luke *f* skylight
Dach′organisation *f* parent company
Dach′pappe *f* roofing paper
Dach′pfanne *f* roof tile
Dach′rinne *f* rain gutter; eaves
Dach′röhre *f* downspout
Dachs [daks] *m* (**–es;–e**) badger; **ein
  frecher D.** a young whippersnapper
Dachs′hund *m* dachshund
Dach′sparren *m* rafter
Dach′stube *f* attic, garret
Dach′stuhl *m* roof framework
dachte ['daxtə] *pret of* denken
Dach′traufe *f* rain gutter
Dach′werk *n* roof
Dach′ziegel *m* roof tile
dadurch [da'durç] *adv* through it;
  thereby; by this means; **dadurch, daß**
  by (*ger*)
dafür [da'fyr] *adv* for it or them; in
  its place; that's why; therefore
Dafür′halten *n*—**nach meinem D.** in
  my opinion
dagegen [da'gegən] *adv* against it or
  them; in exchange for it or them; in
  comparison; on the other hand; **etw
  d. haben** have an objection; **ich bin
  d.** I'm against it
daheim [da'haɪm] *adv* at home
daher [da'her] *adv* from there; therefore; (bei Verben der Bewegung)
  along ‖ ['daher] *adv* that's why
dahin [da'hɪn] *adv* there, to that place;
  (*vergangen*) gone; (bei Verben der
  Bewegung) along; **bis d.** that far, up
  to there; until then; **es steht mir
  bis d.** I'm fed up with it
da′hinauf *adv* up there
da′hinaus *adv* out there
dahin′geben §80 *tr* give away; give up
dahin′gehen §82 *intr* (SEIN) walk along;
  pass; (*sterben*) pass away; **dahinge-
  hend, daß** to the effect that
dahingestellt [da'hɪŋgə∫telt] *adj*—**d.**

sein lassen, ob leave the question
  open whether
dahin′leben *intr* exist from day to day
dahin′raffen *tr* carry off
dahin′scheiden §112 *intr* (SEIN) pass on
dahin′schwinden *intr* (SEIN) dwindle
  away; fade away; pine away
dahin′stehen §146 *impers*—**es steht dahin** it is uncertain
dahin′ten *adv* back there
dahin′ter *adv* behind it or them
dahinterher′ *adv*—**d. sein, daß** be insistent that
dahin′terkommen §99 *intr* (SEIN) find
  out about it; get behind the truth
  of it
dahin′tersetzen *tr* put (*s.o.*) to work
  on it
dahin′welken §113 *intr* (SEIN) fade
  away
dahin′ziehen §163 *intr* (SEIN) move
  along
Dakapo [da'kɑpo] *n* (**–s;–s**) encore
da′lassen §104 *tr* leave behind
dalli ['dalɪ] *interj*—**mach d.!** step on
  it!
damalig ['dɑmalɪç] *adj* of that time
damals ['dɑmals] *adv* then, at that
  time
Damast [da'mast] *m* (**–es;–e**) damask
Dame ['dɑmə] *f* (**–;–n**) lady; (*beim
  Tanz*) partner; (cards, chess) queen;
  (checkers) king; **e-e D. machen**
  crown a checker; **meine D.!** madam!;
  meine Damen und Herrn! ladies and
  gentlemen!
Da′mebrett *n* checkerboard
Da′menbinde *f* sanitary napkin
Da′mendoppelspiel *n* (tennis) women's
  doubles
Da′meneinzelspiel *n* (tennis) women's
  singles
Da′mengesellschaft *f* hen party
Da′menhaft *adj* ladylike
Da′menhemd *n* chemise
Da′menschneider **–in** §6 *mf* dressmaker
Da′menwäsche *f* lingerie
Da′mespiel *n* checkers
damisch ['dɑmɪ∫] *adj* dopey
damit [da'mɪt] *adv* with it or them;
  by it; thereby; **d. hat's noch Zeit**
  that can wait; **es ist nichts d.** it is
  useless ‖ *conj* in order that, to
dämlich ['demlɪç] *adj* dopey
Damm [dam] *m* (**–[e]s;⁼e**) dam; dike;
  embankment; causeway; breakwater;
  pier; (fig) barrier; (anat) perineum;
  auf dem D. sein feel up to it; **wieder
  auf dem D. sein** be on one's feet
  again
Dämmer ['demər] *m* (**–s;**) (poet) twilight
dämmerig ['demərɪç] *adj* dusky, dim
Däm′merlicht *n* dusk, twilight
dämmern ['demərn] *intr* dawn, grow
  light; (*am Abend*) grow dark, become twilight

Däm′merung *f* (-;-en) (*Morgenrot*) dawn; (*am Abend*) dusk, twilight

Dämmplatte [′dɛmplatə] *f* acoustical tile

Dämmstoff [′dɛm/tɔf] *m* insulation

Damm′weg *m* causeway

Dämon [′dɛmɔn] *m* (-s; Dämonen [de′monən] demon

dämonisch [de′monɪʃ] *adj* demoniacal

Dampf [dampf] *m* (-[e]s;⸚e) steam; vapor; (*Angst*) (coll) fear; (*Hunger*) (coll) hunger; (vet) broken wind; **D. dahinter machen** (coll) step on it

dampfen [′dampfən] *intr* steam || *intr* (SEIN) steam along, steam away

dämpfen [′dɛmpfən] *tr* (*dünsten*) steam; (*Lärm*) muffle; (*Farben, Gefühle, Lichter*) subdue; (*Stoß*) absorb; (*Begeisterung*) dampen; **mit gedämpfter Stimme** under one's breath

Dampfer [′dampfər] *m* (-s;-) steamer

Dämpfer [′dɛmpfər] *m* (-s;-) (culin) steamer, boiler; (mach) baffle; (mus) mute; (*beim Klavier*) (mus) damper; **e-n D. aufsetzen** (*dat*) put a damper on

Dampf′heizung *f* steam heat

Dampf′kessel *m* steam boiler, boiler

Dampf′maschine *f* steam engine

Dampf′schiffahrtslinie *f* steamship line

Dämp′fungsfläche *f* (aer) stabilizer

Dampf′walze *f* steam roller

Damspiel [′dam/piːl] *n* var of Damespiel

danach [da′nax] *adv* after it or them; accordingly; according to it or them; afterwards; **d. fragen** ask about it; **d. streben** strive for it; **d. sieht er auch aus** that's just what he looks like

Däne [′dɛnə] *m* (-n;-n) Dane

daneben [da′nebən] *adv* next to it or them || *adv* in addition

dane′bengehen §82 *intr* (SEIN) go amiss

dane′benhauen *intr* miss; (fig) be wrong

Dänemark [′dɛnəmark] *n* (-s;) Denmark

dang [daŋ] *pret* of dingen

danie′derliegen [da′nidərligən] §108 *intr* (fig) be down; **d. an** (*dat*) be laid up with

Dänin [′dɛnɪn] *f* (-;-nen) Dane

dänisch [′dɛnɪʃ] *adj* Danish

dank [daŋk] *prep* (*dat*) thanks to || **Dank** *m* (-[e]s;) thanks; gratitude; **Gott sei D.!** thank God!, thank heaven!

dankbar [′daŋkbar] *adj* thankful; (*lohnend*) rewarding, profitable

Dank′barkeit *f* (-;) gratitude

danken [′daŋkən] *intr* (*dat*) thank; **danke!** thanks!; (*bei Ablehnung*) no, thanks!; **danke schön!** thank you!; **nichts zu d.!** you are welcome!

dan′kenswert *adj* meritorious; rewarding

dank′sagen *intr* return thanks

Danksagung [′daŋkzagʊŋ] *f* (-;) thanksgiving

Dank′sagungstag *m* Thanksgiving Day

Dank′schreiben *n* letter of thanks

dann [dan] *adv* then; **d. und wann** now and then

dannen [′danən] *adv*—**von d.** away

daran [da′ran] *adv* on, at, by, in, onto it or them; **das ist alles d.!** that's great!; **er ist gut d.** he's well off; **er tut gut d. zu** (*inf*) he does well to (*inf*); **es ist nichts d.** there's nothing to it; **ich will wissen, wie ich d. bin** I want to know where I stand; **jetzt bin ich d.** it's my turn; **nahe d. sein zu** (*inf*) be on the point of (*ger*); **was liegt d.?** what does it matter?

daran′gehen §82 *intr* (SEIN) go about it; **d. gehen zu** (*inf*) proceed to (*inf*)

daran′setzen *tr*—**alles d. zu** (*inf*) do one's level best to (*inf*)

darauf [da′rauf] *adv* on it or them; after that; **d. kommt es an** that's what matters; **gerade d. zu** straight towards; **gleich d.** immediately afterwards; **ich lasse es d. ankommen** I'll risk it

daraufhin [darauf′hɪn] *adv* thereupon

daraus [da′raus] *adv* of it, from it; from that; from them; hence; **d. wird nichts!** nothing doing!; **es wird nichts d.** nothing will come of it

darben [′darbən] *intr* live in poverty

darbieten [′darbitən] §58 *tr* present

Dar′bietung *f* (-;-en) presentation; (theat) performance

dar′bringen §65 *tr* present, offer

Dardanellen [darda′nelən] *pl* Dardanelles

darein [da′raɪn] *adv* into it or them

darein′reden *intr* interrupt; **er redet mir in alles d.** he interferes in all that I do

darin [da′rɪn] *adv* in it or them

dar′legen *tr* explain; state

Dar′legung *f* (-;-en) explanation

Darlehn [′darle(ə)n] *n* (-s;-) loan

Dar′leh(e)nskasse *f* loan association

Darm [darm] *m* (-[e]s;⸚e) intestine, gut; (*Wursthaut*) skin

Darm— *comb.fm.* intestinal

Darm′entzündung *f* enteritis

Darm′fäule *f* dysentery

dar′stellen *tr* describe; show, depict, portray; represent; mean; plot, chart; (indust) produce; (theat) play the part of

Dar′steller –in §6 *mf* performer

Dar′stellung *f* (-;-en) representation; portrayal; account, version; (indust) production; (theat) performance

dar′tun §154 *tr* prove; demonstrate

darüber [da′rybər] *adv* over it or them; (*querüber*) across it; (*betreffs*) about that; **d. hinaus** beyond it; moreover; **ich bin d. hinweg** I've gotten over it

darum [da′rum] *adv* around it or them; (*deshalb*) therefore; **er weiß d.** he's aware of it; **es ist mir nur d. tun, daß** all I ask is that

darunter [da′runtər] *adv* below it or them; among them; (*weniger*) less; **d. leiden** suffer from it; **zehn Jahre und d.** ten years and under

das [das] §1 *def art* the || §1 *dem adj* & *dem pron* this, that; **das und das**

such and such ‖ §11 *rel pron* which, that, who

da′sein §139 *intr* (SEIN) be there; be present; exist; **es ist schon alles mal dagewesen** there's nothing new under the sun; **noch nie dagewesen** unprecedented ‖ **Dasein** *n* (-s;) being, existence, life

Da′seinsberechtigung *f* raison d'être

daselbst [da′zɛlpst] *adv* just there; ibidem; **wohnhaft d.** address as above

dasjenige [′dasjenɪɡə] §4,3 *dem adj* that ‖ *dem pron* the one

daß [das] *conj* that; **daß du nicht vergißt!** be sure not to forget!; **daß er doch käme!** I wish he'd come; **es sei denn, daß** unless

dasselbe [das′zɛlbə] §4,3 *dem adj* & *dem pron* the same

da′stehen §146 *intr* stand there; **einzig d.** be unrivaled; **gut d.** be well-off; **wie stehe ich nun da!** how foolish I look now!

Daten [′dɑtən] *pl* data

Da′tenverarbeitung *f* data processing

datieren [da′tirən] *tr* & *intr* date

Dativ [′datif] *m* (-s;-e) dative (case)

dato [′dato] *adv*—**bis d.** to date

Dattel [′datəl] *f* (-;-n) (bot) date

Da·tum [′datum] *n* (-s;-ten [tən]) date; **Daten** data, facts; **heutigen Datums** of today; **neueren Datums** of recent date; **welches D. haben wir heute?** what's today's date?

Daube [′daubə] *f* (-;-n) (barrel) stave

Dauer [′dau·ər] *f* (-;) length, duration; permanence; **auf die D.** in the long run; **für die D. von** for a period of; **von D. sein** last, endure

Dau′erauftrag *m* standing order

Dau′erbelastung *f* constant load

Dau′erertrag *m* constant yield

Dau′erfeuer *n* (mil) automatic fire

Dau′erflug *m* endurance flight

Dau′ergeschwindigkeit *f* cruising speed

dau′erhaft *adj* lasting, durable; (*Farbe*) fast

Dau′erkarte *f* season ticket; (rr) commutation ticket

Dau′erlauf *m* (long-distance) jogging

dauern [′dau·ərn] *tr*—**er dauert mich** I feel sorry for him ‖ *intr* last, continue; **die Fahrt dauert fünf Stunden** the trip takes five hours; **es wird nicht lange d.,** dann it won't be long before; **lange d.** take a long time

Dau′erplissée *n* permanent pleat

Dau′erprobe *f* endurance test

Dau′erschmierung *f* self-lubrication

Dau′erstellung *f* permanent job

Dau′erton *m* (telp) dial tone

Dau′erversuch *m* endurance test

Dau′erwelle *f* permanent wave

Dau′erwirkung *f* lasting effect

Dau′erwurst *f* hard salami

Dau′erzustand *m* permanent condition; **zum D. werden** get to be a regular thing

Daumen [′daumən] *m* (-s;-) thumb; **D. halten!** keep your fingers crossed!; **die D. drehen** twiddle one's thumbs; **über den D. peilen** (or **schätzen**) give a rough estimate of

Dau′menabdruck *m* thumb print

Dau′menindex *m* thumb index

Daune [′daunə] *f* (-;-n) downy feather; **Daunen** down

Dau′nenbett *n* feather bed

Davit [′devɪt] *m* (-s;-s) (naut) davit

davon [da′fɔn] *adv* of it or them; from it or them; about it or them; away

davon′kommen §99 *intr* (SEIN) escape

davon′laufen §105 *intr* (SEIN) run away; ‖ **Davonlaufen** *n*—**es ist zum D.** (coll) it's enough to drive you insane

davon′machen *ref* take off, go away

davon′tragen §132 *tr* carry off; win

davor [da′for] *adv* in front of it or them; of it or them; from it or them

dawider [da′vidər] *adv* against it

dazu [da′tsu] *adv* thereto; to it or them; in addition to that; for that purpose; about it or them; with it or them

dazu′gehörig *adj* belonging to it; proper, appropriate

da′zumal *adv* at that time

dazu′tun §154 *tr* add ‖ **Dazutun** *n*—**ohne sein D.** without any effort on his part

dazwischen [da′tsvɪʃən] *adv* in between; among them

dazwi′schenfahren §71 *intr* (SEIN) jump in to intervene

dazwi′schenfunken *intr* (coll) butt in

dazwi′schenkommen §99 *intr* (SEIN) intervene

Dazwischenkunft [da′tsvɪʃənkunft] *f* (-;) intervention

dazwi′schentreten §152 *intr* (SEIN) intervene

Debatte [de′batə] *f* (-;-n) debate, discussion; **zur D. stehen** be under discussion; **zur D. stellen** open to discussion

debattieren [deba′tirən] *tr* & *intr* debate, discuss

Debet [′debet] *n* (-s;) debit; **im D. stehen** be on the debit side

Debüt [de′by] *n* (-s;-s) debut

Debütantin [debY′tantɪn] *f* (-;-nen) debutante

debütieren [debY′tierən] *intr* make one's debut

Dechant [de′çant] *m* (-en;-en) (educ, R.C.) dean

dechiffrieren [deʃɪf′rirən] *tr* decipher

Deck [dek] *n* (-s;-s) deck

Deck′anstrich *m* final coat

Deck′bett *n* feather bed

Deck′blatt *n* overlay

Decke [′dekə] *f* (-;-n) cover, covering; (*Bett-*) blanket; (*Tisch-*) tablecloth; (*Zimmer-*) ceiling; (*Schicht*) layer; **mit j-m unter e-r D. stecken** be in cahoots with s.o.; **sich nach der D. strecken** make the best of it

Deckel [′dekəl] *m* (-s;-) lid, cap; (*Buch-*) cover; **j-m eins auf den D. geben** (coll) chew s.o. out

decken [′dekən] *tr* cover; (*Tisch*) set; **das Tor d.** guard the goal ‖ *ref* coincide ‖ *intr* cover

Deckenbeleuchtung (Dek′kenbeleuchtung) *f* (-;) ceiling lighting

Deckenlicht (Dek'kenlicht) *n* ceiling light; skylight; (aut) dome light
Deck'farbe *f* one-coat paint
Deck'konto *n* secret account
Deck'mantel *m* pretext, pretense
Deck'name *m* pseudonym; alias; (mil) code name, cover name
Deck'offizier *m* (nav) warrant officer
Deck'plane *f* awning; tarpaulin
Deckung (Dek'kung) *f* (-;-en) covering; protection; roofing; (box) defense; (com) security, surety; collateral
deckungsgleich (dek'kungsgleich) *adj* congruent
defekt [de'fekt] *adj* defective || **Defekt** *m* (-[e]s;-e) defect
defensiv [defen'zif] *adj* defensive || **Defensive** [defen'zivə] *f* (-;-n) defensive
definieren [defɪ'nirən] *tr* define
definitiv [defɪnɪ'tif] *adj* (endgültig) definitive; (bestimmt) definite
Defizit ['defɪtsɪt] *n* (-s;-e) deficit
Degen ['degən] *m* (-s;-) sword; (poet) warrior; (typ) compositor
degradieren [degra'dirən] *tr* demote
Degradie'rung *f* (-;-en) demotion
dehnbar ['denbar] *adj* elastic; (Metall) ductile; (fig) vague, loose
dehnen ['denən] *tr* stretch; extend; expand; (Worte) drawl out; (Vokal) lengthen; (mus) sustain || *ref* stretch out; expand
Deh'nung *f* (-;-en) extension; expansion; dilation; (ling) lengthening
Deich [daɪç] *m* (-[e]s;-e) dike; (Damm) bank, embankment
Deichsel ['daɪksəl] *f* (-;-n) pole
deichseln ['daɪksəln] *tr* (coll) manage
dein [daɪn] §2 *poss adj* your, thy
deinerseits ['daɪnər'zaɪts] *adv* on your part
deinesgleichen ['daɪnəs'glaɪçən] *invar pron* your own kin, your equals, the likes of you
deinethalben ['daɪnət'halbən], **deinetwegen** ['daɪnət'vegən], **deinetwillen** ['daɪnət'vɪlən] *adv* for your sake; because of you, on your account
deinige ['daɪnɪgə] *poss pron* yours
Dekan [de'kan] *m* (-s;-e) dean
deklamieren [dekla'mirən] *tr & intr* declaim; recite
Deklination [deklɪna'tsjon] *f* (-;-en) declension
deklinieren [deklɪ'nirən] *tr* decline
dekolletiert [dekɔle'tirt] *adj* low-necked; (Dame) bare-necked
Dekorateur [dekɔra'tør] *m* (-s;-e) decorator, interior decorator
Dekoration [dekɔra'tsjon] *f* (-;-en) decoration; (theat) scenery
dekorieren [dekɔ'rirən] *tr* decorate
Dekret [de'kret] *n* (-[e]s;-e) decree
delikat [delɪ'kat] *adj* delicate; (lecker) delicious
Delikt [de'lɪkt] *n* (-[e]s;-e) offense
Delle ['delə] *f* (-;-n) dent; dip
Delphin [del'fin] *m* (-s;-e) dolphin
Delta ['delta] *n* (-s;-s) delta
dem [dem] §1 *def art, dem adj & dem pron* || §11 *rel pron*

Demagoge [dema'gogə] *m* (-n;-n) demagogue
Dementi [de'menti] *n* (-s;-s) official denial
dementieren [demen'tirən] *tr* deny (officially)
dem'entsprechend *adj* corresponding || *adv* correspondingly, accordingly
dem'gegenüber *adv* in contrast
dem'gemäß *adv* accordingly
dem'nach *adv* therefore; accordingly
dem'nächst *adv* soon, before long; (theat) (public sign) coming soon
demobilisieren [demɔbɪlɪ'zirən] *tr & intr* demobilize
Demokrat [demo'krat] *m* (-en;-en) democrat
Demokra·tie [demokra'ti] *f* (-;-tien ['ti·ən]) democracy
Demokratin [demo'kratɪn] *f* (-;-nen) democrat
demokratisch [demo'kratɪʃ] *adj* democratic
demolieren [demo'lirən] *tr* demolish
Demonstrant –in [demɔn'strant(ɪn)] §7 *mf* demonstrator
demonstrieren [demɔn'strirən] *tr & intr* demonstrate
Demontage [demɔn'taʒə] *f* (-;) dismantling
demontieren [demɔn'tirən] *tr* dismantle
demselben [dem'zelbən] §4,3 *dem adj & dem pron*
Demut ['demut] *f* (-;) humility
demütig ['demytɪç] *adj* humble
demütigen ['demytɪgən] *tr* humble; (beschämen) humiliate
De'mütigung *f* (-;-en) humiliation
de'mutsvoll *adj* submissive
dem'zufolge *adv* accordingly
den [den] §1 *def art, dem adj & dem pron* || §11 *rel pron* whom
denen ['denən] §11 *rel pron* to whom
Denkarbeit ['deŋkarbaɪt] *f* (-;) brainwork
Denkart ['deŋkart] *f* var of Denkungsart
Denkaufgabe ['deŋkaufgabə] *f* brain twister, problem
denkbar ['deŋkbar] *adj* conceivable; (vorstellbar) imaginable
denken ['deŋkən] §66 *tr* think, consider; **was d. Sie zu tun?** what do you intend to do? || *ref*—**bei sich** (or **für sich**) **d.** think to oneself; **denke dir e–e Zahl** think of a number; **d. Sie sich in ihre Lage** imagine yourself in her place; **sich** [dat] **etw d.** imagine s.th.; **was denkst du dir eigentlich?** what do you think you're doing? || *intr* think; **das gibt mir zu d.** that set me thinking; **d. an** (acc) think about
denk'faul *adj* mentally lazy
Denk'fehler *m* fallacy, false reasoning
Denk'mal *n* (-s;-e & ⁻er) monument
Denk'schrift *f* (pol) memorandum
Denkungsart ['deŋkuŋsart] *f* way of thinking, mentality
Denk'weise *f* way of thinking, mentality
denk'würdig *adj* memorable

Denk'zettel *m—j—m* e—n D. geben teach s.o. a lesson

denn [dɛn] *adv* then; **es sei denn, daß** unless ‖ *conj* for

dennoch ['dɛnɔx] *adv* nevertheless, all the same, (but) still

Dentist –in [dɛn'tɪst(ɪn)] §7 *mf* dentist

Denunziant –in [dɛnun'tsjant(ɪn)] §7 *mf* informer

denunzieren [dɛnun'tsirən] *tr* denounce

Depesche [de'pɛʃə] *f* (–;–n) dispatch

De·ponens [de'ponɛns] *n* (–;-ponenzien** [pə'nɛntsjən]) (gram) deponent

deponieren [depə'nirən] *tr* (com) deposit

deportieren [depɔr'tirən] *tr* deport

Depot [de'po] *n* (–s;-s) depot; warehouse; storage; safe; safe deposit

Depp [dɛp] *m* (–s;-e) (coll) dope

Depression [deprɛ'sjon] *f* (–;-en) depression

der [der] §1 *def art* the ‖ §1 *dem adj & dem pron* this, that; **der und der** such and such, so and so ‖ §11 *rel pron* who, which, that; (to) whom

der'art *adv* so, in such a way; (coll) that

der'artig *adj* such, of that kind

derb [dɛrp] *adj* coarse; tough; rude

Derb'heit *f* (–;-en) coarseness; toughness; crude joke

dereinst' *adv* some day

deren ['derən] §11 *rel pron* whose

derenthalben ['derənt'halbən], **derentwegen** ['derənt'vegən], **derentwillen** ['derənt'vɪlən] *adv* for her sake, for their sake

dergestalt ['dergə'ʃtalt] *adv* so

dergleichen ['der'glaiçən] *invar dem adj* such; similar; of that kind ‖ *invar dem pron* such a thing; **und d. mehr** and so on and the like; **und d. mehr** and so on

derjenige ['derjenɪgə] §4,3 *dem adj* that ‖ *dem pron* the one; he

dermaßen [der'masən] *adv* so, in such a way

derselbe [der'zɛlbə] §4,3 *dem adj & dem pron* the same

derweilen [der'vailən] *adv* meanwhile

derzeit ['der'tsait] *adv* at present

derzeitig ['der'tsaitɪç] *adj* present; then, of that time

des [dɛs] *n* (–;–) (mus) D flat

Desaster [de'zastər] *n* (–s;–) disaster

Deserteur [dezɛr'tør] *m* (–s;-e) deserter

desertieren [dezɛr'tirən] *intr* (SEIN) desert

desgleichen ['dɛs'glaiçən] *invar dem pron* such a thing ‖ *invar rel pron* the likes of which ‖ *adv* likewise

deshalb ['dɛshalp] *adv* therefore

Desinfektion [dɛsɪnfɛk'tsjon] *f* (–;-en) disinfection

Desinfektions'mittel *n* disinfectant

desinfizieren [dɛsɪnfɪ'tsirən] *tr* disinfect

Despot [dɛs'pot] *m* (–en;-en) despot

despotisch [dɛs'potɪʃ] *adj* despotic

Dessin [dɛ'sɛ̃] *n* (–s;-s) design

destillieren [dɛstɪ'lirən] *tr* distill

desto ['dɛsto] *adv* the; **d. besser** the better, all the better

deswegen ['dɛs'vegən] *adv* therefore

Detail [de'tai(l)] *n* (–s;–s) detail; (com) retail

Detail'geschäft *n* retail store

Detail'händler –in §6 *mf* retail dealer

detaillieren [dɛta'jirən] *tr* relate in detail; specify; itemize

Detek·tiv [detɛk'tif] *m* (–s;-tive** ['tivə]) private investigator; (coll) private eye

detonieren [detə'nirən] *intr* detonate; **etw. d. lassen** detonate s.th.

deuchte ['dɔiçtə] *pret of* **dünken**

Deutelei ['dɔitə'lai] *f* (–;-en) quibble

deuteln ['dɔitəln] *intr* (an *dat*) quibble (about), split hairs (over)

deuten ['dɔitən] *tr* interpret; **falsch d.** misinterpret ‖ *intr* (auf *acc*) (& fig) point (to)

deutlich ['dɔitlɪç] *adj* clear, distinct

deutsch [dɔitʃ] *adj* German ‖ **Deutsche** §5 *mf* German

Deu'tung *f* (–;-en) interpretation

Devise [de'vizə] *f* (–;-n) motto; **Devisen** foreign currency

Devi'senbestand *m* foreign-currency reserve

Devi'senbilanz *f* balance of payments

Devi'senkurs *m* rate of exchange

Dezember [de'tsɛmbər] *m* (–s;–) December

dezent [de'tsɛnt] *adj* unobtrusive; (*Licht, Musik*) soft; (*anständig*) decent

Dezernat [detsɛr'nat] *n* (–[e]s;-e) (administrative) department

dezimal [detsɪ'mal] *adj* decimal ‖ **Dezimale** [detsɪ'malə] *f* (–;-n) decimal

Dezimal'bruch *m* decimal fraction

Dezimal'zahl *f* decimal

dezimieren [detsɪ'mirən] *tr* decimate

Dia ['di·a] *n* (–s;–s) (coll) slide

Diadem [di·a'dem] *n* (–s;-e) diadem

Diagnose [di·a'gnozə] *f* (–;-n) diagnosis

diagnostizieren [di·agnɔstɪ'tsirən] *tr* diagnose

diagonal [di·ago'nal] *adj* diagonal ‖ **Diagonale** *f* (–;-n) diagonal

Diagramm [di·a'gram] *n* (–[e]s;e) diagram; graph

Diakon [di·a'kon] *m* (–s;-e & –en;-en) deacon

Dialekt [di·a'lɛkt] *m* (–[e]s;-e) dialect

dialektisch [di·a'lɛktɪʃ] *adj* dialectical

Dialog [di·a'lok] *m* (–s;-e) dialogue

Diamant [di·a'mant] *m* (–en;-en) diamond

Diaposi·tiv [di·apozɪ'tif] *n* (–s;-tive** ['tivə]) slide, transparency

Diät [di'ɛt] *f* (–;-en) diet (*under medical supervision*); **Diäten** daily allowance; **diät leben** be on a diet

Diät- *comb.fm.* dietary

diätetisch [di·ɛ'tetɪʃ] *adj* dietetic

dich [dɪç] §11 *pers pron* you, thee ‖ *reflex pron* yourself, thyself

dicht [dɪçt] *adj* dense; thick; heavy; leakproof; tight ‖ **Dichte** ['dɪçtə] *f* (–;-en) density

dichten ['dɪçtən] *tr* tighten; caulk; compose, write || *intr* write poetry

Dichter ['dɪçtər] *m* (-s;-) (important) writer; poet

Dichterin ['dɪçtərɪn] *f* (-;-nen) poetess

dichterisch ['dɪçtərɪʃ] *adj* poetic(al)

dicht'gedrängt *adj* tightly packed

dicht'halten §90 *intr* keep mum

Dicht'heit *f* (-;), **Dich'tigkeit** *f* (-;) density; compactness; tightness

Dich'kunst *f* poetry

dicht'machen *tr* (coll) close up

Dich'tung *f* (-;-en) gasket; packing; imagination; fiction; poetry; poem;

Dich'tungsring *m*, **Dich'tungsscheibe** *f* washer; gasket

dick [dɪk] *adj* thick; fat; big; (*Luft, Freunde*) close; **dicke Luft** (coll) cheese it!; **sich d. tun** talk big || **Dicke** *f* (-;) thickness, stoutness

Dick'darm *m* (anat) colon

dickfellig ['dɪkfɛlɪç] *adj* thick-skinned

dick'flüssig *adj* viscous

Dickicht ['dɪkɪçt] *n* (-[e]s;-e) thicket

Dick'kopf *m* thick head

dickköpfig ['dɪkkœpfɪç] *adj* thick-headed

dickleibig ['dɪklaɪbɪç] *adj* stout, fat

Dick'schädel *m* thick head

dick'schädelig ['dɪkʃedəlɪç] *adj* thick-headed

die [di] §1 *def art* the || §1 *dem adj* & *dem pron* this, that; **die und die** such and such || §11 *rel pron* who, which, that

Dieb [dip] *m* (-[e]s;-e) thief

Dieberei [dibə'raɪ] *f* (-;-en) thievery; (*Diebstahl*) theft

Diebesbande ['dibəsbandə] *f* pack of thieves

Diebin ['dibɪn] *f* (-;-nen) thief

diebisch ['dibɪʃ] *adj* thievish || *adv*—**sich d. freuen** be tickled pink

Diebstahl ['dip/tal] *m* (-[e]s;-̈) theft, larceny; **leichter D.** petty larceny; **schwerer D.** grand larceny

diejenige ['dijenɪgə] §4,3 *dem adj* that || *dem pron* the one; she

Diele ['dilə] *f* (-;-n) floorboard; (*breiter Flur*) entrance hall; **Dielen** flooring

dienen ['dinən] *intr* (*dat*) serve; **damit ist mir nicht gedient** that doesn't help me any; **womit kann ich d.?** may I help you?

Diener -in ['dinər(ɪn)] §6 *mf* servant

die'nerhaft *adj* servile

dienern ['dinərn] *intr* bow and scrape

Die'nerschaft *f* (-;) domestics, help

dienlich ['dinlɪç] *adj* useful

Dienst [dinst] *m* (-es;-e) service; job; employment; (adm, mil) grade; **außer D.** retired; **im D.** on duty; **j-m e-n D. tun** do s.o. a favor

Dienstag ['dinstak] *m* (-[e]s;-e) Tuesday

Dienst'alter *n* seniority

dienstbar ['dinstbar] *adj* subservient

Dienst'barkeit *f* (-;) servitude, bondage; (jur) easement

dienst'beflissen *adj* eager to serve || *adv* eagerly

Dienst'bote *m* servant, domestic

Dienst'boteneingang *m* service entrance

Dienst'eid *m* oath of office

dienst'eifrig *adj* eager to serve || *adv* eagerly

Dienst'einteilung *f* work schedule; (mil) duty roster

Dienst'fahrt *f* official trip

dienst'frei *adj*—**d. haben** be off duty

Dienst'gebrauch *m*—**nur zum D.** for official use only

Dienst'gespräch *n* business call

Dienst'grad *m* (mil) rank, grade; (nav) rating

dienst'habend *adj* on duty

Dienst'herr *m* employer; (hist) lord

Dienst'leistung *f* service

dienst'lich *adj* official || *adv* officially; on official business

Dienst'mädchen *n* maid

Dienst'pflicht *f* official duty; compulsory military service

Dienst'plan *m* work schedule; (mil) duty roster

Dienst'sache *f* official business

dienst'tauglich *adj* fit for active service

diensttuend ['dinsttu-ənt] *adj* on duty; active; in charge

Dienst'weg *m* official channels

Dienst'wohnung *f* official residence

dies [dis] *dem adj* & *dem pron* var of **dieses**

diese ['dizə] §3 *dem adj* this || *dem pron* this one

dieselbe [di'zelbə] §4,3 *dem adj* & *dem pron* the same

Dieselmotor ['dizəlmotər] *m* diesel engine

dieser ['dizər] §3 *dem adj* this || *dem pron* this one

dieses ['dizəs] §3 *dem adj* this || *dem pron* this one

diesig ['dizɪç] *adj* hazy, misty

dies'jährig *adj* this year's

dies'mal *adv* this time

diesseits ['diszaɪts] *prep* (*genit*) on this side of

Dietrich ['ditrɪç] *m* (-s;-e) skeleton key; (*Einbrecherwerkzeug*) picklock

Differential [dɪferen'tsjal] *n* (-s;-e) (aut, math) differential

Differential— *comb.fm.* (econ, elec, mach, math, phys) differential

Differenz [dɪfe'rents] *f* (-;-en) difference

Diktaphon [dɪkta'fon] *n* (-[e]s;-e) dictaphone

Diktat [dɪk'tat] *n* (-s;-e) dictation; **nach D. schreiben** take dictation

Dik-tator [dɪk'tator] *m* (-s;-tatoren) [ta'torən]) dictator

diktatorisch [dɪkta'torɪʃ] *adj* dictatorial

Diktatur [dɪkta'tur] *f* (-;-en) dictatorship

diktieren [dɪk'tirən] *tr* & *intr* dictate

Dilettant -in [dɪle'tant(ɪn)] §7 *mf* dilettante, amateur

Diner [dɪ'ne] *n* (-s;-s) dinner

Ding [dɪŋ] *n* (-[e]s;-e) thing; **ein D. drehen** (coll) pull a job

dingen ['dɪŋən] §109 & §142 *tr* hire

ding′fest *adj*—**j—n d. machen** arrest s.o.
ding′lich *adj* real
Dings [dɪŋs] *n* (–s;) (coll) thing, doo-dad, thingamajig
Dings′bums *m & n* (–;) var of **Dingsda**
Dings′da *mfn* (–s;) what-d′ye-call-it
Diözese [dɪ.øˈtseːzə] *f* (–;–n) diocese
Diphtherie [dɪfteˈriː] *f* (–;) diphtheria
Dipl.-Ing. *abbr* (**Diplom-Ingenieur**) engineer holding a degree
Diplom [dɪˈploːm] *n* (–s;–e) diploma
Diplom— *comb.fm.* holding a degree
Diplomat [dɪploˈmaːt] *m* (–en;–en) diplomat
Diplomatie [dɪploməˈtiː] *f* (–;) diplomacy
Diplomatin [dɪploˈmaːtɪn] *f* (–;–nen) diplomat
diplomatisch [dɪploˈmaːtɪʃ] *adj* diplomatic
dir [diːr] §11 *pers pron* to or for you, to or for thee || *reflex pron* to or for yourself, to or for thyself
direkt [diˈrɛkt] *adj* direct
Direktion [dɪrɛkˈtsjoːn] *f* (–;) direction; (*Verwaltung*) management
Direk•tor [diˈrɛktor] *m* (–s;–toren [ˈtoːrən]) director; (*e–r Bank*) president; (*e–r Schule*) principal; (*e–s Gefängnisses*) warden
Direktorat [dɪrɛktoˈraːt] *n* (–[e]s;–e) directorship
Direktorin [dɪrɛkˈtoːrɪn] *f* (–;–nen) director; (educ) principal
Direkto•rium [dɪrɛkˈtoːri·um] *n* (–s; –rien [riˑən]) board of directors; executive committee
Direktrice [dɪrɛkˈtriːsə] *f* (–;–n) directress, manager
Dirigent –in [dɪrɪˈgɛnt(ɪn)] §7 *mf* (mus) conductor
dirigieren [dɪrɪˈgiːrən] *tr* direct, manage; (mus) conduct
Dirnd(e)l [ˈdɪrndəl] *n* (–s;–) girl; (*Tracht*) dirndle
Dirne [ˈdɪrnə] *f* (–;–n) girl; (pej) prostitute
Dis [dɪs] *n* (–;–) D sharp
disharmonisch [dɪsharˈmoːnɪʃ] *adj* discordant
Diskont [dɪsˈkɔnt] *m* (–[e]s;–e) discount
diskontieren [dɪskɔnˈtiːrən] *tr* discount
Diskothek [dɪskoˈteːk] *f* (–;–en) discotheque
diskret [dɪsˈkreːt] *adj* discreet
Diskretion [dɪskreˈtsjoːn] *f* (–;–en) discretion
Diskussion [dɪskuˈsjoːn] *f* (–;–en) discussion
diskutieren [dɪskuˈtiːrən] *tr* discuss || *intr*—**d. über** (*acc*) discuss
disponieren [dɪspoˈniːrən] *intr* (**über** *acc*) dispose (of)
Disposition [dɪspɔziˈtsjoːn] *f* (–;–en) disposition; arrangement; disposal
Distanz [dɪsˈtants] *f* (–;–en) distance
distanzieren [dɪstanˈtsiːrən] *tr* (**mit**) beat (by, *e.g.*, *one meter*) || *ref* (**von**) dissociate oneself (from)
distanziert′ *adj* (fig) detached
Distel [ˈdɪstəl] *f* (–;–n) thistle
Dis′telfink *m* goldfinch

Distrikt [dɪsˈtrɪkt] *m* (–[e]s;–e) district
Disziplin [dɪstsɪˈpliːn] *f* (–;–en) discipline
disziplinarisch [dɪstsɪplɪˈnaːrɪʃ] *adj* disciplinary
dito [ˈdiːto] *adv* ditto || **Dito** *n* (–s;–s) ditto
Dividend [dɪviˈdɛnt] *m* (–en;–en), **Dividende** [dɪviˈdɛndə] *f* (–;–n) dividend
dividieren [dɪviˈdiːrən] *tr* divide
Division [dɪviˈzjoːn] *f* (–;–en) division
Diwan [ˈdiːvan] *m* (–s;–e) divan
D-Mark [ˈdeːmark] *f* (–;–) mark (*monetary unit of West Germany*)
doch [dɔx] *adv* yet; of course
Docht [dɔxt] *m* (–[e]s;–e) wick
Dock [dɔk] *n* (–[e]s;–s & –e) dock
docken [ˈdɔkən] *tr & intr* (naut, rok) dock
Dogge [ˈdɔgə] *f* (–;–n) mastiff; **deutsche D.** Great Dane
Dog•ma [ˈdɔgma] *n* (–s;–men [mən]) dogma
Dohle [ˈdoːlə] *f* (–;–n) jackdaw
Dok•tor [ˈdɔktor] *m* (–s;–toren [ˈtoːrən]) doctor
Dok′torarbeit *f* dissertation
Dok′torvater *m* adviser (*for a doctoral dissertation*)
Dokument [dɔkuˈmɛnt] *n* (–[e]s;–e) document; (jur) instrument, deed
Dokumentarfilm [dɔkumɛnˈtarfɪlm] *m* documentary
dokumentarisch [dɔkumɛnˈtaːrɪʃ] *adj* documentary
Dolch [dɔlç] *m* (–[e]s;–e) dagger
Dolch′stoß *m* (pol) stab in the back
Dollar [ˈdɔlar] *m* (–s;–) dollar
dolmetschen [ˈdɔlmɛtʃən] *tr & intr* interpret
Dol′metscher –in §6 *mf* interpreter
Dom [dom] *m* (–[e]s;–e) cathedral; dome
Domäne [doˈmɛːnə] *f* (–;–n) domain
Domino [ˈdɔmino] *n* (–s;–s) domino
Donau [ˈdoːnaʊ] *f* (–;) Danube
Donner [ˈdɔnər] *m* (–s;–) thunder
Don′nerkeil *m* thunderbolt
donnern [ˈdɔnərn] *intr* thunder
Don′nerschlag *m* clap of thunder
Don′nerstag *m* (–[e]s;–e) Thursday
Don′nerwetter *n* thunderstorm; **zum D.!** confound it! || *interj* geez!
doof [dof] *adj* (coll) goofy
dopen [ˈdoːpən] *tr* dope (*a racehorse*)
Doppel [ˈdɔpəl] *n* (–s;–) duplicate; (tennis) doubles
Doppel— *comb.fm.* double, two, bi-, twin
Dop′pelbelichtung *f* double exposure
Dop′pelbild *n* (telv) ghost
Dop′pelbruch *m* compound fracture
Dop′pelehe *f* bigamy
Dop′pelgänger *m* double; second self
Dop′pellaut *m* diphthong
doppeln [ˈdɔpəln] *tr* double
Dop′pelprogramm *n* double feature
Dop′pelpunkt *m* (typ) colon
doppelreihig [ˈdɔpəlraɪ·ɪç] *adj* double-breasted
Dop′pelrendezvous *n* double date

dop′pelseitig adj reversible; (*Lungenentzündung*) double

Dop′pelsinn m double entendre

dop′pelsinnig adj ambiguous

Dop′pelspiel n (fig) double-dealing; (sport) double-header; (tennis) doubles

doppelt [′dɔpəlt] adj double; **doppelter Boden** false bottom; **ein doppeltes Spiel spielen mit** doublecross; **in doppelter Ausführung in** duplicate || adv twice; **ein Buch d. haben** have two copies of a book

Dop′pelverdiener –in §6 mf moonlighter

Dop′pelvokal m diphthong

doppelzüngig [′dɔpəltsʏŋɪç] adj twofaced

Dorf [dɔrf] n (-[e]s;ːer) village

Dorf′bewohner –in §6 mf villager

Dörfchen [′dœrfçən] n (-s;-) hamlet

Dorn [dɔrn] m (-[e]s;-en) thorn; tongue (*of a buckle*); (mach) pin; (sport) spike

Dorn′busch m briar, bramble

dornig [′dɔrnɪç] adj thorny

Dornröschen [′dɔrnrøsçən] n (-s;) Sleeping Beauty

Dörr- [dœr] comb.fm. dried

dorren [′dɔrən] intr (SEIN) dry (up)

dörren [′dœrən] tr dry

Dorschlebertran [′dɔrʃlebərtran] m (-[e]s;) cod-liver oil

dort [dɔrt] adv there, over there

dort′her adv from there

dort′hin adv there, to that place

dor′tig adj in that place, there

Dose [′dozə] f (-;-n) can; box

dösen [′døzən] intr doze

Do′senöffner m can opener

dosieren [do′zirən] tr prescribe (the correct dosage of)

Dosie′rung f (-;-en) dosage

Do-sis [′dozɪs] f (-;-sen [zən]) dose

dotieren [do′tirən] tr endow; **ein Preis mit 100 Mark dotiert** a prize worth 100 marks

Dotter [′dɔtər] m & n (-s;-) yolk

Double [′dubəl] m & n (-s;-s) (cin, theat) stand-in

Dozent –in [do′tsent(ɪn)] §7 (university) instructor, lecturer

Drache [′draxə] m (-n;-n) dragon; (*böses Weib*) battle-ax

Drachen [′draxən] m (-s;-) kite

Dra′chenfliegen n (-s;) hang gliding

Draht [drat] m (-[e]s;ːe) wire; **auf D. sein** (coll) be on the beam

drahten [′dratən] tr telegraph, wire

draht′haarig adj wire-haired

Draht′hindernis n (mil) wire entanglement, barbed wire

drahtig [′dratɪç] adj wiry

draht′los adj wireless

Draht′seil n cable

Draht′seilbahn f cable car, funicular

Draht′zaun m wire fence

drall [dral] adj plump; (*Faden*) sturdy || **Drall** m (-[e]s;-e) rifling

Dra-ma [′drama] n (-s;-men [mən]) drama

Dramatiker –in [dra′matɪkər(ɪn)] §6 mf dramatist, playwright

dramatisch [dra′matɪʃ] adj dramatic

dran [dran] adv var of **daran**

drang [draŋ] pret of **dringen** || **Drang** m (-[e]s;ːe) pressure; urge

drängeln [′drɛŋəln] tr & intr shove

drängen [′drɛŋən] tr & intr push, shove; (*drücken*) press || ref crowd, crowd together; force one's way

Drangsal [′draŋzal] f (-;-e) distress, anguish; hardship

drangsalieren [draŋza′lirən] tr vex

drastisch [′drastɪʃ] adj drastic

drauf [drauf] adv var of **darauf**

drauf′gehen §82 intr (SEIN) (coll) go down the drain

Drauf′gänger m (-s;-) go-getter

drauflos′ adv—d. **arbeiten an** (*dat*) work away at

drauflos′gehen §82 intr (SEIN)—d. **auf** (*acc*) make straight for

drauflos′reden intr ramble on

drauflos′schlagen §132 intr (auf acc) let fly (at)

draußen [′drausən] adv outside; out of doors; (*in der Fremde*) abroad

drechseln [′drɛksəln] tr work (*on a lathe*); (fig) embellish

Dreck [drek] m (-[e]s;) dirt; mud; excrement; (*Abfälle*) trash

dreckig [′drekɪç] adj dirty; muddy

Dreh- [dre] comb.fm. revolving, rotary

Dreh′arbeiten pl (cin) shooting

Dreh′aufzug m dumb waiter

Dreh′bank f (-;ːe) lathe

drehbar [′drebar] adj revolving

Dreh′buch n (mov) script, scenario

drehen [′dre·ən] tr turn; (*Zigaretten*) roll; (coll) wangle; (cin) shoot || ref turn; rotate

Dreh′kreuz n turnstile

Dreh′orgel f hurdy-gurdy

Dreh′orgelspieler m organ grinder

Dreh′punkt m fulcrum; (fig) pivotal point

Dreh′scheibe f potter's wheel; (rr) turntable

Dreh′stuhl m swivel chair

Dre′hung f (-;-en) turn

Dreh′zahl f revolutions per minute

Dreh′zahlmesser m tachometer

drei [drai] adj & pron three || **Drei** f (-;-en) three; (educ) C

dreidimensional [′draidimenzjonal] adj three-dimensional

Dreieck [′drai·ek] n (-[e]s;-e) triangle

drei′eckig adj triangular

drei′fach adj threefold, triple

dreifältig [′draifeltɪç] adj threefold, triple

Dreifaltigkeit [drai′faltɪçkait] f (-;) Trinity

Drei′fuß m tripod

Dreikäsehoch [drai′kezəhoç] m (-s;-) (coll) shrimp, runt

drei′mal adv three times, thrice

Drei′rad n tricycle

Drei′sprung m hop, step, and jump

dreißig [′draisɪç] adj & pron thirty || **Dreißig** f (-;- & -en) thirty

dreißiger [′draisigər] invar adj of the thirties, in the thirties

dreißigste [′draisɪçstə] §9 adj & pron thirtieth

dreist [draɪst] *adj* brazen, bold

dreistimmig ['draɪˌtɪmɪç] *adj* for three voices

drei'zehn *adj* & *pron* thirteen || **Dreizehn** *f* (-;-) thirteen

drei'zehnte §9 *adj* & *pron* thirteenth

dreschen ['drɛʃən] §67 *tr* thresh; (coll) thrash

Dresch'flegel *m* flail

Dresch'tenne *f* threshing floor

dressieren [drɛ'siːrən] *tr* train; (*Pferd*) break in

Dressur [drɛ'suːr] *f* (-;) training

dribbeln ['drɪbəln] *intr* (sport) dribble

drillen ['drɪlən] *tr* drill; train

Drillich ['drɪlɪç] *m* (-s;-e) denim

Dril'lichanzug *m* dungarees; (mil) fatigue uniform, fatigues

Dril'lichhosen *pl* dungarees, jeans

Drilling ['drɪlɪŋ] *m* (-s;-e) triplet

drin [drɪn] *adv* var of **darin**

dringen ['drɪŋən] §142 *intr* (auf *acc*) press (for), insist (on); (in *acc*) pressure, urge || *intr* (SEIN) (aus) break forth (from); (durch) penetrate, pierce; (durch) force one's way (through); (in *acc*) penetrate (into), get (into); **in die Öffentlichkeit d.** leak out; **in j-n d.** press the point with s.o.; **d. bis zu** get as far as

drin'gend *adj* urgent; (*Gefahr*) imminent; (*Verdacht*) strong

dring'lich *adj* urgent

Dring'lichkeit *f* (-;-en) urgency; priority

Drink [drɪŋk] *m* (-s;-s) alcoholic drink

drinnen ['drɪnən] *adv* inside

dritt [drɪt] *adv*—**zu d.** the three of

dritte ['drɪtə] §9 *adj* & *pron* third; **ein Dritter** a disinterested person; (com, jur) a third party

Drittel ['drɪtəl] *n* (-s;-) third (*part*)

drittens ['drɪtəns] *adv* thirdly

dritt'letzt *adj* third from last

droben ['droːbən] *adv* above; up there

Droge ['droːgə] *f* (-;-n) drug

Droge•rie [droːgə'riː] *f* (-;-rien ['riːən) drugstore

Drogist –in [dro'gɪst(ɪn)] §7 *mf* druggist

Droh'brief *m* threatening letter

drohen ['droːən] *intr* (dat) threaten

dro'hend *adj* threatening; impending

Drohne ['droːnə] *f* (-;-n) drone

dröhnen ['drøːnən] *intr* boom, roar; (*Kopf, Motor*) throb

Dro'hung *f* (-;-en) threat

drollig ['drɔlɪç] *adj* amusing, funny

Dromedar [dromə'dar] *n* (-s;-e) dromedary

drosch [drɔʃ] *pret* of **dreschen**

Droschke ['drɔʃkə] *f* (-;-n) cab, hackney; taxi

Drosch'kenkutscher *m* coachman

Drossel ['drɔsəl] *f* (-;-n) thrush; (aut) throttle

Dros'selhebel *m* (aut) throttle

drosseln ['drɔsəln] *tr* (coll) curb, cut; (aut) throttle; (elec) choke

drüben ['dryːbən] *adv* over there

Druck [druk] *m* (-[e]s;̈-e) (& fig) pressure; (*der Hand*) squeeze; (phys) compression, pressure || *m* (-[e]s-e) printing; print, type; (tex) print

Druck'anzug *m* (aer) pressurized suit

Druck'bogen *m* (printed) sheet

druck'dicht *adj* pressurized

Drückeberger ['drykəbɛrgər] *m* (-s;-) shirker; absentee; (mil) goldbrick

drucken ['drukən] *tr* print

drücken ['drykən] *tr* press; squeeze; imprint; (*Preise*) lower; (cards) discard; **die Stimmung d.** be a kill-joy; **j-m die Hand d.** shake hands with s.o. || *intr* (*Schuh*) pinch

Druck'entlastung *f* decompression

Drucker ['drukər] *m* (-s;-) printer

Drücker ['drykər] *m* (-s;-) push button; (e-s *Schlosses*) latch, latch key; (e-s *Gewehrs*) trigger

Druckerei [drukə'raɪ] *f* (-;-en) print shop, press

Druckerschwärze (**Druk'kerschwärze**) *f* printer's ink

Druck'fehler *m* misprint

druck'fertig *adj* ready for the press

druck'fest *adj* pressurized

Druck'kabine *f* pressurized cabin

Druck'knopf *m* push button; (am *Kleid*) snap

Druck'knopfbetätigung *f* push-button control

Druck'luft *f* compressed air

Druckluft- *comb.fm.* pneumatic, air

Druck'luftbremse *f* air brake

Druck'lufthammer *m* jackhammer

Druck'messer *m* pressure gauge

Druck'sache *f* printed matter; **Drucksachen** (com) literature

Druck'schrift *f* type; block letters; publication, printed work; leaflet

drucksen ['druksən] *intr* hem and haw

drum [drum] *adv* var of **darum**

Drüse ['dryːzə] *f* (-;-n) gland

Drüsen- *comb.fm.* glandular

Dschungel ['dʒuŋəl] *m* (-s;-) jungle

du [du] §11 *per pron* you, thou

Dübel ['dyːbəl] *m* (-s;-) dowel

Dublette [du'blɛtə] *f* (-;-n) duplicate; imitation stone

ducken ['dukən] *tr* (den *Kopf*) duck; (coll) take down a peg or two || *ref* duck

Duckmäuser ['dukmɔɪzər] *m* (-s;-) pussyfoot

dudeln ['duːdəln] *tr* hum || *intr* hum, drone; (mus) play the bagpipe

Dudelsack ['duːdəlzak] *m* bagpipe

Duell [du'ɛl] *n* (-s;-e) duel

duellieren [du·ə'liːrən] *recip* duel

Duett [du'ɛt] *n* (-[e]s;-e) duet

Duft [duft] *m* (-[e]s;̈-e) fragrance

duften ['duftən] *intr* be fragrant

duf'tend *adj* fragrant

duftig ['duftɪç] *adj* flimsy, dainty

dulden ['duldən] *tr* (ertragen) bear; (leiden) suffer; (zulassen) tolerate || *intr* suffer

duldsam ['duldzam] *adj* tolerant

Duld'samkeit *f* (-;) tolerance

dumm [dum] *adj* stupid, dumb; foolish

Dumm'heit *f* (-;-en) stupidity; foolishness; (*Streich*) foolish prank

Dumm'kopf *m* dunderhead

dumpf [dumpf] *adj* dull, muffled;

(schwül) muggy; *(moderig)* musty, moldy; *(Ahnung)* vague

dumpfig [ˈdʊmpfɪç] *adj* musty, moldy; muggy

Düne [ˈdynə] *f* (-;-n) sand dune

Dung [dʊŋ] *m* (-[e]s;) dung; *(künstlicher)* fertilizer

düngen [ˈdyŋən] *tr* manure; fertilize

Dünger [ˈdyŋər] *m* (-s;) var of **Dung**

dunkel [ˈdʊŋkəl] *adj* dark; vague; obscure || **Dunkel** *n* (-s;) darkness

Dünkel [ˈdyŋkəl] *m* (-s;) conceit

dün'kelhaft *adj* conceited

Dun'kelheit *f* (-;) darkness; obscurity

Dun'kelkammer *f* (phot) darkroom

Dun'kelmann *m* (-[e]s;ˮer) shady character

dünn [dyn] *adj* thin

Dunst [dʊnst] *m* (-es;ˮe) vapor, mist, haze; *(Rauch)* smoke; *(Dampf)* steam; **in D. und Rauch aufgehen** (fig) go up in smoke; **sich in (blauen) D. auflösen** vanish in thin air

dünsten [ˈdynstən] *tr & intr* stew; steam

dunstig [ˈdʊnstɪç] *adj* steamy; *(Wetter)* misty, hazy

Duplikat [dupliˈkɑt] *n* (-[e]s;-e) duplicate; copy

Dur [dur] *invar n* (mus) major

durch [dʊrç] *adv* throughout; **d. und d.** through and through || *prep (acc)* through, by, by means of

durch'arbeiten *tr* work through || *ref* (durch) work one's way (through); elbow one's way (through)

durchaus' *adv* throughout; entirely; quite, absolutely; **d. nicht** by no means

durch'backen §50 *tr* bake through and through

durch'blättern *tr* thumb through

Durch'blick *m* vista

durch'blicken *intr* be apparent; (durch) look (through); **d. lassen** intimate

durchblutet [dʊrçˈblutət] *adj* supplied with blood

durch'bohren *tr* bore through || **durchboh'ren** *tr* pierce

durch'braten §63 *tr* roast thoroughly

durchbre'chen §64 *tr* break through; *(Vorschriften)* violate; *(mil)* breach || **durch'brechen** *tr* cut *(a hole)*; break in half || *intr* (SEIN) break through

durch'brennen §97 *tr* burn through; *(e-e Sicherung)* blow || *intr* (SEIN) run away; *(Sicherung)* blow

durch'bringen §65 *tr* get through; *(Gesetz)* pass; *(Geld)* spend; *(med)* pull *(a patient)* through || *ref* support oneself; **sich ehrlich d.** make an honest living

Durch'bruch *m* breakthrough; *(Öffnung)* breach, gap; *(der Zähne)* cutting

durch'denken §66 *tr* think through || **durchden'ken** *tr* think out, think over

durch'drängen *ref* push one's way through

durch'drehen *tr* grind; *(Wäsche)* put

through the wringer || *intr* (SEIN) (coll) go mad

durchdrin'gen §142 *tr* penetrate; pervade, imbue || **durch'dringen** *intr* (SEIN) get through; penetrate

durch'drucken *tr* (parl) push through

durchdrungen [dʊrçˈdrʊŋən] *adj.* imbued

durchei'len *tr* rush through || **durch'eilen** (SEIN) (durch) rush through

durcheinan'der *adj & adv* in confusion ||**Durcheinander** *n* (-s;-) mess, muddle

durcheinan'derbringen §65 *tr* muddle

durcheinan'dergeraten §63 *intr* (SEIN) get mixed up

durcheinan'derlaufen §105 *intr* (SEIN) mill about

durcheinan'derreden *intr* speak all at once

durcheinan'derwerfen §160 *tr* throw into confusion, turn upside down

durchfah'ren §71 *tr* travel through; *(Gedanke, Schreck)* strike || **durch'fahren** §71 *intr* (SEIN) go through without stopping

Durch'fahrt *f* passage; **keine D.!** no thoroughfare

Durch'fahrtshöhe *f* clearance

Durch'fall *m* diarrhea; (coll) flop; *(educ)* flunk, failure

durch'fallen §72 *intr* (SEIN) fall through; *(educ)* flunk; *(theat)* flop

durch'fechten §74 *tr* fight through

durch'finden §59 *ref* find one's way

durchflech'ten *tr* interweave

durchfor'schen *tr* examine, make an exhaustive study of

Durchfor'schung *f* exploration; search; thorough research

durch'fressen §70 *tr* eat through; corrode || *ref* (bei) sponge (on); (durch) work one's way (through)

Durchfuhr [ˈdʊrçfur] *f* (-;-en) transit

durchführbar [ˈdʊrçfyrbar] *adj* feasible

durch'führen *tr* lead through or across; *(Auftrag)* carry out; *(Gesetz)* enforce

Durch'gang *m* passage; aisle; (fig) transition; (astr, com) transit; **D. verboten!** no thoroughfare, no trespassing

Durch'gänger *m* (-s;-) runaway

Durch'gangslager *n* transit camp

Durch'gangsverkehr *m* through traffic

Durch'gangszug *m* through train

durch'geben §80 *tr* pass on

durch'gebraten *adj* (culin) well done

durch'gehen §82 *tr* (SEIN) go through; *(durchlesen)* go over || *intr* (SEIN) go through; *(Pferd)* bolt; *(heimlich davonlaufen)* run away; abscond; *(Vorschlag)* pass

durch'gehend(s) *adv* generally; *(durchaus)* throughout

durchgeistigt [dʊrçˈgaɪstɪçt] *adj* highly intellectual

durch'greifen §88 *intr* reach through; (fig) take drastic measures

durch'greifend *adj* vigorous; drastic

durch'halten §90 *tr* keep up || *intr* hold out, stick it out

durch'hauen §93 *tr* chop through;

knock a hole through; (coll) thrash, beat
durch′hecheln tr (coll) run down
durch′helfen §96 intr (dat) (durch) help (through) || ref get by, manage
durch′kämmen tr (& fig) comb through
durch′kochen tr boil thoroughly
durch′kommen §99 intr (SEIN) come through; (durch Krankheit) pull through; (sich durchhelfen) get by; (educ) pass
durchkreu′zen tr cross; (durchstreichen) cross out; (fig) frustrate
Durch·laß [′dʊrçlas] m (–lasses;–lässe) passage; outlet; culvert
durch′lassen §104 tr let through, let pass; (Licht) transmit; (educ) pass
durchlässig [′dʊrçlɛsɪç] adj permeable
Durch′laßschein m pass
durchlau′fen §105 tr run through; look through; (Schule) go through; seine Bahn d. run its course || **durch′laufen** §105 ref—sich [dat] die Schuhe d. wear out one's shoes || §105 intr (SEIN) run through
durchle′ben tr live through
durch′lesen §107 tr read over, peruse
durchleuch′ten tr illuminate; (Gesicht) light up; (Ei) test; X-ray
durch′liegen §108 ref develop bedsores || **Durchliegen** n (–s) bedsores
durchlo′chen tr punch
durch′löchern tr perforate; pierce; (mit Kugeln) riddle
durch′machen tr go through, undergo
Durch′marsch m marching through; (coll) diarrhea, runs
Durch′messer m diameter
durchnäs′sen tr soak, drench
durch′nehmen §116 tr (in der Klasse) do, have
durch′pausen tr trace
durch′peitschen tr whip soundly; (Gesetzentwurf) rush through
durchque′ren tr cross, traverse
durch′rechnen tr check, go over
Durch′reise f passage; auf seiner D. on his way through
durch′reisen intr (SEIN) travel through
Durch′reisende §5 mf transient, transit passenger
durch′reißen §53 tr tear in half || intr (SEIN) tear, break, snap
Durch′sage f special announcement
durch′sagen tr announce
durchschau′en tr (fig) see through || **durch′schauen** intr look through
durch′scheinen §128 intr shine through; show through; be seen
durch′scheuern tr rub through
durchschie′ßen §76 tr shoot through, riddle; (typ) lead || **durch′schießen** §76 intr (durch) shoot (through) || intr (SEIN) dash through
Durch′schlag m carbon copy; (Sieb) (large) strainer, separator; (elec) breakdown; (tech) punch
durchschla′gen §132 tr penetrate || **durch′schlagen** §132 tr knock a hole through; (Holz) split; (Fensterscheibe) smash; (Nagel) drive through; (Kartoffeln, Früchte) strain; (mit Kohlepapier) make a carbon copy of

|| ref fight one's way through; (sich durchhelfen) manage || intr come through; penetrate; take effect; show up || intr (SEIN) (Sicherung) blow
durch′schlagend adj effective; striking
Durch′schlagpapier n carbon paper
durch′schleichen §85 ref & intr (SEIN) creep through
durchschleu′sen tr pass (a ship) through a lock; (Passagiere, Rekruten, usw.) process; (fig) sneak (s.o.) through
durch′schneiden §106 tr cut through; cut in half || **durchschnei′den** §106 tr cut through, cut across || ref cross, intersect
Durch′schnitt m cutting through; average; cross section; über der große D. der Menschen the majority of people; im D. on an average
durch′schnittlich adj average || adv on the average
Durchschnitts– comb.fm. average; mean
Durch′schnittsmensch m average person
durch′schreiben §62 tr make a carbon copy of
durch′sehen §138 tr look over; examine; (flüchtig anschauen) scan; (Papiere, Post) check || intr see through
durch′seihen tr filter; percolate
durchset′zen tr intersperse; penetrate || **durch′setzen** tr carry through; d., daß bring it about that, succeed in (ger) || ref get one's way
Durch′sicht f examination, inspection; (auf acc) view (of)
durch′sichtig adj transparent; clear
durch′sickern intr (SEIN) seep out; (Wahrheit, Gerücht) leak out
durch′sieben tr sift
durch′sprechen §64 tr talk over
durchste′chen §64 tr pierce || **durch′stechen** §64 tr (Nadel) stick through
durch′stehen §146 tr go through
durchstö′bern tr rummage through
durch′stoßen §150 tr push (s.th.) through; (Tür) knock down; (Scheibe) smash in; (Ellbogen) wear through; (mil) penetrate || **durchsto′ßen** §150 tr break through || **durch′stoßen** §150 intr (SEIN) break through
durchstrei′chen §85 tr roam through || **durch′streichen** §85 tr cross out
durchstrei′fen tr wander through
durchsu′chen tr go through, search
durch′treten §152 tr (Sohle) wear a hole in; (Gashebel) floor || intr (SEIN) go through, pass through
durchtrieben [dʊrç′tri:bən] adj sly
durchwa′chen tr remain awake through
durchwach′sen adj gristly
durch′wählen tr & intr dial direct
durchwan′dern tr travel or walk through || **durch′wandern** intr (SEIN) (durch) walk (through), hike (through)
durchwe′ben tr interweave
durch′weg [adv] throughout
durchwei′chen, durch′weichen tr soak
durchwüh′len tr burrow through; (Ge-

päck, Schränke) rummage through ||
durch'wühlen *ref* burrow through;
(fig) work one's way through
durch'wursteln *ref* muddle through
durchzie'hen §163 *tr* pass through,
cross; *(Zimmer)* permeate, fill;
streak; (sew) interweave || **durch'-
ziehen** §163 *tr* pull through || *intr*
(SEIN) pass through; flow through
durchzucken (**durchzuk'ken**) *tr* flash
through the mind of
Durch'zug *m* passage; *(Luftzug)* draft
durch'zwängen *tr* force through || *ref*
squeeze through
dürfen ['dYrfən] §69 *aux* be allowed;
be likely; **darf ich?** may I?; **ich darf
nicht** I must not; **man darf wohl erwarten** it is to be expected
durfte ['dʊrftə] *pret* of **dürfen**
dürftig ['dYrftɪç] *adj* needy; poor,
wretched, miserable, scanty
dürr [dYr] *adj* dry; *(Boden)* arid, barren; *(Holz)* dead, dry; *(Mensch)*
skinny || **Dürre** ['dYrə] *f* (–;) dry-
ness; barrenness; leanness; drought
Durst [dʊrst] *m* (–[e]s;) **(nach)** thirst
(for); **D. haben** be thirsty

dursten ['dʊrstən], **dürsten** ['dYr-
stən] *intr* be thirsty; **(nach)** thirst
(for)
durstig ['dʊrstɪç] *adj* thirsty
Dusche ['du/ə] *f* (–;–n) shower
duschen ['du/ən] *intr* take a shower
Düse ['dyzə] *f* (–;–n) nozzle, jet
Dusel ['duzəl] *m* (–s;–) (coll) fluke
Düsen– *comb.fm.* jet
Dü'senantrieb *m* jet propulsion
Dü'senjäger *m* jet fighter
düster ['dystər] *adj* gloomy; sad; dark
|| **Düster** *n* (–s;) gloom; darkness
Dutzend ['dʊtsənt] *n* (–s;– & –e) dozen
dut'zendmal *adv* a dozen times
dut'zendweise *adv* by the dozen
Duzbruder ['dutsbrudər] *m* buddy
duzen [dutsən] *tr* say **du** to, be on in-
timate terms with
Dynamik [dy'namɪk] *f* (–s;) dynamics
dynamisch [dy'namɪ/] *adj* dynamic
Dynamit [dyna'mit] *n* (–s;–e) dyna-
mite
Dynamo ['dynamo] *m* (–s;–s) dynamo
Dyna·stie [dynas'ti] *f* (–;–stien
['sti·ən] dynasty
D'-Zug *m* through train, express

E

E, e [e] *invar n* E, e; (mus) E
Ebbe ['ɛbə] *f* (–;–n) ebb tide
eben ['ɛbən] *adj* even, level, flat; **zu
ebener Erde** on the ground floor ||
adv just; a moment ago; exactly
|| *interj* exactly!; that's right!
E'benbild *n* image, exact likeness
ebenbürtig ['ɛbənbYrtɪç] *adj* of equal
rank, equal
ebenda ['ɛbən'da] *adv* right there;
(beim Zitieren) ibidem
ebendersel'be §4,3 *adj* self-same
ebendes'wegen *adv* for that very reason
Ebene ['ɛbənə] *f* (–;–n) plain; (fig)
level; (geom) plane
e'benerdig *adj* ground-floor
e'benfalls *adv* likewise, too
E'benholz *n* ebony
E'benmaß *n* right proportions
e'benmäßig *adj* well-proportioned
e'benso *adv* just as; likewise
e'bensogut *adv* just as well
e'bensoviel *adv* just as much
e'bensowenig *adv* just as little
Eber ['ɛbər] *m* (–s;–) boar
E'beresche *f* mountain ash
ebnen ['ɛbnən] *tr* level, even; smooth
Echo ['ɛço] *n* (–s;–s) echo
echoen ['ɛço·ən] *intr* echo
echt [ɛçt] *adj* genuine, real, true
Eck [ɛk] *n* (–[e]s;–e) corner; end
Eck– *comb.fm.* corner; end
Ecke ['ɛkə] *f* (–;–n) corner; edge
Ecker ['ɛkər] *f* (–;–n) beechnut
eckig ['ɛkɪç] *adj* angular; (fig) awkward; **eckige Klammer** bracket
Eck'stein *m* cornerstone; (cards) dia-
monds

Eck'stoß *m* (fb) corner kick
Eck'zahn *m* canine tooth
Eclair [e'kler] *n* (–s;–s) éclair
edel ['edəl] *adj* noble; *(Metall)* pre-
cious; *(Pferd)* thoroughbred; **edle
Teile** vital organs
e'deldenkend *adj* noble-minded
e'delgesinnt *adj* noble-minded
E'del·mann *m* (–[e]s;–leute) noble
e'delmütig *adj* noble-minded
E'delstahl *m* high-grade steel
E'delstein *m* precious stone, gem
E'delweiß *n* (–[e]s;–e) edelweiss
Edikt [ɛ'dɪkt] *n* (–[e]s;–e) edict
Edie ['edlə] §5 *mf* noble
Efeu ['efoɪ] *m* (–s;) ivy
Effekt [ɛ'fɛkt] *m* (–[e]s;–e) effect
Effekten [ɛ'fɛktən] *pl* property; ef-
fects; (fin) securities, stocks
Effek'tenmakler *m* §6 *mf* stock broker
Effekthascherei [ɛfɛktha/ə'raɪ] *f* (–;)
showiness
effektiv [efɛk'tif] *adj* effective; *(wirk-
lich)* actual
Effektiv'lohn *m* take-home pay
Effet [ɛ'fe] *n* (–s;) spin, English
egal [e'gal] *adj* equal; all the same
Egge ['ɛgə] *f* (–;–n) harrow
eggen ['ɛgən] *tr* harrow
Ego ['ego] *n* (–s;) ego
Egoismus [ego'ɪsmʊs] *m* (–;) egoism
Egoist –in [ego'ɪst(ɪn)] §7 *mf* egoist
egoistisch [ego'ɪstɪ/] *adj* egoistic
Egotist –in [ego'tɪst(ɪn)] §7 *mf* egotist
eh [e] *adv* (Aust) anyhow, anyway
ehe ['e·ə] *conj* before || **Ehe** *f* (–;–n)
marriage; matrimony
E'hebrecher *m* (–s;–) adulterer

E'hebrecherin *f* (-;-nen) adulteress
e'hebrecherisch *adj* adulterous
E'hebruch *m* adultery, infidelity
ehedem ['e·ə'dem] *adv* formerly
E'hefrau *f* wife
E'hegatte *m* spouse
E'hegattin *f* spouse
E'hegelöbnis *n* marriage vow
E'hehälfte *f* (coll) better half
E'heleute *pl* married couple
e'helich *adj* marital; (*Kind*) legitimate
e'helos *adj* unmarried, single
E'helosigkeit *f* (-;) celibacy
ehemalig ['e·əmɑlɪç] *adj* former; ex-;
  (*verstorben*) late
ehemals ['e·əmɑls] *adv* formerly
E'hemann *m* husband
E'hepaar *n* married couple
eher ['e·ər] *adv* sooner; rather
E'hering *m* wedding band
ehern ['e·ərn] *adj* brass; (fig) unshakable
E'hescheidung *f* divorce
E'hescheidungsklage *f* divorce suit
E'heschließung *f* marriage
E'hestand *m* married state, wedlock
ehestens ['e·əstəns] *adv* at the earliest;
  as soon as possible
E'hestifter –in §6 *mf* matchmaker
E'heversprechen *n* promise of marriage
Ehrabschneider –in ['erap/naɪdər(ɪn)]
  §6 *mf* slanderer
ehrbar ['erbar] *adj* honorable, respectable
Ehr'barkeit *f* (-;) respectability
Ehre ['erə] *f* (-;-n) honor; glory
ehren ['erən] *tr* honor; **Sehr geehrter
  Herr** Dear Sir
eh'renamtlich *adj* honorary
Eh'rendoktor *m* honorary doctor
Eh'renerklärung *f* apology
eh'renhaft *adj* honorable
ehrenhalber ['erənhalbər] *invar adj*—
  Doktor e. Doctor honoris causa
Eh'renmitglied *n* honorary member
Eh'renrechte *pl*—bürgerliche E. civil
  rights
Eh'rensache *f* point of honor
eh'renvoll *adj* honorable, respectable
eh'renwert *adj* honorable
Eh'renwort *n* word of honor; **auf E.
  entlassen** put on parole
ehrerbietig ['ererbitɪç] *adj* respectful,
  reverent, deferential
Ehrerbietung ['ererbituŋ] *f* (-;), Ehr-
  furcht ['erfurçt] *f* (-;) respect, reverence; (vor *dat*) awe (of)
ehrfürchtig ['erfyrçtɪç], ehrfurchtsvoll
  ['erfurçtsfɔl] *adj* respectful
Ehr'gefühl *n* sense of honor
Ehr'geiz *m* ambition
ehr'geizig *adj* ambitious
ehrlich ['erlɪç] *adj* honest; sincere;
  fair; **j-n e. machen** restore s.o.'s
  good name
Ehr'lichkeit *f* (-;) honesty; candor
ehr'los *adj* dishonorable; (*Frau*) of
  easy virtue; infamous
Ehr'losigkeit *f* (-;) dishonesty; infamy
ehrsam ['erzam] *adj* respectable
Ehr'sucht *f* (-;) ambition
ehr'süchtig *adj* ambitious

Ehr'verlust *m* loss of civil rights
ehr'würdig *adj* venerable; (eccl) reverend
ei [aɪ] *interj* oh!; ah!; ei,ei! oho!; ei je!
  oh dear!; ei was! nonsense! || Ei *n*
  (-[e]s;-er) egg
Eiche ['aɪçə] *f* (-;-n) oak
Eichel ['aɪçəl] *f* (-;-n) acorn; (cards)
  club
eichen ['aɪçən] *adj* oak || *tr* gauge
Ei'chenlaub *n* oak leaf cluster
Eichhörnchen ['aɪçhœrnçən] *n* (-s;-),
  Eichkätzchen ['aɪçketsçən] *n* (-s;-)
  squirrel
Eichmaß ['aɪçmɑs] *n* gauge; standard
Eid [aɪt] *m* (-[e]s;-e) oath
Eid'bruch *m* perjury
eid'brüchig *adj* perjured
Eidechse ['aɪdeksə] *f* (-;-n) lizard
Eiderdaunen ['aɪdərdaunən] *pl* eider
  down
eidesstattlich ['aɪdəs/tatlɪç] *adj* in lieu
  of an oath, solemn
eid'lich *adj* sworn || *adv* under oath
Ei'dotter *m* egg yolk
Ei'erkrem *f* custard
Ei'erkuchen *m* omelet; pancake
Ei'erlandung *f* three-point landing
Ei'erlikör *m* eggnog
Ei'erschale *f* eggshell
Ei'erstock *m* ovary
Eifer ['aɪfər] *m* (-;) zeal, eagerness
Eiferer –in ['aɪfərər(ɪn)] §6 *mf* zealot
Ei'fersucht *f* jealousy
ei'fersüchtig *adj* (auf *acc*) jealous (of)
eifrig ['aɪfrɪç] *adj* zealous; ardent
Ei'gelb *n* (-[e]s;-e) egg yolk
eigen ['aɪgən] *adj* own; of (my, your,
  etc.) own; (*dat*) peculiar (to), characteristic (of) || *invar pron*—etw
  mein e. nennen call s.th. my own
ei'genartig *adj* peculiar; odd, queer
Eigenbrötler ['aɪgənbrøtlər] *m* (-s;-)
  (coll) lone wolf, loner; crank
Ei'gengewicht *n* dead weight
eigenhändig ['aɪgənhendɪç] *adj & adv*
  with or in one's own hand
Ei'genheit *f* (-;-en) peculiarity
Ei'genliebe *f* self-love, egotism
Ei'genlob *n* self-praise
ei'genmächtig *adj* arbitrary, highhanded
Ei'genname *m* proper name
Ei'gennutz *m* self-interest
ei'gennützig *adj* selfish
eigens ['aɪgəns] *adv* expressly
Ei'genschaft *f* (-;-en) quality, property; **in seiner E. als** in his capacity
  as
Ei'genschaftswort *n* (-[e]s;-er) adjective
Ei'gensinn *m* stubbornness
ei'gensinnig *adj* stubborn
eigentlich ['aɪgəntlɪç] *adj* actual || *adv*
  actually, really
Eigentum ['aɪgəntum] *n* (-[e]s;-er)
  property, possession; ownership
Eigentümer –in ['aɪgəntymər(ɪn)] §6
  mf (legal) owner || *m* proprietor || *f*
  proprietress
eigentümlich ['aɪgəntymlɪç] *adj* odd;
  (*dat*) peculiar (to)
Ei'gentümlichkeit *f* (-;-en) peculiarity

Ei'gentumsrecht *n* ownership, title

Ei'genwechsel *m* promissory note

ei'genwillig *adj* independent; (*Stil*) original

eignen ['aɪgnən] *ref* (**für**) be suited (to); (**als**) be suitable (as); (**zu**) be cut out (for)

Eig'nung *f* (-;-en) qualification, aptitude

Ei'gnungsprüfung *f* aptitude test

Eilbrief ['aɪlbrif] *m* special delivery

Eile ['aɪlə] *f* (-;) hurry; **E. haben** or **in E. sein** be in a hurry

eilen ['aɪlən] *ref* hurry (up) || *intr* be urgent || *intr* (SEIN) hurry; **eilt!** (*Briefaufschrift*) urgent! || *impers*—**es eilt mir nicht damit** I'm in no hurry about it

eilends ['aɪlənts] *adv* hurriedly

Eilgut ['aɪlgut] *n* express freight

eilig ['aɪlɪç] *adj* quick, hurried; urgent || *adv* hurriedly; **es e. haben** be in a hurry

Eilpost ['aɪlpɔst] *f* special delivery

Eilzug ['aɪltsuk] *m* (rr) limited

Eimer ['aɪmər] *m* (-s;-) bucket, pail

ein [aɪn] §2,1 *indef art* a, an || §2,1 *num adj* one || *adv* in; **ein und aus in and out**; **nicht ein und aus wissen** not know which way to turn || **einer** *indef pron & num pron* see **einer**

ein-, Ein- *comb.fm.* one-, single

einan'der *invar recip pron* each other; (*unter mehreren*) one another

ein'arbeiten *tr* train (for a job); (**in**) (*acc*) work (into) || *ref* (**in** *acc*) become familiar (with), get the hang (of)

einarmig ['aɪnarmɪç] *adj* one-armed

einäschern ['aɪnɛʃərn] *tr* reduce to ashes, incinerate; (*Leiche*) cremate

ein'atmen *tr & intr* inhale

ein'äugig *adj* one-eyed

einbahnig ['aɪnbanɪç] *adj* single-lane; single-line; one-way

Ein'bahnstraße *f* one-way street

ein'balsamieren *tr* embalm

Ein'band *m* (-[e]s;-̈e) binding; cover

ein'bauen *tr* build in, install

einbegriffen ['aɪnbəgrɪfən] *adj* included, inclusive

ein'behalten §90 *tr* retain; (*Lohn*) withhold

ein'berufen §122 *tr* call, convene; (mil) call up, draft || **Einberufene** §5 *mf* draftee

Ein'berufung *f* (-;-en) (mil) induction

ein'betten *tr* embed

ein'beziehen §163 *tr* include

ein'bilden *ref*—**sich** [*dat*] **etw e.** imagine s.th.

ein'binden §59 *tr* (bb) bind

ein'blenden *tr* (cin) fade in

Ein'blick *m* view; (fig) insight

ein'brechen §64 *tr* break in || *intr* (SEIN) collapse; (*Nacht*) fall; (*Kälte*) set in; (*Dieb*) break in

Ein'brecher –in §6 *mf* burglar

ein'bringen §65 *tr* bring in; earn; yield

Ein'bruch *m* break-in, burglary; invasion; **E. der Nacht** nightfall

Ein'bruchsdiebstahl *m* burglary

ein'bruchsicher *adj* burglarproof

einbürgern ['aɪnbyrgərn] *tr* naturalize || *ref* (fig) take root, become accepted

Ein'bürgerung *f* (-;) naturalization

Ein'buße *f* loss, forfeiture

ein'büßen *tr* lose, forfeit

ein'dämmen *tr* check, contain

ein'decken *tr* cover || *ref* (**mit**) stock up (on)

Eindecker ['aɪndekər] *m* (-s;-) monoplane

ein'deutig *adj* unequivocal, clear

eindeutschen ['aɪndɔɪtʃən] *tr* Germanize

ein'drängen *ref* squeeze in; interfere

ein'dringen §142 *intr* (SEIN) penetrate, come in; **e. auf** (*acc*) crowd in on; **e. in** (*acc*) rush into; penetrate; infiltrate; (mil) invade

ein'dringlich *adj* urgent

Eindringling ['aɪndrɪŋlɪŋ] *m* (-s;-e) intruder, interloper; gate-crasher

ein'drücken *tr* press in; crash, flatten; imprint; (*Fenster*) smash in

Ein'druck *m* imprint; impression

Ein'druckskunst *f* impressionism

ein'drucksvoll *adj* impressive

ein'engen *tr* narrow; (fig) limit

einer ['aɪnər] §2,4 *indef pron & num pron* one || **Einer** *m* (-s;-) (math) unit

einerlei ['aɪnərlaɪ] *invar adj* (*nur attributiv*) one kind of; (*nur prädikativ*) all the same || **Einerlei** *n* (-;) monotony

einerseits ['aɪnərzaɪts], **einesteils** ['aɪnəstaɪls] *adv* on the one hand

ein'fach *adj* single; simple || *adv* simply

einfädeln ['aɪnfedəln] *tr* thread; (fig) engineer

ein'fahren §71 *tr* (*Auto*) break in; (*Ernte*) bring in; (aer) retract || *ref* get driving experience; **die Sache hat sich gut eingefahren** it's off to a good start || *intr* (SEIN) drive in; (rr) arrive

Ein'fahrt *f* entrance; gateway

Ein'fall *m* inroad; (fig) idea; (mil) invasion

ein'fallen §72 *intr* (SEIN) fall in; cave in, collapse; (*in die Rede*) butt in; join in; **e. in** (*acc*) invade; **j-m e.** occur to s.o.; **sich** [*dat*] **etw e. lassen** take s.th. into one's head; think up s.th.; **sich** [*dat*] **nicht e. lassen** not dream of; **was fällt dir ein?** what's the idea?

ein'fallslos *adj* unimaginative

ein'fallsreich *adj* imaginative

Ein'falt *f* simplicity; simple-mindedness

einfältig ['aɪnfeltɪç] *adj* (pej) simple

Ein'faltspinsel *m* sucker, simpleton

ein'farbig *adj* one-colored; plain

ein'fassen *tr* edge, trim; (*einschließen*) enclose; (*Edelstein*) set

Ein'fassung *f* (-;-en) border; mounting

ein'fetten *tr* grease

ein'finden §59 *ref* show up

ein'flechten *tr* plait; (*Haar*) braid; (fig) insert

ein'fliegen §57 *tr* (*Truppen*) fly in;

(*Flugzeug*) flight-test || *intr* (SEIN) fly in

ein′fließen §76 *intr* (SEIN) flow in; **e. in** (*acc*) flow into; **einige Bemerkungen e. lassen** slip in a few remarks

ein′flößen *tr* infuse, instill

Ein′fluß *m* influx; (fig) influence

ein′flußreich *adj* influential

ein′förmig *adj* monotonous

einfried(ig)en [ˈaɪnfriːd(ɪɡ)ən] *tr* enclose, fence in

ein′frieren §77 *tr* (& *fin*) freeze || *intr* (SEIN) freeze (up) || **Einfrieren** *n* (-s;) (fin) freeze

ein′fügen *tr* insert, fit || *ref* fit in; (in *acc*) adapt oneself (to)

ein′fühlen *ref* (in *acc*) relate (to)

Einfuhr [ˈaɪnfuːr] *f* (-;-en) importation; **Einfuhren** imports

ein′führen *tr* import; introduce; (in *ein Amt*) install

Ein′führung *f* (-;-en) introduction

Ein′fuhrwaren *pl* imports

Ein′fuhrzoll *m* import duty

Ein′gabe *f* petition; application

Ein′gang *m* entrance; entry; beginning; introduction; (*von Waren*) arrival; **Eingänge** (com) incoming goods; incoming mail; (fin) receipts

ein′geben §80 *tr* suggest, prompt; (med) administer, give

eingebildet [ˈaɪnɡəbɪldət] *adj* imaginary; self-conceited

eingeboren [ˈaɪnɡəboːrən] *adj* native; only-begotten; (*Eigenschaft*) innate || **Eingeborene** §5 *mf* native

Ein′gebung *f* (-;-en) suggestion; (*höhere*) inspiration

eingedenk [ˈaɪnɡədɛŋk] *adj* (*genit*) mindful (of)

ein′gefallen *adj* (*Backen, Augen*) sunken

eingefleischt [ˈaɪnɡəflaɪʃt] *adj* inveterate

ein′gefroren *adj* icebound

ein′gehen §82 *tr* (HABEN & SEIN) enter into; (*Verpflichtungen*) incur; (*Wette, Geschäft*) make; (*Chance*) take; (*Versicherung*) take out; **e-n Vergleich e.** come to an agreement || *intr* (SEIN) come in; arrive; (*aufhören*) come to an end; fizzle out; (*Stoff*) shrink; (bot, zool) die off; (com) close down; **e. auf** (*acc*) go into, consider; consent to; **e. lassen** drop, discontinue; **es geht mir nicht ein, daß** I can't accept the fact that

ein′gehend *adj* thorough

eingelegt [ˈaɪnɡəleɡt] *adj* inlaid

Eingemachte [ˈaɪnɡəmaxtə] §5 *n* (-n;) preserves

eingemeinden [ˈaɪnɡəmaɪndən] *tr* (*Vorort*) incorporate

eingenommen [ˈaɪnɡənɔmən] *adj* prejudiced; **von sich e.** self-conceited

eingeschnappt [ˈaɪnɡəʃnapt] *adj* (coll) peeved

eingeschneit [ˈaɪnɡəʃnaɪt] *adj* snowed in

Eingesessene [ˈaɪnɡəzɛsənə] §5 *mf* resident

Ein′geständis *n* (-ses;-se) confession

ein′gestehen §146 *tr* confess, admit

Eingeweide [ˈaɪnɡəvaɪdə] *pl* viscera; intestines; (*von Vieh*) entrails

Eingeweihte [ˈaɪnɡəvaɪtə] §5 *mf* insider

ein′gewöhnen *tr* (in *acc*) accustom (to) || *ref* (in *acc*) become accustomed (to)

eingewurzelt [ˈaɪnɡəvurtsəlt] *adj* deep-rooted

ein′gießen §76 *tr* pour in, pour out

eingleisig [ˈaɪnɡlaɪzɪç] *adj* single-track

ein′gliedern *tr* integrate; annex

ein′graben §87 *tr* bury; engrave || *ref* burrow; (mil) dig in

ein′greifen §88 *intr* take action; interfere; (in *j-s Rechte*) encroach; (mach) mesh, be in gear || **Eingreifen** *n* (-s;) interference; (mach) meshing

Ein′griff *m* interference; encroachment; (mach) meshing; (surg) operation

ein′hacken *tr*—**e. auf** (*acc*) peck at; (fig) pick at

ein′haken *tr* (in *acc*) hook (into) || *ref*—**sich bei j-m e.** link arms with s.o. || *intr* (fig) cut in

Ein′halt *m* (-[e]s;) stop, halt; **E. gebieten** (*dat*) put a stop to

ein′halten §90 *tr* stick to; (*Verabredung*) keep; (*Zahlungen*) keep up; **die Zeit e.** be punctual || *intr* stop

ein′händigen *tr* hand over

ein′hängen §92 *tr* (*Türe*) hang; (in *acc*) hook (into); (telp) hang up || *ref*—**sich bei j-m e.** link arms with s.o. || *intr* (telp) hang up

ein′heften *tr* sew in; baste on

ein′heimisch *adj* domestic; local; home-grown; **e. in** (*dat*) native to

einheimsen [ˈaɪnhaɪmzən] *tr* reap

Einheit [ˈaɪnhaɪt] *f* (-;-en) oneness, unity; (math, mil) unit

ein′heitlich *adj* uniform

Einheits- *comb.fm.* standard, uniform; unit; united

ein′heizen *intr* start a fire; **j-m tüchtig e.** (fig) burn s.o. up

einhellig [ˈaɪnhɛlɪç] *adj* unanimous

ein′holen *tr* bring in; (*Flagge*) hawl down; (*Segel*) hawl down; (*im Wettlauf*) catch up with; (*Erkundigungen lauf*) catch up with; (*Erkundigungen*) make; (*Rat, Nachricht, Erlaubnis*) get; (*Verlust*) make good; (*abholen und geleiten*) escort; (*Schiff, Tau*) tow in || *intr* shop

Ein′horn *n* (myth) unicorn

ein′hüllen *tr* wrap up; enclose

einig [ˈaɪnɪç] *adj* united; of one mind; **sich** [*dat*] **e. sein be** in agreement

einige [ˈaɪnɪɡə] §9 *indef adj* & *indef pron* some

einigen [ˈaɪnɪɡən] *tr* unite || *ref* come to terms, agree

einigermaßen [ˈaɪnɪɡərmaːsən] *adv* to some extent; (*ziemlich*) somewhat

ein′niggehen §82 *intr* (SEIN) concur

Ei′nigkeit *f* (-;) unity; harmony; agreement

Ei′nigung f (-;-en) unification; agreement, understanding

ein′impfen tr—j-m Impfstoff e. inoculate s.o. with vaccine; j-m e., daß (fig) drive it into s.o. that

ein′jagen tr (dat) put (e.g., a scare) into

ein′jährig adj one-year-old; (bot) annual

ein′kassieren tr collect

Ein′kauf m purchase; **Einkäufe machen** go shopping

ein′kaufen tr purchase; **e. gehen** go shopping

Ein′käufer –in §6 mf shopper

Ein′kaufspreis m purchase price

Ein′kehr f—E. bei sich halten search one's conscience; E. halten stop off

ein′kehren intr (SEIN) stay overnight; (im Gasthaus) stop off, stay

ein′keilen tr wedge in

ein′kerben tr notch, cut a notch in

einkerkern [′aɪnkɛrkərn] tr imprison

einkesseln [′aɪnkɛsəln] tr encircle

ein′klagen tr sue for (a bad debt)

ein′klammern tr bracket, put in parentheses

Ein′klang m unison; accord

Ein′klebebuch n scrap book

ein′kleben tr (in acc) paste (into)

ein′kleiden tr clothe; vest; (mil) issue uniforms to

ein′klemmen tr jam in, squeeze in

ein′klinken tr & intr engage, catch

ein′knicken tr fold

ein′kochen tr thicken (by boiling); can ‖ intr thicken

ein′kommen §99 intr (SEIN)—bei j-m um etw e. apply to s.o. for s.th. ‖ **Einkommen** n (-s) income, revenue

Ein′kommensteuer f income tax

Ein′kommensteuererklärung f income-tax return

Ein′kommenstufe f income bracket

ein′kreisen tr encircle

Einkünfte [′aɪnkynftə] pl revenue

ein′kuppeln tr let out the clutch

ein′laden §103 tr load; invite

Ein′ladung f (-;-en) invitation

Ein′lage f (-;-n) (im Brief) enclosure; (im Schuh) insole; arch support; (Zwischenfutter) padding; (Kapital-) investment; (Sparkassen-) deposit; (beim Spiel) bet; (culin) solids (in soup); (dent) temporary filling; (mus) musical extra

ein′lagern tr store, store up

Ein′laß [′aɪnlas] m (-lasses;) admission; admittance; (tech) intake

ein′lassen §104 tr let it, admit; (tech) (in acc) sink (into) ‖ ref (auf acc, in acc) let oneself get involved (in)

Ein′laßkarte f admission ticket

Ein′lauf m incoming mail; (e-s Schiffes) arrival; j-m e-n E. machen give s.o. an enema

ein′laufen §105 intr (SEIN) come in, arrive; (Stoff) shrink; das Badewasser e. lassen run the bath; j-m das Haus e. keep running to s.o.'s house ‖ ref warm up (by running)

ein′leben ref (in acc) accustom oneself (to)

Ein′legearbeit f inlaid work

Ein′legebrett n (e-s Tisches) leaf

ein′legen tr put in; (Fleisch, Gurken) pickle; (Geld) deposit; (in e-n Brief) enclose; (Film, Kassette) insert; (Veto) interpose; (Beschwerde) lodge; (Protest) enter; (Berufung) (jur) file; Busse e. put on extra buses

ein′leiten tr introduce; (Buch) write a preface to; (beginnen, eröffnen) start, open; ein Verfahren e. gegen institute proceedings against s.o.

Ein′leitung f (-;-en) introduction; initiation

ein′lenken intr (fig) give in

ein′leuchten intr be evident; (coll) sink in

ein′liefern tr deliver; (ins Gefängnis) put, commit; ins Krankenhaus e. take to the hospital

ein′lösen tr ransom; redeem; (Scheck) cash

ein′machen tr can, preserve

ein′mal adv once; (künftig) one day; auf e. suddenly; all at the same time; einmal...einmal now...now; nicht e. (unstressed) not even; (stressed) not even once

Ein′maleins′ n multiplication table

ein′malig adj unique

Einmann– comb.fm. one-man

Ein′marsch m entry

ein′marschieren intr (SEIN) march in

ein′mauern tr wall in

ein′mengen ref, **ein′mischen** ref (in acc) meddle (with), interfere (with)

Ein′mischung f (-;-en) interference

einmotorig [′aɪnmoˌtoːrɪç] adj single-engine

einmummen [′aɪnmʊmən] ref bundle up

ein′münden intr (in acc) empty (into); (Straßen) run (into)

Ein′mündung f (-;-en) (e-s Flusses) mouth; (e-r Straße) junction

ein′mütig adj unanimous

ein′nähen tr sew in; (Kleid) take in

Ein′nahme f (-;-n) taking; capture; (fin) receipts; **Einnahmen** income

ein′nehmen §116 tr take; capture; (Essen) eat; (Geld) earn; (Steuern) collect; (Stellung) fill; (sew) take in; e-e Haltung e. assume an attitude; e-e hervorragende Stelle e. rank high; j-n für sich e. captivate s.o.; j-n gegen sich e. prejudice s.o. against oneself; seinen Platz e. take one's seat

ein′nicken intr (SEIN) doze off

ein′nisten ref in (dat) settle in; (fig) find a home (at)

Ein′öde f desert, wilderness

ein′ordnen tr put in its place; file; classify ‖ ref fit into place; (sich anstellen) get in line; sich rechts (or links) e. get into the right (or left) lane

ein′packen tr pack up

ein′passen tr (in acc) fit (into)

ein′pauken tr—j-m etw e. drum s.th. into s.o.'s head

ein′pferchen tr pen up; (fig) crowd together

ein'pflanzen *tr* plant; implant
ein'pökeln *tr* pickle; salt
ein'prägen *tr* imprint, impress
ein'quartieren *tr* billet, quarter
ein'rahmen *tr* frame
ein'rammen *tr* ram in, drive in
ein'räumen *tr* (*Recht, Kredit*) grant; (*zugeben*) concede, admit; **e. in** (*acc*) put into
ein'rechnen *tr* include, comprise
Ein'rede *f* objection; (jur) plea
ein'reden *tr—j—m etw e.* talk s.o. into s.th.; **das lasse ich mir nicht e.** I can't believe that || *intr—auf j—n e.* badger s.o.
ein'reiben §62 *tr* rub
ein'reichen *tr* hand in, file; (*Rechnung*) present; (*Abschied*) tender; (*Gesuch*) submit; (*Beschwerde, Klage*) file
ein'reihen *tr* file; rank; enroll; (*Bücher*) shelve || *ref* fall into place; fall in line
ein'reihig *adj* single-breasted
Ein'reise *f* entry
ein'reißen §53 *tr* tear; demolish || *intr* (SEIN) tear; (fig) spread
ein'renken *tr* (*Knochen*) set; (fig) set right
ein'richten *tr* arrange; establish; (*Wohnung*) furnish; (surg) set || *ref* settle down; economize, make ends meet; (**auf** *acc*) make arrangements (for); (**nach**) adapt oneself (to)
Ein'richtung *f* (–;–en) setup; establishment; furniture; equipment
Ein'richtungsgegenstand *m* piece of furniture, piece of equipment
ein'rosten *intr* (SEIN) get rusty
ein'rücken *tr* (*Zeile*) indent; (*Anzeige*) put in || *intr* (SEIN) march in; **in j—s Stelle e.** succeed s.o.; **zum Militär e.** enter military service
Ein'rückung *f* (–;–en) indentation
ein'rühren *tr* (**in** *acc*) stir (into)
eins [ains] *pron* one; one o'clock; **es ist mir eins** it's all the same to me || **Eins** *f* (–;–en) one; (*auf Würfeln*) ace; (educ) A
einsam ['ainzam] *adj* lonely, lonesome
ein'sammeln *tr* gather; (*Geld*) collect
Ein'satz *m* insert, insertion; (*Wette*) bet; (*Risiko*) risk; (*Verwendung*) use; (*für Flaschen*) deposit; (aer) sortie; (mil) action; (mus) starting in, entry; **im E. stehen** be in action; **im vollen E.** in full operation; **unter E. seines Lebens** at the risk of one's life; **zum E. bringen** employ, use; (*Maschinen*) put into operation; (*Polizei*) call out; (mil) throw into action
ein'satzbereit *adj* combat-ready
Ein'satzstück *n* insert
ein'saugen *tr* suck in; (fig) imbibe
ein'säumen *tr* (sew) hem
ein'schalten *tr* insert; (elec) switch on, turn on || *ref* intervene
ein'schärfen *tr—j—m etw e.* impress s.th. on s.o.
ein'schätzen *tr* appraise, value
ein'schenken *tr* pour
ein'schicken *tr* send in
ein'schieben §130 *tr* push in; insert

ein'schießen §76 *tr* (*Gewehr*) test; (*Geld*) contribute; (*Brot in den Ofen*) shove; (fb) score || *ref* (**auf** *acc*) zero in (on)
ein'schiffen *tr & intr* embark
Ein'schiffung *f* (–;–en) embarkation
ein'schlafen §131 *intr* (SEIN) fall asleep; (*Glied*) go to sleep
ein'schläf(e)rig *adj* single (bed)
einschläfern ['ainʃlefərn] *tr* lull to sleep; (vet) put to sleep
Ein'schlag *m* striking; impact; explosion; (*Umschlag*) wrapper; (fig) admixture, element; (golf) putt; (sew) tuck; (tex) weft, woof
ein'schlagen §132 *tr* (*Nagel*) drive in; (*zerbrechen*) smash, bash in; (*einwickeln*) wrap; (*Weg*) take; (*Laufbahn*) enter upon; (*Pflanzen*) stick in the ground; (golf) putt; **die Richtung e. nach** go in the direction of || *intr* (*Blitz*) strike; (*Erfolg haben*) be a success; **nicht e. fail**
einschlägig ['ainʃlegɪç] *adj* relevant
Ein'schlagpapier *n* wrapping paper
ein'schleichen §85 *ref* (**in** *acc*) creep (into), slip (into); (**in** *j—s Gunst*) worm one's way
ein'schleppen *tr* tow in; (*e—e Krankheit*) bring in (*from abroad*)
ein'schleusen *tr* (*Schmuggelwaren*) sneak in; (*Spionen*) plant
ein'schließen §76 *tr* lock up; (**in** *e—m Brief*) enclose; (fig) include; (mil) encircle, surround
ein'schließlich *adv* inclusive(ly) || *prep* (*genit*) inclusive of
ein'schlummern *intr* (SEIN) doze off
Ein'schluß *m* encirclement; **mit E.** (*genit*) including
ein'schmeicheln *ref* (**bei**) ingratiate oneself (with)
ein'schmeichelnd *adj* ingratiating
ein'schmuggeln *tr* smuggle in
ein'schnappen *intr* (SEIN) snap shut; (fig) take offense
ein'schneidend *adj* (fig) incisive
Ein'schnitt *m* cut, incision; (*Kerbe*) notch; (geol) gorge; (pros) caesura
ein'schnüren *tr* tie up; pinch
ein'schränken *tr* (**auf** *acc*) restrict (to), confine (to); (*Ausgaben*) cut; (*Behauptung*) qualify || *ref* economize
Ein'schränkung *f* (–;–en) restriction; **ohne jede E.** without reservation
Ein'schreibebrief *m* registered letter
ein'schreiben §62 *tr* enroll; (*Brief*) register; (*eintragen*) enter; **e—n Brief e. lassen** send a letter by registered mail || *ref* register
ein'schreiten §86 *intr* (SEIN) step in, intervene; (**gegen**) take action (against)
ein'schrumpfen *intr* (SEIN) shrivel up
ein'schüchtern *tr* intimidate, overawe
Ein'schüchterung *f* (–;) intimidation
ein'schulen *tr* enroll in school
Ein'schuß *m* hit (*of a bullet*)
ein'schütten *tr* pour in
ein'segnen *tr* (*neues Gebäude*) consecrate; (*konfirmieren*) confirm
ein'sehen §138 *tr* inspect; (*Akten*) consult; (fig) realize; (mil) observe ||

Einsehen *n*—**ein E. haben** show (some) consideration
ein'seifen *tr* soap; (coll) softsoap
ein'seitig *adj* one-sided
ein'senden §140 *tr* send in, submit
Ein'sender –**in** §6 *mf* sender
ein'senken *tr* (**in** *acc*) sink (into)
ein'setzen *tr* insert, put in; (*Geld*) bet; (*Leben*) risk; (*Polizei*) call out; (*Truppen*) commit; (*Kräfte*) muster; (*Einfluß*) use; (*Beamten*) install; (*er-nennen*) appoint; (*einpflanzen*) plant; (*Artillerie, Tanks, Bomber*) employ; (*Edelsteine*) mount || *ref* (**für**) stand up (for) || *intr* set in, begin; (*mus*) come in
Ein'sicht *f* inspection; (fig) insight
ein'sichtig *adj* understanding
ein'sichtsvoll *adj* understanding
ein'sickern *intr* (SEIN) seep in; (mil) infiltrate
Einsiedelei [aɪnzidə'laɪ] *f* (–;-en) hermitage
Einsiedler –**in** ['aɪnzidlər(ɪn)] §6 *mf* hermit, recluse
einsilbig ['aɪnzɪlbɪç] *adj* monosyllabic; (fig) taciturn
ein'sinken §143 *intr* (SEIN) sink in; (*Erdboden*) subside
ein'sparen *tr* economize on, save
ein'sperren *tr* lock up
ein'springen §142 *intr* (SEIN) jump in; (**für**) substitute (for); (tech) catch
ein'spritzen *tr* inject
Ein'spritzung *f* (–;-en) injection
Ein'spruch *m* objection; (jur) appeal
einspurig ['aɪn/purɪç] *adj* single-track
einst [aɪnst] *adv* once; (*künftig*) someday; **e. wie jezt** (now) as ever
Ein'stand *m* (tennis) deuce
ein'stecken *tr* insert, put in; stick in, pocket; (*Schwert*) sheathe; (*hinneh-men*) take; (coll) lock up, jail
ein'stehen §146 *intr* (SEIN) (**für**) vouch (for), stand up (for); **für die Folgen e.** take the responsibility
ein'steigen §148 *intr* (SEIN) get in; **alle e.!** all aboard!
Ein'steigkarte *f* (aer) boarding pass
Ein'steigloch *n* manhole
einstellbar ['aɪnstelbar] *adj* adjustable
ein'stellen *tr* put in; (*Arbeiter*) hire; (*Gerät*) set, adjust; (*beenden*) stop, quit; (*Sender*) tune in on; (*Fernglas, Kamera*) focus; **die Arbeit e.** go on strike; **etw bei j-m e.** leave s.th. at s.o.'s house; **in die Garage e.** put into the garage; **zum Heeresdienst e.** induct || *ref* show up, turn up; **sich e. auf** (*acc*) attune oneself to
Ein'stellung *f* (–;-en) adjustment; setting; focusing; stoppage; (*der Feind-seligkeiten, Zahlungen*) suspension; hiring; (aut) timing; (mil) induction; **E. des Feuers** cease-fire; **geistige E.** mental attitude
einstig ['aɪnstɪç] *adj* former; (*verstor-ben*) late; (*künftig*) future
ein'stimmen *intr* join in; **e. in** (*acc*) agree to, consent to
einstimmig ['aɪn/tɪmɪç] *adj* unanimous
ein'studieren *tr* study; rehearse
ein'stufen *tr* classify

ein'stürmen *intr* (SEIN) (**auf** *acc*) rush (at); (mil) charge
Ein'sturz *m* (–es;) collapse
ein'stürzen *intr* (SEIN) collapse; **e. auf** (*acc*) (fig) overwhelm
einstweilen ['aɪnstvaɪlən] *adv* for the present; temporarily
einstweilig ['aɪnstvaɪlɪç] *adj* temporary
Ein'tänzer *m* gigolo
ein'tauschen *tr* trade in; **e. gegen** exchange for
ein'teilen *tr* divide; (*austeilen*) distribute; (*einstufen*) classify; (*Geld, Zeit*) budget; (*Arbeit*) plan
eintönig ['aɪntønɪç] *adj* monotonous
Ein'tönigkeit *f* (–;) monotony
Ein'topf *m*, **Ein'topfgericht** *n* one-dish meal
Ein'tracht *f* (–;) harmony, unity
einträchtig ['aɪntreçtɪç] *adj* harmonious
Eintrag ['aɪntrak] *m* (–[e]s;̈e) entry; **E. tun** (*dat*) hurt
ein'tragen §132 *tr* enter, register; (*Ge-winn*) bring in, yield; **j-m etw e.** bring down s.th. on s.o. || *ref* register
einträglich ['aɪntreklɪç] *adj* profitable, lucrative
Ein'tragung *f* (–;-en) entry
ein'treffen §151 *intr* (SEIN) arrive; (*in Erfüllung gehen*) come true
ein'treiben §62 *tr* drive in; (*Geld*) collect || *intr* (SEIN) drift in, sail in
ein'treten §152 *tr* smash in || *ref*—**sich** [*dat*] **e-n Nagel e.** step on a nail || *intr* (SEIN) enter; (*geschehen*) occur; (*Fieber*) develop; (*Fall, Not*) arise; (*Dunkelheit*) fall; **e. für** stand up for, champion; **e. in** (*acc*) join, enter
Ein'tritt *m* (–s;) entry; (*Einlaß*) admittance; (*Anfang*) beginning, onset; (rok) re-entry; **E. frei** free admission; **E. verboten** no admittance
Ein'trittsgeld *n* admission fee
Ein'trittskarte *f* admission ticket
ein'trocknen *intr* (SEIN) dry up
ein'trüben *ref* become overcast
ein'tunken *tr* (**in** *acc*) dip (into)
ein'üben *tr* practice; train, coach
ein'verleiben *tr* incorporate
Einvernahme ['aɪnfernamə] *f* (–;-n) interrogation
Ein'vernehmen *n* (–s;) agreement; **sich mit j-m ins E. setzen** try to come to an understanding with s.o.
einverstanden ['aɪnfer/tandən] *adj* in agreement || *interj* agreed!
Ein'verständnis *n* agreement; approval
ein'wachsen *tr* wax || *intr* (SEIN) (**in** *acc*) grow (into)
Ein'wand *m* (–s;̈e) objection
Ein'wanderer –**in** §6 *mf* immigrant
ein'wandern *intr* (SEIN) immigrate
Ein'wanderung *f* (–;) immigration
ein'wandfrei *adj* unobjectionable; (*ta-dellos*) flawless; (*Alibi, Zustand*) perfect; (*Quelle*) unimpeachable
einwärts ['aɪnverts] *adv* inward(s)
Einweg– *comb.fm.* disposable
ein'weichen *tr* soak
ein'weihen *tr* consecrate, dedicate; **e. in** (*acc*) initiate into; let in on

Ein'weihung *f* (-;-en) dedication; initiation

ein'weisen §118 *tr* install; (*Verkehr*) direct; **e. in** (*acc*) assign to; **j–n in seine Pflichten e.** brief s.o. in his duties; **j–n ins Krankenhaus e.** have s.o. admitted to the hospital

ein'wenden §140 *tr—etw e.* gegen raise an objection to; **nichts einzuwenden haben gegen** have no objections to

Ein'wendung *f* (-;-en) objection

ein'werfen §160 *tr* throw in; (*Fenster*) smash; (*Brief*) mail; (*Münze*) insert; (*fig*) interject

ein'wickeln *tr* wrap (up); (fig) trick

ein'willigen *intr* (**in** *acc*) agree (to)

ein'wirken *intr* (**auf** *acc*) have an effect (on), exercise infuence (on)

Ein'wirkung *f* (-;-en) effect, influence

Ein'wohner –in §6 *mf* inhabitant

Ein'wurf *m* (*Schlitz*) slot; (*e–r Münze*) insertion; (*Einwand*) objection

ein'wurzeln *ref* take root

Ein'zahl *f* (-;) singular

ein'zahlen *tr* pay in; (*in e–e Kasse*) deposit

Ein'zahlung *f* (-;-en) payment; deposit

Ein'zahlungsschein *m* deposit slip

einzäunen ['aɪntsɔɪnən] *tr* fence in

Einzel ['aɪntsəl] *n* (-s;-) singles

Einzel– *comb.fm.* individual; single; isolated; detailed; retail

Ein'zelbild *n* (cin) frame; (phot) still

Ein'zelfall *m* individual case

Ein'zelgänger *m* (coll) lone wolf

Ein'zelhaft *f* solitary confinement

Ein'zelhandel *m* retail trade

Ein'zelheit *f* (-;-en) item; detail, particular; **wegen näherer Einzelheiten** for further particulars

einzellig ['aɪntsɛlɪç] *adj* single-cell

einzeln ['aɪntsəln] *adj* single; particular, individual; separate

Ein'zelperson *f* individual

Ein'zelspiel *n* singles (match)

Ein'zelwesen *n* individual

Ein'zelzimmer *n* single room; (*im Krankenhaus*) private room

ein'ziehen §163 *tr* draw in; retract; (*Flagge*) hawl down; (*Segel*) take in; (*Münzen*) call in; (*eintreiben*) collect; (mil) draft || *intr* (SEIN) move in; **e. in** (*acc*) enter; penetrate

einzig ['aɪntsɪç] *adj & adv* only; **e. darstellen** be unique || *indef pron—* **ein einziger** one only; **kein einziger** not a single one

ein'zigartig *adj* unique; extraordinary

Ein'zug *m* entry; moving in; (*Beginn*) start; (typ) indentation; **seinen E. halten** make one's entry

ein'zwängen *tr* (**in** *acc*) squeeze (into)

Eis [aɪs] *n* (-es;) ice; (*Speise–*) ice cream || ['e·ɪs] *n* (-;-s) (mus) E sharp

Eis'bahn *f* ice-skating rink

Eis'bär *m* polar bear

Eis'bein *n* (culin) pigs feet

Eis'berg *m* iceberg

Eis'beutel *m* (med) ice pack

Eis'blume *f* window frost

Eis'creme *f* ice cream

Eis'diehle *f* ice cream parlor

Eisen ['aɪzən] *n* (-s;-) iron; **altes E.** scrap iron; **heißes E.** (fig) hot potato; **zum alten E. werfen** (fig) scrap

Ei'senbahn *f* railroad; **mit der E.** by train, by rail

Ei'senbahndamm *m* railroad embankment

Ei'senbahner *m* (-s;-) railroader

Ei'senbahnknotenpunkt *m* railroad junction

Ei'senblech *n* sheet iron

Ei'senerz *n* iron ore

Ei'senhütte *f* ironworks

Ei'senwaren *pl* hardware, ironware

Ei'senwarenhandlung *f* hardware store

Ei'senzeit *f* iron age

eisern ['aɪzərn] *adj* iron; (*Fleiß*) unflagging; (*Rationen*) emergency

Eis'glätte *f* icy road conditions

eis'grau *adj* hoary

eisig ['aɪsɪç] *adj* icy; icy-cold

Eis'kappe *f* ice cap

Eis'kunstlauf *m* figure skating

Eis'lauf *m* ice skating

Eis'laufbahn *f* ice-skating rink

eis'laufen §105 *intr* (SEIN) ice-skate

Eis'läufer –in §6 *mf* skater

Eis'meer *n—***Nördliches E.** Arctic Ocean; **Südliches E.** Antarctic Ocean

Eis'pickel *m* ice axe

Eis'schnellauf *m* speed skating

Eis'scholle *f* ice floe

Eis'schrank *m* icebox

Eis'vogel *m* kingfisher

Eis'würfel *m* ice cube

Eis'würfelschale *f* ice-cube tray

Eis'zapfen *m* icicle

Eis'zeit *f* ice age, glacial period

eitel ['aɪtəl] *adj* (*nutzlos*) vain, empty; (*selbstgefällig*) vain; || *invar adj* pure || *adv* merely

Ei'telkeit *f* (-;) vanity

Eiter ['aɪtər] *m* (-s;) pus

Ei'terbeule *f* boil, abscess

eitern ['aɪtərn] *intr* fester, suppurate

Ei'terung *f* (-;-en) festering

eitrig ['aɪtrɪç] *adj* pussy

Ei'weiß *n* (-es;-e) egg white; albumen

Ekel ['ekəl] *m* (-s;) (vor *dat*) disgust (at) || *n* (-s;) (coll) pest

ekelerregend ['ekələregənt] *adj* sickening, nauseating

e'kelhaft *adj* disgusting

ekeln ['ekəln] *impers—***es eket mir** or **mich** I am disgusted || *ref* (vor *dat*) feel disgusted (at)

eklig ['eklɪç] *adj* disgusting, revolting; nasty, beastly

Ekzem [ek'tsem] *n* (-s;-e) eczema

elastisch [e'lastɪʃ] *adj* elastic

Elch [ɛlç] *m* (-[e]s;-e) elk, moose

Elefant [ele'fant] *m* (-en;-en) elephant

Elefan'tenreiber *m* mahout

Elefan'tenzahn *m* elephant's tusk

elegant [ele'gant] *adj* elegant

Eleganz [ele'gants] *f* (-;) elegance

Elektriker [ɛ'lektrɪkər] *m* (-s;-) electrician

elektrisch [ɛ'lektrɪʃ] *adj* electric(al)

elektrisieren [ɛlektri'ziːrən] *tr* electrify

Elektrolyse [elektro'lyːzə] *f* (-;-) electricity

Elektrizitäts– *comb.fm.* electric, electro–

Elektro– [ɛlɛktrə] *comb.fm.* electrical, electro–

Elektrode [ɛlɛk'trodə] *f* (–ʒ–n) electrode

Elek'trogerät *n* electrical appliance

Elektrizität [ɛlɛktrɪtsɪ'tɛt] *f* (–ʒ) electricity

Elek·tron [e'lɛktrɔn] *n* (–ʒ;–tronen ['trɔnən]) electron

Elektronen– [ɛlɛktrɔnən–] *comb.fm.* electronic

Elektronik [ɛlɛk'trɔnɪk] *f* (–ʒ) electronics

Elektrotechnik *f* (–ʒ) electrical engineering

Elektrotech'niker *m* (–s;–) electrical engineer

Element [elɛ'mɛnt] *n* (–[e]s;–e) element; (elec) cell

elementar [elɛmɛn'tar] *adj* elementary

Elementar'buch *n* primer

Elen ['elɛn] *m & n* (–s;–) elk

elend ['elɛnt] *adj* miserable ‖ **Elend** *n* (–[e]s) misery; extreme poverty; **das graue E.** the blues

E'lendsviertel *n* slums

elf [elf] *adj & pron* eleven ‖ **Elf** *f* (–ʒ–en) eleven

Elfe ['ɛlfə] *m* (–n;–n), *f* (–ʒ–n) elf

Elfenbein ['ɛlfənbaɪn] *n* (–s;) ivory

elfte ['ɛlftə] §9 *adj & pron* eleventh

Elftel ['ɛlftəl] *n* (–s;–) eleventh (*part*)

Elite [e'litə] *f* (–ʒ) elite, flower

Ellbogen ['ɛlbogən] *m* (–s;–) elbow

Ell'bogenfreiheit *f* elbowroom

Elsaß ['ɛlzas] *n* (–ʒ) Elsace

elsässisch ['ɛlzɛsɪʃ] *adj* Alsatian

Elster ['ɛlstər] *f* (–ʒ–n) magpie

elterlich ['ɛltərlɪç] *adj* parental

Eltern ['ɛltərn] *pl* parents; **nicht von schlechtern E.** (coll) terrific

El'ternbeirat *m* Parent-Teacher Association

El'ternhaus *n* home

el'ternlos *adj* orphaned; **elternlose Zeugung** spontaneous generation

El'ternschaft *f* parenthood

El'ternteil *m* parent

Email [e'maj] *n* (–s;), **Emaille** [e'maljə] *f* (–ʒ) enamel

Email'geschirr *n* enamelware

Email'lack *m* enamel paint

emaillieren [ema(l)'jirən] *tr* enamel

Email'waren *pl* enamelware

emanzipieren [emantsɪ'pirən] *tr* emancipate

Embargo [ɛm'bargo] *n* (–s;–s) embargo

Embo·lie [ɛmbo'li] *f* (–ʒ–lien ['li·ən]) embolism

Embry·o ['ɛmbry·o] *m* (–s;–onen ['ɔnən]) embryo

Emigrant –in [emɪ'grant(ɪn)] §7 *mf* emigrant

Emission [emɪ'sjon] *f* (–ʒ–en) emission; (fin) issuance; (rad) broadcasting

empfahl [ɛm'pfal] *pret* of **empfehlen**

Empfang [ɛm'pfaŋ] *m* (–[e]s;–̈e) reception; (*Erhalten*) receipt; (*im Hotel*) reception desk

empfangen [ɛm'pfaŋən] §73 *tr* receive; (*Kind*) conceive

Empfänger –in (ɛm'pfɛŋər(ɪn)] §6 *mf* receiver, recipient; addressee

empfänglich [ɛm'pfɛŋlɪç] *adj* (für) susceptible (to)

Empfängnis [ɛm'pfɛŋnɪs] *f* (–ʒ) conception

empfäng'nisverhütend *adj* contraceptive; **empfängnisverhütendes Mittel** contraceptive

Empfäng'nisverhütung *f* contraception

Empfangs'chef *m* desk clerk

Empfangs'dame *f* receptionist; (*im Restaurant*) hostess

Empfangs'schein *m* (com) receipt

empfehlen [ɛm'pfelən] §147 *tr* recommend; **e. Sie mich** (*dat*) remember me to ‖ *ref* say goodbye

empfeh'lenswert *adj* commendable

Empfeh'lung *f* (–ʒ–en) recommendation; (*Gruß*) compliments

empfinden [ɛm'pfɪndən] §59 *tr* feel

empfindlich [ɛm'pfɪntlɪç] *adj* sensitive; delicate, touchy; (*Kälte*) bitter; (gegen) susceptible (to)

Empfind'lichkeit *f* (–ʒ–en) sensitivity, touchiness; susceptibility

empfindsam [ɛm'pfɪntzam] *adj* sensitive, touchy; sentimental

Empfind'samkeit *f* (–ʒ–en) sensibility; sentimentality

Empfin'dung *f* (–ʒ–en) sensation; feeling, sentiment

empfin'dungslos *adj* numb; (fig) callous

Empfin'dungswort *n* (gram) interjection

Emphysem [ɛmfy'zem] *n* (–s;) emphysema

empor [ɛm'por] *adv* up, upwards

empören [ɛm'pørən] *tr* anger, shock ‖ *ref* rebel, revolt; (mil) mutiny

empor'fahren §71 *intr* (SEIN) jump up

empor'kommen §99 *intr* (SEIN) rise up; (*in der Welt*) get ahead

Emporkömmling [ɛm'porkœmlɪŋ] *m* (–s;–e) upstart, parvenu

empor'ragen *intr* tower, rise

empor'steigen §148 *intr* (SEIN) rise

empor'streben *intr* (SEIN) rise, soar; (fig) aspire

Empö'rung *f* (–ʒ–en) revolt; (über *acc*) indignation (at)

emsig ['ɛmzɪç] *adj* industrious, busy

Em'sigkeit *f* (–ʒ) industry; activity

End– [ɛnt] *comb.fm.* final, ultimate

Ende ['ɛndə] *n* (–s;–n) end; ending; outcome; **letzten Endes** in the final analysis; **zu E. gehen** end; **zu E. sein** be over

enden ['ɛndən] *tr & intr* end; **nicht e. wollend** unending

End'ergebnis *n* final result, upshot

End'gerade *f* (–ʒ) home stretch

end'gültig *adj* final, definitive

endigen ['ɛndɪgən] *tr & intr* end; **e. auf** (*acc*) (gram) terminate in

Endivie [ɛn'divjə] *f* (–ʒ–n) endive

End'lauf *m* (sport) final heat

end'lich *adj* final; limited, finite ‖ *adv* finally, at last

end'los *adj* endless

End'runde *f* final round, finals

End'station *f* final stop, terminus
End'summe *f* sum total
End'termin *m* final date; closing date
En'dung *f* (–;–en) ending
Ener·gie [ener'gi] *f* (–;–gien ['gi·ən]) energy
energisch [e'nergɪʃ] *adj* energetic
eng [ɛŋ] *adj* narrow; tight; (*Freunde*) close; (*innig*) intimate; **im engeren Sinne** strictly speaking
engagieren [ãga'zirən] *tr* engage, hire || *ref* commit oneself
Enge ['ɛŋə] *f* (–;–n) narrowness; tightness; (*Meer-*) strait; (fig) tight spot
Engel ['ɛŋəl] *m* (–s;–) angel
en'gelhaft *adj* angelic
eng'herzig *adj* stingy; petty
England ['ɛŋlant] *n* (–s;) England
Engländer ['ɛŋlɛndər] *m* (–s;–) Englishman; **die E.** the English
Engländerin ['ɛŋlɛndərɪn] *f* (–;–nen) Englishwoman
englisch ['ɛŋlɪʃ] *adj* English
Eng'paß *m* pass, defile; (fig) bottleneck
engros [ã'gro] *adv* wholesale
engstirnig ['ɛŋʃtɪrnɪç] *adj* narrow-minded
Enkel ['ɛŋkəl] *m* (–s;–) grandson
Enkelin ['ɛŋkəlɪn] *f* (–;–nen) granddaughter
En'kelkind *n* grandchild
enorm [e'nɔrm] *adj* enormous
Ensemble [ã'sãbl(ə)] *n* (–s;–s) (mus) ensemble; (theat) company, cast
ent- [ɛnt] *insep pref*
entarten [ɛnt'artən] *intr* (SEIN) degenerate
entartet [ɛnt'artət] *adj* degenerate; (fig) decadent
entäu'ßern *ref* (*genit*) divest oneself of
entbehren [ɛnt'berən] *tr* lack, miss; do without; spare; dispense with
entbehr'lich *adj* dispensable; needless, superfluous
Entbeh'rung *f* (–;–en) privation, need
entbin'den §59 *tr* release, absolve; (*Frau*) deliver || *intr* give birth
Entbin'dung *f* (–;–en) dispensation; (*Niederkunft*) delivery, childbirth
Entbin'dungsanstalt *f* maternity hospital
entblät'tern *tr* defoliate || *ref* defoliate; (coll) strip
entblößen [ɛnt'bløsən] *tr* bare; uncover; (mil) expose || *ref* strip; remove one's hat
entbren'nen §97 *intr* (SEIN) flare up
entdecken (**entdek'ken**) *tr* discover || *ref*—**sich j–m e.** confide in s.o.
Entdeckung (**Entdek'kung**) *f* (–;–en) discovery
Ente ['ɛntə] *f* (–;–n) duck; (coll) hoax
enteh'ren *tr* dishonor; (*Mädchen*) violate, deflower
enteh'rend *adj* disgraceful
Enteh'rung *f* (–;–en) disgrace; rape
enteig'nen *tr* dispossess
enteisen [ɛnt'aizən] *tr* defrost; deice
enter'ben *tr* disinherit
Enterich ['ɛntərɪç] *m* (–s;–e) drake
entern ['ɛntərn] *tr* (naut) board
entfachen [ɛnt'faxən] *tr* kindle; (fig) provoke

entfah'ren §71 *intr* (SEIN) (*dat*) slip out (on)
entfal'len §72 *intr* (SEIN) (*dat*) slip (from); **auf j–n e.** fall to s.o.'s share; **entfällt** not applicable
entfal'ten *tr* unfold; display; (mil) deploy || *ref* unfold; develop
entfernen [ɛnt'fernən] *tr* remove || *ref* withdraw, move away; deviate
entfernt [ɛnt'fernt] *adj* distant; **nicht weit davon e. zu** (*inf*) far from (*ger*)
Entfer'nung *f* (–;–en) removal; range; distance; absence
Entfer'nungsmesser *m* (phot) range finder
entfes'seln *tr* unleash
entflam'men *tr* inflame || *intr* (SEIN) ignite; flash; (fig) flare up
entflech'ten *tr* disentangle; (*Kartell*) break up; (mil) disengage
entflie'hen §75 *intr* (SEIN) flee, escape; (*Zeit*) fly
entfremden [ɛnt'fremdən] *tr* alienate
entfrosten [ɛnt'frɔstən] *tr* defrost
entführ'ren *tr* abduct; kidnap; (*Flugzeug*) hijack; (hum) steal
Entführ'rer –in §6 *mf* abductor, kidnaper; (aer) hijacker
Entführ'rung *f* (–;–en) abduction; kidnaping; (aer) hijacking
entge'gen *prep* (*dat*) contrary to; in the direction of, towards
entge'gengehen §82 *intr* (SEIN) (*dat*) go to meet; (*dat*) face, confront
entge'gengesetzt *adj* contrary, opposite
entge'genhalten §90 *tr* hold out; point out, say in answer
entge'genkommen §99 *intr* (SEIN) (*dat*) approach; (*dat*) come to meet; (*dat*) meet halfway || **Entgegenkommen** *n* (–s;) courtesy
entge'genkommend *adj* on-coming; (fig) accommodating
entge'genlaufen §105 *intr* (SEIN) (*dat*) run towards; (*dat*) run counter to
entge'gennehmen §116 *tr* accept, receive
entge'gensehen §138 *intr* (*dat*) look forward to; (*dat*) await; (*dat*) face
entge'gensetzen *tr* put up, offer
entge'genstehen §146 *intr* (*dat*) oppose
entge'genstellen *tr* set in opposition || *ref* (*dat*) oppose, resist
entge'genstrecken *tr* (*dat*) stretch out (toward)
entge'gentreten §152 *intr* (SEIN) (*dat*) walk toward; (fig) (*dat*) confront
entgegnen [ɛnt'gegnən] *tr & intr* reply
Entgeg'nung *f* (–;–en) reply
entge'hen §82 *intr* (SEIN) (*dat*) escape, elude; **sich** [*dat*] **etw e. lassen** let s.th. slip by
Entgelt [ɛnt'gelt] *n* (–[e]s;) compensation, payment
entgel'ten §83 *tr* pay for
entgeistert [ɛnt'gaistərt] *adj* aghast
entgleisen [ɛnt'glaizən] *intr* (SEIN) jump the track; (fig) make a slip
Entglei'sung *f* (–;–en) derailment; (fig) slip
entglei'ten §86 *intr* (SEIN) (*dat*) slip away (from)
entgräten [ɛnt'gretən] *tr* bone (*a fish*)

enthaaren [ɛntˈhɑːrən] *tr* remove the hair from
Enthaa/rungsmittel *n* hair remover
enthal/ten §90 *tr* contain; comprise ‖ *ref* (*genit*) refrain (from); **sich der Stimme e.** (parl) abstain
enthaltsam [ɛntˈhaltzam] *adj* abstinent
Enthalt/samkeit *f* (–;) abstinence
Enthal/tung *f* (–;-en) abstention
enthär/ten *tr* (*Wasser*) soften
enthaupten [ɛntˈhauptən] *tr* behead
enthäuten [ɛntˈhɔɪtən] *tr* skin
enthe/ben §94 *tr* (*genit*) exempt (from), relieve (of); (*e-s Amtes*) remove (*from office*)
enthei/ligen *tr* desecrate, profane
enthül/len *tr* unveil; reveal, expose
Enthül/lung *f* (–;-en) unveiling; (fig) exposé
enthül/sen *tr* shell; (*Mais*) husk
Enthusiasmus [ɛntuziˈasmʊs] *m* (–;) enthusiasm
enthusiastisch [ɛntuziˈastɪʃ] *adj* enthusiastic
entjungfern [ɛntˈjʊŋfərn] *tr* deflower
entkei/men *tr* sterilize; (*Milch*) pasteurize ‖ *intr* (SEIN) sprout
entkernen [ɛntˈkɛrnən] *tr* (*Obst*) pit
entklei/den *tr* undress; (*genit*) strip (of), divest (of) ‖ *ref* undress
Entklei/dungsnummer *f* striptease act
Entklei/dungsrevue *f* striptease show
entkom/men §99 *intr* (SEIN) (*dat*) escape (from) ‖ **Entkommen** *n* (–s;) escape
entkor/ken *tr* uncork, open
entkräften [ɛntˈkrɛftən] *tr* weaken; (*Argument*) refute
entla/den §103 *tr* unload; (*Batterie*) discharge ‖ *ref* (*Gewehr*) go off; (*Sturm*) break; (elec) discharge; **sein Zorn entlud sich** he vented his anger
Entla/dung *f* (–;-en) unloading; discharge; explosion; **zur E. bringen** detonate
entlang/ *adv* along ‖ *prep* (*dat* or *acc* or an *dat*; or after *genit* or *dat*) along
entlarven [ɛntˈlarfən] *tr* expose
entlas/sen §104 *tr* dismiss, fire; set free; (mil) discharge
Entlas/sungspapiere *pl* discharge papers
entla/sten *tr* unburden; (**von**) relieve (of); (jur) exonerate
Entla/stungsstraße *f* bypass
Entla/stungszeuge *m* witness for the defense
entlauben [ɛntˈlaubən] *tr* defoliate
entlaubt/ *adj* leafless
entlau/fen §105 *intr* (SEIN) (*dat*) run away (from); (*mit e-m Liebhaber*) elope
entlausen [ɛntˈlauzən] *tr* delouse
entledigen [ɛntˈleːdɪɡən] *tr* (*genit*) release (from) ‖ *ref* (*genit*) get rid (of), rid oneself (of)
entlee/ren *tr* empty; drain
entle/gen *adj* distant, remote
entleh/nen *tr* borrow
entlei/hen §81 *tr* borrow
entlo/ben *ref* break the engagement
entlocken [ɛntˈlɔkən] *tr* elicit
entloh/nen *tr* pay, pay off
entlüf/ten *tr* ventilate

entmannen [ɛntˈmanən] *tr* castrate
entmilitarisieren [ɛntmɪlɪtariˈziːrən] *tr* demilitarize
entmutigen [ɛntˈmuːtɪɡən] *tr* discourage
entneh/men §116 *tr* (*dat*) take (from); (*Geld*) (*aus*) withdraw (from); (*dat* or *aus*) infer (from), gather (from)
entnerven [ɛntˈnɛrfən] *tr* enervate
entpuppen [ɛntˈpʊpən] *ref* emerge from the cocoon; **sich e. als** (fig) turn out to be
enträtseln [ɛntˈrɛtsəln] *tr* solve; (*Schriftzeichen*) decipher
entrei/ßen §53 *tr* (*dat*) wrest (from)
entrich/ten *tr* pay
entrin/nen §121 *intr* (SEIN) escape (from)
entrol/len *tr* unroll; unfurl ‖ *ref* unroll ‖ *intr* (SEIN) roll down
entrüsten [ɛntˈrʏstən] *tr* anger ‖ *ref*— **sich e. über** (*acc*) become incensed at; be shocked at
Entrü/stung *f* (–;) anger, indignation
entsa/gen *intr* (*dat*) renounce, forego; **dem Thron e.** abdicate
Entsatz/ *m* (–es;) (mil) relief
entschä/digen *tr* compensate; reimburse
Entschä/digung *f* (–;) compensation
Entschä/digungsanspruch *m* damage claim
entschär/fen *tr* defuse
Entscheid [ɛntˈʃaɪt] *m* (–[e]s;-e) (jur) decision
entschei/den §112 *tr*, *ref* & *intr* decide
entschei/dend *adj* decisive
Entschei/dung *f* (–;-en) decision
Entschei/dungsbefugnis *f* jurisdiction
Entschei/dungskampf *m* (sport) finals
Entschei/dungsspiel *n* (cards) rubber game; (sport) finals
Entschei/dungsstunde *f* moment of truth
entschei/dungsvoll *adj* critical ‖
entschieden [ɛntˈʃiːdən] *adj* decided; decisive; firm, resolute
entschla/fen §131 *intr* (SEIN) fall asleep; (*sterben*) pass away, die
entschlei/ern *tr* unveil; (fig) reveal
entschlie/ßen §76 *ref* (zu) decide (on)
Entschlie/ßung *f* (–;-en) (parl) resolution
entschlossen [ɛntˈʃlɔsən] *adj* resolute
entschlüp/fen *intr* (SEIN) (*dat*) slip away (from); (*dat*) slip out (on)
Entschluß/ *m* resolve, decision
entschlüs/seln *tr* decipher
Entschluß/kraft *f* will power
entschulden [ɛntˈʃʊldən] *tr* free of debt
entschuldigen [ɛntˈʃʊldɪɡən] *tr* excuse; exculpate ‖ *ref* apologize; **es läßt sich e.** it's excusable; **sich e. lassen** beg to be excused; **sich mit Unwissenheit e.** plead ignorance
entschul/digend *adj* apologetic
Entschul/digung *f* (–;-en) excuse; apology; **ich bitte um E.** I beg your pardon
Entschul/digungsgrund *m* excuse
entseelt [ɛntˈzeːlt] *adj* lifeless, dead
entsen/den §140 *tr* send off
entset/zen *tr* horrify; (mil) relieve ‖

ref (über *acc*) be horrified (at) || **Ent-setzen** *n* (-s;) horror

entsetz'lich *adj* horrible, appalling || *adv* (coll) awfully

Entset'zung *f* (-;) dismissal; (mil) relief

entsi'chern *tr* take (*a gun*) off safety

entsie'geln *tr* unseal

entsin'nen §121 *ref* (*genit*) recall

entspan'nen *tr* & *ref* relax

Entspan'nung *f* (-;) relaxation; (pol) detente

entspre'chen §64 *intr* (*dat*) correspond (to); (*dat*) meet, suit; (*dat*) be equivalent (to); (*dat*) answer (*a description*)

entspre'chend *adj* corresponding; adequate; equivalent || *adv* accordingly || *prep* (*dat*) according to

entsprin'gen §142 *intr* (SEIN) rise, originate; (*entlaufen*) escape

entstaatlichen [ent'ʃtɑtlɪçən] *tr* free from state control, denationalize

entstam'men *intr* (SEIN) (*dat*) descend (from), originate (from)

entste'hen §146 *intr* (SEIN) originate

Entste'hung *f* (-;) origin

entstel'len *tr* disfigure; deface; (*Tatsachen*) distort

enttäu'schen *tr* disappoint

entthronen [ent'tronən] *tr* dethrone

entvölkern [ent'fœlkərn] *tr* depopulate

entwach'sen §155 *intr* (SEIN) (*dat*) outgrow

entwaff'nen *tr* disarm

entwar'nen *intr* sound the all-clear

entwäs'sern *tr* drain; dehydrate

entweder [ent'vedər] *conj*—**entweder ... oder** either ... or

entwei'chen §85 *intr* (SEIN) escape

entwei'hen *tr* desecrate, profane

entwen'den *tr* steal

entwer'fen §160 *tr* sketch; draft

entwer'ten *tr* (*Geld*) depreciate; (*Briefmarke*) cancel; (*Karten*) punch

entwickeln (entwik'keln) *tr* develop; evolve; (mil) deploy || *ref* develop

Entwick'lung *f* (-;-en) development; evolution; (mil) deployment

Entwick'lungsland *n* developing country

Entwick'lungslehre *f* theory of evolution

entwin'den §59 *tr* (*dat*) wrest (from) || *ref* extricate oneself

entwirren [ent'vɪrən] *tr* & *ref* unravel

entwi'schen *intr* (SEIN) escape; (*dat* or *aus*) slip away (from)

entwöhnen [ent'vønən] *tr* wean; **j—n e.** (*genit*) break s.o. of || *ref* (*genit*) give up

Entwurf' *m* (-s;̈-e) sketch; draft

entwur'zeln *tr* uproot

entzau'bern *tr* disenchant

entzie'hen §163 *tr* (*dat*) withdraw (from), take away (from); (chem) extract; **j—m das Wort z.** (parl) rule s.o. out of order || *ref* (*dat*) shirk, elude

Entzie'hungsanstalt *f* rehabilitation center

entziffern [ent'tsɪfərn] *tr* decipher

entzücken (entzük'ken) *tr* delight

Entzückung (Entzük'kung) *f* (-;-en) delight, rapture

Entzug' *m* (-[e]s;) deprivation

entzündbar [ent'tsyntbɑr] *adj* inflammable

entzün'den *tr* set on fire; (fig) inflame || *ref* catch fire; (pathol) become inflamed

Entzün'dung *f* (-;) kindling; (pathol) inflammation

entzwei' *adv* in two, apart

entzwei'brechen §64 *tr* & *intr* break in two, snap

entzweien [ent'tsvaɪ-ən] *tr* divide

Enzykli·ka [en'tsyklɪkɑ] *f* (-;-ken [kən]) encyclicle

Enzyklopä·die [entsyklɔpɛ'di] *f* (-; -dien ['di·ən]) encyclopedia

Enzym [en'tsym] *n* (-[e]s;-e) enzyme

Epaulette [epɔ'letə] *f* (-;-n) epaulet

ephemer [efe'mer] *adj* ephemeral

Epide·mie [epɪde'mi] *f* (-;-mien ['mi·ən]) epidemic

epidemisch [epɪ'demɪ] *adj* epidemic

Epigramm [epɪ'gram] *n* (-s;-e) epigram

Epik ['epɪk] *f* (-;) epic poetry

Epilog [epɪ'lok] *m* (-s;-e) epilogue

episch ['epɪ] *adj* epic

Episode [epɪ'zodə] *f* (-;-n) episode

Epoche [e'pɔxə] *f* (-;-n) epoch

Epos ['epɔs] *n* (-; **Epen** ['epən]) epic

Equipage [ek(v)ɪ'pɑʒə] *f* (-;-n) carriage; (naut) crew; (sport) team

Equipe [e'k(v)ɪp(ə)] *f* (-;-n) team; group

er [er] §11 *pers pron* he; it

er- [er] *insep pref*

erach'ten *tr* think || **Erachten** *n* (-s;) opinion; **meines Erachtens** in my opinion

erar'beiten *tr* acquire (*by working*)

Erb- [erp] *comb.fm.* hereditary

Erb'anfall *m* inheritance

Erb'anlage *f* (biol) gene

erbarmen [er'barmən] *tr* move to pity || *ref* (*genit*) pity; **erbarme Dich unser** have mercy on us || **Erbarmen** *n* (-s;) pity, mercy

erbar'menswert, **erbar'menswürdig** *adj* pitiable

erbärmlich [er'bermlɪç] *adj* pitiful; wretched, miserable || *adv* awfully

erbar'mungslos *adj* pitiless

erbau'en *tr* erect; (fig) edify || *ref* (an *dat*) be edified (by)

Erbau'er *m* (-s;-) builder

erbau'lich *adj* edifying

Erbau'ung *f* (-;) building; edification

Erbau'ungsbuch *n* book of devotions

erb'berechtigt *adj* eligible as heir

Erbe ['erbə] *m* (-n;-n) heir; **ohne Leibliche Erben** without issue || *n* (-s;) inheritance, heritage; **väterliches E.** patrimony

erbe'ben *intr* (SEIN) tremble

erb'eigen *adj* hereditary

erben ['erbən] *tr* inherit

erbet'teln *tr* get (*by begging*)

erbeuten [er'bɔɪtən] *tr* capture

Erb'feind *m* traditional enemy

Erb'folge *f* succession

erbie'ten §58 *ref* volunteer

Erbin ['ɛrbɪn] *f* (–;–nen) heiress
erbit'ten §60 *ref*—sich [*dat*] etw e. ask for s.th., request s.th.
erbittern [ɛr'bɪtərn] *tr* embitter
Erb'krankheit *f* hereditary disease
erblassen [ɛr'blasən] *intr* (SEIN) turn pale
Erblasser –in ['ɛrplasər(ɪn)] §6 *mf* testator
erbleichen [ɛr'blaɪçən] §85 & §109 *intr* (SEIN) turn pale; (poet) die
erb'lich *adj* hereditary
Erb'lichkeit *f* (–;) heredity
erblicken (erblik'ken) *tr* spot, see
erblinden [ɛr'blɪndən] *intr* (SEIN) go blind
Erblin'dung *f* (–;) loss of sight
Erb'onkel *m* (coll) rich uncle
erbre'chen §64 *tr* break open || *ref* vomit
erbrin'gen §65 *tr* produce
Erb'schaft *f* (–;–en) inheritance
Erbse ['ɛrpsə] *f* (–;–n) pea
Erb'stück *n* heirloom
Erb'sünde *f* original sin
Erb'tante *f* (coll) rich aunt
Erb'teil *m* share (in an inheritance)
Erd– [ert] *comb.fm.* earth, of the earth; geo–; ground
Erd'anschluß *m* (elec) ground
Erd'arbeiten *pl* excavation work
Erd'bahn *f* orbit of the earth
Erd'ball *m* globe
Erd'beben *n* (–s;–) earthquake
Erd'bebenmesser *m* seismograph
Erd'beere *f* strawberry
Erd'boden *m* ground, earth; dem E. gleichmachen raze (to the ground)
Erde ['ɛrdə] *f* (–;–n) earth; ground, soil, land; (elec) ground wire; zu ebener E. on the ground floor
erden ['ɛrdən] *tr* (elec) ground
erden'ken §66 *tr* think up
erdenk'lich *adj* imaginable
Erd'gas *n* natural gas
Erd'geschoß *n* ground floor
erdich'ten *tr* fabricate, think up
Erdich'tung *f* (–;–en) fabrication
erdig ['ɛrdɪç] *adj* earthy
Erd'innere §5 *n* interior of the earth
Erd'klumpen *m* clod
Erd'kreis *m* earth, world
Erd'kugel *f* globe, sphere; world
Erd'kunde *f* geography
Erd'leitung *f* (elec) ground wire
Erd'nuß *f* peanut
Erd'nußbutter *f* peanut butter
Erd'öl *n* petroleum, oil; auf E. stoßen strike oil
erdolchen [ɛr'dɔlçən] *tr* stab
Erd'reich *n* soil
erdreisten [ɛr'draɪstən] *ref* have the nerve, have the audacity
Erd'rinde *f* crust of the earth
erdros'seln *tr* strangle
erdrücken (erdrük'ken) *tr* crush to death
erdrückend (erdrük'kend) *adj* overwhelming
Erd'rutsch *m* land slide
Erd'schicht *f* stratum
Erd'spalte *f* fissure; chasm
Erd'teil *m* continent

erdul'den *tr* suffer
ereifern [ɛr'aɪfərn] *ref* get excited
ereignen [ɛr'aɪgnən] *ref* happen, occur
Ereignis [ɛr'aɪgnɪs] *n* (–ses;–se) event, occurrence
ereig'nislos *adj* uneventful
ereig'nisvoll *adj* eventful
Erektion [erek'tsjon] *f* (–;–en) erection
Eremit [ere'mit] *m* (–en;–en) hermit
erer'ben *tr* inherit
erfah'ren *adj* experienced || §71 *tr* find out; (*erleben*) experience; (*Pflege*) receive
Erfah'rung *f* (–;–en) experience
erfas'sen *tr* grasp; understand; include; register, list
erfin'den §59 *tr* invent
Erfin'der –in §6 *mf* inventor
erfinderisch [ɛr'fɪndərɪʃ] *adj* inventive
Erfin'dung *f* (–;–en) invention
Erfin'dungsgabe *f* inventiveness
erfle'hen *tr* obtain (by entreaty)
Erfolg [ɛr'fɔlk] *m* (–[e]s;–e) success; (*Wirkung*) result
erfol'gen *intr* (SEIN) ensue; occur
erfolg'los *adj* unsuccessful || *adv* in vain
erfolg'reich *adj* successful
Erfolgs'mensch *m* go-getter
erfolg'versprechend *adj* promising
erforderlich [ɛr'fɔrdərlɪç] *adj* required, necessary
erfor'derlichenfalls *adv* if need be
erfordern [ɛr'fɔrdərn] *tr* require
Erfordernis [ɛr'fɔrdərnɪs] *n* (–ses;–se) requirement; exigency
erfor'schen *tr* investigate; (*Land*) explore
Erfor'scher –in §6 *mf* explorer
Erfor'schung *f* (–;–en) investigation; exploration
erfra'gen *tr* ask for; find out
erfreu'en *tr* delight || *ref* (an *dat*) be delighted (at); sich e. (*genit*) enjoy
erfreulich [ɛr'frɔɪlɪç] *adj* delightful; (*Nachricht*) welcome, good
erfreut [ɛr'frɔɪt] *adj* (über *acc*) glad (about); e. zu (*inf*) pleased to (*inf*)
erfrie'ren §77 *intr* (SEIN) freeze to death; (*Pflanzen*) freeze
Erfrie'rung *f* (–;–en) freeze
erfrischen [ɛr'frɪʃən] *tr* refresh
Erfri'schung *f* (–;–en) refreshment
erfül'len *tr* fill; fulfill; (*Aufgabe*) perform; (*Bitte*) comply with; (*Hoffnungen*) live up to || *ref* materialize
Erfül'lung *f* (–;) fulfillment; accomplishment; in E. gehen come true
erfunden [ɛr'fundən] *adj* made-up
ergänzen [ɛr'gentsən] *tr* complete; complement; (*Statue*) restore
ergän'zend *adj* complementary
ergattern [ɛr'gatərn] *tr* (coll) dig up
ergau'nern *tr*—etw von j–m e. cheat s.o. out of s.th.
erge'ben *adj* devoted || §80 *tr* yield; amount to; show || *ref* surrender; (*dat*) devote oneself (to); (aus) result (from); sich dem Trunk e. take to drinking; sich e. in (*acc*) resign oneself to
Erge'benheit *f* (–;) devotion; resignation

ergebenst [er'ge:bənst] *adv* respectfully

Ergebnis [er'ge:pnɪs] *n* (-ses;-se) result, outcome; (*Punktzahl*) score

Erge'bung *f* (-;) submission, resignation; (mil) surrender

erge'hen §82 *intr* (SEIN) come out, be published; **e. lassen** issue, publish; **etw über sich e. lassen** put up with s.th.; **Gnade vor Recht e. lassen** show leniency || *ref* take a stroll; **sich e. in** (*acc*) indulge in; **sich e. über** (*acc*) expatiate on || *impers*—**es ist ihm gut ergangen** things went well for him || **Ergehen** *n* (-s;) state of health

ergiebig [er'gi:bɪç] *adj* productive, fertile; rich, abundant

ergie'ßen §76 *ref* flow; pour out

ergötzen [er'gœtsən] *tr* amuse || *ref* (**an** *dat*) take delight (in)

ergötz'lich *adj* delightful

ergrau'en *intr* (SEIN) turn gray

ergrei'fen §88 *tr* seize; (*Verbrecher*) apprehend; (*Gemüt*) move; (*Beruf, Waffen*) take up; (*Maßnahmen*) take

Ergrei'fung *f* (-;) seizure

ergriffen [er'grɪfən] *adj* moved; **e. von** seized with

Ergriffenheit *f* (-;) emotion

ergrün'den *tr* get to the bottom of

Erguß' *m* discharge; (fig) flood of words

erha'ben *adj* elevated, lofty; **erhabene Arbeit** relief work; **e. sein über** (*acc*) be above

Erhalt' *m* (-es;) receipt

erhal'ten §90 *tr* get, receive; keep, keep up, maintain; conserve; (*Familie*) support; (*Gesundheit*) preserve; **Betrag dankend e.** (*stamped on bills*) paid; **gut e.** well preserved; **noch e. sein** survive || *ref* survive; (von) subsist (on)

erhältlich [er'hɛltlɪç] *adj* obtainable

Erhal'tung *f* (-;) preservation; maintenance; support; (*der Energie, usw.*) conservation

erhän'gen *tr* hang

erhär'ten *tr* harden; (fig) substantiate || *intr* (SEIN) harden

erha'schen *tr* catch; **e-n Blick von ihr e.** catch her eye

erhe'ben §94 *tr* raise; (*erhöhen*) elevate; (*preisen*) exalt; (*Steuern*) collect; (*Anklage*) bring; (*math*) raise || *ref* get up, rise, start; arise

erheblich [er'he:plɪç] *adj* considerable

Erhe'bung *f* (-;-en) elevation; promotion; uprising, revolt; **Erhebungen machen** make inquiries

erheitern [er'haɪtərn] *tr* amuse || *ref* cheer up

erhellen [er'hɛlən] *tr* light up; (fig) shed light on || *ref* grow light(er); light up || *impers*—**es erhellt** it appears

erhitzen [er'hɪtsən] *tr* heat; (fig) inflame || *ref* grow hot; get angry

erhöhen [er'hø:ən] *tr* raise; (fig) heighten || *ref* increase; be enhanced

Erhö'hung *f* (-;-en) rise

erho'len *ref* recover; relax

Erho'lung *f* (-;-en) recovery; relaxation; recreation

erho'lungsbedürftig *adj* in need of rest

Erho'lungsheim *n* convalescent home

erhö'ren *tr* (*Gebet*) hear; (*Bitte*) grant

erinnerlich [er'ɪnərlɪç] *adj*—**das ist mir nicht e.** it slipped my mind; **soviel mir e. ist** as far as I can remember

erinnern [er'ɪnərn] *tr* (**an** *acc*) remind (of) || *ref* (**an** *acc*) remember

Erin'nerung *f* (-;-en) recollection, remembrance; (*Mahnung*) reminder; **zur E. an** (*acc*) in memory of

Erin'nerungsvermögen *n* memory

erkalten [er'kaltən] *intr* (SEIN) cool off; (fig) grow cool

erkälten [er'kɛltən] *ref* catch cold

Erkäl'tung *f* (-;-en) cold

erkennbar [er'kɛnbar] *adj* recognizable

erkennen [er'kɛnən] §97 *tr* make out; recognize; detect; realize; **j-n e. für** (com) credit s.o. with; **sich zu e. geben** disclose one's identity; **j-n e. geben, daß** indicate that || *intr*—**auf e-e Geldstrafe e.** impose a fine; **gegen j-n e.** judge against s.o.

erkenntlich [er'kɛntlɪç] *adj* grateful

Erkennt'lichkeit *f* (-;) gratitude

Erkenntnis [er'kɛntnɪs] *f* (-;-se) insight, judgment, realization, knowledge; (philos) cognition || *n* (-ses; -se) decision, finding

Erker ['ɛrkər] *m* (-s;-) (archit) oriel

Er'kerfenster *n* bay window

erklären [er'klɛrən] *tr* explain, account for; (*aussprechen*) state

Erklä'rer -in §6 *mf* commentator

erklär'lich *adj* explicable

Erklä'rung *f* (-;-en) explanation; statement; commentary; (jur) deposition

erklin'gen §142 *intr* (SEIN) sound; (*widerhallen*) resound

erkor (er'kor) *pret* of **erkiesen**

erkoren [er'korən] *adj* chosen

erkranken [er'krankən] *intr* (SEIN) get sick; (*Pflanzen*) become diseased

erkühnen [er'ky:nən] *ref* dare, venture

erkunden [er'kundən] *tr* & *intr* reconnoiter

erkundigen [er'kundɪgən] *ref* inquire

Erkun'digung *f* (-;-en) inquiry

Erkun'dung *f* (-;) reconnaissance

erlahmen [er'lamən] *intr* (SEIN) tire; (*Kraft*) give out

erlangen [er'laŋən] *tr* reach; (*sich verschaffen*) get; **wieder e.** recover

Er-laß' [er'las] *m* (-lasses;-lässe) remission; exemption; edict, order

erlas'sen §104 *tr* release; (*Schulden*) cancel; (*Strafe*) remit; (*Sünden*) pardon; (*Verordnung*) issue; **e. Sie es mir zu** (*inf*) allow me not to (*inf*), don't ask me to (*inf*)

erläßlich [er'lɛslɪç] *adj* pardonable

erlauben [er'laubən] *tr* allow || *ref*—**sich** [*dat*] **e. zu** (*inf*) take the liberty to (*inf*); **sich** [*dat*] **nicht e.** not be able to afford

Erlaubnis [er'laupnɪs] *f* (-;-se) permission

Erlaub'nisschein *m* permit, license

erlaucht [er'lauxt] *adj* illustrious

erläutern [er'lɔɪtərn] *tr* explain

Erläu'terung *f* (-;-en) explanation

Erle ['ɛrlə] *f* (-;-n) (bot) alder
erle'ben *tr* live to see; experience
Erlebnis [ɛr'lepnɪs] *n* (-ses;-se) experience, adventure; occurrence
erledigen [ɛr'ledɪgən] *tr* settle; (*Post, Einkäufe, Gesuch*) attend to, take care of; **j-n e.** (coll) do s.o. in
erledigt [ɛr'ledɪçt] *adj* (& fig) finished; (*Stellung*) open; (coll) bushed
erle'gen *tr* pay down; (*töten*) kill
erleichtern [ɛr'laɪçtərn] *tr* lighten; make easy; (*Not*) relieve, ease
Erleich'terung *f* (-;) alleviation
erlei'den §106 *tr* suffer
erler'nen *tr* learn
erle'sen *adj* choice || §107 *tr* choose
erleuch'ten *tr* light up; enlighten
erlie'gen §108 *intr* (SEIN) (*dat*) succumb (to), fall victim (to)
erlogen [ɛr'logən] *adj* false
Erlös [ɛr'løs] *m* (-es;) proceeds
erlosch [ɛr'lɔʃ] *pret* of **erlöschen**
erloschen [ɛr'lɔʃən] *pp* of **erlöschen**
erlöschen [ɛr'lœʃən] §110 *intr* (SEIN) go out; (*Vertrag*) expire; (fig) become extinct
erlö'sen *tr* redeem; free; get (*by sale*)
Erlö'ser *m* (-s;-) deliverer; (relig) Redeemer
Erlö'sung *f* (-;) redemption
ermächtigen [ɛr'mɛçtɪgən] *tr* authorize
Ermäch'tigung *f* (-;-en) authorization
ermah'nen *tr* admonish
Ermah'nung *f* (-;-en) admonition
ermangeln [ɛr'maŋəln] *intr* (*genit*) lack; **es an nichts e. lassen** spare no pains; **nicht e. zu** (*inf*) not fail to (*inf*)
Erman'gelung *f—in E.** (*genit*) in default of
ermä'ßigen *tr* reduce
ermatten [ɛr'matən] *tr* tire || *intr* (SEIN) tire; grow weak; slacken
Ermat'tung *f* (-;) fatigue
ermes'sen §70 *tr* judge, estimate; realize; **e. aus** infer from || **Ermessen** *n* (-s;) judgment, opinion; **nach freiem E.** at one's discretion
ermitteln [ɛr'mɪtəln] *tr* ascertain || *intr* conduct an investigation
Ermitt'lung *f* (-;-en) ascertainment; **Ermittlungen** investigation
Ermitt'lungsausschuß *m* fact-finding committee
Ermitt'lungsbeamte *m* investigator
Ermitt'lungsverfahren *n* judicial inquiry
ermöglichen [ɛr'møklɪçən] *tr* enable, make possible
ermorden [ɛr'mɔrdən] *tr* murder
ermüden [ɛr'mydən] *tr* tire || *intr* (SEIN) tire, get tired
Ermü'dung *f* (-;) fatigue
ermuntern [ɛr'muntərn] *tr* cheer up; encourage || *ref* cheer up
Ermun'terung *f* (-;) encouragement
ermutigen [ɛr'mutɪgən] *tr* encourage
ernäh'ren *tr* nourish; (fig) support
Ernäh'rer -in §6 *mf* supporter
Ernäh'rung *f* (-;) nourishment; support; (physiol) nutrition
ernen'nen §97 *tr* nominate, appoint
erneuern [ɛr'nɔɪ-ərn] *tr* renew; reno-

vate; (*Gemälde*) restore; (*Öl*) change; (*Reifen*) retread; (mach) replace
erneu'ert *adj* repeated || *adv* anew
Erneu'erung *f* (-;-en) renewal; renovation; restoration; replacement
erniedrigen [ɛr'nidrɪgən] *tr* lower; (*demütigen*) humble; (*im Rang*) degrade || *ref* humble oneself; debase oneself
ernst [ɛrnst] *adj* earnest; serious || **Ernst** *m* (-[e]s;) seriousness; **im E.** in earnest
Ernst'fall *m—im E.** in case of emergency; (mil) in case of war
ernst'haft *adj* earnest, serious
ernst'lich *adj* earnest; serious
Ernte ['ɛrntə] *f* (-;-n) harvest; crop
ernten ['ɛrntən] *tr* reap, harvest
ernüch'tern *tr* sober; disallusion || *ref* sober up; be disallusioned
Ero'berer -in §6 *mf* conqueror
erobern [ɛr'obərn] *tr* conquer
Ero'berung *f* (-;-en) conquest
eröff'nen *tr* open; (*feierlich*) inaugurate; disclose || *ref* open; present itself; **sich j—m e.** unburden oneself to s.o.
Eröff'nung *f* (-;-en) (grand) opening; inauguration; announcement
erörtern [ɛr'œrtərn] *tr* discuss
erotisch [ɛ'rotɪʃ] *adj* erotic
Erpel ['ɛrpəl] *m* (-s;-) drake
erpicht [ɛr'pɪçt] *adj—e. auf* (*acc*) keen on, dead set on, hell bent on
erpres'sen *tr* extort; (*Person*) blackmail
Erpres'sung *f* (-;-en) extortion; blackmail
erpro'ben *tr* test, try out
erquicken [ɛr'kvɪkən] *tr* refresh
erquick'lich *adj* refreshing; agreeable
errat'en §63 *tr* guess
errech'nen *tr* calculate
erregbar [ɛr'rekbar] *adj* excitable; irritable
erregen [ɛr'regən] *tr* excite; cause || *ref* get excited, get worked up
Erre'gung *f* (-;) excitation; agitation; excitement; **E. öffentlichen Ärgernisses** disorderly conduct
erreichbar [ɛr'raɪçbar] *adj* reachable; available
errei'chen *tr* reach, attain; get to; (*Zug, Bus*) catch; **e., daß** bring it about that
erret'ten *tr* save, rescue
Erret'tung *f* (-;-en) rescue; (relig) Salvation
errich'ten *tr* erect; found
errin'gen §142 *tr* get; attain, achieve
errö'ten *intr* (SEIN) redden; blush
Errungenschaft [ɛr'ruŋənʃaft] *f* (-;-en) achievement; acquisition
Ersatz' *m* (-es;) substitute; replacement; compensation; (mil) recruitment
Ersatz- *comb.fm.* substitute, replacement; spare; alternative; recruiting
Ersatz'mann *m* substitute; alternate
Ersatz'stück *n*, **Ersatz'teil** *n* spare part, spare
erschaf'fen §126 *tr* create
Erschaf'fer -in §6 *mf* creator
Erschaf'fung *f* (-;-en) creation

erschal/len §127 *intr* (SEIN) begin to sound; ring out; resound

erschau/ern *intr* shudder

erschei/nen §128 *intr* (SEIN) appear; (*Buch*) come out, be published

Erschei/nung *f* (-;-en) appearance; apparition; phenomenon

erschie/ßen §76 *tr* shoot (dead)

Erschie/ßung *f* (-;-en) shooting, execution

Erschie/ßungskommando *n* firing squad

erschlaffen [er'∫lafən] *tr* relax; enervate || *intr* (SEIN) relax; weaken

erschla/gen §132 *tr* slay; **wie e.** dead tired

erschlie/ßen §76 *tr* open up; develop; **e. aus** infer from; derive from || *ref* —**sich j—m e.** unburden oneself to s.o.

erschöp/fen *tr* exhaust; (*fig*) deplete

erschrak [er'∫rak] *pret* of **erschrecken**

erschrecken (**erschrek/ken**) *tr* startle; shock || *ref* get scared || §134 *intr* (SEIN) be startled

erschreckend (**erschrek/kend**) *adj* terrifying; alarming; dreadful

erschüt/ten *tr* shake; upset; move deeply

Erschüt/terung *f* (-;-en) tremor; vibration; deep feeling; concussion

erschweren [er'∫veran] *tr* make more difficult; hamper, impede

erschwin/deln *tr*—**etw von j—m e.** cheat s.o. out of s.th.

erschwin/gen §142 *tr* afford

erschwing/lich *adj* within one's means

erse/hen §138 *tr* (**aus**) gather (from)

erseh/nen *tr* long for

ersetzbar [er'zetsbar] *adj* replaceable

erset/zen *tr* replace; (*Schaden*) compensate for; (*Kräfte*) renew; **j—m etw e.** reimburse s.o. for s.th.; **sie ersetzte ihm die Eltern** she was mother and father to him

ersetz/lich *adj* replaceable

ersicht/lich *adj* evident

ersin/nen §121 *tr* think up

erspa/ren *tr* save

Ersparnis [er'∫parnɪs] *f* (-;-se) (an *dat*) saving (in)

ersprießlich [er'∫prisliç] *adj* useful

erst [erst] *adv* first; at first; just; only; not until; **e. recht** really; **e. recht nicht** most certainly not

erstar/ren *intr* (SEIN) grow stiff; (*Finger*) grow numb; (*Blut*) congeal; (*Zement*) set; (*fig*) run cold; **vor Schreck e.** be paralyzed with fear

erstatten [er'∫tatən] *tr* refund, repay; (*Bericht*) file; **Meldung e.** report

Erstat/tung *f* (-;-en) refund; reimbursement; compensation

Erst/aufführung *f* primiere

erstau/nen *tr* astonish || *intr* (SEIN) (*über acc*) be astonished (at) || **Erstaunen** *n* (-s;) astonishment; **in E. setzen** astonish

erstaun/lich *adj* astonishing

Erst/ausfertigung *f* original

erste ['erstə] §9 *adj* first; **der erste beste** the first that comes along; **fürs e.** for the time being; **zum ersten, zum zweiten, zum dritten** going, going, gone

erste/chen §64 *tr* stab

erste/hen §146 *tr* buy, get || *intr* (SEIN) rise; (*Städte*) spring up

erstei/gen §148 *tr* climb

erstel/len *tr* provide, supply; erect

erstens ['erstəns] *adv* first; in the first place

erst/geboren *adj* first-born

ersticken [er'∫tɪkən] *tr* choke, stifle, smother; **im Keim e.** nip in the bud || *intr* (SEIN) choke; **in Arbeit e.** be snowed under

erstklassig ['erstklasɪç] *adj* first-class

Erstling ['erstlɪŋ] *m* (-s;-e) first-born child; (*fig*) first fruits

Erstlings- *comb.fm.* first

Erst/lingsausstattung *f* layette

erstmalig ['erstmalɪç] *adj* first

erstre/ben *tr* strive for

erstrecken (**erstrek/ken**) *ref* extend

ersu/chen *tr* request, ask

ertappen [er'tapən] *tr* surprise, catch

ertei/len *tr* give; confer; (*Auftrag*) place; (*Audienz, Patent*) grant

ertö/nen *intr* (SEIN) sound; resound

ertö/ten *tr* (*fig*) stifle

Ertrag [er'trak] *m* (-[e]s;ːe) yield; proceeds; produce

ertra/gen §132 *tr* stand, bear

erträglich [er'trekliç] *adj* bearable

ertränken [er'trenkən] *tr* drown

erträu/men *tr* dream of

ertrin/ken §143 *intr* (SEIN) drown

ertüchtigen [er'tyçtɪgən] *tr* train

erübrigen [er'ybrɪgən] *tr* save; (*Zeit*) spare || *ref* be superfluous

erwa/chen *intr* (SEIN) wake up

erwach/sen *adj* adult || §155 *intr* (SEIN) grow, grow up; arise || **Erwachsene** §5 *mf* adult, grown-up

erwä/gen §156 *tr* weigh, consider

Erwä/gung *f* (-;-en) consideration

erwäh/len *tr* choose

erwäh/nen *tr* mention

erwäh/nenswert *adj* worth mentioning

Erwäh/nung *f* (-;) mention

erwär/men *tr* warm, warm up

erwar/ten *tr* expect, await; **etw zu e. haben** be in for s.th.

Erwar/tung *f* (-;-en) expectation

erwar/tungsvoll *adj* expectant

erwecken (**erwek/ken**) *tr* wake; (*Hoffnungen*) raise; (*Gefühle*) awaken; **den Anschein e.** give the impression

erweh/ren *ref* (*genit*) ward off; (*genit*) refrain from; (*der Tränen*) hold back

erwei/chen *tr* soften; (*fig*) move, touch; **sich e. lassen** relent

erwei/sen §118 *tr* prove; show; (*Achtung*) show; (*Dienst*) render; (*Ehre, Gunst*) do || *ref*—**sich e. als** prove

erweitern [er'vaɪtərn] *tr & ref* widen; (*vermehren*) increase; extend, expand

Erwerb [er'verp] *m* (-[e]s;ːe) acquisition; (*Verdienst*) earnings; (*Unterhalt*) living

erwer/ben §149 *tr* acquire; gain; (*verdienen*) earn; (*kaufen*) purchase

erwerbs/behindert *adj* disabled

Erwerbs/betrieb *m* business enterprise

erwerbs/fähig *adj* capable of earning a living

erwerbs/los *adj* unemployed

Erwerbs'quelle f source of income
Erwerbs'sinn m acquisitiveness
erwerbs'tätig adj gainfully employed
erwerbs'unfähig adj unable to earn a living
Erwerbs'zweig m line of business
Erwer'bung f (-;-en) acquisition
erwidern [ɛr'vidərn] tr reply; reciprocate, return
Erwi'derung f (-;-en) reply; return; retaliation
erwir'ken tr secure, obtain
erwi'schen tr catch; **ihn hat's erwischt!** (coll) he's had it!
erwünscht [ɛr'vyn/t] adj desired; welcome; (wünschenswert) desirable
erwür'gen tr strangle
Erz [ɛrts] n (-es;-e) ore; brass; bronze
Erz-, erz- comb.fm. ore; bronze; utterly; (fig) arch-
erzählen [ɛr'tsɛlən] tr tell, narrate
Erzäh'lung f (-;-en) story, narrative
Erz'bischof m archbishop
Erz'engel m archangel
erzeu'gen tr beget; manufacture; produce; generate
Erzeugnis [ɛr'tsɔɪknɪs] n (-ses;-se) product; produce
Erzeu'gung f (-;-en) production; manufacture
erzie'hen §163 tr bring up, rear; (geistig) educate
Erzieher [ɛr'tsiːər] m (-s;-) educator; private tutor
Erzieherin [ɛr'tsiː-ərɪn] f (-;-nen) educator; governess
erzieherisch [ɛr'tsiː-ərɪ/] adj educational, pedagogical
Erzie'hung f (-;) upbringing; education; (Lebensart) breeding
Erzie'hungslehre f (educ) education
Erzie'hungswesen n educational system
erzie'len tr achieve, reach; (Gewinn) realize; (sport) score
Erz'lager n ore deposit
Erz'probe f assay
erzür'nen tr anger || ref get angry
erzwin'gen §137 tr force; wring, obtain by force; (Gehorsam) exact
es [ɛs] adv (as expletive) there; **es gibt** there is, there are || §11 pers pron it; he; she || **Es** n (-;-) (mus) E flat; (psychol) id
Esche ['ɛʃə] f (-;-n) ash tree
Esel ['ɛzəl] m (-s;-) donkey, ass
Eselei [ezə'laɪ] f (-;-en) foolish act, foolish remark
E'selsbrücke f (educ) pony
E'selsohr n dog's-ear
eskalieren [ɛska'liːrən] tr & intr escalate
Eskimo ['ɛskɪmo] m (-s;-s) Eskimo
Espe ['ɛspə] f (-;-n) (bot) aspen
eßbar ['ɛsbar] adj edible, eatable
Eßbesteck ['ɛsbə/tɛk] n knife, fork, and spoon
Esse ['ɛsə] f (-;-n) chimney; forge
essen ['ɛsən] §70 tr & intr eat; **zu Mittag e.** eat lunch || **Essen** n (-s;) eating; food, meal
Essenz [ɛ'sɛnts] f (-;-en) essence
Eßgeschirr ['ɛsgə/ɪr] n (-s;) tableware; table service; (mil) mess kit

Eßgier ['ɛsgir] f (-;) gluttony
Essig ['ɛsɪç] m (-s;-e) vinegar
Es'siggurke f pickle, gherkin
Es'sigsäure f acetic acid
Eßlöffel ['ɛslœfəl] m (-s;-) tablespoon
Eßnapf ['ɛsnapf] m dinner pail
Eßsaal ['ɛszɑl] m dining room
Eßstäbchen ['ɛs/tɛpçən] n chopstick
Eßwaren ['ɛsvarən] pl food, victuals
Eßzimmer ['ɛstsɪmər] n (-s;-) dining room
Estland ['ɛstlant] n (-s;) Estonia
Estrade [ɛs'trɑdə] f (-;-n) dais
etablieren [ɛta'bliːrən] tr establish
Etablissement [etablɪs(ə)'mɑ̃] n (-s; -s) establishment
Etage [ɛ'tɑʒə] f (-;-n) floor, story
Eta'genbett n bunk bed
Eta'genwohnung f apartment
Etappe [ɛ'tapə] f (-;-n) (Teilstrecke) leg, stage; (mil) rear eschelon, rear
Etat [ɛ'tɑ] m (-s;-s) budget
Etats'jahr n fiscal year
etepetete [etəpə'tetə] adj overly particular
Ethik ['etɪk] f (-;) ethics
ethisch ['etɪ/] adj ethical
ethnisch ['ɛtnɪ/] adj ethnic
Ethnologie [ɛtnolo'gi] f (-;) ethnology
Etikett [ɛtɪ'kɛt] n (-s;-e) tab, label
Etikette [ɛtɪ'kɛtə] f (-;) etiquette
etikettieren [ɛtɪkɛ'tiːrən] tr label
etliche ['ɛtlɪçə] adj & pron a few
Etui [ɛ'tvi] n (-s;-s) case (for spectacles, cigarettes, etc.)
etwa ['ɛtva] adv about, around; perhaps; by chance; for example
etwaig [ɛt'va:ɪç] adj eventual
etwas ['ɛtvas] adj some, a little || adv somewhat || pron something; anything || **Etwas** n—**ein gewißes E. a** certain something
euch [ɔɪç] pers pron you; to you || reflex pron yourselves
euer ['ɔɪ-ər] adj your
Eukalyp-tus [ɔɪka'lyptus] m (-; & -ten [tən]) eucalyptus
Eule ['ɔɪlə] f (-;-n) owl
Euphorie [ɔɪfo'ri] f (-;) euphoria
euphorisch [ɔɪ'fori/] adj euphoric
eurige ['ɔɪrɪgə] §2,5 pron yours
Europa [ɔɪ'ropa] n (-s;) Europe
Europäer -in [ɔɪro'pɛ-ər(ɪn)] §6 mf European
europäisch [ɔɪro'pɛ-ɪ/] adj European
Euter ['ɔɪtər] n (-s;-) udder
evakuieren [ɛvaku'iːrən] tr evacuate
evangelisch [ɛvan'geli/] adj evangelical; Protestant
Evangelist [ɛvange'lɪst] m (-en;-en) Evangelist
Evange-lium [ɛvan'geljum] n (-s;-lien [ljən]) gospel
eventuell [ɛventu'ɛl] adj eventual || adv possibly
ewig ['evɪç] adj eternal; perpetual
E'wigkeit f (-;-en) eternity
e'wiglich adv forever
exakt [ɛ'ksakt] adj exact
Exa-men [ɛ'ksamən] n (-s;-s & -mina [mɪna]) examination
examinieren [ɛksami'niːrən] tr examine
exekutiv [ɛkseku'tif] adj executive

Exempel [ɛˈksempəl] *n* (-s;-) example; ein E. statuieren an (*dat*) make an example of

Exemplar [ɛksemˈplɑr] *n* (-s;-e) sample, specimen; (*e-s Buches*) copy

exerzieren [ɛkserˈtsirən] *tr & intr* exercise

Exil [ɛˈksil] *n* (-s;-e) exile

Existenz [ɛksɪˈstents] *f* (-;-en) existence; livelihood; personality

Existenz'minimum *n* living wage

existieren [ɛksɪsˈtirən] *intr* exist

exklusiv [ɛksluˈzif] *adj* exclusive

Exkommunikation [ɛkskomʊnɪkaˈtsjon] *f* (-;-en) excommunication

exkommunizieren [ɛkskəmʊnɪˈtsirən] *tr* excommunicate

Exkrement [ɛkskreˈment] *n* (-[e]s;-e) excrement

exmittieren [ɛksmɪˈtirən] *tr* evict

exotisch [ɛˈksotɪʃ] *adj* exotic

expedieren [ɛkspeˈdirən] *tr* send, ship

Expedition [ɛkspedɪˈtsjon] *f* (-;-en) forwarding; (mil) expedition

Experiment [ɛksperɪˈment] *n* (-[e]s; -e) experiment

experimentieren [ɛksperɪmenˈtirən] *intr* experiment

explodieren [ɛksploˈdirən] *intr* (SEIN) explode; blow up

Explosion [ɛksploˈzjon] *f* (-;-en) explosion

exponieren [ɛkspoˈnirən] *tr* expose; (*darlegen*) expound, set forth

Export [ɛksˈpɔrt] *m* (-[e]s;-e) export

exportieren [ɛkspɔrˈtirən] *tr* export

Ex-preß [ɛksˈprɛs] *m* (-presses; -presse) express

Expreß'zug *m* express train

extra [ˈɛkstra] *adv* extra; (coll) on purpose, for spite

Ex'trablatt *n* (journ) extra

extrahieren [ɛkstraˈhirən] *tr* extract

Extrakt [ɛksˈtrakt] *m* (-[e]s;-e) extract; (*aus Büchern*) excerpt

extravagant [ɛkstravaˈgant] *adj* luxurious; wild, fantastic

Extravaganz [ɛkstravaˈgants] *f* (-;-en) luxury

extrem [ɛksˈtrem] *adj* extreme || Extrem *n* (-s;-e) extreme

Exzellenz [ɛkstseˈlents] *f* (-;-en) Excellency

exzentrisch [ɛksˈtsentrɪʃ] *adj* eccentric

Ex-zeß [ɛksˈtses] *m* (-zesses;-zesse) excess

F

F, f [ɛf] *invar n* F, f; (mus) F

Fabel [ˈfɑbəl] *f* (-;-n) fable; story; (*e-s Dramas*) plot

fa'belhaft *adj* fabulous

fabeln [ˈfɑbəln] *intr* tell stories

Fabrik [faˈbrik] *f* (-;-en) factory, mill

Fabrik'anlage *f* manufacturing plant

Fabrikant **-in** [fabrɪˈkant(ɪn)] §7 *mf* manufacturer, maker

Fabrikat [fabrɪˈkɑt] *n* (-[e]s;-e) product; brand, make

Fabrikation [fabrɪkaˈtsjon] *f* (-;) manufacture, manufacturing

Fabrikations'fehler *m* flaw, defect

Fabrikations'nummer *f* serial number

Fabrik'marke *f* trademark

fabrik'mäßig *adj* mass

Fabrik'nummer *f* serial number

Fabrik'waren *pl* manufactured goods

Fabrik'zeichen *n* trademark

fabrizieren [fabrɪˈtsirən] *tr* manufacture

fabulieren [fabuˈlirən] *tr* make up || *intr* tell yarns

fabulös [fabuˈløs] *adj* fabulous

Facette [faˈsetə] *f* (-;-n) facet

Fach [fax] *n* (-[e]s;-̈er) compartment; (*im Schreibtisch*) pigeonhole; (*Bücherbrett*) shelf; (fig) field, department; line, business; (educ) subject; vom F. sein be an expert

Fach'arbeiter **-in** §6 *mf* specialist

Fach'arzt *m*, **Fach'ärztin** *f* (med) specialist

Fach'ausbildung *f* professional training

Fach'ausdruck *m* technical term

fächeln [ˈfɛçəln] *tr* fan

Fächer [ˈfɛçər] *m* (-s;-) fan

Fä'cherpalme *f* palmetto

Fach'gebiet *n* field, line; department

Fach'gelehrte §5 *mf* expert

fach'gemäß *adj* expert, professional

Fach'genosse *m* colleague

Fach'kenntnisse *pl* specialized knowledge

Fach'kreis *m* experts, specialists

fach'kundig *adj* expert, experienced

fach'lich *adj* professional; technical; specialized

Fach'mann *m* (-es;-̈er & -leute) expert, specialist

fachmännisch [ˈfaxmenɪʃ] *adj* expert

Fach'schule *f* vocational school

Fachsimpelei [faxzɪmpəˈlaɪ] *f* (-;-en) shoptalk

fachsimpeln [ˈfaxzɪmpəln] *intr* talk shop

Fach'werk *n* framework; specialized book

Fach'zeitschrift *f* technical journal

Fackel [ˈfakəl] *f* (-;-n) torch

fackeln [ˈfakəln] *intr* flare; (fig) hesitate, dilly-dally

Fackelschein (**Fak'kelschein**) *m* torchlight

Fackelzug (**Fak'kelzug**) *m* torchlight procession

fade [ˈfɑdə] *adj* stale; (fig) dull

Faden [ˈfɑdən] *m* (-s;-̈) (& fig) thread; filament; (naut) fathom; keinen guten F. lassen an (*dat*) tear apart

Fa'denkreuz *n* crosshairs

Fa'dennudeln *pl* vermicelli

fadenscheinig [ˈfadənʃaɪnɪç] *adj* threadbare

Fagott [faˈɡɔt] *n* (-[e]s;-e) bassoon

fähig [ˈfeːɪç] *adj* capable, able

Fä′higkeit *f* (-;-en) ability; talent

fahl [faːl] *adj* pale; faded, washed-out

fahnden [ˈfandən] *intr* (nach) search (for), hunt (for)

Fahn′dung *f* (-;-en) search, hunt

Fahne [ˈfaːnə] *f* (-;-n) flag; pennant; (mil) colors; (typ) galley proof

Fah′nenabzug *m* galley proof

Fah′neneid *m* (mil) swearing in

Fah′nenflucht *f* desertion

fah′nenflüchtig *adj*—**f. werden** desert ‖ **Fahnenflüchtige** §5 *mf* deserter

Fah′nenmast *m* flagpole

Fah′nenträger *m* in §6 *mf* standard bearer

Fähnrich [ˈfeːnrɪç] *m* (-s;-e) officer cadet; **F. zur See** midshipman

Fahrbahn [ˈfarban] *f* (traffic) lane

fahrbar [ˈfarbar] *adj* passable; navigable; mobile

fahrbereit [ˈfarbəraɪt] *adj* in running order

Fahr′bereitschaft *f* (-;-en) motor pool

Fähre [ˈfeːrə] *f* (-;-n) ferry

fahren [ˈfaːrən] §71 *tr* haul; (*lenken*) drive; (*Boot*) sail ‖ *intr* (SEIN) go; travel, drive; ride; **es fuhr mir durch den Sinn** it flashed across my mind; **f. lassen run** (*a boat, train*); let go; (fig) abandon, renounce; **gut f. bei** do well in; **mit der Hand f. über** (*acc*) run one's hand over; **rechts f.** (public sign) keep right; **was ist in ihn gefahren?** what's gotten into him?

fah′renlassen §104 *tr* let go of

Fah′rer –in §6 *mf* driver

Fah′rerflucht *f* hit-and-run case

Fahrgast [ˈfarɡast] *m* passenger

Fahrgeld [ˈfarɡelt] *n* fare

Fahrgelegenheit [ˈfarɡəleɡənhaɪt] *f* transportation (facilities)

Fahrgestell [ˈfarɡəˌtel] *n* (-[e]s;-e) (aer) landing gear; (aut) chassis

fahrig [ˈfarɪç] *adj* fidgety

Fahrkarte [ˈfarkartə] *f* ticket

Fahr′kartenausgabe *f*, **Fahr′kartenschalter** *m* ticket window

fahrlässig [ˈfarlesɪç] *adj* negligent; **fahrlässige Tötung** involuntary manslaughter

Fahr′lässigkeit *f* (-;) negligence

Fahrlehrer –in [ˈfarlerər(ɪn)] §6 *mf* driving instructor

Fahrnis [ˈfarnɪs] *f* (-;-se) movables

Fährnis [ˈfeːrnɪs] *f* (-;-se) (poet) danger

Fahrplan [ˈfarplan] *m* schedule

fahr′planmäßig *adj* scheduled ‖ *adv* on schedule, on time

Fahrpreis [ˈfarpraɪs] *m* fare

Fahrprüfung [ˈfarpryfuŋ] *f* driver's test

Fahrrad [ˈfarrad] *n* bicycle

Fahrrinne [ˈfarrinə] *f* channel

Fahrschein [ˈfarʃaɪn] *m* ticket

Fahrstuhl [ˈfarˌtul] *m* elevator; (med) wheel chair

Fahr′stuhlführer –in §6 *mf* elevator operator

Fahr′stuhlschacht *m* elevator shaft

Fahrstunde [ˈfarʃtundə] *f* driving lesson

Fahrt [fart] *f* (-;-en) ride, drive; trip; **auf F. gehen** go hiking; **F. verlieren** lose speed; **freie F. haben** have the green light; **in F. kommen** pick up speed; (fig) swing into action; **in F. sein** (coll) be keyed up; (coll) be on the warpath; (naut) be under way

Fährte [ˈfertə] *f* (-;-n) track, scent

Fahrt′unterbrechung *f* (-;-en) stopover

Fahrwasser [ˈfarvasər] *n* navigable water; (& fig) wake

Fahrwerk [ˈfarverk] *n* see **Fahrgestell**

Fahrzeug [ˈfartsɔɪk] *n* vehicle; vessel, craft

Fahr′zeugpark *m* (aut) fleet; (rr) rolling stock

fair [fer] *adj* fair

Fairneß [ˈfernes] *f* (-;) fairness

Fäkalien [feˈkaljən] *pl* feces

faktisch [ˈfaktɪʃ] *adj* actual, factual

Faktor [ˈfaktər] *m* (-s;-toren [ˈtoːrən]) factor; foreman; (com) agent

Faktu·ra [fakˈtura] *f* (-;-ren [rən]) invoice

Fakultät [fakʊlˈtet] *f* (-;-en) (educ) department, school

falb [falp] *adj* claybank (*horse*)

Falke [ˈfalkə] *m* (-;-n) falcon; (pol) hawk

Fal′kenjagd *f* falconry

Falkner [ˈfalknər] *m* (-s;-) falconer

Fall [fal] *m* (-[e]s;⸗e) fall, drop; downfall; case; **auf alle Fälle** in any case; **auf keinen F.** in no case; **auf jeden F.** in any case; **gesetzt den F.** supposing; **im besten F.** at best; **im schlimmsten F.** if worst comes to worst; **von F. zu F.** according to circumstances; **zu F. bringen;** (fig) ruin; (parl) defeat; **zu F. kommen** (fig) collapse

Fall′brücke *f* drawbridge

Falle [ˈfalə] *f* (-;-n) (& fig) trap; (fig) pitfall; (*Bett*) (coll) sack

fallen [ˈfalən] §72 *intr* (SEIN) fall, drop; (*Schuß*) be heard; (mil) fall in battle; **j-m ins Wort f.** interrupt s.o. ‖ **Fallen** *n* (-s;) fall, drop; (fig) downfall

fällen [ˈfelən] *tr* (*Bäume*) fell; (*Urteil*) pass; (chem) precipitate

Fallensteller [ˈfalənˌtelər] *m* (-s;-) trapper

Fall′grube *f* trap, pit; (fig) pitfall

fällig [ˈfelɪç] *adj* due; payable

Fäl′ligkeit *f* (-;-en) due date

Fall′obst *n* windfall

Fall′rohr *n* soil pipe; (*e-r Dachrinne*) down spout

falls [fals] *conj* in case, if

Fall′schirm *m* parachute

Fall′schirmabsprung *m* parachute jump

Fall′schirmjäger *m* paratrooper

Fall′schirmspringer –in §6 *mf* parachutist, sky diver

Fall′strick *m* snare

Fall′sucht *f* (pathol) epilepsy

fall′süchtig *adj* (pathol) epileptic

Fall′tür *f* trapdoor

falsch [falʃ] *adj* false; (*verkehrt*) wrong; (*unecht*) counterfeit; **falsches Spiel** double-dealing || *adv* wrongly; **f. gehen** (horol) be off; **f. schreiben** misspell; **f. schwören** perjure oneself; **f. singen** sing off key; **f. spielen** cheat; **f. verbunden** wrong number || **Falsch** *m*—**ohne F.** without guile

fälschen [ˈfelʃən] *tr* falsify; (*Geld*) counterfeit; (*Urkunde*) forge

Fäl′scher **–in** §6 *mf* forger; counterfeiter

Falsch′geld *n* counterfeit money

Falsch′heit *f* (–;-en) falsity; deceitfulness

fälschlich [ˈfelʃlɪç] *adv* falsely

Falsch′münzer *m* counterfeiter

Falsch′spieler **–in** §6 *mf* card sharp

Fäl′schung *f* (–;-en) falsification; forgery; fake

Faltboot [ˈfaltbot] *n* collapsible boat

Falte [ˈfaltə] *f* (–;-n) fold; (*Plissee*) pleat, crease; (*Runzel*) wrinkle

fälteln [ˈfeltəln] *tr* pleat

falten [ˈfaltən] *tr* fold; wrinkle

Fal′tenrock *m* pleated skirt

Falter [ˈfaltər] *m* (–s;–) butterfly; (*Nacht–*) moth

faltig [ˈfaltɪç] *adj* creased; wrinkled

Falz [falts] *m* (–es;–e) fold; (*Kerbe*) notch; (carp) rabbet

familiär [famiˈljer] *adj* intimate; familiar

Familie [faˈmiljə] *f* (–;-n) family

Fami′lienangehörige §5 *mf* member of the family

Fami′lienanschluß *m*—**F. haben** live as one of the family

Fami′lienname *m* last name

Fami′lienstand *m* marital status

Fami′lienstück *n* family heirloom

Fami′lienzuwachs *m* addition to the family

famos [faˈmos] *adj* excellent, swell

Fan [fen] *m* (–s;–s) (sport) fan

Fanatiker **–in** [faˈnatikər(ɪn)] §6 *mf* fanatic; (sport) fan

fanatisch [faˈnatɪʃ] *adj* fanatic

fand [fant] *pret* of **finden**

Fanfare [fanˈfarə] *f* (–;-n) (mus) fanfare

Fang [faŋ] *m* (–[e]s;–̈e) capture; (*Fisch–*) haul, catch; (*Falle*) trap; (*Kralle*) claw

Fang′arm *m* tentacle

Fang′eisen *n* steel trap

fangen [ˈfaŋən] §73 *tr* catch; trap; (*Ohrfeige*) get || *ref* get caught || **Fangen** *n*—**F. spielen** play catch

Fang′frage *f* loaded question

Fang′messer *n* hunting knife

Fang′zahn *m* fang; tusk

Farb– [farp] *comb.fm.* color

Farb′abzug *m* (phot) color print

Farb′aufnahme *f* color photograph

Farb′band *n* (–[e]s;–̈er) typewriter ribbon

Farbe [ˈfarbə] *f* (–;-n) color; dye; (*zum Malen*) paint; (*Gesichts–*) complexion; (cards) suit; **F. bekennen** folow suit; (fig) lay one's cards on the table

färben [ˈferbən] *tr* color, dye, tint ||

ref take on color; change color; **sich rot f.** turn red; blush

far′benprächtig *adj* colorful

Fär′ber **–in** §6 *mf* dyer

Farb′fernsehen *n* color television

Farb′film *m* color film

farbig [ˈfarbɪç] *adj* colored; colorful

Farb′kissen *n* ink pad

Farb′körper *m* pigment

farb′los *adj* colorless

Farb′spritzpistole *f* paint sprayer

Farb′stift *m* colored pencil; crayon

Farb′stoff *m* dye

Farb′ton *m* tone, hue, shade

Fär′bung *f* (–;-en) coloring; hue

Farm [farm] *f* (–;-en) farm

Farmer **–in** [ˈfarmər(ɪn)] §6 *mf* farmer

Farn [farn] *m* (–[e]s;–e) fern

Farn′kraut *n* fern

Fasan [faˈzan] *m* (–s;–e & –en) pheasant

Fasching [ˈfaʃɪŋ] *m* (–s;) carnival

Faschismus [faˈʃɪsmus] *m* (–;) fascism

Faschist **–in** [faˈʃɪst(ɪn)] §7 *mf* fascist

Faselei [fazəˈlaɪ] *f* (–;-en) drivel

Faselhans [ˈfazəlhans] *m* (–̈;-e & –̈e) blabberer; scatterbrain

faseln [ˈfazəln] *intr* talk nonsense

Faser [ˈfazər] *f* (–;-n) fiber; (*im Holz*) grain; (*Fädchen*) thread, string

Fa′serholzplatte *f* fiberboard

fasern [ˈfazərn] *tr* unravel || *ref* fray || *intr* unravel

Fa′serschreiber *m* felt pen

Faß [fas] *n* (**Fasses;Fässer**) barrel, keg; (*Bütte*) vat, tun

Fassade [faˈsadə] *f* (–;-n) façade

faßbar [ˈfasbar] *adj* comprehensible

Faß′bier *n* draft beer

fassen [ˈfasən] *tr* (*packen*) seize; (*erwischen*) apprehend; (*begreifen*) grasp; (*Edelstein*) mount; (*enthalten können*) hold, seat; (*Essen*) (mil) draw; **e-n Gedanken f.** form an idea; **in Worte f.** put into words; **j-n bei der Ehre f.** appeal to s.o.'s honor; **Tritt fassen** fall in step || *ref* get hold of oneself; **in sich f.** include; **sich f. an** (*acc*) put one's hand to, touch; **sich in Geduld f.** exercise patience; **sich kurz f.** be brief || *intr* take hold; (*nach*) grab (for); **es ist nicht zu f.** it is incomprehensible

Faß′hahn *m* tap, faucet

faß′lich *adj* conceivable

Fasson [faˈson] *f* (–;-en) style, cut

Fas′sung *f* (–;-en) composure; (*schriftlich*) draft; (*für Edelsteine*) setting, mounting; (*Brillenrand*) frame; (*Wortlaut*) wording; (*Lesart*) version; (elec) socket; **aus der F. bringen** upset; **außer F. sein** be beside onself

Fas′sungskraft *f* comprehension

fas′sungslos *adj* disconcerted, shaken

Fas′sungsvermögen *n* capacity; (*geistliches*) (powers of) comprehension

fast [fast] *adv* almost, nearly

fasten [ˈfastən] *intr* fast || **Fasten** *n* (–s;) fasting

Fa′stenzeit *f* Lent, Lenten season

Fast′nacht *f* carnival

Fast′tag *m* day of fasting, fast day

faszinieren [fastsɪ'nirən] *tr* fascinate
fatal [fa'tɑl] *adj* disastrous; (*unange-nehm*) unpleasant
fauchen ['fauxən] *intr* hiss; (*Person*) snarl; (*Katze*) spit
faul [faul] *adj* rotten; lazy; bad, nasty; (*verdächtig*) fishy; (*Ausrede, Witz*) lame, poor; (sport) foul || **Faul** *n* (-s;-s) (sport) foul
Fäule ['fɔɪlə] *f* (-;) rot, decay
faulen ['faulən] *intr* rot, decay
faulenzen ['faulentsən] *intr* loaf
Faulenzer ['faulentsər] *m* (-s;-) loafer; (*Liegestuhl*) chaise longue; (*Linienblatt*) ruled sheet of paper
Faul'heit *f* (-;) laziness
faulig ['faulɪç] *adj* rotten, putrid
Fäulnis ['fɔɪlnɪs] *f* (-;) rot; **in F. übergehen** begin to rot
Faul'pelz *m* (coll) loafer
Faust [faust] *f* (-;̈e) fist; **auf eigene F.** on one's own
faust'dick' *adj* (coll) whopping
Faust'handschuh *m* mitten
Faust'kampf *m* boxing match
Fäustling ['fɔɪstlɪŋ] *m* (-[e]s;-e) mitten
Faust'schlag *m* punch, blow
Favorit –in [favo'rit(ɪn)] §7 *mf* favorite
Faxen ['faksən] *pl* antics; faces; **F. machen** fool around; make a fuss; **F. schneiden** make faces
Fazit ['fatsɪt] *n* (-s;-e & -s) result; **das F. ziehen** sum it up
Feber ['febər] *m* (-[s];-) (Aust) February
Februar ['febru·ar] *m* (-[s];-e) February
fechten ['feçtən] §74 *intr* fence; fight; (*betteln*) beg
Feder ['fedər] *f* (-;-n) feather; pen; quill; (mach) spring; **F. und Nut** (carp) tongue and groove
Fe'derball *m* shuttlecock
Fe'derballspiel *n* badminton
Fe'derbett *n* feather bed
Fe'derbusch *m* plume
Fe'derdecke *f* feather quilt
Federfuchser ['fedərfuksər] *m* (-s;-) scribbler; hack writer
fe'derführend *adj* in charge
Fe'dergewicht *n* featherweight division
Federgewichtler ['fedərgəvɪçtlər] *m* (-s;-) featherweight (boxer)
Fe'derhubtor *n* overhead door
Fe'derkernmatratze *f* innerspring mattress
Fe'derkiel *m* quill
Fe'derkraft *f* springiness; tension
Fe'derkrieg *m* paper war, war of words
fe'derleicht' *adj* light as a feather
Fe'derlesen *n*—**ohne viel Federlesen(s)** without much ado
Fe'dermesser *n* penknife
federn ['fedərn] *tr* fit with springs || *intr* be springy; (*Vogel*) moult; (gym) bounce
Fe'derring *m* lock washer
Fe'derstrich *m* stroke of the pen
Fe'derung *f* (-;) (aut) suspension
Fe'derzug *m* stroke of the pen
Fee [fe] *f* (-;Feen ['fe·ən]) fairy

Feg(e)feuer ['feg(ə)fɔɪ·ər] *n* (-s;) purgatory
fegen ['fegən] *tr* sweep; (*Laub*) tear off || *intr* (SEIN) tear along
Fehde ['fedə] *f* (-;-n) feud
fehl [fel] *adj*—**f. am Ort** out of place || **Fehl** *m* (-[e]s;-e) blemish; fault
fehl– *comb.fm.* wide of the mark; mis-, incorrectly, wrongly || **Fehl–** *comb. fm.* missing; vain, unsuccessful; incorrect, wrong; faulty; negative
Fehl'anzeige *f* negative report
Fehl'ball *m* (tennis) fault
fehlbar ['felbar] *adj* fallible
Fehl'betrag *m* shortage, deficit
Fehl'bitte *f* vain request; **e-e F. tun** meet with a refusal
fehlen ['felən] *tr* miss || *intr* be absent; be missing; be lacking; fail, be unsuccessful; sin, err; (*dat*) miss, e.g., **er fehlt mir sehr** I miss him very much; (*dat*) lack, e.g., **ihm fehlt die Zeit** he lacks the time; **was fehlt Ihnen?** what's wrong with you? || *impers*—**es fehlte nicht viel, und ich wäre gefallen** I came close to falling
Fehler ['felər] *m* (-s;-) mistake, error; flaw, imperfection; blunder
feh'lerfrei *adj* faultless, flawless
feh'lerhaft *adj* faulty
feh'lerlos *adj* faultless, flawless
Fehl'geburt *f* miscarriage
Fehl'gehen §82 *intr* (SEIN) go wrong; (*Schuß*) miss
Fehl'gewicht *n* short weight
fehl'greifen §88 *intr* miss one's hold; (fig) make a mistake
Fehl'griff *m* mistake, blunder
Fehl'leistung *f* (Freudian) slip
fehl'leiten *tr* (& fig) misdirect
Fehl'schlag *m* miss; failure, disappointment; (baseball) foul
Fehl'schluß *m* false inference; fallacy
Fehl'spruch *m* miscarriage of justice
Fehl'start *m* false start
Fehl'tritt *m* false step; (fig) slip
Fehl'wurf *m* (*beim Würfeln*) crap
fehl'zünden *intr* backfire
feien ['faɪ·ən] *tr*—**gefeit sein gegen** be immune to; **j–n f. gegen** make s.o. immune to
Feier ['faɪ·ər] *f* (-;-n) celebration; ceremony
Fei'erabend *m* closing time
fei'erlich *adj* solemn
Fei'erlichkeit *f* (-;-en) solemnity; **Feierlichkeiten** festivities; ceremonies
feiern ['faɪ·ərn] *tr* celebrate, observe; honor || *intr* rest from work
Fei'erstunde *f* commemorative ceremony
Fei'ertag *m* holiday; holy day
feig [faɪk] *adj* cowardly
feige ['faɪgə] *adj* cowardly || **Feige** *f* (-;-n) fig
Feig'heit *f* (-;) cowardice
feig'herzig *adj* faint-hearted
Feigling ['faɪklɪŋ] *m* (-s;-e) coward
feil [faɪl] *adj* for sale
feil'bieten §58 *tr* offer for sale
Feile ['faɪlə] *f* (-;-n) file

feilen [ˈfaɪlən] *tr* file

feilschen [ˈfaɪlʃən] *intr* (**um**) haggle (over), dicker (about)

Feilspäne [ˈfaɪlˌpenə] *pl* filings

fein [faɪn] *adj* fine; delicate; fancy

feind [faɪnt] *adj* hostile ‖ **Feind** *m* (-[e]s;-e) enemy, foe

Feind- *comb.fm.* enemy, hostile; against the enemy

Feind'fahrt *f* (nav) operation against the enemy

Feind'flug *m* (aer) combat mission

Feindin [ˈfaɪndɪn] *f* (-;-nen) enemy

feind'lich *adj* hostile

Feind'schaft *f* (-;-en) enmity

feind'selig *adj* hostile

Feind'seligkeit *f* (-;-en) hostility, animosity; hostile action

fein'fühlend, fein'fühlig *adj* sensitive

Fein'gefühl *n* sensitivity

Fein'heit *f* (-;-en) fineness, fine quality; delicacy; subtlety

Fein'mechanik *f* precision engineering

Feinschmecker [ˈfaɪnˌmekər] *m* (-s;-) gourmet, epicure

fein'sinnig *adj* sensitive; subtle

feist [faɪst] *adj* fat, plump

Feld [felt] *n* (-[e]s;-er) field; panel, compartment; (checkers, chess) square; **auf dem Felde** in the field(s); **auf freiem Felde** in the open; **aufs F. gehen** go to (work in) the fields; **das F. behaupten** stand one's ground; **ins F. ziehen** take the field

Feld'bau *m* agriculture

Feld'becher *m* collapsible drinking cup

Feld'bett *n* army cot; camping cot

Feld'blume *f* wild flower

Feld'bluse *f* army jacket

feld'dienstfähig *adj* fit for active duty

Feld'flasche *f* canteen

Feld'geistliche *m* (-n;-n) army chaplain

Feld'gendarm *m* military police

Feld'gendarmerie *f* military police

Feld'geschrei *n* battle cry

Feld'geschütz *n* field gun, field piece

Feld'herr *m* general; commander in chief

Feld'lager *n* bivouac, camp

Feld'lazarett *n* evacuation hospital

Feld'lerche *f* skylark

Feld'marschall *m* field marshal

feld'marschmäßig *adj* with full field pack

Feld'messer *m* surveyor

Feld'meßkunst *f* (-;) surveying

Feld'mütze *f* (mil) overseas cap

Feld'postamt *n* army post office

Feld'schlacht *f* battle

Feld'stecher *m* field glasses

Feldwebel [ˈfeltvebəl] *m* (-s;-) sergeant

Feld'zeichen *n* ensign, standard

Feld'zug *m* campaign

Felge [ˈfelgə] *f* (-;-n) rim

Fell [fel] *n* (-[e]s;-e) pelt, skin; fur; **ein dickes F. haben** be thick-skinned

Fels [fels] *m* (-es & -en;-en) rock; cliff; **zackige Felsen** crags

Fels'block *m* boulder

Felsen [ˈfelzən] *m* (-s;-) rock; cliff

fel'senfest *adj* firm as a rock

Fel'sengebirge *n* Rocky Mountains

Fel'senklippe *f* cliff

Fel'senriff *n* reef

felsig [ˈfelzɪç] *adj* rocky

Fenster [ˈfenstər] *n* (-s;-) window

Fen'sterbrett *n* window sill

Fen'sterflügel *n* casement

Fen'sterladen *m* window shutter

Fen'sterleder *n* chamois

Fen'sterplatz *m* (rr) window seat

Fen'sterrahmen *m* window frame; sash

Fen'sterrosette *f* rose window

Fen'sterscheibe *f* windowpane

Ferien [ˈferjən] *pl* vacation; (parl) recess

Fe'rienreisende §5 *mf* vacationer

Fe'rienstimmung *f* holiday spirit

Ferkel [ˈferkəl] *n* (-s;-) piglet

Ferkelei [ferkəˈlaɪ] *f* (-;-en) obscenity

fern [fern] *adj* far, distant; (*entlegen*) remote; (*weit fort*) far away

Fern'amt *n* long-distance exchange

Fern'anruf *m* long-distance call

Fern'aufklärung *f* long-range reconnaissance

Fern'bedienung *f* remote control

fern'bleiben §62 *intr* (SEIN) (*dat*) stay away (from) ‖ **Fernbleiben** *n* (-s;) absence; absenteeism

Fern'blick *m* distant view, vista

Ferne [ˈfernə] *f* (-;-n) distance

ferner [ˈfernər] *adj* remote, distant ‖ *adv* further; moreover

Fern'fahrer *m* long-distance trucker

Fern'fahrt *f* long-distance trip

Fern'gang *m* (aut) overdrive

Fern'geschoß *n* long-range missile

Fern'geschütz *n* long-range gun

Fern'gespräch *n* long-distance call; toll call

Fern'glas *n* binoculars

fern'halten §90 *tr & ref* keep away

Fern'heizung *f* heating from a central heating plant

Fern'kursus *m* correspondence course

Fern'laster *m* long-distance truck

fern'lenken *tr* guide by remote control

Fern'lenkrakete *f* guided missile

Fern'lenkung *f* (-;-en) remote control

Fern'lenkwaffe *f* guided missile

Fern'licht *n* (aut) high beam

fern'liegen §108 *impers*—**es liegt mir fern zu** (*inf*) I'm far from (*ger*)

Fernmelde- [fernmeldə] *comb.fm.* communications, signal

Fern'meldetruppen *pl* signal corps

Fern'meldewesen *n* telecommunications system

fern'mündlich *adj & adv* by telephone

Fern'objektiv *n* telephoto lens

Fernost- *comb.fm.* Far Eastern

fern'östlich *adj* Far Eastern

Fern'rohr *n* telescope

Fern'rohraufsatz *m* telescopic gun sight

Fern'ruf *m* telephone call; telephone number

Fern'schnellzug *m* long-distance express

Fern'schreiber *m* teletype, telex

Fernseh- [fernze] *comb.fm.* television

Fern'sehansager -in §6 *mf* television announcer

Fern'sehapparat *m* television set

Fern'sehbildröhre f picture tube
fern'sehen §138 intr watch television || **Fernsehen** n (-s;) television
Fern'seher m (-s;-) television set; television viewer
Fern'sehgerät n television set
Fern'sehkanal m television channel
Fern'sehschau f television show
Fern'sehsendung f telecast
Fern'sehteilnehmer -in §6 mf televiewer
Fern'sehübertragung f telecast
Fern'sicht f view, vista; panorama
fern'sichtig adj far-sighted
Fernsprech- [fɛrn'prɛç] comb.fm. telephone
Fern'sprechauftragsdienst m answering service
Fern'sprechautomat m pay phone
Fern'sprecher m telephone
Fern'sprechzelle f telephone booth
fern'stehen §146 intr (dat) have no personal contact (with); (dat) not be close (to)
Fern'stehende §5 mf outsider; disinterested observer
fern'steuern tr guide by remote control
Fern'studium n correspondence course
Ferse ['fɛrzə] f (-;-n) heel
Fer'sengeld n—F. geben take to one's heels
fertig ['fɛrtɪç] adj finished; ready; (kaputt) ruined, done for
fertig-, Fertig- comb.fm. final; finished; finishing; prefabricated
fer'tigbringen §65 tr (inf) have to, bring about; **es glatt f. zu** (inf) be capable of (ger); **es nicht f., ihm das zu sagen** not have the heart to tell him that
fertigen ['fɛrtɪgən] tr manufacture
Fer'tigkeit f (-;-en) skill
Fer'tigrasen m sod
fer'tigstellen tr complete; get ready
Fer'tigung f (-;-en) manufacture, production; copy, draft
Fes [fɛs] n (mus) F flat
fesch [fɛʃ] adj smart, chic
Fessel ['fɛsəl] f (-;-n) fetter, bond; (anat) ankle; (vet) fetlock
Fes'selballon m captive balloon
fesseln ['fɛsəln] tr chain, tie; (bezaubern) captivate, arrest; (mil) contain; **ans Bett gefesselt** confined to bed, bedridden
fes'selnd adj fascinating, gripping; (Personalität) magnetic
fest [fɛst] adj firm; solid; tight; stationary; steady; (Preis, Kost, Einkommen, Gehalt) fixed; (Schlaf) sound; (mil) fortified; **feste Straße** improved road || **Fest** n (-es;-e) feast; festival
fest'backen intr (SEIN) cake (on)
fest'besoldet adj with a fixed salary
fest'binden §59 tr (an dat) tie (to)
Fest'essen n banquet
fest'fahren §71 tr run aground || ref come to a standstill
fest'halten §90 tr hold on to || ref (an dat) cling (to), hold on (to)
festigen ['fɛstɪgən] tr strengthen; consolidate || ref grow stronger

Fe'stigkeit f (-;-en) firmness; steadiness; strength
Fe'stigung f (-;-) strengthening; consolidation; stabilization
Fest'land n continent
fest'legen tr fix, determine, set; (Anordnung) lay down; (fin, naut) tie up; **j-n f. auf** (acc) pin s.o. down on || **ref** (auf acc) commit oneself (to)
fest'lich adj festive
Fest'lichkeit f (-;-en) festivity
fest'liegen §108 intr be stranded
fest'machen tr fix; (fig) settle || **intr** (naut) moor
Fest'mahl n feast
Fest'nahme f (-;-n) arrest
fest'nehmen §116 tr arrest, apprehend
Fest'rede f ceremonial speech
Fest'saal m grand hall, banquet hall
fest'schnallen tr buckle up || **ref** fasten one's seat belt
Fest'schrift f homage volume
fest'setzen tr fix, set || **ref** settle down (in a town, etc.)
fest'sitzen intr fit tight; be stuck
Fest'spiel n play for a festive occasion; **Festspiele** (mus, theat) festival
fest'stehen §146 intr stand firm; (Tatsache) be certain || **impers**—es steht fest it is a fact
fest'stehend adj stationary; (Achse) fixed; (Tatsache) established
feststellbar ['fɛst'tɛlbar] ascertainable
Fest'stellbremse f hand brake
fest'stellen tr ascertain; (unbeweglich machen) lock, secure; (Tatbestand) find out, establish; (angeben) state; (Schaden) assess; (Kurs) (fin) set, fix
Fest'stellschraube f set screw
Fest'tag m feastday; holiday
Fe'stung f (-;-en) fortress
Fe'stungsgraben m moat
Fest'wagen m float
Fest'wert m standard value; (math, phys) constant
Fest'wiese f fairground
fest'ziehen §163 tr pull tight
Fest'zug m procession
Fetisch ['fɛtɪʃ] m (-[e]s;-e) fetish
fett [fɛt] adj fat; (Boden, Milch, Gemisch) rich; (Zeiten, Leben) of plenty || **Fett** n (-[e]s;-e) fat; (Schmalz) lard; (Pflanzen-) shortening; (Schmier-) grease
Fett'auge n speck of fat
Fett'druck m boldface type
fetten ['fɛtən] tr grease, lubricate
Fett'fleck m grease spot
fettig ['fɛtɪç] adj fatty, greasy, oily
Fett'kloß m (coll) fatso
Fett'kohle f bituminous coal
fettleibig ['fɛtlaɪbɪç] adj stout
Fettnäpfchen ['fɛtnɛpfçən] n—**bei j-m ins F. treten** hurt s.o.'s feelings; **ins F. treten** put one's foot in it
Fett'presse f (aut) grease gun
Fett'spritze f (aut) grease gun
Fett'sucht f obesity
Fett'wanst m (sl) fatso
Fetzen ['fɛtsən] m (-s;-) rag; bit; scrap; (Aust) dishcloth; **daß die F. fliegen** violently
feucht [fɔɪçt] adj moist, damp, humid

feuchten ['fɔɪçtən] *tr* moisten, dampen
Feuch'tigkeit *f* (-;) moisture, dampness, humidity
feudal [fɔɪ'dɑl] *adj* feudal; (fig) magnificent
Feudalismus [fɔɪdɑ'lɪsmʊs] *m* (-;) feudalism
Feuer ['fɔɪ·ər] *n* (-s;-) fire
Feu'eralarm *m* fire alarm
Feu'eralarmübung *f* fire drill
feu'erbeständig *adj* fireproof
Feu'erbestattung *f* cremation
Feu'erbrand *m* firebrand
Feu'ereifer *m* enthusiasm, zeal
Feu'ereinstellung *f* cease-fire
feu'erfest *adj* fireproof
Feu'erfliege *f* firefly
feu'erflüssig *adj* molten
feu'ergefährlich *adj* inflammable
Feu'erhahn *m* hydrant, fireplug
Feu'erhaken *m* poker
Feu'erherd *m* fireplace
Feu'erkampf *m* fire fight, gun battle
Feu'erkraft *f* (mil) fire power
Feu'erleiter *f* fire ladder; (*Nottreppe*) fire escape
Feu'erlinie *f* firing line
Feu'erlöscher *m* fire extinguisher
Feu'ermelder *m* fire alarm
Feu'ermeldung *f* fire alarm
feuern ['fɔɪ·ərn] *tr* fire; (coll) fire, sack || *intr* fire, shoot
Feu'erprobe *f* ordeal by fire; acid test
Feu'ersalve *f* fusillade
Feu'erschneise *f* firebreak
Feu'erspritze *f* fire engine
Feu'erstein *m* flint
Feu'ertaufe *f* baptism of fire
Feu'erversicherung *f* fire insurance
Feu'erwache *f* firehouse
Feu'erwalze *f* (mil) creeping barrage
Feu'erwehr *f* fire department
Feu'erwehrmann *m* (-[e]s;-̈er & -leute) fireman
Feu'erwerk *n* fireworks
Feu'erwerkskörper *m* firecracker
Feu'erzange *f* fire tongs
Feu'erzeug *n* cigarette lighter
Feu'erzeugbenzin *n* lighter fluid
feurig ['fɔɪrɪç] *adj* fiery; ardent
Fiasko [fɪ'asko] *n* (-s;-s) fiasco
Fibel ['fibəl] *f* (-;-n) primer; (archeol) fibula
Fiber ['fibər] *f* (-;-n) fiber
Fichte ['fɪçtə] *f* (-;-n) spruce; pine
Fich'tennadel *f* pine needle
fidel [fɪ'del] *adj* jolly, cheerful
Fieber ['fibər] *n* (-s;-) fever; **das F. messen** take the temperature
fie'berhaft *adj* feverish
fieberig ['fibərɪç] *adj* feverish
fie'berkrank *adj* running a fever
fiebern ['fibərn] *intr* be feverish
Fie'berphantasie *f* delirium
Fie'bertabelle *f* temperature chart
Fiedel ['fidəl] *f* (-;-n) fiddle
Fie'delbogen *m* fiddlestick
fiel [fil] *pret of* fallen
Figur [fɪ'gur] *f* (-;-en) figure; (cards) face card
figürlich [fɪ'gyrlɪç] *adj* figurative
fiktiv [fɪk'tif] *adj* fictitious
Filet [fɪ'le] *n* (-s;-s) (culin) fillet

Filiale [fɪl'jɑlə] *f* (-;-n) branch
Filia'lengeschäft *n* chain store
Filigran [fɪlɪ'grɑn] *n* (-s;-e), **Filigran'arbeit** *f* filigree
Film [fɪlm] *m* (-s;-e) film; (cin) movie
Film'atelier *n* motion-picture studio
Film'empfindlichkeit *f* film speed
Film'kulisse *f* (cin) movie set
Film'leinwand *f* movie screen
Film'probe *f* screen test
Film'regisseur *m* (cin) director
Film'wesen *n* motion-picture industry
Filter ['fɪltər] *m & n* (-s;-) filter
Fil'teranlage *f* filtration plant
Fil'terkaffee *m* drip-grind coffee
Fil'termundstück *n* filter tip
filtern ['fɪltərn] *tr* filter, strain
filtrieren [fɪl'triərən] *tr* filter
Filz [fɪlts] *m* (-es;-e) felt; (coll) miser, skinflint
Filz'schreiber *m* felt pen
Fimmel ['fɪməl] *m* (-s;-) craze, fad
-fimmel *m comb.fm.* mania for
Finanz [fɪ'nɑnts] *f* (-;-en) finance
Finanz- *comb.fm.* financial, fiscal
Finanz'amt *n* internal revenue service
Finanz'ausschuß *m* (adm) ways and means committee
Finanzen [fɪ'nɑntsən] *pl* finances
finanziell [fɪnɑn'tsjel] *adj* financial
finanzieren [fɪnɑn'tsirən] *tr* finance
Finanz'minister *m* secretary of the treasury
Finanz'ministerium *n* treasury department
Finanz'wesen *n* finances
Finanz'wirtschaft *f* public finances
Findelkind ['fɪndəlkɪnt] *n* foundling
finden ['fɪndən] §59 *tr* find; **f. Sie nicht?** don't you think so? || *ref* be found; **ach, das wird sich schon f.** oh, we'll see about that; **es fanden sich** there were; **es findet sich** it happens, it turns out; **sich f. in** (*acc*) resign oneself to; **sie haben sich gefunden** they were united || *intr* find one's way
findig ['fɪndɪç] *adj* resourceful
Findling ['fɪntlɪŋ] *m* (-s;-e) foundling; (geol) boulder
fing [fɪŋ] *pret of* fangen
Finger ['fɪŋər] *m* (-s;-) finger
Fin'gerabdruck *m* fingerprint
fin'gerfertig *adj* deft
Fin'gerhut *m* thimble; (bot) foxglove
fingern ['fɪŋərn] *tr* finger
Fin'gerspitze *f* finger tip; **bis in die Fingerspitzen** through and through
Fin'gerspitzengefühl *n* sensitivity
Fin'gersprache *f* sign language
Fingerzeig ['fɪŋərtsaɪk] *m* (-s;-e) hint
fingieren [fɪŋ'girən] *tr* feign
fingiert [fɪŋ'girt] *adj* fictitious
Fink [fɪŋk] *m* (-en;-en) finch
Finne ['fɪnə] *m* (-n;-n) Finn || *f* (-;-n) fin; (*Ausschlag*) pimple
Fin'nenausschlag *m* acne
Finnin ['fɪnɪn] *f* (-;-nen) Finn
finnisch ['fɪnɪʃ] *adj* Finnish
Finnland ['fɪnlɑnt] *n* (-s;) Finland
finster ['fɪnstər] *adj* dark; gloomy
Finsternis ['fɪnstərnɪs] *f* (-;) darkness; gloom

Finte ['fɪntə] f (-;-n) feint; trick

Firlefanz ['fɪrləfants] m (-es;) junk;
F. treiben fool around

Fir·ma ['fɪrma] f (-;-men [mən]) firm

Firmament [fɪrma'mɛnt] n (-[e]s;-e)
firmament

firmen ['fɪrmən] tr (Cath) confirm

Fir'menschild n (com) name plate

Fir'menwert m (com) good will

Firmling ['fɪrmlɪŋ] m (-s;-e) (Cath)
person to be confirmed

Fir'mung f (-;-en) (Cath) confirmation

Fir·nis ['fɪrnɪs] m (-ses;-se) varnish;
mit F. streichen varnish

firnissen ['fɪrnɪsən] tr varnish

First [fɪrst] m (-es;-e) (archit) ridge
(of roof); (poet) mountain ridge

Fis [fɪs] n (-;-) (mus) F sharp

Fisch [fɪʃ] m (-es;-e) fish

fischen ['fɪʃən] tr fish for, catch || intr
(nach) fish (for)

Fi'scher m (-s;-) fisherman

Fischerei [fɪʃə'raɪ] f (-;-en) fishing;
fishery; fishing trade

Fi'schergerät n fishing tackle

Fisch'fang m catch, haul

Fisch'gräte f fishbone

Fisch'grätenmuster n (tex) herringbone

Fisch'händler –in §6 mf fishmonger

fischig ['fɪʃɪç] adj fishy

Fisch'kunde f ichthyology

Fisch'laich m spawn, fish eggs

Fisch'otter m & f otter

Fisch'rogen m roe

Fisch'schuppe f scale (of a fish)

Fisch'zug m (& fig) catch

fiskalisch [fɪs'kalɪʃ] adj fiscal

Fis·kus ['fɪskus] m (-;-kusse & -ken
[kən]) treasury

Fistelstimme ['fɪstəl/tɪmə] f falsetto

Fittich ['fɪtɪç] m (-es;-e) (poet) wing

fix [fɪks] adj (Idee, Preis) fixed;
(flink) smart, sharp; fix und fertig
all set; all in; done for; fix und
fertig mit through with; mach fix!
make it snappy!

fixen ['fɪksən] intr sell short

fixieren [fɪ'ksirən] tr fix, decide upon;
stare fixedly at; (phot) fix

Fixier'mittel n (phot) fixer

flach [flax] adj flat, level; shallow;
(Relief) low; (fig) dull

Fläche ['flɛçə] f (-;-n) surface; plain;
expanse; facet; (geom) area

Flä'cheninhalt m (geom) area

Flä'chenraum m surface area

flach'fallen §72 intr (SEIN) (coll) fall
flat, flop

Flach'heit f (-;) flatness; shallowness

Flach'land n lowland

Flach'relief n low relief, bas-relief

Flach'rennen n flat racing

Flachs [flaks] m (-es;-e) flax

flachsen ['flaksən] intr (coll) kid

flächse(r)n ['flɛksə(r)n] adj flaxen

Flach'zange f pliers

flackern ['flakərn] intr flicker; (Stimme) quaver, shake

Flagge ['flagə] f (-;-n) flag (esp. for
signaling or identification)

Flag'genmast m flagpole

Flag'genstange f flagstaff

Flagg'schiff n flagship

Flak [flak] abbr (Flugzeugabwehr-
kanone) anti-aircraft gun

Flak'feuer n flak

Flakon [fla'kõ] m & n (-s;-s) perfume
bottle

Flamme ['flamə] f (-;-n) flame

flammen ['flamən] intr blaze; be in
flames

flam'mend adj passionate

Fla'mmenwerfer m flame thrower

Flandern ['flandərn] n (-s;) Flanders

flandrisch ['flandrɪʃ] adj Flemish

Flanell [fla'nɛl] m (-s;-e) flannel

Flanke ['flaŋkə] f (-;-n) flank

Flan'kenfeuer n (mil) enfilade; mit F.
bestreichen enfilade

flankieren [flaŋ'kirən] tr flank

Flansch [flanʃ] m (-es;-e) flange

Flasche ['flaʃə] f (-;-n) bottle; (coll)
flop; (mach) pulley

Fla'schengranate f Molotov cocktail

Fla'schenzug m block and tackle; (coll)
pulley

Flaschner ['flaʃnər] m (-s;-) plumber

flatterhaft ['flatərhaft] adj fickle

flattern ['flatərn] intr flutter, flap

flau [flau] adj stale; (schwach) feeble,
faint; (fade) dull, lifeless; (com)
slack; (phot) overexposed; mir ist
f. (im Magen) I feel queezy

Flaum [flaum] m (-[e]s;) down; (am
Gesicht, am Pfirsich) fuzz

flaumig ['flaumɪç] adj downy, fluffy

Flause ['flauzə] f (-;-n) fib; Flausen
funny ideas, nonsense

Flaute ['flautə] f (-;-n) (com) slack
period; (naut) dead calm

fläzen ['flɛtsən] ref sprawl out

Flechse ['flɛksə] f (-;-n) (dial) sinew,
tendon

Flechte ['flɛçtə] f (-;-n) plait; (bot)
lichen; (pathol) ringworm

flechten ['flɛçtən] §74 tr braid, plait;
(Körbe) weave

Fleck [flɛk] m (-[e]s;-e & -en) spot;
blemish; (Flicken, Landstück) patch

Flecken ['flɛkən] m (-s;-) spot; piece
of land; (Markt-) market town

fleckenlos ['flɛkenlos] adj spotless

Fleck'fieber n spotted fever

fleckig ['flɛkɪç] adj spotty; splotchy

fleddern ['flɛdərn] tr (sl) rob

Fledermaus ['fledərmaus] f bat

Flegel ['flegəl] m (-s;-) flail; (coll)
lout, boor

Flegelei [flegə'laɪ] f (-;) rudeness

fle'gelhaft adj uncouth, boorish

Fle'geljahre pl awkward age

flehen ['fle·ən] intr plea; zu j–m f.
implore s.o. || Flehen n (-s;-) sup-
plication

Fleisch [flaɪʃ] n (-es;) flesh; meat;
sich ins eigene F. schneiden cut one's
own throat; wildes F. proud flesh

Fleisch'bank f (-;-e) meat counter

Fleisch'beil n cleaver

Fleisch'beschau f meat inspection

Fleisch'brühe f broth

Flei'scher m (-s;-) butcher

Flei'scheslust f (-;) lust

Fleisch'farbe f flesh color

fleischfressend adj carnivorous

Fleisch'hacker (-s;-) m, **Fleisch'hauer** m (-s;-) butcher
fleischig ['flaɪçiç] adj fleshy; meaty
fleisch'lich adj carnal
Fleisch'markt m meat market
Fleisch'pastete f meat pie
Fleisch'saft m meat juice, gravy
Fleisch'salat m diced-meat salad
Fleisch'speise f meat course
Fleisch'spieß m skewer
Fleischwerdung ['flaɪʃverduŋ] f (-;)
incarnation
Fleisch'wolf m meat grinder
Fleisch'wunde f flesh wound, laceration
Fleisch'wurst f pork sausage
Fleiß [flaɪs] m (-es;) diligence, industry; **mit F.** intentionally
fleißig ['flaɪsɪç] adj diligent, hardworking
flektieren [flɛk'tiːrən] tr inflect
fletschen ['flɛtʃən] tr bare (teeth)
Flexion [flɛk'sjoːn] f (-;-en) (gram) inflection
flicken ['flɪkən] tr patch, repair || **Flicken** m (-s;-) patch
Flick'schuster m cobbler
Flick'werk n patchwork; hotchpotch; (Pfuscherei) bungling job
Flick'zeug n repair kit
Flieder ['fliːdər] m (-s;-) lilac
Fliege ['fliːgə] f (-;-n) fly; (coll) bow tie
fliegen ['fliːgən] §57 tr fly, pilot || intr (SEIN) fly; (coll) get sacked; **in die Luft f.** blow up
Flie'genfenster n window screen
Flie'gengewicht n flyweight division
Fliegengewichtler ['fliːgəngəvɪçtlər] m (-s;-) flyweight (boxer)
Flie'gengitter n screen
Flie'genklappe f, **Flie'genklatsche** f fly swatter
Flie'genpilz m toadstool
Flie'ger m (-s;-) flyer
Flieger- comb.fm. air-force; air, aerial; flying; airman's
Flie'gerabwehr f anti-aircraft defense
Flie'geralarm m air-raid alarm
Flie'gerangriff m air raid
Flie'gerheld m (aer) ace
Flie'gerhorst m air base
Flie'gerin f (-;-nen) flyer
Flie'gerschaden m air-raid damage
fliehen ['fliː-ən] §75 tr run away from; avoid || intr (SEIN) flee
Flieh'kraft f (-;) centrifugal force
Fliese ['fliːzə] f (-;-n) tile
Flie'senleger m tiler, tile man
Fließband ['flɪsbant] n (-[e]s;¨er) assembly line
fließen ['fliːsən] §76 intr (SEIN) flow
flie'ßend adj (Wasser) running; (fig) fluent
Fließheck ['flɪshɛk] n (aut) fastback
Fließpapier ['flɪspapiːr] n blotting paper
flimmern ['flɪmərn] intr glimmer; glisten, shimmer; flicker
flink [flɪŋk] adj nimble, quick; **mach mal f.!** get a move on!
Flinte ['flɪntə] f (-;-n) shotgun; gun
Flin'tenlauf m gun barrel

flirren ['flɪrən] intr shimmer
Flirt [flɪrt] m (-s;-s) flirtation; boyfriend, girlfriend
flirten ['flɪrtən] intr flirt
Flitter ['flɪtər] m (-s;-) sequins; (Scheinglanz) flashiness
Flit'terglanz m flashiness
Flit'tergold m gold tinsel
Flit'terkram m trinkets
Flit'terstaat m flashy clothes
Flit'terwochen pl honeymoon
flitzen ['flɪtsən] intr (SEIN) flit
flocht [floxt] pret of flechten
Flocke ['flɔkə] f (-;-n) flake; tuft
flog [floːk] pret of fliegen
floh [floː] pret of fliehen || **Floh** m (-s;¨e) flea; **j-m e-n F. ins Ohr setzen** put a bug in s.o.'s ear
Floh'hüpfspiel n tiddlywinks
Flor [floːr] m (-s;-e) bloom || m (-s;-e & ¨e) gauze; (tex) nap, pile
Flor'band n (-[e]s;¨er) crepe; mourning band
Florett [floː'rɛt] n (-s;-e) foil
florieren [floː'riːrən] intr flourish
Floskel ['flɔskəl] f (-;-n) rhetorical ornament, flowery phrase
Floß [floːs] n (-es;¨e) raft
Flosse ['flɔsə] f (-;-n) fin; (aer) stabilizer
flößen ['fløːsən] tr float
Flöte ['fløːtə] f (-;-n) flute; (cards) flush
flöten ['fløːtən] tr play on the flute || intr play the flute; **f. gehen** (fig) go to the dogs
flott [flɔt] adj afloat; brisk, lively; gay; chic, dashing
Flotte ['flɔtə] f (-;-n) fleet
Flot'tenstützpunkt m naval base
flott'gehend adj (com) brisk, lively
Flottille [flɔ'tɪljə] f (-;-n) flotilla
flott'machen tr set afloat; (fig) get going again
Flöz [fløːts] n (-es;-e) (min) seam
Fluch [fluːx] m (-[e]s;¨e) curse
fluchen ['fluːxən] intr curse
Flucht [fluxt] f (-;-en) flight; escape; straight line, alignment; (Häuser-) row; (Spielraum) space, leeway; (Zimmer-) suite; **außerhalb der F.** out of line; **in die F. schlagen** put to flight
flüchten ['flʏçtən] ref (an acc, in acc) take refuge (in), have recourse (to) || intr (SEIN) flee; escape; (vor dat) run away (from)
flüchtig ['flʏçtɪç] adj fugitive; fleeting; cursory, superficial; hurried; (chem) volatile; **f. sein** be on the run; **f. werden** escape, flee
Flüch'tigkeitsfehler m oversight, slip
Flüchtling ['flʏçtlɪŋ] m (-s;-) fugitive; refugee
Flücht'lingslager n refugee camp
Flug [fluːk] m (-[e]s;¨e) flight
Flug'abwehr f anti-aircraft defense
Flugabwehr- comb.fm. anti-aircraft
Flug'anschluß m plane connection
Flug'aufgabe f, **Flug'auftrag** m (aer) mission
Flug'bahn f line of flight; trajectory
Flug'blatt n leaflet, flyer

Flügel ['flygəl] *m* (-s;-) wing; (*e-r Doppeltür*) leaf; (mus) grand piano
Flü'geladjutant *m* aide-de-camp
Flü'gelfenster *n* casement window
Flü'gelmutter *f* wing nut
Flü'gelschlag *m* flap of the wings
Flü'gelschraube *f* thumb screw
Flü'geschraubenmutter *f* wing nut
Flü'geltür *f* folding door
Flug'gast *m* (aer) passenger
flügge ['flygə] *adj* (*Vogel*) fledged (fig) ready to go on one's own
Flug'gesellschaft *f* airline company
Flug'hafen *m* airport
Flug'hafenbefeuerung *f* airport lights
Flug'kapitän *m* captain, pilot
Flug'karte *f* plane ticket; aeronautical chart
flug'klar *adj* ready for take-off
Flug'körper *m* missile; space vehicle
Flug'leitung *f* air-traffic control
Flug'linie *f* air route; airline
Flug'meldesystem *n* air-raid warning system
Flug'motor *m* aircraft engine
Flug'ortung *f* (aer) navigation
Flug'plan *m* flight schedule
Flug'platz *m* airfield, airport
Flug'post *f* air mail
Flug'preis *m* air fare
flugs [fluks] *adv* quickly; at once
Flug'schein *m* plane ticket
Flug'schneise *f* air lane
Flug'schrift *f* pamphlet
Flug'strecke *f* flying distance
Flug'stützpunkt *m* air base
flug'tauglich, flug'tüchtig *adj* airworthy
Flug'techniker –in §6 *mf* aeronautical engineer
Flug'verbot *n* (aer) grounding
Flug'verkehr *m* air traffic
Flug'wesen *n* aviation; aeronautics
Flug'wetter *n* flying weather
Flug'zeug *n* airplane, aircraft
Flug'zeugabwehrgeschütz *n*, **Flug'zeugabwehrkanone** *f* anti-aircraft gun
Flug'zeugführer *m* pilot; **zweiter F.** co-pilot, second officer
Flug'zeugführerschein *m* pilot's license
Flug'zeuggeschwader *n* wing (consisting of 3 squadrons of 9 planes each)
Flug'zeugkreuzer *m*, **Flug'zeugmutterschiff** *n* seaplane tender, seaplane carrier
Flug'zeugrumpf *m* fuselage
Flug'zeugstaffel *f* squadron (consisting of 9 planes)
Flug'zeugträger *m* aircraft carrier
Flug'zeugwerk *n* aircraft factory
Flunder ['flundər] *f* (-;-n) flounder
Flunkerer ['fluŋkərər] *m* (-s;-) fibber
flunkern ['fluŋkərn] *intr* fib
Flunsch [flunʃ] *m* (-es;-e) face; **e-n F. ziehen** (or **machen**) make a face
Fluor ['flu·ər] *n* (-s;) fluorine
Fluoreszenz [flu·ɔrɛs'tsɛnts] *f* (-;) fluorescence; fluorescent light
Fluorid [flu·o'rit] *n* (-[e]s;-e) fluoride
Flur [flur] *m* (-[e]s;-e) entrance hall; hallway ‖ *f* (-;-en) open farmland; meadow; community farmland

Flur'garderobe *f* hallway closet
Fluß [flus] *m* (**Flusses; Flüsse**) river; flow; (metal) fusion; (phys) flux
flußab'wärts *adv* downstream
flußauf'wärts *adv* upstream
Fluß'bett *n* riverbed, channel
Flüßchen ['flysçən] *n* (-s;-) rivulet
flüssig ['flysɪç] *adj* liquid; fluid; (*Gelder*) ready; **f. machen** convert into cash ‖ *adv* fluently
Flüs'sigkeit *f* (-;-en) liquid, fluid; (fig) fluency; (fin) liquidity
Flüs'sigkeitsmaß *n* liquid measure
Fluß'pferd *n* hypopotamus
flüstern ['flystərn] *tr & intr* whisper
Flü'sterparole *f* rumor
Flut [flut] *f* (-;-en) flood; waters; high tide
fluten ['flutən] *tr* flood ‖ *intr* (SEIN) flow, pour
Flut'grenze *f* high-water mark
Flut'licht *n* floodlight
Flut'linie *f* high-water mark
Flut'wasser *n* tidewater
Flut'welle *f* tidal wave
Flut'zeit *f* flood tide, high tide
focht [foxt] *pret of* **fechten**
Focksegel ['fɔkzegəl] *n* (-s;-) foresail
fohlen ['folən] *intr* foal ‖ **Fohlen** *n* (-s;-) foal
Folge ['fɔlgə] *f* (-;-n) sequence; consequence; succession; series; (*e-s Romans*) continuation; (*e-r Zeitschrift*) number; **die Folgen tragen** take the consequences; **in der F.** subsequently
folgen ['fɔlgən] *intr* (dat) obey ‖ *intr* (SEIN) (dat) follow; (dat) succeed; (aus) ensue (from)
folgendermaßen ['fɔlgəndərmasən] *adv* in the following manner, as follows
fol'genschwer *adj* momentous, grave
fol'gerichtig *adj* logical, consistent
folgern ['fɔlgərn] *tr* infer, conclude
Fol'gerung *f* (-;-en) inference, conclusion
Fol'gesatz *m* (gram) result clause
fol'gewidrig *adj* inconsistent
Fol'gezeit *f*—**in der F.** in subsequent times
folglich ['fɔlklɪç] *adv* consequently
folgsam ['fɔlkzam] *adj* obedient
Foliant [fol'jant] *m* (-en;-en) folio
Folie ['foljə] *f* (-;-n) (metal) foil
Folter ['fɔltər] *f* (-;-n) torture; rack; **auf die F. spannen** put to the rack; (fig) keep in suspense
Fol'terbank *f* (-;̈-e) rack
foltern ['fɔltərn] *tr* torture
Fol'terqual *f* torture
Fol'terverhör *n* third degree
Fön [føn] *m* (-[e]s;-e) hand hairdryer
Fond [fõ] *m* (-s;-s) background; rear, back; (culin) gravy
Fonds [fõ] *m* (-s [fõs];-s [fõs]) fund
Fontäne [fɔn'tɛnə] *f* (-;-n) fountain
foppen ['fɔpən] *tr* tease; bamboozle
Fopperei [fɔpə'raɪ] *f* (-;-en) teasing
forcieren [fɔr'sirən] *tr* force; speed up
Förderband ['fœdərbant] *n* (-;̈-er) conveyor belt

För'derer *m* (-s;-) promoter; patron
för'derlich *adj* useful; (*dat*) conducive (to)
fordern ['fordərn] *tr* demand; (*Recht*) claim; (*zum Zweikampf*) challenge; (*vor Gericht*) summon
fördern ['fœrdərn] *tr* promote, back; (*Kohle*) produce; **förderndes Mit'glied** social member; **zutage f.** bring to light
For'derung *f* (-;-en) demand, claim; debt; (*zum Zweikampf*) challenge
För'derung *f* (-;-en) promotion; support; encouragement; (min) output
Forelle [fo'rɛlə] *f* (-;-n) trout
Forke ['fɔrkə] *f* (-;-n) pitchfork
Form [fɔrm] *f* (-;-en) form; shape; mold; condition; (gram) voice; **die F. wahren** keep up appearances
formal [fɔr'mɑl] *adj* formal
Formalität [fɔrmali'tɛt] *f* (-;-en) formality
Format [fɔr'mɑt] *n* (-[e]s;-e) size, format; distinction, stature
Formel ['fɔrməl] *f* (-;-n) formula
for'melhaft *adj* (*Wendung, Gebet*) set
formell [fɔr'mɛl] *adj* formal
formen ['fɔrmən] *tr* form, shape, mold
For'menlehre *f* morphology
Form'fehler *m* defect; flaw; (jur) irregularity
formieren [fɔr'mirən] *tr & ref* line up
-förmig [fœrmɪç] *comb.fm.* -shaped
förmlich ['fœrmlɪç] *adj* formal || *adv* virtually; literally; formally
form'los *adj* shapeless; informal; unconventional; rude; (chem) amorphous
form'schön *adj* well-shaped, beautiful
Formular [fɔrmu'lɑr] *n* (-s;-e) form, blank
formulieren [fɔrmu'lirən] *tr* formulate; word, phrase
Formulie'rung *f* (-;-en) formulation; wording
form'vollendet *adj* perfectly shaped
forsch [fɔrʃ] *adj* dashing || *adv* briskly
forschen ['fɔrʃən] *intr* do research; (nach) search (for)
For'scher -in §6 *mf* researcher; scholar; explorer
For'schung *f* (-;-en) research
For'schungsanstalt *f* research center
Forst [fɔrst] *m* (-[e]s;-e) forest
Förster ['fœrstər] *m* (-s;-) forester; forest ranger
Forst'fach *n* forestry
Forst'mann *m* (-es;-leute) forester
Forst'revier *n* forest range
Forst'wesen *n*, **Forst'wirtschaft** *f* forestry
fort [fɔrt] *adv* away; gone, lost; (*weiter*) on; (*vorwärts*) forward; **ich muß f.** I must be off; **in e—m f.** continuously; **und so f.** and so forth || **Fort** [fɔr] *n* (-s;-s) (mil) fort
fortan' *adv* from now on, henceforth
Fort'bestand *m* continued existence
fort'bestehen §146 *intr* continue
fort'bewegen §56 *tr* move along || *ref* get about
fort'bilden *ref* continue one's studies
Fort'bildung *f* continuing education

fort'bleiben §62 *intr* (SEIN) stay away
Fort'dauer *f* continuance
fort'dauern *intr* continue; last
fort'fahren §71 *tr* hawl away; continue (*to say*); **f. zu** (*inf*) continue to (*inf*), go on (*ger*) || *intr* continue, go on || *intr* (SEIN) drive off, leave
Fort'fall *m* omission; discontinuation; **in F. kommen** be discontinued
fort'fallen §72 *intr* (SEIN) drop out; be omitted; be discontinued
fort'führen *tr* lead away; continue; (*Geschäft*) carry on; (*Linie*) extend
Fort'gang *m* departure; continuation; progress
fort'gehen §82 *intr* (SEIN) go away
fort'geschritten *adj* advanced; late
fort'gesetzt *adj* incessant
fort'kommen §99 *intr* (SEIN) go on, make progress; get away; **in der Welt f.** get ahead in the world || **Fortkommen** *n* (-s;) progress
fort'lassen §104 *tr* allow to go; omit
fort'laufen §105 *intr* (SEIN) run away
fort'laufend *adj* continuing; (*Nummer*) consecutive
fort'leben *intr* live on
fort'pflanzen *tr* propagate; spread || *ref* reproduce; propagate; spread
Fort'pflanzung *f* (-;) propagation
fort'reißen §53 *tr* tear away; carry; **j—n mit sich f.** sweep s.o. off his feet; **sich f. lassen** be caried away
fort'schaffen *tr* remove
fort'scheren *ref* (coll) scram
fort'schreiten §86 *intr* (SEIN) progress, advance
Fort'schritt *m* progress; improvement
fort'schrittlich *adj* progressive
fort'setzen *tr* continue; resume
Fort'setzung *f* (-;-en) continuation; sequel; installment; **F. folgt** to be continued
fort'während *adj* continual; lasting, permanent || *adv* all the time, always
Fossil [fo'sil] *n* (-s;-ien [jən]) fossil
foul [faul] *adj* foul, dirty || **Foul** *n* (-s;-) (sport) foul; **ein F. begehen an** (*dat*) commit a foul against
foulen ['faulən] *tr* (sport) foul
Foyer [fwa'je] *n* (-s;-s) foyer; (*im Hotel*) lobby
Fracht [fraxt] *f* (-;-en) freight, cargo
Fracht'brief *m* bill of lading
Frachter ['fraxtər] *m* (-s;-) freighter
Fracht'gut *n* freight, goods
Fracht'raum *m* cargo compartment; cargo capacity
Fracht'stück *n* package
Frack [frak] *m* (-[e]s;⸚e & -s) tails
Frack'schoß *m* coattail
Frage ['frɑgə] *f* (-;-n) question; **außer F. stehen** be out of the question; **e—e F. stellen** ask a question; **in F. stellen** call in question; **kommt nicht in F.!** nothing doing!
Fra'gebogen *m* questionnaire
fragen ['frɑgən] *tr* ask; **j—n f. nach** ask s.o. about; **j—n nach der Zeit f.** ask s.o. the time; **j—n f. um** ask s.o. for || *ref* wonder || *impers ref*—**es fragt sich, ob** the question is whether || *intr* ask

Fra'gesatz *m* interrogative sentence; **abhängiger F.** indirect question

Fragesteller ['frɑːgə'tɛlər] *m* (-s;-) questioner

Fra'gewort *n* (-es;:-er) interrogative

Fra'gezeichen *n* question mark

fraglich ['frɑːklɪç] *adj* questionable

fraglos ['frɑːkloːs] *adv* unquestionably

Fragment [frɑːg'mɛnt] *n* (-[e]s;-e) fragment

frag'würdig *adj* questionable

Fraktion [frɑːk'tsjoːn] *f* (-;-en) (chem) fraction; (pol) faction

fraktionell [frɑːktsə'nɛl] *adj* factional

Fraktur [frɑːk'tuːr] *f* (-;-en) fracture; Gothic type, Gothic lettering; **mit j-m F. reden** talk turkey with s.o.

frank [frɑːŋk] *adv*—**f. und frei** quite frankly

Franke ['frɑːŋkə] *m* (-n;-n) Franconian; (hist) Frank

Franken ['frɑːŋkən] *m* (-[e]s;-) (Swiss) franc ‖ *n* (-s;) Franconia

frankieren [frɑːŋ'kiːrən] *tr* frank, put postage on

Fränkin ['frɛŋkɪn] *f* (-;-nen) Frank

franko ['frɑːŋko] *adv* postage paid; **f. Berlin** freight paid to Berlin; **f. verzollt** free of freight and duty

Frank'reich *n* (-s;) France

Franse ['frɑːnzə] *f* (-;-n) fringe

fransen ['frɑːnzən] *intr* fray

Franzband ['frɑːntsbɑːnt] *m* (-[e]s;:-e) leather binding

Franz'branntwein *m* rubbing alcohol

Franzose [frɑːn'tsoːzə] *m* (-;-n) Frenchman; **die Franzosen** the French

Französin [frɑːn'tsøːzɪn] *f* (-;-nen) Frenchwoman

französisch [frɑːn'tsøːzɪʃ] *adj* French

frappant [frɑː'pɑːnt] *adj* striking

frappieren [frɑː'piːrən] *tr* strike, astonish; (*Wein*) put on ice

fräsen ['frɛːzən] *tr* mill

fraß [frɑːs] *pret* of **fressen** ‖ **Fraß** *m* (-es;) fodder, food; (pel) garbage

Fratz [frɑːts] *m* (-es;-e) brat

Fratze ['frɑːtsə] *f* (-;-n) grimace; (coll) face; **e—e F. schneiden** make a face

frat'zenhaft *adj* grotesque

Frau [frɑʊ] *f* (-;-en) woman; lady; wife; (*vor Namen*) Mrs; **zur F. geben** give in marriage

Frauen— *comb.fm.* of women

Frau'enarzt *m*, **Frau'enärztin** *f* gynecologist

Frau'enheld *m* ladykiller

Frau'enkirche *f* Church of Our Lady

Frau'enkleidung *f* women's wear

Frau'enklinik *f* women's hospital

Frau'enleiden *n* gynecological disorder

Frau'enzimmer *n* (pej) woman, female

Fräulein ['frɔʏlaɪn] *n* (-s;-) young lady; (*vor Namen*) Miss

frau'lich *adj* womanly

frech [frɛç] *adj* brazen; fresh, smart

Frech'dachs *m* smart aleck

Frech'heit *f* (-;-en) impudence

Fregatte [fre'gɑːtə] *f* (-;-n) frigate

frei [frɑɪ] *adj* free; (*Feld*) open; (*offen*) frank; **auf freien Fuß setzen** release; **auf freier Strecke** (rr) outside the station; **die freien Berufe**

the professions; **freie Fahrt** (public sign) resume speed; **freies Spiel haben** have a free hand; **frei werden** (chem) be released; **ich bin so frei** thank you, I will have some; **sich frei machen** take off one's clothes ‖ **Freie** §5 *n*—**im Freien** out of doors; **ins Freie** out of doors, into the open

Frei'bad *n* outdoor swimming pool

Frei'bank *f* (-;:-e) cheap-meat counter

frei'beruflich *adj* freelance

Frei'betrag *m* allowable deduction

Frei'brief *m* charter; (fig) license

Freier ['frɑɪ·ər] *m* (-s;-) suitor

Frei'frau *f* baroness

Frei'gabe *f* release

frei'geben §80 *tr* release; **für den Verkehr f.** open to traffic ‖ *intr*—**j-m f.** give s.o. (*time*) off

freigebig ['frɑɪgeːbɪç] *adj* generous

Frei'gebigkeit *f* (-;) generosity

Frei'geist *m* freethinker

frei'geistig *adj* open-minded

frei'gestellt *adj* optional

frei'haben *intr* be off

Frei'hafen *m* free port

frei'halten §90 *tr* keep open; **j-n f.** pay the tab for s.o.

Frei'heit *f* (-;-en) freedom; **dichterische F.** poetic license

Frei'heitskrieg *m* war of liberation

Frei'heitsstrafe *f* imprisonment

Frei'herr *m* baron

Frei'karte *f* free ticket; (theat) complimentary ticket

Frei'korps *n* volunteer corps

frei'lassen §104 *tr* release, set free

Frei'lauf *m* coasting

frei'legen *tr* lay open, expose

frei'lich *adv* of course

Freilicht— *comb.fm.* open-air

frei'machen *tr* (*Platz*) vacate; (*Straße*) clear; (*Brief*) stamp; **den Arm f.** roll up one's sleeves ‖ *ref* undress

Frei'marke *f* postage stamp

Frei'maurer *m* Freemason

Frei'maurerei *f* freemasonry

Frei'mut *m* frankness

frei'mütig *adj* frank, outspoken

frei'schaffend *adj* freelance

Frei'sinn *m* (pol) liberalism

frei'sinnig *adj* (pol) liberal

frei'sprechen §64 *tr* acquit

Frei'spruch *m* acquittal

frei'stehen §146 *intr*—**es steht Ihnen frei zu** (*inf*) you are free to (*inf*)

frei'stehend *adj* free-standing; (*Gebäude*) detached

Frei'stelle *f* scholarship

frei'stellen *tr* exempt; **j-m etw f.** leave it to s.o.'s discretion

Frei'stoß *m* (fb) free kick

Frei'tag *m* Friday

Frei'tod *m* suicide

Frei'treppe *f* outdoor stairway

Frei'wild *n* (& fig) fair game

frei'willig *adj* voluntary ‖ **Freiwillige** §5 *mf* (& mil) volunteer

Frei'zeichen *n* (telp) dial tone

Frei'zeit *f* spare time, leisure

Frei'zeitgestaltung *f* planning one's leisure time

freizügig ['frɑɪtsyːgɪç] *adj* unhampered

fremd [fremt] *adj* foreign; strange; someone else's; *(Name)* assumed
fremd'artig *adj* strange, odd
Fremde ['fremdə] §5 *mf* foreigner; stranger || *f*—**aus der F.** from abroad; **in der F.** far from home; **in die F. gehen** go far from home; go abroad
Frem'denbuch *n* visitors' book
Frem'denführer –in §6 *mf* tour guide; *(Buch)* guidebook
Frem'denheim *n* boarding house
Frem'denlegion *f* foreign legion
Frem'denverkehr *m* tourism
Frem'denzimmer *n* guest room; spare room
Fremd'herrschaft *f* foreign domination
Fremd'körper *m* foreign body; *(pol)* alien element
fremdländisch ['fremtlendɪ/] *adj* foreign
Fremdling ['fremtlɪŋ] *m* (-s;-) stranger
Fremd'sprache *f* foreign language
Fremd'wort *n* (-es;-̈er) foreign word
frequentieren [frekven'tirən] *tr* frequent
Frequenz [fre'kvents] *f* (-;-en) frequency; *(Besucherzahl)* attendance
Freske ['freskə] *f* (-;-n), **Fres·ko** ['fresko] *n* (-s;-ken [kən]) fresco
Freßbeutel ['fresbɔɪtəl] *m* feed bag
Fresse ['fresə] *f* (-;-n) (sl) puss
fressen ['fresən] §70 *tr (von Tieren)* eat; feed on; (sl) devour; *(ätzen)* corrode, fret; (tech) freeze || *ref*—**sich satt f.** stuff oneself || *intr* (sl) eat; *(an dat)* gnaw (at)
Fresserei [fresə'raɪ] *f* (-;) gluttony
Freude ['frɔɪdə] *f* (-;-n) joy, pleasure
Freu'denbotschaft *f* glad tidings
Freu'denfeier *f*, **Freu'denfest** *n* celebration, happy occasion
Freu'denhaus *n* brothel
Freu'denmädchen *n* prostitute
freudig ['frɔɪdɪç] *adj* joyful, happy
freud'los *adj* joyless, sad
freuen ['frɔɪ·ən] *tr* please || *ref* be happy; *(an dat)* be delighted (by); *(auf acc)* look forward to (to); *(über acc)* be glad (about) || *impers*—**es freut mich** I am glad
Freund [frɔɪnt] *m* (-[e]s;-e) friend; boyfriend; **F. der Musik** music lover
Freundin ['frɔɪndɪn] *f* (-;-nen) friend; girlfriend
freund'lich *adj* friendly; cheerful
Freund'lichkeit *f* (-;) friendliness
Freund'schaft *f* (-;-en) friendship
Frevel ['frefəl] *m* (-s;) outrage; crime; sacrilege
fre'velhaft *adj* wicked
freveln ['frefəln] *intr* commit an outrage; **am Gesetz f.** violate the law
Fre'veltat *f* outrage
Friede ['fridə] *m* (-ns;), **Frieden** ['fridən] *m* (-s;) peace
Frie'densrichter *m* justice of the peace
Frie'densschluß *m* conclusion of peace
Frie'densstifter –in §6 *m* peacemaker
Frie'densverhandlungen *pl* peace negotiations
Frie'densvertrag *m* peace treaty

friedfertig ['fritfertɪç] *adj* peaceable
Friedhof ['frithof] *m* cemetery
friedlich ['fritlɪç] *adj* peaceful
friedliebend ['fritlibant] *adj* peace-loving
frieren ['frirən] §77 *intr* be cold; freeze || *impers*—**es friert mich** I'm freezing
Fries [fris] *m* (-es;-e) frieze
Frikadelle [frika'delə] *f* (-;-n) meatball
frisch [frɪ/] *adj* fresh; *(kühl)* cool; *(munter)* brisk || *adv* freshly; **f. gestrichen** (public sign) wet paint; **f. zu!** on with it! || **Frische** *f* (-;) freshness; coolness; briskness
Frisch'haltepackung *f* vacuum package
Friseur [frɪ'zør] *m* (-s;-e) barber
Friseur'laden *m* barbershop
Friseur'sessel *m* barber chair
Friseuse [frɪ'zøzə] *f* (-;-n) hairdresser
frisieren [frɪ'zirən] *tr (Dokumente)* doctor; (aut) soup up; **j-m die Haare f.** do s.o.'s hair
Frisier'haube *f* hair dryer; hair net
Frisier'kommode *f*, **Frisier'tisch** *m* dresser
Frist [frɪst] *f* (-;-en) time, period, term; (com, jur) grace; **die F. einhalten** meet the deadline
fristen ['frɪstən] *tr*—**das Leben f.** eke out a living
Frisur [frɪ'zur] *f* (-;-en) hairstyle
frivol [frɪ'vol] *adj* frivolous
froh [fro] *adj* glad, happy, joyful
froh'gelaunt *adj* cheerful
fröhlich ['frølɪç] *adj* gay, merry
froh'locken *intr* rejoice
Froh'sinn *m* good humor
fromm [frɔm] *adj* pious, devout
Frömmelei [frœmə'laɪ] *f* (-;-en) sanctimoniousness; sanctimonious act
frommen ['frɔmən] *intr* (dat) profit
Frömmigkeit ['frœmɪçkaɪt] *f* (-;) piety
Frömmler –in ['frœmlər–ɪn] §6 *mf* hypocrite
Fron [fron] *f* (-;) drudgery; (hist) forced labor
frönen ['frønən] *intr (dat)* gratify
Fron'leichnam *m* Corpus Christi
Front [frɔnt] *f* (-;-en) (& mil) front
Front'abschnitt *m* (mil) sector
fror [fror] *pret* of **frieren**
Frosch [frɔʃ] *m* (-es;-̈e) frog; *(Feuerwerkkörper)* firecracker; **sei kein F.!** don't be a party pooper
Frost [frɔst] *m* (-es;-̈e) frost
Frost'beule *f* chilblain
frösteln ['fröstəln] *intr* feel chilly
Frosterfach ['frɔstərfax] *n* freezer compartment *(of refrigerator)*
frostig ['frɔstɪç] *adj* frosty; chilly
Frost'schutzmittel *n* antifreeze
Frottee [frɔ'te] *m & n* (-s;-s) terry cloth
frottieren [frɔ'tirən] *tr* rub down
Frottier'tuch *n* Turkish towel
Frucht [fruxt] *f* (-;-̈e) fruit; foetus
fruchtbar ['fruxtbar] *adj* fruitful
frucht'bringend *adj* productive
Früch'tebecher *m* fruit cup *(as dessert)*
fruchten ['fruxtən] *intr* bear fruit; have effect; be of use

Frucht'folge f rotation of crops
Frucht'knoten m (bot) pistil
frucht'los adj fruitless
Frucht'saft m fruit juice
Frucht'wechsel m rotation of crops
frugal [fru'gɑl] adj frugal
früh [fry] adj early || adv early; in the morning; **von f. bis spät** from morning till night || **Frühe** f (-;) early morning; **in aller F.** very early
früher ['fry·ər] adj earlier; former || adv earlier; sooner; formerly
frühestens ['fry·əstəns] adv at the earliest
Früh'geburt f premature birth
Früh'jahr n, **Frühling** f ['fryliŋ] m (-s; -e) spring
Früh'lingsmüdigkeit f spring fever
früh'reif adj precocious
Früh'schoppen m eye opener (beer, wine)
Früh'stück n breakfast; **zweites F.** lunch
frühstücken ['fry/tykən] intr eat breakfast
früh'zeitig adj & adv (too) early
Fuchs [fuks] m (-es;⁻e) fox; (Pferd) sorrel, chestnut; (educ) freshman
Fuchsie ['fuksjə] f (-;-n) fuchsia
fuchsig ['fuksɪç] adj red; (fig) furious, wild
Fuchs'jagd f fox hunt(ing)
fuchs'rot' adj sorrel
Fuchs'schwanz m foxtail; (bot) amaranth; (carp) hand saw (with tapered blade)
fuchs'teufelswild' adj hopping mad
Fuge ['fugə] f (-;-n) joint; (mus) fugue; **aus allen Fugen gehen** come apart; go to pieces, go to pot
fügen ['fygən] tr join; (verhängen) decree; (carp) joint || ref give in; **es fügte sich** it so happened
fügsam ['fykzɑm] adj compliant; (Haar) manageable
Fü'gung f (-;-en) (gram) construction; **F. des Himmels, F. Gottes** divine providence; **F. des Schicksals** stroke of fate; **göttliche F.** divine providence
fühlbar ['fylbar] adj tangible; noticeable; **sich f. machen** make itself felt
fühlen ['fylən] tr feel, touch; sense || ref feel; feel big || intr—**f. mit** feel for (s.o.); **f. nach** feel for, grope for
–fühlig [fylɪç] comb.fm.—feeling
Füh'lung f (-;) touch, contact; **F. nehmen mit** get in touch with
fuhr [fur] pret of **fahren**
Fuhre ['furə] f (-;-n) wagon load
führen ['fyrən] tr lead; guide; (Artikel) carry, sell; (Besprechungen) hold, conduct; (Bücher) keep; (Geschäft) run, manage; (Krieg) carry on; (Sprache) use; (Titel) bear; (Truppen) command; (Waffe) wield; (Fahrzeug) drive; (aer) pilot; **den Beweis f.** prove; **be aufsicht f. über** (acc) superintend; **j–m den Haushalt f.** keep house for s.o. || ref conduct oneself || intr lead; (sport) be in the lead
Füh'rer –in §6 mf leader, guide; (aer)

pilot; (aut) driver; (com) manager; (sport) captain
Füh'rerschaft f (-;) leadership
Füh'rerschein m driver's license
Füh'rerscheinentzug m suspension of driver's license
Führhund ['fyrhunt] m Seeing Eye dog
Fuhr'park m (aut) fleet
Füh'rung f (-;-en) guidance; leadership; management; guided tour; behavior; (mil) command; (sport) lead
Füh'rungskraft f executive; **die Führungskräfte** management; (pol) authorities; **untere F.** junior executive
Füh'rungsschicht f (com) management
Füh'rungsspitze f top echelon
Fuhr'unternehmen n trucking
Fuhr'werk n cart, wagon; vehicle
Füllbleistift ['fylblaɪ/tɪft] m mechanical pencil
Fülle ['fylə] f (-;) fullness; abundance, wealth; (Körper–) plumpness
füllen ['fylən] tr fill || ref fill up || **Füllen** n (-s;–) foal, colt, filly
Fül'ler m (-s;–) fountain pen
Füll'federhalter m fountain pen
Füll'horn n cornucopia
Füllsel ['fylzəl] n (-s;–) stopgap; (beim Schreiben) padding; (culin) stuffing
Fül'lung f (-;-en) (Zahn–) filling; (Tür–) panel; (culin) stuffing
Fund [funt] m (-[e]s;-e) find; discovery
Fundament [funda'ment] n (-[e]s;-e) foundation
fundamental [fundamen'tɑl] adj fundamental
Fund'büro n lost-and-found department
Fund'grube f (fig) mine, storehouse
fundieren [fun'dirən] tr lay the foundations of; found; establish; (Schuld) fund; **fundiertes Einkommen** unearned income; **gut fundiert** well-established
fünf [fynf] adj & pron five || **Fünf** f (-;-en) five
Fünf'eck n pentagon
fünfte ['fynftə] §9 adj & pron fifth
Fünftel ['fynftəl] n (-s;–) fifth (part)
fünf'zehn adj & pron fifteen || **Fünfzehn** f (-;-en) fifteen
fünf'zehnte §9 adj & pron fifteenth
Fünf'zehntel n (-s;–) fifteenth (part)
fünfzig ['fynftsɪç] adj fifty
fünf'ziger invar adj of the fifties; **die f. Jahre** the fifties
fünfzigste ['fynftsɪçstə] §9 adj & pron fiftieth
fungieren [fuŋ'girən] intr function; **f. als** function as, act as
Funk [fuŋk] m (-s;) radio
Funk'amateur m (rad) ham
Funk'bastler –in §6 (rad) ham
Fünkchen ['fyŋkçən] n (-s;–) small spark; **kein F.** (fig) not an ounce
Funke ['fuŋkə] m (-ns;-n), **Funken** ['fuŋkən] m (-s;–) spark
funkeln ['fuŋkəln] intr sparkle; (Sterne) twinkle
fun'kelnagelneu' adj brand-new

funken ['fuŋkən] *tr* radio, broadcast || *intr* spark
Fun'ker *m* (-s;-) radio operator
Funk'feuer *n* (aer) radio beacon
Funk'leitstrahl *m* radio beam
Funk'meßanlage *f* radar installation
Funk'meßgerät *n* radar
Funk'netz *n* radio network
Funk'peilung *f* radio direction finding
Funk'spruch *m* radiogram
Funk'streifenwagen *m* squad car
Funktionär –in [fuŋktsjɔ'nɛr(ɪn)] §8 *mf* functionary
für [fyr] *prep (acc)* for || **Für** *n*—**das Für und Wider** the pros and cons
Für'bitte *f* intercession
Furche ['furçə] *f* (-;-n) furrow; (*Runzel*) wrinkle; (*Wagenspur*) rut
furchen ['furçən] *tr* furrow; wrinkle
Furcht [furçt] *f* (-;) fear, dread
furchtbar ['furçtbar] *adj* terrible
fürchten ['fyrçtən] *tr* fear, be afraid of || *ref* (**vor** *dat*) be afraid (of)
fürchterlich ['fyrçtərlıç] *adj* terrible, awful
furcht'erregend *adj* awe-inspiring
furcht'los *adj* fearless
furchtsam ['furçtzam] *adj* timid, shy
Furie ['furjə] *f* (-;-n) (myth) Fury
Furnier [fur'nir] *n* (-s;-e) veneer
Furore [fu'rorə] *f* (-;) & *n* (-s;) stir; **F. machen** cause a stir, be a big hit
Für'sorge *f* care; welfare
Für'sorgeamt *n* welfare department
Fürsorger –in ['fyrzɔrgər(ɪn)] §6 *mf* social worker; welfare officer
fürsorglich ['fyrzɔrklıç] *adj* thoughtful
Für'sprache *f* intercession; **F. einlegen** intercede
Für'sprecher –in §6 *mf* intercessor
Fürst [fyrst] *m* (-en;-en) prince
Fürstentum ['fyrstəntum] *n* (-s;-er) principality
Fürstin ['fyrstɪn] *f* (-;-nen) princess
fürst'lich *adj* princely
Furt [furt] *f* (-;-en) ford
Furunkel [fu'runkəl] *m* (-s;-) boil
Für'wort *n* (-[e]s;-er) pronoun

Furz [furts] *m* (-es;-e) (vulg) fart
Fusel ['fuzəl] *m* (-s;) (coll) booze
Fusion [fu'sjon] *f* (-;-en) (com) merger
Fuß [fus] *m* (-es;-e) foot; **auf freien Fuß setzen** set free; **zu Fuß** on foot; **zu Fuß gehen** walk
Fuß'abdruck *m* footprint
Fuß'ball *m* soccer; football
Fuß'bank *f* (-;-e) footstool
Fuß'bekleidung *f* footwear
Fuß'boden *m* floor; flooring
Fussel ['fusəl] *f* (-;-n) fuzz
fußen ['fusən] *intr*—**f. auf** (*dat*) be based on; rely on
Fuß'fall *m* prostration
fuß'fällig *adv* on one's knees
fuß'frei *adj* ankle-length
Fuß'freiheit *f* leg room
Fuß'gänger *m* (-s;-) pedestrian
Fuß'gelenk *n* ankle joint
Fuß'gestell *n* pedestal
–füßig [fysɪç] *comb.fm.* –footed
Fuß'knöchel *m* ankle
Fuß'leiste *f* baseboard, washboard
Füßling ['fyslɪŋ] *m* (-s;-e) foot (*of stocking, sock, etc.*)
Fuß'note *f* footnote
Fuß'pfad *m* footpath
Fuß'pilz *m* athlete's foot
Fuß'spur *f* footprint(s)
Fuß'stapfe *f* footstep
Fuß'steg *m* footbridge; footpath
Fuß'steig *m* footpath; sidewalk
Fuß'tritt *m* step; (*Stoß*) kick
futsch [futʃ] *adj* (coll) gone; (coll) ruined
Futter ['futər] *n* (-s;) fodder, feed; (*e-s Mantels*) lining
Futteral [futə'ral] *n* (-s;-e) case
Fut'terkrippe *f* crib; (sl) gravy train
Fut'terkrippensystem *n* (pol) spoils system
futtern ['futərn] *intr* (coll) eat heartily
füttern ['fytərn] *tr* feed; (*Kleid, Mantel, Pelz*) line
Fut'terneid *m* jealousy
Fut'terstoff *m* lining
Fut'tertrog *m* feed trough

G

G, g [ge] *invar n* G, g; (mus) G
gab [gap] *pret of* geben
Gabardine [gabar'dinə] *m* (-s;-) (tex) gabardine
Gabe ['gabə] *f* (-;-n) gift; donation; talent; (med) dose; **milde G.** alms
Gabel ['gabəl] *f* (-;-n) fork; (arti) bracket; (telp) cradle
Ga'belbein *n* wishbone
Ga'belbissen *m* tidbit
Ga'belfrühstück *n* brunch
gabelig ['gabəlıç] *adj* forked
gabeln ['gabəln] *tr* pick up with a fork || *ref* divide, branch off
Ga'belstapler *m* forklift
Ga'belung *f* (-;-en) fork (*in the road*)

gackeln ['gakəln], **gackern** ['gakərn], **gacksen** ['gaksən] *intr* cackle, cluck
Gage ['gaʒə] *f* (-;-n) salary, pay
gähnen ['gɛnən] *intr* yawn
gaffen ['gafən] *intr* gape; stare
Gala ['gala] *invar f* gala, Sunday best
galant [ga'lant] *adj* courteous; **galantes Abenteuer** love affair
Galante·rie [galantə'ri] *f* (-;-rien ['ri·ən]) courtesy; flattering word
Gala·xis [ga'laksɪs] *f* (-;-xien [ksjən]) galaxy
Galeere [ga'lerə] *f* (-;-n) galley
Gale·rie [galə'ri] *f* (-;-rien ['ri·ən]) gallery
Galgen ['galgən] *m* (-s;-) gallows

Gal'genfrist f (coll) brief respite
Gal'genhumor m grim humor
Gal'genstrick m, **Gal'genvogel** m (coll) good-for-nothing
gälisch ['gɛlɪʃ] adj Gaelic
Galle ['galə] f (-;) gall, bile; (fig) bitterness
Gal'lenblase f gall bladder
Gal'lenstein m gallstone
Gallert ['galərt] n (-[e]s;-e), **Gallerte** [ga'lertə] f (-;-n) gelatine; jelly
gallig ['galɪç] adj bitter; grouchy
Gallone [ga'lonə] f (-;-n) gallon
Galopp [ga'lɔp] m (-[e]s;-s & -e) gallop; **im G. reiten** gallop; **in gestrecktem G.** at full gallop; **in kurzem G.** at a canter
galoppieren [galɔ'pirən] intr (SEIN) gallop
galt [galt] pret of **gelten**
galvanisieren [galvanı'zirən] tr galvanize; electroplate
Gambe ['gambə] f (-;-n) bass viol
gammeln ['gaməln] intr bum around
Gammler ['gamlər] m (-s;-) hippie
Gamsbart ['gamsbart] m goatee
gang [gaŋ] adj—g. und gäbe customary || **Gang** m (-[e]s;-e) walk, gait; (e-r Maschine) running, operation; (im Hause) hallway; (zwischen Reihen) aisle; (Botengang) errand; (Röhre) conduit; (e-r Schraube) thread; (anat) duct, canal; (aut) gear; (box) round; (culin) course; (min) vein, lode; (min) gallery; (mus) run; **außer G. setzen** stop; (aut) put in neutral; **erster G.** low gear; **es ist etw im G.** there is s.th. afoot; **im G. sein** to be in operation; be in progress; **in G. bringen** (or setzen) set in motion; **in vollem G.** in full swing
Gang'art f gait
gangbar ['gaŋbar] adj passable; (Münze) current; (com) marketable
Gängelband ['gɛŋəlbant] n—**am G. führen** (fig) lead by the nose, dominate
-gänger [gɛŋər] comb.fm., e.g., **Fußgänger** pedestrian
gängig ['gɛŋɪç] adj see **gangbar**
Gang'schaltung f (aut) gear shift
Gangster ['gɛŋstər] m (-s;-s) gangster
Ganove [ga'novə] m (-;-n) crook
Gans [gans] f (-;-e) goose
Gänseblümchen ['gɛnzəblymçən] n (-s;-) daisy
Gänsehaut ['gɛnzəhaut] f (coll) goose flesh, goose pimples
Gänseklein ['gɛnzəklaın] n (-s;) (culin) giblets
Gänsemarsch ['gɛnzəmarʃ] m single file
Gänserich ['gɛnzərɪç] m (-s;-e) gander
ganz [gants] adj whole; all; total; intact; **im ganzen** in all || adv entirely, quite; **g. und gar** completely; **g. und gar nicht** not at all || **Ganze** §5 n whole; **aufs G. gehen** go all the way
Ganz'aufnahme f full-length photograph
Gänze ['gɛntsə] f (-;)—**in G.** in its entirety; **zur G.** entirely
Ganz'fabrikat n finished product

Ganz'leinenband m (-[e]s;-e) cloth-bound volume
gänzlich ['gɛntslɪç] adj entire, total
ganz'seitig adj full-page
ganz'tägig adj full-time
gar [gar] adj (culin) well done; (metal) refined || adv quite, very; (sogar) even; **gar nicht** not at all
Garage [ga'raʒə] f (-;-n) garage
Garan-tie [garan'ti] f (-;-tien ['ti-ən]) guarantee
garantieren [garan'tirən] tr guarantee || intr—g. dafür, daß guarantee that
Garaus ['garaus] m (-;) finishing blow
Garbe ['garbə] f (-;-n) sheaf, shock
Garde ['gardə] f (-;-n) guard
Gardenie [gar'denjə] f (-;-n) gardenia
Garderobe [gardə'robə] f (-;-n) wardrobe; (Kleiderablage) cloakroom; (theat) dressing room
Gardero'benmarke f hat or coat check
Gardero'benständer m coatrack, hatrack
Garderobiere [gardəro'bjerə] f (-;-n) cloakroom attendant
Gardine [gar'dinə] f (-;-n) curtain
Gardi'nenhalter m tieback
Gardi'nenpredigt f (coll) dressing down
Gardi'nenstange f curtain rod
gären ['gerən] §78 intr ferment; bubble
Gärmittel ['germıtəl] n ferment; leaven
Garn [garn] n (-[e]s;-e) yarn; thread; snare; (fig) trap; (fig) yarn
Garnele [gar'nelə] f (-;-n) shrimp
garnieren [gar'nirən] tr garnish; trim
Garnison [garnı'zon] f (-;-en) garrison
Garnitur [garnı'tur] f (-;-en) trimming; set (of matching objects); (mach) fittings, mountings; (mil) uniform
garstig ['garstıç] adj ugly; nasty
Garten ['gartən] m (-s;-) garden
Gar'tenanlage f gardens, grounds
Gar'tenarbeit f gardening
Gar'tenarchitekt m landscape gardener
Gar'tenbau m gardening; horticulture
Gar'tenlaube f arbor
Gar'tenmesser n pruning knife
Gärtner ['gertnər] m (-s;-) gardener
Gärtnerei [gertnə'raı] f (-;-en) gardening; truck farm; nursery
Gä'rung f (-;) fermentation
Gas [gas] n (-es;-e) gas; **Gas geben** step on the gas
Gas'anstalt f gasworks
gas'artig adj gaseous
Gas'behälter m gas tank
gas'förmig adj gaseous
Gas'hebel m (aut) accelerator
Gas'heizung f gas heat(ing)
Gas'herd m gas range
Gas'krieg m chemical warfare
Gas'leitung f gas main
Gas'messer m gas meter
Gasse ['gasə] f (-;-n) side street; **über die G. verkaufen** sell takeouts
Gas'sendirne f streetwalker
Gas'senhauer m popular song
Gas'senjunge m urchin

Gast [gast] *m* (-[e]s;:e) guest; boarder; (com) customer; (theat) guest performer; **zu Gast bitten** invite

Gästebuch ['gɛstəbux] *n* guest book; visitors' book

Gast'freund *m* guest

gast'freundlich *adj* hospitable

Gast'freundschaft *f* hospitality

Gast'geber *m* host

Gast'geberin *f* hostess

Gast'haus *n*, **Gast'hof** *m* inn

Gast'hörer **–in §6** *mf* (educ) auditor

gastieren [gas'tirən] *intr* (telv, theat) appear as a guest

gast'lich *adj* hospitable

Gast'mahl *n* feast; banquet

Gast'professor *m* visiting professor

Gast'rolle *f* guest performance; **e–e G. geben** pay a flying visit

Gast'spiel *n* (theat) guest performance

Gast'stätte *f* restaurant

Gast'stube *f* dining room

Gast'wirt *m* innkeeper

Gast'wirtschaft *f* restaurant

Gas'uhr *f* gas meter

Gas'werk *n* gas works

Gas'zähler *m* gas meter

Gatte ['gatə] *m* (-n;-n) husband; **Gatten** married couple

Gatter ['gatər] *n* (-s;-) grating; latticework; iron gate

Gattin ['gatɪn] *f* (-;-nen) wife

Gattung ['gatuŋ] *f* (-;-en) kind, type, species; family; (biol) genus

Gat'tungsname *m* generic name; (gram) common noun

Gau [gau] *m* (-[e]s;-e) district

Gaukelbild ['gaukəlbɪlt] *n* illusion

gaukeln ['gaukəln] *intr* flit, flutter; perform hocus-pocus

Gau'kelspiel *n*, **Gau'kelwerk** *n* sleight of hand; delusion

Gaul [gaul] *m* (-[e]s;:e) horse; nag

Gaumen ['gaumən] *m* (-s;-) palate

Gauner ['gaunər] *m* (-s;-) rogue; swindler

Gaunerei [gaunə'raɪ] *f* (-;-en) swindling; cheating

gaunern ['gaunərn] *intr* swindle

Gau'nersprache *f* thieves' slang

Gaze ['gazə] *f* (-;-n) gauze; cheesecloth

Gazelle [ga'tsɛlə] *f* (-;-n) gazelle

Geächtete [gə'ɛçtətə] §5 *mf* outlaw

Geächze [gə'ɛçtsə] *n* (-s;) moaning

geartet [gə'artət] *adj*—**anders g. sein** be of a different disposition

Gebäck [gə'bɛk] *n* (-s;) baked goods, cookies

geballt [gə'balt] *adj* concentrated; dense; (Schnee) hardened; (Faust) clenched; (Stil) succinct

gebannt [gə'bant] *adj* spellbound

gebar [gə'bar] *pret* of **gebären**

Gebärde [gə'bɛrdə] *f* (-;-n) gesture

gebärden [gə'bɛrdən] *ref* behave

Gebär'denspiel *n* gesticulation

gebaren [gə'barən] *ref* behave, act || **Gebaren** *n* (-s;) behavior

gebären [gə'bɛrən] §79 *tr* bear || **Gebären** *n* (-s;) childbirth; labor

Gebär'mutter *f* (anat) uterus

Gebär'mutterkappe *f* diaphragm

Gebäude [gə'bɔɪdə] *n* (-s;-) building

gebefreudig ['gebəfrɔɪdɪç] *adj* openhanded

Gebein [gə'baɪn] *n* (-[e]s;-e) bones; **Gebeine** bones; mortal remains

Gebell [gə'bɛl] *n* (-[e]s;), **Gebelle** [gə'bɛlə] *n* (-s;) barking

geben ['gebən] §80 *tr* give; yield; (Gelegenheit) afford; (Laut) utter; (Karten) deal; **Feuer g.** give (s.o.) a light; (mil) open fire; **viel g. auf** (acc) set great store by; **von sich g.** utter; throw up; (chem) give off || *ref* give; (Kopfweh, usw.) get better; **sich g. als** pretend to be; **sich gefangen g.** surrender || *impers*—**es gibt** there is, there are; **es wird Regen geben** it's going to rain

Ge'ber **–in §6** *mf* giver, donor

Gebet [gə'bet] *n* (-[e]s;-e) prayer

gebeten [gə'betən] *pp* of **bitten**

Gebiet [gə'bit] *n* (-[e]s;-e) district, territory; (Fläche) area; (Fach) line; (Bereich) field, sphere

gebieten [gə'bitən] §58 *tr* (Stillschweigen) impose; (Ehrfurcht) command; (verlangen) demand; **j–m g., etw zu tun** order s.o. to do s.th. || *intr* (über acc) have control (over); (dat) control

Gebieter [gə'bitər] *m* (-s;-) master; ruler; commander; governor

Gebieterin [gə'bitərɪn] *f* (-;-nen) mistress; (des Hauses) lady

gebieterisch [gə'bitərɪʃ] *adj* imperious

Gebilde [gə'bɪldə] *n* (-s;-) shape, form; structure; (geol) formation

gebildet [gə'bɪldət] *adj* educated

Gebirge [gə'bɪrgə] *n* (-s;-) mountain range, mountains; **festes G.** bedrock

gebirgig [gə'bɪrgɪç] *adj* mountainous

Gebirgs– [gəbɪrks] *comb.fm.* mountain

Gebirgs'bewohner **–in §6** *mf* mountaineer

Gebirgs'kamm *m*, **Gebirgs'rücken** *m* mountain ridge

Gebirgs'zug *m* mountain range

Ge·biß [gə'bɪs] *n* (-bisses;-bisse) teeth; false teeth; (am Zaum) bit

gebissen [gə'bɪsən] *pp* of **beißen**

Gebläse [gə'blezə] *n* (-s;-) bellows; blower; (aut) supercharger

geblieben [gə'blibən] *pp* of **bleiben**

Geblök [gə'bløk] *n* (-[e]s) bleating

geblümt [gə'blymt] *adj* flowered

Geblüt [gə'blyt] *n* (-[e]s;) (& fig) blood

geboren [gə'borən] *pp* of **gebären** || *adj* born; native; **geborene nee**

geborgen [gə'bɔrgən] *pp* of **bergen** || *adj* safe

Gebor'genheit *f* (-;) safety, security

geborsten [gə'bɔrstən] *pp* of **bersten**

Gebot [gə'bot] *n* (-[e]s;-e) order, command; commandment; (Angebot) bid

geboten [gə'botən] *pp* of **bieten** || *adj* requisite; **dringend g.** imperative

Gebr. *abbr.* (Gebrüder) Brothers

gebracht [gə'braxt] *pp* of **bringen**

gebrannt [gə'brant] *pp* of **brennen**

Gebräu [gə'brɔɪ] *n* (-[e]s;-e) brew

Gebrauch [gə'braux] *m* (-s;-̈e) use; usage; (*Sitte*) custom

gebrauchen [gə'brauxən] *tr* use, employ

gebräuchlich [gə'brɔɪçlɪç] *adj* usual; in use; (*gemein*) common

Gebrauchs'anweisung *f* directions

gebrauchs'fertig *adj* ready for use; (*Kaffee, usw.*) instant

Gebrauchs'graphik *f* commercial art

Gebrauchs'gut *n* commodity

Gebrauchs'muster *n* registered pattern

gebraucht [gə'brauxt] *adj* second-hand

Gebraucht'wagen *m* used car

Gebrechen [gə'breçən] *n* (-s;-) physical disability, infirmity

gebrech'lich *adj* frail, weak; rickety

gebrochen [gə'brɔxən] *pp* of **brechen**

Gebrüder [gə'brydr] *pl* brothers

Gebrüll [gə'bryl] *n* (-[e]s;-) roaring; bellowing; lowing

Gebühr [gə'byr] *f* (-;-en) charge, fee; due, what is due; **nach G.** deservedly; **über G.** excessively; **zu ermäßigter G.** at a reduced rate

gebühren [gə'byrən] *intr* (*dat*) be due to || *impers ref*—es gebührt sich it is proper

gebüh'rend *adj* due; (*entsprechend*) appropriate || *adv* duly

gebüh'renfrei *adj* free of charge

gebüh'renpflichtig *adj* chargeable

gebunden [gə'bundən] *pp* of **binden** || *adj* bound; (*Hitze*) latent; (*Preise*) controlled; (*Kapital*) tied-up; **g. an** (*acc*) (chem) combined with; **gebundene Rede** verse

Geburt [gə'burt] *f* (-;-en) birth

Gebur'tenbeschränkung *f* birth control

Gebur'tenregelung *f* birth control

Gebur'tenrückgang *m* decline in births

gebürtig [gə'byrtɪç] *adj* native

Geburts'anzeige *f* announcement of birth; registration of birth

Geburts'fehler *n* congenital defect

Geburts'helfer -in §6 *mf* obstetrician || *f* midwife

Geburts'hilfe *f* obstetrics

Geburts'mal *n* birth mark

Geburts'recht *n* birthright

Geburts'schein *m* birth certificate

Geburts'tag *m* birthday

Geburts'tagskind *n* person celebrating his or her birthday

Geburts'wehen *pl* labor pains

Geburts'zange *f* forceps

Gebüsch [gə'byʃ] *n* (-es;-e) thicket, underbrush; clump of bushes

Geck [gek] *m* (-en;-en) dude

geckenhaft [gek'kenhaft] *adj* flashy

gedacht [gə'daxt] *pp* of **denken**

Gedächtnis [gə'dɛçtnɪs] *n* (-ses;) memory; **aus dem G.** by heart; **im G. behalten** bear in mind; **zum G.** (*genit or an acc*) in memory of

Gedächt'nisfehler *m* lapse of memory

Gedächt'nisrede *f* memorial address

gedämpft [gə'dɛmpft] *adj* muffled; hushed, quiet; (*Licht, Stimme*) subdued; (culin) stewed

Gedanke [gə'daŋkə] *m* (-ns;-n) thought; notion, idea; **etw in Ge-**

danken tun do s.th. absent-mindedly; **in Gedanken sein** be preoccupied; **sich** [*dat*] **Gedanken machen über** (*acc*) worry about

Gedan'kenblitz *m* (iron) brain wave

Gedan'kenfolge *f*, **Gedan'kengang** *m* train of thought

gedan'kenlos *adj* thoughtless; absent-minded; irresponsible

Gedan'kenpunkt *m* suspension point

Gedan'kenstrich *m* (typ) dash

Gedan'kenübertragung *f* telepathy

gedank'lich *adj* mental; intellectual

Gedärme [gə'dɛrmə] *pl* intestines

Gedeck [gə'dek] *n* (-[e]s;-e) cover; table setting; menu

gedeihen [gə'daɪən] §81 *intr* (SEIN) thrive; succeed || **Gedeihen** *n* (-s;) prosperity; success

Gedenk- [gədeŋk] *comb.fm.* memorial; commemorative

gedenken [gə'deŋkən] §66 *intr* (*genit*) think of, be mindful of; remember; mention; **g. zu** (*inf*) intend to (*inf*) || **Gedenken** *n* (-s;) memory

gedeucht [gə'dɔɪçt] *pp* of **dünken**

Gedicht [gə'dɪçt] *n* (-[e]s;-e) poem; (fig) dream

gediegen [gə'digən] *adj* (*Gold*) solid; (*Silber*) sterling; (*Arbeit*) excellent; (*Kenntnisse*) thorough; (*Möbel*) solidly made; (*Charakter*) sterling; (coll) very funny

gedieh [gə'di] *pret* of **gedeihen**

gediehen [gə'di-ən] *pp* of **gedeihen**

Gedränge [gə'dreŋə] *n* (-s;-) pushing; crowd; difficulties; (fb) scrimmage

gedrängt [gə'dreŋt] *adj* crowded, packed; (*Sprache*) concise

gedroschen [gə'drɔʃən] *pp* of **dreschen**

gedrückt [gə'drykt] *adj* depressed

gedrungen [gə'druŋən] *pp* of **dringen** || *adj* compact; stocky; squat; (*Sprache*) concise

Geduld [gə'dult] *f* (-;) patience

gedulden [gə'duldən] *ref* wait (patiently)

geduldig [gə'duldɪç] *adj* patient

Geduld'spiel *n* puzzle

gedungen [gə'duŋən] *pp* of **dingen**

gedunsen [gə'dunzən] *adj* bloated

gedurft [gə'durft] *pp* of **dürfen**

geehrt [gə'ert] *adj*—**Sehr geehrte Herren!** Dear Sirs; **Sehr geehrter Herr X!** Dear Mr. X

geeignet [gə'aɪgnət] *adj* suitable, right; qualified; appropriate

Gefahr [gə'far] *f* (-;-en) danger; (*Wagnis*) risk; **G. laufen zu** (*inf*) run the risk of (*ger*)

gefährden [gə'ferdən] *tr* jeopardize

gefährlich [gə'ferlɪç] *adj* dangerous

gefahr'los *adj* safe

Gefährt [gə'fert] *n* (-[e]s;-e) carriage

Gefährte [gə'fertə] *m* (-n;-n), **Gefährtin** [gə'fertɪn] *f* (-;-nen) companion; spouse

Gefälle [gə'fɛlə] *n* (-s;-) pitch; slope

gefallen [gə'falən] *adj* fallen; (mil) killed in action || §72 *ref*—**sich g. in** (*dat*) take pleasure in || *intr* please; **das gefällt mir** I like this; **das lasse ich mir nicht g.** I won't stand for this || **Gefallen** *m* (**-;-**) favor || *n* (**-s;**) (**an** *dat*) pleasure (in); **j-m etw zu G. tun** do s.th. to please s.o.; **nach G.** as one pleases; at one's descretion

gefällig [gə'fɛlɪç] *adj* pleasing; obliging; kind; **j-m g. sein** do s.o. a favor; **Kaffee g.?** would you care for coffee?; **was ist g.?** what can I do for you?; **würden Sie so g. sein zu** (*inf*)? would you be so kind as to (*inf*)?

Gefäl'ligkeit *f* (**-;-en**) favor

gefälligst [gə'fɛlɪçst] *adv* if you please; please

gefangen [gə'faŋən] *pp* of **fangen** || *adj* captive; **g. nehmen** take prisoner || **Gefangene** §5 *mf* captive, prisoner

Gefan'genenlager *n* prison camp; (mil) prisoner-of-war camp

Gefan'gennahme *f* (**-;**) capture; arrest

gefan'gennehmen §116 *tr* take prisoner

Gefan'genschaft *f* (**-;**) captivity; imprisonment; **in G. geraten** be taken prisoner

gefan'gensetzen *tr* imprison

Gefängnis [gə'fɛŋnɪs] *n* (**-ses;-se**) prison, jail; imprisonment

Gefäng'nisdirektor *m* warden

Gefäng'nisstrafe *f* prison term

Gefäng'niswärter -in §6 *mf* guard

Gefäß [gə'fɛs] *n* (**-es;-e**) vessel; jar

gefaßt [gə'fast] *adj* calm, composed; **g. auf** (*acc*) ready for

Gefecht [gə'fɛçt] *n* (**-[e]s;-e**) fight, battle, action

Gefechts'auftrag *m* (mil) objective

Gefechts'kopf *m* warhead

Gefechts'lage *f* tactical situation

Gefechts'stand *m* command post

gefeit [gə'fat] *adj* (**gegen**) immune (from), proof (against)

Gefieder [gə'fidər] *n* (**-s;-**) plumage

gefleckt [gə'flɛkt] *adj* spotted

geflissentlich [gə'flɪsəntlɪç] *adj* intentional, willful

geflochten [gə'flɔxtən] *pp* of **flechten**

geflogen [gə'flogən] *pp* of **fliegen**

geflohen [gə'flo.ən] *pp* of **fliehen**

geflossen [gə'flɔsən] *pp* of **fließen**

Geflügel [gə'flygəl] *n* (**-s;**) fowl; (*Federvieh*) poultry

Geflü'gelmagen *m* gizzard

Geflunker [gə'fluŋkər] *m* (**-s;**) (coll) fibbing

Geflüster [gə'flystər] *n* (**-s;**) whisper

Gefolge [gə'fɔlgə] *n* (**-s;-**) retinue; **in seinem G.** in its wake

Gefolgschaft [gə'fɔlkʃaft] *f* (**-;-en**) allegiance; followers

gefräßig [gə'frɛsɪç] *adj* gluttonous

Gefrä'ßigkeit *f* (**-;**) gluttony

Gefreite [gə'fratə] §5 *m* private first class; lance corporal (Brit)

gefressen [gə'frɛsən] *pp* of **fressen**

Gefrieranlage [gə'friranlagə] *f* **Gefrierapparat** [gə'friraparat] *m* freezer

gefrieren [gə'friрən] §77 *intr* (SEIN) freeze

Gefrie'rer *m* (**-s;-**) freezer; deepfreeze

Gefrier'fach *n* freezing compartment

Gefrier'punkt *m* freezing point

Gefrier'schutz *m,* **Gefrier'schutzmittel** *n* antifreeze

gefroren [gə'frorən] *pp* of **frieren** || **Gefrorene** §5 *n* ice cream

Gefüge [gə'fygə] *n* (**-s;-**) structure, make-up; arrangement; texture

gefügig [gə'fygɪç] *adj* pliant, pliable

Gefühl [gə'fyl] *n* (**-[e]s;-e**) feeling; feel; touch; sense; sensation

gefühl'los *adj* numb; callous

gefühls-, Gefühls- [gəfyls] *comb.fm.* of the emotions; emotional; sentimental; (anat) sensory

gefühls'betont *adj* emotional

Gefühlsduselei [gə'fylsduzəlaɪ] *f* (**-;**) sentimentalism, mawkishness

gefühls'selig *adj* mawkish

gefühl'voll *adj* sensitive; tender-hearted || *adv* with feeling

gefunden [gə'fundən] *pp* of **finden**

gefurcht [gə'furçt] *adj* furrowed

gegangen [gə'gaŋən] *pp* of **gehen**

gegeben [gə'gebən] *pp* of **geben** || *adj* given; (*Umstände*) existing; **gegebene Methode** best approach; **zu gegebener Zeit** at the proper time

gege'benfalls *adv* if necessary

gegen ['gegən] *prep* (*acc*) towards; against; about; approximately; compared with; contrary to; in exchange for

gegen-, Gegen- *comb.fm.* anti-; counter-; contrary; opposite; back; in return

Ge'genantwort *f* rejoinder

Ge'genbeschuldigung *f* countercharge

Ge'genbild *n* counterpart

Gegend ['gegənt] *f* (**-;-en**) neighborhood, vicinity; region, district

gegeneinan'der *adv* against one another; towards one another

Ge'gengerade *f* back stretch

Ge'gengewicht *n* counterbalance; (am Rad) (aut) weight; **das G. halten** (*dat*) counterbalance

Ge'gengift *n* antidote

Ge'genkandidat -in §7 *mf* rival candidate

Ge'genklage *f* countercharge; counterclaim

Ge'genmittel *n* (**gegen**) remedy (for), antidote (against)

Ge'genrede *f* reply, rejoinder

Ge'gensatz *m* contrast; opposite, antithesis; (*Widerspruch*) opposition

gegensätzlich ['gegənzetslɪç] *adj* contrary, opposite, antithetical

Ge'genschlag *m* counterplot

ge'genseitig *adj* mutual, reciprocal

Ge'genstand *m* object, thing; subject

gegenständlich ['gegən/tentlɪç] *adj* objective; (fa) representational; (log) concrete

ge'genstandslos *adj* baseless; without purpose; irrelevant; (fa) non-representational

Ge'genstoß *m* (box) counterpunch; (mil) counterthrust

Ge'genstück *n* counterpart

Ge'genteil *n* contrary, opposite; **im G.** on the contrary

ge'genteilig *adj* contrary, opposite

gegenü'ber *prep* (*dat*) opposite to; across from; with regard to; compared with

gegenü'berstellen tr (dat) place opposite to; (dat) confront with; (dat)
contrast with
Gegenü'berstellung f confrontation;
comparison; (auf e-r Wache) line-up
Gegenwart ['ge:gənvart] f (-;) present;
present time; (gram) present tense
gegenwärtig ['ge:gənvertiç] adj present,
current || adv at present; nowadays
Ge'genwehr f defense, resistance
Ge'genwind m head wind
Ge'genwirkung f (auf acc) reaction
(to)
ge'genzeichnen tr countersign
Ge'genzug m countermove
geglichen [gə'glıçən] pp of **gleichen**
geglitten [gə'glıtən] pp of **gleiten**
Gegner –in ['gegnər(ın)] §6 mf oppo-
nent, rival || m (mil) enemy
gegnerisch ['gegnərɪʃ] adj adverse;
antagonistic; opposing; (mil) enemy
gegolten [gə'gɔltən] pp of **gelten**
gegoren [gə'go:rən] pp of **gären**
gegossen [gə'gɔsən] pp of **gießen**
gegriffen [gə'grıfən] pp of **greifen**
Gehabe [gə'ha:bə] n (-s;) affectation
gehaben [gə'ha:bən] ref fare; **gehab
dich nicht** so! stop putting on!; **gehab dich wohl!** farewell!
Gehackte [gə'haktə] §5 n hamburger
Gehalt [gə'halt] m (-[e]s;-e) contents;
capacity; standard; **G. an** (dat) per-
centage of || n (-[e]s;-er) salary
Gehalts'stufe f salary bracket
Gehalts'zulage f increment, raise
gehalt'voll adj substantial; profound
Gehänge [gə'hɛŋə] n (-s;–) slope; pendant; festoon; (e-s Degens) sling
gehangen [gə'haŋən] pp of **hängen**
gehässig [gə'hɛsıç] adj spiteful, nasty
Gehäuse [gə'hɔızə] n (-s;–) case, box;
housing; (e-r Schnecke) shell; (e-s
Apfels) core
Gehege [gə'he:gə] n (-s;–) enclosure
geheim [gə'haım] adj secret; **streng g.**
top-secret
geheim'halten §90 tr keep secret
Geheimnis [gə'haımnıs] n (-ses;-se)
secret, mystery
geheim'nisvoll adj mysterious
Geheim'schrift f code; coded message
Geheim'tinte f invisible ink
Geheim'vorbehalt m mental reservation
Geheiß [gə'haıs] n (-es;) bidding
gehen ['ge:ən] §82 intr (SEIN) go;
walk; leave; (Teig) rise; (Maschine)
work; (Uhr) go; (Ware) sell; (Wind)
blow; **das geht nicht** that will not do;
das geht schon it will be all right;
sich g. lassen take it easy; **wieviel
Zoll g. auf einen Fuß?** how many
inches make a foot? || impers—**es
geht mir gut** I am doing well; **es
geht nichts über** (acc) there is nothing like; **es geht um...** is at stake;
wie geht es Ihnen? how are you?
geheuer [gə'hɔɪ-ər] adj—**mir war nicht
recht g. zumute** I didn't feel quite
at ease; **nicht g.** spooky; suspicious;
risky
Geheul [gə'hɔɪl] n (-s;) howling; loud
sobbing

Gehilfe [gə'hɪlfə] m (-n;-n), **Gehilfin**
[gə'hɪlfɪn] f (-;-nen) assistant
Gehirn [gə'hırn] n (-[e]s;-e) brains,
mind; (anat) brain; **sein G. anstren-
gen** rack one's brain
Gehirn– comb.fm. brain; cerebral
Gehirn'erschütterung f concussion
Gehirn'schlag m (pathol) stroke
Gehirn'wäsche f brainwashing
gehoben [gə'ho:bən] pp of **heben** || adj
(Stellung) high; (Stil) lofty; **gehobene
Stimmung** high spirits
Gehöft [gə'hø:ft] n (-[e]s;-e) farm
geholfen [gə'hɔlfən] pp of **helfen**
Gehölz [gə'hœlts] n (-es;-e) grove;
thicket
Gehör [gə'hø:r] n (-s;) hearing; ear
Gehör– comb.fm. of hearing; auditory
gehorchen [gə'hɔrçən] intr (dat) obey
gehören [gə'hø:rən] ref be proper, be
right || intr (dat or zu) belong to;
(in acc) go into, belong in
gehörig [gə'hø:rıç] adj proper, due;
(dat or zu) belonging to || adv prop-
erly; duly; thoroughly
Gehörn [gə'hœrn] n (-s;-e) horns; **Ge-
hörne** sets of horns
gehorsam [gə'ho:rzam] adj obedient ||
adv obediently; **gehorsamst** respect-
fully || **Gehorsam** m (-s;) obedience
Gehor'samverweigerung f disobedience
gehren ['ge:rən] tr (carp) miter
Gehrlade ['ge:rla:də] f (-;-n) miter box
Gehrock ['ge:rɔk] m Prince Albert
Geh'rung f—**auf G., nach der G.** on
the slant; **auf G. verbinden** miter
Geh'rungslade f (-;-n) miter box
Gehsteig ['ge:taık] m sidewalk
Gehweg ['ge:vek] m sidewalk; footpath
Gehwerk ['ge:verk] n clockwork, works
Geier ['gaı-ər] m (-s;–) vulture; **zum
Geier!** what the devil!
Geifer ['gaıfər] m (-s;) drivel; froth,
slaver, foam; (fig) venom
geifern ['gaıfərn] intr slaver
Geige ['gaıgə] f (-;-n) violin, fiddle
geigen ['gaıgən] intr play the violin
Gei'genbogen m bow, fiddlestick
Gei'genharz n rosin
Gei'ger –in §6 mf violinist
geil [gaıl] adj lustful; in heat; (Boden)
rich; (üppig) luxuriant
Geisel ['gaızəl] f (-;-n) hostage
Geiser ['gaızər] m (-s;-) geyser
Geiß [gaıs] f (-;-en) she-goat
Geißel ['gaısəl] f (-;-n) scourge
geißeln ['gaısəln] tr scourge; (fig)
castigate
Geist [gaıst] m (-es;-er) spirit; (Ge-
spenst) ghost; (Verstand) mind, in-
tellect; **im Geiste** in one's imagina-
tion; in spirit
Gei'sterbeschwörung f (-;) necromancy
Gei'sterstadt f ghost town
Gei'sterstunde f witching hour
geistes– [gaıstəs] comb.fm. spiritually;
mentally, intellectually || **Geistes-
comb.fm.** spiritual; mental, intellectual
gei'stesabwesend adj absent-minded
Gei'stesanlagen pl natural gift
Gei'stesarbeit f brainwork
Gei'stesarmut f dullness, stupidity

Gei'stesblitz m brain wave; aphorism

Gei'stesflug m flight of the imagination

Gei'stesfreiheit f intellectual freedom

Gei'stesfrucht f brainchild

gei'stesgegenwärtig adj mentally alert

geistesgestört ['gaɪstəsgə/tørt] adj mentally disturbed

Gei'steshaltung f mentality

gei'steskrank adj insane

gei'stesschwach adj feeble-minded

Gei'stesstörung f mental disorder

Gei'stes- und Natur'wissenschaften pl arts and sciences

Gei'stesverfassung f frame of mind

gei'stesverwandt adj (mit) spiritually akin (to); (mit) congenial (with)

Gei'stesverwirrung f derangement

Gei'steswissenschaften pl humanities

gei'steswissenschaftlich adj humanistic

Gei'steszustand m state of mind

geistig ['gaɪstɪç] adj mental, intellectual; spiritual

geist'lich adj spiritual; (Orden) religious; (kirchlich) sacred, ecclesiastical; der geistliche Stand holy orders; the clergy || Geistliche §5 m clergyman

Geist'lichkeit f (-;) clergy

geist'los adj spiritless; dull; stupid

geist'reich adj witty; ingenious

Geiz [gaɪts] m (-es;) stinginess; avarice

geizen ['gaɪtsən] intr—g. mit be sparing with; nicht g. mit show freely

Geiz'hals m (coll) tightwad

geizig ['gaɪtsɪç] adj stingy, miserly

Geiz'kragen m (coll) tightwad

Gejammer [gə'jamər] n (-s;) wailing

gekannt [gə'kant] pp of kennen

Geklapper [gə'klapər] n (-s;) rattling

Geklatsche [gə'klatʃə] n (-s;) clapping; gossiping

Geklirr [gə'klɪr] n (-[e]s;) rattling

geklommen [gə'kləmən] pp of klimmen

geklungen [gə'klʊŋən] pp of klingen

gekniffen [gə'knɪfən] pp of kneifen

gekonnt [gə'kɔnt] pp of können

Gekreisch [gə'kraɪʃ] n (-es;) screaming; screeching

Gekritzel [gə'krɪtsəl] n (-s;) scribbling

gekrochen [gə'krɔxən] pp of kriechen

Gekröse [gə'krøzə] n (-s;) tripe

gekünstelt [gə'kʏnstəlt] adj affected

Gelächter [gə'lɛçtər] n (-s;) laughter

Gelage [gə'lagə] n (-s;) carousing

Gelände [gə'lɛndə] n (-s;-) terrain; site, lot; (educ) campus; (golf) fairway

Gelän'delauf m crosscountry running

Gelän'depunkt m landmark

Geländer [gə'lɛndər] n (-s;-) railing; guardrail; banister; parapet

gelang [gə'laŋ] pret of gelingen

gelangen [gə'laŋən] intr (SEIN) (an acc, in acc, zu) attain, reach

gelassen [gə'lasən] pp of lassen || adj composed, calm

Gelatine [ʒela'tinə] f (-;) gelatin

geläufig [gə'lɔɪfɪç] adj fluent; (gemein) common; (Zunge) glib

gelaunt [gə'laʊnt] adj—gut gelaunt in good humor; zu etw g. sein be in the mood for s.th.

Geläut [gə'lɔɪt] n (-es;), **Geläute** [gə-'lɔɪtə] n (-s;) ringing; chimes

gelb [gɛlp] adj yellow || **Gelb** n (-s;) yellow

gelb'lich adj yellowish

Gelb'sucht f jaundice

Geld [gɛlt] n (-[e]s;) money; bares G. cash

Geld- comb.fm. money, financial

-geld n comb.fm. money; fee(s); tax, toll; allowance

Geld'anlage f investment

Geld'anleihe f loan

Geld'anweisung f money order; draft

Geld'ausgabe f expense; expenditure

Geld'beutel m pocketbook

Geld'bewilligung f (parl) appropriation

Geld'buße f fine

Geld'einlage f deposit

Geld'einwurf m coin slot

Geld'entwertung f inflation

Geld'erwerb m moneymaking

Geld'geber m investor; mortgagee

Geld'gier f avarice

Geld'mittel pl funds, resources

Geld'onkel m sugar daddy

Geld'schein m bank note, bill

Geld'schrank m safe

Geld'schublade f till (of cash register)

Geld'sendung f remittance

Geld'sorte f (fin) denomination

Geld'spende f contribution, donation

Geld'strafe f fine

Geld'stück n coin

Geld'überhang m surplus (of money)

Geld'währung f currency; monetary standard

Geld'wechsel m money exchange

Geld'wesen n financial system, finance

Gelee [ʒe'le] m & n (-s;-s) jelly

gelegen [gə'legən] pp of liegen || adj located; convenient; opportune; du kommst mir gerade g. you're just the person I wanted to see; es kommt mir gerade gelegen that suits me just fine; mir ist daran g. zu (inf) I'm anxious to (inf); was ist daran g.? what of it?

Gele'genheit f (-;-en) occasion; opportunity, chance; (com) bargain

Gelegenheits- comb.fm. occasional

Gele'genheitsarbeit f odd job

Gele'genheitskauf m good bargain

gele'gentlich adj occasional; casual; chance || adv occasionally || prep (genit) on the occasion of

gelehrig [gə'lerɪç] adj teachable; intelligent

gelehrsam [gə'lerzam] adj erudite

gelehrt [gə'lert] adj learned, erudite || **Gelehrte** §5 mf scholar

Geleise [gə'laɪzə] n (-s;-) rut; (rr) track; totes G. blind alley, deadlock

Geleit [gə'laɪt] n (-[e]s;) escort; freies (or sicheres) G. safe-conduct; j-m das G. geben escort s.o., accompany s.o.; zum G. forward

geleiten [gə'laɪtən] tr escort, accompany; j-n zur Tür g. see s.o. to the door

Geleit′zug m convoy
Geleit′zugsicherung f convoy escort
Gelenk [gə'lɛŋk] n (-[e]s;-e) joint
Gelenk′entzündung f arthritis
gelenkig [gə'lɛŋkɪç] adj jointed; flexible; agile
gelernt [gə'lɛrnt] adj skilled
Gelichter [gə'lɪçtər] n (-s;) riffraff
Geliebte [gə'liptə] §6 mf beloved, sweetheart
geliehen [gə'li·ən] pp of **leihen**
gelieren [ʒe'lirən] intr jell, gel
gelinde [gə'lɪndə] adj soft; gentle, mild || adv gently, mildly; **g. gesagt** to put it mildly
gelingen [gə'lɪŋən] §142 intr (SEIN) succeed || impers (SEIN)—**es gelingt mir I** succeed || **Gelingen** n (-s;) success
gelitten [gə'lɪtən] pp of **leiden**
gell [gɛl] adj shrill || interj say!
gellen ['gɛlən] intr ring out; yell
gel′lend adj shrill, piercing
geloben [gə'lobən] tr solemnly promise, vow; **take the vow of** || ref—**sich** [dat] **g.** vow to oneself
gelogen [gə'logən] pp of **lügen**
gelt [gɛlt] interj say!
gelten ['gɛltən] §83 tr be worth; **wenig g. mean little** || intr be valid; (Münze) be legal tender; (Gesetz) be in force; (Grund) hold true; (Regel) apply; (Mittel) be allowable; (beim Spiel) count; **g. als** or **für** have the force of; be ranked as; pass for, be considered; **g. lassen** acknowledge as correct; **j—m g.** be aimed at s.o. || impers—**es gilt** (acc) be at stake; be a matter of; be worth (s.th.); **es gilt mir gleich, ob** it's all the same to me whether; **es gilt zu** (inf) it is necessary to (inf); **jetzt gilt's!** here goes!
Gel′tung f (-;) validity; value, importance; **zur G. bringen** make the most of; **zur G. kommen** show off well
Gel′tungsbedürfnis n need for recognition
Gelübde [gə'lypdə] n (-s;-) vow
gelungen [gə'luŋən] pp of **gelingen** || adj successful; (Wendung) well-turned; funny
Gelüst [gə'lyst] n (-[e]s;-e) desire
gelüsten [gə'lystən] impers—**es gelüstet mich nach I** could go for
gemach [gə'max] adv slowly, by degrees || **Gemach** n (-[e]s;=er) room; apartment; chamber
gemächlich [gə'mɛçlɪç] adj leisurely; comfortable
Gemahl [gə'mal] m (-[e]s;-e) husband
Gemahlin [gə'malɪn] f (-;-nen) wife
Gemälde [gə'mɛldə] n (-s;-) painting
gemäß [gə'mɛs] prep (dat) according to
gemäßigt [gə'mɛsɪçt] adj moderate
gemein [gə'maɪn] adj common; mean, vile; **sich g. machen mit** associate with || **Gemeine** §5 m (mil) private
Gemeinde [gə'maɪndə] f (-;-n) community; municipality; (eccl) parish
Gemein′deabgaben pl local taxes
Gemein′deanleihen pl municipal bonds

Gemein′dehaus n town hall
gemein′frei adj in the public domain
gemein′gefährlich adj constituting a public danger, dangerous
gemein′gültig adj generally accepted
Gemein′heit f (-;-en) meanness; dirty trick; vulgarity
gemein′hin adv commonly, usually
Gemein′kosten pl overhead
Gemein′nutz m public interest
gemein′nützig adj non-profit
Gemein′platz m platitude
gemeinsam [gə'maɪnzam] adj common, joint; mutual
Gemein′schaft f (-;-en) community; close association
gemein′schaftlich adj common, joint; mutual
Gemein′schaftsanschluß m (telp) party line
Gemein′schaftsarbeit f teamwork
Gemein′schaftsgeist m esprit de corps
Gemein′sinn m public spirit
gemein′verständlich adj popular; **g. darstellen** popularize
Gemein′wesen n community
Gemein′wohl n commonweal
Gemenge [gə'mɛŋə] n (-s;-) mixture; (Kampfgewühl) scuffle, melee
gemessen [gə'mɛsən] pp of **messen** || adj deliberate; precise; dignified; **g. an** (dat) compared with
Gemetzel [gə'mɛtsəl] n (-s;-) massacre
gemieden [gə'midən] pp of **meiden**
Gemisch [gə'mɪʃ] n (-es;-e) mixture
Gemischt′warenhandlung f general store
Gemme ['gɛmə] f (-;-n) gem
gemocht [gə'mɔxt] pp of **mögen**
gemolken [gə'mɔlkən] pp of **melken**
Gemse ['gɛmzə] f (-;-n) chamois
Gemunkel [gə'muŋkəl] n (-s;-) gossip, whispering
Gemurmel [gə'murməl] n (-s;) murmur
Gemüse [gə'myzə] n (-s;-) vegetable; vegetables
Gemü′sebau m (-[e]s;) vegetable gardening
Gemü′sekonserven pl canned vegetables
gemüßigt [gə'mysɪçt] adj—**sich g. fühlen** feel compelled
gemußt [gə'must] pp of **müssen**
Gemüt [gə'myt] n (-[e]s;-er) mind; disposition; person, soul; warmth of feeling; **j—m etw zu Gemüte führen** bring s.th. home to s.o.
gemütlich [gə'mytlɪç] adj good-natured, easy-going; (Wohnung) cosy
Gemüt′lichkeit f (-;) easy-going nature; cosiness
Gemüts′art f disposition, nature
Gemüts′bewegung f emotion
gemüts′krank adj melancholy
Gemüts′mensch m warm-hearted person
Gemüts′ruhe f—**in** (aller) **G.** in peace and quiet
Gemüts′stimmung f mood
Gemüts′verfassung f state of mind
Gemüts′zustand m frame of mind

gemüt′voll *adj* emotional

gen [gen] *prep* (*acc*) (poet) towards ‖

Gen [gen] *n* (–s;–e) (biol) gene

genannt [gə′nant] *pp* of **nennen**

genau [gə′nau] *adj* exact; fussy

genau′genommen *adv* strictly speaking

Genau′igkeit *f* (–;) exactness, accuracy; meticulousness

Gendarm [ʒā′darm] *m* (–en;–en) policeman

Gendarme·rie [ʒādarmə′ri] *f* (–;–rien [′ri·ən]) rural police; rural police station

Genealo·gie [gene·alə′gi] *f* (–;–gien [′gi·ən]) genealogy

genehm [gə′nem] *adj* agreeable; acceptable; (*dat*) convenient (for)

genehmigen [gə′nemigən] *tr* grant; approve; **sich** [*dat*] **etw g.** (coll) treat oneself to s.th.; **genehmigt O.K.**

Geneh′migung *f* (–;–en) grant; approval; permission; permit

geneigt [gə′narkt] *adj* sloping; (**zu**) inclined (to); (*dat*) well-disposed (towards)

Geneigt′heit *f* inclination; good will

General [gene′ral] *m* (–[e]s;–e & ⁼e) general

General′feldmarschall *m* field marshal

General′inspekteur *m* chief of the joint chiefs of staff

Generalität [generalɪ′tet] *f* (–;) body of generals

General′konsul *m* consul general

General′leutnant *m* lieutenant general; (aer) air marshal

General′major *m* major general

General′nenner *m* common denominator

General′probe *f* dress rehearsal

General′stabskarte *f* strategic map

General′vollmacht *f* full power of attorney

Generation [genera′tsjon] *f* (–;–en) generation

generell [gene′rel] *adj* general, blanket

genesen [gə′nezən] §84 *intr* (SEIN) convalesce; (**von**) recover (from)

Gene′sung *f* (–;–en) convalescence

Gene′sungsheim *n* convalescent home

genetisch [gə′netɪʃ] *adj* genetic

Genf [genf] *n* (–s;) Geneva

Gen′forscher –in §6 *mf* genetic engineer

Gen′forschung *f* (–;) genetic engineering

genial [ge′njal] *adj* brilliant, gifted

Genick [gə′nɪk] *n* (–s;–e) nape of the neck

Genick′bruch *m* broken neck

Genick′schlag *m* (box) rabbit punch

Genie [ʒe′ni] *n* (–s;–s) (man of) genius

genieren [ʒe′nirən] *tr* bother; embarrass ‖ *ref* feel embarrassed

genießbar [gə′nisbar] *adj* edible, drinkable; (fig) agreeable

genießen [gə′nisən] §76 *tr* enjoy; eat; drink

Genie′streich *m* stroke of genius

Genitalien [genɪ′taljən] *pl* genitals

Geni·tiv [′genɪtif] *m* (–s;–tive [′tivə]) genitive

genommen [gə′nɔmən] *pp* of **nehmen**

genoß [gə′nɔs] *pret* of **genießen**

Genosse [gə′nɔsə] *m* (–n;–n) companion, buddy; (pol) comrade

–genosse *m comb.fm.* fellow–, –mate

Genos′senschaft *f* (–;–en) association; coöperative

Genossin [gə′nɔsɪn] *f* (–;–nen) companion, buddy; (pol) comrade

genug [gə′nuk] *invar adj* & *adv* enough

Genüge [gə′nygə] *f—j—m* **G. tun** give s.o. satisfaction; **zur G.** enough; only too well

genügen [gə′nygən] *intr* suffice, do ‖ *ref*—**sich** [*dat*] **g. lassen an** (*dat*) be content with

genü′gend *adj* sufficient

genügsam [gə′nykzam] *adj* easily satisfied; frugal

genug′tun §154 *intr* (*dat*) satisfy

Genugtuung [gə′nuktʊ·ʊŋ] *f* (–;) satisfaction

Ge·nuß [gə′nus] *m* (–nusses;–nüsse) enjoyment; pleasure; (*Nutznießung*) use; (*von Speisen*) consumption

Genuß′mittel *n* semi-luxury (as coffee, tobacco, etc.)

genuß′reich *adj* thoroughly enjoyable

genuß′süchtig *adj* pleasure-seeking

Geographie [ge·ogra′fi] *f* (–;) geography

geographisch [ge·o′grafɪʃ] *adj* geographical

Geologe [ge·o′logə] *m* (–n;–n) geologist

Geologie [ge·olo′gi] *f* (–;) geology

Geometer [ge·o′metər] *m* (–s;–) surveyor

Geometrie [ge·ome′tri] *f* (–;) geometry

Geophysik [ge·ofy′zik] *f* (–;) geophysics

Geopolitik [ge·opolɪ′tik] *f* (–;) geopolitics

Georgine [ge·or′ginə] *f* (–;–n) dahlia

Gepäck [gə′pek] *n* (–[e]s;) luggage

Gepäck′abfertigung *f* luggage check-in; luggage counter

Gepäck′ablage *f* luggage rack

Gepäck′anhänger *m* tag; luggage trailer

Gepäck′aufbewahrung *f* baggage room

Gepäck′netz *n* baggage rack (net type)

Gepäck′raum *m* luggage compartment

Gepäck′schein *m* luggage check

Gepäck′träger *m* porter; (aut) roof rack

Gepäck′wagen *m* (rr) baggage car

gepanzert [gə′pantsərt] *adj* armored

gepfeffert [gə′pfefərt] *adj* peppered; (*Worte*) sharp; (*Preis*) exorbitant

Gepfeife [gə′pfaifə] *n* (–s;) whistling

gepfiffen [gə′pfıfən] *pp* of **pfeifen**

gepflogen [gə′pflogən] *pp* of **pflegen**

Geplo′genheit *f* (–;–en) custom, practice

Geplänkel [gə′plenkəl] *n* (–s;) skirmish; (fig) exchange of words

Geplapper [gə′plapər] *n* (–s;) jabber

Geplärr [gə′pler] *n* (–s;) bawling

Geplauder [gə′plaudər] *n* (–s;) small talk, chat

Gepolter [gə′pɔltər] *n* (–s;) rumbling

Gepräge [gə′pregə] *n* (–s;) impression; stamp, character

Gepränge [gə′preŋə] *n* (–s;) pomp

gepriesen [gə'pri:zən] *pp* of **preisen**

gequollen [gə'kvɔlən] *pp* of **quellen**

gerade [gə'ra:də] *adj* straight; even; direct; *(Haltung)* erect; *(aufrichtig)* straightforward || *adv* straight; exactly; just; just now || **Gerade** *f* (-n; -n) straight line; straightaway; (box) straight; **rechte G.** straight right

gerade(n)wegs [gə'ra:də(n)ve:ks] *adv* immediately, straightaway

geradezu' *adv* downright

Geranie [ge'ra:njə] *f* (-;-n) geranium

gerannt [gə'rant] *pp* of **rennen**

Gerassel [gə'rasəl] *n* (-s;) clanking

Gerät [gə'rɛ:t] *n* (-[e]s;-e) device, instrument; tool; (rad, telv) set

geraten [gə'ra:tən] *pp* of **raten** *f* (-;) successful; *(ratsam)* advisable || §63 *intr* (SEIN) *(gut, schlecht, usw.)* turn out; **außer sich g.** be beside oneself; **g. an** *(acc)* come by; **g. auf** *(acc)* get into; get on to; **g. hinter** *(acc)* get behind; find out about; **g. in** *(acc)* get into, fall into; **g. nach** take after; **g. über** *(acc)* come across; **in Bewegung g.** begin to move; **in Brand g.** catch fire; **ins Schleudern g.** begin to skid; **ins Stocken g.** come to a standstill

Gerä'teschuppen *m* tool shed

Geratewohl [gə'ra:təvo:l] *n* (-s;)—**aufs G.** at random

geraum [gə'raum] *adj* considerable

geräumig [gə'rɔɪmɪç] *adj* spacious

Geräusch [gə'rɔɪʃ] *n* (-[e]s;-e) noise

gerben [gerbən] *tr* tan

Gerberei [gerbə'raɪ] *f* (-;-en) tannery

gerecht [gə'reçt] *adj* just, fair; justified; **g. werden** *(dat)* do justice to

Gerech'tigkeit *f* (-;) justice; fairness

Gerede [gə're:də] *n* (-s;) talk; hearsay

gereichen [gə'raɪçən] *intr*—**es gereicht ihm zur Ehre** it does him justice; **es gereicht ihm zum Vorteil** it is to his advantage; **es gereicht mir zur Freude** it gives me pleasure

gereizt [gə'raɪtst] *adj* irritable; irritated

gereuen [gə'rɔɪ-ən] *tr* cause *(s.o.)* regret || *ref*—**sich keine Mühe g. lassen** spare no trouble || *impers*—**es gereut mich I** regret

Geriatrie [geri-a'tri:] *f* (-;) geriatrics

Gericht [gə'rɪçt] *n* (-[e]s;-e) court; courthouse; judgment; (culin) dish; **das Jüngste G.** the Last Judgment

gericht'lich *adj* legal, judicial, court

Gerichtsbarkeit [gə'rɪçtsbarkaɪt] *f* (-;) jurisdiction

Gerichts'bote *m* (jur) bailiff

Gerichts'hof *m* law court; **Oberster G.** Supreme Court

Gerichts'medizin *f* forensic medicine

Gerichts'saal *m* courtroom

Gerichts'schreiber –**in** §6 *mf* (jur) clerk

Gerichts'stand *m* (jur) venue

Gerichts'verhandlung *f* hearing; trial

Gerichts'vollzieher *m* (jur) marshal

Gerichts'wesen *n* judicial system

gerieben [gə'ri:bən] *pp* of **reiben** || *adj* cunning, smart

Geriesel [gə'ri:zəl] *n* (-s;) purling

gering [gə'rɪŋ] *adj* slight, trifling;

small; *(niedrig)* low; *(ärmlich)* poor; *(minderwertig)* inferior; **nicht im geringsten** not in the least

gering'achten *tr* think little of

gering'fügig *adj* insignificant

gering'schätzen *tr* look down on

Gering'schätzung *f* contempt, disdain

gerinnen [gə'rɪnən] §121 *intr* coagulate, clot; *(Milch)* curdle

Gerinnsel [gə'rɪnzəl] *n* (-s;-) clot

Gerippe [gə'rɪpə] *n* (-s;-) skeleton; *(Gerüst)* framework

gerippt [gə'rɪpt] *adj* ribbed; *(Säule)* fluted; *(Stoff)* corded

gerissen [gə'rɪsən] *pp* of **reißen** || *adj* sly

geritten [gə'rɪtən] *pp* of **reiten**

gern(e) ['gern(ə)] *adv* gladly; **g. haben** or **mögen** like; **ich rauche g. I** like to smoke

gerochen [gə'rɔxən] *pp* of **riechen**

Geröll [gə'rœl] *n* (-s;) pebbles

geronnen [gə'rɔnən] *pp* of **gerinnen** & **rinnen**

Gerste ['gerstə] *f* (-;-n) barley

Ger'stenkorn *n* grain of barley; (pathol) sty

Gerte ['gertə] *f* (-;-n) switch, rod

Geruch [gə'rux] *m* (-[e]s;ⁱe) smell

geruch'los *adj* odorless

Gerücht [gə'rʏçt] *n* (-[e]s;-e) rumor

geruhen [gə'ru:-ən] *intr* deign

geruhsam [gə'ru:zam] *adj* quiet; relaxed

Gerümpel [gə'rʏmpəl] *n* (-s;) junk

gerungen [gə'ruŋən] *pp* of **ringen**

Gerüst [gə'rʏst] *n* (-s;-e) scaffold; *(Tragewerk)* frame; (fig) outline

Ges [ges] *n* (-;-) (mus) G flat

gesamt [gə'zamt] *adj* entire, total

gesamt–, Gesamt– *comb.fm.* total, overall; all–; joint; collective

gesandt [gə'zant] *pp* of **senden**

Gesand'te §5 *mf* envoy

Gesandt'schaft *f* (-;-en) legation

Gesang [gə'zaŋ] *m* (-[e]s;ⁱe) singing; song; (lit) canto

Gesang'verein *m* glee club

Gesäß [gə'zɛ:s] *n* (-es;-e) buttocks; (coll) behind

Geschäft [gə'ʃeft] *n* (-[e]s;-e) business; deal, bargain; shop, store

Geschäftemacherei [gə'ʃeftəmaxəraɪ] *f* (-;) commercialism

geschäftig [gə'ʃeftɪç] *adj* busy

Geschäf'tigkeit *f* (-;) hustle, bustle

geschäft'lich *adj* business || *adv* on business

Geschäfts'abschluß *m* contract; deal

Geschäfts'aufsicht *f* receivership

Geschäfts'bedingungen *pl* terms

geschäfts'führend *adj* managing; executive; **geschäftsführende Regierung** caretaker government

Geschäfts'führer –**in** §6 *mf* manager

Geschäfts'haus *n* firm; office building

Geschäfts'inhaber –**in** §6 *mf* proprietor

geschäfts'kundig *adj* with business experience

Geschäfts'lokal *n* business premises; *(Laden)* shop; *(Büro)* office

Geschäfts'mann *m* (-[e]s;–leute) businessman

geschäfts'mäßig *adj* business-like
Geschäfts'ordnung *f* rules of procedure; **zur G.!** point of order!
Geschäfts'reise *f* business trip
Geschäfts'schluß *m* closing time
Geschäfts'stelle *f* office; branch
Geschäfts'träger *m* agent, representative; (pol) chargé d'affaires
geschäfts'tüchtig *adj* sharp
Geschäfts'verbindung *f* business connections
Geschäfts'verkehr *m* business transactions
Geschäfts'viertel *n* business district
Geschäfts'wert *m* (com) good will
Geschäfts'zweig *m* line of business
geschah [gə'ʃa] *pret* of geschehen
geschehen [gə'ʃe·ən] §138 *intr* (SEIN) happen; take place; be done; **das geschieht dir recht!** serves you right! || **Geschehen** *n* (-s;) events
Geschehnis [gə'ʃenɪs] *n* (-ses;-se) event
gescheit [gə'ʃaɪt] *adj* clever; bright; sensible; **er ist wohl nicht ganz g.** he's not all there
Geschenk [gə'ʃɛŋk] *n* (-[e]s;-e) gift
Geschichte [gə'ʃɪçtə] *f* (-;-n) story; history; (coll) affair, thing
geschicht'lich *adj* historical
Geschichts'forscher -in §6 *mf*, Geschichts'schreiber -in §6 *mf* historian
Geschick [gə'ʃɪk] *n* (-[e]s;-e) fate, destiny; dexterity, skill
Geschick'lichkeit *f* (-;) skillfulness
geschickt [gə'ʃɪkt] *adj* skillful
geschieden [gə'ʃidən] *pp* of scheiden
geschienen [gə'ʃinən] *pp* of scheinen
Geschirr [gə'ʃɪr] *n* (-[e]s;-e) dishes; china; pot; (e-s Pferdes) harness
Geschirr'schrank *m* kitchen cabinet
Geschirrspülmaschine [gə'ʃɪr/pylma-ʃinə] *f* dishwasher
Geschirr'tuch *n* dishtowel
geschissen [gə'ʃɪsən] *pp* of scheißen
Geschlecht [gə'ʃlɛçt] *n* (-[e]s;-er) sex; race; family, line; generation; (gram) gender
geschlecht'lich *adj* sexual
Geschlechts'krankheit *f* venereal disease
Geschlechts'teile *pl* genitals
Geschlechts'trieb *m* sexual instinct
Geschlechts'verkehr *m* intercourse
Geschlechts'wort *n* (-[e]s;-̈) (gram) article
geschlichen [gə'ʃlɪçən] *pp* of schleichen
geschliffen [gə'ʃlɪfən] *pp* of schleifen || *adj* (Glas) cut; (fig) polished
geschlissen [gə'ʃlɪsən] *pp* of schleißen
geschlossen [gə'ʃlosən] *pp* of schließen || *adj* closed; enclosed; (Front) united; (Gesellschaft) private; (ling) close; (telv) closed-circuit || *adv* unanimously; **g. hinter j-m stehen** be solidly behind s.o.
geschlungen [gə'ʃluŋən] *pp* of schlingen
Geschmack [gə'ʃmak] *m* (-s;-̈e & -̈er) taste
Geschmacks'richtung *f* vogue

geschmeidig [gə'ʃmaɪdɪç] *adj* pliant; flexible; lithe; (Haar) manageable
Geschmeiß [gə'ʃmaɪs] *n* (-es;) vermin; rabble
geschmissen [gə'ʃmɪsən] *pp* of schmeißen
geschmolzen [gə'ʃmoltsən] *pp* of schmelzen
Geschnatter [gə'ʃnatər] *n* (-s;) cackle
geschniegelt [gə'ʃnigəlt] *adj* spruce
geschnitten [gə'ʃnɪtən] *pp* of schneiden
geschnoben [gə'ʃnobən] *pp* of schnauben
geschoben [gə'ʃobən] *pp* of schieben
gescholten [gə'ʃoltən] *pp* of schelten
Geschöpf [gə'ʃœpf] *n* (-[e]s;-e) creature
geschoren [gə'ʃorən] *pp* of scheren
Ge·schoß [gə'ʃos] *n* (-schosses; -schosse) shot; missile; shell; floor, story
Geschoß'bahn *f* trajectory
geschossen [gə'ʃosən] *pp* of schießen
geschraubt [gə'ʃraubt] *adj* affected; (Stil) stilted
Geschrei [gə'ʃraɪ] *n* (-[e]s;) shouting
Geschreibsel [gə'ʃraɪpsəl] *n* (-s;) scribbling, scrawl
geschrieben [gə'ʃribən] *pp* of schreiben
geschrieen [gə'ʃrɪ·ən] *pp* of schreien
geschritten [gə'ʃrɪtən] *pp* of schreiten
geschunden [gə'ʃundən] *pp* of schinden
Geschütz [gə'ʃyts] *n* (-es;-e) gun
Geschütz'bedienung *f* gun crew
Geschütz'legierung *f* gun metal
Geschütz'stand *m* gun emplacement
Geschwader [gə'ʃvadər] *n* (-s;-) (aer) group (consisting of 27 aircraft); (nav) squadron
Geschwätz [gə'ʃvɛts] *n* (-es;) chatter
geschweige [gə'ʃvaɪgə]—**g. denn** let alone, much less
geschwiegen [gə'ʃvigən] *pp* of schweigen
geschwind [gə'ʃvɪnt] *adj* quick
Geschwin'digkeit *f* (-;-en) speed; velocity; **mit der G. von** at the rate of
Geschwin'digkeitsbegrenzung *f* speed limit
Geschwin'digkeitsmesser *m* speedometer
Geschwind'schritt *m* (mil) double time
Geschwister [gə'ʃvɪstər] *pl* brother and sister, brothers, sisters, brothers and sisters; siblings
geschwollen [gə'ʃvolən] *pp* of schwellen || *adj* turgid
geschwommen [gə'ʃvomən] *pp* of schwimmen
geschworen [gə'ʃvorən] *pp* of schwören || **Geschworene** §5 *mf* juror; **die Geschworenen** the jury
Geschwo'renengericht *n* jury
Geschwulst [gə'ʃvulst] *f* (-;-̈e) swelling; tumor
geschwunden [gə'ʃvundən] *pp* of schwinden
geschwungen [gə'ʃvuŋən] *pp* of schwingen
Geschwür [gə'ʃvyr] *n* (-s;-e) ulcer

Geselle [gə'zɛlə] m (-n;-n) journey-man; companion; lad, fellow

gesellen [gə'zɛlən] ref—sich zu j-m g. join s.o.

gesellig [gə'zɛlɪç] adj gregarious, sociable

Gesell'schaft f (-;-en) society; company; (pej) bunch; (com) company; j-m G. leisten keep s.o. company

Gesell'schafter –in §6 mf companion; shareholder; (com) partner

gesell'schaftlich adj social

Gesell'schaftsspiel n party game

Gesell'schaftswissenschaft f social science; sociology

gesessen [gə'zɛsən] pp of sitzen

Gesetz [gə'zɛts] n (-es;-e) law

Gesetz'buch n legal code

Gesetz'entwurf m (parl) bill

Gesetzes– [gəzɛtsəs] comb.fm. legal, of law, of the law

Geset'zesantrag m, Geset'zesvorlage f (parl) bill

gesetz'gebend adj legislative

Gesetz'geber –in §6 mf legislator

Gesetz'gebung f (-;) legislation

gesetz'lich adj legal

gesetz'los adj lawless

gesetz'mäßig adj legal; legitimate

Gesetz'sammlung f code of laws

gesetzt [gə'zɛtst] adj sedate; (Alter) mature; g. den Fall, daß assuming that || adv in a dignified manner

gesetz'widrig adj illegal, unlawful

Gesicht [gə'zɪçt] n (-[e]s;-er) face; sight; eyesight; (Aussehen) look

Gesichts'farbe f complexion

Gesichts'kreis m horizon; outlook

Gesichts'punkt m point of view, angle

Gesichts'spannung f face lift

Gesichts'zug m feature

Gesims [gə'zɪms] n (-es;-e) molding

Gesindel [gə'zɪndəl] n (-s;) rabble; lichtscheues G. shady characters

gesinnt [gə'zɪnt] adj disposed; -minded

Gesinnung [gə'zɪnʊŋ] f (-;-en) mind; character; convictions

gesin'nungslos adj without definite convictions

gesin'nungsmäßig adv according to one's convictions

gesin'nungstreu, gesin'nungstüchtig adj staunch

gesittet [gə'zɪtət] adj polite; civilized

gesoffen [gə'zɔfən] pp of saufen

gesogen [gə'zogən] pp of saugen

gesonnen [gə'zɔnən] pp of sinnen || adj—g. sein zu (inf) have a mind to (inf), be inclined to (inf)

gesotten [gə'zɔtən] pp of sieden

Gespann [gə'pan] n (-[e]s;-e) team; pair, combination

gespannt [gə'pant] adj stretched; tense; (Aufmerksamkeit) close; (Beziehungen) strained; ich bin g. (coll) I wonder, I am anxious to know

Gespenst [gə'pɛnst] n (-[e]s;-er) ghost, specter

gespen'sterhaft adj ghostly; spooky

gespenstisch [gə'pɛnstɪʃ] adj ghostly

gespie(e)n [gə'pi(ə)n] pp of speien

Gespiele [gə'pilə] m (-n;-n), Gespielin [gə'pilɪn] f (-;-nen) playmate

Gespinst [gə'pɪnst] n (-es;-e) yarn, (Gewebe) web

gesponnen [gə'pɔnən] pp of spinnen

Gespött [gə'pœt] n (-[e]s;) ridicule; laughing stock

Gespräch [gə'prɛç] n (-[e]s;-e) conversation; (telp) call; Gespräche (pol) talks; G. mit Voranmeldung person-to-person call

gesprächig [gə'prɛçɪç] adj talkative

gespreizt [gə'praɪtst] adj outspread; affected || adv—g. tun act big

gesprenkelt [gə'prɛŋkəlt] adj spotted

gesprochen [gə'prɔçən] pp of sprechen

gesprossen [gə'prɔsən] pp of sprießen

gesprungen [gə'prʊŋən] pp of springen

Gestade [gə'tadə] n (-s;-) (river) bank; (sea)shore

Gestalt [gə'talt] f (-;-en) shape; figure; (Wuchs) stature

gestalten [gə'taltən] tr shape; form; arrange || ref take shape; turn out

Gestal'tung f (-;-en) formation; development; arrangement; design

gestanden [gə'tandən] pp of stehen

geständig [gə'tɛndɪç] adj—g. sein admit one's guilt

Geständnis [gə'tɛntnɪs] n (-ses;-se) confession, admission

Gestank [gə'taŋk] m (-[e]s;) stench

Gestapo [gə'tapo] f (-;) (Geheime Staatspolizei) secret state police

gestatten [gə'tatən] tr permit, allow

Geste ['gɛstə] f (-;-n) gesture

gestehen [gə'te∙ən] §146 tr admit

Gestein [gə'taɪn] n (-[e]s;-e) rock

Gestell [gə'tɛl] n (-[e]s;-e) frame; rack; mounting; (coll) beanpole

Gestel'lungsbefehl m (mil) induction orders

gestern ['gɛstərn] adv yesterday; g. abend last evening, last night

gestiefelt [gə'tifəlt] adj in boots

gestiegen [gə'tigən] pp of steigen

gestikulieren [gɛstiku'lirən] intr gesticulate

Gestirn [gə'tɪrn] n (-[e]s;-e) star; (Sternbild) constellation

gestirnt [gə'tɪrnt] adj starry

gestoben [gə'tobən] pp of stieben

Gestöber [gə'tøbər] n (-s;-) snow flurry

gestochen [gə'tɔxən] pp of stechen

gestohlen [gə'tolən] pp of stehlen

gestorben [gə'tɔrbən] pp of sterben

gestoßen [gə'tosən] pp of stoßen

Gesträuch [gə'trɔɪç] n (-[e]s;) bushes, shrubbery

gestreift [gə'traɪft] adj striped

gestrichen [gə'trɪçən] pp of streichen

gestrig ['gɛstrɪç] adj yesterday's

gestritten [gə'trɪtən] pp of streiten

Gestrüpp [gə'trʏp] n (-[e]s;-e) underbrush

gestunken [gə'tʊŋkən] pp of stinken

Gestüt [gə'tyt] n (-[e]s;-e) stud farm

Gestüt'hengst m stallion, studhorse

Gesuch [gə'zux] n (-[e]s;-e) request; application; (jur) petition

gesucht [gə'zuxt] adj wanted; in demand; studied; (Vergleich) farfetched

Gesudel [gə'zudəl] n (-s;) messy job

Gesumme [gə'zumə] n (-s;) humming
gesund [gə'zunt] adj healthy; sound; wholesome; **g. werden** get well
Gesund'beter **-in** §6 mf faith healer
Gesund'brunnen m mineral spring
gesunden [gə'zundən] intr (SEIN) get well again, recover
Gesund'heit f (-;) health; **auf Ihre G.!** to your health!; **G.!** (God) bless you!
Gesund'heitslehre f hygiene
Gesund'heitspflege f hygiene
Gesund'heitsrücksichten pl—**aus G.** for reasons of health
Gesund'heitswesen n public health
gesungen [gə'zuŋən] pp of **singen**
gesunken [gə'zuŋkən] pp of **sinken**
Getäfel [gə'tefəl] n (-s;) wainscoting
getä'felt adj inlaid
getan [gə'tɑn] pp of **tun**
Getöse [gə'tøzə] n (-s;) din, noise
getragen [gə'trɑgən] pp of **tragen** || adj solemn
Getrampel [gə'trampəl] n (-s;) trample
Getränk [gə'treŋk] n (-[e]s;-e) drink
getrauen [gə'trau-ən] ref dare
Getreide [gə'traɪdə] n (-s;-) grain
Getrei'deboden m granary
Getrei'despeicher m grain elevator
getreu [gə'trɔɪ] adj faithful, true
getreu'lich adv faithfully
Getriebe [gə'tribə] n (-s;-) hustle and bustle; (adm) machinery; (aut) transmission
getrieben [gə'tribən] pp of **treiben**
getroffen [gə'trɔmən] pp of **treffen**
getrogen [gə'trɔgən] pp of **trügen**
getrost [gə'trost] adj confident
getrunken [gə'truŋkən] pp of **trinken**
Getue [gə'tu-ə] n (-s;) fuss
Getto ['geto] n (-s;-s) ghetto
Getümmel [gə'tʏmәl] n (-s;) turmoil
getupft [gə'tupft] adj polka-dot
Geviert [gə'firt] n (-[e]s;-e) square
Gewächs [gə'veks] n (-es;-e) growth; plant
gewachsen [gə'vaksən] adj—**g. sein** (dat) be equal to, be up to
Gewächs'haus n greenhouse, hothouse
gewagt [gə'vakt] adj risky; off-color
gewählt [gə'velt] adj choice; refined
gewahr [gə'var] adj—**g. werden** (genit) become aware of
Gewähr [gə'ver] f (-;) guarantee
gewahren [gə'varən] tr notice
gewähren [gə'verən] tr grant
gewähr'leisten tr guarantee, ensure
Gewähr'leistung f (-;-en) guarantee
Gewahrsam [gə'varzam] m (-[e]s; safekeeping, custody || n (-[e]s;-e) prison
Gewährs'mann m (-[e]s;-er & -leute) informant, source
Gewährs'pflicht f warranty
Gewalt [gə'valt] f (-;-en) force; violence; authority; (Aufsicht) control
Gewalt'haber m (-s;-) ruler; tyrant
Gewalt'herrschaft f tyranny
Gewalt'herrscher m tyrant
gewal'tig adj powerful; huge; (coll) awful || adv terribly
Gewalt'kur f drastic measure; (coll) crash program
gewalt'los adj nonviolent

Gewalt'marsch m forced march
Gewalt'mensch m brute, tyrant
gewaltsam [gə'valtzam] adj violent; forcible; drastic || adv by force
Gewalt'samkeit f (-;) violence
Gewalt'streich m bold stroke
Gewalt'tat f act of violence
gewalt'tätig adj violent, brutal
Gewalt'verbrechen n felony
Gewalt'verbrecher **-in** §6 mf felon
Gewand [gə'vant] n (-[e]s;-er) robe; appearance, guise; (eccl) vestment
gewandt [gə'vant] pp of **wenden** || adj agile; clever
gewann [gə'van] pret of **gewinnen**
gewärtig [gə'vertɪç] adj—**g. sein** (genit) be prepared for
Gewäsch [gə'veʃ] n (-es;) nonsense
Gewässer [gə'vesər] n (-s;-) body of water; waters
Gewebe [gə'vebə] n (-s;-) tissue; (tex) fabric
geweckt [gə'vekt] adj bright, sharp
Gewehr [gə'ver] n (-[e]s;-e) rifle
Geweih [gə'vaɪ] n (-[e]s;-e) antlers
Gewerbe [gə'verbə] n (-s;-) trade, business; calling, profession; industry
Gewer'bebetrieb m business enterprise
Gewer'beschule f trade school
gewerblich [gə'verplɪç] adj industrial; commercial, business
gewerbs'mäßig adj professional
Gewerkschaft [gə'verkʃaft] f (-;-en) labor union
gewerk'schaftlich adj union || adv— **sich g. organisieren** unionize
Gewerk'schaftsbeitrag m union dues
gewesen [gə'vezən] pp of **sein**
gewichen [gə'vɪçən] pp of **weichen**
Gewicht [gə'vɪçt] n (-[e]s;-e) (& fig) weight
gewichtig [gə'vɪçtɪç] adj weighty
gewiegt [gə'vigt] adj experienced, smart, shrewd
gewiesen [gə'vizən] pp of **weisen**
gewillt [gə'vɪlt] adj willing
Gewimmel [gə'vɪmәl] n (-s;) swarm; (Menschen-) throng
Gewimmer [gə'vɪmәr] n (-s;) whimpering; whining
Gewinde [gə'vɪndə] n (-s;-) thread (of a screw); (Kranz) garland; skein
Gewinn [gə'vɪn] m (-[e]s;-e) winnings; profit; (Vorteil) advantage
Gewinn'anteil m dividend
Gewinn'aufschlag m (com) markup
Gewinn'beteiligung f profit sharing
gewinn'bringend adj profitable
gewinnen [gə'vɪnən] §121 tr win, gain; reach || intr win; make a profit; improve; **g. an** (dat) gain in; **g. von** or **durch** profit by
gewin'nend adj engaging
Gewinn'spanne f margin of profit
Gewinn'sucht f greed; profiteering
Gewinsel [gə'vɪnzəl] n (-s;) whimpering
Gewirr [gə'vɪr] n (-[e]s;-e) tangle; entanglement; maze
gewiß [gə'vɪs] adj sure, certain || adv certainly; **aber g.!** of course!
Gewissen [gə'vɪsən] n (-s;-) conscience

gewis'senhaft *adj* conscientious

gewis'senlos *adj* unscrupulous

Gewis'sensbisse *pl* pangs of conscience

Gewis'sensnot *f* moral dilemma

gewis'sermaßen *adv* to some extent; so to speak

Gewiß'heit *f* (-;-en) certainty

gewiß'lich *adv* certainly

Gewitter [gə'vɪtər] *n* (-s;-) thunderstorm

gewittern [gə'vɪtərn] *impers*—es gewittert a storm is brewing

Gewit'terregen *m* thundershower

gewitzigt [gə'vɪtsɪçt] *adj*—g. sein to have learned from experience

gewitzt [gə'vɪtst] *adj* bright, smart

gewoben [gə'voːbən] *pp* of weben

gewogen [gə'voːgən] *pp* of wägen & wiegen ‖ *adj* well disposed

Gewo'genheit *f* (-;) favorable attitude

gewöhnen [gə'vøːnən] *tr* (an *acc*) accustom (to) ‖ *ref* (an *acc*) get used (to)

Gewohnheit [gə'voːnhaɪt] *f* (-;-en) habit, custom

gewohn'heitsmäßig *adj* habitual

Gewohn'heitsmensch *m* creature of habit

gewöhnlich [gə'vøːnlɪç] *adj* usual; normal; common, ordinary

gewohnt [gə'voːnt] *adj* usual; g. sein (*acc*) be used to

Gewölbe [gə'vœlbə] *n* (-s;-) vault; arch

gewölbt [gə'vœlpt] *adj* vaulted

Gewölk [gə'vœlk] *n* (-[e]s;) clouds

gewonnen [gə'vonən] *pp* of gewinnen

geworben [gə'vorbən] *pp* of werben

geworden [gə'vordən] *pp* of werden

geworfen [gə'vorfən] *pp* of werfen

gewrungen [gə'vruŋən] *pp* of wringen

Gewühl [gə'vyːl] *n* (-[e]s;) milling crowd

gewunden [gə'vundən] *pp* of winden

gewürfelt [gə'vyrfəlt] *adj* checkered

Gewürm [gə'vyrm] *n* (-[e]s;) vermin

Gewürz [gə'vyrts] *n* (-[e]s;-e) spice

Gewürz'nelke *f* clove

gewußt [gə'vust] *pp* of wissen

Geysir ['gaɪzɪr] *m* (-s;-) geyser

gezackt [gə'tsakt] *adj* jagged; (*Rand*) serrated

gezähnt [gə'tsɛnt] *adj* toothed; (*Rand*) perforated; (bot) dentated

Gezänk [gə'tseŋk] *n* (-[e]s;) squabbling

Gezeiten [gə'tsaɪtən] *pl* tides

Gezeiten- *comb.fm.* tidal

Gezeter [gə'tseːtər] *n* (-s;) yelling

geziehen [gə'tsiːən] *pp* of zeihen

geziemen [gə'tsiːmən] *intr* (*dat*) be proper for ‖ *impers ref*—es geziemt sich für j-n it is right for s.o.

geziert [gə'tsiːrt] *adj* affected, phoney

Gezisch [gə'tsɪʃ] *n* (-es;) hissing

gezogen [gə'tsoːgən] *pp* of ziehen

Gezücht [gə'tsʏçt] *n* (-[e]s;-e) riffraff

Gezwitscher [gə'tsvɪtʃər] *n* (-s;) chirping

gezwungen [gə'tsvuŋən] *pp* of zwingen ‖ *adj* forced; (*Stil*) labored ‖ *adv* stiffly

Gicht [gɪçt] *f* (-;-en) gout

Giebel ['giːbəl] *m* (-s;-) gable

Gier [gir] *f* (-;) greed

gierig ['giːrɪç] *adj* (nach) greedy (for)

Gießbach ['gisbax] *m* torrent

gießen ['gisən] §76 *tr* pour; (*Blumen usw.*) water; (metal) cast, found ‖ *impers*—es gießt it is pouring

Gießer ['gisər] *m* (-s;-) foundryman

Gießerei [gisə'raɪ] *f* (-;-en) foundry

Gieß'form *f* casting mold; (typ) matrix

Gieß'kanne *f* sprinkling can

Gift [gɪft] *n* (-[e]s;-e) poison

giftig ['gɪftɪç] *adj* poisonous; malicious

Gigant [gɪ'gant] *m* (-en;-en) giant

Gilde ['gɪldə] *f* (-;-n) guild

Gimpel ['gɪmpəl] *m* (-s;-) (coll) sucker

ging [gɪŋ] *pret* of gehen

Gipfel ['gɪpfəl] *m* (-s;-) top; peak

Gip'felkonferenz *f* summit meeting

Gips [gɪps] *m* (-es;-e) gypsum; plaster of Paris; (surg) cast

Gips'arbeit *f* plastering

Gips'diele *f* plasterboard

gipsen ['gɪpsən] *tr* plaster

Gips'verband *m* (surg) cast

Giraffe [gɪ'rafə] *f* (-;-n) giraffe

girieren [gi'riːrən] *tr* endorse

Girlande [gɪr'landə] *f* (-;-n) garland

Giro ['ʒiːro] *n* (-s;-s) endorsement

girren ['gɪrən] *intr* coo

Gis [gɪs] *n* (-;) (mus) G sharp

Gischt [gɪʃt] *n* (-es;) foam; spray

Gitarre [gi'tarə] *f* (-;-n) guitar

Gitter ['gɪtər] *n* (-s;-) grating, grille; bars; lattice; railing; trellis; (electron) grid

Git'terbett *n* baby crib

Git'ternetz *n* grid (on map)

Git'tertor *n* wrought-iron gate

Git'terwerk *n* latticework

Glacéhandschuhe [gla'seːhantʃuːə] *pl* (& fig) kid gloves

Gladi•ator [gladɪ'aːtor] *m* (-s;-atoren [a'toːrən]) gladiator

Glanz [glants] *m* (-es;) shine; polish; luster; brilliance

glänzen ['glɛntsən] *tr* polish ‖ *intr* shine; durch Abwesenheit g. be conspicuous by one's absence

glän'zend *adj* bright; glossy; polished; (fig) splendid, brilliant

Glanz'leder *n* patent leather

Glanz'licht *n* (paint) highlight

glanz'los *adj* dull; lackluster

Glanz'punkt *m* highlight

Glanz'stück *n* master stroke

glanz'voll *adj* brilliant, splendid

Glanz'zeit *f* heyday, golden age

Glas [glas] *n* (-es;̈er) glass

Glaser ['glaːzər] *m* (-s;-) glazier

gläsern ['glɛzərn] *adj* glass; glassy

Glas'hütte *f* glassworks

glasieren [gla'ziːrən] *tr* glaze; (*Kuchen*) frost, ice

glasig ['glaːzɪç] *adj* glassy; vitreous

Glas'jalousie *f* jalousie window

Glas'scheibe *f* pane of glass

Glasur [gla'zuːr] *f* (-;-en) enamel (on pots); glaze; (culin) icing

glatt [glat] *adj* smooth; (*eben*) even; (*poliert*) glossy; (*schlüpfrig*) slippery; (*Absage*) flat; (*Lüge*) downright ‖ *adv* smoothly; directly; entirely

Glätte ['glɛtə] *f* (—;) smoothness; slipperiness; (*Politur*) polish

Glatt'eis *n* sheet of ice; **bei G. fahren** drive in icy conditions

glätten ['glɛtən] *tr* smooth; smooth out || *ref* smooth out; become calm

glatt'streichen §85 *tr* smooth out

glatt'weg *adv* outright, point-blank

glattzüngig ['glatstsʏŋɪç] *adj* smooth-talking

Glatze ['glatsə] *f* (—;-n) bald head

glatz'köpfig *adj* baldheaded

Glaube ['glaubə] *m* (—ns;), **Glauben** ['glaubən] *m* (—s;) belief; faith

glauben ['glaubən] *tr* believe; (*annehmen*) suppose || *intr* (*dat*) believe; **g. an** (*acc*) believe in; **j-m aufs Wort glauben** take s.o.'s word

Glau'bensbekenntnis *n* profession of faith; creed

Glau'benslehre *f* Christian doctrine

Glau'benssatz *m* dogma

gläubig ['glɔɪbɪç] *adj* believing || **Gläubige** §5 *mf* believer || **Gläubiger –in** §6 *mf* creditor

glaublich ['glauplɪç] *adj* credible

glaub'würdig *adj* credible; reliable; plausible

Glaukom [glau'kom] *n* (—s;-e) glaucoma

gleich [glaɪç] *adj* (*dat*) like; (**an** *dat*) equal (in); **es ist mir ganz g.** it's all the same to me || *adv* equally; immediately

gleichaltrig ['glaɪçaltrɪç] *adj* of the same age

gleich'artig *adj* similar, homogeneous

gleich'bedeutend *adj* synonymous

Gleich'berechtigung *f* (pol) equality

gleichen ['glaɪçən] §85 *intr* (*dat*) resemble, look like, be like

glei'chermaßen *adv* equally, likewise

gleich'falls *adv* likewise; as well

gleich'förmig *adj* uniform; regular; monotonous

gleich'gesinnt *adj* like-minded

Gleich'gewicht *n* equilibrium

gleich'gültig *adj* indifferent; **es ist mir g.** it's all the same to me

Gleich'heit *f* (—;-en) equality; (*Ähnlichkeit*) likeness

Gleich'klang *m* consonance; unison

gleich'kommen §99 *intr* (SEIN) (*dat*) equal; (*dat*) be tantamount to

gleich'laufend *adj* (mit) parallel (to)

gleich'machen *tr* make equal; standardize; **dem Erdboden g.** raze

Gleich'maß *n* regularity; evenness; balance, equilibrium; proportion

gleich'mäßig *adj* symmetrical; regular

Gleich'mut *m* equanimity, calmness

gleich'mütig *adj* calm

gleichnamig ['glaɪçnamɪç] *adj* of the same name; (phys) like

Gleichnis ['glaɪçnɪs] *n* (—ses;-se) parable; figure of speech; simile

Gleich'richter *m* (elec) rectifier

gleichsam ['glaɪçzam] *adv* so to speak; more or less, practically

gleichschenklig ['glaɪçʃɛŋklɪç] *adj* isosceles

Gleich'schritt *m*—**im G.** in cadence; **im G. marsch!** forward, march!

gleich'seitig *adj* equilateral

gleich'setzen *tr* (*dat* or *mit*) equate (with)

Gleich'setzung *f* (—;), **Gleich'stellung** *f* (—;) equalization

Gleich'strom *m* direct current

gleich'tun §154 *tr*—**es j-m g.** emulate s.o.

Glei'chung *f* (—;-en) (math) equation

gleichviel *adv*—g. wer not matter who

gleich'wertig *adj* evenly matched

gleichwohl' *adv* nevertheless

gleich'zeitig *adj* simultaneous

gleich'ziehen §163 *intr* (mit) catch up (with or to)

Gleis [glaɪs] *n* (—es;-e) (rr) track

Gleitboot ['glaɪtbot] *n* hydrofoil

gleiten ['glaɪtən] §86 *intr* (SEIN) glide; slip, slide

Gleitfläche ['glaɪtflɛçə] *f* (aer) hydroplane

Gleitflugzeug ['glaɪtfluktsɔɪk] *n* (aer) glider

Gleitschutz– *comb.fm.* skid-proof

Gleit'zeit *f* flexitime

Gletscher ['glɛtʃər] *m* (—s;-) glacier

glich [glɪç] *pret* of *gleichen*

Glied [glit] *n* (—[e]s;-er) limb; member; joint; link; (anat) penis; (log, math) term; (mil) rank, file

glie'derlahm *adj* paralyzed

gliedern ['glidərn] *tr* arrange; plan; divide, break down || *ref* (**in** *acc*) consist of

Glie'derung *f* (—;-en) arrangement; construction; division; organization

Gliedmaßen ['glitmasən] *pl* limbs

glimmen ['glɪmən] *intr* §136 & §109 *intr* glimmer; glow

Glim'mer *m* (—s;) glimmer; (min) mica

glimpflich ['glɪmpflɪç] *adj* gentle; (*Strafe*) light, lenient

glitschen ['glɪtʃən] *intr* (SEIN) slip

glitschig ['glɪtʃɪç] *adj* slippery

glitt [glɪt] *pret* of *gleiten*

glitzern ['glɪtsərn] *intr* glitter

global [glo'bal] *adj* global

Glo-bus ['globus] *m* (—bus & —busses; -busse & —ben [bən]) globe

Glöckchen ['glœkçən] *n* (—s;-) small bell

Glocke ['glokə] *f* (—;-n) bell; (e-s *Rocks*) flare

Glockenspiel (Glok'kenspiel) *n* carillon

Glockenstube (Glok'kenstube) *f*, **Glockenturm (Glok'kenturm)** *m* belfry

Glockenzug (Glok'kenzug) *m* bell rope

Glöckner ['glœknər] *m* (—s;-) bell ringer; sexton

glomm [glom] *pret* of *glimmen*

Glorie ['glorjə] *f* (—;-n) glory

Glo'rienschein *m* halo

glorreich ['glorraɪç] *adj* glorious

glotzäugig ['glotsɔɪgɪç] *adj* popeyed

glotzen ['glotsən] *intr* stare, goggle

Glück [glʏk] *n* (—[e]s;) luck; fortune; happiness; **auf gut G.** at random; **zum G.** luckily

glucken ['glʊkən] *intr* cluck

glücken ['glʏkən] *intr* (SEIN) succeed || *impers*—**es glückt mir** I succeed

gluckern ['glʊkərn] *intr* gurgle

glück'lich adj lucky, fortunate; happy; (günstig) auspicious

glück'licherweise adv fortunately

glück'selig adj blissful; blessed; joyful

Glück'seligkeit f (-;) bliss; joy

glucksen ['gluksən] intr gurgle; chuckle

Glücks'fall m stroke of luck; windfall

Glücks'güter pl earthly possessions

Glücks'hafen m raffle drum

Glücks'pilz m (coll) lucky dog

Glücks'spiel n game of chance

Glücks'topf m grab bag

glück'verheißend adj auspicious

Glück'wunsch m good wishes, congratulations

Glück'wunschkarte f greeting card

Glühbirne ['glybɪrnə] f light bulb

glühen ['gly·ən] tr make red-hot; (metal) anneal || intr glow

glü'hendheiß adj red-hot

Glühfaden ['glyfadən] m filament

Glühwurm ['glyvurm] m firefly

Glut [glut] f (-;) embers; fire; scorching heat; (fig) ardor

Glyzerin [glytsə'rin] n (-s;) glycerine

GmbH abbr (Gesellschaft mit beschränkter Haftung) Inc.; Ltd. (Brit)

Gnade ['gnadə] f (-;-n) grace; favor; mercy; **von eigenen Gnaden** self-styled

Gna'denbeweis m token of favor

Gna'denbrot n—**bei j-m das G. essen** to live on s.o.'s charity

Gna'denfrist f grace, e.g., **e-e G. von zwei Monaten** two months' grace

Gna'dengesuch n plea for mercy

Gna'denstoß m coup de grâce, deathblow

gnädig ['gnedɪç] adj gracious, kind; merciful; **gnädige Frau** madam; **Sehr verehrte gnädige Frau** Dear Madam

Gold [gɔlt] n (-[e]s;) gold

Gold'blech n gold foil

Gold'fink m (orn) goldfinch

goldig ['gɔldɪç] adj (coll) cute

Gold'plombe f (dent) gold filling

Gold'schmied m goldsmith

Gold'schnitt m gilt edging

Golf [gɔlf] m (-[e]s;-e) gulf; bay || n (-s;) golf

Golf'platz m golf course

Golf'schläger m golf club

Gondel ['gɔndəl] f (-;-n) gondola

Gon'delführer m gondolier

gönnen ['gœnən] tr not begrudge; allow; **j—m etw nicht g.** begrudge s.o. s.th.

Gön'ner –in §6 mf patron

gön'nerhaft adj patronizing

Gön'nerschaft f (-;) patronage

gor [gor] pret of gären

Gorilla [go'rɪla] m (-s;-s) gorilla

goß [gɔs] pret of gießen

Gosse ['gɔsə] f (-;-n) gutter

Gote ['gotə] m (-n;-n) Goth

gotisch ['gotɪʃ] adj Gothic

Gott [gɔt] m (-[e]s;⸚er) god; God

gottbegnadet ['gɔtbəgnadət] adj gifted

gott'ergeben adj resigned to God's will

Got'tesdienst m divine service; Mass

Got'tesfürchtig adj God-fearing

Got'tesgabe f godsend

got'teslästerlich adj blasphemous

Got'teslästerung f blasphemy

Got'tesurteil n ordeal

gott'gefällig adj pleasing to God

Gott'heit f (-;-en) deity, divinity

Göttin ['gœtɪn] f (-;-nen) goddess

göttlich ['gœtlɪç] adj godlike, divine; (fig) heavenly

gotlob' interj thank goodness!

Gott'mensch m God incarnate

gott'selig adj blessed

gott'verlassen adj godforsaken

Götze ['gœtsə] m (-n;-n) idol

Göt'zenbild n idol

Göt'zendiener –in §6 mf idolater

Göt'zendienst m idolatry

Gouvernante [guvɛr'nantə] f (-;-n) governess

Gouverneur [guvɛr'nør] m (-s;-e) governor

Grab [grap] n (-[e]s;⸚er) grave; tomb

graben ['grabən] §87 tr dig; burrow || **Graben** m (-s;⸚) ditch; trench; moat

Grab'geläute n death knell

Grab'gesang m funeral dirge

Grab'hügel m burial mound

Grab'inschrift f epitaph

Grab'mal n tombstone; tomb, sepulcher

Grab'stätte f burial place

Grab'stelle f burial plot

Grad [grat] m (-[e]s;-e) degree; grade; (mil) rank

grade ['gradə] adv var of gerade

Grad'einteilung f gradation

Grad'messer m graduated scale; (fig) yardstick

grad'weise adv by degrees

Graf [graf] m (-en;-en) count; earl (Brit)

Gräfin ['grɛfɪn] f (-;-nen) countess

gräflich ['grɛflɪç] adj count's; earl's

Graf'schaft f (-;-en) county

gram [gram] adj—**j—m g. sein** be cross with s.o. || **Gram** m (-[e]s;) grief

grämen ['grɛmən] tr sadden, distress || ref (über acc) grieve (over)

grämlich ['grɛmlɪç] adj glum; crabby

Gramm [gram] n (-s;- & -e) gram

Grammatik [gra'matɪk] f (-;-en) grammar

grammatisch [gra'matɪʃ] adj grammatical

Gran [gran] n (-[e]s;) (fig) bit, jot

Granat [gra'nat] m (-[e]s;-e) garnet

Granat'apfel m pomegranate

Granate [gra'natə] f (-;-n) (arti) shell; (mil) grenade

Granat'feuer n shelling

Granat'hülse f shell case

Granat'splitter m shrapnel

Granat'werfer m (mil) mortar

grandios [grandɪ'os] adj grandiose

Granit [gra'nit] m (-[e]s;-e) granite

Graphik ['grafɪk] f (-;-en) graphic arts; print; engraving; woodcut

graphisch ['grafɪʃ] adj graphic

Graphit [gra'fit] m (-s;) graphite

Gras [gras] n (-es;⸚er) grass

grasen ['grazən] intr graze

Gras'halm m blade of grass

Grashüpfer ['grashypfer] m (-s;-) grasshopper

grasig ['grɑːzɪç] *adj* grassy
Gras'mäher *m* lawn mower; grass cutter
Gras'mähmaschine *f* lawn mower
Gras'narbe *f* sod, turf
grassieren [gra'siːrən] *intr* rage
gräßlich ['greslɪç] *adj* grisly
Gras'weide *f* pasture
Grat [grat] *m* (-[e]s;-e) ridge; edge
Gräte ['greːtə] *f* (-;-n) fishbone
Gratifikation [gratɪfɪka'tsjoːn] *f* (-;
  -en) bonus
grätig ['greːtɪç] *adj* full of fishbones;
  (*mürrisch*) crabby
gratis ['grɑːtɪs] *adv* gratis; **g. und
  franko** (coll) for free
Gratulation [gratula'tsjoːn] *f* (-;-en)
  congratulations
gratulieren [gratu'liːrən] *intr*—j—m g.
  zu congratulate s.o. on
grau [grau] *adj* gray, (*Vorzeit*) remote || **Grau** *n* (- & -s;-s) gray
Grau'bär *m* grizzly bear
grauen ['grau·ən] *intr* dawn || *impers*
  —es graut day is breaking; es graut
  mir vor (*dat*) I shudder at || **Grauen**
  n (-s;) (vor *dat*) horror (of)
grau'enhaft, grau'envoll *adj* horrible
gräulich ['grɔɪlɪç] *adj* grayish
Graupe ['graupə] *f* (-;-n) peeled barley
graupeln ['graupəln] *impers*—es graupelt it is sleeting || **Graupeln** *pl* sleet
Graus [graus] *m* (-es;) dread, horror
grausam ['grauzam] *adj* cruel; (coll)
  awful
Grau'schimmel *m* gray horse
grausen ['grauzən] *impers*—es graust
  mir vor (*dat*) I shudder at
grausig ['grauzɪç] *adj* gruesome
Graveur [gra'vøːr] *m* (-s;-e) engraver
gravieren [gra'viːrən] *tr* engrave
gravie'rend *adj* aggravating
gravitätisch [gravɪ'tɛːtɪʃ] *adj* stately
Grazie ['grɑːtsjə] *f* (-;-n) grace, charm
graziös [gra'tsjøːs] *adj* graceful
Greif [graɪf] *m* (-[e]s;-e) griffin
greifbar ['graɪfbar] *adj* tangible; at
  hand
greifen ['graɪfən] §88 *tr* grasp; seize;
  (*Note*) strike || *intr* catch;
  (*Zahnrad*) engage; **ans Herz g.** touch
  deeply; **an j-s Ehre g.** attack s.o.'s
  honor; **g. in** (*acc*) reach into; **g. nach**
  reach for; try to seize; **g. zu** reach
  for; (fig) resort to; **um sich g.** grope
  about; (*Feuer*) spread; **zu den Waffen g.** take up arms
Greis [graɪs] *m* (-es;-e) old man
Grei'senalter *n* old age
grei'senhaft *adj* aged; senile
Greisin ['graɪzɪn] *f* (-;-nen) old lady
grell [grel] *adj* (von *Ton*) shrill; (*Farbe,
  Kleider*) flashy; (*Licht*) glaring
Gre·mium ['gremjum] *n* (-s;-mien
  [mjən]) group, body; committee;
  corporation
Grenze ['grentsə] *f* (-;-n) boundary;
  frontier; borderline; limit
grenzen ['grentsən] *intr* (an *acc*) adjoin, border (on); (fig) verge (on)
gren'zenlos *adj* limitless
Grenz'fall *m* borderline case

Grenz'linie *f* boundary line
Grenz'sperre *f* ban on border traffic;
  frontier barricade
Grenz'stein *m* boundary stone
Greuel ['grɔɪ·əl] *m* (-s;) abhorrence;
  horror, abomination
greulich ['grɔɪlɪç] *adj* horrible
Griebs [grips] *m* (-es;-e) core
Grieche ['griçə] *m* (-n;-n) Greek
Grie'chenland *n* (-s;) Greece
Griechin ['griçɪn] *f* (-;-nen) Greek
griechisch ['griçɪʃ] *adj* Greek
Griesgram ['grisgram] *m* (-[e]s;-e)
  (coll) grouch
Grieß [gris] *m* (-es;-e) grit; gravel
Grieß'mehl *n* farina
griff [grif] *pret* of greifen || **Griff** *m*
  (-[e]s;-e) grip; handle; hilt; (mus)
  touch
Grill [gril] *m* (-s;-s) grill; broiler
Grille ['grilə] *f* (-;-n) cricket; (fig)
  whim
grillen ['grilən] *tr* grill; broil
gril'lenhaft *adj* whimsical
Grimasse [gri'masə] *f* (-;-n) grimace
Grimm [grim] *m* (-[e]s;) anger, fury
grimmig ['grimɪç] *adj* furious
Grind [grint] *m* (-[e]s;-e) scab
grinsen ['grinzən] *intr* grin
Grippe ['gripə] *f* (-;-n) grippe
grob [grop] *adj* coarse, rough; crude
Grobian ['grobjan] *m* (-s;-e) boor
gröblich ['grøplɪç] *adj* gross
grölen ['grøːlən] *intr* shout raucously
Groll [grɔl] *m* (-[e]s;) resentment
grollen ['grɔlən] *intr* rumble; (**über**
  acc) be resentful (about); **j—m g.**
  have a grudge against s.o.
Grönland ['grønlant] *n* (-s;) Greenland
Gros [gros] *n* (-ses;-) gross || [gro]
  n (-;-) bulk; (mil) main forces
Groschen ['grɔʃən] *m* (-s;-) (Aust)
  penny (*one hundredth of a shilling*)
groß [gros] *adj* big, large; tall; great
groß'artig *adj* grand; magnificent
Groß'aufnahme *f* (phot) close-up
groß'äugig *adj* wide-eyed
Groß'betrieb *m* big company
Großbritan'nien *n* Great Britain
Größe ['grøːsə] *f* (-;-n) size, greatness;
  celebrity; (astr) magnitude; (math)
  quantity
Groß'eltern *pl* grandparents
Groß'enkel *m* great-grandson
Groß'enkelin *f* great-granddaughter
großenteils ['grosəntaɪls] *adv* largely
Größenwahn ['grøːsənvan] *m* megalomania
Groß'grundbesitz *m* large estate
Groß'handel *m* wholesale trade; **im G.
  kaufen** buy wholesale
Groß'handels- *comb.fm.* wholesale
Groß'händler –**in** §6 *mf* wholesaler
Groß'handlung *f* (-;-en) wholesale
  business
groß'herzig *adj* big-hearted
Grossist [grɔ'sɪst] *m* (-en;-en) wholesaler
groß'jährig *adj* of legal age
Groß'maul *n* bigmouth
Groß'mut *m* magnanimity

groß'mütig *adj* big-hearted
Groß'mutter *f* grandmother
Groß'onkel *m* great-uncle
Groß'schreibung *f* capitalization
Groß'segel *n* main sail
Groß'sprecher *m* braggart
großspurig ['gros/puriç] *adj* pompous
Groß'stadt *f* large city (*with over 100,000 inhabitants*)
Großstädter ['gros/tetər] *m* (-s;-) (coll) city slicker
Groß'tat *f* achievement
Groß'teil *m* major part
größtenteils ['grøstəntaɪls] *adv* mainly
groß'tun §154 *intr* brag; put on the dog
Groß'vater *m* grandfather
Groß'wild *n* big game
groß'ziehen §163 *tr* bring up, raise
großzügig ['grostsygɪç] *adj* broad-minded, liberal; generous; large-scale
grotesk [gro'tesk] *adj* grotesque
Grotte ['grɔtə] *f* (-;-n) grotto
grub [grup] *pret* of graben
Grübchen ['grypçən] *n* (-s;-) dimple
Grube ['grubə] *f* (-;-n) pit; mine
Grübelei [grybə'laɪ] *f* (-;-en) brooding
grübeln ['grybəln] *intr* brood
Gruben– ['grubən] *comb.fm.* mine, miner's
Gruft [gruft] *f* (-;-e) tomb, vault
grün [gryn] *adj* green; Grüne Minna (sl) paddy wagon ‖ Grün *n* (-s;) green
Grün'anlage *f* public park
Grund [grunt] *m* (-[e]s;-e) ground; land; bottom; foundation, basis; cause, ground; auf G. von on the strength of; G. und Boden property; im Grunde genommen after all; in G. und Boden outright
–grund *m* *comb.fm.* bottom of; –ground; grounds for, reasons for
Grund'anstrich *m* first coat
Grund'ausbildung *f* (mil) basic training
Grund'bedeutung *f* primary meaning
Grund'begriff *m* fundamental principle
Grund'besitz *m* real estate
Grund'buch *n* land register
grund'ehr'lich *adj* thoroughly honest
gründen ['gryndən] *tr* found; g. auf (*acc*) base on ‖ *ref* (auf *acc*) be based (on)
Gründer –in ['gryndər(ɪn)] §6 *mf* founder
grund'falsch *adj* absolutely false
Grund'farbe *f* primary color
Grund'fläche *f* area; (geom) base
grundieren [grun'dirən] *tr* prime; size
Grundier'farbe *f* primer coat
Grundier'schicht *f* primer coat
Grund'kapital *n* capital stock
Grund'lage *f* basis, foundation
grund'legend *adj* basic, fundamental
Grund'legung *f* founding, foundation
gründlich ['gryntlɪç] *adj* thorough
Grund'linie *f* (geom) base; Grundlinien basic features, outlines
Gründon'nerstag *m* Holy Thursday
Grund'riß *m* floor plan; outline

Grund'satz *m* principle
grundsätzlich ['gruntzetslɪç] *adj* basic ‖ *adv* as a matter of principle
Grund'schule *f* primary school
Grund'stein *m* cornerstone
Grund'stellung *f* position of attention; die G. einnehmen come to attention
Grund'steuer *f* real-estate tax
Grund'stoff *m* raw material; (chem) element
Grund'strich *m* downstroke
Grund'stück *n* lot, property
Grund'ton *m* (fig) prevailing mood; (mus) keynote; (paint) ground shade
Grün'dung *f* (-;-en) foundation
grund'verschie'den *adj* entirely different
Grund'wasserspiegel *m* water table
Grund'zahl *f* cardinal number
Grund'zug *m* main feature; Grundzüge fundamentals, essentials
Grüne ['grynə] *n*—ins G. into the country
grün'lich *adj* greenish
Grün'schnabel *m* know-it-all
Grünspan ['gryn/pan] *m* (-[e]s;) verdigris
Grün'streifen *m* grass strip; (auf der Autobahn) median strip
grunzen ['gruntsən] *tr & intr* grunt
Gruppe ['grupə] *f* (-;-n) group; (mil) squad
Grup'penführer *m* group leader; (hist) lieutenant general (*of S.S. troops*); (mil) squad leader
gruppieren [gru'pirən] *tr & ref* group
Gruppie'rung *f* (-;-en) grouping
gruselig ['gruzəlɪç] *adj* creepy
gruseln ['gruzəln] *intr*—j–n g. machen give s.o. the creeps ‖ *ref* have a creepy feeling ‖ *impers*—es gruselt mir (or mich) it gives me the creeps
Gruß [grus] *m* (-es;-e) greeting; salute; greetings, regards; mit freundlichem Gruß, Ihr ... Sincerely yours
grüßen ['grysən] *tr* greet; salute; grüß Gott! hello!; j–n g. lassen send best regards to s.o.
Grütze ['grʏtsə] *f* (-;-n) groats; (coll) brains
gucken ['gukən] *intr* look; peep
Guck'loch *n* peephole
Guerilla [ge'rɪlja] *m* (-s;-s) guerilla
Gulasch ['gula/] *n* (-[e]s;) goulash
gültig ['gʏltɪç] *adj* valid; legal
Gummi ['gumi] *m & n* (-s;-s) gum; rubber
gum'miartig *adj* gummy; rubbery
Gum'miband *n* (-[e]s;-er) rubber band; elastic
Gum'mibaum *m* rubber plant
Gum'mibonbon *m & n* gumdrop
gummieren [gu'mirən] *tr* gum; rubberize
Gum'miknüppel *m* truncheon; billy club
Gummilinse *f* (phot) zoom lens
Gum'mimantel *m* mackintosh
Gum'mireifen *m* tire
Gum'mischuhe *pl* rubbers
Gum'mizelle *f* padded cell
Gunst [gunst] *f* (-;) favor, goodwill; kindness, good turn

Gunst′bezeigung *f* expression of good-will

günstig [′gʏnstɪç] *adj* favorable; *(Bedingungen)* easy

Günstling [′gʏnstlɪŋ] *m* (-s;-e) favorite; (pej) minion

Gurgel [′gurgəl] *f* (-;-n) gullet

gurgeln [′gurgəln] *intr* gurgle; gargle

Gurke [′gurkə] *f* (-;-n) cucumber

Gurt [gurt] *m* (-[e]s;-e) belt, strap

Gürtel [′gʏrtəl] *m* (-s;-) girdle; belt; (geog) zone

gürten [′gʏrtən] *tr* gird

Guß [gus] *m* (Gusses; Güsse) gush; *(Regen)* downpour; *(Gießen)* casting; (culin) icing; (typ) font

gut [gut] *adj* good; **es ist schon gut** it's all right; **mach′s gut!** so long! ‖ *adv* well ‖ **Gut** *n* (-[e]s;″er) good; possessions; estate; (com) commodity; **Güter goods**; assets

Gut′achten *n* (-s;-) expert opinion

gut′artig *adj* good-natured; (pathol) benign

gut′aussehend *adj* good-looking

Gut′dünken *n* (-s;) judgment; discretion; **nach G.** at will, as one pleases; (culin) to taste

Gute [′gutə] §5 *n* good; **alles G.**! best of everything!; **sein Gutes haben** have its good points

Güte [′gytə] *f* (-;) goodness

Güter- [gytər] *comb.fm.* freight; property; (com) of goods

Gü′terabfertigung *f* freight office

Gü′terbahnhof *m* (rr) freight yard

gut′erhalten *adj* in good condition

Gü′terwagen *m* freight car; **geschlossener G.** boxcar; **offener G.** gondola car

Gü′terzug *m* freight train

gut′gelaunt *adj* good-humored

gut′gesinnt *adj* well-disposed

gut′haben §89 *tr* have to one's credit ‖ **Guthaben** *n* (-s;-) credit balance

gut′heißen §95 *tr* approve of

gut′herzig *adj* good-hearted

gütig [′gytɪç] *adj* kind, good

gütlich [′gytlɪç] *adj* amicable

gut′machen *tr*—**wieder g.** make good for

gut′mütig *adj* good-natured

gut′sagen *intr*—**für j-n g.** vouch for s.o.

Gut′schein *m* coupon; credit note

gut′schreiben §62 *tr*—**j-m e-n Betrag g.** credit s.o. with a sum

Gut′schrift *f* credit entry; credit item

Gut′schriftsanzeige *f* credit note

Guts′herr *m* landowner

gut′tun §154 *intr* do good; behave

gut′willig *adj* willing, obliging

Gymnasiast **-in** [gʏm′nazjast(ɪn)] §7 *mf* high school student

Gymna·sium [gʏm′nazjum] *n* (-s;-sien [zjən]) high school *(with academic course)*

Gymnastik [gʏm′nastɪk] *f* (-;) gymnastics

Gynäkologe [gʏnɛko′logə] *m* (-n;-n), **Gynäkologin** [gʏnɛko′logɪn] *f* (-; nen) gynecologist

Gynäkologie [gʏnɛkolo′gi] *f* (-;) gynecology

H

H, h [ha] *invar n* H, h; (mus) B

Haar [har] *n* (-[e]s;-e) hair; (tex) nap, pile; **aufs H.** exactly; **um ein H.** by a hair's breadth

Haar′büschel *n* tuft of hair

haaren [′harən] *intr* lose hair

Haarfärbmittel [′harfɛrpmɪtəl] *n* hair dye

Haar′feder *f* hairspring

haar′genau *adj* exact, precise

haarig [′harɪç] *adj* hairy

haar′klein *adj* (coll) in detail

Haar′locke *f* lock of hair

Haar′nadel *f* hairpin

haar′scharf *adj* razor-sharp

Haar′schneider *m* barber

Haar′schnitt *m* haircut

Haar′spange *f* barrette

Haarspray [′harsprɛ] *m* (-s;-s) hair spray

haar′sträubend *adj* hair-raising

Haar′teil *m* hair piece

Haar′tolle *f* loose curl

Haar′tracht *f* hairdo

Haar′trockner *m*, **Haar′trockenhaube** *f* hair dryer

Haar′wäsche *f* shampoo

Haar′wasser *n* hair tonic

Haar′wickler *m* curler; hair roller

Haar′zwange *f* tweezers

Hab [hap] *invar n*—**Hab und Gut** possessions

Habe [′habə] *f* (-;) possessions

haben [′habən] §89 *tr & aux* have ‖ **Haben** *n* (-s;) credit side

Habe′nichts *m* (-es;-e) have-not

Hab′gier *f* greed, avarice

hab′haft *adj*—**h. werden** *(genit)* get hold of; *(Diebes)* apprehend

Habicht [′habɪçt] *m* (-[e]s;-e) hawk

Ha′bichtsnase *f* aquiline nose

Habilitation [habɪlɪta′tsjon] *f* (-;-en) accreditation as a university lecturer

habilitieren [habɪlɪ′tirən] *ref* be accredited as a university lecturer

Hab′seligkeiten *pl* belongings

Hab′sucht *f* greed, avarice

hab′süchtig *adj* greedy, avaricious

Hackbeil [′hakbaɪl] *n* cleaver

Hacke [′hakə] *f* (-;-n) heel; hoe; pick; pickax; hatchet; mattock

hacken [′hakən] *tr* hack, chop; peck ‖ *intr* **(nach)** peck (at)

Häckerling [′hɛkərlɪŋ] *m* (-s;) chaff

Hackfleisch [′hakflaɪʃ] *n* ground meat

Häcksel [′hɛksəl] *n* (-s;) chaff

Hader ['hɑdər] *m* (**–s;**) strife || *m* (**–s; –n**) rag
hadern ['hɑdərn] *intr* quarrel
Hafen ['hɑfən] *m* (**–s;⸚**) harbor; port; (fig) haven
Ha'fenamt *n* port authority
Ha'fenanlagen *pl* docks
Ha'fenarbeiter *m* longshoreman
Ha'fendamm *m* jetty, mole
Ha'fensperre *f* blockade
Ha'fenstadt *f* seaport
Ha'fenviertel *n* dock area, waterfront
Hafer ['hɑfər] *m* (**–s;–**) oats; **ihn sticht der H.** he's feeling his oats
Ha'fergrütze *f*, **Ha'fermehl** *n* oatmeal
Hafner ['hɑfnər] *m* (**–s;–**) potter
Haft [haft] *f* (**–;**) arrest; custody; imprisonment; **in H.** under arrest; in custody; in prison
haftbar ['haftbɑr] *adj* (jur) liable
Haft'befehl *m* warrant for arrest
haften ['haftən] *intr* (**an** *dat*) cling (to), stick (to); **h. für** vouch for; (jur) be held liable for; (jur) put up bail for
Haft'fähigkeit *f*, **Haft'festigkeit** *f* adhesion
Häftling ['hɛftlɪŋ] *m* (**–s;–e**) prisoner
Haft'lokal *n* (mil) guardhouse
Haft'pflicht *f* liability
haft'pflichtig *adj* (**für**) liable (for)
Haft'pflichtversicherung *f* liability insurance
Haft'richter *m* (jur) magistrate
Haft'schale *f* contact lens
Haf'tung *f* (**–;–en**) liability
Hag [hɑk] *m* (**–[e]s;–e**) enclosure; (*Hain*) grove; (*Buschwerk*) bushes
Hagedorn ['hɑgədɔrn] *m* hawthorn
Hagel ['hɑgəl] *m* (**–s;**) hail
Ha'gelkorn *n* hailstone
hageln ['hɑgəln] *intr* (SEIN) (fig) rain down || *impers*—**es hagelt** it is hailing
Ha'gelschauer *m* hailstorm
hager ['hɑgər] *adj* gaunt, haggard
Hagestolz ['hɑgəʃtɔlts] *m* (**–es;–e**) confirmed bachelor
Häher ['he·ər] *m* (**–s;–**) (orn) jay
Hahn [hɑn] *m* (**–[e]s;⸚e**) rooster; (*Wasser–*) faucet; **den H. spannen** cock the gun; **H. im Korbe sein** rule the roost
Hähnchen ['hençən] *n* (**–s;–**) young rooster
Hah'nenkamm *m* cockscomb
Hah'nenkampf *m* cock fight
Hah'nenschrei *m* crow of the cock
Hahnrei ['hɑnraɪ] *m* (**–s;–e**) cuckold
Hai [haɪ] *m* (**–[e]s;–e**), **Hai'fisch** *m* shark
Hain [haɪn] *m* (**–[e]s;–e**) grove
Haiti [ha'iti] *n* (**–s;**) Haiti
Häkelarbeit ['hekəlarbaɪt] *f* crocheting
häkeln ['hekəln] *tr & intr* crochet || **Häkeln** *n* (**–s;**) crocheting
Haken ['hɑkən] *m* (**–s;–**) hook; (*Spange*) clasp; (fig) snag, hitch
Ha'kenkreuz *n* swastika
Ha'kennase *f* hooknose
halb [halp] *adj & adv* half
halb–, Halb– *comb.fm.* half–, semi–
Halb'blut *n* half-breed
–halber [halbər] *comb.fm.* for the sake of; owing to
halb'fett *adj* (typ) bold
Halb'franzband *m* (bb) half leather
halb'gar *adj* (culin) (medium) rare
Halb'gott *m* demigod
Halbheit ['halphaɪt] *f* (**–;**) half-
Halb'kugel *f* hemisphere
halbieren [hal'birən] *tr* halve, bisect
Halb'insel *f* peninsula
Halb'kettenfahrzeug *n* half-track
Halb'kugel *f* hemisphere
halb'lang *adj* half-length; **halblange Ärmel** half sleeves
halb'laut *adj* low || *adv* in a low voice
Halb'leiter *m* (elec) semiconductor
halb'mast *adv* at half-mast; **auf h.** at half-mast
Halb'messer *m* radius
halbpart ['halppart] *adv*—**mit j–m h. machen** go fifty-fifty with s.o.
Halb'schuh *m* low shoe
Halb'schwergewicht *n* light-heavyweight division
Halb'schwergewichtler *m* light-heavyweight
halb'stündig *adj* half-hour
halb'stündlich *adj* half-hourly || *adv* every half hour
Halb'vers *m* hemistich
halbwegs ['halbveks] *adv* halfway
Halb'welt *f* demimonde
halbwüchsig ['halpvyksɪç] *adj* teenage || **Halbwüchsige** §5 *mf* teenager
Halb'zug *m* (mil) section
Halde ['haldə] *f* (**–;–n**) slope; (*Schutt–*) slag pile
half [half] *pret* of **helfen**
Hälfte ['hɛlftə] *f* (**–;–n**) half
Halfter ['halftər] *f* (**–;–n**) holster || *n* (**–s;–**) halter
Hall [hal] *m* (**–[e]s;–e**) sound; clang
Halle ['halə] *f* (**–;–n**) hall; (*e–s Hotels*) lobby; (aer) hangar; (rr) concourse
hallen ['halən] *intr* sound, resound
Hal'lenbad *n* indoor pool
Hallo [ha'lo] *n* (**–s;**) hullabaloo || *interj* (to attract attention) hey!; (telp) hello
Halm [halm] *m* (**–[e]s;–e**) stem, stalk; blade (*of grass*)
Hals [hals] *m* (**–es;⸚e**) neck; throat; **H. über Kopf** head over heels
Hals'abschneider *m* cutthroat
hals'abschneiderisch *adj* cutthroat
Hals'ader *f* jugular vein
Hals'ausschnitt *m* neckline, neck
Hals'band *n* (**–[e]s;⸚er**) necklace, choker; (*e–s Hundes*) collar
halsbrecherisch ['halsbreçərɪʃ] *adj* breakneck
Hals'entzündung *f* sore throat
Hals'kette *f* necklace, chain
Hals'kragen *m* collar
Hals'krause *f* frilled collar
hals'starrig *adj* stubborn
Hals'weh *n* sore throat
halt [halt] *adv* just, simply || *interj* stop!; (mil) halt! || **Halt** *m* (**–[e]s; –e**) hold; foothold; support; stability; stop, halt
haltbar ['haltbɑr] *adj* durable; tenable

halten ['haltən] §90 *tr* hold; keep; detain; (*Rede*) deliver; (*Vorlesung*) give; (*feiern*) celebrate; **es h. mit** do with; have an affair with; **etw auf sich h.** have self-respect; **j-n h. für** take s.o. for; **viel h. von** think highly of ‖ *ref* keep, last; hold ones own; **an sich h.** restrain oneself; **auf sich h.** be particular about one's appearance; **sich an etw h.** (fig) stick to s.th.; **sich an j-n h.** hold s.o. liable; **sich gesund h.** keep healthy; **sich links h.** keep to the left ‖ *intr* stop; last; **h. auf** (*acc*) pay attention to; **h. nach** head for; **h. zu** stick by; **was das Zeug hält** with might and main
Hal'ter *m* (-s;-) holder; rack; owner
Hal'teriemen *m* strap (*on bus or trolley*)
Hal'testelle *f* bus stop, trolley stop; (rr) stop
Hal'teverbot *n* (public sign) no stopping
–haltig [haltıç] *comb.fm.* containing
halt'los *adj* without support; helpless; unprincipled
halt'machen *intr* stop, halt
Hal'tung *f* (-;-en) pose, posture; attitude
Halte'zeichen *n* stop sign
Halunke [ha'luŋkə] *m* (-;-n) rascal
hämisch ['hemıʃ] *adj* spiteful, malicious
Hammel ['haməl] *m* (-s;-e & ⁻) wether; (coll) mutton-head; (culin) mutton
Ham'melkeule *f* leg of mutton
Hammer ['hamər] *m* (-s;⁻) hammer; gavel; **unter den H. kommen** be auctioned off
hämmern ['hemərn] *tr & intr* hammer
Hämorrhoiden [hemərɔ'idən] *pl* hemorroids, piles
Hampelmann ['hampəlman] *m* (-[e]s; ⁻er) jumping jack
hamstern ['hamstərn] *tr* hoard
Hand [hant] *f* (-;⁻e) hand; **an H. von** with the help of; **auf eigene H.** of one's own accord; **aus erster H.** (*bei Verkauf*) one-owner; **aus erster H. haben** hear first-hand; **aus erster H. kaufen** buy directly; **bei der H.** at hand, handy; **die letzte H.** finishing touches; **die öffentliche H.** the state, public authorities; **es liegt auf der H.** it is obvious; **H. ans Werk legen** get down to work; **H. aufs Herz!** cross my heart!; **Hände hoch!** hands up!; **H. und Fuß haben** make sense; **in die H.** (or **Hände**) **bekommen** get one's hands on; **j-m an die H. gehen** lend s.o. a hand; **j-m die H. drücken** shake hands with s.o.; **j-m etw an** (**die**) **H. geben** quote s.o. a price on s.th.; **j-m zur H. gehen** lend s.o. a hand; **unter der H.** underhandedly; unofficially; **von der H. weisen** reject; **zu Händen Herrn X** Attention Mr. X; **zur H.** at hand, handy
Hand'arbeit *f* manual labor; needlework
Hand'aufheben *n*, **Hand'aufhebung** *f* show of hands

Hand'ausgabe *f* abridged edition
Hand'bedienung *f* manual control
Hand'betrieb *m*—**mit** (or **für**) **H.** hand-operated
Hand'bibliothek *f* reference library
hand'breit *adj* wide as a hand ‖ **Hand'-breit** *f* (-;-) hand's breadth
Hand'bremse *f* (aut) hand brake
Hand'buch *n* handbook, manual
Händedruck ['hendədrʊk] *m* handshake
Händeklatschen ['hendəklatʃən] *n* clapping
Handel ['handəl] *m* (-s;⁻⁻) trade; deal, bargain; business; affair; **e-n H. eingehen** conclude a deal; **e-n H. treiben** carry on business; **H. und Gewerbe** trade and industry; **Händel suchen** pick a quarrel; **im H. sein** be on the market; **in den H. bringen** put on the market
–handel *m comb.fm.* –trade, –business
handeln ['handəln] *intr* act; take action; proceed; **gegen das Gesetz h.** go against the law; **gut an j-m h.** treat s.o. well; **h. über** (*acc*) or **von** deal with; **h. mit** do business with; **im großen h.** do wholesale business ‖ *impers ref*—**es handelt sich um** it is a matter of; **darum handelt es sich nicht** that's not the point
Han'delsabkommen *n* trade agreement
Han'delsartikel *m* commodity
Han'delsbetrieb *m* commercial enterprise; business; firm
Han'delsbilanz *f* balance of trade; **aktive H.** favorable balance of trade
Han'delsdampfer *m* (naut) merchantman
han'delseinig *adj*—**h. werden mit** come to terms with
Han'delsgärtner *m* truck farmer
Han'delskammer *f* chamber of commerce
Han'delsmarine *f* merchant marine
Han'delsmarke *f* trademark
Han'delsminister *m* secretary of commerce
Han'delsministerium *n* department of commerce
Han'delsplatz *m* trade center
Han'delsschiff *n* merchantman
Han'delssperre *f* trade embargo
händelsüchtig ['hendəlzʏçtıç] *adj* quarrelsome
Han'delsvertrag *m* commercial treaty
Han'delswert *m* trade-in value
Han'delszeichen *n* trademark
Hand'exemplar *n* desk copy
Hand'fertigkeit *f* manual dexterity
Hand'fessel *f* handcuff
hand'fest *adj* sturdy; well-founded
Hand'fläche *f* palm of the hand
Hand'geld *n* advance payment; deposit
Hand'gelenk *n* wrist; **aus** (or **mit**) **dem H.** (coll) easy as pie
hand'gemein *adj*—**h. werden** come to blows
Hand'gemenge *n* scuffle
Hand'gepäck *n* hand luggage
Hand'gepäckschließfach *n* locker
Hand'granate *f* hand grenade
hand'greiflich *adj* tangible; obvious;

j-m etw h. machen make s.th. clear to s.o.; h. werden come to blows

Hand'griff m grip; handle; keinen H. tun not lift a finger

Hand'habe f (-;-n) handle; pretext; occasion; er hat keine H. gegen mich he has nothing on me

hand'haben tr handle; (Maschine) operate; (Rechtspflege) administer; (fig) manage

-händig [hendɪç] comb.fm. -handed

Hand'karren m hand cart, push cart

Hand'koffer m suitcase; attaché case

Handlanger ['hantlaŋər] m (-s;-) handyman; (pej) underling

Händler -in ['hendlər(ɪn)] §6 mf dealer, merchant; storekeeper

Hand'lesekunst f palmistry

Hand'leserin f (-;-nen) palm reader

hand'lich adj handy

Hand'lung f (-;-en) shop; act, action

-handlung f comb.fm. business; shop

Hand'lungsgehilfe m clerk, salesman

Hand'lungsweise f conduct

Hand'pflege f manicure

Hand'pflegerin f (-;-nen) manicurist

Hand'rücken m back of the hand

Hand'schaltung f manual shift

Hand'schelle f handcuff

Hand'schlag m handshake

Hand'schreiben n hand-written letter

Hand'schrift f handwriting; manuscript; (sl) slap, box on the ear

Hand'schriftenkunde f paleography

hand'schriftlich adj hand-written

Hand'schuh m glove

Hand'schuhfach n (aut) glove compartment

Hand'streich m (mil) raid

Hand'tasche f handbag, purse

Hand'tuch n towel; schmales H. (sl) beanpole

Hand'tuchhalter m towel rack

Hand'umdrehen n—im. H. in a jiffy

Hand'voll f (-;-) handful

Hand'werk n craft, trade; j-m ins H. pfuschen (sl) stick one's nose in s.o. else's business

Hand'werker m craftsman

Hand'werkzeug n tool kit

Hand'wörterbuch n pocket dictionary

Hand'wurzel f wrist

Hand'zettel m handbill

hanebüchen ['hanəbyçən] adj (coll) incredible; (coll) monstrous

Hanf [hanf] m (-[e]s;) hemp

Hang [haŋ] m (-[e]s;ꞏꞏe) slope; hillside; (fig) inclination, tendency

Hangar ['haŋgar] m (-s;-s) hangar

Hängebacken ['heŋəbakən] pl jowls

Hängebauch ['heŋəbaux] m potbelly

Hängebrücke ['heŋəbrykə] f suspension bridge

Hängematte ['heŋəmatə] f hammock

hängen ['heŋən] tr hang || ref—sich an j-n h. hang on to s.o.; sich ans Telephon h. be on the telephone || §92 intr hang; cling, stick

hän'genbleiben §62 intr (SEIN) stick; be detained, get stuck; (an dat) get caught (on); (educ) stay behind

Hans [hans] m (-' & -ens;) Johnny, Jack

Hans'dampf m (-[e]s;ꞏꞏe) busybody; H. in allen Gassen jack-of-all trades

Hänselei [henzə'laɪ] f (-;-en) teasing

hänseln ['henzəln] tr tease

Hans'narr m fool

Hans'wurst m (-es;-e & ꞏꞏe) clown

Hantel ['hantəl] f (-;-n) dumbell

hantieren [han'tirən] intr (an acc) be busy (with); mit etw h. handle s.th.

hapern ['hapərn] impers—bei mir hapert es an (dat) (or mit) I am short of; bei mir hapert es in (dat) (or mit) I am weak in; damit hapert's that's the hitch

Happen ['hapən] m (-s;-) morsel; mouthful; (fig) good opportunity; fetter H. (coll) big hawl

happig ['hapɪç] adj greedy; (Preis) steep

Härchen ['herçən] n (-s;-) tiny hair

Harem ['harɛm] m (-s;-s) harem

Häresie [here'zi] f (-;-sien ['ziꞏən]) heresy

Häretiker [he'retɪkər] m (-s;-) heretic

Harfe ['harfə] f (-;-n) harp

Harke ['harkə] f (-;-n) rake

harken ['harkən] tr & intr rake

Harm [harm] m (-[e]s;) harm; grief

härmen ['hermən] ref (um) grieve (over)

harm'los adj harmless

Harmonie [harmo'ni] f (-;-nien ['niꞏən]) harmony

harmonieren [harmo'nirən] intr harmonize

Harmonika [har'monɪka] f (-;-kas & -ken [kən]) accordion; harmonica

harmonisch [har'monɪʃ] adj harmonious

Harn [harn] m (-[e]s;-e) urine; H. lassen pass water

Harn'blase f (anat) bladder

harnen ['harnən] intr urinate

Harn'glas n urinal

Harn'grieß m (pathol) gravel

Harnisch ['harnɪʃ] m (-es;-e) armor; in H. geraten über (acc) fly into a rage over; j-n in H. bringen get s.o. hopping mad

Harn'leiter m (anat) ureter; (surg) catheter

Harn'röhre f urethra

harn'treibend adj diuretic

Harpune [har'punə] f (-;-n) harpoon

harpunieren [harpu'nirən] tr harpoon

harren ['harən] intr tarry; hope; (genit or auf acc) wait (for)

harsch [harʃ] adj harsh || Harsch m (-es;), Harsch'schnee m crushed snow

hart [hart] adj hard; severe || adv—h. an (dat) close to, hard by

Härte ['hertə] f (-;) hardness; severity

härten ['hertən] tr, ref & intr harden

Hart'faserplatte f fiber board

Hart'geld n coins

hartgesotten ['hartgəzotən] adj hard-boiled; (Verbrecher) hardened

hart'herzig adj hard-hearted

hart'köpfig adj thick-headed

hart'leibig adj constipated

Hart'leibigkeit f (-;) constipation

hart'löten tr braze

hartnäckig ['hartnɛkɪç] *adj* stubborn
Hart'platz *m* (tennis) hard court
Harz [harts] *n* (-es;-e) resin; rosin
harzig [hartsɪç] *adj* resinous
Hasardspiel [ha'zart/piːl] *n* gambling game; gamble
haschen ['haʃən] *tr* snatch, grab || *intr* (**nach**) try to catch, snatch (at)
Hase ['hazə] *m* (-n;-n) hare; **alter H.** old-timer, veteran
Ha'selnuß ['hazəlnʊs] *f* hazelnut
Hasenfuß *m* (coll) coward
Ha'senherz *n* (coll) yellow belly
Ha'senmaus *f* chinchilla
Hasenpanier ['hazənpanir] *n*—**das H. ergreifen** take to ones heels
ha'senrein *adj*—**nicht ganz h.** (fig) a bit fishy, rather shady
Ha'senscharte *f* harelip
Haspe ['haspə] *f* (-;-n) hasp
Haspel ['haspəl] *f* (-;-n) & *m* (-s;-) reel, spool; winch, windlass
haspeln ['haspəln] *tr* reel, spool
Haß *m* (**Hasses**;) hatred
hassen ['hasən] *tr* hate
has'senswert, has'senswürdig *adj* hateful
häßlich ['hɛslɪç] *adj* ugly; nasty
Hast [hast] *f* (-;) haste
hasten ['hastən] *intr* be in a hurry, act quickly || *intr* (SEIN) hasten, rush
hastig ['hastɪç] *adj* hasty
hätscheln ['hɛtʃəln] *tr* caress, cuddle; (*verzärteln*) coddle, spoil
hatte ['hatə] *pret* of **haben**
Haube ['haʊbə] *f* (-;-n) cap; (aer) cowling; (aut) hood; (orn) crest
Haubitze [haʊ'bɪtsə] *f* (-;-n) howitzer
Hauch [haʊx] *m* (-[e]s;-e) breath; breeze; (*Schicht*) thin layer; (*Spur*) trace
hauch'dünn *adj* paper-thin
hauchen ['haʊxən] *tr* whisper; (ling) aspirate || *intr* breathe
Hauch'laut *m* (ling) aspirate
Haue ['haʊ·ə] *f* (-;-n) hoe; adze; **H. kriegen** get a spanking
hauen ['haʊ·ən] §93 *tr* hack, cut; strike; (*Baum*) fell; (*Stein*) hew || §109 *tr* beat (up) || *intr*—**h. nach** lash out at; **um sich h.** flail
Hauer ['haʊ·ər] *m* (-s;-) tusk
häufeln ['hɔɪfəln] *tr* hill
häufen ['hɔɪfən] *tr* & *ref* pile up
Haufen ['haʊfən] *m* (-s;-) pile, heap
Hau'fenwolke *f* cumulus cloud
häufig ['hɔɪfɪç] *adj* frequent || *adv* frequently
Häu'figkeit *f* (-;) frequency
Häu'fung *f* (-;-en) accumulation
Haupt [haʊpt] *n* (-[e]s;-er) head; top; chief, leader **aufs H. schlagen** vanquish
Haupt- *comb.fm.* head; chief; major; most important; prime; primary, leading
Haupt'altar *m* high altar
haupt'amtlich *adj* full-time
Haupt'bahnhof *m* main train station
Haupt'darsteller *m* leading man
Haupt'darstellerin *f* leading lady
Häuptel ['hɔɪptəl] *n* (-s;-) head
Haupt'fach *n* (educ) major

Haupt'farbe *f* primary color
Haupt'feldwebel *m* first sergeant
Haupt'film *m* (cin) feature
Haupt'gefreite §5 *m* private first class; lance corporal (Brit); seaman; airman second class
Haupt'geschäftsstelle *f* head office
Haupt'gewinn *m* first price
Haupt'haar *n* hair (*on the head*)
Häuptling ['hɔɪptlɪŋ] *m* (-s;-e) chief
häuptlings ['hɔɪptlɪŋs] *adv* head first
Haupt'linie *f* (rr) trunk line
Haupt'mann *m* (-[e]s;-leute) captain
Haupt'masse *f* bulk
Haupt'mast *m* mainmast
Hauptnenner ['haʊptnenər] *m* (-s;-) (math) common denominator
Haupt'probe *f* dress rehearsal
Haupt'quartier *n* headquarters; **Gro-ßes H.** general headquarters
Haupt'rolle *f* leading role, lead
Haupt'sache *f* main thing; (jur) point at issue
haupt'sächlich *adj* main, principal
Haupt'satz *m* (gram) main clause; (phys) principle, law
Haupt'schalter *m* master switch
Haupt'schiff *n* (archit) nave
Haupt'schlagader *f* aorta
Haupt'schlüssel *m* master key, pass key
Haupt'schriftleiter *m* editor in chief
Haupt'spaß *m* great fun; great joke
Haupt'stadt *f* capital
Haupt'straße *f* main street; highway
Haupt'strecke *f* (rr) main line
Haupt'stütze *f* mainstay
Haupt'ton *m* primary accent
Haupt'treffer *m* first prize; jackpot
Haupt'verkehr *m* peak-hour traffic
Haupt'verkehrsstraße *f* main artery
Haupt'verkehrszeit *f* rush hour
Haupt'wort *n* (-[e]s;-er) noun
Haus [haʊs] *n* (-es;-er) house; **ein großes H. führen** do a lot of entertaining; **H. und Hof** house and home; **öffentliches H.** brothel; **nach Hause** home; **sich zu Hause fühlen** feel at home; **von zu Hause** from home
Haus'angestellte §5 *mf* domestic
Haus'apotheke *f* medicine cabinet
Haus'arbeit *f* housework; (educ) homework
Haus'arzt *m* family doctor
Haus'aufgabe *f* homework
haus'backen *adj* homemade; (*Frau*) plain; (fig) provincial
Haus'bedarf *m* household needs; **für den H.** for the home
Haus'brand *m* domestic fuel
Haus'bursche *m* porter
Haus'diener *m* porter
hausen ['haʊzən] *intr* reside; (coll) make a mess; **schlimm h.** wreak havoc
Häuserblock ['hɔɪzərblɔk] *m* block of houses
Häusermakler –in ['hɔɪzərmaklər(ɪn)] §6 *mf* realtor
Haus'flur *m* entrance hall; hallway
Haus'frau *f* housewife; landlady
Haus'freund *m* friend of the family; (coll) wife's lover

Haus'gebrauch *m* family custom; household use
Haus'gehilfin *f* domestic
Haus'genosse *m*, Haus'genossin *f* occupant of the same house
Haus'gesinde *n* domestics
Haus'glocke *f* doorbell
Haus'halt *m* household; budget; den H. führen keep house
haus'halten §90 *intr* keep house; economize
Haushälter –in ['haushɛltər(ɪn)] §6 *mf* housekeeper
haushälterisch ['haushɛltərɪʃ] *adj* economical
Haus'haltsausschuß *m* ways and means committee
Haus'haltsgerät *n* household utensil
Haus'haltsjahr *n* fiscal year
Haus'haltsplan *m* budget
Haus'haltung *f* housekeeping; household; family budget; management
Haus'haltungslehre *f* home economics
Haus'herr *m* master of the house; landlord
Haus'herrin *f* lady of the house; landlady
haus'hoch' *adj* very high; vast
Haus'hofmeister *m* steward
hausieren [hau'zirən] *intr*—mit etw h. peddle s.th.; go around telling everyone about s.th.
Hausierer [hau'zirər] *m* (-s;-) door-to-door salesman
Haus'lehrer –in §6 *mf* private tutor
häuslich ['hɔɪslɪç] *adj* home, domestic; homey; thrifty
Häus'lichkeit *f* (-;) family life; home
Haus'mädchen *n* maid
Haus'meister *m* caretaker, janitor
Haus'mittel *n* home remedy
Haus'mutter *f* mother of the family
Haus'pflege *f* home nursing
Haus'schlüssel *m* front-door key
Haus'schuh *m* slipper
Hausse ['hose] *f* (-;-n) (econ, st. exch.) boom
Haus'sespekulant *m* (st. exch.) bull
Haussier [hos'je] *m* (-s;-) (st. exch.) bull
haussieren [ho'sirən] *tr* (fin) raise ‖ *intr* (fin) go up, rise
Haus'stand *m* household
Haus'suchungsbefehl *m* search warrant
Haus'tier *n* domestic animal; pet
Haus'vater *m* father of the family
Haus'verwalter *m* superintendent
Haus'wesen *n* household
Haus'wirt *m* landlord
Haus'wirtin *f* landlady
Haus'wirtschaft *f* housekeeping
haus'wirtschaftlich *adj* domestic; household
Haus'wirtschaftslehre *f* home economics
Haus'zins *m* house rent
Haut [haut] *f* (-;̈e) skin; hide; aus der H. fahren fly off the handle
Haut'abschürfung *f* skin abrasion
Haut'arzt *m* dermatologist
Haut'ausschlag *m* rash
Häutchen ['hɔɪtçən] (-s;-) membrane; pellicle; film

häuten ['hɔɪtən] *tr* skin ‖ *ref* slough the skin
haut'eng *adj* skin-tight
Haut'farbe *f* complexion
Haut'plastik *f* skin graft
Haut'reizung *f* skin irritation
Haut'transplantation *f*, Haut'verpflanzung *f* skin grafting
havariert [hava'rirt] *adj* damaged
H'-Bombe *f* H-bomb
Hebamme ['hepamə] *f* (-s;-n) midwife
Hebebaum ['hebəbaum] *m* lever
Hebebühne ['hebəbynə] *f* car lift
Hebeisen ['hebə-aɪzən] *n* crowbar
Hebel ['hebəl] *m* (-s;-) lever
heben ['hebən] §94 *tr* lift, raise; (steigern) increase; (fördern) further; (aut) jack up ‖ *ref* rise
Heber ['hebər] *m* (-s;-) siphon; (aut) jack
Hebeschiff ['hebə/ʃf] *n* salvage ship
Hebräer –in [he'bre-ər(ɪn)] §6 *mf* Hebrew
hebräisch [he'bre-ɪʃ] *adj* Hebrew
He'bung *f* (-;-en) lifting; increase; improvement; (mus, pros) stress
Hecht [hɛçt] *m* (-[e]s;-e) (ichth) pike
hechten ['hɛçtən] *intr* dive
Hecht'sprung *m* flying leap; jacknife dive
Heck [hɛk] *n* (-[e]s;-e & -s) stern; (aer) tail; (aut) rear
Heck'antrieb *m* (aut) rear drive
Hecke ['hɛkə] *f* (-;-n) hedge; brood, hatch
hecken ['hɛkən] *tr* & *intr* breed
Heckenhüpfen (Hek'kenhüpfen) *n* (-s;) (aer) hedgehopping
Heckenschütze (Hek'kenschütze) *m* sniper
Heck'fenster *n* (aut) rear window
Heck'licht *n* (aer, aut) tail light
Heck'motor *m* rear engine
Heck'pfennig *m* lucky penny
Heck'schütze *m* (aer) tail gunner
heda ['heda] *interj* hey there!
Heer [her] *n* (-[e]s;-e) army; host
Heeres– [herəs] *comb.fm.* army
Hee'resbericht *m* official army communiqué
Hee'resdienst *m* military service
Hee'resdienstvorschriften *pl* army regulations
Hee'resgeistliche §5 *m* army chaplain
Hee'resmacht *f* armed forces; army
Hee'reszug *m* (mil) campaign
Heer'lager *n* army camp; (pol) faction
Heer'schar *f* host, legion
Heer'zug *m* (mil) campaign
Hefe ['hefə] *f* (-;-n) yeast; dregs
He'feteig *m* leavened dough
Heft [hɛft] *n* (-[e]s;-e) haft, handle; notebook; (e-r Zeitschrift) issue
heften ['hɛftən] *tr* fasten together; sew, stitch; tack, baste; (Blick) fix ‖ *ref* (an *acc*) stick close (to)
heftig ['hɛftɪç] *adj* violent; (Regen) heavy; (Fieber) high; h. werden lose one's temper
Heft'klammer *f* paper clip; staple
Heft'maschine *f* stapler
Heft'stich *m* (sew) tack
Heft'zwecke *f* thumbtack

hegen ['he:gən] *tr* (*Wild*) preserve; (*Zweifel, Gedanken*) have; **h. und pflegen** lavish care on

Hehl [he:l] *n* (-[e]s;) secret

hehlen ['he:lən] *intr* receive stolen goods

Heh'ler **-in** §6 *mf* fence

hehr [he:r] *adj* sublime, noble

Heide ['haɪdə] *m* (-n;-n) heathen; (*Bib*) gentile || *f* (-;-n) heath

Hei'dekraut *n* heather

Heidelbeere ['haɪdəlbe:rə] *f* blueberry

Hei'denangst *f* (coll) jitters

Hei'dengeld *n* (coll) piles of money

Hei'denlärm *m* hullabaloo

hei'denmäßig *adv*—**h. viel** tremendous amount of

Hei'denspaß *m* (coll) great fun

Heidentum ['haɪdəntum] *n* (-s;) heathendom

heidi [haɪ'di] *adj* gone; lost; **h. gehen** get lost; **be all gone** || *interj* quick!

Heidin ['haɪdɪn] *f* (-;-nen) heathen

heidnisch ['haɪdnɪʃ] *adj* heathen

heikel ['haɪkəl] *adj* particular, fastidious; (*Sache*) ticklish

heil [haɪl] *adj* safe, sound; undamaged || **Heil** *n* (-[e]s;) welfare, benefit; salvation || **Heil** *interj* hail!

Heiland ['haɪlant] *m* (-[e]s;) Saviour

Heil'anstalt *f* sanitarium

Heil'bad *n* spa

heilbar ['haɪlbar] *adj* curable

heil'bringend *adj* beneficial, healthful

Heilbutt ['haɪlbut] *m* (-[e]s;-e) (ichth) halibut

heilen ['haɪlən] *tr* heal || *intr* (HABEN & SEIN) heal

Heil'gehilfe *m* male nurse

Heil'gymnastik *f* physical therapy

heilig ['haɪlɪç] *adj* holy, sacred || **Heilige** §5 *mf* saint

Hei'ligabend *m* Christmas Eve

heiligen ['haɪlɪgən] *tr* hallow

Hei'ligenschein *m* halo

Hei'ligkeit *f* (-;) holiness, sanctity

hei'ligsprechen §64 *tr* canonize

Heiligtum ['haɪlɪçtum] *n* (-[e]s;⸚er) sanctuary; shrine; sacred relic

Hei'ligung *f* (-;) sanctification

Heil'kraft *f* healing power

Heil'kraut *n* medicinal herb

Heil'kunde *f* medical science

heil'los *adj* wicked; (coll) awful

Heil'mittel *n* remedy; medicine

Heil'mittellehre *f* pharmacology

heilsam ['haɪlzam] *adj* healthful

Heils'armee *f* Salvation Army

Heil'stätte *f* sanitarium

Hei'lung *f* (-;-en) cure

heim [haɪm] *adv* home || **Heim** *n* (-[e]s;-e) home; (*Alters-*) old-age home

Heimat ['haɪmat] *f* (-;-en) home; hometown; homeland

hei'matlich *adj* native

hei'matlos *adj* homeless

Hei'matort *m* hometown, home village

Hei'matstadt *f* hometown, native city

heim'begeben §80 *ref* head home

Heimchen ['haɪmçən] *n* (-s;-) cricket

Heim'computer *m* home computer

Heim'fahrt *f* homeward journey

heim'finden §59 *intr* find one's way home

Heim'gang *m* going home; passing on

heimisch ['haɪmɪʃ] *adj* local; locally-produced; domestic; **heimische Sprache** vernacular; **h. werden** settle down; become established; **sich h. fühlen** feel at home

Heimkehr ['haɪmke:r] *f* (-;) homecoming

heim'kehren *intr* (SEIN) return home

Heim'kunft *f* homecoming

heim'leuchten *intr* (sl) (*dat*) tell (*s.o.*) where to get off

heim'lich *adj* secret

Heim'lichkeit *f* (-;-en) secrecy; (*Geheimnis*) secret

Heim'reise *f* homeward journey

heim'suchen *tr* afflict, plague

Heim'tücke *f* treachery

heim'tückisch *adj* treacherous

heimwärts ['haɪmverts] *adv* homeward

Heim'weh *n* homesickness; nostalgia

heim'zahlen *tr*—**j—m etw h.** (coll) pay s.o. back for s.th.

Heini ['haɪni] *m* (-s;) Harry; guy

Heinzelmännchen ['haɪntsəlmençən] *pl* (myth) little people

Heirat ['haɪrat] *f* (-;-en) marriage

heiraten ['haɪratən] *tr & intr* marry

Hei'ratsantrag *m* marriage proposal

hei'ratsfähig *adj* marriageable

Hei'ratsgut *n* dowry

Hei'ratskandidat *m* eligible bachelor

Hei'ratsurkunde *f* marriage certificate

Hei'ratsvermittler **-in** §6 *mf* marriage broker

heischen ['haɪʃən] *tr* demand; beg

heiser ['haɪzər] *adj* hoarse

heiß [haɪs] *adj* hot; (fig) ardent

heißen ['haɪsən] §95 *tr* call; ask, bid; mean || *intr* be called; **das heißt** that is, i.e.; **wie h. Sie?** what is your name?

heiß'geliebt *adj* beloved

heiter ['haɪtər] *adj* cheerful; hilarious; serene; (*Wetter*) clear

Heiz- [haɪts] *comb.fm.* heating

Heiz'anlage *f* heating system

Heiz'apparat *m* heater

heizen ['haɪtsən] *tr* heat; **den Ofen mit Kohle h.** burn coal in the stove || *intr* give off heat; heat; turn on the heating; light the fire (or stove)

Hei'zer *m* (-s;) boilerman; (naut) stoker; (rr) fireman

Heiz'faden *m* (elec) filament

Heiz'kissen *n* heating pad

Heiz'körper *m* radiator; heater

Heiz'material *n* fuel

Heiz'platte *f* hot plate

Heiz'raum *m* boiler room

Heiz'schlange *f* heating coil

Hei'zung *f* (-;) heating; (coll) central heating; radiator

Hei'zungskessel *m* boiler

Hei'zungsrohr *n* radiator pipe

Held [hɛlt] *m* (-en;-en) hero

Hel'denalter *n* heroic age

Hel'dengedicht *n* epic

Hel'dengeist *m* heroism

hel'denhaft *adj* heroic

Hel'denmut *m* heroism

hel′denmütig *adj* heroic
Hel′dentat *f* heroic deed, exploit
Heldentum [′hɛldəntum] *n* (-[e]s;) heroism
Heldin [′hɛldɪn] *f* (-;-nen) heroine
helfen [′hɛlfən] *intr* (*dat*) help; **es hilft nichts** it's of no use
Hel′fer –in §6 *mf* helper
Hel′fershelfer *m* accomplice
Helikopter [hɛlɪ′kɔptər] *m* (-s;-) helicopter
hell [hɛl] *adj* clear; bright; lucid; (*Haar*) fair; (*Bier*) light; (*Wahnsinn, usw.*) sheer || **Helle** §5 *f* brightness; lightness; clarity || *n* light; **ein Helles** a glass of light beer
hellenisch [hɛ′lenɪʃ] *adj* Hellenic
Heller [′hɛlər] *m* (-s;-) penny
hellhörig [′hɛlhørɪç] *adj* having sharp ears; **h. werden** prick up one's ears
hellicht [′hɛlɪçt] *adj*—**hellichter Tag** broad daylight
Hel′ligkeit *f* (-;-en) brightness; (astr) magnitude
hell′sehen §138 *intr* be clairvoyant || **Hellsehen** *n* (-s;) clairvoyance
Hell′seher –in §6 *mf* clairvoyant; (coll) mind reader
hell′sichtig *adj* clear-sighted
hell′wach *adj* wide awake
Helm [hɛlm] *m* (-[e]s;-e) helmet; (archit) dome, spire; (naut) helm
Helm′busch *m* crest, plume
Hemd [hɛmt] *n* (-[e]s;-en) shirt
Hemd′brust *f* dickey, shirt front
Hemd′hose *f* union suit
hemmen [′hɛmən] *tr* slow up; stop; **gehemmt** inhibited
Hemmnis [′hɛmnɪs] *n* (-ses;-se) hindrance
Hemmschuh [′hɛmʃu] *m* (fig) hindrance; (rr) brake
Hem′mung *f* (-;-en) inhibition
hem′mungslos *adj* uninhibited
Hengst [hɛŋst] *m* (-es;-e) stallion
Henkel [′hɛŋkəl] *m* (-s;-) handle
henken [′hɛŋkən] *tr* hang (*s.o.*)
Henker [′hɛŋkər] *m* (-s;-) hangman
Henne [′hɛnə] *f* (-;-n) hen
her [her] *adv* hither, here; ago
herab [hɛ′rap] *adv* down, downwards
herab– *comb.fm.* down; down here
herab′drücken *tr* press down; force down; **die Kurse h.** bear the market
herab′lassen §104 *ref* condescend
Herab′lassung *f* (-;) condescension
herab′sehen §138 *intr* (**auf** *acc*) look down (on)
herab′setzen *tr* put down; reduce; belittle, disparage
herab′steigen §148 *intr* (SEIN) climb down; (*vom Pferd*) dismount
herab′würdigen *tr* demean
Heraldik [hɛ′raldɪk] *f* (-;) heraldry
heran [hɛ′ran] *adv* near; up
heran′arbeiten *ref* (**an** *acc*) work one's way (towards)
heran′bilden *tr* (**zu**) train (as)
heran′brechen §64 *intr* (SEIN) (*Tag*) dawn, break; (*Nacht*) fall, come on
heran′gehen §82 *intr* (SEIN) go close; **h. an** (*acc*) approach, go up to
heran′kommen §99 *intr* (SEIN) come

near; **h. an** (*acc*) approach; get at; **h. bis an** (*acc*) reach as far as
heran′machen *ref*—**h. an** (*acc*) apply oneself to; approach
heran′nahen *intr* (SEIN) approach
heran′wachsen §155 *intr* (SEIN) (**zu**) grow up (to be)
heran′wagen *ref* (**an** *acc*) dare to approach
heran′ziehen §163 *tr* pull closer; call on for help; (*Quellen*) consult; (*zur Beratung*) call in; (*Pflanzen*) grow; (*Nachwuchs*) train || *intr* (SEIN) approach
herauf [hɛ′rauf] *adv* up, up here; upstairs
herauf′arbeiten *ref* work one's way up
herauf′bemühen *ref* take the trouble to come up (or upstairs)
herauf′beschwören §137 *tr* conjure up; (*verursachen*) bring on, provoke
herauf′kommen §99 *intr* (SEIN) come up
herauf′setzen *tr* raise, increase
herauf′steigen §148 *intr* (SEIN) climb up; (*Tag*) dawn
herauf′ziehen §163 *tr* pull up || *intr* (SEIN) move upstairs; (*Sturm*) come up
heraus [hɛ′raus] *adv* out, out here
heraus′bekommen §99 *tr* (**aus**) get out (of); (*Wort*) utter; (*Geld*) get back in change; (*Problem*) figure out
heraus′bringen §65 *tr* bring out; (*Wort*) utter; (*Lösung*) work out; (*Buch*) publish; (*Fabrikat*) bring out
heraus′drücken *tr* squeeze out; (*die Brust*) throw out
heraus′fahren §71 *intr* (SEIN) drive out; (*aus dem Bett*) jump out; (*Bemerkung*) slip out
heraus′finden §59 *tr* find out || *ref* (**aus**) find one's way out (of)
heraus′fordern *tr* challenge, call on
heraus′fordernd *adj* defiant || *adv* defiantly; **sich h. anziehen** dress provocatively
Heraus′forderung *f* (-;-en) challenge
heraus′fühlen *tr* sense
Heraus′gabe *f* surrender; (*e–s Buches*) publication; (jur) restitution
heraus′geben §80 *tr* surrender; give back; (*Buch*) publish || *intr* (*dat*) give (*s.o.*) his change; **h. auf** (*acc*) give change for
Heraus′geber *m* publisher; (*Redakteur*) editor
heraus′greifen §88 *tr* single out
heraus′haben §89 *tr* (*s.th.*) figured out; **er hat den Bogen heraus** (coll) he has the knack of it
heraus′halten §90 *tr* hold out || *ref* (**aus**) keep out (of)
heraus′hängen §92 *tr* & *intr* hang out
heraus′kommen §99 *intr* (SEIN) come out
heraus′lesen §107 *tr* pick out; deduce; **zu viel aus e–m Gedicht h.** read too much into a poem
heraus′machen *tr* (*Fleck*) get out; (*Kinder*) turn out well; (*Geschäft*) make out well
heraus′nehmen §116 *tr* take out || *ref*

—sich [dat] zu viel (or **Freiheiten**) h. take liberties

heraus′platzen intr (SEIN)—**mit etw h.** blurt out s.th.

heraus′putzen ref dress up

heraus′reden ref (**aus**) talk one's way out (of)

heraus′rücken tr move out (here); (coll) (Geld) shell out || intr (SEIN) —**mit dem Geld h.** shell out money; **mit der Sprache h.** reveal it, admit it

heraus′schälen ref become apparent

heraus′stehen §146 intr protrude

heraus′steigen §148 intr (SEIN) (**aus**) climb out (of), step out (of)

heraus′stellen tr put out; **groß h.** give a big build-up-to; **klar h.** present clearly || ref emerge, come to light; **sich h. als** prove to be

heraus′streichen §85 tr delete; (fig) praise

heraus′suchen tr pick out

heraus′treten §152 intr (SEIN) come out, step out; bulge, protrude

heraus′winden §59 ref extricate oneself

heraus′wirtschaften tr manage to save; (Profit) manage to make

heraus′ziehen §163 tr pull out

herb [herp] adj harsh; (sauer) sour; (zusammenziehend) tangy; (Wein) dry; (Worte) bitter; (Schönheit) austere || **Herbe** f (-;) harshness; tang; bitterness; austerity

herbei′ adv here (toward the speaker)

herbei- comb.fm. up, along, here (toward the speaker)

herbei′bringen §65 tr bring along

herbei′eilen intr (SEIN) hurry here

herbei′führen tr bring here; cause

herbei′kommen §99 intr (SEIN) come up

herbei′lassen §104 ref condescend

herbei′rufen §122 tr call over; summon

herbei′schaffen tr bring here; procure; (Geld) raise

herbei′sehnen tr long for

herbei′strömen intr (SEIN) come flocking, flock

herbei′winken tr beckon (s.o.) to come over

herbei′wünschen tr long for, wish for

Herberge [′hɛrbɛrgə] f (-;-n) lodging, shelter; hostel; (obs) inn

her′beten tr say mechanically

Herb′heit f (-;), **Her′bigkeit** f (-;) harshness; tang; bitterness; austerity

her′bringen §65 tr bring here

Herbst [hɛrpst] m (-es;-e) autumn

herbst′lich adj autumn, fall

Herd [hɛrt] m (-[e]s;-e) hearth, fireplace; home; kitchen range; center

Herde [′hɛrdə] f (-;-n) herd, flock

herein [hɛ′raɪn] adv in, in here; **h.!** come in!

herein- comb.fm. in, in here (toward the speaker)

herein′bemühen tr ask (s.o.) to come in || ref trouble oneself to come in

herein′bitten §60 tr invite in

Herein′fall m disappointment, letdown

herein′fallen §72 intr (SEIN) fall in; **h. auf** (acc) fall for; **h. in** (acc) fall into

herein′legen tr fool, take in

herein′platzen intr (SEIN) burst in

her′fallen §72 intr (SEIN)—**h. über** (acc) fall upon, attack

her′finden §59 ref & intr find one's way here

Her′gang m background details

her′geben §80 tr hand over; give up || ref—**sich h. zu** be a party to

her′halten §90 tr hold out, extend || intr—**h. müssen** (Person) be the victim; (Sache) have to do (as a makeshift)

Hering [′hɛrɪŋ] m (-s;-e) herring; **sitzen wie die Heringe** be packed in like sardines

her′kommen §99 intr (SEIN) come here; (Wort) originate; **wo kommst du denn her?** where have you come from? || **Herkommen** n (-s;-) origin; custom, tradition, convention

herkömmlich [′hɛrkœmlɪç] adj customary, usual; traditional, conventional

Herkunft [′hɛrkunft] f (-;) origin; birth, family

her′laufen §105 intr (SEIN) walk here; **hinter j-m h.** follow s.o.

her′leiten tr derive; deduce, infer

Her′leitung f (-;-en) derivation

her′machen tr—**viel h. von** make a fuss over || ref—**sich h. über** (acc) attack; (fig) tackle

Hermelin [hɛrmə′liːn] m (-s;-e) ermine || n (-s;-e) (zool) ermine

hermetisch [hɛr′meːtɪʃ] adj hermetic

hernach′ adv afterwards

her′nehmen §116 tr get; **j-n scharf h.** give s.o. a good talking-to

hernie′der adv down, down here

Heroin [hero′iːn] n (-s;) (pharm) heroin

Heroine [hero′iːnə] f (-;-n) heroine

heroisch [he′roːɪʃ] adj heroic

Heroismus [hero′ɪsmus] m (-;) heroism

Herold [′hɛrɔlt] m (-[e]s;-e) herald

Heros [′hɛrɔs] m (-;) **Heroen** [hɛ′roːən] hero

Herr [hɛr] m (-n;-en) lord; master; gentleman; (als Anrede) Sir; (vor Eigennamen) Mr.; (Gott) Lord; **meine Herren!** gentlemen!

her′reichen tr hand, pass

Herren- [hɛrən] comb.fm. man's, men's; gentlemen's

Her′renabend m stag party

Her′renbegleitung f—**in H.** accompanied by a gentleman

Her′rendoppel(spiel) n (tennis) men's doubles

Her′reneinzel(spiel) n (tennis) men's singles

Her′renfahrer m (aut) owner-driver

Her′renfriseur m barber

Her′rengesellschaft f male company; stag party

Her′rengröße f men's size

Her′rengut n domain, manor

Her′renhaus n mansion; House of Lords

Her′renhof m manor

Her′renleben n life of Riley

her′renlos *adj* ownerless
Her′renmensch *m* born leader
Her′renschnitt *m* woman's very short hairstyle
Her′renzimmer *n* study
Herr′gott *m* Lord, Lord God
her′richten *tr* arrange; get ready
Herrin [′hɛrɪn] *f* (–;–nen) lady
herrisch [′hɛrɪʃ] *adj* masterful
herr′lich *adj* splendid
Herr′lichkeit *f* (–;–en) splendor
Herr′schaft *f* (–;–en) rule, domination; mastery; control; lord, master; estate; **meine Herrschaften!** ladies and gentlemen!
herr′schaftlich *adj* ruler's; gentleman's; high-class
herrschen [′hɛrʃən] *intr* rule; prevail; exist
Herr′scher –in §6 *mf* ruler
Herrschsucht [′hɛrʃzʊçt] *f* (–;) thirst for power; bossiness
herrsch′süchtig *adj* power-hungry; autocratic; domineering
her′rühren *intr*—**h. von** come from, originate with
her′sagen *tr* recite, say
her′schaffen *tr* get (here)
her′stammen *intr*—**h. von** come from, be descended from; (*gram*) be derived from
her′stellen *tr* put here; (*erzeugen*) produce; **fabrikmäßig h.** mass-produce; **Verbindung h.** establish contact; (*telp*) put a call through
Her′steller *m* (–s;–) manufacturer
Her′stellung *f* (–;–en) production
Her′stellungsbetrieb *m* factory
Her′stellungsverfahren *n* manufacturing process
herüber [hɛ′rybər] *adv* over, over here, in this direction (*toward the speaker*)
herum [hɛ′rʊm] *adv* around; about
herum′bringen §65 *tr* bring around; (*Zeit*) spend
herum′drehen *tr*, *ref* & *intr* turn around
herum′fragen *intr* make inquiries
herumfuchteln [hɛ′rʊmfʊxtəln] *intr*—**mit den Händen h.** wave one's hands about
herum′führen *tr* show around
herum′greifen §88 *intr*—**h. um** reach around
herum′hacken *intr*—**h. auf** (*dat*) pick on, criticize
herum′kauen *intr* (**an** *dat*, **auf** *dat*) chew away (on)
herum′kommen §99 *intr* (SEIN) get around; **h. um** get around; evade
herum′lungern *intr* loaf around
herum′reiten §86 *intr* (SEIN) ride around; **h. auf** (*dat*) harp on (*s.th.*); pick on (*s.o.*)
herum′schnüffeln *intr* snoop around
herum′streichen §85 *intr* (SEIN) prowl about
herum′streiten §86 *ref* squabble
herum′treiben §62 *tr* drive around ‖ *ref* roam around, knock about
Herum′treiber *m* (–s;–) loafer, tramp
herum′ziehen §163 *tr* pull around; **h. um** draw (*s.th.*) around ‖ *ref*—**sich h. um** surround ‖ *intr* (SEIN) wander

around; **run around**; **h. um** march around
herunter [hɛ′rʊntər] *adv* down, down here (*towards the speaker*); downstairs; **den Berg h.** down the mountain; **ins Tal h.** down into the valley
herun′terbringen §65 *tr* bring down; (*fig*) lower, reduce
herun′tergehen §82 *intr* (SEIN) go down; (*Preis*, *Temperatur*) fall, drop
herun′terhandeln *tr* (*Preis*) beat down
herun′terhauen §93 *tr* chop off; (*Brief*) dash off; **j-m eins h.** clout s.o.
herun′terkommen §99 *intr* (SEIN) come down; come downstairs; deteriorate
herun′terlassen §104 *tr* let down, lower
herun′terleiern *tr* drone
herun′terlesen §107 *tr* (*Liste*) read down; rattle off
herun′termachen *tr* take down; turn down; (*coll*) chew out; (*coll*) pan
herun′terschießen §76 *tr* shoot down
herun′tersein §139 *intr* (SEIN) be rundown
herun′terwirtschaften *tr* ruin (*through mismanagement*)
herun′terwürgen *tr* choke down
hervor [hɛr′for] *adv* out; forth
hervor′bringen §65 *tr* bring out; engender, produce; (*Wort*) utter
hervor′dringen §142 *intr* (SEIN) emerge
hervor′gehen §82 *intr* (SEIN)—**h. aus** come from; emerge from; **to have been trained at**
hervor′heben §94 *tr* highlight
hervor′holen *tr* produce
hervor′kommen §99 *intr* (SEIN) come out
hervor′lugen *intr* peep out
hervor′ragen *intr* jut out; be prominent; **h. über** (*acc*) tower over
hervor′ragend *adj* prominent
hervor′rufen §122 *tr* evoke, cause; (*Schauspieler*) recall
hervor′stechen §64 *intr* stick out; be conspicuous; be prominent
hervor′treten §152 *intr* (SEIN) emerge; come to the fore; become apparent; (*Augen*) bulge; (*Ader*) protrude
hervor′tun §154 *ref* distinguish oneself
hervor′wagen *ref* dare to come out; **sich mit e-r Antwort h.** venture an answer
hervor′zaubern *tr* produce by magic; **ein Essen h.** whip up a meal
Herweg [′hɛrvek] *m* way here; way home
Herz [hɛrts] *n* (–ens;–en) heart; (*als Anrede*) darling; (*cards*) heart(s); **ich bringe es nicht übers H. zu** (*inf*) I haven't the heart to (*inf*); **sich** [*dat*] **ein H. fassen** get up the courage; **seinem Herzen Luft machen** give vent to one's feelings
Herz– *comb.fm.* heart, cardiac
Herz′anfall *m* heart attack
Herz′beschwerden *pl* heart trouble
Herz′blume *f* (bot) bleeding heart
herzen [′hɛrtsən] *tr* hug, embrace
Her′zensgrund *m* bottom of one's heart
her′zensgut *adj* good-hearted

Her′zenslust *f*—nach H. to one's heart's content
herz′ergreifend *adj* moving, touching
Herz′geräusch *n* heart murmur
herz′haft *adj* hearty
herzig [ˈhɛrtsɪç] *adj* sweet, cute
 –herzig *comb.fm.* –hearted
Herzinfarkt [ˈhɛrtsɪnfarkt] *m* (–[e]s; –e) cardiac infarction
herz′innig *adj* heartfelt
herz′inniglich *adv* sincerely
Herz′klappe *f* cardiac valve
Herz′klopfen *n* palpitations
Herz′kollaps *m* heart failure
herz′lich *adj* cordial; sincere ‖ *adv* very; **h. wenige** precious few
herz′los *adj* heartless
Herzog [ˈhɛrtsɔk] *m* (–[e]s;╪e) duke
Herzogin [ˈhɛrtsɔgɪn] *f* (–;–nen) duchess
Herzogtum [ˈhɛrtsɔktum] *n* (–[e]s;╪er) dukedom; duchy
Herz′schlag *m* heartbeat; heart failure
Herz′stück *n* heart, central point
Herz′verpflanzung *f* heart transplant
Herz′weh *n* (& fig) heartache
Hetzblatt [ˈhɛtsblat] *n* scandal sheet
Hetze [ˈhɛtsə] *f* (–;–n) hunting; hurry, rush; vicious campaign; baiting
hetzen [ˈhɛtsən] *tr* hunt; bait; rush; (fig) hound; **e–n Hund auf j–n h.** sic a dog on s.o. ‖ *ref* rush ‖ *intr* stir up trouble; **h. gegen** conduct a vicious campaign against ‖ *intr* (SEIN) race, dash
Het′zer –in §6 *mf* agitator
Hetz′hund *m* hound, hunting dog
Hetz′jagd *f* hunt; baiting; hurry
Hetz′rede *f* inflammatory speech
Heu [hɔɪ] *n* (–[e]s;) hay
Heu′boden *m* hayloft
Heuchelei [hɔɪçəˈlaɪ] *f* (–;–en) hypocrisy; piece of hypocrisy
heucheln [ˈhɔɪçəln] *tr* feign ‖ *intr* be hypocritical
Heuch′ler –in §6 *mf* hypocrite
heuchlerisch [ˈhɔɪçlərɪʃ] *adj* hypocritical
heuen [ˈhɔɪən] *intr* make hay
heuer [ˈhɔɪər] *adv* this year
heuern [ˈhɔɪərn] *tr* hire
Heu′fieber *n* hayfever
Heu′gabel *f* pitchfork
heulen [ˈhɔɪlən] *intr* bawl; (*Wind*) howl
heurig [ˈhɔɪrɪç] *adj* this year's ‖ **Heurige §5** *m* new wine
Heu′schnupfen *m* (–s;) hayfever
Heuschober [ˈhɔɪʃobər] *m* (–s;–) haystack
Heu′schrecke *f* (–;–n) locust
heute [ˈhɔɪtə] *adv* today; **h. abend** this evening; **h. früh** (or **h. morgen**) this morning; **h. vor acht Tagen** a week ago today; **h. in acht Tagen** today a week
heutig [ˈhɔɪtɪç] *adj* today's; present-day; **am heutigen Tage** (or **der heutige Tag** or **mit dem heutigen Tag**) today
heutzutage [ˈhɔɪttsutagə] *adv* nowadays
Hexe [ˈhɛksə] *f* (–s;–n) witch; hag

hexen [ˈhɛksən] *intr* practice witchcraft
He′xenkessel *m* chaos, inferno
He′xenmeister *m* wizard; sorcerer
He′xenschuß *m* lumbago
Hexerei [hɛksəˈraɪ] *f* (–;) witchcraft
Hiatus [hiˈatus] *m* (–;–) (& pros) hiatus
Hibis·kus [hiˈbɪskus] *m* (–;–ken [kən]) hibiscus
hieb [hip] *pret* of **hauen** ‖ **Hieb** *m* (–[e]s;–e) blow, stroke; **Hiebe** thrashing
hieb′–undstich′fest *adj* (fig) watertight
Hieb′wunde *f* gash
hielt [hilt] *pret* of **halten**
hier [hir] *adv* here
hieran′ *adv* at (by, in, on, to) it or them
Hierar·chie [hiˌerarˈçi] *f* (–;–chien [ˈçi·ən]) hierarchy
hierauf′ *adv* on it, on them; then
hieraus′ *adv* out of it (or them); from this (or these)
hierbei′ *adv* near here; here; in this case; in connection with this
hierdurch′ *adv* through it (or them); through here; hereby
hierfür′ *adv* for it (or them)
hierge′gen *adv* against it
hierher′ *adv* hither, here
hier′herum *adv* around here
hierhin′ *adv* here; **bis h.** up to here
hierin′ *adv* herein, in this
hiermit′ *adv* herewith, with it
hiernach′ *adv* after this, then; about this; according to this
Hieroglyphe [hiˌɛroˈglyfə] *f* (–;–n) hieroglyph
hierorts′ [ˈhirɔrts] *adv* in this town
hierü′ber *adv* over it (or them); about it (or this)
hierzu′ *adv* to it; in addition to it; concerning this
hiesig [ˈhizɪç] *adj* local
hieß [his] *pret* of **heißen**
Hilfe [ˈhɪlfə] *f* (–;–n) help, aid; **zu H. nehmen** make use of
Hil′feleistung *f* assistance
Hil′feruf *m* cry for help
hilf′los *adj* helpless
hilf′reich *adj* helpful
Hilfs– [hɪlfs] *comb.fm.* auxiliary
Hilfs′arbeiter –in §6 *mf* unskilled laborer
Hilfs′arzt *m*, **Hilf′ärztin** *f* intern
hilfs′bedürftig *adj* needy
hilfs′bereit *adj* ready to help
Hilfs′dienst *m* help, assistance
Hilfs′gerät *n* labor-saving device
Hilfs′kraft *f* assistant, helper; (mach) auxiliary power
Hilfs′kraftbremse *f* power brake
Hilfs′kraftlenkung *f* power steering
Hilfs′lehrer –in §6 *mf* student teacher
Hilfs′maschine *f* auxiliary engine
Hilfs′mittel *n* aid, device; remedy; financial aid
Hilfs′quellen *pl* material; sources
Hilfs′rakete *f* booster rocket
Hilfs′schule *f* school for the mentally slow

Hilfs'truppen *pl* auxiliaries
Hilfs'werk *n* welfare organization
Hilfs'zeitwort *n* (-[e]s;-̈er) (gram) auxiliary (verb)
Himbeere ['hɪmbərə] *f* (-;-n) raspberry
Himmel ['hɪməl] *m* (-s;-) sky, skies; heaven(s); firmament; (eccl) baldachin; **ach du lieber H.!** good heavens!; **aus heiterem H.** out of the blue; **in den H. heben** praise to the skies
himmelan' *adv* skywards; heavenwards
him'melangst *invar adj*—**mir wird h. I** feel frightened to death
Him'melbett *n* canopy bed
him'melblau *adj* sky-blue
Him'melfahrt *f* ascension; assumption
Him'melfahrtstag *m* Ascension Day
Him'melreich *n* kingdom of heaven
Himmels- *comb.fm.* celestial
him'melschreiend *adj* atrocious
Him'melsgegend *f* region of the sky; point of the compass
Him'melskörper *m* celestial body
Him'melsrichtung *f* point of the compass; direction
Him'melsschrift *f* skywriting
Him'melswagen *m* (astr) Great Bear
Him'melszelt *n* canopy of heaven
himmelwärts ['hɪmlverts] *adv* skywards; heavenwards
himmlisch ['hɪmlɪʃ] *adj* heavenly, celestial; divine; (coll) gorgeous
hin [hɪn] *adv* there (*away from the speaker*); **ganz hin** (coll) bushed; (coll) quite carried away; **hin ist hin** what's done is done; **hin und her** up and down, back and forth; **hin und wieder** now and then; **vor sich hin** to oneself
hinab' *adv* down
hinan' *adv* up; **bis an etw h.** up to s.th., as far as s.th.
hinauf' *adv* up, up there; upstairs; **den Fluß h.** up the river
hinauf'reichen *tr* hand (*s.th.*) up ‖ *intr* reach up
hinauf'schrauben *tr* (*Preis*) jack up
hinauf'setzen *tr* raise, increase
hinauf'steigen §148 *tr* (SEIN) (*Treppe, Berg*) climb ‖ *intr* (SEIN) climb up; (*Temperatur*) rise
hinaus' *adv* out, out there; over; **auf viele Jahre h.** for many years to come
hinaus'beißen §53 *tr* (coll) edge out
hinaus'gehen §82 *intr* (SEIN) go out; **h. auf** (*acc*) look out over; lead to; drive at, imply; **h. über** (*acc*) exceed
hinaus'kommen §99 *intr* (SEIN) come out; **es kommt auf eins** (or **aufs gleiche**) **hinaus** it amounts to the same thing; **h. über** (*acc*) get beyond
hinaus'laufen §105 *intr* (SEIN) run out; **es läuft aufs eins** (or **aufs gleiche**) **hinaus** it amounts to the same thing
hinaus'schieben §130 *tr* push out; (*Termin, usw.*) postpone
hinaus'werfen §160 *tr* throw out; fire
hinaus'wollen §162 *intr* want to go out; **h. auf** (*acc*) be driving at; **hoch h.** aim high, be ambitious
hinaus'ziehen §163 *tr* prolong ‖ *ref*

take longer than expected ‖ *intr* (SEIN) go out; move out
Hin'blick *m*—**im H. auf** (*acc*) in view of
hin'bringen §65 *tr* bring (there); take (there); (*Zeit*) pass
hinderlich ['hɪndərlɪç] *adj* in the way
hindern ['hɪndərn] *tr* block; **h. an** (*dat*) prevent from (*ger*)
Hindernis ['hɪndərnɪs] *n* (-ses;-se) hindrance; obstacle
Hin'dernisbahn *f* obstacle course
Hin'dernislauf *m* (sport) hurdles
Hin'dernisrennen *n* steeplechase; hurdles
hin'deuten *intr* (auf *acc*) point (to)
hindurch' *adv* through; **den ganzen Sommer h.** throughout the summer
hinein' *adv* in, in there
hinein'arbeiten *ref*—**sich h. in** (*acc*) work one's way into
hinein'denken §66 *ref*—**sich h. in** (*acc*) imagine oneself in
hinein'geraten §63 *intr* (SEIN)—**h. in** (*acc*) get into, fall into
hinein'leben *intr*—**in den Tag h.** live for the moment
hinein'tun §154 *tr* put in
Hin'fahrt *f* journey there, out-bound passage
hin'fallen §72 *intr* (SEIN) fall down
hinfällig ['hɪnfɛlɪç] *adj* frail; (*Gesetz*) invalid
hinfort' *adv* henceforth
hing [hɪŋ] *pret* of **hängen**
Hin'gabe *f* (an *acc*) devotion (to)
hin'geben §80 *tr* give up ‖ *ref* (*dat*) abandon oneself (to)
Hin'gebung *f* (-;) devotion
hinge'gen *adv* on the other hand
hin'gehen §82 *intr* (SEIN) go there; pass
hin'halten §90 *tr* hold out; (*Person*) keep waiting, string along; **den Kopf h.** (fig) take the rap
hinken ['hɪŋkən] *intr* limp; **der Vergleich hinkt** that's a poor comparison ‖ *intr* (SEIN) limp
hin'länglich *adj* sufficient
hin'legen *tr* put down ‖ *ref* lie down
hin'nehmen §116 *tr* accept; take, put up with
hin'raffen *tr* snatch away
hin'reichen *tr* (*dat*) pass to, hand to ‖ *intr* reach; suffice
hin'reißen §53 *tr* enchant, carry away
hin'richten *tr* execute; **h. auf** (*acc*) direct towards
Hin'richtung *f* (-;-en) execution
Hin'richtungsbefehl *m* death warrant
hin'setzen *tr* put down ‖ *ref* sit down
Hin'sicht *f* respect, way; **in H. auf** (*acc*) regarding, in regard to
hin'sichtlich *prep* (*genit*) regarding
hin'stellen *tr* put there; put down
hintan'setzen, **hintan'stellen** *tr* put last, consider last
hinten ['hɪntən] *adv* at the back, in the rear; **h. im Zimmer** at the back of the room; **nach h.** to the rear; backwards; **von h.** from the rear
hinter ['hɪntər] *prep* (*dat*) behind; **h. j-m her sein** be after s.o. ‖ *prep* (*acc*) behind; **h. etw kommen** find

out about s.th., get to the bottom of s.th.

Hin'terachse f rear axle

Hin'terbacke f buttock

Hin'terbein n hind leg; **sich auf die Hinterbeine setzen** strain oneself

Hinterbliebene ['hɪntərbliːbənə] §5 mf survivor (of a deceased); **H.** pl next-of-kin

hinterbrin'gen §65 tr—j-m etw h. let s.o. in on s.th.

Hin'terdeck n quarter deck

hinterdrein [hɪntər'draɪn] adv after; subsequently, afterwards

hin'tere §9 adj back, rear || **Hintere** §5 m (coll) behind

hintereinan'der adv one behind the other; in succession; one after the other

Hin'terfuß m hind foot

Hin'tergaumen m soft palate, velum

Hin'tergedanke m ulterior motive

hinterge'hen §82 tr deceive

Hin'tergrund m background

Hin'terhalt m ambush

hinterhältig ['hɪntərheltɪç] adj underhanded

Hin'terhand f hind quarters (of horse)

Hin'terhaus n rear building

hinterher' adv behind; afterwards

Hin'terhof m backyard

Hin'terkopf m back of the head

Hin'terland n hinterland

hinterlas'sen §104 tr leave behind

Hinterlas'senschaft f (–;-en) inheritance

Hin'terlauf m hind leg

hinterle'gen tr deposit

Hinterle'gung f (–;-en) deposit

Hin'terlist f deceit; trick, ruse

Hin'termann m (–[e]s;–er) instigator; wheeler-dealer; (pol) backer

Hintern ['hɪntərn] m (–s;–) (coll) behind

Hin'terradantrieb m rear-wheel drive

hinterrücks ['hɪntərryks] adv from behind; (fig) behind one's back

Hin'tertreffen n—ins **H.** geraten fall behind; **im H. sein** be at a disadvantage

hintertrei'ben §62 tr frustrate

Hintertrei'bung f (–;-en) frustration

Hin'tertreppe f backstairs

Hin'tertür f backdoor

Hinterwäldler ['hɪntərveltlər] m (–s;–) hillbilly

hin'terwäldlerisch adj hillbilly

hinterzie'hen §163 tr evade

Hinterzie'hung f (–;) tax evasion

hinü'ber adv over, over there; across

hinun'ter adv down

hinun'tergehen §82 tr (SEIN) (Treppe) go down || intr (SEIN) go down

hinweg [hɪn'wɛk] adv away; **über etw h.** over s.th., across s.th. || **Hinweg** ['hɪnvɛk] m way there

hinweg'kommen §99 intr (SEIN)—h. über (acc) get over

hinweg'sehen §138 intr—h. über (acc) look over; overlook, ignore

hinweg'setzen ref—sich h. über (acc) ignore, disregard

hinweg'täuschen tr mislead, blind

Hinweis ['hɪnvaɪs] m (–es;-e) reference; hint; announcement

hin'weisen §118 tr—j-n h. auf (acc) point s.th. out to s.o. || intr—h. auf (acc) point to; point out

hin'werfen §160 tr throw down; (coll) dash off, jot down

hin'wirken intr—h. auf (acc) work toward(s)

hin'ziehen §163 tr attract protract || ref drag on; **sich h. an** (dat) run along; **sich h. bis zu** extend to

hin'zielen intr—h. auf (acc) aim at

hinzu' adv there, thither; in addition

hinzu'fügen tr add

hinzu'kommen §99 intr (SEIN) come (upon the scene); be added; **es kamen noch andere Gründe hinzu** besides, there were other reasons

hinzu'setzen tr add

hinzu'treten §152 intr (SEIN) (zu) walk up (to); **es traten noch andere Gründe hinzu** besides, there were other reasons

hinzu'tun §154 tr add

hinzu'ziehen §163 tr (Arzt) call in

Hirn [hɪrn] n (–[e]s;-e) brain; brains; **sein H. anstrengen** rack one's brains

Hirn- comb.fm. brain; cerebral; intellectual

Hirn'anhang m pituitary gland

Hirn'gespinst n figment of the imagination

Hirn'hautentzündung f meningitis

hirn'los adj brainless

Hirn'rinde f (anat) cortex

Hirn'schale f cranium

hirn'verbrannt adj (coll) crazy

Hirsch [hɪrʃ] m (–es;-e) deer, stag

Hirsch'fänger m hunting knife

Hirsch'kalb n fawn, doe

Hirsch'kuh f hind

Hirsch'leder n deerskin, buckskin

Hirt [hɪrt] m (–en;–en) shepherd

–hirte [hɪrtə] m (–n;–n) –herd

Hir'tenbrief m (eccl) pastoral letter

Hirtin ['hɪrtɪn] f (–;-nen) shepherdess

His [hɪs] n (–;) (mus) B sharp

hissen ['hɪsən] tr hoist

Historie [hɪs'toːrjə] f (–;-n) history; story

Historiker –in [hɪs'toːrɪkər(ɪn)] §6 mf historian

historisch [hɪs'toːrɪʃ] adj historical

Hitze ['hɪtsə] f (–;-n) heat

hit'zebeständig adj heat-resistant

Hit'zeferien pl school holiday (because of hot weather)

Hit'zeschild m (rok) heat shield

Hit'zewelle f heat wave

hitzig ['hɪtsɪç] adj hot-tempered

Hitz'kopf m hothead

hitz'köpfig adj hot-headed

Hitz'schlag m heatstroke

hob [hoːp] pret of **heben**

Hobel ['hoːbəl] m (–s;–) (carp) plane

Ho'belbank f carpenter's bench

hobeln ['hoːbəln] tr (carp) plane

hoch [hoːx], **hohe** ['hoːə] §9) adj (**höher** ['høːər], **höchste** ['høçstə] §9) high; noble; (Alter) advanced; **das ist mir zu h.** that's beyond me; **hohes Gericht!** your honor!; mem-

bers of the jury!; **in höchster Not** in
dire need ‖ *adv* high; highly, very;
(math) to the ... power ‖ **Hoch** *n*
(-s;-s) (*Trinkspruch, Heilruf*) cheer;
(meteor) high

hoch— *comb.fm.* up; upwards; highly,
very; high, as high as

hoch'achten *tr* esteem

Hoch'actung *f* (-;) esteem; **mit vor-**
züglicher H., Ihr ... or Ihre ...
Very truly yours, Respectfully yours

hoch'achtungsvoll *adj* respectful ‖ *adv*
—h., Ihr ... or Ihre ... Very truly
yours, Respectfully yours

Hoch'amt *n* (eccl) High Mass

Hoch'antenne *f* outdoor antenna

hoch'arbeiten *ref* work one's way up

hoch'aufgeschossen *adj* tall, lanky

Hoch'bahn *f* el, elevated train

Hoch'bauingenieur *m* structural engineer

hoch'bäumen *ref* rear up

Hoch'behälter *m* water tower; reservoir

Hochbeiner ['hoxbaɪnər] *m* (-s;-)
(ent) daddy-long-legs

hoch'beinig *adj* long-legged

hoch'betagt *adj* advanced in years

Hoch'betrieb *m* bustle, big rush

Hoch'blüte *f* high bloom; (fig) heyday

hoch'bringen §65 *tr* restore to health;
(*Geschäft*) put on its feet; **es h.**
(sport) get a high score

Hoch'burg *f* fortress, citadel

hoch'denkend *adj* noble-minded

hoch'deutsch *adj* High German

Hoch'druck *m* high pressure; (fig)
great pressure; (meteor) high; **mit H.**
(fig) full blast

Hoch'druckgebiet *n* (meteor) high,
high-pressure area

Hoch'ebene *f* plateau

hoch'fahrend *adj* high-handed

hoch'fein *adj* very refined; high-grade

Hoch'flut *m* high tide; (fig) deluge

Hoch'form *f* top form

hochfrequent ['hoxfrekvɛnt] *adj* high-
frequency

Hoch'frequenz *f* high-frequency

Hoch'frisur *f* upsweep

Hoch'gefühl *n* elation

hoch'gemut *adj* cheerful

Hoch'genuß *m* great pleasure

Hoch'gericht *n* place of execution

hoch'gesinnt *adj* noble-minded

hoch'gespannt *adj* (*Hoffnungen*) high;
(elec) high-voltage

hoch'gestellt *adj* high-ranking

Hoch'glanz *m* high polish, high gloss

Hoch'haus *n* high rise (building)

hoch'herzig *adj* generous

hoch'jagen *tr* (*Wild*) ferret out; (*Mo-*
tor) race; (coll) blow up

hochkant ['hoxkant] *adv* on end

Hoch'konjunktur *f* (econ) boom

Hoch'land *n* highlands; plateau

Hoch'leistung *f* (-;-en) high output;
(sport) first-class performance

Hochleistungs— *comb.fm.* high-powered; high-capacity; high-speed;
heavy-duty

Hoch'mut *m* haughtiness, pride

hoch'mütig *adj* haughty, proud

hochnäsig ['hoxnezɪç] *adj* snooty

Hoch'ofen *m* blast furnace

hoch'ragend *adj* towering

hoch'rappeln *ref* (coll) get on one's
feet again, pick up again

hoch'rollen *tr* roll up

Hoch'ruf *m* cheer

Hoch'saison *f* height of the season

Hoch'schule *f* university, academy

Hoch'schüler –in §6 *mf* university student

Hoch'seefischerei *f* deep-sea fishing

hoch'selig *adj* late, of blessed memory

Hoch'spannung *f* high voltage

Hoch'spannungsleitung *f* high-tension
line

hoch'spielen *tr* play up; put into the
limelight

Hoch'sprache *f* standard language;
(die) **deutsche H.** standard German

höchst *adv* see hoch

Höchst— *comb.fm.* maximum, top

Hochstapelei [hoxʃtapə'laɪ] *f* (-;) false
pretenses; fraud

Hochstapler ['hoxʃtaplər] *m* (-s;) confidence man; imposter, swindler

Hoch'start *m* (sport) standing start

Höchst'belastung *f* (-;-en) maximum
load; (elec) peak load

höchstens ['høçstəns] *adv* at best, at
the very most

Höchst'form *f* (sport) top form

Höchst'frequenz *f* ultrahigh frequency

Höchst'geschwindigkeit *f* top speed;
zulässige H. speed limit

Höchst'leistung *f* (-;-en) maximum
output; highest achievement; (sport)
record

Hoch'straße *f* overpass

Hoch'ton *m* (ling) primary stress

hoch'tönend *adj* bombastic

hochtourig ['hoxturɪç] *adj* high-rev-
ving

hoch'trabend *adj* pompous

Hoch'-und Tief'bau *m* (-[e]s;) civil
engineering

hoch'verdient *adj* of great merit

Hoch'verrat *m* high treason

Hoch'verräter –in §6 *mf* traitor

Hoch'wasser *n* flood(s); **der Fluß führt**
H. the river is swollen

hoch'wertig *adj* high-quality

Hoch'wild *n* big game

Hoch'würden *pl* (*als Anrede*) Reverend; **Seine H. ...** the Reverend ...

Hoch'zeit *f* wedding

hoch'zeitlich *adj* bridal; nuptial

Hoch'zeitsfeier *f* wedding ceremony;
wedding reception

Hoch'zeitspaar *n* newly-weds

Hoch'zeitsreise *f* honeymoon

Hocke ['hɔkə] *f* (-;-n) crouch

hocken ['hɔkən] *ref & intr* squat;
(coll) sit down

Hocker ['hɔkər] *m* (-s;-) stool

Höcker ['hœkər] *m* (-s;-) hump; bump

höckerig ['hœkərɪç] *adj* hunchbacked;
(*Weg*) bumpy

Hockey ['hɔki] *n* (-s;) hockey

Ho'ckeyschläger *m* hockey stick

Hode ['hodə] *f* (-;-n) testicle

Ho'densack *m* (anat) scrotum

Hof [hof] *m* (-[e]s;⸚e) courtyard;

yard; barnyard; (*e-s Königs*) court; (astr) halo; corona; **e-m Mädchen den Hof machen** court a girl

Hoffart ['hɔfart] *f* (-;) haughtiness

hoffärtig ['hɔfertɪç] *adj* haughty

hoffen ['hɔfən] *tr*—**das Beste h.** hope for the best ‖ *intr* (**auf** *acc*) hope (for); **auf j-n h.** put one's hopes in s.o

hoffentlich ['hɔfəntlɪç] *adv* as I hope; **h. kommt er bald** I hope he comes soon

Hoffnung ['hɔfnʊŋ] *f* (-;-en) hope

hoff'nungslos *adj* hopeless

hoff'nungsvoll *adj* hopeful; promising

Hof'hund *m* watchdog

hofieren [hɔ'firən] *tr* court

höfisch ['høfɪʃ] *adj* court, courtly

höflich ['høflɪç] *adj* polite, courteous

Höf'lichkeit *f* (-;-en) politeness, courtesy

Höf'lichkeitsformel *f* complimentary close (*in a letter*)

Höfling ['høflɪŋ] *m* (-[e]s;-e) courtier

Hof'meister *m* steward; tutor

Hof'narr *m* court jester

Hof'staat *m* royal household; retinue

hohe ['ho·ə] *adj* see **hoch**

Höhe ['hø·ə] *f* (-;-en) height; altitude; (*Anhöhe*) hill; (mus) pitch; **auf der H. in good shape; das ist die H.!** that's the limit!; **in der H. von** in the amount of; **in die H. up; in die H. fahren** jump up; **wieder in die H. bringen** (com) put back on its feet

Hoheit ['hohart] *f* (-;-en) sovereignty; (*als Titel*) Highness

Ho'heitsbereich *m* (pol), **Ho'heitsgebiet** *n* (pol) territory

Ho'heitsgewässer *pl* territorial waters

Ho'heitsrechte *pl* sovereign rights

ho'heitsvoll *adj* regal, majestic

Ho'heitszeichen *n* national emblem

Hö'henmesser *m* altimeter

Hö'henruder *n* (aer) elevator

Hö'hensonne *f* ultra-violet lamp

Hö'henstrahlen *pl* cosmic rays

Hö'henzug *m* mountain range

Ho'hepriester *m* high priest

Hö'hepunkt *m* climax; height, acme

höher ['hø·ər] *adj* see **hoch**

hohl [hol] *adj* hollow

Höhle ['hølə] *f* (-;-n) cave; grotto; lair, den; hollow, cavity; socket

Höh'lenmensch *m* caveman

hohl'geschliffen [*adj*] hollow-ground

Hohl'heit *f* (-;) hollowness

Hohl'maß *n* dry measure; liquid measure

Hohl'raum *m* hollow, cavity

Hohl'saum *m* hemstitch

Hohl'weg *m* defile, narrow pass

Hohn [hon] *m* (-[e]s;) scorn; sarcasm; **etw j-m Hohn tun** do s.th. in defiance of s.o.

höhnen ['hønən] *intr* jeer; sneer

höhnisch ['hønɪʃ] *adj* scornful

hohn'sprechen §64 *intr* (*dat*) treat with scorn; defy; make a mockery of

Höker -**in** ['høkər(ɪn)] §6 *mf* huckster

hold [hɔlt] *adj* kindly; lovely; sweet

hold'selig *adj* lovely, sweet

holen ['holən] *tr* fetch; get; (*Atem, Luft*) draw; **h. lassen** send for; **sich** [*dat*] **etw h.** (coll) catch s.th.

Holland ['hɔlant] *n* (-s;) Holland

Holländer ['hɔlendər] *m* (-s;-) Dutchman

Holländerin ['hɔlendərɪn] *f* (-;-nen) Dutch woman

holländisch ['hɔlendɪʃ] *adj* Dutch

Hölle ['hœlə] *f* (-;) hell

Höl'lenangst *f* mortal fear

höllisch ['hœlɪʃ] *adj* hellish

Holm [hɔlm] *m* (-[e]s;-e) islet; (*Stiel*) handle; (aer) spar; (gym) parallel bar

holp(e)rig ['hɔlp(ə)rɪç] *adj* bumpy

holpern ['hɔlpərn] *intr* jolt, bump along; (*beim Lesen*) stumble

Holunder [hɔ'lʊndər] *m* (-s;-) (bot) elder

Holz [hɔlts] *n* (-es;ˮer) wood; lumber; timber, trees; **ins H. gehen** go into the woods

Holz'apfel *m* crab apple

Holz'arbeit *f* woodwork; lumbering

Holz'arbeiter *m* woodworker; lumberjack

holz'artig *adj* woody

Holz'blasinstrumente *pl* wood winds

Holz'brei *m* wood pulp

holzen ['hɔltsən] *tr* fell; deforest; (coll) spank ‖ *intr* cut wood

hölzern ['hœltsərn] *adj* wooden; (fig) clumsy

Holzfäller ['hɔltsfelər] *m* (-s;-) lumberjack, logger

Holz'faser *f* wood fiber; wood pulp; grain; **gegen die H.** against the grain

Holz'faserstoff *m* wood pulp

Holzhacker ['hɔltshakər] *m* (-s;-), **Holzhauer** ['hɔltshau·ər] *m* (-s;-) lumberjack; wood chopper

holzig ['hɔltsɪç] *adj* woody, wooded; (*Gemüse*) stringy

Holz'knecht *m* lumberjack

Holz'kohle *f* charcoal

Holz'nagel *m* wooden peg

Holz'platz *m* lumber yard

holz'reich *adj* wooded

Holz'schnitt *m* woodcut; wood engraving

Holz'schuh *m* wooden shoe

Holz'schuppen *m* woodshed

Holz'wolle *f* excelsior

Homi-lie [homɪ'li] *f* (-;-lien ['li·ən]) homily

homogen [homɔ'gen] *adj* homogeneous

Homosexualität [homɔzeksu·alɪ'tet] *f* (-;) homosexuality

homosexuell [homɔzeksu'el] *adj* homosexual ‖ **Homosexuelle** §5 *mf* homosexual

Honig ['honɪç] *m* (-s;) honey

Ho'nigkuchen *m* gingerbread

ho'nigsüß *adj* sweet as honey

Ho'nigwabe *f* honeycomb

Honorar [honɔ'rar] *n* (-s;-e) fee

Honoratioren [honɔratsɪ'orən] *pl* dignitaries

honorieren [honɔ'rirən] *tr* give an honorarium to; pay royalties to; (*Scheck*) honor

Hopfen ['hɔpfən] *m* (-s;) hops

hopp [hɔp] *interj* up!; quick!; **hopp, los!** get going!

hoppla ['hɔpla] *interj* whoops!; **jetzt aber h.!** come on!; look sharp!

hops [hɔps] *adj*—**h. gehen** go to pot; **h. sein** be done for

hopsasa ['hɔpsasa] *interj* upsy-daisy

hopsen ['hɔpsən] *intr* (SEIN) hop

Hop'ser *m* (-s;-) hop

Hörapparat ['hørap, arat] *m* hearing aid

hörbar ['hørbar] *adj* audible

hörbehindert ['hørbəhɪndərt] *adj* hard of hearing

Hörbericht ['hørbərɪçt] *m* radio report; radio commentary

horchen ['hɔrçən] *intr* listen; eavesdrop

Hor'cher –in §6 *mf* eavesdropper

Horch'gerät *n* sound detector; (nav) hydrophone

Horch'posten *m* (mil) listening post

Horde ['hɔrdə] *f* (-;-n) horde

hören ['hørən] *tr* hear; listen to; (*Vorlesung*) attend ‖ *intr* hear; **h.** (*acc*) pay attention to, obey

Hö'rer *m* (-s;-) listener; member of an audience; student; (telp) receiver

Hö'rerbrief *m* letter from a listener

Hö'rerkreis *m* listeners

Hö'rerschaft *f* (-;-en) audience; (educ) enrollment

Hör'folge *f* radio serial

Hör'gerät *n* hearing aid

hörig ['hørɪç] *adj* in bondage ‖ **Hörige** §5 *mf* serf, thrall

Horizont [hɔrɪ'tsɔnt] *m* (-[e]s;-e) horizon

horizontal [hɔrɪtsɔn'tal] *adj* horizontal ‖ **Horizontale** §5 *f* horizontal line

Horn [hɔrn] *n* (-[e]s;⁀er) horn; (mil) bugle; (mus) horn, French horn

Hörnchen ['hœrnçən] *n* (-s;-) crescent roll

Horn'haut *f* (anat) cornea

Hornisse [hɔr'nɪsə] *f* (-;-n) hornet

Hornist [hɔr'nɪst] *m* (-en;-en) bugler

Horn'ochse *f* (coll) dumb ox

Horoskop [hɔrɔ'skop] *n* (-[e]s;-e) horoscope

horrend [hɔ'rent] *adj* (coll) terrible

Hör'rohr *n* stethoscope

Hör'saal *m* lecture room

Hör'spiel *n* radio play

Horst [hɔrst] *m* (-[e]s;-e) (eagle's) nest

Hort [hɔrt] *m* (-[e]s;-e) hoard, treasure; (place of) refuge; protector

Hör'weite *f*—**in H.** within earshot

Hose ['hozə] *f* (-;-n), **Hosen** ['hozən] *pl* pants, trousers; (*Unterhose*) shorts; panties; **sich auf die Hosen setzen** buckle down

Ho'senboden *m* seat (of trousers)

Ho'senklappe *f*, **Ho'senlatz** *m* fly

Ho'senrolle *f* (theat) male role

Ho'senträger *pl* suspenders

Hospitant [hɔspɪ'tant] *m* (-en;-en) (educ) auditor

hospitieren [hɔspɪ'tirən] *intr* (educ) audit a course

Hospiz [hɔs'pits] *n* (-es;-e) hospice

Hostie ['hɔstjə] *f* (-;-n) host, wafer

Hotel [hɔ'tel] *n* (-s;-s) hotel

Hotel'boy *m* bellboy, bellhop

Hotel'diener *m* hotel porter

Hotel'fach *n*, **Hotel'gewerbe** *n* hotel business

Hub [hup] *m* (-[e]s;⁀e) (mach) stroke

hübsch [hypʃ] *adj* pretty; handsome; (coll) good-sized

Hubschrauber ['hup, rraubər] *m* (-s;-) helicopter

huckepack ['hukəpak] *adv* piggyback

hudeln ['hudəln] *intr* be sloppy

Huf [huf] *m* (-[e]s;-e) hoof

Huf'eisen *n* horseshoe

Huf'schlag *m* hoofbeat

Hüfte ['hyftə] *f* (-;-n) hip; **die Arme in die Hüften gestemmt** with arms akimbo

Hüft'gelenk *n* hip joint

Hüft'gürtel *m*, **Hüft'halter** *m* garter belt

Hügel ['hygəl] *m* (-s;-) hill; mound

hügelab' *adv* downhill

hügelauf' *adv* uphill

hügelig ['hygəlɪç] *adj* hilly

Huhn [hun] *n* (-[e]s;⁀er) fowl; hen, chicken

Hühnchen ['hynçən] *n* (-s;-) young chicken; **ein H. zu rupfen haben mit** (fig) have a bone to pick with

Hüh'nerauge *n* (pathol) corn

Hüh'nerdraht *m* chicken wire

Hüh'nerhund *m* bird dog

Huld [hult] *f* (-;) grace, favor

huldigen ['huldɪgən] *intr* (*dat*) pay homage to

Hul'digung *f* (-;) homage

Hul'digungseid *m* oath of allegiance

huld'reich, huld'voll *adj* gracious

Hülle ['hylə] *f* (-;-n) cover; case; wrapper; envelope; (-s *Buches*) jacket; (fig) cloak; **in H. und Fülle** in abundance; **sterbliche H.** mortal remains

hüllen ['hylən] *tr* cover; veil; wrap

Hülse ['hylzə] *f* (-;-n) pod, hull; cartridge case, shell case

Hül'senfrucht *f* legume

human [hu'man] *adj* humane

humanistisch [huma'nɪstɪʃ] *adj* humanistic; classical

humanitär [humanɪ'ter] *adj* humanitarian

Humanität [humanɪ'tet] *f* (-;) humanity; humaneness

Humanitäts'duselei *f* sentimental humanitarianism

Humanitäts'verbrechen *n* crime against humanity

Hummel ['huməl] *f* (-;-n) bumblebee

Hummer ['humər] *m* (-s;-) lobster

Humor [hu'mor] *m* (-s;) humor

humoristisch [humɔ'rɪstɪʃ] *adj* humorous

humpeln ['humpəln] *intr* (SEIN) hobble

Hund [hunt] *m* (-[e]s;-e) dog

Hündchen ['hyntçən] *n* (-s;-) small dog; puppy

Hun'deangst *f*—**e-e H. haben** (coll) be scared stiff

Hun'dearbeit *f* drudgery

Hun'dehütte *f* doghouse

Hun'dekälte *f* severe cold

Hun′demarke *f* dog tag
hun′demü′de *adj* (coll) dog-tired
hundert [′hʊndərt] *invar adj & pron*
hundred ‖ **Hundert** *n* (-s;-e) hundred; **drei von H.** three percent; **im H.** by the hundred ‖ *f* (-;-en) hundred
hun′dertfach *adj* hundredfold
Hundertjahr′feier *f* centennial
Hun′dertsatz *m* percentage
hundertste [′hʊndərtstə] §9 *adj & pron* hundredth
Hun′deschau *f* dog show
Hun′dezwinger *m* dog kennel
Hündin [′hʏndɪn] *f* (-;-nen) bitch
hündisch [′hʏndɪʃ] *adj* (*Benehmen*) servile; (*Angst*) deadly
hunds′gemein *adj* beastly
hunds′miserabel *adj* (sl) lousy
Hunds′stern *m* Dog Star
Hunds′tage *pl* dog days
Hüne [′hynə] *m* (-n;-n) giant
hü′nenhaft *adj* gigantic
Hunger [′hʊŋər] *m* (-s;) hunger; **H. haben** be hungry
Hun′gerkur *f* starvation diet
Hun′gerlohn *m* starvation wages
hungern [′hʊŋərn] *intr* be hungry; go without food; **h. nach** yearn for ‖ *impers*—**es hungert mich** I am hungry
Hun′gersnot *f* famine
Hun′gertod *m* death from starvation
Hun′gertuch *n*—**am H. nagen** go hungry; live in poverty
hungrig [′hʊŋrɪç] *adj* hungry; (*Jahre*) lean
Hunne [′hʊnə] *m* (-n;-n) (hist) Hun
Hupe [′hupə] *f* (-;-n) (aut) horn
hupen [′hupən] *intr* blow the horn
hüpfen [′hʏpfən], **hupfen** [′hʊpfən] *intr* (SEIN) hop, jump
Hürde [′hʏrdə] *f* (-;-n) hurdle
Hure [′hurə] *f* (-;-n) whore
huren [′hurən] *intr* whore around
hurtig [′hʊrtɪç] *adj* nimble, swift
huschen [′huʃən] *intr* (SEIN) scurry
hüsteln [′hystəln] *intr* clear the throat
husten [′hustən] *tr* cough up ‖ *intr* cough; **h. auf** (*acc*) (coll) not give a rap about

Hut [hut] *m* (-[e]s;ᵘe) hat ‖ *f* (-;) protection, care; **auf der Hut sein** be on guard
hüten [′hytən] *tr* guard, protect; tend; **das Bett h.** be confined to bed; **das Haus h.** stay indoors; **Kinder h.** baby-sit ‖ *ref* (*vor dat*) be on guard (against), beware (of); **ich werde mich schön h.** (coll) I'll do no such thing
Hü′ter –in §6 *mf* guardian
Hut′krempe *f* brim of a hat
hut′los *adj* hatless
Hütte [′hytə] *f* (-;-n) hut; cabin; doghouse; glassworks; (Bib) tabernacle; (metal) foundry
Hüt′tenkunde *f*, **Hüt′tenwesen** *n* metallurgy
Hyäne [hy′ɛnə] *f* (-;-n) hyena
Hyazinthe [hya′tsɪntə] *f* (-;-n) hyacinth
Hydrant [hy′drant] *m* (-en;-en) hydrant
Hydraulik [hy′draʊlɪk] *f* (-;) hydraulics; hydraulic system
hydraulisch [hy′draʊlɪʃ] *adj* hydraulic
hydrieren [hy′drirən] *tr* hydrogenate
Hygiene [hy′gjenə] *f* (-;) hygiene
hygienisch [hy′gjenɪʃ] *adj* hygienic
Hymne [′hʏmnə] *f* (-;-n) hymn; anthem
Hyperbel [hy′pɛrbəl] *f* (-;-n) (geom) hyperbola; (rhet) hyperbole
Hypnose [hyp′nozə] *f* (-;-n) hypnosis
hypnotisch [hyp′notɪʃ] *adj* hypnotic
Hypothese [hflpo′tezə] *f* (-;-n) hypothesis
Hypochonder [hypɔ′xɔndər] *m* (-s;-) hypochondriac
Hypothek [hypɔ′tek] *f* (-;-en) mortgage
Hypothe′kengläubiger *m* mortgagee
Hypothe′kenschuldner *m* mortgagor
Hypothese [hypɔ′tezə] *f* (-;-n) hypothesis
hypothetisch [hypɔ′tetɪʃ] *adj* hypothetical
Hysterektomie [hysterektɔ′mi] *f* (-;) hysterectomy
Hysterie [hyste′ri] *f* (-;) hysteria
hysterisch [hʏs′terɪʃ] *adj* hysterical

I

I, i [i] *invar n* I, i
iah [′i′a] *interj* heehaw!
iahen [′i′a.ən] *intr* heehaw, bray
iberisch [i′berɪʃ] *adj* Iberian
ich [ɪç] §11 *pers pron* I
ichbezogen [′ɪçbətsogən] *adj* self-centered, egocentric
Ich′sucht *f* egotism
ideal [ɪde′al] *adj* ideal ‖ **Ideal** *n* (-s; -e) deal
idealisieren [ɪde.alɪ′zirən] *tr* idealize
Idealismus [ɪde.a′lɪsmʊs] *m* (-;) idealism
Idealist –in [ɪde.a′lɪst(ɪn)] §7 *mf* idealist

idealistisch [ɪde.a′lɪstɪʃ] *adj* idealistic
I-dee [ɪ′de] *f* (-;-deen* [′de.ən]) idea
Iden [′idən] *pl* Ides
identifizieren [ɪdentɪfɪ′tsirən] *tr* identify ‖ *ref*—**i. mit** identify with
identisch [ɪ′dentɪʃ] *adj* identical
Identität [ɪdentɪ′tet] *f* (-;-en) identity
Ideolo·gie [ɪde.olɔ′gi] *f* (-;-gien* [′gi.ən]) ideology
Idiom [ɪ′djom] *n* (-s;-e) idiom, dialect, language
idiomatisch [ɪdjɔ′matɪʃ] *adj* idiomatic
Idiosynkra·sie [ɪdjɔzynkra′zi] *f* (-; -sien* [′zi.ən]) idiosyncrasy
Idiot [ɪ′djot] *m* (-en;-en) idiot

Idio·tie [ɪdjɔ'ti] *f* (–;–tien ['ti·ən]) idiocy

Idiotin [ɪdjotɪn] *f* (–;–nen) idiot

Idol [ɪ'dol] *n* (–s;–e) idol

idyllisch [ɪ'dylɪʃ] *adj* idyllic

Igel ['igəl] *m* (–s;–) hedgehog

Ignorant [ɪgnɔ'rant] *m* (–en;–en) ignoramus

ignorieren [ɪgnɔ'rirən] *tr* ignore

ihm [im] §11 *pers pron* (dative of **er** and **es**) (to) him; (to) it

ihn [in] §11 *pers pron* (accusative of **er**) him

ihnen ['inən] §11 *pers pron* (dative of **sie**) (to) them || **Ihnen** §11 *pers pron* (dative of **Sie**) (to) you

ihr [ir] §2,2 *poss adj* her; their || §11 *pers pron* (dative of **sie**) (to) her || **Ihr** §2,2 *poss adj* your

ihrerseits ['irərzaɪts] *adv* on her (or their) part; **Ihrerseits** on your part

ihresgleichen ['irəs'glaɪçən] *pron* the likes of her (or them); her (or their) equal(s); **Ihresgleichen** the likes of you; your equal(s)

ihrethalben ['irət'halbən] *adv* var of ihretwegen

ihretwegen ['irət'vegen] *adv* because of her (or them); for her (or their) sake; **Ihretwegen** because of you, for your sake

ihretwillen ['irət'vɪlən] *adv* var of ihretwegen

ihrige ['irɪgə] §2,5 *poss pron* hers; theirs; **Ihrige** yours

Ikone [ɪ'konə] *f* (–;–n) icon

illegal [ɪle'gal] *adj* illegal

illegitim [ɪlegɪ'tim] *adj* illegitimate

illuminieren [ɪlumɪ'nirən] *tr* illuminate

Illusion [ɪlu'zjon] *f* (–;–en) illusion

illustrieren [ɪlus'trirən] *tr* illustrate

Illustrierte [ɪlus'trirtə] §5 *f* (illustrated) magazine

Iltis ['ɪltɪs] *m* (–ses;–se) polecat

im [ɪm] *contr* in **dem**

Image ['ɪmɪdʒ] *n* (–s;–s) (fig) image

imaginär [ɪmagɪ'ner] *adj* imaginary

Im·biß ['ɪmbɪs] *m* (–bisses;–bisse) snack

Im'bißhalle *f* luncheonette

Im'bißstube *f* snack bar

Imi·tator [ɪmɪ'tatɔr] *m* (–s;–tatoren [ta'torən] imitator; impersonator

Imker ['ɪmkər] *m* (–s;–) beekeeper

immateriell [ɪmate'rjel] *adj* immaterial, spiritual

immatrikulieren [ɪmatrɪku'lirən] *tr* & *intr* register; **sich i. lassen** get registered

immens [ɪ'mens] *adj* immense

immer ['ɪmər] *adv* always; **auf i. und ewig** for ever and ever; **für i.** for good; **i. langsam!** steady now!; **i. mehr** more and more; **i. wieder** again and again; **noch i.** still; **nur i. zu!** keep trying!; **was auch i.** whatever

immerdar' *adv* (Lit) forever

immerfort' *adv* all the time

im'mergrün' *adj* evergreen || **Immergrün** *n* (–s;–e) evergreen

immerhin' *adv* after all, anyhow

immerwäh'rend *adj* perpetual

immerzu' *adv* all the time, constantly

Immobilien [ɪmɔ'biljen] *pl* real estate

Immobi'lienmakler **–in** §6 *mf* real-estate broker

immun [ɪ'mun] *adj* (gegen) immune (to)

immunisieren [ɪmunɪ'zirən] *tr* immunize

Imperativ [ɪmpera'tif] *m* (–s;–e) (gram) imperative

Imperfek·tum [ɪmper'fektum] *n* (–s; –ta [ta]) (gram) imperfect

Imperialismus [ɪmperɪa'lɪsmus] *m* (–;) imperialism

impfen ['ɪmpfen] *tr* vaccinate; inoculate

Impfling ['ɪmpflɪŋ] *m* (–s;–e) person to be vaccinated or inoculated

Impf'schein *m* vaccination certificate

Impf'stoff *m* vaccine

Imp'fung *f* (–;–en) vaccination; inoculation

imponieren [ɪmpɔ'nirən] *intr* (dat) impress

Import [ɪm'pɔrt] *m* (–[e]s;–e) import

importieren [ɪmpɔr'tirən] *tr* import

imposant [ɪmpɔ'zant] *adj* imposing

imprägnieren [ɪmpreg'nirən] *tr* waterproof; creosote

Impresario [ɪmpre'zarjo] *m* (–s;–e) agent, business manager

Impres·sum [ɪm'presum] *n* (–s;–sen [sən]) (journ) masthead

imstande [ɪm'ʃtandə] *adv*—**i. sein zu** (*inf*) be in a position to (*inf*)

in [ɪn] *prep* (position) (dat) in, at; (direction) (acc) in, into

Inangriffnahme [ɪn'angrɪfnamə] *f* (–;) starting; putting into action

Inanspruchnahme [ɪn'an/pruxnamə] *f* (–;) laying claim; demands; utilization

In'begriff *m* essence; embodiment

in'begriffen *adj* included

Inbrunst ['ɪnbrunst] *f* (–;) ardor

inbrünstig ['ɪnbrynstɪç] *adj* ardent

indem [ɪn'dem] *conj* while, as; by (ger)

Inder –in ['ɪndər(ɪn)] §6 *mf* Indian (inhabitant of India)

indes [ɪn'des], **indessen** [ɪn'desən] *adv* meanwhile; however || *conj* while; whereas

Indianer –in [ɪn'djanər(ɪn)] §6 *mf* Indian (of North America)

Indien ['ɪndjən] *n* (–s;) India

Indio ['ɪndɪ·o] *m* (–s;–s) Indian (of Central or South America)

indisch ['ɪndɪʃ] *adj* Indian

indiskret [ɪndɪs'kret] *adj* indiscreet

indiskutabel [ɪndɪsku'tabəl] *adj* out of the question

individuell [ɪndɪvɪdu'el] *adj* individual

Individu·um [ɪndɪ'vidu·um] *n* (–s;–en [ən]) individual; (pej) character

Indizienbeweis [ɪn'ditsjənbəvaɪs] *m* (piece of) circumstantial evidence

Indossament [ɪndɔsa'ment] *n* (–[e]s; –e) indorsement

Indossant [ɪndɔ'sant] *m* (–en;–en) indorser

indossieren [ɪndɔ'sirən] *tr* indorse

industrialisieren [ɪndustrɪ·alɪ'zirən] *tr* industrialize

Indus·trie [ɪndʊs'tri] *f* (-;-**trien** ['tri-ən]) industry
Industrie'anlage *f* industrial plant
Industrie'betrieb *m* industrial establishment
Industrie'kapitän *m* tycoon
industriell [ɪndʊstrɪ'ɛl] *adj* industrial || **Industrielle** §5 *m* industrialist
ineinan'der *adv* into one another; **i. übergehen** merge
ineinan'derfügen *tr* dovetail
ineinan'dergreifen §88 *intr* mesh
ineinan'derpassen *intr* dovetail
infam [ɪn'fam] *adv* (coll) frightfully
Infante·rie [ɪnfantə'ri] *f* (-;-**rien** ['ri-ən]) infantry
Infanterist [ɪnfantə'rɪst] *m* (-en;-en) infantryman
infantil [ɪnfan'til] *adj* infantile
Infektion [ɪnfɛk'tsjon] *f* (-;-en) infection
Infini·tiv [ɪnfɪni'tif] *m* (-s;-**tive** ['tivə]) infinitive
infizieren [ɪnfi'tsirən] *tr* infect
infolge [ɪn'fɔlgə] *prep* (genit) in consequence of, owing to; according to
infolgedes'sen *adv* consequently
Information [ɪnfɔrma'tsjon] *f* (-;-en) (piece of) information
informieren [ɪnfɔr'mirən] *tr* inform
infrarot [ɪnfra'rot] *adj* infrared || **Infrarot** *n* (-s;-) infrared
Ingenieur [ɪnʒɛn'jør] *m* (-s;-e) engineer
Ingenieur'bau *m* (-[e]s;) civil engineering
Ingenieur'wesen *n* engineering
ingeniös [ɪnɡe'njøs] *adj* ingenious
Ingrimm ['ɪnɡrɪm] *m* inner rage
Ingwer ['ɪnvər] *m* (-s;) ginger
Ing'werplätzchen *n* gingersnap
Inhaber -**in** ['ɪnhabər(ɪn)] §6 *mf* owner; bearer; occupant; holder
inhaftieren [ɪnhaf'tirən] *tr* arrest
Inhalierapparat [ɪnha'liraparat] *m* (med) inhalator
inhalieren [ɪnha'lirən] *tr & intr* inhale
Inhalt ['ɪnhalt] *m* (-[e]s;-e) contents; subject matter; (geom) area; volume
In'haltsangabe *f* summary; list of contents
in'haltsarm, in'haltsleer *adj* empty
in'haltsreich *adj* substantive; (*Leben*) full
in'haltsschwer *adj* pregnant with meaning; momentous
In'haltsverzeichnis *n* table of contents
in'haltsvoll *adj* full of meaning
inhibieren [ɪnhi'birən] *tr* inhibit
Initiative [ɪnɪtsja'tivə] *f* (-;-en) initiative
Injektion [ɪnjɛk'tsjon] *f* (-;-en) injection
Injektions'nadel *f* hypodermic needle
injizieren [ɪnji'tsirən] *tr* inject
Inkasso [ɪn'kaso] *n* (-s;-s) bill collecting
Inkas'sobeamte *m* bill collector
inklusive [ɪnklu'zivə] *adj* inclusive || *prep* (genit) including
inkonsequent ['ɪnkɔnzɛkvɛnt] *adj* inconsistent; illogical
Inkraft'treten *n* going into effect

In'land *n* (-[e]s;) home country; interior
Inländer -**in** ['ɪnlɛndər(ɪn)] §6 *mf* native
inländisch ['ɪnlɛndɪʃ] *adj* home, domestic; inland
In'landspost *f* domestic mail
Inlett ['ɪnlɛt] *n* (-[e]s;-e) bedtick
in'liegend *adj* enclosed
inmit'ten *prep* (genit) in the middle of, among
innehaben ['ɪnəhabən] §89 *tr* (*Amt*) hold; (*Wohnung*) occupy, own
innehalten ['ɪnəhaltən] §90 *intr* stop
innen ['ɪnən] *adv* inside; indoors; **nach i.** inwards; **tief i.** deep down
Innen- *comb.fm.* inner, internal; inside, interior; home, domestic
In'nenarchitekt -**in** §7 *mf* interior decorator
In'nenaufnahme *f* (phot) indoor shot
In'nenhof *m* quadrangle
In'nenleben *n* inner life
In'nenminister *m* Secretary of the Interior; Secretary of State for Home Affairs (Brit)
In'nenpolitik *f* domestic policy
In'nenraum *m* interior (*of building*)
In'nenstadt *f* center of town, inner city
inner- [ɪnər] *comb.fm.* internal; intra-
innere ['ɪnərə] §9 *adj* inner, internal; inside; inward; domestic || **Innere** §5 *n* inside, interior
in'nerhalb *adv* on the inside; **i. von** within || *prep* (genit) inside, within
in'nerlich *adj* inner, inward || *adv* inwardly; mentally, emotionally
In'nerlichkeit *f* (-;-en) introspection; inner quality
innerste ['ɪnərstə] §9 *adj* innermost
innesein ['ɪnəzaɪn] §139 *intr* (SEIN) (genit) be aware of
innewerden ['ɪnəverdən] §159 *intr* (SEIN) (genit) become aware of
innig ['ɪnɪç] *adj* close; deep, heartfelt || *adv* deeply
In'nigkeit *f* (-;) intimacy; deep feeling; tender affection
Innung ['ɪnʊŋ] *f* (-;-en) guild
inoffiziell ['ɪnɔfɪtsjɛl] *adj* unofficial
ins *contr* in das
Insasse ['ɪnzasə] *m* (-n;-n), **Insassin** ['ɪnsasɪn] *f* (-;-nen) occupant; (*e-s Gefängnisses*) inmate; (*e-s Autos*) passenger
insbesondere [ɪnsbə'zɔndərə] *adv* in particular, especially
In'schrift *f* inscription
Insekt [ɪn'zɛkt] *n* (-[e]s;-en) insect
Insek'tenbekämpfungsmittel *n* insecticide
Insek'tenkunde *f* entomology
Insek'tenstich *m* insect bite
Insektizid [ɪnzɛktɪ'tsit] *n* (-[e]s;-e) insecticide
Insel ['ɪnzəl] *f* (-;-n) island
Inserat [ɪnzə'rat] *n* (-es;-e) classified advertisement, ad
inserieren [ɪnzə'rirən] *tr* insert || *intr* (in *dat*) advertise (in)
insgeheim [ɪnsɡə'haɪm] *adv* secretly
insgemein [ɪnsɡə'maɪn] *adv* as a whole; in general, generally

insgesamt [ɪnsgə'zamt] *adv* in a body, as a unit; in all, altogether

inso'fern *adv* to this extent || **insofern' conj** in so far as

insoweit' *adv & conj* var of **insofern**

Inspek·tor [ɪn'spɛktɔr] *m* (-s;-toren ['tɔrən]) inspector

inspirieren [ɪnspi'riːrən] *tr* inspire

inspizieren [ɪnspi'tsiːrən] *tr* inspect

Installation [ɪnstala'tsjoːn] *f* (-;-en) installation

installieren [ɪnsta'liːrən] *tr* install

instand [ɪn'ʃtant] *adv*—i. halten keep in good condition; i. setzen repair

Instand'haltung *f* upkeep, maintenance

instāndig [ɪn'ʃtɛndɪç] *adj* insistent

Instand'setzung *f* repair, renovation

Instanz [ɪn'ʃtants] *f* (-;-en) (adm) authority; e-e höhere I. anrufen appeal to a higher court; Gericht der ersten I. court of primary jurisdiction; Gericht der zweiten I. court of appeal; höchste I. court of final appeal

Institut [ɪnsti'tuːt] *n* (-[e]s;-e) institute

instruieren [ɪnstru'iːrən] *tr* instruct

Instruktion [ɪnstrʊk'tsjoːn] *f* (-;-en) instruction

Instrument [ɪnstru'mɛnt] *n* (-[e]s;-e) instrument

Instrumentalist –in [ɪnstrumɛnta'lɪst (ɪn)] §7 *mf* instrumentalist

Insulaner –in [ɪnzu'laːnər(ɪn)] §6 *mf* islander

insular [ɪnzu'laːr] *adj* insular

Insulin [ɪnzu'liːn] *n* (-s;) insulin

inszenieren [ɪnstse'niːrən] *tr* stage

Intellekt [ɪntɛ'lɛkt] *m* (-[e]s;) intellect

intellektuell [ɪntɛlɛktʊ'ɛl] *adj* intellectual || **Intellektuelle** §5 *mf* intellectual

intelligent [ɪntɛli'gɛnt] *adj* intelligent

Intelligenzler [ɪntɛli'gɛntslər] *m* (-s;-) (pej) egghead

Intendant [ɪntɛn'dant] *m* (-en;-en) (theat) director

intensiv [ɪntɛn'ziːf] *adj* intense; intensive

–intensiv *comb.fm.*, e.g., **lohnintensive Güter** goods of which wages constitute a high proportion of the cost

interessant [ɪntɛrɛ'sant] *adj* interesting

Interesse [ɪntɛ'rɛsə] *n* (-s;-n) (an *dat*, für) interest (in)

interes'selos *adj* uninterested

Interes'sengemeinschaft *f* community of interest; (com) syndicate

Interessent –in [ɪntɛrɛ'sɛnt(ɪn)] §7 *mf* interested party

interessieren [ɪntɛrɛ'siːrən] *tr* (für) interest (in) || *ref*—sich i. für be interested in

interimistisch [ɪntɛri'mɪstɪʃ] *adj* provisional

intern [ɪn'tɛrn] *adj* internal

Internat [ɪntɛr'naːt] *n* (-[e]s;-e) boarding school

international [ɪntɛrnatsjə'naːl] *adj* international

Internat(s)schüler –in §6 *mf*, **Interne** [ɪn'tɛrnə] §5 *mf* boarding student

internieren [ɪntɛr'niːrən] *tr* intern

Internist –in [ɪntɛr'nɪst(ɪn)] §7 *mf* (med) internist

Interpret [ɪntɛr'preːt] *m* (-en;-en) interpreter; exponent

interpunktieren [ɪntɛrpʊŋk'tiːrən] *tr* punctuate

Interpunktion [ɪntɛrpʊŋk'tsjoːn] *f* (-;-en) punctuation

Interpunktions'zeichen *n* punctuation mark

Intervall [ɪntɛr'val] *n* (-s;-e) interval

intervenieren [ɪntɛrve'niːrən] *intr* intervene

Interview ['ɪntɛrvjuː] *n* (-s;-s) interview

interviewen [ɪntɛr'vjuː-ən] *tr* interview

intim [ɪn'tiːm] *adj* intimate

Intimitāt [ɪntimi'tɛːt] *f* (-;-en) intimacy

intolerant [ɪntɔle'rant] *adj* intolerant

intonieren [ɪntɔ'niːrən] *tr* intone

intransitiv ['ɪntranzitiːf] *adj* intransitive

intravenös [ɪntrave'nøːs] *adj* intravenous

intrigant [ɪntri'gant] *adj* intriguing, scheming || **Intragant** –in §7 *mf* intriguer; schemer

Intrige [ɪn'triːgə] *f* (-;-n) intrigue

introspektiv [ɪntrɔspɛk'tiːf] *adj* introspective

Introvertierte [ɪntrɔvɛr'tirtə] §5 *mf* introvert

invalide [ɪnva'liːdə] *adj* disabled || **Invalide** §5 *mf* invalid

Invaliditāt [ɪnvalidi'tɛːt] *f* (-;) disability

Invasion [ɪnva'zjoːn] *f* (-;-en) invasion

Inventar [ɪnvɛn'taːr] *n* (-s;-e) inventory

Inventur [ɪnvɛn'tuːr] *f* (-;-en) stock taking; I. machen take stock

inwärts ['ɪnvɛrts] *adv* inwards

inwendig ['ɪnvɛndɪç] *adj* inward, inner

inwiefern' *adv* how far; in what way

inwieweit' *adv* var of **inwiefern**

In'zucht *f* inbreeding

inzwi'schen *adv* meanwhile

Ion [i'oːn] *n* (-s;-en) (phys) ion

ionisieren [i-ɔni'ziːrən] *tr* ionize

Irak [i'raːk] *m* (-s;) Iraq

Iraker –in [i'raːkər(ɪn)] §6 *mf* Iraqi

irakisch [i'raːkɪʃ] *adj* Iraqi

Iran [i'raːn] *n* (-s;) Iran

Iraner –in [i'raːnər(ɪn)] §6 *mf* Iranian

iranisch [i'raːnɪʃ] *adj* Iranian

irden ['ɪrdən] *adj* earthen

irdisch ['ɪrdɪʃ] *adj* earthly, worldly || **Irdische** §5 *n* earthly nature

Ire ['iːrə] *m* (-n;-n) Irishman; die Iren the Irish

irgend ['ɪrgɛnt] *adv*—i. etwas something, anything; i. jemand someone, anyone; nur i. possibly

ir'gendein *adj* some, any || **ingendeiner** *indef pron* someone, anyone

ir'gendeinmal *adv* at some time or other

ir'gendwann *adv* at some time or other

ir'gendwelcher *adj* any; any kind of

ir'gendwer *indef pron* someone

ir'gendwie *adv* somehow or other

ir'gendwo *adv* somewhere or other; anywhere

ir′gendwoher *adv* from somewhere or other

ir′gendwohin *adv* somewhere or other

Irin [′ɪrɪn] *f* (–;-nen) Irish woman

Iris [′ɪrɪs] *f* (–;–) (anat, bot) iris

irisch [′ɪriʃ] *adj* Irish

Irland [′ɪrlant] *n* (–s;) Ireland

Iro·nie [ɪro′ni] *f* (–;-nien [′ni-ən]) irony

ironisch [ɪ′roniʃ] *adj* ironic(al)

irre [′ɪrə] *adj* stray; confused; mad; **i. werden** go astray; get confused; **i. werden an** (*dat*) lose faith in ‖ **Irre** §5 *mf* lunatic ‖ *f* maze; wrong track; **in die I. führen** put on the wrong track; **in die I. gehen** go astray

ir′refahren §71 *intr* (SEIN) lose one's way, go wrong

ir′reführen *tr* mislead

ir′regehen §82 *intr* (SEIN) lose one's way; (fig) go wrong

ir′remachen *tr* confuse; **j-n i. an** (*dat*) make s.o. lose faith in

irren [′ɪrən] *intr* go astray; err ‖ *ref* (in *dat*) be mistaken (about); **sich in der Straße i.** take the wrong road; **sich in der Zeit i.** misjudge the time

Ir′renanstalt *f*, **Ir′renhaus** *n* insane asylum

Ir′renhäusler [′ɪrənhɔɪzlər] *m* (–s;–) inmate of an insane asylum

ir′rereden *intr* rave; talk deliriously

Irrfahrt [′ɪrfart] *f* odyssey

Irrgang [′ɪrgaŋ] *m* winding path

Irrgarten [′ɪrgartən] *m* labyrinth

Irrglaube [′ɪrglaʊbə] *m* heresy

irrgläubig [′ɪrglɔɪbɪç] *adj* heretical

irrig [′ɪrɪç] *adj* mistaken

Irri·gator [ɪrɪ′gator] *m* (–s;-gatoren [ga·torən]) douche

irritieren [ɪrɪ′tirən] *tr* irritate; (coll) confuse

Irrlehre [′ɪrlerə] *f* false doctrine

Irrlicht [′ɪrlɪçt] *n* jack-o'-lantern

Irrsinn [′ɪrzɪn] *m* insanity

irr′sinnig *adj* insane

Irrtum [′ɪrtum] *n* (–s;̈er) error

irrtümlich [′ɪrtymlɪç] *adj* erroneous

Irrweg [′ɪrvek] *m* wrong track

Irrwisch [′ɪrvɪʃ] *m* (–es;-e) jack-o'-lantern; (coll) fireball

Islam [ɪs′lam] *m* (–s;) Islam

Island [′islant] *n* (–s;) Iceland

Iso·lator [ɪzo′lator] *m* (–s;-latoren [la′torən]) (elec) insulator

Isolier– [ɪzo′lir] *comb.fm.* isolation; insulating; insulated

Isolier′band *n* (–[e]s;̈-e) friction tape

isolieren [ɪzo′lirən] *tr* (*Kranke*) isolate; (*abdichten*) insulate

Isolier′haft *f* solitary confinement

Isolier′station *f* isolation ward

Isolie′rung *f* (–;-en) isolation; (elec) insulation

Isotop [ɪzo′top] *n* (–[e]s;-e) isotope

Israel [′isra-ɛl] *n* (– & –s;) Israel

Israeli [ɪsra′eli] *m* (–s;-s) Israeli

israelisch [ɪsra′eliʃ] *adj* Israeli

Israelit –in [ɪsra-e′lit(ɪn)] §7 *mf* Israelite

israelitisch [ɪsra-e′litɪʃ] *adj* Israelite

Ist– [ɪst] *comb.fm.* actual

Ist-′Bestand *m* actual stock; (fin) actual balance; (mil) actual stockpile

Ist-′Stand *m*, **Ist-′Stärke** *f* (mil) effective strength

Italien [ɪ′taljən] *n* (–s;) Italy

Italiener –in [ɪtal′jenər(ɪn)] §6 *mf* Italian

italienisch [ɪtal′jeniʃ] *adj* Italian

J

J, j [jɔt] *invar n* J, j

ja [jɑ] *adv* yes; indeed, certainly; of course ‖ **Ja** *n* (–s;-s) yes

Jacht [jaxt] *f* (–;-en) yacht

Jacke [′jakə] *f* (–;-n) jacket, coat

Jackenkleid (**Jak′kenkleid**) *n* lady's two-piece suit

Jackett [ʒa′kɛt] *n* (–s;-s) jacket

Jagd [jakt] *f* (–;-en) hunt(ing); **auf die J. gehen** go hunting; **J. machen auf** (*acc*) hunt for

Jagd′abschirmung *f* (aer) fighter screen

Jagd′aufseher *m* gamewarden

jagdbar [′jaktbar] *adj* in season, fair (*game*)

Jagd′bomber *m* (aer) fighter-bomber

Jagd′flieger *m* fighter pilot

Jagd′flugzeug *n* (aer) fighter plane

Jagd′gehege *n* game preserve

Jagd′geleit *n* (aer) fighter escort

Jagd′hund *m* hunting dog, hound

Jagd′rennen *n* steeplechase

Jagd′revier *n* hunting ground

Jagd′schein *m* hunting license

Jagd′schutz *m* (aer) fighter protection

Jagd′verband *m* (aer) fighter unit

Jagd′wild *n* game; game bird

jagen [′jagən] *tr* hunt; pursue; chase; (fig) follow close on; **in die Luft j.** blow up ‖ *intr* go hunting; **j. nach** pursue ‖ *intr* (SEIN) rush

Jäger [′jegər] *m* (–s;–) hunter; (aer) fighter plane; (mil) rifleman

Jägerei [jega′raɪ] *f* (–;) hunting

Jä′gerlatein *n* (coll) fish story

Jaguar [′jagu-ar] *m* (–s;-s) jaguar

jäh [je] *adj* sudden; steep ‖ **Jähe** *f* (–;) suddenness; steepness

jählings [′jelɪŋs] *adv* suddenly; steeply

Jahr [jar] *n* (–[e]s;-e) year

jahraus′ adv—j. jahrein year in year out, year after year

Jahr′buch *n* almanac; yearbook; annual

jahrelang [′jarəlaŋ] *adj* long-standing ‖ *adv* for years

jähren [′jerən] *ref* be a year ago

Jahres– [jarəs] *comb.fm.* annual, yearly, of the year

Jah′resfeier *f* anniversary
Jah′resfrist *f* period of a year
Jah′resrente *f* annuity
Jah′restag *m* anniversary
Jah′reszahl *f* date, year
Jah′reszeit *f* season
jah′reszeitlich *adj* seasonal
Jahr′gang *m* age group; class, year; crop; vintage; **er gehört zu meinem J.** he was born in the same year as I
Jahrhun′dert *n* century
–jährig [jɛrɪç] *comb.fm.* –year-old
jährlich [′jɛrlɪç] *adj* yearly, annual
Jahr′markt *m* fair
Jahr′marktplatz *m* fairground
Jahrtau′send *n* millennium
Jahrzehnt [jɑr′tsɛnt] *n* (–[e]s;–e) decade
Jäh′zorn *m* fit of anger; hot temper
jäh′zornig *adj* quick-tempered
Jalou·sie [ʒalu′zi] *f* (–;–sien [′zi·ən]) louvre; Venetian blind
Jammer [′jamər] *m* (–s;) misery; wailing; **es ist ein J.,** daß it's a pity that
Jam′merlappen *m* (pej) jellyfish
jämmerlich [′jɛmərlɪç] *adj* miserable; pitiful; (*Anblick*) sorry
jammern [′jamərn] *tr* move to pity ‖ *intr* (über *acc,* um) moan (about); **j. nach** (or **um**) whimper for
Jam′merschade *adj* deplorable
Jänner [′jɛnər] *m* (–s & –;–) (Aust) January
Januar [′janu·ɑr] *m* (–s & –;–e) January
Japan [′japan] *n* (–s;) Japan
Japaner –**in** [ja′pɑnər(ɪn)] §6 *mf* Japanese
japanisch [ja′panɪʃ] *adj* Japanese
jappen [′japən] *intr* pant, gasp
Jasager [′jazagər] *m* (–s;–) yes-man
jäten [′jɛtən] *tr* weed; **das Unkraut j.** pull out weeds ‖ *intr* weed
Jauche [′jauxə] *f* (–;–n) liquid manure; (sl) slop
jauchen [′jauxən] *tr* manure
Jau′chegrube *f* cesspool
jauchzen [′jauxtsən] *intr* rejoice; **vor Freude j.** shout for joy ‖ **Jauchzen** *n* (–s;) jubilation
Jauch′zer *m* (–s;–) shout of joy
jawohl [ja′vol] *interj* yes, indeed!
Ja′wort *n* (–[e]s;) consent
Jazz [dʒɛz], [jats] *m* (–;) jazz
je [je] *adv* ever; **denn je** than ever; **je länger, je** (or **desto**) **besser** the longer the better; **je nach** according to, depending on; **je nachdem, ob** according to whether; **je Pfund** per pound; **je zwei** two each; two by two, in twos; **seit je** always
Jeans [dʒinz] *pl* jeans
jedenfalls [′jedənfals] *adv* at any rate; **ich j.** I for one
jeder [′jedər] §3 *indef adj* each, every ‖ *indef pron* each one, everyone
jederlei [′jedər′laɪ] *invar adj* every kind of
je′dermann *indef pron* everyone, everybody
je′derzeit *adv* at all times, at any time
je′desmal *adv* each time, every time
jedoch [je′dɔx] *adv* however

jeglicher [′jeklɪçər] §3 *indef adj* each, every ‖ *indef pron* each one, everyone
je′her *adv*—**von j.** since time immemorial
Jelän′gerjelie′ber *m* & *n* honeysuckle
jemals [′jemals] *adv* ever
jemand [′jemant] *indef pron* someone, somebody; anyone, anybody
jener [′jenər] §3 *dem adj* that ‖ *dem pron* that one
jenseitig [′jenzaɪtɪç] *adj* opposite, beyond, otherworldly
jenseits [′jenzaɪts] *prep* (*genit*) on the other side of; beyond ‖ **Jenseits** *n* (–s;) beyond
jetzig [′jetsɪç] *adj* present, current
jetzt [jetst] *adv* now
jeweilig [′jevaɪlɪç] *adj* at that time
jeweils [′jevaɪls] *adv* at that time
jiddisch [′jɪdɪʃ] *adj* Yiddish
Joch [jɔx] *n* (–[e]s;–e) yoke; yoke of oxen; (*e–r Brücke*) span; (*e–s Berges*) saddleback
Joch′bein *n* cheekbone
Joch′brücke *f* pile bridge
Jockei [′dʒɔki] *m* (–s;–s) jockey
Jod [jot] *n* (–s;) iodine
jodeln [′jodəln] *intr* yodel
Jodler –**in** [′jodlər(ɪn)] §6 *mf* yodeler ‖ *m* yodel
Jodtinktur [′jottɪŋktur] *f* (–;) (pharm) iodine
Johannisbeere [jo′hanɪsberə] *f* currant
johlen [′jolən] *intr* yell, boo
jonglieren [ʒɔŋ′(g)lirən] *tr* & *intr* juggle
Journalist –**in** [ʒurna′lɪst(ɪn)] §7 *mf* journalist
jovial [jo′vjal] *adj* jovial
Jubel [′jubəl] *m* (–s;) jubilation
Ju′belfeier *f,* **Ju′belfest** *n* jubilee
Ju′beljahr *n* jubilee year
jubeln [′jubəln] *intr* rejoice; shout for joy
Jubilä·um [jubɪ′le·um] *n* (–s;–en [ən]) jubilee
juche [jux′he] *interj* hurray!
juchei [jux′haɪ] *interj* hurray!
juchzen [′juxtsən] *intr* shout for joy
jucken [′jukən] *tr* itch; scratch ‖ *ref* scratch ‖ *intr* itch ‖ *impers*—**es juckt mich** I feel itchy; **es juckt mir** (or **mich**) **in den Fingern zu** (*inf*) I am itching to (*inf*); **es juckt sie in den Beinen** she is itching to dance
Jude [′judə] *m* (–n;–n) Jew
Ju′denschaft *f* (–;) Jewry
Ju′denstern *m* star of David
Judentum [′judəntum] *n* (–s;) Judaism; **das J.** the Jews
Jüdin [′jydɪn] *f* (–;–nen) Jewish woman
jüdisch [′jydɪʃ] *adj* Jewish
Jugend [′jugənt] *f* (–;) youth
Ju′gendalter *n* youth; adolescence
Ju′gendgericht *n* juvenile court
Ju′gendherberge *f* youth hostel
Ju′gendkriminalität *f* juvenile delinquency
jugendlich [′jugəntlɪç] *adj* youthful ‖ **Jugendliche** §5 *mf* youth, teenager
Ju′gendliebe *f* puppy love
Ju′gendstrich *m* youthful prank

Jugoslawien [jugo'slavjən] *n* (-s;) Yugoslavia

jugoslawisch [jugo'slavɪʃ] *adj* Yugoslav

Juli ['juli] *m* (-[s];-s) July

jung [juŋ] *adj* (jünger ['jyŋər]; jüngste ['jyŋstə] §9) young; (*Erbsen*) green; (*Wein*) new ‖ Junge §5 *m* boy ‖ *n* newly born; young

jungen ['juŋən] *intr* produce young

jun'genhaft *adj* boyish

Jünger ['jyŋər] *m* (-s;-) disciple

Jungfer ['juŋfər] *f* (-;-n) maiden; virgin

jüngeferlich ['jyŋfərlɪç] *adj* maidenly

Jung'fernfahrt *f* maiden voyage

Jung'fernhäutchen *n* hymen

Jung'fernkranz *m* bridal wreath

Jung'fernschaft *f* virginity

Jung'frau *f* virgin

jungfräulich ['juŋfrɔɪlɪç] *adj* maidenly; virgin

Jung'fräulichkeit *f* virginity

Jung'geselle *m* bachelor

Jung'gesellenstand *m* bachelorhood

Jung'gesellin *f* single girl

Jüngling ['jyŋlɪŋ] *m* (-s;-e) young man

jüngst [jyŋst] *adv* recently

jüng'ste *adj* see jung

Juni ['juni] *m* (-[s];-s) June

Junker ['juŋkər] *m* (-s;-) young nobleman; nobleman

Jura ['jura] *pl*—J. studieren study law

Jurist –in [ju'rɪst(ɪn)] §7 *mf* lawyer; (educ) law student

Juristerei [jurɪstə'raɪ] *f* (-;) jurisprudence

juristisch [ju'rɪstɪʃ] *adj* legal, law; juristische Person legal entity, corporation

just [just] *adv* just, precisely

justieren [jus'tirən] *tr* adjust

Justiz [jus'tits] *f* (-;) justice; administration of justice

Justiz'irrtum *m* miscarriage of justice

Justiz'minister *m* minister of justice; attorney general; Lord Chancellor (Brit)

Jutesack ['jutəzak] *m* gunnysack

Juwel [ju'vel] *n* (-s;-en) jewel, gem; Juwelen jewelry

Juwe'lenkästchen *n* jewel box

Juwelier –in [juve'lir(ɪn)] §6 *mf* jeweler

Juwelier'waren *pl* jewelry

Jux [juks] *m* (-es;-e) spoof, joke; aus Jux as a joke; sich [*dat*] e–n Jux mit j–m machen play a joke on s.o.

K

K, k [ka] *invar n* K, k

Kabale [ka'balə] *f* (-;-n) intrigue

Kabarett [kaba'ret] *n* (-[e]s;-e) cabaret; floor show; (*drehbare Platte*) lazy Suzan

Kabel ['kabəl] *n* (-s;-) cable

Ka'belgramm *n* (-es;-e) cablegram

Kabeljau ['kabəljau] *m* (-s;-e) codfish

kabeln ['kabəln] *tr* cable

Kabine [ka'binə] *f* (-;-n) cabin; booth; (aer) cockpit

Kabinett [kabɪ'net] *n* (-s;-e) closet; small room; (& pol) cabinet

Kabriolett [kabrɪ·o'let] *n* (-[e]s;-e) (aut) convertible

Kachel ['kaxəl] *f* (-;-n) glazed tile

kacken ['kakən] *intr* (sl) defecate

Kadaver [ka'davər] *m* (-s;-) cadaver

Kada'vergehorsam *m* blind obedience

Kadenz [ka'dents] *f* (-;-en) cadence

Kader ['kadər] *m* (-s;-) cadre

Kadett [ka'det] *m* (-en;-en) cadet

Käfer ['kefər] *m* (-s;-) beetle

Kaffee ['kafe] *m* (-s;-s) coffee

Kaf'feebohne *f* coffee bean

Kaf'feeklatsch *m* coffee klatsch

Kaf'feemaschine *f* coffee maker

Kaf'feepflanzung *f*, Kaf'feeplantage *f* coffee plantation

Kaf'feesatz *m* coffee grounds

Kaf'feetante *f* coffee fiend

Käfig ['kefɪç] *m* (-[e]s;-e) cage

kahl [kal] *adj* bald; (*Baum*) bare; (*Landschaft*) bleak, barren

kahl'köpfig *adj* bald-headed

Kahm [kam] *m* (-[e]s;-e) mold; scum

kahmig ['kamɪç] *adj* moldy; scummy

Kahn [kan] *m* (-[e]s;·e) boat; barge

Kai [kaɪ], [ke] *m* (-s;-s) quay, wharf

Kaiser ['kaɪzər] *m* (-s;-) emperor

Kaiserin ['kaɪzərɪn] *f* (-;-nen) empress

kai'serlich *adj* imperial

Kai'serreich *n*, Kaisertum ['kaɪzərtum] *n* (-[e]s;··er) empire

Kai'serschnitt *m* Caesarian operation

Kai'serzeit *f* (hist) Empire

Kajüte [ka'jytə] *f* (-;-n) (naut) cabin

Kajü'tenjunge *m* cabin boy

Kajü'tentreppe *f* (naut) companionway

Kakao [ka'ka·o] *m* (-s;) cocoa; j–n durch den K. ziehen pull s.o.'s leg

Kaktee [kak'te·ə] *f* (-;-n), Kaktus ['kaktus] *m* (-;-se) cactus

Kalauer ['kalau·ər] *m* (-s;-) pun

Kalb [kalp] *n* (-[e]s;··er) calf

Kalbe ['kalbə] *f* (-;-n) heifer

kalbern ['kalbərn] *intr* be silly

Kalb'fell *n* calfskin

Kalb'fleisch *n* veal

Kalbs'braten *m* roast veal

Kalbs'kotelett *n* veal cutlet

Kalbs'schnitzel *n* veal cutlet

Kaleidoskop [kalaɪdo'skop] *n* (-s;-e) kaleidoscope

Kalender [ka'lendər] *m* (-s;-) calendar

Kali ['kalɪ] *n* (-s;) potash

Kaliber [ka'libər] *n* (-s;-) caliber

kalibrieren [kalɪ'brirən] *tr* calibrate; gauge

Kaliko ['kalɪko] *m* (-s;-s) calico

Kalium ['kaljum] *n* (-s;) potassium

Kalk [kalk] *m* (–[e]s;-e) lime; calcium
kalken ['kalkən] *tr* whitewash; lime
kalkig ['kalkıç] *adj* limy
Kalk'ofen *m* limekiln
Kalk'stein *m* limestone
Kalk'steinbruch *m* limestone quarry
Kalkül [kal'kyl] *m & n* (–s;-e) calculation; (math) calculus
kalkulieren [kalku'lirən] *tr* calculate
Kal·mar ['kalmar] *m* (–s;-mare ['marə]) squid
Kalo·rie [kalə'ri] *f* (–;-rien ['ri·ən]) calorie
Kalotte [ka'lɔtə] *f* (–;-n) skullcap
kalt [kalt] *adj* (**kälter** ['kɛltər); **kälteste** ['kɛltəstə] §9) cold
kaltblütig ['kaltblytıç] *adj* cold-blooded
Kälte ['kɛltə] *f* (–;) cold, coldness
käl'tebeständig *adj* cold-resistant
Käl'tegrad *m* degree below freezing
kälten ['kɛltən] *tr* chill
Käl'tewelle *f* (meteor) cold wave
Kalt'front *f* cold front
kalt'herzig *adj* cold-hearted
kalt'machen *tr* (sl) bump off
kaltschnäuzig ['kalt'nɔıtsıç] *adj* (coll) callous; (coll) cool, unflappable
kalt'stellen *tr* render harmless
kam [kam] *pret* of **kommen**
Kambodscha [kam'bɔtʒa] *n* (–s;) Cambodia
kambodschanisch [kambə'dʒanıʃ] *adj* Cambodian
Kamel [ka'mel] *n* (–[e]s;-e) camel
Kamel'garn *n* mohair
Kamera ['kamera] *f* (–;-s) camera
Kamerad [kamə'rat] *m* (–en;-en), **Kameradin** [kamə'radın] *f* (–;-nen) comrade
Kamerad'schaft ((–;-en) comradeship
Kamin [ka'min] *m* (–s;-e) chimney; fireplace
Kamin'platte *f* hearthstone
Kamin'sims *m* mantelpiece
Kamm [kam] *m* (–[e]s;̈-e) comb; (e–s Gebirges) ridge; (e–r Welle) crest
kämmen ['kɛmən] *tr* comb; (Wolle) card
Kammer ['kamər] *f* (–;-n) chamber; (adm) board; (anat) ventricle
Kam'merdiener *m* valet
Kämmerer ['kɛmərər] *m* (–s;–) chamberlain; (Schatzmeister) treasurer
Kam'mermusik *f* chamber music
Kamm'garn *n* (tex) worsted
Kamm'rad *n* cogwheel
Kampagne [kam'panjə] *f* (–;-n) campaign
Kämpe ['kɛmpə] *m* (–n;-n) warrior
Kampf [kampf] *m* (–[e]s;̈-e) fight
Kampf'bahn *f* (sport) stadium, arena
kämpfen ['kɛmpfən] *tr & intr* fight
Kampfer ['kampfər] *m* (–s;) camphor
Kämpfer –in ['kɛmpfər(ın)] §6 *mf* fighter
kämpferisch ['kɛmpfərıʃ] *adj* fighting
kampf'erprobt *adj* battle-tested
kampf'fähig *adj* fit to fight; (mil) fit for active service
Kampf'hahn *m* gamecock; (fig) scrapper
Kampf'handlung *f* (mil) action

Kampf'müdigkeit *f* combat fatigue
Kampf'parole *f* (pol) campaign slogan
Kampf'platz *m* battleground
Kampf'raum *m* battle zone
Kampf'richter *m* referee, umpire
Kampf'schwimmer *m* (nav) frogman
Kampf'spiel *n* (sport) competition
Kampf'staffel *f* tactical squadron
kampf'unfähig *adj* disabled; **k. machen** put out of action
Kampf'veranstalter *m* (sport) promotor
Kampf'verband *m* combat unit
Kampf'wert *m* fighting efficiency
Kampf'ziel *n* (mil) objective
kampieren [kam'pirən] *intr* camp
Kanada ['kanada] *n* (–s;) Canada
Kanadier –in [ka'nadjər(ın)] §6 *mf* Canadian || *n* canoe
kanadisch [ka'nadıʃ] *adj* Canadian
Kanaille [ka'naljə] *f* (–;-n) bum; (Pöbel) riffraff
Kanal [ka'nal] *m* (–s;̈e) canal; (für Abwasser) drain, sewer; (agr) irrigation ditch; (anat, elec) duct; (geol, telv) channel
Kanalisation [kanalıza'tsjon] *f* (–;) drainage; sewerage system
Kanalräumer [ka'nalrɔımər] *m* (–s;-) sewer worker
Kanal'wähler *m* (telv) channel selector
Kanapee ['kanape] *n* (–s;-s) sofa
Kanarienvogel [ka'narjənfogəl] *m* canary
Kandare [kan'darə] *f* (–;-n) bit, curb; **j–n an die K. nehmen** take s.o. in hand
Kanda'renkette *f* curb chain
Kandelaber [kandə'labər] *m* (–s;-) candelabrum
Kandidat –in [kandı'dat(ın)] §7 *mf* candidate
Kandidatur [kandıda'tur] *f* (–;-en) candidacy
kandideln [kan'didəln] *ref* get drunk
kandidieren [kandı'dirən] *intr* be a candidate, run for office
Kandis ['kandıs] *m* (–;) rock candy
Kaneel [ka'nel] *m* (–s;-e) cinnamon
Känguruh ['kɛnguru] *n* (–s;-s) kangaroo
Kaninchen [ka'nınçən] *n* (–s;-) rabbit
Kanister [ka'nıstər] *m* (–s;-) canister
Kanne ['kanə] *f* (–;-n) can; pot; jug
Kannelüre [kanə'lyrə] *f* (–;-n) (archit) flute
Kannibale [kanı'balə] *m* (–n;-n), **Kannibalin** [kanı'balın] *f* (–;-nen) cannibal
kannte ['kantə] *pret* of **kennen**
Ka·non ['kanɔn] *m* (–s;-s) (Maßstab; Gebet bei der Messe) canon; (mus) round || *n* (–s;-nones ['nonəs] canon (of Canon Law)
Kanone [ka'nonə] *f* (–;-n) (arti) gun; (hist) canon; (coll) expert; **unter aller K.** indescribably bad
Kano'nenboot *n* gunboat
Kano'nenrohr *n.* gun barrel; **heiliges K.!** holy smokes!
kanonisieren [kanonı'zirən] *tr* canonize
Kante ['kantə] *f* (–;-n) edge

kanten ['kantən] *tr* set on edge; *(beim Schifahren)* cant || **Kanten** *m* (-s;-) end of a loaf, crust

Kanthaken ['kanthakən] *m* grappling hook

kantig ['kantıç] *adj* angular; squared

Kantine [kan'tinə] *f* (-;-n) canteen; (mil) post exchange

Kanton [kan'ton] *m* (-s;-e) canton

Kan·tor ['kantɔr] *m* (-s;-toren ['torən]) choir master; organist

Kanu [ka'nu] *n* (-s;-s) canoe

Kanzel ['kantsəl] *f* (-;-n) pulpit; (aer) cockpit

Kanzlei [kants'laɪ] *f* (-;-en) office; chancellery

Kanzlei′papier *n* official foolscap

Kanzlei′sprache *f* legal jargon

Kanzler ['kantslər] *m* (-s;-) chancellor

Kap [kap] *n* (-s;-s) cape, headland

Kapaun [ka'paun] *m* (-s;-e) capon

Kapazität [kapatsɪ'tɛt] *f* (-;-en) capacity; *(Könner)* authority

Kapelle [ka'pelə] *f* (-;-n) chapel; (mus) band

Kapell′meister *m* band leader; orchestra conductor

kapern ['kapərn] *tr* capture; (coll) nab

kapieren [ka'pirən] *tr* get, understand || *intr* get it; **kapiert?** got it?

kapital [kapɪ'tal] *adj* excellent || **Kapital** *n* (-s;-e & -ien [jən]) (fin) capital; **K. schlagen aus** capitalize on; **K. und Zinsen** principal and interest

Kapital′anlage *f* investment

Kapital′ertragssteuer *f* tax on unearned income

kapitalisieren [kapɪtalɪ'zirən] *tr* (fin) capitalize

Kapitalismus [kapɪta'lɪsmʊs] *m* (-s;) capitalism

Kapitalist –**in** [kapɪta'lɪst(ın)] *m* §7 capitalist

Kapital′verbrechen *n* capital offense

Kapitän [kapɪ'tɛn] *m* (-s;-e) captain, skipper; **K. zur See** (nav) captain

Kapitän′leutnant *m* (nav) lieutenant

Kapitel [ka'pɪtəl] *n* (-s;-) chapter

Kapitell [kapɪ'tel] *n* (-s;-e) (archit) capital

kapitulieren [kapɪtu'lirən] *intr* capitulate, surrender; reenlist

Kaplan [ka'plan] *m* (-s;ꞏꞏe) chaplain; (R.C.) assistant (pastor)

Kapo ['kapo] *m* (-s;-s) prisoner overseer; (mil) (coll) N.C.O.

Kappe ['kapə] *f* (-;-n) cap; hood, cover; **etw auf seine eigene K. nehmen** take the responsibility for s.th.

Käppi ['kɛpɪ] *n* (-s;-s) garrison cap

Kaprice [ka'prisə] *f* (-s;-n) caprice

Kapriole [kaprɪ'olə] *f* (-;-n) caper

kaprizieren [kaprɪ'tsirən] *ref*—**sich k. auf** *(acc)* be dead set on

kapriziös [kaprɪ'tsjøs] *adj* capricious

Kapsel ['kapsəl] *f* (-;-n) capsule; *(e-r Flasche)* cap; *(e-s Sprengkörpers)* detonator

kaputt [ka'put] *adj* (sl) broken; (sl) ruined; (sl) exhausted; (sl) dead

kaputt′gehen §82 *intr* (SEIN) get ruined

kaputt′machen *tr* ruin

Kapuze [ka'putsə] *f* (-;-n) hood; (eccl) cowl

Kapuziner [kapu'tsinər] *m* (-s;-) Capuchin

Kapuzi′nerkresse *f* Nasturtium

Karabiner [kara'binər] *m* (-s;-) carbine

Karabi′nerhaken *m* snap

Karaffe [ka'rafə] *f* (-;-n) carafe

Karambolage [karambo'laʒə] *f* (-;-n) (coll) collision

karambolieren [karambo'lirən] *intr* (coll) collide

Karamelle [kara'melə] *f* (-;-n) caramel

Karat [ka'rat] *n* (-[e]s;) carat

–**karätig** [karetıç] *comb.fm.* –*carat*

Karawane [kara'vanə] *f* (-;-n) caravan

Karbid [kar'bit] *n* (-[e]s;-e) carbide

Karbolsäure [kar'bolzɔɪrə] *f* (-;) carbolic acid

Karbon [kar'bon] *n* (-s;) (geol) carbon

Karbunkel [kar'buŋkəl] *n* (-s;-) carbuncle

Kardinal– [kardɪnal] *comb.fm.* cardinal, principal || **Kardinal** *m* (-s;ꞏꞏe) (eccl, orn) cardinal

Karenzzeit [ka'rentstsaɪt] *f* (ins) waiting period

Karfreitag [kar'fraɪtak] *m* Good Friday

karg [kark] *adj* (karger & kärger ['kergər]; kargste & kärgste ['kerstə] §9) *(ärmlich)* meager; *(Boden)* poor; *(Landschaft)* bleak

kargen ['kargən] *intr* be sparing

Karg′heit *f* (-;) bleakness; meagerness; frugality

kärglich ['kerlıç] *adj* meager, poor

kariert [ka'rirt] *adj* checked, squared

Karikatur [karɪka'tur] *f* (-;-en) caricature; cartoon

karikieren [karɪ'kirən] *tr* caricature

Karl [karl] *m* (-s;) Charles; **Karl der Große** Charlemagne

Karmeliter [karme'litər] *m* (-s;-) Carmelite Friar

Karmelitin [karme'litın] *f* (-;-nen) Carmelite nun

karmesinrot [karme'zinrot], **karminrot** [kar'minrot] *adj* crimson

Karneval ['karnəval] *m* (-s;-e & -e) carnival

Karnickel [kar'nıkəl] *n* (-s;-) (coll) rabbit; *(Sündenbock)* (coll) scapegoat; *(Einfaltspinsel)* simpleton

Karo ['karo] *n* (-s;-s) diamond; check, square; (cards) diamond(s)

Karosse [ka'rosə] *f* (-;-n) state carriage

Karosse·rie [karosə'ri] *f* (-;-rien ['ri·ən] (aut) body

Karotte [ka'rotə] *f* (-;-n) carrot

Karpfen ['karpfən] *m* (-s;-) carp

Karre ['karə] *f* (-;-n), **Karren** ['karən] *m* (-s;-) cart; wheelbarrow; **die alte K.** the old rattletrap

Karriere [ka'rjerə] *f* (-;-n) career; gallop; **K. machen** get ahead

Karte ['kartə] *f* (-;-n) card; ticket; *(Landkarte)* map; *(Speise-)* menu

Kartei [kar'taɪ] *f* (-;-en) card file

Kartei′karte *f* index card

Kartell [kar'tel] *n* (-s;-e) cartel
Kar'tenkunststück *n* card trick
Kartenlegerin ['kartənlegərın] *f* (-;
-nen) fortuneteller
Kar'tenstelle *f* ration board
Kartoffel [kar'tɔfəl] *f* (-;-n) potato
Kartof'felbrei *m* mashed potatoes
Kartoffelpuffer [kar'tɔfəlpufər] *m* (-s;
-) potato pancake
Karton [kar'tɔn] *m* (-s;-s) cardboard;
carton; (paint) cartoon
Kartonage [kartɔ'naʒə] *f* (-;-n) card-
board box
kartoniert [kartɔ'nirt] *adj* (bb) soft-
cover
Karton'papier *n* (thin) cardboard
Kartothek [kartɔ'tek] *f* (-;-en) card
index; card filing system
Kartothek'ausgabe *f* loose-leaf edition
Karussell [karu'sel] *n* (-s;-e) merry-
go-round
Karwoche ['karvɔxə] *f* Holy Week
Karzer ['kartsər] *m* (-s;-) (educ) detention room; **K. bekommen** get a
detention
Kaschmir ['ka/mɪr] *m* (-s;-e) cashmere
Käse ['kezə] *m* (-s;-) cheese; (sl)
baloney
Kaserne [ka'zernə] *f* (-;-n) barracks
käsig ['kezıç] *adj* cheesy; (Gesichtsfarbe) pasty
Kasino [ka'zino] *n* (-s;-s) casino;
(mil) officer's mess
Kas'pisches Meer' ['kaspı/əs] *n* Cas-
pian Sea
Kassa ['kasa] *f*—**per K.** in cash
Kassa- *comb.fm.* cash, spot
Kasse ['kasə] *f* (-;-n) money box; till;
cash register; cashiers desk; (Bar-
geld) cash; (adm) finance depart-
ment; (educ) bursars office; (sport)
ticket window; (theat) box office;
gegen (or **per**) **K.** cash, for cash;
gut bei K. sein (coll) be flush
Kas'senabschluß *m* balancing of ac-
counts
Kas'senbeamte *m* cashier; teller
Kas'senbeleg *m* sales slip
Kas'senbestand *m* cash on hand
Kas'senerfolg *m* (theat) hit
Kas'senführer **-in** §6 *mf* cashier; teller
Kas'senschalter *m* teller's window
Kas'senschrank *m* safe
Kas'senzettel *m* sales slip
Kasserolle [kasə'rɔlə] *f* (-s;-n) casse-
role
Kassette [ka'setə] *f* (-;-n) base, box;
(cin, phot) cassette
kassieren [ka'sirən] *tr* (Geld) take in;
get; (Urteil) annul; (coll) confiscate;
(coll) arrest; (mil) break
Kassie'rer **-in** §6 *mf* cashier; teller
Kastagnette [kastan'jetə] *f* (-;-n)
castanet
Kastanie [kas'tanjə] *f* (-;-n) chestnut
Kästchen ['kestçən] *n* (-s;-) case, box
Kaste ['kastə] *f* (-;-n) caste
kasteien [kas'taı-ən] *tr & ref* mortify;
sein Leib k. mortify the flesh
Kastell [kas'tel] *n* (-s;-e) small fort
Kasten ['kastən] *m* (-s; & -) chest,
case, box; cupboard, cabinet; (Auto)

(coll) crate; (Boot) (coll) tub; (Gefängnis) (coll) jug
Ka'stengeist *m* snobbishness
Ka'stenwagen *m* (aut) panel truck; (rr)
boxcar
Ka'stenwesen *n* caste system
Kastrat [kas'trat] *m* (-en;-en) eunuch
kastrieren [kas'trirən] *tr* castrate
Katakomben [kata'kɔmbən] *pl* cata-
combs
Katalog [kata'lok] *m* (-[e]s;-e) catalogue
katalogisieren [katalɔgi'zirən] *tr* catalogue
Katapult [kata'pult] *m & n* (-[e]s;-e)
catapult
katapultieren [katapul'tirən] *tr* catapult
Katarakt [kata'rakt] *m* (-[e]s;-e) cataract, rapids; (pathol) cataract
Katasteramt [ka'tastəramt] *n* land-
registry office
katastrophal [katastrɔ'fal] *adj* cata-
strophic, disastrous
Katastrophe [kata'strofə] *f* (-;-n)
catastrophe, disaster
Katastro'phengebiet *m* disaster area
Kategorie [kategɔ'ri] *f* (-;-rien
['ri-ən] category
kategorisch [kate'gori/] *adj* categori-
cal
Kater ['katər] *m* (-s;-) tomcat; (coll)
hangover
Katheder [ka'tedər] *n & m* (-s;-)
teacher's desk
Kathe'derblüte *f* teacher's blunder
Kathedrale [kate'dralə] *f* (-;-n) cathe-
dral
Kathode [ka'todə] *f* (-;-n) cathode
Katholik **-in** [katɔ'lik(ın)] §7 *mf*
Catholic
katholisch [ka'toli/] *adj* Catholic
Kattun [ka'tun] *m* (-s;-e) calico
Kätzchen ['ketsçən] *n* (-s;-) kitten
Katze ['katsə] *f* (-;-n) cat; **für die K.**
(coll) for the birds
kat'zenartig *adj* cat-like, feline
Kat'zenauge *n* reflector
Kat'zenbuckel *m* cat's arched back;
vor j-m K. machen lick s.o.'s boots
kat'zenfreundlich *adj* overfriendly
Kat'zenjammer *m* hangover; blues
Kat'zenkopf *m* (coll) cobblestone;
(box) rabbit punch
Kat'zensprung *m* stone's throw
Kauderwelsch ['kaudərvel/] *n* (-es;)
gibberish
kauen ['kau-ən] *tr* chew
kauern ['kau-ərn] *ref & intr* cower
Kauf [kauf] *m* (-[e]s;-e) purchase;
in K. nehmen (fig) take, put up with;
leichten Kaufes davonkommen get
off cheaply; **zum K. stehen** be for
sale
Kauf'auftrag *m* (com) order
kaufen ['kaufən] *tr* purchase, buy
Käufer **-in** ['kɔıfər(ın)] §6 *mf* buyer
Kauf'haus *n* department store
Kauf'kraft *f* purchasing power
käuflich ['kɔıflıç] *adj* for sale; (bestechlich) open to bribes
Kauf'mann *m* (-[e]s;-leute) businessman; salesman

kaufmännisch ['kaufmenɪʃ] *adj* commercial, business
Kauf'mannsdeutsch *n* business German
Kauf'zwang *m* obligation to buy
Kaugummi ['kaugumɪ] *m* chewing gum
kaukasisch [kau'kazɪʃ] *adj* Caucasian
Kaulquappe ['kaulkvapə] *f* (-;-n) tadpole, polliwog
kaum [kaum] *adv* hardly, scarcely
Kautabak ['kautabak] *m* chewing tobacco
Kaution [kau'tsjon] *f* (-;-en) (jur) bond; (*Bürgschaft*) (jur) bail; **gegen K.** on bail
Kautschuk ['kautʃuk] *m* (-s;-e) rubber
Kauz [kauts] *m* (-es;-e) owl; (sl) crackpot
Kavalier [kava'lir] *m* (-s;-e) cavalier; gentleman; beau
Kavalkade [kaval'kadə] *f* (-;-n) cavalcade
Kavalle·rie [kavalə'ri] *f* (-;-rien ['ri·ən]) cavalry
Kavallerist [kavalə'rɪst] *m* (-en;-en) cavalryman, trooper
Kaviar ['kavjar] *m* (-[e]s;-e) caviar
keck [kek] *adj* bold; impudent; cheeky
Kegel ['kegəl] *m* (-s;-) tenpin; (geom) cone; **K. schieben** bowl
Ke'gelbahn *f* bowling alley
kegeln ['kegəln] *intr* bowl
Keg'ler –in §6 *mf* bowler
Kehle ['kelə] *f* (-;-n) throat
kehlig ['kelɪç] *adj* throaty
Kehlkopf ['kelkɔpf] *m* larynx
Kehl'kopfentzündung *f* laryngitis
Kehre ['kerə] *f* (-;-n) turn, bend
kehren ['kerən] *tr* sweep; (*wenden*) turn; **alles zum besten k.** make the best of it; **j-m den Rücken k.** turn one's back on s.o. || *ref* turn; **in sich gekehrt sein** be lost in thought; **sich an nichts k.** not care about anything; **sich k. an** (*acc*) heed || *intr* sweep
Kehricht ['kerɪçt] *m & n* (-[e]s;) sweepings; trash, rubbish
Keh'richteimer *m* trash can
Keh'richtschaufel *f* dustpan
Kehr'maschine *f* street cleaner
Kehr'reim *m* refrain, chorus
Kehr'seite *f* reverse; (fig) seamy side
kehrtmachen ['kertmaxən] *intr* turn around; (mil) about-face
Kehrt'wendung *f* about-face
keifen ['kaifən] *intr* nag
Keiferei [kaifə'rai] *f* (-;-en) nagging; squabble
Keil [kail] *m* (-[e]s;-e) wedge
keilen ['kailən] *tr* wedge; (coll) recruit || *recip* scrap
Keilerei [kailə'rai] *f* (-;-en) scrap
keil'förmig *adj* wedge-shaped; tapered
Keil'hammer *m* sledgehammer
Keil'hose *f* tapered trousers
Keil'schrift *f* cuneiform writing
Keim [kaim] *m* (-[e]s;-e) germ; embryo; (fig) seeds; (bot) bud, sprout; **im K. ersticken** nip in the bud; **im K. vorhanden** at an embryonic stage; **Keime treiben** germinate
keimen ['kaimən] *intr* germinate;

sprout || **Keimen** *n*—**zum K. bringen** cause to germinate
keim'frei *adj* germ-free, sterile
Keimling ['kaimlɪŋ] *m* (-s;-e) embryo; sprout; seedling
keintötend ['kaimtøtənt] *adj* germicidal; antiseptic, sterilizing
Keim'zelle *f* germ cell, sex cell
kein [kain] §2,1 *adj* no, not any
keiner ['kainər] §2,4 *indef pron* none; no one, nobody, not one; **k. von beiden** neither of them
keinerlei ['kainər'lai] *invar adj* no... of any kind, no...whatsoever
keineswegs ['kainəs'veks] *adv* by no means, not at all
Keks [keks] *m & n* (-es;-e) biscuit, cracker; cookie
Kelch [kelç] *m* (-[e]s;-e) cup; (bot) calyx; (eccl) chalice
Kelch'blatt *n* (bot) sepal
Kelle ['kelə] *f* (-;-n) ladle; (hort, mas) trowel
Keller ['kelər] *m* (-s;-) cellar
Kel'lergeschoß *n* basement
Kel'lergewölbe *n* underground vault
Kellner ['kelnər] *m* (-s;-) waiter
Kellnerin ['kelnərɪn] *f* (-;-nen) waitress
Kelte ['keltə] *m* (-n;-n) Celt
Kelter ['keltər] *f* (-;-n) wine press
keltern ['keltərn] *tr* press
Keltin ['keltɪn] *f* (-;-nen) Celt
keltisch ['keltɪʃ] *adj* Celtic
kennbar ['kenbar] *adj* recognizable
kennen ['kenən] §97 *tr* be acquainted with, know
ken'nenlernen *tr* get to know, meet
Ken'ner –in §6 *mf* expert
Ken'nerblick *m* knowing glance
Ken'ner –in §6 *mf* expert
Kennkarte ['kenkartə] *f* identity card
kenntlich ['kentlɪç] *adj* identifiable, recognizable; conspicuous
Kenntnis ['kentnɪs] *f* (-;-se) knowledge; **gute Kenntnisse haben in** (*dat*) be well versed in; **j–n von etw in K. setzen** apprise s.o. of s.th.; **Kenntnisse** knowledge; skills; know-how; **oberflächliche Kenntnisse** a smattering; **von etw K. nehmen** take note of s.th.; **zur K. nehmen** take note of s.th.
Kennwort ['kenvɔrt] *n* (-[e]s;-er) code word; (mil) password
Kennzeichen ['kentsaiçən] *n* distinguishing mark; hallmark; criterion; (aer) marking; (aut) license number
kennzeichnen ['kentsaiçnən] *tr* characterize; identify; brand
Kennziffer ['kentsɪfər] *f* code number
kentern ['kentərn] *intr* (SEIN) capsize
Keramik [ke'ramɪk] *f* (-;) ceramics; pottery
keramisch [ke'ramɪʃ] *adj* ceramic
Kerbe ['kerbə] *f* (-;-n) notch, groove
kerben ['kerbən] *tr* notch, nick; make a groove in; serrate
Kerbholz ['kerphɔlts] *n*—**etw auf dem K. haben** have a crime chalked up against one
Kerbtier ['kerptir] *n* insect
Kerker ['kerkər] *m* (-s;-) jail

Kerl [kɛrl] *m* (-s; -e) fellow, guy; (*Mädchen*) lass

Kern [kɛrn] *m* (-[e]s; -e) `kernel; (*im Obst*) pit, stone, pip; hard core; (*e-s Problems*) crux; (phys) nucleus

Kern- *comb.fm.* core; central, basic; through and through; (phys) nuclear

Kern'aufbau *m* nuclear structure

kern'deutsch' *adj* German through and through

Kern'energie *f* nuclear energy

Kern'fächer *pl* core curriculum

kern'gesund' *adj* perfectly sound

Kern'holz *n* heartwood

kernig ['kɛrnɪç] *adj* full of seeds; robust, vigorous

kern'los *adj* seedless

Kern'physik *f* nuclear physics

Kern'punkt *m* gist, crux; focal point

Kern'schußweite *f* —**auf K.** at point-blank range

Kern'spaltung *f* nuclear fission

Kern'truppen *pl* crack troops

Kern'verschmelzung *f* nuclear fusion

Kern'waffe *f* nuclear weapon

Kerosin [kero'zin] *n* (-s;) kerosene

Kerze ['kɛrtsə] *f* (-;-n) candle; (aut) plug

ker'zengera'de *adj* straight as an arrow ‖ *adv* bolt upright

Kessel ['kɛsəl] *m* (-s;-) kettle; cauldron; boiler; (geog) basin-shaped valley; (mil) pocket

Kes'selpauke *f* kettledrum

Kes'selraum *m* boiler room

Kes'selschmied *m* boilermaker

Kes'selwagen *m* (aut) tank truck; (rr) tank car

Kette ['kɛtə] *f* (-;-n) chain; (*e-s Panzers*) track

ketten ['kɛtən] *intr* (**an** *acc*) chain (to)

Ket'tengeschäft *n* chain store

Ket'tenglied *n* chain link

Ket'tenhund *m* watch dog

Ket'tenrad *n* sprocket

Ket'tenraucher –**in** §6 *mf* chain smoker

Ket'tenstich *m* chain stitch, lock stitch

Ketzer –**in** ['kɛtsər(ɪn)] §6 *mf* heretic

Ketzerei [kɛtsə'raɪ] *f* (-;-en) heresy

ketzerisch ['kɛtsərɪʃ] *adj* heretical

keuchen ['kɔɪçən] *intr* pant, gasp

Keuch'husten *m* (-s;) whooping cough

Keule ['kɔɪlə] *f* (-;-n) club; (culin) leg, drumstick

keusch [kɔɪʃ] *adj* chaste

Keusch'heit *f* (-;) chastity

KG *abbr* (**Kommanditgesellschaft**) Ltd.

Khaki ['kɑki] *m* (-;) (tex) khaki

kichern ['kɪçərn] *intr* giggle

kicken ['kɪkən] *tr* (fb) kick

Kicker ['kɪkər] *m* (-s;-) soccer player

Kiebitz ['kibɪts] *m* (-[e]s;-e) (orn) lapwing; (*Zugucker*) kibitzer

kiebitzen ['kibɪtsən] *intr* kibitz

Kiefer ['kifər] *m* (-s;-) jaw(bone) ‖ *f* (-;-n) pine; **gemeine K.** Scotch pine

Kiel [kil] *m* (-[e]s;-e) (*Feder*) quill; (naut) keel

Kiel'raum *m* hold

Kiel'wasser *n* wake

Kieme ['kimə] *f* (-;-n) gill

Kien ['kin] *m* (-[e]s;-e) pine cone

Kien'span *m* pine torch

Kiepe ['kipə] *f* (-;-n) basket (*carried on one's back*)

Kies [kis] *m* (-es;-e) gravel

Kiesel ['kizəl] *m* (-s;-) pebble

Kilo ['kilo] *n* (-s;-s & -) kilogram

Kilogramm [kɪlo'gram] *n* (-s;-e & -) kilogram

Kilometer [kɪlo'metər] *m & n* (-s;-) kilometer

Kilome'terfresser *m* (coll) speedster

Kilowatt [kɪlo'vat] *n* (-s;-) kilowatt

Kimm [kɪm] *m* (-es;-e) horizon ‖ *f* (-;-e) (naut) bilge

Kimme ['kɪmə] *f* (-;-n) notch; groove; (*e–s Gewehrs*) sight

Kind [kɪnt] *n* (-[e]s;-er) child; baby

Kinder- [kɪndər] *comb.fm.* child's, children's

Kin'derarzt *m*, **Kin'derärztin** *f* pediatrician

Kinderei [kɪndə'raɪ] *f* (-;-en) childish behavior, childish prank

Kin'derfrau *f* nursemaid

Kin'derfräulein *n* governess

Kin'derfürsorge *f* child welfare

Kin'dergarten *m* nursery school, play-school

Kin'dergärtnerin *f* nursery school attendant

Kin'dergeld *n* see **Kinderzulage**

Kin'derheilkunde *f* pediatrics

Kin'derheim *n* children's home

Kin'derhort *m* day nursery

Kin'derlähmung *f* polio

kin'derleicht *adj* easy as pie

Kin'derlied *n* nursery rhyme

kin'derlos *adj* childless

Kin'dermädchen *n* nursemaid

Kin'derpuder *m* baby powder

Kin'derreim *m* nursery rhyme

Kin'derschreck *m* bogeyman

Kin'dersportwagen *m* stroller

Kin'derstube *f* nursery; (*Erziehung*) upbringing

Kin'derstuhl *m* highchair

Kin'derwagen *m* baby carriage

Kin'derzulage *f* family allowance (*paid by the employer*)

Kin'desalter *n* childhood; infancy

Kin'desannahme *f* adoption

Kin'desbeine *pl*—**von Kindesbeinen an** from childhood on

Kin'desentführer –**in** §6 *mf* kidnaper

Kin'desentführung *f*, **Kin'desraub** *m* kidnaping

Kind'heit *f* (-;) childhood

kindisch ['kɪndɪʃ] *adj* childish

kindlich ['kɪntlɪç] *adj* childlike

Kinetik [kɪ'netɪk] *f* (-;) kinetics

kinetisch [kɪ'netɪʃ] *adj* kinetic

Kinkerlitzchen ['kɪŋkərlɪtsçən] *pl* trifles; gimmicks

Kinn [kɪn] *n* (-[e]s;-e) chin

Kinn'backen *m* jawbone

Kinn'haken *m* (box) uppercut

Kinn'kette *f* curb chain

Kino ['kino] *n* (-s;-s) movie theater

Ki'nobesucher –**in** §6 *mf* moviegoer

Ki'nokamera *f* movie camera

Ki'nokasse *f* box office

Kiosk ['kɪʊsk] *m* (-[e]s;-e) stand

Kipfel ['kɪpfəl] *n* (-s;-) (Aust) (culin) crescent roll

Kippe [ˈkɪpə] *f* (-;-n) edge; (*Zigarettenstummel*) butt; **auf der K. stehen** stand on edge; (fig) be touch and go

kippen [ˈkɪpən] *tr* tilt, tip over; dump || *intr* (SEIN) tilt; overturn

Kipper [ˈkɪpər] *m* (-s;-) dump truck

Kirche [ˈkɪrçə] *f* (-;-n) church

Kirchen– [kɪrçən] *comb.fm.* church, ecclesiastical

Kir′chenbann *m* excommunication; **in den K. tun** excommunicate

Kir′chenbau *m* (-[e]s;) building of churches || *m* (-[e]s;-ten) church

Kir′chenbesuch *m* church attendance

Kir′chenbuch *n* parish register

Kir′chendiener *m* sacristan, sexton

Kir′chengut *n* church property

Kir′chenlied *n* hymn

Kir′chenschändung *f* desecration of a church

Kir′chenschiff *n* (archit) nave

Kir′chenspaltung *f* schism

Kir′chenstaat *m* Papal States

Kir′chenstuhl *m* pew

Kir′chentag *m* Church congress

Kirchgang [ˈkɪrçgaŋ] *m* going to church

Kirch′gänger –in §6 *mf* church-goer

Kirch′hof *m* churchyard

kirch′lich *adj* church, ecclesiastical

Kirch′spiel *n* parish

Kirch′turm *m* steeple

Kirch′turmpolitik *f* (pej) parochialism

Kirch′turmspitze *f* spire

Kirchweih [ˈkɪrçvaɪ] *f* (-;-en) church picnic

Kirch′weihe *f* dedication of a church

Kirch′weihfest *n* church picnic

Kirsch [kɪrʃ] *m* (-es;-) cherry brandy

Kirsche [ˈkɪrʃə] *f* (-;-n) cherry

Kirsch′wasser *n* cherry brandy

Kissen [ˈkɪsən] *n* (-s;-) cushion, pillow; (*Polster*) pad

Kis′senbezug *m* pillowcase

Kiste [ˈkɪstə] *f* (-;-n) box, crate, case; (aer) crate; (aut) rattletrap; (naut) tub

Kitsch [kɪtʃ] *m* (-es;) kitsch

kitschig [ˈkɪtʃɪç] *adj* trashy; mawkish

Kitt [kɪt] *m* (-[e]s;-e) putty; cement; **der ganze Kitt** the whole caboodle

Kittchen [ˈkɪtçən] *n* (-s;-) (coll) jail

Kittel [ˈkɪtəl] *m* (-s;-) smock, coat; (Aust) skirt

Kit′telkleid *n* house dress

kitten [ˈkɪtən] *tr* putty; cement; glue; (fig) patch up

Kitzel [ˈkɪtsəl] *m* (-s;) tickle; (fig) itch

kitzeln [ˈkɪtsəln] *tr* tickle

kitzlig [ˈkɪtslɪç] *adj* ticklish

Kladderadatsch [kladəraˈdatʃ] *m* (-es;) crash, bang; mess, muddle

klaffen [ˈklafən] *intr* gape, yawn

kläffen [ˈklɛfən] *intr* yelp

Klafter [ˈklaftər] *f* (-; & -n), *m* & *n* (-s;-) fathom; (*Holz*–) cord

klagbar [ˈklakbar] *adj* (jur) actionable

Klage [ˈklagə] *f* (-;-n) complaint; (jur) (civil) suit

Kla′gelied *n* dirge, threnody

klagen [ˈklagən] *tr*—**j-m seinen Kummer k.** pour out one's troubles to s.o.

|| *intr* complain; **auf Scheidung k.** sue for divorce; **k. über** (*acc*) complain about; **k. um** lament

Kläger –in [ˈklegər(ɪn)] §6 *mf* (jur) plaintiff

Kla′geweib *n* hired mourner

kläglich [ˈkleklɪç] *adj* plaintive, pitiful; (*Zustand*) sorry; (*Ergebnis, Ende*) miserable

klaglos [ˈklaklos] *adv* uncomplainingly

klamm [klam] *adj* (*erstarrt*) numb; (*feuchtkalt*) clammy; **k. an Geld** (coll) short of dough || **Klamm** *f* (-;-en) gorge

Klammer [ˈklamər] *f* (-;-n) clamp; clip; paper clip; (*Schließe*) clasp; clothespin; hair clip, bobby pin; **eckige K.** bracket; **runde K.** parenthesis

klammern [ˈklamərn] *tr* clamp; clasp || *ref*—**sich k. an** (*acc*) cling to

Klamotte [klaˈmɔtə] *f* (-;-n)—**alte K.** oldy; (aer, aut) old crate; **Klamotten** things, clothes

Klampfe [ˈklampfə] *f* (-;-n) guitar

klang [klaŋ] *pret* of **klingen** || **Klang** *m* (-[e]s;ᵘe) tone, sound

Klang′farbe *f* timbre

klang′getreu *adj* high-fidelity

Klang′regler *m* (rad) tone-control knob

Klang′taste *f* tone-control push button

klang′voll *adj* sonorous

Klappe [ˈklapə] *f* (-;-n) flap; (*Mund*) (sl) trap; (anat, mach) valve; **in die K. gehen** (sl) hit the sack

klappen [ˈklapən] *tr* flip || *intr* flap, fold || *impers*—**es klappt** (coll) it clicks, it turns out well

Klapper [ˈklapər] *f* (-;-n) rattle

klap′perdürr *adj* skinny

Klap′pergestell *n* (coll) beanpole; (*Kiste*) (coll) rattletrap

klappern [ˈklapərn] *intr* rattle, clatter; (*Zähne*) chatter

Klap′perschlange *f* rattlesnake

Klap′perstorch *m* stork

Klappflügel [ˈklapflygəl] *m* (aer) folding wing (*of carrier plane*)

Klappmesser [ˈklapmesər] *n* jackknife

klapprig [ˈklaprɪç] *adj* rickety

Klappstuhl [ˈklap/tul] *m* folding chair

Klapptisch [ˈklapti/] *m* drop-leaf table

Klapptür [ˈklaptyr] *f* trap door

Klaps [klaps] *m* (-es;-e) smack, slap; **e-n K. kriegen** (sl) go nuts

klapsen [ˈklapsən] *tr* smack, slap

Klaps′mühle *f* (coll) booby hatch

klar [klar] *adj* clear; **klar zum Start** ready for take-off

Kläranlage [ˈkleranlagə] *f* sewage-disposal plant

klären [ˈklerən] *tr* clear; (*Mißverständnis*) clear up || *ref* become clear

Klar′heit *f* (-;) clearness, clarity

Klarinette [klariˈnetə] *f* (-;-n) clarinet

klar′legen, klar′stellen *tr* clear up

Klärung [ˈkleruŋ] *f* (-;) clarification

Klasse [ˈklasə] *f* (-;-n) class; (educ) grade, class

Klas′senarbeit *f* test

Klas′senaufsatz *m* composition (*written in class*)

klas′senbewußt *adj* class-conscious

Klas'seneinteilung f classification

Klas'senkamerad –in §7 mf classmate

Klas'sentreffen n (–s;–) class reunion

klassifizieren [klasɪfi'tsirən] tr classify

Klassifizie'rung f (–;-en) classification

–klassig [klasɪç] comb.fm. –class, –grade

Klassik ['klasɪk] f (–;) classical antiquity, classical period

Klas'siker –in §6 mf classical author

klassisch ['klasɪʃ] adj classic(al)

Klatsch [klatʃ] m (–es;) clap; gossip

Klatsch'base f gossipmonger; tattletale

Klatsch'blatt n scandal sheet

Klatsche ['klatʃə] f (–;-n) fly swatter; tattletale; (educ) pony

klatschen ['klatʃən] tr smack, slap; **dem Lehrer etw k.** tattletale to the teacher about s.th.; **j–m Beifall k.** applaud s.o. || intr clap; (Regen) patter; (fig) gossip; **in die Hände (or mit den Händen) k.** clap the hands

Klatscherei [klatʃə'raɪ] f (–;-en) gossip

klatsch'naß' adj soaking wet

Klatsch'spalte f gossip column

klauben ['klaubən] tr pick

Klaue ['klau-ə] f (–;-n) claw, talon; (Spalthuf) hoof; (coll) scrawl

klauen ['klau-ən] tr (coll) snitch

Klause ['klauzə] f (–;-n) hermitage; (Schlucht) defile; (coll) den, pad

Klausel ['klauzəl] f (–;-n) clause; (Abmachung) stipulation

Klausner ['klausnər] m (–s;–) hermit

Klausur [klau'zur] f (–;-en) seclusion; (educ) final examination

Klausur'arbeit f final examination

Klaviatur [klavja'tur] f (–;-en) keyboard

Klavier [kla'vir] n (–[e]s;-e) piano

Klavier'auszug m piano score

Klebemittel ['klebəmɪtəl] n (–s;–) adhesive, glue

kleben ['klebən] tr & intr stick

Kleberolle ['klebərələ] f roll of gummed tape

Klebestreifen ['klebə'traɪfən] m adhesive tape; Scotch tape (trademark)

Klebezettel ['klebətsetəl] m label, sticker

klebrig ['klebrɪç] adj sticky

Klebstoff ['kleptof] m adhesive

Klecks [kleks] m (–es;-e) stain; dab

klecksen ['kleksən] tr splash || intr make blotches

Kleckser –in ['kleksər(ɪn)] §6 mf scribbler; dauber

Klee [kle] m (–s;) clover

Klee'blatt n cloverleaf; (fig) trio

Kleid [klaɪt] n (–[e]s;-er) garment; dress; robe; **Kleider** clothes

kleiden ['klaɪdən] tr dress; **j–n gut k.** look good on s.o.

Klei'derablage f cloakroom; (Kleiderständer) clothes rack

Klei'derbestand m wardrobe

Klei'derbügel m coat hanger

Klei'dersack m (mil) duffle bag

Klei'derschrank m clothes closet

Klei'derständer m clothes rack

kleidsam ['klaɪtzam] adj well-fitting, becoming

Klei'dung f (–;) clothing

Kleie ['klaɪ-ə] f (–;-n) bran

klein [klaɪn] adj small, little; short; **ein k. wenig** a little bit || **Kleine** §5 m little boy || f little girl || n little one

Klein'anzeigen pl classified ads

Klein'arbeit f detailed work

Klein'asien n Asia Minor

Klein'bahn f narrow-gauge railroad

Klein'bauer m small farmer

Klein'betrieb m small business

Kleinbild– comb.fm. (phot) 35mm

klein'bürgerlich adj lower middle-class

Klein'geld n change

klein'gläubig adj of little faith

Klein'handel m retail business

Klein'händler –in §6 mf retailer

Klein'hirn n (anat) cerebellum

Klein'holz n kindling; **K. aus j–m machen** (coll) beat s.o. to a pulp

Klein'igkeit f small object; trifle, minor detail; small matter

Klei'nigkeitskrämer m fusspot

kleinkalibrig ['klaɪnkalibrɪç] adj small-bore

Klein'kind n infant

Klein'kinderbewahranstalt f day care center

Klein'kram m odds and ends; details

klein'laut adj subdued

klein'lich adj stingy; (Betrag) paltry; (engstirnig) narrow-minded, pedantic

Klein'mut m despondency; faint-heartedness

klein'mütig adj despondent; faint-hearted

Klei'nod ['klaɪnot] n (–[e]s;-node & –nodien ['nodjən] jewel, gem

klein'schneiden §106 tr chop up

Klein'schreibmaschine f portable typewriter

Kleister ['klaɪstər] m (–s;–) paste

Klemme ['klemə] f (–;-n) clamp, clip; (coll) tight spot, fix; (elec) terminal; (surg) clamp

klemmen ['klemən] tr tuck, put; (stehlen) pinch, swipe || ref—**sich** [dat] **den Finger k.** smash one's finger; **sich hinter die Arbeit k.** get down to business; **sich k. hinter** (acc) get after || intr be stuck

Klempner ['klempnər] m (–s;–) tinsmith; plumber

Klempnerei [klempnə'raɪ] f (–;) plumbing

Kleptomane [klepto'manə] §5 mf kleptomaniac

klerikal [kleri'kal] adj clerical

Kleriker ['klerikər] m (–s;–) clergyman, priest

Klerus ['klerus] m (–;) clergy

Klette ['kletə] f (–;-n) (bot) burr; (coll) pain in the neck

Klet'tergarten m training area (for mountain climbing)

klettern ['kletərn] intr (SEIN) climb

Klet'terpflanze f (bot) creeper

Klet'terrose f rambler

Klet'tertour f climbing expedition

Klient [kli'ent] m (–en;-en) client

Klientel [kli-en'tel] f (–;-en) clientele (of a lawyer)

Klientin [klɪˈɛntɪn] *f* (-;-nen) client

Klima [ˈklima] *n* (-s;-s) climate

Kli'maanlage *f* air conditioner

kli'magerecht *adj* air-conditioned

klimatisch [kliˈmatɪʃ] *adj* climatic

klimatisieren [klimatɪˈziːrən] *tr* air-condition

Klimatisie'rung *f* (-;) air conditioning

Klimbim [klɪmˈbɪm] *m* (-s;) (coll) junk; (coll) racket; (coll) fuss

klimmen [ˈklɪmən] §164 *intr* (SEIN) climb

klimpern [ˈklɪmpərn] *intr* jingle; *(auf der Gitarre)* strum; **mit den Wimpern k.** flutter one's eyelashes

Klinge [ˈklɪŋə] *f* (-;-n) blade; sword, saber; **über die K. springen lassen** put to the sword

Klingel [ˈklɪŋəl] *f* (-;-n) bell

Klin'gelbeutel *m* collection basket

Klin'gelknopf *m* doorbell button

klingeln [ˈklɪŋəln] *intr* ring, tinkle; *(Vers, Reim)* jingle || *impers*—es **klingelt** the doorbell is ringing; there goes the (school) bell; the phone is ringing

kling'klang *interj* ding-dong!

Klinik [ˈkliːnɪk] *f* (-;-en) teaching hospital *(of a university)*; private hospital; nursing home

klinisch [ˈkliːnɪʃ] *adj* clinical; hospital

Klinke [ˈklɪŋkə] *f* (-;-n) door handle; (telp) jack; **Klinken putzen** beg or peddle from door to door

Klippe [ˈklɪpə] *f* (-;-n) rock, reef

klirren [ˈklɪrən] *intr* rattle, clang; *(Gläser)* clink; *(Waffen)* clash

Klischee [klɪˈʃeː] *n* (-s;-s) cliché

Klistier [klɪsˈtiːr] *n* (-s;-e) enema

klistieren [klɪsˈtiːrən] *tr* give an enema to

klitschig [ˈklɪtʃɪç] *adj* doughy

Klo [klo] *n* (-s;-s) (coll) john

Kloake [kloˈaːkə] *f* (-;-n) sewer

Kloben [ˈkloːbən] *m* (-s;-) pulley; *(Holz)* block; *(Schraubenstock)* vise

klobig [ˈkloːbɪç] *adj* clumsy; bulky

klomm [klɔm] *pret of* **klimmen**

klopfen [ˈklɔpfən] *tr (Nagel)* drive; *(Teppich)* beat; *(Fleisch)* pound || *intr* knock; *(Herz)* beat, pound; *(Motor)* ping; **j-m auf die Schulter k.** pat s.o. on the back || *impers*—es **klopft** s.o. is knocking

klopffest [ˈklɔpffɛst] *adj* antiknock

Klöppel [ˈklœpəl] *m* (-s;-) bobbin; *(e-r Glocke)* clapper; (mus) mallet

klöppeln [ˈklœpəln] *tr* make *(lace)* with bobbins

Klops [klɔps] *m* (-es;-e) meatball

Klosett [kloˈzɛt] *n* (-s;-e & -s) (flush) toilet

Klosett'becken *n* toilet bowl

Klosett'brille *f* toilet seat

Klosett'deckel *m* toilet-seat lid

Klosett'papier *n* toilet paper

Kloß [kloːs] *m* (-es;ːe) dumpling; **e-n K. im Hals haben** have a lump in one's throat

Kloster [ˈkloːstər] *n* (-s;ː) monastery; convent

Kloster- *comb.fm.* monastic

Klo'sterbruder *m* lay brother, friar

Klo'sterfrau *f* nun

klösterlich [ˈkløːstərlɪç] *adj* monastic

Klotz [klɔts] *m* (-es;ːe) block; toy building block; (coll) blockhead; **ein K. am Bein** (coll) a drag; **wie ein K. schlafen** sleep like a log

klotzig [ˈklɔtsɪç] *adj* clumsy; uncouth || *adv*—**k. reich** filthy rich

Klub [klup] *m* (-s;-s) club

Klub'jacke *f* blazer

Klub'sessel *m* easy chair

Kluft [kluft] *f* (-;ːe) gorge, ravine; (fig) gulf; (poet) chasm || *f* (-;-en) outfit, uniform

klug [kluk] *adj* (klüger [ˈklyːgər]; klügste [ˈklyːkstə] §9) clever, bright; wise; **aus Schaden k. werden** learn the hard way; **nicht k. werden können aus** be unable to figure out

klügeln [ˈklyːgəln] *intr* quibble

Klug'heit *f* (-;) cleverness; intelligence; wisdom

klüglich [ˈklyːklɪç] *adv* wisely

Klug'redner *m* wise guy, know-it-all

Klumpen [ˈklumpən] *m* (-s;-) lump, clod; *(Haufen)* heap; (min) nugget

Klumpfuß [ˈklumpfuːs] *m* clubfoot

klumpig [ˈklumpɪç] *adj* lumpy

Klüngel [ˈklyːŋəl] *m* (-s;-) clique

knabbern [ˈknabərn] *intr* nibble

Knabe [ˈknaːbə] *m* (-n;-n) boy

Kna'benalter *n* boyhood

kna'benhaft *adj* boyish

knack [knak] *interj* crack!; snap!; click!

knacken [ˈknakən] *tr* crack || *intr* crack; *(Schloß)* click; *(Feuer)* crackle

Knacks [knaks] *m* (-es;-e) crack; snap; click; **e-n K. kriegen** get a crack; **e-n K. weg haben** be badly hit; **sich [dat] e-n K. holen** suffer a blow

Knack'wurst *f* pork sausage; smoked sausage

Knall [knal] *m* (-[e]s;-e) crack, bang; **K. und Fall** on the spot, at once

Knallblättchen [ˈknalblɛtçən] *n* (-s;-) cap *(for a toy pistol)*

Knall'bonbon *m & n* noise maker

Knall'büchse *f* popgun

Knall'dämpfer *m* silencer

Knall'effekt *m* big surprise

knall'rot *adj* fiery red

knapp [knap] *adj* (eng) close, tight; *(Mehrheit)* bare; *(Zeit)* short; *(Stil)* concise; **k. werden** run short, run low

Knappe [ˈknapə] *m* (-n;-n) (hist) squire; (min) miner

Knapp'heit *f* (-;) closeness, tightness; shortage; conciseness

Knapp'schaft *f* (-;-en) miner's union

Knapp'schaftskasse *f* miner's insurance

knarren [ˈknarən] *intr* creek

Knaster [ˈknastər] *m* (-s;-) tobacco

knattern [ˈknatərn] *intr* crackle; *(Maschinengewehr)* rattle || *intr* (SEIN) put-put along

Knäuel [ˈknɔɪəl] *m & n* (-s;-) *(Garn-)* ball; *(Menschen-)* throng

Knauf [knauf] *m* (-[e]s;ːe) knob

Knauser **-in** [ˈknauzər(ɪn)] §6 *mf* tightwad

Knauserei [knauzə'raɪ] *f* (-;) stinginess

knauserig ['knauzərɪç] *adj* stingy

knausern ['knauzərn] *intr* be stingy

knautschen ['knaut/ən] *tr* crumple || *intr* crumple; (coll) wimper

Knebel ['knebəl] *m* (-s;-) gag

Kne'belbart *m* handlebar moustache

knebeln ['knebəln] *tr* gag; (fig) muzzle

Kne'belpresse *f* tourniquet

Kne'belung *f*—K. der Presse muzzling of the press

Knecht [knɛçt] *m* (-[e]s;-e) servant; farmhand; serf; slave

knechten ['knɛçtən] *tr* enslave; oppress

knechtisch ['knɛçtɪ/] *adj* servile

Knecht'schaft *f* (-;) servitude

kneifen ['knaɪfən] §88 & §109 *tr* pinch || §88 *intr* (*Kleid*) be too tight; back out, back down; (fencing) retreat; k. vor (*dat*) shirk, dodge

Kneifzange ['knaɪftsaŋə] *f* (pair of) pincers

Kneipe ['knaɪpə] *f* (-;-n) saloon

kneipen ['knaɪpən] *intr* (coll) booze

Knei'penwirt *m* saloon keeper

Kneiperei [knaɪpə'raɪ] *f* (-;-en) drinking bout

kneten ['knetən] *tr* knead; massage

Knick [knɪk] *m* (-[e]s;-e) bend; (*Bruch*) break; (*Falte*) fold, crease

knicken ['knɪkən] *tr* bend; break; fold; (*Hoffnungen*) dash || *intr* (SEIN) snap

Knicker ['knɪkər] *m* (-s;-) tightwad

Knicks [knɪks] *m* (-es;-e) curtsy

knicksen ['knɪksən] *intr* curtsy

Knie [kni] *n* (-s;- ['kni·ə]) knee

Knie'beuge *f* knee bend

Knie'beugung *f* genuflection

knie'fällig *adj* on one's knees

knie'frei *adj* above-the-knee

Knie'freiheit *f* legroom

Knie'kehle *f* hollow of the knee

knien ['kni·ən] *intr* kneel

Knie'scheibe *f* kneecap

Knie'schützer *m* (sport) kneepad

kniff [knɪf] *pret* of kneifen || **Kniff** *m* (-[e]s;-e) crease, fold; (*Kunstgriff*) knack

kniff(e)lig ['knɪf(ə)lɪç] *adj* tricky

kniffen ['knɪfən] *tr* crease, fold

Knigge ['knɪgə] *m* (-s) (fig) Emily Post

knipsen ['knɪpsən] *tr* (*Karte*) punch; (phot) snap || *intr* snap a picture; mit den Fingern k. snap one's fingers

Knirps [knɪrps] *m* (-es;-e) (coll) shrimp

knirschen ['knɪr/ən] *intr* crunch; mit den Zähnen k. gnash one's teeth

knistern ['knɪstərn] *intr* crackle; (*Seide*) rustle

knitterfest ['knɪtərfɛst] *adj* wrinkleproof

knittern ['knɪtərn] *tr* wrinkle; crumple

knobeln ['knobəln] *intr* play dice; an e-m Problem k. puzzle over a problem

Knoblauch ['knoblaux] *m* (-[e]s;) garlic

Knöchel ['knœçəl] *m* (-s;-) knuckle, joint; ankle

Knochen ['knɔxən] *m* (-s;-) bone

Kno'chenbruch *m* fracture

Kno'chengerüst *n* skeleton

Kno'chenmark *n* marrow

Kno'chenmühle *f* (coll) sweat shop

knöchern ['knœçərn] *adj* bone; bony

knochig ['knɔxɪç] *adj* bony

Knödel ['knødəl] *m* (-s;-) dumpling; e-n K. im Hals haben have a lump in one's throat

Knolle ['knɔlə] *f* (coll) bulbous nose; (bot) tuber

Knollen ['knɔlən] *m* (-s;-) lump; (coll) bulbous nose

knollig ['knɔlɪç] *adj* bulbous

Knopf [knɔpf] *m* (-[e]s;⁻e) button; knob; (e-r *Stechnadel*) head; alter K. old fogey

knöpfen ['knœpfən] *tr* button

Knopf'loch *n* buttonhole

knorke ['knɔrkə] *adj* (coll) super

Knorpel ['knɔrpəl] *m* (-s;-) cartilage

Knorren ['knɔrən] *m* (-s;-) knot, gnarl

knorrig ['knɔrɪç] *adj* gnarled, knotty

Knospe ['knɔspə] *f* (-;-n) bud

knospen ['knɔspən] *intr* bud

knoten ['knotən] *tr & intr* knot || **Knoten** *m* (-s;-) knot; (*Schwierigkeit*) snag; (*Haarfrisur*) chignon; (*Seemeile*) knot; (astr, med, phys) node; (theat) plot

Kno'tenpunkt *m* intersection, interchange; (rr) junction

knotig ['knotɪç] *adj* knotty

Knuff [knuf] *m* (-[e]s;⁻e) (coll) poke

knuffen ['knufən] *tr* (coll) poke

knüllen ['knylən] *tr* crumple

Knüller ['knylər] *m* (-s;-) (coll) hit

knüpfen ['knypfən] *tr* tie, knot; (*Teppich*) weave; (*Bündnis*) form; (befestigen) fasten; k. an (acc) tie in with || *ref*—sich k. an (acc) be tied in with

Knüppel ['knypəl] *m* (-s;-) cudgel; (e-s Polizisten) blackjack; (aer) control stick

knurren ['knurən] *intr* growl, snarl; (Magen) rumble; (fig) grumble

knurrig ['knurɪç] *adj* grumpy

knusprig ['knusprɪç] *adj* crisp; (Mädchen) attractive

Knute ['knutə] *f* (-;-n) whip; (Gewalt) power; (Gewaltherrschaft) tyranny

knutschen ['knut/ən] *tr, recip & intr* (coll) neck, pet

Knüttel ['knytəl] *m* (-s;-) cudgel

Knüt'telvers *m* doggerel

k.o. ['ka'o] *adj* knocked out || *adv*—k.o. schlagen knock out || **K.O.** *m* (-[s];-s) knockout

Koalition [ko·alɪ'tsjon] *f* (-;-en) coalition

Kobalt ['kobalt] *n* (-es;) cobalt

Koben ['kobən] *m* (-s;-) pigsty

Kobold ['kobɔlt] *m* (-[e]s;-e) goblin

Kobolz [ko'bɔlts] *m*—e-n K. schießen do a somersault

Koch [kɔx] *m* (-[e]s;⁻e) cook

Koch'buch *n* cookbook

kochen ['kɔxən] *tr & intr* cook; boil

Kocher ['kɔxər] *m* (-s;-) cooker; boiler

Köcher [ˈkœçər] m (-s;-) quiver; golf bag

Koch′fett n shortening

Koch′geschirr n (mil) mess kit

Koch′herd m kitchen range

Köchin [ˈkœçɪn] f (-;-nen) cook

Koch′löffel m wooden spoon

Koch′salz n table salt

Köder [ˈkøːdər] m (-s;-) bait; lure

ködern [ˈkøːdərn] tr bait; lure

Kodex [ˈkoːdɛks] m (-es;-e) codex; (jur) code

kodifizieren [kodɪfɪˈtsiːrən] tr codify

Koffein [kɔfeˈiːn] n (-s;) caffeine

Koffer [ˈkɔfər] m (-s;-) suitcase; trunk; case (for portable items)

Kof′ferfernseher m portable television

Kof′fergerät n (rad, telv) portable set

Kof′ferraum m (aut) trunk

Kof′ferschreibmaschine f portable typewriter

Kognak [ˈkɔnjak] m (-s;-s) cognac

Kohl [koːl] m (-s;) cabbage; nonsense

Kohle [ˈkoːlə] f (-;-n) coal; (Holzkohle) charcoal

Kohlehydrat [ˈkoːləhydrat] n (-[e]s; -e) carbohydrate

kohlen [ˈkoːlən] tr & intr carbonize

Koh′lenbergbau m coal mining

Koh′lenbergwerk n coal mine

Koh′lendioxyd n carbon dioxide

Koh′lenoxyd n carbon monoxide

Koh′lenrevier n coal field

Koh′lensäure f carbonic acid

Koh′lenstoff m carbon

Koh′lenwagen m coal truck; (rr) coal car

Koh′lepapier n carbon paper

Koh′leskizze f charcoal sketch

kohl′ra′benschwarz′ adj jet black

Koitus [ˈkoːɪtus] m (-;-) coitus

Koje [ˈkoːjə] f (-;-n) bunk, berth

Kojote [koˈjoːtə] m (-;-n) coyote

Kokain [kokaˈiːn] n (-s;) cocaine

Kokerei [kokəˈraɪ] f (-;-en) coking plant

kokett [koˈkɛt] adj flirtatious || **Kokette** f (-;-n) flirt

kokettieren [kokɛˈtiːrən] intr flirt

Kokon [koˈkõ] m (-s;-s) cocoon

Kokosnuß [ˈkokosnus] f coconut

Kokospalme [ˈkokospalmə] f coconut palm, coconut tree

Koks [koks] m (-es;-e) coke; (coll) nonsense; (Geld) (coll) dough

Kolben [ˈkɔlbən] m (-s;-) butt; (Keule) mace; (Löt-) soldering iron; (aut) piston; (chem) flask; (culin) cob; (elec) bulb

Kol′benhub m piston stroke

Kol′benring m piston ring

Kol′benstange f piston rod

Kolchose [kɔlˈçoːzə] f (-;-n) collective farm

Kolibri [ˈkoːlɪbrɪ] m (-s;-s) humming bird

Kolik [ˈkoːlɪk] f (-;-en) colic

Kolkrabe [ˈkɔlkraːbə] m (-n;-n) raven

Kollaborateur [kɔlabɔraˈtøːr] m (-s;-) collaborator (with the enemy)

kollaborieren [kɔlabɔˈriːrən] intr collaborate

Kollaps [kɔˈlaps] m (-es;-e) collapse

kollationieren [kɔlatsjoˈniːrən] tr collate

Kol·leg [kɔˈlek] n (-s;-s & -legien [ˈleːgjən]) lecture; course of lectures; theological college

Kollege [kɔˈleːgə] m (-n;-n) colleague

Kolleg′heft n lecture notes

Kollegin [kɔˈleːgɪn] f (-;-nen) colleague

Kollekte [kɔˈlɛktə] f (-;-n) collection; (eccl) collect

Kollektion [kɔlɛkˈtsjoːn] f (-;-en) collection

kollektiv [kɔlɛkˈtiːf] adj collective || **Kollektiv** n (-s;-e) collective

Koller [ˈkɔlər] m (-s;) rage, temper

kollern [ˈkɔlərn] ref roll about; (vor Lachen) double over || intr (Puter) gobble; (Magen) rumble || intr (SEIN) roll

kollidieren [kɔlɪˈdiːrən] intr (SEIN) collide

Kollier [kɔˈliːr] n (-s;-s) necklace

Kollision [kɔlɪˈzjoːn] f (-;-en) collision

Köln [kœln] n (-s;) Cologne

Kölnischwasser [ˈkœlnɪʃˈvasər] n cologne

kolonial [koloˈnjaːl] adj colonial

Kolonial′waren pl groceries

Kolonial′warengeschäft n grocery store

Kolo·nie [koloˈniː] f (-;-nien [ˈniːən]) colony

Kolonnade [kɔlɔˈnaːdə] f (-;-n) colonnade

Kolonne [koˈlɔnə] f (-;-n) column; (mil) convoy (of vehicles)

kolorieren [koloˈriːrən] tr color

Kolorit [koloˈriːt] n (-[e]s;-e) coloring

Ko·loß [koˈlɔs] m (-losses;-losse) colossus; giant

kolossal [koloˈsaːl] adj colossal

Kolportage [kɔlpɔrˈtaːʒə] f (-;-n) trashy literature; spreading of rumors

kolportieren [kɔlpɔrˈtiːrən] tr peddle; (Gerüchte) spread

Kolumnist -in [kolumˈnɪst(ɪn)] §7 mf columnist

Kombi [ˈkɔmbi] m (-s;-s) (coll) station wagon

Kombination [kɔmbinaˈtsjoːn] f (-; -en) combination; (Flieger-) flying suit; (e-s Monteurs) coveralls; sport suit; reasoning, deduction; conjecture

kombinieren [kɔmbiˈniːrən] tr combine || intr reason

Kom′biwagen m station wagon

Kombüse [kɔmˈbyːzə] f (-;-n) (naut) galley, kitchen

Komik [ˈkoːmɪk] f (-;) humor

Komiker [ˈkoːmɪkər] m (-s;-) comedian

Komikerin [ˈkoːmɪkərɪn] f (-;-nen) comedienne

komisch [ˈkoːmɪʃ] adj funny

Komitee [komiˈteː] n (-s;-s) committee

Komma [ˈkoma] n (-s;-s) comma; (Dezimalzeichen) decimal point

Kommandant [komanˈdant] m (-en; -en) commanding officer; commandant

Kommandantur [kɔmandan'tur] *f* (–;
-en) headquarters
Kommandeur [kɔman'dør] *m* (–s;-e)
commanding officer, commander
kommandieren [kɔman'dirən] *tr* command, order; be in command of;
(mil) detail; (mil) detach ‖ *intr* command, be in command
Kommanditgesellschaft [kɔman'ditgə-
zel/aft] *f* limited partnership; **K. auf
Aktien** partnership limited by shares
Kommando [kɔ'mando] *n* (–s;-s) command, order; (mil) command; (mil)
detachment, detail; **K. zurück!** as
you were!
Komman'dobrücke *f* (nav) bridge
Komman'doraum *m* control room
Komman'dostab *m* baton
Komman'dostand *m*, **Komman'dostelle**
f command post; (nav) bridge
Komman'dotruppe *f* commando unit
Komman'doturm *m* conning tower;
control tower (*of an aircraft carrier*)
kommen ['kɔmən] §99 *intr* (SEIN)
come; (*geschehen*) happen; **auf etw**
[*acc*] **k.** hit on s.th.; **auf jeden k. drei
Mark** each one gets three marks; **das
kommt bloß daher, daß** that's entirely due to; **dazu k.** get around to
it; get hold of it; **hinter etw** [*acc*] **k.**
find s.th. out; **j–m grob k.** be rude
to s.o.; **k. lassen** send for; **nichts k.
lassen auf** (*acc*) defend; **so weit k.,
daß** reach the point where; **ums
Leben k.** lose one's life; **wenn Sie
mir so k.** if you talk like that to me;
weit k. get far; **wieder zu sich k.**
come to, regain consciousness; **wie
kam er denn dazu?** how come he did
it? **wie komme ich zum Bahnhof?**
how do I get to the train station?
Kommentar [kɔmen'tar] *m* (–s;-e)
commentary; **kein K.!** no comment!
Kommen·tator [kɔmen'tator] *m* (–s;
-tatoren [ta'torən]) commentator
kommentieren [kɔmen'tirən] *tr* comment on
Kommers [kɔ'mers] *m* (–es;-e) drinking party
Kommers'buch *n* students' song book
kommerziell [kɔmer'tsjel] *adj* commercial
Kommilitone [kɔmili'tonə] *m* (–n;-n)
fellow student
Kom·mis [kɔ'mi] *m* (–mis ['mis];
–mis ['mis]) clerk
Kom·miß [kɔ'mis] *m* (–misses;) (coll)
army; (coll) army life
Kommissar [kɔmi'sar] *m* (–s;-e) commissioner; (pol) commissar
kommissarisch [kɔmi'sari/] *adj* provisional, temporary
Kommission [kɔmi'sjon] *f* (–;-en)
commission, board; **in K.** (com) on
consignment; on a commission basis
Kommissionär [kɔmisjo'ner] *m* (–s;-e)
agent; wholesale bookseller
Kommissions'gebühr *f* (com) commission
kommissions'weise *adv* on a commission basis
Kommiß'stiefel *m* army boot
kommod [kɔ'mot] *adj* comfortable

Kommode [kɔ'modə] *f* (–;-n) bureau,
chest of drawers
kommunal [kɔmu'nal] *adj* municipal,
local
Kommunal'politik *f* local politics
Kommune [kɔ'munə] *f* (–;-n) municipality; **die K.** the Commies
Kommunikant –in [kɔmuni'kant(in)]
§7 *mf* communicant
Kommunion [kɔmu'njon] *f* (–;-en)
Communion
Kommuniqué [kɔmyni'ke] *n* (–s;-s)
communiqué
Kommunismus [kɔmu'nismus] *m* (–;)
communism
Kommunist –in [kɔmu'nist(in)] §7 *mf*
communist
kommunistisch [kɔmu'nisti/] *adj* communist(ic)
Komödiant [kɔmø'djant] *m* (–en;-en)
comedian; (pej) ham
Komödie [kɔ'mødjə] *f* (–;-n) comedy;
K. spielen (coll) put on an act
Kompagnon [kɔmpan'jõ] *m* (–s;-s)
(business) partner; associate
kompakt [kɔm'pakt] *adj* compact
Kompa·nie [kɔmpa'ni] *f* (–;-nien
['ni-ən]) company
Kompanie'chef *m* company commander
komparativ [kɔmpara'tif] *adj* comparative ‖ **Komparativ** *m* (–s;-e)
comparative
Komparse [kɔm'parzə] *m* (–n;-n)
(theat) extra
Kom·paß ['kɔmpas] *m* (–passes;
–passe) compass
Kompen·dium [kɔm'pendjum] *n* (–s;
–dien [djən]) compendium
Kompensation [kɔmpenza'tsjon] *f* (–;
-en) compensation
Kompensations'geschäft *n* fair-value
exchange
kompensieren [kɔmpen'zirən] *tr* compensate for, offset
Kompetenz [kɔmpe'tents] *f* (–;-en)
(jur) jurisdiction
komplementär [kɔmplemen'ter] *adj*
complementary
Komplet [kɔ̃'ple] *n* (–s;-s) dress with
matching coat
komplett [kɔm'plet] *adj* complete;
everything included
komplex [kɔm'pleks] *adj* complex ‖
Komplex *m* (–es;-e) complex
Komplice [kɔm'plitsə] *m* (–n;-n) accomplice
komplizieren [kɔmpli'tsirən] *tr* complicate
Komplott [kɔm'plɔt] *n* (–[e]s;-e) plot
Komponente [kɔmpo'nentə] *f* (–;-n)
component
komponieren [kɔmpo'nirən] *tr* compose
Komponist –in [kɔmpo'nist(in)] §7 *mf*
composer
Komposition [kɔmpozi'tsjon] *f* (–;-en)
composition
Komposi·tum [kɔm'pozitum] *n* (–s;
–ta [ta] & –ten [tən]) compound
(word)
Kompott [kɔm'pɔt] *n* (–[e]s;-e) stewed fruit

Kompres·sor [kɔm'prɛsər] *m* (-s; -soren ['sorən]) compressor; (aut) supercharger

komprimieren [kɔmprɪ'mirən] *tr* compress

Kompro·miß [kɔmpro'mɪs] *m* (-misses; -misse) compromise

kompromittieren [kɔmprɔmɪ'tirən] *tr* compromise

kondensieren [kɔndɛn'zirən] *tr*, *ref* & *intr* (SEIN) condense

Kondensmilch [kɔn'dɛnsmɪlç] *f* evaporated milk

Kondens′streifen [kɔn'dɛns/traɪfən] *m* contrail

Konditorei [kɔndɪtə'raɪ] *f* (-;-en) pastry shop

Konfekt [kɔn'fɛkt] *n* (-[e]s;) candy, chocolates; fancy cookies

Konfektion [kɔnfɛk'tsjon] *f* (-;) ready-made clothes; manufacture of ready-made clothes

Konfektionär [kɔnfɛktsjo'nɛr] *m* (-s; -e) clothing manufacturer; clothing retailer

konfektionieren [kɔnfɛktsjo'nirən] *tr* manufacture (*clothes*)

Konferenz [kɔnfe'rɛnts] *f* (-;-en) conference

konferieren [kɔnfe'rirən] *intr* confer, hold a conference

Konfession [kɔnfe'sjon] *f* (-;-en) religious denomination; (eccl) confession; confession of faith, creed

konfessionell [kɔnfɛsjo'nɛl] *adj* denominational

konfessions′los *adj* nondenominational

Konfessions′schule *f* denominational school, parochial school

konfirmieren [kɔnfɪr'mirən] *tr* (eccl) (Prot) confirm

konfiszieren [kɔnfɪs'tsirən] *tr* confiscate

Konfitüre [kɔnfɪ'tyrə] *f* (-;-n) jam

Konflikt [kɔn'flɪkt] *m* (-[e]s;-e) conflict

konform [kɔn'fɔrm] *adj* concurring; **mit j-m k. gehen** agree with s.o.

Konfrontation [kɔnfrɔnta'tsjon] *f* (-; -en) confrontation

konfrontieren [kɔnfrɔn'tirən] *tr* confront

konfus [kɔn'fus] *adj* confused, puzzled

Kongruenz [kɔngru'ɛnts] *f* (-;) (geom) congruence; (gram) agreement

König ['kønɪç] *m* (-[e]s;-e) king

Königin ['kønɪgɪn] *f* (-;-nen) queen

kö′niglich *adj* kingly, royal

Kö′nigreich *n* kingdom

Kö′nigsadler *m* golden eagle

Kö′nigsrose *f* (bot) peony

Kö′nigsschlange *f* boa constrictor

kö′nigstreu *adj* royalist

Kö′nigswürde *f* kingship

Königtum ['kønɪçtum] *n* (-s;) royalty, kinship; monarchy

konisch ['konɪʃ] *adj* conical

konjugieren [kɔnju'girən] *tr* conjugate

Konjunktion [kɔnjuŋk'tsjon] *f* (-;-en) conjunction

Konjunktiv [kɔnjuŋk'tif] *m* (-s;-e) subjunctive mood

Konjunktur [kɔnjuŋk'tur] *f* (-;-en)

economic situation; business trend; (*Hochstand*) boom

konkav [kɔn'kaf] *adj* concave

konkret [kɔn'kret] *adj* concrete

Konkurrent –in [kɔnku'rent(ɪn)] §7 *mf* competitor

Konkurrenz [kɔnku'rents] *f* (-;-en) competition; **K. machen** (*dat*) compete with

konkurrenz′fähig *adj* competitive

konkurrieren [kɔnku'rirən] *intr* compete

Konkurs [kɔn'kurs] *m* (-es;-e) bankruptcy; **in K. gehen** (or **geraten**) go bankrupt; **K. anmelden** declare bankruptcy

Konkurs′masse *f* bankrupt company's assets

können ['kœnən] §100 *tr* able to do; know; **ich kann nichts dafür** I can't help it || *intr*—**ich kann nicht hinein** I can't get in || *mod aux* be able to; know how to; be allowed; **das kann sein** that may be; **ich kann nicht sehen** I can't see || **Können** *n* (-s;) ability

Könner ['kœnər] *m* (-s;-) expert

konnte ['kɔntə] *pret* of **können**

konsequent [kɔnze'kvent] *adj* consistent

Konsequenz [kɔnze'kvents] *f* (-;-en) consistency; (*Folge*) consequence

konservativ [kɔnzerva'tif] *adj* conservative

Konservato·rium [kɔnzerva'torjum] *n* (-s;-rien [rjən]) conservatory

Konserve [kɔn'zervə] *f* (-;-n) canned food

Konser′venbüchse *f*, **Konser′vendose** *f* can

Konser′venfabrik *f* cannery

Konser′venöffner *m* can opener

konservieren [kɔnzer'virən] *tr* preserve

Konservie′rung *f* (-;) preservation

Konsisto·rium [kɔnzɪs'torjum] *n* (-s; -rien [rjən]) (eccl) consistory

Konsole [kɔn'zolə] *f* (-;-n) bracket; (archit) console

konsolidieren [kɔnzɔlɪ'dirən] *tr* consolidate

Konsonant [kɔnzo'nant] *m* (-en;-en) consonant

Konsorte [kɔn'zɔrtə] *m* (-n;-n) (pej) accomplice; (fin) member of a syndicate

Konsor·tium [kɔn'zɔrtjum] *n* (-s;-tien [tjən]) (fin) syndicate

konstant [kɔn'stant] *adj* constant || **Konstante** §5 *f* (math, phys) constant

konstatieren [kɔnsta'tirən] *tr* ascertain; state; (med) diagnose

konsterniert [kɔnster'nirt] *adj* stunned

konstituieren [kɔnstɪtu'irən] *tr* constitute || *ref* be established; **sich als Ausschuß k.** form a committee of the whole

konstitutionell [kɔnstɪtutsjo'nɛl] *adj* constitutional

konstruieren [kɔnstru'irən] *tr* construct; (*entwerfen*) design; (gram) construe

Konsul ['kɔnzul] *m* (-s;-n) consul

konsularisch [kɔnzu'larɪʃ] *adj* consular

Konsulat [kɔnzu'lɑt] *n* (-[e]s;-e) consulate; (hist) consulship

Konsulent –**in** [kɔnzu'lent(ɪn)] §7 *mf* (jur) counsel

konsultieren [kɔnzul'tirən] *tr* consult

Konsum [kɔn'zum] *m* (-s;-s) cooperative store; (com) consumption

Konsument –**in** [kɔnzu'ment(ɪn)] §7 *mf* consumer

Konsum′güter *pl* consumer goods

konsumieren [kɔnzu'mirən] *tr* consume

Konsum′verein *m* cooperative society

Kontakt [kɔn'takt] *m* (-[e]s;-e) contact

Kontakt′glas *n*, **Kontakt′schale** *f* contact lens

Konteradmiral ['kɔntəratmɪral] *m* rear admiral

Konterfei [kɔntər'faɪ] *n* (-s;-e) portrait, likeness

kontern ['kɔntərn] *tr* counter

Kontinent ['kɔntinɛnt] *m* (-[e]s;-e) continent

Kontingent [kɔntɪŋ'gɛnt] *n* (-[e]s;-e) quota; (mil) contingent

Kon·to ['kɔnto] *n* (-s;-s & -ten [tən]) account

Kon′toauszug *m* bank statement

Kontor [kɔn'tor] *n* (-s;-e) (com) office

Kontorist –**in** [kɔntə'rɪst(ɪn)] §7 *mf* clerk (*in an office*)

Kontrahent [kɔntra'hɛnt] *m* (-en;-en) contracting party; dueller

kontrahieren [kɔntra'hirən] *tr & intr* contract

Kontrakt [kɔn'trakt] *m* (-[e]s;-e) contract

Kontrapunkt ['kɔntrapuŋkt] *m* (mus) counterpoint

konträr [kɔn'trer] *adj* contrary

Kontrast [kɔn'trast] *m* (-[e]s;-e) contrast

konstrastieren [kɔntras'tirən] *intr* contrast

Kontrast′regelung *f* (telv) contrast button

Kontroll– [kɔntrɔl] *comb.fm.* checking; control

Kontroll′abschnitt *m* stub (*of ticket*)

Kontrolle [kɔn'trɔlə] *f* (-s;-n) control, check, inspection

Kontrolleur [kɔntrə'lør] *m* (-s;-e) inspector, supervisor; (aer) air-traffic controller; (indust) timekeeper

kontrollieren [kɔntrə'lirən] *tr* control, check, inspect; (*Bücher*) audit

Kontroll′kasse *f* cash register

Kontroll′leuchte *f* (aut) warning light (*on dashboard*)

Kontroll′turm *m* (aer) control tower

Kontroverse [kɔntra'vɛrzə] *f* (-s;-n) controversy

Kontur [kɔn'tur] *f* (-s;-en) contour

Konvent [kɔn'vɛnt] *m* (-[e]s;-e) convent; monastery; (*Versammlung*) convention

Konvention [kɔnvɛn'tsjon] *f* (-s;-en) convention

konventionell [kɔnvɛntsjo'nɛl] *adj* conventional

Konversation [kɔnvɛrza'tsjon] *f* (-s;-en) conversation

Konversations′lexikon *n* encyclopedia; **wandelndes K.** (coll) walking encyclopedia

konvertieren [kɔnvɛr'tirən] *tr* convert || *intr* be converted

Konvertit –**in** [kɔnvɛr'tit(ɪn)] §7 *mf* convert

konvex [kɔn'vɛks] *adj* convex

Konvikt [kɔn'vɪkt] *n* (-s;-e) minor seminary

Konvoi ['kɔnvɔɪ] *m* (-s;-s) convoy

Konvolut [kɔnvə'lut] *n* (-[e]s;-e) bundle, roll

Konzentration [kɔntsɛntra'tsjon] *f* (-s;-en) concentration

Konzentrations′lager *n* concentration camp

konzentrieren [kɔntsɛn'trirən] *tr & ref* (auf *acc*) concentrate (*on*)

konzentrisch [kɔn'tsɛntrɪʃ] *adj* concentric

Konzept [kɔn'tsɛpt] *n* (-[e]s;-e) rough draft; **aus dem K. bringen** confuse, throw off; **aus dem K. kommen** lose one's train of thought

Konzept′papier *n* scribbling paper

Konzern [kɔn'tsɛrn] *m* (-s;-e) (com) combine

Konzert [kɔn'tsɛrt] *n* (-[e]s;-e) concert

Konzert′flügel *m* grand piano

Konzession [kɔntsɛ'sjon] *f* (-s;-en) concession; license

konzessionieren [kɔntsɛsjo'nirən] *tr* (com) license

Kon·zil [kɔn'tsil] *n* (-[e]s;-e & -zilien ['tsiljən]) (eccl) council

konziliant [kɔntsɪ'ljant] *adj* conciliatory; understanding

konzipieren [kɔntsɪ'pirən] *tr* conceive

koordinieren [kɔ·ɔrdi'nirən] *tr* coordinate

Kopf [kɔpf] *m* (-es;ᵘe) head; **aus dem Kopfe** by heart; **j-m über den K. wachsen** be taller than s.o.; (fig) be too much for s.o.; **mit dem K. voran** head first; **seinen eigenen K. haben** have a mind of one's own; **seinen K. lassen müssen** lose one's life

Kopf′bedeckung *f* headgear, head wear

Kopf′brett *n* headboard

köpfen ['kœpfən] *tr* behead; (*Baum*) top; (fb) head

Kopf′ende *n* head (*of bed, etc.*)

Kopf′geld *n* reward (*for capture of criminal*)

Kopf′haut *f* scalp

Kopf′hörer *m* headset, earphones

–köpfig [kœpfiç] *comb.fm.* -headed; -man

Kopf′kissen *n* pillow

Kopf′kissenbezug *m* pillowcase

kopf′lastig *adj* top-heavy

Kopf′lehne *f* headrest

Kopf′rechnen *n* (-s;) mental arithmetic

Kopf′salat *m* head lettuce

kopf′scheu *adj* (*Pferd*) nervous; (*Person*) shy; **k. werden** become alarmed

Kopf′schmerzen *pl* headache

Kopf′schuppen *pl* dandruff

Kopf'sprung *m* dive; **e–n K. machen** dive

Kopf'stand *m* handstand; **e–n K. machen** (aer) nose over

Kopf'stärke *f* (mil) strength

kopf'stehen §146 *intr* stand on one's head; (fig) be upside down

Kopf'steinpflaster *n* cobblestones

Kopf'steuer *f* poll tax

Kopf'stimme *f* falsetto

Kopf'stoß *m* butt; (fb) header

Kopf'tuch *n* kerchief, babushka

kopfü'ber *adv* head over heels

kopfun'ter *adv*—**kopfüber k.** head over heels

Kopf'weh *n* headache

Kopf'wellenknall *m* sonic boom

Ko·pie [koˈpiˑ] *f* (–;–pien [ˈpiˑən]) copy, duplicate; (phot) print

kopieren [koˈpirən] *tr* copy; (phot) print

Kopier'maschine *f* copier, photocopying machine

Kopier'papier *n* tracing paper; carbon paper; (phot) printing paper

Kopier'stift *m* indelible pencil

Koppel [ˈkɔpəl] *f* (–;–n) leash; (*Gehege*) enclosure, paddock ‖ *n* (–s;–) (mil) belt

koppeln [ˈkɔpəln] *tr* tie together, yoke; (fig) tie in; (elec) connect; (rad, rr) couple; (rok) dock ‖ **Koppeln** *n* (–s;) (aer, naut) dead reckoning; (rok) docking

Kopplungsgeschäft [ˈkɔplʊŋsgəˌʃɛft] *n* package deal

Koralle [koˈralə] *f* (–;–n) coral

Korb [kɔrp] *m* (–[e]s;¨e) basket; **j–m den K. geben** (fig) give s.o. the brush-off

Korb'ball *m* basketball

Körbchen [ˈkœrpçən] *n* (–s;–) little basket; (*e–s Büstenhalters*) cup

Korb'flasche *f* demijohn

Korb'geflecht *n* wickerwork

Korb'möbel *pl* wicker furniture

Korb'weide *f* (bot) osier

Kordel [ˈkɔrdəl] *f* (–;–n) cord

Kordon [kɔrˈdõ] *m* (–s;–ns) cordon; (*Ordensband*) ribbon

Korea [koˈreˑa] *n* (–s;) Korea

koreanisch [koreˈaniˑ] *adj* Korean

Korinthe [koˈrɪntə] *f* (–;–n) currant

Kork [kɔrk] *m* (–[e]s;–e) cork

Korken [ˈkɔrkən] *m* (–s;–) cork, stopper

Korkenzieher [ˈkɔrkəntsiˑər] *m* (–s;–) corkscrew

Korn [kɔrn] *n* (–[e]s;¨er) grain; seed; (*am Gewehr*) bead; (*Getreide*) rye; (*e–r Münze*) fineness; (phot) graininess; **j–n aufs K. nehmen** draw a bead on s.o.

Korn'ähre *f* ear of grain

Korn'branntwein *m* whiskey

Kornett [kɔrˈnɛt] *n* (–[e]s;–e) (mus) cornet

körnig [ˈkœrnɪç] *adj* granular

Korn'kammer *f* granary; (fig) breadbasket

koronar [koroˈnar] *adj* coronary

Körper [ˈkœrpər] *m* (–s;–) body; (geom, phys) solid

Kör'perbau *m* (–[e]s;) build, physique

kör'perbehindert *adj* physically handicapped

Kör'perbeschaffenheit *f* constitution

Körperchen [ˈkœrpərçən] *n* (–s;–) corpuscle

Kör'perfülle *f* plumpness, corpulence

Kör'pergeruch *m* body odor

Kör'perhaltung *f* posture, bearing

Kör'perkraft *f* physical strength

kör'perlich *adj* physical; (*stofflich*) corporeal

Kör'perpflege *f* personal hygiene

Kör'perpuder *m* talcum powder

Kör'perschaft *f* (–;–en) body (*of persons*); corporation

Kör'perverletzung *f* bodily injury

Korporation [kɔrpəraˈtsjon] *f* (–;–en) corporation

Korps [kor] *n* (– [kors];– [kors]) corps

Korps'geist *m* esprit de corps

Korps'student *m* member of a fraternity

korrekt [kɔˈrɛkt] *adj* correct, proper

Korrek·tor [kɔˈrɛktor] *m* (–s;–toren [ˈtorən]) proofreader

Korrektur [kɔrɛkˈtur] *f* (–;–en) correction; proofreading

Korrektur'bogen *m* page proof

Korrektur'fahne *f* galley proof

Korrelat [kɔreˈlat] *n* (–[e]s;–e) correlative

Korrespondent –**in** [kɔrɛspɔnˈdɛnt(ɪn)] §7 *mf* correspondent

Korrespondenz [kɔrɛspɔnˈdɛnts] *f* (–;–en) correspondence

Korrespondenz'karte *f* (Aust) postcard

Korridor [ˈkɔridor] *m* (–s;–e) corridor

korrigieren [kɔriˈgirən] *tr* correct

korrodieren [kɔroˈdirən] *tr & intr* corrode

Korse [ˈkɔrzə] *m* (–n;–n) Corsican

Korsett [kɔrˈzɛt] *n* (–[e]s;–e & –s) corset

Korsika [ˈkɔrzika] *n* (–s;) Corsica

Korvette [kɔrˈvɛtə] *f* (–;–n) corvette

Kosak [koˈzak] *m* (–en;–en) Cossack

K.-o.-Schlag [kaˈoˈʃlak] *m* knockout punch

kosen [ˈkozən] *tr* fondle, caress

Kosename [ˈkozənaˌmə] *m* pet name

Kosmetik [kɔsˈmetɪk] *f* (–;) beauty treatment; **chirurgische K.** cosmetic surgery, plastic surgery

Kosme'tikartikel *m* cosmetic

Kosmeti·kum [kɔsˈmetikum] *n* (–s;–ka [ka]) cosmetic

kosmisch [ˈkɔsmiʃ] *adj* cosmic

kosmopolitisch [kɔsmopoˈlitiʃ] *adj* cosmopolitan

Kosmos [ˈkɔsmɔs] *m* (–;) cosmos

Kost [kɔst] *f* (–;) food, board

kostbar [ˈkɔstbar] *adj* valuable; costly

Kost'barkeit *f* (–;–en) costliness; (fig) precious thing

kosten [ˈkɔstən] *tr* cost; taste, sip ‖ **Kosten** *pl* costs; **auf K.** (*genit*) at the expense of; **auf seine K. kommen** get one's money's worth; **sich in K. stürzen** go to great expense

Ko'stenanschlag *m* estimate

Ko'stenaufwand *m* expenditure, outlay

Ko'stenberechnung *f* cost accounting

Ko'stenersatz m, **Ko'stenerstattung** f reimbursement of expenses

ko'stenlos adj free of charge

Ko'stenvoranschlag m estimate

Kost'gänger –in §6 mf boarder

köstlich ['kœstlıç] adj delicious; delightful || adv—sich k. amüsieren have a grand time

Kost'probe f sample (to taste)

kostspielig ['kɔst/pilıç] adj expensive woman's suit; fancy dress

Kostüm [kɔs'tym] n (-s;-e) costume; woman's suit; fancy dress

kostümieren [kɔsty'miren] tr & ref dress up

Kostüm'probe f dress rehearsal

Kot [kot] m (-[e]s;) mud, dirt; (tierischer) dirt, dung; excrement

Kotelett [kɔtə'let] n (-[e]s;-e & -s) pork chop; cutlet

Köter ['køtər] m (-s;-) mut, mongrel

Kot'flügel m (aut) fender

kotig ['kotıç] adj muddy, dirty

kotzen ['kɔtsən] intr (sl) puke || Kotzen n—es ist zum K. it's enough to make you throw up

Krabbe ['krabə] f (-;-n) crab; shrimp; (niedliches Kind) little darling

krabbeln ['krabəln] tr & intr tickle || intr (SEIN) crawl

Krach [krax] m (-[e]s;-s & -e) crash, bang; (Lärm) racket; (Streit) row; (fin) crash; K. machen kick up a row

krachen ['kraxən] intr crash, crack

krächzen ['krɛçtsən] intr croak, caw

kraft [kraft] prep (genit) by virtue of || Kraft f (-;̈e) strength, power, force; außer K. setzen repeal; in K. sein be in force; in K. treten come into force

Kraft'anlage f (elec) power plant

Kraft'anstrengung f strenuous effort

Kraft'aufwand m effort

Kraft'ausdruck m swear word; Kraftausdrücke strong language

Kraft'brühe f concentrated broth

Kraft'fahrer –in §6 mf motorist

Kraft'fahrzeug n motor vehicle

kräftig ['kreftıç] adj strong, powerful; (Speise) nutritious || adv hard; heartily

kräftigen ['kreftıgən] tr strengthen

Kraft'leistung f feat of strength

kraft'los adj powerless; weak

Kraft'meier m (coll) bully; (coll) muscle man

Kraft'probe f test of strength

Kraft'protz m (coll) powerhouse

Kraft'rad n motorcycle

Kraft'stoff m fuel

Kraft'stoffleitung f fuel line

kraftstrotzend ['kraft/trɔtsənt] adj strapping

Kraft'übertragung f (aut) transmission

Kraft'wagen m motor vehicle

Kraft'werk n generating plant

Kraft'wort n (-[e]s;̈er) swear word

Kragen ['kragən] m (-s;-) collar

Krähe ['kre·ə] f (-;-n) crow

krähen ['kre·ən] intr crow

Krähenfüße ['kre·ənfysə] pl crow's feet (wrinkles)

Krakeel [kra'kel] m (-s;-e) (coll) rumpus; (lauter Streit) brawl

krakeelen [kra'kelən] intr (coll) kick up a storm

Kralle ['kralə] f (-;-n) claw

Kram [kram] m (-[e]s;) (coll) things, stuff; (coll) business, affairs

kramen ['kramən] intr rummage

Krämer –in ['kremər(ın)] §6 mf shopkeeper || m (pej) philistine

Krä'merseele f philistine

Kram'laden m general store

Krampe ['krampə] f (-;-n) staple

Krampf [krampf] m (-[e]s;̈e) cramp, spasm; convulsion; (Unsinn) nonsense

Krampf'ader f varicose vein

krampf'artig adj spasmodic

krampf'haft adj convulsive

Kran [kran] m (-[e]s;̈e & -e) (mach) crane

Kranich ['kranıç] m (-s;-e) (orn) crane

krank [krank] adj sick, ill || Kranke §5 mf patient

—**krank** comb.fm. suffering from

kränkeln ['krenkəln] intr be sickly

kranken ['krankən] intr—k. an (dat) suffer from

kränken ['krenkən] tr hurt, offend || ref (über acc) feel hurt (at)

Kran'kenanstalt f hospital

Kran'kenbahre f stretcher

Kran'kenbett n hospital bed

Kran'kenfahrstuhl m wheel chair

Kran'kengeld n sick benefit

Kran'kenhaus n hospital; ins K. einweisen hospitalize

Kran'kenkasse f medical insurance plan

Kran'kenlager n sickbed

Kran'kenpflege f nursing

Kran'kenpfleger –in §6 mf nurse

Kran'kenrevier n (mil) sick quarters; (nav) sick bay

Kran'kensaal m hospital ward

Kran'kenschwester f nurse

Kran'kenstube f infirmary

Kran'kenstuhl m wheel chair

Kran'kenurlaub m sick leave

Kran'kenversicherung f health insurance

Kran'kenwagen m ambulance

krank'feiern intr (coll) play sick

krank'haft adj morbid, pathological

Krank'heit f (-;-en) sickness, disease

Krank'heitsbericht m medical bulletin

Krank'heitserscheinung f symptom

kränklich ['krenklıç] adj sickly

Kränk'lichkeit f (-;) poor health

Kränkung ['krenkuŋ] f (-;-en) offense

Kran'wagen m (aut) wrecker, tow truck

Kranz [krants] m (-[e]s;̈e) wreath

Kränzchen ['krentsçən] n (-s;-) small wreath; ladies' circle; informal dance

kränzen ['krentsən] tr wreathe

Krapfen ['krapfən] m (-s;-) doughnut

kraß [kras] adj crass, gross

Krater ['kratər] m (-s;-) crater

Kratzbürste ['krats/byrstə] f wire brush; (fig) stand-offish woman

Krätze ['kretsə] f (-;) itch, scabies

kratzen ['kratsən] tr & intr scratch

Krat'zer m (-s;-) scratch; scraper

krauen ['krau·ən] *tr* scratch gently

kraus [kraus] *adj* (*Haar*) frizzy; (*Gedanken*) confused; **die Stirn k. ziehen** knit one's brows

Krause ['krauzə] *f* (-;-n) ruffle

kräuseln ['krɔɪzəln] *tr* & *ref* curl

Krau'seminze *f* (bot) spearmint

Kraus'haar *n* frizz

Kraut [kraut] *n* (-[e]s;⁼er) herb, plant; leafy top; (*Kohl*) cabbage; **ins K. schießen** run wild

Krawall [kra'val] *m* (-[e]s;-e) riot; (coll) rumpus

Krawatte [kra'vatə] *f* (-;-n) necktie

Krawat'tenhalter *m* tie clip

kraxeln ['kraksəln] *intr* (SEIN) climb

Kreatur [kre·a'tur] *f* (-;-en) creature

Krebs [kreps] *m* (-es;-e) crawfish, crab; (pathol) cancer

krebs'artig *adj* (pathol) cancerous

Kredenz [kre'dɛnts] *f* (-;-en) buffet, credenza, sideboard

kredenzen [kre'dɛntsən] *tr* (*Wein*) serve

Kredit [kre'dit] *m* (-[e]s;-e) credit

Kredit'bank *f* commercial bank

kreditieren [kredi'tirən] *tr* credit ‖ *intr* give credit

Kredit'karte *f* credit card

Kredit'würdigkeit *f* trustworthiness; (com) credit rating

Kreide ['kraɪdə] *f* (-;-n) chalk, piece of chalk, crayon

kreieren [kre'irən] *tr* create

Kreis [kraɪs] *m* (-es;-e) circle; (*Bereich*) field; (*Bezirk*) district; (adm) county; (elec) circuit

Kreis'abschnitt *m* segment

Kreis'amt *n* district office

Kreis'ausschnitt *m* sector

Kreis'bahn *f* orbit

Kreis'bogen *m* (geom) arc

kreischen ['kraɪʃən] *intr* shriek

Kreisel ['kraɪzəl] *m* (-s;-) gyroscope; top (*toy*)

Krei'selbewegung *f* gyration

Krei'selhorizont *m* artificial horizon

kreiseln ['kraɪzəln] *intr* spin, rotate, gyrate; spin the top

Krei'selpumpe *f* centrifugal pump

kreisen ['kraɪzən] *intr* circle; revolve; (*Blut*) circulate

kreis'förmig *adj* circular

Kreis'lauf *m* circulation; cycle

Kreis'laufsstörung *f* circulatory disorder

kreis'rund *adj* circular

Kreis'säge *f* circular saw, buzz saw

kreißen ['kraɪsən] *intr* be in labor

Kreißsaal ['kraɪszal] *m* delivery room

Kreis'stadt *f* (rural) county seat

Kreis'umfang *m* circumference

Kreis'verkehr *m* traffic circle

Krem [krem] *f* (-;-s) & *m* (-s;-s) cream

Kreml ['kreml] *m* (-[e]s;) Kremlin

Krempe ['krempə] *f* (-;-n) brim, rim

Krempel ['krempəl] *m* (-s;) (coll) stuff, junk ‖ *f* (-;-n) (tex) card

Kren [kren] *m* (-[e]s;) horseradish

krepieren [kre'pirən] *intr* (SEIN) (*Tiere*) die; (*Granate*) explode, burst; (sl) kick the bucket

Krepp [krep] *m* (-s;-s) crepe

Kreta ['kreta] *n* (-s;) Crete

Kretonne [kre'tonə] *f* (-;-n) cretonne

kreuz [krɔɪts] *adv—***k. und quer** crisscross ‖ **Kreuz** *n* (-es;-e) cross; (anat) small of the back; (cards) club(s)

Kreuz'abnahme *f* deposition

Kreuz'band *n* (-[e]s;⁼er) mailing wrapper (*for newspapers, etc.*)

kreuz'brav' *adj* (coll) very honest; (coll) very well-behaved

kreuzen ['krɔɪtsən] *tr* cross ‖ *recip* cross; interbreed ‖ *intr* cruise

Kreuzer ['krɔɪtsər] *m* (-s;-) penny; (nav) cruiser

Kreuz'fahrer *m* crusader

Kreuz'fahrt *f* cruise; (hist) crusade

Kreuz'feuer *n* crossfire

kreuz'fidel' *adj* very cheerful

Kreuz'gang *m* (archit) cloister(s)

kreuzigen ['krɔɪtsigən] *tr* crucify

Kreu'zigung *f* (-;-en) crucifixion

Kreuz'otter *f* adder

Kreuz'ritter *m* crusader; Knight of the Teutonic Order

Kreuz'schiff *m* transept (*of church*)

Kreuz'schlitzschraubenzieher *m* Phillips screwdriver

Kreu'zung *f* (-;-en) intersection; crossbreeding; hybrid; (rr) crossing

Kreuz'verhör *n* cross-examination; **j—n ins K. nehmen** cross-examine s.o.

Kreuz'verweis *m* cross reference

Kreuz'weg *m* crossroad; (eccl) stations of the cross

Kreuz'worträtsel *n* crossword puzzle

Kreuz'zeichen *n* (eccl) sign of the cross; (typ) dagger

Kreuz'zug *m* crusade

kribbelig ['krɪbəlɪç] *adj* irritable; (nervös) edgy, on edge

kribbeln ['krɪbəln] *intr* tickle

kriechen ['kriçən] §102 *intr* (SEIN) creep, crawl

kriecherisch ['kriçərɪʃ] *adj* fawning

Kriechtier ['kriçtir] *n* reptile

Krieg [krik] *m* (-[e]s;-e) war

kriegen ['krigən] *tr* (coll) get, catch

Krie'ger *m* (-s;-) warrior

kriegerisch ['krigərɪʃ] *adj* warlike; (*Person*) belligerent

krieg'führend *adj* warring

Kriegs'akademie *f* war college

Kriegs'bemalung *f* war paint

Kriegs'berichter *m*, **Kriegs'berichterstatter** *m* war correspondent

Kriegs'dienst *m* military service

Kriegs'dienstverweigerer *m* conscientious objector

Kriegs'einsatz *m* (mil) action

Kriegs'entschädigung *f* reparations

Kriegs'fall *m—***im K.** in case of war

Kriegs'flotte *f* fleet; naval force

Kriegs'fuß *m—***mit j—m auf K. stehen** be at loggerheads with s.o.

Kriegs'gebiet *n* war zone

Kriegs'gefangene §5 *mf* prisoner of war

Kriegs'gericht *n* court martial

Kriegsgewinnler ['kriksgəvɪnlər] *m* (-s;-) war profiteer

Kriegs'hafen *m* naval base

Kriegs'hetzer *m* warmonger

Kriegs'kamerad *m* fellow soldier
Kriegs'lazarett *n* base hospital
Kriegs'list *f* stratagem
Kriegs'marine *f* navy
Kriegs'ministerium *n* war department
Kriegs'opfer *n* war victim
Kriegs'pfad *m* warpath
Kriegs'rat *m* council of war
Kriegs'recht *n* martial law
Kriegs'rüstung *f* arming for war; war production
Kriegs'schauplatz *m* theater of war
Kriegs'schuld *f* war debt; war guilt
Kriegs'teilnehmer *m* combatant; (*ehemaliger*) ex-serviceman, veteran
Kriegs'verbrechen *n* war crime
Kriegs'versehrte §5 *m* disabled veteran
kriegs'verwendungsfähig *adj* fit for active duty
Kriegs'wesen *n* warfare, war
Kriegs'zug *m* (mil) campaign
Kriegs'zustand *m* state of war
Krim [krɪm] *f* (–;) Crimea
Krimi ['krimi] *m* (–s;–s) & (–;–) (coll) murder mystery; (telv) thriller
kriminal [krɪmɪ'nɑl] *adj* criminal
Kriminal– *comb.fm.* criminal, crime
Kriminal'beamte *m* detective investigator
Kriminal'roman *m* detective novel
Kriminal'stück *n* (telv) thriller
kriminell [krɪmɪ'nel] *adj* criminal ‖ **Kriminelle** §5 *mf* criminal
Krimskrams ['krɪmskrams] *m* (–es;) (coll) junk
Kripo ['kripo] *abbr* (**Kriminalpolizei**) crime squad
Krippe ['krɪpə] *f* (–;–n) crib, manger; day nursery (*for infants up to 3 years*)
Krise ['krizə] *f* (–;–n) crisis
kriseln ['krizəln] *impers*—**es kriselt** there's a crisis, trouble is brewing
Kristall [krɪs'tal] *m* (–s;–e) crystal
Kristalleuchter (**Kristall'leuchter**) *m* crystal chandelier
Kristall'glas *n* crystal
kristallisieren [krɪstalɪ'zirən] *ref* & *intr* crystallize
Kristall'zucker *m* granulated sugar
Krite•rium [krɪ'terjum] *n* (–s;–rien [rjən]) criterion
Kritik [krɪ'tik] *f* (–;–en) criticism; critique; **unter aller K.** abominable
Kritikaster [krɪtɪ'kastər] *m* (–s;–) (pej) faultfinder
Kritiker –in ['kritɪkər(ɪn)] §6 *mf* critic; reviewer
kritik'los *adj* uncritical
kritisch ['kritɪʃ] *adj* critical
kritisieren [krɪtɪ'zirən] *tr* criticize; (*werten*) review
Krittelei ['krɪtə'laɪ] *f* (–;–en) faultfinding; petty criticism
kritteln ['krɪtəln] *intr* (**an** *dat*) find fault (with), grumble (about)
Kritzelei [krɪtsə'laɪ] *f* (–;–en) scribbling, scrawling; scribble, scrawl
kritzeln ['krɪtsəln] *tr* & *intr* scribble
kroch [krɔx] *pret* of **kriechen**
Krokodil [krokə'dil] *n* (–[e]s;–e) crocodile
Krokus ['krokus] *m* (–;– & –se) crocus

Krone ['kronə] *f* (–;–n) crown
krönen ['krønən] *tr* crown
Kronerbe ['kronerbə] *m*, **Kronerbin** ['kronerbɪn] *f* heir apparent
Kronleuchter ['kronlɔɪçtər] *m* chandelier
Kronprinz ['kronprɪnts] *m* crown prince
Kronprinzessin ['kronprɪntsesɪn] *f* crown princess
Krö'nung *f* (–;–en) coronation
Kropf [krɔpf] *m* (–[e]s;⁀e) crop (*of bird*); (pathol) goiter
Kröte ['krøtə] *f* (–;–n) toad; **Kröten** (coll) coins, coppers
Krücke ['krykə] *f* (–;–n) crutch
Krückstock ['krykʃtɔk] *m* walking stick
Krug [kruk] *m* (–[e]s;⁀e) jar, jug; mug; pitcher; (*Wirtshaus*) tavern
Krume ['krumə] *f* (–;–n) crumb; topsoil
Krümel ['kryməl] *m* (–s;–) crumb
krümeln ['kryməln] *tr* & *intr* crumble
krumm [krum] *adj* (**krummer** & **krümmer** ['krymər]; **krummste** & **krümmste** ['krymstə] §9) bent, stooping; crooked
krumm'beinig *adj* bowlegged
krümmen ['krymən] *tr* bend, curve ‖ *ref* (*vor Schmerzen*) writhe; (*vor Lachen*) double up; (*Wurm*) wriggle; (*Holz*) warp; (*Fluß, Straße*) wind
Krümmer ['krymər] *m* (–s;–) (tech) elbow
krumm'nehmen §116 *tr* (coll) take the wrong way, take amiss
Krumm'stab *m* (eccl) crozier
Krüm'mung *f* (–;–en) bend, curve; winding
krumpeln ['krumpəln] *tr* & *intr* (coll) crumple, crease
Krüppel ['krypəl] *m* (–s;–) cripple; **zum K. machen** cripple
krüp'pelhaft *adj* deformed
krüp'pelig *adj* crippled; stunted
Kruste ['krustə] *f* (–;–n) crust
Kru'stentier *n* crustacean
krustig ['krustɪç] *adj* crusty
Kruzifix [krutsɪ'fiks] *n* (–es;–e) crucifix
Kryp•ta ['krypta] *f* (–;–ten [tən]) crypt
Kübel ['kybəl] *m* (–s;–) tub; bucket
Kü'belwagen *m* jeep
kubieren [ku'birən] *tr* (math) cube
Kubik– [kubik] *comb.fm.* cubic
Kubik'maß *n* cubic measure
kubisch ['kubɪʃ] *adj* cubic
Kubismus [ku'bɪsmus] *m* (–;) cubism
Küche ['kyçə] *f* (–;–n) kitchen; (culin) cuisine
Kuchen ['kuxən] *m* (–s;–) cake, pie
Ku'chenblech *n* cookie sheet
Kü'chenchef *m* chef
Kü'chendienst *m* (mil) K.P.
Kü'chenform *f* cake pan
Kü'chengerät *n* kitchen utensil
Kü'chengeschirr *n* kitchen utensils
Kü'chenherd *m* kitchen range, stove
Kü'chenmaschine *f* electric kitchen appliance
Kü'chenmeister *m* chef

Kü'chenzettel m menu

Küchlein ['kyçlaɪn] n (-s;-) chick; (culin) small cake

Kuckuck ['kʊkʊk] m (-s;-e) cuckoo; zum K..gehen (coll) go to hell

Kufe ['kufə] f (-;-n) vat; (Schlitten-) runner

Küfer ['kyfər] m (-s;-) cooper

Kugel ['kugəl] f (-;-n) ball; sphere; (Geschoß) bullet; (sport) shot

ku'gelfest adj bulletproof

ku'gelförmig adj spherical

Ku'gelgelenk n (mach) ball-and-socket joint; (anat) socket joint

Ku'gellager n ball bearing

kugeln ['kugəln] tr roll || ref roll around; sich vor Lachen k. double over with laughter || intr (SEIN) roll

Ku'gelregen m hail of bullets

ku'gelrund adj round; (coll) tubby

Ku'gelschreiber m ball-point pen

Ku'gelstoßen n (sport) shot put

Kuh [ku] f (-;-¨e) cow

Kuh'dorf n hick town

Kuh'fladen m cow dung

Kuh'handel m (pol) horse trading

Kuh'haut f cowhide; das geht auf keine K. but that's a long story

kühl [kyl] adj cool

Kühl'anlage f refrigerator; cooling system; cold storage (room)

Kühle ['kylə] f (-;) cool, coolness

kühlen ['kylən] tr cool; (Wein) chill

Küh'ler m (-s;-) cooler; (aut) radiator

Küh'lerverschluß m radiator cap

Kühl'mittel n coolant

Kühl'schrank m refrigerator

Kühl'truhe f freezer

Kühl'wagen m refrigerator truck; (rr) refrigerator car

Kuh'magd f milkmaid

Kuh'mist m cow dung

kühn [kyn] adj bold, daring

Kühn'heit f (-;) boldness, daring

Kuhpocken ['kupɔkən] pl cowpox

Kuh'stall m cowshed, cow barn

Kujon [ku'jon] m (-s;-e) (pej) louse

kujonieren [kujo'nirən] tr bully

Küken ['kykən] n (-s;-) chick

Kukuruz ['kukʊrʊts] m (-es;) (Aust) corn

kulant [ku'lant] adj obliging; generous

Kuli ['kuli] m (-s;-s) coolie

kulinarisch [kuli'nariʃ] adj culinary

Kulisse [ku'lisə] f (-;-n) (theat) wing; hinter den Kulissen behind the scenes; Kulissen scenery

Kulis'senfieber n stage fright

kullern ['kʊlərn] intr (SEIN) roll

kulminieren [kʊlmi'nirən] intr culminate

Kult [kʊlt] m (-[e]s;-e) cult

kultivieren [kʊlti'virən] tr cultivate

Kultur [kʊl'tur] f (-;-en) culture, civilization; (agr) cultivation; (bact, chem) culture

Kultur'austausch m cultural exchange

kulturell [kʊltu'rɛl] adj cultural

Kultur'erbe n cultural heritage

Kultur'film m educational film

Kultur'geschichte f history of civilization; cultural history

Kultur'volk n civilized people

Kul·tus ['kʊltus] m (-;-te [tə]) cult

Kümmel ['kʏməl] m (-s;-) caraway seed; caraway brandy

Küm'melbrot n seeded rye bread

Kummer ['kʊmər] m (-s;) grief, sorrow; worry, concern, trouble; j-m großen K. bereiten cause s.o. a lot of worry; sich [dat] K. machen über (acc) worry about

kümmerlich ['kʏmərlɪç] adj wretched; (dürftig) needy

Kümmerling ['kʏmərlɪŋ] m (-s;-e) stunted animal; stunted plant

kümmern ['kʏmərn] tr trouble, worry; concern || ref—sich k. um worry about; take care of; sich nicht k. um not bother about; neglect

Kümmernis ['kʏmərnɪs] f (-;-se) worry, trouble

kum'mervoll adj grief-stricken

Kumpan [kʊm'pan] m (-s;-e) companion; buddy

Kumpel ['kʊmpəl] m (-s;-) buddy, sidekick; (min) miner

kund [kʊnt] adj known

kündbar ['kʏntbar] adj (Vertrag) terminable; (fin) redeemable

Kunde ['kʊndə] m (-n;-n) customer; übler K. (fig) tough customer || f (-;) news, information; lore

-kunde f comb.fm. –ology; –graphy; science of; guide to, study of

Kun'dendienst m customer service; warranty service

Kun'denkreis m clientele

kund'geben §80 tr make known, announce

Kundgebung ['kʊntgebuŋ] f (-;-en) manifestation; (pol) rally

kundig ['kʊndɪç] adj well-informed; k. sein (genit) know

-kundig comb.fm. well versed in; able to

kündigen ['kʏndɪgən] tr (Vertrag) give notice to terminate; (Wohnung) give notice to vacate; (Stellung) give notice of quitting; (Kapital) call in; (Hypothek) foreclose on; j-m fristlos k. (coll) sack s.o. || intr (dat) given notice to, release

Kün'digung f (-;-en) (seitens des Arbeitnehmers) resignation; (seitens des Arbeitgebers) notice (of termination); mit monatlicher K. subject to a month's notice

Kün'digungsfrist f period of notice

kund'machen tr make known, announce

Kund'machung f (-;-en) announcement

Kund'schaft f (-;) clientele, customer(s); (mil) reconnaissance

kundschaften ['kʊntʃaftən] intr go on reconnaissance, scout

Kund'schafter m (-s;-) scout, spy

kund'tun §154 tr make known, announce

kund'werden §159 intr (SEIN) become known

künftig ['kʏnftɪç] adj future, to come, next || adv in the future, from now on

künf'tighin' adv from now on, hereafter

Kunst [kunst] f (-;=e) art; skill; **das ist keine K.** it's easy

Kunstbanause ['kunstbanauzə] m (-n; -n) philistine

Kunst'dünger m chemical fertilizer

Künstelei [kynstə'laɪ] f (-;-en) affectation

Kunst'faser f synthetic fiber

Kunst'fehler m—**ärztlicher K.** malpractice

kunst'fertig adj skillful, skilled

Kunst'flieger m stunt pilot

Kunst'flug m stunt flying

Kunst'freund **-in** §8 mf art lover; patron of the arts

Kunst'gegenstand m objet d'art

kunst'gerecht adj skillful; expert

Kunst'gewerbe n arts and crafts

Kunst'glied n artificial limb

Kunst'griff m trick

Kunst'händler **-in** §6 mf art dealer

Kunst'kenner **-in** §6 mf art connoisseur

Kunst'laufen n figure skating

Künstler **-in** ['kynstlər(ɪn)] §6 mf artist; performer

künstlerisch ['kynstlərɪʃ] adj artistic

künstlich ['kynstlɪç] adj artificial; (chem) synthetic

Kunst'liebhaber **-in** §6 mf art lover

kunst'los adj unaffected

Kunst'maler **-in** §6 mf painter, artist

Kunst'pause f pause for effect

kunst'reich adj ingenious

Kunst'reiter m equestrian

Kunst'seide f rayon

Kunst'springen n (sport) diving

Kunst'stoff m plastic material; synthetic material; (tex) synthetic fiber

Kunststoff— comb.fm. plastic; plastics

Kunst'stopfen n invisible mending

Kunst'stück n trick, feat

Kunst'tischler m cabinet maker

Kunstverständige ['kunstfer/tendɪgə] §5 mf art expert

kunst'voll adj elaborate, ornate

Kunst'werk n work of art

kunterbunt ['kuntərbunt] adj chaotic

Kupfer ['kupfər] n (-s;) copper

kupfern ['kupfərn] adj copper

kupieren [ku'pirən] tr (Schwanz, Ohren) cut off; (Spielkarten) cut; (Fahrkarten) punch

Kuppe ['kupə] f (-;-n) top, summit

Kuppel ['kupəl] f (-;-n) cupola

Kuppelei [kupə'laɪ] f (-;-en) procuring

kuppeln ['kupəln] tr couple, connect ‖ intr be a pimp; be a procuress; (aut) operate the clutch

Kuppler ['kuplər] m (-s;-) pimp

Kupplerin ['kuplərɪn] f (-;-nen) procuress

Kupplung ['kuplun] f (-;-en) (aut) clutch; (rr) coupling

Kur [kur] f (-;-en) cure (at a spa); **j-n in die Kur nehmen** give s.o. a talking to

Kuratel [kura'tel] f (-;) guardianship; **j-n unter K. stellen** appoint a guardian for s.o.

Ku·rator [ku'ratər] m (-s;-ratoren [ra'torən]) (e-s Museums) curator; (educ) trustee; (jur) guardian

Kurato·rium [kura'torjum] n (-s;-rien [rjən]) (educ) board of trustees

Kurbel ['kurbəl] f (-;-n) crank, handle, winch

Kurbelei [kurbə'laɪ] f (-;-en) shooting a film; (aer) dogfight

Kur'belgehäuse n (aut) crankcase

kurbeln ['kurbəln] tr crank; (Film) shoot ‖ intr engage in a dogfight

Kur'belstange f (mach) connecting rod

Kur'belwelle f (mach) crankshaft

Kürbis ['kyrbɪs] m (-ses;-se) pumpkin; (Kopf) (sl) bean

küren ['kyrən] §165 & §109 tr elect

Kurfürst ['kurfyrst] m (-en;-en) elector (of the Holy Roman Empire)

Kur'haus n spa; hotel

Kurie ['kurjə] f (-;-n) (eccl) curia

Kurier [ku'rir] m (-s;-e) courier

kurieren [ku'rirən] tr cure

kurios [ku'rjos] adj odd, curious

Kuriosität [kurjozı'tet] f (-;-en) quaintness; curio, curiosity

Kur'ort m health resort, spa

Kurpfuscher ['kurpfuʃər] m (-s;-) quack

Kurrentschrift [ku'rent/rɪft] f cursive script

Kurs [kurs] m (-es;-e) (educ) course; (fin) rate of exchange; (fin) circulation; (naut) course; (st. exch.) price; **außer K. setzen** take out of circulation; **hoch im K. stehen** be at a premium; (fig) rate high; **zum Kurse von** at the rate of

Kurs'bericht m (st. exch.) market report

Kurs'buch n (rr) timetable

Kürschner ['kyr/nər] m (-s;-) furrier

Kurs'entwicklung f price trend

Kurs'gewinn m (st. exch.) gain

kursieren [kur'zirən] intr circulate

Kursive [kur'zivə] f (-;-n), **Kursivschrift** [kur'zif/rɪft] f (-;) italics

Kurs'stand m (st. exch.) price level

Kur·sus ['kurzus] m (-;-se [zə]) (educ) course

Kurs'veränderung f (fin) change in exchange rates; (naut) change of course; (pol) change of policy; (st. exch.) price change

Kurs'wert m (st. exch.) market value

Kurve ['kurvə] f (-;-n) curve; **in die K. gehen** (aer) bank

kurz [kurts] adj (kürzer ['kyrtsər]; kürzeste ['kyrtsəstə] §9) short, brief; **auf das kürzeste** very briefly; **binnen kurzem** within a short time; **in kurzem** before long; **k. und gut** in a word; **seit kurzem** for the last few days or weeks; **über k. oder lang** sooner or later; **zu k. kommen** (coll) get the short end of it ‖ adv shortly; briefly; curtly

kurzatmig ['kurtsatmiç] adj short-winded; (Pferd) broken-winded

Kürze ['kyrtsə] f (-;) shortness; brevity; **in K.** shortly; briefly

kürzen ['kyrtsən] tr shorten; (Gehalt) cut; (math) reduce

kurzerhand adv offhand

Kurz'fassung f abridged version

Kurz'film m (cin) short

kurzfristig [ˈkʊrtsfrɪstɪç] *adj* short-term
Kurz'geschichte *f* short story
kurzlebig [ˈkʊrtsleːbɪç] *adj* short-lived
kürzlich [ˈkʏrtslɪç] *adj* lately, recently
Kurz'meldung *f* news flash
Kurz'nachrichten *pl* news summary
kurz'schließen §76 *tr* short-circuit
Kurz'schluß *m* short circuit
Kurz'schlußbrücke *f* (elec) jumper
Kurz'schrift *f* shorthand
kurz'sichtig *adj* near-sighted; (fig) short-sighted
Kurz'streckenlauf *m* sprint
Kurz'streckenläufer -in §6 *mf* sprinter
kurzum' *adv* in short, in a word
Kür'zung *f* (-;-en) reduction; curtailment; (*e-s Buches*) abridgment
Kurz'waren *pl* sewing supplies
kurz'weg *adv* bluntly, flatly
Kurzweil [ˈkʊrtsvaɪl] *f* (-;) pastime
kurzweilig [ˈkʊrtsvaɪlɪç] *adj* amusing
kusch [kʊʃ] *interj* lie down! (*to a dog*)
kuschen [ˈkʊʃən] *ref* lie down; crouch || *intr* lie down; crouch, cringe; (*Person*) knuckle under, submit
Kusine [kuˈziːnə] *f* (-;-n) female cousin
Kuß [kʊs] *m* (Kusses; Küsse) kiss; **kalter K.** popsicle

küssen [ˈkʏsən] *tr & intr* kiss
Kuß'hand *f*—;-m e-e **K.** zuwerfen throw s.o. a kiss; **mit K.** with pleasure
Küste [ˈkʏstə] *f* (-;-n) coast, shore
Kü'stenfahrer *m* coasting vessel
Kü'stenfischerei *f* inshore fishing
Kü'stengewässer *n* coastal waters
Kü'stenlinie *f* coastline, shoreline
kü'stennah *adj* offshore; coastal
Kü'stenschiffahrt *f* coastal shipping
Kü'stenstreife *f* shore patrol
Küster [ˈkʏstər] *m* (-s;-) sexton
Kustos [ˈkʊstɔs] *m* (-; Kustoden [kʊsˈtoːdən]) custodian
Kutsche [ˈkʊtʃə] *f* (-;-n) coach
Kut'scher *m* (-s;-) coachman
kutschieren [kʊˈtʃiːrən] *intr* drive a coach || *intr* (SEIN) ride in a coach
Kutte [ˈkʊtə] *f* (-;-n) (eccl) cowl
Kutteln [ˈkʊtəln] *pl* tripe
Kutter [ˈkʊtər] *m* (-s;-) (naut) cutter
Kuvert [kuˈvɛrt] *n* (-s;-s) & (-[e]s;-e) envelope; table setting
kuvertieren [kuverˈtiːrən] *tr* put into an envelope
Kux [kʊks] *m* (-es;-e) mining share
Kyklon [kʏˈkloːn] *m* (-s;-e) cyclone
Kyniker [ˈkyːnɪkər] *m* (-s;-) (philos) cynic

L

L, l [ɛl] *invar n* L, l
laben [ˈlaːbən] *tr* refresh
Labial [laˈbjaːl] *n* (-s;-e) labial
labil [laˈbiːl] *adj* unstable
Labor [laˈbɔr] *n* (-s;-s) (coll) lab
Laborant [laboˈrant] (in) §7 *mf* laboratory technician
Laborato-rium [laboraˈtoːrjʊm] *n* (-s; rien [rjən]) laboratory
laborieren [laboˈriːrən] *intr* experiment; **l. an** (*dat*) suffer from
Labsal [ˈlapzaːl] *n* (-[e]s;-e) refreshment
La'bung *f* (-;-en) refreshment
Labyrinth [labyˈrɪnt] *n* (-[e]s;-e) labyrinth
Lache [ˈlaxə] *f* (-;-n) puddle, pool; laugh; **e-e gellende L. anschlagen** break out in laughter
lächeln [ˈlɛçəln] *intr* (über *acc*) smile (at) || **Lächeln** *n* (-s;) smile; **höhnisches L.** sneer
lachen [ˈlaxən] *intr* laugh; **daß ich nicht lache!** don't make me laugh! || **Lachen** *n* (-s;) laugh, laughter; **du hast gut L.!** you can laugh!
lächerlich [ˈlɛçərlɪç] *adj* ridiculous; **l. machen** ridicule; **sich l. machen** make a fool of oneself
lachhaft [ˈlaxhaft] *adj* ridiculous
Lachkrampf [ˈlaxkrampf] *m* fit of laughter
Lachs [laks] *m* (-es;-e) salmon
Lachsalve [ˈlaxzalvə] *f* (-;-n) peal of laughter

Lachs'schinken *m* raw, lightly smoked ham
Lack [lak] *m* (-[e]s;-e) lacquer, varnish
Lackel [ˈlakəl] *m* (-s;-) (coll) dope
lackieren [laˈkiːrən] *tr* lacquer, varnish; (*Autos*) paint
Lack'leder *n* patent leather
Lackmuspapier [ˈlakmuspapiːr] *n* litmus paper
Lack'schuhe *pl* patent-leather shoes
Lade [ˈlaːdə] *f* (-;-n) box, case; (*Schublade*) drawer
La'dearbeiter *m* loader
La'debaum *m* derrick
La'defähigkeit *f* loading capacity
La'dehemmung *f* jamming (*of a gun*); **L. haben** jam
La'deklappe *f* tailgate
La'delüke *f* (naut) hatch
laden [ˈlaːdən] §103 *tr* load; (*Gast*) invite; (elec) charge; (jur) summon; **geladen sein** (coll) be burned up || **Laden** *m* (-s;-) store, shop; (*Fenster-*) shutter; **den L. schmeißen** pull it off, lick it
La'dendieb *m*, **La'dendiebin** *f* shoplifter
La'dendiebstahl *m* shoplifting
La'denhüter *m* drug on the market
La'deninhaber -in §6 *mf* shopkeeper
La'denkasse *f* till
Lä'denmädchen *n* salesgirl
La'denpreis *m* retail price
La'denschluß *m* closing time

La'denschwengel *m* (pej) stupid shop clerk
La'dentisch *m* counter
La'derampe *f* loading platform
La'deschein *m* bill of lading
La'destock *m* ramrod
La'destreifen *m* cartridge clip
La'dung *f* (-;-en) loading; load; (*Güter*) freight; (elec) charge; (jur) summons; (mil) charge; (naut) cargo
Lafette [la'fɛtə] *f* (-;-n) gun mount
Laffe ['lafə] *m* (-n;-n) jazzy dresser
lag [lɑk] *pret* of **liegen**
Lage ['lɑgə] *f* (-;-n) site, location; situation; (*Zustand*) condition, state; (*Haltung*) posture; (*Schicht*) layer, deposit; (*Salve*) volley; (*Bier*) round; (bb) quire; (mil) position; (mus) pitch; **mißliche L.** predicament; **versetzen Sie sich in meine L.** put yourself in my position
Lager ['lɑgər] *n* (-s;-) bed; (*e-s Wildes*) lair; (*Stapelplatz*) dump; (*Partei*) side, camp; (*von Waffen*) cache; (*Vorrat*) stock; (*Warenlager*) stockroom; (geol) stratum, vein; (mach) bearing; (mil) camp; **auf L.** in stock; (fig) up one's sleeve; **ein L. halten von** keep stock of
La'geraufnahme *f* inventory
La'gerbier *n* lager beer
La'gerfähigkeit *f* shelf life
La'gerfeuer *n* campfire
La'gergebühr *f* storage charges
La'gerhalter *m* stock clerk
La'gerhaus *n* warehouse
Lagerist –in [lɑgə'rɪst(ɪn)] §7 *mf* warehouse clerk
La'gerleben *n* camp life
lagern ['lɑgərn] *tr* lay down; (*Waren*) stock, store; (*altern*) season; (mach) mount on bearings ‖ *ref* lie down, rest ‖ *intr* lie down, rest; (*Waren*) be stored; (*Wein*) season; (geol) be deposited; (mil) camp
La'gerort *m*, **La'gerplatz** *m* resting place; (*Stapelplatz*) dump; (mil) camp site
La'gerraum *m* storeroom, stockroom
La'gerstand *m* stock on hand, inventory
La'gerstätte *f*, **La'gerstelle** *f* resting place; (geol) deposit; (mil) camp site
La'gerung *f* (-;-en) storage; (*Alterung*) seasoning; (geol) stratification
La'gervorrat *m* stock, supply
Lagune [la'gunə] *f* (-;-n) lagoon
lahm [lɑm] *adj* lame; paralyzed ‖ **Lahme** §5 *mf* paralytic
lahmen ['lɑmən] *intr* be lame, limp
lähmen ['lɛmən] *tr* paralyze; (*Verkehr*) tie up; (fig) cripple
lahm'legen *tr* cripple, paralyze; (mil) neutralize
Läh'mung *f* (-;-en) paralysis
Laib [laɪp] *m* (-[e]s;-e) loaf
Laich [laɪç] *m* (-[e]s;-e) spawn
laichen ['laɪçən] *intr* spawn
Laie ['laɪə] *m* (-n;-n) layman; **Laien** laity
Lai'enbruder *m* lay brother
lai'enhaft *adj* layman's
Lakai [la'kaɪ] *m* (-en;-en) lackey

Lake ['lɑkə] *f* (-;-n) brine, pickle
Laken ['lɑkən] *n* (-s;-) sheet
lakonisch [la'konɪʃ] *adj* laconic
Lakritze [la'krɪtsə] *f* (-;-n) licorice
Lakune [la'kunə] *f* (-;-n) lacuna
lallen ['lalən] *tr & intr* stammer
lamellenförmig [la'melənfœrmɪç] *adj* laminate
lamentieren [lamen'tirən] *intr* wail
Lametta [la'meta] *n* (-s;) tinsel
Lamm [lam] *n* (-[e]s;"er) lamb
Lamm'braten *m* roast lamb
Lämmerwolke ['lemərvəlkə] *f* cirrus
Lamm'fleisch *n* (culin) lamb
lamm'fromm' *adj* meek as a lamb
Lampe ['lampə] *f* (-;-n) lamp; light
Lam'penfieber *n* stage fright
Lam'penschirm *m* lamp shade
Lampion [lam'pjõ] *m* (-s;-s) Chinese lantern
lancieren [lã'sirən] *tr* launch, promote; (*Kandidaten*) (pol) groom
Land [lant] *n* (-[e]s;"er & -e) land; (*Ackerboden*) ground, soil; (*Staat*) country; (*Provinz*) state; (*Gegensatz: Stadt*) country; **ans L.** ashore; **auf dem Lande** in the country; **aufs L.** into the country; **aus aller Herren Ländern** from everywhere; **außer Landes gehen** go abroad; **zu Lande** by land
Land'arbeiter *m* farm hand
Land'armee *f* land forces
Land'bau *m* farming, agriculture
Land'besitz *m* landed property
Land'besitzer –in §6 *mf* landowner
Landebahn ['landəban] *f* runway
Landedeck ['landədek] *n* flight deck
Land'edelmann *m* (-es;-leute) country gentleman
Landefeuer ['landəfɔɪ-ər] *n* runway lights
land'einwärts *adv* inland
Landekopf ['landəkɔpf] *m* beachhead
landen ['landən] *tr & intr* (SEIN) land
Land'enge *f* isthmus, neck of land
Landeplatz ['landəplats] *m* wharf; (aer) landing field
Länderei [lendə'raɪ] *f* (-;-en) or **Ländereien** *pl* lands, estates
Länderkunde ['lendərkundə] *f* geography
Landes– [landəs] *comb.fm.* national, native, of the land
Lan'desaufnahme *f* land survey
Lan'desbank *f* national bank
Lan'desbeschreibung *f* topography
lan'deseigen *adj* state-owned
Lan'deserzeugnis *n* domestic product
Lan'desfarben *pl* national colors
Lan'desfürst *m* sovereign
Lan'desgesetz *n* law of the land
Lan'desherr *m* sovereign
Lan'desherrschaft *f*, **Lan'deshoheit** *f* sovereignty
Lan'dessprache *f* vernacular
Lan'destracht *f* national costume
Lan'destrauer *f* public mourning
lan'desüblich *adj* customary
Lan'desvater *m* sovereign
Lan'desverrat *m* high treason
Lan'desverräter –in §6 *mf* traitor
Lan'desverteidigung *f* national defense

Land'flucht f rural exodus
land'flüchtig adj exiled, fugitive
Land'friedensbruch m disturbance of the peace
Land'gericht n district court, superior court
Land'gewinnung f land reclamation
Land'gut n country estate
Land'haus n country house
Land'jäger m rural policeman; (culin) sausage
Land'junker m country squire
Land'karte f map
Land'kreis m rural district
land'läufig adj customary
Ländler ['lɛntlər] m (-s;-) waltz
Land'leute pl country folk
ländlich ['lɛntlɪç] adj rural, rustic
Land'luft f country air
Land'macht f land forces
Land'mann m (-[e]s;-leute) farmer
Land'marke f landmark (for travelers and sailors)
Land'maschinen pl farm machinery
Land'messer m surveyor
Land'partie f outing, picnic
Land'plage f nation-wide plague; (coll) big nuisance
Land'rat m regional governor
Land'ratte f (fig) landlubber
Land'recht n common law
Land'regen m steady rain
Land'rücken m ridge
Land'schaft f (-;-en) landscape, scenery; (Bezirk) district, region
land'schaftlich adj scenic; regional
Landser ['lantsər] m (-s;-) G.I.
Lands'knecht m mercenary
Lands'mann m (-[e]s;-leute) fellow countryman
Land'spitze f promontory
Land'straße f highway
Land'streicher m (-s;-) tramp, hobo
Land'strich m tract of land
Land'sturm m home guard
Land'tag m state assembly
landumschlossen ['lantʊmʃlɔsən] adj landlocked
Lan'dung f (-;-en) landing
Lan'dungsboot n landing craft
Lan'dungsbrücke f jetty, pier
Lan'dungsgestell n landing gear
Lan'dungssteg m gangplank
Land'vermessung f surveying
Land'volk n country folk
Land'weg m overland route
Land'wehr f militia, home guard
Land'wirt m farmer
Land'wirtschaft f agriculture; **L. betreiben** farm
land'wirtschaftlich adj farm, agricultural
Land'zunge f spit of land
lang [laŋ] adj (länger ['lɛŋər]); längste ['lɛŋstə] §9) long; (Person) tall || adv—die ganze Woche l. all week; e—e Stunde l. for an hour
langatmig ['laŋatmɪç] adj long-winded
lang'beinig adj long-legged
lange ['laŋə] adv long, a long time; es ist noch l. nicht fertig it is far from ready; schon l. her long ago; schon l. her, daß a long time since;

so l. bis until; so l. wie as long as; wie l.? how long?
Länge ['lɛŋə] f (-;-n) length; long syllable; (geog) longitude; (pros) quantity; auf die L. in the long run; der L. nach lengthwise; in die L. ziehen drag out
langen ['laŋən] tr reach, hand; j-m eine l. (coll) give s.o. a smack || intr be enough; l. nach reach for || impers—es langt mir I have enough; jetzt langt's mir aber! I've had it!
Län'gengrad m degree of longitude
Län'genkreis m meridian
Län'genmaß n linear measure
Lan'geweile f boredom; sich [dat] die L. vertreiben (coll) kill time
Lang'finger m pickpocket
langfingerig ['laŋfɪŋərɪç] adj (fig) thievish
langfristig ['laŋfrɪstɪç] adj long-term
lang'jährig adj long-standing
Lang'lauf m crosscountry skiing
langlebig ['laŋlebɪç] adj long-lived
Lang'lebigkeit f (-;) longevity
lang'legen ref lie down, stretch out
länglich ['lɛŋlɪç] adj oblong
läng'lichrund adj oval, elliptical
Lang'mut f patience
lang'mütig adj patient
Lang'mütigkeit f patience
längs [lɛŋs] prep (genit or dat) along
langsam ['laŋzam] adj slow
Lang'spielplatte f long-playing record
längst [lɛŋst] adv long since, long ago
längstens ['lɛŋstəns] adv at the latest; (höchstens) at the most
Langstrecken— comb.fm. long-range; (sport) long-distance
langweilen ['laŋvaɪlən] tr bore || ref feel bored
Lang'weiler m (-s;-) slowpoke
langweilig ['laŋvaɪlɪç] adj boring
langwierig ['laŋvirɪç] adj lengthy
Lanolin [lano'lin] n (-s;) lanolin
Lanze ['lantsə] f (-;-n) lance, spear
Lan'zenstechen n (-s;) jousting
Lanzette [lan'tsɛtə] f (-;-n) lancet
Lappalie [la'pɑljə] f (-;-n) trifle
Lappen ['lapən] m (-s;-) rag; washrag; (Flicken) patch; (anat) lobe
läppisch ['lɛpɪʃ] adj silly, trifling
Lappland ['laplant] n (-s;) Lapland
Lärche ['lɛrçə] f (-;-n) (bot) larch
Lärm [lɛrm] m (-[e]s;) noise; **L. schlagen** (fig) make a fuss
lärmen ['lɛrmən] intr make noise
lär'mend adj noisy
Larve ['larfə] f (-;-n) mask; larva
las [las] pret of **lesen**
lasch [laʃ] adj limp; (Speise) insipid
Lasche ['laʃə] f (-;-n) (Klappe) flap; (Schuh-) tongue; (rr) fishplate
lasieren [la'zirən] tr glaze
lassen ['lasən] §104 tr let; (erlauben) allow; (bewirken) have, make; leave (behind, undone, open, etc.); **den Film entwickeln l.** have the film developed; **etw fallen l.** drop s.th.; **ich kann es nicht l.** I can't help it; **j-n warten l.** keep s.o. waiting; **kommen l.** send for; **laß den Lärm!** stop

the noise!; **laß es!** cut it out!; **laßt uns gehen** let us go; **sein Leben l.** lose one's life; **sein Leben l.** für sacrifice one's life for || *ref—***das läßt sich denken** I can imagine; **das läßt sich hören!** now you're talking!; **es läßt sich nicht beschreiben** it defies description; **es läßt sich nicht leugnen, daß** it cannot be denied that; **sich** [*dat*] **Zeit l.** take one's time

lässig ['lɛsɪç] *adj* (*faul*) lazy; (*träge*) sluggish; (*nachlässig*) remiss

Läs'sigkeit *f* (–;) laziness; negligence

läßlich ['lɛslɪç] *adj* venial

Last [last] *f* (–;-en) load, weight; (*Bürde*) burden; (*Hypotek*) encumbrance; (aer, naut) cargo, freight; **j—m etw zur L. legen** blame s.o. for s.th.; **L. der Beweise** weight of evidence; **ruhende L.** dead weight; **zur L. fallen** (*dat*) become a burden for

Last'auto *n* truck

lasten ['lastən] *intr* (**auf** *dat*) weigh (on)

la'stenfrei *adj* unencumbered

La'stensegler *m* transport glider

Laster ['lastər] *m* (–s;–) (coll) truck || *n* (–s;–) vice

Lästerer –in ['lɛstərər(ɪn)] §6 *mf* slanderer; blasphemer

la'sterhaft *adj* vicious

La'sterleben *n* life of vice

lästerlich ['lɛstərlɪç] *adj* slanderous; blasphemous

Lästermaul ['lɛstərmaʊl] *n* scandalmonger

lästern ['lɛstərn] *tr* slander; blaspheme

Lä'sterung *f* (–;-en) slander; blasphemy

lästig ['lɛstɪç] *adj* troublesome; **j—m l. fallen** bother s.o.

Last'kahn *m* barge

Last'kraftwagen *m* truck

Last'schrift *f* (acct) debit

Last'tier *n* beast of burden

Last'träger *m* porter

Last'wagen *m* truck

Last'zug *m* tractor-trailer (*consisting of several trailers*)

Lasur [la'zur] *f* (–;) glaze

Latein [la'taɪn] *n* (–s;) Latin

lateinisch [la'taɪnɪʃ] *adj* Latin

Laterne [la'ternə] *f* (–;-n) lantern; lamp

Latrine [la'trinə] *f* (–;-n) latrine

Latri'nenparole *f* scuttlebut

Latsche ['latʃə] *f* (–;-n) (coll) slipper || *n* ['latʃə] *f* (–;-n) (bot) dwarf pine

latschen ['latʃən] *intr* (SEIN) shuffle along

Latte ['latə] *f* (–;-n) lath

Lat'tenkiste *f* crate

Lat'tenzaun *m* picket fence

Lattich ['latɪç] *m* (–[e]s;–e) lettuce

Latz [lats] *m* (–es;–e) bib; (*Klappe*) flap; (*Schürzchen*) pinafore

Lätzchen ['lɛtsçən] *n* (–s;–) bib

lau [laʊ] *adj* lukewarm; (*Wetter*) mild; (fig) half-hearted

Laub [laʊp] *n* (–[e]s;) foliage

Laub'baum *m* deciduous tree

Laube ['laʊbə] *f* (–;-n) arbor; (*Säulen-*

gang) portico; (*Bogengang*) arcade; (theat) box

Lau'bengang *m* arcade

Laub'säge *f* fret saw

Laub'sägearbeit *f* fretwork

Laub'werk *n* foliage

Lauer ['laʊ.ər] *f* (–;) ambush; **auf der L. liegen** lie in wait

lauern ['laʊ.ərn] *intr* lurk; **l. auf** (*acc*) lie in wait for, watch for

lau'ernd *adj* (*Blick*) wary; (*Gefahr*) lurking

Lauf [laʊf] *m* (–[e]s;–e) running; run; (*e–s Flusses*) course; (*Strömung*) current; (*Wettlauf*) race; (*e–s Gewehrs*) barrel; (astr) path, orbit; **den Dingen freien L. lassen** let things take their course; **im Laufe der Zeit** in the course of time; **im vollen Laufe** at full speed

Lauf'bahn *f* career; (astr) orbit; (sport) lane

Lauf'bursche *m* errand boy; office boy

laufen ['laʊfən] §105 *intr* (SEIN) run; (*zu Fuß gehen*) walk; (*leck sein*) leak; (*Zeit*) pass; **die Dinge l. lassen** let things slide; **j—n l. lassen** let s.o. go; (*straflos*) let s.o. off

lau'fend *adj* (*ständig*) steady; (*Jahr, Preis*) current; (*Nummern*) consecutive; (*Wartung, Geschäft*) routine; (*Meter, usw.*) running; **auf dem laufenden** up to date; **laufendes Band** conveyor belt; assembly line

Läufer ['lɔɪfər] *m* (–s;–) runner; (*Teppich*) runner; (chess) bishop; (fb) halfback; (mach) rotor; (mus) run

Lauferei [laʊfə'raɪ] *f* (–;-en) running around

Lauf'feuer *n* (–s;) wildfire

Lauf'fläche *f* tread (*on tire*)

Lauf'gewicht *n* sliding weight

Lauf'gitter *n* playpen

Lauf'graben *m* trench

läufig ['lɔɪfɪç] *adj* in heat

Läu'figkeit *f* (–;) heat

Lauf'junge *m* errand boy; office boy

Lauf'kran *m* (mach) traveling crane

Lauf'kunde *m* chance customer

Lauf'masche *f* run (*in stocking*)

lauf'maschenfrei *adj* runproof

Lauf'paß *m* (coll) walking papers; (coll) brush-off

Lauf'planke *f* gangplank

Lauf'rad *n* (–e–r Turbine) rotor; (aer) landing wheel

Lauf'schritt *m* double-quick time

Lauf'steg *m* footbridge

Laufställchen ['laʊf/tɛlçən] *n* (–s;–) playpen

Lauf'zeit *f* rutting season; (*e–s Vertrags*) term; (cin) running time; (mach) (service) life

Lauge ['laʊgə] *f* (–;-n) lye; (*Salzlauge*) brine; (*Seifenlauge*) suds

Lau'gensalz *n* alkali

lau'gensalzig *adj* alkaline

Laune ['laʊnə] *f* (–;-n) mood, humor; (*Grille*) whim

lau'nenhaft *adj* capricious

launig ['laʊnɪç] *adj* humorous, witty

lau'nisch *adj* moody

Laus [laʊs] *f* (–;–e) louse

Laus'bub m rascal

lauschen ['lauʃən] intr listen; eavesdrop; **l. auf** (acc) listen to

Lau'scher –in §6 mf eavesdropper

lauschig ['lauʃɪç] adj cosy, peaceful

Lau'sebengel m, **Lau'sejunge** m, **Lau'sekerl** m (coll) rascal, brat

lausen ['lauzən] tr pick lice from; **ich denke, mich laust der Affe** (coll) I couldn't believe my eyes

lausig ['lauzɪç] adj lousy

laut [laut] adj loud; (lärmend) noisy; **l. werden** become public; **l. werden lassen** divulge || prep (genit & dat) according to; (com) as per; **l. Bericht** according to the report || **Laut** m (–[e]s;–e) sound

Laute ['lautə] f (–;–n) lute

lauten ['lautən] intr sound; (Worte) read, go, say; **das Urteil lautet auf Tod** the sentence is death

läuten ['lɔɪtən] tr & intr ring, toll || impers—**es läutet** the bell is ringing || **Läuten** n (–s;) toll

lauter ['lautər] adj pure; (aufrecht) sincere || invar adj (nichts als) nothing but

Lau'terkeit f (–;) purity; sincerity

läutern ['lɔɪtərn] tr purify; (Metall, Zucker) refine; (veredeln) ennoble

Laut'gesetz n phonetic law

Laut'lehre f phonetics, phonology

laut'lich adj phonetic

laut'los adj soundless

Laut'malerei f onomatopoeia

Laut'schrift f phonetic spelling

Laut'sprecher m loudspeaker

Laut'sprecheranlage f public address system

Laut'sprecherwagen m sound truck

Laut'stärke f volume

Laut'stärkeregler m volume control

Laut'system n phonetic system

Laut'zeichen n phonetic symbol

lau'warm adj lukewarm

Lava ['lava] f (–;) lava

Lavendel [la'vɛndəl] m (–s;) (bot) lavender

laven'delfarben adj lavender

lavieren [la'virən] intr (fig) maneuver; (naut) tack

Lawine [la'vinə] f (–;–n) avalanche

lax [laks] adj lax

Lax'heit f (–;) laxity

Laxiermittel [la'ksirmɪtəl] n laxative

Layout ['le·aut] n (–s;–s) layout

Lazarett [latsa'rɛt] n (–[e]s;–e) (mil) hospital

Lebedame ['lebədamə] f woman of leisure

Lebehoch [lebə'hox] n (–s;–s) cheer; toast; **ein dreimaliges L.** three cheers

Lebemann ['lebəman] m playboy

leben ['lebən] tr & intr live || **Leben** n (–s;–) life; existence; **am L. bleiben** survive; **am L. erhalten** keep alive; **ins L. rufen** bring into being; **sein L. lang** all his life; **ums L. kommen** lose one's life

lebendig [le'bɛndɪç] adj living, alive; (lebhaft) lively; (Darstellung) vivid

Le'bensalter n age, period of life

Le'bensanschauung f outlook on life

Le'bensart f manners

Le'bensaufgabe f mission in life

Le'bensbaum m (bot) arbor vitae

Le'bensbedingungen pl living conditions

Le'bensbeschreibung f biography

Le'bensdauer f life span

Le'benserwartung f life expectancy

le'bensfähig adj viable

Le'bensfrage f vital question

Le'bensgefahr f mortal danger

le'bensgefährlich adj perilous

Le'bensgefährte m, **Le'bensgefährtin** f life companion, spouse

le'bensgroß adj life-size

Le'benshaltung f standard of living

Le'benshaltungskosten pl cost of living

Le'bensinteressen pl vital interests

Le'benskraft f vitality

Le'benskünstler m—**er ist ein L.** nothing can get him down

lebensläng'lich ['lebɛnsleŋlɪç] adj life

Le'benslauf m curriculum vitae

Le'bensmittel pl groceries

Le'bensmittelgeschäft n grocery store

Le'bensmittelkarte f food ration card

Le'bensmittellieferant m caterer

le'bensmüde adj weary of life

le'bensnotwendig adj vital, essential

Le'bensprozeß m vital function

Le'bensstandard m standard of living

Le'bensstellung f lifetime job; tenure

Le'bensstil m life style

Le'bensunterhalt m livelihood

le'bensuntüchtig adj impractical

Le'bensversicherung f life insurance

Le'benswandel m conduct; life

Le'bensweise f way of life

Le'bensweisheit f worldly wisdom

le'benswichtig adj vital, essential

Le'benszeichen n sign of life

Le'benszeit f lifetime; **auf L.** for life

Leber ['lebər] f (–s;–n) liver; **frei von der L. weg reden** speak frankly

Le'berfleck m mole

Leberkäs ['lebərkɛs] m (–es;) meat loaf (made with liver)

Le'bertran m cod-liver oil

Lebewesen ['lebəvezən] n living being

Lebewohl [lebə'vol] n (–[e]s;–e) farewell

lebhaft ['lephaft] adj lively; full of life; (Farbe) bright; (Straße) busy; (Börse) brisk; (Interesse) keen

Lebkuchen ['lepkuxən] m gingerbread

leblos ['leplos] adj lifeless

Lebtag ['leptak] m—**mein L.** in all my life

Lebzeiten ['leptsaɪtən] pl—**zu meinen L.** in my lifetime

lechzen ['leçtsən] intr (nach) thirst (for)

leck [lek] adj leaky || **Leck** n (–[e]s;–e) leak; **ein L. bekommen** spring a leak

lecken ['lekən] tr lick || intr leak; (naut) have sprung a leak

lecker ['lekər] adj dainty; (köstlich) delicious

Leckerbissen (**Lek'kerbissen**) m delicacy, dainty

Leckerei [lekə'raɪ] f (–;–en) daintiness; sweets

leckerhaft (**lek'kerhaft**) adj dainty

Leckermaul (Lek'kermaul) n—ein L. sein have a sweet tooth

Leder ['ledər] n (-s;) leather

ledern ['ledərn] adj leather; (fig) dull, boring

ledig ['ledɪç] adj single; (Kind) illegitimate; l. (genit) free of; **lediger Stand** single state; celibacy

le'diglich adv merely, only

leer [ler] adj empty, void; (fig) vain || **Leere** f (-;) emptiness, void; vacuum || n—**der Schlag ging ins L.** the blow missed; **ins L. starren** stare into space

leeren ['lerən] tr empty

Leer'gut n empties (bottles, cases)

Leer'lauf m (aut) idling, idle; (Gang) (aut) neutral

leer'laufen §105 intr (SEIN) idle

leer'stehend adj unoccupied, vacant

Leer'taste f (typ) space bar

legal [le'gal] adj legal

legalisieren [legalɪ'zirən] tr legalize

Legat [le'gat] m (-en;-en) legate || n (-[e]s;-e) legacy, bequest

legen ['legən] tr lay, put; **auf die Kette l.** chain, tie up; **j-m ans Herz l.** recommend warmly to s.o.; **Nachdruck l. auf** (acc) emphasize; **Wert l. auf** (acc) attach importance to || ref lie down; go to bed; (Wind) die down; **die Krankheit hat sich ihm auf die Lungen gelegt** his sickness affected his lungs

legendär [legen'der] adj legendary

Legende [le'gendə] f (-;-n) legend

legieren [le'girən] tr alloy

Legie'rung f (-;-en) alloy

Legion [le'gjon] f (-;-en) legion

Legionär [legjo'ner] m (-s;-e) legionnaire, legionary

legislativ [legɪsla'tif] adj legislative || **Legislative** [legɪsla'tivə] f (-;-n) legislature

Legis·lator [legɪs'lator] m (-s;-latoren [la'torən]) legislator

Legislatur [legɪsla'tur] f (-;-en) legislature

legitim [legɪ'tim] adj legitimate

Legitimation [legɪtɪma'tsjon] f (-;-en) proof of identity

legitimieren [legɪtɪ'mirən] tr legitimize; (berechtigen) authorize || ref prove one's identity

Lehen ['leən] n (-s;-) (hist) fief

Le'hensherr m liege lord

Le'hens·mann m (-[e]s;-leute) vassal

Lehm [lem] m (-[e]s;-e) clay, loam

lehmig ['lemɪç] adj clayey, loamy

Lehne ['lenə] f (-;-n) support; (e-s Stuhls) arm, back; (Abhang) slope

lehnen ['lenən] tr, ref & intr lean

Lehnsessel ['lenzesəl] m, **Lehnstuhl** ['len/tul] m armchair, easy chair

Lehn'wort ['lenvort] n (-[e]s;-er) loan word

Lehramt ['leramt] n teaching profession; professorship

Lehranstalt ['leran/talt] f educational institution

Lehrbrief ['lerbrif] m apprentice's diploma

Lehrbube ['lerbubə] m apprentice

Lehrbuch ['lerbux] n textbook

Lehrbursche ['lerbur/ə] m apprentice

Lehre ['lerə] f (-;-n) doctrine, teaching; (Wissenschaft) science; (Theorie) theory; (Unterweisung) instruction; (Warnung) lesson; (e-r Fabel) moral; (Richtschnur) rule, precept; (e-s Lehrlings) apprenticeship; (tech) gauge; **in der L. sein** be serving one's apprenticeship

lehren ['lerən] tr teach, instruct

Lehrer –in ['lerər(ɪn)] §6 mf teacher

Leh'rerbildungsanstalt f teacher's college

Leh'rerkollegium n teaching staff

Lehrfach ['lerfax] n subject

Lehrfilm ['lerfɪlm] m educational film

Lehrgang ['lergaŋ] m (educ) course

Lehrgedicht ['lergədɪçt] n didactic poem

Lehrgegenstand ['lergegən/tant] m (educ) subject

Lehrgeld ['lergelt] n—**L. zahlen** (fig) learn the hard way

lehrhaft ['lerhaft] adj didactic

Lehrjunge ['lerjuŋə] m apprentice

Lehrkörper ['lerkörpər] m teaching staff; faculty (of a university)

Lehrling ['lerlɪŋ] m (-s;-e) apprentice

Lehrmädchen ['lermetçən] n girl apprentice

Lehrmeister ['lermaɪstər] m master, teacher, instructor

Lehrmittel ['lermɪtəl] n teaching aid

Lehrplan ['lerplan] m curriculum

lehrreich ['lerraɪç] adj instructive

Lehrsaal ['lerzal] m lecture hall

Lehrsatz ['lerzats] m (eccl) dogma; (math) theorem

Lehrspruch ['ler/prux] m maxim

Lehrstelle ['ler/telə] f position as an apprentice

Lehrstoff ['ler/tof] m subject matter

Lehrstuhl ['ler/tul] m (educ) chair

Lehrstunde ['ler/tundə] f lesson

Lehrzeit ['lertsaɪt] f apprenticeship

Leib [laɪp] m (-[e]s;-er) body; (Bauch) belly, abdomen; (Taille) waist; (Mutterleib) womb; **am ganzen L. zittern** tremble all over; **bleib mir nur damit vom Leibe!** (coll) don't bother me with that: **e-n harten L. haben** be constipated; **gesegneten Leibes** with child; **L. und Leben** life and limb; **mit L. und Seele** through and through; **sich** [dat] **j-n vom Leibe halten** keep s.o. at arm's length; **zu Leibe gehen** (dat) tackle (s.th.), attack (s.o.)

Leib'arzt m personal physician

Leib'binde f sash

Leibchen ['laɪpçən] n (-s;-) bodice; vest

leib'eigen adj in bondage || **Leibeigene** §5 mf serf

Leib'eigenschaft f (-;) serfdom, bondage

Lei'besbeschaffenheit f (-;-en) constitution

Lei'beserbe m (-n;-n) offspring

Lei'beserziehung f physical education

Lei'besfrucht f fetus

Lei'beskräfte pl—**aus Leibeskräften**

schreien scream at the top of one's lungs
Lei′besübungen *pl* physical education
Lei′besvisitation *f* body search
Leib′garde *f* bodyguard
Leibgardist [ˈlaɪpgardɪst] *m* (-en; -en) bodyguard
Leib′gericht *n* favorite dish
leibhaft(ig) [ˈlaɪphaft(ɪç)] *adj* incarnate, real
leib′lich *adj* bodily, corporal; **leiblicher Vetter** first cousin; **sein leiblicher Sohn** his own son
Leib′rente *f* annuity for life
Leib′schmerzen *pl*, **Leib′schneiden** *n* abdominal pains
Leibstandarte [ˈlaɪpʃtandartə] *f* (-; -n) (hist) SS bodyguard
Leib′wache *f* bodyguard
Leib′wäsche *f* underwear
Leiche [ˈlaɪçə] *f* (-; -n) corpse, body; carcass; (dial) funeral
Leichenbegängnis [ˈlaɪçənbəgɛŋnɪs] *n* (-ses; -se) funeral, interment
Leichenbeschauer [ˈlaɪçənbəʃaʊ-ər] *m* (-s; -) coroner
Leichenbestatter [ˈlaɪçənbəʃtatər] *m* (-s; -) undertaker
Lei′chenbittermiene *f* woe-begone look
Leichenfledderer [ˈlaɪçənfledərər] *m* (-s; -) body stripper
Lei′chengift *n* ptomaine poison
lei′chenhaft *adj* corpse-like
Lei′chenhalle *f* mortuary
Lei′chenöffnung *f* autopsy
Lei′chenräuber *m* body snatcher
Lei′chenrede *f* eulogy
Lei′chenschau *f* post mortem
Lei′chenschauhaus *n* morgue
Lei′chenstarre *f* rigor mortis
Lei′chenträger *m* pallbearer
Lei′chentuch *n* shroud
Lei′chenverbrennung *f* cremation
Lei′chenwagen *m* hearse
Lei′chenzug *m* funeral cortege
Leichnam [ˈlaɪçnam] *m* (-[e]s; -e) corpse
leicht [laɪçt] *adj* light; (*nicht schwierig*) easy; (*gering*) slight; **leichten Herzens** light-heartedly
Leicht′atletik *f* track and field
Leicht′bauweise *f* lightweight construction
Leicht′benzin *n* cleaning fluid
leichtbeschwingt [ˈlaɪçtbəʃvɪŋt] *adj* gay
leicht′blütig *adj* light-hearted
leicht′entzündlich *adj* highly flammable
Leichter [ˈlaɪçtər] *m* (-s; -) (naut) lighter
leicht′fertig *adj* frivolous, flippant; careless
leicht′flüchtig *adj* highly volatile
leicht′flüssig *adj* thin
Leicht′gewicht *n* lightweight division
Leichtgewichtler [ˈlaɪçtgəvɪçtlər] *m* (-s; -) lightweight boxer
leicht′gläubig *adj* gullible
leicht′hin *adv* lightly, casually
Leich′tigkeit *f* (-;) ease
leichtlebig [ˈlaɪçtlebɪç] *adj* easygoing
Leicht′sinn *m* frivolity, irresponsibility;

(*Sorglosigkeit*) carelessness; (*Unbedachtsamkeit*) imprudence
leicht′sinnig *adj* frivolous, irresponsible
leicht′verdaulich *adj* easy to digest
leicht′verderblich *adj* perishable
leid [laɪt] *adj*—**er tut mir l.** I feel sorry for him; **es tut mir l., daß I am sorry that**; **es ist** (or **tut**) **mir l. um I** feel sorry for, I regret; **ich bin es l.** I'm fed up with it || **Leid** *n* (-[e]s;) (*Betrübnis*) sorrow; (*Schaden*) harm; (*Unrecht*) wrong; **j-m ein L. antun** harm s.o.
Leideform [ˈlaɪdəfɔrm] *f* (gram) passive voice
leiden [ˈlaɪdən] §106 *tr* suffer; (*ertragen*) stand || *intr* (an *dat*) suffer (*from*) || **Leiden** *n* (-s; -) suffering; (*Krankheit*) ailment
Lei′denschaft *f* (-; -en) passion
lei′denschaftlich *adj* passionate
lei′denschaftslos *adj* dispassionate
Lei′densgefährte *m*, **Lei′densgefährtin** *f* fellow sufferer
Lei′densgeschichte *f* tale of woe; (relig) Passion
Lei′densweg *m* way of the cross
leider [ˈlaɪdər] *adv* unfortunately
leiderfüllt [ˈlaɪterfʏlt] *adj* sorrowful
leidig [ˈlaɪdɪç] *adj* tiresome
leidlich [ˈlaɪtlɪç] *adv* tolerable; (*halbwegs gut*) passable || *adv* so-so
leidtragend [ˈlaɪttragənt] *adj* in mourning || **Leidtragende** §5 *mf* mourner; **er ist der L. dabei** he is the one that suffers for it
Leid′wesen *n*—**zu meinem L.** to my regret
Leier [ˈlaɪ-ər] *f* (-; -n) (mus) lyre
Lei′erkasten *m* hand organ, hurdygurdy
Lei′ermann *m* (-[e]s; ∸er) organ grinder
leiern [ˈlaɪ-ərn] *tr* (*winden*) crank; (*Gebete, Verse*) drone || *intr* drone
Leih- [laɪ] *comb.fm.* loan, rental
Leih′amt *n*, **Leih′anstalt** *f* loan office
Leih′bibliothek *f* rental library
leihen [ˈlaɪ-ən] *tr* lend, loan out; (*entleihen*) (von) borrow (*from*)
Leih′gebühr *f* rental fee
Leih′haus *n* pawnshop
Leim [laɪm] *m* (-[e]s; -e) glue; birdlime; **aus dem L. gehen** fall apart; **j-m auf den L. gehen** be taken in by s.o.
leimen [ˈlaɪmən] *tr* glue; (*betrügen*) take in, fool
Leim′farbe *f* distemper
leimig [ˈlaɪmɪç] *adj* gluey
Lein [laɪn] *m* (-[e]s; -e) flax
Leine [ˈlaɪnə] *f* (-; -n) line, cord; (*Hunde-*) leash
Leinen [ˈlaɪnən] *n* (-s; -) linen
Lei′neneinband *m* (-[e]s; ∸e) (bb) cloth binding
Lei′nenschuh *m* sneaker, canvas shoe
Lei′nenzeug *n* linen fabric
Lein′öl *n* linseed oil
Lein′tuch *n* sheet
Lein′wand *f* linen cloth; canvas; (cin) screen
leise [ˈlaɪzə] *adj* soft, low; (*sanft*) gentle; (*gering*) faint; (*Schlaf*) light

lei'sestellen *tr* (rad) turn down
Lei'setreter *m* (-s;-) pussyfoot
Leiste ['laɪstə] *f* (-;-n) (*Rand*) border; (anat) groin; (carp) molding
leisten ['laɪstən] *tr* do, perform, accomplish; (*Dienst*) render; (*Eid*) take; (*Abbitte, Hilfe, Widerstand*) offer; **Bürgschaft l. für** put up bail for; **Folge l.** (*dat*), **Gehorsam l.** (*dat*) obey; **Genüge l.** (*dat*) satisfy; **j-m Gesellschaft l.** keep s.o. company; **sich** [*dat*] **etw l. können** be able to afford s.th. ‖ **Leisten** *m* (-s;-) last; **alles über e-n L. schlagen** (fig) be undiscriminating
Lei'stenbruch *m* hernia, rupture
Lei'stung *f* (-;-en) performance; efficiency; ability; feat, achievement; (*Ergebnis*) result; (*Erzeugung*) production; (*Abgabe, Ausstoß*) output; (*Beitrag*) contribution; (*Dienstleistungen*) services rendered; (elec) power, wattage; (indust) output, production; (insur) benefits; (mach) capacity
Lei'stungsanreiz *m* incentive
lei'stungsfähig *adj* (*Person*) efficient; (*Motor*) powerful; (*Fabrik*) productive; (phys) efficient
Lei'stungsfähigkeit *f* efficiency; proficiency; (*e-s Autos*) performance; (*e-s Motors*) power; (mach) output
lei'stungsgerecht *adj* based on merit
Lei'stungsgrenze *f* peak of performance
Leis'tungslohn *m* pay based on performance
Lei'stungszulage *f* bonus
Leit- [laɪt] *comb.fm.* leading, dominant, guiding
Leit'artikel *m* editorial
Leit'bild *n* (good) example, ideal
leiten ['laɪtən] *tr* lead, guide; (*Verkehr*) route; (*Betrieb*) direct, run; (*Versammlung*) preside over; (arti) direct; (elec, mus, phys) conduct
Lei'ter *m* (-s;-) leader; director; (educ) principal; (elec, mus) conductor ‖ *f* (-;-n) ladder
Lei'terin *f* (-;-nen) leader; director
Leit'faden *m* manual, guide
Leit'fähigkeit *f* conductivity
Leit'gedanke *m* main idea, main theme
Leit'hammel *m* (fig) boss, leader
Leit'motiv *n* keynote; (mus) leitmotiv
Leit'satz *m* basic point
Leit'spruch *m* motto
Leit'stelle *f* head office
Leit'stern *m* polestar, lodestar
Lei'tung *f* (-;-en) direction, guidance; (*Beaufsichtigung*) management; (*Rohr*) pipeline; (*für Gas, Wasser*) main; (elec) lead; (phys) conduction; (telp) line; **e-e lange L. haben** be rather dense; **L. besetzt!** line is busy!
Lei'tungsdraht *m* (elec) lead
Lei'tungsmast *m* telephone pole
Lei'tungsnetz *n* (elec) power lines
Lei'tungsrohr *n* pipe, main
Lei'tungsvermögen *n* conductivity
Lei'tungswasser *n* tap water
Leit'werk *n* (aer) tail assembly
Leit'zahl *f* code number

Lektion [lɛk'tsjon] *f* (-;-en) lesson; (fig) lecture, rebuke
Lek·tor ['lɛktor] *m* (-s;-toren ['torən]) lecturer; (*e-s Verlags*) reader
Lektüre [lɛk'tyrə] *f* (-;) reading matter, literature
Lende ['lɛndə] *f* (-;-n) loin; (*Hüfte*) hip
Len'denbraten *m* roast loin, sirloin
len'denlahm *adj* stiff; (*Ausrede*) lame
Len'denschurz *m* loincloth
Len'denstück *n* tenderloin, sirloin
lenkbar ['lɛŋkbar] *adj* manageable; steerable, maneuverable; **lenkbares Luftschiff** dirigible
lenken ['lɛŋkən] *tr* guide, control; (*Wagen*) drive; (*wenden*) turn; (*steuern*) steer; **Aufmerksamkeit l. auf** (*acc*) call attention to
Len'ker **-in** §6 *mf* ruler; (aut) driver
Lenkrad ['lɛŋkrat] *n* steering wheel
Lenksäule ['lɛŋkzɔɪlə] *f* steering column
Lenkstange ['lɛŋkʃtaŋə] *f* handlebar; (aut) connecting rod
Len'kung *f* (-;-en) guidance, control; (aut) steering mechanism
Lenz [lɛnts] *m* (-es;-e) (fig) prime of life; (poet) spring
Lenz'pumpe *f* bilge pump
Lepra ['lepra] *f* (-;) leprosy
Lerche ['lɛrçə] *f* (-;-n) (orn) lark
lernbegierig ['lɛrnbəgiriç] *adj* eager to learn, studious
lernen [‚'lɛrnən] *tr & intr* learn; study
Lesart ['lezart] *f* version
lesbar ['lezbar] *adj* legible; readable
Lesbierin ['lɛsbɪ·ərɪn] *f* (-;-nen) lesbian
lesbisch ['lɛsbɪʃ] *adj* lesbian; **lesbische Liebe** lesbianism
Lese ['lezə] *f* (-;-n) gathering, picking; (*Wein-*) vintage
Lese- [lezə] *comb.fm.* reading; lecture
Le'sebrille *f* reading glasses
Le'sebuch *n* reader
Le'sehalle *f* reading room
lesen ['lezən] §107 *tr* read; gather; (*Messe*) say ‖ *intr* read; lecture; **l. über** (*acc*) lecture on
le'senswert *adj* worth reading
Le'seprobe *f* specimen from a book; (theat) reading rehearsal
Le'ser **-in** §6 *mf* reader; picker
Le'seratte *f* (coll) bookworm
le'serlich *adj* legible
Le'serzuschrift *f* letter to the editor
Le'sestoff *m* reading matter
Le'sezeichen *n* bookmark
Le'sung *f* (-;-en) reading
Lette ['lɛtə] *m* (-n;-n), **Lettin** ['lɛtɪn] *f* (-;-nen) Latvian
lettisch ['lɛtɪʃ] *adj* Latvian
Lettland ['lɛtlant] *n* (-[e]s;) Latvia
letzte ['lɛtstə] §9 *adj* last; (*endgültig*) final, ultimate; (*neueste*) latest; (*Ausweg*) last; **bis ins l.** to the last detail; **in den letzten Jahren** in recent years; **in der letzten Zeit** lately; **letzten Endes** in the final analysis ‖ **Letzte** §5 *pron* last, last one; **am Letzten** on the last of the month; **sein Letztes hergeben** do one's ut-

most; **zu guter Letzt** finally, last but not least
letztens ['lɛtstəns] *adv* lately
letztere ['lɛtstərə] §5 *mfn* latter
letzthin [lɛtst'hɪn] *adv* lately
letztlich ['lɛtstlɪç] *adv* lately, recently; in the final analysis
letztwillig ['lɛtstvɪlɪç] *adj* testamentary
Leucht– [lɔɪçt] *comb.fm.* luminous; illuminating
Leucht'bombe *f* flare bomb
Leuchte ['lɔɪçtə] *f* (–;–n) light, lamp; lantern; (fig) luminary
leuchten ['lɔɪçtən] *intr* shine
leuch'tend *adj* shining, bright; luminous
Leuchter ['lɔɪçtər] *m* (–s;–) candlestick; chandelier
Leucht'farbe *f* luminous paint
Leucht'feuer *n* (aer) flare; (naut) beacon
Leucht'käfer *m* lightning bug
Leucht'körper *m* light bulb; light fixture
Leucht'kugel *n* tracer bullet; flare
Leucht'pistole *f* Very pistol
Leucht'rakete *f* (aer) flare
Leucht'reklame *f* neon sign
Leucht'röhre *f* fluorescent lamp
Leucht'spurgeschoß *n* tracer bullet
Leucht'turm *m* lighthouse
Leucht'zifferblatt *n* luminous dial
leugnen ['lɔɪgnən] *tr* deny; disclaim
Leukoplast [lɔɪko'plast] *n* (–[e]s;–e) adhesive tape
Leumund ['lɔɪmʊnt] *m* (–[e]s;) reputation
Leu'mundszeugnis *n* character reference
Leute ['lɔɪtə] *pl* people, persons, men; (*Dienstleute*) servants
Leu'teschinder *m* oppressor; slave driver
Leutnant ['lɔɪtnant] *m* (–s;–s) lieutenant
Leut'priester *m* secular priest
leut'selig *adj* affable
Lexikograph [lɛksiko'graf] *m* (–en;–en) lexicographer
Lexikon ['lɛksikɔn] *n* (–s;–s) encyclopedia
Libanon ['libanɔn] *n* (–s;) Lebanon
Libelle [li'bɛlə] *f* (–;–n) dragonfly; (carp) level
liberal [libe'ral] *adj* liberal
Liberalismus [libera'lɪsmʊs] *m* (–s;) liberalism
Libyen ['liby·ən] *n* (–s;) Libya
licht [lɪçt] *adj* light, bright; (*durchsichtig*) clear ‖ **Licht** *n* (–[e]s;–er) light; (*Kerze*) candle
licht'beständig *adj* non-fading
Licht'bild *n* photograph
Licht'bildervortrag *m* illustrated lecture
licht'blau *adj* light-blue
Licht'blick *m* (fig) bright spot
Licht'bogen *m* (elec) arc
Licht'bogenschweißung *f* arc welding
Licht'brechung *f* (–;–en) refraction of light
Licht'druck *m* phototype
licht'durchlässig *adj* translucent

licht'echt *adj* non-fading
licht'empfindlich *adj* sensitized; **l. machen** sensitize
Licht'empfindlichkeit *f* (phot) speed
lichten ['lɪçtən] *tr* clear; thin; (*Anker*) weigh
lichterloh ['lɪçtərlo] *adv* ablaze; **l. brennen** be ablaze
Licht'hof *m* (archit) light well, inner court; (phot) halo
Licht'kegel *m* beam of light
Licht'maschine *f* generator, dynamo
Licht'pause *f* blueprint
Licht'punkt *m* (fig) ray of hope
Licht'schacht *m* light well
Licht'schalter *m* light switch
licht'scheu *adj*—**lichtscheues Gesindel** shady characters
Licht'schirm *m* lamp shade
Licht'seite *f* (fig) bright side
Licht'spiele *pl*, **Licht'spielhaus** *n*, **Licht'spieltheater** *n* movie theater
licht'stark *adj* (*Objektiv*) high-powered; (phot) high-speed
Lich'tung *f* (–;–en) clearing
Lid [lit] *n* (–[e]s;–er) eyelid
Lid'schatten *m* eye shadow
lieb [lip] *adj* dear; (*nett*) nice; **der liebe Gott** the good Lord; **es ist mir l., daß** I am glad that; **seien Sie so l. und** please; **sich lieb Kind machen bei** ingratiate oneself with
lieb'äugeln *intr*—**l. mit** (& *fig*) flirt with
Liebchen ['lipçən] *n* (–s;–) darling
Liebe ['libə] *f* (–;) (zu) love (*for, of*)
liebedienerisch ['libədinəriʃ] *adj* fawning
Liebelei [libə'laɪ] *f* (–;–en) flirtation
lieben ['libən] *tr* love, be fond of
lie'bend *adj* loving ‖ *adv*—**l. gern** gladly ‖ **Liebende** §5 *mf* lover
lie'benswert *adj* lovable
lie'benswürdig *adj* lovable; charming; **das ist sehr l. von Ihnen** that's very kind of you
lieber ['libər] *adv* rather, sooner; **l. haben** prefer
Liebes– [libəs] *comb.fm.* love, of love
Lie'besdienst *m* favor, good turn
Lie'beserlebnis *n* romance
Lie'besgabe *f* charitable gift
Lie'beshandel *m* love affair
Lie'besmahl *n* love feast
Lie'besmühe *f*—**verlorene L.** wasted effort
Lie'bespaar *n* couple (of lovers)
Lie'bespfand *n* token of love
Lie'bestrank *m* love potion
Lie'beswerben *n* advances
lie'bevoll *adj* loving, affectionate
Lieb'frauenkirche *f* Church of Our Lady
lieb'gewinnen §121 *tr* grow fond of
lieb'haben §89 *tr* love, be fond of
Liebhaber ['liphabər] *m* (–s;–) lover, beau; amateur; fan, buff; **erster L.** leading man
lieb'kosen *tr* caress, fondle
lieb'lich *adj* lovely, sweet; charming
Liebling ['liplɪŋ] *m* (–s;–e) darling; (*Haustier*) pet; (*Günstling*) favorite
Lieblings– *comb.fm.* favorite

Lieb′lingsgedanke *m* pet idea

Lieb′lingswunsch *m* dearest wish

lieb′los *adj* unkind

lieb′reich *adj* kind, affectionate

Lieb′reiz *m* charm, attractiveness

lieb′reizend *adj* charming

Lieb′schaft *f* (-;-en) love affair

liebste [′lipstə] §9 *adj* favorite; **am liebsten trinke ich Wein** || I like wine best of all

Lied [lit] *n* (-[e]s;-er) song; **er weiß ein L. davon zu singen** he can tell you all about it; **geistliches L.** hymn

liederlich [′li:dərlɪç] *adj* dissolute; (*unordentlich*) disorderly

lief [lif] *pret* of laufen

Lieferant –in [lifə′rant(ɪn)] §7 *mf* supplier; (*Verteiler*) distributor; (*von Lebensmitteln*) caterer

Lieferauto [′lifərauto] *n* delivery truck

lieferbar [′lifərbar] *adj* available, deliverable

Liefergebühr [′lifərgə′byr] *f* delivery charge

liefern [′lifərn] *tr* deliver; (*beschaffen*) supply, furnish; (*Ertrag*) yield; **ich bin geliefert** (coll) I'm done for

Lieferschein [′lifər/ain] *m* delivery receipt

Lie′ferung *f* (-;-en) delivery, shipment; supply; (*e-s Werkes*) installment; number; **zahlbar bei L.** cash on delivery

Lieferwagen [′lifərvagən] *m* delivery truck

Liege [′ligə] *f* (-;-n) couch

Lie′gekur *f* rest cure

liegen [′ligən] §108 *intr* lie, be situated; **gut auf der Straße l.** hug the road; **l. an** (*dat*) lie near; (fig) be due to; **wie die Sache jetzt liegt** as matters now stand || *impers*—**es liegt an ihm zu** (*inf*) it's up to him to (*inf*); **es liegt auf der Hand** it is obvious; **es liegt mir nichts daran** it doesn't matter to me; **es liegt mir (sehr viel) daran** it matters a (great deal) to me

lie′genbleiben §62 *intr* (SEIN) stay in bed; (*Waren*) remain unsold; (*stekkenbleiben*) have a breakdown; (*Arbeit*) be left undone

lie′genlassen §104 *tr* let lie; leave alone; (*Arbeit*) leave undone

Lie′genschaft *f* (-;-en) real estate

Lie′gestuhl *m* deck chair

Lie′gestütz *m* (gym) pushup

lieh [li] *pret* of leihen

ließ [lis] *pret* of lassen

Li•ga [′liga] *f* (-;-gen [gən]) league

Liguster [lɪ′gustər] *m* (-s;-) privet

lieren [lɪ′irən] *ref*—**sich l. mit** ally oneself with

Likör [lɪ′kør] *m* (-s;-e) liqueur

lila [′lila] *adj* lilac

Lilie [′liljə] *f* (-;-n) lily

Limonade [lɪmo′nadə] *f* (-;-n) soft drink, soda

lind [lɪnt] *adj* mild, gentle

Linde [′lɪndə] *f* (-;-n) (bot) linden

lindern [′lɪndərn] *tr* alleviate; (*Übel*) mitigate; (*mildern*) soften

Lindwurm [′lɪntvurm] *m* dragon

Lineal [lɪne′al] *n* (-s;-e) ruler

Linguist –in [lɪŋgu′ɪst(ɪn)] §7 *mf* linguist

Linie [′linjə] *f* (-;-n) line; **auf gleicher L. mit** on a level with; **in erster L.** in the first place

Li′nienpapier *n* lined paper

Li′nienrichter *m* (sport) linesman

Li′nienschiff *n* ship of the line

li′nientreu *adj*—**l. sein** follow the party line

linieren [lɪ′nirən] *tr* line, rule

linke [′lɪŋkə] §9 *adj* left; (*Seite*) wrong, reverse || §5 **Linke** *m* (box) left || §5 *f* left side; left hand; **die L.** (pol) the left

linkisch [′lɪŋkɪ/] *adj* clumsy, awkward

links [lɪŋks] *adv* left; to the left; on the left; (*verkehrt*) inside out; **l. liegenlassen** bypass, ignore; **links um!** left, face!

links′drehend *adj* counterclockwise

linksgängig [′lɪŋksgɛnɪç] *adj* counterclockwise

Linkshänder [′lɪŋkshɛndər] *m* (-s;-) left-hander

links′läufig *adj* counterclockwise

links′stehend *adj* (pol) leftist

Linnen [′lɪnən] *n* (-s;) linen

Linse [′lɪnzə] *f* (-;-n) (bot) lentil; (opt) lens

Lippe [′lɪpə] *f* (-;-n) lip; **e-e L. riskieren** (fig) speak out of turn

Lip′penbekenntnis *n* lip service

Lip′penlaut *m* labial

Lip′penstift *m* lipstick

liquid [lɪ′kvit] *adj* (*Geldmittel*) liquid; (*Gesellschaft*) solvent

Liquidation [lɪkvida′tsjon] *f* (-;-en) liquidation; (*Kostenrechnung*) bill

liquidieren [lɪkvi′dirən] *tr* liquidate; (*Geschäft*) wind up; (*Honorar*) charge

lispeln [′lɪspəln] *tr & intr* lisp; (*flüstern*) whisper

Lissabon [lɪsa′bon] *n* (-s;) Lisbon

List [lɪst] *f* (-;-en) cunning; trick

Liste [′lɪstə] *f* (-;-n) list; **schwarze L.** blacklist

Li′stenwahl *f* block voting

listig [′lɪstɪç] *adj* cunning, sly

Litanei [lɪta′nai] *f* (-;-en) litany

Litauen [′litau·ən] *n* (-s;) Lithuania

litauisch [′litau·ɪ/] *adj* Lithuanian

Liter [′litər] *m & n* (-s;-) liter

literarisch [lɪte′rarɪ/] *adj* literary

Literatur [lɪtera′tur] *f* (-;-en) literature

Litfaßsäule [′lɪtfaszɔilə] *f* advertising pillar

Litur•gie [lɪtur′gi] *f* (-;-gien [′gi·ən]) liturgy

Litze [′lɪtsə] *f* (-;-n) cord; (elec) strand

Li•vree [lɪ′vre] *f* (-;-vreen [′vre·ən]) uniform, livery

Lizenz [lɪ′tsɛnts] *f* (-;-en) license

Lob [lop] *n* (-[e]s;) praise

loben [′lobən] §109 *tr* praise

lo′benswert *adj* praiseworthy

Lobhudelei [lophudə′lai] *f* (-;-en) flattery

lob′hudeln tr heap praise on

löblich [′løplıç] adj commendable

lob′preisen tr extol, praise

Lob′rede f panegyric

Loch [lɔx] n (−es;ⁿer) hole

Loch′bohrer m auger

lochen [′lɔxən] tr punch, perforate

Locher [′lɔxər] m (−s;−) punch

löcherig [′lœçərıç] adj full of holes

Loch′karte f punch card

Lo′chung f (−;−en) perforation

Locke [′lɔkə] f (−;−n) lock, curl

locken [′lɔkən] tr allure, entice; decoy; (Hund) whistle to

locker [′lɔkər] adj loose; (nicht straff) slack; spongy; (moralisch) loose

lockern [′lɔkərn] tr loosen

lockig [′lɔkıç] adj curly, curled

Lock′mittel n, **Lock′speise** f (& fig) bait

Lockspitzel [′lɔk/pıtsəl] m stool-pigeon

Lo′ckung f (−;−en) allurement

Lock′vogel m (& fig) decoy

Loden [′lodən] m (−s;−) coarse woolen cloth

lodern [′lodərn] intr blaze; (fig) glow

Löffel [′lœfəl] m (−s;−) spoon; (culin) spoonful; (coll & hunt) ear; **über den L. balbieren** hoodwink

Löf′felbagger m power shovel

löffeln [′lœfəln] tr spoon out

log [lok] pret of **lügen**

Logbuch [′lɔkbux] n logbook

Loge [′loʒə] f (−;−n) (der Freimaurer) lodge; (theat) box

Lo′genbruder m freemason

Logierbesuch [lo′ʒirbəzux] m houseguest(s)

logieren [lo′ʒirən] intr (bei) stay (with)

Logik [′logık] f (−;) logic

Logis [lo′ʒi] invar n lodgings

logisch [′logıʃ] adj logical

Lohe [′lo·ə] f (−;−n) blaze, flame

Lohgerber [′logərbər] m (−s;−) tanner

Lohn [lon] m (−[e]s;ⁿe) pay, wages; (fig) reward

Lohn′abbau m wage cut

lohnen [′lonən] tr compensate, reward; (Arbeiter) pay; **j−m etw l.** reward s.o. for s.th.; ‖ ref pay, be worthwhile

löhnen [′lønən] tr pay, pay wages to

Lohn′erhöhung f raise, wage increase

Lohn′gefälle n wage differential

Lohn′herr m employer

lohn′intensiv adj with high labor costs

Lohn′liste f payroll

Lohn′satz m pay rate

Lohn′stopp m wage freeze

Lohn′tag m payday

Lohn′tüte f pay envelope

Löh′nung f (−;−en) payment

lokal [lo′kal] adj local ‖ **Lokal** n (−[e]s;−e) locality, premises; (Wirtshaus) restaurant, pub, inn

lokalisieren [lokalı′zirən] tr localize

Lokalität [lokalı′tɛt] f (−;−en) locality

Lokomotive [lokomo′tivə] f (−;−n) locomotive

Lokomotiv′führer m (rr) engineer

Lokus [′lokus] m (−;−se) (coll) john

Lorbeer [′lɔrbər] m (−s;−en) laurel

los [los] adj loose; **es ist etw los** there is s.th. going on; **es ist nichts los** there is nothing going on; **etw los haben** have s.th. on the ball; **j−n** (or **etw**) **los sein** be rid of s.o. (or s.th.); **los!** go on!, scram!; (sprich!) fire away!; (mach schnell!) let's go!; (sport) play ball!; **mit ihm ist nicht viel los** he's no great shakes; **was ist los?** what's the matter? ‖ **Los** n (−[e]s;−e) lot; (Lotterie-) ticket; (Anteil) lot, portion; (Schicksal) fate; **das Große Los** first prize; **das Los ziehen** draw lots; **die Lose sind gefallen** the die is cast

los− comb.fm. un−, e.g., **losmachen** undo

los′arbeiten tr extricate ‖ ref get loose, extricate oneself ‖ intr (auf acc) work away (at)

lösbar [′løsbar] adj solvable

los′binden §59 tr loosen, untie

los′brechen §64 tr break off ‖ intr (SEIN) break loose

Löschblatt [′lœʃ/blat] n blotter

Löscheimer [′lœʃ/aımər] m fire bucket

löschen [′lœʃən] tr put out; (Durst) quench; (Schuld) cancel; (Schrift) blot; (Bandaufnahme) erase; (Firma) liquidate; (Hypotek) pay off; (naut) unload

Lö′scher m (−s;−) blotter; (Feuer−) fire extinguisher

Löschgerät [′lœʃ/gəret] n fire extinguisher

Löschmannschaft [′lœʃ/manʃaft] f fire brigade

Löschpapier [′lœʃ/papir] n blotting paper

Lö′schung f (−;−en) extinction; (Tilgung) cancellation; (naut) unloading

los′drehen tr unscrew, twist off

los′drücken tr fire ‖ intr pull the trigger

lose [′lozə] §9 adj loose

Lösegeld [′løzəgelt] n ransom

loseisen [′losaızən] tr—**Geld l. von** wangle money out of; **j−n l. aus** get s.o. out of; **j−n l. von** get s.o. away from ‖ ref (von) worm one's way (out of)

losen [′lozən] intr draw lots

lösen [′løzən] tr loosen, untie; (abtrennen) sever; (Bremse) release; (Fahrkarte) buy; (loskaufen) ransom; (lossprechen) absolve; (Rätsel) solve; (Schuß) fire; (Verlobung) break off ‖ ref come loose, come undone; dissolve; (sich befreien) free oneself

los′fahren §71 intr (SEIN) drive off; **l. auf** (acc) head for; rush at; attack (verbally)

los′gehen §82 intr (SEIN) (coll) begin; (Gewehr) go off; (sich lösen) come loose; **auf j−n l.** attack s.o.

los′haken tr unhook

los′kaufen tr ransom

los′ketten tr unchain

los′kommen §99 intr (SEIN) come loose, come off; **ich komme nicht davon los** I can't get over it; **l. von** get away from; get rid of

los′lachen intr burst out laughing

los′lassen §104 *tr* let go; release; **den Hund l. auf** (*acc*) sic the dog on
los′legen *intr* (coll) start up, let fly; (*reden*) (coll) open up; **leg los!** (*coll*) fire away!
löslich ['løslɪç] *adj* soluble
los′lösen *tr* detach
los′machen *tr* undo, untie; (*freimachen*) free || *ref* disengage onself
los′platzen *intr* (SEIN) burst out laughing; **l. mit** blurt out
los′reißen §53 *tr* & *ref* break loose
los′sagen *ref*—**sich l. von** renounce
los′schlagen §132 *tr* knock off; (*verkaufen*) dispose of, sell cheaply || *intr* open the attack; **l. auf** (*acc*) let fly at
los′schnallen *tr* unbuckle
los′schrauben *tr* unscrew
los′sprechen §64 *tr* absolve
los′steuern *intr*—**l. auf** (*acc*) head for
Lo′sung *f* (-;-en) (*Kot*) dung; (mil) password; (pol) slogan
Lö′sung *f* (-;-en) solution
Lö′sungsmittel *n* solvent; thinner
los′werden §159 *tr* (SEIN) get rid of
los′ziehen §163 *intr* (SEIN) set out, march away; **l. auf** (*acc*) talk about, run down
Lot [lot] *n* (-[e]s;-e) plummet; plumb line; (*Lötmetall*) solder; (geom) perpendicular; **im Lot** perpendicular; (fig) in order; **ins Lot bringen** (fig) set right
Löteisen ['løtaɪzən] *n* soldering iron
loten ['lotən] *tr* (naut) plumb || *intr* (naut) take soundings
löten ['løtən] *tr* solder
Lötkolben ['løtkɔlbən] *m* soldering iron
Lötlampe ['løtlampə] *f* blowtorch
Lötmetall ['løtmetal] *n* solder
lot′recht *adj* perpendicular
Lotse ['lotsə] *m* (-n;-n) (aer) air traffic controller; (naut) pilot
lotsen ['lotsən] *tr* (*Flugzeuge*) guide in; (naut) pilot
Lotte·rie [lɔtə'ri] *f* (-;-rien ['ri·ən]) lottery, sweepstakes
Lotterie′los *n* lottery ticket
lotterig ['lɔtərɪç] *adj* sloppy
Lotterleben ['lɔtərlebən] *n* dissolute life
Lotto ['lɔto] *n* (-s;-s) state-owned numbers game
Löwe ['løvə] *m* (-n;-n) lion
Lö′wenanteil *m* lion's share
Lö′wenbändiger **-in** §6 *mf* lion tamer
Lö′wengrube *f* lion's den
Lö′wenmaul *n* (bot) snapdragon
Lö′wenzahn *m* (bot) dandelion
Löwin ['løvɪn] *f* (-;-nen) lioness
loyal [lo·a'jal] *adj* loyal
Luchs [lʊks] *m* (-es;-e) lynx
Lücke ['lʏkə] *f* (-;-n) gap, hole; (*Mangel*) deficiency; (*im Gesetz*) loophole; (*Zwischenraum*) interval; **auf L. stehend** staggered
Lückenbüßer ['lʏkənbysər] *m* (-s;-) stop-gap
lückenhaft (lük′kenhaft) *adj* defective, fragmentary
Luder ['ludər] *n* (-s;-) carrion; (coll)

cad; (*Weibsbild*) slut; **das arme L.!** the poor thing!; **dummes L.!** fathead!
Lu′derleben *n* dissolute life
ludern ['ludərn] *intr* lead a dissolute life
Luft [lʊft] *f* (-;-̈e) air; (*Atem*) breath; (*Brise*) breeze; **die L. ist rein** the coast is clear; **es ist dicke L.** there is trouble brewing; **es liegt etw in der L.** (fig) there's s.th. in the air; **frische L. schöpfen** get a breath of fresh air; **in die L. fliegen** be blown up; **in die L. gehen** blow one's top; **in die L. sprengen** blow up; **j-n an die L. setzen** give s.o. the air; **nach L. schnappen** gasp for breath; **seinem Zorn L. machen** give vent to one's anger; **tief L. holen** take a deep breath
Luft′alarm *m* air-raid alarm
Luft′angriff *m* air raid
Luft′ansicht *f* aerial view
Luft′aufklärung *f* air reconnaissance
Luft′bild *n* aerial photograph
Luft′bremse *f* air brake
Luft′brücke *f* airlift
Lüftchen ['lʏftçən] *n* (-s;-) gentle breeze
luft′dicht *adj* airtight
Luft′druck *m* atmospheric pressure; (*e-r Explosion*) blast; (aut) air pressure
Luft′druckbremse *f* air brake
Luft′druckmesser *m* barometer
Luft′druckprüfer *m* tire gauge
Luft′düse *f* air nozzle, air jet
lüften ['lʏftən] *tr* air, ventilate; **den Hut l.** tip one's hat
Luft′fahrt *f* aviation
Luft′fahrzeug *n* aircraft
Luft′flotte *f* air force
luft′förmig *adj* gaseous
Luft′hafen *m* airport
Luft′heizung *f* hot-air heating
Luft′herrschaft *f* air supremacy
Luft′hülle *f* atmosphere
luftig ['lʊftɪç] *adj* airy; (*windig*) windy; (*Person*) flighty; (*Kleidung*) loosely woven, light
Luftikus ['lʊftɪkus] *m* (-;-se) lightheaded person
Luft′klappe *f* air valve
luft′krank *adj* airsick
Luft′kurort *m* mountain resort
Luft′landetruppen *pl* airborne troops
luft′leer *adj* vacuous; **luftleerer Raum** vacuum
Luft′linie *f* beeline; **fünfzig Kilometer L.** 50 kilometers as the crow flies
Luft′loch *n* vent; (aer) air pocket
Luft′parade *f* flyover
Luft′post *f* airmail
Luft′raum *m* atmosphere; air space
Luft′reifen *m* tire
Luft′reklame *f* sky writing
Luft′röhre *f* (anat) windpipe
Luft′schiff *n* airship
Luft′schiffahrt *f* aviation
Luft′schloß *n* castle in the air
Luft′schutz *m* air-raid protection
Luft′schutzkeller *m* air-raid shelter
Luft′schutzwart *m* air-raid warden
Luft′spiegelung *f* mirage

Luft′sprung m caper
Luft′streitkräfte pl air force
Luft′strom m air current
Luft′strudel m (aer) wash
Luft′stützpunkt m air base
luft′tüchtig adj air-worthy
Lüf′tung f (-;) airing, ventilation
Luft′veränderung f change of climate
Luft′verkehrsgesellschaft f, **Luft′ver-
kehrslinie** f airline
Luft′vermessung f aerial survey
Luft′verpestung f (-;), **Luft′ver-
schmutzung** f (-;), **Luft′verunreini-
gung** f (-;) air pollution
Luft′waffe f air force
Luft′warnung f air-raid warning
Luft′weg m air route; **auf dem Luft-
wege** by air
Luft′widerstand m (phys) air resistance
Luft′zug m draft
Lug [luk] m (-[e]s;) lie; **Lug und Trug**
pack of lies
Lüge [′lygə] f (-;-n) lie; **fromme L.**
white lie; **j-n Lügen strafen** prove
s.o. a liar
lugen [′lugən] intr peep
lügen [′lygən] §111 tr—**das Blaue vom
Himmel herunter l.** lie like mad ||
intr lie, tell a lie
Lügendetek·tor [′lygəndetektor] m (-s;
-toren [′torən] lie detector
Lü′gengeschichte f cock-and-bull story
Lü′gengespinst n, **Lü′gengewebe** n tissue of lies
lü′genhaft adj (Person) dishonest, lying; (Nachricht) untrue
Lügner -in [′lygnər(in)] §6 mf liar
lügnerisch [′lygnəriʃ] adj dishonest
Luke [′lukə] f (-;-n) (am Dach) dormer window; (naut) hatch
Lümmel [′lyməl] m (-s;-) lout
Lump [lump] m (-en;-en) scoundrel
lumpen [′lumpən] intr lead a wild life;
sich nicht l. lassen (coll) be gener-
ous || **Lumpen** m (-s;-) rag
Lum′pengeld n measly sum; **für ein L.**
dirtcheap
Lum′pengesindel n mob, rabble
Lum′penhändler m ragman
Lum′penkerl m (coll) bum
Lum′penpack n rabble, riffraff
Lumperei [lumpə′raɪ] f (-;-en) shady
deal; dirty trick; (Kleinigkeit) trifle
lumpig [′lumpɪç] adj ragged; shabby

Lunge [′luŋə] f (-;-n) lung
Lungen- comb.fm. pulmonary
Lun′genentzündung f pneumonia
Lun′genflügel m lung
lun′genkrank adj consumptive || **Lun-
genkranke** §5 mf consumptive
Lun′genschwindsucht f tuberculosis
lungern [′luŋərn] intr (HABEN & SEIN)
loiter about, lounge about
Lunte [′luntə] f (-;-n) fuse; **L. riechen**
smell a rat
Lupe [′lupə] f (-;-n) magnifying glass;
unter die L. nehmen examine closely
lüpfen [′lypfən] tr lift gently
Lust [lust] f (-;⸚e) pleasure; (Verlangen) desire; (Wollust) lust; **L.
haben zu** (inf) feel like (ger); **mit
L. und Liebe** with heart and soul
Lust′barkeit f (-;-en) amusement, entertainment
Lüster [′lystər] m (-s;-) luster
lüstern [′lystərn] adj (nach) desirous
(of); lustful; (Bilder, Späße) lewd
Lü′sternheit f (-;) greediness; lustful-
ness; lewdness
Lust′fahrt f pleasure ride
lustig [′lustɪç] adv gay, jolly; (belu-
stigend) amusing; **du bist vielleicht
l.!** you must be joking!; **l. sein** have
a gay time; **sich l. machen über**
(acc) poke fun at
Lüstling [′lystlɪŋ] m (-s;-e) lecher
lust′los adj listless; (Börse) inactive
Lustmolch [′lustmolç] m (-[e]s;-e)
sex fiend
Lust′mord m sex murder
Lust′reise f pleasure trip
Lust′seuche f venereal disease
Lust′spiel n comedy
lust′wandeln intr (SEIN) stroll
Lutheraner -in [lutə′ranər(in)] §6 mf
Lutheran
lutherisch [′lutərɪʃ] adj Lutheran
lutschen [′lutʃən] tr & intr suck
Lut′scher m (-s;-) nipple, pacifier
Luxus [′luksus] m (-;) luxury
Lu′xusausgabe f deluxe edition
Luzerne [lu′tsernə] f (-;-n) alfalfa
Lymphe [′lymfə] f (-;-n) lymph
lynchen [′lynçən] tr lynch
Lyrik [′lyrɪk] f (-;) lyric poetry
lyrisch [′lyrɪʃ] adj lyric(al)
Lyze·um [ly′tse·um] n (-s;-en [ən])
girls' high school

M

M, m [em] invar n M, m
M abbr (Mark) (fin) mark
Maar [mar] n (-[e]s;-e) crater lake
Maat [mat] m (-[e]s;-e) (naut) mate
Machart [′maxart] f make, type
Mache [′maxə] f (-;) (coll) make-believe; **er hat es schon in der M.** he is
working on it
machen [′maxən] tr make; (tun) do;
(bewirken) produce; (verursachen)
cause; (Prüfung, Reise, Spaziergang)

take; (Begriff) form; (Besuch) pay;
(Freude) give; (Holz) chop; (Konkurrenz) offer; **das macht mir zu
schaffen** that causes me trouble; **das
macht nichts** it doesn't matter; never
mind; **das macht Spaß** that's fun;
Dummheiten m. behave foolishly;
Ernst m. be in earnest; **gemacht!**
right!; O.K.!; **Geschäfte m.** do business; **Geschichten m.** make a fuss;
Hochzeit m. get married; **ich mache**

Spaß I'm joking; **mach dir nichts daraus!** don't worry about it; **mach's gut!** so long!; **wieviel macht es?** how much is it? || *ref* make progress, do all right; **sich auf den Weg m.** set out; **sich** [*dat*] **etw m. lassen** have s.th. made to order; **sich m. an** (*acc*) get down to; **sich** [*dat*] **nichts daraus m.** not care for (or about) || *intr*—**laß nich nur m.!** just leave it to me; **mach, daß . . . !** see to it that . . . !; **m. in** (*dat*) deal in; dabble in; **mach schon** (or **zu**)! get going!; **nichts zu m!** (coll) nothing doing! no dice!

Machenschaften ['maxənʃaftən] *pl* intrigues

Macher ['maxər] *m* (-s;-) instigator; (coll) big shot

Macht [maxt] *f* (-;-̈e) might, power; (*Kraft*) force, strength; **aus eigener M.** on one's own responsibility; **an der Macht** in power; **an die M. kommen** come to power

Macht'ausgleich *m* balance of power

Macht'befugnis *f* authority

Machthaber ['maxthabər] *m* (-s;-) ruler; dictator

machthaberisch ['maxthabərɪʃ] *adj* dictatorial

mächtig ['mɛçtɪç] *adj* mighty, powerful; (*riesig*) huge

macht'los *adj* powerless

Macht'losigkeit *f* (-;) impotence

Macht'politik *f* power politics

Macht'vollkommenheit *f* absolute power; **aus eigener M.** on one's own authority

Macht'wort *n* (-[e]s;-e)—**ein M. sprechen** put one's foot down

Machwerk ['maxverk] *n* bad job

Mädchen ['mɛtçən] *n* (-s;-) girl; maid

mäd'chenhaft *adj* girlish; maidenly

Mäd'chenhandel *m* white slavery

Mäd'chenname *m* maiden name; girl's name

Made ['madə] *f* (-;-n) maggot

Mädel ['medəl] *n* (-s;-) (coll) girl

madig ['madɪç] *adj* wormy

Magazin [maga'tsin] *n* (-s;-e) warehouse; (*Zeitschrift; Fernsehprogramm; am Gewehr*) magazine

Magd [makt] *f* (-;-̈e) maid; (poet) maiden

Magen ['magən] *m* (-s;-̈ & -) stomach; **auf nüchternen M.** on an empty stomach

Ma'genbeschwerden *pl* stomach trouble

Ma'gengrube *f* pit of the stomach

Ma'gensaft *m* gastric juice

Ma'genweh *n* stomach ache

mager ['magər] *adj* lean; (*Ernte*) poor

Magie [ma'gi] *f* (-;) magic

Magier -in ['magiər(ɪn)] §6 *mf* magician

magisch ['magɪʃ] *adj* magic(al)

Magister [ma'gɪstər] *m* (-s;-) school teacher; **M. der freien Künste** Master of Arts

Magistrat [magɪs'trat] *m* (-[e]s;-e) city council; (hist) magistracy

Magnat [mag'nat] *m* (-en;-en) magnate

Magnet [mag'net] *m* (-[e]s;-e) or (-en;-en) magnet

magnetisch [mag'netɪʃ] *adj* magnetic

magnetisieren [magnetɪ'zirən] *tr* magnetize

Magnetismus [magne'tɪsmus] *m* (-;) magnetism

Mahagoni [maha'goni] *n* (-s;) mahogony

Mahd [mat] *f* (-;-en) mowing

Mähdrescher ['medreʃər] *m* (agr) combine

mähen ['me·ən] *tr* mow; (*Getreide*) reap

Mä'her *m* (-s;-) mower; reaper

Mahl [mal] *n* (-[e]s;-̈er) meal

mahlen ['malən] (*pp* **gemahlen**) *tr* grind || *intr* spin

Mahl'zahn *m* molar

Mahl'zeit *f* meal; **prost M.!** that's a nice mess!

Mähmaschine ['memaʃinə] *f* reaper; (*Rasen*-) lawn mower

Mähne ['menə] *f* (-;-n) mane

mahnen ['manən] *tr* (**an** *acc*) remind (of); (**an** *acc*) warn (about or of)

Mahnmal ['manmal] *n* (-s;-e) monument

Mah'nung *f* (-;-en) admonition; (com) reminder, notice

Mähre ['merə] *f* (-;-n) old nag

Mähren ['merən] *n* (-s;) Moravia

Mai [mai] *m* (-[e]s;-e) May

Mai'baum *m* maypole

Mai'blume *f* lily of the valley

Maid [mait] *f* (-;-en) (poet) maiden

Mai'glöckchen *n* lily of the valley

Mai'käfer *m* June bug

Mailand ['mailant] *n* (-[e]s;) Milan

Mais [mais] *m* (-es;) Indian corn

Maische ['maiʃə] *f* (-;) mash

Mais'hülse *f* corn husk

Mais'kolben *m* corncob

Majestät [majes'tet] *f* (-;-en) majesty

majestätisch [majes'tetɪʃ] *adj* majestic

Major [ma'jor] *m* (-s;-e) major

Majoran [majo'ran] *m* (-s;-e) marjoram

majorenn [majo'ren] *adj* of age

Majorität [majorɪ'tet] *f* (-;-en) majority

Makel ['makəl] *m* (-s;-) spot, stain

Mäkelei [mekə'lai] *f* (-;-en) carping

mäkelig ['mekəlɪç] *adj* critical; (*im Essen*) picky

ma'kellos *adj* spotless; (fig) impeccable

mäkeln ['mekəln] *intr* (**an** *dat*) carp (at), find fault (with)

Makkaroni [maka'roni] *pl* macaroni

Makler -in ['maklər(ɪn)] §6 *mf* agent, broker

Mäkler -in ['meklər(ɪn)] §6 *mf* faultfinder

Mak'lergebühr *f* brokerage

Makrele [ma'krelə] *f* (-;-n) mackerel

Makrone [ma'kronə] *f* (-;-n) macaroon

Makulatur [makula'tur] *f* (-;) waste

mal [mal] *adv* (coll) once; (arith) times; **komm mal her!** come here once!; **zwei mal drei** two times three; **zwei mal Spinat** two (orders of) spinach ‖ **Mal** n (-[e]s;-e) mark, sign; (*Mutter*-) birthmark, mole; (*Fleck*) stain; time; **dieses Mal** this time; **manches liebe Mal** many a time; **mit e-m Male** all at once

Malbuch ['malbux] n coloring book

malen ['malən] tr & intr paint

Ma'ler –in §6 mf painter

Malerei [malə'raɪ] f (-;-en) painting

malerisch ['malərɪʃ] adj picturesque

Ma'lerleinwand f canvas

Malkunst ['malkunst] f art of painting

Malstrom ['malʃtrom] m maelstrom

malträtieren [maltre'tirən] tr maltreat

Malve ['malvə] f (-;-n) mallow

Malz [malts] n (-es;) malt

Malz'bonbon m cough drop

Mal'zeichen n multiplication sign

Mama [ma'ma], ['mama] f (-;-s) mom, ma

Mamsell [mam'zel] f (-;-en) miss; (*Wirtschafterin*) housekeeper

man [man] indef pron one, they, people, you; **man hat mir gesagt** I have been told

manch [manç] invar adj—**manch ein** many a ‖ **mancher** §3 adj many a; **manche** pl some, several ‖ pron many a person; many a thing

mancherlei ['mançərlaɪ] invar adj all sorts of, various

Manchester [man'ʃɛstər] m (-s;) corduroy

manch'mal adv sometimes

Mandant –in [man'dant(ɪn)] §7 mf client

Mandarine [manda'rinə] f (-;-n) tangerine

Mandat [man'dat] n (-[e]s;-e) mandate

mandatieren [manda'tirən] tr mandate

Mandel ['mandəl] f (-;-n) almond; (*15 Stück*) fifteen; (anat) tonsil

Man'delentzündung f tonsilitis

Mandoline [mando'linə] f (-;-n) mandolin

Mandschurei [mantʃu'raɪ] f (-;) Manchuria

Mangan [maŋ'gan] n (-s;) manganese

Mangel ['maŋəl] m (-s;⸚) lack, deficiency; (*Knappheit*) shortage; (*Fehler*) shortcoming; **aus M. an** (dat) for lack of; **M. haben an** (dat) be deficient in; **M. leiden an** (dat) be short of ‖ f (-;-n) mangle

Mangel– comb.fm. in short supply

Man'gelberuf m undermanned profession

man'gelhaft adj defective; faulty; unsatisfactory, deficient

Man'gelkrankheit f nutritional deficiency

mangeln ['maŋəln] tr (*Wäsche*) mangle ‖ intr (an dat) be short of, lack ‖ impers—**es mangelt mir an** (dat) I lack

Mängelrüge ['meŋəlrygə] f (-;-n) (com) complaint (*about a shipment*)

mangels ['maŋəls] prep (genit) for want of, for lack of

Ma·nie [ma'ni] f (-;-nien ['ni·ən]) mania

Manier [ma'nir] f (-;-en) manner

maniert [ma'nirt] adj affected

Manieriert'heit f (-;-en) mannerism

manier'lich adj mannerly, polite

Manifest [manɪ'fɛst] n (-es;-e) (aer, naut) manifest; (pol) manifesto

Maniküre [manɪ'kyrə] f (-;-n) manicure; manicurist

maniküren [manɪ'kyrən] tr manicure

manipulieren [manɪpu'lirən] tr manipulate

manisch ['manɪʃ] adj maniacal

Manko ['maŋko] n (-s;-s) deficit; (com) shortage

Mann [man] m (-[e]s;⸚er) man; (*Gatte*) husband; **an den M. bringen** manage to get rid of; **der M. aus dem Volke** the man in the street; **seinen M. stehen** hold one's own

mannbar ['manbar] adj marriageable

Mann'barkeit f (-;) puberty; marriageable age (*of girls*)

Männchen ['mɛnçən] n (-s;-) little man; (*Ehemann*) hubby; (zool) male; **M. machen** sit on its hind legs

Männerchor ['mɛnərkor] m men's choir

Mannesalter ['manəsaltər] n manhood

Manneszucht ['manəstsuxt] f discipline

mann'haft adj manly, valiant

mannigfaltig ['manɪçfaltɪç] adj manifold

Man'nigfaltigkeit f (-;) diversity

männlich ['mɛnlɪç] adj male; (fig) manly; (gram) masculine

Männ'lichkeit f (-;) manhood; virility

Mannsbild ['mansbɪlt] n (pej) man

Mann'schaft f (-;-en) crew; (sport) team, squad; **Mannschaften** (mil) enlisted men

Mann'schaftsführer –in §6 mf (sport) captain

Mann'schaftswagen m (mil) personnel carrier

Mannsleute ['manslɔɪtə] pl menfolk

mannstoll ['manstɔl] adj man-crazy

Manns'tollheit f (-;) nymphomania

Mann'weib n mannish woman

Manometer [mano'metər] n pressure gauge

Manöver [ma'nøvər] n (-s;-) maneuver

manövrieren [manø'vrirən] intr maneuver

manövrier'fähig adj maneuverable

Mansarde [man'zardə] f (-;-n) attic

manschen ['manʃən] tr & intr splash

Manschette [man'ʃɛtə] f (-;-n) cuff

Manschet'tenknopf m cuff link

Mantel ['mantəl] m (-s;⸚) overcoat; (*Fahrrad–*) tire; (*e–s Kabels*) sheathing; (*Geschoß–*) jacket, case; (geol, orn) mantle

manuell [manu'ɛl] adj manual

Manufaktur [manufak'tur] f (-;-en) manufacture

Manufaktur'waren pl manufactured goods

Manuskript [manu'skrɪpt] n (-[e]s;-e) manuscript

Mappe ['mapə] f (-;-n) briefcase; (*Aktendeckel*) folder

Märchen ['mɛrçən] n (-s;-) fairy tale

mär'chenhaft adj legendary; (fig) fabulous

Mär'chenland n fairyland
Marchese [mar'keːzə] m (-;-n) marquis
Marder ['mardər] m (-s;-) marten; (fig) thief
Margarine [marga'rinə] f (-;) margarine
Marienbild [ma'riːənbɪlt] n image of the Virgin
Marienfäden [ma'riːənfeːdən] pl gossamer(s)
Marienglas [ma'riːənglas] n mica
Marienkäfer [ma'riːənkeːfər] m ladybug
Marine [ma'rinə] f (-;-n) (Kriegs-) navy; (Handels-) merchant marine
mari'neblau adj navy-blue
Mari'neflugzeug n seaplane
Mari'neinfanterie f marines
Mari'neminister m secretary of the navy
Mari'neoffizier –in §6 mf naval officer
Mari'nesoldat m marine
marinieren [marɪ'nirən] tr marinate
Marionette [marɪ.ə'netə] f (-;-n) puppet
Marionet'tentheater n puppet show
Mark [mark] f (-;-) (fin) mark; (hist) borderland, march || n (-[e]s;) marrow; (im Holz) pith; **bis ins M.** to the quick; **er hat M.** (fig) he has guts; **j-m durch M. und Bein gehen** (fig) go right through s.o.
markant [mar'kant] adj (einprägsam) marked; (außergewöhnlich) striking; (Geländepunkt) prominent
Marke ['markə] f (-;-n) mark; (Brief-) stamp; (Handelszeichen) trademark; (Sorte) brand; (Fabrikat) make; (Spiel-) counter
mark'erschütternd adj piercing
Marketenderei [markətendə'raɪ] f (-;-en) post exchange, PX
Marketing ['markıtıŋ] n (-s;) (com) marketing
markieren [mar'kirən] tr mark; (spielen) pretend to be
Markise [mar'kizə] f (-;-n) awning
Mark'stein m landmark
Markt [markt] m (-[e]s;ːe) market; (Jahrmarkt) fair
Markt'bude f booth, stall
markten ['marktən] intr (um) bargain (for)
markt'fähig adj marketable
Markt'flecken m market town
marktgängig ['marktgɛŋɪç] adj marketable
Markt'platz m market place
Markt'schreier m quack
Marmelade [marmə'ladə] f (-;-n) jam
Marmor ['marmor] m (-s;-e) marble
Mar'morbruch m marble quarry
marmorn ['marmorn] adj marble
marode [ma'rodə] adj (coll) tired out
Marodeur [maro'dør] m (-s;-e) marauder
marodieren [maro'dirən] intr maraud
Marone [ma'ronə] f (-;-n) chestnut
Maroquin [maro'kɛ̃] m (-s;) morocco
Marotte [ma'rotə] f (-;-n) whim
marsch [marʃ] interj march!; be off!; **m., m.!** on the double || **Marsch** m (-s; ːe) march; **in M. setzen** get

going; **j–m den M. blasen** (coll) chew s.o. out; **(sich) in M. setzen** set out
Marschall ['marʃal] m (-s;ːe) marshal
Mar'schallstab m marshal's baton
Marsch'gepäck n full field pack
marschieren [mar'ʃirən] intr (SEIN) march
Marsch'kompanie f replacement company
Marsch'lied n marching song
Marsch'verpflegung f field rations
Marter ['martər] f (-;-n) torture
martern ['martərn] tr torture, torment
Mar'terpfahl m stake
Märtyrer –in ['mertyrər(ın)] §6 mf martyr
Märtyrertum ['mertyrərtum] n (-s;) martyrdom
März [merts] m (-[es];-e) March
Masche ['maʃə] f (-;-n) mesh; stitch; (fig) trick
Ma'schendraht m chicken wire; screen; wire mesh
ma'schenfest adj runproof
Maschine [ma'ʃinə] f (-;-n) machine; (aer) airplane
maschinell [maʃɪ'nel] adj mechanical || adv by machine
Maschi'nenantrieb m—**mit M.** machinedriven
Maschi'nenbau m (-[e]s;) mechanical engineering
Maschi'nengewehr n machine gun
Maschi'nengewehrschütze m machine gunner
maschi'nenmäßig adj mechanical
Maschi'nenpistole f tommy gun
Maschi'nenschaden m engine trouble
Maschi'nenschlosser m machinist
maschi'nenschreiben tr type || **Maschi'nenschreiben** n (-s;-) typing; typewritten letter
Maschi'nenschrift f typescript
Maschi'nensprache f computer language
Maschinerie [maʃɪnə'ri] f (-;) (& fig) machinery
Maschinist –in [maʃɪ'nɪst(ın)] §7 mf machinist
Masern ['mazərn] pl measles
Maserung ['mazəruŋ] f (-;) grain (in wood)
Maske ['maskə] f (-;-n) mask; (fig) disguise; (theat) make-up
Ma'skenball m masquerade
Maskerade [maskə'radə] f (-;-n) masquerade
maskieren [mas'kirən] tr mask
Maskotte [mas'kotə] f (-;-n) mascot
maskulin [masku'lin] adj masculine
Maskuli•num [masku'linum] n (-s;-na [na]) masculine noun
maß [mas] pret of **messen** || **Maß** n (-es;-e) measure; (Messung) measurement; (Ausdehnung) extent, dimension; (Verhältnis) rate, proportion; (Grad) degree; (Mäßigung) moderation; **das Maß ist voll!** I've had it!; **das Maß überschreiten** go too far; **er hat sein gerütteltes Maß an Kummer gehabt** he had his full share of trouble; **in gewissem Maße** to a certain extent; **in hohem Maße**

highly; **j—m Maß nehmen zu** take s.o.'s measurements for; **Maß halten** observe moderation; **mit Maße** in moderation; **nach Maß angefertigt** custom-made; **ohne Maß und Ziel** without limit; **weder Maß noch Ziel kennen** know no bounds; **zweierlei Maß** double standard || *f* (-ʒ- & -e) quart (*of beer*), stein

massakrieren [masa'kri:rən] *tr* massacre

Maß'anzug *m* tailor-made suit

Maß'arbeit *f* work made to order

Masse ['masə] *f* (-ʒ-n) mass; bulk; (*Menge*) volume; (*Volk*) crowd; (*Hinterlassenschaft*) estate; (elec) ground; **die breite M.** the masses; **the rank and file; e—e Masse...** (coll) lots of

Maß'einheit *f* unit of measure

Masseleisen ['masəlaizən] *n* pigiron

Massen— *comb.fm.* mass, bulk, wholesale

Mas'senabsatz *m* wholesale selling

Mas'senangriff *m* mass attack

Mas'senanziehung *f* gravitation

mas'senhaft *adj* in large quantities

Maß'gabe *f—mit der M.*, **daß** with the understanding that; **nach M.** (genit) in proportion to; according to; (jur) as provided in

maß'gebend, maßgeblich ['masgeplɪç] *adj* standard; authoritative; (*Kreise*) leading, influential; **das ist nicht maßgebend für** that is no criterion for

maß'gerecht *adj* to scale

maß'halten §90 *intr* observe moderation

maß'haltig *adj* precise

massieren [ma'si:rən] *tr* massage; (*Truppen*) mass

massig ['masɪç] *adj* bulky; solid; (*Person*) stout || *adv*—**m. viel** (coll) very much

mäßig ['mɛsɪç] *adj* moderate; frugal; (*Leistung*) mediocre

mäßigen ['mɛsɪgən] *tr* moderate, tone down || *ref* control oneself

Mä'ßigkeit *f* moderation; frugality; temperance

Mä'ßigung *f* (-ʒ) moderation

massiv [ma'si:f] *adj* massive; solid

Maß'krug *m* beer mug, stein

Maß'liebchen *n* daisy

maß'los *adj* immoderate || *adv* extremely

Maß'nahme *f* (-ʒ-n), **Maß'regel** *f* (-ʒ -n) measure, step, move

maß'regeln *tr* reprimand

Maß'schneider *m* custom tailor

Maß'stab *m* ruler; (fig) yardstick, standard; (*auf Landkarten*) scale; **jeden M. verlieren** lose all sense of proportion

maß'voll *adj* moderate; (*Benehmen*) discreet

Mast [mast] *m* (-es;-en & -e) pole; (naut) mast || *f* (-ʒ) (*Schweinfutter*) mast

Mast'baum *m* (naut) mast

Mast'darm *m* rectum

mästen ['mɛstən] *tr* fatten

Mast'korb *m* masthead, crow's nest

Material [materɪ'ɑl] *n* (-s;-ien [ɪ·ən]) material

Materialismus [materɪ·a'lɪsmus] *m* (-ʒ) materialism

materialistisch [materɪ·a'lɪstɪʃ] *adj* materialistic

Material'waren *pl* (Aust) medical supplies

Materie [ma'te:rɪ·ə] *f* (-ʒ-n) matter

materiell [materɪ'el] *adj* material; (*Schwierigkeiten*) financial; (*Recht*) substantive

Mathe ['matə] *f* (-ʒ) (coll) math

Mathematik [matema'tik] *f* (-ʒ) mathematics

Mathematiker –in [mate'matɪkər(ɪn)] §6 *mf* mathematician

mathematisch [mate'matɪʃ] *adj* mathematical

Matratze [ma'tratsə] *f* (-ʒ-n) mattress

Mätresse [me'tresə] *f* (-ʒ-n) mistress

Matrize [ma'tritsə] *f* (-ʒ-n) stencil; (*Stempel*) die, matrix

Matrone [ma'tronə] *f* (-ʒ-n) matron

matro'nenhaft *adj* matronly

Matrose [ma'trozə] *m* (-nʒ-n) sailor

Matro'senanzug *m* sailor's uniform

Matro'senjacke *f* (nav) peacoat

Matsch [matʃ] *m* (-esʒ) (*Brei*) mush; (*Schlamm*) mud; (*halbgetauter Schnee*) slush

matschig ['matʃɪç] *adj* mushy; muddy; slushy

matt [mat] *adj* dull; weak; limp; (*Glas, Birne*) frosted; (*Börse*) slack; (*erschöpft*) exhausted; (*Kugel*) spent; (*Licht*) dim; (*Metall*) tarnished; (phot) matt; **m. machen** dull; tarnish; **m. setzen** checkmate

Matte ['matə] *f* (-ʒ-n) mat; (*Wiese*) Alpine meadow; (poet) mead

Matt'glas *n* frosted glass

Matt'gold *n* dull gold

Matt'heit *f* dullness; fatigue

matt'herzig *adj* faint-hearted

Mat'tigkeit *f* (-ʒ) fatigue

Matura [ma'turɑ] *f* (-ʒ) (Aust) final examination (*before graduation*)

Mätzchen ['metsçən] *n* (-sʒ-) trick; **M. machen** play tricks; put on airs

Mauer ['mau·ər] *f* (-ʒ-n) wall

Mau'erblümchen *n* (fig) wallflower

Mau'erkalk *m* mortar

mauern ['mau·ərn] *tr* build (*in stone or brick*)

Mau'erstein *m* brick

Mau'erwerk *n* brickwork; masonry

Mau'erziegel *m* brick

Maul [maul] *n* (-[e]s;ẅer) mouth; maw; **halt's M.!** (sl) shut up!

Maul'affe *m* gaping fool

Maul'beerbaum *m* mulberry tree

Maul'beere *f* mulberry

maulen ['maulən] *intr* gripe

Maul'esel *m* mule

maul'faul *adj* too lazy to talk

Maul'held *m* braggart

Maul'korb *m* muzzle

Maul'schelle *f* slap in the face

Maul'sperre *f* lock jaw

Maul'tier *n* mule

Maul'trommel *f* Jew's-harp

Maul'- und Klau'enseuche *f* hoof and mouth disease

Maul'werk *n*—**ein großes M. haben** have the gift of gab

Maul'wurf *m* (zool) mole

Maul'wurfshaufen *m*, **Maul'wurfshügel** *m* molehill

Maure ['maurə] *m* (-n;-n) Moor

Maurer ['maurər] *m* (-s;-) mason; bricklayer

Mau'rerkelle *f* trowel

Mau'rerpolier *m* bricklayer foreman

Maus [maus] *f* (-;⸚e) mouse

Mäuschen ['mɔɪsçən] *n* (-s;-) little mouse; (fig) pet, darling; wench

Mau'sefalle *f* mousetrap

mausen ['mauzən] *tr* pilfer, swipe || *intr* catch mice

Mauser ['mauzər] *f* (-;) molting season; **in der M. sein** be molting

mausern ['mauzərn] *ref* molt

mau'setot *adj* dead as a doornail

mausig ['mauzɪç] *adj*—**sich m. machen** put on airs, be stuck-up

Mauso·leum [mauzo'le·um] *n* (-s; -leen ['le·ən]) mausoleum

Maxime [ma'ksimə] *f* (-;-n) maxim

Mayonnaise [majo'nɛzə] *f* (-;) mayonnaise

Mechanik [me'çanɪk] *f* (-;-en) mechanics; (Triebwerk) mechanism

Mechaniker [me'çanɪkər] *m* (-s;-) mechanic

mechanisch [me'çanɪʃ] *adj* mechanical; power-

mechanisieren [meçanɪ'zirən] *tr* mechanize

Mechanis·mus [meça'nɪsmus] *m* (-; -men [mən]) mechanism; (Uhrwerk) works

Meckerer ['mɛkərər] *m* (-s;-) (coll) grumbler

meckern ['mɛkərn] *intr* bleat; (coll) grumble

Medaille [me'daljə] *f* (-;-n) medal

Medaillon [medal'jɔ̃] *n* (-s;-s) medallion; locket

Medikament [medɪka'ment] *n* (-s;-e) medication

Meditation [medɪta'tsjon] *f* (-;-en) meditation

meditieren [medɪ'tirən] *intr* meditate

Medizin [medɪ'tsin] *f* (-;-en) medicine

Medizinalassistent [medɪtsɪ'nalasɪstant(ɪn)] §7 *mf* intern

Medizinalbeamte [medɪtsɪ'nalbə·amtə] *m* health officer

Medizinalbehörde [medɪtsɪ'nalbəhørdə] *f* board of health

Mediziner -in [medɪ'tsinər(ɪn)] §6 *mf* physician; medical student

medizinisch [medɪ'tsinɪʃ] *adj* medical, medicinal; medicated; **medizinische Fakultät** medical school

Meer [mer] *n* (-[e]s;-e) sea; **am Meere** at the seashore; **übers M.** overseas

Meer'busen *m* bay, gulf

Meer'enge *f* straits

Meeres- [merəs] *comb.fm.* sea, marine

Mee'resarm *m* inlet

Mee'resboden *m* bottom of the sea

Mee'resbucht *f* bay

Mee'resgrund *m* bottom of the sea

Mee'reshöhe *f* sea level

Mee'resküste *f* seacoast

Mee'resleuchten *n* phosphorescence

Mee'resspiegel *m* sea level

meer'grün *adj* sea-green

Meer'rettich *m* horseradish

Meer'schaum *m* meerschaum

Meer'schwein *n* porpoise

Meer'schweinchen *n* guinea pig

Meer'ungeheuer *n* sea monster

Meer'weib *n* mermaid

Mehl [mel] *n* (-[e]s;) (grobes) meal; (feines) flour; (Staub) dust, powder

Mehl'kloß *m* dumpling

Mehl'speise *f* pastry; pudding

Mehl'suppe *f* gruel

Mehl'tau *m* mildew

mehr [mer] *invar adj & adv* more; **immer m.** more and more; **kein Wort m.!** not another word!; **m. oder weniger** more or less, give or take; **nicht m.** no more, no longer; **nie m.** never again || **Mehr** *n* (-s;) majority; (Zuwachs) increase; (Überschuß) surplus

Mehr'arbeit *f* extra work; (Überstunden) overtime

Mehr'aufwand *m*, **Mehr'ausgabe** *f* additional expenditure

Mehr'betrag *m* surplus; extra charge

mehr'deutig *adj* ambiguous

mehren ['merən] *tr & ref* increase

mehrere ['merərə] *adj & pron* several

mehr'fach *adj* manifold; repeated, multiple

mehr'farbig *adj* multicolored

Mehr'gebot *n* higher bid

Mehr'gepäck *n* excess luggage

Mehr'gewicht *n* excess weight

Mehr'heit *f* (-;-en) majority; (pol) plurality

Mehr'heitsbeschluß *m*, **Mehr'heitsentscheidung** *f* plurality vote

mehr'jährig *adj* (bot) perennial

Mehr'kosten *pl* extra charges

Mehr'ladegewehr *n* repeater

Mehr'leistung *f* increased performance; (ins) extended benefits

mehrmalig ['mermalɪç] *adj* repeated

mehrmals ['mermals] *adv* several times, on several occasions; repeatedly

Mehr'porto *n* additional postage

Mehr'preis *m* extra charge

mehr'seitig *adj* multilateral; many-sided; (Brief) of many pages

mehrsilbig ['merzɪlbɪç] *adj* polysyllabic

mehrsprachig ['merʃpraxɪç] *adj* polyglot

mehrstöckig ['merʃtœkɪç] *adj* multistory

mehrstufig ['merʃtufɪç] *adj* multistage

Meh'rung *f* (-;) increase, multiplication

Mehr'verbrauch *m* increased consumption

Mehr'wertsteuer *f* added value tax

Mehr'zahl *f* majority; (gram) plural

meiden ['maɪdən] §112 *tr* avoid, shun

Meier ['maɪ·ər] *m* (-s;-) tenant farmer; dairy farmer

Meierei [maɪ·ə'raɪ] *f* (-;-en) dairy

Mei'ergut *n*, **Mei'erhof** *m* dairy farm

Meile ['maɪlə] *f* (-;-n) mile

mei'lenweit *adj* extending for miles, miles and miles of || *adv* far away; **m. auseinander** miles apart

Mei'lenzahl *f* mileage

mein [maɪn] §2,2 *poss adj* my || §2,4,5 *pron* mine; **das Meine** my share; my due; **die Meinen** my family

Meineid ['maɪnaɪt] *m* (-[e]s;) perjury; **e-n M. schwören** (or **leisten**) commit perjury

meineidig ['maɪnaɪdɪç] *adj* perjured; **m. werden** perjure oneself

meinen ['maɪnən] *tr* think; (*im Sinne haben*) mean, intend; **das will ich m.** I should think so; **die Sonne meint es heute gut** the sun is very warm today; **es ehrlich m.** have honorable intentions; **es gut m.** mean well; **ich meinte dich im Recht** I thought you were in the right; **m. Sie das ernst** (or **im Ernst**)? do you really mean it?; **was m. Sie damit?** what do you mean by that?; **was m. Sie dazu?** what do you think of that? || *intr* think; **m. Sie?** do you think so?; **m. Sie nicht auch?** don't you agree?; **wie m. Sie?** I beg your pardon?

meinerseits ['maɪnər'zaɪts] *adv* for my part

meinesgleichen ['maɪnəs'glaɪçən] *pron* people like me, the likes of me

meinethlben ['maɪnət'halbən], **meinetwegen** ['maɪnət'vegən] *adv* for my sake, on my account; for all I care

meinetwillen ['maɪnət'vɪlən] *adv*—**um m.** for my sake, on my behalf

meinige ['maɪnɪgə] §2,5 *pron* mine

Mei'nung *f* (-;-en) opinion; **anderer M. mit j-m sein über** (*acc*) disagree with s.o. about; **der M. sein** be of the opinion; **geteilter M. sein** be of two minds; **j-m die** (or **seine**) **M. sagen** give s.o. a piece of one's mind; **meiner M. nach** in my opinion; **vorgefaßte M.** preconceived idea

Mei'nungsäußerung *f* expression of opinion

Mei'nungsaustausch *m* exchange of views

Mei'nungsbefragung *f*, **Mei'nungsforschung** *f* public opinion poll

Mei'nungsumfrage *f* public opinion poll

Mei'nungsverschiedenheit *f* difference of opinion, disagreement

Meise ['maɪzə] *f* (-;-n) titmouse

Meißel ['maɪsəl] *m* (-s;-) chisel

meißeln ['maɪsəln] *tr & intr* chisel

meist [maɪst] *adj* most; **am meisten** most; **das meiste** the most; **die meisten Menschen** most people; **die meiste Zeit** most of the time; **die meiste Zeit des Jahres** most of the year || *adv* usually, generally

Meist'begünstigungsklausel *f* mostfavored nation clause

Meist'bietende §5 *mf* highest bidder

meistens ['maɪstəns] *adv* mostly

Meister ['maɪstər] *m* (-s;-) master; boss; (*im Betrieb*) foreman; (*sport*) champion

mei'sterhaft *adj* masterly

Meisterin ['maɪstərɪn] *f* (-;-nen) master's wife; (*sport*) champion

mei'sterlich *adj* masterly

meistern ['maɪstərn] *tr* master

Mei'sterschaft *f* (-;-en) mastery; (*sport*) championship

Mei'sterstück *n*, **Mei'sterwerk** *n* masterpiece

Mei'sterzug *m* master stroke

Melancholie [melaŋkə'li] *f* (-;) melancholy

melancholisch [melaŋ'kolɪʃ] *adj* melancholy

Melasse [me'lasə] *f* (-;-n) molasses

Meldeamt ['meldə-amt] *n*. **Meldebüro** ['meldəbyro] *n* registration office

Meldefahrer ['meldəfarər] *m* (mil) dispatch rider

Meldegänger ['meldəgɛŋər] *m* (mil) messenger, runner

melden ['meldən] *tr* report; (*polizeilich*) turn (*s.o.*) in; **den Empfang m.** (*genit*) acknowledge the receipt of; **er hat nichts zu m.** he has nothing to say in the matter; **gemeldet werden zu** (sport) be entered in; **j–m m. lassen, daß** send s.o. word that || *ref* report; (*Alter*) begin to show; (*Gläubiger*) come forward; (*Kind*) cry; (*Magen*) growl; (*polizeilich*) register; (*Winter*) set in; (telp) answer; **sich auf e-e Anzeige m.** answer an ad; **sich krank m.** (mil) go on sick call; **sich m. zu apply for;** (*freiwillig*) volunteer for; (mil) enlist in; (sport) enter; **sich zum Dienst m.** (mil) report for duty; **sich zum Wort m.** ask to speak; (*in der Schule*) hold up the hand

Mel'der *m* (-s;-) (mil) runner

Meldezettel ['meldətsetəl] *m* registration form

Mel'dung *f* (-;-en) report; message, notification; (*Bewerbung*) application

Melkeimer ['melkaɪmər] *m* milk pail

melken ['melkən] §113 *tr* milk

Melo-die [melo'di] *f* (-;-dien ['di-ən]) melody

melodisch [me'lodɪʃ] *adj* melodious

Melone [me'lonə] *f* (-;-n) melon; (coll) derby

Meltau ['meltaʊ] *m* (-[e]s;) honeydew

Membran [mem'bran] *f* (-;-en), **Membrane** [mem'branə] *f* (-;-n) membrane

Memme ['memə] *f* (-;-n) coward

Memoiren [memo'arən] *pl* memoirs

memorieren [memo'rirən] *tr* memorize

Menge ['meŋə] *f* (-;-n) quantity, amount; crowd; **e-e M. a lot of**

mengen ['meŋən] *tr* mix || *ref* (*unter acc*) mingle (with); (**in** *acc*) meddle (in)

Men'genlehre *f* (math) theory of sets

men'genmäßig *adj* quantitative

Mengsel ['meŋzəl] *n* (-s;-) hodgepodge

Mennige ['menɪgə] *f* (-;) rust-preventive paint

Mensch [menʃ] *m* (-en;-en) human being, man; person, individual; **die Menschen** the people; **kein M.** no one || *n* (-es; -er) hussy, slut

Menschen— [menʃən] *comb.fm.* man, of men; human

Men'schenalter *n* generation, age

Men'schenfeind –in §8 *mf* misanthropist

Men'schenfresser *m* cannibal

Men'schenfreund –in §8 *mf* philanthropist

men'schenfreundlich *adj* philanthropic, humanitarian

Men'schengedenken *n*—seit M. since time immemorial

Men'schengeschlecht *n* mankind

Men'schengewühl *n* milling crowd

Men'schenglück *n* human happiness

Men'schenhandel *m* slave trade

Men'schenhaß *m* misanthropy

Men'schenjagd *f* manhunt

Men'schenkenner –in §6 *mf* judge of human nature

Men'schenkind *n* human being; **armes M.** poor soul

men'schenleer *adj* deserted

Men'schenliebe *f* philanthropy

Men'schenmaterial *n* manpower

men'schenmöglich *adj* humanly possible

Men'schenraub *m* kidnaping

Men'schenräuber –in §6 *mf* kidnaper

Men'schenrechte *pl* human rights

men'schenscheu *adj* shy, unsociable

Men'schenschinder *m* oppressor, slave driver

Men'schenschlag *m* race

Men'schenseele *f* human soul; **keine M.** not a living soul

Men'schenskind *interj* man alive!

Men'schensohn *m* (Bib) Son of man

men'schenunwürdig *adj* degrading

Men'schenverächter –in §6 *mf* cynic

Men'schenverstand *m*—guter M. common sense

Men'schenwürde *f* human dignity

men'schenwürdig *adj* decent

Mensch'heit *f* (–;) mankind, humanity

mensch'lich *adj* human; *(human)* humane

Mensch'lichkeit *f* (–;) humanity

Menschwerdung ['menʃverdʊŋ] *f* (–;) incarnation

Menstruation [mentru·aˈtsjon] *f* (–;-en) menstruation

Mensur [menˈzur] *f* (–;-en) measure; *(Meßglas)* measuring glass; students' duel

Mentalität [mentalɪtɛt] *f* (–;-en) mentality

Menuett [menuˈet] *n* (–[e]s;-e) minuet

Meridian [merɪˈdjan] *m* (–s;-e) (astr) meridian

merkbar ['merkbar] *adj* noticeable

Merkblatt ['merkblat] *n* instruction sheet

Merkbuch ['merkbux] *n* notebook

merken ['merkən] *tr* notice; realize; **etw m.** lassen show s.th., betray s.th.; **man merkte es sofort an ihrem Ausdruck, daß** one noticed immediately by her expression that || *ref*—m. **Sie sich** [*dat*], **was ich sage!** mark my word!; **sich** [*dat*] **etw m.** bear s.th. in mind; **sich** [*dat*] **nichts m.** lassen not give oneself away || *intr*—m. **auf** *(acc)* pay attention to, heed

merk'lich *adj* noticeable

Merkmal ['merkmal] *n* (–[e]s;-e) mark, feature, characteristic

Merkur [merˈkur] *m & n* (–s;) mercury

Merk'wort *n* (–[e]s;-̈er) catchword; (theat) cue

merk'würdig *adj* remarkable; *(seltsam)* curious, strange

merkwürdigerweise ['merkvyrdɪgərvaɪzə] *adv* strange to say

Merk'würdigkeit *f* (–;-en) strange thing

Merk'zeichen *n* mark

meschugge [meˈʃuga] *adj* (coll) nuts

Mesner ['mesnər] *m* (–s;-) sexton

Meß— [mes] *comb.fm.* measuring; (eccl) mass

Meß'band *n* (–[e]s;-̈er) measuring tape

meßbar ['mesbar] *adj* measurable

Meß'buch *n* (relig) missal

Meß'diener *m* acolyte

Messe ['mesə] *f* (–;-n) fair; (eccl) mass; (nav) officers' mess

messen ['mesən] §70 *tr* measure; *(Zeit)* time, clock; *(mustern)* size up || *ref* —sich m. mit cope with; *(geistig)* match wits with; **sich nicht m. können mit** be no match for || *intr* measure

Messer ['mesər] *m* (–s;-) gauge; meter || *n* (–s;-) knife; (surg) scalpel; **bis aufs M.** to the death

Mes'serheld *m* (coll) cutthroat

mes'serscharf *adj* razor-sharp

Mes'serschmied *m* cutler

Messerschmiedewaren ['mesərʃmidəvarən] *pl* cutlery

Mes'serschneide *f* knife edge

Meß'gewand *n* (eccl) vestment; chasuble

Meß'hemd *n* (eccl) alb

Messias [meˈsi·as] *invar m* Messiah

Messing ['mesɪŋ] *n* (–s;) brass

messingen ['mesɪŋən] *adj* brass

Meß'opfer *n* sacrifice of the mass

Mes'sung *f* (–;-en) measurement

Metall [meˈtal] *n* (–s;-e) metal

Metall'baukasten *m* erector set

metallen [meˈtalən], **metallisch** [meˈtalɪʃ] *adj* metallic

Metall'säge *f* hacksaw

Metallurgie [metalʊrˈgi] *f* (–;) metallurgy

metall'verarbeitend *adj* metal-processing

Metall'waren *pl* hardware

Metapher [meˈtafər] *f* (–;-n) metaphor

Meteor [meteˈor] *m* (–s;-e) meteor

Meteorologe [mete·oroˈlogə] *m* (–n;-n) meteorologist

Meteorologie [mete·orolоˈgi] *f* (–;) meteorolgy

Meteorologin [mete·oroˈlogɪn] *f* (–;-nen) meteorologist

meteorologisch [mete·oroˈlogɪʃ] *adj* meteorological

Meteor'stein *m* meteorite, aerolite

Meter ['metər] *m & n* (–s;-) meter

Me'termaß *n* tape measure

Methode [meˈtodə] *f* (–;-n) method

methodisch [meˈtodɪʃ] *adj* methodical

Metrik ['metrɪk] *f* (–;) metrics

metrisch ['metrɪʃ] *adj* metrical

Metropole [metrə'polə] *f* (-;-n) metropolis

Mette ['metə] *f* (-;-n) matins

Mettwurst ['metvurst] *f* soft sausage

Metzelei [metsə'laɪ] *f* (-;-en) massacre, slaughter

metzeln ['metsəln] *tr* massacre

Metzger ['metsgər] *m* (-s;-) butcher

Metzgerei [metsgə'raɪ] *f* (-;-en) butcher shop

Meuchelmord ['mɔɪçəlmɔrt] *m* assassination

Meuchelmörder **-in** ['mɔɪçəlmœrdər (ɪn)] §6 *mf* assassin

meucheln ['mɔɪçəln] *tr* murder

meuchlerisch ['mɔɪçlərɪʃ] *adj* murderous

meuchlings ['mɔɪçlɪŋs] *adv* treacherously

Meute ['mɔɪtə] *f* (-;-n) pack (*of hounds*); (fig) horde, gang

Meuterei [mɔɪtə'raɪ] *f* (-;-en) mutiny

meuterisch ['mɔɪtərɪʃ] *adj* mutinous

meutern ['mɔɪtərn] *intr* mutiny

Mexikaner **-in** [meksɪ'kanər(ɪn)] §6 *mf* Mexican

mexikanisch [meksɪ'kanɪʃ] *adj* Mexican

Mexiko ['meksɪko] *n* (-s;) Mexico

miauen [mɪ'au̯.ən] *intr* meow

mich [mɪç] §11 *pers pron* me ‖ §11 *reflex pron* myself

mied [mit] *pret of* **meiden**

Mieder ['midər] *n* (-s;-) bodice

Mie'derwaren *pl* foundation garments

Mief [mif] *n* (-s;) foul air

Miene ['minə] *f* (-;-n) mien; facial expression; **M. machen zu** (*inf*) make a move to (*inf*); **ohne die M. zu verziehen** without flinching

mies [mis] *adj* (coll) miserable, lousy

Mies'macher *m* (-s;-) alarmist

Miet- [mit] *comb.fm.* rental, rented; rent

Miet'auto *n* rented car

Miete ['mitə] *f* (-;-n) rent; (*Zins*) rental; (*Erd-*) pit (*for storing vegetables*); **in M. geben** rent out; **in M. nehmen** rent; **kalte M.** rent not including heat; **zur M. wohnen** live in a rented apartment (or home)

mieten ['mitən] *tr* rent, hire; (*Flugzeug*) charter

Miet'entschädigung *f* allowance for house rent

Mie'ter **-in** §6 *mf* tenant

Miet'ertrag *m* rent, rental

Miet'kontrakt *m* lease

Mietling ['mitlɪŋ] *m* (-s;-e) hireling

Miets'haus *n* apartment building

Miets'kaserne *f* tenement house

Miet'vertrag *m* lease

Miet'wagen *m* rented car

Miet'wohung *f* apartment

Miet'zins *m* rent

Mieze ['mitsə] *f* (-;-n) pussy

Migräne [mɪ'grenə] *f* (-;-n) migraine

Mikrobe [mɪ'krobə] *f* (-;-n) microbe

Mikrofilm ['mikrofɪlm] *m* microfilm

Mikrophon [mikro'fon] *n* (-s;-e) microphone

Mikroskop [mikro'skop] *n* (-s;-e) microscope

mikroskopisch [mikro'skopɪʃ] *adj* microscopic

Milbe ['mɪlbə] *f* (-;-n) (ent) mite

Milch [mɪlç] *f* (-;) milk

Milch'bart *m* sissy

Milch'brot *n*, **Milch'brötchen** *n* French roll

Milch'bruder *m* foster brother

Milch'drüse *f* mammary gland

Milch'eimer *m* milk pail

Milch'geschäft *n* creamery, dairy

Milch'glas *n* milk glass

milchig ['mɪlçɪç] *adj* milky

Milch'mädchen *n* milkmaid

Milch'mädchenrechnung *f* oversimplification

Milch'mixgetränk *n* milkshake

Milch'pulver *n* powdered milk

Milch'reis *m* rice pudding

Milch'schwester *f* foster sister

Milch'straße *f* Milky Way

Milch'tüte *f* carton of milk

Milch'wirtschaft *f* dairy

Milchzähne ['mɪlçtsenə] *pl* baby teeth

mild [mɪlt] *adj* mild; (*nicht streng*) lenient; (*Stiftung*) charitable; (*Wein*) smooth; (*Lächeln*) faint ‖ **Milde** *f* (-;) mildness; leniency; kindness

mildern ['mɪldərn] *tr* soften, alleviate; **mildernde Umstände** extenuating circumstances

Mil'derung *f* (-;) softening, alleviation, mitigation

mild'herzig, mild'tätig *adj* charitable

Militär [mɪlɪ'tɛr] *n* (-s;) military, army; **zum M. gehen** join the army ‖ *m* (-s;-s) professional soldier

Militär'dienst *m* military service

Militär'geistliche §5 *m* chaplain

Militär'gericht *n* military court

militärisch [mɪlɪ'tɛrɪʃ] *adj* military

Militarismus [mɪlɪta'rɪsmus] *m* (-;) militarism

Miliz [mɪ'lɪts] *f* (-;) militia

Miliz'soldat *m* militiaman

Milliardär **-in** [mɪljar'der(ɪn)] §8 *mf* multimillionaire

Milliarde [mɪl'jardə] *f* (-;-n) billion

Milligramm [mɪlɪ'gram] *n* milligram

Millimeter [mɪlɪ'metər] *n & m* millimeter

Millime'terpapier *n* graph paper

Million [mɪl'jon] *f* (-;-en) million

Millionär **-in** [mɪljo'ner(ɪn)] §8 *mf* millionaire

millionste [mɪl'jonstə] §9 *adj & pron* millionth

Milz [mɪlts] *f* (-;) spleen

Mime ['mimə] *m* (-n;-n) mime

Mimiker **-in** ['mimɪkər(ɪn)] §6 *mf* mimic

Mimose [mɪ'mozə] *f* (-;-n) mimosa

minder ['mɪndər] *adj* lesser, smaller; (*geringer*) minor, inferior ‖ *adv* less; **m. gut** inferior; **nicht m.** likewise

min'derbedeutend *adj* less important

min'derbegabt *adj* less talented

min'derbemittelt *adj* of moderate means

Min'derbetrag *m* shortage, deficit

Min'derheit *f* (-;-en) minority

min'derjährig *adj* underage ‖ **Minderjährige** §5 *mf* minor

mindern ['mɪndərn] *tr* lessen, diminish
Min′derung *f* (-;-en) diminution
min′derwertig *adj* inferior
Min′derwertigkeit *f* inferiority
Min′derwertigkeitskomplex *m* inferiority complex
Min′derzahl *f* minority
Mindest– ['mɪndəst] *comb.fm.* minimum
mindeste ['mɪndəstə] §9 *adj* least; (*kleinste*) smallest; **nicht die mindesten Aussichten** not the slightest chance; **nicht im mindesten** not in the least; **zum mindesten** at the very least
mindestens ['mɪndəstəns] *adv* at least
Min′destgebot *n* lowest bid
Min′destlohn *m* minimum wage
Mine ['minə] *f* (-;-n) (*im Bleistift*) lead; (mil, min) mine; **alle Minen springen lassen** (fig) pull out all the stops
Minenleger ['minənlegər] *m* (-s;-) minelayer
Minenräumboot ['minənrɔɪmbot] *n* minesweeper
Mineral [minə′ral] *n* (-s;-e & -ien [jən]) mineral
mineralisch [minə′ralɪʃ] *adj* mineral
Mineralogie [minəralo′gi] *f* (-;) mineralogy
Miniatur [minja′tur] *f* (-;-en) miniature
minieren [mi′nirən] *tr* (fig) undermine; (mil) mine
minimal [mini′mal] *adj* minimal
Minirock ['minirɔk] *m* miniskirt
Minister [mi′nɪstər] *m* (-s;-) minister, secretary
Ministe•rium [minɪs′terjum] *n* (-s; -rien [rjən]) ministry, department
Mini′sterpräsident *m* prime minister
Mini′sterrat *m* (-[e]s;=e) cabinet
Ministrant [minɪs′trant] *m* (-en;-en) altar boy, acolyte
Minne ['minə] *f* (-;) (obs) love
Min′nesänger *m* minnesinger; troubadour
minorenn [minə′ren] *adj* underage
minus ['minus] *adv* minus || **Minus** *n* (-;-) minus; (com) deficit
Minute [mi′nutə] *f* (-;-n) minute
Minu′tenzeiger *m* minute hand
–minutig [minutɪç] *comb.fm.* –minute
Minze ['mintsə] *f* (-;-n) (bot) mint
mir [mir] §11 *pers pron* me, to me, for me; **mir ist kalt** I am cold; **mir nichts, dir nichts** suddenly; **von mir aus** for all I care || §11 *reflex pron* myself, to myself, for myself
Mirabelle [mira′belə] *f* (-;-n) yellow plum
Mirakel [mi′rakəl] *n* (-s;-) miracle
Mira′kelspiel *n* miracle play
Mischehe ['mɪʃ∕e•ə] *f* mixed marriage
mischen ['mɪʃən] *tr* mix, blend; (cards) shuffle
Mischling ['mɪʃlɪŋ] *m* (-es;-e) half-breed; mongrel
Mischmasch ['mɪʃmaʃ] *m* (-es;-e) hodgepodge
Mischpult ['mɪʃpult] *n* (rad, telv) master console

Mischrasse ['mɪʃrasə] *f* cross-breed
Mi′schung *f* (-;-en) mixture, blend
Misere [mi′zerə] *f* (-;-n) misery
Miß–, miß– [mɪs] *comb.fm.* mis–, dis–, amiss; bad, wrong, false
mißach′ten *tr* disregard; (*geringschätzen*) slight
mißartet [mɪs′artət] *adj* degenerate
miß′behagen *intr* (*dat*) displeasure || **Mißbehagen** *n* (-s;) displeasure
miß′bilden *tr* misshape, deform
Miß′bildung *f* (-;-en) deformity
miß′billigen *tr* disapprove
Miß′billigung *f* (-;-en) disapproval
Miß′brauch *m* abuse; (*falsche Anwendung*) misuse
mißbrau′chen *tr* abuse; misuse
mißbräuchlich ['mɪsbrɔɪçlɪç] *adj* improper
mißdeu′ten *tr* misinterpret
missen ['mɪsən] *tr* miss; do without
Miß′erfolg *m* failure, flop
Miß′ernte *f* bad harvest
Missetat ['mɪsətat] *f* misdeed; (*Verstoß*) offense; (*Verbrechen*) felony; (*Sünde*) sin
Missetäter –in ['mɪsətetər(ɪn)] §6 *mf* wrongdoer; offender; felon; sinner
mißfal′len §72 *intr* (*dat*) displease || **Mißfallen** *n* (-s;) displeasure
miß′fällig *adj* displeasing; (*anstößig*) shocking; (*verächtlich*) disparaging
miß′farben, miß′farbig *adj* discolored
Miß′geburt *f* freak
mißgelaunt ['mɪsgəlaunt] *adj* in bad humor, sour
Miß′geschick *n* (-s;) mishap; misfortune
Miß′gestalt *f* deformity; monster
miß′gestaltet *adj* deformed, misshapen
mißgestimmt ['mɪsgəʃtɪmt] *adj* grumpy
mißglücken (mißglük′ken) *intr* (SEIN) fail, not succeed
mißgön′nen *tr* begrudge
Miß′griff *m* mistake
Miß′gunst *f* grudge, jealousy
mißhan′deln *tr* mistreat
Miß′heirat *f* mismarriage
Mißhelligkeit ['mɪshelɪçkaɪt] *f* (-;-en) friction, disagreement
Mission [mɪ′sjon] *f* (-;-en) mission
Missionar [mɪsjo′nar] *m*, **Missionär** [mɪsjo′ner] *m* (-s;-e) missionary
Miß′klang *m* dissonance; (fig) sour note
Miß′kredit *m* discredit, disrepute
mißlang [mɪs′laŋ] *pret of* **mißlingen**
miß′lich *adj* awkward; (*gefährlich*) dangerous; (*bedenklich*) critical
miß′liebig *adj* unpopular
mißlingen [mɪs′lɪŋən] §142 *intr* (SEIN) go wrong, misfire, prove a failure || **Mißlingen** *n* (-s;) failure
Miß′mut *m* bad humor; discontent
miß′mutig *adj* sullen; discontented
mißra′ten §63 *intr* (SEIN) go wrong, misfire; **mißratene Kinder** spoiled children
Miß′stand *m* bad state of affairs; **Mißstände abschaffen** remedy abuses
Miß′stimmung *f* dissension; (*Mißmut*) bad humor
Miß′ton *m* dissonance; (fig) sour note

mißtrau′en *intr* (*dat*) mistrust, distrust || **Miß′trauen** *n* (−s;) mistrust
mißtrauisch ['mɪstrau·iʃ] *adj* distrustful
Miß′vergnügen *n* displeasure
miß′vergnügt *adj* cross; discontented
Miß′verhältnis *n* disproportion
Miß′verständnis *n* misunderstanding
miß′verstehen §146 *tr* & *intr* misunderstand
Miß′wirtschaft *f* mismanagement
Mist [mɪst] *m* (−es;) dung, manure; (*Schmutz*) dirt; (fig) mess, nonsense; **M. machen** (coll) blow the job; (*Spaß machen*) (coll) horse around; **viel M. verzapfen** talk a lot of nonsense
Mist′beet *n* hotbed
Mistel ['mɪstəl] *f* (−;−n) mistletoe
misten ['mɪstən] *tr* (*Stall*) muck; (*Acker*) fertilize
Mist′fink *m* (coll) dirty brat
Mist′haufen *m* manure pile
mistig ['mɪstɪç] *adj* dirty; (*sehr unangenehm*) very unpleasant
mit [mɪt] *adv* along; also, likewise; simultaneously || *prep* (*dat*) with; **mit 18 Jahren** at the age of eighteen
Mit′angeklagte §5 *mf* codefendant
Mit′arbeit *f* cooperation, collaboration
mit′arbeiten *intr* cooperate, collaborate; **m. an** (*dat*) contribute to
Mit′arbeiter −in §6 *mf* co-worker
Mit′arbeiterstab *m* staff
mit′bekommen §99 *tr* receive when leaving; (*verstehen*) get, catch
mit′benutzen *tr* use jointly
Mit′bestimmung *f* share in decision making
mit′bewerben *ref* (**um**) compete (for)
Mit′bewerber −in §6 *mf* competitor
mit′bringen §65 *tr* bring along
Mitbringsel ['mɪtbrɪŋzəl] *n* (−s;−) little present
Mit′bürger −in §6 *mf* fellow citizen
Mit′eigentümer −in §6 *mf* co-owner
miteinan′der *adv* together
mit′empfinden §59 *tr* sympathize with
Mit′erbe *m*, **Mit′erbin** *f* coheir
Mitesser ['mɪtesər] *m* (−s;−) pimple, blackhead
mit′fahren §71 *intr* (SEIN) ride along; **j−n m. lassen** give s.o. a lift
mit′fühlen *tr* share, sympathize with
mit′fühlend *adj* sympathetic
mit′gehen §82 *intr* (SEIN) (**mit**) go along (with)
Mit′gift *f* dowry
Mit′giftjäger *m* fortune hunter
Mit′glied *n* member; **M. auf Lebenszeit** life member
Mit′gliederversammlung *f* general meeting
Mit′gliederzahl *f* membership
Mit′gliedsbeitrag *m* dues
Mit′gliedschaft *f* (−;−en) membership
Mit′gliedskarte *f* membership card
Mit′gliedstaat *m* member nation
Mit′haftung *f* joint liability
mit′halten §90 *intr* be one of a party; **ich halte mit** I'll join you
mit′helfen §96 *intr* help along, pitch in

Mit′helfer −in §6 *mf* assistant
Mit′herausgeber −in §6 *mf* coeditor
Mit′hilfe *f* assistance
mithin′ *adv* consequently
mit′hören *tr* listen in on; (*zufällig*) overhear; (rad, telp) monitor
Mit′inhaber −in §6 *mf* copartner
Mit′kämpfer −in §6 *mf* fellow fighter
mit′klingen §142 *intr* resonate
mit′kommen §99 *intr* (SEIN) come along; (fig) keep up
mit′kriegen *tr* (coll) see **mitbekommen**
Mit′läufer −in §6 *mf* (pol) fellow traveler
Mit′laut *m* consonant
Mit′leid *n* compassion, pity
Mit′leidenschaft *f*—**j−n in M. ziehen** affect s.o.
mit′leidig *adj* compassionate; pitiful
Mit′leidsbezeigung *f* condolences
mit′leidslos *adj* pitiless
mit′leidsvoll *adj* full of pity
mit′machen *tr* participate in, join in on; (*ertragen*) suffer, endure
Mit′mensch *m* fellow man
mit′nehmen §116 *tr* take along; (*erschöpfen*) wear out, exhaust; (*abholen*) pick up; (*Ort, Museum*) visit, take in; **j−n arg m.** treat s.o. roughly
mitnichten ['mɪt′nɪçtən] *adv* by no means, not at all
mit′rechnen *tr* include || *intr* count
mit′reden *tr*—**ein Wort mitzureden haben bei** have a say in || *intr* join in a conversation
Mit′reisende §5 *mf* travel companion
mit′reißen §53 *tr* (& fig) carry away
mit′reißend *adj* stirring
mitsamt [mɪt′zamt] *prep* (*dat*) together with
mit′schreiben §62 *intr* take notes
Mit′schuld *f* (an *dat*) complicity (in)
mit′schuldig *adj* (an *dat*) accessory (to) || **Mitschuldige** §5 *mf* accomplice
Mit′schüler −in §6 *mf* schoolmate
mit′singen §142 *intr* sing along
mit′spielen *intr* play along; (fig) be involved; **j−m arg** (or **übel**) **m.** play s.o. dirty
Mit′spieler −in §6 *mf* partner
Mit′spracherecht *n* right to share in decision making
mit′sprechen §64 *tr* say with (*s.o.*) || *intr* be involved; (*an e−r Entscheidung beteiligt sein*) share in decision making
Mit′tag *m* noon; (poet) South; **M. machen** stop for lunch; **zu M. essen** eat lunch
Mittag– *comb.fm.* midday, noon; lunch
Mit′tagbrot *n*, **Mit′tagessen** *n* lunch
mit′täglich *adj* midday, noontime
mittags ['mɪtaks] *adv* at noon
Mit′tagskreis *m*, **Mit′tagslinie** *f* meridian
Mit′tagsruhe *f* siesta
Mit′tagsstunde *f* noon; lunch hour
Mit′tagstisch *m* lunch table; lunch; **gut bürglicher M.** good home cooking
Mit′tagszeit *f* noontime; lunch hour
Mit′täter −in §6 *mf* accomplice
Mit′täterschaft *f* complicity

Mitte ['mɪtə] ƒ (-;-n) middle, midst; (*Mittelpunkt*) center; **ab durch die M.!** (coll) scram!; **aus unserer M.** from among us; **die goldene M.** the golden mean; **die richtige M. treffen** hit a happy medium; **er ist M. Vierzig** he is in his mid-forties; **in die M. nehmen** take by both arms; (sport) sandwich in; **j—m um die M. fassen** put one's arms around s.o.'s waist

mit′teilbar *adj* communicable

mit′teilen *tr* tell; (*im Vertrauen*) intimate; **ich muß Ihnen leider m.,** **daß** I regret to inform you that

mitteilsam ['mɪttaɪlzam] *adj* communicative

Mit′teilung ƒ (-;-en) communication; information; (*amtliche*) communiqué; (*an die Presse*) release

mittel ['mɪtəl] *adj* medium, average ‖ **Mittel** *n* (-s;-) middle; means; (*Heil—*) remedy; (*Maßnahme*) measure; (*Ausweg*) expedient; (*Durchschnitt*) average; (math) mean; (phys) medium; **im M.** on the average; **ins M. treten** (or **sich ins M. legen**) intervene, intercede; **letztes M.** last resort; **mit allen Mitteln** by every means; **Mittel** *pl* resources, means; funds; **M. und Wege** ways and means; **M. zum Zweck** means to an end; **sicheres M.** reliable method

Mit′telalter *n* Middle Ages

mittelalterlich ['mɪtəlaltərlɪç] *adj* medieval

Mit′telamerika *n* Central America

mittelbar ['mɪtəlbar] *adj* indirect

Mit′telgang *m* center aisle

Mit′telgebirge *n* highlands

Mit′telgewicht *n* (box) middleweight class

Mittelgewichtler ['mɪtəlgəvɪçtlər] *m* (-s;-) middleweight boxer

Mit′telgröße ƒ medium size

mit′telhochdeutsch *adj* Middle High German ‖ **Mittelhochdeutsch** *n* (-es;) Middle High German

Mit′tellage ƒ central position; (mus) middle range

mittelländisch ['mɪtəllendɪʃ] *adj* Mediterranean

Mit′telläufer *m* (fb) center halfback

mit′tellos *adj* penniless, destitute

Mit′telmaß *n* medium; balance; average

mitt′telmäßig *adj* medium, mediocre; (*leidlich*) indifferent, so-so

Mit′telmäßigkeit ƒ mediocrity

Mit′telmast *m* mainmast

Mit′telmeer *n* Mediterranean

Mit′telohr *n* middle ear

Mit′telpreis *m* average price

Mit′telpunkt *m* center

mittels ['mɪtəls] *prep* (*genit*) by means of

Mit′telschiff *n* (archit) nave

Mit′telschule ƒ secondary school

Mit′tels·mann *m* (-[e]s;-̈er & -leute) go-between; (com) middleman

Mit′telsorte ƒ medium quality

Mit′telsperson ƒ see **Mittelsmann**

Mit′telstand *m* middle class

Mit′telstürmer *m* (fb) center forward

Mit′telweg *m* middle course; **der goldene M.** the golden mean; **e—n M. einschlagen** steer a middle course

Mit′telwort *n* (-[e]s;-̈er) (gram) participle

mitten ['mɪtən] *adv*—**m. am Tage** in broad daylight; **m. auf dem Wege** well on the way; **m. auf der Straße;** right in the middle of the street; **m. aus** from the midst of, from among; **m. darin** right in the very center (of it, of them); **m. entzwei brechen** break right in two; **m. im Winter** in the dead of winter; **m. in der Luft** in midair; **m. ins zwanzigste Jahrhundert** well into the twentieth century

Mitternacht ['mɪtərnaxt] ƒ midnight

mitternächtig ['mɪtərneçtɪç], **mitternächtlich** ['mɪtərneçtlɪç] *adj* midnight

Mittler –in ['mɪtlər(ɪn)] §6 *mƒ* mediator; (com) middleman

mittlere ['mɪtlərə] §9 *adj* middle, central; (*durchschnittlich*) average; (*mittelmäßig*) medium; (math) mean; **der Mittlere Osten** the Middle East; **in mittleren Jahren** sein be middleaged; **von mittlerer Größe** medium-sized

mitt′lerweile *adv* in the meantime

mittschiffs ['mɪt/ɪfs] *adv* amidships

Mittwoch ['mɪtvɔx] *m* -[e]s;-e) Wednesday

mitun′ter *adv* now and then

mit′unterzeichnen *tr* & *intr* countersign

mit′verantwortlich *adj* jointly responsible

Mit′verantwortung ƒ joint responsibility

Mit′verschworene §5 *mƒ* co-conspirator

Mit′welt ƒ present generation; our (his, etc.) contemporaries

mit′wirken *intr* (an *dat* or bei) cooperate (in)

Mit′wirkung ƒ cooperation

Mit′wissen *n*—**ohne mein M.** without my knowledge

Mitwisser –in ['mɪtvɪsər(ɪn)] §6 *mƒ* accessory; one in the know

mit′zählen *tr* include ‖ *intr* count along

mixen ['mɪksən] *tr* mix

Mixgetränk ['mɪksgətreŋk] *n* mixed drink

Mixtur [mɪks′tur] ƒ (-;-en) mixture

Möbel ['møbəl] *n* (-s;-) piece of furniture; **Möbel** *pl* furniture

Mö′belstück *n* piece of furniture

Möbeltransporteur ['møbəltransportør] *m* (-s;-e) mover

Mö′belwagen *m* moving van

mobil [mo′bil] *adj* movable; (*flink*) chipper; (mil) mobile

Mobiliar [mobi′ljar] *n* (-[e]s;) furniture

Mobilien [mo′biljən] *pl* movables

mobilisieren [mobɪlɪ′zirən] *tr* mobilize

Mobilisierung [mobɪlɪ′ziruŋ] ƒ (-;) mobilization

mobil'machen tr mobilize

Mobilmachung [mɔ'bilmaxuŋ] f (-;) mobilization

möblieren [mø'blirən] tr furnish; **möbliert wohnen** (coll) live in a furnished room; **neu m.** refurnish

mochte ['mɔxtə] pret of mögen

Mode ['modə] f (-;-n) fashion, style

Mo'debild n fashion plate

Modell [mɔ'dɛl] n (-[e]s;-e) model; (Muster) pattern; (fig) prototype; **M. stehen zu** (dat) model for

modellieren [modɛ'lirən] tr fashion, shape

Modell'puppe f mannequin

modeln ['modəln] tr fashion, shape; **(nach)** model (on) || ref—**zu alt sein, um sich m. zu lassen** be too old to change

Mo'dengeschäft n dress shop

Mo'denschau f fashion show

Mo'denzeitung f fashion magazine

Moder ['modər] m (-;) mold; mustiness; (Schlamm) mud

Mo'derduft m, **Mo'dergeruch** m musty smell

moderig ['modəriç] adj moldy, musty

modern [mɔ'dɛrn] adj modern || ['modərn] intr rot, decay || **Modern** n (-;) decay

modernisieren [modɛrnı'zirən] tr modernize; bring up to date

Mo'deschmuck m costume jewelry

Mo'deschriftsteller –in §6 mf popular writer

Mo'dewaren pl (com) novelties

modifizieren [mɔdıfı'tsirən] tr modify

modisch ['mɔdı∫] adj fashionable

Modistin [mɔ'dıstın] f (-;-nen) milliner

modrig ['modrıç] adj moldy

modulieren [modu'lirən] tr modulate; (Stimme) inflect

Mo·dus ['modus] m (-;-di [di]) mode, manner; (gram) mood

mogeln ['mogəln] intr cheat || **Mogeln** n (-s;) cheating

mögen ['møgən] §114 tr like, care for; **ich mag lieber** I prefer || mod aux may; can; care to; **er mag nicht nach Hause gehen** he doesn't care to go home; **ich möchte lieber bleiben** I'd rather stay; **ich möchte wissen** I should like to know; **mag kommen was da will** come what may; **wer mag das nur sein?** who can that be?; **wie mag das geschehen sein?** how could this have happened?

möglich ['møklıç] adj possible; (ausführbar) feasible; **sein möglichstes tun** do one's utmost || **Mögliche** §5 n possibility; **er muß alles Mögliche bedenken** he must consider every possibility; **im Rahmen des Möglichen** within the realm of possibility

möglichenfalls ['møklıçənfals], **möglicherweise** ['møklıçərvaızə] adv possibly, if possible

Mög'lichkeit f (-;-en) possibility; potentiality; **ist es die M.!** well, I never!; **finanzielle Möglichkeiten** financial means; **nach M.** as far as possible

möglichst ['møklıçst] adv as ... as possible

Mohn [mon] m (-[e]s;-e) poppyseed; (bot) poppy

Mohn'samen m poppyseed

Mohr [mor] m (-en;-en) Moor

Möhre ['mørə] f (-;-n) carrot

Mohr'rübe f carrot

Mokka ['mɔka] m (-s;-s) mocha (coffee)

Molch [mɔlç] m (-[e]s;-e) salamander

Mole ['molə] f (-;-n) mole, breakwater

Molekül [molə'kyl] n (-s;-e) molecule

molekular [molɛku'lar] adj molecular

Molke ['mɔlkə] f (-;) whey

Molkerei [mɔlkə'raı] f (-;-en) dairy

Moll [mɔl] invar n (mus) minor

mollig ['mɔlıç] adj plump; (Frau) buxom; (behaglich) snug, cozy

Moll'tonart f (mus) minor key

Moment [mo'mɛnt] m (-[e]s;-e) moment || n (-[e]s;-e) momentum; (Antrieb) impulse, impetus; (Faktor) factor, point; (Beweggrund) motive

momentan [momɛn'tan] adj momentary

Moment'aufnahme f snapshot; (Bewegungsaufnahme) action shot

Monarch [mo'narç] m (-en;-en) monarch

Monar·chie [monar'çi] f (-;-chien ['çi·ən]) monarchy

Monat ['monat] m (-[e]s;-e) month

monatelang ['monatəlaŋ] adj lasting for months || adv for months

mo'natlich adj monthly

Mo'natsbinde f sanitary napkin

Mo'natsfluß m menstruation

mo'natsweise adv monthly

Mönch [mœnç] m (-[e]s;-e) monk, friar

Mönchs'kappe f monk's cowl

Mönchs'kloster n monastery

Mönchs'kutte f monk's habit

Mönchs'orden m monastic order

Mönchs'wesen n monasticism

Mond [mont] m (-[e]s;-e) moon; **abnehmender M.** waning moon; **zunehmender M.** waxing moon

mondän [mɔn'dɛn] adj sophisticated

Mond'fähre f (rok) lunar lander

Mond'finsternis f lunar eclipse

mond'hell adj moonlit

Mond'jahr n lunar year

Mond'kalb m (fig) born fool

Mond'schein m moonlight

Mond'sichel f crescent moon

Mond'sucht f lunacy; somnambulism

mond'süchtig adj moonstruck

Moneten [mo'netən] pl (coll) dough

monieren [mo'nirən] tr criticize; remind

Monogramm [mono'gram] n (-s;-e) monogram

Monolog [mono'lok] m (-s;-e) monologue

Monopol [mono'pol] n (-s;-e) monopoly

monopolisieren [monɔpolı'zirən] tr monopolize

monoton [mono'ton] adj monotonous

Monotonie [monoto'ni] f (-;) monotony

Monsterfilm [ˈmɔnstərfɪlm] *m* (cin) spectacular
Monstranz [mɔnˈstrants] *f* (–;–en) monstrance
monströs [mɔnˈstrøs] *adj* monstrous
Monstrosität [mɔnstrozɪˈtet] *f* (–;–en) monstrosity
Mon·strum [ˈmɔnstrʊm] *n* (–;-stra [stra]) monster
Monsun [mɔˈzun] *m* (–s;–e) monsoon
Montag [ˈmɔntak] *m* (–[e]s;–e) Monday
Montage [mɔnˈtaʒə] *f* (–;–n) mounting, fitting; (mach) assembly
Montaˈgebahn *f*, **Montaˈgeband** *n* assembly line
Montaˈgehalle *f* assembly room
montags [ˈmɔntaks] *adv* Mondays
Montan– [mɔntan] *comb.fm.* mining
Monteur [mɔnˈtør] *m* (–s;–e) assemblyman, mechanic
Monteurˈanzug *m* coveralls
montieren [mɔnˈtirən] *tr* mount, fit; (zusammenbauen) assemble; (einrichten) install; (aufstellen) set up
Montur [mɔnˈtur] *f* (–;–en) uniform
Moor [mor] *n* (–[e]s;–e) swamp
Moorˈbad *n* mud bath
moorig [ˈmoriç] *adj* swampy
Moos [mos] *n* (–es;) moss; (Geld) (coll) dough
Mop [mɔp] *m* (–s;–s) mop
Moped [ˈmoped] *n* (–s;–s) motor bike, moped
moppen [ˈmɔpən] *tr* mop
mopsen [ˈmɔpsən] *tr* (coll) swipe || *ref* be bored stiff; be upset
Moral [moˈral] *f* (–;) morality; (Nutzwendung) moral; (mil) morale
moralisch [moˈralɪʃ] *adj* moral
moralisieren [moralɪˈzirən] *intr* moralize
Moralität [moralɪˈtet] *f* (–;) morality
Morast [moˈrast] *m* (–es;–e & ⸚e) mire; morass, quagmire
Mord [mɔrt] *m* (–[e]s;–e) murder
Mordˈanschlag *m* murder attempt; (pol) assassination attempt
Mordˈbrennerei *f* arson and murder
Mordˈbube *m* murderer, assassin
morden [ˈmɔrdən] *tr & intr* murder
Mörder –in [ˈmœrdər(ɪn)] §6 murderer
möderisch [ˈmœrdərɪ] *adj* murderous; (coll) awful, terrible
mordˈgierig *adj* bloodthirsty
Mordˈkommission *f* homicide squad
mordˈlustig *adj* bloodthirsty
Mords– [mɔrts] *comb.fm.* huge; terrible, awful; fantastic, incredible
Mordsˈangst *f* mortal fear
Mordsˈgeschichte *f* tall story
Mordsˈgeschrei *n* loud shouting
Mordsˈkerl *m* (coll) great guy
mordsˈmäßig *adv* (coll) awfully
Mordsˈspektakel *n* awful din
Mordˈtat *f* murder
Mordˈwaffe *f* murder weapon
Mores [ˈmores] *pl*—j–n **M.** lehren teach s.o. manners
morgen [ˈmɔrgən] *adv* tomorrow; **m. abend** tomorrow evening (or night); **m. früh** tomorrow morning; **m. in**
acht Tagen (or über acht Tage) a week from tomorrow; **m. mittag** tomorrow noon || **Morgen** *m* (–s;–) morning; acre; **des Morgens** in the morning || *n* (–;) tomorrow
Morˈgenblatt *n* morning paper
Morˈgendämmerung *f* dawn, daybreak
morˈgendlich *adj* morning
Morˈgengabe *f* wedding present
Morˈgengrauen *n* dawn, daybreak
Morˈgenland *n* Orient
Morgenländer –in [ˈmɔrgənlendər(ɪn)] §6 *mf* Oriental
Morˈgenrock *m* house robe
Morˈgenrot *n*, **Morˈgenröte** *f* dawn, sunrise; (fig) dawn, beginning
morgens [ˈmɔrgəns] *adv* in the morning
Morˈgenstern *m* morning star
Morˈgenstunde *f* morning hour
Morˈgenzeitung *f* morning paper
morgig [ˈmɔrgiç] *adj* tomorrow's
Morphium [ˈmɔrfjum] *n* (–s;) morphine
morsch [mɔrʃ] *adj* rotten; (baufällig) dilapidated; (brüchig) brittle; (fig) decadent
Morsealphabet [ˈmɔrzəˌalfabet] *n* Morse code
Mörser [ˈmœrzər] *m* (–s;–) (& mil) mortar
Mörˈserkeule *f* pestle
Mörtel [ˈmœrtəl] *m* (–s;–) mortar, plaster; **mit M. bewerfen** roughcast
Mörˈtelkelle *f* trowel
Mörˈteltrog *m* hod
Mosaik [mozaˈik] *n* (–s;–en) mosaic
mosaisch [moˈza·ɪʃ] *adj* Mosaic
Moschee [moˈʃe] *f* (–;–n) mosque
Moskau [ˈmɔskau] *n* (–s;) Moscow
Moslem [ˈmɔsləm] *m* (–s;–s) Moslem
moslemisch [mɔsˈlemɪʃ] *adj* Moslem
Most [mɔst] *m* (–es;–e) must, grape juice; new wine
Mostrich [ˈmɔstriç] *m* (–[e]s;–e) mustard
Motel [moˈtel] *n* (–s;–s) motel
Motiv [moˈtif] *n* (–[e]s;–e) (Beweggrund) motive; (mus, paint) motif
motivieren [motiˈvirən] *tr* justify
Mo·tor [ˈmotor], [moˈtor] *m* (–s; -toren [ˈtorən] & –tore [ˈtorə]) motor
Moˈtordefekt *m* motor trouble
Moˈtorhaube *f* (aer) cowl; (aut) hood
–motorig [motoriç] *comb.fm.* –motor, –engine
Moˈtorpanne *f* (aut) breakdown
Moˈtorpflug *m* tractor plow
Moˈtorrad *n* motorcycle
Moˈtorradfahrer –in §6 *mf* motorcyclist
Moˈtorrasenmäher *m* power mower
Moˈtorroller *m* motor scooter
Moˈtorsäge *f* power saw
Moˈtorschaden *m* engine trouble
Motte [ˈmɔtə] *f* (–;–n) moth
motˈtenfest *adj* mothproof
Motˈtenkugel *f* mothball
Motto [ˈmɔto] *n* (–s;–s) motto
moussieren [muˈsirən] *intr* fizz; (Wein) sparkle
Möwe [ˈmøvə] *f* (–;–n) sea gull

Mucke ['mʊkə] f (-;-n) whim; (dial) gnat; **Mucken haben** have moods

Mücke ['mʏkə] f (-;-n) gnat; mosquito; (dial) fly

Mucker ['mʊkər] m (-s;-) hypocrite; bigot; grouch; (coll) awkward guy

Muckerei [mʊkə'raɪ] f (-;) hypocrisy

muckerhaft ['mʊkərhaft] adj hypocritical, bigoted

Mucks [mʊks] m (-es;-e) faint sound; **keinen M. mehr!** not another sound!

mucksen ['mʊksən] ref & intr stir, say a word; **nicht gemuckst!** stay pat!

müde ['mydə] adj tired; **zum Umfallen m.** ready to drop

Müdigkeit f (-;) weariness

Muff [mʊf] m (-[e]s;-e) (Handwärmer) muff; (Schimmel) mold; musty smell

Muffe ['mʊfə] f (-;-n) (mach) sleeve

muffeln ['mʊfəln] intr sulk, be grouchy; (anhaltend kauen) munch; mumble

muffig ['mʊfɪç] adj musty; (Person) sulky; (Luft) stale, frowzy

Mühe ['my·ə] f (-;-n) trouble, pains; (Anstrengung) effort; **geben Sie sich keine M.!** don't bother; **j-m M. machen** cause s.o. trouble; **mit M.** with difficulty; **mit M. und Not** barely; **nicht der M. wert** not worthwhile; **sich** [dat] **große M. machen** go to great pains; **verlorene M.** wasted effort

mü'helos adj easy, effortless

muhen ['mu·ən] intr moo, low

mühen ['my·ən] ref take pains

mü'hevoll adj hard, troublesome

Mühewaltung ['my·əvaltʊŋ] f (-;) trouble, efforts; **für Ihre M. dankend, verbleiben wir ...** thanking you for your cooperation, we remain ...

Mühle ['mylə] f (-;-n) mill

Mühlrad ['mylrɑt] n water wheel

Mühlstein ['myl∫taɪn] m millstone

Muhme ['mumə] f (-;-n) aunt; cousin

Mühsal ['myzɑl] f (-;-e) trouble

mühsam ['myzam] adj wearisome; (Leben) hard; (Arbeit) painstaking ‖ adv with effort, with difficulty

mühselig ['myzelɪç] adj (Arbeit) hard; (Leben) miserable, tough

Mulatte [mu'latə] m (-n;-n), **Mulattin** [mu'latɪn] f (-;-nen) mulatto

Mulde ['mʊldə] f (-;-n) trough; (geol) depression, basin

Mull [mʊl] m (-[e]s;) gauze

Müll [myl] m (-[e]s;) dust, ashes; (Abfälle) trash, garbage

Müll'abfuhr f garbage disposal

Müll'abfuhrwagen m garbage truck

Müll'eimer m trash can, garbage can

Müller ['mylər] m (-s;-) miller

Müllerin ['mylərɪn] f (-;-nen) miller's wife; miller's daughter

Müll'fahrer m garbage man

Müll'haufen m scrap heap

Müll'platz m garbage dump

Müll'schaufel f dustpan

Mulm [mʊlm] m (-[e]s;) rotten wood

mul'mig adj rotten; dusty; (Luft) sticky; (Lage) ticklish

Multiplikation [mʊltɪplika'tsjon] f (-;) multiplication

multiplizieren [mʊltɪplɪ'tsirən] tr multiply

Mumie ['mumjə] f (-;-n) mummy

Mumm [mʊm] m (-s;) (coll) drive, grit

Mummelgreis ['mʊmǝlgraɪs] m (coll) old fogey

mummeln ['mʊmǝln] tr & intr mumble

Mund [mʊnt] m (-[e]s;⁀er) mouth; **den M. aufreißen** brag; **den M. halten** shut up; **den M. vollnehmen** talk big; **e-n losen M. haben** answer back; **sich** [dat] **den Mund verbrennen** put one's foot into it; **wie auf den M. geschlagen** dumbfounded

Mund'art f dialect

Mündel ['mʏndǝl] m & n (-s;-) & f (-;-n) ward

Mündelgelder ['mʏndǝlgeldǝr] pl trustfund

mün'delsicher adj gilt-edged; absolutely safe

munden ['mʊndən] intr taste good

münden ['mʏndən] intr—**m. in** (acc) empty into, flow into

mund'faul adj too lazy to talk

mund'gerecht adj palatable

Mund'geruch m halitosis

Mund'harmonika f mouth organ

Mund'höhle f oral cavity

mündig ['mʏndɪç] adj of age

Mün'digkeit f (-;) majority, full age

mündlich ['mʏntlɪç] adj oral, verbal

Mund'pflege f oral hygiene

Mund'sperre f lockjaw

Mund'stück n mouthpiece; (Zigaretten-) tip; (Düse) nozzle

mund'tot adj—**j-n m. machen** (fig) silence s.o.

Mund'tuch n table napkin

Mün'dung f (e-s Flusses) mouth; (e-r Feuerwaffe) muzzle

Mün'dungsfeuer n muzzle flash

Mün'dungsweite f (arti) bore

Mund'vorrat m provisions

Mund'wasser n mouthwash

Mund'werk n (fig) mouth, tongue

Mund'winkel m corner of the mouth

Munition [muni'tsjon] f (-;) ammunition

Munitions'lager n ammunition dump

munkeln ['mʊŋkəln] tr & intr whisper

Münster ['mʏnstər] n (-s;-) cathedral

munter ['mʊntər] adj awake; (lebhaft) lively; (rüstig) vigorous; gay

Münz– ['mʏnts] comb.fm. monetary; of the mint; coin; coinage; coin-operated

Münz'anstalt f mint

Münze ['mʏntsə] f (-;-n) coin; change; (Münzanstalt) mint; (Denkmünze) medal; **bare M.** hard cash; **für bare Münze nehmen** take at face value

Münz'einheit f monetary unit

Münz'einwurf m coin slot

münzen ['mʏntsən] tr coin, mint; **das ist auf ihn gemünzt** that is meant for him ‖ **Münzen** n (-s;) mintage, coinage

Münz'fälscher m counterfeiter

Münz'fernsprecher m public telephone

Münz′kunde f numismatics
Münz′wesen n monetary system
Münz′wissenschaft f numismatics
mürb [mʏrp], **mürbe** [′mʏrbə] adj
(Fleisch) tender; (sehr reif) mellow;
(gut durchgekocht) well done; (Gebäck) crisp and flaky; (brüchig)
brittle; (erschöpft) worn out; (mil)
demoralized; **j-n mürbe machen** (fig)
break s.o. down; **mürbe werden**
soften, give in
Murks [mʊrks] m (-es;) bungling job
murksen [′mʊrksən] intr bungle
Murmel [′mʊrməl] f (-;-n) marble
murmeln [′mʊrməln] tr & intr murmur
Mur′meltier n ground hog, woodchuck
murren [′mʊrən] intr grumble
mürrisch [′mʏrɪʃ] adj grouchy, crabby
Mus [mus] n (-es;-e) purée; sauce
Muschel [′mʊʃəl] f (-;-n) mussel;
(Schale) shell; (anat) concha
Muse [′muzə] f (-;-n) (myth) Muse
Muse•um [mu′ze•ʊm] n (-s;-en) mu-
seum
Musik [mu′zik] f (-;) music
Musikalien [muzɪ′kaljən] pl music
book
musikalisch [muzɪ′kalɪʃ] adj musical
Musikant [muzɪ′kant] m (-en;-en)
musician
Musikan′tenknochen m funny bone
Musik′automat m, **Musikbox** [′mjuzɪk-
bɔks] f (-;-en) juke box
Musiker -in [′muzɪkər(ɪn)] §6 mf
musician
Musik′hochschule f conservatory
Musik′kapelle f band
Musik′korps m military band
Musik′pavillon m bandstand
Musik′schrank m, **Musik′truhe** f radio-
phonograph console
Musi•kus [′muzɪkʊs] m (-;-zi [tsi])
(hum) musician
Musik′wissenschaft f musicology
musisch [′muzɪʃ] adj artistic
musizieren [muzɪ′tsirən] intr play
music
Muskat [mʊs′kat] m (-[e]s;-e) nut-
meg
Muskateller [mʊska′tɛlər] m (-s;)
muscatel
Muskat′nuß f nutmeg
Muskel [′mʊskəl] m (-s;-n) muscle
Mus′kelkater m (coll) charley horse
Mus′kelkraft f brawn
Mus′kelriß m torn muscle
Mus′kelschwund m muscular distrophy
Mus′kelzerrung f pulled muscle
Muskete [mʊs′ketə] f (-;-n) musket
Muskulatur [mʊskula′tur] f (-;-en)
muscles, muscular system
muskulös [mʊsku′løs] adj muscular
Muß [mʊs] invar n must, necessity
Muße [′musə] f (-;) leisure; **mit M.**
at leisure
Muß′ehe f shotgun wedding
Musselin [mʊsə′lin] m (-s;-e) muslin
müssen [′mʏsən] intr—**ich muß nach
Hause** I must go home || mod aux—
ich muß (inf) I must (inf), I have to
(inf); **ich muß nicht** I don't have to;
muß das wirklich sein? is it really
neecessary?; **sie hätten hier sein m.**

they ought to have been here; **sie
müssen bald kommen** they are bound
to come soon
müßig [′mʏsɪç] adj idle; (unnütz) unprofitable; (zwecklos) useless; (überflüssig) superfluous
Mü′ßiggang m idleness
Müßiggänger m loafer
mußte [′mʊstə] pret of müssen
Muster [′mʊstər] n (-s;-) pattern;
(Probestück) sample; (Vorbild) example, model; **das M. e-r Hausfrau**
a model housewife; **nach dem M.
von** along the lines of; **sich** [dat]
ein M. nehmen an (dat) model oneself on
Mu′sterbeispiel n typical example
Mu′sterbild n ideal, paragon
Mu′stergatte m model husband
Mu′stergattin f model wife
mu′stergültig adj model, ideal
Mu′stergut n model farm
mu′sterhaft adj model, ideal
Mu′sterknabe m (pej) sissy
Mu′sterkollektion f (kit of) samples
mustern [′mʊstərn] tr examine, eye,
size up; (mil) inspect, review
Mu′sterprozeß m test case
Mu′sterschüler -in §6 mf model pupil
Mu′sterstück n specimen, sample
Mu′sterstudent -in §7 mf model stu-
dent
Mu′sterung f (-;-en) inspection; ex-
amination; (mil) review
Mu′sterungsbescheid m induction no-
tice
Mu′sterungskommission f draft board
Mu′sterwerk n standard work
Mu′sterwort n (-[e]s;⸗er) (gram) paradigm
Mut [mut] m (-[e]s;) courage; **den
Mut sinken lassen** lose heart; **guten
Mutes sein** feel encouraged; **j-m
den Mut nehmen** discourage s.o.;
nur Mut! cheer up!
Mutation [muta′tsjon] f (-;-en) (biol)
mutation, sport
Mütchen [′mʏtçən] n—**sein M. kühlen
an** (dat) take it out on
mutieren [mu′tirən] intr (Stimme)
change
mutig [′mutɪç] adj courageous, brave
-mütig [mytɪç] comb.fm. -minded,
-feeling
mut′los adj discouraged
Mut′losigkeit f (-;) discouragement
mutmaßen [′mutmasən] tr suppose,
conjecture
mutmaßlich [′mutmaslɪç] adj supposed, alleged; **mutmaßlicher Erbe**
heir presumptive || adv presumably
Mut′maßung f (-;-en) conjecture,
guesswork; **Mutmaßungen anstellen**
conjecture
Mutter [′mutər] f (-;⸗) mother; **wer-
dende M.** expectant mother || f (-;
-n) nut
Mut′terboden m rich soil
Mütterchen [′mʏtərçən] n (-s;-)
mummy; little old lady
Mut′tererde f rich soil; native soil
Mut′terfürsorge f maternity welfare
Mut′terkuchen m (anat) placenta

Mut'terleib *m* womb
Mütterlich ['mʏtərlɪç] *adj* motherly, maternal; **m. verwandt** related on the mother's side
mut'terlos *adj* motherless
Mut'termal *n* birthmark
Mut'terpferd *n* mare
Mut'terschaf *n* ewe
Mut'terschaft *f* (–;) motherhood, maternity
Mut'terschlüssel *m* (mach) wrench
mut'terseelenallein' *adj* all alone
Muttersöhnchen ['mutərzønçən] *n* (–s;) mamma's boy
Mut'tersprache *f* mother tongue
Mut'terstelle *f*—**bei j–m die M. vertreten** be a mother to s.o.
Mut'terstute *f* mare
Mut'tertier *n* (zool) dam
Mut'terwitz *m* common sense
Mutti ['muti] *f* (–;–s) (coll) mom
mut'voll *adj* courageous
Mut'wille *m* mischievousness

mut'willig *adj* mischievous, willful
Mütze ['mʏtsə] *f* (–;–n) cap
Myriade [myrɪ'adə] *f* (–;–n) myriad
Myrrhe ['mʏrə] *f* (–;–n) myrrh
Myrte ['mʏrtə] *f* (–;–n) myrtle
Mysterienspiel [mys'terjən/pil] *n* (theat) mystery play
mysteriös [myste'rjøs] *adj* mysterious
Myste•rium [mys'terjum] *n* (–s;–rien [rjən]) mystery
mystifizieren [mystɪfɪ'tsirən] *tr* mystify; (*täuschen*) hoax
Mystik ['mystɪk] *f* (–;) mysticism
My'stiker –in §6 *mf* mystic
mystisch ['mystɪʃ] *adj* mystic(al)
Mythe ['mytə] *f* (–;–n) myth
mythisch ['mytɪʃ] *adj* mythical
Mytholo•gie ['mytolə'gi] *f* (–;–gien ['gi•ən]) mythology
mythologisch [myto'logɪʃ] *adj* mythological
My•thus ['mytus] *m* (–;–then [tən]) myth

N

N, n [ɛn] *invar n* N, n
na [na] *interj* well!; **na also!** there you are!; **na, so was!** don't tell me!; **na, und ob! I'll** say!; **na, warte!** just you wait!
Nabe ['nabə] *f* (–;–n) hub
Nabel ['nabəl] *m* (–s;–) navel
Na'belschnur *f* umbilical cord
nach [nax] *adv* after; **n. und n.** little by little; **n. wie vor** now as ever || *prep (dat) (Zeit)* after; (*Reihenfolge*) after, behind; (*Ziel, Richtung*) to, towards, for; (*Art, Maß, Vorbild, Richtschnur*) according to, after
Nach-, nach- *comb.fm.* subsequent, additional, supplementary; post-; over, over again, re–; after
nach'äffen *tr* ape, imitate
nachahmen ['naxamən] *tr* imitate, copy
Nach'ahmer –in §6 *mf* imitator
Nach'ahmung *f* (–;–en) imitation, copy
nach'arbeiten *tr* copy; (*ausbessern*) touch up; (*Versäumtes*) make up for
nach'arten *intr* (SEIN) (*dat*) take after
Nachbar ['naxbar] *m* (–s & –n;–n), **Nachbarin** ['naxbarin] *f* (–;–nen) neighbor
nach'barlich *adj* neighborly; neighboring
Nach'barschaft *f* (–;–en) neighborhood; **gute N. halten** be on friendly terms with neighbors
Nach'bau *m* (–s;) imitation, duplication; licensed manufacture; **unerlaubter N.** illegal manufacture
Nach'behandlung *f* (med) follow-up treatment
nach'bestellen *tr* reorder, order more of
Nach'bestellung *f* (–;–en) repeat order
nach'beten *tr & intr* repeat mechanically

nach'bezahlen *tr* pay afterwards; pay the rest of || *intr* pay afterwards
Nach'bild *n* copy
nach'bilden *tr* copy
Nach'bildung *f* (–;–en) copying; (*Kopie*) copy, reproduction; (*Modell*) mock-up; (*Attrappe*) dummy
nach'bleiben §62 *intr* (SEIN) remain behind; (educ) stay in; **hinter j–m n.** lag behind s.o.
nach'blicken *intr* (*dat*) look after
nach'brennen §97 *intr* smolder || **Nachbrennen** *n* (–s;) (rok) afterburn
Nach'brenner *m* (aer) afterburner
nach'datieren *tr* postdate
nachdem [nax'dem] *adv* afterwards; **je n.** as the case may be, it all depends || *conj* after, when; **je n.** according to how, depending on how
nach'denken §66 *intr* think it over; **n. über** (*acc*) think over, reflect on || **Nachdenken** *n* (–s;) reflection; **bei weiterem N.** on second thought
nach'denklich *adj* reflective, thoughtful; (*Buch*) thought-provoking; (*abwesend*) lost in thought
Nach'dichtung *f* (–;–en) free poetical rendering
nach'drängen *intr* (SEIN) (*dat*) crowd after; pursue
nach'dringen §142 *intr* be in hot pursuit; (*dat*) pursue
Nach'druck *m* (*Betonung*) stress, emphasis; energy; (*Raubdruck*) pirated edition; (typ) reprint; **mit N.** emphatically; **N. verboten** all rights reserved
nach'drucken *tr* reprint
nach'drücklich *adj* emphatic; **n. betonen** emphasize
nach'dunkeln *intr* get darker
nach'eifern *intr* (*dat*) emulate

nach'eilen *intr* (SEIN) (*dat*) hasten after, rush after

nacheinan'der *adv* one after another

nach'empfinden §59 *tr* have a feeling for; **j—m etw n.** sympathize with s.o. about s.th.

Nachen ['naxən] *m* (-s;-) (poet) boat

nach'erzählen *tr* repeat, retell

Nachfahr ['naxfar] *m* (-s;-en) descendant

nach'fahren §71 *intr* (SEIN) (*dat*) drive after, follow

nach'fassen *tr* (mil) get a second helping of || *intr* (econ) do a follow-up

Nach'folge *f* succession

nach'folgen *intr* (*dat*) succeed, follow; follow in the footsteps of

nach'folgend *adj* following, subsequent

Nach'folger –in §6 *mf* follower; successor

nach'fordern *tr* charge extra; claim subsequently

nach'forschen *intr* (*dat*) investigate

Nach'frage *f* inquiry; (com) demand

nach'fragen *intr* (nach) ask (about)

Nach'frist *f* time extension

nach'fühlen *tr—j—m etw n.* sympathize with s.o. about s.th.

nach'füllen *tr* refill, fill up

nach'geben §80 *tr* give later; (*beim Essen*) give another helping of; **j—m nichts an Eifer n.** not be outdone by s.o. in zeal || *intr* give way, give; (*schlaff werden*) slacken, give; (*dat*) give in to, yield to

nach'geboren *adj* younger; posthumous

Nach'gebühr *f* postage due

nach'gehen §82 *intr* (SEIN) (*dat*) follow; (*Geschäften*) attend to; (*untersuchen*) investigate, check on

nachgemacht ['naxgəmaxt] *adj* false, imitation; (*künstlich*) artificial

nachgeordnet ['naxgə·ɔrdnət] *adj* subordinate

nach'gerade *adv* by now; (*allmählich*) gradually; (*wirklich*) really

Nach'geschmack *m* aftertaste, bad taste

nachgewiesenermaßen ['naxgəvizənərmasən] *adv* as has been shown (or proved)

nachgiebig ['naxgibɪç] *adj* elastic, yielding, compliant; (*nachsichtig*) indulgent; (st. exch.) declining

nach'gießen §76 *tr* fill up, refill || *intr* add more

nach'glühen *tr* (tech) temper || *intr* smolder

nach'grübeln *intr* (dat or über *acc*) mull (over), ponder (on)

Nach'hall *m* echo, reverberation

nach'hallen *intr* echo, reverberate

nachhaltig ['naxhaltɪç] *adj* lasting

nach'hängen §92 *intr* (*dat*) give free rein to || *impers—es hängt mir nach* I still feel the effects of it

nach'helfen §96 *intr* (*dat*) help along

nach'her *adv* afterwards, later, then; **bis n.!** so long!

nachherig ['naxherɪç] *adj* later

Nach'hilfe *f* assistance, help

Nach'hilfelehrer –in §6 *mf* tutor

Nach'hilfestunde *f* tutoring lesson

Nach'hilfeunterricht *m* tutoring

nach'hinken *intr* (*dat*) lag behind

Nachholbedarf ['naxholbədarf] *m* backlog of unsatisfied demands

nach'holen *tr* make up for

Nach'hut *f* (mil) rear guard

nach'jagen *tr—j—m etw n.* send s.th. after s.o. || *intr* (SEIN) (*dat*) pursue

Nach'klang *m* echo; (fig) reminiscence

nach'klingen §142 *intr* reecho, resound

Nachkomme ['naxkɔmə] *m* (-n;-n) offspring, descendant

nach'kommen §99 *intr* (SEIN) (*dat*) follow; join (s.o.) later; (*Vorschriften, e—m Gesetz*) obey; (*e—m Versprechen*) keep; (*e—r Pflicht*) live up to

Nach'kommenschaft *f* (-;) posterity

Nachkömmling ['naxkœmlɪŋ] *m* (-s; -e) offspring, descendant

Nach'laß ['naxlas] *m* (-lasses;-lässe) remission; (*am Preis*) reduction; (*Erbschaft*) estate; **literarischer N.** unpublished works

nach'lassen §104 *tr* leave behind; (*lockern*) slacken; **j—m 15% vom Preise n.** give s.o. a fifteen percent reduction in price || *intr* (*sich lockern*) slacken; (*sich vermindern*) diminish; (*milder werden*) relent; (*Regen*) let up; (*Kräfte*) give out; (*Wind, Sturm*) die down; (*schlechter werden*) get worse

Nach'laßgericht *n* probate court

nach'lässig *adj* careless, negligent

Nach'lässigkeit *f* carelessness, negligence

nach'laufen §105 *intr* (SEIN) (*dat*) run after, pursue

nach'leben *intr* (*dat*) live up to || **Nach'leben** *n* afterlife

Nach'lese *f* gleanings

nach'lesen §107 *tr* glean; (*Stelle im Buch*) reread, look up

nach'liefern *tr* deliver subsequently

nach'machen *tr* imitate; (*fälschen*) counterfeit; **j—m alles n.** imitate s.o. in everything

nach'malen *tr* copy

nachmalig ['naxmalɪç] *adj* later

nachmals ['naxmals] *adv* afterwards

nach'messen §70 *tr* measure again

Nach'mittag *m* afternoon

nach'mittags *adv* in the afternoon

Nach'mittagsvorstellung *f* matinée

Nach'nahme *f* (-;) C.O.D.

Nach'name *m* last name, family name

nach'plappern *tr* repeat mechanically

Nach'porto *n* postage due

nachprüfbar ['naxpryfbar] *adj* verifiable

nach'prüfen *tr* verify, check out

nach'rechnen *tr* (acct) check

Nach'rede *f* epilogue; **j—n in üble N. bringen** bring s.o. into bad repute; **üble N.** slander; **üble N. verbreiten** spread nasty rumors

nach'reden *tr—j—m etw n.* say s.th. behind s.o.'s back

Nachricht ['naxrɪçt] *f* (-;-en) news; (*Bericht*) report; (*kurzer Bericht*) notice; (*Auskunft*) information; **e—e N. verbreiten** spread the news; **geben Sie mir von Zeit zu Zeit N.!** keep me advised; **Nachrichten** (rad, telv) news, news report; **Nachrichten einholen** make inquiries; **Nachrichten einziehen** gather information; **zur N.!** for your information

Nach'richtenabteilung f (mil) intelligence section

Nach'richtenagentur f news agency

Nach'richtenbüro n news room; news agency

Nach'richtendienst m news service; (mil) army intelligence

Nach'richtensatellit m communications satellite

Nach'richtensendung f newscast

Nach'richtenwesen n communications

nach'rücken intr (SEIN) (im Rang) move up; (mil) (dat) follow up; **j-m n.** move up into s.o.'s position

Nach'ruf m obituary

nach'rufen §122 tr (dat) call after

Nach'ruhm m posthumous fame

nach'rühmen tr—**j-m etw n.** say s.th. nice about s.o.

nach'sagen tr—**j-m etw n.** repeat s.th. after s.o.; say s.th behind s.o.'s back; **das lasse ich mir nicht n.** I won't let that be said of me

Nach'satz m concluding clause

nach'schaffen tr replace

nach'schauen intr (dat) gaze after

nach'schicken tr forward

Nachschlagebuch ['nax/lɑgəbux] n reference book

nach'schlagen §132 tr look up; (Buch) consult || intr (box) counter

Nachschlagewerk ['nɑx/lɑgəverk] n reference work

Nach'schlüssel m skeleton key

nach'schreiben §62 tr copy; take down from dictation

Nach'schrift f postscript

Nach'schub m (mil) supply, fresh supplies; (mil) supply lines

Nach'schublinie f (mil) supply line

Nach'schubstützpunkt m (mil) supply base

Nach'schubweg m supply line

nach'sehen §138 tr (nachschlagen) look up; (nachprüfen) check; (acct) audit; (mach) overhaul; **j-m vieles n.** overlook much in s.o. || intr (dat) gaze after || **Nachsehen** n—**das N. haben** get the short end

nach'senden §140 tr send after, forward

nach'setzen intr (dat) run after

Nach'sicht f patience; **mit j-m N. üben** have patience with s.o.

nach'sichtig, nach'sichtsvoll adj lenient, considerate

Nach'silbe f suffix

nach'sinnen §121 intr (über acc) reflect (on), muse (over)

nach'sitzen intr be kept in after school

Nach'sommer m Indian summer

Nach'speise f dessert

Nach'spiel n (fig) sequel

nach'spüren intr (dat) track down

nächst [neçst] prep (dat) next to

nächst'beste §9 adj second-best

nächstdem' adv thereupon

nächste ['neçstə] §9 adj (super of

nahe) next; (Weg) shortest; (Beziehungen) closest || **Nächste** §5 mf neighbor, fellow man, fellow creature

nach'stehen §146 intr (dat) be inferior to

nach'stehend adj following || adv (mentioned) below

nach'stellen tr (Schraube) reset, adjust; (Uhr) set back || intr (dat) be after; (e-m Mädchen) run after

Nach'stellung f (-;-en) persecution; ambush; (gram) postposition

nächsten ['neçstən] adv one of these days, before long; next time

Näch'stenliebe f charity

nächst'liegend adj nearest

nach'stöbern intr rummage about

nach'stoßen §150 intr (SEIN) (dat) (mil) follow up

nach'streben intr (dat) strive after; (e-r Person) emulate

nach'strömen, nach'strümen, nach'stürzen intr (SEIN) (dat) crowd after

nach'suchen tr search for || intr—**n. um** apply for

Nach'suchung f (-;-en) search, inquiry; petition

Nacht [naxt] f (-;ᵈe) night; **bei N. und Nebel** under cover of night

Nacht'ausgabe f final (edition)

Nacht'teil m disadvantage

nach'teilig adj disadvantageous

Nacht'essen n supper

Nacht'eule f night owl

Nacht'falter m (ent) moth

Nacht'geschirr n chamber pot

Nacht'gleiche f equinox

Nacht'hemd n nightgown

Nachtigall ['naxtigal] f (-;-n) nightingale

nächtigen ['neçtigən] intr pass the night

Nacht'tisch m dessert

Nacht'klub m, **Nacht'lokal** n nightclub

Nacht'lager n accommodations for the night

nächtlich ['neçtliç] adj night, nightly

Nacht'mal n supper

Nacht'musik f serenade

nach'tönen intr resound; (Note) linger

Nacht'quartier n accommodations for the night

Nachtrag ['naxtrak] m (-[e]s;ᵈe) supplement, addition

nach'tragen §132 tr add; **j-m etw n.** carry s.th. after s.o.; (fig) hold s.th. against s.o.

nachträgerisch ['naxtregərɪʃ] adj resentful, vindictive

nachträglich ['naxtrekliç] adj supplementary; (später) subsequent

Nachtrags- comb.fm. supplementary

Nacht'trupp m (-s;) rear guard

nachts [naxts] adv at night

Nacht'schicht f night shift

nacht'schlafend adj—**bei** (or **zu**) **nachtschlafender Zeit** late at night

Nacht'schwärmer -in §6 mf reveler

Nacht'tisch m night table

Nacht'topf m chamber pot

nach'tun §154 tr—**j-m etw n.** imitate s.o. in s.th.

Nacht'wache f night watch, vigil

Nacht'wächter m night watchman

Nachtwandler –in [ˈnaxtvandlər(in)] §6 *mf* sleepwalker, somnambulist
Nacht'zeug *n* overnight things
Nach'urlaub *m* extended leave
nach'wachsen §155 *intr* (SEIN) grow again
Nach'wahl *f* special election
Nachwehen [ˈnaxveˑən] *pl* afterpains; (fig) painful consequences
nach'weinen *tr*—**keine Tränen n.** (dat) waste no tears over || *intr* (dat) cry over
Nachweis [ˈnaxvais] *m* (–es;–e) proof; **den N. bringen** (or **führen**) furnish proof
nach'weisbar *adj* demonstrable
nach'weisen §118 *tr* point, show; (beweisen) prove; (begründen) substantiate; (verweisen) refer to
nach'weislich *adj* demonstrable
Nach'welt *f* posterity
nach'wiegen §57 *tr* verify the weight of
nach'wirken *intr* have an aftereffect
Nach'wirkung *f* (–;–en) aftereffect
Nach'wort *n* (–[e]s;–e) epilogue
Nach'wuchs *m* younger generation; younger set; children
nach'zahlen *tr & intr* pay extra
nach'zählen *tr* count over, check
nach'zeichnen *tr* draw a copy of || *intr* copy
nach'ziehen §163 *tr* drag; tow; (Linien) trace; (Schraube) tighten || *intr* (SEIN) (dat) follow after
nach'zoteln *intr* (SEIN) (coll) trot after
Nachzügler –in [ˈnaxtsyklər(in)] §6 *mf* straggler; latecomer
Nackedei [ˈnakədai] *m* (–[e]s;–e) naked child; nude
Nacken [ˈnakən] *m* (–s;–) nape of the neck
nackend [ˈnakənt] *adj* var of **nackt**
Nackenschlag [ˈnakenʃlag] *m* rabbit punch; (fig) hard blow
–nackig [nakiç] *comb.fm.* –necked
nackt [nakt] *adj* nude, bare; (Tatsache) hard; **sich n. ausziehen** strip bare
Nackt'heit *f* (–;) nudity, nakedness
Nadel [ˈnadəl] *f* (–;–n) needle; pin; **wie auf Nadeln sitzen** be on pins and needles
Na'delbaum *m* coniferous tree
Na'delkissen *n* pin cushion
Nadelöhr [ˈnadəlˀør] *n* (–s;–e) eye of a needle
Na'delstich *m* pinprick; (sew) stitch
Nagel [ˈnagəl] *m* (–s;ⁿ) nail; **an den N. hängen** (fig) shelve; **an den Nägeln kauen** bite one's nails
Na'gelhaut *f* cuticle
nageln [ˈnagəln] *tr & intr* nail
na'gelneu' *adj* brand-new
nagen [ˈnagən] *tr* gnaw; **das Fleisch vom Knochen n.** pick the meat off the bone || *intr* (an *dat*) gnaw (at), nibble (at); (fig) (an *dat*) rankle
Nagetier [ˈnagətiːr] *n* rodent
Nah– [na] *comb.fm.* close-range, short-range
Näh– [ne] *comb.fm.* sewing, needlework
Näh'arbeit *f* sewing, needlework
Näh'aufnahme *f* (phot) close-up

nahe [ˈnaˑə] *adj* (näher [ˈneˑər]; nächste [ˈneçstə] §9) near, close; nearby; (bevorstehend) forthcoming; (Gefahr) imminent || *adv*—**j–m zu n. treten** hurt s.o.'s feelings; **n. an.** (dat or acc), **n. bei** close to; **n. daran sein zu** (inf) be on the point of (ger)
Nähe [ˈneˑə] *f* (–;–n) nearness; vicinity; **in der N.** close by
na'hebei *adv* nearby
na'hebringen §65 *tr* drive home
na'hegehen §82 *intr* (SEIN) (dat) affect, touch, grieve
na'hekommen §99 *intr* (SEIN) approach; (dat) come near to; **der Wahrheit n.** get at the truth
na'helegen *tr* suggest
na'heliegen §108 *intr* be close by; be obvious; be easy
na'heliegend *adj* obvious
nahen [ˈnaˑən] *ref & intr* (SEIN) approach; (dat) draw near to
nähen [ˈneˑən] *tr & intr* sew, stitch
näher [ˈneˑər] *adj* (comp of **nahe**) nearer; **bei näherer Betrachtung** upon further consideration || *adv* closer; **immer n. kommen** close in; **treten Sie n.!** this way, please! || **Nähere** §5 *n* details, particulars; **das N. auseinandersetzen** explain fully; **Näheres erfahren** learn further particulars; **sich des Näheren entsinnen** remember all particulars; **wenn Sie Näheres wissen wollen** if you want details
Näherin [ˈneˑərin] *f* (–;–nen) seamstress
nähern [ˈneˑərn] *ref* approach; (dat) draw near to, approach
Nä'herungswert *m* approximate value
na'hestehen §146 *intr* (dat) share the view of
na'hetreten §152 *intr* (SEIN) (dat) come into close contact with
na'hezu *adv* almost, nearly
Näh'garn *n* thread
Nah'kampf *m* hand-to-hand fighting; (box) in-fighting
nahm [nam] *pret* of **nehmen**
Näh'maschine *f* sewing machine
–nahme [namə] *f* (–;–n) *comb.fm.* taking
Nähr– [ner] *comb.fm.* nutritive
Nähr'boden *m* rich soil; (fig) breeding ground; (biol) culture medium
nähren [ˈneˑrən] *tr* nourish, feed; (Kind) nurse || *ref* make a living; **sich n. von** subsist on || *intr* be nutritious
nahrhaft [ˈnaːrhaft] *adj* nourishing, nutritious, nutritive
Nähr'mittel *pl* (Teigwaren) noodles; (Hülsenfrüchte) beans and peas
Nahrung [ˈnaːrʊŋ] *f* (–;) nourishment; (Kost) diet; (Unterhalt) livelihood
Nah'rungsmittel *pl* food
Nah'rungsmittelvergiftung *f* food poisoning
Nah'rungssorgen *pl* difficulty in making ends meet
Nähr'wert *m* nutritive value
Näh'stube *f* sewing room
Naht [nat] *f* (–;ⁿe) seam

Nah'verkehr *m* local traffic

Näh'zeug *n* sewing kit

naiv [na'if] *adj* naive

Name ['namə] *m* (–ns;–n), **Namen** ['namən] *m* (–s;–) name

na'menlos *adj* nameless; (*unsäglich*) indescribable

namens ['naməns] *adv* named, called || *prep* (*genit*) in the name of, on behalf of

Na'mensschild *n* nameplate

Na'menstag *m* name day

Na'mensvetter *m* namesake

namentlich ['naməntlɪç] *adj*—**namentliche Abstimmung** roll-call vote || *adv* by name, individually; (*besonders*) especially

Na'menverzeichnis *n* index of names; nomenclature

namhaft ['namhaft] *adj* distinguished; (*beträchtlich*) considerable; **n. machen** name, specify

nämlich ['nemlɪç] *adv* namely, that is; (coll) you know, you see

nannte ['nantə] *pret* of **nennen**

nanu [na'nu] *interj* gee!

Napf [napf] *m* (–es;᠆e) bowl

Narbe ['narbə] *f* (–;–n) scar; (*des Leders*) grain; (agr) topsoil

narbig ['narbɪç] *adj* scarred

Narkose [nar'kozə] *f* (–;–n) anesthesia

Narkoti•kum [nar'kotikum] *n* (–s;–ka [ka]) narcotic, dope

narkotisch [nar'kotɪʃ] *adj* narcotic

Narr [nar] *m* (–en;–en) fool; (hist) jester; **j–n zum Narren halten** make a fool of s.o.

Närrchen ['nɛrçən] *n* (–s;–) silly little goose

narren ['narən] *tr* make a fool of

Narrenfest ['narənfest] *n* masquerade

Narrenhaus ['narənhaus] *n* madhouse

Narrenkappe ['narənkapə] *f* cap and bells

narrensicher ['narənzɪçər] *adj* (coll) foolproof

Narren(s)possen ['narən(s)pɔsən] *pl* horseplay; **laß die N.!** stop horsing around!

Narr'heit *f* (–;–en) folly

närrisch ['nerɪʃ] *adj* foolish; (*verrückt*) crazy; (*Kauz*) eccentric; **n. sein auf** (*acc*) be crazy about

Narzisse [nar'tsɪsə] *f* (–;–n) (bot) narcissus; **gelbe N.** daffodil

naschen ['naʃən] *tr* nibble at || *intr* (**an** *dat*, **von**) nibble (on); **gern n.** have a sweet tooth

Näscher –in ['nɛʃər(ɪn)] §6 *mf* nibbler

Näscherei [neʃə'raɪ] *f* (–;–en) snack

naschhaft ['naʃhaft] *adj* sweet-toothed

Naschkatze ['naʃkatsə] *f* nibbler

Naschmaul ['naʃmaul] *n* nibbler

Naschwerk ['naʃverk] *n* sweets, tidbits

Nase ['nazə] *f* (–;–n) nose; **auf der N. liegen** be laid up in bed; **aufgeworfene N.** turned-up nose; **das sticht ihm in die N.** it annoys him; he's itching to have it; **daß du die N. im Gesicht behältst!** keep your shirt on!; **dem Kind die N. putzen** wipe the child's nose; **die N. läuft ihm blau an** his nose is getting red; **die N. rüm-**

pfen über (*acc*) turn up one's nose at; **die N. voll haben von** be fed up with; **e–e tüchtige N. voll bekommen** (or **einstecken müssen**) get chewed out; **faß dich an deine eigene N.!** mind your own business!; **feine N. für** flair for; **immer der N. nach!** follow your nose!; **in der N. bohren** poke one's nose; **j–m e–e lange N. machen** thumb one's nose at s.o.; **j–m e–e N. drehen** outwit s.o.; **j–m die Würmer aus der N. ziehen** worm it out of s.o.; **j–m etw auf die N. binden** divulge s.th. to s.o.; **j–m in die N. fahren** (or **steigen**) annoy s.o.; **j–n an der N. herumführen** lead s.o. by the nose; **man kann es ihm an der N. ansehen** it's written all over his face; **mit langer N. abziehen** be the loser; **pro N.** per head; **sich** [*dat*] **die N. begießen** wet one's whistle

näseln ['nezəln] *intr* speak through the nose || **Näseln** *n* (–s;) nasal twang

nä'selnd *adj* nasal

Na'senbein *n* nasal bone

Na'senbluten *n* (–s;) nosebleed

na'senlang *adv*—**alle n.** constantly

Na'senlänge *f*—**um e–e N. by** a nose

Na'senlaut *m* (phonet) nasal

Na'senloch *n* nostril

Na'senrücken *m* bridge of the nose

Na'senschleim *m* mucus

Na'senschleimhaut *f* mucous membrane

Nasenspray ['nazənspre] *m* (–s;–s) nose spray

Na'sentropfen *m* nose drop

na'seweis *adj* fresh, wise || **Naseweis** *m* (–es;–e) wise guy

Na'seweisheit *f* freshness

nasführen ['nasfyrən] *tr* lead by the nose; (*foppen*) fool

Nashorn ['nashɔrn] *n* (–[e]s;᠆er) rhinoceros

naß [nas] *adj* (**nasser** ['nasər] or **nässer** ['nesər]; **nasseste** ['nasəstə] or **nässeste** ['nesəstə] §9) wet; (*feucht*) moist || **Naß** *n* (**Nasses**;) (poet) liquid

Nassauer ['nasau.ər] *m* (–s;–) sponger, chiseler

nassauern ['nasau.ərn] *intr* (coll) sponge

Nässe ['nesə] *f* (–;) wetness; moisture

nässen ['nesən] *tr* wet; moisten || *intr* ooze

naß'forsch *adj* rash, bold

naß'kalt *adj* raw, cold and damp

Nation [na'tsjon] *f* (–;–en) nation

national [natsjo'nal] *adj* national

National'hymne *f* national anthem

nationalisieren [natsjonali'zirən] *tr* nationalize

Nationalismus [natsjona'lɪsmus] *m* (–;) nationalism

Nationalität [natsjonali'tet] *f* (–;–en) nationality; ethnic minority

National'sozialismus *m* national socialism, Nazism

National'sozialist –in §7 *mf* national socialist, Nazi

National'tracht *f* national costume

Nativität [nativi'tet] *f* (–;–en) horoscope

Natrium ['nɑtrɪ·um] *n* (-s;) sodium
Natter ['natər] *f* (-;-n) adder, viper
Natur [na'tur] *f* (-;-en) nature; (*Körperbeschaffenheit*) constitution; (*Gemütsart*) disposition; (*Art*) character; (*Person*) creature; **von N.** by nature
Natura [na'tura] *f*—in N. in kind
Naturalien [natu'raljən] *pl* produce
naturalisieren [naturali'zirən] *tr* naturalize ‖ *ref*—**sich n. lassen** become naturalized
Natur'anlage *f* disposition
Natur'arzt *m* naturopath
Naturell [natu'rel] *n* (-[e]s;-e) nature, temperament
Natur'erscheinung *f* phenomenon
Natur'forscher -in §6 *mf* naturalist
Natur'gabe *f* natural gift, talent
natur'gemäß *adv* naturally
Natur'geschichte *f* natural history
Natur'gesetz *n* natural law
natur'getreu *adj* life-like
Natur'kunde *f*, **Natur'lehre** *f* natural science
natürlich [na'tyrlɪç] *adj* natural; (*echt*) real; (*ungezwungen*) natural; **das geht aber nicht mit natürlichen Dingen zu** there is s.th. fishy about it; **das geht ganz n. zu** there is nothing strange about it ‖ *adv* naturally, of course
Natur'mensch *m* primitive man; nature enthusiast
Natur'philosoph *m* natural philosopher
Natur'recht *n* natural right
Natur'schutz *m* preservation of natural beauty
Natur'schutzgebiet *n* wildlife preserve
Natur'schutzpark *m* national park
Natur'spiel *n* freak of nature
Natur'theater *n* outdoor theater
Natur'trieb *m* instinct
Natur'verehrung *f* natural religion
Natur'volk *n* primitive people
natur'widrig *adj* contrary to nature
Natur'wissenschaft *f* natural science
Natur'wissenschaftler -in §6 *mf* scientist
naturwüchsig [na'turvyksɪç] *adj* unspoiled by civilization
Natur'zustand *m* natural state
nautisch ['nautɪʃ] *adj* nautical
Navigation [naviga'tsjon] *f* (-;) navigation
navigieren [navi'girən] *intr* navigate
Nazi ['natsi] *m* (-s;-s) Nazi
Nazismus [na'tsɪmus] *m* (-;) Nazism
nazistisch [na'tsɪstɪʃ] *adj* Nazi
Nebel ['nebəl] *m* (-s;-) fog, mist; (*Dunst*) haze
Ne'belbank *f* (-;ⁿe) fog bank
Ne'belfeld *n* patch of fog
Ne'belferne *f* hazy distance; (fig) dim future
Ne'belfleck *m* (astr) nebula
ne'belhaft *adj* foggy, hazy; (*Ferne*) dim
Ne'belhorn *n* foghorn
nebeln ['nebəln] *intr* be foggy
Ne'belscheinwerfer *m* (aut) fog light
Ne'belschicht *f* fog bank
Ne'belschirm *m* smoke screen
Ne'belvorhang *m* smoke screen
neben ['nebən] *prep* (*dat & acc*) by,

beside; side by side with, alongside, close to, next to; (*vergleichen mit*) compared with; (*außer*) besides, aside from; in addition to; extra
Neben- *comb.fm.* secondary, accessory, by-, side-, subordinate
Ne'benabsicht *f* ulterior motive
Ne'benaltar *m* side altar
Ne'benamt *n* additional duties
nebenan' *adv* close by; next-door
Ne'benanschluß *m* (telp) extension; (telp) party line
Ne'benarbeit *f* extra work
Ne'benarm *m* tributary, branch
Ne'benausgaben *pl* incidentals, extras
Ne'benausgang *m* side exit
Ne'benbahn *f* (rr) branch line
Ne'benbedeutung *f* (-;-en) secondary meaning
nebenbei' *adv* close by; (*außerdem*) besides, on the side; (*beiläufig*) incidentally
Ne'benberuf *m* sideline, side job
ne'benberuflich *adj* sideline, spare-time
Ne'benbeschäftigung *f* sideline
Nebenbuhler -in ['nebənbulər(ɪn)] §6 *mf* competitor, rival
ne'benbuhlerisch *adj* rival
Ne'benbending *n* secondary matter
nebeneinan'der *adv* side by side; neck and neck; (*gleichzeitig*) simultaneously; **n. bestehen** coexist
Nebeneinan'derleben *n* coexistence
nebeneinan'derstellen *tr* juxtapose
Ne'beneingang *m* side entrance
Ne'beneinkünfte *pl*, **Ne'beneinnahmen** *pl* extra income
Ne'benerzeugnis *n* by-product
Ne'benfach *n* (educ) minor; **als N. studieren** minor in
Ne'benflügel *m* (archit) wing
Ne'benfluß *m* tributary
Ne'benfrage *f* side issue
Ne'benfrau *f* concubine
Ne'bengang *m* side aisle
Ne'bengasse *f* side street, alley
Ne'bengebäude *n* annex, wing
Ne'bengedanke *m* ulterior motive
Ne'bengericht *n* side dish
Ne'bengeschäft *n* (com) branch
Ne'bengleis *n* (rr) siding, sidetrack
Ne'benhandlung *f* (-;-en) subplot
nebenher' *adv* on the side; besides; along
nebenhin' *adv* incidentally, by the way
Ne'benkosten *pl* incidentals, extras
Ne'benlinie *f* (rr) branch line
Ne'benmann *m* (-[e]s;ⁿer) neighbor
Ne'benprodukt *n* by-product
Ne'benpunkt *m* minor point
Ne'benrolle *f* supporting role
Ne'bensache *f* side issue
ne'bensächlich *adj* subordinate; incidental; (*unwesentlich*) unimportant
Ne'bensächlichkeit *f* unimportance; triviality
Ne'bensatz *m* subordinate clause
Ne'benschaltung *f* (-;-en) (elec) shunt
Ne'benschluß *m* (elec) shunt
Ne'benspesen *pl* additional charges
ne'benstehend *adj* marginal, in the margin ‖ **Nebenstehende** §5 *mf* bystander

Ne′benstelle f branch; (telp) extension
Ne′benstraße f side street
Ne′bentisch m next table
Ne′bentür f side door
Ne′benverdienst m extra pay; side job
Ne′benvorstellung f side show
Ne′benweg m side road
Ne′benwirkung f (-;-en) side effect
Ne′benzimmer n adjoining room
Ne′benzweck m secondary aim
neblig [′neblɪç] adj foggy, misty
nebst [nepst] prep (dat) including
necken [′nekən] tr & recip tease, kid
Neckerei [nekə′raɪ] f (-;-en) teasing
neckisch [′nekɪʃ] adj fond of teasing; (coll) cute
nee [ne] adv (dial) no
Neffe [′nefə] m (-n;-n) nephew
Negation [nega′tsjon] f (-;-en) negation
negativ [nega′tif] adj negative ‖ **Ne-gativ** n (-s;-e) negative
Neger **–in** [′negər(ɪn)] §6 mf black, Negro
Negligé [neglɪ′ʒe] n (-s;-s) negligee
nehmen [′nemən] §116 tr take; (weg-) take away; (anstellen) take on, hire; (Anwalt) retain; (Hindernis) clear, take; (Kurve) negotiate; (Schaden) suffer; **Anfang n.** begin; **Anstand n.** hesitate; **an sich n.** pocket, misappropriate; collect; retrieve; **Anstoß n. an** (dat) take offense at; **auf sich n.** assume, take upon oneself; **das Wort n.** begin to speak; **den Mund voll n.** (coll) talk big; **die Folgen auf sich n.** bear the consequences; **ein Ende n.** come to an end; **ein gutes Ende n.** turn out all right; **er versteht es, die Kunden richtig zu n.** he knows how to handle customers; **etw genau n.** take s.th. literally; **ich lasse es mir nicht n. zu** (inf) I insist on (ger); **im Grunde genommen** basically; an Angriff n. begin; **in Arbeit n.** start making; **in die Hand n.** pick up; (fig) take in hand; **j—m etw n.** take s.th. away from s.o.; deprive s.o. of s.th.; **kein Ende n.** go on endlessly; **man nehme zwei Eier, usw.** (im Kochbuch) take two eggs, etc.; **n. Sie bitte Platz!** please sit down; **n. wir den Fall, daß** let's suppose that; **Rücksicht n. auf** (acc) show consideration for; **sich** [dat] **das Leben n.** take one's life; **sich** [dat] **nichts von seinen Rechten n. lassen** insist on one's rights; **streng genommen** strictly speaking; **Stunden n.** take lessons; **Urlaub n.** take a vacation; (mil) go on furlough; **wie man's nimmt** it all depends; **zu Hilfe n.** use; **zur Ehe n.** marry; **zu sich n.** [dat] **n.** put into one's pocket; (Speise) eat; (Kind) take charge of
Neid [naɪt] m (-es;) envy; (blasser or gelber) **N.** pure envy; **vor N. vergehen** die of envy
neiden [′naɪdən] tr—j—m etw n. envy s.o. for s.th.
Neid′hammel m envious person
nei′dig adj (dial) var of neidisch
neidisch [′naɪdɪʃ] adj (auf acc) envious (of)

neid′los adj free of envy
Neid′nagel m hangnail
Neige [′naɪgə] f (-;-n) slope; (Ab-nahme) decline; (Überbleibsel) sediment, dregs; **zur N. gehen** (Geld, Vorräte) run low; (Sonne) go down; (Tag, Jahr) draw to a close ·
neigen [′naɪgən] tr incline, bend; **geneigt** sloping; (fig) friendly, favorable ‖ ref (vor dat) bow (to); (Ab-hang) slope; **sich zum Ende n.** draw to a close ‖ intr—n. zu be inclined to
Nei′gung f (-s;-en) slope, incline; (des Hauptes) bowing; (e-s Schiffes) list; (in der Straße) dip; (Gefälle) gradient; (Hang) inclination; (Anlage) tendency; (Vorliebe) taste, liking; (Zuneigung) affection; **e-e N. nach rechts haben** lean towards the right; **N. fassen zu** take (a fancy) to
nein [naɪn] adv no ‖ **Nein** n (-s;) no
Nein′stimme f (parl) nay
Nekrolog [nekro′lok] m (-[e]s;-e) obituary
Nektar [′nektar] m (-s;) nectar
Nelke [′nelkə] f (-;-n) carnation; (Ge-würz) clove
Nel′kenöl n oil of cloves
Nel′kenpfeffer m allspice
Nemesis [′nemezɪs] f (-;) Nemesis
nennbar [′nenbar] adj mentionable
nennen [′nenən] §97 tr name, call; (er-wähnen) mention; (benennen) term ‖ ref be called, be named
nen′nenswert adj worth mentioning
Nenner [′nenər] m (-s;-) (math) denominator; **auf e-n gemeinsamen N. bringen** reduce to a common denominator
Nennform [′nenform] f (gram) infinitive
Nenngeld [′nengelt] n entry fee
Nen′nung f (-;) naming; mentioning
Nennwert [′nenvert] m face value
Neologis•mus [ne•olo′gɪsmʊs] m (-;-men [mən]) neologism
Neon [′ne•ɔn] n (-s;) neon
Ne′onlicht n neon light
Nepotismus [nepo′tɪsmʊs] m (-;) nepotism
neppen [′nepən] tr (coll) gyp, clip
Nepplokal [′neplɔkal] n (sl) clip joint
Neptun [nep′tun] m (-s;) Neptune
Nerv [nerf] m (-s;-en) nerve; **die Nerven behalten** keep cool; **die Nerven verlieren** lose one's head; **j—m auf die Nerven gehen** get on s.o.'s nerves; **mit den Nerven herunter sein** be a nervous wreck
Nerven-, nerven– [′nerfən] comb.fm. nervous, neuro–, of nerves
Ner′venarzt m, **Ner′venärztin** f neurologist
ner′venaufreibend adj nerve-racking
Ner′venberuhigungsmittel n sedative
Ner′venbündel n (fig) bundle of nerves
Ner′venentzündung f neuritis
Ner′venfaser f nerve fiber
Ner′venheilanstalt f mental institution
Ner′venheilkunde f neurology
Ner′venkitzel m thrill, suspense
Ner′venknoten m ganglion
ner′venkrank adj neurotic

Ner'venkrieg *m* war of nerves

Ner'venlehre *f* neurology

Ner'vensäge *f* (coll) pain in the neck

Ner'venschmerz *m* neuralgia

Ner'venschwäche *f* nervousness

Ner'venzentrum *n* (fig) nerve center

Ner'venzusammenbruch *m* nervous breakdown

nervig ['nɛrvɪç], ['nɛrfɪç] *adj* sinewy

nervös [nɛr'vøs] *adj* nervous

Nervosität [nɛrvozi'tet] *f* (–;) nervousness

Nerz [nɛrts] *m* (–es;–e) (zool) mink

Nerz'mantel *m* mink coat

Nessel ['nɛsəl] *f* (–;–n) nettle; **sich in die Nesseln setzen** (fig) get oneself into hot water

Nest [nɛst] *n.* (–es;–er) nest; (*Schlupfwinkel*) hideout; small town; dead town; (*Bett*) (coll) bed

nesteln ['nɛstəln] *tr* lace, tie ‖ *intr* —n. an (*dat*) fiddle with, fuss with

Nesthäkchen ['nɛsthɛkçən] *n* (–s;–), **Nestküken** ['nɛstkykən] *n* (–s;–) baby (*of the family*)

nett [nɛt] *adj* nice; (*sauber*) neat; (*niedlich*) cute; **das kann ja n. werden!** (iron) that's going to be just dandy!

netto ['nɛto] *adv* net; clear

Net'togewicht *n* net weight

Net'togewinn *m* clear profit

Net'tolohn *m* take-home pay

Net'topreis *m* net price

Netz [nɛts] *n* (–es;–e) net; network; grid

netzen ['nɛtsən] *tr* wet, moisten

Netz'haut *f* retina

Netz'werk *n* netting, webbing

neu [nɔɪ] *adj* new; (*frisch*) fresh; (*unlängst geschehen*) recent; **aufs neue** anew; **neuere Geschichte** modern history; **neuere Sprachen** modern languages; **von neuem** all over again ‖ *adv* newly; recently; anew; afresh ‖ **Neue §5** *mf* newcomer ‖ **§5** *n*—**was gibt es Neues?** what's new?

Neu-, neu- *comb.fm.* new-, newly; re–; neo–

Neu'anlage *f* new installation; (fin) reinvestment

Neu'anschaffung *f* recent acquisition

neu'artig *adj* novel; modern

Neu'aufführung *f* (–;–en) (theat) revival

Neu'ausgabe *f* new edition, republication; (*Neudruck*) reprint

Neu'bau *m* (–[e]s;–bauten) new building

neu'bearbeiten *tr* revise

Neubelebung ['nɔɪbəlebʊŋ] *f* (–;–en) revival

Neu'bildung *f* (–;–en) new growth; (gram) neologism

Neu'druck *m* reprint

neuerdings ['nɔɪ·ərdɪŋs] *adv* recently; (*vom neuem*) anew

Neuerer –in ['nɔɪ·ərər(ɪn)] **§6** *mf* innovator

Neuerung ['nɔɪ·ərʊŋ] *f* (–;–en) innovation

neuestens ['nɔɪ·əstəns] *adv* recently

Neu'fassung *f* revision

Neufundland [nɔɪ'funtlant] *n* (–s;) Newfoundland

neu'gebacken *adj* fresh-baked; brand-new

neu'geboren *adj* new-born

neu'gestalten *tr* reorganize

Neu'gier *f*, **Neugierde** ['nɔɪgɪrdə] *f* (–;) curiosity, inquisitiveness

neu'gierig *adj* curious, nosey

Neu'gründung *f* (–;–en) reestablishment

Neu'gruppierung *f* (–;–en) regrouping; reshuffling

Neu'heit *f* (–;–en) novelty

neu'hochdeutsch *adj* modern High German

Neu'igkeit *f* (–;–en) news, piece of news

Neu'jahr *n* New Year

Neu'land *n* virgin soil; (fig) new ground

neu'lich *adv* lately

Neuling ['nɔɪlɪŋ] *m* (–[e]s;–e) beginner

neu'modisch *adj* fashionable; new-fangled

neun [nɔɪn] *invar adj & pron* nine ‖ **Neun** *f* (–;–en) nine

Neunmalkluge ['nɔɪnmalklugə] **§5** *mf* wiseacre

neunte ['nɔɪntə] **§9** *adj & pron* ninth

Neuntel ['nɔɪntəl] *n* (–s;–) ninth

neun'zehn *invar adj & pron* nineteen ‖ **Neunzehn** *f* (–;–en) nineteen

neun'zehnte §9 *adj & pron* nineteenth

neunzig ['nɔɪntsɪç] *invar adj & pron* ninety ‖ **Neunzig** *f* (–;–en) ninety

neunziger ['nɔɪntsɪgər] *invar adj* of the nineties; **die n. Jahre** the nineties ‖ **Neunziger** –in **§6** *mf* nonagenarian

neunzigste ['nɔɪntsɪçstə] **§9** *adj & pron* ninetieth

Neu'ordnung *f* (–;–en) reorganization

Neural·gie [nɔɪral'gi] *f* (–;–gien ['gi·ən]) neuralgia

Neu'regelung *f* (–;–en) rearrangement

Neu·ron ['nɔɪron] *n* (–;–ronen ['ro·nən]) neuron

Neurose [nɔɪ'rozə] *f* (–;–n) neurosis

Neurotiker –in [nɔɪ'rotɪkər(ɪn)] **§6** *mf* neurotic

neurotisch [nɔɪ'rotɪʃ] *adj* neurotic

Neusee'land *n* (–s;) New Zealand

Neu'silber *n* German silver

Neusprachler –in ['nɔɪ/praxlər(ɪn)] **§6** *mf* modern-language teacher

Neu'stadt *f* new section of town

Neu'steinzeit *f* neolithic age

neu'steinzeitlich *adj* neolithic

neutral [nɔɪ'tral] *adj* neutral

neutralisieren [nɔɪtralɪ'zirən] *tr* neutralize

Neutralität [nɔɪtrali'tet] *f* (–;) neutrality

Neu·tron ['nɔɪtron] *n* (–;–tronen ['tronən]) neutron

Neu·trum ['nɔɪtrum] *n* (–s;–tra [tra] & –tren [trən]) (gram) neuter

neuvermählt ['nɔɪfermelt] *adj* newly married ‖ **Neuvermählte §5** *pl* newlyweds

Neu'zeit *f* recent times

Nibelung ['nibəluŋ] *m* (–s;) (myth)

(King) Nibelung || *m* (**-en; -en**)
Nibelung

nicht [nɪçt] *adv* not; **auch... nicht** not
... either; **n. doch!** please don't; **n.
einmal** not even, not so much as; **n.
mehr** no longer, no more; **n. um die
Welt** not for the world; **n. wahr?**
isn't it so?, no?, right?

Nicht-, nicht- *comb.fm.* in-, im-, un-,
non-

Nicht'achtung *f* disregard, disrespect;
N. des Gerichts contempt of court

nicht'amtlich *adj* unofficial

Nicht'angriffspakt *m* nonaggression
pact

Nicht'annahme *f* nonacceptance

Nichte ['nɪçtə] *f* (**-; -n**) niece

Nicht'einmischung *f* noninterference

Nicht'eisenmetall *n* nonferrous metal

nichtig ['nɪçtɪç] *adj* invalid; void;
(*eitel*) vain; (*vergänglich*) transitory;
für n. erklären annul

Nich'tigkeit *f* (**-; -en**) invalidity; futility; (*Kleinigkeit*) trifle; **Nichtigkeiten**
trivia

Nich'tigkeitserklärung *f* annulment

Nicht'kämpfer *m* noncombatant

nicht'öffentlich *adj* private; (*Sitzung*)
closed

nicht'rostend *adj* rustproof; (*Stahl*)
stainless

nichts [nɪçts] *indef pron* nothing; **gar
n.** nothing at all; **n. als** nothing but;
n. mehr davon! not another word
about it!; **n. und wieder n.** absolutely
nothing; **soviel wie n.** next to nothing;
um n. for nothing, to no avail; **weiter
n.?** is that all?; **wenn es weiter n. ist!**
if it's nothing worse than that ||
Nichts *n* (**-es**) nothingness; nonentity;
(*Leere*) void; (*Kleinigkeit*) trifle; **vor
dem N. stehen** be faced with utter
ruin

nichtsdestowe'niger *adv* nevertheless

Nichts'könner *m* incompetent person;
ignoramus

Nichts'nutz *m* good-for-nothing

nichts'nutzig *adj* good-for-nothing

nichts'sagend *adj* insignificant; (*Antwort*) vague; noncommittal; (*Gesicht*) vacuous; (*Redensart*) trite

Nichts'tuer -in *§6 mf* loafer

Nichts'wisser -in *§6 mf* ignoramus

nichts'würdig *adj* contemptible

Nicht'zutreffende *§5 n* —**Nichtzutref-
fendes streichen** delete if not applicable

Nickel ['nɪkəl] *n* (**-s; -**) (metal) nickel

nicken ['nɪkən] *intr* nod; (*schlummern*)
nap

Nickerchen ['nɪkərçən] *n* (**-s; -**) nap

nie [ni] *adv* never, at no time

nieder ['nidər] *adj* low; (*gemein*) base
|| *adv* down

nie'derbrechen *§64 tr & intr* (SEIN)
break down

nie'derbrennen *§97 tr & intr* (SEIN)
burn down

nie'derdeutsch *adj* Low German ||
Niederdeutsch *n* Low German ||
Niederdeutsch *§5 mf* North German

nie'derdonnern *tr* (coll) shout down ||
intr go (or come) crashing down

Nie'derdruck *m* low pressure

nie'derdrücken *tr* press down (fig)
weigh down; (*unterdrücken*) oppress;
(*entmutigen*) depress

nie'derfallen *§72 intr* (SEIN) fall down

Nie'derfrequenz *f* low frequency; audio
frequency

Nie'dergang *m* descent; (*der Sonne*)
setting; (fig) decline, fall

nie'dergehen *§82 intr* (SEIN) go down;
(*Flugzeug*) land; (*Regen*) fall; (*Vorhang*) drop

nie'dergeschlagen *adj* dejected

nie'derhalten *§90 tr* hold down, keep
down

nie'derholen *tr* lower, haul down

Nie'derholz *n* underbrush

nie'derkämpfen *tr* (& fig) overcome

nie'derkommen *§99 intr* (SEIN) (**mit**)
give birth (to)

Niederkunft ['nidərkunft] *f* (**-;**) confinement, childbirth

Nie'derlage *f* defeat; (*Lager*) warehouse; (*Filiale*) branch

Niederlande, die ['nidərlandə] *pl* The
Netherlands, Holland

Niederländer ['nidərlendər] *m* (**-s; -**)
Dutchman

niederländisch ['nidərlendɪʃ] *adj* Dutch

nie'derlassen *§104 tr* let down || *ref*
sit down, recline; (*Wohnsitz nehmen*)
settle; (*ein Geschäft eröffnen*) set
oneself up in business; (*Vogel, Flugzeug*) land

Nie'derlassung *f* (**-; -en**) settlement,
colony; establishment; (*e-r Bank*)
branch; (com) plant

nie'derlegen *tr* lay down, put down;
(*Amt*) resign; (*Geschäft*) give up;
(*Krone*) abdicate; (*schriftlich*) set
down in writing; **die Arbeit n.** go on
strike || *ref* lie down; go to bed

nie'dermachen *tr* butcher, massacre

nie'dermähen *tr* mow down

nie'dermetzeln *tr* butcher, massacre

Nie'derschlag *m* (*Bodensatz*) sediment;
(box) knockdown; (chem) precipi-
tate; (meteor) precipitation; **radioaktiver N.** fallout

nie'derschlagen *§132 tr* knock down;
(*Augen*) cast down; (*Aufstand*) put
down; (*vertuschen*) hush up; (*Verfahren*) quash; (*Forderung*) waive;
(*Hoffnungen*) dash; (chem) precipitate

nie'derschmettern *tr* knock to the
ground; (fig) crush

nie'derschreiben *§62 tr* write down

nie'dersetzen *tr* set down || *ref* sit down

nie'dersinken *§143 intr* (SEIN) sink
down

nie'derstimmen *tr* vote down

Nie'dertracht *f* nastiness, meanness

nie'derträchtig *adj* nasty; underhand

Nie'derung *f* (**-; -en**) low ground, depression

niederwärts ['nidərverts] *adv* downward

nie'derwerfen *§160 tr* knock down;
(*Aufstand*) put down || *ref* fall down

Nie'derwild *n* small game

niedlich ['nitlɪç] *adj* nice, cute

Niednagel ['nitnagəl] *m* hangnail

niedrig ['niːdrɪç] *adj* low; (*Herkunft*) humble; (*gemein*) mean, base
niemals ['niːmɑls] *adv* never
niemand ['niːmant] *indef pron* no one, nobody
Nie′mandsland *n* no man's land
Niere ['niːrə] *f* (-;-n) kidney; **das geht mir an die Nieren** (fig) that cuts me deep
nieseln ['niːzəln] *impers*—**es nieselt** it is drizzling
Nie′selregen *m* drizzle
niesen ['niːzən] *intr* sneeze
Niet [niːt] *m* (-[e]s;-e) rivet
Niete ['niːtə] *f* (-;-n) rivet; (*in der Lotterie*) blank; (*Versager*) flop
nieten ['niːtən] *tr* rivet
niet-′ und na′gelfest *adj* nailed down
Nihilismus [nihɪ'lɪsmɪs] *m* (-;) nihilism
Nikotin [niko'tiːn] *n* (-s;) nicotine
nikotin′arm *adj* low in nicotine
Nil [niːl] *m* (-s;) Nile
Nil′pferd *n* hippopotamus
Nimbus ['nɪmbʊs] *m* (-;-se) halo; aura; (*Ansehen*) prestige; (meteor) nimbus
nimmer ['nɪmər] *adv* never; (dial) no more
nim′mermehr *adv* never more; by no means
Nippel ['nɪpəl] *m* (-s;-) (mach) nipple
nippen ['nɪpən] *tr & intr* sip
Nippsachen ['nɪpzaxən] *pl* knicknacks
nirgends ['nɪrgənts] *adv* nowhere
nirgendwo ['nɪrgəntvo] *adv* nowhere
Nische ['niːʃə] *f* (-;-n) niche
nisten ['nɪstən] *intr* nest
Nitrat [ni'traːt] *n* (-[e]s;-e) nitrate
Nitrid [ni'triːt] *n* (-[e]s;-e) nitride
Nitroglyzerin [nitroglytsə'riːn] *n* (-s;) nitroglycerin
Niveau [ni'voː] *n* (-s;-s) level; **N. haben** have class; **unter dem N. sein** be substandard
Niveau′übergang *m* (rr) grade crossing
nivellieren [nive'liːrən] *tr* level
nix [nɪks] *indef pron* (dial) nothing ‖
Nix *m* (-[e]s;-e) water sprite
Nixe ['nɪksə] *f* (-;-n) water nymph
nobel ['noːbəl] *adj* noble; elegant; (*freigebig*) generous
noch [nɔx] *adv* still, yet; even; else; **heute n.** this very day; **n. besser** even bettter; **n. dazu** over and above that; **n. einer** one more, still another; **n. einmal** once more; **n. einmal so viel** twice as much; **n. etwas** one more thing; **n. etwas?** anything else?; **n. heute** even today; **n. immer** still; **n. nicht** not yet; **n. nie** never before; **n. und n.** (coll) over and over; **sei es n. so klein** now matter how small it is; **was denn n. alles?** what next? **wer kommt n.?** who else is coming?
noch′mal *adv* once more
nochmalig ['nɔxmalɪç] *adj* repeated
nochmals ['nɔxmals] *adv* once more
Nocke ['nɔkə] *f* (-;-n) (mach) cam
Nockenwelle (**Nok′kenwelle**) *f* camshaft
Nockerl ['nɔkərl] *n* (-s;- & -n) (Aust) dumpling

Nomade [no'maːdə] *m* (-n;-n) nomad
nominell [nomi'nɛl] *adj* nominal
nominieren [nomi'niːrən] *tr* nominate
Nonne ['nɔnə] *f* (-;-n) nun
Non′nenkloster *n* convent
Noppe ['nɔpə] *f* (-;-n) (tex) nap
Nord [nɔrt] *m* (-[e]s;) North; (poet) north wind
Norden ['nɔrdən] *m* (-s;) North; **im N. von** north of
nordisch ['nɔrdɪʃ] *adj* northern; (*Rasse*) Nordic; (*skandinavisch*) Norse
nördlich ['nœrtlɪç] *adj* northern
Nord′licht *n* northern lights
nordwärts ['nɔrtvɛrts] *adv* northward
Nörgelei [nœrgə'lai] *f* (-;-en) griping
nörgelig ['nœrgəlɪç] *adj* nagging
nörgeln ['nœrgəln] *intr*—**n. an** (dat) gripe about, kick about
Norm [nɔrm] *f* (-;-en) norm, standard
normal [nɔr'maːl] *adj* normal, standard
normalisieren [nɔrmali'ziːrən] *tr* normalize
Normal′zeit *f* standard time
Normanne [nɔr'manə] *m* (-n;-n) Norman
normen ['nɔrmən], **normieren** [nɔr'miːrən] *tr* normalize, standardize
Norwegen ['nɔrveɡən] *n* (-s;) Norway
Norweger **-in** ['nɔrveɡər(ɪn)] §6 *mf* Norwegian
norwegisch ['nɔrveɡɪʃ] *adj* Norwegian
Not [noːt] *f* (-;⁻e) need, want; (*Notlage*) necessity; (*Gefahr*) distress; (*Dringlichkeit*) emergency; **es hat keine Not** there's no hurry about it; **es tut not it is necessary**; **in der Not** in a pinch; **in Not geraten** fall upon hard times; **j-m große Not machen** give s.o. a lot of trouble; **j-m seine Not klagen** cry on s.o.'s shoulders; **mit knapper Not** narrowly; **mit Not** scarcely; **Not haben zu** (*inf*) be scarcely able to (*inf*); **Not leiden** suffer want; **ohne Not** needlessly; **seine liebe Not haben mit** have a lot of trouble with; **sie haben Not auszukommen** they have difficulty making ends meet; **zur Not** if need be, in a pinch
Nota ['noːta] *f* (-;-s) note; **etw in N. geben** place an order for s.th.; **etw in N. nehmen** make a note of s.th.
Notar **-in** [no'taːr(ɪn)] §8 *mf* notary public
Notariat [nota'rjaːt] *n* (-[e]s;-e) notary office
notariell [nota'rjɛl] *adv*—**n. beglaubigen** notarize
Not′ausgang *m* emergency exit
Not′ausstieg *m* escape hatch
Not′behelf *m* makeshift, stopgap
Not′bremse *f* (rr) emergency brake
Not′durft ['noːtdʊrft] *f* (-;) want; necessities of life; **seine N. verrichten** relieve oneself
not′dürftig *adj* scanty, poor; hard up; (*behelfsmäßig*) temporary
Note ['noːtə] *f* (-;-n) note; (*Banknote*) bill; (*Eigenart*) trait; (educ) mark; (mus) note; **in Noten setzen** set to music; **nach Noten** (fig) thoroughly; **persönliche Note** personal

touch; **wie nach Noten** like clock-work

No′tenblatt *n* sheet music

No′tenbuch *n*, **No′tenheft** *n* music book

No′tenlinie *f* (mus) line

No′tenschlüssel *m* (mus) clef

No′tenständer *m* music stand

No′tensystem *n* (mus) staff

Not′fall *m* emergency

notfalls ['nɔtfals] *adv* if necessary

notgedrungen ['nɔtgədruŋən] *adj* compulsory ‖ *adv* of necessity

notieren [nɔ'tirən] *tr* note down; jot down; (*Preise*) quote

Notie′rung *f* (-;-en) noting; (st. exch.) quotation

nötig ['nø̞tɪç] *adj* necessary; **das habe ich nicht n.!** I don't have to stand for that!; **n. haben** need

nötigen ['nø̞tɪgən] *tr* urge; (*zwingen*) force ‖ *ref*—**lassen Sie sich nicht n.!** don't wait to be asked; **sich genötigt sehen zu** (*inf*) feel compelled to (*inf*)

nö′tigenfalls *adv* in case of need

Nö′tigung *f* (-;) compulsion; urgent request; (jur) duress

Notiz [nɔ'tits] *f* (-;-en) notice; (*Vermerk*) note, memorandum; **keine N. nehmen von** take no notice of; **sich** [*dat*] **Notizen machen** jot down notes

Notiz′block *m* scratch pad

Not′lage *f* predicament; emergency

Not′landung *f* emergency landing

Not′lüge *f* white lie

Not′maßnahme *f* emergency measure

Not′nagel *m* (fig) stopgap

notorisch [nɔ'torɪʃ] *adj* notorious

Not′pfennig *m* savings; **sich e-n N. aufsparen** save up for a rainy day

Not′ruf *m* (telp) emergency

Not′signal *n* distress signal

Not′stand *m* state of emergency

Not′standsgebiet *n* disaster area

Not′treppe *f* fire escape

Not′wehr *f*—**aus N.** in self-defense

notwendig ['notvɛndɪç] *adj* necessary

Not′wendigkeit *f* (-;-en) necessity

Not′zeichen *n* distress signal

Not′zucht *f* rape

not′züchtigen *tr* rape, ravish

Nougat ['nugat] *m* & *n* (-s;-s) nougat

Novelle [no'vɛlə] *f* (-;-n) short story; (parl) amendment, rider

November [no'vɛmbər] *m* (-s;-) November

Novität [novi'tɛt] *f* (-;-en) novelty

Novize [no'vitsə] *m* (-n;-n), **Novizin** [no'vitsɪn] *f* (-;-nen), novice

Noviziat [novi'tsjat] *n* (-[e]s;-e) novitiate

Nu [nu] *invar m*—**im Nu** in a jiffy

Nuance [nУ'ãsə] *f* (-;-n) nuance

nüchtern ['nÝçtərn] *adj* fasting; not having had breakfast; (*Magen*) empty; (*nicht betrunken*) sober; (*leidenschaftslos*) cool; (*geistlos*) dry, dull; (*unsentimental*) matter-of-fact

Nudel ['nudəl] *f* (-;-n) noodle; **e-e komische N.** (coll) a funny person

Nu′delholz *n* rolling pin

nudeln ['nudəln] *tr* force-feed

Nugat ['nugat] *m* (-s;-s) nougat

nuklear [nukle'ar] *adj* nuclear

Nukle·on ['nukle·ɔn] *n* (-s;-onen) ['onən]) nucleon

null [nʊl] *adj* null; **n. und nichtig** null and void; **n. und nichtig machen** annul ‖ **Null** *f* (-;-en) naught; zero; (fig) nobody; **in N. Komma nichts** in less than no time, in no time

Null′punkt *m* zero; freezing point; **auf dem N. angekommen sein** hit bottom

Numera·le [nume'ralə] *n* (-s;-lien ljən] & -lia [lja]) numeral

numerieren [nume'rirən] *tr* number; **numerierter Platz** reserved seat

numerisch [nu'merɪʃ] *adj* numerical

Nummer ['nʊmər] *f* (-;-n) number; (*Größe*) size; (*e-r Zeitung*) issue; **auf N. Sicher sitzen** (sl) be in jail; **bei j-m e-e gute N. haben** (coll) be in good with s.o.; **e-e bloße N.** a mere figurehead; **er ist e-e N.** he's quite a character; **laufende N.** serial number; **N. besetzt!** line is busy!

Num′mernfolge *f* numerical order

Num′mernscheibe *f* (telp) dial

Num′mernschild *n* (aut) license plate

nun [nʊn] *adv* now; **nun? well?**; **nun aber** now; **nun also!** well now!; **nun gut!** all right then!; **nun und nimmer(mehr)** never more; **von nun ab** from now on; **wenn er nun käme?** what if he came?

nun′mehr′ *adv* now; from now on

nur [nur] *adv* only, merely, but; (*lauter*) nothing but; **nicht nur ... sondern auch** not only ... but also; **nur daß** except that; **nur eben** scarcely; (*zeitlich*) a moment ago; **nur zu!** go to it!; **wenn nur** if only, provided that

Nürnberg ['nÝrnbɛrk] *n* (-s;) Nuremberg

nuscheln ['nʊʃəln] *intr* (coll) mumble

Nuß [nʊs] *f* (-; **Nüsse**) nut

nuß′braun *adj* nut-brown; (*Augen*) hazel

Nuß′kern *m* kernel

Nußknacker ['nʊsknakər] *m* (-s;-) nutcracker

Nuß′schale *f* nutshell

Nüster ['nÝstər] *f* (-;-n) nostril

Nut [nut] *f* (-;-en), **Nute** ['nutə] *f* (-;-n) groove, rabbet

Nutte ['nʊtə] *f* (-;-n) whore

nutz [nʊts] *adj* useful; **zu nichts n. sein** be good for nothing ‖ **Nutz** *m* (-es;) use; benefit; profit; **zu j-s N. und Frommen** for s.o.'s benefit

Nutz′anwendung *f* utilization

nutzbar ['nʊtsbar] *adj* useful; **sich** [*dat*] **etw n. machen** utilize s.th.

nutz′bringend *adj* useful, profitable

nütze ['nÝtsə] *adj* useful; **nichts n.** of no use; **zu nichts n. sein** be good for nothing

Nutz′effekt *m* efficiency

nutzen ['nʊtsən], **nützen** ['nÝtsən] *tr* make use of; **das kann mir viel (wenig, nichts) n.** this can do me much (little, no) good; **was nützt das**

alles? what's the good of all this? ||
intr do good || *impers*—es **nützt**
nichts it's no use || **Nutzen** *m* (-s;-)
use; benefit; (*Gewinn*) profit; (*Vor-
teil*) advantage; **von N. sein** be of use
Nutz′fahrzeug *n* commercial vehicle
Nutz′garten *m* vegetable garden
Nutz′holz *n* lumber
Nutz′leistung *f* (mech) output

nützlich ['nʏtslɪç] *adj* useful
nutz′los *adj* useless
Nutz′losigkeit *f* (-;) uselessness
Nutz′schwelle *f* break-even point
Nut′zung *f* (-;) use
Nylon ['naɪlɔn] *n* (-s;) nylon
Nymphe ['nʏmfə] *f* (-;-n) nymph
Nymphomanin [nʏmfo'manɪn] *f* (-;
-nen) nymphomaniac

O

O, o [o] *invar n* O, o
Oase [o'azə] *f* (-;-n) oasis
ob [ɔp] *prep* (*dat*) above; (*genit*) on
account of || *conj* whether; **als ob**
as if; **na ob!** rather!; **und ob!** and
how!
Obacht ['obaxt] *f* (-;)—**in O. nehmen**
take care of; **O.!** watch out!; **O.
geben auf** (*acc*) pay attention to;
take care of
Obdach ['ɔpdax] *n* (-[e]s;) shelter
ob′dachlos *adj* homeless
Obduktion [ɔpdʊk'tsjon] *f* (-;-en)
autopsy
obduzieren [ɔpdʊ'tsirən] *tr* perform
an autopsy on
O–Beine ['obaɪnə] *pl* bow legs
O′-beinig *adj* bowlegged
Obelisk [obe'lɪsk] *m* (-en;-en) obelisk
oben ['obən] *adv* above; (*in der Höhe*)
up; (*im Himmelsraum*) on high; (*im
Hause*) upstairs; (*auf der Spitze*) at
the top; (*auf der Oberfläche*) on the
surface; (*Aufschrift auf Kisten*) this
side up; **da o.** up there; **nach o.
gehen** go up, go upstairs; **o. am
Tische sitzen** sit at the head of the
table; **o. auf** (*dat*) at the top of, on
the top of; **von o.** from above; **von
o. bis unten** from top to bottom;
from head to foot; **von o. herab** (fig)
condescendingly; **wie o. angegeben**
as stated above
obenan′ *adv* at the top, at the head
obenauf′ *adv* on top; **immer o. sein**
be always in top spirits
obendrein [obən'draɪn] *adv* on top of
it, into the bargain
o′benerwähnt, o′bengenannt *adj* above-
mentioned
o′bengesteuert *adj* (aut) overhead
obenhin′ *adv* superficially; perfunctorily
obenhinaus′ *adv*—**o. wollen** have big
ideas
o′ben-oh′ne *adj* (coll) topless
o′benstehend *adj* given above
Ober ['obər] *m* (-s;-) (coll) waiter;
Herr O.! waiter!
Ober- *comb.fm.* upper, higher; superior; chief, supreme, head; southern
O′berägypten *n* Upper Egypt
O′berarm *m* upper arm
O′beraufseher *m* inspector general;
superintendent
O′beraufsicht *f* superintendence

O′berbau *m* (-[e]s;-ten) superstructure
O′berbefehl *m* supreme command; **O.
führen** have supreme command
O′berbefehlshaber *m* commander in
chief
O′berbegriff *m* wider concept
O′berdeck *n* upper deck
O′berdeckomnibus *m* double-decker
bus
o′berdeutsch *adj* of southern Germany
obere ['obərə] §9 *adj* higher, upper;
chief, superior; supreme || **Obere** §5
m (eccl) father superior || *n* top
o′berfaul *adj* (fig) fishy
O′berfeldwebel *m* sergeant first class
O′berfläche *f* surface
o′berflächlich *adj* superficial
O′bergefreite §5 *m* corporal
O′bergeschoß *n* upper floor
O′bergewalt *f* supreme authority
o′berhalb *prep* (*genit*) above
O′berhand *f* (fig) upper hand; **die O.
gewinnen über** (*acc*) get the better
of
O′berhaupt *n* head, chief
O′berhaus *n* upper house
O′berhaut *f* epidermis
O′berherr *m* sovereign
O′berherrschaft *f* sovereignty; suprem-
acy
O′berhirte *m* prelate
O′berhofmeister *m* Lord Chamberlain
O′berhoheit *f* supreme authority
Oberin ['obərɪn] *f* (-;-nen) mother
superior; (med) head nurse
O′beringenieur *m* chief engineer
o′berirdisch *adj* above-ground; over-
head
O′berkellner *m* head waiter
O′berkiefer *m* upper jaw
O′berkleidung *f* outer wear
O′berkommando *n* general headquar-
ters
O′berkörper *m* upper part of the body
O′berland *n* highlands
Oberländer –in ['obərlendər(ɪn)] §6
mf highlander
o′berlastig *adj* top-heavy
O′berleder *n* uppers
O′berlehrer –in §6 *mf* secondary school
teacher, high school teacher
O′berleitung *f* supervision; (elec) over-
head line (*of trolley, etc.*)
O′berleutnant *m* first lieutenant

O'berlicht n skylight
O'berliga f (sport) upper division
O'berlippe f upper lip
O'berpostamt n general post office
O'berprima f senior class
Obers ['obərs] m (–ʒ) (Aust) cream
O'berschenkel m thigh
O'berschicht f upper layer; (der Bevölkerung) upper classes; **geistige O.** intelligentsia
O'berschule f high school
O'berschwester f (med) head nurse
O'berseite f topside, right side
Oberst ['obərst] m (–en;–en) colonel
O'berstaatsanwalt m attorney general
oberste ['obərstə] §9 adj (super of **obere**) uppermost, highest, top || **Oberste** §5 mf senior, chief
O'berstimme f treble, soprano
O'berstleutnant m lieutenant colonel
O'berstock m upper floor
O'berwasser n—**O. haben** (fig) have the upper hand
O'berwelt f upper world
O'berwerk n upper manual (of organ)
obgleich' conj though, although
Ob'hut f (–ʒ) care, protection
obig ['obiç] adj above, above-mentioned
Objekt [ɔp'jɛkt] n (–[e]s;–e) object
objektiv [ɔpjɛk'tif] adj objective; (unparteiisch) impartial || **Objektiv** n (–s;–e) objective lens
Objektivität [ɔpjɛktivi'tɛt] f (–ʒ) objectivity; impartiality
Objekt'träger m slide (of microscope)
Oblate [ɔ'blatə] f (–ʒ–n) wafer; (eccl) host
obliegen [ɔp'ligən] §108 intr (dat) apply oneself to, devote oneself to; (dat) be incumbent upon || impers—**es obliegt mir zu** (inf) it's up to me to (inf)
Ob'liegenheit f (–ʒ–en) obligation
obligat [ɔbli'gat] adj obligatory; (unerläßlich) indispensable; (unvermeidlich) inevitable
Obligation [ɔbliga'tsjon] f (–ʒ–en) bond; obligation
obligatorisch [ɔbliga'toriʃ] adj obligatory
Ob'mann ['ɔpman] m (–[e]s;⁻er & –leute) chairman; (jur) foreman
Oboe [ɔ'bo·ə] f (–ʒ–n) oboe
Obrigkeit ['obriçkait] f (–ʒ–en) authority; (coll) authorities
o'brigkeitlich adj government(al)
obschon' conj though, although
Observatorium [ɔpzɛrva'torjum] n (–s;–rien) [rjən] observatory
obsiegen ['ɔpzigən] intr be victorious; (dat) triumph over
obskur [ɔps'kur] adj obscure
Obst [ɔpst] n (–es;) (certain kinds of) fruit (mainly central-European, e.g., apples, plums; but not bananas, oranges); **O. und Südfrüchte** European and (sub)tropical fruit
Obst'garten m orchard
Obst'kern m stone; seed, pip
Obstruktion [ɔpstruk'tsjon] f (–ʒ–en) obstruction; (pol) filibuster; **O. treiben** filibuster

obszön [ɔps'tsøn] adj obscene
Obszönität [ɔpstsøni'tɛt] f (–ʒ–en) obscenity
ob'walten, obwal'ten intr exist; prevail; hold sway
obwohl' conj though, although
Ochse ['ɔksə] m (–n;–n) ox
ochsen ['ɔksən] intr (educ) cram
O'chsenfleisch n beef
O'chsenfrosch m bullfrog
öde ['ødə] adj bleak || **Öde** f (–ʒ–n) wasteland; (fig) bleakness
Ödem [ø'dem] n (–s;–e) edema
oder ['odər] conj or
Öd·land ['øtlant] n (–[e]s;–ländereien [lendə'rai·ən]) wasteland
Ofen ['ofən] m (–s;⁻) stove; (Back–) oven; (Hoch–) furnace; (Brenn–, Dürr–) kiln
O'fenklappe f damper
O'fenrohr n stovepipe
O'fenröhre f warming oven
offen ['ɔfən] adj open; (öffentlich) public; (fig) frank, open
offenbar ['ɔfənbar] adj obvious, manifest
offenbaren [ɔfən'barən] tr reveal
Offenba'rung f (–ʒ–en) revelation
Of'fenheit f (–ʒ) openness
of'fenherzig adj forthright; (Kleid) (hum) low-cut
of'fenkundig adj well-known; (offensichtlich) obvious; (Beweis) clear
of'fensichtlich adj obvious
offensiv [ɔfɛn'zif] adj offensive || **Offensive** [ɔfɛn'zivə] f (–ʒ–n) offensive
öffentlich ['œfəntliç] adj public; (Dienst) civil; **öffentliches Haus** brothel
Öf'fentlichkeit f (–ʒ) public; publicity; **an die Ö. treten** appear in public; **im Licht der Ö.** in the limelight; **in aller Ö.** in public; **sich in die Ö. flüchten** rush into print
offerieren [ɔfə'rirən] tr offer
Offerte [ɔ'fɛrtə] f (–ʒ–n) offer
Offerto·rium [ɔfɛr'torjum] n (–s;–rien [rjən]) offertory
Offiziant [ɔfi'tsjant] m (–en;–en) officiating priest
offiziell [ɔfi'tsjɛl] adj official
Offizier –in [ɔfi'tsir(in)] §6 mf officer
Offiziers'anwärter –in §6 mf officer candidate
Offiziers'bursche m orderly
Offiziers'deck n quarter deck
Offiziers'kasino n officers' club
Offiziers'patent n officer's commission
Offizin [ɔfi'tsin] f (–ʒ–en) drugstore; (Druckerei) print shop, press
offiziös [ɔfi'tsjøs] adj semiofficial
öffnen ['œfnən] tr & ref open
Öff'ner m (–s;–) opener
Öff'nung f (–ʒ–en) opening
oft [ɔft], **öfter(s)** ['œftər(s)] adv often
oftmals ['ɔftmals] adv often(times)
oh [o] interj oh!, O!
Oheim ['ohaim] m (–s;–e) uncle
Ohm [om] m (–s;–e) (poet) uncle || n (–s;–) (elec) ohm
ohne ['onə] prep (acc) without; **o. daß** (ind) without (ger); **o. mich!** count

me out!; **o. weiteres** right off; **o. zu** (*inf*) without (*ger*)

ohnedies' *adv* anyhow, in any case

ohnglei'chen *adj* unequaled

ohnehin' *adv* anyhow, as it is

Ohnmacht ['ɔnmaxt] *f* (–;) faint, unconsciousness; helplessness; **in O. fallen** (or **sinken**) faint, pass out

ohnmächtig ['ɔnmɛçtɪç] *adj* unconscious; helpless; **o. werden** faint

Ohr [ør] *n* (–[e]s;–en) ear; (*im Buch*) dog-ear; **die Ohren spitzen** prick up the ears; **es dick hinter den Ohren haben** be sly; **ganz Ohr sein** be all ears; **j–m in den Ohren liegen** keep dinning it into s.o.'s ears; **j–n hinter die Ohren hauen** box s.o.'s ears; **j–n übers Ohr hauen** cheat s.o.; **sich aufs Ohr legen** take a nap; **zum e–n Ohr hinein, zum anderen wieder hinaus** in one ear and out the other

Öhr [ør] *n* (–[e]s;–e) eye (*of needle*); ax hole, hammer hole

ohrenbetäubend *adj* earsplitting

Oh'renklingen *n* ringing in the ears

Oh'rensausen *n* buzzing in the ear

Oh'renschmalz *n* earwax

Oh'renschmaus *m* treat for the ears

Ohrenschützer *m* earmuff

Ohr'feige *f* (–;–n) box on the ear

ohrfeigen ['ɔrfaɪgən] *tr* box on the ear

Ohrläppchen ['ɔrlɛpçən] *n* (–s;–) earlobe

Ohr'muschel *f* auricle

okkult [ɔ'kult] *adj* occult

Ökologie [økɔlɔ'gi] *f* (–;) ecology

ökologisch [økɔ'logɪʃ] *adj* ecological

Ökonom [økɔ'nom] *m* (–en;–en) economist

Ökono·mie [økɔnɔ'mi] (–;–mien) ['mi-ən]) economy; economics

ökonomisch [økɔ'nomɪʃ] *adj* economical

Oktav [ɔk'taf] *n* (–s;–e) octavo

Oktave [ɔk'tavə] *f* (–;–n) octave

Oktober [ɔk'tobər] *m* (–s;–) October

oktroyieren [ɔktrwa'jirən] *tr* impose

Okular [ɔku'lar] *n* (–s;–e) eyepiece

okulieren [ɔku'lirən] *tr* inoculate

Ökumene [øku'menə] *f* (–;) ecumenism

ökumenisch [øku'menɪʃ] *adj* ecumenical

Okzident ['ɔktsɪdent] *m* (–s;) Occident

Öl [øl] *n* (–[e]s;–e) oil; **Öl ins Feuer gießen** (fig) add fuel to the fire

Öl'baum *m* olive tree

Öl'berg *m* Mount of Olives

Oleander [ɔle'andər] *m* (–s;–) oleander

ölen ['ølən] *tr* oil; (mach) lubricate

Öl'götze *m* (coll) dummy, lout

Öl'heizung *f* oil heat

ölig ['ølɪç] *adj* oily

Oligar·chie [ɔligar'çi] *f* (–;–chien ['çi·ən]) oligarchy

Olive [ɔ'livə] *f* (–;–n) olive

Oli'venöl *n* olive oil

Öl'leitung *f* pipeline

Öl'quelle *f* oil well

Öl'schlick *m* oil slick

Öl'stand *m* (aut) oil level

Öl'standanzeiger *m* oil gauge

Öl'standmesser *m* (aut) oil gauge; dipstick

Ö'lung *f* (–;–en) oiling; anointing; **die Letzte Ö.** extreme unction

Olymp [ɔ'lymp] *m* (–s;) Mt. Olympus

Olympiade [ɔlym'pjadə] *f* (–;–n) olympiad

olympisch [ɔ'lympɪʃ] *adj* Olympian; Olympic; **die Olympischen Spiele** the Olympics

Öl'zweig *m* olive branch

Oma ['oma] *f* (–;–s) (coll) grandma

Omelett [ɔm(ə)'let] *n* (–[e]s;–e & –s) omelette

O·men ['omen] *n* (–s;–mina [mɪna]) omen

ominös [ɔmi'nøs] *adj* ominous

Omnibus ['ɔmnibus] *m* (ses;–se) bus

Onanie [ɔna'ni] *f* (–;) masturbation

ondulieren [ɔndu'lirən] *tr* (Haar) wave

Onkel ['ɔŋkəl] *m* (–s;– & –s) uncle; **der große O.** (coll) the big toe

Opa ['opa] *m* (–s;–s) (coll) grandpa

Oper ['opər] *f* (–;–n) opera

Operateur [ɔpera'tør] *m* (–s;–s) operator; (cin) projectionist; (surg) operating surgeon

Operation [ɔpera'tsjon] *f* (–;–en) operation

Operations'gebiet *n* theater of operations

Operations'saal *m* operating room

operativ [ɔpera'tif] *adj* surgical; operational, strategic

operieren [ɔpe'rirən] *tr* operate on; **sich o. lassen** undergo an operation

O'pernglas *n*, **O'perngucker** *m* opera glasses

O'pernhaus *n* opera house, opera

Opfer ['ɔpfər] *n* (–s;–) sacrifice; victim; **zum O. fallen** (dat) fall victim to

op'ferfreudig *adj* self-sacrificing

Op'fergabe *f* offering

Op'ferkasten *m* poor box

Op'ferlamm *n* sacrificial lamb; **Lamb of God**; (fig) victim

Op'fermut *m* spirit of sacrifice

opfern ['ɔpfərn] *tr* sacrifice, offer up

Op'ferstock *m* poor box

Op'fertier *n* victim

Op'fertod *m* sacrifice of one's life

Op'fertrank *m* libation

Op'ferung *f* (–;–en) offering, sacrifice

op'ferwillig *adj* willing to make sacrifices

opponieren [ɔpo'nirən] *intr* (dat) oppose

opportun [ɔpɔr'tun] *adj* opportune

optieren [ɔp'tirən] *intr*—**o. für** opt for

Optik ['ɔptɪk] *f* (–;) optics

Optiker –in ['ɔptɪkər(ɪn)] §6 *mf* optician

optimistisch [ɔpti'mɪstɪʃ] *adj* optimistic

optisch ['ɔptɪʃ] *adj* optic(al)

Orakel [ɔ'rakəl] *n* (–s;–) oracle

ora'kelhaft *adj* oracular

orange [ɔ'rãʒə] *adj* orange ‖ **Orange** *f* (–;–n) orange

oran'genfarben, oran'genfarbig *adj* orange-colored

oratorisch [ɔra'torɪʃ] *adj* oratorical

Orchester [ɔr'kɛstər] *n* (-s;-) orchestra

orchestral [ɔrçes'tral] *adj* orchestral

orchestrieren [ɔrkes'triːrən] *tr* orchestrate

Orchidee [ɔrçi'de·ə] *f* (-;-n) orchid

Orden ['ɔrdən] *m* (-s;-) medal, decoration; (eccl) order

Or'densband *n* (-[e]s;:-er) ribbon

Or'densbruder *m* monk, friar

Or'denskleid *n* (eccl) habit

Or'densschwester *f* nun, sister

ordentlich ['ɔrdəntlɪç] *adj* orderly; (*aufgeräumt*) tidy; (*anständig*) decent, respectable; (*regelrecht*) regular; (*tüchtig*) sound; (*Frühstück*) solid; (*Mitglied*) active; (*Professor*) full; **e-e ordentliche Leistung** a pretty good job; **in ordentlichem Zustand** in good condition || *adv* thoroughly, properly; (*sehr*) (coll) awfully, very; really

Order ['ɔrdər] *f* (-;-n) (com, mil) order

ordinär [ɔrdi'nɛr] *adj* ordinary; vulgar; rude

Ordina·rius [ɔrdi'narjus] *m* (-;-rien [rjən]) professor; (eccl) ordinary

Ordinär'preis *m* retail price

ordinieren [ɔrdi'niːrən] *tr* ordain || *intr* (med) have office hours

ordnen ['ɔrdnən] *tr* arrange; (*regeln*) put in order; (*säubern*) tidy up

Ord'nung *f* (-;-en) order, arrangement; classification; system; class; rank; regulation; (mil) formation; **aus der O. bringen** disturb; **in bester O. in** tiptop shape; **in O. bringen** set in order; **in O. sein** be all right; **nicht in O. sein** be out of order; be wrong; be out of sorts

ord'nungsgemäß *adv* duly

Ord'nungsliebe *f* tidiness, orderliness

ord'nungsmäßig *adj* orderly, regular || *adv* duly

Ord'nungsruf *m* (parl) call to order

Ord'nungssinn *m* sense of order

Ord'nungsstrafe *f* fine

ord'nungswidrig *adj* irregular, illegal

Ord'nungszahl *f* ordinal number

Ordonnanz [ɔrdɔ'nants] *f* (-;-en) (mil) orderly

Organ [ɔr'gan] *n* (-s;-e) organ

Organisation [ɔrganiza'tsjon] *f* (-;-en) organization

organisch [ɔr'ganɪʃ] *adj* organic; (*Gewebe*) structural || *adv* organically

organisieren [ɔrgani'ziːrən] *tr* organize; (mil) scrounge || *ref* unionize; **organisierter Arbeiter** union worker

Organis·mus [ɔrga'nɪsmus] *m* (-;-men [mən]) organism

Organist -in [ɔrga'nɪst(ɪn)] §7 *mf* organist

Orgas·mus [ɔr'gasmus] *m* (-;-men [mən]) orgasm

Orgel ['ɔrgəl] *f* (-;-n) organ

Or'gelzug *m* organ stop

Orgie ['ɔrgjə] *f* (-;-n) orgy

Orient ['ɔrjent] *m* (-s;) Orient

Orientale [ɔrjen'talə] *m* (-n;-n) Orientalin** [ɔrjen'talɪn] *f* (-;-nen) Oriental

orientalisch [ɔrjen'talɪʃ] *adj* oriental

orientieren [ɔrjen'tiːrən] *tr* orient; (fig) inform, instruct; (mil) brief

Orientie'rung *f* (-;-en) orientation; information, instruction; **die O. verlieren** lose one's bearings

Orientie'rungssinn *m* sense of direction

original [ɔrigi'nal] *adj* original || **Original** *n* (-s;-e) original; (typ) copy

Original'ausgabe *f* first edition

Originalität [ɔriginali'tet] *f* (-;) originality

Original'sendung *f* live broadcast

originell [ɔrigi'nel] *adj* original

Orkan [ɔr'kan] *m* (-[e]s;-e) hurricane

Ornament [ɔrna'ment] *n* (-[e]s;-e) ornament

Ornat [ɔr'nat] *m* (-[e]s;-e) robes

Ort [ɔrt] *m* (-[e]s;-e) place, spot; (*Örtlichkeit*) locality; (*Dorf*) village; **am Ort sein** be appropriate; **an allen Orten** everywhere; **an Ort und Stelle** on the spot; **an Ort und Stelle gelangen** reach one's destination; **höheren Ortes** at higher levels; **Ort der Handlung** scene of action; **vor Ort** on location; **vor Ort arbeiten** (min) work at the face || *m* (-[e]s; :-er) position, locus

Örtchen ['œrtçən] *n* (-s;-) toilet

orten ['ɔrtən] *tr* get the bearing on, locate || *intr* take a bearing

orthodox [ɔrto'dɔks] *adj* orthodox

Orthographie [ɔrtogra'fiː] *f* (-;) orthography

Orthopäde [ɔrto'pedə] *m* (-n;-n), **Orthopädin** [ɔrto'pedin] *f* (-;-nen) orthopedist

orthopädisch [ɔrto'pedɪʃ] *adj* orthopedic

örtlich ['œrtlɪç] *adj* local, topical

Ört'lichkeit *f* (-;-en) locality

Orts-, orts- [ɔrts] *comb.fm.* local

Orts'amt *n* (telp) local exchange

Orts'angabe *f* address

orts'ansässig *adj* resident || **Ortsansässige** §5 *mf* resident

Orts'behörde *f* local authorities

Orts'beschreibung *f* topography

Ort'schaft *f* (-;-en) place; (*Dorf*) village

orts'fremd *adj* nonlocal, out-of-town

Orts'gespräch *n* (telp) local call

Orts'kenntnis *f* familiarity with a place

orts'kundig *adj* familiar with the locality

Orts'name *m* place name

Orts'sinn *m* sense of direction

Orts'veränderung *f* change of scenery

Orts'verkehr *m* local traffic

Orts'zeit *f* local time

Orts'zustellung *f* local delivery

Or'tung *f* (-;-en) (aer, naut) taking of bearings, navigation

Öse ['øzə] *f* (-;-n) loop, eye; (*des Schuhes*) eyelet

Ost [ɔst] *m* (-es;-e) East; (poet) east wind

Ost- *comb.fm.* eastern, East

Osten ['ɔstən] *m* (-s;) East; **der Ferne O.** the Far East; **der Nahe O.** the Near East; **nach O.** eastward

ostentativ [ɔstenta'tif] *adj* ostentatious

Oster– [ostər] *comb.fm.* Easter
O'sterei *n* Easter egg
O'sterfest *n* Easter
O'sterhase *m* Easter bunny
O'sterlamm *n* paschal lamb
Ostern ['ostərn] *n* (–;–) & *pl* Easter
Österreich ['østəraɪç] *n* (–s;) Austria
Österreicher –in ['østəraɪçər(ɪn)] §6 *mf* Austrian
österreichisch ['østəraɪçɪʃ] *adj* Austrian
O'sterzeit *f* Eastertide
Ost'front *f* eastern front
Ost'gote *m* Ostrogoth
östlich ['œstlɪç] *adj* eastern, easterly; Oriental; **ö. von** east of
Ost'mark *f* East-German mark
Ost'see *f* Baltic Sea
ostwärts ['ostverts] *adv* eastward

Otter ['ɔtər] *m* (–s;–) otter ‖ *f* (–;–n) (*Schlange*) adder
Ouvertüre [uver'tyrə] *f* (–;–n) (*mus*) overture
oval [o'val] *adj* oval ‖ **Oval** *n* (–s;–e) oval
Ovar [o'var] *n* (–s;–e & –ien [jən]) ovary
Overall ['ovərol] *m* (–s;–s) overalls
Oxyd [o'ksyt] *n* (–[e]s;–e) oxide
Oxydation [ɔksyda'tsjon] *f* (–;) oxidation
oxydieren [ɔksy'dirən] *tr* & *intr* (SEIN) oxidize
Ozean ['otse·an] *m* (–s;–e) ocean; **der Große (or Stille) O.** the Pacific
Ozeanographie [otse·anogra'fi] *f* (–;) oceanography
Ozon [o'tson] *n* (–s;) ozone

P

P, p [pe] *invar n* P, p
paar [par] *adj* even ‖ *invar adj*—**ein p.** a couple of, a few ‖ **Paar** *n* (–[e]s; –e) pair, couple; **zu Paaren treiben** rout
paaren ['parən] *tr* match, mate ‖ *ref* mate
paarig ['parɪç] *adj* in pairs
paar'laufen §105 *intr* (SEIN) skate as a couple
paar'mal *adv*—**ein p.** a couple of times
Paa'rung *f* (–;) pairing, matching; (*Begattung*) mating
Paa'rungszeit *f* mating season
paar'weise *adv* in pairs, two by two
Pacht [paxt] *f* (–;–en) lease; (*Geld*) rent; **in P. geben** lease out; **in P. nehmen** lease, rent
Pacht'brief *m* lease
pachten ['paxtən] *tr* take a lease on
Pächter –in ['pɛçtər(ɪn)] §6 *mf* tenant
Pacht'ertrag *m*, **Pacht'geld** *n* rent
Pacht'gut *n*, **Pacht'hof** *m* leased farm
Pacht'kontrakt *m* lease
Pach'tung *f* (–;–en) leasing; leasehold
Pacht'vertrag *m* lease
Pacht'zeit *f* term of lease
Pacht'zins *m* rent
Pack [pak] *m* (–[e]s;–e & ⁖e) pack; (*Paket*) parcel; (*Ballen*) bale; **ein P. Spielkarten** a pack of cards ‖ *n* (–[e]s;) rabble; **ein P. von Lügnern** a pack of liars
Päckchen ['pɛkçən] *n* (–s;–) small package; (*Zigaretten–*) pack
packen ['pakən] *tr* pack, pack up; (*fassen*) seize, grab; (*fig*) grip, thrill; **pack dich!** scram! ‖ **Packen** *m* (–s;–) pack; (*Ballen*) bale ‖ *n* (–s;) packing
Pack'esel *m* (fig) drudge
Pack'papier *n* wrapping paper
Pack'pferd *n* packhorse
Pack'tier *n* pack animal
Packung (Pak'kung) *f* (–;–en) packing; (*Paket*) packet; **P. Zigaretten** pack of cigarettes

Pack'wagen *m* (rr) baggage car
Pädadoge [peda'gogə] *m* (–n;–n) pedagogue
Pädagogik [peda'gogɪk] *f* (–;) pedagogy
pädagogisch [peda'gogɪʃ] *adj* pedagogical, educational
Paddel ['padəl] *n* (–s;–) paddle
Pad'delboot *n* canoe
paddeln ['padəln] *intr* paddle, canoe
Pädiatrie [pedi·a'tri] *f* (–;) pediatrics
paff [paf] *interj* bang!
paffen ['pafən] *tr* & *intr* puff
Page ['paʒə] *m* (–n;–n) page
Pa'genfrisur *f*, **Pa'genkopf** *m* pageboy
Pagode [pa'godə] *f* (–;–n) pagoda
Pair [per] *m* (–s;–s) peer
Pak [pak] *f* (–;– & –s) (**Panzerabwehrkanone**) antitank gun
Paket [pa'ket] *n* (–[e]s;–e) parcel; (*Bücher–, Post–*) bundle
Paket'adresse *f* gummed label
Paket'post *f* parcel post
Pakt [pakt] *m* (–[e]s;–e) pact
paktieren [pak'tirən] *intr* make a pact
Paläontologie [pale·ontolo'gi] *f* (–;) paleontology
Palast [pa'last] *m* (–es;⁖e) palace
palast'artig *adj* palatial
Palästina [pale'stina] *n* (–s;) Palestine
Palette [pa'letə] *f* (–;–n) palette
Palisade [palɪ'zadə] *f* (–;–n) palisade
Palme ['palmə] *f* (–;–n) palm tree; palm branch; **j–n auf die P. bringen** (coll) drive s.o. up the wall
Palm'wedel *m*, **Palm'zweig** *m* palm branch
Pampelmuse ['pampəlmuzə] *f* (–;–n) grapefruit
Pamphlet [pam'flet] *n* (–[e]s;–e) lampoon
Panama ['panama] *n* (–s;) Panama
Paneel [pa'nel] *n* (–s;–e) panel
paneelieren [pane'lirən] *tr* panel
Panier [pa'nir] *n* (–s;–e) slogan
panieren [pa'nirən] *tr* (culin) bread

Panik ['pɑnɪk] f (-;) panic

panisch ['pɑnɪʃ] adj panic-stricken

Panne ['panə] f (-;-n) breakdown; (Reifenpanne) blowout; (fig) mishap

Panora·ma [panə'rɑma] n (-s;-men [mən]) panorama

panschen ['pan/ən] tr adulterate, water down || intr splash about; mix

Panther ['pantər] m (-s;-) panther

Pantine [pan'tinə] f (-;-n) clog

Pantoffel [pan'tɔfəl] m (-s;-n) slipper; unter dem P. stehen be henpecked

Pantof'felheld m henpecked husband

Panzer ['pantsər] m (-s;-) armor; armor plating; (mil) tank; (zool) shell

Pan'zerabwehrkanone f antitank gun

pan'zerbrechend adj armor-piercing

Pan'zerfalle f tank trap

Pan'zerfaust f bazooka

Pan'zergeschoß n, Pan'zergranate f armor-piercing shell

Pan'zerhandschuh m gauntlet

Pan'zerhemd n coat of mail

Pan'zerkreuzer m battle cruiser

panzern ['pantsərn] tr armor || ref arm oneself

Pan'zerschrank m safe

Panzerspähwagen ['pantsər/pevagən] m (mil) armored car

Pan'zersperre f antitank obstacle

Pan'zerung f (-;-en) armor plating

Pan'zerwagen m armored car

Papagei [papa'gaɪ] m (-en;-en) & (-[e]s;-e) parrot

Papier [pa'pir] n (-[e]s;-e) paper

Papier'bogen m sheet of paper

papieren [pa'pirən] adj paper

Papier'fabrik f paper mill

Papier'format n size of paper

Papier'korb m wastebasket

Papier'krieg m (fig) red tape

Papier'mühle f paper mill

Papier'schlange f paper streamer

Papier'tüte f paper bag

Papier'waren pl stationery

Papp [pap] m (-[e]s;-e) (Brei) pap; (Kleister) paste

Papp- [pap] comb.fm. sticky; cardboard

Papp'band m (-[e]s;⸚e) paperback

Papp'deckel m piece of cardboard

Pappe ['papə] f (-;) cardboard

Pappel ['papəl] f (-;-n) poplar

päppeln ['pepəln] tr feed lovingly

pappen ['papən] tr paste, glue || intr stick

Pap'penstiel m (coll) trifle; das ist keinen P. wert (coll) this isn't worth a thing

papperlapapp [papərla'pap] interj nonsense!

pap'pig adj sticky

Papp'karton m, Papp'schachtel f cardboard box, cardboard carton

Papp'schnee m sticky snow (for skiing)

Paprika ['paprika] m (-s;) paprika

Pap'rikaschote f (green) pepper

Papst [papst] m (-es;⸚e) pope

päpstlich ['pepstlɪç] adj papal

Papsttum ['papsttum] n (-s;) papacy

Papy·rus [pa'pyrus] m (-;-ri) [ri]) papyrus

Parabel [pa'rabəl] f (-;-n) parable; (geom) parabola

Parade [pa'radə] f (-;-n) parade; (fencing) parry; (mil) review; (fb) save

Para'deanzug m (mil) dress uniform

Paradeiser [para'daɪzər] m (-s;-) (Aust) tomato

Para'depferd n (fig) show-off

Para'deplatz m parade ground

Para'deschritt m goose step

paradieren [para'dirən] intr parade; (fig) show off

Paradies [para'dis] n (-es;-e) paradise

Paradies'apfel m tomato

paradox [para'dɔks] adj paradoxical || Paradox n (-es;-e) paradox

Paraffin [para'fin] n (-s;-e) paraffin

Paragraph [para'graf] m (-en & -s; -en) paragraph; (jur) section

parallel [para'lel] adj parallel || Parallele f (-;-n) parallel

Paralyse [para'lyzə] f (-;-n) paralysis

paralysieren [paraly'zirən] tr paralyze

Paralytiker -in [para'lytikər(ɪn)] §6 mf paralytic

Paranuß ['paranus] f Brazil nut

Parasit [para'zit] m (-en;-en) parasite

parat [pa'rat] adj ready

Pardon [par'dõ] m (-s;) pardon; keinen P. geben (mil) given no quarter

Parenthese [paren'tezə] f (-;-n) parenthesis

Parfüm [par'fym] n (-[e]s;-e) perfume

Parfüme·rie [parfymə'ri] f (-;-rien ['ri·ən]) perfume shop

parfümieren [parfy'mirən] tr perfume

pari ['pari] adv at par || Pari m (- [s];) par; auf P. at par

Paria ['parja] m (-s;-s) pariah

parieren [pa'rirən] tr (Pferd) rein in; (Hieb) parry || intr (dat) obey

Pa'rikurs m (com) parity

Paris [pa'ris] n (-;) Paris

Pariser -in [pa'rizər(ɪn)] §6 mf Parisian

Parität [pari'tet] f (-;) equality; (fin, st. exch.) parity

paritätisch [pari'tetɪʃ] adj on a footing of equality

Park [park] m (-s;-s & -e) park

Park'anlage f park; Parkanlagen grounds

parken ['parkən] tr & intr park

Parkett [par'ket] n (-[e]s;-e) (Fußboden) parquet; (theat) parquet

Parkett'fußboden m parquet flooring

Park'licht n parking light

Park'platz m parking lot

Park'platzwärter m parking lot attendant

Park'uhr f parking meter

Parlament [parla'ment] n (-[e]s;-e) parliament

Parlamentär [parlamen'ter] m (-s;-e) truce negotiator

parlamentarisch [parlamen'tarɪʃ] adj parliamentary

parlamentieren [parlamen'tirən] intr (coll) parley

Paro·die [parə'di] f (-;-dien ['di·ən]) parody

parodieren [parə'dirən] tr parody

Parole [pa'rolə] *f* (-;-n) (mil) password; (pol) slogan
Partei [par'taɪ] *f* (-;-en) party; (*Mieter*) tenant(s); (jur, pol) party; (sport) side; **j-s P. ergreifen** or **P. nehmen für j-n** side with s.o.
Partei/bonze *m* (pol) party boss
Partei/gänger -in §6 *mf* (pol) party sympathizer
Partei/genosse *m*, **Partei/genossin** *f* party member
Partei/grundsatz *m* party plank
parteiisch [par'taɪ·ɪʃ] *adj* partial, biased; (pol) partisan
partei/lich *adj* partisan
Partei/lichkeit *f* (-;) partiality
partei/los *adj* (pol) independent || **Parteilose** §5 *mf* independent
Partei/losigkeit *f* (-;) impartiality; political independence
Partei/nahme *f* (-;) taking sides
Partei/programm *n* party platform
Partei/tag *m* party rally
Partei/zugehörigkeit *f* party affiliation
Parterre [par'ter] *n* (-s;-s) ground floor; (theat) parterre
Par-tie [par'ti] *f* (-;-tien ['ti·ən]) part; (*Gesellschaft*) party; (*Spiel*) game; (*Ausflug*) outing; (com) lot; (theat) role; **e-e gute P. machen** (coll) marry rich; **ich bin mit von der P.!** count me in!
partiell [par'tsjel] *adj* partial || *adv* partly, partially
Partikel [par'tikəl] *f* (-;-n) particle
Partisan -in [partɪ'zan(ɪn)] §7 *mf* partisan
Partitur [partɪ'tur] *f* (-;-en) (mus) score
Partizip [partɪ'tsip] *n* (-s;-ien [jən]) participle
Partner -in ['partnər(ɪn)] §6 *mf* partner
Part/nerschaft *f* (-;-en) partnership
Parzelle [par'tselə] *f* (-;-n) lot
parzellieren [partse'lirən] *tr* parcel out, allot
paschen ['paʃən] *tr* smuggle || *intr* smuggle; (*würfeln*) play dice
Paß [pas] *m* (Passes; Pässe) pass, passport; (geog) mountain pass
passabel [pa'sabəl] *adj* tolerable
Passage [pa'saʒə] *f* (-;-en) passage; (mus) run
Passagier [pasa'ʒir] *m* (-s;-e) passenger; **blinder P.** stowaway
Passagier/dampfer *m* passenger liner
Passagier/gut *n* luggage
Passah ['pasa] *n* (-s;), **Pas/sahfest** *n* Passover
Paß/amt *n* passport office
Passant -in [pa'sant(ɪn)] §7 *mf* passer-by
Paß/ball *m* (sport) pass
Paß/bild *n* passport photograph
passen ['pasən] *ref* be proper || *intr* fit; (*dat*) suit; (cards, fb) pass; **p. auf** (*acc*) watch for, wait for; **p. zu** suit, fit; **sie p. zueinander** they are a good match
pas/send *adj* suitable; .convenient; (*Kleidungsstück*) matching; **für p. halten** think it proper

Paß/form *f*—**e-e gute P. haben** be form-fitting
passierbar [pa'sirbar] *adj* passable
passieren [pa'sirən] *tr* pass, cross; (culin) sift, sieve || *intr* (SEIN) happen
Passier/schein *m* pass, permit
Passion [pa'sjon] *f* (-;-en) passion
passioniert [pasjə'nirt] *adj* ardent
Passions/spiel *n* passion play
passiv [pa'sif] *adj* passive; (*Handelsbilanz*) unfavorable; **passives Wahlrecht** eligibility || **Passiv** *n* (-s;-e) (gram) passive
Passiva [pa'siva] *pl*, **Passiven** [pa'sivən] *pl* debts, liabilities
Paß/kontrolle *f* passport inspection
Paste ['pastə] *f* (-;-n) paste
Pastell [pa'stel] *n* (-s;-e) pastel; crayon
pastell/farben *adj* pastel
Pastell/stift *m* crayon
Pastete [pas'tetə] *f* (-;-en) meat pie, fish pie
pasteurisieren [pastœrɪ'zirən] *tr* pasteurize
Pastille [pa'stɪlə] *f* (-;-n) lozenge
Pa-stor ['pastor] *m* (-s;-storen ['torən]) pastor, minister, vicar
Pate ['patə] *m* (-n;-n) godfather || *f* (-;-n) godmother
Pa/tenkind *n* godchild
patent [pa'tent] *adj* neat; smart; **ein patenter Kerl** quite a fellow || **Patent** *n* (-[e]s;-e) patent; (mil) commission; **P. angemeldet** patent pending
Patent/amt *n* patent office
patentieren [paten'tirən] *tr* patent
Pater ['patər] *m* (-s; Patres ['patres]) (eccl) Father
pathetisch [pa'tetɪʃ] *adj* impassioned; solemn
Pathologe [pato'logə] *m* (-n;-n) pathologist
Pathologie [patolo'gi] *f* (-;) pathology
Pathologin [pato'login] *f* (-;-nen) pathologist
Patient -in [pa'tsjent(ɪn)] §7 *mf* patient
Patin ['patɪn] *f* (-;-nen) godmother
Patriarch [patri'arç] *m* (-en;-en) patriarch
Patriot -in [patri'ot(ɪn)] §7 *mf* patriot
patriotisch [patri'otɪʃ] *adj* patriotic
Patrize [pa'tritsə] *f* (-;-n) die, stamp
Patrizier -in [pa'tritsjər(ɪn)] §6 *mf* patrician
Patron [pa'tron] *m* (-s;-e) patron; (pej) guy
Patronat [patro'nat] *n* (-[e]s;-e) patronage
Patrone [pa'tronə] *f* (-;-n) cartridge
Patro/nengurt *m* cartridge belt
Patro/nenhülse *f* cartridge case
Patronin [pa'tronɪn] *f* (-;-nen) patroness
Patrouille [pa'truljə] *f* (-;-n) patrol
patrouillieren [patru'ljirən] *tr & intr* patrol
Patsche ['patʃə] *f* (-;-en) (*Pfütze*) puddle; (coll) jam, scrape; **in der P. lassen** leave in a lurch; **in e-e P. geraten** get into a jam

patschen ['patʃən] *tr* slap ‖ *intr* splash; **in die Hände p.** clap hands
patsch'naß' *adj* soaking wet
patzig ['patsɪç] *adj* snappy, sassy
Pauke ['pauka] *f* (-;-n) kettledrum; **j–m e–e P. halten** give s.o. a lecture
pauken ['paukən] *tr* (educ) cram ‖ *intr* beat the kettledrum; (educ) cram
Pau'ker *m* (-s;-) (coll) martinet
pausbackig ['pausbakıç], **pausbäckig** ['pausbekıç] *adj* chubby-faced
pauschal [pau'ʃal] *adj* (*Summe*) flat
Pauschal'betrag *m* flat rate
Pauscha·le [pau'ʃalə] *n* (-s;-lien [ljən]) lump sum
Pauschal'preis *m* package price
Pauschal'reise *f* all-inclusive tour
Pauschal'summe *f* flat sum
Pause ['pauzə] *f* (-;-n) pause; (*Pauszeichnung*) tracing; (educ) recess, break; (mus) rest; (theat) intermission; **e–e P. machen** take a break
pausen ['pauzən] *tr* trace
pau'senlos *adj* continuous
Pau'senzeichen *n* (rad) station identification
pausieren [pau'zirən] *intr* pause; rest
Pauspapier ['pauzpapir] *n* tracing paper
Pavian ['pavjan] *m* (-s;-e) baboon
Pavillon ['pavɪljɔ] *m* (-s;-s) pavilion
Pazifik [pa'tsifɪk] *m* Pacific
pazifisch [pa'tsifɪʃ] *adj* Pacific
Pazifist –in [patsɪ'fɪst(ɪn)] §7 *mf* pacifist
Pech [peç] *n* (-[e]s;-e) pitch; **P. haben** (coll) have tough luck
Pech'fackel *f* torch
Pech'kohle *f* bituminous coal
pech'ra'benschwarz' *adj* pitch-black
pech'schwarz' *adj* pitch-dark
Pech'strähne *f* streak of bad luck
Pech'vogel *m* (coll) unlucky fellow
Pedal [pe'dal] *n* (-s;-e) pedal
Pedant [pe'dant] *m* (-en;-en) pedant
pedantisch [pe'dantɪç] *adj* pedantic
Pegel ['pegəl] *m* (-s;-) water gauge
Pe'gelstand *m* water level
Peil- [paɪl] *comb.fm.* direction-finding, sounding
peilen ['paɪlən] *tr* take the bearings of; (*Tiefe*) sound; **über den Daumen p.** (coll) estimate roughly ‖ *intr* take bearings
Pei'lung *f* (-;-en) bearings; taking of bearings; sounding
Pein [paɪn] *f* (-;) pain, torment
peinigen ['paɪnɪgən] *tr* torment
pein'lich *adj* painful; embarrassing; (*genau*) painstaking; (*sorgfältig*) scrupulous ‖ *adv* scrupulously; carefully
Peitsche ['paɪtʃə] *f* (-;-n) whip; **mit der P. knallen** crack the whip
peitschen ['paɪtʃən] *tr* whip
Peit'schenhieb *m* whiplash
Peit'schenknall *m* crack of the whip
Pelerine [pelə'rinə] *f* (-;-n) cape
Pelikan ['pelɪkan] *m* (-s;-e) pelican
Pelle ['pelə] *f* (-;-n) peel, skin
pellen ['pelən] *tr* peel, skin
Pellkartoffeln ['pelkartɔfəln] *pl* potatoes in their jackets

Pelz [pelts] *m* (-es;-e) fur; (*Fell*) pelt; fur coat
Pelz'besatz *m* fur trimming
Pelz'futter *n* fur lining
Pelz'händler –in §6 *mf* furrier
pel'zig *adj* furry; (*Gefühl im Mund*) cottony
Pelz'tier *n* fur-bearing animal
Pelz'tierjäger *m* trapper
Pelz'werk *n* furs
Pendel ['pendəl] *n* (-s;-) pendulum
pendeln ['pendəln] *intr* swing, oscillate; (*zwischen zwei Orten*) commute
Pen'deltür *f* swinging door
Pen'delverkehr *m* commuter traffic; shuttle service
Pen'delzug *m* shuttle train
Pendler ['pentlər] *m* (-s;-) commuter
Penizillin [penɪtsɪ'lin] *n* (-s;) penicillin
Pension [pen'zjon] *f* (-;-en) pension, retirement pay; (*Fremdenhaus*) boarding house; (*Unterkunft und Verpflegung*) room and board; (*Pensionat*) girls' boarding school; **in P. gehen** go on pension
Pensionär [penzjo'ner] *m* (-s;-e) pensioner; boarder
Pensionat [penzjo'nat] *n* (-[e]s;-e) girls boarding school
pensionieren [penzjo'nirən] *tr* put on pension; (mil) retire on half pay; **sich p. lassen** retire
Pensions'kasse *f* pension fund
Pensions'preis *m* price of room and board
Pen·sum ['penzum] *n* (-s;-sen [zən] & -sa [za]) task, assignment; quota
per [per] *prep* (acc) per, by, with; (*zeitlich*) by, until; **per Adresse** care of, c/o; **per sofort** at once
perfekt [per'fekt] *adj* perfect; concluded ‖ **Perfekt** *n* (-[e]s;-e) perfect
Pergament [perga'ment] *n* (-[e]s;-e) parchment
Periode [per'jodə] *f* (-;-n) period
periodisch [per'jodɪʃ] *adj* periodic
Periphe·rie [perife'ri] *f* (-;-rien ['ri·ən]) periphery
Periskop [perɪ'skop] *n* (-s;-e) periscope
Perle ['perlə] *f* (-;-n) pearl; (*aus Glas*) bead; (*Tropfen*) drop, bead; (*Bläschen*) bubble; (fig) gem
perlen ['perlən] *intr* sparkle
Per'lenauster *f* pearl oyster
Per'lenkette *f*, **Per'lenschnur** *f* pearl necklace, string of pearls
Perlhuhn ['perlhun] *n* guinea fowl
perlig ['perlɪç] *adj* pearly
Perl'muschel *f* pearl oyster
Perlmutt ['perlmut] *n* (-s;), **Perl'mutter** *f* mother of pearl
perplex [per'pleks] *adj* perplexed
Persenning [per'zenɪŋ] *f* (-;-en) tarpaulin
Persien ['perzjən] *n* (-s;) Persia
persisch [perzɪʃ] *adj* Persian
Person [per'zon] *f* (-;-en) person; (theat) character; **ich für meine P.** I for one; **klein von P.** small of stature
Personal [perzo'nal] *n* (-s;) personnel
Personal'akte *f* personal file, dossier

Personal'angaben pl personal data
Personal'aufzug m passenger elevator
Personal'ausweis m identity card
Personal'chef m personnel manager
Personalien [perzɔ'nɑljən] pl personal data, particulars
Personal'pronomen n personal pronoun
Perso'nengedächtnis n good memory for names
Perso'nenkraftwagen m passenger car
Perso'nenschaden m personal injury
Perso'nenverzeichnis n list of persons; (theat) dramatis personae, cast
Perso'nenwagen m passenger car
Perso'nenzug m passenger train; (rr) local
personifizieren [perzɔnifɪ'tsirən] tr personify
persönlich [per'zønlɪç] adj personal || adv personally, in person
Persön'lichkeit f (-;-en) personality
Perspektiv [perspɛk'tif] n (-s;-e) telescope
Perücke [pe'rʏkə] f (-;-n) wig
pervers [per'vers] adj perverse
pessimistisch [pesɪ'mɪstɪʃ] adj pessimistic
Pest [pest] f (-;) plague
pest'artig adj pestilential
Pestilenz [pestɪ'lɛnts] f (-;-en) pestilence
Petersilie [petər'ziljə] f (-;) parsley
Petroleum [pe'trole-ʊm] n (-s;) petroleum
Petschaft ['pet∫aft] n (-s;-e) seal
Petting ['petɪŋ] n (-s;) petting
petto ['peto]—**in p. haben** have in reserve; (coll) have up one's sleeve
Petunie [pe'tunjə] f (-;-n) petunia
Petze ['petsə] f (-;-n) tattletale
petzen ['petsən] intr tattle, squeal
Pfad [pfɑt] m (-[e]s;-e) path, track
Pfadfinder ['pfɑtfɪndər] m (-s;-) boy scout
Pfadfinderin ['pfɑtfɪndərɪn] f (-;-nen) girl scout
Pfaffe ['pfafə] m (-n;-n) (pej) priest
Pfahl [pfɑl] m (-[e]s;⸚e) stake; post
Pfahl'bau m (-[e]s;-bauten) lake dwelling
Pfahl'werk n palisade, stockade
Pfahl'wurzel f taproot
Pfahl'zaun m palisade, stockade
Pfälzer -in ['pfɛltsər(ɪn)] §6 mf inhabitant of the Palatinate
Pfand [pfant] n (-[e]s;⸚er) pledge; deposit; (Bürgschaft) security, pawn; (auf Immobilien) mortgage; **zum Pfande geben** (or **setzen**) pawn, mortgage
pfändbar ['pfɛntbɑr] adj (jur) attachable
Pfand'brief m mortgage papers
pfänden ['pfɛndən] tr attach, impound
Pfand'geber m mortgagor
Pfand'gläubiger m mortgagee
Pfand'haus n, **Pfand'leihe** f pawnshop
Pfand'leiher -in §6 mf pawnbroker
Pfand'recht n lien
Pfand'schein m pawn ticket
Pfand'schuldner m mortgagor
Pfän'dung f (-;-en) attachment, confiscation

Pfanne ['pfanə] f (-;-n) pan; (anat) socket; **etw auf der P. haben** (fig) have s.th. up one's sleeve; **in die P. hauen** (fig) make mincemeat of
Pfan'nenstiel m panhandle
Pfann'kuchen m pancake; **Berliner P.** doughnut
Pfarr- [pfar] comb.fm. parish, parochial
Pfarr'amt n rectory
Pfarr'bezirk m parish
Pfarr'dorf n parish seat
Pfarre ['pfarə] f (-;-n) parish; (Pfarrhaus) rectory
Pfarrei [pfa'rai] f (-;-en) parish; (Pfarrhaus) rectory
Pfarrer ['pfarər] m (-s;-) pastor
Pfarr'gemeinde f parish
Pfarr'haus n rectory
Pfarr'kind n parishioner
Pfarr'kirche f parish church
Pfarr'schule f parochial school
Pfau [pfau] m (-[e]s;-en) peacock
Pfau'enhenne f peahen
Pfeffer ['pfefər] m (-s;) pepper
pfefferig ['pfefərɪç] adj peppery
Pfef'ferkorn n peppercorn
Pfef'ferkuchen m gingerbread
Pfef'ferminze f (bot) peppermint
Pfef'ferminzplätzchen n peppermint cookie
pfeffern ['pfefərn] tr pepper
Pfef'fernuß f ginger nut
Pfeife ['pfaifə] f (-;-n) whistle; (Orgel-) pipe; (zum Rauchen) (tobacco) pipe
pfeifen ['pfaifən] tr whistle; **ich pfeife ihm was** he can whistle for it || intr whistle; (Schiedsrichter) blow the whistle; (Maus) squeak; (Vogel) sing; (dat) whistle for or to; **auf dem letzten Loche p.** be on one's last legs; **ich pfeife darauf!** I couldn't care less!
Pfei'fenkopf m pipe bowl
Pfei'fenrohr n pipestem
Pfei'fer -in (-s;-) §6 mf whistler; (mus) piper, fife player
Pfeif'kessel m, **Pfeif'topf** m whistling kettle
Pfeil [pfail] m (-[e]s;-e) arrow, dart; **P. und Bogen** bow and arrow
Pfei'ler m (-s;-) (& fig) pillar; (e-r Brücke) pier
pfeil'gera'de adj straight as an arrow
pfeil'schnell' adj swift as an arrow || adv like a shot
Pfeil'schütze m archer
Pfeil'spitze f arrowhead
Pfennig ['pfenɪç] m (-[e]s;-e & -) pfennig, penny (one hundredth of a mark)
Pfennigfuchser ['pfenɪçfuksər] m (-s;-) penny pincher
Pferch [pferç] m (-[e]s;-e) fold, pen
pferchen ['pferçən] tr herd together, pen in
Pferd [pfert] n (-[e]s;-e) horse; **zu Pferde** on horseback
Pferde- [pferdə] comb.fm. horse
Pfer'deapfel m horse manure
Pfer'debremse f horsefly
Pfer'dedecke f horse blanket

Pfer'defuß m (Kennzeichen des Teufels) cloven hoof; (pathol) clubfoot
Pfer'degeschirr n harness
Pfer'degespann n team of horses
Pfer'deknecht m groom
Pfer'dekoppel f corral
Pfer'delänge f (beim Rennen) length
Pfer'derennbahn f race track
Pfer'derennen n horse racing
Pfer'destärke f horsepower
Pfer'dezucht f horse breeding
pfiff [pfɪf] pret of **pfeifen** || **Pfiff** m (-[e]s;-e) whistle; **den P. heraushaben** (fig) know the ropes
Pfif'ferling ['pfɪfərlɪŋ] m (-s;-e) (bot) chanterelle; **keinen P. wert** not worth a thing
pfiffig ['pfɪfɪç] adj shrewd, sharp
Pfif'fikus ['pfɪfɪkus] m (-;-), (-ses;-se) (coll) sly fox
Pfingsten ['pfɪŋstən] n (-s;) Pentecost
Pfingst'rose f (bot) peony
Pfingst'son'ntag m Whitsunday
Pfirsich ['pfɪrzɪç] m (-[e]s;-e) peach
Pflanze ['pflantsə] f (-;-n) plant
pflanzen ['pflantsən] tr plant
Pflan'zenfaser f vegetable fiber
Pflan'zenfett n vegetable shortening
pflan'zenfressend adj herbivorous
Pflan'zenkost f vegetable diet
Pflan'zenkunde f botany
Pflan'zenleben n plant life, vegetation
Pflan'zenlehre f botany
Pflan'zenöl n vegetable oil
Pflan'zenreich n vegetable kingdom
Pflan'zensaft m sap, juice
Pflan'zenschutzmittel n pesticide
Pflan'zenwelt f flora
Pflan'zer –in §6 mf planter
pflanz'lich adj vegetable
Pflanz'schule f, **Pflanz'stätte** f nursery; (fig) hotbed
Pflan'zung f (-;-en) plantation
Pflaster ['pflastər] n (-s;-) pavement; (Fleck) patch; (med) Band-Aid; **als P.** (fig) in compensation; **ein teueres P.** (fig) an expensive place; **P. treten** (fig) pound the sidewalks
Pflasterer ['pflastərər] m (-s;-) paver
pfla'stermüde adj tired of walking the streets
pflastern ['pflastərn] tr pave
Pfla'sterstein m paving stone; (Kopfstein) cobblestone
Pfla'stertreter m (-s;-) loafer
Pfla'sterung f (-;) paving
Pflaume ['pflaumə] f (-;-n) plum; (spitze Bemerkung) dig
pflaumen ['pflaumən] intr (coll) tease
pflau'menweich adj (fig) spineless
Pflege ['pflegə] f (-;-n) care; (e-s Kranken) nursing; (Wartung) tending; (e-s Gartens, der Künste) cultivation; **gute P. haben** be well cared for; **in P. nehmen** take charge of
Pflegebefohlene ['pflegəbəfolənə] §5 mf charge; foster-child
Pfle'geeltern pl foster parents
Pfle'geheim n nursing home
Pfle'gekind n foster child
pflegen ['pflegən] tr take care of, look after; (Kranken) nurse; (Garten, Kunst) cultivate; (Freundschaft) fos-

ter; **Gesellschaft p.** lead an active social life; **Umgang p. mit** associate with || intr—**p. zu** (inf) be wont to (inf), be in the habit of (ger); **sein Vater pflegte zu sagen** his father used to say; **sie pflegt morgens zeitig aufzustehen** she usually gets up early in the morning || intr (pp **gepflegt & gepflogen**) (genit) carry on; **der Liebe p.** enjoy the pleasures of love; **der Ruhe p.** take a rest; **Rats p. mit** consult with
Pfle'ger –in §6 mf nurse; (jur) guardian
Pfle'gesohn m foster son
Pfle'gestelle f foster home
Pfle'getocher f foster daughter
Pfle'gevater m foster father
pfleglich ['pfleklɪç] adj careful
Pflegling ['pfleklɪŋ] m (-s;-e) foster child; (Pflegebefohlener) charge
Pflegschaft ['pflekʃaft] f (-;-en) (jur) guardianship
Pflicht [pflɪçt] f (-;-en) duty; **sich seiner P. entziehen** evade one's duty
pflicht'bewußt adj conscientious
Pflicht'bewußtsein n conscientiousness
Pflicht'eifer m zeal
pflicht'eifrig adj zealous
Pflicht'erfüllung f performance of duty
Pflicht'fach n (educ) required course
Pflicht'gefühl n sense of duty
pflicht'gemäß adj dutiful
–pflichtig [pflɪçtɪç] comb.fm. obligated, e.g., **schulpflichtig** obligated to attend school
pflicht'schuldig adj duty-bound
pflicht'treu adj dutiful, loyal
pflicht'vergessen adj forgetful of one's duty; (untreu) disloyal
Pflicht'vergessenheit f dereliction of duty; disloyalty
Pflicht'verletzung f, **Pflicht'versäumnis** n neglect of duty
Pflock [pflɔk] m (-[e]s;ᵉe) peg; **e-n P. zurückstecken** (fig) come down a peg
pflog [pflok] pret of **pflegen**
pflücken ['pflʏkən] tr pluck, pick
Pflug [pfluk] m (-[e]s;ᵉe) plow
pflügen ['pflygən] tr & intr plow
Pflug'schar f plowshare
Pforte ['pfɔrtə] f (-;-n) gate
Pförtner –in ['pfœrtnər(ɪn)] §6 mf gatekeeper || m doorman; (anat) pylorus
Pfosten ['pfɔstən] m (-s;-) post; (carp) jamb
Pfote ['pfotə] f (-;-n) paw; **j-m eins auf die Pfoten geben** rap s.o.'s knuckles
Pfriem [pfrim] m (-[e]s;-e) awl
Pfropf [pfrɔpf] m (-[e]s;-e) stopper, plug, cork
pfropfen ['pfrɔpfən] tr cork, plug; (stopfen) cram; (hort) graft || **Pfropfen** m (-s;-) stopper, plug, cork
Pfropf'enzieher m corkscrew
Pfropf'reis n (hort) graft
Pfründe f ['pfrʏndə] f (-;-n) benefice; (ohne Seelsorge) sinecure; **fette P.** (fig) cushy, well-paying job
Pfuhl [pful] m (-[e]s;-e) pool, puddle; (fig) pit

Pfühl [pfyl] *m* (-[e]s;-e) (poet) cushion
pfui [ˈpfuˑ*ɪ*] *interj* phooey!; **p. über dich!** shame on you!
Pfund [pfunt] *n* (-[e]s;-e) pound
pfundig [ˈpfundɪç] *adj* (coll) great
-pfündig [pfʏndɪç] *comb.fm.* -pound
Pfundskerl [ˈpfuntskerl] *m* (coll) great guy
pfund'weise *adv* by the pound
Pfuscharbeit [ˈpfuˈarbaɪt] *f* bungling
pfuschen [ˈpfuʃən] *tr & intr* bungle; **j-m ins Handwerk p.** meddle in s.o.'s business
Pfuscherei [pfuʃəˈraɪ] *f* (-;-en) bungling
Pfütze [ˈpfʏtsə] *f* (-;-n) puddle
Phänomen [fenoˈmen] *n* (-s;-e) phenomenon
phänomenal [fenoˈmeˈnɑl] *adj* phenomenal
Phanta·sie [fantaˈzi] *f* (-;-sien [ˈzi·ən]) imagination
Phantasie'gebilde *n* daydream
phantasieren [fantaˈziˈrən] *intr* daydream; (mus) improvise; (pathol) be delirious
phantasie'voll *adj* imaginative
Phantast **-in** [fanˈtast(ɪn)] §7 *mf* visionary
phantastisch [fanˈtastɪʃ] *adj* fantastic
Phantom [fanˈtom] *n* (-s;-e) phantom
Pharisäer [fariˈzeˑər] *m* (-s;-) Pharisee; (fig) pharisee
pharmazeutisch [farmaˈtsɔɪtɪʃ] *adj* pharmaceutical
Pharmazie [farmaˈtsi] *f* (-;) pharmacy
Phase [ˈfɑzə] *f* (-;-n) phase
Philantrop **-in** [filanˈtrop(ɪn)] §7 *mf* philanthropist
philanthropisch [filanˈtropɪʃ] *adj* philanthropic
Philister [fɪˈlɪstər] *m* (-s;-) Philistine
Phiole [fɪˈolə] *f* (-;-n) vial, phial
Philologe [filoˈlogə] *m* (-n;-n) philologist
Philologie [filoloˈgi] *f* (-;) philology
Philologin [filoˈlogɪn] *f* (-;-nen) philologist
Philosoph [filoˈzof] *m* (-en;-en) philosopher
Philoso·phie [filozoˈfi] *f* (-;-fien [ˈfi·ən]) philosophy
philosophieren [filozoˈfirən] *intr* philosophize
philosophisch [filoˈzofɪʃ] *adj* philosophic(al)
Phlegma [ˈflegma] *n* (-s;) indolence
Phonetik [foˈnetɪk] *f* (-;) phonetics
phonetisch [foˈnetɪʃ] *adj* phonetic
Phönix [ˈfønɪks] *m* (-[e]s;-e) phoenix
Phönizien [føˈnitsjən] *n* (-s;) Phoenicia
Phönizier **-in** [føˈnitsjər(ɪn)] §6 *mf* Phoenician
Phosphor [ˈfosfər] *m* (-s;) phosphorus
phos'phorig *adj* phosphorous
Photo [ˈfoto] *n* (-s;-) photo
Pho'toapparat *m* camera
photogen [fotoˈgen] *adj* photogenic
Photograph [fotoˈgraf] *m* (-en;-en) photographer
Photogra·phie [fotograˈfi] *f* (-;-fien [ˈfi·ən]) photography

photographieren [fotograˈfirən] *tr & intr* photograph; **sich p. lassen** have one's photograph taken
Photographin [fotoˈgrafɪn] *f* (-;-nen) photographer
photographisch [fotoˈgrafɪʃ] *adj* photographic
Photokopie *f* photocopy
photokopie'ren *tr* photocopy
Pho'tozelle *f* photoelectric cell
Phrase [ˈfrazə] *f* (-;-n) phrase; (fig) platitude; **das sind nur Phrasen** that's just talk
phra'senhaft *adj* empty, trite; windy
Physik [fyˈzik] *f* (-;) physics
physikalisch [fyziˈkalɪʃ] *adj* physical
Physiker **-in** [ˈfysɪkər(ɪn)] §6 *mf* physicist
Physiogno·mie [fyzjɔgnoˈmi] *f* (-;-mien [ˈmi·ən]) physiognomy
Physiologie [fyzjɔloˈgi] *f* (-;) physiology
physiologisch [fyzjoˈlogɪʃ] *adj* physiological
physisch [ˈfyzɪʃ] *adj* physical
Pianino [pɪˑaˈnino] *n* (-s;-s) small upright piano
Pianist **-in** [pɪˑaˈnɪst(ɪn)] §7 *mf* pianist
picheln [ˈpɪçəln] *tr & intr* tipple
pichen [ˈpɪçən] *tr* pitch, cover with pitch
Pichler **-in** [ˈpɪçlər(ɪn)] §6 *mf* tippler
Picke [ˈpɪkə] *f* (-;-n) pickax
Pickel [ˈpɪkəl] *m* (-s;-) pimple; (*Picke*) pickax; (*Eispicke*) ice ax
Pickelhaube (**Pik'kelhaube**) *f* spiked helmet
Pickelhering (**Pik'kelhering**) *m* pickled herring
pickelig (**pik'kelig**) *adj* pimply
picken [ˈpɪkən] *tr & intr* peck
picklig [ˈpɪklɪç] *adj* var of pickelig
Picknick [ˈpɪknɪk] *n* (-s;-s) picnic
pieken [ˈpikən] *tr* sting; (coll) prick
piekfein [ˈpikˈfaɪn] *adj* tiptop
pieksauber [ˈpikˈzaʊbər] *adj* spick and span
piepen [ˈpipən] *intr* chirp; (*Maus*) squeal; **bei dir piept's wohl?** are you quite all there? ‖ **Piepen** *n—* **das ist zum P.!** that's ridiculous
Pier [pir] *m* (-s;-e) pier
piesacken [ˈpizakən] *tr* (coll) pester
Pietät [pɪˑeˈtet] *f* (-;) piety
pietät'los *adj* irreverent
pietät'voll *adj* reverent(ial)
Pigment [pɪgˈment] *n* (-[e]s;-e) pigment
Pik [pik], [pɪk] *m* (-s;-s & -e) (*Bergspitze*) peak ‖ *m* (-s;-e) (coll) grudge; **e-n Pik auf j-n haben** hold a grudge against s.o. ‖ *n* (-s;-e) (cards) spade(s)
pikant [pɪˈkant] *adj* piquant, pungent; (*Bermerkung*) suggestive
Pikante·rie [pɪkantəˈri] *f* (-;-rien [ˈri·ən]) piquancy; spicy story, suggestive remark
Pike [ˈpikə] *f* (-;-n) pike, spear; **von der P. auf dienen** (fig) rise through the ranks
pikiert [pɪˈkirt] *adj* (**über** *acc*) piqued (at)

Pikkolo ['pɪkɔlo] *m* (-s;-s) apprentice waiter; (mus) piccolo
Pik'koloflöte *f* (mus) piccolo
Pilger ['pɪlgər] *m* (-s;-) pilgrim
Pil'gerfahrt *f* pilgrimage
Pilgerin ['pɪlgərɪn] *f* (-;-nen) pilgrim
pilgern ['pɪlgərn] *intr* (SEIN) go on a pilgrimage, make a pilgrimage
Pille ['pɪlə] *f* (-;-n) pill; **P. danach** morning-after pill
Pilot –in [pɪ'lot(ɪn)] §7 *mf* pilot
Pilz [pɪlts] *m* (-es;-e) fungus; mushroom
pimp(e)lig ['pɪmp(ə)lɪç] *adj* sickly, delicate; (*verweichlicht*) effeminate
Pinguin [pɪŋgu'in] *m* (-s;-e) penguin
Pinie ['pɪnjə] *f* (-;-n) umbrella pine
Pinke ['pɪŋkə] *f* (-;) (coll) dough
Pinkel ['pɪŋkəl] *m* (-s;-) (coll) dude
pinkeln ['pɪŋkəln] *intr* (sl) pee
Pinne ['pɪnə] *f* (-;-n) pin; tack; (naut) tiller
Pinscher ['pɪnʃər] *m* (-s;-) terrier
Pinsel ['pɪnzəl] *m* (-s;-) brush; (fig) simpleton, dope
Pinselei [pɪnzə'laɪ] *f* (-;-en) daubing; (*schlechte Malerei*) daub
pinseln ['pɪnzəln] *tr & intr* paint
Pinzette [pɪn'tsetə] *f* (-;-n) pair of tweezers, tweezers
Pionier [pi·o'nir] *m* (-s;-e) (fig) pioneer; (mil) engineer
Pionier'arbeit *f* (fig) spadework
Pionier'truppe *f* (mil) engineers
Pirat [pɪ'rat] *m* (-en;-en) pirate
Piraterie [pɪratə'ri] *f* (-;) piracy
Pirol [pɪ'rol] *m* (-s;-e) oriole
Pirsch [pɪrʃ] *f* (-;) hunt
pirschen ['pɪrʃən] *intr* stalk game
Pirsch'jagd *f* hunt
Pistazie [pɪs'tatsjə] *f* (-;-n) pistachio
Piste ['pɪstə] *f* (-;-n) beaten track; ski run; toboggan run; (aer) runway
Pistole [pɪs'tolə] *f* (-;-n) pistol
Pisto'lentasche *f* holster
pitsch(e)naß ['pɪtʃ(ə)'nas] *adj* soaked to the skin
pittoresk [pɪtɔ'resk] *adj* picturesque
Pkw., PKW *abbr* (**Personenkraftwagen**) passenger car
placieren [pla'sirən] *tr* place
placken ['plakən] *tr* pester, plague || *ref* toil, drudge
Plackerei [plakə'raɪ] *f* (-;) drudgery
plädieren [ple'dirən] *intr* plead
Plädoyer [pledwa'je] *n* (-s;-s) plea
Plage ['plagə] *f* (-;-n) trouble, bother; torment; (*Seuche*) plague
Pla'gegeist *m* pest, pain in the neck
plagen ['plagən] *tr* trouble, bother; (*mit Fragen, usw.*) pester
Plagiat [pla'gjat] *n* (-[e]s;-e) plagiarism
Pla'giator [pla'gjatɔr] *m* (-s;-giatoren [gia'torən]) plagiarist
Plakat [pla'kat] *n* (-[e]s;-e) poster
Plakat'träger *m* sandwich man
Plakette [pla'ketə] *f* (-;-n) plaque
plan [plan] *adj* plain, clear; (*eben*) level || **Plan** *m* (-[e]s;-e) plan; (*Stadt-*) map; (poet) battlefield; **auf den P. treten** appear on the scene
Plane ['planə] *f* (-;-n) tarpaulin

Plänemacher ['plenəmaxər] *m* (-s;-) schemer
planen ['planən] *tr* plan
Pläneschmied ['plenə/mit] *m* schemer
Planet [pla'net] *m* (-en;-en) planet
Planeta·rium [plane'tarjum] *n* (-s; -rien [rjən]) planetarium
Planeten– [planetən] *comb.fm.* planetary
Plane'tenbahn *f* planetary orbit
plan'gemäß *adv* according to plan
planieren [pla'nirən] *tr* level, grade
Planier'raupe *f* bulldozer
Planimetrie [planime'tri] *f* (-;) plane geometry
Planke ['plaŋkə] *f* (-;-n) plank
Plänkelei [pleŋkə'laɪ] *f* (-;-en) skirmish, skirmishing
plänkeln ['pleŋkəln] *intr* skirmish
plan'los *adj* aimless; indiscriminate
plan'mäßig *adj* systematic; fixed, regular; (*Verkehr*) scheduled || *adv* according to plan
planschen ['plan/ən] *intr* splash
Plantage [plan'taʒə] *f* (-;-n) plantation
Pla'nung *f* (-;) planning
plan'voll *adj* systematic, methodical
Plan'wagen *m* covered wagon
Plan'wirtschaft *f* planned economy
Plapperei [plapə'raɪ] *f* (-;) chatter
Plappermaul ['plapərmaul] *n* chatterbox
plappern ['plapərn] *intr* chatter; prattle
plärren ['plerən] *intr* (coll) bawl
Plas·ma ['plasma] *n* (-s;-men [mən]) plasma
Plastik ['plastɪk] *f* (-;-en) (*Bildwerk*) sculpture; (surg) plastic surgery || *n* (-s;) plastic
plastisch ['plastɪ/] *adj* plastic; (*anschaulich*) graphic
Platane [pla'tanə] *f* (-;-n) sycamore
Plateau [pla'to] *n* (-s;-s) plateau
Plateau'schuhe *pl* platform shoes
Platin [pla'tin] *n* (-s;) platinum
platin'blond *adj* platinum-blonde
Platoniker [pla'tonɪkər] *m* (-s;-) Platonist
platonisch [pla'toni/] *adj* Platonic
plätschern ['plet/ərn] *intr* splash; (*Bach*) babble
platt [plat] *adj* flat; (*nichtssagend*) trite; (coll) flabbergasted
Plättbrett ['pletbret] *n* ironing board
platt'deutsch *adj* Low German
Platte ['platə] *f* (-;-n) plate; top, surface; slab; (*Präsentierteller*) tray; (*Speise*) dish; (fig) pate, bean; (mus) record; (phot) plate
Plätteisen ['pletaɪzən] *n* flatiron
plätten ['pletən] *tr & intr* iron
Plat'tenjockey *m* disc jockey
Plat'tenspieler *m* record player
Plat'tenteller *m* turntable
Plat'tenwechsler *m* record changer
Platt'form *f* platform
Platt'fuß *m* (aut) flat; **Plattfüße** flat feet
platt'füßig *adj* flat-footed
Platt'heit *f* (-;-en) flatness; (fig) banality

plattieren [pla'tirən] *tr* plate
Plättwäsche ['pletvɛʃə] *f* ironing
Platz [plats] *m* (-es;ℓe) place; spot; locality; square; (*Sitz*) seat; (*Raum*) room, space; (*Stellung*) position; (sport) ground, field; (tennis) court; **auf die Plätze, fertig, los!** on your marks, get set, go! **fester P.** (mil) fortified position; **freier P.** open space; **immer auf dem Platze sein** be always on the alert; **nicht am P. sein** be out of place; be irrelevant; **P. da!** make way; **P. greifen** (fig) take effect, gain ground; **P. machen** make room; **P. nehmen** sit down; **seinen P. behaupten** stand one's ground
Platz'anweiser –in §6 *mf* usher
Plätzchen ['pletsçən] *n* (-s;-) little place; little square; (*Süßware*) candy wafer; (*Gebäck*) cookie, cracker
platzen ['platsən] *intr* (SEIN) burst; split; crack; (*Granate*) explode; (*Luftreifen*) blow out; (fig) come to nothing; **da platzte ihm endlich der Kragen** he finally blew his top; **der Wechsel ist geplatzt** the check bounced
Platz'karte *f* reserved-seat ticket
Platz'kommandant *m* commandant
Platz'konzert *n* open-air concert
Platz'patrone *f* blank cartridge; **mit Platzpatronen schießen** fire blanks
Platz'regen *m* cloudburst
Platz'runde *f* (aer) circuit of a field
Platz'wechsel *m* change of place; (sport) change in lineup
Platz'wette *f* betting on a horse to finish in first, second, or third place, bet to place
Plauderei [plaudə'raɪ] *f* (-;-en) chat; small talk
Plau'derer –in §6 *mf* talker, chatterer
plaudern ['plaudərn] *intr* chat, chatter; **aus der Schule p.** tell tales out of school
Plaudertasche ['plaudartaʃə] *f* chatterbox
Plauderton ['plaudərton] *m* conversational tone
plausibel [plau'zibəl] *adj* plausible
plauz [plauts] *interj* crash!
pleite ['plaɪtə] *adj* (coll) broke || *adv* **—p. gehen** go broke || **Pleite** *f* (-;) (coll) bankruptcy; **P. machen** (coll) go broke
Plenarsitzung [ple'narzıtsuŋ] *f* (-;-en) plenary session
Plenum ['plenum] *n* (-s;) plenary session
Pleuelstange ['plɔɪ-əlʃtaŋə] *f* (mach) connecting rod
Plexiglas ['pleksıglas] *n* (-es;) plexiglass
Plinse ['plınzə] *f* (-;-n) pancake; fritter
Plissee [plɪ'se] *n* (-s;-s) pleat
Plissee'rock *m* pleated skirt
plissieren [plɪ'siren] *tr* pleat
Plombe ['plɔmbə] *f* (-;-n) lead seal; (dent) filling
plombieren [plɔm'biren] *tr* seal with lead; (dent) fill

plötzlich ['plœtslıç] *adj* sudden || *adv* suddenly, all of a sudden
plump [plump] *adj* (*unförmig*) shapeless; (*schwerfällig*) heavy, slow; (*derb*) coarse; (*unbeholfen*) ungainly; (*taktlos*) tactless, blunt
plumps [plumps] *interj* plop! thump!
plumpsen ['plumpsən] *intr* (HABEN & SEIN) plop, flop
Plunder ['plundər] *m* (-s;) junk
plündern ['plyndərn] *tr & intr* plunder
Plural ['plural] *m* (-s;-e) plural
plus [plus] *adv* plus || **Plus** *n* (-;-) plus; (*Überschuß*) surplus; (*Vorteil*) advantage, edge
Plus'pol *m* (elec) positive pole
Plutokrat [pluto'krat] *m* (-en;-en) plutocrat
Plutonium [plu'tonjum] *n* (-s;) plutonium
pneumatisch [pnɔɪ'matıʃ] *adj* pneumatic
Pöbel ['pøbəl] *m* (-s;) mob, rabble
pö'belhaft *adj* rude, rowdy
Pö'belherrschaft *f* mob rule
pochen ['pɔxən] *tr* (min) crush || *intr* knock; (*Herz*) pound; **p. an** (*dat*) knock on; **p. auf** (*acc*) pound on; (fig) insist on
Pochmüle ['pɔxmylə] *f*, **Pochwerk** ['pɔxverk] *n* crushing mill
Pocke ['pɔkə] *f* (-;-n) pockmark; **Pocken** (pathol) smallpox
Pockennarbe [Pok'kennarbe] *f* pockmark
pockennarbig (pok'kennarbig) *adj* pockmarked
Podest [po'dest] *m & n* (-es;-e) pedestal; (*Treppenabsatz*) landing; podium
Po·dium ['podjum] *n* (-s;-dien [djən]) podium, platform
Poesie [po·e'zi] *f* (-;) poetry
Poet [po'et] *m* (-en;-en) poet
Poetik [po'etik] *f* (-;) poetics
poetisch [po'etıʃ] *adj* poetic
Pointe [po'ɛ̃tə] *f* (-;) point (*of joke*)
Pokal [po'kal] *m* (-s;-e) goblet; (sport) cup
Pökel ['pøkəl] *m* (-s;) brine
Pö'kelfleisch *n* salted meat
Pö'kelhering *m* pickled herring
pökeln ['pøkəln] *tr* pickle, salt
Poker ['pokər] *n* (-s;) poker
Pol [pol] *m* (-s;-e) pole
Polar- [polar] *comb.fm.* polar
polarisieren [poları'ziren] *tr* polarize
Polarität [poları'tet] *f* (-;-en) polarity
Polar'kreis *m* polar circle; **nördlicher P.** Arctic Circle; **südlicher P.** Antarctic Circle
Polar'licht *n* polar lights
Polar'stern *m* polestar
Polar'zone *f* frigid zone
Pole ['polə] *m* (-n;-n) Pole
Polemik [po'lemık] *f* (-;) polemics
polemisch [po'lemıʃ] *adj* polemical
Polen ['polən] *n* (-s;) Poland
Police [po'lisə] *f* (-;-n) (ins) policy
Polier [po'lir] *m* (-s;-e) foreman
polieren [po'liren] *tr* polish
Polin ['polın] *f* (-;-nen) Pole
Politik [polı'tik] *f* (-;-en) policy; (*Staatsangelegenheiten*) politics

Politiker –in [pɔ'lɪtɪkər(ɪn)] §6 *mf* politician

Politi·kum [pɔ'litikum] *n* (-s;-ka [ka]) political issue, political matter

politisch [pɔ'liti ʃ] *adj* political

politisieren [pɔlɪtɪ'zirən] *intr* talk politics

Politur [pɔlɪ'tur] *f* (-;-en) polish

Polizei [pɔlɪ'tsaɪ] *f* (-;) police

Polizei'aufgebot *n* posse

Polizei'aufsicht *f*—unter P. stehen have to report periodically to the police

Polizei'beamte §5 *m* police officer

Polizei'büro *n*, **Polizei'dienststelle** *f* police station

Polizei'knüppel *m* billy club

Polizei'kommissar *m* police commissioner

polizei'lich *adj* police

Polizei'präsident *m* chief of police

Polizei'revier *n* police station

Polizei'spion *m*, **Polizei'spitzel** *m* stoolpigeon

Polizei'streife *f* raid; police patrol

Polizei'streifenwagen *m* squad car

Polizei'stunde *f* closing time; curfew

Polizei'wache *f* police station

polizei'widrig *adj* against police regulations

Polizist [pɔlɪ'tsɪst] *m* (-en;-en) policeman

Polizistin [pɔlɪ'tsɪstɪn] *f* (-;-nen) policewoman

Polizze [pɔ'lɪtsə] *f* (-;-n) (Aust) insurance policy

Polka ['pɔlka] *f* (-;-s) polka

polnisch ['pɔlnɪʃ] *adj* Polish

Polo ['polo] *n* (-s;) (sport) polo

Polster ['pɔlstər] *m* & *n* (-s;-) cushion

Pol'stergarnitur *f* living-room suite

Pol'stermöbel *pl* upholstered furniture

polstern ['pɔlstərn] *tr* upholster

Pol'stersessel *m* upholstered chair

Pol'sterstuhl *m* padded chair

Pol'sterung *f* (-;) padding, stuffing

Polterabend ['pɔltərabənt] *m* eve of the wedding day

Poltergeist ['pɔltərgaɪst] *m* poltergeist

poltern ['pɔltərn] *intr* make noise; (*rumpeln*) rumble; (*zanken*) bluster

Polyp [pɔ'lyp] *m* (-en;-en) (pathol, zool) polyp; (*Polizist*) (sl) cop

Polytechni·kum [pɔly'teçnɪkum] *n* (-s; -ka [ka]) polytechnic institute

Pomade [pɔ'madə] *f* (-;-n) pomade

Pomeranze [pɔmə'rantsə] *f* (-;-n) bitter orange

Pommern ['pɔmərn] *n* (-s;) Pomerania

Pommes frites [pɔm'frɪt] *pl* French fries

Pomp [pɔmp] *m* (-es;) pomp

Pompadour ['pɔmpadur] *m* (-s;-e & -s) lady's string-drawn bag

pomp'haft, pompös [pɔm'pøs] *adj* pompous

pontifikal [pɔntifɪ'kal] *adj* pontifical

Pontifikat [pɔntifɪ'kat] *n* (-s;) pontificate

Pontius ['pɔntsjus] *m*—von P. zu Pilatus geschickt werden (coll) get the run-around

Pony ['pɔni] *m* (-s;-s) (*Damenfrisur*) pony ‖ *n* (-s;-s) (*Pferd*) pony

Popo [pɔ'po] *m* (-s;-s) (coll) backside

populär [pɔpu'ler] *adj* popular

Popularität [pɔpulari'tet] *f* (-;) popularity

Pore ['porə] *f* (-;-n) pore

porig ['porɪç] *adj* porous

Pornofilm ['pɔrnofɪlm] *m* (coll) smoker, pornographic movie

Pornoladen ['pɔrnoladən] *m* (coll) porn shop

Pornographie [pɔrnəgra'fi] *f* (-;) pornography

poros [pɔ'ros] *adj* porous

Porphyr ['pɔrfyr] *m* (-s;) porphyry

Porree ['pɔre] *m* (-s;-s) (bot) leek

Portal [pɔr'tal] *n* (-s;-e) portal

Portemonnaie [pɔrtmɔ'ne] *n* (-s;-s) wallet

Portier [pɔr'tje] *m* (-s;-s) doorman

Portion [pɔr'tsjon] *f* (-;-en) portion; (culin) serving, helping; halbe P. (coll) half pint; zwei Portionen Kaffee two cups of coffee

Por·to ['pɔrto] *n* (-s;-ti [ti]) postage

Por'togebühren *pl* postage

Por'tokasse *f* petty cash

Porträt [pɔr'tret] *n* (-s;-s), (-[e]s;-e) portrait

porträtieren [pɔrtre'tirən] *tr* portray

Portugal ['pɔrtugal] *n* (-s;) Portugal

Portugiese [pɔrtu'gizə] *m* (-n;-n), **Portugiesin** [pɔrtu'gizɪn] *f* (-;-nen) Portuguese

portugiesisch [pɔrtu'gizɪʃ] *adj* Portuguese

Porzellan [pɔrtsə'lan] *n* (-s;-e) porcelain; china; Meißener Porzellan Dresden china

Porzellan'brennerei *f* porcelain factory

Posament [pɔza'ment] *n* (-[e]s;-e) trimming, lace

Posaune [pɔ'zaunə] *f* (-;-n) trombone

posaunen [pɔ'zaunən] *intr* play the trombone

Pose ['pozə] *f* (-;-n) pose

posieren [po'zirən] *intr* pose

Position [pɔzi'tsjon] *f* (-;-en) position

Positions'lampe *f* **Positions'licht** *n* (aer, naut) navigation light

positiv [pɔzi'tif] *adj* (*bejahend*) affirmative; (*Kritik*) favorable; (elec, math, med) positive ‖ *adv* in the affirmative; (coll) for certain ‖ **Positiv** *m* (-s;-e) (gram) positive degree ‖ *n* (-s;-e) (mus) small organ; (phot) positive

Positur [pɔzi'tur] *f* (-;-en) posture, attitude; sich in P. setzen (or stellen or werfen) strike a pose

Posse ['pɔsə] *f* (-;-n) (theat) farce

Possen ['pɔsən] *m* (-s;-) trick, practical joke; j-m e-n P. spielen play a practical joke on s.o.; laß die P.! cut out the nonsense; P. treiben (or reißen) crack jokes

pos'senhaft *adj* farcical, comical

Possenreißer ['pɔsənraisər] *m* (-s;-) joker

Pos'senspiel *n* farce, burlesque

possierlich [pɔ'sirlɪç] *adj* funny

Post [pɔst] *f* (-;-en) mail; (*Postgebäude*) post office

postalisch [pɔs'talɪʃ] *adj* postal

Postament [pɔsta'ment] *n* (-[e]s;-e) pedestal
Post'amt *n* post office
Post'anweisung *f* money order
Post'auto *n* mail truck
Post'beamte *m* postal clerk
Post'beutel *m* mailbag
Post'bote *m* mailman
Post'direktor *m* postmaster
Posten ['pɔstən] *m* (-s;-) post; (*Stellung*) position; (acct) entry, item; (com) line, lot; (mil) guard, sentinel; **auf dem P. sein** (fig) be on guard; **auf verlorenem P. kämpfen** (coll) play a losing game; **nicht recht auf dem P. sein** be out of sorts; **P. aufstellen** post sentries; **P. stehen** stand guard; **ruhiger P.** (mil) soft job
Po'stenjäger –in §6 *mf* job hunter
Po'stenkette *f* line of outposts
Post'fach *n* post-office box
Post'gebühr *f* postage
posthum [pɔst'hum] *adj* posthumous
postieren [pɔs'tirən] *tr* post, place
Postille [pɔs'tilə] *f* (-;-n) devotional book
Post'karte *f* post card
Post'kasten *m* mail box
Post'kutsche *f* stagecoach
post'lagernd *adj* general-delivery ‖ *adv* general delivery
Postleitzahl ['pɔstlaɪttsal] *f* zip code
Post'minister *m* postmaster general
Post'nachnahme *f* (-;-n) C.O.D.
Post'sack *m* mailbag
Post'schalter *m* post-office window
Post'scheck *m* postal check
Postschließfach ['pɔst/lisfax] *n* post-office box
Postskript [pɔst'skrɪpt] *n* (-[e]s;-e) postscript
Post'stempel *m* postmark
Post'überweisung *f* money order
post'wendend *adj & adv* by return mail
Post'wertzeichen *n* postage stamp
Post'wesen *n* postal system
potent [po'tent] *adj* potent
Potential [potɛn'tsjal] *n* (-s;-e) potential
Potenz [po'tɛnts] *f* (-;-en) potency; (math) power; **dritte P.** (math) cube; **zweite P.** (math) square
potenzieren [potɛn'tsirən] *tr* raise to a higher power; (fig) intensify
Pottasche ['pɔta/ə] *f* (-;) potash
Pottwal ['pɔtval] *m* sperm whale
potz [pɔts] *interj*—**p. Blitz!** holy smoke!
potztau'send *interj* holy smoke!
poussieren [pu'sirən] *tr* (coll) flirt with; (coll) butter up ‖ *intr* flirt
Pracht [praxt] *f* (-;) splendor, magnificence
Pracht'ausgabe *f* deluxe edition
Pracht'exemplar *n* beauty, beaut
prächtig ['prɛçtɪç] *adj* splendid
Pracht'kerl *m* (coll) great guy
Pracht'stück *n* (coll) beauty, beaut
pracht'voll *adj* gorgeous
Pracht'zimmer *n* stateroom (*in palace*)
Prädikat [predɪ'kat] *n* (-[e]s;-e) title; (educ) mark, grade; (gram) predicate

Prädikatsnomen [predɪ'katsnomən] *n* (-s;-s) (gram) complement
Präfix [prɛ'fɪks] *n* (-es;-e) prefix
Prag [prak] *n* (-s;) Prague
Prägeanstalt ['prɛgə·anstalt] *f* mint
prägen ['prɛgən] *tr* stamp, coin ‖ *ref* —**das hat sich mir tief in das Gedächtnis geprägt** that made a lasting impression on me
Prä'gestempel *m* (mach) die
pragmatisch [prag'matɪʃ] *adj* pragmatic
prägnant [prɛ'gnant] *adj* pithy, terse
Prä'gung *f* (-;-en) coining, minting; (fig) coinage
prahlen ['pralən] *intr* (**mit**) brag (about); (**mit**) show off (with)
Prah'ler *m* (-s;-) braggart; show-off
Prahlerei [pralə'raɪ] *f* (-;-en) bragging, boasting; (*Prunken*) showing off
Prah'lerin *f* (-;-nen) braggart; show-off
prahlerisch ['pralərɪʃ] *adj* bragging
Prahlhans ['pralhans] *m* (-es;-̈e) braggart
Prahm [pram] *m* (-[e]s;-e) flat-bottomed lighter
Praktik ['praktɪk] *f* (-;-en) practice; (*Kniff*) trick
Praktikant –in [praktɪ'kant(ɪn)] §7 *mf* student in on-the-job training
Praktiker ['praktɪkər] *m* (-s;-) practical person
Prakti·kum ['praktɪkum] *n* (-s;-ka [ka]) practical training
Praktikus ['praktɪkus] *m* (-;-se) old hand
praktisch ['praktɪʃ] *adj* practical; **praktischer Arzt** general practitioner
praktizieren [praktɪ'tsirən] *tr* practice; **etw in die Tasche p.** manage to slip s.th. into the pocket
Prälat [prɛ'lat] *m* (-en;-en) prelate
Praline [pra'linə] *f* (-;-n) chocolate
prall [pral] *adj* (*straff*) tight; (*Brüste*) full; (*Backen*) chubby; (*Arme, Beine*) shapely; (*Sonne*) blazing ‖ **Prall** *m* (-[e]s;-e) impact; collision
prallen ['pralən] *intr* (SEIN) bounce, rebound; (*Sonne*) beat down
Prämie ['prɛmjə] *f* (-;-n) award, prize; premium; bonus
prämieren [prɛmɪ'irən] *tr* award a prize to
prangen ['praŋən] *intr* shine; look beautiful
Pranger ['praŋər] *m* (-s;-) pillory
Pranke ['praŋkə] *f* (-;-n) claw
pränumerando [prenumə'rando] *adv* in advance, beforehand
Präparat [prepa'rat] *n* (-[e]s;-e) preparation
präparieren [prepa'rirən] *tr* prepare
Präposition [prepozɪ'tsjon] *f* (-;-en) preposition
Prä·rie [prɛ'ri] *f* (-;-rien ['ri·ən]) prairie
Präsens ['prezɛns] *n* (-; **Präsentia** [prɛ'zɛntsi·a]) (gram) present
präsent [prɛ'zɛnt] *adj* present ‖ **Präsent** *n* (-s;-e) present, gift
präsentieren [prezɛn'tirən] *tr* present
Präsentier'teller *m* tray

Präsenzstärke [prɛ'zɛnts/tɛrkə] f effective strength

Präservativ [prezɛrva'tif] m (-s;-e) prophylactic, condom

Präsident [prɛzɪ'dɛnt] m (-en;-en) president

Präsidenten– [prɛzɪdɛntən] comb.fm. presidential

Präsident'schaft f (-;-en) presidency

präsidieren [prɛzɪ'dirən] intr preside

Präsi·dium [prɛ'zidjʊm] n (-s;-dien [djən]) presidency; chairmanship

prasseln ['prasəln] intr crackle; (Regen) patter

prassen ['prasən] intr lead a dissipated life

Prasserei [prasə'raɪ] f (-;) luxurious living, high life

Prätendent [pretɛn'dɛnt] m (-en;-en) (auf acc) pretender (to)

Pra·xis ['praksɪs] f (-;-xen [ksən]) practice; experience; doctor's office; law office; (jur) clientele; (med) patients

Präzedenzfall [pretsɛ'dɛntsfal] m precedent

präzis [prɛ'tsis] adj precise

Präzision [pretsi'zjon] f (-;) precision

predigen ['predɪgən] tr & intr preach

Prediger ['predɪgər] m (-s;-) preacher

Predigt ['predɪçt] f (-;-en) sermon

Preis [praɪs] m (-es;-e) price, rate, cost; (poet) praise, glory; äußerster P. (coll) rock-bottom price; um jeden P. (fig) at all costs; um keinen P. (fig) on no account; zum P. von at the rate of

Preis'aufgabe f project in a competition

Preis'aufschlag m extra charge

Preis'ausschreiben n competition

Preisdrückerei ['praɪsdrʏkərəɪ] f (-; -en) price cutting

Preiselbeere ['praɪzəlberə] f cranberry

preisen ['praɪzən] tr praise

Preis'ermäßigung f price reduction

Preis'frage f question in a competition; question of price (coll) sixty-four-dollar question

Preis'gabe f abandonment, surrender

preis'geben §80 tr abandon, surrender; (Geheimnis) betray; j-n dem Spott p. hold s.o. up to ridicule

preisgekrönt ['praɪsgəkrønt] adj prize-winning

Preis'gericht n jury

Preis'grenze f price limit; obere P. ceiling; untere P. minimum price

preis'günstig adj worth the money

Preis'lage f price range

Preis'niveau n price level

Preis'notierung f rate of exchange

Preis'richter m judge (in competition)

Preis'schießen n shooting competition

Preis'schild n price tag

Preis'schlager m bargain price

Preis'schrift f prize-winning essay

Preis'stopp m price freezing

Preis'sturz m drop in prices

Preis'träger –in §6 mf prize winner

Preistreiberei [praɪstraɪbə'raɪ] f (-;) price rigging

Preis'überwachung f price control

Preis'verzeichnis n price list

preis'wert, preis'würdig adj worth the money, reasonable

Preis'zuschlag m markup

prekär [pre'ker] adj precarious

Prellbock ['prɛlbɔk] m (rr) buffer

prellen ['prɛlən] tr bump; bounce; toss up· (in a blanket); (um) cheat (out of) || ref–sich [dat] den Arm p. bruise one's arm

Prell'er m (-s;-) bump; ricochet; bilker, cheat

Prellerei [prɛlə'raɪ] f (-;-en) (act of) cheating

Prell'schuß m ricochet

Prell'stein m curbstone

Prell'ung f (-;-en) bruise

Premier [prə'mje] m (-s;-s) premier

Premiere [prə'mjerə] f (-;-n) (theat) premiere, first night, opening

Premier'minister m prime minister

Presbyterianer –in [prɛsbytə'rjanər (ɪn)] §6 mf Presbyterian

presbyterianisch [prɛsbytə'rjanɪʃ] adj Presbyterian

preschen ['preʃən] intr charge

pressant [prɛ'sant] adj pressing

Presse ['presə] f (-;-n) (& journ) press; (educ) cram class

Pres'seagentur f press agency

Pres'seamt n public-relations office

Pres'seausweis m press card

Pres'sebericht m press report

Pres'sechef m press secretary

Pres'sekonferenz f press conference

Pres'semeldung f news item

Pres'sestelle f public-relations office

Pres'severtreter m reporter; public-relations officer

Preßkohle ['preskolə] f briquette

Preßluft ['presluft] f compressed air

Preß'lufthammer m jackhammer

Preuße ['prɔɪsə] m (-n;-n) Prussian

Preußen ['prɔɪsən] n (-s;) Prussia

Preußin ['prɔɪsɪn] f (-;-nen) Prussian

preußisch ['prɔɪsɪʃ] adj Prussian

prickeln ['prɪkəln] intr tingle

Priem [prim] m (-[e]s;-e) plug (of tobacco)

priemen ['primən] intr chew tobacco

pries [pris] pret of preisen

Priester ['pristər] m (-s;-) priest

Prie'steramt n priesthood

Priesterin ['pristərɪn] f (-;-nen) priestess

prie'sterlich adj priestly

Prie'sterrock m cassock

Priestertum ['pristərtum] n (-s;) priesthood

Prie'sterweihe f (eccl) ordination

prima ['prima] invar adj first-class; terrific, swell

primär [prɪ'mer] adj primary || adv primarily

Primat [prɪ'mat] m & n (-[e]s;-e) primacy, priority || m (-en;-en) primate

Primel ['priməl] f (-;-n) primrose

primitiv [prɪmɪ'tif] adj primitive

Prinz [prɪnts] m (-en;-en) prince

Prinzessin [prɪn'tsesɪn] f (-;-nen) princess

Prinz'gemahl m prince consort

Prin·zip [prɪn'tsip] n (-s;-zipien ['tsipjən]) principle
prinzipiell [prɪntsɪ'pjel] adj in principle, fundamentally
Prinzi'pienreiter m (coll) pedant
prinz'lich adj princely
Pri·or ['pri·ɔr] m (-s;-oren ['ɔrən]) (eccl) prior
Priorität [prɪ·ɔrɪ'tet] f (-;-en) priority
Prise ['prizə] f (-;-n) pinch (of salt, etc.); (nav) prize
Pris·ma ['prɪsma] n (-s;-men [men]) prism
privat [prɪ'vat] adj private; personal
Privat'adresse f, **Privat'anschrift** f home address
Privat'dozent –in §7 mf non-salaried university lecturer
Privat'druck m private printing
Privat'eigentum n private property
Privat'gespräch n (telp) personal call
privatim [prɪ'vatɪm] adv privately; confidentially
privatisieren [prɪvatɪ'zirən] intr be financially independent
Privat'lehrer –in §6 mf tutor
Privat'recht n civil law
privat'rechtlich adj (jur) civil
Privi·leg [prɪvɪ'lek] n (-[e]s;-legien ['legjən]) privilege
privilegiert [prɪvɪle'girt] adj privileged
probat [pro'bat] adj tried, tested
Probe ['probə] f (-;-n) (Versuch) trial, experiment; (Prüfung) test; (Muster) sample; (Beweis) proof; (theat) rehearsal; **auf die P. stellen** put to the test; **auf (or zur) P.** on approval
Pro'beabdruck m, **Pro'beabzug** m (typ) proof
Pro'bebild n (phot) proof
Pro'bebogen m proof sheet
Pro'bedruck m (typ) proof
Pro'befahrt f road test, trial run
Pro'beflug m test flight
Pro'belauf m trial run; dry run
Pro'besendung f sample sent on approval
Pro'bestück n sample, specimen
pro'beweise adv on trial; on approval
Pro'bezeit f probation period
probieren [pro'birən] tr try out, test; try, taste; (metal) assay
Probier'glas n test tube
Probier'stein m touch-stone
Problem [pro'blem] n (-s;-e) problem
Produkt [pro'dʊkt] n (-[e]s;-e) product; (des Bodens) produce
Produktion [prodʊk'tsjon] f (-;-en) production; (indust) output
produktiv [prodʊk'tif] adj productive
Produzent [produ'tsɛnt] m (-en;-en) (& cin) producer
produzieren [produ'tsirən] tr produce ‖ ref perform; (pej) show off
profan [pro'fan] adj profane
profanieren [profa'nirən] tr profane
Profession [profe'sjon] f (-;-en) profession
Professional [profesjə'nal] m (-s;-e) (sport) professional
professionell [profesjə'nel] adj professional
Profes·sor [pro'fesɔr] m (-s;-soren

['sorən]), **Professorin** [profe'sorɪn] f (-;-nen) professor; **außerordentlicher P.** associate professor; **ordentlicher P.** full professor
Professur [profe'sur] f (-;-en) professorship
Profi ['profi] m (-s;-s) (coll) pro
Profil [pro'fil] n (-s;-e) profile; (aut) tread; **im P.** in profile
profiliert [profɪ'lirt] adj outstanding
Profit [pro'fit] m (-[e]s;-e) profit
profitabel [profɪ'tabəl] adj profitable
Profit'gier f profiteering
profitieren [profɪ'tirən] tr & intr profit
Prognose [pro'gnozə] f (-;-n) (med) prognosis; (meteor) forecast
Programm [pro'gram] n (-s;-e) program; (pol) platform
programmieren [progra'mirən] tr (data proc) program
Projekt [pro'jɛkt] n (-[e]s;-e) project
Projektil [projɛk'til] n (-s;-e) projectile
Projektion [projɛk'tsjon] f (-;-en) projection
Projektions'apparat m, **Projektions'gerät** n, **Projek·tor** [pro'jɛktɔr] m (-s;-toren ['torən]) projector
projizieren [proji'tsirən] tr project
proklamieren [prokla'mirən] tr proclaim
Prokura [pro'kura] f (-;) power of attorney; **per P.** by proxy
Prolet [pro'let] m (-en;-en) (pej) cad
Proletariat [proleta'rjat] n (-[e]s;-e) proletariat
Proletarier –in [prole'tarjər(ɪn)] §6 mf proletarian
proletarisch [prole'tarɪʃ] adj proletarian
Prolog [pro'lok] m (-[e]s;-e) prologue
prolongieren [proloŋ'girən] tr extend; (cin) hold over
Promenade [promə'nadə] f (-;-n) avenue; (Spaziergang) promenade
promenieren [promə'nirən] intr stroll
prominent [promɪ'nɛnt] adj prominent
Promotion [promo'tsjon] f (-;-en) awarding of the doctor's degree
promovieren [promo'virən] intr attain a doctor's degree
prompt [prompt] adj prompt, quick
Prono·men [pro'nomən] n (-s;-mina [mɪna]) pronoun
Propaganda [propa'ganda] f (-;) propaganda
propagieren [propa'girən] tr propagate
Propeller [pro'pelər] m (-s;-) propeller
Prophet [pro'fet] m (-en;-en) prophet
Prophetin [pro'fetɪn] f (-;-nen) prophetess
prophetisch [pro'fetɪʃ] adj prophetic
prophezeien [profe'tsai·ən] tr prophesy
Prophezei'ung f (-;-en) prophecy
Proportion [propɔr'tsjon] f (-;-en) proportion
proportional [propɔrtsjo'nal] adj proportional
proportioniert [propɔrtsjo'nirt] adj proportionate
Propst [propst] m (-es;-̈e) provost

Prosa ['proza] f (-;) prose
prosaisch [pro'za·ɪʃ] adj prosaic
prosit ['prozɪt] interj to your health!
|| **Prosit** n (-s;-s) toast
Prospekt [pro'spɛkt] m (-[e]s;-e)
prospect, view; brochure, folder
prostituieren [prɔstɪtu'irən] tr prostitute
Prostituierte [prɔstɪtu'irtə] §5 f prostitute
protegieren [prote'girən] tr patronize;
(schützen) protect
Protektion [protek'tsjon] f (-;) pull,
connections
Protest [pro'tɛst] m (-es;-e) protest
Protestant -in [protes'tant(ɪn)] §7 mf
Protestant
protestantisch [protes'tantɪʃ] adj Protestant
protestieren [protes'tirən] tr & intr
protest
Protokoll [proto'kɔl] n (-s;-e) protocol; record, minutes; **P. führen** take
the minutes; **zu P. nehmen** take down
Protokoll'führer -in §6 mf recording
secretary; (jur) clerk
protokollieren [protoko'lirən] tr record
Pro·ton ['proton] n (-s;-tonen
['tonən]) (phys) proton
Protz [prɔts] m (-en;-en) show-off
protzen ['prɔtsən] intr show off
protz'enhaft, protzig ['prɔtsɪç] adj
show-offish
Prozedur [protse'dur] f (-;-en) procedure; (jur) proceeding
Prozent [pro'tsɛnt] n (-[e]s;-e) percent
Prozent'satz m percentage
Pro·zeß [pro'tsɛs] m (-zesses;-zesse)
process; (jur) case, suit; (jur) proceedings; **e-n P. anstrengen** (or
führen) gegen sue; **kurzen P. machen
mit** make short work of
Prozeß'akten pl (jur) record
Prozeß'führer -in §6 mf litigant
prozessieren [protse'sirən] intr go to
court; **p. gegen** sue
Prozession [protse'sjon] f (-;-en) procession
Prozeß'kosten pl (jur) court costs
Prozeß'vollmacht f power of attorney
prüde ['prydə] adj prudish
prüfen ['pryfən] tr test; (nachprüfen)
check, verify; (untersuchen) examine;
(kosten) taste; (acct) audit
Prüfer -in §6 mf examiner; (acct) auditor
Prüfling ['pryflɪŋ] m (-s;-e) examinee
Prüfstein ['pryfʃtaɪn] m touchstone
Prü·fung f (-;-en) test; examination;
check, verification; (acct) audit; (jur)
review
Prü'fungsarbeit f test paper
Prü'fungsausschuß m, **Prü'fungskom-
mission** f examining board
Prügel ['prygəl] m (-s;-) stick, cudgel;
Prügel pl whipping
Prügelei [prygə'laɪ] f (-;-en) brawl;
free-for-all
Prü'gelknabe m whipping boy, scape-
goat
prügeln ['prygəln] tr beat, whip || ref
have a fight

Prü'gelstrafe f corporal punishment
Prunk [pruŋk] m (-[e]s;) pomp, show
prunken ['pruŋkən] intr show off
Prunk'gemach n stateroom
prunk'haft adj showy
Prunk'sucht f ostentatiousness
prunk'süchtig adj ostentatious
prunk'voll adj gorgeous
Prunk'zimmer n stateroom
prusten ['prustən] intr snort
Psalm [psalm] m (-s;-en) psalm
Psalter ['psaltər] m (-s;-) psalter
Pseudonym [psɔɪdo'nym] n (-s;-e)
pseudonym
Psychiater (psyçɪ'atər) m (-s;-) psychiatrist
Psychiatrie [psyçɪ·a'tri] f (-;) psychiatry
psychiatrisch [psyçɪ'atrɪʃ] adj psychi-
atric
psychisch ['psyçɪʃ] adj psychic(al)
Psychoanalyse [psyço·ana'lyzə] f (-;)
psychoanalysis
Psychoanalytiker -in [psyço·ana'lytɪ-
kər(ɪn)] §6 mf psychoanalyst
Psychologe [psyço'logə] m (-n;-n) psychologist
Psychologie [psyçolo'gi] f (-;) psychology
Psychologin [psyço'login] f (-;-nen)
psychologist
psychologisch [psyço'logɪʃ] adj psy-
chological
Psychopath -in [psyço'pat(ɪn)] §7 mf
psychopath
Psychose [psy'çozə] f (-;-n) psychosis
Psychotherapie [psyçotera'pi] f (-;)
psychotherapy
Pubertät [puber'tet] f (-;) puberty
publik [pub'lik] adj public
Publi·kum ['publikum] n (-s;-ka
[ka]) public; (theat) audience
publizieren [publɪ'tsirən] tr publish
Publizist -in [publɪ'tsɪst(ɪn)] §7 mf
(journ) writer on public affairs;
teacher or student of journalism
Publizität [publɪtsɪ'tet] f (-;) publicity
Pudel ['pudəl] m (-s;) poodle; des
Pudels Kern (fig) gist of the matter
Pu'delmütze f fur cap; woolen cap
pu'delnaß adj (coll) soaking wet
Puder ['pudər] m (-s;) powder
Pu'derdose f powder box; compact
Pu'derquaste f powder puff
Pu'derzucker m powdered sugar
Puff [puf] m (-[e]s;ᵉe & -e) (Stoß)
poke; (Knall) pop; (Bausch) puff;
|| m (-s;-s) (coll) brothel
Puff'ärmel m puffed sleeve
puffen ['pufən] tr poke; (coll) prod ||
intr puff; (knallen) pop, bang away
Puffer ['pufər] m (-s;-) buffer; pop-
gun; (culin) potato pancake
Puf'ferbatterie f booster battery
Puf'ferstaat m buffer state
Puff'mais m popcorn
Puff'reis m (-es) puffed rice
Pulli ['puli] m (-s;-s) (coll) sweater
Pullover [pu'lovər] m (-s;-) sweater
Puls [puls] m (-es;-e) pulse
Puls'ader f artery
pulsieren [pul'zirən] intr pulsate
Puls'schlag m pulse beat

Pult [pʊlt] *n* (-[e]s;-e) desk
Pulver ['pʊlfər] *n* (-s;-) powder; (*Schieß*-) gunpowder; (coll) dough
pul'verig *adj* powdery
pulverisieren [pʊlfərɪ'zirən] *tr* pulverize
Pul'verschnee *m* powdery snow
Pummel ['pʊməl] *m* (-s;-) butterball (*chubby child*)
pummelig ['pʊməlɪç] *adj* (coll) chubby
Pump [pʊmp] *m*—**auf P.** (coll) on tick
Pumpe ['pʊmpə] *f* (-;-n) pump
pumpen ['pʊmpən] *tr* pump; (coll) give on tick; (coll) get on tick ‖ *intr* pump
Pum'penschwengel *m* pump handle
Pumpernickel ['pʊmpərnɪkəl] *m* (-s; -) pumpernickel
Pump'hosen *f* pair of knickerbockers
Punkt [pʊŋkt] *m* (-[e]s;-e) point; (*Tüpfelchen*) dot; (*Stelle*) spot; (*Einzelheit*) item; (gram) period; **der tote P.** a deadlock; **dunkler P.** (fig) skeleton in the closet; **nach Punkten siegen** win on points; **P. sechs Uhr** at six o'clock sharp; **springender P.** crux; **strittiger P.** point at issue; **wunder P.** (fig) sore spot
Punkt'gleichheit *f* (sport) tie
punktieren [pʊŋk'tirən] *tr* dot, stipple; **punktierte Linie** dotted line
pünktlich ['pʏŋktlɪç] *adj* punctual
Punkt'sieg *m* (box) winning on points
punktum ['pʊŋktʊm] *interj*—**und damit p.!** and that's it!; period!
Punkt'zahl *f* (sport) score
Punsch [pʊnʃ] *m* (-es;) punch (*drink*)
Punze ['pʊntsə] *f* (-;-n) punch, stamp
punzen ['pʊntsən] *tr* punch, stamp
Pupille [pu'pɪlə] *f* (-;-n) (anat) pupil
Puppe ['pʊpə] *f* (-;-n) doll; puppet; (*Schneider*-) dummy; (zool) pupa
Pup'penspiel *n* puppet show
Pup'penwagen *m* doll carriage
pur [pʊr] *adj* pure, sheer

Püree [pʏ're] *n* (-s;-s) mashed potatoes; puree
purgieren [pʊr'girən] *tr* & *intr* purge
Purpur ['pʊrpʊr] *m* (-s;) purple
pur'purfarben *adj* purple
purpurn [pʊrpʊrn] *adj* purple
Purzelbaum ['pʊrtsəlbaum] *m* somersault; **e-en P. schlagen** do a somersault
purzeln ['pʊrtsəln] *intr* (SEIN) tumble
pusselig ['pʊsəlɪç] *adj* fussy
Puste ['pʊstə] *f* (-;) (coll) breath
Pustel ['pʊstəl] *f* (-;-n) pustule
pusten ['pʊstən] *tr*—**ich puste dir was!** (coll) you may whistle for it! ‖ *intr* puff, pant
Pu'sterohr *n* peashooter
Pute ['pʊtə] *f* (-;-n) turkey (hen)
Puter ['pʊtər] *m* (-s;-) turkey (cock)
Putsch [pʊtʃ] *m* (-es;-e) putsch, uprising
Putz [pʊts] *m* (-es;) finery; trimming; ornaments; plaster
putzen ['pʊtsən] *tr* (*reinigen*) clean; (*Schuhe*) polish; (*Zähne*) brush; (*Person*) dress; (*schmücken*) adorn ‖ *ref* dress; **sich** [*dat*] **die Nase p.** blow one's nose
Put'zer *m* (-s;-) cleaner; (mil) orderly
Putzerei [pʊtsə'raɪ] *f* (-;-s) (Aust) dry cleaner's; (Aust) laundry
Putz'frau *f* cleaning woman
putzig ['pʊtsɪç] *adj* funny
Putz'lappen *m* cleaning cloth
Putz'mittel *n* cleaning agent
Putz'wolle *f* cotton waste
Putz'zeug *n* cleaning things
Pygmäe [pʏg'me·ə] *m* (-n;-n) pygmy
Pyjama [pɪ'dʒama] *m* (-s;-s) pajamas
Pyramide [pʏra'midə] *f* (-;-n) pyramid; (mil) stack
Pyrenäen [pʏra'ne·ən] *pl* Pyrenees
Pyrotechnik [pʏro'tɛçnɪk] *f* (-;) pyrotechnics
Pythonschlange ['pyton/laŋə] *f* python

Q

Q, q [ku] *invar n* Q, q
quabbelig ['kvabəlɪç] *adj* flabby; quivering, jelly-like
quabbeln ['kvabəln] *intr* quiver
Quackelei [kvakə'laɪ] *f* (-;-en) silly talk; (*unnützes Zeug*) rubbish
Quacksalber ['kvakzalbər] *m* (-s;-) quack
Quader ['kvadər] *m* (-s;-) ashlar
Quadrant [kva'drant] *m* (-en;-en) quadrant
Quadrat [kva'drat] *n* (-[e]s;-e) square; **e-e Zahl ins Q. erheben** square a number; **zwei Fuß im Q.** two feet square
quadratisch [kva'dratɪʃ] *adj* square; quadratic
Quadrat'meter *n* square meter
Quadrat'wurzel *f* square root
quadrieren [kva'drirən] *tr* square

quaken ['kvakən] *intr* (*Ente*) quack; (*Frosch*) croak
quäken ['kvekən] *intr* bawl
Qual [kval] *f* (-;-en) torment, agony
quälen ['kvelən] *tr* torment; worry; (*ständig bedrängen*) pester ‖ *ref*—**sich mit e-r Arbeit q.** slave at a job; **sich umsonst q.** labor in vain; **sich zu Tode q.** worry oneself to death
Quälgeist ['kvelgaɪst] *m* pest
Qualifikation [kvalifɪka'tsjon] *f* (-; -en) qualification
qualifizieren [kvalifɪ'tsirən] *tr* & *ref* (zu) qualify (for)
Qualität [kvalɪ'tɛt] *f* (-;-en) quality
Qualitäts– *comb.fm.* high-quality, highgrade, quality
Qualle ['kvalə] *f* (-;-n) jellyfish
Qualm [kvalm] *m* (-[e]s;) smoke; vapor

qualmen ['kvalmən] *tr* smoke || *intr* smoke; (coll) smoke like a chimney
qual'mig *adj* smoky
qual'voll *adj* agonizing
Quantentheorie ['kvantənte·əri] *f* quantum theory
Quantität [kvantɪ'tet] *f* (-;-en) quantity
Quan·tum ['kvantum] *n* (-s;-ten [tən]) quantum; quantity; (*Anteil*) portion
Quappe ['kvapə] *f* (-;-n) tadpole
Quarantäne [kvaran'tɛnə] *f* (-;-n) quarantine
Quark [kvark] *m* (-[e]s;) curds; cottage cheese; (fig) nonsense
Quark'käse *m* cottage cheese
quarren ['kvarən] *intr* (*Frosch*) croak; (fig) groan
Quart [kvart] *n* (-s;-e) quart; quarto || *f* (-;-en) (mus) fourth
Quartal [kvar'tal] *n* (-s;-e) quarter (*of a year*)
Quartals'abrechnung *f* (fin) quarterly statement
Quartals'säufer *m* periodic drunkard
Quart'band *m* (-[e]s;⸗e) quarto volume
Quarte ['kvartə] *f* (-;-n) (mus) fourth
Quartett [kvar'tet] *n* (-[e]s;-e) quartet
Quart'format *n* quarto
Quartier [kvar'tir] *n* (-s;-e) (*Stadtviertel*) quarter; (*Unterkunft*) quarters; (mil) quarters, billet
Quartier'meister *m* (mil) quartermaster
Quarz [kvarts] *m* (-es;-e) quartz
quasseln ['kvasəln] *tr* (coll) talk || *intr* talk nonsense
Quast [kvast] *m* (-[e]s;-e) brush
Quaste ['kvastə] *f* (-;-n) tassel
Quatsch [kvat∫] *m* (-es;) (coll) baloney
quatschen ['kvat∫ən] *intr* chatter; talk nonsense; (*durch Schlamm*) slog
Quecksilber ['kvekzɪlbər] *n* mercury
queck'silbrig *adj* fidgety
Quell [kvɛl] *m* (-[e]s;-e) (poet) var of Quelle
Quelle ['kvɛlə] *f* (-;-n) fountainhead; source; spring
quellen ['kvɛlən] §119 *tr* cause to swell; soak || *intr* (SEIN) spring, gush; (*Tränen*) well up; (*anschwellen*) swell; **ihm quollen die Augen fast aus dem Kopf** his eyes almost popped out
Quel'lenangabe *f* citation; bibliography
quel'lenmäßig *adj* according to the best authorities, authentic
Quel'lenmaterial *n* source material
Quel'lenstudium *n* original research

Quell'fluß *m* source
Quell'gebiet *n* headwaters
Quell'wasser *n* spring water
Quengelei [kvɛŋə'laɪ] *f* (-;-en) nagging
quengeln ['kvɛŋəln] *intr* nag
quer [kver] *adj* cross, transverse || *adv* crosswise; **q. über** (*acc*) across
Quer'balken *m* crossbeam
Quere ['kverə] *f* (-;) diagonal direction; **j-m in die Q. kommen** run across s.o.; (fig) disturb s.o.
queren ['kverən] *tr* traverse, cross
querfeldein' *adv* cross-country
Quer'kopf *m* contrary person
quer'köpfig *adj* contrary
Quer'pfeife *f* (mus) fife
Quer'ruder *n* (aer) aileron
Quer'schiff *n* (archit) transept
Quer'schläger *m* ricochet
Quer'schnitt *m* cross section
Quer'treiber *m* schemer, plotter
querü'ber *adv* straight across
Querulant ·in [kveru'lant(ɪn)] §7 *mf* grumbler, grouch
Quetsche ['kvet∫ə] *f* (-;-n) squeezer; (pej) joint
quetschen ['kvet∫ən] *tr* squeeze, pinch; bruise; (*zerquetschen*) crush, mash
Quetsch'kartoffeln *pl* mashed potatoes
Quet'schung *f* (-;-en) bruise, contusion
Quetsch'wunde *f* bruise
quick [kvɪk] *adj* brisk, lively
quick'lebendig *adj* (coll) very lively
quieken ['kvikən] *intr* squeal, squeak
quietschen ['kvit∫ən] *intr* (*Tür*) creak; (*Ferkel*) squeal; (*Bremsen*) screech
Quintessenz ['kvɪntesents] *f* (-;) quintessence
Quintett [kvɪn'tet] *n* (-[e]s;-e) quintet
Quirl [kvɪrl] *m* (-[e]s;-e) (fig) fidgeter; (culin) whisk, mixer
quirlen ['kvɪrlən] *tr* beat, mix
quitt [kvɪt] *adj* even, square
Quitte ['kvɪtə] *f* (-;-n) quince
quittieren [kvɪ'tirən] *tr* give a receipt for; (*aufgeben*) quit
Quit'tung *f* (-;-en) receipt
Quiz [kvɪs] *n* (-;-) quiz
quoll [kvɔl] *pret* of quellen
Quotation [kvota'tsjon] *f* (-;-en) (st. exch.) quotation
Quote ['kvotə] *f* (-;-en) quota
Quotient [kvo'tsjent] *m* (-en;-en) quotient
quotieren [kvo'tirən] *tr* quote

R

R, r [er] *invar* *n* R, r
Rabatt [ra'bat] *m* (-[e]s;-e) reduction, discount
Rabatt'marke *f* trading stamp
Rabatz [ra'bats] *m*—**R. machen** (coll) raise Cain
Rab·bi ['rabi] *m* (-[s];-s & -binen** ['binən]), **Rabbiner** [ra'binər] *m* (-s;-) rabbi
Rabe ['rabə] *m* (-n;-n) raven; **weißer R.** (fig) rare bird
Ra'benaas *n* (coll) beast
Ra'benmutter *f* hard-hearted mother
ra'benschwarz' *adj* jet-black

rabiat [ra'bjɑt] *adj* rabid, raving
Rache ['raxə] *f* (-;) revenge
Rachen ['raxən] *m* (-s;-) throat; mouth; (fig) jaws
rächen ['reçən] *tr* avenge || *ref* (an *dat*) avenge oneself (on)
Ra'chenhöhle *f* pharynx
Ra'chenkatarrh *m* sore throat
Rä'cher –in §6 *mf* avenger
Rachgier ['raxgir] *f* revengefulness
rach'gierig, rach'süchtig *adj* vengeful
Rad [rɑt] *n* (-[e]s;̈er) wheel; bike; **ein Rad schlagen** turn a cartwheel; (*Pfau*) fan the tail
Radar ['rɑdɑr], [ra'dɑr] *n* (-s;) radar
Ra'dargerät *n* radar
Ra'darschirm *m* radarscope
Radau [ra'dau] *m* (-s;-) (coll) row
Radau'macher *m* rowdy
Rädchen ['retçən] *n* (-s;-) little wheel
Rad'dampfer *m* river boat
radebrechen ['rɑdəbreçən] §64 *tr* murder (*a language*)
radeln ['rɑdəln] *intr* (SEIN) (coll) ride a bike
Rädelsführer ['redəlsfyrər] *m* ringleader
rädern ['redərn] *tr* torture; **wie gerädert sein** (coll) be bushed
Räderwerk ['redərverk] *n* gears; (fig) clockwork
rad'fahren §71 *intr* (SEIN) ride a bicycle
radieren [ra'dirən] *tr* erase; etch
Radie'rer *m* (-s;-) eraser; etcher
Radier'gummi *m* eraser
Radier'kunst *f* art of etching
Radier'messer *n* scraper, eraser
Radie'rung *f* (-;-en) erasure; etching
Radieschen [ra'disçən] *n* (-s;-) radish
radikal [radɪ'kɑl] *adj* radical || **Radikale** §5 *mf* radical, extremist
Radio ['rɑdjo] *n* (-s;-s) radio; **im R.** on the radio; **R. hören** listen to the radio
Ra'dioamateur *m* (rad) ham
Ra'dioapparat *m*, **Ra'diogerät** *n* radio set
Radiologe [radjo'logə] *m* (-n;-n) radiologist
Radiologie [radjolo'gi] *f* (-;) radiology
Ra'dioröhre *f* radio tube
Ra'diosender *m* radio transmitter
Radium ['rɑdjum] *n* (-s;) radium
Ra·dius ['rɑdjus] *m* (-;-dien [djən]) radius
Rad'kappe *f* hubcap
Rad'kranz *m* rim
Radler –in ['rɑdlər(ɪn)] §6 *mf* cyclist
Rad'nabe *f* hub
Rad'rennen *n* bicycle race
–rädrig [redrɪç] *comb.fm.* –wheeled
rad'schlagen §132 *intr* turn a cartwheel
Rad'spur *f* rut, track
Rad'stand *m* wheelbase
Rad'zahn *m* cog
raffen ['rafən] *tr* snatch up, gather up; (sew) take up
Raffgier ['rafgir] *f* rapacity
raffgierig ['rafgirɪç] *adj* rapacious
Raffine·rie [rafɪnə'ri] *f* (-;-rien ['ri-ən]) refinery
raffinieren [rafɪ'nirən] *tr* refine

raffiniert [rafɪ'nirt] *adj* refined; (fig) shrewd, cunning
Raffzahn ['raftsɑn] *m* canine tooth
ragen ['rɑgən] *intr* tower, loom
Ragout [ra'gu] *n* (-s;-s) (culin) stew
Rahe ['rɑ·ə] *f* (-;-n) (naut) yard
Rahm [rɑm] *m* (-[e]s;) cream
Rahmen ['rɑmən] *m* (-s;-) frame; (*Gefüge*) framework; (*Bereich*) scope, limits; (fig) setting; (aut) chassis; **aus dem R. fallen** be out of place; **e-n R. abgeben für** form a setting for; **im R.** (*genit*) in the course of; **im R. von** (or *genit*) within the scope of; within the framework of
Rah'menerzählung *f* story within a story
rahmig ['rɑmɪç] *adj* creamy
Rakete [ra'ketə] *f* (-;-n) rocket
Rake'tenabschußrampe *f* launch pad
Rake'tenbunker *m* silo
Rake'tenstart *m* rocket launch
Rake'tenwerfer *m* rocket launcher
Rake'tenwesen *n* rocketry
Rakett [ra'ket] *n* (-[e]s;-e & -s) (tennis) racket
Rammbär ['rambɛr] *m*, **Rammbock** ['rambɔk] *m*, **Ramme** ['ramə] *f* (-;-n) rammer; pile driver
rammeln ['raməln] *tr* shove; (*zusammenpressen*) pack; (*belegen*) copulate with || *intr* copulate
rammen ['ramən] *tr* ram; (*Beton*) tamp
Rampe ['rampə] *f* (-;-n) ramp; (rok) launch pad; (rr) platform; (theat) apron
Ram'penlicht *n* footlights; (fig) limelight
Ramsch [ramʃ] *m* (-es;) odds and ends; junk; (com) rummage
Ramsch'verkauf *m* rummage sale
Ramsch'waren *pl* junk
Rand [rant] *m* (-[e]s;̈er) edge, border; (*e-s Druckseite*) margin; **am Rande bemerken** note in passing; **außer R. und Band** completely out of control; **bis zum Rande** to the brim; **e-n R. hinterlassen** leave a ring (*e.g., from a wet glass*); **Ränder unter den Augen** circles under the eyes
Rand'auslöser *m* (typ) margin release
Rand'bemerkung *f* marginal note; (fig) snide remark
rändeln ['rendəln], **rändern** ['rendərn] *tr* border, edge; (*Münzen*) mill
Rand'gebiet *n* borderland; (*e-r Stadt*) outskirts
rand'los *adj* rimless
Rand'staat *m* border state
Ranft [ranft] *m* (-[e]s;̈e) crust
rang [raŋ] *pret* of **ringen** || **Rang** *m* (-[e]s;̈e) rank; (theat) balcony; **j-m den R. ablaufen** (fig) run rings around s.o.
Rang'abzeichen *n* insignia of rank
Rang'älteste §5 *mf* ranking officer
Range ['raŋə] *m* (-n;-n) & *f* (-;-n) brat
Rangier'bahnhof *m* (rr) marshaling yard
rangieren [rɑ'ʒirən] *tr* rank; (rr) shunt, switch || *intr* rank

Rang'ordnung f order of precedence
Rang'stufe f rank
rank [raŋk] adj slender
Ranke ['raŋkə] f (-;-n) tendril
Ränke ['rɛŋkə] pl schemes; **R. schmieden** scheme
ranken ['raŋkən] ref & intr creep, climb; **sich r. um** wind around
rän'kevoll adj scheming
rann [ran] pret of **rinnen**
rannte ['rantə] pret of **rennen**
Ranzen ['rantsən] m (-s;-) knapsack; school bag; (Bauch) belly; (mil) field pack
ranzig ['rantsıç] adj rancid
rapid [ra'pit], **rapide** [ra'pidə] adj rapid
Rappe ['rapə] m (-n;-n) black horse
rar [rar] adj rare, scarce
Rarität [rarı'tɛt] f (-;-en) rarity
rasant [ra'zant] adj grazing, point-blank (fire); (fig) impetuous
Rasanz [ra'zants] f (-;) flat trajectory; (fig) impetuosity
rasch [raʃ] adj quick; (hastig) hasty
rascheln ['raʃəln] intr rustle
Rasch'heit f (-;) haste, speed
rasen ['razən] intr rage, rave ‖ intr (SEIN) rush; (aut) speed ‖ **Rasen** m (-s;-) lawn, grass
ra'send adj raging, raving; wild, mad; (Hunger) ravenous; (Wut) towering; (Tempo) break-neck; **r. werden** see red
Ra'sendecke f turf
Ra'senmäher m lawn mower
Ra'senplatz m lawn
Ra'sensprenger m lawn sprinkler
Raserei [razə'raı] f (-;) rage, madness; (aut) reckless driving
Rasier- [razir] comb.fm. shaving, razor
Rasier'apparat m safety razor
rasieren [ra'zirən] tr & ref shave
Rasier'klinge f razor blade
Rasier'messer n straight razor
Rasier'napf m shaving mug
Rasier'pinsel m shaving brush
Rasier'wasser n after-shave lotion
Rasier'zeug n shaving outfit
Raspel ['raspəl] f (-;-n) rasp; (culin) grater
raspeln ['raspəln] tr rasp; grate
Rasse ['rasə] f (-;-n) race; (Zucht) breed, blood, stock; (fig) good breeding
Rassel ['rasəl] f (-;-n) rattle
rasseln ['rasəln] intr rattle; **durchs Examen r.** (coll) flunk the exam
Rassen- ['rasən] comb.fm. racial
Ras'senfrage f racial problem
Ras'senhaß m racism, race hatred
Ras'senkreuzung f miscegenation; crossbreeding
Ras'senkunde f ethnology
ras'senmäßig adj racial
Ras'senmerkmal n racial characteristic
Ras'sentrennung f segregation
Ras'senunruhen pl racial disorders
Ras'sepferd n thoroughbred (horse)
ras'serein adj racially pure; thoroughbred
Ras'sevieh n purebred cattle

rassig ['rasıç] adj racy; thoroughbred
rassisch ['rasıʃ] adj racial
Rast [rast] f (-;-en) rest; station; stage; (mach) notch, groove; (mil) halt; **e-e R. machen** take a rest
rasten ['rastən] intr rest; (mil) halt
rast'los adj restless
Rast'losigkeit f (-;) restlessness
Rast'platz m, **Rast'stätte** f resting place
Rast'tag m day of rest
Rasur [ra'zur] f (-;-en) shave
Rat [rat] m (-[e]s; Ratschläge ['rat-ʃlɛgə]) advice, piece of advice, counsel; (Beratung) deliberation; (Ausweg) means, solution; **auf e-n Rat hören** listen to reason; **sich** [dat] **keinen Rat mehr wissen** be at one's wits' end; **zu Rate ziehen** consult (a person, dictionary, etc.) ‖ m (-[e]s; ̈-e) council, board; (Person) councilor, alderman; advisor; (jur) counsel
Rate ['ratə] f (-;-n) installment; **auf Raten** on the installment plan
raten ['ratən] §63 tr guess; (Rätsel) solve; **das will ich dir nicht geraten haben!** you had better not!; **geraten!** you guessed it!; **j—m etw r.** advise s.o. about s.th.; **komm nicht wieder. das rate ich dir!** take my advice and don't come back! ‖ intr guess; give advice; (dat) advise; **gut r.** take a good guess; **hin und her r.** make random guesses; **j—m gut r.** give s.o. good advice; **j—m zu etw r.** recommend s.th. to s.o. ‖ **Raten** n (-s;) guesswork; advice
ra'tenweise adv by installments
Ra'tenzahlung f payment in installments; **auf R.** on the installment plan
Räterepublik ['rɛtərepublik] f Soviet Union, Soviet Republic
Rat'geber –in §6 mf adviser, counselor
Rat'haus n city hall
ratifizieren [ratıfı'tsirən] tr ratify
Ratifizie'rung f (-;-en) ratification
Ration [ra'tsjon] f (-;-en) ration
rational [ratsjo'nal] adj rational
rationalisieren [ratsjonalı'zirən] tr streamline (operations in industry)
rationell [ratsjo'nel] adj rational
rationieren [ratsjo'nirən] tr ration
rätlich ['retlıç] adj advisable
rat'los adj helpless, perplexed
ratsam ['ratzam] adj advisable
Ratsche ['ratʃə] f (-;-n) rattle; (coll) chatterbox; (tech) ratchet
ratschen ['ratʃən] intr make noise with a rattle; (coll) chat
Rat'schlag m advice, piece of advice
rat'schlagen §132 intr deliberate, consult
Rat'schluß m decision, decree, resolution
Rätsel ['retsəl] n (-s;-) puzzle; (fig) riddle, enigma, mystery
rät'selhaft adj puzzling; mysterious
Ratte ['ratə] f (-;-n) rat
Rat'tenschwanz m rat tail; (fig) tangle; (coll) whole string (of questions, etc.); (Haarzopf) (coll) pigtail
rattern ['ratərn] intr rattle
ratzekahl ['ratsə'kal] adj (Person)

completely bald; (*Landschaft*) completely barren || *adv* completely

Raub [raup] *m* (-[e]s;) robbery; plunder; (*Beute*) prey, spoils; **zum Raube fallen** fall prey, fall victim

Raub– *comb.fm.* predatory, rapacious

Raub'bau *m* (-[e]s;) excessive exploitation (*of natural resources*)

rauben ['raubən] *tr*—j–m etw r. rob s.o. of s.th.; **e–m Mädchen die Unschuld r.** seduce a girl; **e–n Kuß r.** steal a kiss || *intr* rob

Räuber ['rɔɪbər] *m* (-s;-) robber; **R. und Gendarm spielen** play cops and robbers

Räu'berbande *f* gang of robbers

Räu'berhauptmann *m* gang leader

räuberisch ['rɔɪbərɪʃ] *adj* predatory

Raub'fisch *m* predatory fish

Raub'gesindel *n* gang of robbers

Raub'lust *f* rapacity

raub'gierig *adj* rapacious

Raub'lust *f* rapacity

Raub'mord *m* murder with robbery

Raub'mörder *m* robber and murderer

Raub'schiff *n* corsair, pirate ship

Raub'tier *n* beast of prey

Raub'überfall *m* holdup, robbery

Raub'vogel *m* bird of prey

Raub'zug *m* plundering raid

Rauch [raux] *m* (-[e]s;) smoke

rauchen ['rauxən] *tr & intr* smoke

Raucher ['rauxər] *m* (-s;-) smoker

Räucher– [rɔɪxər] *comb.fm.* smoked

Rau'cherabteil *n* smoking section

Räu'cherfaß *n* (eccl) censer

Räu'cherhering *m* smoked herring

Rau'cherhusten *m* cigarette cough

Räu'cherkammer *f* smokehouse

räuchern ['rɔɪxərn] *tr* smoke, cure; (*desinfizieren*) fumigate

Räu'cherschinken *m* smoked ham

Räu'cherung *f* (-;) smoking; fumigation

Rau'cherwagen *m* (rr) smoker

Rauch'fahne *f* trail of smoke

Rauch'fang *m* (*über dem Herd*) hood; (*im Schornstein*) flue

Rauch'fleisch *n* smoked meat

rauchig ['rauxɪç] *adj* smoky

rauch'los *adj* smokeless

Rauch'schleier *m* (mil) smoke screen

Rauch'waren *pl* (*Pelze*) furs; (*Tabakwaren*) tobacco supplies

Räude ['rɔɪdə] *f* (-;) mange

räudig ['rɔɪdɪç] *adj* mangy; **räudiges Schaf** (fig) black sheep

Raufbold ['raufbɔlt] *m* (-[e]s;-e) roughneck, bully

Raufe ['raufə] *f* (-;-n) hayrack

raufen ['raufən] *tr* tear, pull out || *recip & intr* fight, brawl, scuffle

Rauferei [raufə'raɪ] *f* (-;-en) fight, scuffle

Rauf'handel *m* fight, scuffle

rauf'lustig *adj* scrappy, belligerent

rauh [rau] *adj* rough; (*Hals*) hoarse; (*Behandlung*) harsh; **rauhe Wirklichkeit** hard facts

Rauh'bein *n* (fig) roughneck, churl

rauh'beinig *adj* tough, churlish

Rau'heit *f* (-;) roughness; hoarseness

rauhen ['rau·ən] *tr* roughen

Rauh'futter *n* roughage

rauh'haarig *adj* shaggy, hirsute

Rauh'reif *m* hoarfrost

Raum [raum] *m* (-[e]s;–e) room, space; (*Zimmer*) room; (*Bereich*) area; (*e–s Schiffes*) hold; **am Rande R. lassen** (typ) leave a margin; **freier R.** open space; **gebt R.!** make way! **luftleerer R.** vacuum; **R. bieten für** accommodate; **R. einnehmen** take up space; **R. geben** (*dat*) give way to; comply with

Raum'anzug *m* space suit

Räumboot ['rɔɪmbot] *n* minesweeper

Raum'dichte *f* (phys) density by volume

räumen ['rɔɪmən] *tr* clear; (*Wohnung*) vacate; (*Minen*) sweep; (mil) evacuate; **den Saal r.** clear the room; **das Lager r.** (com) clear out the stock; **j–n aus dem Wege r.** (fig) finish s.o. off

Raum'ersparnis *f* economy of space; **der R. wegen** to save space

Raum'fahrer *m* spaceman

Raum'fahrt *f* space travel

Raum'flug *m* space flight

Raum'gestaltung *f* interior decorating

Raum'inhalt *m* volume, capacity

Raum'kunst *f* interior decorating

Raum'lehre *f* geometry

räumlich ['rɔɪmlɪç] *adj* spatial

Räum'lichkeit *f* (-;-en) room

Raum'mangel *m* lack of space

Raum'medizin *f* space medicine

Raum'meter *m* cubic meter

Raum'schiff *n* space ship

Raum'schiffart *f* space travel

Raum'schiffkapsel *f* space capsule

Raum'sonde *f* unmanned space explorer

Raum'ton *m* stereophonic sound

Räu'mung *f* (-;-en) clearing, removal; (com) clearance; (mil) evacuation

Räu'mungsausverkauf *m* clearance sale

Räu'mungsbefehl *m* eviction notice; (mil) evacuation order

raunen ['raunən] *tr & intr* whisper

raunzen ['rauntsən] *intr* grumble

Raupe ['raupə] *f* (-;-n) (ent, mach) caterpillar

Rau'penfahrzeug *n* full-track vehicle

Rau'penkette *f* caterpillar track

Rau'penschlepper *m* caterpillar tractor

Rausch [rau ʃ] *m* (-es;–e) drunkenness; (fig) intoxication, ecstasy; **e–n R. haben** be drunk; **sich** [*dat*] **e–n R. antrinken** get drunk

rauschen ['rau ʃən] *intr* (*Blätter, Seide*) rustle; (*Bach*) murmur; (*Brandung, Sturm*) roar || *intr* (SEIN) strut; rush

rau'schend *adj* rustling; (*Fest*) uproarious; (*Beifall*) thunderous

Rausch'gift *n* drug, dope

Rausch'gifthandel *m* drug traffic

Rausch'giftschieber –in §6 *mf* pusher

Rausch'giftsucht *f* drug addiction

Rausch'giftsüchtige §5 *mf* dope addict

Rausch'gold *n* tinsel

räuspern ['rɔɪspərn] *ref* clear one's throat

Rausschmeißer ['rausʃmaɪsər] *m* (-s;-) (coll) bouncer

Raute ['rautə] *f* (-;-n) (cards) diamond; (geom) rhombus

Rayon [re'jõ] *m* (-s;-s) (*Bezirk*) district, region; (*im Warenhaus*) department

Raz·zia ['ratsja] *f* (-;-zien [tsjən]) police raid

Reagenzglas [re·a'gentsglɑs] *n*· test tube

reagieren [re·a'girən] *intr* (**auf** *acc*) react (to)

Reaktion [re·ak'tsjon] *f* (-;-en) reaction

reaktionär [re·aktsjo'ner] *adj* reactionary || **Reaktionär** *m* (-s;-e) reactionary

Reak·tor [re'aktər] *m* (-s;-toren ['torən]) (phys) reactor

real [re'ɑl] *adj* real

Real'gymnasium *n* high school (*where modern languages, mathematics, or sciences are stressed*)

Realien [re'ɑljən] *pl* real facts, realities; exact sciences

realisieren [re·ɑlɪ'zirən] *tr* realize

Realist -in [re·a'lɪst(ɪn)] §7 *mf* realist

realistisch [re·a'lɪstɪʃ] *adj* realistic

Realität [re·ɑlɪ'tet] *f* (-;-en) reality; **Realitäten** real property

Real'lexikon *n* encyclopedia

Real'lohn *m* purchasing power of wages

Real'schule *f* non-classical secondary school

Rebe ['rebə] *f* (-;-n) vine; tendril

Rebell [re'bel] *m* (-en;-en) rebel

rebellieren [rebe'lirən] *intr* rebel

Rebellin [re'belɪn] *f* (-;-nen) rebel

Rebellion [rebel'jon] *f* (-;-en) rebellion

rebellisch [re'belɪʃ] *adj* rebellious

Re'bensaft *m* (poet) juice of the grape

Rebhuhn ['rephun] *n* partridge

Rebstock ['rep/tok] *m* vine

rechen ['reçən] *tr* rake || **Rechen** *m* (-s;-) rake; grate

Re'chenaufgabe *f* arithmetic problem

Re'chenautomat *m* computer

Re'chenbrett *n* abacus

Re'chenbuch *n* arithmetic book

Re'chenexemplar *n* arithmetic problem

Re'chenkunst *f* arithmetic

Re'chenmaschine *f* calculator

Re'chenpfennig *m* counter

Re'chenschaft *f* (-;) account; **j–n zur R. ziehen** call s.o. to account

Re'chenschaftsbericht *m* report

Re'chenschieber *m* slide rule

rechnen ['reçnən] *tr* reckon, calculate, figure out || *intr* reckon; calculate; **falsch r.** miscalculate; **r. auf** (*acc*) count on; **r. mit** be prepared for; expect; take into account; **r. zu** be counted among || **Rechnen** *n* (-s;) arithmetic; calculation

Rech'ner *m* (-s;-) calculator, computer; **er ist ein guter R.** he is good at numbers

rechnerisch ['reçnərɪʃ] *adj* arithmetical

Rech'nung *f* (-;-en) calculation; account; bill; (*Warenrechnung*) invoice; (*im Restaurant*) check; **auf j–s R. setzen** (or **stellen**) charge to s.o.'s account; **auf R. kaufen** buy on credit; **auf seine R. kaufen** get one's money's worth; **außer R. lassen** overlook; **das geht auf meine R.** this is on me; **die R. begleichen** settle an account (or bill); **j–m in R. stellen** charge to s.o.'s account; **in R. ziehen** take into account; **R. tragen** (*dat*) make allowance for

Rech'nungsabschluß *m* closing of accounts

Rech'nungsauszug *m* (com) statement

Rech'nungsführer -in §6 *mf* accountant

Rech'nungsführung *f* accounting

Rech'nungsjahr *n* fiscal year

Rech'nungsprüfer -in §6 *mf* auditor

Rech'nungswesen *n* accounting

recht [reçt] *adj* right; (*richtig*) correct; (*echt*) real; (*gerecht*) all right, right; (*geziemend*) suitable, proper; **es ist mir nicht r.** I don't like it; **es ist schon r.** that's all right; **mir soll's r. sein** I don't mind; **zur rechten Zeit** at the right moment || *adv* right; quite; (*sehr*) very; **das kommt mir gerade r.** that comes in handy; **erst r.** all the more; **es j–m r. machen** please s.o.; **es geschieht ihm r.** it serves him right; **j–m r. geben** agree with s.o.; **nun erst r.** nicht now less than ever; **r. daran tun zu** (*inf*) do right to (*inf*); **r. haben** be right || **Recht** *n* (-[e]s;-e) right; (*Vorrecht*) privilege; (jur) law; **alle Rechte vorbehalten** all rights reserved; **die Rechte studieren** study law; **mit R.** with good reason; **R. sprechen** dispense justice; **sich** [*dat*] **selbst R. verschaffen** take the law into one's hands; **von Rechts wegen** by rights; **wieder zu seinem Rechte kommen** come into one's own again; **zu R. bestehen** be justified || **Rechte** §5 *mf* right person; **an den Rechten kommen** meet one's match; **du bist mir der R.!** you're a fine fellow! || *f* right hand; (box) right; **die R.** (pol) the right || *n* right; **er dünkt sich** [*dat*] **was Rechtes** he thinks he's somebody; **nach dem Rechten sehen** look after things

Recht'eck *n* rectangle, oblong

recht'eckig *adj* rectangular

recht'fertigen *tr* justify, vindicate

Recht'fertigung *f* (-;-en) justification

recht'gläubig *adj* orthodox

rechthaberisch ['reçthabərɪʃ] *adj* dogmatic

recht'lich *adj* legal, lawful; (*ehrlich*) honest, honorable

Recht'lichkeit *f* (-;) legality; (*Redlichkeit*) honesty

recht'los *adj* without rights

recht'mäßig *adj* legal; legitimate

Recht'mäßigkeit *f* (-;) legality; legitimacy

rechts [reçts] *adv* on the right; right, to the right

Rechts– *comb.fm.* legal

Rechts'angelegenheit *f* legal matter

Rechts'anspruch *m* legal claim

Rechts'anwalt *m* lawyer, attorney

Rechts′ausdruck m legal term
Rechts′auskunft f legal advice
Rechts′außen m (-;-) (fb) right wing
recht′schaffen adj honest
Recht′schaffenheit f (-;) honesty
Recht′schreibung f orthography
Rechts′fall m case, legal case
Rechts′gang m legal procedure
Rechts′gefühl n sense of justice
Rechts′gelehrsamkeit f jurisprudence
Rechts′grund m, legal grounds; (Anspruch) title, claim
rechts′gültig adj legal, valid
Rechts′gültigkeit f legality
Rechts′gutachten n legal opinion
Rechts′handel m lawsuit
rechtshändig [′rɛçtshɛndɪç] adj right-handed
rechts′herum adv clockwise
Rechts′kraft f legal force
rechts′kräftig adj valid
Rechts′lage f legal status
Rechts′lehre f jurisprudence
Rechts′mittel n legal remedy
Rechts′pflege f administration of justice
Recht′sprechung f (-;) administration of justice; **die R.** (coll) the judiciary
Rechts′schutz m legal protection
Rechts′spruch m verdict
Rechts′streit m legal dispute; pending case; difference of opinion in the interpretation of the law
rechtsum′ interj (mil) right face!
rechts′ungültig adj illegal, invalid
rechts′verbindlich adj legally binding
Rechtsverdreher –in [′rɛçtsferdreər(ɪn)] §6 mf pettifogger
Rechts′verletzung f (-;-en) violation of the law; infringement of another's rights
Rechts′weg m recourse to the law; **auf dem Rechtswege** by the courts; **den R. beschreiten** take legal action
Rechts′wissenschaft f jurisprudence
Reck [rɛk] n (-[e]s;-e) horizontal bar
recken [′rɛkən] tr stretch; **den Hals r.** crane one's neck
Redakteur [redak′tør] m (-s;-e) editor
Redaktion [redak′tsjon] f (-;-en) editorship; (Arbeitskräfte) editorial staff; (Arbeitsraum) editorial office
redaktionell [redaktsjo′nɛl] adj editorial
Redaktions′schluß m press time, deadline
Rede [′redə] f (-;-n) speech; (Gespräch) conversation; (Gerücht) rumor; **das ist nicht der R. wert** that is not worth mentioning; **davon kann keine R. sein** that's out of the question; **die in R. stehende Person** the person in question; **e-e R. halten** give a speech; **es geht die R., daß** it is rumored that; **gebundene R.** verse; **gehobene R.** lofty language; **j-m in die R. fallen** interrupt s.o.; **j-m R. und Antwort stehen** explain oneself to s.o.; **j-n zur R. stellen** take s.o. to task; **keine R.!** absolutely not!; **lose Reden führen** engage in loose talk; **ungebundene R.** prose

Re′defigur f figure of speech
Re′defluß m flow of words
Re′defreiheit f freedom of speech
Re′degabe f eloquence, fluency
re′degewandt adj fluent; (iron) glib
Re′degewandtheit f fluency, eloquence
Re′dekunst f eloquence
reden [′redən] tr speak, talk || **refmit sich r. lassen** listen to reason; **sich heiser r.** talk oneself hoarse; **von sich r. machen** cause a lot of talk || intr speak, talk; converse; **du hast gut r.!** it's easy for you to talk; **j-m ins Gewissen r.** appeal to s.o.'s conscience; **j-m nach dem Munde r.** humor s.o.; **mit j-m deutsch r.** (fig) talk turkey to s.o.
Re′densart f phrase, expression; idiom
Rederei [redə′raɪ] f (-;-en) empty talk
Re′deschwall m verbosity
Re′deteil m part of speech
Re′deweise f style of speaking
Re′dewendung f phrase, expression
redigieren [redi′girən] tr edit
redlich [′retlɪç] adj upright, honest || adv—es r. meinen mean well; **sich r. bemühen** make an honest effort
Red′lichkeit f (-;) honesty, integrity
Redner –in [′rednər(ɪn)] §6 mf speaker
Red′nerbühne f podium, platform
Red′nergabe f (gift of) eloquence
rednerisch [′rednərɪʃ] adj rhetorical
Redoute [re′dutə] f (-;-n) masquerade; (mil) redoubt
redselig [′retzelɪç] adj talkative
Reduktion [reduk′tsjon] f (-;-en) reduction
reduplizieren [reduplɪ′tsirən] tr reduplicate
reduzieren [redu′tsirən] tr (auf acc) reduce (to)
Reede [′redə] f (-;-n) (naut) roadstead
Reeder [′redər] m (-s;-) shipowner
Reederei [redə′raɪ] f (-;-en) shipping company; shipping business
reell [re′ɛl] adj honest; (Preis) fair; (Geschäft) sound || adv—r. bedient werden get one's money's worth
Reep [rep] n (-[e]s;-e) (naut) rope
Referat [refə′rat] n (-[e]s;-e) report; (Vortrag) paper; **ein R. halten** give a paper
Referendar [referen′dar] m (-s;-e) junior lawyer; in-service teacher
Referent –in [refe′rent(ɪn)] §7 mf reader of a paper; (Berichterstatter) reporter; (Gutachter) official adviser
Referenz [refe′rɛnts] f (-;-en) reference; **j-n als R. angeben** give s.o. as a reference; **über gute Referenzen verfügen** have good references
referieren [refe′rirən] intr (über acc) give a report (on); (über acc) read a paper (on)
reffen [′refən] tr (naut) reef
reflektieren [reflɛk′tirən] tr reflect || intr reflect; **r. auf** (acc) reflect on; (com) think of buying
Reflek·tor [re′flɛktər] m (-s;-toren [′torən]) reflector
Reflex [re′flɛks] m (-es;-e) reflex
Reflex′bewegung f reflex action

Reflexion [refle'ksjon] f (-;-en) reflection

reflexiv [refle'ksif] adj reflexive

Reform [re'form] f (-;-en) reform

Reformation [reforma'tsjon] f (-;-en) reformation

Refor·mator [refor'mator] m (-s; [ma'toren]) reformer

Reform'haus n health-food store

reformieren [refor'miron] tr reform

Reform'kost f health food

Refrain [re'frɛ̃] m (-s;-s) refrain; **den R. mitsingen** join in the refrain

Regal [re'gal] n (-s;-e) shelf

Regat·ta [re'gata] f (-;-ten) [tən] regatta

rege ['regə] adj brisk, lively

Regel ['regəl] f (-;-n) rule, regulation; (pathol) menstruation; **in der R. as a rule**

re'gellos adj irregular; disorderly

Re'gellosigkeit f (-;-en) irregularity

re'gelmäßig adj regular

Re'gelmäßigkeit f regularity

regeln ['regəln] tr regulate; arrange; control

re'gelrecht adj regular; downright

Re'gelung f (-;-en) regulation; control

re'gelwidrig adj against the rules; (sport) foul

regen ['regən] tr & ref move, stir ‖ **Regen** m (-s;-) rain; **vom R. unter die Traufe kommen** jump out of the frying pan into the fire

re'genarm adj rainless, dry

Re'genbö f rain squall

Re'genbogen m rainbow

Re'genbogenhaut f (anat) iris

re'gendicht adj rainproof

Re'genfall m rainfall

re'genfest adj rainproof

Re'genguß m downpour

Re'genhaut f oilskin coat

Re'genmantel m raincoat

Re'genmenge f amount of rainfall

Re'genmesser m rain gauge

Re'genpfeifer m (orn) plover

Re'genschauer m shower

Re'genschirm m umbrella

Regent –in [re'gent(ɪn)] §7 mf regent

Re'gentag m rainy day

Re'gentropfen m raindrop

Re'genumhang m cape

Re'genwetter n rainy weather

Re'genwurm m earthworm

Re'genzeit f rainy season

Re·gie [re'ʒi] f (-;-gien ['ʒi·ən]) management, administration; (com) state monopoly; (cin, theat) direction

Regie'assistent –in §7 mf (cin, theat) assistant director

Regie'pult n (rad) control console

Regie'raum m (rad) control room

regieren [re'girən] tr govern, rule; (gram) govern, take ‖ intr reign; (fig) predominate

Regie'rung f (-;-en) government, rule; administration; reign

Regie'rungsanleihe f government loan

Regie'rungsantritt m accession

Regie'rungsbeamte §5 m government official

Regie'rungssitz m seat of government

Regie'rungszeit f reign; administration

Regime [re'ʒim] n (-s;-s) regime

Regiment [regɪ'ment] n (-[e]s;-e) rule, government ‖ n (-[e]s;-er) (mil) regiment

Regiments– comb.fm. regimental

Regiments'kommandeur m regimental commander

Region [re'gjon] f (-;-en) region

regional [regjo'nal] adj regional

Regisseur [reʒɪ'sør] m (-s;-e) (cin, theat) director

Register [re'gɪstər] n (-s;-) file clerk; (Inhaltsverzeichnis) index; (Orgel-) stop

Regi·strator [regɪs'trator] m (-s; –stratoren] [stra'torən]) registrar

Registratur [regɪstra'tur] f (-;-en) filing; filing cabinet

registrieren [regɪs'trirən] tr register; (Betrag) ring up

Registrier'kasse f cash register

Registrie'rung f (-;-en) registration

Reglement [reglə'mã] n (-s;-s) regulation(s), rule(s)

Regler ['reglər] m (-s;-) regulator; (mach) governor

reglos ['reklos] adj motionless

regnen ['regnən] impers—**es regnet it is raining**; **es regnet Bindfäden** it is raining cats and dogs; **es regnete Püffe** blows came thick and fast

regnerisch ['regnərɪʃ] adj rainy

Re·greß [re'grɛs] m (-gresses;-gresse) recourse, remedy; **R. nehmen zu** have recourse to

regsam ['rekzam] adj lively; quick

regulär [regu'lɛr] adj regular

regulierbar [regu'lirbar] adj adjustable

regulieren [regu'lirən] tr regulate; adjust

Regung ['regun] f (-;-en) motion, stirring; emotion; impulse

Reh [re] n (-[e]s;-e) deer

rehabilitieren [rehabɪlɪ'tirən] tr rehabilitate

Rehabilitie'rung f (-;-en) rehabilitation

Reh'bock m roebuck

Reh'braten m roast venison

Reh'kalb n fawn

Reh'keule f leg of venison

Rehkitz ['rekɪts] n (-es;-e) fawn

Reh'leder n doeskin

Reibahle ['raɪpalə] f (-;-n) reamer

Reibe ['raɪbə] f (-;-n) (coll) grater

Reibeisen ['raɪparzən] n (culin) grater

reiben ['raɪbən] §62 tr rub; grate; grind ‖ ref—**sich r. an** (dat) take offense at ‖ intr rub

Reiberei [raɪbə'raɪ] f (-;-en) (coll) friction, squabble

Rei'bung f (-;-en) friction

rei'bungslos adj frictionless; (fig) smooth

reich [raɪç] adj wealthy; (an dat) rich (in); (Fang) big; (Phantasie) fertile; (Mahlzeit) lavish ‖ **Reich** n (-[e]s; –e) empire, realm; kingdom

reichen ['raɪçən] tr reach; hand, pass ‖ intr reach, extend; do, manage; **das reicht!** that will do!

reich'haltig adj rich; abundant

reich′lich *adj* plentiful, abundant || *adv* pretty, fairly
Reichs′kanzlei *f* chancellery
Reichs′kanzler *m* chancellor
Reichs′mark *f* reichsmark
Reichts′tag *m* (hist) diet; (hist) Reichstag (*lower house*)
Reichtum [′raɪçtum] *n* (-s;-̈er) riches
Reich′weite *f* reach, range
reif [raɪf] *adj* ripe; (fig) mature || **Reif** *m* (-[e]s;) frost
Reife [′raɪfə] *f* (-;) ripeness; (fig) maturity
reifen [′raɪfən] *intr* (SEIN) ripen; mature || *impers*—**es reift** there is frost || **Reifen** *m* (-s;-) tire; hoop
Rei′fendruckmesser *m* tire gauge
Rei′fenpanne *f*, **Rei′fenschaden** *m* flat tire, blowout
Rei′feprüfung *f* final examination (*as prerequisite for entering university*)
Rei′fezeugnis *n* high school diploma
reif′lich *adj* careful
Reigen [′raɪgən] *m* (-s;-) square dance
Reihe [′raɪ·ə] *f* (-;-n) row, string; set, series; rank, file; turn; **an der R. sein** be next; **an die R. kommen** get one's turn; **aus der R. tanzen** (fig) go one's own way; **die R. ist an mir** it's my turn; **nach der R.** in succession
reihen [′raɪ·ən] *tr* range, rank; (*Perlen*) string
Rei′hendorf *n* one-street village
Rei′henfabrikation *f* assembly-line production
Rei′henfolge *f* succession, sequence
Rei′henhaus *n* row house
Rei′henschaltung *f* (elec) series connection
reih′enweise *adv* in rows
Reiher [′raɪ·ər] *m* (-s;-) heron
Reim [raɪm] *m* (-[e]s;-e) rhyme
reimen [′raɪmən] *tr* (auf *acc*) make rhyme (with) || *ref* rhyme; (fig) make sense; (auf *acc*) rhyme (with) || *intr* rhyme
reim′los *adj* unrhymed, blank
rein [raɪn] *adj* pure; (*sauber*) clean; (*klar*) clear; (*Gewinn*) net; (*Wahrheit*) simple; (*Wahnsinn*) sheer, absolute; **etw ins reine bringen** clear up s.th.; **etw ins reine schreiben** write (or type) a final copy of s.th.; **mit j-m ins reine kommen** come to an understanding with s.o. || *adv* quite, downright; **r. alles** almost everything || **Rein** *f* (-;-en) pan
Reindl [′raɪndəl] *n* (-s;- & -n) pan
Rei′nemachen *n* (-s;) housecleaning
Rein′ertrag *m* clear profit
Rein′fall *m* flop, disappointment
Rein′gewicht *n* net weight
Rein′gewinn *m* net profit
Rein′heit *f* (-;) purity; cleanness
reinigen [′raɪnɪgən] *tr* clean, cleanse; (fig) purify, refine
Rei′nigung *f* (-;-en) cleaning; purification; dry cleaning
Rei′nigungsanstalt *f* dry cleaner's
Rei′nigungsmittel *n* cleaning agent
Reinmachefrau [′raɪnmaxəfrau] *f* cleaning woman
Rein′schrift *f* final copy

reinweg [′raɪn′vɛk] *adv* (coll) flatly, absolutely
rein′wollen *adj* all-wool
Reis [raɪs] *m* (-es;) rice || *n* (-es;-er) twig; (fig) scion
Reis′brei *m* rice pudding
Reise [′raɪzə] *f* (-;-n) trip, tour; (aer) flight; (naut) voyage; **auf der R.** while traveling; **auf Reisen sein** be traveling
Rei′sebericht *m* travelogue
Rei′sebeschreibung *f* travel book
Rei′sebüro *n* travel agency
rei′sefertig *adj* ready to leave
Rei′seführer *m* guidebook
Rei′segefährte *m*, **Rei′segefährtin** *f* travel companion
Rei′segenehmigung *f* travel permit
Rei′segepäck *n* luggage; (rr) baggage
Rei′segesellschaft *f* tour operator(s); travel group
Rei′sehandbuch *n* guidebook
Rei′seleiter –*in* §6 *mf* courier, guide
rei′selustig *adj* fond of traveling
reisen [′raɪzən] *intr* (SEIN) travel
Reisende [′raɪzəndə] §5 *mf* traveler
Rei′sepaß *m* passport
Rei′seplan *m* itinerary
Rei′seprospekt *m* travel folder
Rei′seroute *f* itinerary
Rei′sescheck *m* traveler's check
Rei′seschreibmaschine *f* portable typewriter
Rei′sespesen *pl* travel expenses
Rei′setasche *f* overnight bag, flight bag
Rei′seziel *n* destination
Reisig [′raɪzɪç] *n* (-s;) brushwood
Rei′sigbündel *n* faggot
Reisige [′raɪzɪgə] §5 *m* cavalryman
Reißaus [raɪs′aus] *n*—**R. nehmen** (coll) take to one's heels
Reißbrett [′raɪsbret] *n* drawing board
reißen [′raɪsən] §53 *tr* tear, rip; (*ziehen*) pull, yank; (*wegschnappen*) wrest, snatch || *intr* tear; pull, tug; break, snap; (*sich spalten*) split, burst; **das reißt ins Geld** this is running into money; **mir reißt die Geduld** I am losing all patience || *ref*—**an sich r.** seize; (com) monopolize; **die Führung an sich r.** take the lead; **sich an e-m Nagel r.** scratch oneself on a nail; **sich um etw r.** scramble for s.th. || **Reißen** *n* (-s;) tearing; bursting; sharp pains; rheumatism
rei′ßend *adj* rapid; (*Schmerz*) sharp; (*Tier*) rapacious; **reißenden Absatz finden** (coll) sell like hotcakes
Reißer [′raɪsər] *m* (-s;-) bestseller; (cin) box-office hit; (com) good seller
Reißfeder [′raɪsfedər] *f* drawing pen
Reißleine [′raɪslaɪnə] *f* rip cord
Reißnagel [′raɪsnagəl] *m* thumbtack
Reißschiene [′raɪs′inə] *f* T-square
Reißverschluß [′raɪsfer′lus] *m* zipper
Reißzahn [′raɪstsan] *m* canine tooth
Reißzeug [′raɪstsɔɪk] *n* mechanical-drawing tools
Reißzwecke [′raɪstsvekə] *f* thumbtack
Reit– [raɪt] *comb.fm.* riding
Reit′anzug *m* riding habit

Reit'bahn f riding ring
reiten ['raɪtən] §86 tr ride; **e-n Weg r.** ride along a road; **ihn reitet der Teufel** (coll) he is full of the devil; **krumme Touren r.** (coll) pull shady deals; **Prinzipien r.** (fig) stick rigidly to principles; **über den Haufen r.** knock down || intr (SEIN) go horseback riding; **geritten kommen** come on horseback; **vor Anker r.** ride at anchor
Rei'ter –in §6 mf rider
Rei'terstandbild n equestrian statue
Reit'gerte f riding crop
Reit'hose f riding breeches
Reit'knecht m groom
Reit'kunst f horsemanship
Reit'peitsche f riding crop
Reit'pferd n saddle horse
Reit'schule f riding academy
Reit'stiefel m riding boot
Reit'weg m bridle path
Reiz [raɪts] m (–es;–e) charm, appeal; (Erregung) irritation; (physiol, psychol) stimulus; (acc) attract; **sie läßt ihre Reize spielen** she turns on the charm
reizbar ['raɪtsbar] adj irritable; (empfindlich) sensitive, touchy
reizen ['raɪtsən] tr (entzünden, ärgern) irritate; (locken) allure; (anziehen) attract; (anregen) excite, stimulate; (aufreizen) provoke; (Appetit) whet || intr (cards) bid || impers—**es reizt mich zu** (inf) I'm itching to (inf)
rei'zend adj charming; cute, sweet; (pathol) irritating
Reiz'entzug m sensory deprivation
Reiz'husten m (–s) constant cough
reiz'los adj unattractive; (Kost) bland
Reiz'mittel n stimulant; (fig) incentive
Reiz'stoff m irritant
Rei'zung f (–;–en) irritation; (Lockung) allurement; (Anregung) stimulation; (Aufreizung) provocation
reiz'voll adj charming, attractive; fascinating; (verlockend) tempting
rekeln ['rekəln] ref (coll) lounge
Reklamation [reklama'tsjon] f (–;–en) complaint, protest
Reklame [re'klamə] f (–;–en) advertisement, ad; publicity; **R. machen für** advertise
Rekla'mebüro n advertising agency
Rekla'mefeldzug m advertising campaign
reklamieren [rekla'mirən] tr claim || intr (gegen) protest (against); (wegen) complain (about)
rekognoszieren [rekɔs'tsirən] tr & intr reconnoiter
Rekonvaleszent –in [rekɔnvales'tsent (ɪn)] §7 mf convalescent
Rekonvaleszenz [rekɔnvales'tsents] f (–;) convalescence
Rekord [re'kɔrt] m (–[e]s;–e) record
Rekord'ernte f bumper crop, record crop
Rekordler –in [re'kɔrtlər(ɪn)] §6 mf (coll) record holder
Rekord'versuch m attempt to break the record

Rekrut [re'krut] m (–en;–en) recruit
Rekru'tenausbildung f basic training
Rekru'tenaushebung f recruitment
rekrutieren [rekru'tirən] tr recruit || ref—**sich r. aus** be recruited from
Rek·tor ['rektɔr] m (–s;–toren ['torən]) principal; (e-r Universität) president
Relais [rə'le] n (–lais ['le(s)];–lais ['les]) relay
relativ [rela'tif] adj relative
Relegation [relega'tsjon] f (–;–en) expulsion
relegieren [rele'girən] tr expel
Relief [re'ljef] n (–s;–s & –e) relief
Religion [relɪ'gjon] f (–;–en) religion
Religions'ausübung f practice of religion
Religions'bekenntnis n religious denomination
religiös [relɪ'gjøs] adj religious
Reling ['relɪŋ] f (–s;–s) (naut) rail
Reliquie [re'likvjə] f (–;–n) relic
Reli'quienschrein m reliquary
remis [rə'mi] adj (cards) tied || **Remis** n (–;–) (chess) tie, draw
remittieren [remɪ'tirən] tr (Geld) remit; (Waren) return || intr (Fieber) go down
rempeln ['rempəln] tr bump, jostle || intr (fb) block
Remter ['remtər] m (–s;–) refectory; assembly hall
Ren [ren] (–s;–e) reindeer
Renaissance [rənə'sãs] f (–;–n) renaissance
Rendite [ren'ditə] f (–;–n) return
Renn– [ren] comb.fm. race, racing
Renn'bahn f race track; (aut) speedway
Renn'boot n racing boat
rennen ['renən] §97 tr run; **j-m den Degen durch den Leib r.** run s.o. through with a sword; **über den Haufen r.** run over; **zu Boden r.** knock down || intr (SEIN) run; race || **Rennen** n (–s;–) running; race; (Einzelrennen) heat; **das R. machen** win the race; **totes R.** dead heat, tie
Ren'ner m (–s;–) (good) race horse
Renn'fahrer m (aut) race driver
Renn'pferd n race horse
Renn'platz m race track; (aut) speedway
Renn'rad n racing bicycle, racer
Renn'sport m racing
Renn'strecke f race track; distance (to be raced); (aut) speedway
Renn'wagen m racing car, racer
Renommee [renɔ'me] n (–s;–s) reputation
renommieren [renɔ'mirən] intr (mit) brag (about), boast (about)
renommiert' adj (wegen) renowned (for)
Renommist [renɔ'mɪst] m (–en;–en) braggart
renovieren [reno'virən] tr renovate; redecorate
rentabel [ren'tabəl] adj profitable
Rentabilität [rentabɪlɪ'tet] f (–;–en) (e-r Investition) return; (fin) productiveness

Rente ['rɛntə] ƒ (-;-n) income, reve-nue; pension; annuity
Ren'tenbrief m annuity bond
Ren'tenempfänger –in §6 mƒ pensioner
Rentier [rɛn'tje] m (-s;-s) person of independent means || ['rɛntir] n (-s; -s;) reindeer
rentieren [rɛn'tirən] reƒ pay
Rentner –in ['rɛntnər(ɪn)] §6 mƒ per-son on pension
Reparatur [rɛpara'tur] ƒ (-;-en) repair
Reparatur'werkstatt ƒ repair shop; (aut) garage
reparieren [rɛpa'rirən] tr repair, fix
Reportage [rɛpɔr'taʒə] ƒ (-;-n) report; coverage
Reporter –in [rɛ'pɔrtər(ɪn)] §6 mƒ re-porter
Repräsentant –in [reprɛzɛn'tant(ɪn)] §7 mƒ representative
repräsentieren [reprɛzɛn'tirən] tr rep-resent || intr be a socialite
Repressalie [reprɛ'saljə] ƒ (-;-n) re-prisal
Reprise [re'prizə] ƒ (-;-n) (cin) rerun; (mus) repeat; (theat) revival
reproduzieren [reprodu'tsirən] tr re-produce
Reptil [rɛp'til] n (-s;-ien [jən] & -e) reptile
Republik [repu'blik] ƒ (-;-en) repub-lic
Republikaner –in [republɪ'kanər(ɪn)] §6 mƒ republican
republikanisch [republɪ'kanɪʃ] adj re-publican
Requisit [rekvɪ'zit] n (-[e]s;-en) req-usite; **Requisiten** (theat) props
Reservat [rezɛr'vat] n (-[e]s;-e) reser-vation
Reserve [re'zɛrvə] ƒ (-;-n) reserve
Reser'vebank ƒ (-;-e) (sport) bench
Reser'vereifen m spare tire
Reser'veteil m spare part
Reser'vetruppen pl (mil) reserves
reservieren [rezɛr'virən] tr reserve
Reservie'rung ƒ (-;-en) reservation
Residenz [rezɪ'dɛnts] ƒ (-;-en) resi-dence
Residenz'stadt ƒ capital
residieren [rezɪ'dirən] intr reside
resignieren [rezɪg'nirən] intr resign
Respekt [re'spɛkt] m (-[e]s;) respect
respektabel [respɛk'tabəl] adj respect-able
respektieren [respɛk'tirən] tr respect
respekt'los adj disrespectful
respekt'voll adj respectful
Ressort [re'sor] n (-s;-s) department
Rest [rɛst] m (-es;-e & -er) rest; (Stoff–) remnant; (Zahlungs–) bal-ance; (Bodensatz) residue; (math) re-mainder; **irdische** (or **sterbliche**) **Reste** earthly (or mortal) remains; **j–m den R. geben** (coll) finish s.o. off
Rest'auflage ƒ remainders
Restaurant [rɛstɔ'rã] n (-s;-s) restau-rant
Restauration [restaura'tsjon] ƒ (-;-en) restoration; (Aust) restaurant
Rest'bestand m remainder
Rest'betrag m balance, remainder
Re'steuerkauf m remnant sale

rest'lich adj remaining
rest'los adj complete
Resultat [rezul'tat] n (-[e]s;-e) result; upshot; (sport) score
Ret'ter m (-s;–) rescuer; (Heiland) Savior
Rettich ['rɛtɪç] m (-s;-e) radish
Ret'tung ƒ (-;-en) rescue; salvation
Ret'tungsaktion ƒ rescue operation
Ret'tungsboot n lifeboat
Ret'tungsfloß n life raft
Ret'tungsgürtel m life preserver
Ret'tungsleine ƒ life line
ret'tungslos adj irretrievable
Ret'tungsmannschaft ƒ rescue party
Ret'tungsring m life preserver
Ret'tungsstation ƒ first-aid station
retuschieren [retu'ʃirən] tr retouch
Reue ['rɔɪə] ƒ (-;) remorse
reu'elos adj remorseless, impenitent
reuen ['rɔɪ-ən] tr—**die Tat reut mich** I regret having done it; **die Zeit reut mich** I regret wasting the time || impers—**es reut mich, daß** I regret that, I am sorry that
reu'evoll adj repentant, contrite
Reugeld ['rɔɪgɛlt] n forfeit
reumütig ['rɔɪmytɪç] adj repentant
Revanche [re'vã/ə] ƒ (-;) revenge
Revan'chekrieg m punitive war
revan'chelustig adj vengeful
Revan'chepartie ƒ (sport) return game
revanchieren [revã'ʃirən] reƒ (an dat) take revenge (on); **sich für e–en Dienst r.** return a favor
Revers [re'vers] m (-es;-e) (e–r Münze) reverse; (Erklärung) state-ment || [re'ver] m (Aust) & n (-;-) lapel; cuff
revidieren [revi'dirən] tr revise; (nach-prüfen) check; (com) audit
Revier [re'vir] n (-s;-e) district; quar-ter; hunting ground; police station; (mil) sick quarters
Revier'stube ƒ (mil) sickroom
Revision [revi'zjon] ƒ (-;-en) revision; (com) audit; (jur) appeal
Re'visor [re'vizor] m (-s;-visoren [vɪ'zorən]) reviser; (com) auditor
Revolte [re'voltə] ƒ (-;-n) revolt
revoltieren [revɔl'tirən] intr revolt
Revolution [revolu'tsjon] ƒ (-;-en) revolution
revolutionär [revolutsjo'nɛr] adj revo-lutionary || **Revolutionär –in** §8 mƒ revolutionary
Revolver [re'vɔlvər] m (-s;–) revolver
Revol'verblatt n (coll) scandal sheet
Revol'verschnauze ƒ (coll) lip, sass
Re-vue [re'vy] ƒ (-;-vuen ['vy-ən]) re-view; (theat) revue
Rezensent –in [retsɛn'zɛnt(ɪn)] §7 mƒ reviewer, critic
rezensieren [retsɛn'zirən] tr review
Rezension [retsɛn'zjon] ƒ (-;-en) re-view
Rezept [re'tsɛpt] n (-[e]s;-e) (culin) recipe; (med) prescription
rezitieren [retsɪ'tirən] tr recite
Rhabarber [ra'barbər] m (-s;) rhubarb
Rhapso·die [rapsɔ'di] ƒ (-;-dien ['di·ən]) rhapsody

Rhein [raɪn] m (-[e]s;) Rhine

Rhesusfaktor ['rezʊsfaktər] m (-s;) Rh factor

Rhetorik [re'torɪk] f (-;) rhetoric

rhetorisch [re'torɪʃ] adj rhetorical

rheumatisch [rɔɪ'matɪʃ] adj rheumatic

Rheumatismus [rɔɪma'tɪsmʊs] m (-;) rheumatism

rhythmisch ['rʏtmɪʃ] adj rhythmical

Rhyth·mus ['rʏtmʊs] m (-;-men [mən]) rhythm

Richtbeil ['rɪçtbaɪl] n executioner's ax

Richtblei ['rɪçtblaɪ] n plummet

richten ['rɪçtən] tr arrange, adjust; put in order; (lenken) direct; (Waffe, Fernrohr) (auf acc) point (at), aim (at); (Bitte, Brief, Frage, Rede) (an acc) address (to); (Augenmerk, Streben) (auf acc) concentrate (on), focus (on); (Bett) make; (Essen) prepare; (ausbessern) fix; (gerade biegen) straighten; (jur) judge, sentence; (mil) dress; **zugrunde r.** ruin || ref (auf acc, gegen) be directed (at); **das richtet sich ganz danach, ob** it all depends on whether; **sich** [dat] **die Haare r.** do one's hair; **sich r. nach** follow the example of; **sich selbst r.** commit suicide || intr judge, sit in judgment

Rich'ter m (-s;-) judge

Rich'teramt n judgeship

Rich'terin f (-;-nen) judge

Rich'terkollegium n (jur) bench

rich'terlich adj judicial

Rich'terspruch m judgment; sentence

Rich'terstand m judiciary

Rich'terstuhl m tribunal, bench

richtig ['rɪçtɪç] adj right, correct; (echt) real, genuine; (genau) exact; (Zeit) proper || adv right, really, downright; **die Uhr geht r.** the clock keeps good time; **und r., da kam sie!** and sure enough, there she was!

rich'tiggehend adj (Uhr) keeping good time; (fig) regular

Rich'tigkeit f (-;) correctness; accuracy

rich'tigstellen tr rectify

Richtlinien ['rɪçtlinjən] pl guidelines

Richtlot ['rɪçtlot] n plumbline

Richtmaß ['rɪçtmas] n standard, gauge

Richtplatz ['rɪçtplats] m place of execution

Richtpreis ['rɪçtpraɪs] m standard price

Richtschnur ['rɪçt/nur] f plumbline; (fig) guiding principle

Richtschwert ['rɪçt/vert] n executioner's sword

Richtstätte ['rɪçt/tɛtə] f place of execution

Rich'tung f (-;-en) direction; (Weg) course; (Entwicklung) trend; (Einstellung) slant, view

Rich'tungsanzeiger m (aut) direction signal

Richtwaage ['rɪçtvagə] f level

rieb [rip] pret of reiben

riechen ['riçən] §102 tr smell; (fig) stand; **kein Pulver r. können** have no guts || intr smell; **r. an** (dat) sniff at; **r. nach** smell of

Riechsalz ['riçzalts] n smelling salts

rief [rif] pret of rufen

Riefe ['rifə] f (-;-n) groove; (archit) flute

Riege ['rigə] f (-;-n) (gym) squad

Riegel ['rigəl] m (-s;-) bolt; (Seife) cake; (Schokolade) bar

riegeln ['rigəln] tr bolt, bar

Riemen ['rimən] m (-s;-) strap; (Leib-, Trieb-) belt; (Ruder) oar; (e-s Gewehrs) sling

Rie'menscheibe f pulley

Ries [ris] n (-es;-e) ream (of one thousand sheets)

Riese ['rizə] m (-;-n) giant

rieseln ['rizəln] intr (HABEN & SEIN) trickle; (Bach) purl || impers—es rieselt it is drizzling

Rie'selregen m drizzle

Rie'senbomber m superbomber

Rie'senerfolg m smash hit

rie'sengroß adj gigantic

rie'senhaft adj gigantic

Rie'senrad n Ferris wheel

Rie'senschlange f boa constrictor

Rie'sentanne f (bot) sequoia

riesig ['rizɪç] adj gigantic, huge || adv (coll) awfully

Riesin ['rizɪn] f (-;-nen) giant

riet [rit] pret of raten

Riff [rɪf] n (-[e]s;-e) reef

Rille ['rɪlə] f (-;-n) groove; small furrow; (archit) flute

Rimesse [rɪ'mɛsə] f (-;-n) (com) remittance

Rind [rɪnt] n (-[e]s;-er) head of cattle; **Rinder** cattle

Rinde ['rɪndə] f (-;-n) rind; (Baum-) bark; (Brot-) crust; (anat) cortex

Rin'derbraten m roast beef

Rin'derbremse f horsefly

Rin'derherde f herd of cattle

Rin'derhirt m cowboy

Rind'fleisch n beef

Rinds'leder n cowhide

Rinds'lendenstück n rump steak, tenderloin

Rinds'rückenstück n sirloin of beef

Rind'vieh n cattle; (sl) idiot

Ring [rɪŋ] m (-[e]s;-e) ring; (Kreis) circle; (Kettenglied) link; (Kartell) combine; (astr) halo

Ringel ['rɪŋəl] m (-s;) small ring; (Locke) ringlet, curl

Rin'gelblume f marigold

ringeln ['rɪŋəln] tr & ref curl

Rin'gelreihen m ring-around-the-rosy

Rin'gelspiel n merry-go-round

ringen ['rɪŋən] §142 tr wrestle; (Wäsche, Hände) wring; (herauswinden) wrest || intr wrestle; (fig) struggle

Rin'ger –in §6 mf wrestler

Ring'kampf m wrestling match

Ring'mauer f town wall, city wall

Ring'richter m (box) referee

rings [rɪŋs] adv around; **r. um** all around

Ring'schlüssel m socket wrench

rings'herum', rings'um', rings'umher' adv all around

Rinne ['rɪnə] f (-;-n) groove; (Strombett) channel; (Leitung) duct; (Gosse) gutter; (Erdfurche) furrow

rinnen ['rɪnən] §121 *intr* (SEIN) run, flow; trickle || *intr* (HABEN) leak

Rinnsal ['rɪnzal] *n* (-[e]s;-e) little stream

Rinn'stein *m* gutter; (*Ausgußbecken*) sink; (*unterirdisch*) culvert

Rippchen ['rɪpçən] *n* (-s;-) cutlet

Rippe ['rɪpə] *f* (-;-n) rib; (*Schokolade*) bar; (*archit*) groin

rippen ['rɪpən] *tr* rib, flute

Rip'penfellentzündung *f* pleurisy

Rip'penstoß *m* nudge (in the ribs)

Rip'penstück *n* loin end

Risi·ko ['rizɪko] *n* (-s;-s & -ken [kən]) risk; **ein R. eingehen** take a risk

riskant [rɪs'kant] *adj* risky

riskieren [rɪs'kirən] *tr* risk

riß [rɪs] *pret of* **reißen** || **Riß** *m* (Risses; Risse) tear, rip; (*Bruch*) fracture; (*Lücke*) gap; (*Kratzer*) scratch; (*Spalt*) split, cleft; (*Spaltung*) fissure; (*Sprung*) crack; (*Zeichnung*) sketch; (*eccl*) schism; (*geol*) crevasse

rissig ['rɪsɪç] *adj* torn; cracked; split; (*Haut*) chapped

Rist [rɪst] *m* (-es;-e) wrist; (*des Fußes*) instep

ritt [rɪt] *pret of* **reiten** || **Ritt** *m* (-[e]s; -e) ride

Ritter ['rɪtər] *m* (-s;-) knight; cavalier; **zum R. schlagen** knight

Rit'tergut *n* manor

Rit'terkreuz *n* (mil) Knight's Cross (*of the Iron Cross*)

rit'terlich *adj* knightly; (fig) chivalrous

Rit'terlichkeit *f* (-;) chivalry

Rit'terzeit *f* age of chivalry

rittlings ['rɪtlɪŋs] *adv*—**r. auf** (*dat or acc*) astride

Ritual [rɪtu'al] *n* (-s;-e & -ien [jən]) ritual

rituell [rɪtu'el] *adj* ritual

Ri·tus ['ritus] *m* (-;-ten [tən]) rite

Ritz [rɪts] *m* (-es;-e), **Ritze** ['rɪtsə] *f* (-;-en) crack, crevice; (*Schlitz*) slit; (*Schramme*) scratch

ritzen ['rɪtsən] *tr* scratch; (*Glas*) cut

Rivale [rɪ'valə] *m* (-n;-n), **Rivalin** [rɪ'valɪn] *f* (-;-nen) rival

rivalisieren [rɪvalɪ'zirən] *intr* be in rivalry; **r. mit** rival

Rivalität [rɪvalɪ'tet] *f* (-;-en) rivalry

Rizinusöl ['ritsɪnusøl] *n* castor oil

Robbe ['rɔbə] *f* (-;-n) seal

robben ['rɔbən] *intr* (HABEN & SEIN) (mil) crawl (*using one's elbows*)

Rob'benfang *m* seal hunt

Robe ['rɔbə] *f* (-;-n) robe, gown

Roboter ['rɔbotər] *m* (-s;-) robot

robust [rɔ'bust] *adj* robust

roch [rɔx] *pret of* **riechen**

röcheln ['rœçəln] *tr* gasp out || *intr* rattle (*in one's throat*)

rochieren [rɔ'ʃirən] *intr* (chess) castle

Rock [rɔk] *m* (-[e]s;ⁿe) skirt; jacket

Rock'schoß *m* coattail

Rodel ['rɔdəl] *m* (-s;-) & *f* (-;-n) toboggan; (*mit Steuerung*) bobsled

Ro'delbahn *f* toboggan slide

rodeln ['rɔdəln] *intr* (HABEN & SEIN) toboggan

Ro'delschlitten *m* toboggan; bobsled

roden ['rɔdən] *tr* root out; (*Wald*) clear; (*Land*) make arable

Rogen ['rɔgan] *m* (-s;) roe, spawn

Roggen ['rɔgan] *m* (-s;) rye

roh [ro] *adj* raw; crude; (*Steine*) unhewn; (*Dielen*) bare; (fig) uncouth, brutal

Roh'bau *m* (-[e]s;-ten) rough brickwork

Roh'diamant *m* uncut diamond

Roh'einnahme *f* gross receipts

Roh'eisen *n* pig iron

Roh'heit *f* (-;) rawness, raw state; crudeness; brutality

Roh'entwurf *m* rough sketch

Roh'gewicht *n* gross weight

Roh'gewinn *m* gross profit

Roh'gummi *m* crude rubber

Roh'kost *f* uncooked vegetarian food

Rohling ['rɔlɪŋ] *m* (-s;-e) blank; slug; (fig) thug, hoodlum

Roh'material *n* raw material

Roh'öl *n* crude oil

Rohr [ror] *n* (-[e]s;-e) reed, cane; (*Röhre*) pipe, tube; (*Kanal*) duct, channel; (*Gewehrlauf*) barrel

Rohr'anschluß *m* pipe joint

Rohr'bogen *m* elbow

Röhre ['rørə] *f* (-;-n) tube, pipe; (electron) tube

Röh'renblitz *m* electronic flash

Röh'renblitzgerät *n* electronic flash unit

Rohr'leger *m* pipe fitter

Rohr'leitung *f* pipeline, main

Rohr'schäftung *f* sleeve joint

Rohr'schelle *f* pipe clamp

Rohr'zange *f* pipe wrench

Rohr'zucker *m* cane sugar

Roh'stoff *m* raw material

Rolladen (Roll'laden) *m* sliding shutter; sliding cover

Rollbahn ['rɔlban] *f* (aer) runway; (mil) road leading up to the front

Röllchen ['rœlçən] *n* (-s;-) caster

Rolldach ['rɔldax] *n* (aut) sun roof

Rolle ['rɔlə] *f* (-;-n) roll; (*Walze*) roller; (*Flaschenzug*) pulley; (*Spule*) spool, reel; (*unter Möbeln*) caster; (*Mangel*) mangle; (*Liste*) list, register; (theat) role; **aus der R. fallen** (fig) misbehave; **spielt keine R.!** never mind!, forget it!

rollen ['rɔlən] *tr* roll; (*auf Rädern*) wheel; (*Wäsche*) mangle; || *ref* curl up || *intr* (HABEN & SEIN) roll; (*Flugzeug*) taxi; (*Geschütze*) roar || **Rollen** *n*—**ins. R. kommen** get going

Rol'lenbesetzung *f* (theat) cast

Rol'lenlager *n* roller bearing

Rol'lenzug *m* block and tackle

Rol'ler *m* (-s;-) scooter; motor scooter

Roll'feld *n* (aer) runway

Roll'kragen *m* turtleneck

Roll'mops *m* pickled herring

Rollo ['rɔlo] *n* (-s;-s) (coll) blind, shade

Roll'schuh *m* roller skate; **R. laufen** roller-skate

Roll'schuhbahn *f* roller-skating rink

Roll'stuhl *m* wheelchair

Roll'treppe *f* escalator

Roll'wagen m truck
Rom [rom] n (-s;) Rome
Roman [ro'man] m (-s;-e) novel
Roman'folge f serial
roman'haft adj fictional
romanisch [ro'manɪʃ] adj (Sprache) Romance; (archit) Romanesque
Romanist –**in** [roma'nɪst(ɪn)] §7 mf scholar of Romance languages
Roman'schriftsteller –**in** §6 mf novelist
Romantik [ro'mantɪk] f (-;) Romanticism
romantisch [ro'mantɪʃ] adj romantic
Romanze [ro'mantsə] (-;-n) romance
Römer –**in** ['rømər(ɪn)] §6 mf Roman
römisch ['rømɪʃ] adj Roman
rö'misch-katho'lisch adj Roman Catholic
röntgen ['rœntgən] tr x-ray
Rönt'genapparat m x-ray machine
Rönt'genarzt m, **Rönt'genärztin** f radiologist
Rönt'genaufnahme f, **Rönt'genbild** n x-ray
Rönt'genstrahlen pl x-rays
rosa ['roza] adj pink ‖ **Rosa** n (-s; & -s) pink
Rose ['rozə] f (-;-n) rose
Ro'senkohl m Brussels sprouts
Ro'senkranz m (eccl) rosary
ro'senrot adj rosy, rose-colored
Ro'senstock m rosebush
rosig ['rozɪç] adj (& fig) rosy; (Laune) happy
Rosine [ro'zinə] f (-;-n) raisin
Roß [rɔs] n (Rosses; Rosse) horse; (sl) jerk; (poet) steed
Rost [rɔst] m (-es;) rust; mildew ‖ m (-es;-e) grate; grill; **auf dem R. braten** grill
Rost'braten m roast beef
Röstbrot ['rœstbrot] n toast
rosten ['rɔstən] intr rust
rösten ['rœstən] tr (auf dem Rost) grill; (in der Pfanne) fry; (Brot) toast; (Mais) pop; (Kaffee) roast
Rö'ster m (-s;-) roaster; toaster
Rost'fleck m rust stain
rost'frei adj rust-proof; (Stahl) stainless
rostig ['rɔstɪç] adj rusty, corroded
rot [rot] adj (röter ['røtər], röteste ['røtəstə] §9) red ‖ **Rot** n (-es;) red; (Schminke) rouge
Rotation [rota'tsjon] f (-;-en) rotation
Rotations'maschine f rotary press
rotbäckig ['rotbɛkɪç] adj red-cheeked
Rot'dorn m (bot) pink hawthorn
Röte ['røtə] f (-;) red(ness); blush
Röteln ['røtəln] pl German measles
rotieren [ro'tirən] intr rotate
Rotkäppchen ['rotkɛpçən] n (-s;) Little Red Riding Hood
Rotkehlchen ['rotkelçən] n (-s;-) robin
rötlich ['røtlɪç] adj reddish
Ro·tor ['rotor] m (-s;-toren ['torən] (aer) rotor; (elec) armature
Rot'schimmel m roan (horse)
Rot'tanne f spruce
Rotte ['rɔtə] f (-;-n) gang, mob
Rotz [rɔts] m (-es;-e) (sl) snot
rot'zig adj (sl) snotty

Rouleau [ru'lo] n (-s;-s) window shade
Route ['rutə] f (-;-n) route
Routine [ru'tinə] f (-;) routine; practice, experience
routiniert [ruti'nirt] adj experienced
Rübe ['rybə] f (-;-n) beet; **gelbe R.** carrot; **weiße R.** turnip
Rubin [ru'bin] m (-s;-e) ruby
Rubrik [ru'brik] f (-;-en) rubric; heading; (Spalte) column
ruchbar ['ruxbar] adj known, public
ruchlos ['ruxlos] adj wicked
Ruck [ruk] m (-[e]s;-e) jerk; yank; jolt; **auf e-n R.** at once; **mit e-m R.** in one quick move
Rück-, rück- [ryk] comb.fm. re-, back, rear; return
Rück'ansicht f rear view
Rück'antwort f reply; **Postkarte mit R.** prepaid reply postcard
rück'bezüglich adj (gram) reflexive
Rück'bleibsel n remainder
rücken ['rykən] tr move, shove ‖ intr (SEIN) move; (Platz machen) move over; (marschieren) march; **höher r.** be promoted; **näher r.** approach ‖ **Rücken** m (-s;-) back; (Rückseite) rear; (der Nase) bridge
Rückendeckung (**Rük'kendeckung**) f (fig) backing, support
Rückenlehne (**Rük'kenlehne**) f back rest
Rückenmark (**Rük'kenmark**) n spinal cord
Rückenschwimmen (**Rük'kenschwimmen**) n backstroke
Rückenwind (**Rük'kenwind**) m tail wind
Rückenwirbel (**Rük'kenwirbel**) m (anat) vertebra
rück'erstatten tr reimburse, refund
Rück'fahrkarte f, **Rück'fahrschein** m round-trip ticket
Rück'fahrt f return trip
Rück'fall m relapse
rück'fällig adj habitual, relapsing
rück'federnd adj resilient
Rück'flug m return flight
Rück'frage f further question
Rück'führung f repatriation
Rück'gabe f return, restitution
Rück'gang m return; regression; (der Preise) drop; (econ) recession
rückgängig ['rykgɛnɪç] adj retrogressive; dropping; **r. machen** cancel
rück'gewinnen §121 tr recover
Rück'grat m backbone, spine
Rück'griff m (auf acc) recourse (to)
Rück'halt m backing; (mil) reserves; **e-n R. an j–m haben** have s.o.'s backing; **ohne R.** without reservation
rück'haltlos adj frank, unreserved ‖ adv without reserve
Rück'handschlag m (tennis) back-hand stroke
Rück'kauf m repurchase
Rück'kehr f return; (fig) comeback
Rück'kopplung f (electron) feedback
Rück'lage f reserves, savings
Rück'lauf m reverse; (mil) recoil
Rück'läufer m letter returned to sender
rückläufig ['ryklɔɪfɪç] adj retrograde

Rück'licht n (aut) taillight
rücklings ['rʏklɪŋs] adv backwards
Rück'nahme f withdrawal, taking back
Rück'porto n return postage
Rück'prall m bounce, rebound, recoil
Rück'reise f return trip
Ruck'sack m knapsack
Rück'schau m—**R. halten auf** (acc) look back on
Rück'schlag m back stroke; (e-s Balles) bounce; (fig) setback
Rück'schluß m conclusion, inference
Rück'schritt m backward step; (fig) falling off, retrogression
Rück'seite f back; reverse; wrong side
Rück'sicht f regard, respect, consideration; **aus R. auf** (acc) out of consideration for; **in** (or **mit**) **R. auf** (acc) in regard to; **ohne R. auf** (acc) irrespective of; **R. nehmen auf** (acc) take into account, show consideration for
rück'sichtlich prep (genit) considering
rück'sichtslos adj inconsiderate; reckless; ruthless
rück'sichtsvoll adj considerate
Rück'sitz m (aut) rear seat
Rück'spiegel m (aut) rear-view mirror
Rück'spiel n return match
Rück'sprache f discussion; conference; **R. nehmen mit** consult with
Rück'stand m arrears; (Satz) sediment; (Rest) remainder; (von Aufträgen, usw.) backlog; (chem) residue
rück'ständig adj behind, in arrears; (Geld) outstanding; (Raten) delinquent; (altmodisch) backward
Rück'stau m back-up water
Rück'stelltaste f backspace key
Rück'stoß m repulsion; recoil, kick
Rückstrahler ['rʏkstralər] m (-s;-) reflector
Rück'strahlung f reflection
Rück'tritt m resignation
Rück'trittbremse f coaster brake
Rück'umschlag m return envelope
rückwärts ['rʏkverts] adv backward(s)
Rück'wärtsgang m (aut) reverse
Rück'weg m way back, return
ruck'weise adv by fits and starts
rück'wirken intr react
rück'wirkend adj retroactive
Rück'wirkung f (-;-en) reaction; repercussion
rück'zahlen tr repay, refund
Rück'zug m withdrawal; retreat; **zum R. blasen** sound the retreat
Rück'zugsgefecht n running fight
rüde ['rydə] adj rude, coarse || **Rüde** m (-n;-n) male (wolf, fox, etc.)
Rudel ['rudəl] n (-s;-) herd; flock; (von Wölfen, U-Booten) wolf pack
Ruder ['rudər] n (-s;-) (aer, naut) rudder; (naut) oar
Ru'derblatt n blade of an oar
Ru'derboot n rowboat
Ru'derer -in §6 mf rower
Ru'derklampe f oarlock
rudern ['rudərn] tr & intr row
Ru'derschlag m stroke of the oar
Ru'dersport m (sport) crew
Ruf [ruf] m (-[e]s;-e) call; shout, yell; (Berufung) vocation; (Nach-

rede) reputation; appointment; (com) credit
rufen ['rufən] §122 tr call; shout; **r. lassen** send for || intr call; shout
Ruf'mord m character assassination
Ruf'name m first name
Ruf'nummer f telephone number
Ruf'weite f—**in R.** within earshot
Ruf'zeichen n (rad) station identification; (telp) call sign
Rüge ['rygə] f (-;-n) reprimand
rügen ['rygən] tr reprimand
Ruhe ['ru·ə] f (-;) rest; quiet, calm; (Frieden) peace; (Stille) silence; **immer mit der R.!** (coll) take it easy!
ru'hebedürftig adj in need of rest
Ru'hegehalt n pension
Ru'hekur f rest cure
ru'helos adj restless
ruhen ['ru·ən] intr rest; sleep
Ru'hepause f pause, break
Ru'heplatz m resting place
Ru'hestand m retirement
Rü'hestätte f resting place
Ru'hestörer -in §6 mf disturber of the peace
Ru'hetag m day of rest, day off
Ru'hezeit f leisure
ruhig ['ru·ɪç] adj still, quiet; calm
Ruhm [rum] m (-[e]s;) glory, fame
rühmen ['rymən] tr praise || ref (genit) boast (about)
rühmlich ['rymlɪç] adj praiseworthy
ruhm'los adj inglorious
ruhmredig ['rumredɪç] adj vainglorious
ruhm'reich adj glorious
ruhm'voll adj famous, glorious
ruhm'würdig adj praiseworthy
Ruhr [rur] f (-;) dysentery; **Ruhr** (river)
Rührei ['ryrar] n scrambled egg
rühren ['ryrən] tr stir; touch, move; (Trommel) beat; **alle Kräfte r.** exert every effort || ref stir, move; get a move on; **rührt euch!** (mil) at ease! || intr stir, move; **r. an** (acc) touch; (fig) mention; **r. von** originate in
rührig ['ryrɪç] adj active; agile
Rührlöffel ['ryrlœfəl] m ladle
rührselig ['ryrzelɪç] adj sentimental
Rührstück ['ryrftyk] n soap opera
Rüh'rung f (-;-en) emotion
Ruin [ru'in] m (-s;) ruin; decay
Ruine [ru'inə] f (-;-n) ruins; (fig) wreck
rui'nenhaft adj ruinous
ruinieren [ru·i'nirən] tr ruin
Rülps [rʏlps] m (-es;-e) belch
rülpsen ['rʏlpsən] intr belch
Rülp'ser m (-s;-) belch
Rum [rum] m (-s;-s) rum
Rumäne [ru'menə] m (-n;-n) Rumanian
Rumänien [ru'menjən] n (-s;) Rumania
Rumänin [ru'menɪn] f (-;-nen) Rumanian
rumänisch [ru'menɪʃ] adj Rumanian
Rummel ['ruməl] m (-s;) junk; racket; hustle and bustle; **auf den R. gehen** go to the fair; **den ganzen R. kaufen** (coll) buy the works
Rum'melplatz m amusement park, fair
Rumor [ru'mor] m (-s;) noise, racket.

Rumpel ['rumpəl] f (-;-n) scrub board
Rum'pelkammer f storage room, junk room
Rum'pelkasten m (aut) jalopy
rumpeln ['rumpəln] tr (Wäsche) scrub || intr rumble, rattle
Rumpf [rumpf] m (-[e]s;⁼e) trunk, body; torso; (aer) fuselage; (naut) hull
rümpfen ['rʏmpfən] tr—**die Nase r. über** (acc) turn up one's nose at
rund [runt] adj round; (Absage) flat || adv around; about, approximately; **r. um** ground
Rund'blick m panorama
Rund'brief m circular letter
Runde ['rundə] f (-;-n) round; (box) round; (beim Rennsport) lap
runden ['rundən] tr make round; round off || ref become round
Rund'erlaß m circular
rund'erneuern tr (aut) retread; **runderneuerter Reifen** m retread
Rund'fahrt f sightseeing tour
Rund'flug m (aer) circuit
Rund'frage f questionnaire, poll
Rund'funk m radio; **im R.** on the radio
Rund'funkansage f radio announcement
Rund'funkansager –in §6 mf radio announcer
Rund'funkgerät n radio set
Rund'funkgesellschaft f broadcasting company
Rund'funkhörer –in §6 mf listener
Rund'funknetz n radio network
Rund'funksender m broadcasting station
Rund'funksendung f radio broadcast
Rund'funksprecher –in §6 mf announcer
Rund'funkwerbung f (rad) commercial
Rund'gang m tour; stroll
rund'heraus' adv plainly, flatly
rundherum' adv all around
rund'lich adj round; (dick) plump
Rund'reise f sightseeing tour
Rund'schau f panorama; (journ) news in brief
Rund'schreiben n circular letter
rundweg ['runt'vɛk] adv bluntly, flatly

Runzel ['runtsəl] f (-;-n) wrinkle
runzelig ['runtsəlɪç] adj wrinkled
runzeln ['runtsəln] tr wrinkle; **die Brauen r.** knit one's brows; **die Stirn r.** frown || ref wrinkle
Rüpel ['rypəl] m (-s;-) boor
rü'pelhaft adj rude, boorish
rupfen ['rupfən] tr pluck; (fig) fleece
ruppig ['rupɪç] adj shabby; (fig) rude
Ruprecht ['rupreçt] m (-s;)—**Knecht R.** Santa Claus
Ruß [rus] m (-es;) soot
Russe ['rusə] m (-n;-n) Russian
Rüssel ['rysəl] m (-s;-) snout; (Elephanten-) trunk; (coll) snoot; (ent) proboscis
rußig ['rusɪç] adj sooty
Russin ['rusɪn] f (-;-nen) Russian
russisch ['rusɪʃ] adj Russian
Rußland ['ruslant] n (-s;) Russia
Rüst- [ryst] comb.fm. scaffolding; armament, munition
rüsten ['rystən] tr arm, equip; prepare || ref get ready || intr (zu) get ready (for); **zum Krieg r.** mobilize
Rüster ['rystər] f (-;-n) elm
rüstig ['rystɪç] adj vigorous; alert
Rüst'kammer f armory, arsenal
Rü'stung f (-;-en) preparation; equipment; armament; mobilization; armor; implements; (archit) scaffolding
Rü'stungsbetrieb m munitions factory
Rü'stungsfertigung f war production
Rü'stungsindustrie f war industry
Rü'stungskontrolle f arms control
Rü'stungsmaterial n war materiel
Rü'stungsstand m state of preparedness
Rüst'zeug n kit; (fig) knowledge
Rute ['rutə] f (-;-n) rod; twig; tail; (anat) penis
Rutsch [rutʃ] m (-es;-e) slip, slide
Rutsch'bahn f slide; chute
Rutsche ['rutʃə] f (-;-n) slide; chute
rutschen ['rutʃən] intr (SEIN) slip, slide; (aut) skid
rutschig ['rutʃɪç] adj slippery
rütteln ['rytəln] tr shake; jolt; (Getreide) winnow; (aus dem Schlafe) rouse || intr—**r. an** (acc) cause to rattle; (fig) try to undermine

---

S

S, s [es] invar n S, s
SA abbr (mil) (Sturmabteilung) storm troopers
Saal [zal] m (-[e]s; **Säle** ['zelə]) hall
Saat [zat] f (-;-en) seed; (Säen) sowing; (Getreide auf dem Halm) crop(s); **die S. bestellen** sow
Saat'bestellung f sowing
Saat'kartoffel f seed potato
Sabbat ['zabat] m (-s;-e) Sabbath
Sabberei [zabə'raɪ] f (-;-en) drooling; (Geschwätz) drivel
sabbern ['zabərn] intr drool, drivel

Säbel ['zebəl] m (-s;) saber; **mit dem S. rasseln** (pol) rattle the saber
sä'belbeinig adj bowlegged
säbeln ['zebəln] tr (coll) hack
Sä'belrasseln n (pol) saber rattling
Sabotage [zabo'taʒə] f (-;-n) sabotage
Saboteur [zabo'tør] m (-s;-e) saboteur
sabotieren [zabo'tirən] tr sabotage
Saccharin [zaxa'rin] n (-s;) saccharin
Sach- [zax] comb.fm. of facts, factual
Sach'anlagevermögen n tangible fixed assets
Sach'bearbeiter –in §6 mf specialist

Sach'beschädigung f property damage
Sach'bezüge pl compensation in kind
Sach'buch n nonfiction (work)
Sach'darstellung f statement of facts
sach'dienlich adj relevant, pertinent || adv
Sache ['zaxə] f (-;-n) thing, matter;
cause; (jur) case; **bei der S. sein** be
on the ball; **beschlossene S.** foregone
conclusion; **die S. der Freiheit** the
cause of freedom; **große S.** big affair; **gute S.** good cause; **heikle S.**
delicate point; **in eigner S.** on one's
own behalf; **in Sachen X gegen Y**
(jur) in the case of X versus Y;
meine sieben Sachen all my belongings; **nicht bei der S. sein** not be with
it; **nicht zur S. gehörig** irrelevant;
von der S. abkommen get off the
subject; **zur S.!** come to the point!
(parl) question!
sach'gemäß adj proper, pertinent || adv
in a suitable manner
Sach'kenner –in §6 mf expert
Sach'kenntnis f, **Sach'kunde** f expertise
sach'kundig adj expert || **Sach'kundige**
§5 mf expert
Sach'lage f state of affairs, circumstances
Sach'leistung f payment in kind
sach'lich adj (treffend) to the point;
(gegenständlich) objective; (tatsächlich) factual; (unparteiisch) impar-
tial; (nüchtern) matter-of-fact || adv
to the point
sächlich ['zeçlıç] adj (gram) neuter
Sach'lichkeit f (-;) objectivity; reality;
impartiality; matter-of-factness
Sach'register n index
Sach'schaden m property damage
Sach'schadenersatz m indemnity (for
property damage)
Sachse ['zaksə] m (-n;-n) Saxon
Sachsen ['zaksən] n (-s;) Saxony
sächsisch ['zeksı/] adj Saxon
sacht(e) ['zaxt(ə)] adj soft, gentle;
(langsam) slow || adv gingerly; im-
mer sacht! easy does it!
Sach'verhalt m facts of the case
Sach'vermögen n real property
sach'verständig adj experienced ||
Sachverständige §5 mf expert
Sach'wert m actual value; **Sachwerte**
material assets
Sach'wörterbuch n encyclopedia
Sack [zak] m (-[e]s;-e) sack, bag;
pocket; **j–n in den S. stecken** (coll)
be way above s.o.; **mit S. und Pack**
bag and baggage
Säckel ['zɛkəl] m (-s;-) little bag;
pocket; purse
sacken ['zakən] tr bag || ref be baggy
|| intr (SEIN) sag; (archit) settle;
(naut) founder
Sack'gasse f blind alley, dead end;
(fig) stalemate, dead end
Sack'leinwand f burlap
Sack'pfeife f bagpipe
Sack'tuch n handkerchief
Sadist –in [za'dıst(ın)] §7 mf sadist
sadistisch [za'dıstı/] adj sadistic
säen ['ze·ən] tr & intr sow
Saffian ['zafjan] m (-s;) morocco

Safran ['zafran] m (-s;-e) saffron
Saft [zaft] m (-[e]s;-̈e) juice; sap;
(culin) gravy
saftig ['zaftıç] adj juicy; (Witze) spicy
saft'los adj juiceless; (fig) wishy-washy
saft'reich adj juicy, succulent
Sage ['zagə] f (-;-n) legend, saga
Säge ['zegə] f (-;-n) saw
Sä'geblatt n saw blade
Sä'gebock m sawhorse, sawbuck
Sä'gefisch m sawfish
Sä'gemehl n sawdust
sagen ['zagən] tr say; (mitteilen) tell;
das hat nichts zu s. that's neither
here nor there; **das will nicht s.** that
is not to say; **gesagt, getan** no sooner
said than done; **j–m s. lassen** send
s.o. word; **laß dir gesagt sein** let it
be a warning to you; **sich** [dat]
nichts s. lassen not listen to reason
sägen ['zegən] tr saw || intr saw; (coll)
snore, cut wood
sa'genhaft adj legendary
Sägespäne ['zegə/penə] pl sawdust
Sä'gewerk n sawmill
sah [za] pret of **sehen**
Sahne ['zanə] f (-;) cream
Saison [sɛ'zõ] f (-;-s) season
Saison– comb.fm. seasonal
saison'bedingt, saison'mäßig adj sea-
sonal
Saite ['zaitə] f (-;-n) string, chord
Sai'teninstrument n string instrument
Sakko ['zako] m & n (-s;-s) suit coat
Sak'koanzug m sport suit
Sakrament [zakra'ment] n (-[e]s;-e)
sacrament; **das S. des Altars** the
Eucharist || interj (sl) dammit!
Sakrileg [zakrı'lek] n (-s;-e) sacrilege
Sakristan [zakrıs'tan] m (-s;-e) sac-
ristan
Sakristei [zakrıs'tai] f (-;-en) sacristy
Säkular– [zekular] comb.fm. secular;
centennial
säkularisieren [zekuları'zirən] tr secu-
larize
Salami [za'lami] f (-;-s) salami
Salat [za'lat] m (-[e]s;-e) salad; lettuce; **gemischter S.** tossed salad
Salat'soße f salad dressing
salbadern [zal'badərn] intr talk hypo-
critically, put on the dog
Salbe ['zalbə] f (-;-n) salve
salben ['zalbən] tr put salve on; anoint
Sal'bung f (-;-en) anointing
sal'bungsvoll adj unctuous
saldieren [zal'dirən] tr (com) balance
Sal·do ['zaldo] m (-s;-s & di [di])
(acct) balance; **e–n S. aufstellen** (or
ziehen) strike a balance; **e–n S. ausweisen** show a balance
Saline [za'linə] f (-;-n) saltworks
Salmiak [zal'mjak] m (-s;) ammonium
chloride, sal ammoniac
Salmiak'geist m ammonia
Salon [za'lõ] m (-s;-s) salon; parlor,
living room
salon'fähig adj (Aussehen) presentable;
(Ausdruck) fit for polite company
Salon'held m, **Salon'löwe** m ladies' man
salopp [za'lɔp] adj sloppy; (ungezwungen) casual
Salpeter [zal'petər] m (-s;) saltpeter

salpeterig [zal'petəriç] *adj* nitrous
Salpe'tersäure *f* nitric acid
Salto ['zalto] *m* (-s;-s) somersault
Salut [za'lut] *m* (-[e]s;-e) salute; **S. schießen** fire a salute
salutieren [zalu'tirən] *tr & intr* salute
Salve ['zalvə] *f* (-;-n) volley, salvo
Salz [zalts] *n* (-es;-e) salt
Salz'bergwerk *n* salt mine
Salz'brühe *f* brine
salzen ['zaltsən] *tr* salt
Salz'faß *n* salt shaker
Salz'fleisch *n* salted meat
Salz'gurke *f* pickle
salz'haltig *adj* saline
Salz'hering *m* pickled herring
salzig ['zaltsiç] *adj* salty; saline
Salz'kartoffeln *pl* boiled potatoes
Salz'lake *f* brine
Salz'säure *f* hydrochloric acid, muriatic acid
Salz'sole *f* brine
Salz'werk *n* salt works
Samariter –in [zama'ritər(ın)] §6 *mf* Samaritan
Same ['zamə] *m* (-ns;-n), **Samen** ['zamən] *m* (-s;-) seed; (biol) semen
Sa'menkorn *n* grain of seed
Sa'menstaub *m* pollen
Samentierchen ['zaməntirçən] *n* (-s;-) spermatozoon
sämig ['zemiç] *adj* (culin) thick, creamy
Sämischleder ['zemiʃledər] *n* chamois
Sämling ['zemlıŋ] *m* (-s;-e) seedling
Sammel– [zaməl] *comb.fm.* collecting, collective
Sam'melbatterie *f* storage battery
Sam'melbecken *n* reservoir; storage tank
Sam'melbegriff *m* collective noun
Sam'melbüchse *f* poor box
Sam'mellinse *f* convex lens
sammeln ['zaməln] *tr* gather; collect; (*Aufmerksamkeit, Truppen*) concentrate || *ref* gather; compose oneself; **sich wieder s.** (mil) reassemble
Sam'melname *m* collective noun
Sam'melplatz *m* collecting point; meeting place; (mil) rendezvous
Sam'melverbindung *f* conference call
Sam'melwerk *n* compilation
Sammler ['zamlər] *m* (-s;-) collector; compiler; (elec) storage cell
Samm'lung *f* (-;-en) collection; (*Zusammenstellung*) compilation; (*Fassung*) composure; concentration
Samstag ['zamstak] *m* (-[e]s;-e) Saturday
samt [zamt] *adv*—**s. und sonders** each and everyone, without exception || *prep* (*dat*) together with || **Samt** *m* (-[e]s;-e) velvet
samt'artig *adj* velvety
sämtlich ['zemtliç] *adj* all, complete || *adv* all together
Sanato·rium [zana'torjum] *n* (-s;-rien [rjən]) sanitarium
Sand [zant] *m* (-[e]s;-e) sand; **im Sande verlaufen** (fig) peter out
Sandale [zan'dalə] *f* (-;-n) sandal
Sand'bahn *f* (sport) dirt track
Sand'bank *f* (-;ˑe) sandbank

Sand'boden *m* sandy soil
Sand'düne *f* sand dune
Sand'grube *f* sand pit
sandig ['zandıç] *adj* sandy
Sand'kasten *m* sand box
Sand'korn *n* grain of sand
Sand'mann *m* (-[e]s;) (*fig*) sandman
Sand'papier *n* sandpaper; **mit S. abschleifen** sand, sandpaper
Sand'sack *m* sandbag
Sand'stein *m* sandstone
Sand'steingebäude *n* brownstone
sand'strahlen *tr* sandblast
Sand'sturmgebiet *n* dust bowl
sandte ['zantə] *pret of* **senden**
Sand'torte *f* sponge cake
Sand'uhr *f* hour glass
Sand'wüste *f* sandy desert
sanft [zanft] *adj* soft, gentle
Sänfte ['zenftə] *f* (-;-n) sedan chair
Sanft'mut *f* gentleness, meekness
sanft'mütig *adj* gentle, meek, mild
sang [zaŋ] *pret of* **singen** || **Sang** *m* (-[e]s;ˑe) song; **mit S. und Klang** (fig) with great fanfare
sang–/und klang'los *adv* unceremoniously
Sänger ['zeŋər] *m* (-s;-) singer
Sän'gerchor *m* glee club
Sängerin ['zeŋərın] *f* (-;-nen) singer
Sanguiniker [zaŋ'gwinıkər] *m* (-s;-) optimist
sanguinisch [zaŋ'gwinıʃ] *adj* sanguine
sanieren [za'nirən] *tr* cure; improve the sanitary conditions of; disinfect; (fin) put on a firm basis
Sanie'rung *f* (-;-en) restoration; reorganization
sanitär [zani'ter] *adj* sanitary
Sanitäter [zani'tetər] *m* (-s;-) first-aid-man; (mil) medic
Sanitäts– [zanitets] *comb.fm.* first-aid, medical
Sanitäts'korps *n* army medical corps
Sanitäts'soldat *m* medic
Sanitäts'wache *f* first-aid station
Sanitäts'wagen *m* ambulance
Sanitäts'zug *m* hospital train
sank [zaŋk] *pret of* **sinken**
Sanka ['zaŋka] *m* (-s;-s) (**Sanitätskraftwagen**) field ambulance
Sankt [zaŋkt] *invar mf* Saint
Sanktion [zaŋk'tsjon] *f* (-;-en) sanction
sanktionieren [zaŋktsjo'nirən] *tr* sanction
sann [zan] *pret of* **sinnen**
Saphir ['zafır] *m* (-s;-e) sapphire
sapperment [zapər'mɛnt] *interj* the deuce!
Sardelle [zar'dɛlə] *f* (-;-n) anchovy
Sardine [zar'dinə] *f* (-;-n) sardine
Sardinien [zar'dinjən] (-s;) Sardinia
sardinisch [zar'dinıʃ] *adj* Sardinian
Sarg [zark] *m* (-[e]s;ˑe) coffin
Sarg'tuch *n* pall
Sarkasmus [zar'kasmus] *m* (-;) sarcasm
sarkastisch [zar'kastıʃ] *adj* sarcastic
Sarkophag [zarko'fak] *m* (-s;-e) sarcophagus
saß [zas] *pret of* **sitzen**
Satan ['zatan] *m* (-s;-e) Satan

satanisch [za'tɑnɪʃ] *adj* satanic(al)
Satellit [zate'lit] *m* (-en;-en) satellite
Satin [sa'tɛ̃] *m* (-s;-s) satin
Satire [za'tirə] *f* (-;-n) satire
Satiriker –in [za'tirɪkər(ɪn)] §6 *mf* satirist
satirisch [za'tirɪʃ] *adj* satirical
satt [zat] *adj* satisfied; satiated; (*Farben*) deep, rich; (chem) saturated; **etw s. bekommen** (or **haben**) be fed up with s.th.; **ich bin s.** I've had enough; **sich s. essen** eat one's fill
Sattel ['zatəl] *m* (-s;⸚) saddle
sat'telfest *adj* (fig) well-versed
Sat'telgurt *m* girth
satteln ['zatəln] *tr* saddle
Sat'telschlepper *m* semi-trailer
Sat'teltasche *f* saddlebag
Satt'heit *f* (-;) saturation; (*der Farben*) richness
sättigen ['zɛtɪgən] *tr* satisfy, satiate; saturate
Sät'tigung *f* (-;) satiation; saturation
Sattler ['zatlər] *m* (-s;-) harness maker
sattsam ['zatzam] *adv* sufficiently
saturieren [zatu'rirən] *tr* saturate
Satz [zats] *m* (-es;⸚e) sentence; clause; phrase; (*Behauptung*) proposition; (*Bodensatz*) grounds; sediment; (*Betrag*) amount; (*Tarif*) rate; (*Gebühr*) fee; (*Garnitur*) set; (*Sprung*) leap; (*Wette*) stake; (*Menge*) batch; (math) theorem; (mus) movement; (tennis) set; (typ) typesetting, composition; **e-n S. machen** jump; **e-n S. aufstellen** set down an article of faith; **einfacher S.** simple sentence; **hauptwörtlicher S.** substantive clause; **in S. gehen** go to press; **verkürzter S.** phrase; **zum S. von** at the rate of; **zusammengesetzter S.** compound sentence
Satz'aussage *f* (gram) predicate
Satz'bau *m* (-[e]s;) (gram) construction
Satz'gefüge *n* complex sentence
Satz'gegenstand *m* (gram) subject
Satz'lehre *f* syntax
Satz'teil *m* (gram) part of speech
Sat'zung *f* (-;-en) rule, regulation; (*Vereins-*) bylaw; statute
sat'zungsgemäß, sat'zungsmäßig *adj* statutory, according to the bylaws
Satz'zeichen *n* punctuation mark
Sau [zau] *f* (-;⸚e) sow; (pej) pig; **wie e-e gesengte Sau fahren** drive like a maniac
Sau'arbeit *f* (coll) sloppy work; (coll) tough job; (coll) dirty job
sauber ['zaubər] *adj* clean; exact
säuberlich ['zɔɪbərlɪç] *adj* clean, neat; (*anständig*) decent
sau'bermachen *tr* clean, clean up
säubern ['zɔɪbərn] *tr* clean; (*freimachen*) clear; (*Buch*) expurgate; (mil) mop up; (pol) purge
Säu'berungsaktion *f* (mil) mopping-up operation; (pol) purge
Sau'borste *f* hog bristle
Sauce ['zosə] *f* (-;-n) sauce; gravy; (*Salat-*) dressing
sau'dumm' *adj* (coll) awfully dumb
sauer ['zau·ər] *adj* sour

Sau'erbraten *m* braised beef soaked in vinegar
Sauerei [zau·ə'raɪ] *f* (-;-en) filth, filthy joke
Sau'erkohl *m*, Sau'erkraut *n* sauerkraut
säuerlich ['zɔɪ·ərlɪç] *adj* sourish, acidulous; (*Lächeln*) forced
säuern ['zɔɪ·ərn] *tr* sour; (*Teig*) leaven || *intr* turn sour, acidify
Sau'erstoff *m* (-[e]s;) oxygen
Sau'erstofflasche *f* oxygen tank
Sau'erteig *m* leaven
Sau'ertopf *m* (coll) sourpuss
Sau'erwasser *n* sparkling water
Saufaus ['zaufaus] *m* (-;-), Saufbold ['zaufbɔlt] *m* (-[e]s;-e), Saufbruder ['zaufbrudər] *m* (coll) booze hound
saufen ['zaufən] §124 *tr* drink, guzzle || *intr* drink; (sl) booze
Säufer –in ['zɔɪfər(ɪn)] §6 *mf* drunkard
Saufgelage ['zaufgəlagə] *n* booze party
Sau'fraß *m* terrible food, slop
Säugamme ['zɔɪkamə] *f* wet nurse
saugen ['zaugən] §109 & §125 *tr* suck || *ref*—sich [*dat*] etw aus den Fingern s. invent s.th., make up s.th.
säugen ['zɔɪgən] *tr* suckle, nurse
Sauger ['zaugər] *m* (-s;-) sucker; nipple; pacifier
Säuger ['zɔɪgər] *m* (-s;-), Säugetier ['zɔɪgətir] *n* mammal
Saug'flasche *f* baby bottle
Säugling ['zɔɪklɪŋ] *m* (-s;-e) baby
Säug'lingsausstattung *f* layette
Säug'lingsheim *n* nursery
Sau'glück *n* (coll) dumb luck
Saug'napf *m* suction cup
Saug'pumpe *f* suction pump
Saug'watte *f* absorbent cotton
Saug'wirkung *f* suction
Sau'hund *m* (sl) louse, dirty dog
Sau'igel *m* (sl) dirty guy
sauigeln ['zau·igəln] *intr* (sl) tell dirty jokes
Sau'kerl *m* (sl) cad, skunk
Säule ['zɔɪlə] *f* (-;-n) column; (& fig) pillar; (elec) dry battery; (phys) pile
Säu'lenfuß *m* base of a column
Säu'lengang *m* colonnade, peristyle
Säu'lenhalle *f* portico, gallery
Säu'lenkapitell *n*, Säu'lenknauf *m*, Säu'lenknopf *m* (archit) capital
Säu'lenschaft *m* shaft of a column
Säu'lenvorbau *m* portico, (front) porch
Saum [zaum] *m* (-[e]s;⸚e) seam, hem; (*Rand*) border; (*e-r Stadt*) outskirts
säumen ['zɔɪmən] *tr* hem; border; (*Straßen*) line || *intr* tarry
Sau'mensch *n* (vulg) slut
säumig ['zɔɪmɪç] *adj* tardy
Säumnis ['zɔɪmnɪs] *f* (-;-nisse) dilatoriness; (*Verzug*) delay; (*Nichterfüllung*) default
Saum'pfad *m* mule track
Saum'tier *n* beast of burden
Sau'pech *n* (coll) rotten luck
Säure ['zɔɪrə] *f* (-;-n) sourness; acidity; tartness; (chem) acid
Sauregur'kenzeit *f* slack season
Säu'remesser *m* (aut) battery tester
Saures ['zaurəs] *n*—gib ihm S. (coll) give it to 'im!

Saus [zaus] *m*—**in S. und Braus leben** live high

säuseln ['zɔɪzəln] *intr* rustle; **mit säuselnder Stimme** in whispers

sausen ['zauzən] *intr* (*Wind, Kugel*) whistle; (*Wasser*) gush ‖ *intr* (SEIN) rush, whiz ‖ *impers*—**mir saust es in den Ohren** my ears are ringing ‖ **Sausen** *n* (-s;) rush and roar; humming, ringing (*in the ears*)

Sau'stall *m* pigsty; (fig) terrible mess

Sau'wetter *n* (coll) nasty weather

Sau'wirtschaft *f* (coll) helluva mess

sau'wohl' *adj* (coll) in great shape

Saxophon [zakso'fon] *n* (-s;-e) saxophone

Schabe ['ʃabə] *f* (-;-n) cockroach

Schabeisen ['ʃapaɪzən] *n* scraper

schaben ['ʃabən] *tr* scrape; grate, rasp

Scha'ber *m* (-s;-) scraper

Schabernack ['ʃabərnak] *m* (-[e]s;-e) practical joke

schäbig ['ʃebɪç] *adj* shabby; (fig) mean

Schablone [ʃa'blonə] *f* (-;-n) (*Muster*) pattern, model; (*Matrize*) stencil; (*mechanische Arbeit*) routine; **nach der S.** mechanically

schablo'nenhaft, schablo'nenmäßig *adj* mechanical; (*Arbeit*) routine

Schach [ʃax] *n* (-[e]s) chess; **in S. halten** (fig) keep in check; **S. bieten** (or **geben**) check; (fig) defy; **S. dem König!** check!

Schach'brett *n* chessboard

Schacher ['ʃaxər] *m* (-s;) haggling; **S. treiben** haggle, huckster

Schach'feld *n* (chess) square

Schach'figur *f* chessman; (fig) pawn

schach'matt' *adj* checkmated; (fig) beat

Schach'partie *f*, **Schach'spiel** *n* game of chess

Schacht [ʃaxt] *m* (-[e]s;ⁿe) shaft; manhole

Schacht'deckel *m* manhole cover

Schachtel ['ʃaxtəl] *f* (-;-n) box; (*von Zigaretten*) pack; (fig) frump

Schach'zug *m* (chess & fig) move

schade ['ʃadə] *adj* too bad

Schädel ['ʃedəl] *m* (-s;-) skull; **mir brummt** (or **dröhnt**) **der S.** my head is throbbing

Schä'delbruch *m*, **Schä'delfraktur** *f* skull fracture

Schä'delhaut *f* scalp

Schä'delknochen *m* cranium

Schä'dellehre *f* phrenology

schaden ['ʃadən] *intr* do harm; (*dat*) harm, damage; **das wird ihr nichts s.** it serves her right; **ein Versuch kann nichts s.** there's no harm in trying ‖ *impers*—**es schadet nichts** it doesn't matter ‖ **Schaden** *m* (-s;ⁿ) damage, injury; (*Verlust*) loss; (*Nachteil*) disadvantage; **er will deinen S. nicht** he means you no harm; **j-m S. zufügen** inflict loss on s.o.; (coll) give s.o. a black eye; **mit S. verkaufen** sell at a loss; **S. nehmen** come to grief; **zu meinem S.** to my detriment

Scha'denersatz *m* compensation, damages; (*Wiedergutmachen*) reparation; **S. leisten** pay damages; make amends

Scha'denersatzklage *f* damage suit

Scha'denfreude *f* gloating

scha'denfroh *adj* gloating, malicious

Scha'denversicherung *f* comprehensive insurance

schadhaft ['ʃathaft] *adj* damaged; (*Material*) faulty; (*Zähne*) decayed; (*baufällig*) dilapidated

schädigen ['ʃedɪgən] *tr* inflict financial damage on; (*benachteiligen*) wrong; (*Ruf*) damage; (*Rechte*) infringe on

Schä'digung *f* (-;) damage

schädlich ['ʃetlɪç] *adj* harmful; (*nachteilig*) detrimental; (*verderblich*) noxious; (*Speise*) unwholesome

Schädling ['ʃetlɪŋ] *m* (-s;-e) (*Person*) parasite; (ent) pest; **Schädlinge** vermin

Schäd'lingsbekämpfung *f* pest control

schadlos ['ʃatlos] *adj*—**sich an j-m s. halten** make s.o. pay (*for an injury done to oneself*); **sich für etw s. halten** compensate oneself for s.th., make up for s.th.

Schaf [ʃaf] *n* (-[e]s;-e) sheep; (fig) blockhead, dope

Schaf'bock *m* ram

Schäfchen ['ʃefçən] *n* (-s;-) lamb; (*Wolken*) fleecy clouds

Schäf'chenwolke *f* fleecy cloud

Schäfer ['ʃefər] *m* (-s;-) shepherd

Schä'ferhund *m* sheep dog; **deutscher S.** German shepherd

Schaf'fell *n* sheepskin

schaffen ['ʃafən] §109 *tr* do; get; put; manage, manage to do; (*erreichen*) accomplish; (*liefern*) supply; (*erschaffen*) bring, cause; (*wegbringen*) take; **auf die Seite s.** put aside; (*betrügerisch*) embezzle; **ich schaffe es noch, daß** I'll see to it that; **Rat s.** know what to do; **vom Halse s.** get off one's neck ‖ §126 *tr* create; produce; **wie geschaffen sein für** cut out for ‖ §109 *intr* do; (*arbeiten*) work; **j-m viel zu s. machen** cause s.o. a lot of trouble; **sich zu s. machen** be busy, putter around

schaf'fend *adj* working; (*schöpferisch*) creative; (*produktiv*) productive

Schaf'fensdrang *m* creative urge

Schaf'fenskraft *f* creative power

Schaffner ['ʃafnər] *m* (-s;-) (rr) conductor

Schaf'fung *f* (-;-en) creation

Schaf'hirt *m* shepherd

Schaf'pelz *m* sheepskin coat

Schaf'ferch *m* sheepfold

Schafs'kopf *m* (sl) mutton-head

Schaf'stall *m* sheepfold

Schaft [ʃaft] *m* (-[e]s;ⁿe) shaft; (*e-r Feder*) stem; (*e-s Gewehrs*) stock; (*e-s Ankers*) shank; (bot) stem, stalk

Schaft'stiefel *m* high boot

Schaf'zucht *f* sheep raising

Schakal [ʃa'kal] *m* (-s;-e) jackal

schäkern ['ʃekərn] *intr* joke around; flirt

schal [ʃal] *adj* stale; insipid; (fig) flat ‖ **Schal** *m* (-s;-e & -s) scarf; shawl

Schale ['ʃalə] *f* (-;-n) bowl; (*Tasse*) cup; (*von Obst*) peel, skin; (*Hülse*) shell; (*Schote*) pod; (*Rinde*) bark;

(*Waagschale*) scale; (zool) shell; **sich in S. werfen** (coll) doll up

schälen ['ʃɛlən] *tr* peel; (*Mais*) husk; (*Baumrinde*) bark ‖ *ref* peel off

Scha'lentier *n* (zool) crustacean

Schalk [ʃalk] *m* (-[e]s;-e & ⸚e) rogue

schalk'haft *adj* roguish

Schall [ʃal] *m* (-[e]s;-e & ⸚e) sound; (*Klang*) ring; (*Lärm*) noise

Schall'boden *m* sounding board

Schall'dämpfer *m* (*an Schußwaffen*) silencer; (aut) muffler; (mus) soft pedal

schall'dicht *adj* soundproof

Schall'dose *f* (electron) pickup

Schall'druck *m* sonic boom

Schallehre (**Schall'lehre**) *f* acoustics

schallen ['ʃalən] *intr* sound, resound

Schall'grenze *f* sound barrier

Schall'mauer *f* sound barrier

Schall'meßgerät *n* sonar

Schall'pegel *m* sound level

Schall'platte *f* phonograph record

Schall'plattenaufnahme *f* recording

Schall'wand *f* baffle

Schall'welle *f* sound wave

Schalotte [ʃa'lɔtə] *f* (-;-n) (bot) scallion

schalt [ʃalt] *pret* of **schelten**

Schalt- *comb.fm.* switch; connecting; breaking; shifting

Schalt'bild *n* circuit diagram

Schalt'brett *n* switchboard; control panel; (aut) dashboard

Schalt'dose *f* switch box

schalten ['ʃaltən] *tr* switch; (*anlassen*) start; (*Gang*) (aut) shift ‖ *intr* switch; (*regieren*) be in command; (aut) shift gears; **s. und walten mit** do as one pleases with

Schal'ter *m* (-s;-) switch; (*Ausschalter*) circuit breaker; (*für Kundenverkehr*) window, ticket window

Schal'terdeckel *m* switch plate

Schalt'hebel *m* (aut) gearshift; (elec) switch lever

Schalt'jahr *n* leap year

Schalt'kasten *m* switch box

Schalt'pult *n* (rad, telv) control desk

Schalt'tafel *f* switchboard, instrument panel; (aut) dashboard

Schalt'uhr *f* timer

Schal'tung *f* (-;-en) switching; (elec) connection; (elec) circuit

Schaluppe [ʃa'lupə] *f* (-;-n) sloop

Scham [ʃam] *f* (-;) shame; (anat) genitals

Scham'bein *n* (anat) pubis

schämen ['ʃɛmən] *ref* (**über** *acc*) feel ashamed (of)

Scham'gefühl *n* sense of shame

Scham'haar *n* pubic hair

scham'haft *adj* modest, bashful

scham'los *adj* shameless

Schampun [ʃam'pun] *n* (-s;-s) shampoo

schampunieren [ʃampu'nirən] *tr* shampoo

scham'rot *adj* blushing; **s. werden** blush

Scham'teile *pl* genitals

Schand- [ʃant] *comb.fm.* of shame

schandbar ['ʃantbar] *adj* shameful; infamous

Schande ['ʃandə] *f* (-;) shame, disgrace

schänden ['ʃɛndən] *tr* disgrace; (*entweihen*) desecrate; (*Mädchen*) rape

Schän'der *m* (-s;-) violator; rapist

Schand'fleck *m* stain; (fig) blemish; (fig) good-for-nothing; **der S. der Familie** the disgrace of the family

schändlich ['ʃɛntlɪç] *adj* shameful, disgraceful; scandalous ‖ *adv* (coll) awfully

Schand'mal *n* stigma

Schand'tat *f* shameful deed, crime

Schän'dung *f* (-;-en) desecration; disfigurement; rape

Schank [ʃaŋk] *m* (-[e]s;⸚e) bar, saloon

Schank'bier *n* draft beer

Schank'erlaubnis *f*, **Schank'gerechtigkeit** *f*, **Schank'konzession** *f* liquor license

Schank'stätte *f* bar, tavern

Schank'tisch *m* bar

Schank'wirt *m* bartender

Schank'wirtschaft *f* bar, saloon

Schanzarbeit ['ʃantsarbaɪt] *f* earthwork; **Schanzarbeiten** entrenchments

Schanze ['ʃantsə] *f* (-;-n) entrenchments, trench; (naut) quarter-deck; (sport) take-off ramp (*of ski jump*)

Schanz'gerät *n* entrenching tool

Schar [ʃar] *f* (-;-en) group, bunch; crowd; (*von Vögeln*) flock, flight

Scharade [ʃa'radə] *f* (-;-n) charade

scharen ['ʃarən] *ref* (**um**) gather (around)

scharf [ʃarf] *adj* (**schärfer** ['ʃɛrfər]; **schärfste** ['ʃɛrfstə] §9) sharp; (*Tempo*) fast; (*Bemerkung*) cutting; (*Blick*) hard; (*Brille*) strong; (*Fernrohr*) powerful; (*Geruch*) pungent; (*Munition*) live; (*Pfeffer, Senf*) hot; (*streng*) severe; (*genau*) exact; (*Ton*) shrill; (*wahrnehmend*) keen; **s. machen** sharpen; **s. sein auf** (acc) be keen on ‖ *adv* hard; fast; **j-n s. nehmen** be very strict with s.o.; **s. ansehen** look hard at; **s. geladen** loaded; **s. schießen** shoot with live ammunition; **s. umreißen** define clearly

Scharf'blick *m* (fig) sharp eye

Schärfe ['ʃɛrfə] *f* (-;-n) sharpness; keenness; pungency; severity; accuracy

Scharf'einstellung *f* (phot) focusing

schärfen ['ʃɛrfən] *tr* sharpen, whet; make pointy; (fig) intensify

scharf'kantig *adj* sharp-edged

scharf'machen *tr* stir up; (*Bomben*) arm; (*Zünder*) activate

Scharf'macher *m* demagogue, agitator

Scharf'richter *m* executioner

Scharf'schütze *m* (mil) sharpshooter

scharf'sichtig *adj* sharp-eyed; (fig) clear-sighted

Scharf'sinn *m* sagacity, acumen

scharf'sinnig *adj* sharp, sagacious

Scharlach ['ʃarlax] *m* (-s;-e) scarlet; (pathol) scarlet fever

schar'lachfarben *adj* scarlet

schar'lachrot *adj* scarlet

Scharlatan ['ʃarlatan] *m* (-s;-e) charlatan, quack

scharmant [ʃar'mant] *adj* charming
Scharmützel [ʃar'mytsəl] *n* (-s;-) skirmish
Scharnier [ʃar'nir] *n* (-s;-e) hinge; joint
Schärpe ['ʃerpə] *f* (-;-n) sash
Scharre ['ʃarə] *f* (-;-n) scraper
Scharreisen ['ʃaraɪzən] *n* scraper
scharren ['ʃarən] *tr* scrape, paw ‖ *intr* scrape; (an *acc*) scratch (on); **auf den Boden s.** paw the ground; **mit den Füßen** scrape the feet (*in disapproval*)
Scharte ['ʃartə] *f* (-;-n) nick, dent; (*Kerbe*) notch; (*Kratzer*) scratch; (*Riß*) crack; (*Bergsattel*) gap; (fig) mistake; **e-e S. auswetzen** (fig) make amends
Scharteke [ʃar'tekə] *f* (-;-n) worthless old book; (fig) frump
schartig ['ʃartɪç] *adj* jagged; notched
Schatten ['ʃatən] *m* (-s;-) shade; shadow; **in den S. stellen** throw into the shade
Schat'tenbild *n* silhouette; (fig) phantom
Schat'tendasein *n* shadowy existence
Schat'tengestalt *f* shadowy figure
schat'tenhaft *adj* shadowy
Schat'tenriß *m* silhouette
Schat'tenseite *f* shady side; dark side; (fig) seamy side
schattieren [ʃa'tirən] *tr* shade; (*schraffieren*) hatch; (*abtönen*) tint
Schattie'rung *f* (-;-en) shading; (*Farbton*) shade, tint
schattig ['ʃatɪç] *adj* shadowy; shady
Schatulle [ʃa'tulə] *f* (-;-n) cash box; (*für Schmuck*) jewelry box; (hist) private funds (*of a prince*)
Schatz [ʃats] *m* (-es;ᵉe) treasure; (*Vorrat*) store; (fig) sweetheart
Schatz'amt *n* treasury department
Schatz'anweisung *f* treasury bond
schätzbar ['ʃetsbar] *adj* valuable
schätzen ['ʃetsən] *tr* (*Grundstücke, Häuser, Schaden*) estimate, appraise; (*urteilen, vermuten*) guess; (*achten*) esteem, value; (*würdigen*) appreciate; **er schätzte mich auf 20 Jahre** he took me for 20 years old; **zu hoch s.** overestimate, overrate; **zu s. wissen** appreciate ‖ *ref*—**sich** [*dat*] **es zu Ehre s.** consider it an honor; **sich glücklich s.** consider oneself lucky ‖ *recip*—**sie s. sich nicht** there's no love lost between them
schät'zenswert *adj* valuable
Schät'zer –in §6 *mf* appraiser; (*zur Besteuerung*) assessor
Schatz'kammer *f* treasury; (fig) storehouse
Schatz'meister –in §6 *mf* treasurer
Schät'zung *f* (-;-en) estimate; (*Meinung*) estimation; (*Hochachtung*) esteem; (*Hochschätzung*) appreciation; (*zur Besteuerung*) assessment
schät'zungsweise *adv* approximately
Schät'zungswert *m* estimated value; assessed value; (*des Schadens*) appraisal
Schatz'wechsel *m* treasury bill
Schau [ʃau] *f* (-;-en) view; (*Ausstel-*

lung) exhibition, show; (mil) review; (telv) show; **zur S. stehen** be on display; **zur S. stellen** put on display; **zur S. tragen** feign
Schau'bild *n* diagram, chart
Schauder ['ʃaudər] *m* (-s;-) shudder, shiver; (*Schrecken*) horror, terror
schauderbar ['ʃaudərbar] *adj* terrible
schau'dererregend *adj* horrifying
schau'derhaft *adj* horrible, awful
schaudern ['ʃaudərn] *intr* (vor *dat*) shudder (at) ‖ *impers*—**es schaudert mich** I shudder
schauen ['ʃau.ən] *tr* look at; (*beobachten*) observe ‖ *intr* look
Schauer ['ʃau.ər] *m* (-s;-) shower, downpour; (*Schauder*) shudder, chill; thrill; (*Anfall*) fit, attack; **einzelne S.** scattered showers
Schau'erdrama *n* (theat) thriller
schau'erlich *adj* dreadful, horrible
schauern ['ʃau.ərn] *intr* shudder ‖ *impers*—**es schauert it is pouring;** **schauert mich** (or **mir**) **vor** (*dat*) I shudder at; I shiver with
Schau'erroman *m* thriller
Schaufel ['ʃaufəl] *f* (-;-n) shovel; scoop; (*Rad*–) paddle; (*Turbinen*–) blade, vane
schaufeln ['ʃaufəln] *tr* shovel; (*Grab*) dig ‖ *intr* shovel
Schau'felrad *n* paddle wheel
Schau'fenster *n* display window; **die S. ansehen** go window-shopping
Schau'fensterauslage *f* window display
Schau'fensterbummel *m* window-shopping
Schau'fensterdekoration *f* window dressing
Schau'fliegen *n* stunt flying
Schau'flug *m* air show
Schau'gepränge *n* pageantry
Schau'gerüst *n* grandstand
Schau'kampf *m* (box) exhibition fight
Schau'kasten *m* showcase
Schaukel ['ʃaukəl] *f* (-;-n) swing
Schau'kelbrett *n* seesaw
schaukeln ['ʃaukəln] *tr* swing; rock ‖ *intr* swing; rock; sway
Schau'kelpferd *n* rocking horse
Schau'kelreck *n* trapeze
Schau'kelstuhl *m* rocking chair
Schau'loch *n* peephole
Schaum [ʃaum] *m* (-[e]s;ᵉe) foam, froth; (*Abschaum*) scum; (*Geifer*) slaver; **zu S. schlagen** whip; **zu S. werden** (fig) come to nothing
Schaum'bad *n* bubble bath
schäumen ['ʃɔɪmən] *intr* foam; (*Wein*) sparkle; (*aus Wut*) fume, boil
Schaum'gummi *n* & *m* foam rubber
Schaum'haube *f* head (*on beer*)
schaumig ['ʃaumɪç] *adj* foamy
Schaum'krone *f* whitecap (*on wave*)
Schau'modell *n* mock-up
Schaum'wein *m* sparkling wine
Schau'platz *m* scene, theater
Schau'prozeß *m* mock trial
schaurig ['ʃaurɪç] *adj* horrible
Schau'spiel *n* play, drama; spectacle
Schau'spieler *m* actor
Schau'spielerin *f* actress
schau'spielerisch *adj* theatrical

schauspielern [ˈʃauʃpilərn] *intr* act; (*schwindeln*) act, make believe
Schau′spielhaus *n* theater
Schau′spielkunst *f* dramatic art
Schau′stück *n* show piece; (*Muster*) sample
Scheck [ʃɛk] *m* (-s;-s & -e) check; **e-n S. ausstellen an** (*acc*) **über** (*acc*) write out a check to (*s.o.*) in the amount of; **e-n S. einlösen** cash a check; **e-n S. sperren lassen** stop payment on a check; **offener S.** blank check
Scheck′abschnitt *m* check stub
Scheck′formular *n* blank check
Scheck′heft *n* check book
scheckig [ˈʃɛkɪç] *adj* dappled
Scheck′konto *n* checking account
scheel [ʃel] *adj* squinting; squint-eyed; (fig) envious, jealous
Scheffel [ˈʃɛfəl] *m* (-s;-) bushel
scheffeln [ˈʃɛfəln] *tr* amass
Scheibe [ˈʃaibə] *f* (-;-n) disk; sheet; plate; (*Glas-*) pane; (*Honig-*) honeycomb; (*Ziel*) target; (*Schnitte*) slice; (astr) orb, disk; (mach) washer; (telp) dial
Schei′benbremse *f* disk brake
Schei′benkönig *m* top marksman
Schei′benschießen *n* target practice
Schei′benwäscher *m* windshield washer
Schei′benwischer *m* windshield wiper
Scheide [ˈʃaidə] *f* (-;-n) sheath; border, boundary; (anat) vagina
Schei′debrief *m* farewell letter
Schei′degruß *m* goodbye
scheiden [ˈʃaidən] §112 *tr* separate, divide; (*zerlegen*) decompose; (*Ehe*) dissolve; (*Eheleute*) divorce; (chem) analyze; (chem) refine || *ref* part; **sich s. lassen** get a divorce || *intr* (SEIN) part; depart; (*aus dem Amt*) resign, retire
schei′dend *adj* (*Tag*) closing; (*Sonne*) setting
Schei′dewand *f* partition
Schei′deweg *m* fork, crossroad; (fig) moment of decision
Schei′dung *f* (-;-en) separation; (*Ehe-*) divorce
Schein [ʃain] *m* (-[e]s;-e) shine; (*Licht*) light; (*Schimmer*) gleam, glitter; (*Strahl*) flash; (*Erscheinung*) appearance; (*Anschein*) pretense, show; (*Urkunde*) certificate, papers, license, ticket; (*Geldschein*) bill; (*Quittung*) receipt; **dem Scheine nach** apparently; **den äußeren S. wahren** save face; **sich** [*dat*] **den S. geben** make believe; **zum S.** pro forma
Schein- *comb.fm.* sham, mock, make-believe
scheinbar [ˈʃainbar] *adj* seeming, apparent; likely; (*vorgeblich*) make-believe
Schein′bild *n* illusion; phantom
scheinen [ˈʃainən] §128 *intr* shine; seem, appear || *impers*—**es scheint** it seems
Schein′grund *m* pretext
schein′heilig *adj* sanctimonious, hypocritical
Schein′tod *m* suspended animation

Schein′werfer *m* flashlight; (aer) beacon; (aut) headlight
Scheit [ʃait] *n* (-[e]s;-e) piece of chopped wood; **Holz in Scheite hakken** chop wood
Scheitel [ˈʃaitəl] *m* (-s;-) apex, top; top of the head; (*des Haares*) part; **e-n S. ziehen** make a part
scheiteln [ˈʃaitəln] *tr & ref* part
Schei′telpunkt *m* (fig) summit; (astr) zenith; (math) vertex
Schei′telwinkel *m* opposite angle
Scheiterhaufen [ˈʃaitərhaufən] *m* funeral pile; **auf dem S. sterben** die at the stake
scheitern [ˈʃaitərn] *intr* (SEIN) run aground, be wrecked; (*Plan*) miscarry || **Scheitern** *n* (-s;) shipwreck; (fig) failure
Schelle [ˈʃɛlə] *f* (-;-n) bell; (*Fessel*) handcuff; (*Ohrfeige*) box on the ear
schellen [ˈʃɛlən] *tr & intr* ring
Schel′lenkappe *f* cap and bells
Schellfisch [ˈʃɛlfɪʃ] *m* haddock
Schelm [ʃɛlm] *m* (-[e]s;-e) rogue; (Lit) knave; **armer S.** poor devil
Schel′menstreich *m* prank
schelmisch [ˈʃɛlmɪʃ] *adj* roguish, impish
Schelte [ˈʃɛltə] *f* (-;-n) scolding
schelten [ˈʃɛltən] *tr & intr* scold
Scheltwort [ˈʃɛltvɔrt] *n* (-[e]s;-e & ″er) abusive word; word of reproof
Sche·ma [ˈʃema] *n* (-s;-s & -mata [mata] & -men [mən]) scheme; diagram; (*Muster*) pattern, design
Schemel [ˈʃeməl] *m* (-s;-) stool
Schemen [ˈʃemən] *m* (-s;-) phantom, shadow
sche′menhaft *adj* shadowy
Schenk [ʃɛŋk] *m* (-en;-en) bartender
Schenke [ˈʃɛŋkə] *f* (-;-n) bar, tavern
Schenkel [ˈʃɛŋkəl] *m* (-s;-) thigh; (*e-s Winkels*) side; (*e-r Schere*) blade; (*e-s Zirkels*) leg
schenken [ˈʃɛŋkən] *tr* give, offer; pour (out); (*Aufmerksamkeit*) pay; (*Schuld*) remit; **das ist geschenkt** that's dirt cheap; **das kann ich mir s.** I can pass that up; **das kannst du dir s.!** keep it to yourself! **j-m Beifall s.** applaud s.o.; **j-m das Leben s.** grant s.o. pardon
Schenk′stube *f* taproom, barroom
Schenk′tisch *m* bar
Schen′kung *f* (-;-en) donation
Schenk′wirt *m* bartender
scheppern [ˈʃɛpərn] *intr* (coll) rattle
Scherbe [ˈʃɛrbə] *f* (-;-n), **Scherben** [ˈʃɛrbən] *m* (-s;-) broken piece; potsherd; **in Scherben gehen** go to pieces
Scher′bengericht *n* ostracism
Scherbett [ʃɛrˈbɛt] *m* (-[e]s;-e) sherbe(r)t
Schere [ˈʃerə] *f* (-;-n) (pair of) scissors; shears; (*Draht-*) cutter; (zool) claw
scheren [ˈʃerən] *tr* bother; **was schert dich das?** what's that to you? || §129 *tr* cut, clip, trim; (*Schafe*) shear; || §109 *ref*—**scher dich ins Bett!** off to bed with you!; **scher dich zum Teu-**

fel! the devil with you!; **sich um etw s.** trouble oneself about s.th.

Schererei [ʃerə'raɪ] f (-;-en) trouble

Scherflein ['ʃerflaɪn] n (-s;-) bit; **sein S. beitragen** contribute one's bit

Scherz [ʃerts] m (-es;-e) joke; **im** (or **zum**) **S.** for fun; **S. treiben mit** make fun of

scherzen ['ʃertsən] intr joke, kid

'scherz'haft adj joking, humorous

Scherz'name m nickname

scherz'weise adv in jest, as a joke

scheu [ʃɔɪ] adj shy; **s. machen** frighten; startle || **Scheu** f (-;) shyness

Scheuche ['ʃɔɪçə] f (-;-n) scarecrow

scheuchen ['ʃɔɪçən] tr scare (away)

scheuen ['ʃɔɪən] tr shun; shrink from; fear; (Mühen, Kosten) spare; **ohne die Kosten zu s.** regardless of expenses || ref (vor dat) be afraid (of); **ich s. mich zu** (inf) I am reluctant to (inf) || intr—**s. vor** (dat) shy at

Scheuer ['ʃɔɪ-ər] f (-;-n) barn

Scheu'erbürste f scrub brush

Scheu'erfrau f scrubwoman

Scheu'erlappen m scrub rag

scheuern ['ʃɔɪ-ərn] tr scrub, scour; (reiben) rub

Scheu'erpulver n scouring powder

Scheu'klappe f blinder (for horses)

Scheune ['ʃɔɪnə] f (-;-n) barn

Scheu'nendrescher m—**er ißt wie ein S.** (coll) he eats like a horse

Scheusal ['ʃɔɪzal] n (-s;-e) monster

scheußlich ['ʃɔɪslɪç] adj dreadful, atrocious; (coll) awful, rotten

Scheuß'lichkeit f (-;-en) hideousness; (Tat) atrocity

Schi [ʃi] m (-s;- & -er) ski; **Schi fahren** (or **laufen**) ski

Schicht [ʃɪçt] f (-;-en) layer, film; (Farb-) coat; (Arbeiter-) shift; (Gesellschafts-) class; (geol) stratum; (phot) emulsion; **Leute aus allen Schichten** people from all walks of life; **S. machen** (coll) knock off from work

Schicht'arbeit f shift work

schichten ['ʃɪçtən] tr arrange in layers; laminate; (Holz) stack (up); (in Klassen einteilen) classify; (geol) stratify; (Ladung) (naut) stow

Schich'tenaufbau m, **Schich'tenbildung** f (geol) stratification

–schichtig [ʃɪçtɪç] comb.fm. –layer, –ply

Schicht'linie f contour line

Schicht'linienplan m contour map

Schicht'meister m shift foreman

schicht'weise adv in layers; in shifts

schick [ʃɪk] adj chic, swank || **Schick** m (-[e]s;) (Geschick) skill; (Geschmack) tact, taste; **S. haben für** have a knack for

schicken ['ʃɪkən] tr send || ref—**sich s. für** (or **zu**) be suitable for; **sich s. in** (acc) adapt oneself to; resign oneself to || intr—**nach j-m s.** send for s.o. || impers—**es schickt sich** it is proper; (sich ereignen) come to pass

schick'lich adj proper; decent

Schick'lichkeit f (-;) propriety

Schick'lichkeitsgefühl n sense of propriety

Schicksal ['ʃɪkzal] n (-[e]s;-e) destiny, fate

Schick'salsgefährte m fellow sufferer

Schick'salsglaube m fatalism

Schick'salsgöttinnen pl (myth) Fates

Schick'salsschlag m stroke of fate

Schickung (**Schik'kung**) f (-;-en) (divine) dispensation

Schiebe– [ʃibə] comb.fm. sliding, push

Schie'beleiter f extension ladder

schieben ['ʃibən] §130 tr push, shove; traffic in; **auf die lange Bank s.** put off; **e-e ruhige Kugel s.** have a cushy job; **Kegel s.** bowl; **Wache s.** (mil) pull guard duty || ref move, shuffle || intr shuffle along; profiteer

Schieber ['ʃibər] m (-s;-) slide valve; (Riegel) bolt; (am Schornstein) damper; (fig) racketeer

Schie'bergeschäft f (com) racket

Schiebertum ['ʃibərtum] n (-s;) (com) racketeering

Schie'betür f sliding door

schied [ʃit] pret of **scheiden**

Schieds– [ʃits] comb.fm. of arbitration

Schieds'gericht n board of arbitration; **an ein S. verweisen** refer to arbitration

Schieds'mann m (-[e]s;:̈er) arbitrator

Schieds'richter m arbitrator; (sport) referee, umpire

schieds'richterlich adj of an arbitration board || adv by arbitration

Schieds'spruch m decision; **e-n S. fällen** render a decision

schief [ʃif] adj (abfallend) slanting; (krumm) crooked; (einseitig) lopsided; (geneigt) inclined; (Winkel) oblique; (falsch) false, wrong; **auf die schiefe Ebene geraten** (fig) go downhill; **schiefe Lage** (fig) tight spot; **schiefes Licht** (fig) bad light || adv at an angle; awry; obliquely; wrong; **s. ansehen** look askance at; **s. halten** tip, tilt; **s. nehmen** take amiss

Schiefer ['ʃifər] m (-s;-) slate; (Splitter) splinter

Schie'ferbruch m slate quarry

Schie'feröl n shale oil

Schie'fertafel f (educ) slate

schief'gehen §82 intr (SEIN) go wrong

schief'treten §152 tr—**die Absätze s.** wear down the heels

schieläugig ['ʃilɔɪgɪç] adj squint-eyed; cross-eyed

schielen ['ʃilən] intr squint; **s. nach** squint at; leer at

schie'lend adj squinting; cross-eyed; furtive

schien [ʃin] pret of **scheinen**

Schienbein ['ʃinbaɪn] n shinbone, tibia

Schien'beinschützer m shinguard

Schiene ['ʃinə] f (-;-n) (rr) rail, track; (surg) splint; **aus den Schienen springen** jump the track

schienen ['ʃinən] tr put in splints

Schie'nenbahn f track, rails; streetcar; railroad

Schie'nenfahrzeug n rail car

Schie'nengleis n track

schier [ʃir] *adj* sheer || *adv* almost
Schierling [ˈʃirlɪŋ] *m* (-s;-e) (bot) hemlock
Schieß- [ʃis] *comb.fm.* shooting
Schieß′baumwolle *f* guncotton
Schieß′bedarf *m* ammunition
Schieß′bude *f* shooting gallery
Schieß′eisen *n* (hum) shooting iron
schießen [ˈʃisən] §76 *tr* shoot, fire; **e-n Bock s.** (coll) pull a boner; **ein Tor s.** make a goal || *intr* (**auf** *acc*) shoot (at); **aus dem Hinterhalt s.** snipe; **gut s.** be a good shot; **scharf s.** shoot with live ammunition || *intr* (SEIN) shoot up; spurt; zig, fly; **das Blut schoß ihm ins Gesicht** his face got red; **in Samen s.** go to seed; **ins Kraut s.** sprout || **Schießen** *n* (-s;) shooting; **das ist ja zum s.!** (coll) that's a riot!
Schießerei [ʃisəˈraɪ] *f* (-;-en) gun fight; pointless firing
Schieß′gewehr *n* firearm
Schieß′hund *m* (hunt) pointer
Schieß′lehre *f* ballistics
Schieß′platz *m* firing range
Schieß′prügel *m* (hum) shooting iron
Schieß′pulver *n* gunpowder
Schieß′scharte *f* loophole
Schieß′scheibe *f* target
Schieß′stand *m* shooting gallery; (mil) firing range, rifle range
Schieß′übung *f* firing practice
Schi′fahrer *-in* §6 *mf* skier
Schiff [ʃɪf] *n* (-[e]s;-e) ship; (archit) nave; (typ) galley
Schiffahrt (Schiff′fahrt) *f* navigation
Schiffahrtslinie (Schiff′fahrtslinie) *f* steamship line
Schiffahrtsweg (Schiff′fahrtsweg) *m* shipping lane
schiffbar [ˈʃɪfbar] *adj* navigable
Schiff′bau *m* (-[e]s;) shipbuilding
Schiff′bruch *m* shipwreck
schiff′brüchig *adj* shipwrecked
Schiff′brücke *f* pontoon bridge; (naut) bridge
Schiffchen [ˈʃɪfçən] *n* (-s;-) little ship; (mil) overseas cap; (tex) shuttle
schiffen [ˈʃɪfən] *intr* (vulg) pee || *impers* **es schifft** (vulg) it's pouring
Schiffer [ˈʃɪfər] *m* (-s;-) seaman; skipper; (*Schiffsführer*) navigator
Schiff′erklavier *n* (coll) concertina
Schiffs′journal *n* log, logbook
Schiffs′junge *m* cabin boy
Schiffs′küche *f* galley
Schiffs′ladung *f* cargo
Schiffs′luke *f* hatch
Schiffs′mannschaft *f* crew
Schiffs′ortung *f* dead reckoning
Schiffs′raum *m* hold; tonnage
Schiffs′rumpf *m* hull
Schiffs′schraube *f* propeller
Schiffs′tau *n* hawser
Schiffs′taufe *f* christening of a ship
Schiffs′werft *f* shipyard, dockyard
Schiffs′winde *f* winch, capstan
Schiffs′zimmermann *m* ship's carpenter; (*bei e-r Werft*) shipwright
Schikane [ʃɪˈkanə] *f* (-;-n) chicanery; **mit allen Schikanen** with all the frills; (aut) fully loaded

schikanieren [ʃɪkaˈnirən] *tr* harass
schikanös [ʃɪkaˈnøs] *adj* annoying
Schi′langlauf *m* cross-country skiing
Schi′lauf *m* skiing
schi′laufen §105 *intr* (SEIN) ski || **Schilaufen** *n* (-s;) skiing
Schi′läufer *-in* §6 *mf* skier
Schild [ʃɪlt] *m* (-[e]s;-e) shield; (heral) coat of arms; **etw im Schilde führen** have s.th. up one's sleeve || *n* (-[e]s;-er) sign; road sign; nameplate; (*e-s Arztes, usw.*) shingle; (*Etikett*) label; (*Mützenschirm*) visor, shade
Schild′bürger *m* (fig) dunce
Schild′bürgerstreich *m* boner
Schild′drüse *f* thyroid gland
Schilderhaus [ˈʃɪldərhaus] *n* sentry box
Schil′dermaler *m* sign painter
schildern [ˈʃɪldərn] *tr* depict, describe
Schil′derung *f* (-;-en) description
Schild′kröte *f* tortoise, turtle
Schildpatt [ˈʃɪltpat] *n* (-[e]s;) tortoise shell, turtle shell
Schilf [ʃɪlf] *n* (-[e]s;-e) reed
Schilf′rohr *n* reed
Schi′lift *m* ski lift
Schiller [ˈʃɪlər] *m* (-s;) luster; iridescence
schillern [ˈʃɪlərn] *intr* be iridescent
Schil′lerwein *m* bright-red wine
Schilling [ˈʃɪlɪŋ] *m* (-s;- & -e) shilling; (Aust) schilling
Schimäre [ʃɪˈmɛrə] *f* (-;-n) chimera
Schimmel [ˈʃɪməl] *m* (-s;-) white horse; mildew, mold
schimmelig [ˈʃɪməlɪç] *adj* moldy
schimmeln [ˈʃɪməln] *intr* (HABEN & SEIN) get moldy
Schimmer [ˈʃɪmər] *m* (-s;) glimmer
schimmern [ˈʃɪmərn] *intr* glimmer
schimmlig [ˈʃɪmlɪç] *adj* moldy
Schimpanse [ʃɪmˈpanzə] *m* (-n;-n) chimpanzee
Schimpf [ʃɪmpf] *m* (-[e]s;-e) insult, abuse
schimpfen [ˈʃɪmpfən] *tr* scold, abuse || *intr* be abusive; (**über** *acc* or **auf** *acc*) curse (at), swear (at)
schimpf′lich *adj* disgraceful
Schimpf′name *m* nickname; **j-m Schimpfnamen geben** call s.o. names
Schimpf′wort *n* (-[e]s;-e & ̈er) swear word
Schindaas [ˈʃɪntas] *n* carrion
Schindel [ˈʃɪndəl] *f* (-;-n) shingle
schindeln [ˈʃɪndəln] *tr* shingle
schinden [ˈʃɪndən] §167 *tr* skin; torment; oppress; exploit; **Eindruck s.** try to make an impression; **Eintrittsgeld s.** crash the gate; **Zeilen s.** pad the writing; **Zigaretten s.** bum cigarettes || *ref* break one's back
Schin′der *m* (-s;-) slave driver
Schinderei [ʃɪndəˈraɪ] *f* (-;-en) drudgery, grind
Schindluder [ˈʃɪntludər] *n* carrion; **mit j-m S. treiben** treat s.o. outrageously
Schindmähre [ˈʃɪntmɛrə] *f* old nag
Schinken [ˈʃɪŋkən] *m* (-s;-) ham; (hum) tome; (hum) huge painting
Schinnen [ˈʃɪnən] *pl* dandruff

Schippe [ˈʃɪpə] f (-;-n) shovel, scoop; (cards) spade(s); **e-e S. machen** (or **ziehen**) pout; **j-n auf die S. nehmen** (coll) pull s.o.'s leg

schippen [ˈʃɪpən] tr & intr shovel

Schirm [ʃɪrm] m (-[e]s;-e) screen; umbrella; x-ray screen; lampshade; visor; (fig) protection, shelter; (hunt) blind

Schirm'bild n x-ray

Schirm'bildaufnahme f x-ray

Schirm'dach n lean-to

schirmen [ˈʃɪrmən] tr protect

Schirm'futteral n umbrella case

Schirm'herr m protector, patron

Schirm'herrin f protectress, patroness

Schirm'herrschaft f protectorate; patronage

Schirm'ständer m umbrella stand

Schir'mung f (-;-en) (elec) shielding

schirren [ˈʃɪrən] tr harness

Schis·ma [ˈʃɪsma] n (-;-mata [mata] & -men [mən] schism

Schi'sprung m ski jump

Schi'stock m ski pole

schizophren [ʃɔɪtsoˈfreːn] adj schizophrenic

Schizophrenie [ʃɔɪtsofreˈniː] f (-;) schizophrenia

schlabbern [ˈʃlabərn] tr lap up || intr (geifern) slobber; (fig) babble

Schlacht [ʃlaxt] f (-;-en) battle; **die S. bei** the battle of

schlachten [ˈʃlaxtən] tr slaughter

Schlacht'enbummler m camp follower; (sport) fan

Schlächter [ˈʃlɛçtər] m (-s;-) butcher

Schlacht'feld n battlefield

Schlacht'flieger m combat pilot; close-support fighter

Schlacht'geschrei n battle cry

Schlacht'haus n slaughterhouse

Schlacht'kreuzer m heavy cruiser

Schlacht'opfer n sacrifice; (fig) victim

Schlacht'ordnung f battle array

Schlacht'roß n (hist) charger

Schlacht'ruf m battle cry

Schlacht'schiff n battleship

Schlach'tung f (-;-en) slaughter

Schlacke [ˈʃlakə] f (-;-n) cinder; lava; (metal) slag, dross

schlackig [ˈʃlakɪç] adj sloppy (weather)

Schlaf [ʃlaf] m (-[e]s;) sleep

Schlaf'abteil n sleeping compartment

Schlaf'anzug m pajamas

Schläfchen [ˈʃlɛfçən] n (-s;-) nap; **ein S. machen** take a nap

Schläfe [ˈʃlɛfə] f (-;-n) temple

schlafen [ˈʃlafən] §131 tr sleep || intr sleep; **sich s. legen** go to bed

Schla'fenszeit f bedtime

Schläfer –in [ˈʃlɛfər(ɪn)] §6 mf sleeper

schläfern [ˈʃlɛfərn] impers—es schläfert mich I'm sleepy

schlaff [ʃlaf] adj slack; limp; flabby; (locker) loose

Schlaf'gelegenheit f sleeping accommodations

Schlaf'kammer f bedroom

Schlaf'krankheit f sleeping sickness

schlaf'los adj sleepless

Schlaf'losigkeit f (-;) sleeplessness

Schlaf'mittel n sleeping pill

Schlaf'mütze f nightcap; (fig) sleepyhead

schläfrig [ˈʃlefrɪç] adj sleepy, drowsy

Schläf'rigkeit f (-;) sleepiness, drowsiness

Schlaf'rock m housecoat

Schlaf'saal m dormitory

Schlaf'sack m sleeping bag

Schlaf'stätte f, **Schlaf'stelle** f place to sleep

Schlaf'stube f bedroom

Schlaf'trunk m (hum) nightcap

schlaf'trunken adj still half-asleep

Schlaf'wagen m (rr) sleeping car

schlaf'wandeln intr (SEIN) walk in one's sleep

Schlafwandler –in [ˈʃlafvandlər(ɪn)] §6 mf sleepwalker

Schlaf'zimmer n bedroom

Schlag [ʃlak] m (-[e]s;ːe) blow; stroke; (Puls–) beat; (Faust–) punch; (Hand–) slap; (Donner–) clap; (Tauben–) loft; (Art, Sorte) kind, sort, breed; (e-s Taues) coil; (der Vögel) song; (vom Pferd) kick; (e-r Kutsche) door; (Holz–) cut; (Pendel) swing; (agr) field; (elec) shock; (mil) scoop, ladleful; (pathol) stroke; **ein S. ins Wasser** a vain attempt; **Leute seines Schlages** the likes of him; **S. zwölf Uhr** at the stroke of twelve; **von gutem S.** of the right sort

Schlag'ader f artery

Schlag'anfall m (pathol) stroke

schlag'artig adj sudden, surprise; (heftig) violent || adv all of a sudden; with a bang

Schlag'baum m barrier

Schlag'besen m eggbeater

Schlag'bolzen m firing pin

Schlägel [ˈʃlegəl] m (-s;-) sledge hammer

schlagen [ˈʃlagən] §132 tr hit; strike; beat; (besiegen) defeat; (strafen) spank; (Alarm) sound; (Brücke) build; (Eier) beat; (Geld) coin; (Holz) fell; (Saiten) strike; (Schlacht) fight; **die Augen zu Boden s.** cast down the eyes; **durch ein Sieb s.** strain, sift; **e-e geschlagene Stunde** (coll) a solid hour; **in die Flucht s.** put to flight; **in Fesseln s.** put in chains; **in Papier s.** wrap in paper; **Wurzel s.** take root; **zu Boden s.** knock down || ref come to blows; fight a duel; fence; **sich gut s.** stand one's ground; **sich s. zu side with;** **um sich s.** flail about || intr strike; beat; (Pferd) kick; (Vogel) sing; **mit den Flügeln s.** flap the wings; **nach j-m s.** take a swing at s.o.; (fig) be like s.o., take after s.o.

schla'gend adj striking, impressive; convincing; **schlagende Verbindung** dueling fraternity; **schlagende Wetter** firedamp

Schla'ger m (-s;-) (tolle Sache) hot item; (mus, theat) hit

Schläger [ˈʃlegər] m (-s;-) beater; hitter; batter; baseball bat; golf club; tennis racket; eggbeater; mallet; (Singvogel) warbler; (Raufbold) bully

Schlägerei [ʃlɛgəˈraɪ] *f* (-;-en) fight; fighting; brawl

Schla'gerpreis *m* rock-bottom price

Schla'gersänger -in §6 *mf* pop singer

schlag'fertig *adj* quick with an answer; (*Antwort*) ready

Schlag'holz *n* club, bat

Schlag'instrument *n* percussion instrument

Schlag'kraft *f* striking power

schlag'kräftig *adj* (*Armee*) powerful; (*Beweis*) conclusive

Schlag'licht *n* strong light; glare

Schlag'loch *n* pothole

Schlag'mal *n* (baseball) home plate

Schlag'ring *m* brass knuckles

Schlag'sahne *f* whipped cream

Schlag'schatten *m* deep shadow

Schlag'seite *f* (naut) list; **S. haben** have a list; (hum) be drunk

Schlag'uhr *f* striking clock

Schlag'weite *f* striking distance

Schlag'welle *f* breaker, comber

Schlag'wetter *pl* (min) firedamp

Schlag'wort *n* (-[e]s;⁼er & -e) slogan; key word, subject (*in cataloguing*); (*Phrasendrescherei*) claptrap

Schlag'wörterkatalog *m* (libr) subject index

Schlag'zeile *f* headline

Schlag'zeug *n* percussion instruments

Schlaks [ʃlaks] *m* (-es;-e) lanky person

schlaksig [ˈʃlaksɪç] *adj* lanky

Schlamassel [ʃlaˈmasəl] *m & n* (-s;-) (coll) jam, pickle, mess

Schlamm [ʃlam] *m* (-[e]s;-e) mud, slime; (*im Motor*) sludge; (fig) mire

Schlamm'bad *n* mud bath

schlämmen [ˈʃlɛmən] *tr* dredge; (metal) wash

schlammig [ˈʃlamɪç] *adj* muddy

Schlampe [ˈʃlampə] *f* (-;-n) frump; (sl) slut

Schlamperei [ʃlampəˈraɪ] *f* (-;-en) slovenliness; untidiness, mess

schlampig [ˈʃlampɪç] *adj* sloppy

schlang [ʃlaŋ] *pret* of **schlingen**

Schlange [ˈʃlaŋə] *f* (-;-n) snake; queue, waiting line; (*Wasserschlauch*) hose; **Schlange stehen nach** line up for

schlängeln [ˈʃlɛŋəln] *ref* wind; (*Fluß*) meander; (*sich krümmen*) squirm; wriggle; (fig) worm one's way

Schlan'genbeschwörer -in §6 *mf* snake charmer

Schlan'genlinie *f* wavy line

schlank [ʃlaŋk] *adj* slender, slim; **im schlanken Trabe** at a fast clip

Schlank'heit *f* (-;) slenderness

Schlank'heitskur *f*—e-**e S. machen** diet

schlankweg [ˈʃlaŋkvɛk] *adv* flatly; downright

schlapp [ʃlap] *adj* slack, limp; flabby; (*müde*) washed out ‖ **Schlappe** *f* (-;-n) setback; (*Verlust*) loss

schlappen [ˈʃlapən] *intr* flap; shuffle along ‖ **Schlappen** *m* (-s;-) slipper

schlappern [ˈʃlapərn] *tr* lap up

schlapp'machen *intr* (*zusammenbrechen*) collapse; (*ohnmächtig werden*) faint; (*nicht durchhalten*) call it quits

Schlapp'schwanz *m* (coll) weakling; sissy; (*Feigling*) coward

Schlaraffenland [ʃlaˈrafənlant] *n* paradise

Schlaraffenleben [ʃlaˈrafənlebən] *n* life of Riley

schlau [ʃlaʊ] *adj* sly; clever

Schlauch [ʃlaʊx] *m* (-[e]s;⁼e) hose; tube; (fig) souse; (aut) inner tube; (educ) pony

Schlauch'boot *n* rubber dinghy

schlauchen [ˈʃlaʊxən] *tr* drive hard; (mil) drill mercilessly

Schlauch'ventil *n* (aut) valve

Schläue [ˈʃlɔɪə] *f* (-;) slyness

schlau'erweise *adv* prudently

Schlaufe [ˈʃlaʊfə] *f* (-;-n) loop

Schlau'kopf *m*, **Schlau'meier** *m* sly fox

schlecht [ʃlɛçt] *adj* bad, poor; **mir wird s.** I'm getting sick; **schlechter werden** get worse; **s. werden** go bad ‖ *adv* poorly; **die Uhr geht s.** the clock is off; **s. daran sein** be badly off; **s. und recht** somehow; **s. zu sprechen sein auf** (*acc*) have it in for

schlechterdings [ˈʃlɛçtərdɪŋs] *adv* utterly, absolutely

schlecht'gelaunt *adj* in a bad mood

schlecht'hin *adv* simply, downright

schlecht'machen *tr* talk behind the back of

schlechtweg [ˈʃlɛçtvɛk] *adv* simply, downright

schlecken [ˈʃlɛkən] *tr* lick ‖ *intr* eat sweets, nibble

Schleckerei [ʃlɛkəˈraɪ] *f* (-;-en) sweets

schleckern [ˈʃlɛkərn] *intr* have a sweet tooth ‖ *impers*—**mich schleckert es nach** I have a yen for

Schlegel [ˈʃlegəl] *m* (-s;-) sledge hammer; (*Holz-*) mallet; (culin) leg; (mus) drumstick

schleichen [ˈʃlaɪçən] §85 *ref & intr* (SEIN) sneak

schlei'chend *adj* creeping; furtive; (*Krankheit*) lingering; (*Gift*) slow

Schlei'cher *m* (-s;-) sneak, hypocrite

Schleicherei [ʃlaɪçəˈraɪ] *f* (-;-en) sneaking; underhand dealing

Schleich'gut *n* contraband

Schleich'handel *m* underhand dealing; smuggling; black-marketing

Schleich'weg *m* secret path; **auf Schleichwegen** in a roundabout way

Schleier [ˈʃlaɪ-ər] *m* (-s;-) veil; haze; gauze

schlei'erhaft *adj* hazy; mysterious; (fig) veiled; **das ist mir s.** I don't know what to make of it

Schleif– [ʃlaɪf] *comb.fm.* sliding; grinding, abrasive

Schleif'bürste *f* (elec) brush

Schleife [ˈʃlaɪfə] *f* (-;-n) (*am Kleid, im Haar*) bow; (*in Schnüren*) slipknot; (*er Straße*) hairpin curve; (*-s Flusses*) bend; (*Wende-*) loop; (*mit langen Bändern*) streamer; (*Rutschbahn*) slide, chute; (aer) loop

schleifen [ˈʃlaɪfən] *tr* drag; (*Kleid*) trail along; demolish; raze; (mus) slur ‖ §88 *tr* grind; whet; polish; (*Glas, Edelstein*) cut; (mil) drill hard ‖ §109 *intr* drag, trail

Schleif′mit′tel n abrasive
Schleif′papier n sandpaper
Schleif′rad n emery wheel
Schleif′stein m whetstone
Schleim [ʃlaɪm] m (-[e]s;-e) slime; mucus, phlegm
Schleim′haut f mucous membrane
schleimig [ˈʃlaɪmɪç] adj slimy; mucous
schleißen [ˈʃlaɪsən] §53 tr split; slit; (Federkiele) strip ‖ intr wear out
Schlemm [ʃlɛm] m (-s;-e) (cards) slam
schlemmen [ˈʃlɛmən] intr carouse; gorge oneself; live high
Schlem′mer –in §6 mf glutton, guzzler; gourmet
schlem′merhaft adj gluttonous; (üppig) plentiful, luxurious
Schlem′merlokal n gourmet restaurant
Schlempe [ˈʃlɛmpə] f (-;-n) slop
schlendern [ˈʃlɛndərn] intr (SEIN) stroll
Schlendrian [ˈʃlɛndri-an] m (-s) routine
schlenkern [ˈʃlɛŋkərn] tr dangle, swing ‖ intr dangle; **mit den Armen s.** swing the arms
Schlepp– [ʃlɛp] comb.fm. towing, drag
Schlepp′dampfer m tugboat
Schlepp′dienst m towing service
Schleppe [ˈʃlɛpə] f (-;-n) train
schleppen [ˈʃlɛpən] tr drag; lug, tote; (aer, naut) tow ‖ ref drag along; **sich mit etw s.** be burdened with s.th.
Schlep′penkleid n dress with a train
Schlep′per m (-s;-) hauler; tractor; tugboat; tender, lighter
Schlepp′fischerei f trawling
Schlepp′netz n dragnet, dredge; trawling net
Schlepp′netzboot n trawler
Schlepp′schiff n tugboat
Schlepp′tau n towline; **ins S. nehmen** take in tow
Schleuder [ˈʃlɔɪdər] f (-;-n) sling; slingshot; (aer) catapult; (mach) centrifuge
schleudern [ˈʃlɔɪdərn] tr fling; sling; (aer) catapult ‖ intr (aut) skid; (com) undersell
Schleu′derpreis m cutrate price
Schleu′dersitz m (aer) ejection seat
schleunig [ˈʃlɔɪnɪç] adj speedy ‖ adv in all haste; (sofort) at once
schleunigst [ˈʃlɔɪnɪçst] adv as soon as possible; right away
Schleuse [ˈʃlɔɪzə] f (-;-n) lock, sluice, sluice way; drain, sewer
schleusen [ˈʃlɔɪzən] tr (fig) maneuver
schlich [ʃlɪç] pret of **schleichen** ‖
Schlich [ʃlɪç] m (-[e]s;-e) trick; **alle Schliche kennen** know all the ropes; **j-m auf die Schliche (or hinter j-s Schliche) kommen** be on to s.o.
schlicht [ʃlɪçt] adj smooth; plain
schlichten [ˈʃlɪçtən] tr smooth; (fig) settle, arbitrate
Schlich′ter –in §6 mf arbitrator
Schlich′tung f (-;-en) arbitration; settlement
schlief [ʃlif] pret of **schlafen**
Schließe [ˈʃlisə] f (-;-n) clasp; pin
schließen [ˈʃlisən] §76 tr shut, close; lock; end, conclude; (Betrieb) shut

down; (Bücher) balance; (Konto; Klammer) close; (Bündnis) form; (Frieden; Rede) conclude; (Kompromiß) reach; (Heirat) form; (Geschäft, Handel) strike; (Versammlung) adjourn; (Wette) make; (Reihen) (mil) close; **ans Herz s.** press to one's heart; **aus etw. s., daß** conclude from s.th. that; **den Zug s.** (mil) bring up the rear; **e-n Vergleich s.** come to an agreement; **ins Herz s.** take a liking to; **kurz s.** (elec) short ‖ ref shut, close; **in sich s.** comprise, include; (bedeuten) imply; (umfassen) involve; **von sich auf andere s.** judge others by oneself ‖ intr shut, close; end
Schließ′fach n post office box; safe-deposit box
schließlich [ˈʃlislɪç] adj final, eventual ‖ adv finally
schliff [ʃlɪf] pp of **schleifen** ‖ **Schliff** m (-[e]s;-e) polish; (e-s Diamanten) cut; (fig) polish; (mil) rigorous training
schlimm [ʃlɪm] adj bad; (bedenklich) serious; (traurig) sad; (wund) sore; (eklig) nasty; **am schlimmsten** worst; **immer schlimmer** worse and worse; **s. daran sein** be badly off
schlimmstenfalls [ˈʃlɪmstənfals] adv at worst
Schlinge [ˈʃlɪŋə] f (-;-n) loop; coil; (fig) trap, difficulty; (bot) tendril; (hunt) snare; (surg) sling; **in die S. gehen** (fig) fall into a trap
Schlingel [ˈʃlɪŋəl] m (-s;-) rascal; **fauler S.** lazybones
schlingen [ˈʃlɪŋən] §142 tr tie; twist; wind; wrap; gulp ‖ ref wind, coil; climb, creep ‖ intr gulp down food
Schlingerbewegung [ˈʃlɪŋərbəveguŋ] f (naut) roll
schlingern [ˈʃlɪŋərn] intr (naut) roll
Schlinggewächs [ˈʃlɪŋgəvɛks] n, **Schlingpflanze** [ˈʃlɪŋpflantsə] f climber
Schlips [ʃlɪps] m (-es;-e) necktie
Schlitten [ˈʃlɪtən] m (-s;-) sled; (an der Schreibmaschine) carriage
schlit′tenfahren §71 intr go sleigh riding; **mit j–m s.** make life miserable for s.o.
schlittern [ˈʃlɪtərn] intr (HABEN & SEIN) slide; (Wagen) skid
Schlittschuh [ˈʃlɪt/u] m ice skate; **S. laufen** skate, go ice-skating
Schlitt′schuhläufer –in §6 mf ice skater
Schlitz [ʃlɪts] m (-es;-e) slit, slot; (Hosen–) fly
schlitz′äugig adj slit-eyed, sloe-eyed
schlitzen [ˈʃlɪtsən] tr slit; rip
Schloß [ʃlɔs] n (Schlosses; Schlösser) castle; country mansion; lock; snap, clasp; **hinter S. und Riegel** behind bars; **unter S. und Riegel** under lock and key
Schloße [ˈʃlosə] f (-;-n) hailstone
Schlosser [ˈʃlɔsər] m (-s;-) mechanic; locksmith
Schloß′graben m moat
Schlot [ʃlot] m (-[e]s;-e & ⸚e) chimney, smokestack; (fig) louse

Schlot'baron m (coll) tycoon

Schlot'feger m chimney sweep

schlotterig ['ʃlɔtərɪç] adj loose, dangling; wobbly; (liederlich) slovenly

schlottern ['ʃlɔtərn] intr fit loosely; (baumeln) dangle; (zittern) tremble; (wackeln) wobble

Schlucht [ʃluçt] f (-;-en) gorge; ravine

schluchzen ['ʃluxtsən] intr sob

Schluck [ʃluk] m (-[e]s;-e) gulp; sip

Schluck'auf m (-s;) hiccups

schlucken ['ʃlukən] tr & intr gulp

Schlucker ['ʃlukər] m (-s;-)—armer S. (coll) poor devil

schlucksen ['ʃluksən] intr have the hiccups

schluderig ['ʃludərɪç] adj slipshod

schludern ['ʃludərn] intr do slipshod work

Schlummer ['ʃlumər] m (-s;) slumber

Schlum'merlied n lullaby

schlummern ['ʃlumərn] intr slumber

schlum'mernd adj latent

Schlum'merrolle f cushion

Schlund [ʃlunt] m (-[e]s;-e) gullet; pharynx; (e-s Vulcans) crater; (fig) abyss

Schlund'röhre f esophagus

Schlupf [ʃlupf] m (-[e]s;-e) hole; (elec, mach) slip

schlüpfen ['ʃlypfən] intr (SEIN) slip; sneak

Schlüp'fer m (-s;-) (pair of) panties; (pair of) bloomers

Schlupf'jacke f sweater

Schlupf'loch n hiding place; loophole

schlüpfrig ['ʃlypfrɪç] adj slippery; (obszön) off-color

Schlupf'winkel m hiding place; haunt

schlurfen ['ʃlurfən] intr (SEIN) shuffle

schlürfen ['ʃlyrfən] tr slurp; lap up

Schluß [ʃlus] m (Schlusses; Schlüsse) end, close; (Ablauf) expiration; (Folgerung) conclusion; **S. damit!** time!; cut it out!; **S. folgt** to be concluded; **S. machen** mit put an end to; knock off from (work); break up with (s.o.); **zum S.** in conclusion

Schluß'effekt m upshot

Schlüssel ['ʃlysəl] m (-s;-) key; wrench; quota; code key; (fig) key, clue

Schlüs'selbein n collarbone, clavicle

Schlüs'selblume f cowslip; **helle S.** primrose

Schlüs'selbrett n keyboard

Schlüs'selbund m bunch of keys

schlüs'selfertig adj ready for occupancy

Schlüs'selloch n keyhole

Schluß'ergebnis n final result

Schluß'folge f, **Schluß'folgerung** f conclusion, deduction

Schluß'formel f complimentary close

schlüssig ['ʃlysɪç] adj determined; logical; (Beweis) conclusive; **sich [dat] noch nicht s. sein, ob** be undecided whether

Schluß'licht n (aut) taillight

Schluß'linie f (typ) dash

Schluß'rennen n (sport) final heat

Schluß'runde f (sport) finals

Schluß'schein m sales agreement

Schluß'verkauf m clearance sale

Schmach [ʃmax] f (-;) disgrace, shame; insult; humiliation

schmachten ['ʃmaxtən] intr (vor dat) languish (with); **s. nach** long for

Schmachtfetzen ['ʃmaxtfetsən] m sentimental song or book; melodrama

schmächtig ['ʃmɛçtɪç] adj scrawny

Schmachtriemen ['ʃmaxtrimən] m—**den S. enger schnallen** (fig) tighten one's belt

schmach'voll adj disgraceful; humiliating

schmackhaft ['ʃmakhaft] adj tasty

schmähen ['ʃme·ən] tr revile, abuse; speak ill of

schmählich ['ʃmelɪç] adj disgraceful, scandalous; humiliating

Schmährede ['ʃmeredə] f abuse; diatribe

Schmähschrift ['ʃmeʃrɪft] f libel

schmähsüchtig ['ʃmezyçtɪç] adj abusive

Schmä'hung f (-;-en) abuse; slander

schmal [ʃmal] adj narrow; slim; meager

schmälern ['ʃmelərn] tr curtail; belittle

Schmal'spurbahn f narrow-gauge railroad

Schmalz [ʃmalts] n (-[e]s;) lard, grease; (fig) schmaltz

schmalzen ['ʃmaltsən] tr lard, grease

schmalzig ['ʃmaltsɪç] adj greasy; fatty; (fig) schmaltzy

schmarotzen [ʃma'rɔtsən] intr (bei) sponge (on)

Schmarot'zer m (-s;-) sponger; (zool) parasite

schmarotzerisch [ʃma'rɔtsərɪʃ] adj sponging; (zool) parasitic(al)

Schmarre ['ʃmarə] f (-;-n) scar; scratch

schmarrig ['ʃmarɪç] adj scary

Schmatz [ʃmats] m (-es;-e) hearty kiss

schmatzen ['ʃmatsən] tr (coll) kiss loudly || intr smack one's lips

Schmaus [ʃmaus] m (-es;-e) feast; treat

schmausen ['ʃmauzən] intr (von) feast (on)

schmecken ['ʃmɛkən] tr taste, sample; (fig) stand || intr taste good; **s. nach** taste like

Schmeichelei [ʃmaiçə'lai] f (-;-en) flattery; coaxing

schmeichelhaft ['ʃmaiçəlhaft] adj flattering

schmeicheln ['ʃmaiçəln] ref—**sich [dat] s. zu** (inf) pride oneself on (ger) || intr be flattering; (dat) flatter

Schmeich'ler –in §6 mf flatterer

schmeichlerisch ['ʃmaiçlərɪʃ] adj flattering; complimentary; fawning

schmeißen ['ʃmaisən] §53 tr (coll) throw; (coll) manage; **e-e Runde Bier s.** set up a round of beer || ref—**mit Geld um sich s.** throw money around

Schmelz [ʃmelts] m (-es;-e) enamel; glaze; melodious ring; (fig) bloom

schmelzen ['ʃmeltsən] §133 tr melt; smelt || intr (SEIN) melt; (fig) soften

schmel′zend adj mellow; melodious
Schmelzerei [ˌʃmeltsəˈraɪ] f (-;-en) foundry
schmelz′flüssig adj molten
Schmelz′hütte f foundry
Schmelz′käse m soft cheese
Schmelz′ofen m smelting furnace
Schmelz′punkt m melting point
Schmelz′tiegel m crucible, melting pot
Schmer [ʃmer] m & n (-s;) fat, grease
Schmer′bauch m (coll) potbelly
Schmerz [ʃmerts] m (-es;-en) pain, ache; **mit Schmerzen** (coll) anxiously, impatiently
schmerzen [ˈʃmertsən] tr & intr hurt
schmer′zend adj aching, sore
Schmer′zensgeld n damages (for pain or anguish)
Schmer′zenskind n problem child
schmerz′haft adj painful, aching
schmerz′lich adj painful, severe
schmerz′lindernd adj soothing
schmerz′los adj painless
Schmerz′schwelle f threshold of pain
Schmetterling [ˈʃmetərlɪŋ] m (-s;-e) butterfly
Schmet′terlingsstil m (sport) butterfly
schmettern [ˈʃmetərn] tr smash; **zu Boden s.** knock down || intr (Trompete) blare; (Vogel) warble
Schmied [ʃmit] m (-[e]s;-e) smith
Schmiede [ˈʃmidə] f (-;-n) forge; blacksmith shop
Schmie′deeisen n wrought iron
Schmie′dehammer m sledge hammer
schmieden [ˈʃmidən] tr forge; hammer; (Pläne, usw.) devise, concoct
schmiegen [ˈʃmigən] tr—**das Kinn or die Wange) in die Hand s.** prop one's chin (or cheek) in one's hand || ref (an acc) snuggle up (to); **sich s. und biegen vor** (dat) bow and scrape before
schmiegsam [ˈʃmikzam] adj flexible
Schmier– [ʃmir] comb.fm. grease, lubricating; smearing
Schmiere [ˈʃmirə] f (-;-n) grease; lubricant; salve; (Schmutz) muck; (fig) mess; (fig) spanking; (theat) barnstormers; **S. stehen** be the lookout man
schmieren [ˈʃmirən] tr grease, lubricate; smear; (Butter) spread; (Brot) butter; (bestechen) bribe; **j-m e-e s.** (coll) paste s.o.; **wie geschmiert** like greased lightning || ref—**sich** [dat] **die Kehle s.** (coll) wet one's whistle || intr scribble
Schmie′renkomödiant –**in** §7 mf (theat) barnstormer, ham
Schmiererei [ʃmirəˈraɪ] f (-;-en) greasing; smearing; scribbling
Schmier′fink m scrawler; (Schmutzkerl) dirty fellow
Schmier′geld n (coll) bribe; (coll) hush money; (pol) slush fund
schmierig [ˈʃmirɪç] adj smeary, greasy; oily; (Geschäfte) dirty
Schmier′käse m cheese spread
Schmier′mittel n lubricant
Schmier′pistole f, **Schmier′presse** f grease gun
Schmie′rung f (-;-en) lubrication

Schminke [ˈʃmɪŋkə] f (-;-n) rouge; make-up
schminken [ˈʃmɪŋkən] tr apply make-up to; rouge; **die Lippen s.** put on lipstick || ref put on make-up
Schminkunterlage [ˈʃmɪŋkʊntərlagə] f base
Schmirgel [ˈʃmɪrgəl] m (-s;) emery
Schmir′gelleinen n, **Schmir′gelleinwand** f emery cloth
Schmir′gelpapier n emery paper
Schmir′gelscheibe f emery wheel
Schmiß [ʃmɪs] m (Schmisses; Schmisse) (coll) stroke, blow; (coll) gash; (coll) dueling scar; (coll) zip
schmissig [ˈʃmɪsɪç] adj (coll) snazzy
schmollen [ˈʃmɔlən] intr pout, sulk
schmolz [ʃmɔlts] pret of **schmelzen**
Schmorbraten [ˈʃmorbratən] m braised meat
schmoren [ˈʃmorən] tr braise, stew || intr (fig) swelter; **laß ihn s.!** let him stew!
schmuck [ʃmʊk] adj nice, cute; smart, dapper; (sauber) neat || **Schmuck** m (-[e]s;) ornament; decoration; trimmings; trinket(s); jewelry
schmücken [ˈʃmʏkən] tr adorn; decorate, trim; (Aufsatz) embellish || ref spruce up, dress up
Schmuck′kästchen n jewel box
schmuck′los adj unadorned, plain
Schmuck′waren pl jewelry
Schmuddel [ˈʃmʊdəl] m (-s;-) slob
schmuddelig [ˈʃmʊdəlɪç] adj dirty
Schmuggel [ˈʃmʊgəl] m (-s;), **Schmuggelei** [ʃmʊgəˈlaɪ] f (-;-en) smuggling
schmuggeln [ˈʃmʊgəln] tr & intr smuggle
Schmug′gelware f contraband
Schmuggler –**in** [ˈʃmʊglər(ɪn)] §6 mf smuggler
schmunzeln [ˈʃmʊntsəln] intr grin || **Schmunzeln** n (-s;) big grin
Schmutz [ʃmʊts] m (-es;) dirt, filth; (Zote) smut
schmutzen [ˈʃmʊtsən] tr & intr soil
Schmutz′fink m (coll) slob
Schmutz′fleck m stain, smudge, blotch
schmut′zig adj dirty
Schnabel [ˈʃnabəl] m (-s;⁼) beak, bill; **halt den S.!** (sl) shut up!
Schna′belhieb m peck
schnäbeln [ˈʃnɛbəln] tr & intr peck; (fig) kiss
Schnalle [ˈʃnalə] f (-;-n) buckle; (vulg) whore
schnallen [ˈʃnalən] tr buckle, fasten
schnalzen [ˈʃnaltsən] intr—**mit den Fingern s.** snap one's fingers; **mit der Zunge s.** click one's tongue
schnapp [ʃnap] interj snap!
schnappen [ˈʃnapən] tr grab; (Dieb) nab || intr snap; **ins Schloß s.** snap shut; **mit den Fingern s.** snap one's fingers; **nach Luft s.** gasp for air; **s. nach** snap at
Schnapp′messer n jackknife
Schnapp′schuß m (phot) snapshot
Schnaps [ʃnaps] m (-es;⁼e) hard liquor
Schnaps′brennerei f distillery
Schnaps′bruder m (coll) booze hound

Schnaps'idee f (coll) crazy idea
schnarchen ['ʃnarçən] intr snore
Schnarre ['ʃnarə] f (-;-n) rattle
schnarren ['ʃnarən] intr rattle; (Säge) buzz; (Insekten) drone, buzz
schnattern ['ʃnatərn] intr (Enten) cackle; (Zähne) chatter; (fig) gab
schnauben ['ʃnaubən] intr pant, puff; (Pferd) snort; **nach Rache s.** breathe revenge; **vor Wut s.** fume with rage || ref blow one's nose
schnaufen ['ʃnaufən] intr pant; wheeze
Schnau'fer m (-s;-) (coll) deep breath
Schnauzbart ['ʃnautsbart] m mustache
Schnauze ['ʃnautsə] f (-;-n) snout, muzzle; spout; (sl) snoot; (sl) big mouth
Schnauzer ['ʃnautsər] m (-s;-) schnauzer
schnauzig ['ʃnautsɪç] adj rude
Schnecke ['ʃnekə] f (-;-n) snail; (Nacht-) slug; (e-r Säule) volute; spiral; (anat) cochlea; (mach) worm; (e-r Violine) (mus) scroll
Schneckenhaus (Schnek'kenhaus) n snail shell
Schneckentempo (Schnek'kentempo) n (fig) snail's pace
Schnee [ʃne] m (-s;) snow; whipped egg white
Schnee'besen m eggbeater
Schnee'brett n snow slide, avalanche
Schnee'brille f snow goggles
Schnee'decke f blanket of snow
Schnee'flocke f snowflake
Schnee'gestöber n snow flurry
schneeig ['ʃne.ɪç] adj snowy
Schnee'matsch m slush
Schnee'pflug m snowplow
Schnee'schaufel f, **Schnee'schippe** f snow shovel
Schnee'schläger m eggbeater
Schnee'schmelze f thaw
Schnee'treiben n blizzard
schneeverweht ['ʃnefervet] adj snowbound
Schnee'verwehung f snowdrift
Schnee'wehe f snowdrift
Schneewittchen ['ʃnevɪtçən] n (-s;) Snow White
Schneid [ʃnart] m (-[e]s;) (coll) pluck; (Mut) (coll) guts
Schneid'brenner m cutting torch
Schneide ['ʃnardə] f (-;-n) (cutting) edge; (e-s Hobels) blade; **auf des Messers S.** (fig) on the razor's edge
Schnei'debrett n cutting board
Schnei'demaschine f cutter, slicer
Schnei'demühle f sawmill
schneiden ['ʃnardən] §106 tr cut; (Baum) prune; (Fingernägel) pare; (Hecke) trim; (nicht grüßen) snub; (surg) operate on; (tennis) slice; **Gesichter s.** make faces; **klein s.** cut up || ref (fig) be mistaken; (fig) be disappointed; (math) intersect; **sich in den Finger s.** cut one's finger || intr cut
Schnei'der (-s;-) m cutter; tailor
Schneiderei [ʃnardə'rar] f (-;-en) tailoring; (Werkstatt) tailorshop
Schnei'derin f (-;-nen) dressmaker

schneidern ['ʃnardərn] tr make || intr do tailoring; be a dressmaker
Schnei'derpuppe f dummy
Schnei'dezahn m incisor
schneidig ['ʃnardɪç] adj sharp-edged; energetic; smart, sharp
schneien ['ʃnar-ən] impers—es schneit it is snowing
Schneise ['ʃnarzə] f (-;-n) lane (between rows of trees)
schnell [ʃnel] adj fast, quick
Schnellauf (Schnell'lauf) m race; sprint; speed skating
Schnell'bahn f high-speed railroad
Schnelle ['ʃnelə] f (-;-n) speed; (Strom-) rapids; **auf die S.** (coll) in a hurry, very briefly
schnellen ['ʃnelən] tr let fly || intr (SEIN) spring, jump up; (Preise) shoot up; **mit dem Finger s.** snap one's fingers
Schnell'gang m (aut) overdrive
Schnellhefter ['ʃnelheftər] m (-s;-) folder, file
Schnell'imbiß m snack
Schnell'kraft f elasticity
schnellstens ['ʃnelstəns] adv as fast as possible
Schnell'verfahren n quick process; (jur) summary proceeding
Schnell'zug m express train
Schneppe ['ʃnepə] f (-;-n) spout; (sl) prostitute
schneuzen ['ʃnɔrtsən] ref blow one's nose
schniegeln ['ʃnigəln] ref dress up; **geschniegelt und gebügelt** dressed to kill
schnipfeln ['ʃnɪpfəln] tr & intr snip
Schnippchen ['ʃnɪpçən] n—j-m ein S. schlagen (coll) pull a fast one on s.o.; outwit s.o.
Schnippel ['ʃnɪpəl] m & n (-s;-) chip
schnippeln ['ʃnɪpəln] tr & intr snip
schnippen ['ʃnɪpən] intr—mit den Fingern s. (coll) snap one's fingers
schnippisch ['ʃnɪpɪʃ] adj fresh || adv pertly; **s. erwidern** snap back
schnitt [ʃnɪt] pret of **schneiden** ||
Schnitt m (-[e]s;-e) cut, incision; (Kerbe) notch; (Schnitte) slice; (Quer-) profile, cross section; (Durch-) average; (e-s Anzuges) cut, style; (Gewinn) cut; (agr) reaping; (bb) edge; (cin) editing; (geom) intersection; **welcher Schnitt** (cin) dissolve
Schnitt'ansicht f sectional view
Schnitt'ball m (tennis) slice
Schnitt'blumen pl cut flowers
Schnitt'bohnen pl string beans
Schnittchen ['ʃnɪtçən] n (-s;-) thin slice; sandwich
Schnitte ['ʃnɪtə] f (-;-n) slice
Schnit'ter —in §6 m-f reaper, mower
Schnitt'fläche f (geom) plane
Schnitt'holz n lumber
schnittig ['ʃnɪtɪç] adj smart-looking; (aut) streamlined
Schnitt'lauch ['ʃnɪtlaux] m (-[e]s;) (bot) chive
Schnitt'linie f (geom) secant
Schnitt'meister m (cin) editor

Schnitt'muster n pattern (of dress, etc.)

Schnitt'punkt m intersection

Schnitt'waren pl dry goods

Schnitt'wunde f cut, gash

Schnitz [ʃnɪts] m (-es;-e) cut; slice; chop; chip

Schnitzel ['ʃnɪtsəl] n (-s;-) chip; slice; shred; (Abfälle) parings; (culin) cutlet

schnitzeln ['ʃnɪtsəln] tr cut up; shred; (Holz) whittle

schnitzen ['ʃnɪtsən] tr carve

Schnit'zer m (-s;-) carver; (Fehler) blunder; grober S. boner

Schnitzerei [ʃnɪtsə'raɪ] f (-;-en) wood carving, carved work

schnob [ʃnop] pret of schnauben

schnodderig ['ʃnɔdərɪç] adj brash

schnöde ['ʃnødə] adj vile; disdainful; (Gewinn) filthy

Schnorchel ['ʃnɔrçəl] m (-s;-) snorkel

Schnörkel ['ʃnœrkəl] m (-s;-) (beim Schreiben) flourish; (fig) frills; (archit) scroll

schnorren ['ʃnɔrən] tr (coll) chisel, bum || intr (coll) sponge, chisel

Schnösel ['ʃnøzəl] m (-s;-) wise guy

schnüffeln ['ʃnʏfəln] intr snoop around; (an dat) sniff (at)

Schnüff'ler -in §6 mf (coll) snoop

Schnuller ['ʃnʊlər] m (-s;-) pacifier

Schnultze ['ʃnʊltsə] f (-;-n) (coll) tear-jerker

schnultzig ['ʃnʊltsɪç] adj (coll) corny, mawkish

schnupfen ['ʃnʊpfən] tr snuff || intr take snuff || **Schnupfen** m (-s;-) cold; **den S. bekommen** catch a cold

Schnupftabak ['ʃnʊpftabak] m snuff

schnuppe ['ʃnʊpə] adj—**das ist mir s.** it's all the same to me || **Schnuppe** f (-;-n) shooting star; (e-r Kerze) snuff

Schnur [ʃnur] f (-;-̈e & -en) string; (Band) braid; (elec) flexible cord; **nach der S.** regularly

Schnürband ['ʃnʏrbant] n (-[e]s;-̈er) shoestring; corset lace

Schnürchen ['ʃnʏrçən] n (-s;-) string; **etw am S. haben** have at one's fingertips; **wie am S.** like clockwork

schnüren ['ʃnʏrən] tr tie; lace; (Perlen) string || ref put on a corset

schnur'gerade adj straight || adv straight, as the crow flies

schnurr [ʃnur] interj purr!; buzz!

Schnurrbart ['ʃnurbart] m mustache

schnurren ['ʃnurən] intr (Katze) purr; (Rad) whir; (Maschine) hum; (schnorren) sponge, chisel

schnurrig ['ʃnurɪç] adj funny; queer

Schnürschuh ['ʃnʏrʃu] m oxford shoe

Schnürsenkel ['ʃnʏrzɛŋkəl] m shoestring

schnurstracks ['ʃnur'traks] adv right away; directly; **s. entgegengesetzt** diametrically opposite; **s. losgehen auf** (acc) make a beeline for

schob [ʃop] pret of schieben

Schober ['ʃobər] m (-s;-) stack

Schock [ʃɔk] m (-[e]s;-s) shock || n (-[e]s;-e) threescore

schockant [ʃɔ'kant] adj shocking

schockieren [ʃɔ'kirən] tr shock

schofel ['ʃofəl] adj mean; miserable; (schäbig) shabby; (geizig) stingy

Schöffe ['ʃœfə] m (-n;-n) juror

Schokolade [ʃɔko'ladə] f (-;-n) chocolate

schokoladen [ʃɔko'ladən] adj chocolate

Schokola'dentafel f chocolate bar

scholl [ʃɔl] pret of schallen

Scholle ['ʃɔlə] f (-;-n) clod; sod; stratum; ice floe; (ichth) sole; **heimatliche S.** native soil

schon [ʃon] adv already; as early as; yet, as yet; (sogar) even; (bloß) the bare, the mere; **ich komme s.!** all right, I'm coming!; **s. am folgenden Tage** on the very next day; **s. der Gedanke** the mere thought; **s. früher** before now; **s. gut!** all right!; **s. immer** always; **s. lange** long since, for a long time; **s. wieder** again

schön [ʃøn] adj beautiful; nice; (Künste) fine; (Mann) handsome; (Summe) nice round; (Geschlecht) fair; **schönen Dank!** many thanks!; **schönen Gruß an** (acc) best regards to || adv nicely; **der Hund macht s.** the dog sits up and begs; **s. warm** nice and warm

schonen ['ʃonən] tr spare; take it easy on; treat with consideration || ref take care of oneself

scho'nend adj careful; considerate

schön'färben tr gloss over

Schon'frist f period of grace

Schon'gang m (aut) overdrive

Schön'heit f (-;-en) beauty

Schön'heitsfehler m flaw

Schön'heitskönigin f beauty queen

Schön'heitspflege f beauty treatment

schön'tun §154 intr (dat) flatter; (dat) flirt (with)

Scho'nung f (-;-en) care, careful treatment; mercy; consideration; tree nursery; wild-game preserve

scho'nungslos adj unsparing; merciless; relentless

scho'nungsvoll adj considerate

Schon'zeit f (hunt) closed season

Schopf [ʃɔpf] m (-[e]s;-̈e) tuft of hair; (orn) crest

schöpfen ['ʃœpfən] tr draw; bail; scoop, ladle; (frische Luft) breathe; (Mut) take; **Verdacht s.** become suspicious; **wieder Atem (or Luft) s.** (fig) breathe freely again

Schöp'fer m (-s;-) creator; author; composer; painter; sculptor; dipper, ladle

schöpferisch ['ʃœpfərɪʃ] adj creative

Schöp'ferkraft f creative power

Schöpf'kelle f scoop

Schöpf'löffel m ladle

Schöp'fung f (-;-en) creation

Schoppen ['ʃɔpən] m (-s;-) pint; glass of beer, glass of wine

schor [ʃor] pret of scheren

Schorf [ʃɔrf] m (-[e]s;-e) scab

Schornstein ['ʃɔrnʃtaɪn] m chimney; smokestack

Schorn'steinfeger m chimney sweeper

Schoß [ʃos] m (Schosses; Schosse)

sprout || [ʃos] m (-es;̈-e) lap; womb; (fig) bosom; **die Hände in den S. legen** cross one's arms; (fig) be idle

Schößling ['ʃœslɪŋ] m (-s;̈-e) shoot

Schote ['ʃotə] f (-;-n) pod, shell

Schotte ['ʃotə] m (-n;-n) Scotchman || f (-;-n) (naut) bulkhead

Schotter ['ʃotər] m (-s;-) gravel; macadam, crushed stone; (rr) ballast

Schottin ['ʃotɪn] f (-;-nen) Scotchwoman

schottisch ['ʃotɪʃ] adj Scotch

schraffieren [ʃra'firən] tr hatch

schräg [ʃrek] adj oblique; (abfallend) slanting, sloping; diagonal || adv obliquely; **s. gegenüber von** diagonally across from; **s. geneigt** sloping

Schräg'linie f diagonal

schrak [ʃrɑk] pret of **schrecken**

Schramme ['ʃramə] f (-;-n) scratch, abrasion; scar

schrammen ['ʃramən] tr scratch; skin

Schrank [ʃraŋk] m (-[e]s;̈-e) closet

Schranke ['ʃraŋkə] f (-;-n) barrier; (fig) bounds, limit; (jur) bar; (rr) gate; (sport) starting gate

schran'kenlos adj boundless; exaggerated

Schran'kenwärter m (rr) signalman

Schrank'fach n compartment

Schrank'koffer m wardrobe trunk

Schrapnell [ʃrap'nel] n (-s;-e & -s) shrapnel, piece of shrapnel

Schraubdeckel ['ʃraupdekəl] m screwon cap

Schraube ['ʃraubə] f (-;-n) screw; bolt; (aer, naut) propeller

schrauben ['ʃraubən] tr screw; **in die Höhe s.** raise || ref—**sich in die Höhe s.** circle higher and higher

Schrau'benflügel m propeller blade

Schrau'bengang m, **Schrau'bengewinde** n thread (of a screw)

Schrau'benmutter f (-;-n) nut

Schrau'benschlüssel m wrench; **verstellbarer S.** monkey wrench

Schrau'benstrahl m, **Schrau'benstrom** m (aer) slipstream

Schraubenzieher ['ʃraubəntsi·ər] m (-s;-) screwdriver

Schraubstock ['ʃraupʃtɔk] m vice

Schrebergarten ['ʃrebərgartən] m garden plot (at edge of town)

Schreck [ʃrek] m (-[e]s;-e) var of **Schrecken**

Schreck'bild n frightful sight; boogeyman

schrecken ['ʃrekən] tr frighten, scare || **Schrecken** m (-s;-) fright, fear

Schreckensbotschaft (Schrek'kensbotschaft) f alarming news

Schreckensherrschaft (Schrek'kensherrschaft) f reign of terror

Schreckenskammer (Schrek'kenskammer) f chamber of horrors

Schreckensregiment (Schrek'kensregiment) n reign of teror, terrorism

Schreckenstat (Schrek'kenstat) f atrocity

schreck'haft adj timid

schreck'lich adj frightful, terrible

Schrecknis ['ʃreknɪs] n (-ses;-se) horror

Schreck'schuß m warning shot

Schreck'sekunde f reaction time

Schrei [ʃraɪ] m (-[e]s;-e) cry, shout; **letzter S.** latest fashion

Schreib- [ʃraɪp] comb.fm. writing

Schreib'art f style; spelling

Schreib'bedarf m stationery

Schreib'block m writing pad, note pad

schreiben ['ʃraɪbən] §62 tr write; spell; type; **ins Konzept s.** make a rough draft of; **ins reine s.** make a clean copy; **Noten s.** copy music || ref spell one's name || intr write; spell; type || **Schreiben** n (-s;-) writing; (com) letter

Schrei'ber m (-s;-) writer; clerk; recording instrument, recorder

schreib'faul adj too lazy to write

Schreib'feder f pen

Schreib'fehler m slip of the pen

Schreib'heft n copybook, exercise book

Schreib'mappe f portfolio

Schreib'maschine f typewriter; **mit der S. geschrieben** typed; **S. schreiben** type

Schreib'maschinenfarbband n (-[e]s; ̈-er) typewriter ribbon

Schreib'maschinenschreiber –in §6 mf typist

Schreib'maschinenschrift f typescript

Schreib'materialien pl, **Schreib'papier** n stationery

Schreib'schrift f (typ) script

Schreib'stube f (mil) orderly room

Schreib'tisch m desk

Schrei'bung f (-;-en) spelling

Schreib'unterlage f desk pad

Schreib'waren pl stationery

Schreib'warenhandlung f stationery store

Schreibweise f style; spelling

Schreib'zeug n writing materials

schreien ['ʃraɪ·ən] §135 tr cry, shout, scream, howl || ref—**sich heiser s.** shout oneself hoarse; **sich tot s.** yell one's lungs out || intr cry, shout, scream, howl; (Esel) bray; (Eule) screech; (Schwein) squeal; **s. nach** clamor for; **s. über** (acc) cry out against; **s. vor** (dat) shout for (joy); cry out in (pain); roar with (laughter) || **Schreien** n (-s) shouting; **das ist zum S.!** that's a scream!

schrei'end adj shrill; (Farbe) loud; (Unrecht) flagrant

Schrei'hals m (coll) crybaby

Schrei'krampf m crying fit

Schrein [ʃraɪn] m (-[e]s;-e) reliquary

Schreiner ['ʃraɪnər] m (-s;-) carpenter; cabinetmaker

schreiten ['ʃraɪtən] §86 intr (SEIN) step; stride; **zur Abstimmung s.** proceed to vote; **zur Tat s.** proceed to act

schrie [ʃri] pret of **schreien**

schrieb [ʃrip] pret of **schreiben**

Schrift [ʃrɪft] f (-;-en) writing; handwriting; letter, character; document; book; publication; periodical; (auf Münzen) legend; (typ) type, font; **die Heilige S.** Holy Scripture; **nach der S. sprechen** speak standard German

Schrift'art f type, font
Schrift'auslegung f exegesis
Schrift'bild n type face
Schrift'deutsch n literary German
Schrift'führer –in §6 mf secretary
Schrift'leiter –in §6 mf editor
schrift'lich adj written || adv in writing; s. wiedergeben transcribe
Schrift'satz m (jur) brief; (typ) composition
Schrift'setzer m typesetter
Schrift'sprache f literary language
Schriftsteller –in [ˈʃrɪft/tɛlər(ɪn)] §6 mf writer, author
Schrift'stück n piece of writing; document
Schrifttum [ˈʃrɪfttum] n (–s;) literature
Schrift'verkehr m, **Schrift'wechsel** m correspondence
Schrift'zeichen n letter, character
schrill [ʃrɪl] adj shrill
schrillen [ˈʃrɪlən] intr ring loudly
schritt [ʃrɪt] pret of schreiten ||
Schritt m (–[e]s;–e) step; pace; stride; (e–r Hose) crotch; (fig) step
Schritt'macher m pacemaker
schritt'weise adv gradually; step by step
schroff [ʃrɔf] adj steep; rugged; rude, uncouth; rough, harsh; (Ablehnung, Widerspruch) flat
schröpfen [ˈʃrœpfən] tr (fig) milk, fleece; (med) bleed, cup
Schrot [ʃrot] m & n (–[e]s;–e) scrap; (Getreide) crushed grain, grits; (zum Schießen) buckshot
Schrot'brot n whole grain bread
Schrot'flinte f shotgun
Schrot'korn n, **Schrot'kugel** f pellet
Schrott [ʃrɔt] m (–[e]s;) scrap metal
Schrott'platz m junk yard
schrubben [ˈʃrubən] tr scrub
Schrulle [ˈʃrulə] f (–;–n) (coll) nutty idea
schrul'lenhaft, schrullig [ˈʃrulɪç] adj whimsical
schrumpelig [ˈʃrumpəlɪç] adj crumpled; wrinkled, shriveled
schrumpeln [ˈʃrumpəln] intr shrivel
schrumpfen [ˈʃrumpfən] intr (SEIN) shrink; shrivel; (pathol) atrophy
Schub [ʃup] m (–[e]s;–e) shove, push; batch; (phys) thrust
Schub'fach n drawer
Schub'karre f, **Schub'karren** m wheelbarrow
Schub'kasten m drawer
Schub'kraft f thrust
Schub'lade f drawer
Schub'leistung f thrust
Schubs [ʃups] m (–es;–e) (coll) shove
schubsen [ˈʃupsən] tr & intr shove
Schub'stange f (aut) connecting rod
schüchtern [ˈʃʏçtərn] adj shy, bashful
schuf [ʃuf] pret of schaffen
Schuft [ʃuft] m (–[e]s;–e) cad
schuften [ˈʃuftən] intr drudge, slave
Schufterei [ʃuftə'raɪ] f (–;) drudgery; (Schuftigkeit) meanness
schuftig [ˈʃuftɪç] adj (fig) rotten
Schuh [ʃu] m (–[e]s;–e) shoe; boot
Schuh'band n (–[e]s;–er) shoestring

Schuhflicker [ˈʃuflɪkər] m (–s;–) shoe repairman, shoemaker
Schuh'krem m shoe polish
Schuh'laden m shoe store
Schuh'leisten m last
Schuh'löffel m shoehorn
Schuh'macher m shoemaker
Schuhplattler [ˈʃuplatlər] m (–s;–) Bavarian folk dance
Schuh'putzer m shoeshine boy
Schuh'sohle f sole
Schuhspanner [ˈʃu/panər] m (–s;–) shoetree
Schuh'werk n footwear
Schuh'wichse f shoe polish
Schuh'zeug n footwear
Schul– [ʃul] comb.fm. school
Schul'amt n school board
Schul'arbeit f homework; (Aust) classroom work
Schul'aufsicht f school board
Schul'bank f (–;–e) school desk
Schul'behörde f school board; board of education
Schul'beispiel n (fig) test case
Schul'besuch m attendance at school
Schul'bildung f schooling, education
schuld [ʃult] adj at fault, to blame ||
Schuld f (–;–en) debt; fault; guilt
schuld'bewußt adj conscious of one's guilt
schulden [ˈʃuldən] tr owe
schuld'haft adj culpable || **Schuld'haft** f imprisonment for debt
Schul'diener m school janitor
schuldig [ˈʃuldɪç] adj guilty; responsible; j–m etw s. sein owe s.o. s.th. ||
Schuldige §5 mf culprit; guilty party
Schul'digkeit f (–;–en) duty, obligation; seine S. tun do one's duty
Schul'direktor –in §7 mf principal
schuld'los adj innocent
Schuld'losigkeit f (–;) innocence
Schuldner –in [ˈʃuldnər(ɪn)] §6 mf debtor
Schuld'schein m promissory note, IOU
Schuld'spruch m verdict of guilty
Schuld'verschreibung f promissory note, IOU; (Obligation) bond
Schule [ˈʃulə] f (–;–n) school; auf der S. in school; S. machen (fig) set a precedent; von der S. abgehen quit school
schulen [ˈʃulən] tr train; (pol) indoctrinate
Schüler [ˈʃylər] m (–s;–) pupil (in grammar school or high school); trainee; (Jünger) disciple
Schü'leraustausch m student exchange
Schülerin [ˈʃylərɪn] f (–;–nen) pupil
Schul'film m educational film
Schul'flug m training flight
schul'frei adj—schulfreier Tag holiday; s. haben have off
Schul'gelände n school grounds; campus
Schul'geld n tuition
Schul'gelehrsamkeit f book learning
Schul'hof m schoolyard, playground
Schul'kamerad m school chum
Schul'lehrer –in §6 mf schoolteacher
Schul'mappe f schoolbag
Schul'meister m schoolmaster; pedant
schul'meistern intr criticize

Schul'ordnung f school regulation
Schul'pflicht f compulsory school attendance
schul'pflichtig adj of school age; **schulpflichtiges Alter** school age
Schul'plan m curriculum
Schul'ranzen m schoolbag
Schul'rat m (-[e]s;⁓e) (educ) superintendent
Schul'reise f field trip
Schul'schiff n training ship
Schul'schluß m close of school
Schul'schwester f teaching nun
Schul'stunde f lesson, period
Schul'tasche f schoolbag
Schulter ['ʃultər] f (-;-n) shoulder
Schul'terblatt n shoulder blade
schul'terfrei adj off-the-shoulder; (trägerfrei) strapless
schultern ['ʃultərn] tr shoulder
Schul'terstück n epaulet
Schul'unterricht m instruction; schooling; **im S.** in school
Schul'wesen n school system
Schul'zeugnis n report card
Schul'zimmer n classroom
Schul'zwang m compulsory education
schummeln ['ʃuməln] intr (coll) cheat
schund [ʃunt] pret of **schinden** ||
Schund m (-[e]s;) junk, trash
Schund'literatur f trashy literature
Schund'roman m dime novel
Schupo ['ʃupo] m (-s;-s) (Schutzpolizist) policeman, copy || f (-;)
(Schutzpolizei) police
Schuppe ['ʃupə] f (-;-n) scale; **Schuppen** dandruff
schuppen ['ʃupən] tr scale; scrape ||
Schuppen m (-s;-) shed; (aer) hangar; (aut) garage
schuppig ['ʃupɪç] adj scaly, flaky
Schups [ʃups] m (-es;-e) shove
schupsen ['ʃupsən] tr shove
Schüreisen ['ʃyraɪzən] n poker
schüren ['ʃyrən] tr poke, stir; (fig) stir up, foment
schürfen ['ʃyrfən] tr scratch, scrape; dig for || intr (nach) prospect (for)
schurigeln ['ʃurigəln] tr (coll) bully
Schurke ['ʃurkə] m (-n;-n) bum, punk
Schur'kenstreich m, **Schur'kentat** f, **Schurkerei** [ʃurkə'raɪ] f (-;-en) mean trick
schurkisch ['ʃurkɪʃ] adj mean, low-down
Schürze ['ʃyrtsə] f (-;-n) apron
schürzen ['ʃyrtsən] tr tuck up; tie
Schür'zenband n (-[e]s;⁓er) apron
Schür'zenjäger m skirt chaser, wolf
Schuß [ʃus] m (Schusses; Schüsse) shot; (Ladung) round; (Schußwunde) gunshot wound; (rasche Bewegung) rush; (Brot) batch; (bot) shoot; (culin) dash; (sport) shot; **blinder S.** blank; **e-n S. abgeben** fire a shot; **ein S. ins Blaue** a wild shot; **ein S. in Schwarze** a bull's-eye; **im S. haben** have under control; **im vollen S.** in full swing; **in S. bekommen** get going; **in S. bringen** get (s.th.); **j-m vor den S. kommen** come within s.o.'s range; (fig) come across s.o.; **scharfer S.**

live round; **weit vom S.** out of harm's way
Schüssel ['ʃysəl] f (-;-n) bowl; (fig) dish
schuß'fest, schuß'sicher adj bulletproof
Schuß'waffe f firearm
Schuß'weite f range
Schuster ['ʃustər] m (-s;-) shoemaker; (fig) bungler
schustern ['ʃustərn] intr bungle
Schutt [ʃut] m (-es;) rubbish; rubble
Schutt'abladeplatz m dump
Schüttboden ['ʃytbodən] m granary
Schüttelfrost ['ʃytəlfrɔst] m shivers
schütteln ['ʃytəln] tr shake; **j-m die Hand s.** shake hands with s.o.
schütten ['ʃytən] tr pour, spill || impers —es schüttet it is pouring
Schutz [ʃuts] m (-es;) protection, defense; (Obdach) shelter; (Deckung) cover; (Schirm) screen; (Schutzgeleit) safeguard; **zu S. und Trutz** defensive and offensive
Schutz'brille f safety goggles
Schütze ['ʃytsə] m (-n;-n) marksman, shot; (astr) Sagittarius; (mil) rifleman || f (-;-n) sluice gate
schützen ['ʃytsən] tr (gegen) protect (against), defend (against); (vor dat) preserve (from) || **Schützen** m (-s;-) tex) shuttle
schüt'zend adj protective; tutelary
Schutz'engel m guardian angle
Schüt'zengraben m (mil) foxhole
Schüt'zenkompanie f rifle company
Schüt'zenkönig m crack shot
Schüt'zenloch n (mil) foxhole
Schüt'zenmine f anti-personnel mine
Schutz'geleit n escort; safe conduct; (aer) air cover; (nav) convoy
Schutz'glocke f (aer) umbrella
Schutz'gott m, **Schutz'göttin** f tutelary deity
Schutz'haft f protective custody
Schutzheilige §5 mf patron saint
Schutz'herr m protector; patron
Schutz'herrin f protectress; patroness
Schutz'impfung f immunization
Schutz'insel f traffic island
Schützling ['ʃytslɪŋ] m (-s;-e) ward
schutz'los adj defenseless
Schutz'mann m (-[e]s;⁓er & -leute) policeman
Schutz'marke f trademark
Schutz'mittel n preservative; preventive
Schutz'patron -in §8 mf patron saint
Schutz'polizei f police
Schutz'polizist m policeman, cop
Schutz'scheibe f (aut) windshield
Schutz'staffel f SS troops
Schutz'umschlag m dust jacket
Schutz'-und-Trutz'-Bündnis f defensive and offensive alliance
Schutz'waffe f defensive weapon
Schutz'zoll m protective tariff
Schwabe ['ʃvabə] m (-n;-n) Swabian
Schwaben ['ʃvabən] n (-s;) Swabia
Schwäbin ['ʃvebɪn] f (-;-nen) Swabian
schwäbisch ['ʃvebɪʃ] adj Swabian; **das Schwäbische Meer** Lake Constance
schwach [ʃvax] adj (schwächer ['ʃveçər]; schwächste ['ʃveçstə] §9)

weak; (*Hoffnung, Ton, Licht*) faint; (*unzureichend*) scanty; sparse; (*armselig*) poor

Schwäche ['ʃvɛçə] *f* (-;-n) weakness

Schwach'kopf *m* dunce; sap, dope

schwächlich ['ʃvɛçlɪç] *adj* feeble, delicate

Schwächling ['ʃvɛçlɪŋ] *m* (-s;-e) weakling

schwach'sinnig *adj* feeble-minded ‖ **Schwachsinnige** §5 *mf* dimwit, moron

Schwach'strom *m* low-voltage current

Schwaden ['ʃvadən] *m* (-s;-) swath; cloud (*of smoke, etc.*)

Schwadron [ʃva'dron] *f* (-;-en) squadron

schwadronieren [ʃvadro'nirən] *intr* (coll) brag

schwafeln ['ʃvafəln] *intr* talk nonsense

Schwager ['ʃvagər] *m* (-s;-) brother-in-law

Schwägerin ['ʃvɛgərɪn] *f* (-;-nen) sister-in-law

Schwalbe ['ʃvalbə] *f* (-;-n) swallow

Schwal'bennest *n* (aer) gun turret

Schwal'benschwanz *m* (*Frack*) tails; (carp) dovetail

Schwall [ʃval] *m* -[e]s;-e) flood; (*von Worten*) torrent

schwamm [ʃvam] *pret* of **schwimmen** ‖ **Schwamm** *m* (-[e]s;⁺e) sponge; mushroom; fungus; dry rot; **S. darüber!** skip it!

schwammig ['ʃvamɪç] *adj* spongy

Schwan [ʃvan] *m* (-[e]s;⁺e) swan

schwand [ʃvant] *pret* of **schwinden**

schwang [ʃvaŋ] *pret* of **schwingen**

schwanger ['ʃvaŋər] *adj* pregnant

schwängern ['ʃvɛŋərn] *tr* make pregnant; (fig) impregnate

Schwan'gerschaft *f* (-;-en) pregnancy

Schwan'gerschaftsverhütung *f* contraception

schwank [ʃvaŋk] *adj* flexible; unsteady ‖ **Schwank** *m* (-[e]s;⁺e) prank; joke; funny story; (theat) farce

schwanken ['ʃvaŋkən] *intr* stagger; (*schaukeln*) rock; (*schlingern*) roll; (*stampfen*) pitch; (*Flamme*) flicker; (*pendeln*) oscillate; (*vibrieren*) vibrate; (*wellenartig*) undulate; (*zittern*) shake; (*Preise*) fluctuate; (*zögern*) vacillate, hesitate

Schwanz [ʃvants] *m* (-es;⁺e) tail; (*Gefolge*) train; (vulg) pecker; **kein S.** not a living soul; **mit dem S. wedeln** (or **wippen**) wag its tail

schwänzeln ['ʃvɛntsəln] *intr* wag its tail; **s. um** fawn on

schwänzen ['ʃvɛntsən] *tr—die Schule s.** play hooky from school; **e-e Stunde s.** cut a class ‖ *intr* play hooky

schwappen ['ʃvapən] *intr* slosh around; **s. über** (*acc*) spill over

schwapps [ʃvaps] *interj* slap!; splash!

Schwäre ['ʃvɛrə] *f* (-;-n) abscess

schwären ['ʃvɛrən] *intr* fester

Schwarm [ʃvarm] *m* (-[e]s;⁺e) swarm; flock, herd; (*von Fischen*) school; (fig) idol; (fig) craze; (aer) flight of five aircraft; **sie ist mein S.** (coll) I have a crush on her

schwärmen ['ʃvɛrmən] *intr* swarm; stray; daydream; go out on the town; **s. für** (or **über** *acc* or **von**) rave about

Schwär'mer *m* (-s;-) enthusiast; reveler; daydreamer; firecracker; (religious) fanatic; (ent) hawk moth

Schwärmerei [ʃvɛrmə'raɪ] *f* (-;-en) enthusiasm; daydreaming; revelry; fanaticism

schwärmerisch ['ʃvɛrmərɪʃ] *adj* enthusiastic; gushy; fanatic; fanciful

Schwarte ['ʃvartə] *f* (-;-n) rind, skin; (coll) old book

schwarz [ʃvarts] *adj* black; dark; (*ungesetzlich*) illegal; (*schmutzig*) dirty; (*düster*) gloomy; (*von der Sonne*) tanned; **schwarze Kunst** black magic; **schwarzes Brett** bulletin board ‖ *adv* illegally

Schwarz'arbeit *f* moonlighting; nonunion work; illicit work

Schwarz'brenner *m* moonshiner

Schwärze ['ʃvɛrtsə] *f* (-;-n) blackness; darkness; printer's ink

schwärzen ['ʃvɛrtsən] *tr* darken; blacken

schwarz'fahren §71 *intr* (SEIN) drive without a license; ride without a ticket

Schwarz'fahrer -in §6 *mf* unlicensed driver; rider without a ticket

Schwarz'fahrt *f* joy ride; ride without a ticket

Schwarz'handel *m* black-marketing

Schwarz'händler -in §6 *mf* black marketeer; (*mit Eintrittskarten*) scalper

schwärzlich ['ʃvɛrtslɪç] *adj* blackish

Schwarz'markt *m* black market

Schwarz'seher -in §6 *mf* pessimist

Schwarz'sender *m* illegal transmitter

schwatzen ['ʃvatsən], **schwätzen** ['ʃvɛtsən] *tr* (coll) talk ‖ *intr* (coll) yap, talk nonsense; (coll) gossip

Schwät'zer -in §6 *mf* windbag; gossip

schwatz'haft *adj* talkative

Schwatz'maul *n* blabber mouth

Schwebe ['ʃvebə] *f* (-;) suspense; **in der S. sein** be undecided; be pending

Schwe'bebahn *f* cablecar

Schwe'beflug *m* hovering, soaring

schweben ['ʃvebən] *intr* (HABEN & SEIN) be suspended, hang; float; (*Hubschrauber*) hover; (*Segelflugzeug*) soar; glide; (fig) waver, be undecided; **in Gefahr s.** be in danger; **in Ungewißheit s.** be in suspense

Schwede ['ʃvedə] *m* (-n;-n) Swede

Schweden ['ʃvedən] *n* (-s;) Sweden

Schwedin ['ʃvedɪn] *f* (-;-nen) Swede

schwedisch ['ʃvedɪʃ] *adj* Swedish

Schwefel ['ʃvefəl] *m* (-s;) sulfur

Schwe'felsäure *f* sulfuric acid

Schweif [ʃvaɪf] *m* (-[e]s;-e) tail; (fig) train

schweifen ['ʃvaɪfən] *tr* curve; (*spülen*) rinse ‖ *intr* (SEIN) roam, wander

Schweigegeld ['ʃvaɪgəgɛlt] *n* hush money

schweigen ['ʃvaɪgən] §148 *intr* be silent, keep silent; (*aufhören*) stop; **ganz zu s. von** to say nothing of; **s. zu** make no reply to

schwei′gend adj silent ‖ adv in silence
schweigsam [ˈʃvaɪkzəm] adj taciturn
Schwein [ʃvaɪn] n (-[e]s;-e) pig, hog; **S. haben** be lucky, have luck
Schwei′nebraten m roast pork
Schwei′nefleisch n pork
Schwei′nehund m (pej) filthy swine
Schwei′nekoben m pigsty, pig pen
Schweinerei [ʃvaɪnəˈraɪ] f (-;-en) mess; dirty business
Schwei′nerippchen pl pork chops
Schwei′newirtschaft f dirty mess
Schweins′kotelett n pork chop
Schweiß [ʃvaɪs] m (-es;) perspiration
schweißen [ˈʃvaɪsən] tr weld ‖ intr begin to melt, fuse; (hunt) bleed
Schwei′ßer –in §6 mf welder
Schweißfüße [ˈʃvaɪsfysə] pl sweaty feet
schweißig [ˈʃvaɪsɪç] adj sweaty; (hunt) bloody
Schweiß′perle f bead of sweat
Schweiz [ʃvaɪts] f (-;)—**die S.** Switzerland
Schwei′zer m Swiss; dairyman
schweizerisch [ˈʃvaɪtsərɪʃ] adj Swiss
schwelen [ˈʃvelən] intr smolder
schwelgen [ˈʃvelgən] intr feast; **s. in** (dat) (fig) revel in; wallow in
Schwelgerei [ʃvelgəˈraɪ] f (-;-en) feasting, carousing
schwelgerisch [ˈʃvelgərɪʃ] adj riotous; luxurious
Schwelle [ˈʃvelə] f (-;-n) sill; doorstep; (fig) verge; (psychol) threshold; (rr) railroad tie
schwellen [ˈʃvelən] §119 tr swell ‖ intr (SEIN) swell; (Wasser) rise; (anwachsen) increase
Schwel′lung f (-;-en) swelling
Schwemme [ˈʃvemə] f (-;-n) watering place; (coll) taproom; (com) glut
schwemmen [ˈʃvemən] tr wash off, rinse; (Vieh) water; (Holz) float
Schwengel [ˈʃveŋəl] m (-s;-) pump handle; (e-r Glocke) hammer
schwenkbar [ˈʃveŋkbar] adj rotating
schwenken [ˈʃveŋkən] tr swing; shake; (drohend) brandish; (Hut) wave; (spülen) rinse ‖ intr (SEIN) turn; swivel, pivot; (Geschütz) traverse; (mil) wheel; (pol) change sides
Schwen′kung f (-;-en) turn; wheeling; traversing; (fig) change of mind
schwer [ʃver] adj heavy; difficult, hard; serious; (schwerfällig) ponderous; (Strafe) severe; (Wein) strong; (Speise) rich; (unbeholfen) clumsy; (Kompanie) heavy-weapons; **drei Pfund s. sein** weigh three pounds; **schweres Geld bezahlen** pay a stiff price ‖ adv hard; with difficulty; (coll) very
Schwere [ˈʃverə] f (-;) weight; seriousness; (des Weines) body; difficulty; significance; (phys) gravity
schwe′relos adj weightless
schwer′fällig adj heavy; clumsy, slow
Schwer′gewicht n heavyweight class; (Nachdruck) emphasis
Schwergewichtler –in [ˈʃvergəvɪçtlər (ɪn)] §6 mf (sport) heavyweight
schwer′hörig adj hard of hearing

Schwer′industrie f heavy industry
Schwer′kraft f gravity
schwer′lich adv hardly
Schwer′mut f melancholy, depression
schwer′mütig adj melancholy, depressed
schwer′nehmen §116 tr take hard
Schwer′punkt m center of gravity; crucial point, focal point
Schwert [ʃvert] n (-[e]s;-er) sword
Schwer′verbrecher m §6 mf felon
schwer′verdient adj hard-earned
schwer′wiegend adj weighty
Schwester [ˈʃvestər] f (-;-n) sister; nurse; nun
Schwe′sterhelferin f nurse's aide
schwieg [ʃvik] pret of **schweigen**
Schwieger- [ˈʃvigər] comb.fm. -in-law
Schwie′germutter f mother-in-law
Schwie′gersohn m son-in-law
Schwie′gertochter f daughter-in-law
Schwie′gervater m father-in-law
Schwiele [ˈʃvilə] f (-;-n) callus
schwielig [ˈʃvilɪç] adj callous
schwierig [ˈʃvirɪç] adj hard, difficult
Schwie′rigkeit f (-;-en) difficulty
Schwimm- [ʃvɪm] comb.fm. swimming
Schwimm′anstalt f, **Schwimm′bad** n, **Schwimm′bassin** n, **Schwimm′becken** n swimming pool
schwimmen [ˈʃvɪmən] §136 intr (HABEN & SEIN) swim; float
Schwimm′gürtel m life belt
Schwimm′haut f web
Schwimm′hose f bathing trunks
Schwimm′kraft f buoyancy
Schwimm′panzer m amphibious tank
Schwimm′weste f life jacket
Schwindel [ˈʃvɪndəl] m (-s;-) dizziness; swindle, gyp; (Unsinn) bunk; (pathol) vertigo; **der ganze S.** the whole caboodle
Schwin′delanfall m dizzy spell
Schwin′delfirma f fly-by-night
schwin′delhaft adj fraudulent, bogus
schwindelig [ˈʃvɪndəlɪç] adj dizzy
schwindeln [ˈʃvɪndəln] tr swindle ‖ intr fib ‖ impers—**mir schwindelt** I feel dizzy
Schwin′delunternehmen n fly-by-night
schwinden [ˈʃvɪndən] §59 intr (SEIN) dwindle; decline; (Farbe) fade
Schwind′ler –in §6 mf swindler; fibber
schwindlig [ˈʃvɪntlɪç] adj dizzy
Schwindsucht [ˈʃvɪntzuçt] f tuberculosis
Schwinge [ˈʃvɪŋə] f (-;-n) wing; fan; winnow; (poet) pinion
schwingen [ˈʃvɪŋən] §142 tr swing; wave; brandish; (agr) winnow; (tex) swingle ‖ ref vault; soar ‖ intr swing; sway; oscillate; vibrate
Schwin′ger m (-s;-) oscillator; (box) haymaker
Schwin′gung f (-;-en) oscillation; vibration; swinging
Schwips [ʃvɪps] m—**e-n S. haben** (coll) be tight, be tipsy
schwirren [ˈʃvɪrən] intr (HABEN & SEIN) whiz, whir; buzz; (Gerüchte) fly
Schwitzbad [ˈʃvɪtsbat] n Turkish bath
schwitzen [ˈʃvɪtsən] tr & intr sweat

schwoll [ʃvɔl] *pret of* **schwellen**

schwor [ʃvoːr] *pret of* **schwören**

schwören ['ʃvøːrən] §137 *tr & intr* swear; **auf j-n** (*or* **etw**) **s.** swear by s.o. (or s.th.)

schwul [ʃvuːl] *adj* (vulg) homosexual

schwül [ʃvyːl] *adj* sultry, muggy

Schwulität [ʃvuːli'tɛt] *f* (-;-en) trouble

Schwulst [ʃvulst] *m* (-es;̈-e) bombast

schwülstig ['ʃvylstɪç] *adj* bombastic

schwummerig ['ʃvumərɪç] *adj* (coll) shaky

Schwund [ʃvunt] *m* (-[e]s;) dwindling; shrinkage; loss; leakage; (*des Haares*) falling out; (rad) fading; (pathol) atrophy

Schwung [ʃvuŋ] *m* (-[e]s;̈-e) swing; vault; (*Tatkraft*) zip, go; (*der Phantasie*) flight; **in S. bringen** start; **S. bekommen** gather momentum

schwung/haft *adj* brisk, lively

Schwung/kraft *f* centrifugal force; (fig) zip, pep; (phys) momentum

Schwung/rad *n* (mach) flywheel

schwung/voll *adj* enthusiastic, lively

schwur [ʃvuːr] *pret of* **schwören** ‖ **Schwur** *m* (-[e]s;̈-e) oath

Schwur/gericht *n* jury

sechs [zɛks] *invar adj & pron* six ‖ **Sechs** *f* (-;-en) six

Sechs/eck *n* hexagon

Sechser ['zɛksər] *m* (-s;-) six; (*in der Lotterie*) jackpot

Sechsta/gerennen *n* six-day bicycle race

sechste ['zɛkstə] §9 *adj & pron* sixth

Sechstel ['zɛkstəl] *n* (-s;-) sixth

sech'zehn *invar adj & pron* sixteen ‖ **Sech'zehn** *f* (-;-en) sixteen

sech'zehnte §9 *adj & pron* sixteenth

Sech'zehntel *n* (-s;-) sixteenth

sechzig ['zɛçtsɪç] *invar adj & pron* sixty ‖ **Sechzig** *f* (-;-en) sixty

sechziger ['zɛçtsɪgər] *invar adj* of the sixties; **die s. Jahre** the sixties ‖ **Sechziger** *m* (-s;-) sexagenarian

sechzigste ['zɛçtsɪçstə] §9 *adj & pron* sixtieth

See [ze] *m* (Sees; Seen ['zeːən] lake ‖ *f* (See; ['zeːən]) sea; ocean; **an der See** at the seashore; **an die See gehen** go to the seashore; **auf See** at sea; **in See gehen** (*or* **stechen**) put out to sea; **in See sein** in open water; **Kapitän zur See** navy captain; **zur See gehen** go to sea

See'bad *n* seashore resort

See'bär *m* (fig) sea dog

see'fähig *adj* seaworthy

See'fahrer *m* seafarer

See'fahrt *f* seafaring; voyage

see'fest *adj* seaworthy; **s. werden** get one's sea legs

See'gang *m*—**hoher** (*or* **schwerer** *or* **starker**) **S.** heavy seas

See'hafen *m* seaport

See'handel *m* maritime trade

See'hund *m* (zool) seal

See'jungfer *f*, **See'jungfrau** *f* mermaid

See'kadett *m* naval cadet

See'karte *f* (naut) chart

see'krank *adj* seasick

See'krebs *m* lobster

Seele ['zeːlə] *f* (-;-n) soul; mind; (*Ein-*

wohner) inhabitant, soul; (*e-s Geschützes*) bore; (*e-s Kabels*) core

See'lenangst *f* mortal fear

See'lenfriede *m* peace of mind

See'lenheil *n* salvation

See'lennot *f* mental distress

See'lenpein *f*, **See'lenqual** *f* mental anguish

See'lenruhe *f* peace of mind; composure

see'lensgut *adj* good-hearted

seelisch ['zeːlɪ] *adj* mental, psychic

Seel'sorge *f* (-;) ministry

Seel'sorger *m* (-s;-) minister, pastor

See'macht *f* sea power

See'mann *m* (-[e]s;-leute) seaman

See'meile *f* nautical mile

See'möwe *f* sea gull

See'not *f* (naut) distress

See'ratte *f* (fig) old salt

See'raub *m* piracy

See'räuber *m* pirate; corsair

See'räuberei *f* piracy

See'recht *n* maritime law

See'reise *f* voyage; cruise

See'sperre *f* naval blockade

See'stadt *f* seaport town; coastal town

See'straße *f* shipping lane

See'streitkräfte *pl* naval forces

See'tang *m* seaweed

see'tüchtig *adj* seaworthy

See'warte *f* oceanographic institute

See'weg *m* sea route; **auf dem S. by sea**

See'wesen *n* naval affairs

Segel ['zeːgəl] *n* (-s;-) sail

Se'gelboot *n* sailboat; (sport) yacht

Se'gelfliegen *n* gliding

Se'gelflieger **-in** §6 *mf* glider pilot

Se'gelflug *m* glide, gliding

Se'gelflugzeug *n* glider

Se'gelleinwand *f* sailcloth, canvas

segeln ['zeːgəln] *intr* (HABEN & SEIN) sail; (aer) glide

Se'gelschiff *n* sailing vessel

Se'gelsport *m* sailing

Se'geltuch *n* sailcloth, canvas

Se'geltuchhülle *f*, **Se'geltuchplane** *f* tarpaulin

Segen ['zeːgən] *m* (-s;-) blessing

se'gensreich *adj* blessed, blissful

Segler ['zeːglər] *m* (-s;-) yachtsman; (aer) glider; (naut) sailing vessel

segnen ['zeːgnən] *tr* bless

Seh- [zeː] *comb.fm.* visual, of vision

sehen ['zeːən] §138 *tr* see ‖ *intr* see; look; **s. auf** (*acc*) look at; take care of; face (*a direction*); **s. nach** look for, look around for; **schlecht s.** have poor eyes ‖ **Sehen** *n* (-s;) sight; eyesight, vision; **vom S.** by sight

se'henswert *adj* worth seeing

Se'henswürdigkeit *f* object of interest; **Sehenswürdigkeiten** sights

Seher ['zeːər] *m* (-s;-) seer, prophet

Se'hergabe *f* gift of prophecy

Seh'feld *n* field of vision

Seh'kraft *f* eyesight

Sehne ['zeːnə] *f* (-;-n) tendon, sinew; (*Bogen-*) string; (geom) secant

sehnen ['zeːnən] *ref*—**sich s. nach** long for, crave ‖ **Sehnen** *n* (-s;) longing

Seh'nerv *m* optic nerve

sehnig ['zeniç] *adj* sinewy; *(Fleisch)* stringy

sehnlich ['zenliç] *adj* longing; ardent

Sehnsucht ['zenzuçt] *f* (-;) yearning

sehr [zer] *adv* very; very much

Seh'rohr *n* periscope

Seh'vermögen *n* sight, vision

Seh'weite *f* visual range; **in S.** within sight

seicht [zaiçt] *adj* (& fig) shallow

Seide ['zaidə] *f* (-;-n) silk

seiden ['zaidən] *adj* silk, silky

Sei'denatlas *m* satin

Sei'denpapier *n* tissue paper

Sei'denraupe *f* silkworm

Sei'denspinnerei *f* silk mill

Sei'denstoff *m* silk cloth

seidig ['zaidiç] *adj* silky

Seife ['zaifə] *f* (-;-n) soap

Sei'fenblase *f* soap bubble

Sei'fenbrühe *f* soapsuds

Sei'fenflocken *pl* soap flakes

Sei'fenlauge *f* soapsuds

Sei'fenpulver *n* soap powder

Sei'fenschale *f* soap dish

Sei'fenschaum *m* lather

seifig ['zaifiç] *adj* soapy

seihen ['zai-ən] *tr* strain, filter

Sei'her *m* (-s;-) strainer, filter

Seil [zail] *n* (-[e]s;-e) rope; cable

Seil'bahn *f* cable railway; cable car

seil'springen *intr* jump rope

Seil'tänzer –in §6 *mf* ropewalker

sein [zain] §139 *intr* (SEIN) be; exist; **es ist mir, als wenn I** feel as if; **es sei denn, daß** unless; **lassen Sie das s.!** stop it!; **wenn dem so ist if** that is the case; **wie dem auch sein mag** however that may be || *aux* (to form compound past tenses of intransitive verbs of motion, change of condition, etc.) have, e.g., **ich bin gegangen I** have gone, I went || §2,2 *poss adj* his; its; one's; her || §2,4,5 *poss pron* his; hers; **die Seinen** his family; **er hat das Seine getan** he did his share; **jedem das Seine** to each his own || **Sein** *n* (-s;) being; existence; reality

seinerseits ['zainər'zaits] *adv* for his part

seinerzeit ['zainər'tsait] *adv* in its time; in those days; in due time

seinesgleichen ['zainəs'glaiçən] *pron* people like him, the likes of him

seinethalben ['zainət'halbən], **seinetwegen** ['zainət'vegən] *adv* for his sake; on his account; *(von ihm aus)* for all he cares

seinetwillen ['zainət'vilən] *adv*—**um s.** for his sake, on his behalf

Seinige ['zainigə] §2,5 *pron* his; **das S.** his property, his own; his due; his share; **die Seinigen** his family

seit [zait] *prep* (*dat*) since, for; **s. e-m Jahr** for one year; **s. einiger Zeit** for some time past; **s. kurzem** lately; **s. langem** for a long time; **s. wann** since when || *conj* since

seitdem [zait'dem] *adv* since that time || *conj* since

Seite ['zaitə] *f* (-;-n) side; page; direction; *(Quelle)* source; (mil) flank

Sei'tenansicht *f* side view, profile

Sei'tenbau *m* (-[e]s;-ten) annex

Sei'tenblick *m* side glance

Sei'tenflosse *f* (aer) horizontal stabilizer

Sei'tenflügel *m* (archit) wing

Sei'tengang *m* side aisle

Sei'tengeleise *n* sidetrack

Sei'tenhieb *m* snide remark, dig

sei'tenlang *adj* pages of

Sei'tenriß *m* profile

sei'tens *prep* (*genit*) on the part of

Sei'tenschiff *n* (archit) aisle

Sei'tenschwimmen *n* sidestroke

Sei'tensprung *m* (fig) escapade

Sei'tenstück *n* (fig) counterpart

Sei'tenwind *m* cross wind

seither [zait'her] *adv* since then

-seitig [zaitiç] *comb.fm.* –sided

seit'lich *adj* lateral

seitwärts ['zaitverts] *adv* sideways, sidewards; aside

Sekretär –in [zekre'ter(in)] §8 *mf* secretary

Sekt [zekt] *m* (-[e]s;-e) champagne

Sekte ['zektə] *f* (-;-n) sect

Sek·tor ['zektər] *m* (-s;-toren ['torən]) sector; (fig) field

Sekundant [zekun'dant] *m* (-en;-en) (box) second

sekundär [zekun'der] *adj* secondary

Sekunde [ze'kundə] *f* (-;-n) second

Sekun'denbruchteil *m* split second

Sekun'denzeiger *m* second hand

Sekurit [zeku'rit] *n* (-s;) safety glass

selber ['zelbər] *invar pron* (coll) var of **selbst**

selbst [zelpst] *invar pron* self; in person, personally; *(sogar)* even; by oneself; **ich s.** I myself; **von s.** voluntarily; spontaneously; automatically || *adv* even; **s. ich** even I; **s. wenn** even if, even when

Selbst'achtung *f* self-respect

selbständig ['zelpʃtendiç] *adj* independent

Selbst'bedienung *f* self-service

Selbst'beherrschung *f* self-control

Selbst'beobachtung *f* introspection

Selbst'bestimmung *f* self-determination

Selbst'betrug *m* self-deception

selbst'bewußt *adj* self-confident

Selbst'binder *m* necktie; (agr) combine

Selbst'erhaltung *f* self-preservation

selbst'gebacken *adj* homemade

selbst'gefällig *adj* complacent, smug

Selbst'gefühl *n* self-confidence

selbst'gemacht *adj* homemade

selbst'gerecht *adj* self-righteous

Selbst'gespräch *n* soliloquy

selbst'gezogen *adj* home-grown

selbst'herrlich *adj* high-handed

Selbst'herrschaft *f* autocracy

Selbst'herrscher *m* autocrat

Selbst'kosten *pl* production costs

Selbst'kostenpreis *m* factory price; **zum S. abgeben** sell at cost

Selbstlader ['zelpstladər] *m* (-s;-) automatic (weapon)

Selbst'laut *m* vowel

selbst'los *adj* unselfish

Selbst'mord *m* suicide

selbst'sicher *adj* self-confident

Selbst'steuer *n* automatic pilot

Selbst′sucht *f* egotism, selfishness
selbst′süchtig *adj* egotistical
selbst′tätig *adj* automatic
Selbst′täuschung *f* self-deception
Selbstüberhebung ['zɛlpstybərhebuŋ]
  f (-;) self-conceit, presumption
Selbst′verbrennung *f* spontaneous combustion; self-immolation
Selbst′verlag *m*—im **S.** printed privately
Selbst′verleugnung *f* self-denial
Selbst′versorger *m* (-s;-) self-supporter
selbst′verständlich *adj* obvious; natural || *adv* of course
Selbst′verständlichkeit *f* foregone conclusion, matter of course
Selbst′verteidigung *f* self-defense
Selbst′vertrauen *n* self-confidence
Selbst′verwaltung *f* autonomy
Selbst′wähler *m* (-s;-) dial telephone
Selbst′zucht *f* self-discipline
selbst′zufrieden *adj* self-satisfied
Selbst′zufriedenheit *f* self-satisfaction
Selbst′zweck *m* end in itself
selig ['zeliç] *adj* blessed; (*verstorben*) late; (*fig*) ecstatic; (*fig*) tipsy; **seligen Angedenkens** of blessed memory; **s. werden** attain salvation, be saved
Se′ligkeit *f* (-;) happiness; salvation
Se′ligpreisung *f* (Bib) beatitude
se′ligsprechen §64 *tr* beatify
Sellerie ['zɛləri] *m* (-s;) & *f* (-;) celery (bulb)
selten ['zɛltən] *adj* rare, scarce || *adv* seldom, rarely
Selterswasser ['zɛltərsvasər] *n* seltzer, soda water
seltsam ['zɛltzam] *adj* odd, strange
Semester [ze′mɛstər] *n* (-s;-) semester
Semikolon ['zemɪkolən] *n* semicolon
Seminar [zemɪ′nar] *n* (-s;-e) seminary; (educ) seminar
Seminarist [zemɪna′rɪst] *m* (-en;-en) seminarian
semitisch [ze′mɪtɪʃ] *adj* Semitic
Semmel ['zɛməl] *f* (-;-n) roll
Senat [ze′nat] *m* (-[e]s;-e) senate
Se-nator [ze′natɔr] *m* (-s;-natoren [na′torən]) senator
Sende- [zɛndə] *comb.fm.* transmitting, transmitter, broadcasting
senden ['zɛndən] *tr & intr* transmit, broadcast; telecast || §120 & §140 *tr* send || *intr*—**s. nach** send for
Sen′der *m* (-s;-) (rad, telv) transmitter; (rad) broadcasting station
Sen′deraum *m* broadcasting studio
Sen′dezeichen *n* station identification
Sen′dezeit *f* air time
Sen′dung *f* (-;-en) sending; (fig) mission; (com) shipment; (rad) broadcast; (telv) telecast
Senf [zɛnf] *m* (-[e]s;-e) mustard
sengen ['zɛŋən] *tr* singe, scorch
seng(e)rig ['zɛŋ(ə)rɪç] *adj* burnt; (fig) suspicious, fishy
senil [ze′nil] *adj* senile
Senilität [zenili′tɛt] *f* (-;) senility
senior ['zɛnjər] *adj* senior
Senkblei ['zɛŋkblaɪ] *n* plummet; (naut) sounding lead
Senke ['zɛŋkə] *f* (-;-n) depression
senken ['zɛŋkən] *tr* lower; sink; (*Kopf*)

bow || *ref* sink, settle; dip, slope; (*Mauer*) sag
Senkfüße ['zɛŋkfysə] *pl* flat feet, fallen arches
Senk′fußeinlage *f* arch support
Senkgrube ['zɛŋkgrubə] *f* cesspool
Senkkasten ['zɛŋkkastən] *m* caisson
senkrecht ['zɛŋkrɛçt] *adj* vertical; (geom) perpendicular
Sen′kung *f* (-;-en) sinking; depression; dip, slope; sag; (*der Preise*) lowering
Sensation [zenza′tsjon] *f* (-;-en) sensation
sensationell [zenzatsjo′nɛl] *adj* sensational
Sensations′blatt *n* (pej) scandal sheet
Sensations′lust *f* sensationalism
Sensations′meldung *f*, **Sensations′nachricht** *f* (journ) scoop
Sensations′presse *f* yellow journalism
Sense ['zenzə] *f* (-;-n) scythe
sensibel [zen′zibəl] *adj* sensitive; (*Nerven*) sensory
Sensibilität [zenzibili′tɛt] *f* (-;) sensitivity, sensitiveness
sentimental [zentimen′tal] *adj* sentimental
separat [zepa′rat] *adj* separate
September [zep′tembər] *m* (-[s]s;) September
Serenade [zere′nadə] *f* (-;-n) serenade
Serie ['zerjə] *f* (-;-n) series; line
Se′rienanfertigung *f*, **Se′rienbau** *m*, **Se′rienfabrikation** *f*, **Se′rienherstellung** *f* mass production
se′rienmäßig *adj*—**serienmäßige Herstellung** mass production || *adv*—**s. herstellen** mass-produce
Se′riennummer *f* serial number
Se′rienproduktion *f* mass production
seriös [ze′rjøs] *adj* serious; reliable
Se-rum ['zerum] *n* (-s;-ren [rən] & -ra [ra]) serum
Service [′zɔrvɪs] *m* (Services [′zɔrvɪs(əs)];) (*Kundendienst*) service || [zer′vis] *n* (Services [zer′vis];) **Service** [zer′vis(ə)]) (*Tafelgeschirr*) service
Servierbrett [zer′virbret] *n* tray
servieren [zer′virən] *tr* serve; **es ist serviert!** dinner is ready! || *intr* wait at table
Serviertisch [zer′virtɪʃ] *m* sideboard
Servierwagen [zer′virvagən] *m* serving cart
Serviette [zer′vjetə] *f* (-;-n) napkin
Servo- [zervə] *comb.fm.* booster, auxiliary, servo, power, automatic
Ser′vobremsen *pl* power brakes
Ser′vokupplung *f* automatic transmission
Ser′volenkung *f* power steering
Servus ['zervus] *interj* (Aust) hello!; (coll) so long!
Sessel ['zesəl] *m* (-s;-) easy chair
Ses′sellift *m* chair lift
seßhaft [′zeshaft] *adj* settled; **sich s. machen** settle down
Setzei ['zetsaɪ] *n* fried egg
setzen [′zetsən] *tr* set, put, place; seat; (*beim Spiel*) bet; (*Denkmal*) erect; (*Frist*) fix; (*Junge*) breed; (*Fische*) stock; (*Pflanzen*) plant; (*mus*) com-

pose; (typ) set ‖ *ref* sit down; (*Kaffee*) settle ‖ *intr* set type; s. auf (*acc*) bet on ‖ *intr* (SEIN)—s. über (*acc*) jump over

Set'zer *m* (-s;-) typesetter, compositor

Setz'fehler *m* typographical error

Seuche ['zɔɪçə] *f* (-;-n) epidemic

seufzen ['zɔɪftsən] *intr* sigh

Seuf'zer *m* (-s;-) sigh

Sex [zɛks] *m* (-es;) sex

Sex-Appeal ['zɛks ə'pil] *m* (-s;) sex appeal

Sex'-Bombe *f* (coll) sex pot

Sexual- [zɛksuɑl] *comb.fm.* sex

sexuell [zɛksu'ɛl] *adj* sexual

Sexus ['zɛksus] *m* (-;-) sex

sezieren [ze'tsirən] *tr* dissect

Shampoo [ʃam'pu] *n* (-s;-s) shampoo

Sibirien [zɪ'birjən] *n* (-s;) Siberia

sich [zɪç] §11 *reflex pron* oneself; himself; herself; itself; themselves; **an (und für)** s. in itself; **außer** s. **sein** be beside oneself ‖ *recip pron* each one another

Sichel ['zɪçəl] *f* (-;-n) sickle

sicher ['zɪçər] *adj* sure; positive; reliable; (**vor** *dat*) safe (from), secure (from) ‖ *adv* surely, certainly

Si'cherheit *f* (-;-en) safety, security; (*Gewißheit*) certainty; (*Zuverlässigkeit*) reliability; (*im Auftreten*) assurance; (com) security; (jur) bail

Si'cherheitsgurt *m*, **Si'cherheitsgürtel** *m* (aer, aut) seat belt

Si'cherheitsnadel *f* safety pin

Si'cherheitspolizei *f* security police

Si'cherheitsspielraum *m* margin of safety, leeway

si'cherlich *adv* surely, certainly

sichern ['zɪçərn] *tr* secure; fasten; guarantee; (*Gewehr*) put on safety

Si'cherstellung *f* safekeeping; guarantee

Si'cherung *f* (-;-en) protection; guarantee; (*an Schußwaffe*) safety catch; (elec) fuse; **durchgebrannte** S. blown fuse

Si'cherungskasten *m* fuse box

Sicht [zɪçt] *f* (-;) sight; (*Aussicht*) view; (*Sichtigkeit*) visibility; **auf kurze** S. short-range; **auf** S. at sight

sichtbar ['zɪçtbar] *adj* visible

sichten ['zɪçtən] *tr* sight; (fig) sift

sichtig ['zɪçtɪç] *adj* clear

sicht'lich *adj* visible

Sicht'vermerk *m* visa

sickern ['zɪkərn] *intr* (HABEN & SEIN) trickle, seep, leak

sie [zi] §11 *pers pron* she, her; it; they, them ‖ §11 **Sie** *pers pron* you

Sieb [zip] *n* (-[e]s;-e) sieve, colander; screen; (rad) filter

sieben ['ziban] *invar adj* & *pron* seven ‖ *tr* sift, strain; (fig) screen; (rad) filter ‖ **Sieben** *f* (-;-en) seven

siebente ['zibəntə] §9 *adj* & *pron* seventh

Siebentel ['zibəntəl] *n* (-s;-) seventh

siebte ['ziptə] §9 *adj* & *pron* seventh

Siebtel ['ziptəl] *n* (-s;-) seventh

siebzehn ['ziptsen] *invar adj* & *pron* seventeen ‖ **Siebenzehn** *f* (-;-en) seventeen

siebzehnte ['ziptsentə] §9 *adj* & *pron* seventeenth

Siebzehntel ['ziptsentəl] *n* (-s;-) seventeenth

siebzig ['ziptsɪç] *invar adj* & *pron* seventy ‖ **Siebzig** *f* (-;-en) seventy

siebziger ['ziptsɪgər] *invar adj* of the seventies; **die** s. **Jahre** the seventies ‖ **Siebziger** *m* (-s;-) septuagenarian

siebzigste ['ziptsɪçstə] §9 *adj* & *pron* seventieth

siech [ziç] *adj* sickly

siechen ['ziçən] *intr* be sickly

Siechtum ['ziçtum] *n* (-s;) lingering illness

siedeheiß ['zidə'haɪs] *adj* piping hot

siedeln ['zidəln] *intr* settle

sieden ['zidən] §141 *tr* & *intr* boil

Siedepunkt ['zidəpuŋkt] *m* boiling point

Siedler -in ['zidlər(ɪn)] §6 *mf* settler

Sied'lerstelle *f* homestead

Sied'lung *f* (-;-en) settlement; colony; housing development

Sieg [zik] *m* (-[e]s;-e) victory

Siegel ['zigəl] *n* (-s;-) seal

siegeln ['zigəln] *tr* seal

Sie'gelring *m* signet ring

siegen ['zigən] *intr* win, be victorious

Sie'ger -in §6 *mf* winner, victor; **zweiter Sieger** runner-up

Sieges- [zigəs] *comb.fm.* victory, of victory, triumphal

Sie'gesbogen *m* triumphal arch

sieg'reich *adj* victorious

Signal [zɪg'nal] *n* (-s;-e) signal

signalisieren [zɪgnalɪ'zirən] *tr* signal

Silbe ['zɪlbə] *f* (-;-n) syllable

Sil'bentrennung *f* syllabification

Silber ['zɪlbər] *n* (-s;) silver

silbern ['zɪlbərn] *adj* silver, silvery

Sil'berzeug *n* silver, silverware

Silhouette [zilu'ɛtə] *f* (-;-n) silhouette

Silo ['zilo] *m* (-s;-s) silo

Silvester [zɪl'vɛstər] *m* (-s;-), **Silve'sterabend** *m* New Year's Eve

simpel ['zɪmpəl] *adj* simple ‖ **Simpel** *m* (-s;-) simpleton

Sims [zɪms] *m* & *n* (-es;-e) ledge; (*Fenster*-) sill; (*Kamin*-) mantelpiece

Simulant -in [zimu'lant(ɪn)] §7 *mf* faker; (mil) goldbrick

simulieren [zimu'lirən] *tr* simulate, fake ‖ *intr* loaf

simultan [zimul'tan] *adj* simultaneous

Sinfo·nie [zɪnfo'ni] *f* (-;-nien ['ni·ən) symphony

singen ['zɪŋən] §142 *tr* & *intr* sing

Singsang ['zɪŋzaŋ] *m* (-[e]s;) singsong

Sing'spiel *n* musical comedy, musical

Sing'stimme *f* vocal part

Singular ['zɪŋgular] *m* (-s;-e) singular

sinken ['zɪŋkən] §143 *intr* (SEIN) sink slump, sag; (*Preise*) drop; s. **lassen** lower; (*Mut*) lose

Sinn [zɪn] *m* (-[e]s;-e) sense; mind; meaning; liking, taste

Sinn'bild *n* emblem, symbol

sinn'bildlich *adj* symbolic(al) ‖ *adv* symbolically; s. **darstellen** symbolize

sinnen ['zɪnən] §121 *tr* plan; plot ‖ *intr* (**auf** *acc*) plan, plot; (**über** *acc*)

think (about) || **Sinnen** *n* (-s;) reflection, meditation, reverie
Sin'nend *adj* pensive, reflective
Sin'nenlust *f* sensuality
Sin'nenmensch *m* sensualist
Sin'nenwelt *f* material world
Sin'nesänderung *f* change of mind
Sin'nesart *f* character, disposition
Sin'nestäuschung *f* illusion, hallucination, mirage
sinn'lich *adj* sensual; material
sinn'los *adj* senseless
sinn'reich *adj* ingenious, bright
sinn'verwandt *adj* synonymous
sinn'voll *adj* meaningful; sensible
Sintflut ['zɪntflut] *f* deluge, flood
Sippe ['zɪpə] *f* (-;-n) kin; clan
Sipp'schaft *f* (-;-en) clique, set
Sirup ['zirup] *m* (-s;-e) syrup
Sitte ['zɪtə] *f* (-;-n) custom; habit; usage; **die Sitten** the morals
Sit'tenbild *n*, **Sit'tengemälde** *n* description of the manners (*of an age*)
Sit'tengesetz *n* moral law
Sit'tenlehre *f* ethics
sit'tenlos *adj* immoral
Sit'tenpolizei *f* vice squad
sit'tenrein *adj* chaste
Sit'tenrichter *m* censor
sit'tenstreng *adj* puritanical, prudish
Sittich ['zɪtɪç] *m* (-s;-e) parakeet
sittlich ['zɪtlɪç] *adj* moral, ethical
Sittlichkeit *f* (-;) morality
Sitt'lichkeitsverbrechen *n* indecent assault
sittsam ['zɪtzam] *adj* modest, decent
Situation [zɪtu·a'tsjon] *f* (-;-en) situation
situiert [zɪtu'irt] *adj*—**gut s.** well-to-do
Sitz [zɪts] *m* (-es;-e) seat; residence; (*e-s Kleides*) fit; (*eccl*) see
sitzen ['zɪtsən] §144 *intr* sit; dwell; (*Vögel*) perch; (*Kleider*) fit; (*Hieb*) hit home; (*coll*) be in jail
sit'zenbleiben §62 *intr* (SEIN) remain seated; (*beim Tanzen*) be a wallflower; (*bei der Heirat*) remain unmarried; (*educ*) stay behind, flunk
sit'zenlassen §104 *tr* leave, abandon; (*Mädchen*) jilt
Sitz'gelegenheit *f* seating accommodation
Sitz'ordnung *f* seating arrangement
Sitz'platz *m* seat
Sitz'streik *m* sit-down strike
Sit'zung *f* (-;-en) session
Sit'zungsbericht *m* minutes
Sit'zungsperiode *f* session; (*jur*) term
Sizilien [zɪ'tsiljən] *n* (-s;) Sicily
Ska·la ['skala] *f* (-;-len [lən]) scale
Skandal [skan'dal] *m* (-s;-e) scandal
skandalös [skanda'løs] *adj* scandalous
Skandinavien [skandɪ'navjən] *n* (-s) Scandinavia
Skelett [ske'lɛt] *n* (-[e]s;-e) skeleton
Skepsis ['skɛpsɪs] *f* (-;) skepticism
Skeptiker –in ['skɛptɪkər(ɪn)] §6 *mf* skeptic
skeptisch ['skɛptɪʃ] *adj* skeptical
Ski [ʃi] *m* (-s; **Skier** ['ʃi-ər]) ski
Skizze ['skɪtsə] *f* (-;-n) sketch
skizzieren [skɪ'tsirən] *tr & intr* sketch
Sklave ['sklavə] *m* (-n;-n) slave

Sklaverei [sklavə'raɪ] *f* (-;) slavery
sklavisch ['sklavɪʃ] *adj* slavish
Skonto ['skɔnto] *m & n* (-s;-s) discount
Skrupel ['skrupəl] *m* (-s;-) scruple
skru'pellos *adj* unscrupulous
skrupulös [skrupu'løs] *adj* scrupulous
Skulptur [skʊlp'tur] *f* (-;-en) sculpture
Slalom ['slalom] *m & n* (-s;-s) slalom
Slawe ['slavə] *m* (-n;-n), **Slawin** ['slavɪn] *f* (-;-nen) Slav
slawisch ['slavɪʃ] *adj* Slavic
Smaragd [sma'rakt] *m* (-[e]s;-e) emerald
Smoking ['smokɪŋ] *m* (-s;-s) tuxedo
so [zo] *adv* so; this way, thus; **so ein** such a; **so oder so** by hook or by crook; **so...wie as...as**
sobald' *conj* as soon as
Socke ['zɔkə] *f* (-;-n) sock
Sockenhalter (**Sok'kenhalter**) *m* garter
Soda ['zoda] *f* (-;) & *n* (-s;) soda
sodann' *adv* then
Sodbrennen ['zotbrenən] *n* (-s;) heartburn
soeben [zo'ebən] *adv* just now, just
Sofa ['zofa] *n* (-s;-s) sofa
sofern' *conj* provided, if
soff [zɔf] *pret of* **saufen**
sofort' *adv* at once, right away
sofortig [zo'fortɪç] *adj* immediate
sog [zok] *pret of* **saugen** || **Sog** *m* (-[e]s;) suction; undertow; (*aer*) wash
sogar' *adv* even
so'genannt *adj* so-called; would-be
sogleich' *adv* at once, right away
Sohle ['zolə] *f* (-;-n) sole; bottom
Sohn [zon] *m* (-[e]s;-̈e) son
solang *conj* as long as
solch [zɔlç] *adj* such
Sold [zɔlt] *m* (-[e]s;-e) pay
Soldat [zɔl'dat] *m* (-en;-en) soldier
Söldner ['zœldnər] *m* (-s;-) mercenary
Sole ['zolə] *f* (-;-n) brine
solid [zo'lit] *adj* solid; sound; reliable; steady; respectable; (*Preis*) reasonable; (*com*) sound, solvent
solide [zo'lidə] *adj* var of **solid**
Solist –in [zo'lɪst(ɪn)] §7 *mf* soloist
Soll [zɔl] *n* (-s;-e) quota; (*acct*) debit side; **S. und Haben** debit and credit
Soll- *comb.fm.* estimated; debit
sollen ['zɔlən] §145 *mod* (*inf*) be obliged to (*inf*), have to (*inf*); (*inf*) be supposed to (*inf*); (*inf*) be said to (*inf*)
Soll'wert *m* face value
solo ['zolo] *adv* (*mus*) solo || **So·lo** *n* (-s;-s & -li [li]) solo
somit' *adv* so, consequently
Sommer ['zɔmər] *m* (-s;-) summer
Som'merfrische *f* health resort; **in die S. fahren** go to the country
Sommerfrischler ['zɔmərfrɪʃlər] *m* (-s;-) vacationer
som'merlich *adj* summery
Som'mersprosse *f* freckle
sonach' *adv* consequently, so
Sonate [zo'natə] *f* (-;-n) sonata
Sonde ['zɔndə] *f* (-;-n) probe
Sonder- [zɔndər] *comb.fm.* special, extra; separate

sonderbar ['zɔndərbɑr] *adj* strange, odd; peculiar

son'derlich *adj* special, particular

Sonderling ['zɔndərlɪŋ] *m* (-s;-e) odd person, strange character

sondern ['zɔndərn] *tr* separate; sever; part; sort out; classify ‖ *conj* but

Son'derrecht *n* privilege

Son'derung *f* (-;-en) separation; sorting, sifting; classifying

Son'derverband *m* (mil) task force

Son'derzug *m* (rr) special

sondieren [zɔn'dirən] *tr* probe; (fig) sound out; (naut) sound

Sonnabend ['zɔnɑbənt] *m* (-s;-e) Saturday

Sonne ['zɔnə] *f* (-;-n) sun

sonnen ['zɔnən] *tr* sun ‖ *ref* sun oneself

Son'nenaufgang *m* sunrise

Son'nenbad *n* sun bath

Son'nenblende *f* (aut) sun visor; (phot) lens shade

Sonnenbrand *m* sunburn

Son'nenbräune *f* suntan

Son'nenbrille *f* (pair of) sun glasses

Son'nendach *n* awning

Son'nenenergie *f* solar energy

Son'nenfinsternis *f* eclipse of the sun

Son'nenfleck *m* sunspot

Son'nenjahr *n* solar year

son'nenklar' *adj* sunny; (fig) clear as day

Son'nenlicht *n* sunlight

Son'nenschein *m* sunshine

Son'nenschirm *m* parasol

Son'nensegel *n* awning

Son'nenseite *f* sunny side

Son'nenstich *m* sunstroke

Son'nenstrahl *m* sunbeam

Son'nensystem *n* solar system

Son'nenuhr *f* sundial

Son'nenuntergang *m* sunset

son'nenverbrannt *adj* sunburnt, tanned

Son'nenwende *f* solstice

sonnig ['zɔnɪç] *adj* sunny

Sonntag ['zɔntɑk] *m* (-s;-e) Sunday

sonn'tags *adv* on Sundays

Sonn'tagsfahrer –in §6 *mf* Sunday driver

Sonn'tagskind *n* person born under a lucky star

Sonn'tagsstaat *m* Sunday clothes

sonor [zo'nor] *adj* sonorous

sonst [zɔnst] *adv* otherwise; else; (*ehemals*) formerly; **s. etw** something else; **s. keiner** no one else; **s. nichts** nothing else; **s. noch was?** anything else?; **wie s.** as usual; **wie s. was** (coll) like anything

sonstig ['zɔnstɪç] *adj* other

sonst'wer *pron* someone else

sonst'wie *adv* in some other way

sonst'wo *adv* somewhere else

Sopran [zo'prɑn] *m* (-s;-e) soprano; treble

Sopranist –in [zopra'nɪst(ɪn)] §7 *mf* soprano

Sorge ['zɔrgə] *f* (-;-n) care; worry; **außer S. sein** be at ease; **keine S.!** don't worry; **sich** [*dat*] **Sorgen machen über** (*acc*) or **um** be worried about

sorgen ['zɔrgən] *intr*—**dafür s., daß** take care that, see to it that; **s. für** take care of ‖ *ref* be uneasy; **sich s. über** (*acc*) grieve over; **sich s. um** be worried about

sor'genfrei *adj* carefree; untroubled

Sor'genkind *n* problem child

sor'genlos *adj* carefree

sor'genvoll *adj* uneasy, anxious

Sor'gerecht *n* (für) custody (of)

Sorgfalt ['zɔrkfalt] *f* (-;) care, carefulness; accuracy

sorgfältig ['zɔrkfeltɪç] *adj* careful

sorglich ['zɔrklɪç] *adj* careful

sorglos ['zɔrklos] *adj* careless; thoughtless; carefree

sorgsam ['zɔrkzam] *adj* careful; cautious

Sorte ['zɔrtə] *f* (-;-n) sort, kind

sortieren [zɔr'tirən] *tr* sort out

Sortiment [zɔrtɪ'ment] *n* (-[e]s;-e) assortment

Soße ['zosə] *f* (-;-n) sauce; gravy

sott [zɔt] *pret* of **sieden**

Souffleur [zu'flør] *m* (-s;-s), **Souffleuse** [zu'fløzə] *f* (-;-n) prompter

souffieren [zu'flirən] *intr* (*dat*) prompt

Soutane [zu'tɑnə] *f* (-;-n) cassock

Souvenir [zuvə'nir] *n* (-s;-s) souvenir

souverän [zuvə'ren] *adj* sovereign ‖ **Souverän** *m* (-s;-e) sovereign

Souveränität [zuvərenɪ'tet] *f* (-;) sovereignty

soviel' *adv* so much; **noch einmal s.** twice as much ‖ *conj* as far as

soweit' *conj* as far as

sowie' *conj* as well as

sowieso' *adv* in any case, anyhow

Sowjet [zɔv'jet] *m* (-s;-s) Soviet

sowjetisch [zɔv'jetɪʃ] *adj* Soviet

sowohl' *conj*—**sowohl...als auch** as well as, both...and

sozial [zo'tsjɑl] *adj* social

Sozial'fürsorge *f* social welfare

sozialisieren [zɔtsjali'zirən] *tr* nationalize

Sozialismus [zɔtsja'lɪsmus] *m* (-;) socialism

Sozialist –in [zɔtsja'lɪst(ɪn)] §7 *mf* socialist

sozialistisch [zɔtsja'lɪstɪʃ] *adj* socialistic

Sozial'wissenschaft *f* social science

Soziologie [zɔtsjolo'gi] *f* (-;) sociology

Sozius ['zotsjus] *m* (-;-se) associate, partner; (*auf dem Motorrad*) rider

sozusa'gen *adv* so to speak, as it were

Spachtel ['ʃpaxtəl] *m* (-s;-) & *f* (-;-n) spatula; putty knife

Spach'telmesser *n* putty knife

Spagat [ʃpa'gat] *m* (-[e]s;-e) (gym) split; (dial) string

spähen ['ʃpe-ən] *intr* peer; spy

Spä'her *m* (-s;-) lookout; (mil) scout

Spä'herblick *m* searching glance

Spähtrupp ['ʃpetrup] *m* reconnaissance squad

Späh'wagen *m* reconnaissance car

Spalier [ʃpa'lir] *n* (-s;-e) trellis; double line (*of people*)

Spalt [ʃpalt] *m* (-[e]s;-e) split; crack; slit; (geol) cleft

Spalte ['ʃpaltə] f (-ɜ-n) split; crack; slit; (typ) column

spalten ['ʃpaltən] tr (pp gespaltet or gespalten) split; slit; crack; (Holz) chop

Spal'tung f (-ɜ-en) split; (der Meinungen) division; (chem) decomposition; (eccl) schism; (phys) fission

Span [ʃpan] m (-[e]s;ⁿe) chip; splinter; Späne shavings

Span'ferkel n suckling pig

Spange ['ʃpanə] f (-ɜ-n) clasp; hair clip; (Schnalle) buckle

Spanien ['ʃpanjən] n (-s;) Spain

Spanier -in ['ʃpanjər(ɪn)] §6 mf Spaniard

spanisch ['ʃpanɪʃ] adj Spanish; das kommt mir s. vor (coll) that's Greek to me; spanischer Pfeffer paprika; spanische Wand folding screen

spann [ʃpan] pret of spinnen || Spann m (-sɜ-e) instep

Spanne ['ʃpanə] f (-ɜ-n) span; (com) margin

spannen ['ʃpanən] tr stretch; strain; make tense; (Bogen) bend; (Feder) tighten; (Flinte) cock; (Erwartungen) raise; (Pferde) hitch; straff s. tighten; || intr be (too) tight; s. auf (acc) wait eagerly for; listen closely to

span'nend adj tight; exciting

Spann'kraft f tension; elasticity; (fig) resiliency

spann'kräftig adj elastic

Spann'nung f (-ɜ-en) stress; strain; pressure; close attention; suspense; excitement; strained relations; (elec) voltage

Spar- [ʃpar] comb.fm. savings

Spar'buch n bank book, pass book

Spar'büchse f piggy bank

sparen ['ʃparən] tr & intr save

Spar'flamme f pilot light

Spargel ['ʃpargəl] m (-sɜ-) asparagus

Spar'kasse f savings bank

Spar'konto n savings account

spärlich ['ʃperlɪç] adj scanty; scarce; sparse; frugal; (Haar) thin || adv poorly; scantily; sparsely

Sparren ['ʃparən] m (-sɜ-) rafter

sparsam ['ʃparzam] adj thrifty

Spaß [ʃpas] m (-esɜⁿe) joke; fun; aus S. in fun; S. beiseite! all joking aside; S. haben an (dat) enjoy; S. machen be joking; be fun; viel S.! have fun!; zum S. for fun

spaß'haft, spaßig ['ʃpasɪç] adj funny, facetious

Spaß'macher m joker

Spaßverderber ['ʃpasverderbər] m (-sɜ-) (coll) kill-joy

Spaß'vogel m joker

spät [ʃpet] adj late; wie s. ist es? what time is it? || adv late

Spaten ['ʃpatən] m (-sɜ-) spade

später ['ʃpetər] adv later

späterhin ['ʃpetərhɪn] adv later on

spätestens ['ʃpetəstəns] adv at the latest

Spät'jahr n autumn, fall

Spatz [ʃpats] m (-es & -enɜ-en) sparrow

spazieren [ʃpa'tsirən] intr (SEIN) stroll, take a walk

spazie'renfahren §71 intr (SEIN) go for a drive

spazie'renführen tr walk (e.g., a dog)

spazie'rengehen §82 intr (SEIN) go for a walk

Spazier'fahrt f drive

Spazier'gang m stroll, walk; e-n S. machen take a walk

Spazier'gänger -in §6 mf stroller

Spazier'weg m walk

Specht [ʃpeçt] m (-[e]sɜ-e) woodpecker

Speck [ʃpek] m (-[e]sɜ) fat; bacon; (beim Wal) blubber

Speck'bauch m (coll) potbelly

speckig ['ʃpekɪç] adj greasy, dirty

spedieren [ʃpe'dirən] tr dispatch, ship

Spediteur [ʃpedɪ'tør] m (-sɜ-e) shipper; furniture mover

Spedition [ʃpedɪ'tsjon] f (-ɜ-en) shipment; moving company, movers

Speer [ʃper] m (-[e]sɜ-e) spear; (sport) javelin

Speiche ['ʃpaɪçə] f (-ɜ-n) spoke

Speichel ['ʃpaɪçəl] m (-sɜ) saliva

Spei'chellecker m brown-noser

speicheln ['ʃpaɪçəln] intr drool

Speicher ['ʃpaɪçər] m (-sɜ-) warehouse; grain elevator; attic, loft

speichern ['ʃpaɪçərn] tr store

speien ['ʃpaɪ-ən] §135 tr vomit; spit; (Feuer) belch; (Wasser) spurt || intr vomit, throw up; spit

Speise ['ʃpaɪzə] f (-ɜ-n) food; meal; (Gericht) dish

Speis'eis n ice cream

Speis'ekammer f pantry

Speis'ekarte f menu

speisen ['ʃpaɪzən] tr feed; (fig) supply || intr eat; auswärts s. dine out

Speis'enfolge f menu

Speis'ereste pl leftovers

Speis'erohr n (mach) feed pipe

Speis'eröhre f esophagus

Speis'esaal m dining room

Speis'eschrank m cupboard

Speis'ewagen m (rr) diner

Speis'ezimmer n dining room

Spektakel [ʃpek'takəl] m (-sɜ-) noise, racket

Spekulant -in [ʃpeku'lant(ɪn)] §7 mf speculator

Spekulation [ʃpekula'tsjon] f (-ɜ-en) speculation; venture

spekulieren [ʃpeku'lirən] intr speculate, reflect; (fin) speculate

Spelunke [ʃpe'luŋkə] f (-ɜ-n) (coll) drive, joint

Spende ['ʃpendə] f (-ɜ-n) donation

spenden ['ʃpendən] tr give; donate; (Sakramente) administer; (Lob) bestow; j-m Trost s. comfort s.o.

spendieren [ʃpen'dirən] tr—j-m etw s. treat s.o. to s.th.

Sperling ['ʃperlɪŋ] m (-sɜ-e) sparrow

Sperr- [ʃper] comb.fm. barrage; barred

Sperr'baum m barrier, bar

Sperre ['ʃperə] f (-ɜ-n) shutting; close; blockade; embargo; barricade; catch; lock; (rr) gate

sperren ['ʃperən] tr shut; (Gas, Licht) cut off; (Straße) block off; cordon

off; (*blockieren*) blockade; (*mit Schloß*) lock; (*verriegeln*) bolt; (*Konto, Gelder*) freeze; (*Scheck*) stop payment on; (*verbieten*) stop; (sport) block; (sport) suspend; (typ) space || *intr* jam, be stuck
Sperr′feuer *n* barrage
Sperr′gebiet *n* restricted area
Sperr′holz *n* plywood
sperrig [′ʃperɪç] *adj* bulky
Sperr′sitz *m* (*im Kino*) rear seat; (*im Zirkus*) front seat
Sperr′stunde *f* closing time; curfew
Sper′rung *f* (-;-en) stoppage; blocking; blockade; embargo; suspension (*of telephone service, etc.*)
Spesen [′ʃpezən] *pl* costs, expenses
Spezi [′ʃpetsi] *m* (-s;-s) (coll) buddy
spezial [ʃpe′tsjal] *adj* special
Spezial′arzt *m*, **Spezial′ärztin** *f* specialist
Spezial′fach *n* specialty
Spezial′geschäft *n* specialty shop
spezialisieren [ʃpetsjalɪ′zirən] *ref* (*auf acc*) specialize (in)
Spezialist -in [ʃpetsja′lɪst(ɪn)] §7 *mf* specialist
Spezialität [ʃpetsjalɪ′tet] *f* (-;-en) specialty
speziell [ʃpe′tsjel] *adj* special
spezifisch [ʃpe′tsifɪʃ] *adj* specific
Sphäre [′sferə] *f* (-;-n) sphere
sphärisch [′sferɪʃ] *adj* spherical
Spickaal [′ʃpɪkal] *m* smoked eel
spicken [′ʃpɪkən] *tr* lard; (fig) bribe
spie [ʃpi] *pret* of **speien**
Spiegel [′ʃpigəl] *m* (-s;-) mirror
Spie′gelbild *n* reflection (*in mirror*)
spie′gelblank′ *adj* spick and span
Spie′gelei *n* fried egg
spie′gelglatt′ *adj* glassy
spiegeln [′ʃpigəln] *tr* reflect; mirror || *ref* be reflected || *intr* shine
Spiel [ʃpil] *n* (-[e]s;-e) game; play; set (*of chessmen or checkers*); (cards) deck; (mach) play; (mus) playing; (sport) match; (theat) acting, performance; **auf dem S. stehen** be at stake; **aufs S. setzen** risk; **bei etw im S. sein** be at the bottom of s.th.; **leichtes S. haben** have an easy time with; **S. der Natur** freak of nature
Spiel′art *f* (biol) variety
Spiel′automat *m* slot machine
Spiel′bank *f* (-;-en) gambling table; gambling casino
Spiel′dose *f* music box
spielen [′ʃpilən] *tr & intr* play
Spielerei [ʃpilə′raɪ] *f* (-;-en) fooling around; child′s play
Spiel′ergebnis *n* (sport) score
spielerisch [′ʃpilərɪʃ] *adj* playful
Spiel′feld *n* (sport) playing field
Spiel′film *m* feature film
Spiel′folge *f* program
Spiel′gefährte *m*, **Spiel′gefährtin** *f* playmate
Spiel′karten *pl* (playing) cards
Spiel′leiter *m* (cin, theat) director
Spiel′marke *f* chip, counter
Spiel′plan *m* program
Spiel′platz *m* playground; playing field

Spiel′raum *m* (fig) elbowroom; (mach) play
Spiel′sachen *pl* toys
Spiel′tisch *m* gambling table
Spiel′verderber *m* kill-joy
Spiel′verlängerung *f* overtime
Spiel′waren *pl* toys
Spiel′zeug *n* toy(s)
Spieß [ʃpis] *m* (-es;-e) spear, pike; (sl) top kick; (culin) spit; **den S. umdrehen gegen** turn the tables on
Spieß′bürger *m* Philistine, lowbrow
spieß′bürgerlich *adj* narrow-minded
spießen [′ʃpisən] *tr* spear; spit
Spie′ßer *m* (-s;-) Philistine, lowbrow
Spieß′gesell *m* accomplice
Spießruten [′ʃpisrutən] *pl*—**S. laufen** run the gauntlet
spinal [ʃpi′nal] *adj* spinal; **spinale Kinderlähmung** infantile paralysis
Spinat [ʃpi′nat] *m* (-[e]s;-e) spinach
Spind [ʃpɪnt] *m & n* (-[e]s;-e) wardrobe; (mil) locker
Spindel [′ʃpɪndəl] *f* (-;-n) spindle; (*Spinnrocken*) distaff
spin′deldürr′ *adj* skinny, scrawny
Spinne [′ʃpɪnə] *f* (-;-n) spider
spinnen [′ʃpɪnən] *tr* spin; **Ränke s.** hatch plots || *intr* purr; (*im Gefängnis sitzen*) do time; (sl) be loony
Spin′nengewebe *n* spider web
Spin′ner *m* (-s;-) spinner; (sl) nut
Spinnerei [ʃpɪnə′raɪ] *f* (-;-en) spinning; spinning mill
Spinn′faden *m* spider thread; **Spinnfäden** gossamer
Spinn′gewebe *n* (-s;-) cobweb
Spinn′rad *n* spinning wheel
Spinn′webe *f* (-;-n) (Aust) cobweb
Spion [ʃpi′on] *m* (-[e]s;-e) spy
Spionage [ʃpi·ɔ′naʒə] *f* (-;) spying, espionage
Spiona′geabwehr *f* counterintelligence
spionieren [ʃpi·ɔ′nirən] *intr* spy
Spirale [ʃpi′ralə] *f* (-;-n) spiral
Spirituosen [ʃpirɪtu′ozən] *pl* liquor
Spiritus [′ʃpirɪtus] *m* (-;-se) alcohol
Spital [ʃpi′tal] *n* (-s;-̈er) hospital
spitz [ʃpɪts] *adj* pointed; sharp; (*Winkel*) acute
Spitz′bart *m* goatee
Spitz′bube *m* rascal; thief; swindler
Spitze [′ʃpɪtsə] *f* (-;-n) point; tip; top; summit; (tex) lace; **an der S. liegen** be in the lead; **auf die S. treiben** carry to extremes
Spitzel [′ʃpɪtsəl] *m* (-s;-) spy; stool pigeon; plain-clothes man
spitzen [′ʃpɪtsən] *tr* point; sharpen; (*Ohren*) prick up; **den Mund s.** purse the lips || *ref*—**sich s. auf** (*acc*) look forward to || *intr* be on one′s toes
Spitzen- *comb.fm.* top; peak; leading; topnotch; maximum; (tex) lace
Spit′zenform *f* (sport) top form
Spit′zenleistung *f* top performance
Spit′zenmarke *f* (com) top brand
Spit′zer *m* (-s;-) pencil sharpener
spitz′findig *adj* subtle; sharp
Spitz′hacke *f*, **Spitz′haue** *f* pickax
spitzig [′ʃpɪtsɪç] *adj* pointed; (& fig) sharp

Spitz'marke f (typ) heading
Spitz'name m nickname; pet name
Spitz'nase f pointed nose
spleißen ['ʃplaɪsən] §53 tr splice
spliß [ʃplɪs] pret of **spleißen**
Splitter ['ʃplɪtər] m (-s;-) splinter; chip; fragment
split'ternackt' adj stark-naked
Split'terpartei f splinter party
split'tersicher adj shatterproof
spontan [ʃpɔn'tɑn] adj spontaneous
Spore ['ʃporə] f (-;-n) spore
Sporn [ʃpɔrn] m (-[e]s; **Sporen** ['ʃporən]) spur; (fig) stimulus; (aer) tail skid; (naut) ram
spornen ['ʃpɔrnən] tr spur
Sport [ʃpɔrt] m (-[e]s;-e) sport(s); **S. ausüben** (or **treiben**) play sports
Sport'freund –in §8 mf sports fan
Sport'hose f shorts, trunks
Sport'jacke f sport jacket, blazer
Sport'kleidung f sportswear
Sportler –in ['ʃpɔrtlər(ɪn)] §6 mf athlete
sport'lich adj sportsmanlike; (Figur) athletic; (Kleidung) sport
Sport'wagen m sports car; (Kinderwagen) stroller
Sport'wart m trainer
Spott [ʃpɔt] m (-[e]s;) mockery; scorn
Spott'bild n caricature
spott'bil'lig adj dirt-cheap
Spott'drossel f mockingbird
Spöttelei [ʃpœtə'laɪ] f (-;-en) mockery
spotten ['ʃpɔtən] intr (über acc) scoff (at), ridicule; **das spottet jeder Beschreibung** that defies description
Spötterei [ʃpœtə'raɪ] f (-;-en) mockery
Spott'gebot n (com) ridiculous offer
spöttisch ['ʃpœtɪʃ] adj mocking, satirical; sneering
Spott'name m nickname
Spott'schrift f satire
sprach [ʃprɑx] pret of **sprechen**
Sprach- comb.fm. speech; grammatical; linguistic; philological
Sprache ['ʃprɑxə] f (-;-n) language, tongue; speech; diction; style; idiom
Sprach'eigenheit f, **Sprach'eigentümlichkeit** f idiom, idiomatic expression
Sprach'fehler m speech defect
Sprach'forschung f linguistics
Sprach'führer m phrase book
Sprach'gebrauch m usage
Sprach'gefühl n feeling for a language
sprach'gewandt adj fluent
sprach'kundig adj proficient in languages
Sprach'lehre f grammar
Sprach'lehrer –in §6 mf language teacher
sprach'lich adj grammatical; linguistic
sprach'los adj speechless
Sprach'rohr n megaphone; (fig) mouthpiece
Sprach'schatz m vocabulary
Sprach'störung f speech defect
Sprach'wissenschaft f philology; linguistics
sprang [ʃpraŋ] pret of **springen**
Sprech- [ʃprɛç] comb.fm. speaking
Sprech'art f way of speaking

Sprech'bühne f legitimate theater
sprechen ['ʃprɛçən] §64 tr speak; talk; (Gebet) say; (Urteil) pronounce; speak to, see || intr (über acc, von) speak (about), talk (about); **er ist nicht zu s.** he's not available
Spre'cher –in §6 mf speaker, talker
Sprech'fehler m slip of the tongue
Sprech'funkgerät n walkie-talkie
Sprech'probe f audition
Sprech'sprache f spoken language
Sprech'stunde f office hours
Sprech'stundenhilfe f receptionist
Sprech'zimmer n office (of doctor, etc.)
Spreize ['ʃpraɪtsə] f (-;-n) prop, strut; (gym) split
spreizen ['ʃpraɪtsən] tr spread, stretch out || ref sprawl out; (fig) (mit) boast (of); **sich s. gegen** resist
Spreng- [ʃprɛŋ] comb.fm. high-explosive
Sprengel ['ʃprɛŋəl] m (-s;-) diocese; parish
sprengen ['ʃprɛŋən] tr break, burst; (mit Sprengstoff) blow up; (Tür) force; (Versammlung) break up; (Mine) set off; (bespritzen) sprinkle; (Garten) water || intr (SEIN) gallop
Spreng'kommando n bomb disposal unit
Spreng'kopf m warhead
Spreng'körper m, **Spreng'stoff** m explosive
Spreng'wagen m sprinkling truck
Sprenkel ['ʃprɛŋkəl] m (-s;-) speck
sprenkeln ['ʃprɛŋkəln] tr speckle
Spreu [ʃprɔɪ] f (-;) chaff
Sprichwort ['ʃprɪçvɔrt] n (-[e]s;-̈er) proverb, saying
sprichwörtlich ['ʃprɪçvœrtlɪç] adj proverbial
sprießen ['ʃprisən] §76 intr (SEIN) sprout
Springbrunnen ['ʃprɪŋbrunən] m (-s;-) fountain
springen ['ʃprɪŋən] §142 intr (SEIN) jump; dive; burst; (Eis) crack; (coll) rush, hurry
Sprin'ger m (-s;-) jumper; (chess) knight; (sport) diver
Spring'insfeld m (-[e]s;-e) (coll) live wire
Spring'kraft f (& fig) resiliency
Spring'seil n jumping rope
Sprint [ʃprɪnt] m (-s;-s) sprint
Sprit [ʃprɪt] m (-[e]s;-e) alcohol; (coll) gasoline
Spritze ['ʃprɪtsə] f (-;-n) squirt; (Feuerwehr) fire engine; (med) injection, shot; (med) syringe
spritzen ['ʃprɪtsən] tr squirt; splash; (sprühen) spray; (sprengen) sprinkle; (Wein) mix with soda water; (med) inject || intr spurt, spout || impers— **es spritzt** it is drizzling || intr (SEIN) dash, flit
Spritz'tour f (coll) side trip
spröde ['ʃprødə] adj brittle; (Haut) chapped; (fig) prudish, coy
sproß [ʃprɔs] pret of **sprießen** || **Sproß** m (Sprosses; Sprosse) offspring, descendant; (bot) shoot

Sprosse [ˈʃprɔsə] f (-;-n) rung; prong

sprossen [ˈʃprɔsən] intr (HABEN & SEIN) sprout

Sprößling [ˈʃprœslɪŋ] m (-s;-e) offspring, descendant; (bot) sprout

Spruch [ʃprux] m (-[e]s;⁻e) saying; motto; text, passage; (jur) sentence; (jur) verdict; **e-n S. fällen** give the verdict

Spruch′band n (-[e]s;⁻er) banderole

Sprudel [ˈʃpruːdəl] m (-s;-) mineral water

sprudeln [ˈʃpruːdəln] intr bubble

sprühen [ˈʃpryː.ən] tr emit ‖ intr spray; sparkle; (fig) flash ‖ impers—**es sprüht** it is drizzling

Sprüh′regen m drizzle

Sprüh′teufel m (coll) spitfire

Sprung [ʃpruŋ] m (-[e]s;⁻e) jump; crack; (sport) dive

Sprung′brett n diving board; (fig) stepping stone

Spucke [ˈʃpukə] f (-;) (coll) spit

spucken [ˈʃpukən] tr spit ‖ intr spit; (Motor) sputter

Spuk [ʃpuk] m (-[e]s;-e) ghost, spook; (Lärm) racket; (Alptraum) nightmare

spuken [ˈʃpuːkən] intr linger on ‖ impers—**es spukt hier** this place is haunted

spuk′haft adj spooky

Spülabort [ˈʃpyːlabort] m flush toilet

Spül′becken n sink

Spule [ˈʃpuːlə] f (-;-n) spool, reel; (elec) coil

Spüle [ˈʃpyːlə] f (-;-n) wash basin

spulen [ˈʃpuːlən] tr reel, wind

spülen [ˈʃpyːlən] tr wash, rinse; (Abort) flush; **an Land s.** wash ashore ‖ intr flush the toilet; undulate

Spü′ler m (-s;-) dishwasher

Spülicht [ˈʃpyːlɪçt] n (-[e]s;-e) dishwater; swill, slop

Spül′maschine f dishwasher

Spül′mittel n detergent

Spülwasser n dishwater

Spund [ʃpunt] m (-[e]s;⁻e) bung, plug; (carp) feather, tongue

Spur [ʃpuːr] f (-;-en) trace; track, rut; (hunt) scent; **S. Salz** pinch of salt

spürbar [ˈʃpyːrbar] adj perceptible

spüren [ˈʃpyːrən] tr trace; track, trail; (fühlen) feel; (wahrnehmen) perceive

spur′los adj trackless ‖ adv without a trace

Spür′nase f (coll) good nose

Spür′sinn m flair

Spur′weite f (aut) tread; (rr) gauge

sputen [ˈʃputən] ref hurry up

SS [ˈɛsˈɛs] f (-;) (Schutzstaffel) S.S.

Staat [ʃtaːt] m (-[e]s;-en) state; government; (Aufwand) show; (Putz) finery

Staats- comb.fm. state; government; national; public; political

Staatsangehörigkeit [ˈʃtaːtsangəhøːrɪçkaɪt] f (-;) nationality

Staats′anwalt m district attorney

Staats′bauten pl public works

Staats′beamte m civil servant

Staats′bürger -in §6 mf citizen

Staats′bürgerkunde f civics

Staats′bürgerschaft f citizenship

Staats′dienst m civil service

staats′eigen adj state-owned

Staats′feind m public enemy

staats′feindlich adj subversive

Staats′form f form of government

Staats′gewalt f supreme power

Staats′hoheit f sovereignty

staats′klug adj politic, diplomatic

Staats′klugheit f statecraft

Staats′kunst f statesmanship

Staats′mann m (-[e]s;⁻er) statesman

staats′männisch adj statesmanlike

Staats′oberhaupt n head of state

Staats′papiere pl government bonds

Staats′recht n public law

Staats′streich m coup d'état

Staats′wirtschaft f political economy

Staats′wissenschaft f political science

Stab [ʃtaːp] m (-[e]s;⁻e) staff; rod; bar; (e-r Jalousie) slat; (eccl) crozier; (mil) staff; (mil) headquarters; (mus, sport) baton

stab′hochspringen §142 intr (SEIN) pole-vault

stabil [ʃtaˈbiːl] adj stable, steady

stabilisieren [ʃtabiliˈziːrən] tr stabilize

stach [ʃtax] pret of stechen

Stachel [ˈʃtaxəl] m (-s;-n) prick; quill; (bot) thorn; (ent) sting

Sta′chelbeere f gooseberry

Sta′cheldraht m barbed wire

stachelig [ˈʃtaxəlɪç] adj prickly; (& fig) thorny

Sta′chelschwein n porcupine

Sta·dion [ˈʃtaːdjɔn] n (-s;-dien [djən]) stadium

Sta·dium [ˈʃtaːdjum] n (-s;-dien [djən]) stage

Stadt [ʃtat] f (-;⁻e) city, town

Städtchen [ˈʃtɛtçən] n (-s;-) town

Städtebau [ˈʃtɛtəbau] m (-[e]s;) city planning

Stadt′gemeinde f township

Stadt′gespräch n talk of the town

städtisch [ˈʃtɛtɪʃ] adj municipal

Stadt′plan m map of the city

Stadt′rand m outskirts

Stadt′rat m (-[e]s;⁻e) city council; (Person) city councilor

Stadt′teil m Stadt′viertel n quarter (of the city)

Stafette [ʃtaˈfɛtə] f (-;-n) courier; (sport) relay

Staffel [ˈʃtafəl] f (-;-n) step, rung; (Stufe) degree; (aer) squadron (of nine aircraft); (sport) relay team

Staffelei [ʃtafəˈlaɪ] f (-;-en) easel

Staf′felkeil m (aer) V-formation

Staf′fellauf m relay race

staffeln [ˈʃtafəln] tr graduate; (Arbeitszeit, usw.) stagger

stahl [ʃtaːl] pret of stehlen ‖ Stahl m (-[e]s;⁻e) steel

Stahl′beton m reinforced concrete

stählen [ˈʃtɛːlən] tr temper; (fig) steel

Stahl′kammer f steel vault

Stahlspäne [ˈʃtaːlʃpɛːnə] pl steel wool

stak [ʃtaːk] pret of stecken

Stalag [ˈʃtaːlak] n (-s;-s) (Stammlager) main camp (for P.O.W.'s)

Stall [ʃtal] *m* (-[e]s;̈-e) stable; shed
Stall′knecht *m* groom
Stamm [ʃtam] *m* (-[e]s;̈-e) stem;
stalk; trunk; stock, race; tribe; breed
Stamm′aktie *f* common stock
Stamm′baum *m* family tree; pedigree
stammeln [ˈʃtaməln] *tr* & *intr* stammer
Stamm′eltern *pl* ancestors
stammen [ˈʃtamən] *intr* (SEIN) (aus,
von) come (from); (von) date
(from); (gram) (von) be derived
(from)
Stamm′gast *m* regular customer
stämmig [ˈʃtemɪç] *adj* stocky; husky
Stamm′kneipe *f* favorite bar
Stamm′kunde *m*, **Stamm′kundin** *f* regular customer
Stamm′personal *n* skeleton staff
Stamm′tisch *m* reserved table
Stammutter (**Stamm′mutter**) *f* ances-
tress
Stamm′vater *m* ancestor
stampfen [ˈʃtampfən] *tr* tamp, pound;
(*Kartoffeln*) mash; (*Boden*) paw ||
intr stamp the ground; (*durch
Schnee*) trudge; (naut) pitch
stand [ʃtant] *pret of* **stehen** || **Stand** *m*
(-[e]s;̈-e) stand; footing, foothold;
level, height; condition; status, rank;
class, caste; booth; profession; trade;
(sport) score; **seinen S. behaupten**
hold one's ground
Standard [ˈʃtandart] *m* (-s;-s) standard
Standarte [ʃtanˈdartə] *f* (-;-n) banner;
standard
Stand′bild *n* statue
Ständchen [ˈʃtentçən] *n* (-s;-) serenade; **j-m ein S. bringen** serenade
s.o.
Ständer [ˈʃtendər] *m* (-s;-) stand,
rack; pillar; stud; (mach) column
Stan′desamt *n* bureau of vital statistics
stan′desamtlich *adj* & *adv* before a
civil magistrate
stan′desgemäß *adj* according to rank
Stan′desperson *f* dignitary
stand′fest *adj* stable, steady, sturdy
stand′haft *adj* steadfast
stand′halten §90 *intr* hold out; (*dat*)
withstand
ständig [ˈʃtendɪç] *adj* permanent;
steady, constant
Stand′licht *n* parking light
Stand′ort *m* position; station; (mil)
base; (mil) garrison
Stand′pauke *f* (coll) lecture
Stand′punkt *m* standpoint
Stand′recht *n* martial law
Stand′uhr *f* grandfather's clock
Stange [ˈʃtaŋə] *f* (-;-n) pole; rod, bar;
perch, roost; **e-e S. Zigaretten** a carton of cigarettes; **von der S.** ready-
made (*clothes*)
stank [ʃtaŋk] *pret of* **stinken**
stänkern [ˈʃteŋkərn] *intr* (coll) stink;
(coll) make trouble
Stanniol [ʃtaˈnjol] *n* (-s;-e), **Stan-
niol′papier** *n* tinfoil
Stanze [ˈʃtantsə] *f* (-;-n) stanza;
punch, die, stamp
stanzen [ˈʃtantsən] *tr* (mach) punch
Stapel [ˈʃtapəl] *m* (-s;-) stack; depot;

stock; (naut) slip; (tex) staple; **auf
S. liegen** be in drydock; **vom S.
laufen lassen** launch
Sta′pellauf *m* launching
stapeln [ˈʃtapəln] *tr* stack, pile up
Sta′pelplatz *m* lumberyard; depot
stapfen [ˈʃtapfən] *intr* (SEIN) slog
Star [ʃtar] *m* (-[e]s;-e) (orn) starling;
(pathol) cataract; **grauer S.** cataract;
grüner S. glaucoma || *m* (-s;-s) (cin,
theat) star
starb [ʃtarp] *pret of* **sterben**
stark [ʃtark] *adj* (**stärker** [ˈʃterkər];
stärkste [ˈʃterkstə] §9) strong; stout;
(*Erkältung*) bad; (*Familie*) big;
(*Kälte*) severe; (*Frost*, *Verkehr*)
heavy; (*Wind*) high; (*Stunde*) full ||
adv much; hard; very
Stärke [ˈʃterkə] *f* (-;-n) strength;
force; stoutness; thickness; might;
violence; intensity; (*Anzahl*) number; (fig) forte; (chem) starch
stärken [ˈʃterkən] *tr* strengthen;
(*Wäsche*) starch || *ref* take some
refreshment
Stark′strom *m* high-voltage current
Stär′kung *f* (-s;-en) strengthening; refreshment; (*Imbiß*) snack
starr [ʃtar] *adj* stiff, rigid; fixed; inflexible; obstinate; dumbfounded;
numb || *adv*—**s. ansehen** stare at
starren [ˈʃtarən] *intr* (**auf** *acc*) stare
(at); **s. von** be covered with
Starr′kopf *m* stubborn fellow
starr′köpfig *adj* stubborn
Starr′krampf *m* (-es;) tetanus
Starr′sinn *m* (-[e]s;) stubbornness
Start [ʃtart] *m* (-[e]s;-s & -e) start;
(aer) take-off; (rok) launching
Start′bahn *f* (aer) runway
starten [ˈʃtartən] *tr* start; launch ||
intr (SEIN) start; (aer) take off; (rok)
lift off, be launched
Start′rampe *f* (rok) launch pad
Station [ʃtaˈtsjon] *f* (-;-en) station;
(med) ward; **freie S.** free room and
board
statisch [ˈʃtatɪʃ] *adj* static
Statist **-in** [ʃtaˈtɪst(ɪn)] §7 *mf* (cin)
extra; (theat) supernumerary
Statistik [ʃtaˈtɪstɪk] *f* (-;-en) statistic;
(*Wissenschaft*) statistics
statistisch [ʃtaˈtɪstɪʃ] *adj* statistical
Stativ [ʃtaˈtif] *n* (-s;-e) stand; (phot)
tripod
statt [ʃtat] *prep* (*genit*) instead of; **s.
zu** (*inf*) instead of (*ger*) || **Statt** *f*
(-;) place, stead; **an Kindes S. annehmen** adopt
Stätte [ˈʃtetə] *f* (-;-n) place, spot;
(*Wohnung*) abode; room
statt′finden §59 *intr* take place
statt′haft *adj* admissible; legal
Statthalter [ˈʃtathaltər] *m* (-s;-) governor
statt′lich *adj* stately; imposing
Statue [ˈʃtatʊ-ə] *f* (-;-n) statue
statuieren [ʃtatuˈiːrən] *tr* establish; **ein
Exempel s. an** (*dat*) make an exam-
ple of
Statur [ʃtaˈtuːr] *f* (-;-en) stature
Statut [ʃtaˈtuːt] *n* (-[e]s;-en) statute;
Statuten bylaws

Stau [ʃtau] m (-[e]s;-e) dammed-up
water; updraft; (aut) tie-up
Staub [ʃtaup] m (-[e]s;) dust
Stau′becken n reservoir
stauben [ʹʃtaubən] intr make dust
stäuben [ʹʃtɔɪbən] tr dust; sprinkle,
powder; (Flüssigkeit) spray ‖ intr
make dust; throw off spray
staubig [ʹʃtaubɪç] adj dusty
staub′saugen tr & intr vacuum
Staub′sauger m vacuum cleaner
Staub′wedel m feather duster
Staub′zucker m powdered sugar
stauchen [ʹʃtauçən] tr knock, jolt;
compress; (sl) chew out
Stau′damm m dam
Staude [ʹʃtaudə] f (-;-n) perennial
stauen [ʹʃtau-ən] tr dam up; (Waren)
stow away; (Blut) stanch ‖ ref be
blocked, jam up
Stau′er m (-s;-) stevedore
staunen [ʹʃtaunən] intr (über acc) be
astonished (at) ‖ **Staunen** n (-s;)
astonishment
stau′nenswert adj astonishing
Staupe [ʹʃtaupə] f (-;) (vet) distemper
Stau′see m reservoir
Stau′ung f (-;-en) damming up; blockage; (Engpaß) bottleneck; (Ver-
kehrs-) jam-up; (pathol) congestion
stechen [ʹʃtɛçən] §64 prick; sting, bite;
(mit e-r Waffe) stab; (Torf) cut;
(Star) remove; (Kontrolluhr) punch;
(Wein) draw; (Näherei) stitch; (gravieren) engrave; (cards) trump;
(cards) take (a trick) ‖ intr sting,
bite; (Sonne) be hot; (cards) be
trump; j-m in die Augen s. catch
s.o.'s eye ‖ impers—es sticht mich
in der Brust I have a sharp pain in
my chest
ste′chend adj (Blick) piercing; (Geruch) strong; (Schmerz) sharp, stab-
bing
Stech′karte f timecard
Stech′schritt m goosestep
Stech′uhr f time clock
Steckbrief [ʹʃtɛkbrif] m warrant for
arrest
steck′brieflich adv—s. verfolgen put
out a "wanted" notice for
Steckdose [ʹʃtɛkdozə] f (elec) outlet
stecken [ʹʃtɛkən] tr & intr stick ‖
Stecken m (-s;-) stick
steckenbleiben (stek′kenbleiben) §62
intr (SEIN) get stuck
Steckenpferd (Stek′kenpferd) hobby-
horse; (fig) hobby
Stecker (Stek′ker) m (-s;-) (elec) plug
Steck′kontakt m (elec) plug
Steck′nadel f pin
Steg [ʃtɛk] m (-[e]s;-e) footpath;
footbridge; (e-r Brille, Geige)
bridge; (Landungs-) jetty; (naut)
gangplank
Steg′reif m—aus dem S. extempore
stehen [ʹʃte-ən] §146 tr—e-m Maler
Modell s. sit for a painter; Schlange
s. stand in line; Schmiere s. (coll)
be a lookout; Wache s. stand guard
‖ intr (HABEN & SEIN) stand; stop;
be; (gram) occur, be used; (Kleider)
fit; das steht bei Ihnen that depends

on you; gut s. (dat) fit, suit; gut s.
mit be on good terms with; wie
steht's? (coll) how is it going?
ste′henbleiben §62 intr (SEIN) stop
ste′henlassen §104 tr leave standing;
(nicht anrühren) leave alone; (Fehler) leave uncorrected; (vergessen)
forget; (culin) allow to stand or cool
Ste′her m (-s;-) long-distance cyclist
Stehlampe [ʹʃtelampə] f floor lamp
Stehleiter [ʹʃtelaɪtər] f stepladder
stehlen [ʹʃtelən] §147 tr & intr steal
Stehplatz [ʹʃteplats] m standing room
steif [ʃtaɪf] adj stiff; rigid; (Lächeln)
forced; (förmlich) formal; (starr)
numb
steifen [ʹʃtaɪfən] tr stiffen; (Wäsche)
starch
Steig [ʃtaɪk] m (-[e]s;-e) path
Steig′bügel m stirrup
steigen [ʹʃtaɪgən] §148 tr (Treppen)
climb ‖ intr (SEIN) climb; rise; go
up; (Nebel) lift; (Blut in den Kopf)
rush ‖ **Steigen** n (-s;) rise; increase
steigern [ʹʃtaɪgərn] tr raise, increase;
(verstärken) enhance; (gram) compare ‖ ref increase, go up
Stei′gerung f (-;-en) rising; increase;
intensification; (gram) comparison
Stei′gerungsgrad m (gram) degree of
comparison
Stei′gung f (-;-en) rise; (Hang) slope;
(e-s Propellers) pitch
steil [ʃtaɪl] adj steep
Stein [ʃtaɪn] m (-[e]s;-e) stone; rock;
(horol) jewel; (pathol) stone
stein′alt′ adj old as the hills
Stein′bruch m quarry
Stein′druck m lithography; (Bild)
lithograph
steinern [ʹʃtaɪnərn] adj stone
Stein′gut n earthenware
steinig [ʹʃtaɪnɪç] adj stony, rocky
steinigen [ʹʃtaɪnɪgən] tr stone
Stein′kohle f hard coal
Stein′metz m stonemason
stein′reich′ adj (coll) filthy rich
Stein′salz n rock salt
Stein′schlag m (public sign) falling
rocks
Stein′wurf m stone's throw
Stein′zeit f stone age
Steiß [ʃtaɪs] m (-es;-e) buttocks
Stelldichein [ʹʃtɛldɪçaɪn] n (-[s];
-[s]) (coll) date
Stelle [ʹʃtelə] f (-;-n) place, spot; position; job; agency, department; quotation; (math) digit; an S. von in
place of; auf der S. on the spot; auf
der S. treten (fig & mil) mark time;
freie (or offene) S. opening; zur S.
sein be on hand
stellen [ʹʃtelən] tr put, place; set;
stand; (ein-) regulate, adjust; (anordnen) fix, arrange; (Frage) ask;
(Horoskop) cast; (Diagnose) give;
(Falle, Wecker) set; (Kaution) put
up; (Zeugen) produce; e-n Antrag s.
make a motion; in Dienst s. appoint;
put into service ‖ ref place oneself,
stand; give oneself up; der Preis
stellt sich auf...the price is...; sich
s., als ob act as if

Stel′lenangebot n help wanted
Stel′lenbewerber –in §6 mf applicant
Stel′lengesuch n situation wanted
Stel′lenjagd f job hunting
Stel′lennachweis m, **Stel′lenvermitt-lungsbüro** n employment agency
stel′lenweise adv here and there
–stellig [ʃtelɪç] comb.fm. **–digit**
Stel′schraube f set screw
Stel′lung f (–;–en) position; situation; job; standing; status; rank; posture; (mil) line, position; (mil) emplacement; **S. nehmen zu** express one's opinion on; (erklären) explain; (be-antworten) answer
Stel′lungnahme f (–;–n) attitude, point of view; (Erklärung) comment; (Gut-achten) opinion; (Bericht) report; (Beantwortung) answer; (Entscheid) decision; **sich** [dat] **e-e S. vorbehal-ten** not commit oneself
Stel′lungsgesuch n (job) application
stel′lungslos adj jobless
stell′vertretend adj acting
Stell′vertreter –in §6 mf representa-tive; deputy; proxy; substitute
Stell′vertretung f (–;–en) represen-tation; substitution; **in S.** by proxy
Stelzbein [′ʃteltsbaɪn] n wooden leg
Stelze [′ʃteltsə] f (–;–n) stilt
stelzen [′ʃteltsən] intr (SEIN) stride
Stemmeisen [′ʃtemaɪzən] n crowbar
stemmen [′ʃtemən] tr support; (Ge-wicht) lift; (Loch) chisel ‖ ref—sich s. gegen oppose
Stempel [′ʃtempəl] m (–s;–) stamp; prop; (Kolben) piston; (bot) pistil
Stem′pelkissen n ink pad, stamp pad
stempeln [′ʃtempəln] tr stamp ‖ intr—s. gehen (coll) collect unemployment insurance
Stengel [′ʃteŋəl] m (–s;–) stalk
Steno [′ʃteno] f (–;) stenography
Stenograph [ʃteno′graf] m (–en;–en) stenographer
Stenographie [ʃtenogra′fi] f (–;) ste-nography, shorthand
stenographieren [ʃtenogr′firən] tr take down in shorthand ‖ intr do short-hand
Stenographin [ʃteno′grafɪn] f (–;–nen) stenographer
Stenotypistin [ʃtenotY′pɪstɪn] f (–;–nen) stenographer
Step [ʃtep] m (–s;–) tap dance; **S. tanzen** tap-dance
Steppdecke [′ʃtepdekə] f comforter
Steppe [′ʃtepə] f (–;–n) steppe
steppen [′ʃtepən] tr quilt ‖ intr tap-dance ‖ **Steppen** n (–s;) tap-dancing
Sterbe– [′ʃterbə] comb.fm. dying, death
Ster′befall m death
Ster′begeld n death benefit
Ster′behilfe f euthanasia
sterben [′ʃterbən] §149 intr (SEIN) an [dat] die (of)
sterb′lich adj mortal ‖ adv—s. verliebt in** (acc) head over heals in love with
Sterb′lichkeit f (–;) mortality
Sterb′lichkeitsziffer f death rate
stereotyp [stereo′typ] adj stereotyped
steril [ʃte′ril] adj sterile
sterilisieren [ʃterɪlɪ′zirən] tr sterilize

Stern [ʃtern] m (–[e]s;–e) star; (typ) asterisk
Stern′bild n constellation
Stern′blume f aster
Sterndeuter [′ʃterndɔɪtər] m (–s;–) astrologer
Sterndeuterei [ʃterndɔɪtə′raɪ] f (–;) astrology
Ster′nenbanner n Stars and Stripes
stern′ha′gelvoll adj (sl) dead drunk
stern′hell adj starlit
Stern′himmel m starry sky
Stern′kunde f astronomy
Stern′schuppe f shooting star
Stern′warte f observatory
stet [ʃtet], **stetig** [′ʃtetɪç] adj steady
stets [ʃtets] adv constantly, always
Steuer [′ʃtɔɪ·ər] f (–;–n) tax; duty ‖ n (–s;–) rudder, helm; (aer) controls; (aut) steering wheel; **am S. at** the helm; (aut) behind the wheel
Steu′eramt n tax office
Steu′erbord n (naut) starboard
Steu′ererhebung f levy of taxes
Steu′ererklärung f tax return
Steu′erflosse f vertical stabilizer
Steu′erhinterziehung f tax evasion
Steu′erjahr n fiscal year
Steu′erknüppel m control stick
Steu′er·mann m (–[e]s;–̈er & –leute) helmsman
steuern [′ʃtɔɪ·ərn] tr steer; control; regulate; (aer, naut) pilot; (aut) drive ‖ intr (dat) curb, check
steu′erpflichtig adj taxable; dutiable
Steu′ersäule f (aer) control column; (aut) steering column
Steu′errad n steering wheel
Steu′erruder n rudder, helm
Steu′ersatz m tax rate
Steu′erveranlagung f tax assessment
Steu′erwerk n (aer) controls
Steu′erzahler –in §6 mf tax payer
Steu′erzuschlag m surtax
Steven [′ʃtevən] m (–s;–) (naut) stem
Stewar·deß [′st(j)u·ərdes] f (–;–dessen [desən]) (aer) stewardess
stibitzen [ʃtɪ′bɪtsən] tr snitch
Stich [ʃtɪç] m (–[e]s;–e) prick; (Messer–) stab; (Insekten–) sting, bite; (Stoß) thrust; (Seitenstechen) sharp pain; (Kupfer–) engraving; (cards) trick; (naut) knot; (sew) stitch; **im S. lassen** abandon
Stichelei [ʃtɪçə′laɪ] f (–;–en) taunt
sticheln [′ʃtɪçəln] intr—gegen **j–n s.** (fig) needle s.o.
Stich′flamme f flash
stich′haltig adj valid, sound
Stich′probe f spot check
Stich′tag m effective date; due date
Stich′wahl f run-off election
Stich′wort n (–[e]s;–̈er) key word; dic-tionary entry ‖ n (–[e]s;–e) (theat) cue
Stich′wunde f stab wound
sticken [′ʃtɪkən] tr embroider ‖ intr embroider

Stickerei [ʃtɪkə'raɪ] *f* (-;-en) embroidery

Stick'husten *m* whooping cough

stickig ['ʃtɪkɪç] *adj* stuffy, close

Stick'stoff *m* nitrogen

stieben ['ʃtibən] §130 *intr* (HABEN & SEIN) fly; (*Menge*) disperse

Stief [ʃtif] *comb.fm.* step-

Stief'bruder *m* stepbrother

Stiefel ['ʃtifəl] *m* (-s;-) boot

Stie'felknecht *m* bootjack

Stief'mutter *f* stepmother

Stief'mütterchen *n* (bot) pansy

Stief'vater *m* stepfather

stieg [ʃtik] *pret of* steigen

Stiege ['ʃtigə] *f* (-;-n) staircase

Stiel [ʃtil] *m* (-[e]s;-e) handle; (bot) stalk

stier [ʃtir] *adj* staring, glassy || **Stier** *m* (-[e]s;-e) bull; (astr) Taurus

stieren ['ʃtirən] *intr* (**auf** *acc*) stare (at)

Stier'kampf *m* bullfight

stieß [ʃtis] *pret of* stoßen

Stift [ʃtɪft] *m* (-[e]s;-e) pin; peg; pencil; crayon; (*Zwecke*) tack; (coll) apprentice || *n* (-[e]s;-e & -er) charitable foundation or institution

stiften ['ʃtɪftən] *tr* (*gründen*) found; (*spenden*) donate; (*verursachen*) cause; (*Unruhe*) stir up; (*Frieden*) make; (*Brand*) start; (*e-e Runde Bier*) set up

Stif'ter –in §6 *mf* founder; donor; (fig) author, cause

Stif'tung *f* (-;-en) foundation; donation; grant; **fromme S.** religious establishment; **milde S.** charitable institution

Stif'tungsfest *n* founder's day

Stil [ʃtil] *m* (-[e]s;-e) style

stil'gerecht *adj* in good taste

stilisieren [ʃtili'zirən] *tr* word

stilistisch [ʃti'lɪstɪç] *adj* stylistic

still [ʃtɪl] *adj* still; calm; silent; (com) slack; **im stillen** in secret; **Stiller Ozean** Pacific Ocean || **Stille** *f* (-;) stillness; silence

still'bleiben §62 *intr* (SEIN) keep still

Stilleben (**Still'leben**) *n* still life

stillegen (**still'legen**) *tr* (*Betrieb*) shut down; (*Verkehr*) stop; (*Schiff*) put into mothballs

stillen ['ʃtɪlən] *tr* still; (*Hunger*) appease; (*Durst*) quench; (*Blut*) stanch; (*Begierde*) gratify

stilliegen (**still'liegen**) §108 *intr* lie still; (*Betrieb*) lie idle; (*Verkehr*) be at a standstill

still'schweigen §148 *intr* be silent; **s. zu** acquiesce in || **Stillschweigen** *n* (-s;) silence; secrecy

still'schweigend *adj* silent; (fig) tacit

Still'stand *m* standstill; (*Sackgasse*) stalemate, deadlock

still'stehen §146 *intr* stand still; (*Betrieb*) be idle; (mil) stand at attention; **stillgestanden!** (mil) attention!

Stil'möbel *pl* period furniture

stil'voll *adj* stylish

Stimm– [ʃtɪm] *comb.fm.* vocal; voting

Stimm'abgabe *f* vote, voting

Stimm'band *n* (-[e]s;-er) vocal cord

Stimm'block *m* (parl) bloc

Stimm'bruch *m* change of voice

Stimme ['ʃtɪmə] *f* (-;-n) voice; vote

stimmen ['ʃtɪmən] *tr* make feel (*happy, etc.*); (mus) tune || *intr* be right; vote; (mus) be in tune

Stim'menrutsch *m* (pol) landslide

Stimm'enthaltung *f* abstention

Stimm'gabel *f* tuning fork

Stimm'recht *n* right to vote, suffrage

Stim'mung *f* (-;-en) tone; (*Laune*) mood; (mil) morale; (mus) tuning; (st.exch.) trend

stim'mungsvoll *adj* cheerful

Stimm'zettel *m* ballot

stinken ['ʃtɪŋkən] §143 *intr* stink

Stink'tier *n* skunk

Stipen–dium [ʃtɪ'pɛndjʊm] *n* (-s;-dien [djən]) scholarship, grant

stippen ['ʃtɪpən] *tr* (coll) dunk

Stippvisite ['ʃtɪpvizitə] *f* (-;-n) short visit

Stirn [ʃtɪrn] *f* (-;-en) **Stirne** ['ʃtɪrnə] *f* (-;-n) forehead, brow; (fig) insolence, gall; **die S. runzeln** frown

Stirn'runzeln *n* (-s;) frown(ing)

stob [ʃtop] *pret of* stieben

stöbern ['ʃtøbərn] *tr* (*Wild*) flush; (*aus dem Bett*) yank || *intr* poke around; browse; (*Schnee*) drift

stochern ['ʃtɔxərn] *intr* poke around; **im Essen s.** pick at one's food; **im Feuer s.** stoke the fire; **in den Zähnen s.** pick one's teeth

Stock [ʃtɔk] *m* (-[e]s;-e) stick; cane; wand; baton; stem; vine; tree stump; cleaning rod; beehive; massif; story, floor; **im ersten S.** on the second floor

Stock–, stock– *comb.fm.* thoroughly

stock'blind *adj* stone-blind

stock'dun'kel *adj* pitch-dark

Stöckel ['ʃtœkəl] *m* (-s;-) high heel

stocken ['ʃtɔkən] *intr* stop; (*Geschäft*) slack off; (*Blut*) coagulate; (*in der Rede*) get stuck; (*Milch*) curdle; (*Stimme*) falter; (*stammeln*) get moldy; (*Unterhandlungen*) become deadlocked; (*Verkehr*) get tied up; (*zögern*) hesitate || **Stocken** *n* (-s;) stopping; hesitation; **ins S. bringen** tie up

stock'fin'ster *adj* pitch-black

Stock'fleck *m* mildew

stock'fleckig *adj* mildewy

stockig ['ʃtɔkɪç] *adj* moldy

–stöckig [ʃtœkɪç] *comb.fm.* –story

stock'nüch'tern *adj* dead-sober

stock'steif *adj* stiff as a board

stock'taub' *adj* stone-deaf

Stockung (**Stok'kung**) *f* (-;-en) stoppage; (*des Verkehrs*) tie-up; (*des Blutes*) congestion; (*Unterbrechung*) interruption; (*Verlangsamung*) slow-down; (*Zeitverlust*) delay; (*Pause*) pause; (*Zögern*) hesitation; (*der Unterhandlungen*) deadlock

Stock'werk *n* story, floor

Stoff [ʃtɔf] *m* (-[e]s;-e) stuff, matter; fabric; material; cloth; subject, topic; (chem) substance

stoff'lich *adj* material

Stoff'rest *m* (tex) remnant

Stoff'wechsel m metabolism
stöhnen ['ʃtøːnən] intr groan, moan
Stolle ['ʃtɔlə] f (-;-n) fruit cake
Stollen ['ʃtɔlən] m (-s;-) fruit cake; tunnel; (Pfosten) post; (Stütze) prop
stolpern ['ʃtɔlpərn] intr (SEIN) stumble, trip
stolz [ʃtɔlts] adj (auf acc) proud (of) ‖ **Stolz** m (-es;) pride
stolzieren [ʃtɔl'tsiːrən] intr (SEIN) strut; (Pferd) prance
stopfen ['ʃtɔpfən] tr stuff, cram; (Pfeife) fill; (Strumpf) darn; (mus) mute; **j-m den Mund s.** shut s.o. up ‖ intr be filling; cause constipation
Stopf'garn n darning yarn
Stoppel ['ʃtɔpəl] f (-;-n) stubble
stoppelig ['ʃtɔpəlɪç] adj stubbly
stoppeln ['ʃtɔpəln] tr glean; (fig) patch
stoppen ['ʃtɔpən] tr stop; clock, time ‖ intr stop
Stopp'licht n tail light; stoplight
Stopp'uhr f stopwatch
Stöpsel ['ʃtœpsəl] m (-s;-) stopper, cork; (coll) squirt; (elec) plug
stöpseln ['ʃtœpsəln] tr plug; cork
Storch [ʃtɔrç] m (-[e]s;-̈e) stork
stören ['ʃtøːrən] tr disturb, bother; (Pläne) cross; (Vergnügen) spoil; (mil) harass; (rad) jam
Störenfried ['ʃtøːrənfriːt] m (-[e]s;-e) pain in the neck
störrig ['ʃtœrɪç], **störrisch** ['ʃtœrɪʃ] adj stubborn
Stö'rung f (-;-en) disturbance, trouble; breakdown; interruption; annoyance; intrusion; (rad) static; (rad) jamming
Stoß [ʃtoːs] m (-es;-̈e) push, shove; hit, blow; nudge, poke; (Einschlag) impact; (Erschütterung) shock; (Fecht-) pass; (Feuer-) burst (of fire); (Fuß-) kick; (Haufen) pile, bundle; (Rück-) recoil; (Saum) seam, hem; (Schwimm-) stroke; (Trompeten-) blast; (Wind-) gust; (mil) thrust; (orn) tail
Stoß'dämpfer m shock absorber
Stößel ['ʃtøːsəl] m (-s;-) pestle
stoßen ['ʃtoːsən] §150 tr push, shove; hit, knock; kick; punch; jab, nudge, poke; ram; pound; pulverize; oust ‖ ref bump oneself; **sich s. an** (dat) take offense at; take exception to ‖ intr kick; (mit den Hörnen) butt; (Gewehr) recoil, kick; (Wagen) jolt (Schiff) toss; **in die Trompete s.** blow the trumpet; **s. auf** (acc) swoop down on ‖ intr (SEIN)—**s. an** (acc) bump against; adjoin; be next-door to; **s. auf** (acc) run into; come across; (naut) dash against; **s. durch** (mil) smash through; **vom Lande s.** shove off; **zu j-m s.** side with s.o.
Stoß'stange f (aut) bumper
Stoß'trupp m assault party; **Stoßtruppen** shock troops; commandos, rangers
Stoß'zahn m tusk
stottern ['ʃtɔtərn] tr stutter, stammer ‖ intr stutter, stammer; (aut) sputter
stracks [ʃtraks] adv immediately; (geradeaus) straight ahead
Straf- [ʃtraf] comb.fm. penal; criminal

Straf'anstalt f penal institution
Straf'arbeit f (educ) extra work
Straf'aufschub m reprieve
strafbar ['ʃtrafbar] adj punishable
Strafe ['ʃtrafə] f (-;-n) punishment; penalty; (Geld-) fine; **bei S. von** under pain of; **zur S.** as punishment
strafen ['ʃtrafən] tr punish
straff [ʃtraf] adj tight; (Seil) taut; (gespannt) tense; (aufrecht) erect; (fig) strict; **s. spannen** tighten
straf'fällig adj punishable; culpable
Straf'geld n fine
Straf'gesetzbuch n penal code
sträflich ['ʃtrɛflɪç] adj culpable
Sträfling ['ʃtrɛflɪŋ] m (-s;-e) convict
straf'los adj unpunished
Straf'porto n postage due
Straf'predigt f talking-to, lecture
Straf'raum m (sport) penalty box
Straf'recht n criminal law
Straf'stoß m (sport) penalty kick
Straf'umwandlung f (jur) commutation
Straf'verfahren n criminal proceedings
Strahl [ʃtral] m (-[e]s;-en) ray; beam; flash; jet; (geom) radius
Strahl'antrieb m jet propulsion
strahlen ['ʃtralən] intr beam, shine
Strahl'motor m, **Strahl'triebwerk** n jet engine
Strah'lung f (-;-en) radiation
Strähne ['ʃtrɛnə] f (-;-n) strand; lock; hank, skein
strähnig ['ʃtrɛnɪç] adj wispy
stramm [ʃtram] adj tight; (kräftig) strapping; (Zucht) strict; (Arbeit) hard; (Soldat) smart; (Mädel) buxom ‖ adv—**s. stehen** stand at attention
stramm'ziehen §163 tr draw tight
strampeln ['ʃtrampəln] intr kick
Strand [ʃtrant] m (-[e]s;-̈e) beach, seashore, shore
stranden ['ʃtrandən] intr (SEIN) be beached, run aground, be stranded
Strand'gut n flotsam, jetsam
Strand'gutjäger –in §6 mf beachcomber
Strand'korb m hooded beach chair
Strand'schirm m beach umbrella
Strang [ʃtraŋ] m (-[e]s;-̈e) rope; (Strähne) hank; (Zugseil) trace; (rr) track; **wenn alle Stränge reißen** (fig) if worse comes to worst
Strapaze [ʃtra'patsə] f (-;-n) fatigue; exertion, strain
strapazieren [ʃtrapa'tsiːrən] tr tire out; (Kleider) wear hard
strapazier'fähig adj heavy-duty
strapaziös [ʃtrapa'tsjøs] adj tiring
Straße ['ʃtrasə] f (-;-n) street; road, highway; (Meerenge) strait
Stra'ßenanzug m business suit
Stra'ßenbahn f streetcar, trolley; trolley line
Stra'ßenbahnwagen m streetcar
Stra'ßendirne f streetwalker
Stra'ßengraben m ditch, gutter
Stra'ßenhändler –in §6 mf street vendor
Stra'ßenjunge m urchin
Stra'ßenkarte f street map
Stra'ßenkreuzung f intersection
Stra'ßenlage f (aut) roadability
Stra'ßenrennen n drag race

Stra'ßenrinne f gutter

Stra'ßenschild n street sign

Stra'ßensperrung f (public sign) road closed

Stra'ßenstreife f highway patrol

strategisch [ʃtra'teːgɪʃ] adj strategic

sträuben ['ʃtrɔɪbən] tr ruffle ‖ ref bristle, stand on end; **sich s. gegen** resist, struggle against

Strauch [ʃtraux] m (-[e]s;ⁱer) shrub

straucheln ['ʃtrauxəln] intr (SEIN) stumble, trip; (fig) go wrong

Strauß [ʃtraus] m (-[e]s;ⁱe) bouquet ‖ m (-[e]s;-e) ostrich

Strebe [ʃtreːbə] f (-;-n) prop, strut

Stre'bebogen m flying buttress

streben ['ʃtreːbən] intr (nach) strive (after); (nach) tend (toward) ‖ **Streben** n (-s;-) striving; pursuit; (Hang) tendency; (Anstrengung) endeavor

Stre'ber m (-s;-) go-getter, eager beaver; social climber; (in der Schule) grind

strebsam ['ʃtreːpzam] adj zealous

Streb'samkeit f (-;) zeal; industry

Strecke ['ʃtrekə] f (-;-n) stretch; extent; distance; stage, leg; (geom) straight line; (hunt) bag; (rr) section; **zur S. bringen** catch up with; (box) defeat; (hunt) bag

strecken ['ʃtrekən] tr stretch; (Metalle) laminate; (Wein) dilute; (fig) make last; **die Waffen s.** lay down one's arms ‖ ref stretch (oneself)

Streich [ʃtraɪç] m (-[e]s;-e) blow; (fig) trick, prank

streicheln ['ʃtraɪçəln] tr stroke; pat

streichen ['ʃtraɪçən] §85 tr stroke; (Butter, usw.) spread; (an-) paint; (Geige) play; (Messer) whet; (Rasiermesser) strop; (Streichholz) strike; (Flagge, Segel) lower; (Ärmel) roll down; (Ziegel) make; (mit Ruten) flog; delete; (sport) scratch ‖ intr—**mit der Hand s. über** (acc) pass one's hand over ‖ intr (SEIN) stretch, extend; wander; pass, move; rush

Streich'holz n match

Streich'holzbrief m matchbook

Streich'instrument n stringed instrument

Streich'orchester n string band

Streich'riemen m razor strop

Streif [ʃtraɪf] m (-[e]s;-e) streak, stripe; strip

Streif'band n (-[e]s;ⁱer) wrapper

Streife ['ʃtraɪfə] f (-;-n) raid; (Runde) beat; (mil) patrol

streifen ['ʃtraɪfən] tr stripe; streak; graze; skim over; (abziehen) strip; (grenzen an) verge on; (Thema) touch on ‖ intr (SEIN) roam; (mil) patrol; **s. an** (acc) brush against; (fig) verge on; **s. über** (acc) scan ‖ **Streifen** m (-s;-) stripe; streak; strip; slip; (cin) movie

Strei'fendienst m patrol duty

Strei'fenwagen m patrol car, squad car

streifig ['ʃtraɪfɪç] adj striped

Streif'licht n flash, streak of light; **S. werfen auf** (acc) shed light on

Streif'wunde f scratch

Streif'zug m exploratory trip, look-see

Streik [ʃtraɪk] m (-[e]s;-s) strike, walkout; **wilder S.** wildcat strike

streiken ['ʃtraɪkən] intr go on strike

Strei'kende §5 mf striker

Streik'posten m picket; **S. stehen** picket

Streit [ʃtraɪt] m (-[e]s;-e) fight; argument, quarrel; (jur) litigation

Streit'axt f battle-ax; **die S. begraben** (fig) bury the hatchet

streitbar ['ʃtraɪtbar] adj belligerent

streiten ['ʃtraɪtən] §86 recip & intr quarrel

Streit'frage f point at issue

streitig ['ʃtraɪtɪç] adj controversial; at issue

Streit'kräfte pl (mil) forces, troops

streitlustig adj belligerent, scrappy

Streit'objekt n bone of contention

Streit'punkt m issue, point at issue

streit'süchtig adj quarrelsome

streng [ʃtrɛŋ] adj severe, stern; austere; strict; (Geschmack) sharp ‖ **Strenge** f (-;) severity, sternness; austerity; strictness; sharpness

streng'genommen adv strictly speaking

streng'gläubig adj orthodox

Streu [ʃtrɔɪ] f (-;-en) straw bed

Streu'büchse f shaker

streuen ['ʃtrɔɪən] tr strew, sprinkle; (ausbreiten) spread; (verbreiten) scatter ‖ intr spread, scatter

strich [ʃtrɪç] pret of **streichen** ‖ **Strich** m (-[e]s;-e) stroke; line; (Streif) stripe; (Landstrich) tract; (carp) grain; (tex) nap; (typ) dash; **auf den S. gehen** walk the streets (as prostitute); **gegen den S. gehen** go against the grain; (fig) rub the wrong way

Strich'mädchen n streetwalker

Strich'punkt m semicolon

Strich'regen m local shower

strich'weise adv here and there

Strick [ʃtrɪk] m (-[e]s;-e) rope, cord; (fig) rogue, good-for-nothing

stricken ['ʃtrɪkən] tr & intr knit

Strick'garn n knitting yarn

Strick'jacke f cardigan

Strick'kleid n knitted dress

Strick'leiter f rope ladder

Strick'waren pl knitwear

Strick'zeug n knitting things

Striemen ['ʃtriːmən] m (-s;-) stripe, streak; (in der Haut) weal

Strippe ['ʃtrɪpə] f (-;-n) string; strap; shoestring; (telp) line

stritt [ʃtrɪt] pret of **streiten**

strittig ['ʃtrɪtɪç] adj controversial

Stroh [ʃtroː] n (-[e]s) straw

Stroh'dach n thatched roof

Stroh'halm m straw; drinking straw

Stroh'mann m (-[e]s;ⁱer) scarecrow; (cards) dummy

Stroh'puppe f scarecrow

Stroh'sack m straw mattress; **heiliger S.!** holy smokes!

Strolch [ʃtrɔlç] m (-[e]s;-e) bum

strolchen ['ʃtrɔlçən] intr bum around

Strom [ʃtroːm] m (-[e]s;ⁱe) river; stream; (von Worten) torrent; (& elec) current

stromab'wärts adv downstream
stromauf'wärts adv upstream
Strom'ausfall m (elec) power failure
strömen ['ʃtrømən] intr (HABEN & SEIN) stream; (Regen) pour (down)
Strö'mer m (-s;-) (coll) tramp
Strom'kreis m (elec) circuit
strom'linienförmig adj streamlined
Strom'richter m (elec) converter
Strom'schnelle f rapids
Strom'spannung f (elec) voltage
Strom'stärke f (elec) amperage
Strö'mung f (-;-en) current; trend
Strom'unterbrecher m circuit breaker
Strom'wandler m (elec) transformer
Strom'zähler m electric meter
Strophe ['ʃtrofə] f (-;-n) stanza
strotzen ['ʃtrotsən] intr—s. von or vor (dat) abound in, teem with
Strudel ['ʃtrudəl] m (-s;-) eddy, whirlpool; (fig) maelstrom; (culin) strudel
strudeln ['ʃtrudəln] intr eddy, whirl
Struktur [ʃtruk'tur] f (-;-en) structure; (tex) texture
Strumpf [ʃtrumpf] m (-[e]s;⸚e) stocking
Strumpf'band n (-[e]s;⸚er), **Strumpfhalter** m garter
Strumpf'waren pl hosiery
struppig ['ʃtrupɪç] adj shaggy, unkempt
Stube ['ʃtubə] f (-;-n) room
Stu'benmädchen n chambermaid
stu'benrein adj housebroken
Stubsnase ['ʃtupsnazə] f snub nose
Stuck [ʃtuk] m (-[e]s;) stucco
Stück [ʃtyk] n (-[e]s;-e) piece; lot; plot; stretch distance; (Butter) pat; (Zucker) lump; (Seife) cake; (Vieh) head; (mus) piece, number; (theat) play, show; **pro S.** apiece
stückeln ['ʃtykəln] tr cut or break into small pieces; piece together
stück'weise adv piecemeal
Stück'werk n patchwork
Student [ʃtu'dent] m (-en;-en) college student
Studen'tenheim n dormitory
Studen'tenverbindung f fraternity
Studentin [ʃtu'dentɪn] f (-;-nen) college student, coed
Studie ['ʃtudjə] f (-;-n) (Lit) essay; (paint) study, sketch
Stu'diengang m (educ) course
Stu'dienplan m curriculum
Stu'dienrat m (-[e]s;⸚e) high school teacher
Stu'dienreferendar -in §8 mf practice teacher
Stu'dienreise f (educ) field trip
studieren [ʃtu'dirən] tr & intr study (at college); examine
studiert [ʃtu'dirt] adj college-educated; (gekünstelt) affected
Studier'zimmer n study
Stu-dium ['ʃtudjum] n (-s;-dien [djən]) study (at college); studies
Stufe ['ʃtufə] f (-;-n) step, stair; (e-r Leiter) rung; (Grad) grade; (Niveau) level; stage; (mus) interval
Stu'fenfolge f graduation; succession
Stu'fenleiter f stepladder; (fig) gamut
stu'fenweise adv by degrees

Stuhl [ʃtul] m (-[e]s;⸚e) chair; (Stuhlgang) stool, feces; **der Heilige S.** the Holy See
Stuhl'bein n leg of a chair
Stuhl'drang m urgent call of nature
Stuhl'gang m stool, feces; **S. haben** have a bowel movement
Stuhl'lehne f back of a chair
Stulpe ['ʃtulpə] f (-;-n) cuff
Stülpnase ['ʃtylpnazə] f snub nose
stumm [ʃtum] adj dumb, mute; (schweigend) silent; (gram) mute
Stummel ['ʃtuməl] m (-s;-) (e-s Armes, Baumes, e-r Zigarette) stump
Stümper ['ʃtympər] m (-s;-) bungler
Stümperei [ʃtympə'raɪ] f (-;-en) bungling
stüm'perhaft adj bungling
stümpern ['ʃtympərn] tr & intr bungle
stumpf [ʃtumpf] adj blunt; (& fig) obtuse || **Stumpf** m (-[e]s;⸚e) stump
Stumpf'sinn m apathy, dullness
stumpf'sinnig adj dull, stupid
Stunde ['ʃtundə] f (-;-n) hour; (educ) class, lesson, period
stunden ['ʃtundən] tr grant postponement of
Stun'dengeld n tutoring fee
Stun'dengeschwindigkeit f miles per hour
Stun'denkilometer pl kilometers per hour
stun'denlang adv for hours
Stun'denlohn m hourly wage(s)
Stun'denplan m roster, schedule
stun'denweise adv by the hour
Stun'denzeiger m hour hand
-stündig [ʃtyndɪç] comb.fm. –hour
stündlich ['ʃtyntlɪç] adj hourly
Stun'dung f (-;-en) period of grace
Stunk [ʃtuŋk] m (-[e]s;) stink; **S. machen** (sl) raise a stink
Stups [ʃtups] m (-es;-e) nudge
stupsen ['ʃtupsən] tr nudge
Stups'nase f snub nose
stur [ʃtur] adj stubborn; (Blick) fixed
Sturm [ʃturm] m (-[e]s;⸚e) storm; gale
stürmen ['ʃtyrmən] tr storm || intr rage, roar || intr (SEIN) rush || impers—es stürmt it is stormy
Stürmer ['ʃtyrmər] m (-s;-) (fb) forward
stürmisch ['ʃtyrmɪʃ] adj stormy; impetuous || adv—nicht so s.! not so fast!
Sturm'schritt m (mil) double time
Sturm'trupp m assault party
Sturm'welle f (mil) assault wave
Sturm'wind m gale, hurricane
Sturz [ʃturts] m (-es;⸚e) fall, sudden drop; overthrow; collapse; (archit) lintel; (aut) camber; (com) slump
Sturz'bach m torrent
Sturz'bomber m dive bomber
Stürze ['ʃtyrtsə] f (-;-n) lid
stürzen ['ʃtyrtsən] tr throw down; upset, overturn; overthrow; (tauchen) plunge; **nicht s.!** this side up! || ref rush; plunge || intr (SEIN) fall, tumble; rush; (Tränen) pour; (aer) dive
Sturz'flug m (aer) dive
Sturz'helm m crash helmet

Sturz'regen m downpour
Sturz'see f heavy seas
Stute ['ʃtutə] f (-;-n) mare
Stütze ['ʃtytsə] f (-;-n) support, prop; (fig) help, support
stutzen ['ʃtutsən] tr cut short; (Flügel) clip; (Bäume) prune; (Ohren) crop; (Bart) trim || intr stop short; be startled; (Pferd) shy
stützen ['ʃtytsən] tr support; prop; shore up; (fig) support || ref—**sich s. auf** (acc) lean on; (fig) depend on
Stutzer ['ʃtutsər] m (-s;-) car coat; (coll) snazzy dresser
Stutz'flügel m baby grand piano
stutzig ['ʃtutsɪç] adj suspicious
Stütz'pfeiler m abutment
Stütz'punkt m footing; (mil) base; (phys) fulcrum
Subjekt [zup'jɛkt] n (-[e]s;-e) (coll) guy, character; (gram) subject
subjektiv [zupjɛk'tif] adj subjective
Substantiv ['zupstan'tif] n (-[e]s;-e) (gram) substantive, noun
Substanz [zup'stants] f (-;-en) substance
subtil [zup'til] adj subtle
subtrahieren [zuptra'hirən] tr subtract
Subtraktion [zuptrak'tsjon] f (-;-en) subtraction
Subvention [zupvɛn'tsjon] f (-;-en) subsidy
Such- [zux] comb.fm. search
Such'anzeige f want ad
Such'büro n, **Such'dienst** m missing-persons bureau
Suche ['zuxə] f (-;-en) search; **auf der S. nach** in search of, in quest of
suchen ['zuxən] tr search for, look for; (erstreben) seek; want, desire; (in der Zeitung) advertise for; (Gefahr) court; **das Weite s.** run away || intr search; **nach etw s.** look for s.th.
Sucht [zuxt] f (-;⸚e) passion, mania; (nach) addition (to)
süchtig ['zyçtɪç] adj addicted || **Süchtige §5** mf addict
Sud [zut] m (-[e]s;-e) brewing; brew
Süd [zyt] m (-[e]s;-) south
sudelhaft ['zudəlhaft], **sudelig** ['zudəlɪç] adj slovenly, sloppy
sudeln ['zudəln] tr & intr mess up
Süden ['zydən] m (-s;) south
Sudeten [zu'detən] pl Sudeten mountains (along northern border of Czechoslovakia)
Süd'früchte pl (tropical and subtropical) fruit (e.g., bananas, oranges)
süd'lich adj south, southern, southerly; **s. von** south of || adv south
Südost' m, **Südo'sten** m southeast
südöst' lich adj southeast(ern)
Süd'pol m (-s;) South Pole
südwärts ['zytverts] adv southward
Südwest' m, **Südwe'sten** m southwest
süffig ['zyfɪç] adj tasty
suggerieren [zugə'rirən] tr suggest
suggestiv [zugɛs'tif] adj suggestive
Suggestiv'frage f leading question
suhlen ['zulən] ref wallow
Sühne ['zynə] f (-;) atonement
sühnen ['zynən] tr atone for, expiate
Sülze ['zyltsə] f (-;-n) jellied meat

summarisch [zu'marɪʃ] adj summary
Summe ['zumə] f (-;-n) sum, total
summen ['zumən] tr hum || intr hum; buzz
Sum'mer m (-s;-) buzzer
summieren [zu'mirən] tr sum up, total || ref run up, pile up
Summton ['zumton] m (telp) dial tone
Sumpf [zumpf] m (-[e]s;⸚e) swamp
sumpfig ['zumpfɪç] adj swampy, marshy
Sünde ['zyndə] f (-;-n) sin
Sün'denbock m scapegoat
Sün'denerlaß m absolution
Sün'denfall m original sin
Sün'der m (-s;-) sinner
Sünd'flut ['zyntflut] f Deluge
sünd'haft, sündig ['zyndɪç] adj sinful
sündigen ['zyndɪgən] intr sin
Superlativ ['zuperlatif] m (-s;-e) (gram) superlative
Su'permarkt m supermarket
Suppe ['zupə] f (-;-n) soup
Sup'penschüssel f tureen
surren ['zurən] intr buzz
Surrogat [zuro'gat] n (-[e]s;-e) substitute
suspendieren [zuspɛn'dirən] tr suspend
süß [zys] adj sweet || **Süße** f (-;) sweetness
süßen ['zysən] tr sweeten
Sü'ßigkeit f (-;-en) sweetness; **Süßigkeiten** sweets, candy
Süß'kartoffel f sweet potato
süß'lich adj sweetish; (fig) mawkish
Süß'stoff m artificial sweetener
Süß'waren pl sweets, candy
Süß'wasser n fresh water
Symbol [zym'bol] n (-s;-e) symbol
Symbolik [zym'bolik] f (-;) symbolism
symbolisch [zym'bolɪʃ] adj symbolic(al)
Symme·trie [zyme'tri] f (-;-trien) ['tri·ən]) symmetry
symmetrisch [zy'metrɪʃ] adj symmetrical
Sympa·thie [zympa'ti] f (-;-thien ['ti·ən]) liking
sympathisch [zym'patɪʃ] adj likeable; **er ist mir s.** I like him
sympathisieren [zympatɪ'zirən] intr— **s. mit** sympathize with; like
Sympho·nie [zymfo'ni] f (-;-nien ['ni·ən]) symphony
Symptom [zymp'tom] n (-s;-e) symptom
symptomatisch [zymptə'matɪʃ] adj (für) symptomatic (of)
Synagoge [zyna'gogə] f (-;-n) synagogue
synchronisieren [zynkronɪ'zirən] tr synchronize
Syndikat [zyndɪ'kat] n (-[e]s;-e) syndicate
Syndi·kus ['zyndɪkus] m (-;-kusse & -ki [ki]) corporation lawyer
synonym [zyno'nym] adj synonymous || **Synonym** n (-s;-e) synonym
Syntax ['zyntaks] f (-;) syntax
synthetisch [zyn'tetɪʃ] adj synthetic
Syrien ['zyrjən] n (-s;) Syria

System [zʏs'tem] *n* (-s;-e) system
systematisch [zʏste'matiʃ] *adj* systematic
Szene ['stsenə] *f* (-;-n) scene; **in S.** | setzen stage; **sich in S. setzen** put on an act
Sze'nenaufnahme *f* (cin) take
Szenerie [stenə'ri] *f* (-;) scenery

T

T, t [te] *invar n* T, t
Tabak [ta'bak], ['tɑbak] *m* (-[e]s;-e) tobacco
Tabaks'beutel *m* tobacco pouch
Tabak'trafik *f* (Aust) cigar store
Tabak'waren *pl* tobacco products
tabellarisch [tabe'lɑrɪʃ] *adj* tabular
tabellarisieren [tabelarɪ'zirən] *tr* tabulate
Tabelle [ta'belə] *f* (-;-n) table, chart; graph
Tabernakel [taber'nɑkəl] *m & n* (-s;-) tabernacle
Tablett [ta'blet] *n* (-[e]s;-e) tray
Tablette [ta'bletə] *f* (-;-n) tablet, pill
tabu [ta'bu] *adj* taboo ‖ **Tabu** *n* (-s; -s) taboo
Tachometer [taxo'metər] *n* speedometer
Tadel ['tɑdəl] *m* (-s;-) scolding; (*Schuld*) blame; (educ) demerit
ta'dellos *adj* blameless; flawless
tadeln ['tɑdəln] *tr* scold, reprimand; blame, find fault with
Tafel ['tɑfəl] *f* (-;-n) (*Tisch, Diagramm*) table; (*Anschlag-*) billboard; (*Glas-*) pane; (*Holz-, Schalt-*) panel; (*Mahlzeit*) meal, dinner; (*Metall-*) sheet, plate; (*Platte*) slab; (*Schiefer-*) slate; (*Schreib-*) tablet; (*Schokolade*) bar; (*Wand-*) blackboard; **bei T. at** dinner; **die T. decken** set the table; **offene T. halten** have open house
Ta'felaufsatz *m* centerpiece
Ta'felbesteck *n* knife, fork, and spoon
ta'felförmig *adj* tabular
Ta'felgeschirr *n* table service
Ta'felland *n* tableland, plateau
Ta'felmusik *f* dinner music
tafeln ['tɑfəln] *intr* dine, feast
täfeln ['tɛfəln] *tr* (*Wand*) wainscot, panel; (*Fußboden*) parquet
Ta'felöl *n* salad oil
Ta'felservice *n* tableware
Tä'felung *f* (-;-en) inlay; paneling
Taft [taft] *m* (-[e]s;-e) taffeta
Tag [tɑk] *m* (-[e]s;-e) day; daylight; **am Tage** by day; **am Tage nach** the day after; **an den Tag bringen** bring to light; **bei Tage** by day, in the daytime; **den ganzen Tag** all day long; **e-n Tag um den andern** every other day; **e-s Tages** someday; **es wird Tag** day is breaking; **guten Tag!** hello!; how do you do?; (*bei Verabschiedung*) good day!; goodby!; **Tag der offenen Tür** open house; **unter Tage** (min) underground, below the surface
tagaus', tagein' *adv* day in and day out
Tage- [tɑgə] *comb.fm.* day-, daily

Ta'geblatt *n* daily, daily paper
Ta'gebuch *n* diary, journal
Ta'gegeld *n* per diem allowance
ta'gelang *adv* for days
Tagelöhner -in ['tɑgəlønər(ɪn)] §6 *mf* day laborer
tagen ['tɑgən] *intr* dawn; (*beraten*) meet; (jur) be in session
Ta'gesanbruch *m* daybreak
Ta'gesangriff *m* (aer) daylight raid
Ta'gesbefehl *m* (mil) order of the day
Ta'gesbericht *m* daily report
Ta'geseinnahme *f* daily receipts
Ta'gesgespräch *n* topic of the day
ta'geshell *adj* as light as day
Ta'geskasse *f* (theat) box office
Ta'gesleistung *f* daily output
Ta'geslicht *n* daylight
Ta'geslichtaufnahme *f* (phot) daylight shot
Ta'gesordnung *f* agenda; (coll) order of the day
Ta'gespreis *m* market price
Ta'gespresse *f* daily press
Ta'gesschau *f* (telv) news
Ta'geszeit *f* time of day; daytime; **zu jeder T.** at any hour
Ta'geszeitung *f* daily paper
ta'geweise *adv* by the day
Ta'gewerk *n* day's work
-tägig [tegɪç] *comb.fm.* -day
täglich ['teklɪç] *adj* daily
tags [taks] *adv* —**t. darauf** the following day; **t. zuvor** the day before
Tag'schicht *f* day shift
tags'über *adv* during the day, in the daytime
Tagung ['tɑguŋ] *f* (-;-en) convention, conference, meeting
Ta'gungsort *m* meeting place
Taifun [tar'fun] *m* (-s;-e) typhoon
Taille ['taljə] *f* (-;-n) waist; (*Mieder*) bodice
Takel ['tɑkəl] *n* (-s;-) tackle
Takelage [takə'lɑʒə] *f* (-;-n) rigging
takeln ['tɑkəln] *tr* rig
Ta'kelwerk *n* var of Takelage
Takt [takt] *m* (-[e]s;-e) tact; (mach) stroke; (mus) time, beat; (mus) bar; **den T. schlagen** mark time; **im T.** in time; in step; **T. halten** mark time
takt'fest *adj* keeping good time; (fig) reliable
Taktik ['taktɪk] *f* (-;-en) (& fig) tactics
Tak'tiker *m* (-s;-) tactician
taktisch ['taktɪʃ] *adj* tactical
takt'los *adj* tactless
Takt'messer *m* metronome
Takt'stock *m* baton

Takt′strich m (mus) bar
takt′voll adj tactful
Tal [tɑl] n (-[e]s;⁼er) valley
Talar [ta′lɑr] m (-s;-e) robe, gown
Tal′boden m valley floor
Talent [ta′lent] n (-[e]s;-e) talent
talentiert [talen′tirt] adj talented
Tal′fahrt f descent
Talg [talk] m (-[e]s;-e) suet; tallow
Talg′kerze f, **Talg′licht** n tallow candle
Talisman [′tɑlɪsman] m (-s;-e) talisman
Talk(um)puder [′talk(ʊm)pudər] m talcum powder
Talmi [′talmi] n (-s;) (fig) imitation
Tal′sperre f dam
Tamburin [tambu′rin] n (-s;-e) tambourine
Tampon [tã′põ] m (-s;-s) (med) tampon
Tamtam [tam′tam] n (-s;-s) gong; (fig) fanfare, drum beating
Tand [tant] m (-[e]s;) trifle; tallow
tändeln [′tendəln] intr trifle; flirt
Tang [taŋ] m (-[e]s;-e) seaweed
Tangente [taŋ′gentə] f (-;-n) (geom) tangent
tangieren [taŋ′girən] tr concern
Tango [′taŋgo] m (-s;-s) tango
Tank [taŋk] m (-[e]s;-e & -s) tank
tanken [′taŋkən] intr get gas; refuel
Tan′ker m, **Tank′schiff** n tanker
Tank′stelle f gas (or service) station
Tank′wagen m tank truck; (rr) tank car
Tankwart [′taŋkvart] m (-[e]s;-e) gas station attendant
Tanne [′tanə] f (-;-n) fir (tree)
Tan′nenbaum m fir tree
Tan′nenzapfen m fir cone
Tante [′tantə] f (-;-n) aunt; **T.** Meyer (coll) john
Tantieme [tã′tjemə] f (-;-n) dividend; (com) royalty
Tanz [tants] m (-es;⁼e) dance
Tanz′bein n—das **T. schwingen** (coll) cut a rug
Tanz′diele f dance hall
tänzeln [′tentsəln] intr (HABEN & SEIN) skip about; (Pferd) prance
tanzen [′tantsən] tr & intr dance
Tänzer –in [′tentsər(ɪn)] §6 mf dancer
Tanz′fläche f dance floor
Tanz′kapelle f dance band
Tanz′lokal n dance hall
Tanz′saal m ballroom
Tanz′schritt m dance step
Tanz′stunde f dancing lesson
Tapete [ta′petə] f (-;-n) wallpaper
Tape′tenpapier n wallpaper (in rolls)
Tape′tentür f wallpapered door
Tapezierarbeit [tape′tsirarbaɪt] f paperhanging
tapezieren [tape′tsirən] tr wallpaper
Tapezie′rer m (-s;-) paperhanger
tapfer [′tapfər] adj brave, valiant
Ta′pferkeit f (-;) bravery, valor
tappen [′tapən] intr (HABEN & SEIN) grope about; **t. nach** grope for
täppisch [′tepɪ/] adj clumsy
tapsen [′tapsən] intr (SEIN) clump along

Tara [′tɑra] f (-;) (com) tare
Tarif [ta′rif] m (-s;-e) tariff; price list; wage scale; postal rates
Tarif′lohn m standard wages
Tarif′verhandlung f collective bargaining
Tarif′vertrag m wage agreement
Tarn– [tarn] comb.fm. camouflage
tarnen [′tarnən] tr camouflage
Tarn′kappe f (myth) magic cap (rendering wearer invisible)
Tar′nung f (-;) camouflage
Tasche [′ta/ə] f (-;-n) pocket; handbag; pocketbook; schoolbag; flight bag; pouch; briefcase
Ta′schenausgabe f pocket edition
Ta′schenbuch n paperback
Ta′schendieb m pickpocket
Ta′schendiebstahl m pickpocketing
Ta′schengeld n pocket money
Ta′schenlampe f flashlight
Ta′schenmesser n pocketknife
Ta′schenrechner m pocket calculator
Ta′schenspieler –in §6 mf magician
Ta′schenspielerei f sleight of hand
Ta′schentuch n handkerchief
Ta′schenuhr f pocket watch
Ta′schenwörterbuch n pocket dictionary
Tasse [′tasə] f (-;-n) cup
Tastatur [tasta′tur] f (-;-en) keyboard
Taste [′tastə] f (-;-n) key
tasten [′tastən] tr feel, touch; (telg) send ‖ ref feel one's way ‖ intr (nach) grope (for)
Tastsinn [′tastzɪn] m sense of touch
tat [tat] pret of **tun** ‖ **Tat** f (-;-en) deed, act; (Verbrechen) crime; **auf frischer Tat ertappen** catch redhanded; **in der Tat** in fact; **in die Tat umsetzen** implement
Tat′bestand m facts of the case
Tat′bestandsaufnahme f factual statement
tatenlos [′tatənlos] adj inactive
Ta′tenlosigkeit f (-;) inactivity
Täter –in [′tetər(ɪn)] §6 mf doer, perpetrator; culprit
Tat′form f (gram) active voice
tätig [′tetɪç] adj active; busy; **t. sein bei** be employed by
tätigen [′tetɪgən] tr conclude
Tä′tigkeit f (-;-en) activity; occupation, job, profession
Tä′tigkeitsbericht m progress report
Tä′tigkeitsfeld n field, line
Tä′tigung f (-;-en) transaction
Tat′kraft f energy, strength; vigor
tat′kräftig adj energetic; vigorous
tätlich [′tetlɪç] adj violent; **tätliche Beleidigung** (jur) assault and battery; **t. werden gegen** assault ‖ adv —t. **beleidigen** (jur) assault
Tät′lichkeit f (-;-en) (act of) violence; **es kam zu Tätlichkeiten** it came to blows
Tat′ort m scene of the crime
tätowieren [teto′virən] tr tattoo
Tätowie′rung f (-;-en) tattoo
Tat′sache f fact
Tat′sachenbericht m factual report
tat′sächlich adj actual, real, factual
tätscheln [′tet/əln] tr pet, stroke

Tatterich ['tatərıç] m (-s;) shakes

Tatze ['tatsə] f (-;-n) paw

Tau [tau] m (-[e]s;) dew ‖ n (-[e]s; -e) rope; (naut) hawser

taub [taup] adj deaf; (betäubt) numb; (unfruchtbar) barren; (Gestein) not containing ore; (Nuß) hollow; (Ei) unfertile; (Hafer) wild; **t. gegen** deaf **to; t. vor Kälte** numb with cold

Taube ['taubə] f (-;-n) pigeon; (pol) dove

Tau′benhaus n, **Tau′benschlag** m dovecote

Taub′heit f (-;) deafness; numbness

taub′stumm adj deaf and dumb ‖ **Taubstumme** §5 mf deaf-mute

Tauchboot ['tauxbot] n submarine

tauchen ['tauxən] tr dip, duck, immerse ‖ intr (HABEN & SEIN) dive, plunge; (naut) submerge, dive

Tau′cher –in §6 mf (& orn) diver

Tau′cheranzug m diving suit

Tau′chergerät n aqualung

Tau′cherglocke f diving bell

Tauch′krankheit f bends

Tauch′schwimmer m (nav) frogman

tauen ['tau-ən] tr thaw, melt; (schleppen) tow ‖ intr (HABEN & SEIN) thaw ‖ impers—**es taut** dew is falling ‖ impers (HABEN & SEIN)—**es taut** it is thawing ‖ **Tauen** n (-s;) thaw

Tauf- [tauf] comb.fm. baptismal

Tauf′becken n baptismal font

Tauf′buch n parish register

Taufe ['taufə] f (-;-n) baptism, christening

taufen ['taufən] tr baptize, christen

Täufer ['tɔɪfər] m—**Johannes der T.** John the Baptizer

Täufling ['tɔɪflıŋ] m (-s;-e) child (or person) to be baptized

Tauf′name m Christian name

Tauf′pate m godfather

Tauf′patin f godmother

Tauf′schein m baptismal certificate

taugen ['taugən] intr be of use; **zu etw t.** be good for s.th.

Taugenichts ['taugənıçts] m (-es;-e) good-for-nothing

tauglich ['tauklıç] adj (für, zu) good (for), fit (for), suitable (for); (mil) able-bodied; **t. zu** (inf) able to (inf)

Taumel ['tauməl] m (-s;) giddiness; (Überschwang) ecstasy

taumelig ['tauməlıç] adj giddy; reeling

taumeln ['tauməln] intr (SEIN) reel, stagger; be giddy; be ecstatic

Tausch [tauʃ] m (-es;-e) exchange

tauschen ['tauʃən] tr (gegen) exchange (for) ‖ intr—**mit j-m t.** exchange places with s.o.

täuschen ['tɔɪʃən] tr deceive, fool; (betrügen) cheat; (Erwartungen) disappoint ‖ ref be mistaken

täu′schend adj deceptive, illusory; (Ähnlichkeit) striking

Tausch′geschäft n exchange, swap

Tausch′handel m barter; **T. treiben** barter

Täu′schung f (-;-en) deception, deceit; fraud; **optische T.** optical illusion

Täu′schungsangriff m (mil) feint attack

Täu′schungsmanöver n feint

tausend ['tauzənt] invar adj & pron thousand ‖ **Tausend** m—**ei der T.!** (or **potz T.!**) holy smokes! ‖ f (-; -en) thousand ‖ n (-s;-e) thousand

Tau′sendfuß m, **Tausendfüß(l)er** ['tauzəntfys(l)ər] m (-s;-) centipede

tausendste ['tauzəntstə] §9 adj & pron thousandth

Tausendstel ['tauzəntstəl] n (-s;-) thousandth

Tau′tropfen m dewdrop

Tau′werk n (naut) rigging

Tau′wetter n thaw

Tau′ziehen n tug of war

Taxameter [taksa′metər] m taxi meter

Taxe ['taksə] f (-;-n) tax; (Schätzung) appraisal; (Gebühr) fee; (Taxi) taxi

Taxi ['taksi] n (-s;-s) taxi, cab

taxieren [ta′ksirən] tr appraise; rate

Taxifahrer –in §6 mf taxi driver

Ta′xistand m taxi stand

Taxus ['taksus] m (-;-) (bot) yew

Team [tim] n (-s;-s) team

Technik ['tɛçnık] f (-;-en) technique; workmanship; technology

Tech′niker –in §6 mf technician; engineer

Techni·kum ['tɛçnıkum] n (-s;-ka [ka] & -ken [kən]) technical school; school of engineering

technisch ['tɛçnıʃ] adj technical; **technische Angelegenheit** technicality; **technische Hochschule** technical institute

Technologie [tɛçnɔlə′gi] f (-;) technology

technologisch [tɛçnə′logıʃ] adj technological

Tee [te] m (-s;-s) tea

Tee′gebäck n tea biscuit, cookie

Tee′kanne f teapot

Tee′kessel m teakettle

Tee′löffel m teaspoon; teaspoonful

Teenager ['tinedʒər] m (-s;-) teenager

Teer [ter] m (-[e]s;-e) tar

Teer′decke f tar surface, blacktop

teeren ['terən] tr tar

Teer′pappe f tar paper

Tee′satz m tealeaves

Teich [taıç] m (-[e]s;-e) pond, pool

Teig [taık] m (-[e]s;-e) dough

teigig ['taıgıç] adj doughy

Teig′mulde f kneading trough

Teig′waren pl noodles; pastries

Teil [taıl] m & n (-[e]s;-e) part; piece; portion; (Abschnitt) section; (jur) party; **der dritte T. von** one third of; **edle Teile des Körpers** vital parts; **zu gleichen Teilen** fifty-fifty; **zum größten T.** for the most part; **zum T.** partly, in part

Teil- comb.fm. partial

teilbar ['taılbar] adj divisible

Teilchen ['taılçən] n (-s;-) particle

teilen ['taılən] tr divide; (mit) share (with) ‖ ref (Weg) divide; (Ansichten) differ; **sich t. in** (acc) share (in), share (in)

teil′haben §89 intr (an dat) participate (in), share (in)

Teilhaber –in ['taılhabər(ın)] §6 mf participant; (com) partner

Teil′haberschaft f (-;-en) partnership

-teilig [taɪlɪç] *comb.fm.* -piece

Teil′nahme *f* (-;) participation; sympathy; interest

teilnahmslos [′taɪlnamslos] *adj* indifferent; apathetic

Teil′nahmslosigkeit *f* (-;) indifference; apathy

teilnahmsvoll [′taɪlnamsfɔl] *adj* sympathetic; (*besorgt*) solicitous

teil′nehmen §116 *intr* (**an** *dat*) participate (in), take part (in); (**an** *dat*) attend; (fig) (**an** *dat*) sympathize (with)

Teil′nehmer **-in** §6 *mf* participant; (*Mitglied*) member; (sport) competitor; (telp) customer, party

teils [taɪls] *adv* partly

Teil′strecke *f* section, stage

Tei′lung *f* (-;-en) division; partition; separation; (*Grade*) graduation, scale; (*Anteile*) sharing

teil′weise *adv* partly

Teil′zahlung *f* partial payment; **auf T. kaufen** buy on the installment plan

Teint [tɛ̃] *m* (-s;-s) complexion

Telefon [tele′fon] *n* (-s;-e) telephone

Telegramm [tele′gram] *n* (-s;-e) telegram

Telegraph [tele′graf] *m* (-en;-en) telegraph

Telegra′phenstange *f* telegraph pole

telegraphieren [telegra′firən] *tr & intr* telegraph; (*nach Übersee*) cable

Teleobjektiv [′tele-ɔbjektif] *n* telephoto lens

Telephon [tele′fon] *n* (-s;-e) telephone, phone; **ans T. gehen** answer the phone

Telephon′anruf *m* telephone call

Telephon′anschluß *m* telephone connection

Telephon′gespräch *n* telephone call

Telephon′hörer *m* receiver

telephonieren [telefo′nirən] *intr* telephone; **mit j-m t.** phone s.o.

telephonisch [tele′foniʃ] *adj* telephone || *adv* by telephone

Telephonist **-in** [telefo′nɪst(ɪn)] §7 *mf* telephone operator

Telephon′vermittlung *f* telephone exchange

Telephon′zelle *f* telephone booth

Telephon′zentrale *f* telephone exchange

Teleskop [tele′skop] *n* (-s;-e) telescope

Television [televi′zjon] *f* (-;) television

Teller [′tɛlər] *m* (-s;-) plate

Tel′lereisen *n* trap

Tel′lermine *f* antitank mine

Tel′lertuch *n* dishtowel

Tempel [′tɛmpəl] *m* (-s;-) temple

Temperament [tempəra′mɛnt] *n* (-[e]s;-e) temperament; enthusiasm; **er hat kein T.** he has no life in him; **hitziges T.** hot temper

temperament′los *adj* lifeless, boring

temperament′voll *adj* lively, vivacious

Temperatur [tempera′tur] *f* (-;-en) temperature

Temperenzler [tempe′rɛntslər] *m* (-s;-) teetotaler

temperieren [tempe′rirən] *tr* temper; cool; air-condition; (mus) temper

Tem·po [′tempo] *n* (-s;-s & pi [pi]) tempo; speed; (mus) movement

Tem·pus [′tempʊs] *n* (-;-pora [pɔra]) (gram) tense

Tendenz [ten′dɛnts] *f* (-;-en) tendency

Tender [′tɛndər] *m* (-s;-) (nav, rr) tender

Tenne [′tɛnə] *f* (-;-n) threshing floor

Tennis [′tɛnɪs] *n* (-;) tennis

Ten′nisplatz *m* tennis court

Ten′nisschläger *m* tennis racket

Ten′nistournier *n* tennis tournament

Tenor [′tenɔr] *m* (-s;) (*Wortlaut*) tenor, purport || [te′nor] *m* (-[e]s;⸗e) tenor

Teppich [′tepɪç] *m* (-s;-e) rug, carpet

Teppichkehrmaschine [′tepɪçkermaʃinə] *f* carpet sweeper

Termin [ter′min] *m* (-s;-e) date, time, day; deadline; (com) due date; **er hat heute T.** he is to appear in court today; **äußerster T.** deadline

termin′gemäß *adv* on time, punctually

Termin′geschäft *n* futures

Termin′kalender *m* appointment book; (jur) court calendar

Terminolo·gie [termɪnolɔ′gi] *f* (-;-gien [′gi·ən]) terminology

termin′weise *adv* (com) on time

Terpentin [terpen′tin] *m* (-s;) terpentine

Terrain [te′rɛ̃] *n* (-s;-s) ground; (*Grundstück*) lot; (mil) terrain; **T. gewinnen** (fig & mil) gain ground

Terrasse [te′rasə] *f* (-;-n) terrace

terras′senförmig *adj* terraced

Terrine [te′rinə] *f* (-;-n) tureen

Territo·rium [teri′torjʊm] *n* (-s;-rien [rjən]) territory

Terror [′terɔr] *m* (-s;) terror

terrorisieren [terɔri′zirən] *tr* terrorize

Terrorist **-in** [terɔ′rɪst(ɪn)] §7 *mf* terrorist

Terz [terts] *f* (-;-en) (mus) third

Terzett [ter′tset] *n* (-[e]s;-e) trio

Test [test] *m* (-[e]s;-e & -s) test

Testament [testa′mɛnt] *n* (-[e]s;-e) will; (eccl) Testament

testamentarisch [testamɛn′tarɪʃ] *adj* testamentary || *adv* by will; **t. bestimmen** will

Testaments′vollstrecker **-in** §6 *mf* executor

testen [′testən] *tr* test

teuer [′tɔɪ·ər] *adj* dear, expensive; (*Preis*) high

Teu′erung *f* (-;-en) rise in price

Teu′erungswelle *f* rise in prices

Teu′erungszulage *f* cost-of-living increase

Teufel [′tɔɪfəl] *m* (-s;-) devil; **des Teufels sein** be mad; **wer zum T.?** who the devil?

Teufelei [tɔɪfə′laɪ] *f* (-;-en) deviltry

Teufelsbanner [′tɔɪfəlsbanər] *m* (-s;-) exorcist

Teu′felskerl *m* helluva fellow

teuflisch [′tɔɪflɪʃ] *adj* devilish

Teutone [tɔɪ′tonə] *m* (-n;-n) Teuton

teutonisch [tɔɪ′tonɪʃ] *adj* Teutonic

Text [tekst] *m* (-[e]s;-e) text, words; (cin) script; (mus) libretto; (typ) double pica; **aus dem T. kommen**

lose the train of thought; **j-m den T. lesen** give s.o. a lecture

Text'buch *n* (mus) libretto

Texter **-in** ['tekstər(ın)] §6 *mf* ad writer, ad man; (mus) lyricist

Textil- [tekstil] *comb.fm.* textile

Textilien [teks'tiljən] *pl*, **Textil'waren** *pl* textiles

text'lich *adj* textual

Theater [te'atər] *n* (-s;-) theater; **T. machen** (fig) make a fuss; **T. spielen** (fig) make believe, put on

Thea'terbesucher **-in** §6 *mf* theater-goer

Thea'terdichter **-in** §6 *mf* playwright

Thea'terkarte *f* theater ticket

Thea'terkasse *f* box office

Thea'terprobe *f* rehearsal

Thea'terstück *n* play

Thea'terzettel *m* program

theatralisch [te·a'tralıʃ] *adj* theater; (fig) theatrical

Theke ['teka] *f* (-;-n) counter; bar

The·ma ['tema] *n* (-s;-men [mən] & -mata [mata]) theme, subject

Theologe [te·o'logə] *m* (-n;-n) theologian

Theologie [te·olo'gi] *f* (-;) theology

theologisch [te·o'logıʃ] *adj* theological

theoretisch [te·o'retıʃ] *adj* theoretic(al)

Theo·rie [te·o'ri] *f* (-;-rien ['ri·ən]) theory

Thera·pie [tera'pi] *f* (-;-pien ['pi·ən]) therapy

Thermalbad [ter'malbat] *n* thermal bath

Thermometer [termə'metər] *n* thermometer

Thermome'terstand *m* thermometer reading

Thermosflasche ['termosflaʃə] *f* thermos bottle

Thermostat [termo'stat] *m* (-[e]s;-e) & (-en;-en) thermostat

These ['teza] *f* (-;-n) thesis

Thrombose [trɔm'bozə] *f* (-;-n) thrombosis

Thron [tron] *m* (-[e]s;-e) throne

Thron'besteigung *f* accession to the throne

Thron'bewerber *m* pretender to the throne

Thron'folge *f* succession to the throne

Thron'folger *m* successor to the throne

Thron'himmel *m* canopy, baldachin

Thron'räuber *m* usurper

Thunfisch ['tunfıʃ] *m* tuna

Tick [tık] *m* (-[e]s;-s & -e) tic; (fig) eccentricity; **e-n T. auf j-n haben** have a grudge against s.o.; **e-n T. haben** (coll) be balmy

ticken ['tıkən] *intr* tick

ticktack ['tık'tak] *adv* ticktock ‖ **Ticktack** *n* (-s;) ticktock

tief [tif] *adj* deep; profound; (*niedrig*) low; (*Schlag*) sound; (*Farbe*) dark; (*äußerst*) extreme; **aus tiefstem Herzen** from the bottom of one's heart; **im tiefsten Winter** in the dead of winter ‖ *adv* deeply; **zu t. singen** be flat ‖ **Tief** *n* (-[e]s;-e) (meteor) low

Tief'angriff *m* low-level attack

Tief'bau *m* (-[e]s;) underground engineering; underground work

tief'betrübt *adj* deeply grieved

Tief'druckgebiet *n* (meteor) low

Tiefe ['tifə] *f* (-;-n) depth; profundity

Tief'ebene *f* lowlands, plain

teif'empfunden *adj* heartfelt

Tie'fenanzeiger *m* (naut) depth gauge

Tie'fenschärfe *f* (phot) depth of field

Tief'flug *m* low-level flight

Tief'gang *m* (fig) depth; (naut) draft

tief'gekühlt *adj* deep-freeze

tief'greifend *adj* far-reaching; radical; deep-seated

Tief'kühlschrank *m* deep freeze

Tief'land *n* lowlands

tief'liegend *adj* low-lying; deep-seated; (*Augen*) sunken

Tief'punkt *m* (& fig) low point

Tief'schlag *m* (box) low blow

Tiefsee- [tifze] *comb.fm.* deep-sea

tief'sinnig *adj* pensive; melancholy

Tief'stand *m* low level

Tiegel ['tigəl] *m* (-s;-) saucepan; (*zum Schmelzen*) crucible; (typ) platen

Tier [tir] *n* (-[e]s;-e) animal; (& fig) beast; **großes** (or **hohes**) **T.** (coll) big shot, big wheel

Tier'art *f* species (of animal)

Tier'arzt *m* veterinarian

Tier'bändiger **-in** §6 *mf* wild-animal tamer

Tier'garten *m* zoo

Tier'heilkunde *f* veterinary medicine

tierisch ['tirıʃ] *adj* animal (fig) brutish, bestial

Tier'kreis *m* zodiac

Tier'kreiszeichen *n* sign of the zodiac

Tier'quälerei *f* cruelty to animals

Tier'reich *n* animal kingdom

Tier'schutzverein *m* society for the prevention of cruelty to animals

Tier'wärter *m* keeper (*at zoo*)

Tier'welt *f* animal kingdom

Tiger ['tigər] *m* (-s;-) tiger

Tigerin ['tigərın] *f* (-;-nen) tigress

tilgen ['tılgən] *tr* wipe out; (*ausrotten*) eradicate; (*Schuld*) pay off; (*Sünden*) expiate; (*streichen*) delete

Til'gung *f* (-;-en) eradication, extinction; payment; deletion

Til'gungsfonds *m* sinking fund

Tingeltangel ['tıŋəltaŋəl] *m & n* (-s;-) honky-tonk

Tinktur [tıŋk'tur] *f* (-;-en) tincture

Tinte ['tıntə] *f* (-;-n) ink; **in der T. sitzen** (coll) be in a pickle

Tin'tenfaß *n* inkwell

Tin'tenfisch *m* cuttlefish

Tin'tenfleck *m*, **Tin'tenklecks** *m* ink spot

Tin'tenstift *m* indelible pencil

Tip [tıp] *m* (-s;-s) tip, hint

Tippelbruder ['tıpəlbrudər] *m* tramp

tippeln ['tıpəl] *intr* (SEIN) (coll) tramp; (coll) toddle

tippen ['tıpən] *tr* type ‖ *intr* tap; tap; (*wetten*) bet; **an j-n nicht t. können** not be able to come near s.o. (in performance); **daran kannst du nicht t.** that's beyond your reach; **t. auf** (acc) predict ‖ *ref*—**sich an die Stirn t.** tap one's forehead

Tippfehler ['tɪpfelər] *m* typographical error
Tippfräulein ['tɪpfrɔɪlaɪn] *n* (coll) typist
tipptopp ['tɪp'tɔp] *adj* tiptop
Tirol [tɪ'rol] *n* (-s) Tyrol
Tiroler -in [tɪ'rolər(ɪn)] §6 *mf* Tyrolean
tirolerisch [tɪ'rolərɪʃ] *adj* Tyrolean
Tisch [tɪʃ] *m* (-es;-e) table; (*Mahlzeit*) meal, dinner, supper; **bei T.** during the meal; **nach T.** after the meal; **reinen T. machen** make a clean sweep of it; **unter den T. fallen** be ignored; **vom grünen T.** arm-chair; bureaucratic; **vor T.** before the meal; **zu T., bitte!** dinner is ready
Tisch/aufsatz *m* centerpiece
Tisch/besen *m* crumb brush
Tisch/besteck *n* knife, fork, and spoon
Tisch/blatt *n* leaf of a table
Tisch/decke *f* tablecloth
Tisch/gast *m* dinner guest
Tisch/gebet *n*—**T. sprechen** say grace
Tisch/gesellschaft *f* dinner party
Tisch/glocke *f* dinner bell
Tisch/karte *f* name plate
Tisch/lampe *f* table lamp; desk lamp
Tischler ['tɪʃlər] *m* (-s;-) cabinet maker
Tisch/platte *f* table top
Tisch/rede *f* after-dinner speech
Tisch/tennis *n* Ping-Pong
Tisch/tuch *n* tablecloth
Tisch/zeit *f* mealtime, dinner time
Tisch/zeug *n* table linen and tableware
Titan [tɪ'tan] *m* (-en;-en) Titan || *n* (-s) (chem) titanium
titanisch [tɪ'tanɪʃ] *adj* titanic
Titel ['titəl] *m* (-s;-) title; (*Anspruch*) claim; **e-n T. innehaben** (sport) hold a title
Ti/telbild *n* frontispiece; (*e-r Illustrierten*) cover picture
Ti/telblatt *n* title page
Ti/telkampf *m* (box) title bout
Ti/telrolle *f* title role
titulieren [tɪtu'lirən] *tr* title
Toast [tost] *m* (-es;-e & -s) toast
toasten ['tostən] *tr* (*Brot*) toast || *intr* propose a toast, drink a toast; **auf j-n t.** toast s.o.
toben ['tobən] *intr* rage; (*Kinder*) raise a racket || **Toben** *n* (-s) rage, raging; racket; noise
Tob/sucht *f* frenzy, madness
tob/süchtig *adj* raving, mad; frantic
Tochter ['tɔxtər] *f* (-;-) daughter
Toch/terfirma *f*, **Toch/tergesellschaft** *f* (com) subsidiary, affiliate
Tod [tot] *m* (-es;-e) death; (jur) decease; **des Todes sein** be a dead man; **sich** [*dat*] **den Tod holen** catch a death of a cold
tod/ernst/ *adj* dead serious
Todes- [todəs] *comb.fm.* of death; deadly
To/desanzeige *f* obituary
To/desfall *m* death
To/desgefahr *f* mortal danger
To/deskampf *m* death struggle
To/deskandidat *m* one at death's door
To/desstoß *m* coup de grâce

To/desstrafe *f* death penalty; **bei T.** on pain of death
To/destag *m* anniversary of death
To/desursache *f* cause of death
To/desurteil *n* death sentence
Tod/feind -in §8 *mf* mortal enemy
todgeweiht ['totgəvaɪt] *adj* doomed
tödlich ['tøtlɪç] *adj* deadly, fatal
tod/mü/de *adj* dead tired
tod/schick/ *adj* (coll) very chic
tod/si/cher *adj* (coll) dead sure
Tod/sünde *f* mortal sin
Toilette [twa'letə] *f* (-;-n) toilet
Toilet/tentisch *m* dressing table
tolerant [tole'rant] *adj* (gegen) tolerant (toward)
Toleranz [tole'rants] *f* (-;-en) toleration; (mach) tolerance
tolerieren [tole'rirən] *tr* tolerate
toll [tɔl] *adj* mad, crazy; fantastic, terrific; **das wird noch toller kommen** the worst is yet to come; **er ist nicht so t.** (coll) he's not so hot; **es zu t. treiben** carry it a bit too far; **t. nach** crazy about
tollen ['tɔlən] *intr* (HABEN & SEIN) romp about
Toll/haus *n* (fig) bedlam
Toll/heit *f* (-;) madness
Toll/kopf *m* (coll) crackpot
toll/kühn *adj* foolhardy, rash
Toll/wut *f* rabies
Tolpatsch ['tɔlpatʃ] *m* (-es;-e), **Tölpel** ['tœlpəl] *m* (-s;-) (coll) clumsy ox
töl/pelhaft *adj* clumsy
Tomate [to'matə] *f* (-;-n) tomato
Ton [ton] *m* (-[e]s;=e) tone; sound; tint, shade; (*Betonung*) accent, stress; (fig) fashion; **den Ton angeben** (fig) set the tone; (mus) give the keynote; **e-n anderen Ton anschlagen** change one's tune; **große Töne reden** talk big; **guten Ton** (fig) good taste; **hast du Töne!** can you beat that! || *m* (-s;-e) clay
Ton/abnehmer *m* (electron) pickup
ton/angebend *adj* leading
Ton/arm *m* pickup arm
Ton/art *f* type of clay; (mus) key
Ton/atelier *n* (cin) sound studio
Ton/band *n* (-[e]s;=er) (cin) sound track; (electron) tape
Ton/bandgerät *n* tape recorder
tönen ['tønən] *tr* tint, shade || *intr* sound; (*läuten*) ring
tönern ['tønərn] *adj* clay, of clay
Ton/fall *m* intonation, accent
Ton/farbe *f* timbre
Ton/film *m* sound film
Ton/folge *f* melody
Ton/frequenz *f* audio frequency
Ton/geschirr *n* earthenware
Ton/höhe *f*, **Ton/lage** *f* pitch
Ton/leiter *f* (mus) scale
ton/los *adj* voiceless; unstressed
Ton/malerei *f* onomotopoeia
Ton/meister *m* sound engineer
Tonnage [to'naʒə] *f* (-;-n) (naut) tonnage
Tonne ['tɔnə] *f* (-;-n) barrel; ton
Ton/silbe *f* accented syllable
Ton/spur *f* groove (*of record*)
Ton/streifen *m* (cin) sound track

Tonsur [tɔn'zur] f (-;-en) tonsure
Ton'taube f clay pigeon
Ton'taubenschießen n trapshooting
Tö'nung f (-;-en) tint; (phot) tone
Ton'verstärker m amplifier
Ton'waren pl earthenware
Topas [tɔ'pas] m (-es;-e) topaz
Topf [tɔpf] m (-[e]s;̈-e) pot
Topf'blume f potted flower
Töpfer ['tœpfər] m (-s;-) potter
Töpferei [tœpfə'raɪ] f (-;-en) potter's shop
Töp'ferscheibe f potter's wheel
Töp'ferwaren pl pottery
Topf'lappen m potholder
Topf'pflanze f potted plant
Topp [tɔp] m (-s;-e) (naut) masthead
‖ **topp** interj it's a deal
Tor [tor] m (-en;-en) fool ‖ n (-[e]s; -e) gate; gateway; (sport) goal
Torbogen m archway
Torf [tɔrf] m (-[e]s;) peat
Tor'flügel m door (of double door)
Torf'moos n peat moss
Tor'heit f (-;-en) foolishness, folly
Tor'hüter m gatekeeper; (sport) goalie
töricht ['tørɪçt] adj foolish, silly
Törin ['tørɪn] f (-;-nen) fool
torkeln ['tɔrkəln] intr (HABEN & SEIN) (coll) stagger
Tor'latte f (sport) crossbar
Tor'lauf m slalom
Tor'linie f (sport) goal line
Tornister [tɔr'nɪstər] m (-s;-) knapsack; school bag; (mil) field pack
torpedieren [tɔrpe'dirən] tr torpedo
Torpedo [tɔr'pedo] m (-s;-s) torpedo
Tor'pfosten m doorpost; (fb) goal post
Tor'schluß m—kurz vor T. (fig) at the eleventh hour
Torte ['tɔrtə] f (-;-n) cake; pie
Tortur [tɔr'tur] f (-;-en) torture
Tor'wächter m, **Torwart** ['torvart] m (-[e]s;-e) (sport) goalie
Tor'weg m gateway
tosen ['tozən] intr (HABEN & SEIN) rage, roar ‖ **Tosen** n (-s;) rage, roar
tot [tot] adj dead; (Kapital) idle; (Wasser) stagnant; **toter Punkt** dead center; (fig) snag; **totes Rennen** dead heat; **tote Zeit** dead season
total [to'tal] adj total; all-out
totalitär [totalɪ'ter] adj totalitarian
tot'arbeiten ref work oneself to death
Tote ['totə] §5 mf dead person
töten ['tøtən] tr kill; (Nerv) deaden
To'tenacker m churchyard
To'tenbett n deathbed
to'tenblaß adj deathly pale
To'tenblässe f deathly pallor
to'tenbleich adj deathly pale
To'tengräber m gravedigger
To'tengruft f crypt
To'tenhemd n shroud, winding sheet
To'tenklage f lament
To'tenkopf m skull
To'tenkranz m funeral wreath
To'tenmaske f death mask
To'tenmesse f requiem
To'tenreich n (myth) underworld
To'tenschau f coroner's inquest
To'tenschein m death certificate
To'tenstadt f necropolis

To'tenstarre f rigor mortis
To'tenstille f dead silence
To'tenwache f wake
tot'geboren adj stillborn
Tot'geburt f stillbirth
tot'lachen ref die laughing
Toto ['toto] m (-s;-s) football pool
tot'schießen §76 tr shoot dead
Tot'schlag m manslaughter
tot'schlagen §132 tr strike dead; (Zeit) kill
tot'schweigen §148 tr hush up; keep under wraps ‖ intr hush up
tot'stellen ref feign death, play dead
tot'treten §152 tr trample to death
Tö'tung f (-;-en) killing
Tour [tur] f (-;-en) tour; turn; (Umdrehung) revolution; **auf die krumme T.** by hook or by crook; **auf die langsame T.** very leisurely; **auf höchsten Touren** at full speed; (fig) full blast; **auf Touren bringen** (aut) rev up; **auf Touren kommen** pick up speed; (fig) get worked up; **auf Touren sein** (coll) be in good shape
Tou'renzahl f revolutions per minute
Tourismus [tu'rɪsmus] m (-;) tourism
Tourist [tu'rɪst] m (-en;-en) tourist
Touri'stenverkehr m, **Touristik** [tu'rɪstɪk] f (-;) tourism
Touristin [tu'rɪstɪn] f (-;-nen) tourist
Tour-nee [tur'ne] f (-;-neen ['ne-ən]) (mus, theat) tour
Trab [trap] m (-[e]s;) trot; **im T.** at a trot
Trabant [tra'bant] m (-en;-en) satellite
traben ['trabən] intr (HABEN & SEIN) trot
Tra'ber m (-s;-) trotter
Tra'berwagen m sulky
Trab'rennen n harness racing
Tracht [traxt] f (-;-en) costume; (Last) load; (Ertrag) yield
trachten ['traxtən] intr—t. nach strive for; **t. zu** (inf) endeavor to (inf)
trächtig ['trɛçtɪç] adj pregnant
Tradition [tradɪ'tsjon] f (-;-en) tradition
traditionell [tradɪtsjo'nɛl] adj traditional
traf [traf] pret of treffen
Trafik [tra'fɪk] f (-;-en) (Aust) cigar store
träg [trek] adj var of träge
Tragbahre ['trakbarə] f (-;-n) stretcher, litter
Trag'balken ['trakbalkən] m supporting beam; girder; joist
Tragband ['trakbant] n (-[e]s;̈-er) strap; shoulder strap
tragbar ['trakbar] adj portable; (Kleid) wearable; (fig) bearable
Trage ['tragə] f (-;-n) litter
träge ['tregə] adj lazy; slow; inert
tragen ['tragən] §132 tr carry; bear; endure; support; (Kleider) wear, have on; (hervorbringen) produce, yield; (Bedenken) have; (Folgen) take; (Risiko) run; (Zinsen) yield; **bei sich t.** have on one's person; **getragen sein von** be based on; **zur Schau t.** show off ‖ ref dress; sich

gut t. wear well || *intr* (*Stimme*) carry; (*Schußwaffe*) have a range; (*Baum, Feld*) bear, yield; (*Eis*) be thick enough

Träger ['trɛgər] *m* (-s;-) carrier; porter; (*Inhaber*) bearer; shoulder strap; (archit) girder, beam

Trä'gerflugzeug *n* carrier plane

trä'gerlos *adj* strapless

tragfähig ['tra:kfɛ-ɪç] *adj* strong enough, capable of carrying; **tragfähige Grundlage** (fig) sound basis

Trag'fähigkeit *f* (-;-en) capacity, load limit; (naut) tonnage

Tragfläche ['tra:kflɛçə] *f*, **Tragflügel** ['tra:kfly:gəl] *m* airfoil

Träg'heit ['trɛkhaɪt] *f* (-;) laziness; (phys) inertia

Traghimmel ['tra:khɪməl] *m* canopy

Tragik ['tra:gɪk] *f* (-;) tragedy

tragisch ['tra:gɪʃ] *adj* tragic

Tragödie [tra'gø:djə] *f* (-;-n) tragedy

Tragriemen ['tra:kri:mən] *m* strap

Tragsessel ['tra:kzɛsəl] *m* sedan chair

Tragtasche ['tra:ktaʃə] *f* shopping bag

Tragtier ['tra:kti:r] *n* pack animal

Tragweite ['tra:kvaɪtə] *f* range; (*Bedeutung*) significance, moment

Tragwerk ['tra:kvɛrk] *n* (aer) airfoil

Trainer ['trɛnər] *m* (-s;-) coach

trainieren [trɛ'ni:rən] *tr* & *intr* train; coach

Training ['trɛnɪŋ] *n* (-s;) training

Trai'ningsanzug *m* sweat suit

traktieren [trak'ti:rən] *tr* treat; treat roughly

Trak•tor ['traktor] *m* (-s;-toren ['to:rən]) tractor

trällern ['trɛlərn] *tr* & *intr* hum

trampeln ['trampəln] *tr* trample

Tram'pelpfad *m* beaten path

Tran [tra:n] *m* (-[e]s;-e) whale oil; **im T. sein** to be drowsy; be under the influence of alcohol

tranchieren [trã'ʃi:rən] *tr* carve

Träne ['trɛ:nə] *f* (-;-n) tear

tränen ['trɛ:nən] *intr* water

Trä'nengas *n* tear gas

trank [traŋk] *pret* of **trinken** || **Trank** *m* (-[e]s;⁃e) drink, beverage; potion

Tränke ['trɛŋkə] *f* (-;-n) watering hole

tränken ['trɛŋkən] *tr* give (*s.o.*) a drink; (*Tiere*) water; soak

Transfor•mator [transfor'ma:tor] *m* (-s; -matoren [ma'to:rən] transformer

transformieren [transfor'mi:rən] *tr* transform; step up; step down

Transfusion [transfu'zjo:n] *f* (-;-en) transfusion

Tran•sistor [tran'zɪstor] *m* (-s;-sistoren [zɪs'to:rən]) transistor

transitiv [tranzi'ti:f] *adj* transitive

Transmission [transmɪ'sjo:n] *f* (-;-en) transmission

transparent [transpa'rɛnt] *adj* transparent || **Transparent** *n* (-[e]s;-e) transparency; (*Spruchband*) banderol

transpirieren [transpi'ri:rən] *intr* perspire

Transplantation [transplanta'tsjo:n] *f* (-;-en) (surg) transplant

Transport [trans'pɔrt] *m* (-[e]s;-e) transportation

transportabel [transpɔr'ta:bəl] *adj* transportable

Transporter [trans'pɔrtər] *m* (-s;-) troopship; transport plane

transport'fähig *adj* transportable

transportieren [transpɔr'ti:rən] *tr* transport, ship

Transport'unternehmen *n* carrier

Trapez [tra'pe:ts] *n* (-es;-e) trapeze; (geom) trapezoid

trappeln ['trapəln] *intr* (SEIN) clatter; (*Kinder*) patter

Trassant [tra'sant] *m* (-en;-en) (fin) drawer

Trassat [tra'sat] *m* (-en;-en) drawee

trassieren [tra'si:rən] *tr* trace, lay out; **e-n Wechsel t. auf** (*acc*) write out a check to

trat [tra:t] *pret* of **treten**

Tratsch [tra:tʃ] *m* (-es;) gossip

tratschen ['tra:tʃən] *intr* gossip

Tratte ['tratə] *f* (-;-n) (fin) draft

Trau– [trau] *comb.fm.* wedding, marriage

Traube ['traubə] *f* (-;-n) grape; bunch of grapes; (fig) bunch

Trau'bensaft *m* grape juice

Trau'benzucker *m* glucose

trauen ['trau-ən] *tr* (*Brautpaar*) marry; **sich t. lassen** get married || *ref* dare || *intr* (*dat*) trust (in), have confidence (in)

Trauer ['trau-ər] *f* (-;) grief, sorrow; mourning; (*Trauerkleidung*) mourning clothes; **T. anlegen** put on mourning clothes; **T. haben** be in mourning

Trau'eranzeige *f* obituary

Trau'erbotschaft *f* sad news

Trau'erfall *m* death

Trau'erfeier *f* funeral ceremony

Trau'erflor *m* mourning crepe

Trau'ergefolge *n*, **Trau'ergeleit** *n* funeral procession

Trau'ergottesdienst *m* funeral service

Trau'erkloß *m* (coll) sad sack

Trau'ermarsch *m* funeral march

trauern ['trau-ərn] *intr* (um) mourn (for); (um) wear mourning (for)

Trau'erspiel *n* tragedy

Trau'erweide *f* weeping willow

Trau'erzug *m* funeral cortege

Traufe ['traufə] *f* (-;-n) eaves

träufeln ['trɔɪfəln] *tr* & *intr* drip

Trauf'rinne *f* rain gutter

Trauf'röhre *f* rain pipe

traulich ['traulɪç] *adj* intimate; cozy

Traum [traum] *m* (-[e]s;⁃e) dream; (fig) daydream, reverie

Traum'bild *n* vision, phantom

Traum'deuter –in §6 *mf* interpreter of dreams

träumen ['trɔɪmən] *tr* & *intr* dream

Träu'mer *m* (-s;-) dreamer

Träumerei [trɔɪmə'raɪ] *f* (-;-en) dreaming; daydream

Träumerin ['trɔɪmərɪn] *f* (-;-nen) dreamer

träumerisch ['trɔɪmərɪʃ] *adj* dreamy; absent-minded

Traum'gesicht *n* vision, phantom

traum'haft *adj* dream-like

traurig ['traurɪç] *adj* sad

Trau'ring *m* wedding ring (or band)

Trau'schein m marriage certificate
traut [traut] adj dear; cozy; intimate
Trau'ung f (-;-en) marriage ceremony; **kirchliche T.** church wedding; **standesamtliche T.** civil ceremony
Trau'zeuge m best man
Trecker ['trekər] m (-s;-) tractor
Treff [tref] n (-s;-s) (cards) club(s)
treffen ['trefən] §151 tr hit; (begegnen) meet; (betreffen) concern || ref meet; assemble; **sich t. mit** meet with || intr hit home; (box) land, connect || **Treffen** n (-s;-) meeting; (mil) encounter; (sport) meet
tref'fend adj pertinent; to the point; (Ähnlichkeit) striking
Tref'fer m (-s;-) hit; winner; prize
treff'lich adj excellent
Treff'punkt m rendezvous, meeting place
Treib- [traɪp] comb.fm. moving; driving
treiben ['traɪbən] §62 tr drive; propel; chase, expel; (Beruf) pursue; (Blätter, Blüten) put forth; (Geschäft) run, carry on; (Metall) work; (Musik, Sport) go in for; (Sprachen) study; (Pflanzen) force; **es zu weit t.** go too far; **was treibst du denn?** (coll) what are you doing? || intr blossom; sprout; (Teig) ferment || intr (SEIN) drift, float || **Treiben** n (-s) doings, activity; drifting, floating
Treib'haus n hothouse
Treib'holz n driftwood
Treib'kraft f driving force
Treib'mine f floating mine
Treib'rakete f booster rocket
Treib'riemen m drive belt
Treib'sand m drifting sand; quicksand
Treib'stange f connecting rod
Treib'stoff m fuel; propellant
Treib'stoffbehälter m fuel tank
trennbar ['trenbar] adj separable
trennen ['trenən] tr separate; sever; (Naht) undo; (Ehe) dissolve; (elec, telp) cut off || ref part; separate; (Weg) branch off
Tren'nung f (-;-en) separation; parting; dissolution
Tren'nungsstrich m dividing line; hyphen
Trense ['trenzə] f (-;-n) snaffle
Treppe ['trepə] f (-;-n) stairs, stairway; flight of stairs; **die T. hinauffallen** (coll) be kicked upstairs; **zwei Treppen hoch wohnen** live two flights up
Trep'penabsatz m landing
Trep'penflucht f flight of stairs
Trep'pengeländer n banister
Trep'penhaus n staircase
Trep'penläufer m stair carpet
Trep'penstufe f step, stair
Tresor [tre'zor] m (-s;-e) safe; vault
Tresse ['tresə] f (-;-n) (mil) stripe
treten ['tretən] §152 tr tread; tread on; trample; (Fußhebel) work; (Orgel) pump; **mit Füßen t.** (fig) trample under foot || intr (SEIN) step, walk; tread; **an j-s Stelle t.** succeed s.o.; **auf der Stelle t.** (mil) mark time; **in**

Kraft t. go into effect; **j-m zu nahe t.** offend s.o.; **t. in** (acc) enter (into)
Tretmühle ['tretmylə] f treadmill
treu [trɔɪ] adj loyal, faithful, true
Treu'bruch m breach of faith
Treue ['trɔɪ·ə] f (-;) loyalty, fidelity; allegiance; **j—m die T. halten** remain loyal to s.o.
Treu'eid m oath of allegiance
Treu'hand f (jur) trust
Treuhänder –in ['trɔɪhendər(ɪn)] §6 mf trustee
Treu'handfonds m trust fund
treu'herzig adj trusting; sincere
treu'los adj unfaithful; (gegen) disloyal (to)
Tribüne [trɪ'bynə] f (-;-n) rostrum; (mil) reviewing stand; (sport) grandstand
Tribut [trɪ'but] m (-[e]s;-e) tribute
Trichter ['trɪçtər] m (-s;-) funnel; (Bomben-) crater, pothole; (mus) bell (of wind instrument); **auf den T. kommen** (coll) catch on
Trick [trɪk] m (-s;-s & -e) trick
Trick'film m animated cartoon
trieb [trip] pret of **treiben** || **Trieb** m (-[e]s;-e) sprout, shoot; urge, drive; instinct
Trieb'feder f (horol) mainspring
Trieb'kraft f motive power
trieb'mäßig adj instinctive
Trieb'werk n motor, engine
triefäugig ['trifɔɪgɪç] adj bleary-eyed
triefen ['trifən] §153 intr drip; (Augen) water; (Nase) run
triezen ['tritsən] tr (coll) tease
Trift [trɪft] f (-;-en) pasture land; cattle track; log-running
triftig ['trɪftɪç] adj cogent; valid
Trigonometrie [trɪgɔnome'tri] f (-;) trigonometry
Trikot [trɪ'ko] m & n (-s;-s) knitted cloth; (sport) trunks, tights
Triller ['trɪlər] m (-s;-) trill; (mus) quaver
trillern ['trɪlərn] intr trill; (Vogel) warble
Tril'lerpfeife f whistle
Trink- [trɪŋk] comb.fm. drinking
trinkbar ['trɪŋkbar] adj drinkable
Trink'becher m drinking cup
trinken ['trɪŋkən] §143 tr & intr drink
Trin'ker –in §6 mf drinker
trink'fest adj able to hold one's liquor
Trink'gelage n drinking party
Trink'geld n tip, gratuity
Trink'glas n drinking glass
Trink'halm m straw
Trink'spruch m toast
Trink'wasser n drinking water
Trio ['tri·o] n (-s;-s) trio
trippeln ['trɪpəln] intr (SEIN) patter
Tripper ['trɪpər] m (-s;) gonorrhea
trist [trɪst] adj dreary
tritt [trɪt] pret of **treten** || m (-[e]s; -e) step; kick; pace; footstep; footprint; small stepladder; pedal; **j—m e–n T. versetzen** give s.o. a kick
Tritt'brett n running board
Tritt'leiter f stepladder
Triumph [trɪ'umf] m (-[e]s;-e) triumph

Triumph′bogen *m* triumphal arch
triumphieren [trɪ·um′fi:rən] *intr* triumph
Triumph′zug *m* triumphal procession
trocken [′trɔkən] *adj* dry; arid; **trokkenes Brot** plain bread
Trockenbagger (Trok′kenbagger) *m* (mach) excavator
Trockendock (Trok′kendock) *n* drydock
Trockenei (Trok′kenei) *n* dehydrated eggs
Trockeneis (Trok′keneis) *n* dry ice
Trockenhaube (Trok′kenhaube) *f* hair drier
Trockenheit (Trok′kenheit) *f* (-;) dryness, aridity
trockenlegen (trok′kenlegen) *tr* (*Sumpf*) drain; (*Säugling*) change (the diapers of)
Trockenmaß (Trok′kenmaß) *n* dry measure
Trockenmilch (Trok′kenmilch) *f* powdered milk
Trockenschleuder (Trok′kenschleuder) *f* spin-drier, clothes drier
Trockenübung (Trok′kenübung) *f* dry run
trocknen [′trɔknən] *tr* dry || *intr* (SEIN) dry, dry up
Troddel [′trɔdəl] *f* (-;-n) tassel
Trödel [′trø:dəl] *m* (-s;) secondhand goods; old clothes; junk; (fig) nuisance, waste of time
Trö′delkram *m* junk
trödeln [′trø:dəln] *intr* waste time
Tröd′ler –in §6 *mf* secondhand dealer
troff [trɔf] *pret* of **triefen**
trog [tro:k] *pret* of **trügen** **Trog** *m* (-[e]s;̈e) trough
Trommel [′trɔməl] *f* (-;-n) drum
Trom′melfell *n* drumhead; (anat) eardrum
trommeln [′trɔməln] *tr & intr* drum
Trom′melschlag *m* drumbeat
Trom′melschlegel *m*, **Trom′melstock** *m* drumstick
Trom′melwirbel *m* drum roll
Trommler [′trɔmlər] *m* (-s;-) drummer
Trompete [trɔm′pe:tə] *f* (-;-n) trumpet
trompeten [trɔm′pe:tən] *intr* blow the trumpet; (*Elefant*) trumpet
Trompe′ter –in §6 *mf* trumpeter
Tropen [′tro:pən] *pl* tropics
Tropf [trɔpf] *m* (-[e]s;̈e) simpleton; **armer T.** poor devil
tröpfeln [′trœpfəln] *tr & intr* drip || *intr* (SEIN) trickle || *impers*—**es tröpfelt** it is sprinkling
tropfen [′trɔpfən] *tr & intr* drip || *intr* (SEIN) trickle || **Tropfen** *m* (-s;-) drop; **ein T. auf den heißen Stein** a drop in the bucket
trop′fenweise *adv* drop by drop
Trophäe [tro′fɛ:ə] *f* (-;-n) trophy
tropisch [′tro:pɪʃ] *adj* tropical
Troß [trɔs] *m* (Trosses; Trosse) (coll) load, baggage; (coll) hangers-on
Trosse [′trɔsə] *f* (-;-n) cable; (naut) hawser
Trost [tro:st] *m* (-es;) consolation, comfort; **geringer T.** cold comfort;

wohl nicht bei T. sein not be all there
trösten [′trø:stən] *tr* console, comfort || *ref* cheer up; feel consoled
tröstlich [′trø:stlɪç] *adj* comforting
trost′los *adj* disconsolate; bleak
Trost′preis *m* consolation prize
trost′reich *adj* comforting
Trö′stung *f* (-;-en) consolation
Trott [trɔt] *m* (-[e]s;-e) trot; (coll) routine
Trottel [′trɔtəl] *m* (-s;-) (coll) dope
trotten [′trɔtən] *intr* (SEIN) trot
Trottoir [trɔ′twa:r] *n* (-s;-e & -s) sidewalk
trotz [trɔts] *prep* (*genit*) in spite of; **t. alledem** for all that || **Trotz** *m* (-es;) defiance; **j-m T. bieten** defy s.o.
trotz′dem *adv* nevertheless || *conj* although
trotzen [′trɔtsən] *intr* be stubborn; (*schmollen*) sulk; (*dat*) defy
trotzig [′trɔtsɪç] *adj* defiant; sulky; obstinate
Trotz′kopf *m* defiant child (or adult)
trüb [try:p], **trübe** [′try:bə] *adj* turbid, muddy; (*Wetter*) dreary; (*glanzlos*) dull; (*Erfahrung*) sad
Trubel [′tru:bəl] *m* (-s;) bustle
trüben [′try:bən] *tr* make turbid, muddy; dim; disturb, trouble (*Freude, Stimmung*) spoil || *ref* grow cloudy; become muddy; become strained
Trübsal [′try:pza:l] *f* (-;-en) distress, misery; **T. blasen** be in the dumps
trüb′selig *adj* gloomy, sad
Trüb′sinn *m* (-[e]s;) gloom
trüb′sinnig *adj* gloomy
Trü′bung *f* (-;) muddiness; blurring
trudeln [′tru:dəln] *intr* go into a spin || **Trudeln** *n* (-s;) spin; **ins T. kommen** (aer) go into a spin
trug [tru:k] *pret* of **tragen** || **Trug** *m* (-[e]s;) deceit; fraud; delusion
Trug′bild *n* phantom; illusion
trügen [′try:gən] §111 *tr & intr* deceive
trügerisch [′try:gərɪʃ] *adj* deceptive, illusory; (*verräterisch*) treacherous
Trug′schluß *m* fallacy
Truhe [′tru:ə] *f* (-;-n) trunk, chest
Trulle [′trulə] *f* (-;-n) slut
Trümmer [′trymər] *pl* ruins; rubble
Trumpf [trumpf] *m* (-[e]s;̈e) trump
Trunk [truŋk] *m* (-[e]s;̈e) drinking; **im T.** when drunk
trunken [′truŋkən] *adj* drunk; **t. vor** (*dat*) elated with
Trunkenbold [′truŋkənbɔlt] *m* (-[e]s;-e) drunkard
Trun′kenheit *f* (-;) drunkenness; **T. am Steuer** (jur) drunken driving
trunk′süchtig *adj* alcoholic || **Trunksüchtige** §5 *mf* alcoholic
Trupp [trup] *m* (-s;-s) troop, gang; (mil) detail, detachment
Truppe [′trupə] *f* (-;-n) (mil) troop; (theat) troupe; **Truppen** (mil) troops
Trup′peneinheit *f* unit
Trup′penersatz *m* reserves
Trup′pengattung *f* branch of service
Trup′penschau *f* (mil) review, parade

Trup'pentransporter *m* (aer) troop carrier; (nav) troopship
Trüp'penübung *f* field exercise
Trup'penverband *m* unit; task force
Trup'penverbandplatz *m* (mil) first-aid station
Trust [trʊst] *m* (-[e]s;-e & -s) (com) trust
Truthahn ['truthɑn] *m* turkey (cock)
Truthenne ['truthenə] *f* turkey (hen)
trutzig ['trʊtsɪç] *adj* defiant
Tscheche ['tʃɛçə] *m* (-n;-n), **Tschechin** ['tʃɛçɪn] *f* (-;-nen) Czech
tschechisch ['tʃɛçɪʃ] *adj* Czech
Tschechoslowakei [tʃɛçoslova'kaɪ] *f* (-;)—**die T.** Czechoslovakia
Tube ['tubə] *f* (-;-n) tube; **auf die T. drücken** (aut) step on it
Tuberkulose [tubɛrku'lozə] *f* (-;) tuberculosis
Tuch [tux] *n* (-[e]s;-e) cloth; fabric ‖ *n* (-[e]s;̈er) kerchief; shawl; scarf
tuchen ['tuxən] *adj* cloth, fabric
Tuch'fühlung *f*—**T. haben mit** (mil) stand shoulder to shoulder with; **T. halten mit** keep in close touch with
Tuch'seite *f* right side (*of cloth*)
tüchtig ['tʏçtɪç] *adj* able, capable, efficient; sound, thorough; excellent; good; (*Trinker*) hard; **t. in** (*dat*) good at; **t. zu** qualified for ‖ *adv* very much; hard; soundly, thoroughly; (sl) awfully
Tüch'tigkeit *f* (-;) ability, efficiency; soundness, thoroughness; excellency
Tuch'waren *pl* dry goods
Tücke ['tʏkə] *f* (-;-n) malice; **mit List und T.** by cleverness
tückisch ['tʏkɪʃ] *adj* insidious
tüfteln ['tʏftəln] *intr*—**t. an** (*dat*) (coll) puzzle over
Tugend ['tugənt] *f* (-;-en) virtue
Tugendbold ['tugəntbɔlt] *m* (-[e]s;-e) (pej) paragon of virtue
tu'gendhaft *adj* virtuous
Tulpe ['tʊlpə] *f* (-;-n) tulip
tummeln ['tʊməln] *tr* (*Pferd*) exercise ‖ *ref* hurry; (*Kinder*) romp about
Tum'melplatz *m* playground; (fig) arena
Tümmler ['tʏmlər] *m* (-s;-) dolphin; (*Taube*) tumbler
Tumor ['tumɔr] *m* (-s; Tumoren [tʊ'morən]) tumor
Tümpel ['tʏmpəl] *m* (-s;-) pond
Tumult [tʊ'mʊlt] *m* (-[e]s;-e) uproar; uprising
tun [tun] §154 *tr* do; make; take; **dazu tun** add to it; **e-n Zug tun** take a swig; **es zu tun bekommen mit** have trouble with; **j-n in ein Internat tun** send s.o. to a boarding school ‖ *intr* do; be busy; **alle Hände voll zu tun haben** have one's hands full; **es ist mir darum zu tun** I am anxious about it; **groß tun** talk big; **mir ist sehr darum zu tun zu** (*inf*) it is very important for me to (*inf*); **tun so** pretend that; **spröde tun** be prudish; **stolz tun** be proud; **weh tun** hurt; **zu t. haben** be busy; have one's work cut out; **zu tun haben mit** have trouble with ‖ *impers*—**es tut mir**

leid I am sorry; **es tut nichts** it doesn't matter ‖ **Tun** *n* (-s;) doings; action; **Tun und Treiben** doings
Tünche ['tʏnçə] *f* (-;-n) whitewash
tünchen ['tʏnçən] *tr* whitewash
Tunichtgut ['tunɪçtgut] *m* (- & -[e]s; -e) good-for-nothing
Tunke ['tʊŋkə] *f* (-;-n) sauce; gravy
tunken ['tʊŋkən] *tr* dip, dunk
tunlichst ['tunlɪçst] *adv*—**das wirst du t. bleiben lassen** you had better leave it alone
Tunnel ['tʊnəl] *m* (-s;- & -s) tunnel
Tüpfchen ['tʏpfçən] *n* (-s;-) dot
Tüpfel ['tʏpfəl] *m* & *n* (-s;-) dot
tüpfen ['tʏpfən] *tr* dab; dot ‖ **Tupfen** *m* (-s;-) dot, spot
Tür [tyr] *f* (-;-en) door
Tür'angel *f* door hinge
Tür'anschlag *m* doorstop
Turbine [tur'binə] *f* (-;-n) turbine
Turboprop ['turbɔprɔp] *m* (-s;-s) turboprop
Tür'drücker *m* latch
Tür'flügel *m* door (*of double door*)
Tür'griff *m* door handle; door knob
Türke ['tʏrkə] *m* (-n;-n) Turk
Türkei [tʏr'kaɪ] *f* (-;)—**die T.** Turkey
Türkin ['tʏrkɪn] *f* (-;-nen) Turk
Türkis [tʏr'kis] *m* (-es;-e) turquoise
türkisch ['tʏrkɪʃ] *adj* Turkish
türkisen [tʏr'kizən] *adj* turquoise
Tür'klingel *f* doorbell
Tür'klinke *f* door handle
Turm [tʊrm] *m* (-[e]s;̈e) tower; steeple; turret; (chess) castle
Türmchen ['tʏrmçən] *n* (-s;-) turret
türmen ['tʏrmən] *tr* & *ref* pile up ‖ *intr* (SEIN) run away, bolt
turm'hoch *adj* towering ‖ *adv* (by) far
Turm'spitze *f* spire
Turm'springen *n* high diving
Turn- [tʊrn] *comb.fm.* gymnastic, gym, athletic
turnen ['tʊrnən] *intr* do exercises ‖ **Turnen** *n* (-s;) gymnastics
Tur'ner **-in** §6 *mf* gymnast
turnerisch ['tʊrnərɪʃ] *adj* gymnastic
Turn'gerät *n* gymnastic apparatus
Turn'halle *f* gymnasium, gym
Turn'hemd *n* gym shirt
Turn'hose *f* trunks
Turnier [tʊr'nir] *n* (-s;-e) tournament
Turn'schuhe *pl* sneakers
Tür'pfosten *m* doorpost
Tür'rahmen *m* doorframe
Tür'schild *n* doorplate
Tür'schwelle *f* threshold
Tusche ['tuʃə] *f* (-;-n) (paint) wash; **chinesische T.** India ink
tuscheln ['tuʃəln] *intr* whisper
Tute ['tutə] *f* (-;-n) (aut) horn
Tüte ['tytə] *f* (-;-n) paper bag; paper cone; ice cream cone
tuten ['tutən] *intr* blow the horn; (coll) blare away
Twen [tvɛn] *m* (-s;-s) young man (*in his twenties*)
Typ [typ] *m* (-s;-en) type; (*Bauart*) model
Type ['typə] *f* (-;-n) type; (coll) strange character
Ty'pennummer *f* model number

Typhus ['tyfus] *m* (-;) typhoid
typisch ['typɪʃ] *adj* (für) typical (of)
Tyrann [tʏ'ran] *m* (-en;-en) tyrant
Tyrannei [tʏra'naɪ] *f* (-;-en) tyranny

tyrannisch [tʏ'ranɪʃ] *adj* tyrannical
   —sich ü. overwork oneself
tyrannisieren [tʏranɪ'zirən] *tr* tyrannize, oppress
Tz ['tetset] *n*—bis ins **Tz** thoroughly

U

U, u [u] *invar n* U, u
u.A.w.g. *abbr* (**um Antwort wird gebeten**) R.S.V.P.
U-Bahn ['uban] *f* (**Untergrundbahn**)
subway
übel ['ybəl] *adj* evil; (*schlecht*) bad;
(*unwohl*) queasy, sick; (*Geruch,
usw.*) nasty, foul; **er ist ein übler
Geselle** he's a bad egg; **mir ist ü.**
I feel sick; **ü. daran sein** have it
rough ‖ *adv* badly; **est steht ü. mit
things** don't look good for; **ü. auslegen** misconstrue; **ü. deuten** misinterpret; **ü. ergehen** fare badly; **ü.
gelaunt in bad humor** ‖ **Übel** *n*
(-s;-) evil; ailment
ü'belgelaunt *adj* ill-humored
ü'belgesinnt *adj* evil-minded
Ü'belkeit *f* (-;) nausea
ü'belnehmen §116 *tr* take amiss; take
offense at, resent
ü'belnehmend *adj* resentful
ü'belriechend *adj* foul-smelling
Ü'belstand *m* evil; bad state of affairs
Ü'beltat *f* misdeed, crime, offense
Ü'beltäter –in §6 *mf* wrongdoer; criminal
ü'belwollen §162 *intr* (*dat*) be ill-disposed towards ‖ **Übelwollen** *n* (-s;)
ill will, malevolence
ü'belwollend *adj* malevolent
üben ['ybən] *tr* practice, exercise;
(*e-e Kunst*) cultivate; (*Handwerk*)
pursue; (*Gewalt*) use; (*Verrat*) commit; (*mil*) drill; (*sport*) train; **Barmherzigkeit ü. an** (*dat*) have mercy on;
Gerechtigkeit ü. gegen be fair to;
Nachsicht ü. gegen be lenient towards; **Rache ü. an** (*dat*) take revenge on ‖ *ref*—sich im Schifahren
ü. practice skiing
über ['ybər] *adv*—j–m ü. sein in (*dat*)
be superior to s.o. in; **ü. und ü.**
over and over ‖ *prep* (*dat*) over;
above, on top of ‖ *prep* (*acc*) by way
of, via; (*bei, während*) during; (*nach*)
past; over; across; (*betreffend*)
about, concerning; **Briefe ü. Briefe**
letter after letter; **ein Scheck ü.
10 DM** a check for 10 marks; **es geht
nichts ü.** there is nothing better than;
heute übers Jahr a year from today;
ü. Gebühr more than was due; **ü.
kurz oder lang** sooner or later; **ü.
Land** crosscountry
überall' *adv* everywhere, all over
überall'her' *adv* from all sides
überall'hin' *adv* in every direction
Ü'berangebot *n* over-supply
überan'strengen *tr* overexert, strain ‖
ref overexert oneself, strain oneself

überar'beiten *tr* revise, touch up ‖ *ref*
Überar'beitung *f* (-;-en) revision,
touching up; revised text
ü'beraus *adv* extremely, very
überbacken (überbak'ken) §50 *tr* bake
lightly
Ü'berbau *m* (-[e]s; -e & -ten [tən])
superstructure
ü'berbeanspruchen *tr* overwork
ü'berbelasten *tr* overload
ü'berbelegt *adj* overcrowded
ü'berbelichten *tr* (phot) overexpose
ü'berbetonen *tr* overemphasize
überbie'ten §58 *tr* outbid; (fig) outdo
Ü'berbleibsel ['ybərblaɪpsəl] *n* (-s;-)
remains; leftovers
überblei'dung *f* (cin) dissolve
Ü'berblick *m* survey; (fig) synopsis
überblicken (überblik'ken) *tr* survey
überbrin'gen §65 *tr* deliver; convey
Überbrin'ger –in §6 *mf* bearer
überbrücken (überbrük'ken) *tr* (& fig)
bridge
Überbrückung (Überbrük'kung) *f* (-;
-en) bridging; (rr) overpass
Überbrückungs– *comb.fm.* emergency,
stop-gap
überdachen ['ybər'daxən] *tr* roof over
überdau'ern *tr* outlast
überdecken (überdek'ken) *tr* cover
überden'ken §66 *tr* think over
überdies' *adv* moreover, besides
überdre'hen *tr* (Uhr) overwind
Ü'berdruck *m* excess pressure
Ü'berdruckanzug *m* space suit
Ü'berdruckkabine *f* pressurized cabin
Über'druß ['ybərdrus] *m* (-drusses;)
boredom; (*Übersättigung*) satiety;
(*Ekel*) disgust; **bis zum Ü. ad nau-
seam**
überdrüssig ['ybərdrʏsɪç] *adj* (*genit*)
sick of, disgusted with
ü'berdurchschnittlich *adj* above the
average
Ü'bereifer *m* excessive zeal
ü'bereifrig *adj* overzealous
überei'len *tr* precipitate; rush ‖ *ref*
be in too big a hurry; act rashly
übereilt [ybər'aɪlt] *adj* hasty, rash
übereinan'der *adv* one on top of the
other
übereinan'derschlagen §132 *tr* cross
überein'kommen §99 *intr* (SEIN) come
to an agreement ‖ **Übereinkommen**
n (-s;-) agreement
Überein'kunft *f* agreement
überein'stimmen *intr* be in agreement;
concur; (*Farben, usw.*) harmonize
Überein'stimmung *f* agreement; accord; (*Gleichförmigkeit*) conformity;

(Einklang) harmony; **in Ü. mit** in line with

ü′berempfindlich *adj* oversensitive

überfah′ren §71 *tr* run over, run down; *(Fluß, usw.)* cross; **ein Signal ü.** go through a traffic light; **ü. werden** (coll) be taken in || **ü′berfahren** §71 *tr (über e-n Fluß, usw.)* take across || *intr* (SEIN) drive over, cross

Ü′berfahrt *f* crossing

Ü′berfall *m* surprise attack, assault; *(Raubüberfall)* holdup; *(Einfall)* raid

überfal′len §72 *tr (räuberisch)* hold up; assault; (mil) surprise; (mil) invade, raid; **ü. werden** be overcome *(by sleep)*; be seized *(with fear)*

ü′berfällig *adj* overdue

Ü′berfallkommando *n* riot squad

überflie′gen §57 *tr* fly over; *(Buch)* skim through

ü′berfließen §76 *intr* (SEIN) overflow

überflü′geln [ybər′flygəln] *tr* outflank; (fig) outstrip

Ü′berfluß *m* abundance; excess; **im Ü. vorhanden sein** be plentiful

ü′berflüssig *adj* superfluous

überflu′ten *tr* overflow, flood, swamp || **ü′berfluten** *intr* (SEIN) overflow

überfor′dern *tr* demand too much of; overwork

Ü′berfracht *f* excess luggage

überfüh′ren *tr* carry across; *(Leiche)* transport in state || **überführ′ren** *tr (genit)* convince of; *(genit)* convict of

Überfüh′rung *f* (–;–en) overpass; *(e-s Verbrechers)* conviction

Ü′berfülle *f* superabundance

überfül′len *tr* stuff, jam, pack

Ü′bergabe *f* delivery; *(& mil)* surrender

Ü′bergang *m* passage; crossing; transition; (jur) transfer; (mil) desertion; (paint) blending; (rr) crossing

Ü′bergangshilfe *f* severance pay

Ü′bergangsstadium *n* transition stage

Ü′bergangszeit *f* transitional period

überge′ben §80 *tr* hand over; give up; *(einreichen)* submit; (& mil) surrender; **dem Verkehr ü.** open to traffic || *ref* vomit, throw up

überge′hen §82 *tr* omit; overlook; **mit Stillschweigen ü.** pass over in silence || **ü′bergehen** §82 *intr* (SEIN) go over, cross; *(sich verändern)* (in acc) change (into); **auf j-n ü.** devolve upon s.o.; **in andere Hände ü.** change hands; **in Fäulnis ü.** become rotten

Ü′bergewicht *n* overweight; (fig) preponderance; **das Ü. bekommen** become top-heavy; (fig) get the upper hand

ü′bergießen §76 *tr* spill || **übergie′ßen** §76 *tr* pour over, pour on; *(Braten)* baste; **mit Zuckerguß ü.** (culin) ice

übergrei′fen §88 *intr* (auf acc) spread (to); (auf acc) encroach (on)

Ü′bergriff *m* encroachment

ü′bergroß *adj* huge, colossal; oversize

ü′berhaben §89 *tr* have left; *(Kleider)* have on; (fig) be fed up with

überhand′nehmen §116 *intr* get the upper hand; run riot

ü′berhängen §92 *tr (Mantel)* put on;

(Gewehr) sling over the shoulders || *intr* overhang, project

überhäu′fen *tr* overwhelm, swamp

überhaupt′ *adv* really; anyhow; *(besonders)* especially; *(überdies)* besides; at all; **ü. kein** no...whatever; **ü. nicht** not at all; **wenn ü.** if...at all; if...really

überheb′lich [ybər′heplɪç] *adj* arrogant

überhei′zen, überzhit′zen *tr* overheat

überhö′hen [ybər′hø·ən] *tr (Kurve)* bank; *(Preise)* raise too high

ü′berholen *tr* take across; **die Segel ü.** shift sails || *intr* (naut) heel || **überho′len** *tr* outdistance, outrun; *(ausbessern)* overhaul; *(Fahrzeug)* pass; (fig) outstrip

überholt [ybər′holt] *adj* obsolete, out of date; *(repariert)* reconditioned

überhö′ren *tr* not hear, miss; ignore; misunderstand

ü′berirdisch *adj* supernatural

überkandidelt [′ybərkandidəlt] *adj* (coll) nutty, wacky

ü′berkippen *intr* (SEIN) tilt over

überkle′ben *tr* paper over; **ü. mit** cover with

Ü′berkleid *n* outer garment; overalls

ü′berklug *adj* (pej) wise, smart

ü′berkochen *intr* (SEIN) boil over

überkom′men *adj* traditional || §99 *tr* overcome || *intr* (SEIN) be handed down to

überla′den *adj* overdone || §103 *tr* overload

Ü′berlandbahn *f* interurban trolley line

Ü′berlandleitung *f* (elec) high-tension line; (telp) long-distance line

überlas′sen §104 *tr* yield, leave, relinquish; entrust; (com) sell; **das bleibt ihm ü.** he is free to do as he pleases || *ref (dat)* give way to

Ü′berlast *f* overload; overweight

überla′sten *tr* overload

überlau′fen *adj* overcrowded; (fig) swamped || §105 *tr* overrun; *(belästigen)* pester; **Angst überlief ihn** fear came over him || **ü′berlaufen** §105 *intr* (SEIN) run over, overflow; boil over; (fig & mil) desert; **die Galle läuft mir über** (fig) my blood boils || *impers*—**mich überläuft es kalt** I shudder

Ü′berläufer -in §6 *mf* (mil) deserter; (pol) turncoat

ü′berlaut *adj* too noisy

überle′ben *tr* outlive, survive || *ref* go out of style

überle′bend *adj* surviving || **Überlebende** §5 *mf* survivor

ü′berlebensgroß *adj* bigger than life

überlebt [ybər′lept] *adj* antiquated

überle′gen *adj (dat)* superior (to); (an *dat*) superior (in) || *tr* consider, think over || *ref—sich [dat]* anders **ü.** change one's mind; **sich [dat] ü.** consider, think over || *intr* think it over || **ü′berlegen** *tr* lay across; *(Mantel)* put on

Überle′genheit *f* (–;) superiority

überlegt′ *adj* well considered; (jur) willful

Überle'gung f (-;-en) consideration

überle'sen §107 tr read over, peruse

überlie'fern tr deliver; hand down, transmit; (mil) surrender

Überlie'ferung f (-;-en) delivery; (fig) tradition; (mil) surrender

überli'sten tr outwit, outsmart

überma'chen tr bequeath

Ü'bermacht f superiority; (fig) predominance

ü'bermächtig adj overwhelming; predominant

überma'len tr paint over

übermannen [ybər'manən] tr overpower

Ü'bermaß n excess; **bis zum Ü.** to excess

ü'bermäßig adj excessive || adv excessively; overly

Ü'bermensch m superman

ü'bermenschlich adj superhuman

übermitteln [ybər'mɪtəln] tr transmit, convey, forward

Übermitt'lung f (-;-en) transmission, conveyance, forwarding

ü'bermorgen adv the day after tomorrow

übermüdet [ybər'mydət] adj overtired

Ü'bermut m exuberance, mischievousness

ü'bermütig adj exuberant; haughty

ü'bernächste §9 adj next but one; **am übernächsten Tag** the day after tomorrow; **ü. Woche** week after next

übernach'ten intr spend the night

Übernach'tung f (-;-en) accommodations for the night; spending the night

Ü'bernahme f taking over, takeover

ü'bernatürlich adj supernatural

überneh'men §116 tr take over; assume; undertake; take upon oneself; accept, receive || **ü'bernehmen** §116 tr (Mantel, Schal) put on; (Gewehr) shoulder || **überneh'men** §116 ref overreach oneself; **sich beim Essen ü.** overeat

ü'berordnen tr place over, set over

ü'berparteilich adj nonpartisan

Ü'berproduktion f overproduction

überprü'fen tr examine again, check; verify; (Personen) screen

Überprü'fung f (-;-en) checking; checkup

ü'berquellen §119 intr (SEIN) (Teig) run over; **überquellende Freude** irrepressible joy

überqueren [ybər'kveran] tr cross

überra'gen tr tower over; (fig) surpass

überra'schen tr surprise

Überra'schung f (-;-en) surprise

überrech'nen tr count over

überre'den tr persuade; **j-n zu etw ü.** talk a person into s.th.

Überre'dung f (-;) persuasion

ü'berreich adj (an dat) abounding (in) || adv—**ü. ausgestattet** well equipped

überrei'chen tr hand over, present

ü'berreichlich adj superabundant

ü'berreif adj overripe

überrei'zen tr overexcite; (Augen, Nerven) strain

überreizt' adj overwrought

überren'nen §97 tr overrun; (fig) overwhelm

Ü'berrest m rest, remainder; **irdische Überreste** mortal remains

Ü'berrock m topcoat, overcoat

überrum'peln tr take by surprise

Überrum'pelung f (-;-en) surprise

überrun'den tr (sport) lap

übersät [ybər'zet] adj (fig) strewn, dotted

übersät'tigen tr stuff; cloy; (chem) saturate, supersaturate

Übersät'tigung f (chem) supersaturation

Überschall—comb.fm. supersonic

überschat'ten tr overshadow

überschät'zen tr overestimate

Ü'berschau f survey

überschau'en tr look over, survey; overlook (a scene)

überschla'fen §131 tr (fig) sleep on

Ü'berschlag m rough estimate; (aer) loop; (gym) somersault

überschla'gen adj lukewarm || §132 tr skip, omit; estimate roughly; consider || ref go head over heels; do a somersault; (Auto) overturn; (Boot) capsize; (Flugzeug) do a loop; (beim Landen) nose over; (Stimme) break; (fig) (vor dat) outdo oneself (in) || **ü'berschlagen** §132 tr (Beine) cross; flip over; **ü. in** (acc) (fig) change suddenly to

ü'berschnappen intr (SEIN) (Stimme) squeak; (coll) flip one's lid

überschnei'den §106 ref (Linien) intersect; (& fig) overlap

überschrei'ben §62 tr sign over

überschrei'en §135 tr shout down || ref strain one's voice

überschrei'ten §86 tr cross, step over; (Kredit) overdraw; (Gesetz) violate, transgress; (fig) exceed, overstep

Ü'berschrift f heading, title

Ü'berschuh m overshoe

Ü'berschuß m surplus, excess; profit

ü'berschüssig adj surplus, excess

überschüt'ten tr shower; (& fig) overwhelm, flood

Ü'berschwang m (-[e]s;) rapture

überschwem'men tr flood, inundate

Überschwem'mung f (-;-en) flood, inundation

überschwenglich ['ybər∫vɛnlɪç] adj effusive, gushing

Ü'bersee f (-;) overseas

Ü'berseedampfer m ocean liner

Ü'berseehandel m overseas trade

übersehbar [ybər'zebar] adj visible at a glance

überse'hen §138 tr survey, look over; (nicht bemerken) overlook; (absichtlich) ignore; (erkennen) realize

übersen'den §140 tr send, forward; transmit; (Geld) remit

Übersen'dung f (-;-en) forwarding; transmission; consignment

übersetzen tr ferry across || **übersetz'en** tr translate

Überset'zung f (-;-en) translation; (mach) gear, transmission

Ü'bersicht f survey, review; (Abriß) abstract; (Zusammenfassung) sum-

mary; (*Umriß*) outline; (*Ausblick*) perspective; **jede Ü. verlieren** lose all perspective
ü′bersichtlich *adj* clear; (*Gelände*) open
Ü′bersichtsplan *m* general plan
ü′bersiedeln *intr* (SEIN) move; emigrate
ü′bersinnlich *adj* transcendental
überspan′nen *tr* span; cover; overstrain; (fig) exaggerate
überspannt [ybər′/pant] *adj* eccentric; extravagant
Überspannt′heit *f* (-;-en) eccentricity
Überspan′nung *f* (-;-en) overstraining; (fig) exaggeration; (elec) excess voltage
überspie′len *tr* outplay; outwit; (*Tonbandaufnahme*) transcribe; (*Schüchternheit*) hide
überspitzt [ybər′/pɪtst] *adj* oversubtle
übersprin′gen §142 *tr* jump; (*auslassen*) omit, skip || **ü′berspringen** §142 *intr* (SEIN) jump
ü′bersprudeln *intr* (SEIN) bubble over
ü′berständig *adj* leftover; (*Bier*) flat; (*Obst*) overripe
überste′hen §146 *tr* stand, endure; (*Krankheit, usw.*) get over; (*Operation*) pull through; (*überleben*) survive || **ü′berstehen** §146 *intr* jut out
überstei′gen §148 *tr* climb over; (*Hindernisse*) overcome; (*Erwartungen*) exceed || **ü′bersteigen** §148 *intr* (SEIN) step over
überstim′men *tr* vote down, defeat
überstrah′len *tr* shine upon; (*verdunkeln*) outshine, eclipse
überstrei′chen §85 *tr* paint over
ü′berstreifen *tr* slip on
überströ′men *tr* flood, inundate || **ü′berströmen** *intr* (SEIN) overflow
Ü′berstunde *f* hour of overtime; **Überstunden machen** work overtime
überstür′zen *tr* rush, hurry || *ref* be in too big a hurry; act rashly; (*Ereignisse*) follow one another rapidly
überstürzt [ybər′/tyrtst] *adj* hasty
überteuern [ybər′tɔɪ-ərn] *tr* overcharge
übertölpeln [ybər′tœpəln] *tr* dupe
übertö′nen *tr* drown out
Übertrag [′ybərtrak] *m* (-[e]s;-̈e) (acct) carryover, balance
übertragbar [ybər′trakbar] *adj* transferable; (pathol) contagious
übertra′gen *adj* figurative, metaphorical || §132 *tr* carry over, transfer; (*Amt, Titel*) confer; (*Aufgabe*) assign; (*Vollmacht*) delegate; (*Kurzschrift*) transcribe; (**in** *acc*) translate (into); (acct) transfer; (pathol) spread, communicate; (rad) broadcast, transmit; (**mit** *Relais*) relay; (telv) televise
Übertra′gung *f* (-;-en) carrying over; transfer; assignment; delegation; conferring; transcription; translation; copy; (pathol) spread; (rad) broadcast; relay; (telv) televising
übertref′fen §151 *tr* surpass, outdo
übertrei′ben §62 *tr* overdo; exaggerate; (theat) overact
Übertrei′bung *f* (-;-en) overdoing; exaggeration; (theat) overacting

übertre′ten §152 *tr* (*Gesetz*) transgress, break || *ref*—**sich** [*dat*] **den Fuß ü.** sprain one's ankle || **ü′bertreten** §152 *intr* (SEIN) (sport) go off sides; **ü. zu** (fig) go over to; (relig) be converted to
Übertre′tung *f* (-;-en) violation
Ü′bertritt *m* change, going over; (relig) conversion
übervölkern [ybər′fœlkərn] *tr* overpopulate
Übervöl′kerung *f* (-;) overpopulation
ü′bervoll *adj* brimful; crowded
übervorteilen [ybər′fortaɪlən] *tr* take advantage of, get the better of
überwa′chen *tr* watch over; supervise; (*kontrollieren*) inspect, check; (*polizeilich*) shadow; (rad, telv) monitor
Überwa′chung *f* (-;-en) supervision; inspection; control; surveillance
Überwa′chungsausschuß *m* watchdog committee
überwältigen [ybər′vɛltɪɡən] *tr* overpower (fig) overwhelm
überwei′sen §118 *tr* (*Geld*) send; (**zu** **e-m** *Spezialisten*) refer
Überwei′sung *f* (-;-en) sending, remittance; referral
ü′berweltlich *adj* otherworldly
überwerfen §160 *tr* throw over || **überwer′fen** §160 *ref* (**mit**) have a run-in (with)
überwie′gen §57 *tr* outweigh || *intr* prevail, preponderate || **Überwiegen** *n* (-s;) prevalence, preponderance
überwie′gend *adj* prevailing; (*Mehrheit*) vast || *adv* predominantly
überwin′den §59 *tr* conquer, overcome || *ref*—**sich ü. zu** (*inf*) bring oneself to (*inf*)
überwintern [ybər′vɪntərn] *intr* pass the winter; (bot) survive the winter
überwu′chern *tr* overrun; (fig) stifle
Ü′berwurf *m* wrap; shawl
Ü′berzahl *f* numerical superiority; majority
überzäh′len *tr* & *intr* overpay
überzäh′len *tr* count over, recount
überzählig [′ybərtseliç] *adj* surplus
überzeu′gen *tr* convince || *ref*—**ü. Sie sich selbst davon!** go and see for yourself!
Überzeu′gung *f* (-;-en) conviction
überzie′hen §163 *tr* cover; (**mit** *Farbe*) coat; (*Bett*) put fresh linen on; (*Konto*) overdraw; **ein Land mit Krieg ü.** invade a country || **ü′berziehen** §163 *tr* (*Mantel, usw.*) slip on; **j-m eins ü.** (coll) give s.o. a whack
Ü′berzieher *m* (-s;-) overcoat
überzuckern (**überzuk′kern**) *tr* (& fig) sugarcoat
Ü′berzug *m* coat, film; (*Decke*) cover; (*Hülle*) case; pillow case; (*Kruste*) crust; (*Schale, Rinde*) skin
üblich [′yplɪç] *adj* usual, customary
U′-Boot *n* (*Unterseeboot*) submarine
U′-Bootbunker *m* submarine pen
U′-Bootjäger *m* (aer) antisubmarine aircraft; (nav) subchaser
U′-Bootortungsgerät *n* sonar
U′-Bootrudel *n* (nav) wolf pack
übrig [′ybrɪç] *adj* left (over), remain-

ing, rest (of); **die übrigen** the others, the rest; **ein übriges tun** do more than is necessary; **etw ü. haben für** have a soft spot for; **im übrigen** for the rest, otherwise

ü'brigbehalten §90 *tr* keep, spare

ü'brigbleiben §62 *intr* (SEIN) be left (over) ‖ *impers*—**es blieb mir nichts anderes ü. als zu** (*inf*) I had no choice but to (*inf*)

übrigens ['ybrɪgəns] *adv* moreover; after all; by the way

ü'briglassen §104 *tr* leave, spare

Übung ['ybuŋ] *f* (-;-en) exercise; practice; (*Gewohnheit*) use; (*Ausbildung*) training; (mil) drill

Ü'bungsbeispiel *n* practical example

Ü'bungsbuch *n* composition book; workbook

Ü'bungsgelände *n* training ground; (*für Bomben*) target area

Ü'bungshang *m* (sport) training slope

Ü'bungsheft *n* composition book; workbook

Ufer ['ufər] *n* (-s;-) (*e-s Flusses*) bank; (*e-s Meers*) shore

U'ferdamm *m* embankment, levee

u'ferlos *adj* fruitless

Uhr [ur] *f* (-;-en) clock; watch; o'clock; **um wieviel Uhr?** at what time; **um zwölf Uhr** at twelve o'clock; **wieviel Uhr ist es?** what time is it?

Uhr'armband *n* (-[e]s;-̈er) watchband

Uhr'feder *f* watch spring

Uhr'glas *n* watch crystal

Uhr'macher *m* watchmaker

Uhr'werk *n* works, clockwork

Uhr'zeiger *m* hand

Uhr'zeigerrichtung *f*—**entgegen der U.** counterclockwise; **in der U.** clockwise

Uhr'zeigersinn *m*—**im U.** clockwise

Uhu ['uhu] *m* (-s;-s) owl

Ukraine [u'kraɪnə] *f* (-;)—**die U.** the Ukraine

ukrainisch [u'kraɪnɪʃ] *adj* Ukrainian

UK-Stellung [u'ka/telʊŋ] *f* (-;-en) military deferment

Ulk [ʊlk] *m* (-[e]s;-e) joke, fun

ulken ['ʊlkən] *intr* (coll) make fun

ulkig ['ʊlkɪç] *adj* funny

Ulme ['ʊlmə] *f* (-;-n) elm

Ultima·tum [ʊltɪ'matʊm] *n* (-s;-ten [tən] & -ta [ta]) ultimatum

Ultra-, ultra- [ʊltra] *comb.fm.* ultra-

Ul'trakurzfrequenz *f* ultrashort frequency

ultramontan [ultramɔn'tan] *adj* strict Catholic

Ultraschall- *comb.fm.* supersonic

ul'traviolett [ultravio'lɛt] *adj* ultraviolet

um [ʊm] *adv*—**deine Zeit ist um** your time is up; **je…um so the…the; um so besser** all the better; **um so weniger** all the less; **um und um round and round** ‖ *prep* (acc) around, about; for; at; **um die Hälfte mehr** half as much again; **um die Wette laufen** race; **um ein Jahr älter** one year older; **um etw eintauschen** exchange for s.th.; **um jeden Preis** at

any price; **um…Uhr** at…o'clock; **um…zu** (*inf*) in order to (*inf*)

um'ackern *tr* plow up, turn over

um'adressieren *tr* readdress

um'ändern *tr* change (around)

Um'änderung *f* (-;-en) change, alteration

um'arbeiten *tr* rework; (*Metall*) recast; (*Buch*) revise; (*Haus*) remodel; (*berichtigen*) emend, correct; (*verbessern*) improve

umar'men *tr* embrace, hug

Umar'mung *f* (-;-en) embrace, hug

Um'bau *m* (-[e]s;-e & -ten) rebuilding; alterations, remodeling; reorganization

um'bauen *tr* remodel; reorganize ‖ **umbau'en** *tr* build around; **umbauter Raum** floor space

um'besetzen *tr* (*Stellungen*) switch around; (pol) reshuffle; (theat) recast

um'biegen §47 *tr* bend (over); bend up, bend down

um'bilden *tr* remodel; reconstruct; (adm) reorganize, (pol) reshuffle

Um'bildung *f* (-;-en) remodeling; reconstruction; reorganization; reshuffling

um'binden §59 *tr* (*Schürze, usw.*) put on ‖ **umbin'den** §59 *tr* (*verletztes Glied, usw.*) bandage

um'blättern *tr* turn ‖ *intr* turn the page(s)

um'brechen §64 *tr* (*Bäume, usw.*) knock down; (*Acker*) plow up ‖ **umbre'chen** *tr* make into page proof

um'bringen §65 *tr* kill

Um'bruch *m* upheaval; (typ) page proof

um'buchen *tr* transfer to another account; book for another date

um'denken §66 *tr* rethink

um'dirigieren *tr* redirect

um'disponieren *tr* rearrange

umdrän'gen *tr* crowd around

um'drehen *tr* turn around; (*Hals*) wring; (*j-s Worte*) twist ‖ *ref* turn around ‖ *intr* turn around

Umdre'hung *f* (-;-en) turn; revolution

Um'druck *m* reprint; (typ) transfer

umeinan'der *adv* around each other

um'erziehen §163 *tr* reeducate

um'fahren §71 *tr* run down ‖ **umfah'ren** §71 *tr* drive around; sail around

um'fallen §72 *intr* (SEIN) fall over, fall down; collapse; give in

Um'fang *m* circumference; perimeter; (*Bereich*) range; (*Ausdehnung*) extent; (*des Leibes*) girth; (fig) scope; (mus) range; **im großen U.** on a large scale

umfan'gen §73 *tr* surround; embrace

um'fangreich *adj* extensive; (*körperlich*) bulky; (*geräumig*) spacious

umfas'sen *tr* embrace; clasp; comprise, cover; include; contain; (mil) envelop

umfas'send *adj* comprehensive; extensive

Umfas'sung *f* (-;-en) embrace; clasp; enclosure, fence; (mil) envelopment

Umfas'sungsmauer *f* enclosure
umflat'tern *tr* flutter around
umflech'ten §74 *tr* braid
umflie'gen §57 *tr* fly around || **um'flie-gen** §57 *intr* (SEIN) (coll) fall down
umflie'ßen §76 *tr* flow around
um'formen *tr* reshape; (elec) convert
Um'former *m* (-s;-) (elec) converter
Um'frage *f* inquiry, poll; **öffentliche U.** public opinion poll
umfrieden [um'fri·dən] *tr* enclose
Um'gang *m* round, circuit; revolution, rotation; (*Zug*) procession; association, company; (archit) gallery; ge-schlechtlicher U. sexual intercourse; schlechter U. bad company; U. mit j-m haben (or pflegen) associate with s.o.
umgänglich ['umgɛnlɪç] *adj* sociable
Um'gangsformen *pl* social manners
Um'gangssprache *f* colloquial speech
um'gangssprachlich *adj* colloquial
umgar'nen *tr* (fig) trap
umge'ben §80 *tr* surround
Umgebung [um'ge·buŋ] *f* (-;-en) sur-roundings, environs, neighborhood; company, associates; background; environment
Umgegend ['umge·gənt] *f* (-;) (coll) neighborhood
umgehen §82 *tr* go around; evade; by-pass; (mil) outflank || **um'gehen** §82 *intr* (SEIN) go around; (*Gerücht*) cir-culate; **an** (or **in**) **e-m Ort u.** haunt a place; **mit dem Gedanken** (or **Plan**) **u. zu** (*inf*) be thinking of (*ger*); **u. mit** deal with, handle; manage; be occupied with; hang around with
um'gehend *adj* immediate; **mit umge-hender Post** by return mail; **umge-hende Antwort erbeten!** please an-swer at your earliest convenience || *adv* immediately
Umge'hung *f* (-;-en) going around; bypassing; (fig) evasion; (mil) flank-ing movement
Umge'hungsstraße *f* bypass
umgekehrt ['umgə·kert] *adj* reverse; contrary || *adv* on the contrary; vice versa; upside down; inside out
umgestalten *tr* alter; remodel
um'graben §87 *tr* dig up
umgren'zen *tr* fence in; (fig) limit
Umgren'zung *f* (-;-en) enclosure; (fig) limit, boundary
um'gruppieren *tr* regroup; (pol) re-shuffle
um'gucken *ref* look around
um'haben §89 *tr* have on, be wearing
Um'hang *m* wrap; cape; shawl
um'hängen *tr* put on; (*Gewehr*) sling; (*Bild*) hang elsewhere
Um'hängetasche *f* shoulder bag
um'hauen §93 *tr* cut down; (coll) bowl over
umher' *adv* around, about
umher'blicken *tr* look around
umher'fuchteln *intr* gesticulate
umher'schweifen, umher'streifen *intr* (SEIN) rove, roam about
umhin' *adv*—**ich kann nicht u.** I can't do otherwise; **ich kann nicht u. zu** (*inf*) I can't help (*ger*)

umhül'len *tr* wrap up, cover; envelop
Umhül'lung *f* (-;-en) wrapping
Umkehr ['umker] *f* (-;) return; change; conversion; (elec) reversal
um'kehren *tr* turn around; overturn; (*Tasche*) turn out; (elec) reverse; (gram, math, mus) invert || *intr* (SEIN) turn back, return
Um'kehrung *f* (-;-en) overturning; re-versal; conversion; inversion
um'kippen *tr* upset || *intr* (SEIN) tilt over
umklam'mern *tr* clasp; cling to; (mil) envelop; **einander u.** (box) clinch
Umklam'merung *f* (-;-en) embrace; (box) clinch; (mil) envelopment
umklei'den *tr* clothe || *ref* change around || **um'kleiden** *tr* change the clothes of
Um'kleideraum *m* dressing room
um'kommen §99 *intr* (SEIN) perish; (*Essen*) spoil
Um'kreis *m* circuit; vicinity; (geom) circumference; **5 km im U.** within a radius of 5 km
umkrei'sen *tr* circle, revolve around
um'krempeln *tr* (*Ärmel*) roll up; **völ-lig u.** (coll) change completely
um'laden §103 *tr* reload; transship
Um'lauf *m* circulation; (*Umdrehung*) revolution, rotation; (*Flugblatt*) cir-cular; (*Rundschreiben*) circular let-ter; **in U. setzen** circulate
Um'laufbahn *f* orbit
um'laufen §105 *tr* run down || *intr* (SEIN) circulate || **umlau'fen** §105 *tr* walk around
Um'laut *m* (-es;-e) umlaut, vowel mu-tation; mutated vowel
umlegbar ['umlekbar] *adj* reversible
um'legen *tr* lay down; turn down; (*an-ders legen*) shift; (*Kragen*) put on; (*gleichmäßig verteilen*) apportion; (coll) knock down; (vulg) lay
um'leiten *tr* detour, divert
Um'leitung *f* (-;-en) detour
um'lenken *tr* turn back
um'lernen *tr* relearn, learn anew
um'liegend *adj* surrounding
ummau'ern *tr* wall in
um'modeln *tr* remodel
umnachtet [um'naxtət] *adj* deranged
Umnach'tung *f* (-;)—**geistige U.** men-tal derangement
um'nähen *tr* hem
umne'beln *tr* fog; (fig) dull; **umnebelter Blick** glassy eyes
um'nehmen §116 *tr* put on
um'packen *tr* repack
um'pflanzen *tr* transplant || **umpflan'-zen** *tr*—**etw mit Blumen u.** plant flowers around s.th.
um'pflügen *tr* plow up, turn over
umrah'men *tr* frame
umranden [um'randən] *tr* edge, border
Umran'dung *f* (-;-en) edging, edge
umran'ken *tr* twine around; **mit Efeu umrankt** ivy-clad
um'rechnen *tr* convert; **umgerechnet auf** (*acc*) expressed in
Um'rechnungskurs *m* rate of exchange
Um'rechnungstabelle *f* conversion table
Um'rechnungswert *m* exchange value

um'reißen §53 *tr* pull down; knock down ‖ **umrei'ßen** §53 *tr* outline

umrin'gen *tr* surround

Um'riß *m* outline

Um'rißzeichnung *f* sketch

um'rühren *tr* stir, stir up

um'satteln *tr* resaddle ‖ *intr* change jobs; (educ) change one's course or major; (pol) switch parties

Um'satz *m* turnover, sales

Um'satzsteuer *f* sales tax

umsäu'men *tr* enclose, hem in

um'schalten *tr* switch; (*Strom*) convert ‖ *intr* (*auf acc*) switch back (to)

Um'schalter *m* (elec) switch; (typ) shift key

Um'schaltung *f* (-;-en) switching; shifting

Um'schau *f* look around; **U. halten** have a look around

um'schauen *ref* look around

um'schichten *tr* regroup, reshuffle

umschichtig ['ʊmʃɪçtɪç] *adv* alternately

umschif'fen *tr* circumnavigate; (*ein Kap*) double

Um'schlag *m* (sudden) change, shift; envelope; (*e-s Buches*) cover, jacket; cuff; hem; transshipment; (med) compress

um'schlagen §132 *tr* knock down; (*Ärmel*) roll up; (*Bäume*) fell; (*Saum*) turn up; (*Seite*) turn; (*umladen*) transship ‖ *intr* (SEIN) (*Laune, Wetter*) change; (*Wind*) shift; (*kentern*) capsize

Um'schlagpapier *n* wrapping paper

umschlie'ßen §76 *tr* surround, enclose

umschlin'gen §142 *tr* clasp; embrace; wind around

um'schmeißen §53 *tr* (coll) throw over

um'schnallen *tr* buckle on

um'schreiben §62 *tr* rewrite; (*abschreiben*) transcribe; (*Wechsel*) re-endorse; **u. auf** (*acc*) transfer to ‖ **umschrei'ben** §62 *tr* circumscribe; paraphrase

Um'schreibung *f* (-;-en) transcription; transfer ‖ **Umschrei'bung** *f* (-;-en) paraphrase

Um'schrift *f* transcription; (*e-r Münze*) legend

um'schulen *tr* retrain

um'schütteln *tr* shake (up)

um'schütten *tr* spill; pour into another container

umschwär'men *tr* swarm around; (fig) idolize

Um'schweif *m* digression; **ohne Umschweife** point-blank; **Umschweife machen** beat around the bush

umschweifig [ʊm'ʃvaɪfɪç] *adj* roundabout

um'schwenken *intr* wheel around; (fig) change one's mind

Um'schwung *m* change; (*Drehung*) revolution; (*Umkehrung*) reversal; (*der Gesinnung*) revulsion

umse'geln *tr* sail around; (*Kap*) double

Umse'gelung *f* (-;-en) circumnavigation

um'sehen §138 *ref* (*nach*) look around (for); (fig) (*nach*) look out (for)

um'sein §139 *intr* (SEIN) (*Zeit*) be up; (*Ferien*) be over

um'setzen *tr* shift; transplant; (*Nährstoffe*) assimilate; (*Schüler*) switch around; (*Ware*) sell; (*verwandeln*) convert; (mus) transpose; **Geld u. in** (*acc*) spend money on; **in die Tat u.** translate into action ‖ *ref* —**sich u. in** (*acc*) (biochem) be converted into

Um'sicht *f* (-;) circumspection

umsichtig ['ʊmzɪçtɪç] *adj* circumspect

um'siedeln *tr & intr* (SEIN) resettle

Um'siedlung *f* (-;-en) resettlement

umsonst' *adv* for nothing, gratis; (*vergebens*) in vain

um'spannen *tr* (*Wagenpferde*) change; (elec) transform ‖ **umspan'nen** *tr* span; encompass; include

Um'spanner *m* (-s;-) (elec) transformer

um'springen §142 *intr* (SEIN) (*Wind*) shift; **mit j-m rücksichtslos u.** (coll) treat s.o. thoughtlessly

Um'stand *m* circumstance; factor; fact; (*Einzelheit*) detail; (*Aufheben*) fuss; **in anderen Umständen** (coll) pregnant; **sich** [*dat*] **Umstände machen** go to the trouble; **Umstände machen** be formal; **unter Umständen** under certain conditions

umständehalber ['ʊmʃtɛndəhalbər] *adv* owing to circumstances

umständlich ['ʊmʃtɛntlɪç] *adj* detailed; (*förmlich*) formal; (*zu genau*) fussy; (*verwickelt*) complicated; (*Erzählung*) long-winded, round-about

Um'standskleid *n* maternity dress

Um'standskrämer *m* fusspot

Um'standswort *n* (-[e]s;ᵉer) adverb

um'stehend *adj* (*Seite*) next ‖ **Umstehende** §5 *mf* bystander

Um'steige(fahr)karte *f* transfer

um'steigen §148 *intr* (SEIN) transfer

um'stellen *tr* put into a different place, shift; (*Möbel*) rearrange; (*auf acc*) convert (to) ‖ *ref* (*auf acc*) adjust (to) ‖ **umstel'len** *tr* surround

Um'stellung *f* (-;-en) change of position, shift; conversion; readjustment

um'stimmen *tr* tune to another pitch; **make** (s.o.) change his mind

um'stoßen §150 *tr* knock down; (*Pläne*) upset; (*Vertrag*) annul; (*Urteil*) reverse

umstricken (umstrik'ken) *tr* ensnare

umstritten [ʊm'ʃtrɪtən] *adj* contested; controversial

Um'sturz *m* overthrow

um'stürzen *tr* overturn; overthrow; (*Mauer*) tear down; (*Plan*) change, throw out ‖ *intr* (SEIN) fall down

Umstürzler —in ['ʊmʃtʏrtslər(ɪn)] §6 *mf* revolutionary, subversive

umstürzlerisch ['ʊmʃtʏrtslərɪʃ] *adj* revolutionary; subversive

Um'tausch *m* exchange

um'tauschen *tr* (*gegen*) exchange (for)

um'tun §154 *tr* (*Kleider*) put on ‖ *ref* —**sich u. nach** look around for

um'wälzen *tr* roll around; (fig) revolutionize ‖ *ref* roll around

umwäl'zend *adj* revolutionary

Umwäl'zung *f* (-;-en) revolution

umwandelbar ['ʊmvandəlbɑr] *adj* (com) convertible

um'wandeln *tr* change; (elec, fin) convert; (jur) commute

Um'wandlung *f* (–;-en) change; (elec, fin) conversion; (jur) commutation

um'wechseln *tr* exchange; (fin) convert

Um'weg *m* detour; **auf Umwegen** indirectly

um'wehen *tr* knock down ‖ **umwe'hen** *tr* blow around

Um'welt *f* environment

Um'weltverschmutzung *f* ecological pollution

um'wenden §140 *tr* turn over ‖ *ref* & *intr* turn around

umwer'ben §149 *tr* court, go with

um'werfen §160 *tr* throw down; upset; (*Plan*) ruin; (*Kleider*) throw about one's shoulders

umwickeln (umwik'keln) *tr* (*mit Band*) tape

umwin'den *tr* wreathe

umwölken [ʊm'vœlkən] *ref* & *intr* cloud over

umzäunen [ʊm'tsɔɪnən] *tr* fence in

um'ziehen §163 *ref* change one's clothes ‖ *intr* (SEIN) move ‖ **umzie'hen** §163 *ref—der Himmel hat sich umzogen** the sky has become overcast

umzingeln [ʊm'tsɪŋəln] *tr* encircle

Um'zug *m* procession, parade; (*Wohnungswechsel*) moving; (pol) march

un– [ʊn] *comb.fm.* un–, in–, ir–, non–

unabän'derlich *adj* unalterable

un'abhängig *adj* (von) independent (of) ‖ **Unabhängige** §5 *mf* (pol) independent

Un'abhängigkeit *f* independence

unabkömm'lich *adj* unavailable; indispensable; (mil) essential (*on the homefront*); **ich bin augenblicklich u.** I can't get away at the moment

unablässig ['ʊnaplesɪç] *adj* incessant

unablösbar [ʊnap'løsbɑr], **unablöslich** [ʊnap'løslɪç] *adj* unpayable

unabseh'bar *adj* unforeseeable; immense

unabsetz'bar *adj* irremovable

unabsicht'lich *adj* unintentional

unabwendbar [ʊnap'ventbɑr] *adj* inevitable

un'achtsam *adj* careless, inattentive

um'ähnlich *adj* dissimilar, unlike

unanfecht'bar *adj* indisputable

un'angebracht *adj* out of place

un'angefochten *adj* undisputed

un'angemessen *adj* improper; inadequate; unsuitable

un'angenehm *adj* unpleasant, disagreeable; awkward

un'annehmbar *adj* unacceptable

Un'annehmlichkeit *f* unpleasantness; annoyance, inconvenience; **Unannehmlichkeiten** trouble

un'ansehnlich *adj* unsightly; (*unscheinbar*) plain, inconspicuous

un'anständig *adj* indecent; obscene

un'antastbar *adj* unassailable

un'appetitlich *adj* unappetizing; (*ekelhaft*) unsavory

Un'art *f* bad habit; (*Ungezogenheit*)

naughtiness; (*schlechte Manieren*) bad manners

un'artig *adj* ill-behaved, naughty

un'aufdringlich *adj* unostentatious; unobtrusive

un'auffällig *adj* inconspicuous

unauffindbar ['ʊnauffɪntbɑr] *adj* not to be found

unaufgefordert ['ʊnaufgəfordərt] *adj* unasked, uncalled for ‖ *adv* spontaneously

unaufhaltbar ['ʊnaufhaltbɑr], **unaufhaltsam** ['ʊnaufhaltzɑm] *adj* irresistible; relentless

unaufhörlich ['ʊnaufhørlɪç] *adj* incessant

un'aufmerksam *adj* inattentive

un'aufrichtig *adj* insincere

unaufschiebbar ['ʊnauf'ʃipbɑr] *adj* not to be postponed, urgent

unausbleiblich ['ʊnausblaɪplɪç] *adj* inevitable

unausführbar ['ʊnausfyrbɑr] *adj* unfeasible, impracticable

unausgeglichen ['ʊnausgəglɪçən] *adj* uneven; (fig) unbalanced

unauslöschbar ['ʊnauslœ/bɑr], **unauslöschlich** ['ʊnauslœ/lɪç] *adj* inextinguishable; (*Tinte*) indelible

unaussprechlich ['ʊnaus/preçlɪç] *adj* unspeakable, ineffable

unausstehlich ['ʊnaus/telɪç] *adj* intolerable, insufferable

unbändig ['ʊnbendɪç] *adj* wild

un'barmherzig *adj* unmerciful

un'beabsichtigt *adj* unintentional

un'beachtet *adj* unobserved, unnoticed

unbeanstandet ['ʊnbə·an/tandət] *adj* unopposed, unhampered

unbearbeitet ['ʊnbə·arbaɪtət] *adj* unworked; (*roh*) raw; (*Land*) untilled; (mach) unfinished

unbebaut ['ʊnbəbaut] *adj* uncultivated; (*Gelände*) undeveloped

unbedacht ['ʊnbədaxt] *adj* thoughtless

un'bedenklich *adj* unhesitating; unswerving; unobjectionable, harmless ‖ *adv* without hesitation

un'bedeutend *adj* unimportant; slight

un'bedingt *adj* unconditional, unqualified; implicit

un'befahrbar *adj* impassable

un'befangen *adj* unembarrassed; (*unparteiisch*) impartial; natural, unaffected

unbefleckt ['ʊnbəflekt] *adj* immaculate

un'befriedigend *adj* unsatisfactory

un'befriedigt *adj* unsatisfied

un'befugt *adj* unauthorized; (jur) incompetent ‖ **Unbefugte** §5 *mf* unauthorized person

un'begabt *adj* untalented

unbegreif'lich *adj* incomprehensible

un'begrenzt *adj* unlimited

un'begründet *adj* unfounded

Un'behagen *n* discomfort, uneasiness

un'behaglich *adj* uncomfortable

unbehelligt ['ʊnbəhelɪçt] *adj* undisturbed, unmolested

unbehindert ['ʊnbəhɪndərt] *adj* unhindered; unrestrained

unbeholfen ['ʊnbəhɔlfən] *adj* clumsy

unbeirrbar ['ʊnbə·ɪrbɑr] *adj* unwavering

unbeirrt ['ʊnbə·ɪrt] *adj* unswerving

un'bekannt *adj* unknown; unfamiliar; unacquainted; (*Ursache*) unexplained || **Unbekannte** §5 *mf* stranger || *f* (math) unknown quantity

unbekümmert ['ʊnbəkʏmərt] *adj* (**um**) unconcerned (about)

un'beladen *adj* unloaded

unbelastet ['ʊnbəlɑstət] *adj* unencumbered; (*Wagen*) unloaded; carefree

un'belebt *adj* inanimate; (*Straße*) quiet; (com) slack

unbelichtet ['ʊnbəlɪçtət] *adj* (*Film*) unexposed

un'beliebt *adj* unpopular, disliked

unbemannt ['ʊnbəmant] *adj* unmanned

un'bemerkbar *adj* imperceptible

un'bemittelt *adj* poor

un'benommen *adj*—**es bleibt Ihnen u. zu** (*inf*) you are free to (*inf*); **es ist mir u., ob** it's up to me whether

unbenutzbar ['ʊnbənʊtsbɑr] *adj* unusable

unbenutzt ['ʊnbənʊtst] *adj* unused

un'bequem *adj* inconvenient; uncomfortable

unberechenbar ['ʊnbərɛçənbɑr] *adj* incalculable; unpredictable

un'berechtigt *adj* unauthorized; unjustified

unbeschadet ['ʊnbəʃɑdət] *prep* (*genit*) without prejudice to

unbeschädigt ['ʊnbəʃɛdɪçt] *adj* unhurt; undamaged

un'bescheiden *adj* pushy

unbescholten ['ʊnbəʃɔltən] *adj* of good reputation

un'beschränkt *adj* unlimited; absolute

unbeschreiblich ['ʊnbəʃraɪplɪç] *adj* indescribable

unbesehen ['ʊnbəze·ən] *adv* sight unseen

un'besetzt *adj* unoccupied, vacant

unbesiegbar ['ʊnbəzikbɑr] *adj* invincible

unbesoldet ['ʊnbəzɔldət] *adj* unsalaried

un'besonnen *adj* thoughtless; careless; rash

un'besorgt *adj* unconcerned; carefree

un'beständig *adj* unsteady, inconstant; (*Preise*) fluctuating; (*Wetter*) changeable; (*Person*) fickle, unstable

unbestätigt ['ʊnbəʃtetɪçt] *adj* unconfirmed

un'bestechlich *adj* incorruptible

un'bestimmt *adj* indeterminate; vague; (*unsicher*) uncertain; (*unentschieden*) undecided; (gram) indefinite

unbestraft ['ʊnbəʃtrɑft] *adj* unpunished

unbestreit'bar *adj* indisputable

unbestritten ['ʊnbəʃtrɪtən] *adj* undisputed, uncontested

unbeteiligt ['ʊnbətaɪlɪçt] *adj* uninterested; indifferent; impartial

un'beträchtlich *adj* trifling, slight

unbeugsam ['ʊnbɔɪkzɑm] *adj* inflexible

unbewacht ['ʊnbəvaxt] *adj* unguarded

unbewaffnet ['ʊnbəvafnət] *adj* unarmed; (*Auge*) naked

un'beweglich *adj* immovable; motionless

unbewiesen ['ʊnbəvizən] *adj* unproved

unbewohnt ['ʊnbəvont] *adj* uninhabited

un'bewußt *adj* unconscious; involuntary

unbezähmbar [ʊnbə'tsembɑr] *adj* untamable; (fig) uncontrollable

Un'bilden *pl*—**U. der Witterung** inclement weather

Un'bildung *f* lack of education

un'billig *adj* unfair

unbotmäßig ['ʊnbotmesɪç] *adj* unruly; insubordinate

unbrauch'bar *adj* useless, of no use

un'bußfertig *adj* unrepentant

un'christlich *adj* unchristian

und [ʊnt] *conj* and; **und?** so what? **und wenn** even if

Un'dank *m* ingratitude

un'dankbar *adj* ungrateful; thankless

Un'dankbarkeit *f* ingratitude

undatiert ['ʊndatirt] *adj* undated

undenk'bar *adj* unthinkable

undenklich [ʊn'dɛŋklɪç] *adj*—**seit undenklichen Zeiten** from time immemorial

un'deutlich *adj* unclear, indistinct

un'deutsch *adj* un-German

un'dicht *adj* not tight; leaky

Un'ding *n* nonsense, absurdity

un'duldsam *adj* intolerant

undurchdring'lich *adj* (**für**) impervious (to); **undurchdringliche Miene** poker face

undurchführ'bar *adj* not feasible

un'durchlässig *adj* (**für**) impervious (to)

un'durchsichtig *adj* opaque; (*Beweggründe*) hidden; (*Machenschaften*) shady

un'eben *adj* uneven; bumpy; **nicht u.!** (coll) not bad!

un'echt *adj* false, spurious; artificial, imitation; (*Farbe*) fading

un'edel *adj* ignoble; (*Metall*) base

un'ehelich *adj* illegitimate

Un'ehre *f* dishonor

un'ehrenhaft *adj* dishonorable

un'ehrerbietig *adj* disrespectful

un'ehrlich *adj* dishonest; underhand

un'eigennützig *adj* unselfish

un'einig *adj* disunited; at odds

Un'einigkeit *f* disagreement

uneinnehm'bar *adj* impregnable

un'eins *adj* at odds, at variance

un'empfänglich *adj* (**für**) insusceptible (to)

un'empfindlich *adj* (**gegen**) insensitive (to); (**gegen**) insensible (to)

unend'lich *adj* endless; infinite; **auf u. einstellen** (phot) set at infinity || *adv* endlessly; infinitely; **u. viele an** endless number of

unentbehr'lich *adj* indispensible

unentrinnbar [ʊnɛnt'rɪnbɑr] *adj* inescapable

un'entschieden *adj* undecided; (*schwankend*) indecisive; (sport) tie || **Unentschieden** *n* (**-s;-**) (sport) tie

Un'entschiedenheit *f* indecision

un'entschlossen *adj* irresolute

Un'entschlossenheit *f* indecision
unentschuld'bar *adj* inexcusable
unentwegt ['unentvekt] *adj* staunch; unswerving || *adv* continuously; untiringly || **Unentwegte** §5 *mf* die-hard
unentwirrbar ['unentvɪrbɑr] *adj* inextricable
unerbittlich [uner'bɪtlɪç] *adj* inexorable; *(Tatsache)* hard
un'erfahren *adj* inexperienced
unerfindlich [uner'fɪntlɪç] *adj* incomprehensible, mysterious
unerforschlich [uner'fɔrʃlɪç] *adj* inscrutable
unerfreulich ['unerfrɔɪlɪç] *adj* unpleasant
unerfüllbar [uner'fʏlbɑr] *adj* unattainable
un'ergiebig *adj* unproductive
un'ergründlich *adj* unfathomable
un'erheblich *adj* insignificant; **(für)** irrelevant (to)
unerhört [uner'hørt] *adj* unheard-of, unprecedented; outrageous || **un'erhört** *adj (Bitte)* unanswered
un'erkannt *adj* unrecognized || *adv* incognito
unerklär'lich *adj* inexplicable
unerläßlich [uner'leslɪç] *adj* indispensable
un'erlaubt *adj* illicit, unauthorized
un'erledigt *adj* unsettled, unfinished
unermeßlich [uner'meslɪç] *adj* immense
unermüdlich [uner'mydlɪç] *adj* untiring; *(Person)* indefatigable
unerquicklich [uner'kvɪklɪç] *adj* unpleasant
unerreich'bar *adj* unattainable, out of reach
unerreicht ['unerraɪçt] *adj* unrivaled
unersättlich [uner'zetlɪç] *adj* insatiable
unerschlossen ['unerʃlɔsən] *adj* undeveloped; *(Boden)* unexploited
unerschöpflich [uner'ʃøpflɪç] *adj* inexhaustible
unerschrocken ['unerʃrɔkən] *adj* intrepid, fearless
unerschütterlich [uner'ʃʏterlɪç] *adj* unshakable; imperturbable
unerschwing'lich *adj* unattainable; beyond one's means; exorbitant
unersetz'bar, unersetz'lich *adj* irreplaceable; *(Schaden)* irreparable
unerträg'lich *adj* intolerable
unerwähnt ['unervent] *adj* unmentioned; **u. lassen** pass over in silence
unerwartet ['unervartət] *adj* unexpected, sudden
unerweis'lich *adj* unprovable
un'erwünscht *adj* undesired; unwelcome
unerzogen ['unertsogən] *adj* ill-bred
un'fähig *adj* incapable, unable; unqualified, inefficient
Un'fähigkeit *f* inability; inefficiency
Un'fall *m* accident, mishap
Un'fallflucht *f* hit-and-run offense
Un'fallstation *f* first-aid station
Un'falltod *m* accidental death
Un'fallversicherung *f* accident insurance
Un'fallziffer *m* accident rate

unfaß'bar, unfaß'lich *adj* incomprehensible; inconceivable
unfehl'bar *adj* infallible; unfailing
Unfehl'barkeit *f* infallibility
un'fein *adj* coarse; indelicate
un'fern *adj* near; **u. von** not far from || *prep (genit)* not far from
un'fertig *adj* not ready; not finished; immature
Unflat ['unflɑt] *m* (-s;) dirt, filth
unflätig ['unfletɪç] *adj* dirty, filthy
un'folgsam *adj* disobedient
Un'folgsamkeit *f* disobedience
unförmig ['unfœrmɪç] *adj* shapeless
un'förmlich *adj* informal
unfrankiert ['unfraŋkirt] *adj* unfranked, unstamped
un'frei *adj* not free; unstamped || *adv* —**u. schicken** send c.o.d.
un'freiwillig *adj* involuntary
un'freundlich *adj* unfriendly, unkind
Un'friede *m* dissension, discord
un'fruchtbar *adj* unfruitful, sterile; *(fig)* fruitless
Unfug ['unfuk] *m* (-[e]s;) nuisance, disturbance; mischief; misdemeanor; **U. treiben** cause mischief
ungang'bar *adj* impassable; unsalable
Ungar ['uŋgar] *m* (-;-n), **Ungarin** ['uŋgarɪn] *f* (-;-nen) Hungarian
ungarisch ['uŋgarɪʃ] *adj* Hungarian
Ungarn ['uŋgarn] *n* (-s;) Hungary
un'gastlich *adj* inhospitable
ungeachtet ['uŋgə-axtət] *adj* not esteemed || *prep (genit)* regardless of
ungeahnt ['uŋgə-ant] *adj* unexpected
ungebärdig ['uŋgəberdɪç] *adj* unruly
ungebeten ['uŋgəbetən] *adj* unbidden
ungebeugt ['uŋgəbɔɪkt] *adj* unbowed; *(gram)* uninflected
un'gebildet *adj* uneducated
un'gebräuchlich *adj* unusual; *(veraltet)* obsolete
un'gebraucht *adj* unused
Un'gebühr *f* indecency, impropriety
un'gebührlich *adj* indecent, improper
ungebunden ['uŋgəbundən] *adj* unbound; *(ausschweifend)* loose, dissolute; *(frei)* unrestrained; **ungebundene Rede** prose
ungedeckt ['uŋgədekt] *adj* uncovered; *(Tisch)* unset; *(Haus)* roofless; *(Kosten)* unpaid; *(Scheck)* overdrawn
Un'geduld *f* impatience
un'geduldig *adj* impatient
un'geeignet *adj* unfit, unsuitable; unqualified
ungefähr ['uŋgəfer] *adj* approximate || *adv* approximately, about; **nicht von u.** on purpose
ungefährdet ['uŋgəferdət] *adj* safe, unendangered
un'gefährlich *adj* not dangerous
un'gefällig *adj* discourteous
un'gefüge *adj* monstrous; clumsy
un'gefügig *adj* unyielding, inflexible
ungefüttert ['uŋgəfʏtərt] *adj* unlined
un'gehalten *adj (Versprechen)* unkept, broken; **(über** *acc)* indignant (at)
ungeheißen ['uŋgəhaɪsən] *adv* of one's own accord
ungehemmt ['uŋgəhemt] *adj* unchecked

ungeheuer ['ʊngəhɔɪ-ər] *adj* huge; monstrous || *adv* tremendously ||
Ungeheuer *n* (-s;-) monster

un'geheuerlich *adj* monstrous || *adv* (coll) tremendously

ungehobelt ['ʊngəhobəlt] *adj* unplaned; (fig) uncouth

un'gehörig *adj* improper; (*Stunde*) ungodly

Un'gehörigkeit *f* (-;-en) impropriety

un'gehorsam *adj* disobedient || **Ungehorsam** *m* (-s;) disobedience

un'gekünstelt *adj* unaffected, natural

un'gekürzt *adj* unabridged

un'gelegen *adj* inconvenient

Un'gelegenheiten *pl* inconvenience

un'gelehrig *adj* unteachable

un'gelenk *adj* clumsy; stiff

un'gelernt *adj* (coll) unskilled

Un'gemach *n* discomfort; trouble

un'gemein *adj* uncommon

un'gemütlich *adj* uncomfortable; (*Zimmer*) dreary; (*Person*) disagreeable

un'genannt *adj* anonymous

un'genau *adj* inaccurate, inexact

ungeniert ['ʊnʒenirt] *adj* informal || *adv* freely

ungenieß'bar *adj* inedible; undrinkable; (& fig) unpalatable

un'genügend *adj* insufficient; **u. bekommen** get a failing grade

ungepflastert ['ʊngəpflastərt] *adj* unpaved, dirt

un'gerade *adj* uneven; crooked; (*Zahl*) odd

un'geraten *adj* spoiled

un'gerecht *adj* unjust, unfair

Un'gerechtigkeit *f* injustice

ungereimt ['ʊngəraɪmt] *adj* unrhymed; (*unvernünft*) absurd; **ungereimtes Zeug reden** talk nonsense

un'gern *adv* unwillingly, reluctantly

ungerührt ['ʊngəryrt] *adj* (fig) unmoved

un'geschehen *adj* undone; **u. machen** undo

ungescheut ['ʊngəʃɔɪt] *adv* without fear

Un'geschick *n*, **Un'geschicklichhkeit** *f* awkwardness

un'geschickt *adj* awkward, clumsy

un'geschlacht ['ʊngəʃlaxt] *adj* uncouth

ungeschliffen ['ʊngəʃlɪfən] *adj* unpolished; (*Messer*) blunt; (*Edelstein*) uncut; (fig) rude

ungeschminkt ['ʊngəʃmɪŋkt] *adj* without makeup; (*Wahrheit*) unvarnished

un'gesellig *adj* unsociable

un'gesetzlich *adj* illegal

ungesittet ['ʊngəzɪtət] *adj* unmannerly; uncivilized

ungestört ['ʊngəʃtørt] *adj* undisturbed

ungestraft ['ʊngəʃtraft] *adj* unpunished || *adv* scot-free

ungestüm ['ʊngəʃtym] *adj* impetuous, violent || **Ungestüm** *n* (-[e]s;) impetuosity, violence

un'gesund *adj* unhealthy; unwholesome

ungeteilt ['ʊngətaɪlt] *adj* undivided

un'getreu *adj* disloyal, untrue

ungetrübt ['ʊngətrypt] *adj* cloudless; clear; (fig) untroubled

Ungetüm ['ʊngətym] *n* (-[e]s;-e) monster

ungeübt ['ʊngə-ypt] *adj* untrained; (*Arbeiter*) inexperienced

un'gewandt *adj* unskillful; clumsy

un'gewiß *adj* uncertain; **j-n im ungewissen lassen** keep s.o. in suspense

Un'gewißheit *f* uncertainty

Un'gewitter *n* storm

un'gewöhnlich *adj* unusual

un'gewohnt *adj* unusual; (*genit*) unaccustomed (to)

ungezählt ['ʊngətselt] *adj* countless

Ungeziefer ['ʊngətsifər] *n* (-s;) vermin, bugs

ungeziemend ['ʊngətsimənt] *adj* improper; (*frech*) impudent

un'gezogen *adj* rude; naughty

ungezügelt ['ʊngətsygəlt] *adj* unbridled

un'gezwungen *adj* unforced; natural, easy-going

Un'glaube *m* disbelief, unbelief

un'gläubig *adj* incredulous; (*heidnisch*) infidel || **Ungläubige** §5 *mf* infidel

unglaub'lich *adj* incredible

un'glaubwürdig *adj* untrustworthy; incredible

un'gleich *adj* uneven, unequal; (*unähnlich*) unlike, dissimilar; (*Zahl*) odd || *adv* much, far, by far

un'gleichartig *adj* heterogeneous

un'gleichförmig *adj* unequal; irregular

Un'gleichheit *f* inequality; difference, dissimilarity; unevenness

un'gleichmäßig *adj* disproportionate

Unglimpf ['ʊnglɪmpf] *m* (-[e]s;-e) harshness; wrong, insult

un'glimpflich *adj* harsh

Un'glück *n* (-s;) bad luck; (*Unfall*) accident; disaster, calamity

un'glücklich *adj* unlucky; unfortunate; unhappy

un'glücklicherweise *adv* unfortunately

Un'glücksbote *m* bearer of bad news

Un'glücksbringer *m* (-s;-) jinx

un'glückselig *adj* miserable; disastrous

Un'glücksfall *m* accident, misfortune

Un'glücksmensch *m* unlucky person

Un'glücksrabe *m*, **Un'glücksvogel** *m* unlucky fellow

Un'gnade *f* (-;) disfavor, displeasure

un'gnädig *adj* ungracious; **etw u. aufnehmen** take s.th. amiss

un'gültig *adj* null and void, invalid; **für u. erklären** nullify, void

Un'gültigkeit *f* invalidity

Un'gültigkeitserklärung *f* annulment

Un'gunst *f* disfavor; **zu meinen Ungunsten** to my disadvantage

un'günstig *adj* unfavorable, bad, adverse

un'gut *adj* unkind; **nichts für u.!** no offense!; **ungutes Gefühl** misgivings

un'haltbar *adj* not durable; untenable

un'handlich *adj* unwieldy, unhandy

Un'heil *n* disaster; mischief; **U. anrichten** cause mischief; **U. heraufbeschwören** ask for trouble

unheil'bar *adj* incurable; irreparable

un'heilvoll *adj* ominous; disastrous

un'heimlich *adj* uncanny; sinister

un'höflich *adj* impolite, uncivil

Un'höflichkeit f impoliteness
un'hold adj unkind || Unhold m (-[e]s; -e) fiend
un'hörbar adj inaudible
un'hygienisch adj unsanitary
Uni ['uni] f (-;-s) (Universität) (coll) university
uniform [uni'fɔrm] adj uniform || Uniform f (-;-en) uniform
Uni-kum ['unikum] n (-s;-s & -ka [ka]) unique example; (coll) queer duck
un'interessant adj uninteresting
un'interessiert adj (an dat) uninterested (in)
Union [un'jon] f (-;-en) union
universal [univer'zal] adj universal
Universal'mittel n panacea, cure-all
Universal'schlüssel m monkey wrench
Universität [universi'tet] f (-;-en) university
Universitäts'auswahlmannschaft f varsity (team)
Universum [uni'verzum] n (-s;) universe
Unke ['uŋkə] f (-;-n) toad
unken ['uŋkən] intr (coll) be a prophet of doom
un'kenntlich adj unrecognizable; u. machen disguise
Un'kenntnis f (-;) ignorance
Un'kenruf m croak
un'keusch adj unchaste
un'kindlich adj precocious; (Verhalten) disrespectful
un'kirchlich adj secular, worldly
un'klar adj unclear; muddy; misty; im unklaren sein über (acc) be in the dark about
Un'klarheit f obscurity
un'kleidsam adj unbecoming
un'klug adj unwise, imprudent
Un'klugheit f imprudence; foolish act
un'kontrollierbar adj unverifiable
un'körperlich adj incorporeal
Un'kosten pl expenses, costs; overhead; sich in U. stürzen go to great expense
Un'kraut n weed, weeds; U. jäten pull weeds
Un'krautvertilgungsmittel n weed killer
un'kündbar adj binding; (Darlehen) irredeemable; (Stellung) permanent
un'kundig adj (genit) ignorant (of), unacquainted (with)
unlängst ['unleŋst] adv recently, the other day
un'lauter adj unfair
un'leidlich adj intolerable
un'lenksam adj unruly
unles'bar, unle'serlich adj illegible
unleugbar ['unlɔikbar] adj indisputable, undeniable
un'lieb adj disagreeable; es ist mir u. I am sorry
un'logisch adj illogical
unlös'bar adj (Problem) unsolvable; (untrennbar) inseparable; (chem) insoluble
unlös'lich adj (chem) insoluble
Un'lust f reluctance; listlessness
un'lustig adj reluctant; listless

un'manierlich adj impolite
un'männlich adj unmanly
Un'maß n excess; im U. to excess
Un'masse f (coll) vast amount, lots
un'maßgeblich adj unauthoritative; irrelevant; nach meiner unmaßgeblichen Meinung in my humble opinion
un'mäßig adj immoderate; excessive
Un'menge f (coll)—e-e U. von lots of
Un'mensch m brute, monster
un'menschlich adj inhuman, brutal
Un'menschlichkeit f brutality
un'merklich adj imperceptible
un'methodisch adj unmethodical
un'mißverständlich adj unmistakable
un'mittelbar adj direct, immediate
un'möbliert adj unfurnished
un'modern adj outmoded
un'möglich, unmög'lich adj impossible
Un'möglichkeit f impossibility
Un'moral f immorality
un'moralisch adj immoral
un'mündig adj underage
un'musikalisch adj unmusical
Un'mut m (über acc) displeasure (at)
un'mutig adj displeased, annoyed
unnachahmlich ['unnaxamliç] adj inimitable
un'nachgiebig adj unyielding
un'nachsichtig adj unrelenting, inexorable; strict
unnahbar [un'nabar] adj inaccessible
un'natürlich adj unnatural
unnenn'bar adj inexpressible
un'nötig adj unnecessary
unnütz ['unnyts] adj useless; vain
un'ordentlich adj disorderly; untidy
Un'ordnung f disorder; mess; in U. bringen throw into disorder
un'organisch adj inorganic
un'paar, un'paarig adj unpaired, odd
un'parteisch, un'parteilich adj impartial, disinterested
Un'parteilichkeit f impartiality
un'passend adj unsuitable; (unschicklich) improper; (unzeitgemäß) untimely
un'passierbar adj impassable
unpäßlich ['unpesliç] adj indisposed, ill
un'patriotisch adj unpatriotic
un'persönlich adj impersonal
un'politisch adj nonpolitical
un'populär adj unpopular
un'praktisch adj impractical; (unerfahren) unskillful
Un'rast f restlessness
Un'rat m (-[e]s;) garbage; dirt; U. wittern (coll) smell a rat
un'rätlich, un'ratsam adj inadvisable
un'recht adj wrong || Unrecht n (-[e]s;) —im U. sein be in the wrong; j-m U. geben decide against s.o.; mit (or zu) U. wrongly; unjustly; illegally
un'redlich adj dishonest
Un'redlichkeit f dishonesty
un'reell adj unfair
un'regelmäßig adj irregular
Un'regelmäßigkeit f irregularity
un'reif adj unripe, green; (fig) immature
Un'reife f unripeness; immaturity
un'rein adj unclean; (& fig) impure;

ins u. schreiben make a rough copy of

Un'reinheit f uncleanness; (& fig) impurity

un'reinlich adj dirty

un'rentabel adj unprofitable

un'rettbar adj irrecoverable

un'richtig adj incorrect, wrong

un'ritterlich adj unchivalrous

Un'ruh f (-;-en) (horol) balance wheel

Un'ruhe f restlessness; uneasiness; (Aufruhr) commotion, riot; (Störung) disturbance; (Besorgnis) anxiety

un'ruhig adj restless; uneasy; (laut) noisy; (Pferd) restive; (Meer) choppy; (nervös) jumpy

un'rühmlich adj inglorious

Un'ruhstifter –in §6 mf agitator, troublemaker; (Wirrkopf) screwball

uns [ʊns] pers pron us; to us || reflex pron ourselves; **wir sind doch unter uns** we are by ourselves || recip pron each other, one another; **wir sehen uns später** we'll meet later

un'sachgemäß adj inexpert

un'sachlich adj subjective; personal

unsagbar [ʊn'zakbar], **unsäglich** [ʊn'zeːklɪç] adj unspeakable; (fig) immense

un'sauber adj unclean; (unlauter) unfair, dirty

un'schädlich adj harmless

un'scharf adj (Apparat) out of focus; (Bild) blurred; (Begriff) poorly defined

un'schätzbar adj inestimable, invaluable

un'scheinbar adj inconspicuous, insignificant

un'schicklich adj unbecoming; indecent

Un'schicklichkeit f impropriety

un'schlüssig adj indecisive

Un'schlüssigkeit f indecision, hesitation

un'schmackhaft adj insipid, unpalatable

un'schön adj unlovely; plain, homely; (Angelegenheit) unpleasant

Un'schuld f innocence; **ich wasche meine Hände in U.** I wash my hands of it

un'schuldig adj innocent; (keusch) chaste; harmless; **sich für u. erklären** (jur) plead not guilty

un'schwer adj not difficult

Un'segen m adversity; (Fluch) curse

un'selbständig adj dependent, helpless

un'selig adj unfortunate; (Ereignis) fatal

unser ['ʊnzər] §2,3 poss adj our || §2,4 poss pron ours || pers pron us; of us; **erinnerst du dich unser noch?** do you still remember us?; **es waren unser vier** there were four of us

unseresgleichen ['ʊnzərəs'glaɪçən] pron people like us; the likes of us

unsrige ['ʊnzərɪɡə] §2,5 pron ours

unserthalben ['ʊnzərt'halbən], **unsertwegen** ['ʊnzərt'veːɡən] adv for our sake, on our behalf, on our account

un'sicher adj unsafe; shaky; precarious

Un'sicherheit f unsafeness; shakiness; insecurity; precariousness

un'sichtbar adj invisible

Un'sinn m (-[e]s;) nonsense, rubbish; **U. machen** fool around

un'sinnig adj nonsensical

Un'sitte f bad habit

un'sittlich adj immoral, indecent

Un'sittlichkeit f immorality

un'solid(e) adj unsolid; (Person) loose; (Firma) unreliable, shaky

unsortiert ['ʊnzɔrtirt] adj unsorted

un'sozial adj antisocial

un'sportlich adj unsportsmanlike

unsererseits ['ʊnzər'zaɪts] adv as for us, for our part

unsrige ['ʊnzrɪɡə] §2,5 poss pron ours

un'ständig adj impermanent, temporary

un'statthaft adj inadmissible; forbidden

unsterb'lich adj immortal

Unsterb'lichkeit f immortality

Un'stern m unlucky star; (fig) disaster

un'stet adj unsteady; restless; changeable

un'stillbar adj unappeasable; (Durst) unquenchable; (Hunger) unsatiable

unstimmig ['ʊn'tɪmɪç] adj discrepant; inconsistent

Un'stimmigkeit f (-;-en) discrepancy; inconsistency; (Widerspruch) disagreement

un'sträflich adj blameless; guileless

un'streitig adj indisputable

Un'summe f enormous sum

un'symmetrisch adj asymmetrical

un'sympathisch adj unpleasant; **er ist mir u.** I don't like him

un'tadelhaft adj blameless; flawless

Un'tat f crime

un'tätig adj inactive

un'tauglich adj unfit, unsuitable; useless; (Person) incompetent; **u. machen** disqualify

un'teilbar adj indivisible

unten ['ʊntən] adv below, beneath; downstairs; **da u.** down there; **er ist bei ihnen u. durch** they are through with him; **nach u.** downstairs; downwards; **tief u.** far below; **u. am Berge** at the foot of the mountain; **u. an der Seite** at the bottom of the page; **von u. her** from underneath

unter ['ʊntər] prep (dat) under, below; beneath, underneath; (zwischen) among; (während) during; **ganz u. uns gesagt** just between you and me; **u. aller Kritik** beneath contempt; **u. anderem** among other things; **u. diesem Gesichtspunkt** from this point of view; **u. Null** below zero; **was versteht man unter...?** what is meant by...? || prep (acc) under, below; beneath, underneath; among || **Unter** m (-s;-) (cards) jack

Unter-, unter- comb.fm. under-, sub-; lower

Un'terabteilung f subdivision

Un'terarm m forearm

Un'terart f subspecies

Un'terausschuß m subcommittee

Un'terbau m (-[e]s;-ten) foundation

un'terbelichten tr underexpose

un'terbewußt adj subconscious

Un'terbewußtsein n subconscious

unterbie'ten §58 tr undercut, undersell; underbid

un'terbinden §59 tr tie underneath || **unterbin'den** §59 tr (Verkehr) tie up; (Blutgefäß) tie off; (verhindern) prevent; (Angriff) neutralize

Unterbin'dung f stoppage; (surg) ligature

unterblei'ben §62 intr (SEIN) remain undone; not take place; be discontinued; **das muß u.** that must be stopped

unterbre'chen §64 tr interrupt; (einstellen) suspend; (Schweigen, Stille, Kontakt) break; (Verkehr) hold up; (telp) disconnect; **die Reise in München u.** have a stopover in Munich || ref stop short

Unterbre'cher m (elec) circuit breaker

Unterbre'chung f interruption; disconnection; (e-r Fahrt) stopover

unterbrei'ten tr submit

un'terbringen §65 tr provide a place for; find room for; (Gäste) accommodate, put up; (Stapeln) store; (Anleihe) place; (Geld) invest; (Pferde) stable; (Wagen) park; (Truppe) billet; **e-n Artikel bei e-r Zeitung u.** have an article published in a newspaper; **j-n auf e-m Posten** (or **in e-r Stellung**) **u.** find s.o. a job, place s.o.

Un'terbringung f (-; -en) accommodations, housing; billet; storage; investment; placement

Un'terbringungsmöglichkeiten pl accommodations

unterdes [untər'des], **unterdessen** [untər'desən] adv meanwhile

Un'terdruck m low pressure

unterdrücken (unterdrük'ken) tr suppress; (Aufstand) quell; (bedrücken) oppress; (ersticken) stifle; (Seufzer) repress

Un'terdruckgebiet n low-pressure area

Unterdrückung (Unterdrük'kung) f (-;) oppression; suppression

untere ['untərə] §9 adj lower, inferior

untereinan'der adv among one another; mutually; reciprocally

unterentwickelt ['untərentvɪkəlt] adj underdeveloped

unterernährt ['untərernert] adj undernourished

Un'terernährung f (-;) undernourishment

Un'terfamilie f subfamily

unterfer'tigen tr sign

Unterfüh'rung f (-; -en) underpass

unterfüt'tern tr line

Un'tergang m setting; (fig) decline, fall; (naut) sinking

unterge'ben adj (dat) subject (to), inferior (to) || **Untergebene** §5 mf subordinate

un'tergehen §82 intr (SEIN) go down, sink; (fig) perish; (astr) set

untergeordnet ['untərgə·ɔrdnət] adj subordinate || **Untergeordnete** §5 mf subordinate

Un'tergeschoß n ground floor; (Kellergeschoß) basement

Un'tergestell n undercarriage

Un'tergewand n underwear

un'tergliedern tr subdivide

untergra'ben §87 tr undermine

Un'tergrund m subsoil

Un'tergrundbahn f subway

Un'tergrundbewegung f underground movement

un'terhalb prep (genit) below

Un'terhalt m (-[e]s;) support; maintenance, upkeep; livelihood

un'terhalten §90 tr hold under || **unterhal'ten** §90 tr maintain; support; (Briefwechsel) keep up; (Feuer) feed; entertain, amuse || ref enjoy oneself, have a good time; amuse oneself; **sich u. mit** talk with

unterhaltsam [untər'haltzam] adj entertaining, amusing, enjoyable

Un'terhaltsbeitrag m alimony; (für Kinder) support

Unterhaltsberechtigte ['untərhaltsbəreçtɪgtə] §5 mf dependent

Un'terhaltskosten pl living expenses

Unterhal'tung f (-; -en) entertainment, amusement; (Gespräch) conversation; (Aufrechterhaltung) upkeep; (Unterstützung) support

Unterhal'tungskosten pl maintenance cost, maintenance

Unterhal'tungslektüre f light reading

unterhan'deln intr negotiate

Un'terhändler -in §6 mf negotiator; (Vermittler) mediator

Unterhand'lung f (-; -en) negotiation

Un'terhaus n (parl) lower house

Un'terhemd n undershirt

unterhöh'len tr undermine

Un'terholz n undergrowth, underbrush

Un'terhose f shorts; panties; **in Unterhosen zeigen** (coll) debunk

un'terirdisch adj underground, subterranean; (myth) of the underworld

Un'terjacke f vest

unterjo'chen tr subjugate

Unterjo'chung f (-;) subjugation

Un'terkiefer m lower jaw

Un'terkinn n double chin

Un'terkleid n slip

Un'terkleidung f (-;) underwear

un'terkommen §99 intr (SEIN) find accommodations; find employment || **Unterkommen** n (-s;) accommodations; (Stellung) job

Un'terkörper m lower part of the body

un'terkriegen tr (coll) get the better of; **er läßt sich nicht u.** he won't knuckle under

Unterkunft ['untərkunft] f (-;⁼e) accommodations; apartment; (Obdach) shelter, place to stay; (mil) quarters; **U. und Verpflegung** room and board

Un'terlage f foundation; base; pad; desk pad; rubber pad (for a bed); (Teppich-) underpad; (Beleg) voucher; (Urkunde) document; (archit) support; (geol) substratum; **keine Unterlagen haben** have nothing to go on; **Unterlagen** documentation; data

Un'terland n lowland

Unterlaß ['ʊntərlas] *m*—**ohne U.** without letup

unterlas'sen §104 *tr* omit; neglect; skip; stop, cut out

Unterlas'sung *f* (-;-en) omission; neglect; failure

Unterlas'sungssünde *f* sin of omission

unterlau'fen *adj*—**blau u.** black-and-blue; **mit Blut u.** bloodshot ‖ **un'terlaufen** §105 *intr* (SEIN) (*Fehler*) slip in

un'terlegen *tr* lay under, put under; (*Bedeutung, Sinn*) attach; **der Musik Worte u.** set words to music ‖ **unterle'gen** *adj* defeated; (*dat*) inferior (to) ‖ **Unterlegene** §5 *mf* loser

Unterle'genheit *f* (-;) inferiority

Unterlegring ['ʊntərlekrɪŋ] *m*, **Unterlegscheibe** ['ʊntərlekʃaɪbə] *f* washer

Un'terleib *m* abdomen

Unterleibs- *comb.fm.* abdominal

unterlie'gen §108 *intr* (SEIN) (*dat*) be beaten (by), lose (to); **e-m Rabatt u.** be subject to discount ‖ *impers* (SEIN)—**es unterliegt keinem Zweifel, daß** there is no doubt that

Un'terlippe *f* lower lip

unterma'len *tr* put the primer on; **mit Musik u.** accompany with music

untermau'ern *tr* support

Un'termiete *f* (-;) subletting; **in U. abgeben** sublet; **in U. wohnen bei** sublet from

Un'termieter –in §6 *mf* subtenant

unterminie'ren *tr* (fig) undermine

unterneh'men §116 *tr* undertake; (*versuchen*) attempt; **Schritte u.** (fig) take steps ‖ **Unternehmen** *n* (-s;-) undertaking; venture; enterprise; (mil) operation

unterneh'mend *adj* enterprising

Unterneh'mensberater *m* management consultant

Unterneh'mer –in §6 *mf* entrepreneur; (*Arbeitgeber*) employer; (*Bau*–) contractor

Unterneh'mung *f* (-;-en) undertaking; enterprise, business; (mil) operation

Unterneh'mungsgeist *m* initiative

unterneh'mungslustig *adj* enterprising

Un'teroffizier *m* noncommissioned officer, N.C.O.

un'terordnen *tr* (*dat*) subordinate (to) ‖ *ref* (*dat*) submit (to)

unterre'den *ref* (mit) confer (with)

Unterre'dung *f* (-;-en) conference

Unterricht ['ʊntərrɪçt] *m* (-[e]s;-e) instruction, lessons

unterrich'ten *tr* instruct; **u. von** (or **über** *acc*) inform (of, about)

Un'terrichtsfach *n* subject, course

Un'terrichtsfilm *m* educational film; (mil) training film

Un'terrichtsministerium *n* department of public instruction

Un'terrichtsstunde *f* (educ) period

Un'terrichtswesen *n* education; teaching

Un'terrock *m* slip

untersa'gen *tr* forbid, prohibit

Un'tersatz *m* saucer; support; (*Gestell*) stand; (archit) socle; (log) minor premise

unterschät'zen *tr* underrate, underestimate; undervalue

unterschei'den §112 *tr* distinguish ‖ *ref* (von) differ (from)

Unterschei'dung *f* (-;-en) difference, distinction

Un'terschenkel *m* shank

un'terschieben §130 *tr* shove under; (*statt genit*) substitute (for); (*dat*) impute (to), foist (on)

Unterschied ['ʊntər∫it] *m* (-[e]s;-e) difference, distinction; **zum U. von** as distinct from, unlike

un'terschiedlich *adj* different; varying

un'terschiedslos *adj* indiscriminate

unterschla'gen §132 *tr* embezzle; (*Nachricht*) suppress; (*Brief*) intercept

Unterschla'gung *f* (-;-en) embezzlement; suppression; interception

Unterschlupf ['ʊntər∫lʊpf] *m* (-[e]s;) shelter; hide-out

unterschrei'ben §62 *tr* sign; (fig) subscribe to, agree to

Un'terschrift *f* signature

Un'terseeboot *n* submarine

unterseeisch ['ʊntərze·ɪ∫] *adj* submarine

Un'terseekabel *n* transoceanic cable

Un'terseite *f* underside

untersetzt [ʊntər'zetst] *adj* stocky

Un'tersetzung *f* (-;-en) (mech) reduction

un'tersinken §143 *intr* (SEIN) go down

Un'terstand *m* (mil) dugout

unterste ['ʊntərstə] §9 *adj* lowest, bottom

unterste'hen §146 *ref* dare; **untersteh dich!** don't you dare! ‖ *intr* (*dat*) be under (*s.o.*) ‖ **un'terstehen** §146 *intr* take shelter

un'terstellen *tr* place under; (*Auto*) put into the garage ‖ *ref* take cover ‖ **unterstel'len** *tr* assume, suppose; (*dat*) impute (to); (mil) (*dat*) put under the command (of)

Unterstel'lung *f* (-;-en) assumption; imputation

unterstrei'chen §85 *tr* underline

unterstüt'zen *tr* support, back; help

Unterstüt'zung *f* (-;-en) support, backing; assistance; (*Beihilfe durch Geld*) relief; (ins) benefit

untersu'chen *tr* examine, inspect; investigate; study, do research on; (chem) analyze

Untersu'chung *f* (-;-en) examination; inspection; investigation; study, research; (chem) analysis

Untersu'chungsausschuß *m* fact-finding committee

Untersu'chungsgericht *n* court of inquiry

Untersu'chungshaft *f* (jur) detention

Untersu'chungsrichter *m* examining judge

Untertagebau [ʊntər'tagəbau] *m* (-[e] s;) mine

Untertan ['ʊntərtan] *m* (-s & -en;-en) subject

untertänig [ʊntər'tenɪç] *adj* submissive

Un'tertasse *f* saucer; **fliegende U.** flying saucer

un'tertauchen *tr* submerge; duck || *intr* (SEIN) dive; (fig) disappear || **Unter-tauchen** *n* (-s;) dive; disappearance
Un'terteil *m & n* lower part, bottom
untertei'len *tr* subdivide
Untertei'lung *f* (-;-en) subdivision
Un'tertitel *m* subtitle; caption
Un'terton *m* undertone
un'tertreten §152 *intr* (SEIN) take cover
un'tervermieten *tr* sublet
Un'tervertrag *m* subcontract
unterwan'dern *tr* infiltrate
Un'terwäsche *f* underwear
Unterwasser– *comb.fm.* underwater, submarine
Un'terwasserbombe *f* depth charge
Un'terwasserhorchgerät *n* hydrophone
Un'terwasserortungsgerät *n* sonar
unterwegs [ʊntər'veks] *adv* on the way; (com) in transit
unterwei'sen §118 *tr* instruct
Unterwei'sung *f* (-;-en) instruction
Un'terwelt *f* underworld; (myth) lower world
unterwer'fen §160 *tr* subjugate; (*dat*) subject (to) || *ref* (*dat*) submit to, subject oneself to; **sich** [*dat*] **ein Volk u.** subjugate a people
Unterwer'fung *f* (-;) subjugation; submission
unterworfen [ʊntər'vorfən] *adj* subject
unterwürfig ['ʊntərvyrfɪç] *adj* submissive, subservient
unterzeich'nen *tr* sign
Unterzeich'ner **–in** §6 *mf* signer; signatory
Unterzeichnete [ʊntər'tsaɪçnətə] §5 *mf* undersigned
Unterzeich'nung *f* (-;-en) signing; signature
un'terziehen §163 *tr* put on underneath || **unterzie'hen** §163 *tr* (*dat*) subject (to) || *ref*—**sich der Mühe u. zu** (*inf*) take the trouble to (*inf*); **sich e-r Operation u.** have an operation; **sich e-r Prüfung u.** take an examination
un'tief *adj* shallow || **Untiefe** *f* (-;-n) shoal
Un'tier *n* (& fig) monster
untilg'bar *adj* inextinguishable; (*Tinte*) indelible; (*Anleihe*) irredeemable
untrag'bar *adj* unbearable; (*Kleidung*) unwearable; (*Kosten*) prohibitive
untrenn'bar *adj* inseparable
un'treu *adj* unfaithful || **Untreue** *f* unfaithfulness; infidelity
untröst'lich *adj* inconsolable
untrüg'lich *adj* unerring, infallible
un'tüchtig *adj* incapable; inefficient
Un'tugend *f* bad habit, vice
un'überlegt *adj* thoughtless; rash
unübersehbar *adj* vast, huge; incalculable || *adv* very
unübersetz'bar *adj* untranslatable
un'übersichtlich *adj* unclear; (*Kurve*) blind
unübersteig'bar, unübersteig'lich *adj* insurmountable
unübertreff'bar *adj* unsurpassable
unübertroffen [ʊnybər'trɔfən] *adj* unsurpassed
unüberwind'lich *adj* invincible; (*Schwierigkeiten*) insurmountable

unumgäng'lich *adj* indispensable
unumschränkt ['ʊnʊm'reŋkt] *adj* unlimited; (pol) absolute
unumstößlich ['ʊnʊm'tøslɪç] *adj* irrefutable; (*unwiderruflich*) irrevocable
unumwunden ['ʊnʊmvʊndən] *adj* blunt
un'unterbrochen *adj* continuous
unverän'derlich *adj* unchangeable, invariable
unverant'wortlich *adj* irresponsible
unveräu'ßerlich *adj* inalienable
unverbesserlich [ʊnfer'besərlɪç] *adj* incorrigible
unverbind'lich *adj* without obligation; (*Verhalten*) proper, formal; (*Antwort*) noncommittal
un'verblümt *adj* blunt, plain
unverbürgt [ʊnfer'byrkt] *adj* unwarranted; (*Nachricht*) unconfirmed
un'verdächtig *adj* unsuspected
un'verdaulich *adj* indigestible
unverderbt ['ʊnferderpt], **unverdorben** ['ʊnferdorbən] *adj* unspoiled
unverdient ['ʊnferdint] *adj* undeserved
un'verdrossen *adj* indefatigable
un'verdünnt ['ʊnferdynt] *adj* undiluted
unverehelicht ['ʊnfere·əlɪçt] *adj* unmarried, single
un'vereinbar *adj* incompatible; contradictory
unverfälscht ['ʊnferfel/t] *adj* genuine; (*Wein*) undiluted
un'verfänglich *adj* innocent
un'verfroren *adj* brash
un'vergänglich *adj* imperishable
un'vergeßlich *adj* unforgettable
unvergleich'bar *adj* incomparable
unvergleichlich ['ʊnferglaɪçlɪç] *adj* incomparable
un'verhältnismäßig *adj* disproportionate
un'verheiratet *adj* unmarried
unvergolten ['ʊnfergɔltən] *adj* unrewarded
unverhofft ['ʊnferhɔft] *adj* unhoped-for
unverhohlen ['ʊnferholən] *adj* unconcealed; (fig) open
un'verkäuflich *adj* unsalable
unverkennbar ['ʊnferkenbar] *adj* unmistakable
unverkürzt ['ʊnferkyrtst] *adj* unabridged
unverlangt ['ʊnferlaŋt] *adj* unsolicited
un'verletzbar, un'verletzlich *adj* undamageable; (fig) inviolable
unverletzt ['ʊnferletst] *adj* safe and sound, unharmed; (*Sache*) undamaged
unvermeid'lich *adj* inevitable
unvermindert ['ʊnfermɪndərt] *adj* undiminished
unvermittelt ['ʊnfermɪtəlt] *adj* sudden
Un'vermögen *n* inability; impotence
un'vermögend *adj* poor; impotent
unvermutet ['ʊnfermutət] *adj* unexpected
un'vernehmlich *adj* imperceptible
Un'vernunft *f* unreasonableness; folly
un'vernünftig *adj* unreasonable; foolish
un'verschämt *adj* brazen, shameless

unverschuldet [ˈʊnferˌʃʊldət] *adj* un-encumbered; (*unverdient*) unde-served
un'versehens *adv* unawares, suddenly
unversehrt [ˈʊnferzeːrt] *adj* undamaged (*Person*) unharmed
unversichert [ˈʊnferzɪçərt] *adj* unin-sured
unversiegbar [ʊnferˈziːkbaːr] **unversieg-lich** [ʊnferˈziːklɪç] *adj* inexhaustible
unversiegelt [ˈʊnferziːgəlt] *adj* unsealed
un'versöhnlich *adj* irreconcilable
unversorgt [ˈʊnferzɔrkt] *adj* unpro-vided for
Un'verstand *m* lack of judgment
un'verständig *adj* foolish
un'verständlich *adj* incomprehensible
unversucht [ˈʊnferzuːxt] *adj* untried
un'verträglich *adj* unsociable; quarrel-some; incompatible, contradictory
un'verwandt *adj* steady, unflinching
unverwelklich [ʊnferˈvelklɪç] *adj* un-fading
un'verwendbar *adj* unusable
unverweslich [ˈʊnfervezlɪç] *adj* incor-ruptible
unverwindbar [ʊnferˈvɪntbaːr] *adj* ir-reparable; (*Enttäuschung*) lasting
un'verwundbar *adj* invulnerable
unverwüstlich [ˈʊnfervyːstlɪç] *adj* in-destructible; (*Stoff*) durable; (fig) irrepressible
unverzagt [ˈʊnfertsaːkt] *adj* undaunted
un'verzeihlich *adj* unpardonable
unverzerrt [ˈʊnfertsert] *adj* undistorted
unverzinslich [ˈʊnfertsɪnslɪç] *adj* (fin) without interest
unverzüglich [ˈʊnfertsyːklɪç] *adj* prompt, immediate || *adv* without delay
unvollendet [ˈʊnfɔlendət] *adj* unfin-ished
un'vollkommen *adj* imperfect
Un'vollkommenheit *f* imperfection
un'vollständig *adj* incomplete; (gram) defective
un'vorbereitet *adj* unprepared; (*Rede*) extemporaneous || *adv* extempore
un'voreingenommen *adj* unbiased
un'vorhergesehen *adj* unforeseen
un'vorsätzlich *adj* unintentional
un'vorsichtig *adj* incautious; careless
un'vorteilhaft *adj* disadvantageous; unprofitable; (*Kleid*) unflattering
un'wahr *adj* untrue
un'wahrhaftig *adj* untruthful
Un'wahrheit *f* untruth, falsehood
un'wahrnehmbar *adj* imperceptible
un'wahrscheinlich *adj* unlikely, improb-able
unwan'delbar *adj* unchangeable
unwegsam [ˈʊnvekzaːm] *adj* impass-able
unweigerlich [ʊnˈvaɪɡərlɪç] *adj* un-hesitating; (*Folge*) necessary || *adv* without fail
un'weit *adj—u. von* not far from || *prep* (*genit*) not far from
Un'wesen *n* mischief; **sein U. treiben** be up to one's old tricks
un'wesentlich *adj* unessential; unim-portant; (für) immaterial (to)
Un'wetter *n* storm

un'wichtig *adj* unimportant
unwiederbringlich [ʊnviːdərˈbrɪŋlɪç] *adj* irretrievable, irreparable
unwiderleg'bar *adj* irrefutable
un'widerruf'lich *adj* irrevocable
unwidersteh'lich *adj* irresistible
Un'wille *m*, **Un'willen** *m* indignation, displeasure; reluctance
un'willig *adj* (über *acc*) indignant (at), displeased (at); **u. zu** (*inf*) reluctant to (*inf*)
un'willkommen *adj* unwelcome
un'willkürlich *adj* involuntary
un'wirklich *adj* unreal
un'wirksam *adj* ineffective; inefficient; (chem) inactive; (jur) null and void
Un'wirksamkeit *f* ineffectiveness; inef-ficiency; (chem) inactivity
unwirsch [ˈʊnvɪrʃ] *adj* surly
un'wirtlich *adj* inhospitable
un'wirtschaftlich *adj* uneconomical
unwissend [ˈʊnvɪsənt] *adj* ignorant
Unwissenheit [ˈʊnvɪsənhaɪt] *f* (–;) ig-norance
un'wissenschaftlich *adj* unscientific
un'wissentlich *adv* unwittingly
un'wohl *adj* sickish; **ich fühle mich u.** I don't feel well
un'wohnlich *adj* uninhabitable; (*un-behaglich*) uncomfortable
un'würdig *adj* unworthy
Un'zahl *f* (von) huge number (of)
unzähl'bar, unzählig [ʊnˈtseːlɪç] *adj* countless, innumerable
un'zart *adj* indelicate
Unze [ˈʊntsə] *f* (–;-n) ounce
Un'zeit *f* wrong time
un'zeitgemäß *adj* out-of-date
un'zeitig *adj* untimely; (*Obst*) unripe
unzerbrech'lich *adj* unbreakable
unzerstör'bar *adj* indestructible
unzertrennlich [ʊntserˈtrenlɪç] *adj* in-separable
unziemend [ˈʊntsiːmənt], **un'ziemlich** *adj* unbecoming, unseemly
Un'zucht *f* unchastity; lewdness
un'züchtig *adj* unchaste; lewd
un'zufrieden *adj* dissatisfied
un'zugänglich *adj* inaccessible; aloof
un'zulänglich *adj* inadequate
un'zulässig *adj* inadmissible; (*Beein-flussung, Einmischung*) undue
un'zurechnungsfähig *adj* unaccountable
un'zureichend *adj* inadequate
un'zusammenhängend *adj* incoherent
un'zuträglich *adj* (dat) bad (for)
un'zutreffend *adj* not applicable
un'zuverlässig *adj* unreliable
un'zweckmäßig *adj* inappropriate; un-suitable; impractical
un'zweideutig *adj* unambiguous
un'zweifelhaft *adj* undoubted
üppig [ˈʏpɪç] *adj* luxurious, plush; (*Mahl*) sumptuous; (*Pflanzenwuchs*) luxuriant; (*sinnlich*) voluptuous
Ur-, ur- [uːr] *comb.fm.* original; very
ur'alt *adj* very old, ancient
Uran [uˈraːn] *n* (–s;) uranium
Ur'aufführung *f* world première
urbar [ˈuːrbaːr] *adj* arable; **u. machen** reclaim
Urbarmachung [ˈuːrbaːrmaːxʊŋ] *f* (–;) reclamation

Ur'bewohner pl aborigines
Ur'bild n prototype; original
ur'deutsch adj hundred-percent German
ur'eigen adj one's very own; original
Ur'einwohner pl aborigines
Ur'eltern pl ancestors
Ur'enkel m great-grandson
Ur'geschichte f prehistory
Ur'großmutter f great-grandmother
Ur'großvater m great-grandfather
Urheber **–in** ['urhebər(ın)] §6 mf originator, author
Ur'heberrecht n copyright
Ur'heberschaft f (–;-e) authorship
Urin [u'rin] m (–s;) urine
urinieren [urı'nirən] intr urinate
ur'ko'misch adj very funny
Urkunde ['urkundə] f (–;-n) document; deed; (Vertrag) instrument
Ur'kundenmaterial n documentation
urkundlich ['urkuntlıç] adj documentary; (verbürgt) authentic
Urlaub ['urlaup] m (–[e]s;-e) vacation; (mil) furlough
Ur'lauber **–in** §6 mf vacationer
Ur'laubsschein m (mil) pass
Ur'laubstag m day off
Urne ['urnə] f (–;-n) urn; ballot box; zur U. gehen go to the polls
Ur'nengang m balloting

ur'plötz'lich adj sudden || adv all of a sudden
Ur'sache f cause, reason; keine U.! don't mention it!
ur'sächlich adj causal
Ur'schleim m (–es;) protoplasm
Ur'schrift f original text, original
Ur'sprung m origin, source; beginning; (Ursache) cause
ursprünglich ['ur'sprynlıç] adj original
Ur'stoff m primary matter; (chem) element
Ur'teil n judgment; (Ansicht) view, opinion; (jur) verdict; (Strafmaß) (jur) sentence
urteilen ['urtaılən] intr judge; u. nach judge by
Ur'teilskraft f discernment
Ur'teilsspruch m verdict; sentence
Ur'text m original text
Ur'tier n protozoon
Ur'volk n aborigines
Ur'wald m virgin forest; jungle
ur'weltlich adj primeval
urwüchsig ['urvyksıç] adj original; (fig) rough
Ur'zeit f remote antiquity
Utensilien [uten'ziljən] pl utensils
Uto·pie [uto'pi] f (–;-pien ['pi·ən]) utopia; pipe dream
uzen ['utsən] tr tease, kid

V

V, v [fau] invar n V, v
vag [vak] adj vague
Vagabund [vaga'bunt] m (–en;-en) vagabond, tramp, bum
vagabundieren [vagabun'dirən] intr (HABEN & SEIN) bum around
vage ['vagə] adj vague
vakant [va'kant] adj vacant
Vakanz [va'kants] f (–;-en) vacancy
Vaku·um ['vaku·um] n (–s;-ua [u·a]) vacuum
Vakzine [vak'tsinə] f (–;-n) vaccine
vakzinieren [vaktsı'nirən] tr vaccinate
Valet [va'let] n (–s;-s) farewell
Valu·ta [va'luta] f (–;-ten [tən]) value; (foreign) currency
Vampir ['vampir] m (–s;-e) vampire
Vandale [van'dalə] m (–n;-n) Vandal; (fig) vandal
Vanille [va'nıljə] f (–;) vanilla
Variante [varı'antə] f (–;-n) variant
Varietät [varı·ɛ'tet] f (–;-en) variety
Varieté [varı·ɛ'te] n (–s;-s) vaudeville; vaudeville stage
variieren [varı'irən] tr & intr vary
Vase ['vazə] f (–;-n) vase
Vaselin [vaze'lin] n (–s;-e), **Vaseline** [vaze'linə] f (–;-n) vaseline
Vater ['fatər] m (–s;ⁿ) father
Va'terland n (native) country
vaterländisch ['fatərlendıʃ] adj national || adv—gesinnt patriotic
Va'terlandsliebe f patriotism
väterlich ['fetərlıç] adj fatherly

väterlicherseits ['fetərlıçər'zaıts] adv on the father's side
Va'terliebe f paternal love
Va'terschaft f (–;) fatherhood
Va'terschaftsklage f paternity suit
Va'tersname m family name, last name
Va'terstadt f home town
Va'terstelle f—bei j-m V. vertreten be a father to s.o.
Vaterun'ser n (–s;–) Lord's Prayer
Vati ['fati] m (–s;-s) dad, daddy
Vatikan [vatı'kan] m (–s;) Vatican
v. Chr. abbr (vor Christus) B.C.
Vegetarier **–in** [vege'tarjər(ın)] §6 mf vegetarian
Vegetation [vegeta'tsjon] f (–;) vegetation
vegetieren [vege'tirən] intr vegetate
Veilchen ['faılçən] n (–s;–) (bot) violet
Vene ['venə] f (–;-n) (anat) vein
Venedig [ve'nedıç] n (–s;) Venice
venerisch [ve'nerıʃ] adj venereal; venerisches Leiden venereal disease
Ventil [ven'til] n (–s;-e) valve; (bei der Orgel) stop; (fig) outlet
Ventilation [ventıla'tsjon] f (–;) ventilation
Venti·lator [ventı'lator] m (–s;-latoren [la'torən]) ventilator; fan
ver– [fer] pref up, e.g., **verbrauchen** use up; away, e.g., **verjagen** chase away; mis-, wrongly, e.g., **verstellen** misplace, **verdrehen** turn the wrong

way; (to form verbs from other parts of speech) **verwirklichen** realize, **vergöttern** deify; (to express a sense opposite that of the simple verb) **verlernen** forget, **verkaufen** sell; (to indicate consumption or waste through the action of the verb) **verschreiben** use up in writing; (to indicate intensification or completion) **verhungern** die of hunger; (to indicate cessation of action) **vergären** cease to ferment; (to indicate conversion to another state) **verflüssigen** liquify

verabfolgen [fɛr'apfɔlgən] tr hand over; deliver; (Arznei) give, administer

verabreden [fɛr'apredən] tr agree upon; **schon anderweitig verabredet sein** have a prior engagement ‖ ref make an appointment

Verab'redung f (-;-en) agreement; appointment

verabreichen [fɛr'apraɪçən] tr give

verabsäumen [fɛr'apzɔɪmən] tr var of **versäumen**

verabscheuen [fɛr'apʃɔɪ-ən] tr detest, loath, abhor

verab'scheuenswert, verab'scheuenswürdig detestable

verabschieden [fɛr'apʃidən] tr dismiss; (Beamte) put on pension; (Gesetz) pass; (mil) disband ‖ ref (von) take leave (of), say goodbye (to)

Verab'schiedung f (-;-en) dismissal; pensioning; (mil) disbanding; (parl) passing, enactment

verach'ten tr despise; **nicht zu v.** not to be sneezed at

verächtlich [fɛr'ɛçtlɪç] adj contemptuous; (verachtungswert) contemptible

Verach'tung f (-;) contempt

veralbern [fɛr'albərn] tr tease

verallgemeinern [fɛralgə'maɪnərn] tr & intr generalize

Verallgemei'nerung f (-;-en) generalization

veralten [fɛr'altən] intr become obsolete; (Kleider) go out of style

veraltet [fɛr'altət] adj obsolete; out of date, old-fashioned

Veran•da [ve'randa] f (-;-den [dən]) veranda, porch

veränderlich [fɛr'ɛndərlɪç] adj changeable; (math) variable

Verän'derlichkeit f (-;-en) changeableness; fluctuation; instability

verän'dern [fɛr'ɛndərn] tr change; vary ‖ ref change; look for a new job

Verän'derung f (-;-en) change

verängstigt [fɛr'ɛŋstɪçt] adj intimidated

verankern [fɛr'aŋkərn] tr anchor, moor

Veran'kerung f (-;-en) anchorage, mooring

veranlagen [fɛr'anlagən] tr (zu e-r Steuer) assess; **gut veranlagt** highly talented; **künstlerisch veranlagt** artificially inclined; **schlecht veranlagt** poorly endowed

Veran'lagung f (-;-en) talents; disposition; (fin) assessment

veran'lassen tr cause, occasion, make; (bereden) induce

Veran'lassung f (-;-en) cause, occasion; **auf V. von** at the suggestion of; **ohne jede V.** without provocation; **V. geben zu** give rise to

veranschaulichen [fɛr'anʃaulɪçən] tr make clear, **illust**rate

veran'schlagen §132 tr rate, value; (im voraus berechnen) estimate; **zu hoch v.** overrate

Veran'schlagung f (-;) estimate

veranstalten [fɛr'anʃtaltən] tr organize, arrange; (Empfang) give; (Sammlung) take up; (Versammlung) hold

Veran'stalter –in §6 mf organizer

Veran'staltung f (-;-en) organization, arrangement; affair; performance; show; meeting; (sport) event, meet

veran'tworten tr answer for, account for; (verteidigen) defend ‖ ref defend oneself, justify oneself

verantwortlich [fɛr'antvɔrtlɪç] adj responsible, answerable; **für etw v. zeichnen** sign for s.th.

Verant'wortlichkeit f (-;) responsibility; (jur) liability

Verant'wortung f (-;-en) responsibility; (Rechtfertigung) justification; **auf eigene V.** at one's own risk; **die V. abwälzen auf** (acc) pass the buck to; **zur V. ziehen** call to account

Verant'wortungsbewußtsein n sense of responsibility

verant'wortungsfreudig adj willing to assume responsibility

verant'wortungsvoll adj responsible

veräppeln [fɛr'ɛpəln] tr (coll) tease

verar'beiten tr manufacture, process; (zu) make (into); (verdauen) digest; (fig) assimilate

verar'beitend adj manufacturing

Verar'beitung f (-;-en) manufacturing; digestion; (fig) assimilation

verargen [fɛr'argən] tr—**j-m etw v.** blame s.o. for s.th.

verär'gern tr annoy

verarmen [fɛr'armən] intr (SEIN) grow poor

verästeln [fɛr'ɛstəln] ref branch out

verausgaben [fɛr'ausgabən] tr pay out ‖ ref run short of money

veräußern [fɛr'ɔɪsərn] tr sell

Verb [vɛrp] n (-s;-en) verb

verbal [vɛr'bal] adj verbal

Verband [fɛr'bant] m (-[e]s;-̈e) association, union, federation; (aer, nav) formation; (mil) unit; (surg) bandage, dressing; **sich aus dem V. lösen** (aer) peel off

Verband'kasten m first-aid kit

Verband'päckchen n first-aid pack

Verband'platz m first-aid station

Verband'stoff m bandage, dressing

verbannen [fɛr'banən] tr banish, exile

Verbannte [fɛr'bantə] §5 mf exile

Verban'nung f (-;-en) banishment; place of exile

verbarrikadie'ren tr barricade

verbau'en tr (Gelände) build up; use up (in building); (Geld) spend (in building); build poorly; **j-m den Weg v. zu** bar s.o.'s way to

verbei'ßen §53 *tr* swallow, suppress ||
ref (in *acc*) stick (to)
verber'gen §54 *tr* & *ref* hide
verbes'sern *tr* improve; correct; (*Aufsatz*) grade; (*Gesetz*) amend; (*Tat-
sache*) rectify || *ref* improve; better
oneself
Verbes'serung *f* (–;-en) improvement;
correction; amendment
verbeu'gen *ref* bow
Verbeu'gung *f* (–;-en) bow; curtsy
verbeulen [fer'bɔilən] *tr* dent; batter
verbie'gen §57 *tr* bend || *ref* warp
verbie'ten §58 *tr* forbid
verbil'den *tr* spoil; educate badly
verbil'ligen *tr* reduce the price of
Verbil'ligung *f* (–;-en) reduction
verbin'den §59 *tr* tie, tie up; join,
unite; (*verketten*) link; (*zu Dank verpflichten*) obligate; (chem) combine;
(med) bandage; (telp) connect
(with), put through (to); **j–m die
Augen v.** blindfold s.o. || *ref* unite
verbindlich [fer'bɪntlɪç] *adj* obliging;
binding; **verbindlichsten Dank!** thank
you ever so much!
Verbind'lichkeit *f* (–;-en) obligation;
commitment; polite way; (*e–s Vertrags*) binding force
Verbin'dung *f* (–;-en) union; association; alliance; combination; contact;
touch; (*Fuge, Gelenk*) joint; (chem)
compound; (educ) fraternity; (mach,
rr, telp) connection; (mil) liaison;
die V. verlieren mit lose touch with;
e–e V. eingehen (chem) form a compound; **er hat gute Verbindungen** he
has good connections; **in V. mit** in
conjunction with; **sich in V. setzen
mit** get in touch with; **unmittelbare
V.** (telp) direct call
Verbin'dungsbahn *f* connecting train
Verbin'dungsleitung *f* (telp) trunk line
Verbin'dungslinie *f* line of communication
Verbin'dungsoffizier *m* liaison officer
Verbin'dungspunkt *m*, **Verbin'dungs-
stelle** *f* joint, juncture
Verbin'dungsstück *n* joint, coupling
verbissen [fer'bɪsən] *adj* dogged, grim;
(*Zorn*) suppressed; **v. sein in** (*dat*)
stick doggedly to
Verbis'senheit *f* (–;) doggedness, grimness
verbitten [fer'bɪtən] §60 *ref–sich
[dat] etw v.* not stand for s.th.
verbittern [fer'bɪtərn] *tr* embitter
Verbit'terung *f* (–;) bitterness
verblassen [fer'blasən] *intr* (SEIN)
grow pale; (fig) fade
verblättern [fer'blɛtərn] *tr–die Seite
v.* lose the page
Verbleib [fer'blaɪp] *m* (–[e]s;) whereabouts
verblei'ben §62 *intr* (SEIN) remain, be
left; (**bei**) persist (in); **wir sind so
verblieben, daß** we finally agreed
that
verblei'chen §85 *intr* (SEIN) fade
verblen'den *tr* blind; dazzle; (*Mauer*)
face; (*Fenster*) wall up
Verblen'dung *f* (–;-en) blindness, infatuation; (archit) facing

verblichen [fer'blɪçən] *adj* faded
verblödet [fer'blødət] *adj* idiotic
verblüffen [fer'blʏfən] *tr* dumbfound,
flabbergast; bewilder, perplex
Verblüf'fung *f* (–;) bewilderment
verblü'hen *intr* (SEIN) wither; fade
verblümt [fer'blymt] *adj* euphemistic
verblu'ten *ref* & *intr* (SEIN) bleed to
death
verbocken [fer'bɔkən] *tr* bungle
verboh'ren *ref–sich v. in* (*acc*) stick
stubbornly to
verbohrt [fer'bort] *adj* stubborn; odd
verbolzen [fer'bɔltsən] *tr* bolt
verbor'gen *adj* secret; latent; hidden ||
tr lend out || **Verborgene** §5 *n–im
Verborgenen** in secret, on the sly
Verbor'genheit *f* (–;) secrecy; concealment; seclusion
Verbot [fer'bot] *n* (–[e]s;-e) prohibition; (jur) injunction
verboten [fer'botən] *adj* forbidden;
Eintritt v.! no admittance; **Plakatan-
kleben v.!** post no bills!; **Stehenbleiben v.!** no loitering
verbrämen [fer'bremən] *tr* trim, edge;
(fig) sugar-coat
verbrannt [fer'brant] *adj* burnt; torrid; **Politik der verbrannten Erde**
scorched-earth policy
Verbrauch' *m* (–[e]s;) use, consumption
verbrau'chen *tr* use up, consume;
waste; (*abnutzen*) wear out
Verbrau'cher *m* (–s;–) consumer; (*Be-
nützer*) user; (*Kunde*) customer
Verbrau'chergenossenschaft *f* co-op
Verbrauchs'güter *pl* consumer goods
verbraucht' *adj* used up, consumed;
worn out; (*Geld*) spent; (*Luft*) stale
verbre'chen §64 *tr* commit, do || **Ver-
brechen** *n* (–s;–) crime
Verbre'cher *m* (–s;–) criminal
Verbre'cheralbum *n* rogues' gallery
Verbre'cherin *f* (–;-nen) criminal
verbrecherisch [fer'breçərɪʃ] *adj* criminal
Verbre'cherkolonie *f* penal colony
verbreiten [fer'braɪtən] *tr* spread;
(*Frieden, Licht*) shed || *ref* spread;
sich v. über (*acc*) expatiate on
verbreitern [fer'braɪtərn] *tr* & *ref*
widen, broaden
Verbrei'terung *f* (–;) widening, broad-
ening
Verbrei'tung *f* (–;) spreading; dissemi-
nation; diffusion
verbren'nen §97 *tr* burn; scorch; (*bräu-
nen*) tan; (*Leichen*) cremate || *ref*
burn oneself; **sich** [*dat*] **die Finger
v.** (& fig) burn one's fingers
Verbren'nung *f* (–;-en) burning, combustion; cremation; (*Brandwunde*)
burn
Verbren'nungskraftmaschine *f*, **Verbren'nungsmotor** *m* internal combustion engine
Verbren'nungsraum *m* combustion
chamber
verbrin'gen §65 *tr* spend, pass; (*wegbringen*) take away
verbrüdern [fer'brydərn] *ref* (**mit**) fraternize (with)

Verbrü'derung f (-;) fraternizing
verbrü'hen tr scald
verbu'chen tr book; **etw als Erfolg v.** chalk s.th. up as a success
Ver·bum ['verbum] n (-s;-ba [ba]) verb
verbunden [fer'bundən] adj connected; **falsch v.!** sorry, wrong number!; **untereinander v.** interconnected; **zu Dank v.** obligated
verbünden [fer'byndən] ref—**sich mit j-m v.** ally oneself with s.o.
Verbun'denheit f (-;) connection, ties; solidarity, union
Verbündete [fer'byndətə] §5 mf ally
verbür'gen tr guarantee, vouch for || ref—**sich v. für** vouch for
verbürgt [fer'byrkt] adj authenticated
verbüßen [fer'bysən] tr atone for, pay for; **seine Strafe v.** serve one's time
verchromen [fer'kromən] tr chromeplate
Verchro'mung f (-;-en) chromeplating
Verdacht [fer'daxt] m (-[e]s;) suspicion; **in V. kommen** come under suspicion; **V. hegen gegen** have suspicions about; **V. schöpfen** get suspicious
verdächtig [fer'deçtiç] adj suspicious; (genit) suspected (of)
verdächtigen [fer'deçtigən] tr cast suspicion on; (genit) suspect (of)
Verdäch'tigung f (-;-en) insinuation
verdammen [fer'damən] tr condemn; damn
Verdammnis [fer'damnis] f (-;) damnation, perdition
verdammt' adj (sl) damn || interj (sl) damn it!
verdamp'fen tr & intr (SEIN) evaporate
Verdampf'fung f (-;) evaporation
verdan'ken tr—**j-m etw v.** be indebted to s.o. for s.th.
verdarb [fer'darp] pret of **verderben**
verdattert [fer'datərt] adj (coll) shook up
verdauen [fer'dau·ən] tr digest
verdaulich [fer'dauliç] adj digestible
Verdau'ung f (-;) digestion
Verdau'ungsbeschwerden pl **Verdau'ungsstörung** f indigestion
Verdau'ungswerkzeug n digestive track
Verdeck [fer'dek] n (-[e]s;-e) hood (of baby carriage); (aut) convertible top; (naut) deck
verdecken (verdek'ken) tr cover; hide
verden'ken §66 tr—**j-m etw v.** blame s.o. for s.th.
Verderb [fer'derp] m (-[e]s;) ruin; decay
verderben [fer'derbən] §149 tr spoil; ruin; (Magen) upset; (verführen) corrupt || intr (SEIN) spoil, go bad; (fig) go to pot || **Verderben** (-s;) ruin; **j-n ins V. stürzen** ruin s.o.
verderblich [fer'derpliç] adj ruinous; (Lebensmittel) perishable
Verderbnis [fer'derpnis] f (-;) depravity
verderbt [fer'derpt] adj depraved
Verderbt'heit f (-;) depravity
verdeutlichen [fer'dɔitliçən] tr make plain, explain

verdeutschen [fer'dɔit/ən] tr translate into (or express in) German
verdich'ten tr condense, thicken || ref condense; solidify; thicken; (Nebel, Rauch) grow thicker; (Verdacht) become stronger, grow
verdicken [fer'dikən] tr & ref thicken
verdie'nen tr deserve; (Geld) earn
Verdienst [fer'dinst] m (-es;-e) earnings; gain, profit || n (-es;-e) merit; deserts; **es ist dein V., daß** it is owing to you that; **nach V.** deservedly; **nach V. behandelt werden** get one's due; **sich** [dat] **als** (or **zum**) **V. anrechnen** take credit for it; **V. um** services to
Verdienst'ausfall m loss of wages
verdienst'lich adj meritorious
Verdienst'spanne f margin of profit
verdienst'voll adj meritorious
verdient [fer'dint] adj—**sich um j-n v. machen** serve s.o. well
verdol'metschen tr translate orally; interpret
Verdol'metschung f (-;) oral translation; interpretation
verdonnern [fer'dɔnərn] tr (coll) condemn
verdop'peln tr & ref double
verdorben [fer'dɔrbən] adj spoiled; (Luft) foul; (Magen) upset; (moralisch) depraved
verdorren [fer'dɔrən] intr (SEIN) dry up, wither
verdrän'gen tr push aside, crowd out; dislodge; (phys) displace; (psychol) repress, inhibit
Verdrän'gung f (-;-en) (phys) displacement; (psychol) repression, inhibition
verdre'hen tr twist; (Augen) roll; (Glied) sprain; (fig) distort; **j-m den Kopf v.** make s.o. fall in love with one
verdreht' adj twisted; (fig) distorted; (fig) (verrückt) cracked
verdreifachen [fer'draifaxən] tr triple
verdre'schen §67 tr (coll) spank
verdrießen [fer'drisən] §76 tr bother, annoy, get down; **laß es dich nicht v.!** don't let it get you down; **sich keine Mühe v. lassen** spare no pains || impers—**es verdrießt mich, daß** it bothers me that
verdrießlich [fer'drisliç] adj glum; tiresome, depressing; annoyed
verdroß [fer'drɔs] pret of **verdrießen**
verdro'ßen adj cross; (mürrisch) surly; (lustlos) listless
verdrucken (verdruk'ken) tr misprint
verdrücken (verdrük'ken) tr wrinkle; (coll) eat up, polish off || ref (coll) sneak away
Ver·druß [fer'drus] m (-drusses; -drusse) annoyance, vexation; **j-m etw zum V. tun** do s.th. to spite s.o.
verduften [fer'duftən] intr (SEIN) lose its aroma; (coll) take off, scram
verdummen [fer'dumən] tr make stupid || intr (SEIN) become stupid
verdunkeln [fer'duŋkəln] tr darken; obscure; (Glanz) dull; (fig) cloud; (astr) eclipse; (mil) black out || ref darken; (Himmel) cloud over

Verdun'kelung f (-;-en) darkening; (astr) eclipse; (mil) blackout

verdünnen [fɛr'dʏnən] tr thin; dilute; (Gase) rarefy

verdun'sten intr (SEIN) evaporate

Verdun'stung f (-;) evaporation

verdur'sten intr (SEIN) die of thirst

verdutzen [fɛr'dʊtsən] tr bewilder

veredeln [fɛr'edəln] tr ennoble; (verfeinen) refine; (Rohstoff) process; (Boden) enrich; (Pflanze, Tier) improve

Vere'delung f (-;) refinement; processing; enrichment; improvement

verehelichen [fɛr'e-əliçən] ref get married

verehren [fɛr'erən] tr revere; worship; (fig) adore; **j-m etw v.** present s.o. with s.th.

Vereh'rer –in §6 mf worshiper; (Liebhaber) admirer

verehrt [fɛr'ert] adj—**Sehr verehrte gnädige Frau!** Dear Madam; **Sehr verehrter Herr!** Dear Sir; **Verehrte Anwesende** (or **Gäste**)! Ladies and Gentlemen!

Vereh'rung f (-;) reverence, veneration; worship, adoration

vereiden [fɛr'aɪdən], **vereidigen** [fɛr'aɪdɪgən] tr swear in

Verein [fɛr'aɪn] m (-[e]s;-e) society

vereinbar [fɛr'aɪnbar] adj compatible

vereinbaren [fɛr'aɪnbarən] tr agree to, agree upon || ref—**das läßt sich mit meinen Grundsätzen nicht v.** that is inconsistent with my principles

Verein'barkeit f (-;) compatibility

Verein'barung f (-;) agreement, arrangement; terms; **nur nach V.** by appointment only

vereinen [fɛr'aɪnən] tr unite, join

vereinfachen [fɛr'aɪnfaxən] tr simplify

Verein'fachung f (-;-en) simplification

vereinheitlichen [fɛr'aɪnhaɪtlɪçən] tr standardize

vereinigen [fɛr'aɪnɪgən] tr unite, join; (verbinden) combine; (verschmelzen) merge; (versammeln) assemble || ref unite, join; (Flüsse) meet; **sich v. mit** team up with; **sich v. lassen mit** be compatible with, square with

Verei'nigten Staa'ten pl United States

Verein'igung f (-;-en) union; combination; society, association

vereinnahmen [fɛr'aɪnamən] tr take in

vereinsamen [fɛr'aɪnzamən] intr (SEIN) become lonely; become isolated

Verein'samung f (-;) loneliness; isolation

Vereins'meier –in §6 mf (coll) joiner

vereinzeln [fɛr'aɪntsəln] tr isolate

verein'zelt adj isolated; sporadic

vereisen [fɛr'aɪsən] tr (surg) freeze || intr (SEIN) become covered with ice; (aer) ice up

vereiteln [fɛr'aɪtəln] tr frustrate; baffle

verekeln [fɛr'ekəln] tr—**j—m etw v.** spoil s.th. for s.o.

veren'den intr (SEIN) die

verengen [fɛr'eŋən] tr & ref narrow

verer'ben tr bequeath, leave; (über-** mitteln) hand down; (Krankheit) transmit || ref run in the family

Verer'bung f (-;-en) inheritance; transmission; heredity

Verer'bungslehre f genetics

verewigen [fɛr'evigən] tr perpetuate

verewigt [fɛr'evɪçt] adj late, deceased

verfah'ren adj bungled, messed up || §71 tr bungle; (Geld, Zeit) spend (on travel) || ref lose one's way, take a track || intr (SEIN) proceed; act || **wrong turn**; (fig) be on the wrong

Verfahren n (-s;-) procedure, method; system; (chem) process; (jur) proceedings, case

Verfall m (-[e]s;) deterioration, decay; decline, downfall; (Fristablauf) expiration; (von Wechseln) maturity; **in V. geraten** become delapidated

verfal'len adj delapidated; **e-m Rauschgift v. sein** be addicted to a drug || §72 intr (SEIN) decay, go to ruin, decline; (ablaufen) expire; (Kranker) waste away; (Recht) lapse; (Pfand) be forfeited; (Wechsel) mature

Verfall'tag m due date; date of maturity

verfäl'schen tr falsify; (Geld) counterfeit; (Wein) adulterate; (Urkunde) forge

Verfäl'schung f (-;-en) falsification; forging; adulteration

verfan'gen §73 ref become entangled || intr (bei) have an effect (on)

verfänglich [fɛr'fɛnlɪç] adj (Frage) loaded; (Situation) awkward

verfär'ben ref change color

verfas'sen tr compose, write

Verfas'ser –in §6 mf author

Verfas'sung f (-;-en) constitution; (Zustand) condition; frame of mind, mood

verfas'sungsgemäß, verfas'sungsmäßig adj constitutional

verfas'sungswidrig adj unconstitutional

verfau'len intr (SEIN) rot

verfech'ten §74 tr defend, stand up for

Verfech'ter m (-s;-) champion

verfeh'len tr (Abzweigung, Ziel, Zug) miss; (Wirkung) fail to achieve, not have; **ich werde nicht v. zu** (inf) I will not fail to (inf) || recip—**wir haben uns verfehlt** we missed each other

verfehlt [fɛr'felt] adj wrong

Verfeh'lung f (-;-en) offense; mistake

verfeinden [fɛr'faɪndən] recip become enemies

verfeinern [fɛr'faɪnərn] tr refine, improve || ref become refined, improve

verfertigen [fɛr'fertɪgən] tr manufacture, make

Verfer'tigung f (-;) manufacture

verfilmen [fɛr'filmən] tr adapt to the screen, make into a movie

Verfil'mung f (-;-en) film version

verfilzen [fɛr'filtsən] ref get tangled

verfinstern [fɛr'fɪnstərn] ref get dark

verflachen [fɛr'flaxən] tr flatten || ref & intr (SEIN) flatten out

verflech'ten §74 tr interweave; (fig) implicate, involve

verflie'gen §57 ref (aer) lose one's

bearings || *intr* (SEIN) fly away; (*Zeit*) fly; evaporate; (fig) vanish
verflie'ßen §76 *intr* (SEIN) flow off; (*Frist*) run out, expire; (*Farben*) blend; (*Begriffe, Grenzen*) overlap
verflixt [fɛr'flɪkst] *adj* (sl) darn
verflossen [fɛr'flɔsən] *adj* past; former
verflu'chen *tr* curse, damn
verflucht' *adj* (sl) damn || *interj* (sl) damn it!
verflüchtigen [fɛr'flʏçtɪgən] *tr* volatilize || *ref* evaporate; (fig) disappear
verflüssigen [fɛr'flʏsɪgən] *tr* & *ref* liquefy
Verfolg [fɛr'fɔlk] *m* (-s;) course; **im V.** (*genit*) in pursuance of
verfol'gen *tr* pursue; follow up; persecute; haunt; (hunt) track; (jur) prosecute; **j-n steckbrieflich v.** send out a warrant for the arrest of s.o.
Verfol'ger **-in** §6 *mf* pursuer; persecutor
Verfol'gung *f* (-;-en) pursuit; persecution; (jur) prosecution
Verfol'gungswahn *m*, **Verfol'gungswahnsinn** *m* persecution complex
verfrachten [fɛr'fraxtən] *tr* ship; (coll) bundle off
Verfrach'ter **-in** §6 *mf* shipper
verfrühen [fɛr'fry·ən] *ref* be too early
verfügbar [fɛr'fykbar] *adj* available, at one's disposal
verfü'gen *tr* decree, order || *ref*—**sich v. nach** betake oneself to || *intr*—**v. über** (*acc*) have at one's disposal, have control over
Verfü'gung *f* (-;-en) decree, order; disposal; **einstweilige V.** (jur) injunction; **j-m zur V. stehen** be at s.o.'s disposal; **j-m zur V. stellen** put at s.o.'s disposal; **letztwillige V.** last will and testament
verfüh'ren *tr* mislead; (*zum Irrtum*) lead; (*verlocken*) seduce
Verfüh'rer **-in** §6 *mf* seducer
verführerisch [fɛr'fyrərɪʃ] *adj* seductive, tempting
Verfüh'rung *f* (-;-en) seduction
vergaffen [fɛr'gafən] *ref* (coll) (**in** *acc*) fall in love (with)
vergammeln [fɛr'gaməln] *intr* (SEIN) (coll) go to the dogs
vergangen [fɛr'gaŋən] *adj* past; (*Schönheit*) faded
Vergan'genheit *f* (-;) past; background; (gram) past tense
vergänglich [fɛr'gɛŋlɪç] *adj* transitory
vergasen [fɛr'gazən] *tr* gas
Verga'ser *m* (-s;-) carburetor
vergaß [fɛr'gas] *pret* of **vergessen**
verge'ben §80 *tr* forgive (*s.th.*); give away; (*Chance*) miss, pass up; (*Amt, freie Stelle*) fill; (*Auftrag*) place; (*Karten*) misdeal; (*verleihen*) confer; **v. sein** have a previous engagement; be engaged (*to a man*) || *ref*—**sich** (*dat*) **etw v.** compromise on s.th. || *intr* (*dat*) forgive (*s.o.*)
verge'bens [fɛr'gebəns] *adv* in vain
vergeb'lich [fɛr'geplɪç] *adj* vain, futile
Verge'bung *f* (-;) forgiveness; bestowal
vergegenwärtigen [fɛr'gegənvɛrtɪgən] *ref*—**sich** (*dat*) **etw. v.** visualize s.th.

verge'hen §82 *ref*—**sich an j–m v.** offend s.o.; (*sexuell*) violate s.o. || *intr* (SEIN) pass, go away; fade || **Vergehen** *n* (-s;-) offense, misdemeanor
vergel'ten §83 *tr* requite; **vergelt's Gott!** (coll) thank you!
Vergel'tung *f* (-;) repayment; retaliation, reprisal
Vergel'tungswaffe *f* V-1 or V-2
vergesellschaften [fɛrgə'zɛlʃaftən] *tr* socialize; nationalize
vergessen [fɛr'gesən] §70 *tr* forget
Verges'senheit *f* (-;)—**in V. geraten** fall (or sink) into oblivion
vergeßlich [fɛr'geslɪç] *adj* forceful
Vergeß'lichkeit *f* (-;) forgetfulness
vergeuden [fɛr'gɔidən] *tr* waste
Vergeu'dung *f* (-;) waste, squandering
vergewaltigen [fɛrgə'valtɪgən] *tr* do violence to; (*Mädchen*) rape
Vergewal'tigung *f* (-;-en) rape
vergewerkschaften [fɛrgə'vɛrkʃaftən] *tr* unionize
vergewissern [fɛrgə'vɪsərn] *ref* (*genit*) make sure of, ascertain
vergie'ßen §76 *tr* spill; (*Tränen*) shed
vergiften [fɛr'gɪftən] *tr* (& fig) poison; (*verseuchen*) contaminate || *ref* take poison
Vergif'tung *f* (-;-en) poisoning; contamination
vergipsen [fɛr'gɪpsən] *tr* plaster
Vergißmeinnicht [fɛr'gɪsmaɪnnɪçt] *n* (-[e]s;-e) forget-me-not
vergittern [fɛr'gɪtərn] *tr* bar up
Vergleich [fɛr'glaɪç] *m* (-[e]s;-e) comparison; (*Verständigung*) agreement; (*Ausgleich*) settlement; **e-n V. anstellen zwischen** make a comparison between; **e-n V. treffen** reach a settlement, come to an agreement
vergleichbar [fɛr'glaɪçbar] *adj* comparable
verglei'chen [fɛr'glaɪçən] §85 *tr* (**mit**) compare (with, to) || *ref* (**mit**) come to an agreement (with)
Vergleichs'grundlage *f* basis for comparison
vergleichs'weise *adv* by way of comparison
Verglei'chung *f* (-;-en) comparison; matching; contrasting
verglü'hen *intr* (SEIN) cease to glow
vergnügen [fɛr'gnygən] *tr* amuse, delight || *ref* enjoy oneself, amuse oneself || **Vergnügen** *n* (-s;-) delight, pleasure; **mit V.** with pleasure; **V. finden an** (*dat*) take delight in; **viel V.!** (coll) have fun!; **zum V.** for fun
vergnügt [fɛr'gnykt] *adj* cheerful, gay; (**über** *acc*) delighted (with)
Vergnü'gung *f* (-;-en) pleasure, amusement
Vergnü'gungspark *m* amusement park
Vergnü'gungsreise *f* pleasure trip
Vergnü'gungssteuer *f* entertainment tax
vergnü'gungssüchtig *adj* pleasure-loving
vergolden [fɛr'gɔldən] *tr* gild
Vergol'dung *f* (-;) gilding
vergönnen [fɛr'gœnən] *tr* not begrudge
vergöttern [fɛr'gœtərn] *tr* deify; (fig) idolize
vergra'ben §87 *tr* (& fig) bury

vergrämen [fɛr'grɛmən] *tr* annoy, anger

vergrämt [fɛr'grɛmt] *adj* haggard

vergrei'fen §88 *ref* (mus) hit the wrong note; **sich v. an** (*dat*) lay violent hands on; (*fremdem Gut*) encroach on; (*Geld*) misappropriate; (*Mädchen*) assault; **sich im Ausdruck v.** express oneself poorly

vergreisen [fɛr'graizən] *intr* (SEIN) age; become senile

vergriffen [fɛr'grifən] *adj* sold out; (*Buch*) out of print

vergröbern [fɛr'grøbərn] *tr* roughen ‖ *ref* become coarser

vergrößern [fɛr'grøsərn] *tr* enlarge; increase; (*ausdehnen*) expand; (opt) magnify ‖ *ref* become larger

Vergrö'ßerung *f* (–;-en) enlargement; increase; expansion; (opt) magnification

Vergrö'ßerungsapparat *m* (phot) enlarger

Vergrö'ßerungsglas *m* magnifying glass

Vergünstigung [fɛr'gynstiɡuŋ] *f* (–;-en) privilege; (*bevorzugte Behandlung*) preferential treatment

vergüten [fɛr'ɡytən] *tr* make good; (*Stahl*) temper; **j–m etw v.** reimburse (or compensate) s.o. for s.th.

Vergü'tung *f* (–;-en) reimbursement, compensation; tempering

verhaften [fɛr'haftən] *tr* apprehend

Verhaf'tung *f* (–;-en) apprehension

verhal'ten *adj* (*Atem*) bated; (*Stimme*) low ‖ §90 *tr* hold back; (*Atem*) hold; (*Lachen*) suppress; (*Stimme*) keep down; **den Schritt v.** slow down; (*stehenbleiben*) stop ‖ *ref* behave, act; be; **A verhält sich zu B wie X zu Y** A is to B as X is to Y; **sich anders v.** be different; **sich ruhig v.** keep quiet ‖ *impers ref*—**wenn es sich so verhält** if that's the case ‖ **Verhalten** *n* (–s;) conduct, behavior; attitude

Verhältnis [fɛr'hɛltnis] *n* (–ses;-se) proportion, ratio; (*Beziehung*) relation; (*Liebes-*) love affair; **aus kleinen Verhältnissen** of humble birth; **bei sonst gleichen Verhältnissen** other things being equal; **das steht in keinem V. zu** that is all out of proportion to; **Verhältnisse** circumstances, conditions; matters; means

verhält'nismäßig *adj* proportionate ‖ *adv* relatively, comparatively

Verhält'nismaßregeln *pl* instructions

Verhält'niswahl *f* proportional representation

verhält'niswidrig *adj* disproportionate

Verhält'niswort *n* (–[e]s;-⸚er) preposition

verhan'deln *tr* discuss; (*Waren*) sell ‖ *intr* negotiate; argue; (*beraten*) confer; (jur) plead a case; **gegen j–n wegen etw v.** (jur) try s.o. for s.th.

Verhand'lung *f* (–;-en) negotiation; discussion; proceedings, trial

verhangen [fɛr'haŋən] *adj* overcast

verhän'gen *tr* (*Fenster*) put curtains on; (*Strafe*) impose; (*Untersuchung*) order; (*Belagerungszustand*) proclaim; **mit verhängtem Zügel** at full speed

Verhängnis [fɛr'hɛŋnis] *n* (–ses;-se) destiny, fate; (*Unglück*) disaster

verhäng'nisvoll *adj* fateful; disastrous

verhärmt [fɛr'hɛrmt] *adj* haggard

verharren [fɛr'harən] *intr* (HABEN & SEIN) remain; (**auf** *dat*, **in** *dat*, **bei**) stick (to)

verhärten [fɛr'hɛrtən] *tr & ref* harden

verhaßt [fɛr'hast] *adj* hated, hateful

verhätscheln [fɛr'hɛtʃəln] *tr* pamper

Verhau [fɛr'hau] *m* (–[e]s;-e) barbwire entanglement

verhau'en §93 *tr* lick, beat up; (*Kind*) spank; (*Auftrag, Ball, usw.*) muff ‖ *ref* make a blunder

verheddern [fɛr'hedərn] *ref* get tangled up

verheeren [fɛr'herən] *tr* devastate

verhee'rend *adj* terrible; (coll) awful

Verhee'rung *f* (–;) devastation

verhehlen [fɛr'helən] *tr* conceal

verhei'len *intr* (SEIN) heal up

verheimlichen [fɛr'haimliçən] *tr* keep secret, conceal

Verheim'lichung *f* (–;) concealment

verhei'raten *tr* marry; (*Tochter*) give away ‖ *ref* (**mit**) get married (to)

Verhei'ratung *f* (–;) marriage

verhei'ßen §95 *tr* promise

Verhei'ßung *f* (–;-en) promise

verhei'ßungsvoll *adj* promising

verhel'fen §96 *intr*—**j–m zu etw v.** help s.o. to acquire s.th.

verherrlichen [fɛr'herliçən] *tr* glorify

Verherr'lichung *f* (–;) glorification

verhet'zen *tr* instigate

verhexen [fɛr'heksən] *tr* bewitch, hex

verhimmeln [fɛr'himəln] *tr* praise to the skies; (*Schauspieler*) idolize

verhin'dern *tr* prevent

Verhin'derung *f* (–;) prevention; **im Falle seiner V.** in case he's unavailable

verhohlen [fɛr'holən] *adj* hidden

verhöh'nen *tr* jeer at; make fun of

Verhöh'nung *f* (–;) jeering; ridicule

Verhör [fɛr'høːr] *n* (–s;-e) interrogation, questioning, hearing

verhö'ren *tr* interrogate, question ‖ *ref* hear wrong

verhudeln [fɛr'hudəln] *tr* (coll) bungle

verhüllen [fɛr'hylən] *tr* cover, veil; wrap up; disguise

Verhül'lung *f* (–;-en) cover; disguise

verhun'gern *intr* (SEIN) starve to death

verhunzen [fɛr'huntsən] *tr* (coll) botch

verhü'ten *tr* prevent, avert

verinnerlicht [fɛr'inərliçt] *adj* introspective

verir'ren *ref* lose one's way; (*Augen, Blick*) wander; (fig) make a mistake

verirrt [fɛr'irt] *adj* stray

verja'gen *tr* chase away

verjähren [fɛr'jɛrən] *intr* (SEIN) fall under the statute of limitations

verjubeln [fɛr'jubəln] *tr* squander

verjüngen [fɛr'jyŋən] *tr* rejuvenate; reduce in scale; taper ‖ *ref* be rejuvenated; taper, narrow

Verjün'gung *f* (–;) rejuvenation; tapering; scaling down

verkatert [fɛrˈkɑtərt] *adj* suffering from a hangover

Verkauf *m* (-[e]s;-e) sale

verkau'fen *tr* sell

Verkäu'fer -in §6 *mf* seller; salesclerk; vendor || *m* salesman || *f* salesgirl, saleswoman

verkäuf'lich *adj* salable

Verkaufs'anzeige *f* for-sale ad

Verkaufs'automat *m* vending machine

Verkaufs'leiter -in §6 *mf* sales manager

Verkaufs'schlager *m* good seller

Verkaufs'steigerung *f* sales promotion

Verkaufs'vertrag *m* agreement of sale

Verkehr [fɛrˈker] *m* (-s;) traffic; commerce; company, association; (*sexuell*) intercourse; (aer, rr) service; (fin) circulation

verkeh'ren reverse, invert; turn upside down; convert, change; (*Sinn, Worte*) twist || *intr* (*Fahrzeug*) run, run regularly; **mit j–m geschlechtlich v.** have intercourse with s.o.; **mit j–m v.** associate with s.o.

Verkehrs'ader *f* main artery

Verkehrs'ampel *f* traffic light

Verkehrs'andrang *m* heavy traffic

Verkehrs'betrieb *m* public transportation company

Verkehrs'delikt *n* traffic violation

Verkehrs'flugzeug *n* airliner

Verkehrs'insel *f* traffic island

Verkehrs'mittel *n* means of transportation

Verkehrs'ordnungen *pl* traffic regulations

Verkehrs'polizist -in §7 *mf* traffic cop

verkehrs'reich *adj* crowded, congested

verkehrs'stark *adj* busy

Verkehrs'stockung *f*, **Verkehrs'störung** *f* traffic jam

Verkehrs'unfall *m* traffic accident

Verkehrs'unternehmen *n* transportation company

Verkehrs'vorschrift *f* traffic regulation

Verkehrs'wesen *n* traffic, transportation

Verkehrs'zeichen *n* traffic sign

verkehrt [fɛrˈkert] *adj* reversed; upside down; inside out; wrong

verken'nen §97 *tr* misunderstand; (*Person*) misjudge, mistake

verketten [fɛrˈketən] *tr* chain together; (fig) link

Verket'tung *f* (-;) chaining; (fig) concatenation; (fig) coincidence

verkit'ten *tr* cement; putty; seal, bond

verkla'gen *tr* accuse; (jur) sue

Verklagte [fɛrˈklɑktə] §5 *mf* defendant

verklat'schen *tr* (coll) slander; (educ) squeal on

verkle'ben *tr* glue, cement; **v. mit** cover with

verklei'den *tr* disguise, dress up; (*täfeln*) panel; line, face; (mil) camouflage

Verklei'dung *f* (-;-en) disguise; paneling; lining, facing; (mil) camouflage

verkleinern [fɛrˈklaɪnərn] *tr* lessen, diminish; (fig) disparage; (math) reduce; **maßstäblich v.** scale down

Verklei'nerung *f* (-;-en) diminution, reduction; (fig) detraction

Verklei'nerungsform *f* diminutive

verklin'gen §142 *intr* (SEIN) die away

verkloppen [fɛrˈklɔpən] *tr* (coll) beat up

verknacken [fɛrˈknakən] *tr* (coll) sentence

verknallt [fɛrˈknalt] *adj*—**in j–n v. sein** (coll) have a crush on s.o.

verknappen [fɛrˈknapən] *intr* (SEIN) run short, run low

Verknap'pung *f* (-;) shortage

verknei'fen §88 *ref*—**sich** [*dat*] **etw v.** deny oneself s.th.

verkniffen [fɛrˈknɪfən] *adj* wry

verknip'sen *tr* (*Film*) waste

verknöchern [fɛrˈknœçərn] *intr* (SEIN) ossify; (*Glieder*) become stiff

verknöchert [fɛrˈknœçərt] *adj* pedantic; (*Junggeselle*) inveterate

verknoten [fɛrˈknotən] *tr* snarl, tie up

verknüp'fen *tr* tie together; (fig) connect, combine, relate

verknusen [fɛrˈknuzən] *tr* (coll) stand

verkohlen [fɛrˈkolən] *tr* carbonize; char; **j–n v.** (coll) pull s.o.'s leg

verkom'men *adj* decayed; degenerate; (*Gebäude*) squalid || §99 *intr* (SEIN) decay, spoil; (fig) go to the dogs; **v. zu** degenerate into

Verkom'menheit *f* (-;) depravity

verkop'peln *tr* couple; (*Interessen*) (com) consolidate

verkorken [fɛrˈkɔrkən] *tr* cork up

verkorksen [fɛrˈkɔrksən] *tr* (coll) bungle || *ref*—**sich** [*dat*] **den Magen v.** (coll) upset one's stomach

verkörpern [fɛrˈkœrpərn] *tr* embody, personify; (*Rolle*) play

Verkör'perung *f* (-;-en) embodiment, incarnation

verkra'chen *ref*—**sich mit j–m v.** have an argument with s.o. || *intr* (SEIN) (coll) go bankrupt

verkrampft [fɛrˈkrampft] *adj* cramped

verkrie'chen §102 *ref* hide; (& fig) crawl into a hole; **neben ihm kannst du dich v.!** you're no match for him!

verkrümeln [fɛrˈkryməln] *tr* crumble || *ref* (fig) disappear

verkrüm'men *tr* & *ref* bend

Verkrüm'mung *f* (-;) bend, crookedness; curvature

verkrüppeln [fɛrˈkrypəln] *tr* cripple || *intr* (SEIN) become crippled; (*verkümmern*) become stunted

verkrustet [fɛrˈkrʊstət] *adj* caked

verküh'len *ref* catch a cold

verküm'mern *intr* (SEIN) become stunted; (pathol) atrophy

Verküm'merung *f* (-;) atrophy

verkünden [fɛrˈkyndən], **verkündigen** [fɛrˈkyndɪgən] *tr* announce, proclaim; (*Urteil*) pronounce

Verkün'digung *f* (-;-en), **Verkün'dung** *f* (-;-en) announcement, proclamation; pronouncement; **Mariä Verkündigung** (feast of the) Annunciation

verkup'peln *tr* couple; (*Mädchen, Mann*) procure; (*Tochter*) sell into prostitution

verkür′zen tr shorten; abridge; (*beschränken*) curtail; (*Zeit*) pass

Verkür′zung f (–;-en) shortening; abridgement; curtailment

verla′chen tr laugh at

verla′den §103 tr load, ship

Verlag [fer′lak] m (–[e]s;-e) publisher; **im V. von** published by

verla′gern tr shift; (*aus Sicherheitsgründen*) evacuate || ref shift

Verla′gerung f (–;-en) shift, shifting; evacuation

Verlags′anstalt f publisher

Verlags′buchhandlung f publisher and dealer

Verlags′recht n copyright

verlangen [fer′laŋən] tr demand, require; want, ask || intr—v. nach ask for; long for || **Verlangen** n (–s;) demand; request; wish; claim; (*Sehnsucht*) longing, yearning; **auf V.** upon demand, upon request

verlängern [fer′leŋərn] tr lengthen; prolong, extend; **seinen Paß v. lassen** have one's passport renewed

Verlän′gerung f (–;-en) lengthening; prolongation, extension; (sport) overtime

Verlän′gerungsschnur f extension cord

verlangsamen [fer′laŋzamən] tr slow down

verläppern [fer′lepərn] tr (coll) fritter away

Ver-laß [fer′las] m (–lasses;) reliance; **es ist kein V. auf ihn** you can't rely on him

verlas′sen adj abandoned, deserted; lonesome || §104 tr leave; forsake, desert || ref—**sich v. auf** (acc) rely on

Verlas′senheit f (–;) loneliness

verläßlich [fer′leslıç] adj reliable

verlästern [fer′lestərn] tr slander

Verlä′sterung f (–;-en) slander

Verlaub [fer′laup] m—**mit V. with your permission; mit V. zu sagen if I may say so**

Verlauf′ m (–[e]s;) course; e—n guten **V. haben** turn out well; **nach V. von** after a lapse of

verlau′fen §105 intr (SEIN) (*Zeit*) pass, lapse; (*ablaufen*) turn out, come off; (*vorgehen*) proceed, run || ref lose one's way; (*Wasser*) run off; (*Menschenmenge*) disperse

verlau′ten intr (SEIN) become known, be reported; **kein Wort davon v. lassen** not breathe a word about it; **wie verlautet** as reported || impers— **es verlautet** it is reported

verle′ben tr spend, pass

verlebt [fer′lept] adj haggard

verle′gen adj embarrassed; confused; **v. um** (e—e *Antwort*) at a loss for; (*Geld*) short of || tr move, shift; transfer; misplace; (*Buch*) publish; (*Geleise, Kabel, Rohre*) lay; (*sperren*) block; (*vertagen*) postpone || ref—**sich v. auf** (acc) apply onself to; devote oneself to; resort to

Verle′genheit f (–;) embarrassment; difficulties; predicament; **in V. bringen** embarrass

Verle′ger m (–s;-) publisher

Verle′gung f (–;-en) move, shift; transfer; postponement; (*von Kabeln, usw.*) laying

verlei′den tr spoil, take the joy out of

Verleih [fer′laı] m (–s;-e) rental service

verlei′hen §81 tr lend out, loan; rent out; (*Gunst*) grant; (*Titel*) confer; (*Auszeichnung*) award

Verlei′her –in §6 mf lender; grantor; (*von Filmen*) distributor

Verlei′hung f (–;-en) lending out; rental; grant; bestowal

verlei′ten tr mislead; (*zur Sünde, zum Trunk*) lead; (jur) suborn

verler′nen tr unlearn, forget

verle′sen §107 tr read out; (*Namen*) read off; (*Salat*) clean; (*Gemüse*) sort out || ref misread

verletzen [fer′letsən] tr (& fig) injure, hurt; (*kränken*) offend; (*Gesetz*) break; (*Recht*) violate

verlet′zend adj offensive

Verletzte [fer′letstə] §5 mf injured party

Verlet′zung f (–;-en) injury; offense; (e–s *Gesetzes*) breaking; (e–s *Rechtes*) violation

verleug′nen tr deny; (*Kind*) disown; (*Glauben*) renounce || ref—**sich selbst v.** act contrary to one's nature; **sich vor Besuchern v. lassen** refuse to see visitors

Verleug′nung f (–;-en) denial; renunciation; disavowal

verleumden [fer′lɔımdən] tr slander

verleumderisch [fer′lɔımdərıʃ] adj slanderous, libelous

Verleum′dung f (–;-en) slander

verlie′ben ref—**sich in j–n v.** fall in love with s.o.

verliebt [fer′lipt] adj in love

verlieren [fer′lirən] §77 tr lose || ref lose one's way; disappear; disperse

Verlies [fer′lis] n (–es;-e) dungeon

verlo′ben ref (mit) become engaged (to)

Verlöbnis [fer′løpnıs] n (–ses;-se) engagement

Verlobte [fer′lɔptə] §5 m fiancé; **die Verlobten** the engaged couple || f fiancée

Verlo′bung f (–;-en) engagement

verlocken (verlok′ken) tr lure, tempt; (*verführen*) seduce

verlockend (verlok′kend) adj tempting

Verlockung (Verlok′kung) f (–;-en) allurement, temptation

verlogen [fer′logən] adj dishonest

verlohn′nen impers ref—**es verlohnt sich nicht** it doesn't pay || impers—**es verlohnt der Mühe nicht** it is not worth the trouble

verlor [fer′lor] pret of **verlieren**

verloren [fer′lorən] pp of **verlieren** || adj lost; (*hilflos*) forlorn; (*Ei*) poached; **der verlorene Sohn** the prodigal son

verlo′rengehen §180 tr give up for lost

verlo′rengehen §82 intr (SEIN) be lost

verlö′schen §110 tr extinguish; (*Schrift*) erase || intr (SEIN) (*Licht, Kerze*) go out; (*Zorn*) cease

verlo'sen tr raffle off, draw lots for
verlö'ten tr solder; **e–n v.** (coll) belt one down
verlottern [fer'lɔtərn] intr (coll) go to the dogs
verlumpen [fer'lumpən] tr (coll) blow, squander || intr (coll) go to the dogs
Verlust [fer'lust] m (-[e]s;-e) loss; **in V. geraten** get lost; **Verluste** (mil) casualties
Verlust'liste f (mil) casualty list
verma'chen tr bequeath, leave
Vermächtnis [fer'mɛçtnɪs] n (-ses;-se) bequest, legacy
vermählen [fer'mɛlən] tr marry || ref (mit) get married (to)
Vermäh'lung f (-;-en) marriage, wedding
vermah'nen tr admonish, warn
Vermah'nung f (-;-en) admonition
vermaledeien [fermalɛ'daɪ.ən] tr curse
vermanschen [fer'man/ən] tr (coll) make a mess of
vermasseln [fer'masəln] tr (coll) bungle, muff
vermassen [fer'masən] intr (SEIN) lose one's individuality
vermauern [fer'mau.ərn] tr wall up
vermehren [fer'merən] tr & ref increase; (an Zahl) multiply; **vermehrte Auflage** enlarged edition
vermei'den tr avoid
vermeidlich [fer'maɪtlɪç] adj avoidable
Vermei'dung f (-;) avoidance
vermei'nen tr suppose; presume, allege
vermeintlich [fer'maɪntlɪç] adj supposed, alleged; (gedacht) imaginary
vermel'den tr (poet) announce
vermen'gen tr mix, mingle; confound || ref (mit) meddle (with)
Vermerk [fer'merk] m (-[e]s;-e) note
vermer'ken tr note, record
vermes'sen adj daring, bold || §70 tr measure; (Land) survey || ref measure wrong; **sich v. zu** (inf) have the nerve to (inf)
Vermes'sung f (-;-en) surveying
vermie'ten tr rent out; lease out
Vermie'ter –in §6 mf (jur) lessor || m landlord || f landlady
vermindern [fer'mɪndərn] tr diminish, lessen; (beschränken) reduce, cut || ref diminish, decrease
Vermin'derung f (-;-en) diminution, decrease; reduction, cut
verminen [fer'minən] tr (mil) mine
vermi'schen tr & ref mix
Vermi'schung f (-;-en) mixture
vermissen [fer'misən] tr miss
vermißt [fer'mɪst] adj (mil) missing in action || **Vermißte** §5 mf missing person
vermitteln [fer'mɪtəln] tr negotiate; arrange, bring about; (beschaffen) get, procure || intr mediate; intercede
vermittels [fer'mɪtəls] prep (genit) by means of, through
Vermitt'ler –in §6 mf mediator, go-between; (com) agent
Vermitt'lung f (-;-en) negotiation; mediation; procuring, providing; intercession; (Mittel) means; agency;

brokerage; (telp) exchange; **durch gütige V.** (genit) through the good offices of
Vermitt'lungsamt n (telp) exchange
Vermitt'lungsgebühr f, **Vermitt'lungsprovision** f commission; brokerage
vermo'dern intr (SEIN) rot, decay
vermöge [fer'møgə] prep (genit) by virtue of
vermö'gen §114 tr be able to do; **j–n v. zu** (inf) induce s.o. to (inf); **sie vermag bei ihm viel** (or **wenig**) she has great (or little) influence with him; **v. zu** (inf) be able to (inf), have the power to (inf) || **Vermögen** n (-s;-) ability; capacity, power; fortune, means; property; (fin) capital, assets; **nach bestem V.** to the best of one's ability
vermö'gend adj well-to-do, well-off
Vermö'genslage f financial situation
Vermö'gensteuer f property tax
vermorscht [fer'mɔr/t] adj rotten
vermottet [fer'mɔtət] adj moth-eaten
vermummen [fer'mumən] tr disguise || ref disguise oneself
vermuten [fer'mutən] tr suppose, presume
vermutlich [fer'mutlɪç] adj presumable || adv presumably, I suppose
Vermu'tung f (-;-en) guess, conjecture
vernach'lässigen [fer'naxlɛsɪgən] tr neglect
Vernach'lässigung f (-;) neglect
verna'geln tr nail up; board up
vernä'hen tr sew up
vernarben [fer'narbən] intr (SEIN) heal up
vernarren [fer'narən] ref—**sich v. in** (acc) be crazy about, be stuck on
verna'schen tr spend on sweets; (Mädchen) make love to
vernebeln [fer'nebəln] tr (mil) screen with smoke; (fig) hide, cover over
vernehmbar [fer'nembar] adj perceptible
verneh'men §116 tr perceive; (erfahren) hear, learn; (jur) question; **sich v. lassen** be heard, express an opinion || **Vernehmen** n (-s;-)—**dem V. nach** reportedly, according to the report
vernehmlich [fer'nemlɪç] adj perceptible, audible; distinct
Verneh'mung f (-;-en) interrogation
verneigen [fer'naɪgən] ref bow; curtsy
Verneigung f (-;-en) bow; curtsy
verneinen [fer'naɪnən] tr say no to; reject, refuse; disavow
vernei'nend adj negative
Vernei'nung f (-;-en) negation; denial
vernichten [fer'nɪçtən] tr destroy, annihilate; (Hoffnung) dash
vernich'tend adj (Kritik) scathing; (Niederlage) crushing
Vernich'tung f (-;) destruction
vernickeln [fer'nɪkəln] tr nickel-plate
vernie'ten tr rivet
Vernunft [fer'nunft] f (-;) reason; good sense; senses; **die gesunde V.** common sense; **V. annehmen** listen to reason; **zur V. bringen** bring to one's senses

Vernunft'ehe f marriage of convenience

vernunft'gemäß adj reasonable

vernünftig [fer'nynftıç] adj rational; reasonable; sensible, level-headed

vernunft'los adj senseless

vernunft'mäßig adj rational; reasonable

veröden [fer'ødən] intr (SEIN) become desolate

veröffentlichen [fer'œfəntlıçən] tr publish; announce

Veröf'fentlichung f (-;-en) publication; announcement

verord'nen tr decree; (med) prescribe

Verord'nung f (-;-en) decree, order; (med) prescription

verpach'ten tr farm out; lease, rent out

Verpäch'ter -in §6 mf lessor

verpacken (verpak'ken) tr pack up

Verpackung (Verpak'kung) f (-;-en) packing (material); wrapping

verpas'sen tr (Gelegenheit, Anschluß, usw.) miss; j-m e-n Anzug v. fit s.o. with a suit; j-m e-e v. (coll) give s.o. a smack

verpatzen [fer'patsən] tr (coll) make a mess of

verpesten [fer'pestən] tr infect, contaminate

verpet'zen tr (coll) squeal on

verpfän'den tr pawn; mortgage; **sein Wort v.** give one's word of honor

verpflan'zen tr (bot, surg) transplant

Verpflan'zung f (-;-en) (bot, surg) transplant

verpfle'gen tr feed; (mil) supply

Verpfle'gung f (-;) feeding; board; (mil) rations, supplies

verpflichten [fer'pflıçtən] tr obligate, bind; **zu Dank v.** put under obligation

Verpflich'tung f (-;-en) obligation; commitment; (jur) liability

verpfuschen [fer'pfu/ən] tr (coll) botch, bungle, muff

verplap'pern ref blab out a secret

verplau'dern tr waste in chatting

verpönt [fer'pønt] adj taboo

verprü'geln tr (coll) wallop, thrash

verpuf'fen intr (SEIN) fizzle; (fig) fizzle out

verpulvern [fer'pulfərn] tr (coll) waste, fritter away

verpum'pen tr (coll) loan

verpusten [fer'pustən] ref (coll) catch one's breath

Verputz [fer'puts] m (-es;-e) finishing coat (of plaster)

verput'zen tr plaster; (aufessen) polish off; (coll) stand

verquicken [fer'kvıkən] tr interrelate

verquollen [fer'kvolən] adj (Augen) swollen; (Gesicht) puffy; (Holz) warped

verrammeln [fer'raməln] tr barricade

verramschen [fer'ram/ən] tr (coll) sell dirt-cheap

verrannt [fer'rant] adj—**v. sein in** (acc) be stuck on

Verrat' m (-[e]s;) betrayal; treason

verra'ten §63 tr betray

Verräter -in [fer'retər(ın)] §6 mf traitor; betrayer

verräterisch [fer'retərı/] adj treacherous; (Spur, usw.) telltale

verrau'chen tr spend on smokes

verräu'chern tr fill with smoke

verrech'nen tr (ausgleichen) balance; (Scheck) deposit; (fin) clear || ref miscalculate; (fig) be mistaken

Verrech'nung f (-;-en) miscalculation; (fin) clearing; **nur zur V.** for deposit only

Verrech'nungsbank f, **Verrech'nungskasse** f clearing house

verrecken [fer'rekən] intr (SEIN) die; (sl) croak; **verrecke!** drop dead!

verreg'nen tr spoil with too much rain

verrei'sen intr (SEIN) go on a trip; **v. nach** depart for

verreist [fer'raıst] adj out of town

verren'ken tr wrench, dislocate || ref—**sich** [dat] **den Arm v.** wrench one's arm; **sich** [dat] **den Hals v.** (coll) crane one's neck

Verren'kung f (-;-en) dislocation

verrich'ten tr do; (Gebet) say; **seine Notdurft v.** ease oneself

Verrich'tung f (-;-en) performance; task, duty

verrie'geln tr bolt, bar

verringern [fer'rıŋərn] tr diminish, reduce || ref diminish; be reduced

Verrin'gerung f (-;-en) diminution; reduction

verrin'nen §121 intr (SEIN) run off; (Zeit) pass

verro'sten intr (SEIN) rust

verrotten [fer'rotən] intr (SEIN) rot

verrucht [fer'ruxt] adj wicked

verrücken (verrük'ken) tr move, shift

verrückt [fer'rykt] adj crazy; **v. auf etw** or **etw about s.th.; v. nach** j-m crazy about s.o. || **Verrückte** §5 mf lunatic

Verrückt'heit f (-;-en) craziness, madness; crazy action or act

Verruf' m (-[e]s;) discredit, disrepute

verru'fen adj disreputable

verrüh'ren tr stir thoroughly

verrut'schen intr (SEIN) slip

Vers [fers] m (-es;-e) verse

versa'gen tr refuse; **versagt sein** have a previous engagement || ref—**sich** [dat] **etw v.** deny oneself s.th.; **ich kann es mir nicht v. zu** (inf) I can't refrain from (ger) || intr fail; (Beine, Stimme, usw.) give out; (Gewehr) misfire; (Motor) fail to start; **bei e-r Prüfung v.** flunk a test || **Versagen** n (-s;-) failure, flop; misfire

Versa'ger m (-s;-) failure, flop; (Patrone) dud

versal'zen tr oversalt; (fig) spoil

versam'meln tr gather together, assemble; convoke || ref gather, assemble

Versamm'lung f (-;-en) assembly, meeting

Versand [fer'zant] m (-[e]s;) shipment; mailing

Versand'abteilung f shipping department

versanden [fer'zandən] intr (SEIN) silt up; (fig) bog down

Versand'geschäft n, **Versand'haus** n mail-order house

versäu'men tr (Gelegenheit, Schule, Zug) miss; (Geschäft, Pflicht) neglect; **v. zu** (inf) fail to (inf)

Versäumnis [fɛr'zɔɪmnɪs] f (-;-se), n (-ses;-se) omission, neglect; (educ) absence; (jur) default

verschaf'fen tr get, obtain || ref—sich [dat] etw **v.** get; **sich** [dat] **Geld v.** raise money; **sich** [dat] **Respekt v.** gain respect

verschämt [fɛr'ʃɛmt] adj bashful, coy

Verschämt'heit f (-;) bashfulness

verschandeln [fɛr'ʃandəln] tr deface

verschan'zen tr fortify || ref entrench oneself; **sich v. hinter** (dat) (fig) hide behind

Verschan'zung f (-;-en) entrenchment

verschär'fen tr intensify; aggravate; **verschärfter Arrest** detention on a bread-and-water diet || ref get worse

verschei'den §112 intr (SEIN) pass away

verschen'ken tr give away

verscher'zen tr—sich [dat] etw **v.** throw away, lose (frivolously)

verscheu'chen tr scare away

verschicken (verschik'ken) tr send away; (deportieren) deport

Verschie'bebahnhof m marshaling yard

verschie'ben §130 tr postpone; shift; displace; black-market; (rr) shunt, switch || ref shift

Verschie'bung f (-;-en) postponement; shift, shifting

verschieden [fɛr'ʃidən] adj different, various; distinct

verschie'denartig adj of a different kind

verschiedenerlei [fɛr'ʃidənərlaɪ] invar adj different kinds of

Verschie'denheit f (-;-en) difference, variety, diversity

verschiedentlich [fɛr'ʃidəntlɪç] adv repeatedly; at times, occasionally

verschie'ßen §76 tr (Schießvorrat) use up, expend || intr (SEIN) (Farbe) fade

verschif'fen tr ship

Verschif'fung f (-;) shipment

verschim'meln intr (SEIN) get moldy

verschla'fen adj sleepy, drowsy || §131 tr miss by sleeping; (Zeit) sleep away || intr oversleep

Verschla'fenheit f (-;) sleepiness

Verschlag' m partition; crate

verschla'gen sly; (lau) lukewarm || §132 tr partition off; board up; (Kisten) nail shut; (Seite im Buch) lose; (naut) drive off course; (tennis) misserve; **j—m den Atem v.** take s.o.'s breath away; **j—m die Sprache** (or **Rede, Stimme**) **v.** make s.o. speechless; **v. werden auf** (acc) (or **in** acc) be driven to || impers— **es verschlägt nichts** it doesn't matter

verschlammen [fɛr'ʃlamən] intr (SEIN) silt up

verschlampen [fɛr'ʃlampən] tr ruin (through neglect); (verlegen) misplace || intr get slovenly

verschlechtern [fɛr'ʃlɛçtərn] tr make worse || ref get worse, deteriorate

Verschlech'terung f (-;) deterioration

verschleiern [fɛr'ʃlaɪ·ərn] tr veil; (Tatsachen) cover up; (Stimme) disguise; (mil) screen; **die Bilanz v.** juggle the books || ref cloud up

verschleiert [fɛr'ʃlaɪ·ərt] adj hazy; (Stimme) husky; (Augen) misty

Verschlei'erung f (-;) coverup; camouflaging; (jur) suppression of evidence

verschlei'ßen §88 tr slur, slur over

Verschleiß [fɛr'ʃlaɪs] m (-es;) wear and tear; (Aust) retail trade

verschlei'ßen §53 tr wear out; (Aust) retail || ref wear out

verschleiß'fest adj durable

verschlep'pen tr drag off; abduct; (im Krieg) displace; (Verhandlungen) drag out; (Seuche) spread; (verzögern) delay

verschleu'dern tr waste, squander; (Waren) sell dirt-cheap

verschlie'ßen §76 tr shut; lock; put under lock and key || ref (dat) close one's mind to

verschlimmern [fɛr'ʃlɪmərn] tr make worse; (fig) aggravate || ref get worse

verschlin'gen §142 tr devour, wolf down; (verflechten) intertwine

verschlissen [fɛr'ʃlɪsən] adj frayed

verschlossen [fɛr'ʃlɔsən] adj shut; (fig) reserved, tight-lipped

verschlucken (verschluk'ken) tr swallow || ref swallow the wrong way

verschlungen [fɛr'ʃluŋən] adj (Weg) winding; (fig) intricate

Ver·schluß' m (-schlusses;-schlüsse) fastener; (Schnapp-) catch; (Schloß) lock; (e—r Flasche) stopper; (Stöpsel) plug; (Plombe) seal; (e—s Gewehrs) breechlock; (phot) shutter; **unter V.** under lock and key

verschlüsseln [fɛr'ʃlʏsəln] tr code

Verschluß'laut m (ling) stop, plosive

verschmach'ten intr (SEIN) pine away; **vor Durst v.** be dying of thirst

verschmä'hen tr disdain

verschmel'zen §133 tr & intr (SEIN) fuse, merge; blend

Verschmel'zung f (-;-en) fusion; (com) merger

verschmer'zen tr get over

verschmie'ren tr smear; soil, dirty; (verwischen) blur

verschmitzt [fɛr'ʃmɪtst] adj crafty

verschmut'zen tr dirty || intr (SEIN) get dirty

verschnap'pen ref give oneself away

verschnau'fen ref & intr stop for breath

verschnei'den §106 tr clip, trim; cut wrong; castrate; (Branntwein, Wein) blend

verschneit [fɛr'ʃnaɪt] adj snow-covered

Verschnitt' m (-[e]s;) blend

verschnup'fen tr annoy; **verschnupft sein** have a cold; (coll) be annoyed

verschnü'ren tr tie up

verschollen [fɛr'ʃɔlən] adj missing, never heard of again; (jur) presumed dead

verscho'nen tr spare; **j—n mit etw v.** spare s.o. s.th.

verschönern [fɛr'ʃønərn] tr beautify

verschossen [fɛr'ʃɔsən] *adj* faded, discolored; (**in** *acc*) (coll) be madly in love (with)

verschränken [fɛr'ʃrɛŋkən] *tr* fold (one's arms)

verschrau'ben *tr* screw tight

verschrei'ben §62 *tr* use up (*in writing*); (jur) make over; (med) prescribe ‖ *ref* make a mistake (*in writing*)

Verschrei'bung *f* (–;-en) prescription

verschrei'en §135 *tr* decry

verschrien [fɛr'ʃriːən] *adj*—**v. sein als** have the reputation of being

verschroben [fɛr'ʃroːbən] *adj* eccentric

Verschro'benheit *f* (–;-en) eccentricity

verschrotten [fɛr'ʃrɔtən] *tr* scrap

verschüch'tern *tr* intimidate

verschul'den *tr* encumber with debts; **etw v.** be guilty of s.th.; be the cause of s.th. ‖ **Verschulden** *n* (-s;) fault

verschuldet [fɛr'ʃʊldət] *adj* in debt

Verschul'dung *f* (–;-en) indebtedness; encumbrance

verschüt'ten *tr* spill; (*ausfüllen*) fill up; (*Person*) bury alive

verschwägert [fɛr'ʃvɛːgərt] *adj* related by marriage

verschwei'gen §148 *tr* keep secret; **j–m etw v.** keep s.th. from s.o.

Verschwei'gung *f* (–;) concealment

verschwei'ßen *tr* weld (together)

verschwenden [fɛr'ʃvɛndən] *tr* (**an** *acc*) waste (on), squander (on)

Verschwen'der –in §6 *mf* spendthrift

verschwenderisch [fɛr'ʃvɛndərɪʃ] *adj* wasteful; lavish, extravagant

Verschwen'dung *f* (–;) waste; extravagance

verschwiegen [fɛr'ʃviːgən] *adj* discreet; reserved, reticent

Verschwie'genheit *f* (–;) discretion; reticence; secrecy

verschwim'men §136 *intr* (SEIN) become blurred; (fig) fade

verschwin'den §59 *intr* (SEIN) disappear; **ich muß mal v.** (coll) I have to go (to the toilet); **v. lassen** put out of the way; spirit off ‖ **Verschwinden** *n* (-s;) disappearance

verschwistert [fɛr'ʃvɪstərt] *adj* closely related

verschwit'zen *tr* sweat up; (coll) forget

verschwollen [fɛr'ʃvɔlən] *adj* swollen

verschwommen [fɛr'ʃvɔmən] *adj* hazy, indistinct; (*Bild*) blurred

Verschwom'menheit *f* (–;) haziness

verschwö'ren §137 *tr* forswear ‖ *ref* (**gegen**) plot (against); **sich zu etw v.** plot s.th.

Verschwö'rer –in §6 *mf* conspirator

Verschwö'rung *f* (–;-en) conspiracy

verse'hen §138 *tr* (*Amt, Stellung*) hold; (*Dienst, Pflicht*) perform; (*Haushalt, usw.*) look after; (**mit**) provide (with); (eccl) administer the last rites to; **j–s Dienst v.** fill in for s.o.; **mit e–m Saum v.** hem; **mit Giro v.** endorse; **mit Unterschrift v.** sign ‖ *ref* make a mistake; **ehe man es sich versieht** before you know it; **sich v.** (*genit*) expect ‖ **Versehen** *n* (-s;–) mistake, slip; oversight; **aus V.** by mistake

versehentlich [fɛr'zeː-əntlɪç] *adv* by mistake, erroneously, inadvertently

versehren [fɛr'zeːrən] *tr* injure

Versehrte [fɛr'zeːrtə] §5 *mf* disabled person

versen'den §140 *tr* send; ship; **ins Ausland v.** export

versen'gen *tr* scorch; (*Haar*) singe

versen'ken *tr* sink; submerge; lower; (*Kabel*) lay; (*Schraube*) countersink; (naut) scuttle ‖ *ref*—**sich v. in** (*acc*) become engrossed in

Versen'kung *f* (–;-en) sinking; (theat) trapdoor; **in der V. verschwinden** (fig) vanish into thin air

versessen [fɛr'zɛsən] *adj*—**v. auf** (*acc*) crazy about, obsessed with

verset'zen *tr* move, shift; (*Pflanze*) transplant; (*Schulkind*) promote; (*Beamte*) transfer; (*Schlag*) deal, give; (*verpfänden*) pawn; (*vermischen*) mix; (*Metall*) alloy; (*erwidern*) reply; (*vergeblich warten lassen*) (coll) stand up; (mus) transpose; **in Angst v.** terrify; **in Erstaunen v.** amaze; **in den Ruhestand v.** retire; **in Zorn v.** anger ‖ *ref*—**v. Sie sich in meine Lage** put yourself in my place

Verset'zung *f* (–;-en) moving, shifting; transplanting; transfer; mixing; alloying; (educ) promotion

Verset'zungszeichen *n* (mus) accidental

verseuchen [fɛr'zɔɪçən] *tr* infect, contaminate

Verseu'chung *f* (–;) infection; contamination

Vers'fuß *m* (pros) foot

versicherbar [fɛr'zɪçərbar] *adj* insurable

versichern [fɛr'zɪçərn] *tr* assure; assert, affirm; insure ‖ *ref* (*genit*) assure oneself

Versicherte [fɛr'zɪçərtə] §5 *mf* insured

Versi'cherung *f* (–;-en) assurance; affirmation; insurance

Versi'cherungsanstalt *f* insurance company

Versi'cherungsbeitrag *m* premium

versi'cherungsfähig *adj* insurable

Versi'cherungsgesellschaft *f* insurance company

Versi'cherungsleistung *f* insurance benefit

Versi'cherungsmathematiker –in §6 *mf* actuary

Versi'cherungsnehmer –in §6 *mf* insured

versi'cherungspflichtig *adj* subject to mandatory insurance

Versi'cherungspolice *f*, **Versi'cherungsschein** *m* insurance policy

Versi'cherungsträger *m* underwriter

Versi'cherungszwang *m* compulsory insurance

versickern (versik/kern) *intr* (SEIN) seep out, trickle away

versie'geln *tr* seal (up); (jur) seal off

Versie'gelung *f* (–;) sealing (off)

versie'gen *intr* (SEIN) dry up

versil'bern *tr* silver-plate; (coll) sell

Versil'berung *f* (–;) silver-plating

versin′ken §143 *intr* (SEIN) (**in** *acc*) sink (into); (fig) (**in** *acc*) lapse (into)

versinnbildlichen [fɛrˈzɪnbɪltlɪçən] *tr* symbolize

Version [verˈzjon] *f* (–ʒ–en) version

versippt [fɛrˈzɪpt] *adj* (**mit**) related (to)

versklaven [fɛrˈsklavən] *tr* enslave

Vers′kunst *f* versification

Vers′macher –in §6 *mf* versifier

Vers′maß *n* meter

versoffen [fɛrˈzɔfən] *adj* (coll) drunk

versohlen [fɛrˈzolən] *tr* (coll) give (*s.o.*) a good licking

versöhnen [fɛrˈzønən] *tr* (**mit**) reconcile (with) || *ref* become reconciled

versöhnlich [fɛrˈzønlɪç] *adj* conciliatory

Versöh′nung *f* (–ʒ) reconciliation

Versöh′nungstag *m* Day of Atonement

versonnen [fɛrˈzɔnən] *adj* wistful

versor′gen *tr* look after; provide for; (mit) supply (with), provide (with)

Versor′ger –in §6 *mf* provider, breadwinner

Versor′gung *f* (–ʒ) providing, supplying; (*Unterhalt*) maintenance; (*Alters– und Validen–*) social security

Versor′gungsbetrieb *m* public utility

Versor′gungstruppen *pl* service troops

Versor′gungswege *pl* supply lines

verspan′nen *tr* guy, brace

verspäten [fɛrˈpɛtən] *ref* come late; (rr) be behind schedule

verspätet [fɛrˈpɛtət] *adj* belated, late

Verspä′tung *f* (–ʒ–en) lateness, delay; **mit e–r Stunde V.** one hour behind schedule; **V. haben** be late

verspei′sen *tr* eat up

verspekulie′ren *tr* lose on a gamble || *ref* lose all through speculation

versper′ren *tr* bar, block, obstruct; (*Tür*) lock

verspie′len *tr* lose, gamble away || *intr* **–bei j–m v.** lose favor with s.o.

verspielt [fɛrˈpilt] *adj* playful; frivolous

versponnen [fɛrˈpɔnən] *adj*—**in Gedanken versponnen** lost in thought

verspot′ten *tr* mock, deride

Verspot′tung *f* (–ʒ) mockery, derision

verspre′chen §64 *tr* promise || *ref* make a mistake in speaking; **ich verspreche mir viel davon** I expect a lot from that || **Versprechen** *n* (–sʒ–) promise; slip of the tongue

Verspre′chung *f* (–ʒ–en) promise

versprengen *tr* scatter, disperse

Versprengte [fɛrˈprɛntə] §5 *mf* (mil) straggler

versprit′zen *tr* squirt, spatter

versprü′hen *tr* spray

verspü′ren *tr* feel, sense

verstaatlichen [fɛrˈtatlɪçən] *tr* nationalize

Verstaat′lichung *f* (–ʒ) nationalization

verstädtern [fɛrˈtɛtərn] *tr* urbanize

Verstäd′terung *f* (–ʒ) urbanization

Verstand′ *m* (–[e]sʒ) understanding; intellect; intelligence; brains; (*Vernunft*) reason; (*Geist*) mind; senses; sense; **den V. verlieren** lose one's

mind; **gesunder V.** common sense; **klarer V.** clear head; **nicht bei V. sein** be out of one's mind

Verstan′deskraft *f* intellectual power

verstan′desmäßig *adj* rational

Verstan′desmensch *m* matter-of-fact person

verstän′dig *adj* intelligent; sensible, reasonable; wise

verständigen [fɛrˈtɛndɪgən] *tr* (**von**) inform (about), notify (of) || *ref*—**sich v. mit** make oneself understood to; come to an understanding with

Verstän′digung *f* (–ʒ) understanding; information; communication; (telp) quality of reception

verständlich [fɛrˈtɛntlɪç] *adj* understandable, intelligible; **sich v. machen** make oneself understood

Verständnis [fɛrˈtɛntnɪs] *n* (–sesʒ–se) (**für**) understanding (of), appreciation (for)

verständ′nislos *adj* uncomprehending

verständ′nisinnig *adj* with deep mutual understanding; (*Blick*) knowing

verständ′nisvoll *adj* understanding; appreciative; (*Blick*) knowing

verstän′kern *tr* stink up

verstär′ken *tr* strengthen; (*steigern*) intensify; (elec) boost; (mil) reinforce; (rad) amplify

Verstär′ker *m* (–sʒ–) (rad) amplifier

Verstär′kung *f* (–ʒ–en) strengthening; intensification; (mil) reinforcement; (rad) amplification

verstatten [fɛrˈtatən] *tr* permit

verstau′ben *intr* (SEIN) get dusty

verstäu′ben *intr* atomize

verstaubt [fɛrˈtaupt] *adj* dusty; (fig) antiquated

verstau′chen *tr* sprain

Verstau′chung *f* (–ʒ–en) sprain

verstau′en *tr* stow away

Versteck [fɛrˈtek] *m* (–[e]sʒ–e) hiding place; hideout; **V. spielen** play hide-and-seek

verstecken (versteck′ken) *tr* & *ref* hide

versteckt [fɛrˈtekt] *adj* hidden, veiled; (*Absicht*) ulterior

verste′hen §146 *tr* understand, see; make out; realize; (*Sprache*) know; **e–n Spaß v.** take a joke; **ich verstehe es zu** (*inf*) I know how to (*inf*); **falsch v.** misunderstand; **verstanden?** get it?; **v. Sie mich recht!** don't get me wrong!; **was v. Sie unter** (*dat*)? what do you mean by? || *ref*—(**das**) **versteht sich!** that's understood!; **das versteht sich von selbst!** that goes without saying; **sich gut v. mit** get along well with; **sich v. auf** (*acc*) be skilled in; **sich zu etw v.** (*sich zu etw entschließen*) bring oneself to do s.th.; (*in etw einwilligen*) agree to s.th. || *recip* understand each other

verstei′fen *tr* stiffen; strut, brace, reinforce || *ref* stiffen; **sich v. auf** (*acc*) insist on

verstei′gen §148 *ref* lose one's way in the mountain; **sich dazu v., daß** go so far as to (*inf*)

Verstei′gerer *m* (–sʒ–) auctioneer

verstei′gern *tr* auction off

Verstei'gerung f (-;-en) auction
verstei'nern intr (SEIN) become petrified; (fig) be petrified
verstell'bar adj adjustable
verstel'len tr (regulieren) adjust; (versperren) block; (Stimme, usw.) disguise; (Weiche) throw; (Verkehrsampel) switch; (Zeiger e-r Uhr) move; misplace; **j–m den Weg v.** block s.o.'s way ‖ ref put on an act
Verstel'lung f (-;-en) adjusting; disguise
versteu'ern tr pay taxes on
Versteu'erung f (-;) paying of taxes
verstiegen [fer'ʃtigən] adj (Idee, Plan) extravagant, fantastic
verstim'men tr put out of tune; (fig) put out of humor
verstimmt [fer'ʃtɪmt] adj out of tune; (Magen) upset; **v. über** (acc) upset over
Verstim'mung f (-;) bad humor; (zwischen zweien) bad feeling, bad blood
verstockt [fer'ʃtɔkt] adj stubborn; (Verbrecher) hardened; (eccl) impenitent
Verstockt'heit f (-;) stubbornness; (eccl) impenitence
verstohlen [fer'ʃtolən] adj furtive
verstop'fen tr stop up, clog; (Straße) block, jam; (Leib) constipate
Verstop'fung f (-;) stopping up, clogging; congestion; (pathol) constipation
verstorben [fer'ʃtɔrbən] adj late, deceased ‖ **Verstorbene** §5 mf deceased
verstört [fer'ʃtørt] adj shaken, bewildered, distracted
Verstört'heit f (-;) bewilderment
Verstoß' m (gegen) violation (of), offense (against)
versto'ßen §150 tr disown ‖ intr—**v. gegen** violate, break
verstre'ben tr prop, brace
verstrei'chen §85 tr (Butter) spread; (Risse) plaster up ‖ intr (SEIN) pass, elapse; (Gelegenheit) slip by; (Frist) expire
verstreu'en tr scatter, disperse, strew
verstricken (verstrik'ken) tr use up in knitting; (fig) involve, entangle ‖ ref get entangled
verstümmeln [fer'ʃtymǝln] tr mutilate; (Funkspruch) garble
Verstüm'melung f (-;-en) mutilation; (rad) garbling
verstummen [fer'ʃtumən] intr (SEIN) become silent; (vor Erstaunen) be dumbstruck; (Geräusch) cease
Versuch [fer'zux] m (-[e]s;-e) try, attempt; (Probe) test, trial; (wissenschaftlich) experiment; **e–n V. machen mit** have a try at
versu'chen tr try; tempt; (kosten) taste
Versuchs'anstalt f research institute
Versuchs'ballon m (& fig) trial balloon
Versuchs'flieger m test pilot
Versuchs'flug m test flight
Versuchs'kaninchen n (fig) guinea pig
Versuchs'reihe f series of tests
versuchs'weise adv by way of a test; on approval
Versu'chung f (-;-en) temptation

versumpfen [fer'zumpfən] intr (SEIN) become marshy; (coll) go to the dogs
versün'digen ref (an dat) sin (against)
versunken [fer'zuŋkən] adj sunk; **v. in** (acc) (fig) lost in
versü'ßen tr sweeten
verta'gen tr & ref (auf acc) adjourn (till), recess (till)
Verta'gung f (-;-en) adjournment
vertändeln [fer'tɛndəln] tr trifle away
vertäuen [fer'tɔɪ.ən] tr (naut) moor
vertau'schen tr (gegen) exchange (for)
Vertau'schung f (-;-en) exchange
verteidigen [fer'taɪdɪgən] tr defend
Vertei'diger –in §6 mf defender; (Befürworter) advocate; (jur) counsel for the defense ‖ m (fb) back
Vertei'digung f (-;-en) defense
Vertei'digungsbündnis n defensive alliance
Vertei'digungsminister m secretary of defense
Vertei'digungsministerium n department of defense
Vertei'digungsschrift f written defense
Vertei'digungsstellung f defensive position
vertei'len tr distribute; (zuteilen) allot; (über e–e große Fläche) scatter; (steuerlich) spread out; (Rollen) (theat) cast ‖ ref spread out
Vertei'ler m (-s;-) distributer; (Anschriftenliste) mailing list; (von Durchschlägen) distribution; (aut) distributor
Vertei'lung f (-;-en) distribution; allotment; (theat) casting
verteuern [fer'tɔɪ.ərn] tr raise the price of
verteufelt [fer'tɔɪfəlt] adj devilish; a devil of a
vertiefen [fer'tifən] tr make deeper; (fig) deepen ‖ ref—**sich v. in** (acc) become absorbed in
Vertie'fung f (-;-en) deepening; (Höhlung) hollow, depression; (Nische) niche; (Loch) hole; (fig) absorption
vertiert [fer'tirt] adj bestial
vertikal [vertɪ'kal] adj vertical ‖ **Vertikale** f (-;-n) vertical
vertil'gen tr exterminate, eradicate; (aufessen) (coll) eat, polish off
Vertil'gung f (-;) extermination
vertip'pen tr type incorrectly ‖ ref make a typing error
verto'nen tr set to music
Verto'nung f (-;-en) musical arrangement
vertrackt [fer'trakt] adj (coll) odd, strange; (coll) blooming
Vertrag [fer'trak] m (-[e]s;-e) contract, agreement; (dipl) treaty
vertra'gen §132 tr stand, take; tolerate ‖ recip agree, be compatible; (Farben) harmonize; (Personen) get along
vertrag'lich [fer'traklɪç] adj contractual ‖ adv by contract, as stipulated; **sich v. verpflichten zu** (inf) contract to (inf)
verträglich [fer'trɛklɪç] adj sociable, personable; (Speise) digestible
Vertrags'bruch m breach of contract
vertragsbrüchig [fer'traksbrʏçɪç] adj —**v. werden** break a contract

vertrags′gemäß *adj* contractual

vertrags′widrig *adj* contrary to the terms of a contract or treaty

vertrau′en *intr* (*dat*) trust; **v. auf** (*acc*) trust in, have confidence in ‖ **Vertrauen** *n* (**-s;**) trust, confidence; **ganz im V.** just between you and me; **im V.** confidentially

vertrau′enerweckend *adj* inspiring confidence

Vertrau′ensbruch *m* breach of trust

Vertrau′ens·mann *m* (**-[e]s;-er &** **-leute**) confidential agent; (*Vertrauter*) confidant; (*Sprecher*) spokesman; (*Gewährsmann*) informant

Vertrau′ensposten *m*, **Vertrau′ensstellung** *f* position of trust

vertrau′ensvoll *adj* confident; trusting

Vertrau′ensvotum *n* vote of confidence

vertrau′enswürdig *adj* trustworthy

vertrauern [fer′trau·ərn] *tr* spend in mourning

vertraulich [fer′traulıç] *adj* confidential; intimate

Vertrau′lichkeit *f* (**-;-en**) intimacy, familiarity; **sich** [*dat*] **Vertraulichkeiten herausnehmen** take liberties

verträu′men *tr* dream away

verträumt [fer′trɔımt] *adj* dreamy

vertraut [fer′traut]*adj* familiar; friendly, intimate ‖ **Vertraute** §5 *mf* intimate friend ‖ *m* confidant ‖ *f* confidante

Vertraut′heit *f* (**-;**) familiarity

vertrei′ben §62 *tr* drive away, expel; (*aus dem Hause*) chase out; (*aus dem Lande*) banish; (*Ware*) sell, market; (*Zeit*) pass, kill

Vertrei′bung *f* (**-;**) expulsion

vertre′ten §152 *tr* represent; substitute for; (*Ansicht, usw.*) advocate ‖ *ref* **—sich** [*dat*] **den Fuß v.** sprain one's ankle; **sich** [*dat*] **die Beine v.** (coll) stretch one's legs

Vertre′ter **-in** §6 *mf* representative; substitute; (*Bevollmächtigte*) proxy; (*im Amt*) deputy; (*Fürsprecher*) advocate; (com) agent

Vertre′tung *f* (**-;-en**) representation; substitution; (com) agency; (pol) mission; **in V.** by proxy; **in V.** (*genit*) signed for

Vertrieb′ *m* (**-[e]s;-e**) sale, turnover; retail trade; sales department

Vertriebs′abkommen *n* franchise agreement

Vertriebs′abteilung *f* sales department

Vertriebs′kosten *pl* distribution costs

Vertriebs′leiter **-in** §6 *mf* sales manager

Vertriebs′recht *n* franchise

vertrin′ken §143 *tr* drink up

vertrock′nen *intr* (SEIN) dry up

vertrödeln [fer′trødəln] *tr* fritter away

vertrö′sten *tr* string along; **auf später v.** put off till later

vertun′ §154 *tr* waste ‖ *ref* (coll) make a mistake

vertu′schen *tr* hush up

verübeln [fer′ybəln] *tr* take (*s.th.*) the wrong way; **j-m etw v.** blame s.o. for s.th.

verü′ben *tr* commit, perpetrate

verul′ken *tr* (coll) kid

verunehren [fer′unerən] *tr* dishonor

veruneinigen [fer′unaınıgən] *tr* disunite ‖ *recip* fall out, quarrel

verunglimpfen [fer′unglımpfən] *tr* slander, defame

verunglücken [fer′unglykən] *intr* (SEIN) have an accident; (coll) fail

Verunglückte [fer′unglyktə] §5 *mf* victim, casualty

verunreinigen [fer′unraınıgən] *tr* soil, dirty; (*Luft, Wasser*) pollute

Verun′reinigung *f* (**-;**) pollution

verunstalten [fer′un/taltən] *tr* disfigure, deface

veruntreuen [fer′untrɔı·ən] *tr* embezzle

Verun′treuung *f* (**-;**) embezzlement

verunzieren [fer′untsirən] *tr* mar

verursachen [fer′urzaxən] *tr* cause

verur′teilen *tr* condemn; sentence

Verur′teilung *f* (**-;-en**) condemnation; sentence

vervielfachen [fer′filfaxən] *tr* multiply ‖ *ref* increase considerably

vervielfältigen [fer′filfeltıgən] *tr* multiply; duplicate; mimeograph; (*nachbilden*) reproduce

Verviel′fältigung *f* (**-;-en**) duplication; mimeographing; reproduction; (phot) printing

Verviel′fältigungsapparat *m* duplicator

vervollkommnen [fer′folkəmnən] *tr* improve on, perfect

Vervoll′kommnung *f* (**-;**) improvement, perfection

vervollständigen [fer′fol/tendıgən] *tr* complete

Vervoll′ständigung *f* (**-;**) completion

verwach′sen *adj* overgrown; deformed; hunchbacked; **mit etw v. sein** (fig) be attached to s.th. ‖ *intr* (SEIN) grow together; become deformed; (*Wunde*) heal up; **zu e-r Einheit v.** form a whole

Verwach′sung *f* (**-;-en**) deformity

verwackelt [fer′vakəlt] *adj* (phot) blurred

verwah′ren *tr* keep; **v. vor** (*dat*) protect against ‖ *ref*—**sich v. gegen** protest against

verwahrlosen [fer′varlozən] *tr* neglect ‖ *intr* (SEIN) (*Gebäude*) deteriorate; (*Kinder*) run wild; (*Personen*) go to the dogs

verwahrlost [fer′varlost] *adj* uncared-for; (*Person*) unkempt; (*sittlich*) degenerate; (*Garten*) overgrown with weeds

Verwahr′losung *f* (**-;**) neglect

Verwah′rung *f* (**-;**) care, safekeeping; custody; (fig) protest; **etw in V. nehmen** take care of s.th.; **j-m in V. geben** entrust to s.o.'s care

verwaisen [fer′vaızən] *intr* (SEIN) become an orphan, be orphaned

verwaist [fer′vaıst] *adj* orphaned; (fig) deserted

verwalten [fer′valtən] *tr* administer, manage

Verwal′ter **-in** §6 *mf* administrator, manager

Verwal′tung *f* (**-;-en**) administration; management

Verwal'tungsapparat *m* administrative machinery

Verwal'tungsbeamte *m* civil service worker; administrative official

Verwal'tungsdienst *m* civil service

Verwal'tungsrat *m* advisory board; (*e-r Aktiengesellschaft*) board of directors; (*e-s Instituts*) board of trustees

verwan'deln *tr* change, turn, convert; (*Strafe*) commute || *ref* change, turn

Verwand'lung *f* (*-;-en*) change, transformation; (jur) commutation

verwandt [fɛr'vant] *adj* (mit) related (to); (*Wissenschaften*) allied; (*Wörter*) cognate; (*Seelen*) kindred || **Verwandte** §5 *mf* relative, relation

Verwandt'schaft *f* (*-;-en*) relationship; relatives; (chem) affinity

verwandt'schaftlich *adj* kindred

Verwand'schaftsgrad *m* degree of relationship

verwanzt [fɛr'vantst] *adj* (coll) full of bugs, lousy

verwar'nen *tr* warn, caution

Verwar'nung *f* (*-;-en*) warning, caution

verwa'schen *adj* washed-out, faded; (*verschwommen*) vague, fuzzy

verwäs'sern *tr* dilute; (fig) water down

verwe'ben §94 *tr* interweave

verwe'chseln *tr* confuse, get (*various items*) mixed up; (*Hüte, Mäntel*) take by mistake || **Verwechseln** *n* (*-s;*)—**sie sehen sich zum V. ähnlich** they are as alike as two peas

Verwechs'lung *f* (*-;-en*) mix-up

verwegen [fɛr'vegən] *adj* bold, daring

verwe'hen *tr* (*Blätter*) blow away; (*Spur*) cover up (with snow) || *intr* (SEIN) be blown in all directions; (*Spur*) be covered up; (*Worte*) drift away

verweh'ren *tr*—**j-m etw v.** refuse s.o. s.th.; prevent s.o. from getting s.th.

Verwe'hung *f* (*-;-en*) (snow)drift

verweichlichen [fɛr'vaɪçlɪçən] *tr* make effeminate; (*Kind*) coddle || *ref & intr* become effeminate; grow soft

verweichlicht [fɛr'vaɪçlɪçt] *adj* effeminate; soft, flabby

Verweich'lichung *f* (*-;*) effeminacy

verwei'gern *tr* refuse, deny, turn down

Verwei'gerung *f* (*-;-en*) refusal

verweilen [fɛr'vaɪlən] *intr* linger, tarry; (fig) dwell

verweint [fɛr'vaɪnt] *adj* red with tears

Verweis [fɛr'vaɪs] *m* (*-es;-e*) reprimand, rebuke; (*Hinweis*) reference

verwei'sen §118 *tr* banish; (*Schüler*) expel; **j-m etw v.** reprimand s.o. for s.th.; **j-n an j-n v.** refer s.o. to s.o.; **j-n auf etw v.** refer s.o. to s.th.

Verwei'sung *f* (*-;-en*) banishment, expulsion; (**an** *acc*) referral (to); (**auf** *acc*) reference (to)

verwel'ken *intr* (SEIN) wither, wilt

verweltlichen [fɛr'vɛltlɪçən] *tr* secularize

verwendbar [fɛr'vɛntbɑr] *adj* applicable; available; usable

Verwend'barkeit *f* (*-;*) availability; usefulness

verwen'den §140 *tr* use, employ; (**auf** *acc*, **für**) apply (to); **Zeit und Mühe v. auf** (*acc*) spend time and effort on || *ref*—**sich bei j-m v. für** intercede with s.o. for

Verwen'dung *f* (*-;-en*) use, employment; application; **keine V. haben für** have no use for; **vielseitige V.** versatility

verwen'dungsfähig *adj* usable

verwer'fen §160 *tr* reject; (*Plan*) discard; (*Berufung*) turn down; (*Klage*) dismiss; (*Urteil*) overrule || *ref* (*Holz*) warp; (geol) fault

verwerf'lich *adj* objectionable

Verwer'fung *f* (*-;-en*) rejection; warping; (geol) fault

verwer'ten *tr* utilize

Verwer'tung *f* (*-;-en*) utilization

verwesen [fɛr'vezən] *intr* (SEIN) rot

verweslich [fɛr'vezlɪç] *adj* perishable

Verwe'sung *f* (*-;*) decay

verwet'ten *tr* lose (*in betting*)

verwich'sen *tr* (coll) clobber

verwickeln [fɛr'vɪkəln] *tr* snarl, entangle; complicate; (fig) involve || *ref*—**sich v. in** (*acc*) get entangled in; (fig) get involved in

Verwick'lung *f* (*-;-en*) snarl, tangle; involvement; complexity; complication

verwil'dern *intr* become overgrown; (*Person*) become depraved; (*Kind*) run wild, go wild

verwildert [fɛr'vɪldərt] *adj* wild, savage; weed-grown

verwin'den §59 *tr* get over; (*Verlust*) recover from

verwir'ken *tr* forfeit; (*Strafe*) incur || *ref*—**sich** [*dat*] **j-s Gunst v.** lose favor with s.o.

verwirklichen [fɛr'vɪrklɪçən] *tr* realize, make come true || *ref* come true

Verwirk'lichung *f* (*-;*) realization

Verwir'kung *f* (*-;-en*) forfeiture

verwirren [fɛr'vɪrən] *tr* throw into disorder; (*Haar*) muss up; confuse

verwirrt [fɛr'vɪrt] *adj* confused

Verwir'rung *f* (*-;-en*) confusion; **in V. geraten** become confused

verwirt'schaften *tr* squander

verwi'schen *tr* wipe out; (*teilweise*) blur; (*verschmieren*) smear; (*Spuren*) cover || *ref* become blurred

verwit'tern *intr* (SEIN) become weatherbeaten; (*zerfallen*) crumble away

verwittert [fɛr'vɪtərt] *adj* weatherbeaten

verwitwet [fɛr'vɪtvət] *adj* widowed

verwöhnen [fɛr'vønən] *tr* pamper, spoil

verworfen [fɛr'vɔrfən] *adj* depraved

Verwor'fenheit *f* (*-;*) depravity

verworren [fɛr'vɔrən] *adj* confused

verwundbar [fɛr'vuntbɑr] *adj* vulnerable

verwun'den *tr* wound

verwunderlich [fɛr'vundərlɪç] *adj* remarkable, astonishing

verwun'dern *tr* astonish || *ref* (**über** *acc*) be astonished (at), wonder (at)

Verwun'derung *f* (*-;*) astonishment; **j-n in V. setzen** astonish s.o.

verwundet [fɛr'vundət] *adj* wounded

|| **Verwundete** §5 *mf* wounded person

verwunschen [fɛr'vunʃən] *adj* enchanted

verwün'schen *tr* damn, curse; (*in Märchen*) bewitch, put a curse on

verwünscht [fɛr'vynʃt] *adj* confounded, darn || *interj* darn it!

Verwün'schung *f* (-;-en) curse

verwurzelt [fɛr'vurtsəlt] *adj* deeply rooted

verwüsten [fɛr'vystən] *tr* devastate

Verwü'stung *f* (-;-en) devastation

verzagen [fɛr'tsagən] *intr* (SEIN) lose heart, despair; **v. an** (*dat*) give up on

verzagt [fɛr'tsakt] *adj* despondent

Verzagt'heit *f* (-;) despondency

verzäh'len *ref* miscount

verzärteln [fɛr'tsertəln] *tr* pamper

verzau'bern *tr* bewitch, charm; **v. in** (*acc*) change into

Verzehr [fɛr'tser] *m* (-[e]s;) consumption

verzeh'ren *tr* consume; (*Geld*) spend; (*Mahlzeit*) eat || *ref* (**in** *dat*, **vor** *dat*) pine away (with); (**nach**) yearn (for)

verzeh'rend *adj* (*Blick*) longing; (*Fieber*) wasting; (*Leidenschaft*) burning

Verzeh'rung *f* (-;) consumption

verzeich'nen *tr* draw wrong; make a list of; register; catalogue; (opt) distort

Verzeichnis [fɛr'tsaɪçnɪs] *n* (-ses;-se) list; catalogue; (*im Buch*) index; (*Inventar*) inventory; (*Tabelle*) table; (telp) directory

verzeihen [fɛr'tsaɪ-ən] §81 *tr* forgive, pardon (*s.th.*); condone || *intr* (*dat*) forgive, pardon (*s.o.*)

verzeihlich [fɛr'tsaɪlɪç] *adj* pardonable

Verzei'hung *f* (-;) pardon

verzer'ren *tr* distort; contort

Verzer'rung *f* (-;-en) distortion; contortion; grimace

verzetteln [fɛr'tsetəln] *tr* fritter away; catalogue || *ref* spread oneself too thin

Verzicht [fɛr'tsɪçt] *m* (-[e]s;) renunciation; **V. leisten auf** (*acc*) waive

verzichten [fɛr'tsɪçtən] *intr*—**v. auf** (*acc*) do without; (*verabsäumen*) pass up; (*aufgeben*) give up, renounce; (*Rechte*) waive

verzieh [fɛr'tsi] *pret* of **verzeihen**

verzie'hen §163 *tr* distort; (*Kind*) spoil; **den Mund v.** make a face; **ohne e-e Miene zu v.** without batting an eye || *ref* disappear; (*Schmerz*) go away; (*Menge, Wolken*) disperse; (*Holz*) warp; (*durch Druck*) buckle; (coll) sneak off

verzie'ren *tr* decorate

Verzie'rung *f* (-;-en) decoration; (*Schmuck*) ornament

verzinsen [fɛr'tsɪnzən] *tr* pay interest on; **e-e Summe zu 6% v.** pay 6% interest on a sum || *ref* yield interest; **sich mit 6% v.** yield 6% interest

verzinslich [fɛr'tsɪnslɪç] *adj* bearing interest || *adv*—**v. anlegen** put out at interest

Verzin'sung *f* (-;) interest

verzog [fɛr'tsok] *pret* of **verziehen**

verzogen [fɛr'tsogən] *adj* distorted; (*Kind*) spoiled; (*Holz*) warped

verzö'gern *tr* delay; put off, postpone || *ref* be late

Verzö'gerung *f* (-;-en) delay; postponement

verzollen [fɛr'tsɔlən] *tr* pay duty on; (naut) clear; **haben Sie etw zu v.?** do you have anything to declare?

verzückt [fɛr'tsʏkt] *adj* ecstatic

Verzückung [fɛr'tsʏkuŋ] *f* (-;) ecstasy

Verzug' *m* (-[e]s;) delay; (*in der Leistung*) default; **in V. geraten mit** fall behind in; **ohne V.** without delay

verzwei'feln *intr* (HABEN & SEIN) (**an** *dat*) despair (of) || **Verzweifeln** *n*—**es ist zum V.** it's enough to drive one to despair

verzweifelt [fɛr'tsvaɪfəlt] *adj* desperate

Verzweif'lung *f* (-;) despair

verzweigen [fɛr'tsvaɪgən] *ref* branch out

verzweigt [fɛr'tsvaɪkt] *adj* having many branches; (fig) complex

verzwickt [fɛr'tsvɪkt] *adj* (coll) tricky, ticklish

Vestibül [vɛstɪ'byl] *n* (-s;-e) vestibule; (theat) lobby

Veteran [vete'ran] *m* (-en;-en) veteran, ex-serviceman

Veterinär -**in** [veterɪ'ner(ɪn)] §8 *mf* veterinarian

Veto ['veto] *n* (-s;-s) veto

Vetter ['fɛtər] *m* (-s;-) cousin

Vet'ternwirtschaft *f* nepotism

Vexierbild [vɛ'ksɪrbɪlt] *n* picture puzzle

vexieren [vɛ'ksɪrən] *tr* tease; pester

V-förmig ['faʊfœrmɪç] *adj* V-shaped

vibrieren [vɪ'brirən] *intr* vibrate

Vieh [fi] *n* (-[e]s;) livestock; cattle; animal, beast

Vieh'bestand *m* livestock

Vieh'bremse *f* horsefly

viehisch ['fi·ɪʃ] *adj* brutal

Vieh'tränke *f* water hole

Vieh'wagen *m* (rr) cattle car

Vieh'weide *f* cow pasture

Vieh'zucht *f* cattle breeding

Vieh'züchter -**in** §6 *mf* rancher

viel [fil] *adj* much; many; a lot of || *adv* much; a lot || *pron* much; many

viel'beschäftigt *adj* very busy

viel'deutig *adj* ambiguous

Viel'eck *n* polygon

vielerlei ['filər'laɪ] *invar adj* many kinds of

viel'fach *adj* multiple; manifold || *adv* (coll) often

Vielfach- *comb.fm.* multiple

viel'fältig *adj* manifold, various

Viel'fältigkeit *f* (-;) multiplicity; variety

vielleicht' *adv* maybe, perhaps

vielmalig ['filmalɪç] *adj* oft repeated

vielmals ['filmals] *adv* frequently; **danke v.!** many thanks!

vielmehr' *adv* rather, on the contrary

viel'sagend *adj* suggestive

viel'seitig *adj* many-sided; versatile

vielstufig ['fil'tufɪç] *adj* multistage

viel'teilig *adj* of many parts

viel'versprechend *adj* very promising

vier [fir] *adj* four; **unter vier Augen** confidentially || *pron* four; **auf allen vieren** on all fours || **Vier** *f* (-;-en) four

vier′beinig *adj* four-legged

Vier′eck *n* quadrangle

vier′eckig *adj* quadrangular

viererlei [′firər′laɪ] *invar adj* four different kinds of

vier′fach, vier′fältig *adv* fourfold, quadruple

Vierfüßer [′firfysər] *m* (-s;-) quadruped

vierhändig [′firhɛndɪç] *adv*—**v. spielen** (mus) play a duet

Vierlinge [′firlɪŋə] *pl* quadruplets

vier′mal *adv* four times

vierschrötig [′fir′ʃrøtɪç] *adj* stocky

vierstrahlig [′fir′ʃtraːlɪç] *adj* four-engine (jet)

viert [firt] *pron*—**zu v.** in fours; **wir gehen zu v.** the four of us are going

Viertakter [′firtaktər] *m* (-s;-), **Viertaktmotor** [′firtaktmotor] *m* four-cycle engine

Vierte [′firtə] §9 *adj & pron* fourth

vier′teilen *tr* quarter

Viertel [′firtəl] *n* (-s;-) quarter; fourth (*part*); (*Stadtteil*) quarter, section

Vierteljahr′ *n* quarter (*of a year*)

vierteljäh′rig, vierteljähr′lich *adj* quarterly

vierteln [′firtəln] *tr* quarter

Vier′telnote *f* (mus) quarter note

Viertelpfund′ *n* quarter of a pound

Viertelstun′de *f* quarter of an hour

viertens [′firtəns] *adv* fourthly

vier′zehn *invar adj & pron* fourteen || **Vierzehn** *f* (-;-en) fourteen

vier′zehnte §9 *adj & pron* fourteenth

Vier′zehntel *n* (-s;-) fourteenth (*part*)

vierzig [′fɪrtsɪç] *invar adj & pron* forty || **Vierzig** *f* (-;-en) forty

vierziger [′fɪrtsɪgər] *invar adj* of the forties; **die v. Jahre** the forties

vierzigste [′fɪrtsɪçstə] §9 *adj & pron* fortieth

Vikar [vɪ′kɑr] *m* (-s;-e) vicar

Vil·la [′vɪla] *f* (-;-len [lən]) villa

violett [vɪ·o′lɛt] *adj* violet

Violine [vɪ·o′linə] *f* (-;-n) violin

Violin′schlüssel *m* treble clef

Viper [′vipər] *f* (-;-n) viper

viril [vɪ′ril] *adj* virile

virtuos [vɪrtu′os] *adj* masterly || **Virtuose** [vɪrtu′ozə] *m* (-n;-n), **Virtuosin** [vɪrtu′ozɪn] *f* (-;-nen) virtuoso

Vi·rus [′virus] *n* (-;-ren [rən]) virus

Visage [vɪ′zaʒə] *f* (-;-n) (coll) mug

Visier [vɪ′zir] *n* (-s;-e) visor; (*am Gewehr*) sight

visieren [vɪ′zirən] *tr* (*eichen*) gauge; (*Paß*) visa

Vision [vɪ′zjon] *f* (-;-en) vision

visionär [vɪzjo′ner] *adj* visionary || **Visionär** *m* (-s;-e) visionary

Visitation [vɪzɪta′tsjon] *f* (-;-en) inspection; search

Visite [vɪ′zitə] *f* (-;-n) formal call; **Visiten machen** (med) make the rounds

Visi′tenkarte *f* calling card

visuell [vɪzu′ɛl] *adj* visual

Vi·sum [′vizum] *n* (-s;-sa [za]) visa

vital [vɪ′tal] *adj* energetic

Vitalität [vɪtalɪ′tet] *f* (-;) vitality

Vitamin [vɪta′min] *n* (-s;-e) vitamin

Vitamin′mangel *m* vitamin deficiency

Vitrine [vɪ′trinə] *f* (-;-n) showcase

Vize- [fitsə], [vitsə] *comb.fm.* vice-

Vi′zekönig *m* viceroy

Vlies [flis] *n* (-es;-e) fleece

Vogel [′fogəl] *m* (-s;::) bird; (coll) chap, bird; **den V. abschießen** (coll) bring down the house; **du hast e-n V.!** (coll) you're cuckoo!

Vo′gelbauer *n* birdcage

Vogelbeerbaum [′fogəlberbaum] *m* mountain ash

vo′gelfrei *adj* outlawed

Vo′gelfutter *n* birdseed

Vo′gelkunde *f* ornithology

Vo′gelmist *m* bird droppings

vögeln [′føgəln] *tr & intr* (vulg) screw

Vo′gelperspektive *f*, **Vo′gelschau** *f* bird's-eye view

Vo′gelpfeife *f* bird call

Vo′gelscheuche *f* scarecrow

Vo′gelstange *f* perch

Vogel-Strauß′-Politik *f* burying one's head in the sand; **V. betreiben** bury one's head in the sand

Vo′gelstrich *m*, **Vo′gelzug** *m* migration of birds

Vöglein [′føglaɪn] *n* (-s;-) little bird

Vogt [fokt] *m* (-[e]s;::e) (obs) steward; (obs) governor, prefect, magistrate

Vokabel [vo′kabəl] *f* (-;-n) vocabulary word

Vokal [vo′kal] *m* (-s;-e) vowel

Volk [folk] *n* (-[e]s;::er) people, nation; lower classes; (von Bienen) swarm; (von Rebhühnern) covey

Völker- [fœlkər] *comb.fm.* international

Völ′kerbund *m* League of Nations

Völ′kerfriede *m* international peace

Völ′kerkunde *f* ethnology

Völ′kermord *m* genocide

Völ′kerrecht *n* international law

Völ′kerschaft *f* (-;-en) tribe

Völ′kerwanderung *f* barbarian invasions

volk′reich *adj* populous

Volks′abstimmung *f* plebiscite

Volks′aufwiegler *m* rabble rouser

Volks′ausdruck *m* household expression

Volks′befragung *f* public opinion poll

Volks′begehren *n* national referendum

Volks′bibliotek *f* free library

Volks′charakter *m* national character

Volks′deutsche §5 *mf* German national

Volks′dichter *m* popular poet

volks′eigen *adj* state-owned

Volks′entscheid *m* referendum

Volks′feind *m* public enemy

Volks′gunst *f* popularity

Volks′haufen *m* crowd, mob

Volks′herrschaft *f* democracy

Volks′hochschule *f* adult evening school

Volks′justiz *f* lynch law

Volks'küche f soup kitchen
Volks'kunde f folklore
Volks'lied n folksong
volks'mäßig adj popular
Volks'meinung f popular opinion
Volks'menge f populace, crowd of people
Volks'musik f popular music
Volks'partei f people's party
Volks'republik f people's republic
Volks'schule f grade school
Volks'sitte f national custom
Volks'sprache f vernacular
Volks'stamm m tribe; race
Volks'stimme f popular opinion
Volks'stimmung f mood of the people
Volks'tracht f national costume
Volkstum ['fɔlkstum] n (-s;) nationality
volkstümlich ['fɔlkstymlɪç] ᾱ adj national; popular
Volks'verführer –in §6 mf demagogue
Volks'versammlung f public meeting
Volks'vertreter –in §6 mf representative
Volks'wirt m political economist
Volks'wirtschaft f national economy
Volks'wirtschaftslehre f (educ) political economy
Volks'wohl n public good
Volks'wohlfahrt f public welfare
Volks'zählung f census
voll [fɔl] adj full, filled; whole, entire; (Tageslicht) broad; (coll) drunk; **aus dem vollen schöpfen** have unlimited resources; **j–n für v. ansehen** (or **nehmen**) take s.o. seriously || adv fully, in full; **v. und ganz** fully
vollauf' adv—**das genügt v.** that's quite enough; **v. beschäftigt** plenty busy; **v. zu tun haben** have plenty to do
Voll'beschäftigung f full employment
Voll'besitz m full possession
Voll'blut n, **Voll'blutpferd** n thoroughbred
voll'blütig ['fɔlblytɪç] adj full-blooded
vollbrin'gen §65 tr achieve
vollbusig ['vɔlbuzɪç] adj big-breasted
Voll'dampf m full steam; **mit V.** (fig) at full blast, full speed
vollenden [fɔl'ɛndən] tr bring to a close, finish, complete; (vervollkommnen) perfect; **er hat sein Leben vollendet** (poet) he died
vollendet [fɔl'ɛndət] adj perfect
vollends ['fɔlɛnts] adv completely
Vollen'dung f (-;) finishing, completing; (Vollkommenheit) perfection
Völlerei [fœlə'raɪ] f (-;) gluttony
voll'führen tr carry out, execute
voll'füllen tr fill up
Voll'gas n full throttle
Voll'gefühl n—**im V.** (genit) fully conscious of
Voll'genuß m full enjoyment
vollgepfropft ['fɔlgəpfrɔpft] adj jammed, packed
voll'gießen §76 tr fill up
völlig ['fœlɪç] adj full, complete
voll'jährig adj of age
Voll'jährigkeit f legal age, majority
vollkom'men, **voll'kommen** adj perfect || adv (coll) absolutely

Vollkom'menheit f (-;) perfection
Voll'kornbrot n whole-grain bread
Voll'kraft f full vigor, prime
voll'machen tr fill up; (coll) dirty
Voll'macht f full authority; (jur) power of attorney; **in V.** for... (prefixed to the signature of another at end of letter)
Voll'matrose m able-bodied seaman
Voll'milch f whole milk
Voll'mond m full moon
Voll'pension f full board and lodging
voll'saftig adj juicy, succulent
voll'schenken tr fill up
voll'schlagen §132 ref—**sich** [dat] **den Bauch v.** (coll) stuff oneself
voll'schlank adj well filled out
Voll'sitzung f plenary session
Voll'spur f (rr) standard-gauge track
voll'ständig adj full; complete, entire || adv completely, quite
Voll'ständigkeit f (-;) completeness
voll'stopfen tr stuff, cram
vollstrecken (vollstrek'ken) tr (Urteil) carry out; (Testament) execute; **ein Todesurteil an j–m v.** execute s.o.
Vollstreckung (Vollstrek'kung) f. (-;) execution
voll'tanken tr (aut) fill up || intr (aut) fill it up
volltönend ['fɔltønənt] adj (Stimme) rich; (Satz) well-rounded
Voll'treffer m direct hit
Voll'versammlung f plenary session
Voll'waise f (full) orphan
voll'wertig adj of full value; complete, perfect
vollzählig ['fɔltselɪç] adj complete; **sind wir v.?** are we all here? || adv in full force
vollzie'hen §163 tr execute, carry out, effect; (Vertrag) ratify; (Ehe) consummate || ref take place
vollzie'hend adj executive
Vollzie'hung f, **Vollzug'** m execution, carrying out
Vollzugs'ausschuß m executive committee
Volontär –in [vɔlɔn'ter(ɪn)] §8 mf volunteer; trainee
volontieren [vɔlɔn'tirən] intr work as a trainee
Volt [vɔlt] n (-[e]s;–) (elec) volt
Volu·men [vo'lumən] n (-s;– & –mina [mina]) (Band; Rauminhalt) volume
vom [fɔm] abbr **von dem**
von [fɔn] prep (dat) (beim Passiv) by; **für den Genitiv** of; (räumlich, zeitlich) from; (über) about, of; **von... an** from...on; **von Holz** (made) of wood; **von Kindheit auf** from earliest childhood; **von mir aus as far as I am concerned; von selbst** automatically
voneinan'der adv from each other; of each other; apart
vonnöten [fɔn'nøtən] invar adj—**v. sein** be necessary
vonstatten [fɔn'tatən] adv—**gut v. gehen** go well; **v. gehen** take place
vor [for] prep (dat) (örtlich) in front of, before; (zeitlich) before, prior to; (Abwehr) against, from; (wegen) of,

with, for; **etw vor sich haben** face s.th.; **heute vor acht Tagen** today a week ago; **vor sich gehen** take place, occur; **vor sich hin** to oneself || *prep* (*acc*) in front of

vorab′ *adv* in advance

Vor′abend *m*—**am V.** (*genit*) on the eve of

Vor′ahnung *f* (coll) hunch, idea

voran′ *adv* in front, out ahead || *interj* go ahead!, go on!

voran′gehen §82 *intr* (SEIN) go on ahead, take the lead; (fig) set an example; **die Arbeit geht gut voran** the work is coming along well

voran′kommen §99 *intr* (SEIN) make progress; **gut v.** come along well

Vor′anschlag *m* rough estimate

Vor′anzeige *f* preliminary announcement; (cin) preview of coming attractions

Vor′arbeit *f* preliminary work

vor′arbeiten *intr* do the work in advance; do the preliminary work

vorauf′ *adv* ahead, in front

voraus′ *adv* in front; (*dat*) ahead (of) || **vor′aus** *adv*—**im v.** in advance

Voraus′abteilung *f* (mil) vanguard

voraus′bedingen §142 *tr* stipulate beforehand

voraus′bestellen *tr* reserve

voraus′bestimmen *tr* predetermine

voraus′bezahlen *tr* pay in advance

voraus′eilen *intr* (SEIN) rush ahead

vorausgesetzt [fo′rausgəzetst] *adj*—**v., daß** provided that

Voraus′sage *f* prediction; prophecy; (*des Wetters*) forecast; (*Wink*) tip

voraus′sagen *tr* predict; prophesy; (*Wetter*) forecast

Voraus′sagung *f* var of **Voraussage**

voraus′schauen *intr* look ahead

voraus′schicken *tr* send ahead; (fig) mention beforehand

voraus′sehen §138 *tr* foresee

voraus′setzen *tr* presume, presuppose

Voraus′setzung *f* assumption; prerequisite; premise

Voraus′sicht *f* foresight

voraus′sichtlich *adj* probable, presumable || *adv* probably, presumably, the way it looks

Voraus′zahlung *f* advance payment

Vor′bau *m* (-[e]s;-ten) projection; balcony, porch

vor′bauen *tr* build out || *intr* (*dat*) take precautions against

vor′bedacht *adj* premeditated || **Vorbedacht** *m* (-[e]s;)—**mit V.** on purpose; **ohne V.** unintentionally

vor′bedeuten *tr* forebode

Vor′bedeutung *f* (-;-en) foreboding, omen, portent

Vor′bedingung *f* (-;-en) precondition

Vorbehalt [′forbəhalt] *m* (-[e]s;-e) reservation; proviso; **mit allem V. hinnehmen!** take it for what it's worth!; **mit** (*or* **unter**) **dem V., daß** with the proviso that; **stiller** (*or* **innerer**) **V.** mental reservation; **unter V. aller Rechte** all rights reserved

vor′behalten §90 *tr* reserve; **Änderungen v.!** subject to change without

notice || *ref*—**sich** [*dat*] **etw v.** reserve s.th. for oneself

vor′behaltlich *prep* (*genit*) subject to

vor′behaltlos *adj* unreserved, unconditional

vorbei′ *adv* over, past, gone; **es ist drei Uhr v.** it's past three o'clock; **v. an** (*dat*) past, by; **v. ist v.** done is done; **v. können** be able to pass

vorbei′eilen *intr* (SEIN)—**an j—m v.** rush past s.o.

vorbei′fahren §71 *intr* (SEIN) drive by

vorbei′fliegen §57 *intr* (SEIN) fly past

vorbei′fließen §76 *intr* (SEIN) flow by

vorbei′gehen §82 *intr* (SEIN) pass; **an j—m v.** pass by s.o. || **Vorbeigehen** *n*—**im V.** in passing

vorbei′gelingen §142 *intr* (SEIN) fail

vorbei′kommen §99 *intr* (SEIN) pass by; (coll) stop in

vorbei′lassen §104 *tr* let pass

Vorbei′marsch *m* parade

vorbei′marschieren *intr* (SEIN) march by

Vor′bemerkung *f* (-;-en) preliminary remark; (parl) preamble

vorbenannt [′forbənant] *adj* aforementioned

vor′bereiten *tr* prepare || *ref* (**auf** *acc*, **für**) get ready (for)

vor′bereitend *adj* preparatory

Vor′bereitung *f* (-;-en) preparation

Vor′bericht *m* preliminary report

Vor′besprechung *f* (-;-en) preliminary discussion

vor′bestellen *tr* order in advance; (*Zimmer*, *usw.*) reserve

Vor′bestellung *f* (-;-en) advance order; reservation

vor′bestraft *adj* previously convicted

vor′beten *tr* keep repeating || *intr* lead in prayer

vor′beugen *ref* bend forward || *intr* (*dat*) prevent

vor′beugend *adj* preventive

Vor′beugung *f* (-;-en) prevention

Vor′beugungsmittel *n* preventive

Vor′bild *n* model; (*Beispiel*) example

vor′bildlich *adj* exemplary, model

Vor′bildung *f* (-;-en) educational background

Vor′bote *m* forerunner; (fig) harbinger

vor′bringen §65 *tr* bring forward, produce; (*Gründe*) give; (*Plan*) propose; (*Klagen*) prefer; (*Wunsch*) express

vor′buchstabieren *tr* spell out

Vor′bühne *f* apron, proscenium

vor′datieren *tr* antedate

vordem [for′dem] *adv* formerly

Vorder- [fordər] *comb.fm.* front, fore-

Vor′derachse *f* front axle

Vor′derarm *m* forearm

Vor′derbein *n* foreleg

vordere [′fordərə] §9 *adj* front

Vor′derfront *f* front; (fig) forefront

Vor′derfuß *m* front foot

Vor′dergrund *m* foreground

vor′derhand *adv* for the time being

vor′derlastig *adj* (aer) nose-heavy

Vor′derlauf *m* (hunt) foreleg

Vor′dermann *m* (-[e]s;-̈er) man in front; **j—n auf V. bringen** (coll) put s.o. straight; **V. halten** keep in line

Vor'derpfote f front paw
Vor'derrad n front wheel
Vor'derradantrieb m front-wheel drive
Vor'derreihe f front row; front rank
Vor'dersicht f front view
Vor'derseite f front side, front; (e-r Münze) obverse, heads
Vor'dersitz m front seat
vorderste ['fɔrdərstə] §9 adj farthest front
Vor'dersteven m (naut) stem
Vor'derteil m & n front section; (naut) prow
Vor'dertür f front door
Vor'derzahn m front tooth
Vor'derzimmer n front room
vor'drängen tr & ref press forward
vor'dringen §142 intr (SEIN) forge ahead, advance
vor'dringlich adj urgent
Vor'druck m printed form, blank
vor'ehelich adj premarital
vor'eilig adj hasty, rash
Vor'eiligkeit f (–;) haste, rashness
vor'eingenommen adj biased, prejudiced
Vor'eingenommenheit f (–;-en) bias, prejudice
Vor'eltern pl ancestors, forefathers
vor'enthalten §90 tr—j-m etw v. withhold s.th. from s.o.
Vor'entscheidung f (–;-en) preliminary decision
vor'erst adv first of all; for the time being, for the present
vorerwähnt ['fɔrervent] adj aforesaid
Vorfahr ['fɔrfar] m (–en;-en) forebear
vor'fahren §71 intr (SEIN) (bei) drive up (to)
Vor'fahrt f, **Vor'fahrt(s)recht** n right of way
Vor'fall m incident; event
vor'fallen §72 intr (SEIN) happen
Vor'feld n (aer) apron (of airport); (mil) approaches
vor'finden §59 tr find there
Vor'freude f anticipation
Vor'frühling m early spring
vor'fühlen intr—bei j-m v. feel s.o. out, put out feelers to s.o.
Vorführdame ['fɔrfyrdamə] f mannequin
vor'führen tr bring forward, produce; display, demonstrate; (Kleider) model; (Film) show; (Stück) (theat) present
Vor'führer –in §6 mf projectionist
Vor'führung f (–;-en) production; demonstration; showing; show, performance
Vor'gabe f points, handicap
Vor'gaberennen n handicap (race)
Vor'gabespiel n handicap
Vor'gang m event, incident, phenomenon; (Verfahren) process, procedure; (Präzedenzfall) precedent; (in den Akten) previous correspondence
Vor'gänger –in §6 mf predecessor
Vor'garten m front yard
vor'geben §80 tr pretend; give as an excuse; j-m zehn Punkte v. give s.o. ten points odds || intr—j-m v. give

s.o. odds || **Vorgeben** n (–s;–) pretext
Vor'gebirge n foothills; (Kap) cape
vorgeblich ['fɔrgeplɪç] adj ostensible
vorgefaßt ['fɔrgəfast] adj preconceived
Vor'gefühl n inkling; banges V. misgivings; im V. von or genit in anticipation of
vor'gehen §82 intr (SEIN) advance; go first; act; take action, proceed; (sich ereignen) go on, happen; (Uhr) be fast; (dat) take precedence (over); die Arbeit geht vor work comes first; was geht hier vor? what's going on here? || **Vorgehen** n (–s;) advance; action, proceeding; gemeinschaftliches V. concerted action
vorgelagert ['fɔrgəlagərt] adj offshore
Vor'gelände n foreground
vorgenannt ['fɔrgənant] adj aforementioned
Vor'gericht n appetizer
Vor'geschichte f previous history; (Urgeschichte) prehistory
vor'geschichtlich adj prehistoric
Vor'geschmack m foretaste
Vorgesetzte ['fɔrgəzetstə] §5 mf superior; boss; (mil) senior officer
vor'gestern adv day before yesterday
vor'gestrig adj of the day before yesterday
vorgetäuscht ['fɔrgətɔɪʃt] adj makebelieve
vor'greifen §88 intr (dat) anticipate
Vor'griff m anticipation
vor'gucken intr (Unterkleid) show
vor'haben §89 tr have in mind, plan; intend to do; (ausfragen) question; (schelten) scold; (Schürze) (coll) have on || **Vorhaben** n (–s;–) intention, plan; project
Vor'halle f entrance hall; lobby
vor'halten §90 tr—j-m etw v. hold s.th. in front of s.o.; (fig) reproach s.o. with s.th. || intr last
Vor'haltung f (–;-en) reproach; j-m Vorhaltungen machen über (acc) reproach s.o. for
Vor'hand f (cards) forehand; (tennis) forehand stroke; die V. haben (cards) lead off
vorhanden [for'handən] adj present, at hand, available; (com) in stock; v. sein exist
Vorhan'densein n existence; presence
Vor'hang m (–[e]s;-̈e) curtain; (theat) (coll) curtain call; Eiserner V. iron curtain
Vorhängeschloß ['fɔrheŋəʃlɔs] n padlock
Vor'hangstange f curtain rod
Vor'hangstoff m drapery material
Vor'haut f foreskin
Vor'hemd n dicky, shirt front
vor'her adv before, previously; (im voraus) in advance
vorher'bestellen tr reserve
vorher'bestimmen tr predetermine; (eccl) predestine
Vorher'bestimmung f predestination
vorher'gehend, vorherig [for'heriç] adj preceding, previous; prior
Vor'herrschaft f predominance

vor'herrschen *intr* predominate, prevail

vor'herrschend *adj* predominant, prevailing

Vorher'sage *f* prediction; forecast

vorher'sagen *tr* predict, foretell; (*Wetter*) forecast

vorhin' *adv* a little while ago

vor'historisch *adj* prehistoric

Vor'hof *m* front yard; (anat) auricle

Vor'hut *f* (mil) vanguard

vorige ['fɔrɪgə] §9 *adj* previous, former; **voriges Jahr** last year

Vor'jahr *n* preceding year

vor'jährig *adj* last year's

Vor'kammer *f* (anat) auricle; (aut) precombustion chamber

Vor'kampf *m* (box) preliminary bout; (sport) heat

Vor'kämpfer –in §6 *mf* pioneer

Vorkehrung ['fɔrkerʊŋ] *f* (–;–en) precaution; **Vorkehrungen treffen** take precautions

Vor'kenntnis *f* (von) basic knowledge (of); **Vorkenntnisse** rudiments, basics; **Vorkenntnisse nicht erforderlich** no previous experience necessary

vor'knöpfen *ref*—**sich** [*dat*] **j–n v.** (coll) chew s.o. out

Vor'kommando *n* (mil) advance party

vor'kommen §99 *intr* (SEIN) happen; (*Fall*) come up; (*als Besucher*) be admitted; (*scheinen*) seem, look; (*sich finden*) be found; (*zu Besuch*) call on || *ref*—**er kam sich** [*dat*] **dumm vor** he felt silly || *impers*—**es kommt dir nur so vor** you are just imagining it; **es kommt mir vor** it seems to me || **Vorkommen** *n* (–s;–) occurrence; (min) deposit

Vorkommnis ['fɔrkɔmnɪs] *n* (–ses;–se) event, occurrence

Vorkriegs– *comb.fm.* prewar

vor'laden §103 *tr* (jur) summon; (*unter Strafandrohung*) (jur) subpoena

Vor'ladung *f* (–;–en) (jur) summons; (*unter Strafandrohung*) (jur) subpoena

Vor'lage *f* submission, presentation; proposal; (*Muster*) pattern; bedside carpet; (fb) forward pass; (parl) bill

vor'lassen §104 *tr* let go ahead; (*Auto*) let pass; (*zulassen*) admit

Vor'lauf *m* (sport) qualifying heat

Vor'läufer –in §6 *mf* forerunner

vor'läufig *adj* preliminary; temporary || *adv* provisionally; temporarily, for the time being

vor'laut *adj* forward, fresh

Vor'leben *n* past life, former life

Vorlegebesteck ['fɔrlegəbə/tɛk] *n* carving set

Vorlegegabel ['fɔrlegəgabəl] *f* carving fork

Vor'legelöffel ['fɔrlegəlœfəl] *m* serving spoon

Vorlegemesser ['fɔrlegəmesər] *n* carving knife

vor'legen *tr* put forward; propose; (*Ausweis, Paß*) show; (*Essen*) serve; (*zur Prüfung, usw.*) submit, present; **den Ball v.** (fb) pass the ball; **ein scharfes Tempo v.** (coll) speed it up;

—j–m e–e Frage v. ask s.o. a question || *ref* lean forward

Ver'leger *m* (–s;–) throw rug

Vorlegeschloß ['fɔrlegə/lɔs] *n* padlock

vor'lesen §107 *tr*—**j–m etw v.** read s.th. to s.o.

Vor'lesung *f* (–;–en) reading; lecture; **e–e V. halten über** (*acc*) give a lecture on

Vor'lesungsverzeichnis *n* university catalogue

vor'letzte §9 *adj* second last; (gram) penultimate

Vor'liebe *f* preference

vorliebnehmen [for'lipnemən] §116 *intr* take pot luck; **v. mit** put up with

vor'liegen §108 *intr* be present; exist; be under consideration; **dem Richter v.** be up before the judge; **heute liegt nichts vor** there's nothing doing today; **mir liegt e–e Beschwerde vor** I have a complaint here; **was liegt gegen ihn vor?** what is the charge against him?

vor'liegend *adj* present, at hand

vor'lügen §111 *tr*—**j–m etw v. über** (*acc*) tell s.o. lies about

vor'machen *tr*—**du kannst mir doch nichts v.** you can't put anything over on me; **j–m etw v.** show s.o. how to do s.th. || *ref*—**er läßt sich** [*dat*] **nichts v.** he's nobody's fool; **sich** [*dat*] **selbst etw v.** fool oneself

Vor'macht *f* leading power; supremacy

Vor'machtstellung *f* (position of) supremacy

vormalig ['fɔrmalɪç] *adj* former

vormals ['fɔrmals] *adv* formerly

Vor'marsch *m* advance

vor'merken *tr* note down; reserve; **sich v. lassen für** put in for

Vor'mittag *m* forenoon, morning

vor'mittags *adv* in the forenoon

Vor'mund *m* guardian

Vor'mundschaft *f* (–;–en) guardianship

vor'mundschaftlich *adj* guardian's

Vor'mundschaftsgericht *n* orphans' court

vorn [fɔrn] *adv* in front; ahead; **ganz v.** all the way up front; **nach v.** forward; **nach v. heraus wohnen** live in the front part of the house; **nach v. liegen** face the front; **von v.** from the front; **von v. anfangen** begin at the beginning

Vor'nahme *f* undertaking

Vor'name *m* first name

vorne ['fɔrnə] *adv* (coll) var of **vorn**

vornehm ['fɔrnem] *adj* distinguished, high-class; **vornehme Welt** high society; **vornehmste Aufgabe** principal task || *adv*—**v. tun** put on airs

vor'nehmen §116 *tr* (*umbinden*) put on; undertake, take up; (*Änderungen*) make; **wieder v.** resume || *ref*—**sich** [*dat*] **ein Buch v.** take up a book; **sich** [*dat*] **etw v.** decide upon s.th.; **sich** [*dat*] **j–n v.** take s.o. to task; **sich** [*dat*] **v. zu** (*inf*) make up one's mind to (*inf*); **sich** [*dat*] **zuviel v.** bite off more than one can chew

Vor'nehmheit *f* (–;) distinction, high rank; distinguished bearing

vor'nehmlich adv especially

vor'neigen ref bend forward

vorn'herein adv—**von v.** from the first

vorweg ['fɔrvɛk], (fɔrn'vɛk) adv— **er ist weit v.** he is way out in front; **mit dem Kopf v.** head first; **mit dem Mund v. sein** be fresh

Vor'ort m suburb

Vorort— comb.fm. suburban

Vor'ortbahn f (rr) suburban line

Vor'ortzug m commuter train

Vor'platz m front yard; (Diele) entrance hall; (Vorfeld) (aer) apron

Vor'posten m (mil) outpost

Vor'rang m precedence; priority; pre-eminence; **den V. vor j—m haben** have precedence over s.o.

Vor'rat m (—[e]s;÷e) (an dat) stock (of), supply (of): **auf V. kaufen** buy in quantity; **e–n V. anlegen an** (dat) stock

vorrätig ['fɔrretiç] adj in stock

Vor'ratskammer f pantry, storeroom

Vor'ratsraum m storeroom

Vor'ratsschrank m pantry

Vor'raum m anteroom

vor'rechnen tr—j—m etw v. figure out s.th. for s.o.; **j—m seine Fehler v.** enumerate s.o.'s mistakes to s.o.

Vor'recht n privilege, prerogative

Vor'rede f preface, introduction

vor'reden tr—j—m etw v. try to make s.o. believe s.th.

Vor'redner –in §6 mf previous speaker

Vor'richtung f (—;—en) preparation; (Gerät) device, appliance, mechanism; (mach) fixture

vor'rücken tr move forward ‖ intr (SEIN) (Truppen) advance; (Polizei) move in; (im Dienst) be promoted

Vor'runde f (sport) play-offs

vors [fɔrs] abbr vor das

vor'sagen tr—j—m etw v. recite s.th. to s.o. ‖ intr (dat) prompt

Vor'sager –in §6 mf prompter

Vor'satz m purpose, intention; (jur) premeditation; **den V. fassen zu** (inf) make up one's mind to (inf); **mit V.** on purpose; **seinen V. ausführen** gain one's ends

Vor'satzblatt n (bb) end paper

Vor'satzgerät n adapter

vorsätzlich ['fɔrzetsliç] adj deliberate; (Mord) premeditated

Vor'schau f (cin) preview

vor'schieben §130 tr push forward; offer as an excuse; (fig) plead; **den Riegel v.** (dat) (fig) prevent; **Truppen v.** move troops forward

vor'schießen §76 tr (Geld) (coll) advance ‖ intr (SEIN) dart ahead

Vor'schiff n (naut) forecastle

Vor'schlag m proposal; (Angebot) offer; (Anregung) suggestion; (Empfehlung) recommendation; (mus) grace note; (parl) motion; **in V. bringen** propose; (parl) move

vor'schlagen §132 tr propose; suggest; recommend; **zur Wahl v.** nominate

Vor'schlagsliste f slate of candidates

Vor'schlußrunde f (sport) semifinal

vor'schnell adj rash, hasty

vor'schreiben §62 tr prescribe, order;

specify; write out; **ich lasse mir nichts v.** I take orders from no one

vor'schreiten §86 intr (SEIN) step forward; advance

Vor'schrift f order, direction; regulation; (med) prescription

vor'schriftsmäßig adj & adv according to regulations

vor'schriftswidrig adj & adv against regulations

Vor'schub m assistance; (mach) feed; **V. leisten** (dat) encourage; (jur) aid and abet

Vor'schule f prep school; (Elementarschule) elementary school

Vor'schuß m (Geld–) advance; (jur) retainer

vor'schützen tr pretend, plead

Vor'schützung f (—;) pretense

vor'schweben intr—**mir schwebte etw anderes vor** I had s.th. else in mind; **das schwebt mir dunkel vor** I have a dim recollection of it

vor'schwindeln tr—j—m etw v. fool s.o. about s.th.

vor'sehen §138 tr schedule, plan; provide; (fin) earmark; **das Gesetz sieht vor, daß** the law provides that ‖ ref be careful, take care; **sich mit etw v.** provide oneself with s.th.; **sich v. vor** (dat) be on one's guard against

Vor'sehung f (—;) Providence

vor'setzen tr put forward; (Silbe) prefix; **j—m etw v.** set s.th. before s.o. (to eat); **j—m j—n v.** set s.o. over s.o.

Vor'sicht f caution, care; (Umsicht) prudence; **V.!** watch out! (auf Kisten) handle with care!; **V., Stufe!** watch your step!

vor'sichtig adj cautious, careful

Vor'sichtigkeit f (—;) caution

vorsichtshalber ['fɔrziçtshalbər] adv to be on the safe side, as a precaution

Vor'sichtsmaßnahme f, **Vor'sichtsmaßregel** f precaution

Vor'silbe f prefix

vor'singen §142 tr—j—m etw v. sing s.th. to s.o. ‖ intr lead the choir

Vor'sitz m chairmanship, chair; presidency; **den V. haben** (or **führen**) **bei** preside over; **unter V. von** presided over by

Vorsitzende ['fɔrzitsəndə] §5 mf chairperson; president

Vor'sorge f provision; **V. tragen** (or **treffen**) **für** make provision for, provide for

vor'sorgen intr (für) provide (for)

vorsorglich ['fɔrzɔrkliç] adv as a precaution, just in case

Vor'spann m (cin) credits; (Kurzfilm) (cin) short

Vor'speise f appetizer

vor'spiegeln tr—j—m etw v. delude s.o. with s.th.; **j—m falsche Tatsachen v.** misrepresent facts to s.o.

Vor'spiegelung f (—;) sham; pretense; **V. falscher Tatsachen** misrepresentation of facts

Vor'spiel n prelude; (beim Geschlechtsverkehr) foreplay; (mus) overture; (theat) curtain raiser; **das**

war nur das V.! (fig) that was only the beginning!

vor'spielen tr—j—m etw v. play s.th. for s.o.

vor'sprechen §64 tr—j—m etw v. pronounce s.th. for s.o.; teach s.o. how to pronounce s.th. || intr—bei j—m v. drop in on s.o.; j—m v. audition before s.o.

vor'springen §142 intr (SEIN) leap forward; (aus dem Versteck) jump out; (vorstehen) stick out, protrude

Vor'sprung m projection; (Sims) ledge; (Vorteil) advantage; (sport) head start; (sport) lead

Vor'stadt f suburb

vor'städtisch adj suburban

Vor'stand m board of directors; executive committee, executive board; (Person) chairman of the board

vor'stehen §146 intr protrude; (dat) be at the head of, direct, manage

Vor'steher m (—s;—) head, director, manager; (educ) principal

Vor'steherdrüse f prostate gland

Vor'steherin f (—;—nen) head, director, manager; (educ) principal

vor'stellen tr place in front, put ahead; (Uhr) set ahead; (einführen) introduce, present; (darstellen) represent; (bedeuten) mean; (hinweisen auf) point out || ref—sich [dat] etw v. imagine s.th., picture s.th.

Vor'stellung f (—;—en) introduction, presentation; (Begriff) idea; (Einspruch) remonstrance, protest; (cin) show; (theat) performance

Vor'stellungsvermögen n imagination

Vor'stoß m (fig & mil) thrust, drive

vor'stoßen §150 tr push forward || intr (SEIN) push forward, advance

Vor'strafe f previous conviction

Vor'strafenregister n previous record

vor'streeken tr stretch out; (Geld) advance

Vor'stufe f preliminary stage

Vor'tag m previous day

vor'täuschen tr pretend, put on

Vor'teil m advantage; profit; (tennis) advantage

vor'teilhaft adj advantageous; profitable

Vortrag ['fortrɑk] m (—[e]s;—e) performance; (Bericht) report; (e—s Gedichtes) recitation; (e—r Rede) delivery; (Vorlesung) lecture; (acct) balance (carried over); (mus) recital; e—n V. halten über (acc) give a lecture on

vor'tragen §132 tr perform; present

Vortragende ['fortragəndə] §5 mf performer; speaker; lecturer

Vor'tragsfolge f program

vortrefflich ['fortreflɪç] adj excellent

vor'treten §152 intr (SEIN) step forward; (fig) stick out, protrude

Vor'tritt m (—[e]s;) precedence

vorü'ber adv past, by, along; (zeitlich) over, gone by

vorü'bergehen §82 intr (SEIN) pass; (an dat) pass by; (fig) disregard

vorü'bergehend adj passing, transitory || **Vorübergehende** §5 mf passer-by

vorü'berziehen §163 intr (SEIN) march by; (Gewitter) blow over

Vor'übung f warmup

Vor'untersuchung f preliminary investigation

Vor'urteil n prejudice

vor'urteilsfrei, vor'urteilslos adj unprejudiced

Vor'vergangenheit f (gram) past perfect

Vor'verkauf m advance sale; (theat) advance reservation

vor'verlegen tr advance, move up

Vor'wahl f (pol) primary

vor'wählen intr dial the area code

Vor'wählnummer f (telp) area code

Vor'wand m (—[e]s;—e) pretext; excuse

vorwärts ['forverts] adv forward, on, ahead || interj go on!

vor'wärtsbringen §65 tr bring forward; (fig) advance

vor'wärtsgehen §82 intr (SEIN) progress

vor'wärtskommen §99 intr (SEIN) go ahead; progress, make headway

vorweg [for'vek] adv beforehand; out in front

Vorweg'nahme f anticipation

vorweg'nehmen §116 tr anticipate; presuppose, assume

vor'weisen §118 tr produce, show

Vor'welt f prehistoric world

vor'weltlich adj primeval

vor'werfen §160 tr—j—m etw v. throw s.th. to s.o.; (fig) throw s.th. up to s.o.

vorwiegend ['forvigənt] adj predominant || adv predominantly, chiefly

Vor'wissen n foreknowledge

vor'witzig adj inquisitive; brash

Vor'wort n (—[e]s;—e) foreword

Vor'wurf m reproach, blame; (e—s Dramas) subject; j—m Vorwürfe machen blame s.o.

vor'wurfslos adj irreproachable

vor'wurfsvoll adj reproachful

vor'zählen tr enumerate

Vor'zeichen n omen; (math) sign; (mus) accidental; negatives V. minus sign

vor'zeichnen tr—j—m etw v. draw or sketch s.th. for s.o.

Vor'zeichnung f (—;—en) drawing; (mus) signature

vor'zeigen tr produce, show; (Wechsel) present

Vor'zeiger —in §6 mf bearer

Vor'zeigung f (—;—en) producing, showing; presentation

Vor'zeit f remote antiquity

vor'zeiten adv in days of old

vor'zeitig adj premature

vor'ziehen §163 tr draw forth; pull out; prefer; (mil) move up

Vor'zimmer n anteroom; entrance hall

Vor'zug m preference; (Vorteil) advantage; (Überlegenheit) superiority; (Vorrang) priority; (Vorrecht) privilege; (Vorzüglichkeit) excellence; e—r Sache den V. geben prefer s.th.

vorzüglich ['fortsyklɪç] adj excellent, first-rate || adv especially

Vor'züglichkeit f (—;) excellence

Vor'zugsaktie f preferred stock

Vor'zugsbehandlung *f* preferential treatment
Vor'zugspreis *m* special price
Vor'zugsrecht *n* priority; privilege
vor'zugsweise *adv* preferably
votieren [vo'ti:rən] *intr* vote
Votiv- [vo'ti:f] *comb.fm.* votive
Vo•tum ['vo:tum] *n* (-s;-ten [tən] & -ta [ta]) vote

vulgär [vʊl'gɛːr] *adj* vulgar
Vulkan [vʊl'kaːn] *m* (-s;-e) volcano
Vulkan'ausbruch *m* eruption
vulkanisch [vʊl'kaːnɪʃ] *adj* volcanic
vulkanisieren [vʊlkanɪ'ziːrən] *tr* vulcanize
Vulkan'schlot *m* volcanic vent
VW *abbr* (Volkswagen) VW
V-Waffe *f* (Vergeltungswaffe) V-1, V-2

W

W, w [ve] *invar n* W, w
Waage ['vaːgə] *f* (-;-n) (pair of) scales; (astr) Libra; (gym) horizontal position; **die beiden Dinge halten sich [dat] die W.** the two things balance each other; **die W. halten** (*dat*) counterbalance; **j-m die W. halten** be a match for s.o.
waa'gerecht, waagrecht ['vaːkreçt] *adj* horizontal, level
Waagschale ['vaːkʃaːlə] *f* scale(s); **in die W. fallen** carry weight; **in die W. werfen** bring to bear
wabbelig ['vabəlɪç] *adj* (coll) flabby
Wabe ['vaːbə] *f* (-;-n) honeycomb
wach [vax] *adj* awake; (*lebhaft*) lively; (*Geist*) alert; **ganz w.** wide awake
Wach'ablösung *f* changing of the guard
Wach'dienst *m* guard duty
Wache ['vaxə] *f* (-;-n) guard, watch; (*Wachstube*) guardroom; (*Wachlokal*) guardhouse; (*Polizei-*) police station; (*Wachdienst*) guard duty; (*Posten*) guard, sentinel; **auf W.** on guard; **auf W. ziehen** mount guard; **W. schieben** (coll) pull guard duty
wachen ['vaxən] *intr* be awake; **bei j-m w.** sit up with s.o.; **w. über** (*acc*) watch over, guard
wach'habend *adj* on guard duty
wach'halten §90 *tr* keep awake; (fig) keep alive
Wach'hund *m* watchdog
Wach'lokal *n* guardroom; police station
Wach'mann *m* (-[e]s;-leute) (Aust) policeman
Wach'mannschaft *f* (mil) guard detail
Wacholder [va'xɔldər] *m* (-s;-) juniper
Wachol'derbranntwein *m* gin
Wach'posten *m* sentry
wach'rufen §122 *tr* wake up; (*Erinnerung*) bring back
Wachs [vaks] *n* (-es;-e) wax
wachsam ['vaxzam] *adj* vigilant
Wach'samkeit *f* (-) vigilance
Wachs'bohne *f* wax bean
wachsen ['vaksən] *tr* wax || §155 *intr* (SEIN) grow; (an *dat*) increase (in)
wächsern ['vɛksərn] *adj* wax; (fig) waxy
Wachs'figurenkabinett *n* wax museum
Wachs'kerze *f*, **Wachs'licht** *n* wax candle
Wachs'leinwand *f* oilcloth

Wach'stube *f* guardroom
Wachs'tuch *n* oilcloth
Wachstum ['vaxstuːm] *n* (-s;) growth; increase
Wacht [vaxt] *f* (-;-en) guard, watch
Wächte ['veçtə] *f* (-;-n) snow cornice
Wachtel ['vaxtəl] *f* (-;-n) quail
Wach'telhund *m* spaniel
Wächter ['veçtər] *m* (-s;-) guard
Wacht'meister *m* police sergeant
Wach'traum *m* daydream
Wacht'turm *m* watchtower
wackelig ['vakəlɪç] *adj* wobbly; (*Zahn*) loose; (fig) shaky
Wackelkontakt ['vakəlkɔntakt] *m* (elec) loose connection, poor contact
wackeln ['vakəln] *intr* wobble; shake; (*locker sein*) be loose
wacker ['vakər] *adj* decent, honest; (*tapfer*) brave || *adv* heartily
wacklig ['vaklɪç] *adj* var of **wackelig**
Wade ['vaːdə] *f* (-;-n) (anat) calf
Wa'denbein *n* (anat) fibula
Wa'denkrampf *m* leg cramp
Wa'denstrumpf *m* calf-length stocking
Waffe ['vafə] *f* (-;-n) weapon; branch of service; **die Waffen strecken** surrender; (fig) give up; **zu den Waffen greifen** take up arms
Waffel ['vafəl] *f* (-;-n) waffle
Waf'fenbruder *m* comrade in arms
waf'fenfähig *adj* capable of bearing arms
Waf'fengang *m* armed conflict
Waf'fengattung *f* branch of service
Waf'fengewalt *f* force of arms
Waf'fenkammer *f* armory
Waf'fenlager *n* ordnance depot; **heimliches W.** cache of arms
waf'fenlos *adj* unarmed
Waf'fenruhe *f* truce
Waf'fenschein *m* gun permit
Waf'fenschmied *m* gunsmith
Waf'fenschmuggel *m* gunrunning
Waf'fenstillstand *m* armistice
Waf'fen-SS *f* (-;) SS combat unit
Wagehals ['vaːgəhals] *m* daredevil
Wagemut ['vaːgəmuːt] *m* daring
wagen ['vaːgən] *tr* dare; risk || *ref* venture, dare || **Wagen** *m* (-s;-) wagon; (*Fahrzeug*; Teil e-r Schreibmaschine*) carriage; (aut, rr) car; **der Große Wagen** the Big Dipper; **j-m an den W. fahren** (fig) step on s.o.'s toes
wägen ['vɛːgən] *tr* (& fig) weigh
Wa'genabteil *n* (rr) compartment

Wa'genburg f barricade of wagons
Wa'genheber m (aut) jack
Wa'genpark m fleet of cars
Wa'genpflege f (aut) maintenance
Wa'genschlag m car door, carriage door
Wa'genschmiere f (aut) grease
Wa'genspur f wheel track, rut
Wa'genwäsche f car wash
Wagestück ['vagəʃtyk] n hazardous venture, daring deed
Waggon [va'gõ] m (-s;-s) railroad car
waghalsig ['vakhalziç] adj foolhardy
Wagnis ['vaknis] n (-ses;-se) risk
Wahl [val] f (-;-en) choice, option; (Auswahl) selection; (Alternative) alternative; (pol) election; e-e W. treffen make a choice; vor der W. stehen have the choice
wählbar ['velbar] adj eligible
Wähl'barkeit f (-;) eligibility
Wahl'beeinflussung f interference with the election process
wahl'berechtigt adj eligible to vote
Wahl'beteiligung f election turnout
Wahl'bezirk m ward
wählen ['velən] tr choose; select; (pol) elect; (telp) dial || intr vote
Wäh'ler m (-s;-) voter
Wahl'ergebnis n election returns
Wäh'lerin f (-;-nen) voter
wählerisch ['velərɪʃ] adj choosy, particular
Wäh'lerschaft f (-;-en) constituency
Wäh'lerscheibe f (telp) dial
Wahl'fach n (educ) elective
wahl'fähig adj eligible for election; having a vote
wahl'frei adj (educ) elective
Wahl'gang m ballot
Wahl'kampf m election campaign
Wahl'kreis m constituency; district
Wahl'leiter m campaign manager
Wahl'list f (pol) slate, ticket
Wahl'lokal n polling place
Wahl'lokomotive f (coll) vote getter
wahl'los adj indiscriminate
Wahl'parole f campaign slogan
Wahl'programm n (pol) platform
Wahl'recht n right to vote, suffrage
Wahl'rede f campaign speech
Wahl'spruch m motto; (com, pol) slogan
Wahl'urne f ballot box
Wahl'versammlung f campaign rally
wahl'verwandt adj congenial
Wahl'zelle f voting booth
Wahl'zettel m ballot
Wahn [van] m (-[e]s;) delusion; error; folly; madness
Wahn'bild n phantom, delusion
wähnen ['venən] tr fancy, imagine
Wahn'idee f delusion; (coll) crazy idea
Wahn'sinn m (& fig) madness
wahn'sinnig adj (vor dat) mad (with); (coll) terrible || adv madly; (coll) awfully || **Wahnsinnige** §5 mf lunatic
Wahn'vorstellung f hallucination
Wahn'witz m (& fig) madness
wahn'witzig adj mad; (unverantwortlich) irresponsible
wahr [var] adj true; (wirklich) real; (echt) genuine; nicht w.? right?

wahren ['varən] tr keep; (Anschein) keep up; (vor dat) protect (against)
während ['verən] intr last
während ['verənt] prep (genit) during; (jur) pending || conj while; whereas
wahr'haben §89 tr admit
wahr'haft, wahr'haftig adj true, truthful; (wirklich) real || adv actually
Wahr'haftigkeit f (-;) truthfulness
Wahr'heit f (-;-en) truth; j-m die W. sagen give s.o. a piece of one's mind
wahr'heitsgemäß, wahr'heitsgetreu adj true, faithful; truthful
Wahr'heitsliebe f truthfulness
wahr'heitsliebend adj truthful
wahr'lich adv truly; (Bib) verily
wahrnehmbar ['varnembar] adj noticeable
wahr'nehmen §116 tr notice; (benutzen) make use of; (Interesse) protect; (Recht) assert
Wahr'nehmung f (-;) observation, perception; (der Interessen) safeguarding
wahr'sagen ref—sich [dat] w. lassen have one's fortune told || intr prophesy; tell fortunes
Wahr'sagerin f (-;-nen) fortuneteller
wahrscheinlich [var'ʃainlɪç] adj probable, likely || adv probably
Wahrschein'lichkeit f (-;) probability
Wahr'spruch m verdict
Wäh'rung f (-;) safeguarding
Wäh'rung f (-;-en) currency; standard
Wäh'rungsabwertung f devaluation
Wäh'rungseinheit f monetary unit
Wahr'zeichen n landmark
Walse ['vaizə] f (-;-n) orphan
Wai'senhaus n orphanage
Wal [val] m (-[e]s;-e) whale
Wald [valt] m (-[e]s;-̈er) forest, woods
Wald– comb.fm. forest; sylvan; wild
Wald'aufseher m forest ranger
Wald'brand m forest fire
waldig ['valdiç] adj wooded
Waldung ['valduŋ] f (-;-en) forest
Wald'wirtschaft f forestry
Wal'fang m whaling
Wal'fänger m (-s;-) whaler
walken ['valkən] tr full
Wal'ker m (-s;-) fuller
Wall [val] m (-[e]s;-̈e) mound; embankment; (mil) rampart
Wallach ['valax] m (-[e]s;-e) gelding
wallen ['valən] intr (sieden) boil; (sprudeln) bubble; (Gewand, Haar) flow, fall in waves || intr (SEIN) go on a pilgrimage; travel, wander
wall'fahren insep intr (SEIN) go on a pilgrimage
Wall'fahrer –in §6 mf pilgrim
Wall'fahrt f pilgrimage
Wall'graben m moat
Wal'lung f (-;) simmering, boiling; bubbling; flow; flutter; (Blutandrang) congestion; in W. bringen enrage; in W. geraten fly into a rage; **Wallungen** hot flashes
Walnuß ['valnus] f walnut
Walroß ['valros] n walrus
Wal'speck m blubber
walten ['valtən] intr rule; hold sway;

Gnade w. lassen show mercy; **seines Amtes w.** attend to one's duties
Wal'tran *m* whale oil
Walze ['valtsə] *f* (–;–n) cylinder; drum; roll, roller; (*der Schreibmaschine*) platen
walzen ['valtsən] *tr* roll
wälzen ['vɛltsən] *tr* roll; (*Bücher*) pore over; (*Gedanken*) turn over in one's mind; **die Schuld auf j–n w.** shift the blame to s.o. else || *ref* roll, toss; (*im Kot*) wallow; (*im Blut*) welter
Wal'zer *m* (–s;–) waltz
Wäl'zer *m* (–s;–) (coll) thick tome
Walz'werk *n* rolling mill
Wamme ['vamə] *f* (–;–n) dewlap; (coll) potbelly
Wampe ['vampə] *f* (–;–n) (coll) potbelly
wand [vant] *pret of* **winden** || **Wand** *f* (–;–e) wall; partition; (*Fels–*) cliff; **spanische W.** folding screen
Wand'apparat *m* (telp) wall phone
Wand'bekleidung *f* wainscot
Wandel ['vandəl] *m* (–s;) change
wandelbar ['vandəlbɑr] *adj* changeable
Wan'delgang *m*, **Wan'delhalle** *f* lobby
wandeln ['vandəln] *tr* change || *ref* (in *acc*) change (into) || *intr* (SEIN) (poet) wander; (poet) walk
Wan'derer –in §6 *mf* wanderer; hiker
Wan'derlust *f* wanderlust, itch to travel
wandern ['vandərn] *intr* (SEIN) wander; hike; (*Vögel*) migrate
Wan'derniere *f* floating kidney
Wan'derpreis *m* challenge trophy
Wan'derschaft *f* (–;) travels, wanderings
Wan'derstab *m* walking stick
Wan'derung *f* (–;–en) hike; migration
Wan'dervogel *m* migratory bird; (coll) rover
Wand'gemälde *n* mural
Wand'karte *f* wall map
Wand'leuchter *m* sconce
Wand'lung *f* (–;–en) change, transformation; (eccl) consecration
Wand'malerei *f* wall painting
Wand'pfeiler *m* pilaster
Wand'schirm *m* folding screen
Wand'schrank *m* wall shelves
Wand'spiegel *m* wall mirror
Wand'steckdose *f*, **Wand'stecker** *m* (elec) wall outlet
Wand'tafel *f* blackboard
wandte ['vantə] *pret of* **wenden**
Wand'teppich *m* tapestry
Wange ['vaŋə] *f* (–;–n) cheek
–wangig [vaŋɪç] *comb.fm.* –cheeked
Wan'kelmut *m* fickleness
wan'kelmütig *adj* fickle
wanken ['vaŋkən] *intr* stagger; sway, rock; (fig) waver
wann [van] *adv & conj* when; **w. immer** anytime, whenever
Wanne ['vanə] *f* (–;–n) tub
Wanst [vanst] *m* (–es;–e) belly, paunch
–wanstig [vanstɪç] *comb.fm.* –bellied
Wanze ['vantsə] *f* (–;–n) bedbug
Wappen ['vapən] *n* (–s;–) coat of arms
Wap'penkunde *f* heraldry

Wap'penschild *m* escutcheon
wappnen ['vapnən] *ref* arm oneself; **sich mit Geduld w.** have patience
war [vɑr] *pret of* **sein**
warb [varp] *pret of* **werben**
ward [vart] *pret of* **werden**
Ware ['vɑrə] *f* (–;–n) ware; article; commodity; **Waren** goods, merchandise
–waren [vɑrən] *pl comb.fm.* –ware
Wa'renaufzug *m* freight elevator
Wa'renausgabe *f* wrapping department
Wa'renbestand *m* stock
Wa'renbörse *f* commodity market
Wa'renhaus *n* department store
Wa'renlager *n* warehouse; stockroom
Wa'renmarkt *m* commodity market
Wa'renmuster *n*, **Wa'renprobe** *f* sample
Wa'renrechnung *f* invoice
Wa'renzeichen *n* trademark
warf [varf] *pret of* **werfen**
warm [varm] *adj* (**wärmer** ['vɛrmər]; **wärmste** ['vɛrmstə] §9) warm
Warmblüter ['varmblytər] *m* (–s;–) warm-blooded animal
warmblütig ['varmblytɪç] *adj* warm-blooded
Wärme ['vɛrmə] *f* (–;) warmth, heat
wär'mebeständig *adj* heatproof
Wär'meeinheit *f* thermal unit; calory
Wär'megrad *m* degree of heat, temperature
wärmen ['vɛrmən] *tr* warm, heat
Wär'meplatte *f*—**elektrische W.** hotplate
Warm'flasche *f* hot-water bottle
warm'halten §90 *tr* keep warm
warm'herzig *adj* warm-hearted
warm'laufen §105 *intr*—**den Motor w. lassen** let the motor warm up
Warmluft'heizung *f* hot-air heating
Warmwas'serbehälter *m* hot-water tank
Warmwas'serheizung *f* hot-water heating
Warmwas'serspeicher *m* hot-water tank
Warn– [varn] *comb.fm.* warning
Warn'anlage *f* warning system
warnen ['varnən] *tr* (**vor** *dat*) warn (of), caution (against)
Warn'gebiet *n* danger zone
Warn'schuß *m* warning shot
Warn'signal *n* warning signal
War'nung *f* (–;–en) warning, caution; **zur W.** as a warning
War'nungsschild *n*, **Warn'zeichen** *n* danger sign
Warschau ['varʃau] *n* (–s;) Warsaw
Warte ['vartə] *f* (–;–n) watchtower, lookout
War'tefrau *f* attendant; nurse
War'tefrist *f* waiting period
warten ['vartən] *tr* tend, attend to; (*pflegen*) nurse || *intr* (**auf** *acc*) wait (for)
Wärter ['vɛrtər] *m* (–s;–) attendant; (*Pfleger*) male nurse; (*Aufseher*) caretaker; (*Gefängnis–*) guard; (rr) signalman
War'teraum *m* waiting room
Wärterin ['vɛrtərɪn] *f* (–;–nen) attendant; nurse

War'tesaal m, **War'tezimmer** n waiting room

War'tung f (-;) maintenance

warum [va'rum] adv why

Warze ['vartsə] f (-;-n) wart; (Brust-) nipple

was [vas] indef pron something; **na, so was!** well, I never! || interr pron what; **ach was!** go on! **was für ein** what kind of, what sort of; **was haben wir gelacht!** how we laughed! || rel pron what; which; that; **was auch immer** no matter what; **was immer** whatever

Wasch- [vaʃ] comb.fm. wash, washing

waschbar ['vaʃbar] adj washable

Wasch'bär m racoon

Wasch'becken n sink

Wasch'benzin n cleaning fluid

Wasch'blau n bluing

Wasch'bütte f washtub

Wäsche ['veʃə] f (-;-n) wash, laundry; linen; underwear

Wä'schebeutel m laundry bag

wasch'echt adj washable; (fig) genuine

Wä'scheklammer f clothespin

Wä'schekorb m clothesbasket

Wä'scheleine f clothesline

waschen ['vaʃə] f §158 tr wash; launder; (Gold) pan; (Haar) shampoo; (reinigen) purify || ref wash; **sich** [dat] **die Hände w.** wash one's hands || intr wash

Wä'scher ['veʃər] m (-s;-) washer; laundryman

Wäscherei [veʃə'rai] f (-;-en) laundry

Wäscherin ['veʃərin] f (-;-nen) washerwoman, laundress

Wä'scherolle f mangle

Wä'scheschleuder f spin-drier

Wä'scheschrank m linen closet

Wä'schezeichen n laundry mark

Wasch'frau f laundress

Wasch'haus n laundry

Wasch'korb m clothesbasket

Wasch'küche f laundry

Wasch'lappen m washcloth; (fig) wishy-washy person

Wasch'maschine f washmachine, washer

Wasch'mittel n detergent

Wasch'raum m washroom, lavatory

Wasch'schüssel f wash basin

Wasch'tisch m washstand

Wasch'trog m washtub

Wa'schung f (-;-en) washing; ablution

Wasch'weib n (coll) gossip (woman)

Wasch'zettel m laundry list; (am Schutzumschlag) blurb

Wasser ['vasər] n (-s;-) water; **das W. läuft mir im Mund zusammen** my mouth is watering; **j—m das W. abgraben** pull the rug out from under s.o.; **mit allen Wassern gewaschen** sharp as a needle

was'serabstoßend adj water-repellent

was'serarm adj arid

Was'serball m water polo

Was'serbau m (-[e]s;) harbor and canal construction

Was'serbehälter m water tank; reservoir; cistern

Was'serblase f bubble; (auf der Haut) blister

Was'serbombe f depth charge

Was'serbüffel m water buffalo

Was'serdampf m steam

was'serdicht adj watertight, waterproof

Was'sereimer m bucket

Was'serfall m waterfall, cascade

Was'serfarbe f watercolor

Was'serflasche f water bottle

Was'serflugzeug n seaplane

Was'sergeflügel n waterfowl

Was'sergraben m drain; moat

Was'serhahn m faucet, spigot

Was'serhose f waterspout

wässerig ['vesəric] adj watery

Was'serjungfer f dragonfly

Was'serkessel m cauldron

Was'serklosett n toilet

Was'serkraftwerk n hydroelectric plant

Was'serkrug m water jug, water pitcher

Was'serkur f spa

Was'serland'flugzeug n amphibian plane

Was'serland'panzerwagen m amphibian tank

Was'serlauf m watercourse

Was'serleitung f water main; aqueduct

Was'sermangel m water shortage

Was'sermann m (-[e]s;) (astr) Aquarius

Was'sermelone f watermelon

wassern ['vasərn] intr land on water; (rok) splash down

wässern ['vesərn] tr water; irrigate; (phot) wash || intr (Augen, Mund) water

Was'serratte f water rat; (fig) old salt

Was'serrinne f gutter

Was'serrohr n water pipe

was'serscheu adj afraid of water

Was'serscheide f watershed, divide

Was'serschi m water ski

Was'serschlauch m hose

Wasserspeier ['vasərʃpai-ər] m (-s;-) gargoyle

Was'serspiegel m surface; water level

Was'sersport m aquatics

Was'serstand m water level

Was'serstiefel m rubber boots

Was'serstoff m hydrogen

was'serstoffblond adj peroxide-blond

Was'serstoffbombe f hydrogen bomb

Was'serstrahl m jet of water

Was'serstraße f waterway

Was'sersucht f dropsy

Was'serung f (-;-en) (aer) landing on water; (rok) splashdown

Wäs'serung f (-;) watering; irrigation

Was'serverdrängung f displacement

Was'serversorgung f water supply

Was'servogel m waterfowl

Was'serwaage f (carp) level

Was'serweg m waterway; **auf dem W.** by water

Was'serwerk n waterworks

Was'serzähler m water meter

Was'serzeichen n watermark

wässrig ['vesric] adj watery

waten ['vatən] intr (SEIN) wade

Watsche ['vatʃə] f (-;-n) slap

watscheln ['vatʃəln] intr (SEIN) waddle

watschen ['vatʃən] tr slap

Watt [vat] n (-s;-) (elec) watt
Watte ['vatə] f (-;-en) absorbent cotton; wadding
Wat'tebausch m swab
Wat'tekugel f cotton ball
Wat'tenmeer n shallow coastal waters
Wat'testäbchen n Q-tip, cotton swab
wattieren [va'tirən] tr pad, wad
Wattie'rung f (-;-en) padding, wadding
wauwau ['vau'vau] interj bow-wow! || **Wauwau** m (-s;-s) bow-wow, doggy
weben ['vebən] §109 & §94 tr & intr weave
We'ber m (-s;-) weaver
Weberei [vebə'raɪ] f (-;-en) weaving
We'berin f (-;-nen) weaver
We'berknecht m daddy-long-legs
Webstuhl ['vep/tul] m loom
Webwaren ['vepvarən] pl textiles
Wechsel ['veksəl] m (-s;-) change, shift; (für Studenten) allowance; (agr) rotation (of crops); (fin) bill of exchange; (hunt) run, beaten track; **gezogener W.** draft; **offener W.** letter of credit; **trockener** (or **eigener**) **W.** promissory note
Wech'selbeziehung f correlation
Wechselfälle ['veksəlfelə] pl ups and downs, vicissitudes
Wech'selfieber n intermittent fever; malaria
Wech'selfrist f period of grace (before bill of exchange falls due)
Wech'selgeld n change, small change
Wech'selgesang m antiphony
Wech'selgespräch n dialogue
wech'selhaft adj changeable
Wech'selkurs m rate of exchange
Wech'selmakler -in §6 mf bill-broker
wechseln ['veksəln] tr change; vary; (austauschen) exchange; **den Besitzer w.** change hands; **die Zähne w.** get one's second set of teeth; **seinen Wohnsitz w.** move || intr change; vary
Wech'selnehmer m (fin) payee
Wech'selnotierung f foreign exchange rate
Wech'selrichter m (elec) vibrator (producing a.c.)
wech'selseitig adj mutual, reciprocal
Wech'selseitigkeit f (-;) reciprocity
Wech'selspiel n interplay
Wech'selsprechanlage f intercom
Wech'selstrom m alternating current
Wech'selstube f money-exchange office
Wech'seltierchen n amoeba
wech'selvoll adj (Landschaft) changing; (Leben) checkered; (Wetter) changeable
wech'selweise adv mutually; alternately
Wech'selwirkung f interaction
Wech'selwirtschaft f crop rotation
wecken ['vekən] tr wake, awaken, rouse
Wecker (Wek'ker) m (-s;-) alarm clock
Weck'ruf m (mil) reveille
Wedel ['vedəl] m (-s;-) brush, whisk; (Schwanz) tail; (eccl) sprinkler
wedeln ['vedəln] tr brush away || intr

—mit dem Fächer w. fan oneself; mit dem Schwanz w. wag its tail
weder ['vedər] conj—**weder...noch** neither...nor
weg [vek] adv away, off; gone; lost || **Weg** [vek] m (-[e]s;-e) way, path; road; route, course; (Art und Weise) way; (Mittel) means; **am Wege** by the roadside; **auf dem besten Wege sein** be well on the way; **auf gütlichem Wege** amicably; **auf halbem Wege** halfway; **aus dem Weg räumen** remove; (fig) bump off; **etw in die Wege leiten** prepare the way for s.th.; introduce s.th.; **j-m aus dem Wege gehen** make way for s.o.; steer clear of s.o.; **Weg und Steg kennen** know every turn in the road
weg'bekommen §99 tr (Fleck) get out; (Krankheit) catch; (verstehen) get the hang of; **e-e w.** (coll) get a crack
weg'bleiben §62 intr (SEIN) stay away; be omitted
weg'blicken intr glance away
weg'bringen §65 tr take away; (Fleck) get out
Wegebau ['vegəbau] m (-[e]s;) road building
Wegegeld ['vegəgelt] n mileage allowance; turnpike toll
wegen ['vegən] prep (genit) because of, on account of; for the sake of; (mit Rücksicht auf) in consideration of; (infolge) in consequence of; (jur) on (the charge of); **von Amts w.** officially; **von Rechts w.** by right
Wegerecht ['vegəreçt] n right of way
weg'essen §70 tr eat up
weg'fahren §71 tr remove || intr (SEIN) drive away, leave
weg'fallen §72 intr (SEIN) fall away, fall off; (ausgelassen werden) be omitted; (aufhören) cease; (abgeschafft werden) be abolished
weg'fangen §73 tr snap away, snatch
weg'fliegen §57 intr (SEIN) fly away
weg'fressen §70 tr devour
weg'führen tr lead away
Weggang ['vekgaŋ] m departure
weg'geben §80 tr give away
weg'gehen §82 intr (SEIN) go away; **w. über** (acc) pass over; **wie warme Semmeln w.** go like hotcakes
weg'haben §89 tr get rid off; (Schläge, usw.) have gotten one's share of; (verstehen) catch on to; **der hat eins weg** (sl) he has a screw loose; (sl) he's loaded
weg'jagen tr chase away
weg'kehren tr sweep away; (Gesicht) avert || ref turn away
weg'kommen §99 intr (SEIN) come away; get away (verlorengehen) get lost; **nicht w. über** (acc) not get over
weg'können §100 intr—**nicht w.** not be able to get away
Wegkreuzung ['vekkrɔɪtsuŋ] f (-;-en) crossing, intersection
weg'kriegen tr get; (Fleck) get out
weg'lassen §104 tr leave out; let go; cross out; (gram) elide; (math) cancel
weg'legen tr put aside

weg′machen *tr* take away; (*Fleck*) take out

wegmüde ['vekmydə] *adj* travel-weary

weg′müssen §115 *intr* have to go

Wegnahme ['veknɑmə] *f* (–;–n) taking away; confiscation; (mil) capture

weg′nehmen §116 *tr* take away; (*Raum, Zeit*) take up; (*beschlagnahmen*) confiscate; (mil) capture

weg′packen *tr* pack away || *ref* pack off

weg′raffen *tr* snatch away

Wegrand ['vekrant] *m* wayside

weg′räumen *tr* clear away

weg′reißen §53 *tr* tear off, tear away

weg′rücken *tr* move away

weg′schaffen *tr* remove; get rid of

weg′scheren §129 *tr* clip || *ref* scram

weg′scheuchen *tr* scare away

weg′schicken *tr* send away

weg′schleichen §85 *ref* & *intr* (SEIN) sneak away, steal away

weg′schmeißen §53 *tr* (coll) throw away

weg′schneiden §106 *tr* cut away

weg′sehen §138 *intr* look away; **w. über** (*acc*) shut one's eyes to

weg′setzen *tr* put away || *ref*—**sich w. über** (*acc*) not mind; feel superior to || *intr* (SEIN)—**w. über** (*acc*) jump over

weg′spülen *tr* wash away; (geol) erode

weg′stehlen §147 *ref* slip away

weg′stellen *tr* put aside

weg′stoßen §150 *tr* shove aside

weg′streichen §85 *tr* cross out

weg′treten §152 *intr* (SEIN) step aside; (mil) break ranks; **weggetreten!** (mil) dismissed!; **w. lassen** (mil) dismiss

weg′tun §154 *tr* put away

Wegweiser ['vekvaizər] *m* (–s;–) roadsign; (*Buch, Reiseführer*) guide

weg′wenden §120 & §140 *tr* & *ref* turn away

weg′werfen §160 *tr* throw away || *ref* degrade oneself

weg′werfend *adj* disparaging

weg′wischen *tr* wipe away

weg′zaubern *tr* spirit away

weg′ziehen §163 *tr* pull away || *intr* (SEIN) move; (mil) pull out

weh [ve] *adj* painful, sore; **mir ist weh ums Herz** I am sick at heart || *adv*—**sich** [*dat*] **weh tun** hurt oneself; **weh tun ache** || *interj* woe! weh! woe is me! || **Weh** *n* (–[e]s;–e) pain, ache

wehe ['ve·ə] *adj, adv, & interj* var of **weh** || **Wehe** *f* (–;–n) drift

wehen ['ve·ən] *tr* blow; (*Schnee*) drift || (*Wind*) blow; (*Fahne, Kerzenflamme*) flutter || **Wehen** *pl* labor, labor pains; (fig) travail

Weh′geschrei *n* wails, wailing

Weh′klage *f* wail

weh′klagen *intr* (**über** *acc*) wail (over); **w. um** lament for

weh′leidig *adj* complaining, whining; **W. tun** whine

Weh′mut *f* (–;) melancholy; nostalgia

weh′mütig *adj* melancholy; nostalgic

Wehr [ver] *f* (–;–en) weapon; (*Abwehr*) defense, resistance; (*Brüstung*) parapet; **sich zur W. setzen** offer resistance || **Wehr** *n* (–[e]s;–e) dam

Wehr′dienst *m* military service

wehr′dienstpflichtig *adj* subject to military service

Wehr′dienstverweigerer *m* (–s;–) conscientious objector

wehren ['veran] *tr*—**j–m etw w.** keep s.o. (away) from s.th. || *ref* defend oneself; resist, put up a fight; **sich seiner Haut w.** save one's skin || *intr* (*dat*) resist; (*dat*) check

wehr′fähig *adj* fit for military service

wehr′haft *adj* (*Person*) full of fight; (*Burg*) strong

wehr′los *adj* defenseless

Wehr′macht *f* (hist) German armed forces

Wehr′meldeamt *n* draft board

Wehr′paß *m* service record

Wehr′pflicht *f* compulsory military service; **allgemeine W.** universal military training

wehr′pflichtig *adj* subject to military service

Weib [vaip] *n* (–[e]s;–er) woman; wife; **ein tolles W.** a luscious doll

Weibchen ['vaipçən] *n* (–s;–) (*Tier*) female; (*Ehefrau*) little woman

Weiberfeind ['vaibərfaint] *m* womanhater

Weiberheld ['vaibərhelt] *m* ladies' man

Weibervolk ['vaibərfolk] *n* womenfolk

weibisch ['vaibiʃ] *adj* womanish, effeminate

weib′lich *adj* female; womanly; (& gram) feminine

Weib′lichkeit *f* (–;) womanhood; feminine nature; **die holde W.** (hum) the fair sex

Weibs′bild *n* female; (pej) wench

Weibs′stück *n* (sl) woman

weich [vaiç] *adj* soft; (*Ei*) soft-boiled; (*zart*) tender; (*schwach*) weak; **w. machen** soften up; **w. werden** (& fig) soften; relent

Weich′bild *n* urban area, outskirts

Weiche ['vaiçə] *f* (–;–n) (anat) side, flank; (rr) switch; **Weichen stellen** throw the switch

weichen ['vaiçən] *tr* & *intr* soften; soak || §85 *intr* (SEIN) yield; give ground; (*Boden*) give way; (*dat*) give in to; **j–m nicht von der Seite w.** not leave s.o.'s side; **nicht von der Stelle w.** not budge from the spot; **von j–m w.** leave s.o.

Weichensteller ['vaiçənstelər] *m* (–s;–) (rr) switchman

Weich′heit *f* (–;) softness; tenderness

weich′herzig *adj* soft-hearted

Weich′käse *m* soft cheese

weich′lich *adj* soft; tender; flabby; insipid; (*weibisch*) effeminate; (*lässig*) indolent

Weichling ['vaiçlɪŋ] *m* (–s;–e) weakling

Weich′tier *n* mollusk

Weide ['vaidə] *f* (–;–n) pasture; (bot) willow

Wei′deland *n* pasture land

weiden ['vaidən] *tr* graze; (*Augen*)

feast || *ref—***sich w. an** (*dat*) feast one's eyes on || *intr* graze
Wei'denkorb *m* wicker basket
weidlich ['vaɪtlɪç] *adv* heartily
weidmännisch ['vaɪtmɛnɪʃ] *adj* (hunt) sportsmanlike
weigern ['vaɪgərn] *ref—***sich w. zu** (*inf*) refuse to (*inf*)
Wei'gerung *f* (–;–en) refusal
Weihe ['vaɪə] *f* (–;–en) consecration; (*e–s Priesters*) ordination
weihen ['vaɪən] *tr* consecrate; (*zum Priester*) ordain; (*widmen*) dedicate; **dem Tode geweiht** doomed to death || *ref* devote oneself
Wei'her *m* (–s;–) pond
wei'hevoll *adj* solemn
Weihnachten ['vaɪnaxtən] *n* (–s;) & *pl* Christmas; **zu W.** for or at Christmas
Weih'nachtsabend *m* Christmas Eve
Weih'nachtsbaum *m* Christmas tree; (coll) bombing markers
Weih'nachtsbescherung *f* exchange of Christmas presents
Weih'nachtsfeier *f* Christmas celebration; (*in Betrieben*) Christmas party
Weih'nachtsfest *n* feast of Christmas
Weih'nachtsgeschenk *n* Christmas present
Weih'nachtsgratifikation *f* Christmas bonus
Weih'nachtslied *n* Christmas carol
Weih'nachtsmann *m* (–[e]s;) Santa Claus
Weih'nachtsmarkt *m* Christmas fair (*at which Christmas decorations are sold*)
Weih'nachtag *m* Christmas day
Weih'rauch *m* incense
Weih'rauchfaß *n* censer
Weih'wasser *n* holy water
Weih'wedel *m* (eccl) sprinkler
weil [vaɪl] *conj* because, since
weiland ['vaɪlant] *adv* formerly
Weilchen ['vaɪlçən] *n* (–s;) little while
Weile ['vaɪlə] *f* (–;) while
weilen ['vaɪlən] *intr* stay, linger
Wein [vaɪn] *m* (–[e]s;–e) wine; (*Pflanze*) vine
Wein'bau *m* (–[e]s;) winegrowing
Wein'bauer –in §6 *mf* winegrower
Wein'beere *f* grape
Wein'berg *m* vineyard
Wein'blatt *n* vine leaf
Wein'brand *m* brandy
weinen ['vaɪnən] *tr* (*Tränen*) shed || *intr* cry, weep; **vor Freude w.** weep for joy; **w. um** cry over
weinerlich ['vaɪnərlɪç] *adj* tearful; (*Stimme*)) whining
Wein'ernte *f* vintage
Wein'essig *m* wine vinegar
Wein'faß *n* wine barrel
Wein'händler *m* wine merchant
Wein'jahr *n* vintage year
Wein'karte *f* wine list
Wein'keller *m* wine cellar
Wein'kelter *f* wine press
Wein'kenner *m* connoisseur of wine
Wein'krampf *m* crying fit
Wein'laub *n* vine leaves
Wein'lese *f* grape picking
Wein'presse *f* wine press

Wein'ranke *f* vine tendril
Wein'rebe *f* grapevine
wein'selig *adj* tipsy, tight
Wein'stock *m* vine
Wein'traube *f* grape; bunch of grapes
weise ['vaɪzə] *adj* wise || **Weise** §5 *m* wise man, sage || *f* (–;–n) way; (*Melodie*) tune; **auf diese W.** in this way
-weise *comb.fm.* –wise; by, e.g., **dutzendweise** by the dozen; –ly, e.g., **glücklicherweise** luckily
weisen ['vaɪzən] §118 *tr* point out, show; (*aus dem Lande*) banish; (*aus der Schule*) expel; **j–n w. an** (*acc*) refer s.o. to; **j–n w. nach** direct s.o. to; **j–n w. von** order s.o. off (*premises, etc.*); **von der Hand w.** refuse; **weit von der Hand w.** have nothing to do with || *ref—***von sich w.** refuse || *intr—***w. auf** (*acc*) point to
Weis'heit *f* (–;–en) wisdom; wise saying; **Weisheiten** words of wisdom
Weis'heitszahn *m* wisdom tooth
weis'lich *adv* wisely, prudently
weismachen ['vaɪsmaxən] *tr—***j–m etw w.** put s.th. over on s.o.; **mach das anderen weis!** tell it to the marines!
weiß [vaɪs] *adj* white
weissagen ['vaɪszagən] *tr* foretell
Weiß'blech *n* tin plate, tin
Weiß'blechdose *f* tincan
weiß'bluten *tr* bleed white
Weiß'brot *n* white bread
Weiß'dorn *m* (bot) hawthorn
Weiße ['vaɪsə] *f* (–;–n) whiteness; (Berlin) ale || §5 *m* white man || *f* white woman || *n* (*im Auge, im Ei*) white
weißen ['vaɪsən] *tr* whiten; (*tünchen*) whitewash
weiß'glühend *adj* white-hot
Weiß'glut *f* white heat, incandescence
Weiß'kohl *m*, **Weiß'kraut** *n* cabbage
weiß'lich *adj* whitish
Weiß'metall *n* pewter; Babbitt metal
Weiß'waren *pl* linens
Weiß'wein *m* white wine
Wei'sung *f* (–;–en) directions, instructions; directive
weit [vaɪt] *adj* far, distant; (*ausgedehnt*) extensive; (*breit*) wide, broad; (*geräumig*) large; (*Gewissen*) elastic; (*Herz*) big; (*Kleid*) full, big; (*Meer*) broad; (*Reise, Weg*) long; (*Welt*) wide; **bei weitem besser** better by far; **von weitem** from afar || *adv* far, way; widely; greatly; **w. besser** far better
weit'ab' *adv* (**von**) far away (from)
weit'aus' *adv* by far
Weit'blick *m* farsightedness
weit'blickend *adj* farsighted
Weite ['vaɪtə] *f* (–;–n) width, breadth; (*Ferne*) distance; (*Umfang*) size; (*Ausdehnung*) extent; (*Durchmesser*) diameter; (fig) range; **in die W. ziehen** go out into the world
weiten ['vaɪtən] *tr* widen; (*Loch*) enlarge; (*Schuh*) stretch || *ref* widen
weiter ['vaɪtər] *adj* farther; further; wider; **bis auf weiteres** until further notice; **des weiteren** furthermore;

ohne weiteres without further ado ‖ *adv* farther; further; furthermore; *(voran)* on; **er kann nicht w.** he can't go on; **nur s. w.!** keep it up!; **und so w.** and so forth, and so on

weiter– *comb.fm.* on; keep on, continue to

wei′terbefördern *tr* forward

Wei′terbestand *m* continued existence

wei′terbestehen §146 *intr* survive

wei′terbilden *tr* develop ‖ *ref* continue one's studies

wei′tererzählen *tr* spread *(rumors)*

wei′terfahren §71 *intr* (SEIN) drive on

wei′tergeben §80 *tr* pass on, relay

wei′tergehen §82 *intr* (SEIN) go on

wei′terhin′ *adv* furthermore; again

wei′terkommen §99 *intr* (SEIN) get ahead, make progress

wei′terkönnen §100 *intr* be able to go on; **ich kann nicht weiter** I'm stuck

wei′terleben *intr* live on, survive

wei′termachen *tr & intr* continue ‖ *interj* (mil) as you were!, carry on!

weit′gehend *adj* far-reaching

weit′gereist *adj* widely traveled

weit′greifend *adj* far-reaching

weit′her′ *adv*—**von w.** from afar

weit′her′geholt *adj* far-fetched

weit′herzig *adj* broad-minded

weit′hin′ *adv* far off

weitläufig [′vaɪtlɔɪfɪç] *adj* lengthy, detailed; complicated; *(Verwandte)* distant; *(geräumig)* roomy ‖ *adv* at length, in detail

weit′reichend *adj* far-reaching

weitschweifig [′vaɪt/vaɪfɪç] *adj* detailed, lengthy; long-winded

weit′sichtig *adj* (& fig) far-sighted

Weit′sprung *m* (sport) long jump

Weit′streckenflug *m* long-distance flight

weit′tragend *adj* long-range; (fig) far-reaching

Weit′winkelobjektiv *n* wide-angle lens

Weizen [′vaɪtsən] *m* (–s;–) wheat

Wei′zenmehl *n* wheat flour

welch [velç] *interr adj* which ‖ *interr pron* which one; *(in Ausrufen)* what …!; **mit welcher** (or **mit welch einer**) **Begeisterung arbeitet er!** with what enthusiasm he works! ‖ *indef pron* any; some ‖ *rel pron* who, which, that

welcherlei [′velçər′laɪ] *invar adj* what kind of; whatever

welk [velk] *adj* withered; *(Haut, Lippen)* wrinkled; (fig) faded

welken [′velkən] *intr* (SEIN) wither; (fig) fade

Wellblech [′velbleç] *n* corrugated iron

Well′blechhütte *f* Quonset hut

Welle [′velə] *f* (–;–n) wave; *(Wellbaum)* shaft; (gym) circle *(around horizontal bar)*; (mach) shaft

wellen [′velən] *tr & ref* wave

Wel′lenbereich *m* wave band

Wel′lenberg *m* crest *(of wave)*

Wel′lenbewegung *f* undulation

Wel′lenbrecher *m* breakwater

wel′lenförmig *adj* wavy

Wel′lenlänge *f* wavelength

Wel′lenlinie *f* wavy line

wel′lenreiten §86 *intr* surf; waterski ‖

Wellenreiten *n* (–s;) surfing, surfboard riding; waterskiing

Wel′lenreiter –**in** §6 *mf* surfer; waterskier

Wel′lenreiterbrett *n* surfboard; water ski

Wel′lental *n* trough *(of wave)*

wellig [′velɪç] *adj* wavy

Well′pappe *f* corrugated cardboard

Welt [velt] *f* (–;–en) world

Welt′all *n* universe; outer space

Welt′anschauung *f* outlook on life; ideology

Welt′ausmaß *m*—**im W.** on a global scale

Welt′ausstellung *f* world's fair

welt′bekannt, welt′berühmt *adj* world-renowned

Wel′tenbummler *m* globetrotter

welt′erfahren *adj* sophisticated

Weltergewicht [′veltərgəvɪçt] *n* welterweight class

Weltergewichtler [′veltərgəvɪçtlər] *m* (–s;–) welterweight boxer

welt′erschütternd *adj* earth-shaking

welt′fremd *adj* secluded; innocent

Welt′friede *m* world peace

Welt′geistlicher *m* secular priest

welt′gewandt *adj* worldly-wise

Welt′karte *f* map of the world

welt′klug *adj* worldly-wise

Welt′körper *m* heavenly body

Welt′krieg *m* world war

Welt′kugel *f* globe

Welt′lage *f* international situation

welt′lich *adj* worldly; secular

Welt′macht *f* world power

Welt′mann *m* (–[e]s;¨er) man of the world

welt′männisch *adj* sophisticated

Welt′meer *n* ocean

Welt′meinung *f* world opinion

Welt′meister –**in** §6 *mf* world champion

Welt′meisterschaft *f* world championship

Welt′ordnung *f* cosmic order

Welt′postverein *m* postal union

Welt′priester *m* secular priest

Welt′raum *m* (–[e]s;) outer space

Welt′raumfahrer *m* spaceman

Welt′raumfahrt *f* space travel

Welt′raumfahrzeug *n* spacecraft

Welt′raumforschung *f* exploration of outer space

Welt′raumgeschoß *n* space shot

Welt′raumkapsel *f* space capsule

Welt′raumstation *f* space station

Welt′raumstrahlen *pl* cosmic rays

Welt′reich *n* world empire

Welt′reise *f* trip around the world

Welt′rekord *m* world record

Welt′ruf *m* world-wide renown

Welt′ruhm *m* world-wide fame

Welt′schmerz *m* world-weariness

Welt′sicherheitsrat *m* U.N. Security Council

Welt′stadt *f* metropolis *(city with more than one million inhabitants)*

Welt′teil *m* continent

welt′umfassend *adj* world-wide

Welt′weisheit *f* philosophy

wem [vem] *interr & rel pron* to whom

Wem'fall *m* dative case

wen [ven] *interr & rel pron* whom

Wende ['vendə] *f* (-;-n) turn; turning point; (gym) face vault, front vault

Wen'dekreis *m* (geog) tropic

Wendeltreppe ['vendəltrepə] *f* spiral staircase

Wen'demarke *f* (aer) pylon; (sport) turn post

wenden ['vendən] §140 *tr* turn; turn around; turn over; (*Geld, Mühe*) spend || *ref* turn; (*Wind, Wetter*) change || *intr* turn, turn around

Wen'depunkt *m* turning point

wendig ['vendɪç] *adj* maneuverable; (*Person*) versatile, resourceful

Wen'dung *f* (-;-en) turn; change; (*Redensart*) idiomatic expression

Wen'fall *m* accusative case

wenig ['venɪç] *adj* little; **ein w.** a little, a bit of; **wenige** few, a few, some || *adv* little; not very; seldom || *indef pron* little; **wenige** few, a few

weniger ['venɪgər] *adj* fewer; less; (arith) minus

We'nigkeit *f* (-;) fewness; smallness; pittance; trifle; **meine W.** (coll) poor little me

wenigste ['venɪçstə] §9 *adj* least; very few, fewest; **am wenigsten** least of all

wenigstens ['venɪçstəns] *adv* at least

wenn [ven] *conj* if, in case; (*zeitlich*) when, whenever; **auch w. even if; außer w.** except when, except if, unless; **w. anders** provided that; **w. auch** although, even if; **w. schon, denn schon** go all the way || **Wenn** *n* (-;-) if

wenngleich', wennschon' *conj* although

Wenzel ['ventsəl] *m* (-s;-) (cards) jack

wer [ver] *interr pron* who, which one; **wer auch immer** whoever; **wer da?** who goes there? || *rel pron* he who, whoever || *indef pron* somebody, anybody

Werbe- [verbə] *comb.fm.* advertising; publicity; commercial

Wer'befernsehen *n* commercial television

Wer'befilm *m* commercial

Wer'befläche *f* advertising space

Wer'begraphik *f* commercial art

Wer'begraphiker —in §6 *mf* commercial artist

werben ['verbən] §149 *tr* (*neue Kunden*) try to get; (mil) recruit || *intr* advertise; **für e–n neuen Handelsartikel w.** advertise a new product; **um ein Mädchen w.** court a girl

Wer'beschrift *f* folder

Wer'bestelle *f* advertising agency

Wer'bung *f* (-;-en) advertising; publicity; courting; recruiting

Werdegang ['verdəgaŋ] *m* career, background; (*Entwicklung*) development; (*Wachstum*) growth; (*Ablauf der Herstellung*) process of production

werden ['verdən] §159 *intr* (SEIN) become, grow, get, turn; **w. zu** change into; **zu nichts w.** come to nought ||

aux (SEIN) (to form the future) **er wird gehen** he will go; (to form the passive) **er wird geehrt** he is being honored || **Werden** *n* (-s;) becoming, growing; (*Entstehung*) evolution; (*Wachstum*) growth; **im W. sein** be in the process of development; be in the making

wer'dend *adj* nascent; (*Mutter*) expectant; (*Arzt*) future

Werder ['verdər] *m* (-s;-) islet

Wer'fall *m* subjective case

werfen ['verfən] §160 *tr* throw, cast; (*Junge*) produce; (*Blasen*) form, blow; **Falten w.** wrinkle || *ref* (*Holz*) warp; **sich hin und her w.** toss; **sich in die Brust w.** throw out one's chest || *intr* throw; (*Tieren*) produce young

Werft [verft] *f* (-;-e) shipyard

Werft'halle *f* (aer) repair hangar

Werg [verk] *n* (-[e]s;) oakum, tow

Werk [verk] *n* (-[e]s;-e) work; (*Tat*) deed; (*Erzeugnis*) production; (*Leistung*) performance; (*Unternehmen*) undertaking; (*Fabrik*) works, plant, mill; (horol) clockwork; **das ist dein W.** that's your doing; **gutes W.** good deed; **im Werke sein** be in the works; **zu Werke gehen** go to it

Werk'anlage *f* plant, works

Werk'bank *f* (-;-e) workbench

werk'fremd *adj* (*Personen*) unauthorized

Werk'meister *m* foreman

Werk'nummer *f* factory serial number

Werks'angehörige §5 *mf* employee

Werk'schutz *m* security force

Werks'kantine *f* factory cafeteria

Werk'statt *f*, **Werk'stätte** *f* workshop

Werk'stattwagen *m* maintenance truck

Werk'stoff *m* manufacturing material

Werk'stück *n* (indust) piece

Werk'tag *m* weekday; working day

werk'tägig *adj* workaday, ordinary

werk'tags *adv* (on) weekdays

werk'tätig *adj* working; practical

Werk'zeug *n* tool

Werk'zeugmaschine *f* machine tool

Wermut ['vermut] *m* (-[e]s;) vermouth; (bot) wormwood

wert [vert] *adj* worth; worthy; esteemed; **etw** [*genit or acc*] **w. sein** be worth s.th.; **nicht der Rede w. sein** not worth mentioning; **nichts w.** good for nothing; **Werter Herr X** Dear Mr. X || **Wert** *m* (-[e]s;-e) worth, value; price, rate; (*Wichtigkeit*) importance; (chem) valence; **äußerer W.** face value; **im W. von** valued at; **innerer W.** intrinsic value; **Werte** (com) assets; (phys) data

Wert'angabe *f* valuation

wert'beständig *adj* of lasting value; (*Währung*) stable

Wert'bestimmung *f* appraisal

Wert'brief *m* insured letter

werten ['vertən] *tr* (*bewerten*) value; (*nach Leistung*) rate; (*auswerten*) evaluate

Wert'gegenstand *m* valuable article; **Wertgegenstände** valuables

—wertig [vertɪç] *comb.fm.* —value, —quality, e.g., **geringwertig** low-qual-

ity; (chem) –valent, e.g., **zweiwertig** bivalent
Wer'tigkeit *f* (–;–en) (chem) valence
wert'los *adj* worthless
Wert'papiere *pl* securities
Wert'sachen *pl* valuables
wert'voll *adj* valuable
Wert'zeichen *n* stamp; (*Briefmarke*) postage stamp; (*Banknote*) bill
Wesen ['vezən] *n* (–s;–) being, creature; entity; (*inneres Sein, Kern*) essence; (*Betragen*) conduct, way; (*Getue*) fuss; (*Natur*) nature, character; **einnehmendes W.** pleasing personality; **höchtes W.** Supreme Being
–wesen *n comb.fm.* system
we'senhaft *adj* real; characteristic
we'senlos *adj* unreal; incorporeal
wesentlich ['vezentlɪç] *adj* essential; (*beträchtlich*) substantial
Weser ['vezər] *f* (–;) Weser (River)
Wes'fall *m* genitive case
weshalb [ves'halp] *adv* why; wherefore
Wespe ['vespə] *f* (–;–n) wasp
wessen ['vesən] *interr pron* whose
West [vest] *m* (–s;) west; (poet) west wind
Weste ['vestə] *f* (–;–n) vest; **e–e reine W.** a clean slate
Westen ['vestən] *m* (–s;) west; **im W. von** west of; **nach W.** westward
Westfalen [vest'falən] *n* (–s;) Westphalia
westfälisch [vest'felɪʃ] *adj* Westphalian
West'gote *m* (–n;–n) Visigoth
Westindien [vest'ɪndjən] *n* (–s;) the West Indies
west'lich *adj* west, western; westerly
Westmächte ['vestmeçtə] *pl* Western Powers
westwärts ['vestverts] *adv* westward
weswegen [ves'vegən] *adv* why; wherefore
wett [vet] *adj* even, quits
Wett– *comb.fm.* competitive
Wett'bewerb *m* (–s;–e) competition, contest; (*Treffen*) meet
Wett'bewerber –in §6 *mf* competitor
Wette ['vetə] *f* (–;–n) bet, wager; **e–e W. abschließen** (or **eingehen**) make a bet; **mit j–m um die W. laufen** race s.o.; **was gilt die W.?** what do you bet?
Wett'eifer *m* competitiveness, rivalry
wetteifern ['vetaɪfərn] *insep intr* compete; **w. um** compete for
Wetter ['vetər] *n* (–s;) weather; (min) ventilation; **alle W.!** holy smokes!
wet'terbeständig, wet'terfest *adj* weatherproof
Wet'terglas *n* barometer
wet'terhart *adj* hardy
Wet'terkunde *f* meteorology
Wet'terlage *f* weather conditions
wet'terleuchten *insep impers*—es wetterleuchtet there is summer lightning ‖ **Wetterleuchten** *n* (–s;) summer lightning, heat lightning
Wet'terverhältnisse *pl* weather conditions
Wet'tervorhersage *f* weather forecast

Wet'terwarte *f* meteorological station
Wet'terwechsel *m* change in the weather
wetterwendisch ['vetərvendɪʃ] *adj* moody
Wett'fahrer –in §6 *mf* racer
Wett'fahrt *f* race
Wett'kampf *m* competition, contest
Wett'kämpfer –in §6 *mf* competitor, contestant
Wett'lauf *m* race, foot race
Wett'läufer –in §6 *mf* runner
wett'machen *tr* make up for
Wett'rennen *n* race
Wett'rudern *n* boat race
Wett'rüsten *n* armaments race
Wett'schwimmen *n* swimming meet
Wett'segeln *n* regatta
Wett'spiel *n* game, match
Wett'streit *n* contest, match, game
Wett'zettel *n* betting ticket
wetzen ['vetsən] *tr* whet, sharpen
Wetzstein ['vets/taɪn] *m* whetstone
Whisky ['vɪski] *m* (–s;–s) whiskey
wich [vɪç] *pret* of **weichen**
Wichs [vɪks] *m* (es–;–e) gala; **in vollem W.** in full dress; **sich in W. werfen** dress up
Wichse ['vɪksə] *f* (–;–n) shoepolish ‖ *f* (–;) (coll) spanking
wichsen ['vɪksən] *tr* polish; (coll) spank, beat up
Wicht [vɪçt] *m* (–[e]s;–e) elf; dwarf
Wichtel ['vɪçtəl] *m* (–s;–) dwarf
wichtig ['vɪçtɪç] *adj* important ‖ *adv* **–w. tun** act important
Wich'tigkeit *f* (–;) importance
Wichtigtuer ['vɪçtɪçtu–ər] *m* (–s;–) busybody
wichtigtuerisch ['vɪçtɪçtu–ərɪʃ] *adj* officious
Wicke ['vɪkə] *f* (–;–n) (bot) vetch
Wickel ['vɪkəl] *m* (–s;–) wrapper; curler, roller; (*von Garn*) ball; (med) compress
wickeln ['vɪkəln] *tr* wrap; wind (*Haar*) curl; (*Kind*) diaper; (*Zigaretten*) roll
Widder ['vɪdər] *m* (–s;–) ram; (astr) Ram
wider ['vidər] *prep* (*acc*) against, contrary to
wider– *comb.fm.* re–, con–, un–, counter–, contra–, anti–, with–
wi'derborstig *adj* stubborn, contrary
widerfah'ren §71 *intr* (SEIN) (*dat*) befall, happen to
Wi'derhaken *m* barb
Wi'derhall *m* echo, reverberation; (fig) response, reaction
wi'derhallen *intr* echo, resound
Wi'derlager *n* abutment
widerle'gen *tr* refute
wi'derlich *adj* repulsive
wi'dernatürlich *adj* unnatural
widerra'ten §63 *tr*—j–m etw **w.** dissuade s.o. from s.th.
wi'derrechtlich *adj* illegal
Wi'derrede *f* contradiction
Wi'derruf *m* recall; cancellation; retraction; denial; **bis auf W.** until further notice
widerru'fen §122 *tr* revoke; (*Auftrag*)

cancel; (*Befehl*) countermand; (*Behauptung*) retract

Widersacher –in ['vidərzaxər(ın)] §6 *mf* adversary

Wi'derschein *m* reflection

widerset'zen *ref* (*dat*) oppose, resist

widersetz'lich *adj* insubordinate

wi'dersinnig *adj* absurd, nonsensical

widerspenstig ['vidər/penstıç] *adj* refractory, contrary; (*Haar*) stubborn

wi'derspiegeln *tr* reflect || *ref* (**in** *dat*) be reflected (in)

Wi'derspiel *n* contrary, reverse

widerspre'chen §64 *intr* (*dat*) contradict; (*dat*) oppose

widerspre'chend *adj* contradictory

Wi'derspruch *m* contradiction; opposition; **auf heftigen W. stoßen bei** meet with strong opposition from

widersprüchlich ['vidər/pryçlıç] *adj* contradictory

wi'derspruchsvoll *adj* full of contradictions

Wi'derstand *m* resistance; opposition; (elec) resistance; (elec) resistor

Wi'derstandsnest *n* pocket of resistance

widerste'hen §146 *intr* (*dat*) withstand, resist; (*dat*) be repugnant to

widerstre'ben *intr* (*dat*) oppose, resist; (*dat*) be repugnant to || *impers*—**es widerstrebt mir zu** (*inf*) I hate to (*inf*)

widerstre'bend *adj* reluctant

Wi'derstreit *m* opposition, antagonism; (fig) conflict, clash

widerstrei'ten §86 *intr* (*dat*) clash with

widerwärtig ['vidər/vertıç] *adj* nasty

Wi'derwille *m* (**gegen**) dislike (of, for), aversion (to); (*Widerstreben*) reluctance; **mit W.** reluctantly

wi'derwillig *adj* reluctant, unwilling

widmen ['vıtmən] *tr* dedicate, devote || *ref* (*dat*) devote oneself to

Wid'mung *f* (–;-en) dedication

widrig ['vidrıç] *adj* contrary; (*ungünstig*) unfavorable, adverse

wid'rigenfalls *adv* otherwise, or else

wie [vi] *adv* how; (*vergleichend*) as, such as, like; **so...wie as...as; und wie!** and how!; **wie, bitte?** what did you say?; **wie dem auch sei** be that as it may; **wie wäre es mit...?** how about...?

wieder ['vidər] *adv* again; anew; (*zurück*) back; (*als Vergeltung*) in return

wieder- *comb.fm.* re-

Wie'derabdruck *m* reprint

wiederan'knüpfen *tr* resume

Wiederauf'bau *m* (–[e]s) rebuilding

wiederauf'bauen *tr* rebuild, reconstruct

wiederauf'erstehen §146 *intr* (SEIN) rise from the dead

Wiederauf'erstehung *f* resurrection

Wiederauf'führung *f* (theat) revival

wiederauf'kommen §99 *intr* (SEIN) (*Kranker*) recover; (*Mode*) come in again

Wiederauf'nahme *f* resumption; (jur) reopening

Wiederauf'nahmeverfahren *n* retrial

Wiederauf'rüstung *f* rearmament

Wie'derbeginn *m* reopening

wie'derbekommen §99 *tr* recover

wie'derbeleben *tr* revive, resuscitate

wie'derbeschaffen *tr* replace

wie'derbringen §65 *tr* bring back; restore, give back

wiederein'bringen §65 *tr* make up for

wiederein'setzen *tr* (**in** *acc*) reinstate (in); **in Rechte w.** restore to former rights

wiederein'stellen *tr* rehire; (mil) reenlist

Wie'dereintritt *m* (rok) reentry

wie'derergreifen §88 *tr* recapture

wie'dererhalten §90 *tr* get back

wie'dererkennen §97 *tr* recognize

wie'dererlangen *tr* recover, retrieve

wie'dererstatten *tr* restore; (*Geld*) refund

Wie'dergabe *f* return; reproduction; rendering

wie'dergeben §80 *tr* give back; (*Ton*) reproduce; (*spielen, übersetzen*) render; (*Ehre, Gesundheit*) restore

Wie'dergeburt *f* rebirth

wie'dergenesen §84 *intr* (SEIN) recover

wie'dergewinnen §52 *tr* regain

wiedergut'machen *tr* make good

Wiedergut'machung *f* (–;-en) reparation

wiederher'stellen *tr* restore

wie'derholen *tr* bring back; take back || **wiederho'len** *tr* repeat

wiederholt [vidər'holt] *adv* repeatedly

Wiederho'lung *f* (–;-en) repetition

Wiederho'lungszeichen *n* dittomarks; (mus) repeat

Wie'derhören *n*—**auf W.!** (telp) goodbye!

wie'derimpfen *tr* give (s.o.) a booster shot

wiederinstand'setzen *tr* repair

wiederkäuen ['vidərkɔı̯·ən] *tr* ruminate; (fig) repeat over and over || *intr* chew the cud

Wiederkehr ['vidərker] *f* (–;) return; recurrence; anniversary

wie'derkehren *intr* (SEIN) return; recur

wie'derkommen §99 *intr* (SEIN) come back

Wiederkunft ['vidərkunft] *f* (–;) return

wie'dersehen §138 *tr* see again || *recip* meet again || **Wiedersehen** *n* (–s;–) meeting again; **auf W.!** see you!

Wie'dertäufer *m* Baptist

wie'dertun §154 *tr* do again, repeat

wie'derum *adv* again; on the other hand

wie'dervereinigen *tr* reunite; reunify

Wie'dervereinigung *f* reunion; (pol) reunification

wie'derverheiraten *tr & recip* remarry

Wie'derverkäufer –in §6 *mf* retailer

Wie'derwahl *f* reelection

wie'derwählen *tr* reelect

wiederzu'lassen §104 *tr* readmit

Wiege ['vigə] *f* (–;-n) cradle

wiegen ['vigən] *tr* (*schaukeln*) rock || *ref*—**sich in den Hüften w.** sway one's hips; **sich w. in** (*acc*) lull oneself into || §57 *tr & intr* weigh

Wie'gendruck *m* incunabulum

Wie'genlied *n* lullaby

wiehern ['viːərn] *intr* neigh; **wiehern-des Gelächter** horselaugh

Wien [viːn] *n* (-s;) Vienna

Wiener –in ['viːnər(ın)] §6 *mf* Viennese

wienerisch ['viːnərıʃ] *adj* Viennese

wies [viːs] *pret* of **weisen**

Wiese ['viːzə] *f* (-;-n) meadow

Wiesel ['viːzəl] *n* (-s;-) weasel

Wie'senland *n* meadowland

wieso' *adv* why, how come

wieviel' *adj* how much; **w. Uhr ist es?** what time is it? || *adv & pron* how much || **vieviele** *adj & pron* how many

wievielte [vi'filtə] §9 *adj* which, what; **den wievielten haben wir?** (or **der w. ist heute?**) what day of the month is it?

wiewohl' *conj* although

wild [vılt] *adj* wild; savage; (*grausam*) ferocious; (*Flucht*) headlong; (*auf acc*) wild (about); **wilde Ehe** concubinage; **wilder Streik** wildcat strike || **Wild** *n* (-es;) game

Wild'bach *m* torrent

Wild'braten *m* roast venison

Wildbret ['vıltbret] *n* (-s;) game; venison

Wild'dieb *m* poacher

Wilde ['vıldə] §5 *mf* savage; **wie ein Wilder** like a madman

Wild'ente *f* wild duck

Wilderer ['vıldərər] *m* (-s;-) poacher

wildern ['vıldərn] *intr* poach

Wild'fleisch *n* game; venison

wild'fremd *adj* completely strange

Wild'hüter *m* game warden

Wild'leder *n* doeskin, buckskin; chamois; suede

Wildnis ['vıltnıs] *f* (-;) wilderness

Wild'schwein *n* wild boar

Wild'wasser *n* rapids

Wild'west'film *m* western

wildwüchsig ['vıltvyksıç] *adj* wild

Wille ['vılə] *m* (-ns;-n), **Willen** ['vılən] *m* (-s;-) will; (*Absicht*) intention; **mit W.** on purpose; **um j-s willen** for s.o.'s sake; **wider Willen** unwillingly; unintentionally; **willens sein zu** (*inf*) be willing to (*inf*)

wil'lenlos *adj* irresolute; unstable

Wil'lensfreiheit *f* free will

Wil'lenskraft *f* will power

wil'lensschwach *adj* weak-willed

wil'lensstark *adj* strong-willed

willfah'ren *intr* (*dat*) comply with

willig ['vılıç] *adj* willing, ready

Wil'ligkeit *f* (-;) willingness

willkom'men *adj* welcome; **j-n w. heißen** welcome s.o. || **Willkommen** *m & n* (-s;) welcome

Willkür ['vılkyr] *f* (-;) arbitrariness

will'kürlich *adj* arbitrary

wimmeln ['vıməln] *intr* (**von**) team (with)

wimmern ['vımərn] *intr* whimper

Wimpel ['vımpəl] *m* (-s;-) streamer; pennant

Wimper ['vımpər] *f* (-;-n) eyelash; **ohne mit der W. zu zucken** without batting an eye

Wim'perntusche *f* mascara

Wind [vınt] *m* (-[e]s;-e) wind; flatulence; (*hunt*) scent

Wind'beutel *m* (fig) windbag; (aer) windsock; (culin) cream puff

Winde ['vındə] *f* (-;-n) winch, windlass; reel; (naut) capstan

Windel ['vındəl] *f* (-;-n) diaper

win'delweich *adj*—**w. schlagen** (coll) beat to a pulp

winden ['vındən] §59 *tr* wind; twist, coil; (*Kranz*) weave, make || *ref* wriggle; (*Fluß*) wind; (*vor Schmerzen*) writhe

Wind'fang *m* storm porch

Wind'hose *f* tornado

Wind'hund *m* greyhound; (coll) windbag

windig ['vındıç] *adj* windy; (fig) flighty

Wind'kanal *m* wind tunnel

Wind'licht *n* hurricane lamp

Wind'mühle *f* windmill

Wind'pocken *pl* chicken pox

Wind'sack *m* windsock

Wind'schatten *m* lee

Wind'schutzscheibe *f* windshield

Wind'stärke *f* wind velocity

wind'still *adj* calm || **Windstille** *f* calm

Wind'stoß *m* gust

Wind'strömung *f* air current

Win'dung *f* (-;-en) winding, twisting; (*Kurve*) bend; (*e-r Schlange*) coil; (*e-r Schraube*) thread, worm; (*e-r Muschel*) whorl

Wind'zug *m* air current, draft

Wink [vıŋk] *m* (-[e]s;-e) sign; (*Zwinkern*) wink; (*mit der Hand*) wave; (*mit dem Kopfe*) nod; (*Hinweis*) hint, tip; **W. mit dem Zaunpfahl** broad hint

Winkel ['vıŋkəl] *m* (-s;-) corner; (carp) square; (geom) angle; (mil) chevron

winkelig ['vıŋkəlıç] *adj* angular; (*Straße*) crooked

Win'kellinie *f* diagonal

Win'kelmaß *n* (carp) square

Win'kelzug *m* subterfuge; evasion

winken ['vıŋkən] *intr* signal; **mit der Hand** wave; (*mit dem Kopfe*) nod; (*mit dem Auge*) wink; **mit dem Taschentuch w.** wave the handkerchief

Win'ker *m* (-s;-) signalman; (aut) direction signal

winseln ['vınzəln] *intr* whimper, whine

Winter ['vıntər] *m* (-s;-) winter

win'terfest *adj* winterized; (*Pflanzen*) hardy

win'terlich *adj* wintry

Win'terschlaf *m* hibernation; **W. halten** hibernate

Win'tersonnenwende *f* winter solstice

Winzer ['vıntsər] *m* (-s;-) vinedresser; (*Traubenleser*) grape picker

winzig ['vıntsıç] *adj* tiny

Wipfel ['vıpfəl] *m* (-s;-) treetop

Wippe ['vıpə] *f* (-;-n) seesaw

wippen ['vıpən] *intr* seesaw; rock; balance oneself

wir [vir] §11 *pers pron* we

Wirbel ['vırbəl] *m* (-s;-) whirl; eddy; whirlpool; (*Trommel-*) roll; (*Violin-*)

peg; (anat) vertebra; **e-n W. machen**
(coll) raise Cain
wirbelig ['vɪrbəlɪç] adj whirling; giddy
Wir'belknochen m (anat) vertebra
wir'bellos adj spineless, invertebrate
wirbeln ['vɪrbəln] tr warble || intr
whirl; (Wasser) eddy; (Trommel)
roll; (Lerche) warble; **mir wirbelt
der Kopf** my head is spinning
Wir'belsäule f spinal column, spine
Wir'belsturm m hurricane, typhoon
Wir'beltier n vertebrate
Wir'belwind m whirlwind
wirken ['vɪrkən] tr work, bring about,
effect; (Teig) knead; (Teppich)
weave; (Pullover) knit; **Gutes w.** do
good; **Wunder w.** work wonders ||
intr work; be active; function; look,
appear; (Worte) tell, hit home; **als
Arzt w.** be a doctor; **an e-r Schule
(als Lehrer) w.** teach school; **anregend w.** act as a stimulant; **berauschend w. auf** (acc) intoxicate; **beruhigend w. auf** (acc) have a soothing
effect on; **gut w.** work well; **lächerlich w.** look ridiculous; **stark w. auf**
(acc) touch deeply; **w. auf** (acc)
affect, have an effect on; **w. bei** (acc)
have an effect on; **w. für** work for; **w. ge-
gen** work against, counteract ||
Wirken n (-s;) action, performance;
operation
wirk'lich adj real, actual; true || adv
really, actually; truly
Wirk'lichkeit f (-;-en) reality; actual
fact
Wirk'lichkeitsform f indicative mood
wirksam ['vɪrkzɑm] adj active; effective; (Hieb) telling; **w. für** good for
Wirk'samkeit f (-;) effectiveness
Wirk'stoff m metabolic substance
(vitamin, hormone, or enzyme)
Wir'kung f (-;-en) effect; result; operation, action; influence, impression
Wir'kungsbereich m scope; effective
range; (mil) zone of fire
wir'kungsfähig adj active; effective;
efficient
Wir'kungskreis m domain, province
wir'kungslos adj ineffective; inefficient
wir'kungsvoll adj effective; efficacious
Wirk'waren pl knitwear
wirr [vɪr] adj confused; (verworren)
chaotic; (Haar) disheveled
Wirren ['vɪrən] pl disorders, troubles
Wirr'kopf m scatterbrain
Wirrwarr ['vɪrvar] m (-s;) mix-up,
mess
Wirt [vɪrt] m (-[e]s;-e) host; innkeeper; landlord; (biol) host
Wirtin ['vɪrtɪn] f (-;-nen) hostess;
innkeeper, innkeeper's wife; landlady
wirt'lich adj hospitable
Wirt'schaft f (-;-en) economy; business; industry and trade; (Haushal-
tung) housekeeping; (Hauswesen)
household; (Gasthaus) inn; (Treiben)
goings-on; (Durcheinander) mess;
(Umstände) fuss, trouble; **die W. besorgen** (or **führen**) keep house; **ge-
lenkte W.** planned economy
wirtschaften ['vɪrtʃaftən] intr keep

house; economize; (herumhantieren)
bustle about; **gut w.** manage well
Wirt'schafter –in §6 mf manager || f
housekeeper
Wirt'schaftler –in §6 mf economist;
economics teacher
wirt'schaftlich adj economical, thrifty;
economic; industrial; (vorteilhaft)
profitable
Wirt'schaftsgeld n housekeeping
money
Wirt'schaftshilfe f economic aid
Wirt'schaftsjahr n fiscal year
Wirt'schaftslehre f economics
Wirt'schaftspolitik f economic policy
Wirt'schaftsprüfer –in §6 mf certified
public accountant, CPA
Wirts'haus n inn, restaurant; bar
wischen ['vɪʃən] tr wipe
Wisch'lappen m dustcloth
Wisch'tuch n dishtowel
wispern ['vɪspərn] tr & intr whisper
Wißbegierde ['vɪsbəgɪrdə] f (-;) crav-
ing for knowledge; curiosity
wissen ['vɪsən] tr & intr know ||
Wissen n (-s;) knowledge; learning;
know-how; **meines Wissens** as far as
I know
Wis'senschaft f (-;-en) knowledge;
science
Wis'senschaftler –in §6 mf scientist
wis'senschaftlich adj scientific; scholarly; learned
Wis'sensdrang m, **Wis'sensdurst** m
thirst for knowledge
Wis'sensgebiet n field of knowledge
wis'senswert adj worth knowing
wis'sentlich adj conscious; willful ||
adv knowingly; on purpose
wittern ['vɪtərn] tr scent, smell
Wit'terung f (-;-en) weather; (hunt)
scent; **bei günstiger W.** weather per-
mitting; **e-e feine W. haben** have a
good nose
Wit'terungsverhältnisse pl weather
conditions
Witwe ['vɪtvə] f (-;-n) widow
Witwer ['vɪtvər] m (-s;-) widower
Witz [vɪts] m (-es;-e) joke; wisecrack;
wit; wittiness; **das ist der ganze W.**
that's all; **Witze machen** (or **reißen**)
crack jokes
Witz'blatt n comics
Witzbold ['vɪtsbolt] m (-[e]s;-e) joker
witzig ['vɪtsɪç] adj witty; funny
wo [vo] adv where; wo auch (or **wo
immer**) wherever; **wo nicht** if not;
wo nur wherever
woan'ders adv somewhere else
wob [vop] pret of **weben**
wobei' adv whereby; whereat; whereto;
at which; in the course of which
Woche ['vɔxa] f (-;-n) week; **heute in
e-r W.** a week from today; **in den
Wochen** sein be in labor; **in die
Wochen kommen** go into labor;
unter der W. (coll) during the week
Wo'chenbeihilfe f maternity benefits
Wo'chenbett n post-natal period
Wo'chenblatt n weekly (newspaper)
Wo'chenende n weekend
Wo'chengeld n weekly allowance; (für
Mütter) maternity benefits

wo′chenlang *adj* lasting many weeks ‖ *adv* for weeks

Wo′chenlohn *m* weekly wages

Wo′chenschau *f* (cin) newsreel

wöchentlich [′vœçəntlıç] *adj* weekly ‖ *adv* every week; **einmal w.** once a week

-wöchig [vœçıç] *comb.fm.* -week

Wöchnerin [′vœçnərın] *f* (-;-nen) recent mother

Wodka [′vɔtka] *m* (-s;) vodka

wodurch′ *adv* whereby, by which; how

wofern′ *conj* provided that; **w. nicht** unless

wofür′ *adv* wherefore, for which; what for; **w. halten Sie mich?** what do you take me for?

wog [vok] *pret* of **wägen & wiegen**

Woge [′vogə] *f* (-;-n) billow; **Wogen der Erregung** waves of excitement

woge′gen *adv* against what; against which; in exchange for what

wogen [′vogən] *intr* billow, surge, heave; (*Getreide*) wave; **hin und her w.** fluctuate

woher′ *adv* from where; **w. wissen Sie das?** how do you know this?

wohin′ *adv* whereto, where

wohinge′gen *conj* whereas

wohl [vol] *adj* well ‖ *adv* well; (*freilich*) to be sure, all right; I guess; possibly, probably; perhaps; **es sich** [*dat*] **w. sein lassen** have a good time; **nun w.!** well!; **w. daran tun zu** (*inf*) do well to (*inf*); **w. dem, der** happy he who; **w. kaum** hardly; **w. oder übel** willy-nilly ‖ **Wohl** *n* (-[e]s;) good health, well-being; (*Wohlfahrt*) welfare; (*Gedeihen*) prosperity; **auf Ihr W.!** to your health! **gemeines W.** common good

wohlan′ *interj* all right then!

wohlauf′ *adj* in good health, well ‖ *interj* all right then!

wohlbedacht [′volbədaxt] *adj* well-thought-out

Wohl′befinden *n* (-s;) well-being

Wohl′behagen *n* comfort, contentment

wohl′behalten *adj* safe and sound

wohl′bekannt *adj* well-known

wohl′beschaffen *adj* in good condition

Wohl′ergehen *n* well-being

wohl′erzogen *adj* well-bred

Wohl′fahrt *f* (-;) welfare

Wohl′fahrtsarbeit *f* social work

wohl′feil *adj* cheap

Wohl′gefallen *n* (-s;) pleasure, satisfaction

wohl′gefällig *adj* pleasant, agreeable

wohl′gemeint *adj* well-meant

wohlgemut [′volgəmut] *adj* cheerful

wohl′genährt *adj* well-fed

wohl′geneigt *adj* affectionate

Wohl′geruch *m* fragrance, perfume

wohl′gesinnt *adj* well-disposed

wohl′habend *adj* well-to-do

wohlig [′volıç] *adj* comfortable

Wohl′klang *m* melodious sound

wohl′klingend *adj* melodious

Wohl′leben *n* good living, luxury

wohl′riechend *adj* fragrant

wohl′schmeckend *adj* tasty

Wohl′sein *n* good health, well-being

Wohl′stand *m* prosperity, wealth

Wohl′tat *f* benefit; (*Gunst*) kindness, good deed; **e-e W. sein** hit the spot

Wohl′täter -in §6 *mf* benefactor

wohl′tätig *adj* charitable; beneficent

Wohl′tätigkeit *f* charity

wohltuend [′voltu-ənt] *adj* pleasant

wohl′tun §154 *intr* do good; (*dat*) be pleasant (to)

wohl′unterrichtet *adj* well-informed

wohl′verdient *adj* well-deserved

wohl′verstanden *interj* mark my words!

wohl′weislich *adv* very wisely

wohl′wollen §162 *intr* (*dat*) be well-disposed towards ‖ **Wollwollen** *n* (-s;) good will; (*Gunst*) favor

Wohn- [von] *comb.fm.* residential; dwelling, living

Wohn′anhänger *m* house trailer

Wohn′block *m* block of apartments

wohnen [′vonən] *intr* live, reside; (*als Mieter*) room

wohn′haft *adj* residing, living

Wohn′haus *n* dwelling; apartment house

Wohn′küche *f* efficiency apartment

Wohn′laube *f* garden house

wohn′lich *adj* livable; cozy

Wohn′möglichkeit *f* living accommodations

Wohn′ort *m* place of residence; (jur) domicile; **ständiger W.** permanent address

Wohn′raum *m* living space; room (*of a house*)

Wohn′sitz *m* place of residence

Woh′nung *f* (-;-en) dwelling, home; apartment; room; accommodations

Woh′nungsamt *n* housing authority

Woh′nungsbau *m* (-[e]s;) housing construction

Woh′nungsfrage *f* housing problem

Woh′nungsinhaber *m* §6 *mf* occupant

Woh′nungsmangel *m*, **Woh′nungsnot** *f* housing shortage

Wohn′viertel *n* residential district

Wohn′wagen *m* mobile home

Wohn′wagenparkplatz *m* trailer camp

Wohn′zimmer *n* living room

wölben [′vœlbən] *tr* vault, arch ‖ *ref* (*über dat or acc*) arch (over)

Wöl′bung *f* (-;-en) curvature; vault

Wolf [vɔlf] *m* (-[e]s;⸚e) wolf; (*Fleisch-*) meat grinder; (astr) Lupus; (pathol) lupus

Wolfram [′vɔlfram] *n* (-s;) tungsten

Wolke [′vɔlkə] *f* (-;-n) cloud

Wol′kenbildung *f* cloud formation

Wol′kenbruch *m* cloudburst

Wol′kendecke *f* cloudcover

Wol′kenfetzen *m* wispy cloud

Wol′kenhöhe *f* (meteor) ceiling

Wol′kenkratzer *m* (-s;-) skyscraper

Wol′kenwand *f* cloud bank

wolkig [′vɔlkıç] *adj* cloudy, clouded

Wolldecke [′vɔldɛkə] *f* woolen blanket

Wolle [′vɔlə] *f* (-;-n) wool

wollen [′vɔlən] *adj* woolen, wool ‖ §162 *tr* want, wish; mean, intend; (*gern haben*) like ‖ *intr* wish, like; **dem sei, wie ihm wolle** be that as it may; **wie Sie w.** as you please ‖ *mod aux* want (to), wish (to), intend (to);

be going (to) || **Wollen** *n* (-s;) will; volition

Wollfett ['vɔlfet] *n* lanolin

Wollgarn ['vɔlgarn] *n* worsted

wollig ['vɔliç] *adj* woolly

Wolljacke ['vɔljakə] *f* cardigan

Wollsachen ['vɔlzaxən] *pl* woolens

Wollstoff ['vɔl/tɔf] *m* woolen fabric

Wollust ['vɔllust] *f* (-;ə̈e) lust

wollüstig ['vɔllʏstıç] *adj* voluptuous; *(geil)* lewd, lecherous

Wollüstling ['vɔllʏstlıŋ] *m* (-s;-e) voluptuary

Wollwaren ['vɔlvarən] *pl* woolens

womit' *adv* with which; with what; wherewith; **w. kann ich dienen?** (com) can I help you?

womög'lich *adv* possibly, if possible

wonach' *adv* after which, whereupon; according to which

Wonne ['vɔnə] *f* (-;-n) delight; bliss

Won'negefühl *n* blissful feeling

Won'neschauer *m* thrill of delight

won'netrunken *adj* enraptured

won'nevoll, wonnig ['vɔnıç] *adj* blissful

woran' *adv* at which; at what; **ich weiß nicht, w. ich bin** I don't know where I stand

worauf' *adv* on which; on what; whereupon; **w. warten Sie?** what are you waiting for?

woraus' *adv* out of what, from what; out of which, from which; **w. ist das gemacht?** what is this made of?

worden ['vɔrdən] *pp* of **werden**

worin' *adv* in what; in which

Wort [vɔrt] *n* (-[e]s;ə̈er) word *(individual; literal)* || *n* (-[e]s;-e) word *(expression; figurative)*; *(Ausspruch)* saying; *(Ehrenwort)* word *(of honor)*; **auf ein W.!** may I have a word with you!; **auf mein W.!** word of honor!; **aufs W.** implicitly, to the letter; **das W. ergreifen** begin to speak; (parl) take the floor; **das W. erhalten** (or **haben**) be allowed to speak; (parl) have the floor; **das W. führen** be the spokesman; **hast du Worte!** (coll) can you beat that!; **in Worten** in writing; **j-m das W. erteilen** allow s.o. to speak; **j-m ins W. fallen** cut s.o. short

Wort'art *f* (gram) part of speech

Wort'bedeutungslehre *f* semantics

Wort'beugung *f* declension

Wort'bildung *f* word formation

wort'brüchig *adj*—**w. werden** break one's word

Wörterbuch ['vœrtərbux] *n* dictionary

Wörterverzeichnis ['vœtərfertsaıçnıs] *n* word index; vocabulary; glossary

Wort'folge *f* word order

Wort'führer **-in** §6 *mf* spokesman

Wort'gefecht *n* dispute

wort'getreu *adj* literal; verbatim

wort'karg *adj* taciturn

Wortklauber **-in** ['vɔrtklaubər(ın)] §6 *mf* quibbler, hairsplitter

Wort'laut *m* wording; (fig) letter

wörtlich ['vœrtlıç] *adj* word-for-word; literal; *(Rede)* direct

wort'los *adv* without saying a word

Wort'register *n* word index

Wort'schatz *m* vocabulary

Wort'schwall *m* flood of words, verbiage

Wort'spiel *n* pun

Wort'stamm *m* stem

Wort'stellung *f* word order

Wort'streit *m*, **Wort'wechsel** *m* argument

worüber [vo'rybər] *adv* over what, over which

worum [vo'rum] *adv* about what, about which

worunter [vo'runtər] *adv* under what, under which; among which

wovon' *adv* from what, of what, from which, of which; **w. ist die Rede?** what are they talking about?

wovor' *adv* of what; before which

wozu' *adv* for what; why; to which

Wrack [vrak] *n* (-[e]s;-e & -s) (& fig) wreck

Wrack'gut *n* wreckage

wrang [vraŋ] *pret* of **wringen**

wringen ['vrıŋən] §142 *tr* wring

Wringmaschine ['vrıŋma∫inə] *f* wringer

Wucher ['vuxər] *m* (-s;) profiteering; **das ist ja W.!** (coll) that's highway robbery!; **W. treiben** profiteer

Wu'cherer **-in** §6 *mf* profiteer; loan shark

Wu'chergewinn *m* excess profit

wu'cherhaft, wucherisch ['vuxərı∫] *adj* profiteering, exorbitant

Wu'chermiete *f* excessive rent

wuchern ['vuxərn] *intr* grow luxuriantly; *(Wucher treiben)* profiteer

Wu'cherung *f* (-;-en) (bot) rank growth; (pathol) growth

Wu'cherzinsen *pl* excessive interest

wuchs [vuks] *pret* of **wachsen** || **Wuchs** *m* (-es;) growth; groß von W. tall

-wüchsig ['vyksıç] *comb.fm.* -growing, -grown

Wucht [vuxt] *f* (-;-en) weight, force

wuchten ['vuxtən] *tr* lift with effort

wuchtig ['vuxtıç] *adj* heavy; massive

Wühlarbeit ['vylarbaıt] *f* subversive activity

wühlen ['vylən] *intr* dig, burrow; *(Schwein)* root about; *(suchend)* rummage about; (pol) engage in subversive activities; **im Geld w.** be rolling in money; **in Schmutz w.** wallow in filth

Wüh'ler **-in** §6 *mf* subversive, agitator

Wulst [vulst] *m* (-es;ə̈e) & *f* (-;ə̈e) bulge; (aut) rim (of tire)

wulstig ['vulstıç] *adj* bulging; *(Lippen)* thick

wund [vunt] *adj* sore; (poet) wounded

Wunde ['vundə] *f* (-;-n) wound; sore

Wunder ['vundər] *n* (-s;-) wonder; miracle; **W. wirken** work wonders

wunderbar ['vundərbar] *adj* wonderful; *(& fig)* miraculous

Wun'derding *n* marvel

Wun'derdoktor *m* faith healer

Wun'derkind *n* child prodigy

Wun'derkraft *f* miraculous power

wun'derlich *adj* queer, odd

wundern ['vundərn] *tr* amaze || *ref*

(über *acc*) be amazed (at) ‖ *impers* —**es sollte mich w., wenn** I'd be surprised if; **es wundert mich, daß I am** surprised that

wun'derschön' *adv* lovely, gorgeous

Wun'dertat *f* miracle

Wun'dertäter –in §6 *mf* wonder worker

wundertätig *adj* miraculous

wun'dervoll *adj* wonderful, marvelous

Wun'derwerk *n* (& *fig*) miracle

Wun'derzeichen *n* omen, prodigy

Wund'klammer *f* (surg) clamp

wund'liegen §108 *ref* get bedsores

Wund'mal *n* scar, sore; (relig) wound

wund'reiten §86 *ref* become saddlesore

Wunsch [vʊnʃ] *m* (**-es;¨e**) wish; (nach) desire (for); **auf W.** upon request; **ein frommer W.** wishful thinking; **nach W.** as desired

Wünschelrute ['vʏnʃəlrutə] *f* divining rod

Wün'schelrutengänger *m* dowser

wünschen ['vʏnʃən] *tr* wish; wish for, desire; **was w. Sie?** (com) may I help you? ‖ *intr* wish, please

wün'schenswert *adj* desirable

Wunsch'form *f* (gram) optative

Wunsch'konzert *n* (rad) request program

wunsch'los *adj* contented ‖ *adv*—**w. glücklich** perfectly happy

wuppdich ['vʊpdɪç] *interj* zip!, in a flash!; all of a sudden!

wurde ['vʊrdə] *pret* of **werden**

Würde ['vʏrdə] *f* (**-;-n**) honor; title; dignity; post, office; **akademische W.** academic degree; **unter aller W.** beneath contempt

wür'delos *adj* undignified

Wür'denträger –in §6 *mf* dignitary

wür'devoll *adj* dignified

würdig ['vʏrdɪç] *adj* dignified; (genit) worthy (of), deserving (of)

würdigen ['vʏrdɪgən] *tr* appreciate, value; (genit) deem worthy (of)

Wurf [vʊrf] *m* (**-[e]s;¨e**) throw, cast, pitch; (fig) hit, success; (zool) litter, brood

Wurf'anker *m* grapnel

Würfel ['vʏrfəl] *m* (**-s;-**) die; cube,

square; (geom) cube; **W. spielen** play dice

Wür'felbecher *m* dice box

würfelig ['vʏrfəlɪç] *adj* cube-shaped; (*Muster*) checkered

würfeln ['vʏrfəln] *intr* play dice

Wür'felzucker *m* cube sugar

Wurf'geschoß *n* projectile, missile

Wurf'pfeil *m* dart

würgen ['vʏrgən] *tr* choke; strangle ‖ *intr* choke; **am Essen w.** gag on food

Wurm [vʊrm] *m* (**-s;¨er**) (& mach) worm

wurmen ['vʊrmən] *tr* (coll) bug

wurmig ['vʊrmɪç] *adj* wormy; wormeaten

wurmstichig ['vʊrmʃtɪçɪç] *adj* wormeaten

Wurst [vʊrst] *f* (**-;¨e**) sausage; **es geht um die W.** now or never; **es ist mir W.** I couldn't care less

Würstchen ['vʏrstçən] *n* (**-s;-**), **Würstel** ['vʏrstəl] *n* (**-s;-n**) hotdog

wursteln ['vʊrstəln] *intr* muddle along

Würze ['vʏrtsə] *f* (**-;-n**) spice, seasoning; (fig) zest

Wurzel ['vʊrtsəl] *f* (**-;-n**) root; **W. fassen** (or **schlagen**) take root

wurzeln ['vʊrtsəln] *intr* take root; **w. in** (dat) be rooted in

würzen ['vʏrtsən] *tr* spice, season

würzig ['vʏrtsɪç] *adj* spicy; aromatic

Würz'stoff *m* seasoning

wusch [vuʃ] *pret* of **waschen**

wußte ['vʊstə] *pret* of **wissen**

Wust [vʊst] *m* (**-es;**) jumble, mess

wüst [vyst] *adj* desert, waste; (roh) coarse; (wirr) confused

Wüste ['vystə] *f* (**-;-en**) desert

Wüstling ['vystlɪŋ] *m* (**-s;-e**) debauchee

Wut [vut] *f* (**-;**) rage, fury; madness

Wut'anfall *m* fit of rage

wüten ['vytən] *intr* rage

wü'tend *adj* (auf *acc*) furious (at)

Wüterich ['vytərɪç] *m* (**-s;-e**) madman; bloodthirsty villain

wut'schäumend *adj* foaming with rage

wut'schnaubend *adj* in a towering rage

Wut'schrei *m* shout of anger

X

X, x [ɪks] *invar n* X, x

X'-Beine *pl* knock-knees

x'-beinig *adj* knock-kneed

x'-beliebig *adj* any, whatever ‖ **X-beliebige** §5 *m*—**jeder X.** every Tom, Dick, and Harry

x'-fach *adj* (coll) hundredfold

x'-mal *adv* umpteen times

X'-Strahlen *pl* x-rays

X'-Tag *m* D-day

x-te ['ɪkstə] §9 *adj* umpteenth; **die x-te Potenz** (math) the nth power

Xylophon [ksylə'fon] *n* (**-s;-e**) xylophone

Y

Y, y [ypsɪlən] *invar n* Y, y

Yacht [jaxt] *f* (**-;-en**) yacht

Yamswurzel ['jamsvʊrtsəl] *f* (**-;-**) (bot) yam

Yankee ['jɛŋki] *m* (**-s;-s**) Yankee

Yoghurt ['jogurt] *m* & *n* (**-s;**) yogurt

Yo-Yo ['jo'jo] *n* (**-s;-s**) yo-yo

Ypsilon ['ypsɪlən] *n* (**-[s];-s**) y

Z

Z, z [tset] *invar n* Z, z
Zacke ['tsakə] *f* (-;-n) sharp point; (*Zinke*) prong; (*Fels–*) crag; (*e–s Kamms, e–r Säge*) tooth; (*am Kleid*) scallop
zacken ['tsakən] *tr* notch; scallop ‖ **Zacken** *m* (-s;-) var of **Zacke**
zackig ['tsakıç] *adj* toothed; notched; (*Felsen*) jagged; (*spitz*) pointed; (*Kleid*) scalloped; (fig) sharp
zagen ['tsagən] *intr* be faint-hearted
zaghaft ['tsakhaft] *adj* timid
zäh [tse] *adj* tough; (*klebig*) viscous; (*beharrlich*) persistent; (*Gedächtnis*) tenacious; (*halsstarrig*) dogged
zäh'flüssig *adj* viscous
Zäh'flüssigkeit *f* (-;) viscosity
Zä'higkeit *f* (-;) toughness; tenacity; viscosity; doggedness
Zahl [tsal] *f* (-;-en) number; (*Betrag, Ziffer*) figure; **an Z. übertreffen** outnumber; **arabische Z.** Arabic numeral; **der Z. nach** in number; **ganze Z.** integer; **gebrochene Z.** fraction; **gerade Z.** even number; **in roten Zahlen stecken** be in the red; **ungerade Z.** odd number; **wenig an der Z.** few in number
zahlbar ['tsalbar] *adj* payable; **z. bei Lieferung** cash on delivery
zählebig ['tselebıç] *adj* hardy
zahlen ['tsalən] *tr* pay; (*Schuld*) pay off ‖ *intr* pay
zählen ['tselən] *tr* count; number, amount to ‖ *intr* count; be of importance, count; **nach Tausenden z.** number in the thousands; **z. auf** (*dat*) count on; **z. zu** be numbered among, belong to
Zah'lenangaben *pl* figures
Zah'lenfolge *f* numerical order
zah'lenmäßig *adj* numerical
Zah'ler –in §6 *mf* payer
Zäh'ler (-s;-) counter; recorder; (*für Gas, Elektrizität*) meter; (math) numerator; (parl) teller; (sport) scorekeeper
Zählerableser ['tselərapleзər] *m* (-s;-) meter man
Zahl'karte *f* money-order form
zahl'los *adj* countless, innumerable
Zahl'meister *m* paymaster; (mil) pay officer; (nav) purser
zahl'reich *adj* numerous
Zähl'rohr *n* Geiger counter
Zahl'stelle *f* cashier's window; (*e–r Bank*) branch office
Zahl'tag *m* payday
Zah'lung *f* (-;-en) payment; (*e–r Schuld*) settlement
Zäh'lung *f* (-;-en) counting; computation
Zah'lungsanweisung *f* draft; check; postal money order
Zah'lungsausgleich *m* balance of payments
Zah'lungsbedingungen *pl* (fin) terms
Zah'lungsbestätigung *f* receipt

Zah'lungsbilanz *f* balance of payments; **aktive** (or **passive**) **Z.** favorable (or unfavorable) balance of payments
zah'lungsfähig *adj* solvent
Zah'lungsfähigkeit *f* (-;) solvency
Zah'lungsfrist *f* due date
Zah'lungsmittel *n* medium of exchange; **gesetzliches Z.** legal tender; **bargeldloses Z.** instrument of credit
Zah'lungsschwierigkeiten *pl* financial embarrassment
Zah'lungssperre *f* stoppage of payments
Zah'lungstermin *m* date of payment; (fin) date of maturity
Zah'lungsverzug *m* (fin) default
Zähl'werk *n* meter
Zahl'wort *n* (-[e]s;ːer) numeral
Zahl'zeichen *n* figure, cipher
zahm [tsam] *adj* tame; domesticated
zähmen ['tsemən] *tr* tame; domesticate; (fig) control ‖ *ref* control oneself
Zäh'mung *f* (-;) taming; domestication
Zahn [tsan] *m* (-[e]s;ːe) tooth; (mach) tooth, cog; **j–m auf den Z. fühlen** sound s.o. out; **mit den Zähnen knirschen** grind one's teeth
Zahn'arzt *m*, **Zahn'ärztin** *f* dentist
Zahn'bürste *f* toothbrush
Zahn'creme *f* toothpaste
zahnen ['tsanən] *intr* cut one's teeth
Zahn'ersatz *m* denture
Zahn'fäule *f* tooth decay, caries
Zahn'fleisch *n* gum
Zahn'füllung *f* (dent) filling
Zahn'heilkunde *f* dentistry
Zahn'klammer *f* (-;-n) (dent) brace
Zahn'krem *f* toothpaste
Zahn'krone *f* (dent) crown
Zahn'laut *m* (phonet) dental
Zahn'lücke *f* gap between the teeth
Zahn'paste *f* toothpaste
Zahn'pflege *f* dental hygiene
Zahn'pulver *n* tooth powder
Zahn'rad *n* cog wheel; (*Kettenrad*) sprocket
Zahn'radbahn *f* cog railway
Zahn'schmerz *m* toothache
Zahn'spange *f* (-;-n) (dent) brace
Zahn'stein *m* (dent) tartar
Zahnstocher ['tsan/toxər] *m* (-s;-) toothpick
Zahn'techniker –in §6 *mf* dental technician
Zahn'weh *n* toothache
Zange ['tsaŋə] *f* (-;-en) (pair of) pliers; (pair of) tongs; (*Pinzette*) (pair of) tweezers; (dent, surg, zool) forceps; **j–n in die Z. nehmen** corner s.o. (*with tough questioning*)
Zank ['tsaŋk] *m* (-[e]s;) quarrel, fight
Zank'apfel *m* apple of discord
zanken ['tsaŋkən] *tr* scold ‖ *recip & intr* quarrel, fight
zank'haft, zänkisch ['tseŋkı/], **zank'-süchtig** *adj* quarrelsome

Zäpfchen ['tsepfçən] *n* (-s;-) little peg; (anat) uvula; (med) suppository
zapfen ['tsapfən] *tr* (*Bier, Wein*) tap || **Zapfen** *m* (-s;-) plug, bung; (*Stift*) stud; (*Drehpunkt*) pivot; (*Eis-*) icicle; (*Tannen-*) cone; (carp) tenon; (mach) pin; (mach) journal
Zapf'fenstreich *m* (mil) taps
Zapf'hahn ['tsapfhɑn] *m* tap, spigot
Zapf'säule ['tsapfzɔɪlə] *f* (-;-n) (aut) gasoline pump
Zapf'stelle ['tsapf/tɛlə] *f* (-;-n) (aut) service station, gas station
Zapf'wart ['tsapfvart] *m* (-[e]s;-e) (aut) service station attendant
zappelig ['tsapəlɪç] *adj* fidgety
zappeln ['tsapəln] *intr* fidget; squirm; (*im Wasser*) founder
Zar [tsɑr] *m* (-en;-en) czar
Zarge ['tsargə] *f* (-;-n) border; frame
zart [tsart] *adj* tender; (*Farbe, Haut*) soft; (*Gesundheit*) delicate
zart'fühlend *adj* tender; sensitive
Zart'gefühl *n* sensitivity; tact
Zart'heit *f* (-;) tenderness
zärtlich ['tsertlɪç] *adj* tender, affectionate
Zärt'lichkeit *f* (-;-en) tenderness; (*Liebkosung*) caress
Zaster ['tsastər] *m* (-s;) (coll) dough
Zauber ['tsaʊbər] *m* (-s;-) spell; magic; (fig) charm, glamor
Zauber– *comb.fm.* magic
Zauberei [tsaʊbə'raɪ] *f* (-;-en) magic; witchcraft, sorcery
Zau'berer *m* (-s;-) magician; sorcerer
Zau'berformel *f* incantation, spell
zau'berhaft *adj* magic; enchanting
Zau'berin *f* (-;-nen) sorceress, witch; enchantress
zauberisch ['tsaʊbərɪʃ] *adj* magic
Zau'berkraft *f* magic power
Zau'berkunst *f* magic
Zau'berkünstler –in §6 *mf* magician
Zau'berkunststück *n* magic trick
Zau'berland *n* fairyland
zaubern ['tsaʊbərn] *tr* produce by magic || *intr* practice magic; do magic tricks
Zau'berspruch *m* incantation, spell
Zau'berstab *m* magic wand
Zau'bertrank *m* magic potion
Zau'berwerk *n* witchcraft
Zau'berwort *n* (-[e]s;-e) magic word
zaudern ['tsaʊdərn] *intr* procrastinate; hesitate; linger
Zaum [tsaʊm] *m* (-[e]s;ːe) bridle; **im Z. halten** keep in check
zäumen ['tsɔɪmən] *tr* bridle
Zaun [tsaʊn] *m* (-[e]s;ːe) fence; **e–n Streit vom Z. brechen** pick a quarrel
Zaun'gast *m* non-paying spectator
Zaun'könig *m* (orn) wren
Zaun'pfahl *m* fence post
zausen ['tsaʊzən] *tr* tug at; tousle, ruffle || *recip* tug at each other
Zebra ['tsebra] *n* (-s;-s) zebra
Ze'brastreifen *m* zebra stripe; (*auf der Fahrbahn*) passenger crossing
Zech– [tsɛç] *comb.fm.* drinking
Zech'bruder *m* boozehound
Zeche ['tsɛçə] *f* (-;-n) (*Wirtshausrechnung*) check; (min) mine **die Z.**

prellen (coll) sneak out without paying the bill
zechen ['tsɛçən] *intr* booze
Ze'cher –in §6 *mf* heavy drinker
Zech'gelage *n* drinking party
Zechpreller ['tsɛçprɛlər] *m* (-s;-) cheat, bilker
Zech'tour *f* binge; **e–e Z. machen** go on a binge
Zecke ['tsɛkə] *f* (-;-n) (ent) tick
Zeder ['tsedər] *f* (-;-n) cedar
Zehe ['tse·ə] *f* (-;-n) toe; (*Knoblauch-*) clove
Ze'hennagel *m* toenail
Ze'henspitze *f* tip of the toe; **auf den Zehenspitzen** (on) tiptoe
zehn [tsen] *invar adj & pron* ten || **Zehn** *f* (-;-en) ten
Zehner ['tsenər] *m* (-s;-) ten; tenmark bill
zehn'fach, zehn'fältig *adj* tenfold
Zehnfin'gersystem *n* touch-type system
Zehn'kampf *m* decathlon
zehn'mal *adv* ten times
zehnte ['tsentə] §9 *adj & pron* tenth || **Zehnte** §5 *mfn* tenth
Zehntel ['tsentəl] *n* (-s;-) tenth (*part*)
zehren ['tseren] *intr* be debilitating; **an den Kräften z.** drain one's strength; **an der Gesundheit z.** undermine one's health; **z. an** (*dat*) (fig) gnaw at; **z. von** live on, live off
Zeh'rung *f* (-s) provisions; expenses
Zeichen ['tsaɪçən] *n* (-s;-) sign; signal; token; (*Merkmal*) distinguishing mark; (*Beweis*) proof; symbol; (astr) sign; (com) brand; (med) symptom; (rad) call sign; **er ist seines Zeichens Anwalt** he is a lawyer by profession; **zum Z., daß** as proof that
Zei'chenbrett *n* drawing board
Zei'chenbuch *n* sketchbook
Zei'chengerät *n* drafting equipment
Zei'chenheft *n* sketchbook
Zei'chenlehrer –in §6 *mf* art teacher
Zei'chenpapier *n* drawing paper
Zei'chensetzung *f* punctuation
Zei'chensprache *f* sign language
Zei'chentisch *m* drawing board
Zei'chentrickfilm *m* animated cartoon
Zei'chenunterricht *m* drawing lesson
zeichnen ['tsaɪçnən] *tr* draw; sketch; (*entwerfen*) design; (*brandmarken*) brand; (*Anleihe*) take out; (*Aktien*) buy; (*Geld*) pledge; (*Wäsche*) mark; (*Brief*) sign || *intr* draw; sketch; (hunt) leave a trail of blood; **z. für** sign for
Zeich'ner –in §6 *mf* draftsman; (*Mode-*) designer; (*e–r Anleihe*) subscriber
zeichnerisch ['tsaɪçnərɪʃ] *adj* (*Begabung*) for drawing; (*Darstellung*) graphic
Zeich'nung *f* (-;-en) drawing; sketch; design; picture, illustration; diagram; signature; (*e–r Anleihe*) subscription; (*des Holzes*) grain
zeich'nungsberechtigt *adj* authorized to sign
Zeigefinger ['tsaɪgəfɪŋər] *m* index finger
zeigen ['tsaɪgən] *tr* show, indicate;

(*in e-r Rede*) point out; (*zur Schau stellen*) display; (*beweisen*) prove; (*dartun*) demonstrate || *ref* appear, show up; prove to be || *intr* point; **z. auf** (*acc*) point to; **z. nach** point toward || *impers ref*—**es zeigt sich, daß** it turns out that; **es wird sich ja z., ob** we shall see whether

Zei'ger *m* (**-s;-**) pointer; indicator; (*e-r Uhr*) hand

Zeigestock ['tsaɪgəʃtɔk] *m* pointer

Zeile ['tsaɪlə] *f* (**-;-n**) line; (*Reihe*) row

Zeit [tsaɪt] *f* (**-;-en**) time; **auf Z.** (com) on credit, on time; **in der letzten Z.** lately; **in jüngster Z.** quite recently; **mit der Z.** in time, in the course of time; **vor Zeiten** in former times; **zu meiner Z.** in my time; **zu rechter Z.** in the nick of time; on time; **zur Z.** at present; **zur Z.** (*genit*) at the time of

Zeit'abschnitt *m* period, epoch

Zeit'abstand *m* interval of time

Zeit'alter *n* age

Zeit'angabe *f* time; date; exact date and hour; **ohne Z.** undated

Zeit'ansage *f* (rad) (giving of) time

Zeit'aufnahme *f* (phot) time exposure

Zeit'aufwand *m* loss of time; (**für**) time spent (on)

Zeit'dauer *f* term, period of time

Zeit'einteilung *f* timetable; timing

Zei'tenfolge *f* sequence of tenses

Zei'tenwende *f* beginning of the Christian era

Zeit'folge *f* chronological order

Zeit'form *f* tense

Zeit'geist *m* spirit of the times

zeit'gemäß *adj* timely; up-to-date

Zeit'genosse *m*, **Zeit'genossin** *f* contemporary

zeitgenössisch ['tsaɪtgənœsɪʃ] *adj* contemporary

Zeit'geschichte *f* contemporary history

zeitig ['tsaɪtɪç] *adj* early; (*reif*) mature, ripe

zeitigen ['tsaɪtɪgən] *tr* ripen

Zeit'karte *f* commuter ticket

Zeit'lage *f* state of affairs

Zeit'lang *f—e-e Z.* for some time

Zeit'lauf *m* course of time

zeit'lebens *adv* during my (his, your, etc.) life

zeit'lich *adj* temporal; chronological || *adv* in time || **Zeitliche §5** *n*—**das Z. segnen** depart this world

zeit'los *adj* timeless

Zeit'lupe *f* (cin) slow motion

Zeit'mangel *m* lack of time

Zeit'maß *n* (mus) tempo; (pros) quantity

Zeit'nehmer –in §6 *mf* timekeeper

Zeit'ordnung *f* chronological order

Zeit'punkt *m* point of time, moment

Zeitraffer ['tsaɪtrafər] *m* (**-s;**) time-lapse photography

zeit'raubend *adj* time-consuming

Zeit'raum *m* space of time, period

Zeit'rechnung *f* era

Zeit'schaltgerät *n* timer

Zeit'schrift *f* periodical, magazine

Zeit'spanne *f* span (of time)

Zeit'tafel *f* chronological table

Zei'tung *f* (**-;-en**) newspaper; journal

Zei'tungsarchiv *n* (journ) morgue

Zei'tungsartikel *m* newspaper article

Zei'tungsausschnitt *m* newspaper clipping

Zei'tungsbeilage *f* supplement

Zei'tungsdeutsch *n* journalese

Zei'tungsente *f* (journ) hoax, spoof

Zei'tungskiosk *m* newsstand

Zei'tungsmeldung *f*, **Zei'tungsnotiz** *f* newspaper item

Zei'tungspapier *n* newsprint

Zei'tungsverkäufer –in §6 *mf* newsvendor

Zei'tungswesen *n—das Z.* the press

Zeit'vergeudung *f* waste of time

zeit'verkürzend *adj* entertaining

Zeit'verlust *m* loss of time

Zeit'vermerk *m* date

Zeit'verschwendung *f* waste of time

Zeit'vertreib *m* pastime

zeitweilig ['tsaɪtvaɪlɪç] *adj* temporary; periodic || *adv* temporarily; at times, from time to time

Zeit'wende *f* beginning of a new era

Zeit'wert *m* current value

Zeit'wort *n* (**-[e]s;⸗er**) verb

Zeit'zeichen *n* time signal

Zeit'zünder *m* time fuse

Zelle ['tsɛlə] *f* (**-;-n**) cell; (aer) fuselage; (telp) booth

Zel'lenlehre *f* cytology

Zellophan [tsɛlo'fɑn] *n* (**-s;**) cellophane

Zellstoff ['tsɛlʃtɔf] *m* cellulose

Zelluloid [tsɛlʊ'lɔɪt] *n* (**-s;**) celluloid

Zellulose [tsɛlʊ'lozə] *f* (**-;**) cellulose

Zelt ['tsɛlt] *n* (**-[e]s;-e**) tent

zelten ['tsɛltən] *intr* camp out

Zelt'leinwand *f* canvas

Zelt'pfahl *m* tent pole

Zelt'pflock *m* tent peg, tent stake

Zelt'stange *f*, **Zelt'stock** *m* tent pole

Zement [tse'mɛnt] *m* (**-[e]s;**) cement

zementieren [tsemɛn'tirən] *tr* cement

Zenit [tse'nit] *m* (**-[e]s;**) zenith

zensieren [tsɛn'zirən] *tr* censor; (educ) mark, grade

Zen·sor ['tsɛnzɔr] *m* (**-s;-soren** ['zorən]) censor

Zensur [tsɛn'zur] *f* (**-;-en**) censorship; (educ) grade, mark

Zentimeter [tsɛntɪ'metər] *m & n* centimeter

Zentner ['tsɛntnər] *m* (**-s;-**) hundredweight

Zent'nerlast *f* (fig) heavy load

zentral [tsɛn'tral] *adj* central

Zentral'behörde *f* central authority

Zentrale [tsɛn'tralə] *f* (**-;-n**) central office; telephone exchange, switchboard; (elec) power station

Zentral'heizung *f* central heating

Zen·trum ['tsɛntrʊm] *n* (**-s;-tren** [trən]) center

Zephir ['tsefɪr] *m* (**-s;-e**) zephyr

Zepter ['tsɛptər] *n* (**-s;-**) scepter

zer– [tser] *pref* up, to pieces, apart

zerbei'ßen §53 *tr* bite to pieces

zerber'sten §55 *intr* (SEIN) split apart

zerbre'chen §64 *tr* break to pieces, shatter, smash || *ref*—**sich** [*dat*] **den**

Kopf z. über (acc) rack one's brains over || intr (SEIN) shatter

zerbrech′lich adj fragile, brittle

zerbröckeln (zerbrök′keln) tr & intr (SEIN) crumble

zerdrücken (zerdrük′ken) tr crush; (Kleid) wrinkle; (Kartoffeln) mash

Zeremonie [tseremo′ni] f (-;-nien [′ni-ən]) ceremony

zeremoniell [tseremo′njel] adj ceremonial || **Zeremoniell** n (-s;-e) ceremonial

Zeremo′nienmeister m master of ceremonies

zerfah′ren adj (Weg) rutted; (zerstreut) absent-minded; (konfus) scatterbrained

Zerfall′ m (-s;) decay, ruin; disintegration; (geistig) decadence

zerfal′len adj—z. sein mit be at variance with || §72 intr (SEIN) fall into ruin; decay; disintegrate; z. in (acc) divide into; z. mit fall out with

zerfa′sern tr unravel || intr fray

zerfet′zen tr tear to shreds

zerflei′schen tr mangle; lacerate

zerflie′ßen §76 intr (SEIN) melt; (Farben) run

zerfres′sen §70 tr eat away, chew up; erode, eat a hole in; corrode

zerge′hen §82 intr (SEIN) melt

zerglie′dern tr dissect; analyze

zerhacken (zerhak′ken) tr chop up

zerkau′en tr chew well

zerkleinern [tser′klainərn] tr cut into small pieces; chop up

zerklop′fen tr pound

zerklüftet [tser′klyftət] adj jagged

zerknirscht [tser′knirʃt] adj contrite

Zerknir′schung f (-;) contrition

zerknit′tern (Papier) crumple; (Kleider) rumple

zerknül′len tr crumple up

zerko′chen tr overcook

zerkrat′zen tr scratch up

zerkrü′meln tr & intr (SEIN) crumble

zerlas′sen §104 tr melt, dissolve

zerlegbar [tser′lekbar] adj collapsible; (chem) decomposable; (math) divisible

zerle′gen tr take apart; (zerstücken) cut up; (Braten) carve; (Licht) disperse; (anat) dissect; (chem) break down; (geom, mus) resolve; (gram & fig) analyze; (mach) tear down

zerle′sen adj well-thumbed

zerlö′chern tr riddle with holes

zerlumpt [tser′lumpt] adj tattered

zermah′len tr grind

zermal′men tr crush

zermür′ben tr wear down

Zermür′bung f (-;) attrition, wear

zerna′gen tr gnaw, chew up; (chem) corrode

zerplat′zen intr (SEIN) burst; explode

zerquet′schen tr crush; (culin) mash

Zerrbild [′tserbilt] n distorted picture; caricature

zerrei′ben §62 tr grind, pulverize

zerrei′ßen §95 tr tear; tear up; (zerfleischen) mangle; (fig) split; (pathol) rupture; j-m das Herz z. break s.o.'s heart || ref—sich z. für

(fig) knock oneself out for || intr (SEIN) tear

zerren [′tserən] tr drag; (Sehne) pull || intr (an dat) tug (at)

zerrin′nen §121 intr (SEIN) melt away

zerrissen [tser′risən] adj torn

Zer′rung f (-;-en) strain, muscle pull

zerrütten [tser′rytən] tr disorganize; (Geist) unhinge; (Gesundheit) undermine; (Nerven) shatter; (Ehe) wreck

zersä′gen tr saw up

zerschel′len intr (SEIN) be wrecked; (Schiff) break up

zerschie′ßen §76 tr shoot up

zerschla′gen adj battered, broken; exhausted, beat || §132 tr beat up; break to pieces; smash; batter

zerschmel′zen tr & intr (SEIN) melt

zerschmet′tern tr smash, crush

zerschnei′den §106 tr cut up; mince

zerset′zen tr decompose; electrolyze; (fig) undermine || ref decompose, disintegrate

zerspal′ten tr split

zersplit′tern tr split up; splinter; (Menge) disperse; (Kraft, Zeit) fritter away || ref spread oneself thin

zerspren′gen tr blow up; (Kette) break; (mil) rout

zersprin′gen §142 intr (SEIN) break, burst; (Glas) crack; (Saite) snap; (Kopf) split; (vor Wut) explode; (vor Freude) burst

zerstamp′fen tr crush, pound; trample

zerstäu′ben tr pulverize, spray

Zerstäu′ber m (-s;-) sprayer; (für Parfüm) atomizer

zerste′chen §64 tr sting; bite

zerstie′ben intr §130 intr (SEIN) scatter

zerstö′ren tr destroy; (Fernsprechleitung) disrupt; (Leben, Ehe, usw.) ruin; (Illusionen) shatter

Zerstö′rer m (-s;-) (& nav) destroyer

Zerstö′rung f (-;-en) destruction; ruin; disruption

Zerstö′rungswerk n work of destruction

Zerstö′rungswut f vandalism

zersto′ßen §150 tr pound, crush

zerstreu′en tr scatter, disperse; (Bedenken, Zweifel) dispel; (ablenken) distract; (Licht) diffuse || ref scatter; amuse oneself

zerstreut′ adj dispersed; (Licht) diffused; (fig) absent-minded

Zerstreut′heit f (-;) absent-mindedness

Zerstreu′ung f (-;) scattering; diffusion; diversion; absent-mindedness

zerstückeln [tser′ʃtykəln] tr chop up; (Körper) dismember; (Land) parcel out

zertei′len tr divide; (zerstreuen) disperse; (Braten, usw.) cut up || ref divide, separate

Zertifikat [tsertifi′kat] n (-[e]s;-e) certificate

zertren′nen tr sever

zertre′ten §152 tr trample, squash; (Feuer) stamp out

zertrümmern [tser′trymərn] tr smash, demolish; (Atome) split

zerwüh′len tr root up; (Haar) dishevel; (Bett, Kissen) rumple

Zerwürfnis [tsɛr'vʏrfnɪs] *n* (-ses;-se) disagreement, quarrel

zerzau'sen *tr* (*Haar*) muss; (*Federn*) ruffle

Zeter ['tsetər] *n* (-s;)—**Z. und Mordio schreien** (coll) cry bloody murder

zetern ['tsetərn] *intr* cry out, raise an outcry

Zettel ['tsetəl] *m* (-s;-) slip of paper; note; (*Anschlag*) poster; (*zum Ankleben*) sticker; (*zum Anhängen*) tag

Zet'telkartei *f*, **Zet'telkasten** *m*, **Zet'-telkatalog** *m* card file

Zeug [tsɔɪk] *n* (-[e]s;-e) stuff, material; (*Stoff*) cloth, fabric; (*Sachen*) things; (*Waren*) goods; (*Geräte*) tools; (*Plunder*) junk; **dummes Z.** silly nonsense; **er hat das Z.** he has what it takes

-zeug *n comb.fm.* stuff; tools; equipment; tackle; instrument; things; -wear

Zeuge ['tsɔɪgə] *m* (-n;-n) witness; **als Z. aussagen** testify

zeugen ['tsɔɪgən] *tr* beget; (fig) produce, generate ‖ *intr* produce offspring; testify; **z. für** testify in favor of; **z. von** bear witness to

Zeu'gung *f* (-;) procreation; breeding

Zeu'genaussage *f* deposition

Zeu'genbank *f* witness stand

Zeu'genbeeinflussung *f* suborning of witnesses

Zeu'genstand *m* witness stand

Zeugin ['tsɔɪgɪn] *f* (-;-nen) witness

Zeugnis ['tsɔɪknɪs] *n* (-ses;-se) evidence, testimony; proof; (*Schein*) certificate; (educ) report card; **j-m ein Z. ausstellen** (or **schreiben**) write s.o. a letter of recommendation; **Z. ablegen** testify; **zum Z. dessen** in witness whereof

Zeu'gung *f* (-;) procreation; breeding

Zeu'gungstrieb *m* sexual drive

zeu'gungsunfähig *adj* impotent

Zicke ['tsɪkə] *f* (-;-n) (pej) old nanny goat; **Zicken machen** (coll) play tricks

Zicklein ['tsɪklaɪn] *n* (-s;-) kid

Zickzack ['tsɪktsak] *m* (-[e]s;-e) zigzag; **im Z. laufen** run zigzag

Zick'zackkurs *m*—**im Z. fahren** zigzag

Ziege ['tsigə] *f* (-;-n) she-goat

Ziegel ['tsigəl] *m* (-s;-) brick; (*Dach-*) tile

Zie'gelbrenner *m* brickmaker; tilemaker

Zie'gelbrennerei *f* brickyard; tileworks

Zie'geldach *n* tiled roof

Zie'gelstein *m* brick

Zie'genbart *m* goatee

Zie'genbock *m* billy goat

Zie'genhirt *m* goatherd

Zie'genpeter *m* (pathol) mumps

Zieh- [tsi] *comb.fm.* draw; tow-; foster

Zieh'brunnen *m* well

ziehen ['tsi·ən] §163 *tr* pull; (*Folgerung, Kreis, Linie, Los, Schwert, Seitengewehr, Vorhang, Wechsel*) draw; (*Glocke*) ring; *aus der Tasche*) pull out; (*Zahn*) extract, pull; (*züchten*) grow, breed; (*Kinder*) raise; (*beim Schach*) move; (*den*

Hut) tip; (*Graben*) dig; (*Mauer*) build; (*Schiff*) tow; (*Blasen*) raise; (*Vergleich*) make; (*Gewehrlauf*) rifle; (math) extract; **auf Fäden z.** string (*pearls*); **auf Flaschen z.** bottle; **auf seine Seite z.** win over to one's side; **den kürzeren z.** get the short end of it; **die Bilanz z.** balance accounts; **die Stirn kraus z.** knit the brows; **Grimassen z.** make faces; **ins Vertrauen z.** take into confidence; **j-n auf die Seite z.** take s.o. aside; **Nutzen z.** derive benefit; **Wasser z.** leak ‖ *ref* (*Holz*) warp; (*Stoff*) stretch; (geog) extend, run; **an sich** (or **auf sich**) **z.** attract; **sich in die Länge z.** drag on ‖ *intr* ache; (an *dat*) pull (on); (theat) (coll) pull them in; **an e-r Zigarette z.** puff on a cigarette ‖ *intr* (SEIN) go; march; (*Vögel*) migrate; (*Wohnung wechseln*) move ‖ *impers*—**es zieht** there is a draft; **es zieht mich nach I** feel drawn to ‖ **Ziehen** *n* (-s;) drawing; cultivation; growing; raising; breeding; migration

Zieh'harmonika *f* accordion

Zieh'kind *n* foster child

Zie'hung *f* (-;-en) drawing (*of lots*)

Ziel [tsil] *n* (-[e]s;-e) aim; mark; goal; (*beim Rennsport*) finish line; (*e-r Reise*) destination; (*beim Schießen*) target; (*Grenze*) limit, boundary; (*Zweck*) end, object; (*des Spottes*) butt; (*Frist*) term; (mil) objective; **auf Z.** (com) on credit; **durchs Z. gehen** pass the finish line; **gegen zwei Jahre Z.** (or **mit zwei Jahren Z.**) with two years to pay; **j-m zwei Jahre Z. gewähren** give s.o. two years to pay; **seinem Ehrgeiz ein Z. setzen** set a limit to one's ambition

Ziel'anflug *m* (aer) bomb run

Ziel'band *n* (-[e]s;⸚er) (sport) tape

ziel'bewußt *adj* purposeful; single-minded

zielen ['tsilən] *intr* take aim; **z. auf** (*acc*) or **nach** aim at

Ziel'fernrohr *n* telescopic sight

Ziel'gerade *f* homestretch

Ziel'gerät *n* gunsight; (aer) bombsight

Ziel'landung *f* pinpoint landing

Ziel'linie *f* (sport) finish line

ziel'los *adj* aimless

Ziel'photographie *f* photo finish

Ziel'punkt *m* objective; bull's-eye

Ziel'scheibe *f* target; (fig) butt

Ziel'setzung *f* objective, target

ziel'sicher *adj* steady, unerring

Ziel'sprache *f* target language

zielstrebig ['tsil/trebɪç] *adj* single-minded, determined

Ziel'sucher *m* (rok) homing device

Ziel'vorrichtung *f* gunsight; bombsight

ziemen ['tsimən] *ref* be proper; **sich für j-n z.** become s.o. ‖ *intr* (*dat*) be becoming to

ziemlich ['tsimlɪç] *adj* fit, suitable; (*leidlich*) middling; (*mäßig*) fair; (*beträchtlich*) considerable ‖ *adv* pretty, rather, fairly; (*fast*) almost, practically

Zier [tsir] *f* (-;), **Zierat** ['tsirɑt] *m* (-s;) ornament, decoration
Zierde ['tsirdə] *f* (-;-n) ornament decoration; (fig) credit, honor
zieren ['tsirən] *tr* decorate, adorn || *ref* be affected, be coy; (*beim Essen*) need to be coaxed; **zier dich doch nicht so!** don't be coy!
Zier'leiste *f* trim(ming)
zier'lich *adj* delicate; (*nett*) nice
Zier'pflanze *f* ornamental plant
Zier'puppe *f* glamour girl
Ziffer ['tsifər] *f* (-;-n) digit, figure
Zif'ferblatt *n* face (*of a clock*)
zig [tsiç] *invar adj* (coll) umpteen
Zigarette [tsiga'retə] *f* (-;-n) cigarette
Zigaret'tenautomat *m* cigarette machine
Zigaret'tenetui *n* cigarette case
Zigaret'tenspitze *f* cigarette holder
Zigaret'tenstummel *m* cigarette butt
Zigarre [tsi'garə] *f* (-;-n) cigar
Zigeuner -**in** [tsi'gɔɪnər(ɪn)] §6 *mf* gipsy
Zimbel ['tsɪmbəl] *f* (-;-n) cymbal
Zimmer ['tsɪmər] *n* (-s;-) room
Zim'merantenne *f* indoor antenna
Zim'merarbeit *f* carpentry
Zim'merdienst *m* room service
Zim'mereinrichtung *f* furniture
Zim'merer *m* (-s;-) carpenter
Zim'merflucht *f* suite
Zim'mermädchen *n* chambermaid
Zim'mer-mann *m* (-[e]s;-leute) carpenter
zimmern ['tsɪmərn] *tr* carpenter, build || *intr* carpenter
Zim'mervermieter *m* landlord
-**zimmrig** [tsɪmrɪç] *comb.fm.* -roomed
zimperlich ['tsɪmpərlɪç] *adj* prudish; fastidious; (*gegen Kälte*) oversensitive
Zimt [tsɪmt] *m* (-[e]s;) cinnamon
Zink [tsɪŋk] *m* & *n* (-[e]s;) zinc
Zinke ['tsɪŋkə] *f* (-;-n) prong; (*e-s Kammes*) tooth; (carp) dovetail
zinken ['tsɪŋkən] *tr* dovetail; (*Karten*) mark || **Zinken** *m* (-s;-) (sl) schnozzle
-**zinkig** [tsɪŋkɪç] *comb.fm.* -pronged
Zinn [tsɪn] *n* (-[e]s;) tin
Zinne ['tsɪnə] *f* (-;-n) pinnacle; battlement
zinnoberrot [tsɪ'nobərrot] *adj* vermilion
Zins [tsɪns] *m* (-es;-en) interest; (*Miete*) rent; **auf Zinsen anlegen** put out at interest; **j-m mit Zinsen (und Zinseszinsen) heimzahlen** (coll) pay s.o. back in full; **Zinsen berechnen** charge interest
zins'bringend *adj* interest-bearing
Zin'senbelastung *f* interest charge
Zinseszinsen ['tsɪnzəstsɪnzən] *pl* compound interest
zins'frei *adj* rent-free; interest-free
Zins'fuß *m*, **Zins'satz** *m* rate of interest
Zins'schein *m* (interest) coupon; dividend warrant
Zionismus [tsi-ɔ'nɪsmus] *m* (-;) Zionism
Zipfel ['tsɪpfəl] *m* (-s;-) tip, point;

edge; (*Ecke*) corner; (*e-r Wurst*) end piece
Zip'felmütze *f* nightcap, tasseled cap
zirka ['tsɪrka] *adv* approximately
Zirkel ['tsɪrkəl] *m* (-s;-) circle; (*Reißzeug*) compass; (fig) circle
Zir'kelschluß *m* vicious circle
Zirkon [tsɪr'kon] *m* (-s;-e) zircon
zirkulieren [tsɪrku'lirən] *intr* (SEIN) circulate; **z. lassen** circulate
Zirkus ['tsɪrkus] *m* (-;-se) circus
zirpen ['tsɪrpən] *intr* chirp
zischeln ['tsɪʃəln] *tr & intr* whisper
zischen ['tsɪʃən] *intr* hiss; sizzle; (*schwirren*) whiz || **Zischen** *n* (-s;) hissing; sizzle; whiz
Zisch'laut *m* hissing sound; (phonet) sibilant
ziselieren [tsize'lirən] *tr* chase
Zisterne [tsɪs'ternə] *f* (-;-n) cistern
Zitadelle [tsita'delə] *f* (-;-n) citadel
Zitat [tsɪ'tat] *n* (-[e]s;-e) quotation
Zither ['tsɪtər] *f* (-;-n) zither
zitieren [tsɪ'tirən] *tr* quote; **j-n vor Gericht z.** issue s.o. a summons
Zitronat [tsɪtro'nat] *n* (-[e]s;-e) candied lemon peel
Zitrone [tsɪ'tronə] *f* (-;-n) lemon
Zitro'nenlimonade *f* lemonade; (*mit Sodawasser*) lemon soda
Zitro'nenpresse *f* lemon squeezer
Zitro'nensaft *m* lemon juice
Zitro'nensäure *f* citric acid
zitterig ['tsɪtərɪç] *adj* shaky
zittern ['tsɪtərn] *intr* quake, tremble; quiver; (*flimmern*) dance; (**vor** *dat*) shake (with), shiver (with); **beim dem Gedanken an etw** [*acc*] **z.** shudder at the thought of s.th.
Zit'terpappel ['tsɪtərpapəl] *f* aspen
Zitze ['tsɪtsə] *f* (-;-n) teat
zivil [tsɪ'vil] *adj* civil; civilian; (*Preise*) reasonable || **Zivil** *n* (-s;) civilians; **in Z.** in plain clothes
Zivil'courage *f* courage of one's convictions, moral courage
Zivil'ehe *f* civil marriage
Zivilisation [tsɪvɪliza'tsjon] *f* (-;-en) civilization
zivilisieren [tsɪvɪli'zirən] *tr* civilize
Zivilist -**in** [tsɪvɪ'lɪst(ɪn)] §7 *mf* civilian
Zivil'klage *f* (jur) civil suit
Zivil'kleidung *f* civilian clothes
Zivil'person *f* civilian
Zobel ['tsobəl] *m* (-s;-) (zool) sable
Zofe ['tsofə] *f* (-;-n) lady-in-waiting
zog [tsok] *pret* of **ziehen**
zögern ['tsøgərn] *intr* hesitate; delay || **Zögern** *n* (-s;) hesitation; delay
Zögling ['tsøklɪŋ] *m* (-s;-e) pupil
Zölibat [tsølɪ'bat] *m & n* (-[e]s;) celibacy
Zoll [tsɔl] *m* (-[e]s;-̈e) duty, customs; (*Brückenzoll*) toll; (*Maß*) inch
Zoll'abfertigung *f* customs clearance
Zoll'amt *n* customs office
Zoll'beamte §5 *m* customs official
zollen ['tsɔlən] *tr* give, pay; **j-m Achtung z.** show s.o. respect; **j-m Beifall z.** applaud s.o.; **j-m Dank z.** thank s.o.; **j-m Lob z.** praise s.o.
Zoll'erklärung *f* customs declaration

zoll'frei adj duty-free

Zoll'grenze f customs frontier

–zöllig ['tsœlɪç] comb.fm. –inch

Zoll'kontrolle f customs inspection

zoll'pflichtig adj dutiable

Zoll'schein m customs clearance

Zoll'schranke f customs barrier

Zoll'stab m, **Zoll'stock** m foot rule

Zoll'tarif m tariff

Zone ['tsonə] f (–;–n) zone; **blaue Z.** limited-parking area; **Z. der Windstille** doldrums

Zoo [tso] m (– & –s;–s) zoo

Zoologe [tso·o'logə] m (–n;–n) zoologist

Zoologie [tso·olo'gi] f (–;) zoology

Zoologin [tso·o'login] f (–;–nen) zoologist

zoologisch [tso·o'logɪʃ] adj zoological

Zopf [tsɔpf] m (–[e]s;⸗e) plait of hair; pigtail; twisted (bread) roll; **alter Z.** outdated custom

zopfig ['tsɔpfɪç] adj pedantic; old-fashioned

Zorn [tsɔrn] m (–[e]s;) anger, rage

Zorn'anfall m fit of anger

Zorn'ausbruch m outburst of anger

zornig ['tsɔrnɪç] adj (**auf** acc) angry (at)

zorn'mütig adj hotheaded

Zote ['tsotə] f (–;–n) obscenity; dirty joke; **Zoten reißen** crack dirty jokes; talk dirty

zo'tenhaft, zotig ['tsotɪç] adj obscene, dirty

Zotte ['tsotə] f (–;–n) tuft of hair; strand of hair

Zottel ['tsotəl] f (–;–n) strand of hair

Zot'telhaar n stringy hair

zottelig ['tsotəlɪç] adj stringy (hair)

zotteln ['tsotəln] intr (SEIN) (coll) saunter

zottig ['tsotɪç] adj shaggy; matted

zu [tsu] adj closed, shut || adv too; immer zu! (or nur zu!) go on! || prep (dat) at, in, on; to; along with; in addition to; beside, near; **zu Anfang** at the beginning; **zu dritt** in threes; **zu Wasser und zu Lande** by land and by sea

zuallererst [tsu-alər'ɛrst] adv first of all

zuallerletzt [tsu-alər'letst] adv last of all

zuballern ['tsubalərn] tr (coll) slam

zu'bauen tr wall up, wall in

Zubehör ['tsubəhør] m & n (–s;) accessories; fittings; trimmings; **Wohnung mit allem Z.** apartment with all utilities

Zu'behörteil m accessory, attachment, component

zu'beißen §53 intr bite; snap at people

zu'bekommen §99 tr get in addition; (Tür, usw.) manage to close

zu'bereiten tr prepare; (Speise) cook; (Getränk) mix

Zu'bereitung f (–;–en) preparation

zu'billigen tr grant, allow, concede

zu'binden §59 tr tie up; **j–m die Augen z.** blindfold s.o.

zu'bleiben §62 intr (SEIN) remain closed

zu'blinzeln intr (dat) wink at

zu'bringen §65 tr (Zeit) spend; (coll) manage to shut; (tech) feed

Zu'bringer m (–s;–) (tech) feeder

Zu'bringerdienst m shuttle service

Zu'bringerstraße f access road

Zucht [tsuxt] f (–;) breeding; rearing; (Rasse) race, stock; (Pflanzen–) cultivation; (Schul–) education; discipline; training, drill; **Z. halten** maintain discipline

züchten ['tsyçtən] tr breed; rear, raise; (bot) grow, cultivate

Züch'ter –in §6 mf breeder; grower

Zucht'haus n penitentiary, hard labor; **lebenslängliches Z.** life imprisonment

Zuchthäusler –in ['tsuxthɔɪzlər(ɪn)] §6 mf convict, prisoner at hard labor

Zucht'hengst m studhorse

züchtig ['tsyçtɪç] adj modest, chaste

züchtigen ['tsyçtɪgən] tr chastise

zucht'los adj undisciplined

Zucht'losigkeit f (–;) lack of discipline

Zucht'meister m disciplinarian

Zucht'perle f cultured pearl

Züch'tung f (–;) breeding; rearing; growing, cultivation

zucken ['tsukən] tr (Achseln) shrug || intr twitch, jerk; (Blitz) flash; (vor Schmerzen) wince; **mit keiner Wimper z.** not bat an eye; **ohne zu z.** without wincing || impers—**es zuckte mir in den Fingern zu** (inf) my fingers were itching to (inf) || **Zucken** n (–s;) twitch

zücken ['tsykən] tr (Schwert) draw

Zucker ['tsukər] m (–s;) sugar

Zuckerdose (Zuk'kerdose) f sugar bowl

Zuckererbse (Zuk'kererbse) f sweet pea

Zuckerguß (Zuk'kerguß) m frosting

Zuckerharnruhr (Zuk'kerharnruhr) f diabetes

Zuckerhut (Zuk'kerhut) m sugar loaf

zuckerig ['tsukərɪç] adj sugary

zuckerkrank (zuk'kerkrank) adj diabetic || **Zuckerkranke** §5 mf diabetic

Zuckerkrankheit (Zuk'kerkrankheit) f diabetes

Zuckerlecken (Zuk'kerlecken) n (–s;) (fig) pushover, picnic

Zuckerrohr (Zuk'kerrohr) n sugar cane

Zuckerrübe (Zuk'kerrübe) f sugar beet

zuckersüß (zuk'kersüß') adj sweet as sugar

Zuckerwerk (Zuk'kerwerk) n, **Zuckerzeug** (Zuk'kerzeug) n candy

Zuckung (Zuk'kung) f (–;–en) twitch, spasm, convulsion

Zu'decke f (coll) bed covering

zu'decken tr cover up

zudem [tsu'dem] adv moreover, besides

zu'denken §66 tr—**j–m etw z.** intend s.th. as a present for s.o.

Zu'drang m crowding, rush

zu'drehen tr turn off; **j–m den Rücken z.** turn one's back on s.o.

zu'dringlich adj obtrusive; **z. werden** make a pass

zu'drücken tr close, shut

zu'eignen tr dedicate

Zu'eignung f (–;–en) dedication

zu'erkennen §97 *tr* confer, award; (jur) adjudge, award

zuerst' *adv* first; at first

zu'erteilen *tr* award; confer, bestow

zu'fahren §71 *intr* (SEIN) drive on; z. auf (*acc*) drive in the direction of (*s.th.*); rush at (*s.o.*)

Zu'fahrt *f* access

Zu'fahrtsrampe *f* on-ramp

Zu'fahrtsstraße *f* access road

Zu'fall *m* chance; coincidence; accident; **durch Z.** by chance

zu'fallen §72 *intr* (SEIN) close, shut; **j-m z.** fall to s.o.'s share

zufällig ['tsufeliç] *adj* chance, fortuitous; accidental; casual ‖ *adv* by chance; accidentally

zu'fälligerweise *adv* by chance

Zufalls– *comb.fm.* chance

zu'fassen *intr* set to work; lend a hand; (*e-e Gelegenheit wahrnehmen*) seize the opportunity

Zu'flucht *f* refuge; (fig) recourse; seine Z. nehmen zu take refuge in; have recourse to

Zu'fluß *m* influx; (*Nebenfluß*) tributary; (mach) feed

zu'flüstern *intr* (*dat*) whisper to

zufolge [tsu'folgə] *prep* (*genit & dat*) in consequence of; according to

zufrieden [tsu'fridən] *adj* satisfied; **j-n z. lassen** leave s.o. alone

zufrie'dengeben §80 *ref* (mit) be satisfied (with), acquiesce (in)

Zufrie'denheit *f* (–;) satisfaction

zufrie'denstellen *tr* satisfy

zufrie'denstellend *adj* satisfactory

Zufrie'denstellung *f* satisfaction

zu'frieren §77 *intr* (SEIN) freeze up

zu'fügen *tr* add; (*Niederlage*) inflict; (*Kummer, Schaden, Schmerz*) cause

Zufuhr ['tsufur] *f* (–;) supply; importation; supplies; (mach) feed

zu'führen *tr* convey, bring; (*Waren*) supply; (mach) feed

Zu'führung *f* (–;–en) conveyance; supply; importation; (elec) lead; (mach) feed

Zug [tsuk] *m* (–[e]s;–e) train; pull, tug; drawing, pulling; (*Spannung*) tension; strain; (*beim Rauchen*) puff; (*beim Atmen*) breath, gasp; (*Schluck*) drink, gulp, swig, (*Luft–*) draft; (*Reihe*) row, line; (*Um–*) procession; parade; (*Kriegs–*) campaign; (*Geleit*) escort; (*von Vögeln*) flock; flight, migration; (*von Fischen*) school; (*Rudel*) pack; (*Trupp*) platoon; (*Gespann*) team, yoke; (*Gesichts–*) feature; (*Charakter–*) trait; characteristic; (*Neigung*) trend, tendency; (*im Gewehrlauf*) groove, rifling; (*Strich*) stroke; (*Schnörkel*) flourish; (*Umriß*) outline; (*beim Brettspiel*) move; **auf dem Zuge** on the march; **auf e–n Zug** in one gulp; at one stroke; at a stretch; **du bist am Zug** (& fig) it's your move; **e–n guten Zug haben** drink like a fish; **e–n Zug tun** take a puff; make a move; take a drink; **gut im Zuge sein** (or **im besten Zuge sein**) be going strong; **in e–m Zuge** in one

gulp; in one breath; at one stroke; at a stretch; **in großen Zügen** in broad outlines; **in vollen Zügen** thoroughly; **in Zug bringen** start; **nicht zum Zug kommen** not get a chance; **ohne rechten Zug** half-heartedly; **Zug um Zug** in rapid succession

Zu'gabe *f* addition; (theat) encore

Zu'gang *m* access; approach; entrance; (*Zunahme*) increase; (libr) accession

zugänglich ['tsugeŋlɪç] *adj* accessible; (*Person*) affable; (*benutzbar*) available; (*dat, für*) open (to); **nicht z. für** proof against

Zug'artikel *m* (com) popular article

Zug'brücke *f* drawbridge

zu'geben §80 *tr* add; (*erlauben*) allow; (*anerkennen*) admit, concede; (*eingestehen*) confess; (com) throw into the bargain

zugegen [tsu'gegən] *adj* (bei) present (at)

zu'gehen §82 *intr* (SEIN) go on; walk faster; (*sich schließen*) shut; **auf j-n z.** go up to s.o.; **j-m etw z. lassen** send s.th. to s.o.

zu'gehören *intr* (*dat*) belong to

zu'gehörig *adj* (*dat*) belonging to

Zu'gehörigkeit *f* (–;) (zu) membership (in)

Zügel ['tsygəl] *m* (–s;–) rein; bridle; (fig) curb

zü'gellos *adj* (& fig) unbridled; (*ausschweifig*) dissolute

Zü'gellosigkeit *f* (–;) licentiousness

zügeln ['tsygəln] *tr* bridle; (fig) curb

Zu'geständnis *n* admission, concession

zu'gestehen §146 *tr* admit, concede

zu'getan *adj* (*dat*) fond of

Zug'feder *f* tension spring

Zug'führer *m* (mil) platoon leader; (rr) chief conductor

zu'gießen §76 *tr* add

zugig ['tsugɪç] *adj* drafty

zügig ['tsygɪç] *adj* speedy, fast

Zug'klappe *f* damper

Zug'kraft *f* tensile force; (fig) drawing power

zug'kräftig *adj* attractive, popular

zugleich' *adv* at the same time; **z. mit** together with

Zug'luft *f* draft

Zug'maschine *f* tractor

Zug'mittel *n* (fig) attraction, draw

zu'graben §87 *tr* cover up

zu'greifen §88 *intr* grab hold; lend a hand; (fig) go into action; **greifen Sie zu!** (bei Tisch) help yourself!; (*bei Reklamen*) don't miss this opportunity!

Zu'griff *m* grip; (fig) clutches

zugrunde [tsu'grundə] *adv*—**z. gehen** go to ruin; **z. legen** (*dat*) take as a basis (for); **z. liegen** (*dat*) underlie

Zug'tier *n* draft animal

zu'gucken *intr* (coll) look on

zugunsten [tsu'gunstən] *prep* (*genit*) in favor of; for the benefit of

zugute [tsu'gutə] *adv*—**j-m etw z. halten** make allowance to s.o. for s.th.; **j-m z. kommen** stand s.o. in good stead

Zug'verkehr *m* train service

Zug′vogel *m* migratory bird
zu′haben §89 *tr* (*Augen*) have closed; (*Mantel*) have buttoned up ‖ *intr* (*Geschäft*) be closed
zu′halten §90 *tr* keep closed; (*Ohren*) shut ‖ *intr*—z. auf (*acc*) head for
Zuhälter [′tsuhɛltər] *m* (-s;-) pimp
Zuhälterei [tsuhɛltə′raɪ] *f* (-;) pimping
zuhanden [tsu′handən] *prep* (*genit*) (*auf Briefumschlägen*) Attn:
Zuhause [tsu′hauzə] *n* (-s;) home
zu′heilen *intr* (SEIN) heal up
zu′hören *intr* (*dat*) listen (to)
Zu′hörer **-in** §6 *mf* hearer, listener; **die Z.** the audience
Zu′hörerschaft *f* (-;) audience
zu′jauchzen, zu′jubeln *intr* cheer
zu′klappen *tr* shut, slam shut
zu′kleben *tr* glue up, paste up
zu′knallen *tr* bang, slam shut
zu′kneifen §88 *tr*—**die Augen z.** blink; **ein Auge z.** wink
zu′knöpfen *tr* button up
zu′kommen §99 *intr* (SEIN) (*dat*) reach; (*dat*) be due to; **auf j-n z.** come up to s.o.; **das kommt dir nicht zu** you're not entitled to it; **j-m etw z. lassen** let s.o. have s.th.; send s.th. to s.o. ‖ *impers*—**mir kommt es nicht zu zu** (*inf*) it's not up to me to (*inf*)
zu′korken *tr* put the cork on
Zu′kost *f* vegetables; trimmings
Zukunft [′tsukʊnft] *f* (-;) future; (*gram*) future (tense)
zukünftig [′tsukʏnftɪç] *adj* future ‖ *adv* in the future ‖ **Zukünftige** §5 *m* (coll) fiancé ‖ *f* (coll) fiancée
Zu′kunftsmusik *f* wishful thinking
Zu′kunftsroman *m* science fiction
zu′lächeln *intr* (*dat*) smile at; (*dat*) smile on
Zu′lage *f* extra pay; pay raise
zulande [tsu′landə] *adv*—**bei uns z.** in my (or our) country
zu′langen *intr* suffice, do; (*bei Tisch*) help oneself
zu′länglich *adj* adequate, sufficient
zu′lassen §104 *tr* admit; (*erlauben*) allow; (*Tür*) leave shut; (*Fahrzeug*) license; (*Zweifel*) admit of
zulässig [′tsulɛsɪç] *adj* permissible; **zulässige Abweichung** allowance, tolerance
Zu′lassung *f* (-;-en) admission; permission; approval; license
Zu′lassungsprüfung *f* college entrance examination
Zu′lassungsschein *m* registration card
Zu′lauf *m* crowd, rush; **Z. haben** be popular; (theat) have a long run
zu′laufen §105 *intr* (SEIN) run on; run faster; (*dat*) flock to; **auf j-n z.** run up to s.o.; **spitz z.** end in a point
zu′legen *tr* add; **etw z.** up one's offer ‖ *ref*—**sich** [dat] **etw. z.** (coll) get oneself s.th.
zuleide [tsu′laɪdə] *adv*—**j-m etw z. tun** hurt s.o., do s.o. wrong
zu′leiten *tr* (*Wasser*) (*dat*) let in (to); (*dat*) direct (s.o.) (to); (*Schreiben*) (*dat*) pass on (to); **auf dem Amtsweg**) channel (to); (tech) feed

Zu′leitung *f* (-;-en) feed pipe; (elec) lead-in wire; (elec) conductor
zuletzt [tsu′lɛtst] *adv* last; at last; finally; after all
zuliebe [tsu′libə] *prep* (*dat*) for (*s.o.′s*) sake
zum [tsum] *abbr* **zu dem**; **es ist zum ...it's** enough to make one...
zu′machen *tr* shut; (*Loch*) close up; (*zuknöpfen*) button up
zumal [tsu′mal] *adv* especially; **z. da** all the more because
zu′mauern *tr* wall up
zumindest [tsu′mɪndəst] *adv* at least
zumute [tsu′mutə] *adv*—**mir ist gut** (or **wohl**) **z.** I feel good; **mir ist nicht zum Lachen z.** I don't feel like laughing
zumuten [′tsumutən] *tr*—**j-m etw z.** expect s.th. of s.o. ‖ *ref*—**sich** [dat] **zuviel z.** attempt too much
Zu′mutung *f* (-;-en) imposition
zunächst [tsu′nɛçst] *adv* first, at first, first of all; (*erstens*) to begin with; (*vorläufig*) for the time being ‖ *prep* (*dat*) next to
zu′nageln *tr* nail up, nail shut
zu′nähen *tr* sew up
Zu′nahme *f* (-;-n) increase; growth; rise
Zu′name *m* last name, family name
Zünd- [tsʏnt] *comb.fm.* ignition
zünden [′tsyndən] *tr* ignite; kindle; (*Sprengstoff*) detonate ‖ *intr* ignite, catch fire; (fig) catch on
Zün′der *m* (-s;-) fuse; detonator
Zünd′flamme *f* pilot light
Zünd′holz *n* match
Zünd′kerze *f* (aut) spark plug
Zünd′nadel *f* firing pin
Zünd′satz *m* primer
Zünd′schlüssel *m* ignition key
Zünd′schnur *f* fuse
Zünd′stein *m* flint
Zünd′stoff *m* fuel
Zün′dung *f* (-;-en) (aut) ignition
zu′nehmen §116 *intr* (an and *dat*) increase (in); (*steigen*) rise; grow longer
zu′neigen *tr* (*dat*) tilt toward ‖ *ref & intr* (*dat*) incline toward(s); **sich dem Ende z.** draw to a close
Zu′neigung *f* (-;) (für, zu) liking (for)
Zunft [tsunft] *f* (-;-en) guild
Zunge [′tsuŋə] *f* (-;-n) tongue
züngeln [′tsʏŋəln] *intr* dart out the tongue; (*Flamme*) dart, leap up
Zun′genbrecher *m* tongue twister
zun′genfertig *adj* glib
Zun′genspitze *f* tip of the tongue
zunichte [tsu′nɪçtə] *adv*—**z. machen** destroy; (*Plan*) spoil; (*Theorie*) explode; **z. werden** come to nothing
zu′nicken *intr* (*dat*) nod to
zunutze [tsu′nutsə] *adv*—**sich etw z. machen** utilize s.th.
zuoberst [tsu′obərst] *adv* at the top
zupfen [′tsupfən] *tr* pull; pluck ‖ *intr* (an *dat*) tug (at)
zu′prosten *intr* (*dat*) toast
zur [tsur] *abbr* **zu der**
zu′rechnen *tr* add; (*dat*) number among, classify with; (*dat*) attribute to

zu'rechnungsfähig *adj* accountable; responsible; of sound mind
Zu'rechnungsfähigkeit *f* responsibility; sound mind
zurecht– [tsuˈrɛçt] *comb.fm.* right, in order; at the right time
zurecht'biegen §57 *tr* straighten out
zurecht'bringen §65 *tr* set right
zurecht'finden §59 *ref* find one's way; (fig) see one's way
zurecht'kommen §99 *intr* (SEIN) come on time; get on, manage; turn out all right; mit etw nicht z. make a mess of s.th.; mit j–m z. get along with s.o.
zurecht'legen *tr* lay out in order || *ref*–sich [*dat*] z. figure out
zurecht'machen *tr & ref* get ready
zurecht'schneiden §106 *tr* cut to size
zurecht'setzen *tr* set right, fix, adjust
zurecht'weisen §118 *tr* reprimand
zu'reden *intr* (*dat*) try to persuade; (*dat*) encourage
zu'reichen *tr* reach, pass || *intr* do
zu'reichend *adj* sufficient
zu'reiten §86 *tr* break in
zu'richten *tr* prepare; cook
zu'riegeln *tr* bolt
zürnen [ˈtsʏrnən] *intr* (*dat*) be angry (with)
zurren [ˈtsʊrən] *tr* (naut) lash down
Zurschau'stellung *f* display
zurück [tsuˈrʏk] *adv* back; backward; behind; ein paar Jahre z. a few years ago || *interj* back up!
zurück– *comb.fm.* back; behind; re–
zurück'behalten §90 *tr* keep back
zurück'bekommen §99 *tr* get back
zurück'bleiben §62 *intr* (SEIN) stay behind; fall behind; (*Uhr*) lose time; (hinter *dat*) fall short (of)
Zurück'blenden *n* (cin) flashback
zurück'blicken *intr* look back
zurück'bringen §65 *tr* bring back; z. auf (*acc*) (math) reduce to
zurück'datieren *tr* antedate
zurück'drängen *tr* force back; repress
zurück'dürfen §69 *intr* be allowed to return
zurück'erobern *tr* reconquer, win back
zurück'erstatten *tr* return; (*Ausgaben*) refund; (*Kosten*) reimburse
zurück'fahren §71 *tr* drive back || *intr* (SEIN) drive back, ride back; (*vor Schreck*) recoil, start
zurück'finden §59 *ref* find one's way back
zurück'fordern *tr* reclaim, demand back
zurück'führen *tr* lead back; trace back; z. auf (*acc*) refer to; attribute to
zurück'geben §80 *tr* give back, return
zurück'gehen §82 *intr* (SEIN) go back; (*Fieber, Preise*) drop; (*Geschwulst*) go down; (mil) fall back
zurück'gezogen *adj* secluded
zurück'greifen §88 *intr*—z. auf (*acc*) (fig) fall back on
zurück'halten §90 *tr* hold back; j–n davon z. zu (*inf*) keep s.o. from (*ger*) || *intr* mit etw z. conceal s.th.
zurück'haltend *adj* reserved; shy
Zurück'haltung *f* (–;–en) reserve

zurück'kehren *intr* (SEIN) return
zurück'kommen §99 *intr* (SEIN) return; z. auf (*acc*) come back to, revert to; (*hinweisen*) refer to
zurück'können §100 *intr* be able to return
zurück'lassen §104 *tr* leave behind; outstrip, outrun
zurück'legen *tr* (*Kopf*) lean back; (*Geld*) put aside; (*Jahre*) complete; (*Strecke*) cover; (*Ware*) lay away || *ref* lean back
zurück'lehnen *ref* lean back
zurück'liegen §108 *intr* belong to the past || *impers*—es liegt jetzt zehn Jahre zurück, daß it's ten years now that
zurück'müssen §115 *intr* have to return
zurück'nehmen §116 *tr* take back; (*widerrufen*) revoke; (*Auftrag*) cancel; (*Vorwurf*) retract; (*Klage*) withdraw; (*Versprechen*) go back on; (*Truppen*) pull back; das Gas z. slow down
zurück'prallen *intr* (SEIN) rebound; (*vor Schreck*) start, be startled
zurück'rufen §122 *tr* call back, recall
zurück'schauen *intr* look back
zurück'schicken *tr* send back
zurück'schlagen §132 *tr* beat back, throw back || *intr* strike back
zurück'schrecken *intr* frighten away; (*von*) deter (from) || §109 & §134 *intr* (SEIN) (*von, vor dat*) shrink back (from)
zurück'sehnen *ref* yearn to return
zurück'sein §139 *intr* (SEIN) be back; (in *dat*) be behind (in)
zurück'setzen *tr* put back; (*im Preis*) reduce; (fig) snub || *ref* sit back
zurück'stecken *tr* put back
zurück'stellen *tr* (*Uhr*) set back; (*Plan*) shelve; (mil) defer
zurück'stoßen §150 *tr* push back; repel
zurück'strahlen *tr* reflect
zurück'streifen *tr* (*Ärmel*) roll up
zurück'treten §152 *intr* (SEIN) step back; (vom *Amt*) resign; (*Wasser, Berge*) recede
zurück'tun §154 *tr* put back
zurück'verfolgen *tr* (*Schritte*) retrace; (fig) trace back
zurück'verweisen §118 *tr* (an *acc*) refer back (to); (parl) remand (to)
zurück'weichen §85 *intr* (SEIN) fall back, make way; (*Hochwasser*) recede; (*vor dem Feind*) give ground; z. vor (*dat*) shrink from
zurück'weisen §118 *tr* turn back; (*ablehnen*) turn down; (*Angriff*) repel || *intr*—z. auf (*acc*) refer to
Zurück'weisung *f* (–;–en) rejection
zurück'wenden §140 *tr & ref* turn back
zurück'werfen §160 *tr* throw back; (*e–n Patienten*) set back; (*Strahlen*) reflect; (*Feind*) hurl back
zurück'wirken *intr* (auf *acc*) react (on); (*Gesetz*) be retroactive
zurück'zahlen *tr* pay back; (fin) refund
zurück'ziehen §163 *tr* draw back; (*Antrag*) withdraw; (*Geld*) call in; (*Truppen*) pull back; (sport) scratch || *ref* withdraw; (*schlafengehen*) re-

tire; (mil) pull back || *intr* (SEIN) move back; (mil) fall back, retreat

Zu′ruf *m* call; cheer; (parl) acclamation

zu′rufen §122 *tr—j—m etw z.* shout s.th. to s.o.

Zu′sage *f* (–;–n) assent; promise

zu′sagen *tr* promise || *intr* accept an invitation; (*dat*) please; (*dat*) agree (with) ·

zusammen [tsu′zamən] *adv* together; in common; at the same time

Zusam′menarbeit *f* cooperation

zusam′menarbeiten *intr* cooperate

zusam′menballen *tr* (*Faust*) clench

zusam′menbeißen §53 *tr—die Zähne z.* grit one's teeth

zusam′menbinden §59 *tr* tie together

zusam′menbrauen *tr* concoct || *ref* (*Sturm*) brew

zusam′menbrechen §64 *intr* (SEIN) break down; collapse

Zusam′menbruch *m* collapse; breakdown

zusam′mendrängen *tr* crowd together

zusam′mendrücken *tr* compress

zusam′menfahren §71 *intr* (SEIN) be startled; (mit) collide (with)

zusam′menfallen §72 *intr* (SEIN) fall in, collapse; (*Teig*) fall; (*Person*) lose weight; (mit) coincide (with)

Zusam′menfall *m* coincidence

zusam′menfalten *tr* fold

zusam′menfassen *tr* (*in sich fassen*) comprise; (*verbinden*) combine; (*Macht, Funktionen*) concentrate; (*Bericht*) summarize

zusam′menfassend *adj* comprehensive; summary

Zusam′menfassung *f* (–;–en) summary, résumé

zusam′menfinden §59 *ref* meet

zusam′menfügen *tr* join together; (*Scherben, Teile*) piece together

zusam′mengehen §82 *intr* (SEIN) go together; match; close; shrink

zusam′mengehören *intr* belong together

zusam′mengeraten §63 *intr* (SEIN) collide

zusammengewürfelt [tsu′zamengevʏrfəlt] *adj* mixed, motely

Zusam′menhalt *m* cohesion; consistency

zusam′menhalten §90 *tr* hold together; compare || *intr* stick together

Zusam′menhang *m* connection, relation; context; coherence

zusam′menhängend *adj* coherent; allied

zusam′menklappen *tr* fold up; **die Hacken z.** click one's heels || *intr* (SEIN) collapse

zusam′menkommen §99 *intr* (SEIN) come together

Zusammenkunft [tsu′zamənkunft] *f* (–;″e) meeting

zusam′menlaufen §105 *intr* (SEIN) run together; come together; flock; (*Milch*) curdle; (*Farben*) run; (*einschrumpfen*) shrink up; (geom) converge

zusammenlegbar [tsu′zamənlekbɑr] *adj* collapsible

zusam′menlegen *tr* put together; (*fal-*

ten) fold; (*Geld*) pool; (*vereinigen*) combine, consolidate || *intr* pool money

zusam′mennehmen §116 *tr* gather up; (*Gedanken*) collect; (*Kräfte, Mut*) muster; **alles zusammengenommen** considering everything || *ref* pull oneself together

zusam′menpacken *tr* pack up

zusam′menpassen *tr & intr* match

zusam′menpferchen *tr* crowd together

Zusam′menprall *m* collision; (fig) (mit) impact (on)

zusam′menprallen *intr* collide

zusam′menraffen *tr* collect in haste; (*ein Vermögen*) amass; (*Kräfte*) summon up, marshal || *ref* pull oneself together

zusam′menreißen §53 *ref* (coll) pull oneself together

zusam′menrollen *tr* roll up

zusam′menrotten *ref* band together, form a gang; (*Aufrührer*) riot

zusam′menrücken *tr* push together || *intr* (SEIN) move closer together

zusam′menschießen *tr* (*Stadt*) shoot up; (*Menschen*) shoot down; (*Geld*) pool

zusam′menschlagen §132 *tr* smash up; (*Absätze*) click; (*Beine, Zeitung*) fold; (*Hände*) clap; (*zerschlagen*) beat up; **die Hände über den Kopf z.** (fig) throw up one's hands || *intr* (SEIN)—**aneinander z.** clash

zusam′menschließen §76 *tr* join; link together || *ref* join together, unite

Zusam′menschluß *m* union; alliance

zusam′menschmelzen *intr* (SEIN) fuse; melt away; (fig) dwindle

zusam′menschnüren *tr* tie up

zusam′menschrumpfen *intr* (SEIN) shrivel; (*Geld*) (coll) dwindle away

zusam′mensetzen *tr* put together; (*mach*) assemble || *ref* sit down together; **sich z. aus** consist of

Zusam′mensetzung *f* (–;–en) composition; (*Bestandteile*) ingredients; (*Struktur*) structure; (chem, gram) compound

Zusam′menspiel *n* teamwork

zusam′menstauchen *tr* browbeat, chew out

zusam′menstellen *tr* put together; (*Liste*) compile; (*Farben*) match; organize

Zusam′menstoß *m* collision; (*der Meinungen*) clash; (*Treffen*) encounter; (mil) engagement

zusam′menstoßen §150 *tr* knock together; (*Gläser*) touch || *intr* adjoin; **mit den Gläsern z.** clink glasses || *intr* (SEIN) collide; (*Gegner*) clash

zusam′menstückeln *tr* piece together

zusam′menstürzen *intr* (SEIN) collapse

zusam′mentragen §132 *tr* collect

zusam′mentreffen §151 *intr* (SEIN) meet; coincide || **Zusammentreffen** *n* (–s;) encounter, meeting; coincidence

zusam′mentreiben §62 *tr* round up; (*Geld*) scrape up

zusam′mentreten §152 *intr* (SEIN) meet

zusam′menwirken *intr* cooperate; collaborate; interact ‖ **Zusammen-wirken** n (-s;) cooperation; inter-action

zusam'menzählen tr count up, add up

zusam'menziehen §163 tr draw together, contract; (*Lippen*) pucker; (*Brauen*) knit; (*Summe*) add up; (*kürzen*) shorten; (*Truppen*) concentrate ‖ ref contract; (*Gewitter*) brew ‖ intr (SEIN)—**mit j-m z.** move in with s.o.

Zu'satz m addition; (*Ergänzung*) supplement; (*Anhang*) appendix; (*Nachschrift*) postscript; (*Beimischung*) admixture; (zu e-m *Testament*) codicil; (parl) rider; **unter Z. von** with the addition of

Zu'satzgerät n attachment

zusätzlich ['tsuzetslıç] adj additional, extra ‖ adv in addition

zuschanden [tsu'/andən] adv—**z. machen** ruin; **z. werden** go to ruin

zu'schauen intr look on; (*dat*) watch

Zu'schauer -in §6 mf spectator

Zu'schauerraum m auditorium

zu'schicken tr (dat) send (to)

zu'schieben §130 tr close, shut; (*Riegel*) push forward; **j-m die Schuld z.** push the blame on s.o.

Zu'schlag m extra charge; **den Z. erhalten** get the contract (on a bid)

zu'schlagen §132 tr (*Tür*) slam; (*Buch*) shut; (auf *Auktionen*) knock down; (*hinzurechnen*) add ‖ intr hit hard

zu'schließen §76 tr shut, lock

zu'schnallen tr buckle up

zu'schnappen intr snap shut; **z. lassen** snap shut

zu'schneiden §106 tr cut out; (*Anzug*) cut to size

Zu'schnitt m cut; (fig) style

zu'schnüren tr lace up

zu'schrauben tr screw tight

zu'schreiben §62 tr ascribe; (*Bedeutung*) attach; (*Grundstück*, usw.) transfer, sign over ‖ ref—**er hat es sich** [dat] **selbst zuzuschreiben** he has himself to thank for it

Zu'schrift f letter, communication

zuschulden [tsu'/uldən] adv—**sich** [dat] **etw. z. kommen lassen** take the blame for it

Zu'schuß m subsidy; grant; allowance

zu'schütten tr add; (*Graben*) fill up

zu'sehen §138 intr look on; (*dat*) watch; **z., daß** see to it that

zusehends ['tsuze-ənts] adv visibly

zu'senden §120 & §140 tr (dat) send to

zu'setzen tr add; (*Geld*) lose ‖ intr (dat) pester; (*dat*) be hard on; (mil) (*dat*) put pressure on

zu'sichern tr—**j-m etw z.** assure s.o. of s.th.

Zu'sicherung f (-;-en) assurance

zu'siegeln tr seal up

Zu'speise f side dish

zu'sperren tr lock

zu'spielen tr—**j-m den Ball z.** pass the ball to s.o.; **j-m etw z.** slip s.th. to s.o.

zu'spitzen tr sharpen, make pointy ‖ ref (*Lage*) come to a head

zu'sprechen §64 tr (& jur) award

Zu'spruch m consolation, encouragement; (com) customers, clientele

zu'springen §142 intr (SEIN) snap shut

Zu'stand m state, condition; gegenwärtiger Z. status quo; **in gutem Z.** in good condition; **Zustände** state of affairs

zustande [tsu'/tandə] adv—**z. bringen** bring about; put across; get away with; **z. kommen** come about, come off; happen; be realized; (*Gesetz*) pass; (*Vertrag*) be reached

zu'ständig adj competent; (*Behörde*) proper; (*verantwortlich*) responsible

Zu'ständigkeit f (-;) jurisdiction

zustatten [tsu'/tatən] adv—**z. kommen** come in handy

zu'stehen §146 intr (dat) be due to

zu'stellen tr deliver; (jur) serve

Zu'stellung f (-;-en) delivery; (jur) serving

zu'steuern tr (*Geld*) contribute, kick in ‖ intr (dat, auf acc) head for

zu'stimmen intr (dat) agree to, approve of (s.th.); (dat) agree with (s.o.)

Zu'stimmung f (-;) consent, approval

zu'stopfen tr plug up

zu'stoßen §150 tr slam ‖ intr (SEIN) lunge; (dat) happen to

zu'streben intr (dat) strive for

zutage [tsu'tagə] adv to light; **z. liegen** be evident

Zutaten ['tsutatən] pl ingredients

zuteil [tsu'taıl] adv—**j-m z. werden** fall to s.o.'s share

zu'teilen tr allot; ration; award; (*gewähren*) grant; confer; (mil) assign

Zu'teilung f (-;-en) allotment, allocation; rationing; (mil) assignment

zu'tragen §132 tr carry; (*Neuigkeiten*) report ‖ ref happen

zuträglich ['tsutreklıç] adj advantageous; (*Klima*) healthful; (*Nahrung*) wholesome; **j-m z. sein** agree with s.o.

zu'trauen tr—**j-m etw z.** give s.o. credit for s.th.; imagine s.o. capable of s.th. ‖ **Zutrauen** n (-s;) (zu) confidence (in)

zu'traulich adj trustful; (*zahm*) tame

zu'treffen §151 intr (SEIN) prove right; come true; hold true, be conclusive; **z. auf** (acc) apply to

zu'treffend adj correct; to the point; (*anwendbar*) applicable

zu'trinken §143 intr (dat) drink to

Zu'tritt m access; admission, entrance; **kein Z.!** no admittance!

zu'tun §154 tr close; (*hinzufügen*) add

zu'verlässig adj reliable; **von zuverlässiger Seite** on good authority

Zu'verlässigkeit f (-;) reliability

Zuversicht ['tsuferzıçt] f (-;) confidence

zu'versichtlich adj confident

zuviel [tsu'fil] adv & indef pron too much; **einer z.** one too many

zuvor [tsu'for] adv before, previously; first (of all); **kurz z.** shortly before

zuvor– comb.fm. beforehand

zuvor'kommen §99 intr (SEIN) (dat) anticipate; **j-m z.** get the jump on s.o.

zuvor′kommend *adj* obliging; polite

zuvor′tun §154 *tr*—es j–m z. outdo s.o.

Zu′wachs *m* increase; growth; **auf Z.** (big enough) to allow for growth

zu′wachsen §155 *intr* (SEIN) grow together; (*Wunde*) heal up; (*dat*) accrue (to)

Zu′wachsrate *f* rate of increase

zuwege [tsu′vegə] *adv*—z. **bringen** bring about; achieve; finish; **gut z. sein** be fit as a fiddle

zuweilen [tsu′vaɪlən] *adv* sometimes

zu′weisen §118 *tr* assign, allot

zu′wenden §120 & §140 *tr* (*dat*) turn (*s.th.*) towards; (*dat*) give (*s.th.*) to, devote (*s.th.*) to ‖ *ref* (*dat*) devote oneself to, concentrate on

Zu′wendung *f* (–;–en) gift, donation

zuwenig [tsu′veniç] *adv* & *pron* too little

zu′werfen §160 *tr* (*Tür*) slam; (*Blick*) cast; (*Grube*) fill up; j–m etw z. throw s.o. s.th.

zuwider [tsu′vidər] *adj* (*dat*) distasteful (to) ‖ *prep* (*dat*) contrary to

zuwi′derhandeln *intr* (*dat*) go against

Zuwi′derhandlung *f* (–;–en) violation

zu′winken *intr* (*dat*) wave to; beckon to

zu′zahlen *tr* pay extra

zu′zählen *tr* add

zuzeiten [tsu′tsaɪtən] *adv* at times

zu′ziehen §163 *tr* (*Vorhang*) draw; (*Knoten*) tighten; (*Arzt, Experten*) call in ‖ *ref*—sich [*dat*] etw z. incur s.th.; contract s.th. ‖ *intr* (SEIN) move in; move (*to a city*)

Zu′ziehung *f*—unter Z. (*genit* or *von*) in consultation with

zuzüglich [′tsutsyklıç] *prep* (*genit*) plus; including

zwang [tsvaŋ] *pret* of **zwingen** ‖ **Zwang** *m* (–[e]s;) coercion, force; restraint; obligation; (*Druck*) pressure; (jur) duress; **auf j–n Z. ausüben** put pressure on s.o. ‖ *ref*—sich [*dat*] **keinen Z. antun** (or **auferlegen**) relax

zwängen [′tsveŋən] *tr* force, squeeze ‖ *ref* (*durch*) squeeze (through)

zwang′los *adj* free and easy; informal

Zwang′losigkeit *f* (–;) ease; informality

Zwangs– [tsvaŋs] *comb.fm.* force, compulsory

Zwangs′arbeit *f* hard labor

Zwangs′arbeitslager *n* labor camp

Zwangs′jacke *f* strait jacket

Zwangs′lage *f* tight spot

zwangs′läufig *adj* inevitable

zwangs′mäßig *adj* forced; coercive

Zwangs′maßnahme *f*—zu Zwangsmaßnahmen greifen resort to force

Zwangs′verschleppte §5 *mf* displaced person

Zwangs′verwaltung *f* receivership

Zwangs′vorstellung *f* hallucination

zwangs′weise *adv* by force

Zwangs′wirtschaft *f* (econ) government control, controlled economy

zwanzig [′tsvantsıç] *invar adj* & *pron* twenty ‖ **Zwanzig** *f* (–;–en) twenty

zwanziger [′tsvansıgər] *invar adj* of the twenties; **die z. Jahre** the twenties

zwanzigste [′tsvantsıçstə] §9 *adj* & *pron* twentieth

Zwanzigstel [′tsvantsıçstəl] *n* (–s;–) twentieth (*part*)

zwar [tsvar] *adv* indeed, no doubt, it is true; **und z.** namely, that is

Zweck [tsvek] *m* (–[e]s;–e) purpose, aim, object, point; **es hat keinen Z.** there's no point to it

zweck′dienlich *adj* serviceable, useful

Zwecke [′tsvekə] *f* (–;–n) tack; thumbtack

zweck′entfremden *tr* misuse

zweck′entsprechend *adj* appropriate

zweck′los *adj* pointless

zweck′mäßig *adj* serving its purpose; (*Möbel*) functional

zwecks [tsveks] *prep* (*genit*) for the purpose of

zwei [tsvaɪ] *adj* & *pron* two; **alle z.** (coll) both; **zu zweien** in twos, two by two, in pairs; **zu zweien hintereinander** in double file ‖ **Zwei** *f* (–;–en) two

zwei′beinig *adj* two-legged

Zwei′bettzimmer *n* double room

Zweidecker [′tsvaɪdekər] *m* (–s;–) biplane

zweideutig [′tsvaɪdɔɪtıç] *adj* ambiguous; (*Witz*) off-color; (*schlüpfrig*) suggestive

zweierlei [′tsvaɪ·ər′laɪ] *invar adj* two kinds of; **das ist z.** (coll) that's different

zwei′fach, zwei′fältig *adj* twofold, double; **in zweifacher Ausfertigung** in duplicate

Zweifami′lienhaus *n* duplex

zwei′farbig *adj* two-tone

Zweifel [′tsvaɪfəl] *m* (–s;–) doubt; **in Z. stellen** (or **ziehen**) call into question; **über allen Zweifeln erhaben** beyond reproach

zwei′felhaft *adj* doubtful; questionable; (*Persönlichkeit*) suspicious

zwei′fellos *adj* doubtless

zweifeln [′tsvaɪfəln] *intr* be in doubt; waver, hesitate; **z. an** (*dat*) doubt

Zwei′felsfall *m*—im Z. in case of doubt

Zweif′ler –in §6 *mf* skeptic

Zweig [tsvaɪk] *m* (–[e]s;–e) branch

Zweig′anstalt *f*, **Zweig′geschäft** *n* (com) branch

Zweig′gesellschaft *f* (com) affiliate

Zweig′niederlassung *f*, **Zweig′stelle** *f* (com) branch

Zwei′kampf *m* duel, single combat

zwei′mal *adv* twice

zweimalig [′tsvaɪmalıç] *adj* repeated

zweimotorig [′tsvaɪmɔtorıç] *adj* two-engine, twin-engine

zweireihig [′tsvaɪraɪ·ıç] *adj* (*Sakko*) double-breasted

zwei′schneidig *adj* double-edged

zwei′seitig *adj* bilateral; reversible

zweisprachig [′tsvaɪpraxıç] *adj* bilingual

Zweistär′kenglas *n* bifocal lens; (*Brille*) bifocals

zwei′stimmig *adj* for two voices

zweistufig [′tsvaɪtufıç] *adj* (rok) two-stage

zwei′stündig *adj* two-hour

zwei'stündlich *adj & adv* every two hours

zweit [tsvaɪt] *adv*—**zu z.** by twos; **wir sind zu z.** there are two of us

Zwei'taktmotor *m* two-cycle engine

Zweit'ausfertigung *f* duplicate

zweit'beste §9 *adj* second-best

zweite ['tsvaɪtə] §9 *adj & pron* second; another; **aus zweiter Hand** second-hand; at second hand; **zum zweiten** secondly || **Zweite** §5 *mf* (sport) runner-up

zwei'teilig *adj* two-piece; two-part

zweitens ['tsvaɪtəns] *adv* secondly

zweit'klassig *adj* second-class

Zwerchfell ['tsvɛrçfɛl] *n* diaphragm

Zwerg [tsvɛrk] *m* (–[e]s;–e) dwarf

zwer'genhaft *adj* dwarfish

Zwetsche ['tsvɛtʃə] *f* (–;–n), **Zwetsch-ge** ['tsvɛtʃgə] *f* (–;–n) plum

Zwetsch'genwasser *n* plum brandy

zwicken ['tsvɪkən] *tr* pinch

Zwicker (**Zwik'ker**) *m* (–s;–) pince-nez

Zwickmühle ['tsvɪkmylə] *f* (fig) fix

zwie– [tsvi] *comb.fm.* dis–, two–, double

Zwieback ['tsvibak] *m* (–s;ⁿe & –e) zwieback

Zwiebel ['tsvibəl] *f* (–;–n) onion; (*Blumen–*) bulb

Zwie'gespräch *n* dialogue

Zwie'licht *n* twilight

Zwiesel ['tsvizəl] *f* (–;–n) fork (*of tree*)

Zwie'spalt *m* dissension; schism; discrepancy; **im Z. sein mit** be at variance with

zwiespältig ['tsvispɛltɪç] *adj* disunited, divided; divergent

Zwie'tracht *f* (–;) discord

Zwilling ['tsvɪlɪŋ] *m* (–s;–e) twin; **eineiige Zwillinge** identical twins

Zwil'lingsbruder *m* twin brother

Zwil'lingsschwester *f* twin sister

Zwinge ['tsvɪŋə] *f* (–;–n) ferrule; clamp; (*Schraubstock*) vise

zwingen ['tsvɪŋən] §142 *tr* force, compel; (*schaffen*) accomplish, swing

zwin'gend *adj* forceful, cogent

Zwin'ger *m* (–s;–) dungeon; cage; dog kennel; bear pit; lists

zwinkern ['tsvɪŋkərn] *intr* blink

Zwirn [tsvɪrn] *m* (–[e]s;–e) thread

Zwirns'faden *m* thread

zwischen ['tsvɪʃən] *prep* (*dat & acc*) between, among

Zwi'schenbemerkung *f* interruption

Zwi'schendeck *n* steerage

Zwi'schending *n* cross, mixture

zwischendurch' *adv* in between; at times

Zwi'schenergebnis *n* incomplete result

Zwi'schenfall *m* (unexpected) incident

Zwi'schenhändler –**in** §6 *mf* middleman

Zwi'schenlandung *f* stopover

Zwi'schenlauf *m* (sport) quarterfinal; (sport) semifinal

Zwi'schenpause *f* break, intermission

Zwi'schenraum *m* space, interval

Zwi'schenruf *m* boo; interruption

Zwi'schenrunde *f* (sport) quarterfinal; (sport) semifinal

Zwi'schenspiel *n* interlude

zwi'schenstaatlich *adj* international; interstate

Zwi'schenstation *f* (rr) way station

Zwi'schenstecker *m* (elec) adapter

Zwi'schenstellung *f* (–;–en) intermediate position

Zwi'schenstück *n* insert; (*Verbindung*) connection; (elec) adapter

Zwi'schenstufe *f* intermediate stage

Zwi'schenträger –**in** §6 *mf* gossip

Zwi'schenwand *f* partition wall

Zwi'schenzeit *f* interval, meanwhile

Zwist [tsvɪst] *m* (–es;–e) discord; quarrel; (*Feindschaft*) enmity

Zwist'igkeit *f* (–;–en) hostility

zwitschern ['tsvɪtʃərn] *tr*—**e–n z.** (coll) have a shot of liquor || *intr* chirp

Zwitter ['tsvɪtər] *m* (–s;–) hermaphrodite

Zwit'terfahrzeug *n* (mil) half-track

zwo [tsvo] *adj & pron* (coll) two

zwölf ['tsvœlf] *invar adj & pron* twelve || **Zwölf** *f* (–;–en) twelve

Zwölffin'gerdarm *m* duodenum

zwölfte ['tsvœlftə] §9 *adj & pron* twelfth

Zwölftel ['tsvœlftəl] *n* (–s;–) twelfth (*part*)

Zyklon [tsʏ'klon] *m* (–s;–e), **Zyklone** [tsʏ'klonə] *f* (–;–n) cyclone

Zyk·lus ['tsyklus] *m* (–;–len [lən]) cycle; (*Reihe*) series, course

Zylinder [tsʏ'lɪndər] *m* (–s;–) cylinder (*e–r Lampe*) chimney; (*Hut*) top hat

zylindrisch [tsʏ'lɪndrɪʃ] *adj* cylindrical

Zyniker ['tsynɪkər] *m* (–s;–) cynic; (philos) Cynic

zynisch ['tsynɪʃ] *adj* cynical

Zypern ['tsypərn] *n* (–s;) Cyprus

Zypresse [tsʏ'prɛsə] *f* (–;–n) cypress

Zyste ['tsʏstə] *f* (–;–n) cyst

GRAMMATICAL EXPLANATIONS

German Pronunciation

All the German letters and their variant spellings are listed below (in column 1) with their IPA symbols (in column 2), a description of their sounds (in column 3), and German examples with phonetic transcription (in column 4).

VOWELS

SPELLING	SYMBOL	APPROXIMATE SOUND	EXAMPLES
a	[a]	Like *a* in English *swat*	Apfel ['apfəl], lassen ['lasən], Stadt [ʃtat]
a	[ɑ]	Like *a* in English *father*	Vater ['fɑtər], laden ['lɑdən]
aa	[ɑ]	" "	Paar [pɑr], Staat [ʃtat]
ah	[ɑ]	" "	Hahn [hɑn], Zahl [tsɑl]
ä	[ɛ]	Like *e* in English *met*	Äpfel ['ɛpfəl], lässig ['lɛsɪç], Städte ['ʃtɛtə]
ä	[e]	Like *e* in English *they* (without the following sound of *y*)	mäßig ['mesɪç], Väter ['fetər]
äh	[e]	" "	ähnlich ['enlɪç], Zähne ['tsenə]
e	[ə]	Like *e* in English *system*	Bitte ['bɪtə], rufen ['rufən]
e	[ɛ]	Like *e* in English *met*	Kette ['kɛtə], messen ['mɛsən]
e	[e]	Like *e* in English *they* (without the following sound of *y*)	Feder ['fedər], regnen ['regnən]
ee	[e]	" "	Meer [mer], Seele ['zelə]
eh	[e]	" "	Ehre ['erə], zehn [tsen]
i	[ɪ]	Like *i* in English *sin*	bin [bɪn], Fisch [fɪʃ]
i	[i]	Like *i* in English *machine*	Maschine [ma'ʃinə], Lid [lit]
ih	[i]	" "	ihm [im], ihr [ir]
ie	[i]	" "	dieser ['dizər], tief [tif]
o	[ɔ]	Like *o* in English *often*	Gott [gɔt], offen ['ɔfən]
o	[o]	Like *o* in English *note*, but without the diphthongal glide	holen ['holən], Rose ['rozə]
oo	[o]	" "	Boot [bot], Moos [mos]
oh	[o]	" "	Bohne ['bonə], Kohle ['kolə]
ö	[œ]	The lips are rounded for [ɔ] and held without moving while the sound [ɛ] is pronounced.	Götter ['gœtər], öffnen ['œfnən]

3a

SPELLING	SYMBOL	APPROXIMATE SOUND	EXAMPLES
ö	[ø]	The lips are rounded for [o] and held without moving while the sound [e] is pronounced.	böse ['bøzə], Löwe ['løvə]
öh	[ø]	" "	Röhre ['rørə], Söhne ['zønə]
u	[ʊ]	Like *u* in English *bush*	Busch [bʊʃ], muß [mʊs], Hund [hʊnt]
u	[u]	Like *u* in English *rule*	Schule ['ʃulə], Gruß [grus]
uh	[u]	" "	Uhr [ur], Ruhm [rum]
ü	[Y]	The lips are rounded for [ʊ] and held without moving while the sound [ɪ] is pronounced.	Hütte ['hYtə], müssen ['mYsən]
ü	[y]	The lips are rounded for [u] and held without moving while the sound [i] is pronounced.	Schüler ['ʃylər], Grüße ['grysə]
üh	[y]	" "	Mühle ['mylə], kühn [kyn]
y	[Y]	Like *ü* [Y] above	Mystik ['mYstɪk]
y	[y]	Like *ü* [y] above	Mythe ['mytə]

DIPHTHONGS

SPELLING	SYMBOL	APPROXIMATE SOUND	EXAMPLES
ai	[aɪ]	Like *i* in English *night*	Saite ['zaɪtə], Mais [maɪs]
au	[aʊ]	Like *ou* in English *ouch*	kaufen ['kaʊfən], Haus [haʊs]
äu	[ɔɪ]	Like *oy* in English *toy*	träumen ['trɔɪmən], Gebäude [gə'bɔɪdə]
ei	[aɪ]	Like *i* in English *night*	Zeit [tsaɪt], nein [naɪn]
eu	[ɔɪ]	Like *oy* in English *toy*	heute ['hɔɪtə], Eule ['ɔɪlə]

CONSONANTS

SPELLING	SYMBOL	APPROXIMATE SOUND	EXAMPLES
b	[b]	Like *b* in English *boy*	Buch [bux], haben ['habən]
b	[p]	Like *p* in English *lap*	gelb [gelp], lieblich ['liplɪç]
c	[k]	Like *c* in English *car*	Clown [klaʊn], Café [ka'fe]
c	[ts]	Like *ts* in English *its*	Cäsar ['tsezar], Centrale [tsen'tralə]
ch	[x]	This sound is made by breathing through a space between the back of the tongue and the soft palate.	auch [aux], Buche ['buxə]
ch	[ç]	This sound is made by breathing through a space left when the front of the tongue is pressed close to the hard palate with the tip of the tongue behind the lower teeth.	ich [ɪç], Bücher ['byçər], Chemie [çe'mi], durch [durç]

4a

SPELLING	SYMBOL	APPROXIMATE SOUND	EXAMPLES
ch	[k]	Like *k* in English *key*	**Charakter** [ka'raktər], **Chor** [kor]
ch	[ʃ]	Like *sh* in English *shall*	**Chef** [ʃef], **Chassis** [ʃa'si]
chs	[ks]	Like *x* in English *box*	**sechs** [zeks], **Wachs** [vaks]
ck	[k]	Like *k* in English *key* When *ck* in a vocabulary entry in this Dictionary has to be divided by an accent mark, the word is first spelled with *ck* and is then repeated in parentheses with the *ck* changed to *kk* in accordance with the principle which requires this change when the division comes at the end of the line, e.g., **Deckenlicht (Dek′kenlicht)**.	**wecken** ['vɛkən], **Ruck** [rʊk]
d	[d]	Like *d* in English *door*	**laden** ['lɑdən], **deutsch** [dɔɪtʃ]
d	[t]	Like *t* in English *time*	**Freund** [frɔɪnt], **Hund** [hʊnt]
dt	[t]	" "	**verwandt** [fɛr'vant], **Stadt** [ʃtat]
f	[f]	Like *f* in English *five*	**Fall** [fal], **auf** [aʊf]
g	[g]	Like *g* in English *go*	**geben** ['gebən], **Regen** ['regən]
g	[k]	Like *k* in English *key*	**Krieg** [krik], **Weg** [vek]
g	[ç]	See **ch** [ç] above	**wenig** ['venɪç], **häufig** ['hɔɪfɪç]
h	[h]	Like *h* in English *hat*	**Haus** [haʊs], **Freiheit** ['fraɪhaɪt]
j	[j]	Like *y* in English *yet*	**Jahr** [jɑr], **jener** ['jenər]
k	[k]	Like *k* in English *key*	**Kaffee** [ka'fe], **kein** [kaɪn]
l	[l]	This sound is made with the tip of the tongue against the back of the upper teeth and the side edges of the tongue against the side teeth.	**laden** ['lɑdən], **fahl** [fɑl]
m	[m]	Like *m* in English *man*	**mehr** [mer], **Amt** [amt]
n	[n]	Like *n* in English *neck*	**Nase** ['nɑzə], **kaufen** ['kaʊfən]
n	[ŋ]	Like *n* in English *sink*	**sinken** ['zɪŋkən], **Funke** ['fʊŋkə]
ng	[ŋ]	" "	**Finger** ['fɪŋər], **Rang** [raŋ]
p	[p]	Like *p* in English *pond*	**Perle** ['pɛrlə], **Opfer** ['ɔpfər]
ph	[f]	Like *f* in English *five*	**Phase** ['fɑzə], **Graphik** ['grɑfɪk]
qu	[kv]	Does not occur in English.	**Quelle** ['kvɛlə], **bequem** [bə'kvem]
r	[r]	This sound is a trilled sound made by vibrating the tip of the tongue against the upper gums or by vibrating the uvula.	**rufen** ['rufən], **Rede** ['redə]

5a

SPELLING	SYMBOL	APPROXIMATE SOUND	EXAMPLES
s	[s]	Like s in English sock	Glas [glɑs], erst [erst]
s	[z]	Like z in English zest	sind [zɪnt], Eisen ['aɪzən]
sch	[ʃ]	Like sh in English shall	Schuh [ʃu], Schnee [ʃne]
sp	[ʃp]	Does not occur in English in the initial position.	sparen ['ʃpɑrən], Spott [ʃpɔt]
ss	[s]	This spelling is used only in the intervocalic position and when the preceding vowel sound is one of the following: [a], [ɛ], [ɪ], [ɔ], [œ], [ʊ], [ʏ]	Klasse ['klasə], essen ['ɛsən], wissen ['vɪsən], Gosse ['gɔsə], Rössel ['rœsəl], Russe ['rʊsə], müssen ['mʏsən]
ß	[s]	This spelling is used instead of ss (a) when in the final position in a word or component, (b) when followed by a consonant, or (c) when intervocalic and preceded by a diphthong or one of the following vowel sounds: [ɑ], [e], [i], [o], [ø], [u], [y]	(a) Fluß [flʊs], Flußufer ['flʊsufər], (b) läßt [lest], (c) dreißig ['draɪsɪç], Straße ['ʃtrɑsə], mäßig ['mesɪç], schießen ['ʃisən], stoßen ['ʃtosən], Stößel ['ʃtøsəl], Muße ['musə], müßig ['mysɪç]
st	[ʃt]	Does not occur in English in the initial position.	Staub [ʃtaʊp], stehen ['ʃte‧ən]
t	[t]	Like t in English time	Teller ['tɛlər], Tau [taʊ]
th	[t]	" "	Theater [tɛ'ɑtər], Thema ['tema]
ti+ vowel	[tsj]	Does not occur in English.	Station [sta'tsjon], Patient [pa'tsjent]
tz	[ts]	Like ts in English its	schätzen ['ʃɛtsən], jetzt [jetst]
v	[f]	Like f in English five	Vater ['fɑtər], brav [brɑf]
v	[v]	Like v in English vat	November [nɔ'vɛmbər], Verb [verp]
w	[v]	" "	Wasser ['vasər], wissen ['vɪsən]
x	[ks]	Like x in English box	Export [eks'pɔrt], Taxe ['taksə]
z	[ts]	Like ts in English its	Zahn [tsɑn], reizen ['raɪtsən]

German Grammar References

§1. Declension of the Definite Article

	SINGULAR			PLURAL
	MASC	FEM	NEUT	MASC, FEM, NEUT
NOM	der	die	das	die
ACC	den	die	das	die
DAT	dem	der	dem	den
GENIT	des	der	des	der

§2. Declension of the Indefinite Article and the Numeral Adjective

	SINGULAR			PLURAL
1.	MASC	FEM	NEUT	MASC, FEM, NEUT
NOM	ein	eine	ein	
ACC	einen	eine	ein	
DAT	einem	einer	einem	
GENIT	eines	einer	eines	

2. Other words that are declined like **ein** are: **kein** *no, not any* and the possessive adjectives **mein** *my;* **dein** *thy, your;* **sein** *his; her; its;* **ihr** *her; their;* **Ihr** *your;* **unser** *our;* **euer** *your.* Unlike **ein**, they have plural forms, as shown in the following paradigm.

	SINGULAR			PLURAL
	MASC	FEM	NEUT	MASC, FEM, NEUT
NOM	kein	keine	kein	keine
ACC	keinen	keine	kein	keine
DAT	keinem	keiner	keinem	keinen
GENIT	keines	keiner	keines	keiner

3. The **e** of **er** of **unser** and **euer** is generally dropped when followed by an ending, as shown in the following paradigm. And instead of the **e** of **er** dropping, the **e** of final **em** and **en** in these words may drop.

	SINGULAR			PLURAL
	MASC	FEM	NEUT	MASC, FEM, NEUT
NOM	unser	uns(e)re	unser	uns(e)re
ACC	uns(e)ren or unsern	uns(e)re	unser	uns(e)re
DAT	uns(e)rem or unserm	uns(e)rer	uns(e)rem or unserm	uns(e)ren or unsern
GENIT	uns(e)res	uns(e)rer	uns(e)res	uns(e)rer

All adjectives that follow these words are declined in the mixed declension.

4. The pronouns **einer** and **keiner**, as well as all the possessive pronouns, are declined according to the strong declension of adjectives. The neuter forms **eines** and **keines** have the variants **eins** and **keins.**

5. When the possessive adjectives are used as possessive pronouns, they are declined according to the strong declension of adjectives. When preceded by the definite article, they are declined according to the weak declension of adjectives. There are also possessive pronouns with the infix **ig** which are always preceded by the definite article and capitalized and are declined according to the declension of adjectives, e.g., **der, die, das Meinige** *mine.*

§3. Declension of the Demonstrative Pronoun

	SINGULAR			PLURAL
	MASC	FEM	NEUT	MASC, FEM, NEUT
NOM	dieser	diese	dieses or dies	diese
ACC	diesen	diese	dieses or dies	diese
DAT	diesem	dieser	diesem	diesen
GENIT	dieses	dieser	dieses	dieser

Other words that are declined like **dieser** are **jeder** *each;* **jener** *that;* **mancher** *many a;* **welcher** *which.* All adjectives that come after these words are declined in the weak declension.

§4. Declension of Adjectives.
Adjectives have three declensions: 1) the strong declension, 2) the weak declension, and 3) the mixed declension. On both sides of this Dictionary, adjectives occurring in the expressions consisting solely of an adjective and a noun are entered in their weak forms.

1. The strong declension of adjectives, whose endings are shown in the following table, is used when the adjective is not preceded by **der** or by **dieser** or any of the other words listed in §3 or by **ein** or any of the other words listed in §2.

	SINGULAR			PLURAL
	MASC	FEM	NEUT	MASC, FEM, NEUT
NOM	–er	–e	–es	–e
ACC	–en	–e	–es	–e
DAT	–em	–er	–em	–en
GENIT	–en	–er	–en	–er

2. The weak declension of adjectives, whose endings are shown in the following table, is used when the adjective is preceded by **der** or **dieser** or any of the other words listed in §3.

	SINGULAR			PLURAL
	MASC	FEM	NEUT	MASC, FEM, NEUT
NOM	–e	–e	–e	–en
ACC	–en	–e	–e	–en
DAT	–en	–en	–en	–en
GENIT	–en	–en	–en	–en

3. The **der** component of **derselbe** and **derjenige** is the article **der** and is declined like it, while the **–selbe** and **–jenige** components are declined according to the weak declension of adjectives.

4. The mixed declension of adjectives, whose endings are shown in the following table, is used when the adjective is preceded by **ein** or **kein** or any of the other words listed in §2.

8a

	SINGULAR			PLURAL
	MASC	FEM	NEUT	MASC, FEM, NEUT
NOM	–er	–e	–es	–en
ACC	–en	–e	–es	–en
DAT	–en	–en	–en	–en
GENIT	–en	–en	–en	–en

§5. Adjectives Used as Nouns. When an adjective is used as a masculine, feminine, or neuter noun, it is spelled with an initial capital letter and is declined as an adjective in accordance with the principles set forth in §4. We have, for example, **der** or **die Fremde** the foreigner; **der** or **die Angestellte** *the employee;* **ein Angestellter** *a (male) employee,* **eine Angestellte** *a (female) employee;* **das Deutsche** *German* (i.e., *language*). These nouns are entered on both sides of this Dictionary in the weak form of the adjective and their genitives and plurals are not shown.

§6. Many masculine nouns ending in **–er** and **–ier** have feminine forms made by adding **–in.** The masculine forms have genitives made by adding **s** and remain unchanged in the plural, while the feminine forms remain unchanged in the singular and have plurals made by adding **–nen.** For example:

	MASC	FEM
NOM SG	**Verkäufer** *salesperson (salesman)*	**Verkäuferin** *salesperson (saleslady)*
GENIT SG	**Verkäufers**	**Verkäuferin**
NOM PL	**Verkäufer**	**Verkäuferinnen**

§7. Many masculine nouns ending in **–at** (e.g., **Advokat**), or in **–ant** (e.g., **Musikant**), or in **–ist** (*e.g.,* **Artist**), or in **–ent** (e.g., **Student**), or in **–graph** (e.g., **Choreograph**), or in **–ot** (e.g., **Pilot**), or in **–et** (e.g., **Analphabet**), or in **–it** (e.g., **Israelit**), or in **–ast** (e.g., **Phantast**), etc., have feminine forms made by adding **–in.** The masculine forms have genitives and plurals made by adding **–en,** while the femine forms remain unchanged in the singular and have plurals made by adding **–nen.** For example:

	MASC	FEM
NOM SG	**Advokat** *attorney*	**Advokatin** *attorney*
GENIT SG	**Advokaten**	**Advokatin**
NOM PL	**Advokaten**	**Advokatinnen**

§8. Many masculine nouns ending in **–ar** (e.g., **Antiquar**) or in **–är** (e.g., **Milliardär**) have feminine forms made by adding **–in.** The masculine forms have genitives made by adding **–(e)s** and plurals made by adding **–e,** while the feminine forms remain unchanged in the singular and have plurals made by adding **–nen.** For example:

	MASC	FEM
NOM SG	**Antiquar** *antique dealer*	**Antiquarin** *antique dealer*
GENIT SG	**Antiquar(e)s**	**Antiquarin**
NOM PL	**Antiquare**	**Antiquarinnen**

§9. Adjectives are generally given in their uninflected form, the form in which they appear in the predicate, e.g., **billig, reich, alt.** However, those adjectives which do not occur in an uninflected form are given with the weak ending **–e,** which in the nominative is the same for all genders, e.g., **andere, besondere, beste, hohe.**

9a

§10. Adjectives which denote languages may be used as adverbs. When so used with **sprechen, schreiben, können,** and a few others, they are translated in English by the corresponding noun, and actual and immediate action is implied, e.g., **deutsch sprechen** *to speak German* (i.e., to be speaking German right now). Adjectives which denote languages may be capitalized and used as invariable nouns, and when so used with **sprechen, schreiben, können,** and a few other verbs, general action is implied, e.g., **Deutsch sprechen** *to speak German* (i.e., to know how to speak German, to be a speaker of German).

With other verbs, these adjectives used as adverbs are translated by the corresponding noun preceded by "auf" or "in", e.g., **sich auf** (or **in**) **deutsch unterhalten** *to converse in German.*

811. Personal and Reflexive Pronouns

PERSONS	SUBJECT	PERSONAL DIRECT OBJECT	PERSONAL INDIRECT OBJECT	REFLEXIVE DIRECT OBJECT	REFLEXIVE INDIRECT OBJECT
SG					
1	ich *I*	mich *me*	mir *(to) me*	mich *myself*	mir *(to) myself*
2	du *you*	dich *you*	dir *(to) you*	dich *yourself*	dir *(to) yourself*
3 MASC	er *he; it*	ihn *him; it*	ihm *(to) him; (to) it*	sich *himself; itself*	sich *(to) himself; (to) itself*
3 FEM	sie *she; it*	sie *her; it*	ihr *(to) her; (to) it*	sich *herself; itself*	sich *(to) herself; (to) itself*
3 NEUT	es *it; she; he*	es *it; her; him*	ihm *(to) it; (to) her (to) him*	sich *itself; herself; himself*	sich *(to) itself; (to) herself; (to) himself*
PL					
1	wir *we*	uns *us*	uns *(to) us*	uns *ourselves*	uns *(to) ourselves*
2	ihr *you*	euch *you*	euch *(to) you*	euch *yourselves*	euch *(to) yourselves*
3	sie *they*	sie *them*	ihnen *(to) them*	sich *themselves*	sich *(to) themselves*
2 FORMAL SG & PL	Sie *you*	Sie *you*	Ihnen *(to) you*	sich *yourself; yourselves*	sich *(to) yourself; (to) yourselves*

er means *it* when it stands for a masculine noun that is the name of an animal or a thing, as **Hund, Tisch.** **sie** means *it* when it stands for a feminine noun that is the name of an animal or a thing, as **Hündin, Feder.** **es** means *she* when it stands for a neuter noun that is the name of a female person, as **Fräulein, Mädchen, Weib;** it means *he* when it stands for a neuter noun that is the name of a male person, as **Söhnchen, Söhnlein.** The dative means also *from me, from you,* etc., with certain verbs expressing separation such as **entnehmen.**

11a

§12. Separable and Inseparable Prefixes. Many verbs can be compounded either with a prefix, which is always inseparable and unstressed, or with a combining form (conventionally called also a prefix), which can be separable and stressed or inseparable and unstressed. Exceptions are indicated by the abbreviations *sep* and *insep.*

1. The inseparable prefixes are **be–, emp–, ent–, er–, ge–, ver–,** and **zer–,** e.g., **beglei′ten, erler′nen, verste′hen.** They are never stressed.

2. The separable prefixes (i.e., combining forms) are prepositions, e.g., **auf–** as in **auf′tragen,** adverbs, e.g., **vorwärts–** as in **vor′wärtsbringen,** adjectives, e.g., **tot–** as in **tot′schlagen,** nouns, e.g., **maschine–** as in **maschi′neschreiben,** or other verbs, e.g., **stehen–** as in **ste′henbleiben.** They are always stressed except as provided for those listed in the following section.

3. The prefixes (combining forms) **durch, hinter, über, um, unter, wider,** and **wieder,** when their meaning is literal, are separable and stressed, e.g. **durch′schneiden** *cut through, cut in two,* and, when their meaning is figurative or derived, are inseparable and unstressed, e.g., **durchschnei′den** *cut across, traverse.*

4. A compound prefix is (a) inseparable if it consists of an inseparable prefix plus a separable prefix, e.g., **beauf′tragen,** (b) separable if it consists of a separable prefix plus an inseparable prefix, e.g.,**vor′bereiten—er bereitet etwas vor,** and (c) separable if it consists of two separable prefixes, e.g., **vorbei′laufen—sie lief vorbei.** Although verbs falling under (b) are separable, they do not take **–ge–** in the past participle, e.g., **vor′bereitet** (past participle of **vorbereiten**). But they do take the infix **–zu–** in the infinitive, e.g., **vor′-zubereiten.** Note that compound prefixes falling under (c) are stressed on the second of the two separable components.

§13. German verbs are regarded as reflexive regardless of whether the reflexive pronoun is the direct or indirect object of the verb.

§14. The declension of German nouns is shown by giving the genitive singular followed by the nominative plural, in parentheses after the abbreviation indicating gender. This is done by presenting the whole noun by a hyphen with which the ending and/or the umlaut may or may not be shown according to the inflection; e.g., **Stadt** [ʃtat] *f* (–;⸚e) means **der Stadt** and **die Städte.** If the noun has no plural, the closing parenthesis comes immediately after the semicolon following the genitive singular, e.g., **Kleidung** [ˈklaɪdʊŋ] *f* (–;). In loan words in which the ending changes in the plural, the centered period is used to mark off the portion of the word that has to be detached before the portion showing the plural form is added, e.g., **Da·tum** [ˈdatʊm] *n* (–s;-ten [tən]).

When a vowel is added to a word ending in ß, the ß remains if it is preceded by a diphthong or one of the following vowel sounds: [ɑ], [e], [i], [o], [ø], [y], e.g., **Stoß** [ʃtos], plural: **Stöße; Strauß,** plural: **Sträuße,** but changes to **ss** if it is preceded by one of the following vowel sounds: [a], [ɛ], [ɪ], [ɔ], [œ], [ʊ], [ʏ], e.g., **Roß** [rɔs], plural **Rosses.** In this Dictionary the inflection of words in which ß does not change is shown in the usual way, e.g., **Stoß** [ʃtos] *m* (–es;⸚e); **Strauß** [ʃtraʊs] *m* (–es;⸚e), while the inflection of words in which ß changes to **ss** is shown in monosyllables by repeating the full word in its inflected forms, e.g., **Roß** [rɔs] *n* (**Rosses; Rosse**) and in polysyllables by marking off with a centered dot the final syllable and then repeating it in its inflected forms, e.g., **Ver·laß** [fɛrˈlas] *m* (–lasses;).

§15. When a word ending in a double consonant is combined with a following word beginning with the same single consonant followed by a vowel, the resultant group of three identical consonants is shortened to two, e.g., **Schiff** combined with **Fahrt** makes **Schiffahrt** and **Schall** combined with **Lehre** makes

Schallehre.[1] However, when such a compound as a vocabulary entry has to be divided by an accent mark, the word is first spelled with two identical consonants and is then repeated in parentheses with three identical consonants, e.g., **Schiffahrt (Schiff′fahrt)**. Furthermore, when such a compound has to be divided because the first component comes at the end of a line and is followed by a hyphen and the second component begins the following line, the three consonants are used, e.g., **Schiff–fahrt** and **Schall–lehre**.

When the medial group **ck** in a vocabulary entry has to be divided by an accent mark, the word is first spelled with **ck** and is then repeated in parentheses with the **ck** changed to **kk** in accordance with the orthographic principle which requires this change when the division comes at the end of the line, e.g., **Deckenlicht (Dek′kenlicht)**.

---

[1] If the intial consonant of the following word is followed by a consonant instead of a vowel, the group of three identical consonants remains, e.g., **Fetttropfen, Rohstofffrage.**

German Model Verbs

These verbs are models for all the verbs that appear as vocabulary entries in the German-English part of this Dictionary. If a section number referring to this table is not given with an entry, it is understood that the verb is a weak verb conjugated like **loben, reden, handeln,** or **warten.** If a section number is given, it is understood that the verb is a strong, mixed, or irregular verb and that it is identical in all forms with the model referred to in its radical vowel or diphthong and the consonants that follow the radical. Thus **schneiden** is numbered §106 to refer to the model **leiden.** Such words include the model itself, e.g., **denken,** numbered §66 to refer to the model **denken,** compounds of the model, e.g., **bekommen,** numbered §99 to refer to the model **kommen,** and verbs that have the same radical component, e.g., **empfehlen,** numbered §51 to refer to the model **befehlen.**

If a strong or mixed verb in a given function (transitive or intransitive) and/or meaning may be conjugated also as a weak verb, this is indicated by the insertion of the section number of the appropriate weak verb (**loben, handeln, reden,** or **warten**) after the section number of the model strong verb, e.g., **dingen** §142 & §109.

If a strong or mixed verb in a different function is conjugated as a weak verb, this is indicated by dividing the two functions by parallels and showing the conjungation of each by the insertion of the appropriate section numbers, e.g., **hängen** §92 *tr* . . . ‖ §109 *intr.*

If a strong or mixed verb in a different meaning is conjugated as a weak verb, this is indicated by dividing the two meanings by parallels and showing the conjungation of each by the insertion of the appropriate section numbers, e.g., **bewegen** *tr* move, set in motion . . . ‖ §56 *tr* move, induce.

It is understood that verbs with inseparable prefixes, verbs with compound separable prefixes of which the first component is separable and the second inseparable, and verbs ending in –ieren do not take **ge** in the past participle.

No account is taken here of the auxiliary used in forming compound tenses. The use of SEIN is indicated in the body of the Dictionary.

Alternate forms are listed in parentheses immediately below the corresponding principal part of the model verb.

	INFINITIVE	3D SG PRESENT INDICATIVE	IMPERFECT INDICATIVE	IMPERFECT SUBJUNCTIVE	PAST PARTICIPLE
§50	backen	bäckt	buk	büke	gebacken
§51	befehlen	befiehlt	befahl	beföhle	befohlen
§52	beginnen	beginnt	begann	begönne (begänne)	begonnen
§53	beißen	beißt	biß	bisse	gebissen
§54	bergen	birgt	barg	bärge (bürge)	geborgen
§55	bersten	birst (berstet)	barst	bärste (börste)	geborsten
§56	bewegen	bewegt	bewog	bewöge	bewogen
§57	biegen	biegt	bog	böge	gebogen
§58	bieten	bietet	bot	böte	geboten
§59	binden	bindet	band	bände	gebunden
§60	bitten	bittet	bat	bäte	gebeten
§61	blasen	bläst	blies	bliese	geblasen
§62	bleiben	bleibt	blieb	bliebe	geblieben
§63	braten	brät	briet	briete	gebraten
§64	brechen	bricht	brach	bräche	gebrochen
§65	bringen	bringt	brachte	brächte	gebracht
§66	denken	denkt	dachte	dächte	gedacht
§67	dreschen	drischt	drosch (drasch)	drösche (dräsche)	gedroschen
§68	dünken	dünkt (deucht)	dünkte (deuchte)	dünkte (deuchte)	gedünkt (gedeucht)

15a

	INFINITIVE	3D SG PRESENT INDICATIVE	IMPERFECT INDICATIVE	IMPERFECT SUBJUNCTIVE	PAST PARTICIPLE
§69	dürfen	darf	durfte	dürfte	gedurft (dürfen)
§70	essen	ißt	aß	äße	gegessen
§71	fahren	fährt	fuhr	führe	gefahren
§72	fallen	fällt	fiel	fiele	gefallen
§73	fangen	fängt	fing	finge	gefangen
§74	fechten	ficht	focht	föchte	gefochten
§75	fliehen	flieht	floh	flöhe	geflohen
§76	fließen	fließt	floß	flösse	geflossen
§77	frieren	friert	fror	fröre	gefroren
§78	gären	gärt	gor	göre	gegoren
§79	gebären	gebiert	gebar	gebäre	geboren
§80	geben	gibt	gab	gäbe	gegeben
§81	gedeihen	gedeiht	gedieh	gediehe	gediehen
§82	gehen	geht	ging	ginge	gegangen
§83	gelten	gilt	galt	gälte (gölte)	gegolten
§84	genesen	genest	genas	genäse	genesen
§85	gleichen	gleicht	glich	gliche	geglichen
§86	gleiten	gleitet	glitt	glitte	geglitten
§87	graben	gräbt	grub	grübe	gegraben
§88	greifen	greift	griff	griffe	gegriffen
§89	haben	hat	hatte	hätte	gehabt
§90	halten	hält	hielt	hielte	gehalten

	INFINITIVE	3D SG PRESENT INDICATIVE	IMPERFECT INDICATIVE	IMPERFECT SUBJUNCTIVE	PAST PARTICIPLE
§91	handeln	handelt	handelte	handelte	gehandelt
§92	hängen	hängt	hing	hinge	gehangen
§93	hauen	haut	hieb	hiebe	gehauen
§94	heben	hebt	hob	höbe	gehoben
§95	heißen	heißt	hieß	hieße	geheißen
§96	helfen	hilft	half	hälfe (hülfe)	geholfen
§97	kennen	kennt	kannte	kennte	gekannt
§98	kiesen	kiest	kor	köre	gekoren
§99	kommen	kommt	kam	käme	gekommen
§100	können	kann	konnte	könnte	gekonnt (können)
§101	kreischen	kreischt	kreischte (krisch)	kreischte (krische)	gekreischt (gekrischen)
§102	kriechen	kriecht	kroch	kröche	gekrochen
§103	laden	lädt	lud	lüde	geladen
§104	lassen	läßt	ließ	ließe	gelassen
§105	laufen	läuft	lief	liefe	gelaufen
§106	leiden	leidet	litt	litte	gelitten
§107	lesen	liest	las	läse	gelesen
§108	liegen	liegt	lag	läge	gelegen
§109	loben	lobt	lobte	lobte	gelobt
§110	löschen	lischt	losch	lösche	geloschen
§111	lügen	lügt	log	löge	gelogen

	INFINITIVE	3D SG PRESENT INDICATIVE	IMPERFECT INDICATIVE	IMPERFECT SUBJUNCTIVE	PAST PARTICIPLE
§112	meiden	meidet	mied	miede	gemieden
§113	melken	melkt	molk	mölke	gemolken
§114	mögen	mag	mochte	möchte	gemocht (mögen)
§115	müssen	muß	mußte	müßte	gemußt (müssen)
§116	nehmen	nimmt	nahm	nähme	genommen
§117	pflegen	pflegt	pflog	pflöge	gepflogen
§118	preisen	preist	pries	priese	gepriesen
§119	quellen	quillt	quoll	quölle	gequollen
§120	reden	redet	redete	redete	geredet
§121	rinnen	rinnt	rann	ränne (rönne)	geronnen
§122	rufen	ruft	rief	riefe	gerufen
§123	salzen	salzt	salzte	salzte	gesalzen
§124	saufen	säuft	soff	söffe	gesoffen
§125	saugen	saugt	sog	söge	gesogen
§126	schaffen	schafft	schuf	schüfe	geschaffen
§127	schallen	schallt	scholl	schölle	geschollen
§128	scheinen	scheint	schien	schiene	geschienen
§129	scheren	schert (schiert)	schor	schöre	geschoren
§130	schieben	schiebt	schob	schöbe	geschoben
§131	schlafen	schläft	schlief	schliefe	geschlafen

18a

	INFINITIVE	3D SG PRESENT INDICATIVE	IMPERFECT INDICATIVE	IMPERFECT SUBJUNCTIVE	PAST PARTICIPLE
§132	schlagen	schlägt	schlug	schlüge	geschlagen
§133	schmelzen	schmilzt	schmolz	schmölze	geschmolzen
§134	schrecken	schrickt	schrak	schräke	geschrocken
§135	schreien	schreit	schrie	schriee	geschrie(e)n
§136	schwimmen	schwimmt	schwamm	schwämme (schwömme)	geschwommen
§137	schwören	schwört	schwur (schwor)	schwüre	geschworen
§138	sehen	sieht	sah	sähe	gesehen
§139	sein	ist	war	wäre	gewesen
§140	senden	sendet	sandte	sendete	gesandt
§141	sieden	siedet	sott	sötte	gesotten
§142	singen	singt	sang	sänge	gesungen
§143	sinken	sinkt	sank	sänke	gesunken
§144	sitzen	sitzt	saß	säße	gesessen
§145	sollen	soll	sollte	sollte	gesollt (sollen)
§146	stehen	steht	stand	stände (stünde)	gestanden
§147	stehlen	stiehlt	stahl	stähle (stöhle)	gestohlen
§148	steigen	steigt	stieg	stiege	gestiegen
§149	sterben	stirbt	starb	stürbe	gestorben
§150	stoßen	stößt	stieß	stieße	gestoßen

	INFINITIVE	3D SG PRESENT INDICATIVE	IMPERFECT INDICATIVE	IMPERFECT SUBJUNCTIVE	PAST PARTICIPLE
§151	treffen	trifft	traf	träfe	getroffen
§152	treten	tritt	trat	träte	getreten
§153	triefen	trieft	troff	tröffe	getroffen
§154	tun	tut	tat	täte	getan
§155	wachsen	wächst	wuchs	wüchse	gewachsen
§156	wägen	wiegt	wog	wöge	gewogen
§157	warten	wartet	wartete	wartete	gewartet
§158	waschen	wäscht	wusch	wüsche	gewaschen
§159	werden	wird	wurde (ward)	würde	geworden (worden)
§160	werfen	wirft	warf	würfe	geworfen
§161	wissen	weiß	wußte	wüßte	gewußt
§162	wollen	will	wollte	wollte	gewollt (wollen)
§163	ziehen	zieht	zog	zöge	gezogen
§164	klimmen	klimmt	klomm	klömme	geklommen
§165	küren	kürt	kor	köre	gekoren
§166	schinden	schindet	schund	schünde	geschunden

20a

Die Aussprache des Englischen

Die nachstehenden Lautzeichen bezeichnen fast alle Laute der englischen Sprache:

VOKALE

LAUTZEICHEN	UNGEFÄHRER LAUT	BEISPIEL
[æ]	Offener als *ä* in *hätte*	hat [hæt]
[ɑ]	Wie *a* in *Vater* Wie *a* in *Mann*	father ['fɑðər] proper ['prɑpər]
[ɛ]	Wie *e* in *Fett*	met [mɛt]
[e]	Offener als *eej* in *Seejungfrau*	fate [fet] they [ðe]
[ə]	Wie *e* in *finden*	haven ['hevən] pardon ['pɑrdən]
[i]	Wie *ie* in *sie*	she [ʃi] machine [məˈʃin]
[ɪ]	Offener als *i* in *bitte*	fit [fɪt] beer [bɪr]
[o]	Offenes *o* mit anschließendem kurzem (halbvokalischem) *u*	nose [noz] road [rod] row [ro]
[ɔ]	Wie *o* in *oft*	bought [bɔt] law [lɔ]
[ʌ]	Wie *er* in *jeder* (umgangssprachlich)	cup [kʌp] come [kʌm] mother ['mʌðər]
[ʊ]	Wie *u* in *Fluß*	pull [pʊl] book [bʊk] wolf [wʊlf]
[u]	Wie *u* in *Fluß*	move [muv] tomb [tum]

DIPHTHONGE

LAUTZEICHEN	UNGEFÄHRER LAUT	BEISPIEL
[aɪ]	Wie *ei* in *nein*	night [naɪt] eye [aɪ]
[aʊ]	Wie *au* in *Haus*	found [faʊnd] cow [kaʊ]
[ɔɪ]	Wie *eu* in *heute*	voice [vɔɪs] oil [ɔɪl]

KONSONANTEN

LAUTZEICHEN	UNGEFÄHRER LAUT	BEISPIEL
[b]	Wie *b* in *bin*	bed [bɛd] robber ['rɑbər]

LAUTZEICHEN	UNGEFÄHRER LAUT	BEISPIEL
[d]	Wie *d* in *du*	dead [dɛd] add [æd]
[dʒ]	Wie *dsch* in *Dschungel*	gem [dʒɛm] jail [dʒel]
[ð]	*d* als Reibelaut ausgesprochen	this [ðɪs] Father ['faðər]
[f]	Wie *f* in *fett*	face [fes] phone [fon]
[g]	Wie *g* in *gehen*	go [go] get [gɛt]
[h]	Wie *h* in *Haus*	hot [hɑt] alcohol ['ælkə,hɔl]
[j]	Wie *j* in *ja*	yes [jɛs] unit ['junɪt]
[k]	Wie *k* in *kann*	cat [kæt] chord [kɔrd] kill [kɪl]
[l]	Wie *l* in *lang*, aber mit angehobenem Zungenrücken	late [let] allow [ə'lau]
[m]	Wie *m* in *mehr*	more [mor] command [kə'mænd]
[n]	Wie *n* in *Nest*	nest [nɛst] manner ['mænər]
[ŋ]	Wie *ng* in *singen*	king [kɪŋ] conquer ['kɑŋkər]
[p]	Wie *p* in *Pech*	pen [pɛn] cap [kæp]
[r]	Im Gegensatz zum deutschen gerollten Zungenspitzen- oder Zäpfchen-r, ist das englische *r* mit retroflexer Zungenstellung und gerundeten Lippen zu artikulieren.	run [rʌn] far [far] art [ɑrt] carry ['kæri]
[s]	Wie *s* in *es*	send [sɛnd] cellar ['sɛlər]
[ʃ]	Wie *sch* in *Schule*	shall [ʃæl] machine [mə'ʃin] nation ['neʃən]
[t]	Wie *t* in *Tee*	ten [tɛn] dropped [drɑpt]
[tʃ]	Wie *tsch* in *deutsch*	child [tʃaɪld] much [mʌtʃ] nature ['netʃər]
[θ]	Ist als stimmloser linguadentaler Lispellaut zu artikulieren	think [θɪŋk] truth [truθ]
[v]	Wie *w* in *was*	vest [vɛst] over ['ovər] of [ɑv]
[w]	Ist als Halbvokal zu artikulieren	work [wʌrk] tweed [twid] queen [kwin]
[z]	Ist stimmhaft zu artikulieren wie *s* in *so*	zeal [zil] busy ['bɪzi] his [hɪz] winds [wɪndz]
[ʒ]	Wie *j* in *Jalousie*	azure ['eʒər] measure ['mɛʒər]

Aussprache der zusammengesetzten Wörter

Im englisch-deutschen Teil dieses Wörterbuches ist die Aussprache aller einfachen englischen Wörter in einer Neufassung der Lautzeichen des Internationalen Phonetischen Alphabets in eckigen Klammern angegeben.

Außer den mit Präfixen, Suffixen und Wortbildungselementen gebildeten Zusammensetzungen gibt es im Englischen drei Arten von zusammengesetzten Wörtern: (1) zusammengeschriebene, z.B. **bookcase** Bücherregal, (2) mit Bindestrich geschriebene, z.B. **short-circuit** kurzschließen, und (3) getrennt geschriebene, z.B. **post card** Postkarte. Die Aussprache der englischen zusammengesetzten Wörter ist nicht angegeben, sofern die Aussprache der Bestandteile an der Stelle angegeben ist, wo sie als selbständige Stichwörter erscheinen; angegeben ist jedoch die Betonung durch Haupt- und Nebentonakzent und zwar jeweils am Ende der betonten Silben, z.B. **book′case′**, **short′-cir′cuit**, **post′ card′**.

In Hauptwörtern, in denen der Nebenton auf den Bestandteilen **–man** und **–men** liegt, wird der Vokal dieser Bestandteile wie in den Wörtern **man** und **men** ausgesprochen, z.B. **mailman** [′mel͵mæn] und **mailmen** [′mel͵men]. In Hauptwörtern, in denen diese Bestandteile unbetont bleiben, wird der Vokal beider Bestandteile als schwa ausgesprochen, z.B. **policeman** [pə′lismən] und **policemen** [pə′lismən]. Es gibt Hauptwörter, in denen diese Bestandteile entweder mit dem Nebenton oder unbetont ausgesprochen werden, z.B. **doorman** [′dor͵mæn] oder [′dormən] und **doormen** [′dor͵men] oder [′dormən]. In diesem Wörterbuch ist die Lautschrift für diese Wörter nicht angegeben, sofern sie für den ersten Bestandteil dort angeführt ist, wo er als Stichwort erscheint; angegeben sind jedoch Haupt- und Nebenton:

> mail′man *s* (–men′)
> police′man *s* (–men)
> door′man′ & door′man *s* (–men′ & –men)

Aussprache des Partizip Perfekt

Bei Wörtern, die auf **–ed** (oder **–d** nach stummem e) enden und nach den nachstehenden Regeln ausgesprochen werden, ist die Aussprache in diesem Wörterbuch nicht angegeben, sofern sie für die endungslose Form dort angegeben ist, wo diese als Stichwort erscheint. Die Doppelschreibung des Schlußkonsonanten nach einfachem betontem Vokal hat keinen Einfluß auf die Aussprache der Endung **–ed**.

Die Endung **–ed** (oder **–d** nach stummem e) der Vergangenheit, des Partizip Perfekt und gewisser Adjektive hat drei verschiedene Aussprachen je nach dem Klang des Konsonanten am Stammende.

1) Wenn der Stamm auf einen stimmhaften Konsonanten mit Ausnahme von [d] ausgeht, nämlich [b], [g], [l], [m], [n], [ŋ], [r], [v], [z], [ʒ], oder auf einen Vokal, wird **–ed** als [d] ausgesprochen.

KLANG DES STAMMENDES	INFINITIV	VERGANGENHEIT UND PARTIZIP PERFEKT
[b]	ebb [ɛb]	ebbed [ɛbd]
	rob [rɑb]	robbed [rɑbd]
	robe [rob]	robed [robd]
[g]	egg [ɛg]	egged [ɛgd]
	sag [sæg]	sagged [sægd]
[l]	mail [mel]	mailed [meld]
	scale [skel]	scaled [skeld]
[m]	storm [stɔrm]	stormed [stɔrmd]
	bomb [bɑm]	bombed [bɑmd]
	name [nem]	named [nemd]
[n]	tan [tæn]	tanned [tænd]
	sign [saɪn]	signed [saɪnd]
	mine [maɪn]	mined [maɪnd]
[ŋ]	hang [hæŋ]	hanged [hæŋd]
[r]	fear [fɪr]	feared [fɪrd]
	care [ker]	cared [kerd]
[v]	rev [rɛv]	revved [rɛvd]
	save [sev]	saved [sevd]
[z]	buzz [bʌz]	buzzed [bʌzd]
[ð]	smooth [smuð]	smoothed [smuðd]
	bathe [beð]	bathed [beðd]
[ʒ]	massage [mə′sɑʒ]	massaged [mə′sɑʒd]
[dʒ]	page [pedʒ]	paged [pedʒd]
Klang des Vokals	key [ki]	keyed [kid]
	sigh [saɪ]	sighed [saɪd]
	paw [pɔ]	pawed [pɔd]

23a

2) Wenn der Stamm auf einen stimmlosen Konsonanten mit Ausnahme von [t] ausgeht, nämlich: [f], [k], [p], [s], [θ], [ʃ] oder [tʃ], wird –ed als [t] ausgesprochen.

KLANG DES STAMMENDES	INFINITIV	VERGANGENHEIT UND PARTIZIP PERFEKT
[f]	loaf [lof] knife [naɪf]	loafed [loft] knifed [naɪft]
[k]	back [bæk] bake [bek]	backed [bækt] baked [bekt]
[p]	cap [kæp] wipe [waɪp]	capped [kæpt] wiped [waɪpt]
[s]	hiss [hɪs] mix [mɪks]	hissed [hɪst] mixed [mɪkst]
[θ]	lath [læθ]	lathed [læθt]
[ʃ]	mash [mæʃ]	mashed [mæʃt]
[tʃ]	match [mætʃ]	matched [mætʃt]

3) Wenn der Stamm auf einen Dentallaut ausgeht, nämlich: [t] oder [d], wird –ed als [ɪd] oder [əd] ausgesprochen.

KLANG DES STAMMENDES	INFINITIV	VERGANGENHEIT UND PARTIZIP PERFEKT
[t]	wait [wet] mate [met]	waited ['wetɪd] mated ['metɪd]
[d]	mend [mɛnd] wade [wed]	mended ['mɛndɪd] waded ['wedɪd]

Es ist zu beachten, daß die Doppelschreibung des Schlußkonsonanten nach einem einfachen betonten Vokal die Aussprache der Endung **–ed** nicht beeinflußt: **batted** ['bætɪd], **dropped** [drɒpt], **robbed** [rɒbd].

Diese Regeln gelten auch für zusammengesetzte Adjektive, die auf **–ed** enden. Für diese Adjektive ist nur die Betonung angegeben, sofern die Aussprache der beiden Bestandteile ohne die Endung **–ed** dort angegeben ist, wo sie als Stichwörter erscheinen, z.B. **o′pen-mind′ed.**

Es ist jedoch zu beachten, daß bei manchen Adjektiven, deren Stamm auf einen anderen Konsonanten als [d] oder [t] ausgeht, das **–ed** als [ɪd] ausgesprochen wird; in diesem Fall ist die volle Aussprache in phonetischer Umschrift angegeben, z.B. **blessed** ['blɛsɪd], **crabbed** ['kræbɪd].

PART TWO

English-German

A

A, a [e] *s* erster Buchstabe des englischen Alphabets; (mus) A *n*; **A flat** As *n*; **A sharp** Ais *n*

a [e], [ə] *indef art* ein || *prep* pro; **once a year** einmal im Jahr

abandon [ə'bændən] *s*—**with a.** rückhaltlos || *tr (forsake)* verlassen; *(give up)* aufgeben; *(a child)* aussetzen; *(a position)* (mil) überlassen; **a. oneself to** sich ergeben (*dat*)

abase [ə'bes] *tr* demütigen

abasement [ə'besmənt] *s* Demütigung *f*

abashed [ə'bæʃt] *adj* fassungslos

abate [ə'bet] *tr* mäßigen || *intr* nachlassen

abbess ['æbɪs] *s* Äbtissin *f*

abbey ['æbi] *s* Abtei *f*

abbot ['æbət] *s* Abt *m*

abbreviate [ə'brivɪ ‚et] *tr* abkürzen

abbreviation [ə ‚brivɪ'eʃən] *s* Abkürzung *f*

ABC's [‚e ‚bi'siz] *spl* Abc *n*

abdicate ['æbdɪ ‚ket] *tr* niederlegen; *(a right, claim)* verzichten auf (*acc*) || *intr* abdanken

abdomen ['æbdəmən] *s* Unterleib *m*

abdominal [æb'dɑmɪnəl] *adj* Unterleibs-

abduct [æb'dʌkt] *tr* entführen

abet [ə'bet] *v* (*pret & pp* **abetted**; *ger* **abetting**) *tr (a person)* aufhetzen; *(a crime)* Vorschub leisten (*dat*)

abeyance [ə'be·əns] *s*—**in a.** in der Schwebe

ab·hor [æb'hɔr] *v* (*pret & pp* **–horred**; *ger* **–horring**) *tr* verabscheuen

abhorrent [æb'hɔrənt] *adj* verhaßt

abide [ə'baɪd] *v* (*pret & pp* **abode** [ə'bod] & **abided**) *intr*—**a. by** *(an agreement)* sich halten an (*acc*); *(a promise)* halten

ability [ə'bɪlɪti] *s* Fähigkeit *f*; **to the best of one's a.** nach bestem Vermögen

abject [æb'dʒekt] *adj (servile)* unterwürfig; *(poverty)* äußerst

ablative ['æblətɪv] *s* Ablativ *m*

ablaze [ə'blez] *adj* in Flammen; **(with)** glänzend (vor *dat*); *(excited)* **(with)** erregt (vor *dat*)

able ['ebəl] *adj* fähig, tüchtig; **be a. to** *(inf)* können *(inf)*

able-bodied ['ebəl'bɑdɪd] *adj* kräftig; (mil) wehrfähig; **a. seaman** Vollmatrose *m*

ably ['ebli] *adv* mit Geschick

abnormal [æb'nɔrməl] *adj* abnorm

abnormality [‚æbnɔr'mælɪti] *s* Ungewöhnlichkeit *f*; (pathol) Mißbildung *f*

abnor'mal psychol'ogy *s* Psychopathologie *f*

aboard [ə'bord] *adv* an Bord; **all a.!** *(a ship)* alles an Bord! *(a bus, plane, train)* alles einsteigen! || *prep (a ship)* an Bord *(genit)*; *(a bus, train)* in *(dat)*

abode [ə'bod] *s* Wohnsitz *m*

abolish [ə'bɑlɪʃ] *tr* aufheben, abschaffen

abominable [ə'bɑmɪnəbəl] *adj* abscheulich

aborigines [‚æbə'rɪdʒɪ ‚niz] *spl* Ureinwohner *pl*, Urvolk *n*

abort [ə'bɔrt] *tr* (rok) vorzeitig zur Explosion bringen || *intr* fehlgebären; (fig) fehlschlagen

abortion [ə'bɔrʃən] *s* Abtreibung *f*

abortive [ə'bɔrtɪv] *adj* (fig) mißlungen; **prove a.** fehlschlagen

abound [ə'baund] *intr* reichlich vorhanden sein; **a. in** reich sein an (*dat*)

about [ə'baut] *adv* umher, herum; *(approximately)* ungefähr, etwa; **be a. to** *(inf)* im Begriff sein zu *(inf)* || *prep (around)* um (*acc*); *(concerning)* über (*acc*); *(approximately at)* gegen (*acc*)

about' face' *interj* kehrt!

about'-face' *s*—**do an a.** (fig) umschwenken; **complete a.** (fig) völliger Umschwung *m*

above [ə'bʌv] *adj* obig || *adv* oben, droben || *prep (position)* über (*dat*); *(direction)* über (*acc*); *(physically)* oberhalb *(genit)*; **a. all** vor allem

above' board' *adj & adv* ehrlich, redlich

above'-men'tioned *adj* obenerwähnt, obig

abrasion [ə'breʒən] *s* Abschleifen *n*; *(of the skin)* Abschürfung *f*

abrasive [ə'bresɪv] *adj* abschleifend; *(character)* auf die Nerven gehend || *s* Schleifmittel *n*

abreast [ə'brest] *adj & adv* nebeneinander; **keep a. of** Schritt halten mit

abridge [ə'brɪdʒ] *tr* verkürzen

abridgement [ə'brɪdʒmənt] *s* Verkürzung *f*

abroad [ə'brɔd] *adv* im Ausland; *(direction)* ins Ausland; *(out of doors)* draußen

abrogate ['æbrə ‚get] *tr* abschaffen

abrupt [ə'brʌpt] *adj (sudden)* jäh; *(curt)* schroff; *(change)* unvermittelt; *(style)* abgerissen

abscess ['æbses] *s* Geschwür *n*, Abszeß *m*

abscond [æb'skɑnd] *intr* **(with)** durchgehen (mit)

absence ['æbsəns] *s* Abwesenheit *f*; *(lack)* Mangel *m*; **in the a. of** in Ermangelung von (or *genit*)

ab'sence without' leave' *s* unerlaubte Entfernung *f* von der Truppe

absent ['æbsənt] *adj* abwesend; **be a. fehlen** || [æb'sent] *tr*—**a. oneself** (*stay away*) fernbleiben; (*go away*) sich entfernen

absentee [,æbsən'ti] *s* Abwesende *mf*

ab'sent-mind'ed *adj* geistesabwesend

absolute ['æbsə,lut] *adj* absolut

absolutely ['æbsə,lutli] *adv* absolut, völlig || ['æbsə'lutli] *adv* (*coll*) ganz bestimmt, jawohl; **a. not!** keine Rede!

absolve [æb'salv] *tr* (*from sin, an obligation*) lossprechen; (*sins*) vergeben

absorb [æb'sɔrb] *tr* aufsaugen; (*a shock*) dämpfen; (*engross*) ganz in Anspruch nehmen; **be absorbed in** vertieft sein in (*acc*)

absorbent [æb'sɔrbənt] *adj* aufsaugend **absor'bent cot'ton** *s* Verbandswatte *f*

absorb'ing *adj* (fig) packend

abstain [æb'sten] *intr* (**from**) sich enthalten (*genit*); (parl) sich der Stimme enthalten

abstention [æb'stenʃən] *s* (**from**) Enthaltung *f* (von); (parl) Stimmenthaltung *f*

abstinence ['æbstɪnəns] *s* Enthaltsamkeit *f*; (**from**) Enthaltung *f* (von)

abstinent ['æbstɪnənt] *adj* enthaltsam

abstract ['æbstrækt] *adj* abstrakt || *s* (*summary*) Abriß *m*; **in the a.** im und für sich (betrachtet) || [æb'strækt] *tr* (*the general from the specific*) abstrahieren; (*summarize*) kurz zusammenfassen; (*purloin*) entwenden

abstruse [æb'strus] *adj* dunkel

absurd [æb'sʌrd] *adj* unsinnig

absurdity [æb'sʌrdɪti] *s* Unsinn *m*

abundance [ə'bʌndəns] *s* (**of**) Fülle *f* (von), Überfluß *m* (an *dat*, von)

abundant [ə'bʌndənt] *adj* reichlich; **a. in** reich an (*dat*)

abuse [ə'bjus] *s* (*misuse*) Mißbrauch *m*; (*insult*) Beschimpfung *f*; (*physical ill-treatment*) Mißhandlung *f* || [ə'bjuz] *tr* mißbrauchen; (*insult*) beschimpfen; (*ill-treat*) mißhandeln; (*a girl*) schänden

abusive [ə'bjusɪv] *adj* mißbräuchlich; (*treatment*) beleidigend; **a. language** Schimpfworte *pl*; **become a.** ausfällig werden

abut [ə'bʌt] *v* (*pret & pp* **abutted;** *ger* **abutting**) *intr*—**a. on** grenzen an (*acc*)

abutment [ə'bʌtmənt] *s* (*of arch*) Strebepfeiler *m*; (*of bridge*) Widerlager *n*

abyss [ə'bɪs] *s* Abgrund *m*

academic [,ækə'demɪk] *adj* akademisch

academ'ic gown' *s* Talar *m*

academy [ə'kædəmi] *s* Akademie *f*

accede [æk'sid] *intr* beistimmen; **a. to** (*s.o.'s wishes*) gewähren; (*an agreement*) beitreten (*dat*); **a. to the throne** den Thron besteigen

accelerate [æk'selə,ret] *tr & intr* beschleunigen

accelerator [æk'selə,retər] *s* Gashebel *m*

accent ['æksent] *s* (*stress*) Betonung *f*; (*peculiar pronunciation*) Akzent *m* || [æk'sent] *tr* betonen

ac'cent mark' *s* Tonzeichen *n*, Akzent *m*

accentuate [æk'sentʃu,et] *tr* betonen

accept [æk'sept] *tr* annehmen; (*one's fate, blame*) auf sich [*acc*] nehmen; (*put up with*) hinnehmen; (*recognize*) anerkennen

acceptable [æk'septəbəl] *adj* annehmbar; (*pleasing*) angenehm; (*welcome*) willkommen

acceptance [æk'septəns] *s* Annahme *f*; (*recognition*) Anerkennung *f*

access ['ækses] *s* Zugang *m*; (*to a person*) Zutritt *m*; (data proc) Zugriff *m*

accessible [æk'sesɪbəl] *adj* (**to**) zugänglich (für)

accession [æk'seʃən] *s* (*to an office*) Antritt *m*; **a. to the throne** Thronbesteigung *f*

accessory [æk'sesəri] *adj* (*subordinate*) untergeordnet; (*additional*) zusätzlich || *s* Zubehörteil *n*; (*to a crime*) Teilnehmer –in *mf*; (*after the fact*) Begünstiger –in *mf*; (*before the fact*) Anstifter –in *mf*

ac'cess road' *s* Zufahrtsstraße *f*; (*on a turnpike*) Zubringerstraße *f*

accident ['æksɪdənt] *s* (*mishap*) Unfall *m*; (*chance*) Zufall *m*; **by a.** zufälligerweise; **have an a.** verunglücken

accidental [,æksɪ'dentəl] *adj* zufällig; **a. death** Unfalltod *m* || *s* (mus) Versetzungszeichen *n*

acclaim [ə'klem] *s* Beifall *m* || *tr* (*e.g., as king*) begrüßen, akklamieren

acclamation [,æklə'meʃən] *s* Beifall *m*

acclimate ['æklɪ,met] *tr* akklimatisieren || *intr* (**to**) sich gewöhnen (an *acc*)

accommodate [ə'kamə,det] *tr* (*oblige*) aushelfen (*dat*); (*have room for*) Platz haben für

accom'modating *adj* gefällig

accommodation [ə,kamə'deʃən] *s* (*convenience*) Annehmlichkeit *f*; (*adaptation, adjustment*) Anpassung *f*; (*willingness to please*) Gefälligkeit *f*; (*compromise*) Übereinkommen *n*; **accommodations** (*lodgings*) Unterkunft *f*

accompaniment [ə'kʌmpənɪmənt] *s* Begleitung *f*

accompanist [ə'kʌmpənɪst] *s* Begleiter –in *mf*

accompany [ə'kʌmpəni] *v* (*pret & pp* **-nied**) *tr* begleiten

accomplice [ə'kamplɪs] *m* Mitschuldige *mf*

accomplish [ə'kamplɪʃ] *tr* (*a task*) vollenden; (*a goal*) erreichen

accom'plished *adj* (*skilled*) ausgezeichnet

accomplishment [ə'kamplɪʃmənt] *s* (*completion*) Vollendung *f*; (*achievement*) Leistung *f*

accord [ə'kɔrd] *s* Übereinstimmung *f*; **in a. with** übereinstimmend mit; **of**

one's own a. aus eigenem Antriebe || *tr* gewähren || *intr* übereinstimmen

accordingly [ə'kɔrdɪŋli] *adv* demgemäß

accord'ing to' *prep* gemäß (*dat*), laut (*genit* or *dat*), nach (*dat*)

accordion [ə'kɔrdɪ-ən] *s* Akkordeon *m*

accost [ə'kɔst] *tr* ansprechen

account [ə'kaunt] *s* Rechnung *f*; (*narrative*) Erzählung *f*; (*report*) Bericht *m*; (*importance*) Bedeutung *f*; (*com*) Konto *n*; **by all accounts** nach allem, was man hört; **call to a.** zur Rechenschaft ziehen; **on a. of** wegen; **on no a.** auf keinen Fall; **render an a. of s.th. to s.o.** j-m Rechenschaft von etw ablegen; **settle accounts with** (*coll*) abrechnen mit; **take into a.** in Betracht ziehen

accountable [ə'kauntəbəl] *adj* (*explicable*) erklärlich; (*responsible*) (**for**) verantwortlich (für)

accountant [ə'kauntənt] *s* Rechnungsführer –in *mf*, Buchhalter –in *mf*

account'ing *s* Rechnungswesen *n*

accouterments [ə'kutərmənts] *spl* Ausrüstung *f*

accredit [ə'kredɪt] *tr* (*e.g., an ambassador*) beglaubigen; (*a school*) bestätigen; (*a story*) als wahr anerkennen; (*give credit for*) gutschreiben

accrue [ə'kru] *intr* anwachsen; (*said of interest*) auflaufen || *intr* sich anhäufen

accumulation [ə,kjumjə'leʃən] *s* Anhäufung *f*

accuracy [ˈækjərəsi] *s* Genauigkeit *f*

accurate [ˈækjərɪt] *adj* genau

accursed [ə'kʌrsɪd], [ə'kʌrst] *adj* verwünscht

accusation [,ækjə'zeʃən] *s* Anschuldigung *f*; (*jur*) Anklage *f*

accusative [ə'kjuzətɪv] *s* Akkusativ *m*

accuse [ə'kjuz] *tr* (**of**) beschuldigen (*genit*); (*jur*) (**of**) anklagen (wegen)

accustom [ə'kʌstəm] *tr* (**to**) gewöhnen (an *acc*); **become accustomed to** sich gewöhnen an (*acc*)

ace [es] *s* (aer, cards) As *n*

acetate [ˈæsɪ,tet] *s* Azetat *n*; (tex) Azetatseide *f*

ace'tic ac'id [ə'sitɪk] *s* Essigsäure *f*

acetone [ˈæsɪ,ton] *s* Azeton *n*

acet'ylene torch' [ə'setɪ,lin] *s* Schweißbrenner *m*

ache [ek] *s* Schmerz *m* || *intr* schmerzen; **a. for** (coll) sich sehnen nach

achieve [ə'tʃiv] *tr* erlangen; (*success*) erzielen; (*a goal*) erreichen

achievement [ə'tʃivmənt] *s* (*something accomplished*) Leistung *f*; (*great deed*) Großtat *f*; (*heroic deed*) Heldentat *f*; (*of one's object*) Erreichung *f*

achieve'ment test' *s* Leistungsprüfung *f*

Achil'les' ten'don [ə'kɪlis] *s* Achillessehne *f*

acid [ˈæsɪd] *adj* sauer || *s* Säure *f*

acidity [ə'sɪdɪti] *s* Säure *f*, Schärfe *f*; (*of the stomach*) Magensäure *f*

ac'id test' *s* (fig) Feuerprobe *f*

acidy [ˈæsɪdi] *adj* säuerlich, säurig

acknowledge [æk'nɑlɪdʒ] *tr* anerken-

nen; (*admit*) zugeben; (*receipt*) bestätigen

acknowledgment [æk'nɑlɪdʒmənt] *s* Anerkennung *f*; (*e.g., of a letter*) Bestätigung *f*

acme [ˈækmi] *s* Höhepunkt *m*

acne [ˈækni] *s* (pathol) Akne *f*

acolyte [ˈækə,laɪt] *s* Ministrant *m*

acorn [ˈekɔrn] *s* Eichel *f*

acoustic(al) [ə'kustɪk(əl)] *adj* akustisch, Gehör–, Hör–

acous'tical tile' *s* Dämmplatte *f*

acoustics [ə'kustɪks] *s & spl* Akustik *f*

acquaint [ə'kwent] *tr*—**a. s.o. with s.th.** j-n mit etw bekanntmachen, j-m etw mitteilen; **be acquainted with** kennen; **get acquainted with** kennenlernen

acquaintance [ə'kwentəns] *s* Bekanntschaft *f*; (*person*) Bekannte *mf*

acquiesce [,ækwɪ'es] *intr* (**in**) einwilligen (in *acc*)

acquiescence [,ækwɪ'esəns] *s* (**in**) Einwilligung *f* (in *acc*)

acquire [ə'kwaɪr] *tr* erwerben, sich [*dat*] anschaffen; **a. a taste for** Geschmack gewinnen an (*dat*)

acquisition [,ækwɪ'zɪʃən] *s* Anschaffung *f*

acquisitive [ə'kwɪzɪtɪv] *adj* gewinnsüchtig

acquit [ə'kwɪt] *v* (*pret & pp* **acquitted**; *ger* **acquitting**) *tr* freisprechen

acquittal [ə'kwɪtəl] *s* Freispruch *m*

acre [ˈekər] *s* Acre *m*

acreage [ˈekrɪdʒ] *s* Fläche *f*

acrid [ˈækrɪd] *adj* beißend, scharf

acrobat [ˈækrə,bæt] *s* Akrobat –in *mf*

acrobatic [,ækrə'bætɪk] *adj* akrobatisch || **acrobatics** *spl* Akrobatik *f*; (aer) Kunstflug *m*

acronym [ˈækrənɪm] *s* Akronym *n*

across [ə'krɔs] *adv* herüber, hinüber; **a. from** gegenüber (*dat*); **ten feet a.** zehn Fuß im Durchmesser || *prep* (quer) über (*acc*); (*on the other side of*) jenseits (*genit*); **come a.** (*a person*) treffen; (*a thing*) stoßen auf (*acc*); **come a. with it!** (say it!) heraus damit!; (*give it!*) her damit!

across'-the-board' *adj* allgemein

acrostic [ə'krɔstɪk] *s* Akrostichon *n*

act [ækt] *s* Tat *f*, Handlung *f*; (coll) Theater *n*; (jur) Gesetz *n*; (telv) Nummer *f*; (theat) Akt *m*, Aufzug *m*; **catch in the act** auf frischer Tat ertappen || *tr* spielen; || *intr* (*take action*) handeln; (*function*) wirken; (*behave*) (**like**) sich benehmen (wie); (theat & fig) Theater spielen; **act as** dienen als; **act as if** so tun, als ob; **act on** (*follow*) befolgen; (*affect*) (ein)wirken auf (*acc*)

act'ing *adj* stellvertretend; (theat) Bühnen– || *s* (*as an art*) Schauspielkunst *f*

action [ˈækʃən] *s* Tätigkeit *f*, Tat *f*; (*effect*) Wirkung *f*; (jur) Klage *f*; (mil) Gefecht *n*; (tech) Wirkungsweise *f*; **go into a.** eingreifen; **put out of a.** (mil) außer Gefecht setzen; (tech) außer Betrieb setzen; **see a.** (mil) an der Front kämpfen

activate ['æktı‚vet] *tr* aktivieren; (mil) aufstellen

active ['æktıv] *adj* tätig; (*member*) ordentlich; (gram, mil) aktiv

ac'tive voice' *s* Tätigkeitsform *f*

activist ['æktıvıst] *s* Aktivist –in *mf*

activity [æk'trvıti] *s* Tätigkeit *f*

act' of God' *s* höhere Gewalt *f*

act' of war' *s* Angriffshandlung *f*

actor ['æktər] *s* Schauspieler *m*

actress ['æktrıs] *s* Schauspielerin *f*

actual ['ækt/υ-əl] *adj* wirklich

actually ['ækt/υ-əli] *adv* (*really*) wirklich; (*as a matter of fact*) eigentlich

actuary ['ækt/υ‚εri] *s* Aktuar –in *mf*

actuate ['ækt/υ‚et] *tr* in Bewegung setzen; (*incite*) antreiben

acumen [ə'kjumən] *s* Scharfsinn *m*

acupuncture ['ækjə‚pʌŋkt/ər] *s* Akupunktur *f*

acute [ə'kjut] *adj* (*stage, appendicitis*) akut; (*pain*) scharf; (*need*) vordringlich; (*vision*) scharf; (*hearing*) fein; (*problem*) brennend; (*shortage*) bedenklich; (*angle*) spitz

A.D. *abbr* n. Chr. (*nach Christus*)

ad [æd] *s* (coll) Anzeige *f*; **put an ad in the papers** inserieren

adage ['ædıdʒ] *s* Sprichwort *n*

adamant ['ædəmənt] *adj* unnachgiebig

Ad'am's ap'ple ['ædəmz] *s* Adamsapfel *m*

adapt [ə'dæpt] *tr* (to) anpassen (*dat* or an *acc*); **a. to the stage** für die Bühne bearbeiten; **a. to the screen** verfilmen ‖ *intr* sich anpassen

adaptation [‚ædæp'te/ən] *s* (*adjustment*) (to) Anpassung *f* (an *acc*); (*reworking, rewriting*) (for) Bearbeitung *f* (für)

adapter [ə'dæptər] *s* Zwischenstück *n*; (elec) Zwischenstecker *m*

add [æd] *tr* hinzufügen; (math) addieren; **add** (*e.g., 10%*) **to the price** auf den Preis aufschlagen; **add up** zusammenrechnen ‖ *intr* (math) addieren; **add to** (*in number*) vermehren; (*in size*) vergrößern; **add up** (coll) stimmen; **add up to** betragen

adder ['ædər] *s* Natter *f*, Otter *f*

addict ['ædıkt] *s* Süchtige *mf* ‖ [ə'dıkt] *tr—a. oneself to* sich ergeben (*dat*)

addict'ed *adj* ergeben; **a. to drugs** rauschgiftsüchtig

addiction [ə'dık/ən] *s* (to) Sucht *f* (nach)

add'ing machine' *s* Addiermaschine *f*

addition [ə'dı/ən] *s* Hinzufügung *f*, Zusatz *m*; (*to a family, possessions*) Zuwachs *m*; (*to a building*) Anbau *m*; (math) Addition *f*; **in a.** außerdem; **in a. to** außer

additional [ə'dı/ənəl] *adj* zusätzlich

additive ['ædıtıv] *s* Zusatz *m*

address [ə'dres], ['ædres] *s* Adresse *f*, Anschrift *f* ‖ ['ædres] *s* Rede *f*; **deliver an a.** e–e Rede halten ‖ *tr* (*a letter*) (to) adressieren (an *acc*); (*words, a question*) (to) richten (an *acc*); (*an audience*) e–e Ansprache halten an (*acc*)

adduce [ə'd(j)us] *tr* anführen

adenoids ['ædə‚nɔıdz] *spl* Polypen *pl*

adept [ə'dept] *adj* (**in**) geschickt (in *dat*)

adequate ['ædıkwıt] *adj* angemessen; (**to**) ausreichend (für)

adhere [æd'hır] *intr* (**to**) haften (an *dat*); (fig) (**to**) festhalten (an *dat*)

adherence [æd'hırəns] *s* (**to**) Festhalten *n* (an *dat*); (fig) (**to**) Festhalten *n* (an *dat*), Beharren *n* (bei)

adherent [æd'hırənt] *s* Anhänger –in *mf*

adhesion [æd'hiʒən] *s* (*sticking*) Ankleben *n*; (*loyalty*) Anhänglichkeit *f*; (pathol, phys) Adhäsion *f*

adhesive [æd'hısıv] *adj* anklebend ‖ *s* Klebemittel *n*, Klebstoff *m*

adhe'sive tape' *s* Heftpflaster *m*

adieu [ə'd(j)u] *s* (**adieus** & **adieux**) Lebewohl *n* ‖ *interj* lebe wohl!

adjacent [ə'dʒesənt] *adj* (**to**) angrenzend (an *acc*); (*angles*) Neben-

adjective ['ædʒıktıv] *s* Eigenschaftswort *n*, Adjektiv *n*

adjoin [ə'dʒɔın] *tr* angrenzen an (*acc*) ‖ *intr* angrenzen, naheliegen

adjoin'ing *adj* angrenzend; **a. rooms** Nebenzimmer *pl*

adjourn [ə'dʒʌrn] *tr* vertagen ‖ *intr* sich vertagen

adjournment [ə'dʒʌrnmənt] *s* Vertagung *f*

adjudge [ə'dʒʌdʒ] *tr* (*a prize*) zusprechen; **a. s.o. guilty** j–n für schuldig erklären

adjudicate [ə'dʒudı‚ket] *tr* gerichtlich entscheiden

adjunct ['ædʒʌŋkt] *s* (**to**) Zusatz *m* (zu)

adjust [ə'dʒʌst] *tr* (*to the right position*) einstellen; (*to an alternate position*) verstellen; (*fit*) (**to**) anpassen (*dat* or an *acc*); (*differences*) ausgleichen; (*an account*) bereinigen; (ins) berechnen ‖ *intr* (**to**) sich anpassen (*dat* or an *acc*)

adjustable [ə'dʒʌstəbəl] *adj* verstellbar

adjuster [ə'dʒʌstər] *s* (ins) Schadenssachverständiger –in *mf*

adjustment [ə'dʒʌstmənt] *s* (**to**) Anpassung *f* (*dat* or an *acc*); (*of an account*) Bereinigung *f*; (ins) Berechnung *f*; (mach) Einstellung *f*

adjutant ['ædʒətənt] *s* Adjutant *m*

ad-lib [‚æd'lıb] *v* (*pret* & *pp*) **–libbed**; *ger* **–libbing**) *tr* & *intr* improvisieren

ad-man ['ædmən] *s* (**–men**) Werbefachmann *m*; (*writer*) Werbetexter *m*

administer [æd'mınıstər] *tr* verwalten; (*help*) leisten; (*medicine*) eingeben; (*an oath*) abnehmen; (*punishment*) verhängen; (*a sacrament*) spenden; **a. justice** Recht sprechen ‖ *intr—a. to* dienen (*dat*)

administration [æd‚mınıs'tre/ən] *s* (*of an institution*) Verwaltung *f*; (*of an official*) Amtsführung *f*; (*government*) Regierung *f*; (*period of government*) Regierungszeit *f*; (*of a president*) Amtszeit *f*; (*of tests*) Durchführung *f*; (*of an oath*) Abnahme *f*; (*of a sacrament*) Spendung *f*; **a. of justice** Rechtspflege *f*

administrator [æd'mɪnɪs‚tretər] s Verwalter –in *mf*

admiral ['ædmɪrəl] s Admiral *m*

admiration [‚ædmɪ're∫ən] s Bewunderung *f*

admire [æd'maɪr] *tr* (**for**) bewundern (wegen)

admirer [æd'maɪrər] s Bewunderer –in *mf*; (*of a woman*) Verehrer *m*

admissible [æd'mɪsɪbəl] *adj* (& *jur*) zulässig

admission [æd'mɪ∫ən] s (*entry*) Eintritt *m*; (*permission to enter*) Eintrittserlaubnis *f*; (*entry fee*) Eintrittsgebühr *f*; (*of facts*) Anerkennung *f*; (*of guilt*) Eingeständis *n*; (*enrollment*) (**to, into**) Aufnahme *f* (in *acc*); (**to**) (*a profession*) Zulassung *f* (zu)

ad‧mit [æd'mɪt] *v* (*pret & pp* **-mitted;** *ger* **-mitting**) *tr* (hin)einlassen; (**to**) (*a hospital, a society*) aufnehmen (in *acc*); (**to**) (*a profession*) zulassen (zu); (*accept*) anerkennen; (*concede*) zugeben; (*a crime, guilt*) eingestehen || *intr*—**a. of** zulassen

admittance [æd'mɪtəns] s Eintritt *m*; **no a.** Eintritt verboten

admittedly [æd'mɪtɪdli] *adv* anerkanntermaßen

admixture [æd'mɪkst∫ər] s Beimischung *f*

admonish [æd'mɑnɪ∫] *tr* ermahnen

admonition [‚ædmə'nɪ∫ən] s Ermahnung *f*

ado [ə'du] s Getue *n*; **much ado about nothing** viel Lärm um nichts; **without further ado** ohne weiteres

adobe [ə'dobi] s Lehmstein *m*

adolescence [‚ædə'lesəns] s Jugendalter *n*

adolescent [‚ædə'lesənt] *adj* jugendlich || s Jugendliche *mf*

adopt [ə'dɑpt] *tr* (*a child*) adoptieren; (*an idea*) annehmen

adopt′ed child′ s Adoptivkind *n*

adoption [ə'dɑp∫ən] s (*of a child*) Adoption *f*; (*of an idea*) Annahme *f*

adorable [ə'dorəbəl] *adj* anbetungswürdig; (*coll*) entzückend

adore [ə'dor] *tr* anbeten; (*coll*) entzückend finden

adorn [ə'dɔrn] *tr* schmücken

adornment [ə'dɔrnmənt] s Schmuck *m*

adrenaline [ə'drenəlɪn] s Adrenalin *n*

adrift [ə'drɪft] *adj*—**be a.** treiben; (*fig*) weder aus noch ein wissen

adroit [ə'drɔɪt] *adj* geschickt, gewandt

adulation [‚ædjə'le∫ən] s Schmeichelei *f*

adult [ə'dʌlt], ['ædʌlt] *adj* erwachsen || s Erwachsene *mf*

adult′ educa′tion s Erwachsenenbildung *f*

adulterate [ə'dʌltə‚ret] *tr* verfälschen; (*e.g., wine*) panschen

adulterer [ə'dʌltərər] s Ehebrecher *m*

adulteress [ə'dʌltərɪs] s Ehebrecherin *f*

adulterous [ə'dʌltərəs] *adj* ehebrecherisch

adultery [ə'dʌltəri] s Ehebruch *m*

advance [æd'væns] s Fortschritt *m*; (*money*) Vorschuß *m*; **in a.** im vor-

aus; **make advances to** (*e.g., a girl*) Annäherungsversuche machen bei || *tr* vorrücken; (*a clock*) vorstellen; (*money*) vorschießen; (*a date*) aufschieben; (*an opinion*) vorbringen; (*s.o.'s interests*) fördern; (*in rank*) befördern || *intr* vorrücken

advancement [æd'vænsmənt] s Fortschritt *m*; (*promotion*) Beförderung *f*; (*of a cause*) Förderung *f*

advance′ pay′ment s Voraus(be)zahlung *f*

advantage [æd'væntɪdʒ] s Vorteil *m*; **be of a.** nützlich sein; **take a. of** ausnutzen; **to a.** vorteilhaft

advantageous [‚ædvən'tedʒəs] *adj* vorteilhaft

advent ['ædvent] s Ankunft *f*; **Advent** Advent *m*, Adventszeit *f*

adventure [æd'vent∫ər] s Abenteuer *n*

adventurer [æd'vent∫ərər] s Abenteurer *m*

adventuress [æd'vent∫ərɪs] s Abenteurerin *f*

adventurous [æd'vent∫ərəs] *adj* (*person*) abenteuerlustig; (*undertaking*) abenteuerlich

adverb ['ædvʌrb] s Umstandswort *n*

adverbial [æd'vʌrbɪəl] *adj* adverbial

adversary ['ædvər‚seri] s Gegner –in *mf*

adverse [æd'vʌrs], ['ædvʌrs] *adj* ungünstig, nachteilig

adversity [æd'vʌrsɪti] s Unglück *n*, Not *f*

advertise ['ædvər‚taɪz] *tr* Reklame machen für || *intr* Reklame machen; **a. for** durch Inserat suchen

advertisement [‚ædvər'taɪzmənt], [æd'vʌrtɪsmənt] s Anzeige *f*, Reklame *f*

ad′vertising a′gency s Reklamebüro *n*

ad′vertising campaign′ s Werbfeldzug *m*

ad′vertising man′ s (*solicitor*) Anzeigenvermittler *m*; (*writer*) Werbetexter *m*

advice [æd'vaɪs] s Rat *m*, Ratschlag *m*; **a piece of a.** ein Rat *m*; **get a. from** sich [*dat*] Rat holen bei; **give a. to** raten (*dat*)

advisable [æd'vaɪzəbəl] *adj* ratsam

advise [æd'vaɪz] *tr* raten (*dat*); (**of**) benachrichtigen (von); (**on**) beraten (über *acc*); **a. s.o. against s.th.** j–m von etw abraten

advisement [æd'vaɪzmənt] s—**take under a.** in Betracht ziehen

adviser [æd'vaɪzər] s Berater –in *mf*

advisory [æd'vaɪzəri] *adj* Beratungs-

advi′sory board′ s Beirat *m*

advocate ['ædvə‚ket] s Fürsprecher –in *mf*; (*jur*) Advokat –in *mf* || *tr* befürworten

aeon ['i‧ən], ['i‧ɑn] s Äon *m*

aerial ['erɪ‧əl] *adj* Luft– || s Antenne *f*

aerodynamic [‚erodaɪ'næmɪk] *adj* aerodynamisch || **aerodynamics** s Aerodynamik *f*

aeronautic(al) [‚erə'nɔtɪk(əl)] *adj* aeronautisch || **aeronautics** s Aeronautik *f*, Luftfahrt *f*

aerosol ['erə‚sɔl] s Sprühdose *f*

aerospace ['erəspes] *adj* Raum–
aesthetic [es'θetɪk] *adj* ästhetisch ||
  aesthetics *s* Ästhetik *f*
afar [ə'faɪ] *adv*—**a.** off weit weg; **from
  a.** von weit her
affable ['æfəbəl] *adj* leutselig
affair [ə'fer] *s* Angelegenheit *f*; (*event,
  performance*) Veranstaltung *f*; (*romantic involvement*) Verhältnis *n*
affect [ə'fekt] *tr* (*influence*) berühren;
  (*injuriously*) angreifen; (*pretend*)
  vortäuschen
affectation [,æfek'teʃən] *s* Geziertheit
  f
affect'ed *adj* affektiert
affection [ə'fekʃən] *s* (*for*) Zuneigung
  f (*zu*); (*pathol*) Erkrankung *f*
affectionate [ə'fekʃənɪt] *adj* liebevoll
affidavit [,æfɪ'devɪt] *s* (*schriftliche*)
  eidesstattliche Erklärung *f*
affiliate [ə'fɪlɪ,et] *s* Zweiggesellschaft
  f || *tr* angliedern || *intr* sich anglie-
  dern
affinity [ə'fɪnɪti] *s* Verwandtschaft *f*
affirm [ə'fʌrm] *tr & intr* behaupten
affirmation [,æfər'meʃən] *s* Behauptung *f*
affirmative [ə'fʌrmətɪv] *adj* bejahend
  || *s* Bejahung *f*; **in the a.** bejahend,
  positiv
affix [ə'fɪks] *tr* (*a seal*) aufdrücken;
  (**to**) befestigen (**an** *dat*), anheften (**an**
  acc)
afflict [ə'flɪkt] *tr* plagen; **afflicted with**
  erkrankt an (*dat*)
affliction [ə'flɪkʃən] *s* Elend *n*, Leiden
  n; (*grief*) Betrübnis *f*
affluence ['æflu·əns] *s* Wohlstand *m*
affluent ['æflu·ənt] *adj* wohlhabend
af'fluent socie'ty *s* Wohlstandsgesell-
  schaft *f*
afford [ə'fɔrd] *tr* (*confer*) gewähren;
  (*time*) erübrigen; (*be able to meet
  the expense of*) sich [*dat*] leisten
affront [ə'frʌnt] *s* Beleidigung *f* || *tr*
  beleidigen
afire [ə'faɪr] *adj & adv* in Flammen
aflame [ə'flem] *adj & adv* in Flammen
afloat [ə'flot] *adj* flott, schwimmend;
  (*awash*) überschwemmt; (*at sea*) auf
  dem Meer; (*in circulation*) im Umlauf; **keep a.** (& fig) über Wasser
  halten; **stay a.** (& fig) sich über
  Wasser halten
afoot [ə'fut] *adj & adv* (*on foot*) zu
  Fuß; (*in progress*) im Gange
aforesaid [ə'for,sed] *adj* vorerwähnt
afoul [ə'faul] *adj* (*entangled*) ver-
  wickelt || *adv*—**run a. of the law** mit
  dem Gesetz in Konflikt geraten
afraid [ə'fred] *adj* ängstlich; **be a.** (**of**)
  (*inf*) sich scheuen zu (*inf*)
afresh [ə'freʃ] *adv* aufs neue
Africa ['æfrɪkə] *s* Afrika *n*
African ['æfrɪkən] *adj* afrikanisch ||
  s Afrikaner –in *mf*
aft [æft] *adv* (*nach*) achtern
after ['æftər] *adj* später; (*naut*) achter
  || *adv* nachher, darauf || *prep* nach
  (*dat*); **a. all** immerhin; **a. that** da-
  rauf; **be a. s.o.** hinter j–m her sein ||
  conj nachdem
af'ter-din'ner speech' *s* Tischrede *f*

af'tereffect' *s* Nachwirkung *f*; **have an
  a.** nachwirken
af'terlife' *s* (*later life*) zukünftiges
  Leben *n*; (*life after death*) Leben *n*
  nach dem Tode
aftermath ['æftər,mæθ] *s* Nach-
  wirkungen *pl*; (*agr*) Grummet *n*
af'ternoon' *s* Nachmittag *m*; **in the a.**
  am Nachmittag, nachmittags; **this a.**
  heute nachmittag
af'ter-shave' lo'tion *s* Rasierwasser *n*
af'tertaste' *s* Nachgeschmack *m*
af'terthought' *s* nachträglicher Einfall
  m
afterward(s) ['æftərwərd(z)] *adv* später
af'terworld' *s* Jenseits *n*
again [ə'gen] *adv* wieder, noch einmal;
  half as much a. anderthalbmal so
  viel; **what's his name a.?** wie heißt
  er doch schnell?
against [ə'genst] *prep* gegen (*acc*); **a.
  it** dagegen; **a. the rules** regelwidrig;
  be up a. it (coll) in der Klemme sein
age [edʒ] *s* Alter *n*, Lebensalter *n*;
  (*period of history*) Zeitalter *n*; **at the
  age of** mit, im Alter von; **come of
  age** mündig werden; **for ages** e–e
  Ewigkeit; **of age** volljährig; **of the
  same age** gleichaltrig; **twenty years
  of age** zwanzig Jahre alt || *tr* alt
  machen; (*wine*) ablagern || *intr*
  altern; (*said of wine*) lagern
aged [edʒd] *adj* alt, e.g., **a. three** drei
  Jahre alt || ['edʒɪd] *adj* bejahrt
age' lim'it *s* Altersgrenze *f*
agency ['edʒənsi] *s* (*instrumentality*)
  Vermittlung *f*; (*activity*) Tätigkeit
  f; (*adm*) Behörde *f*; (*com*) Agentur *f*
agenda [ə'dʒendə] *s* Tagesordnung *f*
agent ['edʒənt] *s* Handelnde *mf*; (*biol,
  chem*) Agens *n*; (*com*) Agent –in *mf*
agglomeration [ə,glamə'reʃən] *s* Anhäufung *f*
aggravate ['ægrə,vet] *tr* erschweren,
  verschärfen; (*coll*) ärgern
aggravation [,ægrə've'ʃən] *s* Erschwe-
  rung *f*, Verschärfung *f*; (*coll*) Ärger
  m
aggregate ['ægrɪ,get] *adj* gesamt || *s*
  Aggregat *n*; **in the a.** im ganzen || *tr*
  anhäufen
aggression [ə'greʃən] *s* Agression *f*
aggressive [ə'gresɪv] *adj* aggressiv
aggressor [ə'gresər] *s* Aggressor *m*
aggrieved [ə'grivd] *adj* (*saddened*) betrübt; (*jur*) geschädigt
aghast [ə'gæst] *adj* entsetzt
agile ['ædʒɪl] *adj* flink; (*mind*) rege
agility [ə'dʒɪlɪti] *s* Flinkheit *f*; (*of the
  mind*) Regsamkeit *f*
agitate ['ædʒɪ,tet] *tr* hin und her be-
  wegen; (*fig*) beunruhigen || *intr* agi-
  tieren
agitator ['ædʒɪ,tetər] *s* Unruhestifter
  –in *mf*; (*in a washer*) Rührapparat *m*
aglow [ə'glo] *adj & adv* (er)glühend
agnostic [æg'nɑstɪk] *adj* agnostisch ||
  s Agnostiker –in *mf*
ago [ə'go] *adv* vor (*dat*), e.g., **a year
  ago** vor e–m Jahr; **long ago** vor langer Zeit
agog [ə'gag] *adv* gespannt, erpicht
agonize ['ægə,naɪz] *intr* sich quälen

ag′onizing adj qualvoll
agony [′ægəni] s Qual f; (death struggle) Todeskampf m
agrarian [ə′grɛrɪ·ən] adj landwirtschaftlich, agrarisch
agree [ə′gri] intr übereinstimmen; a. on (or upon) sich einigen über (acc); a. to zustimmen (dat); a. to (inf) übereinkommen zu (inf); a. with (& gram) übereinstimmen mit; (affect one's health) bekommen (dat)
agreeable [ə′gri·əbəl] adj angenehm
agreed′ interj abgemacht!, einverstanden!
agreement [ə′grimənt] s Abkommen n, Vereinbarung f; (contract) Vertrag m; (& gram) Übereinstimmung f
agriculture [′ægrɪ‚kʌltʃər] s Landwirtschaft f, Ackerbau m
aground [ə′graʊnd] adv gestrandet; run a. stranden, auf Grund laufen
ahead [ə′hɛd] adj & adv in (the front) vorn; (to the front) nach vorn; (in advance) voraus; (forward) vorwärts; a. of vor (dat); get a. vorwärtskommen; go a. vorangehen; go a.! los!; go a. with fortfahren mit; look a. an die Zukunft denken
ahoy [ə′hɔɪ] interj ahoi!
aid [ed] s Hilfe f, Beihilfe f ‖ tr helfen (dat); aid and abet Vorschub leisten (dat)
aide [ed] s Gehilfe m
aide-de-camp [′ɛddə′kæmp] s (aides-de-camp) Adjutant m
ail [el] tr schmerzen; what ails you? was fehlt Ihnen? ‖ intr (have pain) Schmerzen haben; (be ill) erkrankt sein
ail′ing adj leidend, kränklich
ailment [′elmənt] s Leiden n
aim [em] s Ziel n; (fig) Ziel n, Zweck m; is your aim good? zielen Sie gut?; take aim zielen ‖ tr (a gun, words) (at) richten auf (acc); aim to (inf) beabsichtigen zu (inf) ‖ intr zielen; aim at (& fig) zielen auf (acc); aim for streben nach
aimless [′emlɪs] adj ziellos, planlos
air [ɛr] s Luft f; (mus) Melodie f; be on the air (an announcer) senden; (a program) gesendet werden; be up in the air (fig) in der Luft hängen; by air per Flugzeug; go off the air die Sendung beenden; go on the air die Sendung beginnen; in the open air im Freien; put on airs groß tun; walk on air sich wie im Himmel fühlen ‖ tr lüften
air′base′ s Flugstützpunkt m
airborne [′ɛr‚bɔrn] adj aufgestiegen; a. troops Luftlandetruppen pl
air′brake′ s Druckluftbremse f
air′-condi′tion tr klimatisieren
air′ condi′tioner s Klimaanlage f
air′ cov′er s Luftsicherung f
air′craft′ s (pl aircraft) Flugzeug n
air′craft car′rier s Flugzeugträger m
air′ cur′rent s Luftströmung f
air′ fare′ s Flugpreis m
air′field′ s Flugplatz m
air′ force′ s Luftstreitkräfte pl
air′ing s Lüftung f

air′ lane′ s Flugschneise f
air′lift′ s Luftbrücke f ‖ tr auf dem Luftwege transportieren
air′line(s)′ s Luftverkehrsgesellschaft f
air′line pi′lot s Flugkapitän m
air′lin′er s Verkehrsflugzeug n
air′mail′ s Luftpost f
air′-mail let′ter s Luftpostbrief m
air′-mail stamp′ s Luftpostbriefmarke f
air′plane′ s Flugzeug n
air′ pock′et s Luftloch n
air′ pollu′tion s Luftverunreinigung f
air′port′ s Flughafen m, Flugplatz m
air′ raid′ s Fliegerangriff m
air′-raid drill′ s Luftschutzübung f
air′-raid shel′ter s Luftschutzraum m
air′-raid war′den s Luftschutzwart m
air′-raid warn′ing s Fliegeralarm m
air′ recon′naissance s Luftaufklärung f
air′show′ s Flugvorführung f
air′sick′ adj luftkrank
air′sleeve′, air′sock′ s Windsack m
air′strip′ s Start- und Landestreifen m
air′ suprem′acy s Luftherrschaft f
air′tight′ adj luftdicht
air′ time′ s (rad, telv) Sendezeit f
air′-traffic control′ s Flugsicherung f
air′waves′ spl Rundfunk m; on the a. im Rundfunk
air′way′ s Luft(verkehrs)linie f
air′wor′thy adj lufttüchtig
airy [′ɛri] adj (room) luftig; (lively) lebhaft; (flippant) leichtsinnig
aisle [aɪl] s Gang m; (archit) Seitenschiff n
ajar [ə′dʒɑr] adj angelehnt
akimbo [ə′kɪmbo] adj—with arms a. die Arme in die Hüften gestemmt
akin [ə′kɪn] adj verwandt; a. to ähnlich (dat)
alabaster [′ælə‚bæstər] s Alabaster m
alacrity [ə′lækrɪti] s Bereitwilligkeit f
alarm [ə′lɑrm] s Alarm m; (sudden fear) Bestürzung f; (apprehension) Unruhe f ‖ tr alarmieren
alarm′ clock′ s Wecker m
alas [ə′læs] interj o weh!
Albania [æl′beni·ə] s Albanien n
Albanian [æl′beni·ən] adj albanisch ‖ s Alban(i)er –in mf
albatross [′ælbə‚trɔs] s Albatros m
album [′ælbəm] s Album n
albumen [æl′bjumən] s Eiweiß n
alchemy [′ælkɪmi] s Alchimie f
alcohol [′ælkə‚hɔl] s Alkohol m
alcoholic [‚ælkə′hɑlɪk] adj alkoholisch ‖ s Alkoholiker –in mf
alcove [′ælkov] s Alkoven m
alder [′ɔldər] s (bot) Erle f
al′der·man s (–men) Stadtrat m
ale [el] s Ale n, englisches Bier n
alert [ə′lʌrt] adj wachsam ‖ s (state of readiness) Alarmbereitschaft f; on the a. alarmbereit; (fig) auf der Hut ‖ tr alarmieren
alfalfa [æl′fælfə] s Luzerne f
algae [′ældʒi] spl Algen pl
algebra [′ældʒɪbrə] s Algebra f
Algeria [æl′dʒɪrɪ·ə] s Algerien n
Algerian [æl′dʒɪrɪ·ən] adj algerisch ‖ s Algerier –in mf
Algiers [æl′dʒɪrz] s Algier n

alias ['elɪ·əs] *adv* alias, sonst...genannt || *s* Deckname *m*

ali·bi ['ælɪ ,baɪ] *s* (–bis) Alibi *n*; (*excuse*) Ausrede *f*

alien ['eljən], ['elɪ·ə] *adj* fremd || *s* Fremde *mf*, Ausländer –in *mf*

alienate ['eljə ,net], ['elɪ·ə ,net] *tr* entfremden; (*jur*) übertragen

alight [ə'laɪt] *v* (*pret & pp* **alighted &alit** [ə'lɪt]) *intr* aussteigen; (*said of a bird*) (**on**) sich niederlassen (auf *dat* or *acc*); (aer) landen

align [ə'laɪn] *tr* (**with**) ausrichten (nach); (aut) einstellen; **a. oneself with** sich anschließen an (**acc**) || *intr* —a. with sich ausrichten nach

alignment [ə'laɪnmənt] *s* Ausrichten *n*; (pol) Ausrichtung *f*; **bring into a.** gleichschalten; **out of a.** schlecht ausgerichtet

alike [ə'laɪk] *adj* gleich, ähnlich; **look a.** sich [*dat*] ähnlich sehen; (*resemble completely*) gleich aussehen

alimony ['ælɪ ,moni] *s* Unterhaltskosten *pl*

alive [ə'laɪv] *adj* lebendig; (*vivacious*) lebhaft; **keep a.** am Leben bleiben; **keep s.o. a.** j–n am Leben erhalten

alka·li ['ælkə ,laɪ] *s* (–lis & –lies) Laugensalz *n*, Alkali *n*

alkaline ['ælkə ,laɪn] *adj* alkalisch

all [əl] *adj* all, ganz; **all day long** den ganzen Tag; **all kinds of** allerlei; **all the time** fortwährend; **for all that** trotzdem || *adv* ganz, völlig; **all along** schon immer; **at once** auf einmal; **all gone alie; all in** (coll) völlig erschöpft; **all over** (*everywhere*) überall; (*ended*) ganz vorbei; **all right** gut, schön; **all the better** um so besser; **all the same** dennoch; **not be all there** (coll) nicht ganz richtig im Kopf sein || *s*—after all schließlich; **all in all** im großen und ganzen; **and all** gesamt, e.g., he went, family and **all** er ging mit gesamter Familie; **in all** insgesamt; **not at all** überhaupt nicht, gar nicht || *indef pron* alle; (*everything*) alles

all'-around' *adj* vielseitig

allay [ə'le] *tr* beschwichtigen; (*hunger, thirst*) stillen

all'-clear' *s* Entwarnung *f*

allege [ə'ledʒ] *tr* behaupten; (*advance as an excuse*) vorgeben

alleged' *adj* angeblich, mutmaßlich

allegiance [ə'lidʒəns] *s* Treue *f*

allegoric(al) [,ælɪ'gɔrɪk(əl)] *adj* allegorisch

allegory ['ælɪ ,gori] *s* Allegorie *f*

allergic [ə'lɑrdʒɪk] *adj* allergisch

allergy ['ælərdʒɪ] *s* Allergie *f*

alleviate [ə'livɪ ,et] *tr* lindern

alley ['ælɪ] *s* Gasse *f*; (*for bowling*) Kegelbahn *f*

alliance [ə'laɪ·əns] *s* Bündnis *n*

allied' *adj* (*field*) benachbart; (*science*) verwandt; (mil, pol) alliiert

alligator ['ælɪ ,getər] *s* Alligator *m*

all'-inclu'sive *adj* Pauschal-

alliteration [ə ,lɪtə're/ən] *s* Stabreim *m*, Alliteration *f*

all'-know'ing *adj* allwissend

allocate ['ælə ,ket] *tr* zuteilen

al·lot [ə'lɑt] (*pret & pp* **–lotted; ger–lotting**) *tr* zuteilen, austeilen

all'-out' *adj* vollkommen, total

allow [ə'lau] *tr* erlauben, gestatten; (*admit*) zugeben; (*e.g., a discount*) gewähren; **be allowed to** (*inf*) dürfen (*inf*) || *intr*—a. for bedenken

allowable [ə'lau·əbəl] *adj* zulässig

allowance [ə'lau·əns] *s* (*tolerance*) Duldung *f*; (*permission*) Erlaubnis *f*; (*ration*) Zuteilung *f*, Ration *f*; (*pocket money*) Taschengeld *n*; (*discount*) Abzug *m*; (*salary for a particular expense*) Zuschuß *m*, Zulage *f*; (*for groceries*) Wirtschaftsgeld *n*; (*mach*) Toleranz *f*; **make a. for** berücksichtigen

alloy ['ælɔɪ] *s* Legierung *f* || [ə'lɔɪ] *tr* legieren

all'-pow'erful *adj* allmächtig

all' right' *adj*—be a. in Ordnung sein || *interj* schon gut!

All' Saints'' Day' *s* Allerheiligen *n*

All' Souls'' Day' *s* Allerseelen *n*

all'spice' *s* Nelkenpfeffer *m*

all'-star' *adj* (*sport*) aus den besten Spielern bestehend

allude [ə'lud] *intr*—a. to anspielen auf (*acc*)

allure [ə'lur] *s* Charme *m* || *tr* anlocken

allurement [ə'lurmənt] *s* Verlockung *f*

allur'ing *adj* verlockend

allusion [ə'luʒən] *s* (**to**) Anspielung *f* (*auf acc*)

al·ly ['ælaɪ], [ə'laɪ] *s* Alliierte *mf*, Verbündete *mf* || [ə'laɪ] *v* (*pret & pp* **–lied**) *tr*—a. oneself with sich verbünden mit

almanac ['ɔlmə ,næk] *s* Almanach *m*

almighty [ɔl'maɪtɪ] *adj* allmächtig

almond ['amənd] *s* Mandel *f*

almost ['ɔlmost], [ɔl'most] *adv* fast

alms [amz] *s & spl* Almosen *n*

aloft [ə'lɔft] *adv* (*position*) oben; (*direction*) nach oben; **raise a.** emporheben

alone [ə'lon] *adj* allein; **let a.** (*not to mention*) geschweige denn; (*not bother*) in Ruhe lassen || *adv* allein

along [ə'lɔŋ] *adv* vorwärts, weiter; **all a.** schon immer; **a. with** zusammen mit; **get a. with** sich gut vertragen mit; **go a. with** mitgehen mit; (*agree with*) sich einverstanden erklären mit || *prep* (*direction*) entlang (*acc*); (*position*) an (*dat*), längs (*genit*)

along'side' *adv* (naut) längsseits; **a. of** im Vergleich zu || *prep* neben (*dat*); (naut) längsseits (*genit*)

aloof [ə'luf] *adj* zurückhaltend || *adv*—keep a. (**from**) sich fernhalten (von); **stand a.** für sich bleiben

aloud [ə'laud] *adv* laut

alphabet ['ælfə ,bet] *s* Alphabet *n*

alphabetic(al) [,ælfə'betɪk(əl)] *adj* alphabetisch

alpine ['ælpaɪn] *adj* alpin, Alpen-

Alps [ælps] *spl* Alpen *pl*

already [ɔl'redɪ] *adv* schon, bereits

Alsace [æl'ses], ['ælsæs] *s* Elsaß *n*

Alsatian [æl'se/ən] *adj* elsässisch || *s*

Elsässer –in *mf;* (*dog*) deutscher Schäferhund *m*

also [ˈɔlso] *adv* auch

altar [ˈɔltər] *s* Altar *m*

al'tar boy' *s* Ministrant *m*

alter [ˈɔltər] *tr* ändern; (*castrate*) kastrieren || *intr* sich ändern

alteration [ˌɔltəˈreʃən] *s* Änderung *f;* **alterations** (*in construction*) Umbau *m*

alternate [ˈɔltərnɪt] *adj* abwechselnd || *s* Ersatzmann *m* || [ˈɔltərˌnet] *tr* (ab)wechseln; (*e.g., hot and cold compresses*) zwischen (*dat*) und (*dat*) abwechseln || *intr* miteinander abwechseln

al'ternating cur'rent *s* Wechselstrom *m*

alternative [ɔlˈtʌrnətɪv] *adj* Ausweich-, Alternativ- || *s* Alternative *f*

although [ɔlˈðo] *conj* obgleich, obwohl

altimeter [ælˈtɪmɪtər] *s* Höhenmesser *m*

altitude [ˈæltɪˌt(j)ud] *s* Höhe *f*

al-to [ˈælto] *s* (**-tos**) Alt *m,* Altstimme *f;* (*singer*) Altist *m*

altogether [ˌɔltəˈgeðər] *adv* durchaus; (*in all*) insgesamt

altruist [ˈæltrʊ-ɪst] *s* Altruist –in *mf*

alum [ˈæləm] *s* Alaun *m*

aluminum [əˈlumɪnəm] *s* Aluminium *n*

alu'minum foil' *s* Aluminiumfolie *f*

alum·na [əˈlʌmnə] *s* (**-nae** [ni]) ehemalige Studentin *f*

alum·nus [əˈlʌmnəs] *s* (**-ni** [naɪ]) ehemaliger Student *m*

always [ˈɔlwɪz], [ˈɔlwez] *adv* immer

A.M. *abbr* (*ante meridiem*) vormittags; (*amplitude modulation*) Amplitudenmodulation *f*

amalgam [əˈmælgəm] *s* Amalgam *n;* (*fig*) Mischung *f,* Gemenge *n*

amalgamate [əˈmælgəˌmet] *tr* amalgamieren || *intr* sich amalgamieren

amass [əˈmæs] *tr* aufhäufen, ansammeln

amateur [ˈæmətʃər] *adj* Amateur- || *s* Amateur *m,* Liebhaber *m*

amaze [əˈmez] *tr* erstaunen

amaz'ing *adj* erstaunlich

Amazon [ˈæməˌzɑn] *s* (*river*) Amazonas *m;* (*fig*) Mannweib *n;* (*myth*) Amazone *f*

ambassador [æmˈbæsədər] *s* Botschafter –in §6 *mf;* (*fig*) Bote *m*

ambassadorial [æmˌbæsəˈdorɪ-əl] *adj* Botschafts-

amber [ˈæmbər] *adj* Bernstein-; (*in color*) bernsteinfarben || *s* Bernstein *m*

ambiguity [ˌæmbɪˈgju-ɪti] *s* Doppelsinn *m,* Zweideutigkeit *f*

ambiguous [æmˈbɪgjʊ-əs] *adj* doppelsinnig, zweideutig

ambit [ˈæmbɪt] *s* Bereich *m*

ambition [æmˈbɪʃən] *s* Ehrgeiz *m;* (*aim, object*) Ambition *f*

ambitious [æmˈbɪʃəs] *adj* ehrgeizig

ambivalent [æmˈbɪvələnt] *adj* (chem) ambivalent; (psychol) zwiespältig

amble [ˈæmbəl] *s* (*of a person*) gemächlicher Gang *m;* (*of a horse*) Paßgang *m* || *intr* schlendern; (*said of a horse*) im Paßgang gehen

ambulance [ˈæmbjələns] *s* Krankenwagen *m*

ambulatory [ˈæmbjələˌtori] *adj* gehfähig

ambuscade [ˌæmbəsˈked] *s* Hinterhalt *m*

ambush [ˈæmbʊʃ] *s* Hinterhalt *m* || *tr* aus dem Hinterhalt überfallen

ameliorate [əˈmiljəˌret] *tr* verbessern || *intr* besser werden

amen [ˈeˌmen], [ˈɑˈmen] *s* Amen *n* || *interj* amen!

amenable [əˈmenəbəl] *adj* (*docile*) fügsam; **a. to** (*e.g., flattery*) zugänglich (*dat*); (*e.g., laws*) unterworfen (*dat*)

amend [əˈmend] *tr* (*a law*) (ver)bessern; (*one's ways*) (ab)ändern || *intr* sich bessern

amendment [əˈmendmənt] *s* Änderungsantrag *m;* (by addition) Zusatzantrag *m;* (*to the constitution*) Zusatzartikel *m*

amends [əˈmendz] *s & spl* Genugtuung *f;* **make a. for** wiedergutmachen

amenity [əˈmenɪti] *s* (*pleasantness*) Annehmlichkeit *f;* **amenities** (*of life*) Annehmlichkeiten *pl*

America [əˈmerɪkə] *s* Amerika *n*

American [əˈmerɪkən] *adj* amerikanisch || *s* Amerikaner –in *mf*

Americanize [əˈmerɪkəˌnaɪz] *tr* amerikanisieren

amethyst [ˈæmɪθɪst] *s* Amethyst *m*

amiable [ˈemɪ-əbəl] *adj* liebenswürdig

amicable [ˈæmɪkəbəl] *adj* freundschaftlich, gütlich

amid [əˈmɪd] *prep* inmitten (*genit*)

amidships [əˈmɪdˌʃɪps] *adv* mittschiffs

amiss [əˈmɪs] *adj* (*improper*) unpassend; (*wrong*) verkehrt; **there is s.th. a.** etwas stimmt nicht || *adv* verkehrt; **go a.** danebengehen; **take a.** übelnehmen

amity [ˈæmɪti] *s* Freundschaft *f*

ammo [ˈæmo] *s* (sl) Muni *m*

ammonia [əˈmonɪ-ə] *s* (*gas*) Ammoniak *n;* (*solution*) Salmiakgeist *m*

ammunition [ˌæmjəˈnɪʃən] *s* Munition *f*

amnesia [æmˈniʒɪ-ə] *s* Amnesie *f*

amnes·ty [ˈæmnɪsti] *s* Amnestie *f* || *v* (*pret & pp.* **-tied**) *tr* begnadigen

amoeba [əˈmibə] *s* Amöbe *f*

among [əˈmʌŋ] *prep* (*position*) unter (*dat*); (*direction*) unter (*acc*); **a. other things** unter anderem

amorous [ˈæmərəs] *adj* amourös

amortize [ˈæmərˌtaɪz] *tr* tilgen

amount [əˈmaʊnt] *s* (*sum*) Betrag *m;* (*quantity*) Menge *f* || *intr*—**a. to** betragen

ampere [ˈæmpɪr] *s* Ampere *n*

amphibian [æmˈfɪbɪ-ən] *s* Amphibie *f*

amphibious [æmˈfɪbɪ-əs] *adj* amphibisch

amphitheater [ˈæmfɪˌθi-ətər] *s* Amphitheater *n*

ample [ˈæmpəl] *adj* (*sufficient*) genügend; (*spacious*) geräumig

amplifier [ˈæmplɪˌfaɪ-ər] *s* Verstärker *m*

ampli·fy [ˈæmplɪˌfaɪ] *v* (*pret & pp* **-fied**) *tr* (*a statement*) erweitern; (electron, rad, phys) verstärken

amplitude ['æmplɪ,t(j)ud] s Weite f; (electron, rad, phys) Amplitude f

am'plitude modula'tion s Amplitudenmodulation f

amputate ['æmpjə,tet] tr amputieren

amputee [,æmpje'ti] s Amputierte mf

amuck [ə'mʌk] adv—run a. Amok laufen

amulet ['æmjəlɪt] s Amulett n

amuse [ə'mjuz] tr amüsieren, belustigen

amusement [ə'mjuzmənt] s Vergnügen n

amuse'ment park' s Vergnügungspark m

amus'ing adj amüsant

an [æn], [ən] indef art ein

anachronism [ə'nækrə,nɪzəm] s Anachronismus m

analogous [ə'næləgəs] adj (to) analog (dat), ähnlich (dat)

analogy [ə'nælədʒi] s Analogie f

analy·sis [ə'nælɪsɪs] s (–ses [,siz]) Analyse f; (of a literary work) Zergliederung f

analyst ['ænəlɪst] s Analytiker –in mf

analytic(al) [,ænə'lɪtɪk(əl)] adj analytisch

analyze ['ænə,laɪz] tr analysieren

anarchist ['ænərkɪst] s Anarchist –in mf

anarchy ['ænərki] s Anarchie f

anatomic(al) [,ænə'tɑmɪk(əl)] adj anatomisch

anatomy [ə'nætəmɪ] s Anatomie f

ancestor ['ænsestər] s Vorfahr m, Ahne m

ancestral [æn'sestrəl] adj angestammt, Ahnen–; (inherited) Erb–, ererbt

ancestry ['ænsestri] s Abstammung f

anchor ['æŋkər] s Anker m; cast a. vor Anker gehen; weigh a. den Anker lichten || tr verankern || intr ankern

anchorage ['æŋkərɪdʒ] s Ankerplatz m

anchovy ['æntʃovi] s Anschovis f

ancient ['entʃənt] adj (very old) uralt; (civilization) antik || the ancients spl die alten Griechen und Römer

an'cient his'tory s alte Geschichte f

and [ænd], [ənd] conj und; and how! und ob! and so forth und so weiter

andiron ['ænd,aɪ·ərn] s Kaminbock m

anecdote ['ænɪk,dot] s Anekdote f

anemia [ə'nimɪ·ə] s Anämie f

anemic [ə'nimɪk] adj anämisch, blutarm

anesthesia [,ænɪs'θiʒə] s Anästhesie f; general a. Vollnarkose f; local a. Lokalanästhesie f

anesthetic [,ænɪs'θetɪk] adj betäubend || s Betäubungsmittel n; local a. örtliches Betäubungsmittel n

anesthetize [æ'nesθɪ,taɪz] tr betäuben

anew [ə'n(j)u] adv von neuem, aufs neue

angel ['endʒəl] s Engel m; (financial backer) Hintermann m

angelic(al) [æn'dʒelɪk(əl)] adj engelgleich, engelhaft

anger ['æŋgər] s Zorn m || tr erzürnen

angina pectoris [æn'dʒaɪnə'pektərɪs] s Brustbeklemmung f, Herzbräune f

angle ['æŋgəl] s Winkel m; (point of view) Gesichtswinkel m; (ulterior motive) Hintergedanken m; (side) Seite f

angler ['æŋglər] s Angler –in mf

angry ['æŋgri] adj zornig, böse; (wound) entzündet; a. at (s.th.) zornig über (acc); a. with (s.o.) zornig auf (acc)

anguish ['æŋgwɪʃ] s Qual f, Pein f

angular ['æŋgjələr] adj kantig

animal ['ænɪməl] adj tierisch, Tier— || s Tier n

animate ['ænɪmɪt] adj belebt; (lively) lebhaft || ['ænɪ,met] tr beleben, beseelen; (make lively) aufmuntern

an'imated cartoon' s Zeichentrickfilm m

animation [,ænɪ'meʃən] s Lebhaftigkeit f; (cin) Herstellung f von Zeichentrickfilm

animosity [,ænɪ'mɑsɪti] s Feindseligkeit f

anion ['æn,aɪ·ən] s Anion n

anise ['ænɪs] s Anis m

anisette [,ænɪ'set] s Anisett m

ankle ['æŋkəl] s Fußknöchel m

an'kle support' s Knöchelstütze f

anklet ['æŋklɪt] s (ornament) Fußring m; (sock) Söckchen n

annals ['ænəlz] spl Annalen pl

anneal [ə'nil] tr ausglühen; (the mind) stählen

annex ['æneks] s (building) Anbau m, Nebengebäude n; (supplement) Zusatz m || [ə'neks] tr annektieren

annexation [,æneks'eʃən] s Einverleibung f; (pol) Annexion f

annihilate [ə'naɪ·ɪ,let] tr vernichten; (fig) zunichte machen

annihilation [ə,naɪ·ɪ'leʃən] s Vernichtung f

anniversary [,ænɪ'vʌrsəri] s Jahrestag m

annotate ['ænə,tet] tr mit Anmerkungen versehen

annotation [,ænə'teʃən] s Anmerkung f

announce [ə'nauns] tr ankündigen, anmelden; (rad) ansagen, melden

announcement [ə'naunsmənt] s Ankündigung f; (rad) Durchsage f

announcer [ə'naunsər] s Ansager –in mf

annoy [ə'nɔɪ] tr ärgern; be annoyed at sich ärgern über (acc)

annoyance [ə'nɔɪ·əns] s Ärger m

annoy'ing adj ärgerlich

annual ['ænjʊ·əl] adj jährlich, Jahres–; (plant) einjährig || s (book) Jahrbuch n; (bot) einjährige Pflanze f

annuity [ə'n(j)u·ɪti] s Jahresrente f

an·nul [ə'nʌl] v (pret & pp –nulled; ger –nulling) tr annullieren

annulment [ə'nʌlmənt] s Annullierung f; (of marriage) Nichtigkeitserklärung f

anode ['ænod] s Anode f

anoint [ə'nɔɪnt] tr salben

anomaly [ə'nɑməli] s Anomalie f

anonymous [ə'nɑnɪməs] adj anonym

another [ə'nʌðər] adj (a different) ein anderer; (an additional) noch ein; a. Caesar ein zweiter Cäsar || pron *(a different one)* ein anderer; *(an additional one)* noch einer

answer ['ænsər] *s* Antwort *f;* *(to a problem)* Lösung *f* || *tr (a person)* antworten *(dat); (a question, letter)* beantworten; *(need, description)* entsprechen *(dat); (enemy fire)* antworten auf *(acc);* **a. an ad** sich auf e–e Anzeige melden; **a. the door** die Tür öffnen; **a. the telephone** ans Telefon gehen || *intr* antworten; (telp) sich melden; **a. back** e–n losen Mund haben; **a. for** verantworten; **a. to** *(a description)* entsprechen *(dat)*

an'swering serv'ice *s* Fernsprechauftragsdienst *m*

ant [ænt] *s* Ameise *f*

antagonism [æn'tægə‚nızəm] *s* Feindseligkeit *f*

antagonize [æn'tægə‚naız] *tr* sich *[dat]* zum Gegner machen

antarctic [ænt'ɑrktık] *adj* antarktisch || **the Antarctic** *s* die Antarktis

Antarc'tic Cir'cle *s* südlicher Polarkreis *m*

Antarc'tic O'cean *s* südliches Eismeer *n*

ante ['ænti] *s* (cards) Einsatz *m;* (com) Scherflein *n* || *tr* (cards) einsetzen || *intr (in a joint venture)* sein Scherflein beitragen; *(pay up)* (coll) blechen; (cards) einsetzen

antecedent [‚æntı'sidənt] *adj* vorhergehend || *s* (gram) Beziehungswort *n;* **antecedents** Antezedenzien *pl*

antechamber ['æntı‚tʃembər] *s* Vorzimmer *n*

antelope ['æntı‚lop] *s* Antilope *f*

anten·na [æn'tɛnə] *s* (–nae [ni]) (ent) Fühler *m* || *s* (–nas) (rad) Antenne *f*

antepenult [‚æntı'pınʌlt] *s* drittletzte Silbe *f*

anthem ['ænθəm] *s* Hymne *f*

ant'hill' *s* Ameisenhaufen *m*

anthology [æn'θɑlədʒı] *s* Anthologie *f*

anthropology [‚ænθrə'pɑlədʒı] *s* Anthropologie *f,* Lehre *f* vom Menschen

antiaircraft [‚æntı'ɛr‚kræft] *adj* Flak–, Flugabwehr– || *s* Flak *f*

antiair'craft gun' *s* Flak *f*

antibiotic [‚æntıbaı'ɑtık] *s* Antibiotikum *n*

antibody ['æntı‚bɑdi] *s* Antikörper *m*

anticipate [æn'tısı‚pet] *tr (expect)* erwarten; *(remarks, criticism, etc.)* vorwegnehmen; *(trouble)* vorausahnen; *(pleasure)* vorausempfinden; *(s.o.'s wish or desire)* zuvorkommen *(dat)*

anticipation [æn‚tısı'peʃən] *s* Erwartung *f,* Vorfreude *f*

antics ['æntıks] *spl* Possen *pl*

antidote ['æntı‚dot] *s* Gegengift *n*

antifreeze ['æntı‚friz] *s* Gefrierschutzmittel *n*

antiknock [‚æntı'nɑk] *adj* klopffest || *s* Antiklopfmittel *n*

antipathy [æn'tıpəθı] *s* Abneigung *f,* Antipathie *f*

antiquarian [‚æntı'kwɛrı·ən] *adj* altertümlich || *s* Altertumsforscher –in *mf*

antiquated ['æntı‚kwetıd] *adj* veraltet

antique [æn'tik] *adj* (ur)alt, antik || *s* Antiquität *f*

antique' deal'er *s* Antiquitätenhändler –in *mf*

antique' shop' *s* Antiquitätenladen *m*

antiquity [æn'tıkwıtı] *s* Altertum *n,* Vorzeit *f;* **antiquities** Antiquitäten *pl,* Altertümer *pl*

antirust [‚æntı'rʌst] *adj* Rostschutz–

anti-Semitic [‚æntısı'mıtık] *adj* antisemitisch, judenfeindlich

antiseptic [‚æntı'sɛptık] *adj* antiseptisch || *s* Antiseptikum *n*

antitank [‚æntı'tæŋk] *adj* Panzer–: *(unit)* Panzerjäger–

antitank' mine' *s* Tellermine *f*

antithe·sis [æn'tıθısıs] *s* (–ses [‚siz]) Gegensatz *m,* Antithese *f*

antitoxin [‚æntı'tɑksın] *s* Gegengift *n*

antitrust [‚æntı'trʌst] *adj* Antitrust–

antiwar [‚æntı'wɔr] *adj* antimilitaristisch

antler ['æntlər] *s* Geweihsprosse *f;* **(pair of) antlers** Geweih *n*

antonym ['æntənım] *s* Antonym *n*

anus ['enəs] *s* After *m*

anvil ['ænvıl] *s* Amboß *m*

anxiety [æŋ'zaı·ətı] *s* **(over)** Besorgnis *f* (um); (psychol) Beklemmung *f*

anxious ['æŋk/əs] *adj (about)* besorgt (um or wegen); **(for)** gespannt (auf *acc*), begierig (auf *acc*); **I am a. to** *(inf)* es liegt mir daran zu *(inf)*

any ['ɛni] *indef adj* irgendein, irgendwelch; *(a little)* etwas; **any (possible)** etwaig; **any (you wish)** jeder beliebige; **do you have any money on you?** haben Sie Geld bei sich?; **I do not have any money** ich habe kein Geld || *adv*—any more *(e.g., coffee)* noch etwas; *(e.g., apples)* noch ein paar; **not any better** keinwegs besser; **not ...any longer** nicht mehr; **not...any more** nicht mehr

an'ybod'y *indef pron* var of **anyone**

an'yhow' *adv* sowieso, trotzdem; *(in any event)* jedenfalls

an'yone' *indef pron* (irgend)jemand, irgendeiner; **a. but you** jeder andere als du; **a. else** sonstnochwer; **ask a.** frag wen du willst; **I don't see a.** ich sehe niemand

an'yplace' *adv* (coll) var of **anywhere**

an'ything' *indef pron* (irgend)etwas, (irgend)was; **a. but** alles andere als; **a. else?** noch etwas?, sonst etwas?; **a. you want** was du willst; **not...a.** nichts; **not for a. in the world** um keinen Preis

an'ytime' *adv* zu jeder (beliebigen) Zeit; *(at some unspecified time)* irgendwann

an'yway' *adv* sowieso, trotzdem

an'ywhere' *adv (position)* irgendwo; *(everywhere)* an jedem beliebigen Ort; (direction) irgendwohin; *(everywhere)* an jeden beliebigen Ort; *(to any extent)* einigermaßen, e.g., **a. near** correct einigermaßen richtig; **get a.** *(achieve success)* es zu etwas bringen

apace [ə'pes] *adv* schnell, rasch

apart [ə'pɑrt] *adv (to pieces)* auseinander; (*separately*) einzeln, für sich; **a. from** abgesehen von

apartment [ə'pɑrtmənt] *s* Wohnung *f*

apart'ment house' *s* Apartmenthaus *n*

apathetic [,æpə'θetɪk] *adj* apathisch, teilnahmslos

apathy ['æpəθɪ] *s* Apathie *f*

ape [ep] *s* Affe *m* ‖ *tr* nachäffen

aperture ['æpərtʃər] *s* Öffnung *f*; (phot) Blende *f*

apex ['epeks] *s* (**apexes & apices** ['æpɪ,siz]) Spitze *f*; (fig) Gipfel *m*

aphid ['æfɪd] *s* Blattlaus *f*

aphorism ['æfə,rɪzəm] *s* Aphorismus *m*

apiary ['epɪ,erɪ] *s* Bienenhaus *n*

apiece [ə'pis] *adv* pro Stück; (*per person*) pro Person

aplomb [ə'plɑm] *s* sicheres Auftreten *n*

apogee ['æpə,dʒi] *s* Erdferne *f*

apologetic [ə,pɑlə'dʒetɪk] *adj* (*remark*) entschuldigend; (*letter, speech*) Entschuldigungs–; **be a. (about)** Entschuldigungen vorbringen (für)

apologize [ə'pɑlə,dʒaɪz] *intr* sich entschuldigen; **a. to s.o. for s.th.** sich bei j–m wegen etw entschuldigen

apology [ə'pɑlədʒɪ] *s* (*excuse*) Entschuldigung *f*; (*apologia*) Verteidigung *f*

apoplec'tic stroke' [,æpə'plektɪk] *s* Schlaganfall *m*

apoplexy ['æpə,pleksɪ] *s* Schlaganfall *m*

apostle [ə'pɑsəl] *s* Apostel *m*

apostolic [,æpəs'tɑlɪk] *adj* apostolisch

apostrophe [ə'pɑstrəfɪ] *s* (gram) Apostroph *m*; (rhet) Anrede *f*

apothecary [ə'pɑθɪ,kerɪ] *s* (*druggist*) Apotheker *m*; (*drugstore*) Apotheke *f*

appall [ə'pɔl] *tr* entsetzen

appall'ing *adj* entsetzlich

appara·tus [,æpə'retəs], [,æpə'rætəs] *s* (**-tus & -tuses**) Apparat *m*

apparel [ə'pærəl] *s* Kleidung *f*, Tracht *f*

apparent [ə'pærənt] *adj* (*visible*) sichtbar; (*obvious*) offenbar; (*seeming*) scheinbar

apparition [,æpə'rɪʃən] *s* Erscheinung *f*; (*ghost*) Gespenst *n*

appeal [ə'pil] *s* (*request*) Appell *m*, dringende Bitte *f*; (*to reason, etc.*) Appell *m*; (*charm*) Anziehungskraft *f*; (jur) Berufung *f* (an *acc*) ‖ *tr*–**a. a case** Berufung einlegen in e–r Rechtssache ‖ *intr*–**a. to** (*entreat*) dringend bitten; (*be attractive to*) reizen; (jur) appellieren an (*acc*)

appear [ə'pɪr] *intr* erscheinen; (*seem*) scheinen; (*come before the public*) sich zeigen; (jur) sich stellen; (theat) auftreten; **a. as a guest** (telv) gastieren

appearance [ə'pɪrəns] *s* Erscheinen *n*; (*outward look*) Aussehen *n*; (*semblance*) Anschein *m*; (*on the stage*) Auftreten *n*; (jur) Erscheinen *n*; **for the sake of appearances** anstandshalber; **to all appearances** allem Anschein nach

appease [ə'piz] *tr* beruhigen; (*hunger*)

stillen; (*pain*) mildern; (dipl) beschwichtigen

appeasement [ə'pizmənt] *s* Beruhigung *f*; (*of hunger*) Stillung *f*; (dipl) Beschwichtigung *f*

appel'late court' [ə'pelɪt] *s* Berufungsgericht *n*

append [ə'pend] *tr* anhängen; (*a signature*) hinzufügen

appendage [ə'pendɪdʒ] *s* Anhang *m*

appendectomy [,æpən'dektəmɪ] *s* Blinddarmoperation *f*

appendicitis [ə,pendɪ'saɪtɪs] *s* Blinddarmentzündung *f*, Appendizitis *f*

appen·dix [ə'pendɪks] *s* (**-dixes & -dices** [dɪ,siz]) Anhang *m*; (anat) Appendix *m*

appertain [,æpər'ten] *intr* (**to**) gehören (zu), gebühren (*dat*)

appetite ['æpɪ,taɪt] *s* (**for**) Appetit *m* (auf *acc*)

appetizer ['æpɪ,taɪzər] *s* Vorspeise *f*

ap'petizing *adj* appetitlich

applaud [ə'plɔd] *tr* Beifall klatschen (*dat*); (*praise*) billigen ‖ *intr* Beifall klatschen

applause [ə'plɔz] *s* Beifall *m*, Applaus *m*

apple ['æpəl] *s* Apfel *m*

ap'plecart' *s*—**upset the a.** die Pläne über den Haufen werfen

ap'ple of one's eye' *s* Augapfel *m*

ap'ple pie' *s* gedeckte Apfeltorte *f*

ap'ple-pol'isher *s* (coll) Speichellecker *m*

ap'plesauce' *s* Apfelmus *n*

ap'ple tree' *s* Apfelbaum *m*

appliance [ə'plaɪ·əns] *s* Gerät *n*, Vorrichtung *f*

applicable ['æplɪkəbəl] *adj* (**to**) anwendbar (auf *acc*); **not a.** nicht zutreffend

applicant ['æplɪkənt] *s* Bewerber –in *mf*

application [,æplɪ'keʃən] *s* (*use*) Anwendung *f*; (*for a job*) Bewerbung *f*; (*for a grant*) Antrag *m*; (*zeal*) Fleiß *m*; (med) Anlegen *n*

applica'tion blank' *s* (*for a job*) Bewerbungsformular *n*; (*for a grant*) Antragsformular *n*

applied' *adj* angewandt

apply [ə'plaɪ] *v* (pret & pp **-plied**) *tr* anwenden; (med) anlegen; **a. oneself to** sich befleißigen (*genit*); **a. the brakes** bremsen ‖ *intr* gelten; **a. for** (*a job*) sich bewerben um; (*a grant*) beantragen

appoint [ə'pɔɪnt] *tr* (*a person*) ernennen; (*a time, etc.*) festsetzen

appointment [ə'pɔɪntmənt] *s* Ernennung *f*; (post) Stelle *f*; (*engagement*) Verabredung *f*; **by a. only** nur nach Vereinbarung; **have an a. with** (*e.g., a dentist*) bestellt sein zu

appoint'ment book' *s* Terminkalender *m*

apportion [ə'pɔrʃən] *tr* zumessen

appraisal [ə'prezəl] *s* Abschätzung *f*

appraise [ə'prez] *tr* (ab)schätzen

appraiser [ə'prezər] *s* Schätzer –in *mf*

appreciable [ə'priʃɪ·əbəl] *adj* (*notice-*

able) merklich; (*considerable*) erheblich

appreciate [ə'priʃɪ,et] *tr* dankbar sein für; (*danger*) erkennen; (*regard highly*) hochschätzen || *intr* (im Werte) steigen

appreciation [ə,priʃɪ'eʃən] *s* (*gratitude*) Dank *m*. Anerkennung *f*; (*for art*) Verständnis *n*; (*high regard*) Schätzung *f*; (*increase in value*) Wertzuwachs *m*

appreciative [ə'priʃɪ·ətɪv] *adj* (*of*) dankbar (für)

apprehend [,æprɪ'hɛnd] *tr* verhaften, ergreifen; (*understand*) begreifen

apprehension [,æprɪ'hɛnʃən] *s* (*arrest*) Verhaftung *f*; (*fear*) Befürchtung *f*; (*comprehending*) Begreifen *n*

apprehensive [,æprɪ'hɛnsɪv] *adj* (*of*) besorgt (um)

apprentice [ə'prɛntɪs] *s* Lehrling *m*

appren'ticeship' *s* Lehre *f*; **serve an a.** in der Lehre sein

apprise, apprize [ə'praɪz] *tr* (*of*) benachrichtigen (von)

approach [ə'protʃ] *s* Annäherung *f*; (*e.g., a road*) Zugang *m*, Zufahrt *f*; (*e.g., to a problem*) Behandlung *f*; (*tentative sexual approach*) Annäherungsversuch *m*; (*aer*) Anflug *m* || *tr* sich nähern (*dat*); (*e.g., a problem*) behandeln; (*perfection*) nahekommen (*dat*); (*aer*) anfliegen || *intr* sich nähern

approachable [ə'protʃəbəl] *adj* zugänglich

approbation [,æprə'beʃən] *s* (*approval*) Beifall *m*; (*sanction*) Billigung *f*

appropriate [ə'propri·ɪt] *adj* (to) angemessen (*dat*) || [ə'propri,et] *tr* (*take possession of*) sich [*dat*] aneignen; (*authorize*) bewilligen

approval [ə'pruvəl] *s* (*approbation*) Beifall *m*; (*sanction*) Billigung *f*; **meet with s.o.'s a.** j-s Beifall finden; **on a.** auf Probe

approve [ə'pruv] *tr* (*sanction*) genehmigen; (*judge favorably*) billigen; (*a bill*) (parl) annehmen || *intr*—**a. of** billigen

approvingly [ə'pruvɪŋli] *adv* beifällig

approximate [ə'prɑksɪmɪt] *adj* annähernd || [ə'prɑksɪ,met] *tr* (*come close to*) nahekommen (*dat*); (*estimate*) schätzen; (*simulate closely*) täuschend nachahmen

approximately [ə'prɑksɪmɪtli] *adv* ungefähr, etwa

apricot ['eprɪ,kɑt] *s* Aprikose *f*

ap'ricot tree' *s* Aprikosenbaum *m*

April ['eprɪl] *s* April *m*

A'pril fool' *interj* April, April!

A'pril Fools'' Day' *s* der erste April *m*

apron ['eprən] *s* Schürze *f*; (*aer*) Vorfeld *n*; (theat) Vorbühne *f*

apropos [,æprə'po] *adj* passend || *adv*—**a. of** in Bezug auf (*acc*)

apse [æps] *s* Apsis *f*

apt [æpt] *adj* (*suited to the occasion*) passend; (*suited to the purpose*) geeignet; (*metaphor*) zutreffend; **be apt to** (*inf*) (*be prone to*) dazu neigen zu

(*inf*); **he is apt to believe it** er wird es wahrscheinlich glauben

aptitude ['æptɪ,t(j)ud] *s* Eignung *f*

ap'titude test' *s* Eignungsprüfung *f*

aqualung ['ækwə,lʌŋ] *s* Tauchergerät *n*

aquamarine [,ækwəmə'rin] *adj* blaugrün || *s* Aquamarin *m*

aquari·um [ə'kwɛrɪ·əm] *s* (**-ums & -a** [ə]) Aquarium *n*

aquatic [ə'kwætɪk] *adj* Wasser– || **aquatics** *spl* Wassersport *m*

aqueduct ['ækwə,dʌkt] *s* Aquädukt *n*

aq'uiline nose' ['ækwɪ,laɪn]–*s* Adlernase *f*

Arab ['ærəb] *adj* arabisch || *s* Araber –in *mf*

Arabia [ə'rebɪ·ə] *s* Arabien *n*

Arabic ['ærəbɪk] *adj* arabisch || *s* Arabisch *n*

arable ['ærəbəl] *adj* urbar, Acker–

arbiter ['ɑrbɪtər] *s* Schiedsrichter *m*

arbitrary ['ɑrbɪ,trɛri] *adj* (*act*) willkürlich; (*number*) beliebig; (*person, government*) tyrannisch

arbitrate ['ɑrbɪ,tret] *tr* schlichten || *intr* als Schiedsrichter fungieren

arbitration [,ɑrbɪ'treʃən] *s* Schlichtung *f*

arbitrator ['ɑrbɪ,tretər] *s* Schiedsrichter *m*

arbor ['ɑrbər] *s* Laube *f*; (mach) Achse *f*

arbore·tum [,ɑrbə'ritəm] *s* (**-tums & -ta** [tə]) Baumgarten *m*

arc [ɑrk] *s* (astr, geom, mach) Bogen *m*; (elec) Lichtbogen *m*

arcade [ɑr'ked] *s* Bogengang *m*, Arkade *f*

arcane [ɑr'ken] *adj* geheimnisvoll

arch [ɑrtʃ] *adj* (*liar, etc.*) abgefeimt || *s* Bogen *m* || *tr* wölben; (*span*) überwölben || *intr* sich wölben

archaeologist [,ɑrkɪ'ɑlədʒɪst] *s* Archäolog(e) *m*, Archäologin *f*

archaeology [,ɑrkɪ'ɑlədʒi] *s* Archäologie *f*

archaic [ɑr'ke·ɪk] *adj* (*word*) veraltet; (*manner, notion*) antiquiert

archangel ['ɑrk,endʒəl] *s* Erzengel *m*

archbishop ['ɑrtʃ'bɪʃəp] *s* Erzbischof *m*

archduke ['ɑrtʃ'd(j)uk] *s* Erzherzog *m*

archenemy ['ɑrtʃ,ɛnmi] *s* Erzfeind *m*

archer ['ɑrtʃər] *s* Bogenschütze *m*

archery ['ɑrtʃəri] *s* Bogenschießen *n*

archipela·go [,ɑrkɪ'pɛləgo] *s* (**-gos & -goes**) Inselmeer *n*; (*group of islands*) Inselgruppe *f*, Archipel *m*

architect ['ɑrkɪ,tɛkt] *s* Architekt –in *mf*

architecture ['ɑrkɪ,tɛktʃər] *s* Architektur *f*, Baukunst *f*

archives ['ɑrkaɪvz] *spl* Archiv *n*

arch'way' *s* Bogengang *m*, Torbogen *m*

arctic ['ɑrktɪk] *adj* arktisch, nördlich || **the Arctic** die Arktis

Arc'tic Cir'cle *s* nördlicher Polarkreis *m*

arc' weld'ing *s* Lichtbogenschweißung *f*

ardent ['ɑrdənt] *adj* feurig, eifrig

ardor ['ɑrdər] *s* Eifer *m*, Inbrust *f*

arduous ['ɑːdʒʊ·əs] *adj* mühsam
area ['ɛrɪ·ə] *s* (*surface*) Fläche *f*; (*district*) Gegend *f*; (*field of enterprise*) Bereich *m*, Gebiet *n*; (*of danger*) Zone *f*
arena [ə'riːnə] *s* Arena *f*, Kampfbahn *f*
Argentina [ˌɑːdʒən'tiːnə] *s* Argentinien *n*
argue ['ɑːgjuː] *tr* erörtern; (*maintain*) behaupten; **a. into** (*ger*) dazu überreden zu (*inf*) ‖ *intr* (*with*) streiten (*mit*); **a. for** (or *against*) s.th. für (or gegen) etw eintreten; **don't a.!** keine Widerrede!
argument ['ɑːgjəmənt] *s* (*discussion*) Erörterung *f*; (*point*) Beweisgrund *m*; (*disagreement*) Auseinandersetzung *f*; (*theme*) Thema *n*
argumentative [ˌɑːgjə'mɛntətɪv] *adj* streitsüchtig
aria ['ɑːrɪ·ə], ['ɛrɪ·ə] *s* Arie *f*
arid ['ærɪd] *adj* trocken, dürr
aridity [ə'rɪdɪtɪ] *s* Trockenheit *f*
arise [ə'raɪz] *v* (*pret* **arose** [ə'roːz]; *pp* **arisen** [ə'rɪzən]) *intr* (*come into being*) (**from**) entstehen (aus); (*get out of bed*) aufstehen; (*from a seat*) sich erheben; (*occur*) aufkommen, auftauchen; (*said of an opportunity*) sich bieten; (*stem*) (**from**) stammen (von)
aristocracy [ˌærɪs'tɑːkrəsɪ] *s* Aristokratie *f*
aristocrat [ə'rɪstəˌkræt] *s* Aristokrat –in *mf*
aristocratic [əˌrɪstə'krætɪk] *adj* aristokratisch
arithmetic [ə'rɪθmətɪk] *s* Arithmetik *f*
arithmetical [ˌærɪθ'mɛtɪkəl] *adj* arithmetisch, rechnerisch
ark [ɑːk] *s* Arche *f*
ark′ of the cov′enant *s* Bundeslade *f*
arm [ɑːm] *s* Arm *m*; (*of a chair*) Seitenlehne *f*; (*weapon*) Waffe *f*; **keep s.o. at arm's length** sich j–m vom Leibe halten; **take up arms** zu den Waffen greifen; **up in arms** in Aufruhr ‖ *tr* bewaffnen; ‖ *intr* sich bewaffnen
armament ['ɑːməmənt] *s* Kriegsausrüstung *f*, Bewaffnung *f*
ar′maments race′ *s* Rüstungswettlauf *m*
armature ['ɑːməˌtʃər] *s* (*of doorbell or magnet*) Anker *m*; (*of a motor or dynamo*) Läufer *m*; (*biol*) Panzer *m*
arm′chair′ *s* Lehnsessel *m*; (*unpadded*) Lehnstuhl *m*
armed′ for′ces *spl* Streitkräfte *pl*
armed′ rob′bery *s* bewaffneter Raubüberfall *m*
Armenia [ɑːr'miːnɪ·ə] *s* Armenien *n*
armful ['ɑːmˌfʊl] *s* Armvoll *m*
armistice ['ɑːmɪstɪs] *s* Waffenstillstand *m*
armor ['ɑːmər] *s* Panzer *m* ‖ *tr* panzern
ar′mored car′ *s* Panzerwagen *m*
armor-piercing ['ɑːmərˌpɪrsɪŋ] *adj* panzerbrechend
ar′mor plat′ing ['pleɪtɪŋ] *s* Panzerung *f*
armory ['ɑːmərɪ] *s* (*large arms storage*) Arsenal *n*; (*arms repair and storage room of a unit*) Waffenkam-

mer *f*; (*arms factory*) Waffenfabrik *f*; (*drill hall*) Exerzierhalle *f*
arm′pit′ *s* Achselhöhle *f*
arm′rest′ *s* Armlehne *f*
army ['ɑːmɪ] *adj* Armee–, Heeres– ‖ *s* Armee *f*, Heer *n*; **join the a.** zum Militär gehen
aroma [ə'roːmə] *s* Aroma *n*, Duft *m*
aromatic [ˌærə'mætɪk] *adj* aromatisch
around [ə'raʊnd] *adv* ringsherum; **be a.** in der Nähe sein; **get a.** viel herumkommen; **get a. to** (*inf*) dazukommen zu (*inf*) ‖ *prep* um (*acc*) herum; (*approximately*) etwa; (*near*) bei (*dat*); **a. town** in der Stadt
arouse [ə'raʊz] *tr* aufwecken; (*fig*) erwecken
arraign [ə'reɪn] *tr* (*accuse*) anklagen; (*jur*) vor Gericht stellen
arrange [ə'reɪndʒ] *tr* arrangieren; (*in a certain order*) (an)ordnen; (*a time*) festsetzen; (*mus*) bearbeiten ‖ *intr*— **a. for** Vorkehrungen treffen für
arrangement [ə'reɪndʒmənt] *s* Anordnung *f*; (*agreement*) Vereinbarung *f*; (*mus*) Bearbeitung *f*; **make arrangements to** (*inf*) ‖ Vorbereitungen treffen, um zu (*inf*)
array [ə're] *s* (*of troops, facts*) Ordnung *f*; (*large number or quantity*) Menge *f*; (*apparel*) Staat *m* ‖ *tr* ordnen; (*dress up*) putzen
arrears [ə'rɪrz] *spl* Rückstand *m*; **in a.** rückständig
arrest [ə'rɛst] *s* Verhaftung *f*; **make an a.** e–e Verhaftung vornehmen; **place under a.** in Haft nehmen; **under a.** verhaftet ‖ *tr* verhaften; (*attention*) fesseln; (*a disease, progress*) hemmen
arrival [ə'raɪvəl] *s* Ankunft *f*; (*of merchandise*) Eingang *m*; (*a person*) Ankömmling *m*
arrive [ə'raɪv] *intr* ankommen; (*said of time, an event*) kommen; **a. at** (*a conclusion, decision*) erlangen
arrogance ['ærəgəns] *s* Anmaßung *f*
arrogant ['ærəgənt] *adj* anmaßend
arrogate ['ærəˌget] *tr* sich (*dat*) anmaßen
arrow ['æro] *s* Pfeil *m*
ar′rowhead′ *s* Pfeilspitze *f*
arsenal ['ɑːrsənəl] *s* Arsenal *n*
arsenic ['ɑːrsɪnɪk] *s* Arsen *n*
arson ['ɑːrsən] *s* Brandstiftung *f*
arsonist ['ɑːrsənɪst] *s* Brandstifter –in *mf*
art [ɑːt] *s* Kunst *f*
artery ['ɑːrtərɪ] *s* Pulsader *f*; (*highway*) Verkehrsader *f*
artful ['ɑːrtfəl] *adj* (*cunning*) schlau, listig; (*skillful*) kunstvoll
arthritic [ɑːr'θrɪtɪk] *adj* arthritisch, gichtisch ‖ *s* Arthritiker –in *mf*
arthritis [ɑːr'θraɪtɪs] *s* Arthritis *f*
artichoke ['ɑːrtɪˌtʃok] *s* Artischocke *f*
article ['ɑːrtɪkəl] *s* (*object*) Gegenstand *m*; (*com, gram, journ, jur*) Artikel *m*
articulate [ɑːr'tɪkjəlɪt] *adj* deutlich ‖ [ɑːr'tɪkjəˌlet] *tr* & *intr* deutlich aussprechen
artifact ['ɑːrtɪˌfækt] *s* Artefakt *n*
artifice ['ɑːrtɪfɪs] *s* Kunstgriff *m*
artificial [ˌɑːrtɪ'fɪʃəl] *adj* Kunst–,

künstlich; (*emotion, smile*) gekünstelt

artillery [ɑr'tɪləri] *s* Artillerie *f*

artil'lery-man *s* (-men) Artillerist *m*

artisan ['ɑrtɪzən] *s* Handwerker –in *mf*

artist ['ɑrtɪst] *s* Künstler –in *mf*

artistic [ɑr'tɪstɪk] *adj* künstlerisch

artistry ['ɑrtɪstri] *s* Kunstfertigkeit *f*

artless ['ɑrtlɪs] *adj* (*lacking art*) unkünstlerisch; (*made without skill*) stümperhaft; (*ingenuous*) unbefangen

arts' and crafts' *spl* Kunstgewerbe *n*

arts' and sci'ences *spl* Geistes– und Naturwissenschaften *pl*

arty ['ɑrti] *adj* (coll) gekünstelt

Aryan ['ɛrɪ·ən], ['ɑrjən] *adj* arisch || *s* Arier –in *mf*; (*language*) Arisch *n*

as [æz], [əz] *adv* wie; as...as (eben)so ...wie; as far as **Berlin** bis nach Berlin; as far as I know soviel ich weiß; as far back as **1900** schon im Jahre 1900; as for me was mich betrifft; as if als ob; as long as solange; (*with the proviso that*) vorausgesetzt, daß; as soon as sobald wie; as though als ob; as well ebensogut, auch; as yet bis jetzt || *rel pron* wie, was || *prep* als; as a rule in der Regel || *conj* wie; (*while*) als, während; (*because*) da, weil, indem; as it were sozusagen

asbestos [æs'bɛstəs] *adj* Asbest– || *s* Asbest *m*

ascend [ə'sɛnd] *tr* (*stairs*) hinaufsteigen; (*a throne, mountain*) besteigen || *intr* emporsteigen; (*said of a balloon, plane*) aufsteigen

ascendancy [ə'sɛndənsi] *s* Überlegenheit *f*

ascension [ə'sɛnʃən] *s* Aufsteigen *n*

Ascen'sion Day' *s* Himmelfahrtstag *m*

ascent [ə'sɛnt] *s* (*on foot*) Besteigung *f*; (*by vehicle*) Auffahrt *f*; (*upward slope*) Steigung *f*; (& fig) Aufstieg *m*

ascertain [ˌæsər'ten] *tr* feststellen

ascetic [ə'sɛtɪk] *adj* asketisch || *s* Asket –in *mf*

ascribe [ə'skraɪb] *tr*—a. to zuschreiben (*dat*)

aseptic [ə'sɛptɪk] *adj* aseptisch

ash [æʃ] *s* Asche *f*; (*tree*) Esche *f*; **ashes** Asche *f*; (*mortal remains*) sterbliche Überreste *pl*

ashamed [ə'ʃemd] *adj*—be (or feel) a. (of) sich schämen (*genit*)

ash'can' *s* Ascheneimer *m*

ashen ['æʃən] *adj* aschgrau

ashore [ə'ʃor] *adv* (*position*) am Land; (*direction*) ans Land

ash'tray' *s* Aschenbecher *m*

Ash' Wednes'day *s* Aschermittwoch *m*

Asia ['eʒə], ['eʃə] *s* Asien *n*

A'sia Mi'nor *s* Kleinasien *n*

aside [ə'saɪd] *adv* zur Seite; a. from außer || *s* (theat) Seitenbemerkung *f*

asinine ['æsɪˌnaɪn] *adj* eselhaft

ask [æsk] *tr* (*request*) bitten; (*demand*) auffordern; (*a high price*) fordern; (*inquire of*) fragen; **ask a question** (of s.o.) (j–m) e–e Frage stellen; **ask in** hereinbitten; **that is asking too much** das ist zuviel verlangt || *intr*

fragen; **ask for** bitten um; **ask for trouble** sich [*dat*] selbst Schwierigkeiten machen

askance [əs'kæns] *adv*—**look a. at** schief ansehen

askew [ə'skju] *adv* schräg

ask'ing *s*—**for the a.** umsonst

asleep [ə'slip] *adj* schlafend; (*numb*) eingeschlafen; **be a.** schlafen; **fall a.** einschlafen

asp [æsp] *s* Natter *f*

asparagus [ə'spærəgəs] *s* Spargel *m*

aspect ['æspɛkt] *s* Gesichtspunkt *m*

aspen ['æspən] *s* Espe *f*

aspersion [ə'spɑrʒən] *s* (eccl) Besprengung *f*; **cast aspersions on** verleumden

asphalt ['æsfɔlt], ['æsfælt] *s* Asphalt *m* || *tr* asphaltieren

asphyxiate [æs'fɪksɪˌet] *tr & intr* ersticken

aspirant [ə'spaɪrənt] *s* Bewerber –in *mf*

aspirate ['æspɪrɪt] *s* Hauchlaut *m* || ['æspɪˌret] *tr* behauchen

aspire [ə'spaɪr] *intr* (after, to) streben (nach); **a. to** (*inf*) danach streben zu (*inf*)

aspirin ['æspɪrɪn] *s* Aspirin *n*

ass [æs] *s* Esel *m*; (vulg) Arsch *m*; **make an ass of oneself** (sl) sich lächerlich machen

assail [ə'sel] *tr* angreifen, anfallen; (*with questions*) bestürmen

assassin [ə'sæsɪn] *s* Meuchelmörder –in *mf*

assassinate [ə'sæsɪˌnet] *tr* ermorden

assassination [əˌsæsɪ'neʃən] *s* Meuchelmord *m*, Ermordung *f*

assault [ə'sɔlt] *s* Überfall *m*; (*rape*) Vergewaltigung *f*; (*physical violence*) (jur) tätlicher Angriff *m*; (*threat of violence*) (jur) unmittelbare Bedrohung *f*; (mil) Sturm *m* || *tr* (er)stürmen, anfallen; (jur) tätlich beleidigen

assault' and bat'tery *s* schwere tätliche Beleidigung *f*

assay [ə'se], ['æse] *s* Prüfung *f* || [ə'se] *tr* prüfen

assemble [ə'sɛmbəl] *tr* versammeln; (mach) montieren || *intr* sich versammeln

assembly [ə'sɛmbli] *s* Versammlung *f*; (mach) Montage *f*; (pol) Unterhaus *n*

assem'bly line' *s* Fließband *n*

assent [ə'sɛnt] *s* Zustimmung *f* || *intr* (to) zustimmen (*dat*)

assert [ə'sʌrt] *tr* behaupten; **a. oneself** sich behaupten

assertion [ə'sʌrʃən] *s* Behauptung *f*; (*of rights*) Geltendmachung *f*

assess [ə'sɛs] *tr* (*damage*) festsetzen; (*property*) (at) (ab)schätzen (auf *acc*); **assessed value** Schätzungswert *m*

assessment [ə'sɛsmənt] *s* (*of damage*) Festsetzung *f*; (*valuation*) Einschätzung *f*; (*of real estate*) Veranlagung *f*

assessor [ə'sɛsər] *s* Steuereinschätzer *m*

asset ['æset] *s* Vorzug *m; (com)* Aktivposten *m;* **assets** Vermögenswerte *pl;* **assets and liabilities** Aktiva und Passiva *pl*

assiduous [ə'sɪdʒʊ·əs] *adj* emsig

assign [ə'saɪn] *tr* zuweisen; *(homework)* aufgeben; *(transfer)* (jur) abtreten; (mil) zuteilen

assignment [ə'saɪnmənt] *s* Zuweisung *f; (homework)* Aufgabe *f; (task)* Auftrag *m,* Aufgabe *f; (transference)* (jur) Abtretung *f; (to a unit)* (mil) Zuteilung *f*

assimilate [ə'sɪmɪ,let] *tr* angleichen ‖ *intr* sich angleichen

assimilation [ə,sɪmɪ'leʃən] *s* Assimilierung *f,* Angleichung *f*

assist [ə'sɪst] *s* (sport) Zuspiel *n* ‖ *tr* beistehen *(dat)* ‖ *intr*—a. in beistehen bei, behilflich sein bei

assistance [ə'sɪstəns] *s* Hilfe *f*

assistant [ə'sɪstənt] *adj* Hilfs-, Unter- ‖ *s (helper)* Gehilfe *m,* Gehilfin *f*

associate [ə'soʃɪ·ɪt] *adj* Mit-, beigeordnet; *(member)* außerordentlich ‖ *s (companion)* Gefährte *m,* Gefährtin *f; (colleague)* Kollege *m,* Kollegin *f;* (com) Partner –in *mf* ‖ [ə'soʃɪ,et] *tr* verbinden ‖ *intr* (with) verkehren (mit)

asso′ciate profes′sor *s* außerordentlicher Professor *m*

association [ə,soʃɪ'eʃən] *s (connection)* Verbindung *f; (social intercourse)* Verkehr *m; (society)* Verband *m; (suggested ideas, feelings)* Assoziation *f*

assonance ['æsənəns] *s* Assonanz *f*

assorted [ə'sɔrtɪd] *adj* verschieden

assortment [ə'sɔrtmənt] *s* Sortiment *n*

assuage [ə'swedʒ] *tr (pain)* lindern; *(hunger)* befriedigen; *(thirst)* stillen

assume [ə's(j)um] *tr (a fact as true; a certain shape, property, habit)* annehmen; *(a duty)* auf sich nehmen; *(office)* antreten; *(power)* ergreifen; **assuming that** vorausgesetzt, daß

assumed′ *adj (feigned)* erheuchelt; **a. name** Deckname *m*

assumption [ə'sʌmpʃən] *s (supposition)* Annahme *f; (e.g., of power)* Übernahme *f*

assurance [ə'ʃʊrəns] *s* Versicherung *f*

assure [ə'ʃʊr] *tr* versichern

aster ['æstər] *s* Aster *f*

asterisk ['æstə,rɪsk] *s* Sternchen *n*

astern [ə'stɜrn] *adv* achtern, achteraus

asthma ['æzmə] *s* Asthma *n*

astonish [ə'stɑnɪʃ] *tr* in Erstaunen setzen; **be astonished at** staunen über *(acc),* sich wundern über *(acc)*

aston′ishing *adj* erstaunlich

astonishment [ə'stɑnɪʃmənt] *s* Erstaunen *n,* Verwunderung *f*

astound [ə'staund] *tr* überraschen

astound′ing *adj* erstaunlich

astray [ə'stre] *adv*—**go a.** irregehen; **lead a.** irreführen

astride [ə'straɪd] *adv* rittlings ‖ *prep (a road)* an beiden Seiten *(genit); (a horse)* rittlings auf *(dat)*

astringent [əs'trɪndʒənt] *adj* stopfend ‖ *s* Stopfmittel *n*

astrology [ə'strɑlədʒɪ] *s* Astrologie *f*

astronaut ['æstrə,nɔt] *s* Astronaut *m*

astronautics [,æstrə'nɔtɪks] *s* Raumfahrtwissenschaft *f,* Astronautik *f*

astronomer [ə'strɑnəmər] *s* Astronom –in *mf*

astronomic(al) [,æstrə'nɑmɪk(əl)] *adj* astronomisch

astronomy [ə'strɑnəmɪ] *s* Astronomie *f*

astute [ə'st(j)ut] *adj* scharfsinnig; *(cunning)* schlau

asunder [ə'sʌndər] *adv* auseinander

asylum [ə'saɪləm] *s (refuge)* Asyl *n; (for the insane)* Irrenhaus *n*

at [æt], [ət] *prep (position)* an *(dat),* auf *(dat),* in *(dat),* bei *(dat),* zu *(dat); (direction)* auf *(acc),* gegen *(acc),* nach *(dat),* zu *(dat); (manner, circumstance)* auf *(acc),* in *(dat),* unter *(dat),* bei *(dat),* zu *(dat); (time)* um *(acc),* bei *(dat),* auf *(dat)* zu *(dat);* **at all** *(in questions)* überhaupt; **at high prices** zu hohen Preisen; **even at that** sogar so

atheism ['eθɪ,ɪzəm] *s* Atheismus *m*

atheist ['eθɪ·ɪst] *s* Atheist –in *mf*

Athens ['æθɪns] *s* Athen *n*

athlete ['æθlit] *s* Sportler –in *mf*

ath′lete′s foot′ *s* Fußflechte *f*

athletic [æθ'letɪk] *adj* athletisch, Sport-, Turn- ‖ **athletics** *s* Athletik *f*

Atlantic [æt'læntɪk] *adj* atlantisch ‖ *s* Atlantik *m*

atlas ['ætləs] *s* Atlas *m*

atmosphere ['ætməs,fɪr] *s* (& fig) Atmosphäre *f*

atmospheric [,ætməs'ferɪk] *adj* atmosphärisch

atom ['ætəm] *s* Atom *n*

atomic [ə'tɑmɪk] *adj* atomisch, atomar, Atom-

atom′ic age′ *s* Atomzeitalter *n*

atom′ic bomb′ *s* Atombombe *f*

atom′ic pow′er *s* Atomkraft *f;* **atomic powers** (pol) Atommächte *pl*

atomizer ['ætə,maɪzər] *s* Zerstäuber *m*

atone [ə'ton] *intr*—**a. for** büßen

atonement [ə'tonmənt] *s* Buße *f*

atrocious [ə'troʃəs] *adj* gräßlich

atrocity [ə'trɑsɪtɪ] *s* Greueltat *f*

atro-phy ['ætrəfɪ] *s* Verkümmerung *f,* Atrophie *f* ‖ *v (pret & pp —phied) tr* auszehren ‖ *intr* verkümmern

attach [ə'tætʃ] *tr (with glue, stitches, tacks)* (to) anheften (an *acc); (connect)* (to) befestigen (an *acc); (importance)* (to) beimessen *(dat);* (a person) (jur) verhaften; *(a thing)* (jur) beschlagnahmen; (mil) (to) zuteilen *(dat);* **a. oneself to** sich anschließen an *(acc);* **be attached to** festhalten an *(dat);* (fig) verwachsen sein mit

attaché [,ætə'ʃe] *s* Attaché *m*

attaché′ case′ *s* Aktenköfferchen *n*

attachment [ə'tætʃmənt] *s* Befestigung *f; (regard)* (to) Zuneigung *f* (zu); *(device)* Zusatzgerät *n; (of a person)* (jur) Verhaftung *f; (of a thing)* (jur) Beschlagnahme *f*

attack [ə'tæk] *s* Angriff *m;* (pathol)

Anfall *m* ‖ *tr & intr* angreifen; (pathol) überfallen

attain [ə'ten] *tr* erreichen, erzielen ‖ *intr*—**a. to** erreichen

attainment [ə'tenmənt] *s* Erreichen *n*; **attainments** Fertigkeiten *pl*

attempt [ə'tempt] *s* Versuch *m*; (*assault*) Attentat *n* ‖ *tr* versuchen

attend [ə'tend] *tr* beiwohnen (*dat*); (*school, church*) besuchen; (*accompany*) begleiten; (*a patient*) behandeln ‖ *intr*—**a. to** nachgehen (*dat*), erledigen

attendance [ə'tendəns] *s* Besuch *m*; (*number in attendance*) Besucherzahl *f*; (med) Behandlung *f*

attendant [ə'tendənt] *s* (*servant, waiter*) Diener –in *mf*; (*keeper*) Wärter –in *mf*; (*at a gas station*) Tankwart *m*; (*escort*) Begleiter –in *mf*

attention [ə'tenʃən] *s* Aufmerksamkeit *f*; Acht *f*; **a. Mr. X.** zu Händen von Herrn X; **call a. to** hinweisen auf (*acc*); **call s.o.'s a. to** j–n aufmerksam machen auf (*acc*); **pay a.** achtgeben; **pay a. to** achten auf (*acc*); **stand at a.** stillstehen ‖ *interj* (mil) Achtung!

attentive [ə'tentɪv] *adj* aufmerksam

attenuate [ə'tenjʊ‚et] *tr* (*dilute, thin*) verdünnen; (*weaken*) abschwächen

attest [ə'test] *tr* bezeugen ‖ *intr*—**a. to** bezeugen

attic ['ætɪk] *s* Dachboden *m*; (*as living quarters*) Mansarde *f*

attire [ə'taɪr] *s* Putz *m* ‖ *tr* kleiden

attitude ['ætɪ‚t(j)ud] *s* Haltung *f*; (aer, rok) Lage *f*

attorney [ə'tʌrni] *s* Rechtsanwalt *m*

attor'ney gen'eral *s* (**attorneys general**) Justizminister *m*

attract [ə'trækt] *tr* anziehen, reizen; (*attention*) erregen

attraction [ə'trækʃən] *s* Anziehungskraft *f*; (*that which attracts*) Anziehungspunkt *m*; (*in a circus, variety show*) Attraktion *f*; (theat) Zugstück *n*

attractive [ə'træktɪv] *adj* reizvoll; (*price, offer*) günstig

attribute ['ætrɪ‚bjut] *s* Attribut *n* ‖ [ə'trɪbjut] *tr* (**to**) zuschreiben (*dat*)

attrition [ə'trɪʃən] *s* Abnutzung *f*, Verschleiß *m*

attune [ə't(j)un] *tr* (**to**) abstimmen (auf *acc*)

auburn ['ɔbərn] *adj* kastanienbraun

auction ['ɔkʃən] *s* Auktion *f* ‖ *tr*—**a. off** versteigern; **be auctioned off** unter den Hammer kommen

auctioneer [‚ɔkʃən'ɪr] *s* Versteigerer –in *mf*

audacious [ə'deʃəs] *adj* (*daring*) kühn; (*brazen*) keck

audacity [ə'dæsɪti] *s* (*daring*) Kühnheit *f*; (*insolence*) Unverschämtheit *f*

audience ['ɔdɪəns] *s* (*spectators*) Publikum *n*; (*formal hearing*) Audienz *f*; (rad) Zuhörerschaft *f*; (telv) Fernsehpublikum *n*

au'dio fre'quency ['ɔdɪ‚o] *s* Tonfrequenz *f*, Hörfrequenz *f*

au'dio-vis'ual *adj* audiovisuell; **a. aids** Lehrmittel *pl*

audit ['ɔdɪt] *s* Rechnungsprüfung *f* ‖ *tr* prüfen, revidieren; (*a lecture*) als Gasthörer belegen

audition [ɔ'dɪʃən] *s* Hörprobe *f* ‖ *tr* vorspielen (or vorsingen) lassen ‖ *intr* vorspielen, vorsingen

auditor ['ɔdɪtər] *s* (com) Rechnungsprüfer –in *mf*; (educ) Gasthörer –in *mf*

auditorium [‚ɔdɪ'tɔrɪ‚əm] *s* Hörsaal *m*

auger ['ɔgər] *s* Bohrer *m*

augment [ɔg'ment] *tr* (*in size*) vergrößern; (*in number*) vermehren ‖ *intr* sich vergrößern; sich vermehren

augur ['ɔgər] *s* Augur *m* ‖ *intr* weissagen; **a. well for** Gutes versprechen für

augury ['ɔgəri] *s* Weissagung *f*

august [ɔ'gʌst] *adj* erhaben ‖ **August** ['ɔgəst] *s* August *m*

aunt [ænt], [ɑnt] *s* Tante *f*

auricle ['ɔrɪkəl] *s* äußeres Ohr *n*; (*of the heart*) Herzohr *n*

auspices ['ɔspɪsɪz] *spl* Auspizien *pl*

auspicious [əs'pɪʃəs] *adj* glückverheißend

austere [ɔs'tɪr] *adj* (*stern*) streng; (*simple*) einfach; (*frugal*) genügsam; (*style*) schmucklos

Australia [ɔ'streljə] *s* Australien *n*

Australian [ɔ'streljən] *adj* australisch ‖ *s* Australier –in *mf*

Austria ['ɔstrɪ‚ə] *s* Österreich *n*

Austrian ['ɔstrɪ‚ən] *adj* österreichisch ‖ *s* Österreicher –in *mf*; (*dialect*) Österreichisch *n*

authentic [ə'θentɪk] *adj* authentisch

authenticate [ə'θentɪ‚ket] *tr* (*establish as genuine*) als echt erweisen; (*a document*) beglaubigen

author ['ɔθər] *s* (*of a book*) Autor –in *mf*; (*creator*) Urheber –in *mf*

authoritative [ə'θɔrɪ‚tetɪv] *adj* maßgebend

authority [ə'θɔrɪti] *s* (*power; expert*) Autorität *f*; (*right*) Recht *n*; (*approval*) Genehmigung *f*; (*source*) Quelle *f*; (*commanding influence*) Ansehen *n*; (*authoritative body*) Behörde *f*; **on one's own a.** auf eigene Verantwortung; **the authorities** die Behörden

authorize ['ɔθə‚raɪz] *tr* autorisieren

au'thorship' *s* Autorschaft *f*

au·to ['ɔto] *s* (**-tos**) Auto *n*

autobiography [‚ɔtobaɪ'ɑgrəfi] *s* Selbstbiographie *f*

autocratic [‚ɔtə'krætɪk] *adj* autokratisch

autograph ['ɔtə‚græf] *s* Autogramm *n* ‖ *tr* autographieren

automat ['ɔtə‚mæt] *s* Automatenrestaurant *n*

automatic [‚ɔtə'mætɪk] *adj* automatisch ‖ *s* Selbstladepistole *f*

automat'ic transmis'sion *s* Automatik *f*

automation [‚ɔtə'meʃən] *s* Automation *f*

automa·ton [ɔ'tʌmə‚tɑn] *s* (**-tons** & **-ta** [tə]) Automat *m*

automobile [ˌɔtəmoˈbil] s Automobil n

automotive [ˌɔtəˈmotɪv] adj Auto–

autonomous [ɔˈtʌnəməs] adj autonom

autonomy [ɔˈtɑnəmi] s Autonomie f

autopsy [ˈɔtɑpsi] s Obduktion f

autumn [ˈɔtəm] adj Herbst– || s Herbst m

autumnal [ɔˈtʌmnəl] adj herbstlich

auxiliary [ɔgˈzɪljəri] adj Hilfs– || s (helper) Helfer –in m|f; (gram) Hilfszeitwort n; **auxiliaries** (mil) Hilfstruppen pl

avail [əˈvel] s—**to no a.** nutzlos; **without a.** vergeblich || tr nützen (dat); **a. oneself of** sich bedienen (genit) || intr nützen

available [əˈveləbəl] adj vorhanden; (articles, products) erhältlich; (e.g., documents) zugänglich; **be a.** (for consultation, etc.) zu sprechen sein; **make a.** (to) zur Verfügung stellen (dat)

avalanche [ˈævəˌlæntʃ] s Lawine f

avarice [ˈævərɪs] s Habsucht f, Geiz m

avaricious [ˌævəˈrɪʃəs] adj geizig

avenge [əˈvendʒ] tr (a person) rächen; (a crime) ahnden; **a. oneself on** sich rächen an (dat)

avenger [əˈvendʒər] s Rächer –in m|f

avenue [ˈævəˌn(j)u] s (wide street) Straße f; (fig) Weg m

average [ˈævərɪdʒ] adj Durchschnitts– || s Durchschnitt m; (naut) Havarie f; **on the a.** im Durchschnitt || tr (amount to, as a mean quantity) durchschnittlich betragen; (find the average of) den Durchschnitt berechnen von; (earn on the average) durchschnittlich verdienen; (travel on the average) durchschnittlich zurücklegen

averse [əˈvʌrs] adj (to) abgeneigt (dat)

aversion [əˈvʌrʒən] s (to) Abneigung f (gegen)

avert [əˈvʌrt] tr abwenden

aviary [ˈevɪˌɛri] s Vogelhaus n

aviation [ˌevɪˈeʃən] s Flugwesen n

aviator [ˈevɪˌetər] s Flieger –in m|f

avid [ˈævɪd] adj gierig

avocation [ˌævəˈkeʃən] s Nebenbeschäftigung f

avoid [əˈvɔɪd] tr (a person) meiden; (a thing) vermeiden

avoidable [əˈvɔɪdəbəl] adj vermeidbar

avoidance [əˈvɔɪdəns] s (of a person) Meidung f; (of a thing) Vermeidung f

avow [əˈvau] tr bekennen, gestehen

avowal [əˈvauəl] s Bekenntnis n

avowed adj (declared) erklärt; (acknowledged) offen anerkannt

await [əˈwet] tr erwarten

awake [əˈwek] adj wach, munter || v (pret & pp **awoke** [əˈwok] & **awaked**) tr wecken; (fig) erwecken || intr erwachen

awaken [əˈweken] tr wecken; (fig) erwecken || intr erwachen

awak′ening s Erwachen n; **a rude a.** ein unsanftes Erwachen

award [əˈwɔrd] s Preis m, Prämie f || tr (to) zuerkennen (dat)

aware [əˈwer] adj—**be a. of** sich [dat] bewußt sein (genit)

awareness [əˈwernɪs] s Bewußtsein n

awash [əˈwɑʃ] adj überschwemmt

away [əˈwe] adj abwesend; (on a trip) verreist; (sport) Auswärts– || adv fort, (hin)weg; **do a. with** abschaffen; **make a. with** (kill) umbringen

awe [ɔ] s (of) Ehrfurcht f (vor dat); **stand in awe of s.o.** vor j–m Ehrfurcht haben

awesome [ˈɔsəm] adj ehrfurchtgebietend

awful [ˈɔfəl] adj ehrfurchtgebietend; (coll) furchtbar

awfully [ˈɔfəli] adv (coll) furchtbar

awhile [əˈhwaɪl] adv eine Zeitlang

awkward [ˈɔkwərd] adj ungeschickt; (situation) peinlich

awl [ɔl] s Ahle f, Pfriem m

awning [ˈɔnɪŋ] s Markise f

awry [əˈraɪ] adv—**go a.** schiefgehen

ax [æks] s Axt f, Beil n

axiom [ˈæksɪəm] s Axiom n

axiomatic [ˌæksɪəˈmætɪk] adj axiomatisch

axis [ˈæksɪs] s (axes [ˈæksiz]) Achse f

axle [ˈæksəl] s Achse f

ay(e) [aɪ] adv (yes) ja; **aye, aye, sir!** zu Befehl, Herr (Leutnant, etc.) || s Ja n, Jastimme f; **the ayes have it** die Mehrheit ist dafür

azalea [əˈzeljə] s Azalee f

azure [ˈəʒər] adj azurblau || s Azur m

B

B, b [bi] zweiter Buchstabe des englischen Alphabets; (mus) H n; **B flat** B n; **B sharp** His n

babble [ˈbæbəl] s Geschwätz n; (of brook) Geplätscher n || tr schwätzen || intr schwätzen; (said of a brook) plätschern

babe [beb] s Kind n; (naive person) Kindskopf m; (pretty girl) Puppe f

baboon [bæˈbun] s (zool) Pavian m

ba·by [ˈbebi] s Baby n; (youngest child) Nesthäkchen n || v (pret & pp –bied) tr verzärteln

ba′by bot′tle s Saugflasche f

ba′by car′riage s Kinderwagen m

ba′by grand′ s Stutzflügel m

ba′by pow′der s Kinderpuder m

ba′by-sit′ v (pret & pp –sat; ger –sitting) intr Kinder hüten

ba·by-sit′ter s Babysitter m

ba′by talk′ s Babysprache f
ba′by teeth′ spl Milchzähne pl
baccalaureate [ˌbækəˈlɔrɪ‧ɪt] s (bach-elor's degree) Bakkalaureat n; (serv-ice) Gottesdienst m bei der akade-mischen Promotion
bacchanal [ˈbækənəl] s (devotee) Bac-chantin f; (orgy) Bacchanal n
bachelor [ˈbætʃələr] s Junggeselle m
bach′elorhood′ s Junggesellenstand m
Bach′elor of Arts′ s Bakkalaureus m der Geisteswissenschaften
Bach′elor of Sci′ence s Bakkalaureus m der Naturwissenschaften
bacil·lus [bəˈsɪləs] s (–li [laɪ]) Ba-zillus m, Stäbchenbakterie f
back [bæk] adj Hinter-, Rück- ‖ s (of a man, animal) Rücken m, Kreuz n; (of a hand, book, knife, mountain) Rücken m; (of a head, house, door, picture, sheet) Rückseite f; (of a fabric) linke Seite f; (of a seat) Rückenlehne f; (of a coin) Kehrseite f; (of clothing) Rückenteil m; (sport) Verteidiger m; **at the b. of** (e.g., a room) hinten in (dat); **b. to b.** (coll) nacheinander; **behind s.o.'s b.** hinter j–s Rücken; **have one's b. to the wall** an die Wand gedrückt sein; **turn one's b. on s.o.** (& fig) j–m den Rücken kehren ‖ adv zurück; **b. and forth** hin und her; **b. home** bei uns (zulande); ‖ tr (a person) den Rücken decken (dat); (a candidate, product) befürworten; (a horse) set-zen auf (acc); **b. up** (a car) rückwärts laufen lassen; **b. water** rückwärts rudern; das Schiff rückwärts fahren lassen; (fig) sich zurückziehen ‖ intr —**b. down** klein beigeben; **b. down from** abstehen von; **b. out of** zurück-treten von; **b. up** zurückfahren; zurückgehen; (said of a sewer) zurückfließen
back′ache′ s Rückenschmerzen pl
back′bit′ing s Anschwärzerei f
back′bone′ s Rückgrat n; (fig) Willens-kraft f
back′break′ing adj mühsam
back′ door′ s Hintertür f
back′drop′ s (fig & theat) Hintergrund m
backer [ˈbækər] s Förderer m, Unter-stützer m; (com) Hintermann m
back′fire′ s Fehlzündung f ‖ intr fehl-zünden; (fig) nach hinten losgehen
back′ground′ adj Hintergrund- ‖ s (& fig) Hintergrund m; (e.g., of an ap-plicant) Vorbildung f, Erfahrung f
back′hand′ s (tennis) Ruckhandschlag m
back′hand′ed adj Rückhand-; (compli-ment) zweideutig
back′ing s Unterstützung f; (material) versteifende Ausfütterung f
back′lash′ s (& fig) Rückschlag m; (mach) toter Gang m
back′log′ s Rückstand m
back′ or′der s rückständiger Auftrag m
back′ pay′ s rückständiger Lohn m
back′ seat′ s Rücksitz m
back′side′ s Rückseite f; (coll) Gesäß n

back′space′ intr den Wagen zurück-schieben
back′space key′ s Rücktaste f
back′spin′ s Rückeffet n
back′stage′ adv hinten auf der Bühne
back′ stairs′ spl Hintertreppe f
back′stop′ s (baseball) Ballfang m
back′ stretch′ s Gegengerade f
back′stroke′ s Rückenschwimmen n
back′swept′ adj pfeilförmig
back′ talk′ s freche Antworten pl
back′track′ intr denselben Weg zurück-gehen; (fig) e–n Rückzieher machen
back′up′ s (stand-by) Beistand m; (in traffic) Verkehrsstauung f
back′up light′ s (aut) Rückfahrschein-werfer m
backward [ˈbækwərd] adj rückwärts gerichtet, Rück–; (country) rück-ständig; (in development) zurückge-blieben; (shy) zurückhaltend ‖ adv rückwärts, zurück; (fig) verkehrt; **b. and forward** vor und zurück
backwardness [ˈbækwərdnɪs] s Rück-ständigkeit f; (shyness) Zurückhal-tung f
back′wash′ s zurücklaufende Strömung f
back′wa′ter s Rückstau m; (fig) Öde f
back′woods′ spl Hinterwälder pl
back′yard′ s Hinterhof m
bacon [ˈbekən] s Speck m; **bring home the b.** (sl) es schaffen
bacteria [bækˈtɪrɪ‧ə] spl Bakterien pl
bacteriological [bækˌtɪrɪ‧əˈlɑdʒɪkəl] adj bakteriologisch
bacteriology [bækˌtɪrɪ‧əˈlɑdʒi] s Bak-teriologie f, Bakterienkunde f
bacteri·um [bækˈtɪrɪ‧əm] s (–a [ə]) Bakterie f
bad [bæd] adj schlecht, schlimm; (un-favorable) ungünstig; (risk) zweifel-haft; (debt) uneinbringlich; (check) ungedeckt; (blood) böse; (breath) übelriechend; (language) anstößig; (pain) stark; **bad for** schädlich (dat); **from bad to worse** immer schlimmer; **I feel bad about it** es tut mir leid; **too bad!** schade!
bad′ egg′ s (sl) übler Kunde m
badge [bædʒ] s Abzeichen n
badger [ˈbædʒər] s Dachs m ‖ tr quälen
bad′ luck′ s Unglück n, Pech n
badly [ˈbædli] adv schlecht, übel; (coll) dringend; **b. wounded** schwer-verwundet; **be b. off** übel dran sein
badminton [ˈbædmɪntən] s Federball-spiel n
bad′-tem′pered adj schlecht gelaunt
baffle [ˈbæfəl] s Sperre f; (on loud-speaker) Schallwand f ‖ tr verwir-ren; (gas) drosseln
baf′fling adj verwirrend
bag [bæg] s Sack m; (for small items) Tüte f; (for travel) Reisetasche f; (sl) Frauenzimmer n; (hunt) Strecke f; **bag and baggage** mit Sack und Pack; **it's in the bag** das haben wir in der Tasche ‖ v (pret & pp bagged; ger bagging) tr einsacken; (hunt) zur Strecke bringen ‖ intr sich bauschen
baggage [ˈbægɪdʒ] s Gepäck n

bag′gage car′ s Gepäckwagen m

bag′gage check′ s Gepäckschein m

bag′gage count′er s Gepäckabfertigung f

bag′gage room′ s Gepäckaufbewahrung f

baggy ['bægi] adj bauschig

bag′pipe′ s Dudelsack m; play the b. dudeln

bail [bel] s Kaution f; be out on b. gegen Kaution auf freiem Fuß sein; put up b. for bürgen für || tr—b. out (water) ausschöpfen; (fig) retten; (jur) durch Kaution aus der Haft befreien || intr Wasser schöpfen; b. out (aer) abspringen

bailiff ['belɪf] s (agr) Gutsverwalter m; (jur) Gerichtsvollzieher m

bailiwick ['belɪwɪk] s (fig) Spezialgebiet n; (jur) Amtsbezirk m

bait [bet] s (& fig) Köder m || tr (traps) mit Köder versehen; (lure) ködern; (harass) quälen

bake [bek] tr (bread) backen; (meat) braten; (in a kiln) brennen || intr backen; (meat) braten

baked′ goods′ spl Gebäck n, Backwaren pl

baked′ pota′to s gebackene Pellkartoffel f

baker ['bekər] s Bäcker –in mf

bakery ['bekəri] s Bäckerei f

bak′ing pow′der s Backpulver n

bak′ing so′da s Backpulver n

balance ['bæləns] s (equilibrium) Gleichgewicht n; (remainder) Rest m; (scales) Waage f; (in a bank account) Bankguthaben n; (fig) Fassung f; (com) Bilanz f; || tr balancieren; (offset) abgleichen; (make come out even) ausgleichen || intr balancieren

bal′ance of pay′ments s Devisenbilanz f

bal′ance of pow′er s Gleichgewicht n der Kräfte

bal′ance sheet′ s Bilanz f

bal′ance wheel′ s (horol) Unruh f

balcony ['bælkəni] s Balkon m; (theat) Rang m

bald [bɔld] adj kahl; (eagle) weißköpfig; (fig) unverblümt

bald′head′ed adj kahlköpfig

baldness ['bɔldnɪs] s Kahlheit f

bald′ spot′ s Kahlstelle f

bale [bel] s Ballen m || tr in Ballen verpacken

baleful ['belfəl] adj unheilvoll

balk [bɔk] intr (at) scheuen (vor dat)

Balkan ['bɔlkən] adj Balkan– || s— the Balkans der Balkan

balky ['bɔki] adj störrisch

ball [bɔl] s Ball m; (dance) Ball m; (of yarn) Knäuel m & n; (of the foot) Ballen m; be on the b. (coll) bei der Sache sein; have a lot on the b. (coll) viel auf dem Kasten haben

ballad ['bæləd] s Ballade f

ball′-and-sock′et joint′ s Kugelgelenk n

ballast ['bæləst] s (aer, naut) Ballast m; (rr) Schotter m || tr (aer, naut) mit Ballast beladen; (rr) beschottern

ball′ bear′ing s Kugellager n

ballerina [,bælə'rinə] s Ballerina f

ballet [bæ'le] s Ballett n

ball′ han′dling s (sport) Balltechnik f

ballistic [bə'lɪstɪk] adj ballistisch || ballistics s Ballistik f

balloon [bə'lun] s Ballon m

ballot ['bælət] s Stimmzettel m || intr abstimmen

bal′lot box′ s Wahlurne f

ball′-point pen′ s Kugelschreiber m

ball′room′ s Ballsaal m, Tanzsaal m

ballyhoo ['bælɪ,hu] s Tamtam n || tr Tamtam machen um

balm [bɑm] s (& fig) Balsam m

balmy ['bɑmi] adj mild, lind; be b. (coll) e–n Tick haben

baloney [bə'loni] s (sausage) (coll) Bolognawurst f; (sl) Quatsch m

balsam ['bɔlsəm] s Balsam m

Baltic ['bɔltɪk] adj baltisch || s Ostsee f

baluster ['bæləstər] s Geländersäule f

balustrade ['bæləs,tred] s Brüstung f

bamboo [bæm'bu] s Bambus m, Bambusrohr n

bamboozle [bæm'buzəl] tr (cheat) anschmieren; (mislead) irreführen; (perplex) verwirren

ban [bæn] s Verbot n; (eccl) Bann m; || v (pret & pp banned; ger banning) tr verbieten

banal [bə'nɑl] adj banal

banana [bə'nænə] s Banane f; (tree) Bananenbaum m

band [bænd] s (e.g., of a hat) Band n; (stripe) Steifen m; (gang) Bande f; (mus) Musikkapelle f; (rad) Band n || intr—b. together sich zusammenrotten

bandage ['bændɪdʒ] s Verband m || tr verbinden

Band′-Aid′ s (trademark) Schnellverband m

bandit ['bændɪt] s Bandit m

band′lead′er s Kapellmeister m

band′ saw′ s Bandsäge f

band′stand′ s Musikpavillon m

band′wag′on s—climb the b. mitlaufen

bane [ben] s Ruin m

baneful ['benfəl] adj verderblich

bang [bæŋ] s Knall m; bangs Ponyfrisur f; with a b. mit Krach || tr knallen lassen; (a door) zuschlagen; || intr knallen; (said of a door) zuschlagen; || interj bums! paff!

bang′-up′ adj (sl) tipptopp, prima

banish ['bænɪʃ] tr verbannen

banishment ['bænɪʃmənt] s Verbannung f

banister ['bænɪstər] s Geländer n

bank [bæŋk] s Bank f; (of a river) Ufer n; (in a road) Überhöhung f; (aer) Schräglage f; (rr) Böschung f; || tr (money) in e–r Bank deponieren; (a road) überhöhen; (aer) in Schräglage bringen || intr (at) ein Bankkonto haben (bei); (aer) in die Kurve gehen; b. on bauen auf (acc)

bank′ account′ s Bankkonto n

bank′ bal′ance s Bankguthaben n

bank′book′ s Sparbuch n, Bankbuch n

banker ['bæŋkər] s Bankier –in mf

bank'ing s Bankwesen n
bank' note' s Geldschein m
bank'roll' s Rolle f von Geldscheinen || tr (sl) finanzieren
bankrupt ['bæŋkrʌpt] adj bankrott; go b. Pleite machen || tr bankrott machen
bankruptcy ['bæŋkrʌptsi] s Bankrott m
bank' state'ment s Bankausweis m
banner ['bænər] s Fahne f, Banner n
banquet ['bæŋkwɪt] s Bankett n || intr tafeln
banter ['bæntər] s Neckerei f || intr necken
baptism ['bæptɪzəm] s Taufe f
baptismal [bæp'tɪzməl] adj Tauf-
baptis'mal certi'ficate s Taufschein m
bap'tism of fire' s Feuertaufe f
Baptist ['bæptɪst] s Baptist –in mf, Wiedertäufer m
baptistery ['bæptɪstəri] s Taufkapelle f
baptize [bæp'taɪz] tr taufen
bar [bar] s Stange f; (of a door, window) Riegel m; (of gold, etc.) Barren m; (of chocolate, soap) Riegel m; (barroom) Bar f; (counter) Schanktisch m; (obstacle) (to) Schranke f (gegen); (jur) Gerichtshof m, Anwaltschaft f; (bar line) (mus) Taktstrich m; (measure) Takt m; (naut) Barre f; be admitted to the bar zur Advokatur zugelassen werden; behind bars hinter Gittern; || prep— bar none ohne Ausnahme || v (pret & pp barred; ger barring) tr (a door) verriegeln; (a window) vergittern; (the way) versperren; bar s.o. from j–n hindern an (dat)
barb [barb] s Widerhaken m; (fig) Stachelrede f; (bot) Bart m
barbarian [bar'berɪ·ən] s Barbar m
barbaric [bar'bærɪk] adj barbarisch
barbarism ['barbə,rɪzəm] s Barbarei f; (gram) Barbarismus m
barbarity [bar'berɪti] s Barbarei f
barbarous ['barbərəs] adj barbarisch
barbecue ['barbɪ,kju] s am Spieß (or am Rost) gebratenes Fleisch n; (grill) Bratrost m; (outdoor meal) Gartengrillfest n || tr am Spieß (or am Rost) braten
barbed' wire' s Stacheldraht m
barbed'-wire entan'glement s Drahtverhau m
barber ['barbər] s Friseur m
bar'ber chair' s Friseursessel m
bar'bershop' s Friseurladen m
bard [bard] s Barde m
bare [ber] adj nackt, bloß; (tree, wall) kahl; (facts) nackt; (majority) knapp || tr entblößen; (heart, thoughts) offenbaren; (teeth) fletschen
bare'back' adj & adv sattellos
bare'faced' adj unverschämt
bare'foot' adj & adv barfuß
bare'head'ed adj & adv barhäuptig
barely ['berli] adv kaum, bloß
bar'fly' s Kneipenhocker m
bargain ['bargɪn] s (deal) Geschäft n; (cheap purchase) Sonderangebot n; into the b. obendrein; it's a b.! abge-

macht! || tr—b. away mit Verlust verkaufen || intr handeln; b. for verhandeln über (acc)
bar'gain price' s Preisschlager m
bar'gain sale' s Sonderverkauf m
barge [bardʒ] s Lastkahn m; || intr— b. in hereinstürzen; b. into stürzen in (acc)
baritone ['berɪ,ton] s Bariton m
barium ['berɪ·əm] s Barium n
bark [bark] s (of a tree) Rinde f; (of a dog) Bellen n, Gebell n; (boat) Barke f; tr—b. out bellend hervorstoßen || intr bellen; b. at anbellen
barker ['barkər] s Anreißer m
barley ['barli] s Gerste f; grain of b. Graupe f
bar'maid' s Schankmädchen n, Bardame f
barn [barn] s Scheune f; (for animals) Stall m
barnacle ['barnəkəl] s Entenmuschel f
barn'storm' intr auf dem Lande Theateraufführungen veranstalten; (pol) auf dem Lande Wahlreden halten
barn'yard' s Scheunenhof m
barometer [bə'ramɪtər] s Barometer n
barometric [,bærə'metrɪk] adj barometrisch
baron ['bærən] s Baron m
baroness ['bærənɪs] s Baronin f
baroque [bə'rok] adj barock || s (style, period) Barock m & n
barracks ['bærəks] s (temporary wooden structure) Baracke f; (mil) Kaserne f
barrage [bə'raʒ] s Sperrfeuer n; moving b. Sperrfeuerwalze f
barrel ['bærəl] s Faß n, Tonne f; (of a gun) Lauf m; (of money, fun) große Menge f; have over the b. (sl) in der Gewalt haben || intr (coll) rasen, sausen
barren ['bærən] adj dürr, unfruchtbar; (landscape) kahl
barricade ['bærɪ,ked] s Barrikade f || tr verbarrikadieren
barrier ['bærɪ·ər] s Schranke f, Schlagbaum m; (e.g., on a street) Sperre f
bar'room' s Schenkstube f, Bar f
bartend ['bar,tend] intr Getränke ausschenken
bar'tend'er s Schankwirt m, Barmixer m
barter ['bartər] s Tauschhandel m || tr tauschen || intr Tauschhandel treiben
basalt [bə'sɔlt], ['bæsɔlt] s Basalt m
base [bes] adj gemein, niedrig; (metal) unedel || s (cosmetic) Schminkunterlage f; (fig) Grundlage f; (archit) Basis f, Fundament n; (baseball) Mal n; (chem) Base f; (geom) Grundlinie f, Grundfläche f; (math) Basis f; (mil) Stützpunkt m || tr (mil) stationieren; b. on stützen auf (acc), gründen auf (acc)
base'ball' s Baseball m
base'board' s Wandleiste f
basement ['besmənt] s Kellergeschoß n
bash [bæʃ] s heftiger Schlag m
bashful ['bæʃfəl] adj schüchtern

basic ['besɪk] *adj* grundsätzlich; (*e.g.,
salary*) Grund–; (chem) basisch
basically ['besɪkəli] *adv* grundsätzlich
ba'sic train'ing *s* Grundausbildung *f*
basilica [bə'sɪlɪkə] *s* Basilika *f*
basin ['besɪn] *s* Becken *n*; (geol) Mulde *f*; (naut) Bassin *n*
ba·sis ['besɪs] *s* (–ses [siz]) Basis *f*,
Grundlage *f*; b. of comparison Ver-
gleichsgrundlage *f*; put on a firm b.
(fin) sanieren
bask [bæsk] *intr* (& fig) sich sonnen
basket ['bæskɪt] *s* (& sport) Korb *m*
bas'ketball' *s* Basketball *m*, Korbball *m*
bas-relief [,bɑrɪ'lif] *s* Flachrelief *n*
bass [bes] *adj* Baß– ‖ *s* (mus) Baß *m*
‖ [bæs] *s* (ichth) Flußbarsch *m*, See-
barsch *m*
bass' clef' *s* Baßschlüssel *m*
bass' drum' *s* große Trommel *f*
bass' fid'dle *s* Baßgeige *f*
bassoon [bə'sun] *s* Fagott *n*
bass viol ['bes 'vaɪ·əl] *s* Gambe *f*
bastard ['bæstərd] *adj* Bastard–; (*illegitimate in birth*) unehelich ‖ *s*
Bastard *m*; (vulg) Schweinehund *m*
baste [best] *tr* (*thrash*) verprügeln;
(*scold*) schelten; (culin) begießen;
(*sew*) lose (an)heften
bastion ['bæstʃən] *s* Bastion *f*
bat [bæt] *s* (sport) Schläger *m*; (zool)
Fledermaus *f*; go to bat for s.o. (fig)
für j–n eintreten ‖ *v* (*pret & pp
batted; ger batting*) *tr* schlagen;
without batting an eye ohne mit der
Wimper zu zucken
batch [bætʃ] *s* Satz *m*, Haufen *m*; (*of
bread*) Schub *m*; (*of letters*) Stoß *m*
bated ['betɪd] *adj*–with b. breath mit
verhaltenem Atem
bath [bæθ] *s* Bad *n*; take a b. ein Bad
nehmen
bathe [beð] *tr & intr* baden
bather ['beðər] *s* Badende *mf*
bath'house' *s* Umkleideräume *pl*
bath'ing *s* Baden *n*, Bad *n*
bath'ing cap' *s* Badehaube *f*
bath'ing suit' *s* Badeanzug *m*
bath'ing trunks' *spl* Badehose *f*
bath'robe' *s* Bademantel *m*
bath'room' *s* Badezimmer *n*
bath'room fix'tures *spl* Armaturen *pl*
bath'room scales *spl* Personenwaage *f*
bath' tow'el *s* Badetuch *n*
bath'tub' *s* Badewanne *f*
baton [bæ'tɑn] *s* (mil) Kommandostab
m; (mus) Taktstock *m*
battalion [bə'tæljən] *s* Bataillon *n*
batter ['bætər] *s* Teig *m*; (baseball)
Schläger –in *mf* ‖ *tr* zerschlagen;
(aer) bombardieren; **b. down** niederschlagen; **b. in** einschlagen
bat'tering ram' *s* Sturmbock *m*
battery ['bætəri] *s* Batterie *f*; (*secondary cell*) Akkumulator *m*; (arti) Batterie *f*; (nav) Geschützgruppe *f*
battle ['bætəl] *s* Schlacht *f*; (& fig)
Kampf *m*; **do b.** kämpfen; **in b.** im
Felde ‖ *tr* bekämpfen ‖ *intr* kämpfen
bat'tle array' *s* Schlachtordnung *f*
bat'tleax' *s* Streitaxt *f*; (fig) Drachen
m
bat'tle cruis'er *s* Schlachtkreuzer *m*

bat'tle cry' *s* Schlachtruf *m*; (fig)
Schlagwort *n*
bat'tle fatigue' *s* Kriegsneurose *f*
bat'tlefield' *s* Schlachtfeld *n*
bat'tlefront' *s* Front *f*, Hauptkampf-
linie *f*
bat'tleground' *s* Kampfplatz *m*
battlement ['bætəlmənt] *s* Zinne *f*
bat'tle scar' *s* Kampfmal *n*
bat'tleship' *s* Schlachtschiff *n*
bat'tle wag'on *s* (coll) Schlachtschiff *n*
batty ['bæti] *adj* (sl) doof
bauble ['bobəl] *s* Tand *m*; (*jester's
staff*) Narrenstab *m*
Bavaria [bə'verɪ·ə] *s* Bayern *n*
Bavarian [bə'verɪ·ən] *adj* bayerisch ‖
s Bayer –in *mf*
bawd [bɔd] *s* Dirne *f*
bawdy ['bɔdi] *adj* unzüchtig
bawl [bɔl] *s* Geplärr *n* ‖ *tr*–b. out
(*names, etc.*) ausschreien; (*scold*) an-
schnauzen ‖ *intr* (coll) plärren
bay [be] *adj* kastanienbraun ‖ *s* Bucht
f; (*horse*) Rotfuchs *m*; (bot) Lorbeer
m; keep at bay in Schach halten ‖
intr laut bellen; **bay at** anbellen
bayo·net ['be·ənɪt] *s* Bajonett *n*, Seitengewehr *n*; with fixed bayonets mit
aufgepflanztem Bajonett ‖ *v* (*pret &
pp* –net(t)ed; *ger* –net(t)ing) *tr* mit
dem Bajonett erstechen
bay' win'dow *s* Erkerfenster *n*
bazaar [bə'zɑr] *s* Basar *m*, Markt *m*
bazooka [bə'zukə] *s* Panzerfaust *f*
be [bi] *v* (*pres am* [æm], *is* [ɪz], *are*
[ɑr]; *pret was* [wɑz], [wʌz], *were*
[wʌr]; *pp been* [bɪn]) *intr* sein; be
about in der Nähe sein; be about to
(*inf*) im Begriff sein zu (*inf*); be
after s.o. hinter j–m her sein; be
along hier sein; be behind in im
Rückstand sein mit; be behind s.o.
j–m den Rücken decken; be from
(*a country*) stammen aus, sein aus;
be in zu Hause sein; be in for zu
erwarten haben; be in for it in der
Patsche sitzen; be in on dabei sein
bei; be off weggehen; be on to s.o.
j–m auf die Schliche kommen; be
out nicht zu Hause sein, aus sein;
be out for s.th. auf der Suche nach
etw sein; be up auf sein; be up to
s.th. etw im Sinn haben; how are
you? wie geht es Ihnen?, wie befin-
den Sie sich?; how much is that?
wieviel kostet das?; there are, there
is es gibt (*acc*) ‖ *aux*—he is studying
er studiert; he is to go er soll gehen;
he was hit er ist getroffen worden ‖
impers—how is it that...? wie
kommt es, daß...?; it is cold es ist
kalt; it is to be seen that es ist darauf zu sehen, daß
beach [bitʃ] *s* Strand *m*; on the b. am
Strand, an der See ‖ *tr* auf den
Strand ziehen; be beached stranden
beach'comb'er *s* Strandgutjäger *m*;
(*wave*) Strandwelle *f*
beach'head' *s* Landekopf *m*
beach' tow'el *s* Badetuch *n*
beach' umbrel'la *s* Strandschirm *m*
beacon ['bikən] *s* Leuchtfeuer *n*, Bake
f; (*lighthouse*) Leuchtturm *m*; (aer)

Scheinwerfer *m* || *tr* lenken || *intr* leuchten

bead [bid] (*of glass, wood, sweat*) Perle *f*; (*of a gun*) Korn *n*; **beads** (eccl) Rosenkranz *m*; **draw a b. on** zielen auf (*acc*)

beagle ['bigel] *s* Spürhund *m*

beak [bik] *s* Schnabel *m*; (*nose*) (sl) Rübe *f*

beam [bim] *s* (*of wood*) Balken *m*; (*of light, heat, etc.*) Strahl *m*; (*fig*) Glanz *m*; (aer) Leitstrahl *m*; (*width of a vessel*) (naut) größte Schiffsbreite *f*; (*horizontal structural member*) (naut) Deckbalken *m*; **b. of light** Lichtkegel *m*; **off the b.** (sl) auf dem Holzweg; **on the b.** (sl) auf Draht || *intr* strahlen; **b. at** anstrahlen

bean [bin] *s* Bohne *f*; (*head*) (sl) Birne *f*; **spill the beans** (sl) alles ausquatschen

bean'pole' *s* (& coll) Bohnenstange *f*

bear [ber] *adj* (*market*) flau, Baisse– || *s* Bär *m*; (st. exch.) Baissier *m* || *v* (*pret* **bore** [bor]; *pp* **borne** [born]) *tr* (*carry*) tragen; (*endure*) dulden, ertragen; (*children*) gebären; (*date*) tragen; (*a name, sword*) führen; (*a grudge, love*) hegen; (*a message*) überbringen; (*the consequences*) auf sich [*acc*] nehmen; **bear in mind** bedenken, beachten; **bear fruit** Früchte tragen; (fig) Frucht tragen; **bear out** bestätigen || *intr*—**bear down on** losgehen auf (*acc*); (naut) zufahren auf (*acc*); **bear left** sich links halten; **bear on** sich beziehen auf (*acc*); **bear up** (well) against gut ertragen; **bear with** Geduld haben mit

bearable ['berəbəl] *adj* erträglich

beard [bɪrd] *s* Bart *m*

beard'ed *adj* bärtig

beardless ['bɪrdlɪs] *adj* bartlos

bearer ['berər] *s* Träger –in *mf*; (*of a message*) Überbringer –in *mf*; (com) Inhaber –in *mf*

bear' hug' *s* (coll) Knutsch *m*

bear'ing *s* Körperhaltung *f*; (mach) Lager *n*; (on) Beziehung *f* (auf *acc*); **bearings** (aer, naut) Lage *f*, Richtung *f*, Peilung *f*; **lose one's bearings** die Richtung verlieren

bear'skin' *s* Bärenfell *n*

beast [bist] *s* Tier *n*; (fig) Bestie *f*

beastly ['bistli] *adj* bestialisch; **b. weather** Hundewetter *n*

beast' **of bur'den** *s* Lasttier *n*

beat [bit] *adj* (sl) erschöpft || *s* (*of the heart*) Schlag *m*; (*of a policeman*) Runde *f*, Revier *n*; (mus) Takt *m* || *v* (*pret* **beat**; *pp* **beat & beaten**) *tr* (*eggs, a child, record, team, etc.*) schlagen; (*a carpet*) ausklopfen; (*metal*) hämmern; (*a path*) treten; **b. it!** hau ab!; **b. one's brains out** sich [*dat*] den Kopf zerbrechen; **b. s.o. to** j-m zuvorkommen; **b. up** verprügeln || *intr* schlagen, klopfen; **b. against** peitschen gegen; **b. down** niederprallen

beati·fy [bɪ'ætɪ,faɪ] *v* (*pret & pp* **–fied**) *tr* seligsprechen

beat'ing *s* Prügel *pl*

beatitude [bɪ'ætɪ,t(j)ud] *s* Seligpreisung *f*

beau [bo] *s* (**beaus & beaux** [boz]) Liebhaber *m*

beautician [bju'tɪʃən] *s* Kosmetiker –in *mf*; (*hairdresser*) Friseuse *f*

beautiful ['bjutɪfəl] *adj* schön

beauti·fy ['bjutɪ,faɪ] *v* (*pret & pp* **–fied**) *tr* verschönern

beauty ['bjuti] *s* (*quality; woman*) Schönheit *f*; (coll) Prachtexemplar *n*

beau'ty queen' *s* Schönheitskönigin *f*

beau'ty shop' *s* Frisiersalon *m*

beau'ty sleep' *s* Schönheitsschlaf *m*

beau'ty spot' *s* Schönheitsmal *n*

beaver ['bivər] *s* Biber *m*

because [bɪ'kɔz] *conj* weil, da || *interj* darum!

because' **of** *prep* wegen (genit)

beck [bek] *s* Wink *m*; **be at s.o.'s beck and call** j-m ganz zu Diensten sein

beckon ['bekən] *tr* zuwinken (*dat*); (*summon*) heranwinken || *intr* winken; **b. to s.o.** j-m zuwinken

become [bɪ'kʌm] *v* (*pret* **–came**; *pp* **–come**) *tr* (*said of clothes*) gut anstehen (*dat*); (*said of conduct*) sich schicken für || *intr* werden; **what has b. of him?** was ist aus ihm geworden?

becom'ing *adj* (*said of clothes*) kleidsam; (*said of conduct*) schicklich

bed [bed] *s* (*for sleeping; of a river*) Bett *n*; (*of flowers*) Beet *n*; (*of straw*) Lager *n*; (geol) Lager *n*; (rr) Unterbau *m*; **put to bed** zu Bett bringen

bed'bug' *s* Wanze *f*

bed'clothes' *spl* Bettwäsche *f*

bed'ding *s* Bettzeug *n*; (*for animals*) Streu *f*

bed'fel'low *s*—**strange bedfellows** ein seltsames Paar *n*

bedlam ['bedləm] *s* (fig) Tollhaus *n*; **there was b.** es ging zu wie im Tollhaus

bed' lin'en *s* Bettwäsche *f*

bed'pan' *s* Bettschüssel *f*

bed'post' *s* Bettpfosten *m*

bedraggled [bɪ'drægəld] *adj* beschmutzt

bedridden ['bed,rɪdən] *adj* bettlägerig

bed'rock' *s* Grundgestein *n*; (fig) Grundlage *f*

bed'room' *s* Schlafzimmer *n*

bed'side' *s*—**at s.o.'s b.** an j–s Bett

bed'sore' *s* wundgelegene Stelle *f*; **get bedsores** sich wundliegen

bed'spread' *s* Bettdecke *f*, Tagesdecke *f*

bed'spring' *s* (*one coil*) Sprungfeder *f*; (*framework of springs*) Sprungfedermatratze *f*

bed'stead' *s* Bettgestell *n*

bed'time' *s* Schlafenszeit *f*; **it's past b.** es ist höchste Zeit, zu Bett zu gehen

bee [bi] *s* Biene *f*

beech [bitʃ] *s* Buche *f*

beech'nut' *s* Buchecker *f*

beef [bif] *s* Rindfleisch *n*; (*brawn*) (coll) Muskelkraft *f*; (*human flesh*) (coll) Fleisch *n*; (*complaint*) (sl) Gemecker *n* || *tr*—**b. up** (coll) verstärken ‖ *intr (complain)* (sl) meckern

beef′ broth′ *s* Kraftbrühe *f*

beef′steak′ *s* Beefsteak *n*

beefy [ˈbifi] *adj* muskulös

bee′hive′ *s* Bienenstock *m*, Bienenkorb *m*

bee′line′ *s*—**make a b. for** schnurstracks losgehen auf *(acc)*

beer [bɪr] *s* Bier *n*

bee′ sting′ *s* Bienenstich *m*

beeswax [ˈbiz͵wæks] *s* Bienenwachs *n*

beet [bit] *s* Rübe *f*

beetle [ˈbitəl] *s* Käfer *m*

be•fall [bɪˈfɔl] *v (pret* **–fell** [ˈfɛl]; *pp* **–fallen** [ˈfɔlən]) *tr* betreffen, zustoßen ‖ *intr* sich ereignen

befit′ting *adj* passend

before [bɪˈfor] *adv* vorher, früher ‖ *prep (position or time)* vor *(dat)*; *(direction)* vor *(acc)*; **b. long** binnen kurzem; **b. now** schon früher ‖ *conj* bevor, ehe

before′hand′ *adv* zuvor, vorher

befriend [bɪˈfrɛnd] *tr* sich *[dat]* *(j–n)* zum Freund machen, sich anfreunden mit

befuddle [bɪˈfʌdəl] *tr* verwirren

beg [bɛg] *v (pret & pp* begged; *ger* begging) *tr* bitten um; *(a meal)* betteln um; **beg s.o. to** *(inf)* j–n bitten zu *(inf)*; **I beg your pardon** (ich bitte um) Verzeihung! ‖ *intr* betteln; *(said of a dog)* Männchen machen; **beg for** bitten um, flehen um; **beg off** absagen

be•get [bɪˈgɛt] *v (pret* **–got** [ˈgɑt]; *pp* **–gotten & –got**; *ger* **–getting**) *tr* erzeugen

beggar [ˈbɛgər] *s* Bettler –in *mf*

be•gin [bɪˈgɪn] *v (pret* **–gan** [ˈgæn]; *pp* **–gun** [ˈgʌn]; *ger* **–ginning** [ˈgɪnɪŋ]) *tr* beginnen, anfangen ‖ *intr* beginnen, anfangen; **to b. with** zunächst

beginner [bɪˈgɪnər] *s* Anfänger –in *mf*

begin′ning *s* Beginn *m*, Anfang *m*

begrudge [bɪˈgrʌdʒ] *tr*—**b. s.o. s.th.** j–m etw mißgönnen

beguile [bɪˈgaɪl] *tr (mislead)* verleiten; *(charm)* betören

behalf [bɪˈhæf] *s*—**on b. of** zugunsten *(genit),* für; *(as a representative of)* im Namen *(genit),* im Auftrag von

behave [bɪˈhev] *intr* sich benehmen

behavior [bɪˈhevjər] *s* Benehmen *n*

behead [bɪˈhɛd] *tr* enthaupten

behind [bɪˈhaɪnd] *adj (in arrears)* (in) im Rückstand (mit); **the clock is ten minutes b.** die Uhr geht zehn Minuten nach ‖ *adv (in the rear)* hinten, hinterher; *(to the rear)* nach hinten, zurück; **from b.** von hinten ‖ *s* (sl) Hintern *m*, Popo *m* ‖ *prep (position)* hinter *(dat)*; *(direction)* hinter *(acc)*; **be b. schedule** sich verspäten; **b. time** zu spät sein; **b. the times** hinter dem Mond

be•hold [bɪˈhold] *v (pret & pp* **–held** [ˈhɛld]) *tr* betrachten ‖ *interj* schau!

behoove [bɪˈhuv] *impers*—**it behooves me** es geziemt mir

beige [beʒ] *adj* beige ‖ *s* Beige *n*

be′ing *adj*—**for the time b.** einstweilen

‖ *s* Dasein *n*; *(creature)* Wesen *n*; **come into b.** entstehen

belabor [bɪˈlebər] *tr* herumreiten auf *(dat)*

belated [bɪˈletɪd] *adj* verspätet

belch [bɛltʃ] *s* Rülpser *m* ‖ *tr (fire)* ausspeien ‖ *intr* rülpsen

beleaguer [bɪˈligər] *tr* belagern

belfry [ˈbɛlfri] *s* Glockenturm *m*

Belgian [ˈbɛlʒən] *adj* belgisch ‖ *s* Belgier –in *mf*

Belgium [ˈbɛldʒəm] *s* Belgien *n*

belief [bɪˈlif] *s* **(in)** Glaube(n) *m* (an *acc)*

believable [bɪˈlivəbəl] *adj* glaublich

believe [bɪˈliv] *tr (a thing)* glauben; *(a person)* glauben *(dat)* ‖ *intr* glauben; **b. in** glauben an *(acc)*; **I don't b. in war** ich halte nicht viel vom Kriege

believer [bɪˈlivər] *s* Gläubige *mf*

belittle [bɪˈlɪtəl] *tr* herabsetzen

bell [bɛl] *s* Glocke *f*; *(small bell)* Klingel *f*; *(of a wind instrument)* Schalltrichter *m*; *(box)* Gong *m*

bell′boy′ *s* Hotelboy *m*

bell′hop′ *s* (sl) Hotelpage *m*

belligerent [bəˈlɪdʒərənt] *adj* streitlustig ‖ *s* kriegführender Staat *m*

bell′ jar′ *s* Glasglocke *f*

bellow [ˈbɛlo] *s* Gebrüll *n*; **bellows** Blasebalg *m*; (phot) Balgen *m* ‖ *tr & intr* brüllen

bell′ tow′er *s* Glockenturm *m*

bel•ly [ˈbɛli] *s* Bauch *m*; *(of a sail)* Bausch *m* ‖ *v (pret & pp* **–lied**) *intr* bauschen

bel′lyache′ *s* (coll) Bauchweh *n* ‖ *intr* (sl) jammern

bel′ly but′ton *s* Nabel *m*

bel′ly danc′er *s* Bauchtänzerin *f*

bel′ly flop′ *s* Bauchklatscher *m*

bellyful [ˈbɛli͵ful] *s*—**have a b. of** die Nase voll haben von

bel′ly-land′ing *s* Bauchlandung *f*

belong [bɪˈlɔŋ] *intr* **b. to** *(designating ownership)* gehören *(dat)*; *(designating membership)* gehören zu; **where does this table b.?** wohin gehört dieser Tisch?

belongings [bɪˈlɔŋɪŋz] *spl* Sachen *pl*

beloved [bɪˈlʌvɪd], [bɪˈlʌvd] *adj* geliebt ‖ *s* Geliebte *mf*

below [bɪˈlo] *adv (position)* unten; *(direction)* nach unten, hinunter ‖ *prep (position)* unter *(dat),* unterhalb *(genit)*; *(direction)* unter *(acc)*

belt [bɛlt] *s* Riemen *m*, Gurt *m*, Gürtel *m*; (geol) Gebiet *n*; (mach) Treibriemen *m*; **tighten one's b.** den Riemen enger schnallen *(fig)* ‖ *tr* (sl) e–n heftigen Schlag versetzen *(dat)*

belt′ buck′le *s* Gürtelschnalle *f*

belt′way′ *s* Verkehrsgürtel *m*

bemoan [bɪˈmon] *tr* betrauern, beklagen

bench [bɛntʃ] *s* Bank *f*; (jur) Gerichtshof *m*; (sport) Reservebank *f*, Bank *f*

bend [bɛnd] *s* Biegung *f*, *(in a road)* Kurve *f*; **bends** (pathol) Tauchkrankheit *f* ‖ *v (pret & pp* bent [bɛnt]) *tr* biegen, beugen; *(a bow)* spannen ‖

intr sich biegen, sich beugen; **b. down** sich bücken; **b. over backwards** (fig) sich [*dat*] übergroße Mühe geben

beneath [bɪ'niθ] *adv* unten || *prep* (*position*) unter (*dat*), unterhalb (*genit*); (*direction*) unter (*acc*); **b. me** unter meiner Würde

benediction [,benɪ'dɪk/ən] *s* Segen *m*

benefactor ['benɪ,fæktər] *s* Wohltäter –in *mf*

beneficence [bɪ'nefɪsəns] *s* Wohltätigkeit *f*

beneficent [bɪ'nefɪsənt] *adj* wohltätig

beneficial [,benɪ'fɪ/əl] *adj* heilbringend, gesund; **(to)** nützlich (*dat*)

beneficiary [,benɪ'fɪ/ɪ,erɪ] *s* Begünstigte *mf*; (ins) Bezugsberechtigte *mf*

benefit ['benɪfɪt] *s* Nutzen *m*; (*fundraising performance*) Benefiz *n*; (ins) Versicherungsleistung *f*

benevolence [bɪ'nevələns] *s* Wohlwollen *n*

benevolent [bɪ'nevələnt] *adj* wohlwollend

benign [bɪ'naɪn] *adj* gütig; (pathol) gutartig

bent [bent] *adj* krumm, verbogen; **b. on** versessen auf (*acc*) || *s* Hang *m*

benzene ['ben'zin] *s* Benzol *n*

bequeath [bɪ'kwið] *tr* vermachen

bequest [bɪ'kwest] *s* Vermächtnis *n*

berate [bɪ'ret] *tr* ausschelten, rügen

be·reave [bɪ'riv] *v* (*pret & pp* **–reaved & –reft** ['reft]) *tr* (*of*) berauben (*genit*)

bereavement [bɪ'rivmənt] *s* Trauerfall *m*

beret [bə're] *s* Baskenmütze *f*

Berlin [bər'lɪn] *adj* Berliner, berlinerisch || *s* Berlin *n*

Berliner [bər'lɪnər] *s* Berliner –in *mf*

berry ['berɪ] *s* Beere *f*

berserk [bər'sʌrk] *adj* wütend || *adv*— **go b.** wütend werden

berth [bʌrθ] *s* Schlafkoje *f*; (naut) Liegeplatz *m*; (rr) Bett *n*; **give s.o. wide b.** um j–n e–n weiten Bogen machen || *tr* am Kai festmachen

be·seech [bɪ'sit/] *v* (*pret & pp* **–sought** ['sɔt] & **–seeched**) *tr* anflehen

be·set [bɪ'set] *v* (*pret & pp* **–set**; *ger* **–setting**) *tr* bedrängen, umringen

beside [bɪ'saɪd] *prep* (*position*) neben (*dat*), bei (*dat*); (*direction*) neben (*acc*); **be b. oneself with** außer sich [*dat*] sein vor (*dat*)

besides [bɪ'saɪdz] *adv* überdies, außerdem || *prep* außer (*dat*)

besiege [bɪ'sidʒ] *tr* belagern

besmirch [bɪ'smʌrt/] *tr* beschmutzen

be·speak [bɪ'spik] *v* (*pret* **–spoke** ['spok]; *pp* **–spoken** ['spokən]) *tr* bezeigen

best [best] *adj* beste; **b. of all, very b.** allerbeste || *adv* am besten; **had b. es wäre am besten, wenn** || *s*—**at b.** bestenfalls; **be at one's b.** in bester Form sein; **for the b.** zum Besten; **make the b. of** sich abfinden mit; **to the b. of one's ability** nach bestem Vermögen

bestial ['best/əl] *adj* bestialisch

best' man' *s* Brautführer *m*

bestow [bɪ'sto] *tr* verleihen

bestowal [bɪ'sto·əl] *s* Verleihung *f*

best' sel'ler *s* (*book*) Bestseller *m*

bet [bet] *s* Wette *f*; **make a bet** e–e Wette abschließen (or eingehen) || *v* (*pret & pp* **bet & betted**; *ger* **betting**) *tr* (**on**) wetten (auf *acc*) || *intr* wetten; **you bet!** aber sicher!

betray [bɪ'tre] *tr* verraten; (*a secret*) preisgeben; (*ignorance*) offenbaren; (*a trust*) mißbrauchen

betrayal [bɪ'tre·əl] *s* Verrat *m*

betrayer [bɪ'tre·ər] *s* Verräter –in *mf*

better ['betər] *adj* besser; **the b. part of** der größere Teil (*genit*) || *s*— **change for the b.** sich zum Besseren wenden; **get the b. of** übervorteilen; **one's betters** die Höherstehenden *pl*; || *adv* besser; **all the b.** um so besser; **b. off** besser daran; (*financially*) wohlhabender; **so much the b.** desto besser; **you had b. do it at once** am besten tust du es sofort; **you had b. not** das will ich dir nicht geraten haben || *tr* verbessern; **b. oneself** sich verbessern

bet'ter half' *s* (coll) bessere Hälfte *f*

betterment ['betərmənt] *s* Besserung *f*

bettor ['betər] *s* Wettende *mf*

between [bɪ'twin] *adv*—**in b.** dazwischen || *prep* (*position*) zwischen (*dat*); (*direction*) zwischen (*acc*); **just b. you and me** ganz unter uns gesagt

bev·el ['bevəl] *adj* schräg || *s* schräge Kante *f*; || *v* (*pret & pp* **–el(l)ed**; *ger* **–el(l)ing**) *tr* abschrägen

beverage ['bevərɪdʒ] *s* Getränk *n*

bevy ['bevɪ] *s* Schar *f*

bewail [bɪ'wel] *tr* beklagen

beware [bɪ'wer] *intr* sich hüten; **b.! gib acht!**; **b. of** sich hüten vor (*dat*); **b. of imitations** vor Nachahmungen wird gewarnt

bewilder [bɪ'wɪldər] *tr* verblüffen

bewilderment [bɪ'wɪldərmənt] *s* Verblüffung *f*

bewitch [bɪ'wɪt/] *tr* (fig) bezaubern

beyond [bɪ'jɔnd] *adv* jenseits || *s*— **the b.** das Jenseits || *prep* jenseits (*genit*), über (*acc*) hinaus; (fig) über *acc*), außer (*dat*); **he is b. help** ihm ist nicht mehr zu helfen; **that's b. me** das geht über meinen Verstand

B' girl' *s* (coll) Animiermädchen *n*

bias ['baɪ·əs] *s* Voreingenommenheit *f* || *tr* (**against**) einnehmen (**gegen**)

bi'ased *adj* voreingenommen

bib [bɪb] *s* Latz *m*, Lätzchen *n*

Bible ['baɪbəl] *s* Bibel *f*

biblical ['bɪblɪkəl] *adj* biblisch

bibliographer [,bɪblɪ'ɑgrəfər] *s* Bibliograph –in *mf*

bibliography [,bɪblɪ'ɑgrəfɪ] *s* Bücherverzeichnis *n*; (*science*) Bücherkunde *f*

bi·ceps ['baɪseps] *s* (**–cepses** [sepsɪz] **& –ceps**) Bizeps *m*

bicker ['bɪkər] *intr* (sich) zanken

bick'ering *s* Gezänk *n*

bicuspid [baɪ'kʌspɪd] *s* kleiner Backenzahn *m*

bicycle ['baɪsɪkəl] *s* Fahrrad *n*

bid [bɪd] *s* Angebot *n*; (cards) Meldung *f*; (com) Kostenvoranschlag *m* || *v* (pret **bade** [bæd] & **bid**; pp **bidden** ['bɪdən]) *tr* (ask) heißen; (at auction) bieten; (cards) melden, reizen || *intr* (cards) reizen; (com) ein Preisangebot machen; **bid for** sich bewerben um

bidder ['bɪdər] *s* (at an auction) Bieter –in *mf*; **highest b.** Meistbietende *mf*

bid'ding *s* (at an auction) Bieten *n*; (request) Geheiß *n*; (cards) Reizen *n*

bide [baɪd] *tr*—**b. one's time** seine Gelegenheit abwarten

biennial [baɪ'enɪ·əl] *adj* zweijährig

bier [bɪr] *s* Totenbahre *f*

bifocals [baɪ'fokəlz] *spl* Zweistärken-brille *f*

big [bɪg] *adj* (**bigger**; **biggest**) groß

bigamist ['bɪgəmɪst] *s* Bigamist *m*

bigamous ['bɪgəməs] *adj* bigamisch

bigamy ['bɪgəmi] *s* Bigamie *f*

big'-boned' *adj* starkknochig

big' busi'ness *s* das große Geschäft; (collectively) Großunternehmertum *n*

Big' Dip'per *s* Großer Bär *m*

big' game' *s* Hochwild *n*

big'-heart'ed *adj* großherzig

big'mouth' *s* (sl) Großmaul *n*

bigot ['bɪgət] *s* Fanatiker –in *mf*

bigoted ['bɪgətɪd] *adj* bigott, fanatisch

bigotry ['bɪgətri] *s* Bigotterie *f*

big' shot' *s* (coll) hohes Tier *n*, Bonze *m*

big'-time' *adj* groß, erstklassig; **b. operator** Großschieber –in *mf*

big' toe' *s* große Zehe *f*

big' top' *s* (coll) großes Zirkuszelt *n*

big' wheel' *s* (coll) hohes Tier *n*

big'wig' *s* (coll) Bonze *m*

bike [baɪk] *s* (coll) Rad *n*

bikini [bɪ'kini] *s* Bikini *m*

bilateral [baɪ'lætərəl] *adj* beiderseitig verbindlich

bile [baɪl] *s* Galle *f*

bilge [bɪldʒ] *s* Bilge *f*, Kielraum *m*

bilge' wat'er *s* Bilgenwasser *n*

bilingual [baɪ'lɪŋgwəl] *adj* zweisprachig

bilk [bɪlk] *tr* (out of) prellen (um)

bill [bɪl] *s* Rechnung *f*; (paper money) Geldschein *m*, Schein *m*; (of a bird) Schnabel *m*; (parl) Gesetzesvorlage *f*; **pass a b.** ein Gesetz verabschieden || *tr* in Rechnung stellen

bill'board' *s* Anschlagtafel *f*

bill' collec'tor *s* Einkassierer –in *mf*

billet ['bɪlɪt] *s* (mil) Quartier *n* || *tr* (mil) einquartieren, unterbringen

bill'fold' *s* Brieftasche *f*

bil'liard ball' *s* Billardkugel *f*

billiards ['bɪljərdz] *s* Billard *n*

bil'liard ta'ble *s* Billardtisch *m*

billion ['bɪljən] *s* Milliarde *f*; (Brit) Billion *f* (million million)

bill' of exchange' *s* Tratte *f*, Wechsel *m*

bill' of fare' *s* Speisekarte *f*

bill' of health' *s* Gesundheitszeugnis *n*; **he gave me a clean b.** (fig) er hat mich für einwandfrei befunden

bill' of lad'ing ['ledɪŋ] *s* Frachtbrief *m*

bill' of rights' *s* erste zehn Zusatzartikel *pl* zur Verfassung (der U.S.A.)

bill' of sale' *s* Kaufurkunde *f*

billow ['bɪlo] *s* Woge *f* || *intr* wogen

bil'ly club' ['bɪli] *s* Polizeiknüppel *m*

bil'ly goat' *s* (coll) Ziegenbock *m*

bind [baɪnd] *s*—**in a b.** in der Klemme || *v* (pret & pp **bound** [baʊnd]) *tr* binden; (obligate) verpflichten; (bb) einbinden

binder ['baɪndər] *s* Binder –in *mf*; (e.g., cement) Bindemittel *n*; (for loose papers) Aktendeckel *m*; (mach) Garbenbinder *m*

bindery ['baɪndəri] *s* Buchbinderei *f*

bind'ing *adj* (on) verbindlich (für) || *s* Binden *n*; (for skis) Bindung *f*; (bb) Einband *m*

binge [bɪndʒ] *s* (sl) Zechtour *f*; **go on a b.** (sl) e–e Zechtour machen

binoculars [baɪ'nakjələrz] *spl* Fernglas *n*

biochemistry [ˌbaɪ·ə'kemɪstri] *s* Biochemie *f*

biographer [baɪ'agrəfər] *s* Biograph –in *mf*

biographic(al) [ˌbaɪ·ə'græfɪk(əl)] *adj* biographisch

biography [baɪ'agrəfi] *s* Biographie *f*

biologic(al) [ˌbaɪ·ə'ladʒɪk(əl)] *adj* biologisch

biologist [baɪ'alədʒɪst] *s* Biologe *m*, Biologin *f*

biology [baɪ'alədʒi] *s* Biologie *f*

biophysics [ˌbaɪ·ə'fɪzɪks] *s* Biophysik *f*

biopsy ['baɪ·apsi] *s* Biopsie *f*

bipartisan [baɪ'partɪzən] *adj* Zweiparteien–

biped ['baɪped] *s* Zweifüßer *m*

bird [bɪrd] *s* Vogel *m*; **for the birds** für die Katz; **kill two birds with one stone** zwei Fliegen mit e–r Klappe schlagen

bird'cage' *s* Bauer *n*, Vogelkäfig *m*

bird' call' *s* Vogelruf *m*, Lockpfeife *f*

bird' dog' *s* Hühnerhund *m*

bird' of prey' *s* Raubvogel *m*

bird'seed' *s* Vogelfutter *n*

bird's'-eye view' *s* Vogelperspektive *f*

birth [bɪrθ] *s* Geburt *f*; (origin) Herkunft *f*; **give b. to** gebären

birth' certi'ficate *s* Geburtsurkunde *f*

birth' control' *s* Geburtenbeschränkung *f*

birth'day' *s* Geburtstag *m*

birth'day cake' *s* Geburtstagskuchen *m*

birth'day par'ty *s* Geburtstagsfeier *f*

birth'day pres'ent *s* Geburtstagsgeschenk *n*

birth'day suit' *s* (hum) Adamskostüm *n*

birth'mark' *s* Muttermal *n*

birth'place' *s* Geburtsort *m*

birth' rate' *s* Geburtenziffer *f*

birth'right' *s* Geburtsrecht *n*

biscuit ['bɪskɪt] *s* Keks *m*

bisect [baɪ'sekt] *tr* halbieren || *intr* sich teilen

bishop ['bɪʃəp] *s* Bischof *m*; (chess) Läufer *m*

bison ['baɪsən] *s* Bison *m*

bit [bɪt] *s* Bißchen *n*; (of food) Stückchen *n*; (*of time*) Augenblick *m*; (*part of a bridle*) Gebiß *n*; (*drill*) Bohrer *m*; **a bit** (*somewhat*) ein wenig; **a little bit** ein klein wenig; **bit by bit** brockenweise; **bits and pieces** Brocken *pl*; **every bit as** ganz genauso

bitch [bɪtʃ] *s* Hündin *f*; (*vulg*) Weibsbild *n*

bite [baɪt] *s* Biß *m*; (*wound*) Bißwunde *f*; (*of an insect*) Stich *m*; (*of a snake*) Biß *m*; (*snack*) Imbiß *m*; (*fig*) Bissigkeit *f*; **I have a b.** (*in fishing*) es beißt e-r an || *v* (*pret* **bit** [bɪt]; *pp* **bit** & **bitten** ['bɪtən]) *tr* beißen; (*said of insects*) stechen; (*said of snakes*) beißen; **b. one's nails** an den Nägeln kauen || *intr* beißen; (*said of fish*) anbeißen; (*said of the wind*) schneiden; **b. into** anbeißen

bit'ing *adj* (*remark*) bissig; (*cold, wind*) schneidend

bit' part *s* kleine Rolle *f*

bitter ['bɪtər] *adj* (& *fig*) bitter; (*Person, Blick*) bitterböse

bitterly ['bɪtərli] *adv* bitterlich

bitterness ['bɪtərnɪs] *s* Bitterkeit *f*

bitters ['bɪtərz] *spl* Magenbitter *m*

bitu'minous coal' [bɪ't(j)uminəs] *s* Fettkohle *f*

bivouac ['bɪvwæk] *s* Biwak *n* || *intr* biwakieren

bizarre [bɪ'zar] *adj* bizarr

blab [blæb] *v* (*pret* & *pp* **blabbed**; *ger* **blabbing**) *tr* ausplaudern || *intr* plaudern

blabber ['blæbər] *intr* schwatzen

blab'bermouth' *s* Schwatzmaul *n*

black [blæk] *adj* schwarz || *s* Schwarz *n*; (*black person*) Neger –in *mf*, Schwarze *mf* || *tr* schwärzen; **b. out** (*mil*) verdunkeln || *intr*—**b. out** die Besinnung verlieren

black'-and-blue' *adj* blau unterlaufen; **beat s.o. b.** j-n grün und blau schlagen

black' and white' *s*—**in b.** schwarz auf weiß, schriftlich

black'-and-white' *adj* schwarzweiß

black'ball' *tr* (*ostracize*) ausschließen; (*vote against*) stimmen gegen

black'ber'ry *s* Brombeere *f*

black'berry bush' *s* Brombeerstrauch *m*

black'bird' *s* Amsel *f*

black'board' *s* Tafel *f*, Wandtafel *f*

blacken ['blækən] *tr* schwärzen; (*a name*) anschwärzen

black' eye' *s* blaues Auge *n*; **give s.o. a b.** (*fig*) j-m Schaden zufügen

black'head' *s* Mitesser *m*

blackish ['blækɪʃ] *adj* schwärzlich

black'jack' *s* (*club*) Totschläger *m*; (*cards*) Siebzehnundvier *n* || *tr* niederknüppeln

black'list' *s* schwarze Liste *f* || *tr* auf die schwarze Liste setzen

black' mag'ic *s* schwarze Kunst *f*

black'mail' *s* Erpressung *f* || *tr* erpressen

blackmailer ['blæk,melər] *s* Erpresser –in *mf*

black' mar'ket *s* Schwarzmarkt *m*

black' marketeer' *s* Schwarzhändler –in *mf*

black'out' *s* (*fainting*) Bewußtlosigkeit *f*; (*of memory*) kurze Gedächtnisstörung *f*; (*of news*) Nachrichtensperre *f*; (*mil*) Verdunkelung *f*; (*telv*) Sperre *f*; (*theat*) Auslöschen *n* aller Rampenlichter

black' sheep' *s* (*fig*) schwarzes Schaf *n*

black'smith' *s* Grobschmied *m*; (*person who shoes horses*) Hufschmied *m*

bladder ['blædər] *s* Blase *f*

blade [bled] *s* (*of a sword, knife*) Klinge *f*; (*of grass*) Halm *m*; (*of a saw, ax, shovel, oar*) Blatt *n*; (*of a propeller*) Flügel *m*

blame [blem] *s* Schuld *f* || *tr* die Schuld geben (*dat*); **b. s.o. for** j-m Vorwürfe machen wegen; **I don't b. you for laughing** ich nehme es Ihnen nicht übel, daß Sie lachen

blameless ['blemlɪs] *adj* schuldlos

blame'wor'thy *adj* tadelnswert, schuldig

blanch [blæntʃ] *tr* erbleichen lassen; (*celery*) bleichen; (*almonds*) blanchieren || *intr* erbleichen

bland [blænd] *adj* sanft, mild

blandish ['blændɪʃ] *tr* schmeicheln (*dat*)

blank [blæŋk] *adj* (*cartridge*) blind; (*piece of paper, space, expression*) leer; (*form*) unausgefüllt; (*tape*) unbespielt; (*nonplussed*) verblüfft; **my mind went b.** ich konnte mich an nichts erinnern || *s* (*cartridge*) Platzpatrone *f*; (*unwritten space*) leere Stelle *f*; (*form*) Formular *n*; (*unfinished piece of metal*) Rohling *m* || *tr* (*sport*) auf Null halten

blank' check' *s* Blankoscheck *m*

blanket ['blæŋkɪt] *adj* generell, umfassend || *s* Decke *f*

blank' verse' *s* Blankvers *m*

blare [bler] *s* Lärm *m*; (*of trumpets*) Geschmetter *n* || *intr* schmettern; (*aut*) laut hupen

blasé [bla'ze] *adj* blasiert; **b. attitude** Blasiertheit *f*

blaspheme [blæs'fim] *tr* & *intr* lästern

blasphemous ['blæsfɪməs] *adj* lästerlich

blasphemy ['blæsfɪmi] *s* Lästerung *f*

blast [blæst] *s* (*of an explosion*) Luftdruck *m*; (*of a horn, trumpet, air*) Stoß *m*; (*of air*) Luftzug *m*; **at full b.** (*fig*) auf höchsten Touren || *tr* (*e.g., a tunnel*) sprengen; (*ruin*) (*fig*) verderben; (*criticize*) wettern gegen; (*blight*) versengen; **b. it!** verdammt! || *intr*—**b. off** (*rok*) starten

blast' fur'nace *s* Hochofen *m*

blast'-off' *s* (*rok*) Start *m*

blatant ['bletənt] *adj* (*lie, infraction*) eklatant; (*nonsense*) schreiend

blaze [blez] *s* Brand *m*; **b. of color** Farbenpracht *f*; **b. of glory** Ruhmesglanz *m*; **b. of light** Lichterglanz *m*; **go to blazes!** (*sl*) geh zum Teufel!; **like blazes** wie verrückt || *tr*—**b. a trail** e-n Weg markieren; (*fig*) e-n Weg bahnen || *intr* lodern; **b. away at** drauflosschießen auf (*acc*)

blazer ['blezər] s Sportjacke f
blaz'ing adj (sun) prall
bleach [blitʃ] s Bleichmittel n || tr
bleichen; (hair) blondieren || intr
bleichen
bleachers ['blitʃərs] spl Zuschauersitze
pl im Freien
bleak [blik] adj öde, trostlos
bleary-eyed ['blɪri ,aɪd] adj triefäugig
bleat [blit] s Blöken n || intr blöken;
(said of a goat) meckern
bleed [blid] v (pret & pp bled [bled])
tr (brakes) entlüften; (med) zur
Ader lassen; **b. white** (fig) zum
Weißbluten bringen || intr bluten;
b. to death verbluten
blemish ['blemɪʃ] s Fleck m, Makel m;
(fig) Schandfleck m
blend [blend] s Mischung f; (liquor)
Verschnitt m || v (pret & pp blended
& blent [blent]) tr mischen; (wine,
liquor) verschneiden || intr sich ver-
mischen; (said of colors) zueinander
passen, zusammenpassen
bless [bles] tr segnen; **God b. you!**
(after a sneeze) Gesundheit!
blessed ['blesɪd] adj selig
bless'ing s Segen m, Gnade f; **b. in
disguise** Glück n im Unglück
blight [blaɪt] s (fig) Gifthauch m;
(agr) Brand m, Mehltau m || tr (fig)
verderben; (agr) schädigen
blight'ed adj brandig
blimp [blɪmp] s unstarres Luftschiff n
blind [blaɪnd] adj blind; (curve) un-
übersichtlich; **go b. erblinden** || s
Jalousie f; (hunt) Attrappe f || tr
blenden; (fig) verblenden
blind' al'ley s (& fig) Sackgasse f
blind' date' s Verabredung f mit e-r
(or e-m) Unbekannten
blinder ['blaɪndər] s Scheuklappe f
blind' fly'ing s Blindflug m
blind'fold adj mit verbundenen Augen
|| adv blindlings || tr die Augen ver-
binden (dat)
blind' man' s Blinder m
blind'man's' bluff' s Blindekuhspiel n
blindness ['blaɪndnɪs] s Blindheit f
blink [blɪŋk] s Blinken n; (with the
eyes) Blinzeln n; **on the b.** (sl) kaputt
|| tr—**b. one's eyes** mit den Augen
zwinkern || intr (said of a light)
blinken; (said of the eyes) blinzeln
blinker ['blɪŋkər] s (for horses) Scheuklappe f; (aut) Blinker m
blip [blɪp] s (radar) Leuchtfleck m
bliss [blɪs] s Wonne f
blissful ['blɪsfəl] adj glückselig
blister ['blɪstər] s Blase f; (from a
burn) Brandblase f || intr (said of
the skin) Blasen ziehen; (said of
paint) Blasen werfen
blithe [blaɪð] adj fröhlich
blitzkrieg ['blɪts ,krig] s Blitzkrieg m
blizzard ['blɪzərd] s Blizzard m
bloat [blot] tr aufblähen || intr an-
schwellen
bloc [blak] s (parl) Stimmblock m;
(pol) Block m
block [blak] s (of wood) Klotz m;
(toy) Bauklotz m; (for chopping)
Hackklotz m; (of houses) Häuser-

block m; (of seats) Reihe f; (mach)
Rolle f; (sport) Block m; **five blocks
from here** fünf Straßen weiter || tr
versperren; (traffic, a street, a player) blockieren; (a ball) abfangen; (a
hat) aufdämpfen; **be blocked** sich
stauen; **b. off** (a street) absperren;
b. up verstopfen, versperren
blockade [bla'ked] s Blockade f,
Sperre f || tr blockieren, sperren
blockade' run'ner s Blockadebrecher m
blockage ['blakɪdʒ] s Stockung f
block' and tac'kle s Flaschenzug m
block'head' s Klotz m, Dummkopf m
blond [bland] adj blond || s Blonde m
blonde [bland] s Blondine f
blood [blʌd] s Blut n; (lineage) Geblüt
n; **in cold b.** kaltblütig
blood' circula'tion s Blutkreislauf m
blood' clot' s Blutgerinnsel n
bloodcurdling ['blʌd ,kʌrdlɪŋ] adj
haarsträubend
blood' do'nor s Blutspender –in mf
blood'hound' s (& fig) Bluthund m
bloodless ['blʌdlɪs] adj blutlos; (revolution) unblutig
blood' poi'soning s Blutvergiftung f
blood' pres'sure s Blutdruck m
blood' rela'tion s Blutsverwandte mf
blood'shed' s Blutvergießen n
blood'shot' adj blutunterlaufen
blood'stain' s Blutfleck m, Blutspur f
blood'stained' adj blutbefleckt
blood'stream' s Blutstrom m
blood'suck'er s (& fig) Blutsauger m
blood' test' s Blutprobe f
blood'thirst'y adj blutdürstig
blood' transfu'sion s Blutübertragung f
blood' type' s Blutgruppe f
blood' ves'sel s Blutgefäß n
blood-y ['blʌdi] adj blutig; (blood-
stained) blutbefleckt || v (pret & pp
-ied) tr mit Blut beflecken
bloom [blum] s Blüte f || intr blühen
blossom ['blasəm] s Blüte f || intr
blühen
blot [blat] s Fleck m; (fig) Schand-
fleck m || v (pret & pp blotted) ger
blotting) tr (smear) beschmieren;
(with a blotter) (ab)löschen; **b. out**
ausstreichen; (fig) auslöschen || intr
(said of ink) klecksen
blotch [blatʃ] s Klecks m; (on the
skin) Ausschlag m
blotter ['blatər] s Löscher m
blot'ting pa'per s Löschpapier n
blouse [blaus] s Bluse f
blow [blo] s Schlag m, Hieb m; (fig)
Schlag m; **come to blows** handge-
mein werden || v (pret blew [blu];
pp blown) tr blasen; (money) (sl)
verschwenden; (a fuse) durchbren-
nen; **b. a whistle** pfeifen; **b. off
steam** sich austoben; **b. one's top**
(coll) hochgehen; **b. out** (a candle)
ausblasen; **b. up** (inflate) aufblasen;
(with explosives) sprengen; (phot)
vergrößern || intr blasen; **b. out** (said
of a candle) auslöschen; (said of a
tire) platzen; **blow over** vorüber-
ziehen; **b. up** (& fig) in die Luft
gehen
blower ['blo·ər] s Gebläse n, Bläser m

blow'out' s (sl) Gelage n; (aut) Reifenpanne f
blow'pipe' s Blasrohr n
blow'torch' s Lötlampe f
blubber ['blʌbər] s Tran m || intr (cry
noisily) jaulen
bludgeon ['blʌdʒən] s Knüppel m || tr
mit dem Knüppel bearbeiten
blue [blu] adj blau; (fig) bedrückt || s
Blau n; **blues** (mus) Blues m; **have
the blues** trüb gestimmt sein; **out of
the b.** aus heiterem Himmel
blue'ber'ry s Heidelbeere f
blue'bird' s Blaukehlchen n
blue' chip' s (cards) blaue Spielmarke
f; (fin) sicheres Wertpapier n
blue'-col'lar work'er s Arbeiter m
blue' jeans' spl Jeans pl
blue' moon' s—once in a b. alle Jubel-
jahre einmal
blue'print' s Blaupause f
blue' streak' s—talk a b. (coll) in e-r
Tour reden
bluff [blʌf] adj schroff; (person) derb
|| s (coll) Bluff m; (geol) Steilküste
f; **call s.o.'s b.** j-m beim Wort neh-
men || tr & intr bluffen
bluffer ['blʌfər] s Bluffer m
blu'ing s Waschblau n
bluish ['blu·ɪʃ] adj bläulich
blunder ['blʌndər] s Schnitzer m; ||
intr e-n Schnitzer machen; **b. into**
stolpern in (acc); **b. upon** zufällig
geraten auf (acc)
blunt [blʌnt] adj stumpf; (fig) plump,
unverblümt || tr abstumpfen
bluntly ['blʌntli] adv unverblümt
blur [blʌr] s Verschwommenheit f || v
(pret & pp blurred; ger blurring) tr
verwischen || intr verschwommen
werden
blurb [blʌrb] s Reklametext m
blurred adj verschwommen; (vision)
unscharf
blurt [blʌrt] tr—b. out herausplatzen
blush [blʌʃ] s Röte f, Schamröte f ||
intr (at) erröten (über acc)
bluster ['blʌstər] s Prahlerei f || intr
(said of a person) prahlen, poltern;
(said of wind) toben
blustery ['blʌstəri] adj stürmisch
boa constrictor ['bo·ə kən'strɪktər] s
Abgottschlange f, Königsschlange f
boar [bor] s Eber m; (wild boar) Wildschwein n
board [bord] s Brett n; (of administra-
tors) Ausschuß m, Behörde f, Rat m;
(meals) Kost f; (educ) Schultafel f;
above b. offen; **on b.** an Bord || tr
(a ship) besteigen; (a plane, train)
einsteigen in (acc); (paying guests)
beköstigen; **b. up** mit Brettern ver-
nageln || intr (with) in Kost sein
(bei)
boarder ['bordər] s Kostgänger –in mf
board'inghouse' s Pension f
board'ing pass' s Bordkarte f
board'ing school' s Internat n
board'ing stu'dent s Interne mf
board' of direc'tors s Verwaltungsrat
m, Aufsichtsrat m
board' of educa'tion s Unterrichtsmi-
nisterium n

board' of health' s Gesundheitsbehörde
f
board' of trade' s Handelskammer f
board' of trustees' s Verwaltungsrat m
board'walk' s Strandpromenade f
boast [bost] s Prahlerei f; (cause of
pride) Stolz m || tr sich rühmen
(genit) || intr (about) prahlen (mit)
boastful ['bostfəl] adj prahlerisch
boat [bot] s Boot n; **in the same b.**
(fig) in der gleichen Lage
boat'house' s Bootshaus n
boat'ing s Bootsfahrt f; **go b.** e–e Boot-
fahrt machen
boat'race' s Bootrennen n
boat' ride' s Bootsfahrt f
boatswain ['bosən] s Hochbootsmann
m
bob [bab] s (jerky motion) Ruck m;
(hairdo) Bubikopf m; (of a fishing
line) Schwimmer m; (of a plumb
line) Senkblei n || v (pret & pp
bobbed; ger bobbing) tr (hair) kurz
schneiden || intr sich hin und her be-
wegen; **bob up and down** sich auf
und ab bewegen
bobbin ['babɪn] s Klöppel m
bobble ['babəl] tr (coll) ungeschickt
handhaben
bob'by pin' ['babi] s Haarklammer f
bob'sled' s Bob m, Rennschlitten m
bode [bod] tr bedeuten
bodily ['badɪli] adj leiblich; **b. injury**
Körperverletzung f || adv leibhaftig
body ['badi] s Körper m; (of a person
or animal) Körper m; (corpse) Leiche
f; (collective group) Körperschaft f;
(of a plane, ship) Rumpf m; (of a
vehicle) Karosserie f; (of beer, wine)
Schwere f; (of a letter) Text m; **b. of
water** Gewässer n; **in a b.** geschlossen
bod'yguard' s Leibgarde f
bod'y o'dor s Körpergeruch m
bog [bag] s Sumpf m || v (pret & pp
bogged; ger bogging) intr—**bog down**
steckenbleiben
bogey'man' ['bogi‚mæn] s (–men) Kin-
derschreck m
bogus ['bogəs] adj schwindelhaft
Bohemia [bo'himɪ·ə] s Böhmen n
Bohemian [bo'himɪ·ən] adj böhmisch
|| s (person) Böhme m, Böhmin f;
(fig) Bohemien m; (language) Böhmisch n
boil [bɔɪl] s (pathol) Geschwür n;
bring to a b. zum Sieden bringen ||
tr kochen, sieden || intr kochen, sie-
den; **b. away** verkochen; **b. over**
überkochen
boiled' ham' s gekochter Schinken m
boiled' pota'toes spl Salzkartoffeln pl
boiler ['bɔɪlər] s (electrical water
tank) Boiler m; (kettle) Kessel m
boil'ermak'er s Kesselschmied m
boil'er room' s Heizraum m
boil'ing adj siedend || adv—**be b. mad**
vor Zorn kochen; **b. hot** siedeheiß
boil'ing point' s Siedepunkt m
boisterous ['bɔɪstərəs] adj ausgelassen
bold [bold] adj kühn, gewagt; (outlines) deutlich
bold'face' s Fettdruck m

boldness ['boldnɪs] s Kühnheit f
Bolshevik ['bɔl/əvɪk] adj bolsche-
wistisch || s Bolschewik –in mf
bolster ['bolstər] s Nackenrolle f || tr
unterstützen
bolt [bolt] s Bolzen m; (door lock)
Riegel m; (of cloth) Stoffballen m;
(of lightning) Blitzstrahl m; **b. out of
the blue** Blitz m aus heiterem Him-
mel || tr (a door) verriegeln; (a po-
litical party) im Stich lassen; (food)
hinunterschlingen || intr davonstür-
zen; (said of a horse) durchgehen
bomb [bam] s (dropped from the air)
Bombe f; (planted) Sprengladung f;
(fiasco) (sl) Versager m || tr (from
the air) bombardieren; (blow up)
sprengen || intr (sl) versagen
bombard [bam'bard] tr bombardieren,
beschießen; (fig) bombardieren
bombardier [,bambər'dɪr] s Bomben-
schütze m
bombardment [bam'bardmənt] s Bombardement n, Beschießung f
bombast ['bambæst] s Schwulst m
bombastic [bam'bæstɪk] adj schwülstig
bomb' bay' s Bombenschacht m
bomb' cra'ter s Bombentrichter m
bomber ['bamər] s Bomber m
bomb'ing s Bombenabwurf m
bomb'ing run' s Bomben(ziel)anflug m
bomb'proof' adj bombenfest, bomben-
sicher
bomb'shell' s (& fig) Bombe f
bomb' shel'ter s Bombenkeller m
bomb'sight' s Bombenzielgerät n
bomb' squad' s Entschärfungskom-
mando n
bona fide ['bonə,faɪd] adj ehrlich,
echt; (offer) solide
bonanza [bo'nænzə] s Goldgrube f
bond [band] s Fessel f; (fin) Obligation f
bondage ['bandɪdʒ] s Knechtschaft f
bond'hold'er s Inhaber –in mf e–r Obligation
bonds·man ['bandzmən] s (-men)
Bürge m
bone [bon] s Knochen m, Bein n; (of
fish) Gräte f; **bones** Gebein n; (mortal remains) Gebeine pl; **have a b. to
pick with** ein Hühnchen zu rupfen
haben mit; **make no bones about it**
nicht viel Federlesens machen mit;
to the b. bis ins Mark || tr (meat)
ausbeinen; (fish) ausgräten || intr—
b. up for (sl) büffeln für
bone'-dry' adj knochentrocken
bone'head' s Dummkopf m
boneless ['bonlɪs] adj ohne Knochen;
(fish) ohne Gräten
boner ['bonər] s (coll) Schnitzer m;
pull a b. (coll) e–n Schnitzer machen
bonfire ['ban,faɪr] s Freudenfeuer n
bonnet ['banɪt] s Haube f
bonus ['bonəs] s Gratifikation f
bony ['boni] adj knochig; (fish) grätig
boo [bu] s Pfuiruf m || tr niederbrüllen
|| intr Pfui rufen || interj (to jeer)
pfui!; (to scare someone) huhl
boob [bub] s (sl) Blödkopf m
booby ['bubi] s (sl) Blödkopf m
boo'by hatch' s (sl) Affenkasten m

boo'by prize' s Trostpreis m
boo'by trap' s Minenfalle f
boogey·man ['bugi,mæn], ['bogi-
,mæn] s (-men') Schreckgespenst n
book [buk] s Buch n; (of stamps, tickets, matches) Heftchen n; **keep books**
Bücher führen || tr buchen; (e.g.,
seats) vorbestellen
book'bind'er s Buchbinder –in mf
book'bind'ery s Buchbinderei f
book'bind'ing s Buchbinderei f
book'case' s Bücherschrank m
book' end' s Bücherstütze f
bookie ['buki] s (coll) Buchmacher –in
mf
book'ing s Buchung f
bookish ['bukɪʃ] adj lesefreudig
book'keep'er s Buchhalter –in mf
book'keep'ing s Buchhaltung f
book' learn'ing s Schulweisheit f
booklet ['buklɪt] s Büchlein n
book'mak'er s Buchmacher –in mf
book'mark' s Lesezeichen n
book'rack' s Büchergestell n
book' review' s Buchbesprechung f
book'sel'ler s Buchhändler –in mf
book'shelf' s (-shelves) Bücherregal n
book'stand' s Bücher(verkaufs)stand m
book'store' s Buchhandlung f
book'worm' s (& fig) Bücherwurm m
boom [bum] s (noise) dumpfes Dröhnen n; (of a crane) Ausleger m; (cin,
telv) Galgen m; (econ) Boom m,
Hochkonjunktur f; (naut) Baum m,
Spiere f; (st.exch.) Hausse f || intr
dröhnen; (said of an organ) brummen
boomerang ['bumə,ræŋ] s Bumerang
m
boon [bun] s Wohltat f, Segen m
boon' compan'ion s Zechkumpan m
boor [bur] s Rüpel m
boorish ['burɪʃ] adj flegelhaft
boost [bust] s (push) Auftrieb m; (in
pay) Gehaltserhöhung f || tr fördern;
(prices) in die Höhe treiben; (elec)
verstärken; **b. business** die Wirtschaft ankurbeln
booster ['bustər] s (backer) Förderer
m, Förderin f
boost'er rock'et s Hilfsrakete f
boost'er shot' s (med) Nachimpfung f
boot [but] s Stiefel m; (kick) Fußtritt
m; **to b.** noch dazu; **you can bet your
boots on that** (sl) darauf kannst du
Gift nehmen || tr (sl) stoßen; (fb)
kicken; **b. out** (sl) 'rausschmeißen
booth [buθ] s (at a fair) Marktbude f;
(for telephone, voting) Zelle f
boot'leg' adj geschmuggelt || v (pret &
pp -legged; ger -legging) tr (make
illegally) illegal brennen; (smuggle)
schmuggeln
bootlegger ['but,legər] s Alkohol-
schmuggler m, Bootlegger m
bootlicker ['but,lɪkər] s (sl) Kriecher
m
booty ['buti] s Beute f
booze [buz] s (coll) Schnaps m || intr
(coll) saufen
booze' hound' s Saufbold m, Saufaus m
border ['bɔrdər] s Rand m; (of a country) Grenze f; (of a dress, etc.) Saum

m, Borte *f* ‖ *tr* umranden, begrenzen; **be bordered by** grenzen an (*acc*)
‖ *intr*—**b. on** (& *fig*) grenzen an
(*acc*)
bor'derline' *s* Grenzlinie *f*
bor'derline case' *s* Grenzfall *m*
bore [bor] *s* (*drill hole*) Bohrloch *n*;
(*of a gun*) Bohrung *f*; (*of a cylinder*)
innerer Zylinderdurchmesser *m*; (*fig*)
langweiliger Mensch *m* ‖ *tr* bohren;
(*fig*) langweilen
boredom ['bordəm] *s* Langeweile *f*
bor'ing *adj* langweilig ‖ *s* Bohren *n*
born [bɔrn] *adj* geboren; **he was b.**
(*said of a living person*) er ist geboren; (*said of a deceased person*) er
war geboren
borough ['bʌro] *s* Städtchen *n*
borrow ['bɑro] *tr* leihen
borrower ['bɑro•ər] *s* Entleiher—in *mf*;
(fin) Kreditnehmer—in *mf*
bor'rowing *s* Borgen *n*; (fin) Kredit-
aufnahme *f*; (ling) Lehnwort *n*
bosom ['buzəm] *s* Busen *m*; (fig)
Schoß *m*
bos'om friend' *s* Busenfreund *m*
boss [bɔs] *s* (coll) Chef *m*, Boß *m*; (*of
a shield*) Buckel *m*; (pol) Bonze *m*
‖ *tr* (*around*) herumkommandieren
bossy ['bɔsi] *adj* herrschsüchtig
botanical [bə'tænɪkəl] *adj* botanisch
botanist ['bɑtənɪst] *s* Botaniker—in *mf*
botany ['bɑtəni] *s* Botanik *f*
botch [bɑt/] *tr* (coll) verpfuschen
both [boθ] *adj & pron* beide ‖ *conj*—
both…and sowohl… als auch
bother ['bɑðər] *s* Belästigung *f*, Mühe
f ‖ *tr* (*annoy*) belästigen, stören;
(*worry*) bedrücken; (*said of a conscience*) quälen ‖ *intr* sich bemühen;
b. about sich bekümmern um; **b.
with** (*a thing*) sich befassen mit; (*a
person*) verkehren mit
bothersome ['bɑðərsəm] *adj* lästig
bottle ['bɑtəl] *s* Flasche *f* ‖ *tr* in Flaschen abfüllen; **bottled up** aufgestaut
bot'tleneck' *s* Flaschenhals *m*; (fig)
Engpaß *m*, Stauung *f*
bot'tle o'pener *s* Flaschenöffner *m*
bottom ['bɑtəm] *adj* niedrigste, unterste ‖ *s* Boden *m*; (*of a well, shaft,
river, valley*) Sohle *f*; (*of a mountain*) Fuß *m*; (*of an affair*) Grund
m; (*buttocks*) Hintern *m*; **at the b.
of the page** unten auf der Seite; **bot-
toms up!** prosit, ex!; **get to the b. of
a problem** e—r Frage auf den Grund
gehen; **reach b.** (fig) den Nullpunkt
erreichen
bottomless ['bɑtəmlɪs] *adj* bodenlos
bough [bau] *s* Ast *m*
bouillon ['buljɑn] *s* Kraftbrühe *f*
bouil'lon cube' *s* Bouillonwürfel *m*
boulder ['boldər] *s* Felsblock *m*
bounce [bauns] *s* Aufprall *m*; (fig)
Schwung *m* ‖ *tr* (*a ball*) aufprallen
lassen; (*throw out*) (sl) 'rausschmeißen ‖ *intr* aufprallen, aufspringen;
(*said of a check*) (coll) platzen
bouncer ['baunsər] *s* (sl) Rausschmeißer *m*
bounc'ing *adj* (*baby*) stramm
bound [baund] *adj* gebunden, gefes-

selt; (*book*) gebunden; (*in duty*) verpflichtet; **be b. for** unterwegs sein
nach; **be b. up with** eng verbunden
sein mit; **I am b. to** (*inf*) ich muß
(*inf*) ‖ *s* Sprung *m*, Satz *m*; **bounds**
Grenzen *pl*, Schranken *pl*; **in bounds**
(sport) in; **keep within bounds** in
Schranken halten; **know no bounds**
weder Maß noch Ziel kennen; **out of
bounds** (sport) aus; **within the
bounds of** im Bereich (*genit*) ‖ *tr*
begrenzen ‖ *intr* aufprallen, aufspringen
boundary ['baundəri] *s* Grenze *f*; (fig)
Umgrenzung *f*
boun'dary line' *s* Grenzlinie *f*
boun'dary stone' *s* Grenzstein *m*
boundless ['baundlɪs] *adj* grenzenlos
bountiful ['bauntɪfəl] *adj* (*generous*)
freigebig; (*ample*) reichlich
bounty ['baunti] *s* (*generosity*) Freigebigkeit *f*; (*gift*) Geschenk *n*; (*reward*)
Prämie *f*
bouquet [bu'ke] *s* Strauß *m*; (*aroma*)
Blume *f*
bout [baut] *s* (*box*) Kampf *m*; (fencing) Gang *m*; (pathol) Anfall *m*
bow [bau] *s* Verbeugung *f*; (naut) Bug
m ‖ *intr* sich verbeugen; **bow and
scrape** beide sich schmiegen und
biegen vor (*dat*); **bow down** sich
bücken; **bow out** sich geschickt zurückziehen; **bow to** sich (ver)neigen
vor (*dat*) ‖ [bo] *s* (*weapon*) Bogen
m; (*of a violin*) Geigenbogen *m*;
(*bowknot*) Schleife *f*; **bow and arrow** Pfeil *m* und Bogen *m* ‖ *intr*
(mus) geigen
bowel ['bau•əl] *s* Darm *m*; **bowels**
Eingeweide *pl*; **bowels of the earth**
Erdinnere *n*
bow'el move'ment *s* Stuhlgang *m*
bowl [bol] *s* Napf *m*, Schüssel *f*; (*of a
pipe*) Kopf *m*; (*washbowl, toilet
bowl*) Becken *n*; (*of a spoon*) Höhlung *f*; (sport) Stadion *n* ‖ *tr* umhauen; (fig) umwerfen ‖ *intr* kegeln
bowlegged ['bo ,leg(ɪ)d] *adj* O-beinig
bowler ['bolər] *s* Kegler—in *mf*
bowl'ing *s* Kegeln *n*
bowl'ing al'ley *s* Kegelbahn *f*
bowl'ing ball' *s* Kegelkugel *f*
bowl'ing pin' *s* Kegel *m*
bowstring ['bo ,strɪŋ] *s* Bogensehne *f*
bow' tie' [bo] *s* Schleife *f*, Fliege *f*
bow' win'dow [bo] *s* Bogenfenster *n*
bowwow ['bau'wau] *interj* wauwau!
box [bɑks] *s* (*small and generally of
cardboard*) Schachtel *f*; (*larger and
generally of cardboard*) Karton *m*;
(*generally of wood*) Kasten *m*;
(*larger and generally of wood*) Kiste
f; (*of strips of wood*) Spanschachtel
f; (theat) Loge *f*; (typ) Kasten *m*;
box of candy Bonbonniere *f*; **box on
the ear** Ohrfeige *f* ‖ *tr* (sport) boxen;
box in einschließen; **box s.o.'s ears**
j—n ohrfeigen ‖ *intr* (sport) boxen
box'car' *s* geschlossener Güterwagen *m*
boxer ['bɑksər] *s* (sport, zool) Boxer
m
box'ing *s* Boxen *n*, Boxsport *m*
box'ing glove' *s* Boxhandschuh *m*

box′ing match′ s Boxkampf m

box′ kite′ s Kastendrachen m

box′ of′fice s (cin, theat) Kasse f

box′ seat′ s Logenplatz m

box′wood′ s Buchsbaum m

boy [bɔɪ] s Junge m; (servant) Boy m

boycott [′bɔɪkɑt] s Boykott m ‖ tr boykottieren

boy′friend′ s Freund m

boy′hood′ s Knabenalter n

boyish [′bɔɪ·ɪʃ] adj jungenhaft

boy′ scout′ s Pfadfinder m

bra [brɑ] s (coll) BH m

brace [bres] s (carp) Strebe f, Stütze f; (dent) Zahnklammer f, Zahnspange f; (hunt) Paar n; (med) Schiene f; (typ) geschweifte Klammer f ‖ tr verstreben; (fig) stärken; **b. oneself** sich zusammenreißen; **b. oneself against** sich stemmen gegen; **b. oneself for** seinen Mut zusammennehmen für; **b. up** (fig) aufpulvern

brace′ and bit′ s Bohrwinde f

bracelet [′breslɪt] s Armband n

brac′ing adj (invigorating) erfrischend

bracket [′brækɪt] s Winkelstütze f, Konsole f; (wall bracket) Wandarm m; (mounting clip) Befestigungsschelle f; (typ) eckige Klammer f ‖ tr einklammern; (arti) eingabeln

brackish [′brækɪʃ] adj brackig

brag [bræg] v (pret & pp **bragged**; ger **bragging**) intr (about) prahlen (mit)

braggart [′brægərt] s Prahler –in m f

brag′ging s prahlerisch ‖ s Prahlerei f

braid [bred] s (of hair) Flechte f; (flat trimming) Tresse f, Litze f; (round trimming) Kordel f ‖ tr (hair, rope) flechten; (trim with braid) mit Tresse (or Borten) besetzen

braille [brel] s Blindenschrift f

brain [bren] s Hirn n; **brains** Hirn n; (fig) Grütze f ‖ tr (coll) den Schädel einschlagen (dat)

brain′child′ s Geistesfrucht f

brainless [′brenlɪs] adj hirnlos

brain′storm′ s (coll) Geistesblitz m

brain′wash′ tr Gehirnwäsche vornehmen bei

brain′wash′ing s Gehirnwäsche f

brain′ wave′ s Hirnwelle f; (fig) Geistesblitz m

brain′work′ s Gehirnarbeit f

brainy [′breni] adj geistreich

braise [brez] tr schmoren, dünsten

brake [brek] s Bremse f; **put on the brakes** bremsen ‖ intr bremsen

brake′ drum′ s Bremstrommel f

brake′ light′ s Bremslicht n

brake′ lin′ing s Bremsbelag m

brake′man s (–men) Bremser m

brake′ped′al s Bremspedal n

brake′ shoe′ s (aut) Bremsbacke f

bramble [′bræmbəl] s Dornbusch m

bran [bræn] s Kleie f

branch [bræntʃ] s (of a tree) Ast m; (smaller branch; of lineage) Zweig m; (of river) Arm m; (of a road, railroad) Abzweigung f; (of science, work, a shop) Branche f, Unterabteilung f; (com) Filiale f, Nebenstelle f ‖ intr—**b. off** abzweigen; **b. out** sich verzweigen

branch′ line′ s Seitenlinie f

branch′ of′fice s Zweigstelle f

branch′ of serv′ice s Truppengattung f

brand [brænd] s (kind) Marke f; (trademark) Handelsmarke f; (on cattle) Brandmal n; (branding iron) Brandeisen n; (dishonor) Schandfleck m ‖ tr (& fig) brandmarken

brand′-new′ adj nagelneu

brandish [′brændɪʃ] tr schwingen; (threateningly) schwenken

brandy [′brændi] s Branntwein m

brash [bræʃ] adj schnodd(e)rig, frech

brass [bræs] adj Messing– ‖ s Messing n; (mil) hohe Offiziere pl; (mus) Blechinstrumente pl

brass′ band′ s Blechblaskapelle f

brassiere [brə′zɪr] s Büstenhalter m

brass′ knuck′les spl Schlagring m

brass′ tacks′ spl—**get down to b.** (coll) zur Sache kommen

brat [bræt] s (coll) Balg m

bravado [brə′vɑdo] s Bravour f, Angabe f

brave [brev] adj tapfer, mutig ‖ s indianischer Krieger m ‖ tr trotzen (dat)

bravery [′brevəri] s Tapferkeit f

bra·vo [′brɑvo] s (–vos) Bravo n ‖ interj bravo!

brawl [brɔl] s Rauferei f ‖ intr raufen

brawler [′brɔlər] s Raufbold m

brawn [brɔn] s Muskelkraft f

brawny [′brɔni] adj muskulös, kräftig

bray [bre] s Eselsschrei m ‖ intr schreien, iahen

braze [brez] tr (brassplate) mit Messing überziehen; (solder) hartlöten

brazen [′brezən] adj Messing–, ehern; (fig) unverschämt ‖ tr—**b. it out** unverschämt durchsetzen

Brazil [brə′zɪl] s Brasilien n

Brazilian [brə′zɪljən] adj brasilianisch, brasilisch ‖ s Brasilier –in m f

Brazil′ nut′ s Paranuß f

breach [britʃ] s Bruch m; (mil) Bresche f ‖ tr (mil) durchbrechen

breach′ of con′tract s Vertragsbruch m

breach′ of prom′ise s Verlöbnisbruch m

breach′ of the peace′ s Friedensbruch m

breach′ of trust′ s Vertrauensbruch m

bread [bred] s Brot n; (money) (sl) Pinke f ‖ tr (culin) panieren

bread′ and but′ter s Butterbrot n; (livelihood) Lebensunterhalt m

bread′ box′ s Brotkasten m

bread′ crumb′ s Brotkrume f

bread′ed adj paniert

bread′ed veal′ cut′let s Wiener Schnitzel n

bread′ knife′ s Brotmesser n

breadth [bredθ] s Breite f

bread′win′ner s Brotverdiener –in m f

break [brek] s Bruch m; (split, tear) Riß m; (crack) Sprung m; (in relations) Bruch m; (in a forest) Lichtung f; (in the clouds) Lücke f; (recess) Pause f; (rest from work)

Arbeitspause *f;* (*luck*) Glück *n;* (*chance*) Chance *f;* (box) Lösen *n;* **bad b.** Pech *n;* **b. in the weather** Wetterumschlag *m;* **give s.o. a b.** j—m e—e Chance geben; **make a b. for** losstürzen auf (*acc*); **take a b.** e—e Pause machen; **tough b.** Pech *n;* **without a b.** ohne Unterbrechung ‖ *v* (*pret* **broke** [brok]; *pp* **broken** ['brokən]) *tr* (& fig) brechen; (*snap*) zerreißen; (*a string*) durchreißen; (*a dish*) zerbrechen; (*an appointment*) nicht einhalten; (*contact*) unterbrechen; (*an engagement*) auflösen; (*a law, limb*) verletzen; (*monotony*) auflockern; (*a record*) brechen; (*a seal*) erbrechen; (*a window*) einschlagen; (*one's word, promise*) nicht halten; **b. down** (*into constituents*) zerlegen; (*s.o.'s resistance*) überwinden; (*mach*) abmontieren; **b. in** (*a horse*) zureiten; (*a car*) einfahren; (*a person*) anlernen; **b. loose** losreißen; **b. off** abbrechen, losbrechen; (*an engagement*) auflösen; **b. open** aufbrechen; **b. s.o. from s.th.** j—m etw abgewöhnen; **b. the news (to)** die Nachricht eröffnen (*dat*), die Nachricht beibringen (*dat*); **b. to pieces** zerbrechen; (*a meeting*) auflösen; (*forcibly*) sprengen; **break wind** e—n Darmwind abgehen lassen ‖ *intr* brechen; (*snap*) reißen; (*said of the voice*) mutieren; (*said of waves*) sich brechen; (*said of large waves*) sich überschlagen; (*said of the weather*) umschlagen; **b. down** zusammenbrechen; (*mach*) versagen; **b. even** gerade die Unkosten decken; **b. loose** losbrechen, sich losreißen; **b. out** (*said of fire, an epidemic, prisoner*) ausbrechen; **b. up** (*said of a meeting*) sich auflösen

breakable ['brekəbəl] *adj* zerbrechlich
breakage ['brekɪdʒ] *s* Bruch *m;* (*cost of broken articles*) Bruchschaden *m*
break'down' *s* (*of health, discipline, morals*) Zusammenbruch *m;* (*disintegration*) Zersetzung *f;* (*of costs, etc.*) Aufgliederung *f;* (aut) Panne *f;* (chem) Analyse *f;* (elec) Durchschlag *m;* (*of a piece of equipment*) (mach) Versagen *n;* (*e.g., of power supply, factory equipment*) Betriebsstörung *f*
breaker ['brekər] *s* Sturzwelle *f;* **breakers** Brandung *f*
breakfast ['brekfəst] *s* Frühstück *n* ‖ *intr* frühstücken
break'neck' *adj* halsbrecherisch
break' of day' *s* Tagesanbruch *m*
break'through' *s* Durchbruch *m*
break'up' *s* Aufbrechen *n;* (*of a meeting*) Auflösung *f*
break'wa'ter *s* Wellenbrecher *m*
breast [brest] *s* Brust *f;* (*of a woman*) Brust *f,* Busen *m;* **beat one's b.** sich an die Brust schlagen; **make a clean b. of sth** [*dat*] vom Herzen reden
breast'bone' *s* Brustbein *n*
breast' feed'ing *s* Stillen *n*
breast'plate' *s* Brustharnisch *m*
breast'stroke' *s* Brustschwimmen *n*

breath [brɛθ] *s* Atem *m;* (*single inhalation*) Atemzug *m;* (fig) Hauch *m;* **b. of air** Lüftchen *n;* **gasp for b.** nach Luft schnappen; **have bad b.** aus dem Mund riechen; **in the same b.** im gleichen Atemzug; **save one's b.** sich [*dat*] seine Worte ersparen; **take a deep b.** tief Luft holen; **take one's b. away** j—m den Atem verschlagen; **waste one's b.** in den Wind reden
breathe [brið] *tr* atmen, schöpfen; **b. a sigh of relief** aufatmen; **b. life into** beseelen; **b. one's last** die Seele aushauchen; **b. out** ausatmen; **not b. a word about it** kein Wort davon verlauten lassen ‖ *intr* atmen, hauchen; **b. again** aufatmen; **b. on** anhauchen
breath'ing space' *s* Atempause *f*
breathless ['brɛθlɪs] *adj* atemlos
breath'-tak'ing *adj* atemberaubend
breech [brit] *s* Verschlußstück *n*
breed [brid] *s* Zucht *f,* Stamm *m;* (*sort, group*) Schlag *m;* (*of animals*) Rasse *f* ‖ *v* (*pret & pp* **bred** [bred]) *tr* (*beget*) erzeugen; (*raise*) züchten; (fig) hervorrufen ‖ *intr* sich vermehren
breeder ['bridər] *s* Züchter –in *mf*
breed'ing *s* (*of animals*) Züchtung *f,* Aufzucht *f;* (fig) Erziehung *f*
breeze [briz] *s* Lüftchen *n,* Brise *f* ‖ *intr*—**b. by** vorbeiflitzen; **b. in** frisch und vergnügt hereinkommen
breezy ['brizi] *adj* luftig; (fig) keß
brevity ['breviti] *s* Kürze *f*
brew [bru] *s* Brühe *f;* (*of beer*) Bräu *m* ‖ *tr* (*tea, coffee*) aufbrühen; (*beer*) brauen ‖ *intr* ziehen; (*said of a storm*) sich zusammenbrauen; **something is brewing** etwas ist im Anzuge
brewer ['bru·ər] *s* Brauer –in *mf*
brewery ['bru·əri] *s* Brauerei *f*
bribe [braɪb] *s* Bestechungsgeld *n* ‖ *tr* bestechen
bribery ['braɪbəri] *s* Bestechung *f*
brick [brɪk] *s* Ziegelstein *m*
bricklayer ['brɪk ,le·ər] *s* Maurer *m*
brick'work' *s* Mauerwerk *n*
brick'yard' *s* Ziegelei *f*
bridal ['braɪdəl] *adj* Braut–, Hochzeits–
brid'al gown' *s* Brautkleid *n*
brid'al veil' *s* Brautschleier *m*
bride [braɪd] *s* Braut *f*
bride'groom' *s* Bräutigam *m*
brides'maid' *s* Brautjungfer *f*
bridge [brɪdʒ] *s* (*over a river*) Brücke *f;* (*of eyeglasses*) Steg *m;* (*of a nose*) Nasenrücken *m;* (cards) Bridge *n;* (dent) Zahnbrücke *f;* (naut) Kommandobrücke *f* ‖ *tr* (& fig) überbrücken
bridge'head' *s* Brückenkopf *m*
bridge'work' *s* (dent) Brückenarbeit *f*
bridle ['braɪdəl] *s* Zaum *m,* Zügel *m* ‖ *tr* aufzäumen, zügeln
bri'dle path' *s* Reitweg *m*
brief [brif] *adj* kurz; **be b.** sich kurz fassen ‖ *s* (jur) Schriftsatz *m* ‖ *tr* einweisen, orientieren
brief' case' *s* Aktentasche *f*

brief'ing s Einsatzbesprechung f

brier ['braɪ·ər] s Dornbusch m

brig [brɪg] s (naut) Brigg f; (nav) Knast m

brigade [brɪ'ged] s Brigade f

brigadier' gen'eral [,brɪgə'dɪr] s Brigadegeneral m

brigand ['brɪgənd] s Brigant m

bright [braɪt] adj hell; (color) lebhaft; (face) strahlend; (weather) heiter; (smart) gescheit, aufgeweckt ∥ adv —b. and early in aller Frühe

brighten ['braɪtən] tr aufhellen ∥ intr sich aufhellen

bright'-eyed' adj hellaügig

brightness ['braɪtnɪs] s Helle f

bright' side' s (fig) Lichtseite f

bright' spot' s (fig) Lichtblick m

brilliance ['brɪljəns], **brilliancy** ['brɪljənsi] s Glanz m

brilliant ['brɪljənt] adj (& fig) glänzend

brim [brɪm] s Rand m; (of a hat) Krempe f; **to the b.** bis zum Rande ∥ v (pret & pp **brimmed**; ger **brimming**) intr—b. over (with) (fig) überschäumen (vor dat)

brimful ['brɪm,ful] adj übervoll

brim'stone' s Schwefel m

brine [braɪn] s Salzwasser n, Sole f; (for pickling) Salzlake f

bring [brɪŋ] v (pret & pp **brought** [brɔt]) tr bringen; **b.** about zustande bringen; **b. back** zurückbringen; (memories) zurückrufen; **b. down** herunterbringen; (shoot down) abschießen; **b. down the house** (fig) Lachstürme entfesseln; **b. forth** hervorbringen; **b. forward** vorbringen; **b. it about** that es durchsetzen, daß; **b. on** herbeiführen; **b. oneself to** (inf) sich überwinden zu (inf); **b. to** wieder zu sich bringen; **b. together** zusammenbringen; **b. up** (children) erziehen; (a topic) zur Sprache bringen

bring'ing-up' s Erziehung f

brink [brɪŋk] s (& fig) Rand m

brisk [brɪsk] adj (pace, business) flott; (air) frisch, scharf

bristle ['brɪsəl] s Borste f ∥ intr sich sträuben

bristly ['brɪsli] adj borstig

Britain ['brɪtən] s Britannien n

British ['brɪtɪʃ] adj britisch ∥ **the B.** spl die Briten pl

Britisher ['brɪtɪʃər] s Brite m, Britin f

Briton ['brɪtən] s Brite m, Britin f

Brittany ['brɪtəni] s die Bretagne f

brittle ['brɪtəl] adj brüchig, spröde

broach [brotʃ] tr zur Sprache bringen

broad [brɔd] adj breit; (daylight) hellicht; (outline) grob; (sense) weit; (view) allgemein, umfassend

broad'cast' s Sendung f, Übertragung f ∥ v (pret & pp –cast) tr (rumors, etc.) ausposaunen ∥ (pret & pp –cast & –casted) tr & intr senden, übertragen

broadcaster ['brɔd,kæstər] s Rundfunksprecher –in mf

broad'casting sta'tion s Sender m

broad'casting stu'dio s Senderaum m

broad'cloth' s feiner Wäschestoff m

broaden ['brɔdən] tr verbreitern ∥ intr sich verbreitern

broad'-gauge' adj (rr) breitspurig

broad'-mind'ed adj großzügig

broad'-shoul'dered adj breitschultrig

broad'side' s (guns on one side of ship) Breitseite f; (fig) Schimpfkanonade f

brocade [bro'ked] s Brokat m

broccoli ['brakəli] s Spargelkohl m

brochure [bro'ʃur] s Broschüre f

broil [brɔɪl] tr am Rost braten, grillen

broiler ['brɔɪlər] s Bratrost m

broke [brok] adj (coll) abgebrannt, pleite; **go b.** (coll) pleite gehen

broken ['brokən] adj zerbrochen; (limb, spirit, English) gebrochen; (home) zerrüttet; (line) gestrichelt

bro'ken-down' adj erschöpft; (horse) abgearbeitet

bro'ken-heart'ed adj mit gebrochenem Herzen

broker ['brokər] s Makler –in mf

brokerage ['brokərɪdʒ] s Maklergeschäft n; (fee) Maklergebühr f

bromide ['bromaɪd] s Bromid n; (coll) Binsenweisheit f

bromine ['bromin] s Brom n

bronchial ['braŋkɪ·əl] adj bronchial

bron'chial tube' s Luftröhre f, Bronchie f

bronchitis [braŋ'kaɪtɪs] s Bronchitis f

bron·co ['braŋko] s (–cos) kleines halbwildes Pferd n

bronze [branz] adj Bronze– ∥ s Bronze f ∥ tr bronzieren ∥ intr sich bräunen

brooch [brotʃ], [brutʃ] s Brosche f

brood [brud] s Brut f, Junge pl ∥ tr ausbrüten ∥ intr brüten; (coll) sinnieren; **b. over** grübeln über (acc)

brook [bruk] s Bach m ∥ tr dulden

broom [brum] s Besen m

broom'stick' s Besenstiel m

broth [brɔθ] s Brühe f

brothel ['braθəl] s Bordell n

brother ['brʌðər] s Bruder m; **brother(s) and sister(s)** Geschwister pl

broth'erhood' s (& relig) Brüderschaft f

broth'er-in-law' s (brothers-in-law) Schwager m

brotherly ['brʌðərli] adj brüderlich

brow [brau] s Stirn f

brow'beat' v (pret –beat; pp –beaten) tr einschüchtern

brown [braun] adj braun ∥ s Bräune f ∥ tr & intr bräunen

brownish ['braunɪʃ] adj bräunlich

brown'-nose' tr (sl) kriechen (dat)

brown' sug'ar s brauner Zucker m

browse [brauz] intr grasen, weiden; (through books) schmökern, stöbern; (through a store) herumsuchen

bruise [bruz] s Quetschung f ∥ tr quetschen

brunette [bru'net] adj brünett ∥ s Brünette f

brunt [brʌnt] s Anprall m; **bear the b.** die Hauptlast tragen

brush [brʌʃ] s Bürste f; (of an artist; for shaving) Pinsel m; (brief encoun-

ter) kurzer Zusammenstoß *m; (light touch)* leichte Berührung *f; (bot)* Gebüsch *n; (elec)* Bürste *f;* || br bürsten; **b. aside** beiseite schieben; **b. off** abbürsten; *(devour)* verschlingen; *(make light of)* abwimmeln || *intr*—**b. against** streifen; **b. up on** auffrischen

brush'-off' *s* (coll) Laufpaß *m*

brush'wood' *s* Unterholz *n*, Niederwald *m*

brusque [brʌsk] *adj* brüsk

Brussels ['brʌsəlz] *s* Brüssel *n*

Brus'sels sprouts' *spl* Rosenkohl *m*

brutal ['brutəl] *adj* brutal

brutality [bru'tælɪti] *s* Brutalität *f*

brute [brut] *adj* viehisch; *(strength)* roh || *s* Tier *n; (fig)* Unmensch *m*

brutish ['brutɪʃ] *adj* tierisch, roh

bubble ['bʌbəl] *s* Blase *f*, Bläschen *n* || *intr* sprudeln; **b. over (with)** übersprudeln (vor *dat)*

bub'ble bath' *s* Schaumbad *n*

bub'ble gum' *s* Knallkaugummi *m*

bubbly ['bʌbli] *adj* sprudelnd; *(Person)* lebhaft

buck [bʌk] *s* Bock *m; (sl)* Dollar *m;* **pass the b.** (coll) die Verantwortung abschieben || *tr* (fig) kämpfen gegen; **b. off** abwerfen || *intr* bocken; **b. for** *(a promotion)* sich bemühen um

bucket ['bʌkɪt] *s* Eimer *m*

buck'et seat' *s* Schalensitz *m*

buckle ['bʌkəl] *s* Schnalle *f; (bend)* Ausbuchtung *f* || *tr* zuschnallen || *intr (from heat, etc.)* zusammensacken; **b. down** sich auf die Hosen setzen

buck' pri'vate *s* gemeiner Soldat *m*

buckram ['bʌkrəm] *s* Buckram *n*

buck'shot' *s* Rehposten *m*

buck'tooth' *s* **(-teeth)** vorstehender Zahn *m*

buck'wheat' *s* Buchweizen *m*

bud [bʌd] *s* Knospe *f*, Keim *m;* **nip in the bud** (fig) im Keime ersticken || *v (pret & pp* budded*; ger* budding) *intr* knospen, keimen, ausschlagen

buddy ['bʌdi] *s* (coll) Kumpel *m*

budge [bʌdʒ] *tr* (von der Stelle) bewegen || *intr* sich (von der Stelle) bewegen

budget ['bʌdʒɪt] *s* Budget *n*, Haushaltsplan *m; (of a state)* Staatshaushalt *m* || *tr* einteilen, vorausplanen

budgetary ['bʌdʒɪ,teri] *adj* Budget-

buff [bʌf] *adj* lederfarben || *s* Lederfarbe *f;* (coll) Schwärmer –in *mf* || *tr* polieren

buffa·lo ['bʌfə,lo] *s* **(-loes & -los)** Büffel *m*

buffer ['bʌfər] *s* Puffer *m; (polisher)* Polierer *m;* (rr) Prellbock *m*

buff'er state' *s* Pufferstaat *m*

buffet [bu'fe] *s (meal)* Büfett *n; (furniture)* Kredenz *f* || ['bʌfɪt] *tr* herumstoßen

buffoon [bə'fun] *s* Hanswurst *m*

bug [bʌg] *s* Insekt *n*, Käfer *m; (defect)* (coll) Defekt *m; (electron)* Abhörgerät *n*, Wanze *f;* **bugs** Ungeziefer *n* || *v (pret & pp* bugged*; ger* bugging) *tr (annoy)* (sl) ärgern;

(electron) (sl) Abhörgeräte einbauen in *(dat)*

bug'-eyed' *adj* (sl) mit großen Augen

buggy ['bʌgi] *adj* verwanzt; *(crazy)* (sl) verrückt || *s* Wagen *m*

bugle ['bjugəl] *s* Signalhorn *n*

bu'gle call' *s* Signal *n*

bugler ['bjuglər] *s* Hornist –in *mf*

build [bɪld] *s* Bauart *f*, Gestalt *f; (of a person)* Körperbau *m* || *v (pret & pp* built [bɪlt]) *tr* bauen; *(a bridge)* schlagen; *(with stone or brick)* mauern; *(a fire)* anmachen; **b. up** aufbauen; *(an area)* ausbauen; *(hopes)* erwecken

builder ['bɪldər] *s* Baumeister *m*

build'ing *s* Gebäude *n*

build'ing and loan' associa'tion *s* Bausparkasse *f*

build'ing block' *s* Zementblock *m; (for children)* Bauklötzchen *n*

build'ing con'tractor *s* Bauunternehmer *m*

build'ing in'dustry *s* Bauindustrie *f*

build'ing lot' *s* Bauplatz *m*, Grundstück *n*

build'ing mate'rial *s* Baustoff *m*

build'-up' *s* (coll) Propaganda *f*

built'-in' *adj* Einbau-

built'-up' *adj* bebaut

bulb [bʌlb] *s* (bot) Knolle *f*, Zwiebel *f; (elec)* Glühbirne *f; (phot)* Blitzlampe *f*

Bulgaria [bʌl'gɑrɪ·ə] *s* Bulgarien *n*

Bulgarian [bʌl'gɑrɪ·ən] *adj* bulgarisch || *s* Bulgare *m*, Bulgarin *f; (language)* Bulgarisch *n*

bulge [bʌldʒ] *s* Ausbauchung *f*, Beule *f; (of a sail)* Bausch *m; (mil)* Frontvorsprung *m* || *intr* sich bauschen; *(said of eyes)* hervortreten

bulg'ing *adj (belly, muscles)* hervorspringend; *(eyes)* hervorquellend; *(sails)* gebläht; **b. with** bis zum Platzen gefüllt mit

bulk [bʌlk] *adj* Massen–, unverpackt || *s* Masse *f; (main part)* Hauptteil *m;* **in b.** unverpackt || *intr*—**b. large** e–e große Rolle spielen

bulk'head' *s* (aer) Spant *m; (naut)* Schott *n*

bulky ['bʌlki] *adj* sperrig

bull [bul] *s* Bulle *m*, Stier *m; (sl)* Quatsch *m; (eccl)* Bulle *f; (st. exch.)* Haussier *m;* **like a b. in a china shop** wie ein Elefant im Porzellanladen; **shoot the b.** (sl) quatschen; **take the b. by the horns** den Stier an den Hörnern packen; **throw the b.** (sl) aufschneiden

bull'dog' *s* Bulldogge *f*

bull'doze' *tr* planieren; (fig) überfahren

bulldozer ['bʌl,dozər] *s* Planierraupe *f*

bullet ['bulɪt] *s* Kugel *f*

bul'let hole' *s* Schußöffnung *f*

bulletin ['bulətɪn] *s (report)* Bulletin *n; (flyer)* Flugschrift *f*

bul'letin board' *s* Anschlagbrett *n*

bul'letproof' *adj* kugelsicher

bull'fight' *s* Stierkampf *m*

bull'fighter *s* Stierkämpfer –in *mf*

bull'frog' *s* Ochsenfrosch *m*

bull'-head'ed *adj* dickköpfig

bull' horn' *s* Richtungslautsprecher *m*

bullion ['buljən] *s* Barren *m*; (mil, nav) Kordel *f*

bull' mar'ket *s* Spekulationsmarkt *m*

bullock ['bulək] *s* Ochse *m*

bull'pen' *s* Stierpferch *m*; (baseball) Übungsplatz *m* für Reservewerfer

bull'ring' *s* Stierkampfarena *f*

bull' ses'sion *s* (sl) zwanglose Diskussion *f*

bull's'-eye' *s* (of a target) Schwarze *n*; (round window) Bullauge *n*; **hit the b.** ins Schwarze treffen

bul·ly ['buli] *adj*—**b. for you!** großartig! || *s* Raufbold *m* || *v* (pret & pp **-lied**) *tr* tyrannisieren

bulrush ['bul ˌrʌʃ] *s* Binse *f*

bulwark ['bulwərk] *s* Bollwerk *n*

bum [bʌm] *s* (sl) Strolch *m*; **give s.o. the bum's rush** j-n auf den Schub bringen || *v* (pret & pp **bummed**; ger **bumming**) *tr* (sl) schinden, schnorren || *intr*—**bum around** bummeln

bumblebee ['bʌmbəl ˌbi] *s* Hummel *f*

bump [bʌmp] *s* Stoß *m*, Bums *m*; (swelling) Beule *f*; (in the road) holp(e)rige Stelle *f* || *tr* (an)stoßen; **b. off** (sl) abknallen; **b. one's head against s.th.** mit dem Kopf gegen etw stoßen || *intr* zusammenstoßen; **b. against** stoßen an (acc); **b. into** stoßen gegen; (meet unexpectedly) in die Arme laufen (dat)

bumper ['bʌmpər] *s* Stoßstange *f*

bumpkin ['bʌmpkɪn] *s* Tölpel *m*

bumpy ['bʌmpi] *adj* holperig; (aer) böig

bum' steer' *s*—**give s.o. a b.** (coll) nasführen

bun [bʌn] *s* Kuchenbrötchen *n*; (of hair) Haarknoten *m*

bunch [bʌntʃ] *s* Bündel *n*; (of grapes) Traube *f*; (group) Schar *f*, Bande *f*; **b. of flowers** Blumenstrauß *m*; **b. of grapes** Weintraube *f* || *tr*—**b. together** zusammenfassen || *intr*—**b. together** sich zusammendrängen

bundle ['bʌndəl] *s* Bündel *n*; (heap) Stoß *m*; (of straw) Schütte *f*; **b. of nerves** Nervenbündel *n* || *tr* bündeln; **b. off** (coll) verfrachten; **b. up** sich warm anziehen

bung [bʌŋ] *s* Spund *m* || *tr* verspunden

bungalow ['bʌŋgə ˌlo] *s* Bungalow *m*

bung'hole' *s* Spundloch *n*

bungle ['bʌŋgəl] *s* Pfuscherei *f* || *tr* verpfuschen || *intr* pfuschen

bungler ['bʌŋglər] *s* Pfuscher –*in* *mf*

bun'gling *adj* stümperhaft || *s* Stümperei *f*

bunk [bʌŋk] *s* Schlafkoje *f*; (sl) Unsinn *m* || *intr* (with) schlafen (mit)

bunk' bed' *s* Etagenbett *n*

bunker ['bʌŋkər] *s* Bunker *m*

bunny ['bʌni] *s* Kaninchen *n*

bunt'ing *s* (cloth) Fahnentuch *n*; (decoration) Fahnenschmuck *m*; (orn) Ammer *f*

buoy [bɔɪ] *s* Boje *f* || *tr*—**b. up** flott erhalten; (fig) Auftrieb geben (dat)

buoyancy ['bɔɪ·ənsi] *s* Auftrieb *m*; (fig) Spannkraft *f*

buoyant ['bɔɪ·ənt] *adj* schwimmend; (fig) lebhaft

burden ['bʌrdən] *s* Bürde *f*, Last *f*; (fig) Belastung *f* || *tr* belasten

bur'den of proof' *s* Beweislast *f*

burdensome ['bʌrdənsəm] *adj* lästig

bureau ['bjuro] *s* Kommode *f*; (office) Büro *n*; (department) Amt *n*

bureaucracy [bju'rakrəsi] *s* Bürokratie *f*, Beamtenschaft *f*

bureaucrat ['bjurə ˌkræt] *s* Bürokrat –*in* *mf*

bureaucratic [ˌbjurə'krætɪk] *adj* bürokratisch

burglar ['bʌrglər] *s* Einbrecher –*in* *mf*

bur'glar alarm' *s* Einbruchssicherung *f*

burglarize ['bʌrglə ˌraɪz] *tr* einbrechen in (acc)

bur'glarproof' *adj* einbruchssicher

burglary ['bʌrgləri] *s* Einbruchdiebstahl *m*

Burgundy ['bʌrgəndi] *s* Burgund *n*; (wine) Burgunder *m*

burial ['bɛri·əl] *s* Beerdigung *f*

bur'ial ground' *s* Begräbnisplatz *m*

burlap ['bʌrlæp] *s* Sackleinwand *f*

burlesque [bər'lɛsk] *adj* burlesk *f* || *tr* burlesk behandeln

burlesque' show' *s* Varieté *n*

burly ['bʌrli] *adj* stämmig, beleibt

Burma ['bʌrmə] *s* Birma *n*

Bur·mese [bər'miz] *adj* birmanisch || *s* (**-mese**) (person) Birmane *m*, Birmanin *f*; (language) Birmanisch *n*

burn [bʌrn] *s* Brandwunde *f*; || *v* (pret & pp **burned** & **burnt** [bʌrnt]) *tr* (ver)brennen; **be burned up** (coll) fauchen; **b. down** niederbrennen; **b. up** (coll) wütend machen || *intr* (ver)brennen; (said of food) anbrennen; **b. out** ausbrennen; (elec) durchbrennen; **b. up** ganz verbrennen; (during reentry) verglühen

burner ['bʌrnər] *s* Brenner *m*

burn'ing *adj* (& fig) brennend

burnish ['bʌrnɪʃ] *tr* polieren

burn'out' *s* (rok) Brennschluß *m*

burnt *adj* verbrannt; (smell) brenzlig

burp [bʌrp] *s* Rülpser *m* || *tr* rülpsen lassen || *intr* rülpsen

burr [bʌr] *s* (growth on a tree) Auswuchs *m*; (in metal) Grat *m*; (bot) Klette *f*

burrow ['bʌro] *s* Bau *m* || *tr* graben || *intr* sich eingraben, wühlen

bursar ['bʌrsər] *s* Schatzmeister *m*

burst [bʌrst] *s* Bersten *n*; (split) Riß *m*; Bruch *m*; **b. of gunfire** Feuerstoß *m* || *v* (pret & pp **burst**) *tr* (auf)sprengen, zum Platzen bringen || *intr* bersten, platzen; (split) reißen; (said of a boil) aufgehen; **b. into** (e.g., a room) hereinstürzen in (acc); **b. into tears** in Tränen ausbrechen; **b. open** aufplatzen; **b. out laughing** loslachen

bur·y ['bɛri] *v* (pret & pp **-led**) *tr* beerdigen, begraben; **be buried in thought** in Gedanken versunken sein; **b. alive** verschütten

bus [bʌs] *s* (busses & buses) Autobus *m*, Bus *m* || *v* (pret & pp) **bussed** &

bused; *ger* bussing & busing) *tr* & *intr* mit dem Bus fahren

bus′ boy′ *s* Pikkolo *m*

bus′ driv′er *s* Autobusfahrer –in *mf*

bush [buʃ] *s* Busch *m*; **beat around the b.** um die Sache herumreden

bushed *adj* (coll) abgeklappert

bushel [′buʃəl] *s* Scheffel *m*; **by the b.** scheffelweise

bush′ing *s* Buchse *f*

bushy [′buʃi] *adj* strauchbewachsen; (*brows*) buschig

business [′bɪznɪs] *adj* Geschäfts- || *s* Geschäft *n*; (*company*) Firma *f*, Betrieb *m*; (*employment*) Beruf *m*, Gewerbe *n*; (*duty*) Pflicht *f*; (*right*) Recht *n*; (coll) Sache *f*; **be in b.** geschäftlich tätig sein; **do b. with** Geschäfte machen mit; **get down to b.** (coll) zur Sache kommen; **go about one′s b.** seiner Arbeit nachgehen; **he means b.** (coll) er meint es ernst; **know one′s b.** seine Sache verstehen; **make s.th. one′s b.** sich [*dat*] etw angelegen sein lassen; **mind your own b.** kümmere dich um deine eigenen Sachen; **that′s none of your b.** das geht dich gar nichts an; **the whole b.** die ganze Geschichte; **you have no b. here** du hast hier nichts zu suchen

busi′ness call′ *s* Dienstgespräch *n*

busi′ness card′ *s* Geschäftskarte *f*

busi′ness cen′ter *s* Geschäftszentrum *n*

busi′ness col′lege *s* Handelsschule *f*

busi′ness dis′trict *s* Geschäftsviertel *n*

busi′ness expens′es *spl* Geschäftsspesen *pl*

busi′ness hours′ *s* Geschäftszeit *f*

busi′ness let′ter *s* Geschäftsbrief *m*

busi′nesslike *adj* sachlich; (pej) geschäftsmäßig

busi′ness·man′ *s* (**–men′**) Geschäftsmann *m*

busi′ness reply′ card′ *s* Rückantwortkarte *f*

busi′ness suit′ *s* Straßenanzug *m*

busi′ness·wom′an *s* (**–wom′en**) Geschäftsfrau *f*

bus′ line′ *s* Autobuslinie *f*

bus′ stop′ *s* Autobushaltestelle *f*

bust [bʌst] *s* (*chest*) Busen *m*; (*measurement*) Oberweite *f*; (*statue*) Brustbild *n*; (*blow*) (sl) Faustschlag *m*; (*failure*) (sl) Platzen *n*; (*binge*) (sl) Sauftour *f* || *tr* (sl) kaputtmachen; (mil) degradieren || *intr* (*break*) (sl) kaputtgehen

bustle [′bʌsəl] *s* (*activity*) Hochbetrieb *m*, Trubel *m* || *intr* umherhasten; **b. about** herumsausen

bus′tling *adj* geschäftig

bus·y [′bɪzi] *adj* tätig, beschäftigt; (*day, life*) arbeitsreich; (*street*) lebhaft, verkehrsstark; (telp) belegt, besetzt; **be b.** (*be occupied*) zu tun haben; (*be unavailable*) nicht zu sprechen sein || *v* (*pret & pp* –**ied**) *tr* beschäftigen

bus′ybod′y *s* Wichtigtuer –in *mf*

bus′y sig′nal *s* (telp) Besetztzeichen *n*

but [bʌt] *adv* nur, lediglich, bloß; (*just, only*) erst; **all but** beinahe ||

außer (*dat*); (*after negatives*) als; **all but one** alle bis auf einen || *conj* aber; (*after negatives*) sondern

butcher [′butʃər] *s* Fleischer –in *mf*, Metzger –in *mf*; (fig) Schlächter –in *mf* || *tr* schlachten; (fig) abschlachten

butch′er knife′ *s* Fleischermesser *n*

butch′er shop′ *s* Metzgerei *f*

butchery [′butʃəri] *s* (*slaughterhouse*) Schlachthaus *n*; (fig) Gemetzel *n*

butler [′bʌtlər] *s* Haushofmeister *m*

butt [bʌt] *s* (*of a gun*) Kolben *m*; (*of a cigarette*) Stummel *m*; (*with the horns, head*) Stoß *m*; (*of ridicule*) Zielscheibe *f* || *tr* stoßen || *intr* stoßen; **b. in** (sl) sich einmischen, dazwischenfahren

butter [′bʌtər] *s* Butter *f* || *tr* mit Butter bestreichen; (*bread*) schmieren; **b. s.o. up** (coll) j-m Honig um den Mund schmieren

but′terball′ *s* Butterkugel *f*; (*chubby child*) Pummelchen *n*

but′tercup′ *s* Butterblume *f*, Hahnenfuß *m*

but′ter dish′ *s* Butterdose *f*

but′terfly′ *s* Schmetterling *m*; (sport) Schmetterlingsstil *m*

but′ter knife′ *s* Buttermesser *n*

but′termilk′ *s* Buttermilch *f*

buttocks [′bʌtəks] *spl* Hinterbacken *pl*

button [′bʌtən] *s* Knopf *m* || *tr* knöpfen; **button up** zuknöpfen

but′tonhole′ *s* Knopfloch *n* || *tr* im Gespräch festhalten

buttress [′bʌtrɪs] *s* Strebepfeiler *m*; (fig) Stütze *f* || *tr* (durch Strebepfeiler) stützen; (fig) (unter)stützen

butt′-weld′ *tr* stumpfschweißen

buxom [′bʌksəm] *adj* beleibt

buy [baɪ] *s* Kauf *m* || *v* (*pret & pp* **bought** [bɔt]) *tr* kaufen; (*bus ticket, train ticket*) lösen; (*accept, believe*) glauben; **buy off** (*bribe*) bestechen; **buy out** auskaufen; **buy up** aufkaufen

buyer [′baɪ·ər] *s* Käufer –in *mf*

buzz [bʌz] *s* Summen *n*, Surren *n*; (telp) (coll) Anruf *m* || *tr* (coll) (aer) dicht vorbeisausen an (*dat*); (telp) (coll) anrufen || *intr* summen, surren; **b. around** herumsausen

buzzard [′bʌzərd] *s* Bussard *m*

buzz′ bomb′ *s* Roboterbombe *f*, V-Waffe *f*

buzzer [′bʌzər] *s* Summer *m*; **did the b. sound?** ist der Summer ertönt

buzz′ saw′ *s* Kreissäge *f*, Rundsäge *f*

by [baɪ] *adv* vorüber, vorbei; **by and by** nach und nach; **by and large** im großen und ganzen || *prep* (*agency*) von (*dat*), durch (*acc*); (*position*) bei (*dat*), an (*dat*), neben (*dat*); (*no later than*) bis spätestens; (*in division*) durch (*acc*); (*indicating mode of transportation*) mit (*dat*); (*indicating authorship*) von (*dat*); (*according to*) nach (*dat*); (*past*) an (*dat*) vorbei; (*by means of*) mit (*dat*); **by** (ger) indem (ind); **by an inch** um e-n Zoll; **by day** bei Tag; **by far** bei weitem; **by heart** auswendig; **by itself** (*automatically*) von selbst; **by land** zu Lande; **by mail**

per Post; **by myself** ganz allein; **by nature** von Natur aus; **by now** schon; **by the pound** per Pfund; **two by four** zwei mal vier
bye [baɪ] s (sport) Freilos n
bye'bye' interj Wiedersehen!
bygone ['baɪ ˌgɔn] adj vergangen || **s—let bygones be bygones** laß(t) das Vergangene ruhen
by'law' s Satzung f; **bylaws** (*of an organization*) Statuten pl, Satzungen pl
by'-line' s (journ) Verfasserangabe f

by'pass' s Umgehungsstraße f, Umleitung f; (elec) Nebenschluß m || tr umgehen
by'prod'uct s Nebenprodukt n
bystander ['baɪ ˌstændər] s Umstehende mf
by'way' s Seitenweg m
by'word' s Sprichwort n
Byzantine ['bɪzən ˌtin], [bɪ'zæntin] adj byzantinisch || s Byzantiner –in mf
Byzantium [bɪ'zænʃɪˌəm], [bɪ'zæntɪˌəm] s Byzanz f

C

C, c [si] s dritter Buchstabe des englischen Alphabets; (mus) C n; **C flat** Ces n; **C sharp** Cis n
cab [kæb] s Taxi n; (*of a truck*) Fahrerkabine f
cabaret [ˌkæbə're] s Kabarett n
cabbage ['kæbɪdʒ] s Kohl m, Kraut n
cab'driv'er s Taxifahrer –in mf
cabin ['kæbɪn] s Hütte f; (aer) Kabine f; (naut) Kajüte f, Kabine f
cab'in boy' s Schiffsjunge m
cabinet ['kæbɪnɪt] adj Kabinetts– || s (*in a kitchen*) Küchenschrank m; (*for a radio*) Gehäuse n; (pol) Kabinett n, Ministerrat m
cab'inetmak'er s Tischler m
cable ['kebəl] s Kabel n, Seil n; (naut) Tau m; (telg) Kabelnachricht f || tr & intr kabeln
ca'ble car' s Seilbahn f, Schwebebahn f
ca'blegram' s Kabelnachricht f
caboose [kə'bus] s (rr) Dienstwagen m
cab'stand' s Taxistand m
cache [kæʃ] s Geheimlager n, Versteck n; **c. of arms** Waffenlager n
cachet [kæ'ʃe] s Siegel n; (fig) Stempel m; (pharm) Kapsel f
cackle ['kækəl] s (*of chickens*) Gegacker n; (*of geese*) Geschnatter n || intr gackern, gackeln; schnattern
cac·tus ['kæktəs] s (–tuses & –ti [taɪ]) Kaktus m
cad [kæd] s (sl) Saukerl m, Schuft m
cadaver [kə'dævər] s Kadaver m, Leiche f
caddie ['kædi] s Golfjunge m || intr die Schläger tragen
cadence ['kedəns] s (*rhythm*) Rhythmus m; (*flow of language*) Sprechrhythmus m; (mus) Kadenz f
cadet [kə'det] s Offizier(s)anwärter –in mf
cadre ['kædri] s Kader m
Caesar'ean opera'tion [sɪ'zɛrɪˌən] s Kaiserschnitt m
café [kæ'fe] s Café n
cafeteria [ˌkæfə'tɪrɪ·ə] s Selbstbedienungsrestaurant n
caffeine [kæ'fin] s Koffein n
cage [kedʒ] s Käfig m || tr in e–n Käfig sperren
cagey ['kedʒi] adj (coll) schlau

cahoots [kə'huts] s—**be in c.** (sl) unter e–r Decke stecken
Cain [ken] s—**raise C.** Krach schlagen
caisson ['kesən] s Senkkasten m
cajole [kə'dʒol] tr beschwatzen
cake [kek] s Kuchen m; (*round cake*) Torte f; (*of soap*) Riegel m; **he takes the c.** (coll) er schießt den Vogel ab; **that takes the c.** (coll) das ist die Höhe || intr zusammenbacken; **c. on** anbacken
calamitous [kə'læmɪtəs] adj unheilvoll
calamity [kə'læmɪti] s Unheil n
calci·fy ['kælsɪˌfaɪ] v (pret & pp –fied) tr & intr verkalken
calcium ['kælsɪˌəm] s Kalzium n
calculate ['kælkjəˌlet] tr berechnen || intr rechnen
cal'culated risk' s—**take a c.** ein bewußtes Risiko eingehen
cal'culating adj berechnend
calculation [ˌkælkjə'le/ən] s Berechnung f; **rough c.** Überschlagsrechnung f
calculator ['kælkjəˌletər] s Rechenmaschine f; (data proc) Rechner m
calcu·lus ['kælkjələs] s (–luses & –li [ˌlaɪ]) (math) Differenzial– und Integralrechnung f; (pathol) Stein m
caldron ['kɔldrən] s Kessel m
calendar ['kæləndər] s Kalender m
calf [kæf] s (**calves** [kævz]) (*of a cow*) Kalb n; (*of certain other mammals*) Junge n; (anat) Wade f
calf'skin' s Kalbleder n
caliber ['kælɪbər] s (& fig) Kaliber n
calibrate ['kælɪˌbret] tr kalibrieren
cali·co ['kælɪˌko] s (–coes & –cos) Kaliko m
calisthenics [ˌkælɪs'θenɪks] spl Leibesübungen pl
calk [kɔk] tr abdichten, kalfatern
calk'ing s Kalfaterung f
call [kɔl] s Ruf m; (*visit*) Besuch m; (*reason*) Grund m; (com) (*for*) Nachfrage f (nach); (naut) Anlaufen n; (telp) Anruf m; **on c.** auf Abruf || tr rufen; (*name*) nennen; (*wake*) wecken; (*a meeting*) einberufen; (*a game*) absagen; (*a strike*) ausrufen; (*by phone*) anrufen; (*a witness*) vorladen; (*a doctor; taxi*) kommen las-

sen; **be called** heißen; **c. down** (coll) herunterputzen; **c. in** (*a doctor, specialist*) hinzuziehen; (*for advice*) zu Rate ziehen; (*currency*) einziehen; (*capital*) kündigen; **c. it a day** (coll) Schluß machen; **c. off** absagen; **c. out** ausrufen; (*the police*) einsetzen; **c. s.o. names** j-n beschimpfen; **c. up** (mil) einberufen; (telp) anrufen || *intr* rufen; (cards) ansagen; **c. for** (*require*) erfordern; (*fetch*) abholen; (*help*) rufen um; (*a person*) rufen nach; **c. on** (*a pupil*) aufrufen; (*visit*) e-n Besuch machen bei; **c. to s.o.** j-m zurufen; **c. upon** jem auffordern

call' bell' *s* Rufglocke *f*
call' boy' *s* Hotelpage *m*; (theat) Inspezientengehilfe *m*
caller ['kɔlər] *s* Besucher –in *mf*
call' girl' *s* Callgirl *n*
call'ing *s* Beruf *m*; (relig) Berufung *f*
call'ing card' *s* Visitenkarte *f*
call'ing-down' *s* (coll) Standpauke *f*
call' num'ber *s* (libr) Standortnummer
callous ['kæləs] *adj* schwielig; (fig) gefühllos, abgestumpft
call'up' *s* (mil) Einberufung *f*
callus ['kæləs] *s* Schwiele *f*
calm [kɑm] *adj* ruhig || *s* Ruhe *f*; (naut) Flaute *f* || *tr* beruhigen; **c. down** beruhigen || *intr*—**c. down** sich beruhigen
calorie ['kæləri] *s* Kalorie *f*
calumny ['kæləmni] *s* Verleumdung *f*
Calvary ['kælvəri] *s* Golgatha *n*
calve [kæv] *intr* kalben
cam [kæm] *s* Nocken *m*
camel ['kæməl] *s* Kamel *n*
camellia [kə'miljə] *s* Kamelie *f*
came·o ['kæmɪ‚o] *s* (–os) Kamee *f*
camera ['kæmərə] *s* Kamera *f*
cam'era·man' *s* (–men') Kameramann *m*
camouflage ['kæmə‚flɑʒ] *s* Tarnung *f* || *tr* tarnen
camp [kæmp] *s* (& fig) Lager *n* || *intr* kampieren, lagern, campen
campaign [kæm'pen] *s* (& fig) Feldzug *m*; (pol) Wahlfeldzug *m* || *intr* an e–m Feldzug teilnehmen; **c. for** (pol) Wahlpropaganda machen für
campaigner [kæm'penər] *s* (*for a specific cause*) Befürworter –in *mf*; (pol) Wahlredner –in *mf*
campaign' slo'gan *s* Wahlparole *f*
campaign' speech' *s* Wahlrede *f*
camper ['kæmpər] *s* Camper *m*
camp'fire' *s* Lagerfeuer *n*
camp'ground *s* Campingplatz *m*
camphor ['kæmfər] *s* Kampfer *m*
camp'ing *s* Camping *n*
campus ['kæmpəs] *s* Universitätsgelände *n*
cam'shaft' *s* Nockenwelle *f*
can [kæn] *s* Dose *f*, Büchse *f*; (*for gasoline, water*) Kanister *m* || *v* (*pret & pp* **canned**; *ger* **canning**) *tr* einmachen; (sl) 'rausschmeißen || *v* (*pret & cond*) (**could**) *aux*—**I can come** ich kann kommen; **I cannot come** ich kann nicht kommen
Canada ['kænədə] *s* Kanada *n*

Canadian [kə'nedɪ‚ən] *adj* kanadisch || *s* Kanadier –in *mf*
canal [kə'næl] *s* Kanal *m*; (anat) Gang *m*
canary [kə'neri] *s* Kanarienvogel *m* || **the Canaries** *spl* die Kanarischen Inseln *pl*
can·cel ['kænsəl] *v* (*pret & pp* **–el(l)ed**; *ger* **–el(l)ing**) *tr* (*an event*) absagen; (*an order*) rückgängig machen; (*something written*) (aus)streichen, annulieren; (*stamps*) entwerten; (*a debt*) tilgen; (*a newspaper*) abbestellen; (math) streichen; **c. out** ausgleichen
cancellation [‚kænsə'leʃən] *s* (*of an event*) Absage *f*; (*of an order*) Annullierung *f*; (*of something written*) Streichung *f*; (*of a debt*) Tilgung *f*; (*of a stamp*) Entwertung *f*; (*of a newspaper*) Abbestellung *f*
cancer ['kænsər] *s* Krebs *m*
cancerous ['kænsərəs] *adj* krebsartig
candela·brum [‚kændə'lɑbrəm] *s* (**–bra** [brə] & **–brums**) Armleuchter *m*
candid ['kændɪd] *adj* offen
candidacy ['kændɪdəsi] *s* Kandidatur *f*
candidate ['kændɪ‚det] *s* (**for**) Kandidat –in *mf* (für)
candied ['kændɪd] *adj* kandiert
candle ['kændəl] *s* Kerze *f*
can'dlelight' *s* Kerzenlicht *n*
can'dlepow'er *s* Kerzenstärke *f*
can'dlestick' *s* Kerzenhalter *m*
candor ['kændər] *s* Offenheit *f*
can·dy ['kændi] *s* Süßwaren *pl*; **piece of c.** Bonbon *m* & *n* || *v* (*pret & pp* **–died**) *tr* glacieren, kandieren
can'dy store' *s* Süßwarengeschäft *n*
cane [ken] *s* (*plant; stem*) Rohr *n*; (*walking stick*) Stock *m* || *tr* mit e–m Stock züchtigen
cane' sug'ar *s* Rohrzucker *m*
canine ['kenaɪn] *adj* Hunde– || *s* (*tooth*) Eckzahn *m*, Reißzahn *m*
canister ['kænɪstər] *s* Dose *f*
canker ['kæŋkər] *s* (bot) Brand *m*; (pathol) Mundgeschwür *n*
canned' goods' *spl* Dosenkonserven *pl*
canned' mu'sic *s* Konservenmusik *f*
canned' veg'etables *spl* Gemüsekonserven *pl*
cannery ['kænəri] *s* Konservenfabrik *f*
cannibal ['kænɪbəl] *s* Kannibale *m*
can'ning *adj* Konserven– || *s* Konservenfabrikation *f*
cannon ['kænən] *s* Kanone *f*
cannonade [‚kænə'ned] *s* Kanonade *f*, Beschießung *f* || *tr* beschießen
can'nonball' *s* Kanonenkugel *f*
canny ['kæni] *adj* (*shrewd*) schlau; (*sagacious*) klug
canoe [kə'nu] *s* Kanu *n*
canoe'ing *s* Kanufahren *n*
canoeist [kə'nu·ɪst] *s* Kanufahrer *m*
canon ['kænən] *s* Kanon *m*; (*of a cathedral*) Domherr *m*
canonical [kə'nɑnɪkəl] *adj* kanonisch || **canonicals** *spl* kirchliche Amtstracht *f*

canonize [ˈkænəˌnaɪz] *tr* heiligsprechen

can'on law' *s* kanonisches Recht *n*

can' o'pener *s* Dosenöffner *m*

canopy [ˈkænəpi] *s* Baldachin *m*; *(above a king or pope)* Thronhimmel *m*; *(of a bed)* Betthimmel *m*

cant [kænt] *s (insincere statements)* unaufrichtiges Gerede *n*; *(jargon of thieves)* Gaunersprache *f*; *(technical phraseology)* Jargon *m*

cantaloupe [ˈkæntəˌlop] *s* Kantalupe *f*

cantankerous [kænˈtæŋkərəs] *adj* mürrisch, zänkisch

cantata [kənˈtɑtə] *s* Kantate *f*

canteen [kænˈtin] *s (service club, service store)* Kantine *f*; *(flask)* Feldflasche *f*

canter [ˈkæntər] *s* kurzer Galopp *m* || *intr* im kurzen Galopp reiten

canticle [ˈkæntɪkəl] *s* Lobgesang *m*

canton [ˈkæntən] *s* Kanton *m*

canvas [ˈkænvəs] *s* Leinwand *f*; *(naut)* Segeltuch *n*; *(a painting)* Gemälde *n*

canvass [ˈkænvəs] *s (econ)* Werbefeldzug *m*; *(pol)* Wahlfeldzug *m* || *tr (a district)* (pol) bearbeiten; *(votes)* (pol) werben

canyon [ˈkænjən] *s* Schlucht *f*

cap [kæp] *s* Kappe *f*, Mütze *f*; *(of a jar)* Deckel *m*; *(twist-off type)* Kapsel *f*; *(for a toy pistol)* Knallblättchen *n*; *(typ)* großer Buchstabe *m*; **use caps** *(typ)* großschreiben || *v (pret & pp capped; ger capping) tr (a bottle)* mit e-r Kapsel versehen; *(e.g., with snow)* bedecken; *(outdo)* übertreffen; *(success)* krönen

capability [ˌkepəˈbɪlɪti] *s* Fähigkeit *f*

capable [ˈkepəbəl] *adj* tüchtig; **c. of** fähig *(genit)*; *(ger)* fähig zu *(inf)*

capacious [kəˈpeʃəs] *adj* geräumig

capacity [kəˈpæsɪti] *adj* maximal, Kapazitäts– || *s (ability)* Fähigkeit *f*; *(content)* Fassungsvermögen *n*; *(of a truck, bridge)* Tragfähigkeit *f*; *(tech)* Kapazität *f*; **in my c. as** in meiner Eigenschaft als

cap' and gown' *s* Barett *n* und Talar *m*

cape [kep] *s* Umhang *m*; *(geog)* Kap *n*

Cape' of Good' Hope' *s* Kap *n* der Guten Hoffnung

caper [ˈkepər] *s* Luftsprung *m*; *(prank)* Schabernack *m*; *(culin)* Kaper *f* || *intr* hüpfen

capita [ˈkæpɪtə] *spl*—**per c.** pro Kopf, pro Person

capital [ˈkæpɪtəl] *adj (importance)* äußerste, höchste; *(city)* Haupt–; *(crime)* Kapital– || *s (city)* Hauptstadt *f*; *(archit)* Kapitell *n*; *(fin)* Kapital *n*; *(typ)* Großbuchstabe *m*

cap'ital gains' *spl* Kapitalzuwachs *m*

capitalism [ˈkæpɪtəˌlɪzəm] *s* Kapitalismus *m*

capitalist [ˈkæpɪtəlɪst] *s* Kapitalist –in *mf*

capitalistic [ˌkæpɪtəˈlɪstɪk] *adj* kapitalistisch

capitalize [ˈkæpɪtəˌlaɪz] *tr (fin)* kapitalisieren; *(typ)* groß schreiben (or drucken) || *intr*—**c. on** Nutzen ziehen aus

cap'ital let'ter *s* Großbuchstabe *m*

cap'ital pun'ishment *s* Todesstrafe *f*

capitol [ˈkæpɪtəl] *s* Kapitol *n*

capitulate [kəˈpɪtʃəˌlet] *intr* kapitulieren

capon [ˈkepɑn] *s* Kapaun *m*

caprice [kəˈpris] *s* Grille *f*, Kaprice *f*

capricious [kəˈprɪʃəs] *adj* kapriziös

capsize [ˈkæpsaɪz] *tr* zum Kentern bringen || *intr* kentern

capsule [ˈkæpsəl] *s* Kapsel *f*

captain [ˈkæptən] *s (of police, of firemen, in the army)* Hauptmann *m*; *(naut, sport)* Kapitän *m*; *(nav)* Kapitän *m* zur See; *(sport)* Mannschaftsführer *m*

caption [ˈkæpʃən] *s (heading of an article)* Überschrift *f*; *(wording under a picture)* Bildunterschrift *f*; *(cin)* Untertitel *m*

captivate [ˈkæptɪˌvet] *tr* fesseln

captive [ˈkæptɪv] *adj* gefangen || *s* Gefangene *mf*

cap'tive au'dience *s* unfreiwillige Zuhörerschaft *f*

captivity [kæpˈtɪvɪti] *s* Gefangenschaft *f*

captor [ˈkæptər] *s* Fänger –in *mf*

capture [ˈkæptʃər] *s* Fangen *n*, Gefangennahme *f*; *(naut)* Kaperung *f* || *tr (animals)* fangen; *(soldiers)* gefangennehmen; *(a ship)* kapern; *(a town)* erobern; *(a prize)* gewinnen

car [kɑr] *s (aut, rr)* Wagen *m*

carafe [kəˈræf] *s* Karaffe *f*

caramel [ˈkærəməl] *s* Karamelle *f*

carat [ˈkærət] *s* Karat *n*

caravan [ˈkærəˌvæn] *s* Karawane *f*

car'away seed' [ˈkærəˌwe] *s* Kümmelkorn *n*

carbide [ˈkɑrbaɪd] *s* Karbid *n*

carbine [ˈkɑrbɪn] *s* Karabiner *m*

carbohydrate [ˌkɑrboˈhaɪdret] *s* Kohlenhydrat *n*

carbol'ic ac'id [kɑrˈbɑlɪk] *s* Karbolsäure *f*

carbon [ˈkɑrbən] *s (chem)* Kohlenstoff *m*; *(elec)* Kohlenstift *m*

carbonated [ˈkɑrbəˌnetɪd] *adj* kohlensäurehaltig, Brause–

car'bon cop'y *s* Durchschlag *m*; **make a c.** of durchschlagen

car'bon diox'ide *s* Kohlendioxyd *n*

car'bon monox'ide *s* Kohlenoxyd *n*

car'bon pa'per *s* Kohlepapier *n*

carbuncle [ˈkɑrbʌŋkəl] *s (stone)* Karfunkel *m*; *(pathol)* Karbunkel *m*

carburetor [ˈkɑrb(j)əˌretər] *s* Vergaser *m*

carcass [ˈkɑrkəs] *s* Kadaver *m*, Aas *n*; *(without effort)* Rumpf *m*

car' coat' *s* Stutzer *m*

card [kɑrd] *s* Karte *f*; *(person)* (coll) Kerl *m*; *(text)* Krempel *f* || *tr (text)* kardätschen

card'board' *s* Kartonpapier *n*; *(thick pasteboard)* Pappe *f*; **piece of c.** Papp(en)deckel *m*

card'board box' *s* Pappkarton *m*, Pappschachtel *f*

card' cat'alogue *s* Kartothek *f*

card′ file′ s Kartei f
cardiac [′kɑrdɪˌæk] adj Herz– ‖ s (remedy) Herzmittel n; (patient) Herzkranke mf
cardinal [′kɑrdɪnəl] adj Kardinal– ‖ s (eccl, orn) Kardinal m
card′ in′dex s Karthotek f, Kartei f
card′sharp′ s Falschspieler –in mf
card′ trick′ s Kartenkunststück n
care [ker] s (accuracy) Sorgfalt f; (worry) Sorge f, Kummer m; (prudence) Vorsicht f; (upkeep) Pflege f; **be under a doctor's c.** unter der Aufsicht e–s Arztes stehen; **c. of** (on letters) bei; **take c.** aufpassen; **take c. not to** (inf) sich hüten zu (inf); **take c. of s.o.** (provide for s.o.) für j–n sorgen; (attend to) sich um j–n kümmern; **take c. of s.th.** etw besorgen; (e.g., one's clothes) schonen ‖ intr—**c. about** sich kümmern um; **c. for** (like) mögen, gern haben; (have concern for) sorgen für; (attend to) pflegen; **c. to** (inf) Lust haben zu (inf); **for all I c.** von mir aus
careen [kə′rin] tr auf die Seite legen ‖ intr (aut) sich in die Kurve neigen
career [kə′rɪr] adj Berufs– ‖ s Karriere f
career′ wo′man s berufstätige Frau f
care′free′ adj unbelastet, sorgenfrei
careful [′kerfəl] adj (cautious) vorsichtig; (accurate) sorgfältig; **b. c.!** gib acht!
careless [′kerlɪs] adj (incautious) unvorsichtig; (remark) unbedacht; (inaccurate) nachlässig
carelessness [′kerlɪsnɪs] s Unvorsichtigkeit f; Nachlässigkeit f
caress [kə′res] s Liebkosung f ‖ tr liebkosen
caret [′kærət] s Auslassungszeichen n
caretaker [′kerˌtekər] s Verwalter m
care′worn′ adj abgehärmt, vergrämt
car′fare′ s Fahrgeld n
car′go [′kɑrgo] s (–goes & –gos) Fracht f
car′go compart′ment s Frachtraum m
car′go plane′ s Frachtflugzeug n
Caribbean [ˌkærɪ′biˌən], [kə′rɪbɪ–ən] adj karibisch ‖ s Karibisches Meer n
caricature [′kærɪkətʃər] s Karikatur f ‖ tr karikieren
caries [′kɛrɪz] s (dent) Karies f
carillon [′kærɪˌlɑn] s Glockenspiel n
car′ lift′ s (aut) Hebebühne f
car′load′ s Wagenladung f
carnage [′kɑrnɪdʒ] s Blutbad n
carnal [′kɑrnəl] adj fleischlich
car′nal know′ledge s Geschlechtsverkehr m
carnation [kɑr′neʃən] s Nelke f
carnival [′kɑrnɪvəl] s Karneval m
carnivorous [kɑr′nɪvərəs] adj fleischfressend
car-ol [′kærəl] s Weihnachtslied n ‖ v (pret & pp –ol(l)ed; ger –l(l)ing) intr Weihnachtslieder singen
carom [′kærəm] s (billiards) Karambolage f ‖ intr (fig) zusammenstoßen; (billiards) karambolieren
carouse [kə′rauz] intr zechen

carp [kɑrp] s Karpfen m ‖ intr nörgeln
carpenter [′kɑrpəntər] s Zimmermann m
carpentry [′kɑrpəntri] s Zimmerei f
carpet [′kɑrpɪt] s Teppich m ‖ tr mit Teppichen belegen
car′pet sweep′er s Teppichkehrmaschine f
car′port′ s Autoschuppen m
car′-ren′tal serv′ice s Autovermietung f
carriage [′kærɪdʒ] s Kutsche f; (of a typewriter) Wagen m; (bearing) Körperhaltung f; (econ) Transportkosten pl
car′ ride′ s Autofahrt f
carrier [′kærɪ–ər] s Träger m; (company) Transportunternehmen n
car′rier pig′eon s Brieftaube f
carrion [′kærɪ–ən] s Aas n
carrot [′kærət] s Karotte f, Mohrrübe f
carrousel [ˌkærə′zɛl] s Karussell n
car-ry [′kæri] v (pret & pp –ried) tr tragen; (wares) führen; (a message) überbringen; (a tune) halten; (said of transportation) befördern; (insurance) haben; (math) übertragen; (parl) durchbringen; **be carried** (said of a motion, bill) angenommen werden; **be carried away by** (& fig) mitgerissen werden von; **c. away** (an audience) mitreißen; **c. off** (a prize) davontragen; **c. on** weiterführen; (a business) betreiben, führen; **c. out** hinaustragen; (a duty) erfüllen; (measures) durchführen; (a sentence) vollstrecken; (an order) ausführen; **c. over** (acct) übertragen; **c. s.th. too far** etw übertreiben; **c. through** durchsetzen; ‖ intr (said of sounds) tragen; (parl) durchgehen; **c. on** (continue) weitermachen; (act up) (coll) toben; **c. on with** ein Verhältnis haben mit
car′rying char′ges spl Kreditgebühren pl
car′ry-o′ver s Überbleibsel n; (acct) Übertrag m
cart [kɑrt] s Karren m ‖ tr mit dem Handwagen befördern; **c. away** (or **c. off**) abfahren
cartel [kɑr′tel] s Kartell n
cartilage [′kɑrtɪlɪdʒ] s Knorpel m
carton [′kɑrtən] s Karton m; **a c. of cigarettes** e–e Stange Zigaretten
cartoon [kɑr′tun] s Karikatur f; (comic strip) Karikaturenreihe f; (cin) Zeichentrickfilm m; (paint) Entwurf m natürlicher Größe ‖ tr karikieren
cartoonist [kɑr′tunɪst] s Karikaturenzeichner –in mf
cartridge [′kɑrtrɪdʒ] s Patrone f; (phot) Filmpatrone f
car′tridge belt′ s Patronengurt m
cart′wheel′ s Wagenrad n; **turn a c.** ein Rad schlagen
carve [kɑrv] tr (wood) schnitzen; (meat) tranchieren, vorschneiden; (stone) meißeln; **c. out** (e.g., a career) aufbauen

carver ['kɑrvər] s (at table) Vor-schneider –in mf

carv/ing knife/ s Tranchiermesser n

car/ wash/ s Wagenwäsche f

cascade [kæs'ked] s Kaskade f || intr kaskadenartig herabstürzen

case [kes] s (instance) Fall m; (situation) Sache f; (box) Kiste f; (for a knife, etc.) Hülle f; (for cigarettes) Etui n; (for eyeglasses) Futteral n; (for shipping) Schutzkarton m; (of a watch) Gehäuse n; (of sickness) Krankheitsfall m; (sick person) Patient –in mf; (gram) Fall m; (jur) Fall m, Sache f, Prozeß m; (typ) Setzkasten m; as the c. may be je nachdem; have a strong c. schlüssige Beweise haben; if that's the c. wenn es sich so verhält; in any c. auf jeden Fall, jedenfalls; in c. falls; in c. of im Falle (genit); in c. of emergency im Notfall; in no c. keinesfalls || tr (sl) genau ansehen; the c. at issue der vorliegende Fall

case/ his/tory s Vorgeschichte f; (med) Krankengeschichte f

casement ['kesmənt] s Fensterflügel m

case/ment win/dow s Flügelfenster n

cash [kæʃ] adj Bar- || s Bargeld n; (cash payment) Barzahlung f; c. and carry nur gegen Barzahlung und eigenen Transport; in c. per Kasse; out of c. nicht bei Kasse; pay c. for bar bezahlen || tr einlösen || intr—c. in on (coll) Nutzen ziehen aus

cash/box/ s Schatulle f, Kasse f

cash/ dis/count s Kassaskonto n

cashew/ nut/ [kə'ʃu], ['kæʃu] s Kaschunuß f

cashier [kæ'ʃɪr] s Kassierer –in mf

cashmere ['kæʃmɪr] s Kaschmir m

cash/ on deliv/ery adv per Nachnahme

cash/ reg/ister m Registrierkasse f

cas/ing s (wrapping) Verpackung f; (housing) Gehäuse n; (of a window or door) Futter n; (of a tire) Mantel m; (of a sausage) Wurstdarm m

casi-no [kə'sino] s (-nos) Kasino n

cask [kæsk] s Faß n, Tonne f

casket ['kæskɪt] s Sarg m

casserole ['kæsə,rol] s Kasserolle f

cassette [kæ'set] s Kassette f

cassock ['kæsək] s (eccl) Soutane f

cast [kæst] s (throw) Wurf m; (act of molding) Guß m; (mold) Gußform f; (object molded) Abguß m; (hue) Abtönung f; (surg) Gipsverband m; (theat) Rollenbesetzung f || v (pret & pp cast) tr werfen; (a net, anchor) auswerfen; (a ballot) abgeben; (lots) ziehen; (skin, horns) abwerfen; (a shadow, glance) werfen; (metal) gießen; (a play or motion picture) die Rollen besetzen in (dat); be c. down niedergeschlagen sein; c. aside (reject) verwerfen; || intr (angl) die Angel auswerfen; c. off (naut) loswerfen

castanet [,kæstə'net] s Kastagnette f

cast/away/ adj verworfen; (naut) schiffbrüchig || s (naut) Schiffbrüchige mf

caste [kæst] s Kaste f

caster ['kæstər] s (under furniture) Rolle f; (shaker) Streuer m

castigate ['kæstɪ,get] tr züchtigen; (fig) geißeln

cast/ing s Wurf m; (act of casting) (metal) Guß m; (the object cast) (metal) Gußstück n; (theat) Rollenverteilung f

cast/ing rod/ s Wurfangel f

cast/ i/ron s Gußeisen n

cast/-i/ron adj gußeisern; (fig) eisern

castle ['kæsəl] s Schloß n, Burg, f; (chess) Turm m || intr (chess) rochieren

cast/off/ adj abgelegt || s (e.g., dress) abgelegtes Kleidungsstück n; (person) Verstoßene mf

cas/tor oil/ ['kæstər] s Rizinusöl n

castrate ['kæstret] tr kastrieren

casual ['kæʒʊəl] adj (cursory) beiläufig; (occasional) gelegentlich; (incidental) zufällig; (informal) zwanglos; (unconcerned) gleichgültig

casualty ['kæʒʊəlti] s (victim) Opfer n; (accident) Unfall m; (person injured) Verunglückte mf; (person killed) (mil) Gefallene mf; (person wounded) (mil) Verwundete mf; casualties (in an accident) Verunglückte pl; (in war) Verluste pl

cas/ualty list/ s Verlustliste f

cat [kæt] s Katze f; (guy) (sl) Typ m; (malicious woman) (sl) falsche Katze f

catacomb ['kætə,kom] s Katakombe f

catalog(ue) ['kætə,lɔg] s Katalog m; (list) Verzeichnis n; (of a university) Vorlesungsverzeichnis n || tr katalogisieren

catalyst ['kætəlɪst] s Katalysator m

catapult ['kætə,pʌlt] s Katapult m & n || tr katapultieren, abschleudern

cataract ['kætə,rækt] s Katarakt m; (pathol) grauer Star m; remove s.o.'s c. j-m den Star stechen

catastrophe [kə'tæstrəfi] s Katastrophe f

cat/call/ s Auspfeifen n || tr auspfeifen

catch [kætʃ] s Fang m; (of fish) Fischfang m; (device) Haken m, Klinke f; (desirable partner) Partie f; (fig) Haken m; || v (pret & pp caught [kɔt]) tr fangen; (s.o. or s.th. falling) auffangen; (by pursuing) abfangen; (s.o. or s.th. that has escaped) einfangen; (by surprise) ertappen, erwischen; (in midair) aufschnappen; (take hold of) fassen; (said of a storm) überraschen; (e.g., a train) erreichen; c. a cold sich erkälten; c. fire in Brand geraten; c. hold of ergreifen; c. it (coll) sein Fett kriegen; c. one's breath wieder Atem schöpfen; c. one's eye j-m ins Auge fallen; get caught on hängenbleiben an (dat) || intr (said of a bolt, etc.) einschnappen; c. on (said of an idea) Anklang finden; c. on to (fig) kapieren; catch up aufholen; c. up on nachholen; c. up with einholen

catch/ing adj (disease) ansteckend; (attractive) anziehend

catch'word' s (*slogan*) Schlagwort n; (*actor's cue*) Stichwort n; (pol) Parteiparole f

catchy ['kætʃi] adj einschmeichelnd

catechism ['kætɪˌkɪzəm] s Katechismus m

category ['kætɪˌgori] s Kategorie f

cater ['ketər] tr Lebensmittel liefern für || intr—c. to schmeicheln (dat); (*deliver food to*) Lebensmittel liefern für

cater-corner ['kætərˌkɔrnər] adj & adv diagonal

caterer ['ketərər] s Lebensmittellieferant –in mf

caterpillar ['kætərˌpɪlər] s (ent, mach) Raupe f

cat'fish' s Katzenwels m, Katzenfisch m

cat'gut' s (mus) Darmseite f; (surg) Katgut n

cathedral [kə'θidrəl] s Dom m

catheter ['kæθɪtər] s Katheter n

cathode ['kæθod] s Kathode f

catholic ['kæθəlɪk] adj universal; Catholic katholisch || Catholic s Katholik –in mf

cat'nap' s Nickerchen n

catnip ['kætnɪp] s Baldrian m

catsup ['kætsəp], ['ketʃəp] s Ketchup m

cattle ['kætəl] spl Vieh n

cat'tle car' s (rr) Viehwagen m

cat'tle·man s (–men) Viehzüchter m

cat'tle ranch' s Viehfarm f

catty ['kæti] adj boshaft

cat'walk' s Steg m, Laufplanke f

Caucasian [kɔ'keʒən] adj kaukasisch || s Kaukasier –in mf

caucus ['kɔkəs] s Parteiführerversammlung f

cauliflower ['kɔlɪˌflau·ər] s Blumenkohl m

cause [kɔz] s (*origin*) Ursache f; (*reason*) Grund m; (*person*) Urheber –in mf; (*occasion*) Anlaß m; for a good c. für e-e gute Sache || tr verursachen; c. s.o. to (*inf*) j-n veranlassen zu (*inf*)

cause'way' s Dammweg m

caustic ['kɔstɪk] adj (& fig) ätzend

cauterize ['kɔtəˌraɪz] tr verätzen

caution ['kɔʃən] s (*carefulness*) Vorsicht f; (*warning*) Warnung f || tr (*against*) warnen (vor dat)

cautious ['kɔʃəs] adj vorsichtig

cavalcade ['kævəlˌked] s Kavalkade f

cavalier [ˌkævə'lɪr] adj hochmütig || s Kavalier m

cavalry ['kævəlri] s Kavallerie f

cav'alry·man s (–men) Kavallerist m

cave [kev] s Höhle f || intr—c. in (*collapse*) einstürzen

cave'–in' s Einsturz m

cave' man' s Höhlenmensch m

cavern ['kævərn] s (*große*) Höhle f

caviar ['kævɪˌar] s Kaviar m

cav·il ['kævɪl] v (*pret* & *pp* –l(l)ed; *ger* –l(l)ing) intr (at, about) herumnörgeln (an dat)

cavity ['kævɪti] s Hohlraum m; (anat) Höhle f; (dent) Loch n

cavort [kə'vɔrt] intr (coll) herumtollen

caw [kɔ] s Krächzen n || intr krächzen

cease [sis] s—without c. unaufhörlich || tr einstellen; (ger) aufhören (zu inf); c. fire das Feuer einstellen || intr aufhören

cease'fire' s Feuereinstellung f

ceaseless ['sislɪs] adj unaufhörlich

cedar ['sidər] s Zeder f

cede [sid] tr abtreten, überlassen

cedilla [sɪ'drlə] s Cedille f

ceiling ['silɪŋ] s Decke f; (fin) oberste Grenze f; hit the c. (coll) platzen

ceil'ing light' s Deckenlicht n

ceil'ing price' s Höchstpreis m

celebrant ['selɪbrənt] s Zelebrant m

celebrate ['selɪˌbret] tr (a feast) feiern; (mass) zelebrieren || intr feiern; (eccl) zelebrieren

cel'ebrat'ed adj (for) berühmt (wegen)

celebration [ˌselɪ'breʃən] s Feier f; (eccl) Zelebrieren n; in c. of zur Feier (genit)

celebrity [sɪ'lebrɪti] s Berühmtheit f; (person) Prominente m

celery ['seləri] s Selleriestengel m

celestial [sɪ'lestʃəl] adj himmlisch; (astr) Himmels–

celibacy ['selɪbəsi] s Zölibat m & n

celibate ['selɪbɪt] adj ehelos

cell [sel] s Zelle f

cellar ['selər] s Keller m

cellist ['tʃelɪst] s Cellist –in mf

cel·lo ['tʃelo] s (–los) Cello n

cellophane ['seləˌfen] s Zellophan n

celluloid ['seljəˌlɔɪd] s Zelluloid n

Celt [selt], [kelt] s Kelte m, Keltin f

Celtic ['seltɪk], ['keltɪk] adj keltisch

cement [sɪ'ment] s (glue) Bindemittel n; (used in building) Zement m || tr zementieren; (glue) kitten; (fig) (be)festigen

cement' mix'er s Betonmischmaschine f

cemetery ['semɪˌteri] s Friedhof m

censer ['sensər] s Räucherfaß n

censor ['sensər] s (of printed matter, films) Zensor m; (of morals) Sittenrichter m || tr zensieren

cen'sorship' s Zensur f

censure ['senʃər] s Tadel m || tr tadeln

census ['sensəs] s Volkszählung f

cent [sent] s Cent m

centaur ['sentɔr] s Zentaur m

centennial [sen'tenɪ·əl] adj hundertjährig || s Hundertjahrfeier f

center ['sentər] s Zentrum n, Mittelpunkt m; (pol) Mitte f || tr in den Mittelpunkt stellen; (tech) zentrieren || intr—c. on sich konzentrieren auf (acc)

cen'ter aisle' s Mittelgang m

cen'ter cit'y s Stadtmitte f

cen'terpiece' s Tischaufsatz m

centigrade ['sentɪˌgred] s Celsius, e.g., one degree c. ein Grad Celsius

centimeter ['sentɪˌmitər] s Zentimeter m

centipede ['sentɪˌpid] s Hundertfüßler m

central ['sentrəl] adj zentral

Cen'tral Amer'ica s Mittelamerika n

centralize ['sentrəˌlaɪz] tr zentralisieren

centri′fugal force′ [sen ′trɪfjəgəl] *s* Fliehkraft *f*

centrifuge [′sentrɪ ,fjudʒ] *s* Zentrifuge *f*

century [′sentʃəri] *s* Jahrhundert *n*

ceramic [sɪ′ræmɪk] *adj* keramisch ‖ **ceramics** *s* (art) Keramik *f*; *spl* Töpferwaren *pl*

cereal [′sɪri·əl] *adj* Getreide– ‖ *s* (grain) Getreide *n*; (dish) Getreide- flockengericht *n*

cerebral [′serɪbrəl] *adj* Gehirn—

ceremonial [,serɪ ′moni·əl] *adj* zere- moniell, feierlich

ceremonious [,serɪ ′moni·əs] *adj* zere- moniös, umständlich

ceremony [′serɪ ,moni] *s* Zeremonie *f* *n*

certain [′sʌrtən] *adj* (sure) sicher, be- stimmt; (particular but unnamed) gewiß; **be c.** feststehen; **for c.** gewiß; **make c.** of sich vergewissern (genit); **make c.** that sich vergewissern, daß

certainly [′sʌrtənli] *adv* sicher(lich); (as a strong affirmative) allerdings

certainty [′sʌrtənti] *s* Sicherheit *f*

certificate [sər′tɪfɪkɪt] *s* Schein *m*; (educ) Abgangszeugnis *n*

certification [,sʌrtɪfɪ′keʃən] *s* Be- scheinigung *f*, Beglaubigung *f*

cer′tified *adj* beglaubigt

cer′tified check′ *s* durch Bank be- stätigter Scheck *m*

cer′tified pub′lic account′ant *s* amt- lich zugelassener Wirtschaftsprüfer *m*

certi·fy [′sʌrtɪ ,faɪ] *v* (pret & pp –fied) bescheinigen, beglaubigen

cervix [′sʌrvɪks] *s* (cervices [sər- ′vaɪsiz]) Genick *n*

cessation [se′seʃən] *s* (of territory) Abtretung *f*; (of activities) Einstel- lung *f*

cesspool [′ses ,pul] *s* Senkgrube *f*

chafe [tʃef] *tr* (the skin) wund- scheuern ‖ *intr* (rub) scheuern; (be- come sore) sich wundreiben; (be irritated) (at) sich ärgern über (acc)

chaff [tʃæf] *s* Spreu *f*

chaf′ing dish′ *s* Speisenwärmer *m*

chagrin [ʃə′grɪn] *s* Verdruß *m* ‖ *tr* verdrießen

chain [tʃen] *s* Kette *f* ‖ *tr* (to) an- ketten (an acc)

chain′ gang′ *s* Kettensträflinge *pl*

chain′ reac′tion *s* Kettenreaktion *f*

chain′ smok′er *s* Kettenraucher –in *mf*

chain′ store′ *s* Kettenladen *m*

chair [tʃer] *s* Stuhl *m*; (upholstered) Sessel *m*; (of the presiding officer) Vorsitz *m*; (presiding officer) Vor- sitzende *mf*; (educ) Lehrstuhl *m* ‖ *tr* den Vorsitz führen von

chair′la′dy *s* Vorsitzende *f*

chair′ lift′ *s* Sessellift *m*

chair′man *s* (–men) Vorsitzende *m*

chair′manship′ *s* Vorsitz *m*

chalice [′tʃælɪs] *s* Kelch *m*

chalk [tʃɔk] *s* Kreide *f* ‖ *tr*—**c. up** ankreiden; (coll) verbuchen

challenge [′tʃælɪndʒ] *s* Aufforderung *f*; (to a duel) Herausforderung *f*; (jur) Ablehnung *f*; (mil) Anruf *m* ‖ *tr* auffordern; (to a duel) herausfor-

dern; (a statement, right) bestreiten; (jur) ablehnen; (mil) anrufen

chamber [′tʃembər] *s* Kammer *f*; (parl) Sitzungssaal *m*

chamberlain [′tʃembərlɪn] *s* Kammer- herr *m*

cham′bermaid′ *s* Stubenmädchen *n*

cham′ber of com′merce *s* Handels- kammer *f*

chameleon [kə′mili·ən] *s* Chamäleon *n*

chamfer [′tʃæmfər] *s* Schrägkante *f* ‖ *tr* abschrägen; (furrow) auskehlen

cham·ois [′ʃæmi] *s* (-ois) Sämischle- der *n*; (zool) Gemse *f*

champ [tʃæmp] *s* (coll) Meister *m* ‖ *tr* kauen; **champ the bit am** Gebiß kauen

champagne [ʃæm′pen] *s* Champagner *m*, Sekt *m*

champion [′tʃæmpi·ən] *s* (of a cause) Verfechter –in *mf*; (sport) Meister –in *mf* ‖ *tr* eintreten für

cham′pionship′ *s* Meisterschaft *f*

chance [tʃæns] *adj* zufällig ‖ *s* (acci- dent) Zufall *m*; (opportunity) Chance *f*, Gelegenheit *f*; (risk) Risiko *n*; (possibility) Möglichkeit *f*; (lottery ticket) Los *n*; **by c.** zufällig; **c. of a lifetime** einmalige Gelegenheit *f*; **chances are** (that) aller Wahrschein- lichkeit nach; **on the c. that** für den Fall, daß; **take a c.** ein Risiko ein- gehen; **take no chances** nichts riskie- ren; ‖ *tr* riskieren ‖ *intr* sich ereignen; **c. upon** stoßen auf (acc)

chancel [′tʃænsəl] *s* Altarraum *m*

chancellery [′tʃænsələri] *s* Kanzlei *f*

chancellor [′tʃænsələr] *s* Kanzler *m*; (hist) Reichskanzler *m*

chandelier [,ʃændə′lɪr] *s* Kronleuch- ter *m*

change [tʃendʒ] *s* Veränderung *f*; (in times, styles, etc.) Wechsel *m*; (in attitude, relations, etc.) Wandel *m*; (small coins) Kleingeld *n*; (of weath- er) Umschlag *m*; **c. for the better** Verbesserung *f*; **c. for the worse** Verschlechterung *f*; **for a c.** zur Ab- wechslung; **give c. for a dollar** auf e–n Dollar herausgeben; **need a c.** Luftveränderung brauchen ‖ *tr* ver- ändern; (plans) ändern; (money, subject, oil) wechseln; (a baby) trockenlegen; (stations, channels) umschalten; **c. around** umändern; **c. hands** den Besitzer wechseln; **c. one's mind** sich anders besinnen; **c. trains** (or buses, streetcars) umstei- gen ‖ *intr* sich verändern; (said of a mood, wind, weather) umschlagen; (said of a voice) mutieren; (change clothes) sich umziehen **change into** sich wandeln in (acc)

changeable [′tʃendʒəbəl] *adj* veränder- lich

changeless [′tʃendʒlɪs] *adj* unveränder- lich

change′ of heart′ *s* Sinnesänderung *f*

change′ of life′ *s* Wechseljahre *pl*

change′ of scen′ery *s* Ortsveränderung *f*

change′-o′ver *s* Umstellung *f*

chan·nel ['tʃænəl] s (strait) Kanal m; (of a river) Fahrrinne f; (groove) Rinne f; (furrow) Furche f; (fig) Weg m; (telv) Kanal m; **through official channels** auf dem Amtswege || v (pret & pp **-nel(l)ed**; ger **-nel-(l)ing**) tr lenken; (furrow) kanalisieren

chant [tʃænt] s Gesang m; (singsong) Singsang m; (eccl) Kirchengesang m || tr singen

chanter ['tʃæntər] s Kantor m

chaos ['ke·as] s Chaos n

chaotic [ke'atɪk] adj chaotisch

chap [tʃæp] s (in the skin) Riß m; (coll) Kerl m || v (pret & pp **chapped**; ger **chapping**) tr (the skin) rissig machen || intr rissig werden, aufspringen

chapel ['tʃæpəl] s Kapelle f

chaperon ['ʃæpə,ron] s Begleiter –in mf; (of a young couple) Anstandsdame f || tr als Anstandsdame begleiten

chaplain ['tʃæplɪn] s Kaplan n; (of an organization) Ortsgruppe f

chapter ['tʃæptər] s Kapitel n; (of an organization) Ortsgruppe f

char [tʃar] v (pret & pp **charred**; ger **charring**) tr verkohlen

character ['kærɪktər] s Charakter m; (letter) Schriftzeichen n; (typewriter space) Anschlag m; (coll) Kauz m; (theat) handelnde Person f; **be out of c.** nicht passen

characteristic [,kærɪktə'rɪstɪk] adj (of) charakteristisch (für) || s Charakterzug m, Kennzeichen n

characterize ['kærɪktə,raɪz] tr charakterisieren, kennzeichnen

charade [ʃə'red] s Scharade f

charcoal ['tʃar,kol] s Holzkohle f; (for sketching) Zeichenkohle f

charge [tʃardʒ] s (accusation) Anklage f; (fee) Gebühr f; (custody) Obhut f; (responsibility) Pflicht f; (ward) Pflegebefohlene mf; (of an explosive or electricity) Ladung f; (assault) Ansturm m; (of a judge to the jury) Rechtsbelehrung f; **be in c. of** verantwortlich sein für; **charges** Spesen pl; **take c. of** die Verantwortung übernehmen für; **there is no c.** es kostet nichts; **under s.o.'s c.** unter j–s Aufsicht || tr (a battery) (auf)laden; (with) anklagen (wegen); (a jury) belehren; (mil) stürmen; **c. s.o. ten marks for** j–m zehn Mark berechnen für; **c. s.o.'s account** auf j–s Rechnung setzen || intr (mil) anrennen für; **c. to s.o.'s account** auf j–s Rechnung setzen || intr (mil) anstürmen

charge' account' s laufendes Konto m

charger ['tʃardʒər] s (elec) Ladevorrichtung f; (hist) Schlachtroß m

chariot ['tʃærɪ·ət] s Kampfwagen m

charitable ['tʃærɪtəbəl] adj (generous) freigebig; (lenient) nachsichtig; **c. institution** wohltätige Stiftung f

charity ['tʃærɪti] s (giving of alms) Wohltätigkeit f; (alms) Almosen n; (institution) Wohlfahrtsinstitut n; (love of neighbor) Nächstenliebe f

charlatan ['ʃarlətən] s Scharlatan m

Charles [tʃarlz] s Karl m

char'ley horse' ['tʃarli] s (coll) Muskelkater m

charm [tʃarm] s Charme m; (trinket) Amulett n || tr verzaubern; (fig) entzücken

charm'ing adj scharmant, reizend

chart [tʃart] s Karte f; (table) Tabelle f; (naut) Seekarte f || tr entwerfen, auf e–r Karte graphisch darstellen

charter ['tʃartər] adj (plane, etc.) Charter– || s Freibrief m, Charter m; (of an organization) Gründungsurkunde f und Satzungen pl || tr chartern

char'ter mem'ber s gründendes Mitglied n

char·woman ['tʃar,wumən] s (–women [,wɪmɪn] Putzfrau f

chase [tʃes] s (pursuit) Verfolgung f; (hunt) Jagd f || tr jagen; (girls) nachsteigen (dat); **c. away** verjagen; **c. out** vertreiben || intr—**c. after** nachlaufen (dat)

chasm ['kæzəm] s (& fig) Abgrund m

chas·sis ['tʃæsi] s (–sis [siz]) Chassis n; (aut) Fahrgestell n

chaste [tʃest] adj keusch

chasten ['tʃesən] tr züchtigen

chastise [tʃæs'taɪz] tr züchtigen

chastity ['tʃæstɪti] s Keuschheit f

chat [tʃæt] s Plauderei f || v (pret & pp **chatted**; ger **chatting**) intr plaudern

chattel ['tʃætəl] s Sklave m; **chattels** Hab und Gut n

chatter ['tʃætər] s (talk) Geplapper n; (of teeth) Klappern n || intr (talk) plappern; (said of teeth) klappern

chat'terbox' s (coll) Plappermaul n

chauffeur ['ʃofər], [ʃo'fʌr] s Chauffeur m || tr fahren

cheap [tʃip] adj (inexpensive) billig; (shoddy) minderwertig; (base) gemein; (stingy) geizig; **feel c.** sich verlegen fühlen || adv billig; **get off c.** mit e–m blauen Auge davonkommen

cheapen ['tʃipən] tr herabsetzen

cheat [tʃit] s Betrüger –in mf || tr (out of) betrügen (um) || intr schwindeln; (at cards) mogeln; **c. on** (e.g., a wife) betrügen

cheat'ing s Betrügerei f; (at cards) Mogelei f

check [tʃek] s (of a bank) Scheck m; (for luggage) Schein m; (in a restaurant) Rechnung f; (inspection) Kontrolle f; (test) Nachprüfung f; (repulse) Rückschlag m; (restraint) (on) Hemmnis n (für); (square) Karo n; (chess) Schach n; **hold in c.** in Schach halten || tr (restrain) hindern; (inspect) kontrollieren; (test) nachprüfen, überprüfen; (a hat, coat) abgeben; (luggage) aufgeben; (figures) nachrechnen; (chess) Schach bieten (dat); **c. off** abhaken || intr (agree) übereinstimmen; **c. out** (of a hotel) sich abmelden; **c. up on** überprüfen; (a person) sich erkundigen über (*acc*); **c. with** (*correspond to*) übereinstimmen mit; (*consult*) sich besprechen mit ‖ *interj* Schach!

check′book′ *s* Scheckbuch *n*, Scheckheft *n*

checker [′tʃɛkər] *s* Kontrolleur *m*; (*in checkers*) Damestein *m*; **checkers** Damespiel *n*

check′erboard′ *s* Damebrett *n*

check′ered *adj* kariert; (*life, career*) wechselvoll

check′ing account′ *s* Scheckkonto *n*

check′ list′ *s* Kontrolliste *f*

check′mate′ *s* Schachmatt *n*; (fig) Niederlage *f* ‖ *tr* (& fig) matt setzen ‖ *interj* schachmatt!

check′-out count′er *s* Kasse *f*

check′point′ *s* Kontrollstelle *f*

check′room′ *s* Garderobe *f*

check′up′ *s* Überprüfung *f*; (med) ärztliche Untersuchung *f*

cheek [tʃik] *s* Backe *f*, Wange *f*; (coll) Frechheit *f*

cheek′bone′ *s* Backenknochen *m*

cheek′ by jowl′ *adv* Seite an Seite

cheeky [′tʃiki] *adj* (coll) frech

cheer [tʃɪr] *s* (*applause*) Beifallsruf *m*; (*encouragement*) Ermunterung *f*; (sport) Ermunterungsruf *m*; **three cheers for** ein dreifaches Hoch auf (*acc*) ‖ *tr* zujubeln (*dat*); **c. on** anfeuern; **c. up** aufmuntern; **c. up!** nur Mut!

cheerful [′tʃɪrfəl] *adj* heiter; (*room, surroundings*) freundlich

cheer′lead′er *s* Anführer –in *mf* beim Beifallsrufen

cheerless [′tʃɪrlɪs] *adj* freudlos

cheese [tʃiz] *s* Käse *m*

cheeseburger [′tʃiz͵bɑrgər] *s* belegtes Brot *n* mit Frikadelle und überbackenem Käse

cheese′cake′ *s* Käsekuchen *m*

cheese′ cloth′ *s* grobe Baumwollgaze *f*

cheesy [′tʃizi] *adj* (sl) minderwertig

chef [ʃɛf] *s* Küchenchef *m*

chemical [′kɛmɪkəl] *adj* chemisch; (*fertilizer*) Kunst– ‖ *s* Chemikalie *f*

chemist [′kɛmɪst] *s* Chemiker –in *mf*

chemistry [′kɛmɪstri] *s* Chemie *f*

cherish [′tʃɛrɪʃ] *tr* (*hold dear*) schätzen; (*hopes, thoughts*) hegen

cherry [′tʃɛri] *s* Kirsche *f*

cher′ry tree′ *s* Kirschbaum *m*

cher·ub [′tʃɛrəb] *s* (*–ubim* [əbɪm]) Cherub *m* ‖ *s* (**–ubs**) Engelskopf *m*

chess [tʃɛs] *s* Schach *n*

chess′board′ *s* Schachbrett *n*

chess′man′ *s* (**–men′**) Schachfigur *f*

chest [tʃɛst] *s* Truhe *f*; (anat) Brust *f*

chestnut [′tʃɛsnət] *adj* kastanienbraun ‖ *s* Kastanie *f*; (*tree*) Kastanienbaum *m*; (*horse*) Rotfuchs *m*

chest′ of drawers′ *s* Kommode *f*

chevron [′ʃɛvrən] *s* (mil) Winkel *m*

chew [tʃu] *s* Kauen *m*; (*stick of tobacco*) Priem *m* ‖ *tr* kauen; **c. the cud** wiederkäuen; **c. the rag** (sl) schwatzen

chew′ing gum′ *s* Kaugummi *m*

chew′ing tobac′co *s* Kautabak *m*

chic [ʃik] *adj* schick ‖ *s* Schick *m*

chicanery [ʃɪ′kenəri] *s* Schikane *f*

chick [tʃɪk] *s* Küken *n*; (*girl*) (sl) kesse Biene *f*

chicken [′tʃɪkən] *adj* Hühner–; (sl) feig(e) ‖ *s* Huhn *n*, Hühnchen *n*

chick′en coop′ *s* Hühnerstall *m*

chick′en-heart′ed *adj* feig(e)

chick′en pox′ *s* Windpocken *pl*

chick′en wire′ *s* Maschendraht *m*

chick′pea′ *s* Kichererbse *f*

chicory [′tʃɪkəri] *s* Zichorie *f*

chide [tʃaɪd] *v* (*pret* & *pp* **chided** & **chid** [tʃɪd]; *pp* **chided**) *tr* tadeln

chief [tʃif] *adj* Haupt–, Ober–, oberste; (*leading*) leitend ‖ *s* Chef *m*, Oberhaupt *n*; (*of an Indian tribe*) Häuptling *m*

chief′ exec′utive *s* Regierungsoberhaupt *n*

chief′ jus′tice *s* Vorsitzender *m* des obersten Gerichtshofes

chiefly [′tʃifli] *adv* vorwiegend

chief′ of police′ *s* Polizeipräsident *m*

chief′ of staff′ *s* Generalstabschef *m*

chief′ of state′ *s* Staatschef *m*

chieftain [′tʃiftən] *s* Häuptling *m*

chiffon [ʃɪ′fɑn] *s* Chiffon *m*

child [tʃaɪld] *s* (**children** [′tʃɪldrən]) Kind *n*; **with c.** schwanger

child′ abuse′ *s* Kindermißhandlung *f*

child′birth′ *s* Niederkunft *f*

child′hood′ *s* Kindheit *f*

childish [′tʃaɪldɪʃ] *adj* kindisch

childless [′tʃaɪldlɪs] *adj* kinderlos

child′like′ *adj* kindlich

child′ prod′igy *s* Wunderkind *n*

child′s′ play′ *s* (fig) Kinderspiel *n*

child′ support′ *s* Alimente *pl*

child′ wel′fare *s* Jugendfürsorge *f*

Chile [′tʃɪli] *s* Chile *n*

chili [′tʃɪli] *s* Cayennepfeffer *m*

chil′i sauce′ *s* Chillisoße *f*

chill [tʃɪl] *s* (*coldness*) Kälte *f*; (*sensation of cold or fear*) Schau(d)er *m*; **chills** Fieberschauder *m* ‖ *tr* kühlen; (*hopes, etc.*) dämpfen; (*metals*) abschrecken; **be chilled to the bone** durchfrieren ‖ *intr* abkühlen

chilly [′tʃɪli] *adj* (& fig) frostig; **feel chilly** frösteln

chime [tʃaɪm] *s* Geläut *n*; **chimes** Glockenspiel *n* ‖ *intr* (*said of bells*) läuten; (*said of a doorbell*) ertönen; (*said of a clock*) schlagen; **c. in** (coll) beipflichten

chimera [kaɪ′mɪrə] *s* Hirngespinst *n*

chimney [′tʃɪmni] *s* Schornstein *m*; (*of a lamp*) Zylinder *m*

chimpanzee [͵tʃɪm′pænzi] *s* Schimpanse *m*

chin [tʃɪn] *s* Kinn *n*; **keep one's c. up** die Ohren steifhalten; **up to the c.** bis über die Ohren

china [′tʃaɪnə] *s* Porzellan *n* ‖ **China** *s* China *n*

chi′na clos′et *s* Porzellanschrank *m*

chi′na·man *s* (**–men**) (pej) Chinese *m*

chin′aware′ *s* Porzellanwaren *pl*

Chi·nese [tʃaɪ′niz] *adj* chinesisch ‖ *s* (**–nese**) Chinese *m*, Chinesin *f*; (*language*) Chinesisch *n*

Chi′nese lan′tern *s* Lampion *m*

chink [tʃɪŋk] *s* Ritze *f*; (*of coins or*

glasses) Klang *m* || *tr* (*glasses*) anstoßen

chin'-up' *s* Klimmzug *m*

chip [tʃɪp] *s* Span *m*, Splitter *m*; (*in china*) angestoßene Stelle *f*; (*in poker*) Spielmarke *f*; **a c. off the old block** (coll) ganz der Vater; **have a c. on one's shoulder** (coll) vor Zorn geladen sein || *v* (*pret & pp* **chipped**; *ger* **chipping**) *tr* (*e.g., a cup*) anschlagen; **c. in** (coll) beitragen; **c. off** abbrechen || *intr* (leicht) abbrechen; **c. in** (with) einspringen (mit); **c. off** (*said of paint*) abblättern

chipmunk [ˈtʃɪpˌmʌŋk] *s* Streifenhörnchen *n*

chipper [ˈtʃɪpər] *adj* (coll) munter

chiropodist [kaɪˈrɑpədɪst], [kɪˈrɑpədɪst] *s* Fußpfleger –in *mf*

chiropractor [ˈkaɪroˌpræktər] *s* Chiropraktiker –in *mf*

chirp [tʃʌrp] *s* Gezwitscher *n* || *intr* zwitschern

chis∙el [ˈtʃɪzəl] *s* Meißel *m* || *v* (*pret & pp* -el[l]ed; *ger* -il[l]ing) *tr* meißeln; (sl) bemogeln || *intr* meißeln; (sl) mogeln

chiseler [ˈtʃɪzələr] *s* (sl) Mogler *m*

chitchat [ˈtʃɪtˌtʃæt] *s* Schnickschnack *m*

chivalrous [ˈʃɪvəlrəs] *adj* ritterlich

chivalry [ˈʃɪvəlri] *s* Rittertum *n*; (*politeness*) Ritterlichkeit *f*

chive [tʃaɪv] *s* Schnittlauch *m*

chloride [ˈklɔraɪd] *s* Chlorid *n*

chlorine [ˈklɔrin] *s* Chlor *n*

chloroform [ˈklɔrəˌfɔrm] *s* Chloroform *n* || *tr* chloroformieren

chlorophyll [ˈklɔrəfɪl] *s* Chlorophyll *n*

chock-full [ˈtʃɑkˈful] *adj* zum Bersten voll

chocolate [ˈtʃɔkəlɪt] *adj* Schokoladen–; (*in color*) schokoladenfarben || *s* Schokolade *f*; (*chocolate-covered candy*) Praline *f*

choc'olate bar' *s* Schokoladentafel *f*

choice [tʃɔɪs] *adj* (aus)erlesen || *s* Wahl *f*; (*selection*) Auswahl *f*

choir [kwaɪr] *s* Chor *m*; (archit) Chor *m*

choir'boy' *s* Chorknabe *m*

choir' loft' *s* Chorgalerie *f*

choir'mas'ter *s* Chordirigent *m*

choke [tʃok] *s* (aut) Starterklappe *f* || *tr* erwürgen, ersticken; **c. back** (*tears*) herunterschlucken; **c. down** herunterwürgen; **c. up** verstopfen || *intr* ersticken; **c. on** ersticken an (*dat*)

choker [ˈtʃokər] *s* enges Halsband *n*

cholera [ˈkɑlərə] *s* Cholera *f*

cholesterol [kəˈlestəˌrol] *s* Blutfett *n*

choose [tʃuz] *v* (*pret* **chose** [tʃoz]; *pp* **chosen** [ˈtʃozən]) *tr & intr* wählen

choosy [ˈtʃuzi] *adj* (coll) wählerisch

chop [tʃɑp] *s* Hieb *m*; (culin) Kotelett *n*, Schnitzel *n*; **chops** (sl) Maul *n* || *v* (*pret & pp* **chopped**; *ger* **chopping**) *tr* hacken; **c. down** niederhauen; **c. off** abhacken; **c. up** zerhacken

chopper [ˈtʃɑpər] *s* (ax) Hackbeil *n*; (coll) Hubschrauber *m*

chop'ping block' *s* Hackklotz *m*

choppy [ˈtʃɑpi] *adj* (sea) bewegt

chop'stick' *s* Eßstäbchen *n*

choral [ˈkorəl] *adj* Chor–, Sänger–

chorale [koˈral] *s* Choral *m*

chord [kɔrd] *s* (anat) Band *n*; (geom) Sehne *f*; (*combination of notes*) (mus) Akkord *m*; (mus & fig) Saite *f*

chore [tʃor] *s* Hausarbeit *f*

choreography [ˌkɔriˈɑgrəfi] *s* Choreographie *f*

chorus [ˈkorəs] *s* Chor *m*; (*refrain*) Kehrreim *m*

cho'rus girl' *s* Revuetänzerin *f*

chowder [ˈtʃaudər] *s* Fischsuppe *f*

Christ [kraɪst] *s* Christus *m*

Christ' child' *s* Christkind *n*

christen [ˈkrɪsən] *tr* taufen

Christendom [ˈkrɪsəndəm] *s* Christenheit *f*

chris'tening *s* Taufe *f*; **c. of a ship** Schiffstaufe *f*

Christian [ˈkrɪstʃən] *adj* christlich || *s* Christ –in *mf*

Chris'tian E'ra *s* christliche Zeitrechnung *f*

Christianity [ˌkrɪstiˈænɪti] *s* (*faith*) Christentum *n*; (*all Christians*) Christenheit *f*

Chris'tian name' *s* Taufname *m*

Christmas [ˈkrɪsməs] *adj* Weihnachts– || *s* Weihnachten *pl*, Weihnachtsfest *n*

Christ'mas card' *s* Weihnachtskarte *f*

Christ'mas car'ol *s* Weihnachtslied *n*

Christ'mas Eve' *s* Heiliger Abend *m*

Christ'mas gift' *s* Weihnachtsgeschenk *n*

Christ'mas tree' *s* Christbaum *m*

Christ'mas tree' lights' *spl* Weihnachtskerzen *pl*

Christopher [ˈkrɪstəfər] *s* Christoph *m*

chromatic [kroˈmætɪk] *adj* chromatisch

chrome [krom] *adj* Chrom– || *s* Chrom *n* || *tr* verchromen

chrome'plate' *tr* verchromen

chromium [ˈkromɪ-əm] *s* Chrom *n*

chromosome [ˈkroməˌsom] *s* Chromosom *n*

chronic [ˈkrɑnɪk] *adj* chronisch

chronicle [ˈkrɑnɪkəl] *s* Chronik *f* || *tr* aufzeichnen

chronicler [ˈkrɑnɪklər] *s* Chronist –in *mf*

chronological [ˌkrɑnəˈlɑdʒɪkəl] *adj* chronologisch

chronology [krəˈnɑlədʒi] *s* Chronologie *f*

chronometer [krəˈnɑmɪtər] *s* Chronometer *n*

chrysanthemum [krɪˈsænθɪməm] *s* Chrysantheme *f*

chubby [ˈtʃʌbi] *adj* pummelig

chuck [tʃʌk] *s* (culin) Schulterstück *n*; (mach) Klemmfutter *n* || *tr* schmeißen

chuckle [ˈtʃʌkəl] *s* Glucksen *n* || *intr* glucksen

chug [tʃʌg] *s* Tuckern *n* || *v* (*pret & pp* **chugged**; *ger* **chugging**) *intr* tuckern; **c. along** tuckernd fahren

chum [tʃʌm] s (coll) Kumpel m ‖ v (pret & pp **chummed**; ger **chumming**) intr—c. **around with** sich eng anschließen an (acc)

chummy ['tʃʌmi] adj eng befreundet

chump [tʃʌmp] s (coll) Trottel m

chunk [tʃʌŋk] s Klotz m, Stück n

church [tʃʌrtʃ] adj Kirchen-, kirchlich ‖ s Kirche f

churchgoer ['tʃʌrtʃ,go·ər] s Kirchgänger –in mf

church' pic'nic s Kirchweih f

church'yard' s Kirchhof m

churl [tʃʌrl] s Flegel m

churlish ['tʃʌrlɪʃ] adj flegelhaft

churn [tʃʌrn] s Butterfaß n ‖ tr (cream) buttern; c. **up** aufwühlen ‖ intr sich heftig bewegen

chute [ʃut] s (for coal, etc.) Rutsche f; (for laundry, etc.) Abwurfschacht m; (sliding board) Rutschbahn f; (in a river) Stromschnelle f; (aer) Fallschirm m

cider ['saɪdər] s Apfelwein m

cigar [sɪˈgɑr] s Zigarre f

cigarette [,sɪgəˈret] s Zigarette f

cigarette' cough' s Raucherhusten m

cigarette' light'er s Feuerzeug n

cigar' store' s Rauchwarenladen m

cinch [sɪntʃ] s Sattelgurt m; (sure thing) totsichere Sache f; (snap) (sl) Kinderspiel n; (likely candidate) totsicherer Kandidat m ‖ tr (sl) sich [dat] sichern

cinder ['sɪndər] s (ember) glühende Kohle f; (slag) Schlacke f; **cinders** Asche f

Cinderella [,sɪndəˈrelə] s Aschenbrödel n

cin'der track' s (sport) Aschenbahn f

cinema ['sɪnəmə] s Kino n

cinematography [,sɪnəməˈtɑgrəfi] s Kinematographie f

cinnamon ['sɪnəmən] s Zimt m

cipher ['saɪfər] s Ziffer f; (zero) Null f; (code) Chiffre f ‖ tr chiffrieren

circle ['sʌrkəl] s Kreis m; **circles under the eyes** Ränder pl unter den Augen ‖ tr einkreisen; (go around) umkreisen ‖ intr kreisen

circuit ['sʌrkɪt] s (course) Kreislauf m; (elec) Stromkreis m; (jur) Bezirk m

cir'cuit break'er s Ausschalter m

cir'cuit court' s Bezirksgericht n

circuitous [sərˈkjuˌɪtəs] adj weitschweifig

circular ['sʌrkjələr] adj kreisförmig; (saw) Kreis– ‖ s Rundschreiben n

circulate ['sʌrkjəˌlet] tr in Umlauf setzen; (a rumor) verbreiten; (fin) girieren ‖ intr umlaufen; (said of blood) kreisen; (said of a rumor) umgehen

circulation [,sʌrkjəˈleʃən] s (of blood) Kreislauf m; (of a newspaper) Auflage f; (of money) Umlauf m

circumcize ['sʌrkəm,saɪz] tr beschneiden

circumference [sərˈkʌmfərəns] s Umfang m

circumflex ['sʌrkəm,fleks] s Zirkumflex m

circumlocution [,sʌrkəmloˈkjuʃən] s Umschreibung f

circumscribe ['sʌrkəmˌskraɪb] tr (geom) umschreiben; (fig) umgrenzen

circumspect ['sʌrkəmˌspekt] adj umsichtig

circumstance ['sʌrkəmˌstæns] s Umstand m; **circumstances** (financial situation) Verhältnisse pl

cir'cumstan'tial ev'idence [,sʌrkəmˈstænʃəl] s Indizienbeweis m

circumvent [,sʌrkəmˈvent] tr umgehen

circus ['sʌrkəs] s Zirkus m

cistern ['sɪstərn] s Zisterne f

citadel ['sɪtədəl] s Burg f

citation [saɪˈteʃən] s Zitat n; (jur) Vorladung f; (mil) Belobung f

cite [saɪt] tr (quote) anführen; (jur) vorladen; (mil) belobigen

citizen ['sɪtɪzən] s Bürger –in mf

cit'izenship' ['sɪtɪzənˌʃɪp] s Staatsangehörigkeit f

cit'rus fruit' ['sɪtrəs] s Zitrusfrucht f

city ['sɪti] s Stadt f

cit'y coun'cil s Stadtrat m

cit'y fa'ther s Stadtrat m

cit'y hall' s Rathaus n

cit'y plan'ning s Stadtplanung f

civic ['sɪvɪk] adj bürgerlich, Bürger– ‖ **civics** s Staatsbürgerkunde f

civil ['sɪvɪl] adj (life, duty) bürgerlich; (service) öffentlich; (polite) höflich; (jur) privatrechtlich

civ'il cer'emony s standesamtliche Trauung f

civ'il defense' s zivile Verteidigung f

civ'il engineer'ing s Hoch– und Tiefbau m

civilian [sɪˈvɪljən] adj bürgerlich, Zivil– ‖ s Zivilist –in mf

civilization [,sɪvɪlɪˈzeʃən] s Zivilisation f, Kultur f

civilize ['sɪvɪˌlaɪz] tr zivilisieren

civ'il rights' spl Bürgerrechte pl

civ'il serv'ant s Staatsbeamte m, Staatsbeamtin f

civ'il serv'ice s Staatsdienst m

civ'il war' s Bürgerkrieg m

claim [klem] s Anspruch m; (assertion) Behauptung f; (for public land) beanspruchtes Land n ‖ tr beanspruchen; (assert) behaupten; (attention) erfordern; c. **to be** sich ausgeben für

claim' check' s Aufgabeschein m

clairvoyance [klerˈvɔɪ·əns] s Hellsehen n

clairvoyant [klerˈvɔɪ·ənt] adj hellseherisch; **be c.** hellsehen ‖ s Hellseher –in mf

clam [klæm] s eßbare Meermuschel f

clamber ['klæmər] intr klettern

clammy ['klæmi] adj feuchtkalt

clamor ['klæmər] s Geschrei n ‖ intr (for) schreien (nach)

clamorous ['klæmərəs] adj schreiend

clamp [klæmp] s Klammer f; (surg) Klemme f ‖ tr (ver)klammern ‖ intr —c. **down on** einschreiten gegen

clan [klæn] s Stamm m; (pej) Sippschaft f

clandestine [klænˈdestɪn] adj heimlich

clang [klæŋ] s Geklirr n ‖ intr klirren

clank [klæŋk] s Geklirr n, Gerassel n ‖ intr klirren, rasseln

clannish ['klænɪʃ] adj stammesbewußt

clap [klæp] s (of the hands) Klatschen n; (of thunder) Schlag m ‖ v (pret & pp clapped; ger clapping) tr (a tax, fine, duty) (on) auferlegen (dat); **clap hands** in die Hände klatschen ‖ intr Beifall klatschen

clapper ['klæpər] s Klöppel m

clap'trap' s Phrasendrescherei f

claque [klæk] s Claque f

clari·fy ['klærɪ‚faɪ] v (pret & pp -fied) tr erklären

clarinet [‚klærɪ'nɛt] s Klarinette f

clarity ['klærɪti] s Klarheit f

clash [klæʃ] s (sound) Geklirr n; (of interests, etc.) Widerstreit m ‖ intr (conflict) kollidieren; (said of persons) aufeinanderstoßen; (said of ideas) im Widerspruch stehen; (said of colors) nicht zusammenpassen

clasp [klæsp] s (fastener) Schließe f, Spange f; (on a necktie) Klammer f; (embrace) Umarmung f; (of hands) Händedruck m ‖ tr umklammern; **c. s.o.'s hand** j–m die Hand drücken

class [klæs] s (group) Klasse f; (period of instruction) Stunde f; (year) Jahrgang m; **have c.** (sl) Niveau haben ‖ tr einstufen

classic ['klæsɪk] adj klassisch ‖ s Klassiker m

classical ['klæsɪkəl] adj klassisch; **c. antiquity** Klassik f; **c. author** Klassiker m

classicist ['klæsɪsɪst] s Kenner –in mf der Klassik

classification [‚klæsɪfɪ'keʃən] s Klassifikation f, Anordnung f

clas'sified ad' s kleine Anzeige f

clas'sified ad' s kleine Anzeige f

classi·fy ['klæsɪ‚faɪ] v (pret & pp -fied) tr klassifizieren

class'mate' s Klassenkamerad m

class' reun'ion s Klassentreffen n

class'room' s Klassenzimmer n

classy ['klæsi] adj (sl) pfundig

clatter ['klætər] s Geklapper n ‖ intr klappern

clause [klɔz] s Satzteil m; (jur) Klausel f

clavicle ['klævɪkəl] s Schlüsselbein n

claw [klɔ] s Klaue f, Kralle f; (of a crab) Schere f ‖ tr zerkratzen; (a hole) scharren ‖ intr kratzen

clay [kle] adj tönern ‖ s Ton m, Lehm m

clay' pig'eon s Tontaube f

clean [klin] adj sauber, rein; (cut) glatt; (features) klar ‖ adv (coll) völlig ‖ tr reinigen, putzen; **c. out** (clear out by force) räumen; (empty) ausleeren; (sl) ausbeuten; **c. up** (a room) aufräumen ‖ intr putzen; **c. up** sich zurechtmachen; (in gambling) (sl) schwer einheimsen

clean'-cut' adj (also) (person) ordentlich; (clearly outlined) klar umrissen

cleaner ['klinər] s (person, device) Reiniger m; **cleaners** (establishment) Reinigungsanstalt f

clean'ing flu'id s flüssiges Reinigungsmittel n

clean'ing wo'man s Reinemachefrau f

cleanliness ['klɛnlɪnɪs] s Sauberkeit f

cleanse [klɛnz] tr reinigen

cleanser ['klɛnzər] s Reinigungsmittel n

clean'-shav'en adj glattrasiert

clean'up' s Reinemachen n; (e.g., of vice, graft) Säuberungsaktion f

clear [klɪr] adj klar; (sky, weather) heiter; (light) hell; (profit) netto; (conscience) rein; (proof) offenkundig ‖ adv (coll) völlig; (fin) netto ‖ tr klären; (streets) freimachen; (the table) abräumen; (a room) räumen; (a forest) roden; (the air) reinigen; (an obstacle without touching it) setzen über (acc); (a path) bahnen; (as profit) rein gewinnen; (at customs) zollamtlich abfertigen; (one's name) reinwaschen; **c. away** wegräumen; (doubts) beseitigen; **c. up** klarlegen ‖ intr sich klären; **c. out** (coll) sich davonmachen; **c. up** sich aufklären

clearance ['klɪrəns] s (approval) Genehmigung f; (at customs) Zollabfertigung f; (of a bridge) lichte Höhe f; (aer) Starterlaubnis f; (mach) Spielraum m

clear'ance sale' s Räumungsverkauf m

clear'-cut' adj klar, eindeutig

clear'-head'ed adj verständig

clear'ing s (in a woods) Lichtung f

clear'ing house' s Abstimmungszentrale f; (fin) Verrechnungsstelle f

clear'-sight'ed adj scharfsichtig

cleat [klit] s Stollen m

cleavage ['klivɪdʒ] s Spaltung f

cleave [kliv] v (pret & pp cleft [klɛft] & cleaved) tr zerspalten ‖ intr (split) sich spalten; (to) kleben (an dat)

cleaver ['klivər] s Hackbeil n

clef [klɛf] s Notenschlüssel m

cleft [klɛft] s Riß m, Spalt m

clemency ['klɛmənsi] s Milde f; (jur) Begnadigung f

clement ['klɛmənt] adj mild

clench [klɛntʃ] tr (a fist) ballen; (the teeth) zusammenbeißen

clerestory ['klɪr‚stori] s Lichtgaden m

clergy ['klɛrdʒi] s Geistlichkeit f

cler'gy·man s (–men) Geistliche m

cleric ['klɛrɪk] s Kleriker m

clerical ['klɛrɪkəl] adj Schreib–, Büro–; (eccl) geistlich

cler'ical er'ror s Schreibfehler m

cler'ical staff' s Schreibkräfte pl

cler'ical work' s Büroarbeit f

clerk [klʌrk] s (in a store) Verkäufer –in mf; (in an office) Büroangestellte mf; (in a post office) Schalterbeamte m; (jur) Gerichtsschreiber –in mf

clever ['klɛvər] adj (intelligent) klug; (adroit) geschickt; (witty) geistreich; (ingenious) findig

cleverness ['klɛvərnɪs] s (intelligence) Klugheit f; (adroitness) Geschicklichkeit f; (ingeniousness) Findigkeit f

cliché [kli'ʃe] s Klischee n

click [klɪk] *s* Klicken *n*; *(of the tongue)* Schnalzen *n*; *(of a lock)* Einschnappen *n* ‖ *tr* klicken lassen; **c. one's heels** die Hacken zusammenschlagen ‖ *intr* klicken; *(said of heels)* knallen; *(said of a lock)* einschnappen ‖ *impers*—**it clicks** (coll) es klappt

client ['klaɪ‧ənt] *s (customer)* Kunde *m*, Kundin *f*; *(of a company)* Auftraggeber –in *mf*; *(jur)* Klient –in *mf*

clientele [‚klaɪ‧ən'tel] *s* Kundschaft *f*; (com, jur) Klientel *f*

cliff [klɪf] *s* Klippe *f*, Felsen *m*

climate ['klaɪmɪt] *s* Klima *n*

climax ['klaɪmæks] *s* Höhepunkt *m*

climb [klaɪm] *s* Aufstieg *m*, Besteigung *f*; (aer) Steigungsflug *m* ‖ *tr* ersteigen, besteigen; *(stairs)* hinaufsteigen; **climb a tree** auf e–n Baum klettern; ‖ *intr* steigen, klettern; *(said of a street)* ansteigen

climber ['klaɪmər] *s* Kletterer –in *mf*; *(of a mountain)* Bergsteiger –in *mf*; (bot) Kletterpflanze *f*

clinch [klɪntʃ] *s* (box) Clinch *m* ‖ *tr* *(settle)* entscheiden ‖ *intr* clinchen

clincher ['klɪntʃər] *s* (coll) Trumpf *m*

cling [klɪŋ] *v (pret & pp* **clung** [klʌŋ]) *intr* haften; **c. to** sich anklammern an *(acc)*; *(said of a dress)* sich anschmiegen an *(acc)*; (fig) festhalten an *(dat)*

clinic ['klɪnɪk] *s* Klinik *f*

clinical ['klɪnɪkəl] *adj* klinisch

clink [klɪŋk] *s* Klirren *n*; *(prison)* (sl) Kittchen *n* ‖ *tr*—**c. glasses** mit den Gläsern anstoßen ‖ *intr* klirren

clip [klɪp] *s* Klammer *f*; **go at a good c.** ein scharfes Tempo gehen ‖ *v (pret & pp* **clipped**; *ger* **clipping)** *tr (a hedge)* beschneiden; *(hair)* schneiden; *(wings)* stutzen; *(sheep)* scheren; *(from newspapers, etc.)* ausschneiden; *(syllables)* verschlucken; (sl) schröpfen; **c. together** zusammenklammern

clip′board′ *s* Manuskripthalter *m*

clip′ joint′ *s* (sl) Nepplokal *n*

clipper ['klɪpər] *s* (aer) Klipperflugzeug *n*; (naut) Klipper *m*; **clippers** Haarschneidemaschine *f*

clip′ping *s (act)* Stutzen *n*; *(from newspapers)* Ausschnitt *m*; **clippings** *(of paper)* Schnitzel *pl*; *(scraps)* Abfälle *pl*

clique [klik] *s* Sippschaft *f*

cliquish ['klikɪʃ] *adj* cliquenhaft

cloak [klok] *s* Umhang *m*; (fig) Deckmantel *m*; **under the c. of darkness** im Schutz der Dunkelheit ‖ *tr* (fig) bemänteln

cloak′-and-dag′ger *adj* Spionage–

cloak′room′ *s* Garderobe *f*

clobber ['klɑbər] *tr* (coll) verwichsen

clock [klɑk] *s* Uhr *f* ‖ *tr (a runner)* abstoppen

clock′mak′er *s* Uhrmacher –in *mf*

clock′ tow′er *s* Uhrturm *m*

clock′wise′ *adv* im Uhrzeigersinn

clock′work′ *s* Uhrwerk *n*; **like c.** wie am Schnürchen

clod [klɑd] *s* Klumpen *m*, Scholle *f*

clodhopper ['klɑd‚hɑpər] *s* Bauerntölpel *m*

clog [klɑg] *s* Verstopfung *f*; *(shoe)* Holzschuh *m* ‖ *v (pret & pp* **clogged**; *ger* **clogging)** *tr* verstopfen ‖ *intr* sich verstopfen

cloister ['klɔɪstər] *s* Kloster *n*; *(covered walk)* Kreuzgang *m*

close [klos] *adj (near)* nahe; *(tight)* knapp; *(air)* schwül; *(ties; friend)* eng; *(attention)* gespannt; *(game)* beinahe gleich; *(observer)* scharf; *(surveillance)* streng; *(supervision)* genau; *(inspection)* eingehend; *(resemblance; competition)* stark; *(shave)* glatt; *(translation)* wortgetreu; *(stingy)* geizig; *(order)* (mil) geschlossen; **c. to** *(position)* nahe an *(dat)*, neben *(dat)*; *(direction)* nahe an *(acc)*, neben *(acc)* ‖ *adv* dicht, eng; **from c. up** in der Nähe ‖ [kloz] *s* Schluß *m*, Ende *n*; **bring to a c.** zu Ende bringen; **draw to a c.** zu Ende gehen ‖ *tr* schließen; *(an account, deal)* abschließen; **c. down** stillegen; **c. off** abschließen; *(a road)* sperren; **c. out** (com) ausverkaufen; **c. up** zumachen ‖ *intr* sich schließen; **c. in** immer näher kommen; **c. in on** umschließen

close-by ['klos'baɪ] *adj* nebenan

close-cropped ['klos'krɑpt] *adj* kurz geschoren

closed [klozd] *adj* geschlossen; **c. today** (public sign) heute Betriebsruhe

closed′ shop′ *s* Unternehmen *n* mit Gewerkschaftszwang

closefisted ['klos'fɪstəd] *adj* geizig

close-fitting ['klos'fɪtɪŋ] *adj* eng anliegend

close-mouthed ['klos'mauðd] *adj* verschwiegen

close′ or′der drill′ [klos] *s* (mil) geschlossenes Exerzieren *n*

closeout ['kloz‚aut] *s* Räumungsausverkauf *m*

close′ shave′ [klos] *s* glatte Rasure *f*; (fig) knappes Entkommen *n*; **have a c.** mit knapper Not davonkommen

closet ['klɑzɪt] *s* Schrank *m*

close-up ['klos‚ʌp] *s* Nahaufnahme *f*

clos′ing *adj* Schluß–; *(day)* scheidend ‖ *s* Schließung *f*; *(of an account)* Abschluß *m*; *(of a factory)* Stillegung *f*; *(of a road)* Sperrung *f*

clos′ing price′ *s* Schlußkurs *m*

clos′ing time′ *s (of a shop)* Geschäftsschluß *m*; *(of bars)* Polizeistunde *f*

clot [klɑt] *s* Klumpen *m*; *(of blood)* Gerinnsel *n* ‖ *v (pret & pp* **clotted**; *ger* **clotting)** *intr* gerinnen

cloth [klɔθ] *s* Stoff *m*, Tuch *n*; *(for cleaning, etc.)* Lappen *m*; **the c.** die Geistlichkeit

clothe [kloð] *v (pret & pp* **clothed** & **clad** [klæd]) *tr* ankleiden, (be)kleiden; (fig) (in) einhüllen in *(acc)*

clothes [kloz], [kloðz] *spl* Kleider *pl*; **change one's clothes** sich umziehen; **put on one's clothes** sich anziehen

clothes′bas′ket *s* Wäschekorb *m*

clothes′brush′ *s* Kleiderbürste *f*

clothes′ clos′et *s* Kleiderschrank *m*

clothes′ dri′er s Wäschetrockner m
clothes′ hang′er s Kleiderbügel m
clothes′line′ s Wäscheleine f
clothes′pin′ s Wäscheklammer f
clothier [′kloðjər] s Kleiderhändler m; (cloth maker) Tuchmacher m; (cloth dealer) Tuchhändler m
clothing [′kloðɪŋ] s Kleidung f
cloud [klaud] s Wolke f; **be up in the clouds** (fig) in höheren Regionen schweben ‖ tr bewölken; (a liquid) trüben; (fig) verdunkeln ‖ intr—**c. over** (or **up**) sich bewölken
cloud′burst′ s Wolkenbruch m
cloud′-capped′ adj von Wolken bedeckt
cloudiness [′klaudɪnɪs] s Bewölktheit f
cloudless [′klaudlɪs] adj unbewölkt
cloudy [′klaudi] adj bewölkt; (liquid) trüb(e)
clout [klaut] s (blow) (coll) Hieb m; (influence) (coll) Einfluß m ‖ tr—**c. s.o.** (coll) j-m eins herunterhauen
clove [klov] s Gewürznelke f; **c. of garlic** Knoblauchzehe f
clo′ven hoof′ [′klovən] s (as a sign of the devil) Pferdefuß m
clover [′klovər] s Klee m
clo′ver·leaf′ s (-leaves) Kleeblatt n
clown [klaun] s Clown m, Hanswurst m
clownish [′klaunɪʃ] adj närrisch
cloy [klɔɪ] tr übersättigen
club [klʌb] s (weapon) Keule f; (organization) Klub m; (cards) Kreuz n; (golf) Schläger m ‖ (pret & pp **clubbed**; ger **clubbing**) tr verprügeln
club′ car′ s (rr) Salonwagen m
club′house′ s Klubhaus n
cluck [klʌk] s Glucken n ‖ intr glucken
clue [klu] s Schlüssel m, Anhaltspunkt m
clump [klʌmp] s (of earth) Klumpen m; (of hair, grass) Büschel n; (of trees) Gruppe f; (heavy tramping sound) schwerer Tritt m; **c. of bushes** Gebüsch n ‖ intr—**c. along** trapsen
clumsy [′klʌmzi] adj ungeschickt, plump; **c. ox** Tölpel m
cluster [′klʌstər] s (bunch growing together) Büschel n; (of grapes) Traube f; (group) Gruppe f ‖ intr—**c. around** sich zusammendrängen um
clutch [klʌtʃ] s Griff m; (aut) Kupplung f; **fall into s.o.'s clutches** j-m in die Klauen geraten; **let out the c.** einkuppeln; **step on the c.** auskuppeln ‖ tr packen
clutter [′klʌtər] s Durcheinander n ‖ tr—**c. up** vollstopfen
Co. abbr (**Company**) Gesellschaft f
c/o abbr (**care of**) per Adresse, bei
coach [kotʃ] s Kutsche f; (rr) Personenwagen m; (sport) Trainer m ‖ tr Nachhilfeunterricht geben (dat); (sport) trainieren ‖ intr (sport) trainieren
coach′ing s Nachhilfeunterricht m; (sport) Training n
coach′man s (–men) Kutscher m

coagulate [ko′ægjə‚let] tr gerinnen lassen ‖ intr gerinnen
coal [kol] s Kohle f
coal′bin′ s Kohlenkasten m
coal′-black′ adj kohlrabenschwarz
coal′ car′ s (rr) Kohlenwagen m
coal′deal′er s Kohlenhändler m
coalesce [‚ko·ə′les] intr zusammenwachsen, sich vereinigen
coalition [‚ko·ə′lɪʃən] s Koalition f
coal′ mine′ s Kohlenbergwerk n
coal′min′ing s Kohlenbergbau m
coal′ oil′ s Petroleum n
coal′yard′ s Kohlenlager n
coarse [kors] adj (& fig) grob
coast [kost] s Küste f; **the c. is clear** (coll) die Luft ist rein ‖ intr im Leerlauf fahren; **c. along** (fig) sich mühelos fortbewegen
coastal [′kostəl] adj küstennah, Küsten-
coaster [′kostər] s (for a glass) Untersatz m; (naut) Küstenfahrer m
coast′guard′ s Küstenwachdienst m
coast′line′ s Küstenlinie f
coat [kot] s (of a suit) Jacke f, Rock m; (topcoat) Mantel m; (of fur) Fell n; (of enamel, etc.) Belag m; (of paint) Anstrich m ‖ tr (e.g., with teflon) beschichten; (e.g., with chocolate) überziehen; (e.g., with oil) beschmieren
coat′ed adj überzogen; (tongue) belegt
coat′ hang′er s Kleiderbügel m
coat′ing s Belag m, Überzug m
coat′ of arms′ s Wappen n
coat′rack′ s Kleiderständer m
coat′room′ s Garderobe f
coat′tail′ s Rockschoß m; (of formal wear) Frackschoß m
coauthor [′ko‚ɔθər] s Mitautor m
coax [koks] tr schmeicheln (dat); **c. s.o. to** (inf) j-n überreden zu (inf)
cob [kɑb] s Kolben m
cobalt [′kobɔlt] s Kobalt m
cobbler [′kɑblər] s Flickschuster m
cobblestone [′kɑbəl‚ston] s Pflasterstein m, Kopfstein m
cobra [′kobrə] s Kobra f
cob′web′ s Spinn(en)gewebe n
cocaine [ko′ken] s Kokain n
cock [kɑk] s Hahn m; (faucet) Wasserhahn m; (of a gun) Gewehrhahn m ‖ tr (one's ears) spitzen; (one's hat) schief aufsetzen; (the firing mechanism) spannen
cock-a-doodle-doo [′kɑkə‚dudəl′du] s Kikeriki n
cock′-and-bull′ sto′ry s Lügengeschichte f
cockeyed [′kɑk‚aɪd] adj (cross-eyed) nach innen schielend; (slanted to one side) (sl) schief; (drunk) (sl) blau; (absurd) (sl) verrückt
cock′fight′ s Hahnenkampf m
cock′pit′ s Hahnenkampfplatz m; (aer) Kabine f, Kanzel f
cock′roach′ s Schabe f
cock′sure′ adj todsicher
cock′tail′ s Cocktail m
cock′tail dress′ s Cocktailkleid n
cock′tail par′ty s Cocktailparty f

cock′tail shak′er s Cocktailmischgefäß n

cocky [′kɑki] adj (coll) frech

cocoa [′koko] s Kakao m

coconut [′kokə‚nʌt] s Kokosnuß f

co′conut palm′, co′conut tree′ s Kokospalme f

cacoon [kə′kun] s Kokon m

C.O.D., c.o.d. abbr (**cash on delivery**) per Nachnahme

cod [kɑd] s Kabeljau m

coddle [′kɑdəl] tr hätscheln

code [kod] s Geheimschrift f; (jur) Kodex m ‖ tr verschlüsseln, chiffrieren

codefendant [‚kodɪ′fendənt] s Mitangeklagte mf

code′ name′ s Deckname m

code′ of hon′or s Ehrenkodex m

code′ of laws′ s Gesetzsammlung f

code′ word′ s Kennwort n

codex [′kodeks] s (**codices** [′kodɪ‚siz]) Kodex m

cod′fish′ s Kabeljau m

codicil [′kɑdɪsɪl] s Kodizill n

codi•fy [′kɑdɪ‚faɪ] v (pret & pp –fied) tr kodifizieren

cod′-liver oil′ s Lebertran m

coed, co-ed [′ko‚ed] s Studentin f

coeducation [‚ko‚edʒə′keʃən] s Koedukation f

coeducational [‚ko‚edʒə′keʃənəl] adj Koedukations-

coefficient [‚ko•ɪ′fɪʃənt] s Koeffizient m

coerce [ko′ʌrs] tr zwingen

coercion [ko′ʌrʃən] s Zwang m

coexist [‚ko•ɪg′zɪst] intr koexistieren

coexistence [‚ko•ɪg′zɪstəns] s Koexistenz f

coffee [′kɔfɪ] s Kaffee m

cof′fee bean′ s Kaffeebohne f

cof′fee break′ s Kaffeepause f

cof′fee fiend′ s Kaffeetante f

cof′fee grounds′ spl Kaffeesatz m

cof′fee pot′ s Kaffeekanne f

cof′fee shop′ s Kaffeestube f

coffer [′kɔfər] s Truhe f; (archit) Deckenfeld n; **coffers** Schatzkammer f

cof′ferdam′ s (caisson) Kastendamm m; (naut) Kofferdamm m

coffin [′kɔfɪn] s Sarg m

cog [kɑg] s Zahn m; (cogwheel) Zahnrad n

cogency [′kɑdʒənsɪ] s Beweiskraft f

cogent [′kɑdʒənt] adj triftig

cognac [′konjæk], [′kɑnjæk] s Kognak m

cognizance [′kɑgnɪzəns] s Kenntnis f; take c. of s.th. etw zur Kenntnis nehmen

cognizant [′kɑgnɪzənt] adj—be c. of Kenntnis haben von

cog′wheel′ s Zahnrad n

cohabit [ko′hæbɪt] intr in wilder Ehe leben

coheir [ko′er] s Miterbe m, Miterbin f

cohere [ko′hɪr] intr zusammenhängen

cohesion [ko′hiʒən] s Kohäsion f

coiffeur [kwɑ′fʌr] s Friseur m

coiffure [kwɑ′fjur] s Frisur f

coil [kɔɪl] s (something wound in a spiral) Spirale f, Rolle f; (of tubing) Schlange f; (single wind) Windung f; (elec) Spule f ‖ tr aufrollen; (naut) aufschießen ‖ intr—c. up sich zusammenrollen

coil′ spring′ s Spiralfeder f

coin [kɔɪn] s Münze f, Geldstück n ‖ tr münzen, (& fig) prägen

coinage [′kɔɪnɪdʒ] s (minting) Prägen n; (coins collectively) Münzen pl; (fig) Prägung f

coincide [‚ko•ɪn′saɪd] intr (with) zusammentreffen (mit); (in time) (with) gleichzeitig geschehen (mit)

coincidence [ko′ɪnsɪdəns] s Zufall m; by mere c. rein zufällig

coin′ machine′ s Münzautomat m

coin′ slot′ s Münzeinwurf m

coition [ko′ɪʃən], **coitus** [′ko•ɪtəs] s Koitus m, Beischlaf m

coke [kok] s Koks m; (coll) Coca-Cola n

colander [′kʌləndər] s Sieb n

cold [kold] adj kalt ‖ s Kälte f; (indisposition) Erkältung f

cold′ blood′ s—in c. kaltblütig

cold′-blood′ed adj kaltblütig

cold′ chis′el s Kaltmeißel m

cold′ com′fort s (fig) geringer Trost m

cold′ cream′ s Cold Cream n

cold′ cuts′ spl kalter Aufschnitt m

cold′ feet′ spl—have c. (fig) Angst haben

cold′ front′ s Kaltfront f

cold′-heart′ed adj kaltherzig

coldness [′koldnɪs] s Kälte f

cold′ shoul′der s—give s.o. the c. j—m die kalte Schulter zeigen

cold′ snap′ s plötzlicher Kälteeinbruch m

cold′ stor′age s Lagerung f im Kühlraum

cold′ war′ s kalter Krieg m

cold′ wave′ s (meteor) Kältewelle f

coleslaw [′kol‚slɔ] s Krautsalat m

colic [′kɑlɪk] s Kolik f

coliseum [‚kɑlɪ′si•əm] s Kolosseum n

collaborate [kə′læbə‚ret] intr mitarbeiten; (pol) kollaborieren

collaboration [kə‚læbə′reʃən] s Mitarbeit f; (pol) Kollaboration f

collaborator [kə′læbə‚retər] s Mitarbeiter –in m; (pol) Kollaborateur m

collapse [kə′læps] s (of a bridge, etc.) Einsturz m; (com) Krach m; (pathol) Zusammenbruch m, Kollaps m ‖ intr einstürzen; (fig) zusammenbrechen

collapsible [kə′læpsɪbəl] adj zusammenklappbar

collaps′ible boat′ s Faltboot n

collar [′kɑlər] s Kragen m; (of a dog) Halsband n; (of a horse) Kummet n; (mach) Ring m, Kragen m

col′larbone′ s Schlüsselbein n

collate [kə′let] tr kollationieren

collateral [kə′lætərəl] adj kollateral, Seiten- ‖ s (fin) Deckung f

collation [kə′leʃən] s Kollation f

colleague [′kɑlig] s Kollege m, Kollegin f

collect [′kɑlekt] s (eccl) Kollekte f ‖ [kə′lekt] adj—make a c. call ein R-

Gespräch führen ‖ *adv*—**call c.** ein R-Gespräch führen; **send c.** gegen Nachnahme schicken ‖ *tr (money)* (ein)kassieren; *(stamps, coins)* sammeln; *(e.g., examination papers)* einsammeln; *(taxes)* abheben; *(one's thoughts)* zusammennehmen; **c. oneself** sich fassen ‖ *intr* sich (ver)-sammeln; *(pile up)* sich anhäufen

collect'ed *adj (works)* gesammelt; *(self-possessed)* gefaßt

collection [kə'lekʃən] *s (of stamps, etc.)* Sammlung *f*; *(accumulation)* Ansammlung *f*; *(of money)* Einziehung *f*; *(in a church)* Kollekte *f*; *(of mail)* Leerung *f* des Briefkastens; *(com)* Kollektion *f*

collec'tion a'gency *s* Inkassobüro *n*

collec'tion bas'ket *s* Klingelbeutel *m*

collective [kə'lektɪv] *adj* kollektiv, Sammel-, Gesamt- ‖ *s* (pol) Kollektiv *n*

collec'tive bar'gaining *s* Tarifverhandlungen *pl*

collec'tive farm' *s* Kolchose *f*

collector [kə'lektər] *s (e.g., of stamps)* Sammler –in *mf*; *(bill collector)* Einkassierer –in *mf*; *(of taxes)* Einnehmer –in *mf*; *(of tickets)* Fahrkartenabnehmer –in *mf*

college ['kalɪdʒ] *s* College *n*; *(e.g., of cardinals)* Kollegium *n*

collide [kə'laɪd] *intr* zusammenstoßen

collie ['kali] *s* Collie *m*

collision [kə'lɪʒən] *s* Zusammenstoß *m*

colloquial [kə'lokwɪ-əl] *adj* umgangssprachlich, Umgangs-

colloquialism [kə'lokwɪ-ə‚lɪzəm] *s* Ausdruck *m* der Umgangssprache

colloquy ['kaləkwɪ] *s* Gespräch *n*

collusion [kə'luʒən] *s* Kollusion *f*; **be in c.** kolludieren

colon ['kolən] *s* (anat) Dickdarm *m*; (gram) Doppelpunkt *m*

colonel ['kʌrnəl] *s* Oberst *m*

colonial [kə'lonɪ-əl] *adj* Kolonial- ‖ *s* Einwohner –in *mf* e-r Kolonie

colonialism [kə'lonɪ-ə‚lɪzəm] *s* Kolonialismus *m*

colonize ['kalə‚naɪz] *tr* besiedeln

colonnade [‚kalə'ned] *s* Säulengang *m*

colony ['kalənɪ] *s* Kolonie *f*

color ['kʌlər] *adj (film, photo, photography, slide, television)* Farb- ‖ *s* Farbe *f*; **lend c.** to beleben; **show one's colors** sein wahres Gesicht zeigen; **the colors** die Flagge; **with flying colors** glänzend ‖ *tr* färben; (fig) (schön)färben ‖ *intr* sich verfärben; *(become red)* erröten

col'or-blind' *adj* farbenblind

col'ored *adj* farbig

col'or-fast' *adj* farbecht

colorful ['kʌlərfəl] *adj* bunt, farbenreich; (fig) farbig

col'oring *s* Kolorit *n*, Färbung *f*

col'oring book' *s* Malbuch *n*

colorless ['kʌlərlɪs] *adj* farblos

col'or ser'geant *s* Fahnenträger *m*

colossal [kə'lasəl] *adj* kolossal

colossus [kə'lasəs] *s* Koloß *m*

colt [kolt] *s* Füllen *n*

Columbus [kə'lʌmbəs] *s* Kolumbus *m*

column ['kaləm] *s* Säule *f*; *(syndicated article)* Kolumne *f*; (mil) Kolonne *f*; (typ) Spalte *f*, Rubrik *f*; **c. of smoke** Rauchsäule *f*

columnist ['kaləmɪst] *s* Kolumnist –in *mf*

coma ['komə] *s* Koma *n*

comb [kom] *s* Kamm *m*; *(honeycomb)* Wabe *f*; *(of a rooster)* Kamm *m* ‖ *tr* kämmen; *(an area)* absuchen

com•bat ['kambæt] *s (e.g., pilot, strength, unit, zone)* Kampf- ‖ *s* Kampf *m*, Streit *m* ‖ ['kambæt], [kəm'bæt] *v (pret & pp* -bat[t]ed; *ger* -bat[t]ing) *tr* bekämpfen ‖ *intr* kämpfen

combatant ['kambətənt] *s* Kämpfer –in *mf*

com'bat fatigue' *s* Kriegsneurose *f*

combative ['kambətɪv] *adj* streitsüchtig

comber ['komər] *s* Sturzwelle *f*

combination [‚kambɪ'neʃən] *s* Verbindung *f*; (com) Konzern *m*

combine ['kambaɪn] *s* (agr) Mähdrescher *m*; (com) Interessengemeinschaft *f* ‖ [kəm'baɪn] *tr* kombinieren, verbinden

combustible [kəm'bʌstɪbəl] *adj* (ver)brennbar ‖ *s* Brennstoff *m*

combustion [kəm'bʌstʃən] *s* Verbrennung *f*

combus'tion cham'ber *s* Brennkammer *f*

combus'tion en'gine *s* Verbrennungsmaschine *f*

come [kʌm] *v (pret* came [kem]; *pp* come) *intr* kommen; **c. about** geschehen, sich ereignen; **c. across** *(discover)* stoßen auf *(acc)*; *(said of a speech, etc.)* ankommen; **c. across with** (coll) blechen; **c. after** folgen *(dat)*; *(fetch)* holen kommen; **c. along** mitkommen; (coll) vorwärtskommen; **c. apart** auseinanderfallen; **c. around** herumkommen; *(said of a special day)* wiederkehren; *(improve)* wieder zu sich kommen; *(change one's view)* von e-r Ansicht abgehen; **c. back** zurückkehren; *(recur to the mind)* wieder einfallen; **c. between** treten zwischen *(acc)*; **c. by** vorbeikommen; *(acquire)* geraten an *(acc)*; **c. clean** (sl) mit der Wahrheit herausrücken; **c. down** *(said of prices)* sinken; (& fig) herunterkommen; **c. down with** erkranken an *(dat)*; **c. first** *(have priority)* zuerst an die Reihe kommen; **c. for** abholen; **c. forward** vortreten; **c. from** herkommen; *(e.g., a rich family)* stammen aus; *(e.g., school)* kommen aus; **c. in** hereinkommen; **c. in for** (coll) erhalten; **c. in second** den zweiten Platz belegen; **c. off** *(said of a button)* abgehen; *(come loose)* losgehen; *(said of an event)* verlaufen; **c. on!** los!; **c. out** herauskommen; *(said of a spot)* herausgehen; *(said of a publication)* erscheinen; **c. out against** (or for) sich erklären gegen (or für); **c. over** *(said of fear, etc.)* überlaufen; **c. to** *(amount to)* betragen; (after fainting) wieder zu sich kommen; **c. together** zusammenkommen; **c. true** in Erfüllung gehen; **c. up** (occur) vorkommen; (said of a number) herauskommen; (said of plants) aufgehen; (in conversation) zur Sprache kommen; (said of a storm) heranziehen; **c. upon** kommen auf (acc); **c. up to** entsprechen (dat); **for years to c.** auf Jahre hinaus; **how c.?** (coll) wieso?; **it comes easy to me** es fällt mir leicht

come'back' s Comeback n

comedian [kə'mɪdɪ-ən] s Komiker m; (pej) Komödiant –in mf

comedienne [kə,mɪdɪ'en] s Komikerin f

come'down' s (coll) Abstieg m

comedy ['kɑmədi] s Komödie f

comely ['kʌmli] adj anmutig

come'-on' s (sl) Lockmittel n

comet ['kɑmɪt] s Komet m

comfort ['kʌmfərt] s (solace) Trost m; (of a room, etc.) Behaglichkeit f; (person or thing that comforts) Tröster m; (bed cover) Steppdecke f || tr trösten

comfortable ['kʌmfərtəbəl] adj behaglich, bequem; (income) ausreichend; **be** (or **feel**) **c.** sich wohl fühlen

comforter ['kʌmfərtər] s Tröster m; (bed cover) Steppdecke f

com'forting adj tröstlich

com'fort sta'tion s Bedürfnisanstalt f

comic ['kɑmɪk] adj komisch || s Komiker m; **comics** Comics pl, Witzblatt n

comical ['kɑmɪkəl] adj komisch

com'ic op'era s Operette f

com'ic strip' s Bildstreifen m

com'ing adj künftig, kommend; **c. soon** (notice at theater) demnächst || s Kommen n, Ankunft f; **c. of age** Mündigwerden n

comma ['kɑmə] s Komma n, Beistrich m

command [kə'mænd] s (order) Befehl m; (of language) Beherrschung f; (mil) Kommando n; (jurisdiction) (mil) Kommandobereich m; **at s.o.'s c.** auf j–s Befehl; **be in c. of** (mil) das Kommando führen über (acc); **have a good c. of** gut beherrschen; **take c. of** (mil) das Kommando übernehmen über (acc) || tr (a person) befehlen (dat); (respect, silence) gebieten; (troops) führen; (a high price) erzielen || intr (mil) kommandieren

commandant [,kɑmən'dænt] s Kommandant m

commandeer [,kɑmən'dɪr] tr (coll) organisieren; (mil) requirieren

commander [kə'mændər] s Truppenführer m; (of a company) Chef m; (of a military unit from battalion to corps) Kommandeur m; (of an army) Befehlshaber m; (nav) Fregattenkapitän m

comman'der in chief' s Oberbefehlshaber m

command'ing adj (appearance) eindrucksvoll; (view) weit; (position) beherrschend; (general) kommandierend

command'ing of'ficer s Einheitsführer m

commandment [kə'mændmənt] s Gebot n

command' post' s Befehlsstand m

commemorate [kə'meməˌret] tr gedenken (genit), feiern

commemoration [kə,memə'reʃən] s Gedenkfeier f; **in c. of** zum Gedächtnis von

commence [kə'mens] tr & intr anfangen

commencement [kə'mensmənt] s Anfang m; (educ) Schulentlassungsfeier f

commend [kə'mend] tr (praise) (& mil) belob(ig)en; (entrust) empfehlen

commendable [kə'mendəbəl] adj lobenswert

commendation [,kɑmən'deʃən] s Belobigung f

comment ['kɑmənt] s Bemerkung f, Stellungnahme f; **no c.!** kein Kommentar! || intr Bemerkungen machen; **c. on** kommentieren

commentary ['kɑmənˌteri] s Kommentar m

commentator ['kɑmənˌtetər] s Kommentator –in mf; (of a text) Erklärer –in mf

commerce ['kɑmərs] s Handel m

commercial [kə'mɑrʃəl] adj Handels–, Geschäfts–, kommerziell || s (rad, telv) Werbesendung f

commer'cial art' s Gebrauchsgraphik f

commercialism [kə'mɑrʃəˌlɪzəm] s Handelsgeist m

commercialize [kə'mɑrʃəˌlaɪz] tr kommerzialisieren

commiserate [kə'mɪzəˌret] intr—**c. with** bemitleiden

commissar ['kɑmɪˌsɑr] s (pol) Kommissar m

commissary ['kɑmɪˌseri] s (deputy) Kommissar m; (store) Militärversorgungsstelle f

commission [kə'mɪʃən] s (order) Auftrag m; (of a crime) Begehung f; (committee) Kommission f; (percentage) Provision f; (mil) Offizierspatent n; **out of c.** außer Betrieb; || tr beauftragen; (a work) bestellen; (a ship) in Dienst stellen; (mil) ein Offizierspatent verleihen (dat)

commis'sioned of'ficer s Offizier –in mf

commissioner [kə'mɪʃənər] s Kommissar –in mf

com–mit [kə'mɪt] v (pret & pp –mitted; ger –mitting) tr (a crime) begehen; (entrust) anvertrauen; (give over) übergeben; (to an institution) einweisen; **c. oneself** to sich festlegen auf (acc); **c. to memory** auswendig lernen; **c. to writing** zu Papier bringen

commitment [kə'mɪtmənt] s (to) Festlegung f (auf acc); (to an asylum) Anstaltsüberweisung f

committee [kə'mɪti] s Ausschuß m

commode [kə'mod] s Kommode f

commodious [kə'modɪ·əs] adj geräumig

commodity [kə'modɪtɪ] s Ware f

common ['kɒmən] adj (language, property, interest) gemeinsam; (general) allgemein; (people) einfach; (soldier) gemein; (coarse, vulgar) gemein; (frequent) häufig ‖ s—in c. gemeinsam

com'mon denom'inator s gemeinsamer Nenner m; **reduce to a c.** auf e-n gemeinsamen Nenner bringen

commoner ['kɒmənər] s Bürger –in mf

com'mon-law mar'riage s wilde Ehe f

Com'mon Mar'ket s Gemeinsamer Markt m

com'mon noun' s Gattungsname m

com'monplace' adj alltäglich ‖ s Gemeinplatz m

com'mon sense' s gesunder Menschenverstand m

com'mon stock' s Stammaktien pl

commonweal ['kɒmən,wil] s Gemeinwohl n

com'monwealth' s (republic) Republik f; (state in U.S.A.) Bundesstaat m

commotion [kə'moʃən] s Aufruhr m

commune ['kɒmjun] s Kommune f ‖ [kə'mjun] intr sich vertraulich besprechen

communicable [kə'mjunɪkəbəl] adj übertragbar

communicant [kə'mjunɪkənt] s Kommunikant –in mf

communicate [kə'mjunɪ,ket] tr mitteilen; (a disease) (to) übertragen (auf acc) ‖ intr sich besprechen

communication [kə,mjunɪ'keʃən] s Mitteilung f; (message) Nachricht f; **communications** Nachrichtenwesen n; (mil) Fernmeldewesen n

communicative [kə'mjunɪ,ketɪv] adj mitteilsam

communion [kə'mjunjən] s Gemeinschaft f; (Prot) Abendmahl n; (R. C.) Kommunion f

commun'ion rail' s Altargitter n

communiqué [kə,mjunɪ'ke] s Kommuniqué n

communism ['kɒmjə,nɪzəm] s Kommunismus m

communist ['kɒmjənɪst] s kommunistisch ‖ s Kommunist –in mf

community [kə'mjunɪtɪ] s Gemeinschaft f; (people living together) Gemeinde f

communize ['kɒmjə,naɪz] tr kommunistisch machen

commutation [,kɒmjə'teʃən] s (jur) Umwandlung f

commuta'tion tick'et s Zeitkarte f

commutator ['kɒmjə,tetər] s (elec) Kommutator m, Kollektor m

commute [kə'mjut] tr (jur) umwandeln ‖ intr pendeln

commuter [kə'mjutər] s Pendler –in mf

commut'er train' s Pendelzug m

compact [kəm'pækt] adj kompakt, dicht ‖ ['kɒmpækt] s (for cosmetics) Kompaktdose f; (agreement) Vertrag m; (aut) Kompaktwagen m

companion [kəm'pænjən] s Kumpan –in mf; (one who accompanies) Begleiter –in mf

companionable [kəm'pænjənəbəl] adj gesellig

compan'ionship' s Gesellschaft f

compan'ionway' s Kajütstreppe f

company ['kʌmpənɪ] s (companions) Umgang m; (& com) Gesellschaft f; (mil) Kompanie f; (theat) Truppe f; **keep c. with** verkehren mit; **keep s.o. c.** j-m Gesellschaft leisten

com'pany command'er s Kompaniechef m

comparable ['kɒmpərəbəl] adj vergleichbar

comparative [kəm'pærətɪv] adv vergleichend; (gram) komparativ ‖ s (gram) Komparativ m

comparatively [kəm'pærətɪvlɪ] adv verhältnismäßig

compare [kəm'per] s—beyond c. unvergleichlich ‖ tr (with, to) vergleichen (mit); (gram) steigern; **as compared with** im Vergleich zu

comparison [kəm'pærɪsən] s Vergleich m; (gram) Steigerung f

compartment [kəm'partmənt] s Fach n; (rr) Abteil n

compass ['kʌmpəs] s Kompaß m; (geom) Zirkel m; **within the c. of** innerhalb (genit)

com'pass card' s Kompaßrose f

compassion [kəm'pæʃən] s Mitleid n

compassionate [kəm'pæʃənɪt] adj mitleidig

compatible [kəm'pætɪbəl] adj vereinbar

com·pel [kəm'pel] v (pret & pp –pelled; ger –pelling) tr zwingen, nötigen

compendious [kəm'pendɪ·əs] adj gedrängt

compendi·um [kəm'pendɪ·əm] s (–ums & -a [ə]) Abriß m, Kompendium n

compensate ['kɒmpən,set] tr entschädigen ‖ intr—c. for Ersatz leisten (or bieten) für

compensation [,kɒmpən'seʃən] s (for damages) Entschädigung f; (remuneration) Entgeld n

compete [kəm'pit] intr (with) konkurrieren (mit); (for) sich mitbewerben (um); (sport) am Wettkampf teilnehmen

competence ['kɒmpɪtəns] s (mental state) Zurechnungsfähigkeit f; (ability) (in) Fähigkeit f (zu)

competent ['kɒmpɪtənt] adj (able) fähig, tüchtig; (witness) zulässig

competition [,kɒmpɪ'tɪʃən] s Wettbewerb m; (com) Konkurrenz f; (sport) Wettkampf m

competitive [kəm'petɪtɪv] adj (bidding) Konkurrenz–; (prices) konkurrenzfähig; (person) ehrgeizig; (exam) Auslese–

competitor [kəm'petɪtər] s Mitbewerber –in mf; (com) Konkurrent –in mf; (sport) Wettkämpfer –in mf

compilation [,kɒmpɪ'leʃən] s Zusammenstellung f; (book) Sammelwerk n

compile [kəm'paɪl] *tr* zusammenstellen, kompilieren; (*Material*) zusammentragen

complacence [kəm'pleɪsəns], **complacency** [kəm'pleɪsənsi] *s* Selbstgefälligkeit *f*

complacent [kəm'pleɪsənt] *adj* selbstgefällig

complain [kəm'pleɪn] *intr* klagen; **c. to s.o. about** sich bei j-m beklagen über (*acc*)

complaint [kəm'pleɪnt] *s* Klage *f*; (*ailment*) Beschwerde *f*

complement ['kɑmplɪmənt] *s* (& *gram*) Ergänzung *f*; (*geom*) Komplement *n*; (*nav*) Bemannung *f* || ['kɑmplɪ,ment] *tr* ergänzen

complete [kəm'pliːt] *adj* ganz, vollkommen, vollständig; (*works*) sämtlich || *tr* (*make whole*) vervollständigen; (*make perfect*) vollenden; (*finish*) beenden; (*a job*) erledigen

completely [kəm'pliːtli] *adv* völlig

completion [kəm'pliːʃən] *s* Vollendung *f*

complex [kəm'pleks], ['kɑmpleks] *adj* verwickelt || ['kɑmpleks] *s* Komplex *m*

complexion [kəm'plekʃən] *s* Gesichtsfarbe *f*; (*appearance*) Aussehen *n*

complexity [kəm'pleksɪti] *s* Kompliziertheit *f*

compliance [kəm'plaɪəns] *s* Einwilligung *f*; **in c. with your wishes** Ihren Wünschen gemäß

complicate ['kɑmplɪ,ket] *tr* komplizieren

com'plicat'ed *adj* kompliziert

complication [,kɑmplɪ'keʃən] *s* Verwicklung *f*; (& *pathol*) Komplikation *f*

complicity [kəm'plɪsɪti] *s* (**in**) Mitschuld *f* (an *dat*)

compliment ['kɑmplɪmənt] *s* Kompliment *n*; (*praise*) Lob *n*; **compliments** Empfehlungen *pl*; **pay s.o. a (high) c.** j-m ein (großes) Lob spenden || *tr* (**on**) beglückwünschen (zu)

complimentary [,kɑmplɪ'mentəri] *adj* (*remark*) schmeichelhaft; (*free*) Frei-

com·ply [kəm'plaɪ] *v* (*pret* & *pp* –**plied**) *intr* sich fügen; **c. with** einwilligen in (*acc*); **c. with the rules** sich an die Vorschriften halten

component [kəm'ponənt] *adj* Teil- || *s* Bestandteil *m*; (*math, phys*) Komponente *f*

compose [kəm'poz] *tr* (*writings*) verfassen; (*a sentence*) bilden; (*mus*) komponieren; (*typ*) setzen; **be composed of** bestehen aus; **c. oneself** sich fassen

composed' *adj* ruhig, gefaßt

composer [kəm'pozər] *s* Verfasser –in *mf*; (*mus*) Komponist –in *mf*

composite [kəm'pɑzɪt] *adj* zusammengesetzt || *s* Zusammensetzung *f*

composition [,kɑmpə'zɪʃən] *s* (*chem*) Zusammensetzung *f*; (*educ*) Aufsatz *m*; (*mus, paint*) Komposition *f*; (*typ*) Schriftsatz *m*

compositi'on book' *s* Übungsheft *n*

compositor [kəm'pɑzɪtər] *s* Setzer –in *mf*

composure [kəm'poʒər] *s* Fassung *f*

compote ['kɑmpot] *s* (*stewed fruit*) Kompott *n*; (*dish*) Kompottschale *f*

compound ['kɑmpaʊnd] *adj* zusammengesetzt; (*fracture*) kompliziert || *s* Zusammensetzung *f*; (*enclosure*) umzäumtes Gelände *n*; (*chem*) Verbindung *f*; (*gram*) Kompositum *n*; (*mil*) Truppenlager *n* || [kəm'paʊnd] *tr* zusammensetzen

com'pound in'terest *s* Zinseszinsen *pl*

comprehend [,kɑmprɪ'hend] *tr* auffassen

comprehensible [,kɑmprɪ'hensɪbəl] *adj* faßlich, begreiflich

comprehension [,kɑmprɪ'henʃən] *s* Auffassung *f*; (*ability to understand*) Fassungskraft *f*

comprehensive [,kɑmprɪ'hensɪv] *adj* umfassend

compress ['kɑmpres] *s* (*med*) Kompresse *f* || [kəm'pres] *tr* komprimieren

compressed' *adj* komprimiert; (*air*) Druck-; (*fig*) gedrängt

compression [kəm'preʃən] *s* Kompression *f*, Druck *m*

comprise [kəm'praɪz] *tr* umfassen; **be comprised of** bestehen aus

compromise ['kɑmprə,maɪz] *s* Kompromiß *m* || *tr* kompromittieren; (*principles*) preisgeben || *intr* (**on**) e-n Kompromiß schließen (über *acc*)

comptroller [kəm'trolər] *s* Rechnungsprüfer *m*

compulsion [kəm'pʌlʃən] *s* Zwang *m*

compulsive [kəm'pʌlsɪv] *adj* triebhaft

compulsory [kəm'pʌlsəri] *adj* obligatorisch, Zwangs-; **c. military service** allgemeine Wehrpflicht *f*

compute [kəm'pjut] *tr* berechnen || *intr* rechnen

computer [kəm'pjutər] *s* Computer *m*

comput'er lan'guage *s* Maschinensprache *f*

comrade ['kɑmræd] *s* Kamerad *m*

con [kɑn] *s* (*pret* & *pp* **conned**; *ger* **conning**) *tr* beschwindeln

concave [kɑn'kev] *adj* konkav

conceal [kən'sil] *tr* verheimlichen

concealment [kən'silmənt] *s* Verheimlichung *f*; (*place*) Versteck *n*

concede [kən'sid] *tr* zugestehen, zubilligen; **c. victory** (*pol*) den Wahlsieg überlassen || *intr* nachgeben

conceit [kən'sit] *s* (*vanity*) Einbildung *f*, Dünkel *m*; (*witty expression*) Witz *m*

conceit'ed *adj* eingebildet

conceivable [kən'sivəbəl] *adj* denkbar

conceive [kən'siv] *tr* begreifen; (*a desire*) hegen; (*a child*) empfangen

concentrate ['kɑnsən,tret] *tr* konzentrieren; (*troops*) zusammenziehen || *intr* (**on**) sich konzentrieren (auf *acc*); (*gather*) sich sammeln

concentration [,kɑnsən'treʃən] *s* Konzentration *f*

concentric [kən'sentrɪk] *adj* konzentrisch

concept ['kɑnsept] *s* Begriff *m*

conception [kən'sepʃən] *s* (*idea*) Vorstellung *f;* (*design*) Entwurf *m;* (biol) Empfängnis *f*

concern [kən'sʌrn] *s* (*worry*) Besorgnis *f;* (*matter*) Angelegenheit *f;* (com) Firma *f;* **that is no c. of mine** das geht mich nichts an ‖ *tr* betreffen, angehen; **as far as I am concerned** von mir aus; **c. oneself about** sich bekümmern um; **c. oneself with** sich befassen mit; **to whom it may c.** Bescheinigung

concern'ing *prep* betreffend (*acc*), betreffs (*genit*), über (*acc*)

concert [ˈkɑnsərt] *s* (mus) Konzert *n;* **in c. (with)** im Einvernehmen (mit) ‖ [kənˈsʌrt] *tr* zusammensetzen

concession [kənˈseʃən] *s* Konzession *f*

conciliate [kənˈsɪlɪˌet] *tr* versöhnen

conciliatory [kənˈsɪlɪ·əˌtori] *adj* versöhnlich

concise [kənˈsais] *adj* kurz, bündig

conclude [kənˈklud] *tr* schließen; **c. from s.th.** that aus etw schließen, daß; **to be concluded** Schluß folgt ‖ *intr* (**with**) schließen (mit)

conclusion [kənˈkluʒən] *s* Schluß *m;* **draw conclusions from** Schlüsse ziehen aus; **in c.** zum Schluß; **jump at conclusions** voreilige Schlüsse ziehen

conclusive [kənˈklusɪv] *adj* (*decisive*) entscheidend; (*proof*) schlagkräftig

concoct [kənˈkɑkt] *tr* (*brew*) zusammenbrauen; (*plans*) schmieden

concoction [kənˈkɑkʃən] *s* Gebräu *n*

concomitant [kənˈkɑmɪtənt] *adj* begleitend ‖ *s* Begleitumstand *m*

concord [ˈkɑŋkərd] *s* Eintracht *f*

concordance [kənˈkɔrdəns] *s* Übereinstimmung *f;* (*book*) Konkordanz *f*

concourse [ˈkɑŋkors] *s* (*of people*) Zusammenlaufen *n*, Anlauf *m;* (*of rivers*) Zusammenfluß *m;* (rr) Bahnhofshalle *f*

concrete [ˈkɑnkrit], [kɑnˈkrit] *adj* (*not abstract*) konkret; (*solid*) fest; (*evidence*) schlüssig; (*of concrete*) Beton–; (math) benannt ‖ *s* Beton *m* ‖ *tr* betonieren

con'crete block' *s* Betonblock *m*

con'crete noun' *s* Konkretum *n*

concubine [ˈkɑŋkjəˌbain] *s* Nebenfrau *f;* (*mistress*) Konkubine *f*

con·cur [kənˈkʌr] *v* (*pret* & *pp* **–curred;** *ger* **–curring**) *intr* (*agree*) übereinstimmen; (*coincide*) (**with**) zusammenfallen (mit); **c. in** (*an opinion*) beistimmen (*dat*)

concurrence [kənˈkʌrəns] *s* (*agreement*) Einverständis *n;* (*coincidence*) Zusammentreffen *n;* (geom) Schnittpunkt *m*

condemn [kənˈdem] *tr* verdammen; (& jur) verurteilen; (*a building*) für unbewohnlich erklären

condemnation [ˌkɑndemˈneʃən] *s* Verurteilung *f;* (*of a building, ship, plane*) Untauglichkeitserklärung *f*

condense [kənˈdens] *tr* (*make thicker*) verdichten; (*writing*) zusammendrängen; ‖ *intr* kondensieren

condenser [kənˈdensər] *s* Kondensator *m*

condescend [ˌkɑndɪˈsend] *intr* sich herablassen

condescend'ing *adj* herablassend

condescension [ˌkɑndɪˈsenʃən] *s* Herablassung *f*

condiment [ˈkɑndɪmənt] *s* Würze *f*

condition [kənˈdɪʃən] *s* (*state*) Zustand *m;* (*state of health*) Verfassung *f;* (*stipulation*) Bedingung *f;* **conditions** (*e.g. for working; of the weather*) Verhältnisse *pl;* **on c.** that unter der Bedingung, daß ‖ *tr* (*impose stipulations on*) bedingen; (*accustom*) **(to)** gewöhnen (an *acc*); (sport) in Form bringen

conditional [kənˈdɪʃənəl] *adj* bedingt

condi'tional clause' *s* Bedingungssatz *m*

conditionally [kənˈdɪʃənəli] *adv* bedingungsweise

condole [kənˈdol] *intr* (**with**) kondolieren (*dat*)

condolence [kənˈdoləns] *s* Beileid *n*

condom [ˈkɑndəm] *s* Präservativ *n*

condominium [ˌkɑndəˈmɪnɪ·əm] *s* Eigentumswohnung *f*

condone [kənˈdon] *tr* verzeihen

conducive [kənˈd(j)usɪv] *adj*—**c. to** förderlich (*dat*)

conduct [ˈkɑndʌkt] *s* (*behavior*) Betragen *n;* (*guidance*) Führung *f* ‖ [kənˈdʌkt] *tr* (*business, a campaign, a tour*) führen; (elec, phys) leiten; (mus) dirigieren; **c. oneself** sich betragen ‖ *intr* (mus) dirigieren

conductor [kənˈdʌktər] *s* (elec, phys) Leiter *m;* (mus) Dirigent *m;* (rr) Schaffner *m*

conduit [ˈkɑnd(u)ɪt] *s* Röhre *f;* (elec) Isolierrohr *n*

cone [kon] *s* (*ice cream cone; paper cone*) Tüte *f;* (bot) Zapfen *m;* (geom) Kegel *m*, Konus *m*

confection [kənˈfekʃən] *s* Konfekt *n*

confectioner [kənˈfekʃənər] *s* Zuckerbäcker –in *mf*

confec'tioner's sug'ar *s* Puderzucker *m*

confectionery [kənˈfekʃəˌneri] *s* (*shop*) Konditorei *f;* (*sweets*) Zuckerwerk *n*

confederacy [kənˈfedərəsi] *s* Bündnis *n;* (*conspiracy*) Verschwörung *f*

confederate [kənˈfedərɪt] *adj* verbündet ‖ *s* Bundesgenosse *m*, Bundesgenossin *f;* (*accomplice*) Helfershelfer –in *mf* ‖ [kənˈfedəˌret] *tr* verbünden ‖ *intr* sich verbünden

confederation [kənˌfedəˈreʃən] *s* Bund *m*

con·fer [kənˈfʌr] *v* (*pret* & *pp* **–ferred;** *ger* **–ferring**) *tr* (*on, upon*) verleihen (*dat*) ‖ *intr* sich besprechen, konferieren

conference [ˈkɑnfərəns] *s* Konferenz *f;* (sport) Verband *m*

con'ference call' *s* Sammelverbindung *f*

confess [kənˈfes] *tr* (ein)gestehen, bekennen; (*sins*) beichten ‖ *intr* gestehen

confession [kənˈfeʃən] *s* Geständnis *n*, Bekenntnis *n;* (*of sins*) Beichte *f;* **go to c.** beichten

confessional [kən'feʃənəl] *s* Beicht-stuhl *m*

confes'sion of faith' *s* Glaubensbe-kenntnis *n*

confessor [kən'fesər] *s* Beichtvater *m*

confidant [‚kɑnfi'dænt] *s* Vertraute *mf*

confide [kən'faɪd] *tr* (to) anvertrauen (*dat*) ‖ *intr*—**c. in** vertrauen (*dat*)

confidence ['kɑnfɪdəns] *s* (*trust*) (in) Vertrauen *n* (auf *acc*, zu); (*assurance*) Zuversicht *f*; **in c.** im Vertrauen

con'fidence man' *s* Bauernfänger *m*

confident ['kɑnfɪdənt] *adj* zuversicht-lich; **be c. of** sich [*dat*] sicher sein (*genit*)

confidential [‚kɑnfɪ'dɛnʃəl] *adj* ver-traulich

confine ['kɑnfaɪn] *s*—**the confines** die Grenzen *pl* ‖ *tr* [kən'faɪn] *tr* (*limit*) (to) beschränken (auf *acc*); (*shut in*) einsperren; **be confined** (*in pregnancy*) niederkommen; **be confined to bed** bettlägerig sein

confinement [kən'faɪnmənt] *s* Be-schränkung *f*; (*arrest*) Haft *f*; (*childbirth*) Niederkunft *f*

confirm [kən'fʌrm] *tr* bestätigen; (Prot) konfirmieren; (R.C.) firmen; **confirm in writing** verbriefen

confirmation [‚kɑnfər'meʃən] *s* Be-stätigung *f*; (Prot) Konfirmation *f*; (R.C.) Firmung *f*

confirmed' *adj* (*e.g., report*) bestätigt; (*inveterate*) unverbesserlich; **c. bachelor** Hagestolz *m*

confiscate ['kɑnfɪs‚ket] *tr* beschlag-nahmen, konfiszieren

confiscation [‚kɑnfɪs'keʃən] *s* Be-schlagnahme *f*

conflagration [‚kɑnflə'greʃən] *s* Brand *m*, Feuerbrunst *f*

conflict ['kɑnflɪkt] *s* (*of interests, of evidence*) Konflikt *m*; (*fight*) Zu-sammenstoß *m* ‖ [kən'flɪkt] *intr* (with) im Widerspruch stehen (zu)

conflict'ing *adj* einander widerspre-chend

con'flict of in'terest *s* Interessenkon-flikt *m*, Interessenkollision *f*

confluence ['kɑnflu‚əns] *s* Zusammen-fluß *m*

conform [kən'fɔrm] *tr* anpassen ‖ *intr* übereinstimmen; (to) sich anpassen (*dat*)

conformity [kən'fɔrmɪti] *s* (*adaptation*) (to) Anpassung *f* (an *acc*); (*agreement*) (**with**) Übereinstimmung *f* (mit)

confound [kɑn'faʊnd] *tr* (*perplex*) ver-blüffen; (*throw into confusion*) ver-wirren; (*erroneously identify*) (with) verwechseln (mit) ‖ ['kɑn'faʊnd] *tr*—**c. it!** zum Donnerwetter!

confound'ed *adj* (coll) verwünscht

confrere ['kɑnfrer] *s* Kollege *m*

confront [kən'frʌnt] *tr* (*face*) gegen-überstehen (*dat*); (a problem, an enemy) entgegentreten (*dat*); **be confronted with** gegenüberstehen (*dat*); **c. s.o. with** j-n konfrontieren mit

confrontation [‚kɑnfrən'teʃən] *s* Kon-frontation *f*; (*of witnesses*) Gegen-überstellung *f*

confuse [kən'fjuz] *tr* (*e.g., names*) verwechseln; (*persons*) verwirren

confused' *adj* konfus, verwirrt, wirr

confusion [kən'fjuʒən] *s* Verwechs-lung *f*; (*disorder, chaos*) Verwirrung *f*

confute [kən'fjut] *tr* widerlegen

congeal [kən'dʒil] *tr* erstarren lassen ‖ *intr* erstarren

congenial [kən'dʒinjəl] *adj* (*person*) sympathisch; (*surroundings*) ange-nehm

congenital [kən'dʒenɪtəl] *adj* angebo-ren

congen'ital de'fect *s* Geburtsfehler *m*

congest [kən'dʒest] *tr* überfüllen

congest'ed *adj* überfüllt; (*area*) über-völkert; (*with traffic*) verkehrsreich

congestion [kən'dʒestʃən] *s* Über-füllung *f*; (*of traffic*) Verkehrs-stockung *f*; (*of population*) Über-völkerung *f*; (*pathol*) Blutandrang *m*

congratulate [kən'grætʃə‚let] *tr* gratu-lieren (*dat*); **c. s.o. on** j-m gratulie-ren zu

congratulations [kən‚grætʃə'leʃənz] *spl* Glückwunsch *m*; **c.!** ich gratu-liere!

congregate ['kɑŋgrɪ‚get] *intr* sich (ver)sammeln, zusammenkommen

congregation [‚kɑŋgrɪ'geʃən] *s* Ver-sammlung *f*; (eccl) Gemeinde *f*

congress ['kɑŋgres] *s* Kongreß *m*

congressional [kən'greʃənəl] *adj* Kon-greß-

congress·man ['kɑŋgrɪsmən] *s* (–men) Abgeordnete *m*

con'gress·wom'an *s* (–wom'en) Ab-geordnete *f*

congruent ['kɑŋgru‚ənt] *adj* kongruent

conical ['kɑnɪkəl] *adj* kegelförmig

conjecture [kən'dʒekʃər] *s* Vermutung *f*, Mutmaßung *f* ‖ *tr* & *intr* vermuten

conjugal ['kɑndʒəgəl] *adj* ehelich

conjugate ['kɑndʒə‚get] *tr* abwandeln

conjugation [‚kɑndʒə'geʃən] *s* Ab-wandlung *f*

conjunction [kən'dʒʌŋkʃən] *s* Binde-wort *n*; **in c. with** in Verbindung mit

conjure [kən'dʒur] *tr* (*appeal solemnly to*) beschwören ‖ ['kɑndʒər] *tr*—**c. away** wegzaubern; **c. up** herauf-beschwören

conk [kɑŋk] *tr* (sl) hauen ‖ *intr*—**c. out** (sl) versagen

connect [kə'nekt] *tr* verbinden; (& fig) verknüpfen; (elec) (to) anschlie-ßen (an *acc*); (telp) (with) verbinden (mit) ‖ *intr* verbunden sein; (*said of trains, etc.*) (with) Anschluß haben (an *acc*); (box) treffen

connect'ing *adj* Verbindungs-, Binde-; (*trains, buses*) Anschluß-; (*rooms*) mit Zwischentür

connect'ing rod' *s* Schubstange *f*

connection [kə'nekʃən] *s* (*e.g., of a pipe*) Verbindung *f*; (*of ideas*) Ver-knüpfung *f*; (*context*) Zusammen-hang *m*; (*part that connects*) Ver-bindungsteil *m*; (*elec*) Schaltung *f*;

(mach, rr, telp) Verbindung *f*; **con-nections** Beziehungen *pl*; **in c. with** in Zusammenhang mit

con'ning tow'er ['kɑnɪŋ] *s* Kommandoturm *m*

connive [kə'naɪv] *intr*—**c. at** ein Auge zudrücken bei; **c. with** im geheimen Einverständnis stehen mit

connotation [‚kɑno'teʃən] *s* Nebenbedeutung *f*

connote [kə'not] *tr* mitbezeichnen

conquer ['kɑŋkər] *tr* (*win in war*) erobern; (*overcome*) überwinden

conquerer ['kɑŋkərər] *s* Eroberer *m*

conquest ['kɑŋkwest] *s* Eroberung *f*

conscience ['kɑnʃəns] *s* Gewissen *n*

conscientious [‚kɑnʃɪ'enʃəs] *adj* gewissenhaft, pflichtbewußt

conscien'tious objec'tor [əb'dʒektər] *s* Wehrdienstverweigerer *m*

conscious ['kɑnʃəs] *adj* bei Bewußtsein; **c. of** bewußt (*genit*)

consciousness ['kɑnʃəsnɪs] *s* Bewußtsein *n*; (*awareness*) (**of**) Kenntnis *f* (*genit* or von); **regain c.** wieder zu sich kommen

conscript ['kɑnskrɪpt] *s* Dienstpflichtige *m*; (*mil*) Wehrdienstpflichtige *m* || [kən'skrɪpt] *tr* ausheben

conscription [kən'skrɪpʃən] *s* Dienstpflicht *f*; (*draft*) Aushebung *f*

consecrate ['kɑnsɪ‚kret] *tr* weihen

consecration [‚kɑnsɪ'kreʃən] *s* Einweihung *f*; (*at Mass*) Wandlung *f*

consecutive [kən'sekjətɪv] *adj* aufeinanderfolgend

consensus [kən'sensəs] *s* allgemeine Übereinstimmung *f*; **the c. of opinion** die übereinstimmende Meinung

consent [kən'sent] *s* Zustimmung *f*; **by common c.** mit allgemeiner Zustimmung || *intr* zustimmen; **c. to** (*inf*) sich bereit erklären zu (*inf*)

consequence ['kɑnsɪ‚kwens] *s* Folge *f*; (*influence*) Einfluß *m*; **in c. of** infolge (*genit*); **it is of no c.** es hat nichts auf sich; **suffer the consequences** die Folgen tragen

consequently ['kɑnsɪ‚kwentli] *adv* folglich, infolgedessen, mithin

conservation [‚kɑnsər'veʃən] *s* Bewahrung *f*; (*of energy, etc.*) Erhaltung *f*; (*supervision of natural resources*) Naturschutz *m*; (*ecology*) Umweltschutz *m*

conservatism [kən'sɑrvə‚tɪzəm] *s* Konservatismus *m*

conservative [kən'sɑrvətɪv] *adj* konservativ; (*estimate*) vorsichtig || *s* Konservative *mf*

conservatory [kən'sɑrvə‚tori] *s* Treibhaus *n*; (*mus*) Konservatorium *n*

conserve [kən'sɑrv] *tr* sparsam umgehen mit

consider [kən'sɪdər] *tr* (*take into account*) berücksichtigen; (*show consideration for*) Rücksicht nehmen auf (*acc*); (*reflect on*) sich [*dat*] überlegen; (*regard as*) halten für, betrachten als; **all things considered** alles in allem

considerable [kən'sɪdərəbəl] *adj* beträchtlich, erheblich

considerate [kən'sɪdərɪt] *adj* (**towards**) rücksichtsvoll (gegen)

consideration [kən‚sɪdə're ʃən] *s* (*taking into account*) Berücksichtigung *f*; (*regard*) (**for**) Rücksicht *f* (auf *acc*); **be an important c.** e-e wichtige Rolle spielen; **be under c.** in Betracht gezogen werden; **for a c.** entgeltlich; **in c. of** in Anbetracht (*genit*); **take into c.** in Betracht ziehen; **with c.** rücksichtsvoll

consid'ering *adv* (coll) den Umständen nach || *prep* in Anbetracht (*genit*)

consign [kən'saɪn] *tr* (*ship*) versenden; (*address*) adressieren

consignee [‚kɑnsaɪ'ni] *s* Adressat –in *mf*

consignment [kən'saɪnmənt] *s* (*act of sending*) Versand *m*; (*merchandise sent*) Sendung *f*; **on c.** in Kommission

consist [kən'sɪst] *intr*—**c. in** bestehen in (*dat*); **c. of** bestehen aus

consistency [kən'sɪstənsi] *s* Konsequenz *f*; (*firmness*) Festigkeit *f*; (*viscosity*) Dickflüssigkeit *f*; (*agreement*) Übereinstimmung *f*; (*steadfastness*) (**in**) Beständigkeit *f* (in *dat*)

consistent [kən'sɪstənt] *adj* (*performer*) stetig; (*performance*) gleichmäßig; (*free from contradiction*) konsequent; **c. with** in Übereinstimmung mit

consistory [kən'sɪstəri] *s* Konsistorium *n*

consolation [‚kɑnsə'leʃən] *s* Trost *m*

console ['kɑnsol] *s* (*for radio or record player*) Musiktruhe *f*; (*of an organ*) Spieltisch *m*; (*television*) Fernsehtruhe *f* || [kən'sol] *tr* trösten

consolidate [kən'sɑlɪ‚det] *tr* (*a position*) festigen; (*debts*) konsolidieren; (*combine*) zusammenlegen

consonant ['kɑnsənənt] *adj* (**with**) im Einklang (mit) || *s* Mitlaut *m*

consort ['kɑnsort] *s* (*male*) Gemahl *m*; (*female*) Gemahlin *f* || [kən'sort] *intr* (**with**) Umgang haben (mit)

consortium [kən'sortɪ‚əm] *s* (-a [ə]) Konsortium *n*

conspicuous [kən'spɪkjuˌəs] *adj* auffallend, auffällig; **c. for** bemerkenswert wegen

conspiracy [kən'spɪrəsi] *s* Verschwörung *f*

conspirator [kən'spɪrətər] *s* Verschwörer –in *mf*

conspire [kən'spaɪr] *intr* sich verschwören

constable ['kɑnstəbəl] *s* Gendarm *m*

constancy ['kɑnstənsi] *s* Beständigkeit *f*

constant ['kɑnstənt] *adj* (*continuous*) dauernd, ständig; (*faithful*) treu; (*resolute*) standhaft; (*element, time element*) fest; (fig & tech) konstant || *s* (math, phys) Konstante *f*

constantly ['kɑnstəntli] *adv* immerfort

constellation [‚kɑnstə'leʃən] *s* Sternbild *n*

consternation [‚kɑnstər'neʃən] *s* Bestürzung *f*

constipate ['kɒnstɪ,peɪt] *tr* verstopfen
constipation [,kɒnstɪ'peɪʃən] *s* Verstopfung *f*
constituency [kən'stɪtʃʊ-ənsi] *s* Wählerschaft *f*
constituent [kən'stɪtʃʊ-ənt] *adj* wesentlich; **c. part** Bestandteil *m* ‖ *s* Komponente *f*; (pol) Wähler –in *mf*
constitute ['kɒnstɪ,t(j)uːt] *tr* (make up) ausmachen, bilden; (found) gründen
constitution [,kɒnstɪ't(j)uːʃən] *s* (of a country or organization) Verfassung *f*; (bodily condition) Konstitution *f*; (composition) Zusammensetzung *f*
constitutional [,kɒnstɪ't(j)uːʃənəl] *adj* (according to a constitution) konstitutionell; (crisis, amendment, etc.) Verfassungs-
constrain [kən'streɪn] *tr* zwingen
constraint [kən'streɪnt] *s* Zwang *m*; (jur) Nötigung *f*
constrict [kən'strɪkt] *tr* zusammenziehen
construct [kən'strʌkt] *tr* errichten; (eng, geom, gram) konstruieren
construction [kən'strʌkʃən] *s* (act of building) Errichtung *f*; (manner of building) Bauweise *f*; (interpretation) Auslegung *f*; (eng, geom, gram) Konstruktion *f*; **under c.** im Bau
constructive [kən'strʌktɪv] *adj* konstruktiv
construe [kən'struː] *tr* (interpret) auslegen; (gram) konstruieren
consul ['kɒnsəl] *s* Konsul *m*
consular ['kɒns(j)ələr] *adj* konsularisch
consulate ['kɒns(j)əlɪt] *s* Konsulat *n*
con'sul gen'eral *s* Generalkonsul *m*
consult [kən'sʌlt] *tr* konsultieren, um Rat fragen; (a book) nachschlagen ‖ *intr*—**c. with** sich beraten mit
consultant [kən'sʌltənt] *s* Berater –in *mf*
consultation [,kɒnsəl'teɪʃən] *s* Beratung *f*; (& med) Konsultation *f*
consume [kən's(j)uːm] *tr* verzehren; (use up) verbrauchen; (time) beanspruchen
consumer [kən's(j)uːmər] *s* Konsument –in *mf*, Verbraucher –in *mf*
consum'er goods' *spl* Konsumgüter *pl*
consummate [kən'sʌmɪt] *adj* vollendet; (pej) abgefeimt ‖ ['kɒnsə,meɪt] *tr* vollziehen
consumption [kən'sʌmpʃən] *s* (of food) Verzehr *m*; (econ) (of) Verbrauch *m* (an *dat*); (pathol) Schwindsucht *f*
consumptive [kə'sʌmptɪv] *adj* schwindsüchtig ‖ *s* Schwindsüchtige *mf*
contact ['kɒntækt] *s* Kontakt *m*, Berührung *f*; (fig) (with) Verbindung *f* (mit); (elec) Kontakt *m* ‖ *tr* (coll) sich in Verbindung setzen mit
con'tact lens' *s* Haftschale *f*
contagion [kən'teɪdʒən] *s* Ansteckung *f*
contagious [kən'teɪdʒəs] *adj* ansteckend
contain [kən'teɪn] *tr* enthalten; (an

enemy) aufhalten; (one's feelings) verhalten; **c. oneself** sich beherrschen
container [kən'teɪnər] *s* Behälter *m*
containment [kən'teɪnmənt] *s* (mil, pol) Eindämmung *f*
contaminate [kən'tæmɪ,neɪt] *tr* verunreinigen; (fig) vergiften
contamination [kən,tæmɪ'neɪʃən] *s* Verunreinigung *f*; (fig) Vergiftung *f*
contemplate ['kɒntəm,pleɪt] *tr* betrachten; (intend) beabsichtigen ‖ *intr* nachdenken
contemplation [,kɒntəm'pleɪʃən] *s* Betrachtung *f*; (consideration) Erwägung *f*
contemporaneous [kən,tempə'reɪnɪ-əs] *adj* (with) gleichzeitig (mit)
contemporary [kən'tempə,reri] *adj* zeitgenössisch; (modern) modern ‖ *s* Zeitgenosse *m*, Zeitgenossin *f*
contempt [kən'tempt] *s* Verachtung *f*; **beneath c.** unter aller Kritik
contemptible [kən'temptɪbəl] *adj* verachtungswürdig
contempt' of court' *s* Mißachtung *f* des Gerichtes
contemptuous [kən'temptʃʊ-əs] *adj* verachtungsvoll, verächtlich
contend [kən'tend] *tr* behaupten ‖ *intr* (for) sich bewerben (um); (with) kämpfen (mit)
contender [kən'tendər] *s* (for) Bewerber –in *mf* (um)
content [kən'tent] *adj* (with) zufrieden (mit); **c. to** (inf) bereit zu (inf) ‖ *s* Zufriedenheit *f*; **to one's heart's c.** nach Herzenslust ‖ ['kɒntənt] *s* Inhalt *m*; (chem) Gehalt *m*; **contents** Inhalt *m* ‖ [kən'tent] *tr* zufriedenstellen; **c. oneself with** sich begnügen mit
content'ed *adj* zufrieden
contention [kən'tenʃən] *s* (strife) Streit *m*; (assertion) Behauptung *f*
contest ['kɒntest] *s* (for) Wettkampf *m* (um); (written competition) Preisausschreiben *n* ‖ [kən'test] *tr* (argue against) bestreiten; (a will) anfechten; (mil) kämpfen um; **contested** umstritten
contestant [kən'testənt] *s* Bewerber –in *mf*; (sport) Wettkämpfer –in *mf*
context ['kɒntekst] *s* Zusammenhang *m*
contiguous [kən'tɪgjʊ-əs] *adj* einander berührend; (to) angrenzend (an *acc*)
continence ['kɒntɪnəns] *s* Enthaltsamkeit *f*
continent ['kɒntɪnənt] *adj* enthaltsam ‖ *s* Kontinent *m*
continental [,kɒntɪ'nentəl] *adj* kontinental, Kontinental-
contingency [kən'tɪndʒənsi] *s* Zufall *m*
contingent [kən'tɪndʒənt] *adj* (upon) abhängig (von) ‖ *s* (mil) Kontingent *n*
continual [kən'tɪnjʊ-əl] *adj* immer wiederkehrend
continuation [kən,tɪnjʊ'eɪʃən] *s* Fortsetzung *f*; (continued existence) Fortdauer *f*
continue [kən'tɪnjuː] *tr* fortsetzen; **c.**

to (*inf*) fortfahren zu (*inf*); weiter–, e.g., **c. to read** weiterlesen; **to be continued** Fortsetzung folgt || *intr* fortfahren; (*said of things*) anhalten

continuity [‚kɑntɪ'n(j)u·ɪti] *s* Stetigkeit *f*

continuous [kən'tɪnju·əs] *adj* ununterbrochen, anhaltend

contortion [kən'tɔrʃən] *s* Verzerrung *f*

contour ['kɑntur] *s* Kontur *f*

con'tour line' *s* Schichtlinie *f*

con'tour map' *s* Landkarte *f* mit Schichtlinien

contraband [‚kɑntrə'bænd] *adj* Schmuggel– || *s* Konterbande *f*, Schmuggelware *f*

contraceptive [‚kɑntrə'sɛptɪv] *adj* empfängnisverhütend || *s* Empfängnisverhütungsmittel *n*

contract ['kɑntrækt] *s* Vertrag *m*, Kontrakt *m*; (*order*) Auftrag *m* || [kən'trækt] *tr* (*marriage*) (ab)schließen; (*a disease*) sich [*dat*] zuziehen; (*e.g., a muscle*) zusammenziehen; (*debts*) geraten in (*acc*); (ling) kontrahieren || *intr* (*shrink*) sich zusammenziehen; **c. to** (*inf*) sich vertraglich verpflichten zu (*inf*)

contract'ing *adj* vertragsschließend

contraction [kən'trækʃən] *s* (& ling) Zusammenziehung *f*, Kontraktion *f*; (*contracted word*) Verkürzung *f*

contractor ['kɑntræktər] *s* (*supplier*) Lieferant *m*; (*builder*) Bauunternehmer *m*

contradict [‚kɑntrə'dɪkt] *tr* widersprechen (*dat*)

contradiction [‚kɑntrə'dɪkʃən] *s* Widerspruch *m*

contradictory [‚kɑntrə'dɪktəri] *adj* widerspruchsvoll

contrail ['kɑn‚trel] *s* Kondensstreifen *m*

contral·to [kən'trælto] *s* (–tos) (*person*) Altistin *f*; (*voice*) Alt *m*

contraption [kən'træpʃən] *s* (coll) Vorrichtung *f*; (*car*) (coll) Kiste *f*

contrary ['kɑntrɛri] *adj* konträr, gegensätzlich; (*person*) querköpfig; **c. to** entgegen (*dat*); **c. to nature** naturwidrig || *s* Gegenteil *n*; **on the c.** im Gegenteil

contrast ['kɑntræst] *s* Gegensatz *m* || [kən'træst] *tr* (**with**) gegenüberstellen (*dat*) || *intr* (**with**) im Gegensatz stehen (zu)

contravene [‚kɑntrə'vin] *tr* zuwiderhandeln (*dat*)

contribute [kən'trɪbjut] *tr* beitragen, spenden || *intr*—**c. to** beitragen zu; (*with help*) mitwirken an (*dat*)

contribution [‚kɑntrɪ'bjuʃən] *s* Beitrag *m*; (*of money*) Spende *f*

contributor [kən'trɪbjutər] *s* Spender –in *mf*; (*to a periodical*) Mitarbeiter –in *mf*

contrite [kən'traɪt] *adj* reuig

contrition [kən'trɪʃən] *s* Reue *f*

contrivance [kən'traɪvəns] *s* (*device*) Vorrichtung *f*; (*expedient*) Kunstgriff *m*; (*act of contriving*) Aushecken *n*

contrive [kən'traɪv] *tr* (*invent*) erfinden; (*devise*) ersinnen; **c. to** (*inf*) es fertig bringen zu (*inf*) || *intr* Anschläge ausbecken

con·trol [kən'trol] *s* Kontrolle *f*, Gewalt *f*; (*mach*) Steuerung *f*; (*mach*) (*devise*) Regler *m*; **be out of c.** nicht zu halten sein; **be under c.** in bester Ordnung sein; **controls** (aer) Steuerwerk *n*; **gain c. over** die Herrschaft gewinnen über (*acc*); **have c. over s.o.** über j–n Gewalt haben; **keep under c.** im Zaume halten || *v* (*pret* & *pp* –trolled; *ger* –trolling) *tr* (*dominate*) beherrschen; (*verify*) kontrollieren; (*contain*) eindämmen, (*steer*) steuern; (*regulate*) regeln; **c. oneself** sich beherrschen

control' pan'el *s* Schaltbrett *n*

control' room' *s* Kommandoraum *m*; (rad) Regieraum *m*

control' stick' *s* (aer) Steuerknüppel *m*

control' tow'er *s* (*at an airport*) Kontrollturm *m*; (*on an aircraft carrier*) Kommandoturm *m*

controversial [‚kɑntrə'vɑrʃəl] *adj* umstritten, strittig; **c. subject** Streitfrage *f*

controversy ['kɑntrə‚vɑrsi] *s* Kontroverse *f*, Auseinandersetzung *f*

controvert [‚kɑntrə'vɑrt] *tr* (*argue against*) bestreiten; (*argue about*) streiten über (*acc*)

contusion [kən't(j)uʒən] *s* Quetschung *f*

convalesce [‚kɑnvə'lɛs] *intr* genesen

convalescence [‚kɑnvə'lɛsəns] *s* Genesung *f*

convalescent [‚kɑnvə'lɛsənt] *s* Genesende *mf*

convales'cent home' *s* Genesungsheim *n*

convene [kən'vin] *tr* versammeln || *intr* sich versammeln

convenience [kən'vinjəns] *s* Bequemlichkeit *f*; **at one's c.** nach Belieben; **at your earliest c.** möglichst bald; **modern conveniences** moderner Komfort *m*

convenient [kən'vinjənt] *adj* gelegen

convent ['kɑnvənt] *s* Nonnenkloster *n*

convention [kən'vɛnʃən] *s* (*professional meeting*) Tagung *f*; (*political meeting*) Konvent *m*; (*accepted usage*) Konvention *f*

conventional [kən'vɛnʃənəl] *adj* konventionell, herkömmlich

converge [kən'vɑrdʒ] *intr* zusammenlaufen; **c. on** sich stürzen auf (*acc*)

conversation [‚kɑnvər'seʃən] *s* Gespräch *n*

conversational [‚kɑnvər'seʃənəl] *adj* Gesprächs–

converse ['kɑnvɑrs] *adj* gegenteilig || *s* (of) Gegenteil *n* (von) || [kən'vɑrs] *intr* sich unterhalten

conversion [kən'vɑrʒən] *s* (*into*) Umwandlung *f* (in *acc*); (*of a factory*) (**to**) Umstellung *f* (auf *acc*); (*of a building*) (**into**) Umbau *m* (zu); (*of currency*) (**into**) Umwechslung *f* (in *acc*); (elec) (**to**) Umformung *f* (in *acc*); (math) Umrechnung *f*; (phys) Umsetzung *f*; (relig) Bekehrung *f*

convert ['kɑnvʌrt] s (to) Bekehrte mf (zu) ‖ [kən'vʌrt] tr (into) umwandeln (in acc); (a factory) (to) umstellen (auf acc); (a building) (into) umbauen (zu); (currency) (into) umwechseln (in acc); (biochem) (into) umsetzen (in acc); (chem) (into) umwandeln (in acc), verwandeln (in acc); (elec) (to) umformen (in acc); (math) (to) umrechnen (in acc); (phys) (to) umsetzen (in acc); (relig) (to) bekehren (zu) ‖ intr to sich bekehren (zu)

converter [kən'vʌrtər] s (elec) Umformer m, Stromrichter m

convertible ['kɑnvrkt] adj umwandelbar; (fin) konvertierbar ‖ s (aut) Kabriolett n

convex ['kɑnveks], [kɑn'veks] adj konvex

convey [kən've] tr (transport) befördern; (greetings, message) übermitteln; (sound) fortpflanzen; (meaning) ausdrücken; (a property) abtreten

conveyance [kən've·əns] s (act) Beförderung f; (means) Transportmittel n; (jur) Abtretung f

conveyor [kən've·ər] s Beförderer –in mf

convey'or belt' s Förderband n

convict ['kɑnvrkt] s Sträfling m ‖ [kən'vrkt] tr (of) überführen (genit)

conviction [kən'vrkʃən] s (of a crime) Verurteilung f; (certainty) Überzeugung f; convictions Gesinnung f

convince [kən'vrns] tr (of) überzeugen (von)

convivial [kən'vrvi·əl] adj gesellig

convocation [,kɑnvə'keʃən] s Zusammenberufung f; (educ) Eröffnungsfeier f

convoke [kən'vok] tr zusammenberufen

convoy ['kɑnvɔr] s (of vehicles) Kolonne f, Konvoi m; (nav) Geleitzug m

convulse [kən'vʌls] tr erschüttern

convulsion [kən'vʌlʃən] s Krampf m; go into convulsions Krämpfe bekommen

coo [ku] intr girren

cook [kʊk] s Koch m, Köchin f ‖ tr braten, backen; (boil) kochen; c. up (fig) zusammenbrauen ‖ intr braten, backen; (boil) kochen

cook'book' s Kochbuch n

cookie ['kʊki] s Plätzchen n, Keks m & n; cookies pl Gebäck n

cook'ing s Kochen n; do one's own c. sich selbst beköstigen

cool [kul] adj (& fig) kühl; keep c.! ruhig Blut!; keep one's c. (coll) ruhig Blut bewahren ‖ s Kühle f ‖ tr kühlen; c. down (fig) beruhigen; c. off abkühlen ‖ intr (& fig) sich abkühlen

cooler ['kulər] s Kühler m; (sl) Kittchen n

cool'-head'ed adj besonnen

coolie ['kuli] s Kuli m

coolness ['kulnɪs] s (& fig) Kühle f

coon [kun] s (zool) Waschbär m

coop [kup] s (building) Hühnerstall m; (enclosure) Hühnerhof m; (jail) (sl) Kittchen n; fly the c. (sl) auskneifen ‖ tr—c. up einsperren

co-op ['ko·ɑp] s Konsumverein m

cooper ['kupər] s Küfer m, Böttcher m

cooperate [ko'ɑpə,ret] intr (in) mitwirken (an dat, bei); (with) mitarbeiten (mit)

cooperation [ko,ɑpə're(ə)n] s Mitwirkung f, Mitarbeit f

cooperative [ko'ɑpə,retɪv] adj hilfsbereit

coordinate [ko'ɔrdɪnɪt] adj gleichrangig; (gram) beigeordnet ‖ s (math) Koordinate f ‖ [ko'ɔrdɪ,net] tr koordinieren

coordination [ko,ɔrdɪ'neʃən] s Koordination f; (gram) Beiordnung f

cootie ['kuti] s (sl) Laus f

co-owner ['ko,onər] s Miteigentümer –in mf

cop [kɑp] s (sl) Bulle m ‖ v (pret & pp copped; ger copped) tr (catch) (sl) erwischen; (steal) (sl) klauen ‖ intr—cop out (coll) auskneifen

copartner [ko'pɑrtnər] s Mitinhaber –in mf

cope [kop] intr—c. with sich messen mit, aufkommen gegen

cope'stone' s Schlußstein m

copier ['kɑpɪ·ər] s Kopiermaschine f

copilot ['ko,pɑɪlət] s Kopilot m

coping ['kopɪŋ] s Mauerkappe f

copious ['kopɪ·əs] adj reichlich

cop'-out' s (act) Kneifen n; (person) Drückeberger m

copper ['kɑpər] adj kupfern, Kupfer-; (color) kupferrot ‖ s Kupfer n; (coin) Kupfermünze f; (sl) Schupo m

cop'persmith' s Kupferschmied m

copter ['kɑptər] s (coll) Hubschrauber m

copulate ['kɑpjə,let] intr sich paaren

cop·y ['kɑpi] s Kopie f; (of a book) Exemplar n; (typ) druckfertiges Manuskript n ‖ v (pret & pp -ied) tr kopieren; (in school) abschreiben

cop'ybook' s Schreibheft n, Heft n

cop'ycat' s (imitator) Nachäffer –in mf

cop'yright' s Urheberrecht n, Verlagsrecht n ‖ tr urheberrechtlich schützen, verlagsrechtlich schützen

cop'ywrit'er s Texter –in mf

coquette [ko'ket] s Kokette f

coquettish [ko'ketɪʃ] adj kokett

coral ['kɑrəl] adj Korallen– ‖ s Koralle f

cor'al reef' s Korallenriff n

cord [kɔrd] s Schnur f, Strick m; (of wood) Klafter n; (elec) Leitungsschnur f

cordial ['kɔrdʒəl] adj herzlich ‖ s Likör m; (med) Herzstärkung f

cordiality [kɔr'dʒælɪti] s Herzlichkeit f

cordon ['kɔrdən] s Kordon m, Absperrkette f ‖ tr—c. off absperren m

corduroy ['kɔrdə,rɔr] s Kordsamt m; corduroys Kordsamthose f

core [kor] s (of fruit) Kern m; (of a

cable) Seele *f*; (fig) Kern *m*, Mark *n*; (elec) Spulenkern *m*

cork [kɔrk] *s* Kork *m*; (*stopper*) Pfropfen *m*, Korken *m* ‖ *tr* verkorken

corker ['kɔrkər] *s* (sl) Schlager *m*

cork'ing *adj* (sl) fabelhaft

cork'oak', **cork' tree'** *s* Korkeiche *f*

cork'screw' *s* Korkenzieher *m*

corn [kɔrn] *s* (*Indian corn*) Mais *m*; (*on a foot*) Hühnerauge *n*; (*joke*) (sl) Kalauer *m*

corn'bread' *s* Maisbrot *n*

corn'cob' *s* Maiskolben *m*

corn'cob pipe' *s* Maiskolbenpfeife *f*

corn'crib' *s* Maisspeicher *m*

cornea ['kɔrnɪ·ə] *s* Hornhaut *f*

corned' beef' ['kɔrnd] *s* Pökelfleisch *n*

corner ['kɔrnər] *adj* Eck– ‖ *s* Ecke *f*; (*secluded spot*) Winkel *m*; (*curve*) Kurve *f*; **c. of the eye** Augenwinkel *m*; **from all corners of the world** von allen Ecken und Enden; **turn the c.** um die Ecke biegen ‖ *tr* (*a person*) in die Zange nehmen; (*the market*) aufkaufen

cor'nerstone' *s* Eckstein *m*; (*of a new building*) Grundstein *m*

cornet [kɔr'nɛt] *s* (mus) Kornett *n*

corn' exchange' *s* Getreidebörse *f*

corn'field' *s* Maisfeld *n*; (*grain field*) (Brit) Kornfeld *n*

corn'flakes' *spl* Maisflocken *pl*

corn' flour' *s* Maismehl *n*

corn'flow'er *s* Kornblume *f*

corn'frit'ter *s* Maispfannkuchen *m*

corn'husk' *s* Maishülse *f*

cornice ['kɔrnɪs] *s* Gesims *n*

corn' liq'uor *s* Maisschnaps *m*

corn' meal' *s* Maismehl *n*

corn' on the cob' *s* Mais *m* am Kolben

corn' silk' *s* Maisfasern *pl*

corn'stalk' *s* Maisstengel *m*

corn'starch' *s* Maisstärke *f*

cornucopia [ˌkɔrnə'kopɪ·ə] *s* Füllhorn *n*

corny ['kɔrni] *adj* (*sentimental*) rührselig; (*joke*) blöd

corollary ['kɔrəˌlɛri] *s* (to) Folge *f* (von)

coron·a [kə'ronə] *s* (–nas & –nae [ni]) (astr) Hof *m*, Korona *f*; (archit) Kranzleiste *f*

coronary ['kɔrəˌnɛri] *adj* koronar

coronation [ˌkɔrə'neʃən] *s* Krönung *f*

coroner ['kɔrənər] *s* Gerichtsmediziner *m*

cor'oner's in'quest *s* Totenschau *f*

coronet ['kɔrəˌnɛt] *s* Krönchen *n*; (*worn by the nobility*) Adelskrone *f*; (*worn by women*) Diadem *n*

corporal ['kɔrpərəl] *adj* körperlich ‖ *s* (mil) Obergefreite *m*

corporate ['kɔrpərɪt] *adj* korporativ

corporation [ˌkɔrpə'reʃən] *s* (fin) Aktiengesellschaft *f*; (jur) Körperschaft *f*

corpora'tion law'yer *s* Syndikus *m*

corporeal [kɔr'porɪ·əl] *adj* körperlich

corps [kɔr] *s* (*corps* [kɔrz]) Korps *n*

corpse [kɔrps] *s* Leiche *f*, Leichnam *m*

corps'man *s* (–men) Sanitäter *m*

corpulent ['kɔrpjələnt] *adj* beleibt

corpuscle ['kɔrpəsəl] *s* Blutkörperchen *n*

cor·ral [kə'ræl] *s* Pferch *m* ‖ *v* (*pret & pp* –ralled; *ger* –ralling) *tr* zusammenpferchen

correct [kə'rɛkt] *adj* richtig; (*manners*) korrekt; (*time*) genau; **be c.** (*said of a thing*) stimmen; (*said of a person*) recht haben ‖ *tr* korrigieren; (*examination papers*) verbessern; (*beat*) züchtigen; (*scold*) zurechtweisen; (*an unjust situation*) ausgleichen

correction [kə'rɛkʃən] *s* Berichtigung *f*; (*of examination papers*) Verbesserung *f*, Korrektur *f*; (*punishment*) Bestrafung *f*

corrective [kə'rɛktɪv] *adj* (*measures*) Gegen–; (*lenses, shoes*) Ausgleichs–

correctness [kə'rɛktnɪs] *s* Richtigkeit *f*; (*in manners*) Korrektheit *f*

correlate ['kɔrəˌlɛt] *tr* in Wechselbeziehung bringen ‖ *intr* in Wechselbeziehung stehen

correlation [ˌkɔrə'leʃən] *s* Wechselbeziehung *f*, Korrelation *f*

correlative [kə'rɛlətɪv] *adj* korrelativ ‖ *s* Korrelat *n*

correspond [ˌkɔri'spand] *intr* einander übereinstimmen; (**to, with**) entsprechen (dat); (*exchange letters*) (**with**) im Briefwechsel stehen (mit)

correspondence [ˌkɔri'spandəns] *s* (*act of corresponding*) Übereinstimmung *f*; (*instance of correspondence*) Entsprechung *f*; (*exchange of letters; letters*) Korrespondenz *f*

correspon'dence course' *s* Fernkursus *m*

correspondent [ˌkɔri'spandənt] *s* Briefpartner –in *mf*; (journ) Korrespondent –in *mf*

correspond'ing *adj* entsprechend

corridor ['kɔrɪdər] *s* Korridor *m*

corroborate [kə'rabəˌrɛt] *tr* bestätigen

corrode [kə'rod] *tr* & *intr* korrodieren

corrosion [kə'roʒən] *s* Korrosion *f*

corrosive [kə'rosɪv] *adj* ätzend; (*influence*) schädigend ‖ *s* Ätzmittel *n*

cor'rugated card'board ['kɔrəˌgetɪd] *s* Wellpappe *f*

cor'rugated i'ron *s* Wellblech *n*

corrupt [kə'rʌpt] *adj* (*text*) verderbt; (*morally*) verdorben; (*open to bribes*) bestechlich ‖ *tr* verderben; (*bribe*) bestechen

corruption [kə'rʌpʃən] *s* Verderbtheit *f*; (*bribery*) Korruption *f*

corsage [kɔr'saʒ] *s* Blumensträußchen *n* zum Anstecken

corsair ['kɔrsɛr] *s* Korsar *m*

corset ['kɔrsɪt] *s* Korsett *n*

Corsica ['kɔrsɪkə] *s* Korsika *n*

Corsican ['kɔrsɪkən] *adj* korsisch

cortege [kɔr'tɛʒ] *s* Gefolge *n*; (*at a funeral*) Leichenzug *m*

cor·tex ['kɔrˌtɛks] *s* (–tices [tɪˌsiz]) Rinde *f*, Kortex *m*

cortisone ['kɔrtɪˌson] *s* Cortison *n*

corvette [kɔr'vɛt] *s* (naut) Korvette *f*

cosmetic [kaz'mɛtɪk] *adj* kosmetisch ‖ *s* Kosmetikum *n*; **cosmetics** Kosmetikartikel *pl*

cosmic ['kɑzmɪk] *adj* kosmisch
cosmonaut ['kɑzmə,nɔt] *s* Kosmonaut
–in *mf*
cosmopolitan [,kɑzə'pɑlɪtən] *adj* kosmopolitisch ‖ *s* Kosmopolit –in *mf*
cosmos ['kɑzməs] *s* Kosmos *m*
cost [kɔst] *s* Preis *m*; **at all costs** (fig) um jeden Preis; **at c.** zum Selbstkostenpreis; **at the c. of** auf Kosten (*genit*); **costs** Kosten *pl*; (jur) Gerichtskosten *pl* ‖ *v* (*pret & pp* **cost**) *intr* kosten
cost′ account′ing *s* Kostenrechnung *f*
costly ['kɔstlɪ] *adj* kostspielig; (*of great value*) kostbar
cost′ of liv′ing *s* Lebenshaltungskosten *pl*
costume ['kɑst(j)um] *s* Kostüm *n*; (*national dress*) Tracht *f*
cos′tume ball′ *s* Kostümball *m*
cos′tume jew′elry *s* Modeschmuck *m*
cot [kɑt] *s* Feldbett *n*
coterie ['kotərɪ] *s* Klüngel *m*, Koterie *f*
cottage ['kɑtɪdʒ] *s* Hütte *f*; (*country house*) Landhaus *n*
cot′tage cheese′ *s* Quark *m*, Quarkkäse *m*
cot′ter pin′ ['kɑtər] *s* Schließbolzen *m*
cotton ['kɑtən] *s* (*fiber, yarn*) Baumwolle *f*; (*unspun cotton*) Watte *f*; (*sterilized cotton*) Verbandswatte *f*
cot′ton field′ *s* Baumwollfeld *n*
cot′ton gin′ *s* Entkörnungsmaschine *f*
cot′ton mill′ *s* Baumwollspinnerei *f*
cot′ton pick′er ['pɪkər] *s* Baumwollpflücker –in *mf*; (*machine*) Baumwollpflückmaschine *f*
cot′tonseed oil′ *s* Baumwollsamenöl *n*
cot′ton waste′ *s* Putzwolle *f*
couch [kautʃ] *s* Couch *f*, Liege *f* ‖ *tr* (*words*) fassen; (*thoughts*) ausdrücken
cougar ['kugər] *s* Puma *m*
cough [kɔf] *s* Husten *m* ‖ *tr*—**c. up** aushusten; (*money*) (sl) blechen ‖ *intr* husten; (*in order to attract attention*) sich räuspern
cough′ drop′ *s* Hustenbonbon *m & n*
cough′ syr′up *s* Hustentropfen *pl*
could [kud] *aux*—**he c.** (*was able*) er konnte; **if he c.** (*were able*) wenn er könnte
council ['kaunsəl] *s* Rat *m*; (eccl) Konzil *n*
coun′cil·man *s* (–men) Stadtratsmitglied *n*
councilor ['kaunsələr] *s* Rat *m*
coun·sel ['kaunsəl] *s* Rat *m*; (*for the defense*) Verteidiger –in *mf*; (*for the prosecution*) Anklagevertreter –in *mf* ‖ *v* (*pret & pp* –sel[l]ed; *ger* –sel[l]ing) *tr* raten (*dat*) ‖ *intr* Rat geben
counselor ['kaunsələr] *s* Berater –in *mf*
count [kaunt] *s* Zahl *f*; (*nobleman*) Graf *m*; (jur) Anklagepunkt *m*; **lose c.** sich verzählen ‖ *tr* zählen; (*the costs*) berechnen; **c. in** einschließen; **c. off** abzählen; **c. out** (money, a boxer) auszählen ‖ *intr* zählen; **c. for little** (*or* much) wenig (*or* viel)

gelten; c. off (mil) abzählen; **c. on** zählen auf (*acc*)
count′down′ *s* Countdown *m & n*
countenance ['kauntɪnəns] *s* Antlitz *n* ‖ *tr* (*tolerate*) zulassen; (*approve*) billigen
counter ['kauntər] *adj* Gegen– ‖ *adv*—**c. to** wider; **run c. to** zuwiderlaufen (*dat*) ‖ *s* Zähler *m*; (*in games*) Spielmarke *f*; (*in a store*) Ladentisch *m*, Theke *f*; (*in a restaurant*) Büffet *n*; (*in a bank*) Schalter *m*; **under the c.** (fig) heimlich ‖ *tr* widerstreben (*dat*); (*in speech*) widersprechen (*dat*) ‖ *intr* Gegenmaßnahmen treffen; (box) kontern, nachschlagen
coun′teract′ *tr* entgegenwirken (*dat*)
coun′terattack′ *s* Gegenangriff *m* ‖ **coun′terattack′** *tr* e–n Gegenangriff machen auf (*acc*) ‖ *intr* e–n Gegenangriff machen
coun′terbal′ance *s* Gegengewicht *n* ‖ **coun′terbal′ance** *tr* das Gegengewicht halten (*dat*)
coun′terclock′wise *adj* linksläufig ‖ *adv* entgegen der Uhrzeigerrichtung
coun′teres′pionage *s* Gegenspionage *f*
counterfeit ['kauntərfɪt] *adj* gefälscht ‖ *s* Fälschung *f*; (*money*) Falschgeld *n* ‖ *tr* fälschen
counterfeiter ['kauntər,fɪtər] *s* Falschmünzer –in *mf*
coun′terfeit mon′ey *s* Falschgeld *n*
coun′terintel′ligence *s* Spionageabwehr *f*
countermand ['kauntər,mænd] *s* Gegenbefehl *m* ‖ *tr* widerrufen
coun′termeas′ure *s* Gegenmaßnahme *f*
coun′teroffen′sive *s* Gegenoffensive *f*
coun′terpart′ *s* Gegenstück *n*; (*person*) Ebenbild *n*
coun′terpoint′ *s* (mus) Kontrapunkt *m*
coun′terrevolu′tion *s* Konterrevolution *f*
coun′tersign′ *s* Gegenzeichen *n* ‖ *tr & intr* mitunterzeichnen
coun′tersink′ *v* (*pret & pp* –sunk) *tr* (*a screw*) versenken; (*a hole*) ausfräsen
coun′terspy′ *s* Gegenspion –in *mf*
coun′terstroke′ *s* Gegenstoß *m*
coun′terweight′ *s* Gegengewicht *n*
countess ['kauntɪs] *s* Gräfin *f*
countless ['kauntlɪs] *adj* zahllos
countrified ['kʌntrɪ,faɪd] *adj* ländlich; (*boorish*) bäu(e)risch
country ['kʌntrɪ] *adj* (air, house, life, road) Land– ‖ *s* (*state; rural area*) Land *n*; (*land of birth*) Heimatland *n*; **in the c.** auf dem Lande; **to the c.** aufs Land
coun′try club′ *s* exklusiver Klub *m* auf dem Lande
coun′tryfolk′ *spl* Landvolk *n*
coun′try gen′tleman *s* Landedelmann *m*
coun′try·man *s* (–men) Landsmann *m*
coun′tryside′ *s* Landschaft *f*, Land *n*
coun′try-wide′ *adj* über das ganze Land verbreitet (*or* ausgedehnt)
county ['kauntɪ] *s* Kreis *m*
coun′ty seat′ *s* Kreisstadt *f*

coup [ku] s Coup m

coup d'état [ku de 'ta] s Staatsstreich m

coupe [ku'pe], [kup] s Coupé n

couple ['kʌpəl] s Paar n; (of lovers) Liebespaar n; (man and wife) Ehepaar n; (phys) Kräftepaar n; **a c. of** ein paar, e.g., **a c. of days ago** vor ein paar Tagen || tr koppeln || intr sich paaren

couplet ['kʌplɪt] s Verspaar n

coupling ['kʌplɪŋ] s Verbindungsstück n; (rad) Kopplung f; (rr) Kupplung f

coupon ['kj(j)upan] s Gutschein m

courage ['kʌrɪdʒ] s Mut m, Courage f; **get up the c. to** (inf) sich [dat] ein Herz fassen zu (inf)

courageous [kə'redʒəs] adj mutig

courier ['kʌrɪ-ər] s Eilbote m; (tour guide) Reiseleiter –in mf

course [kors] s (direction) Richtung f, Kurs m; (of a river, of time) Lauf m; (method of procedure) Weg m, Weise f, Kurs m; (in racing) Bahn f; (archit) Schicht f; (culin) Gang m; (educ) Kurs m; **c. of action** Handlungsweise f; **go off c.** (aer) sich verfliegen; **in due c.** zur rechten Zeit; **in the c. of** im Verlaufe von (or genit); (with expressions of time) im Laufe (genit); **of c.** natürlich; **run its c.** seinen Verlauf nehmen

court [kort] s (of a king) Hof m; (of justice) Gericht n; (yard) Hof m; (tennis) Platz m; **in c.** (or into c. or to c.) vor Gericht; **out of c.** außergerichtlich || tr (a girl) werben um; (danger) suchen; (disaster) heraufbeschwören

courteous ['kʌrtɪ-əs] adj höflich

courtesan ['kʌrtɪzən] s Kurtisane f

courtesy ['kʌrtɪsi] s Höflichkeit f; **by c. of** freundlicherweise zur Verfügung gestellt von

court'house' s Gerichtsgebäude n

courtier ['kortɪ-ər] s Höfling m

court' jest'er s Hofnarr m

courtly ['kortli] adj höfisch

court'-mar'tial s (courts-martial) Kriegsgericht n || v (pret & pp –tial[l]ed; ger –tial[l]ing) tr vor ein Kriegsgericht stellen

court'room' s Gerichtssaal m

court'ship' s Werbung f

court'yard' s Hof m

cousin ['kʌzɪn] s Vetter m; (female) Kusine f

cove [kov] s Bucht f

covenant ['kʌvənənt] s Vertrag m; (Bib) Bund m

cover ['kʌvər] s Decke f; (lid) Deckel m; (wrapping) Hülle f; (e.g., of a bed) Bezug m; (of a book) Einband m; (protection) Schutz m; (mil) Deckung f; **from c. to c.** von vorn bis hinten; **take c.** sich unterstellen; **under c.** im Geheimen; **under c. of night** im Schutz der Dunkelheit || tr bedecken, decken; (conceal) verdecken; (distances) zurücklegen; (a sales territory) bearbeiten; (a bet) die gleiche Summe setzen gegen; (ex-

penses, losses) decken; (upholstered furniture) beziehen; (deal with) behandeln; (include) umfassen; (material in class) durchnehmen; (said of a reporter) berichten über (acc); (said of plants) bewachsen; (with insurance) versichern, decken; (protect with a gun) sichern; (threaten with a gun) in Schach halten; (have within range) beherrschen; **c. up** zudecken; (conceal) verheimlichen || intr—**c. for** einspringen für

coverage ['kʌvɪrɪdʒ] s (area covered) Verbreitungsgebiet n; (of news) Berichterstattung f; (ins) Versicherungsschutz m; (rad, telv) Sendebereich m

coveralls ['kʌvər,olz] spl Monteuranzug m

cov'ered wag'on s Planwagen m

cov'er girl' s Covergirl n

cov'ering s Decke f, Bedeckung f

covert ['kovərt] adj verborgen

cov'erup' s Beschönigung f, Bemäntelung f

covet ['kʌvɪt] tr begehren

covetous ['kʌvɪtəs] adj begehrlich

covetousness ['kʌvɪtəsnɪs] s Begehrlichkeit f

covey ['kʌvi] s (brood) Brut f; (small flock) Schwarm m; (bevy) Schar f

cow [kau] s Kuh f || tr einschüchtern

coward ['kau-ərd] s Feigling m, Memme f

cowardice ['kau-ərdɪs] s Feigheit f

cowardly ['kau-ərdli] adj feig(e)

cow'bell' s Kuhglocke f

cow'boy' s Cowboy m

cower ['kau-ər] intr kauern

cow'herd' s Kuhhirt m

cow'hide' s Rindsleder n

cowl [kaul] s (on a chimney) Schornsteinkappe f; (aer) Motorhaube f; (eccl) Kapuze f

cowling ['kaulɪŋ] s (aer) Motorhaube f

co-worker ['ko ,wʌrkər] s Mitarbeiter –in mf

cowpox ['kau ,paks] s Kuhpocken pl

coxswain ['kaksən] s Steuermann m

coy [kɔɪ] adj spröde

coyote [kaɪ'oti], ['kaɪ-ot] s Kojote m, Präriewolf m, Steppenwolf m

cozy ['kozi] adj gemütlich

C.P.A. ['si'pi'e] s (certified public accountant) amtlich zugelassener Wirtschaftsprüfer m

crab [kræb] s Krabbe f; (grouch) Sauertopf m

crab' ap'ple s Holzapfel m

crabbed ['kræbɪd] adj mürrisch; (handwriting) unleserlich; (style) schwer verständlich, verworren

crabby ['kræbi] adj mürrisch, grämlich

crack [kræk] adj erstklassig; (troops) Elite– || s Riß m, Sprung m; (of a whip or rifle) Knall m; (blow) (sl) Klaps m; (opportunity) (sl) Gelegenheit f; (try) (sl) Versuch m; (cutting remark) (sl) Seitenhieb m; **at the c. of dawn** bei Tagesanbruch; **take a c. at** (sl) versuchen || tr spalten; (a nut, safe) knacken; (an egg) aufschlagen;

(*a code*) entziffern; (*hit*) (sl) e-n
Klaps geben (*dat*); (chem) spalten;
c. a joke e-n Witz reißen; **c. a smile**
lächeln ‖ *intr* (*make a cracking
sound*) knacken, krachen; (*develop
a crack*) rissig werden; (*said of a
whip or rifle*) knallen; (*said of a
voice*) umschlagen; (*said of ice*)
(zer) springen; **c. down on scharf**
vorgehen gegen; **c. up** (coll) überschnappen; (aut) aufknallen

cracked *adj* (*split*) rissig; (*crazy*) (sl)
übergeschnappt

cracker ['krækər] *s* Keks *m* & *n*

crack'erjack' *adj* (coll) erstklassig ‖ *s*
(coll) Kanone *f*

crackle ['krækəl] *s* Krakelierung *f* ‖
tr krakelieren ‖ *intr* prasseln

crack'pot' *adj* (sl) verrückt ‖ *s* (sl)
Verrückte *m*

crack' shot' *s* Meisterschütze *m*

crack'-up' *s* (aut) Zusammenstoß *m*

cradle ['kredəl] *s* Wiege *f*; (telp) Gabel *f* ‖ *tr* in den Armen wiegen

craft [kræft] *s* Handwerk *n*, Gewerbe
n; (naut) Fahrzeug *n*; **by c.** durch
List ‖ *spl* Fahrzeuge *pl*, Schiffe *pl*;
small c. kleine Schiffe *pl*

craftiness ['kræftɪnɪs] *s* List *f*

crafts·man ['kræftsmən] *s* (–men)
Handwerker *m*

crafts'manship' *s* Kunstfertigkeit *f*

crafty ['kræftɪ] *adj* arglistig

crag [kræg] *s* Felszacke *f*

cram [kræm] *v* (*pret & pp* crammed;
ger cramming) *tr* vollstopfen; **c. into**
hineinstopfen in (*acc*) ‖ *intr* (educ)
büffeln, ochsen; **c. into** sich hinein-
zwängen in (*acc*)

cram' course' *s* Presse *f*

cramp [kræmp] *s* Krampf *m*; (*clamp*)
Klammer *f* ‖ *tr* einschränken, beengen

cramped *adj* eng

cranberry ['kræn,berɪ] *s* Preiselbeere
f

crane [kren] *s* (mach) Kran *m*; (orn)
Kranich *m* ‖ **—c. one's neck** den Hals
recken

crani·um ['krenɪ·əm] *s* (–a [ə]) *s*
Hirnschale *f*, Schädel *m*

crank [kræŋk] *s* Kurbel *f*; (*grouch*)
(coll) Griesgram *m*; (*eccentric*) (coll)
Sonderling *m* ‖ *tr* kurbeln; **c. up**
ankurbeln

crank'case' *s* Kurbelgehäuse *n*

crank'shaft' *s* Kurbelwelle *f*

cranky ['kræŋkɪ] *adj* launisch

cranny ['krænɪ] *s* Ritze *f*

crap [kræp] *s* (*nonsense*) (sl) Unsinn
m; **craps** Würfel *pl*; **shoot craps**
Würfel spielen

crash [kræʃ] *s* Krach *m*; (aer) Absturz
m; (aut) Zusammenstoß *m*; (econ)
Zusammenbruch *m* ‖ *tr* zerschmettern; (*a party*) hineinplatzen in
(*acc*); (aer) zum Absturz bringen ‖
intr (*produce a crashing sound*)
krachen; (*shatter*) zerbrechen; (*collapse*) zusammenstürzen; (aer) abstürzen; (aut) zusammenstoßen; **c.
into** fahren gegen

crash' dive' *s* Schnelltauchen *n*

crash'-dive' *intr* schnelltauchen

crash' hel'met *s* Sturzhelm *m*

crash' land'ing *s* Bruchlandung *f*

crash' pro'gram *s* Gewaltkur *f*

crass [kræs] *adj* kraß

crate [kret] *s* Lattenkiste *f*; (*old car,
old plane*) (coll) Kiste *f* ‖ *tr* in e-r
Lattenkiste verpacken

crater ['kretər] *s* Krater *m*; (*of a
bomb*) Trichter *m*

crave [krev] *tr* ersehnen ‖ *intr*—**c. for**
verlangen nach

craven ['krevən] *adj* feige ‖ *s* Feigling
m

craving *s* (for) Verlangen *n* (nach)

craw [krɔ] *s* Kropf *m*

crawl [krɔl] *s* Kriechen *n* ‖ *intr* kriechen; (*said of the skin*) kribbeln;
(*said of a swimmer*) kraulen; (*said
of cars*) schleichen; **c. along** im
Schneckentempo gehen (or fahren);
c. into a hole (& fig) sich verkrie-
chen; **c. with** wimmeln von

crayon ['kre·ən] *s* (*wax crayon*)
Wachsmalkreide *f*; (*colored pencil*)
Farbstift *m*; (*artist's crayon*) Zei-
chenkreide *f*

craze [krez] *s* Mode *f*, Verrücktheit *f*
‖ *tr* verrückt machen

crazy ['krezɪ] *adj* verrückt; (*senseless*)
sinnlos; **c. about** verrückt nach; **c.
idea** Wahnidee *f*; **drive c.** verrückt
machen

cra'zy bone' *s* Musikantenknochen *m*

creak [krik] *s* (*high-pitched sound*)
Quietschen *n*; (*low-pitched sound*)
Knarren *n* ‖ *intr* quietschen; knarren

creaky ['krikɪ] *adj* quietschend; knar-
rend

cream [krim] *adj* Sahne–, Rahm–; *s*
(*color*) creme, cremefarben ‖ *s*
Sahne *f*, Rahm *m*; (*cosmetic*) Creme
f; (*color*) Cremefarbe *f*; (fig) Creme
f ‖ *tr* (*milk*) abrahmen; (*trounce*)
(sl) schlagen

cream' cheese' *s* Rahmkäse *m*, Sahne-
käse *m*

creamery ['krimərɪ] *s* Molkerei *f*

cream' pitch'er *s* Sahnekännchen *n*

cream' puff' *s* Windbeutel *m*

cream' sep'arator ['sepə,retər] *s*
Milchschleuder *f*, Milchzentrifuge *f*

creamy ['krimɪ] *adj* sahnig

crease [kris] *s* Falte *f*; (*in trousers*)
Bügelfalte *f* ‖ *tr* falten; (*trousers*)
bügeln ‖ *intr* knittern

create [krɪ'et] *tr* (er)schaffen; (*excitement, an impression*) hervorrufen;
(*noise*) verursachen; (*appoint*) ernennen, machen zu; (*a role, fashions*) kreieren

creation [krɪ'eʃən] *s* Schaffung *f*; (*of
the world*) Schöpfung *f*; (*in fashions*) Modeschöpfung *f*

creative [krɪ'etɪv] *adj* schöpferisch

creator [krɪ'etər] *s* Schöpfer *m*

creature ['kritʃər] *s* Kreatur *f*, Geschöpf *n*; **every living c.** jedes Lebewesen *n*

credence ['kridəns] *s* Glaube *m*

credentials [krɪ'denʃəlz] *spl* Beglaubigungsschreiben *n*, Akkreditiv *n*

credenza [krɪ'denzə] *s* Kredenz *f*

credibility [ˌkredɪˈbɪlɪti] s Glaubwürdigkeit f

credibil′ity gap′ s Vertrauenslücke f

credible [ˈkredɪbəl] adj glaubwürdig

credit [ˈkredɪt] s (credence) Glaube m; (honor) Ehre f; (recognition) Anerkennung f; (educ) Anrechnungspunkt m; (fin) Kredit m; (credit balance) (fin) Guthaben n; **be a c. to** Ehre machen (dat); **credits** (cin) Vorspann m; **give s.o. c. for s.th.** j-m etw hoch anrechnen; **on c.** auf Kredit; **on thirty days′** c. auf dreißig Tage Ziel; **take c. for** sich [dat] als Verdienst anrechnen; **to s.o.′s c.** zu j-s Ehre ‖ tr (believe) glauben (dat); (an account) gutschreiben (dat); **c. s.o. with s.th.** j-m etw hoch anrechnen

creditable [ˈkredɪtəbəl] adj ehrenwert

cre′dit card′ s Kreditkarte f

cre′dit hour′ s (educ) Anrechnungspunkt m

creditor [ˈkredɪtər] s Gläubiger –in mf

cre′dit rat′ing s Bonität f

credulous [ˈkredʒələs] adj leichtgläubig

creed [krid] s (& fig) Glaubensbekenntnis n

creek [krik] s Bach m

creep [krip] s Kriechen n; (sl) Spinner m; **it gives me the creeps** mir gruselt ‖ v (pret & pp **crept** [krept]) intr kriechen, schleichen; (said of plants) kriechen; **c. along** dahinschleichen; **c. up on** heranschleichen an (acc); **it makes my flesh c.** es macht mich schaudern

creeper [ˈkripər] s Kletterpflanze f

creepy [ˈkripi] adj schaudererregend; (sensation) gruselig; **have a c. feeling** gruseln

cremate [ˈkrimet] tr einäschern

cremation [krɪˈmeʃən] s Einäscherung f

crematory [ˈkriməˌtori] s Krematorium n

crepe [krep] s Krepp m; (mourning band) Trauerflor m

crepe′ pa′per s Kreppapier n

crescent [ˈkresənt] s Mondsichel f

cres′cent roll′ s Hörnchen n

cress [kres] s (bot) Kresse f

crest [krest] s (of a hill, wave, or rooster) Kamm m; (of a helmet) Helmbusch m; (of a bird) Federbüschel n

crestfallen [ˈkrestˌfɔlən] adj niedergeschlagen

Crete [krit] s Kreta n

crevice [ˈkrevɪs] s Riß m

crew [kru] s Gruppe f; (aer, nav) Besatzung f; (of a boat) (sport) Mannschaft f; (rowing) (sport) Rudersport m

crew′ cut′ s Bürstenschnitt m

crib [krɪb] s (manger) Krippe f; (for children) Kinderbettstelle f; (bin) Speicher m; (student's pony) Eselsbrücke f ‖ v (pret & pp **cribbed**; ger **cribbing**) tr & intr abbohren

cricket [ˈkrɪkɪt] s (ent) Grille f;

(sport) Kricketspiel n; **not c.** (coll) nicht fair

crime [kraɪm] s Verbrechen n

criminal [ˈkrɪmɪnəl] adj verbrecherisch; (act, case, code, court, law) Straf-; (investigation, trial, police) Kriminal- ‖ s Verbrecher –in mf

crim′inal charge′ s Strafanzeige f

crim′inal neg′ligence s grobe Fahrlässigkeit f

crim′inal offense′ s strafbare Handlung f

crim′inal rec′ord s Strafregister n

crimp [krɪmp] s Welle f; **put a c. in** (coll) e-n Dämpfer aufsetzen (dat) ‖ tr wellen, riffeln

crimson [ˈkrɪmzən] adj karmesinrot ‖ s Karmesin n

cringe [krɪndʒ] intr sich krümmen; (fawn) kriechen

crinkle [ˈkrɪŋkəl] s Runzel f ‖ tr runzeln; (one's nose) rümpfen

cripple [ˈkrɪpəl] s Krüppel m ‖ tr verkrüppeln; (fig) lähmen, lahmlegen

cri·sis [ˈkraɪsɪs] s (-ses [siz]) Krise f

crisp [krɪsp] adj (brittle) knusprig; (firm and fresh) mürb; (air, clothes) frisch; (manner) forsch

crisscross [ˈkrɪsˌkrɔs] adj & adv kreuz und quer ‖ tr kreuz und quer markieren ‖ intr sich kreuzen

criteri·on [kraɪˈtɪrɪən] s (-a [ə] & -ons) Kennzeichen n, Kriterium n

critic [ˈkrɪtɪk] s Kritiker –in mf

critical [ˈkrɪtɪkəl] adj kritisch

criticism [ˈkrɪtɪˌsɪzəm] s Kritik f

criticize [ˈkrɪtɪˌsaɪz] tr kritisieren

critique [krɪˈtik] s (review) Rezension f; (critical discussion) Kritik f

croak [krok] s (of a frog) Quaken n; (of a raven) Krächzen n ‖ intr quaken; krächzen; (die) (sl) verrecken

cro·chet [kroˈʃe] s Häkelarbeit f ‖ v (pret & pp **-cheted** [ˈʃed]; ger **-cheting** [ˈʃe·ɪŋ]) tr & intr häkeln

crochet′ nee′dle s Häkelnadel f

crock [krak] s irdener Topf m, Krug m

crockery [ˈkrakəri] s irdenes Geschirr n

crocodile [ˈkrakəˌdaɪl] s Krokodil n

croc′odile tears′ spl Krokodilstränen pl

crocus [ˈkrokəs] s (bot) Krokus m

crone [kron] s altes Weib n

crony [ˈkroni] s alter Kamerad m

crook [kruk] s (of a shepherd) Hirtenstab m; (sl) Gauner m ‖ tr krümmen

crooked [ˈkrukɪd] adj krumm; (dishonest) unehrlich

croon [krun] tr & intr schmalzig singen

crooner [ˈkrunər] s Schnulzensänger m

crop [krap] s Ernte f; (whip) Peitsche f; (of a bird) Kropf m; (large number) Menge f; **the crops** die ganze Ernte ‖ v (pret & pp **cropped**; ger **cropping**) tr stutzen; (said of an animal) abfressen ‖ intr—**c. up** auftauchen

crop′ fail′ure s Mißernte f

croquet [kroˈke] s Krocket n

croquette [kro'ket] *s* (culin) Krokette *f*

crosier ['krozər] *s* Bischofsstab *m*

cross [krɒs] *adj* Quer-, Kreuz-; (biol) Kreuzungs-; (angry) (with) ärgerlich (auf *acc*, über *acc*) ‖ *s* (& fig) Kreuz *n*; (biol) Kreuzung *f* ‖ *tr* (arms, legs, streets, plans, breeds) kreuzen; (a mountain) übersteigen; (oppose) in die Quere kommen (*dat*); **c. my heart!** Hand aufs Herz!; **c. oneself** sich bekreuzigen; **c. s.o.'s mind** j—m durch den Kopf gehen; **c. out** ausstreichen ‖ *intr* sich kreuzen; **c. over to** hinübergehen zu

cross′bones′ *spl* gekreuzte Skelettknochen *pl*

cross′bow′ *s* (hist) Armbrust *f*

cross′breed′ *v* (pret & pp **–bred**) *tr* kreuzen

cross′-coun′try *adj* (vehicle) geländegängig ‖ **cross′-coun′try** *s* (sport) Langlauf *m*

cross′cur′rent *s* Gegenströmung *f*

cross′-exam′ine *tr* ins Kreuzverhör nehmen

cross′-examina′tion *s* Kreuzverhör *n*

cross′-eyed′ *adj* schieläugig

cross′fire′ *s* Kreuzfeuer *n*

cross′ing *s* (of streets) Kreuzung *f*; (of the ocean) Überfahrt *f*, Überquerung *f*; (rr) Übergang *m*

cross′piece′ *s* Querstück *n*

cross′-pur′pose *s*—**be at cross-purposes** einander entgegenarbeiten

cross′ ref′erence *s* Querverweis *m*

cross′road′ *s* Querweg *m*; **crossroads** Straßenkreuzung *f*; (fig) Scheideweg *m*

cross′ sec′tion *s* Querschnitt *m*

cross′wind′ *s* Seitenwind *m*

cross′wise′ *adj & adv* quer, in die Quere

cross′word puz′zle *s* Kreuzworträtsel *n*

crotch [krɒtʃ] *s* (of a tree) Gabelung *f*; (of a body or trousers) Schritt *m*

crotchety ['krɒtʃɪti] *adj* verschroben

crouch [kraʊtʃ] *s* Hocke *f* ‖ *intr* hocken

croup [krup] *s* (of a horse) Kruppe *f*; (pathol) Halsbräune *f*

croupier ['krupɪ·ər] *s* Croupier –in *mf*

crouton ['krutɑn] *s* gerösteter Brotwürfel *m*

crow [kro] *s* (cry) Krähen *n*; (bird) Krähe *f*; **as the c. flies** schnurgrade; **eat c.** klein beigeben ‖ *intr* krähen

crow′bar′ *s* Stemmeisen *n*

crowd [kraʊd] *s* Menge *f*; (mob) Masse *f*; (set) Gesellschaft *f* ‖ *tr* vollstopfen; (push) stoßen; **c. out** verdrängen ‖ *intr* (around) sich drängen (um); **c. into** sich hineindrängen in (*acc*)

crowd′ed *adj* überfüllt; (street) belebt

crown [kraʊn] *s* Krone *f*; (dent) Zahnkrone *f* ‖ *tr* krönen, bekränzen; (checkers) zur Dame machen; (sl) eins aufs Dach geben (*dat*); (dent) überkronen

crown′ jew′els *spl* Kronjuwelen *pl*

crown′ prince′ *s* Kronprinz *m*

crown′ prin′cess *s* Kronprinzessin *f*

crow′s′-feet′ *spl* (wrinkles) Krähenfüße *pl*

crow′s′-nest′ *s* (naut) Krähennest *n*

crucial ['kruʃəl] *adj* entscheidend; (point) springend; **c. question** Gretchenfrage *f*; **c. test** Feuerprobe *f*

crucible ['krusɪbəl] *s* Schmelztiegel *m*

crucifix ['krusɪfɪks] *s* Kruzifix *n*

crucifixion [ˌkrusɪ'fɪkʃən] *s* Kreuzigung *f*

cruci·fy ['krusɪˌfaɪ] *v* (pret & pp **–fied**) *tr* kreuzigen

crude [krud] *adj* (raw, unrefined) roh; (person) grob, ungeschliffen; **c. joke** plumper Scherz *m*

crudity ['krudɪti] *s* Roheit *f*

cruel ['kru·əl] *adj* (to) grausam (gegen)

cruelty ['kru·əlti] *s* Grausamkeit *f*; **c. to animals** Tierquälerei *f*

cruet ['kru·ɪt] *s* Fläschchen *n*; (relig) Meßkännchen *n*

cruise [kruz] *s* Kreuzfahrt *f* ‖ *intr* (aer) mit Reisegeschwindigkeit fliegen; (aut) herumfahren; (naut) kreuzen

cruiser ['kruzər] *s* (nav) Kreuzer *m*

cruise′ ship′ *s* Vergnügungsdampfer *m*

cruller ['krʌlər] *s* Krapfen *m*

crumb [krʌm] *s* Krümel *m*; (& fig) Bröckchen *n*; (sl) Schweinehund *m*

crumble ['krʌmbəl] *tr & intr* zerbröckeln

crumbly ['krʌmbli] *adj* bröcklig

crummy ['krʌmi] *adj* (sl) schäbig

crumple ['krʌmpəl] *tr* zerknittern ‖ *intr* (said of clothes) faltig werden; (collapse) zusammenbrechen

crunch [krʌntʃ] *s* Knacken *n*; (of snow) Knirschen *n*; (tight situation) Druck *m* ‖ *tr* knirschend kauen ‖ *intr* (said of snow) knirschen; **c. on** knirschend kauen

crusade [kru'sed] *s* Kreuzzug *m*

crusader [kru'sedər] *s* Kreuzfahrer *m*

crush [krʌʃ] *s* Gedränge *n*; **have a c. on s.o.** (coll) in j—n vernarrt sein ‖ *tr* (zer)quetschen, zerdrücken; (grain) schroten; (stone) zerkleinern; (suppress) unterdrücken; (oppress) bedrücken; (hopes) knicken; (overwhelm) zerschmettern; (min) pochen; **c. out** (a cigarette) ausdrücken ‖ *intr* zerdrückt werden

crush′ing *adj* (victory) entscheidend; (defeat) vernichtend; (experience) überwältigend

crust [krʌst] *s* Kruste *f*; (sl) Frechheit *f*

crustacean [krʌs'teʃən] *s* Krebstier *n*

crustaceous [krʌs'teʃəs] *adj* Krebs-

crusty ['krʌsti] *adj* krustig, rösch; (surly) mürrisch

crutch [krʌtʃ] *s* (& fig) Krücke *f*

crux [krʌks] *s* Kern *m*, Kernpunkt *m*

cry [kraɪ] *s* (cries) (shout) Schrei *m*, Ruf *m*; (weeping) Weinen *n*; **a far cry from** etw ganz anderes als; **cry for help** Hilferuf *m*; **have a good cry** sich ordentlich ausweinen ‖ *v* (pret & pp **cried**) *tr* schreien, rufen; **cry one's eyes out** sich [*dat*] die Augen aus dem Kopf weinen ‖ *intr* (weep) weinen; *(shout)* schreien; **cry for help** um Hilfe rufen; **cry on s.o.'s shoulder** j—m seine Not klagen; **cry out against** scharf verurteilen; **cry out in** *(pain)* schreien vor *(dat)*; **cry over** nachweinen *(dat)*

cry'ba'by s *(-bies)* Schreihals *m*

cry'ing *adj* —**c.** jag Schreikrampf *m*; **c. shame** schreiende Ungerechtigkeit *f* ‖ *s* Weinen *n*; **for c. out loud!** um Himmels willen!

crypt [krɪpt] *s* Totengruft *f*, Krypta *f*

cryptic(al) ['krɪptɪk(əl)] *adj (secret)* geheim; *(puzzling)* rätselhaft; *(coded)* verschlüsselt

crystal ['krɪstəl] *adj* Kristall— ‖ *s* Kristall *m*; *(cut glass)* Kristallglas *n*; *(of a watch)* Uhrglas *n*

crys'tal ball' *s* Kristall *m*

crystalline ['krɪstəlɪn], ['krɪstə,laɪn] *adj* kristallinisch, kristallen

crystallize ['krɪstə,laɪz] *tr* kristallisieren ‖ *intr* kristallisieren; *(fig)* feste Form annehmen

cub [kʌb] *s* Junge *n*

Cuba ['kjubə] *s* Kuba *n*

Cuban ['kjubən] *adj* kubanisch ‖ *s* Kubaner —in *mf*

cubbyhole ['kʌbɪ,hol] *s* gemütliches Zimmerchen *n*

cube [kjub] *s* Würfel *m*; *(math)* dritte Potenz *f* ‖ *tr* in Würfel schneiden; *(math)* kubieren

cubic ['kjubɪk] *adj* Raum—; *(math)* kubisch; **c. foot** Kubikfuß *m*

cub' report'er *s* unerfahrener Reporter *m*

cub' scout' *s* Wölfling *m*

cuckold ['kʌkəld] *s* Hahnrei *m* ‖ *tr* zum Hahnrei machen

cuckoo ['kuku] *adj* (sl) verrückt ‖ *s* Kuckuck *m*

cuck'oo clock' *s* Kuckucksuhr *f*

cucumber ['kjukʌmbər] *s* Gurke *f*

cud [kʌd] *s*—**chew the cud** wiederkäuen

cuddle ['kʌdəl] *tr* herzen ‖ *intr* sich kuscheln; **c. up** sich behaglich zusammenkuscheln

cudg·el ['kʌdʒəl] *s* Prügel *m* ‖ *v (pret & pp* **-el[l]ed;** *ger* **-el[l]ing)** *tr* verprügeln

cue [kju] *s* Hinweis *m*; *(billiards)* Billardstock *m*; *(theat)* Stichwort *n*; **take the cue from s.o.** sich nach j—m richten ‖ *tr* das Stichwort geben *(dat)*

cuff [kʌf] *s (of a shirt)* Manschette *f*; *(of trousers)* Aufschlag *m*; *(blow)* Ohrfeige *f*; **off the c.** aus dem Handgelenk

cuff' link' *s* Manschettenknopf *m*

cuisine [kwɪ'zin] *s* Küche *f*

culinary ['kjulɪ,nerɪ] *adj* kulinarisch, Koch—; **c. art** Kochkunst *f*

cull [kʌl] *tr (choose)* auslesen; *(pluck)* pflücken

culminate ['kʌlmɪ,net] *intr* (in) kulminieren (in *dat*), gipfeln (in *dat*)

culmination [,kʌlmɪ'neʃən] *s* Gipfel *m*

culpable ['kʌlpəbəl] *adj* schuldhaft

culprit ['kʌlprɪt] *s* Schuldige *mf*

cult [kʌlt] *s* Kult *m*, Kultus *m*

cultivate ['kʌltɪ,vet] *tr (soil)* bearbeiten; *(plants)* ziehen; *(activities)* betreiben; *(an art)* pflegen; *(friendship)* hegen

cul'tivat'ed *adj* kultiviert

cultivation [,kʌltɪ'veʃən] *s (of the soil)* Bearbeitung *f*; *(of the arts)* Pflege *f*; *(of friendship)* Hegen *n*; **under c.** bebaut

cultivator ['kʌltɪ,vetər] *s (mach)* Kultivator *m*

cultural ['kʌltʃərəl] *adj* kulturell, Kultur—

culture ['kʌltʃər] *s* Kultur *f*

cul'tured *adj* kultiviert

cul'ture me'dium *s* Nährboden *m*

culvert ['kʌlvərt] *s* Rinnstein *m*

cumbersome ['kʌmbərsəm] *adj (unwieldy)* unhandlich; *(slow-moving)* schwerfällig; *(burdensome)* lästig

cunning ['kʌnɪŋ] *adj (arg)*listig ‖ *s* List *f*, Arglist *f*, Schlauheit *f*

cup [kʌp] *s* Tasse *f*; *(of a bra)* Körbchen *n*; *(fig, bot, relig)* Kelch *m*; *(sport)* Pokal *m* ‖ *v (pret & pp* **cupped;** *ger* **cupping)** *tr (the hands)* wölben; *(med)* schröpfen

cupboard ['kʌbərd] *s* Schrank *m*

cupidity [kju'pɪdɪti] *s* Habgier *f*

cupola ['kjupələ] *s* Kuppel *f*

cur [kʌr] *s* Köter *m*; *(pej)* Halunke *m*

curable ['kjurəbəl] *adj* heilbar

curate ['kjurɪt] *s* Kaplan *m*

curative ['kjurətɪv] *adj* heilend, Heil—

curator ['kju,retər] *s* Kustos *m*

curb [kʌrb] *s (of a street)* Randstein *m*; *(of a horse)* Kandare *f* ‖ *tr (& fig)* zügeln; *(a person)* an die Kandare nehmen

curb'stone' *s* Bordstein *m*

curd [kʌrd] *s* Quark *m*; **curds** Quark *m*

curdle ['kʌrdəl] *tr* gerinnen lassen; *(fig)* erstarren lassen ‖ *intr* gerinnen, stocken; *(fig)* erstarren

cure [kjur] *s (restoration to health)* Heilung *f*; *(remedy)* Heilmittel *n*; *(treatment)* Kur *f* ‖ *tr (a disease, evil)* heilen; *(by smoking)* räuchern; *(by drying)* trocknen; *(by salting)* einsalzen ‖ *intr* heilen

cure'-all' *s* Allheilmittel *n*

curfew ['kʌrfju] *s* Ausgehverbot *n*; *(enforced closing time)* Polizeistunde *f*

curi·o ['kjurɪ,o] *s (-os)* Kuriosität *f*

curiosity [,kjurɪ'ɑsɪti] *s* Neugier *f*; *(strange article)* Kuriosität *f*

curious ['kjurɪ·əs] *adj* neugierig; *(odd)* kurios, merkwürdig

curl [kʌrl] *s (of hair)* Locke *f*; *(of smoke)* Rauchkringel *m* ‖ *tr* locken; *(lips)* verächtlich schürzen ‖ *intr* sich kräuseln; **c. up** sich zusammenrollen; *(said of an edge)* sich umbiegen

curler ['kʌrlər] *s* Haarwickler *m*

curlicue ['kʌrlɪ,kju] *s* Schnörkel *m*

curly ['kʌrli] *adj* lockig; *(leaves, etc.)* gekräuselt

currant ['kʌrənt] *s (raisin)* Korinthe *f*; *(genus Ribes)* Johannisbeere *f*

currency [ˈkʌrənsi] *s* (*money*) Währung *f*; (*circulation*) Umlauf *m*; **foreign c.** Devisen *pl*; **gain c.** in Gebrauch kommen

current [ˈkʌrənt] *adj* (*year, prices, account*) laufend; (*events*) aktuell, Tages–; **be c.** Gültigkeit haben; (*said of money*) gelten ‖ *s* (& elec) Strom *m*

currently [ˈkʌrəntli] *adv* gegenwärtig

curriculum [kəˈrɪkjələm] *s* (**–lums &** **–la** [lə]) Lehrplan *m*

curry [ˈkʌri] *s* Curry *m* ‖ *v* (*pret &* *pp* **–ried**) *tr* (*a horse*) striegeln; **c.** **favor with s.o.** sich bei j–m einzuschmeicheln suchen

currycomb *s* Striegel *m*

curry powder *s* Currypulver *m*

curse [kʌrs] *s* Fluch *m*; **put a c. on** verwünschen ‖ *tr* verfluchen ‖ *intr* (**at**) fluchen (auf *acc*)

cursed [ˈkʌrsɪd], [kʌrs] *adj* verflucht

curse word *s* Fluchwort *n*, Schimpfwort *n*

cursive [ˈkʌrsɪv] *adj* Kurrent–

cursory [ˈkʌrsəri] *adj* flüchtig

curt [kʌrt] *adj* barsch, schroff

curtail [kərˈtel] *tr* einschränken

curtain [ˈkʌrtɪn] *s* Gardine *f*; (*drape*) Vorhang *m*; (theat) Vorhang *m* ‖ *tr*—**c.** off mit Vorhängen abteilen

curtain call *s* Vorhang *m*, Hervorruf *m*

curtain rod *s* Gardinenstange *f*

curtsy [ˈkʌrtsi] *s* Knicks *m* ‖ *v* (*pret* *& pp* **–sied**) *intr* (**to**) knicksen (vor *dat*)

curvaceous [kʌrˈveʃəs] *adj* kurvenreich

curvature [ˈkʌrvətʃər] *s* (*of the spine*) Verkrümmung *f*; (*of the earth*) Krümmung *f*

curved *adj* krumm

cushion [ˈkuʃən] *s* Kissen *n*, Polster *m & n*; (billiards) Bande *f* ‖ *tr* polstern; (*a shock*) abfedern

cuss [kʌs] *s* (sl) Kerl *m*; (*curse*) (sl) Fluch *m* ‖ *tr* (sl) verfluchen ‖ *intr* (sl) fluchen

cussed [ˈkʌsɪd] *adj* (sl) verflucht

cussedness [ˈkʌsɪdnɪs] *s* (sl) Bosheit *f*

custard [ˈkʌstərd] *s* Eierkrem *f*

custodian [kəˈstodɪ·ən] *s* (*e.g., of records*) Verwalter *m*; (*of inmates*) Wärter *m*; (*caretaker*) Hausmeister *m*

custody [ˈkʌstədi] *s* Verwahrung *f*, Obhut *f*; (jur) Gewahrsam *m*; **c. of** (*children*) Sorgerecht für; **in the c. of** in der Obhut (*genit*); **take into c.** in Gewahrsam nehmen

custom [ˈkʌstəm] *s* Brauch *m*, Sitte *f*; (*habit*) Gewohnheit *f*; **customs** Zollkontrolle *f*; **pay customs on s.th.** für etw Zoll bezahlen

customary [ˈkʌstə‚meri] *adj* gebräuchlich

custom-built *adj* nach Wunsch gebaut

customer [ˈkʌstəmər] *s* Kunde *m*, Kundin *f*; (*in a restaurant*) Gast *m*; (telp) Teilnehmer –in *mf*

custom-made *adj* nach Maß angefertigt

customs clearance *s* Zollabertigung *f*

customs declaration *s* Zollerklärung *f*; (*form*) Abfertigungsschein *m*

customs inspection *s* Zollkontrolle *f*

customs office *s* Zollamt *n*

customs officer *s* Zollbeamte *m*, Zollbeamtin *f*

custom tailor *s* Maßschneider *m*

cut [kʌt] *adj* (*glass*) geschliffen; **cut** **flowers** Schnittblumen *pl*; **cut out** **for** wie geschaffen für (or zu) ‖ *s* Schnitt *m*; (*piece cut off*) Abschnitt *m*; (*slice*) Schnitte *f*; (*wound*) Schnittwunde *f*; (*of a garment*) Schnitt *m*, Fasson *f*; (*of the profits*) Anteil *m*; (*in prices, pay*) Kürzung *f*, Senkung *f*; (*absence from school*) Schwänzen *n*; (*of meat*) Stück *n*; (cards) Abheben *n*; (tennis) Drehschlag *m*; **a cut above** e–e Stufe besser als ‖ *v* (*pret & pp* **cut**; *ger* **cutting**) *tr* schneiden; (*glass, precious stones*) schleifen; (*grass*) mähen; (*hedges*) stutzen; (*hay*) machen; (*a tunnel*) bohren; (*a motor*) abstellen; (*production*) drosseln; (*pay*) kürzen, vermindern; (*class*) (coll) schwänzen; (*prices*) herabsetzen, kürzen; (*whiskey*) (coll) panschen; (*cards*) abheben; (tennis) schneiden; **cut back** (*plants*) stutzen; (fig) abbauen; **cut down** fällen; **cut** **it out!** Schluß damit!; **cut off** abschneiden; (*a tail*) kupieren; (*gas,* *telephone, electricity*) absperren; (*troops*) absprengen; **cut one's finger** sich in den Finger schneiden; **cut** **out the nonsense!** laß den Quatsch!; **cut short** (*e.g., a vacation*) abkürzen; (*a person*) das Wort abschneiden (*dat*); **cut up** zerstückeln ‖ *intr* schneiden; **cut down on** einschränken, verringern; **cut in** sich einmischen; (*at a dance*) ablösen; **cut** **in ahead of s.o.** vor j–m einbiegen; **cut up** (sl) wild darauf losschießen

cut-and-dried [ˈkʌtənˈdraɪd] *adj* fix und fertig

cutaway *s* Cut *m*

cutback *s* Einschränkung *f*

cute [kjut] *adj* (*pretty*) niedlich; (*shrewd*) (coll) klug

cut glass *s* geschliffenes Glas *n*

cuticle [ˈkjutɪkəl] *s* Nagelhaut *f*

cutie [ˈkjuti] *s* (sl) flotte Biene *f*

cutlass [ˈkʌtləs] *s* Entermesser *n*

cutlery [ˈkʌtləri] *s* Schneidwerkzeuge *pl*

cutlet [ˈkʌtlɪt] *s* Schnitzel *n*

cut-off *s* (*turn-off*) Abzweigung *f*; (*cut-off point*) (acct) gemeinsamer Endpunkt *m*; (elec) Ausschaltvorrichtung *f*; (mach) Absperrvorrichtung *f*

cut-off date *s* Abschlußtag *m*

cut-out *s* Ausschnitt *m*; (*design to be* *cut out*) Ausschneidemuster *n*; (aut) Auspuffklappe *f*

cut-rate *adj* (*price*) Schleuder–

cutter [ˈkʌtər] *s* (naut) Kutter *m*

cutthroat *adj* halsabschneiderisch ‖ *s* Halsabschneider –in *mf*

cutting *adj* schneidend; (*tools*)

Schneide–; (*remark*) scharf || *s* Abschnitt *m*; (*of prices*) Herabsetzung *f*; (hort) Steckling *m*; **cuttings** Abfälle *pl*

cut'ting board' *s* Schneidebrett *n*

cut'ting edge' *s* Schnittkante *f*

cut'ting room' *s* (cin) Schneideraum *m*

cuttlefish ['kʌtəl.fɪʃ] *s* Tintenfisch *m*

cyanamide ['saɪænə.maɪd] *s* (chem) Zyanamid *n*; (com) Kalkstickstoff *m*

cycle ['saɪkəl] *s* Kreis *m*; (*of an internal combustion engine*) Takt *m*; (phys) Periode *f* || *intr* radeln

cyclic(al) ['sɪklɪk(əl)] *adj* zyklisch, kreisförmig

cyclist ['saɪklɪst] *s* Radfahrer –in *mf*

cyclone ['saɪklon] *s* Zyklon *m*

cyclotron ['saɪklə.tran] *s* Zyklotron *n*, Beschleuniger *m*

cylinder ['sɪlɪndər] *s* Zylinder *m*

cyl'inder block' *s* Zylinderblock *m*

cyl'inder bore' *s* Zylinderbohrung *f*

cyl'inder head' *s* Zylinderkopf *m*

cylindric(al) [sɪ'lɪndrɪk(əl)] *adj* zylindrisch

cymbal ['sɪmbəl] *s* Becken *n*

cynic ['sɪnɪk] *adj* (philos) zynisch || *s* Menschenverächter –in *mf*; (philos) Zyniker *m*

cynical ['sɪnɪkəl] *adj* zynisch

cynicism ['sɪnɪ.sɪzəm] *s* Zynismus *m*; (*cynical remark*) zynische Bemerkung *f*

cypress ['saɪprəs] *s* Zypresse *f*

Cyprus ['saɪprəs] *s* Zypern *n*

Cyrillic [sɪ'rɪlɪk] *adj* kyrillisch

cyst [sɪst] *s* Zyste *f*

czar [zar] *s* Zar *m*

czarina [za'rinə] *s* Zarin *f*

Czech [tʃɛk] *adj* tschechisch || *s* Tscheche *m*, Tschechin *f*; (*language*) Tschechisch *n*

Czechoslovakia [.tʃɛkəslo'vækɪ.ə] *s* die Tschechoslowakei *f*

D

D, d [di] *s* vierter Buchstabe des englischen Alphabets; (mus) D; **D flat** Des *n*; **D sharp** Dis *n*

D.A. *abb* (**District Attorney**) Staatsanwalt *m*

dab [dæb] *s* (*of color*) Klecks *m*; (*e.g., of butter*) Stückchen *n* || *v* (*pret & pp* **dabbed**; *ger* **dabbing**) *tr* betupfen || *intr*—**dab at** betupfen

dabble ['dæbəl] *tr* bespritzen || *intr* (*splash about*) plantschen; **d. in** herumstümpern in (*dat*)

dachshund ['daks.hund] *s* Dachshund *m*

dad [dæd] *s* (coll) Vati *m*

daddy ['dædi] *s* (coll) Vati *m*

dad'dy-long'legs' *s* (–legs) Weberknecht *m*

daffodil ['dæfədɪl] *s* gelbe Narzisse *f*

daffy ['dæfi] *adj* (coll) doof

dagger ['dægər] *s* Dolch *m*; (typ) Kreuzzeichen *n*; **look daggers at s.o.** j–n mit Blicken durchbohren

dahlia ['dæljə] *s* Georgine *f*, Dahlie *f*

daily ['deli] *adj* täglich, Tages– || *adv* täglich || *s* Tageszeitung *f*

dainty ['denti] *adj* zart; (*food*) lecker; (*finiky*) wählerisch

dairy ['dɛri] *s* Molkerei *f*

dair'y farm' *s* Meierei *f*

dair'y farm'er *s* Meier –in *mf*

dais ['de·ɪs] *s* Tribüne *f*

daisy ['dezi] *s* Gänseblümchen *n*

dal·ly ['dæli] *v* (*pret & pp* –**lied**) *intr* (*delay*) herumtrödeln; (*play amorously*) liebäugeln

dam [dæm] *s* Damm *m*; (*female quadruped*) Muttertier *f* || *v* (*pret & pp* **dammed**; *ger* **damming**) *tr* eindämmen; **dam up** anstauen

damage ['dæmɪdʒ] *s* Schaden *m*; **damages** (jur) Schadenersatz *m*; **do d.** Schaden anrichten; **sue for damages**

auf Schadenersatz klagen || *tr* beschädigen; (*a reputation*) beeinträchtigen

dam'aging *adj* (*influence*) schädlich; (*evidence*) belastend

dame [dem] *s* Dame *f*; (sl) Weibsbild *n*

damn [dæm] *adj* (sl) verflucht || *s*— **I don't give a d. about it** (sl) ich mache mir e–n Dreck daraus; **not be worth a d.** (sl) keinen Pfifferling wert sein || *tr* verdammen; (*curse*) verfluchen; **d. it!** (sl) verflucht!

damnation [dæm'neʃən] *s* Verdammnis *f*

damned *adj* verdammt; (sl) verflucht || *adv* (sl) verdammt || **the d.** *spl* die Verdammten *pl*

damp [dæmp] *adj* feucht || *s* Feuchtigkeit *f* || *tr* (be)feuchten; (*a fire; enthusiasm*) dämpfen; (elec, mus, phys) dämpfen

dampen ['dæmpən] *tr* befeuchten; (fig) dämpfen

damper ['dæmpər] *s* (*of a fireplace*) Schieber *m*; (*of a stove*) Ofenklappe *f*; (mus) Dämpfer *m*; **put a d. on** e–n Dämpfer aufsetzen (*dat*)

dampness ['dæmpnɪs] *s* Feuchtigkeit *f*

damsel ['dæmzəl] *s* Jungfrau *f*

dance [dæns] *s* Tanz *m* || *tr & intr* tanzen

dance' band' *s* Tanzkapelle *f*

dance' floor' *s* Tanzfläche *f*

dance' hall' *s* Tanzsaal *m*, Tanzlokal *n*

dancer ['dænsər] *s* Tänzer –in *mf*

dance' step' *s* Tanzschritt *m*

danc'ing part'ner *s* Tanzpartner –in *mf*

dandelion ['dændɪ.laɪ·ən] *s* Löwenzahn *m*

dandruff ['dændrəf] *s* Schuppen *pl*

dandy ['dændɪ] *adj* (coll) pfundig, nett ‖ *s* Stutzer *m*

Dane [den] *s* Däne *m*, Dänin *f*

danger ['dendʒər] *s* (to) Gefahr *f* (für)

dan′ger list′ *s*—be on the d. in Lebensgefahr sein

dangerous ['dendʒərəs] *adj* gefährlich

dangle ['dæŋgəl] *tr* schlenkern, baumeln lassen ‖ *intr* baumeln

Danish ['denɪʃ] *adj* dänisch ‖ *s* (language) Dänisch *n*

Dan′ish pas′try *s* feines Hefegebäck *n*

dank [dæŋk] *adj* feucht

Danube ['dænjub] *s* Donau *f*

dapper ['dæpər] *adj* schmuck

dappled ['dæpəld] *adj* scheckig, bunt

dare [der] *s* Herausforderung *f* ‖ *tr* wagen; (a person) herausfordern; **d. to** (inf) es wagen zu (inf); **don′t you d. go** unterstehen Sie sich, wegzugehen!; **I d. say** ich darf wohl behaupten ‖ *intr*—**don′t you d.!** unterstehen Sie sich!

dare′dev′il *s* Waghals *m*, Draufgänger *m*

dar′ing *adj* (deed) verwegen; (person) wagemutig ‖ *s* Wagemut *m*

dark [dark] *adj* finster; (color, beer, complexion) dunkel; (fig) düster ‖ *s* Finsternis *n*, Dunkel *n*; **be in the d. about** im unklaren sein über (acc)

Dark′ A′ges, *spl* frühes Mittelalter *n*

dark-complexioned ['darkkəm'plekʃənd] *adj* dunkelhäutig

darken ['darkən] *tr* (a room) verfinstern ‖ *intr* sich verfinstern; (fig) sich verdüstern

dark′-eyed′ *adj* schwarzäugig

dark′ horse′ *s* Außenseiter *m*

darkly ['darkli] *adv* geheimnisvoll

darkness ['darknɪs] *s* Finsternis *f*

dark′room′ *s* (phot) Dunkelkammer *f*

darling ['darlɪŋ] *adj* lieb ‖ *s* Liebchen *n*

darn [darn] *adj* (coll) verwünscht ‖ *adv* (coll) verdammt ‖ *s*—**I don′t give a d. about it** ich pfeif drauf! ‖ *tr* (stockings) stopfen; **d. it!** (coll) verflixt!; **I′ll be darned if** der Kukkuck soll mich holen, wenn

darn′ing nee′dle *s* Stopfnadel *f*

dart [dart] *s* Wurfspieß *m*, Pfeil *m*; (sew) Abnäher *m*; **darts** (game) Pfeilwerfen *n*; **play darts** Pfeile werfen ‖ *intr* huschen; **d. ahead** vorschießen; **d. off** davonstürzen

dash [dæʃ] *s* (rush) Ansturm *m*; (smartness) Schneidigkeit *f*; (spirit) Schwung *m*; (of solids) Prise *f*; (of liquids) Schuß *m*; (sport) Kurzstreckenlauf *m*; (typ) Gedankenstrich *m*; **make a d. for** losstürzen auf (acc) ‖ *tr* (throw) schleudern; (hopes) niederschlagen, knicken; **d. off** (a letter) hinwerfen ‖ *intr* stürmen, stürzen

dash′board′ *s* (aut) Armaturenbrett *n*

dash′ing *adj* schneidig, forsch

dastardly ['dæstərdli] *adj* feige

data ['detə] *s* or *spl* Daten *pl*, Angaben *pl*

da′ta proc′essing *s* Datenverarbeitung *f*

date [det] *s* Datum *n*; (fixed time) Termin *m*; (period) Zeitraum *m*; (appointment) (coll) Verabredung *f*; (person on a date) Freund –in *mf*; (bot) Dattel *f*; (jur) Termin *m*; **have a d. with** verabredet sein mit; **make a d. with** sich verabreden mit; **out of d.** veraltet; **to d.** bis heute; **what is the d. today?** der wievielte ist heute? ‖ *tr* datieren; (coll) ausgehen mit ‖ *intr*—**d. back to** zurückgehen auf (acc); **d. from** stammen aus

dat′ed *adj* (provided with a date) datiert; (out-of-date) zeitgebunden

date′ line′ *s* Datumsgrenze *f*

date′line′ *s* (journ) Datumszeile *f*

date′ palm′ *s* Dattelpalme *f*

dative ['detɪv] *s* Dativ *m*, Wemfall *m*

daub [dɔb] *s* Bewurf *m* ‖ *tr* (a canvas) beschmieren; (a wall) bewerfen; (e.g. mud, plaster) (on) schmieren (auf acc) ‖ *intr* (paint) klecksen

daughter ['dɔtər] *s* Tochter *f*

daugh′ter-in-law′ *s* (**daughters-in-law**) Schwiegertochter *f*

daunt [dɔnt] *tr* einschüchtern

dauntless ['dɔntlɪs] *adj* furchtlos

davenport ['dævən,pɔrt] *s* Diwan *m*

davit ['devɪt] *s* (naut) Bootskran *m*

daw [dɔ] *s* (orn) Dohle *f*

dawdle ['dɔdəl] *intr* trödeln, bummeln

dawn [dɔn] *s* Morgendämmerung *f*; (fig) Anbeginn *m* ‖ *intr* dämmern; **d. on s.o.** j–m zum Bewußtsein kommen

day [de] *adj* Tage–, Tages– ‖ *s* Tag *m*; (specific date) Termin *m*; **all day long** den ganzen Tag; **by day** am Tage, bei Tage; **by the day** tageweise; **call it a day** (coll) Feierabend machen; **day after day** Tag für Tag; **day by day** Tag für Tag; **day in, day out** tagaus, tagein; **day off** Urlaubstag *m*, Ruhetag *m*; **every other day** jeden zweiten Tag; **in days of old** in alten Zeiten; **in his day** zu seiner Zeit; **in those days** damals; **one day** e–s Tages; **one of these days** demnächst; **the day after** am folgenden Tag; **the day after tomorrow** übermorgen; **the day before** am Vortag; **the day before yesterday** vorgestern; **the other day** neulich, unlängst; **these days** heutzutage; **to this very day** bis auf den heutigen Tag; **what day of the week is it?** welchen Wochentag haben wir?

day′ bed′ *s* Ruhebett *n*, Liege *f*

day′break′ *s* Tagesanbruch *m*

day′-by-day′ *adj* tagtäglich, Tag für Tag

day′-care cen′ter *s* Kindertagesstätte *f*, Kindergarten *m*

day′ coach′ *s* (rr) Personenwagen *m*

day′dream′ *s* Träumerei *f*, Wachtraum *m*; (wild ideas) Phantasterei *f* ‖ *intr* mit offenen Augen träumen

day′dream′er *s* Träumer –in *mf*

day′ la′borer *s* Tagelöhner –in *mf*

day′light′ *adj* Tageslicht–; *s* Tageslicht *n*; **in broad d.** am hellichten Tag; **knock the daylights out of** (sl) zur Sau machen

day′light-sav′ing time′ s Sommerzeit f
day′ nurs′ery s Kleinkinderbewahranstalt f
day′ of reck′oning s Jüngster Tag m
day′ shift′ s Tagschicht f
day′time′ s Tageszeit f; **in the d.** bei Tage, am Tage
daze [dez] s Benommenheit f; **be in a d.** benommen sein || tr betäuben
dazzle ['dæzəl] s Blenden n || tr (& fig) blenden
dazz′ling adj blendend
D-day ['di ,de] s X-Tag m; (hist) Invasionstag m
deacon ['dikən] s Diakon m
deaconess ['dikənɪs] s Diakonisse f
dead [dɛd] adj tot; (plant) abgestorben, dürr; (faint, sleep) tief; (numb) gefühllos; (volcano, fire) erloschen; (elec) stromlos; (sport) tot, nicht im Spiel; **d. as a doornail** mausetot; **d. shot** unfehlbarer Schütze m; **d. stop** völliger Stillstand m; **d. silence** Totenstille f || adv völlig, tod- || s—**in the d. of night** mitten in der Nacht; **in the d. of winter** im tiefsten Winter
dead′ beat′ s (sl) Nichtstuer –in mf
dead′ bolt′ s Absteller m
dead′ calm′ s Windstille f
dead′ cen′ter s genaue Mitte f; (dead point) (mach) toter Punkt m
deaden ['dɛdən] tr (pain) betäuben; (a nerve) abtöten; (sound) dämpfen
dead′ end′ s (& fig) Sackgasse f
dead′head′ s Dummkopf m
dead′ heat′ s totes Rennen n
dead′-let′ter of′fice s Abteilung f für unbestellbare Briefe
dead′line′ s (letzter) Termin m; (journ) Redaktionsschluß m; **meet the d.** den Termin einhalten; **set a d. for** terminieren
dead′lock′ s Stillstand m; **break the d.** den toten Punkt überwinden; **reach a d.** steckenbleiben || tr zum völligen Stillstand bringen; **become deadlocked** stocken
deadly ['dɛdli] adj (fatal) tödlich; **d. enemy** Todfeind –in mf; **d. fear** Todesangst f || adv—**d. dull** sterbenlangweilig; **d. pale** leichenblaß
dead′ly sins′ spl Todsünden pl
dead′pan′ adj (look) ausdruckslos; (person) schafsgesicht
dead′ pan′ s (coll) Schafsgesicht n
dead′ reck′oning s (naut) Koppelkurs m
dead′ ring′er ['rɪŋər] s (coll) Doppelgänger m
dead′wood′ s (& fig) totes Holz n
deaf [dɛf] adj taub; **d. and dumb** taubstumm; **d. to** (fig) taub gegen; **turn a d. ear to** taube Ohren haben für
deafen ['dɛfən] tr betäuben
deaf′ening adj ohrenbetäubend
deaf′-mute′ adj taubstumm || s Taubstumme mf
deafness ['dɛfnɪs] s Taubheit f
deal [dil] s (business transaction) Geschäft n; (underhanded agreement) Schiebung f; (cards) Austeilen n, Geben n; **a good d. of** (coll) ziemlich

viel; **a good d. worse** (coll) viel (or weit) schlechter; **a great d. of** (coll) sehr viel; **give s.o. a good d.** (be fair to s.o.) j–n fair behandeln; (make s.o. a good offer) j–m ein gutes Angebot machen; **give s.o. a raw d.** j–m übel mitspielen; **it is my d.** (cards) ich muß geben; **it's a d.!** abgemacht!; **make a d.** (coll) ein Abkommen treffen || v (pret & pp dealt [dɛlt]) tr (a blow) versetzen; (cards) austeilen, geben || intr (cards) geben; **d. at** (a store) kaufen bei; **d. in** handeln mit; **d. with** (settle) erledigen; (occupy oneself or itself with) sich befassen mit; (treat, e.g., fairly) behandeln; (patronize) in Geschäftsbeziehungen stehen mit; **I'll d. with you later** mit Ihnen werde ich später abrechnen!
dealer ['dilər] s Geber –in mf; (com) Händler –in mf
deal′ings spl (business dealings) Handel m; (relations) Umgang m; **I'll have no d. with** ich will nichts zu tun haben mit
dean [din] s (eccl, educ) Dekan m
dean′ship′ s (eccl, educ) Dekanat n
dear [dɪr] adj lieb, traut; (expensive) teuer; **Dear Madam** Sehr verehrte gnädige Frau!; **Dear Mrs. X** Sehr geehrte Frau X; **Dear Mr. X** Sehr geehrter Herr X!; **Dear Sir** Sehr geehrter Herr! || s Liebling m, Schatz m || interj—**oh d.!** ach herrje!
dearie ['dɪri] s (coll) Liebchen n
dearth [dɐrθ] s (of) Mangel m (an dat)
death [dɛθ] s Tod m; (in the family) Todesfall m; **at death's door** sterbenskrank; **catch a d. of a cold** sich [dat] den Tod holen; **he'll be the d. of me yet** er bringt mich noch ins Grab; **put to d.** hinrichten; **to the d.** bis aufs Messer; **work to d.** totarbeiten
death′bed′ s Totenbett n, Sterbebett n
death′blow′ s Gnadenstoß m; (fig) Todesstoß m
death′ certif′icate s Totenschein m
death′ house′ s Todeshaus n
death′ knell′ s Grabgeläute n
deathless ['dɛθlɪs] adj unsterblich
deathly ['dɛθli] adj tödlich, Todes-, Toten- || adv toten-
death′ mask′ s Totenmaske f
death′ pen′alty s Todesstrafe f
death′ rate′ s Sterblichkeitsziffer f
death′ rat′tle s Todesröcheln n
death′ sen′tence s Todesurteil n
death′ strug′gle s Todeskampf m
death′ trap′ s (fig) Mausefalle f
death′ war′rant s Hinrichtungsbefehl m
debacle [de'bakəl] s Zusammenbruch m
de-bar [dɪ'bar] v (pret & pp –barred; ger –barring) tr (from) ausschließen (aus)
debark [dɪ'bark] tr ausschiffen || intr sich ausschiffen, an Land gehen
debarkation [,dibar'ke/ən] s Ausschiffung f

debase [dɪ'bes] *tr* entwürdigen; (*currency*) entwerten

debatable [dɪ'betəbəl] *adj* strittig

debate [dɪ'bet] *s* Debatte *f* || *tr & intr* debattieren

debauch [dɪ'bɔtʃ] *s* Schwelgerei *f* || *tr* verderben; (*seduce*) verführen; **d. oneself** verkommen

debauched' *adj* ausschweifend

debauchee [,debə't/i] *s* Wüstling *m*

debauchery [dɪ'bɔtʃəri] *s* Schwelgerei *f*

debenture [dɪ'bentʃər] *s* (*bond*) Obligation *f*; (*voucher*) Schuldschein *m*

debilitate [dɪ'bɪlɪ,tet] *tr* entkräften

debility [dɪ'bɪlɪti] *s* Schwäche *f*

debit ['debɪt] *s* Debet *n*, Soll *n*; (*as entry*) Belastung *f*

de'bit bal'ance *s* Sollsaldo *n*

de'bit side' *s* Soll *n*, Sollseite *f*

debonair [,debə'ner] *adj* (*courteous*) höflich; (*carefree*) heiter und sorglos

debris [de'bri] *s* Trümmer *pl*

debt [det] *s* Schuld *f*; **be in s.o.'s d.** j–m verpflichtet sein; **run into d.** in Schulden geraten

debtor ['detər] *s* Schuldner –in *mf*

de·bug [dɪ'bʌg] *v pret & pp* –bugged; *ger* –bugging) *tr* (*remove defects from*) bereinigen; (*electron*) Abhörgeräte entfernen aus

debut [de'bju] *s* Debüt *n*; **make one's d.** debütieren

debutante ['debju,tɑnt] *s* Debütantin *f*

decade ['deked] *s* Jahrzehnt *n*, Dekade *f*

decadence ['dekədəns] *s* Dekadenz *f*

decadent ['dekədənt] *adj* dekadent; (*art*) entartet

decal ['dikæl] *s* Abziehbild *n*

decanter [dɪ'kæntər] *s* Karaffe *f*

decapitate [dɪ'kæpɪ,tet] *tr* enthaupten

decathlon [dɪ'kæθlɑn] *s* Zehnkampf *m*

decay [dɪ'ke] *s* (*rotting*) Verwesung *f*; (fig) Verfall *m*; (dent) Karies *f*; **fall into d.** (& fig) in Verfall geraten || *intr* verfaulen; (fig) verfallen

decease [dɪ'sis] *s* Ableben *n*

deceased' *adj* verstorben || *s* Verstorbene *mf*

deceit [dɪ'sit] *s* Betrügerei *f*

deceitful [dɪ'sitfəl] *adj* betrügerisch

deceive [dɪ'siv] *tr* betrügen || *intr* trügen

decelerate [dɪ'selə,ret] *tr* verlangsamen || *intr* seine Geschwindigkeit verringern

December [dɪ'sembər] *s* Dezember *m*

decency ['disənsi] *s* Anstand *m*; **decencies** Anstandsformen *pl*

decent ['disənt] *adj* anständig

decentralize [dɪ'sentrə,laɪz] *tr* dezentralisieren

deception [dɪ'sepʃən] *s* (*act of deceiving*) Betrug *m*; (*state of being deceived*) Täuschung *f*

deceptive [dɪ'septɪv] *adj* trügerisch; (*misleading*) irreführend; (*similarity*) täuschend

decide [dɪ'saɪd] *tr* entscheiden || *intr* (**on**) sich entscheiden, sich entschließen (über *acc*, für)

deciduous [dɪ'sɪdʒʊ·əs] *adj* blattabwerfend; **d. tree** Laubbaum *m*

decimal ['desɪməl] *adj* dezimal || *s* Dezimalzahl *f*

dec'imal place' *s* Dezimalstelle *f*

dec'imal point' *s* (*in German the comma is used to separate the decimal fraction from the integer*) Komma *n*

decimate ['desɪ,met] *tr* dezimieren

decipher [dɪ'saɪfər] *tr* entziffern

decision [dɪ'sɪʒən] *s* Entscheidung *f*, Entschluß *m*; (jur) Urteil *n*

decisive [dɪ'saɪsɪv] *adj* entscheidend

deck [dek] *s* (*of cards*) Spiel *n*; (data proc) Kartensatz *m*; (naut) Deck *n*, Verdeck *n* || *tr* (coll) zu Boden schlagen; **d. out** ausschmücken

deck' chair' *s* Liegestuhl *m*

deck' hand' *s* gemeiner Matrose *m*

deck' land'ing *s* (aer) Trägerlandung *f*

declaim [dɪ'klem] *s* & *intr* deklamieren

declaration [,deklə'reʃən] *s* Erklärung *f*; (at customs) Zollerklärung *f*

declarative [dɪ'klærətɪv] *adj*—**d. sentence** Aussagesatz *m*

declare [dɪ'kler] *tr* erklären; (*tourist's belongings*) verzollen; (*commercial products*) deklarieren; **d. oneself against** sich aussprechen gegen

declension [dɪ'klenʃən] *s* Deklination *f*

declinable [dɪ'klaɪnəbəl] *adj* deklinierbar

decline [dɪ'klaɪn] *s* (*decrease*) Abnahme *f*; (*in prices*) Rückgang *m*; (*deterioration*) Verschlechterung *f*; (*slope*) Abhang *m*; (fig) Niedergang *m*; **be on the d.** in Abnahme begriffen sein || *tr* (*refuse*) ablehnen; (gram) deklinieren || *intr* (*refuse*) ablehnen; (*descend*) sich senken; (*sink*) sinken; (*draw to a close*) zu Ende gehen

declivity [dɪ'klɪvɪti] *s* Abhang *m*

decode [di'kod] *tr* entschlüsseln

decompose [,dikəm'poz] *tr* zerlegen || *intr* sich zersetzen, verwesen

decomposition [,dikampə'zɪʃən] *s* Zersetzung *f*, Verwesung *f*

decompression [,dikəm'preʃən] *s* Dekompression *f*

decontamination [,dikan,tæmɪ'neʃən] *s* Entseuchung *f*

décor [de'kɔr] *s* Dekor *m*

decorate ['dekə,ret] *tr* dekorieren, (aus)schmücken; (*a new room*) einrichten; (*e.g., with a badge*) auszeichnen

decoration [,dekə'reʃən] *s* Schmuck *m*; (medal) Orden *m*, Ehrenzeichen *n*, Dekoration *f*

decorative ['dekərətɪv] *adj* dekorativ

decorator ['dekə,retər] *s* Dekorateur –in *mf*

decorous ['dekərəs] *adj* schicklich

decorum [dɪ'korəm] *s* Schicklichkeit *f*

decoy ['dikɔr] *s* (*bird or person*) Lockvogel *m*; (*anything used as a lure*) Lockmittel *n* || [dɪ'kɔɪ] *tr* locken

decrease ['dikris] *s* Abnahme *f* ||

[dɪ'kris] *tr* verringern || *intr* abnehmen

decree [dɪ'kri] *s* Dekret *n*, Verordnung *f* || *tr* dekretieren, verordnen

decrepit [dɪ'krepɪt] *adj* (*age-worn*) altersschwach; (*frail*) gebrechlich

de-cry [dɪ'kraɪ] *v* (*pret & pp* –**cried**) *tr* (*disparage*) herabsetzen; (*censure openly*) kritisieren

dedicate ['dedɪˌket] *tr* (*a book, one's life*) (**to**) widmen (*dat*); (*a building*) einweihen

dedication [ˌdedɪ'keʃən] *s* Widmung *f*; (*of a building, etc.*) Einweihung *f*; (**to**) Hingabe *f* (an *acc*)

deduce [dɪ'd(j)us] *tr* (**from**) schließen (aus)

deduct [dɪ'dʌkt] *tr* abziehen, abrechnen

deduction [dɪ'dʌkʃən] *s* Abzug *m*; (*conclusion*) Schluß *m*, Folgerung *f*

deed [did] *s* (*act*) Tat *f*; (*jur*) Besitzurkunde *f*

deem [dim] *tr* halten für; **d. s.o. worthy of my confidence** j-n meines Vertrauens für würdig halten

deep [dip] *adj* tief; (*recondite*) dunkel; (*impression*) tiefgehend; (*color, sound*) tief, dunkel; **be d. in debt** tief in Schulden stecken; **four** (**ranks**) **d.** in Viererreihen; **in d. water** (fig) in Schwierigkeiten; **that's too d. for me** das ist mir zu hoch || *adv* tief; **d. down in** tief innen in (*dat*) || *s* Tiefe *f*, Meer *n*

deepen ['dipən] *tr* (& fig) vertiefen || *intr* sich vertiefen

deep'-freeze' *v* (*pret* –**freezed** & –**froze**; *pp* –**freezed** & –**frozen**) *tr* tiefkühlen

deep'-fry' *v* (*pret & pp* –**fried**) *tr* fritieren

deep'-laid' *adj* schlau angelegt

deep' mourn'ing *s* tiefe Trauer *f*

deep'-root'ed *adj* tiefsitzend

**deep'-set' *adj* (*eyes*) tiefliegend

deer [dɪr] *s* Hirsch *m*, Reh *n*, Rotwild *n*

deer'skin' *s* Hirschleder *n*, Wildleder *n*

deface [dɪ'fes] *tr* (*disfigure*) verunstalten; (*make illegible*) unleserlich machen

defacement [dɪ'fesmənt] *s* Verunstaltung *f*

de facto [di'fækto] *adj & adv* tatsächlich, de facto

defamation [ˌdefə'meʃən] *s* Verleumdung *f*

defame [dɪ'fem] *tr* verleumden

default [dɪ'fɔlt] *s* (*in duties*) Unterlassung *f*; (fin) Verzug *m*; **by d.** (jur) durch Nichterscheinen; (sport) durch Nichtantreten; **in d. of** in Ermangelung (*genit*) || *tr* nicht erfüllen; (fin) nicht zahlen || *intr* seinen Verpflichtungen nicht nachkommen; (fin) in Verzug sein

defeat [dɪ'fit] *s* Niederlage *f*; (parl) Niederstimmen *n*; **admit d.** sich geschlagen geben || *tr* besiegen, schlagen; (*frustrate*) hilflos machen; (*plans*) zunichte machen; (*a bill*) niederstimmen; **d. the purpose** den Zweck verfehlen

defeatism [dɪ'fitɪzəm] *s* Defätismus *m*

defeatist [dɪ'fitɪst] *s* Defätist –in *mf*

defecate ['defɪˌket] *intr* Stuhl haben

defect ['difekt] *s* Defekt *m*; (*physical or mental defect*) Gebrechen *n*; (*imperfection*) Mangel *m*; (*in manufacture*) Fabrikationsfehler *m* || [dɪ'fekt] *intr* (**from**) (*a religion*) abfallen (von); (*a party*) abtrünnig werden (von); (**to**) überlaufen (zu)

defection [dɪ'fekʃən] *s* Abfall *m*; (**to**) Übertritt *m* (zu)

defective [dɪ'fektɪv] *adj* fehlerhaft; (gram) unvollständig; (tech) defekt

defector [dɪ'fektər] *s* (pol) Abtrünnige *mf*, Überläufer –in *mf*

defend [dɪ'fend] *tr* verteidigen

defendant [dɪ'fendənt] *s* (*in civil suit*) Beklagte *mf*; (*in criminal suit*) Angeklagte *mf*

defender [dɪ'fendər] *s* Verteidiger –in *mf*; (sport) Titelverteidiger –in *mf*

defense [dɪ'fens] *s* (& jur, sport) Verteidigung *f*; (*tactical*) (mil) Abwehr *f*; **d. against** (*e.g., disease*) Schutz *m* vor (*dat*)

defenseless [dɪ'fenslɪs] *adj* schutzlos

defensible [dɪ'fensɪbəl] *adj* verteidigungsfähig; (*argument, claim*) verfechtbar

defensive [dɪ'fensɪv] *adj* defensiv; (mil) Verteidigungs-, Abwehr- || *s* Defensive *f*; (*tactical*) Abwehr *f*; **be on the d.**—sich in der Defensive befinden

de-fer [dɪ'fʌr] *v* (*pret & pp* –**ferred**; *ger* –**ferring**) *tr* verschieben; (mil) zurückstellen || *intr*—**d.** to nachgeben (*dat*)

deference ['defərəns] *s* (*courteous regard*) Ehrerbietung *f*; (*yielding*) Nachgiebigkeit *f*; **in d.** to aus Rücksicht gegen; **with all due d.** to bei aller Achtung vor (*dat*)

deferential [ˌdefə'renʃəl] *adj* ehrerbietig, rücksichtsvoll

deferment [dɪ'fʌrmənt] *s* Aufschub *m*; (mil) Zurückstellung *f*

defiance [dɪ'faɪəns] *s* Trotz *m*; **in d. of s.o.** j-m zum Trotz

defiant [dɪ'faɪ-ənt] *adj* trotzig

deficiency [dɪ'fɪʃənsi] *s* (**of**) Mangel *m* (an *dat*); (*shortcoming*) Defekt *m*; (*deficit*) Defizit *n*

deficient [dɪ'fɪʃənt] *adj* mangelhaft; **be d. in** Mangel haben an (*dat*); **mentally d.** schwachsinnig

deficit ['defɪsɪt] *s* Defizit *n*

defilade [ˌdefɪ'led] *s* Deckung *f* || *tr* gegen Feuer sichern

defile [dɪ'faɪl], ['dɪfaɪl] *s* Hohlweg *m* || [dɪ'faɪl] *tr* beflecken

defilement [dɪ'faɪlmənt] *s* Befleckung *f*

define [dɪ'faɪn] *tr* definieren, bestimmen; (*e.g., boundaries*) festlegen

definite ['defɪnɪt] *adj* bestimmt

definition [ˌdefɪ'nɪʃən] *s* Definition *f*, Bestimmung *f*; (opt) Bildschärfe *f*

definitive [dɪ'fɪnɪtɪv] *adj* endgültig

deflate [dɪ'flet] *tr* Luft ablassen aus; (*prices*) herabsetzen; (*s.o.'s ego, hopes*) e-n Stoß versetzen (*dat*)

deflation [dɪ'fleʃən] s (fin) Deflation f

deflect [dɪ'flekt] tr ablenken || intr (from) abweichen (von)

deflection [dɪ'flekʃən] s Ablenkung f; Abweichung f; (of an indicator) Ausschlag m; (of light rays) Beugung f; (radar, telv) Ablenkung f

deflower [dɪ'flaʊ-ər] tr entjungfern

defoliate [di'folɪ,et] tr entblättern

deforest [di'forɪst] tr abholzen

deform [dɪ'form] tr entstellen

deformed' adj verwachsen, mißförmig

deformity [dɪ'fɔrmɪti] s (state of being deformed) Mißgestalt f; (deformed part) Verwachsung f; (ugliness) Häßlichkeit f

defraud [dɪ'frɔd] tr (of) betrügen (um)

defray [dɪ'fre] tr tragen, bestreiten

defrock [di'frak] tr das Priesteramt entziehen (dat)

defrost [dɪ'frɔst] tr entfrosten

defroster [dɪ'frɔstər] s Entfroster m

deft [deft] adj flink, fingerfertig

defunct [dɪ'fʌŋkt] adj (person) verstorben; (no longer in operation) stillgelegt; (no longer in effect) außer Kraft (befindlich); (newspaper) eingegangen

de•fy [dɪ'faɪ] v (pret & pp –fied) tr trotzen (dat); (challenge) herausfordern; **d. description** sich nicht beschreiben lassen

degeneracy [dɪ'dʒenərəsi] s Entartung f

degenerate [dɪ'dʒenərɪt] adj entartet, verkommen || [dɪ'dʒenə,ret] intr entarten; (into) ausarten (in acc)

degrade [dɪ'gred] tr degradieren; (bring into low esteem) entwürdigen

degrad'ing adj entwürdigend

degree [dɪ'gri] s Grad m; (gram) Steigerungsstufe f; **by degrees** gradweise; **d. of latitude** Breitengrad m; **d. of longitude** Längengrad m; **take one's d.** promovieren; **to a d.** einigermaßen; **to a high d.** in hohem Maße

dehumanize [dɪ'hjumə,naɪz] tr entmenschlichen

dehumidifier [,dihju'mɪdɪ,faɪ-ər] s Luftentfeuchter m

dehumidi•fy [,dihju'mɪdɪ,faɪ] v (pret & pp –fied) tr entfeuchten

dehydrate [di'haɪdret] tr (vegetables) dörren, das Wasser entziehen (dat); (chem) dehydrieren || intr das Wasser verlieren

dehy'drated adj (vegetables) Trocken–; (body) dehydriert

deice [di'aɪs] tr enteisen

dei•fy ['di-ɪ,faɪ] v (pret & pp –fied) tr (a man) zum Gott erheben; (a woman) zur Göttin erheben

deject'ed adj niedergeschlagen

dejection [dɪ'dʒekʃən] s Niedergeschlagenheit f, Mutlosigkeit f

delay [dɪ'le] s Aufschub m, Verzögerung f; **without d.** unverzüglich || (postpone) aufschieben; (detain) aufhalten || intr zögern

delectable [dɪ'lektəbəl] adj ergötzlich

delegate ['delɪ,get], ['delɪgɪt] s Delegierte mf || ['delɪ,get] tr delegieren; (authority) übertragen

delegation [,delɪ'geʃən] s (persons delegated) Delegation f; (e.g., of authority) Übertragung f

delete [dɪ'lit] tr tilgen

deletion [dɪ'liʃən] s Tilgung f

deliberate [dɪ'lɪbərɪt] adj (intentional) vorsätzlich, bewußt; (slow) gemessen, bedächtig || [dɪ'lɪbə,ret] intr überlegen; (said of several persons) beratschlagen; **d. on** sich beraten über (acc)

deliberately [dɪ'lɪbərɪtli] adv mit Absicht

deliberation [dɪ,lɪbə'reʃən] s Überlegung f; (by several persons) Beratung f; (slowness) Bedächtigkeit f

delicacy ['delɪkəsi] s Zartheit f; (fine food) Delikatesse f

delicate ['delɪkɪt] adj fein, delikat; (situation) heikel; (health) zart

delicatessen [,delɪkə'tesən] s (food) Delikatessen pl; (store) Delikatessengeschäft n

delicious [dɪ'lɪʃəs] adj köstlich

delight [dɪ'laɪt] s Freude f; (high degree of pleasure) Entzücken n; **take d. in** Freude finden an (dat) || tr entzücken, erfreuen; **be delighted by** sich freuen an (dat); **I'll be delighted to come** ich komme mit dem größten Vergnügen || intr–**d. in** sich ergötzen an (dat)

delightful [dɪ'laɪtfəl] adj entzückend

delimit [dɪ'lɪmɪt] tr abgrenzen

delineate [dɪ'lɪnɪ,et] tr zeichnen

delinquency [dɪ'lɪŋkwənsi] s Pflichtvergessenheit f; (misdeed) Vergehen n

delinquent [dɪ'lɪŋkwənt] adj pflichtvergessen; (guilty) straffällig; (overdue) rückständig; (in default) säumig || s Straffällige mf

delirious [dɪ'lɪrɪ-əs] adj irre; (with) rasend (vor dat)

delirium [dɪ'lɪrɪ-əm] s Fieberwahn m

deliver [dɪ'lɪvər] tr liefern; (a message) überreichen; (free) befreien; (mail) zustellen; (a speech) halten; (a blow) versetzen; (a verdict) aussprechen; (a child) zur Welt bringen; (votes) bringen; (a ball) werfen; (relig) erlösen

deliverance [dɪ'lɪvərəns] s Erlösung f

delivery [dɪ'lɪvəri] s Lieferung f; (freeing) Befreiung f; (of mail) Zustellung f; (of a speaker, actor, singer) Vortragsweise f; (of a pitcher) Wurf m; (childbirth) Entbindung f

deliv'ery-man' s (–men') Austräger m

deliv'ery room' s Kreißsaal m

deliv'ery truck' s Lieferwagen m

dell [del] s enges Tal n

delouse [di'laʊs] tr entlausen

delta ['deltə] s Delta n

delude [dɪ'lud] tr täuschen

deluge ['deljudʒ] s Überschwemmung f; (fig) Hochflut f; **Deluge** (Bib) Sintflut f || tr überschwemmen; (with letters, etc.) überschütten

delusion [dɪ'luʒən] s (state of being deluded) Täuschung f; (misconcep-

tion) Wahnvorstellung *f*; (*psychiatry*) Wahn *m*; **delusions of grandeur** Größenwahn *m*

deluxe [dɪˈluks], [dɪˈlʌks] *adj* Luxus-

delve [delv] *intr*—**d. into** sich vertiefen in (*acc*)

demagogue [ˈdeməˌgɑg] *s* Volksverführer –in *mf*

demand [dɪˈmænd] *s* Verlangen *n*; (*com*) (*for*) Nachfrage *f* (nach); **in** (*great*) **d.** (sehr) gefragt; **make demands on** Ansprüche erheben auf (*acc*); **on d.** auf Verlangen ‖ *tr* (*from or of*) verlangen (von), fordern (von)

demand/ing *adj* anspruchsvoll; (*strict*) streng

demarcation line/ [ˌdimɑrˈkeʃən] *s* Demarkationslinie *f*

demean [dɪˈmin] *tr* erniedrigen

demeanor [dɪˈminər] *s* Benehmen *n*

demented [dɪˈmentɪd] *adj* wahnsinnig

demerit [dɪˈmerɪt] *s* (*fault*) Fehler *m*; (*deficiency mark*) Minuspunkt *m*

demigod [ˈdemɪˌgɑd] *s* Halbgott *m*

demijohn [ˈdemɪˌdʒɑn] *s* Korbflasche *f*

demilitarize [diˈmɪlɪtəˌraɪz] *tr* entmilitarisieren

demise [dɪˈmaɪz] *s* Ableben *n*

demitasse [ˈdemɪˌtæs], [ˈdemɪˌtɑs] *s* Mokkatasse *f*

demobilize [diˈmobɪˌlaɪz] *tr & intr* demobilisieren

democracy [dɪˈmɑkrəsi] *s* Demokratie *f*

democrat [ˈdeməˌkræt] *s* Demokrat –in *mf*

democratic [ˌdeməˈkrætɪk] *adj* demokratisch

demolish [dɪˈmɑlɪʃ] *tr* (*raze*) niederreißen; (*destroy*) zertrümmern; (*an argument*) vernichten; (*devour*) (coll) verschlingen

demolition [ˌdeməˈlɪʃən], [ˌdimə-ˈlɪʃən] *s* (*act of razing*) Abbruch *m*; (*by explosives*) Sprengung *f*; **demolitions** Sprengstoff *m*

demoli/tion squad/ *s* Sprengkommando *n*

demoli/tion work/ *s* Sprengarbeiten *pl*

demon [ˈdimən] *s* Dämon *m*, böser Geist *m*

demonstrable [dɪˈmɑnstrəbəl] *adj* beweisbar

demonstrate [ˈdemənˌstret] *tr* (*prove*) beweisen; (*explain*) dartun; (*display*) zeigen; (*a product, process*) vorführen ‖ *intr* (pol) demonstrieren

demonstration [ˌdemənˈstreʃən] *s* (com) Vorführung *f*; (pol) Demonstration *f*

demonstrative [dɪˈmɑnstrətɪv] *adj* (*showing emotions*) gefühlvoll; (*illustrative*) anschaulich; (gram) hinweisend

demonstrator [ˈdemənˌstretər] *s* (*of products*) Vorführer –in *mf*; (*model used in demonstration*) Vorführmodell *n*; (pol) Demonstrant –in *mf*

demoralize [dɪˈmɔrəˌlaɪz] *tr* demoralisieren

demote [dɪˈmot] *tr* (*an employee*) her-

abstufen; (*a student*) zurückversetzen; (mil) degradieren

demotion [dɪˈmoʃən] *s* (*of an employee*) Herabstufung *f*; (*of a student*) Zurückversetzung *f*; (mil) Degradierung *f*

de-mur [dɪˈmʌr] *v* (*pret & pp* –murred; *ger* –murring) *intr* Einwände erheben

demure [dɪˈmjur] *adj* zimperlich

den [den] *s* (*of animals; of thieves*) Höhle *f*; (*comfortable room*) Freizeitraum *m*

denaturalize [diˈnætʃərəˌlaɪz] *tr* ausbürgern

denial [dɪˈnaɪəl] *s* (*of an assertion*) Leugnung *f*; (*of guilt*) Leugnen *n*; (*of a request*) Ablehnung *f*; (*of faith*) Ableugnung *f*; (*of rights*) Verweigerung *f*; (*of a report*) Dementi *n*

denigrate [ˈdenɪˌgret] *tr* anschwärzen

denim [ˈdenɪm] *s* Drillich *m*

denizen [ˈdenɪzən] *s* Bewohner –in *mf*

Denmark [ˈdenmɑrk] *s* Dänemark *n*

denomination [dɪˌnɑmɪˈneʃən] *s* Bezeichnung *f*; (*class, kind*) Klasse *f*; (*of money*) Nennwert *m*; (*of shares*) Stückelung *f*; (relig) Konfession *f*, Bekenntnis *n*; **in denominations of five and ten dollars** in Fünf- und Zehndollarnoten

denotation [ˌdinoˈteʃən] *s* Bedeutung *f*

denote [dɪˈnot] *tr* (*mean*) bedeuten; (*indicate*) anzeigen

dénouement [deˈnumɑ̃] *s* Auflösung *f*

denounce [dɪˈnauns] *tr* (*inform against*) denunzieren; (*condemn openly*) brandmarken, anprangern; (*a treaty*) kündigen

dense [dens] *adj* dicht; (coll) beschränkt

density [ˈdensɪti] *s* Dichte *f*

dent [dent] *s* Beule *f* ‖ *tr* einbeulen

dental [ˈdentəl] *adj* Zahn–; (ling) dental ‖ *s* (ling) Zahnlaut *m*

den/tal hygiene/ *s* Zahnpflege *f*

den/tal surgeon *s* Zahnarzt *m*, Zahnärztin *f*

dentifrice [ˈdentɪfrɪs] *s* Zahnputzmittel *n*

dentist [ˈdentɪst] *s* Zahnarzt *m*, Zahnärztin *f*

dentistry [ˈdentɪstri] *s* Zahnheilkunde *f*

denture [ˈdentʃər] *s* künstliches Gebiß *n*

denunciation [dɪˌnʌnsɪˈeʃən] *s* (*informing against*) Denunzierung *f*; (*public condemnation*) Brandmarkung *f*

de-ny [dɪˈnaɪ] *v* (*pret & pp* –nied) *tr* (*a statement*) leugnen; (*officially*) dementieren; (*a request*) ablehnen; (*one's faith*) ableugnen; (*rights*) verweigern; **d. oneself s.th.** sich [*dat*] etw versagen; **d. s.o. s.th.** j–m etw aberkennen

deodorant [diˈodərənt] *s* Deodorant *n*

deodorize [diˈodəˌraɪz] *tr* desodorieren

deoxidize [diˈɑksɪˌdaɪz] *tr* desoxydieren

depart [dɪ'pɑrt] *intr* (*on foot*) fortgehen; (*in a vehicle or boat*) abfahren; (*by plane*) abfliegen; (*on horseback*) abreiten; (*on a trip*) abreisen; (*deviate*) abweichen

department [dɪ'pɑrtmənt] *s* (*subdivision*) Abteilung *f*; (*field*) Fach *n*; (*principal branch of government*) Ministerium *n*; (*government office*) Amt *n*; (*educ*) Abteilung *f*

depart'ment head' *s* Abteilungsleiter –in *mf*

depart'ment store' *s* Kaufhaus *n*, Warenhaus *n*

departure [dɪ'pɑrtʃər] *s* (*on foot*) Weggehen *n*; (*by car, boat, train*) Abfahrt *f*, Abreise *f*; (*by plane*) Abflug *m*; (*deviation*) Abweichung *f*

depend [dɪ'pɛnd] *intr* (**on**) abhängen (von); (*rely on*) sich verlassen (auf *acc*); **depending on** je nach; **depending on how** je nachdem; **it all depends** (coll) es kommt darauf an

dependable [dɪ'pɛndəbəl] *adj* zuverlässig

dependence [dɪ'pɛndəns] *s* Abhängigkeit *f*

dependency [dɪ'pɛndənsi] *s* Schutzgebiet *n*

dependent [dɪ'pɛndənt] *adj* (**on**) abhängig (von) || *s* Abhängige *mf*; (*for tax purposes*) Unterhaltsberechtigte *mf*

depict [dɪ'pɪkt] *tr* schildern

deplete [dɪ'plit] *tr* entleeren; (fig) erschöpfen

deplorable [dɪ'plorəbəl] *adj* (*situation*) beklagenswert; (*regrettable*) bedauerlich; (*bad*) schlecht

deplore [dɪ'plor] *tr* bedauern

deploy [dɪ'plɔɪ] *tr* entfalten || *intr* sich entfalten

deployment [dɪ'plɔɪmənt] *s* Entfaltung *f*

depolarize [di'polə‚raɪz] *tr* depolarisieren

deponent [dɪ'ponənt] *s* (gram) Deponens *n*; (jur) Deponent –in *mf*

depopulate [di'pɑpjə‚let] *tr* entvölkern

deport [dɪ'port] *tr* deportieren; **d. oneself** sich benehmen

deportation [‚dipor'teʃən] *s* Deportation *f*

deportment [dɪ'portmənt] *s* Benehmen *n*

depose [dɪ'poz] *tr* (*from office*) absetzen; (jur) bezeugen || *intr* (jur) unter Eid aussagen; (*in writing*) (jur) eidesstattlich versichern

deposit [dɪ'pɑzɪt] *s* (*partial payment*) Anzahlung *f*; (*at a bank*) Einlage *f*; (*for safekeeping*) Hinterlegung *f*; (geol) Ablagerung *f*; (min) Vorkommen *n*; **for d. only** nur zur Verrechnung || *tr* (*set down*) niederlegen; (*money at a bank*) einlegen; (*a check*) verrechnen; (*as part payment*) anzahlen; (*for safekeeping*) deponieren; (geol) ablagern; (*a coin*) (telp) einwerfen

depositor [dɪ'pɑzɪtər] *s* Einzahler –in *mf*; (*of valuables*) Hinterleger –in *mf*

depos'it slip' *s* Einzahlungsbeleg *m*

depot ['dipo], ['depo] *s* (*bus station; storage place*) Depot *n*; (*train station*) Bahnhof *m*

depraved [dɪ'prevd] *adj* verworfen

depravity [dɪ'prævɪti] *s* Verworfenheit *f*

deprecate ['dɛprɪ‚ket] *tr* mißbilligen

depreciate [dɪ'priʃɪ‚et] *tr* (*money, stocks*) abwerten; (*for tax purposes*) abschreiben; (*value or price*) herabsetzen; (*disparage*) geringschätzen || *intr* im Wert sinken

depreciation [dɪ‚priʃɪ'eʃən] *s* (*decrease in value*) Wertminderung *f*; (*of currency or stocks*) Abwertung *f*; (*for tax purposes*) Abschreibung *f*

depress [dɪ'prɛs] *tr* niederdrücken; (*sadden*) deprimieren; (*cause to sink*) herunterdrücken

depressed' *adj* (*saddened*) niedergeschlagen; (*market*) flau

depressed' ar'ea *s* Notstandsgebiet *n*

depress'ing *adj* deprimierend

depression [dɪ'prɛʃən] *s* (*mental state; economic crisis*) Depression *f*; (geol) Vertiefung *f*

deprive [dɪ'praɪv] *tr*—**d. s.o. of s.th.** j-m etw entziehen; (*withhold*) j-m etw vorenthalten

depth [dɛpθ] *s* Tiefe *f*; **go beyond one's d.** den Boden unter den Füßen verlieren; **in d.** gründlich

depth' charge' *s* Wasserbombe *f*

depth' of field' *s* (phot) Tiefenschärfe *f*

deputation [‚dɛpjə'teʃən] *s* Abordnung *f*

deputize ['dɛpjə‚taɪz] *tr* abordnen

deputy ['dɛpjəti] *s* Vertreter –in *mf*; (pol) Abgeordnete *mf*

derail [dɪ'rel] *tr* zum Entgleisen bringen || *intr* entgleisen

derailment [dɪ'relmənt] *s* Entgleisung *f*

deranged [dɪ'rendʒd] *adj* geistesgestört

derangement [dɪ'rendʒmənt] *s* Geistesgestörtheit *f*

derby ['dɑrbi] *s* (*hat*) Melone *f*; (*race*) Derbyrennen *n*

derelict ['dɛrɪlɪkt] *adj* (*negligent*) (**in**) nachlässig (in *dat*); (*abandoned*) herrenlos || *s* (*ship; bum*) Wrack *n*

dereliction [‚dɛrɪ'lɪkʃən] *s* (*neglect*) Vernachlässigung *f*

deride [dɪ'raɪd] *tr* verspotten

derision [dɪ'rɪʒən] *s* Spott *m*

derivation [‚dɛrɪ'veʃən] *s* (gram, math) Ableitung *f*

derivative [dɪ'rɪvətɪv] *adj* abgeleitet || *s* (chem) Derivat *n*; (gram, math) Ableitung *f*

derive [dɪ'raɪv] *tr* (*obtain*) gewinnen; (gram, math) ableiten; **d. pleasure from s.th.** Freude an etw finden || *intr* (**from**) herstammen (von)

dermatologist [‚dʌrmə'tɑlədʒɪst] *s* Hautarzt *m*, Hautärztin *f*

derogatory [dɪ'rɑgə‚tori] *adj* abfällig

derrick ['dɛrɪk] *s* (*over an oil well*) Bohrturm *m*; (naut) Ladebaum *m*

dervish ['dʌrvɪʃ] *s* Derwisch *m*

desalinization [di‚sɛlɪnɪ'zeʃən] *s* Entsalzung *f*

desalt [di'sɔlt] *tr* entsalzen
descend [dɪ'send] *tr* hinuntergehen ‖ *intr* (*dismount, alight*) absteigen; (*said of a plane*) niedergehen; (*from a tree, from heaven*) herabsteigen; (*said of a road*) sich senken; (*pass by inheritance*) (**to**) übergehen (auf *acc*); **be descended from** abstammen von; **d. upon** hereinbrechen über (*acc*)
descendant [dɪ'sendənt] *s* Abkömmling *m*, Nachkomme *m*; **descendants** Nachkommenschaft *f*
descendent [dɪ'sendənt] *adj* absteigend
descent [dɪ'sent] *s* Abstieg *m*; (*lineage*) Herkunft *f*; (*of a plane or parachute*) Niedergehen *n*; (*slope*) Abhang *m*; (*hostile raid*) (**on**) Überfall *m* (auf *acc*)
describe [dɪ'skraɪb] *tr* beschreiben
description [dɪ'skrɪpʃən] *s* Beschreibung *f*; (*type*) Art *f*; **beyond d.** unbeschreiblich
descriptive [dɪ'skrɪptɪv] *adj* beschreibend
de•scry [dɪ'skraɪ] *v* (*pret* & *pp* **–scried**) *tr* erspähen, erblicken
desecrate ['desɪˌkret] *tr* entweihen
desecration [ˌdesɪ'kreʃən] *s* Entweihung *f*
desegregate [di'segrɪˌget] *tr* die Rassentrennung aufheben in (*dat*)
desegregation [diˌsegrɪ'geʃən] *s* Aufhebung *f* der Rassentrennung
desert ['dezərt] *adj* öde, wüst; (*sand, warfare, etc.*) Wüsten– ‖ *s* Wüste *f*; (*fig*) Öde *f* ‖ [dɪ'zʌrt] *s* Verdienst *m*; **get one's just deserts** seinen wohlverdienten Lohn empfangen ‖ *tr* verlassen ‖ *intr* (mil) desertieren; (**to**) überlaufen (zu)
deserter [dɪ'zʌrtər] *s* Deserteur *m*
desertion [dɪ'zʌrʃən] *s* Verlassen *n*; (*of a party*) Abfall *m*; (mil) Fahnenflucht *f*
deserve [dɪ'zʌrv] *tr* verdienen
deservedly [dɪ'zʌrvɪdli] *adv* mit Recht
deserv′ing *adj* (**of**) würdig (*genit*)
design [dɪ'zaɪn] *s* (*outline*) Entwurf *m*; (*pattern*) Muster *n*; (*plan*) Plan *m*; (*plot*) Anschlag *m*; (*of a building, etc.*) Bauart *f*; (*aim*) Absicht *f*; **designs on** böse Absichten auf (*acc*) ‖ *tr* (*make a preliminary sketch of*) entwerfen; (*draw up detailed plans for*) konstruieren; **designed for** gedacht für
designate ['dezɪgˌnet] *tr* (**as**) bezeichnen (als); (**to**) ernennen (zu)
designation [ˌdezɪg'neʃən] *s* (*act of designating*) Kennzeichnung *f*; (*title*) Bezeichnung *f*; (*appointment*) Ernennung *f*
designer [dɪ'zaɪnər] *s* (*of patterns*) Musterzeichner –in *mf*; (*of fashions*) Modeschöpfer –in *mf*; (theat) Dekorateur –in *mf*
design′ing *adj* intrigant; (*calculating*) berechnend
desirable [dɪ'zaɪrəbəl] *adj* wünschenswert, begehrenswert
desire [dɪ'zaɪr] *s* (*wish*) Wunsch *m*; (*interest*) Lust *f*; (*craving*) Begierde

f; (*thing desired*) Gewünschte *n* ‖ *tr* wünschen
desirous [dɪ'zaɪrəs] *adj* (**of**) begierig (nach)
desist [dɪ'zɪst] *intr* (**from**) ablassen (von)
desk [desk] *s* Schreibtisch *m*; (*of a teacher*) Pult *n*; (*of a pupil*) Schulbank *f*; (*in a hotel*) Kasse *f*
desk′ cop′y *s* Freiexemplar *n*
desk′ lamp′ *s* Tischlampe *f*
desk′ pad′ *s* Schreibunterlage *f*
desolate ['desəlɪt] *adj* (*barren*) öde; (*joyless*) trostlos; (*deserted*) verlassen; (*delapidated*) verfallen ‖ ['desəˌlet] *tr* verwüsten
desolation [ˌdesə'leʃən] *s* (*devastation*) Verwüstung *f*; (*dreariness*) Trostlosigkeit *f*
despair [dɪs'per] *s* Verzweiflung *f* ‖ *intr* (**of**) verzweifeln (an *dat*)
despair′ing *adj* verzweifelt
despera•do [ˌdespə'rado], [ˌdespə'redo] *s* (**–does** & **–dos**) Desperado *m*
desperate ['despərɪt] *adj* verzweifelt
desperation [ˌdespə'reʃən] *s* Verzweiflung *f*
despicable ['despɪkəbəl] *adj* verächtlich, verachtungswürdig
despise [dɪ'spaɪz] *tr* verachten
despite [dɪ'spaɪt] *prep* trotz (*genit*)
despondency [dɪ'spandənsi] *s* Kleinmut *m*
despondent [dɪ'spandənt] *adj* kleinmütig
despot ['despat] *s* Despot –in *mf*
despotic [des'patɪk] *adj* despotisch
despotism ['despəˌtɪzəm] *s* Despotie *f*; (*as a system*) Despotismus *m*
dessert [dɪ'zʌrt] *s* Nachtisch *m*
destination [ˌdestɪ'neʃən] *s* (*of a trip*) Bestimmungsort *m*, Reiseziel *n*; (*purpose*) Bestimmung *f*
destine ['destɪn] *tr* (**for**) bestimmen (zu or für)
destiny ['destɪni] *s* Schicksal *n*; (*doom*) Verhängnis *n*
destitute ['destɪˌt(j)ut] *adj* mittellos; **d. of** ohne
destitution [ˌdestɪ't(j)uʃən] *s* äußerste Armut *f*
destroy [dɪ'strɔɪ] *tr* vernichten, zerstören; (*animals, bacteria*) töten
destroyer [dɪ'strɔɪ-ər] *s* (nav) Zerstörer *m*
destroy′er es′cort *s* Zerstörergeleitschutz *m*
destruction [dɪ'strʌkʃən] *s* Zerstörung *f*; (*of species*) Ausrottung *f*
destructive [dɪ'strʌktɪv] *adj* zerstörend; (*criticism*) vernichtend; (*tendency*) destruktiv
desultory ['desəlˌtori] *adj* (*without plan*) planlos; (*fitful*) sprunghaft; (*remark*) deplaciert
detach [dɪ'tætʃ] *tr* ablösen; (*along a perforation*) abtrennen; (mil) abkommandieren
detachable [dɪ'tætʃəbəl] *tr* abnehmbar, ablösbar
detached′ *adj* (*building*) alleinstehend; (*objective*) objektiv; (*aloof*) distanziert

detachment [dɪˈtætʃmənt] s Objektivität f; (aloofness) Abstand m; (mil) Trupp m, Kommando n

detail [dɪˈtel], [ˈditel] s Enzelheit f, Detail n; (mil) Kommando n, Trupp m; **details** (pej) Kleinkram m; **in d.** ausführlich || [dɪˈtel] (relate in detail) ausführlich berichten; (list) einzeln aufzählen; (mil) abkommandieren

de'tail draw'ing s Detailzeichnung f

detailed' adj ausführlich; **d. work** Kleinarbeit f

detain [dɪˈten] tr zurückhalten; (jur) in Haft behalten

detect [dɪˈtekt] tr (discover) entdecken; (catch) ertappen

detection [dɪˈtekʃən] s Entdeckung f

detective [dɪˈtektɪv] s Detektiv m

detec'tive sto'ry s Kriminalroman m

detector [dɪˈtektər] s (e.g., of smoke) Spürgerät n; (of objects) Suchgerät n; (rad) Detektor m

détente [deˈtɑnt] s Entspannung f, Détente f

detention [dɪˈtenʃən] s (jur) Haft f

deten'tion camp' s Internierungslager n

deten'tion home' s Haftanstalt f

de-ter [dɪˈtʌr] v (pret & pp **–terred**; ger **–terring**) tr (from) abschrecken (von), abhalten (von)

detergent [dɪˈtʌrdʒənt] s Reinigungsmittel n; (in a washer) Waschmittel n

deteriorate [dɪˈtɪrɪ·əˌret] tr verschlechtern || intr sich verschlechtern

deterioration [dɪˌtɪrɪ·əˈreʃən] s Verschlechterung f, Verfall m

determination [dɪˌtʌrmɪˈneʃən] s Bestimmung f, (resoluteness) Entschlossenheit f; (of boundaries) Festlegung f

determine [dɪˈtʌrmɪn] tr (fix conclusively) bestimmen; (boundaries) festlegen; (decide) entscheiden

deter'mined adj entschlossen

deterrent [dɪˈtʌrənt] adj abschreckend || s Abschreckungsmittel n

detest [dɪˈtest] tr verabscheuen

detestable [dɪˈtestəbəl] adj abscheulich

dethrone [dɪˈθron] tr entthronen

detonate [ˈdetəˌnet] tr explodieren lassen || intr explodieren

detour [ˈditur] s (for cars) Umleitung f; (for pedestrians) Umweg m || tr umleiten || intr e-n Umweg machen

detract [dɪˈtrækt] tr ablenken || intr—**d. from** beeinträchtigen

detraction [dɪˈtrækʃən] s Beeinträchtigung f

detractor [dɪˈtræktər] s Verleumder –in mf

detrain [dɪˈtren] tr ausladen || intr aussteigen

detriment [ˈdetrɪmənt] s Nachteil m

detrimental [ˌdetrɪˈmentəl] adj (to) nachteilig (für), schädlich (für)

deuce [d(j)us] s (in cards or dice) Zwei f; (in tennis) Einstand m; **what the d.?** was zum Teufel?

devaluate [diˈvælju·ˌet] tr abwerten

devaluation [diˌvælju·ˈeʃən] s Abwertung f

devastate [ˈdevəsˌtet] tr verheeren

develop [dɪˈveləp] tr entwickeln; (one's mind) (aus)bilden; (a habit) annehmen; (a disease) sich [dat] zuziehen; (cracks) bekommen; (land) nutzbar machen; (a mine) ausbauen; (phot) entwickeln || intr sich entwickeln; (said of habits) sich herausbilden; **d. into** sich entwickeln zu

developer [dɪˈveləpər] s (of land) Spekulant –in mf; (phot) Entwickler m

development [dɪˈveləpmənt] s Entwicklung f; (of relations, of a mine) Ausbau m; (of land) Nutzbarmachung f; (of housing) Siedlung f; (an event) Ereignis n; (educ) Ausbildung f; (phot) Entwicklung f

deviate [ˈdivɪ·ˌet] intr abweichen

deviation [ˌdivɪˈeʃən] s Abweichung f

device [dɪˈvaɪs] s Vorrichtung f, Gerät n; (means) Mittel n; (crafty scheme) Kniff m; (literary device) Kunstgriff m; (heral) Sinnbild n; **leave s.o. to his own devices** j–n sich [dat] selbst überlassen

dev-il [ˈdevəl] s Teufel m; **a d. of a** (coll) verteufelt; **between the d. and the deep blue sea** zwischen zwei Feuern; **poor d.** armer Teufel; **the d. with you!** (coll) scher dich zum Teufel!; **what** (who, etc.) **the d.?** was (wer, etc.) zum Teufel? || v (pret & pp **–il[l]ed**; ger **–il[l]ing**) tr (culin) mit viel Gewürz zubereiten

devilish [ˈdev(ə)lɪʃ] adj teuflisch

dev'il-may-care' adj (informal) wurstig; (reckless) verwegen

devilment [ˈdevɪlmənt] s Unfug m

deviltry [ˈdevɪltri] s Unfug m

devious [ˈdivɪ·əs] adj abweichend; (tricky) unredlich; (reasoning) abwegig

devise [dɪˈvaɪz] tr ersinnen; (jur) vermachen

devoid [dɪˈvɔɪd] adj—**d. of** ohne

devolve [dɪˈvɑlv] intr—**d. on** zufallen (dat)

devote [dɪˈvot] tr widmen

devot'ed adj (dedicated) ergeben; (affectionate) liebevoll

devotee [ˌdevəˈti] s Anhänger –in mf

devotion [dɪˈvoʃən] s Ergebenheit f; (devoutness) Frömmigkeit f; (special prayer) (to) Gebet n (zu); **devotions** Andacht f

devour [dɪˈvaur] tr verschlingen; (said of fire) verzehren

devout [dɪˈvaut] adj fromm; (e.g., hope) innig

dew [d(j)u] s Tau m; **dew is falling es** taut

dew'drop' s Tautropfen m

dew'lap' s Wamme f

dewy [ˈd(j)u·i] adj tauig

dexterity [deksˈterɪti] s Geschicklichkeit f, Handfertigkeit f

dexterous [ˈdekstərəs] adj handfertig

dextrose [ˈdekstroz] s Traubenzucker m

diabetes [ˌdaɪ·əˈbitɪs] s Zuckerkrankheit f

diabetic [‚daɪ·ə'betɪk] *adj* zucker- krank *mf*

diabolic(al) [‚daɪ·ə'bɑlɪk(ə)l] *adj* teuf- lisch

diacritical [‚daɪ·ə'krɪtɪkəl] *adj* dia- kritisch

diadem ['daɪ·ə‚dem] *s* Diadem *n*

diaere·sis [daɪ'erɪsɪs] *s* (**-ses** [‚sɪz] Diäresis *f*; (*mark*) Trema *n*

diagnose [‚daɪ·əg'nos], [‚daɪ·əg'noz] *tr* diagnostizieren

diagno·sis [‚daɪ·əg'nosɪs] *s* (**-ses** [siz]) Diagnose *f*

diagonal [daɪ'ægənəl] *adj* diagonal || *s* Diagonale *f*

diagonally [daɪ'ægənəli] *adv*—d. **across from** schräg gegenüber von

diagram ['daɪ·ə‚græm] *s* Diagramm *n*

di·al ['daɪ·əl] *s* Zifferblatt *n*; (tech) Skalenscheibe *f*; (telp) Wählscheibe *f* || *v* (*pret & pp* **-alled;** *ger* **-al[l]ing**) *tr & intr* (telp) wählen

di'aling *s* (telp) Wählen *n* der Nummer

dialogue ['daɪ·ə‚ləg] *s* Dialog *m*

di'al tel'ephone *s* Selbstanschlußtele- fon *n*

di'al tone' *s* Summton *m*, Amtszeichen *n*

diameter [daɪ'æmɪtər] *s* Durchmesser *m*

diamond ['daɪmənd] *adj* diamanten; (*in shape*) rautenförmig || *s* Diamant *m*; (*cut diamond*) Brillant *m*; (*rhom- bus*) Raute *f*; (baseball) Spielfeld *n*; (cards) Karo *n*

dia'mond ring' *s* Brillantring *m*

diaper ['daɪpər] *s* Windel *f*; **change the diapers of** trockenlegen, wickeln

diaphanous [daɪ'æfənəs] *adj* durch- sichtig, durchscheinend

diaphragm ['daɪ·ə‚fræm] *s* (*for birth control*) Gebärmutterkappe *f*; (anat) Zwerchfell *n*; (phot) Blende *f*; (tech, telp) Membran *f*

diarrhea [‚daɪ'ri·ə] *s* Durchfall *m*

diary ['daɪ·əri] *s* Tagebuch *n*

diastole [daɪ'æstəli] *s* Diastole *f*

diatribe ['daɪ·ə‚traɪb] *s* Schmährede *f*

dice [daɪs] *spl* Würfel *pl* || *tr* in Wür- fel schneiden

dice'box' *s* Würfelbecher *m*

dichotomy [daɪ'katəmi] *s* Zweiteilung *f*; (bot) Gabelung *f*

dicker ['dɪkər] *intr* feilschen (*about*) (um)

dickey ['dɪki] *s* Hemdbrust *f*

dictaphone ['dɪktə‚fon] *s* Diktaphon *n*

dictate ['dɪktet] *s* Diktat *n*; **the dic- tates of conscience** das Gebot des Gewissens || *tr & intr* diktieren

dictation [dɪk'teʃən] *s* Diktat *n*

dictator ['dɪktetər] *s* Diktator *m*

dictatorial [‚dɪktə'tɔrɪ·əl] *adj* dikta- torisch; (*power*) unumschränkt

dic'tatorship' *s* Diktatur *f*

diction ['dɪkʃən] *s* Ausdrucksweise *f*

dictionary ['dɪkʃə‚neri] *s* Wörterbuch *n*

dic·tum ['dɪktəm] *s* (**-ta** [tə]) (*saying*) Spruch *m*; (*pronouncement*) Aus- spruch *m*

didactic [daɪ'dæktɪk] *adj* lehrhaft

die [daɪ] *s* (**dice** [daɪs]) Würfel *m*; **the die is cast** die Würfel sind ge- fallen || *s* (**dies**) (*coining die*) Präge- stempel *m*; (*casting die*) Form *f*; (*forging die*) Gesenk *n*; (*threader*) Schneidkopf *m* || *v* (*pret & pp* **died;** *ger* **dying**) *tr*—**die a natural death** e-s natürlichen Todes sterben || *intr* sterben; (*said of plants and animals*) eingehen; **be dying for** (coll) sich sehnen nach; **die down** (*said of the wind*) sich legen; (*said of noise*) er- sterben; (*said of fire*) sterben an (*dat*); **die laughing** sich totlachen; **die of hunger** verhungern; **die of thirst** ver- dursten; **die out** aussterben; (*said of fire*) erlöschen; **I am dying to** (*inf*) (coll) ich würde schrecklich gern (*inf*)

die'-hard' *s* Unentwegte *mf*

die'sel en'gine ['dizəl] *s* Dieselmotor *m*

die'sel oil' *s* Dieselöl *n*

die'stock' *s* Gewindeschneidkluppe *f*

diet ['daɪ·ət] *s* Kost *f*; (*special menu*) Diät *f*; (parl) Reichstag *m*; **be on a d.** diät leben; **put on a d.** auf Diät setzen || *intr* diät leben

dietary ['daɪ·ə‚teri] *adj* Diät–; **d. laws** rituelle Diätvorschriften *pl*

dietetic [‚daɪ·ə'tetɪk] *adj* diätetisch || **dietetics** *spl* Diätetik *f*

dietitian [‚daɪ·ə'tɪʃən] *s* Diätspezialist –in *mf*

differ ['dɪfər] *intr* sich unterscheiden; (*said of opinions*) auseinandergehen; **d. from** abweichen von; **d. in** ver- schieden sein in (*dat*); **d. with** an- derer Meinung sein als

difference ['dɪfərəns] *s* Unterschied *m*; (*argument*) Streit *m*; (math) Dif- ferenz *f*; **d. of opinion** Meinungsver- schiedenheit *f*; **it makes no d. to me** es ist mir gleich; **split the d.** den Rest teilen

different ['dɪfərənt] *adj* verschieden; **a d. kind of** e-e andere Art von; **d. from** anders als, verschieden von; **d. kinds of** verschiedene

differential [‚dɪfə'renʃəl] *adj* (econ, elec, mach, math, phys) Differential– || *s* (*difference*) Unterschied *m*; (mach) Differentialgetriebe *n*; (math) Differential *n*

differentiate [‚dɪfə'renʃɪ‚et] *tr* unter- scheiden; (math) differenzieren || *intr* —**d. between** unterscheiden zwischen (*dat*)

difficult ['dɪfɪ‚kʌlt] *adj* schwierig, schwer

difficulty ['dɪfɪ‚kʌlti] *s* Schwierigkeit *f*; **I have d. in** (*ger*) es fällt mir schwer zu (*inf*); **with d.** mit Mühe

diffuse [dɪ'fjus] *adj* (weit) zerstreut; (*style*) diffus || [dɪ'fjuz] *tr* (*spread*) verbreiten; (*pour out*) ausgießen; (phys) diffundieren || *intr* sich zer- streuen

diffusion [dɪ'fjuʃən] *s* (*spread*) Ver- breitung *f*; (phys) Diffusion *f*

dig [dɪg] *s* (*jab*) Stoß *m*; (*sarcasm*)

Seitenhieb *m*; (archeol) Ausgrabung *f* || *v* (*pret & pp* dug [dʌg] & digged; *ger* digging) *tr* graben; (*a ditch*) auswerfen; (*potatoes*) ausgraben; (*understand*) (sl) kapieren; (*look at*) (sl) anschauen; (*appreciate*) (sl) schwärmen für; **dig up** ausgraben; (*find*) auftreiben; (*information*) ausfindig machen; (*money*) aufbringen; || *intr* graben, wühlen; **dig in** (*with the hands*) hineinfassen; (*work hard*) (coll) schuften; (mil) sich eingraben; **dig for** (*e.g., gold*) schürfen nach

digest [ˈdaɪdʒɛst] *s* Zusammenfassung *f*; (jur) Gesetzessammlung *f* || [daɪˈdʒɛst] *tr* verdauen; (*in the mind*) verarbeiten || *intr* verdauen

digestible [daɪˈdʒɛstɪbəl] *adj* verdaulich, verträglich

digestion [daɪˈdʒɛstʃən] *s* Verdauung *f*

digestive [daɪˈdʒɛstɪv] *adj* Verdauungs-; **d. tract** Verdauungsapparat *m*

digit [ˈdɪdʒɪt] *s* (math) Ziffer *f* (unter zehn); (math) Stelle *f*

digital [ˈdɪdʒɪtəl] *adj* digital, Digital-

dig'ital comput'er *s* digitale Rechenanlage *f*

digitalis [dɪdʒɪˈtælɪs] *s* Digitalis *n*

dignified [ˈdɪgnɪˌfaɪd] *adj* würdig

digni-fy [ˈdɪgnɪˌfaɪ] *v* (*pret & pp* -fied) *tr* ehren

dignitary [ˈdɪgnɪˌteri] *s* Würdenträger –in *mf*

dignity [ˈdɪgnɪti] *s* Würde *f*; **d. of man** Menschenwürde *f*; **stand on one's d.** sich [*dat*] nichts vergeben

digress [daɪˈgres] *intr* (**from**) abschweifen (von)

digression [daɪˈgreʃən] *s* Abschweifung *f*

dike [daɪk] *s* Deich *m*

dilapidated [dɪˈlæpɪˌdetɪd] *adj* baufällig

dilate [daɪˈlet] *tr* ausdehnen || *intr* sich ausdehnen

dilation [daɪˈleʃən] *s* Ausdehnung *f*

dilatory [ˈdɪləˌtori] *adj* saumselig; (*tending to cause delay*) hinhaltend

dilemma [dɪˈlemə] *s* Dilemma *n*

dilettan-te [ˌdɪləˈtænti], [ˌdɪləˈtɑnt] *s* (-tes & -ti [ti]) Dilettant –in *mf*

diligence [ˈdɪlɪdʒəns] *s* Fleiß *m*

diligent [ˈdɪlɪdʒənt] *adj* fleißig

dill [dɪl] *s* Dill *m*

dillydal-ly [ˈdɪlɪˌdæli] *v* (*pret & pp* -lied) *intr* herumtrödeln

dilute [dɪˈlut], [daɪˈlut] *adj* verdünnt || [dɪˈlut] *tr* verdünnen; (*with water*) verwässern || *intr* sich verdünnen

dilution [dɪˈluʃən] *s* Verdünnung *f*; (*with water*) Verwässerung *f*

dim [dɪm] *adj* (dimmer; dimmest) *adj* (*light, eyesight*) schwach; (*poorly lighted*) schwach beleuchtet; (*dull*) matt; (*chances, outlook*) schlecht; (*indistinct*) undeutlich; **take a dim view of** (*disapprove of*) mißbilligen; (*be pessimistic about*) sich [*dat*] etw schwarz ausmalen || *v* (*pret & pp* dimmed; *ger* dimming) *tr* trüben; (*lights*) abblenden || *intr* sich ver-

dunkeln; (*said of lights, hopes*) verblassen

dime [daɪm] *s* Zehncentstück *n*

dime′ nov′el *s* Groschenroman *m*

dimension [dɪˈmɛnʃən] *s* Maß *n*, Ausdehnung *f*; **dimensions** Ausmaß *n*

diminish [dɪˈmɪnɪʃ] *tr* (ver)mindern, verringern || *intr* sich vermindern

diminutive [dɪˈmɪnjətɪv] *adj* winzig; (gram) Verkleinerungs- || *s* Verkleinerungsform *f*

dimmer [ˈdɪmər] *s* (aut) Abblendvorrichtung *f*

dimple [ˈdɪmpəl] *s* Grübchen *n*

dim′wit′ *s* Schwachsinnige *mf*

din [dɪn] *s* Getöse *n* || *v* (*pret & pp* dinned; *ger* dinning) *tr* betäuben; **din s.th. into s.o.** j-m etw einhämmern

dine [daɪn] *intr* speisen; **d. out** auswärts speisen

diner [ˈdaɪnər] *s* Tischgast *m*; (*small restaurant*) speisewagenähnliches Speiselokal *n*; (rr) Speisewagen *m*

dinette [daɪˈnet] *s* Speisenische *f*

dingbat [ˈdɪŋˌbæt] *s* (sl) (*person*) Dingsda *m*; (*thing*) Dingsda *n*

ding-dong [ˈdɪŋˌdɔŋ] *interj* bimbam!, klingklang!

dinghy [ˈdɪŋgi] *s* Beiboot *n*; **rubber d.** Schlauchboot *n*

dingy [ˈdɪndʒi] *adj* (*gloomy*) düster; (*shabby*) schäbig

din′ing car′ *s* (rr) Speisewagen *m*

din′ing hall′ *s* Speisesaal *m*

din′ing room′ *s* Eßzimmer *n*

dinner [ˈdɪnər] *s* (*supper*) Abendessen *n*; (*main meal*) Hauptmahlzeit *f*; (*formal meal*) Diner *n*; **after d.** nach Tisch; **at d.** bei Tisch; **before d.** vor Tisch

din′ner guest′ *s* Tischgast *m*

din′ner jac′ket *s* Smoking *m*

din′ner mu′sic *s* Tafelmusik *f*

din′ner par′ty *s* Tischgesellschaft *f*

din′ner time′ *s* Tischzeit *f*

dinosaur [ˈdaɪnəˌsɔr] *s* Dinosaurier *m*

dint [dɪnt] *s*—**by d.** of kraft (*genit*)

diocesan [daɪˈɑsɪsən] *adj* Diözesan-

diocese [ˈdaɪəˌsis] *s* Diözese *f*

diode [ˈdaɪˌod] *s* (electron) Diode *f*

dioxide [daɪˈɑksaɪd] *s* Dioxyd *n*

dip [dɪp] *s* (*in the road*) Neigung *f*; (*short swim*) kurzes Bad *n*; (*dunk*) Eintauchen *n*; (*sauce*) Tunke *f*; (*of ice cream*) Portion *f* || *v* (*pret & pp* dipped; *ger* dipping) *tr* eintauchen; (*e.g., doughnuts*) eintunken; (*a flag*) senken || *intr* sich senken; **dip into** (*e.g., reserves*) angreifen; **dip into one's pockets** (fig) in die Tasche greifen

diphtheria [dɪfˈθɪrɪ·ə] *s* Diphtherie *f*

diphthong [ˈdɪfθɔŋ] *s* Doppelvokal *m*

diploma [dɪˈplomə] *s* Diplom *n*

diplomacy [dɪˈploməsi] *s* Diplomatie *f*

diplomat [ˈdɪpləˌmæt] *s* Diplomat –in *mf*

diplomatic [ˌdɪpləˈmætɪk] *adj* (& fig) diplomatisch

dipper [ˈdɪpər] *s* Schöpflöffel *m*

dipsomania [ˌdɪpsəˈmenɪ·ə] *s* Trunksucht *f*

dip′ stick′ s (aut) Ölstandmesser m
dire [daɪr] adj (terrible) gräßlich; (need) äußerste
direct [dɪ'rɛkt] adj direkt, unmittelbar; (frank) unverblümt; (quotation) wörtlich || tr (order) beauftragen; (a company) leiten; (traffic) regeln; (a movie, play) Regie führen bei; (an orchestra) dirigieren; (attention, glance) (to) richten (auf acc); (a person) (to) verweisen (an acc); (words, letter) (to) richten (an acc)
direct′ call′ s Selbstwählverbindung f
direct′ cur′rent s Gleichstrom m
direct′ dis′course s direkte Rede f
direct′ hit′ s Volltreffer m
direction [dɪ'rɛkʃən] s Richtung f; (order) Anweisung f; (leadership) Leitung f, Führung f; (cin, theat) Regie f; (mus) Stabführung f; **directions** Weisungen pl; (for use) Gebrauchsanweisung f; **in all directions** nach allen Richtungen
directional [dɪ'rɛkʃənəl] adj Richt-
direc′tion find′er s Peilgerät n
direc′tion sig′nal s (aut) Richtungsanzeiger m
directive [dɪ'rɛktɪv] s Anweisung f
direct′ ob′ject s direktes Objekt n
direct′ op′posite s genaues Gegenteil n
director [dɪ'rɛktər] s Leiter –in mf, Direktor –in mf; (cin, theat) Regisseur –in mf; (mus) Dirigent –in mf; (rad, telv) Sendeleiter –in mf
direc′torship′ s Direktorat n
directory [dɪ'rɛktəri] s Verzeichnis n
dirge [dʌrdʒ] s Trauergesang m
dirigible ['dɪrɪdʒɪbəl] s lenkbares Luftschiff n
dirt [dʌrt] s Schmutz m, Dreck m; (moral filth) Schmutz m; (soil) Erde f
dirt′-cheap′ adj spottbillig
dirt′ farm′er s kleiner Farmer m
dirt′ road′ s unbefestigte Straße f
dirt·y ['dʌrti] adj schmutzig, dreckig; (morally) schmutzig; **d. business** Schweinerei f; **d. dog** Sauhund m; **d. joke** Zote f; **d. lie** gemeine Lüge f; **d. linen** schmutzige Wäsche f; **d. look** böser Blick m; **d. trick** übler Streich m; **that′s a d. shame** das ist e–e Gemeinheit! || v (pret & pp –ied) tr beschmutzen
disability [,dɪsə'bɪlɪti] s Invalidität f
disable [dɪs'ebəl] tr (e.g., a worker) arbeitsunfähig machen; (mil) kampfunsuited for combat) kampfunfähig machen; (jur) rechtsunfähig machen
disa′bled adj invalide; (mil) kampfunfähig; **d. veteran** Kriegsversehrte mf; **d. person** Invalide mf
disabuse [,dɪsə'bjuz] tr—**d. of** befreien von
disadvantage [,dɪsəd'væntɪdʒ] s Nachteil m; **place at a d.** benachteiligen
disadvantageous [dɪs,ædvən'tedʒəs] adj nachteilig
disagree [,dɪsə'gri] intr nicht übereinstimmen; (be contradictory) einander widersprechen; (quarrel) (sich) streiten; **d. with** (said of food) nicht bekommen (dat); **d. with s.o. on**

anderer Meinung über (acc) als j–d sein
disagreeable [,dɪsə'grɪ·əbəl] adj unangenehm
disagreement [,dɪsə'grimənt] s (unlikeness) Verschiedenheit f; (dissention) Uneinigkeit f; (quarrel) Meinungsverschiedenheit f
disappear [,dɪsə'pɪr] intr verschwinden
disappearance [,dɪsə'pɪrəns] s Verschwinden n
disappoint [,dɪsə'pɔɪnt] tr enttäuschen; **be disappointed at (or with)** enttäuscht sein über (acc)
disappointment [,dɪsə'pɔɪntmənt] s Enttäuschung f
disapproval [,dɪsə'pruvəl] s Mißbilligung f
disapprove [,dɪsə'pruv] tr mißbilligen; (e.g., an application) nicht genehmigen || intr—**d. of** mißbilligen
disarm [dɪs'ɑrm] tr (& fig) entwaffnen; (a bomb) entschärfen || intr abrüsten
disarmament [dɪs'ɑrməmənt] s Abrüstung f
disarm′ing adj (fig) entwaffnend
disarray [,dɪsə're] s Unordnung f || tr in Unordnung bringen, verwirren
disassemble [,dɪsə'sɛmbəl] tr zerlegen
disaster [dɪ'zæstər] s Unheil n
disas′ter ar′ea s Katastrophengebiet n
disastrous [dɪ'zæstrəs] adj unheilvoll
disavow [,dɪsə'vau] tr ableugnen
disavowal [,dɪsə'vau·əl] s Ableugnung f
disband [dɪs'bænd] tr auflösen || intr sich auflösen
dis-bar [dɪs'bɑr] v (pret & pp –barred; ger –barring) tr aus dem Anwaltsstand ausschließen
disbelief [,dɪsbɪ'lif] s Unglaube m
disbelieve [,dɪsbɪ'liv] tr & intr nicht glauben
disburse [dɪs'bʌrs] tr auszahlen
disbursement [dɪs'bʌrsmənt] s Auszahlung f
disc [dɪsk] s var of **disk**
discard [dɪs'kɑrd] s Ablegen n || tr (clothes, cards, habits) ablegen; (a plan) verwerfen
discern [dɪ'sʌrn] tr (perceive) wahrnehmen; **be able to d. right from wrong** zwischen Gut und Böse unterscheiden können
discern′ing adj scharfsinnig
discernment [dɪ'sʌrnmənt] s Scharfsinn m
discharge [dɪs't ʃɑrdʒ] s (of a gun) Abfeuern n; (of a battery) Entladung f; (of water) Abfluß m; (of smoke) Ausströmen n; (of duties) Erfüllung f; (of debts) Tilgung f; (of employees, patients, soldiers) Entlassung f; (of a prisoner) Freilassung f; (pathol) Ausfluß m || tr (a gun) abfeuern; (e.g., water) ergießen; (smoke) ausstoßen; (debts) tilgen; (duties) erfüllen; (an office) verwalten; (an employee, patient, soldier) entlassen || intr (said of a gun) losgehen; (said of a battery)

sich entladen; (*pour out*) abfließen; (*pathol*) eitern

disciple [dɪ'saɪpəl] *s* Jünger *m*

disciplinarian [ˌdɪsɪplɪ'nɛrɪ·ən] *s* Zuchtmeister *m*

disciplinary ['dɪsɪplɪˌnɛri] *adj* Disziplinar-

discipline ['dɪsɪplɪn] *s* Disziplin *f*; (*punishment*) Züchtigung *f* || *tr* disziplinieren; (*punish*) züchtigen

disclaim [dɪs'klem] *tr* leugnen; (*jur*) verzichten auf (*acc*)

disclose [dɪs'kloz] *tr* enthüllen

disclosure [dɪs'kloʒər] *s* Enthüllung *f*

discolor [dɪs'kʌlər] *tr* verfärben || *intr* sich verfärben

discoloration [dɪsˌkʌlə'reʃən] *s* Verfärbung *f*

discomfiture [dɪs'kʌmfɪtʃər] *s* (*defeat*) Niederlage *f*; (*frustration*) Enttäuschung *f*; (*confusion*) Verwirrung *f*

discomfort [dɪs'kʌmfərt] *s* Unbehagen *n* || *tr* Unbehagen verursachen (*dat*)

disconcert [ˌdɪskən'sʌrt] *tr* aus der Fassung bringen

dis'concert'ed *adj* fassungslos

disconnect [ˌdɪskə'nɛkt] *tr* trennen; (*elec*) ausschalten; (*mach*) auskuppeln; (*telp*) unterbrechen

disconsolate [dɪs'kɑnsəlɪt] *adj* trostlos

discontent [ˌdɪskən'tɛnt] *s* Unzufriedenheit *f* || *tr* unzufrieden machen

dis'content'ed *adj* (with) mißvergnügt (über *acc*)

discontinue [ˌdɪskən'tɪnju] *tr* (*permanently*) einstellen; (*temporarily*) aussetzen; (*a newspaper*) abbestellen; **d.** (*ger*) aufhören zu (*inf*)

discord ['dɪskɔrd] *s* Mißklang *m*; (*dissention*) Zwietracht *f*

discordance [dɪs'kɔrdəns] *s* Uneinigkeit *f*

discotheque [ˌdɪsko'tɛk] *s* Diskothek *f*

discount ['dɪskaʊnt] *s* (*in price*) Rabatt *m*; (*cash discount*) Kassaskonto *n*; (*deduction from nominal value*) Diskont *m*; **at a d.** mit Rabatt; (*st. exch.*) unter pari || *tr* (*disregard*) außer acht lassen; (*minimize*) geringen Wert beimessen (*dat*); (*for cash payment*) e-n Abzug gewähren auf (*acc*); (*e.g., a promissory note*) diskontieren

dis'count store' *s* Rabattladen *m*

discourage [dɪs'kʌrɪdʒ] *tr* (*dishearten*) entmutigen; **d. s.o. from** (*ger*) (*deter*) j-n davon abschrecken zu (*inf*); (*dissuade*) j-m davon abraten zu (*inf*)

discour'aged *adj* mutlos

discouragement [dɪs'kʌrɪdʒmənt] *s* (*act*) Entmutigung *f*; (*state*) Mutlosigkeit *f*; (*deterrent*) Abschreckung *f*

discourse ['dɪskɔrs] *s* (*conversation*) Gespräch *n*; (*formal treatment*) Abhandlung *f*; (*lecture*) Vortrag *m* || [dɪs'kɔrs] *intr* (on) sich unterhalten (über *acc*)

discourteous [dɪs'kʌrtɪ·əs] *adj* unhöflich

discourtesy [dɪs'kʌrtəsi] *s* Unhöflichkeit *f*

discover [dɪs'kʌvər] *tr* entdecken

discovery [dɪs'kʌvəri] *s* Entdeckung *f*

discredit [dɪs'krɛdɪt] *s* (*disrepute*) Mißkredit *m*; (*disbelief*) Zweifel *m* || *tr* (*destroy confidence in*) in Mißkredit bringen; (*disbelieve*) anzweifeln; (*disgrace*) in Verruf bringen

discreditable [dɪs'krɛdɪtəbəl] *adj* schändlich

discreet [dɪs'krit] *adj* diskret

discrepancy [dɪs'krɛpənsi] *s* Unstimmigkeit *f*

discretion [dɪs'krɛʃən] *s* Diskretion *f*, Besonnenheit *f*; **at one's d.** nach Belieben; **leave to s.o.'s d.** in j-s Belieben stellen

discriminate [dɪs'krɪmɪˌnet] *tr* voneinander unterscheiden || *intr*—**d. against** diskriminieren

discrimination [dɪsˌkrɪmɪ'neʃən] *s* (*distinction*) Unterscheidung *f*; (*prejudicial treatment*) Diskriminierung *f*

discriminatory [dɪs'krɪmɪnəˌtori] *adj* diskriminierend

discus ['dɪskʌs] *s* Diskus *m*

discuss [dɪs'kʌs] *tr* besprechen, diskutieren; (*formally*) erörtern

discussion [dɪs'kʌʃən] *s* Diskussion *f*; (*formal consideration*) Erörterung *f*

disdain [dɪs'den] *s* Geringschätzung *f* || *tr* geringschätzen

disdainful [dɪs'denfəl] *adj* geringschätzig; **be d. of** geringschätzen

disease [dɪ'ziz] *s* Krankheit *f*

diseased' *adj* krank, erkrankt

disembark [ˌdɪsɛm'bɑrk] *tr* ausschiffen, landen || *intr* an Land gehen, landen

disembarkation [dɪsˌɛmbɑr'keʃən] *s* Ausschiffung *f*

disembowel [ˌdɪsɛm'baʊ·əl] *v* (*pret & pp* -el[l]ed; *ger* -el[l]ing) *tr* ausweiden

disenchant [ˌdɪsɛn'tʃænt] *tr* ernüchtern

disenchantment [ˌdɪsɛn'tʃæntmənt] *s* Ernüchterung *f*

disengage [ˌdɪsɛn'gedʒ] *tr* (*a clutch*) ausrücken; (*the enemy*) sich absetzen von; (*troops*) entflechten; **d. the clutch** auskuppeln || *intr* loskommen; (mil) sich absetzen

disengagement [ˌdɪsɛn'gedʒmənt] *s* Lösung *f*; (mil) Truppenentflechtung *f*

disentangle [ˌdɪsɛn'tæŋgəl] *tr* entwirren

disentanglement [ˌdɪsɛn'tæŋgəlmənt] *s* Entwirrung *f*

disfavor [dɪs'fevər] *s* Ungunst *f*

disfigure [dɪs'fɪgjər] *tr* entstellen

disfigurement [dɪs'fɪgjərmənt] *s* Entstellung *f*

disfranchise [dɪs'fræntʃaɪz] *tr* die Bürgerrechte entziehen (*dat*)

disgorge [dɪs'gɔrdʒ] *tr* ausspeien || *intr* sich ergießen

disgrace [dɪs'gres] *s* Schande *f*; (*of a family*) Schandfleck *m* || *tr* in Schande bringen; (*a girl*) schänden; **be disgraced** in Schande kommen

disgraceful [dɪsˈgresfəl] *adj* schändlich, schimpflich

disgruntled [dɪsˈgrʌntəld] *adj* mürrisch

disguise [dɪsˈgaɪz] *s* (*clothing*) Verkleidung *f*; (*insincere manner*) Verstellung *f* ‖ *tr* (*by dress*) verkleiden; (*e.g., the voice*) verstellen

disgust [dɪsˈgʌst] *s* (at) Ekel *m* (vor *dat*) ‖ *tr* anekeln

disgust'ing *adj* ekelhaft

dish [dɪʃ] *s* Schüssel *f*, Platte *f*; (*food*) Gericht *n*; **do the dishes** das Geschirr spülen ‖ *tr*—**d. out** (coll) austeilen

dish'cloth' *s* Geschirrlappen *m*

dishearten [dɪsˈhɑrtən] *tr* entmutigen

disheveled [dɪˈʃevəld] *adj* unordentlich

dishonest [dɪsˈɑnɪst] *adj* unehrlich

dishonesty [dɪsˈɑnɪsti] *s* Unehrlichkeit *f*

dishonor [dɪsˈɑnər] *s* Unehre *f* ‖ *tr* verunehren

dishonorable [dɪsˈɑnərəbəl] *adj* (*person*) ehrlos; (*action*) unehrenhaft

dishon'orable dis'charge *s* Entlassung *f* wegen Wehrunwürdigkeit

dish'pan' *s* Aufwaschschüssel *f*

dish'rack' *s* Abtropfkörbchen *n*

dish'rag' *s* Spüllappen *m*

dish'tow'el *s* Geschirrtuch *n*

dish'wash'er *s* (*person*) Aufwäscher -in *mf*; (*appliance*) Geschirrspülmaschine *f*

dish'wa'ter *s* Spülwasser *n*

disillusion [ˌdɪsɪˈluʒən] *s* Ernüchterung *f* ‖ *tr* ernüchtern

disillusionment [ˌdɪsɪˈluʒənmənt] *s* Ernüchterung *f*

disinclination [dɪsˌɪnklɪˈneʃən] *s* Abneigung *f*, Abgeneigtheit *f*

disinclined [ˌdɪsɪnˈklaɪnd] *adj* abgeneigt

disinfect [ˌdɪsɪnˈfekt] *tr* desinfizieren

disinfectant [ˌdɪsɪnˈfektənt] *adj* desinfizierend ‖ *s* Desinfektionsmittel *n*

disinherit [ˌdɪsɪnˈherɪt] *tr* enterben

disintegrate [dɪsˈɪntɪˌgret] *tr* (& fig) zersetzen ‖ *intr* zerfallen

disintegration [dɪsˌɪntɪˈgreʃən] *s* (& fig) Zerfall *m*

disin-ter [ˌdɪsɪnˈtʌr] *v* (*pret & pp* **-terred;** *ger* **-terring**) *tr* ausgraben

disinterested [dɪsˈɪntəˌrestɪd] *adj* (*unbiased*) unparteiisch; (*uninterested*) desinteressiert

disjunctive [dɪsˈdʒʌŋktɪv] *adj* disjunktiv

disk [dɪsk] *s* Scheibe *f*

disk' brake' *s* Scheibenbremse *f*

disk' jock'ey *s* Schallplattenjockei *m*

dislike [dɪsˈlaɪk] *s* (of) Abneigung *f* (gegen) ‖ *tr* nicht mögen

dislocate [ˈdɪsloˌket] *tr* verschieben; (*a shoulder*) verrenken; (fig) stören

dislocation [ˌdɪsloˈkeʃən] *s* Verschiebung *f*; (*of a shoulder*) Verrenkung *f*; (fig) Störung *f*

dislodge [dɪsˈlɑdʒ] *tr* losreißen; (mil) aus der Stellung werfen

disloyal [dɪsˈlɔɪ·əl] *adj* untreu

disloyalty [dɪsˈlɔɪ·əlti] *s* Untreue *f*

dismal [ˈdɪzməl] *adj* trübselig, düster

dismantle [dɪsˈmæntəl] *tr* demontieren

dismay [dɪsˈme] *s* Bestürzung *f* ‖ *tr* bestürzen

dismember [dɪsˈmembər] *tr* zerstückeln

dismiss [dɪsˈmɪs] *tr* verabschieden; (*an employee*) (from) entlassen (aus); (*a case*) (jur) abweisen; (mil) wegtreten lassen; **d. as** abtun als; **dismissed!** (mil) wegtreten!

dismissal [dɪsˈmɪsəl] *s* Entlassung *f*; (jur) Abweisung *f*

dismount [dɪsˈmaunt] *tr* (*throw down*) abwerfen; (mach) abmontieren ‖ *intr* (*from a carriage*) herabsteigen; (*from a horse*) absitzen

disobedience [ˌdɪsəˈbidi·əns] *s* Ungehorsam *m*, Unfolgsamkeit *f*

disobedient [ˌdɪsəˈbidi·ənt] *adj* ungehorsam, unfolgsam

disobey [ˌdɪsəˈbe] *tr* nicht gehorchen (*dat*) ‖ *intr* nicht gehorchen

disorder [dɪsˈɔrdər] *s* Unordnung *f*; (*public disturbance*) Unruhe *f*; (pathol) Erkrankung *f*; **throw into d.** in Unordnung bringen

disorderly [dɪsˈɔrdərli] *adj* unordentlich, liederlich

disor'derly con'duct *s* ungebührliches Benehmen *n*

disor'derly house' *s* Bordell *n*; (*gambling house*) Spielhölle *f*

disorganize [dɪsˈɔrgəˌnaɪz] *tr* zerrütten, desorganisieren

disown [dɪsˈon] *tr* verleugnen

disparage [dɪˈspærɪdʒ] *tr* herabsetzen, geringschätzen

disparate [ˈdɪspərɪt] *adj* ungleichartig

disparity [dɪˈspærɪti] *s* (*inequality*) Ungleichheit *f*; (*difference*) Unterschied *m*

dispassionate [dɪsˈpæʃənɪt] *adj* leidenschaftslos

dispatch [dɪˈspætʃ] *s* Abfertigung *f*; (*message*) Depesche *f*; **with d. in Eile** ‖ *tr* (*send off*) absenden; (*e.g., a truck*) abfertigen; (*e.g., a task*) schnell erledigen; (*kill*) töten; (*eat fast*) (coll) verputzen

dispatcher [dɪˈspætʃər] *s* (*of vehicles*) Fahrbereitschaftsleiter –in *mf*

dis·pel [dɪˈspel] *v* (*pret & pp* **-pelled;** *ger* **-pelling**) *tr* vertreiben; (*thoughts, doubts*) zerstreuen

dispensary [dɪˈspensəri] *s* Arzneiausgabestelle *f*; (mil) Krankenrevier *n*

dispensation [ˌdɪspenˈseʃən] *s* (eccl) (from) Dispens *m* (von); **by divine d.** durch göttliche Fügung

dispense [dɪˈspens] *tr* (*exempt*) (from) entbinden (von); (pharm) zubereiten und ausgeben; **d. justice** Recht sprechen ‖ *intr*—**d. with** verzichten auf (*acc*)

dispersal [dɪˈspʌrsəl] *s* Auflockerung *f*

disperse [dɪˈspʌrs] *tr* zerstreuen; (*a crowd*) zersprengen; (*one's troops*) auflockern; (*the enemy*) auseinandersprengen ‖ *intr* (*said of clouds, etc.*) sich verziehen; (*said of crowds*) auseinandergehen

dispirited [dɪˈspɪrɪtɪd] *adj* niedergeschlagen

displace [dɪs'ples] *tr (people in war)* verschleppen; *(phys)* verdrängen
displacement [dɪs'plesmənt] *s* Vertreibung *f*; *(phys)* Verdrängung *f*
display [dɪ'sple] *s (of energy, wealth)* Entfaltung *f*; *(of goods)* Ausstellung *f*; *(pomp)* Aufwand *m*; **on d.** zur Schau || *tr (wares)* ausstellen; *(reveal)* entfalten; *(flaunt)* protzen mit
display' case *s* Vitrine *f*
display' room' *s* Ausstellungsraum *m*
display' win'dow *s* Schaufenster *n*
displease [dɪs'pliz] *tr* mißfallen *(dat)*; **be displeased with** Mißfallen finden an *(dat)* || *intr* mißfallen
displeas'ing *adj* mißfällig
displeasure [dɪs'plɛʒər] *s* Mißfallen *n*
disposable [dɪ'spozəbəl] *adj* Einweg-
disposal [dɪ'spozəl] *s (riddance)* Beseitigung *f*; *(of a matter)* Erledigung *f*; *(distribution)* Anordnung *f*; **be at s.o.'s d.** j–m zur Verfügung stehen; **have at one's d.** verfügen über *(acc)*; **put at s.o.'s d.** j–m zur Verfügung stellen
dispose [dɪ'spoz] *tr (incline)* **(to)** geneigt machen (zu); *(arrange)* anordnen || *intr*—**d. of** *(a matter)* erledigen; *(get rid of)* loswerden
disposed' *adj* gesinnt; **d. to** *(ger)* geneigt zu *(inf)*
disposition [,dɪspə'zɪʃən] *s (settlement)* Erledigung *f*; *(nature)* Gemütsart *f*; *(inclination)* Neigung *f*
dispossess [,dɪspə'zɛs] *tr*—**d. s.o. of s.th.** j–m etw enteignen
disproof [dɪs'pruf] *s* Widerlegung *f*
disproportionate [,dɪsprə'porʃənɪt] *adj* unverhältnismäßig; **be d. to** im Mißverhältnis stehen zu
disprove [dɪs'pruv] *tr* widerlegen
dispute [dɪs'pjut] *s (quarrel)* Streit *m*; *(debate)* Wortgefecht *n*; **beyond d.** unstreitig; **in d.** umstritten || *tr* bestreiten || *intr* disputieren
disqualification [dɪs,kwɑlɪfɪ'keʃən] *s* Disqualifizierung *f*
disquali·fy [dɪs'kwɑlɪ,faɪ] *v (pret & pp –fied) tr (make unfit)* **(for)** untauglich machen (für); *(declare ineligible)* disqualifizieren
disquiet [dɪs'kwaɪ·ət] *tr* beunruhigen
disqui'eting *adj* beunruhigend
disregard [,dɪsrɪ'gɑrd] *s (lack of attention)* Nichtbeachtung *f*; *(disrespect)* Mißachtung *f* || *tr (not pay attention to)* nicht beachten; *(treat without due respect)* mißachten
disrepair [,dɪsrɪ'pɛr] *s* Verfall *m*; **fall into d.** verfallen
disreputable [dɪs'rɛpjətəbəl] *adj* verrufen
disrepute [,dɪsrɪ'pjut] *s* Verruf *m*
disrespect [,dɪsrɪ'spɛkt] *s* Nichtachtung *f*, Mißachtung *f* || *tr* nicht achten
disrespectful [,dɪsrɪ'spɛktfəl] *adj* respektlos, unehrerbietig
disrobe [dɪs'rob] *tr* entkleiden || *intr* sich entkleiden
disrupt [dɪs'rʌpt] *tr (throw into confusion)* in Verwirrung bringen; *(interrupt)* unterbrechen; *(cause to*

break down) zum Zusammenbruch bringen
dissatisfaction [,dɪssætɪs'fækʃən] *s* Unzufriedenheit *f*
dissat'isfied' *adj* unzufrieden
dissatis·fy [dɪs'sætɪs,faɪ] *v (pret & pp –fied) tr* nicht befriedigen
dissect [dɪ'sɛkt] *tr (fig)* zergliedern; *(anat)* sezieren
dissection [dɪ'sɛkʃən] *s (fig)* Zergliederung *f*; *(anat)* Sektion *f*
dissemble [dɪ'sɛmbəl] *tr* verbergen || *intr* heucheln
disseminate [dɪ'sɛmɪ,net] *tr* verbreiten
dissension [dɪ'sɛnʃən] *s* Uneinigkeit *f*
dissent [dɪ'sɛnt] *s* abweichende Meinung *f* || *intr (from)* anderer Meinung sein (als)
dissenter [dɪ'sɛntər] *s* Andersdenkende *mf*; *(relig)* Dissident –in *mf*
dissertation [,dɪsər'teʃən] *s* Dissertation *f*
disservice [dɪ'sʌrvɪs] *s* schlechter Dienst *m*; **do s.o. a d.** j–m e–n schlechten Dienst erweisen
dissidence ['dɪsɪdəns] *s* Meinungsverschiedenheit *f*
dissident ['dɪsɪdənt] *adj* andersdenkend || *s* Dissident –in *mf*
dissimilar [dɪ'sɪmɪlər] *adj* unähnlich
dissimilate [dɪ'sɪmɪ,let] *tr (phonet)* dissimilieren
dissimulate [dɪ'sɪmjə,let] *tr* verheimlichen || *intr* heucheln
dissipate ['dɪsɪ,pet] *tr (squander)* vergeuden; *(scatter)* zerstreuen; *(dissolve)* auflösen || *intr (scatter)* sich zerstreuen; *(dissolve)* sich auflösen
dis'sipat'ed *adj* ausschweifend
dissipation [,dɪsɪ'peʃən] *s (squandering)* Vergeudung *f*; *(dissolute mode of life)* Ausschweifung *f*; *(phys)* Dissipation *f*
dissociate [dɪ'soʃɪ,et] *tr* trennen; **d. oneself from** abrücken von
dissolute ['dɪsə,lut] *adj* ausschweifend
dissolution [,dɪsə'luʃən] *s* Auflösung *f*
dissolve [dɪ'zɑlv] *s (cin)* Überblendung *f* || *tr* auflösen; *(cin)* überblenden || *intr* sich auflösen; *(cin)* überblenden
dissonance ['dɪsənəns] *s* Mißklang *m*
dissuade [dɪ'swed] *tr (from)* abbringen (von); **d. s.o. from** *(ger)* j–n davon abbringen zu *(inf)*
dissyllabic [,dɪsɪ'læbɪk] *adj* zweisilbig
distaff ['dɪstæf] *s* Spinnrocken *m*; *(fig)* Frauen *pl*
dis'taff side' *s* weibliche Linie *f*
distance ['dɪstəns] *s* Entfernung *f*; *(between two points)* Abstand *m*; *(stretch)* Strecke *f*; *(of a race)* Rennstrecke *f*; **from a d.** aus einiger Entfernung; **go the d.** bis zum Ende aushalten; **in the d.** in der Ferne; **keep one's d.** zurückhaltend sein; **keep your d.** bleib mir vom Leib!; **within easy d. of** nicht weit weg von; **within walking d. of** zu Fuß erreichbar von
distant ['dɪstənt] *adj* entfernt; *(reserved)* zurückhaltend

distaste [dɪs'test] *s* (**for**) Abneigung *f* (gegen), Ekel *m* (vor *dat*)

distasteful [dɪs'testfəl] *adj* (*unpleasant*) (**to**) unangenehm (*dat*); (*offensive*) (**to**) ekelhaft (*dat*)

distemper [dɪs'tempər] *s* (*of dogs*) Staupe *f*; (*paint*) Temperafarbe *f*

distend [dɪs'tend] *tr* (*swell*) aufblähen; (*extend*) ausdehnen ‖ *intr* (*swell*) anschwellen; (*extend*) (aus)dehnen

distension [dɪs'tenʃən] *s* Aufblähung *f*; Ausdehnung *f*

distill [dɪ'stɪl] *tr* destillieren; (*e.g., whiskey*) brennen

distillation [‚dɪstɪ'leʃən] *s* Destillation *f*; (*of whiskey*) Brennen *n*

distiller [dɪs'tɪlər] *s* Brenner *m*

distillery [dɪs'tɪləri] *s* Brennerei *f*

distinct [dɪ'stɪŋkt] *adj* (*clear*) deutlich; (*different*) verschieden; **as d. from** zum Unterschied von; **keep d.** auseinanderhalten

distinction [dɪs'tɪŋkʃən] *s* (*difference*) Unterschied *m*; (*differentiation*) Unterscheidung *f*; (*honor*) Auszeichnung *f*; (*eminence*) Vornehmheit *f*; **have the d. of** (*ger*) den Vorzug haben zu (*inf*)

distinctive [dɪs'tɪŋktɪv] *adj* (*distinguishing*) unterscheidend; (*characteristic*) kennzeichnend

distinguish [dɪs'tɪŋgwɪʃ] *tr* (*differentiate*) unterscheiden; (*classify*) einteilen; (*honor*) auszeichnen; (*characterize*) kennzeichnen; (*discern*) erkennen ‖ *intr* (**between**) unterscheiden (zwischen *dat*)

distin'guished *adj* (*eminent*) prominent; (**for**) berühmt (wegen)

distort [dɪs'tort] *tr* verzerren; (*the truth*) entstellen; **distorted picture** Zerrbild *n*

distortion [dɪs'torʃən] *s* Verzerrung *f*; (*of the truth*) Entstellung *f*

distract [dɪ'strækt] *tr* ablenken

distraction [dɪ'strækʃən] *s* (*diversion of attention*) Ablenkung *f*; (*entertainment*) Zerstreuung *f*; **drive s.o. to d.** j-n zum Wahnsinn treiben

distraught [dɪ'strot] *adj* (*bewildered*) verwirrt; (*deeply agitated*) (**with**) aufgewühlt (von); (*crazed*) (**with**) rasend (vor *dat*)

distress [dɪ'stres] *s* (*anxiety*) Kummer *m*; (*mental pain*) Betrübnis *f*; (*danger*) Notstand *m*, Bedrängnis *f*; (*naut*) Seenot *f* ‖ *tr* betrüben

distress'ing *adj* betrüblich

distress' signal *s* Notzeichen *n*

distribute [dɪ'strɪbjut] *tr* verteilen; (*divide*) einteilen; (*apportion*) (*jur*) aufteilen

distribution [‚dɪstrɪ'bjuʃən] *s* Verteilung *f*; (*geographic range*) Verbreitung *f*; (*of films*) Verleih *m*; (*marketing*) Vertrieb *m*; (*of dividends*) Ausschüttung *f*; (*jur*) Aufteilung *f*

distributor [dɪ'strɪbjətər] *s* Verteiler –in *mf*; (*of films*) Verleiher –in *mf*; (*dealer*) Lieferant –in *mf*; (*aut*) Verteiler *m*

distri'butorship' *s* Vertrieb *m*

district ['dɪstrɪkt] *s* Bezirk *m*

dis'trict attor'ney *s* Staatsanwalt *m*

distrust [dɪs'trʌst] *s* Mißtrauen *n* ‖ *tr* mißtrauen (*dat*)

distrustful [dɪs'trʌstfəl] *adj* (**of**) mißtrauisch (gegen)

disturb [dɪs'tʌrb] *tr* stören; (*disquiet*) beunruhigen; **d. the peace** die öffentliche Ruhe stören

disturbance [dɪs'tʌrbəns] *s* (*interruption*) Störung *f*; (*breach of peace*) Unruhe *f*

disunited [‚dɪsju'naɪtɪd] *adj* uneinig

disunity [dɪs'junɪti] *s* Uneinigkeit *f*

disuse [dɪs'jus] *s* Nichtverwendung *f*; **fall into d.** außer Gebrauch kommen

ditch [dɪtʃ] *s* Graben *m* ‖ *tr* (*discard*) (sl) wegschmeißen; (aer) (coll) auf dem Wasser notlanden mit ‖ *intr* (aer) (coll) notwassern

dither ['dɪðər] *s*—**be in a d.** verdattert sein

dit'to ['dɪto] *adj* (coll) dito ‖ *s* (**-tos**) Kopie *f* ‖ *tr* vervielfältigen

dit'to mark' *s* Wiederholungszeichen *n*

ditty ['dɪti] *s* Liedchen *n*

diva ['divɑ] *s* (mus) Diva *f*

divan ['daɪvæn], ['daɪvæn] *s* Diwan *m*

dive [daɪv] *s* Kopfsprung *m*; (coll) Spelunke *f*; (aer) Sturzflug *m*; (nav) Tauchen *n*; (sport) Kunstsprung *m*; **make a d. for** (fig) sich stürzen auf (*acc*) ‖ *v* (*pret & pp* **dived** & **dove** [dov]) *intr* (*submerge*) tauchen; (*plunge head first*) e-n Kopfsprung machen; (aer) e-n Sturzflug machen; (nav) (unter)tauchen; (sport) e-n Kunstsprung machen

dive'-bomb' *tr & intr* im Sturzflug mit Bomben angreifen

dive' bomb'er *s* Sturzkampfbomber *m*

diver ['daɪvər] *s* Taucher –in *mf*; (orn) Taucher *m*; (sport) Kunstspringer –in *mf*

diverge [daɪ'vʌrdʒ] *intr* (*said of roads, views*) sich teilen; (*from the norm*) abweichen; (geom, phys) divergieren

diverse [daɪ'vʌrs] *adj* (*different*) verschieden; (*of various kinds*) vielförmig

diversi·fy [daɪ'vʌrsɪ‚faɪ] *v* (*pret & pp* **-fied**) *tr* abwechslungsreich gestalten

diversion [daɪ'vʌrʒən] *s* Ablenkung *f*; (*recreation*) Zeitvertreib *m*; (mil) Ablenkungsmanöver *n*

diversity [daɪ'vʌrsɪti] *s* Mannigfaltigkeit *f*

divert [daɪ'vʌrt] *tr* (*attention*) ablenken; (*traffic*) umleiten; (*a river*) ableiten; (*money*) abzweigen; (*entertain*) zerstreuen

divest [daɪ'vest] *tr*—**d. oneself of** sich entäußern (*genit*); **d. s.o. of** (*e.g., office, power*) j-n entkleiden (*genit*); (*e.g., rights, property*) j-m (*seine Rechte, etc.*) entziehen

divide [dɪ'vaɪd] *s* (geol) Wasserscheide *f* ‖ *tr* teilen; (*cause to disagree*) entzweien; (math) (**by**) teilen (durch); **d. into** einteilen in (*acc*); **d. off** (*a room*) abteilen; **d. up** (*among*) aufteilen (unter *acc*) ‖ *intr* (*said of a road*) sich teilen; **d. into** sich teilen in (*acc*)

dividend ['dɪvɪ,dend] *s* Dividende *f*; (math) Dividend *m*; **pay dividends** Dividenden ausschütten; (fig) sich lohnen

divid'ing line' *s* Trennungsstrich *m*

divination [,dɪvɪ'neʃən] *s* Weissagung *f*

divine [dɪ'vaɪn] *adj* göttlich || *s* Geistlicher *m* || *tr* (er)ahnen

divine' prov'idence *s* göttliche Vorsehung *f*

divine' right' of kings' *s* Königtum *n* von Gottes Gnaden

div'ing *s* Tauchen *n* (sport) Kunstspringen *n*

div'ing bell' *s* Taucherglocke *f*

div'ing board' *s* Sprungbrett *n*

div'ing suit' *s* Taucheranzug *m*

div'ing rod' *s* Wünschelrute *f*

divinity [dɪ'vɪnɪti] *s* (*divine nature*) Göttlichkeit *f*; (*deity*) Gottheit *f*

divisible [dɪ'vɪzɪbəl] *adj* teilbar

division [dɪ'vɪʒən] *s* Teilung *f*; (*dissention*) Uneinigkeit *f*; (adm) Abteilung *f*; (math, mil) Division *f*; (sport) Sportklasse *f*

divisor [dɪ'vaɪzər] *s* (math) Teiler *m*; Divisor *m*

divorce [dɪ'vors] *s* Scheidung *f*; **apply for a d.** die Scheidungsklage einreichen; **get a d.** sich scheiden lassen || *tr* (*said of a spouse*) sich scheiden lassen von; (*said of a judge*) scheiden; (*separate*) trennen

divorcee [dɪvor'si] *s* Geschiedene *f*

divulge [dɪ'vʌldʒ] *tr* ausplaudern

dizziness ['dɪzɪnɪs] *s* Schwindel *m*

dizzy ['dɪzɪ] *adj* schwindlig; (*causing dizziness*) schwindelerregend; (*mentally confused*) benommen; (*foolish*) damisch; (*feeling, spell*) Schwindel-

do [du] *v* (*3d pers does* [dʌz]; *pret* **did** [dɪd]; *pp* **done** [dʌn]; *ger* **doing** ['du·ɪŋ] *tr* tun, machen; (*damage*) anrichten; (*one's hair*) frisieren; (*an injustice*) antun; (*a favor, disservice*) erweisen; (*time in jail*) absitzen; (*miles per hour*) fahren; (*tour*) (coll) besichtigen; (*Shakespeare, etc., in class*) durchnehmen; **do duty as** dienen als; **do in** (sl) umbringen; **do over** (*with paint*) neu anstreichen; (*with covering*) neu überziehen; **what can I do for you?** womit kann ich dienen? || *intr* tun, machen; (*suffice*) genügen; **do away with** abschaffen; (*persons*) aus dem Wege räumen; **do away with oneself** sich [*dat*] das Leben nehmen; **do without** auskommen ohne; **I am doing well es geht** mir gut; (*financially*) ich verdiene gut; (*e.g., in history*) ich komme gut voran; **I'll make it do** ich werde schon damit auskommen; **nothing doing!** ausgeschlossen! **that will do!** genug davon!; **that won't do!** das geht nicht! || *aux* used in English but not specifically expressed in German: 1) in questions, e.g., **do you speak German?** sprechen Sie deutsch?; 2) in negative sentences,

e.g., **I do not live here** ich wohne hier nicht; 3) for emphasis, e.g., **I do feel better** ich fühle mich wirklich besser; 4) in imperative sentences, e.g., **do come again** besuchen Sie mich doch wieder!; 5) in elliptical sentences, e.g., **I like Berlin. So do I** Mir gefällt Berlin. Mir auch.; **he drinks, doesn't he?** er trinkt, nicht wahr?; 6) in inversions after adverbs such as hardly, rarely, scarcely, little, e.g., **little did she realize that...** sie hatte keine Ahnung, daß... || *impers*—**it doesn't do to** (*inf*) es ist unklug zu (*inf*); **it won't do you any good to stay here** es wird Ihnen nicht viel nützen, hier zu bleiben

docile ['dɑsɪl] *adj* gelehrig; (*easy to handle*) fügsam, lenksam

dock [dɑk] *s* Anlegeplatz *m*; (jur) Anklagebank *f*; **docks** Hafenanlagen *pl*; **in the d.** (jur) auf der Anklagebank || *tr* (*a ship, space vehicle*) docken; (*a tail*) stutzen; (*pay*) kürzen; **d. an employee (for)** e-m Arbeitnehmer den Lohn kürzen (um) || *intr* (naut) (am Kai) anlegen; (rok) docken, koppeln

docket ['dɑkɪt] *s* (*agenda*) Tagesordnung *f*; (jur) Prozeßliste *f*

dock' hand' *s* Hafenarbeiter *m*

dock'ing *s* (naut) Anlegen *n*; (rok) Andocken *n*

dock' work'er *s* Dockarbeiter *m*

dock'yard' *s* Werft *f*

doctor ['dɑktər] *s* Doktor *m*; (*physician*) Arzt *m*, Ärztin *f* || *tr* (*records*) frisieren; (*adapt, e.g., a play*) zurechtmachen || *intr* (coll) in ärztlicher Behandlung stehen

doctorate ['dɑktərɪt] *s* Doktorwürde *f*

doctrine ['dɑktrɪn] *s* Doktrin *f*, Lehre *f*

document ['dɑkjəmənt] *s* Urkunde *f* || ['dɑkjə,ment] *tr* dokumentieren

documentary [,dɑkjə'mentərɪ] *adj* dokumentarisch || *s* Dokumentarfilm *m*

documentation [,dɑkjəmen'teʃən] *s* Dokumentation *f*

doddering ['dɑdərɪŋ] *adj* zittrig

dodge [dɑdʒ] *s* Winkelzug *m* || *tr* (*e.g., a blow*) ausweichen (*dat*); (*e.g., a responsibility*) sich drücken vor (*dat*) || *intr* ausweichen

do-do ['dodo] *s* (**-does** & **-dos**) (coll) Depp *m*

doe [do] *s* Rehgeiß *f*, Damhirschkuh *f*

doer ['du·ər] *s* Täter –in *mf*

doe'skin' *s* Rehleder *n*

doff [dɑf] *tr* (*a hat*) abnehmen; (*clothes*) ausziehen; (*habits*) ablegen

dog [dɔg] *s* Hund *m*; **dog eats dog** jeder für sich; **go to the dogs** (coll) vor die Hunde gehen; **lucky dog!** (coll) Glückspilz!; **put on the dog** (coll) großtun || *v* (*pret* & *pp* **dogged**; *ger* **dogging**) *tr* nachspüren (*dat*)

dog' bis'cuit *s* Hundekuchen *m*

dog' days' *spl* Hundstage *pl*

dog'-eared' *adj* mit Eselsohren

dog'face' *s* (mil) Landser *m*

dog'fight' *s* (aer) Kurbelei *f*
dogged ['dɔgɪd] *adj* verbissen
doggerel ['dɔgərəl] *s* Knittelvers *m*
doggone ['dɔg'gɔn] *adj* (sl) verflixt
dog'house' *s* Hundehütte *f*; **in the d.** (fig) in Ungnade
dog' ken'nel *s* Hundezwinger *m*
dogma ['dɔgmə] *s* Dogma *n*
dogmatic [dɔg'mætɪk] *adj* dogmatisch
do-gooder ['du'gʊdər] *s* Humanitäts-apostel *m*
dog' show' *s* Hundeschau *f*
dog's' life' *s* Hundeleben *n*
Dog' Star' *s* Hundestern *m*
dog' tag' *s* Hundemarke *f*; (mil) Erkennungsmarke *f*
dog'-tired' *adj* hundemüde
dog'wood' *s* Hartriegel *m*
doily ['dɔɪlɪ] *s* Zierdeckchen *n*
do'ing *s* Werk *n*; **doings** Tun und Treiben *n*; (*events*) Ereignisse *pl*
doldrums ['dɔldrəmz] *spl* Kalmengürtel *m*; **in the d.** (fig) deprimiert
dole [dol] *s* Spende *f*; **be on the d.** stempeln gehen || *tr*—**d. out** verteilen
doleful ['dolfəl] *adj* trübselig
doll [dal] *s* Puppe *f* || *tr*—**d. up** (coll) aufdonnern || *intr* (coll) sich aufdonnern
dollar ['dalər] *s* Dollar *m*
doll' car'riage *s* Puppenwagen *m*
dolly ['dalɪ] *s* Püppchen *n*; (*cart*) Schiebkarren *m*
dolphin ['dalfɪn] *s* Delphin *m*
dolt [dolt] *s* Tölpel *m*
domain [do'men] *s* (& fig) Domäne *f*
dome [dom] *s* Kuppel *f*
dome' light' *s* (aut) Deckenlicht *n*
domestic [də'mɛstɪk] *adj* (*of the home*) Haus-, häuslich, Haushalts-; (*produced at home*) einheimisch, inländisch, Landes-; (*tame*) Haus-; (*e.g., policy*) Innen-, innere || *s* Hausange-stellte *mf*
domesticate [də'mɛstɪ,ket] *tr* zähmen
domicile ['damɪ,saɪl] *s* Wohnsitz *m*
dominance ['damɪnəns] *s* Vorherrschaft *f*
dominant ['damɪnənt] *adj* vorherrschend; (*factor*) entscheidend
dominate ['damɪ,net] *tr* beherrschen || *intr* (over) herrschen (über *acc*)
domination [,damɪ'neʃən] *s* Beherrschung *f*, Herrschaft *f*
domineer [,damɪ'nɪr] *tr & intr* tyrannisieren
domineer'ing *adj* tyrannisch
dominion [də'mɪnjən] *s* (*sovereignty*) (over) Gewalt *f* (über *acc*); (*domain*) Domäne *f*; (*of British Empire*) Dominion *n*
domi-no ['damɪ,no] *s* (-noes & nos) Dominostein *m*; **dominoes** *ssg* Dominospiel *n*
don [dan] *s* Universitätsprofessor *m* || *v* (*pret & pp* donned; *ger* donning) *tr* anlegen; (*a hat*) sich [*dat*] aufsetzen
donate ['donet] *tr* schenken, spenden
donation [do'neʃən] *s* Schenkung *f*; (*small contribution*) Spende *f*
done [dʌn] *adj* erledigt; (culin) gar, fertig; **d. for** kaputt; **d. with** (com-

pleted) fertig; **get** (*s.th.*) **d.** fertigbe-kommen; **well d.** (culin) durchge-braten
donkey ['dʌŋkɪ] *s* Esel *m*
donor ['donər] *s* Spender –in *mf*
doodad ['dudæd] *s* (*gadget*) Dings *n*; (*decoration*) Tand *m*
doodle ['dudəl] *s* Gekritzel *n* || *tr* be-kritzeln || *intr* kritzeln
doom [dum] *s* Verhängnis *n* || *tr* ver-dammen, verurteilen
doomed *adj* todgeweiht
doomsday ['dumz,de] *s* der Jüngste Tag
door [dor] *s* Tür *f*; **from d. to d.** von Haus zu Haus; **out of doors** draußen, im Freien; **show s.o. the d.** j–m die Tür weisen; **two doors away** zwei Häuser weiter
door'bell' *s* Türklingel *f*; **the d. is ring-ing** es klingelt
door'bell but'ton *s* Klingelknopf *m*
door'frame' *s* Türrahmen *m*
door'han'dle *s* Türgriff *m*, Türklinke *f*
door'jamb' *s* Türpfosten *m*
door'knob' *s* Türknopf *m*
door'man' *s* (–men) Portier *m*
door'mat' *s* Abtreter *m*, Türmatte *f*
door'nail' *s*—dead **as a d.** mausetot
door'post' *s* Türpfosten *m*
door'sill' *s* Türschwelle *f*
door'step' *s* Türstufe *f*
door'stop' *s* Türanschlag *m*
door'-to-door' sales'man *s* Hausierer *m*
door'-to-door sel'ling *s* Hausieren *n*
door'way' *s* Türöffnung *f*; (fig) Weg *m*
dope [dop] *s* (*drug*) (sl) Rauschgift *n*; (*information*) (sl) vertraulicher Tip *m*; (*fool*) (sl) Trottel *m*; (aer) Lack *m* || *tr* (*a racehorse*) (sl) dopen; (*a person*) (sl) betäuben, verdrogen; (aer) lackieren; **d. out** (sl) heraus-finden, ausarbeiten; **d. up** (sl) ver-drogen
dope' ad'dict *s* (sl) Rauschgiftsüchtige *mf*
dope' push'er *s* (sl) Rauschgiftschieber –in *mf*
dope'sheet' *s* (sl) vertraulicher Bericht *m*
dope' traf'fic *s* (sl) Rauschgifthandel *m*
dopey ['dopɪ] *adj* (*dopier; dopiest*) (sl) dämlich; (*from sleep*) (coll) schlaftrunken
dormant ['dɔrmənt] *adj* ruhend, un-tätig; (bot) in der Winterruhe
dormer ['dɔrmər] *s* Bodenfenster *n*; (*the whole structure*) Mansarde *f*
dor'mer win'dow *s* Bodenfenster *n*
dormitory ['dɔrmɪ,torɪ] *s* (*building*) Studentenheim *n*; (*room*) Schlafsaal *m*
dormouse ['dɔr,maʊs] *s* (*mice* [,maɪs]) Haselmaus *f*
dor'sal fin' ['dɔrsəl] *s* Rückenflosse *f*
dosage ['dosɪdʒ] *s* Dosierung *f*
dose [dos] *s* (& fig) Dosis *f*
dossier ['dɑsɪ,e] *s* Dossier *m*
dot [dat] *s* Punkt *m*, Tupfen *m*; **on the dot** auf die Sekunde; **three o'clock on the dot** Punkt drei Uhr || *v* (*pret*

& *pp* dotted; *ger* dotting) *tr* punktieren; tüpfeln; **dot** (the) *s* i's den Punkt aufs i setzen; (fig) übergenau sein

dotage ['dotɪdʒ] *s*—**be in one's d.** senil sein

dotard ['dotərd] *s* kindischer Greis *m*

dote [dot] *intr*—**d. on** vernarrt sein in (*acc*)

dot'ing *adj* (**on**) vernarrt (in *acc*)

dots' and dash'es *spl* (telg) Punkte und Striche *pl*

dot'ted *adj* (*pattern*) getüpfelt; (*with flowers, etc.*) übersät; (*line*) punktiert

double ['dʌbəl] *adj* doppelt ‖ *s* Doppelte *n*; (*person*) Doppelgänger *m* (cin, theat) Double *n*; (tennis) Doppel *n*; **on the d.** im Geschwindschritt ‖ *tr* (ver)doppeln; (*the fist*) ballen; (cards) doppeln; (naut) umsegeln ‖ *intr* sich verdoppeln; (cards) doppeln; **d. back** umkehren; **d. up with** sich biegen vor (*dat*)

dou'ble-bar'reled *adj* (*gun*) doppelläufig; (fig) mit zweifacher Wirkung

dou'ble bass' [bes] *s* Kontrabaß *m*

dou'ble bed' *s* Doppelbett *n*

dou'ble-breast'ed *adj* doppelreihig

dou'ble' chin' *s* Doppelkinn *n*

dou'ble cross' *s* Schwindel *m*

dou'ble-cross' *tr* beschwindeln

dou'ble-cross'er *s* Schwindler –in *mf*

dou'ble date' *s* Doppelrendezvous *n*

dou'ble-deal'er *s* Betrüger –in *mf*

dou'ble-deal'ing *s* Doppelzüngigkeit *f*

dou'ble-deck'er *s* (*ship, bus*) Doppeldecker *m*; (*sandwich*) Doppelsandwich *n*; (*bed*) Etagenbett *n*

dou'ble-edged' *adj* (& fig) zweischneidig

double entendre ['dʌbələn'tandrə] *s* (*ambiguity*) Doppelsinn *m*; (*ambiguous term*) doppelsinniger Ausdruck *m*

dou'ble en'try *s* (com) doppelte Buchführung *f*

dou'ble expo'sure *s* Doppelbelichtung *f*

dou'ble fea'ture *s* Doppelprogramm *n*

dou'blehead'er *s* Doppelspiel *n*

dou'ble-joint'ed *adj* mit Gummigelenken

dou'blepark' *tr* & *intr* falsch parken

dou'ble-spaced' *adj* mit doppeltem Zeilenabstand

dou'ble stand'ard *s* zweierlei Maß *n*

doublet ['dʌblɪt] *s* (*duplicate; counterfeit stone*) Dublette *f*; (hist) Wams *m*; (ling) Doppelform *f*

dou'ble take' *s* (fig) Spätzündung *f*

dou'ble-talk' *s* zweideutige Rede *f*

dou'ble time' *s* (*wage rate*) doppelter Lohn *m*; (mil) Eilschritt *m*

dou'ble track' *s* (rr) doppelgleisige Bahnlinie *f*

doubly ['dʌbli] *adv* doppelt

doubt [daut] *s* Zweifel *m*; **be still in d.** (*said of things*) noch zweifelhaft sein; **beyond d.** ohne (jeden) Zweifel; **in case of d.** im Zweifelsfalle; **no d.** zweifellos; **raise doubts** Bedenken

erregen; **there is no d. that** es unterliegt keinem Zweifel, daß ‖ *tr* bezweifeln ‖ *intr* zweifeln

doubter ['dautər] *s* Zweifler –in *mf*

doubtful ['dautfəl] *adj* zweifelhaft

doubtless ['dautlɪs] *adj* & *adv* zweifellos

douche [duʃ] *s* (*device*) Irrigator *m*; (*act of cleansing*) Spülung *f* ‖ *tr* & *intr* spülen

dough [do] *s* Teig *m*; (sl) Pinke *f*

dough'boy' *s* (sl) Landser *m*

dough'nut' *s* Krapfen *m*

doughty ['dauti] *adj* wacker

doughy ['do-i] *adj* teigig

dour [daur], [dur] *adj* mürrisch

douse [daus] *tr* eintauchen; (**with**) übergießen (mit); (*a fire*) auslöschen

dove [dʌv] *s* (& pol) Taube *f*

dovecote ['dʌv̩,kot] *s* Taubenschlag *m*

dove'tail' *s* (carp) Schwalbenschwanz *m* ‖ *tr* verzinken; (fig) ineinanderfügen ‖ *intr* ineinanderpassen

dowager ['dau-ədʒər] *s* Witwe *f* (von Stand); (coll) Matrone *f*

dowdy ['daudi] *adj* schlampig

dow·el ['dau-əl] *s* Dübel *m* ‖ *v* (*pret* & *pp* -el[l]ed; *ger* -el[l]ing) *tr* (ein)dübeln

down [daun] *adj* (*prices*) gesunken; (*sun*) untergegangen; **be d. for** vorgemerkt sein für; **be d. on** auf j-m herumtrampeln; **be d. three points** (sport) drei Punkte zurück sein; **be d. with a cold** mit e-r Erkältung im Bett liegen; **d. and out** völlig erledigt; **d. in the mouth** niedergedrückt ‖ *adv* herunter, hinunter; **d. from** von... herab; **d. there** da unten; **d. to** bis hinunter zu; **d. to the last man** bis zum letzten Mann; **d. with...!** nieder mit...! ‖ *s* (*of fowl*) Daune *f*; (*fine hair*) Flaum *m*; **downs** grasbedecktes Hügelland *n* ‖ *prep* (postpositive) (*acc*) herunter, hinunter; **a little way d. the road** etwas weiter auf der Straße; **d. the river** flußabwärts ‖ *tr* niederschlagen; (*a glass of beer*) (coll) hinunterstürzen; (aer) abschießen

down'cast' *adj* niedergeschlagen

down'draft' *s* Abwind *m*, Fallwind *m*

down'fall' *s* Untergang *m*

down'grade' *s* Gefälle *n*; **on the d.** (fig) im Niedergang ‖ *tr* herabsetzen; niedriger einstufen

down'heart'ed *adj* niedergeschlagen

down'hill' *adj* bergabgehend; (*in skiing*) Abfahrts– ‖ *adv* bergab; **he's going d.** (coll) mit ihm geht es abwärts

down' pay'ment *s* Anzahlung *f*

down'pour' *s* Regenguß *m*, Sturzregen *m*

down'right' *adj* ausgesprochen; (*lie*) glatt; (*contradiction*) schroff ‖ *adv* ausgesprochen

down'spout' *s* Fallrohr *n*

down'stairs' *adj* unten befindlich ‖ *adv* (*position*) unten; (*direction*) nach unten

down'stream' *adv* stromabwärts

down'stroke' s (*in writing*) Grundstrich m; (*of a piston*) Abwärtshub m

down'-the-line' adj vorbehaltlos

down-to-earth' adj nüchtern

down'town' adj im Geschäftsviertel gelegen || adv (*position*) im Geschäftsviertel; (*direction*) ins Geschäftsviertel, in die Stadt || s Geschäftsviertel n

down'trend' s Baissestimmung f

downtrodden ['daʊn‚trɑdən] adj unterdrückt

downward ['daʊnwərd] adj Abwärts- || adv abwärts

downwards ['daʊnwərdz] adv abwärts

downy ['daʊni] adj flaumig; (*soft*) weich wie Flaum

dowry ['daʊri] s Mitgift f

dowser ['daʊzər] s (*rod*) Wünschelrute f; (*person*) Wünschelrutengänger m

doze [doz] s Schläfchen n || intr dösen

dozen ['dʌzən] s Dutzend n; a d. times dutzendmal

Dr. abbr (*Doctor*) Dr.; (*in addresses: Drive*) Str.

drab [dræb] adj (**drabber; drabbest**) graubraun; (*fig*) trüb

drach·ma ['drækmə] s (**-mas & -mae** [mi]) Drachme f

draft [dræft] s (*of air, drink*) Zug m; (*sketch*) Entwurf m; (*fin*) Tratte f; (*mil*) Einberufung f; **on d.** vom Faß || tr (*sketch*) entwerfen, abfassen; (*mil*) einberufen

draft' age' s wehrpflichtiges Alter n

draft' beer' s Schankbier n

draft' board' s Wehrmeldeamt n

draft' dodg'er ['dɑdʒər] s Drückeberger m

draftee [‚dræf'ti] s Dienstpflichtige mf

draft'ing s (*of a document*) Abfassung f; (*mechanical drawing*) Zeichnen n; (*mil*) Aushebung f

draft'ing board' s Zeichenbrett n

draft'ing room' s Zeichenbüro n

drafts·man ['dræftsmən] s (**-men**) Zeichner m

drafty ['dræfti] adj zugig

drag [dræg] s (*sledge*) Lastschlitten m; (*in smoking*) (coll) Zug m; (*boring person*) langweiliger Mensch m; (*s.th. tedious*) etwas langweiliges; (*encumbrance*) (on) Hemmschuh m (für); (aer) Luftwiderstand m; (*for recovering objects*) (naut) Schleppnetz n; (*for retarding motion*) (naut) Schleppanker m || v (*pret & pp* **dragged; ger dragging**) tr schleppen, schleifen; **d. one's feet** schlurfen, (fig) sich [dat] Zeit lassen; **d. out** dahinschleppen; (*protract*) verschleppen; **d. through the mud** (fig) in den Schmutz zerren; **d. up** (coll) aufwärmen || intr (*said of a long dress, etc.*) schleifen; (*said of time*) dahinschleichen; **d. on** (*be prolonged*) sich hinziehen

drag'net' s Schleppnetz n

dragon ['drægən] s Drache m

drag'onfly' s Libelle f

dragoon [drə'gun] s Dragoner m || tr (*coerce*) zwingen

drag' race' s Straßenrennen n; (sport) Kurzstreckenrennen n

drain [dren] s (*sewer*) Kanal m; (*under a sink*) Abfluß m; (fig) (**on**) Belastung f (*genit*); (surg) Drain m; **down the d.** (fig) zum Fenster hinaus || tr (*land*) entwässern; (*water*) ableiten; (*a cup, glass*) austrinken; (fig) verzehren || intr ablaufen; (culin) abtropfen

drainage ['drenɪdʒ] s Ableitung f; (*e.g., of land*) Entwässerung f; (surg) Drainage f

drain'age ditch' s Abflußgraben m

drain' cock' s Entleerungshahn m

drain'pipe' s Abflußrohr n

drain' plug' s Abflußstöpsel m

drake [drek] s Enterich m

dram [dræm] s Dram n

drama ['drɑmə] s Drama n; (*art and genre*) Dramatik f

dra'ma crit'ic s Theaterkritiker –in mf

dramatic ['drə'mætɪk] adj dramatisch || **dramatics** s Dramatik f; spl (pej) Schauspielerei f

dramatist ['dræmətɪst] s Dramatiker –in mf

dramatize ['dræmə‚taɪz] tr dramatisieren

drape [drep] s Vorhang m; (*hang of a drape or skirt*) Faltenwurf m || tr drapieren

drapery ['drepəri] s Vorhänge pl

dra'pery mate'rial s Vorhangstoff m

drastic ['dræstɪk] adj drastisch

draught [dræft] s & tr var of **draft**

draw [drɔ] s (*in a lottery*) Ziehen n; (*that which attracts*) Schlager m; (*power of attraction*) Anziehungskraft f; **end in a d.** unentschieden ausgehen || v (*pret drew* [dru]; pp **drawn** [drɔn]) tr (*pictures*) zeichnen; (*a line, comparison, parallel, conclusion, lots, winner, sword, wagon*) ziehen; (*a crowd*) anlocken; (*a distinction*) machen; (*blood*) vergießen; (*curtains*) zuziehen; (*a check*) ausstellen; (*water*) schöpfen; (*cards*) nehmen; (*rations*) (mil) in Empfang nehmen; **d. a blank** (coll) e-e Niete ziehen; **d. aside** beiseiteziehen; **d. attention to die Aufmerksamkeit lenken auf** (*acc*); **d. into** (*e.g., an argument*) hineinziehen in (*acc*); **d. lots for** losen um; **d. out** (*protract*) in die Länge ziehen; (*money from a bank*) abheben; **d. s.o. out** j–n ausholen; **d. the line** (fig) e–e Grenze ziehen; **d. up** (*a document*) entwerfen || intr zeichnen; **d. away** sich entfernen; **d. back** sich zurückziehen; **d. near** herannahen; **d. on** zurückgreifen auf (*acc*); **d. to a close** sich dem Ende zuneigen

draw'back' s Nachteil m

draw'bridge' s Zugbrücke f

drawee [‚drɔ'i] s Trassat –in mf

drawer ['drɔ·ər] s Zeichner –in mf; (com) Trassant –in mf || [drɔr] s Schublade f; **drawers** Unterhose f

draw'ing s (*of pictures*) Zeichnen n;

(picture) Zeichnung *f*; *(in a lottery)* Ziehung *f*, Verlosung *f*

draw'ing board' *s* Reißbrett *n*

draw'ing card' *s* Zugnummer *f*

draw'ing room' *s* Empfangszimmer *n*

drawl [drɔl] *s* gedehntes Sprechen *n* ‖ *intr* gedehnt sprechen

drawn [drɔn] *adj (face)* **(with)** verzerrt (vor *dat*); *(sword)* blank

dray [dre] *s* niedriger Rollwagen *m*; *(sledge)* Schleife *f*

dread [dred] *adj* furchtbar ‖ *s* Furcht *f* ‖ *tr* fürchten

dreadful ['dredfəl] *adj* furchtbar

dream [drim] *s* Traum *m*; *(aspiration, ambition)* Wunschtraum *m*; *(ideal)* (coll) Gedicht *n* ‖ *v (pret & pp* dreamed & dreamt [dremt] *tr* träumen; **d. away** verträumen; **d. up** zusammenträumen ‖ *intr* träumen; **d. of** *(long for)* sich [*dat*] entraumen; **I dreamt of her** mir träumte von ihr

dreamer ['drimər] *s* Träumer –in *mf*

dream'land' *s* Traumland *n*

dream'-like' *adj* traumhaft

dream'world' *s* Traumwelt *f*

dreamy ['drimi] *adj (place)* verträumt; *(eyes)* träumerisch

dreary ['drɪri] *adj* trüb, trist

dredge [dredʒ] *s* Bagger *m* ‖ *tr* (aus-)baggern ‖ *intr* baggern

dredger ['dredʒər] *s* Bagger *m*

dredg'ing *s* Baggern *n*

dregs [dregz] *spl* Bodensatz *m*; *(of society)* Abschaum *m*, Auswurf *m*

drench [drentʃ] *tr* durchnässen

Dres'den chi'na ['drezdən] *s* Meißner Porzellan *n*

dress [dres] *s* Kleidung *f*; *(woman's dress)* Kleid *n* ‖ *tr* anziehen; *(a store window)* dekorieren; *(skins)* gerben; *(a salad, goose, chicken)* zubereiten; *(vines)* beschneiden; *(stones)* behauen; *(ore)* aufbereiten; *(wounds)* verbinden; *(hair)* frisieren; *(tex)* appretieren; **d. down** (coll) ausschimpfen; **d. ranks** die Glieder ausrichten; **get dressed** sich anziehen ‖ *intr* sich anziehen; **d. up** sich fein machen

dress' affair' *s* Galaveranstaltung *f*

dresser ['dresər] *s* Frisierkommode *f*; **be a good d.** sich gut kleiden

dress'ing *s (stuffing for fowl)* Füllung *f*; *(for salad)* Soße *f*; *(surg)* Verband *m*

dress'ing down' *s* Gardinenpredigt *f*

dress'ing room' *s* Umkleideraum *m*; (theat) Garderobe *f*

dress'ing sta'tion *s* Verbandsplatz *m*

dress'ing ta'ble *s* Frisierkommode *f*

dress'mak'er *s* Schneiderin *f*

dress'mak'ing *s* Modenschneiderei *f*

dress' rehear'sal *s* Kostümprobe *f*

dress' shirt' *s* Frackhemd *n*

dress' shop' *s* Modenhaus *n*, Modengeschäft *n*

dress' suit' *s* Frackanzug *m*, Frack *m*

dress' un'iform *s* Paradeuniform *f*

dressy ['dresi] *adj (showy)* geschniegelt; *(stylish)* modisch; *(for formal affairs)* elegant

dribble ['drɪbəl] *s (trickle)* Getröpfel

n; *(sport)* Dribbeln *n* ‖ *tr & intr* tröpfeln; *(sport)* dribbeln

driblet ['drɪblɪt] *s* Bißchen *n*

dried [draɪd] *adj* Trocken-, Dörr-

dried' beef' *s* Dörrfleisch *n*

dried' fruit' *s* Dörrobst *n*

dried'-up' *adj* ausgetrocknet, verdorrt

drier ['draɪ·ər] *s* Trockner *m*; *(for the hair)* Haartrockenhaube *f*; *(hand model)* Fön *m*

drift [drɪft] *s (of sand, snow)* Wehe *f*; *(tendency)* Richtung *f*, Neigung *f*; *(intent)* Absicht *f*; *(meaning)* Sinn *m*; *(aer, naut, rad)* Abtrift *f*; *(flow of the ocean current)* (naut) Drift *f* ‖ *intr (said of sand, snow)* sich anhäufen; *(said of a boat)* treiben; **d. away** *(said of sounds)* verwehen; *(said of a crowd)* sich verlaufen; **d. shut** verweht werden

drifter ['drɪftər] *s* zielloser Mensch *m*

drift' ice' *s* Treibeis *n*

drift'wood' *s* Treibholz *n*

drill [drɪl] *s (tool)* Bohrer *m*; *(exercise)* Drill *m*; *(tex)* Drillich *m* ‖ *tr* bohren; *(exercise)* drillen; **d. s.th. into s.o.** j–m etw einpauken ‖ *intr* bohren; *(exercise)* drillen

drill'mas'ter *s* (mil) Ausbilder *m*

drill' press' *s* Bohrpresse *f*

drink [drɪŋk] *s* Trunk *m* ‖ *v (pret* drank [dræŋk]; *pp* drunk [drʌŋk] *tr* trinken; *(said of animals)* saufen; (pej) saufen; **d. away** *(money)* versaufen; **d. down** hinunterspülen; **d. in** *(air)* einschlürfen; *(s.o.'s words)* verschlingen ‖ *intr* trinken; *(excessively)* saufen; **d. to** trinken auf *(acc)*; **d. up** austrinken

drinkable ['drɪŋkəbəl] *adj* trinkbar

drinker ['drɪŋkər] *s* Trinker –in *mf*; **heavy drinker** Zecher –in *mf*

drink'ing foun'tain *s* Trinkbrunnen *m*

drink'ing par'ty *s* Zechgelage *n*

drink'ing song' *s* Trinklied *n*

drink'ing straw' *s* Strohhalm *m*

drink'ing trough' *s* Viehtränke *f*

drink'ing wa'ter *s* Trinkwasser *n*

drip [drɪp] *s* Tröpfeln *n* ‖ *v (pret & pp* dripped; *ger* dripping) *tr & intr* tröpfeln

drip' cof'fee *s* Filterkaffee *m*

drip'-dry' *adj* bügelfrei

drip' pan' *s* Bratpfanne *f*

drip'pings *spl* Bratenfett *n*

drive [draɪv] *s (in a car)* Fahrt *f*; *(road)* Fahrweg *m*; *(energy)* Schwungkraft *f*; *(inner urge)* Antrieb *m*; *(campaign)* Aktion *f*; *(for raising money)* Spendeaktion *f*; (golf) Treibschlag *m*; *(mach)* Antrieb *m*; (mil) Vorstoß *m*; (tennis) Treibschlag *m*; **go for a d.** spazierenfahren ‖ *v (pret* drove [drov]; *pp* driven ['drɪvən]) *tr (a car, etc.)* fahren; *(e.g., cattle)* treiben; *(a tunnel)* vortreiben; **d. a hard bargain** zäh um den Preis feilschen; **d. away** abtreiben; *(oneself, a horse)* hard abjagen; **d. home** nahebringen; **d. in** *(a nail)* einschlagen; **d. off** *Of course* (naut) verschlagen; **d. on** antreiben; **d. out** austreiben; **d. s.o. to** *(inf)* j–n dazu bringen zu (inf); **d. to despair** zur Verzweiflung treiben ‖ intr fahren; **d. along** mitfahren; **d.** at abzielen auf (acc); **d. away** wegfahren; **d. by** vorbeifahren an (dat); **d. in** einfahren; **d. on** weiterfahren; **d. out** herausfahren; **d. up** anfahren

drive' belt' s Treibriemen m

drive'-in' s Autorestaurant n; (cin) Autokino n

driv·el ['drɪvəl] s (slobber) Geifer m; (nonsense) Faselei f ‖ v (pret & pp -el[l]ed; ger -el[l]ing) intr sabbern; (fig) faseln

driver ['draɪvər] s (of a car) Fahrer –in mf; (of a locomotive, streetcar) Führer m; (golf) Treibschläger m; (mach) Treibhammer m

driv'er's li'cense s Führerschein m

drive' shaft' s Antriebswelle f

drive'way' s Einfahrt f

drive'-yourself' serv'ice s Autovermietung f an Selbstfahrer

driv'ing adj (rain) stürmisch ‖ s (aut) Steuerung f

driv'ing instruc'tor s Fahrlehrer –in mf

driv'ing les'son s Fahrstunde f

driv'ing school' s Autofahrschule f

drizzle ['drɪzəl] s Nieselregen m ‖ impers—**it is drizzling** es nieselt

droll [drol] adj drollig

dromedary ['drɑmə‚derɪ] s Dromedar n

drone [dron] s (bee; loafer) Drohne f; (buzz) Gesumme n; (monotonous speech) Geleier n ‖ tr (e.g., prayers) leiern ‖ intr summen; (fig) leiern

drool [drul] intr sabbern

droop [drup] s Herabhängen n; (stoop) gebeugte Haltung f ‖ intr herabhängen; (said of flowers) zu welken beginnen; (fig) den Kopf hängen lassen

droopy ['drupɪ] adj (saggy) schlaff herabhängend; (dejected) mutlos; (shoulders) abfallend; (flowers) welkend

drop [drɑp] s (of liquid) Tropfen m; (candy) Fruchtbonbon m & n; (fall) Fall m; (height differential) Gefälle n; (reduction) Abnahme f; (in prices) Rückgang m; (in temperature) Sturz m; (of bombs or supplies) Abwurf m; (of paratroopers) Absprung m; **a fifty-meter d.** ein Fall m aus e-r Höhe von fünfzig Metern; **b. by d.** tropfenweise; **d. in the bucket** Tropfen m auf e-n heißen Stein ‖ v (pret & pp dropped; ger dropping) tr (let fall) fallenlassen; (bombs, supplies) abwerfen; (a subject, remarks, hints) fallenlassen; (the eyes, voice) senken; (anchor; young of animals) werfen; (money in gambling) (sl) verlieren; (terminate) einstellen; (from membership roll) ausschließen; (paratroopers) absetzen; **d. it!** laß das!; **d. s.o. a line** j–m ein paar Zeilen schreiben ‖ intr fallen; (drip) tropfen; (said of prices, temperature) sinken, fallen; (keel over) umfallen; (said of a curtain) niedergehen; **d. behind** zurück-

fallen; **d. dead!** (sl) laß dich begraben!; **d. in on s.o.** auf e–n Sprung bei j–m vorbeikommen; **d. off to sleep** einschlafen; (sport) ausscheiden; **d. out of school** von der Schule abgehen

drop'ar'ea s (aer) Abwurfraum m

drop'cur'tain s (bemalter) Vorhang m

drop'ham'mer s Fallhammer m

drop'-leaf ta'ble s Tisch m mit herunterklappbaren Flügeln

drop'light' s Hängelampe f

drop'out' s Gescheiterte mf; (educ) Abgänger –in mf

dropper ['drɑpər] s (med) Tropfer m

drop'ping adj (prices) rückgängig ‖ s (of bombs, supplies) Abwurf m; **droppings** tierischer Kot m

dropsy ['drɑpsɪ] s Wassersucht f

drop' ta'ble s Klapptisch m

dross [drɔs] s (slag) Schlacke f; (waste) Abfall m

drought [draut] s Dürre f

drove [drov] s Herde f

drown [draun] tr (& fig) ertränken; **d. out** übertönen ‖ intr ertrinken

drowse [drauz] intr dösen

drowsiness ['drauzɪnɪs] s Schläfrigkeit f

drowsy ['drauzɪ] adj schläfrig, dösig

drub [drʌb] v (pret & pp drubbed; ger drubbing) tr (flog) verprügeln; (sport) entscheidend schlagen

drudge [drʌdʒ] s Packesel m ‖ intr sich placken, schuften

drudgery ['drʌdʒərɪ] s Plackerei f

drug [drʌg] s Droge f, Arznei f; (narcotic) Betäubungsmittel n; (addictive narcotic) Rauschgift n ‖ v (pret & pp drugged; ger drugging) tr betäuben

drug' ad'dict s Rauschgiftsüchtige mf

drug' addic'tion s Rauschgiftsucht f

drug'store' s Apotheke f, Drogerie f

drug' traf'fic s Rauschgifthandel m

druid ['dru·ɪd] s Druide m

drum [drʌm] s (musical instrument; container) Trommel f ‖ v (pret & pp drummed; ger drumming) tr trommeln; **d. s.th. into s.o.** j–m etw einpauken; **d. the table** auf den Tisch trommeln; **d. up** zusammentrommeln ‖ intr trommeln

drum' and bu'gle corps' s Musikzug m

drum'beat' s Trommelschlag m

drum'fire' s (mil) Trommelfeuer n

drum'head' s Trommelfell n

drum' ma'jor s Tambourmajor m

drum' majorette' s Tambourmajorin f

drummer ['drʌmər] s Trommler –in mf

drum'stick' s Trommelschlegel m; (culin) Unterschenkel m

drunk [drʌŋk] adj betrunken ‖ s Säufer –in mf

drunkard ['drʌŋkərd] s Trunkenbold m

drunken ['drʌŋkən] adj betrunken

dry [draɪ] adj trocken; (boring) trocken; (wine) herb; (thirsty) durstig; (rainless) regenarm; (wood) dürr ‖ v (pret & pp –dried) tr (ab)trocknen;

(*e.g., fruit*) dörren; **dry off** abtrocknen; **dry out** austrocknen; **dry up** austrocknen; (fig) erschöpfen ‖ *intr* trocknen; **dry out** austrocknen; **dry up** vertrocknen; (*said of grass, flowers*) verdorren; (fig) versiegen; (*keep quiet*) (sl) die Klappe halten

dry' bat'tery *s* Trockenbatterie *f*
dry' cell' *s* Tockenelement *n*
dry'-clean' *tr* (*chemically*) reinigen
dry' clean'er *s* Reinigungsanstalt *f*
dry' clean'ing *s* chemische Reinigung *f*
dry' dock' *s* Trockendock *n*
dry'-eyed' *adj* ungerührt
dry' goods' *spl* Schnittwaren *pl*
dry' ice' *s* Trockeneis *n*
dry' land' *s* fester Boden *m*
dry' meas'ure *s* Trockenmaß *n*
dryness ['draɪnɪs] *s* Trockenheit *f*, Dürre *f*; (fig) Nüchternheit *f*
dry' nurse' *s* Säuglingsschwester *f*
dry' rot' *s* Trockenfäule *f*
dry' run' *s* Vorübung *f*; (*test run*) Probelauf *m*; (*with blank ammunition*) Zielübung *f*
dry' sea'son *s* Trockenzeit *f*
dual ['d(j)u-əl] *adj* Zwei-, doppelt; (tech) Doppel-
dualism ['d(j)u-ə‚lɪzəm] *s* Dualismus *m*
du'al-pur'pose *adj* e-m doppelten Zweck dienend
dub [dʌb] *v* (*pret & pp* **dubbed;** *ger* **dubbing**) *tr* (*nickname*) betiteln; (cin) synchronisieren; (golf) schlecht treffen; (hist) zum Ritter schlagen
dub'bing *s* (cin) Synchronisierung *f*
dubious ['d(j)ubɪ-əs] *adj* zweifelhaft
ducal ['d(j)ukəl] *adj* herzoglich
duchess ['dʌt/ɪs] *s* Herzogin *f*
duchy ['dʌt/i] *s* Herzogtum *n*
duck [dʌk] *s* Ente *f* ‖ *tr* (*the head*) ducken; (*in water*) (unter)tauchen; (*evade*) sich drücken vor (*dat*) ‖ *intr* ducken; (*go under the surface*) untertauchen
duck'ing *s*—**give s.o. a d.** j-n untertauchen
duck' pond' *s* Ententeich *m*
duck' soup' *s* (sl) Kinderspiel *n*
ducky ['dʌki] *adj* (coll) nett, lieb
duct [dʌkt] *s* Rohr *n*, Kanal *m*, Leitung *f*; (anat, elec) Kanal *m*
duct'less gland' ['dʌktlɪs] *s* endokrine Drüse *f*
duct'work' *s* Rohrleitungen *pl*
dud [dʌd] *s* (sl & mil) Versager *m*, Blindgänger *m*; **duds** (coll) Klamotten *pl*
dude [d(j)ud] *s* (*dandy*) Geck *m*
dude' ranch' *s* Vergnügungsfarm *f*
due [d(j)u] *adj* (*payment; bus, train*) fällig; (*proper*) gehörig; (*consideration*) reichlich; **be due to** (*as a cause*) beruhen auf (*dat*); (*said of an honor*) gebühren (*dat*); (*said of money*) zustehen (*dat*); **be due to** (inf) sollen, müssen; **in due course** im gegebenen Moment; **in due time** zur rechten Zeit ‖ *adv* (naut) genau ‖ *s*—**dues** Beitrag *m*; **get one's due** nach Verdienst behandelt werden; **give every-**

one his due jedem geben, was ihm gebührt
due' date' *s* (*of a payment*) Termin *m*
duel ['d(j)u-əl] *s* Duell *n*; **fight a d.** sich duellieren ‖ *v* (*pret & pp* **duel[l]ed;** *ger* **duel[l]ing**) *intr* sich duellieren
dues-paying ['d(j)uz‚pe-ɪŋ] *adj* beitragzahlend
duet [d(j)u'et] *s* Duett *n*
due' to' *prep* wegen (*genit*)
duf'fle bag' ['dʌfəl] *s* (mil) Kleidersack *m*
dug'out' *s* (*boat*) Einbaum *m*; (baseball, mil) Unterstand *m*
duke [d(j)uk] *s* Herzog *m*
dukedom ['d(j)ukdəm] *s* Herzogtum *n*
dull [dʌl] *adj* (*not sharp*) stumpf; (*pain*) dumpf; (*not shining*) glanzlos, matt; (*uninteresting*) nüchtern, geistlos; (*stupid*) stumpfsinnig; (*open*) flau ‖ *tr* stumpf machen; (fig) abstumpfen ‖ *intr* stumpf werden; (fig) abstumpfen
dullard ['dʌlərd] *s* Dummkopf *m*
dullness ['dʌlnɪs] *s* (*of a blade*) Stumpfheit *f*; (*of color*) Mattheit *f*; (*of a speech, etc.*) Stumpfsinn *m*
duly ['d(j)uli] *adv* ordnungsgemäß
dumb [dʌm] *adj* (*mute*) stumm; (*stupid*) dumm ‖ *adv*—**play d.** sich unwissend stellen
dumb'bell' *s* Hantel *f*; (sl) Dummkopf *m*
dumbstruck ['dʌm‚strʌk] *adj* wie auf den Mund geschlagen
dumb' wait'er *s* (*elevator*) Speiseaufzug *m*; (*serving table*) Serviertisch *m*
dumdum ['dʌm‚dʌm] *s* Dumdumgeschoß *n*
dumfound ['dʌm‚faund] *tr* verblüffen
dummy ['dʌmi] *adj* (*not real*) Schein-; (mil) blind, Übungs- ‖ *s* (*representation for display*) Attrappe *f*; (*clothes form*) Schneiderpuppe *f*; (*dolt*) Ölgötze *m*; (cards) Strohmann *m*; (mil) Übungspatrone *f*; (typ) Blindband *m*
dump [dʌmp] *s* (*trash heap*) Schuttabladeplatz *m*; (sl) Bude *f*; (mil) Lager *n*; **be down in the dumps** (coll) Trübsal blasen ‖ *tr* (aus)kippen; (*fling down*) hinplumpsen; (*garbage*) abladen; (com) verschleudern; **be dumped** (*be fired*) entlassen werden; **no dumping** (*public sign*) Schuttabladen verboten
dumpling ['dʌmplɪŋ] *s* Kloß *m*, Knödel *m*
dump' truck' *s* Kipper *m*
dumpy ['dʌmpi] *adj* rundlich
dun [dʌn] *adj* schwarzbraun ‖ *v* (*pret & pp* **dunned;** *ger* **dunning**) *tr* drängen
dunce [dʌns] *s* Schwachkopf *m*
dunce' cap' *s* Narrenkappe *f*
dune [d(j)un] *s* Düne *f*
dung [dʌŋ] *s* Dung *m*, Mist *m* ‖ *tr* düngen
dungarees [‚dʌŋgə'riz] *spl* Drillichhose *f*, Drillichanzug *m*
dungeon ['dʌndʒən] *s* Verlies *n*; (hist) Bergfried *m*

dung'hill' s Düngerhaufen m
dunk [dʌŋk] tr eintunken
duo ['d(j)u·o] s (duet) Duett n; (a pair) Duo n
duode·num [ˌd(j)u·ə'dinəm] s (-na [nə]) Zwölffingerdarm m
dupe [d(j)up] s Düpierte mf || tr düpieren, übertölpeln
duplex ['d(j)uplɛks] s Doppelhaus n
duplicate ['d(j)uplɪkɪt] adj Duplikat-; (parts) Ersatz-; **d. key** Nachschlüssel m || s Duplikat n, Abschrift f; **in d.** abschriftlich || ['d(j)uplɪˌket] tr (make a copy of) kopieren; (make many copies of) vervielfältigen; (reproduce by writing) abschreiben; (repeat) wiederholen; (perform again) nachmachen
duplication [ˌd(j)uplɪ'keʃən] s Vervielfältigung f
duplicator ['d(j)uplɪˌketər] s Vervielfältigungsapparat m
duplicity [d(j)u'plɪsɪti] s Duplizität f
durable ['d(j)urəbəl] adj dauerhaft
duration [d(j)u'reʃən] s Dauer f
duress ['d(j)ures] s (jur) Nötigung f
during ['d(j)urɪŋ] prep während (genit), bei (dat); **d. the meal** bei Tisch; **the day** tagsüber
dusk [dʌsk] s Abenddämmerung f
dust [dʌst] s Staub m; **cover with d.** bestauben; **make d.** stauben || tr (free of dust) abstauben; (sprinkle, spray with insecticides) bestäuben
dust' bowl' s Staubsturmgebiet n
dust' cloth' s Staubtuch n
dust' collec'tor s Staubfänger m
duster ['dʌstər] s (feather duster) Staubwedel m; (for insecticides) Zerstäuber m
dust'ing pow'der s Streupulver n
dust' jack'et s Schutzumschlag m
dust' mop' s Mop m
dust'pan' s Kehrichtschaufel f
dust'proof' adj staubdicht
dust' rag' s Staublappen m
dusty ['dʌsti] adj staubig
Dutch [dʌtʃ] adj niederländisch; **go D.** (coll) getrennt bezahlen || s (language) Niederländisch n; **in D.** (coll)

in der Patsche; the D. die Niederländer
Dutch'man s (-men) Niederländer m
Dutch' treat' s (coll) Beisammensein n bei getrennter Kasse
dutiable ['d(j)utɪ·əbəl] adj steuerpflichtig
dutiful ['d(j)utɪfəl] adj pflichtgetreu
duty ['d(j)uti] s (to) Pflicht f (gegenüber dat); (service) Dienst m; (task) Aufgabe f; (tax) Zoll m, Abgabe f; **be in d.** bound to (inf) pflichtgemäß müssen (inf); **do d. as** (said of a thing) dienen als; (said of a person) Dienst tun als; **off d.** außer Dienst, dienstfrei; **on. d.** im Dienst; **pay d.** on verzollen
du'ty-free' adj zollfrei
du'ty ros'ter s (mil) Diensteinteilung f
dwarf [dwɔrf] adj zwergenhaft, Zwerg- || s Zwerg m || tr (stunt) in der Entwicklung behindern; (fig) in den Schatten stellen
dwell [dwɛl] v (pret & pp dwelled & dwelt [dwɛlt]) intr wohnen; **d. on** verweilen bei
dwell'ing s Wohnung f
dwell'ing house' s Wohnhaus n
dwindle ['dwɪndəl] intr schwinden, abnehmen; **d. away** dahinschwinden
dye [daɪ] s Farbe f || v (pret & pp dyed; ger dyeing) tr färben
dyed'-in-the-wool' adj (fig) in der Wolle gefärbt
dye'ing s Färben n
dyer ['daɪ·ər] s Färber -in mf
dy'ing adj (person) sterbend; (words) letzte || s Sterben n
dynamic [daɪ'næmɪk] adj dynamisch || **dynamics** s Dynamik f; **dynamics** spl (fig) Triebkraft f
dynamite ['daɪnəˌmaɪt] s Dynamit n || tr sprengen
dyna·mo ['daɪnəˌmo] s (-mos) Dynamo m
dynastic [daɪ'næstɪk] adj dynastisch
dynasty ['daɪnəsti] s Dynastie f
dysentery ['dɪsənˌteri] s Ruhr f
dyspepsia [dɪs'pepsɪ·ə] s Verdauungsstörung f

E

E, e [i] s fünfter Buchstabe des englischen Alphabets; (mus) E n; **E flat** Es n; **E sharp** Eis n
each [itʃ] indef adj jeder; **e. and every** jeder einzelne || adv je, pro Person, pro Stück || indef pron jeder; **e. other** einander, sich
eager ['igər] adj eifrig; **e. for** begierig nach; **e. to** (inf) begierig zu (inf)
ea'ger bea'ver s (coll) Streber -in mf
eagerness ['igərnɪs] s Eifer m
eagle ['igəl] s Adler m
ea'gle-eyed' adj adleräugig
ear [ɪr] s Ohr n; (of corn, wheat) Ähre f; (fig) Gehör n; **be all ears**

ganz Ohr sein; **bend s.o.'s ears** (sl) j-m die Ohren vollreden; **be up to one's ears** in bis über die Ohren stecken in (dat); **by ear** nach Gehör; **ear for music** musikalisches Gehör n; **fall on deaf ears** kein Gehör finden; **in one ear and out the other** zu e-m Ohr hinein und zum anderen hinaus; **turn a deaf ear to** taub sein gegen
ear'ache' s Ohrenschmerzen pl
ear'drops' spl (med) Ohrentropfen pl
ear'drum' s Trommelfell n
earl [ʌrl] s Graf m
ear'lobe' s Ohrläppchen n

early ['ʌrli] adj früh; (reply) baldig; (far back in time) Früh–; **at the earliest possible moment** baldigst; **at your earliest convenience** bei erster Gelegenheit; **be too e.** sich verfrühen || adv früh, frühzeitig; (too soon) zu früh; **as e. as** schon

ear'ly bird' s Frühaufsteher –in mf

ear'ly ris'er s Frühaufsteher –in mf

ear'ly warn'ing sys'tem s Vorwarnungssystem n

ear'mark' s (fig) Kennzeichen n || tr (mark out) kennzeichnen; (e.g., funds) (for) bestimmen (für)

ear'muffs' spl Ohrenschützer m

earn [ʌrn] tr (money) verdienen; (a reputation) sich [dat] erwerben; (interest) einbringen

earnest ['ʌrnɪst] adj ernst, ernsthaft || s—**are you in e.?** ist das Ihr Ernst?; **be in e. about** es ernst meinen mit; **in e.** im Ernst

ear'phone' s Kopfhörer m

ear'piece' s (earphone) Hörer m; (of eyeglasses) Bügel m

ear'ring' s Ohrring m

ear'shot' s—**within e.** in Hörweite

ear'split'ting adj ohrenbetäubend

earth [ʌrθ] s Erde f; **come down to e.** auf den Boden der Wirklichkeit zurückkehren; **on e.** (coll) in aller Welt

earthen ['ʌrθən] adj irden

earth'enware' s Tonwaren pl

earthly ['ʌrθli] adj irdisch; **be of no e. use** völlig unnütz sein; **e. possessions** Glücksgüter pl

earth'quake' s Erdbeben n

earth'shak'ing adj welterschütternd

earth'work' s Schanze f

earth'worm' s Regenwurm m

earthy ['ʌrθi] adj erdig; (fig) deftig

ear'wax' s Ohrenschmalz m

ease [iz] s (facility) Leichtigkeit f; (comfort) Bequemlichkeit f; (informality) Zwanglosigkeit f; **at e.!** (mil) rührt euch!; **feel at e. with s.o.** sich in j–s Gegenwart wohl fühlen; **put at e.** beruhigen; **with e.** mühelos || tr (work) erleichtern; (pain) lindern; (move carefully) lavieren; **e. out** (of a job) hinausmanövrieren || intr—**e. up** nachlassen; **e. up on** (work) es sich [dat] leichter machen mit

easel ['izəl] s Staffelei f

easement ['izmənt] s (jur) Dienstbarkeit f

easily ['izəli] adv leicht, mühelos; **e. satisfied** genügsam

easiness ['izinɪs] s Leichtigkeit f

east [ist] adj Ost–, östlich || adv ostwärts, nach Osten; **e. of** östlich von || s Osten m; **the East** der Osten

east'bound' adj nach Osten fahrend

Easter ['istər] adj Oster– || s Ostern n & pl

easterly ['istərli] adj österlich

eastern ['istərn] adj Ost–

East'ertide' s Osterzeit f

East'-Ger'man mark' s Ostmark f

eastward ['istwərd] adv ostwärts

easy ['izi] adj leicht; (terms) günstig; (virtue) locker; (pace) gemächlich; **e. on the eye** knusprig; **e. to digest**

leichtverdaulich; **have an e. time of it** leichtes Spiel haben; **it's e. for you to talk** du hast gut reden!; **make e.** erleichtern || adv—**e. come, e. go** wie gewonnen, so zerronnen; **get off e.** gnädig davonkommen; **take it e.** (relax) es sich [dat] leicht machen; (take one's time) sich [dat] Zeit lassen; (in parting) mach's gut! (remain calm) reg dich nicht auf!; **take it e. on** (a person) schonend umgehen mit; (a thing) sparsam umgehen mit

eas'y chair' s Lehnsessel m

eas'ygo'ing adj ungeniert, ungezwungen

eas'y mark' s (coll) leichte Beute f

eat [it] s—**eats** pl (coll) Essen n || v (pret ate [et]; pp eaten ['itən]) tr essen; (said of animals) fressen; **eat away** zerfressen; **eat one's fill** sich satt essen; **eat one's heart out** sich in Kummer verzehren; **eat one's words** das Gesagte zurücknehmen; **eat up** aufessen; **what's eating him?** was hat er denn? || intr essen; **eat out** auswärts essen

eatable ['itəbəl] adj eßbar

eaves [ivz] spl Dachrinne f, Traufe f

eaves'drop' v (pret & pp –dropped; ger –dropping) intr horchen; **e. on** belauschen

eaves'drop'per s Horcher –in mf

ebb [eb] s Ebbe f; **at a low ebb** sehr heruntergekommen || intr ebben; (fig) nachlassen

ebb' and flow' s Ebbe und Flut f

ebb' tide' s Ebbe f

ebony ['ebəni] s Ebenholz n

ebullient [ɪ'bʌljənt] adj überschwenglich, hochbegeistert

eccentric [ek'sentrɪk] adj (& fig) exzentrisch || s Sonderling m, Kauz m; (mach) Exzenter m

eccentricity [,eksen'trɪsɪti] s Verschrobenheit f, Tick m

ecclesiastic [ɪ,klizɪ'æstɪk] adj kirchlich; (law) Kirchen– || s Geistlicher m

echelon ['eʃə,lɑn] s (level) Befehlsebene f; (group occupying a particular level) Stabsführung f; (flight formation) Staffel f; **in echelons** staffelförmig || tr staffeln

ech·o ['eko] s (–oes) Echo n || tr (sounds) zurückwerfen; (fig) nachsprechen || intr widerhallen, echoen

éclair [e'kler] s Eclair n

eclectic [ek'lektɪk] adj eklektisch || s Eklektiker –in mf

eclipse [ɪ'klɪps] s Verfinsterung f; **go into e.** sich verfinstern; **in e.** im Schwinden || tr verfinstern; (fig) in den Schatten stellen

eclogue ['eklɔg] s Ekloge f

ecological [,ekə'lɑdʒɪkəl] adj ökologisch

ecology [ɪ'kɑlədʒi] s Ökologie f

economic [,ikə'nɑmɪk], [,ekə'nɑmɪk] adj wirtschaftlich, Wirtschafts–

economical [,ikə'nɑmɪkəl], [,ekə'nɑmɪkəl] adj sparsam

economics [,ikə'nɑmɪks], [,ekə'nɑmɪks] s Wirtschaftswissenschaften pl

economist [ɪ'kɑnəmɪst] *s* Volkswirt-schaftler –in *mf*

economize [ɪ'kɑnə,maɪz] *intr* sparen

economy [ɪ'kɑnəmi] *s* Wirtschaft *f;* *(thriftiness)* Sparsamkeit *f; (a saving)* Ersparnis *f*

ecstasy ['ɛkstəsi] *s* Verzückung *f;* **go into e.** in Verzückung geraten

ecstatic [ɛk'stætɪk] *adj* verzückt

ecumenic(al) [,ɛkjə'mɛnɪk(əl)] *adj* ökumenisch

eczema [ɛg'zimə] *s* Ausschlag *m*

ed·dy ['ɛdi] *s* Strudel *m* || *v (pret & pp* –died) *intr* strudeln

edelweiss ['ɛdəl,vaɪs] *s* Edelweiß *n*

edge [ɛdʒ] *s (of a knife)* Schneide *f; (of a forest, town, water, road)* Rand *m; (e.g., of a table)* Kante *f; (keenness)* Schärfe *f;* (bb) Schnitt *m;* **have an e.** on s.o. den Vorteil gegenüber j–m haben; **on e.** *(said of a person or teeth)* kribbelig; *(said of nerves)* aufs äußerste gespannt; **take the e. off** abstumpfen; (fig) die Schärfe nehmen *(dat)* || *tr (a lawn)* beschneiden; *(put a border on)* einfassen; **e. out** (sport) knapp schlagen || *intr* —**e. forward** langsam vorrücken

edge'wise' *adv*—**not get a word in e.** nicht zu Worte kommen können

edg'ing *s* Umrandung *f,* Besatz *m*

edgy ['ɛdʒi] *adj* kribbelig

edible ['ɛdɪbəl] *adj* eßbar, genießbar

edict ['idɪkt] *s* Edikt *n,* Erlaß *m*

edification [,ɛdɪfɪ'keʃən] *s* Erbauung *f*

edifice ['ɛdɪfɪs] *s* Bauwerk *n,* Gebäude *n*

edi·fy ['ɛdɪ,faɪ] *v (pret & pp* –fied) *tr* erbauen; **be edified by** sich erbauen an *(dat)*

ed'ifying *adj* erbaulich

edit ['ɛdɪt] *tr (a book)* herausgeben; *(a newspaper)* redigieren; (cin) schneiden

edition [ɛ'dɪʃən] *s* Ausgabe *f*

editor ['ɛdɪtər] *s (of a newspaper or magazine)* Redakteur –in *mf; (of a book)* Herausgeber –in *mf; (of editorials)* Leitartikler –in *mf;* (cin) Schnittmeister –in *mf*

editorial [,ɛdɪ'torɪ·əl] *adj* redaktionell, Redaktions– || *s* Leitartikel *m*

editorialize [,ɛdɪ'torɪ·ə,laɪz] *intr* (on) seine Meinung zum Ausdruck bringen *(über acc); (report with a slant)* tendenziös berichten

edito'rial of'fice *s* Redaktion *f*

edito'rial staff *s* Redaktion *f*

ed'itor in chief *s* Chefredakteur –in *mf*

educate ['ɛdʒʊ,ket] *tr* bilden, erziehen

education [,ɛdʒʊ'keʃən] *s* Bildung *f,* Erziehung *f;* (educ) Pädagogik *f*

educational [,ɛdʒʊ'keʃənəl] *adj* Bildungs–; **e. background** Vorbildung *f;* **e. film** Lehrfilm *m;* **e. institution** Lehranstalt *f*

educator ['ɛdʒʊ,ketər] *s* Erzieher –in *mf*

educe [ɪ'd(j)us] *tr* hervorholen

eel [il] *s* Aal *m*

eerie, eery ['ɪri] *adj* unheimlich

efface [ɪ'fes] *tr* austilgen; **e. oneself** sich zurückhalten

effect [ɪ'fɛkt] *s* (on) Wirkung *f (auf acc); (consequence)* (on) Auswirkung *f (auf acc); (impression)* Eindruck *m;* **effects** *(movable property)* Habe *f;* **for e.** zum Effekt; **go into e.** in Kraft treten; **have an e. on** wirken auf *(acc);* **in e.** praktisch; **put into e.** in Kraft setzen; **take e.** zur Geltung kommen; **to the e. that** des Inhalts, daß || *tr* bewirken

effective [ɪ'fɛktɪv] *adj* wirkungsvoll; *(actual)* effektiv; **e. against** wirksam gegen; **e. date** Tag *m* des Inkrafttretens; **e. from** mit Wirkung von; **e. immediately** mit sofortiger Wirkung; **e. strength** (mil) Iststärke *f*

effectual [ɪ'fɛktʊ·əl] *adj* wirksam

effectuate [ɪ'fɛktʊ,et] *tr* bewirken

effeminacy [ɪ'fɛmɪnəsi] *s* Verweichlichung *f*

effeminate [ɪ'fɛmɪnɪt] *adj* verweichlicht

effervesce [,ɛfər'vɛs] *intr* aufbrausen

effervescence [,ɛfər'vɛsəns] *s* Aufbrausen *n,* Moussieren *n*

effervescent [,ɛfər'vɛsənt] *adj (liquid; personality)* aufbrausend

effete [ɪ'fit] *adj* entkräftet

efficacious [,ɛfɪ'keʃəs] *adj* wirksam

efficacy ['ɛfɪkəsi] *s* Wirksamkeit *f,* Wirkungskraft *f*

efficiency [ɪ'fɪʃənsi] *s* Tüchtigkeit *f;* (phys) Nutzeffekt *m;* (tech) Leistungsfähigkeit *f*

efficient [ɪ'fɪʃənt] *adj* tüchtig; (tech) leistungsfähig

effigy ['ɛfɪdʒi] *s* Abbild *n;* **hang in e.** symbolisch hängen

effort ['ɛfərt] *s (exertion)* Mühe *f; (attempt)* Bestreben *n;* **efforts** Bemühungen *pl;* **make an honest e. to** *(inf)* sich redlich bemühen zu *(inf)*

effortless ['ɛfərtlɪs] *adj* mühelos

effrontery [ɪ'frʌntəri] *s* Frechheit *f,* Unverschämtheit *f*

effusion [ɪ'fjuʒən] *s* Erguß *m*

effusive [ɪ'fjusɪv] *adj* überschwenglich

egg [ɛg] *s* Ei *n;* **bad egg** (sl) übler Geselle *m;* **good egg** (sl) feiner Kerl *m;* **lay an egg** ein Ei legen; (fig) **e-e völlige Niete sein** || *tr*—**egg on** anstacheln

egg'beat'er *s* Schneeschläger *m*

egg'cup' *s* Eierbecher *m*

egg'head' *s* (coll) Intelligenzler –in *mf*

egg'nog ['ɛg,nɑg] *s* Eierlikör *m,* Egg-Nog *m*

egg'plant' *s* Eierfrucht *f*

egg'shell' *s* Eierschale *f*

egg' white' *s* Eiweiß *n*

egg' yolk' *s* Eigelb *n,* Eidotter *m*

ego ['igo] *s* Ego *n,* Ich *n;* (coll) Ichsucht *f*

egocentric [,igo'sɛntrɪk] *adj* egozentrisch

egoism ['igo,ɪzəm] *s* Selbstsucht *f*

egoist ['igo·ɪst] *s* Egoist *m*

egotism ['igo,tɪzəm] *s* Ichsucht *f*

egotistic(al) [,igo'tɪstɪk(əl)] *adj* egotistisch, geltungsbedürtig

egregious [ɪ'griʤəs] *adj* unerhört

egress ['igres] *s* Ausgang *m*

Egypt ['idʒɪpt] *s* Ägypten *n*

Egyptian [ɪ'dʒɪpʃən] *adj* ägyptisch || *s* Ägypter –in *mf*; (*language*) Ägyptisch *n*

eiderdown ['aɪdər‚daun] *s* Eiderdaunen *pl*; (*cover*) Daunenbett *n*

eight [et] *adj & pron* acht || *s* Acht *f*

eight'ball' *s*—be behind the e. (sl) in der Klemme sitzen

eighteen ['et'tin] *adj & pron* achtzehn || *s* Achtzehn *f*

eighteenth ['et'tinθ] *adj* achtzehnte || *s* (*fraction*) Achtzehntel *n*; the e. (*in dates or in a series*) der Achzehnte

eighth [etθ] *adj* achte || *s* (*fraction*) Achtel *n*; the e. (*in dates or in a series*) der Achte

eighth' note' *s* (mus) Achtelnote *f*

eightieth ['et·ɪ·θ] *adj* achtzigste || *s* (*fraction*) Achtzigstel *n*; the e. der Achtzigste

eighty ['eti] *adj & pron* achtzig || *s* Achtzig *f*; the eighties die achtziger Jahre *pl*

eigh'ty-one' *adj & pron* einundachtzig

either ['iðər], ['aɪðər] *adj*—e. one is correct beides ist richtig; e. way auf die e–e oder andere Art; in e. case in jedem der beiden Fälle; on e. side auf beiden Seiten || *adv*—not . . . e. auch nicht || *pron* einer von beiden; e. of you einer von euch beiden; I didn't see e. ich habe beide nicht gesehen || *conj*—e. . . . . or entweder . . . oder

ejaculate [ɪ'dʒækjə‚let] *tr* ausstoßen; (physiol) ejakulieren

eject [ɪ'dʒekt] *tr* ausstoßen; (*from a property*) (from) hinauswerfen (aus)

ejection [ɪ'dʒekʃən] *s* Ausstoßung *f*

ejec'tion seat' *s* Schleudersitz *m*

eke [ik] *tr*—eke out a living das Leben fristen

el [el] *s* (coll) Hochbahn *f*

elaborate [ɪ'læbərɪt] *adj* (*detailed*) weitläufig; (*ornate*) kunstvoll; (*idea*) compliziert || [ɪ'læbə‚ret] *tr* ausarbeiten || *intr*—e. on sich verbreiten über (*acc*)

elaboration [ɪ‚læbə'reʃən] *s* Ausarbeitung *f*

elapse [ɪ'læps] *intr* verrinnen

elastic [ɪ'læstɪk] *adj* elastisch; (*conscience*) weit || *s* Gummiband *n*

elasticity [‚ilæs'tɪsɪti] *s* Elastizität *f*

elated [ɪ'letɪd] *adj* freudig erregt

elation [ɪ'leʃən] *s* Hochgefühl *m*

elbow ['elbo] *s* Ellbogen *m*; (*of a pipe*) Rohrknie *n*; at one's e. bei der Hand; rub elbows with s.o. mit j–m in nähere Berührung kommen || *tr*—e. one's way sich [*dat*] seinen Weg bahnen

el'bow grease' *s* (coll) Knochenschmalz *n*

el'bowroom' *s* Spielraum *m*

elder ['eldər] *adj* älter || *s* Ältere *mf*; (bot) Holunder *m*; (eccl) Kirchenälteste *mf*

el'derber'ry *s* Holunderbeere *f*

elderly ['eldərli] *adj* ältlich

el'der states'man *s* profilierter Staatsmann *m*

eldest ['eldɪst] *adj* älteste

elect [ɪ'lekt] *adj* erlesen; (*elected but not yet installed*) zukünftig; (relig) auserwählt || the e. *spl* die Auserwählten *pl* || *tr* wählen; e. s.o. president j–n zum Präsidenten wählen

election [ɪ'lekʃən] *adj* Wahl– || *s* Wahl *f*

elec'tion campaign' *s* Wahlkampf *m*

elec'tion day' *s* Wahltag *m*

electioneer [ɪ‚lekʃə'nɪr] *intr* Stimmen werben

elective [ɪ'lektɪv] *adj* (educ) wahlfrei; (pol) Wahl– || *s* (educ) Wahlfach *n*

electoral [ɪ'lektərəl] *adj* Wahl–

elec'toral col'lege *s* Wahlmänner *pl*

electorate [ɪ'lektərɪt] *s* Wählerschaft *f*

electric(al) [ɪ'lektrɪk(əl)] *adj* elektrisch, Elektro–

elec'trical appli'ance *s* Elektrogerät *n*

elec'trical engineer' *s* Elektroingenieur *m*

elec'trical engineer'ing *s* Elektrotechnik *f*

elec'tric blan'ket *s* Heizdecke *f*

elec'tric bulb' *s* Glühbirne *f*

elec'tric chair' *s* elektrischer Stuhl *m*; (*penalty*) Hinrichtung *f* auf dem elektrischen Stuhl

elec'tric cir'cuit *s* Stromkreis *m*

elec'tric eel' *s* Zitteraal *m*

elec'tric eye' *s* Photozelle *f*

elec'tric fan' *s* Ventilator *m*

elec'tric fence' *s* elektrisch geladener Drahtzaun *m*

electrician [ɪ‚lek'trɪʃən] *s* Elektriker –in *mf*

electricity [‚ɪlek'trɪsɪti] *s* Elektrizität *f*; (*current*) Strom *m*

elec'tric light' *s* elektrisches Licht *n*

elec'tric me'ter *s* Stromzähler *m*

elec'tric saw' *s* Motorsäge *f*

elec'tric shav'er *s* elektrischer Rasierapparat *m*

elec'tric storm' *s* Gewittersturm *m*

elec'tric stove' *s* Elektroherd *m*

electri·fy [ɪ'lektrɪ‚faɪ] *v* (*pret & pp* –fied*) *tr* (& fig) elektrisieren; (a *streetcar, railroad*) elektrifizieren

electrocute [ɪ'lektrə‚kjut] *tr* durch elektrischen Strom töten; (jur) auf dem elektrischen Stuhl hinrichten

electrode [ɪ'lektrod] *s* Elektrode *f*

electrolysis [ɪ‚lek'tralɪsɪs] *s* Elektrolyse *f*

electrolyte [ɪ'lektrə‚laɪt] *s* Elektrolyt *m*

electromagnet [ɪ‚lektrə'mægnət] *s* Elektromagnet *m*

electromagnetic [ɪ‚lektrəmæg'netɪk] *adj* elektromagnetisch

electron [ɪ'lektrɑn] *s* Elektron *n*

electronic [ɪ‚lek'trɑnɪk] *adj* elektronisch, Elektronen– || **electronics** *s* Elektronik *f*

electron'ic flash' *s* Röhrenblitz *m*; (*device*) Blitzgerät *n*

electronic [ɪ‚lek'trɑnɪk] *adj* elektroplattieren, galvanisieren

electrostatic [ɪ ˌlektrə'stætɪk] *adj* elektrostatisch

electrotype [ɪ'lektrə ˌtaɪp] *s* Galvano *n* || *tr* galvanoplastisch vervielfältigen

elegance ['elɪgəns] *s* Eleganz *f*

elegant ['elə ˌgənt] *adj* elegant

elegiac [ˌelɪ'dʒaɪˌæk] *adj* elegisch

elegy ['elɪdʒɪ] *s* Elegie *f*

element ['elɪmənt] *s* (& fig) Element *n*; (e.g., of truth) Körnchen *n*

elementary [ˌelɪ'mentərɪ] *adj* elementar, grundlegend

elemen'tary school' *s* Grundschule *f*

elephant ['elɪfənt] *s* Elefant *m*

elevate ['elɪ ˌvet] *tr* erheben, erhöhen

el'evated *adj* (eyes) erhoben; (style) erhaben || *s* (coll) Hochbahn *f*

elevation [ˌelɪ've ʃən] *s* (height) Höhe *f*; (hill) Anhöhe *f*; (above sealevel) Seehöhe *f*; (archit) Aufriß *m*; (arti) Richthöhe *f*; (astr, relig) Elevation *f*

elevator ['elɪ ˌvetər] *s* Aufzug *m*, Fahrstuhl *m*; (aer) Höhenruder *n*; (agr) Getreidespeicher *m*

el'evator op'erator *s* Fahrstuhlführer –in *mf*

el'evator shaft' *s* Fahrstuhlschacht *m*

eleven [ɪ'levən] *adj & pron* elf || *s* Elf *f*

eleventh [ɪ'levənθ] *adj* elfte || *s* (fraction) Elftel *n*; **the e.** (in dates and in a series) der Elfte

elev'enth hour' *s*—at the e. (fig) kurz vor Torschluß

elf [elf] *s* (elves [elvz]) Elf *m*, Elfe *f*

elicit [ɪ'lɪsɪt] *tr* hervorlocken; (an answer) entlocken

elide [ɪ'laɪd] *tr* elidieren

eligible ['elɪdʒɪbəl] *adj* qualifiziert; (entitled) berechtigt; (for office) wählbar; (for marriage) heiratsfähig

el'igible bach'elor *s* Heiratskandidat *m*

eliminate [ɪ'lɪmɪ ˌnet] *tr* ausscheiden; (alg) eliminieren

elimination [ɪ ˌlɪmɪ'ne ʃən] *s* Ausscheidung *f*

elimina'tion bout' *s* Ausscheidungskampf *m*

elision [ɪ'lɪʒən] *s* Auslassung *f*

elite [e'lit] *adj* Elite– || *s* Elite *f*

elixir [ɪ'lɪksər] *s* Elixier *n*

elk [elk] *s* Elch *m*

ellipse [ɪ'lɪps] *s* (geom) Ellipse *f*

ellip·sis [ɪ'lɪpsɪs] *s* (–ses [siz]) (gram) Ellipse *f*

elliptic(al) [ɪ'lɪptɪk(əl)] *adj* elliptisch

elm [elm] *s* Ulme *f*

elocution [ˌelə'kju ʃən] *s* (art) Vortragskunst *f*; (style) Vortragsweise *f*

elope [ɪ'lop] *intr* ausreißen

elopement [ɪ'lopmənt] *s* Ausreißen *n*

eloquence ['eləkwəns] *s* Beredsamkeit *f*

eloquent ['eləkwənt] *adj* beredt

else [els] *adj* sonst; **someone else's house** das Haus e–s anderen; **what e.?** was sonst?; (in addition) was noch? || *adv* sonst, anders; **nowhere e.** sonst nirgends; **or e.** sonst, andernfalls; **where e.?** wo sonst?

else'where' *adv* (position) woanders;

(direction) sonstwohin; **from e.** andersdaher

elucidate [ɪ'lusɪ ˌdet] *tr* erläutern

elucidation [ɪ ˌlusɪ'de ʃən] *s* Erläuterung *f*

elude [ɪ'lud] *tr* entgehen (dat)

elusive [ɪ'lusɪv] *adj* schwer zu fassen; (memory) unzuverlässig

emaciated [ɪ'meʃɪ ˌetɪd] *adj* abgezehrt

emanate ['emə ˌnet] *intr*—**e. from** (said of gases) ausströmen aus; (said of rays) ausstrahlen aus; (fig) ausgehen von

emancipate [ɪ'mænsɪ ˌpet] *tr* emanzipieren

emasculate [ɪ'mæskjə ˌlet] *tr* (& fig) entmannen

embalm [em'bam] *tr* einbalsamieren

embankment [em'bæŋkmənt] *s* Damm *m*

embar·go [em'bargo] *s* (–goes) Sperre *f*, Embargo *n* || *tr* sperren

embark [em'bark] *intr* (for) sich einschiffen (nach); **e. upon** sich einlassen auf (acc)

embarkation [ˌembar'ke ʃən] *s* Einschiffung *f*

embarrass [em'bærəs] *tr* in Verlegenheit bringen

embar'rassed *adj* verlegen; **feel e.** sich genieren

embar'rassing *adj* peinlich

embarrassment [em'bærəsmənt] *s* Verlegenheit *f*

embassy ['embəsɪ] *s* Botschaft *f*

em·bed [em'bed] *v* (pret & pp –bedded; ger –bedding) *tr* einbetten; **e. in concrete** einbetonieren

embellish [em'belɪʃ] *tr* verschönern

embellishment [em'belɪʃmənt] *s* Verschönerung *f*

ember ['embər] *s* glühende Kohle *f*; **embers** Glut *f*

Em'ber day' *s* Quatember *m*

embezzle [em'bezəl] *tr* unterschlagen

embezzlement [em'bezəlmənt] *s* Unterschlagung *f*, Veruntreuung *f*

embezzler [em'bezlər] *s* Veruntreuer –in *mf*

embitter [em'bɪtər] *tr* verbittern

emblazon [em'blezən] *tr* (decorate) verzieren; (extol) verherrlichen; (heral) heraldisch darstellen

emblem ['embləm] *s* Sinnbild *n*

emblematic(al) [ˌemblə'mætɪk(əl)] *adj* sinnbildlich

embodiment [em'badɪmənt] *s* Verkörperung *f*

embod·y [em'badɪ] *v* (pret & pp –ied) *tr* verkörpern

embolden [em'boldən] *tr* ermutigen

embolism ['embə ˌlɪzəm] *s* Embolie *f*

emboss [em'bos] *tr* bossieren

embossed' *adj* getrieben

embrace [em'bres] *s* Umarmung *f* || *tr* umarmen; (include) umfassen; (a religion, idea) annehmen || *intr* sich umarmen

embrasure [em'breʒər] *s* Schießscharte *f*

embroider [em'brɔɪdər] *tr* sticken

embroidery [em'brɔɪdərɪ] *s* Stickerei *f*

embroi'dery nee'dle *s* Sticknadel *f*

embroil [ɛm'brɔɪl] *tr* verwickeln
embroilment [ɛm'brɔɪlmənt] *s* Verwicklung *f*
embry∙o ['ɛmbrɪ‚o] *s* (**-os**) Embryo *m*
embryology [‚ɛmbrɪ'ɑlədʒi] *s* Embryologie *f*
embryonic ['ɛmbrɪ'ɑnɪk] *adj* embryonal
emend [ɪ'mɛnd] *tr* berichtigen
emendation [‚imen'deʃən] *s* Berichtigung *f*
emerald ['ɛmərəld] *adj* smaragdgrün || *s* Smaragd *m*
emerge [ɪ'mʌrdʒ] *intr* (*come forth*) hervortreten; (*surface*) auftauchen; (*result*) herauskommen (bei)
emergence [ɪ'mʌrdʒəns] *s* Hervortreten *n*; (*surfacing*) Auftauchen *n*
emergency [ɪ'mʌrdʒənsi] *adj* Not- || *s* Notlage *f*; **in case of e.** im Notfall
emeritus [ɪ'mɛrɪtəs] *adj* emeritiert
emersion [ɪ'mʌrʒən] *s* Auftauchen *n*
emery ['ɛməri] *s* Schmirgel *m*
em'ery cloth' *s* Schmirgelleinwand *f*
em'ery wheel' *s* Schmirgelrad *n*
emetic [ɪ'mɛtɪk] *adj* Brech– || *s* Brechmittel *n*
emigrant ['ɛmɪgrənt] *s* Auswanderer –in *mf*
emigrate ['ɛmɪ‚gret] *intr* auswandern
emigration [‚ɛmɪ'greʃən] *s* Auswanderung *f*
eminence ['ɛmɪnəns] *s* (*height*) Anhöhe *f*; (*fame*) Berühmtheit *f*; **Eminence** (*title of a cardinal*) Eminenz *f*; **rise to e.** zu Ruhm und Würde gelangen
eminent ['ɛmɪnənt] *adj* hervorragend
emissary ['ɛmɪ‚sɛri] *s* Abgesandte *mf*
emission [ɪ'mɪʃən] *s* (*biol*) Erguß *m*; (*phys*) Austrahlung *f*, Ausströmung *f*
emis'sion control' *s* Abgasentgiftung *f*
emit [ɪ'mɪt] *v* (*pret & pp* **emitted;** *ger* **emitting**) *tr* von sich geben; (*rays*) austrahlen; (*gases*) ausströmen; (*sparks*) sprühen
emolument [e'mɑljəmənt] *s* Vergütung *f*
emotion [ɪ'moʃən] *s* Gemütsbewegung *f*
emotional [ɪ'moʃənəl] *adj* (*e.g., disorder*) Gemüts–; (*person*) gefühlvoll; (*e.g., sermon*) ergreifend; (*mawkish*) rührselig
emperor ['ɛmpərər] *s* Kaiser *m*
empha∙sis ['ɛmfəsɪs] *s* (**-ses** [‚siz]) Betonung *f*
emphasize ['ɛmfə‚saɪz] *tr* betonen
emphatic [ɛm'fætɪk] *adj* nachdrücklich
emphysema [‚ɛmfɪ'simə] *s* Emphysem *n*
empire ['ɛmpaɪr] *s* Reich *n*; (*Roman period*) Kaiserzeit *f*
Em'pire fur'niture *s* Empiremöbel *pl*
empiric(al) [ɛm'pɪrɪk(əl)] *adj* erfahrungsmäßig, empirisch
empiricist [ɛm'pɪrɪsɪst] *s* Empiriker –in *mf*
emplacement [ɛm'plesmənt] *s* Stellung *f*
employ [ɛm'plɔɪ] *s* Dienst *m* || *tr* (*hire*) anstellen; (*keep in employ-*

ment) beschäftigen; (*use*) verwenden; (*troops, police*) einsetzen
employee [ɛm'plɔɪ‚i], [‚ɛmplɔɪ'i] *s* Arbeitnehmer –in *mf*
employer [ɛm'plɔɪ∙ər] *s* Arbeitgeber –in *mf*
employment [ɛm'plɔɪmənt] *s* (*work*) Beschäftigung *f*, Arbeit *f*; (*use*) Verwendung *f*; (*e.g., of troops*) Einsatz *m*; **out of e.** arbeitslos
employ'ment a'gency *s* Arbeitsvermittlung *f*
empower [ɛm'pau∙ər] *tr* ermächtigen
empress ['ɛmprɪs] *s* Kaiserin *f*
emptiness ['ɛmptɪnɪs] *s* Leere *f*; (fig) Nichtigkeit *f*
emp∙ty ['ɛmpti] *adj* leer; **e. talk** leere Worte *pl*; **on an e. stomach** auf nüchternen Magen || **empties** *spl* Leergut *n* || *v* (*pret & pp* **–tied**) *tr* (*aus*)leeren || *intr*—**e. into** münden in (*acc*)
emp'ty-hand'ed *adj* mit leeren Händen
emp'ty-head'ed *adj* hohlköpfig
emulate ['ɛmjə‚let] *s* nacheifern (*dat*)
emulation [‚ɛmjə'leʃən] *s* Nacheiferung *f*
emulator [‚ɛmjə'letər] *s* Nacheiferer –in *mf*
emulsi∙fy [ɪ'mʌlsɪ‚faɪ] *v* (*pret & pp* **–fied**) *tr* emulgieren
emulsion [ɪ'mʌlʃən] *s* Emulsion *f*; (phot) Schicht *f*
enable [ɛn'ebəl] *tr* befähigen
enact [ɛn'ækt] *tr* erlassen
enactment [ɛn'æktmənt] *s* Erlassen *n*
enam∙el [ɪ'næməl] *s* Email *n*; (dent) Zahnschmelz *m* || *v* (*pret & pp* **–el[l]ed;** *ger* **–el[l]ing**) *tr* emaillieren
enam'el paint' *s* Emaillack *m*
enam'elware' *s* Emailwaren *pl*
enamored [e'næmərd] *adj*—**be e. of** verliebt sein in (*acc*)
encamp [ɛn'kæmp] *tr* in ein Lager unterbringen || *intr* lagern, sich lagern
encampment [ɛn'kæmpmənt] *s* (*camping*) Lagern *n*; (*campsite*) Lager *n*
encase [ɛn'kes] *tr* einschließen
enchant [ɛn't∫ænt] *tr* verzaubern; (fig) bezaubern
enchanter [ɛn't∫æntər] *s* Zauberer –in *mf*
enchanting *adj* bezaubernd
enchantment [ɛn't∫æntmənt] *s* (*state*) Verzauberung *f*; (*cause of enchantment*) Zauber *m*
enchantress [ɛn't∫æntrɪs] *s* Zauberin *f*
encircle [ɛn'sʌrkəl] *tr* umgeben; (mil) einschließen
encirclement [ɛn'sʌrkəlmənt] *s* (mil) Einschließung *f*
enclave ['ɛnklev] *s* Enklave *f*
enclitic [ɛn'klɪtɪk] *adj* enklitisch || *s* Enklitikon *n*
enclose [ɛn'kloz] *tr* einschließen; (*land*) umzäunen; (*in a letter*) beilegen; **e. in parentheses** einklammern; **please find enclosed** in der Anlage erhalten Sie
enclosure [ɛn'kloʒər] *s* Umzäunung *f*; (*in a letter*) Anlage *f*

encomi-um [ɛnˈkomɪ-əm] *s* (**-ums &** **-a** [ə]) Lobpreisung *f*, Enkomion *n*

encompass [ɛnˈkʌmpəs] *tr* umfassen

encore [ˈɑnkor] *s* (*performance*) Zugabe *f*; (*recall*) Dakaporuf *m* || *interj* da capo!; noch einmal!

encounter [ɛnˈkauntər] *s* Begegnung *f*; (*hostile meeting*) Zusammenstoß *m*; (*mil*) Gefecht *n* || *tr* begegnen (*dat*)

encourage [ɛnˈkʌrɪdʒ] *tr* ermutigen

encouragement [ɛnˈkʌrɪdʒmənt] *s* Ermutigung *f*

encroach [ɛnˈkrotʃ] *intr*—e. on übergreifen auf (*acc*); (*rights*) beeinträchtigen

encroachment [ɛnˈkrotʃmənt] *s* Übergriff *m*

encrust [ɛnˈkrʌst] *tr* überkrusten

encumber [ɛnˈkʌmbər] *tr* belasten; (*with debts*) verschulden

encumbrance [ɛnˈkrʌmbrəns] *s* Belastung *f*

encyclical [ɛnˈsɪklɪkəl] *s* Enzyklika *f*

encyclopedia [ɛn ˌsaɪkləˈpidɪ-ə] *s* Enzyklopädie *f*

encyclopedic [ɛn ˌsaɪkləˈpidɪk] *adj* enzyklopädisch

end [ɛnd] *s* Ende *n*; (*purpose*) Zweck *m*; (*goal*) Ziel *n*; (*closing*) Schluß *m*; (*outcome*) Ausgang *m*, Ergebnis *n*; **at the end of one's strength** am Rande seiner Kraft; **come to a bad end** ein schlimmes Ende finden; **come to an end** zu Ende gehen; **end in itself** Selbstzweck *m*; **gain one's ends** seinen Vorsatz ausführen; **go off the deep end** sich unnötig aufregen; **in the end** schließlich; **make both ends meet** gerade auskommen; **no end of** unendlich viel(e); **on end** hochkant; (*without letup*) ununterbrochen; **put an end to** ein Ende machen (*dat*); **that will be the end of me** das überlebe ich nicht; **to no end** vergebens || *tr* beenden || *intr* enden; (*gram*) auslauten; **end in a point** spitz zulaufen; **end up (in)** (*coll*) landen (in *dat*); **end up with** beenden mit

end'-all' *s* Schluß *m* vom Ganzen

endanger [ɛnˈdendʒər] *tr* gefährden

endear [ɛnˈdɪr] *tr*—e. s.o. to j-n einschmeicheln bei

endear'ing *adj* gewinnend

endearment [ɛnˈdɪrmənt] *s* Beliebtheit *f*

endeavor [ɛnˈdevər] *s* Bestreben *n* || *intr*—e. to (*inf*) sich bestreben zu (*inf*), versuchen zu (*inf*)

endemic [ɛnˈdemɪk] *adj* endemisch || *s* Endemie *f*, endemische Krankheit *f*

end'ing *s* Beendigung *f*, Abschluß *m*; (*gram*) Endung *f*

endive [ˈɛndaɪv] *s* Endivie *f*

endless [ˈɛndlɪs] *adj* endlos; **an e. number of** unendlich viele

end'most' *adj* entfernteste

endocrine [ˈɛndoˌkraɪn] *adj* endokrin

endorse [ɛnˈdors] *tr* (*confirm*) bestätigen; (*a check*) indossieren

endorsee [ˌɛndərˈsi] *s* Indossat –in *mf*

endorsement [ɛnˈdorsmənt] *s* Indossament *n*; (*approval*) Bestätigung *f*

endorser [ɛnˈdorsər] *s* Indossant –in *mf*; (*backer*) Hintermann *m*

endow [ɛnˈdau] *tr* (*provide with income*) dotieren; (*with talent*) begaben

endowment [ɛnˈdaumənt] *s* Dotierung *f*; (*talent*) Begabung *f*

endow'ment fund' *s* Stiftungsvermögen *n*

endurance [ɛnˈd(j)urəns] *s* Dauer *f*; (*ability to hold out*) Ausdauer *f*

endur'ance test' *s* Dauerprobe *f*

endure [ɛnˈd(j)ur] *tr* aushalten || *intr* fortdauern

endur'ing *adj* dauerhaft

enema [ˈɛnəmə] *s* Einlauf *m*

enemy [ˈɛnəmi] *adj* feindlich, Feind- || *s* Feind *m*; **become enemies** sich verfeinden

energetic [ˌɛnərˈdʒɛtɪk] *adj* energisch

energy [ˈɛnərdʒi] *s* Energie *f*

enervate [ˈɛnərˌvet] *tr* entkräften

enfeeble [ɛnˈfibəl] *tr* entkräften

enfilade [ˈɛnfɪˌled] *s* (*mil*) Flankenfeuer *n* || *tr* mit Flankenfeuer bestreichen

enfold [ɛnˈfold] *tr* einhüllen

enforce [ɛnˈfors] *tr* durchsetzen; (*obedience*) erzwingen

enforcement [ɛnˈforsmənt] *s* Durchsetzung *f*

enfranchise [ɛnˈfræntʃaɪz] *tr* (*admit to citizenship*) einbürgern; (*give the right to vote to*) das Wahlrecht verleihen (*dat*)

engage [ɛnˈgedʒ] *tr* (*hire*) anstellen; (*reserve*) vorbestellen; (*attention*) fesseln; (*gears*) einrücken; (*one's own troops*) einsetzen; (*the enemy*) angreifen; **be engaged in** beschäftigt sein mit; **e. in** verwickeln in (*acc*) || *intr* (*mach*) (ein)greifen; **e. in** sich einlassen in (*acc*)

engaged' *adj* verlobt; **get e. (to)** sich verloben mit

engaged' cou'ple *s* Brautleute *pl*

engagement [ɛnˈgedʒmənt] *s* (*betrothal*) Verlobung *f*; (*appointment*) Verabredung *f*; (*obligation*) Verpflichtung *f*; (*mil*) Gefecht *n*; **have a previous e.** verabredet sein

engage'ment ring' *s* Verlobungsring *m*

engag'ing *adj* gewinnend

engender [ɛnˈdʒɛndər] *tr* hervorbringen

engine [ˈɛndʒɪn] *s* Maschine *f*; (*aer*, *aut*) Motor *m*; (*rr*) Lokomotive *f*

engineer [ˌɛndʒəˈnɪr] *s* Ingenieur *m*, Techniker *m*; (*mil*) Pionier *m*; (*rr*) Lokomotivführer *m*; **engineers** (*mil*) Pioniertruppe *f* || *tr* errichten; (*fig*) bewerkstelligen

engineer'ing *s* Ingenieurwesen *n*

engineer'ing school' *s* Technikum *n*

en'gine house' *s* Spritzenhaus *n*

en'gine room' *s* Maschinenraum *m*

England [ˈɪŋɡlənd] *s* England *n*

English [ˈɪŋɡlɪʃ] *adj* englisch || *s* (*spin*) Effet *n*; (*language*) Englisch *n*; **in plain E.** unverblümt; **the E.** die Engländer

Eng'lish Chan'nel s Ärmelkanal m
Eng'lish horn' s Englischhorn n
Eng'lish·man s (–men) Engländer m
Eng'lish-speak'ing adj englischsprechend
Eng'lish·wom'an s (–wom'en) Engländerin f
engraft [ɛn'græft] tr aufpropfen; (fig) einprägen
engrave [ɛn'grev] tr gravieren
engraver [ɛn'grevər] s Graveur m
engrav'ing s Kupferstich m
engross [ɛn'gros] tr in Anspruch nehmen; (a document) mit großen Buchstaben schreiben; **become engrossed in** sich versenken in (acc)
engross'ing adj fesselnd
engulf [ɛn'gʌlf] tr (fig) verschlingen
enhance [ɛn'hæns] tr erhöhen; **be enhanced** sich erhöhen
enhancement [ɛn'hænsmənt] s Erhöhung f
enigma [ɪ'nɪgmə] s Rätsel n
enigmatic(al) [ˌɪnɪg'mætɪk(əl)] adj rätselhaft
enjoin [ɛn'dʒɔɪn] tr (forbid) (from ger) verbieten (dat) (zu inf); e. s.o. to (inf) j-m auferlegen zu (inf)
enjoy [ɛn'dʒɔɪ] tr (take pleasure in) Gefallen finden an (dat); (have the advantage of) genießen, sich erfreuen (genit); e. **doing s.th.** gern etw tun; **e. oneself** sich gut unterhalten; **e. to the full** auskosten; **I e. the wine** mir schmeckt der Wein
enjoyable [ɛn'dʒɔɪ·əbəl] adj erfreulich; **thoroughly e.** genußreich
enjoyment [ɛn'dʒɔɪmənt] s Genuß m
enkindle [ɛn'kɪndəl] tr entzünden
enlarge [ɛn'lɑrdʒ] tr vergrößern ‖ intr sich vergrößern; **e. upon** näher eingehen auf (acc)
enlargement [ɛn'lɑrdʒmənt] s Vergrößerung f
enlarger [ɛn'lɑrdʒər] s (phot) Vergrößerungsapparat m
enlighten [ɛn'laɪtən] tr aufklären
enlightenment [ɛn'laɪtənmənt] s (act) Aufklärung f; (state) Aufgeklärtheit f
enlist [ɛn'lɪst] tr (services) in Anspruch nehmen; (mil) anwerben; **e. s.o. in a cause** j-n für e-e Sache gewinnen ‖ intr (in) sich freiwillig melden (zu)
enlist'ed man' s Soldat m; **enlisted men** Mannschaften pl
enlistment [ɛn'lɪstmənt] s Anwerbung f; (period of service) Militärdienstzeit f
enliven [ɛn'laɪvən] tr beleben
enmesh [ɛn'mɛʃ] tr verstricken
enmity [ɛn'mɪti] s Feindschaft f
ennoble [ɛn'nobəl] tr veredeln, adeln
ennui [ɑn'wi] s Langeweile f
enormity [ɪ'nɔrmɪti] s Ungeheuerlichkeit f
enormous [ɪ'nɔrməs] adj enorm, ungeheuer
enough [ɪ'nʌf] adj & adv genug, genügend; **be e.** genügen; **I have e. of it** ich bin es satt; **it's e. to drive one crazy** es ist zum Verrücktwerden

enounce [ɪ'naʊns] tr (declare) verkünden; (pronounce) aussprechen
enrage [ɛn'redʒ] tr wütend machen
enraged' adj (at) wütend (über acc)
enrapture [ɛn'ræptʃər] tr hinreißen
enrich [ɛn'rɪtʃ] tr (a person with money; the mind, a program) bereichern; (soil) fruchtbar machen; (food, metals, gases) anreichern
enrichment [ɛn'rɪtʃmənt] s Bereicherung f; (of food, metals, gases) Anreicherung f
enroll [ɛn'rol] tr als Mitglied aufnehmen ‖ intr (educ) sich immatrikulieren lassen
enrollment [ɛn'rolmənt] s (in a course or school) Schülerzahl f; (of a society) Mitgliederzahl f
en route [ɑn 'rut] adv unterwegs
ensconce [ɛn'skɑns] tr verbergen
ensemble [ɑn'sɑmbəl] s Ensemble n
ensign ['ɛnsɪn] s (flag) (mil) Fahne f; (flag) (nav) Flagge f; (emblem) Abzeichen n; (nav) Leutnant m zur See
enslave [ɛn'slev] tr versklaven
enslavement [ɛn'slevmənt] s Versklavung f
ensnare [ɛn'snɛr] tr (fig) umgarnen
ensue [ɛn's(j)u] intr (from) (er)folgen (aus)
ensu'ing adj darauffolgend
ensure [ɛn'ʃʊr] tr gewährleisten
entail [ɛn'tel] tr mit sich bringen
entangle [ɛn'tæŋgəl] tr verwickeln; **get entangled** sich verwickeln
entanglement [ɛn'tæŋgəlmənt] s Verwicklung f; (mil) Drahtverhau m
enter ['ɛntər] tr (a room) betreten, treten in (acc); (political office) antreten; (a university) beziehen; (a protest) erheben; (a career) einschlagen; (in the records) eintragen; **e. the army** Soldat werden ‖ intr eintreten, hereinkommen; (by car) einfahren; (sport) melden; (theat) auftreten; **e. into** (an agreement) treffen; (a contract) abschließen; **e. upon** anfangen; (a career) einschlagen; (an office, inheritance) antreten; (year of life) eintreten in (acc)
enterprise ['ɛntər‚praɪz] s Unternehmen n; (spirit) Unternehmungsgeist m
en'terprising adj unternehmungslustig
entertain [‚ɛntər'ten] tr unterhalten; (guests) bewirten; (doubts, hopes, suspicions) hegen ‖ intr Gäste haben
entertainer [‚ɛntər'tenər] s Unterhaltungskünstler –in mf
entertain'ing adj unterhaltsam ‖ s—do a lot of e. ein großes Haus führen
entertainment [‚ɛntər'tenmənt] s Unterhaltung f
entertain'ment tax' s Vergnügungssteuer f
enthrall [ɛn'θrɔl] tr bezaubern, fesseln
enthrone [ɛn'θron] tr auf den Thron setzen; **be enthroned** thronen
enthuse [ɛn'θ(j)uz] tr (coll) begeistern
enthusiasm [ɛn'θ(j)uzɪ‚æzəm] s Begeisterung f, Schwärmerei f

enthusiast [ɛn'θ(j)uzɪ‚æst] *s* Schwärmer –in *mf*

enthusiastic [ɛn‚θ(j)uzɪ'æstɪk] *adj* (**about**) begeistert (über *acc* or von)

entice [ɛn'taɪs] *tr* (ver)locken

enticement [ɛn'taɪsmənt] *s* Verlockung *f*

entic'ing *adj* verlockend

entire [ɛn'taɪr] *adj* ganz, gesamt; (*trust*) voll

entirely [ɛn'taɪrli] *adv* ganz, gänzlich

entirety [ɛn'taɪrti] *s*—**in its e.** in seiner Gesamtheit

entitle [ɛn'taɪtəl] *tr* (*call*) betiteln; (**to**) berechtigen (zu); **be entitled to** Anspruch haben auf (*acc*); **be entitled to** (*inf*) berechtigt sein zu (*inf*)

entity ['ɛntɪti] *s* Wesen *n*

entomb [ɛn'tum] *tr* bestatten

entombment [ɛn'tummənt] *s* Bestattung *f*

entomology [‚ɛntə'malədʒi] *s* Entomologie *f*

entourage [‚antu'raʒ] *s* Begleitung *f*

entrails ['ɛntrɛlz] *spl* Eingeweide *pl*

entrain [ɛn'tren] *tr* verladen ‖ *intr* einsteigen

entrance ['ɛntrəns] *s* Eingang *m*; (*drive*) Einfahrt *f*; (*of a home*) Flur *m*; (*upon office*) Antritt *m*; (*theat*) Auftritt *m*; **make one's e.** eintreten ‖ [ɛn'træns] *tr* mitreißen

en'trance examina'tion *s* Aufnahmeprüfung *f*

en'trance fee' *s* Eintrittspreis *m*

entrant ['ɛntrənt] *s* (**in**) Teilnehmer –in *mf* (**an** *dat*)

en-trap [ɛn'træp] *v* (*pret & pp* **-trapped;** *ger* **-trapping**) *tr* verleiten

entreat [ɛn'trit] *tr* anflehen

entreaty [ɛn'triti] *s* dringende Bitte *f*; **at his e.** auf seine Bitte

entrée ['antre] *s* (*access*) Zutritt *m*; (*before main course*) Vorspeise *f*; (*between courses*) Zwischengericht *n*; (*main course*) Hauptgericht *m*

entrench [ɛn'trɛnt∫] *tr* verschanzen; **be entrenched in** (fig) eingewurzelt sein in (*dat*)

entrenchment [ɛn'trɛnt∫mənt] *s* (*activity*) Schanzbau *m*; (*the result*) Verschanzung *f*

entrepreneur [antrəprə'nʌr] *s* Unternehmer –in *mf*

entrust [ɛn'trʌst] *tr* (**to**) anvertrauen (*dat*)

entry ['ɛntri] *s* Eintritt *m*; (*by car*) Einfahrt *f*; (*door*) Eingang *m*, Eingangstür *f*; (*into a country*) Einreise *f*; (*into office*) Antritt *m*; (*in a dictionary*) Stichwort *n*; (*into a race*) Nennung *f*; (*contestant*) Bewerber –in *mf*; (com) Buchung *f*; (theat) Auftritt *m*; **unlawful e.** Hausfriedensbruch *m*

entwine [ɛn'twaɪn] *tr* umwinden

enumerate [ɪ'n(j)umə‚ret] *tr* aufzählen

enunciate [ɪ'nʌnsɪ‚et] *tr* aussprechen ‖ *intr* deutlich aussprechen

envelop [ɛn'vɛləp] *tr* (*said of crowds, waves*) verschlingen; (*said of mist, clouds, darkness*) umhüllen; (mil) umfassen

envelope ['ɛnvə‚lop] *s* Umschlag *m*

envelopment [ɛn'vɛləpmənt] *s* Umhüllung *f*; (mil) Umfassung *f*

envenom [ɛn'vɛnəm] *tr* vergiften

enviable ['ɛnvɪ‚əbəl] *adj* beneidenswert

envious ['ɛnvɪ‚əs] *adj* (**of**) neidisch (**auf** *acc*)

environment [ɛn'vaɪrənmənt] *s* (*ecological condition*) Umwelt *f*; (*surroundings*) Umgebung *f*

environmental [ɛn‚vaɪrən'mɛntəl] *adj* Umwelt–; umgebend, Umgebungs–

environmentalist [ɛn‚vaɪrən'mɛntəlɪst] *s* Umweltschützer –in *mf*

environs [ɛn'vaɪrənz] *spl* Umgebung *f*

envisage [ɛn'vɪzɪdʒ] *tr* ins Auge fassen

envoy ['ɛnvɔɪ] *s* Gesandte *mf*

en-vy ['ɛnvi] *s* Neid *m* ‖ *v* (*pret & pp* **-vied**) *tr* (**for**) beneiden (**um**)

enzyme ['ɛnzaɪm] *s* Enzym *n*

epaulet, epaulette ['ɛpə‚lɛt] *s* Epaulette *f*, Schulterstück *n*

ephemeral [ɪ'fɛmərəl] *adj* flüchtig

epic ['ɛpɪk] *adj* episch; **e. poetry** Epik *f* ‖ *s* Epos *n*, Heldengedicht *n*

epicure ['ɛpɪ‚kjur] *s* Feinschmecker –in *mf*

epicurean [‚ɛpɪkju'ri‚ən] *adj* genußsüchtig; (philos) epikureisch ‖ *s* Genußmensch *m*; (philos) Epikureer *m*

epidemic [‚ɛpɪ'dɛmɪk] *adj* epidemisch ‖ *s* Epidemie *f*, Seuche *f*

epidermis [‚ɛpɪ'dʌrmɪs] *s* Oberhaut *f*

epigram ['ɛpɪ‚græm] *s* Epigramm *n*

epigraph ['ɛpɪ‚græf] *s* Inschrift *f*

epigraphy [ɛ'pɪgrəfi] *s* Inschriftenkunde *f*

epilepsy ['ɛpɪ‚lɛpsi] *s* Epilepsie *f*

epileptic [‚ɛpɪ'lɛptɪk] *adj* epileptisch ‖ *s* Epileptiker –in *mf*

epilogue ['ɛpɪ‚lɔg] *s* Nachwort *n*

Epiphany [ɪ'pɪfəni] *s* Dreikönigsfest *n*

episcopal [ɪ'pɪskəpəl] *adj* bischöflich

Episcopalian [ɪ‚pɪskə'pelɪ‚ən] *adj* Episkopal– ‖ *s* Episkopale *m*, Episkopalin *f*

epis'copal see' *s* Bischofssitz *m*

episcopate [ɪ'pɪskə‚pet] *s* Bischofsamt *n*

episode ['ɛpɪ‚sod] *s* Episode *f*

epistemology [ɪ‚pɪstə'malədʒi] *s* Epistemologie *f*, Erkenntnistheorie *f*

epistle [ɪ'pɪsəl] *s* Epistel *f*

epitaph ['ɛpɪ‚tæf] *s* Grabinschrift *f*

epithet ['ɛpɪ‚θɛt] *s* Beiwort *n*

epitome [ɪ'pɪtəmi] *s* Auszug *m*; (fig) Verkörperung *f*

epitomize [ɪ'pɪtə‚maɪz] *tr*—**e–n** Auszug machen von or aus; (fig) verkörpern

epoch ['ɛpək], ['ipak] *s* Epoche *f*

epochal ['ɛpəkəl] *adj* epochal

e'poch-mak'ing *adj* bahnbrechend

Ep'som salts' ['ɛpsəm] *spl* Bittersalz *n*

equable ['ɛkwəbəl] *adj* gleichmäßig; (*disposition*) ausgeglichen

equal ['ikwəl] *adj* gleich; (*in birth or status*) ebenbürtig; (*in worth*) gleichwertig; (*in kind*) gleichartig; **be e. to** (*e.g., a task*) gewachsen sein (*dat*); **be on e. terms** (*be on the same level*) auf gleichem Fuß stehen; **other**

things being e. bei sonst gleichen Verhältnissen ‖ *s* Gleiche *mfn;* **her or their e.(s)** ihresgleichen; **my (your, etc.) e.(s)** meines– (deines–, etc.) gleichen ‖ *v (pret & pp* **equal[l]ed;** *ger* **equal[l]ing** *tr* gleichkommen *(dat); (a record)* erreichen; *(math)* ergeben

equality [ɪˈkwɑlɪti] *s* Gleichheit *f; (in standing)* Gleichberechtigung *f*

equalize [ˈikwə‚laɪz] *tr* gleichmachen

equally [ˈikwəli] *adv* gleich, ebenso

equanimity [‚ikwəˈnimiti] *s* Gleichmut *m*

equate [iˈkwet] *tr* **(to or with)** gleichsetzen *(dat or* mit*)*

equation [iˈkweʒən] *s* Gleichung *f*

equator [iˈkwetər] *s* Äquator *m*

equatorial [‚ikwəˈtorɪ‑əl] *adj* äquatorial

equestrian [ɪˈkwestrɪ‑ən] *adj* Reiter–; **e. statue** Reiterstandbild *n* ‖ *s* Kunstreiter –in *mf*

equilateral [‚ikwɪˈlætərəl] *adj* gleichseitig

equilibrium [‚ikwɪˈlɪbrɪ‑əm] *s* Gleichgewicht *n; (fig)* Gleichmaß *n*

equinox [ˈikwɪ‚nɑks] *s* Tagundnachtgleiche *f*

equip [ɪˈkwɪp] *v (pret & pp* **equipped;** *ger* **equipping)** *tr* ausrüsten, ausstatten

equipment [ɪˈkwɪpmənt] *s* Ausrüstung *f,* Ausstattung *f*

equipoise [ˈikwɪ‚pɔɪz] *s* Gleichgewicht *n*

equitable [ˈεkwɪtəbəl] *adj* gerecht

equity [ˈεkwɪti] *s (fairness)* Unparteilichkeit *f; (fin)* Nettowert *m*

equivalent [ɪˈkwɪvələnt] *adj* gleichwertig; **(to)** gleichbedeutend (mit) ‖ *s* Gegenwert *m; (of)* Äquivalent *n* *(für)*

equivocal [ɪˈkwɪvəkəl] *adj* zweideutig

equivocate [ɪˈkwɪvə‚ket] *intr* zweideutig reden

equivocation [ɪ‚kwɪvə‚keʃən] *s* Zweideutigkeit *f*

era [ˈɪrə], [ˈirə] *s* Zeitalter *n*

eradicate [ɪˈrædɪ‚ket] *tr* ausrotten

erase [ɪˈres] *tr* ausradieren; *(a tape recording)* löschen; *(a blackboard)* abwischen; *(fig)* auslöschen

eraser [ɪˈresər] *s* Radiergummi *m; (for a blackboard)* Tafelwischer *m*

erasure [ɪˈreʒər], [ɪˈreʒər] *s (action)* Ausradieren *n; (erased spot)* Rasur *f*

ere [er] *prep (poet)* vor *(dat)* ‖ *conj (poet)* ehe, bevor

erect [ɪˈrekt] *adj* aufrecht, straff; *(hair)* gesträubt; **with head e.** erhobenen Hauptes ‖ *tr* errichten

erection [ɪˈrekʃən] *s* Errichtung *f; (of sexual organs)* Erektion *f*

erg [ʌrg] *s* Erg *n*

ermine [ˈʌrmɪn] *s* Hermelinpelz *m*

erode [ɪˈrod] *tr (corrode)* zerfressen; *(fig)* unterhöhlen; *(geol)* erodieren ‖ *intr* zerfressen werden

erosion [ɪˈroʒən] *s (corrosion)* Zerfressen *n; (fig)* Unterhöhlung *f; (geol)* Erosion *f*

erotic [ɪˈrɑtɪk] *adj* erotisch

err [ʌr] *intr* irren, sich irren

errand [ˈerənd] *s* Besorgung *f;* **run an e.** e–e Besorgung machen

er′rand boy′ *s* Laufbursche *m*

erratic [ɪˈrætɪk] *adj* regellos, ziellos; *(geol)* erratisch

erroneous [ɪˈronɪ‑əs] *adj* irrtümlich

erroneously [ɪˈronɪ‑əsli] *adv* irrtümlicherweise, versehentlich

error [ˈerər] *s* Fehler *m,* Irrtum *m*

erudite [ˈer(j)ʊ‚daɪt] *adj* gelehrt

erudition [‚er(j)ʊˈdɪʃən] *s* Gelehrsamkeit *f*

erupt [ɪˈrʌpt] *intr* ausbrechen

eruption [ɪˈrʌpʃən] *s* Ausbruch *m; (pathol)* Ausschlag *m*

escalate [ˈeskə‚let] *tr & intr* eskalieren

escalation [‚eskəˈleʃən] *s* Eskalierung *f*

escalator [ˈeskə‚letər] *s* Rolltreppe *f*

es′calator clause′ *s* Indexklausel *f*

escapade [ˈeskə‚ped] *s* Eskapade *f*

escape [esˈkep] *s* Flucht *f; (of gas or liquid)* Ausströmen *n;* **have a narrow e.** mit knapper Not davonkommen ‖ *intr (said of gas or liquid)* ausströmen; *(from)* flüchten (aus)

escape′ clause′ *s* Ausweichklausel *f*

escapee [‚eskəˈpi] *s* Flüchtling *m*

escape′ hatch′ *s* Notausstieg *m*

escapement [esˈkepmənt] *s* (horol) Hemmung *f*

escape′ wheel′ *s* (horol) Hemmungsrad *n*

escapism [esˈkepɪzəm] *s* Wirklichkeitsflucht *f*

escarpment [esˈkɑrpmənt] *s* (geol) Steilabhang *m; (mil)* Abdachung *f*

eschew [esˈtʃu] *tr (vor)meiden*

escort [ˈeskɔrt] *s* Geleit *n,* Schutzgeleit *n; (person)* Begleiter *m; (mil)* Begleitmannschaft *f,* Bedeckung *f; (nav)* Geleitschutz *m* ‖ [esˈkɔrt] *tr* begleiten; *(mil, nav)* geleiten

es′cort ves′sel *s* Geleitschiff *n*

escutcheon [esˈkʌtʃən] *s* Wappenschild *m; (doorplate)* Schlüssellochschild *n*

Eskimo [ˈeskɪ‚mo] *adj* Eskimo– ‖ *s (–mos & –mo)* Eskimo *m*

esophagus [iˈsɑfəgəs] *s (–gi* [‚dʒaɪ]*)* Speiseröhre *f*

esoteric [‚esoˈterɪk] *adj* esoterisch

especial [esˈpeʃəl] *adj* besondere

especially [esˈpeʃəli] *adv* besonders

espionage [‚espɪ‑əˈnɑʒ] *s* Spionage *f*

espousal [esˈpauzəl] *s (of)* Annahme *f* (von)

espouse [esˈpauz] *tr* annehmen

esprit de corps [esˈpri də ˈkɔr] *s* Korpsgeist *m,* Gemeinschaftsgeist *m*

espy [esˈpaɪ] *v (pret & pp* **espied)** *tr* erspähen

essay [ˈese] *s* Aufsatz *m,* Essay *n* ‖ [eˈse] *tr* probieren

essayist [ˈese‑ɪst] *s* Essayist –in *mf*

essence [ˈesəns] *s* Wesenheit *f; (scent)* Duft *m; (extract)* Essenz *f; (philos)* inneres Wesen *n;* **in e.** im wesentlichen

essential [eˈsenʃəl] *adj* **(to)** wesentlich (für) ‖ *s* Hauptsache *f;* **the essentials** die Grundzüge *pl*

establish [es'tæblɪʃ] *tr* (*found*) gründen; (*a business, an account*) eröffnen; (*relations, connections*) herstellen; (*order*) schaffen; (*a record*) aufstellen; (*a fact*) feststellen

establishment [es'tæblɪʃmənt] *s* (*act*) Gründung *f*; (*institution*) Anstalt *f*; (*business*) Unternehmen *n*; **the Establishment** das Establishment

estate [es'tet] *s* (*landed property*) Landgut *n*; (*possessions*) Vermögen *n*; (*property of deceased person*) Nachlaß *m*; (*social station*) Stand *m*

esteem [es'tim] *s* Hochachtung *f*; **hold in e.** achten || *tr* achten

esthete ['esθit] *s* Ästhetiker –in *mf*

esthetic [es'θetɪk] *adj* ästhetisch || **esthetics** *s* Ästhetik *f*

estimable ['estɪməbəl] *adj* schätzenswert

estimate ['estɪ,met], ['estɪmɪt] *s* Kostenanschlag *m*; (*judgment of value*) Schätzung *f*; **rough e.** Überschlag *m* || ['estɪ,met] *tr* (*costs*) veranschlagen; (*the value*) abschätzen; (*homes, damages*) schätzen; (**at**) beziffern (auf *acc*); **e. roughly** überschlagen

estimation [,estɪ'meʃən] *s* Schätzung *f*; **in my e.** nach meiner Schätzung

Estonia [es'tonɪ-ə] *s* Estland *n*

estrangement [es'trendʒmənt] *s* Entfremdung *f*

estuary ['estʃʊ,erɪ] *s* (*of a river*) Mündung *f*; (*inlet*) Meeresarm *m*

etch [etʃ] *tr* radieren, ätzen

etcher ['etʃər] *s* Radierer –in *mf*

etch′ing *s* Radierung *f*; (*as an art*) Radierkunst *f*

eternal [ɪ'tʌrnəl] *adj* ewig

eternity [ɪ'tʌrnɪti] *s* Ewigkeit *f*

ether ['iθər] *s* Äther *m*

ethereal [ɪ'θɪrɪ-əl] *adj* ätherisch

ethical ['eθɪkəl] *adj* ethisch, sittlich

ethics ['eθɪks] *s* Ethik *f*, Sittenlehre *f*

Ethiopia [,iθɪ'opɪ-ə] *s* Äthiopien *n*

Ethiopian [,iθɪ'opɪ-ən] *adj* äthiopisch || *s* Äthiopier –in *mf*; (*language*) Äthiopisch *n*

ethnic(al) ['eθnɪk(əl)] *adj* völkisch; **e. group** Volksgruppe *f*

ethnography [eθ'nɑgrəfi] *s* Ethnographie *f*

ethnology [eθ'nɑlədʒi] *s* Völkerkunde *f*

ethyl ['eθɪl] *s* Äthyl *m*

ethylene ['eθɪ,lin] *s* Äthylen *n*

etiquette ['etɪ,ket] *s* Etikette *f*

etymology [,etɪ'mɑlədʒi] *s* Etymologie *f*

ety·mon ['etɪ,mɑn] *s* (**-mons** & **-ma** [mə]) Etymon *n*

eucalyp·tus [,jukə'lɪptəs] *s* (**-tuses** & **-ti** [taɪ]) Eukalyptus *m*

Eucharist ['jukərɪst] *s*—**the E.** das heilige Abendmal, die Eucharistie *f*

eugenics [ju'dʒenɪks] *s* Rassenhygiene *f*

eulogize ['julə,dʒaɪz] *tr* lobpreisen

eulogy ['julədʒi] *s* Lobrede *f*

eunuch ['junək] *s* Eunuch *m*

euphemism ['jufɪ,mɪzəm] *s* Euphemismus *m*

euphemistic [,jufə'mɪstɪk] *adj* euphemistisch, verblümt

euphonic [ju'fɑnɪk] *adj* wohlklingend

euphony ['jufəni] *s* Wohlklang *m*

euphoria [ju'forɪ-ə] *s* Euphorie *f*

euphoric [ju'forɪk] *adj* euphorisch

euphuism ['jufju,ɪzəm] *s* gezierte Ausdrucksweise *f*

Europe ['jurəp] *s* Europa *n*

European [,jurə'pi-ən] *adj* europäisch || *s* Europäer –in *mf*

Europe′an plan′ *s* Hotelpreis *m* ohne Mahlzeiten

euthanasia [,juθə'neʒə] *s* Euthanasie *f*

evacuate [ɪ'vækju,et] *tr* evakuieren; (*med*) entleeren; (*an area*) räumen || *intr* sich zurückziehen

evacuation [ɪ,vækju'eʃən] *s* Evakuierung *f*; (*med*) Entleerung *f*

evade [ɪ'ved] *tr* ausweichen (*dat*); (*duties*) vernachlässigen; (*laws*) umgehen; (*prosecution, responsibility*) sich entziehen (*dat*); (*taxes*) hinterziehen

evaluate [ɪ'vælju,et] *tr* (*e.g., jewels*) (ab)schätzen; (*e.g., a performance*) beurteilen

evaluation [ɪ,vælju'eʃən] *s* Abschätzung *f*; (*judgment*) Beurteilung *f*

evangelic(al) [,iven'dʒelɪk(əl)], [,evən'dʒelɪk(əl)] *adj* evangelisch

Evangelist [ɪ'vændʒəlɪst] *s* Evangelist *m*

evaporate [ɪ'væpə,ret] *tr* eindampfen || *intr* (*above boiling point*) verdampfen; (*below boiling point*) verdunsten; (*fig*) sich verflüchtigen

eva′porated milk′ *s* Kondensmilch *f*

evasion [ɪ'veʒən] *s* (*dodge*) Ausweichen *n*; (*of the law*) Umgehung *f*; (*of responsibility*) Vernachlässigung *f*; (*in speech*) Ausflucht *f*

evasive [ɪ'vesɪv] *adj* ausweichend

eve [iv] *s* Vorabend *m*

even ['ivən] *adj* (*smooth*) eben, gerade; (*number*) gerade; (*uniform*) gleichmäßig; (*chance*) gleich; (*temperament*) ruhig, ausgeglichen; **an e. break** gleiche Aussichten *pl*; **an e. dozen** genau ein Dutzend; **be e.** (coll) quitt sein; **e. with** auf gleicher Höhe mit; **get e. with** j–m abrechnen || *adv* selbst, sogar; (*before comparatives*) noch; (*as intensifier before nouns and pronouns*) selbst; **break e.** gerade auf seine Kosten kommen; **e. if** selbst wenn, wenn auch; **e. so** trotzdem; **e. though** obgleich; **e. today** noch heute; **e. when** selbst wenn || *tr* ebnen; **e. up** ausgleichen

e′ven-hand′ed *adj* unparteiisch

evening ['ivnɪŋ] *adj* Abend– || *s* Abend *m*; **in the e.** am Abend; **this e.** heute abend

eve′ning gown′ *s* Abendkleid *n*

eve′ning pa′per *s* Abendblatt *n*

eve′ning school′ *s* Abendschule *f*

evenly ['ivənlɪ] *adv* gleichmäßig; **e. matched** (sport) gleichwertig

ev′en-mind′ed *adj* gleichmütig

evenness ['ivənnɪs] *s* (*smoothness*)

Ebenheit *f*; *(uniformity)* Gleich-
mäßigkeit *f*

event [ɪˈvent] *s* Ereignis *n*; *(sport)*
Veranstaltung *f*; **at all events, in any
e.** auf jeden Fall; **in the e. of** im
Falle *(genit)*

eventful [ɪˈventfəl] *adj* ereignisvoll

eventual [ɪˈventʃʊ‐əl] *adj* schließlich

eventuality [ɪˌventʃʊˈælɪti] *s* Möglichkeit *f*

eventually [ɪˈventʃʊˌəli] *adj* schließlich

ever [ˈevər] *adv* je, jemals; *(before
comparatives)* immer; **did you e.!** hat
man schon sowas gehört!; **e. after**
die ganze Zeit danach; **e. so** noch
so; **e. so much** (coll) sehr; **hardly e.**
fast nie

ev'ergreen' *adj* immergrün ‖ *s* Immergrün *n*

ev'erlast'ing *adj* ewig; *(continual)*
fortwährend; *(iron)* ewig

ev'ermore' *adv* immer; **for e.** in Ewigkeit

every [ˈevri] *adj* jeder, *(confidence)*
voll; **e. bit** (coll) völlig; **e. now and
then** ab und zu; **e. once in a while**
dann und wann; **e. other day** alle
zwei Tage; **e. time (that)** jedesmal
(wenn)

ev'erybod'y *indef pron* jeder, jedermann

ev'eryday' *adj* alltäglich, Alltags‐

ev'eryone', ev'ery one' *indef pron* (of)
jeder (von); **e. else** alle anderen

ev'erything' *indef pron* alles

ev'erywhere' *adv* *(position)* überall;
(direction) überallhin

evict [ɪˈvɪkt] *tr* delogieren

eviction [ɪˈvɪkʃən] *s* Delogierung *f*

evidence [ˈevɪdəns] *s* Beweismaterial
n, Beweise *pl*; *(piece of evidence)*
Beweis *m*; **as e. of** zum Beweis
(genit); **for lack of e.** wegen Mangels
an Beweisen; **give e.** aussagen; **in e.**
sichtbar

evident [ˈevɪdənt] *adj* *(obvious)* offensichtlich; *(visible)* ersichtlich; **be e.**
zutage liegen

evidently [ˈevɪdəntli] *adv* offenbar

evil [ˈivəl] *adj* übel, böse ‖ *s* Übel *n*

e'vildo'er *s* Übeltäter ‐in *mf*

e'vildo'ing *s* Missetat *f*

e'vil eye' *s* böser Blick *m*

e'vil‐mind'ed *adj* übelgesinnt

E'vil One' *s* Böse *m*

evince [ɪˈvɪns] *tr* bekunden

evoke [ɪˈvok] *tr* hervorrufen

evolution [ˌevəˈluʃən] *s* Evolution *f*

evolve [ɪˈvɑlv] *tr* entwickeln, entfalten
‖ *intr* sich entwickeln, sich entfalten

ewe [ju] *s* Mutterschaf *n*

ewer [ˈjuˌər] *s* Wasserkanne *f*

exact [egˈzækt] *adj* genau ‖ *tr* *(e.g.,
money)* beitreiben; *(obedience)* erzwingen

exact'ing *adj* *(strict)* streng; *(task)*
aufreibend; *(picky)* anspruchsvoll

exactly [egˈzæktli] *adv* genau

exactness [egˈzæktnɪs] *s* Genauigkeit *f*

exact' sci'ences *spl* Realien *pl*

exaggerate [egˈzædʒəˌret] *tr* übertreiben

exaggeration [egˌzædʒəˈreʃən] *s* Übertreibung *f*

exalt [egˈzɔlt] *tr* erheben

exam [egˈzæm] *s* (coll) Prüfung *f*

examination [egˌzæmɪˈneʃən] *s* Prüfung *f*, Examen *n*; *(jur)* Verhör *n*,
Vernehmung *f*; *(med)* Untersuchung
f; **direct e.** *(jur)* direkte Befragung
f; **fail an e.** bei e‐r Prüfung durchfallen; **on closer e.** bei näherer Prüfung; **pass an e.** e‐e Prüfung bestehen; **take an e.** e‐e Prüfung ablegen

examine [egˈzæmɪn] *tr* prüfen; *(jur)*
verhören, vernehmen; *(med)* untersuchen

examinee [egˌzæmɪˈni] *s* Prüfling *m*

examiner [egˈzæmɪnər] *s* *(educ)* Prüfer ‐in *mf*; *(med)* Untersucher ‐in *mf*

example [egˈzæmpəl] *s* Beispiel *n*; **for
e.** zum Beispiel; **make an e. of** ein
Exempel statuieren an *(dat)*; **set a
good e.** mit gutem Beispiel vorangehen

exasperate [egˈzæspəˌret] *tr* reizen

excavate [ˈekskəˌvet] *tr* ausgraben

excavation [ˌekskəˈveʃən] *s* Ausgrabung *f*

excavator [ˈekskəˌvetər] *s* *(archeol)*
Ausgräber ‐in *mf*; *(mach)* Trockenbagger *m*

exceed [ekˈsid] *tr* überschreiten

exceedingly [ekˈsidɪŋli] *adv* außerordentlich

ex·cel [ekˈsel] *v* *(pret & pp —celled;
ger —celling)* *tr* übertreffen ‖ *intr*
(in) sich auszeichnen (in *dat*)

excellence [ˈeksələns] *s* Vorzüglichkeit *f*

excellency [ˈeksələnsi] *s* Vorzüglichkeit *f*; **Your Excellency** Eure Exzellenz

excellent [ˈeksələnt] *adj* ausgezeichnet

excelsior [ekˈselsiˌər] *s* Holzwolle *f*

except [ekˈsept] *adv*—**e. for** abgesehen
von; **e. if** außer wenn; **e. that** außer
daß; **e. when** außer wenn ‖ *prep*
außer *(dat)*, ausgenommen *(acc)* ‖
tr ausnehmen, ausschließen

exception [ekˈsepʃən] *s* Ausnahme *f*;
by way of e. ausnahmsweise; **take e.
to** Anstoß nehmen an *(dat)*; **without
e.** ausnahmslos; **with the e. of** mit
Ausnahme von

exceptional [ekˈsepʃənəl] *adj* außergewöhnlich, Sonder‐

excerpt [ˈeksˌʌrpt] *s* Auszug *m* ‖ [ekˈsʌrpt] *tr* exzerpieren

excess [ekˈses], [ˈekˌses] *adj* überschüssig ‖ [ekˈses] *s* *(surplus)*
Überschuß *m*; *(immoderate amount)*
(of) Übermaß *n* (von or an *dat*);
carry to e. übertreiben; **excesses**
Ausschreitungen *pl*; **in e. of** mehr
als; **to e.** übermäßig

ex'cess bag'gage *s* Überfracht *f*

excessive [ekˈsesɪv] *adj* übermäßig

ex'cess‐prof'its tax' *s* Mehrgewinnsteuer *f*

exchange [eksˈtʃendʒ] *s* Austausch *m*;
(e.g., of purchases) Umtausch *m*;
(of words) Wechselgespräch *n*; *(of*

money) Geldwechsel *m;* (fin) Börse *f;* (mil) Kantine *f;* (telp) Vermittlung *f;* e. of letters Briefwechsel *m;* in e. dafür; in e. for für || *tr* (*trade*) tauschen; (*replace*) auswechseln; e. for umtauschen gegen; e. places with s.o. mit j–m tauschen

exchequer [eks'tʃekər] *s* Staatskasse *f;* (*department*) Schatzamt *n*

ex'cise tax' ['eksaɪz] *s* Verbrauchssteuer *f*

excitable [ek'saɪtəbəl] *adj* erregbar

excite [ek'saɪt] *tr* erregen, aufregen

excitement [ek'saɪtmənt] *s* Erregung *f*, Aufregung *f*

excit'ing *adj* erregend, aufregend

exclaim [eks'klem] *tr & intr* ausrufen

exclamation [ˌekskləˈmeʃən] *s* Ausruf *m*

exclama'tion point' *s* Ausrufungszeichen *n*

exclude [eks'klud] *tr* ausschließen

exclusion [eks'kluʒən] *s* Ausschließung *f*, Ausschluß *m;* to the e. of unter Ausschluß (*genit*)

exclusive [eks'klusɪv] *adj* (*rights, etc.*) alleinig, ausschließlich; (*club*) exklusiv; (*shop*) teuer; e. of ausschließlich (*genit*)

excommunicate [ˌekskəˈmjunɪˌket] *tr* exkommunizieren

excommunication [ˌekskəˌmjunɪˈkeʃən] *s* Exkommunikation *f*, Kirchenbann *m*

excoriate [eks'korɪˌet] *tr* (fig) heruntermachen

excrement ['ekskrəmənt] *s* Exkremente *pl*

excrescence [eks'kresəns] *s* Auswuchs *m*

excruciating [eks'kruʃɪˌetɪŋ] *adj* qualvoll

exculpate ['ekskʌlˌpet] *tr* entschuldigen

excursion [eks'kʌrʒən] *s* (*side trip*) Abstecher *m;* (*short trip*) Ausflug *m*

excusable [eks'kjuzəbəl] *adj* entschuldbar, verzeihlich

excuse [eks'kjus] *s* Ausrede *f;* give as an e. vorgeben; make excuses sich ausreden *f* [eks'kjuz] *tr* entschuldigen; e. me! entschuldigen Sie!; you may be excused now Sie können jetzt gehen

execute ['eksɪˌkjut] *tr* (*a condemned man*) hinrichten; (*by firing squad*) erschießen; (*perform*) durchführen, vollziehen; (*a will, a sentence*) vollstrecken; (*mus*) vortragen

execution [ˌeksɪˈkjuʃən] *s* Hinrichtung *f;* (*by firing squad*) Erschießung *f;* (*performance*) Durchführung *f*, Vollziehung *f;* (mus) Vortrag *m*

executioner [ˌeksɪˈkjuʃənər] *s* Scharfrichter *m*

executive [eg'zekjətɪv] *adj* vollziehend, exekutiv || *s* (com) Manager *m*, leitender Angestellte *mf;* the Executive (pol) die Exekutive *f*

exec'utive commit'tee *s* Vollzugsausschuß *m*, Vorstand *m*

exec'utive or'der *s* Durchführungsverordnung *f*

executor [eg'zekjətər] *s* Vollstrecker *m*

executrix [eg'zekjətrɪks] *s* Vollstreckerin *f*

exemplary [eg'zempləri] *adj* vorbildlich, mustergültig

exempli·fy [eg'zemplɪˌfaɪ] *v* (*pret & pp* –fied) *tr* (*demonstrate*) an Beispielen erläutern; (*embody*) als Beispiel dienen für

exempt [eg'zempt] *adj* (**from**) befreit (von) || *tr* befreien; (mil) freistellen

exemption [eg'zempʃən] *s* Befreiung *f;* (mil) Freistellung *f*

exercise ['eksərˌsaɪz] *s* Übung *f;* (*of the body*) Bewegung *f;* (*of power*) Ausübung *f;* (mil) Exerzieren *n;* take e. sich [*dat*] Bewegung machen || *tr* üben; (*the body, a horse*) bewegen; (*power, influence*) ausüben; (mil) exerzieren || *intr* üben; (mil) exerzieren

exert [eg'zart] *tr* ausüben; e. every effort alle Kräfte rühren; e. oneself sich anstrengen

exertion [eg'zarʃən] *s* Anstrengung *f;* (*e.g., of power*) Ausübung *f*

exhalation [ˌekshəˈleʃən] *s* Ausatmung *f;* (*of gases*) Gasabgabe *f*

exhale [eks'hel] *tr & intr* ausatmen

exhaust [eg'zost] *s* (aut) Auspuff *m* || *tr* erschöpfen

exhaust'ed *adj* erschöpft

exhaust' fan' *s* Absaugventilator *m*

exhaust' gas' *s* Abgas *n*

exhaust'ing *adj* anstrengend, mühselig

exhaustion [eg'zostʃən] *s* Erschöpfung *f*

exhaustive [eg'zostɪv] *adj* erschöpfend

exhaust' pipe' *s* Auspuffrohr *n*

exhaust' valve' *s* Auspuffventil *n*

exhibit [eg'zɪbɪt] *s* (*exhibition*) Ausstellung *f;* (*object exhibited*) Ausstellungsstück *n;* (jur) Beleg *m* || *tr* zur Schau stellen; (*wares*) ausstellen; (*e.g., courage*) zeigen

exhibition [ˌeksɪˈbɪʃən] *s* Ausstellung *f*

exhilarating [eg'zɪləˌretɪŋ] *adj* erheiternd

exhort [eg'zort] *tr* ermahnen

exhume [eks'hjum] *tr* exhumieren

exigency ['eksɪdʒənsi] *s* (*demand, need*) Erfordnis *n;* (*state of urgency*) Dringlichkeit *f*

exigent ['eksɪdʒənt] *adj* dringlich

exile ['egzaɪl] *s* Exil *n;* (*person*) Verbannte *mf* || *tr* verbannen

exist [eg'zɪst] *intr* existieren; (*continue to be*) bestehen; e. from day to day dahinleben

existence [eg'zɪstəns] *s* Existenz *f*, Dasein *n;* be in e. bestehen; come into e. entstehen

existential [ˌegzɪsˈtenʃəl] *adj* existentiell

existentialism [ˌegzɪsˈtenʃəˌlɪzəm] *s* Existentialismus *m*

exit ['egzɪt] *s* Ausgang *m;* (*by car*) Ausfahrt *f;* (theat) Abgang *m* || *intr* (theat) abtreten

exodus ['eksədəs] *s* Abwanderung *f*

exonerate [eg'zɑnəˌret] *tr* entlasten

exorbitant [eg'zɔrbɪtənt] *adj* schwindelhaft; **e. price** Wucherpreis *m*

exorcise ['eksɔr,saɪz] *tr* exorzieren

exotic [eg'zatɪk] *adj* exotisch

expand [eks'pænd] *tr* (aus)dehnen; (*enlarge*) erweitern; (*math*) entwickeln ‖ *intr* sich ausdehnen

expanse [eks'pæns] *s* Weite *f*, Fläche *f*

expansion [eks'pænʃən] *s* Ausdehnung *f*; (*expanded part*) Erweiterung *f*

expansive [eks'pænsɪv] *adj* expansiv; (*fig*) mitteilsam

expatiate [eks'peʃɪ,et] *intr* (**on**) sich verbreiten (über *acc*)

expatriate [eks'petrɪ.ɪt] *adj* ausgebürgert ‖ *s* Ausgebürgerte *mf* ‖ [eks'petrɪ,et] *tr* ausbürgern

expect [eks'pekt] *tr* erwarten ‖ *intr*—**she's expecting** (coll) sie ist in anderen Umständen

expectancy [eks'pektansi] *s* Ewartung *f*

expectant [eks'pektənt] *adj* erwartungsvoll; (*mother*) werdende

expectation [,ekspek'teʃən] *s* Erwartung *f*

expectorate [eks'pektə,ret] *tr & intr* spucken

expediency [eks'pidɪ.ənsi] *s* Zweckmäßigkeit *f*

expedient [eks'pidɪ.ənt] *adj* zweckmäßig ‖ *s* Mittel *n*, Hilfsmittel *f*

expedite ['ekspɪ ,daɪt] *tr* beschleunigen; (*a document*) ausstellen

expedition [,ekspɪ'dɪʃən] *s* Expedition *f*

expedi'tionary force' [,ekspɪ'dɪʃə,neri] *s* (mil) Expeditionsstreitkräfte *pl*

expeditious [,ekspɪ'dɪʃəs] *adj* schleunig

ex•pel [eks'pel] *v* (*pret & pp* **–pelled**; *ger* **–pelling**) *tr* (aus)treiben; (*a student*) (**from**) verweisen (von)

expend [eks'pend] *tr* (*time, effort, etc.*) aufwenden; (*money*) ausgeben

expendable [eks'pendəbəl] *adj* entbehrlich

expenditure [eks'pendɪtʃər] *s* Aufwand *m*; (*of money*) Ausgabe *f*

expense [eks'pens] *s* Ausgabe *f*; **at s.o.'s e.** (& fig) auf j–s Kosten; **expenses** Unkosten *pl*; **go to great e.** sich in Unkosten stürzen

expense' account' *s* Spesenkonto *n*

expensive [eks'pensɪv] *adj* kostspielig

experience [eks'pɪrɪ.əns] *s* Erfahrung *f*; (*an event*) Erlebnis *n*; **no previous e. necessary** Vorkenntnisse nicht erforderlich ‖ *tr* erfahren; (*pain*) erdulden; (*loss*) erleiden

expe'rienced *adj* erfahren

experiment [eks'perɪmənt] *s* Experiment *n*, Versuch *m* ‖ [eks'perɪ,ment] *intr* experimentieren, Versuche anstellen

experimental [eks,perɪ'mentəl] *adj* experimentell, Versuchs–

expert ['eksprt] *adj* fachmännisch, erfahren; **e. advice** Gutachten *n* ‖ *s* Fachmann *m*; (jur) Sachverständige *mf*

expertise [,eksper'tiz] *s* (*opinion*) Gutachten *n*; (*skill*) Sachkenntnis *f*

expiate ['ekspɪ,et] *tr* sühnen, büßen

expiation [,ekspɪ'eʃən] *s* Sühnung *f*

expiration [,ekspɪ'reʃən] *s* Verfall *m*

expira'tion date' *s* Verfalltag *m*

expire [eks'paɪr] *tr* ausatmen ‖ *intr* verfallen; (*die*) verscheiden

explain [eks'plen] *tr* erklären, erläutern; (*justify*) rechtfertigen

explanation [,eksplə'neʃən] *s* Erklärung *f*, Erläuterung *f*

explanatory [eks'plænə,tori] *adj* erklärend, erläuternd

expletive ['eksplɪtɪv] *s* Füllwort *n*

explicit [eks'plɪsɪt] *adj* ausdrücklich

explode [eks'plod] *tr* explodieren lassen; (*a theory*) verwerfen ‖ *intr* explodieren; (*said of a grenade*) krepieren; (**with**) platzen (vor *dat*)

exploit ['eksplɔɪt] *s* Heldentat *f*, Großtat *f* ‖ [eks'plɔɪt] *tr* ausnutzen; (pej) ausbeuten; (min) abbauen

exploitation [,eksplɔɪ'teʃən] *s* Ausnutzung *f*; (pej) Ausbeutung *f*; (min) Abbau *m*

exploration [,eksplə'reʃən] *s* Erforschung *f*

explore [eks'plor] *tr* erforschen

explorer [eks'plorər] *s* Forscher –in *mf*

explosion [eks'ploʒən] *s* Explosion *f*

explosive [eks'plosɪv] *adj* explosiv, Spreng– ‖ *s* (*explosive substance*) Sprengstoff *m*; (*device*) Sprengkörper *m*

explo'sive charge' *s* Sprengladung *f*

exponent [eks'ponənt] *s* Exponent *m*

export ['eksport] *adj* Ausfuhr– ‖ *s* Ausfuhr *m*, Export *m*; **exports** Ausfuhrgüter *pl* ‖ [eks'port] *tr* ausführen

exportation [,ekspor'teʃən] *s* Ausfuhr *m*

exporter ['eksportər], [eks'portər] *s* Ausfuhrhändler –in *mf*, Exporteur –in *mf*

expose [eks'poz] *tr* (*to danger, ridicule, sun*) aussetzen; (*bare*) entblößen; (*a person*) (**as**) bloßstellen (als), entlarven (als); (phot) belichten

exposé [,ekspo'ze] *s* Enthüllung *f*

exposition [,ekspə'zɪʃən] *s* Ausstellung *f*; (rhet) Exposition *f*

expostulate [eks'pastʃə,let] *intr* protestieren; **e. with s.o. about** j–m ernste Vorhaltungen machen über (*acc*)

exposure [eks'poʒər] *s* (*of a child*) Aussetzung *f*; (*laying bare*) Entblößung *f*; (*unmasking*) Entlarvung *f*; (*of a building*) Lage *f*; (phot) Belichtung *f*

expo'sure me'ter *s* Belichtungsmesser *m*

expound [eks'paund] *tr* erklären

express [eks'pres] *adj* ausdrücklich ‖ *s* (rr) Expreß *m*; **by e.** als Eilgut *n* ‖ *tr* ausdrücken; (*feelings*) zeigen; **e. oneself** sich äußern

express' com'pany *s* Paketpostgesellschaft *f*

expression [eks'preʃən] *s* Ausdruck *m*

expressive [ɛks'presɪv] *adj* ausdrucksvoll

express' train' *s* Expreßzug *m*

express'way' *s* Schnellverkehrsstraße *f*

expropriate [ɛks'propri,et] *tr* enteignen

expulsion [ɛks'pʌlʃən] *s* Austreibung *f*; (*from school or a game*) Verweisung *f*

expunge [ɛks'pʌndʒ] *tr* ausstreichen

expurgate ['ɛkspər,get] *tr* säubern

exquisite ['ɛkskwɪzɪt], [ɛks'kwɪzɪt] *adj* exquisit, vorzüglich

ex-service-man [,ɛks'sɑrvɪs,mæn] *s* (**-men'**) ehemaliger Soldat *m*

extant ['ɛkstənt] *adj* noch bestehend

extemporaneous [ɛks,tempə'reni·əs] *adj* aus dem Stegreif, unvorbereitet

extempore [ɛks'tempəri] *adj* unvorbereitet ‖ *adv* aus dem Stegreif

extemporize [ɛks'tempə,raɪz] *tr & intr* extemporieren

extend [ɛks'tend] *tr* (*expand*) ausdehnen; (*a line*) fortführen; (*time*) verlängern; (*congratulations, invitation*) aussprechen; (*one's hand*) ausstrecken; (*a building*) ausbauen ‖ *intr* (**to**) sich erstrecken (bis); **e. beyond** hinausgehen über (*acc*)

extension [ɛks'tenʃən] *s* Ausdehnung *f*; (*of time, credit*) Verlängerung *f*; (*archit*) Anbau *m*; (*telp*) Nebenanschluß *m*

exten'sion cord' *s* Verlängerungsschnur *f*

exten'sion lad'der *s* Ausziehleiter *f*

exten'sion ta'ble *s* Ausziehtisch *m*

extensive [ɛks'tensɪv] *adj* umfassend

extent [ɛks'tent] *s* Umfang *m*, Ausmaß *n*; **to some e.** eingermaßen; **to the full e.** in vollem Umfang; **to what e.** inwiefern

extenuating [ɛks'tenju,etɪŋ] *adj* mildernd

exterior [ɛks'tɪrɪ·ər] *adj* Außen-, äußere ‖ *s* Äußere *n*

exterminate [ɛks'tʌrmɪ,net] *tr* vertilgen, ausrotten

extermination [ɛks,tʌrmɪ'neʃən] *s* Vertilgung *f*; (*of vermin*) Raumentwesung *f*

exterminator [ɛks'tʌrmɪ,netər] *s* Raumentweser *m*

external [ɛks'tʌrnəl] *adj* Außen-, äußerlich ‖ **externals** *spl* Äußerlichkeiten *pl*

extinct [ɛks'tɪŋkt] *adj* (*volcano*) erloschen; (*animal*) ausgestorben; **become e.** aussterben

extinguish [ɛks'tɪŋgwɪʃ] *tr* auslöschen; **be extinguished** erlöschen

extinguisher [ɛks'tɪŋgwɪʃər] *s* Löschgerät *n*

extirpate ['ɛkstər,pet] *tr* ausrotten

ex-tol [ɛks'tol] *v* (*pret & pp* **-tolled;** *ger* **-tolling**) *tr* erheben, lobpreisen

extort [ɛks'tort] *tr* erpressen

extortion [ɛks'torʃən] *s* Erpressung *f*

extortionate [ɛks'tor/ənɪt] *adj* überhöht

extra ['ɛkstrə] *adj* übrig; (*special*) Sonder-, Extra-; **meals are e.** Mahlzeiten werden zusätzlich berechnet

‖ *adv* extra, besonders ‖ *s* (cin) Statist –in *mf*; (journ) Sonderausgabe *f*; (theat) Komparse *m*; **extras** (*expenses*) Nebenausgaben *pl*; (*accessories*) Zubehör *n*

extract ['ɛkstrækt] *s* Extrakt *m*, Auszug *m*; (*excerpt*) Ausschnitt *m* ‖ [ɛks'trækt] *tr* extrahieren, ausziehen; (dent, math) ziehen

extraction [ɛks'trækʃən] *s* (*lineage*) Abstammung *f*; (dent) Zahnziehen *n*; (min) Gewinnung *f*

extracurricular [,ɛkstrəkə'rɪkjələr] *adj* außerplanmäßig

extradite ['ɛkstrə,daɪt] *tr* ausliefern

extradition [,ɛkstrə'dɪʃən] *s* Auslieferung *f*

ex'tra in'come *s* Nebeneinkünfte *pl*

ex'tramar'ital *adj* außerehelich

extramural [,ɛkstrə'mjurəl] *adj* außerhalb der Schule stattfindend

extraneous [ɛks'treni·əs] *adj* unwesentlich

extraordinary [,ɛks'trordɪ,neri] *adj* außerordentlich

ex'tra pay' *s* Zulage *f*

extrapolate [ɛks'træpə,let] *tr & intr* extrapolieren

extrasensory [,ɛkstrə'sensəri] *adj* übersinnlich

extravagance [ɛks'trævəgəns] *s* Verschwendung *f*

extravagant [ɛks'trævəgənt] *adj* verschwenderisch, extravagant; (*idea, plan*) überspannt

extreme [ɛks'trim] *adj* äußerst; (*radical*) extrem; (*old age*) höchst; (*necessity*) dringend ‖ *s* Äußerste *n*; **at the other e.** am entgegengesetzten Ende; **carry to extremes** auf die Spitze treiben; **in the e.** äußerst

extremely [ɛks'trimli] *adj* äußerst

extreme' unc'tion *s* die Letzte Ölung

extremist [ɛks'trimɪst] *s* Extremist –in *mf*

extremity [ɛks'tremɪti] *s* Äußerste *n*, äußerstes Ende *n*; **be reduced to extremities** aus dem letzten Loch pfeifen; **extremities** (*hands and feet*) Extremitäten *pl*

extricate ['ɛkstrɪ,ket] *tr* befreien

extrinsic [ɛks'trɪnsɪk] *adj* äußerlich

extrovert ['ɛkstrə,vʌrt] *s* Extravertierte *mf*

extrude [ɛks'trud] *tr* ausstoßen

exuberant [ɛg'z(j)ubərənt] *adj* (*luxuriant*) üppig; (*lavish*) überschwenglich

exude [ɛg'zud] *tr* ausschwitzen; (fig) ausstrahlen

exult [ɛg'zʌlt] *intr* jauchzen

exultant [ɛg'zʌltənt] *adj* jauchzend

eye [aɪ] *s* Auge *n*; (*of a needle*) Öhr *n*; **an eye for an eye** Auge um Auge; **be all eyes** große Augen machen; **by eye** nach dem Augenmaß; **close one's eyes to** die Augen schließen vor (*dat*); **have an eye for** Sinn haben für; **have good eyes** gut sehen; **in my eyes** nach meiner Ansicht; **in the eyes of the law** vom Standpunkt des Gesetzes aus; **keep a close eye on** s.o. j-m auf die Finger sehen; **keep an eye on** s.th. ein wachsames Auge auf etw [*acc*] haben; **keep one's eyes peeled** scharf aufpassen; **lay eyes on** zu Gesicht bekommen; **makes eyes at** verliebte Blicke zuwerfen (*dat*); **see eye to eye with** völlig übereinstimmen mit; **with an eye to** mit Rücksicht auf (*acc*) ‖ *v* (*pret & pp* **eyed**; *ger* **eying & eyeing**) *tr* mustern, schielen nach

eye'ball' *s* Augapfel *m*

eye'brow' *s* Augenbraue *f*

eye'brow pen'cil *s* Augenbrauenstift *m*

eye' cat'cher *s* Blickfang *m*

eye'cup' *s* Augenspülglas *n*

eye' drops' *spl* Augentropfen *pl*

eyeful ['aɪful] *s*—**get an e.** etw Hübsches sehen

eye'glass' *s* Augenglas *n*; **eyeglasses** Brille *f*

eye'lash' *s* Wimper *f*

eyelet ['aɪlɪt] *s* Öse *f*

eye'lid' *s* Lid *n*, Augenlid *n*

eye'o'pener *s* (*surprise*) Überraschung *f*; (*liquor*) Schnäpschen *n*

eye'piece' *s* Okular *n*

eye'shade' *s* Augenschirm *m*

eye' shad'ow *s* Lidschatten *m*

eye'shot' *s*—**within e.** in Sehweite

eye'sight' *s* Augenlicht *n*, Sehkraft *f*; (*range*) Sehweite *f*; **have bad (or good) e.** schlechte (or gute) Augen haben

eye' sock'et *s* Augenhöhle *f*

eye'sore' *s* (fig) Dorn *m* im Auge

eye'strain' *s* Überanstrengung *f* der Augen

eye'tooth' *s* (–**teeth**) Augenzahn *m*; **cut one's eyeteeth** (fig) erfahrener werden

eye'wash' *s* Augenwasser *n*; (sl) Schwindel *m*

eye'wit'ness *s* Augenzeuge *m*, Augenzeugin *f*

F

F, f [ɛf] *s* sechster Buchstabe des englischen Alphabets; (mus) F *n*; **F flat** Fes *n*; **F sharp** Fis *n*

fable ['febəl] *s* Fabel *f*, Märchen *n*

fabric ['fæbrɪk] *s* Gewebe *n*; (*cloth*) Stoff *m*; (fig) Gefüge *n*

fabricate ['fæbrɪ,ket] *tr* herstellen; (*lies*) erfinden

fabrication [,fæbrɪ'keʃən] *s* Herstellung *f*; (fig) Erfindung *f*

fabulous ['fæbjələs] *adj* fabelhaft

façade [fə'sɑd] *s* Fassade *f*

face [fes] *s* Gesicht *n*; (*dial*) Zifferblatt *n*; (tex) rechte Seite *f*; (typ) Satzspiegel *m*; **f. to f. with** Auge in Auge mit; **in the f. of** angesichts (*genit*); **lose f.** sich blamieren; **make faces at s.o.** j-m Gesichter schneiden; **on the f. of it** augenscheinlich; **save f.** das Gesicht wahren; **show one's f.** sich blicken lassen ‖ *tr* (& fig) ins Auge sehen (*dat*); (*said of a building*) liegen nach; (*e.g.,* with brick) verkleiden; **be faced with** stehen vor (*dat*); **facing** gegenüber (*dat*); **have to f. the music** die Suppe löffeln müssen ‖ *intr* (*in some direction*) liegen; **about f.!** (mil) kehrt!; **he faced up to it like a man** er stellte seinen Mann

face' card' *s* Bildkarte *f*, Figur *f*

face' cream' *s* Gesichtskrem *f*

face' lift'ing *s* Gesichtsstraffung *f*; (*of a building*) Schönheitsreparatur *f*

face' pow'der *s* Gesichtspuder *m*

facet ['fæsɪt] *s* Facette *f*; (fig) Aspekt *m*

facetious [fə'siʃəs] *adj* scherzhaft

face' val'ue *s* Nennwert *m*; **take at f.** (fig) für bare Münze nehmen

facial ['feʃəl] *adj* Gesichts–; **f. expression** Miene *f* ‖ *s* Gesichtspflege *f*

facilitate [fə'sɪlɪ,tet] *tr* erleichtern

facility [fə'sɪlɪti] *s* (*ease*) Leichtigkeit

f; (*skill*) Geschicklichkeit *f*; **facilities** Einrichtungen *pl*

fac'ing *s* (archit) Verkleidung *f*; (sew) Besatz *m*

facsimile [fæk'sɪmɪli] *s* Faksimile *n*

fact [fækt] *s* Tatsache *f*; **apart from the f. that** abgesehen davon, daß; **facts of the case** Tatbestand *m*; **in f.** tatsächlich; **it is a f. that** es steht fest, daß

fact'-find'ing *adj* Untersuchungs–

faction ['fækʃən] *s* Clique *f*

factional ['fækʃənəl] *adj* klüngelhaft

factor ['fæktər] *s* (& math) Faktor *m*

factory ['fæktəri] *s* Fabrik *f*

factual ['fæktʃʊ-əl] *adj* sachlich

faculty ['fækəlti] *s* Vermögen *n*; (educ) Lehrkörper *m*

fad [fæd] *s* Mode *f*; **latest fad** letzter Schrei *m*

fade [fed] *tr* verblassen lassen; **f. in** einblenden; **f. out** ausblenden ‖ *intr* (*said of colors, memories*) verblassen; (*said of cloth, wallpaper, etc.*) verschießen; (*said of flowers*) verwelken; **f. away** (*said of sounds*) abklingen; **f. in** (cin, rad, telv) einblenden; **f. out** (cin, rad, telv) ausblenden

fade'-in' *s* (cin, rad, telv) Einblenden *n*

fade'-out' *s* (cin, rad, telv) Ausblenden *n*

fag [fæg] *s* (*cigarette*) (sl) Glimmstengel *m*; (*homosexual*) (sl) Schwuler *m* ‖ *v* (*pret & pp* **fagged**; *ger* **fagging**) *tr*—**fag out** (sl) auspumpen

fagged *adj* (sl) erschöpft

fagot ['fægət] *s* Reisigbündel *n*

fail [fel] *s*—**without f.** ganz bestimmt ‖ *tr* (*an examination*) durchfallen bei; (*a student*) durchfallen lassen; (*friends*) im Stich lassen; (*a father*) enttäuschen; **failing this** widrigenfalls; **I f. to see** ich kann nicht einsehen; **words f. me** mir fehlen die

Worte || *intr* (*said of a person or device*) versagen; (*said of a project, attempt*) fehlschlagen; (*said of crops*) schlecht ausfallen; (*said of strength*) abnehmen; (*said of health*) sich verschlechtern; (com) in Konkurs geraten

failure ['feljər] *s* Versagen *n*; (*person*) Versager –in *mf*; (*lack of success, unsuccessful venture*) Mißerfolg *m*; (*omission*) Versäumnis *n*; (*deterioration*) Schwäche *f*; (*educ*) ungenügende Zensur *f*; (com) Konkurs *m*

faint [fent] *adj* schwach; (*slight*) leise; feel f. sich schwach fühlen || *s* Ohnmacht *f* || *intr* ohnmächtig werden

faint'-heart'ed *adj* kleinmütig

faint'ing spell' *s* Ohnmachtsanfall *m*

fair [fer] *adj* (*just*) gerecht, fair; (*blond*) blond; (*complexion*) hell; (*weather*) heiter; (*chance, knowledge*) mittelmäßig; (*warning*) rechtzeitig; f. to middling gut bis mäßig || *s* Jahrmarkt *m*, Messe *f*

fair' game' *s* (& fig) Freiwild *n*

fair'ground' *s* Jahrmarktplatz *m*

fairly ['ferli] *adv* ziemlich

fair'-mind'ed *adj* unparteiisch

fairness ['fernɪs] *s* Gerechtigkeit *f*; in f. to s.o. um j–m Gerechtigkeit widerfahren zu lassen

fair' play' *s* fair Play *n*

fair' sex', the *s* das schöne Geschlecht

fair'way' *s* (golf) Spielbahn *f*; (naut) Fahrwasser *n*

fair'-weath'er *adj* (*friend*) unzuverlässig

fairy ['feri] *adj* Feen– || *s* Fee *f*; (sl) Schwule *mf*

fair'y god'mother *s* gute Fee *f*

fair'yland' *s* Märchenland *n*

fair'ytale' *s* (& fig) Märchen *n*

faith [feθ] *s* Glaube(n) *m*; (in) Vertrauen *n* (auf *acc* or zu); on the f. of im Vertrauen auf (*acc*); put one's f. in Glauben schenken (*dat*)

faithful ['feθfəl] *adj* (to) (ge)treu (*dat*); (*exact*) genau, wahrheitsgemäß || the f. *spl* die Gläubigen

faith' heal'er *s* Gesundbeter –in *mf*

faithless ['feθlɪs] *adj* treulos

fake [fek] *adj* verfälscht || *s* Fälschung *f*; (*person*) Simulant –in *mf* || *tr* vortäuschen, simulieren; (*forge*) fälschen

faker ['fekər] *s* Simulant –in *mf*

falcon ['fɔ(l)kən] *s* Falke *m*

falconer ['fɔ(l)kənər] *s* Falkner *m*

fall [fɔl] *adj* Herbst– || *s* Fall *m*; (*of prices, of a government*) Sturz *m*; (*moral*) Verfall *m*; (*of water*) Fall *m*; (*autumn*) Herbst *m*; (Bib) Sündenfall *m*; || *v* (*pret* fell [fel]; *pp* fallen ['fɔlən] *intr* (*said of a person, object, rain, snow, holiday, prices, temperature*) fallen; (*said of a town*) gestürzt werden; f. apart auseinanderfallen; f. away wegfallen; f. back zurückfallen; (mil) sich zurückziehen; f. back on zurückgreifen auf (*acc*); f. behind (in) zurückbleiben (mit); f. below unterschreiten; f. down umfallen; (*said only of persons*) hinfallen; f. down on the job versagen; f. due fällig werden; f. flat (coll) flachfallen; f. for reinfallen auf (*acc*); f. from abfallen von; f.. from grace in Ungnade fallen; f. in (*said of a roof*) einstürzen; (mil) antreten; f. in step Tritt fassen; f. into (*e.g., a hole*) hereinfallen in (*acc*); (*e.g., trouble*) geraten in (*acc*); f. into ruin zerfallen; f. in with s.o. j–n zufällig treffen; f. off abfallen; (com) zurückgehen; f. out (*said of hair*) ausfallen; f. out with sich verfeinden mit; f. over umfallen; f. short knapp werden; (arti) kurz gehen; f. short of zurückbleiben hinter (*dat*); f. through durchfallen; f. to s.o.'s share j–m zufallen; f. under s.o.'s influence unter j–s Einfluß geraten; f. upon herfallen über (*acc*)

fallacious [fə'leʃəs] *adj* trügerisch

fallacy ['fæləsi] *s* Trugschluß *m*, Fehlschluß *m*

fall' guy' *s* (sl) Sündenbock *m*

fallible ['fælɪbəl] *adj* fehlbar

fall'ing off' *s* Rückschritt *m*

fall'ing rocks' *spl* (public sign) Steinschlag *m*

fall'ing star' *s* Sternschnuppe *f*

fall'out' *s* radioaktiver Niederschlag *m*

fallow ['fælo] *adj* (agr) brach; lie f. (& fig) brachliegen

false [fɔls] *adj* falsch, Miß–; (*start, step*) Fehl–; (*bottom*) doppelt; (*ceiling*) Zwischen–

false' alarm' *s* blinder Alarm *m*; (fig) Schreckschuß *m*

false' face' *s* Maske *f*

false' front' *s* (fig) (coll) Mache *f*

false'-heart'ed *adj* treulos

false'hood' *s* Unwahrheit *f*

false' pretens'es *spl* Hochstapelei *f*

false' teeth' *spl* (künstliches) Gebiß *n*

falsetto [fɔl'seto] *s* (–tos) Falsett *n*

falsi-fy ['fɔlsɪ͵faɪ] *v* (*pret* & *pp* –fied) *tr* (ver)fälschen

falsity ['fɔlsɪti] *s* Falschheit *f*

falter ['fɔltər] *intr* schwanken; (in speech) stocken

fame [fem] *s* Ruf, *m*, Ruhm *m*

famed *adj* (for) berühmt (wegen, durch)

familiar [fə'mɪljər] *adj* bekannt; (*expression*) geläufig; (*e.g., sight*) gewohnt; (*close*) vertraut; become f. with sich bekannt machen mit

familiarity [fə͵mɪlɪ'ɛrti] *s* Vertrautheit *f*; (*closeness*) Vertraulichkeit *f*

familiarize [fə'mɪljə͵raɪz] *tr* bekannt machen

family ['fæm(ɪ)li] *adj* Familien–; in a f. way in anderen Umständen || *s* Familie *f*

fam'ily doc'tor *s* Hausarzt *m*

fam'ily man' *s* häuslicher Mann *m*

fam'ily name' *s* Familienname *m*

fam'ily tree' *s* Stammbaum *m*

famine ['fæmɪn] *s* Hungersnot *f*

famish ['fæmɪʃ] *tr* (ver)hungern lassen || *intr* verhungern

fam'ished *adj* ausgehungert

famous ['feməs] *adj* (**for**) berühmt (wegen, durch)

fan [fæn] *s* Fächer *m*, Wedel *m*; (*electric*) Ventilator *m*; (*sl*) Fan *m* ‖ *v* (*pret & pp* **fanned**; *ger* **fanning**) *tr* fächeln; (*a fire*) anfachen; (*passions*) entfachen ‖ *intr*—**fan out** (*said of roads*) fächerförmig auseinandergehen; (*mil*) ausschwärmen

fanatic [fə'nætɪk] *adj* fanatisch ‖ *s* Fanatiker –in *mf*

fanatical [fə'nætɪkəl] *adj* fanatisch

fanaticism [fə'nætɪˌsɪzəm] *s* Fanatismus *m*

fan' belt' *s* (aut) Keilriemen *m*

fan'cied *adj* eingebildet

fancier ['fænsɪ-ər] *s* Liebhaber –in *mf*

fanciful ['fænsɪfəl] *adj* phantastisch

fan·cy ['fænsi] *adj* (extra)fein; (*e.g., dress*) Luxus–; (*sport*) Kunst–; **f. price** Phantasiepreis *m* ‖ *s* Phantasie *f*; passing f. vorübergehender Spleen *m*; **take a f. to** Gefallen finden an (*dat*) ‖ *v* (*pret & pp* –**cied**) *tr* sich [*dat*] vorstellen

fan'cy foods' *spl* Feinkost *f*

fan'cy-free' *adj* ungebunden

fan'fare' *s* Fanfare *f*; (*fuss*) Tamtam *n*

fang [fæŋ] *s* Fangzahn *m*; (*of a snake*) Giftzahn *m*

fan' mail' *s* Verehrerbriefe *pl*

fantastic(al) [fæn'tæstɪk(əl)] *adj* phantastisch, toll

fantasy ['fæntəsi] *s* Phantasie *f*

far [fɑr] *adj* (& fig) weit; **at the far end** am anderen Ende; **far cry from** etw ganz anderes als; **far side** andere Seite *f*; **in the f. future** in der fernen Zukunft ‖ *adv* weit; **as far as** soweit; (*up to*) bis zu, bis an (*acc*); **as far as I am concerned** was mich anbelangt; **as far as I know** soviel ich weiß; **as far as that goes** was das betrifft; **by far** weitaus, bei weitem; **far and away** weitaus; **far away** weit entfernt; **far below** tief unten; **far better** weit besser; **far from it!** weit gefehlt!; **far from ready** noch lange nicht fertig; **far into the night** tief in die Nacht hinein; **far out** (sl) ausgefallen; **from far** von weitem; (*from a distant place*) von weit her; **go far** es weit bringen; **go far towards** (*ger*) viel beitragen zu (*inf*); **go too far** das Maß überschreiten; **not far from** unweit von; **so far** soweit, bisher

far'away' *adj* weit entfernt; (fig) träumerisch

farce [fɑrs] *s* Possenspiel *n*, Farce *f*; (fig) Posse *f*, Schwank *m*

farcical ['fɑrsɪkəl] *adj* possenhaft

fare [fer] *s* (*travel price*) Fahrpreis *m*; (*money for travel*) Fahrgeld *n*; (*passenger*) Fahrgast *m*; (*food*) Kost *f* ‖ *intr* (er)gehen; **how did you f., well or ill?** wie ist es Ihnen ergangen, gut oder schlecht?

Far' East', **the** *s* der Ferne Osten

Far' East'ern *adj* fernöstlich

fare'well' *s* Valet *n*, Lebewohl *n*; **bid s.o. f.** j–m Lebewohl sagen ‖ *interj* lebe wohl!; lebt wohl!

farewell' din'ner *s* Abschiedsschmaus *m*

farewell' par'ty *s* Abschiedsfeier *f*

far-fetched ['fɑr'fetʃt] *adj* gesucht

far-flung ['fɑr'flʌŋ] *adj* weit ausgedehnt

farina [fə'rinə] *s* Grießmehl *n*

farm [fɑrm] *adj* landwirtschaftlich ‖ *s* Farm *f*, Bauernhof *m* ‖ *tr* bebauen, bewirtschaften ‖ *intr* Landwirtschaft betreiben, Bauer sein

farm' hand' *s* Landarbeiter *m*

farm'house' *s* Bauernhaus *n*

farm'ing *adj* landwirtschaftlich ‖ *s* Landwirtschaft *f*

farm'land' *s* Ackerland *n*

farm' machin'ery *s* Landmaschinen *pl*

farm'yard' *s* Bauernhof *m*

far'-off' *adj* fernliegend

far'-reach'ing *adj* weitreichend; (*decision*) folgenschwer

far'sight'ed *adj* weitsichtig; (fig) weitblickend

farther ['fɑrðər] *adj & adv* weiter

farthest ['fɑrðɪst] *adj* weiteste ‖ *adv* am weitesten

farthing ['fɑrðɪŋ] *s*—**not worth a f.** keinen Pfifferling wert

fascinate ['fæsɪˌnet] *tr* faszinieren

fas'cinating *adj* faszinierend

fascination [ˌfæsɪ'neʃən] *s* Faszination *f*

fascism ['fæʃɪzəm] *s* Faschismus *m*

fascist ['fæʃɪst] *s* Faschist –in *mf*

fashion ['fæʃən] *s* Mode *f*; (*manner*) Art *f*, Weise *f*; **after a f.** in gewisser Weise; **in f.** in Mode; **out of f.** aus der Mode ‖ *tr* gestalten, bilden

fashionable ['fæʃənəbəl] *adj* (*modern*) modisch; (*elegant*) elegant

fash'ion magazine' *s* Modenzeitschrift *f*

fash'ion plate' *s* Modedame *f*

fash'ion show' *s* Mode(n)schau *f*

fast [fæst] *adj* schnell; (*dye*) dauerhaft; (*company*) flott; (*life*) locker; (*phot*) lichtstark; **be f.** (*said of a clock*) vorgehen; **f. train** Schnellzug *m*; **pull a f. one on s.o.** (coll) j–m ein Schnippchen schlagen ‖ *adv* schnell; (*firmly*) fest; **as f. as possible** schnellstens; **be f. asleep** im tiefen Schlaf liegen; **hold f.** festhalten; **not so f.!** nicht so stürmisch! ‖ *s* Fasten *n* ‖ *intr* fasten

fast' day' *s* Fasttag *m*

fasten ['fæsən] *tr* festmachen, sichern; (*a buckle*) schnallen; (**to**) befestigen (an *dat*); **f. one's seat belt** sich anschnallen; **f. the blame on** die Schuld zuschieben (*dat*) ‖ *intr*—**f. upon** sich heften an (*acc*)

fastener ['fæsənər] *s* Verschluß *m*

fastidious [fæs'tɪdɪ-əs] *adj* wählerisch

fast'ing *s* Fasten *n*

fat [fæt] *adj* (**fatter; fattest**) fett; (*plump*) dick, fett; (*profits*) reich ‖ *s* Fett *n*; **chew the fat** (sl) schwatzen

fatal ['fetəl] *adj* tödlich; (*mistake*) verhängnisvoll; **f. to** verhängnisvoll für

fatalism ['fetə ˌlɪzəm] *s* Fatalismus *m*

fatalist ['fetəlɪst] *s* Fatalist –in *mf*

fatality [fə'tælɪti] *s* Todesfall *m*; (*accident victim*) Todesopfer *n*; (*disaster*) Unglück *n*

fat' cat' *s* (sl) Geldgeber –in *mf*

fate [fet] *s* Schicksal *n*, Verhängnis *n*; **the Fates** die Parzen *pl*

fated ['fetɪd] *adj* vom Schicksal bestimmt

fateful ['fetfəl] *adj* verhängnisvoll

fat'head' *s* (coll) dummes Luder *n*

father ['faðər] *s* Vater *m*; (eccl) Pater *m* ‖ *tr* (*beget*) erzeugen; (*originate*) hervorbringen

fa'therhood' *s* Vaterschaft *f*

fa'ther-in-law' *s* (fathers-in-law) Schwiegervater *m*

fa'therland' *s* Vaterland *n*

fatherless ['faðərlɪs] *adj* vaterlos

fatherly ['faðərli] *adj* väterlich

Fa'ther's Day' *s* Vatertag *m*

fathom ['fæðəm] *s* Klafter *f* ‖ *tr* sondieren; (fig) ergründen

fathomless ['fæðəmlɪs] *adj* unergründlich

fatigue [fə'tig] *s* Ermattung *f*; (mil) Arbeitsdienst *m*; **fatigues** (mil) Arbeitsanzug *m* ‖ *tr* abmatten

fat·so ['fætso] *s* (–sos & –soes) (coll) Fettkloß *m*

fatten ['fætən] *tr* mästen ‖ *intr*—**f. up** (coll) sich mästen

fatty ['fæti] *adj* fettig, fett; **f. tissue** Fettgewebe *n* ‖ *s* (coll) Dicke *mf*

fatuous ['fætʃʊ·əs] *adj* albern

faucet ['fɔsɪt] *s* Wasserhahn *m*

fault [fɔlt] *s* (*blame*) Schuld *f*; (*misdeed*) Vergehen *n*, Fehler *m*; (*defect*) Defekt *m*; (geol) Verwerfung *f*; (tennis) Fehlball *m*; **at f.** schuld; **find f.** with etw zu tadeln finden an (*dat*); **to a f.** allzusehr ‖ *intr* (geol) sich verwerfen

fault'find'er *s* Krittler –in *mf*

fault'find'ing *adj* tadelsüchtig ‖ *s* Krittelei *f*

faultless ['fɔltlɪs] *adj* fehlerfrei

faulty ['fɔlti] *adj* fehlerhaft

faun [fɔn] *s* (myth) Faun *m*

fauna ['fɔnə] *s* Fauna *f*

favor ['fevər] *s* (*kind act*) Gefallen *m*; (*good will*) Gunst *f*; **in f. of** zugunsten (*genit*), für; **in s.o.'s f.** zu j–s Gunsten; **lose f. with s.o.** sich [*dat*] j–s Gunst verwirken; **speak in f. of s.th.** für etw aussprechen ‖ *tr* begünstigen; (*prefer*) bevorzugen; (*a sore limb*) schonen

favorable ['fevərəbəl] *adj* günstig; (*criticism*) positiv; (*report*) beifällig

favorite ['fevərɪt] *adj* Lieblings– ‖ *s* Liebling *m*; (sport) Favorit –in *mf*

favoritism ['fevərɪ‚tɪzəm] *s* Günstlingswirtschaft *f*

fawn [fɔn] *s* Rehkalb *n* ‖ *intr*—**f. on** schmeicheln (*dat*)

fawn'ing *adj* schmeichlerisch

faze [fez] *tr* (coll) auf die Palme bringen

FBI [‚εf‚bi'aɪ] *s* (**Federal Bureau of Investigation**) Bundessicherheitspolizei *f*

fear [fɪr] *s* (of) Furcht *f* (vor *dat*), Angst *f* (vor *dat*); **for f. of** aus Angst

vor (*dat*); **for f. of** (*ger*) um nicht zu (*inf*); **stand in f.** of sich fürchten vor (*dat*) ‖ *tr* fürchten, sich fürchten vor (*dat*); **f. the worst** das Schlimmste befürchten ‖ *intr* sich fürchten; **f. for** besorgt sein um

fearful ['fɪrfəl] *adj* (*afraid*) furchtsam; (*terrible*) furchtbar

fearless ['fɪrlɪs] *adj* furchtlos

feasible ['fizɪbəl] *adj* durchführbar

feast [fist] *s* Fest *n*; (*sumptuous meal*) Schmaus *m* ‖ *tr*—**f. one's eyes on** seine Augen weiden an (*dat*) ‖ *intr* schwelgen; **f. on** sich gütlich tun an (*dat*)

feast'day' *s* Festtag *m*

feast'ing *s* Schmauserei *f*

feat [fit] *s* Kunststück *n*; **f. of arms** Waffentat *f*

feather ['fɛðər] *s* Feder *f*; **a f. in his cap** ein Triumph für ihn ‖ *tr* mit Federn versehen; (aer) auf Segelstellung fahren; (crew) flach drehen; **f. one's nest** sich warm betten

feath'er bed' *s* Federbett *n*

feath'erbed'ding *s* Anstellung *f* unnötiger Arbeitskräfte

feath'erbrain' *s* Schwachkopf *m*

feath'er dust'er *s* Staubwedel *m*

feath'eredge' *s* feine Kante *f*

feath'erweight' *adj* Federgewichts– ‖ *s* (boxer) Federgewichtler *m*

feathery ['fɛðəri] *adj* federartig; (*light as feathers*) federleicht

feature ['fitʃər] *s* (*of the face*) Gesichtszug *m*; (*characteristic*) Merkmal *n*; **f. film** Spielfilm *m*; **main f.** Grundzug *m*; (cin) Hauptfilm *m* ‖ *tr* als Hauptschlager herausbringen; (cin) in der Hauptrolle zeigen

fea'ture writ'er *s* Sonderberichterstatter –in *mf*

February ['fɛbru‚eri] *s* Februar *m*

feces ['fisiz] *spl* Kot *m*, Stuhl *m*

feckless ['fɛklɪs] *adj* (*incompetent*) unfähig; (*ineffective*) unwirksam; (*without spirit*) geistlos

fecund ['fikənd] *adj* fruchtbar

federal ['fɛdərəl] *adj* Bundes–, bundesstaatlich; **f. government** Bundesregierung *f*

federate ['fɛdə‚ret] *adj* verbündet ‖ *tr* zu e–m Bund vereinigen ‖ *intr* sich verbünden

federation [‚fɛdə'reʃən] *s* Staatenbund *m*

fed' up' [fɛd] *adj*—**be f.** die Nase voll haben; **be f. with s.th.** etw satt haben

fee [fi] *s* Gebühr *f*; (*of a doctor*) Honorar *n*

feeble ['fibəl] *adj* schwächlich

fee'ble-mind'ed *adj* schwachsinnig

feed [fid] *s* Futter *n*; (mach) Zuführung *f* ‖ *v* (*pret & pp* **fed** [fɛd]) *tr* (*animals*) füttern; (*persons*) zu Essen geben; (*in a restaurant*) verpflegen; (*e.g., a nation*) nähren; (*a fire*) unterhalten; (mach) zuführen ‖ *intr* fressen; **f. on** sich ernähren von

feed'back' *s* Rückwirkung *f*; (electron) Rückkoppelung *f*

feed' bag' *s* Futtersack *m*; **put on the f.** (sl) futtern

feeder ['fidər] s (elec) Speiseleitung f; (mach) Zubringer m

feed'er line' s (aer, rr) Zubringerlinie f

feed'ing s (of animals) Fütterung f; (& mach) Speisung f

feed' trough' s Futtertrog m

feed' wire' s (elec) Zuleitungsdraht m

feel [fil] s Gefühl n; get the f. of sich gewöhnen an (acc) || v (pret & pp felt [fɛlt]) tr fühlen; (a pain) spüren; f. one's way sich vortasten; (fig) sondieren; f. s.o. out bei j-m vorfühlen || intr (sick, tired, well) sich fühlen; f. about for herumtasten nach; f. for s.o. mit j-m fühlen; f. like (ger) Lust haben zu (inf); f. up to sich gewachsen fühlen (dat); his head feels hot sein Kopf fühlt sich heiß an; how do you f. about it? was halten Sie davon?; I don't quite f. myself ich fühle mich nicht ganz wohl; I f. as if es ist mir, als wenn; make itself felt sich fühlbar machen

feeler ['filər] s (ent) Fühler m; put out feelers to vorfühlen bei

feel'ing s Gefühl n; bad f. Verstimmung f; good f. Wohlwollen n; have a f. for Sinn haben für; have a f. that das Gefühl haben, daß; with f. gefühlsvoll

feign [fen] tr vortäuschen; f. death sich totstellen

feint [fent] s Finte f, Scheinangriff m

feldspar ['fɛld,spɑr] s Feldspat m

feline ['filaɪn] adj katzenartig

fell [fɛl] adj grausam || tr fällen

fellow ['fɛlo] s (coll) Kerl m; (of a society) Mitglied n

fel'low be'ing s Mitmensch m

fel'low cit'izen s Mitbürger –in mf

fel'low coun'tryman s Landsmann m

fel'low crea'ture s Mitgeschöpf n

fel'lowman' s (–men') Mitmensch m

fel'low mem'ber s Mitglied n

fel'lowship' s Kameradschaft f; (educ) Stipendium n

fel'low stu'dent s Kommilitone m

fel'low trav'eler s Mitreisende mf; (pol) Mitläufer –in mf

felon ['fɛlən] s Schwerverbrecher –in mf

felony ['fɛləni] s Schwerverbrechen n

felt [fɛlt] adj Filz– || s Filz m

felt' pen' s Filzschreiber m, Faserstift m

female ['fimel] adj weiblich || s (of animals) Weibchen n; (pej) Weibsbild n

feminine ['fɛmɪnɪn] adj weiblich

feminism ['fɛmɪ,nɪzəm] s Feminismus m

fen [fɛn] s Bruch m & n

fence [fɛns] s Zaun m; (of stolen goods) Hehler m; on the f. (fig) unentschlossen || tr—f. in einzäunen; f. off abzäunen || intr (sport) fechten

fence' post' s Zaunpfahl m

fenc'ing s Fechten n

fend [fɛnd] tr—f. off abwehren || intr —f. for oneself für sich selbst sorgen

fender ['fɛndər] s (aut) Kotflügel m

fennel ['fɛnəl] s Fenchel m

ferment ['fɑrmɛnt] s Gärmittel n; (fig) Unruhe f || [fər'mɛnt] tr in Gärung bringen || intr gären

fermentation [,fɑrmən'teʃən] s Gärung f

fern [fɑrn] s Farn m

ferocious [fə'roʃəs] adj wild

ferocity [fə'rɑsɪti] s Wildheit f

ferret ['fɛrɪt] s Frettchen n || tr—f. out aufspüren

Fer'ris wheel' ['fɛrɪs] s Riesenrad n

ferrule ['fɛrul], ['fɛrəl] s Stockzwinge f, Zwinge f

fer·ry ['fɛri] s Fähre f || v (pret & pp –ried) tr übersetzen

fer'ryboat' s Fährboot n

fer'ry·man s (–men') Fährmann m

fertile ['fʌrtɪl] adj fruchtbar

fertility [fər'tɪlɪti] s Fruchtbarkeit f

fertilization [,fʌrtɪlɪ'zeʃən] s Befruchtung f; (of soil) Düngung f

fertilize ['fʌrtɪ,laɪz] tr (a field) düngen; (an egg) befruchten

fertilizer ['fʌrtɪ,laɪzər] s Kunstdünger m

fervent ['fʌrvənt] adj inbrünstig

fervid ['fʌrvɪd] adj brennend

fervor ['fʌrvər] s Inbrunst f

fester ['fɛstər] intr schwären, eitern; (fig) nagen

festival ['fɛstɪvəl] adj festlich, Fest– || s Fest n; (mus, theat) Festspiele pl

festive ['fɛstɪv] adj festlich

festivity [fɛs'tɪvɪti] s Feierlichkeit f

festoon [fɛs'tun] s Girlande f || tr mit Girlanden schmücken

fetch [fɛtʃ] tr holen, abholen

fetch'ing adj entzückend

fete [fɛt] s Fest n

fetid ['fɛtɪd], [fitɪd] adj stinkend

fetish ['fɛtɪʃ], ['fitɪʃ] s Fetisch m

fetlock ['fɛtlɑk] s Köte f; (tuft of hair) Kötenzopf m

fetter ['fɛtər] s Fessel f || tr fesseln

fettle ['fɛtəl] s—in fine f. in Form

fetus ['fitəs] s Leibesfrucht f

feud [fjud] s Fehde f

feudal ['fjudəl] adj feudal

feudalism ['fjudə,lɪzəm] s Feudalismus m

fever ['fivər] s Fieber n

feverish ['fivərɪʃ] adj fieberig; be f. fiebern

few [fju] adj & pron wenige; a few ein paar

fiancé [,fi·ɑn'se] s Verlobte m

fiancée [,fi·ɑn'se] s Verlobte f

fias·co [fɪ'æsko] s (–cos & –coes) Fiasko n

fib [fɪb] s Flunkerei f || v (pret & pp fibbed; ger fibbing) intr flunkern

fibber ['fɪbər] s Flunkerer –in mf

fiber ['faɪbər] s Faser f

fibrous ['faɪbrəs] adj faserig

fickle ['fɪkəl] adj wankelmütig

fickleness ['fɪkəlnɪs] s Wankelmut m

fiction ['fɪkʃən] s Dichtung f, Romanliteratur f

fictional ['fɪkʃənəl] adj romanhaft

fic'tion writ'er s Romanschriftsteller –in mf

fictitious [fɪk'tɪʃəs] adj fingiert

fiddle ['fɪdəl] s Fiedel f, Geige f || tr fiedeln; f. away (time) vergeuden ||

intr fiedeln; **f. with** herumfingern an (*dat*)

fiddler ['fɪdlər] *s* Fiedler –in *mf*

fid'dlestick' *s* Fiedelbogen *m* || **fiddle-sticks** *interj* Quatsch!

fidelity [fɪ'delɪtɪ] *s* Treue *f*

fidget ['fɪdʒɪt] *intr* zappeln; **f. with** nervös spielen mit

fidgety ['fɪdʒɪtɪ] *adj* zappelig

fiduciary [fɪ'd(j)uʃɪ,erɪ] *adj* treuhänderisch; (*note*) ungedeckt || *s* Treuhänder –in *mf*

fief [fif] *s* (hist) Lehen *n*

field [fild] *adj* (artillery, jacket, hospital, kitchen) Feld– || *s* Feld *n*; (*under cultivation*) Acker *m*; (*contestants collectively*) Wettbewerbsteilnehmer *pl*; (*specialty*) Gebiet *n*; (aer) Flugplatz *m*; (elec) Feld *n*; (*of a motor*) (elec) Magnetfeld *n*; (sport) Spielfeld *n*

field' am'bulance *s* Sanitätskraftwagen *m*

field' day' *s* (fig) großer Tag *m*

fielder ['fildər] *s* Feldspieler *m*

field' ex'ercise *s* Truppenübung *f*

field' glass'es *spl* Feldstecher *m*

field' hock'ey *s* Rasenhockey *n*

field'mar'shal *s* Feldmarschall *m*

field' mouse' *s* Feldmaus *f*

field' of vi'sion *s* Blickfeld *n*

field' pack' *s* (mil) Tornister *m*

field' piece' *s* Feldgeschütz *n*

field' trip' *s* Studienfahrt *f*

field' work' *s* praktische Arbeit *f*

fiend [find] *s* (devil) Teufel *m*; (wicked person) Unhold *m*; (addict) Süchtige *mf*

fiendish ['findɪʃ] *adj* teuflisch

fierce [fɪrs] *adj* wild, wütend; (vehement) heftig; (menacing) drohend; (heat) glühend

fiery ['faɪrɪ], ['faɪ.ərɪ] *adj* feurig

fife [faɪf] *s* Querpfeife *f*

fifteen ['fɪf'tin] *adj & pron* fünfzehn || *s* Fünfzehn *f*

fifteenth ['fɪf'tinθ] *adj & pron* fünfzehnte || *s* (fraction) Fünfzehntel *n*; **the f.** (*in dates or a series*) der Fünfzehnte

fifth [fɪfθ] *adj & pron* fünfte || *s* (fraction) Fünftel *n*; **the f.** (*in dates or a series*) der Fünfte

fifth' col'umn *s* (pol) Fünfte Kolonne *f*

fiftieth ['fɪftɪ-ɪθ] *adj & pron* fünfzigste || *s* (fraction) Fünfzigstel *n*

fifty ['fɪftɪ] *adj & pron* fünfzig || *s* Fünfzig *f*; **the fifties** die fünfziger Jahre

fif'ty-fif'ty *adv* halbpart; **go f. with s.o.** mit j–m halbpart machen

fig [fɪg] *s* Feige *f*; (fig) Pfifferling *m*

fight [faɪt] *s* Kampf *m*, Gefecht *n*; (quarrel) Streit *m*; (brawl) Rauferei *f*; (box) Boxkampf *m*; **pick a f.** Zank suchen || *tr* bekämpfen; (a case) durchkämpfen; **f. back** (tears) niederkämpfen; **f. it out** ausfechten; **f. one's way out** sich durchkämpfen || *intr* kämpfen; (quarrel) streiten; (brawl) raufen

fighter ['faɪtər] *adj* (aer) Jagd– || *s*

Kämpfer –in *mf*; (aer) Jäger *m*; (box) Boxkämpfer *m*

fight'er pi'lot *s* Jagdflieger *m*

fight'ing *s* Schlägerei *f*; (quarreling) Streiten *m*; (mil) Kampfhandlungen *pl*

fig' leaf' *s* Feigenblatt *n*

figment ['fɪgmənt] *s*—**f. of the imagination** Hirngespinst *n*

fig' tree' *s* Feigenbaum *m*

figurative ['fɪgjərətɪv] *adj* bildlich; (meaning) übertragen

figure ['fɪgjər] *s* Figur *f*; (personage) Persönlichkeit *f*; (number) Zahl *f*; **be good at figures** ein guter Rechner sein; **cut a fine** (or **poor**) **f.** e–e gute (or schlechte) Figur abgeben; **run into three figures** in die Hunderte gehen || *tr* (coll) glauben, meinen; **f. out** ausknobeln || *intr*—**f. large** e–e große Rolle spielen; **f. on** rechnen mit

fig'urehead' *s* Strohmann *m*; (naut) Bugfigur *f*; **a mere f.** e–e bloße Nummer

fig'ure of speech' *s* Redewendung *f*

fig'ure skat'ing *s* Kunstlauf *m*

figurine [,fɪgjə'rin] *s* Figurine *f*

filament ['fɪləmənt] *s* Faser *f*, Faden *m*; (elec) Glühfaden *m*

filbert ['fɪlbərt] *s* Haselnuß *f*

filch [fɪltʃ] *tr* mausen

file [faɪl] *s* (tool) Feile *f*; (record) Akte *f*; (cards) Kartei *f*; (row) Reihe *f*; **put on f.** zu den Akten legen || *tr* (with a tool) feilen; (letters, etc.) ablegen, abheften; (a complaint) erheben; (a report) erstatten; (a claim) anmelden; (a petition) einreichen; **f. suit** e–n Prozeß anstrengen || *intr*—**f. for** sich bewerben um; **f. out** im Gänsemarsch herausmarschieren; **f. past** vorbeidefilieren (an *dat*)

file' cab'inet *s* Aktenschrank *m*

file' card' *s* Karteikarte *f*

filial ['fɪlɪ-əl] *adj* kindlich

filibuster ['fɪlɪ,bʌstər] *s* Obstruktion *f* || *intr* Obstruktion treiben

filigree ['fɪlɪ,gri] *s* Filigran *n*

fil'ing *s* Feilen *n*; (of records) Ablegen *n* von Akten; (of a claim) Anmeldung *f*; (of a complaint) Erhebung *f*; (of a petition) Einreichung *f*; **filings** Feilspäne *pl*

Filipi·no [,fɪlɪ'pino] *adj* filipinisch || *s* (–nos) Filipino *m*

fill [fɪl] *s* (fullness) Fülle *f*; (land fill) Aufschüttung *f*; **eat one's f.** sich satt essen; **I have had my f. of it** ich habe es satt || *tr* füllen; (an order) ausführen; (a pipe) stopfen; (a position) besetzen; (dent) plombieren, füllen; **f. full** vollfüllen; **f. in** (empty space) ausfüllen; (one's name) einsetzen; (a hole, grave) zuwerfen; **f. it up** (aut) volltanken; **f. up** auffüllen; (a tank) nachfüllen; (a bag) anfüllen; (a glass) vollschenken; **f. with smoke** verräuchern || *intr* sich füllen; (said of sails) sich blähen; **f. in for** einspringen für; **f. out** rund werden; **f. up** sich füllen

filler ['fɪlər] *s* Füller *m*; (of a cigar)

Einlage *f*; (journ) Lückenbüßer *m*; (paint) Grundierfirnis *m*
fillet ['fɪlət] *s* (headband) Kopfbinde *f*; (archit) Leiste *f* ‖ [fɪ'le] *s* (culin) Filet *n* ‖ *tr* filetieren
fillet' of beef' *s* Rinderfilet *n*
fillet' of sole' *s* Seezungenfilet *n*
fill'ing *s* (culin, dent) Füllung *f*
fill'ing sta'tion *s* Tankstelle *f*
fillip ['fɪlɪp] *s* Schnippchen *n*; (on the nose) Nasenstüber *m*
filly ['fɪli] *s* Stutenfüllen *n*
film [fɪlm] *s* (thin layer) Schicht *f*; (cin, phot) Film *m*; **f. of grease** Fettschicht *f*
film' fes'tival *s* Filmfestspiele *pl*
film' li'brary *s* Filmarchiv *n*
film' speed' *s* Filmempfindlichkeit *f*
film' star' *s* Filmstar *m*
film'strip' *s* Bildstreifen *m*
filmy ['fɪlmi] *adj* trüb
filter ['fɪltər] *s* Filter *m*; (rad) Sieb *n* ‖ *tr* filtern; (rad) sieben
fil'tering *s* Filtrierung *f*
fil'ter pa'per *s* Filterpapier *n*
fil'ter tip' *s* Filtermundstück *n*; (coll) Filterzigarette *f*
filth [fɪlθ] *s* Schmutz *m*; (fig) Unflätigkeit *f*, Zote *f*
filthy ['fɪlθi] *adj* schmutzig (talk) unflätig; (lucre) schnöd(e) ‖ *adv*—**f. rich** (sl) klotzig reich
filtrate ['fɪltret] *s* Filtrat *n* ‖ *tr & intr* filtrieren
filtration [fɪl'treʃən] *s* Filtrierung *f*
fin [fɪn] *s* Flosse *f*; (of a shark or whale) Finne *f*; (of a bomb) Steuerschwanz *m*; (aer) Flosse *f*
final ['faɪnəl] *adj* End-, Schluß-, (definitive) endgültig ‖ *s* (educ) Abschlußprüfung *f*; **finals** (sport) Endrunde *f*, Endspiel *n*
finale [fɪ'nɑli] *s* Finale *n*
finalist ['faɪnəlɪst] *s* Finalist –in *mf*
finality [faɪ'nælɪti] *s* Endgültigkeit *f*
finally ['faɪnəli] *adv* schließlich
finance ['faɪnæns], [fɪ'næns] *s* Finanz *f*; **finances** Finanzwesen *n* ‖ *tr* finanzieren
financial [fɪ'nænʃəl], [faɪ'nænʃəl] *adj* (e.g., policy, situation, crisis, aid) Finanz–; (e.g., affairs, resources, embarrassment) Geld–
financier [ˌfɪnən'sɪr], [ˌfaɪnən'sɪr] *s* Finanzmann *m*
financ'ing, fi'nancing *s* Finanzierung *f*
finch [fɪntʃ] *s* Fink *m*
find [faɪnd] *s* Fund *m*; (archeol) Bodenfund *m* ‖ *v* (pret & pp found [faʊnd]) *tr* finden; (math) bestimmen; **f. one's way** sich zurechtfinden; **f. one's way back** zurückfinden; **f. out** herausfinden; **f. s.o. guilty** j–n für schuldig erklären ‖ *intr*—**f. out about s.th.** hinter etw [acc] kommen
finder ['faɪndər] *s* Finder –in *mf*
find'ing *s* Finden *n*; **findings** Tatbestand *m*
fine [faɪn] *adj* fein; (excellent) hervorragend; (weather) schön; **f.! gut!** ‖ *s* Geldstrafe *f* ‖ *tr* mit e-r Geldstrafe belegen
fine' arts' *spl* schöne Künste *pl*

fineness ['faɪnnɪs] *s* Feinheit *f*; (of a coin or metal) Feingehalt *m*
fine' point' *s* Feinheit *f*
fine' print' *s* Kleindruck *m*
finery ['faɪnəri] *s* Putz *m*, Staat *m*
fine-spun ['faɪnˌspʌn] *adj* feingesponnen
finesse [fɪ'nes] *s* Finesse *f*; (cards) Impaß *m* ‖ *tr & intr* impassieren
fine-toothed ['faɪnˌtuθt] *adj* feingezahnt; **go over with a f. comb** unter die Lupe nehmen
fine' touch' *s* Feinheit *f*
fine' tun'ing *s* Feineinstellung *f*
finger ['fɪŋgər] *s* Finger *m*; **have a f. in the pie** die Hand im Spiel haben; **keep your fingers crossed** halten Sie mir die Daumen; **not lift a f.** keinen Finger rühren; **put the f. on s.o.** (sl) j–n verpetzen; **snap one's fingers** mit den Fingern schnellen; **twist around one's little f.** um den kleinen Finger wickeln ‖ *tr* befingern
fin'ger bowl' *s* Fingerschale *f*
fin'gering *s* (mus) Fingersatz *m*
fin'gernail' *s* Fingernagel *m*
fin'gernail pol'ish *s* Nagellack *m*
fin'gerprint' *s* Fingerabdruck *m* ‖ *tr*—**f. s.o.** j–m die Fingerabdrücke abnehmen
fin'gertip' *s* Fingerspitze *f*; **have at one's fingertips** parat haben
finicky ['fɪnɪki] *adj* wählerisch
finish ['fɪnɪʃ] *s* Ende *n*, Abschluß *m*; (polish) Lack *m*, Politur *f*; **put a f. on** fertig bearbeiten ‖ *tr* beenden; (complete) vollenden; (put a finish on) fertig bearbeiten; (smooth) glätten; (polish) polieren; (ruin) kaputt machen; **f. drinking** austrinken; **f. eating** aufessen; **f. off** (supplies) aufbrauchen; (food) aufessen; (a drink) austrinken; (kill) (sl) erledigen; **f. reading** (a book) auslesen
fin'ished *adj* beendet, fertig; **be all f.** fix und fertig sein
fin'ished pro'duct *s* Fertigprodukt *n*
fin'ishing coat' *s* Deckanstrich *m*
fin'ishing mill' *s* Nachwalzwerk *n*
fin'ishing school' *s* Mädchenpensionat *n*
fin'ishing touch'es *spl*—**put the f. to** die letzte Hand legen an (acc)
fin'ish line' *s* Ziel *n*, Ziellinie *f*
finite ['faɪnaɪt] *adj* endlich
fi'nite verb' *s* Verbum *n* finitum
fink [fɪŋk] *s* (informer) (sl) Verräter –in *mf*; (strikebreaker) (sl) Streikbrecher –in *mf*
Finland ['fɪnlənd] *s* Finnland *n*
Finn [fɪn] *s* Finne *m*, Finnin *f*
Finnish ['fɪnɪʃ] *adj* finnisch ‖ *s* (language) Finnisch *n*
fir [fʌr] *s* Tanne *f*
fir' cone' *s* Tannenzapfen *m*
fire [faɪr] *s* Feuer *n*; (conflagration) Brand *m*; (mil) Feuer *n*; **come under f.** unter Beschuß geraten; **on f.** in Brand; **open f.** Feuer eröffnen; **set on f.** in Brand stecken ‖ *tr* (a gun, pistol, shot) abfeuern; (bricks, ceramics) brennen; (an oven) befeuern; (an employee) entlassen; (throw

hard) feuern; **f. questions at s.o.** j-n mit Fragen bombardieren; **f. up** (& fig) anfeuern ‖ *intr* feuern, schießen; **f. away!** schieß los!; **f. on** (mil) beschießen

fire′ alarm′ *s* Feuermeldung *f*; *(box)* Feuermelder *m*
fire′arm′ *s* Schußwaffe *f*
fire′ball′ *s* Feuerball *m*; *(hustler)* Draufgänger *m*
fire′bomb′ *s* Brandbombe *f* ‖ *tr* mit Brandbomben belegen
fire′brand′ *s* (fig) Aufwiegler –in *mf*
fire′break′ *s* Feuerschneise *f*
fire′ brigade′ *s* Feuerwehr *f*
fire′bug′ *m* (coll) Brandstifter –in *mf*
fire′ chief′ *s* Branddirektor *m*
fire′ com′pany *s* Feuerwehr *f*
fire′crack′er *s* Knallfrosch *m*
fire′damp′ *s* Schlagwetter *pl*
fire′ depart′ment *s* Feuerwehr *f*
fire′ drill′ *s* Feueralarmübung *f*; *(by a fire company)* Feuerwehrübung *f*
fire′ en′gine *s* Spritze *f*
fire′ escape′ *s* Feuerleiter *f*
fire′ extin′guisher *s* Feuerlöscher *m*
fire′fly′ *s* Glühwurm *m*
fire′ hose′ *s* Spritzenschlauch *m*
fire′house′ *s* Feuerwache *f*
fire′ hy′drant *s* Hydrant *m*
fire′ insur′ance *s* Brandversicherung *f*
fire′ i′rons *spl* Kamingeräte *pl*
fire′lane′ *s* Feuer(schutz)schneise *f*
fire′man *s* (**–men**) Feuerwehrmann *m*; *(stoker)* Heizer *m*
fire′place′ *s* Kamin *m*, Herd *m*
fire′plug′ *s* Hydrant *m*
fire′ pow′er *s* (mil) Feuerkraft *f*
fire′proof′ *adj* feuerfest ‖ *tr* feuerfest machen
fire′ sale′ *s* Ausverkauf *m* von feuerbeschädigten Waren
fire′ screen′ *s* Feuervorhang *m*
fire′side′ *s* Kamin *m*, Herd *m*
fire′trap′ *s* feuergefährdetes Gebäude *n*
fire′ wall′ *s* Brandmauer *f*
fire′wa′ter *s* (coll) Feuerwasser *n*
fire′wood′ *s* Brennholz *n*
fire′works′ *spl* Feuerwerk *n*
fir′ing *s* *(of a weapon)* Abfeuern *n*; *(of an employee)* Entlassung *f*
fir′ing line′ *s* Feuerlinie *f*
fir′ing range′ *s* Schießstand *m*
fir′ing squad′ *s* Erschießungskommando *n*; *(for ceremonies)* Ehrensalutkommando *n*; **put to the f. an die Wand stellen**
firm [fʌrm] *adj* fest ‖ *s* (com) Firma *f*
firmament [′fʌrməmənt] *s* Firmament *n*
firmness [′fʌrmnɪs] *s* Festigkeit *f*
first [fʌrst] *adj* erste; **very f.** allererste ‖ *adv* erst, erstens; **f. of all zunächst** ‖ *s* (aut) erster Gang *m*; **at f. zuerst**; **f. come, f. served** wer zuerst kommt, mahlt zuerst; **from the f.** von vornherein; **the f.** *(in dates or in a series)* der Erste
first′ aid′ *s* Erste Hilfe *f*
first′-aid′ kit′ *s* Verbandpäckchen *n*
first′-aid′ sta′tion *s* Unfallstation *f*; (mil) Verbandplatz *m*

first′-born′ *adj* erstgeboren
first′-class′ *adj* erstklassig ‖ *adv* erster Klasse
first′-class′ mail′ *s* Briefpost *f*
first′-class′ tic′ket *s* Fahrkarte *f* (or Flugkarte *f*) erster Klasse
first′ cous′in *s* leiblicher Vetter *m*, leibliche Cousine *f*
first′-degree′ *adj* ersten Grades
first′ draft′ *s* Konzept *n*
first′ fin′ger *s* Zeigefinger *m*
first′ floor′ *s* Parterre *n*, Erdgeschoß *n*
first′ fruits′ *spl* Erstlinge *pl*
first′ lieuten′ant *s* Oberleutnant *m*
firstly [′fʌrstli] *adv* erstens
first′ mate′ *s* Obersteuermann *m*
first′ name′ *s* Vorname *m*
first′ night′ *s* (theat) Erstaufführung *f*
first-nighter [′fʌrst′naɪtər] *s* (theat) Premierenbesucher –in *mf*
first′ offend′er *s* noch nicht Vorbestrafte *mf*
first′ of′ficer *s* erster Offizier *m*
first′ prize′ *s* Hauptgewinn *m*, Haupttreffer *m*
first′-rate′ *adj* erstklassig
first′ ser′geant *s* Hauptfeldwebel *m*
fir′ tree′ *s* Tannenbaum *m*
fiscal [′fɪskəl] *adj* *(period, year)* Rechnungs–; *(policy)* Finanz–
fish [fɪʃ] *s* Fisch *m*; **drink like a f.** wie ein Bürstenbinder saufen; **like a f. out of water** nicht in seinem Element ‖ *tr* fischen ‖ *intr* fischen; **f. for** angeln nach
fish′bone′ *s* Gräte *f*, Fischgräte *f*
fish′ bowl′ *s* Fischglas *n*
fisher [′fɪʃər] *s* Fischer –in *mf*
fish′er·man *s* (**–men**) Angler *m*
fishery [′fɪʃəri] *s* Fischerei *f*
fish′hook′ *s* Angelhaken *m*
fish′ing *adj* Fisch–, Angel– ‖ *s* Fischen *n*
fish′ing line′ *s* Angelschnur *f*
fish′ing reel′ *s* Angelschnurrolle *f*
fish′ing rod′ *s* Angelrute *f*
fish′ing tack′le *s* Fischgerät *n*
fish′ mar′ket *s* Fischmarkt *m*
fishmonger [′fɪʃ ‚mʌŋgər] *s* Fischhändler –in *mf*
fish′pond′ *s* Fischteich *m*
fish′ sto′ry *s* Jägerlatein *n*
fish′tail′ *s* (aer) Abbremsen *n* ‖ *intr* (aer) abbremsen
fishy [′fɪʃi] *adj* fischig; *(eyes, look)* ausdruckslos; *(suspicious)* anrüchig; **there's s.th. f. about it** das geht nicht mit rechten Dingen zu
fission [′fɪʃən] *s* (phys) Spaltung *f*
fissionable [′fɪʃənəbəl] *adj* spaltbar
fissure [′fɪʃər] *s* Riß *m*, Spalt *m*
fist [fɪst] *s* Faust *f*; **make a f. die Faust ballen**; **shake one's f. at s.o.** j-m mit der Faust drohen
fist′ fight′ *s* Handgemenge *n*
fisticuffs [′fɪstɪ ‚kʌfs] *spl* Faustschläge *pl*
fit [fɪt] *adj* (**fitter; fittest**) gesund; *(for)* tauglich (für, zu); (sport) gut in Form; **be fit as a fiddle** kerngesund sein; **be fit to be tied** Gift und Galle spucken; **feel fit** auf der Höhe sein; **fit for military service**

diensttauglich; **fit to eat** genießbar;
fit to drink trinkbar; **keep fit in
Form bleiben; see fit to** (*inf*) es für
richtig halten zu (*inf*) ‖ *s* (*of
clothes*) Sitz *m*; **by fits and starts**
ruckweise; **fit of anger** Wutanfall *m*;
fit of laughter Lachkrampf *m*; **give
s.o. fits** j-n auf die Palme bringen;
it is a good (or **a bad**) **fit** es sitzt
gut (or schlecht); **throw a fit** e-n
Wutanfall kriegen ‖ *v* (*pret* & *pp*
fitted; *ger* **fitting**) *tr* passen (*dat*);
fit in (*for an appointment*) einschie-
ben; **fit out** ausrüsten, ausstatten ‖
intr passen; **fit into** sich einfügen in
(*acc*); **fit in with** passen zu; **fit together** zusammenpassen

fitful ['fɪtfəl] *adj* unregelmäßig

fitness ['fɪtnɪs] *s* Tauglichkeit *f*; **physical f.** gute körperliche Verfassung *f*

fit'ting *adj* passend, angemessen ‖ *s*
(*of a garment*) Anprobe *f*; (*mach*)
Montage *f*; **fittings** Armaturen *pl*

five [faɪv] *adj* & *pron* fünf ‖ *s* Fünf *f*

five'-year plan' *s* Fünfjahresplan *m*

fix [fɪks] *s* (*determination of a position*) Standortbestimmung *f*; (*position*) Standort *m*; (*injection of heroin*) (sl) Schuß *m*; **be in a fix** (coll)
in der Klemme sein ‖ *tr* befestigen;
(*a price, time*) festsetzen; (*repair*)
reparieren, wieder in Ordnung bringen; (*get even with*) (sl) erledigen,
das Handwerk legen (*dat*); (*one's
glance*) (**on**) heften (auf *acc*); (*the
blame*) (**on**) zuschreiben (*dat*); (*a
game*) (sl) auf unehrliche Weise beeinflussen; (*bayonets*) aufpflanzen;
(phot) fixieren

fixed *adj* (*unmovable*) unbeweglich;
(*stare*) starr; (*income*) fest; (*idea,
cost*) fix; **f. date** Termin *m*

fixer ['fɪksər] *s* (phot) Fixiermittel *n*

fix'ing *s* (*making fast*) Befestigung *f*;
(*of a date, etc.*) Festsetzung *f*; **fix-
ings** (culin) Zutaten *pl*

fix'ing bath' *s* (phot) Fixierbad *n*

fixture ['fɪkstʃər] *s* Installationsteil *m*;
he is a permanent f. er gehört zum
Inventar

fizz [fɪz] *s* Zischen *n* ‖ *intr* zischen

fizzle ['fɪzəl] *s* (coll) Pleite *f* ‖ *intr*
aufzischen; **f. out** verpuffen

flabbergast ['flæbər͵gæst] *tr* verblüffen

flabby ['flæbi] *adj* schlaff, schlapp

flag [flæg] *s* Fahne *f*, Flagge *f* ‖ *v*
(*pret* & *pp* **flagged;** *ger* **flagging**) *tr*
signalisieren ‖ *intr* nachlassen

flag'pole' *s* Fahnenmast *m*

flagrant ['flegrənt] *adj* schreiend

flag'ship' *s* Flaggschiff *n*

flag'staff' *s* Flaggenmast *m*

flag'stone' *s* Steinfliese *f*

flag' stop' *s* (rr) Bedarfshaltestelle *f*

flail [flel] *s* Dreschflegel *m* ‖ *tr* dreschen ‖ *intr*—**f. about** um sich schlagen

flair [fler] *s* Spürsinn *m*, feine Nase *f*

flak [flæk] *s* Flak *f*, Flakfeuer *n*

flake [flek] *s* (*thin piece*) Schuppe *f*;
(*of snow, soap*) Flocke *f* ‖ *intr*
Schuppen bilden; **f. off** abblättern

flaky ['fleki] *adj* (*skin*) schuppig;
(*pastry*) blätterig; (sl) überspannt

flamboyant [flæm'bɔɪ·ənt] *adj* (*person*)
angeberisch; (*style*) überladen

flame [flem] *s* Flamme *f*; **be in flames**
in Flammen stehen; **burst into flames**
in Flammen aufgehen ‖ *intr* flammen

flamethrower ['flem͵θro·ər] *s* Flam-
menwerfer *m*

flam'ing *adj* flammend

flamin·go [flə'mɪŋgo] *s* (**~gos** &
~goes) (orn) Flamingo *m*

flammable ['flæməbəl] *adj* brennbar

Flanders ['flændərz] *s* Flandern *n*

flange [flændʒ] *s* (*of a pipe*) Flansch
m; (*of a wheel*) Spurkranz *m*

flank [flæŋk] *s* (anat, mil, zool) Flanke *f*
f ‖ *tr* flankieren

flank'ing move'ment *s* (mil) Umgehung *f*

flannel ['flænəl] *adj* flanellen ‖ *s*
Flanell *m*

flap [flæp] *s* Klappe *f*; **f. of the wing**
Flügelschlag *m* ‖ *v* (*pret* & *pp*
flapped; *ger* **flapping**) *tr*—**f. the
wings** mit den Flügeln schlagen ‖
intr flattern

flare [fler] *s* Leuchtsignal *n*; (*of anger,
excitement*) Aufbrausen *n*; (*of a
skirt*) Glocke *f*; (mil) Leuchtrakete
f, Leuchtbombe *f* ‖ *intr* flackern;
(*said of a skirt*) glockenförmig abstehen; **f. up** auflodern; (fig) aufbrausen

flare'-up' *s* Auflodern *n*; (*of anger*)
Aufbrausen *n*

flash [flæʃ] *s* Blitz *m*; (*of a gun*) Mündungsfeuer *n*; (phot) Blitzlicht *n*; **f.
of genious** Geistesblitz *m*; **f. of light**
Lichtstrahl *m*; **f. of lightning** Blitzstrahl *m*; **in a f.** im Nu ‖ *tr* (*a
glance*) zuwerfen; (*a message*) funkeln; **f. a light in s.o.'s face** j-m ins
Gesicht leuchten ‖ *intr* blitzen; (*said
of eyes*) funkeln; **f. by** vorbeisausen;
f. on aufleuchten; **f. through one's
mind** j-m durch den Kopf schießen

flash'back' *s* (cin) Rückblende *f*

flash' bulb' *s* Blitzlichtbirne *f*

flash' cube' *s* Blitzlichtwürfel *m*

flash' flood' *s* plötzliche Überschwemmung *f*

flash' gun' *s* Blitzlichtgerät *n*

flash'light' *s* Taschenlampe *f*

flash' pic'ture, flash' shot' *s* Blitzlicht-
aufnahme *f*

flashy ['flæʃi] *adj* auffällig; (*clothes*)
protzig; (*colors*) grell

flask [flæsk] *s* Taschenflasche *f*; (*for
laboratory use*) Glaskolben *m*

flat [flæt] *adj* (**flatter; flattest**) platt,
flach; (*food*) fad(e); (*rate*) Pau-
schal–; (*tire*) platt; (*color*) matt;
(*beer, soda*) schal; (*lie*) glatt; (*denial*) entschieden; (mus) erniedrigt;
be f. (mus) zu tief singen ‖ *adv*
(*e.g., in exactly ten minutes*) genau;
fall f. (fig) flachfallen; **go f.** schal
werden; **lie f.** flach liegen ‖ *s* (*apartment*) Wohnung *f*; (*tire*) Reifenpanne *f*

flat'boat' *s* Flachboot *n*

flat-broke ['flæt'brok] *adj* (coll) völlig pleite

flat'car' *s* Plattformwagen *m*

flat' feet' *spl* Plattfüße *pl*

flat'-foot'ed *adj* plattfüßig; **catch f.** auf frischer Tat ertappen

flat'i'ron *s* Bügeleisen *n*

flatly ['flætli] *adv* rundweg, reinweg

flatten ['flætən] *tr* (*paper, cloth*) glattstreichen; (*raze*) einebnen; **f. out** abplatten; (aer) abfangen || *intr* sich verflachen; (aer) ausschweben

flatter ['flætər] *tr* schmeicheln (*dat*); **be flattered** sich geschmeichelt fühlen; **f. oneself** sich [dat] einbilden

flatterer ['flætərər] *s* Schmeichler –in *mf*

flat'tering *adj* schmeichelhaft

flattery ['flætəri] *s* Schmeichelei *f*

flat' tire' *s* Reifenpanne *f*

flat'top' *s* (coll) Flugzeugträger *m*

flat' trajec'tory *s* Rasanz *f*

flatulence ['flætʃələns] *s* Blähung *f*

flat'ware' *s* (*silverware*) Eßbestecke *pl*

flaunt [flɔnt] *tr* prunken mit

flavor ['flevər] *s* Aroma *n* || *tr* würzen

fla'voring *s* Würze *f*

flavorless ['flevərlɪs] *adj* fad(e)

flaw [flɔ] *s* Fehler *m*; (*crack*) Riß *m*; (*in glass, precious stone*) Blase *f*

flawless ['flɔlɪs] *adj* tadellos

flax [flæks] *s* Flachs *m*, Lein *m*

flaxen ['flæksən] *adj* flachsen

flax'seed' *s* Leinsamen *m*

flay [fle] *tr* ausbalgen

flea [fli] *s* Floh *m*

flea'bag' *s* (*sleeping bag*) (coll) Flohkiste *f*; (*hotel*) (coll) Penne *f*

flea'bite' *s* Flohbiß *m*

flea'mar'ket *s*, Flohmarkt *m*

fleck [flɛk] *s* Fleck *m*

fledgling ['fledʒlɪŋ] *s* eben flügge gewordener Vogel *m*; (fig) Grünschnabel *m*

flee [fli] *v* (*pret & pp* **fled** [flɛd]) *intr* fliehen

fleece [flis] *s* Vlies *n* || *tr* (coll) rupfen

fleecy ['flisi] *adj* wollig; **f. clouds** Schäfchenwolken *pl*

fleet [flit] *adj* flink || *s* Flotte *f*; (aer) Geschwader *n*; (nav) Kriegsflotte *f*; **f. of cars** Wagenpark *m*

fleet'ing *adj* flüchtig

Flemish ['flemɪʃ] *adj* flämisch || *s* Flämisch *n*

flesh [flɛʃ] *s* Fleisch *n*; **in the f.** leibhaftig

flesh'-col'ored *adj* fleischfarben

fleshiness ['fleʃinɪs] *s* Fleischigkeit *f*

flesh' wound' *s* Fleischwunde *f*

fleshy ['fleʃi] *adj* fleischig

flex [flɛks] *tr* biegen; (*muscles*) anspannen

flexible ['fleksɪbəl] *adj* biegsam

flex(i)time ['fleks(ɪ) ˌtaɪm] *s* Gleitzeit *f*

flick [flɪk] *s* Schnippen *n* || *tr* (*away*) wegschnippen

flicker ['flɪkər] *s* (*of a flame*) Flakkern *n*; (*of eyelids*) Zucken *n* || *intr* flackern

flier ['flaɪ·ər] *s* Flieger –in *mf*; (*handbill*) Flugblatt *n*

flight [flaɪt] *s* Flug *m*; (*fleeing*) Flucht *f*; (*of birds, geese*) Schar *f*; (*of stairs*) Treppe *f*; **f. of stairs** Treppenflucht *f*; **f. of the imagination** Geistesschwung *m*; **live two flights up** zwei Treppen hoch wohnen; **put to f.** in die Flucht schlagen; **take to f.** sich davonmachen

flight' bag' *s* (aer) Reisetasche *f*

flight' deck' *s* (nav) Landedeck *n*

flight' engineer' *s* Bordmechaniker *m*

flight' instruc'tor *s* Fluglehrer –in *mf*

flight' path' *s* Flugstrecke *f*

flighty ['flaɪti] *adj* leichtsinnig

flim-flam ['flɪm ˌflæm] *s* (*nonsense*) Unsinn *m*; (*deception*) Betrügerei *f* || *v* (*pret & pp* **-flammed**) *ger* **-flamming**) *tr* (coll) betrügen

flimsy ['flɪmzi] *adj* (*material*) hauchdünn; (*excuse, construction*) schwach

flinch [flɪntʃ] *intr* (at) zurückweichen (vor *dat*), zusammenfahren (vor *dat*)

flinch'ing—**without f.** ohne mit der Wimper zu zucken

fling [flɪŋ] *s* Wurf *m*; **go on** (or **have**) **a f.** sich austoben; **have a f. at versuchen** || *v* (*pret & pp* **flung** [flʌŋ]) *tr* schleudern; **f. off** abschleudern; **f. open** aufreißen

flint [flɪnt] *s* Feuerstein *m*

flinty ['flɪnti] *adj* steinhart; (fig) hart

flip [flɪp] *adj* leichtfertig || *s* (*of a coin*) Hochwerfen *n*; (*somersault*) Purzelbaum *m* || *v* (*pret & pp* **flipped**; *ger* **flipping**) *tr* schnellen; (*a coin*) hochwerfen; **f. one's lid** (sl) rasend werden; **f. over** umdrehen

flippancy ['flɪpənsi] *s* Leichtfertigkeit *f*

flippant ['flɪpənt] *adj* leichtfertig

flipper ['flɪpər] *s* Flosse *f*

flirt [flʌrt] *s* Flirt *m* || *intr* kokettieren, flirten; (*with an idea*) liebäugeln

flirtation [flʌr'teʃən] *s* Liebelei *f*

flit [flɪt] *v* (*pret & pp* **flitted**; *ger* **flitting**) *intr* flitzen; **f. by** vorbeiflitzen; (*said of time*) verfliegen

float [flot] *s* Schwimmkörper *m*; (*of a fishing line*) Schwimmer *m*; (*raft*) Floß *n*; (*in parades*) Festwagen *m* || *tr* (*logs*) flößen; (*a loan*) auflegen || *intr* schwimmen; (*in the air*) schweben; **f. about** herumtreiben

float'ing kid'ney *s* Wanderniere *f*

float'ing mine' *s* Treibmine *f*

flock [flak] *s* (*of sheep*) Herde *f*; (*of birds*) Schar *f*, Schwarm *m*; (*of people*) Menge *f* || *intr* herbeiströmen; **come flocking** herbeigeströmt kommen; **f. around** sich scharen um; **f. into** strömen in (*acc*); **f. to** zulaufen (*dat*); **f. together** sich zusammenscharen

floe [flo] *s* Eisscholle *f*

flog [flag] *v* (*pret & pp* **flogged**; *ger* **flogging**) *tr* prügeln

flood [flʌd] *s* Flut *f*; (*caused by heavy rains*) Überschwemmung *f*; (*sudden rise of a river*) Hochwasser *n*; (fig) Schwall *m*; (Bib) Sintflut *f* || *tr* (& fig) überschwemmen; (*e.g., with mail*) überschütten

flood'gate' s (& fig) Schleusentor n
flood'light' s Flutlicht n || tr anstrahlen
flood' tide' s Flut f; at f. zur Zeit der Flut
flood' wa'ters spl Flutwasser n
floor [flor] s Fußboden m; (story) Stock m; (parl) Sitzungssaal m; **have the f.** das Wort haben; **may I have the f.?** ich bitte ums Wort; **on the third f.** im zweiten Stock || tr zu Boden strecken; (coll) verblüffen
floor'board' s Diele f
floor'ing s Fußbodenbelag m
floor' lamp' s Stehlampe f
floor' plan' s Grundriß m
floor' pol'ish s Bohnermasse f
floor' sam'ple s Vorführungsmuster n
floor' show' s Kabarett n
floor' tile' s Bodenfliese f
floor'walk'er s Abteilungsaufseher –in mf
floor' wax' s Bohnerwachs n
flop [flɑp] s (coll) Mißerfolg m; (person) Niete f; (fall) (coll) Plumps m; **take a f.** (coll) plumpsen || v (pret & pp **flopped**; ger **flopping**) intr (fall) (coll) plumpsen; (jail) (coll) versagen; (theat) (coll) durchfallen; **f. down in** (coll) sich plumpsen lassen in (acc)
flora [ˈflorə] s Pflanzenwelt f
floral [ˈflorəl] adj Blumen–
Florence [ˈflorəns] s Florenz n
florescence [floˈrɛsəns] s Blüte f
florid [ˈflorɪd] adj (ornate) überladen; (complexion) blühend
florist [ˈflorɪst] s Blumenhändler –in mf
floss [flɔs] s Rohseide f; (of corn) Narbenfäden pl
floss' silk' s Florettseide f
flossy [ˈflɔsi] adj seidenweich
flotilla [floˈtɪlə] s Flotille f
flotsam [ˈflɑtsəm] s Wrackgut n
flot'sam and jet'sam s Treibgut n; (trifles) Kleinigkeiten pl
flounce [flaʊns] s Volant m || tr mit Volants besetzen || intr erregt stürmen
flounder [ˈflaʊndər] s Flunder f || intr taumeln; (fig) ins Schwimmen kommen
flour [flaʊr] s Mehl n
flourish [ˈflʌrɪʃ] s (in writing) Schnörkel m; (in a speech) Floskel f; (gesture) große Geste f; (mus) Tusch m; **f. of trumpets** Trompetengeschmetter n || tr (banners) schwenken; (swords) schwingen || intr blühen, gedeihen
flour'ishing adj blühend; (business) schwunghaft
flour' mill' s Mühle f
floury [ˈflaʊri] adj mehlig
flout [flaʊt] tr verspotten || intr—f. at spotten über (acc)
flow [flo] s Fluß m || intr fließen, rinnen; (said of hair, clothes) wallen; **f. by** vorbeifließen; **f. into** zuströmen (dat)
flower [ˈflaʊər] s Blume f; **cut flowers** Schnittblumen pl || intr blühen

flow'er bed' s Blumenbeet n
flow'er gar'den s Blumengarten m
flow'er girl' s Blumenmädchen n
flow'erpot' s Blumentopf m
flow'er shop' s Blumenladen m
flow'er show' s Blumenausstellung f
flow'er stand' s Blumenstand m
flowery [ˈflaʊəri] adj blumig; (fig) geziert; **f. phrase** Floskel f
flu [flu] s (coll) Grippe f
flub [flʌb] v (pret & pp **flubbed**; ger **flubbing**) tr (coll) verkorksen
fluctuate [ˈflʌktʃ/ʊˌet] intr schwanken
fluctuation [ˌflʌktʃ/ʊˈeʃ/ən] s Schwankung f
flue [flu] s Rauchrohr n
fluency [ˈflu-ənsi] s Geläufigkeit f
fluent [ˈflu-ənt] adj (speaker) redegewandt; (speech) fließend
fluently [ˈflu-əntli] adv fließend
fluff [flʌf] s Staubflocke f; (blunder) Schnitzer m || tr verpfuschen; **f. up** (a pillow) schütteln; (a rug) aufrauhen
fluffy [ˈflʌfi] adj flaumig
fluid [ˈflu-ɪd] adj flüssig || s Flüssigkeit f
fluke [fluk] s Ankerflügel m; (coll) Dusel m
flunk [flʌŋk] s Durchfallen n || tr (a test) (coll) durchfallen in (dat); (a student) (coll) durchfallen lassen || intr (coll) durchfallen
flunky [ˈflʌŋki] s Schranze mf
fluorescent [floˈrɛsənt] adj fluoreszierend
fluores'cent light' s Leuchtstofflampe f
fluores'cent tube' s Leuchtröhre f
fluoridate [ˈflorɪˌdet] tr mit e–m Fluorid versetzen
fluoride [ˈflorɑɪd] s Fluorid n
fluorine [ˈflorin] s Fluor n
fluorite [ˈflorɑɪt] s Flurkalzium n
fluoroscope [ˈfloraˌskop] s Fluoroskop n
flurry [ˈflʌri] s (of snow) Schneegestöber m; (st. exch.) kurzes Aufflackern n; **f. of activity** fieberhafte Tätigkeit f
flush [flʌʃ] adj (even) eben, glatt; (well-supplied) gut bei Kasse; (full to overflowing) übervoll || adv direkt || s (on the cheeks) Erröten n; (of youth) Blüte f; (of a toilet) Spülung f; (cards) Flöte f; **f. of victory** Siegesrausch m || tr (a toilet) spülen; (hunt) auftreiben; **f. down** hinunterspülen; **f. out** (animals) auftreiben || intr erröten
flush' switch' s Unterputzschalter m
flush' tank' s Spülkasten m
flush' toi'let s Spülklosett n
fluster [ˈflʌstər] s Verwirrung f || tr verwirren
flute [flut] s (archit) Kannelüre f; (mus) Flöte f || tr riffeln
flut'ing s (archit) Kannelierung f
flutist [ˈflutɪst] s Flötist –in mf
flutter [ˈflʌtər] s (excitement) Aufregung f || tr—f. one's eyelashes mit den Wimpern klimpern || intr flattern

flux [flʌks] s (*flow*) Fließen n, Fluß m; (*for fusing metals*) Schmelzmittel n; **in f.** im Fluß

fly [flai] s Fliege f; (*of trousers*) Schlitz m; (*angl*) künstliche Fliege f; **flies** (theat) Soffitten pl; **fly in the ointment** Haar n in der Suppe ‖ v (*pret* **flew** [flu]; *pp* **flown** [flon]) *tr* fliegen ‖ *intr* fliegen; (*rush*) stürzen; (*said of rumors*) schwirren; (*said of time*) verfliegen; (*e.g., the globe*) umherfliegen; **fly around** umherfliegen; **fly at s.o.** auf j-n losgehen; **fly away** abfliegen; **fly in all directions** nach allen Seiten zerstieben; **fly low** tief fliegen; **fly off the handle** (fig) aus der Haut fahren; **fly open** aufspringen; **fly over** überfliegen; **fly past** vorbeifliegen (an *dat*); **let fly** (*e.g., an arrow*) schnellen

fly' ball' s (baseball) Flugball m
fly'-by-night' adj unverläßlich ‖ s (coll) Schwindelunternehmen n
fly' cast'ing s Fischen n mit der Wurfangel
flyer ['flai·ər] s var of **flier**
fly'-fish' *intr* mit künstlichen Fliegen angeln
fly'ing adj fliegend; (*boat, field, time*) Flug–; (*suit, club, school*) Flieger– ‖ s Fliegen n
fly'ing but'tress s Strebebogen m
fly'ing col'ors spl—**come through with f.** e-n glänzenden Sieg erringen
fly'ing sau'cer s fliegende Untertasse f
fly'leaf' s (**–leaves'**) Vorsatzblatt n
fly'pa'per s Fliegenfänger m
fly' rod' s Angelrute f
fly'speck' s Fliegendreck m
fly' swat'ter [ˌswatər] s Fliegenklappe f
fly'trap' s Fliegenfalle f
fly'wheel' s Schwungrad n
foal [fol] s Fohlen n ‖ *intr* fohlen
foam [fom] s Schaum m; (*of waves*) Gischt m; (*from the mouth*) Geifer m ‖ *intr* schäumen; (*said of waves*) branden
foam' rub'ber s Schaumgummi m
foamy ['fomi] adj (*full of foam*) schaumig; (*beer*) schäumend; (*foamlike*) schaumartig
F.O.B., f.o.b. [ˌɛfˌoˈbi] adv (free on board) frei an Bord
focal ['fokəl] adj fokal; **be the f. point** im Brennpunkt stehen; **f. point** (fig & opt) Brennpunkt m
fo·cus ['fokəs] s (**–cuses** & **–ci** [sai]) (math, opt) Brennpunkt m; (pathol) Herd m; **bring into f.** richtig (or scharf) einstellen; **in f.** scharf eingestellt; **out of f.** unscharf ‖ v (*pret & pp* **–cus[s]ed;** *ger* **–cus[s]ing**) *tr* (*a camera*) einstellen; (*attention, etc.*) (**on**) richten (auf *acc*) ‖ *intr* sich scharf einstellen
fo'cusing s Scharfeinstellung f
fodder ['fadər] s Futter n
foe [fo] s Feind –m
fog [fag] s Nebel m; (fig) Verwirrung f; (phot) Grauschleier m ‖ v (*pret & pp* **fogged;** *ger* **fogging**) *tr* vernebeln; (fig) umnebeln ‖ *intr* (phot) verschleiern; **fog up** beschlagen

fog' bank' s Nebelbank f
fog' bell' s Nebelglocke f
fog'-bound' adj durch Nebel festgehalten
fogey ['fogi] s Kauz m
foggy ['fagi] adj neblig, nebelhaft; (phot) verschleiert; **he hasn't the foggiest idea** er hat nicht die leiseste Ahnung
fog'horn' s Nebelhorn n
fog' light' s (aut) Nebelscheinwerfer m
foible ['foibəl] s Schwäche f
foil [foil] s (*of metal*) Folie f; (*of a mirror*) Spiegelbelag m; (fig) (**to**) Hintergrund m (für); (fencing) Florett n ‖ *tr* (*a plan*) durchkreuzen; (*an attempt*) vereiteln
foist [foist] *tr*—**f. s.th. on s.o.** j-m etw anhängen
fold [fold] s Falte f; (*in stiff material*) Falz m; (*for sheep*) Pferch m; (*flock of sheep*) Schafherde f; (relig) Herde f ‖ *tr* falten; (*stiff material*) falzen; (*e.g., a chair*) zusammenklappen; (*the arms*) kreuzen; (*the wash*) zusammenlegen ‖ *intr* sich (zusammen) falten; (*brochure*) Prospekt m
folder ['folder] s (*loose-leaf binder*) Schnellhefter m; (*manila folder*) Mappe f; (*brochure*) Prospekt m
fold'ing adj (*bed, chair, camera, wing*) Klapp–
fold'ing door' s Falttür f
fold'ing screen' s spanische Wand f
foliage ['foli·idʒ] s Laubwerk n, Laub n
foli·o ['foliˌo] adj Folio–, in Folio ‖ s (**–os**) (*page*) Folioblatt n; (*book*) Foliant m ‖ *tr* paginieren
folk [fok] adj Volks– ‖ **folks** spl (*people*) Leute pl; (*family*) Angehörige pl
folk' dance' s Volkstanz m
folk'lore' s Volkskunde f
folk' mu'sic s Volksmusik f
folk' song' s Volkslied n
folksy ['foksi] adj (*person*) leutselig; (*speech, expression*) volkstümlich
folk' tale' s Volkssage f
folk'ways' spl volkstümliche Lebensweise f
follicle ['falikəl] s Follikel m
follow ['falo] *tr* folgen (dat); (*instructions*) befolgen; (*a goal, events, news*) verfolgen; (*in office*) folgen auf (acc); (*a profession*) ausüben; (*understand*) folgen können (dat); **f. one another** aufeinanderfolgen; (*said of events*) sich überstürzen; **f. up** nachgehen (dat); **f. your nose!** immer der Nase nach! ‖ *intr* (nach)folgen; **as follows** folgendermaßen; **f. after** nachfolgen (dat); **f. through** (sport) ganz durchziehen; **f. upon** folgen auf (acc); **it follows that** daraus folgt, daß
follower ['falo·ər] s Anhänger –in mf
fol'lowing adj nachstehend, folgend ‖ s Gefolgschaft f
fol'low-up' adj Nach– ‖ s weitere Verfolgung f

folly ['fɑli] s Torheit f; **follies** (theat) Revue f
foment [fo'ment] tr schüren, anstiften
fond [fɑnd] adj (hope, wish) sehnlich; **become f. of** lieb gewinnen; **be f. of** gern haben; **be f. of reading** gern lesen
fondle ['fɑndəl] tr liebkosen
fondness ['fɑndnɪs] s Verliebtheit f; (for) Hang m (zu), Vorliebe f (für)
font [fɑnt] s (for holy water) Weihwasserbecken n; (for baptism) Taufbecken n; (typ) Schriftart f
food [fud] adj Nähr-, Speise- ‖ s (on the table) Essen n; (in a store) Lebensmittel pl; (requirement for life) Nahrung f; (for animals) Futter n; (for plants) Nährstoff m; **f. and drink** Speis' und Trank; **f. for thought** Stoff m zum Nachdenken
food′ poi′soning s Nahrungsmittelvergiftung f
food′stuffs′ spl Nahrungsmittel pl
food′ val′ue s Nährwert m
fool [ful] s Narr m; **born f.** Mondkalb n; **make a f. of oneself** sich blamieren ‖ tr täuschen, anführen ‖ intr— **f. around** herumtrödeln; **f. around with** herumspielen mit; (romantically) sich herumtreiben mit
fool′har′dy adj tollkühn
fool′ing s Späße pl; **f. around** Firlefanz m; **no f.!** na, so was!
foolish ['fulɪʃ] adj töricht, albern
foolishness ['fulɪʃnɪs] s Torheit f
fool′-proof′ adj narrensicher
fools′cap′ s Narrenkappe f; (paper size) Kanzleipapier n
foot [fut] s (feet [fit]) Fuß m; **be (back) on one's feet** (wieder) auf den Beinen sein; **f. of the bed** Fußende n des Bettes; **on f.** zu Fuß; **put one's best f. forward** sich ins rechte Licht setzen; **put one's f. down** (fig) ein Machtwort sprechen; **put one's f. in it** (coll) ins Fettnäpfchen treten; **stand on one's own two feet** auf eigenen Füßen stehen ‖ tr—**f. the bill** blechen
footage ['fʊtɪdʒ] s Ausmaß n in Fuß
foot′-and-mouth′ disease′ s Maul- und Klauenseuche f
foot′ball′ s Fußball m
foot′board′ s (in a car) Trittbrett n; (of a bed) Fußbrett n
foot′bridge′ s Steg m
foot′fall′ s Schritt m
foot′hills′ spl Vorgebirge n
foot′hold′ s (& fig) Halt m; **gain a f.** festen Fuß fassen
foot′ing s Halt m; **lose one's f.** ausgleiten; **on an equal f. with** auf gleichem Fuße mit
foot′lights′ spl Rampenlicht n
foot′man s (-men) Lakai m
foot′note′ s Fußnote f
foot′path′ s Fußpfad m, Fußsteig m
foot′print′ s Fußstapfe f
foot′ race′ s Wettlauf m
foot′rest′ s Fußraste f
foot′ rule′ s Zollstock m
foot′ sol′dier s Infanterist m
foot′sore′ adj fußkrank

foot′step′ s Tritt m; **follow in s.o.'s footsteps** in j-s Fußstapfen treten
foot′stool′ s Schemel m
foot′wear′ s Schuhwerk n
foot′work′ s (sl) Lauferei f; (sport) Beinarbeit f
foot′worn′ adj abgetreten
fop [fɑp] s Geck m
for [fɔr] prep für; (a destination) nach (dat); (with an English present perfect tense) schon (acc), e.g., **I have been living here for a month** ich wohne hier schone e-n Monat (or seit e-m Monat; (with an English future tense) für or auf (acc); **for good** für immer; **for joy** vor Freude; **for years** jahrelang ‖ conj denn
forage ['fɔrɪdʒ] s Furage f ‖ intr furagieren
foray ['fɔre] s (raid) Raubzug m; (e.g., into politics) Streifzug m ‖ intr plündern
for·bear [fɔr'bɛr] v (pret –bore ['bor]; pp –borne ['born]) tr unterlassen ‖ intr ablassen
forbearance [fɔr'bɛrəns] s (patience) Geduld f; (leniency) Nachsicht f
for·bid [fɔr'bɪd] v (pret –bade ['bæd] & –bad ['bæd]; pp –bidden ['bɪdən]) tr verbieten
forbid′ding adj abschreckend; (dangerous) gefährlich
force [fɔrs] s (strength) Kraft f; (compulsion) Gewalt f; (phys) Kraft f; **be in f.** in Kraft sein; **by f.** gewaltsam; **come into f.** in Kraft treten; **forces** (mil) Streitkräfte pl; **have the f. of** gelten als; **resort to f.** zu Zwangsmaßnahmen greifen; **with full f.** mit voller Wucht ‖ tr zwingen; (plants) treiben; (a door) aufsprengen; (e.g., an issue) forcieren; (into) zwängen (in acc); **f. down** hinunterdrücken; (aer) zur Landung zwingen; **f. one's way** sich drängen; **f. s.th. on s.o.** j-m etw aufdrängen
forced′ land′ing s Notlandung f
forced′ march′ s Gewaltmarsch m
forceful ['fɔrsfəl] adj eindrucksvoll
for·ceps ['fɔrseps] s (-ceps & -cipes [sɪ‚piz]) (dent, surg, zool) Zange f
forcible ['fɔrsɪbəl] adj (strong) kräftig; (violent) gewaltsam
ford [fɔrd] s Furt f ‖ tr durchwaten
fore [fɔr] adj Vorder- ‖ adv (naut) vorn ‖ s—**come to the f.** hervortreten ‖ interj (golf) Achtung!
fore′ and aft′ adv längsschiffs
fore′arm′ s Vorderarm m, Unterarm m
fore′bears′ spl Vorfahren pl
forebode [fɔr'bod] tr vorbedeuten
forebod′ing s (omen) Vorzeichen n; (presentiment) Vorahnung f
fore′cast′ s Voraussage f ‖ v (pret & pp –cast & –casted) tr voraussagen
forecastle ['fɔksəl] s Back f
foreclose tr (a mortgage) für verfallen erklären; (shut out) ausschließen
foredoom′ tr im voraus verurteilen
fore′fa′thers spl Vorfahren pl
fore′fin′ger s Zeigefinger m
fore′front′ s Spitze f
fore′go′ing adj vorhergehend

fore'gone' conclu'sion *s* ausgemachte Sache *f*
fore'ground' *s* Vordergrund *m*
forehead ['fɔrɪd] *s* Stirn(e) *f*
foreign ['fɔrɪn] *adj* (e.g., aid, product) Auslands–; (e.g., body, language, word, worker) Fremd–; (e.g., minister, office, policy, trade) Außen–; (e.g., affairs, service) auswärtig
foreigner ['fɔrɪnər] *s* Ausländer –in *mf*
for'eign exchange' *s* Devisen *pl*
fore'leg' *s* Vorderbein *n*
fore'lock' *s* Stirnlocke *f*
fore'man *s* (–men) Vorarbeiter *m;* (jur) Obmann *m;* (min) Steiger *m*
foremast ['fɔr,mæst] *s* Fockmast *m*
fore'most' *adj* vorderste ‖ *adv* zuerst
fore'noon' *s* Vormittag *m*
fore'part' *s* vorderster Teil *m*
fore'paw' *s* Vorderpfote *f*
fore'quart'er *s* Vorderviertel *n*
fore'run'ner *s* Vorbote *m*
fore'sail' *s* Focksegel *n*
fore·see' *v* (pret –saw'; pp –seen') *tr* voraussehen
foreseeable [for'si·əbəl] *adj* absehbar
foreshad'ow *tr* ahnen lassen
foreshort'en *tr* verkürzen
fore'sight' *s* Voraussicht *f*
fore'sight'ed *adj* umsichtig
fore'skin' *s* Vorhaut *f*
forest ['fɔrɪst] *s* Wald *m*, Forst *m*
forestall' *tr* zuvorkommen (dat)
for'est fire' *s* Waldbrand *m*
for'est rang'er *s* Forstbeamte *m*
forestry ['fɔrɪstri] *s* Forstwirtschaft *f*
fore'taste' *s* Vorgeschmack *m*
fore·tell' *v* (pret & pp –told') *tr* vorhersagen, weissagen
fore'thought' *s* Vorsorge *f*, Vorbedacht *m*
forev'er *adv* ewig, für immer; **f. and ever** auf immer und ewig
forewarn' *tr* (of) vorher warnen (vor dat)
fore'word' *s* Vorwort *n*
forfeit ['fɔrfɪt] *s* Einbuße *f* ‖ *tr* einbüßen, verwirken
forfeiture ['fɔrfɪtʃər] *s* Verwirkung *f*
forgather [for'gæðər] *intr* sich treffen
forge [fɔrdʒ] *s* Schmiede *f* ‖ *tr* schmieden; (documents) fälschen ‖ *intr*— **forge ahead** vordringen
forger ['fɔrdʒər] *s* Fälscher –in *mf*
forgery ['fɔrdʒəri] *s* Fälschung *f;* (coin) Falschgeld *n*
for·get [fər'gɛt] *v* (pret –got; pp –got & –gotten; ger –getting) *tr* vergessen; **f. it!** spielt keine Rolle!; **f. oneself** sich vergessen
forgetful [fər'gɛtfəl] *adj* vergeßlich
forgetfulness [fər'gɛtfəlnɪs] *s* Vergeßlichkeit *f*
forget'-me-not' *s* Vergißmeinnicht *n*
forgivable [fər'gɪvəbəl] *adj* verzeihlich
for·give [fər'gɪv] *v* (pret –gave; pp –given) *tr* (a person) vergeben (dat); (a thing) vergeben
forgiveness [fər'gɪvnɪs] *s* Vergebung *f*
forgiv'ing *adj* versöhnlich
for·go [fər'go] *v* (pret –went; pp –gone) *tr* verzichten auf (acc)

fork [fɔrk] *s* Gabel *f;* (in the road) Gabelung *f;* (of a tree) Astgabelung *f* ‖ *tr* gabeln; **f. over** (coll) übergeben
forked *adj* gabelförmig; (tongue) gespalten
fork'lift truck' *s* Gabelstapler *m*
forlorn [fɔr'lɔrn] *adj* (forsaken) verlassen; (wretched) elend; (attempt) verzweifelt
forlorn' hope' *s* aussichtsloses Unternehmen *n*
form [fɔrm] *s* Form *f*, Gestalt *f;* (paper to be filled out) Formular *n* ‖ *tr* formen, bilden; (a plan) fassen; (a circle, alliance) schließen; (suspicions) schöpfen; (a habit) annehmen; (blisters) werfen ‖ *intr* sich bilden
formal ['fɔrməl] *adj* formell, förmlich
for'mal call' *s* Höflichkeitsbesuch *m*
for'mal educa'tion *s* Schulbildung *f*
formality [fɔr'mælɪti] *s* Formalität *f;* **without f.** ohne Umstände
format ['fɔrmæt] *s* Format *n*
formation [fɔr'meʃən] *s* Bildung *f;* (aer) Verband *m;* (geol, mil) Formation *f*
former ['fɔrmər] *adj* ehemalig, früher; **the f.** jener
formerly ['fɔrmərli] *adv* ehemals, früher
form'-fit'ting *adj*—**be f.** e–e gute Paßform haben
formidable ['fɔrmɪdəbəl] *adj* (huge) gewaltig; (dreadful) schrecklich
formless ['fɔrmlɪs] *adj* formlos
form' let'ter *s* Rundbrief *m*
formu·la ['fɔrmjələ] *s* (–las & –lae [,li]) Formel *f;* (baby food) Kindermilch *f*
formulate ['fɔrmjə,let] *tr* formulieren
formulation [,fɔrmjə'leʃən] *s* Formulierung *f*
fornicate ['fɔrnɪ,ket] *intr* Unzucht treiben
fornication [,fɔrnɪ'keʃən] *s* Unzucht *f*
for·sake [fɔr'sek] *v* (pret –sook ['sʊk]; pp –saken ['sekən]) *tr* verlassen
fort [fɔrt] *s* Burg *f;* (mil) Fort *n*
forte ['fɔrt] *s* Stärke *f*
forth [fɔrθ] *adv* hervor; **and so f.** und so fort; **from that day f.** von dem Tag an
forth'com'ing *adj* bevorstehend
forth'right' *adj* ehrlich, offen
forth'with' *adv* sofort
fortieth ['fɔrtɪ·ɪθ] *adj* & *pron* vierzigste ‖ *s* (fraction) Vierzigstel *n;* (in a series) Vierzigste *mfn*
fortification [,fɔrtɪfɪ'keʃən] *s* Befestigung *f*
forti·fy ['fɔrtɪ,faɪ] *v* (pret & pp –fied) *tr* (a place) befestigen; (e.g., with liquor) kräftigen; (encourage) ermutigen
fortitude ['fɔrtɪ,t(j)ud] *s* Seelenstärke *f*
fortnight ['fɔrtnaɪt] *s* vierzehn Tage *pl*
fortress ['fɔrtrɪs] *s* Festung *f*
fortuitous [fɔr't(j)u·ɪtəs] *adj* zufällig
fortunate ['fɔrt/ənɪt] *adj* glücklich
fortunately ['fɔrt/ənɪtli] *adv* glücklicherweise

fortune ['fɔrtʃən] s Glück n; (money) Vermögen n; **make a f.** sich [dat] ein Vermögen erwerben; **have one's f. told** sich [dat] wahrsagen lassen; **tell fortunes** wahrsagen

for'tune hunt'er s Mitgiftjäger –in mf

for'tunetell'er s Wahrsagerin f

forty ['fɔrtɪ] adj & pron vierzig || s Vierzig f; **the forties** die vierziger Jahre

fo·rum ['fɔrəm] s (–rums & –ra [rə]) (& fig) Forum n

forward ['fɔrwərd] adj vordere, Vorwärts–; (person) keck; (mil) vorgeschoben || adv vorwärts, nach vorn; **bring f.** (an idea) vorschlagen; (a proposal) vorbringen; **come f.** sich melden; **look f. to** sich freuen auf (acc); **put f.** vorlegen || s (fb) Stürmer m || tr befördern; **please f.** bitte nachsenden || interj—**f., march!** im Gleichschritt, marsch!

fossil ['fɑsɪl] adj versteinert || s Fossil n

foster ['fɔstər] adj (child, father, mother, home) Pflege–; (brother, sister) Milch– || tr pflegen

foul [faul] adj übel; (in smell) übelriechend; (air, weather) schlecht; (language) unflätig; (means) unfair || s (sport) Foul n || tr (make dirty) besudeln; (the lines) verwickeln; (sport) foulen; **f. up** durcheinanderbringen || intr (sport) foulen

foul' line' s (baseball) Grenzlinie f; (basketball) Freiwurflinie f

foul-mouthed ['faul‚mauðd], ['faul‚mauθt] adj zotige Reden führend

foul' play' s unfaires Spiel n; (crime) Verbrechen n, Mord m

found [faund] tr gründen; (cast) gießen

foundation [faun'deʃən] s (act) Gründung f; (of a structure) Fundament n; (fund) Stiftung f; (fig) Grundlage f; **lay the foundation of** (& fig) den Grund legen zu

founda'tion gar'ments spl Miederwaren pl

founda'tion wall' s Grundmauer f

founder ['faundər] s Gründer –in mf; (metal) Gießer –in mf || intr (said of a ship) sinken; (fail) scheitern

foundling ['faundlɪŋ] s Findling m

foundry ['faundrɪ] s Gießerei f

found'ry·man s (–men) Gießer m

fount [faunt] s Quelle f

fountain ['fauntən] s Springbrunnen m

foun'tainhead' s Urquell m

foun'tain pen' s Füller m

four [fɔr] adj & pron vier || s Vier f; **on all fours** auf allen vieren

four'-cy'cle adj (mach) Viertakt–

four'-en'gine adj viermotorig

fourflusher ['fɔr‚flʌʃər] s Angeber m

four'foot'ed adj vierfüßig

four' hun'dred adj & pron vierhundert || spl—**the Four Hundred** die oberen Zehntausend

four'lane' adj Vierbahn–

four'-leaf' adj vierblätterig

four'-leg'ged adj vierbeinig

four'-letter word' s unanständiges Wort n

foursome ['fɔrsəm] s Viererspiel n; (group of four) Quartet n

fourteenth [fɔr'tinθ] adj & pron vierzehnte || s (fraction) Vierzehntel n; **the f.** (in dates and in a series) der Vierzehnte

fourth [fɔrθ] adj & pron vierte || s (fraction) Viertel n; **the f.** (in dates and in a series) der Vierte

fourth' estate' s Presse f

fowl [faul] s Huhn n, Geflügel n

fox [fɑks] s (& fig) Fuchs m

fox'glove' s (bot) Fingerhut m

fox'hole' s (mil) Schützenloch n

fox' hound' s Hetzhund m

fox' hunt' s Fuchsjagd f

fox' ter'rier s Foxterrier m

fox' trot' s Foxtrott m

foyer ['fɔɪ·ər] s (of a theater) Foyer n; (of a house) Diele f

fracas ['frekəs] s Aufruhr m

fraction ['frækʃən] s Bruchteil m; **fractions** Bruchrechnung f

fractional ['frækʃənəl] adj Bruch–

fracture ['fræktʃər] s Bruch m || tr sich [dat] brechen

fragile ['frædʒɪl] adj zerbrechlich

fragment ['frægmənt] s Bruchstück n; (of writing) Fragment n

fragmentary ['frægmən‚terɪ] adj bruchstückhaft; (writing) fragmentarisch

fragmenta'tion bomb' [‚frægmən'teʃən] s Splitterbombe f

fragrance ['fregrəns] s Duft m

fragrant ['fregrənt] adj duftend; **be f.** duften

frail [frel] adj schwach, hinfällig; (fragile) zerbrechlich

frailty ['freltɪ] s Schwachheit f

frame [frem] s (e.g., of a picture, door) Rahmen m; (of glasses) Fassung f; (of a house) Balkenwerk n; (structure) Gestell n; (anat) Körperbau m; (cin, telv) Bild n; (naut) Spant n || tr (a picture) einrahmen; (a plan) ersinnen; (sl) reinhängen

frame' house' s Holzhaus n

frame' of mind' s Gemütsverfassung f

frame' of ref'erence s Bezugspunkte pl

frame'-up' s abgekartete Sache f

frame'work' s Gebälk n, Fachwerk n; (fig) Rahmen m; (aer) Aufbau m

franc [fræŋk] s Franc m; (Swiss) Franken m

France [fræns] s Frankreich n

Frances ['frænsɪs] s Franziska f

franchise ['fræntʃaɪz] s Konzession f; (right to vote) Wahlrecht n

Francis ['frænsɪs] s Franz m

Franciscan [fræn'sɪskən] adj Franziskaner– || s Franziskaner m

frank [fræŋk] adj offen || s Freivermerk m; **Frank** (masculine name) Franz m; (medieval German person) Franke m, Frankin f || tr franieren

frankfurter ['fræŋkfərtər] s Würstel n

frankincense ['fræŋkɪn‚sens] s Weihrauch m

Frankish ['fræŋkɪʃ] adj fränkisch

frankness ['fræŋknɪs] s Offenheit f; (bluntness) Freimut m

frantic ['fræntɪk] adj (with) außer sich (vor dat); (efforts) krampfhaft

fraternal [frə'tʌrnəl] *adj* brüderlich; (*twins*) zweieiig

fraternity [frə'tʌrnɪti] *s* Bruderschaft *f*; (*educ*) Studentenverbindung *f*

fraternize ['frætər ,naɪz] *intr* (**with**) sich anfreunden (mit)

fraud [frɔd] *s* Betrug *m*; (*person*) (coll) Betrüger –in *mf*

fraudulent ['frɔdjələnt] *adj* betrügerisch

fraught [frɔt] *adj*—**f. with** voll mit; **f. with danger** gefahrvoll

fray [fre] *s* Schlägerei *f*; (*battle*) Kampf *m* || *tr* ausfranzen; (*the nerves*) aufreiben || *intr* (*said of edges*) sich ausfranzen; (*become threadbare*) sich durchscheuern

freak [frik] *s* Mißbildung *f*; (*whimsy*) Laune *f*; (*enthusiast*) Enthusiast –in *mf*; (*abnormal person*) verrückter Kerl *m*; **f. of nature** Monstrum *n*

freakish ['frikɪʃ] *adj* grotesk; (*capricious*) launisch

freckle ['frɛkəl] *s* Sommersprosse *f*

freckled ['frɛkəld], **freckly** ['frɛkli] *adj* sommersprossig

Frederick ['frɛdərɪk] *s* Friedrich *m*

free [fri] *adj* (**freer** ['fri·ər]; **freest** ['fri·ɪst]) frei; (*off duty*) dienstfrei; **for f.** (coll) gratis; **f. with** (*e.g., money, praise*) freigebig mit; **go f.** frei ausgehen; **he is f. to** (*inf*) es steht ihm frei zu (*inf*); **set f.** freilassen || *adv* umsonst, kostenlos || *v* (*pret & pp* **freed** [frid]; *ger* **freeing** ['fri·ɪŋ]) *tr* (*liberate*) befreien; (*untie*) losmachen

free' and ea'sy *adj* zwanglos

freebooter ['fri ,butər] *s* Freibeuter *m*

free'born' *adj* freigeboren

freedom ['fridəm] *s* Freiheit *f*

free'dom of assem'bly *s* Versammlungsfreiheit *f*

free'dom of speech' *s* Redefreiheit *f*

free'dom of the press' *s* Pressefreiheit *f*

free'dom of wor'ship *s* Glaubensfreiheit *f*

free' en'terprise *s* freie Wirtschaft *f*

free'-for-all' *s* allgemeine Prügelei *f*

free' hand' *s* freie Hand *f*

free'-hand draw'ing *s* (*activity*) Freihandzeichnen *n*; (*product*) Freihandzeichnung *f*

free'hand'ed *adj* freigebig

free'hold' *s* (jur) Freigut *n*

free' kick' *s* (fb) Freistoß *m*

free'-lance' *adj* freiberuflich || *intr* freiberuflich tätig sein

free-lancer ['fri ,lænsər] *s* Freiberufliche *mf*

free' li'brary *s* Volksbibliothek *f*

free'man *s* (**-men**) Ehrenbürger *m*

Free'ma'son *s* Freimaurer *m*

Free'ma'sonry *s* Freimaurerei *f*

free' of charge' *adj & adv* kostenlos

free' on board' *adv* frei an Bord

free' play' *s* (fig & mach) Spielraum *m*

free' port' *s* Freihafen *m*

free' sam'ple *s* (of food) Gratiskostprobe *f*; (of products) Gratismuster *n*

free' speech' *s* Redefreiheit *f*

free'-spo'ken *adj* freimütig

free'stone' *adj* mit leicht auslösbarem Kern

free'think'er *s* Freigeist *m*

free' thought' *s* Freigeisterei *f*

free' trade' *s* Freihandel *m*

free'way' *s* Autobahn *f*

free' will' *s* Willensfreiheit *f*; **of one's own f.** aus freien Stücken

freeze [friz] *s* Frieren *n* || *v* (*pret* **froze** [froz]; *pp* **frozen** ['frozən]) *tr* frieren; (*assets*) einfrieren; (*prices*) stoppen; (*food*) tiefkühlen; (surg) vereisen || *intr* (ge)frieren; (*e.g., with fear*) erstarren; **f. over** zufrieren; **f. to death** erfrieren; **f. up** vereisen

freeze'-dry' *v* (*pret & pp* **-dried**) *tr* gefriertrocknen

freezer ['frizər] *s* (*chest*) Tiefkühltruhe *f*; (*cabinet*) Tiefkühlschrank *m*

freez'er compart'ment *s* Gefrierfach *n*

freez'ing *s* Einfrieren *n*; **below f.** unter dem Gefrierpunkt

freight [fret] *s* (*load*) Fracht *f*; (*cargo*) Frachtgut *n*; (*fee*) Frachtgebühr *f*; **by f.** als Frachtgut || *tr* beladen

freight' car' *s* Güterwagen *m*

freight' el'evator *s* Warenaufzug *m*

freighter ['fretər] *s* Frachter *m*

freight' of'fice *s* Güterabfertigung *f*

freight' train' *s* Güterzug *m*

freight' yard' *s* Güterbahnhof *m*

French [frɛntʃ] *adj* französisch || *s* (*language*) Französisch *n*; **the F.** die Franzosen

French' doors' *spl* Glastüre *pl*

French' fries' *spl* Pommes frites *pl*

French' horn' *s* (mus) Waldhorn *n*

French' leave' *s*—**take F.** sich französisch empfehlen

French'man *s* (**-men**) Franzose *m*

French' roll' *s* Schrippe *f*

French' toast' *s* arme Ritter *pl*

French' win'dow *s* Flügelfenster *n*

French' wom'an *s* (**-wom'en**) Französin *f*

frenzied ['frɛnzid] *adj* rasend

frenzy ['frɛnzi] *s* Raserei *f*

frequency ['frikwənsi] *s* Häufigkeit *f*; (phys) Frequenz *f*

fre'quency modula'tion *s* Frequenzmodulation *f*

frequent ['frikwənt] *adj* häufig || [fri'kwɛnt] *tr* besuchen, frequentieren

frequently ['frikwəntli] *adv* häufig

fres·co ['frɛsko] *s* (**-coes & -cos**) Fresko *n*, Freskogemälde *n*

fresh [frɛʃ] *adj* frisch; (coll) frech || *adv* neu, kürzlich

fresh'-baked' *adj* neugebacken

freshen ['frɛʃən] *tr* erfrischen; **f. up** auffrischen || *intr*—**f. up** sich auffrischen

freshet ['frɛʃɪt] *s* Hochwasser *n*; (*fresh-water stream*) Fluß *m*

fresh'man *s* (**-men**) Fuchs *m*

freshness ['frɛʃnɪs] *s* Frische *f*; (coll) Naseweisheit *f*

fresh' wa'ter *s* Süßwasser *n*

fresh'-wa'ter *adj* Süßwasser-

fret [frɛt] *s* Verdruß *m*; (carp) Laubsägewerk *n*; (mus) Bund *n* || *v* (*pret*

& *pp* **fretted;** *ger* **fretting**) *tr* gitterförmig verzieren || *intr* sich ärgern

fretful ['frɛtfəl] *adj* verdrießlich

fret'work' *s* Laubsägewerk *n*

Freudian ['frɔɪdɪ·ən] *adj* Freudsch || *s* Freudianer –in *mf*

friar ['fraɪ·ər] *s* Klosterbruder *m*

fricassee [,frɪkə'si] *s* Frikassee *n*

friction ['frɪk/ən] *s* Reibung *f*; (fig) Reiberei *f*, Mißhelligkeit *f*

fric'tion tape' *s* Isolierband *n*

Friday ['fraɪdi] *s* Freitag *m*

fried [fraɪd] *adj* gebraten, Brat–, Back–

fried' chick'en *s* Backhuhn *n*

fried' egg' *s* Spiegelei *n*

fried' pota'toes *spl* Bratkartoffeln *pl*

friend [frɛnd] *s* Freund –in *mf*; **be (close) friends** (eng) befreundet sein; **make friends (with)** sich anfreunden (mit)

friendliness ['frɛndlɪnɪs] *s* Freundlichkeit *f*

friendly ['frɛndli] *adj* freundlich; **on f. terms with** in freundschaftlichem Verhältnis mit

friend'ship' *s* Freundschaft *f*

frieze [friz] *s* Fries *m*

frigate ['frɪgɪt] *s* Fregatte *f*

fright [fraɪt] *s* Schrecken *m*

frighten ['fraɪtən] *tr* schrecken; **be frightened** erschrecken; **f. away** verscheuchen, vertreiben

frightful ['fraɪtfəl] *adj* schrecklich

frigid ['frɪdʒɪd] *adj* eiskalt; (pathol) Frigid

frigidity [frɪ'dʒɪdɪti] *s* Kälte *f*; (pathol) Frigidität *f*

Frig'id Zone' *s* kalte Zone *f*

frill [frɪl] *s* (ruffle) Volant *m*, Krause *f*; (frippery) Schnörkel *m*; **put on frills** sich aufgeblasen benehmen; **with all the frills** mit allen Schikanen

fringe [frɪndʒ] *s* Franse *f* || *tr* mit Fransen besetzen; (fig) einsäumen

fringe' ar'ea *s* Randgebiet *n*

fringe' ben'efit *s* zusätzliche Sozialleistung *f*

frippery ['frɪpəri] *s* (cheap finery, trifles) Flitterkram *m*

frisk [frɪsk] *tr* (sl) durchsuchen || *intr* —**f. about** herumtollen

frisky ['frɪski] *adj* ausgelassen

fritter ['frɪtər] *s* Beignet *m* || *tr*—**f. away** vertrödeln, verzetteln

fritz [frɪts] *s*—**on the f.** kaputt

frivolous ['frɪvələs] *adj* leichtfertig; (object) geringfügig

friz [frɪz] *s* (frizzes) Kraushaar *n* || *v* (pret & pp **frizzed;** ger **frizzing**) *tr* kräuseln || *intr* sich kräuseln

frizzle ['frɪzəl] *s* Kraushaar *n* || *tr* (hair) kräuseln; (food) knusprig braten || *intr* sich kräuseln; (sizzle) zischen

frizzy ['frɪzi] *adj* kraus

fro [fro] *adv*—**to and fro** hin und her

frock [frak] *s* Kleid *n*; (eccl) Mönchskutte *f*

frog [frag] *s* (animal; slight hoarseness) Frosch *m*

frog'man' *s* (–men') Froschmann *m*

frol·ic ['fralɪk] *s* Spaß *m* || *v* (pret &

pp –**icked;** ger –**icking**) *intr* Spaß machen; (frisk about) herumtollen

frolicsome ['fralɪksəm] *adj* ausgelassen

from [frʌm] *prep* von (dat), aus (dat), von (dat) aus; **f. afar** von weitem; **f. now on** künftig; **f. ... on** von ... an

front [frʌnt] *adj* Vorder–, vordere || *s* (façade) Vorderseite *f*; (of a shirt, dress) Einsatz *m*; (cover-up) Aushängeschild *n*; (meteor, mil) Front *f*; **from the f.** von vorn; **in f.** vorn; **in f. of** vor (dat or acc); **in the f. of the book** vorn im Buch; **put on a bold f.** Mut zeigen; **they put on a big f.** alles Fassade! || *tr* gegenüberliegen (dat) || *intr*—**f. for s.o.** j-m als Strohmann dienen; **f. on** mit der Front liegen nach

frontage ['frʌntɪdʒ] *s* Straßenfront *f*

frontal ['frʌntəl] *adj* Frontal–; (anat) Stirn–

fron'tal view' *s* Vorderansicht *f*

front'-door' *s* Haustür *f*

front' foot' *s* Vorderfuß *m*

frontier [frʌn'tɪr] *s* (border) Grenze *f*; (area) Grenzland *n*; (fig) Grenzbereich *m*

frontiers'man *s* (–men) Pionier *m*

frontispiece ['frʌntɪs,pis] *s* Titelbild *n*

front' line' *s* Front *f*, Frontlinie *f*

front'-line' *adj* Front–, Gefechts–

front' page' *s* Titelseite *f*

front' porch' *s* Veranda *f*

front' rank' *s* (mil) vorderes Glied *n*; **be in the f.** (fig) im Vordergrund stehen

front' row' *s* erste Reihe *f*

front' run'ner *s* (pol) Spitzenkandidat –in *mf*

front' seat' *s* Vordersitz *m*

front' steps' *spl* Vordertreppe *f*

front' yard' *s* Vorgarten *m*, Vorplatz *m*

frost [frɔst] *s* (freezing) Frost *m*; (frozen dew) Reif *m* || *tr* mit Reif überziehen; (culin) glasieren

frost'bite' *s* Erfrierung *f*

frost'bit'ten *adj* erfroren

frost'ed glass' *s* Mattglas *n*

frost'ing *s* Glasur *f*

frost' line' *s* Frostgrenze *f*

frosty ['frɔsti] *adj* (& fig) frostig

froth [frɔθ] *s* (foam) Schaum *m*; (slaver) Geifer *m* || *intr* schäumen; geifern

frothy ['frɔθi] *adj* schäumend

froward ['froward] *adj* eigensinnig

frown [fraun] *s* Stirnrunzeln *n* || *intr* die Stirn runzeln; **f. at** böse anschauen; **f. on** mißbilligen

frowsy, frowzy ['frauzi] *adj* (slovenly) schlampig; (ill-smelling) muffig

froz'en as'sets ['frozən] *spl* eingefrorene Guthaben *pl*

froz'en foods' *spl* tiefgekühlte Lebensmittel *pl*

frugal ['frugəl] *adj* frugal

fruit [frut] *s* (tree) Obst–, Südfrucht– || *s* Frucht *f*, Obst *n*, Südfrüchte *pl*; (fig) Frucht *f*

fruit' cake' *s* Stolle *f*, Stollen *m*

fruit′ cup′ s gemischte Früchte pl
fruit′ fly′ s Obstfliege f
fruitful [ˈfruːtfəl] adj fruchtbar
fruition [fruˈɪʃən] s Reife f; **come to f.** zur Reife gelangen
fruit′ jar′ s Konservenglas n
fruit′ juice′ s Fruchtsaft m, Obstsaft m
fruitless [ˈfruːtlɪs] adj (& fig) fruchtlos
fruit′ sal′ad s Obstsalat m
fruit′ stand′ s Obststand m
frump [frʌmp] s Scharteke f
frumpish [ˈfrʌmpɪʃ] adj schlampig
frustrate [ˈfrʌstret] tr (discourage) frustrieren; (an endeavor) vereiteln
frustration [frʌsˈtreʃən] s Frustration f; (of an endeavor) Vereitelung f
fry [fraɪ] s Gebratenes n || v (pret & pp fried) tr & intr braten
fry′ing pan′ s Bratpfanne f; **jump out of the f. into the fire** vom Regen unter die Traufe kommen
fuchsia [ˈfjuːə] s (bot) Fuchsie f
fudge [fʌdʒ] s weiches, milchhaltiges, mit Kakao versetztes Zuckerwerk n
fuel [ˈfjuːəl] s Brennstoff m; (for engines) Treibstoff m; (fig) Nahrung f; **add f. to the flames** Öl ins Feuer gießen || v (pret & pp fuel[l]ed) ger fuel[l]ing tr mit Brennstoff versorgen || intr tanken
fu′el dump′ s Treibstofflager n
fu′el gauge′ s Benzinuhr f
fu′el tank′ s Treibstoffbehälter m
fugitive [ˈfjudʒɪtɪv] adj flüchtig || s Flüchtling m
fugue [fjug] s (mus) Fuge f
ful·crum [ˈfʌlkrəm] s (-crums & -cra [krə]) Stützpunkt m, Drehpunkt m
fulfill [fʊlˈfɪl] tr erfüllen
fulfillment [fʊlˈfɪlmənt] s Erfüllung f
full [fʊl] adj voll; (with food) satt; (clothes) weit; (hour) ganz; (life) inhaltsreich; (voice) wohlklingend; (professor) ordentlich; **f. of** voller, voll von; **too f.** übervoll; **work f. time** ganztägig arbeiten || adv—**f. well** sehr gut || s—**in f.** voll, ganz || tr (tex) walken
full′back′ s (fb) Außenverteidiger m
full′-blood′ed adj vollblütig
full-blown [ˈfʊlˈblon] adj (flower) voll aufgeblüht; (fig) voll erblüht
full′-bod′ied adj (wine) stark, schwer
full′ dress′ s Gesellschaftsanzug m; (mil) Paradeanzug m
full′-dress′ adj Gala-, formell
full′-faced′ adj pausbackig; (portrait) mit voll zugewandtem Gesicht
full-fledged [ˈfʊlˈfledʒd] adj richtiggehend
full-grown [ˈfʊlˈɡron] adj voll ausgewachsen
full′ house′ s (cards) Full house n; (theat) volles Haus n
full′-length′ adj (dress) in voller Größe; (portrait) lebensgroß; (movie) abendfüllend
full′ moon′ s Vollmond m
full′-page′ adj ganzseitig
full′ pay′ s volles Gehalt n
full′ profes′sor s Ordinarius m
full′-scale′ adj in voller Größe
full′-sized′ adj in natürlicher Größe

full′ speed′ adv auf höchsten Touren
full′ stop′ s (gram) Punkt m; **come to a f.** völlig stillstehen
full′ swing′ s—**in f.** in vollem Gange
full′ throt′tle s Vollgas n
full′ tilt′ adv auf höchsten Touren
full′-time′ adj ganztägig
full′ view′ s—**in f.** direkt vor den Augen
fully [ˈfʊl(l)i] adj völlig; **be f. booked** ausverkauft sein
fulsome [ˈfʊlsəm] adj (excessive) übermäßig; (offensive) widerlich
fumble [ˈfʌmbəl] tr (a ball) fallen lassen || intr fummeln; **f. for** umherfühlen nach
fume [fjum] s Gas n, Dampf m || intr dampfen; (smoke) rauchen; **f. with rage** vor Wut schnauben
fumigate [ˈfjumɪˌɡet] tr ausräuchern
fun [fʌn] s Spaß m; **be (great) fun** (viel) Spaß machen; **for fun** zum Spaß; **for the fun of it** spaßeshalber; **have fun!** viel Spaß!; **make fun of** sich lustig machen über (acc); **poke fun at** witzeln über (acc)
function [ˈfʌŋkʃən] s Funktion f; (office) Amt n; (formal occasion) Feier f || intr funktionieren; (officiate) fungieren
functional [ˈfʌŋkʃənəl] adj (practical) Zweck-, zweckmäßig; (disorder) funktionell, Funktions-
functionary [ˈfʌŋkʃəˌneri] s Funktionär –in mf
fund [fʌnd] s Fonds m; (fig) Vorrat m; **funds** Geldmittel pl || tr fundieren
fundamental [ˌfʌndəˈmentəl] adj grundlegend, Grund– || s Grundbegriff m
fundamentalist [ˌfʌndəˈmentəlɪst] s Fundamentalist –in mf
fundamentally [ˌfʌndəˈmentəli] adv im Grunde, prinzipiell
funeral [ˈfjunərəl] adj Leichen–, Trauer–, Begräbnis– || s Begräbnis n
fu′neral direc′tor s Bestattungsunternehmer –in mf
fu′neral home′ s Aufbahrungshalle f
fu′neral proces′sion s Trauergefolge m
fu′neral serv′ice s Trauergottesdienst m
fu′neral wreath′ s Totenkranz m
funereal [fjuˈnɪrɪəl] adj düster
fungus [ˈfʌŋɡəs] s (funguses & fungi [ˈfʌndʒaɪ]) Pilz m, Schwamm m
funicular [fjuˈnɪkjələr] s Drahtseilbahn f
funk [fʌŋk] s (fear) Mordsangst f; **be in a f.** niedergeschlagen sein
fun·nel [ˈfʌnəl] s Trichter m; (naut) Schornstein m || v (pret & pp -nel[l]ed; ger -nel[l]ing) tr durch e–n Trichter gießen; (fig) (into) konzentrieren (auf acc)
funnies [ˈfʌniz] spl Witzseite f
funny [ˈfʌni] adj komisch; (strange, suspicious) sonderbar; **don't try anything f.** mach mir keine Dummheiten!
fun′ny bone′ s Musikantenknochen m
fun′ny bus′iness s dunkle Geschäfte pl
fun′ny ide′as spl Flausen pl

fun'ny pa'per s Witzblatt n
fur [fʌr] adj (coat, collar) Pelz– ‖ s Pelz m; (on the tongue) Belag m
furbish ['fɜrbɪʃ] tr aufputzen
furious ['fjurɪ-əs] adj (at) wütend (auf acc); **be f.** wüten
furl [fʌrl] tr zusammenrollen
fur'-lined' adj pelzgefüttert
furlong ['fʌrlɔŋ] s Achtelmeile f
furlough ['fʌrlo] s (mil) Urlaub m; **go on f.** auf Urlaub kommen ‖ tr beurlauben
furnace ['fʌrnɪs] s Ofen m
furnish ['fʌrnɪʃ] tr (a room) möblieren; (e.g., an office) ausstatten; (proof) liefern; (supply) (with) versehen (mit)
fur'nished room' s möbliertes Zimmer n
furnishings ['fʌrnɪʃɪŋz] spl Ausstattung f
furniture ['fʌrnɪtʃər] s Möbel pl; **piece of f.** Möbelstück n
fur'niture store' s Möbelhandlung f
furor ['fjurɔr] s (rage) Wut f; (uproar) Furore f; (vogue) Mode f; **cause a f.** Furore machen
furrier ['fʌrɪ-ər] s Pelzhändler –in mf
furrow ['fʌro] s Furche f ‖ tr furchen
furry ['fʌri] adj pelzig
further ['fʌrðər] adj weiter; (particulars) näher ‖ adv weiter ‖ tr fördern
furtherance ['fʌrðərəns] s Förderung f
fur'thermore' adv überdies, außerdem
furthest ['fʌrðɪst] adj weiteste ‖ adv am weitesten
furtive ['fʌrtɪv] adj verstohlen

fury ['fjuri] s Wut f; **Fury** (myth) Furie f
fuse [fjuz] s (of an explosive) Zünder m; (elec) Sicherung f; **blown f.** durchgebrannte Sicherung f ‖ tr verschmelzen ‖ intr verschmelzen; (fig) sich vereinigen
fuse' box' s Sicherungskasten m
fuselage ['fjuzəlɪdʒ] s (aer) Rumpf m
fusible ['fjuzɪbəl] adj schmelzbar
fusillade ['fjusə‚led] s Feuersalve f; (fig) Hagel m
fusion ['fjuʒən] s Verschmelzung f; (pol, phys) Fusion f
fuss [fʌs] s Getue n; **make a f. over** viel Aufhebens machen von ‖ intr sich aufregen; **f. around** herumwirtschaften; **f. over** viel Aufhebens machen von; **f. with** herumspielen mit
fuss' bud'get, fuss'pot' s Umstandskrämer m
fussy ['fʌsi] adj (given to detail) umständlich; (fastidious) heikel; (irritable) reizbar; **be f.** Umstände machen
fustian ['fʌstʃən] s (bombast) Schwulst m; (tex) Barchent m
fusty ['fʌsti] adj (musty) muffig; (old-fashioned) veraltet
futile ['fjutəl] adj vergeblich, nutzlos
futility [fju'tɪlɪti] s Nutzlosigkeit f
future ['fjutʃər] adj (zu)künftig ‖ s Zukunft f; **futures** (econ) Termingeschäfte pl; **in the f.** künftig
fuzz [fʌz] s (from cloth) Fussel f; (on peaches) Flaum m
fuzzy ['fʌzi] adj flaumig; (unclear) unklar; (hair) kraus

G

G, g [dʒi] s siebenter Buchstabe des englischen Alphabets
gab [gæb] s (coll) Geschwätz n ‖ v (pret & pp **gabbed;** ger **gabbing**) intr schwatzen
gabardine ['gæbər‚din] s Gabardine m
gabble ['gæbəl] s Geschnatter n ‖ intr schnattern
gable ['gebəl] s Giebel m
ga'ble end' s Giebelwand f
ga'ble roof' s Giebeldach n
gad [gæd] v (pret & pp **gadded;** ger **gadding**) intr—**gad about** umherstreifen
gad'about' s Bummler –in mf
gad'fly' s Viehbremse f; (fig) Störenfried m
gadget ['gædʒɪt] s (coll) Gerät n
Gaelic ['gelɪk] adj gälisch ‖ s (language) Gälisch n
gaff [gæf] s Fischhaken m
gag [gæg] s (something put into the mouth) Knebel m; (joke) Witz m; (hoax, trick) amüsanter Trick m ‖ v (pret & pp **gagged;** ger **gagging**) tr knebeln; (said of a tight collar) würgen; (fig) mundtot machen ‖ intr (on food) würgen

gage [gedʒ] s (challenge) Fehdehandschuh m; (pawn) Pfand m
gaiety ['ge-ɪti] s Fröhlichkeit f
gaily ['geli] adv fröhlich
gain [gen] s Gewinn m; (advantage) Vorteil m; **g. in weight** Gewichtszunahme f ‖ tr gewinnen; (pounds) zunehmen; (a living) verdienen; (a victory) erringen; **g. a footing** festen Fuß fassen; **g. ground** (mil & fig) Terrain gewinnen; **g. speed** schneller werden; **g. weight** an Gewicht zunehmen ‖ intr (said of a car) aufholen; (said of a clock) vorgehen; **g. from** Gewinn haben von; **g. in** gewinnen an (dat); **g. on s.o.** j–m den Vorteil abgewinnen
gainful ['genfəl] adj einträglich
gainfully ['genfəli] adv—**g. employed** erwerbstätig
gain'say' v (pret & pp –**said** [‚sed], [‚sed]) tr (a thing) verneinen; (a person) widersprechen (dat)
gait [get] s Gang m, Gangart f
gala ['gælə], ['gelə] adj festlich ‖ s (celebration) Feier f; (dress) Gala f
galaxy ['gæləksi] s Galaxis f; (fig) glänzende Versammlung f

gale [gel] *s* Sturm *m*, Sturmwind *m*; **gales of laughter** Lachensalven *pl*

gale′ warn′ing *s* Sturmwarnung *f*

gall [gol] *s* Galle *f*; (*audacity*) Unverschämtheit *f* ‖ *tr* (*rub*) wundreiben; (*vex*) ärgern, belästigen

gallant ['gælənt] *adj* (*tapfer*); (*stately*) stattlich ‖ [gə'lænt] *adj* galant ‖ *s* Galan *m*

gallantry ['gæləntri] *s* (*bravery*) Tapferkeit *f*; (*courteous behavior*) Ritterlichkeit *f*

gall′ blad′der *s* Gallenblase *f*

galleon ['gælɪ·ən] *s* Galeone *f*

gallery ['gæləri] *s* (*arcade*) Säulenhalle *f*; (*art, theat*) Galerie *f*; (*min*) Stollen *m*; **play to the g.** (coll) Effekthascherei treiben

galley ['gæli] *s* (*a ship*) Galeere *f*; (*a kitchen*) Kombüse *f*; (*typ*) Setzschiff *n*

gal′ley proof′ *s* (typ) Fahne *f*

gal′ley slave′ *s* Galeerensklave *m*

Gallic ['gælɪk] *adj* gallisch

gall′ing *adj* verdrießlich

gallivant ['gælɪˌvænt] *intr* bummeln

gallon ['gælən] *s* Gallone *f*

galloon [gə'lun] *s* Tresse *f*

gallop ['gæləp] *s* Galopp *m*; **at full g.** in gestrecktem Galopp ‖ *tr* in Galopp setzen ‖ *intr* galoppieren

gal·lows ['gæloz] *s* (–lows & –lowses) Galgen *m*

gal′lows bird′ *s* (coll) Galgenvogel *m*

gall′stone′ *s* Gallenstein *m*

galore [gə'lor] *adv* im Überfluß

galosh [gə'lɑʃ] *s* Galosche *f*

galvanize ['gælvəˌnaɪz] *tr* galvanisieren

gambit ['gæmbɪt] *s* (fig) Schachzug *m*; (chess) Gambit *n*

gamble ['gæmbəl] *s* Hasardspiel *n*; (*risk*) Risiko *n*; (com) Spekulationsgeschäft *n* ‖ *tr*—**g. away** verspielen ‖ *intr* spielen, hasardieren

gambler ['gæmblər] *s* Spieler –in *mf*; (fig) Hasardeur *m*, Hasardeuse *f*

gam′bling *s* Spielen *n*, Spiel *n*

gam′bling house′ *s* Spielhölle *f*

gam′bling ta′ble *s* Spieltisch *m*

gam·bol ['gæmbəl] *s* Luftsprung *m* ‖ *v* (*pret & pp* –bol[l]ed; *ger* –bol[l]ing) *intr* umhertollen

gambrel ['gæmbrəl] *s* (*hock*) Hachse *f*; (*in a butcher shop*) Spriegel *m*

gam′brel roof′ *s* Mansardendach *n*

game [gem] *adj* bereit; (*fight*) tapfer; (*leg*) lahm; (hunt) Wild–, Jagd– ‖ *s* Spiel *n*; (*e.g., of chess*) Partie *f*; (fig) Absicht *f*; (culin) Wildbret *n*; (hunt) Wild *n*, Jagdwild *n*; **have the g. in the bag** den Sieg in der Tasche haben; **play a losing g.** auf verlorenem Posten kämpfen; **the g. is up** das Spiel ist aus

game′ bird′ *s* Jagdvogel *m*

game′ board′ *s* Spielbrett *n*

game′cock′ *s* Kampfhahn *m*

gameness ['gemnɪs] *s* Tapferkeit *f*

game′ of chance′ *s* Glücksspiel *n*

game′ preserve′ *s* Wildpark *m*

game′ war′den *s* Jagdaufseher *m*

gamut ['gæmət] *s* Skala *f*

gamy ['gemi] *adj* nach Wild riechend; **g. flavor** Wildgeschmack *m*

gander ['gændər] *s* Gänserich *m*; **take a g. at** (coll) e–n Blick werfen auf (*acc*)

gang [gæŋ] *s* (*group of friends*) Gesellschaft *f*; (*antisocial group*) Bande *f*; (*of workers*) Kolonne *f* ‖ *intr*— **g. up (on)** sich zusammenrotten (gegen)

gangling ['gæŋglɪŋ] *adj* schlaksig

gangli·on ['gæŋglɪ·ən] *s* (–ons & –a [ə]) (*cystic tumor*) Überbein *n*; (*of nerves*) Nervenknoten *m*

gangly ['gæŋgli] *adj* schlaksig

gang′plank′ *s* Laufplanke *f*, Steg *m*

gangrene ['gæŋgrin] *s* Gangrän *n*, Brand *m* ‖ *intr* brandig werden

gangrenous ['gæŋgrɪnəs] *adj* brandig

gangster ['gæŋstər] *s* Gangster *m*

gang′way′ *s* (*passageway*) Durchgang *m*; (naut) Laufplanke *f* ‖ *interj* aus dem Weg!

gantlet ['gɔntlət] *s* (rr) Gleisverschlingung *f*

gantry ['gæntri] *s* (rok) Portalkran *m*; (rr) Signalbrücke *f*

gan′try crane′ *s* Portalkran *m*

gap [gæp] *s* Lücke *f*; (*in the mountains*) Schlucht *f*; (mil) Bresche *f*

gape [gep] *s* Riß *m*, Sprung *m*; (*gaping*) Gaffen *n* ‖ *intr* gaffen; (*said of wounds, etc.*) klaffen; **g. at** angaffen

garage [gə'rɑʒ] *s* Garage *f*; (*repair shop*) Reparaturwerkstatt *f*; **put into the g.** unterstellen

garb [garb] *s* Tracht *f*

garbage ['garbɪdʒ] *s* Müll *m*; (*nonsense*) Unsinn *m*

gar′bage can′ *s* Mülltonne *f*

gar′bage dispos′al *s* Müllabfuhr *f*

gar′bage dump′ *s* Müllplatz *m*

gar′bage man′ *s* Müllfahrer *m*

gar′bage truck′ *s* Müllabfuhrwagen *m*

garble ['garbəl] *tr* verstümmeln

garden ['gardən] *s* Garten *m*; **gardens** Gartenanlage *f*

gardener ['gardənər] *s* Gärtner –in *mf*

gar′den hose′ *s* Gartenschlauch *m*

gardenia [gar'dɪnɪ·ə] *s* Gardenie *f*

gar′dening *s* Gartenarbeit *f*

gar′den par′ty *s* Gartengesellschaft *f*

gargle ['gargəl] *s* Mundwasser *n* ‖ *tr & intr* gurgeln

gargoyle ['gargɔɪl] *s* Wasserspeier *m*

garish ['gerɪʃ], ['gærɪʃ] *adj* grell

garland ['garlənd] *s* Girlande *f*

garlic ['garlɪk] *s* Knoblauch *m*

garment ['garmənt] *s* Kleidungsstück *n*

garner ['garnər] *tr* (*grain*) aufspeichern; (*gather*) ansammeln

garnet ['garnɪt] *s* Granat *m*

garnish ['garnɪʃ] *s* Verzierung *f*; (culin) Garnierung *f* ‖ *tr* verzieren; (culin) garnieren

garret ['gærɪt] *s* Dachstube *f*

garrison ['gærɪsən] *s* (*troops*) Garnison *f*, Besatzung *f*; (*fort*) Festung *f* ‖ *tr* mit e–r Garnison versehen; (*troops*) in Garnison stationieren

gar′rison cap′ *s* Schiffchen *n*

garrote ['garo̱t], [gə'rot] *s* Garrotte *f* ‖ *tr* garrottieren

garrulous ['gær(j)ələs] *adj* schwatzhaft

garter ['gɑrtər] *s* Strumpfband *n*

gar'ter belt' *s* Strumpfhaltergürtel *m*

gas [gæs] *adj* (*e.g., generator, light, main, meter*) Gas– || *s* Gas *n;* (coll) Benzin *n*, Sprit *m;* (*empty talk*) (sl) leeres Geschwätz *n;* **get gas** (coll) tanken; **step on the gas** (coll) Gas geben || *v* (*pret & pp* **gassed; *ger* gassing**) *tr* vergasen || *intr* (sl) schwatzen; **gas up** (coll) volltanken

gas' attack' *s* Gasangriff *m*

gas' burn'er *s* Gasbrenner *m*

gas' en'gine *s* Gasmotor *m*

gaseous ['gæsɪ·əs], ['gæʃəs] *adj* gasförmig

gas' fit'ter *s* Gasinstallateur *m*

gash [gæʃ] *s* tiefe Schnittwunde *f* || e–e tiefe Schnittwunde beibringen (*dat*)

gas' heat' *s* Gasheizung *f*

gas'hold'er *s* Gasbehälter *m*

gasi•fy ['gæsɪˌfaɪ] *v* (*pret & pp* **–fied**) *tr* in Gas verwandeln || *intr* zu Gas werden

gas' jet' *s* Gasflamme *f*

gasket ['gæskɪt] *s* Dichtung *f*

gas' mask' *s* Gasmaske *f*

gasoline [ˌgæsə'lin] *s* Benzin *n*

gasoline' pump' *s* Benzinzapfsäule *f*

gasp [gæsp] *s* Keuchen *n* || *tr* (out) hervorstoßen || *intr* keuchen; **g. for air** nach Luft schnappen; **g. for breath** nach Atem ringen

gas' range' *s* Gasherd *m*

gas' sta'tion *s* Tankstelle *f*

gas' sta'tion attend'ant *s* Tankwart *m*

gas' stove' *s* Gasherd *m*

gas' tank' *s* Benzintbehälter *m*

gastric ['gæstrɪk] *adj* gastrisch

gas'tric juice' *s* Magensaft *m*

gastronomy [gæs'trɑnəmɪ] *s* Gastronomie *f*

gas'works' *spl* Gasanstalt *f*

gate [get] *s* Tor *n*, Pforte *f;* (rr) Sperre *f;* (sport) eingenommenes Eintrittsgeld *n;* **crash the g.** ohne Eintrittskarte durchschlupfen

gate' crash'er [ˌkræʃər] *s* unberechtigter Zuschauer *m*

gate'keep'er *s* Pförtner –in *mf*

gate'post' *s* Torpfosten *m*

gate'way' *s* Tor *n*, Torweg *m*

gather ['gæðər] *tr* (*things*) sammeln; (*people*) versammeln; (*flowers, fruit, peas*) pflücken; (*courage*) aufbringen; (*the impression*) gewinnen; (*information*) einziehen; (*strength, speed*) zunehmen an (*dat*); (*conclude*) (**from**) schließen (aus); **g. together** versammeln; **g. up** aufheben; (*curtains, dress*) raffen || *intr* sich (an)sammeln; (*said of clouds*) sich zusammenziehen; **g. around** sich scharen um

gath'ered *adj* (*skirt*) gerafft

gath'ering *s* Versammlung *f;* (sew) Kräuselfalten *pl*

gaudy ['gɔdɪ] *adj* (*overdone*) überladen; (*color*) grell

gauge [gedʒ] *s* (*instrument*) Messer *m*, Anzeiger *m;* (*measurement*) Eichmaß *n;* (*of wire*) Stärke *f;* (*of a shot-*

gun) Kaliber *n;* (fig) Maß *n;* (mach) Lehre *f;* (rr) Spurweite *f* || *tr* messen; (*check for accuracy*) eichen; (fig) abschätzen

Gaul [gɔl] *s* Gallien *n;* (*native*) Gallier –in *mf*

Gaulish ['gɔlɪʃ] *adj* gallisch

gaunt [gɔnt] *adj* hager

gauntlet ['gɔntlɪt] *s* Panzerhandschuh *m;* (fig) Fehdehandschuh *m;* **run the g.** Spießruten laufen

gauze [gɔz] *s* Gaze *f*

gavel ['gævəl] *s* Hammer *m*

gawk [gɔk] *s* (coll) Depp *m* || *intr*—**g. at** (coll) blöde anstarren

gawky ['gɔki] *adj* schlaksig

gay [ge] *adj* lustig; (*homosexual*) schwul

gay' blade' *s* lebenslustiger Kerl *m*

gaze [gez] *intr* starren; **g. at** anstarren; (*in astonishment*) anstaunen

gazelle [gə'zɛl] *s* Gazelle *f*

gazetteer [ˌgæzə'tɪr] *s* Ortslexikon *n*

gear [gɪr] *s* (*equipment*) Ausrüstung *f;* (aut) Schaltgetriebe *n*, Gang *m;* (mach) Zahnrad *n;* **gears** Räderwerk *n;* **in g.** eingeschaltet; **in high g.** im höchsten Gang; (fig) auf Touren; **shift gears** umschalten; **throw into g.** einschalten; **throw out of g.** (fig) aus dem Gleichgewicht bringen || *tr*—**g. to** anpassen (*dat*)

gear'box' *s* Schaltgetriebe *n*

gear'shift' *s* Gangschaltung *f;* (*lever*) Schalthebel *m*

gear'wheel' *s* Zahnrad *n*

gee [dʒi] *interj* nanu!

Geiger counter ['gaɪgərˌkauntər] *s* Geigerzähler *m*

gel [dʒɛl] *s* Gel *n* || *v* (*pret & pp* **gelled; *ger* gelling**) *intr* gelieren; (coll) klappen

gelatin ['dʒɛlətɪn] *s* Gelatine *f*

geld [gɛld] *v* (*pret & pp* **gelded & gelt** [gɛlt]) *tr* kastrieren

geld'ing *s* Wallach *m*

gem [dʒɛm] *s* Edelstein *m;* (fig) Perle *f*

Gemini ['dʒɛmɪˌnaɪ] *s* (astr) Zwillinge *pl*

gender ['dʒɛndər] *s* Geschlecht *n*

gene [dʒin] *s* Gen *n*, Erbanlage *f*

genealogical [ˌdʒinɪ·ə'lɑdʒɪkəl] *adj* genealogisch, Stamm–

genealog'ical ta'ble *s* Stammtafel *f*

genealog'ical tree' *s* Stammbaum *m*

genealogy [ˌdʒinɪ'ælədʒɪ] *s* Genealogie *f*

general ['dʒɛnərəl] *adj* allgemein, Gesamt– || *s* General *m;* **in g.** im allgemeinen

Gen'eral Assem'bly *s* Vollversammlung *f*

gen'eral deliv'ery *adv* postlagernd

gen'eral head'quarters *spl* Oberkommando *n*

generalissi•mo [ˌdʒɛnərə'lɪsɪmo] *s* (**–mos**) Generalissimus *m*

generality [ˌdʒɛnə'rælɪtɪ] *s* Allgemeingültigkeit *f;* **generalities** Gemeinplätze *pl*

generalization [ˌdʒɛnərəlɪ'zeʃən] *s* Verallgemeinerung *f*

generalize ['dʒɛnərə‚laɪz] *tr* & *intr* verallgemeinern

generally ['dʒɛnərəli] *adv* im allgemeinen; *(usually)* gewöhnlich; *(mostly)* meistens

gen′eral man′ager *s* Generaldirektor –in *mf*

gen′eral plan′ *s* Übersichtsplan *m*

gen′eral post′ of′fice *s* Oberpostamt *n*

gen′eral practi′tioner *s* praktischer Arzt *m*

gen′eralship′ *s* Führereingenschaften *pl*

gen′eral staff′ *s* Generalstab *m*

gen′eral store′ *s* Gemischtwarenhandlung *f*

gen′eral strike′ *s* Generalstreik *m*

generate ['dʒɛnə‚ret] *tr* *(procreate)* zeugen; (fig) verursachen; (elec) erzeugen; (geom) bilden

gen′erating sta′tion *s* Kraftwerk *n*

generation [‚dʒɛnə'reʃən] *s* Generation *f*; present g. Mitwelt *f*; younger g. junge Generation *f*

genera′tion gap′ *s* Generationsproblem *n*

generator ['dʒɛnə‚retər] *s* Erzeuger *m*; (chem, elec) Generator *m*; (elec) Stromerzeuger *m*

generic [dʒɪ'nɛrɪk] *adj* generisch, Gattungs–; g. name Gattungsname *m*

generosity [‚dʒɛnə'rɑsɪti] *s* Freigebigkeit *f*

generous ['dʒɛnərəs] *adj* freigebig

gene·sis ['dʒɛnɪsɪs] *s* (–ses [‚siz]) Genese *f*, Entstehung *f*; **Genesis** (Bib) Genesis *f*

genetic [dʒɪ'nɛtɪk] *adj* genetisch

genet′ic engineer′ *s* Gen-Ingineur *m*

genet′ic engineer′ing *s* Gen-Manipulation *f*

genetics [dʒɪ'nɛtɪks] *s* Genetik *f*, Vererbungslehre *f*

Geneva [dʒɪ'nivə] *adj* Genfer ‖ *s* Genf *n*

Genevieve ['dʒɛnə‚viv] *s* Genoveva *f*

genial ['dʒinɪ‚əl] *adj* freundlich

genie ['dʒini] *s* Kobold *m*

genital ['dʒɛnɪtəl] *adj* Genital– ‖ **genitals** *spl* Genitalien *pl*

genitive ['dʒɛnɪtɪv] *s* Genitiv *m*, Wesfall *m*

genius ['dʒinɪ‚əs] *s* (**geniuses**) Genie *n* ‖ *s* (**genii** ['dʒini‚aɪ]) Genius *m*

Genoa ['dʒɛnoʊ‚ə] *s* Genua *n*

genocidal [‚dʒɛnə'saɪdəl] *adj* rassenmörderisch

genocide ['dʒɛnə‚saɪd] *s* Rassenmord *m*

genre ['ʒɑnrə] *s* Genre *n*

genteel [dʒɛn'til] *adj* vornehm

gentile ['dʒɛntaɪl] *adj* nichtjüdisch; *(pagan)* heidnisch ‖ *s* Nichtjude *m*, Nichtjüdin *f*; *(pagan)* Heide *m*, Heidin *f*

gentility [dʒɛn'tɪlɪti] *s* Vornehmheit *f*

gentle ['dʒɛntəl] *adj* sanft, mild; *(tame)* zahm

gen′tle·man *s* (–men) Herr *m*, Gentleman *m*

gentlemanly ['dʒɛntəlmənli] *adj* weltmännisch

gen′tleman's agree′ment *s* Kavaliersab-

kommen *n*, Gentleman's Agreement *n*

gentleness ['dʒɛntəlnɪs] *s* Sanftmut *f*

gen′tle sex′ *s* zartes Geschlecht *n*

gentry ['dʒɛntri] *s* feine Leute *pl*

genuflection [‚dʒɛnju'flɛkʃən] *s* Kniebeugung *f*

genuine ['dʒɛnju‚ɪn] *adj* echt

genus ['dʒinəs] *s* (**genera** ['dʒɛnərə] & **genuses**) (biol, log) Gattung *f*

geographer [dʒɪ'ɑɡrəfər] *s* Geograph –in *mf*

geographic(al) [‚dʒɪ‚ə'ɡræfɪk(əl)] *adj* geographisch

geography [dʒɪ'ɑɡrəfi] *s* Geographie *f*

geologic(al) [‚dʒɪ‚ə'lɑdʒɪk(əl)] *adj* geologisch

geolog′ical e′ra *s* Erdalter *n*

geologist [dʒɪ'ɑlədʒɪst] *s* Geologe *m*, Geologin *f*

geology [dʒɪ'ɑlədʒi] *s* Geologie *f*

geometric(al) [‚dʒɪ‚ə'mɛtrɪk(əl)] *adj* geometrisch

geometrician [dʒɪ‚ɑmɪ'trɪʃən] *s* Geometer –in *mf*

geometry [dʒɪ'ɑmɪtri] *s* Geometrie *f*

geophysics [‚dʒɪ‚ə'fɪzɪks] *s* Geophysik *f*

geopolitics [‚dʒɪ‚ə'pɑlɪtɪks] *s* Geopolitik *f*

George [dʒɔrdʒ] *s* Georg *m*

geranium [dʒɪ'renɪ‚əm] *s* Geranie *f*

geriatrics [‚dʒɛrɪ'ætrɪks] *s* Geriatrie *f*

germ [dʒʌrm] *s* Keim *m*

German ['dʒʌrmən] *adj* & *adv* deutsch ‖ *s* Deutsche *mf*; *(language)* Deutsch *n*; **in G.** auf deutsch

germane [dʒɛr'men] *adj* (**to**) passend (zu)

Germanize ['dʒʌrmə‚naɪz] *tr* eindeutschen

Ger′man mea′sles *s* & *spl* Röteln *pl*

Ger′man shep′herd *s* deutscher Schäferhund *m*

Ger′man sil′ver *s* Alpaka *n*, Neusilber *n*

Germany ['dʒʌrməni] *s* Deutschland *n*

germ′ cell′ *s* Keimzelle *f*

germicidal [‚dʒʌrmɪ'saɪdəl] *adj* keimtötend

germicide ['dʒʌrmɪ‚saɪd] *s* Keimtöter *m*

germinate ['dʒʌrmɪ‚net] *intr* keimen

germ′ war′fare *s* bakteriologische Kriegsführung *f*

gerontology [‚dʒɛrən'tɑlədʒɪ] *s* Gerontologie *f*

gerund ['dʒɛrənd] *s* Gerundium *n*

gerundive [dʒɪ'rʌndɪv] *s* Gerundiv *n*

gestation [dʒɛs'teʃən] *s* Schwangerschaft *f*; *(in animals)* Trächtigkeit *f*

gesticulate [dʒɛs'tɪkjə‚let] *intr* gestikulieren, sich gebärden

gesticulation [dʒɛs‚tɪkjə'leʃən] *s* Gebärdenspiel *n*, Gestikulation *f*

gesture ['dʒɛstʃər] *s* Geste *f* ‖ *intr* Gesten machen

get [ɡɛt] *v* (*pret* **got** [ɡɑt]; *pp* **got** & **gotten** ['ɡɑtən]; *ger* **getting**) *tr* (*acquire*) bekommen; (*receive*) erhalten; (*procure*) beschaffen, besorgen; (*fetch*) holen; (*understand*) (coll) kapieren; (*s.o. to do s.th.*) dazu

bringen; (*reach by telephone*) erreichen; (*make, e.g., dirty*) machen;
(*convey, e.g., a message*) übermitteln; **get across** klarmachen; **get back**
zurückbekommen; **get down** (*depress*) verdrießen; (*swallow*) hin-
unterwürgen; **get going** in Gang setzen; **get hold of** (*a person*) erwischen; (*a thing*) erlangen; (*grip*)
ergreifen; **get off** (*e.g., a lid*) ab-
bekommen; **get one's way** sich durchsetzen; **get out** (*e.g., a spot*) heraus-
bekommen; **get s.o. used to** j-n gewöhnen an (*acc*); **get s.th. into one's
head** sich [*dat*] etw in den Kopf setzen; **get the hang of** (coll) wegbe-
kommen; **get the jump on s.o.** j-m
zuvorkommen; **get the worst of it**
am schlechtesten dabei wegkommen;
get (*s.th.*) **wrong** falsch verstehen;
you're going to get it! (coll) du wirst
es kriegen! || *intr* (*become*) werden;
get about sich fortbewegen; **get
ahead in the world** in der Welt fort-
kommen; **get along** auskommen; **get
along with** zurechtkommen mit; **get
around** herumkommen; **get around
to it** dazu kommen; **get at** herankom-
men an (*acc*); (*e.g., the real reason*)
herausfinden; **get away** (*run away*)
entlaufen; (*escape*) entkommen; **get
away from me!** geh weg von mir!;
get away with davonkommen mit;
get back at s.o. es j-m heimzahlen;
get by (*e.g., the guards*) vorbeikommen an (*dat*); (*on little money*)
durchkommen; **get down** (*step
down*) absteigen; **get down to brass
tacks** (*or* business) zur Sache kommen; **get going** sich auf den Weg
machen; **get going!** mach, daß du
weiter kommst!; **get into** (*a vehicle*)
einsteigen in (*acc*); (*trouble, etc.*)
geraten in (*acc*); **get loose** sich losmachen; **get lost** verloren gehen, abhanden kommen; (*lose one's way*)
sich verirren; **get lost!** (sl) hau ab!;
get off aussteigen; **get off with** (*a
light sentence*) davonkommen mit;
get on (*e.g., a train*) einsteigen (in
acc); **get on one's feet again** sich
hochrappeln; **get on with** (*s.o.*) zurechtkommen mit; **get out** aussteigen;
get out of a tight spot sich aus der
Schlinge ziehen; **get over** (*a hurdle*)
nehmen; (*a misfortune*) überwinden;
(*a sickness*) überstehen; **get ready**
sich fertig machen; **get through**
durchkommen; **get through to s.o.**
sich verständlich machen (*dat*); (telp)
erreichen; **get to be** werden; **get together** (*meet*) sich treffen; (*agree*)
(on) sich einig werden (über *acc*);
get to the bottom of ergründen; **get
up** aufstehen; **get used to** sich gewöhnen an (*acc*); **get well** gesund
werden; **get with it!** (coll) zur
Sache!

get'away' s Entkommen *n*; (sport)
Start *m*; **make one's g.** entkommen
get'away car' s Fluchtwagen *m*
get'-togeth'er s zwangloses Treffen *n*
get'up' s (coll) Aufzug *m*

get' up' and go' s Unternehmungsgeist
m
gewgaw ['g(j)ugɔ] s Plunder *m*
geyser ['gaɪzər] s Geiser *m*
ghastly ['gæstlɪ] adj (*ghostly*) gespenstisch; (*e.g., crime*) grausig; (*in-
tensely unpleasant*) schrecklich
gherkin ['gʌrkɪn] s Essiggurke *f*
ghet•to ['geto] s (*-tos*) Getto *n*
ghost [gost] s Gespenst *n*, Geist *m*;
(telv) Doppelbild *n*; **give up the g.**
den Geist aufgeben; **not a g. of a
chance** nicht die geringste Aussichten
ghostly ['gostlɪ] adj gespenstisch
ghost' sto'ry s Spukgeschichte *f*
ghost' town' s Geisterstadt *f*
ghost' writ'er s Ghostwriter *m*
ghoul [gul] s (& fig) Unhold *m*
ghoulish ['gulɪʃ] adj teuflisch
GHQ ['dʒɪ'et∫'kju] s (**General Headquarters**) Oberkommando *n*
GI ['dʒɪ'aɪ] s (**GI's**) (coll) Landser *m*
giant ['dʒaɪ-ənt] adj riesig, Riesen– ||
s Riese *m*, Riesin *f*
giantess ['dʒaɪ-əntɪs] s Riesin *f*
gibberish ['dʒɪbərɪʃ], ['gɪbərɪʃ] s
Klauderwelsch *n*
gibbet ['dʒɪbɪt] s Galgen *m* || *tr* hän-
gen
gibe [dʒaɪb] s Spott *m* || *intr* spotten;
g. at verspotten
giblets ['dʒɪblɪts] spl Gänseklein *n*
giddiness ['gɪdɪnɪs] s Schwindelgefühl
n; (*frivolity*) Leichtsinn *m*
giddy ['gɪdɪ] adj (*dizzy*) schwindlig;
(*height*) schwindelerregend; (*frivolous*) leichtsinnig
gift [gɪft] s Geschenk *n*; (*natural ability*) Begabung *f*
gift'ed adj begabt
gift'horse' s—**never look a g. in the
mouth** e-m geschenkten Gaul schaut
man nicht ins Maul
gift' of gab' s (coll) gutes Mundwerk *n*
gift' shop' s Geschenkartikelladen *m*
gift'-wrap' v (*pret & pp* **-wrapped**; *ger*
-wrapping) *tr* als Geschenk verpacken
gift'wrap'ping s Geschenkverpackung
f
gigantic [dʒaɪ'gæntɪk] adj riesig
giggle ['gɪgəl] s Gekicher *n* || *intr*
kichern
gigly ['gɪglɪ] adj allezeit kichernd
gigo•lo ['dʒɪgə‚lo] s (**-los**) Gigolo *m*
gild [gɪld] v (*pret & pp* **gilded & gilt**
[gɪlt]) *tr* vergolden
gild'ing s Vergoldung *f*
gill [gɪl] s (*of a fish*) Kieme *f*; (*of a
cock*) Kehllappen *m*
gilt [gɪlt] adj vergoldet || s Vergol-
dung *f*
gilt' edge' s Goldschnitt *m*
gilt'-edged' adj mit Goldschnitt versehen; (*first-class*) (coll) erstklassig
gimlet ['gɪmlɪt] s Handbohrer *m*
gimmick ['gɪmɪk] s(coll) Trick *m*
gin [dʒɪn] s Wacholderbranntwein *m*,
Gin *m*; (*snare*) Schlinge *f* || v (*pret
& pp* **ginned**; *ger* **ginning**) *tr* ent-
körnen
ginger ['dʒɪndʒər] s Ingwer *m*

gin'ger ale' s Ingwerlimonade f

gin'gerbread' s Pfefferkuchen m

gingerly ['dʒɪndʒərli] adv sacht(e)

gin'gersnap' s Ingwerplätzchen n

gingham ['gɪŋəm] s Gingham m

giraffe [dʒɪ'ræf] s Giraffe f

gird [gʌrd] v (pret & pp girt [gʌrt] & girded) tr gürten; **g. oneself with a sword** sich [dat] ein Schwert umgürten

girder ['gʌrdər] s Tragbalken m

girdle ['gʌrdəl] s Gürtel m

girl [gʌrl] s Mädchen n, Mädel n

girl' friend' s Freundin f, Geliebte f

girl'hood' s Mädchenzeit f

girlish ['gʌrlɪʃ] adj mädchenhaft

girl' scout' s Pfadfinderin f

girth [gʌrθ] s Umfang m; (for a horse) Sattelgurt m

gist [dʒɪst] s Kernpunkt m; **g. of the matter** des Pudels Kern

give [gɪv] v s Elastizität f; (yielding) Nachgeben n || v (pret gave [gev]; pp given ['gɪvən]) tr geben; (a gift, credence) schenken; (free of charge) verschenken; (contribute) spenden; (hand over) übergeben; (a report) erstatten; (a reason, the time) angeben; (attention, recognition) zollen; (a lecture) halten; (an award) zusprechen; (homework) aufgeben; (a headache, etc.) verursachen; (joy) machen; (a reception) veranstalten; (a blow) versetzen; **g. away** weggeben; (divulge) verraten; **g. away the bride** Brautvater sein; **g. back** zurückgeben; **g. ground** zurückweichen; **g. it to 'em!** (coll) hau zu!; **g. off** von sich geben; (steam) ausströmen lassen; **g. oneself away** sich verplappern; **g. oneself up** sich stellen; **g. or take** mehr oder weniger; **g. out** ausgeben; **g. rise to** Anlaß geben zu; **g. up** aufgeben; (a business) schließen; **g. up for lost** verlorengeben; **g. way** weichen; **g. way to** sich überlassen (dat) || intr (yield) nachgeben; (collapse) einstürzen; **g. in to** nachgeben (dat), weichen (dat); **g. out** (said of the voice, legs) versagen; (said of strength) nachlassen; **g. up** aufgeben; (mil) die Waffen strecken; **g. up on** verzagen an (dat)

give'-and-take' s Kompromiß m & n; (exchange of opinion) Meinungsaustausch m

give'away' s (betrayal of a secret) unbeabsichtigte Preisgabe f; (promotional article) Gratisprobe f

give'away show' s Preisrätselsendung f

given ['gɪvən] adj gegeben; (time) festgesetzt; (math, philos) gegeben; **g. to drinking** dem Trunk ergeben

giv'en name' s Vorname m

giver ['gɪvər] s Geber –in mf; (of a contribution) Spender –in mf

gizzard ['gɪzərd] s Geflügelmagen m

gla'cial pe'riod s Eiszeit f

glacier ['gleʃər] s Gletscher m

glad [glæd] adj (gladder; gladdest) froh; **be g.** (about) sich freuen (über acc); **g. to** (inf) erfreut zu (inf); **g. to meet you** sehr erfreut!, sehr ange-

nehm!; **I'll be g. to do it for you** ich werde das gern für Sie tun

gladden ['glædən] tr erfreuen

glade [gled] s Waldwiese f, Waldlichtung f

gladiator ['glædɪ,etər] s Gladiator m

gladiola [,glædɪ'olə] s Gladiole f

gladly ['glædli] adv gern(e)

gladness ['glædnɪs] s Freude f

glad' rags' spl (sl) Sonntagsstaat m

glad' tid'ings spl Freundenbotschaft f

glamorous ['glæmərəs] adj bezaubernd

glamour ['glæmər] s (of a girl) Zauber m; (of an event) Glanz m

glam'our girl' s gefeierte Schönheit f; (pej) Zierpuppe f

glance [glæns] s Blick m; **at a g.**, **at first g.** auf den ersten Blick; || intr (at) blicken (auf acc or nach); **g. around** umherblicken; **g. off** abgleiten an (dat); **g. through** (or over) flüchtig durchsehen; **g. up** aufblicken

gland [glænd] s Drüse f

glanders ['glændərz] spl Rotzkrankheit f

glare [gler] s grelles Licht n; (look) böser Blick m || intr blenden; (look) böse starren; **g. at** böse anstarren

glar'ing adj (light) grell; (fig) schreiend, aufdringlich

glass [glæs] adj gläsern, Glas– || s Glas n; **glasses** Brille f

glass' bead' s Glasperle f

glass' blow'er ['blo·ər] s Glasbläser –in mf

glass' blow'ing s Glasbläserei f

glass' case' s Schaukasten m

glass' cut'ter s Glasschleifer –in mf; (tool) Glasschneider m

glassful ['glæsful] s Glas m

glass'ware' s Glaswaren pl

glass' wool' s Glaswolle f

glass'works' s Glasfabrik f, Glashütte f

glassy ['glæsi] adj (surface) spiegelglatt; (eyes) glasig

glaucoma [glau'komə] s Glaukom n, grüner Star m

glaze [glez] s (on ceramics) Glasur f; (on paintings) Lasur f; (of ice) Glatteis n || tr (ceramics, baked goods) glasieren; (a window) verglasen; (a painting) lasieren

glazed adj (ceramics, baked goods) glasiert; (eyes) glasig; **g. tile** Kachel f

glazier ['gleʒər] s Glaser –in mf

gleam [glim] s Lichtstrahl m; **g. of hope** Hoffnungsschimmer m || intr strahlen

glean [glin] tr & intr auflesen; (fig) zusammentragen

gleanings ['glinɪŋz] spl Nachlese f

glee [gli] s Frohsinn m

glee' club' s Gesangverein m

glen [glɛn] s Bergschlucht f

glib [glɪb] adj (glibber; glibbest) (tongue) beweglich; (person) zungenfertig

glide [glaɪd] s Gleiten n; (aer) Gleitflug m; (with a glider) (aer) Segelflug m; (ling) Gleitlaut m; (mus) Glissando n || intr gleiten

glider ['glaɪdər] s (porch swing) Schaukelbett n; (aer) Segelflugzeug n

glid'er pi'lot s Segelflieger –in mf

glid'ing s Segelfliegen n

glimmer ['glɪmər] s Schimmer m; **g. of hope** Hoffnungsschimmer m || intr schimmern

glim'mering adj flimmernd || s Flimmern n

glimpse [glɪmps] s flüchtiger Blick m; **catch a g. of** flüchtig zu sehen bekommen || tr flüchtig erblicken || intr—**g. at** e-n flüchtigen Blick werfen auf (acc)

glint [glɪnt] s Lichtschimmer m || intr schimmern

glisten ['glɪsən] s Glanz m || intr glänzen

glitter ['glɪtər] s Glitzern n, Glanz m || intr glitzern, glänzen

gloat [glot] intr schadenfroh sein; **g. over** sich weiden an (dat)

gloat'ing s Schadenfreude f

global ['global] adj global, Welt-

globe [glob] s Erdkugel f, Globus m

globe'-trot'ter s Weltenbummler –in mf

globule ['glɑbjul] s Kügelchen n

glockenspiel ['glɑkən ‚spil] s Glockenspiel n

gloom [glum] s Düsternis f; (fig) Trübsinn m

gloominess ['glumɪnɪs] s Düsterkeit f; (fig) Trübsinn m

gloomy ['glumi] adj düster; (depressing) bedrückend; (depressed) trübsinning

glorification ['glorɪfɪ‚keʃən] s Verherrlichung f

glori·fy ['glorɪ ‚faɪ] v (pret & pp –fied) tr verherrlichen

glorious ['glorɪ·əs] adj (full of glory) glorreich; (magnificent) herrlich

glo·ry ['glori] s Ruhm m; (magnificence) Herrlichkeit f; **be in one's g.** im siebenten Himmel sein || v (pret & pp –ried) intr—**g.** in frohlocken über (acc)

gloss [glɔs] s (shine) Glanz m; (notation) Glosse f || tr glossieren; **g. over** verschleiern

glossary ['glɔsəri] s Glossar n

glossy ['glɔsi] adj glänzend

glottis ['glɑtɪs] s Stimmritze f

glove [glʌv] s Handschuh m; **fit like a g.** wie angegossen passen

glove' compart'ment s Handschuhfach n

glow [glo] s Glühen n || intr glühen; **g. with** (fig) (er)glühen vor (dat)

glower ['glau·ər] s finsterer Blick m || intr finster blicken; **g. at** finster anblicken

glow'ing adj glühend; (account) begeistert

glow'worm' s Glühwurm m

glucose ['glukos] s Glukose f

glue [glu] s Leim m, Klebmittel n || tr (wood) leimen; (paper) kleben

gluey ['glu·i] adj leimig

glum [glʌm] adj (glummer; glummest) verdrießlich

glut [glʌt] s Übersättigung f; **a g. on the market** e-e Überschwemmung des Marktes || v (pret & pp glutted; ger glutting) tr übersättigen; (com) überschwemmen

glutton ['glʌtən] s Vielfraß m

gluttonous ['glʌtənəs] adj gefräßig

gluttony ['glʌtəni] s Gefräßigkeit f

glycerine ['glɪsərɪn] s Glyzerin n

gnarled [nɑrld] adj knorrig

gnash [næʃ] tr—**g. one's teeth** mit den Zähnen knirschen

gnat [næt] s Mücke f

gnaw [nɔ] tr zernagen; **g. off** abnagen || intr (on) nagen (an dat)

gnome [nom] s Gnom m, Berggeist m

go [go] s—**be on the go** auf den Beinen sein; **have a lot of go** viel Mumm in den Knochen haben; **it's no go** es geht nicht; **let's have a go at it** probieren wir's mal; **make a go of it** es zu e-m Erfolg machen || v (pret **went** [wɛnt]) pp **gone** [gɔn]) tr—**go it alone** es ganz allein(e) machen || intr gehen; (depart) weggehen; (travel) fahren, reisen; (operate) arbeiten; (belong) gehören; (turn out) verlaufen; (collapse) zusammenbrechen; (fail, go out of order) kaputtgehen; (said of words) lauten; (said of bells) läuten; (said of a buzzer) ertönen; (said of awards) zugeteilt werden; (said of a road) führen; **be going to**, e.g., **I am going to study** ich werde studieren; **go about** umhergehen; (a task) in Angriff nehmen; **go about it** darangehen; **go after** (run after) nachlaufen; (strive for) streben nach; **go against the grain** gegen den Strich gehen; **go ahead** vorausgehen; **go ahead!** voran!; **go along with** (accompany) mitgehen mit; (agree with) zustimmen mit; **go and see for yourself** überzeugen Sie sich selbst davon!; **go around** herumgehen; (suffice) (aus)reichen; (an obstacle) umgehen; **go at** (a person) losgehen auf (acc); (a thing) herangehen an (acc); **go away** weggehen; **go bad** schlecht werden; **go back** zurückkehren; (ride back) zurückfahren; **go back on** (one's word) brechen; **go beyond** überschreiten; **go by** (pass by) vorbeigehen (an dat); (said of time) vergehen; (act according to) sich richten nach; **go down** niedergehen; (said of the sun or a ship) untergehen; (said of a swelling) zurückgehen; (said of a fever or a price) sinken; **go down in history** in die Geschichte eingehen; **go for** (fetch) holen; (apply to) gelten für; (be enthusiastic about) schwärmen für; (have a crush on) verknallt sein in (acc); (be sold for) verkauft werden für; (attack) losgehen auf (acc); **go in** hineingehen; (said of the sun) verschwinden; **go in for** schwärmen für; (sport) treiben; **go into** eintreten in (acc); (arith) enthalten sein in (dat); **go**

into detail ins Detail gehen; **go in with s.o. on** sich beteiligen mit j–m an (dat); **go off** (depart) weggehen; (said of a gun) losgehen; (said of a bomb) explodieren; **go on** (happen) vorgehen; (continue) weitergehen; **(with)** fortfahren (mit); (theat) auftreten; **go on!** (expressing encouragement) nur zu!; (expressing disbelief) ach was!; **go on reading** weiterlesen; **go on to** (another theme) übergehen auf (acc); **go over** (check) überprüfen; (review) noch einmal durchgehen; (figures) nachrechnen; (be a success) einschlagen; **go over to** hinübergehen zu; (the enemy) übergehen zu; **go out** (e.g., of the house) hinausgehen; (on an errand or socially; said of a light) ausgehen; **go out of one's way** sich besonders anstrengen; **go out to dinner** auswärts essen; **go through** (penetrate) durchdringen; (a traffic signal) überfahren; (endure) durchmachen; **go through with** zu Ende führen; **go to** (said of a prize) zugeteilt werden (dat); **go together** zueinanderpassen; **go to it!** los!; **go to show** ein Beweis sein für; **go with** (fit, match) passen zu; (associate with) verkehren mit; **go without** entbehren; **go under an assumed name** e–n angenommenen Namen führen; **go up to s.o.** auf j–n zugehen

goad [god] s Stachel m || tr antreiben; **g. on** (fig) anstacheln

go'-ahead sig'nal n freie Bahn f

goal [gol] s Ziel n; (sport) Tor n; **make a goal** (sport) ein Tor schießen

goalie ['goli] s Torwart m

goal'keep'er s Torwart m

goal' line' s Torlinie f

goal' post' s Torpfosten m

goat [got] s Ziege f, Geiß f; (male goat) Ziegenbock m; **get s.o.'s g.** (sl) j–n auf die Palme bringen

goatee [go'ti] s Ziegenbart m, Spitzbart m

goat'herd' s Ziegenhirt m

goat'skin' s Ziegenfell n

gob [gab] s (coll) Klumpen m; (sailor) (coll) Blaujacke f; **gobs of money** (coll) ein Haufen m Geld

gobble ['gabəl] s Kollern m || tr verschlingen; **g. up** (food) herunterschlingen; (e.g., land) zusammenraffen || intr (said of a turkey) kollern

gobbledegook ['gabəldɪ‚guk] s (coll) Amtssprache f

gobbler ['gablər] s (coll) Fresser –in mf; (orn) (coll) Puter m, Truthahn m

go'-between' s Vermittler –in mf, Unterhändler –in mf

goblet ['gablɪt] s Kelchglas n

goblin ['gablɪn] s Kobold m

go'cart' s (walker) Laufstuhl m; (stroller) Sportwagen m; (small racer) Go-Kart m; (handcart) Handwagen m

god [gad] s Gott m; **God forbid!** Gott bewahre!; **God knows** weiß Gott; **my God!** du lieber Gott!; **so help me God!** so wahr mir Gott helfe!; **ye gods!** heiliger Strohsack!

god'child' s (–chil'dren) Patenkind n

goddess ['gadɪs] s Göttin f

god'fa'ther s Pate m; **be a g.** Pate stehen

God'-fear'ing adj gottesfürchtig

god'forsak'en adj gottverlassen

god'head' s Göttlichkeit f; **Godhead** Gott m

godless ['gadlɪs] adj gottlos

god'like' adj göttlich

godly ['gadli] adj gottselig

god'moth'er s Patin f; **be a g.** Patin stehen

god'send' s Segen m

God'speed' s—**wish s.o. G.** j–m Lebewohl sagen

go-getter ['go‚gɛtər] s Draufgänger m

goggle ['gagəl] intr glotzen

gog'gle-eyed' adj glotzäugig

goggles ['gagəlz] spl Schutzbrille f

go'ing adj (rate) gültig, üblich; **g. on** (e.g., six o'clock) gegen; **I'm g. to do it** ich werde es tun

go'ing concern' s schwunghaftes Geschäft n

go'ing-o'ver s Überprüfung f; (beating) Prügel pl

go'ings on' spl Treiben n, Wirtschaft f

goiter ['gɔɪtər] s Kropf m

gold [gold] adj Gold– || s Gold n

gold' bar' s Goldbarren m

gold'brick' s (mil) Drückeberger m

gold'-brick' intr faulenzen

gold'-brick'ing s (mil) Drückebergerei f

gold'crest' s Goldhähnchen n

gold' dig'ger ['dɪgər] s Goldgräber m; (sl) Vamp m

golden ['goldən] adj golden; (opportunity) günstig

gold'en age' s Glanzzeit f, Goldenes Zeitalter n

gold'en calf', the s das Goldene Kalb

gold'en ea'gle s Goldadler m

Gold'en Fleece', the (myth) das Goldene Vlies

gold'en mean' s goldene Mitte f

gold'en rule' s goldene Regel f

gold'en wed'ding s goldene Hochzeit f

gold'-filled' adj vergoldet

gold' fill'ing s (dent) Goldplombe f

gold'finch' s Goldfink m, Stieglitz m

gold'fish' s Goldfisch m

goldilocks ['goldɪ‚laks] s (bot) Hahnenfuß m

gold' leaf' s Blattgold n

gold'mine' s Goldbergwerk n

gold' nug'get s Goldklumpen m

gold' plate' s Goldgeschirr n

gold'-plate' tr vergolden

gold'smith' s Goldschmied –in mf

gold' stand'ard s Goldwährung f

golf [galf] s Golf n || intr Golf spielen

golf' bag' s Köcher m

golf' club' s Golfschläger m; (organization) Golfklub m

golf' course' s Golfplatz m

golfer ['galfər] s Golfspieler –in mf

golf' links' spl Golfplatz m

gondola ['gandələ] s Gondel f

gon'dola car' s offener Güterwagen m

gondolier [ˌgɑndə'lɪr] s Gondelführer m

gone [gɔn] adj hin, weg; (ruined) futsch; all g. ganz weg; (sold out) ausverkauft; he is g. er ist fort

goner ['gɔnər] s (coll) verlorener Mensch m

gong [gɔŋ] s Gong m, Tamtam n

gonorrhea [ˌgɑnə'ri·ə] s Tripper m

goo [gu] s (sl) klebrige Masse f

good [gud] adj (better; best) gut; (well behaved) brav, artig; (in health) gesund; (valid) gültig; as g. as so gut wie; be g. enough to (inf) so gut sein und; g. and recht, e.g., g. and cheap recht billig; g. at gut in (dat); g. for (suited to) geeignet zu; (effective against) wirksam für; (valid for) gültig für; g. for you! (serves you right!) das geschieht dir recht!; (expressing congratulations) ich gratuliere!, bravo!; make g. wiedergutmachen; (losses) vergüten; (a promise) erfüllen; || s Gut n; (welfare) Wohl n; (advantage) Nutzen m; (philos) Gut n, das Gute; be up to no g. nichts Gutes im Schilde führen; catch with the goods auf frischer Tat ertappen; do g. wohltun; for g. für immer; goods Waren pl; to the g. als Nettogewinn; what g. is it?, what's the g. of it? was nutzt es?

good'-by', good'-bye' s Lebewohl n; say g. (to) sich verabschieden (von) || interj auf Wiedersehen!; (on the telephone) auf Wiederhören!

good' day' interj guten Tag!

good' deed' s Wohltat f

good' egg' s (sl) feiner Kerl m

good' eve'ning interj guten Abend!

good' fel'low s netter Kerl m

good'-fel'lowship s gute Kameradschaft f

good'-for-noth'ing || s Taugenichts m, Nichtsnutz m

Good' Fri'day s Karfreitag m

good' grac'es spl—be in s.o.'s g. in j-s Gunst stehen

good'-heart'ed adj gutherzig

good'-hu'mored adj gutgelaunt, gutmütig

good'-look'ing adj gutaussehend, hübsch

goodly ['gudli] adj beträchtlich; a g. number of viele

good' morn'ing interj guten Morgen!

good'-na'tured adj gutmütig

goodness ['gudnɪs] s Güte f; for g. sake! um Himmels willen!; g. knows weiß Gott; thank g. Gott sei Dank!

good' night' interj gute Nacht!

good' sense' s Sinn m; (common sense) gesunder Menschenverstand m; make g. Sinn haben

good'-sized' adj ziemlich groß

good'-tem'pered adj ausgeglichen

good' time'—have a g. sich gut unterhalten; keep g. taktfest sein

good' turn' s Gefallen m; one g. deserves another e–e Hand wäscht die andere

good' will' s Wohlwollen n; (com) Geschäftswert m

goody ['gudi] s Näscherei f || interj pfundig!

gooey ['gu·i] adj klebrig

goof [guf] s (person) (sl) Depp m; (mistake) (sl) Schnitzer m || tr (sl) verpfuschen || intr (sl) e–n Schnitzer machen; g. off (sl) faulenzen

goof'ball' s (pill) (sl) Beruhigungspille f; (eccentric person) (sl) Sonderling m

goofy ['gufi] adj (sl) dämlich; g. about (sl) vernarrt in (acc)

goon [gun] s (sl) Dummkopf m; (in strikes) bestellter Schläger m

goose [gus] s (geese [gis]) Gans f; (culin) Gänsebraten m; cook s.o.'s g. j–n erledigen

goose'ber'ry s Stachelbeere f

goose' egg' s Gänseei n; (sl) Null f

goose' flesh' s Gänsehaut f

goose'neck' s Schwanenhals m

goose' pim'ples spl Gänsehaut f

goose' step' s Stechschritt m

goose'-step' v (pret & pp –stepped; ger –stepping) intr im Stechschritt marschieren

gopher ['gofər] s Taschenratte f

gore [gor] s geronnenes Blut n || tr aufspießen

gorge [gɔrdʒ] s Schlucht f || tr vollstopfen || intr schlingen

gorgeous ['gɔrdʒəs] adj prachtvoll

gorilla [gə'rɪlə] s Gorilla m

gorse [gɔrs] s Stechginster m

gory ['gori] adj blutig

gosh [gɑʃ] interj herrjeh!

Gospel ['gɑspəl] s Evangelium n

gos'pel truth' s reine Wahrheit f

gossamer ['gɑsəmər] s Sommerfäden pl

gossip ['gɑsɪp] s Klatsch m; (woman) Klatschweib n; (man) Schwätzer m || intr klatschen, tratschen

gos'sip col'umn s Klatschspalte f

gossipmonger ['gɑsɪpˌmʌŋgər] s Klatschbase f

gossipy ['gɑsɪpi] adj tratschsüchtig

Goth [gɑθ] s Gote m, Gotin f

Gothic ['gɑθɪk] adj gotisch || s (language) Gotisch n

Goth'ic arch' s Spitzbogen m

gouge [gaudʒ] s (tool) Hohlmeißel m; (hole made by a gouge) ausgemeißelte Vertiefung f || tr aushöhlen; (overcharge) übervorteilen; g. out (eyes) herausdrücken

gouger ['gaudʒər] s Wucherer –in mf

goulash ['gulɑʃ] s Gulasch n

gourd [gord], [gurd] s Kürbis m

gourmand ['gurmənd] s (glutton) Schlemmer –in mf; (gourmet) Feinschmecker m

gourmet ['gurme] s Feinschmecker m

gout [gaut] s Gicht f

govern ['gʌvərn] tr regieren; (fig) beherrschen; (gram) regieren || intr regieren

governess ['gʌvərnɪs] s Gouvernante f

government ['gʌvərnmənt] adj Regierungs–, Staats– || s Regierung f gov'ernment con'tract s Staatsauftrag m

gov'ernment control' s Zwangsbewirtschaftung f

gov'ernment employ'ee s Staatsbeamte m, Staatsbeamtin f

gov'ernment grant' s Staatszuschuß m

gov'ernment-in-ex'ile s Exilregierung f

gov'ernor ['gʌvərnər] s Statthalter m, Gouverneur m; (mach) Regler m

gov'ernorship' s Statthalterschaft f

gown [gaun] s Damenkleid n; (of a judge, professor) Robe f, Talar m

grab [græb] s—make a g. for grapschen nach || v (pret & pp grabbed; ger grabbing) tr schnappen; g. hold of anpacken || intr—g. for greifen nach

grab' bag' s Glückstopf m

grace [gres] s (mercy, divine favor) Gnade f; (charm) Grazie f; (table prayer) Tischgebet n; (charm) Grazie f; Graces (myth) Grazien pl

graceful ['gresfəl] adj graziös, anmutig

gracious ['greʃəs] adj gnädig; (living) angenehm || interj lieber Himmel!

gradation [gre'deʃən] s Stufenfolge f

grade [gred] s (level) Stufe f, Grad m; (quality) Qualität f; (class year) Schulklasse f; (mark in a course, test) Zensur f; (slope) Steigung f; (mil) Dienstgrad m || tr (sort) einstufen; (evaluate) bewerten; (make level) planieren; (educ) zensieren

grade' cross'ing s (rr) Schienenübergang m

grade' school' s Grundschule f

gradient ['gredɪ·ənt] s Neigung f

gradual ['grædʒʊ·əl] adj allmählich

graduate ['grædʒʊ·ɪt] adj (student) graduiert; (course) Graduierten- || s Promovierte mf; (from a junior college) Abiturient –in mf; (from a university) Absolvent –in mf || ['grædʒʊ‚et] tr & intr graduieren, promovieren; g. from absolvieren

grad'uated adj (tax) abgestuft; (marked by divisions of measurement) graduiert; g. scale Gradmesser m

graduation [‚grædʒʊ'eʃən] s Graduierung f, Promotion f; (marking on a vessel or instrument) Gradeinteilung f

gradua'tion ex'ercises spl Schlußfeier f

graft [græft] s (illegal gain) Schiebung f; (money involved in graft) Schmiergeld n; (twig) (hort) Pfropfreis n; (place where scion is inserted) (hort) Propfstelle f; (organ transplanted) (surg) verpflanztes Gewebe n; (transplanting) (surg) Gewebeverpflanzung f || tr (hort) pfropfen; (surg) verpflanzen

gra'ham bread' ['gre·əm] s Grahambrot n

gra'ham crack'er s Grahamplätzchen n

gra'ham flour' s Grahammehl m

grain [gren] s Korn n; (of leather) Narbe f; (in wood, marble) Maserung f; (unit of weight) Gran n; (cereals) Getreide n; (phot) Korn n; against the g. (& fig) gegen den Strich; g. of truth Körnchen n Wahrheit

grain' el'evator s Getreidesilo m

grain'field' s Saatfeld n, Kornfeld n

gram [græm] s Gramm n

grammar ['græmər] s Grammatik f

gram'mar school' s Grundschule f

grammatical [grə'mætɪkəl] adj grammatisch, grammatikalisch

gramophone ['græmə‚fon] s Grammophon n

granary ['grenəri] s Getreidespeicher m

grand [grænd] adj großartig; (large and striking) grandios; (lofty) erhaben; (wonderful) (coll) herrlich

grand'aunt' s Großtante f

grand'child' s (-chil'dren) Enkelkind n

grand'daugh'ter s Enkelin f

grand' duch'ess s Großfürstin f, Großherzogin f

grand' duch'y s Großfürstentum n, Großherzogtum n

grand' duke' s Großfürst m, Großherzog m

grandee [græn'di] s Grande m

grandeur ['grændʒər] ['grændʒʊr] s Großartigkeit f, Erhabenheit f

grand'fath'er s Großvater m

grand'father's clock' s Standuhr f

grandiose ['grændɪ‚os] adj grandios

grand' ju'ry s Anklagekammer f

grand' lar'ceny s schwerer Diebstahl m

grand' lodge' s Großloge f

grandma ['græn(d)‚ma], ['græm‚ma] s (coll) Oma f

grand'moth'er s Großmutter f

grand'neph'ew s Großneffe m

grand'niece' s Großnichte f

grandpa ['græn(d)‚pa], ['græm‚pa] s (coll) Opa m

grand'par'ents spl Großeltern pl

grand' pian'o s Konzertflügel m

grand' slam' s Schlemm m

grand'son' s Enkel m

grand'stand' s Tribüne f

grand' to'tal s Gesamtsumme f

grand'un'cle s Großonkel m

grand' vizier' s Großwesir m

grange [grendʒ] s Farm f; (organization) Farmervereinigung f

granite ['grænɪt] adj Granit- || s Granit m

granny ['græni] s (coll) Oma f

grant [grænt] s (of money) Beihilfe f; (of a pardon) Gewährung f; (of an award) Verleihung f || tr (permission) geben; (credit) bewilligen; (a favor) gewähren; (a request) erfüllen; (a privilege, award) verleihen; (admit) zugeben; granted that angenommen, daß; take for granted als selbstverständlich hinnehmen

grantee [græn'ti] s Empfänger –in mf

grant'-in-aid' s (grants-in-aid) (by the government) Subvention f; (educ) Stipendium n

grantor ['græntər] s Verleiher –in mf

granular ['grænjələr] adj körnig

granulate ['grænjə‚let] tr körnen

gran'ulated sug'ar s Streuzucker m
granule ['grænjul] s Körnchen n
grape [grep] s Weintraube f
grape' ar'bor s Weinlaube f
grape'fruit' s Pampelmuse f
grape' juice' s Most m, Traubensaft m
grape' pick'er s Weinleser –in mf
grape'vine' s Weinstock m; **through the g.** gerüchteweise
graph [græf] s Diagramm n
graphic(al) ['græfɪk(əl)] adj graphisch; (description) anschaulich, bildhaft
graph'ic arts' spl Graphik f
graphite ['græfaɪt] s Graphit m
graph' pa'per s Millimeterpapier n
grapnel ['græpnəl] s Wurfanker m
grapple ['græpəl] s Enterhaken m; (fight) Handgemenge n || tr packen || intr (use a grapple) (naut) e–n Enterhaken gebrauchen; **g. with** (& fig) ringen mit
grap'pling hook', grap'pling i'ron s Wurfanker m; (naut) Enterhaken m
grasp [græsp] s Griff m; (control) Gewalt f; (comprehension) Verständnis n; (reach) Reichweite f; **have a good g. of** gut beherrschen || tr (& fig) fassen || intr—**g. at** schnappen nach
grasp'ing adj habgierig, geldgierig
grass [græs] s Gras n; (lawn) Rasen m; (pasture land) Weide f
grass' court' s Rasenspielplatz m
grass'hop'per s Grashüpfer m
grass' land' s Weideland n, Grasland n
grass'-roots' adj (coll) volkstümlich
grass' seed' s Grassamen m
grass' wid'ow s Strohwitwe f
grassy ['græsi] adj grasig
grate [gret] s (on a window) Gitter n; (of a furnace) Rost m || tr (e.g., cheese) reiben; **g. the teeth** mit den Zähnen knirschen || intr knirschen; **g. on one's nerves** an den Nerven reißen
grateful ['gretfəl] adj dankbar
grater ['gretər] s (culin) Reibeisen n
grati-fy ['grætɪ,faɪ] v (pret & pp –fied) tr befriedigen; **be gratified by** sich freuen über (acc)
grat'ifying adj erfreulich
grat'ing adj knirschend || s Gitter n
gratis ['grætɪs], ['gretɪs] adj & adv unentgeltlich
gratitude ['grætɪ,t(j)ud] s Dankbarkeit f
gratuitous [grə't(j)u·ɪtəs] adj unentgeltlich; (undeserving) unverdient
gratuity [grə't(j)u·ɪti] s Trinkgeld n
grave [grev] adj (face) ernst; (condition) besorgniserregend; (mistake) folgenschwer; (sound) tief || s Grab n; (accent) Gravis m
gravedigger ['grev,dɪgər] s Totengräber m
gravel ['grævəl] s (rounded stones) Kies m; (crushed stones) Schotter m; (pathol) Harngrieß m || tr mit Kies (or Schotter) bestreuen
gravelly ['grævəli] adj heiser
grav'el pit' s Kiesgrube f
grav'el road' s Schotterstraße f

grave'stone' s Grabstein m
grave'yard' s Friedhof m
gravitate ['grævɪ,tet] intr gravitieren; **g. towards** (fig) neigen zu
gravitation [,grævɪ'teʃən] s Gravitation f, Massenanziehung f
gravitational [,grævɪ'teʃənəl] adj Gravitations–, Schwer–
gravita'tional force' s Schwerkraft f
gravita'tional pull' s Anziehungskraft f
gravity ['grævɪti] s (seriousness) Ernst m; (of a situation) Schwere f; (phys) Schwerkraft f
gravy ['grevi] s Soße f; (coll) leichter Gewinn m
gra'vy boat' s Soßenschüssel f
gra'vy train' s (sl) Futterkrippe f
gray [gre] adj grau || s Grau n || intr ergrauen
gray'beard' s Graubart m
gray'-haired' adj grauhaarig
grayish ['gre·ɪʃ] adj gräulich
gray' mat'ter s graue Substanz f
graze [grez] tr (said of a bullet) streifen; (cattle) weiden lassen || intr weiden
graz'ing land' s Weide f
grease [gris] s Fett n, Schmiere f || [gris], [griz] tr (aut) schmieren
grease' gun' [gris] s Schmierpresse f
grease' paint' s Schminke f
grease' pit' s (aut) Schmiergrube f
grease' spot' s Fettfleck m
greasy ['grisi], ['grizi] adj fett(ig)
great [gret] adj groß; (wonderful) (coll) großartig; **a g. many (of)** e–e große Anzahl von; **g. fun** Heidenspaß m; **g. guy** Prachtkerl m
great'-aunt' s Großtante f
Great' Bear' s Großer Bär m
Great' Brit'ain s Großbritannien n
Great' Dane' s deutsche Dogge f
great'-grand'child' s (–chil'dren) Urenkel m
great'-grand'daugh'ter s Urenkelin f
great'-grand'fa'ther s Urgroßvater m
great'-grand'moth'er s Urgroßmutter f
great'-grand'par'ents spl Urgroßeltern pl
great'-grand'son' s Urenkel m
greatly ['gretli] adv sehr, stark
great'-neph'ew s Großneffe m
greatness ['gretnɪs] s Größe f
great'-niece' s Großnichte f
great'-un'cle s Großonkel m
Grecian ['griʃən] adj griechisch
Greece [gris] s Griechenland n
greed [grid] s Habgier f, Gier f
greediness ['gridɪnɪs] s Gierigkeit f
greedy ['gridi] adj (for) gierig (nach)
Greek [grik] adj griechisch || s (person) Grieche m, Griechin f; (language) Griechisch n; **that's G. to me** das kommt mir spanisch vor
green [grin] adj grün; (unripe) unreif; (inexperienced) unerfahren, neu; **become g.** grünen; **turn g. with envy** grün vor Neid werden || s (& golf) Grün n; **greens** Blattgemüse n
green'back' s (coll) Geldschein m
greenery ['grinəri] s Grün n

green'-eyed' *adj* grünäugig; *(fig)* neidisch

green'gro'cer *s* Obst- und Gemüsehändler –in *mf*

green'horn' *s* Ausländer –in *mf*

green'house' *s* Gewächshaus *n*

greenish ['grinɪʃ] *adj* grünlich

Green'land *s* Grönland *n*

green' light' *s* *(fig)* freie Fahrt *f*

greenness ['grinnɪs] *s* Grün *n*; *(inexperience)* Unerfahrenheit *f*

green' pep'per *s* Paprikaschote *f*

green'room' *s* *(theat)* Aufenthaltsraum *m*

greensward ['grin͵swɔrd] *s* Rasen *m*

green' thumb' *s*—**have a g.** gärtnerisches Geschick besitzen

greet [grit] *tr* grüßen; *(welcome)* begrüßen

greet'ing *s* Gruß *m*; *(welcoming)* Begrüßung *f*; **greetings** Grüße *pl*

greet'ing card' *s* Glückwunschkarte *f*

gregarious [grɪ'gɛrɪ-əs] *adj* gesellig

Gregor'ian cal'endar [grɪ'gorɪ-ən] *s* Gregorianischer Kalender *m*

Gregor'ian chant' *s* Gregorianischer Gesang *m*

grenade [grɪ'ned] *s* Granate *f*

grenade' launch'er *s* Gewehrgranatgerät *n*

grey [gre] *adj*, *s*, & *intr* var of **gray**

grey'hound' *s* Windhund *m*

grid [grɪd] *s* *(on a map)* Gitternetz *n*; *(culin)* Bratrost *m*; *(electron)* Gitter *n*

griddle ['grɪdəl] *s* Bratpfanne *f*; *(cookie sheet)* Backblech *n*

grid'dlecake' *s* Pfannkuchen *m*

grid'i'ron *s* Bratrost *m*; *(sport)* Spielfeld *n*; *(theat)* Schnürboden *m*

grid' leak' *s* *(electron)* Gitterwiderstand *m*

grief [grif] *s* Kummer *m*; **come to g.** zu Fall *(or* Schaden*)* kommen, scheitern

grief'-strick'en *adj* gramgebeugt

grievance ['grivəns] *s* Beschwerde *f*

grieve [griv] *tr* bekümmern ‖ *intr* *(over)* sich grämen *(über acc)*

grievous ['grivəs] *adj* *(causing grief)* schmerzlich; *(serious)* schwerwiegend

griffin ['grɪfɪn] *s* Greif *m*

grill [grɪl] *s* Grill *m* ‖ *tr* grillen; *(an accused person)* scharf verhören

grille [grɪl] *s* Gitter *n*

grim [grɪm] *adj* *(grimmer; grimmest)* grimmig; **g. humor** Galgenhumor *m*

grimace ['grɪməs], [grɪ'mes] *s* Grimasse *f* ‖ *intr* Grimassen schneiden

grime [graɪm] *s* Schmutz *m*, Ruß *m*

grimness ['grɪmnɪs] *s* Grimmigkeit *f*

grimy ['graɪmi] *adj* schmutzig, rußig

grin [grɪn] *s* Grinsen *n*, Schmunzeln *n* ‖ *v* *(pret & pp* grinned; *ger* grinning*)* *intr* grinsen, schmunzeln; **I had to g. and bear it** ich mußte gute Miene zum bösen Spiel machen

grind [graɪnd] *s* *(of coffee, grain)* Mahlen *n*; *(hard work)* Schinderei *f*; *(a student)* Streber –in *mf*; **the daily g.** der graue Alltag ‖ *v* *(pret & pp* ground [graʊnd]) *tr* *(coffee,*

grain) mahlen; *(glass, tools)* schleifen; *(meat)* zermahlen; *(in a mortar)* stampfen; **g. down** zerreiben; **g. one's teeth** mit den Zähnen knirschen; **g. out** *(e.g., articles)* ausstoßen; *(tunes)* leiern

grinder ['graɪndər] *s* *(molar)* (dent) Backenzahn *m*; *(mach)* Schleifmaschine *f*

grind'stone' *s* Schleifstein *m*

grip [grɪp] *s* Griff *m*; *(handle)* Handgriff *m*; *(handbag)* Reisetasche *f*; *(power)* Gewalt *f*; **come to grips with** in Angriff nehmen; **have a good g. on** *(fig)* sicher beherrschen; **lose one's g.** *(fig)* den Halt verlieren ‖ *v* *(pret & pp* gripped; *ger* gripping*)* *tr* *(& fig)* packen

gripe [graɪp] *s* Meckerei *f* ‖ *intr* *(about)* meckern *(über acc)*

grippe [grɪp] *s* *(pathol)* Grippe *f*

grip'ping *adj* fesselnd, packend

grisly ['grɪzli] *adj* gräßlich

grist [grɪst] *s* Mahlkorn *n*; **that's g. for his mill** das ist Wasser auf seine Mühle

gristle ['grɪsəl] *s* Knorpel *m*

gristly ['grɪsli] *adj* knorpelig

grist'mill' *s* Getreidemühle *f*

grit [grɪt] *s* *(abrasive particles)* Grieß *m*; *(pluck)* (coll) Mumm *m*; **grits** Schrotmehl *n* ‖ *v* *(pret & pp* gritted; *ger* gritting*)* *tr* *(one's teeth)* zusammenbeißen

gritty ['grɪti] *adj* grießig

grizzly ['grɪzli] *adj* gräulich

griz'zly bear' *s* Graubär *m*

groan [gron] *s* Stöhnen *n*; **groans** Geächze *n* ‖ *intr* stöhnen; *(grumble)* (coll) brumen

grocer ['grosər] *s* Lebensmittelhändler –in *mf*

grocery ['grosəri] *s* *(store)* Lebensmittelgeschäft *n*; **groceries** Lebensmittel *pl*

gro'cery store' *s* Lebensmittelgeschäft *n*

grog [grɑg] *s* Grog *m*

groggy ['grɑgi] *adj* benommen

groin [grɔɪn] *s* *(anat)* Leiste *f*, Leistengegend *f*; *(archit)* Rippe *f*

groom [grum] *s* Bräutigam *m*; *(stableboy)* Reitknecht *m* ‖ *tr* *(a person, animal)* pflegen; *(for a position)* heranziehen

groove [gruv] *s* Kerbe *f*; *(for letting off water)* Rinne *f*; *(of a record)* Rille *f*; *(in a barrel)* Zug *m*; **in the g.** (fig) im richtigen Fahrwasser

grope [grop] *tr*—**g. one's way** sich vorwärtstasten ‖ *intr* tappen; **g. about** herumtappen; **g. for** tappen nach, tasten nach

gropingly ['gropɪŋli] *adv* tastend

gross [gros] *adj* *(coarse, vulgar)* roh, derb; *(mistake)* grob; *(crass, extreme)* kraß; *(without deductions)* Brutto– ‖ *s* Gros *n* ‖ *tr* e-n Bruttogewinn haben von

grossly ['grosli] *adv* sehr, stark

gross' na'tional prod'uct *s* Bruttosozialprodukt *n*

gross′ receipts′ *spl* Bruttoeinnahmen *pl*

grotesque [gro′tesk] *adj* grotesk

grot·to [′grɑto] *s* (**-toes** & **-tos**) Grotte *f*, Höhle *f*

grouch [grautʃ] *s* (coll) Brummbär *m*, Griesgram *m* ‖ *intr* brummen

grouchy [′grautʃi] *adj* (coll) brummig

ground [graund] *s* Grund *m*, Boden *m*; (*reason*) Grund *m*; (elec) Erde *f*; **every inch of g.** jeder Fußbreit Boden; **grounds** (*e.g., of an estate*) Anlagen *pl*; (*reasons*) Gründe *pl*; (*of coffee*) Satz *m*; **break g.** mit dem Bau beginnen; **gain g.** (an) Boden gewinnen; **hold one's g.** seinen Standpunkt behaupten; **level to the g.** dem Erdboden gleichmachen; **lose g.** (an) Boden verlieren; **low g.** Niederung *f*; **new g.** (fig) Neuland *n*; **on the grounds that** mit der Begründung, daß; **run into the g.** (fig) bis zum Überdruß wiederholen; **stand one's g.** standhalten; **yield g.** (fig) nachgeben ‖ *tr* (*a pilot*) Startverbot erteilen (*dat*); (*a ship*) auflaufen lassen; (elec) erden; **be grounded by bad weather** wegen schlechten Wetters am Starten gehindert werden

ground′ connec′tion *s* (elec) Erdung *f*

ground′ crew′ *s* (aer) Bodenmannschaft *f*

ground′ floor′ *s* Parterre *n*, Erdgeschoß *n*

ground′ glass′ *s* Mattglas *n*

ground′ hog′ *s* Murmeltier *n*

groundless [′graundlɪs] *adj* grundlos

ground′ meat′ *s* Hackfleisch *n*

ground′ plan′ *s* Grundriß *m*; (fig) Entwurf *m*

ground′ speed′ *s* Geschwindigkeit *f* über Grund

ground′ swell′ *s* Dünung *f*; (fig) wogende Erregung *f*

ground′-to-air′ *adj* Boden-Bord-

ground′ wa′ter *s* Grundwasser *n*

ground′ wire′ *s* (elec) Erdleitung *f*

ground′work′ *s* Grundlage *f*

group [grup] *adj* Gruppen- ‖ *s* Gruppe *f*; (*consisting of 18 aircraft*) Geschwader *n* ‖ *tr* gruppieren ‖ *intr* sich gruppieren

group′ing *s* Gruppierung *f*

group′ insur′ance *s* Gruppenversicherung *f*

group′ ther′apy *s* Gruppentherapie *f*

grouse [graus] *s* Waldhuhn *n* ‖ *intr* (sl) meckern

grout [graut] *s* dünner Mörtel *m* ‖ *tr* verstreichen

grove [grov] *s* Gehölz *n*, Hain *m*

grov·el [′grʌvəl], [′grɑvəl] *v* (*pret & pp* **-el[l]ed**; *ger* **-el[l]ing**) *intr* (& fig) kriechen; **g. in filth** in Schmutz wühlen

grow [gro] *v* (*pret* **grew** [gru]; *pp* **grown** [gron]) *tr* (*plants*) planzen, züchten; (*grain*) anbauen; (*a beard*) sich [*dat*] wachsen lassen; **the ram grows horns** dem Widder wachsen Hörner ‖ *intr* wachsen; (*become*) werden; (*become bigger*) größer wer-

den; **g. fond of** liebgewinnen; **g. luxuriantly** wuchern; **g. older** an Jahren zunehmen; **g. on s.o.** j-m ans Herz wachsen; **g. out of** (*clothes*) herauswachsen aus; (fig) entstehen aus; **g. pale** erblassen; **g. together** zusammenwachsen; (*close*) zuwachsen; **g. up** aufwachsen; **g. wild** (*luxuriantly*) wuchern; (*in the wild*) wild wachsen

grower [′gro·ər] *s* Züchter –in *mf*

growl [graul] *s* (*of a dog, stomach*) Knurren *n*; (*of a bear*) Brummen *n* ‖ *tr* (*words*) brummen ‖ *intr* knurren; (*said of a bear*) brummen; **g. at** anknurren

grown [gron] *adj* erwachsen

grown′-up′ *adj* erwachsen ‖ *s* (**grown-ups**) Erwachsene *mf*

growth [groθ] *s* Wachstum *n*; (*increase*) Zuwachs *m*; (pathol) Gewächs *n*; **full g.** volle Größe *f*

grub [grʌb] *s* Larve *f*, Made *f*; (sl) Fraß *m* ‖ *v* (*pret & pp* **grubbed**; *ger* **grubbing**) *tr* ausjäten ‖ *intr* wühlen; **g. for** graben nach

grubby [′grʌbi] *adj* (*dirty*) schmutzig

grudge [grʌdʒ] *s* Mißgunst *f*, Groll *m*; **bear** (**or have**) **a g. against s.o.** j-m grollen ‖ *tr* mißgönnen

grudg′ing *adj* mißgünstig

grudg′ingly *adv* (nur) ungern

gruel [′gru·əl] *s* Haferschleim *m*

gruel′ing *adj* strapaziös

gruesome [′grusəm] *adj* grausig

gruff [grʌf] *adj* barsch

grumble [′grʌmbəl] *s* Murren *n* ‖ *intr* (**over**) murren (über)

grumbler [′grʌmblər] *s* Brummbär *m*

grumpy [′grʌmpi] *adj* übellaunig

grunt [grʌnt] *s* Grunzen *n* ‖ *tr* & *intr* grunzen

G′-string′ *s* (*of a dancer*) letzte Hülle *f*; (*of a native*) Lendenschurz *m*

guarantee [,gærən′ti] *s* Garantie *f* ‖ *tr* garantieren für

guarantor [′gærən,tɔr] *s* Garant –in *mf*

guaranty [′gærənti] *s* Garantie *f* ‖ *v* (*pret & pp* **-tied**) *tr* garantieren

guard [gɑrd] *s* (*watch; watchman*) Wache *f*; (*person*) Wächter –in *mf*; (fb) Verteidiger *m*; (mach) Schutzvorrichtung *f*; (*soldier*) (mil) Posten *m*; (*soldiers*) (mil) Wachmannschaft *f*, Wache *f*; **be on g. against** sich hüten vor (*dat*); **be on one's g.** auf der Hut sein; **keep under close g.** scharf bewachen; **mount g.** Wache beziehen; **relieve the g.** die Wache ablösen; **stand g.** Posten (or Wache) stehen; (*during a robbery*) Schmiere stehen ‖ *tr* bewachen; (fig) hüten; **g. one's tongue** seine Zunge im Zaum halten ‖ *intr*—**g.** against sich vorsehen gegen; **g. over** wachen über (*acc*)

guard′ de′tail *s* Wachmannschaft *f*

guard′ du′ty *s* Wachdienst *m*; **pull g.** Wache schieben

guard′house′ *s* (*building used by guards*) Wache *f*; (*military jail*) Arrestlokal *n*

guardian ['gɑrdɪ·ən] s (*custodian*) Wächter –in *mf*; (jur) Vormund *m*

guard'ian an'gel s Schutzengel *m*

guard'ianship s Obhut *f*; (jur) Vormundschaft *f*

guard'rail s Geländer *n*

guard'room s Wachstube *f*, Wachlokal *n*

guerrilla [gə'rɪlə] s Guerillakämpfer –in *mf*

gueril'la war'fare s Guerillakrieg *m*

guess [ges] s Vermutung *f*; **anybody's g.** reine Vermutung *f*; **take a good g.** gut raten || *tr* vermuten; **you guessed it!** geraten! || *intr* raten; **g. at** schätzen

guesser ['gesər] s Rater –in *mf*

guess'work s Raten *n*, Mutmaßung *f*

guest [gest] *adj* Gast–, Gäste– || s Gast *m*; **be a g. of** zu Gaste sein bei

guest' book' s Gästebuch *n*

guest' perform'ance s Gastspiel *n*; **give a g.** (theat) gastieren

guest' perform'er s Gast *m*

guest' room' s Gästezimmer *n*

guest' speak'er s Gastredner –in *mf*

guffaw [gə'fɔ] s Gewieher *n* || *intr* wiehern

guidance ['gaɪdəns] s Leitung *f*, Führung *f*; (educ) Studienberatung *f*; **for your g.** zu Ihrer Orientierung

guid'ance coun'selor s Studienberater –in *mf*

guide [gaɪd] s Führer –in *mf*; (*book*) Reiseführer *m*; (*tourist escort*) Reiseführer –in *mf*; (*for gardening, etc.*) Leitfaden *m* || *tr* führen; (rok) lenken

guide'book' s Reiseführer *m*, Führer *m*

guid'ed mis'sile s Fernlenkkörper *m*

guid'ed tour' s Führung *f*

guide'line s Richtlinie *f*

guide'post' s Wegweiser *m*

guide' word' s Stichwort *n*

guild [gɪld] s Zunft *f*, Gilde *f*

guile [gaɪl] s Arglist *f*

guileful ['gaɪlfəl] *adj* arglistig

guileless ['gaɪllɪs] *adj* arglos

guillotine ['gɪlə·tin] s Fallbeil *n*, Guillotine *f* || *tr* mit dem Fallbeil (or mit der Guillotine) hinrichten

guilt [gɪlt] s Schuld *f*

guilt'-rid'den *adj* schuldbeladen

guilty ['gɪlti] *adj* (of) schuldig (*genit*); (*conscience*) schlecht; **plead g.** sich schuldig bekennen; **plead not g.** sich für nicht schuldig erklären

guil'ty par'ty s Schuldige *mf*

guil'ty ver'dict s Schuldspruch *m*

guin'ea fowl' ['gɪni] s, **guin'ea hen'** s Perlhuhn *n*

guin'ea pig' s Meerschweinchen *n*; (fig) Versuchskaninchen *n*

guise [gaɪz] s Verkleidung *f*; **under the g. of** unter dem Schein (*genit*)

guitar [gɪ'tɑr] s Gitarre *f*

guitarist [gɪ'tɑrɪst] s Gitarrenspieler –in *mf*

gulch [gʌltʃ] s Bergschlucht *f*

gulf [gʌlf] s Golf *m*; (fig) Kluft *f*

Gulf' Stream' s Golfstrom *m*

gull [gʌl] s Möwe *f*; (coll) Tölpel *m* || *tr* übertölpeln

gullet ['gʌlɪt] s Gurgel *f*, Schlund *m*

gullible ['gʌlɪbəl] *adj* leichtgläubig

gully ['gʌli] s Wasserrinne *f*

gulp [gʌlp] s Schluck *m*, Zug *m*; **at one g.** in e–m Zuge || *tr* schlucken; **g. down** schlingen || *intr* schlucken

gum [gʌm] s Gummi *m* & *n*; (*chewing gum*) Kaugummi *m* & *n*; (anat) Zahnfleisch *n* || *v* (*pret & pp* **gummed**; *ger* **gumming**) *tr* (*e.g., labels*) gummieren; **gum up the works** (coll) die Arbeit (or das Spiel) vermasseln

gum' ar'abic s Gummiarabikum *n*

gum'boil' s (pathol) Zahngeschwür *n*

gum'drop' s Gummibonbon *m* & *n*

gummy ['gʌmi] *adj* klebrig

gumption ['gʌmpʃən] s Unternehmungsgeist *m*, Mumm *m*

gun [gʌn] s Gewehr *n*; (*handgun*) Handfeuerwaffe *f*; (arti) Geschütz *n*; **stick to one's guns** bei der Stange bleiben || *v* (*pret & pp* **gunned**; *ger* **gunning**) *tr*—**gun down** niederschießen; **gun the engine** Gas geben || *intr* auf die Jagd gehen; **be out gunning for** auf dem Korn haben; **gun for game** auf die Jagd gehen

gun' bar'rel s Gewehrlauf *m*; (arti) Geschützrohr *n*

gun' bat'tle s Feuerkampf *m*

gun' belt' s Wehrgehänge *n*

gun'boat' s Kanonenboot *n*

gun' car'riage s Lafette *f*

gun'cot'ton s Schießbaumwolle *f*

gun' crew' s Bedienungsmannschaft *f*

gun' emplace'ment s Geschützstand *m*

gun' fight' s Schießerei *f*

gun'fire' s Geschützfeuer *n*

gun'man s (–men) bewaffneter Bandit *m*

gun' met'al s Geschützlegierung *f*

gun' mount' s Lafette *f*; (*of swivel type*) Schwenklafette *f*

gunner ['gʌnər] s Kanonier *m*; (aer) Bordschütze *m*

gunnery ['gʌnəri] s Geschützwesen *n*

gun'nery prac'tice s Übungsschießen *n*

gunnysack ['gʌnɪ‚sæk] s Jutesack *m*

gun' per'mit s Waffenschein *m*

gun'point' s—**at g.** mit vorgehaltenem Gewehr

gun'pow'der s Schießpulver *n*

gun'run'ning s Waffenschmuggel *m*

gun'shot' s Schuß *m*; (*range*) Schußweite *f*

gun'shot wound' s Schußwunde *f*

gun'-shy' *adj* schußscheu

gun'sight' s Visier *n*

gun'smith' s Büchsenmacher *m*

gun'stock' s Gewehrschaft *m*

gun' tur'ret s Geschützturm *m*; (aer) Schwalbennest *n*

gunwale ['gʌnəl] s Schandeckel *m*

guppy ['gʌpi] s Millionenfisch *m*

gurgle ['gʌrgəl] s Glucksen *n*, Gurgeln *n* || *intr* glucksen, gurgeln

gush [gʌʃ] s Guß *m*; (fig) Erguß *m* || *intr* sich ergießen; **g. out** hervorströmen; **g. over** (fig) viel Aufhebens machen von

gusher ['gʌʃər] s Schwärmer –in *mf*; (*oil well*) sprudelnde Ölquelle *f*

gush'ing *adj* (fig) überschwenglich

gushy ['gʌ/i] *adj* schwärmerisch

gusset ['gʌsɪt] *s* Zwickel *m*

gust [gʌst] *s* Stoß *m*; (*of wind*) Windstoß *m*, Bö *f*

gusto ['gʌsto] *s* Gusto *m*

gusty ['gʌsti] *adj* böig

gut [gʌt] *s* Darm *m*; **guts** Eingeweide *pl*; (coll) Schneid *m* ‖ *v* (*pret & pp* **gutted;** *ger* **gutting**) *tr* ausbrennen; **be gutted** ausbrennen

gutter ['gʌtər] *s* Gosse *f*; (*of a roof*) Dachrinne *f*

gut'tersnipe' *s* (coll) Straßenjunge *m*

guttural ['gʌtərəl] *adj* kehlig; (ling) Kehl– ‖ *s* (ling) Kehllaut *m*

guy [gaɪ] *s* Halteseil *n*; (*of a tent*) Spannschnur *f*; (coll) Kerl *m*; **dirty guy** (coll) Sauigel *m*; **great guy** Prachtkerl *m* ‖ *tr* verspannen

guy' wire' *s* Spanndraht *m*

guzzle ['gʌzəl] *tr & intr* saufen

guzzler ['gʌzlər] *s* Säufer –in *mf*

gym [dʒɪm] *adj* (coll) Turn– ‖ *s* (coll) Turnhalle *f*

gym' class' *s* (coll) Turnstunde *f*

gymnasi·um [dʒɪm'nezɪ·əm] *s* (**–ums** & **–a** [ə]) Turnhalle *f*

gymnast ['dʒɪmnæst] *s* Turner –in *mf*

gymnastic [dʒɪm'næstɪk] *adj* Turn–, gymnastisch; **g. exercise** Turnübung *f* ‖ **gymnastics** *spl* Gymnastik *f*, Turnen *n*

gynecologist [ˌgaɪnə'kɑlədʒɪst] *s* Gynäkologe *m*, Gynäkologin *f*

gynecology [ˌgaɪnə'kɑlədʒi] *s* Gynäkologie *f*

gyp [dʒɪp] *s* (sl) Nepp *m*; (*person*) Nepper *m*; **that's a gyp** das ist Nepp! ‖ *v* (*pret & pp* **gypped;** *ger* **gypping**) *tr* neppen

gyp' joint' *s* Nepplokal *n*

gypper ['dʒɪpər] *s* Nepper *m*

gypsy ['dʒɪpsi] *adj* Zigeuner– ‖ *s* Zigeuner –in *mf*

gyp'sy moth' *s* Großer Schwammspinner *m*

gyrate ['dʒaɪret] *intr* sich drehen; kreiseln

gyration [dʒaɪ're/ən] *s* Kreiselbewegung *f*

gyroscope ['dʒaɪrəˌskop] *s* Kreisel *m*

H

H, h [et/] *s* achter Buchstabe des englischen Alphabets

haberdasher ['hæbər‚dæ/ər] *s* Inhaber –in *mf* e-s Herrenmodengeschäfts

haberdashery ['hæbər‚dæ/əri] *s* Herrenmodengeschäft *n*

habit ['hæbɪt] *s* Gewohnheit *f*; (eccl) Ordenskleid *n*; **be in the h. of** (*ger*) pflegen zu (*inf*); **break s.o. of that h. of smoking** j–m das Rauchen abgewöhnen; **from h.** aus Gewohnheit; **get into the h. of smoking** sich [*dat*] das Rauchen angewöhnen; **make a h, of it** es zur Gewohnheit werden lassen

habitat ['hæbɪ‚tæt] *s* Wohngebiet *n*

habitation [ˌhæbɪ'te/ən] *s* Wohnort *m*

habitual [hə'bɪt/ʊ·əl] *adj* gewohnheitsmäßig, Gewohnheits–

hack [hæk] *s* (*blow*) Hieb *m*; (*notch*) Kerbe *f*; (*rasping cough*) trockener Husten *m*; (*worn-out horse*) Schindmähre *f*; (*hackney*) Droschke *f*; (*taxi*) (coll) Taxi *n*; (*writer*) (coll) Schreiberling *m* ‖ *tr* hacken, hauen; (basketball) auf den Arm schlagen ‖ *intr* Taxi fahren

hackney ['hækni] *s* (*carriage*) Droschke *f*; (*horse*) gewöhnliches Gebrauchspferd *n*

hackneyed ['hæknid] *adj* abgedroschen

hack'saw' *s* Metallsäge *f*, Bügelsäge *f*

haddock ['hædək] *s* Schellfisch *m*

haft [hæft] *s* Griff *m*

hag [hæg] *s* Vettel *f*; (*witch*) Hexe *f*

haggard ['hægərd] *adj* hager

haggle ['hægəl] *intr* (*over*) feilschen (um)

hag'gling *s* Feilschen *n*

Hague, the [heg] *s* den Haag *m*

hail [hel] *s* Hagel *m*; **h. of bullets** Kugelhagel *m* ‖ *tr* (*a taxi, ship*) anrufen; (*acclaim*) preisen; (as) begrüßen (als) ‖ *intr* hageln; **h. from** stammen aus (or von) ‖ *interj* Heil!

Hail' Mar'y *s* Ave Maria *n*

hail'stone' *s* Hagelkorn *n*, Schloße *f*

hail'storm' *s* Hagelschauer *m*

hair [her] *s* (*single hair*) Haar *n*; (*collectively*) Haare *pl*; **by a h.** um ein Haar; **do s.o.'s h.** j–n frisieren; **get in s.o.'s h.** j–m auf die Nerven gehen lassen; **split hairs** Haarspalterei treiben

hair'breadth' *s*—**by a h.** um Haaresbreite

hair'brush' *s* Haarbürste *f*

hair' clip' *s* Spange *f*, Klammer *f*

hair'cloth' *s* Haartuch *n*

hair'curl'er *s* Lockenwickler *m*

hair'cut' *s* Haarschnitt *m*; **get a h.** sich [*dat*] die Haare schneiden lassen

hair'do' *s* (**–dos**) Frisur *f*

hair'dress'er *s* Friseur *m*, Friseuse *f*

hair'dri'er *s* Haartrockner *m*

hair' dye' *s* Haarfärbemittel *n*

hairiness ['herɪnɪs] *s* Behaartheit *f*

hairless ['herlɪs] *adj* haarlos

hair'line' *s* Haaransatz *m*

hair' net' *s* Haarnetz *n*

hair' oil' *s* Haaröl *n*

hair'piece' *s* Haarteil *m*

hair'pin' *s* Haarnadel *f*

hair'pin curve' *s* Haarnadelkurve *f*

hair'-rais'ing *adj* haarsträubend

hair' rinse' *s* Spülmittel *n*

hair'roll'er s Haarwickler m
hair' set' s Wasserwelle f
hair' shirt' s Büßerhemd n
hair'split'ting s Haarspalterei f
hair' spray' s Haarspray m
hair'spring' s Haarfeder f, Spirale f
hair'style' s Frisur f
hair' ton'ic s Haarwasser n
hairy ['heri] adj haarig, behaart
Haiti ['heti] s Haiti n
halberd ['hælbərd] s Hellebarde f
hal'cyon days' ['hælsɪ·ən] spl (fig)
  glückliche Zeit f
hale [hel] adj gesund; h. and hearty
  gesund und munter
half [hæf] adj halb; at h. price zum
  halben Preis; have h. a mind to (inf)
  halb und halb entschlossen sein zu
  (inf); one and a h. eineinhalb || adv
  halb; h. as much as nur halb so wie;
  h. as much again um die Hälfte mehr;
  h. past three halb vier; not h. durch-
  aus nicht || s (halves [hævz]) Hälfte
  f; cut in h. in die Hälfte schneiden;
  go halves with halbpart machen mit
half'-and-half' adj & adv halb und
  halb || s Halb-und-halb-Mischung f
half'back' s (fb) Läufer m
half'-baked' adj halb gebacken; (plans,
  etc.) halbfertig; (person) unerfahren
half'-blood' s Halbblut n
half'-breed' s Halbblut n, Mischling m
half' broth'er s Halbbruder m
half'-cocked' adv (coll) nicht ganz
  vorbereitet
half'-day' adv halbtags
half'-full' adj halbvoll
half'-heart'ed adj zaghaft
half'-hour' adj halfstündig || s halbe
  Stunde f; every h. halbstündlich
half' leath'er s (bb) Halbleder n
half'-length' adj halblang; (portrait) in
  Halbfigur
half'-length por'trait s Brustbild n
half'-light' s Halbdunkel n
half'-mast' s—at h. auf halbmast
half'-meas'ure s Halbheit f
half'-moon' s Halbmond m
half' note' s (mus) halbe Note f
half' pay' s Wartegeld n; be on h.
  Wartegeld beziehen
half' pint' s (sl) Zwerg m
half' sis'ter s Halbschwester f
half' sleeves' spl halblange Ärmel pl
half' sole' s Halbsohle f
half'-staff' s—at h. auf halbmast
half'-tim'bered adj Fachwerk—
half' time' s (sport) Halbzeit f
half'-time' adj Halbzeit—
half' ti'tle s (typ) Schmutztitel m
half'tone' s (mus, paint, typ) Halbton
  m
half'-track' s Halbkettenfahrzeug n
half'-truth' s halbe Wahrheit f
half'way' adj auf halbem Wege liegend
  || adv halbwegs, auf halbem Wege;
  meet s.o. h. j-m auf dem halben
  Wege entgegenkommen
half'way meas'ure s Halbheit f
half'-wit' s Schwachkopf m
half'-wit'ted adj blöd
halibut ['hælɪbət] s Heilbutt m

halitosis [,hælɪ'tosɪs] s Mundgeruch m
hall [hɔl] s (entranceway) Diele f, Flur
  m; (passageway) Gang m; (large
  meeting room) Saal m; (building)
  Gebäude n
hall'mark' s Kennzeichen n
hal·lo [hə'lo] s (—los) Hallo n || interj
  hallo!
hall' of fame' s Ruhmeshalle f
hallow ['hælo] tr heiligen
hallucination [hə,lusɪ'neʃən] s Sinnes-
  täuschung f, Halluzination f
hall'way' s Flur m, Diele f; (passageway) Gang m
ha·lo ['helo] s (—los) Glorienschein m;
  (astr) Ring m, Hof m
halogen ['hælədʒən] s Halogen n
halt [hɔlt] s Halt m, Stillstand m; (rest)
  Rast f; bring to a h. zum Stillstand
  bringen; call a h. to halten lassen;
  come to a h. stehenbleiben || tr an-
  halten || intr halten; (rest) rasten ||
  interj halt!
halter ['hɔltər] s (for a horse) Halfter
  m; (noose) Strick m
halt'ing adj (gait) hinkend; (voice)
  stockend
halve [hæv] tr halbieren
halyard ['hæljərd] s Fall n
ham [hæm] s (pork) Schinken m; (back
  of the knee) Kniekehle f; (actor)
  (sl) Schmierenschauspieler –in mf;
  (rad) (sl) Funkamateur m
hamburger ['hæm,bɑrgər] s Hackfleisch n, deutsches Beefsteak n
hamlet ['hæmlɪt] s Dörfchen n
hammer ['hæmər] s Hammer m; (of a
  bell) Klöppel m; (sport) Wurfham-
  mer m || tr hämmern; h. in (a nail)
  einschlagen; (e.g., rules) einhäm-
  mern; h. out aushämmern || intr
  hämmern; h. away at (fig) herum-
  arbeiten an (dat)
hammock ['hæmək] s Hängematte f
hamper ['hæmpər] s Wäschebehälter
  m || tr behindern
hamster ['hæmstər] s Hamster m
ham'string' s Kniesehne f || v (pret &
  pp –strung) tr (fig) lähmen
hand [hænd] s Hand f; (applause) Beifall m; (handwriting) Handschrift f;
  (of a clock) Zeiger m; (help) Hilfe
  f; all hands on deck! (naut) alle
  Mann an Deck!; at first h. aus erster
  Hand; at h. vorhanden, zur Hand;
  at the hands of von seiten (genit);
  be on h. zur Stelle sein; by h. mit
  der Hand; change hands in andere
  Hände übergehen; fall into s.o.'s
  hands in j-s Hände fallen; from h.
  to mouth von der Hand in den Mund;
  get one's hands on in die Hände
  bekommen; get the upper h. die
  Oberhand gewinnen; give s.o. a free
  h. j-m freies Spiel lassen; give s.o. a
  h. (help s.o.) j-m helfen; (applaud
  s.o.) j-m Beifall spenden; go h. in h.
  with (fig) Hand in Hand gehen mit;
  h. and foot eifrig; h. in h. Hand in
  Hand; hands off! Hände weg!; hands
  up! Hände hoch!; have a good h.
  (cards) gute Karten haben; have a h.

in die Hand im Spiel haben bei; **have one's hands full** alle Hände voll zu tun haben; **have well in h.** gut in der Hand haben; **hold hands** sich bei den Händen halten; **in one's own h.** eigenhändig; **I wash my hands of it** ich wasche meine Hände in Unschuld; **join hands** (fig) sich zusammenschließen; **new h.** Neuling *m*; **on all hands** auf allen Seiten; **on h.** (com) vorrätig; **on one h. ... on the other** einerseits ... andererseits; **out of h.** außer Rand und Band; **play into s.o.'s hands** j–m in die Hände spielen; **put one's h. on** (fig) finden; **show one's h.** (fig) seine Karten aufdecken; **take a h. in** mitarbeiten an (*dat*); **throw up one's hands** verzweifelt die Hände hochwerfen; **try one's h. at** versuchen; **win hands down** spielend gewinnen; **with a heavy h.** streng || *tr* (zu)reichen; **h. down** (*to s.o. below*) herunterreichen; (*e.g., traditions*) überliefern; **h. in** (*e.g., homework*) abgeben; (*an application*) einreichen; **h. out** austeilen; **h. over** übergeben; (*relinquish*) aushändigen, hergeben; **I have to h. it to you** (coll) ich muß dir recht geben

hand'bag' *s* Handtasche *f*, Tasche *f*
hand'ball' *s* Handball *m*
hand'bill' *s* Handzettel *m*
hand'book' *s* Handbuch *n*
hand' brake' *s* (aut) Handbremse *f*
hand'breadth' *s* Handbreit *f*
hand' cart' *s* Handkarren *m*
hand'clasp' *s* Händedruck *m*
hand'cuff' *s* Handschelle *f* || *tr* Handschellen anlegen (*dat*)
–handed [ˌhændɪd] *suf* –händig
handful [ˈhændˌful] *s* Handvoll *f*; (*a few*) ein paar; (fig) Nervensäge *f*
hand'glass' *s* Leselupe *f*
hand' grenade' *s* Handgranate *f*
handi·cap [ˈhændɪˌkæp] *s* Handikap *n*, Benachteiligung *f* || *v* (*pret & pp* **–capped;** *ger* **–capping**) *tr* handikapen, benachteiligen
hand'icap race' *s* Vorgaberennen *n*
handicraft [ˈhændɪˌkræft] *s* Handwerk *n*
handily [ˈhændɪli] *adv* (*dexterously*) geschickt; (*easily*) mit Leichtigkeit
handiwork [ˈhændɪˌwʌrk] *s* Handarbeit *f*; (fig) Werk *n*, Schöpfung *f*
handkerchief [ˈhæŋkərtʃɪf] *s* Taschentuch *n*
handle [ˈhændəl] *s* Griff *m*; (*of a pot*) Henkel *m*; (*of a frying pan, broom, etc.*) Stiel *m*; (*of a crank*) Handkurbel *f*; (*of a pump*) Schwengel *m*; (*of a door*) Drücker *m*; (*name*) (coll) Name *m*; (*title*) (coll) Titelkram *m*; **fly off the h.** vor Wut platzen || *tr* (*touch*) berühren; (*tools, etc.*) handhaben; (*operate*) bedienen; (fig) erledigen; (com) handeln mit; **h. with care!** Vorsicht!; **know how to h. customers** es verstehen, mit Kunden umzugehen || *intr*—**h. well** sich leicht lenken lassen

han'dlebars' *spl* Lenkstange *f*, (*mustache*) (coll) Schnauzbart *m*
handler [ˈhændlər] *s* (sport) Trainer *m*
han'dling *s* (*e.g., of a car*) Lenkbarkeit *f*; (*of merchandise, theme, ball*) Behandlung *f*; (*of a tool*) Handhabung *f*
han'dling charg'es *spl* Umschlagspesen *pl*
hand' lug'gage *s* Handgepäck *n*
hand'made' *adj* handgemacht
hand'-me-downs' *spl* getragene Kleider *pl*
hand' mir'ror *s* Handspiegel *m*
hand'-op'erated *adj* mit Handbetrieb
hand' or'gan *s* Drehorgel *f*
hand'out' *s* milde Gabe *f*; (*sheet*) Handzettel *m*
hand'-picked' *adj* handgepflückt; (fig) ausgesucht
hand'rail' *s* Geländer *n*
hand'saw' *s* Handsäge *f*
hand'shake' *s* Handschlag *m*, Händedruck *m*
handsome [ˈhænsəm] *adj* schön
hand'-to-hand' fight'ing *s* Nahkampf *m*
hand'-to-mouth' *adj* von der Hand in den Mund
hand'work' *s* Handarbeit *f*
hand'writ'ing *s* Handschrift *f*
handwritten [ˈhændˌrɪtən] *adj* handschriftlich; **h. letter** Handschreiben *n*
handy [ˈhændi] *adj* handlich; (*practical*) praktisch; (*person*) geschickt; **come in h.** gelegen kommen; **have h.** zur Hand haben
hand'y·man' *s* (**–men'**) Handlanger *m*
hang [hæŋ] *s* (*of curtains, clothes*) Fall *m*; **get the h. of** (coll) sich einarbeiten in (*acc*); **I don't give a h. about it** (coll) es ist mir Wurst || *v* (*pret & pp* **hung** [hʌŋ]) *tr* hängen; (*a door*) einhängen; (*wallpaper*) ankleben; **h. one's head** den Kopf hängen lassen; **h. out** heraushängen; **h. up** aufhängen; (*the receiver*) (telp) auflegen; **I'll be hanged if** ich will mich hängen lassen, wenn || *intr* hängen; (*float*) schweben; **h. around** herumlungern; **h. around the bar** sich in der Bar herumtreiben; **h. around with** umgehen mit; **h. back** sich zurückhalten; **h. by** (*a thread, rope*) hängen an (*dat*); **h. down** niederhängen; **h. in the balance** in der Schwebe sein; **h. on** durchhalten; **h. on s.o.'s words** an j–s Worten hängen; **h. on to** festhalten; (*retain*) behalten; **h. together** zusammenhalten; **h. up** (telp) einhängen || *v* (*pret & pp* **hanged & hung**) *tr* hängen
hangar [ˈhæŋər] *s* Hangar *m*
hang'-dog look' *s* Armesündergesicht *n*
hanger [ˈhæŋər] *s* Kleiderbügel *m*
hang'er-on' *s* (**hangers-on**) Mitläufer –in *mf*
hang'ing *adj* (herab)hängend || *s* Hängen *n*
hang'man *s* (**–men**) Henker *m*
hang'nail' *s* Niednagel *m*

hang'out' s Treffpunkt m
hang'o'ver s (coll) Kater m
hank [hæŋk] s Strähne f
hanker ['hæŋkər] intr (**for**) sich sehnen (nach)
hanky-panky ['hæŋki'pæŋki] s (coll) Schwindel m
haphazard [,hæp'hæzərd] adj wahllos
haphazardly [,hæp'hæzərdli] adv aufs Geratewohl
hapless ['hæplɪs] adj unglücklich
happen ['hæpən] intr geschehen; **h. to see** zufällig sehen; **h. upon** zufällig stoßen auf (acc); **what happens now?** was soll nun werden?
hap'pening s Ereignis n
happily ['hæpɪli] adv glücklich
happiness ['hæpɪnɪs] s Glück n
happy ['hæpi] adj glücklich; **be h. about s.th.** über etw erfreut sein; **be h. to** (inf) sich freuen zu (inf); **h. as a lark** quietschvergnügt
Hap'py Birth'day interj Herzlichen Glückwunsch zum Geburtstag!
hap'py-go-luck'y adj unbekümmert
hap'py me'dium s—**strike a h.** e-n glücklichen Ausgleich treffen
Hap'py New' Year' interj Glückliches Neujahr!
harangue [hə'ræŋ] s leidenschaftliche Rede f ‖ tr e-e leidenschaftliche Rede halten an (acc)
harass [hə'ræs], ['hærəs] tr schikanieren; (mil) stören
harass'ing fire' s (mil) Störungsfeuer n
harassment [hə'ræsmənt], ['hærəsmənt] s Schikane f; (mil) Störung f
harbinger ['harbɪndʒər] s Vorbote m ‖ tr anmelden
harbor ['harbər] adj Hafen— ‖ s Hafen m ‖ tr (give refuge to) beherbergen; (hide) verbergen; (thoughts) hegen
har'bor mas'ter s Hafenmeister m
hard [hard] adj (substance, water, words) hart; (problem) schwierig; (worker) fleißig; (blow, times, work) schwer; (life) mühsam; (fact) nackt; (rain) heftig; (winter) streng; (drinks) alkoholisch; **be h. on s.o.** j–m schwer zusetzen; **have a h. time** Schwierigkeiten haben; **h. to believe** kaum zu glauben; **h. to please** anspruchsvoll; **h. to understand** schwer zu verstehen ‖ adv hart; (energetically) fleißig; **he was h. put to** (inf) es fiel ihm schwer zu (inf); **rain h.** stark regnen; **take h.** schwer nehmen; **try h.** mit aller Kraft versuchen
hard'-and-fast' adj fest
hard-bitten ['hard,bɪtn] adj verbissen
hard'-boiled' adj (egg) hartgekocht; (coll) hartgesotten
hard' can'dy s Bonbons pl
hard' cash' s bare Münze f
hard' ci'der s Apfelwein m
hard' coal' s Steinkohle f
hard'-earned' adj schwer verdient
harden ['hardən] tr & intr (er)härten
hard'ened adj (criminal) hartgesotten
hard'ening s Verhärtung f
hard'-hearted adj (fig) hartherzig
hard'-heart'ed adj hartherzig

hardihood ['hardɪ,hʊd] s Kühnheit f; (insolence) Frechheit f
hardiness ['hardɪnɪs] s Ausdauer f, Widerstandsfähigkeit f
hard' la'bor s Zwangsarbeit f
hard' luck' s Pech n
hardly ['hardli] adv kaum, schwerlich; **h. ever** fast gar nicht
hardness ['hardnɪs] s Härte f
hard'-of-hear'ing adj schwerhörig
hard'-pressed' adj schwer bedrängt
hard'-shell' adj hartschalig; (coll) unnachgiebig
hard'ship s Mühsal f
hard'top' s (aut) Hardtop n
hard' up' adj (for money) schlecht bei Kasse; **h. for** in Verlegenheit um
hard'ware s Eisenwaren pl; (e.g., on doors, windows) Beschläge pl; **military h.** militärische Ausrüstung f
hard'ware store' s Eisenwarenhandlung f
hard'wood' s Hartholz n
hard'wood floor' s Hartholzboden m
hard'-work'ing adj fleißig
hardy ['hardi] adj (plants) winterfest; (person) widerstandsfähig
hare [her] s Hase m
hare'brained' adj unbesonnen
hare'lip' s Hasenscharte f
harem ['herəm] s Harem m
hark [hark] intr horchen; **h. back to** zurückgehen auf (acc)
harlequin ['harləkwɪn] s Harlekin m
harlot ['harlət] s Hure f
harm [harm] s Schaden m; **do h.** Schaden anrichten; **I meant no h. by it** ich meinte es nicht böse; **out of harm's way** in Sicherheit; **there's no h. in trying** ein Versuch kann nicht schaden ‖ tr beschädigen; (e.g., a reputation, chances) schaden (dat); **h. s.o.** (physically) j–m etw zuleide tun; (fig) schaden (dat)
harmful ['harmfəl] adj schädlich
harmless ['harmlɪs] adj unschädlich
harmonic [har'manɪk] adj harmonisch ‖ s (mus) Oberton m
harmonica [har'manɪkə] s Harmonika f
harmonious [har'manɪ-əs] adj harmonisch
harmonize ['harmə,naɪz] intr harmonieren
harmony ['harməni] s Harmonie f; **be in h. with** im Einklang stehen mit
harness ['harnɪs] s Geschirr n; **die in the h.** in den Sielen sterben ‖ tr anschirren; (e.g., a river, power) nutzbar machen
har'ness mak'er s Sattler m
har'ness rac'ing s Trabrennen n
harp [harp] s Harfe f ‖ intr—**h. on** herumreiten auf (dat)
harpist ['harpɪst] s Harfner –in mf
harpoon [har'pun] s Harpune f ‖ tr harpunieren
harpsichord ['harpsɪ,kɔrd] s Cembalo n
harpy ['harpi] s (myth) Harpyie f
harrow ['hæro] s Egge f ‖ tr eggen
har'rowing adj schrecklich

har·ry ['hæri] v (pret & pp **–ried**) tr martern

Harry ['hæri] s Heinz m

harsh [hɑrʃ] adj (conditions) hart; (tone) schroff; (light) grell; (treatment) rauh

harshness ['hɑrʃnɪs] s Härte f; Schroffheit f; Grelle f; Rauheit f

hart [hɑrt] s Hirsch m

harum-scarum ['hɛrəm'skɛrəm] adj wild || adv wie ein Wilder

harvest ['hɑrvɪst] s Ernte f; **bad h.** Mißernte f || tr & intr ernten

harvester ['hɑrvɪstər] s Schnitter –in mf; (mach) Mähmaschine f

har′vest moon′ s Erntemond m

has-been ['hæz,bɪn] s (coll) Gestrige mf

hash [hæʃ] s Gehacktes n; **make h. of** (coll) verwursteln || tr zerhacken

hashish ['hæʃiʃ] s Haschisch n

hasp [hæsp] s Haspe f

hassle ['hæsəl] s (coll) Streit m

hassock ['hæsək] s Hocker m

haste [hest] s Hast f, Eile f; **in (all) h.** in (aller) Eile; **make h.** sich beeilen

hasten ['hesən] tr beschleunigen || intr hasten, eilen

hasty ['hesti] adj eilig; (rash) hastig

hat [hæt] s Hut m; **keep under one's h.** für sich behalten

hat′band′ s Hutband n

hat′block′ s Hutform f

hat′box′ s Hutschachtel f

hatch [hætʃ] s (opening) (aer, naut) Luke f; (cover) (naut) Lukendeckel m || tr (eggs) ausbrüten; (a scheme) aushecken; (mark with strokes) schraffieren || intr Junge ausbrüten; (said of chicks) aus dem Ei kriechen

hat′check girl′ s Garderobe(n)fräulein n

hatchet ['hætʃɪt] s Beil n; **bury the h.** die Streitaxt begraben

hatch′ing s Schraffierung f

hatch′way′ s (naut) Luke f

hate [het] s Haß m || tr hassen; **I h. to** (inf) es widerstrebt mir zu (inf)

hateful ['hetfəl] adj verhaßt

hatless ['hætlɪs] adj hutlos

hat′pin′ s Hutnadel f

hat′rack′ s Hutständer m

hatred ['hetrɪd] s Haß m

haughtiness ['hɔtɪnɪs] s Hochmut m

haughty ['hɔti] adj hochmütig

haul [hɔl] s Schleppen n; (hauling distance) Transportstrecke f; (amount caught) Fang m; **make a big h.** (fig) reiche Beute machen; **over the long h.** auf die Dauer || tr (tug) schleppen; (transport) transportieren; **h. ashore** an Land ziehen; **h. down** (a flag) einholen; **h. into court** vor Gericht schleppen; **h. out of bed** aus dem Bett herausholen || intr—**h. off** (naut) abdrehen; **h. off and hit** ausholen um zu schlagen

haulage ['hɔlɪdʒ] s Transport m; (costs) Transportkosten pl

haunch [hɔntʃ] s (hip) Hüfte f; (hind quarter of an animal) Keule f

haunt [hɔnt] s Aufenthaltsort m || tr verfolgen; **h. a place** an e–m Ort umgehen; **this place is haunted** es spukt hier

haunt′ed house′ s Haus n in dem es spukt

have [hæv] s—**the haves and the have-nots** die Besitzenden und die Besitzlosen || v (pret & pp **had** [hæd]) tr haben; (a baby) bekommen; (a drink) trinken; (food) essen; **h. back** (coll) zurückhaben; **h. in mind** vorhaben; **h. it in for s.o.** j–n auf dem Strich haben; **h. it out with s.o.** sich mit j–m aussprechen; **h. it your way** meinetwegen machen Sie es, wie Sie wollen; **h. left** übrig haben; **h. on** (clothes) anhaben; (a hat) aufhaben; (e.g., a program) vorhaben; **h. on one's person** bei sich tragen; **h. to do with s.o.** mit j–m zu tun haben; **h. what it takes** das Zeug dazu haben; **I've had it!** jetzt langt's mir aber!; **I will not h. it!** ich werde es nicht dulden!; **you had better** es wäre besser, wenn Sie; **what would you h. me do?** was soll ich machen? || intr—**h. done with it** fertig sein damit; **h. off** frei haben || aux (to form compound past tenses) haben, e.g., **he has paid the bill** er hat die Rechnung bezahlt; (to form compound past tenses of certain intransitive verbs of motion and change of condition, of the verb **bleiben**, and of the transitive verb **eingehen**) sein, e.g., **she has gone to the theater** sie ist ins Theater gegangen; **they h. become rich** sie sind reich geworden; **you h. stayed too long** Sie sind zu lange geblieben; **I h. assumed an obligation** ich bin e–e Verpflichtung eingegangen; (to express causation) lassen, e.g., **I am having a new suit made** ich lasse mir e–n neuen Anzug machen; (to express necessity) müssen, e.g., **I h. to study now** jetzt muß ich studieren; **that will h. to do** das wird genügen müssen

haven ['hevən] s Hafen m

haversack ['hævər,sæk] s Brotbeutel m

havoc ['hævək] s Verwüstung f; **wreak h. on** verwüsten

haw [hɔ] s (bot) Mehlbeere f; (in speech) Äh n || tr nach links lenken || intr nach links gehen || interj (to a horse) hü!

Hawaii [hə'waɪ·i] s Hawaii n

Hawaiian [hə'waɪjən] adj hawaiisch

Hawai′ian Is′lands spl Hawaii-Inseln pl

hawk [hɔk] s Habicht m || tr (wares) verhökern; **h. up** aushusten || intr sich räuspern

hawker ['hɔkər] s Straßenhändler –in mf

hawse [hɔz] s (hole) (naut) Klüse f; (prow) (naut) Klüsenwand f

hawse′hole′ s (naut) Klüse f

hawser ['hɔzər] s (naut) Trosse f, Tau n

hawthorn ['hɔθɔrn] s Weißdorn m

hay [he] s Heu n; **hit the hay** (sl) sich

in die Falle hauen; **make hay** Heu machen

hay'fe'ver *s* Heufieber *n*

hay'field' *s* Kleefeld *n*

hay'fork' *s* Heugabel *f*

hay'loft' *s* Heuboden *m*

hay'mak'er *s* (box) Schwinger *m*

hay'rack' *s* Heuraufe *f*

hayrick ['heɪˌrɪk] *s* Heuschober *m*

hay'ride' *s* Ausflug *m* in e-m teilweise mit Heu gefüllten Wagen

hay'seed' *s* (coll) Bauerntölpel *m*

hay'stack' *s* Heuschober *m*

hay'wire' *adj* (sl) übergeschnappt; **go h.** (go wrong) schiefgehen; (go insane) überschnappen

hazard ['hæzərd] *s* (danger) Gefahr *f*; (risk) Risiko *n* || *tr* riskieren

hazardous ['hæzərdəs] *adj* gefährlich

haze [hez] *s* Dunst *m*; (fig) Unklarheit *f* || *tr* (students) piesacken

hazel ['hezəl] *adj* (eyes) nußbraun || *s* (bush) Hasel *f*

ha'zelnut' *s* Haselnuß *f*

haziness ['hezɪnɪs] *s* Dunstigkeit *f*; (fig) Verschwommenheit *f*

haz'ing *s* (of students) Piesacken *n*

hazy ['hezɪ] *adj* dunstig; (recollection) verschwommen

H-bomb ['et∫ˌbɑm] *s* Wasserstoffbombe *f*

he [hi] *pers pron* er; **he who** wer || *s* Männchen *n*

head [hed] *s* Kopf–; (chief) Haupt–, Ober–, Chef– || *s* (of a body, cabbage, nail, lettuce, pin) Kopf *m*; (of a gang, family) Haupt *m*; (of a school) Direktor –in *mf*; (of a department) Leiter –in *mf*; (of a bed) Kopfende *n*; (of a coin) Bildseite *f*; (of a glass of beer) Blume *f*; (of cattle) Stück *n*; (of stairs) oberer Absatz *m*; (of a river) Quelle *f*; (of a parade, army) Spitze *f*; (toilet) Klo *n*; a **h.** pro Person, pro Kopf; **at the h. of** an der Spitze *f* (genit); **be at the h. of** vorstehen (dat); **be h. and shoulders above** s.o. haushoch über j–m stehen; (be far superior to s.o.) j–m haushoch überlegen sein; **be over one's h.** über j–s Verstand gehen; **bring to a h.** zur Entscheidung bringen; **by a h.** um e–e Kopflänge; **from h. to foot** von Kopf bis Fuß; **go over s.o.'s h.** über j–s Verstand gehen; (adm) über j–s Kopf hinweg handeln; **go to s.o.'s h.** j–m zu Kopfe steigen; **have a good h. for** begabt sein für; **h. over heels** kopfüber; (in love) bis über die Ohren; (in debt) bis über den Hals; **heads or tails?** Kopf oder Wappen?; **heads up!** aufpassen!; **keep one's h.** kaltes Blut behalten; **keep one's h. above water** sich über Wasser halten; **lose one's h.** den Kopf verlieren; **my h.** is spinning es schwindelt mir; **not be able to make h. or tail of** nicht klug werden aus; **out of one's h.** nicht ganz richtig im Kopf; **per h.** pro Kopf; **put heads together** die Köpfe zusammenstecken; **talk over**

s.o.'s **h.** über j–s Kopf hinwegreden; **talk s.o.'s h. off** j–n dumm und dämlich reden; **take it into one's h.** es sich [dat] in den Kopf setzen || *tr* (be in charge of) leiten; (a parade, army, expedition) anführen; (steer, guide) lenken; **h. a list** als erster auf e–r Liste stehen; **h. off** abwehren; **h. up** (a committee) vorsitzen (dat) || *intr*—**h. back** zurückkehren; **h. for** auf dem Wege sein nach; (aer) anfliegen; (naut) ansteuern; **h. home** sich heimbegeben; **where are you heading?** wo wollen Sie hin?

head'ache' *s* Kopfweh *n*, Kopfschmerzen *pl*

head'band' *s* Kopfband *n*

head'board' *s* Kopfbrett *n*

head'cold' *s* Schnupfen *m*

head' doc'tor *s* Chefarzt *m*, Chefärztin *f*

head'dress' *s* Kopfputz *m*

–headed [ˌhedɪd] *suf* –köpfig

head first *adv* kopfüber; (fig) Hals über Kopf

head'gear' *s* Kopfbedeckung *f*

head'hunt'er *s* Kopfjäger *m*

head'ing *s* Überschrift *f*; (aer) Steuerkurs *m*

headland ['hedlənd] *s* Landspitze *f*

headless ['hedlɪs] *adj* kopflos; (without a leader) führerlos

head'light' *s* (aut) Scheinwerfer *m*

head'line' *s* (in a newspaper) Schlagzeile *f*; (at the top of a page) Überschrift *f*; **hit the headlines** (coll) Schlagzeilen liefern

head'lin'er *s* Hauptdarsteller –in *mf*

head'long' *adj* stürmisch || *adv* kopfüber

head'man' *s* (–men) Häuptling *m*, Chef *m*

head'mas'ter *s* Direktor *m*

head'mis'tress *s* Direktorin *f*

head' nurse' *s* Oberschwester *f*

head' of'fice *s* Hauptgeschäftsstelle *f*

head' of gov'ernment *s* Regierungschef *m*

head' of hair' *s*—**beautiful h.** schönes volles Haar *n*

head' of the fam'ily *s* Familienoberhaupt *n*

head'-on' *adj* Frontal– || *adv* frontal

head'phones' *spl* Kopfhörer *pl*

head'piece' *s* Kopfbedeckung *f*; (brains) (coll) Kopf *m*; (typ) Zierleiste *f*

head'quar'ters *s* Hauptquartier *n*; (of police) Polizeidirektion *f*; (mil) Hauptquartier *n*, Stabsquartier *n*

head'quarters com'pany *s* Stabskompanie *f*

head'rest' *s* Kopflehne *f*; (aut) Kopfstütze *f*

head' restrain'er *s* (aut) Kopfstütze *f*

head'set' *s* Kopfhörer *m*

head' shrink'er *s* (coll) Psychiater –in *mf*

head'stand' *s* Kopfstand *m*

head' start' *s* Vorsprung *m*

head'stone' *s* Grabstein *m*

head'strong' *adj* starrköpfig

head′ wait′er s Oberkellner m
head′wa′ters spl Quellflüsse pl
head′way′ s Vorwärtsbewegung f; (fig) Fortschritte pl
head′wear′ s Kopfbedeckung f
head′wind′ s Gegenwind m
head′work′ s Kopfarbeit f
heady [ˈhɛdi] adj (wine) berauschend; (news) spannend; (impetuous) unbesonnen
heal [hil] tr & intr heilen; **h. up** zuheilen
healer [ˈhilər] s Heilkundige mf
heal′ing s Heilung f
health [hɛlθ] s Gesundheit f; **drink to s.o.'s h.** auf j-s Wohl trinken; **in good h.** gesund; **in poor h.** kränklich; **to your h.!** auf Ihr Wohl!
health′ certi′ficate s Gesundheitspaß m
healthful [ˈhɛlθfəl] adj heilsam; (climate) bekömmlich
health′ insur′ance s Krankenversicherung f
health′ resort′ s Kurort m
healthy [ˈhɛlθi] adj gesund; (respect) gehörig; **keep h.** sich gesund halten
heap [hip] s Haufen m; **in heaps** haufenweise || tr beladen; **h.** (e.g., praise) **on s.o.** j-n überhäufen mit; **h. up** anhäufen
hear [hɪr] v (pret & pp heard [hʌrd]) tr hören; (find out) erfahren; (get word) Bescheid bekommen; **h. s.o.'s lessons** j-n überhören; **h. s.o. out** j-n ganz ausreden lassen || intr hören; **h. about** hören über (acc) or von; **h. from** Nachricht bekommen von; **h. of** hören von; **h. wrong** sich verhören; **he wouldn't h. of it** er wollte nichts davon hören
hearer [ˈhɪrər] s Hörer –in mf; **hearers** Zuhörer pl
hear′ing s Hören n, Gehör n; (jur) Verhör n; **within h.** in Hörweite
hear′ing aid′ s Hörgerät n, Hörapparat m
hear′say′ s Hörensagen n; **know s.th. by h.** etw nur vom Hörensagen kennen; **that's mere h.** das ist bloßes Gerede
hearse [hʌrs] s Leichenwagen m
heart [hɑrt] s Herz n; **after my own h.** nach meinem Herzen; **at h.** im Grunde genommen; **be the h. and soul of** die Seele sein (genit); **by h.** auswendig; **cross my h.!** Hand aufs Herz!; **cry one's h. out** sich ausweinen; **eat one's h. out** sich vor Kummer verzehren; **get to the h. of** auf den Grund kommen (dat); **have a h.** (coll) ein Herz haben; **have one's h. in s.th.** mit dem Herzen bei etw sein; **have the h. to** (inf) es übers Herz bringen zu (inf); **h. and soul** mit Leib und Seele; **hearts** (cards) Herz n; **lose h.** den Mut verlieren; **lose one's h. to** sein Herz verlieren an (acc); **set one's h. on** sein Herz hängen an (acc); **take h.** Mut fassen; **take to h.** beherzigen; **to one's heart's content** nach Herzenslust; **wear one's h. on one's sleeve** das Herz auf der Zunge tragen; **with all one's h.** mit ganzem Herzen
heart′ache′ s Herzweh n
heart′ attack′ s Herzanfall m
heart′beat′ s Herzschlag m
heart′break′ s Herzeleid n
heart′break′er s Herzensbrecher –in mf
heartbroken [ˈhɑrt‚brokən] adj trostlos
heart′burn′ s Sodbrennen n
heart′ disease′ s Herzleiden n
–hearted [‚hɑrtɪd] suf –herzig
hearten [ˈhɑrtən] tr ermutigen
heart′ fail′ure s Herzschlag m
heartfelt [ˈhɑrt‚fɛlt] adj herzinnig, tiefempfunden; (wishes) herzlich
hearth [hɑrθ] s Herd m
hearth′stone′ s Kaminplatte f
heartily [ˈhɑrtɪli] adv (with zest) herzhaft; (sincerely) von Herzen
heartless [ˈhɑrtlɪs] adj herzlos
heart′ mur′mur s Herzgeräusch n
heart′-rend′ing adj herzzerreißend
heart′sick′ adj tief betrübt
heart′ strings′ spl—**pull at s.o.'s h.** j-m ans Herz greifen
heart′ throb′ s Schwarm m
heart′ trans′plant s Herzverpflanzung f
heart′ trou′ble s Herzbeschwerden pl
heart′wood′ s Kernholz n
hearty [ˈhɑrti] adj herzhaft; (meal) reichlich; (eater) stark; (appetite) gut
heat [hit] s Hitze f, Wärme f; (heating) Heizung f; (sexual) Brunst f; (in the case of dogs) Läufigkeit f; (of battle) Eifer m; (sport) Rennen n, Einzelrennen n; **be in h.** brunsten (said of dogs) läufig sein; **final h.** Schlußrennen n; **put the h. on** (sl) unter Druck setzen; **qualifying h.** Vorlauf m || tr (e.g., food) wärmen; (fluids) erhitzen; (a house) heizen; **h. up** aufwärmen || intr—**h.** (up) warm (or heiß) werden
heat′ed adj erhitzt; (fig) erregt
heater [ˈhitər] s Heizkörper m; (oven) Heizofen m
heath [hiθ] s Heide f
hea·then [ˈhiðən] adj heidnisch || s (–then & –thens) Heide m, Heidin f
heathendom [ˈhiðəndəm] s Heidentum n
heather [ˈhɛðər] s Heiderkraut n
heat′ing s Heizung f
heat′ing pad′ s Heizkissen n
heat′ing sys′tem s Heizanlage f
heat′ light′ning s Wetterleuchten n
heat′ prostra′tion s Hitzekollaps m
heat′-resis′tant adj hitzebeständig
heat′ shield′ s (rok) Hitzeschild m
heat′stroke′ s Hitzschlag m
heat′ treat′ment s Wärmebehandlung f
heat′ wave′ s Hitzewelle f
heave [hiv] s Hub m; (throw) Wurf m; **heaves** (vet) schweres Atmen n || v (pret & pp heaved & hove [hov]) tr heben; (throw) werfen; (a sigh) ausstoßen; (the anchor) lichten || intr (said of the breast or sea) wogen; (retch) sich übergeben; **h. in sight** auftauchen; **h. to** (naut) stoppen

heaven ['hevən] s Himmel m; **for heaven's sake** um Himmels willen; **good heavens!** ach du lieber Himmel; **the heavens** der Himmel

heavenly ['hevənlɪ] adj himmlisch

hea'venly bod'y s Himmelskörper m

heavenwards ['hevənwərdz] adv himmelwärts

heavily ['hevɪlɪ] adv schwer; **h. in debt** überschuldet

heavy ['hevɪ] adj schwer; (food) schwer verdaulich; (fine, price) hoch; (walk) schwerfällig; (heart) bedrückt, schwer; (traffic, frost, rain) stark; (fog) dicht; (role) (theat) ernst, düster; **h. drinker** Gewohnheitstrinker –in mf; **h. seas** Sturzsee f; **h. with sleep** schlaftrunken

heavy'-armed' adj schwerbewaffnet

heav'y-du'ty adj Hochleistungs–, Schwerlast–

heav'y-du'ty truck' s Schwerlastwagen m

heav'y-heart'ed adj bedrückt

heav'y in'dustry s Schwerindustrie f

heav'yset' adj untersetzt

heav'y weight' adj Schwergewicht– || s Schwergewichtler m

Hebrew ['hibru] adj hebräisch || s Hebräer –in mf; (language) Hebräisch n

hecatomb ['hekə,tom] s Hekatombe f

heck [hek] s—**give s.o. h.** (sl) j–m tüchtig einheizen; **what the h. are you doing?** (sl) was zum Teufel tust du? || interj verflixt!

heckle ['hekəl] tr durch Zwischenrufe belästigen

heckler ['heklər] s Zwischenrufer –in mf

hectic ['hektɪk] adj hektisch

hectograph ['hektə,græf] s Hektograph m || tr hektographieren

hedge [hedʒ] s Hecke f || tr—**h. in** (or **h. off**) einhegen || intr sich den Rücken decken

hedge'hog' s Igel m

hedge'hop' v (pret & pp –hopped) ger hopping) intr (aer) heckenspringen

hedge'hop'ping s (aer) Heckenhüpfen n

hedge'row' s Hecke f

hedonism ['hidə,nɪzəm] s Hedonismus m

hedonist ['hidənɪst] s Hedonist –in mf

heed [hid] s Acht f; **pay h. to** achtgeben auf (acc); **take h.** achtgeben || tr beachten || intr achtgeben

heedful ['hidfəl] adj (of) achtsam (auf acc)

heedless ['hidlɪs] adj achtlos; **h. of** ungeachtet (genit)

heehaw ['hi,hɔ] s Iah n || interj iah!

heel [hil] s (of the foot) Ferse f; (of a shoe) Absatz m; (of bread) Brotende n; (sl) Schurke m; **down at the h.** abgerissen; **cool one's heels** sich [dat] die Beine in den Bauch stehen; **take to one's heels** Fersengeld geben || intr (said of a dog) auf den Fersen folgen

hefty ['heftɪ] adj (heavy) schwer; (muscular) stämmig; (blow) zünftig

heifer ['hefər] s Färse f

height [haɪt] s Höhe f; (e.g., of power) Gipfel m; **h. of the season** Hochsaison f

heighten ['haɪtən] tr erhöhen; (fig) verschärfen

heinous ['henəs] adj abscheulich

heir [er] s Erbe; m; **become h. to** erben; **become s.o.'s h.** j–n beerben

heir' appar'ent s (heirs apparent) Thronerbe m

heiress ['erɪs] s Erbin f

heir'loom' s Erbstück n

heir' presump'tive s (heirs presumptive) mutmaßlicher Erbe m

Helen ['helən] s Helene f

helicopter ['helɪ,kɑptər] s Hubschrauber m

heliport ['helɪ,port] s Hubschrauberlandeplatz m

helium ['hilɪ-əm] s Helium n

helix ['hilɪks] s (helixes & helices ['helɪ,siz]) Spirale f; (archit) Schnecke f

hell [hel] s Hölle f

hell'bent' adj—**h. on** (sl) erpicht auf (acc)

hell'cat' s (shrew) Hexe f

Hellene ['helin] s Hellene m, Hellenin f

Hellenic [he'lenɪk] adj hellenisch

hell'fire' s Höllenfeuer n

hellish ['helɪʃ] adj höllisch

hel-lo [he'lo] s (–los) Hallo n || interj guten Tag!; (in southern Germany and Austria) Grüß Gott!; (to get s.o.'s attention and in answering the telephone) hallo!

helm [helm] s (& fig) Steuerruder n

helmet ['helmɪt] s Helm m

helms'man s (–men) Steuermann m

help [help] s Hilfe f; (domestic) Hilfe f, Hilfskraft f; (temporary) Aushilfe f; **h. wanted** (in newspapers) Stellenangebot n; **there's no h. for it** da ist nicht zu helfen; **with the h. of** mit Hilfe (genit) || tr helfen (dat); **can I h. you?** womit kann ich (Ihnen) dienen?; **h. along** nachhelfen (dat); **h. down from** herunterhelfen (dat) von (dat); **h. oneself** sich bedienen; (at table) zugreifen; **h. oneself to** sich [dat] nehmen; **h. out** aushelfen (dat); **h. s.o. on** (or **off**) **with the coat** j–m in den (or aus dem) Mantel helfen; **I cannot h.** (ger), **I cannot h. but** (inf) ich kann nicht umhin zu (inf); **sorry, that can't be helped** es tut mir leid, aber es geht nicht anders || intr helfen || interj Hilfe!

helper ['helpər] s Gehilfe m, Gehilfin f

helpful ['helpfəl] adj (person) hilfsbereit; (e.g., suggestion) nützlich

help'ing s Portion f

help'ing hand' s hilfreiche Hand f

helpless ['helplɪs] adj hilflos, ratlos

helter-skelter ['heltər'skeltər] adj wirr || adv holterdiepolter

hem [hem] s Saum m || v (pret & pp hemmed; ger hemming) tr säumen; **hem in** umringen || intr stocken; **hem**

and **haw** nicht mit der Sprache her-
auswollen || *interj* hm!
hemisphere ['hemɪ‚sfɪr] *s* Halbkugel *f*
hemistich ['hemɪ‚stɪk] *s* Halbvers *m*
hem'line' *s* Rocklänge *f*
hem'lock' *s* (*conium*) Schierling *m;*
(*poison*) Schierlingsgift *n;* (*Tsuga
canadensis*) Kanadische Hemmlock-
tanne *f*
hemoglobin [‚himə'globɪn] *s* Blutfarb-
stoff *m,* Hämoglobin *n*
hemophilia [‚himə'fɪlɪ-ə] *s* Bluter-
krankheit *f,* Hämophilie *f*
hemorrhage ['hemərɪdʒ] *s* Blutung *f*
hemorrhoids ['hemə‚rɔɪdz] *spl* Hämorrhoiden *pl*
hemostat ['himə‚stæt] *s* Unterbin-
dungsssklemme *f*
hemp [hemp] *s* Hanf *m*
hem'stitch' *s* Hohlsaum *m* || *tr* mit e-m
Hohlsaum versehen
hen [hen] *s* Henne *f,* Huhn *n*
hence [hens] *adv* von hier; (*therefore*)
daher, daraus; **a year h.** in e-m Jahr
hence'forth' *adv* hinfort, von nun an
hench-man ['hentʃmən] *s* (**-men**) Anhänger *m;* (*gang member*) Helfershelfer *m*
hen'house' *s* Hühnerstall *m*
henna ['henə] *s* Henna *f*
hen' par'ty *s* (coll) Damengesellschaft
f
hen'peck' *tr* unter dem Pantoffel haben; **be henpecked** unter dem Pantoffel stehen; **henpecked husband**
Pantoffelheld *m*
Henry ['henrɪ] *s* Heinrich *m*
hep [hɛp] *adj* (**to**) eingeweiht (in *acc*)
her [hʌr] *poss adj* ihr; (if the antece-
dent is neuter, e.g., Fräulein) sein ||
pers pron sie; (if the antecedent is
neuter) es; (indirect object) ihr; (if
the antecedent is neuter) ihm
herald ['herəld] *s* Herold *m;* (fig) Vor-
bote *m* || *tr* ankündigen; **h.** in ein-
führen
heraldic [he'rældɪk] *adj* heraldisch; **h.**
figure Wappenbild *n;* **h. motto**
Wappenspruch *m*
heraldry ['herəldrɪ] *s* Wappenkunde *f*
herb [(h)ʌrb] *s* Kraut *n,* Gewürz *n;*
(pharm) Arzneikraut *n*
herculean [hʌrkju'li-ən] *adj* herkulisch
herd [hʌrd] *s* Herde *f;* (of game) Rudel
n; **the common h.** der Pöbel || *tr*
hüten; **h. together** zusammenpfer-
chen || *intr* in e-r Herde gehen (or
leben)
herds'man *s* (**-men**) Hirt *m*
here [hɪr] *adv* (position) hier; (direction) hierher, her; **h. and there**
hie(r) und da; **h. below** in diesem
Leben; **h. goes!** jetzt gilt's!; **here's
to you!** auf Ihr Wohl!; **neither h. nor
there** belanglos || *interj* hier!
hereabouts ['hɪrə‚bauts] *adv* hier in
der Nähe
hereaf'ter *adv* hiernach || *s* Jenseits *n*
hereby' *adv* hierdurch
hereditary [hɪ'redɪ‚terɪ] *adj* erblich,
Erb–; **be h.** sich vererben
heredity [hɪ'redɪtɪ] *s* Vererbung *f*

herein' *adv* hierin
hereof' *adv* hiervon
hereon' *adv* hierauf
heresy ['herəsɪ] *s* Ketzerei *f*
heretic ['herətɪk] *s* Ketzer –in *mf*
heretical [hɪ'retɪkəl] *adj* ketzerisch
heretofore [‚hɪrtʊ'for] *adv* zuvor
here'upon' *adv* daraufhin
herewith' *adv* hiermit; (in a letter) anbei, in der Anlage
heritage ['herɪtɪdʒ] *s* Erbe *n*
hermet'ically sealed' [hʌr'metɪkəlɪ]
adj hermetisch verschlossen
hermit ['hʌrmɪt] *s* Einsiedler –in *mf;*
(eccl) Eremit *m*
hermitage ['hʌrmɪtɪdʒ] *s* Eremitage *f*
herni-a ['hʌrnɪ-ə] *s* (**-as & -ae** [‚i])
Bruch *m*
he-ro ['hɪro] *s* (**-roes**) Held *m*
heroic [hɪ'ro-ɪk] *adj* heldenhaft,
Helden–; (pros) heroisch || **heroics**
spl Heldentaten *pl*
hero'ic age' *s* Helden(zeit)alter *n*
hero'ic coup'let *s* heroisches Reim-
paar *n*
hero'ic verse' *s* heroisches Vermaß *n*
heroin ['hero-ɪn] *s* Heroin *n*
heroine ['hero-ɪn] *s* Heldin *f*
heroism ['hero‚ɪzəm] *s* Heldenmut *m*
heron ['herən] *s* (orn) Fischreiher *m*
he'ro wor'ship *s* Heldenverehrung *f*
herring ['herɪŋ] *s* Hering *m*
her'ringbone' *s* (pattern) Grätenmuster
n; (parquetry) Riemenparkett *n*
hers [hʌrz] *poss pron* der ihre (or
ihrige), ihrer
herself' *reflex pron* sich; **she's not h.
today** sie ist heute gar nicht wie sonst
|| *intens pron* selbst, selber
hesitancy ['hezɪtənsɪ] *s* Zaudern *n*
hesitant ['hezɪtənt] *adj* zögernd
hesitate ['hezɪ‚tet] *intr* zögern
hesitation [‚hezɪ'teʃən] *s* Zögern *n*
heterodox ['hetərə‚daks] *adj* anders-
gläubig, heterodox
heterodyne ['hetərə‚daɪn] *adj* Über-
lagerungs– || *tr & intr* überlagern
heterogeneous [‚hetərə'dʒɪnɪ-əs] *adj*
heterogen
hew [hju] *v* (*pret* **hewed**) (*pp* **hewed &
hewn**) *tr* (stone) hauen; (trees) fällen; **hew down** umhauen
hex [heks] *s* (spell) Zauber *m;* (witch)
Hexe *f;* **put a hex on** (coll) behexen
|| *tr* (coll) behexen
hexagon ['heksəgan] *s* Hexagon *n*
hey [he] *interj* hei!; **hey there!** heda!
hey'day' *s* Hochblüte *f,* Glanzzeit *f*
H'-hour' *s* (mil) X-Zeit *f*
hi [haɪ] *interj* he!; **hi there!** heda!
hia-tus [haɪ'etəs] *s* (**-tuses & -tus**)
Lücke *f;* (ling) Hiatus *m*
hibernate ['haɪbər‚net] *intr* (& fig)
Winterschlaf halten
hibernation [‚haɪbər'neʃən] *s* Winterschlaf *m*
hibiscus [haɪ'bɪskəs] *s* Hibiskus *m*
hiccough, hiccup ['hɪkəp] *s* Schluckauf
m
hick [hɪk] *s* Tölpel *m*
hickory ['hɪkərɪ] *s* Hickorybaum *m*
hick' town' *s* Kuhdorf *n*

hidden ['hɪdən] *adj* verborgen, versteckt; *(secret)* geheim
hide [haɪd] *s* Haut *f*, Fell *n* ‖ *v (pret* **hid** [hɪd]; *pp* **hid & hidden** ['hɪdən] *tr* verstecken; *(a view)* verdecken; *(fig)* verbergen; **h. from** verheimlichen vor *(dat)* ‖ *intr* (**out**) sich verstecken
hide'-and-seek' *s* Versteckspiel *n*; **play h.** Versteck spielen
hide'away *s* Schlupfwinkel *m*
hide'bound *adj* engherzig
hideous ['hɪdɪ·əs] *adj* gräßlich
hide'out' *s* (coll) Versteck *n*
hid'ing *s* Verstecken *n*; **be in h.** sich versteckt halten; **get a h.** (coll) Prügel bekommen
hid'ing place' *s* Versteck *n*
hierarchy ['haɪ·ə‚rɑrki] *s* Hierarchie *f*
hieroglyphic [‚haɪ·ərə'glɪfɪk] *adj* Hieroglphen– ‖ *s* Hieroglyphe *f*
hi-fi ['haɪ'faɪ] *adj* Hifi– ‖ *s* Hi-Fi *n*
high [haɪ] *adj* hoch; *(wind)* stark; *(hopes)* hochgespannt; *(fever)* heftig *(spirits)* gehoben; **h. and dry** auf dem Trockenen; **h. and mighty** hochfahrend; **it is h. time** es ist höchste Zeit ‖ *adv* hoch; **h. and low** weit und breit ‖ *s (e.g., in prices)* Hochstand *m*; (aut) höchster Gang *m*; (meteor) Hoch *n*; **on h.** oben; **shift into h.** den höchsten Gang einschalten
high' al'tar *s* Hochaltar *m*
high'ball' *s* Highball *m*
high'born' *adj* hochgeboren
high'boy' *s* hochbeinige Kommode *f*
high'brow' *adj* intellektuell ‖ *s* Intellektuelle *mf*
high' chair' *s* Kinderstuhl *m*
High' Church' *s* Hochkirche *f*
high'-class' *adj* vornehm, herrschaftlich
high' command' *s* Oberkommando *n*
high' cost' of liv'ing *s* hohe Lebenshaltungskosten *pl*
high' div'ing *s* Turmspringen *n*
high'er edduca'tion *s* Hochschulbildung *f*
high'er-up' *s* (coll) hohes Tier *n*
high'est bid' ['haɪ·ɪst] *s* Meistgebot *n*
high'est bid'der *s* Meistbietende *mf*
high' explo'sive *s* hochexplosiver Sprengstoff *m*
highfalutin [‚haɪfə'lutən] *adj* hochtönend
high' fidel'ity *s* äußerst getreue Tonwiedergabe *f*, High Fidelity *f*
high'-fidel'ity *adj* klanggetreu
high' fre'quency *s* Hochfrequenz *f*
high'-fre'quency *adj* hochfrequent
high' gear' *s* höchster Gang *m*; **shift into h.** den höchsten Gang einschalten; (fig) auf Hochtouren gehen
High' Ger'man *s* Hochdeutsch *n*
high'-grade' *adj* hochfein, Qualitäts–
high'-grade steel' *s* Edelstahl *m*
high'-hand'ed *adj* anmaßend
high' heel' *s* Stöckel *m*
high'-heeled shoe' *s* Stöckelschuh *m*
high' horse' *s*—**come off one's h.** klein beigeben; **get up on one's h.** sich aufs hohe Roß setzen

high' jinks' [‚dʒɪŋks] *spl* Ausgelassenheit *f*
high' jump' *s* (sport) Hochsprung *m*
highland ['haɪlənd] *s* Hochland *n*; **highlands** Hochland *n*
highlander ['haɪləndər] *s* Hochländer –in *mf*
high' life' *s* Prasserei *f*, Highlife *n*
high'light' *s (big moment)* Höhepunkt *m*; *(in a picture)* Glanzlicht *n* ‖ *tr* hervorheben; *(in a picture)* Glanzlichter aufsetzen *(dat)*
highly ['haɪli] *adv* hoch, hoch–, höchst; **h. sensitive** hochempfindlich; **speak h. of** in den höchsten Tönen sprechen von; **think h. of** große Stücke halten auf *(acc)*
High' Mass' *s* Hochamt *n*
high'-mind'ed *adj* hochgesinnt
high'-necked' *adj* hochgeschlossen
highness ['haɪnɪs] *s* Höhe *f*; **Highness** *(title)* Hoheit *f*
high' noon' *s*—**at h.** am hellen Mittag
high'-oc'tane *adj* mit hoher Oktanzahl
high'-pitched' *adj (voice)* hoch; *(roof)* steil
high'-pow'ered *adj* starkmotorig; **h. engine** Hochleistungsmotor *m*
high' pres'sure *s* Hochdruck *m*
high'-pres'sure *adj* Hochdruck–; **h. area** Hochdruckgebiet *n* ‖ *tr* (com) bearbeiten
high'-priced' *adj* kostspielig
high' priest' *s* Hohe(r)priester *m*
high'-qual'ity *adj* Qualitäts–, hochwertig
high'-rank'ing *adj* hochgestellt
high' rise' *s* Hochbau *m*, Hochhaus *n*
high'road' *s* (fig) sicherer Weg *m*
high' school' *s* Oberschule *f*
high' sea' *s*—**on the high seas** auf offenem Meer
high' soci'ety *s* vornehme Welt *f*, High Society *f*
high'-sound'ing *adj* hochtönend
high'-speed' *adj* Schnell–; (phot) lichtstark
high'-speed steel' *s* Schnelldrehstahl *m*
high'-spir'ited *adj* hochgemut; *(horse)* feurig
high' spir'its *spl* gehobene Stimmung *f*
high-strung ['haɪ'strʌŋ] *adj* überempfindlich
high' ten'sion *s* Hochspannung *f*
high'-ten'sion *adj* Hochspannungs–
high'-test' gas'oline *s* Superbenzin *n*
high' tide' *s* Flut *f*
high' time' *s* höchste Zeit *f*; (sl) Heidenspaß *m*
high' trea'son *s* Hochverrat *m*
high' volt'age *s* Hochspannung *f*
high'-volt'age *adj* Hochspannungs–
high'-wa'ter mark' *s* Hochwassermarke *f*; (fig) Höhepunkt *m*
high'way' *s* Landstraße *f*, Chaussee *f*
high'way'man *s* (**-men**) Straßenräuber *m*
high'way patrol' *s* Straßenstreife *f*
high'way rob'bery *s* Straßenraub *m*
hijack ['haɪ‚dʒæk] *tr (a truck)* überfallen und rauben; *(a plane)* entführen

hijacker [ˈhaɪ ˌdʒækər] *s (of a truck)* Straßenräuber –in *mf; (of a plane)* Entführer –in *mf*

hi'jack'ing *s* Entführung *f*

hike [haɪk] *s* Wanderung *f; (in prices)* Erhöhung *f* || *tr (prices)* erhöhen || *intr* wandern

hiker [ˈhaɪkər] *s* Wanderer –in *mf*

hik'ing *s* Wandern *n*

hilarious [hɪˈlɛrɪ-əs] *adj* heiter

hill [hɪl] *s* Hügel *m;* **go over the h.** (mil) ausbüxen; **over the h.** (coll) auf dem absteigenden Ast || *tr* häufeln

hill'bil'ly *adj* hinterwäldlerisch || *s* Hinterwäldler –in *mf*

hill' coun'try *s* Hügelland *n*

hillock [ˈhɪlək] *s* Hügelchen *n*

hill'side' *s* Hang *m*

hilly [ˈhɪli] *adj* hügelig

hilt [hɪlt] *s* Griff *m;* **armed to the h.** bis an die Zähne bewaffnet; **to the h.** (fig) gründlich

him [hɪm] *pers pron (dative)* ihm; *(accusative)* ihn

himself' *reflex pron* sich; **he is not h. today** er ist heute gar nicht wie sonst || *intens pron* selbst, selber

hind [haɪnd] *adj* Hinter– || *s* Hirschkuh *f*

hinder [ˈhɪndər] *tr* (ver)hindern

hind'most' *adj* hinterste

hind'quar'ter *s* Hinterviertel *n; (of a horse)* Hinterhand *f; (of venison)* Ziemer *m*

hindrance [ˈhɪndrəns] *s* (to) Hindernis *n* (für)

hind'sight' *s* späte Einsicht *f*

Hindu [ˈhɪndu] *adj* Hindu– || *s* Hindu *m*

hinge [hɪndʒ] *s* Scharnier *n; (of a door)* Angel *f* || *intr*—**h. on** abhängen von

hint [hɪnt] *s* Wink *m,* Andeutung *f;* **give a broad h.** e–n Wink mit dem Zaunpfahl geben; **take the h.** den Wink verstehen || *intr*—**h. at** andeuten

hinterland [ˈhɪntər ˌlænd] *s* Hinterland *n*

hip [hɪp] *adj (sl)* im Bild || *s* Hüfte *f; (of a roof)* Walm *m*

hip'bone' *s* Hüftbein *n*

hip'joint' *s* Hüftgelenk *n*

hipped *adj*—**h. on** (coll) erpicht auf *(acc)*

hippopota·mus [ˌhɪpəˈpɑtəməs] *s* (-muses & -mi [ˌmaɪ]) Nilpferd *n*

hip' roof' *s* Walmdach *n*

hire [haɪr] *s* Miete *f; (salary)* Lohn *m;* **for h.** zu vermieten || *tr (workers)* anstellen; *(rent)* mieten; **h. out** sich verdingen bei; **h. out** vermieten

hired' hand' *s* Lohnarbeiter –in *mf*

hireling [ˈhaɪrlɪŋ] *s* Mietling *m*

his [hɪz] *poss adj* sein || *poss pron* seiner, der seine (*or* seinige)

Hispanic [hɪsˈpænɪk] *adj* hispanisch

hiss [hɪs] *s* Zischen *n* || *tr* auszischen || *intr* zischen

hiss'ing *s* Zischen *n,* Gezisch *n*

hiss'ing sound' *s* Zischlaut *m*

hist [hɪst] *interj* st!

historian [hɪsˈtɔri-ən] *s* Historiker –in *mf*

historic [hɪsˈtɔrɪk] *adj* historisch bedeutsam

historical [hɪsˈtɔrɪkəl] *adj* historisch, geschichtlich

history [ˈhɪstəri] *s* Geschichte *f*

historionic [ˌhɪstrɪˈɑnɪk] *adj* schauspielerisch; (fig) übertrieben || **histrionics** *spl* theatralisches Benehmen *n*

hit [hɪt] *s* Schlag *m,* Stoß *m; (a success)* Schlager *m;* (sport) Treffer *m;* (theat) Zugstück *n* || *v (pret & pp* **hit;** *ger* **hitting)** *tr (e.g., with the fist)* schlagen; *(a note, target)* treffen; **hit bottom** *(fig)* auf dem Nullpunkt angekommen sein; **hit it off** gut miteinander auskommen; **hit one's head against** mit dem Kopf stoßen gegen; **hit s.o. hard** *(said of misfortunes, etc.)* schwer treffen; **hit the road** sich auf den Weg machen; **hit the sack** sich hinhauen || *intr* schlagen; **hit on** (*or* **upon**) kommen auf *(acc)*

hit'-and-run' *adj (driver)* flüchtig; **h. accident** Unfall *m* mit Fahrerflucht; **h. attack** Zerstörangriff *m*

hitch [hɪtʃ] *s (difficulty)* Haken *m; (knot)* Stich *m;* (term of service) Dienstzeit *f;* **that's the h.** das ist ja gerade der Haken; **without a h.** reibungslos || *tr* spannen; **h. a ride (to)** per Anhalter fahren (nach); **h. to the wagon** vor (or an) den Wagen spannen; **h. up** *(horses)* anspannen; *(trousers)* hochziehen

hitch'hike' *intr* per Anhalter fahren

hitch'ing post' *s* Pfosten *m* (zum Anbinden von Pferden)

hither [ˈhɪðər] *adv* her, hierher; **h. and thither** hierhin und dorthin

hitherto' *adv* bisher

hit' or miss' *adv* aufs Geratewohl

hit'-or-miss' *adj* planlos

hitter [ˈhɪtər] *s* Schläger *m*

hive [haɪv] *s* Bienenstock *m;* **hives** (pathol) Nesselausschlag *m*

hoard [hɔrd] *s* Hort *m* || *tr & intr* horten; *(food)* hamstern

hoarder [ˈhɔrdər] *s* Hamsterer –in *mf*

hoard'ing *s* Horten *n; (of food)* Hamstern *n*

hoarfrost [ˈhɔr ˌfrɔst] *s* Rauhreif *m*

hoarse [hɔrs] *adj* heiser

hoarseness [ˈhɔrsnɪs] *s* Heiserkeit *f*

hoary [ˈhɔri] *adj* ergraut; (fig) altersgrau

hoax [hoks] *s* Schnabernack *m* || *tr* anführen

hob [hɑb] *s* Kamineinsatz *m*

hobble [ˈhɑbəl] *s* Humpeln *n* || *intr* humpeln

hobby [ˈhɑbi] *s* Hobby *n*

hob'byhorse' *s (stick with horse's head)* Steckenpferd *n; (rocking horse)* Schaukelpferd *n*

hob'gob'lin *s* Kobold *m; (bogy)* Schreckgespenst *n*

hob'nail' *s* grober Schuhnagel *m*

hob·nob [ˈhɑbˌnɑb] v (pret & pp -nobbed; ger -nobbing) intr—**h. with** freundschaftlich verkehren mit

ho·bo [ˈhobo] s (-bos & -boes) Landstreicher m

hock [hɑk] s (of a horse) Sprunggelenk n; in h. verpfändet ‖ tr (hamstring) lähmen; (pawn) (coll) verpfänden

hockey [ˈhɑki] s Hockey n

hoc′key stick′ s Hockeystock m

hock′shop′ s (coll) Leihhaus n

hocus-pocus [ˈhokəsˈpokəs] s Hokuspokus m

hod [hɑd] s Mörteltrog m

hodgepodge [ˈhɑdʒˌpɑdʒ] s Mischmasch m

hoe [ho] s Hacke f, Haue f ‖ tr hacken

hog [hɔg] s Schwein n ‖ v (pret & pp hogged; ger hogging) tr (sl) gierig an sich reißen; **hog the road** rücksichtlos fahren

hog′back′ s scharfer Gebirgskamm m

hog′ bris′tle s Schweinsborste f

hoggish [ˈhɔgɪʃ] adj schweinisch, gefräßig

hog′wash′ s (nonsense) Quatsch m

hoist [hɔɪst] s (apparatus for lifting) Hebezeug n; (act of lifting) Hochwinden n ‖ tr hochwinden; (a flag, sail) hissen

hokum [ˈhokəm] s (nonsense) (coll) Quatsch m; (flimflam) (coll) Effekthascherei f

hold [hold] s Halt m, Griff m; (naut) Raum m; (sport) Griff m; **get h. of** (catch) erwischen; (acquire) erwerben; **get h. of oneself** sich fassen; **take h. of** anfassen ‖ v (pret & pp held [hɛld]) tr halten; (contain) enthalten; (regard as) halten für; (one's breath) anhalten; (an audience) fesseln; (a meeting, election, court) abhalten; (an office, position) bekleiden, innehaben; (talks) führen; (a viewpoint) vertreten; (a meet) (sport) veranstalten; **able to h. one's liquor** trinkfest; **h. back** zurückhalten; (news) geheimhalten; **h. dear** werthalten; **h. down** niederhalten; **h. in contempt** verachten; **h. it!** halt!; **h. off** abhalten; **h. office** amtieren; **h. one's ground** die Stellung halten; **h. one's own** seinen Mann stehen; **h. one's own against** sich behaupten gegen; **h. one's tongue** den Mund halten; **h. open** (a door) aufhalten; **h. out** (a hand) hinhalten; (proffer) vorhalten; **h. over** (e.g., a play) verlängern; **h. s.th. against s.o.** j-m etw nachtragen; **h. sway** walten; **h. under** niederhalten; **h. up** (raise) hochhalten; (detain) aufhalten; (traffic) behindern; (rob) (räuberisch) überfallen; **h. up to ridicule** dem Spott preisgeben; **h. the line** (telp) am Apparat bleiben; **h. the road well** e-e gute Straßenlage haben; **h. together** zusammenhalten; **h. water** (fig) stichhaltig sein ‖ intr (said of a knot) halten; **h. back** sich zurückhalten; **h. forth** (coll) dozieren; **h. on** warten; **h. on to** festhalten, sich

festhalten an (dat); **h. out** aushalten; **h. out for** abwarten; **h. true** gelten; **h. true for** zutreffen auf (acc); **h. up** (wear well) halten

holder [ˈholdər] s (device) Halter m; (e.g., of a title) Inhaber –in mf

hold′ing s (of a meeting) Abhaltung f; (of an office) Bekleidung f; **holdings** Besitz m, Bestand m

hold′ing com′pany s Holdinggesellschaft f

hold′ing pat′tern s (aer) Platzrunde f

hold′-o′ver s Überbleibsel n

hold′up′ s (delay) Aufenthalt m; (robbery) Raubüberfall m; (in traffic) Verkehrsstauung f

hold′up man′ s Räuber m

hole [hol] s Loch n; (of animals) Bau m; **h. in the wall** Loch n; **in a h. in** der Patsche; **in the h.** hängengeblieben, e.g., **I am ten dollars in the h.** ich bin mit zehn Dollar hängengeblieben; **pick holes in** (fig) herumkritisieren an (dat); **wear holes in** völlig abtragen ‖ intr—**h. out** (golf) ins Loch spielen; **h. up** sich vergraben; (fig) sich verstecken

holiday [ˈhɑlɪˌde] s Feiertag m; (vacation) Ferien pl; **take a h.** e-n freien Tag machen, Urlaub nehmen

hol′iday mood′ s Ferienstimmung f

holiness [ˈholɪnɪs] s Heiligkeit f; **His Holiness** Seine Heiligkeit

Holland [ˈhɑlənd] s Holland n

Hollander [ˈhɑləndər] s Holländer –in mf

hollow [ˈhɑlo] adj hohl ‖ s Höhle f, Höhlung f; (geol) Talmulde f ‖ tr—**h. out** aushöhlen

hol′low-cheeked′ adj hohlwangig

hol′low-eyed′ adj hohläugig

holly [ˈhɑli] s Stechpalme f

holm′ oak′ [hom] s Steineiche f

holocaust [ˈhɑləˌkɔst] s Brandopfer n; (disaster) Brandkatastrophe f

holster [ˈholstər] s Pistolentasche f

holy [ˈholi] adj heilig; **h. smokes!** (coll) heiliger Strohsack!

Ho′ly Commun′ion s Kommunion f, das Heilige Abendmahl

ho′ly day′ s Feiertag m

Ho′ly Ghost′ s Heiliger Geist m

Ho′ly of Ho′lies s Allerheiligste n

ho′ly or′ders spl Priesterweihe f

Ho′ly Scrip′ture s die Heilige Schrift

Ho′ly See′ s Heiliger Stuhl m

Ho′ly Sep′ulcher s Heiliges Grab n

Ho′ly Spir′it s Heiliger Geist m

ho′ly wa′ter s Weihwasser n

Ho′ly Week′ s Karwoche f

Ho′ly Writ′ s die Heilige Schrift

homage [ˈ(h)ɑmɪdʒ] s Huldigung f; **pay h. to** huldigen (dat)

home [hom] adj inländisch, Innen– ‖ adv nach Hause, heim; **bring h. to s.o.** j-m beibringen ‖ s Heim n; (house) Haus n, Wohnung f; (place of residence) Wohnort m; (institution) Heim n; **at h.** zu Hause, daheim; **at h. and abroad** im In– und Ausland; **feel at h.** sich zu Hause fühlen; **for the h.** für den Hausbe-

darf; **from h.** von zu Hause; **h. for the aged** Altersheim *n;* **h. for the blind** Blindenheim *n;* **h. of one's own** Zuhause *n*
home′ address′ *s* Privatadresse *f*
home′-baked′ *adj* hausbacken
home′ base′ *s* (aer) Heimatflughafen *m*
home′bod′y *s* Stubenhocker –in *mf*
homebred ['hom ,bred] *adj* einheimisch
home′-brew′ *s* selbstgebrautes Getränk *n*
home′-brewed′ *adj* selbstgebraut
home′com′ing *s* Heimkehr *f*
home′ comput′er *s* Heimcomputer *m*
home′ coun′try *s* Heimatstaat *m*
home′ econom′ics *s* Hauswirtschaftslehre *f*
home′-fried pota′toes *spl,* **home′ fries′** [,fraiz] *spl* Bratkartoffeln *pl*
home′ front′ *s* Heimatfront *f*
home′-grown′ *adj* selbstgezogen
home′ guard′ *s* Landsturm *m*
home′land′ *s* Heimatland *n*
homeless ['homlis] *adj* obdachlos ‖ *s* Obdachlose *mf*
home′like′ *adj* anheimelnd
homely ['homli] *adj* unschön
home′made′ *adj* selbstgemacht; (culin) selbstgebacken
home′mak′er *s* Hausfrau *f*
home′ of′fice *s* Hauptbüro *n*
home′ own′er *s* Hausbesitzer –in *mf*
home′ plate′ *s* Schlagmal *n*
home′ rem′edy *s* Hausmittel *n*
home′ rule′ *s* Selbstverwaltung *f*
home′ run′ *s* (baseball) Vier-Mal-Lauf *m*
home′sick′ *adj*—**be h.** Heimweh haben
home′sick′ness *s* Heimweh *n*
homespun ['hom ,spʌn] *adj* selbstgemacht; (fig) einfach
home′stead′ *s* Siedlerstelle *f*
home′stretch′ *s* Zielgerade *f*
home′ team′ *s* Ortsmannschaft *f*
home′town′ *adj* Heimat– ‖ *s* Heimatstadt *f*
homeward ['homwərd] *adv* heimwärts
home′ward jour′ney *s* Heimreise *f*
home′work′ *s* Hausaufgabe *f*
homey ['homi] *adj* anheimelnd
homicidal [,homi'saidəl] *adj* mörderisch
homicide ['homi ,said] *s* (act) Totschlag *m;* (person) Totschläger –in *mf*
hom′icide squad′ *s* Mordkommission *f*
homily ['homili] *s* Homilie *f*
hom′ing device′ ['homiŋ] *s* Zielsucher *m*
hom′ing pi′geon *s* Brieftaube *f*
homogeneous [,homə'dʒini·əs] *adj* homogen
homogenize [hə'madʒə ,naiz] *tr* homogenisieren
homonym ['hamənim] *s* Homonym *n*
homosexual [,homə'sɛk/ʊ·əl] *adj* homosexuell ‖ *s* Homosexuelle *mf*
hone [hon] *s* Wetzstein *m* ‖ *tr* honen
honest ['anist] *adj* ehrlich, aufrecht
honestly ['anistli] *adv* ehrlich; **to tell you h.** offengestanden ‖ *interj* auf mein Wort!

honesty ['anisti] *s* Ehrlichkeit *f*
hon·ey ['hʌni] *s* Honig *m;* (as a term of endearment) Schatz *m,* Liebling *m* ‖ *v* (pret & pp –eyed & –ied) *tr* versüßen; (speak sweetly to) schmeicheln (dat)
hon′eybee′ *s* Honigbiene *f*
hon′eycomb′ *s* Honigwabe *f* ‖ *tr* (e.g., a hill) wabenartig durchlöchern
hon′eyed *adj* mit Honig gesüßt; (fig) honigsüß
hon′ey lo′cust *s* Honigdorn *m*
hon′eymoon′ *s* Flitterwochen *pl* ‖ *intr* die Flitterwochen verbringen
hon′eysuck′le *s* Geißblatt *n*
honk [hɔŋk] *s* (aut) Hupensignal *n* ‖ *tr*—**h. the horn** hupen ‖ *intr* hupen
honkytonk ['hɔŋki ,tɔŋk] *s* (sl) Tingeltangel *m & n*
honor ['anər] *s* Ehre *f;* (award) Auszeichnung *f;* (chastity) Ehre *f;* **be held in h.** in Ehren gehalten werden; **consider it an h.** es sich [dat] zur Ehre anrechnen; **do the honors** die Honneurs machen; **have the h. of** (ger) sich beehren zu (inf); **in s.o.'s h.** j–m zu Ehren; **your Honor** Euer Gnaden ‖ *tr* ehren; (favor) beehren; (a check) honorieren; **feel honored** sich geehrt fühlen
honorable ['anərəbəl] *adj* (person) ehrbar; (intentions) ehrlich; (peace treaty) ehrenvoll
honorari·um [,anə'rɛri·əm] *s* (–ums & –a [ə]) Honorar *n;* **give an h. to** honorieren
hon′orary degree′ *s* Ehrendoktorat *n*
honorific [,anə'rifik] *adj* ehrend, Ehren– ‖ *s* Ehrentitel *m*
hooch [hut/] *s* (sl) Fusel *m,* Schnaps *m*
hood [hʊd] *s* Haube *f;* (of a monk) Kapuze *f;* (of a baby carriage) Verdeck *n;* (sl) Gangster *m;* (aut) Motorhaube *f;* (culin) Rauchabzug *m;* (educ) Talarüberwurf *m* ‖ *tr* mit e–r Haube versehen; (fig) verhüllen
hoodlum ['hudləm] *s* Ganove *m*
hoodoo ['hudu] *s* Unglücksbringer *m* ‖ *tr* Unglück bringen (dat)
hood′wink′ *tr* täuschen
hooey ['hu·i] *s* (sl) Quatsch *m*
hoof [huf], [hʊf] *s* Huf *m* ‖ *tr*—**h. it** auf Schusters Rappen reiten
hoof′beat′ *s* Hufschlag *m*
hook [hʊk] *s* Haken *m;* (angl) Angelhaken *m;* (baseball) Kurvball *m;* (box) Haken *m;* (golf) Hook *m;* **by h. or by crook** so oder so; **h., line, and sinker** mit allem Drum und Dran; **off the h.** (coll) aus der Schlinge; **on one's own h.** (coll) auf eigene Faust ‖ *tr* festhaken, einhaken; (e.g., a boyfriend) angeln; (steal) schnappen; (box) e–n Haken versetzen (dat); (golf) nach links verziehen; **h. up** zuhaken; (elec) anschließen ‖ *intr* sich krümmen; **h. up with s.o.** sich j–m anschließen
hook′ and eye′ *s* Haken *m* und Öse *f*
hook′-and-lad′der truck′ *s* Feuerwehrfahrzeug *n* mit Drehleiter

hooked *adj* hakenförmig; **h. on drugs** rauschgiftsüchtig

hooker ['hukər] *s* (sl) Nutte *f*

hook'nose' *s* Hakennase *f*

hook'up' *s* (elec, electron) Schaltung *f*; (electron) Schaltbild *n*; (rad, telv) Gemeinschaftsschaltung *f*

hook'worm' *s* Hakenwurm *m*

hooky ['huki] *s*—**play h.** schwänzen

hooligan ['huligən] *s* Straßenlümmel *m*

hoop [hup] *s* Reifen *m* || *tr* binden

hoop' skirt' *s* Reifrock *m*

hoot [hut] *s* Geschrei *n*; **not give a h. about** keinen Pfifferling geben für || *intr* schreien; **h. at** anschreien

hoot' owl' *s* Waldkauz *m*

hop [hap] *s* Hopser *m*; (*dance*) Tanz *m*; **hops** (bot) Hopfen *m* || *v* (*pret & pp* **hopped**; *ger* **hopping**) *tr* (*e.g., a train*) aufspringen auf (*acc*); **hop a ride** (coll) mitfahren || *intr* hüpfen; **hop around** herumhüpfen

hope [hop] *s* (of) Hoffnung *f* (auf *acc*); **beyond h.** hoffnungslos; **not get up one's hopes** sich [*dat*] keine Hoffnungen machen || *tr* hoffen || *intr* hoffen; **h. for** hoffen auf (*acc*); **h. for the best** das Beste hoffen; **I h.** (parenthetical) hoffentlich

hope' chest' *s* Aussteuertruhe *f*

hopeful ['hopfəl] *adj* hoffnungsvoll || *s* (pol) Kandidat –in *mf*

hopefully ['hopfəli] *adv* hoffentlich

hopeless ['hoplis] *adj* hoffnungslos

hopper ['hapər] *s* Fülltrichter *m*; (*in a toilet*) Spülkasten *m*; (*storage container*) Vorratsbehälter *m*; (data proc) Kartenmagazin *n*

hop'per car' *s* (rr) Selbstentladewagen *m*

hop'ping mad' *adj* fuchsteufelswild

hop'scotch' *s* Himmel und Hölle

horde [hord] *s* Horde *f*

horehound ['hor,haund] *s* (*lozenge*) Hustenbonbon *m*; (bot) Andorn *m*

horizon [hə'raizən] *s* Horizont *m*

horizontal [,hari'zantəl] *adj* horizontal, waagerecht || *s* Horizontale *f*

horizon'tal bar' *s* (gym) Reck *n*

horizon'tal controls' *spl* (aer) Seitenleitwerk *n*

horizon'tal sta'bilizer *s* (aer) Höhenflosse *f*

hormone ['hormon] *s* Hormon *n*

horn [horn] *s* (*of an animal; wind instrument*) Horn *n*; (aut) Hupe *f*; **blow one's own h.** (coll) ins eigene Horn stoßen; **blow the h.** (aut) hupen; **horns** (*of an animal*) Geweih *n* || *intr*—**h. in (on)** (coll) sich eindrängen (in *acc*)

hornet ['hornit] *s* Hornisse *f*

hor'net's nest' *s*—**stir up a h.** in ein Wespennest stechen

horn' of plen'ty *s* Füllhorn *n*

horn'-rimmed glass'es *spl* Hornbrille *f*

horny ['horni] *adj* (*callous*) schwielig; (*having horn-like projections*) verhornt; (sl) geil

horoscope ['horə,skop] *s* Horoskop *n*; **cast s.o.'s h.** j-m das Horoskop stellen

horrible ['horibəl] *adj* (& coll) schrecklich

horrid ['horid] *adj* abscheulich

horri·fy ['hori,fai] *v* (*pret & pp* **–fied**) *tr* erschrecken, entsetzen

horror ['horər] *s* Schrecken *m*, Entsetzen *n*

hor'ror sto'ry *s* Schauergeschichte *f*

hors d'oeuvre [or'dʌrv] *s* (**hors d'oeuvres** [or'dʌrvz]) Vorspeise *f*

horse [hors] *s* Pferd *n*; (carp) Sägebock *m*; **back the wrong h.** (fig) auf's falsche Pferd setzen; **bet on a h.** auf ein Pferd setzen; **hold your horses** immer mit der Ruhe!; **h. of another color** e–e andere Sache; **mount a h.** zu Pferd steigen; **straight from the horse's mouth** direkt von der Quelle || *intr*—**h. around** (sl) herumalbern; **stop horsing around** laß den Unsinn!

horse'back' *s*—**on h.** zu Pferd || *adv*—**ride h.** reiten

horse'back rid'ing *s* Reiten *n*

horse' blan'ket *s* Pferdedecke *f*

horse' chest'nut *s* Roßkastanie *f*

horse' col'lar *s* Kummet *n*

horse' doc'tor *s* (coll) Roßarzt *m*

horse'fly' *s* Pferdebremse *f*

horse'hair' *s* Roßhaar *n*, Pferdehaar *n*

horse'laugh' *s* wieherndes Gelächter *n*

horse'man *s* (–men) Reiter *m*

horse'manship' *s* Reitkunst *f*

horse' meat' *s* Pferdefleisch *n*

horse' op'era *s* (coll) Wildwestfilm *m*

horse'play' *s* grober Unfug *m*

horse'pow'er *s* Pferdestärke *f*

horse' race' *s* Pferderennen *n*

horse'rad'ish *s* Meerrettich *m*, Kren *m*

horse' sense' *s* gesunder Menschenverstand *m*

horse' shoe' *s* Hufeisen *n* || *tr* beschlagen

horse'shoe mag'net *s* Hufeisenmagnet *m*

horse' show' *s* Pferdeschau *f*

horse' tail' *s* Pferdeschwanz *m*

horse' trad'er *s* Pferdehändler *m*; (fig) Kuhhändler *m*

horse' trad'ing *s* Pferdehandel *m*; (fig) Kuhhandel *m*

horse'whip' *s* Reitpeitsche *f* || *v* (*pret & pp* **–whipped**; *ger* **–whipping**) *tr* mit der Reitpeitsche schlagen

horse'wom'an *s* (–wom'en) Reiterin *f*

horsy ['horsi] *adj* pferdeartig; (*horseloving*) pferdeliebend

horticultural [,horti'kʌltʃərəl] *adj* Gartenbau–

horticulture ['horti,kʌltʃər] *s* Gartenbau *m*, Gärtnerei *f*

hose [hoz] *s* Schlauch *m* || *s* (**hose**) Strumpf *m*; (*collectively*) Strümpfe *pl*

hosiery ['hoʒəri] *s* Strumpfwaren *pl*; (*mill*) Strumpffabrik *f*

hospice ['haspis] *s* Hospiz *n*

hospitable ['haspitəbəl], [has'pitəbəl] *adj* gastlich, gastfreundlich

hospital ['haspitəl] *s* Hospital *n*, Krankenhaus *n*; (mil) Lazarett *n*

hospitality [,haspi'tæliti] *s* Gastfreundschaft *f;* **show s.o. h.** j-m Gastfreundschaft gewähren

hospitalize ['hɑspɪtə‚laɪz] *tr* ins Krankenhaus einweisen

hos'pital ship' *s* Lazarettschiff *f*

hos'pital train' *s* Sanitätszug *m*

hos'pital ward' *s* Kranken(haus)station *f*

host [host] *s* Gastgeber *m;* (*at an inn*) Wirt *m;* (*in a television show*) Leiter *m;* (*multitude*) Heerschar *f;* (*army*) Heer *n;* **Host** (relig) Hostie *f*

hostage ['hɑstɪdʒ] *s* Geisel *mf*

hostel ['hɑstəl] *s* Herberge *f*

hostelry ['hɑstəlrɪ] *s* Gasthaus *n*

hostess ['hostɪs] *s* Gastgeberin *f;* (*at an inn*) Wirtin *f;* (*on an airplane*) Stewardeß *f;* (*in a restaurant*) Empfangsdame *f;* (*in a television show*) Leiterin *f*

hostile ['hɑstɪl] *adj* feindlich; (**to**) feindselig (gegen)

hostility [hɑs'tɪlɪtɪ] *s* Feindseligkeit *f;* **hostilities** Feindseligkeiten *pl*

hot [hɑt] *adj* heiß; (*spicy*) scharf; (*meal*) warm; (*stolen, sought by the police, radioactive; jazz, tip*) heiß; (*trail, scent*) frisch; (*in heat*) geil; **be hot** (*said of the sun*) stechen; **get into hot water** in die Patsche geraten; **hot and bothered** aufgeregt; **hot from the press** frisch von der Presse; **hot on s.o.'s trail** j-m dicht auf der Spur; **hot stuff** (sl) toller Kerl *m;* **I am hot** mir ist heiß; **I don't feel so hot** (coll) ich fühle mich nicht besonders; **she's not so hot** (coll) sie is nicht so toll

hot' air' *s* Heißluft *f;* (sl) blauer Dunst *m*

hot'-air heat' *s* Heißluftheizung *f*

hot'bed' *s* Frühbeet *n;* (fig) Brutstätte *f*

hot'-blood'ed *adj* heißblütig

hot' cake' *s* Pfannkuchen *m;* **sell like hot cakes** wie warme Semmeln weggehen

hotchpotch ['hɑtʃ‚pɑtʃ] *s* (coll) Mischmasch *m*

hot' dog' *s* warmes Würstel *n*

hotel [ho'tɛl] *adj* Hotel– || *s* Hotel *n;* (*small hotel*) Gasthof *m*

hotel' busi'ness *s* Hotelgewerbe *n*

hotel'man' *s* (**–men**) Hotelbesitzer *m*

hot'foot' *adv* in aller Eile || *tr*—**h. it** schleunigst eilen; **h. it after s.o.** j-m nacheilen

hot'head' *s* Hitzkopf *m*

hot'-head'ed *adj* hitzköpfig

hot'house' *s* Treibhaus *n,* Gewächshaus *n*

hot' line' *s* (telp) heißer Draht *m*

hot' mon'ey *s* (sl) Fluchtkapital *n*

hot' pep'per *s* scharfe Paprikaschote *f*

hot' plate' *s* Heizplatte *f*

hot' pota'to *s* (coll) schwieriges Problem *n*

hot' rod' *s* (sl) frisiertes altes Auto *n*

hot' rod'der [‚rɑdər] *s* (sl) Fahrer *m* e-s frisierten Autos

hot' seat' *s* (sl) elektrischer Stuhl *m*

hot' springs' *spl* Thermalquellen *pl*

hot' tem'per *s* hitziges Temperament *n*

hot'-tem'pered *adj* hitzig, hitzköpfig

hot' war' *s* Schießkrieg *m*

hot' wa'ter *s* Heißwasser *n;* **be in h.** (fig) in der Tinte sitzen; **get into h.** (fig) in die Patsche geraten

hot'-wa'ter bot'tle *s* Gummiwärmflasche *f*

hot'-wa'ter heat'er *s* Heißwasserbereiter *m*

hot'-wa'ter heat'ing *s* Heißwasserheizung *f*

hot'-wa'ter tank' *s* Heißwasserspeicher *m*

hound [haund] *s* Jagdhund *m* || *tr* hetzen

hour [aur] *s* Stunde *f;* **after hours** nach Arbeitsschluß; **at any h.** zu jeder Tageszeit; **by the h.** stundenweise; **every h.** stündlich; **for an h.** e–e Stunde lang; **for a solid h.** e–e geschlagene Stunde lang; **for hours** stundenlang; **h. of death** Todesstunde *f;* **h. overtime** Überstunde *f;* **in the small hours** in den frühen Morgenstunden; **keep late hours** spät zu Bett gehen; **keep. regular hours** zur Zeit aufstehen und schlafengehen; **on the h.** zur vollen Stunde

–hour *suf* –stündig

hour'glass' *s* Stundenglas *n*

hour' hand' *s* Stundenzeiger *m*

hourly ['aurlɪ] *adj* stündlich; **h. rate** Stundensatz *m;* **h. wages** Stundenlohn *m* || *adv* stündlich

house [haus] *adj* (*boat, dress*) Haus– || *s* (**houses** ['hauzɪz]) Haus *n;* **h. and home** Haus und Hof; **h. for rent** Haus *n* zu vermieten; **keep h. (for s.o.)** (j–m) den Haushalt führen; **on the h.** auf Kosten des Wirts; **put one's h. in order** (fig) seine Angelegenheiten in Ordnung bringen || [hauz] *tr* unterbringen

house' arrest' *s* Hausarrest *m*

house'boat' *s* Hausboot *n*

house'break'ing *s* Einbruchsdiebstahl *m*

housebroken ['haus‚brokən] *adj* stubenrein

house' clean'ing *s* Hausputz *m;* (fig) Säuberungsaktion *f*

house'fly' *s* Stubenfliege *f*

houseful ['haus‚ful] *s* Hausvoll *n*

house'guest' *s* Logierbesuch *m*

house'hold' *adj* Haushalts– || *s* Haushalt *m*

house'hold'er *s* Haushaltsvorstand *m*

house'hold fur'nishings *spl* Hausrat *m*

house'hold needs' *spl* Hausbedarf *m*

house'hold word' *s* Alltagswort *n*

house' hunt'ing *s* Wohnungssuche *f*

house'keep'er *s* Haushälterin *f*

house'keep'ing *s* Hauswirtschaft *f*

house'maid' *s* Dienstmädchen *n*

house'moth'er *s* Hausmutter *f*

house' of cards' *s* Kartenhaus *n*

House' of Com'mons *s* Unterhaus *n*

house' of correc'tion *s* Zuchthaus *n,* Besserungsanstalt *f*

house' of ill' repute' *s* öffentliches Haus *n*

House' of Lords' *s* Oberhaus *n*

house' physi'cian s Krankenhausarzt m; (in a hotel) Hausarzt m
house'-to-house' adv von Haus zu Haus; **sell h.** hausieren
house'warm'ing s Einzugsfest n
house'wife' s (wives') Hausfrau f
house'work' s Hausarbeit f
hous'ing s Unterbringung f, Wohnung f; (mach) Gehäuse n
hous'ing devel'opment s Siedlung f
hous'ing pro'ject s Sozialsiedlung f
hous'ing short'age s Wohnungsnot f
hous'ing un'it s Wohneinheit f
hovel ['hʌvəl], ['hɑvəl] s Hütte f
hover ['hʌvər] intr schweben; (fig) pendeln; **h. about** sich herumtreiben in der Nähe von
Hov'ercraft' s (trademark) Schwebefahrzeug n
how [hau] adv wie; **and how!** und wie!; **how about ...?** (would you care for ...?) wie wäre es mit ...?; (what's the progress of ...?) wie steht es mit ...?; (what do you think of ...?) was halten Sie von ...?; **how are you?** wie befinden Sie sich?; **how beautiful!** wie schön!; **how come?** wieso?, wie kommt es?; **how do you do?** (as a greeting) guten Tag!; (at an introduction) freut mich sehr!; **how many** wie viele; **how much** wieviel; **how on earth** wie in aller Welt; **how the devil** wie zum Teufel || s Wie n
how-do-you-do ['haudəjə'du] s—that's a fine h.! (coll) das ist e-e schöne Geschichte!
however adv jedoch, aber; (with adjectives and adverbs) wie ... auch immer; **h. it may be** wie es auch sein mag
howitzer ['hau·ɪtsər] s Haubitze f
howl [haul] s Geheul n, Gebrüll n || tr heulen, brüllen; **h. down** (a speaker) niederschreien; **h. out** hinausbrüllen || intr (said of a dog, wolf, wind, etc.) heulen; (in pain, anger) brüllen; **h. with laughter** vor Lachen brüllen
howler ['haulər] s (coll) Schnitzer m
hub [hʌb] s Nabe, f, Radnabe f
hubbub ['hʌbʌb] s Rummel m
hubby ['hʌbi] s (coll) Mann m
hub'cap' s Radkappe f
huckleberry ['hʌkəl,beri] s Heidelbeere f
huckster ['hʌkstər] s (hawker) Straßenhändler m; (peddler) Hausierer m; (adman) Reklamefachmann m || tr verhökern
huddle ['hʌdəl] s (fb) Zusammendrängen n; **go into a h.** die Köpfe zusammenstecken || intr sich zusammendrängen; (fb) sich um den Mannschaftsführer drängen
hue [hju] s Farbton m
hue' and cry' s Zetergeschrei n
huff [hʌf] s Aufbrausen n; **in a h.** beleidigt
huffy ['hʌfi] adj übelnehmerisch
hug [hʌg] s Umarmung f; **give s.o. a hug** j-n an sich drücken || v (pret & pp hugged; ger hugging) tr umar-

men; **hug the road** gut auf der Straße liegen; **hug the shore** sich dicht an der Küste halten || intr einander herzen
huge [hjudʒ] adj riesig, ungeheuer; **h. success** (theat) Bombenerfolg m
hulk [hʌlk] s (body of an old ship) Schiffsrumpf m; (old ship used as a warehouse, etc.) Hulk m & f; **h. of a man** Koloß m
hulk'ing adj ungeschlacht
hull [hʌl] s (of seed) Schale f; (naut) Schiffsrumpf m || tr schälen
hullabaloo [,hʌləbə'lu] s Heidenlärm m
hum [hʌm] s Summen n || v (pret & pp hummed; ger humming) tr summen; **hum** (e.g., a tune) **to oneself** vor sich hin summen || intr summen; (fig) in lebhafter Bewegung sein
human ['hjumən] adj menschlich, Menschen-
hu'man be'ing s Mensch m, menschliches Wesen n
humane [hju'men] adj human
humaneness [hju'mennɪs] s Humanität f
humanistic [hjumə'nɪstɪk] adj humanistisch
humanitarian [hju,mænɪ'terɪ·ən] adj menschenfreundlich || s Menschenfreund –in mf
humanity [hju'mænɪti] s (mankind) Menschheit f; (humaneness) Humanität f, Menschlichkeit f; **humanities** Geisteswissenschaften pl; (Greek and Latin studies) klassische Philologie f
humanize ['hjumə,naɪz] tr zivilisieren
hu'mankind' s Menschengeschlecht n
humanly ['hjumənli] adv menschlich; **h. possible** menschenmöglich; **h. speaking** nach menschlichen Begriffen
hu'man na'ture s menschliche Natur f
hu'man race' s Menschengeschlecht n
humble ['(h)ʌmbəl] adv demütig; (origens) niedrig; **in my h. opinion** nach meiner unmaßgeblichen Meinung || tr demütigen
hum'ble pie' s—eat h. sich demütigen
hum'bug' s Humbug m
hum'drum' adj eintönig
humer·us ['hjumərəs] s (-i [,aɪ]) Oberarmknochen m
humid ['hjumɪd] adj feucht
humidifier [hju'mɪdɪ,faɪ·ər] s Verdunster m
humidity [hju'mɪdɪti] s Feuchtigkeit f
humiliate [hju'mɪlɪ,et] tr erniedrigen
humil'iating adj schmachvoll
humiliation [hju,mɪlɪ'e/ən] s Erniedrigung f
hum'mingbird' s Kolibri m
humor ['(h)jumər] s (comic quality) Komik f; (frame of mind) Laune f; **in bad (or good) h.** bei schlechter (or guter) Laune || tr bei guter Laune halten
humorist ['(h)jumərɪst] s Humorist –in mf
humorous ['(h)jumərəs] adj humorvoll
hump [hʌmp] s Buckel m; (of a camel)

Höcker m; (slight elevation) kleiner Hügel m; **over the h.** (fig) über den Berg ‖ tr—**h. its back** (said of an animal) e-n Buckel machen

hump'back' s Buckel m; (person) Bucklige mf

Hun [hʌn] s (hist) Hunne m, Hunnin f

hunch [hʌntʃ] s (hump) Buckel m; (coll) Ahnung f ‖ intr—**h. over** sich bücken über (acc)

hunch'back' s Bucklige mf

hunch'backed' adj bucklig

hunched adj—**h. up** zusammengekauert

hundred ['hʌndrəd] adj & pron hundert ‖ s Hundert n; **by the h.**(s) hundertweise; **hundreds (and hundreds) of** Hunderte (und aber Hunderte) von

hun'dredfold' adj & adv hundertfach

hundredth ['hʌndrədθ] adj & pron hundertste; **for the h. time** (fig) zum X-ten Male; **h. anniversary** Hundertjahrfeier f ‖ s (fraction) Hundertstel n

hun'dredweight' s Zentner m

Hungarian [hʌŋ'gɛrɪ·ən] adj ungarisch ‖ s (person) Ungar –in mf; (language) Ungarisch n

Hungary ['hʌŋgəri] s Ungarn n

hunger ['hʌŋgər] s Hunger m ‖ intr hungern; **h. for** hungern nach

hun'ger strike' s Hungerstreik m

hungry ['hʌŋgri] adj hungrig; **be h.** Hunger haben; **be h. for** (fig) begierig sein nach; **go h.** am Hungertuch nagen; **I feel h.** es hungert mich

hunk [hʌŋk] s großes Stück n

hunt [hʌnt] s Jagd f; (search) (for) Suche f (nach); **on the h. for** auf der Suche nach ‖ tr jagen; (a horse) jagen mit; (look for) suchen; **h. down** erjagen ‖ intr jagen; **h. for** suchen; (game) jagen; (a criminal) fahnden nach; **go hunting** auf die Jagd gehen

hunter ['hʌntər] s Jäger –in mf; (horse) Jagdpferd n

hunt'ing adj (e.g., dog, knife, season) Jagd– ‖ s Jägerei f; (on horseback) Parforcejagd f

hunt'ing ground' s Jagdrevier n

hunt'ing li'cense s Jagdschein m

hunt'ing lodge' s Jagdhütte f

huntress ['hʌntrɪs] s Jägerin f

hunts'man s (–men) Weidmann m

hurdle ['hʌrdəl] s Hürde f; (fig) Hindernis n; **hurdles** (sport) Hürdenlauf m ‖ tr überspringen; (fig) überwinden

hurdygurdy ['hʌrdi'gʌrdi] s Drehorgel f

hurl [hʌrl] s Wurf m ‖ tr scheudern; **h. abuse at s.o.** j–m Beleidigungen ins Gesicht schleudern; **h. down** zu Boden werfen

hurrah [hə'rɑ], **hurray** [hə're] s Hurra n ‖ interj hurra!

hurricane ['hʌrɪ‚ken] s Orkan m

hur'ricane lamp' s Sturmlaterne f

hurried ['hʌrid] adj eilig, flüchtig

hurriedly ['hʌridli] adv eilig, eilends

hur-ry ['hʌri] s Eile f; **be in too much of a h.** sich übereilen; **in a h.** in Eile; **there's no h.** es hat keine Eile ‖ v

(pret & pp –ried) tr (prod) antreiben; (expedite) beschleunigen; (an activity) zu schnell tun; (to overhasty action) drängen ‖ intr eilen; **h. away** wegeilen; **h. over s.th.** etw flüchtig erledigen; **h. up** sich beeilen

hurt [hʌrt] adj (injured, offended) verletzt; **feel h.** (about) sich verletzt (or gekränkt) fühlen (durch) ‖ s Verletzung f ‖ v (pret & pp hurt) tr (a person, animal, feelings) verletzen; (e.g., a business) schaden (dat); **it hurts him to think of it** es schmerzt ihn, daran zu denken ‖ intr (& fig) weh tun, schmerzen; **my arm hurts** mir tut der Arm weh; **that won't h.** das schadet nichts; **will it h. if I'm late?** macht es etw aus, wenn ich zu spät komme?

hurtle ['hʌrtəl] tr schleudern ‖ intr stürzen

husband ['hʌzbənd] s Ehemann m; **my h.** mein Mann m ‖ tr haushalten mit

hus'bandman s (–men) Landwirt m

husbandry ['hʌzbəndri] s Landwirtschaft f

hush [hʌʃ] s Stille f ‖ tr zur Ruhe bringen; **h. up** (suppress) vertuschen ‖ intr schweigen ‖ interj still!

hush'-hush' adj streng vertraulich und geheim

hush' mon'ey s Schweigegeld n

husk [hʌsk] s Hülse f; (of corn) Maishülse f ‖ tr enthülsen

husky ['hʌski] adj stämmig; (voice) belegt ‖ s Eskimohund m

hussy ['hʌsi] s (prostitute) Dirne f; (saucy girl) Fratz m

hustle ['hʌsəl] s (coll) Betriebsamkeit f; **h. and bustle** Getriebe n ‖ tr (jostle, rush) drängen; (wares, girls) an den Mann bringen; (customers) bearbeiten; (money) betteln ‖ intr rührig sein; (shove) sich drängen; (hasten) hasten; (make money by fraud) Betrügereien verüben; (engage in prostitution) Prostitution betreiben

hustler ['hʌslər] s rühriger Mensch m

hut [hʌt] s Hütte f; (mil) Baracke f

hutch [hʌtʃ] s Stall m

hyacinth ['haɪ‚əsɪnθ] s Hyazinthe f

hybrid ['haɪbrɪd] adj hybrid ‖ s Kreuzung f

hydrant ['haɪdrənt] s Hydrant m

hydrate ['haɪdret] s Hydrat n ‖ tr hydratisieren, hydrieren

hydraulic [haɪ'drɔlɪk] adj hydraulisch ‖ **hydraulics** s Hydraulik f

hydrau'lic brakes' spl Öldruckbremsen pl

hydrocarbon [‚haɪdrə'kɑrbən] s Kohlenwasserstoff m

hydrochlor'ic ac'id [‚haɪdrə'klorɪk] s Salzsäure f

hydroelectric [‚haɪdro·ɪ'lektrɪk] adj hydroelektrisch

hydroelec'tric plant' s Wasserkraftwerk n

hydrofluo'ric ac'id [‚haɪdrəflu'ɔrɪk] s Flußsäure f

hydrofoil ['haɪdrə‚fɔɪl] s Tragflügelboot n

hydrogen ['haɪdrədʒən] s Wasserstoff m

hy'drogen bomb' s Wasserstoffbombe f

hy'drogen perox'ide s Wasserstoffsuperoxyd n

hydrometer [haɪ'drɑmɪtər] s Hydrometer m

hydrophobia [,haɪdrə'fobɪ·ə] s Wasserscheu f; (rabies) Tollwut f

hydrophone ['haɪdrə,fon] s Unterwasserhorchgerät n, Hydrophon n

hydroplane ['haɪdrə,plen] s (aer) Wasserflugzeug n; (aer) Gleitfläche f; (naut) Gleitboot n; (in a submarine) (nav) Tiefenruder n

hydroxide [haɪ'drɑksaɪd] s Hydroxyd n

hyena [haɪ'inə] s Hyäne f

hygiene ['haɪdʒin] s Hygiene f; (educ) Gesundheitslehre f

hygienic [haɪ'dʒɪnɪk] adj hygienisch

hymn [hɪm] s Hymne f; (eccl) Kirchenlied n

hymnal ['hɪmnəl] s Gesangbuch n

hymn'book' s Gesangbuch n

hyperacidity [,haɪpərə'sɪdɪti] s Übersäuerung f

hyperbola [haɪ'pʌrbələ] s Hyperbel f

hyperbole [haɪ'pʌrbəli] s Hyperbel f

hypersensitive [,haɪpər'sɛnsɪtɪv] adj (to) überempfindlich (gegen)

hypertension [,haɪpər'tɛnʃən] s Hypertonie f

hyphen ['haɪfən] s Bindestrich m

hyphenate ['haɪfə,net] tr mit Bindestrich schreiben

hypnosis [hɪp'nosɪs] s Hypnose f

hypnotic [hɪp'nɑtɪk] adj hypnotisch

hypnotism ['hɪpnə,tɪzəm] s Hypnotismus m

hypnotist ['hɪpnətɪst] s Hypnotiseur m

hypnotize ['hɪpnə,taɪz] tr hypnotisieren

hypochondriac [,haɪpə'kɑndrɪ,æk] s Hypochonder m

hypocrisy [hɪ'pɑkrəsi] s Heuchelei f

hypocrite ['hɪpəkrɪt] s Heuchler –in mf; be a h. heucheln

hypocritical [,hɪpə'krɪtɪkəl] adj heuchlerisch

hypodermic [,haɪpə'dʌrmɪk] adj subkutan || s (injection) subkutane Spritze f

hypoderm'ic nee'dle s Injektionsnadel f

hypotenuse [haɪ'pɑtɪ,n(j)us] s Hypotenuse f

hypothe•sis [haɪ'pɑθɪsɪs] s (–ses [,siz]) Hypothese f

hypothetic(al) [,haɪpə'θɛtɪk(əl)] adj hypothetisch

hysterectomy [,hɪstə'rɛktəmi] s Hysterektomie f

hysteria [hɪs'tɪrɪ·ə] s Hysterie f

hysteric [hɪs'tɛrɪk] adj hysterisch || hysterics spl Hysterie f; go into hysterics e–n hysterischen Anfall bekommen

hysterical [hɪs'tɛrɪkəl] adj hysterisch

I

I, i [ai] s elfter Buchstabe des englischen Alphabets

I pers pron ich

iambic [aɪ'æmbɪk] adj jambisch

Iberian [aɪ'bɪrɪ·ən] adj iberisch

ibex ['aɪbɛks] s (ibexes & ibices ['ɪbɪ,siz]) Steinbock m

ice [aɪs] s Eis n; break the ice (coll) das Eis brechen; cut no ice (coll) nicht ziehen || tr (a cake) glasieren || intr—ice up vereisen

ice' age' s Eiszeit f

iceberg ['aɪs,bʌrg] s Eisberg m

ice'boat' s (sport) Segelschlitten m

ice'bound' adj (boat) eingefroren; (port, river) zugefroren

ice'box' s Eisschrank m; (refrigerator) Kühlschrank m

ice'break'er s Eisbrecher m

ice' buck'et s Sektkübel m

ice'cap' s Eiskappe f

ice' cream' s Eis n, Eiskrem f

ice'-cream cone' s Tüte f Eis

ice' cube' s Eiswürfel m

ice'-cube tray' s Eiswürfelschale f

iced' tea' s Eistee m

ice' floe' s Eisscholle f

ice' hock'ey s Eishockey n

Iceland ['aɪslənd] s Island n

Icelander ['aɪs,lændər] s Isländer –in mf

Icelandic [aɪs'lændɪk] adj isländisch || s (language) Isländisch n

ice'man' s (–men') Eismann m

ice' pack' s (geol) Packeis n; (med) Eisbeutel m

ice' pick' s Eispfriem m; (mount) Eispickel m

ice' skate' s Schlittschuh m

ice'-skate' intr eislaufen

ichthyology [,ɪkθɪ'ɑlədʒi] s Ichthyologie f, Fischkunde f

icicle ['aɪsɪkəl] s Eiszapfen m

icing ['aɪsɪŋ] s Glasur f, Zuckerguß m; (aer) Vereisung f

icon ['aɪkɑn] s Ikone f

iconoclast [aɪ'kʌnə,klæst] s Bilderstürmer –in mf

icy ['aɪsi] adj (& fig) eisig

id [ɪd] s (psychol) Es n

I.D. card ['aɪ'di'kɑrd] s Ausweis m

idea [aɪ'di·ə] s Idee f, Vorstellung f; (intimation) Ahnung f; crazy i. Schnapsidee f; have big ideas große Rosinen im Kopf haben; that's the i.! so ist's richtig!; the i.! na so was!; what's the i.? wie kommen Sie darauf?

ideal [aɪ'di·əl] *adj* ideal || *s* Ideal *n*

idealism [aɪ'di·ə‚lɪzəm] *s* Idealismus *m*

idealist [aɪ'di·əlɪst] *s* Idealist –in *mf*

idealistic [aɪ‚di·əl'ɪstɪk] *adj* idealistisch

idealize [aɪ'di·ə‚laɪz] *tr* idealisieren

identical [aɪ'dɛntɪkəl] *adj* identisch

identification [aɪ'dɛntɪfɪ'keʃən] *s* Identifizierung *f*

identifica'tion tag' *s* Erkennungsmarke *f*

identi·fy [aɪ'dɛntɪ‚faɪ] *v* (*pret & pp* –fied) *tr* identifizieren; **i.** oneself sich ausweisen || *intr*—**i.** with sich einfühlen in (*acc*)

identity [aɪ'dɛntɪti] *s* Identität *f*; **prove one's i.** sich ausweisen

iden'tity card' *s* Ausweis *m*

ideological [‚aɪdɪ·ə'lɑdʒɪkəl] *adj* ideologisch

ideology [‚aɪdɪ'ɑlədʒi] *s* Ideologie *f*

idiocy ['ɪdɪ·əsi] *s* Idiotie *f*

idiom ['ɪdɪ·əm] *s* (*phrase*) Redewendung *f*; (*language, style*) Idiom *n*

idiomatic [‚ɪdɪ·ə'mætɪk] *adj* idiomatisch; **i. expression** (idiomatische) Redewendung *f*

idiosyncrasy [‚ɪdɪ·ə'sɪnkrəsi] *s* Idiosynkrasie *f*

idiot ['ɪdɪ·ət] *s* Idiot *m*, Trottel *m*

idiotic [‚ɪdɪ'ɑtɪk] *adj* idiotisch

idle ['aɪdəl] *adj* (*person, question, hours*) müßig; (*machine, factory*) stillstehend; (*capital*) tot; (*talk, threats*) leer; **lie i.** stilliegen; **stand i.** stillstehen || *s* (aut) Leerlauf *m* || *tr* arbeitslos machen; **i. away** vertrödeln || *intr* (aut) leerlaufen

idleness ['aɪdəlnɪs] *s* Müßiggang *m*

idler ['aɪdlər] *s* Müßiggänger *m*

i'dling *s* (aut) Leerlauf *m*

idol ['aɪdəl] *s* Abgott *m*; (fig) Idol *n*

idolatry [aɪ'dɑlətri] *s* Abgötterei *f*

idolize ['aɪdə‚laɪz] *tr* verhimmeln

idyll ['aɪdəl] *s* Idyll *n*, Idylle *f*

idyllic [aɪ'dɪlɪk] *adj* idyllisch

if [ɪf] *s* Wenn *n* || *conj* wenn; (*whether*) ob

igloo ['ɪglu] *s* Schneehütte *f*, Iglu *m* & *n*

ignite [ɪg'naɪt] *tr & intr* zünden

ignition [ɪg'nɪʃən] *adj* Zünd– || *s* Entzünden *n*; (aut) Zündung *f*

igni'tion key' *s* Zündschlüssel *m*

igni'tion switch' *s* Zündschloß *n*

ignoble [ɪg'nobəl] *adj* unedel

ignominious [‚ɪgnə'mɪnɪ·əs] *adj* schmachvoll, schändlich

ignoramus [‚ɪgnə'reməs] *s* Ignorant –in *mf*

ignorance ['ɪgnərəns] *s* Unwissenheit *f*; (of) Unkenntnis *f* (*genit*)

ignorant ['ɪgnərənt] *adj* unwissend; **be i. of** nicht wissen

ignore [ɪg'nor] *tr* ignorieren; (*words*) überhören; (*rules*) nicht beachten

ilk [ɪlk] *s*—**of that ilk** derselben Art

ill [ɪl] *adj* (*worse* [wʌrs]) *adj*; **worst** [wʌrst]) krank; (*repute*) schlecht; (*feelings*) feindselig; **fall** (*or* **take)**

ill krank werden || *adv* schlecht; **he can ill afford to** (*inf*) er kann es sich [*dat*] kaum leisten zu (*inf*); **take s.th.** ill etw übelnehmen

ill'-advised' *adj* (*person*) schlecht beraten; (*action*) unbesonnen

ill'-at-ease' *adj* unbehaglich

ill'-bred' *adj* ungezogen

ill'-consid'ered *adj* unbesonnen

ill'-disposed' *adj*—**be i. towards** übelgesinnt sein (*dat*)

illegal [ɪ'ligəl] *adj* illegal

illegible [ɪ'lɛdʒɪbəl] *adj* unlesbar

illegitimate [‚ɪlɪ'dʒɪtɪmɪt] *adj* unrechtmäßig; (*child*) illegitim

ill'-fat'ed *adj* unglücklich

illgotten ['ɪl‚gɑtən] *adj* unrechtmäßig erworben

ill' health' *s* Kränklichkeit *f*

ill'-hu'mored *adj* übelgelaunt

illicit [ɪ'lɪsɪt] *adj* unerlaubt

illiteracy [ɪ'lɪtərəsi] *s* Analphabetentum *n*

illiterate [ɪ'lɪtərɪt] *adj* analphabetisch || *s* Analphabet –in *mf*

ill'-man'nered *adj* ungehobelt

ill'-na'tured *adj* bösartig

illness ['ɪlnɪs] *s* (& fig) Krankheit *f*

illogical [ɪ'lɑdʒɪkəl] *adj* unlogisch

ill'-spent' *adj* verschwendet

ill'-starred' *adj* unglücklich

ill'-suit'ed *adj* (to) unpassend (*dat*)

ill'-tem'pered *adj* schlechtgelaunt

ill'-timed' *adj* unpassend

ill'-treat' *tr* mißhandeln

illuminate [ɪ'lumɪ‚net] *tr* beleuchten; (*public buildings, manuscripts*) illuminieren; (*enlighten*) erleuchten; (*explain*) erklären

illumination [ɪ‚lumɪ'neʃən] *s* Beleuchten *n*; Erleuchtung *f*; Illuminierung *f*

illusion [ɪ'luʒən] *s* Illusion *f*

illusive [ɪ'lusɪv] *adj* trügerisch

illusory [ɪ'lusəri] *adj* illusorisch

illustrate ['ɪləs‚tret] *tr* (*exemplify*) erläutern; (*a book*) illustrieren; **illustrated lecture** Lichtbildervortrag *m*; **richly illustrated** bilderreich

illustration [‚ɪləs'treʃən] *s* Erläuterung *f*; (*in a book*) Abbildung *f*

illustrative [ɪ'lʌstrətɪv] *adj* erläuternd; **i. material** Anschauungsmaterial *n*

illustrator ['ɪləs‚tretər] *s* Illustrator *m*

illustrious [ɪ'lʌstrɪ·əs] *adj* berühmt

ill' will' *s* Feindschaft *f*

image ['ɪmɪdʒ] *s* Bild *n*; (*reflection*) Spiegelbild *n*; (*statue*) Standbild *n*; (*before the public*) Image *n*; (opt, phot, telv) Bild *n*; **the spitting i. of his father** ganz der Vater

imagery ['ɪmɪdʒ(ə)ri] *s* Bildersprache *f*

imaginable [ɪ'mædʒɪnəbəl] *adj* erdenklich

imaginary [ɪ'mædʒɪ‚neri] *adj* imaginär

imagination [ɪ‚mædʒɪ'neʃən] *s* Phantasie *f*, Einbildungskraft *f*; **that's pure i.** das ist pure Einbildung

imaginative [ɪ'mædʒɪnətɪv] *adj* phantasievoll

imagine [ɪ'mædʒɪn] *tr* sich [*dat*] vorstellen, sich [*dat*] denken; **i. oneself**

in sich hineindenken in (acc); **you're only imagining things** das bilden Sie sich [*dat*] nur ein || *intr*—**I can i.** das läßt sich denken; **I i.** so ich glaube schon; **just i.** denken Sie nur mal!

imbecile ['ɪmbɪsɪl] *adj* geistesschwach || *s* Geistesschwache *mf*

imbecility [ˌɪmbɪ'sɪlɪti] *s* Geistesschwäche *f*, Blödheit *f*

imbibe [ɪm'baɪb] *tr* aufsaugen; (coll) trinken; (fig) (geistig) aufnehmen

imbue [ɪm'bju] *tr* durchfeuchten; (fig) (**with**) durchdringen (mit)

imitate ['ɪmɪˌtet] *tr* nachahmen, nachmachen; **i. s.o. in everything** j-m alles nachmachen

imitation [ˌɪmɪ'teʃən] *adj* unecht, nachgemacht || *s* Nachahmung *f*; **in i. of** nach dem Muster (*genit*)

imita'tion leath'er *s* Kunstleder *n*

imitator ['ɪmɪˌtetər] *s* Nachahmer –in *mf*

immaculate [ɪ'mækjəlɪt] *adj* makellos; (*sinless*) unbefleckt

immaterial [ˌɪmə'tɪrɪ·əl] *adj* immateriell, unkörperlich; (*unimportant*) unwesentlich; **it's i. to me** es is mir gleichgültig

immature [ˌɪmə'tjur] *adj* unreif

immaturity [ˌɪmə'tjurɪti] *s* Unreife *f*

immeasurable [ɪ'meʒərəbəl] *adj* unermeßlich

immediacy [ɪ'midɪ·əsi] *s* Unmittelbarkeit *f*

immediate [ɪ'midɪ·ɪt] *adj* sofortig; (*direct*) unmittelbar

immediately [ɪ'midɪ·ɪtli] *adv* sofort; **i. afterwards** gleich darauf

immemorial [ˌɪmɪ'morɪ·əl] *adj* uralt; **since time i.** seit Menschengedenken

immense [ɪ'mɛns] *adj* unermeßlich

immensity [ɪ'mɛnsɪti] *s* Unermeßlichkeit *f*

immerse [ɪ'mʌrs] *tr* (unter)tauchen; **immersed in** (*books, thought, work*) vertieft in (*acc*); **i. oneself in** sich vertiefen in (*acc*)

immersion [ɪ'mʌrʒən] *s* Untertauchen *n*; (fig) Versunkenheit *f*

immigrant ['ɪmɪgrənt] *adj* einwandernd || *s* Einwanderer –in *mf*

immigrate ['ɪmɪˌgret] *intr* einwandern

immigration [ˌɪmɪ'greʃən] *s* Einwanderung *f*

imminent ['ɪmɪnənt] *adj* drohend

immobile [ɪ'mobɪl] *adj* unbeweglich

immobilize [ɪ'mobɪˌlaɪz] *tr* unbeweglich machen; (*tanks*) bewegungsunfähig machen; (*troops*) fesseln; (med) ruhigstellen

immoderate [ɪ'madərɪt] *adj* unmäßig

immodest [ɪ'madɪst] *adj* unbescheiden

immolate ['ɪməˌlet] *tr* opfern

immoral [ɪ'morəl] *adj* unsittlich

immorality [ˌɪmə'rælɪti] *s* Unsittlichkeit *f*

immortal [ɪ'mortəl] *adj* unsterblich

immortality [ˌɪmor'tælɪti] *s* Unsterblichkeit *f*

immortalize [ɪ'mortəˌlaɪz] *tr* unsterblich machen

immovable [ɪ'muvəbəl] *adj* unbeweglich

immune [ɪ'mjun] *adj* (*free, exempt*) (**from**) immun (gegen); (*not responsive*) (**to**) gefeit (gegen); (med) (**to**) immun (gegen)

immunity [ɪ'mjunɪti] *s* Immunität *f*

immunization [ˌɪmjunɪ'zeʃən] *s* Schutzimpfung *f*, Immunisierung *f*

immunize ['ɪmjəˌnaɪz] *tr* (**against**) immunisieren (gegen)

immutable [ɪ'mjutəbəl] *adj* unwandelbar

imp [ɪmp] *s* Schlingel *m*

impact ['ɪmpækt] *s* Anprall *m*; (*of a shell*) Aufschlag *m*; (fig) Einwirkung *f*

impair [ɪm'pɛr] *tr* beeinträchtigen

impale [ɪm'pel] *tr* pfählen

impan·el [ɪm'pænəl] *v* (*pret & pp* **-el[l]ed;** *ger* **-el[l]ing**) *tr* in die Geschworenenliste eintragen

impart [ɪm'part] *tr* mitteilen

impartial [ɪm'parʃəl] *adj* unparteiisch

impassable [ɪm'pæsɪbəl] *adj* (*on foot*) ungangbar; (*by car*) unbefahrbar

impasse ['ɪmpæs] *s* Sackgasse *f*; **reach an i.** in e-e Sackgasse geraten

impassible [ɪm'pæsɪbəl] *adj* (**to**) unempfindlich (für)

impassioned [ɪm'pæʃənd] *adj* leidenschaftlich

impassive [ɪm'pæsɪv] *adj* (*person*) teilnahmslos; (*expression*) ausdruckslos

impatience [ɪm'peʃəns] *s* Ungeduld *f*

impatient [ɪm'peʃənt] *adj* ungeduldig

impeach [ɪm'pitʃ] *tr* (*an official*) wegen Amtsmißbrauchs unter Anklage stellen; (*a witness, motives*) in Zweifel ziehen

impeachment [ɪm'pitʃmənt] *s* (*of an official*) öffentliche Anklage *f*; (*of a witness, motives*) Anzweiflung *f*

impeccable [ɪm'pɛkəbəl] *adj* makellos

impecunious [ˌɪmpɪ'kjunɪ·əs] *adj* mittellos

impede [ɪm'pid] *tr* behindern, erschweren

impediment [ɪm'pɛdɪmənt] *s* Behinderung *f*; (*of speech*) Sprachfehler *m*

im·pel [ɪm'pɛl] *v* (*pret & pp* **-pelled;** *ger* **-pelling**) *tr* antreiben

impending [ɪm'pɛndɪŋ] *adj* nahe bevorstehen; (*threatening*) drohend

impenetrable [ɪm'pɛnətrəbəl] *adj* undurchdringlich; (fig) unergründlich

impenitent [ɪm'pɛnɪtənt] *adj* unbußfertig

imperative [ɪm'pɛrətɪv] *adj* dringend nötig || *s* Imperativ *m*

imper'ative mood' *s* Befehlsform *f*

imperceptible [ˌɪmpər'sɛptɪbəl] *adj* nicht wahrnehmbar, unmerklich

imperfect [ɪm'pʌrfɪkt] *adj* unvollkommen || *s* (gram) Imperfekt(um) *n*

imperfection [ˌɪmpər'fɛkʃən] *s* Unvollkommenheit *f*; (*flaw*) Fehler *m*

imperial [ɪm'pɪrɪ·əl] *adj* kaiserlich

imperialism [ɪm'pɪrɪ·əˌlɪzəm] *s* Imperialismus *m*

imperialist [ɪm'pɪrɪ·əlɪst] *adj* imperialistisch || *s* Imperialist –in *mf*

imper·il [ɪm'perɪl] v (pret & pp -il[l]ed; ger -il[l]ing) tr gefährden

imperious [ɪm'perɪ·əs] adj herrisch, anmaßend

imperishable [ɪm'perɪʃəbəl] adj unvergänglich

impersonal [ɪm'pʌrsənəl] adj unpersönlich

impersonate [ɪm'pʌrsə͵net] tr (imitate) nachahmen; (e.g., an officer) sich ausgeben als; (theat) darstellen

impersonator [ɪm'pʌrsə͵netər] s Imitator -in mf

impertinence [ɪm'pʌrtɪnəns] s Ungezogenheit f

impertinent [ɪm'pʌrtɪnənt] adj ungezogen

imperturbable [͵ɪmpʌr'tʌrbəbəl] adj unerschütterlich

impetuous [ɪm'petʃʊ·əs] adj ungestüm

impetus ['ɪmpɪtəs] s (& fig) Antrieb m

impiety [ɪm'paɪ·əti] s Gottlosigkeit f

impinge [ɪm'pɪndʒ] intr—i. on (an) stoßen an (acc); (said of rays) fallen auf (acc); (fig) eingreifen in (acc)

impious ['ɪmpɪ·əs] adj gottlos

impish ['ɪmpɪʃ] adj spitzbübisch

implant [ɪm'plænt] tr einpflanzen

implement ['ɪmplɪmənt] s Werkzeug n, Gerät n || ['ɪmplɪ͵ment] tr durchführen

implicate ['ɪmplɪ͵ket] tr (in) verwickeln (in acc)

implication [͵ɪmplɪ'keʃən] s (involvement) Verwicklung f; (implying) Andeutung f; **implications** Folgerungen pl

implicit [ɪm'plɪsɪt] adj (approval) stillschweigend; (trust) unbedingt

implied [ɪm'plaɪd] adj stillschweigend

implore [ɪm'plor] tr anflehen

im·ply [ɪm'plaɪ] v (pret & pp -plied) tr (express indirectly) andeuten; (involve) in sich schließen; (said of words) besagen

impolite [͵ɪmpə'laɪt] adj unhöflich

import ['ɪmport] s Import m, Einfuhr f; (meaning) Bedeutung f; **imports** Einfuhrwaren pl || [ɪm'port], ['ɪmport] tr importieren, einführen

importance [ɪm'portəns] s Wichtigkeit f; **a man of i.** ein Mann m von Bedeutung; **of no i.** unwichtig

important [ɪm'portənt] adj wichtig

im'port du'ty s Einfuhrzoll m

importer [ɪm'portər] s Importeur m

importune [͵ɪmpor't(j)un] adj aufdringlich || tr bestürmen

impose [ɪm'poz] tr (on, upon) auferlegen (dat) || intr—i. on über Gebühr beanspruchen

impos'ing adj imposant

imposition [͵ɪmpə'zɪʃən] s (of hands, of an obligation) Auferlegung f; (taking unfair advantage) Zumutung f

impossible [ɪm'pɑsɪbəl] adj unmöglich

impostor [ɪm'pɑstər] s Hochstapler m

imposture [ɪm'pɑstʃər] s Hochstapelei f

impotence ['ɪmpətəns] s Machtlosigkeit f; (pathol) Impotenz f

impotent ['ɪmpətənt] adj machtlos; (pathol) impotent

impound [ɪm'paʊnd] tr beschlagnahmen

impoverish [ɪm'pɑvərɪʃ] tr arm machen; **become impoverished** verarmen

impracticable [ɪm'præktɪkəbəl] adj unausführbar

impractical [ɪm'præktɪkəl] adj unpraktisch

impregnable [ɪm'pregnəbəl] adj uneinnehmbar

impregnate [ɪm'pregnet] tr (saturate) imprägnieren; (& fig) schwängern

impresari·o [͵ɪmprɪ'sɑrɪ͵o] s (-os) Impresario m

impress [ɪm'pres] tr (affect) imponieren (dat), beeindrucken; (imprint, emphasize) einprägen; **i. s.th. on s.o.** j-m etw einprägen

impression [ɪm'preʃən] s Eindruck m; (stamp) Gepräge n; **try to make an i.** Eindruck schinden

impressive [ɪm'presɪv] adj eindrucksvoll

imprint ['ɪmprɪnt] s Aufdruck m; (fig) Eindruck m || [ɪm'prɪnt] tr (on) aufdrucken (auf acc); **i. on s.o.'s memory** j-m ins Gedächtnis einprägen

imprison [ɪm'prɪzən] tr einsperren

imprisonment [ɪm'prɪzənmənt] s Haft f; (penalty) Freiheitsstrafe f; (captivity) Gefangenschaft f

improbable [ɪm'prɑbəbəl] adj unwahrscheinlich

impromptu [ɪm'prɑmpt(j)u] adj & adv aus dem Stegreif || s Stegreifstück n

improper [ɪm'prɑpər] adj ungehörig, unschicklich; (use) unzulässig

improve [ɪm'pruv] tr verbessern; (relations) ausbauen; (land) kultivieren; (a salary) aufbessern; **i. oneself** sich bessern; (financially) sich verbessern || intr bessern; (com) sich erholen; **i. on** Verbesserungen vornehmen an (dat)

improvement [ɪm'pruvmənt] s Verbesserung f; (reworking) Umarbeitung f; (of money value) Erholung f; (of a salary) Aufbesserung f; (in health) Besserung f; **be an i. on** ein Fortschritt sein gegenüber

improvident [ɪm'prɑvɪdənt] adj unbedacht

improvise ['ɪmprə͵vaɪz] tr improvisieren || intr improvisieren; (mus) phantasieren

imprudence [ɪm'prudəns] s Unklugheit f

imprudent [ɪm'prudənt] adj unklug

impudence ['ɪmpjədəns] s Unverschämtheit f

impudent ['ɪmpjədənt] adj unverschämt

impugn [ɪm'pjun] tr bestreiten

impulse ['ɪmpʌls] s Impuls m; **act on i.** impulsiv handeln

impulsive [ɪm'pʌlsɪv] adj impulsiv

impunity [ɪm'pjunɪti] s Straffreiheit f; **with i.** ungestraft

impure [ɪm'pjur] adj (& fig) unrein

impurity [ɪmˈpjʊrɪti] *s* (& fig) Unreinheit *f*
impute [ɪmˈpjut] *tr* (**to**) unterstellen (*dat*)
in [ɪn] *adv* (*position*) drin, drinnen; (*direction away from the speaker*) hinein; (*direction toward the speaker*) herein; **be all in** ganz erschöpft sein; **be in** da sein; (*said of a political party*) an der Macht sein; (*be in style*) in Mode sein; **be in for** zu erwarten haben; **have it in for** auf dem Strich haben || *s*—**the ins and outs of** die Einzelheiten (*genit*) || *prep* (*position*) in (*dat*); (*direction*) in (*acc*); (*e.g., the morning, afternoon, evening*) am; (*a field, the country; one eye*) auf (*dat*); (*one's opinion; all probability*) nach (*dat*); (*circumstances; a reign*) unter (*dat*); (*ink; one stroke*) mit (*dat*); (*because of pain, joy, etc.*) vor (*dat*); **he doesn't have it in him to** (*inf*) er hat nicht das Zeug dazu zu (*inf*); **in German** auf deutsch
inability [ˌɪnəˈbɪlɪti] *s* Unfähigkeit *f*; **i. to pay** Zahlungsunfähigkeit *f*
inaccessible [ˌɪnækˈsesɪbəl] *adj* unzugänglich
inaccuracy [ɪnˈækjərəsi] *s* Ungenauigkeit *f*
inaccurate [ɪnˈækjərɪt] *adj* ungenau
inaction [ɪnˈækʃən] *s* Untätigkeit *f*
inactive [ɪnˈæktɪv] *adj* untätig; (*chem*) unwirksam; (*st. exch.*) lustlos
inactivity [ˌɪnækˈtɪvɪti] *s* Untätigkeit *f*
inadequate [ɪnˈædɪkwɪt] *adj* unangemessen
inadmissible [ˌɪnədˈmɪsɪbəl] *adj* unstatthaft, unzulässig
inadvertent [ˌɪnədˈvʌrtənt] *adj* versehentlich
inadvisable [ˌɪnədˈvaɪzəbəl] *adj* nicht ratsam
inalienable [ɪnˈeljənəbəl] *adj* unveräußerlich
inane [ɪnˈen] *adj* leer, unsinnig
inanimate [ɪnˈænɪmɪt] *adj* unbeseelt
inappropriate [ˌɪnəˈproprɪ·ɪt] *adj* unangemessen
inarticulate [ˌɪnɑrˈtɪkjəlɪt] *adj* unartikuliert, undeutlich
inartistic [ˌɪnɑrˈtɪstɪk] *adj* unkünstlerisch, kunstlos
inasmuch as [ˌɪnəzˈmʌtʃˌæz] *conj* da
inattentive [ˌɪnəˈtentɪv] *adv* (**to**) unaufmerksam (or unachtsam) (gegenüber)
inaudible [ɪnˈɔdɪbəl] *adj* unhörbar
inaugural [ɪnˈɔɡ(j)ərəl] *adj* Antritts–
inaugurate [ɪnˈɔɡ(j)əˌret] *tr* feierlich eröffnen; (*a new policy*) einleiten
inauguration [ɪnˌɔɡ(j)əˈreʃən] *s* Eröffnung *f*; (*of an official*) Amtsantritt *m*
inauspicious [ˌɪnɔˈspɪʃəs] *adj* ungünstig
inborn [ˈɪnˌbɔrn] *adj* angeboren
inbred [ˈɪnˌbred] *adj* angeboren, ererbt
in'breed'ing *s* Inzucht *f*

incalculable [ɪnˈkælkjələbəl] *adj* unberechenbar
incandescent [ˌɪnkənˈdesənt] *adj* Glüh–
incantation [ˌɪnkænˈteʃən] *s* Beschwörung *f*
incapable [ɪnˈkepəbəl] *adj* untüchtig; **i. of** (*ger*) nicht fähig zu (*inf*)
incapacitate [ˌɪnkəˈpæsɪˌtet] *tr* unfähig machen; (*jur*) für geschäftsunfähig erklären
incarcerate [ɪnˈkɑrsəˌret] *tr* einkerkern
incarnate [ɪnˈkɑrnet] *adj*—**God i.** Gottmensch *m*; **the devil i.** der Teufel in Menschengestalt
incarnation [ˌɪnkɑrˈneʃən] *s* (fig) Verkörperung *f*; (eccl) Fleischwerdung *f*
incendiary [ɪnˈsendɪˌeri] *adj* Brand–; (fig) aufhetzend || *s* Brandstifter –in *mf*
incense [ˈɪnsəns] *s* Weihrauch *m* || *tr* (eccl) beräuchern || [ɪnˈsens] *tr* erzürnen
in'cense burn'er *s* Räuchergefäß *n*
incentive [ɪnˈsentɪv] *s* Anreiz *m*
inception [ɪnˈsepʃən] *s* Anfang *m*
incessant [ɪnˈsesənt] *adj* unaufhörlich
incest [ˈɪnsest] *s* Blutschande *f*
incestuous [ɪnˈsestʃʊ·əs] *adj* blutschänderisch
inch [ɪntʃ] *s* Zoll *m*; **beat within an i. of one's life** fast zu Tode prügeln; **by inches** nach und nach; **not yield an i.** keinen Fußbreit nachgeben || *intr*—**i. along** dahinschleichen; **i. forward** langsam vorrücken
incidence [ˈɪnsɪdəns] *s* Vorkommen *n*
incident [ˈɪnsɪdənt] *s* Vorfall *m*; (*adverse event*) Zwischenfall *m*
incidental [ˌɪnsɪˈdentəl] *adj* zufällig; **i. to** gehörig zu || **incidentals** *spl* Nebenausgaben *pl*
incidentally [ˌɪnsɪˈdentəli] *adv* übrigens
incinerate [ɪnˈsɪnəˌret] *tr* einäschern
incinerator [ɪnˈsɪnəˌretər] *s* Verbrennungsofen *m*
incipient [ɪnˈsɪpɪ·ənt] *adv* beginnend
incision [ɪnˈsɪʒən] *s* Schnitt *m*
incisive [ɪnˈsaɪsɪv] *adj* (*biting*) beißend; (*penetrating*) durchdringend; (*sharp*) scharf
incisor [ɪnˈsaɪzər] *s* Schneidezahn *m*
incite [ɪnˈsaɪt] *tr* aufreizen, aufhetzen
inclement [ɪnˈklemənt] *adj* ungünstig
inclination [ˌɪnkliˈneʃən] *s* (& fig) Neigung *f*
incline [ˈɪnklaɪn] *s* Abhang *m* || [ɪnˈklaɪn] *tr* neigen || *intr* (**towards**) sich neigen (nach or zu); (fig) (**towards**) neigen (zu); **the roof inclines sharply** das Dach fällt steil ab
include [ɪnˈklud] *tr* einschließen; **i. among** rechnen unter (*acc*); **i. in** einrechnen in (*acc*)
includ'ed *adj* (mit) inbegriffen
includ'ing *prep* einschließlich (*genit*)
inclusive [ɪnˈklusɪv] *adj* umfassend, gesamt; **all i.** alles inbegriffen; **from ... to ... i.** von ... zu ... einschließlich (or inklusive); **i. of** einschließlich (*genit*)

incognito [ɪn'kɑgnɪ‚to] *adv* inkognito

incoherent [‚ɪnko'hɪrənt] *adj* unzusammenhängend; **be i.** (*said of a person*) nicht ganz bei sich sein

incombustible [‚ɪnkəm'bʌstɪbəl] *adj* unverbrennbar

income ['ɪnkʌm] *s* (**from**) Einkommen *n* (aus)

in′come tax′ *s* Einkommensteuer *f*

in′come-tax return′ *s* Einkommensteuererklärung *f*

in′com′ing *adj* (*e.g., tide*) hereinkommend; (*bus, train*) ankommend; (*official*) neu eintretend; **i. goods, i. mail** Eingänge *pl*

incomparable [ɪn'kɑmpərəbəl] *adj* unvergleichlich

incompatible [‚ɪnkəm'pætɪbəl] *adj* (**with**) unvereinbar (mit); (*persons*) unverträglich

incompetent [ɪn'kɑmpɪtənt] *adj* untauglich; (*not legally qualified*) nicht zuständig; (*not legally capable*) geschäftsunfähig; (*inadmissible*) unzulässig ‖ *s* Nichtkönner –in *mf*

incomplete [‚ɪnkəm'plit] *adj* unvollständig

incomprehensible [‚ɪnkɑmprɪ'hensɪbəl] *adj* unbegreiflich

inconceivable [‚ɪnkən'sivəbəl] *adj* undenkbar

inconclusive [‚ɪnkən'klusɪv] *adj* (*not convincing*) nicht überzeugend; (*leading to no result*) ergebnislos

incongruous [ɪn'kɑŋgru‚əs] *adj* nicht übereinstimmend

inconsequential [ɪn‚kɑnsɪ'kwenʃəl] *adj* belanglos

inconsiderate [‚ɪnkən'sɪdərɪt] *adj* unüberlegt; (**towards**) rücksichtslos (gegen)

inconsistency [‚ɪnkən'sɪstənsɪ] *s* (*lack of logical connection*) Inkonsequenz *f*; (*contradiction*) Unstimmigkeit *f*; (*instability*) Unbeständigkeit *f*

inconsistent [‚ɪnkən'sɪstənt] *adj* inkonsequent; (*uneven*) unbeständig

inconspicuous [‚ɪnkən'spɪkju‚əs] *adj* unauffällig

inconstant [ɪn'kɑnstənt] *adj* unbeständig

incontinent [ɪn'kɑntɪnənt] *adj* zügellos

incontrovertible [‚ɪnkɑntrə'vʌrtɪbəl] *adj* unwiderlegbar

inconvenience [‚ɪnkən'vini‚əns] *s* Ungelegenheit *f* ‖ *tr* bemühen, belästigen

inconvenient [‚ɪnkən'vini‚ənt] *adj* ungelegen

incorporate [ɪn'kɔrpə‚ret] *tr* einverleiben; (*an organization*) zu e-r Körperschaft machen ‖ *intr* e-e Körperschaft werden

incorporation [ɪn‚kɔrpə'reʃən] *s* Einverleibung *f*; (*jur*) Körperschaftsbildung *f*

incorrect [‚ɪnkə'rekt] *adj* unrichtig, falsch; (*conduct*) unschicklich

incorrigible [ɪn'kɔrɪdʒɪbəl] *adj* unverbesserlich

increase ['ɪnkris] *s* Zunahme *f*; **be on the i.** steigen; **i. in costs** Kostensteigerung *f*; **i. in pay** Gehaltser-

höhung *f*; (mil) Solderhöhung *f*; **i. in population** Bevölkerungszunahme *f*; **i. in prices** Preiserhöhung *f*; **i. in rent** Mieterhöhung *f*; **i. in taxes** Steuererhöhung *f*; **i. in value** Wertsteigerung *f*; **i. in weight** Gewichtszunahme *f* ‖ [ɪn'kris] *tr* (*in size*) vergrößern; (*in height*) erhöhen; (*in quantity*) vermehren; (*in intensity*) verstärken; (*prices*) heraufsetzen ‖ *intr* zunehmen, sich vergrößern; (*rise*) sich erhöhen; (*in quantity*) sich vermehren; (*in intensity*) sich verstärken; **i. in** zunehmen an (*dat*)

increasingly [ɪn'krisɪŋlɪ] *adv* immer mehr; **i. more difficult** immer schwieriger

incredible [ɪn'kredɪbəl] *adj* unglaublich

incredulous [ɪn'kredʒələs] *adj* ungläubig

increment ['ɪnkrɪmənt] *s* Zunahme *f*, Zuwachs *m*; (*in pay*) Gehaltszulage *f*

incriminate [ɪn'krɪmɪ‚net] *tr* belasten

incrust [ɪn'krʌst] *tr* überkrusten

incubate ['ɪnkjə‚bet] *tr & intr* brüten

incubator ['ɪnkjə‚betər] *s* Brutapparat *m*

inculcate [ɪn'kʌlket], ['ɪnkʌl‚ket] *tr* (**in**) einprägen (*dat*)

incumbency [ɪn'kʌmbənsɪ] *s* (*obligation*) Obliegenheit *f*; (*term of office*) Amtszeit *f*

incumbent [ɪn'kʌmbənt] *adj—be i. on** obliegen (*dat*) ‖ *s* Amtsinhaber –in *mf*

incunabula [‚ɪnkjʊ'næbjələ] *spl* (typ) Wiegendrucke *pl*

in-cur [ɪn'kʌr] *v* (*pret & pp* –**curred**; *ger* –**curring**) *tr* sich (*dat*) zuziehen; (*debts*) machen; (*a loss*) erleiden; (*a risk*) eingehen

incurable [ɪn'kjʊrəbəl] *adj* unheilbar ‖ *s* unheilbarer Kranke *m*

incursion [ɪn'kʌrʒən] *s* Einfall *m*

indebted [ɪn'detɪd] *adj* (**to**) verschuldet (bei); **be i. to s.o. for s.th.** j–m etw zu verdanken haben

indecency [ɪn'disənsɪ] *s* Unsittlichkeit *f*

indecent [ɪn'disənt] *adj* unsittlich; **i. assault** Sittlichkeitsvergehen *n*

indecision [‚ɪndɪ'sɪʒən] *s* Unentschlossenheit *f*

indecisive [‚ɪndɪ'saɪsɪv] *adj* (*person*) unentschlossen; (*battle*) nicht entscheidend

indeclinable [‚ɪndɪ'klaɪnəbəl] *adj* undeklinierbar

indeed [ɪn'did] *adv* ja, zwar ‖ *interj* jawohl!

indefatigable [‚ɪndɪ'fætɪgəbəl] *adj* unermüdlich

indefensible [‚ɪndɪ'fensɪbəl] *adj* nicht zu verteidigen(d); (*argument*) unhaltbar; (*behavior*) unentschuldbar

indefinable [‚ɪndɪ'faɪnəbəl] *adj* undefinierbar

indefinite [ɪn'defɪnɪt] *adj* (*unlimited*) unbegrenzt; (*not exact*) unbestimmt; (*answer*) ausweichend; (*vague*) undeutlich; (gram) unbestimmt

indelible [ɪnˈdɛlɪbəl] *adj* (*ink, pencil*) wasserfest; (fig) unauslöschlich

indelicate [ɪnˈdɛlɪkɪt] *adj* unzart

indemnification [ɪnˌdɛmnɪfɪˈkeʃən] *s* Schadenersatzleistung *f*

indemni·fy [ɪnˈdɛmnɪˌfaɪ] *v* (*pret & pp* –**fied**) *tr* entschädigen

indemnity [ɪnˈdɛmnɪtɪ] *s* Schadenersatz *m*

indent [ɪnˈdɛnt] *tr* (*notch*) einkerben; (*the coast*) tiefe Einschnitte bilden in (*dat*); (typ) einrücken ‖ *intr* (typ) einrücken

indentation [ˌɪndɛnˈteʃən] *s* Kerbe *f*; (typ) Absatz *m*

indenture [ɪnˈdɛntʃər] *s* (*service contract*) Arbeitsvertrag *m*; (*apprentice contract*) Lehrvertrag *m* ‖ *tr* vertraglich binden

independence [ˌɪndɪˈpɛndəns] *s* Unabhängigkeit *f*

independent [ˌɪndɪˈpɛndənt] *adj* (**of**) unabhängig (von) ‖ *s* Unabhängige *mf*

indescribable [ˌɪndɪˈskraɪbəbəl] *adj* unbeschreiblich

indestructible [ˌɪndɪˈstrʌktɪbəl] *adj* unzerstörbar

index [ˈɪndɛks] *s* (**indexes & indices** [ˈɪndɪˌsiz]) (*in a book*) Register *n*; (fig) (**to**) Hisweis *m* (auf *acc*); **Index Index** *m* ‖ *tr* registrieren; (*a book*) mit e-m Register versehen

in′dex card′ *s* Karteikarte *f*

in′dex fin′ger *s* Zeigefinger *m*

India [ˈɪndɪ·ə] *s* Indien *n*

In′dia ink′ *s* chinesische Tusche *f*

Indian [ˈɪndɪ·ən] *adj* indisch; (*e.g., chief, tribe*) Indianer– ‖ *s* (*of India*) Inder –in *mf*; (*of North America*) Indianer –in *mf*; (*of Central or South America*) Indio *m*

In′dian corn′ *s* Mais *m*

In′dian file′ *adv* in Gänsemarsch

In′dian O′cean *s* Indischer Ozean *m*

In′dian sum′mer *s* Altweibersommer *m*

indicate [ˈɪndɪˌket] *tr* angeben, anzeigen

indication [ˌɪndɪˈkeʃən] *s* Angabe *f*; (*of s.th. imminent*) (**of**) Anzeichen *n* (für); **give i. of** anzeigen

indicative [ɪnˈdɪkətɪv] *adj* (gram) indikativ; **be i. of** hindeuten auf (*acc*) ‖ *s* (gram) Wirklichkeitsform *f*, Indikativ *m*

indicator [ˈɪndɪˌketər] *s* Zeiger *m*

indict [ɪnˈdaɪt] *tr* (**for**) anklagen (wegen)

indictment [ɪnˈdaɪtmənt] *s* Anklage *f*

indifference [ɪnˈdɪfərəns] *s* (**to**) Gleichgültigkeit *f* (gegen or gegenüber)

indifferent [ɪnˈdɪfərənt] *adj* (*mediocre*) mittelmäßig; (**to**) gleichgültig (gegen)

indigenous [ɪnˈdɪdʒɪnəs] *adj* (**to**) einheimisch (in *dat*)

indigent [ˈɪndɪdʒənt] *adj* bedürftig

indigestible [ˌɪndɪˈdʒɛstɪbəl] *adj* unverdaulich

indigestion [ˌɪndɪˈdʒɛstʃən] *s* Verdauungsstörung *f*, Magenverstimmung *f*

indignant [ɪnˈdɪgnənt] *adj* (**at**) empört (über *acc*)

indignation [ˌɪndɪgˈneʃən] *s* (**at**) Empörung *f* (über *acc*)

indignity [ɪnˈdɪgnɪtɪ] *s* Beleidigung *f*

indigo [ˈɪndɪˌgo] *adj* Indigo– ‖ *s* Indigo *m & n*

indirect [ˌɪndɪˈrɛkt] *adj* indirekt

in′direct dis′course *s* indirekte Rede *f*

in′direct ques′tion *s* indirekter Fragesatz *m*

indiscreet [ˌɪndɪsˈkrit] *adj* indiskret

indiscretion [ˌɪndɪsˈkrɛʃən] *s* Indiskretion *f*

indiscriminate [ˌɪndɪsˈkrɪmɪnɪt] *adj* unterschiedslos

indispensable [ˌɪndɪsˈpɛnsəbəl] *adj* unentbehrlich

indisposed *adj* (*ill*) unpäßlich; **i. to** abgeneigt (*dat*)

indissoluble [ˌɪndɪˈsɑljəbəl] *adj* unauflösbar

indistinct [ˌɪndɪsˈtɪŋkt] *adj* undeutlich

individual [ˌɪndɪˈvɪdʒʊ·əl] *adj* individuell, Einzel–, einzeln ‖ *s* Individuum *n*

individ′ual case′ *s* Einzelfall *m*

individuality [ˌɪndɪˌvɪdʒʊˈælɪtɪ] *s* Individualität *f*

individually [ˌɪndɪˈvɪdʒʊ·əli] *adv* einzeln

indivisible · [ˌɪndɪˈvɪzɪbəl] *adj* unteilbar

Indochina [ˈɪndoˈtʃaɪnə] *s* Indochina *n*

indoctrinate [ɪnˈdɑktrɪˌnet] *tr* (**in**) schulen (in *dat*), unterweisen (in *dat*)

indoctrination [ˌɪndɑktrɪˈneʃən] *s* Schulung *f*, Unterweisung *f*

Indo-European [ˈɪndoˌjurəˈpi·ən] *adj* indogermanisch ‖ *s* (*language*) Indogermanisch *n*

indolence [ˈɪndələns] *s* Trägheit *f*

indolent [ˈɪndələnt] *adj* träge

Indonesia [ˌɪndoˈniʒə] *s* Indonesien *n*

Indonesian [ˌɪndoˈniʒən] *adj* indonesisch ‖ *s* Indonesier –in *mf*

indoor [ˈɪnˌdor] *adj* Haus–, Zimmer–, Innen–; (sport) Hallen–

indoors [ɪnˈdorz] *adv* innen, drin(nen)

in′door shot′ *s* (phot) Innenaufnahme *f*

induce [ɪnˈd(j)us] *tr* veranlassen, bewegen; (*bring about*) verursachen; (elec, phys) induzieren

inducement [ɪnˈd(j)usmənt] *s* Anreiz *m*

induct [ɪnˈdʌkt] *tr* (**into**) einführen (in *acc*); (mil) (**into**) einberufen (zu)

inductee [ˌɪnˈdʌkti] *s* Einberufene *mf*

induction [ɪnˈdʌkʃən] *s* Einführung *f*; (elec, log) Induktion *f*; (mil) Einberufung *f*

induc′tion coil′ *s* Induktionsspule *f*

indulge [ɪnˈdʌldʒ] *tr* (*a desire*) frönen (*dat*); (*a person*) befriedigen; (*children*) verwöhnen; **i. oneself** in schwelgen in (*dat*) ‖ *intr* (coll) trinken; **i. in s.th.** sich (*dat*) etw gestatten

indulgence [ɪnˈdʌldʒəns] *s* (*of a desire*) Frönen *n*; (*tolerance*) Duldung *f*; (relig) Ablaß *m*; **ask s.o.'s i.** j–n um Nachsicht bitten

indulgent [ɪnˈdʌldʒənt] *adj* schonend; (**toward**) nachsichtig (gegen)

industrial [ɪnˈdʌstrɪ·əl] *adj* (*e.g., bank,*

center, alcohol, product, worker) Industrie–; *(e.g., accident, medicine)* Betriebs–; *(e.g., revolution)* industriell; *(e.g., school, engineering)* Gewerbe–
industrialist [ɪn'dʌstrɪ·əlɪst] *s* Industrielle *mf*
industrialize [ɪn'dʌstrɪ·ə,laɪz] *tr* industrialisieren
indus'trial man'agement *s* Betriebswirtschaft *f*
industrious [ɪn'dʌstrɪ·əs] *adj* fleißig
industry ['ɪndəstrɪ] *s* Industrie *f; (energy)* Fleiß *m*
inebriated [ɪn'ibrɪ,etɪd] *adj* betrunken
inedible [ɪn'edɪbəl] *adj* ungenießbar
ineffable [ɪn'efəbəl] *adj* unaussprechlich
ineffective [,ɪnɪ'fektɪv] *adj* unwirksam; *(person)* untüchtig
ineffectual [,ɪnɪ'fektʃʊ·əl] *adj* unwirksam
inefficient [,ɪnɪ'fɪʃənt] *adj* untüchtig; *(process, procedure)* unrationell; *(mach)* nicht leistungsfähig
ineligible [ɪn'elɪdʒɪbəl] *adj* nicht wählbar; *(not suitable)* ungeeignet
inept [ɪn'ept] *adj* ungeschickt
inequality [,ɪnɪ'kwɑlɪtɪ] *s* Ungleichheit *f*
inequity [ɪn'ekwɪtɪ] *s* Ungerechtigkeit *f*
inertia [ɪn'ʌrʃə] *s* Trägheit *f*
inescapable [,ɪnes'kepəbəl] *adj* unentrinnbar, unabwendbar
inevitable [ɪn'evɪtəbəl] *adj* unvermeidlich, unausweichlich
inexact [,ɪneg'zækt] *adj* ungenau
inexcusable [,ɪneks'kjuzəbəl] *adj* unentschuldbar
inexhaustible [,ɪneg'zɔstɪbəl] *adj* unerschöpflich
inexorable [ɪn'eksərəbəl] *adj* unerbittlich
inexpensive [,ɪnek'spensɪv] *adj* billig
inexperience [,ɪnek'spɪrɪ·əns] *s* Unerfahrenheit *f*
inexpe'rienced *adj* unerfahren
inexplicable [ɪn'eksplɪkəbəl] *adj* unerklärlich
inexpressible [,ɪnek'spresɪbəl] *adj* unaussprechlich
infallibility [,ɪnfælɪ'bɪlɪtɪ] *s* Unfehlbarkeit *f*
infallible [ɪn'fælɪbəl] *adj* unfehlbar
infamous ['ɪnfəməs] *adj* schändlich
infamy ['ɪnfəmɪ] *s* Schändlichkeit *f*
infancy ['ɪnfənsɪ] *s* Kindheit *f;* **be still in its i.** (fig) noch in den Kinderschuhen stecken
infant ['ɪnfənt] *adj* Säuglings– ‖ *s* Kleinkind *n*, Säugling *m*
infantile ['ɪnfən,taɪl] *adj* infantil
in'fantile paral'ysis *s* Kinderlähmung *f*
infantry ['ɪnfəntrɪ] *s* Infanterie *f*
in'fantry·man *s* (–men) Infanterist *m*
infatuated [ɪn'fætʃʊ,etɪd] *adj* betört
infatuation [ɪn,fætʃʊ'eʃən] *s* Betörung *f*
infect [ɪn'fekt] *tr* anstecken, infizieren; **become infected** sich anstecken
infection [ɪn'fekʃən] *s* Ansteckung *f*

infectious [ɪn'fekʃəs] *adj (& fig)* ansteckend
in·fer [ɪn'fʌr] *v (pret & pp* **–ferred;** *ger* **–ferring)** *tr* folgern
inference ['ɪnfərəns] *s* Folgerung *f*
inferior [ɪn'fɪrɪ·ər] *adj (in rank)* niedriger; *(in worth)* minderwertig; **(to)** unterlegen *(dat)*
inferiority [ɪn,fɪrɪ'ɑrɪtɪ] *s* Unterlegenheit *f; (in worth)* Minderwertigkeit *f*
inferior'ity com'plex *s* Minderwertigkeitskomplex *m*
infernal [ɪn'fʌrnəl] *adj* höllisch
infest [ɪn'fest] *tr* in Schwärmen überfallen; **be infested with** wimmeln von
infidel ['ɪnfɪdəl] *adj* ungläubig ‖ *s* Ungläubige *mf*
infidelity [,ɪnfɪ'delɪtɪ] *s* Untreue *f*
in'field' *s* (baseball) Innenfeld *n*
infiltrate [ɪn'fɪltret], ['ɪnfɪl,tret] *tr (filter through)* infiltrieren; *(mil)* durchsickern durch; *(pol)* unterwandern ‖ *intr* infiltrieren
infinite ['ɪnfɪnɪt] *adj* unendlich
infinitive [ɪn'fɪnɪtɪv] *s* (gram) Nennform *f*, Infinitiv *m*
infinity [ɪn'fɪnɪtɪ] *s* Unendlichkeit *f;* **to i.** endlos
infirm [ɪn'fʌrm] *adj* schwach; *(from age)* altersschwach
infirmary [ɪn'fʌrmərɪ] *s* Krankenstube *f;* (mil) Revier *n*
infirmity [ɪn'fʌrmɪtɪ] *s* Schwachheit *f*
inflame [ɪn'flem] *tr (fig & pathol)* entzünden; **become inflamed** sich entzünden
inflammable [ɪn'flæməbəl] *adj* entzündbar, feuergefährlich
inflammation [,ɪnflə'meʃən] *s* Entzündung *f*
inflammatory [ɪn'flæmə,torɪ] *adj* aufrührerisch; (pathol) Entzündungs–
inflate [ɪn'flet] *tr* aufblasen; *(tires)* aufpumpen
inflation [ɪn'fleʃən] *s* (econ) Inflation *f*
inflationary [ɪn'fleʃə,nerɪ] *adj* inflationistisch
inflect [ɪn'flekt] *tr (the voice)* modulieren; (gram) flektieren
inflection [ɪn'flekʃən] *s (of the voice)* Tonfall *m;* (gram) Flexion *f*
inflexible [ɪn'fleksɪbəl] *adj* unbiegsam; *(person)* unbeugsam; *(law)* unabänderlich
inflict [ɪn'flɪkt] *tr (punishment)* **(on)** auferlegen *(dat); (a defeat)* **(on)** zufügen *(dat); (a wound)* **(on)** beibringen *(dat)*
influence ['ɪnflu·əns] *s* **(on)** Einfluß *m* (auf *acc*) ‖ *tr* beeinflussen
influential [ɪnflu'enʃəl] *adj* einflußreich, maßgebend
influenza [,ɪnflu'enzə] *s* Grippe *f*
influx ['ɪnflʌks] *s* Zufluß *m*
inform [ɪn'fɔrm] *tr* **(of)** benachrichtigen (von) ‖ *intr*—**i. against** anzeigen
informal [ɪn'fɔrməl] *adj* zwanglos
informant [ɪn'fɔrmənt] *s* Gewährsmann *m*
information [,ɪnfər'meʃən] *s* Nachricht *f*, Auskunft *f; (items of information)*

Informationen *pl;* **a piece of i.** e–e Auskunft *f;* **for your i.** zu Ihrer Information

informa′tion desk′ *s* Auskunftsstelle *f*

informative [ɪn′fɔrmətɪv] *adj* belehrend

informed′ *adj* unterrichtet

informer [ɪn′fɔrmər] *s* Denunziant –in *mf*

infraction [ɪn′frækʃən] *s* (**of**) Verstoß *m* (gegen)

infrared [ˌɪnfrə′red] *adj* infrarot

infrequent [ɪn′frikwənt] *adj* selten

infringe [ɪn′frɪndʒ] *tr* verletzen ‖ *intr* **—i. on** eingreifen in (*acc*)

infringement [ɪn′frɪndʒmənt] *s* (*of a law*) Verletzung *f;* (*of a right*) Eingriff *m* (in *acc*)

infuriate [ɪn′fjurɪˌet] *tr* wütend machen

infuse [ɪn′fjuz] *tr* (& *fig*) (**into**) einflößen (*dat*)

infusion [ɪn′fjuʒən] *s* (& *fig*) Einflößung *f;* (med) Infusion *f*

ingenious [ɪn′dʒinɪ·əs] *adj* erfinderisch

ingenuity [ˌɪndʒɪ′n(j)u·ɪti] *s* Erfindungsgabe *f,* Scharfsinn *m*

ingenuous [ɪn′dʒenjʊ·əs] *adj* aufrichtig; (*naive*) naiv

ingest [ɪn′dʒest] *tr* zu sich nehmen

inglorious [ɪn′glorɪ·əs] *adj* (*shameful*) unrühmlich; (*without honor*) ruhmlos

ingot [′ɪŋgət] *s* Block *m;* (*of gold or silver*) Barren *m*

ingrained′, in′grained *adj* eingewurzelt

ingrate [′ɪngret] *s* Undankbare *mf*

ingratiate [ɪn′greʃɪˌet] *tr*—**i. oneself with** sich einschmeicheln bei

ingra′tiating *adj* einschmeichelnd

ingratitude [ɪn′grætɪˌt(j)ud] *s* Undankbarkeit *f,* Undank *m*

ingredient [ɪn′gridɪ·ənt] *s* Bestandteil *m;* (culin) Zutat *f*

in′grown′ *adj* eingewachsen

inhabit [ɪn′hæbɪt] *tr* bewohnen

inhabitant [ɪn′hæbɪtənt] *s* Bewohner –in *mf,* Einwohner –in *mf*

inhale [ɪn′hel] *tr* & *intr* einatmen; inhalieren

inherent [ɪn′hɪrənt] *adj* innewohnend; (*right*) angeboren

inherit [ɪn′herɪt] *tr* (biol, jur) erben

inheritance [ɪn′herɪtəns] *s* Erbschaft *f*

inher′itance tax′ *s* Erbschaftssteuer *f*

inheritor [ɪn′herɪtər] *s* Erbe *m,* Erbin *f*

inhibit [ɪn′hɪbɪt] *tr* hemmen, inhibieren

inhibition [ˌɪnɪ′bɪʃən] *s* Hemmung *f*

inhospitable [ɪn′hɑspɪtəbəl] *adj* ungastlich; (*place*) unwirtlich

inhuman [ɪn′hjumən] *adj* unmenschlich

inhumane [ˌɪnju′men] *adj* inhuman

inhumanity [ˌɪnhju′mænɪti] *s* Unmenschlichkeit *f*

inimical [ɪ′nɪmɪkəl] *adj* (**to**) abträglich (*dat*)

iniquity [ɪ′nɪkwɪti] *s* Niederträchtigkeit *f,* Ungerechtigkeit *f*

ini·tial [ɪn′ɪʃəl] *adj* anfänglich ‖ *s* Anfangsbuchstabe *m,* Initiale *f* ‖ *v*

(*pret & pp* **–tial[l]ed;** *ger* **–tial[l]ing**) *tr* mit den Initialen unterzeichnen

initially [ɪ′nɪʃəli] *adv* anfangs

initiate [ɪ′nɪʃɪˌet] *tr* einführen; (*reforms*) einleiten; (**into**) aufnehmen in (*acc*)

initiation [ɪˌnɪʃɪ′eʃən] *s* Einführung *f;* (**into**) Aufnahme *f* (in *acc*)

initiative [ɪ′nɪʃ(ɪ)ətɪv] *s* Unternehmungsgeist *m;* **take the i.** die Initiative ergreifen

inject [ɪn′dʒekt] *tr* (*a needle*) einführen; (*a word*) dazwischenwerfen; (*e.g., bigotry into a campaign*) einfließen lassen; (*a liquid*) (med) injizieren

injection [ɪn′dʒekʃən] *s* (mach) Einspritzung *f;* (med) Injektion *f*

injudicious [ˌɪndʒu′dɪʃəs] *adj* unverständig

injunction [ɪn′dʒʌŋkʃən] *s* Gebot *n;* (jur) gerichtliche Verfügung *f*

injure [′ɪndʒər] *tr* verletzen; (fig) schädigen

injurious [ɪn′dʒurɪ·əs] *adj* schädlich

injury [′ɪndʒəri] *s* Verletzung *f;* (**to**) Schädigung *f* (*genit*)

injustice [ɪn′dʒʌstɪs] *s* Ungerechtigkeit *f*

ink [ɪŋk] *s* Tinte *f* ‖ *tr* schwärzen

inkling [′ɪŋklɪŋ] *s* leise Ahnung *f*

ink′ pad′ *s* Stempelkissen *n*

ink′ spot′ *s* Tintenklecks *m*

inky [′ɪŋki] *adj* tiefschwarz

inlaid [′ɪnˌled] *adj* eingelegt

in′laid floor′ *s* Parkettfußboden *m*

inland [′ɪnlənd] *adj* Binnen– ‖ *adv* landeinwärts ‖ *s* Binnenland *n*

in′-laws′ *spl* angeheiratete Verwandte *pl*

inlay [′ɪnˌle] *s* Einlegearbeit *f;* (dent) gegossene Plombe *f*

in′let *s* Meeresarm *m;* (*opening*) Öffnung *f*

in′mate *s* Insasse *m,* Insassin *f*

inn [ɪn] *s* Gasthaus *n,* Wirtshaus *n*

innards [′ɪnərdz] *spl* (coll) Innere *n*

innate [ɪ′net] *adj* angeboren

inner [′ɪnər] *adj* innere, inwendig, Innen–

in′nermost′ *adj* innerste

in′nerspring mat′tress *s* Federkernmatratze *f*

in′ner tube′ *s* Schlauch *m*

inning [′ɪnɪŋ] *s* Runde *f*

inn′keep′er *s* Wirt *m,* Wirtin *f*

innocence [′ɪnəsəns] *s* Unschuld *f;* (*of a crime*) Schuldlosigkeit *f*

innocent [′ɪnəsənt] *adj* (**of**) unschuldig (an *dat*); (*harmless*) harmlos; (*guileless*) arglos ‖ *s* Unschuldige *mf*

innocuous [ɪ′nɑkju·əs] *adj* harmlos

innovation [ˌɪnə′veʃən] *s* Neuerung *f*

innovative [′ɪnəˌvetɪv] *adj* (*person*) neuerungssüchtig; (*thing*) Neuerungs–

innuen·do [ˌɪnju′endo] *s* (**–does**) Unterstellung *f*

innumerable [ɪ′n(j)umərəbəl] *adj* unzählbar, unzählig

inoculate [ɪn′akjəˌlet] *tr* impfen

inoculation [ɪn′akjə′leʃən] *s* Impfung *f*

inoffensive [ˌɪnəˈfensɪv] *adj* unschädlich

inopportune [ɪnˌɔpərˈt(j)un] *adj* ungelegen

inordinate [ɪnˈɔrdɪnɪt] *adj* übermäßig

inorganic [ˌɪnɔrˈgænɪk] *adj* unorganisch; (chem) anorganisch

in'put' *adj* (data proc) Eingabe- ‖ *s* (in production) Aufwand *m*; (data proc) Eingabe *f*, Eingangsinformation *f*; (elec) Stromzufuhr *f*

inquest [ˈɪnkwest] *s* Untersuchung *f*

inquire [ɪnˈkwaɪr] *intr* anfragen; **i. about** sich erkundigen nach; **i. into** untersuchen; **i. of** sich erkundigen bei

inquiry [ɪnˈkwaɪri], [ˈɪnkwɪri] Anfrage *f*; (investigation) Untersuchung *f*; **make inquiries (about)** Erkundigungen einziehen (über *acc*)

inquisition [ˌɪnkwɪˈzɪʃən] *s* Inquisition *f*

inquisitive [ɪnˈkwɪzɪtɪv] *adj* wißbegierig

in'road *s* (raid) Einfall *m*; (fig) Eingriff *m*

ins' and outs' *spl* alle Kniffe *pl*

insane [ɪnˈsen] *adj* wahnsinnig; (absurd) unsinnig

insane' asy'lum *s* Irrenanstalt *f*

insanity [ɪnˈsænɪti] *s* Wahnsinn *m*

insatiable [ɪnˈseʃəbəl] *adj* unersättlich

inscribe [ɪnˈskraɪb] *tr* (a name) einschreiben; (a book) widmen; (a monument) mit e-r Inschrift versehen

inscription [ɪnˈskrɪpʃən] *s* Inschrift *f*; (of a book) Widmung *f*

inscrutable [ɪnˈskrutəbəl] *adj* unerforschlich

insect [ˈɪnsekt] *s* Insekt *n*, Kerbtier *n*

insecticide [ɪnˈsektɪˌsaɪd] *s* Insektenvertilgungsmittel *n*, Insektizid *n*

insecure [ˌɪnsɪˈkjur] *adj* unsicher

insecurity [ˌɪnsɪˈkjurɪti] *s* Unsicherheit *f*

insensitive [ɪnˈsensɪtɪv] *adj* (to) unempfindlich (gegen)

inseparable [ɪnˈsepərəbəl] *adj* untrennbar; (friends) unzertrennlich

insert [ˈɪnsʌrt] *s* Einsatzstück *n* ‖ [ɪnˈsʌrt] *tr* einfügen; (a coin) einwerfen

insertion [ɪnˈsʌrʃən] *s* Einfügung *f*; (of a coin) Einwurf *m*

in'set' (of a map) Nebenkarte *f*; (inserted piece) Einsatz *m*

in'shore' *adj* Küsten- ‖ *adv* auf die Küste zu

in'side' *adj* innere, Innen-; (information) vertraulich ‖ *adv* innen, drinnen; **come i.** hereinkommen; **i. of** innerhalb von; **i. out** verkehrt; **know i. out** in- und auswendig kennen; **turn i. out** umdrehen ‖ *s* Innenseite *f*, Innere *n*; **on the i.** innen ‖ *prep* innerhalb (genit)

insider [ɪnˈsaɪdər] *s* Eingeweihte *mf*

in'side track' *s* (sport) Innenbahn *f*; **have the i.** (fig) im Vorteil sein

insidious [ɪnˈsɪdɪˌəs] *adj* hinterlistig

in'sight' *s* Einsicht *f*

insigni•a [ɪnˈsɪgnɪˌə] *s* (-a & -as) Abzeichen *n*; **i. of office** Amtsabzeichen *pl*; **i. of rank** Rangabzeichen *pl*

insignificant [ˌɪnsɪgˈnɪfɪkənt] *adj* bedeutungslos, geringfügig

insincere [ˌɪnsɪnˈsɪr] *adj* unaufrichtig

insincerity [ˌɪnsɪnˈserɪti] *s* Unaufrichtigkeit *f*

insinuate [ɪnˈsɪnjuˌet] *tr* andeuten

insipid [ɪnˈsɪpɪd] *adj* (& fig) fad(e)

insist [ɪnˈsɪst] *intr*—**i. on** bestehen auf (dat); **i. on** (ger) darauf bestehen zu (inf)

insistent [ɪnˈsɪstənt] *adj* beharrlich

insofar as [ˌɪnsoˈfar ˌæz] *conj* insoweit als

insolence [ˈɪnsələns] *s* Unverschämtheit *f*

insolent [ˈɪnsələnt] *adj* unverschämt

insoluble [ɪnˈsaljəbəl] *adj* unlösbar

insolvency [ɪnˈsalvənsi] *s* Zahlungsunfähigkeit *f*, Insolvenz *f*

insolvent [ɪnˈsalvənt] *adj* zahlungsunfähig

insomnia [ɪnˈsamnɪˌə] *s* Schlaflosigkeit *f*

insomuch as [ˌɪnsoˈmʌtʃəz] *conj* insofern als

inspect [ɪnˈspekt] *tr* (view closely) besichtigen; (check) kontrollieren; (aut) untersuchen; (mil) besichtigen

inspection [ɪnˈspekʃən] *s* Besichtigung *f*; Kontrolle *f*; (aut) Untersuchung *f*; (mil) Truppenbesichtigung *f*

inspector [ɪnˈspektər] *s* Kontrolleur *m*; (of police) Inspektor *m*

inspiration [ˌɪnspɪˈreʃən] *s* Begeisterung *f*

inspire [ɪnˈspaɪr] *tr* begeistern; (feelings) erwecken

inspir'ing *adj* begeisternd

instability [ˌɪnstəˈbɪlɪti] *s* Unbeständigkeit *f*

install [ɪnˈstɔl] *tr* (appliances) installieren; (in office) einführen

installation [ˌɪnstəˈleʃən] *s* (of appliances) Installation *f*; (mil) Anlage *f*

installment [ɪnˈstɔlmənt] *s* Installation *f*; (in a serialized story) Fortsetzung *f*; (partial payment) Rate *f*; **in installments** ratenweise

install'ment plan' *s* Teilzahlungsplan *m*

instance [ˈɪnstəns] *s* (case) Fall *m*; (example) Beispiel *n*; (jur) Instanz *f*; **for i.** zum Beispiel

instant [ˈɪnstənt] *adj* augenblicklich; (foods) gebrauchsfertig ‖ *s* Augenblick *m*; **this i.** sofort

instantaneous [ˌɪnstənˈtenɪˌəs] *adj* augenblicklich, sofortig

instead [ɪnˈsted] *adv* statt dessen

instead' of *prep* (an)statt (genit); (ger) anstatt zu (inf)

in'step' *s* Rist *m*

instigate [ˈɪnstɪˌget] *tr* anstiften

instigation [ˌɪnstɪˈgeʃən] *s* Anstiftung *f*

instigator [ˈɪnstɪˌgetər] *s* Anstifter –in *mf*

instill [ɪnˈstɪl] *tr* einflößen

instinct [ˈɪnstɪŋkt] *s* Trieb *m*, Instinkt *m*; **by i.** instinktiv

instinctive [ɪnˈstɪŋktɪv] *adj* instinktiv

institute ['ɪnstɪ‚t(j)ut] *s* Institut *n* || *tr* einleiten

institution [‚ɪnstɪ't(j)uʃən] *s* Anstalt *f*

instruct [ɪn'strʌkt] *tr* anweisen, beauftragen; (*teach*) unterrichten

instruction [ɪn'strʌkʃən] *s* (*teaching*) Unterricht *m*; **instructions** Anweisungen *pl*; **instructions for use** Gebrauchsanweisung *f*

instructive [ɪn'strʌktɪv] *adj* lehrreich

instructor [ɪn'strʌktər] *s* Lehrer –in *mf*; (*at a university*) Dozent –in *mf*

instrument ['ɪnstrəmənt] *s* Instrument *n*; (*tool*) Werkzeug *n*; (*jur*) Dokument *n*

instrumental [‚ɪnstrə'mentəl] *adj* (*mus*) instrumental; **he was i. in my getting an award** er war mir behilflich, e–n Preis zu erhalten

instrumentality [‚ɪnstrəmən'tælɪtɪ] *s* Vermittlung *f*

in'strument land'ing *s* Instrumentenlandung *f*

in'strument pan'el *s* Armaturenbrett *n*

insubordinate [‚ɪnsə'bɔrdɪnɪt] *adj* widersetzlich

insubordination [‚ɪnsəbɔrdɪ'neʃən] *s* Widersetzlichkeit *f*

insufferable [ɪn'sʌfərəbəl] *adj* unausstehlich

insufficient [‚ɪnsə'fɪʃənt] *adj* ungenügend, unzureichend

insular ['ɪns(j)ələr] *adj* insular

insulate ['ɪnsə‚let] *tr* isolieren

insulation [‚ɪnsə'leʃən] *s* Isolierung *f*; (*insulating material*) Isolierstoff *m*

insulator ['ɪnsə‚letər] *s* Isolator *m*

insulin ['ɪnsəlɪn] *s* Insulin *n*

insult ['ɪnsʌlt] *s* Beleidigung *f* || [ɪn'sʌlt] *tr* beleidigen, beschimpfen

insurance [ɪn'ʃʊrəns] *adj* Versicherungs– || *s* Versicherung *f*

insure [ɪn'ʃʊr] *tr* versichern

insured' *adj* (*letter, package*) Wert– || *s* Versicherungsnehmer –in *mf*

insurer [ɪn'ʃʊrər] *s* Versicherer –in *mf*

insurgent [ɪn'sʌrdʒənt] *adj* aufständisch || *s* Aufständische *mf*

insurmountable [‚ɪnsər'maʊntəbəl] *adj* unübersteigbar; (*fig*) unüberwindlich

insurrection [‚ɪnsə'rekʃən] *s* Aufstand *m*

intact [ɪn'tækt] *adj* unversehrt

in'take *s* (aut) Einlaß *m*; **i. of food** Nahrungsaufnahme *f*

in'take valve' *s* Einlaßventil *n*

intangible [ɪn'tændʒɪbəl] *adj* immateriell

integer ['ɪntɪdʒər] *s* ganze Zahl *f*

integral ['ɪntɪgrəl] *adj* wesentlich; (math) Integral– || *s* Integral *n*

integrate ['ɪntɪ‚gret] *tr* eingliedern; (*a school*) die Rassentrennung aufheben in (*dat*); (& math) integrieren

integration [‚ɪntɪ'greʃən] *s* Integration *f*; (*of schools*) Aufhebung *f* der Rassentrennung

integrity [ɪn'tegrɪtɪ] *s* Redlichkeit *f*

intellect ['ɪntə‚lekt] *s* Intellekt *m*

intellectual [‚ɪntə'lektʃʊ‚əl] *adj* intellektuell; (*freedom, history*) Geistes– || *s* Intellektuelle *mf*

intelligence [ɪn'telɪdʒəns] *s* Intelligenz *f*, Klugheit *f*; (*information*) Nachricht *f*; (*department*) Nachrichtendienst *m*; **gather i.** Nachrichten einziehen

intel'ligence quo'tient *s* Intelligenz-Quotient *m*

intel'ligence test' *s* Begabungsprüfung *f*

intelligent [ɪn'telɪdʒənt] *adj* intelligent, klug

intelligentsia [ɪn‚telɪ'dʒɛntsɪ‚ə] *s* Intelligenz *f*, geistige Oberschicht *f*

intelligible [ɪn'telɪdʒɪbəl] *adj* (to) verständlich (*dat*)

intemperate [ɪn'tempərɪt] *adj* unmäßig; (*in drink*) trunksüchtig

intend [ɪn'tend] *tr* beabsichtigen; **be intended for** bestimmt sein für, gemünzt sein auf (*acc*) **i. by** bezwecken mit; **i. for s.o.** j–m zudenken

intend'ed *s* (coll) Verlobte *mf*

intense [ɪn'tens] *adj* intensiv, stark

intensi·fy [ɪn'tensɪ‚faɪ] *v* (*pret & pp* –fied*) *tr* steigern, verstärken || *intr* sich steigern, stärker werden

intensity [ɪn'tensɪtɪ] *s* Stärke *f*

intensive [ɪn'tensɪv] *adj* intensiv; (gram) verstärkend

inten'sive care' *s* Intensivstation *f*

intent [ɪn'tent] *adj* (on) erpicht (auf *acc*) || *s* Absicht *f*; **to all intents and purposes** praktisch genommen

intention [ɪn'tenʃən] *s* Absicht *f*; **good i.** guter Wille *m*; **have honorable intentions** es ehrlich meinen; **with the i. of** (*ger*) in der Absicht zu (*inf*)

intentional [ɪn'tenʃənəl] *adj* absichtlich

intently [ɪn'tentlɪ] *adv* gespannt

in·ter [ɪn'tʌr] *v* (*pret & pp* –terred*; *ger* –terring*) *tr* beerdigen

interact [‚ɪntər'ækt] *intr* zusammenwirken, aufeinander wirken

interaction [‚ɪntər'ækʃən] *s* Wechselwirkung *f*

inter·breed [‚ɪntər'brid] *v* (*pret & pp* –bred*) *tr* kreuzen || *intr* sich kreuzen

intercede [‚ɪntər'sid] *intr* Fürsprache einlegen; **i. for s.o. with** Fürsprache einlegen für j–n bei

intercept [‚ɪntər'sept] *tr* (*a letter, aircraft*) abfangen; (*a radio message*) abhören; (*cut off, check*) den Weg abschneiden (*dat*)

interceptor [‚ɪntər'septər] *s* (aer) Abfangjäger *m*

intercession [‚ɪntər'seʃən] *s* Fürsprache *f*; (relig) Fürbitte *f*

interchange ['ɪntər‚tʃendʒ] *s* Wechsel *m*; (*on a highway*) Anschlußstelle *f* || [‚ɪntər'tʃendʒ] *tr* auswechseln || *intr* (with) abwechseln (mit)

interchangeable [‚ɪntər'tʃendʒəbəl] *adj* auswechselbar, austauschbar

intercom ['ɪntər‚kʌm] *s* Wechselsprachanlage *f*

intercourse ['ɪntər‚kors] *s* Verkehr *m*; (*sexual*) Geschlechtsverkehr *m*

interdependent [‚ɪntərdɪ'pendənt] *adj* voneinander abhängig

interdict ['ɪntər‚dɪkt] *s* Verbot *n*; (eccl) Interdikt *n* || [‚ɪntər'dɪkt] *tr* verbieten; **i. s.o. from** (ger) j—m verbieten zu (inf)

interest ['int(ə)rist] s (in) Interesse n (an dat, für); (fin) Zinsen pl; **at i.** gegen Zinsen; **be in s.o.'s i.** in j-s Interesse liegen; **have an i. in** beteiligt sein an (dat) or bei; **interests** Belange pl; **pay i.** (bring in interest) Zinsen abwerfen; (pay out interest) Zinsen zahlen; **take an i. in** sich interessieren für; **with i.** (& fig) mit Zinsen || tr (in) interessieren (für)

in'terested adj—**i. in** interessiert an (dat); **the i. parties** die Beteiligten pl

in'teresting adj interessant

in'terest rate' s Zinsfuß m, Zinssatz m

interfere [,intər'fir] intr (said of a thing) dazwischenkommen; (said of a person) eingreifen; **(in** or **with)** sich (ein)mengen (in acc); **i. with** (rad, telv) stören; **i. with s.o.'s work** j-n bei seiner Arbeit stören

interference [,intər'firəns] s Einmischung f; (phys) Interferenz f; (rad, telv) Störung f

interim ['intərim] adj Zwischen– || s Zwischenzeit f

interior [in'tiri·ər] adj innere, Innen– || s Innere n; (of a building) Innenraum m; (of a country) Inland n

inte'rior dec'orator s Innenarchitekt –in mf

interject [,intər'dʒekt] tr dazwischenwerfen

interjection [,intər'dʒekʃən] s Zwischenwurf m; (gram) Interjektion f

interlard [,intər'lard] tr (& fig) spicken

interlinear [,intər'lini·ər] adj Interlinear–

interlock [,intər'lak] tr miteinander verbinden || intr sich ineinanderschließen

interloper [,intər'lopər] s Eindringling m

interlude ['intər,lud] s (interval) Pause f; (fig, mus, theat) Zwischenspiel n

intermediary [,intər'midi·,eri] adj vermittelnd || s Vermittler –in mf

intermediate [,intər'midi·it] adj zwischenliegend, Zwischen–

interment [in'tarmənt] s Beerdigung f

intermez·zo [,intər'metso] s (–zos & zi [tsi]) Intermezzo n

intermingle [,intər'miŋgəl] tr vermischen || intr sich vermischen

intermission [,intər'miʃən] s Unterbrechung f; (theat) Pause f

intermittent [,intər'mitənt] adj intermittierend

intermix [,intər'miks] tr vermischen || intr sich vermischen

intern ['intarn] s Assistenzarzt m, Assistenzärztin f

internal [in'tarnəl] adj innere, intern; (domestic) einheimisch; (trade, rhyme) Binnen–

inter'nal-combus'tion en'gine s Verbrennungsmotor m

inter'nal med'icine s innere Medizin f

inter'nal rev'enue s Steueraufkommen n

international [,intər'næ/ənəl] adj international

interna'tional date' line' s internationale Datumsgrenze f

interna'tional law' s Völkerrecht n

interne'cine war' s gegenseitiger Vernichtungskrieg m

internee [,intər'ni] s Internierte mf

internment [in'tarnmənt] s Internierung f

in'ternship' s Pflichtzeit f als Assistenzarzt (or Assistenzärztin)

interoffice [,intər'afis] adj Haus–

interplanetary [,intər'plæni,teri] adj interplanetarisch

interplay ['intər,ple] s Wechselspiel n

interpolate [in'tarpə,let] tr interpolieren

interpose [,intər'poz] tr (an obstacle) dazwischensetzen; (a remark) einwerfen

interpret [in'tarprit] tr (& mus) interpretieren; (translate) verdolmetschen || intr dolmetschen

interpretation [in,tarpri'te/ən] s (& mus) Interpretation f

interpreter [in'tarpritər] s Dolmetscher –in mf; **act as i.** dolmetschen

interrogate [in'terə,get] tr ausfragen; (jur) verhören, vernehmen

interrogation [in,terə'ge/ən] s Verhör n

interrogative [,intə'ragətiv] adj Frage–

interrupt [,intə'rʌpt] tr unterbrechen

interruption [,intə'rʌp/ən] s Unterbrechung f; (in industry) Betriebsstörung f

intersect [,intər'sekt] tr durchschneiden || ref sich kreuzen

intersection [,intər'sek/ən] s Straßenkreuzung f; (math) Schnittpunkt m

intersperse [,intər'spʌrs] tr durchsetzen

interstate ['intər,stet] adj zwischenstaatlich

interstellar [,intər'stelər] adj interstellar

interstice [in'tarstis] s Zwischenraum m

intertwine [,intər'twain] tr verflechten || intr sich verflechten

interval ['intərvəl] s Abstand m; (mus) Stufe f, Intervall n

intervene [,intər'vin] intr dazwischenkommen; (interfere) eingreifen; (intercede) intervenieren

intervention [,intər'ven/ən] s Dazwischenkommen n; Eingreifen n; Intervention f

interview ['intər,vju] s Interview n || tr interviewen

inter-weave [,intər'wiv] v (pret –wove & –weaved; pp –wove, –woven & –weaved) tr durchweben, durchflechten

intestate [in'testet] adj ohne Testament

intestine [in'testin] s Darm m; **intestines** Gedärme pl

intimacy ['intiməsi] s Vertraulichkeit f; **intimacies** Intimitäten pl

intimate ['intimit] adj intim, vertraut

|| *s* Vertraute *mf* || ['ɪntɪ ˌmet] *tr* andeuten

intimation [ˌɪntɪ'meʃən] *s* Andeutung *f*

intimidate [ɪn'tɪmɪ ˌdet] *tr* einschüchtern

intimidation [ˌɪntɪmɪ'deʃən] *s* Einschüchterung *f*

into ['ɪntu], ['ɪntu] *prep* in (*acc*)

intolerable [ɪn'talərəbəl] *adj* unerträglich

intolerance [ɪn'talərəns] *s* (**of**) Intoleranz *f* (gegen)

intolerant [ɪn'talərənt] *adj* (**of**) intolerant (gegen)

intonation [ˌɪnto'neʃən] *s* Tonfall *m*

intone [ɪn'ton] *tr* intonieren

intoxicate [ɪn'taksɪ ˌket] *tr* berauschen; (*poison*) vergiften

intoxication [ɪn ˌtaksɪ'keʃən] *s* (& fig) Rausch *m*; (*poisoning*) Vergiftung *f*

intractable [ɪn'træktəbəl] *adj* (*person*) störrisch; (*thing*) schwer zu bearbeiten(d)

intransigent [ɪn'trænsɪdʒənt] *adj* unversöhnlich

intransitive [ɪn'trænsɪtɪv] *adj* intransitiv

intravenous [ˌɪntrə'vinəs] *adj* intravenös

intrepid [ɪn'trepɪd] *adj* unerschrocken

intricate ['ɪntrɪkɪt] *adj* verwickelt

intrigue [ɪn'trig], ['ɪntrɪg] *s* Intrige *f* || [ɪn'trig] *tr* fesseln || *intr* intrigieren

intrigu'ing *adj* fesselnd

intrinsic(al) [ɪn'trɪnsɪk(əl)] *adj* innere, innerlich; (*value*) wirklich

introduce [ˌɪntrə'd(j)us] *tr* einführen; (*strangers*) vorstellen

introduction [ˌɪntrə'dʌkʃən] *s* Einführung *f*; (*of strangers*) Vorstellung *f*; (*in a book*) Einleitung *f*

introductory [ˌɪntrə'dʌktəri] *adj* (*offer, price*) Einführungs–; (*remarks*) einleitend

introspection [ˌɪntrə'spekʃən] *s* Selbstbeobachtung *f*

introspective [ˌɪntrə'spektɪv] *adj* introspektiv

introvert ['ɪntrə ˌvʌrt] *s* Introvertierte *mf*

intrude [ɪn'trud] *intr* (**on**) sich aufdrängen (dat); **am I intruding?** störe ich?

intruder [ɪn'trudər] *s* Eindringling *m*

intrusion [ɪn'truʒən] *s* Eindrängen *n*, Stören *n*

intrusive [ɪn'trusɪv] *adj* störend, lästig

intuition [ˌɪnt(j)u'ɪ/ən] *s* Intuition *f*

inundate ['ɪnən ˌdet] *tr* überschwemmen

inundation [ˌɪnən'deʃən] *s* Überschwemmung *f*

inure [ɪn'jur] *tr* (**to**) abhärten (gegen)

invade [ɪn'ved] *tr* (*a country*) eindringen in (*acc*); (*rights*) verletzen; (*privacy*) stören

invader [ɪn'veder] *s* Eindringling *m*; (mil) Angreifer *m*

invalid [ɪn'vælɪd] *adj* ungültig || ['ɪnvəlɪd] *adj* kränklich || *s* Invalide *m*

invalidate [ɪn'vælɪ ˌdet] *tr* ungültig machen; (*a law*) außer Kraft setzen

invalidity [ˌɪnvə'lɪdɪti] *s* Ungültigkeit *f*

invaluable [ɪn'vælju·əbəl] *adj* unschätzbar

invariable [ɪn'verɪ·əbəl] *adj* unveränderlich

invasion [ɪn'veʒən] *s* Invasion *f*

invective [ɪn'vektɪv] *s* Schmähung *f*

inveigh [ɪn'veɪ] *intr*—**i. against** schimpfen über (*acc*) or auf (*acc*)

inveigle [ɪn'vigel] *tr* verleiten; **i. s.o. into** (*ger*) j–n verleiten zu (*inf*)

invent [ɪn'vent] *tr* erfinden; (*a story*) sich [dat] ausdenken

invention [ɪn'venʃən] *s* Erfindung *f*

inventive [ɪn'ventɪv] *adj* erfinderisch

inventiveness [ɪn'ventɪvnɪs] *s* Erfindungsgabe *f*

inventor [ɪn'ventər] *s* Erfinder –in *mf*

inven·tory ['ɪnvən ˌtɔri] *s* (*stock*) Inventar *n*; (*act*) Inventur *f*; (*list*) Bestandsverzeichnis *n*; **take i.** Inventur machen || *v* (*pret & pp* –**ried**) *tr* inventarisieren

inverse [ɪn'vʌrs] *adj* umgekehrt

inversion [ɪn'vʌrʒən] *s* Umkehrung *f*; (gram) Umstellung *f*

invert [ɪn'vʌrt] *tr* umkehren; (gram) umstellen

invertebrate [ɪn'vʌrtɪ ˌbret] *adj* wirbellos || *s* wirbelloses Tier *n*

invest [ɪn'vest] *tr* (**in**) investieren (in *acc*); (mil) belagern; **i. with** ausstatten mit

investigate [ɪn'vestɪ ˌget] *tr* untersuchen

investigation [ɪn ˌvestɪ'geʃən] *s* Untersuchung *f*

investigator [ɪn'vestɪ ˌgetər] *s* Untersucher –in *mf*

investment [ɪn'vestmənt] *s* Anlage *f*, Investition *f*; (*with an office*) Amtseinführung *f*; (mil) Belagerung *f*

investor [ɪn'vestər] *s* Investor –in *mf*

inveterate [ɪn'vetərɪt] *adj* (*habitual*) eingefleischt; (*firmly established*) eingewurzelt

invidious [ɪn'vɪdɪ·əs] *adj* haßerregend

invigorate [ɪn'vɪgə ˌret] *tr* beleben

invig'orating *adj* belebend

invincible [ɪn'vɪnsɪbəl] *adj* unbesiegbar

invisible [ɪn'vɪzɪbəl] *adj* unsichtbar

invis'ible ink' *s* Geheimtinte *f*

invitation [ˌɪnvɪ'teʃən] *s* Einladung *f*

invite [ɪn'vaɪt] *tr* einladen; **i. in** hereinbitten

invit'ing *adj* lockend

invocation [ˌɪnvə'keʃən] *s* Anrufung *f*; (relig) Bittgebet *n*

invoice ['ɪnvɔɪs] *s* Faktura *f*, Warenrechnung *f*; **as per i.** laut Rechnung || *tr* fakturieren

invoke [ɪn'vok] *tr* anrufen; (*cite*) zitieren

involuntary [ɪn'valən ˌteri] *adj* (*against one's will*) unfreiwillig; (*without one's will*) unwillkürlich

invol'untary man'slaughter *s* unbeabsichtigte Tötung *f*

involve [ɪn'vɑlv] *tr* verwickeln; (*include*) einschließen; (*affect*) betreffen; (*entail*) zur Folge haben

involved' *adj* verwickelt, kompliziert; **be i. in** (*e.g., construction*) beschäftigt sein bei; (*e.g., a crime*) verwickelt sein in (*acc*); **be i. with** (*e.g., a married person*) e-e Affäre haben mit

involvement [ɪn'vɑlʌmənt] *s* Verwicklung *f*

invulnerable [ɪn'vʌlnərəbəl] *adj* unverwundbar

inward ['ɪnwərd] *adj* inner(lich) ‖ *adv* nach innen

inwardly ['ɪnwərdli] *adv* innerlich

iodine ['aɪə‚diŋ] *s* (chem) Jod *n* ‖ ['aɪə‚daɪn] *s* (pharm) Jodtinktur *f*

ion ['aɪɑn], ['aɪən] *s* Ion *n*

ionize ['aɪə‚naɪz] *tr* ionisieren

IOU ['aɪ‚o'ju] *s* (**I owe you**) Schuldschein *m*

I.Q. ['aɪ'kju] *s* (**intelligence quotient**) Intelligenz-Quotient *m*

Iran [ɪ'rɑn], [aɪ'ræn] *s* Iran *m*

Iranian [aɪ'reni‧ən] *adj* iranisch ‖ *s* Iran(i)er –in *mf*

Iraq [ɪ'rɑk] *s* Irak *m*

Ira‧qi [ɪ'rɑki] *adj* irakisch ‖ *s* (**–qis**) Iraker –in *mf*

irascible [ɪ'ræsɪbəl] *adj* jähzornig

irate ['aɪret], [aɪ'ret] *adj* zornig

ire [aɪr] *s* Zorn *m*

Ireland ['aɪrlənd] *s* Irland *n*

iris ['aɪrɪs] *s* (anat, bot) Iris *f*

Irish ['aɪrɪʃ] *adj* irisch ‖ *s* (*language*) Irisch *n*; **the I.** die Iren *pl*

I'rish‧man *s* (**–men**) Ire *m*

I'rishwom'an *s* (**–wom'en**) Irin *f*

irk [ʌrk] *tr* ärgern

irksome ['ʌrksəm] *adj* ärgerlich

iron ['aɪ‧ərn] *adj* (& fig) eisern ‖ *s* Eisen *n*; (*for pressing clothes*) Bügeleisen *n* ‖ *tr* bügeln; **i. out** ausbügeln; (fig) ins Reine bringen

ironclad ['aɪ‧ərn‚klæd] *adj* (fig) unumstößlich

i'ron cur'tain *s* eiserner Vorhang *m*

ironic(al) [aɪ'rɑnɪk(əl)] *adj* ironisch

i'roning *s* (*act*) Bügeln *n*; (*clothes*) Bügelwäsche *f*

i'roning board' *s* Bügelbrett *n*

i'ron lung' *s* eiserne Lunge *f*

i'ron ore' *s* Eisenerz *n*

irony ['aɪrəni] *s* Ironie *f*

irradiate [ɪ'redi‚et] *tr* bestrahlen; (*light*) ausstrahlen; (*a face*) aufheitern

irrational [ɪ'ræʃənəl] *adj* irrational

irreconcilable [‚ɪrekən'saɪləbəl] *adj* unversöhnlich

irredeemable [‚ɪrɪ'dimʌbəl] *adj* (*loan, bond*) nicht einlösbar; (*hopeless*) hoffnungslos

irrefutable [‚ɪrɪ'fjutəbəl] *adj* unwiderlegbar

irregular [ɪ'regjələr] *adj* unregelmäßig

irregularity [ɪ‚regjə'lærɪti] *s* Unregelmäßigkeit *f*

irrelevant [ɪ'reləvənt] *adj* (**to**) nicht anwendbar (auf *acc*)

irreligious [‚ɪrɪ'lɪdʒəs] *adj* irreligiös

irreparable [ɪ'repərəbəl] *adj* unersetzlich

irreplaceable [‚ɪrɪ'plesɪbəl] *adj* unersetzlich

irrepressible [‚ɪrɪ'presɪbəl] *adj* unbezähmbar

irreproachable [‚ɪrɪ'protʃəbəl] *adj* untadelig

irresistible [‚ɪrɪ'zɪstɪbəl] *adj* unwiderstehlich

irresolute [ɪ'rezəlut] *adj* unentschlossen, unschlüßig

irrespective [‚ɪrɪ'spektɪv] *adj*—**i. of** ohne Rücksicht auf (*acc*)

irresponsible [‚ɪrɪ'spɑnsɪbəl] *adj* unverantwortlich

irretrievable [‚ɪrɪ'trivəbəl] *adj* unwiederbringlich, unrettbar

irreverent [ɪ'revərənt] *adj* unehrerbietig

irrevocable [ɪ'revəkəbəl] *adj* unwiderruflich

irrigate ['ɪrɪ‚get] *tr* verwässern; (med) irrigieren

irrigation [‚ɪrɪ'geʃən] *s* Bewässerung *f*

irritable ['ɪrɪtəbəl] *adj* reizbar

irritant ['ɪrɪtənt] *s* Reizstoff *m*

irritate ['ɪrɪ‚tet] *tr* reizen, irritieren

ir'ritating *adj* ärgerlich

irritation [‚ɪrɪ'teʃən] *s* Reizung *f*

irruption [ɪ'rʌpʃən] *s* Einbruch *m*

isinglass ['aɪzɪŋ‚glæs] *s* Fischleim *m*; (*mica*) Glimmer *m*

Islam ['ɪsləm] *s* Islam *m*

island ['aɪlənd] *s* Insel *f*

islander ['aɪləndər] *s* Insulaner –in *mf*

isle [aɪl] *s* kleine Insel *f*

isolate ['aɪsə‚let] *tr* isolieren

isolation [‚aɪsə'leʃən] *s* Isolierung *f*

isolationist [‚aɪsə'leʃənɪst] *s* Isolationist –in *mf*

isola'tion ward' *s* Isolierstation *f*

isometric [‚aɪsə'metrɪk] *adj* isometrisch

isosceles [aɪ'sɑsə‚liz] *adj* gleichschenklig

isotope ['aɪsə‚top] *s* Isotop *n*

Israel ['ɪzrɪ‧əl] *s* Israel *n*

Israe‧li [ɪz'reli] *adj* israelisch ‖ *s* (**–li**) Israeli *m*

Israelite ['ɪzrɪ‧ə‚laɪt] *adj* israelitisch ‖ *s* Israelit –in *mf*

issuance ['ɪ/u‧əns] *s* Ausgabe *f*

issue ['ɪ/u] *s* (*of a magazine*) Nummer *f*; (*result*) Ausgang *m*; (*e.g., of securities*) Ausgabe *f*, Emission *f*; (*under discussion*) Streitpunkt *m*; (*offspring*) Nachkommenschaft *f*; **avoid the i.** der Frage ausweichen; **be at i.** zur Debatte stehen; **make an i. of it** e-e Streitfrage daraus machen; **take i. with** anderer Meinung sein als ‖ *tr* (*orders, supplies, stamps, stocks*) ausgeben; (*a pass*) ausstellen ‖ *intr* (**from**) herauskommen (aus)

isthmus ['ɪsməs] *s* Landenge *f*

it [ɪt] *pron* es; **about it** darüber, davon; **it is I** ich bin es

Italian [ɪ'tæli‧ən] *adj* italienisch ‖ *s* (*person*) Italiener –in *mf*; (*language*) Italienisch *n*

italicize [ɪ'tælɪ‚saɪz] *tr* kursiv drucken

italics [ɪ'tælɪks] *spl* Kursivschrift *f*
Italy ['ɪtəli] *s* Italien *n*
itch [ɪtʃ] *s* Jucken *n*; (pathol) Krätze *f* || *intr* jucken; **I am itching to** (*inf*) es reizt mich zu (*inf*); **my nose itches me** es juckt mich in der Nase
itchy ['ɪtʃi] *adj* juckend; (pathol) krätzig
item ['aɪtəm] *s* Artikel *m*; (*in a list*) Punkt *m*; (com) Posten *m*; (journ) Nachricht *f*; **hot i.** (coll) Schlager *m*
itemize ['aɪtə,maɪz] *tr* einzeln aufführen

itinerant [aɪ'tɪnərənt], [ɪ'tɪnərənt] *adj* Wander–, reisend || *s* Reisende *mf*
itinerary [aɪ'tɪnə,reri] *s* Reiseplan *m*
its [ɪts] *poss adj* sein
itself *reflex pron* sich; **in i.** an und für sich || *intens pron* selbst, selber
ivied ['aɪvid] *adj* efeubewachsen
ivory ['aɪvəri] *adj* elfenbeinern, Elfenbein–; (*color*) kremfarben || *s* Elfenbein *n*; **tickle the ivories** in die Tasten greifen
i'vory tow'er *s* (fig) Elfenbeinturm *m*
ivy ['aɪvi] *s* Efeu *m*

J

J, j [dʒe] *s* zehnter Buchstabe des englischen Alphabets
jab [dʒæb] *s* Stoß *m*; (box) Gerade *f* || *v* (*pret & pp* **jabbed;** *ger* **jabbing**) *tr* stoßen; (box) mit der Gerade stoßen
jabber ['dʒæbər] *tr & intr* plappern
jack [dʒæk] *s* (*money*) (sl) Pinke *f*; (aut) Wagenheber *m*; (cards) Bube *m*; (telp) Klinke *f*; **Jack** Hans *m* || *tr*—**j. up** (aut) heben; (*prices*) hinaufschrauben
jackal ['dʒækəl] *s* Schakal *m*
jack'ass' *s* Esel *m*
jacket ['dʒækɪt] *s* Jacke *f*; (*of a book*) Umschlag *m*; (*of a potato*) Schale *f*
Jack' Frost' *s* Herr Winter *m*
jack'ham'mer *s* Preßlufthammer *m*
jack'-in-the-box' *s* Kastenteufel *m*
jack'knife' *s* (–knives) Klappmesser *n*; (*dive*) Hechtbeuge *f* || *intr* zusammenklappen
jack'-of-all'-trades' *s* Hansdampf *m* in allen Gassen
jack'pot' *s* Jackpot *m*; **hit the j.** das Große Los gewinnen
jack' rab'bit *s* Hase *m*
Jacob ['dʒekəb] *s* Jakob *m*
jade [dʒed] *adj* jadegrün ·|| *s* (*stone*) Jade *m*; (*color*) Jadegrün *n*; (*horse*) Schindmähre *f*
jad'ed *adj* ermattet
jag [dʒæg] *s* Zacke *f*; **have a jag on** (sl) e–n Schwips haben
jagged ['dʒægɪd] *adj* zackig, schartig
jaguar ['dʒægwar] *s* Jaguar *m*
jail [dʒel] *s* Gefängnis *n*, Untersuchungsgefängnis *n*; **be in j.** sitzen || *tr* einsperren
jail'bird' *s* Knastbruder *m*
jailer ['dʒelər] *s* Gefängniswärter *m*
jalopy [dʒə'lɑpi] *s* Rumpelkasten *m*
jal'ousie win'dow ['dʒæləsi] *s* Glasjalousie *f*
jam [dʒæm] *s* Marmelade *f*; **be in a jam** (coll) in der Patsche sitzen || *v* (*pret & pp* **jammed;** *ger* **jamming**) *tr* (*a room*) überfüllen; (*a street*) verstopfen; (*a finger*) quetschen; (rad) stören; **be jammed in** eingezwängt sein; **jam on the brakes** auf die Bremsen drücken; **jam s.th. into**

etw stopfen in (*acc*) || *intr* (*said of a window*) klemmen; (*said of gears*) sich verklemmen; (*said of a gun*) Ladehemmung haben; **jam into** sich hineinquetschen in (*acc*)
jamb [dʒæm] *s* Pfosten *m*
jamboree [,dʒæmbə'ri] *s* Trubel *m*; (*of scouts*) Pfadfindertreffen *n*
James [dʒemz] *s* Jakob *m*
jam'ming *s* (rad) Störung *f*
Jane [dʒen] *s* Johanna *f*
Janet ['dʒænɪt] *s* Hanna *f*
jangle ['dʒæŋgəl] *s* Rasseln *n* || *tr* rasseln lassen; **j. s.o.'s nerves** j–m auf die Nerven gehen || *intr* rasseln
janitor ['dʒænɪtər] *s* Hausmeister *m*
January ['dʒænju,eri] *s* Januar *m*
Japan [dʒə'pæn] *s* Japan *n*
Japanese [,dʒæpə'niz] *adj* japanisch || *s* Japaner –*in* *mf*; (*language*) Japanisch *n*
Jap'anese bee'tle *s* Japankäfer *m*
jar [dʒar] *s* Krug *m*; (*e.g., of jam*) Glas *n*; (*jolt*) Stoß *m* || *v* (*pret & pp* **jarred;** *ger* **jarring**) *tr* (*jolt*) anstoßen; (fig) erschüttern || *intr* nicht harmonieren; **jar on the nerves** auf die Nerven gehen
jargon ['dʒargən] *s* Jargon *m*
jasmine ['dʒæzmɪn] *s* Jasmin *m*
jaundice ['dʒɔndɪs] *s* Gelbsucht *f*
jaun'diced *adj* gelbsüchtig
jaunt [dʒɔnt] *s* Ausflug *m*
jaunty ['dʒɔnti] *adj* (*sprightly*) lebhaft; (*clothes*) fesch
javelin ['dʒæv(ə)lɪn] *s* Speer *m*
jaw [dʒɔ] *s* Kiefer *m*; **the jaws of death** die Klauen des Todes
jaw'bone' *s* Kiefer *m* || *intr* (sl) sich stark machen
jay [dʒe] *s* (orn) Häher *m*
jay'walk' *intr* verkehrswidrig die Straße überqueren
jazz [dʒæz] *s* Jazz *m* || *tr*—**j. up** (coll) aufmöbeln
jazz' band' *s* Jazzband *f*
jazzy ['dʒæzi] *adj* bunt, grell
jealous ['dʒɛləs] *adj* (*of*) eifersüchtig (*auf acc*)
jealousy ['dʒɛləsi] *s* Eifersucht *f*
jeans [dʒinz] *spl* Jeans *pl*

jeep [dʒip] s Jeep m

jeer [dʒɪr] s Hohn m || tr verhöhnen || intr höhnen; **j. at** verhöhnen

Jeffrey ['dʒefri] s Gottfried m

Jehovah [dʒɪ'hovə] s Jehova m

jell [dʒel] s Gelee n || intr gelieren; (fig) zum Klappen kommen

jellied ['dʒelid] adj geliert

jelly ['dʒeli] s Gallerte f

jel'lyfish' s Qualle f; (pej) Waschlappen m

jeopardize ['dʒepər‚daɪz] tr gefährden

jeopardy ['dʒepərdi] s Gefahr f

jerk [dʒʌrk] s Ruck m; (sl) Knülch m || tr ruckweise ziehen || intr zucken

jerky ['dʒʌrki] adj ruckartig

jersey ['dʒʌrzi] s (material) Jersey m; (shirt) Jersey n; (sport) Trikot n

jest [dʒest] s Scherz m; **in j.** scherzweise || intr scherzen

jester ['dʒestər] s Hofnarr m; (joker) Spaßvogel m

Jesuit ['dʒeʒʊ‚ɪt] adj Jesuiten– || s Jesuit m

Jesus ['dʒizəs] s Jesus m

jet [dʒet] adj Düsen– || s (stream) Strahl m; (nozzle) Düse f; (plane) Jet m, Düsenflugzeug n || v (pret & pp jetted; ger jetting) herausströmen; (aer) jetten

jet'-black' adj rabenschwarz

jet' propul'sion s Düsenantrieb m

jetsam ['dʒetsəm] s Seewurfgut n

jet' stream' s Strahlströmung f

jettison ['dʒetɪsən] s Seewurf m || tr (aer) abwerfen; (naut) über Bord werfen

jetty ['dʒeti] s (warf) Landungsbrücke f; (breakwater) Hafendamm m

Jew [dʒu] s Jude m, Jüdin f

jewel ['dʒu·əl] s (& fig) Juwel n; (in a watch) Stein m

jew'el box' s Schmuckkästchen n

jewel(l)er ['dʒu·ələr] s Juwelier –in mf

jewelry ['dʒu·əlri] s Jewelen pl; **piece of j.** Schmuckstück n

jew'elry store' s Juweliergeschäft n

Jewish ['dʒu·ɪʃ] adj jüdisch

Jew's' harp' s Maultrommel f

jib [dʒɪb] s Ausleger m; (naut) Klüver m

jibe [dʒaɪb] intr (coll) übereinstimmen

jiffy ['dʒɪfi] s—**in a j.** im Nu

jig [dʒɪg] s (dance) Gigue f; (tool) Spannvorrichtung f; **the jig is up** (sl) das Spiel ist aus

jigger ['dʒɪgər] s Schnapsglas n; (gadget) Dingsbums n; (naut) Besan f

jiggle ['dʒɪgəl] tr & intr rütteln

jig'saw' s Laubsäge f

jig'saw puz'zle s Puzzlespiel n

jilt [dʒɪlt] tr (a girl) sitzenlassen; (a boy) den Laufpaß geben (dat)

jim·my ['dʒɪmi] s Brecheisen n || v (pret & pp –mied) tr mit dem Brecheisen aufbrechen

jingle ['dʒɪŋgəl] s (of coins) Klimpern n; (bell) Schelle f; (verse) Verseklingel n || tr klimpern mit || intr klimpern; (said of verses) klingeln

jin·go ['dʒɪŋgo] s (–goes) Chauvinist –in mf; **by j.!** alle Wetter!

jinx [dʒɪŋks] s Unglücksrabe m || tr Pech bringen (dat); **be jinxed** vom Pech verfolgt sein

jitters ['dʒɪtərz] spl—**have the j.** wahnsinnig nervös sein; **give s.o. the j.** j–n wahnsinnig nervös machen

jittery ['dʒɪtəri] adj durchgedreht

Joan [dʒon] s Johanna f

job [dʒab] s (employment) Job m; (task, responsibility) Aufgabe f; **bad job** Machwerk n; **do a good job** gute Arbeit leisten; **fall down on the job** seine Pflicht nicht erfüllen; **know one's job** seine Sache verstehen; **on the job** bei der Arbeit; (fig) auf Draht; **out of a job** arbeitslos

jobber ['dʒabər] s (middleman) Zwischenhändler –in mf; (pieceworker) Akkordarbeiter –in mf

job'hold'er s Stelleninhaber –in mf

jobless ['dʒablɪs] adj stellungslos

jockey ['dʒaki] s Jockei m || tr manövrieren

jog [dʒag] s Dauerlauf m; (of a horse) Trott m || v (pret & pp jogged; ger jogging) tr (shake) rütteln; (the memory) auffrischen || intr trotten; (for exercise) langsam rennen, Dauerlauf machen

John [dʒan] s Johann m; **john** (sl) Klo n

Johnny ['dʒani] s Hans m

John'ny-come'-late'ly s Neuling m, Nachzügler m

join [dʒɔɪn] tr verbinden; (a club) beitreten (dat); (a person) sich anschließen (dat); (two parts) zusammenfügen; **j. the army** zum Militär gehen || intr sich verbinden; **j. in** sich beteiligen an (dat); **j. up** (mil) einrücken

joiner ['dʒɔɪnər] s (coll) Vereinsmeier m; (carp) Tischler m

joint [dʒɔɪnt] adj (account, venture) gemeinschaftlich; (return) gemeinsam; (committee) gemischt; (heir, owner) Mit– || s Verbindungspunkt m; (in plumbing) Naht f; (sl) Bumslokal n; (anat, bot, mach) Gelenk n; (carp) Fuge f; (culin) Bratenstück n; **throw out of j.** auskugeln

jointly ['dʒɔɪntli] adv gemeinsam

joint'-stock' com'pany s Aktiengesellschaft f

joist [dʒɔɪst] s Tragbalken m

joke [dʒok] s Witz m; **he can't take a j.** er versteht keinen Spaß; **make a j. of** ins Lächerliche ziehen; **play a j. on** e–n Streich spielen (dat) || intr Spaß machen; **j. about** witzeln über (acc); **j. around** schäkern; **joking aside** Spaß beiseite

joker ['dʒokər] s Spaßvogel m; (pej) Knülch m; (cards) Joker m

jolly ['dʒali] adj lustig

jolt [dʒolt] s Stoß m || tr stoßen || intr holpern; **j. along** dahinholpern

Jordan ['dʒɔrdən] s (country) Jordanien n; (river) Jordan m

josh [dʒaʃ] tr & intr hänseln

jostle ['dʒasəl] tr & intr drängeln

jot [dʒat] s—**not a jot** kein Jota || v

(pret & pp **jotted;** ger **jotting**) tr— **jot down** notieren

journal ['dʒɜrnəl] s (daily record) Tagebuch n; (magazine) Zeitschrift f

journalism ['dʒɜrnə͵lɪzəm] s Journalismus m, Zeitungswesen n

journalist ['dʒɜrnəlɪst] s Journalist –in mf

journey ['dʒɜrni] s Reise f; **go on a j.** verreisen ‖ intr reisen

jour'ney·man adj tüchtig ‖ s (–men) Geselle m

joust [dʒaʊst] s Tjost f ‖ intr turnieren

jovial ['dʒovɪ·əl] adj jovial

jowls [dʒaʊlz] spl Hängebacken pl

joy [dʒɔɪ] s Freude f

joyful ['dʒɔɪfəl] adj froh, freudig

joyless ['dʒɔɪlɪs] adj freudlos

joy' ride' s (coll) Schwarzfahrt f

joy' stick' s (aer) Steuerknüppel m

Jr. abbr (**Junior**) jr., jun.

jubilant ['dʒubɪlənt] adj frohlockend

jubilation [͵dʒubɪ'le/ən] s Jubel m

jubilee ['dʒubɪ͵li] s Jubiläum n

Judaea [dʒu'di·ə] s Judäa n

Judaic [dʒu'de·ɪk] adj jüdisch

Judaism ['dʒudə͵ɪzəm] s Judaismus m

judge [dʒʌdʒ] s (in a competition) Preisrichter –in mf; (box) Punktrichter m; (jur) Richter –in mf ‖ tr (by) beurteilen (nach); (distances) abschätzen; (jur) richten ‖ intr urteilen; (jur) richten; **judging by his words** seinen Worten nach zu urteilen

judge' ad'vocate s Kriegsgerichtsrat m

judgment ['dʒʌdʒmənt] s (& jur) Urteil n; **in my j.** meines Erachtens; **show good j.** ein gutes Urteilsvermögen haben; **sit in j. over** zu Gericht sitzen über (acc)

Judg'ment Day' s Tag m des Gerichts

judicial [dʒu'dɪ/əl] adj Rechts-

judiciary [dʒu'dɪ/ɪ ͵ɛri] adj richterlich ‖ s (branch) richterliche Gewalt f; (judges) Richterstand m

judicious [dʒu'dɪ/əs] adj klug

judo ['dʒudo] s Judo n

jug [dʒʌg] s Krug m; (jail) Kittchen n

juggle ['dʒʌgəl] tr jonglieren; (accounts) frisieren ‖ intr jonglieren

juggler ['dʒʌglər] s Gaukler –in mf

Jugoslav ['jugo ͵slɑv] adj jugoslawisch ‖ s Jugoslawe m, Jugoslawin f

Jugoslavia [͵jugo'slɑvɪ·ə] s Jugoslawien n

jug'ular vein' ['dʒʌgjələr] s Halsader f

juice [dʒus] s Saft m

juicy ['dʒusi] adj saftig

jukebox ['dʒuk ͵bɑks] s Musikautomat m

July [dʒu'laɪ] s Juli m

jumble ['dʒʌmbəl] s Wust m ‖ tr durcheinanderwerfen

jumbo ['dʒʌmbo] adj Riesen-

jump [dʒʌmp] s Sprung m; (aer) Absprung m; **get the j. on** zuvorkommen (dat) ‖ tr überspringen; (attack) überfallen; (a hurdle) nehmen; (in checkers) schlagen; **j. bail** die Kaution verfallen lassen; **j. channels** den amtlichen Weg nicht einhalten; **j. rope** seilspringen; **j. ship** vom Schiff weglaufen; (sport) zu früh starten; **j. the gun** übereilt handeln; (sport) zu früh starten; **j. the track** entgleisen ‖ intr springen; (be startled) auffahren; **j. at** (a chance) stürzen auf (acc); **j. down s.o.'s throat** j–n anfahren

jump' ball' s (basketball) Sprungball m

jumper ['dʒʌmpər] s (dress) Jumper m; (elec) Kurzschlußbrücke f

jump'-off' s Beginn m; (sport) Start m

jump' rope' s Springseil n

jumpy ['dʒʌmpi] adj unruhig, nervös

junction ['dʒʌŋk/ən] s Verbindung f; (of roads, rail lines) Knotenpunkt m

juncture ['dʒʌŋkt/ər] s Verbindungsstelle f; **at this j.** in diesem Augenblick

June [dʒun] s Juni m

June' bug' s Maikäfer m

jungle ['dʒʌŋgəl] s Dschungel m, n & f

junior ['dʒunjər] adj jünger ‖ s Student –in mf im dritten Studienjahr

juniper ['dʒunɪpər] s Wacholder m

junk [dʒʌŋk] s Altwaren pl; (scrap iron) Schrott m; (useless stuff) Plunder m; (naut) Dschunke f

junket ['dʒʌŋkɪt] s Vergnügungsreise f auf öffentlichen Kosten

junk' mail' s Wurfsendung f

junk'yard' s Schrottplatz m

junta ['hʌntə], [dʒʌntə] s Junta f

jurisdiction [͵dʒʊrɪs'dɪk/ən] s Zuständigkeit f; **have j. over** zuständig sein für

jurisprudence [͵dʒʊrɪs'prudəns] s Rechtswissenschaft f

jurist ['dʒʊrɪst] s Jurist –in mf

juror ['dʒʊrər] s Geschworene mf

jury ['dʒʊri] s Geschworene pl

ju'ry box' s Geschworenenbank f

ju'ry tri'al s Schwurgerichtsverfahren n

just [dʒʌst] adj gerecht ‖ adv gerade; (only) nur; (simply) einfach

justice ['dʒʌstɪs] s Gerechtigkeit f; (of a claim) Berechtigung f; (judge) Richter m; **bring to j.** vor Gericht bringen; **do j. to** (a meal) wacker zusprechen (dat); (said of a picture) gerecht werden (dat)

jus'tice of the peace' s Friedensrichter m

justification [͵dʒʌstɪfɪ'ke/ən] s Rechtfertigung f

justi·fy ['dʒʌstɪ ͵faɪ] v (pret & pp –fied) tr rechtfertigen

justly ['dʒʌstli] adv mit Recht

jut [dʒʌt] v (pret & pp **jutted;** ger **jutting**) intr—**jut out** hervorragen

juvenile ['dʒuvə ͵naɪl] adj (books, court) Jugend-; (childish) unreif

ju'venile delin'quency s Jugendkriminalität f

ju'venile delin'quent s jugendlicher Verbrecher m

juxtapose [͵dʒʌkstə'poz] tr nebeneinanderstellen

K

K, k [ke] *s* elfter Buchstabe des englischen Alphabets

kale [kel] *s* Grünkohl *m*

kaleidoscopic [kə͵laɪdə'skɑpɪk] *adj* (& fig) kaleidoskopisch

kangaroo [͵kæŋgə'ru] *s* Känguruh *n*

kangaroo court' *s* Scheingericht *n*

kashmir ['kaeʃmɪr] *s* (tex) Kaschmir *m*

kayo ['ke'o] *s* K.O. *m* ‖ *tr* k.o. schlagen

keel [kil] *s* Kiel *m;* **on an even k.** (fig) gleichmäßig ‖ *intr*—**k. over** umkippen; (naut) kentern

keen [kin] *adj* (*sharp*) scharf; (*interest*) lebhaft; **k. on** scharf auf (*acc*)

keenness ['kinnɪs] *s* Schärfe *f*

keep [kip] *s* Unterhalt *m;* (*of a castle*) Bergfried *m;* **for keeps** (*forever*) für immer; (*seriously*) im Ernst ‖ *v* (*pret & pp* **kept** [kept]) *tr* (*retain*) behalten; (*detain*) aufhalten; (*save for s.o.*) aufbewahren; (*a secret*) bewahren; (*a promise*) (ein)halten; (*animals*) halten; (*books*) (acct) führen; **be kept in school** nachsitzen müssen; **k. at arm's length** vom Leibe halten; **k. at bay** sich erwehren (*genit*); **k. away** fernhalten; **k. back** zurückhalten; (*retain*) zurückbehalten; **k.** (*s.o.*) **company** Gesellschaft leisten (*dat*); **k. down** (*one's head*) niederhalten; (*one's voice*) (*prices*) niedrig halten; **k. from** abhalten von; **k. from** (*ger*) daran hindern zu (*inf*); **k. going** im Gange halten; **k. good time** gut geben; **k. guard** Wache halten; **k. house** den Haushalt führen; **k. in good condition** instand halten; **k. in mind** sich [*dat*] merken; **k. it up!** nur so weiter; **k. on** (*a garment*) anbehalten; (*a hat*) aufbehalten; **k. oneself from** (*ger*) es fertigbringen nicht zu (*inf*); **k. one's temper** sich beherrschen; **k. out** ausschließen; (*light*) nicht durchlassen; (*rain*) abhalten; **k. posted** auf dem laufenden halten; **k. score** die Punktliste führen; **k. secret** geheimhalten; **k. step** Tritt halten; **k. s.th. from s.o.** j-m etw verschweigen; **k. track of** sich [*dat*] merken; **k. under wraps** (coll) totschweigen; **k. up** instand halten; (*appearances*) wahren; (*correspondence*) unterhalten; **k. up the good work!** arbeiten Sie weiter so gut!; **k. waiting** warten lassen; **k. warm** warm halten; **k. your shirt on!** (coll) daß du die Nase im Gesicht behältst! ‖ *intr* (*said of food*) sich halten; **k. at** beharren bei; **k. at it!** bleib dabei!; **k. away** sich fernhalten; **k. cool** (fig) die Nerven behalten; **k. cool!** ruhig Blut!; **k. from** sich enthalten (*genit*); **k. from** (*ger*) es unterlassen zu (*inf*); **k. from laughing** sich das Lachen verkneifen;

k. going weitermachen; **k. moving** weitergehen; **k. on** (*ger*) weiter (*inf*), e.g., **k. on driving** weiterfahren; **k. out!** Eintritt verboten! **k. out of** sich fernhalten von; **k. quiet** sich ruhig verhalten; **k. quiet!** sei still!; **k. to the right** sich rechts halten; **k. up with** (*work*) nachkommen mit; **k. up with the Joneses** mit den Nachbarn Schritt halten; **k. within** bleiben innerhalb (*genit*)

keeper ['kipər] *s* (*of animals*) Halter –in *mf;* (*at a zoo*) Tierwärter –in *mf;* (*watchman*) Wächter *m*

keep'ing *s* Verwahrung *f;* **in k. with** in Einklang mit

keep'sake' *s* Andenken *n*

keg [keg] *s* Faß *n*

ken [ken] *s* Gesichtskreis *m*

kennel ['kenəl] *s* Hundezwinger *m*

kep·i ['kepi], ['kepi] *s* (–is) Kappi *n*

kerchief ['kʌrtʃɪf] *s* (*for the head*) Kopftuch *n;* (*for the neck*) Halstuch *n*

kernel ['kʌrnəl] *s* (*of fruit*) Kern *m;* (*of grain*) Korn *n;* (fig) Kern *m*

kerosene [͵kerə'sin] *s* Petroleum *n*

kerplunk [kər'plʌŋk] *interj* bums!

ketchup ['ketʃəp] *s* Ketchup *m & n*

kettle ['ketəl] *s* Kessel *m*

ket'tledrum' *s* Kesselpauke *f*

key [ki] *adj* (*ring, hole, industry, position*) Schlüssel– ‖ *s* (& fig) Schlüssel *m;* (*of a map*) Zeichenerklärung *f;* (*of a typewriter, piano, organ*) Taste *f;* (*of windinstrument*) Klappe *f;* (*reef*) Riff *n;* (*low island*) Insel *f;* (mus) Tonart *f;* **key of C major** C-dur; **off key** falsch ‖ *tr* (mach) festkeilen

key'board' *s* Tastatur *f*

keyed *adj*—**k. to** gestimmt auf (*acc*); **k. up** in Hochspannung

key'man' *s* Schlüsselfigur *f*

key'note' *s* Grundgedanke *m;* (mus) Tonika *f*

key'note address' *s* programmatische Rede *f*

keynoter ['kɪ͵notər] *s* Programmatiker –in *mf*

keypuncher ['ki͵pʌntʃər] *s* Locher –in *mf*

key'stone' *s* Schlußstein *m;* (fig) Grundlage *f*

key' word' *s* Stichwort *n*

kha·ki ['kæki] *adj* Khaki– ‖ *s* (–kis) Khaki *m;* **khakis** Khakiuniform *f*

kibitz ['kɪbɪts] *intr* (coll) kiebitzen

kibitzer ['kɪbɪtsər] *s* (coll) Kiebitz *m*

kick [kɪk] *s* Fußtritt *m;* (*of a rifle*) Rückstoß *m;* (*of a horse*) Schlag *m;* (*final spurt*) (sport) Endspurt *m;* **give s.o. a k.** j-m e-n Fußtritt versetzen; **I get a (great) k. out of him** er macht mir (riesigen) Spaß ‖ *tr* treten, stoßen; (fb) kicken; **be kicked upstairs** (coll) die Treppe hinauffallen;

I could k. myself ich könnte mich ohrfeigen; **k. a goal** (fb) ein Tor schießen; **k.** (s.o.) **around** schlecht behandeln; (e.g., an idea) beschwatzen; **k. in** (money) beisteuern; **k. open** (a door) aufstoßen; **k. out** (coll) rausschmeißen; **k. s.o. in the shins** j-n gegen das Schienbein treten; **k. the bucket** (sl) krepieren; **k. up a storm** Krach schlagen || intr (said of a gun) stoßen; (said of a horse) ausschlagen; (complain) (about) meckern (über acc); **k. around Europe** in Europa herumbummeln; **k. off** (fb) anspielen

kick'back' s Schmiergeld n

kick'off' s (commencement) Beginn m; (fb) Anstoß m

kid [kɪd] s Zicklein n; (coll) Kind n || v (pret & pp **kidded**; ger **kidding**) tr necken || intr scherzen; **no kidding!** mach keine Witze!

kid' gloves' spl Glacéhandschuhe pl; **handle with k.** (fig) mit Glacéhandschuhen anfassen

kid'nap' v (pret & pp –nap(p)ed; ger –nap(p)ing) tr kidnappen, entführen

kid'nap(p)er [ˈkɪdˌnæpər] s Kidnapper m

kid'nap(p)ing s Kidnapping s

kidney [ˈkɪdni] s Niere f

kid'ney bean' s rote Bohne f

kid'ney-shaped' adj nierenförmig

kid'ney stone' s Nierenstein m

kid'ney trans'plant s Nierenverpflanzung f; (transplanted kidney) verpflanzte Niere f

kid'ney trou'ble s Nierenleiden n

kid' stuff' s (coll) Kinderei f

kill [kɪl] s (aer) Abschuß m; (hunt) Jagdbeute f; (nav) Versenkung f || tr töten; (murder) ermorden, killen; (plants) zum Absterben bringen; (time) totschlagen; (a proposal, plans, competition) zu Fall bringen; (the motor) abwürgen; (the ball) stark schlagen; (a bottle) austrinken; **be killed in action** (im Felde) fallen; **it won't k. you** (coll) es wird dich nicht umbringen; **k. off** abschlachten; **k. oneself** sich umbringen; **k. two birds with one stone** zwei Fliegen mit e-r Klappe schlagen; **she is dressed to k.** sie ist totschick angezogen

killer [ˈkɪlər] s Totschläger –in mf, Killer m

kill'er whale' s Schwertwal m

kill'ing s Tötung f; **make a k.** e-n unerhofften Gewinn erzielen

kill'joy' s Spaßverderber m

kiln [ˈkɪl(n)] s Brennofen m

kil·o [ˈkilo], [ˈkɪlo] s (–os) Kilo n

kilocycle [ˈkɪləˌsaɪkəl] s Kilohertz n

kilogram [ˈkɪləˌgræm] s Kilogramm n

kilohertz [ˈkɪləˌhɑrts] s Kilohertz n

kilometer [kɪˈlɑmɪtər] s Kilometer m; **kilometers per hour** Stundenkilometer pl

kilowatt [ˈkɪləˌwɑt] s Kilowatt n

kil'owatt'-hour' s Kilowattstunde f

kilt [kɪlt] s Kilt m

kilter [ˈkɪltər] s—**out of k.** nicht in Ordnung

kimo·no [kɪˈmono] s (–nos) Kimono m

kin [kɪn] s Sippe f; **the next of kin** die nächsten Angehörigen

kind [kaɪnd] adj liebenswürdig; **(to)** gütig (zu), freundlich (zu); **would you be so k. as to** (inf)? würden Sie so gefällig sein zu (inf)?; **with k. regards** mit freundlichen Grüßen || s Art f, Sorte f; **all kinds of** allerlei; **another k. of** ein anderer; **any k. of** irgendwelcher; **every k. of** jede Art von; **in k.** (fig) auf gleiche Weise; **k. of** (coll) etwas; **nothing of the k.** nichts dergleichen; **that k. of** derartig; **two (three) kinds of** zweierlei (dreierlei); **what k. of** was für ein

kindergarten [ˈkɪndərˌgɑrtən] s Vorschule f, Vorschuljahr n

kind'-heart'ed adj gutmütig

kindle [ˈkɪndəl] tr anzünden; (fig) erwecken || intr sich entzünden

kindling [ˈkɪndlɪŋ] s Entzündung f; (wood) Kleinholz n

kindly [ˈkaɪndli] adj gütig, freundlich || adv freundlich; (please) bitte

kindness [ˈkaɪndnɪs] s Freundlichkeit f; (deed) Gefälligkeit f

kindred [ˈkɪndrɪd] adj verwandtschaftlich; (fig) verwandt || s Verwandtschaft f

kinescope [ˈkɪnɪˌskop] s (trademark) Fernsehempfangsröhre f

kinetic [kɪˈnɛtɪk] adj kinetisch || **kinetics** s Kinetik f

king [kɪŋ] s König m; (cards, chess) König m; (checkers) Dame f

kingdom [ˈkɪŋdəm] s Königreich n; (of animals, etc.) Reich n; **k. of heaven** Himmelreich n

king'fish'er s Königsfischer m

kingly [ˈkɪŋli] adj königlich

king'pin' s (coll) Boß m; (bowling) König m

king'ship' s Königtum n

king'-size' adj übergroß

kink [kɪŋk] s (in a wire) Knick m; (in the hair) Kräuselung f; (in a muscle) Muskelkrampf m; (flaw) Fehler m

kinky [ˈkɪŋki] adj gekräuselt

kin'ship' s Verwandtschaft f

kins'man s (–men) Blutsverwandte m

kins'wom'an s (–wom'en) Blutsverwandte f

kipper [ˈkɪpər] s Räucherhering m || tr einsalzen und räuchern

kiss [kɪs] s Kuß m || tr & intr küssen

kisser [ˈkɪsər] s (sl) Fresse f

kit [kɪt] s (equipment) Ausrüstung f; (tool kit) Werkzeugkasten m; (for models) Modellsatz m; (e.g., for a convention) Mappe f; **the whole kit and caboodle** (things) der ganze Kram; (persons) die ganze Sippschaft

kitchen [ˈkɪtʃən] s Küche f

kitchenette [ˌkɪtʃəˈnɛt] s Kochnische f

kit'chen knife' s Küchenmesser n

kit'chen police' s (mil) Küchendienst m

kit'chen range' s Herd m, Kochherd m

kit′chen sink′ *s* Ausguß *m*

kit′chenware′ *s* Küchengeschirr *n*

kite [kaɪt] *s* Drachen *m;* (orn) Weih *m;* **fly a k.** e-n Drachen steigen lassen; **go fly a k.!** (coll) scher dich zum Kuckuck!

kith′ and kin′ [kɪθ] *spl* Freunde and Verwandte *pl*

kitten [′kɪtən] *s* Kätzchen *n*

kitty [′kɪti] *s* Kätzchen *n;* (cards) gemeinsame Kasse *f;* **Kitty** Käthchen *n*

kleptomaniac [ˌklɛptə′menɪˌæk] *s* Kleptomane *m,* Kleptomanin *f*

knack [næk] *s*—**have a k. for** Talent haben für; **have the k. of it** den Griff heraus haben

knapsack [′næpˌsæk] *s* Rucksack *m*

knave [nev] *s* Schelm *m;* (cards) Bube *m*

knavery [′nevəri] *s* Schelmenstreich *m*

knead [nid] *tr* kneten

knead′ing trough′ *s* Teigmulde *f*

knee [ni] *s* Knie *n;* **bring s.o. to his knees** j-n auf die Knie zwingen; **go down on one’s knees** niederknien; **on bended knees** kniefällig

knee′ bend′ *s* Kniebeuge *f*

knee′ breech′es *spl* Kniehose *f*

knee′cap′ *s* Kniescheibe *f*

knee′-deep′ *adj* knietief

knee′-high′ *adj* kniehoch

knee′ jerk′ *s* Patellarreflex *m*

kneel [nil] *v* (*pret & pp* knelt [nelt] & kneeled) *intr* knien

knee′-length′ *adj* kniefreit

knee′pad′ *s* (sport) Knieschützer *m*

knee′pan′ *s* Kniescheibe *f*

knee′ swell′ *s* (of organ) Knieschweller *m*

knell [nel] *s* Totengeläute *n*

knickers [′nɪkərz] *spl* Knickerbockerhosen *pl*

knickknack [′nɪkˌnæk] *s* Nippsache *f*

knife [naɪf] *s* (knives [naɪvz]) Messer *n* || *tr* erstechen

knife′ sharp′ener *s* Messerschleifer *m*

knife′ switch′ *s* (elec) Messerschalter *m*

knight [naɪt] *s* Ritter *m;* (chess) Springer *m* || *tr* zum Ritter schlagen

knight′hood′ *s* Ritterschaft *f*

knightly [′naɪtli] *adj* ritterlich

knit [nɪt] *v* (*pret & pp* knitted & knit; *ger* knitting) *tr* stricken; **k. one’s brows** die Brauen runzeln || *intr* stricken; (*said of bones*) zusammenheilen

knit′ goods′ *spl* Trikotwaren *pl*

knit′ted dress′ *s* Strickkleid *n*

knit′ting *s* (act) Strickerei *f;* (*materials*) Strickzeug *n*

knit′ting machine′ *s* Strickmaschine *f*

knit′ting nee′dle *s* Stricknadel *f*

knit′ting yarn′ *s* Strickgarn *n*

knit′wear′ *s* Strickwaren *pl*

knob [nab] *s* (of a door) Drücker *m;* (lump) Auswuchs *m;* (in wood) Knorren *m;* (of a radio) Knopf *m*

knock [nak] *s* (& aut) Klopfen *n* || *tr* (*criticize*) tadeln; **k. a hole through** durchbrechen; **k. around** herumstoßen; (*mistreat*) unsanft behandeln;

k. down niederschlagen; (with a car) umfahren; (trees) umbrechen; (at auctions) zuschlagen; **k. it off!** (sl) hör mal auf!; **k. oneself out over** sich [dat] die Zähne ausbeißen an (dat); **k. one’s head against the wall** mit dem Kopf gegen die Wand rennen; **k. out** ausschlagen; (exhaust) (coll) strapazieren; (a tank) abschießen; (box) k.o. schlagen; **k. over** umwerfen; **k. together** (build hurriedly) schnell zusammenhauen; **k. to the ground** zu Boden schlagen; **k. up a girl** (sl) e-m Mädchen ein Kind anhängen || *intr* (an)klopfen; (aut) klopfen; **k. about** herumbummeln; **k. against** stoßen an (acc); **k. off** (from) (coll) aufhören

knock′down′ *s* (box) Niederschlag *m*

knocker [′nakər] *s* Türklopfer *m;* **knockers** (sl) Brüste *pl*

knock-kneed [′nakˌnid] *adj* x-beinig

knock′-knees′ *spl* X-beine *pl*

knock′out′ *s* (woman) (coll) Blitzmädel *n;* (box) Knockout *m*

knock′-out drops′ *spl* Betäubungsmittel *n*

knock′-out punch′ *s* K.o.-Schlag *m*

knoll [nol] *s* Hügel *m*

knot [nat] *s* Knoten *m;* (in wood) Knorren *m;* (of people) Gruppe *f;* (naut) Knoten *m;* **tie a k.** e-n Knoten machen; **tie the k.** (coll) sich verheiraten || *tr* e-n Knoten machen in (acc); (two ends) zusammenknoten

knot′hole′ *s* Astloch *n*

knotty [′nati] *adj* knorrig; (problem) knifflig

know [no] *s*—**be in the k.** Bescheid wissen || *v* (*pret* knew [n(j)u]; *pp* known) *tr* (facts) wissen; (be familiar with) kennen; (a language) können; **come to k.** erfahren; **get to k.** kennenlernen; **known** bekannt; **k. one’s way around** sich auskennen; **k. the ropes** (coll) Bescheid wissen; **k. what’s what** (coll) den Rummel kennen || *intr* wissen; **he ought to k.** better er sollte mehr Verstand haben; **k. about** wissen über (acc); **k. of** wissen von; **not that I k. of** (coll) nicht, daß ich wüßte; **you k.** (coll) wissen Sie

knowable [′no-əbəl] *adj* kenntlich

know′-how′ *s* Sachkenntnis *f*

know′ing *adj* (glance) vielsagend

knowingly [′no-ɪŋli] *adv* wissentlich; (intentionally) absichtlich

know′-it-all′ *s* Naseweis *m*

knowledge [′nalɪdʒ] *s* Wissen *n,* Kenntnisse *pl;* (information) (of) Kenntnis *f* (von); **basic k. of** Grundkenntnisse *pl* in (dat); **come to s.o.’s k.** j-m zur Kenntnis kommen; **to my k.** soweit (or soviel) ich weiß; **to the best of my k.** nach bestem Wissen; **without my k.** ohne mein Mitwissen; **working k. of** praktisch verwertbare Kenntnisse *pl* (genit)

knowledgeable [′nalɪdʒəbəl] *adj* kenntnisreich

known [non] *adj* bekannt; **become k.**

kundwerden; **k. all over town** stadt-
bekannt; **make k.** bekanntgeben
know'-noth'ing s Nichtswisser m
knuckle ['nʌkəl] s Knöchel m, Finger-
knöchel m; (mach) Gelenkstück n;
k. of ham Eisbein n || intr—**k. down
to work** sich ernsthaft an die Arbeit
machen; **k. under** klein beigeben
k.o. ['ke'o] s K.o. m || tr k.o.-schlagen
Koran [ko'ræn] s Koran m
Korea [ko'ri·ə] s Korea n

Korean [ko'ri·ən] adj koreanisch || s
Koreaner –in mf; (language) Koreanisch n
kosher ['koʃər] adj (& coll) koscher
kowtow ['kau'tau] intr e–n Kotau
machen; **k. to** kriechen vor (dat)
K.P. ['ke'pi] s (**kitchen police**) (mil)
Küchendienst m
Kremlin ['kremlɪn] s Kreml m
kudos ['k(i)udɑs] s (coll) Ruhm m,
Renommee n

L

L, l [εl] s zwölfter Buchstabe des englischen Alphabets
lab [læb] s (coll) Labor n
la·bel ['lebəl] s Etikett n; (brand)
Marke f; (fig) Bezeichnung f || v
(pret & pp **-bel[l]ed**; ger **—bel[l]ing**)
tr etikettieren; (fig) bezeichnen
labial ['lebɪ·əl] adj Lippen– || s Lip-
penlaut m, Labial m
labor ['lebər] adj Arbeits–, Arbeiter–
|| s Arbeit f; (toil) Mühe f; **be in
l.** in den Wehen liegen || tr (a point)
ausführlich eingehen auf (acc) || intr
sich abmühen; (at) arbeiten (an dat);
(exert oneself) sich anstrengen; (said
of a ship) stampfen; **l. under** zu leiden haben unter (dat)
la'bor and man'agement spl Arbeitnehmer und Arbeitgeber pl
laboratory ['læbərə,tori] s Laborato-
rium n
lab'oratory techni'cian s Laborant –in
mf
la'bor camp' s Zwangsarbeitslager n
la'bor con'tract s Tarifvertrag m
la'bor dis'pute s Arbeitsstreitigkeit f
la'bored adj (e.g., breathing) mühsam;
(style) gezwungen
laborer ['lebərər] s Arbeiter –in mf;
(unskilled) Hilfsarbeiter –in mf
la'bor force' s Arbeitskräfte pl
laborious [lə'borɪ·əs] adj mühsam,
schwierig
la'bor law' s Arbeitsrecht n
la'bor lead'er s Arbeiterführer –in mf
la'bor mar'ket s Arbeitsmarkt m
la'bor move'ment s Arbeiterbewegung
f
la'bor pains' spl Geburtswehen pl
la'bor-sav'ing adj arbeitssparend; **l.
device** Hilfsgerät n
la'bor short'age s Mangel m an Arbeits-
kräften
la'bor supply' s Arbeitsangebot n
la'bor un'ion s Gewerkschaft f
laburnum [lə'bʌrnəm] s Goldregen m
labyrinth ['læbɪrɪnθ] s Labyrinth n
lace [les] adj (collar, dress) Spitzen–
|| s Spitze f; (shoestring) Schnür-
senkel m || tr (e.g., shoes) schnüren;
(braid) flechten; (drinks) (coll) mit
e–m Schuß Branntwein versetzen;
(beat) (coll) prügeln; **l. up** zuschnü-
ren

lacerate ['læsə,ret] tr zerfleischen
laceration [,læsə'reʃən] s Fleischwunde f
lace' trim'ming s Spitzenbesatz m
lace'work' s Spitzenarbeit f
lachrymose ['lækrɪ,mos] adj tränen-
reich
lac'ing s Schnürung f; (coll) Prügel pl
lack [læk] s (of) Mangel m (an dat);
for l. of aus Mangel an (dat); **l. of
space** Raummangel m; **l. of time**
Zeitmangel m || tr—**I l.** es mangelt
mir an (dat) || intr—**be lacking** feh-
len; **he is lacking in courage** ihm
fehlt der Mut
lackadaisical [,lækə'dezɪkəl] adj teilnahmslos, gleichgültig
lackey ['læki] s Lakai m
lack'ing prep mangels (genit)
lack'lus'ter adj glanzlos
laconic [lə'kɑnɪk] adj lakonisch
lacquer ['lækər] s Lack m || tr lackie-
ren
lac'quer ware' s Lackwaren pl
lacrosse [lə'krɔs] s Lacrosse n
lacu·na [lə'kjunə] s (**-nas** & **-nae** [ni])
Lücke f, Lakune f
lacy ['lesi] adj spitzenartig
lad [læd] s Bube m
la'dies' man' s Weiberheld m, Salonlöwe m
la'dies' room' s Damentoilette f
ladle ['ledəl] s Schöpflöffel m || tr
ausschöpfen
lady ['ledi] s Dame f; **ladies and gentlemen** meine Damen und Herren!
la'dybird', la'dybug' s Marienkäfer m
la'dy compan'ion s Gesellschaftsdame
f
la'dyfin'ger s Löffelbiskuit m & n
la'dy-in-wait'ing s (**ladies-in-waiting**)
Hofdame f
la'dy-kil'ler s Schwerenöter m
la'dylike' adj damenhaft
la'dylove' s Geliebte f
la'dy of the house' s Hausherrin f
la'dy's maid' s Zofe f
la'dy's man' s var of **ladies' man**
lag [læg] s Zurückbleiben n; (aer)
Rücktrift f; (phys) Verzögerung f ||
v (pret & pp **lagged**; ger **lagging**) intr
(behind) zurückbleiben (hinter dat)
la'ger beer' s ['lɑgər] s Lagerbier n
laggard ['lægərd] s Nachzügler m

lagoon [lə'gun] *s* Lagune *f*
laid' up' *adj* (**with**) bettlägerig (infolge von); **be l. in bed** auf der Nase liegen
lair [lɛr] *s* Höhle *f*, Lager *n*
laity ['le·ɪti] *s* Laien *pl*
lake [lek] *s* See *m*
Lake' Con'stance ['kɑnstəns] *s* der Bodensee
lamb [læm] *s* Lamm *n;* (culin) Lammfleisch *n*
lambaste [læm'best] *tr* (*berate*) (coll) herunterputzen; (*beat*) (coll) verdreschen
lamb' chop' *s* Hammelrippchen *n*
lambkin ['læmkɪn] *s* Lammfell *n*
lame [lem] *adj* (*person, leg; excuse*) lahm; **be l. in one leg** auf e–m Bein lahm sein || *tr* lähmen
lament [lə'mɛnt] *s* Jammer *m;* (*dirge*) Klagelied *n* || *tr* beklagen || *intr* wehklagen
lamentable ['læməntəbəl] *adj* beklagenswert; (pej) jämmerlich
lamentation [,læmə'teʃən] *s* Wehklage *f*
laminate ['læmɪ,net] *tr* schichten
lamp [læmp] *s* Lampe *f*
lamp' chim'ney *s* Lampenzylinder *m*
lamp'light' *s* Lampenlicht *n*
lamp'light'er *s* Laternenanzünder *m*
lampoon [læm'pun] *s* Schmähschrift *f* || *tr* mit e–r Schmähschrift verspotten
lamp'post' *s* Laternenpfahl *m*
lamp'shade' *s* Lampenschirm *m*
lance [læns] *s* Lanze *f;* (surg) Lanzette *f* || *tr* (surg) aufstechen
lance' cor'poral *s* (Brit) Hauptgefreite *m*
lancet ['lænsɪt] *s* Lanzette *f*
land [lænd] *s* (*dry land; country*) Land *n;* (*ground*) Boden *m;* **by l.** zu Lande || *tr* (*a plane, troops, punch*) landen; (*a ship, fish*) an Land bringen; (*a job*) (coll) kriegen; **l. s.o. in trouble** j–n in Schwierigkeiten bringen || *intr* (aer, naut, & fig) landen; (*said of a blow*) treffen; **l. on s.o.'s head** j–m auf den Kopf fallen; **l. on water** auf dem Wasser aufsetzen
land' breeze' *s* Landwind *m*
land'ed prop'erty *s* Landbesitz *m*
land'fall' *s* (*sighting of land*) Sichten *n* von Land; **make l.** landen
land' forc'es *spl* Landstreitkräfte *pl*
land'ing *s* Landung *f;* (*of a staircase*) Absatz *m;* **l. on the moon** Mondlandung *f*
land'ing craft' *s* Landungsboot *n*
land'ing field' *s* Landeplatz *m*
land'ing force' *s* Landekorps *n*
land'ing gear' *s* Fahrgestell *n*
land'ing par'ty *s* Landeabteilung *f*
land'ing stage' *s* Landungssteg *m*
land'ing strip' *s* Start– und Landestreifen *m*
land'la'dy *s* (*of an apartment*) Hauswirtin *f;* (*of an inn*) Gastwirtin *f*
land'locked' *adj* landumschlossen
land'lord' *s* (*of an apartment*) Hauswirt *m;* (*of an inn*) Gastwirt *m*
landlubber ['lænd,lʌbər] *s* Landratte *f*
land'mark' *s* Landmarke *f;* (*cardinal event*) Markstein *m*
land' of'fice *s* Grundbuchamt *n*
land'-office bus'iness *s* (fig) Bombengeschäft *n*
land'own'er *s* Grundbesitzer –in *mf*
landscape ['lænd,skep] *s* Landschaft *f;* (paint) Landschaftsbild *n* || *tr* landschaftlich gestalten
land'scape ar'chitect *s* Landschaftsarchitekt –in *mf*
land'scape paint'er *s* Landschaftsmaler –in *mf*
land'slide' *s* Bergrutsch *m;* (pol) Stimmenrutsch *m*
landward ['lændwərd] *adv* landwärts
land' wind' [wɪnd] *s* Landwind *m*
lane [len] *s* Bahn *f;* (*country road*) Feldweg *m;* (aer) Flugschneise *f;* (aut) Fahrbahn *f;* (naut) Fahrtroute *f;* (sport) Laufbahn *f;* (sport) Schwimmbahn *f*
language ['læŋgwɪdʒ] *s* Sprache *f*
lan'guage instruc'tion *s* Sprachunterricht *m*
lan'guage teach'er *s* Sprachlehrer –in *mf*
languid ['læŋgwɪd] *adj* schlaff
languish ['læŋgwɪʃ] *intr* schmachten
languor ['læŋgər] *s* Mattigkeit *f*
languorous ['læŋgərəs] *adj* matt
lank [læŋk] *adj* schlank; (*hair*) glatt
lanky ['læŋki] *adj* schlaksig
lanolin ['lænəlɪn] *s* Lanolin *n*
lantern ['læntərn] *s* Laterne *f*
lan'tern slide' *s* Diapositiv *n*
lanyard ['lænjərd] *s* (*around the neck*) Halsschnur *f;* (naut) Taljereep *n*
Laos ['le·ɑs] *s* Laos *n*
Laotian [le'oʃən] *adj* laotisch || *s* Laote *m*, Laotin *f;* (*language*) Laotisch *n*
lap [læp] *s* (*of the body or clothing*) Schoß *m;* (*of the waves*) Plätschern *n;* (sport) Runde *f* || *v* (*pret & pp* **lapped;** *ger* **lapping**) *tr* schlappen; (sport) überrunden; **lap up** auf(sch)lecken || *intr*—**lap against** (*e.g., a boat, shore*) plätschern gegen; **lap over** hinausragen über (*acc*)
lap' dog' *s* Schoßhund *m*
lapel [lə'pɛl] *s* Aufschlag *m*
Lap'land' *s* Lappland *n*
Laplander ['læp,lændər] *s* Lappländer –in *mf*
Lapp [læp] *s* Lappe *m*, Lappin *f;* (*language*) Lappisch *n*
lapse [læps] *s* (*error*) Versehen *n;* (*of time*) Ablauf *m;* **after a l. of** nach Ablauf von; **l. of duty** Pflichtversäumnis *f;* **l. of memory** Gedächtnislücke *f* || *intr* (*said of a right, an insurance policy*) verfallen; (*said of time*) ablaufen; **l. into** verfallen in (*acc*); **l. into unconsciousness** das Bewußtsein verlieren
lap'wing' *s* Kiebitz *m*
larceny ['lɑrsəni] *s* Diebstahl *m*
larch [lɑrtʃ] *s* (bot) Lärche *f*
lard [lɑrd] *s* Schmalz *n* || *tr* spicken
larder ['lɑrdər] *s* Speisekammer *f*
large [lɑrdʒ] *adj* groß; **at l.** (*as a whole*) gesamt; (*at liberty*) auf freiem

Fuß; (said of an official) zur beson-
deren Verfügung; become larger sich
vergrößern; on a l. scale in großem
Umfang

large' intes'tine s Dickdarm m

largely ['lɑrdʒli] adv größtenteils

largeness ['lɑrdʒnɪs] s Größe f

large'-scale' adj Groß–; (map) in großem Maßstab; (production) Serien–

largesse ['lɑrdʒɛs] s (generosity) Freigebigkeit f; (handout) Geldverteilung
f

lariat ['lærɪ-ət] s Lasso m & n; (for
grazing animals) Halteseil n

lark [lɑrk] s (orn) Lerche f; for a l.
zum Spaß

lark'spur' s (bot) Rittersporn m

lar•va ['lɑrvə] s (–vae [vi]) Larve f

laryngitis [ˌlærɪn'dʒaɪtɪs] s Kehlkopf-
entzündung f, Laryngitis f

larynx ['lærɪŋks] s (larynxes & laryn-
ges [lə'rɪndʒiz]) Kehlkopf m

lascivious [lə'sɪvɪ-əs] adj wollüstig

lasciviousness [lə'sɪvɪ-əsnɪs] s Wol-
lüstigkeit f

laser ['lezər] s Laser m

lash [læʃ] s Peitsche f; (as a punishment) Peitschenhieb m; (of the eye)
Wimper f ‖ tr (whip) peitschen;
(bind) (to) anbinden (an acc); (said
of rain, storms) peitschen ‖ intr—
l. out (at) ausschlagen (nach)

lass [læs] s Mädel n

lassitude ['læsɪˌt(j)ud] s Mattigkeit f

last [læst] adj letzte; very l. allerletzte
‖ adv zuletzt; l. of all zuallerletzt ‖
s Letzte mfn; (of a cobbler) Schuh-
leisten m; at l. schließlich; at long l.
zu guter Letzt; look one's l. on zum
letzten Mal blicken auf (acc); see the
l. of s.o. j–n nicht mehr wiedersehen;
to the l. bis zum Letzten ‖ intr (remain unchanged) anhalten; (for a
specific time) dauern; (said of money,
supplies) reichen; (said of a person)
aushalten

last'ing adj dauerhaft, andauernd; l.
effect Dauerwirkung f; l. for months
monatelang

Last' Judg'ment s Jüngstes Gericht n

lastly ['læstli] adv zuletzt

last'-min'ute adj in letzter Minute

last'-minute news' s neueste Nachrichten pl

last' night' adv gestern abend

last' quar'ter s (astr) abnehmendes
Mondviertel n; (com) letztes Quartal
n

last' resort' s letztes Mittel n

last' sleep' s Todesschlaf m

last' straw' s—that's the l. das schlägt
dem Faß den Boden aus

Last' Sup'per, the s das Letzte Abendmahl

last' week' adv vorige Woche

last' will' and test'ament s letztwillige
Verfügung f

last' word' s letztes Wort n; the l.
(fig) der letzte Schrei

latch [lætʃ] s Klinke f ‖ tr zuklinken
‖ intr einschnappen; l. on to (coll)
spitzkriegen

latch'key' s Hausschlüssel m

late [let] adj (after the usual time)
spät; (at a late hour) zu später Stunde; (deceased) verstorben; be l. sich
verspäten; (said of a train) Verspätung haben; keep l. hours spät
aufbleiben ‖ adv spät; come l. zu
spät kommen; of l. kürzlich; see you
later (coll) bis später!

latecomer ['let͵kʌmər] s Nachzügler m

lateen' sail' ['læ'tin] s Lateinsegel n

lateen' yard' s Lateinrah f

lately ['letli] adv neulich, unlängst

lateness ['letnɪs] s Verspätung f

latent ['letənt] adj latent, verborgen

later ['letər] adj später ‖ adv später,
nachher; l. on späterhin

lateral ['lætərəl] adj seitlich, Seiten–

lath [læθ] s Latte f ‖ tr belatten

lathe [leð] s Drehbank f; turn on a l.
drechseln

lather ['læðər] s Seifenschaum m; (of
a horse) schäumender Schweiß m ‖
tr einseifen ‖ intr schäumen

lathing ['læθɪŋ] s Lattenwerk n

Latin ['lætɪn] adj lateinisch ‖ s
(Romance-speaking person) Romane
m, Romanin f; (language) Lateinisch
n

La'tin Amer'ica s Lateinamerika n

La'tin-Amer'ican adj lateinamerika-
nisch ‖ s Lateinamerikaner –in mf

latitude ['lætɪˌt(j)ud] s Breite f; (fig)
Spielraum m

latrine [lə'trin] s Latrine f

latter ['lætər] adj (later) später; (final)
End–; (recent) letzte; in the l. part
of (e.g., the year) in der zweiten
Hälfte (genit); the l. dieser

lat'ter-day' adj (later) später; (recent)
letzte

Lat'ter-day Saint' s Heilige mf der
Jüngsten Tage

lattice ['lætɪs] s Gitter n ‖ tr vergittern

lat'ticework' s Gitterwerk n

Latvia ['lætvɪ-ə] s Lettland n

Latvian ['lætvɪ-ən] adj lettisch ‖ s
Lette m, Lettin f; (language) Lettisch
n

laud [lɔd] tr loben, preisen

laudable ['lɔdəbəl] adj löblich

laudanum ['lɔd(ə)nəm] s Opiumtink-
tur f

laudatory ['lɔdəˌtɔri] adj Lob–

laugh [læf] s Lachen n, Gelächter n;
for laughs zum Spaß; have a good l.
sich auslachen ‖ tr—l. off sich lachend hinwegsetzen über (acc) ‖ intr
lachen; it's easy for you to l. Sie
haben leicht lachen!; l. about lachen
über (acc); l. at (deride) auslachen;
(find amusement in) lachen über
(acc)

laughable ['læfəbəl] adj lächerlich

laugh'ing adj lachend; it's no l. matter
es ist nichts zum Lachen

laugh'ing gas' s Lachgas n

laugh'ingstock' s Gespött m

laughter ['læftər] s Gelächter n, Lachen n; roar with l. vor Lachen
brüllen

launch [lɔntʃ] s (open boat) Barkasse

f ‖ *tr* (*a boat*) aussetzen; (*a ship*) vom Stapel laufen lassen; (*a plane*) katapultieren; (*a rocket*) starten; (*a torpedo*) abschießen; (*an offensive*) beginnen; **be launched** (naut) vom Stapel laufen; (rok) starten ‖ *intr*—**l. into** sich stürzen in (*acc*)

launch′ing *s* (*of a ship*) Stapellauf *m*; (*of a torpedo*) Ausstoß *m*; (*of a rocket*) Abschuß *m*, Start *m*

launch′ pad′ *s* (rok) Startrampe *f*

launder [′lɔndər] *tr* waschen

laundress [′lɔndrɪs] *s* Wäscherin *f*

laundry [′lɔndrɪ] *s* (*clothes*) Wäsche *f*; (*room*) Waschküche *f*; (*business*) Wäscherei *f*

laun′drybag′ *s* Wäschebeutel *m*

laun′drybas′ket *s* Wäschekorb *m*

laun′dry list′ *s* Waschzettel *m*

laun′dry·man′ *s* (−men′) Wäscher *m*

laun′dry·wom′an *s* (−wom′en) Wäscherin *f*

laurel [′lɔrəl] *s* Lorbeer *m*

lau′rel tree′ *s* Lorbeerbaum *m*

lava [′lɑvə] *s* Lava *f*

lavatory [′lævə‚torɪ] *s* Waschraum *m*; (*toilet*) Toilette *f*

lavender [′lævəndər] *adj* lavendelfarben ‖ *s* (bot) Lavendel *m*

lavish [′lævɪʃ] *adj* (*person*) verschwenderisch; (*dinner*) üppig ‖ *tr*—**l. care on** hegen und pflegen; **l. s.th. on s.o.** j-n mit etw überhäufen

lavishness [′lævɪ/nɪs] *s* Üppigkeit *f*

law [lɔ] *s* Gesetz *n*; (*system*) Recht *n*; (*as a science*) Rechtswissenschaft *f*; (*relig*) Gebot *n*; **according to law** dem Recht entsprechend; **act within the law** sich ans Gesetz halten; **against the law** gesetzwidrig; **become law** Gesetzkraft erlangen; **by law** gesetzlich; **go against the law** gegen das Gesetz handeln; **lay down the law** gebieterisch auftreten; **practice law** den Anwaltsberuf ausüben; **study law** Jura studieren; **take the law into one's own hands** sich [*dat*] selbst sein Recht verschaffen; **under the law** nach dem Gesetz

law′-abid′ing *adj* friedlich

law′ and or′der *s* Ruhe und Ordnung *pl*

law′-and-or′der *adj* für Ruhe und Ordnung

law′break′er *s* Rechtsbrecher −in *mf*

law′break′ing *s* Rechtsbruch *m*

law′court′ *s* Gerichtshof *m*, Gericht *n*

lawful [′lɔfəl] *adj* gesetzmäßig

lawless [′lɔlɪs] *adj* gesetzlos

lawlessness [′lɔlɪsnɪs] *s* Gesetzlosigkeit *f*

law′mak′er *s* Gesetzgeber *m*

lawn [lɔn] *s* Rasen *m*; (tex) Batist *m*

lawn′ mow′er *s* Rasenmäher *m*

lawn′ par′ty *s* Gartenfest *n*

lawn′ sprin′kler *s* Rasensprenger *m*

law′ of dimin′ishing returns′ *s* Gesetz *n* der abnehmenden Erträge

law′ of′fice *s* Anwaltsbüro *n*

law′ of na′tions *s* Völkerrecht *n*

law′ of na′ture *s* Naturgesetz *n*

law′ of probabil′ity *s* Wahrscheinlichkeitsgesetz *n*

law′ of supply′ and demand′ *s* Gesetz *n* von Angebot und Nachfrage

law′ of the land′ *s* Landesgesetz *n*

law′ school′ *s* juristische Fakultät *f*

law′ stu′dent *s* Student −in *mf* der Rechtswissenschaft

law′suit′ *s* Klage *f*, Prozeß *m*

lawyer [′lɔjər] *s* Advokat −in *m*, Anwalt −in *mf*

lax [læks] *adj* lax, nachlässig

laxative [′læksətɪv] *s* Abführmittel *n*

laxity [′læksɪtɪ] *s* Laxheit *f*

lay [le] *adj* (*not of the clergy*) Laien-, weltlich; (*non-expert*) laienhaft ‖ *s* (*poem*) Lied *n* ‖ *v* (*pret & pp* **laid** [led]) *tr* legen; (*eggs; foundation, bricks, lineoleum*) legen; (*cables, pipes, tracks*) verlegen; (vulg) umlegen; **be laid up with** das Bett hüten müssen wegen (*genit*); **I'll lay you two to one** ich wette mit dir zwei zu eins; **lay aside** beiseite legen; (*save*) sparen; **lay bare** bloßlegen; **lay down** niederlegen; (*principles*) aufstellen; **lay claim to** Anspruch erheben auf (*acc*); **lay it on thick** dick auftragen; **lay low** (*said of an illness*) bettlägerig machen; **lay off** (*workers*) vorübergehend entlassen; **lay open** freilegen; **lay out** auslegen; (*a garden*) anlegen; (*money*) aufwenden; (*a corpse*) aufbahren; (surv) abstecken; **lay siege to** belagern; **lay waste** verwüsten ‖ *intr* (*said of hens*) legen; **lay for** auflauern (*dat*); **lay into** (*beat*) (coll) verdreschen; (*scold*) (coll) heruntermachen; **lay off** (*abstain from*) sich enthalten (*genit*); (*let alone*) in Ruhe lassen; **lay over** (*on a trip*) sich aufhalten; **lay to** (naut) stillegen

lay′ broth′er *s* Laienbruder *m*

layer [′le·ər] *s* Schicht *f*; (bot) Ableger *m*; **in layers** schichtenweise; **l. of fat** Fettschicht *f*; **thin l.** Hauch *m*

lay′er cake′ *s* Schichttorte *f*

layette [le′ɛt] *s* Babyausstattung *f*

lay′ fig′ure *s* Gliederpuppe *f*

layman [′lemən] *s* (−men) Laie *m*; **layman's** laienhaft

lay′off′ *s* vorübergehende Entlassung *f*

lay′ of the land′ *s* Gestaltung *f* des Terrains; (fig) Gesichtspunkt *m* der Angelegenheit

lay′out′ *s* Anlage *f*, Anordnung *f*; (typ) Layout *n*; **l. of rooms** Raumverteilung *f*

laziness [′lezɪnɪs] *s* Faulheit *f*

lazy [′lezɪ] *adj* faul

la′zybones′ *s* (coll) Faulpelz *m*

la′zy Su′san *s* drehbares Tablett *n*

lea [li] *s* (poet) Aue *f*

lead [led] *adj* Blei- ‖ *s* Blei *n*; (*in a pencil*) Mine *f*; (*plumb line*) Bleilot *n* ‖ *v* (*pret & pp* **leaded**; *ger* **leading**) *tr* verbleien; (typ) durchschießen [lid] *s* Führung *f*; (cards) Vorhand *f*; (elec) Zuführung *f*; (theat) Hauptrolle *f*; **be in the l.** an der Spitze stehen; **have the l.** die Führung haben; **take the l.** die Führung übernehmen ‖ *v* (*pret & pp*

led [led]) *tr* führen, leiten; *(to error, drinking, etc.)* verleiten; *(a parade)* anführen; *(a life)* führen; **l. astray** verführen; **l. away** wegführen; *(e.g., a criminal)* abführen; **l. back** zurückführen; **l. by the nose** an der Nase herumführen; **l. on** weiterführen; *(deceive)* täuschen; **l. the way** vorangehen ‖ *intr* führen; *(cards)* anspielen; **l. nowhere** zu nichts führen; **l. off** den Anfang machen; **l. to** hinausgehen auf *(acc)*; **l. up to** hinauswollen auf *(acc)* **where will all this l. to?** wo soll das alles hinführen?

leaden [ˈledən] *adj* bleiern; *(in color)* bleifarbig; *(sluggish)* schwerfällig; **l. sky** bleierner Himmel *m*

leader [ˈlidər] *s* Führer –in *mf*; *(of a band)* Dirigent –in *mf*; *(of a film)* Vorspann *m*; *(lead article)* Leitartikel *m*

lead′ership′ *s* Führung *f*

leading [ˈlidɪŋ] *adj (person, position, power)* führend

lead′ing ide′a *s* Leitgedanke *m*
lead′ing la′dy *s* Hauptdarstellerin *f*
lead′ing man′ *s* Hauptdarsteller *m*
leading′ ques′tion *s* Suggestivfrage *f*
lead′ing role′ *s* Hauptrolle *f*
lead′-in wire′ *s* Zuleitungsdraht *m*
lead′ pen′cil [led] *s* Bleistift *m*
lead′ pipe′ [led] *s* Bleirohr *n*
lead′ poi′soning [led] *s* Bleivergiftung *f*

leaf [lif] *s* (**leaves** [livz]) Blatt *n*; *(of a folding door)* Flügel *m*; *(of a folding table)* Tischklappe *f*; *(insertable table board)* Einlegebrett *n*; **turn over a new l.** ein neues Leben anfangen ‖ *intr*—**l. through** durchblättern

leafage [ˈlifɪdʒ] *s* Laubwerk *n*
leafless [ˈliflɪs] *adj* blattlos
leaflet [ˈliflɪt] *s* Werbeprospekt *m*, Flugblatt *n*; *(bot)* Blättchen *n*
leafy [ˈlifi] *adj (abounding in leaves)* belaubt; *(e.g., vegetables)* Blatt–

league [lig] *s* Bund *m*; *(unit of distance)* Meile *f*; *(sport)* Liga *f*; **in l. with** verbündet mit ‖ *tr* verbünden ‖ *intr* sich verbünden

League′ of Na′tions *s* Völkerbund *m*

leak [lik] *s* Leck *n*; **spring a l.** Leck bekommen; **take a l.** *(vulg)* schiffen ‖ *tr (e.g., a story to the press)* durchsickern lassen ‖ *intr (said of a container)* leck sein; *(said of a boat)* lecken; *(said of a fluid)* auslaufen; *(said of a spigot)* tropfen; **l. out** (& fig) durchsickern

leakage [ˈlikɪdʒ] *s* Lecken *n*; *(& fig)* Durchsickern *n*; *(com)* Schwund *m*; *(elec)* Streuung *f*

leaky [ˈliki] *adj* leck

lean [lin] *adj* mager ‖ *v (pret & pp* **leaned** & **leant** [lent]) *tr (against)* lehnen (an *acc* or gegen) ‖ *intr* lehnen; **l. against** sich anlehnen an *(acc)*; **l. back** sich zurücklehnen; **l. forward** sich vorbeugen; **l. on** sich stützen auf *(acc)*; **l. over** *(e.g., a railing)* sich neigen über *(acc)*; **l. toward** (fig) neigen zu

lean′ing *adj* sich neigend; *(tower)* schief ‖ *s* **(toward)** Neigung *f* (zu)

leanness [ˈlinnɪs] *s* Magerkeit *f*

lean′-to′ *s* (**-tos**) Anbau *m* mit Pultdach

lean′ years′ *spl* magere Jahre *pl*

leap [lip] *s* Sprung *m*, Satz *m*; **by leaps and bounds** sprungweise; **l. in the dark** (fig) Sprung *m* ins Ungewisse ‖ *v (pret & pp* **leaped** & **leapt** [lept]) *tr* überspringen ‖ *intr* springen; **l. at** anspringen; **l. at an opportunity** e-e Gelegenheit beim Schopf ergreifen; **l. forward** vorspringen; **l. up** emporschnellen

leap′frog′ *s* Bocksprung *m*; **play l.** Bocksprünge machen

leap′ year′ *s* Schaltjahr *n*

learn [lʌrn] *v (pret & pp* **learned** & **learnt** [lʌrnt]) *tr* lernen; *(find out)* erfahren; **l. s.th. from s.o.**

learned [ˈlʌrnɪd] *adj (person, word)* gelehrt; *(for or of scholars)* Gelehrten–

learn′ed jour′nal *s* Gelehrtenzeitschrift *f*

learn′ed soci′ety *s* Gelehrtenvereinigung *f*

learn′ed world′ *s* Gelehrtenwelt *f*

learn′ing *s (act)* Lernen *n*; *(erudition)* Gelehrsamkeit *f*

lease [lis] *s* Mietvertrag *m*; *(of land)* Pachtvertrag *m* ‖ *tr (in the role of landlord)* vermieten; *(land)* verpachten; *(in the role of tenant)* mieten; *(land)* pachten

lease′hold′ *adj* Pacht– ‖ *s* Pachtbesitz *m*

leash [liʃ] *s* Leine *f*, Hundeleine *f*; **keep on the l.** an der Leine führen; **strain at the l.** (fig) an der Leine zerren ‖ *tr* an die Leine nehmen

leas′ing *s* Miete *f*; *(of land)* Pachtung *f*; **l. out** Vermietung *f*; *(of land)* Verpachtung *f*

least [list] *adj* mindeste, wenigste ‖ *adv* am wenigsten; **l. of all** am wenigsten von allen ‖ *s* Geringste *mfn*; **at l.** mindestens, wenigstens; **at the very l.** zum mindesten; **not in the l.** nicht im mindesten

leather [ˈleðər] *adj* ledern ‖ *s* Leder *n*

leath′er bind′ing *s* Ledereinband *m*

leath′erbound′ *adj* ledergebunden

leath′erneck′ *s* (sl) Marineinfanterist *m*

leathery [ˈleðəri] *adj (e.g., steak)* (coll) lederartig

leave [liv] *s (permission)* Erlaubnis *f*; *(mil)* Urlaub *m*; **on l.** auf Urlaub; **take l. (from)** Abschied nehmen (von); **take l. of one's senses** (coll) den Verstand verlieren ‖ *v (pret & pp* **left** [left]) *tr (go away from)* verlassen; *(undone, open, etc.)* lassen; *(a message, bequest)* hinterlassen; *(a job)* aufgeben; *(a scar)* zurücklassen; *(forget)* liegenlassen, stehenlassen; *(e.g., some food for s.o.)* übriglassen; **be left** übrig sein; **l. alone** (a thing) bleibenlassen; *(a person)* in Frieden lassen; **l. behind** *(said of a deceased person)* hinterlassen; (*forget*) liegenlassen; **l. home** von zu Hause fortgehen; **l. it at that!** überlaß es mir!; **l. lying about** herumliegen lassen; **l. nothing to chance** nichts dem Zufall überlassen; **l. nothing undone** nichts unversucht lassen; **l. open** offen lassen; **l. out** auslassen; **l. standing** stehenlassen; **l.** (*e.g., work*) **undone** liegenlassen || *intr* fortgehen; (*on travels*) abreisen; (*said of vehicles*) abfahren; (*aer*) abfliegen; **l. off** (*e.g., from reading*) aufhören

leaven ['lɛvən] *s* Treibmittel *n* || *tr* säuern

leav'ening *s* Treibstoff *m*

leave' of ab'sence *s* Urlaub *m*

leave'-tak'ing *s* Abschiednehmen *n*

leavings ['livɪŋz] *spl* Überbleibsel *pl*

Leba•nese [,lɛbə'niz] *adj* libanesisch || *s* (**–nese**) Libanese *m*, Libanesin *f*

Lebanon ['lɛbənən] *s* Libanon *n*

lecher ['lɛtʃər] *s* Lüstling *m*

lecherous ['lɛtʃərəs] *adj* wollüstig

lechery ['lɛtʃəri] *s* Wollust *f*

lectern ['lɛktərn] *s* Lesepult *n*

lector ['lɛktər] *s* (eccl) Lektor *m*

lecture ['lɛktʃər] *s* Vorlesung *f*, Vortrag *m*; (coll) Standpauke *f*; **give a l. on** e–n Vortrag halten über (*acc*); **give s.o. a l.** j–m den Text lesen || *tr* (coll) abkanzeln || *intr* lesen

lecturer ['lɛktʃərər] *s* Vortragende *mf*; (*at a university*) Dozent –in *mf*

lec'ture room' *s* Hörsaal *m*

ledge [lɛdʒ] *s* Sims *m* & *n*; (*of a cliff*) Felsenriff *n*

ledger ['lɛdʒər] *s* (acct) Hauptbuch *n*

lee [li] *s* Lee *f*

leech [litʃ] *s* Blutegel *m*; (fig) Blutsauger –in *mf*

leek [lik] *s* (bot) Porree *m*, Lauch *m*

leer [lɪr] *s* lüsterner Seitenblick *m* || *intr* (**at**) lüstern schielen (nach)

leery ['lɪri] *adj* mißtrauisch; **be l. of** mißtrauen (*dat*)

lees [liz] *spl* Hefe *f*

lee' side' *s* Leeseite *f*

leeward ['liwərd] *adv* leewärts || *s* Leeseite *f*

Lee'ward Is'lands *spl* Inseln *pl* unter dem Winde

lee'way' *s* (coll) Spielraum *m*; (aer, naut) Abtrift *f*

left [lɛft] *adj* linke; (*left over*) übrig || *adv* links; **l. face!** (mil) links um! || *s* (*left hand*) Linke *f*; **on our l.** zu unserer Linken; **the l.** (pol) die Linke; **the third street to the l.** die dritte Querstraße links; **to the l.** nach links; **to the l. of** links von

left' field' *s* (baseball) linkes Außenfeld *n*

left' field'er ['fildər] *s* Spieler *m* im linken Außenfeld

left'-hand drive' *s* Linkssteuerung *f*

left'-hand'ed *adj* linkshändig; (*compliment*) fragwürdig; (*counterclockwise*) linksgängig; (*clumsy*) linkisch

left-hander ['lɛft'hændər] *s* Linkshänder –in *mf*

leftish ['lɛftɪʃ] *adj* linksgerichtet

leftist ['lɛftɪst] *s* Linksradikaler *m*; (pol) Linkspolitiker –in *mf*

left'o'ver *adj* übriggeblieben || **leftovers** *spl* Überbleibsel *pl*

left'-wing' *adj* Links-

left' wing' *s* (pol) linker Flügel *m*; (sport) Linksaußen *m*

left-winger ['lɛft'wɪŋər] *s* (coll) Linkspolitiker –in *mf*

lefty ['lɛfti] *adj* (coll) linkshändig || *s* (coll) Linkshänder –in *mf*

leg [lɛg] *s* (*of a body, of furniture, of trousers*) Bein *n*; (*stretch*) Etappe *f*; (*of a compass*) Schenkel *m*; (*of a boot*) Schaft *m*; **be on one's last legs** auf dem letzten Loche pfeifen; **pull s.o.'s leg** (coll) j–n auf die Schippe nehmen; **run one's legs off** sich abrennen; **you don't have a leg to stand on** Sie haben keinerlei Beweise

legacy ['lɛgəsi] *s* Vermächtnis *n*

legal ['ligəl] *adj* (*according to the law*) gesetzlich, legal; (*pertaining to or approved by law*) Rechts-, juristisch); **take l. action** den Rechtsweg beschreiten; **take l. steps against s.o.** gerichtlich gegen j–n vorgehen

le'gal advice' *s* Rechtsberatung *f*

le'gal advis'er *s* Rechtsberater –in *mf*

le'gal age' *s* Volljährigkeit *f*; **of l.** großjährig

le'gal aid' *s* Rechtshilfe *f*

le'gal ba'sis *s* Rechtsgrundlage *f*

le'gal case' *s* Rechtsfall *m*

le'gal claim' *s* Rechtsanspruch *m*

le'gal en'tity *s* juristische Person *f*

le'gal force' *s* Rechtskraft *f*

le'gal grounds' *spl* Rechtsgrund *m*

le'gal hol'iday *s* gesetzlicher Feiertag *m*

legality [lɪ'gælɪti] *s* Gesetzlichkeit *f*, Rechtlichkeit *f*

legalize ['ligə,laɪz] *tr* legalisieren

le'gal jar'gon *s* Kanzleisprache *f*

le'gal profes'sion *s* Rechtsanwaltsberuf *m*

le'gal rem'edy *s* Rechtsmittel *n*

le'gal ten'der *s* gesetzliches Zahlungsmittel *n*; **be l.** gelten

le'gal ti'tle *s* Rechtsanspruch *m*

legate ['lɛgɪt] *s* Legat –in *mf*

legatee [,lɛgə'ti] *s* Legatar –in *mf*

legation [lɪ'geʃən] *s* Gesandtschaft *f*

legend ['lɛdʒənd] *s* Legende *f*

legendary ['lɛdʒən,dɛri] *adj* legendär

legerdemain [,lɛdʒərdɪ'men] *s* Taschenspielerei *f*

leggings ['lɛgɪŋz] *spl* hohe Gamaschen *pl*

leggy ['lɛgi] *adj* langbeinig

Leg'horn' *s* (*chicken*) Leghorn *n*; (*town in Italy*) Livorno *n*

legibility [,lɛdʒɪ'bɪlɪti] *s* Lesbarkeit *f*

legible ['lɛdʒɪbəl] *adj* lesbar

legion ['lidʒən] *s* Legion *f*; (fig) Heerschar *f*

legionnaire [,lidʒə'nɛr] *s* Legionär *m*

legislate ['lɛdʒɪs,let] *tr* durch Gesetzgebung bewirken || *intr* Gesetze geben

legislation [,lɛdʒɪs'leʃən] *s* Gesetzgebung *f*

legislative ['ledʒɪs‚letɪv] *adj* gesetzgebend

legislator ['ledʒɪs‚letər] *s* Gesetzgeber –in *mf*

legislature ['ledʒɪs‚letʃər] *s* Legislatur *f*

legitimacy [lɪ'dʒɪtɪməsi] *s* Rechtmäßigkeit *f*

legitimate [lɪ'dʒɪtɪmɪt] *adj* gesetzmäßig, legitim; *(child)* ehelich ‖ [lɪ'dʒɪtɪ‚met] *tr* legitimieren

legit'imate the'ater *s* literarisch wertvolles Theater *n*

legitimize [lɪ'dʒɪtɪ‚maɪz] *tr* legitimieren

leg' of lamb' *s* Lammkeule *f*

leg' of mut'ton *s* Hammelkeule *f*

leg' room' *s* Beinfreiheit *f*

leg'work' *s* Vorarbeiten *pl*

leisure ['liʒər] *s* Muße *f*; **at l.** mit Muße; **at s.o.'s l.** wenn es j–m paßt

lei'sure class' *s* wohlhabende Klasse *f*

lei'sure hours' *spl* Mußestunden *pl*

leisurely ['liʒərli] *adj & adv* gemächlich

lei'sure time' *s* Freizeit *f*

lemon ['lemən] *adj* Zitronen– ‖ *s* Zitrone *f*; (sl) Niete *f*

lemonade [‚lemɪ'ned] *s* Zitronenlimonade *f*

lem'on squeez'er *s* Zitronenpresse *f*

lend [lend] *v (pret & pp* **lent** [lent]) *tr* leihen, borgen; **l. at five percent interest** zu fünf Prozent Zinsen anlegen; **l. itself to** sich eignen zu or für; **l. oneself to** sich hergeben zu; **l. out** ausleihen, verborgen; **l. s.o. a hand** j–m zur Hand gehen

lender ['lendər] *s* Verleiher –in *mf*

lend'ing li'brary *s* Leihbücherei *f*

length [leŋθ] *s* Länge *f*; *(of time)* Dauer *f*; *(in horse racing)* Pferdelänge *f*; **at great l.** sehr ausführlich; **at l.** ausführlich; *(finally)* schließlich; **at some l.** ziemlich ausführlich; **go to any l.** alles Erdenkliche tun; **go to great lengths** sich bemühen; **keep s.o. at arm's l.** zu j–m Abstand wahren; **stretch out full l.** sich der Länge nach ausstrecken

lengthen ['leŋθən] *tr* verlängern; *(a vowel)* dehnen

length'ening *s* Verlängerung *f*; (ling) Dehnung *f*

length'wise' *adj & adv* der Länge nach

lengthy ['leŋθi] *adj* langwierig

leniency ['lini‚ənsi] *s* Milde *f*

lens [lenz] *s* Linse *f*; *(combination of lenses)* Objektiv *n*

Lent [lent] *s* Fastenzeit *f*

Lenten ['lentən] *adj* Fasten–

lentil ['lentɪl] *s* (bot) Linse *f*

leopard ['lepərd] *s* Leopard *m*

leper ['lepər] *s* Aussätzige *mf*

leprosy ['leprəsi] *s* Aussatz *m*, Lepra *f*

lesbian ['lezbɪ‚ən] *adj* lesbisch ‖ *s* Lesbierin *f*

lesbianism ['lezbɪ‚ə‚nɪzəm] *s* lesbische Liebe *f*

lesion ['liʒən] *s* Wunde *f*

less [les] *comp adj* weniger, geringer;

l. and l. immer weniger ‖ *adv* weniger, minder; **l. than** weniger als ‖ *s*—**do with l.** mit weniger auskommen; **for l.** billiger; **in l. than no time** in Null Komma nichts ‖ *prep* abzüglich *(genit* or *acc)*; (arith) weniger *(acc)*, minus *(acc)*

lessee [le'si] *s* Mieter –in *mf*; *(of land)* Pächter –in *mf*

lessen ['lesən] *tr* vermindern ‖ *intr* sich vermindern, abnehmen

lesser ['lesər] *comp adj* minder, geringer

lesson ['lesən] *s* Unterrichtsstunde *f*, Stunde *f*; *(in a textbook)* Lektion *f*; *(warning)* Lehre *f*; **learn a l. from** e–e Lehre ziehen aus; **let that be l. to you!** lassen Sie sich das e–e Lehre sein

lessor ['lesər] *s* Vermieter –in *mf*; *(of land)* Verpächter –in *mf*

lest [lest] *conj* damit nicht; (after expressions of fear) daß

let [let] *v (pret & pp* **let;** *ger* **letting)** *tr* lassen; **I really let him have it!** (coll) ich hab's ihm ordentlich gegeben!; **let alone** in Ruhe lassen; *(not to mention)* geschweige denn; **let down** herunterlassen; *(disappoint)* enttäuschen; **let drop** fallen lassen; **let fly** fliegen lassen; (coll) loslassen; **let go** fortlassen, loslassen; **let go ahead** vorlassen; **let in** hereinlassen; *(water)* zuleiten; **let in on** (e.g., a *secret)* einweihen in *(acc)*; **let it go,** e.g., **I'll let it go** this time diesmal werde ich es noch hingehen lassen; **let lie** liegenlassen; **let know** wissen lassen, Bescheid geben *(dat)*; **let off** *(e.g., at the next corner)* absetzen; **let off easy** noch so davonkommen lassen; **let off scot-free** straflos laufen lassen; **let one's hair down** (fig) sich gehenlassen; **let out** *(seams, air, water)* auslassen; *(e.g., a yell)* von sich geben; **let pass** durchlassen; **let s.o. have s.th.** j–m etw zukommen lassen; **let stand** (fig) gelten lassen; **let through** durchlassen; **let things slide** die Dinge laufen lassen; **let things take their course** den Dingen ihren Lauf lassen; **let's go! los!;** **let us** (or **let's)** *(inf)*, e.g., **let's** (or **let us) sing** singen wir ‖ *intr* be rented out) *(for)* vermietet werden (für); **let fly with** (coll) loslegen mit; **let go of** loslassen; **let on that** sich *[dat]* anmerken lassen, daß; **let up** nachlassen; **let up on** (coll) ablassen von

let'down' *s* Hereinfall *m*

lethal ['liθəl] *adj* tödlich

lethargic [lɪ'θɑrdʒɪk] *adj* lethargisch

lethargy ['leθərdʒi] *s* Lethargie *f*

letter ['letər] *s* Brief *m*, Schreiben *n*; *(of the alphabet)* Buchstabe *m*; **by l.** brieflich, schriftlich; **to the l.** aufs Wort ‖ *tr* beschriften

let'ter box' *s* Briefkasten *m*

let'ter car'rier *s* Briefträger –in *mf*

let'ter drop' *s* Briefeinwurf *m*

let'tered *adj* gelehrt

let'ter file' *s* Briefordner *m*

let'terhead' s Briefkopf m
let'tering s (act) Beschriften n; (inscription) Beschriftung f
let'ter of condol'ence s Beileidsbrief m
let'ter of cred'it s Kreditbrief m
let'ter of recommenda'tion s Empfehlungsbrief m
letter o'pener s Brieföffner m
let'terper'fect adj buchstabengetreu
let'terpress' s (typ) Hochdruck m
let'ter scales' spl Briefwaage f
let'ter to the ed'itor s Leserbrief m
lettuce ['lɛtɪs] s Salat m
let'up' s Nachlassen n; without l. ohne Unterlaß
leukemia [luˈkimɪ·ə] s Leukämie f
Levant [lɪˈvænt] s Levante f
Levantine [lɪˈvæntɪn] adj levantinisch || s Levantiner –in mf
levee ['lɛvi] s Uferdamm m
lev·el ['lɛvəl] adj eben, gerade; (flat) flach; (spoonful) gestrichen; be l. with so hoch sein wie; do one's l. best sein Möglichstes tun; have a l. head ausgeglichen sein; keep a l. head e–n klaren Kopf behalten || s (& fig) Niveau n; (tool) Wasserwaage f; at higher levels höheren Ortes; be up to the usual l. (fig) auf der gewöhnlichen Höhe sein; on a l. with (& fig) auf gleicher Höhe mit; on the l. (fig) ehrlich || v (pret & pp –el[l]ed; ger –el[l]ing tr (a street, ground) planieren; l. (e.g., a rifle) at richten auf (acc); (e.g., complaints) richten gegen; l. off nivellieren; (aer) abfangen; l. to the ground dem Erdboden gleichmachen || intr—l. off sich verflachen; (said of prices) sich stabilisieren; (aer) in Horizontalflug übergehen; l. with s.o. mit j–m offen sein
lev'elhead'ed adj besonnen, vernünftig
lever ['livər] s Hebel m, Brechstange f || tr mit e–r Brechstange fortbewegen
leverage ['livərɪdʒ] s Hebelkraft f; (fig) Einfluß m
leviathan [lɪˈvaɪ·əθən] s Leviathan m
levitate ['lɛvɪˌtet] tr schweben lassen || intr frei schweben
levitation [ˌlɛvɪˈteʃən] s Schweben n
levity ['lɛvɪti] s Leichtsinn m
lev·y ['lɛvi] s Truppenaushebung f; (of taxes) Erhebung f; (tax) Steuer f || v (pret & pp –vied) tr (troops) ausheben; (taxes) erheben; l. war on Krieg führen gegen
lewd [lud] adj unzüchtig
lewdness ['ludnɪs] s Unzucht f
lexical ['lɛksɪkəl] adj lexikalisch
lexicographer [ˌlɛksɪˈkɑgrəfər] s Lexikograph –in mf
lexicographic(al) [ˌlɛksɪkəˈgræfɪk(əl)] adj lexikographisch
lexicography [ˌlɛksɪˈkɑgrəfi] s Lexikographie f
lexicology [ˌlɛksɪˈkɑlədʒi] s Wortforschung f, Lexikologie f
lexicon ['lɛksɪkən] s Wörterbuch n
liability [ˌlaɪ·əˈbɪlɪti] s (ins) Haftpflicht f; (jur) Haftung f; liabilities Schulden pl; (acct) Passiva pl

liabil'ity insur'ance s Haftpflichtversicherung f
liable ['laɪ·əbəl] adj (jur) (for) haftbar (für); be l. to (inf) (coll) leicht können (inf); l. for damages schadenersatzpflichtig
liaison [liˈɛzən] s Verbindung f; (illicit affair) Liaison f; (ling) Bindung f
liai'son of'ficer s Verbindungsoffizier m
liar ['laɪ·ər] s Lügner –in mf
libation [laɪˈbeʃən] s Opfertrank m
li·bel ['laɪbəl] s Verleumdung f; (in writing) Schmähschrift f || v (pret & pp –bel[l]ed; ger –bel[l]ing) tr verleumden
libelous ['laɪbələs] adj verleumderisch
li'bel suit' s Verleumdungsklage f
liberal ['lɪbərəl] adj (views) liberal, freisinnig; (with money) freigebig; (gift) großzügig; (interpretation) weitherzig; (education) allgemeinbildend; (pol) liberal || s Liberale mf
lib'eral arts' spl Geisteswissenschaften pl
liberalism ['lɪbərəˌlɪzəm] s Liberalismus m
liberality [ˌlɪbəˈrælɪti] s Freigebigkeit f, Großzügigkeit f
liberate ['lɪbəˌret] tr befreien; (chem) freimachen
liberation [ˌlɪbəˈreʃən] s Befreiung f; (chem) Freimachen n
liberator ['lɪbəˌretər] s Befreier –in mf
libertine ['lɪbərˌtin] s Wüstling m
liberty ['lɪbərti] s Freiheit f; take liberties sich [dat] Freiheiten herausnehmen; you are at l. to (inf) es steht Ihnen frei zu (inf)
libidinous [lɪˈbɪdɪnəs] adj wollüstig
libido [lɪˈbido] s Libido f
librarian [laɪˈbrɛrɪ·ən] s Bibliothekar –in mf
library ['laɪˌbrɛri] s Bibliothek f
li'brary card' s Benutzerkarte f
libret·to [lɪˈbreto] s (–tos) Operntext m, Libretto n
Libya ['lɪbɪ·ə] s Libyen n
Libyan ['lɪbɪ·ən] adj libysch || s Libyer –in mf
license ['laɪsəns] s Lizenz f, Genehmigung f; (document) Zulassungsschein m; (for a business, restaurant) Konzession f; (to drive) Führerschein m; (excessive liberty) Zügellosigkeit f || tr konzessionieren; (aut) zulassen
li'cense num'ber s (aut) Kennzeichen n
li'cense plate' or **tag'** s Nummernschild n
licentious [laɪˈsɛnʃəs] adj unzüchtig
lichen ['laɪkən] s (bot) Flechte f
lick [lɪk] s Lecken n || tr lecken; (thrash) (coll) wichsen; (defeat) (coll) schlagen; (said of a flame) züngeln an (dat); l. clean auslecken; l. into shape auf Hochglanz bringen; l. off ablecken; l. one's chops sich [dat] die Lippen lecken; l. s.o.'s boots vor j–m kriechen; l. up auflecken
lick'ing s Prügel pl; give s.o. a good l. j–n versohlen

licorice ['lıkərıs] s Lakritze f
lid [lıd] s Deckel m
lie [laɪ] s Lüge f; give the lie to s.o.
(or s.th.) j-n (or etw) Lügen strafen;
tell a lie lügen || v (pret & pp lied;
ger lying) tr—lie one's way out of
sich herauslügen aus || intr lügen;
lie like mad das Blaue vom Himmel
herunter lügen; lie to belügen || v
(pret lay [le]; pp lain [len]; ger
lying) intr liegen; lie down sich hin-
legen; lie down! (to a dog) leg dich!;
lie in wait auf der Lauer liegen; lie
in wait for auflauern (dat); lie low
sich versteckt halten; (bide one's
time) abwarten; take s.th. lying down
etw widerspruchslos hinnehmen
lie' detec'tor s Lügendetektor m
lien [lin] s Pfandrecht n
lieu [lu] s—in l. of statt (genit)
lieutenant [lu'tenənt] s Leutnant m;
(nav) Kapitänleutnant m
lieuten'ant colo'nel s Oberstleutnant m
lieuten'ant comman'der s Korvetten-
kapitän m
lieuten'ant gen'eral s Generalleutnant
m
lieuten'ant gov'ernor s Vizegouverneur
m
lieuten'ant jun'ior grade' s (nav) Oberleutnant m zur See
lieuten'ant sen'ior grade' s (nav) Kapitänleutnant m
life [laɪf] adj (imprisonment) lebens-
länglich || s (lives [laɪvz]) Leben n;
(e.g., of a car) Lebensdauer f; all
my l. mein ganzes Leben lang; as big
as l. in voller Lebensgröße; bring
back to l. wieder zum Bewußtsein
bringen; bring to l. ins Leben bringen; for dear l. ums liebe Leben;
for l. auf Lebenszeit; full of l. voller
Leben; I can't for the l. of me ich
kann beim besten Willen nicht; lives
lost Menschenleben pl; not on your
l. auf keinen Fall; put l. into beleben; such is l.! so ist nun mal das
Leben; take one's l. sich [dat] das
Leben nehmen; upon my l.! so wahr
ich lebe!; you can bet your l. on
that! darauf kannst du Gift nehmen!
life'-and-death' adj auf Leben und Tod
life' annu'ity s Lebensrente f
life' belt' s Schwimmgürtel m
life'blood' s Lebensblut n
life'boat' s Rettungsboot n
life' buoy' s Rettungsboje f
life' expect'ancy s Lebenserwartung f
life' guard' s (at a pool) Bademeister
–in mf; (at the shore) Strandwärter
–in mf
life' impris'onment s lebenslängliche
Haft f
life' insur'ance s Lebensversicherung f
life' jack'et s Schwimmweste f
lifeless ['laɪflıs] adj leblos; (fig)
schwunglos
life'-like' adj naturgetreu, lebensecht
life' line' s Rettungsleine f; (for a
diver) Signalleine f; (supply line)
Lebensader f
life'long' adj lebenslänglich

life' mem'ber s Mitglied n auf Lebenszeit
life' of lei'sure s Wohlleben n
life' of plea'sure s Wohlleben n
life' of Ri'ley ['raɪli] s Herrenleben n
life' of the par'ty s—be the l. die ganze
Gesellschaft unterhalten
life' preserv'er [prɪ'zɜrvər] s Rettungs-
ring m
lifer ['laɪfər] s (sl) Lebenslängliche mf
life' raft' s Rettungsfloß n
lifesaver ['laɪf‚sevər] s Rettungs-
schwimmer –in mf; (fig) rettender
Engel m
life' sen'tence s Verurteilung f zu le-
benslänglicher Haft
life'-size(d)' adj lebensgroß
life' span' s Lebensdauer f
life' style' s Lebensweise f
life'time' adj lebenslänglich || s Leben
n; for a l. auf Lebenszeit; once in a
l. einmal im Leben
life' vest' s Schwimmweste f
life'work' s Lebenswerk n
lift [lıft] s (elevator) Aufzug m; (aer
& fig) Auftrieb m; give s.o. a l. j-n
im Wagen mitnehmen || tr heben;
(gently) lüpfen; (with effort) wuchten; (weights) stemmen; (the receiver) abnehmen; (an embargo) aufheben; (steal) (sl) klauen; l. up aufheben; (the eyes) erheben; not l. a
finger keinen Finger rühren || intr
(said of a mist) steigen; l. off (rok)
starten
lift'-off' s (rok) Start m
lift' truck' s Lastkraftwagen m mit
Hebevorrichtung
ligament ['lɪgəmənt] s Band n
ligature ['lɪgətʃər] s (mus) Bindung f;
(act) (surg) Abbinden n; (filament)
(surg) Abbindungsschnur f; (typ)
Ligatur f
light [laɪt] adj (clothing, meal, music,
heart, wine, sleep, punishment,
weight) leicht; (day, beer, color,
complexion, hair) hell; as l. as day
tageshell; l. as a feather federleicht;
make l. of auf die leichte Schulter
nehmen; (belittle) als bedeutungslos
hinstellen || s Licht n; according to
his lights nach dem Maß seiner Einsicht; bring to l. ans Licht bringen;
come to l. ans Licht kommen; do
you have a l.? haben Sie Feuer?;
in the l. of im Lichte (genit), angesichts (genit); put in a false l. in ein
falsches Licht stellen; see the l. of
day (be born) das Licht der Welt
erblicken; shed l. on Licht werfen
auf (acc); throw quite a different l.
on ein ganz anderes Licht werfen
auf (acc) || v (pret & pp lighted &
lit [lıt]) tr (a fire, cigarette) anzünden; (an oven) anheizen; (a
street) beleuchten; (a hall) erleuch-
ten; (a face) aufleuchten lassen ||
intr sich entzünden; l. up (said of a
face) aufleuchten; (light a cigarette)
sich [dat] e-e Zigarette anstecken
light'-blue' adj lichtblau, hellblau
light' bulb' s Glühbirne f

light-complexioned [ˈlaɪtkəmˈplekʃənd] *adj* von heller Hautfarbe

lighten [ˈlaɪtən] *tr* (*in weight*) leichter machen; (*brighten*) erhellen; (fig) erleichtern || *intr* (*become brighter*) sich aufhellen; (*during a storm*) blitzen

lighter [ˈlaɪtər] *s* Feuerzeug *n*; (naut) Leichter *m*

ligh'ter flu'id *s* Feuerzeugbenzin *n*

light'-fin'gered *adj* geschickt; (*thievish*) langfingerig

light'-foot'ed *adj* leichtfüßig

light'-head'ed *adj* leichtsinnig; (*dizzy*) schwindlig

light'-heart'ed *adj* leichtherzig

light'-heav'y weight' *adj* (box) Halbschwergewichts– || *s* Halbschwergewichtler *m*

light'house' *s* Leuchtturm *m*

light'ing *s* Beleuchtung *f*

light'ing effects' *spl* Lichteffekte *pl*

light'ing fix'ture *s* Beleuchtungskörper *m*

lightly [ˈlaɪtli] *adv* leicht; (*without due consideration*) leichthin; (*disparagingly*) geringschätzig

light' me'ter *s* Lichtmesser *m*

lightness [ˈlaɪtnɪs] *s* (*in weight*) Leichtigkeit *f*; (*in shade*) Helligkeit *f*

lightning [ˈlaɪtnɪŋ] *s* Blitz *m* || *impers* —**it is l.** es blitzt

light'ning arrest'er [əˌrestər] *s* Blitzableiter *m*

light'ning bug' *s* Leuchtkäfer *m*

light'ning rod' *s* Blitzableiter *m*

light'ning speed' *s* Windeseile *f*

light' op'era *s* Operette *f*

light' read'ing *s* Unterhaltungslektüre *f*

light'ship' *s* Leuchtschiff *n*

light' sleep' *s* Dämmerschlaf *m*

light' switch' *s* Lichtschalter *m*

light' wave' *s* Lichtwelle *f*

light'weight' *adj* (box) Leichtgewichts– || *s* (coll) geistig Minderbemittelter *m*; (box) Leichtgewichtler *m*

light'-year' *s* Lichtjahr *n*

likable [ˈlaɪkəbəl] *adj* sympathisch, lieb

like [laɪk] *adj* gleich, ähnlich; **be l. gleichen** (*dat*) || *adv*—**l. crazy** (coll) wie verrückt || *s*—**and the l.** und dergleichen; **likes and dislikes** Neigungen und Abneigungen *pl* || *tr* gern haben, mögen; **I l. him** er ist mir sympathisch; **I l. the picture** das Bild gefällt mir; **I l. the food** das Essen schmeckt mir; **l. to** (*inf*), e.g., **I l. to read** ich lese gern || *intr*— **as you l.** wie Sie wollen; **if you l.** wenn Sie wollen || *prep* wie; **feel l.** (*ger*) Lust haben zu (*inf*); **feel l. hell** (sl) sich elend fühlen; **it looks l.** es sieht nach ... aus; **l. greased lightning** wie geschmiert; **that's just l. him** das sieht ihm ähnlich; **there's nothing l. traveling** es geht nichts übers Reisen

likelihood [ˈlaɪklɪˌhʊd] *s* Wahrscheinlichkeit *f*

likely [ˈlaɪkli] *adj* wahrscheinlich; **a l. story!** (iron) e–e glaubhafte Ge-

schichte!; **it's l. to rain** es wird wahrscheinlich regen

like'-mind'ed *adj* gleichgesinnt

liken [ˈlaɪkən] *tr* (**to**) vergleichen (mit)

likeness [ˈlaɪknɪs] *s* Ähnlichkeit *f*; **a good l. of** ein gutes Portrait (genit)

like'wise' *adv* gleichfalls, ebenso

lik'ing *s* (**for**) Zuneigung *f* (zu); **not to my l.** nicht nach meinem Geschmack; **take a l. to** Zuneigung fassen zu

lilac [ˈlaɪlək] *adj* lila || *s* Flieder *m*

lilt [lɪlt] *s* rhythmischer Schwung *m*; (*lilting song*) lustiges Lied *n*

lily [ˈlɪli] *s* Lilie *f*

lil'y of the val'ley *s* Maiglöckchen *n*

lil'y pad' *s* schwimmendes Seerosenblatt *n*

lil'y-white' *adj* lilienweiß

li'ma bean' [ˈlaɪmə] *s* Limabohne *f*

limb [lɪm] *s* Glied *n*; (*of a tree*) Ast *m*; **go out on a l.** (fig) sich exponieren; **limbs** Gliedmaßen *pl*

limber [ˈlɪmbər] *adj* geschmeidig || *tr* —**l. up** geschmeidig machen || *intr*— sich geschmeidig machen

lim·bo [ˈlɪmbo] *s* (**–bos**) Vorhölle *f*; (fig) Vergessenheit *f*

lime [laɪm] *s* Kalk *m*; (bot) Limonelle *f*

lime'kiln' *s* Kalkofen *m*

lime'light' *s* (& fig) Rampenlicht *n*

limerick [ˈlɪmərɪk] *s* Limerick *m*

lime'stone' *adj* Kalkstein– || *s* Kalkstein *m*

limit [ˈlɪmɪt] *s* Grenze *f*; **go the l.** zum Äußersten gehen; **off limits** Zutritt verboten; **set a l. to** e–e Grenze ziehen (*dat*); **that's the l.!** das ist denn doch die Höhe!; **there's a l. to everything** alles hat seine Grenzen; **within limits** in Grenzen; **without l.** schrankenlos || *tr* begrenzen; (**to**) beschränken (auf *acc*)

limitation [ˌlɪmɪˈteʃən] *s* Begrenzung *f*, Beschränkung *f*

lim'ited *adj* (**to**) beschränkt (auf acc)

lim'ited-ac'cess high'way *s* Autobahn *f*

lim'ited mon'archy *s* konstitutionelle Monarchie *f*

limitless [ˈlɪmɪtlɪs] *adj* grenzenlos

limousine [ˈlɪməˌzin], [ˌlɪməˈzin] *s* Limousine *f*

limp [lɪmp] *adj* (& fig) schlaff || *s* Hinken *n*; **walk with a l.** hinken || *intr* (& fig) hinken

limpid [ˈlɪmpɪd] *adj* durchsichtig

linchpin [ˈlɪntʃˌpɪn] *s* Achsnagel *m*

linden [ˈlɪndən] *s* Linde *f*, Lindenbaum *m*

line [laɪn] *s* Linie *f*, Strich *m*; (*boundary*) Grenze *f*; (*of a page*) Zeile *f*; (*of verse*) Verszeile *f*; (*of a family*) Zweig *m*; (*sphere of activity*) Fach *n*; (*e.g., of a streetcar*) Linie *f*, Strecke *f*; (*wrinkle*) Furche *f*; (*of articles for sale*) Sortiment *n*; (*for wash*) Leine *f*; (*queue*) Schlange *f*; (sl) zungenfertiges Gerede *n*; (angl) Schnur *f*; (mil) Linie *f*, Front *f*; (telp) Leitung *f*; **all along the l.** (fig) auf der ganzen Linie; **along the lines** *m* of nach dem Muster von; **draw the l.** (at) (fig) e-e Grenze ziehen (bei); **fall into l.** sich einfügen; **forget one's lines** (theat) steckenbleiben; **form a l.** sich in e-r Reihe aufstellen; **get a l. on** (coll) herausklamüsern; **give s.o. a l.** (sl) j-m schöne Worte machen; **hold the l.** die Stellung halten; (telp) am Apparat bleiben; **in l. of duty** im Dienst; **in l. with** in Übereinstimmung mit; **keep in l.** in der Reihe bleiben; **keep s.o. in l.** j-n im Zaum halten; **stand in l.** Schlange stehen; **the l. is busy** (telp) Leitung besetzt! ‖ *tr* linieren; (*e.g.*, *a coat*) füttern; (*a face*) furchen; (*a drawer*) ausschlagen; (*a wall*) verkleiden; **l. one's purse** sich [*dat*] den Beutel spicken; **l. the streets** in den Straßen Spalier bilden; **l. up** ausrichten; (mil) aufstellen ‖ *intr*—**l. up** Schlange stehen; (mil) antreten; **l. up for** sich anstellen nach

lineage ['lɪnɪ-ɪdʒ] *s* Abkunft *f*, Abstammung *f*

lineal ['lɪnɪ-əl] *adj* (*descent*) direkt; (*linear*) geradlinig

lineaments ['lɪnɪ-əmənts] *spl* Gesichtszüge *pl*

linear ['lɪnɪ-ər] *adj* (*arranged in a line*) geradlinig; (*involving a single dimension*) Längen-; (*using lines*) Linien-; (math) linear

lined' pa'per *s* Linienpapier *n*

line'man *s* (-men) (rr) Streckenwärter *m*; (telp) Telephonarbeiter *m*

linen ['lɪnən] *adj* Leinen- ‖ *s* Leinen *n*; (*in the household*) Wäsche *f*; (*of the bed*) Bettwäsche *f*; **linens** Weißzeug *n*; **put fresh l. on the bed** das Bett überziehen

lin'en clos'et *s* Wäscheschrank *m*

lin'en cloth' *s* Leinwand *f*

lin'en goods' *spl* Weißwaren *pl*

line' of approach' *s* (aer) Anflugschneise *f*

line' of bus'iness *s* Geschäftszweig *m*

line' of communica'tion *s* Verbindungslinie *f*

line' of fire' *s* Schußlinie *f*

line' of sight' *s* (*of a gun*) Visierlinie *f*; (astr) Sichtlinie *f*

liner ['laɪnər] *s* Einsatz *m*; (naut) Linienschiff *n*

lines'man *s* (-men) (sport) Linienrichter *m*

line'up' *s* (*at a police station*) Gegenüberstellung *f*; (sport) Aufstellung *f*

linger ['lɪŋgər] *intr* (*tarry*) verweilen; (*said of memories*) nachwirken; (*said of a melody*) nachtönen; **l. over** verweilen bei

lingerie [ˌlænʒə'ri] *s* Damenunterwäsche *f*

lin'gering *adj* (*disease*) schleichend; (*tune*) nachklingend; (*memory, taste, feeling*) nachwirkend

lingo ['lɪŋgo] *s* Kauderwelsch *n*

linguist ['lɪŋgwɪst] *s* Sprachwissenschaftler –in *mf*

linguistic [lɪŋ'gwɪstɪk] *adj* (*e.g.*, *skill*) sprachlich; (*of linguistics*) sprach-

wissenschaftlich ‖ **linguistics** *s* Sprachwissenschaft *f*

liniment ['lɪnɪmənt] *s* Einreibemittel *n*

lin'ing *s* (*of a coat*) Futter *n*; (*of a brake*) Bremsbelag *m*; (*e.g.*, *of a wall*) Verkleidung *f*

link [lɪŋk] *s* Glied *n*; (fig) Bindeglied *n* ‖ *tr* verbinden; (fig) verketten; **l. to** verbinden mit; (fig) in Verbindung bringen mit ‖ *intr*—**l. up** (rok) dokken; **l. up with** sich anschließen an (acc)

linnet ['lɪnɪt] *s* (orn) Hänfling *m*

linoleum [lɪ'nolɪ-əm] *s* Linoleum *n*

linotype ['laɪnə,taɪp] *s* (trademark) Linotype *f*

lin'seed oil' ['lɪn,sid] *s* Leinöl *n*

lint [lɪnt] *s* Fussel *f*

lintel ['lɪntəl] *s* Sturz *m*

lion ['laɪ-ən] *s* Löwe *m*

li'on cage' *s* Löwenzwinger *m*

lioness ['laɪ-ənɪs] *s* Löwin *f*

lionize ['laɪ-ə,naɪz] *tr* zum Helden des Tages machen

li'ons' den' *s* Löwengrube *f*

li'on's share' *s* Löwenanteil *m*

li'on tam'er *s* Löwenbändiger –in *mf*

lip [lɪp] *s* Lippe *f*; (*edge*) Rand *m*; **bite one's lips** sich auf die Lippen beißen; **smack one's lips** sich [*dat*] die Lippen lecken

lip' read'ing *s* Lippenlesen *n*

lip' serv'ice *s* Lippenbekenntnis *n*; **pay l.** to ein Lippenbekenntnis ablegen zu

lip'stick' *s* Lippenstift *m*

lique-fy ['lɪkwɪ,faɪ] *v* (*pret & pp* –fied) *tr* verflüssigen ‖ *intr* sich verflüssigen

liqueur [lɪ'kʌr] *s* Likör *m*

liquid ['lɪkwɪd] *adj* flüssig; (*clear*) klar ‖ *s* Flüssigkeit *f*

liq'uid as'sets *spl* flüssige Mittel *pl*

liquidate ['lɪkwɪ,det] *tr* (*a debt*) tilgen; (*an account*) abrechnen; (*a company*) liquidieren

liquidation [ˌlɪkwɪ'deʃən] *s* (*of a debt*) Tilgung *f*; (*of an account*) Abrechnung *f*; (*of a company*) Liquidation *f*

liquidity [lɪ'kwɪdɪti] *s* flüssiger Zustand *m*; (fin) Liquidität *f*

liq'uid meas'ure *s* Hohlmaß *n*

liquor ['lɪkər] *s* Spirituosen *pl*, Schnaps *m*; **have a shot of l.** einen zwitschern

liquorice ['lɪkərɪs] *s* Lakritze *f*

li'quor li'cense *s* Schankerlaubnis *f*

Lisbon ['lɪzbən] *s* Lissabon *n*

lisp [lɪsp] *s* Lispeln *n* ‖ *tr & intr* lispeln

lissome ['lɪsəm] *adj* biegsam, gelenkig

list [lɪst] *s* Liste *f*, Verzeichnis *n*; (naut) Schlagseite *f*; **enter the lists** (& fig) in die Schranken treten; **make a l.** of verzeichnen ‖ *tr* verzeichnen ‖ *intr* (naut) Schlagseite haben

listen ['lɪsən] *intr* horchen, zuhören; **l. closely** die Ohren aufsperren; **l. for** achten auf (acc); **l. in** mithören; **l. to** zuhören (*dat*); (*a thing*) horchen auf (acc); (*obey*) gehorchen (*dat*); (*take advice from*) hören auf (acc); **l. to reason** auf e-n Rat hören; **l. to the radio** Radio hören

listener ['lɪsənər] *s* Zuhörer –in *mf;* (rad) Rundfunkhörer –in *mf*

lis'tening *adj* Abhör–, Horch–

lis'tening post' *s* Horchposten *m*

listless ['lɪstlɪs] *adj* lustlos

list' price' *s* Listenpreis *m*

litany ['lɪtəni] *s* (& fig) Litanei *f*

liter ['litər] *s* Liter *m & n*

literacy ['lɪtərəsi] *s* Kenntnis *f* des Lesens und Schreibens

literal ['lɪtərəl] *adj* buchstäblich; (*person*) pedantisch; **l. sense** wörtlicher Sinn *m*

literally ['lɪtərəli] *adv* buchstäblich

literary ['lɪtə,reri] *adj* literarisch; **l. language** Literatursprache *f;* **l. reference** Schrifttumsangabe *f*

literate ['lɪtərɪt] *adj* des Lesens und des Schreibens kundig; (*educated*) gebildet || *s* Gebildete *mf*

literati [,lɪtə'rɑti] *spl* Literaten *pl*

literature ['lɪtərət/ər] *s* Literatur *f;* (com) Drucksachen *pl*

lithe [laɪð] *adj* gelenkig

lithia ['lɪθɪ·ə] *s* (chem) Lithiumoxyd *n*

lithium ['lɪθɪ·əm] *s* Lithium *n*

lithograph ['lɪθə,græf] *s* Steindruck *m* || *tr* lithographieren

lithographer [lɪ'θɑgrəfər] *s* Lithograph –in *mf*

lithography [lɪ'θɑgrəfi] *s* Steindruck *m*, Lithographie *f*

Lithuania [,lɪθu'eni·ə] *s* Litauen *n*

Lithuanian [,lɪθu'eni·ən] *adj* litauisch || *s* Litauer –in *mf;* (*language*) Litauisch *n*

litigant ['lɪtɪgənt] *adj* prozessierend; **the l. parties** die streitenden Parteien || *s* Prozeßführer –in *mf*

litigate ['lɪtɪ,get] *tr* prozessieren gegen || *intr* prozessieren

litigation [,lɪtɪ'geʃən] *s* Rechtsstreit *m*

lit'mus pa'per ['lɪtməs] *s* Lackmuspapier *n*

litter ['lɪtər] *s* (*stretcher*) Tragbahre *f;* (*bedding for animals*) Streu *f;* (*of pigs, dogs*) Wurf *m;* (*trash*) herumliegender Abfall *m;* (hist) Sänfte *f* || *tr* verunreinigen || *intr* (*bear young*) werfen; (*strew litter*) Abfälle wegwerfen; **no littering!** das Wegwerfen von Abfällen ist verboten!

lit'terbug' *s*—**don't be a l.** wirf keine Abfälle weg

little ['lɪtəl] *adj* (*in size*) klein; (*in amount*) wenig || *adv* wenig; **l. by l.** nach und nach || *s*—**after a l.** nach kurzer Zeit; **a l.** ein wenig, ein bißchen; **make l. of** wenig halten von

Lit'tle Bear' *s* Kleiner Bär *m*

Lit'tle Dip'per *s* Kleiner Wagen *m*, Kleiner Bär *m*

lit'tle fin'ger *s* kleiner Finger *m*

lit'tle peo'ple *s* kleine Leute *pl;* (myth) Heinzelmännchen *pl*

Lit'tle Red Rid'inghood' *s* Rotkäppchen *n*

lit'tle slam' *s* (cards) Klein-Schlemm *m*

liturgic(al) [lɪ'tʌrdʒɪk(əl)] *adj* liturgisch

liturgy ['lɪtərdʒi] *s* Liturgie *f*

livable ['lɪvəbəl] *adj* (*place*) wohnlich; (*life*) erträglich

live [laɪv] *adj* lebendig; (*coals*) glühend; (*ammunition*) scharf; (elec) stromführend; (rad, telv) live; **l. program** Originalsendung *f* || *adv* (rad, telv) live || [lɪv] *tr* leben; (*a life*) führen; **l. down** durch einwandfreien Lebenswandel vergessen machen; **l. it up** (coll) das Leben genießen; **l. out** (*survive*) überleben || *intr* (*reside*) wohnen; (*reside temporarily*) sich aufhalten; **l. and learn!** man lernt nie aus!; **l. for the moment** in den Tag hineinleben; **l. high off the hog** in Saus und Braus leben; **l. off s.o.** j–m auf der Tasche liegen; **l. on** (*subsist on*) sich nähren von; (*continue to live*) fortleben; **l. through** durchmachen; **l. to see** erleben; **l. up to** gerecht werden (*dat*)

livelihood ['laɪvlɪ,hʊd] *s* Lebensunterhalt *m*

liveliness ['laɪvlɪnɪs] *s* Lebhaftigkeit *f*

livelong ['lɪv,lɔŋ] *adj*—**all the l. day** den lieben langen Tag

lively ['laɪvli] *adj* lebhaft; (*street*) belebt

liven ['laɪvən] *tr* aufmuntern || *intr* munter werden

liver ['lɪvər] *s* (anat) Leber *f*

liverwurst ['lɪvər,wʌrst] *s* Leberwurst *f*

livery ['lɪvəri] *s* Livree *f*

liv'ery sta'ble *s* Mietstallung *f*

live' show' [laɪv] *s* Originalsendung *f*, Livesendung *f*

livestock ['laɪv,stɑk] *s* Viehstand *m*

live' wire' [laɪv] *s* geladener Draht *m;* (coll) energiegeladener Mensch *m*

livid ['lɪvɪd] *adj* bleifarben; (*enraged*) wütend

living ['lɪvɪŋ] *adj* lebend, lebendig; (*for living*) Wohn–; **not a l. soul** keine Muttersele *f* || *s* Unterhalt *n;* **good l.** Wohlleben *n;* **make a l.** (as) sein Auskommen haben (als); **what do you do for a l.?** wie verdienen Sie Ihren Lebensunterhalt?

liv'ing accommoda'tions *spl* Unterkunft *f*

liv'ing be'ing *s* Lebewesen *n*

liv'ing condi'tions *spl* Lebensbedingungen *pl*

liv'ing expens'es *spl* Unterhaltskosten *pl*

liv'ing quar'ters *spl* Unterkunft *f*

liv'ing room' *s* Wohnzimmer *n*

liv'ing-room set' (or **suite'**) *s* Polstergarnitur *f*

liv'ing space' *s* Lebensraum *m*

liv'ing wage' *s* Existenzminimum *n*

lizard ['lɪzərd] *s* Eidechse *f*

load [lod] *s* Last *f,* Belastung *f;* (*in a truck*) Fuhre *f;* **get a l. of that!** schau dir das mal an!; **have a l. on** (sl) einen sitzen haben; **loads of** (coll) Mengen von; **that's a l. off my mind** mir ist dabei ein Stein vom Herzen gefallen || *tr* (*a truck, gun*) laden; (*cargo on a ship*) einladen; (*with work*) überladen; (*with worries*) belasten; **l. down** belasten; **l. the cam-**

era den Film einlegen; **l. up** aufladen || *intr* das Gewehr laden

load′ed *adj* (*rifle*) scharf geladen; (*dice*) falsch; (*question*) verfänglich; (*very rich*) (sl) steinreich; (*drunk*) (sl) sternhagelvoll; **fully l.** (aut) mit allen Schikanen

loader [′lodər] *s* (*worker*) Ladearbeiter –in *mf*; (*device*) Verladevorrichtung *f*

load′ing *s* Ladung *f*, Verladung *f*

load′ing plat′form *s* Ladebühne *f*

load′ing ramp′ *s* Laderampe *f*

load′ lim′it *s* Tragfähigkeit *f*; (elec) Belastungsgrenze *f*

load′stone′ *s* Magneteisenstein *m*

loaf [lof] *s* (**loaves** [lovz]) Laib *m* || *intr* faulenzen; **l. around** herumlungern

loafer [′lofər] *s* Faulenzer *m*

loaf′ing *s* Faulenzen *n*

loam [lom] *s* Lehm *m*

loamy [′lomi] *adj* lehmig

loan [lon] *s* Anleihe *f*, Darlehe(n) *n* || *tr* (ver)leihen, borgen; **l. out** leihen

loan′ com′pany *s* Leihanstalt *f*

loan′ shark′ *s* (coll) Wucherer *m*

loan′ word′ *s* Lehnwort *n*

loath [loθ] *adj*—**be l. to** (*inf*) abgeneigt sein zu (*inf*)

loathe [loð] *tr* verabscheuen

loathing [′loðɪŋ] *s* (*for*) Abscheu *m* (vor *dat*)

loathsome [′loðsəm] *adj* abscheulich

lob [lab] *s* (tennis) Lobball *m* || *v* (*pret & pp* **lobbed**; *ger* **lobbing**) *tr* lobben, hochschlagen

lob·by [′labi] *s* (*of a hotel or theater*) Vorhalle *f*, Foyer *n*; (pol) Interessengruppe *f* || *v* (*pret & pp* –**bied**) *intr* antichambrieren

lob′bying *s* Beeinflussung *f* von Abgeordneten, Lobbying *n*

lobbyist [′labɪ·ɪst] *s* Lobbyist –in *mf*

lobe [lob] *s* (anat) Lappen *m*

lobster [′labstər] *s* Hummer *m*; **red as a l.** (fig) krebsrot

local [′lokəl] *adj* örtlich, Orts–; (*produce*) heimisch || *s* (*group*) Ortsgruppe *f*; (rr) Personenzug *m*

lo′cal anesthe′sia *s* Lokalanästhese *f*

lo′cal call′ *s* (telp) Ortsgespräch *n*

lo′cal col′or *s* Lokalkolorit *n*

lo′cal deliv′ery *s* Ortszustellung *f*

locale [lo′kæl] *s* Ort *m*

lo′cal gov′ernment *s* Gemeindeverwaltung *f*

locality [lo′kælɪti] *s* Örtlichkeit *f*

localize [′lokə‚laɪz] *tr* lokalisieren

lo′cal news′ *s* Lokalnachrichten *pl*

lo′cal pol′itics *s* Kommunalpolitik *f*

lo′cal show′er *s* Strichregen *m*

lo′cal tax′ *s* Gemeindesteuer *f*

lo′cal time′ *s* Ortszeit *f*

lo′cal traf′fic *s* Nahverkehr *m*, Ortsverkehr *m*

locate [lo′ket], [′loket] *tr* (*find*) ausfindig machen; (*a ship, aircraft*) orten; (*the trouble*) finden, feststellen; (*set up, e.g., an office*) errichten; **be located** liegen, gelegen sein || *intr* sich niederlassen

location [lo′keʃən] *s* Lage *f*; **on l.** (cin) auf Außenaufnahme

lock [lak] *s* Schloß *n*; (*of hair*) Locke *f*; (*of a canal*) Schleuse *f*; **l., stock, and barrel** mit allem Drum und Dran; **under l. and key** unter Verschluß || *tr* zusperren; (*arms*) verschränken; **l. in** einsperren; **l. out** aussperren; **l. up** (*a house*) zusperren; (*imprison*) einsperren || *intr* (*said of a lock*) zuschnappen; (*said of brakes*) sperren; **l. together** (*said of bumpers*) sich ineinander verhaken

locker [′lakər] *s* (*as in a gym or barracks*) Spind *m & n*; (*for luggage*) Schließfach *n*

lock′er room′ *s* Umkleideraum *m*

locket [′lakɪt] *s* Medaillon *n*

lock′jaw′ *s* Maulsperre *f*

lock′ nut′ *s* Gegenmutter *f*

lock′out′ *s* Aussperrung *f*

lock′smith′ *s* Schlosser –in *mf*

lock′smith shop′ *s* Schlosserei *f*

lock′ step′ *s* Marschieren *n* in dicht geschlossenen Gliedern

lock′ stitch′ *s* Kettenstich *m*

lock′up′ *s* (coll) Gefängnis *n*

lock′ wash′er *s* Sicherungsring *m*

locomotion [‚lokə′moʃən] *s* (act) Fortbewegung *f*; (*power*) Fortbewegungsfähigkeit *f*

locomotive [‚lokə′motɪv] *s* Lokomotive *f*

lo·cus [′lokəs] *s* (–**ci** [saɪ]) Ort *m*; (geom) geometrischer Ort *m*

locust [′lokəst] *s* (*black locust*) (bot) Robinie *f*; (*carob*) (bot) Johannisbrotbaum *m*; (Cicada) (ent) Zikade *f*

lode [lod] *s* (min) Gang *m*

lode′star′ *s* Leitstern *m*

lodge [ladʒ] *s* (*of Masons*) Loge *f*; (*for hunting*) Jagdhütte *f*; (*for weekending*) Wochenendhäuschen *n*; (*summer house*) Sommerhäuschen *n* || *tr* unterbringen; **l. a complaint** e–e Beschwerde einreichen || *intr* wohnen; (*said of an arrow, etc.*) steckenbleiben

lodger [′ladʒər] *s* Untermieter –in *mf*

lodg′ing *s* Unterkunft *f*; **lodgings** Logis *n*

loft [laft] *s* Speicher *m*; (*for hay*) Heuboden *m*; (*of a church*) Chor *m*; (*of a golf club*) Hochschlaghaltung *f* || *tr* (*a golf club*) in Hochschlaghaltung bringen; (*a golf ball*) hochschlagen

loftiness [′loftɪnɪs] *s* Erhabenheit *f*

lofty [′lofti] *adj* (*style*) erhaben; (*high*) hochragend; (*elevated in rank*) gehoben; (*haughty*) anmaßend

log [lag] *s* (*trunk*) Baumstamm *m*; (*for the fireplace*) Holzklotz *m*; (*record book*) Tagebuch *n*; (aer, naut) Log *n*; **sleep like a log** wie ein Klotz schlafen || *v* (*pret & pp* **logged**; *ger* **logging**) *tr* (*trees*) fällen und abästen; (*cut into logs*) in Klötze schneiden; (*an area*) abholzen; (*enter into a logbook*) in das Logbuch eintragen; (*traverse*) zurücklegen

logarithm [′logə‚rɪðəm] *s* Logarithmus *m*

log'book' *s* (aer, naut) Logbuch *n*
log' cab'in *s* Blockhaus *n*, Blockhütte *f*
logger ['lɔgər] *s* Holzfäller *m*
log'gerhead' *s*—**at loggerheads** auf Kriegsfuß
log'ging *s* Holzarbeit *f*
logic ['lɑdʒɪk] *s* Logik *f*
logical ['lɑdʒɪkəl] *adj* logisch
logician [lo'dʒɪʃən] *s* Logiker –in *mf*
logistic(al) [lo'dʒɪstɪk(əl)] *adj* logistisch
logistics [lo'dʒɪstɪks] *s* Logistik *f*
log'jam' *s* aufgestaute Baumstämme *pl;* (fig) völlige Stockung *f*
log'wood' *s* Kampescheholz *n*
loin [lɔɪn] *s* (*of beef*) Lendenstück *n;* (anat) Lende *f;* **gird up one's loins** (fig) sich rüsten
loin'cloth' *s* Lendentuch *n*
loin' end' *s* (*of pork*) Rippenstück *n*
loiter ['lɔɪtər] *tr*—**l. away** vertrödeln ‖ *intr* trödeln; (*hang around*) herumlungern
loiterer ['lɔɪtərər] *s* Bummler –in *mf*
loi'tering *s* Trödelei *f;* **no l.** Herumlungern verboten!
loll [lɑl] *intr* sich bequem ausstrecken
lollipop ['lɑlɪ‚pɑp] *s* Lutschbonbon *m & n*
Lombardy ['lʌmbərdi] *s* die Lombardei
London ['lʌndən] *adj* Londoner ‖ *s* London *n*
Londoner ['lʌndənər] *s* Londoner –in *mf*
lone [lon] *adj* (*sole*) alleinig; (*solitary*) einzelstehend
loneliness ['lonlɪnɪs] *s* Einsamkeit *f*
lonely ['lonli] *adj* einsam; **become l.** vereinsamen
loner ['lonər] *s* Einzelgänger *m*
lonesome ['lonsəm] *adj* einsam; **be l. for** sich sehnen nach
lone' wolf' *s* (fig) Einzelgänger *m*
long [lɔŋ] *adj* (**longer** ['lɔŋgər]; **longest** ['lɔŋgɪst]) lang; (*way, trip*) weit; (*detour*) groß; **a l. time** lange; **a l. time since** schon lange her, daß; **in the l. run** auf die Dauer ‖ *adv* lange; **as l. as** so lange wie; **but not for l.** aber nicht lange; **l. after** lange nach; **l. ago** vor langer Zeit; **l. live ...!** es lebe ...!; **l. since** längst; **so l.!** bis dann! ‖ *intr*—**l. for** sich sehnen nach; **l. to** (*inf*) sich danach sehnen zu (*inf*)
long'boat' *s* Pinasse *f*
long' dis'tance *s* (telp) Ferngespräch *n;* **call l.** ein Ferngespräch anmelden
long'-dis'tance *adj* (sport) Langstrecken-
long'-dis'tance call' *s* Ferngespräch *n*
long'-dis'tance flight' *s* Langstreckenflug *m*
long'-drawn'-out' *adj* ausgedehnt; (*story*) langatmig
longevity [lɑn'dʒɛvɪti] *s* Langlebigkeit *f*
long' face' *s* langes Gesicht *n*
long'hair' *adj* (fig) intellektuell ‖ *s* (fig) Intellektueller *m;* (mus) (coll) konservativer Musiker *m*
long'hand' *s* Langschrift *f;* **in l.** mit der Hand geschrieben

long'ing *adj* sehnsüchtig ‖ *s* (**for**) Sehnsucht *f* (nach)
longitude ['lɑndʒɪ‚t(j)ud] *s* Länge *f*
longitudinal [‚lɑndʒɪ't(j)udɪnəl] *adj* Longitudinal–
long' jump' *s* Weitsprung *m*
long-lived ['lɔŋ'laɪvd] *adj* langlebig
long'-play'ing rec'ord *s* Langspielplatte *f*
long'-range' *adj* (*plan*) auf lange Sicht; (aer) Langstrecken-
long'shore'man *s* (**–men**) Hafenarbeiter *m*
long' shot' *s* (coll) riskante Wette *f;* **by a l.** bei weitem
long'stand'ing *adj* althergebracht, alt
long'-suf'fering *adj* langmütig
long' suit' *s* (fig) Stärke *f;* (cards) lange Farbe *f*
long'-term' *adj* langfristig
long-winded ['lɔŋ'wɪndɪd] *adj* langatmig
look [lʊk] *s* (*glance*) Blick *m;* (*appearance*) Aussehen *n;* (*expression*) Ausdruck *m;* **from the looks of things** wie die Sache aussieht; **give a second l.** sich [*dat*] genauer ansehen; **have a l. around** Umschau halten; **have a l. at s.th.** sich [*dat*] etw ansehen; **I don't like the looks of it** die Sache gefällt mir nicht; **looks** Ansehen *n;* **new l.** verändertes Aussehen *n;* (*latest style*) neueste Mode *f;* **take a l. at s.th.** sich [*dat*] etw ansehen ‖ *intr* **l. his age** man sieht ihm sein Alter an; **l. one's best** sich in bester Verfassung zeigen; **l. one's last at** zum letzten Mal ansehen; **l. s.o. in the eye** j–m in die Augen sehen; **l. s.o. over** j–n mustern; **l. s.th. over** etw (über)prüfen (or durchsehen); **l. up** (*e.g., a word*) nachschlagen; (*e.g., a friend*) aufsuchen; **l. up and down** von oben bis unten mustern ‖ *intr* (*appear, seem*) aussehen; **l. after** (*e.g., children*) betreuen; (*a household, business*) besorgen; (*a departing person*) nachblicken (*dat*); **l. ahead** vorausschauen; **l. around** (**for**) sich [*dat*] umsehen (nach); **l. at** anschauen (*acc*); **l. back (on)** zurücksehen (auf *acc*); **l. down** herabsehen; (*cast the eyes down*) die Augen niederschlagen; **l. down on** herabsehen auf (*acc*); (*in contempt*) über die Achseln ansehen; **l. for** suchen; (*e.g., a criminal*) fahnden nach; **l. forward to** sich freuen auf (*acc*); **l. hard at** scharf ansehen; **l. into** (*a mirror, the future*) blicken in (*acc*); (*a matter*) nachgehen (*dat*); **l. like** gleichen (*dat*); (*e.g., rain*) aussehen nach; **l. on** zuschauen; **l. on s.o. as** j–n betrachten als; **l. out** aufpassen; **l. out for** ausschauen nach; **l. out on** (*a view*) hinausgehen auf (*acc*); **l. over** hinwegsehen über (*acc*); **l. sharp!** jetzt aber hoppla!; **l. through** (*s.o. or s.o.'s motives*) durchschauen; **l. up** (*raise one's gaze*) aufschauen; **l. up to s.o.** zu j–m hinaufsehen; **things**

are beginning to l. up es wird langsam besser; **things don't l. so good for** est steht übel mit; **what does he l. like?** wie sieht er aus?

look'ing glass' s Spiegel m

look'out' s (*watchman*) Wachposten m; (*observation point*) Ausguck m; (*matter of concern*) Sache f; **be a l.** Schmiere stehen; **be on the l. (for)** Auschau halten (*nach*)

look'out' man' s—**be the l.** Schmiere stehen

look'out tow'er s Aussichtsturm m

loom [lum] s Webstuhl m || intr undeutlich und groß auftauchen; **l. large** von großer Bedeutung scheinen

loon [lun] s (orn) Taucher m

loony ['luni] adj verrückt; **be l.** spinnen

loop [lup] s Schleife f, Schlinge f; (e.g., on a dress for a hook) Öse f; (aer) Looping m; **do a l.** (aer) e-n Looping drehen || tr schlingen || intr Schlingen (or Schleifen) bilden

loop'hole' s Guckloch n; (in a fortification) Schießscharte f; (in a law) Lücke f

loose [lus] adj locker, los; (wobbly) wackelig; (morally) locker, unsolid; (unpacked) unverpackt; (translation) frei; (interpretation) frei; (dress, tongue) lose; (skin) schlaff; **l. connection** (elec) Wackelkontakt m || adv—**break l.** (from an enclosure) ausbrechen; (e.g., from a hitching) sich losmachen; (said of a storm, hell) losbrechen; **come l.** losgehen; **cut l.** (act up) (coll) außer Rand und Band geraten; **turn l.** befreien; **work l.** sich lockern; (said of a button) abgehen; (said of a brick, stone, shoestring) sich lösen || s—**on the l.** ungehemmt, frei || tr (a boat) losmachen; (a knot) lösen

loose' change' s Kleingeld n

loose' end' s (fig) unerledigte Kleinigkeit f; **at loose ends** im ungewissen

loose'-leaf note'book s Loseblattbuch n

loosen ['lusən] tr lockern, locker machen || intr locker werden

looseness ['lusnɪs] s Lockerheit f

loot [lut] s Beute f || tr erbeuten; (plunder) plündern; (e.g., art treasures) verschleppen

lop [lap] v (pret & pp lopped; ger lopping) tr—**lop off** abhacken

lope [lop] s Trab m || intr—**l. along** in großen Schritten laufen

lop'sid'ed adj schief; (score) einseitig

loquacious [loˈkweʃəs] adj geschwätzig

lord [lɔrd] s Herr m; (Brit) Lord m; **Lord Herrgott** m || tr—**l. it over** sich als Herr aufspielen über (acc)

lordly ['lɔrdli] adj würdig; (haughty) hochmütig

Lord's' Day' s Tag m des Herrn

lord'ship' s Herrschaft f

Lord's' Prayer' s Vaterunser n

Lord's' Sup'per s heiliges Abendmahl n

lore [lor] s Kunde f; (traditional wisdom) überlieferte Kunde f

lorry ['lɔri] s (Brit) Lastkraftwagen m

lose [luz] v (pret & pp lost [lɔst]) tr verlieren; (several minutes, as a clock does) zurückbleiben; (in betting) verwetten; (in gambling) verspielen; (the page in a book) verblättern; **l. one's way** sich verirren; (on foot) sich verlaufen; (by car) sich verfahren || intr verlieren; (sport) geschlagen werden; **l. to** (sport) unterliegen (dat)

loser ['luzər] s Unterlegene mf; **be the l.** im länger Nase abziehen

los'ing adj verlierend; (com) verlustbringend || **losings** spl Verluste pl

los'ing game' s aussichtsloses Spiel n

loss [lɔs] s (in) Verlust m (an dat); **at a l.** in Verlegenheit; (com) mit Verlust; **be at a l. for words** nach Worten suchen; **inflict l. on s.o.** j-m Schaden zufügen; **l. of appetite** Appetitlosigkeit f; **l. of blood** Blutverlust m; **l. of face** Blamage f; **l. of life** Verluste pl an Menschenleben; **l. of memory** Gedächtnisverlust m; **l. of sight** Erblindung f; **l. of time** Zeitverlust m; **straight l.** Barverlust m

lost [lɔst] adj verloren; **be l.** (said of a thing) verlorengehen; (not know one's way) sich verirrt haben; **be l. on s.o.** auf j-n keinen Eindruck machen; **get l. in** Verlust geraten; **get l.!** hau ab!; **l. in thought** in Gedanken versunken

lost'-and-found' depart'ment s Fundbüro n

lost' cause' s aussichtslose Sache f

lot [lat] s (fate) Los n, Schicksal n; (in a drawing) Los n; (portion of land) Grundstück n; (cin) Filmgelände n; (com) Posten m, Partie f; **a lot** viel, sehr; **a lot of** (or **lots of**) viel(e); **the lot** das Ganze

lotion ['loʃən] s Wasser n

lottery ['latəri] s Lotterie f

lot'tery tick'et s Lotterielos n

lotto ['lato] s Lotto n

lotus ['lotəs] s Lotos m

loud [laʊd] adj laut; (colors) schreiend

loud-mouthed ['laʊdˌmaʊðd] adj laut

loud'speak'er s Lautsprecher m

lounge [laʊndʒ] s Aufenthaltsraum m || intr sich recken; **l. around** herumlungern

lounge' chair' s Klubsessel m

lounge' liz'ard s (sl) Salonlöwe m

louse [laʊs] s (lice [laɪs]) Laus f; (sl) Sauhund m || tr—**l. up** (sl) versauen

lousy ['laʊzi] adj verlaust; (sl) lausig; **l. with** (people) wimmelnd von; **l. with money** stinkreich

lout [laʊt] s Lümmel m

louver ['luvər] s Jalousie f

lovable ['lʌvəbəl] adj liebenswürdig

love [lʌv] adj Liebes- || s (for, of) Liebe f (zu); **be in l. with** verliebt sein in (acc); **for the l. of God** um Gottes willen; **fall (madly) in l. with** sich (heftig) verlieben in (acc); **Love** (at the end of a letter) herzliche Grüße; **l. at first sight** Liebe f auf den ersten Blick; **make l. to** herzen;

(sl) geschlechtlich verkehren mit; not for l. or money nicht für Gold und gute Worte; **there's no l.** lost between them sie schätzen sich nicht || *tr* lieben; *(like)* gern haben; **l. to dance** sehr gern tanzen

love′ affair′ s Liebeshandel m, Liebesverhältnis n

love′birds′ spl (coll) Unzertrennlichen pl

love′ child′ s Kind n der Liebe

love′ feast′ s (eccl) Liebesmahl n

love′ game′ s (tennis) Nullpartie f

love′ knot′ s Liebesschleife f

loveless [′lʌvlɪs] adj lieblos

love′ let′ter s Liebesbrief m

lovelorn [′lʌv‚lɔrn] adj vor Liebe vergehend

lovely [′lʌvli] adj lieblich

love′-mak′ing s Geschlechtsverkehr m

love′ match′ s Liebesheirat f

love′ po′em s Liebesgedicht n

love′ po′tion s Liebestrank m

lover [′lʌvər] s Liebhaber m; **lovers** Liebespaar n

love′ scene′ s Liebesszene f

love′ seat′ s Sofasessel n

love′sick′ adj liebeskrank

love′ song′ s Liebeslied n

love′ to′ken s Liebespfand n

lov′ing adj liebevoll; **Your l. ...** Dich liebender ...

lov′ing-kind′ness s Herzensgüte f

low [lo] adj *(building, mountain, forehead, birth, wages, estimate, prices, rent)* niedrig; *(number)* nieder; *(altitude, speed)* gering; *(not loud)* leise; *(vulgar)* gemein; *(grades, company)* schlecht; *(fever)* leicht; *(pulse, pressure)* schwach; *(ground)* tiefgelegen; *(bow, voice)* tief; *(almost empty)* fast leer; *(supplies, funds)* knapp; **be low** *(said of the sun, water)* niedrigstehen; **be low in funds** knapp bei Kasse sein; **feel low** niedergeschlagen sein; **have a low opinion** of e-e geringe Meinung haben von || *adv* niedrig; **lay low** über den Haufen werfen; **lie low** sich versteckt halten; *(bide one's time)* abwarten; **run low** knapp werden; **sing low** tief singen; **sink low** tief sinken || s *(low point)* (fig) Tiefstand m; *(meteor)* Tief n || *intr* muhen, brüllen

low′ blow′ s (box) Tiefschlag m

low′born′ adj von niederer Herkunft

low′brow′ s Spießbürger m

low′-cost hous′ing s sozial geförderter Wohnungsbau m

Low′ Coun′tries, the spl die Niederlande

low′-cut′ adj tiefausgeschnitten

low′-down′ adj schurkisch || s *(unadorned facts)* unverblümte Wahrheit f; *(inside information)* Geheimnachrichten pl

lower [′lo·ər] comp adj untere; *(e.g., deck, house, jaw, lip)* Unter– || *tr* herunterlassen; *(the eyes, voice, water level, temperature)* senken; *(prices)* herabsetzen; *(a flag, sail)* streichen; *(lifeboats)* aussetzen; **l.**

oneself sich herablassen || [′lau·ər] *intr* finster blicken; **l. at** finster anblicken

low′er ab′domen [′lo·ər] s Unterbauch m

low′er berth′ [′lo·ər] s untere Koje f

low′er case′ [′lo·ər] s Kleinbuchstaben pl

lower-case [′lo·ər′kes] adj klein

low′er course′ [′lo·ər] s *(of a river)* Unterlauf m

low′er mid′dle class′ [′lo·ər] s Kleinbürgertum n

lowermost [′lo·ər‚most] adj niedrigste

low′er world′ [′lo·ər] s Unterwelt f

low′-fly′ing adj tieffliegend

low′ fre′quency s Niederfrequenz f

low′-fre′quency adj Niederfrequenz–

low′ gear′ s erster Gang m

low′-grade′ adj minderwertig

low′ing s Gebrüll n

lowland [′loland] s Flachland n; **Lowlands** *(in Scotland)* Unterland n

low′ lev′el s Tiefstand m

low′-lev′el attack′ s Tiefangriff m

low′-lev′el flight′ s Tiefflug m

lowly [′loli] adj bescheiden; *(humble in spirit)* niederträchtig

low′-ly′ing adj tiefliegend

Low′ Mass′ s stille Messe f

low′-mind′ed adj niedrig gesinnt

low′ neck′ s *(of a dress)* Ausschnitt m

low′-necked′ adj tief ausgeschnitten pl

low′-pitched′ adj *(sound)* tief; *(roof)* mit geringer Neigung

low′-pres′sure adj Tiefdruck–, Unterdruck–

low′-priced′ adj billig

low′ shoe′ s Halbschuh m

low′-speed′ adj mit geringer Geschwindigkeit; *(film)* unempfindlich

low′-spir′ited adj niedergeschlagen

low′ spir′its spl Niedergeschlagenheit f; **be in l.** niedergeschlagen sein

low′ tide′ s Ebbe f; (fig) Tiefstand m

low′ wa′ter s Niedrigwasser n

low′-wa′ter mark′ s (fig) Tiefpunkt m

loyal [′lɔɪ·əl] adj treu, loyal

loyalist [′lɔɪ·əlɪst] s Regierungstreue mf

loyalty [′lɔɪ·əlti] s Treue f

lozenge [′lɑzɪndʒ] s Pastille f

LP [′el′pi] s (trademark) **(long-playing record)** Langspielplatte f

Ltd. abbr (Brit) **(Limited)** Gesellschaft f mit beschränkter Haftung

lubricant [′lubrɪkənt] s Schmiermittel n

lubricate [′lubrɪ‚ket] tr (ab)schmieren

lubrication [‚lubrɪ′keʃən] s Schmierung f

lucerne [lu′sʌrn] s (bot) Luzerne f; **Lucerne** Luzern n

lucid [′lusɪd] adj *(clear)* klar, deutlich; *(bright)* hell

luck [lʌk] s Glück n; *(chance)* Zufall m; **as l. would have it** wie es der Zufall wollte; **be down on one's l.** an seinem Glück verzagen; **be in l.** Glück haben; **be out of l.** Unglück haben; **dumb l.** (coll) Sauglück n; **have tough l.** (coll) Pech haben;

rotten l. (coll) Saupech n; **try one's l.** sein Glück versuchen; **with l. you should win** wenn Sie Glück haben, werden Sie gewinnen

luckily ['lʌkɪli] adv zum Glück

luckless ['lʌklɪs] adj glücklos

lucky ['lʌki] adj glücklich; **be l.** Glück haben; **l. dog** (coll) Glückspilz m; **l. penny** Glückspfennig m

luck'y shot' s Glückstreffer m

lucrative ['lukrətɪv] adj gewinnbringend

ludicrous ['ludɪkrəs] adj lächerlich

lug [lʌg] s (pull, tug) Ruck m; (lout) (sl) Lümmel m; (elec) Öse f || v (pret & pp lugged; ger lugging) tr schleppen

luggage ['lʌgɪdʒ] s Gepäck n; **excess l.** Mehrgepäck n; **piece of l.** Gepäckstück n

lug'gage car'rier s Gepäckträger m

lug'gage compart'ment s (aer) Frachtraum m

lug'gage rack' s Gepäckablage f; (on the roof of a car) Dachgepäckträger m

lug'gage receipt' s Aufgabeschein m

lugubrious [lu'g(j)ubrɪ-əs] adj tieftraurig

lukewarm ['luk‚wɔrm] adj lau, lauwarm

lull [lʌl] s Windstille f; (com) Flaute f || tr einlullen; (e.g., fears) beschwichtigen; **l. to sleep** einschläfern || intr nachlassen

lullaby ['lʌlə‚baɪ] s Wiegenlied n

lumbago [lʌm'bego] s Hexenschluß m

lumber ['lʌmbər] s Bauholz n || intr sich schwerfällig fortbewegen

lum'berjack' s Holzfäller m

lum'ber·man' s (-men') (dealer) Holzhändler m; (lumberjack) Holzfäller m

lum'beryard' s Holzplatz m

luminary ['lumɪ‚neri] s Leuchtkörper m; (fig) Leuchte f

luminescent [‚lumɪ'nesənt] adj lumineszierend

luminous ['lumɪnəs] adj leuchtend, Leucht–

lu'minous di'al s Leuchtzifferblatt n

lu'minous paint' s Leuchtfarbe f

lummox ['lʌməks] s Lümmel m

lump [lʌmp] s (e.g., of clay) Klumpen m; (on the body) Beule f; **have a l. in one's throat** e-n Kloß (or Knödel) im Hals haben; **l. of sugar** Würfel m Zucker || tr—**l. together** (fig) zusammenwerfen

lumpish ['lʌmpɪ/] adj klumpig

lump' sug'ar s Würfelzucker m

lump' sum' s Pauschalbetrag m

lumpy ['lʌmpi] adj klumpig; (sea) bewegt

lunacy ['lunəsi] s Irrsinn m

lu'nar eclipse' ['lunər] s Mondfinsternis f

lu'nar land'ing s Mondlandung f

lu'nar mod'ule s (rok) Mondfähre f

lu'nar year' s Mondjahr n

lunatic ['lunətɪk] s Irre mf

lu'natic asy'lum s Irrenhaus n

lu'natic fringe' s Extremisten pl

lunch [lʌnt/] s (at noon) Mittagessen n, Lunch m; (light meal) Zwischenmahlzeit f; **eat l.** zu Mittag essen; **have** (s.th.) **for l.** zum Mittagessen haben || intr zu Mittag essen, lunchen

lunch' coun'ter s Theke f

luncheon ['lʌnt/ən] s gemeinsames Mittagessen n

luncheonette [‚lʌnt/ə'net] s Imbißstube f

lunch' hour' s Mittagsstunde f

lunch' room' s Imbißhalle f

lunch'time' s Mittagszeit f

lung [lʌŋ] s Lunge f; **at the top of one's lungs** aus voller Kehle

lunge ['lʌndʒ] s Sprung m vorwärts; (fencing) Ausfall m || tr (a horse) an der Longe laufen lassen || intr—e-n Sprung vorwärts machen; (with a sword) (at) e-n Ausfall machen (gegen); **l. at** losstürzen auf (acc)

lurch [lʌrt/] s Torkeln n, Taumeln n; **leave in a l.** im Stich lassen || intr torkeln; (said of a ship) zur Seite rollen

lure [lur] s Köder m || tr ködern; (fig) verlocken; **l. away** weglocken

lurid ['lurɪd] adj (light) gespenstisch; (sunset) düsterrot; (gruesome) grausig; (pallid) fahl

lurk [lʌrk] intr lauern

luscious ['lʌ/əs] adj köstlich; **a l. doll** (coll) ein tolles Weib

lush [lʌ/] adj üppig

lust [lʌst] s Wollust f; (for) Begierde f (nach) || intr (after, for) gieren (nach)

luster ['lʌstər] s Glanz m; (e.g., chandelier) Lüster m

lusterless ['lʌstərlɪs] adj matt

lus'terware' s Tongeschirr n mit Lüster

lustful ['lʌstfəl] adj lüstern, geil

lustrous ['lʌstrəs] adj glänzend

lusty ['lʌsti] adj kräftig

lute [lut] s Laute f

Lutheran ['luθərən] adj lutherisch || s Lutheraner –in mf

luxuriance [lʌg'ʒurɪ-əns] s Üppigkeit f

luxuriant [lʌg'ʒurɪ-ənt] adj üppig

luxuriate [lʌg'ʒurɪ‚et] intr (thrive) gedeihen; (delight) (in) schwelgen (in dat)

luxurious [lʌg'ʒurɪ-əs] adj luxuriös; **l. living** Prasserei f

luxury ['lʌgʒəri] s Extravaganz f, Luxus m; (object of luxury) Luxusartikel m; **live a life of l.** im vollen Leben

lye [laɪ] s Lauge f

ly'ing adj lügenhaft || s Lügen n

ly'ing-in' hos'pital s Entbindungsanstalt f

lymph [lɪmf] s Lymphe f

lymphatic [lɪm'fætɪk] adj lymphatisch

lynch [lɪnt/] tr lynchen

lynch'ing s Lynchen n

lynch' law' s Lynchjustiz f

lynx [lɪŋks] s Luchs m

lynx'-eyed' adj luchsäugig

lyre [laɪr] s (mus) Leier f
lyric ['lɪrɪk] adj lyrisch; **l. poetry** Lyrik f ‖ s lyrisches Gedicht n; (of a song) Text m

lyrical ['lɪrɪkəl] adj lyrisch
lyricism ['lɪrɪ ˌsɪzəm] s Lyrik f
lyricist ['lɪrɪsɪst] s (of a song) Texter –in mf; (poet) lyrischer Dichter m

M

M, m [em] s dreizehnter Buchstabe des englischen Alphabets
ma [mɑ] s (coll) Mama f
ma'am [mæm] s (coll) gnädige Frau f
macadam [mə'kædəm] s Makadamdecke f
macadamize [mə'kædə ˌmaɪz] tr makadamisieren
maca'dam road' s Straße f mit Makadamdecke
macaroni [ˌmækə'roni] spl Makkaroni pl
macaroon [ˌmækə'run] s Makrone f
macaw [mə'kɔ] s (orn) Ara m
mace [mes] s Stab m, Amtsstab m
mace'bear'er s Träger m des Amtstabes
machination [ˌmækɪ'neʃən] s Intrige f; **machinations** Machenschaften pl
machine [mə'ʃin] s Maschine f; (pol) Apparat m; **by m.** maschinell ‖ tr spannabhebend formen
machine'-driv'en adj mit Maschinenantrieb
machine' gun' s Maschinengewehr n
machine'-gun' v (pret & pp -gunned; ger -gunning) tr unter Maschinengewehrfeuer nehmen
machine' gun'ner s Maschinengewehrschütze m
machine'-made' adj maschinell hergestellt
machinery [mə'ʃinəri] s (& fig) Maschinerie f
machine' screw' s Maschinenschraube f
machine' shop' s Maschinenhalle f
machine' tool' s Werkzeugmaschine f
machinist [mə'ʃinɪst] s (maker and repairer of machines) Maschinenbauer m; (machine operator) Maschinenschlosser –in mf
mackerel ['mækərəl] s Makrele f
mad [mæd] adj (madder; maddest) verrückt; (angry) böse; **be mad about** vernarrt sein in (acc); **be mad at** böse sein auf (acc); **drive mad** verrückt machen (acc); **go mad** verrückt werden
madam ['mædəm] s gnädige Frau f; (of a brothel) (sl) Bordellmutter f
mad'cap' adj ausgelassen ‖ s Wildfang m
madden ['mædən] tr verrückt machen; (make angry) zornig machen
made'-to-or'der adj nach Maß angefertigt
made'-up' adj (story) erfunden; (artificial) künstlich; (with cosmetics) geschminkt

mad'house' s Irrenhaus n, Narrenhaus n
madly ['mædli] adv (coll) wahnsinnig
mad'man' s (–men') Verrückter m
madness ['mædnɪs] s Wahnsinn m
Madonna [mə'dɑnə] s Madonna f
maelstrom ['melstrəm] s (& fig) Strudel m
magazine [ˌmægə'zin] s (periodical) Zeitschrift f; (illustrated) Illustrierte f; (warehouse for munitions; cartridge container) Magazin n; (for a camera) Kassette f
magazine' rack' s Zeitschriftenständer m
Maggie ['mægi] s Gretchen n
maggot ['mægət] s Made f
Magi ['medʒaɪ] spl—**the three M.** (Bib) die drei Weisen pl aus dem Morgenland
magic ['mædʒɪk] adj (enchanting) zauberhaft; (trick, word, wand) Zauber– ‖ s Zauberkunst f
magician [mə'dʒɪʃən] s Zauberer –in mf
ma'gic lan'tern s Laterna magica f
magisterial [ˌmædʒɪs'tɪriəl] adj (of a magistrate) obrigkeitlich; (authoritative) autoritativ; (pompous) anmaßend
magistrate ['mædʒɪs ˌtret] s Polizeirichter m
magnanimous [mæg'nænɪməs] adj großmütig
magnate ['mægnet] s Magnat m
magnesium [mæg'nizɪ əm] s Magnesium n
magnet ['mægnɪt] s Magnet m
magnetic [mæg'netɪk] adj magnetisch; (personality) fesselnd
magnetism ['mægnɪ ˌtɪzəm] s Magnetismus m; (fig) Anziehungskraft f
magnetize ['mægnɪ ˌtaɪz] tr magnetisieren
magnificence [mæg'nɪfɪsəns] s Pracht f
magnificent [mæg'nɪfɪsənt] adj prächtig
magnifier ['mægnɪ ˌfaɪ ˌər] s (electron) Verstärker m
magni·fy ['mægnɪ ˌfaɪ] v (pret & pp -fied) tr vergrößern; (fig) übertreiben
mag'nifying glass' s Lupe f
magnitude ['mægnɪ ˌt(j)ud] s (& astr) Größe f
magno'lia tree' [mæg'noli·ə] s Magnolia f
magpie ['mæg ˌpaɪ] s (& fig) Elster f
mahlstick ['mɑl ˌstɪk] s Malerstock m

mahogany [mə'hagəni] s Mahagoni n
mahout [mə'haut] s Elefantentreiber m
maid [med] s Dienstmädchen n
maiden ['medən] s Jungfer f; (poet) Maid f
maid'enhair' s (bot) Jungfernhaar n
maid'enhead' s Jungfernhäutchen n
maid'enhood' s Jungfräulichkeit f
maidenly ['medənli] adj jungfräulich
maid'en name' s Mädchenname m
maid'en voy'age s Jungfernfahrt f
maid'-in-wait'ing s (maids-in-waiting) Hofdame f
maid' of hon'or s erste Brautjungfer f
maid'serv'ant s Dienstmädchen n
mail [mel] adj Post– || s Post f; (armor) Kettenpanzer m; by m. brieflich; by return m. postwendend || tr (put into the mail) aufgeben; (send) abschicken; m. to zuschicken (dat)
mail'bag' s Postsack m
mail'boat' s Postschiff n
mail'box' s Briefkasten m
mail' car'rier s Briefträger –in mf
mail' deliv'ery s Postzustellung f
mail' drop' s Briefeinwurf m
mailer ['melər] s (phot) Versandbeutel m
mail'ing s Absendung f
mail'ing list' s Postversandliste f
mail'ing per'mit s Zulassung f zum portofreien Versand
mail'man' s (–men') Briefträger m
mail' or'der s Bestellung f durch die Post
mail'-order house' s Versandhaus n
mail' plane' s Postflugzeug n
mail' train' s Postzug m
mail' truck' s Postauto n
maim [mem] tr verstümmeln
main [men] adj Haupt– || s Hauptleitung f; in the main hauptsächlich
main' clause' s (gram) Hauptsatz m
main' course' s Hauptgericht n
main' deck' s Hauptdeck n
main' floor' s Erdgeschoß n
mainland ['men,lænd] s Festland n
main' line' s (rr) Hauptstrecke f
mainly ['menli] adv größtenteils
mainmast ['men,mæst] s Großmast m
main' of'fice s Hauptbüro n, Zentrale f
main' point' s springender Punkt m
mainsail ['men,sel] s Großsegel m
main'spring' s (horol & fig) Triebfeder f
main'stay' s (fig) Hauptstütze f; (naut) Großstag n
main' street' s Hauptstraße f
maintain [men'ten] tr aufrechterhalten; (e.g., a family) unterhalten; (assert) behaupten; (one's reputation) wahren; (e.g., in good condition) bewahren; (order, silence) halten; (a road) instand halten
maintenance ['mentinəns] s (upkeep) Instandhaltung f; (support) Unterhalt m; (e.g., of an automobile) Wardirektor m
maître d'hôtel [,metərdo'tel] s (head waiter) Oberkellner m; (owner)

Hotelbesitzer m; (manager) Hoteltung f
majestic [mə'dʒestık] adj majestätisch
majesty ['mædʒısti] s Majestät f
major ['medʒər] adj Haupt–; (mus) –Dur || s (educ) Hauptfach n; (mil) Major m || intr—m. in als Hauptfach studieren
majordomo ['medʒər'domo] s Haushofmeister m
ma'jor gen'eral s Generalmajor m
majority [mə'dʒorıti] adj Mehrheits– || s Mehrheit f; (full age) Mündigkeit f; (mil) Majorsrang m; (parl) Stimmenmehrheit f; be in the m. in der Mehrheit sein; in the m. of cases in der Mehrzahl der Fälle; the m. of people die meisten Menschen
major'ity vote' s Mehrheitsbeschluß m
ma'jor league' s Oberliga f
make [mek] s Fabrikat n, Marke f || tr machen; (in a factory) herstellen; (cause) lassen; (force) zwingen; (clothes) anfertigen; (money) verdienen; (a reputation, name) erwerben; (a choice) treffen; (a confession) ablegen; (a report) erstatten; (plans) schmieden; (changes) vornehmen; (a movie) drehen; (contact) herstellen; (a meal) (zu)bereiten; (conditions) stellen; (rules, assertions) aufstellen; (a bet, compromise, peace) schließen; (excuses, requests, objections) vorbringen; (a protest) erheben; (a goal) schießen (or erzielen); (a comparison) ziehen; (a speech) halten; (e.g., a good father) abgeben; (be able to fit through, e.g., a window) gehen durch; (e.g., a train, bus, destination) erreichen; (e.g., ten miles) zurücklegen; (a girl) (sl) verführen; (arith) machen; m. (s.o.) believe weismachen (dat); m. into verarbeiten zu; m. of halten von; m. out (e.g., writing) entziffern; (e.g., a person at a distance) erkennen; (understand) kapieren; (a blank or form) ausfüllen; (a check, receipt) ausstellen; m. over to (jur) überschreiben auf (acc); m. s.o. out to be a liar j-n als Lügner hinstellen; m. s.th. of oneself es weit bringen; m. the most of ausnutzen; m. time Zeit gewinnen; m. time with (a woman) (coll) flirten mit; m. up (e.g., a list) zusammenstellen; (a bill) ausstellen; (a sentence) bilden; (a story) sich [dat] ausdenken; m. up one's mind (about) sich [dat] schlüssig werden (über acc); m. way! Platz da!; m. way for ausweichen vor (dat) || intr—m. believe schauspielern; m. believe that nur so tun, als ob; m. do with sich behelfen mit; m. for losteuern auf (acc); m. off with durchbrennen mit; m. out well gut auskommen; m. sure of sich vergewissern (genit); m. sure that vergewissern, daß; m. up (after a quarrel) sich versöhnen; m. up for (past mistakes) wieder gutmachen; (lost time) wieder einbringen

make'-believe' *adj* Schein-, vorgetäuscht ‖ *s* Schein *m*, Mache *f*
maker ['mekər] *s* Hersteller –in *mf*; Maker Schöpfer *m*
make'shift' *adj* behelfsmäßig, Behelfs– ‖ *s* Notbehelf *m*
make'-up' *s* Aufmachung *f*; (*cosmetic*) Make-up *n*, Schminke *f*; (*of a team*) Aufstellung *f*; (*theat*) Maske *f*; (*typ*) Umbruch *m*; **apply m.** sich schminken
make'weight' *s* Gewichtszugabe *f*
mak'ing *s* Herstellung *f*; **be in the m.** im Werden sein; **have the makings of** das Zeug haben zu; **this is of his own m.** dies ist sein eigenes Werk
maladjusted [,mælə'dʒʌstɪd] *adj* unausgeglichen
maladroit [,mælə'drɔɪt] *adj* ungeschickt
malady ['mælədɪ] *s* (& *fig*) Krankheit *f*
malaise [mæ'lez] *s* (*physical*) Unwohlsein *n*; (*mental*) Unbehagen *n*
malaria [mə'lɛrɪ·ə] *s* Malaria *f*
Malaya [mə'le·ə] *s* Malaya *f*
Malaysia [mə'leʒɪ·ə] *s* Malaysia *n*
malcontent ['mælkən,tɛnt] *adj* unzufrieden ‖ *s* Unzufriedene *mf*
male [mel] *adj* männlich ‖ *s* Mann *m*; (*bot*) männliche Pflanze *f*; (*zool*) Männchen *n*
malediction [,mælɪ'dɪkʃən] *s* Verwünschung *f*
malefactor ['mælɪ,fæktər] *s* Übeltäter –in *mf*
male' nurse' *s* Pfleger *m*
malevolence [mæ'lɛvələns] *s* Böswilligkeit *f*
malevolent [mə'lɛvələnt] *adj* böswillig
malfeasance [,mæl'fizəns] *s* strafbare Handlung *f*; **m. in office** Amtsvergehen *n*
malfunction [mæl'fʌŋkʃən] *s* technische Störung *f*
malice ['mælɪs] *s* Bosheit *f*
malicious [mə'lɪʃəs] *adj* boshaft
malign [mə'laɪn] *adj* böswillig ‖ *tr* verleumden
malignancy [mə'lɪgnənsɪ] *s* (*pathol*) Bösartigkeit *f*
malignant [mə'lɪgnənt] *adj* böswillig; (*pathol*) bösartig
malinger [mə'lɪŋgər] *intr* simulieren
malingerer [mə'lɪŋgərər] *s* Simulant –in *mf*
mall [mɔl] *s* (*promenade*) Laubenpromenade *f*; (*shopping center*) überdachtes Einkaufszentrum *n*, Mall *f*
mallard ['mælərd] *s* Stockente *f*
malleable ['mælɪ·əbəl] *adj* schmiedbar
mallet ['mælɪt] *s* Schlegel *m*
mallow ['mælo] *s* Malve *f*
malnutrition [,mæln(j)u'trɪʃən] *s* Unterernährung *f*
malodorous [mæl'odərəs] *adj* übelriechend
malpractice [mæl'præktɪs] *s* ärztlicher Kunstfehler *m*
malt [mɔlt] *s* Malz *n*
maltreat [mæl'trit] *tr* mißhandeln
mamma ['mɑmə] *s* Mama *f*, Mutti *f*

mammal ['mæməl] *s* Säugetier *n*
mammalian [mæ'melɪ·ən] *adj* Säugetier– ‖ *s* Säugetier *n*
mam'mary gland' ['mæməri] *s* Milchdrüse *f*
mam'ma's boy' *s* Muttersöhnchen *n*
mammoth ['mæməθ] *adj* ungeheuer (groß) ‖ *s* (*zool*) Mammut *n*
man [mæn] *s* (*men* [mɛn]) (*adult male*) Mann *m*; (*human being*) Mensch *m*; (*servant*) Diener *m*; (*worker*) Arbeiter *m*; (*mankind*) die Menschheit *f*; (*checkers*) Stein *m*; **man alive!** Menschenskind! ‖ *v* (*pret* & *pp* **manned;** *ger* **manning**) *tr* besetzen; (*nav*, rok) bemannen
man' about town' *s* weltgewandter Mann *m*
manacle ['mænəkəl] *s* Handschelle *f* ‖ *tr* fesseln
manage ['mænɪdʒ] *tr* (*a business, household*) leiten; (*an estate*) verwalten; (*tools, weapons*) handhaben; (*e.g., a boat, car*) völlig in der Gewalt haben; (*children*) fertig werden mit; **I'll m. it** ich werde es schon schaffen; **m. the situation** die Sache deichseln ‖ *intr* zurechtkommen; (*with, on*) auskommen (mit); **m. to** (*inf*) es fertigbringen zu (*inf*)
manageable ['mænɪdʒəbəl] *adj* handlich; (*hair*) fügsam
management ['mænɪdʒmənt] *s* Unternehmensführung *f*; (*group which manages*) Direktion *f*; (*as opposed to labor*) Management *n*
man'agement consul'tant *s* Unternehmungsberater –in *mf*
manager ['mænɪdʒər] *s* Manager *m*, Geschäftsführer –in *mf*; (*of a bank or hotel*) Direktor –in *mf*; (*of an estate*) Verwalter –in *mf*; (*of a department*) Abteilungsleiter –in *mf*; (*of a star, theater, athlete*) Manager *m*
managerial [,mænə'dʒɪrɪ·əl] *adj* Leitungs-, Führungs-
man'aging *adj* geschäftsführend
man'aging direc'tor *s* Geschäftsführer –in *mf*
Manchuria [mæn'tʃurɪ·ə] *s* Mandschurei *f*
man'darin or'ange ['mændərɪn] *s* Mandarine *f*
mandate ['mændet] *s* Mandat *n* ‖ *tr* (to) zuweisen (*dat*)
mandatory ['mændə,torɪ] *adj* verbindlich
mandolin ['mændəlɪn] *s* Mandoline *f*
mandrake ['mændrek] *s* (*bot*) Alraune *f*
mane [men] *s* Mähne *f*
maneuver [mə'nuvər] *s* Manöver *n*; **go on maneuvers** (*mil*) ins Manöver ziehen ‖ *tr* manövrieren; **m. s.o. into** (*ger*) j–n dazubringen zu (*inf*)
maneuverability [mə,nuvərə'bɪlɪtɪ] *s* Manövrierbarkeit *f*
maneuverable [mə'nuvərəbəl] *adj* manövrierfähig
manful ['mænfəl] *adj* mannhaft
manganese ['mæŋgə,niz] *s* Mangan *n*

mange [mendʒ] *s* Räude *f*

manger ['mendʒər] *s* Krippe *f*

mangle ['mæŋgəl] *s* Mangel *f* ‖ *tr* (*tear apart*) zerfleischen; (*wash*) mangeln

mangy ['mendʒi] *adj* räudig; (fig) schäbig

man'han'dle *tr* grob behandeln

man'hole' *s* Kanalschacht *m*, Mannloch *n*

man'hole cov'er *s* Schachtdeckel *m*

man'hood' *s* (*virility*) Männlichkeit *f*; (*age*) Mannesalter *n*

man'-hour' *s* Arbeitsstunde *f* pro Mann

man'hunt' *s* Fahndung *f*

mania ['meni·ə] *s* Manie *f*

maniac ['meni‚æk] *s* Geisteskranke *mf*

maniacal [mə'naɪ·əkəl] *adj* manisch

manicure ['mæni‚kjur] *s* Maniküre *f*, Handpflege *f* ‖ *tr* maniküren

manicurist ['mæni‚kjurɪst] *s* Maniküre *f*

manifest ['mæni‚fest] *adj* offenkundig, offenbar ‖ *s* (aer, naut) Manifest *n* ‖ *tr* bekunden, bezeigen

manifestation [‚mænifes'teʃən] *s* (*manifesting*) Offenbarung *f*; (*indication*) Anzeichen *n*

manifes·to [‚mæni'festo] *s* (-toes) Manifest *n*

manifold ['mæni‚fold] *adj* mannigfaltig ‖ *s* (aut) Rohrverzweigung *f*

manikin ['mænikɪn] *s* Männchen *n*; (*for teaching anatomy*) anatomisches Modell *n*; (*mannequin*) Mannequin *n*

man' in the moon' *s* Mann *m* im Mond

man' in the streets' *s* Durchschnittsmensch *m*

manipulate [mə'nɪpjə‚let] *tr* manipulieren

man'kind' *s* Menschheit *f*

manliness ['mænlɪnɪs] *s* Männlichkeit *f*

manly ['mænli] *adj* mannhaft, männlich

man'-made' *adj* künstlich

manna ['mænə] *s* Manna *n*, Himmelsbrot *n*

manned' space'craft *s* bemanntes Raumfahrzeug *n*

mannequin ['mænikɪn] *s* (*clothes model*) Mannequin *n*; (*in a display window*) Schaufensterpuppe *f*

manner ['mænər] *s* Art *f*, Weise *f*; (*custom*) Sitte *f*; **after the m.** of nach der Art von; **by all m. of means** auf jeden Fall; **by no m. of means** auf keinen Fall; **in a m.** gewissermaßen; **in a m. of speaking** sozusagen; **in like m.** gleicherweise; **in the following m.** folgendermaßen; **in this m.** auf diese Weise; **it's bad manners to** (*inf*) es schickt sich nicht zu (*inf*); **m. of death** Todesart *f*; **manners** Manieren *pl*

mannerism ['mænə‚rɪzəm] *s* Manieriertheit *f*

mannerly ['mænərli] *adj* manierlich

mannish ['mænɪʃ] *adj* männisch; (*woman*) unweiblich

man' of let'ters *s* Literat *m*

man' of the world' *s* Weltmann *m*

man' of war' *s* Kriegsschiff *n*

manor ['mænər] *s* Herrengut *n*

man'or house' *s* Herrenhaus *n*

man'pow'er *s* Arbeitskräfte *pl*; (mil) Kriegsstärke *f*

man'serv'ant *s* (*menservants*) Diener *m*

mansion ['mænʃən] *s* Herrenhaus *n*

man'slaugh'ter *s* Totschlag *m*

mantel ['mæntəl] *s* Kaminsims *m* & *n*

man'telpiece' *s* Kaminsims *m* & *n*

mantilla [mæn'tɪlə] *s* Mantille *f*

mantle ['mæntəl] *s* (& fig) Mantel *m*; (*of a gaslight*) Glühstrumpf *m*; (geol) Mantel *m* ‖ *tr* verhüllen

manual ['mænju·əl] *adj* manuell, Hand– ‖ *s* (*book*) Handbuch *n*, Leitfaden *m*; (mus) Manual *n*

man'ual control' *s* Handbedienung *f*

man'ual dexter'ity *s* Handfertigkeit *f*

man'ual la'bor *s* Handarbeit *f*

man'ual of arms' *s* (mil) Dienstvorschrift *f*

man'ual train'ing *s* Werkunterricht *m*

manufacture [‚mænjə'fækt/ər] *s* Herstellung *f*; (*production*) Erzeugnis *n* ‖ *tr* herstellen; (*clothes*) konfektionieren

manufac'tured goods' *spl* Fertigwaren *pl*

manufacturer [‚mænjə'fækt/ərər] *s* Hersteller –in *mf*

manure [mə'n(j)ur] *s* Mist *m* ‖ *tr* misten

manuscript ['mænjə‚skrɪpt] *adj* handschriftlich ‖ *s* Manuskript *n*

many ['meni] *adj* viele; **a good** (or **great**) **m.** sehr viele; **how m.** wieviele; **in so m. words** ausdrücklich; **m. a** mancher, manch ein; **m. a person** manch einer; **m. a time** manchmal; **twice as m.** noch einmal so viele ‖ *pron* viele; **as m. as ten** nicht weniger als zehn; **how m.** wieviele

man'y-sid'ed *adj* vielseitig

map [mæp] *s* Karte *f*, Landkarte *f*; (*of a city*) Plan *m*; (*of a local area*) Spezialkarte *f*; **map of the world** Weltkarte *f*; **put on the map** (coll) ausposaunen ‖ *v* (*pret & pp* **mapped**; *ger* **mapping**) *tr* kartographisch aufnehmen; **map out** planen

maple ['mepəl] *s* Ahorn *m*

ma'ple sug'ar *s* Ahornzucker *m*

ma'ple syr'up *s* Ahornsirup *m*

mar [mɑr] *v* (*pret & pp* **marred**; *ger* **marring**) *tr* (*detract from the beauty of*) verunzieren; (*e.g., a reputation*) beeinträchtigen

marathon ['mærə‚θɑn] *s* Dauerwettbewerb *m*

mar'athon race' *s* Marathonlauf *m*

maraud [mə'rɔd] *tr* & *intr* plündern

marauder [mə'rɔdər] *s* Plünderer *m*

marble ['mɑrbəl] *adj* marmorn ‖ *s* Marmor *m*; (*little glass ball*) Murmel *f*; **marbles** (*game*) Murmelspiel *n* ‖ *tr* marmorieren

mar'ble quar'ry *s* Marmorbruch *m*

march [mɑrt/] *s* Marsch *m*; (*festive parade*) Umzug *m*; **March** März *m*; **on the m.** auf dem Marsch; **steal a**

m. on s.o. j-m den Rang ablaufen; **the m. of time** der Lauf der Zeit ‖ *tr* marschieren ‖ *intr* marschieren; **m. by** vorbeimarschieren (an *dat*); **m. off** abmarschieren ‖ *interj* marsch!

marchioness ['marʃənɪs] *s* Marquise *f*

mare [mer] *s* Stute *f*

Margaret ['margərɪt] *s* Margarete *f*

margarine ['mardʒərɪn] *s* Margarine *f*

margin ['mardʒɪn] *s* (of a page) Rand *m*; (leeway) Spielraum *m*; (fin) Spanne *f*; **by a narrow m.** mit knappem Abstand; **leave a m.** am Rande Raum lassen; **m. of profit** Gewinnspanne *f*; **m. of safety** Sicherheitsfaktor *m*; **win by a ten-second m.** mit zehn Sekunden Abstand gewinnen; **write in the m.** an dem Rand schreiben

marginal ['mardʒɪnəl] *adj* (costs, profits, case) Grenz–; (in the margin) Rand–

mar'ginal note' *s* Randbemerkung *f*

mar'gin release' *s* Randauslöser *m*

mar'gin set'ter *s* Randsteller *m*

marigold ['mærɪ‚gold] *s* Ringelblume *f*

marijuana [‚marɪ'hwanə] *s* Marihuana *n*

marinate ['mærɪ‚net] *tr* marinieren

marine [mə'rin] *adj* See–, Meer(es)– ‖ *s* (fleet) Marine *f*; (fighter) Marineinfanterist *m*; **marines** Marinetruppen *pl*

Marine' Corps' *s* Marineinfanteriekorps *n*

mariner ['mærɪnər] *s* Seemann *m*

marionette [‚mærɪ‑ə'net] *s* Marionette *f*

marital ['mærɪtəl] *adj* ehelich, Gatten–

mar'ital sta'tus *s* Familienstand *m*

maritime ['mærɪ‚taɪm] *adj* See–

marjoram ['mardʒərəm] *s* Majoran *m*

mark [mark] *s* (& fig) Zeichen *n*; (stain, bruise) Fleck *m*, Mal *n*; (German unit of currency) Mark *f*; (educ) Zensur *f*; **be an easy m.** (coll) leicht reinzulegen sein; **hit the m.** ins Schwarze treffen; **make one's m.** sich durchsetzen; **m. of confidence** Vertrauensbeweis *m*; **m. of favor** Gunstbezeichnung *f*; **m. of respect** Zeichen *n* der Hochachtung; **on your marks!** auf die Plätze!; **wide of the m.** am Ziel vorbei ‖ *tr* (aus)zeichnen, bezeichnen; (student papers) zensieren; (cards) zinken; (labels) beschriften; (laundry) zeichnen; (the score) anschreiben; **m. down** aufschreiben, niederschreiben; (com) im Preis herabsetzen; **m. my words!** merken Sie sich, was ich sage!; **m. off** abgrenzen; (surv) abstecken; **m. time** (mil & fig) auf der Stelle treten; (mus) den Takt schlagen; **m. up** (e.g., a wall) beschmieren; (com) im Preis heraufsetzen

mark'down' *s* Preisnachlaß *m*

marked *adj* (difference) merklich; **a m. man** ein Gezeichneter *m*

marker ['markər] *s* (of scores) Anschreiber –in *mf*; (commemorative marker) Gedenktafel *f*; (on a firing range) Anzeiger *m*; (bombing marker) Leuchtbombe *f*; (felt pen) Filzschreiber *m*

market ['markɪt] *s* Markt *m*; (grocery store) Lebensmittelgeschäft *n*; (stock exchange) Börse *f*; (ready sale) Absatz *m*; **be in the m. for** Bedarf haben an (dat); **be on the m.** zum Verkauf stehen; **put on the m.** auf den Markt bringen ‖ *tr* verkaufen

marketable ['markɪtəbəl] *adj* marktfähig

mar'ket anal'ysis *s* Marktanalyse *f*

mar'keting *s* (econ) Marketing *n*; **do the m.** Einkäufe machen

mar'keting research' *s* Absatzforschung *f*

mar'ketplace' *s* Marktplatz *m*

mar'ket price' *s* Marktpreis *m*

mar'ket town' *s* Marktflecken *m*

mar'ket val'ue *s* Marktwert *m*; (st. exch.) Kurswert *m*

mark'ing *s* Kennzeichen *n*

marks·man ['marksmən] *s* (–men) Schütze *m*

marks'manship' *s* Schießkunst *f*

mark'up' *s* (com) Gewinnaufschlag *m*

marl [marl] *s* Mergel *m* ‖ *tr* mergeln

marmalade ['marmə‚led] *s* Marmelade *f*

maroon [mə'run] *adj* rotbraun, kastanienbraun ‖ *s* Kastanienbraun *n* ‖ *tr* aussetzen; **be marooned** von der Außenwelt abgeschnitten sein

marquee [mar'ki] *s* Schutzdach *n*

marquess ['markwɪs] *s* Marquis *m*

marquis ['markwɪs] *s* Marquis *m*

marquise [mar'kiz] *s* Marquise *f*

marriage ['mærɪdʒ] *s* Heirat *f*; (state) Ehe *f*, Ehestand *m*; **by m.** angeheiratet, schwägerlich; **give in m.** verheiraten

marriageable ['mærɪdʒəbəl] *adj* heiratsfähig; **m. age** (of a girl) Mannbarkeit *f*

mar'riage brok'er *s* Heiratsvermittler –in *mf*

mar'riage cer'emony *s* Trauung *f*

mar'riage li'cense *s* Heiratsurkunde *f*

mar'riage of conven'ience *s* Vernunftehe *f*

mar'riage por'tion *s* Mitgift *f*

mar'riage propo'sal *s* Heiratsantrag *m*

mar'riage vow' *s* Ehegelöbnis *n*

mar'ried cou'ple *s* Ehepaar *n*

mar'ried state' *s* Ehestand *m*

marrow ['mæro] *s* Knochenmark *n*; (fig) Mark *n*

mar·ry ['mæri] *v* (pret & pp –ried) *tr* heiraten; (said of a priest or minister) trauen; **m. off (to)** verheiraten (mit) ‖ *intr* heiraten; **m. rich** e–e gute Partie machen

Mars [marz] *s* Mars *m*

marsh [marʃ] *s* Sumpf *m*

mar·shal ['marʃəl] *s* Zeremonienmeister *m*; (police officer) Bezirkspolizeichef *m*; (mil) Marschall *m* ‖ *v* (pret & pp –shal[l]ed; ger –shal[l]ing) *tr* (troops) ordnungsgemäß aufstellen; (strength) zusammenraffen

marsh′land′ s Sumpfland n

marsh′ mal′low s (bot) Eibisch m

marsh′mal′low s (candy) Konfekt n aus Stärkesirup, Zucker, Stärke, Gelatine, und geschlagenem Eiweiß

marshy [′mɑrʃi] adj sumpfig

mart [mɑrt] s Markt m

marten [′mɑrtən] s (zool) Marder m

Martha [′mɑrθə] s Martha f

martial [′mɑrʃəl] adj Kriegs-

mar′tial law′ s Standrecht n; **declare m.** das Standrecht verhängen; **under m.** standrechtlich

martin [′mɑrtɪn] s Mauerschwalbe f; **Martin** Martin m

martinet [,mɑrtɪ′nɛt] s Pauker –in mf; (mil) Schleifer m

martyr [′mɑrtər] s Märtyrer –in mf || tr martern

martyrdom [′mɑrtərdəm] s Märtyrertum n

mar•vel [′mɑrvəl] s Wunder n || v (pret & pp -vel[l]ed; ger -vel[l]ing) intr (at) sich wundern (über acc)

marvelous [′mɑrvələs] adj wundervoll; (coll) pfundig

Marxist [′mɑrksɪst] adj marxistisch || Marxist –in mf

marzipan [′mɑrzɪ,pæn] s Marzipan n

mascara [mæs′kærə] s Lidtusche f

mascot [′mæskɑt] s Maskotte f

masculine [′mæskjəlɪn] adj männlich

mash [mæʃ] s Brei m; (in brewing) Maische f || tr zerquetschen; (potatoes) zerdrücken

mashed′ pota′toes spl Kartoffelbrei m

mask [mæsk] s Maske f || tr maskieren

masked′ ball′ s Maskenball m

mason [′mesən] s Maurer m; **Mason** Freimaurer m

Masonic [mə′sɑnɪk] adj Freimaurer-

masonite [′mesə,naɪt] s Holzfaserplatte f

masonry [′mesənri] s Mauerwerk n; **Masonry** Freimaurerei f

masquerade [,mæskə′red] s (& fig) Maskerade f || intr (& fig) sich maskieren; **m. as** sich ausgeben als

mass [mæs] adj Massen- || s Masse f; (eccl) Messe; **the masses** die breite Masse f || tr massieren || intr sich ansammeln

massacre [′mæsəkər] s Massaker n || tr massakrieren, niedermetzeln

massage [mə′sɑʒ] s Massage f || tr massieren

masseur [mæ′sʌr] s Masseur m

masseuse [mæ′suz] s Masseuse f

massif [′mæsɪf] s Gebirgsstock m

massive [′mæsɪv] adj massiv

mass′ me′dia [′mɪdɪ•ə] spl Massenmedien pl

mass′ meet′ing s Massenversammlung f

mass′ mur′der s Massenmord m

mass′-produce′ tr serienmäßig herstellen

mass′ produc′tion s Serienherstellung f

mast [mæst] s Mast m; (food for swine) Mast f

master [′mæstər] adj (bedroom, key, switch, cylinder) Haupt- || s Herr m,

Meister m; (male head of a household) Hausherr m; (of a ship) Kapitän m || tr beherrschen

mas′ter build′er s Baumeister m

mas′ter car′penter s Zimmermeister m

mas′ter cop′y s Originalkopie f

masterful [′mæstərfəl] adj herrisch; (masterly) meisterhaft

masterly [′mæstərli] adj meisterhaft

mas′ter mechan′ic s Schlossermeister m

mas′termind′ s führender Geist m || tr planen und überwachen

Mas′ter of Arts′ s Magister m der freien Künste

Mas′ter of cer′emonies s Zeremonienmeister m

mas′ter of the house′ s Hausherr m

mas′terpiece′ s Meisterstück n

mas′ter ser′geant s Oberfeldwebel m

mas′ter stroke′ s Meisterstreich m

mas′terwork′ s Meisterwerk n

mastery [′mæstəri] s (of) Beherrschung f (genit); **gain m. over** die Oberhand gewinnen über (acc)

mast′head′ s (naut) Topp m; (typ) Impressum n

masticate [′mæstɪ,ket] tr zerkauen || intr kauen

mastiff [′mæstɪf] s Mastiff m

masturbate [′mæstər,bet] intr onanieren

masturbation [,mæstər′beʃən] s Onanie f

mat [mæt] s (for a floor) Matte f; (before the door) Türvorleger m; (under cups, vases, etc.) Zierdeckchen n || v (pret & pp matted; ger matting) tr (cover with matting) mit Matten belegen; (the hair) verfilzen || intr sich verfilzen

match [mætʃ] s Streichholz n; (for marriage) Partie f; (sport) Match n; **be a good m.** zueinanderpassen; **be a m.** for gewachsen sein (dat); **be no m.** for sich nicht messen können mit; **meet one's m.** seinen Mann finden || tr (fit together) zusammenstellen; (harmonize with) passen zu; (equal) (in) gleichkommen (in dat); (funds) in gleicher Höhe aufbringen; (adapt) in Übereinstimmung bringen mit; **be well matched** auf gleicher Höhe sein; **m. up** zusammenpassen; **m. wits with** sich geistig messen mit || intr zueinanderpassen

match′book′ s Streichholzbrief m

match′ box′ s Streichholzschachtel f

match′ing adj (clothes) passend; (funds) in gleicher Höhe || s Paarung f

match′mak′er s Heiratsvermittler –in mf; (sport) Veranstalter m

mate [met] s Genosse m, Kamerad m; (in marriage) Ehepartner m; (one of a pair, e.g., of gloves) Gegenstück n; (especially of birds) Männchen n, Weibchen n; (naut) Maat m || tr paaren || intr sich paaren

material [mə′tɪrɪ,əl] adj materiell; (important) wesentlich || s Material n, Stoff m; (tex) Stoff m

materialist [məˈtɪrɪ‑əlɪst] s Materialist –in mf

materialistic [mə‚tɪrɪ‑əˈlɪstɪk] adj materialistisch

materialize [məˈtɪrɪ‑ə‚laɪz] intr sich verwirklichen

materiel [mə‚tɪrɪˈel] s Material n; (mil) Kriegsmaterial n

maternal [məˈtʌrnəl] adj mütterlich; (relatives) mütterlicherseits

maternity [məˈtʌrnɪti] s Mutterschaft f

mater′nity dress′ s Umstandskleid n

mater′nity hos′pital s Wöchnerinnenheim n

mater′nity ward′ s Wöchnerinnenstation f

math [mæθ] s (coll) Mathe f

mathematical [‚mæθɪˈmætɪkəl] adj mathematisch

mathematician [‚mæθɪməˈtɪʃən] s Mathematiker –in mf

mathematics [‚mæθɪˈmætɪks] s Mathematik f

matinée [‚mætɪˈne] s Nachmittagsvorstellung f

mat′ing sea′son s Paarungszeit f

matins [ˈmætɪnz] spl Frühmette f

matriarch [ˈmetrɪ‚ɑrk] s Stammesmutter f

matriarchal [‚metrɪˈɑrkəl] adj matriarchalisch

matriarchy [ˈmetrɪ‚ɑrki] s Matriarchat n

matricide [ˈmætrɪ‚saɪd] s (act) Muttermord m; (person) Muttermörder –in mf

matriculate [məˈtrɪkjə‚let] tr immatrikulieren ‖ intr sich immatrikulieren

matriculation [mə‚trɪkjəˈleʃən] s Immatrikulation f

matrimonial [‚mætrɪˈmonɪ‑əl] adj Ehe-

matrimony [ˈmætrɪ‚moni] s Ehestand m

ma‧trix [ˈmetrɪks] s (–trices [trɪ‚siz] & –trixes) (mold) Gießform f; (math) Matrix f; (typ) Matrize f

matron [ˈmetrən] s Matrone f

matronly [ˈmetrənli] adj matronenhaft, gesetzt

matt [mæt] adj (phot) matt

matter [ˈmætər] s Stoff m; (affair) Sache f, Angelegenheit f; (pus) Eiter m; (phys) Materie f; as a m. of course routinemäßig; as matters now stand wie die Sache jetzt liegt; for that m. was das betrifft; it's a m. of es handelt sich um; it's a m. of life and death es geht um Leben und Tod; m. of opinion Ansichtssache f; m. of taste Geschmackssache f; something is the m. with his heart er hat was am Herz; no laughing m. nichts zum Lachen; no m. ganz gleich; what's the m. (with)? was ist los (mit)? ‖ intr von Bedeutung sein; it doesn't m. es macht nichts (aus); it doesn't m. to me es liegt mir nichts daran; it matters a great deal to me es liegt mir sehr viel daran

mat′ter of fact′ s Tatsache f; as a m. tatsächlich

mat′ter-of-fact′ adj sachlich, nüchtern

Matthew [ˈmæθju] s Matthäus m

mattock [ˈmætək] s Breithacke f

mattress [ˈmætrɪs] s Matratze f

mature [məˈtʃʊr] adj (& fig) reif ‖ tr reifen lassen ‖ intr reifen; (fin) fällig werden

maturity [məˈtʃʊrɪti] s Reife f; (fin) Verfall m

maudlin [ˈmɔdlɪn] adj rührselig

maul [mɔl] tr schlimm zurichten

maulstick [ˈmɔl‚stɪk] s Mahlstock m

mausole‧um [‚mɔsəˈli‑əm] s (–ums & –a [ə]) Mausoleum n

maw [mɔ] s (mouth of an animal) Rachen m; (stomach of an animal) Tiermagen m; (of birds) Kropf m

mawkish [ˈmɔkɪʃ] adj rührselig

maxim [ˈmæksɪm] s Maxime f, Lehrspruch m

maximum [ˈmæksɪməm] adj Höchst‑; m. load Höchstbelastung f ‖ s Maximum n

May [me] s Mai m ‖ **may** v (pret **might** [maɪt]) aux (expressing possibility) mögen, können; (expressing permission) dürfen; (expressing a wish) mögen; be that as it may wie dem auch sei; come what may komme, was da wolle; it may be too late es ist vielleicht zu spät; that may be das kann (or mag) sein

maybe [ˈmebi] adv vielleicht

May′ Day′ s der erste Mai

mayhem [ˈmehəm] s Körperverletzung f

mayonnaise [‚me‑əˈnez] s Mayonnaise f

mayor [mer] s Bürgermeister m; (of a large city) Oberbürgermeister m

May′pole′ s Maibaum m

May′ queen′ s Maikönigin f

maze [mez] s Irrgarten m; (fig) Gewirr n

me [mi] pers pron (direct object) mich; (indirect object) mir; this one is on me das geht auf meine Rechnung

mead [mid] s (hist) Met m; (poet) Aue f

meadow [ˈmedo] s Wiese f

mead′owland′ s Wiesenland n

meager [ˈmigər] adj karg, kärglich

meal [mil] s Mahl n, Mahlzeit f; (grain) grobes Mehl n

meal′ tick′et s Gutschein m für e‑e Mahlzeit

meal′time′ s Essenszeit f

mealy [ˈmili] adj mehlig

mealy-mouthed [ˈmili‚maʊðd] adj zurückhaltend

mean [min] adj (nasty) bösartig; (lowly) gemein, niedrig; (shabby) schäbig; (in statistics) mittlere; no m. kein schlechter ‖ s (log) Mittelbegriff m; (math) Mittel n; by all means unbedingt; by every means mit allen Mitteln; by fair means or foul ganz gleich wie; by lawful means auf dem Rechtswege; by means of mittels (*genit*); **by no means** keineswegs; **live beyond one's means** über seine Verhältnisse leben; **live within one's means** seinen Verhältnissen entsprechend leben; **means** (*way*) Mittel *n*; (*resources*) Mittel *pl*, Vermögen *n*; **means of transportation** Verkehrsmittel *n*; **means to an end** Mittel *pl* zum Zweck; **of means** bemittelt ‖ *v* (*pret & pp* meant [ment]) *tr* (*intend, intend to say*) meinen; (*signify*) bedeuten; **be meant for** (*said, e.g., of a remark*) gelten (*dat*); (*said, e.g., of a gift*) bestimmt sein für; **it means a lot to me to** (*inf*) mir liegt viel daran zu (*inf*); **m. business** es ernst meinen; **m. little** (or **much**) wenig (or viel) gelten; **m. no harm** es nicht böse meinen; **m. s.o. no harm** j-n nicht verletzen wollen; **m. the world to s.o.** j-m alles bedeuten; **what is meant by ...?** was versteht man unter ...? ‖ *intr*—**m. well** es gut meinen

meander [mɪˈændər] *intr* sich winden

mean'ing *s* Bedeutung *f*; **take on m. e-n** Sinn bekommen; **what's the m. of this?** was soll das heißen?

meaningful [ˈmiːnɪŋfəl] *adj* sinnvoll

meaningless [ˈmiːnɪŋlɪs] *adj* sinnlos

mean'-look'ing *adj* bösartig aussehend

meanness [ˈmiːnnɪs] *s* Gemeinheit *f*; (*nastiness*) Bösartigkeit *f*

mean'time', mean'while' *adv* mittlerweile ‖ *s*—**in the m.** mittlerweile, in der Zwischenzeit

measles [ˈmiːzəlz] *s* Masern *pl*; (*German measles*) Röteln *pl*

measly [ˈmiːzli] *adj* kümmerlich, lumpig

measurable [ˈmɛʒərəbəl] *adj* meßbar

measure [ˈmɛʒər] *s* Maß *n*; (*step*) Maßnahme *f*; (*law*) Gesetz *n*; (*mus*) Takt *m*; **beyond m.** übermäßig; **for good m.** obendrein; **in a great m.** in großem Maß; **to some m.** gewissermaßen; **take drastic measures** durchgreifen; **take measures to** (*inf*) Maßnahmen ergreifen um zu (*inf*); **take s.o.'s m.** (*fig*) j-n einschätzen ‖ *tr* messen; **m. off** abmessen; **m. out** ausmessen ‖ *intr* messen; **m. up to** gewachsen sein (*dat*)

measurement [ˈmɛʒərmənt] *s* (*measured dimension*) Maß *n*; (*measuring*) Messung *f*; **measurements** Maße *pl*; **take s.o.'s measurements for** j-m Maß nehmen zu

meas'uring cup' *s* Meßbecher *m*

meas'uring tape' *s* Meßband *n*

meat [mit] *s* Fleisch *n*; (*of a nut, of the matter*) Kern *m*

meat'ball' *m* Fleischklößchen *n*

meat' grind'er *s* Fleischwolf *m*

meat'hook' *s* Fleischhaken *m*

meat'mar'ket *s* Fleischmarkt *m*

meat' pie' *s* Fleischpastete *f*

meaty [ˈmiti] *adj* fleischig; (fig) kernig

Mecca [ˈmɛkə] *s* Mekka *n*

mechanic [məˈkænɪk] *s* Mechaniker *m*, Schlosser *m*; (aut) Autoschlosser *m*; **mechanics** Mechanik *f*

mechanical [məˈkænɪkəl] *adj* mechanisch

mechan'ical engineer' *s* Maschinenbauingenieur *m*

mechan'ical engineer'ing *s* Maschinenbau *m*

mechanism [ˈmɛkəˌnɪzəm] *s* Mechanismus *m*

mechanize [ˈmɛkəˌnaɪz] *tr* mechanisieren

medal [ˈmɛdəl] *s* Medaille *f*, Orden *m*

medallion [mɪˈdæljən] *s* Medaillon *n*

meddle [ˈmɛdəl] *intr* sich einmischen; **m. with** sich abgeben mit

meddler [ˈmɛdlər] *s* zudringliche Person *f*

meddlesome [ˈmɛdəlsəm] *adj* zudringlich

media [ˈmidɪə] *spl* Medien *pl*

median [ˈmidɪən] *adj* mittlere, Mittel- ‖ *s* (arith) Mittelwert *m*; (geom) Mittellinie *f*

me'dian strip' *s* Mittelstreifen *m*

mediate [ˈmidɪˌet] *tr & intr* vermitteln

mediation [ˌmidɪˈeʃən] *s* Vermittlung *f*

mediator [ˈmidɪˌetər] *s* Vermittler –in *mf*

medic [ˈmɛdɪk] *s* (mil) Sanitäter *m*

medical [ˈmɛdɪkəl] *adj* (*of a doctor*) ärztlich; (*of medicine*) medizinisch; (*of the sick*) Kranken-

med'ical bul'letin *s* Krankheitsbericht *m*

med'ical corps' *s* Sanitätstruppe *f*

med'ical profes'sion *s* Arztberuf *m*

med'ical school' *s* medizinische Fakultät *f*

med'ical sci'ence *s* Heilkunde *f*

med'ical stu'dent *s* Medizinstudent –in *mf*

medication [ˌmɛdɪˈkeʃən] *s* Medikament *n*

medicinal [məˈdɪsɪnəl] *adj* medizinisch

medicine [ˈmɛdɪsən] *s* Medizin *f*, Arznei *f*; (*profession*) Medizin *f*; **practice m.** den Arztberuf ausüben

med'icine cab'inet *s* Hausapotheke *f*

med'icine kit' *s* Reiseapotheke *f*

med'icine man' *s* Medizinmann *m*

medic-o [ˈmɛdɪˌko] *s* (–cos) (coll) Mediziner –in *mf*

medieval [ˌmidɪˈivəl], [ˌmɛdɪˈivəl] *adj* mittelalterlich

mediocre [ˌmidɪˈokər] *adj* mittelmäßig

mediocrity [ˌmidɪˈakrɪti] *s* Mittelmäßigkeit *f*

meditate [ˈmɛdɪˌtet] *tr* vorhaben ‖ *intr* (on) meditieren (über *acc*)

meditation [ˌmɛdɪˈteʃən] *s* Meditation *f*

Mediterranean [ˌmɛdɪtəˈrenɪən] *adj* Mittelmeer- ‖ *s* Mittelmeer *n*

medi-um [ˈmidɪəm] *adj* Mittel-, mittlere ‖ *s* (–ums & –a [ə]) Mittel *n*; (*culture*) Nährboden *m*; (*in spiritualism, communications*) Medium *n*; **through the m. of** vermittels (*genit*)

me'dium of exchange' *s* Tauschmittel *n*

me'dium-rare' *adj* halb durchgebraten

me'dium size' *s* Mittelgröße *f*

med′ium-sized′ *adj* mittelgroß

medley [′medli] *s* Mischmasch *m*; (mus) Potpourri *n*

medul·la [mɪ′dʌlə] *s* (–las & –lae [li]) Knochenmark *n*, Mark *n*

meek [mik] *adj* sanftmütig; **m. as a lamb** lammfromm

meekness [′miknɪs] *s* Sanftmut *m*

meerschaum [′mɪrʃəm] *s* Meerschaum *m*

meet [mit] *adj* passend ‖ *s* (sport) Treffen *n*, Veranstaltung *f* ‖ *v* (*pret* & *pp* **met** [met]) *tr* begegnen (*dat*), treffen; (*make the acquaintance of*) kennenlernen; (*demands*) befriedigen; (*obligations*) nachkommen (*dat*); (*wishes*) erfüllen; (*a deadline*) einhalten; **m. s.o. at the train** j-n von der Bahn abholen; **m. s.o. halfway** j-m auf halbem Wege entgegenkommen; **m. the train** zum Zug gehen; **pleased to m. you** freut mich sehr, sehr angenehm ‖ *intr* (*said of persons, of two ends*) zusammenkommen; (*said of persons*) sich treffen; (*in conference*) tagen; (*said of roads, rivers*) sich vereinigen; **make both ends m.** gerade mit dem Geld auskommen; **m. again** sich wiedersehen; **m. up with s.o.** j-n einholen; **m. with** zusammentreffen mit; **m. with an accident** verunglücken; **m. with a refusal** e-e Fehlbitte tun; **m. with approval** Beifall finden; **m. with success** Erfolg haben

meet′ing *s* (*of an organization*) Versammlung *f*; (*e.g., of a committee*) Sitzung *f*; (*of individuals*) Zusammenkunft *f*

meet′ing place′ *s* Treffpunkt *m*

megacycle [′megə‚saɪkəl], **megahertz** [′megə‚hʌrts] *s* (elec) Megahertz *n*

megalomania [‚megəlo′menɪ-ə] *s* Größenwahn *m*

megaphone [′megə‚fon] *s* Sprachrohr *n*

megohm [′meg‚om] *s* Megohm *n*

melancholy [′melən‚kɑli] *adj* schwermütig ‖ *s* Schwermut *f*

melee [′mele], [′mele] *s* Gemenge *n*

mellow [′melo] *adj* (*very ripe*) mürb(e); (*wine*) abgelagert; (*voice*) schmelzend; (*person*) gereift ‖ *tr* zur Reife bringen; (fig) mildern ‖ *intr* mürb(e) werden; (fig) mild werden

melodic [mɪ′lɑdɪk] *adj* melodisch

melodious [mɪ′lodɪ-əs] *adj* melodisch

melodrama [′melo‚drɑmə] *s* (& fig) Melodrama *n*

melody [′melədi] *s* Melodie *f*

melon [′melən] *s* Melone *f*

melt [melt] *tr* & *intr* schmelzen

melt′ing point′ *s* Schmelzpunkt *m*

melt′ing pot′ *s* (& fig) Schmelztiegel *m*

member [′membər] *s* Glied *n*; (*person*) Mitglied *n*, Angehörige *mf*; **m. of the family** Familienangehörige *mf*

mem′bership′ *s* Mitgliedschaft *f*; (*collectively*) Mitglieder *pl*; (*number of members*) Mitgliederzahl *f*

mem′bership card′ *s* Mitgliedskarte *f*

membrane [′membren] *s* Häutchen *n*, Membran(e) *f*

memen·to [mɪ′mento] *s* (–tos & –toes) Erinnerung *f*, Memento *n*

mem·o [′memo] *s* (–os) (coll) Notiz *f*

mem′o book′ *s* Notizbuch *n*, Agenda *f*

memoirs [′memwarz] *spl* Memoiren *pl*

mem′o pad′ *s* Notizblock *m*, Agenda *f*

memorable [′memərəbəl] *adj* denkwürdig

memoran·dum [‚memə′rændəm] *s* (–dums & –da [də]) Notiz *f*, Vermerk *m*; (dipl) Memorandum *n*

memorial [mɪ′morɪ-əl] *adj* Gedächtnis–. Erinnerungs– ‖ *s* Denkmal *n*

Memor′ial Day′ *s* Gefallenengedenktag *m*

memorialize [mɪ′morɪ-ə‚laɪz] *tr* gedenken (*genit*)

memorize [′memə‚raɪz] *tr* auswendig lernen

memory [′meməri] *s* (*faculty*) Gedächtnis *n*; (*of*) Gedenken *n* (an *acc*), Erinnerung *f* (an *acc*); **commit to m.** auswendig lernen; **escape one's m.** seinem Gedächtnis entfallen; **from m.** aus dem Gedächtnis; **in m. of** zur Erinnerung an (*acc*); **of blessed m.** seligen Angedenkens; **within the m. of men** seit Menschengedenken

menace [′menɪs] *s* (to) Drohung *f* (*genit*) ‖ *tr* bedrohen

menagerie [mə′nædʒəri] *s* Menagerie *f*

mend [mend] *s* Besserung *f*; **on the m.** auf dem Wege der Besserung ‖ *tr* (*clothes*) ausbessern; (*socks*) stopfen; (*repair*) reparieren

mendacious [men′deʃəs] *adj* lügnerisch

mendicant [′mendɪkənt] *adj* Bettel– ‖ *s* Bettelmönch *m*

menfolk [′men‚fok] *spl* Mannsleute *pl*

menial [′minɪ-əl] *adj* niedrig ‖ *s* Diener –in *mf*

menopause [′menə‚pɔz] *s* Wechseljahre *pl*

menses [′mensiz] *spl* Monatsfluß *m*

men′s′ room′ *s* Herrentoilette *f*

men′s′ size′ *s* Herrengröße *f*

men′s′ store′ *s* Herrenbekleidungsgeschäft *n*

menstruate [′menstru‚et] *intr* menstruieren

menstruation [‚menstru′eʃən] *s* Menstruation *f*

men′s′ wear′ *s* Herrenbekleidung *f*

mental [′mentəl] *adj* geistig, Geistes–

men′tal an′guish *s* Seelenpein *f*

men′tal arith′metic *s* Kopfrechnen *n*

men′tal capac′ity *s* Fassungskraft *f*

men′tal disor′der *s* Geistesstörung *f*

men′tal institu′tion *s* Nervenheilanstalt *f*

mentality [men′tælɪti] *s* Mentalität *f*

mentally [′mentəli] *adv* geistig, Geistes–; **m. alert** geistesgegenwärtig; **m. disturbed** geistesgestört; **m. lazy** denkfaul

men′tal reserva′tion *s* geistiger Vorbehalt *m*

men′tal teleg′athy *s* Gedankenübertragung *f*

mention [′menʃən] *s* Erwähnung *f*;

make m. of erwähnen || *tr* erwähnen, nennen; be mentioned zur Sprache kommen; **don't m. it!** keine Ursache!; **not worth mentioning** nicht der Rede wert

menu ['menju] *s* Speisekarte *f*

meow [mi'aʊ] *s* Miauen *n* || *intr* miauen

mercantile ['mʌrkən,til], ['mʌrkən,taɪl] *adj* Handels-, kaufmännisch

mercenary ['mʌrsə,neri] *adj* gewinnsüchtig || *s* Söldner *m*

merchandise ['mʌrtʃən,daɪz] *s* Ware *f* || *tr* handeln

mer'chandising *s* Verkaufspolitik *f*

merchant ['mʌrtʃənt] *s* Händler, Kaufmann *m*

mer'chant-man *s* (-men) Handelsschiff *n*

mer'chant marine' *s* Handelsmarine *f*

mer'chant ves'sel *s* Handelsschiff *n*

merciful ['mʌrsɪfəl] *adj* barmherzig

merciless ['mʌrsɪlɪs] *adj* erbarmungslos

mercurial [mer'kjʊrɪ-əl] *adj* quecksilbrig

mercury ['mʌrkjəri] *s* Quecksilber *n*

mercy ['mʌrsi] *s* Barmherzigkeit *f*; **be at s.o.'s m.** in j-s Gewalt sein; **be at the m. of** (*e.g., the wind, waves*) preisgegeben sein (*dat*); **beg for m.** um Gnade flehen; **show no m.** keine Gnade walten lassen; **show s.o. m.** sich j-s erbarmen; **throw oneself on the m. of** sich auf Gnade und Ungnade ergeben (*dat*); **without m.** ohne Gnade

mere [mɪr] *adj* bloß, rein

merely ['mɪrli] *adv* nur, lediglich

meretricious [,meri'trɪʃəs] *adj* (*tawdry*) flitterhaft; (*characteristic of a prostitute*) dirnenhaft

merge [mʌrdʒ] *tr* verschmelzen || *intr* sich verschmelzen

merger ['mʌrdʒər] *s* (com) Fusion *f*; (jur) Verschmelzung *f*

meridian [mə'rɪdɪ-ən] *s* (astr) Meridian *m*; (geog) Meridian *m*, Längenkreis *m*

meringue [mə'ræŋ] *s* (*topping*) Eierschnee *m*; (*pastry*) Schaumgebäck *n*

merit ['merɪt] *s* Verdienst *n*; **of great m.** hochverdient || *tr* verdienen

meritorious [,merə'tori-əs] *adj* verdienstvoll

merlin ['mʌrlɪn] *s* (orn) Merlinfalke *m*

mermaid ['mʌr,med] *s* Seejungfer *f*

merriment ['meriment] *s* Fröhlichkeit *f*

merry ['meri] *adj* fröhlich, heiter

Mer'ry Christ'mas *s* fröhliche Weihnachten *pl*

mer'ry-go-round' *s* Karussell *n*

mer'rymak'er *s* Zecher –in *mf*

mesh [meʃ] *s* Masche *f*; (network) Netzwerk *n*; (mach) Ineinandergreifen *n*; **meshes** (fig) Schlingen *pl* || *intr* ineinandergreifen

mesmerize ['mesmə,raɪz] *tr* hypnotisieren

mess [mes] *s* (*disorder*) Durcheinander *n*; (*dirty condition*) Schweinerei *f*; (*for officers*) Messe *f*; **a nice m.!** e-e schöne Wirtschaft!; **get into a m.** in die Klemme geraten; **make a m.** Schmutz machen; **make a m. of** verpfuschen; **what a m.!** nette Zustände! || *tr*—**m. up** (*dirty*) beschmutzen; (*put into disarray*) in Unordnung bringen || *intr*—**m. around** herumtrödeln; **m. around with** herummurksen an (*dat*)

message ['mesɪdʒ] *s* Botschaft *f*

messenger ['mesəndʒər] *s* Bote *m*, Botin *f*

mess' hall' *s* Messe *f*

Messiah [mə'saɪ-ə] *s* Messias *m*

mess' kit' *s* Eßgeschirr *n*

messy ['mesi] *adj* (*disorderly*) unordentlich; (*dirty*) dreckig

metabolism [mə'tæbə,lɪzəm] *s* Stoffwechsel *m*

metal ['metəl] *s* Metall *n*

metallic [mɪ'tælɪk] *adj* metallisch

metallurgy ['metə,lʌrdʒi] *s* Hüttenwesen *n*, Metallurgie *f*

met'alwork' *s* Metallarbeit *f*

metamorpho-sis [,metə'mɔrfəsɪs] *s* (-ses [,siz]) Verwandlung *f*

metaphor ['metə,fɔr] *s* Metapher *f*

metaphorical [,metə'fɔrɪkəl] *adj* bildlich

metaphysical [,metə'fɪzɪkəl] *adj* metaphysisch

metaphysics [,metə'fɪzɪks] *s* Metaphysik *f*

metathe-sis [mɪ'tæθɪsɪs] *s* (-ses [,siz]) Metathese *f*, Lautversetzung *f*

mete [mit] *tr*—**m. out** austeilen

meteor ['mitɪ-ər] *s* Meteor *m*

meteoric [,mitɪ'ɔrɪk] *adj* meteorisch; (fig) kometenhaft

meteorite ['mitɪ-ə,raɪt] *s* Meteorit *m*

meteorologist [,mitɪ-ə'ralədʒɪst] *s* Meteorologe *m*, Meteorologin *f*

meteorology [,mitɪ-ə'ralədʒi] *s* Meteorologie *f*, Wetterkunde *f*

meter ['mitər] *s* Meter *m* & *n*; (*instrument*) Messer *m*, Zähler *m*; (pros) Versmaß *n*

me'ter read'er *s* Zählerableser –in *mf*

methane ['meθen] *s* Methan *n*, Sumpfgas *n*

method ['meθəd] *s* Methode *f*

methodic(al) [mɪ'θadɪk(əl)] *adj* methodisch

Methodist ['meθədɪst] *s* Methodist –in *mf*

methodology [,meθə'dalədʒi] *s* Methodenlehre *f*

Methuselah [mɪ'θuzələ] *s* Methusalem *m*

meticulous [mɪ'tɪkjələs] *adj* übergenau

metric(al) ['metrɪk(əl)] *adj* metrisch

metrics ['metrɪks] *s* Metrik *f*

metronome ['metrə,nom] *s* Metronom *n*

metropolis [mɪ'trapəlɪs] *s* Metropole *f*

metropolitan [,metrə'palɪtən] *adj* großstädtisch || *s* (eccl) Metropolit *m*

mettle ['metəl] *s* (*temperament*) Veranlagung *f*; (*courage*) Mut *m*

mettlesome ['metəlsəm] *adj* mutig

mew [mju] s Miau n || intr miauen

Mexican ['meksɪkən] adj mexikanisch || s Mexikaner –in mf

Mexico ['meksɪ‚ko] s Mexiko n

mezzanine ['mezə‚nin] s Zwischengeschoß n

mica ['maɪkə] s Glimmer m, Marienglas n

Michael ['maɪkəl] s Michel m

microbe ['maɪkrob] s Mikrobe f

microbiology [‚maɪkrəbaɪ'alədʒi] s Mikrobiologie f

microcosm ['maɪkrə‚kazəm] s Mikrokosmos m

microfilm ['maɪkrə‚fɪlm] s Mikrofilm m || tr mikrofilmen

microgroove ['maɪkrə‚gruv] s Mikrorille f

mic′rogroove rec′ord s Schallplatte f mit Mikrorillen

microphone ['maɪkrə‚fon] s Mikrophon n

microscope ['maɪkrə‚skop] s Mikroskop n

microscopic [‚maɪkrə'skapɪk] adj mikroskopisch

microwave ['maɪkrə‚wev] s Mikrowelle f

mid [mɪd] adj mittlere

midair′ s—in m. mitten in der Luft

mid′day′ adj mittäglich, Mittags– || s Mittag m

middle ['mɪdəl] adj mittlere || s Mitte f, Mittel n; in the m. of inmitten (genit), mitten in (dat)

mid′dle age′ s mittleres Lebensalter n; Middle Ages Mittelalter n

middle-aged ['mɪdəl‚edʒd] adj mittleren Alters

mid′dle class′ s Mittelstand m

mid′dle-class′ adj bürgerlich

mid′dle dis′tance s Mittelgrund m

mid′dle ear′ s Mittelohr n

Mid′dle East′, the s der Mittlere Osten

mid′dle fin′ger s Mittelfinger m

Mid′dle High′ Ger′man s Mittelhochdeutsch n

Mid′dle Low′ Ger′man s Mittelniederdeutsch n

mid′dle-man′ s (–men′) Mittelsmann m, Zwischenhändler m

mid′dleweight box′er s Mittelgewichtler m

mid′dleweight divi′sion s Mittelgewicht n

middling ['mɪdlɪŋ] adj mittelmäßig || adv leidlich, ziemlich

middy ['mɪdi] s (nav) Fähnrich m zur See

midget ['mɪdʒɪt] s Zwerg m

mid′get rail′road s Liliputbahn f

mid′get submarine′ s Kleinst-U-Boot n

midland ['mɪdlənd] adj binnenländisch

mid′night′ adj mitternächtlich; burn the m. oil bis in die tiefe Nacht arbeiten || s Mitternacht f; at m. um Mitternacht

midriff ['mɪdrɪf] s (of a dress) Mittelteil m; (diaphragm) Zwerchfell n; (middle part of the body) Magengrube f; have a bare m. die Taille frei lassen

mid′shipman′ s (–men′) Fähnrich m zur See

midst [mɪdst] s Mitte f; from our m. aus unserer Mitte; in the m. of mitten in (dat)

mid′stream′ s—in m. in der Mitte des Stromes

mid′sum′mer s Mittsommer m

mid′-term′ adj mitten im Semester || midterms spl Prüfungen pl mitten im Semester

mid′way′ adj in der Mitte befindlich || adv auf halbem Weg || s Mitte f des Weges; (at a fair) Mittelstraße f

mid′week′ s Wochenmitte f

mid′wife′ s (–wives′) Hebamme f

mid′win′ter s Mittwinter m

mid′year′ adj in der Mitte des Studienjahres || midyears spl Prüfungen pl in der Mitte des Studienjahres

mien [min] s Miene f

miff [mɪf] s kleine Auseinandersetzung f || tr ärgern

might [maɪt] s Macht f, Kraft f; with m. and main mit aller Kraft || aux used to form the potential mood, e.g., she m. lose her way sie könnte sich verirren; we m. as well go es ist wohl besser, wenn wir gehen

mightily ['maɪtəli] adv gewaltig; (coll) enorm

mighty ['maɪti] adj mächtig || adv (coll) furchtbar

migraine ['maɪgren] s Migräne f

mi′grant work′er ['maɪgrənt] s Wanderarbeiter –in mf

migrate ['maɪgret] intr wandern, ziehen

migration [maɪ'greʃən] s Wanderung f; (e.g., of birds) Zug m

migratory ['maɪgrə‚tori] adj Wander-

mi′gratory bird′ s Zugvogel m

Milan [mɪ'læn] s Mailand n

mild [maɪld] adj mild, lind

mildew ['mɪl‚d(j)u] s Mehltau m

mildly ['maɪldli] adv leicht, schwach; to put it m. gelinde gesagt

mildness ['maɪldnɪs] s Milde f

mile [maɪl] s Meile f; for miles meilenweit; miles apart meilenweit auseinander; miles per hour Stundengeschwindigkeit f

mileage ['maɪlɪdʒ] s Meilenzahl f; (charge) Meilengeld n

mile′post′ s Wegweiser m mit Entfernungsangabe

mile′stone′ s (& fig) Meilenstein m

militancy ['mɪlɪtənsi] s Kampfgeist m

militant ['mɪlɪtənt] adj militant || s Kämpfer –in mf

militarism ['mɪlɪtə‚rɪzəm] s Militarismus m

militarize ['mɪlɪtə‚raɪz] tr auf den Krieg vorbereiten

military ['mɪlə‚teri] adj militärisch; (academy, band, government) Militär– || s Militär n

mil′itary campaign′ s Feldzug m

mil′itary cem′etery s Soldatenfriedhof m

mil′itary obliga′tions spl Wehrpflicht f

mil′itary police′ s Militärpolizei f

mil′itary police′man *s* (**–men**) Militär-
polizist *m*

mil′itary sci′ence *s* Kriegswissenschaft
f

militate [′mɪlɪ‚tet] *intr* (**against**) entgegenwirken (*dat*)

militia [mɪ′lɪʃə] *s* Miliz *f*

mili′tia-man *s* (**–men**) Milizsoldat *m*

milk [mɪlk] *s* Milch *f* || *tr* (& *fig*)
melken

milk′ bar′ *s* Milchbar *f*

milk′ car′ton *s* Milchtüte *f*

milk′maid′ *s* Milchmädchen *n*

milk′man *s* (**–men′**) Milchmann *m*

milk′ pail′ *s* Melkeimer *m*

milk′shake′ *s* Milchmischgetränk *n*

milk′sop′ *s* Milchbart *m*

milk′ tooth′ *s* Milchzahn *m*

milk′weed′ *s* Wolfsmilch *f*, Seiden-
pflanze *f*

milky [′mɪlki] *adj* milchig

Milk′y Way′ *s* Milchstraße *f*

mill [mɪl] *s* Mühle *f*; (*factory*) Fabrik
f, Werk *n*; **put through the m.** (coll)
durch e-e harte Schule schicken || *tr*
(*grain*) mahlen; (*coins*) rändeln;
(*with a milling machine*) fräsern;
(*chocolate*) quirlen || *intr*—**m. around**
durcheinanderlaufen

millenial [mɪ′lenɪ-əl] *adj* tausendjährig

millenni-um [mɪ′lenɪ-əm] *s* (**–ums &**
–a [ə]) Jahrtausend *n*

miller [′mɪlər] *s* Müller *m*

millet [′mɪlɪt] *s* Hirse *f*

milligram [′mɪlɪ‚græm] *s* Milligramm
n

millimeter [′mɪlɪ‚mɪtər] *s* Millimeter
n

milliner [′mɪlɪnər] *s* Putzmacher –in
mf

mil′linery shop′ [′mɪlɪ‚nerɪ] *s* Damen-
hutgeschäft *n*

mill′ing *s* (*of grain*) Mahlen *n*; (*of*
wood or metal) Fräsen *n*

mill′ing machine′ *s* Fräsmaschine *f*

million [′mɪljən] *adj*—**one m. people**
e-e Million Menschen; **two m. people**
zwei Millionen Menschen || *s* Million
f

millionaire [‚mɪljən′er] *s* Millionär –in
mf

millionth [′mɪljənθ] *adj & pron* mil-
lionste || *s* (*fraction*) Millionstel *n*

mill′pond′ *s* Mühlteich *m*

mill′stone′ *s* Mühlstein *m*

mill′ wheel′ *s* Mühlrad *n*

mime [maɪm] *s* Mime *m*, Mimin *f* || *tr*
mimen

mimeograph [′mɪmɪ-ə‚græf] *s* Verviel-
fältigungsapparat *m* || *tr* vervielfäl-
tigen

mim-ic [′mɪmɪk] *s* Mimiker –in *mf* ||
v (*pret & pp* **–icked**; *ger* **–icking**) *tr*
nachäffen

mimicry [′mɪmɪkrɪ] *s* Nachäffen *n*;
(*zool*) Mimikry *f*

mimosa [mɪ′mosə] *s* Mimose *f*

minaret [‚mɪnə′ret] *s* Minarett *n*

mince [mɪns] *tr* (*meat*) zerhacken; **not**
m. words kein Blatt vor den Mund
nehmen

mince′meat′ *s* Pastetenfüllung *f*;

(*chopped meat*) Hackfleisch *n*; **make**
m. of (fig) in die Pfanne hauen

mind [maɪnd] *s* Geist *m*; **bear in m.**
denken an (*acc*); **be of one m.** ein
Herz und e-e Seele sein; **be of two**
minds geteilter Meinung sein; **be out**
of one's m. nicht bei Trost sein;
call to m. erinnern; (*remember*) sich
erinnern; **change one's m.** sich anders besinnen; **give s.o. a piece of**
one's m. j–m gründlich die Meinung
sagen; **have a good m. to** (*inf*) große
Lust haben zu (*inf*); **have in m.** im
Sinn haben zu (*inf*); **have one's m.**
on s.th. ständig an etw denken
müssen; **I can't get her out of my m.**
sie will mir nicht aus dem Sinn;
know one's own m. wissen, was man
will; **of sound m.** zurechnungsfähig;
put s.th. out of one's m. sich [*dat*]
etw aus dem Sinn schlagen; **set one's**
m. on sein Sinnen und Trachten
richten auf (*acc*); **slip s.o.'s m.** j–m
entfallen; **to my m.** meines Erach-
tens || *tr* (*watch over*) aufpassen auf
(*acc*); (*obey*) gehorchen (*dat*); (*be*
troubled by; take care of) sich kümmern um; **do you m. if I smoke?**
macht es Ihnen etw aus, wenn ich
rauche?; **do you m. the smoke?** macht
Ihnen der Rauch etw aus?; **I don't**
m. your smoking ich habe nichts dagegen, daß (or wenn) Sie rauchen;
m. your own business! kümmere dich
um deine Angelegenheit!; **m. you!**
wohlgemerkt! || *intr*—**I don't m.** es
macht mir nichts aus; **I don't m. if**
I do (coll) ja, recht gern; **never m.!**
schon gut!

–minded [‚maɪndɪd] *suf* –mütig, -ge-
sinnt, –sinnig

mindful [′maɪndfəl] *adj* (**of**) eingedenk
(*genit*); **be m.** of achten auf (*acc*)

mind′ read′er *s* Gedankenleser –in *mf*

mind′ read′ing *s* Gedankenlesen *n*

mine [maɪn] *s* Bergwerk *n*, Mine *f*;
(fig) Fundgrube *f*; (mil) Mine *f* ||
poss pron meiner || *tr* (*e.g., coal*)
abbauen; (mil) verminen || *intr*—**m.**
for graben nach

mine′ detec′tor *s* Minensuchgerät *n*

mine′field′ *s* Minenfeld *n*

minelayer [′maɪn‚le-ər] *s* Minenleger
m

miner [′maɪnər] *s* Bergarbeiter *m*

mineral [′mɪnərəl] *adj* mineralisch,
Mineral– || *s* Mineral *n*

mineralogy [‚mɪnə′rɑlədʒɪ] *s* Mineralogie *f*

min′eral resourc′es *spl* Bodenschätze
pl

min′eral wa′ter *s* Mineralwasser *n*

mine′sweep′er *s* Minenräumboot *n*

mingle [′mɪŋgəl] *tr* vermengen || *intr*
(**with**) sich mischen (unter *acc*)

miniature [′mɪnɪ-ət/ər], [′mɪnɪt/ər]
adj Miniatur–, Klein– || *s* Miniatur *f*

minimal [′mɪnɪməl] *adj* minimal, Mindest–

minimize [′mɪnə‚maɪz] *tr* auf das
Minimum herabsetzen; (fig) bagatellisieren

minimum ['mɪnɪməm] *adj* minimal, Mindest– ‖ *s* Minimum *n; (lowest price)* untere Preisgrenze *f*

min'imum wage' *s* Mindestlohn *m*

min'ing *adj* Bergbau– ‖ *s* Bergbau *m*, Bergwesen *n; (mil)* Minenlegen *n*

minion ['mɪnjən] *s* Günstling *m*

miniskirt ['mɪnɪˌskɑrt] *s* Minirock *m*

minister ['mɪnɪstər] *s* (eccl) Geistlicher *m;* (pol) Minister *m* ‖ *intr*—m. to dienen (*dat*); *(aid)* Hilfe leisten (*dat*)

ministerial [ˌmɪnɪs'tɪrɪ·əl] *adj* (eccl) geistlich; (pol) ministeriell

ministry ['mɪnɪstri] *s* *(office)* (eccl) geistliches Amt *n; (the clergy)* (eccl) geistlicher Stand *m;* (pol) Ministerium *n*

mink [mɪŋk] *s* (zool) Nerz *m; (fur)* Nerzfell *n*

mink' coat' *s* Nerzmantel *m*

minnow ['mɪno] *s* Pfrille *f,* Elritze *f*

minor ['maɪnər] *adj* minder, geringer, Neben– ‖ *s (person)* Minderjährige *mf;* (educ) Nebenfach *n;* (log) Untersatz *m;* (mus) Moll *n* ‖ *intr*—m. in als Nebenfach studieren

minority [mɪ'nɔrɪti] *adj* Minderheits– ‖ *s* Minderheit *f; (of votes)* Stimmenminderheit *f; (ethnic group)* Minorität *f*

mi'nor key' *s* Molltonart *f;* in a m. in Moll

minstrel ['mɪnstrəl] *s* (hist) Spielmann *m*

mint [mɪnt] *s* Münzanstalt *f;* (bot) Minze *f* ‖ *tr* münzen

mintage ['mɪntɪdʒ] *s* Prägung *f*

minuet [ˌmɪnju'et] *s* Menuett *n*

minus ['maɪnəs] *adj* negativ ‖ *prep* minus, weniger; *(without)* (coll) ohne *(acc)*

mi'nus sign' *s* Minuszeichen *n*

minute [maɪ'n(j)ut] *adj* winzig ‖ ['mɪnɪt] *s* Minute *f;* **minutes** Protokoll *n;* take the minutes das Protokoll führen

–minute [mɪnɪt] *suf* –minutig

min'ute hand' *s* Minutenzeiger *m*

minutiae [mɪ'n(j)uʃɪ·i] *spl* Einzelheiten *pl*

minx [mɪŋks] *s* Range *f*

miracle ['mɪrəkəl] *s* Wunder *n*

mir'acle play' *s* Mirakelspiel *n*

miraculous [mɪ'rækjələs] *adj* wunderbar; *(e.g., power)* Wunder–

mirage [mɪ'rɑʒ] *s* Luftspiegelung *f;* (fig) Luftbild *n,* Täuschung *f*

mire [maɪr] *s* Morast *m,* Schlamm *m*

mirror ['mɪrər] *s* Spiegel *m* ‖ *tr* spiegeln

mirth [mʌrθ] *s* Fröhlichkeit *f*

miry ['maɪri] *adj* sumpfig, schlammig

misadventure [ˌmɪsəd'ventʃər] *s* Mißgeschick *n*

misanthrope ['mɪsənˌθrop] *s* Menschenfeind *m*

misapprehension [ˌmɪsæprɪ'henʃən] *s* Mißverständnis *n*

misappropriate [ˌmɪsə'proprɪˌet] *tr* sich *[dat]* widerrechtlich aneignen

misbehave [ˌmɪsbɪ'hev] *intr* sich schlecht benehmen

misbehavior [ˌmɪsbɪ'hevɪ·ər] *s* schlechtes Benehmen *n*

miscalculate [mɪs'kælkjəˌlet] *tr* falsch berechnen ‖ *intr* sich verrechnen

miscalculation [ˌmɪskælkjə'leʃən] *s* Rechenfehler *m*

miscarriage [mɪs'kærɪdʒ] *s* Fehlgeburt *f;* (fig) Fehlschlag *m*

miscar'riage of jus'tice *s* Justizirrtum *m*

miscar-ry [mɪs'kæri] *v (pret & pp –ried) intr* e-e Fehlgeburt haben; *(said of a plan)* scheitern, fehlschlagen

miscellaneous [ˌmɪsə'lenɪ·əs] *adj* vermischt

miscellany ['mɪsəˌleni] *s* Gemisch *n; (of literary works)* Sammelband *m*

mischief ['mɪstʃɪf] *s* Unfug *m;* be up to m. e–n Unfug im Kopf haben; cause m. Unfug treiben; get into m. etw anstellen

mis'chief-mak'er *s* Störenfried *m*

mischievous ['mɪstʃɪvəs] *adj* mutwillig

misconception [ˌmɪskən'sepʃən] *s* falsche Auffassung *f*

misconduct [mɪs'kɑndʌkt] *s* schlechtes Benehmen *n;* m. in office Amtsvergehen *n* ‖ [ˌmɪskən'dʌkt] *tr* schlecht verwalten; m. oneself sich schlecht benehmen

misconstrue [ˌmɪskən'stru] *tr* falsch auffassen

miscount [mɪs'kaunt] *s* Rechenfehler *m* ‖ *tr* falsch zählen ‖ *intr* sich verzählen

miscreant ['mɪskrɪ·ənt] *s* Schurke *m*

miscue [mɪs'kju] *s* (fig) Fehler *m;* (billiards) Kicks *m* ‖ *intr* (billiards) kicksen; (theat) den Auftritt verpassen

mis-deal ['mɪsˌdil] *s* falsches Geben *n* ‖ [mɪs'dil] *v (pret & pp –dealt [delt]) tr* falsch geben ‖ *intr* sich vergeben

misdeed [mɪs'did] *s* Missetat *f*

misdemeanor [ˌmɪsdɪ'minər] *s* Vergehen *n*

misdirect [ˌmɪsdɪ'rekt], [ˌmɪsdaɪ'rekt] *tr (& fig)* fehlleiten

misdoing [mɪs'du·ɪŋ] *s* Missetat *f*

miser ['maɪzər] *s* Geizhals *m*

miserable ['mɪzərəbəl] *adj* elend; feel m. sich elend fühlen; make life m. for s.o. j-m das Leben sauer machen

miserly ['maɪzərli] *adj* geizig

misery ['mɪzəri] *s* Elend *n*

misfeasance [mɪs'fizəns] *s* (jur) Amtsmißbrauch *m*

misfire [mɪs'faɪr] *s* Versagen *n* ‖ *intr* versagen

misfit ['mɪsfɪt] *s (clothing)* schlecht sitzendes Kleidungsstück *n; (person)* Gammler *m*

misfortune [mɪs'fɔrtʃən] *s* Unglück *n*

misgiving [mɪs'gɪvɪŋ] *s* böse Ahnung *f;* full of misgivings ahnungsvoll

misgovern [mɪs'gʌvərn] *tr* schlecht verwalten

misguidance [mɪs'gaɪdəns] *s* Irreführung *f*

misguide [mɪs'gaɪd] *tr* irreleiten

misguid'ed *adj* irregeleitet

mishap ['mɪshæp] *s* Unfall *m*

mishmash ['mɪʃ‚mæʃ] *s* Mischmasch *m*

misinform [‚mɪsɪn'fɔrm] *tr* falsch informieren, falsch unterrichten

misinterpret [‚mɪsɪn'tɑrprɪt] *tr* mißdeuten, falsch auffassen

misjudge [mɪs'dʒʌdʒ] *tr* (*e.g., a person, situation*) falsch beurteilen; (*distance*) falsch schätzen

mis·lay [mɪs'le] *v* (*pret & pp* **–laid**) *tr* verlegen, verkramen

mis·lead [mɪs'lid] *v* (*pret & pp* **–led**) *tr* irreführen

mislead'ing *adj* irreführend

mismanage [mɪs'mænɪdʒ] *tr* schlecht verwalten; (*funds*) verwirtschaften

mismanagement [mɪs'mænɪdʒmənt] *s* Mißwirtschaft *f*, schlechte Verwaltung *f*

mismarriage [mɪs'mærɪdʒ] *s* Mißheirat *f*

misnomer [mɪs'nomər] *s* Felhbezeichnung *f*

misplace [mɪs'ples] *tr* verlegen

misprint ['mɪs‚prɪnt] *s* Druckfehler *m* ‖ [mɪs'prɪnt] *tr* verdrucken

mispronounce [‚mɪsprə'nauns] *tr* falsch aussprechen

mispronunciation [‚mɪsprənʌnsɪ'eʃən] *s* falsche Aussprache *f*

misquote [mɪs'kwot] *tr* falsch zitieren

mis·read [mɪs'rid] *v* (*pret & pp* **–read** ['red]) *tr* falsch lesen ‖ *intr* sich verlesen

misrepresent [mɪsreprɪ'zent] *tr* falsch darstellen; **m. the facts to s.o.** j-m falsche Tatsachen vorspiegeln

miss [mɪs] *s* Fehlschlag *m*, Versager *m*; **Miss** Fräulein *n*; **Miss America** die Schönheitskönigin von Amerika ‖ *tr* (*a target; one's calling; a person, e.g., at the station; a town along the road; one's way*) verfehlen; (*feel the lack of*) verpassen; (*school, a train, an opportunity*) versäumen; **m. one's step** fehltreten; **m. the mark** vorbeischießen; (fig) sein Ziel verfehlen; **m. the point** die Pointe nicht verstanden haben ‖ *intr* fehlen; (*in shooting*) vorbeischießen

missal ['mɪsəl] *s* Meßbuch *n*

misshapen [mɪs'ʃepən] *adj* mißgestaltet

missile ['mɪsɪl] *s* Geschoß *n*; (rok) Rakete *f*

missing ['mɪsɪŋ] *adj*—**be m.** fehlen; (*said, e.g., of a child*) vermißt werden; **m. in action** vermißt

miss'ing per'son *s* Vermißte *mf*

miss'ing-per'sons bu'reau *s* Suchdienst *m*

mission ['mɪʃən] *s* Mission *f*; **m. in life** Lebensaufgabe *f*

missionary ['mɪʃən‚erɪ] *adj* Missions– ‖ *s* Missionar –in *mf*

missis ['mɪsɪz] *s*—**the m.** (*the wife*) die Frau; (*of the house*) (coll) die Frau des Hauses

missive ['mɪsɪv] *s* Sendschreiben *n*

mis·spell [mɪs'spel] *v* (*pret & pp* **–spelled** & **–spelt**) *tr & intr* falsch schreiben

misspell'ing *s* Schreibfehler *m*

misspent [mɪs'spent] *adj* vergeudet

misstate [mɪs'stet] *tr* falsch angeben

misstatement [mɪs'stetmənt] *s* falsche Angabe *f*

misstep [mɪs'step] *s* (& fig) Fehltritt *m*

mist [mɪst] *s* feiner Nebel *m* ‖ *tr* umnebeln ‖ *intr* (*said of the eyes*) sich trüben; **mist over** nebeln

mis·take [mɪs'tek] *s* Fehler *m*; **by m.** aus Versehen ‖ *v* (*pret* **–took** ['tʊk]; *pp* **–taken**) *tr* verkennen; **m. s.o. for s.o. else** j-n mit e-m anderen verwechseln

mistaken [mɪs'tekən] *adj* falsch, irrig; **be m. (about)** sich irren (in *dat*); **unless I'm m.** wenn ich mich nicht irre

mistakenly [mɪs'tekənli] *adv* versehentlich

mister ['mɪstər] *s* Herr *m* ‖ *interj* (pej) Herr!

mistletoe ['mɪsəl‚to] *s* Mistel *f*

mistreat [mɪs'trit] *tr* mißhandeln

mistreatment [mɪs'tritmənt] *s* Mißhandlung *f*

mistress ['mɪstrɪs] *s* Herrin *f*; (*lover*) Mätresse *f*, Geliebte *f*

mistrial [mɪs'traɪ·əl] *s* fehlerhaft geführter Prozeß *m*

mistrust [mɪs'trʌst] *s* Mißtrauen *n* ‖ *tr* mißtrauen (*dat*)

misty ['mɪsti] *adj* neblig; (*eyes*) umflort; (fig) unklar

misunder·stand [‚mɪsʌndər'stænd] *v* (*pret & pp* **–stood**) *tr & intr* mißverstehen

misunderstanding [‚mɪsʌndər'stændɪŋ] *s* Mißverständnis *n*

misuse [mɪs'jus] *s* Mißbrauch *m* ‖ [mɪs'juz] *tr* mißbrauchen; (*mistreat*) mißhandeln

misword [mɪs'wʌrd] *tr* in falsche Worte fassen

mite [maɪt] *s* (ent) Milbe *f*

miter ['maɪtər] *s* Bischofsmütze *f* ‖ *tr* auf Gehrung verbinden

mi'ter box' *s* Gehrlade *f*

mitigate ['mɪtɪ‚get] *tr* lindern

mitigation [‚mɪtɪ'geʃən] *s* Linderung *f*

mitt [mɪt] *s* Fausthandschuh *m*; (sl) Flosse *f*; (baseball) Fängerhandschuh *m*

mitten ['mɪtən] *s* Fausthandschuh *m*

mix [mɪks] *s* Mischung *f*, Gemisch *n* ‖ *tr* (ver)mischen; (*a drink*) mixen; (*a cake*) anrühren; **mix in** beimischen; **mix up** vermischen; (*confuse*) verwirren ‖ *intr* sich (ver)mischen; **mix with** vekehren mit

mixed *adj* vermischt; (*feelings, company, doubles*) gemischt

mixed' drink' *s* Mixgetränk *n*

mixed' mar'riage *s* Mischehe *f*

mixer ['mɪksər] *s* Mischer –in *mf*; (*of cocktails*) Mixer –in *mf*; (mach) Mischmaschine *f*; **a good m.** ein guter Gesellschafter

mixture ['mɪkstʃər] *s* (*e.g., of gases*)

Gemisch *n;* (*e.g., of tobacco, coffee*) Mischung *f;* (pharm) Mixtur *f*

mix'-up' *s* Wirrwar *m,* Verwechslung *f*

mizzen ['mɪzən] *s* Besan *m*

mnemonic [nə'manɪk] *s* Gedächtnishilfe *f*

moan [mon] *s* Stöhnen *n* ‖ *intr* stöhnen; **m. about** jammern über (*acc*) or um

moat [mot] *s* Schloßgraben *m*

mob [mab] *s* (*populace*) Pöbel *m;* (*crush of people*) Andrang *m;* (*gang of criminals*) Verbrecherbande *f* ‖ *v* (*pret & pp* **mobbed**) *ger* **mobbing**) *tr* (*crowd into*) lärmend eindringen in (*acc*); (*e.g., a consulate*) angreifen; (*a celebrity*) umringen

mobile ['mobɪl] *adj* fahrbar; (mil) motorisiert

mo'bile home' *s* Wohnwagen *m*

mobility [mo'bɪlɪti] *s* (& mil) Beweglichkeit *f*

mobilization [ˌmobɪlɪ'zeʃən] *s* Mobilisierung *f*

mobilize ['mobɪˌlaɪz] *tr* mobilisieren; (*strength*) aufbieten

mob' rule' *s* Pöbelherrschaft *f*

mobster ['mabstər] *s* Gangster *m*

moccasin ['makəsɪn] *s* Mokassin *m;* (*snake*) Mokassinschlange *f*

Mo'cha cof'fee ['mokə] *s* Mokka *m*

mock [mak] *adj* Schein– ‖ *tr* verspotten; (*imitate*) nachäffen ‖ *intr* spotten; **m. at** sich lustig machen über (*acc*); **m. up** improvisieren

mocker ['makər] *s* Spötter –in *mf*

mockery ['makəri] *s* Spott *m,* Spötterei *f;* **make a m.** of hohnsprechen (*dat*)

mock'ing *adj* spöttisch

mock'ingbird' *s* Spottdrossel *f*

mock' tri'al *s* Schauprozeß *m*

mock' tur'tle soup' *s* falsche Schildkrötensuppe *f*

mock'-up' *s* Schaumodell *n*

modal ['modəl] *adj* modal, Modal–

mode [mod] *s* Modus *m;* (mus) Tonart *f*

mod·el ['madəl] *adj* vorbildlich; (*student, husband*) Muster– ‖ *s* (*e.g., of a building*) Modell *n;* (*at a fashion show*) Vorführdame *f;* (*for art or photography*) Modell *n;* (*example for imitation*) Vorbild *n,* Muster *n;* (*make*) Typ *m,* Bauart *f* ‖ *v* (*pret & pp* –el[l]ed) *ger* –el[l]ing) *tr* (*clothes*) vorführen; **m. oneself on** sich [*dat*] ein Muster nehmen an (*dat*); **m. s.th. on** etw formen nach; (fig) etw gestalten nach ‖ *intr* (for) Modell stehen (zu *dat*)

mod'el air'plane *s* Flugzeugmodell *n*

mod'el num'ber *s* (aut) Typennummer *f*

moderate ['madərɪt] *adj* (*climate*) gemäßigt; (*demand*) maßvoll; (*price*) angemessen; (*e.g., in drinking*) mäßig; **of m. means** minderbemittelt ‖ ['madəˌret] *tr* mäßigen; (*a meeting*) den Vorsitz führen über (*acc*) or bei; (*a television show*) moderieren ‖ *intr* sich mäßigen

moderation [ˌmadə'reʃən] *s* Mäßigung

f, Maß *n;* **in m.** mit Maß; **observe m.** Maß halten

moderator ['madəˌretər] *s* Moderator *m*

modern ['madərn] *adj* modern, zeitgemäß

mod'ern Eng'lish *s* Neuenglisch *n*

mod'ern his'tory *s* Neuere Geschichte *f*

modernize ['madərˌnaɪz] *tr* modernisieren

mod'ern lan'guages *spl* neuere Sprachen *pl*

mod'ern times' *spl* die Neuzeit *f*

modest ['madɪst] *adj* bescheiden

modesty ['madɪsti] *s* Bescheidenheit *f*

modicum ['madɪkəm] *s* bißchen; **a m. of truth** ein Körnchen Wahrheit

modification [ˌmadɪfɪ'keʃən] *s* Abänderung *f*

modifier ['madɪˌfaɪər] *s* (gram) nähere Bestimmung *f*

modi·fy ['madɪˌfaɪ] *v* (*pret & pp* –fied) *tr* abändern; (gram) näher bestimmen

modish ['modɪʃ] *adj* modisch

modulate ['madʒəˌlet] *tr & intr* modulieren

modulation [ˌmadʒə'leʃən] *s* Modulation *f*

mohair ['mo ˌher] *s* Mohair *m*

Mohammedan [mo'hæmɪdən] *adj* mohammedanisch ‖ *s* Mohammedaner –in *mf*

Mohammedanism [mo'hæmɪdəˌnɪzəm] *s* Mohammedanismus *m*

moist [mɔɪst] *adj* feucht; (*eyes*) tränenfeucht

moisten ['mɔɪsən] *tr* anfeuchten; (*lips*) befeuchten ‖ *intr* feucht werden

moisture ['mɔɪstʃər] *s* Feuchtigkeit *f*

molar ['molər] *s* Backenzahn *m*

molasses [mə'læsɪz] *s* Melasse *f*

mold [mold] *s* Form *f;* (*mildew*) Schimmel *m;* (typ) Matrize *f* ‖ *tr* formen ‖ *intr* (ver)schimmeln

molder ['moldər] *s* Former –in *mf;* (fig) Bildner –in *mf* ‖ *intr* modern

mold'ing *s* Formen *n;* (carp) Gesims *n*

moldy ['moldi] *adj* mod(e)rig, schimmlig

mole [mol] *s* (*breakwater*) Hafendamm *m;* (*blemish*) Muttermal *n;* (zool) Maulwurf *m*

molecular [mə'lɛkjələr] *adj* molekular

molecule ['malɪˌkjul] *s* Molekül *n*

mole'skin' *s* (*fur*) Maulwurfsfell *n;* (tex) Englischleder *n*

molest [mə'lɛst] *tr* belästigen

molli·fy ['malɪˌfaɪ] *v* (*pret & pp* –fied) *tr* besänftigen

mollusk ['maləsk] *s* Weichtier *n*

mollycoddle ['malɪˌkadəl] *s* Weichling *m* ‖ *tr* verweichlichen

Mol'otov cock'tail ['malətof] *s* Flaschengranate *f*

molt [molt] *s intr* sich mausern

molten ['moltən] *adj* schmelzflüssig

molybdenum [mə'lɪbdɪnəm] *s* Molybdän *n*

mom [mam] *s* (coll) Mama *f,* Mutti *f*

moment ['momənt] *s* Moment *m,* Augenblick *m;* **a m. ago** nur eben; **at a moment's notice** jeden Augenblick; **at any m.** jederzeit; **at the m.** im Augenblick, zur Zeit; **of great m.** von großer Tragweite; **the very m. I spotted her** sobald ich sie erblickte

momentarily ['momən,terɪli] *adv* momentan; *(in a moment)* gleich

momentary ['momən,teri] *adj* vorübergehend

momentous [mo'mɛntəs] *adj* folgenschwer

momen·tum [mo'mɛntəm] *s* (**–tums** *&* **–ta** [tə]) (phys) Moment *n;* (fig) Schwung *m;* **gather m.** Schwung bekommen

monarch ['mɑnərk] *s* Monarch *m*

monarchical [mə'nɑrkɪkəl] *adj* monarchisch

monarchy ['mɑnərki] *s* Monarchie *f*

monastery ['mɑnəs,teri] *s* Kloster *n*

monastic [mə'næstɪk] *adj* Kloster–, Mönchs–

monasticism [mə'næstɪ,sɪzəm] *s* Mönchswesen *n*

Monday ['mʌndi], ['mʌnde] *s* Montag *m;* **on M.** am Montag

monetary ['mɑnɪ,teri] *adj* (*e.g., crisis, unit*) Währungs–; (*e.g., system, value*) Geld–

mon'etary stand'ard *s* Münzfuß *m*

money ['mʌni] *adj* Geld– ‖ *s* Geld *n;* **big m.** schweres Geld; **get one's money's worth** reell bedient werden; **make m.** (**on**) Geld verdienen (an *dat*); **put m. on** Geld setzen auf (*acc*)

mon'eybag' *s* Geldbeutel *m;* **moneybags** (coll) Geldsack *m*

mon'ey belt' *s* Geldgürtel *m*

moneychanger ['mʌni,tʃendʒər] *s* Wechsler –in *mf*

moneyed ['mʌnɪd] *adj* vermögend

mon'ey exchange' *s* Geldwechsel *m*

mon'eylend'er *s* Geldverleiher –in *mf*

mon'eymak'er *s* (fig) Goldgrube *f*

mon'ey or'der *s* Postanweisung *f*

Mongol ['mɑŋgəl] *adj* mongolid ‖ *s* Mongole *m,* Mongolin *f*

Mongolian [mɑŋ'golɪ·ən] *adj* mongolisch ‖ *s* (*language*) Mongolisch *n*

mon·goose' ['mɑŋgus] *s* (**–gooses**) Mungo *m*

mongrel ['mʌŋgrəl] *s* Bastard *m*

monitor ['mɑnɪtər] *s* (*at school*) Klassenordner *m;* (rad, telv) Überwachungsgerät *n,* Monitor *m* ‖ *tr* überwachen

monk [mʌŋk] *s* Mönch *m*

monkey ['mʌŋki] *s* Affe *m;* (*female*) Äffin *f;* **make a m. of** zum Narren halten ‖ *intr—***m. around** (*trifle idly*) herumalbern; **m. around with s.o.** es mit j–m treiben; **m. around with s.th.** an etw [*dat*] herummurksen

mon'keybusi'ness *s* (*underhanded conduct*) Gaunerei *f;* (*frivolous behavior*) (sl) Unfug *m*

mon'keyshine' *s* (sl) Possen *m*

mon'key wrench' *s* Engländer *m*

monocle ['mɑnəkəl] *s* Monokel *n*

monogamous [mə'nɑgəməs] *adj* monogam

monogamy [mə'nɑgəmi] *s* Einehe *f*

monogram ['mɑnə,græm] *s* Monogramm *n*

monograph ['mɑnə,græf] *s* Monographie *f*

monolithic [,mɑnə'lɪθɪk] *adj* (& fig) monolithisch

monologue ['mɑnə,lɔg] *s* Monolog *m*

monomania [,mɑnə'meni·ə] *s* Monomanie *f*

monoplane ['mɑnə,plen] *s* Eindecker *m*

monopolize [mə'nɑpə,laɪz] *tr* monopolisieren

monorail ['mɑnə,rel] *s* Einschienenbahn *f*

monosyllable ['mɑnə,sɪləbəl] *s* einsilbiges Wort *n*

monotheism [,mɑnə'θi·ɪzəm] *s* Monotheismus *m*

monotonous [mə'nɑtənəs] *adj* eintönig

monotony [mə'nɑtəni] *s* Eintönigkeit *f*

monotype ['mɑnə,taɪp] *s* Monotype *f*

monoxide [mə'nɑksaɪd] *s* Monoxyd *n*

monsignor [mɑn'sinjər] *s* (**monsignors** *&* **monsignori** [,mɑnsi'njori]) (eccl) Monsignore *m*

monsoon [mɑn'sun] *s* Monsun *m*

monster ['mɑnstər] *s* (& fig) Ungeheuer *n*

monstrance ['mɑnstrəns] *s* Monstranz *f*

monstrosity [mɑns'trɑsɪti] *s* Monstrosität *f,* Ungeheuerlichkeit *f*

monstrous ['mɑnstrəs] *adj* ungeheuer(lich)

month [mʌnθ] *s* Monat *m*

monthly ['mʌnθli] *adj* & *adv* monatlich ‖ *s* Monatszeitschrift *f*

monument ['mɑnjəmənt] *s* Denkmal *n*

monumental [,mɑnjə'mɛntəl] *adj* monumental

moo [mu] *s* Muhen *n* ‖ *intr* muhen

mood [mud] *s* Laune *f,* Stimmung *f;* (gram) Aussageweise *f,* Modus *m;* **be in a bad m.** schlechtgelaunt sein; **be in the m. for s.th.** zu etw gelaunt sein

moody ['mudi] *adj* launisch

moon [mun] *s* Mond *m* ‖ *intr—***m. about** herumlungern

moon'beam' *s* Mondstrahl *m*

moon'light' *s* Mondschein *m* ‖ *intr* schwarzarbeiten

moon'light'er *s* Doppelverdiener –in *mf*

moon'light'ing *s* Schwarzarbeit *f*

moon'lit' *adj* mondhell

moon'shine' *s* Mondschein *m;* (sl) schwarz gebrannter Whisky *m*

moonshiner ['mun,ʃaɪnər] *s* Schwarzbrenner –in *mf*

moon'shot' *s* Mondgeschoß *n*

moor [mur] *s* Moor *n,* Heidemoor *n;* **Moor** Mohr *m* ‖ *tr* (naut) vertäuen ‖ *intr* (naut) festmachen

moor'ing *s* (act) Festmachen *n;* **moorings** (*cables*) Vertäuung *f;* (*place*) Liegeplatz *m*

Moorish ['murɪʃ] *adj* maurisch

moose [mus] *s* (**moose**) amerikanischer Elch *m*

moot [mut] *adj* umstritten

mop [mɑp] *s* Mop *m*; *(of hair)* Wust *m* ‖ *v (pret & pp* mopped; *ger* mopping) *tr* mit dem Mop wischen; **mop up** mit dem Mop aufwischen; *(mil)* säubern

mope [mop] *intr* Trübsal blasen

moped ['moped] *s* Moped *n*

mop′ping-up′ opera′tion *s* (mil) Säuberungsaktion *f*

moral ['mɔrəl] *adj* moralisch ‖ *s* Moral *f;* **morals** Sitten *pl*

morale [mə'ræl] *s* Moral *f*

morality [mə'rælɪti] *s* Sittlichkeit *f*

moralize ['mɔrə‚laɪz] *intr* moralisieren

morass [mə'ræs] *s* Morast *m*

moratori·um [‚mɔrə'tori·əm] *s* (**-ums** & a– [ə]) Moratorium *n*

Moravia [mə'revi·ə] *s* Mähren *n*

morbid ['mɔrbɪd] *adj* krankhaft, morbid

mordacious [mɔr'deʃəs] *adj* bissig

mordant ['mɔrdənt] *adj* beißend

more [mor] *comp adj* mehr; **one m. minute** noch e–e Minute ‖ *comp adv* mehr; **all the m.** erst recht; **all the m. because** zumal, da; **m. and m.** immer mehr; **m. and m. expensive** immer teurer; **m. or less** gewissermaßen; **m. than anything** über alles; **no m.** nicht mehr; **not any m.** nicht mehr; **once m.** noch einmal; **the more ... the** (expressing quantity) je mehr ... desto; (expressing frequency) je öfter ... desto ‖ *s* mehr; **see m. of s.o.** j–n noch öfter sehen; **what's m.** außerdem ‖ *pron* mehr

more′o′ver *adv* außerdem, übrigens

morgue [mɔrg] *s* Leichenschauhaus *n*; (journ) Archiv *n*, Zeitungsarchiv *n*

morning ['mɔrnɪŋ] *adj* Morgen– ‖ *s* Morgen *m*; **from m. till night** von früh bis spät; **in the early m.** in früher Morgenstunde; **in the m.** am Morgen; **this m.** heute morgen; **tomorrow m.** morgen früh

morn′ing-af′ter pill′ *s* Pille *f* danach

morn′ing-glo′ry *s* Trichterwinde *f*

morn′ing sick′ness *s* morgendliches Erbrechen *n*

morn′ing star′ *s* Morgenstern *m*

Moroccan [mə'rɑkən] *adj* marokkanisch ‖ *s* Marokkaner –in *mf*

morocco [mə'rɑko] *s* *(leather)* Saffian *m*; **Morocco** Marokko *n*

moron ['mɔrɑn] *s* Schwachsinnige *mf*

morose [mə'ros] *adj* mürrisch

morphine ['mɔrfin] *s* Morphium *n*

morphology [mɔr'fɑlədʒi] *s* Morphologie *f*

morrow ['mɔro] *s*—**on the m.** am folgenden Tag

Morse′ code′ [mɔrs] *s* Morsealphabet *n*

morsel ['mɔrsəl] *s* Bröckchen *n*

mortal ['mɔrtəl] *adj* sterblich ‖ *s* Sterbliche *mf*

mor′tal dan′ger *s* Lebensgefahr *f*

mor′tal en′emy *s* Todfeind *m*

mor′tal fear′ *s* Heidenangst *f*

mortality [mɔr'tælɪti] *s* Sterblichkeit *f*

mortally ['mɔrtəli] *adv* tödlich

mor′tal remains′ *spl* irdische Überreste *pl*

mor′tal sin′ *s* Todsünde *f*

mor′tal wound′ *s* Todeswunde *f*

mortar ['mɔrtər] *s* *(vessel)* Mörser *m*; (archit) Mörtel *m*; (mil) Granatwerfer *m*

mor′tarboard′ *s* Mörtelbrett *n*

mor′tar fire′ *s* Granatwerferfeuer *m*

mor′tar shell′ *s* Granate *f*

mortgage ['mɔrgɪdʒ] *s* Hypothek *f* ‖ *tr* mit e–r Hypothek belasten

mortgagee [‚mɔrgɪ'dʒi] *s* Hypothekengläubiger –in *mf*

mortgagor ['mɔrgɪdʒər] *s* Hypothekenschuldner –in *mf*

mortician [mɔr'tɪʃən] *s* Leichenbestatter –in *mf*

morti·fy ['mɔrtɪ‚faɪ] *v (pret & pp* **-fied)** *tr (the flesh)* abtöten; *(humiliate)* demütigen; **m. oneself** sich kasteien

mortise ['mɔrtɪs] *s* (carp) Zapfenloch *n* ‖ *tr* (carp) verzapfen

mortuary ['mɔrtʃu‚ɛri] *s* Leichenhalle *f*

mosaic [mo'ze·ɪk] *adj* mosaisch ‖ *s* Mosaik *n*

Moscow ['mɑsko], ['mɑskau] *s* Moskau *n*

Moses ['moziz], ['mozis] *s* Moses *m*

mosey ['mozi] *intr* (coll) dahinschlürfen

Mos·lem ['mɑzləm] *adj* muselmanisch ‖ *s* (**-lems** & **-lem**) Moslem –in *mf*

mosque [mɑsk] *s* Moschee *f*

mosqui·to [məs'kito] *s* (**-toes** & **-tos**) Moskito *m*, Mücke *f*

mosqui′to net′ *s* Moskitonetz *n*

moss [mɔs] *s* Moos *n*

mossy ['mɔsi] *adj* bemoost

most [most] *super adj* meist ‖ *super adv* am meisten; *(very)* höchst; **m. of all** am allermeisten ‖ *s*—**at (the) m.** höchstens; **make the m. of** möglichst gut ausnützen; **m. of** die meisten; **m. of the day** der größte Teil des Tages; **the m.** das meiste, das Höchste ‖ *pron* die meisten

mostly ['mostli] *adv* meistens

motel [mo'tɛl] *s* Motel *n*

moth [mɔθ] *s* Nachtfalter *m*; *(clothes moth)* Motte *f*

moth′ball′ *s* Mottenkugel *f*; **put into mothballs** (nav) stillegen, einmotten ‖ *tr* (& fig) einmotten

moth-eaten ['mɔθ‚itən] *adj* mottenzerfressen

mother ['mʌðər] *s* Mutter *f* ‖ *tr (produce)* gebären; *(take care of as a mother)* bemuttern

moth′er coun′try *s* Mutterland *n*

moth′erhood′ *s* Mutterschaft *f*

moth′er-in-law′ *s* (**mothers-in-law**) Schwiegermutter *f*

motherless ['mʌðərlɪs] *adj* mutterlos

motherly ['mʌðərli] *adj* mütterlich

mother-of-pearl ['mʌðərəv'pʌrl] *adj* perlmutten ‖ *s* Perlmutter *f*

Moth′er's Day′ *s* Muttertag *m*

moth′er's help′er *s* Stütze *f* der Hausfrau

moth′er supe′rior s (Schwester) Oberin f

moth′er tongue′ s Muttersprache f

moth′ hole′ s Mottenfraß m

mothy [ˈmoθi] adj mottenzerfressen

motif [moˈtiːf] s (mus, paint) Motiv n

motion [ˈmoʃən] s Bewegung f; (parl) Antrag m; **make a m.** e–n Antrag stellen; **set in m.** in Bewegung setzen || tr zuwinken (dat); **m. s.o. to** (inf) j–n durch e–n Wink auffordern zu (inf)

motionless [ˈmoʃənlɪs] adj bewegungslos

mo′tion pic′ture s Film m; **be in motion pictures** beim Film sein

mo′tion-pic′ture adj Film–

mo′tion-pic′ture the′ater s Kino n

motivate [ˈmotɪˌvet] tr begründen, motivieren

motive [ˈmotɪv] s Anlaß m, Beweggrund m

mo′tive pow′er s Triebkraft f

motley [ˈmɑtli] adj bunt zusammengewürfelt

motor [ˈmotər] adj Motor– || s Motor m

motorcade [ˈmotərˌked] s Wagenkolonne f

mo′torcy′cle s Motorrad n

mo′torcy′list s Motorradfahrer –in mf

mo′toring s Autofahren n

motorist [ˈmotərɪst] s Autofahrer –in mf

motorize [ˈmotəˌraɪz] tr motorisieren

mo′tor launch′ s Motorbarkasse f

mo′tor-man s (–men) Straßenbahnführer m

mo′tor pool′ s Fahrbereitschaft f

mo′tor scoot′er s Motorroller m

mo′tor ve′hicle s Kraftfahrzeug n

mottle [ˈmɑtəl] tr sprenkeln

mot·to [ˈmɑto] s (–toes & –tos) Motto n

mound [maʊnd] s Wall m, Erdhügel m

mount [maʊnt] s (mountain) Berg m; (riding horse) Reittier n || tr (a horse, mountain) besteigen; (stairs) hinaufgehen; (e.g., a machinegun) in Position bringen; (a precious stone) fassen; (photographs in an album) einkleben; (photographs on a backing) aufkleben; m. (e.g., a gun) on montieren auf (acc)

mountain [ˈmaʊntən] s Berg m; **down the m.** bergab; **up the m.** bergauf

moun′tain climb′er s Bergsteiger –in mf

moun′tain climb′ing s Bergsteigen n

mountaineer [ˌmaʊntəˈnɪr] s Bergbewohner –in mf

mountainous [ˈmaʊntənəs] adj gebirgig

moun′tain pass′ s Gebirgspaß m, Paß m

moun′tain rail′road s Bergbahn f

moun′tain range′ s Gebirge n

moun′tain scen′ery s Berglandschaft f

mountebank [ˈmaʊntəˌbæŋk] s Quacksalber m; (charlatan) Scharlatan m

mount′ing s Montage f; (of a precious stone) Fassung f

mourn [morn] tr betrauren || intr

trauern; **mourn for** betrauern, trauern um

mourner [ˈmornər] s Leidtragende mf

mournful [ˈmornfəl] adj traurig

mourn′ing s Trauer f; **be in m.** Trauer tragen

mourn′ing band′ s Trauerflor m

mourn′ing clothes′ spl Trauerkleidung f; **wear m.** Trauer tragen

mouse [maʊs] s (mice [maɪs]) Maus f

mouse′hole′ s Mauseloch n

mouse′trap′ s Mausefalle f

moustache [məsˈtæʃ] s Schnurrbart m

mouth [maʊθ] s (mouths [maʊðz]) Mund m; (of an animal) Maul n; (of a gun, bottle, river) Mündung f; (sl) Maul n; **keep one's m. shut** den Mund halten; **make s.o.'s m. water** j–m das Wasser im Munde zusammenlaufen lassen

mouthful [ˈmaʊθˌful] s Mundvoll m; (sl) großes Wort n

mouth′ or′gan s Mundharmonika f

mouth′piece′ s (of an instrument) Ansatz m; (box) Mundstück n; (fig) Sprachrohr n

mouth′wash′ s Mundwasser n

movable [ˈmuvəbəl] adj beweglich, mobil || **movables** spl Mobilien pl

move [muv] s (movement) Bewegung f; (step, measure) Maßnahme f; (resettlement) Umzug m; (checkers) Zug m; (parl) Vorschlag m; **be on the m.** unterwegs sein; **don't make a m.!** keinen Schritt!; **get a m. on** (coll) sich rühren; **it's your m.** (& fig) du bist am Zug; **she won't make a m. without him** sie macht keinen Schritt ohne ihn || tr bewegen; (emotionally) rühren; (shove) rücken; (checkers) e–n Zug machen mit; (parl) beantragen; **m. the bowels** abführen; **m. up** (mil) vorschieben || intr (stir) sich bewegen; (change residence) umziehen; (in society) verkehren; (checkers) ziehen; (com) Absatz haben; **m. away** wegziehen; **m. back** zurückziehen; **m. for** (e.g., a new trial) beantragen; **m. in** zuziehen; **m. into** (a home) beziehen; **m. on** fortziehen; **m. out** (of) ausziehen (aus); **m. over** (make room) zur Seite rücken; **m. up** (to a higher position) vorrücken; (into a vacated position) nachrücken; (said of a team) aufsteigen

movement [ˈmuvmənt] s (& fig) Bewegung f; (mus) Satz m

mover [ˈmuvər] s Möbeltransporteur m; (parl) Antragsteller –in mf

movie [ˈmuvi] adj (actor, actress, camera, projector) Film– || s (coll) Film m; **movies** Kino n; **go to the movies** ins Kino gehen

mov′ie cam′era s Filmkamera f

moviegoer [ˈmuviˌgo·ər] s Kinobesucher –in mf

mov′ie house′ s Kino n

mov′ie screen′ s Filmleinwand f

mov′ie set′ s Filmkulisse f

mov′ie the′ater s Kino n

mov′ing adj beweglich; (force) trei-

bend; (fig) herzergreifend ‖ s
(*change of residence*) Umzug m

mov′ing pic′ture s Lichtspiel n, Film m

mov′ing spir′it s führender Kopf m

mow [mo] v (pret **mowed**; pp **mowed
& mown**) tr mähen; **mow down** (*enemies*) niedermähen

mower [′moˌər] s Mäher m

m.p.h. [′emˈpiˈetʃ] spl (miles per hour)
Stundenmeilen; **drive sixty m.p.h.**
mit sechzig Stundenmeilen fahren

Mr. [mɪstər] s Herr m

Mrs. [′mɪsɪz] s Frau f

Ms. [mɪz] s Fräulein n

much [mʌtʃ] adj, adv & pron viel; **as
m. again** noch einmal soviel; **how m.**
wieviel; **m. less** (*not to mention*) geschweige denn; **not so m. as** nicht
einmal; **so m. so so sehr**; **so m. the
better** um so besser; **very m.** sehr

mucilage [′mjusɪlɪdʒ] s Klebstoff m

muck [mʌk] s (& fig) Schmutz m

muck′rake′ intr (coll) Korruptionsfälle
enthüllen

muckraker [′mʌkˌrekər] s (coll) Kor-
ruptionsschnüffler –in mf

mucky [′mʌki] adj schmutzig

mucous [′mjukəs] adj schleimig

muc′ous mem′brane s Schleimhaut f

mucus [′mjukəs] s Schleim m

mud [mʌd] s Schlamm m; **drag through
the mud** (fig) in den Schmutz ziehen

mud′ bath′ s Schlammbad n, Moorbad
n

muddle [′mʌdəl] s Durcheinander n ‖
tr durcheinanderbringen ‖ intr—**m.
through** sich durchwursteln

mud′dlehead′ s Wirrkopf m

mud-dy [′mʌdi] adj schlammig; (fig)
trüb ‖ v (pret & pp **–died**) trüben

mud′hole′ s Schlammloch n

mudslinging [′mʌdˌslɪŋɪŋ] s (fig) Verleumdung f

muff [mʌf] s Muff m ‖ tr (coll) verpfuschen

muffin [′mʌfɪn] s Teekuchen m aus
Backpulverteig

muffle [′mʌfəl] tr (*sounds*) dämpfen;
m. up (*wrap up*) einhüllen

muf′fled adj dumpf

muffler [′mʌflər] s (*scarf*) Halstuch n;
(aut) Auspufftopf m

mufti [′mʌfti] s Zivil n

mug [mʌg] s Krug m; (*for beer*) Seidel
n; (*thug*) (sl) Rocker m; (*face*) (sl)
Fratze f ‖ v (pret & pp **mugged**; ger
mugging) tr (sl) photographieren;
(*assault*) (sl) überfallen ‖ intr (sl)
Gesichter schneiden

muggy [′mʌgi] adj schwül

mug′ shot′ s (sl) Polizeiphoto n

mulat-to [məˈlæto] s (**–toes**) Mulatte
m, Mulattin f

mulberry [′mʌlˌberi] s Maulbeere f

mul′berry tree′ s Maulbeerbaum m

mulch [mʌltʃ] s Streu n

mulct [mʌlkt] tr (of) betrügen (um)

mule [mjul] s Maulesel m, Maultier n

mulish [′mjulɪʃ] adj störrisch

mull [mʌl] intr—**m. over** nachgrübeln
über (*acc*)

mullion [′mʌljən] s Mittelpfosten m

multicolored [′mʌltɪˌkələrd] adj bunt

multigraph [′mʌltɪˌgræf] s (trademark) Vervielfältigungsmaschine f ‖
tr vervielfältigen

multilateral [ˌmʌltɪˈlætərəl] adj mehr-
seitig

multimillionaire [′mʌltɪˌmɪljəˈner] s
vielfacher Millionär m

multiple [′mʌltɪpəl] adj mehrfach,
Vielfach– ‖ s (math) Vielfaches n

multiplication [ˌmʌltɪplɪˈkeʃən] s Ver-
mehrung f; (arith) Multiplikation f

multiplica′tion ta′ble s Einmaleins n

multiplicity [ˌmʌltɪˈplɪsɪti] s Vielfäl-
tigkeit f

multi-ply [′mʌltɪˌplaɪ] v (pret & pp
–plied) tr vervielfältigen; (biol) vermehren; (math) multiplizieren ‖ intr
sich vervielfältigen; (biol) sich vermehren

multistage [′mʌltɪˌstedʒ] adj mehrstufig

multistory [′mʌltɪˌstori] adj mehrstöckig

multitude [′mʌltɪˌt(j)ud] s (*large number*) Vielheit f; (*of people*) Masse f

mum [mʌm] adj still; **keep mum about**
Stillschweigen beobachten über (*acc*);
mum's the word! Mund halten!

mumble [′mʌmbəl] tr & intr murmeln

mummery [′mʌməri] s Hokuspokus m

mummy [′mʌmi] s Mumie f

mumps [mʌmps] s Ziegenpeter m,
Mumps m

munch [mʌntʃ] tr & intr geräuschvoll
kauen

mundane [mʌnˈden] adj irdisch

municipal [mjuˈnɪsɪpəl] adj städtisch

muni′cipal bond′ s Kommunalobliga-
tion f

municipality [mjuˌnɪsɪˈpælɪti] s Stadt
f, Gemeinde f; (*governing body*)
Stadtverwaltung f

munificent [mjuˈnɪfɪsənt] adj freigebig

munificence [mjuˈnɪfɪsəns] s Freigebigkeit f

munitions [mjuˈnɪʃəns] s Kriegsmaterial n, Munition f

muni′tions dump′ s Munitionsdepot n

muni′tions fac′tory s Rüstungsfabrik f

mural [′mjurəl] s Wandgemälde n

murder [′mʌrdər] s Mord m ‖ tr
(er)morden; (*a language*) radebrechen

murderer [′mʌrdərər] s Mörder m

murderess [′mʌrdərɪs] s Mörderin f

mur′der mys′tery s Krimi m

murderous [′mʌrdərəs] adj mörderisch

mur′der plot′ s Mordanschlag m

murky [′mʌrki] adj düster

murmur [′mʌrmər] s Gemurmel n ‖
tr & intr murmeln

muscle [′mʌsəl] s Muskel m; **muscles**
Muskulatur f

muscular [′mʌskjələr] adj muskulös

Muse [mjuz] s Muse f ‖ **muse** intr
(*over*) nachsinnen (über *acc*)

museum [mjuˈziˌəm] s Museum n

mush [mʌʃ] s (*corn meal*) Maismehl-
brei m; (*soft mass*) Matsch m; (*sentimental talk*) Süßholzraspeln n

mush′room′ s Pilz m, Champignon m

|| *intr* wie Pilze aus dem Boden schießen

mushy ['mʌʃi] *adj* matschig; (*sentimental*) rührselig

music ['mjuːsɪk] *s* Musik *f*; (*score*) Noten *pl*; **face the m.** die Sache ausbaden; **set to m.** vertonen

musical ['mjuːzɪkəl] *adj* musikalisch || *s* (cin) Singspielfilm *m*; (theat) Musical *n*, Singspiel *n*

mu'sical in'strument *s* Musikinstrument *n*

musicale [,mjuːzɪ'kæl] *s* Musikabend *m*

mu'sic box' *s* Spieldose *f*

musician [mjuˈzɪʃən] *s* Musikant –in *mf*; (*accomplished artist*) Musiker –in *mf*

musicology [,mjuːzɪ'kɑlədʒi] *s* Musikwissenschaft *f*

mu'sic stand' *s* Notenständer *m*

mus'ing *s* Grübelei *f*

musk [mʌsk] *s* Moschus *m*

musket ['mʌskɪt] *s* Muskete *f*

musk'rat' *s* Bisamratte *f*

muslin ['mʌzlɪn] *s* Musselin *m*

muss [mʌs] *tr* (*hair*) zerzausen; (*dirty*) schmutzig machen; (*rumple*) zerknittern

mussel ['mʌsəl] *s* Muschel *f*

mussy ['mʌsi] *adj* (*hair*) zerzaust; (*clothes*) zerknittert

must [mʌst] *s* (*a necessity*) Muß *n*; (*new wine*) Most *m*; (*mold*) Moder *m* || *mod*—**I m.** (*inf*) ich muß (*inf*)

mustache [məsˈtæʃ] *s* Schnurrbart *m*

mustard ['mʌstərd] *s* Senf *m*

mus'tard plas'ter *s* Senfpflaster *n*

muster ['mʌstər] *s* Appell *m*; **pass m. die Prüfung bestehen** || *tr* (*troops*) antreten lassen; (*courage, strength*) aufbringen; **m. out** ausmustern

musty ['mʌsti] *adj* mod(e)rig

mutation [mjuˈteʃən] *s* (biol) Mutation *f*

mute [mjuːt] *adj* (& ling) stumm || *s* (ling) stummer Buchstabe *m*; (mus) Dämpfer *m* || *tr* (mus) dämpfen

mutilate ['mjuːtɪ,let] *tr* verstümmeln

mutineer [,mjutɪ'nɪr] *s* Meuterer *m*

mutinous ['mjutɪnəs] *adj* meuterisch

muti·ny ['mjutɪni] *s* Meuterei *f* || *v* (*pret & pp* –**nied**) *intr* meutern

mutt [mʌt] *s* (coll) Köter *m*

mutter ['mʌtər] *s* Gemurmel *n* || *tr* & *intr* murmeln

mutton ['mʌtən] *s* (culin) Hammel *m*

mut'ton-head' *s* (sl) Hammel *m*

mutual ['mjutʃu·əl] *adj* gegenseitig; (*friends*) gemeinsam

mu'tual fund' *s* Investmentfond *m*

mu'tual insur'ance com'pany *s* Versicherungsgesellschaft *f* auf Gegenseitigkeit

mutually ['mjutʃu·əli] *adv* gegenseitig

muzzle ['mʌzəl] *s* Maulkorb *m*; (*of a gun*) Rohrmündung *f*; (*snout*) Schnauze *f* || *tr* (*an animal*) e–n Maulkorb anlegen (*dat*); (*e.g., the press*) mundtot machen

muz'zle flash' *s* Mündungsfeuer *n*

my [maɪ] *poss adj* mein

myopic [maɪ'ɑpɪk] *adj* kurzsichtig

myriad ['mɪrɪ·əd] *adj* Myriade *f*

myrrh [mʌr] *s* Myrrhe *f*

myrtle ['mʌrtəl] *s* Myrte *f*

myself ['maɪ'sɛlf] *reflex pron* mich; (*indirect object*) mir || *intens pron* selbst, selber

mysterious [mɪs'tɪrɪ·əs] *adj* mysteriös

mystery ['mɪstəri] *s* Geheimnis *n*; (fi) Rätsel *n*; (relig) Mysterium *n*

mys'tery nov'el *s* Kriminalroman *m*

mys'tery play' *s* Mysterienspiel *n*

mystic ['mɪstɪk] *adj* mystisch || *s* Mystiker –in *mf*

mystical ['mɪstɪkəl] *adj* mystisch

mysticism ['mɪstɪ,sɪzəm] *s* Mystik *f*

mystification [,mɪstɪfɪ'keʃən] *s* Verwirrung *f*

mysti·fy ['mɪstɪ,faɪ] *v* (*pret & pp* –**fied**) *tr* verwirren

myth [mɪθ] *s* Mythe *f*, Mythos *m*; (*ill-founded belief*) Märchen *n*

mythical ['mɪθɪkəl] *adj* mythisch

mythological [,mɪθə'lɑdʒɪkəl] *adj* mythologisch

mythology [mɪ'θɑlədʒi] *s* Mythologie *f*

N

N, n [ɛn] *s* vierzehnter Buchstabe des englischen Alphabets

nab [næb] *v* (*pret & pp* **nabbed**; *ger* –**nabbing**) *tr* (coll) schnappen

nadir ['nedɪr] *s* (fig) Tiefpunkt *m*; (astr) Nadir *m*

nag [næg] *s* Gaul *m*; **old nag** Schindmähre *f* || *v* (*pret & pp* **nagged**; *ger* **nagging**) *tr* zusetzen (*dat*) || *intr* nörgeln; **nag at** herumnörgeln an (*dat*)

nag'ging *adj* nörgelnd || *s* Nörgelei *f*

naiad ['naɪ·æd] *s* Najade *f*

nail [nel] *s* Nagel *m*; **hit the n. on the head** den Nagel auf den Kopf treffen || *tr* (to) annageln (an *acc*); (*catch*)

(coll) erwischen; (box) (coll) treffen; **n. down** (fig) festnageln; **n. shut** zunageln

nail' clip'pers *spl* Nagelzange *f*

nail' file' *s* Nagelfeile *f*

nail' pol'ish *s* Nagellack *m*

nail' scis'sors *s* & *spl* Nagelschere *f*

naïve [nɑ'iv] *adj* naiv

naked ['nekɪd] *adj* nackt; (*eye*) bloß

nakedness ['nekɪdnɪs] *s* Nacktheit *f*

name [nem] *s* Name *m*; (*reputation*) Name *m*, Ruf *m*; **by n.** dem Namen nach; **by the n. of** namens; **in n. only** nur dem Namen nach; **of the same n.** gleichnamig; **spell one's n.** sich

schreiben; **what is your n.?** wie hei-
ßen Sie? || *tr* nennen; *(nominate)*
ernennen; **be named after** heißen
nach; **n. after** nennen nach; **named**
namens
name'-call'ng *s* Beschimpfung *f*
name' day' *s* Namenstag *m*
nameless ['nemlɪs] *adj* namenlos
namely ['nemli] *adv* nämlich, und
zwar
name'plate' *s* Namensschild *n*
name'sake' *s* Namensvetter *m*
nanny ['næni] *s* Kindermädchen *n*
nan'ny goat' *s* (coll) Ziege *f*
nap [næp] *s* Schläfchen *n;* (tex) Noppe
f; **take a nap** ein Schläfchen machen
|| *v (pret & pp* **napped;** *ger* **napping)**
intr schlummern; **catch s.o. napping**
(fig) j-n überrumpeln
napalm ['nepɑm] *s* Napalm *n*
nape [nep] *s—n.* **of the neck** Nacken
m
naphtha ['næfθə] *s* Naphtha *f & n*
napkin ['næpkɪn] *s* Serviette *f*
nap'kin ring' *s* Serviettenring *m*
narcissism ['nɑrsɪˌsɪzəm] *s* Narzißmus
m
narcissus [nɑr'sɪsəs] *s* (bot) Narzisse *f*
narcotic [nɑr'kɑtɪk] *adj* narkotisch ||
s (med) Betäubungsmittel *n*, Narko-
tikum *n; (addictive drug)* Rauschgift
n; (addict) Rauschgiftsüchtige *mf*
narrate [næ'ret] *tr* erzählen
narration [næ're/ən] *s* Erzählung *f*
narrative ['nærətɪv] *adj* erzählend || *s*
Erzählung *f*
narrator [næ'retər] *s* Erzähler *m;* (telv)
Moderator *m*
narrow ['næro] *adj* eng, schmal; *(e.g.,
margin)* knapp || **narrows** *spl*
Meerenge *f* || *tr* verengen || *intr* sich
verengen
nar'row escape' *s—***have a n.** mit
knapper Not entkommen
nar'row-gauge rail'road *s* Schmalspur-
bahn *f*
narrowly ['næroli] *adv* mit knapper
Not
nar'row-mind'ed *adj* engstirnig
nasal ['nezəl] *adj (of the nose)* Nasen-;
(sound) näselnd || *s* (phonet) Nasen-
laut *m*
nasalize ['nezəˌlaɪz] *tr* nasalieren ||
intr näseln
na'sal twang' *s* Näseln *n*
nascent ['nesənt] *adj* werdend
nastiness ['næstɪnɪs] *s* Ekligkeit *f*
nasturtium [nə'stʌr/əm] *s* Kapuziner-
kresse *f*
nasty ['næsti] *adj (person, smell, taste)*
ekelhaft; *(weather)* scheußlich; *(dog,
accident, tongue)* böse; **n. to** garstig
zu or gegen
nation ['ne/ən] *s* Nation *f*, Volk *n*
national ['næ/ənəl] *adj* national, Landes- || *s* Staatsangehörige *mf*
na'tional an'them *s* Nationalhymne *f*
na'tional defense' *s* Landesverteidigung
f
nationalism ['næ/ənəˌlɪzəm] *s* Nationalismus *m*
nationality [ˌnæ/ə'nælɪti] *s (citizen-*

ship) Staatsangehörigkeit *f; (ethnic
identity)* Nationalität *f*
nationalization [ˌnæ/ənəlɪ'ze/ən] *s*
Verstaatlichung *f*
nationalize ['næ/ənəˌlaɪz] *tr* verstaatlichen
na'tional park' *s* Naturschutzpark *m*
na'tional so'cialism *s* Nationalsozialis-
mus *m*
na'tionwide' *adj* im ganzen Land
native ['netɪv] *adj* eingeboren; *(prod-
ucts)* heimisch, Landes- || *s* Eingebo-
rene *mf;* **be a n. of** beheimatet sein
in *(dat)*
na'tive coun'try *s* Vaterland *n*
na'tive land' *s* Heimatland *n*
na'tive tongue' *s* Muttersprache *f*
nativity [nə'tɪvɪti] *s* Geburt *f;* (astrol)
Nativität *f;* **the Nativity** die Geburt
Christi
NATO ['neto] *s* **(North Atlantic Treaty
Organization)** NATO *f*
natty ['næti] *adj* elegant
natural ['næt/ərəl] *adj* natürlich; *(be-
havior)* ungezwungen || *s* (mus)
weiße Taste *f; (symbol)* (mus) Auf-
lösungszeichen *n;* **a n.** *(person)* (coll)
ein Naturtalent *n; (thing)* (coll) e-e
totsichere Sache *f*
na'tural his'tory *s* Naturgeschichte *f*
naturalism ['næt/ərəˌlɪzəm] *s* Natura-
lismus *m*
naturalist ['næt/ərəlɪst] *s (student of
natural history)* Naturforscher -in
mf; (paint, philos) Naturalist -in *mf*
naturalization [ˌnæt/ərəlɪ'ze/ən] *s* Ein-
bürgerung *f*
naturalize ['næt/ərəˌlaɪz] *tr* einbürgern
na'tural law' *s* Naturgesetz *n*
na'tural phenom'enon *s (occurring in
nature)* Naturereignis *n; (not supernatural)* natürliche Erscheinung *f*
na'tural re'sources *spl* Bodenschätze *pl*
na'tural sci'ence *s* Naturwissenschaft *f*
na'tural state' *s* Naturzustand *m*
nature ['net/ər] *s* die Natur; *(quali-
ties)* Natur *f*, Beschaffenheit *f;* **by n.**
von Natur aus
naught [nɔt] *s* Null *f;* **all for n.** ganz
umsonst; **bring to n.** zuschanden machen; **come to n.** zunichte werden
naughty ['nɔti] *adj* unartig, ungezogen
nausea ['nɔ/ɪ-ə], ['nɔsɪ-ə] *s* Übelkeit *f*
nauseate ['nɔ/ɪˌet], ['nɔsɪˌet] *tr* Übelkeit erregen *(dat)*
naus'eating *adj* Übelkeit erregend
nauseous ['nɔ/ɪ-əs], ['nɔsɪ-əs] *adj
(causing nausea)* Übelkeit erregend;
I feel n. mir ist übel
nautical ['nɔtɪkəl] *adj* See-, nautisch
nau'tical mile' *s* ['nɔtɪkəl] *s* Seemeile *f*
nau'tical term' *s* Ausdruck *m* der See-
mannssprache *f*
naval ['nevəl] *adj (e.g., battle, blockade, cadet, victory)* See-; *(unit)*
Flotten-; *(academy, officer)* Marine-
na'val base' *s* Flottenstützpunkt *m*
na'val cap'tain *s* Kapitän *m* zur See
na'val engage'ment *s* Seegefecht *n*
na'val forc'es *spl* Seestreitkräfte *pl*
na'val suprem'acy *s* Seeherrschaft *f*

nave [nev] *s* (*of a church*) Schiff *n*; (*of a wheel*) Nabe *f*

navel ['nevəl] *s* Nabel *m*

na'vel or'ange *s* Navelorange *f*

navigable ['nævɪgəbəl] *adj* schiffbar

navigate ['nævɪ‚get] *tr* (*traverse*) befahren; (*steer*) steuern || *intr* (aer, naut) navigieren

navigation [‚nævɪ'geʃən] *s* (*plotting courses*) Navigation *f*; (*sailing*) Schiffahrt *f*

naviga'tion chart' *s* Navigationskarte *f*

naviga'tion light' *s* (aer, naut) Positionslicht *n*

navigator ['nævɪ‚getər] *s* Seefahrer *m*; (aer) Navigator *m*

navy ['nevi] *adj* Marine- || *s* Kriegsmarine *f*

na'vy bean' *s* Weiße Bohne *f*

na'vy blue' *adj* marineblau || *s* Marineblau *n*

na'vy yard' *s* Marinewerft *f*

nay [ne] *adv* nein || *s* Nein *n*; (parl) Neinstimme *f*; **the nays have it** die Mehrheit stimmt dagegen

Nazarene [‚næzə'rin] *adj* aus Nazareth || *s* Nazarener *m*

Nazi ['nɑtsi] *adj* Nazi– || *s* Nazi *m*

Nazism ['nɑtsɪzəm] *s* Nazismus *m*

N.C.O. ['ɛn'si'o] *s* (**noncommissioned officer**) Unteroffizier *m*

neap' tide' [nip] *s* Nippflut *f*

near [nɪr] *adj* nahe(liegend); (*escape*) knapp; **n. at hand** zur Hand || *adv* nahe; **draw n. (to)** sich nähern (*dat*); **live n.** (*e.g., a church*) in der Nähe wohnen (*genit*) || *prep* nahe (*dat*), nahe an (*dat*), bei (*dat*); **n. here** hier in der Nähe

near'by' *adj* nahe(gelegen) || *adv* in der Nähe

Near' East', the *s* der Nahe Osten

nearly ['nɪrli] *adv* beinahe, fast

nearness ['nɪrnɪs] *s* Nähe *f*

near'-sight'ed *adj* kurzsichtig

near'-sight'edness *s* Kurzsichtigkeit *f*

neat [nit] *adj* sauber, ordentlich; (*simple but tasteful*) nett; (*cute*) niedlich; (*tremendous*) (coll) prima

neatness ['nitnɪs] *s* Sauberkeit *f*

nebu·la ['nɛbjələ] *s* (**-lae** [‚li] **& -las**) (astr) Nebelfleck *m*

nebulous ['nɛbjələs] *adj* nebelhaft; (astr) Nebel-

necessarily [‚nɛsɪ'sɛrɪli] *adv* notwendigerweise, unbedingt

necessary ['nɛsɪ‚sɛri] *adj* notwendig, nötig; (*consequence*) zwangsläufig; **if n.** notfalls

necessitate [nɪ'sɛsɪ‚tet] *tr* notwendig machen, enfordern

necessity [nɪ'sɛsɪti] *s* (*state of being necessary*) Notwendigkeit *f*; (*something necessary*) Bedürfnis *n*; (*poverty*) Not *f*; **in case of n.** im Notfall; **necessities of life** Lebensbedürfnisse *pl*; **of n.** notwendigerweise

neck [nɛk] *s* Hals *m*; (*of a dress*) Halsausschnitt *m*; **break one's n.** (& fig) sich [*dat*] den Hals brechen; **get it in the n.** (sl) eins aufs Dach kriegen; **get s.o. off one's n.** sich [*dat*] j–n

vom Halse schaffen; **n. and n.** Seite an Seite || *intr* (coll) sich knutschen

-necked [‚nɛkt] *suf* –halsig, –nackig

neckerchief ['nɛkərtʃɪf] *s* Halstuch *n*

neck'ing *s* Abknutscherei *f*

necklace ['nɛklɪs] *s* Halsband *n*; (*metal chain*) Halskette *f*

neck'line *s* Halsausschnitt *m*; **with a low n.** tief ausgeschnitten

neck'tie' *s* Krawatte *f*, Schlips *m*

necrology [nɛ'krɑlədʒi] *s* (*list of the dead*) Totenliste *f*; (*obituary*) Nekrolog *m*

necromancer ['nɛkrə‚mænsər] *s* Geistesbeschwörer –in *mf*

necromancy ['nɛkrə‚mænsi] *s* Geistesbeschwörung *f*

necropolis [nɛ'krɑpəlɪs] *s* Nekropolis *f*

nectar ['nɛktər] *s* (bot, myth) Nektar *m*

nectarine [‚nɛktə'rin] *s* Nektarine *f*

nee [ne] *adj* geborene, e.g., **Mrs. Mary Schmidt, nee Müller** Frau Maria Schmidt, geborene Müller

need [nid] *s* Bedarf *m*, Bedürfnis *n*; **be in n.** in Not sein; **be in n. of repair** reparaturbedürftig sein; **be in n. of s.th.** etw nötig haben; **if n. be** erforderlichenfalls; **meet s.o.'s needs** j–s Bedarf decken; **needs** Bedarfsartikel *pl* || *tr* benötigen, brauchen; **as needed** nach Bedarf

needful ['nidfəl] *adj* nötig

needle ['nidəl] *s* Nadel *f* || *tr* (*prod*) anstacheln; **n. s.o. about** gegen j–n sticheln wegen

nee'dlepoint', nee'dlepoint lace' *s* Nadelspitze *f*

needless ['nidlɪs] *adj* unnötig; **n. to say** es erübrigt sich zu sagen

nee'dlework' *s* Näharbeit *f*

needy ['nidi] *adj* bedürftig

ne'er [nɛr] *adv* nie

ne'er-do-well' *s* Tunichtgut *m*

nefarious [nɪ'fɛri‚əs] *adj* ruchlos

negate [nɪ'get] *tr* verneinen

negation [nɪ'geʃən] *s* Verneinung *f*

negative ['nɛgətɪv] *adj* negativ || *s* Verneinung *f*; (elec) negativer Pol *m*; (gram) Verneinungswort *n*; (phot) Negativ *n*

neglect [nɪ'glɛkt] *s* Vernachlässigung *f* || *tr* vernachlässigen; **n. to** (*inf*) unterlassen zu (*inf*)

négligée, negligee [‚nɛglɪ'ʒe] *s* Negligé *n*

negligence ['nɛglɪdʒəns] *s* Fahrlässigkeit *f*

negligent ['nɛglɪdʒənt] *adj* fahrlässig

negligible ['nɛglɪdʒɪbəl] *adj* geringfügig

negotiable [nɪ'goʃɪ‚əbəl] *adj* diskutierbar; (fin) übertragbar, bankfähig

negotiate [nɪ'goʃɪ‚et] *tr* (*a contract*) abschließen; (*a curve*) nehmen || *intr* verhandeln

negotiation [nɪ‚goʃɪ'eʃən] *s* Verhandlung *f*; **carry on negotiations with** in Verhandlungen stehen mit; **enter negotiations with** in Verhandlungen treten mit

negotiator [nɪ'goʃɪˌetər] s Unterhändler –in mf

Ne·gro ['nigro] s (–groes) Neger –in mf

neigh [ne] s Wiehern n || intr wiehern

neighbor ['nebər] s Nachbar –in mf; (fellow man) Nächste m || tr angrenzen an (acc) || intr—n. on angrenzen an (acc)

neigh'borhood' s Nachbarschaft f; (vicinity) Umgebung f; in the n. of (coll) etwa

neigh'boring adj benachbart, Nachbar–, angrenzend

neighborliness ['nebərlɪnɪs] s gutnachbarliche Beziehungen pl

neighborly ['nebərli] adj (gut)nachbarlich

neither [niðər] indef adj keiner || indef pron (of) keiner (von); n. of them keiner von beiden || conj noch, ebensowenig; auch nicht, e.g., n. do I ich auch nicht; neither ... nor weder ... noch; that's n. here nor there das hat nichts zu sagen

neme·sis ['neməsɪs] s (–ses [ˌsiz]) Nemesis f

Neolith'ic Age' [ˌni·ə'lɪθɪk] s Neusteinzeit f

neologism [ni'ɑlə ˌdʒɪzəm] s Neubildung f, Neologismus m

neon ['ni·ɑn] s Neon n

ne'on light' s Neonröhre f

ne'on sign' s Neonreklame f

neophyte ['ni·ə ˌfaɪt] s Neuling m; (relig) Neubekehrte mf

nephew ['nefju] s Neffe m

nepotism ['nepə ˌtɪzəm] s Nepotismus m

Neptune ['nept(j)un] s Neptun m

neptunium [nep't(j)unɪ·əm] s Neptunium n

nerve [nʌrv] adj Nerven– || s Nerv m; (courage) Wagemut m; (gall) (coll) Unverfrorenheit f; get on s.o.'s nerves j–m auf die Nerven gehen; lose one's n. die Nerven verlieren; nerves of steel Nerven pl wie Drahtseile

nerve' cen'ter s Nervenzentrum n

nerve'-rack'ing adj nervenaufreibend

nervous ['nʌrvəs] adj nervös; (system) Nerven–; (horse) kopfscheu; be a n. wreck mit den Nerven herunter sein

ner'vous break'down s Nervenzusammenbruch m

nervousness ['nʌrvəsnɪs] s Nervosität f

nervy ['nʌrvi] adj (brash) unverschämt; (courageous) mutig

nest [nest] s Nest n || intr nisten

nest' egg' s (fig) Sparpfennig m

nestle ['nesəl] intr (up to) sich anschmiegen (an acc)

net [net] adj Rein– || adv netto, rein || s Netz n; (for fire victims) Sprungtuch n || v (pret & pp netted; ger netting) tr (e.g., fish, butterflies) mit dem Netz fangen; (said of an enterprise) netto einbringen; (said of a person) rein verdienen

net'ball' s (tennis) Netzball m

Netherlander ['neðər ˌlændər] s Niederländer –in mf

Netherlands, the ['neðərləndz] s & spl die Niederlande

net'ting s Netzwerk n

nettle ['netəl] s Nessel f || tr reizen

net'work' s Netzwerk n; (rad, telv) Sendergruppe f

neuralgia [n(j)u'rældʒə] s Neurologie f

neuritis [n(j)u'raɪtɪs] s Nervenentzündung f

neurologist [n(j)u'rɑlədʒɪst] s Nervenarzt m, Nervenärztin f

neurology [n(j)u'rɑlədʒi] s Nervenheilkunde f, Neurologie f

neuron ['n(j)urɑn] s Neuron n

neuro·sis [n(j)u'rosɪs] s (–ses [siz]) Neurose f

neurotic [n(j)u'rɑtɪk] adj neurotisch || s Neurotiker –in mf

neuter ['n(j)utər] adj (gram) sächlich || s (gram) Neutrum n

neutral ['n(j)utrəl] adj neutral || s Neutrale mf; (aut) Leerlauf m

neutrality [n(j)u'trælɪti] s Neutralität f

neutralize ['n(j)utrə ˌlaɪz] tr (a bomb) entschärfen; (& chem) neutralisieren; (troops) lahmlegen; (an attack) unterbinden

neutron ['n(j)utrɑn] s Neutron n

never ['nevər] adv nie(mals); n. again nie wieder; n. before noch nie; n. mind! spielt keine Rolle!

ne'vermore' adv nimmermehr

ne'verthele'ss adv nichtsdestoweniger

new [n(j)u] adj neu; (wine) jung; (inexperienced) unerfahren; what's new? was gibt's Neues?

new' arriv'al s Neuankömmling m

new'born' adj neugeboren

New'cas'tle s—carry coals to N. Eulen nach Athen tragen

newcomer ['n(j)u ˌkʌmər] s Neuankömmling m

newel ['n(j)u·əl] s Treppenspindel f

new'el post' s Geländerpfosten m

newfangled ['n(j)u ˌfæŋgəld] adj neumodisch

Newfoundland ['n(j)ufənd ˌlænd] s Neufundland n || [n(j)u'faundlənd] s (dog) Neufundländer m

newly ['n(j)uli] adv neu, Neu–

new'lyweds' spl Neuvermählten pl

new' moon' s Neumond m

new-mown ['n(j)u ˌmon] adj frischgemäht

newness ['n(j)unɪs] s Neuheit f

news [n(j)uz] s Nachricht f; (rad, telv) Nachrichten pl; that's not n. to me das ist mir nicht neu; piece of n. Neuigkeit f

news' a'gency s Nachrichtenagentur f

news'boy' s Zeitungsjunge m

news' bul'letin s Kurznachricht f

news'cast' s Nachrichtensendung f

news'cast'er s Nachrichtensprecher –in mf

news'deal'er s Zeitungshändler –in mf

news' ed'itor s Nachrichtenredakteur –in mf

news′let′ter s Rundschreiben n
news′man′ s (-men′) Journalist m; (dealer) Zeitungshändler m
news′pa′per adj Zeitungs– || s Zeitung f
news′paper clip′ping s Zeitungsausschnitt m
news′paper·man′ s (-men′) Journalist m; (dealer) Zeitungshändler m
news′paper se′rial s Zeitungsroman m
news′print s Zeitungspapier n
news′reel′ s Wochenschau f
news′ report′ s Nachrichtensendung f
news′ report′er s Zeitungsreporter –in mf
news′ room′ s Nachrichtenbüro n
news′stand′ s Zeitungskiosk m
news′wor′thy adj berichtenswert
New′ Tes′tament s Neues Testament n
New′ World′ s Neue Welt f
New′ Year′ s Neujahr n; **happy N.!** glückliches Neues Jahr!
New′ Year′s′ Eve′ s Silvesterabend m
New′ Zea′land [′zilənd] s Neuseeland n
next [nekst] adj nächste; **be n.** an der Reihe sein; **come n.** folgen; **in the n. place** darauf; **n. best** nächstbeste; **n. time** das nächste Mal; **n. to** (locally) gleich neben (dat); (almost) sogut wie; **the n. day** am nächsten Tag || adv dann, danach; **what should I do n.?** was soll ich als Nächstes tun?
next′-door′ adj—**n. neighbor** unmittelbarer Nachbar m || **next′-door′** adv nebenan; **n. to** direkt neben (dat)
next′ of kin′ s (pl: next of kin) nächster Angehöriger m
niacin [′naɪ-əsɪn] s Niacin n
Niag′ara Falls′ [naɪ′ægrə] s Niagarafall m
nib [nɪb] s Spitze f; (of a pen) Federspitze f
nibble [′nɪbəl] tr knabbern || intr (on) knabbern (an dat)
Nibelung [′nibəluŋ] s (myth) Nibelung m
nice [naɪs] adj nett; (pretty) hübsch; (food) lecker; (well-behaved) artig; (distinction) fein; **have a n. time** sich gut unterhalten; **n. and warm** schön warm
nicely [′naɪsli] adv nett; **he′s doing n.** es geht ihm recht gut; **that will do n.** das paßt gut
nicety [′naɪsəti] s Feinheit f; **niceties of life** Annehmlichkeiten pl des Lebens
niche [nɪtʃ] s Nische f; (fig) rechter Platz m
nick [nɪk] s Kerbe f, Scharte f; **in the n. of time** gerade im rechten Augenblick || tr kerben
nickel [′nɪkəl] s Nickel n; (coin) Fünfcentstück n || tr vernickeln
nick′el-plate′ tr vernickeln
nick′name′ s Spitzname m || tr e-n Spitznamen geben (dat)
nicotine [′nɪkə‚tin] s Nikotin n; **low in n.** nikotinarm
niece [nis] s Nichte f
nifty [′nɪfti] adj (coll) fesch, prima

niggard [′nɪgərd] s Knauser –in mf
niggardly [′nɪgərdli] adj knauserig
night [naɪt] adj (light, shift, train, watch) Nacht– || s Nacht f; **all n.** (long) die ganze Nacht (über); **at n.** nachts; **last n.** gestern abend; **n. after n.** Nacht für Nacht; **n. before last** vorgestern abend
night′ cap′ s Nachtmütze f; (drink) Schlummertrunk m
night′ club′ s Nachtklub m
night′fall′ s Anbruch m der Nacht; **at n.** bei Anbruch der Nacht
night′gown′ s Damennachthemd n
nightingale [′naɪtən‚gel] s Nachtigall f
night′light′ s Nachtlicht n
night′long′ adj & adv die ganze Nacht dauernd
nightly [′naɪtli] adj & adv allnächtlich
night′mare′ s Alptraum m
nightmarish [′naɪt‚merɪʃ] adj alpartig
night′ owl′ s (coll) Nachteule f
night′ school′ s Abendschule f
night′time′ s Nachtzeit f; **at n.** zur Nachtzeit
night′ watch′man s Nachtwächter m
nihilism [′naɪ-ɪ‚lɪzəm] s Nihilismus m
nil [nɪl] s Nichts n, Null f
Nile [naɪl] s Nil m
nimble [′nɪmbəl] adj flink
nincompoop [′nɪnkəm‚pup] s Trottel m
nine [naɪn] adj & pron neun || s Neun f
nineteen [′naɪn′tin] adj & pron neunzehn || s Neunzehn f
nineteenth [′naɪn′tinθ] adj & pron neunzehnte || s (fraction) Neunzehntel n; **the nineteenth** (in dates or in a series) der Neunzehnte
ninetieth [′naɪntɪ-ɪθ] adj & pron neunzigste || s (fraction) Neunzigstel n
ninety [′naɪnti] adj & pron neunzig || s Neunzig f; **the nineties** die neunziger Jahre
nine′ty-first′ adj & pron einundneunzigste
nine′ty-one′ adj & pron einundneunzig
ninny [′nɪni] s (coll) Trottel m
ninth [naɪnθ] adj & pron neunte || s (fraction) Neuntel n; **the n.** (in dates or in a series) der Neunte
nip [nɪp] s (pinch) Kneifen n; (of cold weather) Schneiden n; (of liquor) Schluck m || v (pret & pp nipped; ger nipping) tr (pinch) kneifen; (alcohol) nippen; **nip in the bud** im Keime ersticken
nippers [′nɪpərz] spl Zwickzange f
nipple [′nɪpəl] s (of a nursing bottle) Lutscher m; (anat) Brustwarze f; (mach) Schmiernippel m
nippy [′nɪpi] adj schneidend
nirvana [nɪr′vɑnə] s Nirwana n
nit [nɪt] s (ent) Nisse f
niter [′naɪtər] s Salpeter m
nit′pick′er s (coll) Pedant –in mf
nitrate [′naɪtret] s Nitrat n || tr nitrieren
ni′tric ac′id [′naɪtrɪk] s Salpetersäure f

nitride ['naɪtraɪd] s Nitrid n
nitrogen ['naɪtrədʒən] s Stickstoff m
nitroglycerin [ˌnaɪtrə'glɪsərɪn] s Nitroglyzerin n
ni'trous ac'id ['naɪtrəs] s salpetrige Säure f
ni'trous ox'ide s Stickstoffoxydul n
nit'wit' s Trottel m
no [no] adj kein; **no admittance** Zutritt verboten; **no ... of any kind** keinerlei; **no offense!** nichts für ungut!; **no parking** Parkverbot; **no smoking** Rauchen verboten; **no thoroughfare** Durchgang verboten; **no ... whatever** überhaupt kein || adv kein; **no?** nicht wahr?; **no longer** (or **no more**) nicht mehr || s Nein n; **give no for an answer** mit (e-m) Nein antworten
No'ah's Ark' ['no·əz] s Arche f Noah(s)
nobility [no'bɪlɪti] s (nobleness; aristocracy) Adel m; (noble rank) Adelsstand m; **n. of mind** Seelenadel m
noble ['nobəl] adj (rank) ad(e)lig; (character, person) edel || s Adliger m; **nobles** Edelleute pl
no'ble-man s (-men) Edelmann m
no'blemind'ed adj edelsinnig
nobleness ['nobəlnɪs] s Vornehmheit f
no'ble-wom'an s (-wom'en) Edelfrau f
nobody ['no‚badi] s indef pron niemand, keiner; **n. else** sonst keiner || s (coll) Null f
nocturnal [nak'tʌrnəl] adj nächtlich
nod [nad] s Kopfnicken n || v (pret & pp **nodded**; ger **nodding**) tr—**nod one's head** mit dem Kopf nicken || intr nicken; **nod to** zunicken (dat)
node [nod] s (anat, astr, math, phys) Knoten m
nodule ['nadʒul] s Knötchen n; (bot) Knollen m
noise [nɔɪz] s Geräusch n; (disturbingly loud) Lärm m || tr—**n. abroad** ausposaunen
noiseless ['nɔɪzlɪs] adj geräuschlos
noisy ['nɔɪzi] adj lärmend, geräuschvoll
nomad ['nomæd] s Nomade m, Nomadin f
no' man's' land' s Niemandsland n
nomenclature ['nomən‚kletʃər] s Nomenklatur f
nominal ['namɪnəl] adj nominell
nominate ['namɪ‚net] tr ernennen; **n. as candidate** als Kandidaten aufstellen
nomination [ˌnamɪ'neʃən] s Ernennung f; (of a candidate) Aufstellung f
nominative ['namɪnətɪv] s Nominativ m
nominee [ˌnamɪ'ni] s Designierte mf
non- [nan] pref Nicht-, nicht-
non'accept'ance s Nichtannahme f
non'belli'gerent adj nicht am Krieg teilnehmend
non'break'able adj unzerbrechlich
non'-Cath'olic nichtkatholisch || s Nichtkatholik -in mf
nonchalant [ˌnanʃə'lant] adj zwanglos

noncom ['nan‚kam] s (coll) Kapo m
non'com'batant s Nichtkämpfer m
non'commis'sioned of'ficer s Unteroffizier m
noncommittal [ˌnankə'mɪtəl] adj nichtssagend; (person) zurückhaltend
nondescript ['nandɪ‚skrɪpt] adj unbestimmbar
none [nʌn] adv—**n. too** keineswegs zu || indef pron keiner; **that's n. of your business** das geht dich nichts an
nonen'tity s Nichts m; (fig) Null f
non'exis'tent adj nichtexistent
nonfic'tion s Sachbücher pl
nonfulfill'ment s Nichterfüllung f
non'interven'tion s Nichteinmischung f
non'met'al s Nichtmetall n, Metalloid n
non'nego'tiable adj unübertragbar; (demands) unabdingbar
nonpar'tisan adj überparteilich
nonpay'ment s Nichtbezahlung f
non'polit'ical adj unpolitisch
non-plus [nan'plʌs] s Verlegenheit f || v (pret & pp **-plus[s]ed**; ger **-plus[s]ing**) tr verblüffen
nonprof'it adj gemeinnützig
nonres'ident adj nich ansässig || s Nichtansässige mf
non'return'able adj (bottles, etc.) Einweg-; (merchandise) nicht rücknehmbar
non'scienti'fic adj nichtwissenschaftlich
non'sectar'ian adj keiner Sekte angehörend
nonsense ['nansəns] s Unsinn m
nonsen'sical adj unsinnig, widersinnig
non'skid' adj rutschsicher
nonsmok'er s Nichtraucher –in mf
non'stop' adj & adv ohne Zwischenlandung
nonvi'olence s Gewaltlosigkeit f
nonvi'olent adj gewaltlos
noodle ['nudəl] s Nudel f; (head) (coll) Birne f
noo'dle soup' s Nudelsuppe f
nook [nʊk] s Ecke f; (fig) Winkel m
noon [nun] s Mittag m; **at n.** zu Mittag
no' one', no'-one' indef pron niemand, keiner; **n. else** kein anderer
noon' hour' s Mittagsstunde f
noon'time' adj mittäglich || s Mittagszeit f
noose [nus] s Schlinge f
nor [nɔr] conj (after **neither**) noch; auch nicht, e.g., **nor do I** ich auch nicht
Nordic ['nɔrdɪk] adj nordisch
norm [nɔrm] s Norm f
normal ['nɔrməl] adj normal
normalcy ['nɔrməlsi] s Normalzustand m
normalize ['nɔrmə‚laɪz] tr normalisieren
Norman ['nɔrmən] adj normannisch || s Normanne m, Normannin f
Normandy ['nɔrməndi] s die Normandie
Norse [nɔrs] adj altnordisch || s (language) Altnordisch n; **the N.** die Skandinavier pl
Norse'man s (-men) Nordländer m

north [nɔrθ] *adj* nördlich, Nord– ‖ *adv* nach Norden ‖ *s* Norden *m*; **to the n. of** im Norden von

North' Amer'ica *s* Nordamerika *n*

North' Amer'ican *adj* nordamerikanisch ‖ *s* Nordamerikaner –in *mf*

north'east' *adj & adv* nordöstlich ‖ *s* Nordosten *m*

north'east'er *s* Nordostwind *m*

northerly ['nɔrðərli] *adj* nördlich

northern ['nɔrðərn] *adj* (*direction*) nördlich; (*race*) nordisch

north'ern expo'sure *s* Nordseite *f*

North'ern Hem'isphere *s* nördliche Halbkugel *f*

north'ern lights' *spl* Nordlicht *n*

nor'thernmost' *adj* nördlichst

North' Pole' *s* Nordpol *m*

North' Sea' *s* Nordsee *f*

northward ['nɔrθwərd] *adv* nach Norden

north'west' *adj & adv* nordwestlich ‖ *s* Nordwesten *m*

north' wind' *s* Nordwind *m*

Norway ['nɔrwe] *s* Norwegen *n*

Norwegian [nɔr'widʒən] *adj* norwegisch ‖ *s* Norweger –in *mf*; (*language*) Norwegisch *n*

nose [noz] *s* Nase *f*, (aer) Nase *f*, Bug *m*; **by a n.** (sport) um e-e Nasenlänge; **blow one's n.** sich schneuzen; **lead around by the n.** an der Nase herumführen; **pay through the n.** e-n zu hohen Preis bezahlen; **turn one's n. up at** die Nase rümpfen über (*acc*) ‖ *tr*—**n. out** (fig) mit knappem Vorsprung besiegen; (sport) um e-e Nasenlänge schlagen ‖ *intr*—**n. about** herumschnüffeln; **n. over** (aer) sich überschlagen

nose'bleed' *s* Nasenbluten *n*

nose' cone' *s* (rok) Raketenspitze *f*

nose' dive' *s* (aer) Sturzflug *m*

nose'-dive' *intr* e-n Sturzflug machen

nose' drops' *spl* Nasentropfen *pl*

nose'gay' *s* Blumenstrauß *m*

nose'-heav'y *adj* (aer) vorderlastig

nostalgia [nɑ'stældʒə] *s* Heimweh *n*

nostalgic [nɑ'stældʒɪk] *adj* wehmütig

nostril ['nɑstrɪl] *s* (anat) Nasenloch *n*; (zool) Nüster *f*

nostrum ['nɑstrəm] *s* Allheilmittel *n*

nosy ['nozi] *adj* neugierig

not [nɑt] *adv* nicht; **not at all** überhaupt nicht; **not even** nicht einmal; **not one** keiner; **not only … but also** nicht nur … sondern auch

notable ['notəbəl] *adj* bemerkenswert ‖ *s* Standesperson *f*

notarial [no'tɛrɪ-əl] *adj* notariell

notarize ['notə‚raɪz] *tr* notariell beglaubigen

no'tary pub'lic ['notəri] *s* (**notaries public**) Notar *m*, Notarin *f*

notation [no'teʃən] *s* (*note*) Aufzeichnung *f*; (*system of symbols*) Bezeichnung *f*; (*method of noting*) Schreibweise *f*

notch [nɑtʃ] *s* Kerbe *f*; (*in a belt*) Loch *n*; (*degree, step*) Grad *m*; (*of a wheel*) Zahn *m* ‖ *tr* einkerben

note [not] *s* Notiz *f*; (*to a text*) An-

merkung *f*; (*slip*) Zettel *m*; (*e.g., of doubt*) Ton *m*; (mus) Note *f*; **jot down notes** sich [*dat*] Notizen machen; **make a n. of** sich [*dat*] notieren; **take n. of** zur Kenntnis nehmen; **take notes** sich [*dat*] Notizen machen ‖ *tr* beachten; **n. down** notieren; **n. in passing** am Rande bemerken

note'book' *s* Heft *n*, Notizbuch *n*

note' pad' *s* Schreibblock *m*

note'wor'thy *adj* beachtenswert

nothing ['nʌθɪŋ] *indef pron* nichts; **be for n.** vergebens sein; **come to n.** platzen; **for n.** (*gratis*) umsonst; **have n. to go on** keine Unterlagen haben; **next to n.** soviel wie nichts; **n. at all** gar nichts; **n. but** lauter; **n. doing!** kommt nicht in Frage!; **n. else** sonst nichts; **n. new** nichts Neues; **there is n. like** es geht nichts über (*acc*)

nothingness ['nʌθɪŋnɪs] *s* (*non-existence*) Nichts *n*; (*utter insignificance*) Nichtigkeit *f*

notice ['notɪs] *s* (*placard*) Anschlag *m*; (*in the newspaper*) Anzeige *f*; (*attention*) Beachtung *f*; (*announcement*) Ankündigung; (*notice of termination*) Kündigung *f*; **at a moment's n.** jeden Moment; **escape s.o.'s n.** j-m entgehen; **give s.o. a week's n.** j-m acht Tage vorher kündigen; **take n. of** Notiz nehmen von; **until further n.** bis auf weiteres ‖ *tr* (be)merken, wahrnehmen; **be noticed by s.o.** j-m auffallen; **n. s.th. about s.o.** j-m etw anmerken

noticeable ['notɪsəbəl] *adj* wahrnehmbar

notification [‚notɪfɪ'keʃən] *s* Benachrichtigung *f*

noti•fy ['notɪ‚faɪ] *v* (*pret & pp* –**fied**) *tr* (*about*) benachrichtigen (von)

notion ['noʃən] *s* (*idea*) Vorstellung *f*; **I have a good n. to** (*inf*) ich habe gute Lust zu (*inf*); **notions** Kurzwaren *pl*

notoriety [‚notə'raɪ-ɪti] *s* Verruf *m*

notorious [no'torɪ-əs] *adj* (**for**) notorisch (wegen)

no'-trump' *adj* ohne Trumpf ‖ *s* Ohne-Trumpf-Ansage *f*

notwithstanding [‚nɑtwɪθ'stændɪŋ] *adv* trotzdem ‖ *prep* trotz (genit)

noun [naʊn] *s* Hauptwort *n*

nourish ['nʌrɪʃ] *tr* (er)nähren

nour'ishing *adj* nahrhaft, Nähr-

nourishment ['nʌrɪʃmənt] *s* (*feeding*) Ernährung *f*; (*food*) Nahrung *f*

Nova Scotia ['novə'skoʃə] *s* Neuschottland *n*

novel ['nɑvəl] *adj* neuartig ‖ *s* Roman *m*

novelist ['nɑvəlɪst] *s* Romanschriftsteller –in *mf*

novelty ['nɑvəlti] *s* Neuheit *f*

November [no'vɛmbər] *s* November *m*

novena [no'vinə] *s* Novene *f*

novice ['nɑvɪs] *s* Neuling *m*; (eccl) Novize *m*, Novizin *f*

novitiate [no'vɪʃɪ-ɪt] *s* Noviziat *n*

novocaine ['novə‚ken] *s* Novokain *n*, Novocain *n*

now [naʊ] *adv* jetzt; (*without tem-*

poral force) nun; **before now** schon früher; **by now** nachgerade; **from now on** von nun ab, fortan; **now and then** dann und wann; **now ... now** bald ... bald; **now or never** jetzt oder nie

nowadays ['nau·ə‚dez] *adv* heutzutage

no'way', **no'ways'** *adv* keineswegs

no'where' *adv* nirgends

noxious ['nɑk/əs] *adj* schädlich

nozzle ['nɑzəl] *s* Düse *f*; (*on a can*) Schnabel *m*

nth [ɛnθ] *adj*—**nth times** zig mal; **to the nth degree** (fig) im höchsten Maße

nuance ['n(j)u·ɑns] *s* Nuance *f*

nub [nʌb] *s* Knoten *m*; (*gist*) Kernpunkt *m*

nuclear ['n(j)uklɪ·ər] *adj* nuklear; (*energy, fission, fusion, physics, reactor, weapon*) Kern—

nu'clear pow'er *s* Atomkraft *f*

nu'clear pow'er plant' *s* Atomkraftwerk *n*

nucleolus [n(j)u'kli·ələs] *s* Nukleolus *m*

nucleon ['n(j)ukli·ɑn] *s* Nukleon *n*

nucle·us ['n(j)ukli·əs] *s* (**-uses** & **i-** [‚aɪ]) Kern *m*

nude [n(j)ud] *adj* nackt ‖ *s* (*nude figure*) Akt *m*; **in the n.** nackt

nudge [nʌdʒ] *s* Stups *m* ‖ *tr* stupsen

nudist ['n(j)udɪst] *s* Nudist –in *mf*

nudity ['n(j)udɪti] *s* Nacktheit *f*

nugget ['nʌgɪt] *s* Klumpen *m*

nuisance ['n(j)usəns] *s* Ärgernis *n*; **be a n.** lästig sein

nui'sance raid' *s* Störungsangriff *m*

null' and void' [nʌl] *adj* null und nichtig

nulli·fy ['nʌlɪ‚faɪ] *v* (*pret* & *pp* **–fied**) *tr* (*e.g., a law*) für ungültig erklären; (*e.g., the effects*) aufheben

numb [nʌm] *adj* taub; (**with**) starr (vor *dat*); (fig) betäubt; **grow n.** erstarren ‖ *tr* (& fig) betäuben; (*said of cold*) starr machen

number ['nʌmbər] *s* Nummer *f*; (*count*) Zahl *f*, Anzahl *f*; (*article*) (com) Artikel *m*; (gram) Zahl *f*; (mus) Stück *n*; **in n.** der Zahl nach; **get s.o.'s n.** (coll) j-m auf die Schliche kommen ‖ *tr* (*e.g., pages*) numerieren; (*amount to*) zählen; **be numbered among** zählen zu; **n. among** zählen zu

numberless ['nʌmbərlɪs] *adj* zahllos

num'bers game' *s* Zahlenlotto *n*

numbness ['nʌmnɪs] *s* Taubheit *f*; (*from cold*) Starrheit *f*

numeral ['n(j)umərəl] *adj* Zahl– ‖ *s* Zahl *f*, Ziffer *f*; (gram) Zahlwort *n*

numerator ['n(j)umə‚retər] *s* Zähler *m*

numerical [n(j)u'mɛrɪkəl] *adj* numerisch; **n. order** Zahlenfolge *f*; **n. superiority** Überzahl *f*; **n. value** Zahlenwert *m*

numerous ['n(j)umərəs] *adj* zahlreich

numismatic [‚n(j)umɪz'mætɪk] *adj* numismatisch ‖ **numismatics** *s* Münzkunde *f*

numskull ['nʌm‚skʌl] *s* Dummkopf *m*

nun [nʌn] *s* Nonne *f*

nunci·o ['nʌn/ɪ·o] *s* (**-os**) Nuntius *m*

nuptial ['nʌp/əl] *adj* Braut–, Hochzeits– ‖ **nuptials** *spl* Trauung *f*

Nuremberg ['n(j)urəm‚bʌrg] *s* Nürnberg *n*

nurse [nʌrs] *s* Krankenschwester *f*; (*male*) Krankenpfleger *m*; (*wet nurse*) Amme *f* ‖ *tr* (*the sick*) pflegen; (*a child*) stillen; (*hopes*) hegen; **n. a cold** e–e Erkältung kurieren

nurse'maid' *s* Kindermädchen *n*

nursery ['nʌrsəri] *s* Kinderstube *f*; (*for day care*) Kindertagesstätte *f*; (hort) Baumschule *f*, Pflanzschule *f*

nurs'ery·man *s* (**-men**) Kunstgärtner *m*

nurs'ery rhyme' *s* Kinderlied *n*

nurs'ery school' *s* Kindergarten *m*

nurse''s aide' *s* Schwesternhelferin *f*

nurs'ing *s* (*as a profession*) Krankenpflege *f*; (*of a person*) Pflege *f*; (*of a baby*) Stillen *n*

nurs'ing home' *s* Pflegeheim *n*

nurture ['nʌrt/ər] *s* Nahrung *f* ‖ *tr* (er)nähren

nut [nʌt] *s* Nuß *f*; (sl) verrückter Kerl *m*; (mach) Mutter *f*, Schraubenmutter *f*; **be nuts** (sl) verrückt sein; **be nuts about** (sl) vernarrt sein in (*acc*); **go nuts** (sl) e–n Klaps kriegen

nut'crack'er *s* Nußknacker *m*

nutmeg ['nʌt‚mɛg] *s* (*spice*) Muskatnuß *f*; (*tree*) Muskat *m*

nutrient ['nutrɪ·ənt] *s* Nährstoff *m*

nutriment ['n(j)utrɪmənt] *s* Nährstoff *m*

nutrition [n(j)u'trɪʃən] *s* Ernährung *f*

nutritious [n(j)u'trɪʃəs] *adj* nahrhaft

nutritive ['n(j)utrɪtɪv] *adj* nahrhaft, Nähr–

nut'shell' *s* Nußschale *f*; **in a n.** mit wenigen Worten

nutty ['nʌti] *adj* nußartig; (sl) spleenig, verrückt

nuzzle ['nʌzəl] *tr* sich mit der Schnauze (or Nase) reiben an (*dat*) ‖ *intr* (*burrow*) mit der Schnauze wühlen; **n. up to** sich anschmiegen an (*acc*)

nylon ['naɪlɑn] *s* Nylon *n*

nymph [nɪmf] *s* Nymphe *f*

nymphomaniac [‚nɪmfə'menɪ·æk] *s* Nymphomanin *f*

O

O, o [o] fünfzehnter Buchstabe des englischen Alphabets

oaf [of] *s* Tölpel *m*

oak [ok] *adj* eichen ‖ *s* Eiche *f*

oak' leaf' clus'ter *s* Eichenlaub *n*

oak' tree' *s* Eichbaum *m*

oakum ['okəm] *s* Werg *n*

oar [or], [ər] *s* Ruder *n*, Riemen *m*

oar'lock' s Ruderdolle f
oars'man' s (**-men'**) Ruderer m
oa·sis [o'esɪs] s (**-ses** [siz]) Oase f
oath [oθ] s (**oaths** [oðz]) Eid m; **o. of allegiance** Treueid m; **o. of office** Amtseid m; **under o.** eidlich
oat'meal' s Hafergrütze f, Hafermehl n
oats [ots] spl Hafer m; **he's feeling his o.** (coll) ihn sticht der Hafer; **sow one's wild o.** (coll) sich [dat] die Hörner ablaufen
obbligato [,ɑblɪ'gɑto] adj hauptstimmig || s Obligato m
obdurate ['ɑbdjərɪt] adj verstockt
obedience [o'bidɪ·əns] s (**to**) Gehorsam m (gegenüber dat, gegen); **blind o.** Kadavergehorsam m
obedient [o'bidɪ·ənt] adj (**to**) gehorsam (dat)
obeisance [o'bisəns] s Ehrerbietung f
obelisk ['ɑbəlɪsk] s Obelisk m
obese [o'bis] adj fettleibig
obesity [o'bisti] s Fettleibigkeit f
obey [o'be] tr gehorchen (dat); (a law, order) befolgen || intr gehorchen
obfuscate [ɑb'fʌsket] tr verdunkeln
obituary [o'bɪtʃu,eri] adj Todes- || s Todesanzeige f, Nachruf m
object ['ɑbdʒɪkt] s Gegenstand m; (aim) Ziel n, Zweck m; (gram) Ergänzung f, Objekt n; **money is no o.** Geld spielt keine Rolle || [ɑb'dʒɛkt] intr (**to**) Einwände erheben (gegen)
objection [ɑb'dʒɛkʃən] s Einwand m; **I have no o. to his staying** ich habe nichts dagegen (einzuwenden), daß er bleibe
objectionable [ɑb'dʒɛkʃənəbəl] adj nicht einwandfrei
objective [ɑb'dʒɛktɪv] adj sachlich, objektiv || s Ziel n
objec'tive case' s Objektsfall m
ob'ject les'son s Lehre f
obligate ['ɑblɪ,get] tr verpflichten; **be obligated to s.o.** j-m zu Dank verbunden sein
obligation [,ɑblɪ'geʃən] s Verpflichtung f
obligatory ['ɑblɪgə,tori], [ə'blɪgə,tori] adj verpflichtend, obligatorisch
oblige [ə'blaɪdʒ] tr (bind) verpflichten; (do a favor to) gefällig sein (dat); **be obliged to** (inf) müssen (inf); **feel obliged to** (inf) sich bemüßigt fühlen zu (inf); **I'm much obliged to you** ich bin Ihnen sehr verbunden
oblig'ing adj gefällig
oblique [ə'blik] adj schief
obliterate [ə'blɪtə,ret] tr auslöschen; (traces) verwischen; (writing) unleserlich machen
oblivion [ə'blɪvɪ·ən] s Vergessenheit f
oblivious [ə'blɪvɪ·əs] adj—**be o. of** sich [dat] nicht bewußt sein (genit)
oblong ['ɑblɔŋ] adj länglich || s Rechteck n
obnoxious [ɑb'nɑkʃəs] adj widerlich
oboe ['obo] s Oboe f
oboist ['obo·ɪst] s Oboist –in mf
obscene [ɑb'sin] adj obszön

obscenity [ɑb'senɪti] s Obszönität f
obscure [əb'skjur] adj dunkel, obskur || tr verdunkeln
obscurity [əb'skjurɪti] s Dunkelheit f
obsequies ['ɑbsɪkwiz] spl Totenfeier f
obsequious [əb'sikwɪ·əs] adj unterwürfig
observance [əb'zʌrvəns] s Beachtung f, Befolgung f; (celebration) Feier f
observant [əb'zʌrvənt] adj beobachtend
observation [,ɑbzər've/ən] s Beobachtung f; **keep under o.** beobachten
observa'tion tow'er s Aussichtsturm m
observatory [əb'zʌrvə,tori] s Sternwarte f, Observatorium n
observe [əb'zʌrv] tr (a person, rules) beobachten; (a holiday) feiern; **o. silence** Stillschweigen bewahren
obsess [əb'ses] tr verfolgen; **obsessed (by)** besessen (von)
obsession [əb'seʃən] s Besessenheit f
obsolescent [,ɑbsə'lesənt] adj veraltend
obsolete ['ɑbsə,lit] adj veraltet; **become o.** veralten
obstacle ['ɑbstəkəl] s Hindernis n
ob'stacle course' s Hindernisbahn f
obstetrical [ɑb'stetrɪkəl] adj Geburtshilfe-, Entbindungs-
obstetrician [,ɑbstə'trɪʃən] s Geburtshelfer –in mf
obstetrics [ɑb'stetrɪks] s Geburtshilfe f
obstinacy ['ɑbstɪnəsi] s Starrheit f
obstinate ['ɑbstɪnɪt] adj starr
obstreperous [əb'strepərəs] adj (clamorous) lärmend; (unruly) widerspenstig
obstruct [əb'strʌkt] tr (e.g., a pipe) verstopfen; (a view, way) versperren; (traffic) behindern; **o. justice** die Rechtspflege behindern
obstruction [əb'strʌkʃən] s (of a view, way) Versperrung f; (of traffic) Behinderung f; (obstacle) Hindernis n; (parl, pathol) Obstruktion f
obtain [əb'ten] tr erhalten, erlangen || intr bestehen
obtrusive [əb'trusɪv] adj aufdringlich
obtuse [əb't(j)us] adj (& fig) stumpf
obviate ['ɑbvɪ,et] tr erübrigen
obvious ['ɑbvɪ·əs] adj naheliegend; **it is o.** es liegt auf der Hand
occasion [ə'keʒən] s Gelegenheit f; (reason) Anlaß m; **on o.** gelegentlich; **on the o. of** anläßlich (genit) || tr veranlassen
occasional [ə'keʒənəl] adj gelegentlich
occasionally [ə'keʒənəli] adv gelegentlich, zuweilen
occident ['ɑksɪdənt] s Abendland n
occidental [,ɑksɪ'dentəl] adj abendländisch || s Abendländer –in mf
occlusion [ə'kluʒən] s Okklusion f
occult [ə'kʌlt, ɑ'kʌlt] adj geheim, okkult
occupancy ['ɑkjəpənsi] s Besitz m, Besitzergreifung f; (of a home) Einzug m
occupant ['ɑkjəpənt] s Besitzer –in mf; (of a home) Inhaber –in mf; (of a car) Insasse m, Insassin f
occupation [,ɑkjə'peʃən] s (employ-

ment) Beruf *m*, Beschäftigung *f*; (mil) Besetzung *f*, Besatzung *f*

occup'ational disease' [ˌɑkjəˈpeʃənəl] *s* Berufskrankheit *f*

occupa'tional ther'apy *s* Beschäftigungstherapie *f*

occupa'tion troops' *spl* Besatzungstruppen *pl*

occu•py [ˈɑkjəˌpaɪ] *v* (*pret & pp* **–pied**) *tr* in Besitz nehmen; (*a house*) bewohnen; (*time*) in Anspruch nehmen; (*keep busy*) beschäftigen; (mil) besetzen; **occupied** (*said of a seat or toilet*) besetzt; (*said of a person*) beschäftigt; **o. oneself with** sich befassen mit

oc•cur [əˈkʌr] *v* (*pret & pp* **–curred**; *ger* **–curring**) *intr* sich ereignen; (*come to mind*) (**to**) einfallen (*dat*)

occurrence [əˈkʌrəns] *s* Ereignis *n*; (*e.g., of a word*) Vorkommen *n*

ocean [ˈoʃən] *s* Ozean *m*

oceanic [ˌoʃiˈænɪk] *adj* Ozean-, ozeanisch

o'cean lin'er *s* Ozeandampfer *m*

oceanography [ˌoʃənˈɑgrəfi] *s* Ozeanographie *f*

ocher [ˈokər] *s* Ocker *m & n*

o'clock [əˈklɑk] *adv* Uhr; **at . . . o'clock** um . . . Uhr

octane [ˈɑkten] *s* Oktan *n*

oc'tane num'ber *s* Oktanzahl *f*

octave [ˈɑktɪv], [ˈɑktev] *s* Oktave *f*

October [ɑkˈtobər] *s* Oktober *m*

octogenarian [ˌɑktədʒɪˈnɛriˌən] *s* Achtzige *mf*

octo•pus [ˈɑktəpəs] *s* (**–puses & –pi** [ˌpaɪ]) Seepolyp *m*

ocular [ˈɑkjələr] *adj* Augen-

oculist [ˈɑkjəlɪst] *s* Augenarzt *m*, Augenärztin *f*

odd [ɑd] *adj* (*strange*) seltsam, eigenartig; (*number*) ungerade; (*e.g., glove*) einzeln; **two hundred odd pages** etwas über zweihundert Seiten ‖ **odds** *spl* (*probability*) Wahrscheinlichkeit *f*; (*advantage*) Vorteil *m*; (*in gambling*) Vorgabe *f*; **at odds** uneinig; **lay** (*or* **give**) **odds** vorgeben; **the odds are two to one** die Chancen stehen zwei zu eins

odd' ball' *s* (sl) Sonderling *m*

oddity [ˈɑdɪti] *s* Seltsamkeit *f*

odd' jobs' *spl* Gelegenheitsarbeit *f*; (*chores*) kleine Aufgaben *pl*

odds' and ends' *spl* Kleinkram *m*

ode [od] *s* Ode *f*

odious [ˈodiˌəs] *adj* verhaßt

odor [ˈodər] *s* Duft *m*, Geruch *m*; **be in bad o.** in schlechtem Ruf stehen

odorless [ˈodərlɪs] *adj* geruchlos

odyssey [ˈɑdɪsi] *s* Irrfahrt *f*; **Odyssey** Odyssee *f*

of [ɑv], [əv] *prep* von (*dat*); genit, e.g., **the name of the dog** der Name des Hundes

off [ɔf] *adj* (*free from work*) dienstfrei; (*poor, bad*) schlecht; (*electric current*) ausgeschaltet, abgeschaltet; **be badly off** in schlechten Verhältnissen sein; **be off** (*said of a clock*) nachgehen; (*said of a measurement*)

falsch sein; (*said of a person*) im Irrtum sein; (*be crazy*) nicht ganz richtig im Kopf sein; **be well off** in guten Verhältnissen sein; **the deal** (*or* **party**) **is off** es ist aus mit dem Geschäft (or mit der Party) ‖ *adv* (*distant*) weg; **he was off in a flash** er war im Nu weg; **I must be off** ich muß fort ‖ *prep* von (*dat*); **off duty** außer Dienst; **off limits** Zutritt verboten

offal [ˈɔfəl] *s* (*refuse*) Abfall *m*; (*of butchered meat*) Innereien *pl*

off' and on' *adv* ab und zu

off'beat' *adj* (sl) ungewöhnlich

off' chance' *s* geringe Chance *f*

off'-col'or *adj* schlüpfrig

off'-du'ty *adj* außerdienstlich

offend [əˈfend] *tr* beleidigen ‖ *intr*— **o. against** verstoßen gegen

offender [əˈfendər] *s* Missetäter –in *mf*; **first o.** nicht Vorbestrafte *mf*; **second o.** Vorbestrafte *mf*

offense [əˈfens] *s* (**against**) Vergehen *n* (gegen); **give o.** Anstoß geben; **no o.!** nichts für ungut!; **take o.** (**at**) Anstoß nehmen (an *dat*)

offensive [əˈfensɪv] *adj* anstößig; (*odor*) ekelhaft; (*action*) offensiv ‖ *s* Offensive *f*; **take the o.** die Offensive ergreifen

offer [ˈɔfər] *s* Angebot *n* ‖ *tr* anbieten; (*a price*) bieten; (*help, resistance*) leisten; (*friendship*) schenken; **o. an excuse** e–e Entschuldigung vorbringen; **o. as an excuse** als Entschuldigung vorbringen; **o. for sale** feilbieten; **o. one's services** sich anbieten; **o. up** aufopfern ‖ *intr*—**o. to** (*inf*) sich erbieten zu (*inf*)

of'fering *s* (*act*) Opferung *f*; (*gift*) Opfergabe *f*

offertory [ˈɔfərˌtori] *s* Offertorium *n*

off'hand' *adj* (*excuse*) unvorbereitet; (*manner*) lässig ‖ *adv* kurzerhand

office [ˈɔfɪs] *s* (*room*) Büro *n*, Amt *n*; (*position*) Amt *n*; (*of a doctor*) Sprechzimmer *n*; **be in o.** amtieren; **through the good offices of** durch die freundliche Vermittlung (*genit*); **run for o.** für ein Amt kandidieren

of'fice boy' *s* Bürojunge *m*

of'fice build'ing *s* Bürogebäude *n*

of'ficehold'er *s* Amtsträger –in *mf*

of'fice hours' *spl* Dienststunden *pl*; (*of a doctor, lawyer*) Sprechstunde *f*

officer [ˈɔfɪsər] *s* (adm) Beamte *m*, Beamtin *f*; (com) Direktor –in *mf*; (mil) Offizier –in *mf*

of'ficer can'didate *s* Offiziersanwärter –in *mf*

of'ficers' mess' *s* Offizierskasino *n*; (nav) Offiziersmesse *f*

of'fice seek'er *s* Amtsbewerber –in *mf*

of'fice supplies' *spl* Bürobedarf *m*

of'fice work' *s* Büroarbeit *f*

official [əˈfɪʃəl] *adj* amtlich; (*in line of duty*) Dienst–; (*visit*) offiziell; (*document*) öffentlich; **on o. business** dienstlich ‖ *s* Beamte *m*, Beamtin *f*; **top officials** Spitzenkräfte *pl*

offi'cial busi'ness *s* Dienstsache *f*

offi'cial call' *s* (telp) Dienstgespräch *n*

officialdom [ə'fɪʃ/əldəm] *s* Beamtentum *n*

officialese [ə,fɪʃə'liz] *s* Amtssprache *f*

officially [ə'fɪʃ/əli] *adv* offiziell

offi'cial use' *s* Dienstgebrauch *m*

officiate [ə'fɪʃɪ,et] *intr* amtieren; **o. at a marriage** e–n Traugottesdienst halten

officious [ə'fɪʃəs] *adj* dienstbeflissen

offing ['ɔfɪŋ] *s*—**in the o.** in Aussicht

off'-lim'its *adj* gesperrt

off'print' *s* Abdruck *m*, Sonderdruck *m*

off'-seas'on *adj*—**o. prices** Preise *pl* während der Vor– und Nachsaison || *s* Vor– und Nachsaison *f*

off'set' *s* (compensation) Ausgleich *m*; (typ) Offsetdruck *m* || **off'set'** *v* (pret –set; ger –setting) *tr* ausgleichen

off'set press' *s* Offsetdruck *m*

off'shoot' *s* Ableger *m*

off'shore' *adj* küstennah

off'side' *adv* (sport) abseits

off'spring' *s* Sprößling *m*

off'stage' *adj* hinter der Bühne befindlich || *adv* hinter der Bühne

off'-the-cuff' *adj* aus dem Stegreif

off'-the-rec'ord *adj* im Vertrauen

often ['ɔfən] *adv* oft, häufig; **every so o.** von Zeit zu Zeit; **quite o.** öfters

of'tentimes' *adv* oftmals

ogive ['odʒaɪv] *s* (diagonal vaulting rib) Gratrippe *f*; (pointed arch) Spitzbogen *m*

ogle ['ogəl] *tr* liebäugeln mit || *intr* liebäugeln

ogre ['ogər] *s* Scheusal *n*; (myth) Menschenfresser *m*

oh [o] *interj* oh!; **oh, dear!** o weh!

ohm [om] *s* Ohm *n*

oil [ɔɪl] *s* Öl *n*; **strike oil** auf Öl stoßen || *tr* ölen

oil' burn'er *s* Ölbrenner *m*

oil'can' *s* Ölkanne *f*

oil'cloth' *s* Wachsleinwand *f*

oil' col'or *s* Ölfarbe *f*

oil' drum' *s* Ölfaß *n*

oil' field' *s* Ölfeld *n*

oil' gauge' *s* Ölstandsanzeiger *m*

oil' heat' *s* Ölheizung *f*

oil' lev'el *s* Ölstand *m*

oil'man' *s* (–men') Ölhändler *m*

oil' paint'ing *s* Ölgemälde *n*

oil' pres'sure *s* Öldruck *m*

oil' rig' *s* Ölbohrinsel *f*

oil' shale' *s* Ölschiefer *m*

oil' slick' *s* Öllache *f*

oil' tank' *s* Ölbehälter *m*

oil' tank'er *s* Öltanker *m*

oil' well' *s* Ölquelle *f*

oily ['ɔɪli] *adj* ölig; (unctious) salbungsvoll

ointment ['ɔɪntmənt] *s* Salbe *f*

O.K. ['o'ke] *adj* in Ordnung, okay || *s* Billigung *f* || *v* (pret & pp O.K.'d; ger O.K.'ing) *tr* billigen || *intr* okay!

old [old] *adj* alt; **as old as the hills** uralt; (said of a person) steinalt

old' age' *s* Alter *n*, Greisenalter *n*

old'-age' home' *s* Altersheim *n*

old' coun'try *s* Heimatland *n*

olden ['oldən] *adj* alt

old'-fash'ioned *adj* altmodisch

Old' fog'(e)y ['fogi] *s* alter Kauz *m*

Old' Glo'ry *s* Sternenbanner *n*

old' hand' *s* alter Hase *m*

old' hat' *adj* bärtig

old' la'dy *s* Greisin *f*; (wife) (pej) Alte *f*

old' maid' *s* alte Jungfer *f*

old' man' *s* Greis *m*; (mil) Alter *m*

old' mas'ter *s* (paint) alter Meister *m*

old' moon' *s* letztes Viertel *n*

old' salt' *s* alter Seebär *m*

oldster ['oldstər] *s* alter Knabe *m*

Old' Tes'tament *s* Altes Testament *n*

old'-time' *adj* altväterisch

old'-tim'er *s* (coll) alter Hase *m*

old' wives'' tale' *s* Altweibergeschichte *f*

Old' World' *s* alte Welt *f*

oleander [,olɪ'ændər] *s* Oleander *m*

olfactory [al'fæktori] *adj* Geruchs–

oligarchy ['olɪ,garki] *s* Oligarchie *f*

olive ['alɪv] *s* Olive *f*

ol'ive branch' *s* Ölzweig *m*

ol'ive grove' *s* Olivenhain *m*

ol'ive oil' *s* Olivenöl *n*

ol'ive tree' *s* Ölbaum *m*, Olivenbaum *m*

olympiad [o'lɪmpɪ,æd] *s* Olympiade *f*

Olympian [o'lɪmpɪ-ən] *adj* olympisch

Olympic [o'lɪmpɪk] *adj* olympisch || **the Olympics** *spl* die Olympischen Spiele

omelet, omelette ['amə,let] *s* Eierkuchen *m*, Omelett *n*

omen ['omən] *s* Omen *n*, Vorzeichen *n*

ominous ['amɪnəs] *adj* ominös, unheilvoll

omission [o'mɪʃən] *s* Auslassung *f*; (of a deed) Unterlassung *f*

omit [o'mɪt] *v* (pret & pp omitted; ger omitting) *tr* (a word) auslassen; (a deed) unterlassen; **be omitted** ausfallen; **o. (ger)** es unterlassen zu (inf)

omnibus ['amnɪ,bʌs] *adj* Sammel–, Mantel– || *s* Omnibus *m*, Autobus *m*

omnipotent [am'nɪpətənt] *adj* allmächtig

omnipresent [,amnɪ'prezənt] *adj* allgegenwärtig

omniscient [am'nɪʃənt] *adj* allwissend

on [on] *adj* (in progress) im Gange; (light, gas, water) an; (radio, television) angestellt; (switch) eingeschaltet; (brakes) angezogen; **be on to s.o.** j–n durchsehen; **be on to s.th.** über etw [acc] im Bilde sein || *adv* weiter; **on and off** dann und wann; **on and on** in e–m fort || *prep* auf (dat or acc), an (dat or acc); (concerning) über (acc)

once [wʌns] *adv* einmal; (formerly) einst; **at o.** auf einmal; (immediately) sofort; **not o.** nicht ein einziges Mal; **o. and for all** ein für allemal; **o. before** früher einmal; **o. in a while** ab und zu; **o. more** noch einmal; **o. upon a time there was** es war einmal || *s*—**this o.** dieses (eine) Mal || *conj* sobald

once'-o'ver *s*—**give (s.o. or s.th.) the o.** rasch mustern

one [wʌn] *adj* ein; (one certain, e.g.,

Mr. Smith) ein gewisser; **for one thing** zunächst; **her one care** ihre einzige Sorge; **it's all one to me** es ist mir ganz gleich; **one and a half hours** anderthalb Stunden; **one day** e–s Tages; **one more** noch ein; **one more thing** noch etwas; **one o'clock** ein Uhr, eins; **on the one hand ... on the other** einerseits ... andererseits ‖ *s* Eins *f* ‖ *pron* einer; **I for one** was mich betrifft, ich jedenfalls; **one after another** einer nach dem anderen; **one after the other** nacheinander; **one another** einander, sich; **one at a time, please!** einer nach dem anderen, bitte! **one behind the other** hintereinander; **one by one** einer nach dem anderen; **one of these days** früher oder später; **one on top of the other** übereinander, aufeinander; **one to nothing** eins zu Null; **this one** dieser da, der da; **with one another** miteinander ‖ *indef pron* man; **one's** sein

one'-armed' *adj* einarmig
one'-eyed' *adj* einäugig
one'-horse town' *s* Kuhdorf *n*
one'-leg'ged *adj* einbeinig
onerous ['ɑnərəs] *adj* lästig
oneself' *reflex pron* sich; **be o.** sein, wie man immer ist; **by o.** allein; **to o.** vor sich [*acc*] hin
one'-sid'ed *adj* (& fig) einseitig
one'-track' *adj* eingleisig; (fig) einseitig
one'-way street' *s* Einbahnstraße *f*
one'-way tick'et *s* einfache Fahrkarte *f*
one'-week' *adj* achttägig
onion ['ʌnjən] *s* Zwiebel *f*; **know one's onions** (coll) Bescheid wissen
on'ionskin' *s* Durchschlagpapier *n*
on'look'er *s* Zuschauer –in *mf*
only ['onli] *adj* (son, hope) einzig ‖ *adv* nur; **not only ... but also** nicht nur ... sondern auch; **o. too** nur (all)zu; **o. too well** zur Genüge; **o. yesterday** erst gestern ‖ *conj* aber; **o. that** nur daß
on'ly-begot'ten *adj* eingeboren
onomatopoeia [,ɑnə,mætə'pi-ə] *s* Lautmalerei *f*
on'-ramp' *s* Zufahrtsrampe *f*
on'rush' *s* Ansturm *m*
on'set' *s* Anfang *m*; (attack) Angriff *m*
onslaught ['ɑn,slɔt] *s* Angriff *m*
on'to *prep* auf (*acc*) hinauf; **be o. s.o.** hinter j–s Schliche kommen; **be o. s.th.** über etw [*acc*] im Bilde sein
onus ['onəs] *s* Last *f*; **o. of proof** Beweislast *f*
onward(s) ['ɑnwərd(z)] *adv* vorwärts
onyx ['ɑnɪks] *s* Onyx *m*
oodles ['udəlz] *spl* (coll) (of) Unmengen *pl* (von)
ooze [uz] *s* Sickern *n*; (mud) Schlamm *m* ‖ *tr* ausschwitzen ‖ *intr* sickern; **o. out** durchsickern
opal ['opəl] *s* Opal *m*
opaque [o'pek] *adj* undurchsichtig; (stupid) stumpf
open ['opən] *adj* (window, position, sea, question, vowel) offen; (air, field, seat) frei; (business, office)

geöffnet; (seam) geplatzt; (account) laufend; (meeting) öffentlich; **be o.** offenstehen; **get o.** aufbekommen; **have an o. mind about s.th.** sich noch nicht auf etw [*acc*] festgelegt haben; **keep o.** offenhalten; **lay oneself o. to** sich aussetzen (*dat*); **o. to** (the public) zugänglich (*dat*); (criticism) ausgesetzt (*dat*); (doubt) unterworfen (*dat*); **o. to bribery** bestechlich; **o. to question** strittig ‖ *s*—**come out into the o.** (fig) mit seinen Gedanken herauskommen; **in the o.** im Freien ‖ *tr* öffnen, aufmachen; (a business, account, meeting, hostilities, fire) eröffnen; (a book) aufschlagen; (eyes in surprise) aufreißen; (a box, bottle) anbrechen; (an umbrella) aufspannen; **o. the attack** losschlagen; **o. to traffic** dem Verkehr übergeben; **o. wide** weit aufreißen ‖ *intr* sich öffnen, aufgehen; (said of a school, speech, play) beginnen; **o. onto** hinausgehen auf (*acc*); **o. up** sich auftun; **o. with hearts** (cards) Herz ausspielen
o'pen-air' *adj* Freiluft–; (theat) Freilicht–; **o. concert** Konzert *n* im Freien
opener ['opənər] *s* Öffner *m*, **for openers** (coll) für den Anfang
o'pen-eyed' *adj* mit offenen Augen
o'pen-hand'ed *adj* freigebig
o'pen-heart'ed *adj* offenherzig
o'pen house' *s* allgemeiner Besuchstag *m*
o'pening *adj* (scene) erste; (remarks) Eröffnungs– ‖ *s* Öffnung *f*; (of a speech, play) Anfang *m*; (of a store, etc.) Eröffnung *f*; (vacant job) freie (or offene) Stelle *f*; (in the woods) Lichtung *f*; (good opportunity) günstige Gelegenheit *f*; (theat) Erstaufführung *f*
o'pening night' *s* Eröffnungsvorstellung *f*, Premiere *f*
o'pening num'ber *s* erstes Stück *n*
o'pen-mind'ed *adj* aufgeschlossen
openness ['opənnɪs] *s* Offenheit *f*
o'pen sea'son *s* Jagdzeit *f*
o'pen se'cret *s* offenes Geheimnis *n*
o'pen shop' *s* offener Betrieb *m* (für den kein Gewerkschaftszwang besteht)
opera ['ɑpərə] *s* Oper *f*
op'era glass'es *spl* Opernglas *n*
op'era house' *s* Opernhaus *n*
operate ['ɑpə,ret] *tr* (a machine, gun) bedienen; (a tool) handhaben; (a business) betreiben; **be operated by electricity** elektrisch betrieben werden ‖ *intr* (said of a device, machine) funktionieren, laufen; (surg) operieren; **o. on** (surg) operieren
operatic [,ɑpə'rætɪk] *adj* opernhaft
op'erating costs' *spl* Betriebskosten *pl*
op'erating instruc'tions *spl* Bedienungsanweisung *f*
op'erating room' *s* Operationssaal *m*
op'erating ta'ble *s* Operationstisch *m*
operation [,ɑpə're/ən] *s* (process) Verfahren *n*; (of a machine) Bedie-

nung *f*; (*of a business*) Leitung *f*; (mil) Operation *f*, Aktion *f*; (surg) Operation *f*; **be in o.** (*said of a machine*) in Betrieb sein; (*said of a law*) in Kraft sein; **have** (or **undergo**) **an o.** sich e-r Operation unterziehen; **in a single o.** in e-m einzigen Arbeitsgang; **put into o.** in Betrieb setzen

operational [‚ɑpə'reʃənəl] *adj* (*ready to be used*) betriebsbereit; (*pertaining to operations*) Betriebs– Arbeits–; (mil) Einsatz–, Operations–

opera'tions room' *s* (aer) Bereitschaftsraum *m*

operative ['ɑpərətɪv] *adj* funktionsfähig, wirkend; **become o.** in Kraft treten ‖ *s* Agent –in *mf*

operator ['ɑpə‚retər] *s* (*of a machine*) Bedienende *mf*; (*of an automobile*) Fahrer –in *mf*; (sl) Schieber –in *mf*; (telp) Telephonist –in *mf*; **o.!** (telp) Zentrale!

op'erator's li'cense *s* Führerschein *m*

operetta [‚ɑpə'retə] *s* Operette *f*

ophthalmologist [‚ɑfθəl'mɑlədʒɪst] *s* Augenarzt *m*, Augenärztin *f*

ophthalmology [‚ɑfθəl'mɑlədʒɪ] *s* Augenheilkunde *f*, Ophthalmologie *f*

opiate ['opɪ‚et] *s* Opiat *n*; (fig) Betäubungsmittel *n*

opinion [ə'pɪnjən] *s* Meinung *f*; **be of the o.** der Meinung sein; **give an o. on** begutachten; **have a high o. of** große Stücke halten auf (*acc*); **in my o.** meiner Meinung nach, meines Erachtens

opinionated [ə'pɪnjə‚netɪd] *adj* von sich eingenommen

opin'ion poll' *s* Meinungsumfrage *f*

opium ['opɪ‚əm] *s* Opium *n*

o'pium den' *s* Opiumhöhle *f*

o'pium pop'py *s* Schlafmohn *m*

opossum [ə'pɑsəm] *s* Opossum *n*

opponent [ə'ponənt] *s* Gegner –in *mf*

opportune [‚ɑpər't(j)un] *adj* gelegen

opportunist [‚ɑpər't(j)unɪst] *s* Opportunist –in *mf*

opportunity [‚ɑpər't(j)unɪtɪ] *s* Gelegenheit *f*

oppose [ə'poz] *tr* sich widersetzen (*dat*); (*for comparison*) gegenüberstellen; **be opposed to s.th.** gegen etw sein

oppos'ing *adj* (*team, forces*) gegnerisch; (*views*) entgegengesetzt

opposite ['ɑpəsɪt] *adj* (*side, corner*) gegenüberliegend; (*meaning*) entgegengesetzt; (*view*) gegenteilig; **o. angle** (geom) Gegenwinkel *m*; **o. to** gegenüber (*dat*) ‖ *s* Gegensatz *m*, Gegenteil *n* ‖ *prep* gegenüber (*dat*)

op'posite num'ber *s* Gegenstück *n*, Gegenspieler –in *mf*

opposition [‚ɑpə'zɪʃən] *s* Widerstand *m*; (pol) Opposition *f*; **meet with stiff o.** auf heftigen Widerstand stoßen; **offer o.** Widerstand leisten

oppress [ə'pres] *tr* unterdrücken

oppression [ə'preʃən] *s* Unterdrückung *f*

oppressive [ə'presɪv] *adj* bedrückend

oppressor [ə'presər] *s* Unterdrücker –in *mf*

opprobrious [ə'probrɪ‚əs] *adj* schändlich

opprobrium [ə'probrɪ‚əm] *s* Schande *f*

opt [ɑpt] *intr*—**opt for** optieren für

optic ['ɑptɪk] *adj* Augen– ‖ **optics** *s* Optik *f*

optical ['ɑptɪkəl] *adj* optisch

op'tical illus'ion *s* optische Täuschung *f*

optician [ɑp'tɪʃən] *s* Optiker –in *mf*

op'tic nerve' *s* Augennerv *m*

optimism ['ɑptɪ‚mɪzəm] *s* Optimismus *m*

optimist ['ɑptɪmɪst] *s* Optimist –in *mf*

optimistic [‚ɑptɪ'mɪstɪk] *adj* optimistisch

option ['ɑpʃən] *s* (*choice*) Wahl *f*; (*alternative*) Alternative *f*; (ins) Option *f*

optional ['ɑpʃənəl] *adj* wahlfrei; **be o.** freistehen

optometrist [ɑp'tɑmɪtrɪst] *s* Augenoptiker –in *mf*

optometry [ɑp'tɑmɪtrɪ] *s* Optometrie *f*

opulent ['ɑpjələnt] *adj* (*wealthy*) reich; (*luxurious*) üppig

or [ər] *conj* oder

oracle ['ɔrəkəl] *s* Orakel *n*

oracular [o'rækjələr] *adj* orakelhaft

oral ['orəl] *adj* mündlich

o'ral hygiene' *s* Mundpflege *f*

orange ['ɔrɪndʒ] *adj* orange ‖ *s* Orange *f*, Apfelsine *f*

orangeade [‚ɔrɪndʒ'ed] *s* Orangeade *f*

or'ange blos'som *s* Orangenblüte *f*

or'ange grove' *s* Orangenhain *m*

or'ange tree' *s* Orangenbaum *m*

orang-outang [o'ræŋu‚tæŋ] *s* Orang-Utan *m*

oration [o'reʃən] *s* Rede *f*

orator ['ɔrətər] *s* Redner –in *mf*

oratorical [‚ɔrə'tɔrɪkəl] *adj* rednerisch

oratori·o [‚ɔrə'torɪ‚o] *s* (**-os**) Oratorium *n*

oratory ['ɔrə‚torɪ] *s* Redekunst *f*

orb [ɔrb] *s* Kugel *f*; (*of the moon or sun*) Scheibe *f*

orbit ['ɔrbɪt] *s* Umlaufbahn *f*; **send into o.** in die Umlaufbahn schicken ‖ *tr* umkreisen

orbital ['ɔrbɪtəl] *adj* Kreisbahn–

orchard ['ɔrtʃərd] *s* Obstgarten *m*

orchestra ['ɔrkɪstrə] *s* Orchester *n*

or'chestra pit' *s* Orchesterraum *m*

orchestrate ['ɔrkɪ‚stret] *tr* orchestrieren

orchid ['ɔrkɪd] *s* Orchidee *f*

ordain [ɔr'den] *tr* verordnen; (eccl) ordinieren, zum Priester weihen

ordeal [ɔr'dil] *s* Qual *f*; (hist) Gottesurteil *n*; **o. by fire** Feuerprobe *f*

order ['ɔrdər] *s* (*command*) Befehl *m*; (*decree*) Verordnung *f*; (*order, arrangement*) Ordnung *f*; (*medal*) Orden *m*; (*sequence*) Reihenfolge *f*; (archit, bot, zool) Ordnung *f*; (com) (**for**) Auftrag *m* (auf *acc*), Bestellung *f* (auf *acc*); (eccl) Orden *m*; (jur) Beschluß *m*; **according to orders** befehlsgemäß; **be in good o.** in gutem

Zustand sein; **be the o. of the day**
(coll) an der Tagesordnung sein; **be
under orders to** (*inf*) Befehl haben
zu (*inf*); **by o. of** auf Befehl von (or
genit); **call to o.** (*a meeting*) für
eröffnet erklären; (*reestablish order*)
zur Ordnung rufen; **in o.** (*function-
ing*) in Ordnung; (*proper, in place*)
angebracht; **in o. of** geordnet nach;
in o. that damit; **in o. to** (*inf*) um
... zu (*inf*); **make to o.** nach Maß
machen; **of a high o.** von ausgezeich-
neter Art; **on o.** (com) in Auftrag;
o.!, o.! zur Ordnung! **out of o.** (*defective*) außer Betrieb; (*not function-
ing at all*) nicht in Ordnung; (*dis-
arranged*) in Unordnung; (parl) im
Widerspruch zur Geschäftsordnung,
unzulässig; **put in o.** in Ordnung bringen; **restore to o.** die Ordnung wiederherstellen; **you are out of o.** Sie
haben nicht das Wort || *tr* (*com-
mand*) befehlen, anordnen; (*decree*)
verordnen; (com) bestellen; **as ordered** auftragsgemäß; **o. around** herin-
umkommandieren; **o. in advance**
vor(her)bestellen; **o. more of** nachbestellen; **o. s.o. off** (*e.g., the premises*) j-n weisen von

or'der blank' *s* Auftragsformular *n*
orderliness ['ɔrdərlɪnɪs] *s* (*of a person*)
Ordnungsliebe *f*; (*of a room, etc.*)
Ordnung *f*
orderly ['ɔrdərli] *adj* ordentlich || *s*
(med) Krankenwärter *m*; (mil)
Bursche *m*
or'derly room' *s* (mil) Schreibstube *f*
or'der slip' *s* Bestellzettel *m*
ordinal ['ɔrdɪnəl] *adj* Ordnungs– || *s*
Ordnungszahl *f*
ordinance ['ɔrdɪnəns] *s* Verfügung *f*;
(*of a city*) Verordnung *f*
ordinary ['ɔrdɪ‚nɛri] *adj* gewöhnlich;
(*member*) ordentlich; **o. person** All-
tagsmensch *m* || *s* Gewöhnliche *n*;
(eccl) Ordinarius *m*; **nothing out of
the o.** nichts Ungewöhnliches; **out of
the o.** außerordentlich
ordination [‚ɔrdɪ'neʃən] *s* Priesterweihe *f*
ordnance ['ɔrdnəns] *s* Waffen und
Munition *pl*; (arti) Geschützwesen *n*
ore [or] *s* Erz *n*
organ ['ɔrgən] *s* (*means*) Werkzeug *n*;
(*publication*) Organ *n*; (adm, biol)
Organ *n*; (mus) Orgel *f*
organdy ['ɔrgəndi] *s* Organdy *m*
or'gan grind'er *s* Drehorgelspieler *m*
organic [ɔr'gænɪk] *adj* organisch
organism ['ɔrgə‚nɪzəm] *s* Organismus
m
organist ['ɔrgənɪst] *s* Organist –in *mf*
organization [‚ɔrgənɪ'zeʃən] *s* Organisation *f*
organizational [‚ɔrgənɪ'zeʃənəl] *adj*
organisatorisch
organize ['ɔrgə‚naɪz] *tr* organisieren
organizer ['ɔrgə‚naɪzər] *s* Organisator
–in *mf*
or'gan loft' *s* Orgelbühne *f*
orgasm ['ɔrgæzəm] *s* Orgasmus *m*
orgy ['ɔrdʒi] *s* Orgie *f*

Orient ['ɔrɪ‚ənt] *s* Orient *m* || **orient**
['ɔrɪ‚ent] *tr* orientieren
oriental [‚ɔrɪ'entəl] *adj* orientalisch ||
Oriental *s* Orientale *m*, Orientalin *f*
orientation [‚ɔrɪ‚ən'teʃən] *s* Orientierung *f*; (*of new staff members*) Einführung *f*
orifice ['ɔrɪfɪs] *s* Öffnung *f*
origin ['ɔrɪdʒɪn] *s* Ursprung *m*; (*of a
person or word*) Herkunft *f*
original [ə'rɪdʒɪnəl] *adj* ursprünglich;
(*first*) Ur–; (*novel, play*) originell;
(*person*) erfinderisch || *s* Original *n*
originality [ə‚rɪdʒɪ'nælɪti] *s* Originalität *f*
ori'ginal research' *s* Quellenstudium *n*
ori'ginal sin *s* Erbsünde *f*, Sündenfall
m
originate [ə'rɪdʒɪ‚net] *tr* hervorbrin-
gen || *intr* (*from*) entstehen (aus);
o. in seinen Ursprung haben in (*dat*)
originator [ə'rɪdʒɪ‚netər] *s* Urheber
–in *mf*
oriole ['ɔrɪ‚ol] *s* Goldamsel *f*, Pirol *m*
ormolu ['ɔrmə‚lu] *s* Malergold *n*
ornament ['ɔrnəmənt] *s* Verzierung *f*,
Schmuck *m* || ['ɔrnə‚ment] *tr* ver-
zieren
ornamental [‚ɔrnə'mentəl] *adj* Zier–
ornamentation [‚ɔrnəmən'teʃən] *s* Verzierung *f*
ornate [ɔr'net] *adj* überladen; (*speech*)
bilderreich
ornery ['ɔrnəri] *adj* (*cantankerous*)
mürrisch; (*vile*) gemein
ornithology [‚ɔrnɪ'θalədʒɪ] *s* Vogel-
kunde *f*, Ornithologie *f*
orphan ['ɔrfən] *s* Waise *f*; **become an
o.** verwaisen
orphanage ['ɔrfənɪdʒ] *s* Waisenhaus *n*
or'phaned *adj* verwaist; **be o.** verwaisen
or'phans' court' *s* Vormundschaftsge-
richt *n*
orthodox ['ɔrθə‚daks] *adj* orthodox
orthography [ɔr'θagrəfi] *s* Orthographie *f*, Rechtschreibung *f*
orthopedist [‚ɔrθə'pidɪst] *s* Orthopäde
m, Orthopädin *f*
oscillate ['asɪ‚let] *intr* schwingen
oscillation [‚asɪ'leʃən] *s* Schwingung *f*
oscillator ['asɪ‚letər] *s* Oszillator *m*
osier ['oʒər] *s* Korbweide *f*
osmosis [as'mosɪs] *s* Osmose *f*
osprey ['aspri] *s* Fischadler *m*
ossi·fy ['asɪ‚faɪ] *v* (*pret & pp* –fied)
tr verknöchern lassen || *intr* verknö-
chern
ostensible [as'tensɪbəl] *adj* vorgeblich
ostentation [‚asten'teʃən] *s* Zurschau-
stellung *f*, Prahlerei *f*
ostentatious [‚asten'teʃəs] *adj* prahlerisch, prunksüchtig
osteopath [‚astɪ‚ə‚pæθ] *s* Osteopath
–in *mf*
osteopathy [‚astɪ'apəθi] *s* Osteopathie
f
ostracism ['astrə‚sɪzəm] *s* Ächtung *f*;
(hist) Scherbengericht *n*
ostracize ['astrə‚saɪz] *tr* verfemen
ostrich ['astrɪtʃ] *s* Strauß *m*
Ostrogoth ['astrə‚gaθ] *s* Ostgote *m*

other ['ʌðər] *adj* andere, sonstig; among o. things unter anderem; every o. day jeden zweiten Tag; none o. than he kein anderer als er; on the o. hand andererseits; o. things being equal unter gleichen Voraussetzungen; someone or o. irgend jemand; some ... or o. irgendein; the o. day unlängst || *adv*—o. than anders als || *indef pron* andere; the others die anderen

otherwise ['ʌðər,waɪz] *adj* sonstig || *adv* sonst; I can't do o. ich kann nicht umhin; o. engaged anderweitig beschäftigt; think o. anders denken

otter ['ɑtər] *s* Otter *m*; (*snake*) Otter *f*

Ottoman ['ɑtəmən] *adj* osmanisch || **ottoman** *s* (*couch*) Ottomane *m*; (*cushioned stool*) Polsterschemel *m*; **O.** Osmane *m*

ouch [aʊtʃ] *interj* au!

ought [ɔt] *aux* used to express obligation, e.g., you o. to tell her Sie sollten es ihr sagen; they o. to have been here sie hätten hier sein sollen

ounce [aʊns] *s* Unze *f*

our [aʊr] *poss adj* unser

ours [aʊrz] *poss pron* der uns(e)rige, der uns(e)re, uns(e)rer; a friend of o. ein Freund von uns; this is o. das gehört uns

ourselves [aʊr'sɛlvz] *reflex pron* uns; we are by o. wir sind doch unter uns || *intens pron* selbst, selber

oust [aʊst] *tr* (from) verdrängen (aus); o. from office seines Amtes entheben

ouster ['aʊstər] *s* Amtsenthebung *f*

out [aʊt] *adj*—an evening out ein Ausgehabend *m*; be out (*of the house*) ausgegangen sein; (*said of a light, fire*) aus sein; (*said of a new book*) erschienen sein; (*said of a secret*) enthüllt sein; (*said of flowers*) aufgeblüht sein; (*said of a dislocated limb*) verrenkt sein; (*be out of style*) aus der Mode sein; (*be at an end*) aus sein; (*be absent from work*) der Arbeit fernbleiben; (*be on strike*) streiken; be out after s.o. hinter j-m her sein; be out for a good time dem Vergnügen nachgehen; be out on one's feet (coll) erledigt sein; be out ten marks zehn Mark eingebüßt haben; be out to (*inf*) darauf ausgehen (or aus sein) zu (*inf*); that's out das kommt nicht in Frage; the best thing out das Beste, was es gibt || *adv* (gone forth; ended, terminated) aus; out of (*curiosity, pity, etc.*) aus (*dat*); (*fear*) vor (*dat*); (*a certain number*) von (*dat*); (*deprived of*) beraubt (*genit*); out of breath außer Atem; out of money ohne Geld; out of place verlegt; (*not appropriate or proper*) unpassend; out of the window zum Fenster hinaus || *s* (*pretext*) Ausweg *m*; be on the outs with s.o. mit j-m auf gespanntem Fuße sein || *prep* aus (*dat*) || *interj* (sport) aus!; out with it! heraus damit!

out′ and away′ *adv* bei weitem

out′-and-out′ *adj* abgefeimt

out′-ar′gue *tr* in Grund und Boden argumentieren

out′bid′ *v* (*pret* –bid; *pp* –bid & –bidden; *ger* –bidding) *tr* überbieten

out′board mo′tor *s* Außenbordmotor *m*

out′bound′ *adj* nach auswärts bestimmt; (*traffic*) aus der Stadt fließend

out′break′ *s* Ausbruch *m*

out′build′ing *s* Nebengebäude *n*

out′burst′ *s* Ausbruch *m*; o. of anger Zornausbruch *m*

out′cast′ *adj* ausgestoßen || *s* Ausgestoßene *mf*

out′come′ *s* Ergebnis *n*

out′cry′ *s* Ausruf *m*; raise an o. ein Zetergeschrei erheben

out-dat′ed *adj* zeitlich überholt

out′dis′tance *tr* hinter sich [*dat*] lassen

out′do′ *v* (*pret* –did; *pp* –done) *tr* überbieten, übertreffen; not to be outdone by s.o. in zeal j-m nichts an Eifer nachgeben; o. oneself in sich überbieten in (*dat*)

out′door′ *adj* Außen-

out′doors′ *adv* draußen, im Freien || *s*—in the outdoors im Freien

out′door shot′ *s* (*phot*) Außenaufnahme *f*

out′door swim′ming pool′ *s* Freibad *n*

out′door the′ater *s* Naturtheater *n*

out′door toil′et *s* Abtritt *m*

outer ['aʊtər] *adj* äußere, Außen-

out′er ear′ *s* Ohrmuschel *f*

out′er gar′ment *s* Oberkleid *n*

out′ermost′ *adj* äußerste

out′er space′ *s* Weltall *n*, Weltraum *m*

out′field′ *s* (baseball) Außenfeld *n*

out′fit′ *s* (*equipment*) Ausrüstung *f*; (*set of clothes*) Ausstattung *f*; (*uniform*) Kluft *f*; (*business firm*) Gesellschaft *f*; (*mil*) Einheit *f* || *v* (*pret* –fitted; *ger* –fitting) *tr* (*with equipment*) ausrüsten; (*with clothes*) neu ausstaffieren

out′flank′ *tr* überflügeln, umfassen

out′flow′ *s* Ausfluß *m*

out′go′ing *adj* (*sociable*) gesellig; (*officer*) bisherig; (*tide*) zurückgehend; (*train, plane*) abgehend

out′grow′ *v* (*pret* –grew; *pp* –grown) *tr* herauswachsen aus; (fig) entwachsen (*dat*)

out′growth′ *s* Auswuchs *m*; (fig) Folge *f*

out′ing *s* Ausflug *m*

outlandish [aʊt′lændɪʃ] *adj* fremdartig; (*prices*) überhöht

out′last′ *tr* überdauern

out′law′ *s* Geächtete *mf* || *tr* ächten

out′lay′ *s* Auslage *f*, Kostenaufwand *m* || **out′lay′** *v* (*pret & pp* –laid) *tr* auslegen

out′let′ *s* (*for water*) Abfluß *m*, Ausfluß *m*; (fig) (*for*) Ventil *n* (für); (com) Absatzmarkt *m*; (elec) Steckdose *f*; find an o. for (fig) Luft machen (*dat*); no o. Sackgasse *f*

out′line′ *s* (*profile*) Umriß *m*; (*sketch*) Umrißzeichnung *f*; (*summary*) Grundriß *m*; rough o. knapper Umriß *m* || *tr* umreißen

out'live' *tr* überleben

out'look' *s* (*place giving a view*) Aus-guck *m*; (*view from a place*) Ausblick *m*; (*point of view*) Anschauung *f*; (*prospects*) Aussichten *pl*

out'ly'ing *adj* Außen—

out'maneu'ver *tr* ausmanövrieren; (fig) überlisten

outmoded [,aut'modɪd] *adj* unmodern

out'num'ber *tr* an Zahl übertreffen

out'-of-bounds' *adj* (fig) nicht in den Schranken; (sport) im Aus

out'-of-court' **set'tlement** *s* außerge-richtlicher Vergleich *m*

out'-of-date' *adj* veraltet

out'-of-door' *adj* Außen—

out'-of-doors' *adj* Außen— || *adv* im Freien, draußen || *s*—in the o. im Freien

out'-of-pock'et *adj*—o. expenses Bar-auslagen *pl*

out'of print' *adj* vergriffen

out'-of-the-way' *adj* abgelegen

out'of tune' *adj* verstimmt

out' of work' *adj* arbeitslos, erwerbs-los

out'pace' *tr* überholen

out'pa'tient *s* ambulant Behandelte *mf*

out'patient clin'ic *s* Ambulanz *f*

out'play' *tr* überspielen

out'point' *tr* (sport) nach Punkten schlagen

out'post' *s* (mil) Vorposten *m*

out'pour'ing *s* (& fig) Erguß *m*

out'put' *s* (*of a machine or factory*) Arbeitsleistung *f*; (*of a factory*) Pro-duktion *f*; (mech) Nutzleistung *f*; (min) Förderung *f*

out'rage' *s* Unverschämtheit *f*; (against) Verletzung *f* (genit) || *tr* gröblich beleidigen

outrageous [aut'redʒəs] *adj* unver-schämt

out'rank' *tr* im Rang übertreffen

out'rid'er *s* Vorreiter *m*

outrigger ['aut,rɪgər] *s* Ausleger *m*; (*of a racing boat*) Outrigger *m*

out'right' *adj* (lie, refusal) glatt; (loss) total; (frank) offen || *adv* (com-pletely) völlig; (without reserve) ohne Vorbehalt; (at once) auf der Stelle; buy o. per Kasse kaufen; refuse o. glatt ablehnen

out'run' *v* (pret —ran; pp —run; ger —running) *tr* hinter sich [dat] lassen

out'sell' *v* (pret & pp —sold) *tr* e-n größeren Umsatz haben als

out'set' *s* Anfang *m*

out'shine' *v* (pret & pp —shone) *tr* überstrahlen

out'side' *adj* (help, interference) von außen; (world, influence, impres-sions) äußere; (lane, work) Außen— || *adv* draußen || *s* Außenseite *f*, Äußere *n*; at the (very) o. (aller—) höchstens; from the o. von außen || *prep* außerhalb (genit)

outsider [,aut'saɪdər] *s* Außenste-hende *mf*; (sport) Außenseiter *m*

out'size' *adj* übergroß || *s* Übergröße *f*

out'skirts' *spl* Randgebiet *n*, Stadtrand *m*

out'smart' *tr* überlisten

out'spo'ken *adj* freimütig

out'spread' *adj* (legs) gespreizt; (arms, wings) ausgebreitet

out'stand'ing *adj* hervorragend, profi-liert; (money, debts) ausstehend

out'strip' *v* (pret & pp —stripped; ger —stripping) *tr* (& fig) hinter sich [dat] lassen

out'vote' *tr* überstimmen

outward ['autwərd] *adj* äußerlich, äu-ßere || *adv* auswärts, nach außen

outwardly ['autwərdli] *adv* äußerlich

outwards ['autwərdz] *adv* auswärts

out'weigh' *tr* an Gewicht übertreffen; (fig) überwiegen

out'wit' *v* (pret & pp —witted; ger —witting) *tr* überlisten

oval ['ovəl] *adj* oval || *s* Oval *n*

ovary ['ovəri] *s* Eierstock *m*

ovation [o'veʃən] *s* Huldigung *f*, Ova-tion *f*

oven ['ʌvən] *s* Ofen *m*; (*for baking*) Backofen *m*

over ['ovər] *adj* (ended) vorbei, aus; it's all o. with him es ist vorbei mit ihm; o. and done with total erledigt || *adv*—all o. (everywhere) überall; (on the body) über und über; chil-dren of twelve and o. Kinder von zwölf Jahren und darüber; come o.! komm herüber!; o.! (turn the page) bitte wenden!; o. again noch einmal; o. against gegenüber (dat); o. and above obendrein; o. and out! (rad) Ende!; o. and o. again immer wie-der; o. in Europe drüben in Europa; o. there dort, da drüben || *prep* (po-sition) über (dat); (motion) über (acc); (because of) wegen (genit); (in the course of, e.g., a cup of tea) bei (dat); (during; more than) über (acc); all o. town (position) in der ganzen Stadt; (direction) durch die ganze Stadt; be o. s.o. über j-m stehen; b. o. s.o.'s head j-m zu hoch sein; from all o. Germany aus ganz Deutschland; o. and above außer (genit); o. the radio im Radio

o'veract' *tr* & *intr* (theat) übertreiben

o'verac'tive *adj* übermäßig tätig

overage ['ovər'edʒ] *adj* über das vor-geschriebene Alter hinaus

o'verall' *adj* Gesamt— || **o'veralls'** *spl* Monteuranzug *m*; (trousers) Über-ziehhose *f*

o'verambi'tious *adj* allzu ehrgeizig

o'veranx'ious *adj* überängstlich; (over-eager) übereifrig

o'verawe' *tr* einschüchtern

o'verbear'ing *adj* überheblich

o'verboard' *adv* über Bord; go o. about sich übermäßig begeistern für

o'vercast' *adj* bewölkt, bedeckt; be-come o. sich bewölken || *s* Bewöl-kung *f*

o'vercharge' *s* Überteuerung *f*; (elec) Überladung *f* || **o'vercharge'** *tr* e-n Überpreis abverlangen (dat); (elec) überladen

o'vercoat' *s* Mantel *m*, Überrock *m*

o'ver·come' *v* (pret —came; pp —come)

tr überwältigen; **be o. with joy** vor Freude hingerissen sein

o'vercon'fidence *s* zu großes Selbstvertrauen *n*

o'vercon'fident *adj* zu vertrauensvoll

o'vercook' *tr* (*overboil*) zerkochen; (*overbake*) zu lange backen, zu lange braten

o'vercrowd' *tr* überfüllen; (*a room, hotel, hospital*) überbelegen

o'ver·do' *v* (*pret* –did; *pp* –done) *tr* übertreiben; **o. it** sich überanstrengen

o'verdone' *adj* (culin) übergar

o'verdose' *s* Überdosis *f*

o'verdraft' *s* Überziehung *f*

o'ver·draw' *v* (*pret* –drew; *pp* –drawn) *tr* überziehen

o'verdress' *intr* sich übertrieben kleiden

o'verdrive' *s* (aut) Schongang *m*

o'verdue' *adj* überfällig

o'ver·eat' *v* (*pret* –ate; *pp* –eaten) *intr* sich überessen

o'verem'phasis *s* Überbetonung *f*

o'verem'phasize *tr* überbetonen

o'veres'timate *tr* überschätzen

o'verexcite' *tr* überreizen

o'verexert' *tr* überanstrengen

o'verexer'tion *s* Überanstrengung *f*

o'verexpose' *tr* (phot) überbelichten

o'verexpo'sure *s* Überbelichtung *f*

o'verextend' *tr* übermäßig ausweiten

o'verflow' *s* (*inundation*) Überschwemmung *f*; (*surplus*) Überschuß *m*; (*outlet for surplus liquid*) Überlauf *m*; **filled to o.** bis zum Überfließen gefüllt || o'verflow' *tr* überfluten; **o. the banks** über die Ufer treten || *intr* überfließen

o'ver·fly' *v* (*pret* –flew; *pp* –flown) *tr* überfliegen

o'verfriend'ly *adj* katzenfreundlich

o'vergrown' *adj* überwachsen; (*child*) lang hinaufgeschossen; **become o.** (said *of a garden*) verwildern; **become o. with** überwuchert werden von

o'verhang' *s* Überhang *m* || o'ver·hang' *v* (*pret & pp* –hung) *tr* hervorragen über (*acc*); (*threaten*) bedrohen || *intr* überhängen

o'verhaul' *s* Überholung *f* || o'verhaul' *tr* (*repair; overtake*) überholen

o'verhead' *adj* (*line*) oberirdisch; (*valve*) obengesteuert || *adv* droben || *s* (econ) Gemeinkosten *pl*, laufende Unkosten *pl*

o'verhead door' *s* Federhubtor *n*

o'verhead line' *s* (*of a trolley*) Oberleitung *f*

o'ver·hear' *v* (*pret & pp* –heard) *tr* mitanhören; **be o.** belauscht werden

o'verheat' *tr* überhitzen; (*a room*) überheizen || *intr* heißlaufen

o'verindulge' *tr* verwöhnen || *intr* (in) sich allzusehr ergehen (in *dat*)

o'verkill' *s* Overkill *m*

overjoyed [ˌovərˈdʒɔɪd] *adj* überglücklich

overland ['ovər ˌlænd] *adj* Überland–; **o. route** Landweg *m* || *adv* über Land

o'verlap' *s* Überschneiden *n* || o'verlap' *v* (*pret & pp* –lapped; *ger* –lapping)

tr sich überschneiden mit || *intr* (& fig) sich überschneiden

o'verlap'ping *s* (& fig) Überschneidung *f*

o'verlay' *s* Auflage *f*; (*for a map*) Planpause *f*; **o. of gold** Goldauflage *f*

o'verload' *s* Überbelastung *f*; (elec) Überlast *f* || o'verload' *tr* überlasten; (*a truck*) überladen; (*in radio communications*) übersteuern; (elec) überlasten

o'verlook' *tr* (*by mistake*) übersehen; (*a mistake*) hinwegsehen über (*acc*); (*a view*) überblicken

overly ['ovərli] *adv* übermäßig

o'vernight' *adj*—**o. stop** Aufenthalt *m* von e–r Nacht; **o. things** Nachtzeug *n* || *adv* über Nacht; **stay o.** übernachten

o'vernight' bag' *s* Nachtzeugtasche *f*

o'verpass' *s* Überführung *f*

o'ver·pay' *v* (*pret & pp* –paid) *tr & intr* überbezahlen

o'verpay'ment *s* Überbezahlung *f*

o'verpop'ulat'ed *adj* übervölkert

o'verpop'ula'tion *s* Übervölkerung *f*

o'verpow'er *tr* (& fig) überwältigen

o'verproduc'tion *s* Überproduktion *f*

o'verrate' *tr* zu hoch schätzen

o'verreach' *tr* (*extend beyond*) hinausragen über (*acc*); (*an arm*) zu weit ausstrecken; **o. oneself** sich übernehmen

o'verrefined' *adj* überspitzt

o'verripe' *adj* überreif

o'verrule' *tr* (*an objection*) zurückweisen; (*a proposal*) verwerfen; (*a person*) überstimmen

o'verrun' *s* Überproduktion *f* || o'ver·run' *v* (*pret* –ran; *pp* –run; *ger* –running) *tr* überrennen; (*said of a flood*) überschwemmen; **o. with** (*weeds*) überwuchert von; (*tourists*) überlaufen von; (*vermin*) wimmeln von

o'versalt' *tr* versalzen

o'versea(s)' *adj* Übersee– || *adv* nach Übersee

o'ver·see' *v* (*pret & pp* –saw; *pp* –seen) *tr* beaufsichtigen

o'verse'er *s* Aufseher –in *mf*

o'versen'sitive *adj* überempfindlich

o'vershad'ow *tr* überschatten; (fig) in den Schatten stellen

o'vershoe' *s* Überschuh *m*

o'ver·shoot' *v* (*pret & pp* –shot) *tr* (& fig) hinausschießen über (*acc*)

o'versight' *s* Versehen *n*; **through an o.** aus Versehen

o'versimplifica'tion *s* allzu große Vereinfachung *f*

o'versize' *adj* übergroß || *s* Übergröße *f*

o'ver·sleep' *v* (*pret & pp* –slept) *tr & intr* verschlafen

o'verspe'cialized *adj* überspezialisiert

o'verstaffed' *adj* (mit Personal) übersetzt

o'verstay' *tr* überschreiten

o'ver·step' *v* (*pret & pp* –stepped; *ger* –stepping) *tr* überschreiten

o'verstock' tr überbevorraten
o'verstrain' tr überanstrengen
o'verstuffed' adj überfüllt; (furniture) überpolstert
o'versupply' s zu großer Vorrat m; (com) Überangebot n || o'versup-ply' v (pret & pp –plied) tr überreichlich versehen; (com) überreichlich anbieten
overt ['ovərt], [o'vʌrt] adj offenkundig
o'ver-take' v (pret –took; pp –taken) tr (catch up to) einholen; (pass) überholen; (suddenly befall) überfallen
o'vertax' tr überbesteuern; (fig) überfordern, übermäßig in Anspruch nehmen
o'ver-the-coun'ter adj (pharm) rezeptfrei; (st. exch.) freihändig
o'verthrow' s Sturz m || o'ver-throw' (pret –threw; pp –thrown) tr stürzen
o'vertime' adj Überstunden– || adv—work o. Überstunden arbeiten; work five hours o. fünf Überstunden machen || s Überstunden pl; (sport) Spielverlängerung f
o'vertired' adj übermüdet
o'vertone' s (fig) Nebenbedeutung f; (mus) Oberton m
o'vertrump' tr überstechen
overture ['ovərtʃər] s Antrag m; (mus) Ouvertüre f
o'verturn' tr umstürzen || intr umkippen; (aut) sich überschlagen
overweening [,ovər'winɪŋ] adj hochmütig
o'verweight' adj zu schwer || s Übergewicht n; (of freight) Überfracht f
overwhelm [,ovər'whelm] tr (with some feeling) überwältigen; (e.g., with questions, gifts) überschütten; (with work) überbürden
o'verwhelm'ing adj überwältigend
overwind [,ovər'waɪnd] v (pret & pp –wound) tr überdrehen
o'verwork' s Überarbeitung f, Überanstrengung f || o'verwork' tr überfordern || intr sich überarbeiten
o'verwrought' adj überreizt

o'verzeal'ous adj übereifrig
ow [au] interj au!
owe [o] tr schulden (dat), schuldig sein (dat); he owes her everything er verdankt ihr alles
ow'ing adj—it is o. to you that es ist dein Verdienst, daß; o. to infolge (genit)
owl [aul] s Eule f; (barn owl, screech owl) Schleiereule f
own [on] adj eigen || s—be left on one's own sich [dat] selbst überlassen sein; be on one's own auf eigenen Füßen stehen; come into one's own zu seinem Recht kommen; hold one's own sich behaupten; of one's own für sich allein; on one's own (initiative) aus eigener Initiative; (responsibility) auf eigene Faust || tr besitzen; (acknowledge) anerkennen; who owns this house? wem gehört dieses Haus? || intr—own to sich bekennen zu; own up to zugeben (dat)
owner ['onər] s Eigentümer –in mf
own'ership' s Eigentum n; (legal right of possession) Eigentumsrecht n; under new o. unter neuer Leitung
ox [aks] s (oxen ['aksən]) Ochse m
ox'cart' s Ochsenkarren m
oxfords ['aksfərdz] spl Halbschuhe pl
oxide ['aksaɪd] s Oxyd n
oxidize ['aksɪ,daɪz] tr & intr oxydieren
oxydation [,aksɪ'deʃən] s Oxydation f
oxygen ['aksɪdʒən] s Sauerstoff m
oxygenate ['aksɪdʒə,net] tr mit Sauerstoff anreichern
ox'ygen mask' s Sauerstoffmaske f
ox'ygen tank' s Sauerstoffflasche f
ox'ygen tent' s Sauerstoffzelt n
oxytone ['aksɪ,ton] adj oxytoniert || s Oxytonon f
oyster ['ɔɪstər] s Auster f
oys'ter bed' s Austernbank f
oys'ter farm' s Austernpark m
oys'ter-man s (–men) Austernfischer m
oys'tershell' s Austernschale f
oys'ter stew' s Austernragout n
ozone ['ozon] s Ozon n
O'zone layer' s Ozonschicht f

P

P, p [pi] s sechzehnter Buchstabe des englischen Alphabets
pace [pes] s Schritt m; (speed) Tempo n; at a fast p. in schnellem Tempo; keep p. with Schritt halten mit; put s.o. through his paces j–n auf Herz und Nieren prüfen; set the p. das Tempo angeben; (sport) Schrittmacher sein || tr (the room, floor) abschreiten; p. off abschreiten || intr—p. up and down (in) auf und ab schreiten (in dat)
pace'mak'er s Schrittmacher m
pacific [pə'sɪfɪk] adj pazifisch; the

Pacific Ocean der Pazifische (or Stille) Ozean || s—the Pacific der Pazifik
pacifier ['pæsɪ,faɪ·ər] s Friedensvermittler –in mf; (for a baby) Schnuller m
pacifism ['pæsɪ,fɪzəm] s Pazifismus m
pacifist ['pæsɪfɪst] s Pazifist –in mf
paci-fy ['pæsɪ,faɪ] v (pret & pp –fied) tr (a country) befrieden; (a person) beruhigen
pack [pæk] s Pack m, Packen m; (of a soldier) Gepäck n; (of wolves, submarines) Rudel n; (of hounds) Meute

f; (of cigarettes) Päckchen *n*, Schachtel *f; (on pack animals)* Last *f; (med)* Packung *f*; **p. of cards** Spiel *n* Karten; **p. of lies** Lug und Trug || *tr (a trunk)* packen; *(clothes)* einpacken; *(seal)* abdichten; **p. in** *(above normal capacity)* einpferchen; **p. up** zusammenpacken || *intr* packen; **send s.o. packing** j-m Beine machen

package ['pækɪdʒ] *adj (price, tour, agreement)* Pauschal– || *s* Paket *n* || *tr* (ver)packen

pack′age deal′ *s* Koppelgeschäft *n*

pack′ an′imal *s* Packtier *n*

packet ['pækɪt] *s* Paket *n*, Päckchen *n; (naut)* Postschiff *n*

pack′ing *s (act)* Packen *n; (seal)* Dichtung *f; (wrapper)* Verpackung *f*

pack′ing case′ *s* Packkiste *f*

pack′ing house′ *s* Konservenfabrik *f*

pack′sad′dle *s* Packsattel *m*

pact [pækt] *s* Pakt *m*; **make a p.** paktieren

pad [pæd] *s (of writing paper)* Block *m; (ink pad)* Stempelkissen *n; (cushion)* Kissen *n; (of butter)* Stück *n; (under a rug)* Unterlage *f; (living quarters)* Bude *f; (rok)* Abschußrampe *f; (sport)* Schützer *m; (surg)* Bausch *m* || *v (pret & pp* **padded;** *ger* **padding)** *tr (e.g., the shoulders)* wattieren; *(writing)* ausbauschen

pad′ded cell′ *s* Gummizelle *f*

pad′ding *s* Wattierung *f; (coll)* Ballast *m*

paddle ['pædəl] *s (of a canoe)* Paddel *n; (for table tennis)* Schläger *m* || *tr* paddeln; *(spank)* prügeln || *intr* paddeln

pad′dle wheel′ *s* Schaufelrad *n*

paddock ['pædək] *s* Pferdekoppel *f; (at the races)* Sattelplatz *m*

pad′dy wag′on ['pædi] *s (sl)* Grüne Minna *f*

pad′lock′ *s* Vorhängeschloß *n* || *tr* mit e-m Vorhängeschloß verschließen

paean ['pi-ən] *s* Siegeslied *n*

pagan ['pegən] *adj* heidnisch || *s* Heide *m*, Heidin *f*

paganism ['pegə,nɪzəm] *s* Heidentum *n*

page [pedʒ] *s* Seite *f; (in a hotel or club; at court)* Page *m* || *tr (summon)* über den Lautsprecher (or durch Pagen) holen lassen || *intr*—**p. through** durchblättern

pageant ['pædʒənt] *s* Festspiel *n; (procession)* Festzug *m*

pageantry ['pædʒəntri] *s* Schaugepränge *n*

page′boy′ *s* Pagenfrisur *f*

page′ proof′ *s* Umbruchabzug *m*

pagoda [pə'godə] *s* Pagode *f*

paid′ in full′ [ped] *adj* voll bezahlt

paid′-up′ *adj (debts)* abgezahlt; *(policy, capital)* voll eingezahlt

pail [pel] *s* Eimer *m*

pain [pen] *s* Schmerz *m*; **on p. of death** bei Todesstrafe; **take pains** sich bemühen || *tr & intr* schmerzen || *impers*—**it pains me** to *(inf)* es fällt mir schwer zu *(inf)*

painful ['penfəl] *adj* schmerzhaft; *(fig)* peinlich

pain′ in the neck′ *s (coll)* Nervensäge *f*

pain′kill′er *s* schmerzstillendes Mittel *n*

painless ['penlɪs] *adj* schmerzlos

pains′tak′ing *adj (work)* mühsam; *(person)* sorgfältig

paint [pent] *s* Farbe *f; (for a car)* Lack *m* || *tr (e.g.)* malen; *(e.g., a house)* (an)streichen; *(a car)* lackieren; *(with watercolors)* aquarellieren; *(fig)* schildern; **p. the town red** tüchtig auf die Pauke hauen || *intr* malen; *(with house paint)* überstreichen

paint′box′ *s* Malkasten *m*

paint′brush′ *s* Pinsel *m*

paint′ can′ *s* Farbendose *f*

painter ['pentər] *s* Maler –in *mf; (of houses, etc.)* Anstreicher –in *mf*

paint′ing *s* Malerei *f; (picture)* Gemälde *n*

paint′ remov′er *s* Farbenabbeizmittel *n*

paint′ spray′er *s* Farbspritzpistole *f*

pair [per] *s* Paar *n*; **a p. of glasses** e–e Brille *f*; **a p. of gloves** ein Paar *n* Handschuhe; **a p. of pants** e–e Hose *f*; **a p. of scissors** e–e Schere *f*; **a p. of twins** ein Zwillingspaar *n*; **in pairs** paarweise || *tr* paaren; **p. off** paarweise ordnen; *(coll)* verheiraten || *intr*—**p. off** sich paarweise absondern

pajamas [pə'dʒɑməz] *s* Pyjama *s*

Pakistan ['pækɪ,stæn] *s* Pakistan *n*

Pakista·ni [,pækɪ'stæni] *adj* pakistanisch || *s* (**–nis**) Pakistaner –in *mf*

pal [pæl] *s* Kamerad *m* || *v (pret & pp* **palled;** *ger* **palling)** *intr*—**pal around with** dick befreundet sein mit

palace ['pælɪs] *s* Palast *m*

palatable ['pælətəbəl] *adj (& fig)* mundgerecht

palatal ['pælətəl] *adj* Gaumen– || *s (phonet)* Gaumenlaut *m*

palate ['pælɪt] *s* Gaumen *m*

palatial [pə'leʃəl] *adj* palastartig

Palatinate [pə'lætɪ,net] *s* Rheinpfalz *f*

pale [pel] *adj (face, colors, recollection)* blaß; **turn pale** erblassen, erbleichen || *s* Pfahl *m* || *intr* erblassen; **pale beside** *(fig)* verblassen neben *(dat)*

pale′face′ *s* Bleichgesicht *n*

Palestine ['pælɪs,taɪn] *s* Palästina *f*

palette ['pælɪt] *s* Palette *f*

palisade [,pælɪ'sed] *s* Palisade *f; (line of cliffs)* Flußklippen *pl*

pall [pɔl] *s* Bahrtuch *n; (of smoke, gloom)* Hülle *f* || *intr (on)* zuviel werden *(dat)*

pall′bear′er *s* Sargträger *m*

pallet ['pælɪt] *s* Lager *n*

palliate ['pælɪ,et] *tr* lindern; *(fig)* bemänteln

pallid ['pælɪd] *adj* blaß, bleich

pallor ['pælər] *s* Blässe *f*

palm [pɑm] *s (of the hand)* Handfläche *f; (tree)* Palme *f*; **grease s.o.'s palm** j-n schmieren; **palm of victory** Siegespalme *f* || *tr (a card)* in der Hand verbergen; **palm s.th. off on s.o.** j-m etw andrehen

palmette [pæl'mɛt] *s* Palmette *f*
palmet·to [pæl'mɛto] *s* (**-tos** & **-toes**) Fächerpalme *f*
palmist ['pɑmɪst] *s* Wahrsager –in *mf*
palmistry ['pɑmɪstri] *s* Handlesekunst *f*
palm' leaf' *s* Palmblatt *n*
Palm' Sun'day *s* Palmsonntag *m*
palm' tree' *s* Palme *f*
palpable ['pælpəbəl] *adj* greifbar
palpitate ['pælpɪ̩tet] *intr* klopfen
palsied ['pɔlzid] *adj* lahm, gelähmt
palsy ['pɔlzi] *s* Lähmung *f*
paltry ['pɔltri] *adj* armselig
pamper ['pæmpər] *tr* verwöhnen
pamphlet ['pæmflɪt] *s* Flugschrift *f*
pan [pæn] *s* Pfanne *f*; (sl) Visage *f* || *tr* (*gold*) waschen; (*a camera*) schwenken; (*criticize sharply*) (coll) verreißen || *intr* (cin) panoramieren; **pan out** glücken, klappen
panacea [ˌpænə'si·ə] *s* Allheilmittel *n*
Panama ['pænəmɑ] *s* Panama *n*
Pan'ama Canal' *s* Panamakanal *m*
Pan-American [ˌpænə'mɛrɪkən] *adj* panamerikanisch
pan'cake' *s* (flacher) Pfannkuchen *m* || *intr* (aer) absacken, bumslanden
pan'cake land'ing *s* Bumslandung *f*
panchromatic [ˌpænkro'mætɪk] *adj* panchromatisch
pancreas ['pænkrɪ·əs] *s* Bauchspeicheldrüse *f*
pandemic [pæn'dɛmɪk] *adj* pandemisch
pandemonium [ˌpændə'moni·əm] *s* Höllenlärm *m*
pander ['pændər] *s* Kuppler *m* || *intr* kuppeln; **p. to** Vorschub leisten (*dat*)
pane [pen] *s* Scheibe *f*
panegyric [ˌpæni'dʒɪrɪk] *s* Lobrede *f*
pan·el ['pænəl] *s* Tafel *f*, Feld *n*; (*in a door*) Füllung *f*; (*for instruments*) Schlattafel *f*; (*of experts*) Diskussionsgruppe *f*; (archit) Paneel *n*; (jur) Geschworenenliste *f* || *v* (*pret & pp* **-el[l]ed**; *ger* **-el[l]ing**) *tr* täfeln
pan'el discus'sion *s* Podiumsdiskussion *f*
pan'eling *s* Täfelung *f*
panelist ['pænəlɪst] *s* Diskussionsteilnehmer –in *mf*
pang [pæŋ] *s* stechender Schmerz *m*; (fig) Angst *f*; **pangs of conscience** Gewissensbisse *pl*; **pangs of hunger** nagender Hunger *m*
pan'han'dle *s* Pfannenstiel *m*; (geog) Landzunge *f* || *intr* (sl) betteln
pan'han'dler *s* (sl) Bettler –in *mf*
pan·ic ['pænɪk] *s* Panik *f* || *v* (*pret & pp* **-icked**; *ger* **-icking**) *tr* in Panik versetzen || *intr* von panischer Angst erfüllt werden
pan'ic-strick'en *adj* von panischem Schrecken erfaßt
panicky ['pænɪki] *adj* übernervös
panoply ['pænəpli] *s* Pracht *f*; (*full suit of armor*) vollständige Rüstung *f*
panorama [ˌpænə'ræmə] *s* Panorama *n*
pansy ['pænzi] *s* Stiefmütterchen *n*
pant [pænt] *s* Keuchen *n*; **pants** Hose

f, Hosen *pl* || *intr* keuchen; **p. for** or **after** gieren nach
pantheism ['pænθɪ̩ɪzəm] *s* Pantheismus *m*
pantheon ['pænθɪ̩ɑn] *s* Pantheon *n*
panther ['pænθər] *s* Panther *m*
panties ['pæntiz] *spl* Schlüpfer *m*
pantomime ['pæntə̩maɪm] *s* Pantomime *f*
pantry ['pæntri] *s* Speisekammer *f*
pap [pæp] *s* Brei *m*, Kleister *m*
papa ['pɑpə] *s* Papa *m*, Vati *m*
papacy ['pepəsi] *s* Papsttum *n*
papal ['pepəl] *adj* päpstlich
Pa'pal State' *s* Kirchenstaat *m*
paper ['pepər] *s* (*money, plate, towel*) Papier– || *s* Papier *n*; (*before a learned society*) Referat *n*; (*newspaper*) Zeitung *f*; **papers** (*documents*) Papiere *pl* || *tr* tapezieren
pa'perback' *s* Taschenbuch *n*, Pappband *m*
pa'per bag' *s* Papiertüte *f*, Tüte *f*
pa'perboy' *s* Zeitungsjunge *m*
pa'per clip' *s* Büroklammer *f*
pa'per cone' *s* Tüte *f*
pa'per cup' *s* Papierbecher *m*
pa'per cut'ter *s* Papierschneidemaschine *f*
pa'perhang'er *s* Tapezierer –in *mf*
pa'perhang'ing *s* Tapezierarbeit *f*
pa'pering *s* Tapezieren *n*
pa'per mill' *s* Papierfabrik *f*
pa'per nap'kin *s* Papierserviette *f*
pa'perweight' *s* Briefbeschwerer *m*
pa'perwork' *s* Schreibarbeit *f*
papier-mâché [ˌpepərmə'ʃe] *s* Papiermaché *n*, Pappmaché *n*
paprika [pæ'prikə] *s* Paprika *m*
papy·rus [pə'paɪrəs] *s* (**-ri** [raɪ]) Papyrus *m*
par [pɑr] *s* (fin) Pari *n*; (golf) festgesetzte Schlagzahl *f*; **at par** pari, auf Pari; **on a par with** auf gleicher Stufe mit; **up to par** (coll) auf der Höhe
parable ['pærəbəl] *s* Gleichnis *n*
parabola [pə'ræbələ] *s* Parabel *f*
parachute ['pærə̩ʃut] *s* Fallschirm *m* || *tr* mit dem Fallschirm abwerfen || *intr* abspringen
par'achute jump' *s* Fallschirmabsprung *m*
parachutist ['pærə̩ʃutɪst] *s* Fallschirmspringer –in *mf*
parade [pə'red] *s* Parade *f* || *tr* zur Schau stellen || *intr* paradieren; (mil) aufmarschieren
paradigm ['pærədɪm], ['pærə̩daɪm] *s* Musterbeispiel *n*, Paradigma *n*
paradise ['pærə̩daɪs] *s* Paradies *n*
paradox ['pærə̩dɑks] *s* Paradox *n*
paradoxical [ˌpærə'dɑksɪkəl] *adj* paradox
paraffin ['pærəfɪn] *s* Paraffin *n*
paragon ['pærə̩gɑn] *s* Musterbild *n*
paragraph ['pærə̩græf] *s* Absatz *m*, Paragraph *m*
parakeet ['pærə̩kit] *s* Sittich *m*
paral·lel ['pærə̩lɛl] *adj* parallel; **be (or run) p. to** parallel verlaufen zu || *s* Parallele *f*; (*of latitude*) Breiten-

kreis *m*; (fig) Gegenstück *n*; **without p.** ohnegleichen ‖ *v* (*pret & pp* -lel[l]ed; *ger* -lel[l]ing) *tr* parallel verlaufen zu; (*match*) gleichkommen (*dat*); (*correspond to*) entsprechen (*dat*)

par′allel bars′ *spl* Barren *m*

paraly•sis [pə′rælɪsɪs] *s* (-ses [‚siz]) Lähmung *f*, Paralyse *f*

paralytic [‚pærə′lɪtɪk] *adj* paralytisch ‖ *s* Paralytiker -in *mf*

paralyze [′pærə‚laɪz] *tr* lähmen, paralysieren; (*traffic*) lahmlegen

parameter [pə′ræmɪtər] *s* Parameter *m*

paramilitary [‚pærə′mɪlɪ‚teri] *adj* halbmilitärisch

paramount [′pærə‚maunt] *adj* oberste; **be p.** an erster Stelle stehen; **of p. importance** von äußerster Wichtigkeit

paranoia [‚pærə′nɔɪ•ə] *s* Paranoia *f*

paranoiac [‚pærə′nɔɪ‚æk] *adj* paranoisch ‖ *s* Paranoiker -in *mf*

paranoid [′pærə‚nɔɪd] *adj* paranoid

parapet [′pærə‚pet] *s* (*of a wall*) Brustwehr *f*; (*of a balcony*) Geländer *n*

paraphernalia [‚pærəfər′neli•ə] *s* Zubehör *n*, Ausrüstung *f*

paraphrase [′pærə‚frez] *s* Umschreibung *f* ‖ *tr* umschreiben

parasite [′pærə‚saɪt] *s* (& fig) Parasit *m*

parasitic(al) [‚pærə′sɪtɪk(əl)] *adj* parasitisch

parasol [′pærə‚sɔl] *s* Sonnenschirm *m*

paratrooper [′pærə‚trupər] *s* Fallschirmjäger *m*

par•cel [′pɑrsəl] *s* Paket *n*; (com) Posten *m* ‖ *v* (*pret & pp* -cel[l]ed; *ger* -cel[l]ing) *tr*—**p. out** aufteilen

par′cel post′ *s* Paketpost *f*

parch [pɑrtʃ] *tr* ausdörren; **my throat is parched** mir klebt die Zunge am Gaumen

parchment [′pɑrtʃmənt] *s* Pergament *n*

pardon [′pɑrdən] *s* Verzeihung *f*; (jur) Begnadigung *f*; **I beg your p.** ich bitte um Entschuldigung; **p.?** wie, bitte? ‖ *tr* (*a person*) verzeihen (*dat*); (*an act*) verzeihen; (*officially*) begnadigen

pardonable [′pɑrdənəbəl] *adj* verzeihlich

pare [per] *tr* (*nails*) schneiden; (*e.g., potatoes*) (ab)schälen; (*costs*) beschneiden

parent [′perənt] *s* Elternteil *m*; **parents** Eltern *pl*

parentage [′perəntɪdʒ] *s* Abstammung *f*

parental [pə′rentəl] *adj* elterlich

parenthe•sis [pə′renθɪsɪs] *s* (-ses [‚siz]) Klammer *f*; (*expression in parentheses*) Parenthese *f*

parenthetic(al) [‚perən′θetɪk(əl)] *adj* parenthetisch

parenthood [′perənt‚hʊd] *s* Elternschaft *f*

pariah [pə′raɪ•ə] *s* Paria *m*

par′ing knife′ *s* Schälmesser *n*

Paris [′pærɪs] *s* Paris *n*

parish [′pærɪʃ] *adv* Pfarr- ‖ *s* Pfarrgemeinde *f*

parishioner [pə′rɪ/ənər] *s* Gemeindemitglied *n*, Pfarrkind *n*

Parisian [pə′rɪʒən] *adj* Pariser ‖ *s* Pariser -in *mf*

parity [′pærɪti] *s* Parität *f*

park [pɑrk] *s* Park *m* ‖ *tr* abstellen, parken ‖ *intr* parken

park′ing *s* Parken *n*; **no p.** (public sign) Parken verboten

park′ing light′ *s* Parklicht *n*

park′ing lot′ *s* Parkplatz *m*

park′ing lot′ atten′dant′ *s* Parkplatzwärter -in *mf*

park′ing me′ter *s* Parkuhr *f*

park′ing place′, park′ing space *s* Parkplatz *m*, Parkstelle *f*

park′ing tick′et *s* gebührenpflichtige Verwarnung *f* (wegen falschen Parkens)

park′way′ *s* Aussichtsautobahn *f*

parley [′pɑrli] *s* Unterhandlung *f* ‖ *intr* unterhandeln

parliament [′pɑrləmənt] *s* Parlament *n*

parliamentary [‚pɑrlə′mentəri] *adj* parlamentarisch

parlor [′pɑrlər] *s* Salon *m*; (*living room*) Wohnzimmer *n*

par′lor game′ *s* Gesellschaftsspiel *n*

parochial [pə′roki•əl] *adj* Pfarr-; (fig) beschränkt

paro′chial school′ *s* Pfarrschule *f*

paro•dy [′pærədi] *s* Parodie *f* ‖ *v* (*pret & pp* -died) *tr* parodieren

parole [pə′rol] *s* bedingte Strafaussetzung *f*; **be out on p.** bedingt entlassen sein ‖ *tr* bedingt entlassen

par•quet [pɑr′ke], [pɑr′ket] *v* (*pret & pp* -queted [′ked]; *ger* -queting [′ke•ɪŋ]) *tr* parkettieren

parquetry [′pɑrkɪtri] *s* Parkettfußboden *m*

parrot [′pærət] *s* Papagei *m* ‖ *tr* nachplappern

par•ry [′pæri] *s* Parade *f* ‖ *v* (*pret & pp* -ried) *tr* parieren

parse [pɑrs] *tr* zergliedern

parsimonious [‚pɑrsɪ′moni•əs] *adj* sparsam

parsley [′pɑrsli] *s* Petersilie *f*

parsnip [′pɑrsnɪp] *s* Pastinak *m*

parson [′pɑrsən] *s* Pfarrer *m*

parsonage [′pɑrsənɪdʒ] *s* Pfarrhaus *n*

part [pɑrt] *adv*—**p. ... p.** zum Teil ... zum Teil ‖ *s* Teil *m & n*; (*section*) Abschnitt *m*; (*spare part*) Ersatzteil *m*; (*of a machine, etc.*) Bestandteil *m*; (*share*) Anteil *m*; (*of the hair*) Scheitel *m*; (mus) Partie *f*; (theat) Rolle *f*; **do one's p.** das Seinige tun; **for his p.** seinerseits; **for the most p.** größtenteils; **have a p. in** Anteil haben an (*dat*); **in p.** zum Teil, teilweise; **make a p.** (*in the hair*) e-n Scheitel ziehen; **on his p.** seinerseits; **p. and parcel** ein wesentlicher Bestandteil *m*; **take p.** (in) teilnehmen (an *dat*); **take s.o.'s p.** j-s Partei ergreifen ‖ *tr* (ab)scheiden; (*the hair*) scheiteln; **p. company** von

einander scheiden || *intr* sich tren-
nen; **p. with** hergeben

par·take [par'tek] *v* (*pret* ~**took;** *pp*
taken) *intr*—**p. in** teilnehmen an
(*dat*); **p. of** zu sich nehmen

partial ['parʃəl] *adj* Teil-, partiell;
(*prejudiced*) parteiisch; **be p. to** bevorzugen

partiality [‚parʃɪ'ælɪti] *s* Parteilichkeit *f*, Befangenheit *f*

partially ['parʃəli] *adv* teilweise

participant [par'tɪsɪpənt] *s* Teilnehmer –in *mf*

participate [par'tɪsɪ‚pet] *intr* (**in**) teilnehmen (an *dat*)

participation [par‚tɪsɪ'peʃən] *s* (**in**)
Teilnahme *f* (*an* dat)

participle ['partɪ‚sɪpəl] *s* Mittelwort
n, Partizip *n*

particle ['partɪkəl] *s* Teilchen *n*; (gram,
phys) Partikel *f*

particular [par'tɪkjələr] *adj* (*specific*)
bestimmt; (*individual*) einzeln; (*meticulous*) peinlich genau; (*especial*)
peinlich genau; (*choosy*) heikel || *s*
Einzelheit *f*; **in p.** insbesondere

partisan ['partɪzən] *adj* parteiisch || *s*
(mil) Partisan –in *mf*; (pol) Partei-
gänger –in *mf*

partition [par'tɪʃən] *s* Teilung *f*; (*wall*)
Scheidewand *f* || *tr* (auf)teilen; **p. off**
abteilen

partly ['partli] *adv* teils, teilweise

partner ['partnər] *s* Partner –in *mf*

part′nership′ *s* Partnerschaft *f*

part′ of speech′ *s* Wortart *f*

partridge ['partrɪdʒ] *s* Rebhuhn *n*

part′-time′ *adj* & *adv* nicht vollzeitlich

part′-time work′ *s* Teilzeitarbeit *f*

party ['parti] *s* Gesellschaft *f*, Party *f*;
(jur) Partei *f*; (mil) Kommando *n*;
(pol) Partei *f*; (telp) Teilnehmer –in
mf; **be a p. to** sich hergeben zu

par′ty affilia′tion *s* Parteizugehörigkeit
f

par′ty line′ *s* (pol) Parteilinie *f*; (telp)
Gemeinschaftsanschluß *m*

par′ty mem′ber *s* Parteigenosse *m*, Par-
teigenossin *f*

par′ty pol′itics *s* Parteipolitik *f*

paschal ['pæskəl] *adj* Oster-

pass [pæs] *s* (*over a mountain; permit*) Paß *m*; (*erotic advance*) An-
näherungsversuch *m*; (fencing) Stoß
m; (fb) Paßball *m*; (mil) Urlaubs-
schein *m*; (theat) Freikarte *f*; **make
a p. at** (*flirt with*) e-n Annäherungs-
versuch machen bei; (aer) vorbeiflie-
gen an (*dat*) || *tr* (*go by*) vorbeigehen
an (*dat*), passieren; (*a test*) bestehen;
(*a student in a test*) durchlassen; (*a
bill*) verabschieden; (*hand over*)
reichen; (*judgment*) abgeben; (*sentence*) sprechen; (*time*) verbringen;
(*counterfeit money*) in Umlauf bringen; (*a car*) überholen; (*e.g., a kidney stone*) ausscheiden; (*a ball*)
weitergeben; (*to*) zuspielen (*dat*); **p.
around** herumgehen lassen; **p. away**
(*time*) vertreiben; **p. in** einhändigen;
p. off as ausgeben als; **p. on** weiter-
leiten; (*e.g., news*) weitersagen; **p.

out** ausgeben; **p. over in silence** unerwähnt lassen; **p. up** verzichten auf
(*acc*) || *intr* (by) vorbeikommen (an
dat), vorbeigehen (an *dat*); (*in a car*)
(by) vorbeifahren (an *dat*); (*in a
test*) durchkommen; (*e.g., from father
to son*) übergehen; (cards) passen;
(parl) zustandekommen; **bring to p.**
herbeiführen; **come to p.** geschehen;
p.! (cards) passe!; **p. away** verscheiden; **p. for** gelten als; **p. on** ab-
scheiden; **p. out** ohnmächtig werden;
p. over (*disregard*) hinweggehen über
(*acc*); **p. through** durchgehen (*durch*);
(*said of an army*) durchziehen
(durch); (*said of a train*) berühren

passable ['pæsəbəl] *adj* (*road*) gangbar; (*by car*) befahrbar; (*halfway
good*) leidlich, passabel

passage ['pæsɪdʒ] *s* Korridor *m*, Gang
m; (*crossing*) Überfahrt *f*; (*in a
book*) Stelle *f*; (*of a law*) Annahme
f; (*of time*) Ablauf *m*; **book p. for**
e-e Schiffskarte bestellen nach

pas′sageway′ *s* Durchgang *m*, Passage *f*

pass′book′ *s* Sparbuch *n*

passenger ['pæsəndʒər] *s* Passagier –in
mf; (*in public transportation*) Fahrgast *m*; (*in a car*) Insasse *m*, Insassin *f*

pas′senger car′ *s* Personenkraftwagen
m

pas′senger plane′ *s* Passagierflugzeug *n*

pas′senger train′ *s* Personenzug *m*

passer-by ['pæsər'baɪ] *s* (**passers-by**)
Passant –in *mf*

pass′ing *adj* vorübergehend; **a p. grade**
die Note „befriedigend" || *s* (*act of
passing*) Vorbeigehen *n*; (*of a law*)
Verabschiedung *f*; (*of time*) Verstreichen *n*; (*dying*) Hinscheiden *n*;
in p. im Vorbeigehen; (*as under-
statement*) beiläufig; **no p.** (public
sign) Überholen verboten

passion ['pæʃən] *s* Leidenschaft *f*; (*of
Christ*) Passion *f*; **fly into a p.** in
Zorn geraten; **have a p. for** e-e
Vorliebe haben für

passionate ['pæʃənɪt] *adj* leidenschaftlich

pas′sion play′ *s* Passionsspiel *n*

passive ['pæsɪv] *adj* (& gram) passiv
|| *s* Passiv(um) *n*

pass′key′ *s* (*master key*) Hauptschlüssel
m; (*skeleton key*) Nachschlüssel *m*

Pass′o′ver *s* Passah *n*

pass′port *s* Paß *m*, Reisepaß *m*

pass′port of′fice *s* Paßamt *n*

pass′word′ *s* (mil) Kennwort *n*

past [pæst] *adj* (*e.g., week*) vergangen;
(*e.g., president*) ehemalig, früher;
(*gone*) vorbei; **for some time p.** seit
einiger Zeit || *s* Vergangenheit *f* ||
prep (*e.g., one o'clock*) nach; (*beyond*) über (*acc*) hinaus; **get p.** (*an
opponent*) (sport) umspielen; **go p.**
vorbeigehen an (*dat*); **it's way p.
bedtime** es ist schon längst Zeit zum
Schlafengehen

paste [pest] *s* (*glue*) Kleister *m*; (culin)
Brei *m*, Paste *f* || *tr* (*e.g., a wall*)
(**with**) bekleben (mit); **p. on** aufkle-

ben auf (acc); **p. together** zusammenkleben

paste′board′ s Pappe f

pastel [pæs′tel] adj pastellfarben || s
Pastell n

pastel′ col′or s Pastellfarbe f

pasteurize [′pæstə‚raɪz] tr pasteurisieren

pastime [′pæs‚taɪm] s Zeitvertreib m

past′ mas′ter s Experte m

pastor [′pæstər] s Pastor m

pastoral [′pæstərəl] adj Schäfer-,
Hirten-; (eccl) Hirten-, pastoral ||
s Schäfergedicht n

pas′toral let′ter s Hirtenbrief m

pastorate [′pæstərɪt] s Pastorat n

pastry [′pestri] s Gebäck n; **pastries**
Backwaren pl

pas′try shop′ s Konditorei f

past′ tense′ s Vergangenheit f

pasture [′pæst∫ər] s Weide f || tr &
intr weiden

pas′ture land′ s Weideland n

pasty [′pesti] adj (sticky) klebrig;
(complexion) bläßlich

pat [pæt] adj (answer) treffend; **have
s.th. down pat** etw in- und auswen-
dig wissen || adv—**stand pat** bei der
Stange bleiben || s Klaps m; (of but-
ter) Klümpchen n || tr tätscheln; **pat
s.o. on the back** j-m auf die Schulter
klopfen; (fig) j-n beglückwünschen

patch [pæt∫] s (of clothing, land, color)
Fleck m; (garden bed) Beet n; (of
clothing, inner tube) Flicken m; (over
the eye) Binde f; (for a wound) Pfla-
ster n || tr flicken; **p. together** (&
fig) zusammenflicken; **p. up** (a
friendship) kitten; (differences) beilegen

patch′work′ s Flickwerk n; (fig) Stück-
werk n

patch′work quilt′ s Flickendecke f

pate [pet] s (coll) Schädel m

patent [′petənt] adj öffentlich ||
[′pætənt] adj Patent-, e.g., **p. lawyer**
Patentanwalt m || s Patent n; **p.
pending** Patent angemeldet || tr
patentieren

pa′tent leath′er [′pætənt] s Lackleder
n

pa′tent-leath′er shoe′ s Lackschuh m

pat′ent med′icine [′pætənt] s rezept-
freies Medikament n

pat′ent rights′ [′pætənt] spl Schutz-
rechte pl

paternal [pə′tʌrnəl] adj väterlich

paternity [pə′tʌrnɪti] s Vaterschaft f

path [pæθ] s Pfad m; (astr) Lauf m;
clear a p. e–n Weg bahnen; **cross
s.o.'s p.** j–s Weg kreuzen

pathetic [pə′θetɪk] adj (moving) rührend; (evoking contemptuous pity)
kläglich

path′find′er s Pfadfinder m; (aer) Be-
leuchter m

pathologist [pə′θɑlədʒɪst] s Pathologe
m, Pathologin f

pathology [pə′θɑlədʒi] s Pathologie f

pathos [′peθɑs] s Pathos n

path′way′ s Weg m, Pfad m

patience [′pe∫əns] s Geduld f

patient [′pe∫ənt] adj geduldig || s Pa-
tient –in mf

pati·o [′pæti·o] s (–os) Terasse f

patriarch [′petri‚ɑrk] s Patriarch m

patrician [pə′tri∫ən] adj patrizisch ||
Patrizier –in mf

patricide [′pætri‚saɪd] s (act) Vater-
mord m; (person) Vatermörder –in
mf

patrimony [′pætri‚moni} s väterliches
Erbe n

patriot [′petri·ət] s Patriot –in mf

patriotic [‚petri′ɑtik] adj patriotisch

patriotism [′petri·ə‚tizəm] s Patrio-
tismus m

pa·trol [pə′trol] s Patrouille f, Streife
f || v (pret & pp –trolled; ger –trol-
ling) tr & intr patrouillieren

patrol′ car′ s Streifenwagen m

patrol′man s (–men) Polizeistreife f

patrol′ wag′on s Gefangenenwagen m

patron [′petrən] s Schützherr m;
(com) Kunde m, Kundin f; (eccl)
Schutzpatron m

patronage [′petrənɪdʒ] s Patronat n

patroness [′petrənɪs] s Schutzherrin f;
(eccl) Schutzpatronin f

patronize [′petrə‚naɪz] tr beschützen,
protegieren; (com) als Kunde besuchen; (theat) regelmäßig besuchen

pa′tronizing adj gönnerhaft

pa′tron saint′ s Schutzheilige mf

patter [′pætər] s (of rain) Prasseln n;
(of feet) Getrappel n || intr (said of
rain) prasseln; (said of feet) trappeln

pattern [′pætərn] s Muster n; (sew)
Schnittmuster n

patty [′pæti] s Pastetchen n

paucity [′pɔsɪti] s Knappheit f

paunch [pɔnt∫] s Wanst m

paunchy [′pɔn/i] adj dickbäuchig

pauper [′pɔpər] s Arme mf; (person on
welfare) Unterstützte mf

pause [pɔz] s Pause f; (mus) Fermate
f || intr pausieren

pave [pev] tr pflastern; **p. the way for**
(fig) anbahnen

pavement [′pevmənt] s Pflaster n;
(sidewalk) Bürgersteig m, Trottoir n

pavilion [pə′vɪljən] s Pavillon m

pav′ing s Pflasterung f

pav′ing stone′ s Pflasterstein m

paw [pɔ] s Pfote f || tr (scratch) krat-
zen; (coll) befummeln; **paw the
ground** auf dem Boden scharren ||
intr (said of a horse) mit dem Huf
scharren

pawl [pɔl] s Sperrklinke f

pawn [pɔn] s Pfand n; (fig) Schach-
figur f; (chess) Bauer m || tr ver-
pfänden

pawn′brok′er s Pfandleiher –in mf

pawn′shop′ s Pfandhaus n

pawn′ tick′et s Pfandschein m

pay [pe] s Lohn m; (mil) Sold m || v
(pret & pp **paid** [ped]) tr bezahlen;
(a visit) abstatten; (a dividend) ausschütten; (a compliment) machen;
pay back zurückzahlen; **pay damages**
Schadenersatz leisten; **pay down** an-
zahlen; **pay extra** nachzahlen; **pay in
advance** vorausbezahlen; **pay in full**

begleichen; **pay interest on** verzinsen; **pay off** (*a debt*) abbezahlen; (*a person*) entlohnen; **pay one's way** ohne Verlust arbeiten; **pay out** auszahlen; **pay s.o. back for s.th.** j-m etw heimzahlen; **pay taxes on** versteuern; **pay up** (*a debt*) abbezahlen; (*ins*) voll einzahlen ‖ *intr* zahlen; (*be worthwhile*) sich lohnen; **pay extra** zuzahlen; **pay for** (*a purchase*) (be)zahlen für; (*suffer for*) büßen

payable ['pe·əbəl] *adj* fällig, zahlbar
pay' check' *s* Lohnscheck *m*
pay'day' *s* Zahltag *m*
pay' dirt' *s*—**hit p.** sein Glück machen
payee [pe'i] *s* (*of a draft*) Zahlungsempfänger *–in mf;* (*of a check*) Wechselnehmer *–in mf*
pay' en'velope *s* Lohntüte *f*
payer ['pe·ər] *s* Zahler *–in mf*
pay'load' *s* Nutzlast *f;* (*explosive energy*) Sprengladung *f*
pay'mas'ter *s* Zahlmeister *m*
payment ['pemənt] *s* Zahlung *f;* **in p. of** zur Bezahlung (*genit*)
pay' phone' *s* Münzfernsprecher *m*
pay' raise' *s* Gehaltserhöhung *f*
pay' rate' *s* Lohnsatz *m*
pay'roll' *s* Lohnliste *f;* (*money paid*) gesamte Lohnsumme *f*
pay' sta'tion *s* Telephonautomat *m*
pea [pi] *s* Erbse *f*
peace [pis] *s* Friede(n) *m;* (*quiet*) Ruhe *f;* **be at p. with** in Frieden leben mit; **keep the p.** die öffentliche Ruhe bewahren
peaceable ['pisəbəl] *adj* friedfertig
Peace' Corps' *s* Friedenskorps *n*
peace'-lov'ing *adj* friedliebend
peace'mak'er *s* Friedenstifter *–in mf*
peace' nego'tia'tions *spl* Friedensverhandlungen *pl*
peace' of mind' *s* Seelenruhe *f*
peace'pipe' *s* Friedenspfeife *f*
peace'time' *adj* Friedens– ‖ *s*—**in p.** in Friedenszeiten
peace' trea'ty *s* Friedensvertrag *m*
peach [pitʃ] *s* Pfirsich *m*
peach' tree' *s* Pfirsichbaum *m*
peachy ['pitʃi] *adj* (*coll*) pfundig
pea'cock' *s* Pfau *m*
pea'hen' *s* Pfauenhenne *f*
pea' jack'et *s* (*nav*) Matrosenjacke *f*
peak [pik] *adj* Spitzen– ‖ *s* (& *fig*) Gipfel *m;* (*of a cap*) Mützenschirm *m;* (*elec*) Leistungsspitze *f;* (*phys*) Scheitelwert *m*
peak' hours' *spl* (*of traffic*) Hauptverkehrszeit *f;* (*elec*) Stoßzeit *f*
peak' load' *s* (*elec*) Spitzenlast *f*
peak' vol'tage *s* Spitzenspannung *f*
peal [pil] *s* Geläute *n* ‖ *intr* erschallen
peal' of laugh'ter *s* Lachsalve *f*
peal' of thun'der *s* Donnergetöse *n*
pea'nut' *s* Erdnuß *f;* **peanuts** (*coll*) kleine Fische *pl*
pea'nut but'ter *s* Erdnußbutter *f*
pear [per] *s* Birne *f*
pearl [pʌrl] *adj* Perlen– ‖ *s* Perle *f*
pearl' neck'lace *s* Perlenkette *f*
pearl' oys'ter *s* Perlenauster *f*
pear' tree' *s* Birnbaum *m*

peasant ['pezənt] *adj* Bauern–, bäuerlich ‖ *s* Bauer *m*, Bäuerin *f*
peasantry ['pezəntri] *s* Bauernstand *m*
pea'shoot'er *s* Blasrohr *n*
pea' soup' *s* Erbsensuppe *f;* (*fig*) Waschküche *f*
peat [pit] *s* Torf *m*
peat' moss' *s* Torfmull *m*
pebble ['pebəl] *s* Kiesel *m;* **pebbles** Geröll *n*
peck [pɛk] *s* (*measure*) Viertelscheffel *m;* (*e.g., of a bird*) Schnabelhieb *n;* (*kiss*) (*coll*) flüchtiger Kuß *m;* (*of trouble*) (*coll*) Menge *f* ‖ *tr* hacken; (*food*) aufpicken ‖ *intr* hacken, picken; (*eat food*) picken; **p. at** hacken nach; (*food*) (*coll*) herumstochern in (*dat*)
peculation [,pekjə'leʃən] *s* Geldunterschlagung *f*
peculiar [pɪ'kjuljər] *adj* eigenartig, absonderlich; **p. to** eigen (*dat*)
peculiarity [,pɪkjulɪ'ærɪti] *s* Eigenheit *f*, Absonderlichkeit *f*
pedagogic(al) [,pedə'gadʒɪk(əl)] *adj* pädagogisch, erzieherisch
pedagogue ['pedə,gag] *s* Pädagoge *m*, Erzieher *m*
pedagogy ['pedə,gadʒi] *s* Pädagogik *f*, Erziehungskunde *f*
ped·al ['pedəl] *s* Pedal *n* ‖ *v* (*pret* & *pp* **-al[l]ed;** *ger* **-al[l]ing**) *tr* fahren ‖ *intr* die Pedale treten
pedant ['pedənt] *s* Pedant *–in mf*
pedantic [pɪ'dæntɪk] *adj* pedantisch
pedantry ['pedəntri] *s* Pedanterie *f*
peddle ['pedəl] *tr* hausieren mit ‖ *intr* hausieren
peddler ['pedlər] *s* Hausierer *–in mf*
pedestal ['pedɪstəl] *s* Sockel *m*, Postament *n;* **put s.o. on a p.** (*fig*) j–n aufs Podest erheben
pedestrian [pɪ'destrɪ·ən] *adj* Fußgänger–; (*fig*) schwunglos ‖ *s* Fußgänger *–in mf*
pediatrician [,pidɪ·ə'trɪʃən] *s* Kinderarzt *m*, Kinderärztin *f*
pediatrics [,pidɪ'ætrɪks] *s* Kinderheilkunde *f*
pediment ['pedɪmənt] *s* Giebelfeld *n*
peek [pik] *s* schneller Blick *m* ‖ *intr* gucken; **p. at** angucken
peekaboo ['pikə,bu] *adj* durchsichtig ‖ *interj* guck, guck!
peel [pil] *s* Schale *f* ‖ *tr* schälen; **p. off** abschälen ‖ *intr* sich schälen; (*said of paint*) abbröckeln; **p. off** (*aer*) sich aus dem Verband lösen
peep [pip] *s* schneller Blick *m;* heimlicher Blick *m;* **not another p. out of you!** kein Laut mehr aus dir! ‖ *intr* gucken; (*look carefully*) lugen; **p. out** hervorlugen
peep'hole' *s* Guckloch *n*
peep' show' *s* Fleischbeschau *f*
peer [pɪr] *s* Gleichgestellte *mf* ‖ *intr* blicken; **p. at** mustern
peerless ['pɪrlɪs] *adj* unvergleichlich
peeve [piv] *s* (*coll*) Beschwerde *f* ‖ *tr* (*coll*) ärgern
peeved *adj* verärgert
peevish ['pivɪʃ] *adj* sauertöpfisch

peg [peg] *s* Pflock *m*; (*for clothes*) Haken *m*; (*e.g., of a violin*) Wirbel *m*; **take down a peg or two** ducken ‖ *v* (*pret & pp* **pegged**; *ger* **pegging**) *tr* festpflocken; (*prices*) festlegen; (*throw*) (*sl*) schmeißen; (*identify*) (*sl*) erkennen

peg'board' *s* Klammerplatte *f*

Peggy ['pegɪ] *s* Gretchen *n*, Gretl *f & n*

peg' leg' *s* Stelzbein *n*

Pekin-ese [ˌpikɪ'niz] *s* (**-ese**) Pekinese *m*

pelf [pelf] *s* (pej) Mammon *m*

pelican ['pelɪkən] *s* Pelikan *m*

pellet ['pelɪt] *s* Kügelchen *n*; (*bullet*) Schrotkugel *f*, Schrotkorn *n*

pell-mell ['pel'mel] *adj* verworren ‖ *adv* durcheinander

pelt [pelt] *s* Fell *n*, Pelz *m*; (*whack*) Schlag *m* ‖ *tr* (*with*) bewerfen (mit); (*with questions*) bombardieren

pelvis ['pelvɪs] *s* Becken *n*

pen [pen] *s* Feder *f*; (*fountain pen*) Füllfederhalter *m*; (*enclosure*) Pferch *m*; (*prison*) (sl) Kittchen *n* ‖ *v* (*pret & pp* **penned**; *ger* **penning**) *tr* (*a letter*) verfassen ‖ (*pret & pp* **penned & pent**; *ger* **penning**) *tr*—**pen in** pferchen

penal ['pinəl] *adj* strafrechtlich, Straf-

pe'nal code' *s* Strafgesetzbuch *n*

penalize ['pinəˌlaɪz] *tr* bestrafen; (box) mit Strafpunkten belegen

penalty ['penltɪ] *s* Strafe *f*; (*point deducted*) (sport) Strafpunkt *m*; **under p. of death** bei Todesstrafe

pen'alty ar'ea *s* (sport) Strafraum *m*

pen'alty box' *s* Strafbank *f*

pen'alty kick' *s* Strafstoß *m*

penance ['penəns] *s* Buße *f*

penchant ['penʃənt] *s* (**for**) Hang *m* (zu)

pen-cil ['pensəl] *s* Bleistift *m* ‖ *v* (*pret & pp* **-cil[l]ed**; *ger* **-cil[l]ing**) *tr* mit Bleistift anzeichnen

pen'cil push'er *s* (coll) Schreiberling *m*

pen'cil sharp'ener *s* Bleistiftspitzer *m*

pendant ['pendənt] *s* Anhänger *m*; (*electrical fixture*) Hängeleuchter *m*

pendent ['pendənt] *adj* (herab)hängend

pend'ing *adj* schwebend; **be p. in** (der) Schwebe sein ‖ *prep* (*during*) während (*genit*); (*until*) bis zu (*dat*)

pendulum ['pendʒələm] *s* Pendel *n*

pen'dulum bob' *s* Pendelgewicht *n*

penetrate ['penɪˌtret] *tr* eindringen in (*acc*) ‖ *intr* eindringen

penetration [ˌpenɪ'treʃən] *s* Durchdringen *n*; (of, *e.g., a country*) Eindringen *n* (in *acc*); (*in ballistics*) Durchschlagskraft *f*

penguin ['peŋgwɪn] *s* Pinguin *m*

penicillin [ˌpenɪ'sɪlɪn] *s* Penizillin *n*

peninsula [pə'nɪnsələ] *s* Halbinsel *f*

pe-nis ['pinɪs] *s* (**-nes** [niz] **& -nises**) Penis *m*

penitence ['penɪtəns] *s* Bußfertigkeit *f*

penitent ['penɪtənt] *adj* bußfertig ‖ *s* Büßer **-in** *mf*; (eccl) Beichtkind *n*

penitentiary [ˌpenɪ'tenʃərɪ] *s* Zuchthaus *n*

pen'knife' *s* (**-knives'**) Federmesser *n*

penmanship ['penmən ˌʃɪp] *s* Schreibkunst *f*

pen' name' *s* Schriftstellername *m*

pennant ['penənt] *s* Wimpel *m*; (nav) Stander *m*

penniless ['penɪlɪs] *adj* mittellos

penny ['penɪ] *s* Pfennig *m*; (*U.S.A.*) Cent *m*

pen'ny pinch'er [ˌpɪnt/ər] *s* Pfennigfuchser *m*

pen' pal' *s* Schreibfreund **-in** *mf*

pension ['penʃən] *s* Pension *f*, Rente *f*; **put on p.** pensionieren ‖ *tr* pensionieren

pensioner ['penʃənər] *s* Pensionär **-in** *mf*; (ins) Rentenempfänger **-in** *mf*

pen'sion fund' *s* Pensionskasse *f*

pensive ['pensɪv] *adj* sinnend

pentagon ['pentəˌgɑn] *s* Fünfeck *n*; **the Pentagon** das Pentagon

Pentecost ['pentɪˌkɔst] *s* Pfingsten *n*

penthouse ['pent ˌhaʊs] *s* Wetterdach *n*; (*exclusive apartment*) Penthouse *n*

pent-up ['pent'ʌp] *adj* verhalten

penult ['pinʌlt] *s* vorletzte Silbe *f*

penurious [pɪ'nʊrɪ-əs] *adj* karg

penury ['penjərɪ] *s* Kargheit *f*

peony ['pi-ənɪ] *s* Pfingstrose *f*

people ['pipəl] *spl* Leute *pl*, Menschen *pl*; **his p.** die Seinen; **p. like him** seinesgleichen; **p. say** man sagt, die Leute sagen ‖ *s* (**peoples**) Volk *n* ‖ *tr* bevölkern

pep [pep] *s* (coll) Schwungkraft *f* ‖ *v* (*pret & pp* **pepped**; *ger* **pepping**) *tr*— **pep up** aufpulvern

pepper ['pepər] *s* (*spice*) Pfeffer *m*; (*plant*) Paprika *f*; (*vegetable*) Paprikaschote *f* ‖ *tr* pfeffern

pep'per mill' *s* Pfeffermühle *f*

pep'permint' *adj* Pfefferminz- ‖ *s* Pfefferminze *f*

pep'per shak'er *s* Pfefferstreuer *m*

peppery ['pepərɪ] *adj* pfefferig

per [pʌr] *prep* pro (*acc*); **as per** laut (*genit & dat*)

perambulator [pər'æmbjəˌletər] *s* Kinderwagen *m*

per capita [pər'kæpɪtə] pro Kopf

perceivable [pər'sivəbəl] *adj* wahrnehmbar

perceive [pər'siv] *tr* wahrnehmen

percent [pər'sent] *s* Prozent *n*

percentage [pər'sentɪdʒ] *s* Prozentsatz *m*; **p. of** (*e.g., the profit*) Anteil *m* an (*dat*); (*e.g., of a group*) Teil *m* (*genit*)

perceptible [pər'septəbəl] *adj* wahrnehmbar

perception [pər'sepʃən] *s* Wahrnehmung *f*

perch [pʌrtʃ] *s* Stange *f*; (ichth) Barsch *m* ‖ *tr* setzen ‖ *intr* sitzen

percolate ['pʌrkəˌlet] *tr* durchseihen; (*coffee*) perkolieren ‖ *intr* durchsickern

percolator ['pʌrkəˌletər] *s* Perkolator *m*

percussion [pər'kʌʃən] *s* Schlag *m*; (med) Perkussion *f*

percus'sion in'strument *s* Schlaginstrument *n*

per di'em allow'ance [pər'daɪ·əm] s Tagegeld n

perdition [pər'dɪʃən] s Verdammnis f

perennial [pə'renɪ·əl] adj immerwährend; (bot) ausdauernd ‖ s ausdauernde Pflanze f

perfect ['pʌrfɪkt] adj perfekt, vollkommen; **he is a p. stranger to me** er ist mir völlig fremd ‖ s (gram) Perfekt(um) n ‖ [pər'fekt] tr vervollkommnen

perfection [pər'fekʃən] s Vollkommenheit f; **to p.** vollkommen

perfectionist [pər'fekʃənɪst] s Perfektionist –in mf

perfectly ['pʌrfɪktli] adv völlig, durchaus; **p. well** ganz genau

perfidious [pər'fɪdɪ·əs] adj treulos

perfidy ['pʌrfɪdi] s Treubruch m

perforate ['pʌrfə‚ret] tr durchlöchern

per'forated line' s durchlochte Linie f

perforation [‚pʌrfə'reʃən] s gelochte Linie f

perforce [pər'fɔrs] adv notgedrungen

perform [pər'fɔrm] tr ausführen; (an operation) vornehmen; (theat) aufführen ‖ intr (öffentlich) auftreten; (mach) funktionieren

performance [pər'fɔrməns] s Ausführung f; (mach) Leistung f; (theat) Aufführung f

performer [pər'fɔrmər] s Künstler –in mf

perform'ing arts' spl darstellende Künste pl

perfume ['pʌrfjum] s Parfüm n ‖ tr parfümieren

perfunctorily [pər'fʌŋktərɪli] adv oberflächlich

perfunctory [pər'fʌŋktəri] adj oberflächlich

perhaps [pər'hæps] adv vielleicht

per hour' pro Stunde, in der Stunde

peril ['perɪl] s Gefahr f; **at one's own p.** auf eigene Gefahr

perilous ['perɪləs] adj gefährlich

perimeter [pə'rɪmɪtər] s (math) Umfang m; (mil) Rand m

period ['pɪrɪ·əd] s Periode f, Zeitabschnitt m; (menstrual period) Periode f; (educ) Stunde f; (gram) Punkt m; (sport) Viertel n; **extra p.** (sport) Verlängerung f; **for a p. of** für die Dauer von; **p.!** und damit punktum!; **p. of grace** Frist f; **p. of life** Lebensalter n; **p. of time** Zeitdauer f

pe'riod fur'niture s Stilmöbel pl

periodic [‚pɪrɪ'adɪk] adj zeitweilig

periodical [‚pɪrɪ'adɪkəl] s Zeitschrift f

peripheral [pə'rɪfərəl] adj peripher

periphery [pə'rɪfəri] s Peripherie f

periscope ['perɪ‚skop] s Periskop n

perish ['perɪʃ] intr umkommen; (said of wares) verderben

perishable ['perɪʃəbəl] adj vergänglich; (food) leicht verderblich

perjure ['pʌrdʒər] tr—**p. oneself** Meineid begehen

perjury ['pʌrdʒəri] s Meineid m; **commit p.** e–n Meineid leisten

perk [pʌrk] tr—**p. up** (the head) aufwerfen; (the ears) spitzen ‖ intr

(percolate) (coll) perkolieren; **p. up** lebhaft werden

permanence ['pʌrmənəns] s Dauer f

permanent ['pʌrmənənt] adj (fort)dauernd, bleibend ‖ s Dauerwelle f

per'manent address' s ständiger Wohnort m

per'manent job' s Dauerstellung f

per'manent wave' s Dauerwelle f

permeable ['pʌrmɪ·əbəl] adj durchlässig

permeate ['pʌrmɪ‚et] tr durchdringen ‖ intr durchsickern

permissible [pər'mɪsɪbəl] adj zulässig

permission [pər'mɪʃən] s Erlaubnis f; **with your p.** mit Verlaub

permissive [pər'mɪsɪv] adj nachsichtig

per-mit ['pʌrmɪt] s Erlaubnis f; (document) Erlaubnisschein m ‖ [pər'mɪt] v (pret & pp –mitted; ger –mitting) tr erlauben, gestatten; **be permitted to** (inf) dürfen (inf)

permute [pər'mjut] tr umsetzen; (math) permutieren

pernicious [pər'nɪʃəs] adj **(to)** schädlich (für)

perox'ide blonde' [pə'raksaɪd] s Wasserstoffblondine f

perpendicular [‚pʌrpən'dɪkjələr] adj senkrecht ‖ s Senkrechte f

perpetrate ['pʌrpɪ‚tret] tr verüben

perpetual [pər'petʃu·əl] adj (everlasting) ewig; (continual) unaufhörlich

perpetuate [pər'petʃu‚et] tr verewigen

perplex [pər'pleks] tr verblüffen

perplexed' adj verblüfft

perplexity [pər'pleksɪti] s Verblüffung f

persecute ['pʌrsɪ‚kjut] tr verfolgen

persecution [‚pʌrsɪ'kjuʃən] s Verfolgung f

persecutor ['pʌrsɪ‚kjutər] s Verfolger –in mf

perseverance [‚pʌrsɪ'vɪrəns] s Ausdauer f, Beharrlichkeit f

persevere [‚pʌrsɪ'vɪr] intr ausdauern; **p. in** (cling to) beharren auf (acc); (e.g., efforts, studies) fortfahren mit

Persia ['pʌrʒə] s Persien n

Persian ['pʌrʒən] adj persisch ‖ s Perser –in mf; (language) Persisch n

Per'sian rug' s Perserteppich m

persimmon [pər'sɪmən] s Persimone f

persist [pər'sɪst] intr andauern; **p. in** verbleiben bei

persistent [pər'sɪstənt] adj andauernd

person ['pʌrsən] s Person f; **in p.** persönlich; **per p.** pro Person

personable ['pʌrsənəbəl] adj (attractive) ansehnlich; (good-natured) verträglich

personage ['pʌrsənɪdʒ] s Persönlichkeit f

personal ['pʌrsənəl] adj persönlich; (private) Privat–; **become p.** anzüglich werden

per'sonal da'ta spl Personalien pl

per'sonal hygiene' s Körperpflege f

per'sonal in'jury s Personenschaden m

personality [‚pʌrsə'nælɪti] s Persönlichkeit f

personally ['pʌrsənəli] adv persönlich

per'sonal pro'noun s Personalpronomen n

personi•fy [pər'sɑnɪ ˌfaɪ] v (pret & pp –fied) tr personifizieren, verkörpern

personnel [ˌpʌrsə'nel] s Personal n

per'son-to-per'son call' s Gespräch n mit Voranmeldung

perspective [pər'spɛktɪv] s Perspektive f

perspicacious [ˌpʌrspɪ'keʃəs] adj scharfsinnig

perspiration [ˌpʌrspɪ'reʃən] s Schweiß m; (perspiring) Schwitzen n

perspire [pər'spaɪr] intr schwitzen

persuade [pər'swed] tr überreden

persuasion [pər'sweʒən] s Überredung f

persuasive [pər'swesɪv] adj redegewandt

pert [pʌrt] adj keck; (sprightly) lebhaft

pertain [pər'ten] intr—p. to betreffen, sich beziehen auf (acc)

pertinacious [ˌpʌrtɪ'neʃəs] adj beharrlich

pertinent ['pʌrtɪnənt] adj einschlägig; be p. to sich beziehen auf (acc)

perturb [pər'tʌrb] tr beunruhigen

peruse [pə'ruz] tr sorgfältig durchlesen

pervade [pər'ved] tr durchdringen

perverse [pər'vʌrs] adj (abnormal) pervers; (obstinate) verstockt

perversion [pər'vʌrʒən] s Perversion f; (of truth) Verdrehung f

perversity [pər'vʌrsɪti] s Perversität f

pervert ['pʌrvərt] s perverser Mensch m || [pər'vʌrt] tr (corrupt) verderben; (twist) verdrehen; (misapply) mißbrauchen

pesky ['peski] adj (coll) lästig

pessimism ['pɛsɪ ˌmɪzəm] s Pessimismus m

pessimist ['pɛsɪmɪst] s Pessimist –in mf

pessimistic [ˌpɛsɪ'mɪstɪk] adj pessimistisch

pest [pɛst] s (insect) Schädling m; (annoying person) Plagegeist m; (pestilence) Pest f

pest' control' s Schädlingsbekämpfung f

pester ['pɛstər] tr piesacken; (with questions) belästigen

pesticide ['pɛstɪ ˌsaɪd] s Pestizid n

pestilence ['pɛstɪləns] s Pestilenz f

pestle ['pɛsəl] s Stößel m

pet [pɛt] adj Lieblings– || s (animal) Haustier n; (person) Liebling m; (favorite child) Schoßkind n || v (pret & pp petted; ger petting) tr streicheln || intr sich abknutschen

petal ['pɛtəl] s Blumenblatt n

Peter ['pitər] s Peter m || intr—peter out im Sande verlaufen

pet' ide'a s Lieblingsgedanke m

petition [pɪ'tɪʃən] s Eingabe f; (jur) Gesuch n || tr (s.o.) ersuchen

pet' name' s Kosename m

petri•fy ['pɛtrɪ ˌfaɪ] v (pret & pp –fied) tr (& fig) versteinern; be petrified versteinern; (fig) zu Stein werden

petroleum [pə'troliˑəm] s Petroleum n

pet' shop' s Tierhandlung f

petticoat ['pɛtɪ ˌkot] s Unterrock m

pet'ting s Petting n

petty ['pɛti] adj klein, geringfügig; (narrow) engstirnig

pet'ty cash' s Handkasse f

pet'ty lar'ceny s geringer Diebstahl m

pet'ty of'ficer m (nav) Bootsmann m

petulant ['pɛtjələnt] adj verdrießlich

petunia [pə't(j)uni·ə] s Petunie f

pew [pju] s Bank f, Kirchenstuhl m

pewter ['pjutər] s Weißmetall n

Pfc. ['pi'ɛf'si] s (private first class) Gefreiter m

phalanx ['fælæŋks] s Phalanx f

phantasm ['fæntæzəm] s Trugbild n

phantom ['fæntəm] s Phantom n

Pharaoh ['fɛro] s Pharao m

Pharisee ['færɪ ˌsi] s Pharisäer m

pharmaceutical [ˌfɑrmə'sutɪkəl] adj pharmazeutisch

pharmacist ['fɑrməsɪst] s Apotheker –in mf

pharmacy ['fɑrməsi] s Apotheke f; (science) Pharmazie f

pharynx ['færɪŋks] s Rachenhöhle f

phase [fez] s Phase f || tr in Phasen einteilen; p. out abwickeln

pheasant ['fɛzənt] s Fasan m

phenobarbital [ˌfino'bɑrbɪ ˌtæl] s Phenobarbital n

phenomenal [fɪ'nɑmɪnəl] adj phänomenal

phenome•non [fɪ'nɑmɪ ˌnɑn] s (–na [nə]) (& fig) Phänomen n, Erscheinung f

phial ['faɪ·əl] s Phiole f

philanderer [fɪ'lændərər] s Schürzenjäger m

philanthropist [fɪ'lænθrəpɪst] s Menschenfreund –in mf, Philanthrop –in mf

philanthropy [fɪ'lænθrəpi] s Menschenliebe f, Philanthropie f

philately [fɪ'lætəli] s Briefmarkenkunde f

Philippine ['fɪlɪ ˌpin] adj philippinisch || the Philippines spl die Philippinen

Philistine ['fɪlɪstɪn] adj (& fig) philisterhaft || s (& fig) Philister m

philologist [fɪ'lɑlədʒɪst] s Philologe m, Philologin f

philology [fɪ'lɑlədʒi] s Philologie f

philosopher [fɪ'lɑsəfər] s Philosoph m

philosophic(al) [ˌfɪlə'sɑfɪk(əl)] adj philosophisch

philosophy [fɪ'lɑsəfi] s Philosophie f

phlebitis [flɪ'baɪtɪs] s Venenentzündung f

phlegm [flɛm] s Schleim m

phlegmatic(al) [flɛg'mætɪk(əl)] adj phlegmatisch

phobia ['fobɪ·ə] s Phobie f

Phoenicia [fɪ'nɪʃə] s Phönizien s

Phoenician [fɪ'nɪʃən] adj phönizisch || s Phönizier m

phoenix ['finɪks] s Phönix m

phone [fon] s (coll) Telephon n; on the p. am Apparat || tr (coll) anrufen || intr telephonieren

phone' call' s (coll) Anruf m

phonetic [fo'netɪk] *adj* phonetisch, Laut– ‖ **phonetics** *s* Lautlehre *f*, Phonetik *f*

phonograph ['fonə‚græf] *s* Grammophon *n*

pho'nograph rec'ord *s* Schallplatte *f*

phonology [fə'nɑlədʒɪ] *s* Lautlehre *f*

phony ['foni] *adj* falsch, Schein– ‖ *s* Schwindler –in *mf*

phosphate ['fɑsfet] *s* Phosphat *n*

phosphorescent [‚fɑsfə'resənt] *adj* phosphoreszierend

phospho·rus ['fɑsfərəs] *s* (–ri [‚raɪ]) Phosphor *m*

pho·to ['foto] *s* (–tos) (coll) Photo *n*

pho'tocop'y *s* Photokopie *f* ‖ *v* (*pret & pp* –ied) *tr* photokopieren

pho'toengrav'ing *s* Lichtdruckverfahren *n*

pho'to fin'ish *s* Zielphotographie *f*

photogenic [‚foto'dʒenɪk] *adj* photogen

photograph ['fotə‚græf] *s* Photographie *f* ‖ *tr & intr* photographieren

photographer [fə'tɑgrəfər] *s* Photograph –in *mf*

photography [fə'tɑgrəfi] *s* Photographie *f*

photostat ['fotə‚stæt] *s* (trademark) Photokopie *f* ‖ *tr* photokopieren

phrase [frez] *s* Sinngruppe *f* ‖ *tr* formulieren; (mus) phrasieren

phrenology [frə'nɑlədʒɪ] *s* Schädellehre *f*

physic ['fɪzɪk] *s* Abführmittel *n*; **physics** *s* Physik *f*

physical ['fɪzɪkəl] *adj* körperlich, physisch ‖ *s* (*examination*) ärztliche Untersuchung *f*

phys'ical condi'tion *s* Gesundheitszustand *m*

phys'ical de'fect *s* körperliches Gebrechen *n*

phys'ical educa'tion *s* Leibeserziehung *f*

phys'ical ex'ercise *s* Leibesübungen *pl*; (*calisthenics*) Bewegung *f*

phys'ical hand'icap *s* Körperbehinderung *f*

physician [fɪ'zɪʃən] *s* Arzt *m*, Ärztin *f*

physicist ['fɪzɪsɪst] *s* Physiker –in *mf*

physics ['fɪzɪks] *s* Physik *f*

physiognomy [‚fɪzɪ'ɑgnəmi] *s* Gesichtsbildung *f*, Physiognomie *f*

physiological [‚fɪzɪ·ə'lɑdʒɪkəl] *adj* physiologisch

physiology [‚fɪzɪ'ɑlədʒɪ] *s* Physiologie *f*

physique [fɪ'zik] *s* Körperbau *m*

pi [paɪ] *s* (math) Pi *n* ‖ *tr* (typ) zusammenwerfen

pianist ['pi·ənɪst] *s* Pianist –in *mf*

pian·o [pɪ'æno] *s* (–os) Klavier *n*

pian'o stool' *s* Klavierschemel *m*

picayune [‚pɪkə'jun] *adj* (paltry) geringfügig; (*person*) kleinlich

picco·lo ['pɪkəlo] *s* (–los) Pikkoloflöte *f*

pick [pɪk] *s* (*tool*) Spitzhacke *f*; (*choice*) Auslese *f*; **the p. of the crop** das Beste von allem ‖ *tr* (*choose*) sich [*dat*] aussuchen; (*e.g., fruit*) pflücken; (*one's teeth*) stochern in (*dat*); (*one's nose*) bohren in (*dat*); (*a lock*) mit e–m Dietrich öffnen; (*a quarrel*) suchen; (*a bone*) abnagen; **p. off** abpflücken; (*shoot*) (coll) abknallen; **p. out** auswählen; **p. s.o.'s brains** j–s Ideen klauen; **p. s.o.'s pocket** j–m die Tasche ausräumen; **p. up** (*lift up*) aufheben; (*a girl*) (coll) aufgabeln; (*a suspect*) aufgreifen; (*with a car*) abholen; (*passengers; the scent*) aufnehmen; (*a language; news*) aufschnappen; (*a habit*) annehmen; (*a visual object*) erkennen; (*strength*) wieder erlangen; (*weight*) zunehmen an (*dat*); **p. up speed** in Fahrt kommen ‖ *intr*—**p. and choose** wählerisch suchen; **p. at** herumstochern in (*dat*); **p. on** herumreiten auf (*dat*); **p. up** (*improve in health or business*) sich (wieder) erholen

pick'ax' *s* Picke *f*, Pickel *m*

picket ['pɪkɪt] *s* Holzpfahl *m*; (*of strikers*) Streikposten *m* ‖ *tr* durch Streikposten absperren, Streikposten stehen vor (*dat*) ‖ *intr* Streikposten stehen

pick'et fence' *s* Lattenzaun *m*

pick'et line' *s* Streikkette *f*

pickle ['pɪkəl] *s* Essiggurke *f*; **be in a p.** (coll) im Schlamassel sitzen ‖ *tr* (ein)pökeln

pick'led *adj* (sl) blau

pick'led her'ring *s* Rollmops *m*

pick'pock'et *s* Taschendieb *m*

pick'up' *s* (*of a car*) Beschleunigungsvermögen *n*; (*girl*) Straßenbekanntschaft *f*; (*restorative*) Stärkungsmittel *n*, Erfrischung *f*; (*a stop to pick up*) Abholung *f*; (*of a phonograph*) Schalldose *f*

pick'up truck' *s* offener Lieferwagen *m*

picky ['pɪki] *adj* wählerisch

pic·nic ['pɪknɪk] *s* Picknick *n* ‖ *v* (*pret & pp* –nicked; *ger* –nicking) *intr* picknicken

pictorial [pɪk'torɪ·əl] *adj* illustriert ‖ *s* Illustrierte *f*

picture ['pɪktʃər] *s* Bild *n*; (fig) Vorstellung *f*; **look the p. of health** kerngesund aussehen ‖ *tr* sich [*dat*] vorstellen

pic'ture gal'lery *s* Gemäldegalerie *f*

pic'ture post'card *s* Ansichtspostkarte *f*

picturesque [‚pɪktʃə'resk] *adj* malerisch, pittoresk; (*language*) bilderreich

pic'ture tube' *s* Bildröhre *f*

pic'ture win'dow *s* Panoramafenster *n*

piddling ['pɪdlɪŋ] *adj* lumpig

pie [paɪ] *s* Torte *f*; (*meat-filled*) Pastete *f*; **pie in the sky** Luftschloß *n*

piece [pis] *s* Stück *n*; (checkers) Stein *m*; (chess) Figur *f*; (mil) Geschütz *n*; (mus, theat) Stück *n*; **a p. of advice** ein Rat *m*; **a p. of bad luck** ein unglücklicher Zufall *m*; **a p. of furniture** ein Möbelstück *n*; **a p. of luggage** ein Gepäckstück *n*; **a p. of**

news e–e Neuigkeit f; **a p. of paper** ein Blatt Papier; **a p. of toast** e–e geröstete Brotscheibe f; **say one's p.** seine Meinung sagen
piece'meal' adv stückweise
piece'work' s Akkordarbeit f; **do p. in Akkord** arbeiten
piece'work'er s Akkordarbeiter –in mf
pier [pɪr] s Landungsbrücke f, Pier m & f; (of a bridge) Pfeiler m
pierce [pɪrs] tr durchstechen, durchbohren
pierc'ing adj (look, pain) scharf, stechend; (cry) gellend; (cold) schneidend
piety ['paɪ·əti] s Frömmigkeit f
pig [pɪg] s Schwein n
pigeon ['pɪdʒən] s Taube f
pi'geonhole' s Fach n || tr auf die lange Bank schieben
pi'geon loft' s Taubenschlag m
pi'geon-toed' adj & adv mit einwärts gerichteten Zehen
piggish ['pɪgɪʃ] adj säuisch
piggyback ['pɪgɪ,bæk] adv huckepack
pig'gy bank' s Sparschweinchen n
pig'head·ed adj dickköpfig
pig' i'ron s Roheisen n
pigment ['pɪgmənt] s Pigment n
pig'pen' s Schweinekoben m
pig'skin' s Schweinsleder n; (sport) (coll) Fußball m
pig'sty' s Schweinestall m
pig'tail' s (hair style) Rattenschwanz m
pike [paɪk] s Pike f, Spieß m; (highway) Landstraße f; (ichth) Hecht m
piker ['paɪkər] s (coll) Knicker m
pilaster [pɪ'læstər] s Wandpfeiler m
pile [paɪl] s (heap) Haufen m; (e.g., of papers) Stoß m; (stake) Pfahl m; (fortune) (coll) Menge f; (atom. phys) Meiler m, Reaktor m; (elec, phys) Säule f; (tex) Flor m; **piles** (pathol) Hämorrhoiden pl; **piles of money** (coll) Heidengeld n || tr anhäufen, aufhäufen; **p. it on** (coll) dick auftragen || intr—**p. into** sich drängen in (acc); **p. on** sich übereinander stürzen; **p. out of** sich hinausdrängen aus; **p. up** sich (an)häufen '
pile' driv'er s Pfahlramme f, Rammbär m
pilfer ['pɪlfər] tr mausen, stibitzen
pilgrim ['pɪlgrɪm] s Pilger –in mf
pilgrimage ['pɪlgrɪmɪdʒ] s Pilgerfahrt f; **go on a p.** pilgern
pill [pɪl] s (& fig) Pille f
pillar ['pɪlər] s Pfeiler m, Säule f
pill'box' s Pillenschachtel f; (mil) Bunker m
pillo·ry ['pɪləri] s Pranger m || v (pret & pp –ried) tr an den Pranger stellen; (fig) anprangern
pillow ['pɪlo] s Kopfkissen n
pil'lowcase' s Kopfkissenbezug m
pilot ['paɪlət] adj (experimental) Versuchs– || s (aer) Pilot m, Flugzeugführer –in mf; (naut) Lotse m || tr (aer) steuern, führen; (naut) steuern, lotsen
pi'lothouse' s (naut) Ruderhaus n
pi'lot light' s Sparflamme f

pi'lot's li'cense s Flugzeugführerschein m
pimp [pɪmp] s Zuhälter m || intr kuppeln
pimp'ing s Zuhälterei f
pimple ['pɪmpəl] s Pickel m
pimply ['pɪmpli] adj pickelig
pin [pɪn] s Stecknadel f; (ornament) Anstecknadel f; (bowling) Kegel m; (mach) Pinne f, Zapfen m; **be on pins and needles** wie auf Nadeln sitzen || v (pret & pp pinned); ger pinning) tr (fasten with a pin) mit e–r Nadel befestigen; (e.g., a dress) abstecken; (e.g., under a car) einklemmen; (e.g., against the wall) drücken; (in wrestling) auf die Schultern legen; **pin down** (a person) festlegen; (troops) niederhalten; **pin one's hopes on** seine Hoffnungen setzen auf (acc); **pin s.th. on s.o.** (fig) j–m etw anhängen; **pin up** (a sign) anschlagen; (the hair, a dress) aufstecken
pinafore ['pɪnə,for] s Latz m
pin'ball machine' s Spielautomat m
pin' boy' s Kegeljunge m
pincers ['pɪnsərz] s & spl Kneifzange f
pinch [pɪntʃ] s Kneifen n; (of salt) Prise f; **give s.o. a p.** j–n kneifen; **in a p.** zur Not, in der Not || tr kneifen, zwicken; (steal) (sl) klauen; (arrest) (coll) schnappen; **I got my finger pinched in the door** ich habe mir den Finger in der Tür geklemmt; **p. and scrape every penny** sich [dat] jeden Groschen vom Munde absparen; **p. off** abzwicken || intr (said of shoe) (& fig) drücken
pinchers ['pɪntʃərz] s & spl Kneifzange f
pinch'-hit' v (pret & pp –hit; ger –hitting) intr einspringen
pinch' hit'ter s Ersatzmann m
pin'cush'ion s Nadelkissen n
pine [paɪn] adj Kiefern– || s Kiefer f || intr—**p. away** sich abzehren; **p. for** sich sehnen nach
pine'ap'ple s Ananas f
pine' cone' s Kiefernzapfen m
pine' nee'dle s Kiefernnadel f
ping [pɪŋ] s Päng n; (of a motor) Klopfen n || intr (aut) klopfen
ping-pong ['pɪŋ,paŋ] s Ping-pong n
pin'head' s (& fig) Stecknadelkopf m
pink [pɪŋk] adj rosa || s Rosa n
pin' mon'ey s Nadelgeld n
pinnacle ['pɪnəkəl] s Zinne f
pin'point' adj haarscharf; **p. landing** Ziellandung f || tr markieren
pin'prick' s Nadelstich m
pint [paɪnt] s Schoppen m, Pinte f
pin'up girl' s Pin-up-Girl n
pin'wheel' s (toy) Windmühle f; (fireworks) Feuerrad n
pioneer [,paɪ·ə'nɪr] s Bahnbrecher –in mf; (fig & mil) Pionier m || tr (fig) den Weg freimachen für || intr (fig) Pionierarbeit leisten
pious ['paɪ·əs] adj fromm
pip [pɪp] s (in fruit) Kern m; (on dice) Punkt m; (on a radarscope) Leuchtpunkt m; (of chickens) Pips m

pipe [paɪp] s Rohr n; (for smoking; of an organ) Pfeife f || tr durch ein Rohr (weiter)leiten || intr pfeifen; **p. down** (sl) das Maul halten; **p. up** (coll) anfangen zu sprechen, loslegen

pipe′ clean′er s Pfeifenreiniger m

pipe′ dream′ s Wunschtraum m

pipe′ joint′ s Rohranschluß m

pipe′ line′ s Rohrleitung f, Pipeline f; (of information) Informationsquelle f

pipe′ or′gan s Orgel f

piper [′paɪpər] s Pfeifer –in mf

pipe′ wrench′ s Rohrzange f

piping [′paɪpɪŋ] adv—**p. hot** siedend heiß || s Rohrleitung f; (on uniforms) Biese f; (sew) Paspel f

piquancy [′pikənsi] s Pikanterie f

piquant [′pikənt] adj pikant

pique [pik] s Pik m || tr verärgern; **be piqued** at pikiert sein über (acc)

piracy [′paɪrəsi] s Seeräuberei f

pirate [′paɪrɪt] s Seeräuber m || tr (a book) (ungesetzlich) nachdrucken

pirouette [,pɪru′et] s Pirouette f

pista′chio nut′ [pɪs′tæʃɪ.o] s Pistazien-nuß f

pistol [′pɪstəl] s Pistole f

pis′tol point′ s—**at p.** mit vorgehaltener Pistole

piston [′pɪstən] s Kolben m

pis′ton ring′ s Kolbenring m

pis′ton rod′ s Kolbenstange f

pis′ton stroke′ s Kolbenhub m

pit [pɪt] s Grube f; (in fruit) Kern m; (trap) Fallgrube f; (in the skin) Narbe f; (from corrosion) Rostgrübchen n; (in auto racing) Box f; (for cockfights) Kampfplatz m; (min) Schacht m; (theat) Parkett n; (mus) Orchester m; **pit of the stomach** Magengrube f || v (pret & pp pitted; ger pitting) tr (a face) mit Narben bedecken; (fruit) entkernen; (through corrosion) anfressen; **pit A against B** A gegen B ausspielen; **pit one′s strength against s.th.** seine Kraft mit etw messen

pitch [pɪtʃ] s Pech n; (of a roof) Dachschräge f; (downward slope) Gefälle n; (of a ship) Stampfen n; (of a screw, thread) Teilung f; (of a propeller) Steigung f; (throw) Wurf m; (sales talk) Verkaufsgespräch n; (mus) Tonhöhe f || tr (seal with pitch) verpichen; (a tent) aufschlagen; (a ball) dem Schläger zuwerfen; (hay) mit der Heugabel werfen || intr (naut) stampfen; **p. and toss** schlingern; **p. in** mithelfen

pitch′ ac′cent s musikalischer Tonakzent m

pitch′-black′ adj pechrabenschwarz

pitcher [′pɪtʃər] s (jug) Krug m

pitch′fork′ s Heugabel f

pitch′ing s (naut) Stampfen n

pit′fall′ s Fallgrube f; (fig) Falle f

pith [pɪθ] s (& fig) Mark n

pithy [′pɪθi] adj (& fig) markig

pitiable [′pɪtɪ.əbəl] adj erbarmenswert

pitiful [′pɪtɪfəl] adj erbärmlich

pitiless [′pɪtɪlɪs] adj erbarmungslos

pit′ted adj (by corrosion) angefressen; (fruit) entkernt

pit·y [′pɪti] s Erbarmen n, Mitleid n; **have p. on** Mitleid haben mit; **it′s a p. that** (es ist) schade, daß; **move to p. jammern; what a p.!** wie schade! || v (pret & pp –ied) tr sich erbarmen (genit), bemitleiden

pivot [′pɪvət] s Drehpunkt m || intr (on) sich drehen (um); (mil) schwenken

placard [′plækərd] s Plakat n

placate [′pleket] tr begütigen

place [ples] s (seat; room) Platz m; (area, town, etc.) Ort m, Ortschaft f; (in a book; in a room) Stelle f; (situation) Lage f; (spot to eat in, dance in, etc.) Lokal n; **all over the p.** überall; **at your p.** (coll) bei Ihnen; **in my p.** an meiner Stelle; **in p. of** anstelle von (or genit); **in the first p.** erstens; **know one′s p.** wissen, wohin man gehört; **out of p.** (& fig) nicht am Platz; **p. to stay** Unterkunft f; **put s.o. in his p.** j–n in seine Schranken verweisen; **take one′s p.** antreten; **take p.** stattfinden; **take s.o.′s p.** an j–s Stelle treten || tr setzen, stellen; (an advertisement) aufgeben; (an order) erteilen; (find a job for) unterbringen; **I can′t p. him** ich weiß nicht, wo ich ihn hintun soll; **p. a call** (telp) ein Gespräch anmelden || intr (in horseracing) sich als Zweiter placieren; (sport) sich placieren

place·bo [plə′sibo] s (–bos & –boes) Placebo n

place′ card′ s Tischkarte f

place′ mat′ s Tischmatte f

placement [′plesmənt] s Unterbringung f

place′-name′ s Ortsname m

place′ of birth′ s Geburtsort m

place′ of employ′ment s Arbeitsstätte f

place′ of res′idence s Wohnsitz m

placid [′plæsɪd] adj ruhig, sanftmütig

plagiarism [′pledʒə,rɪzəm] s Plagiat n

plagiarist [′pledʒərɪst] s Plagiator –in mf

plagiarize [′pledʒə,raɪz] intr ein Plagiat begehen

plague [pleg] s Seuche f || tr heimsuchen

plaid [plæd] adj buntkariert || s Schottenkaro n

plain [plen] adj (simple) einfach; (clear) klar; (fabric) einfarbig; (homely) unschön; (truth) rein; (food) bürgerlich; (paper) unlin(i)iert; (speech) unverblümt; (alcohol) unverdünnt || s Ebene f

plain′ clothes′ spl—**in p.** in Zivil

plain′-clothes′ man′ s Geheimpolizist m

plaintiff [′plentɪf] s Kläger –in mf

plaintive [′plentɪv] adj Klage-, klagend

plait [plet], [plæt] s Flechte f; **p. of hair** Zopf m || tr flechten

plan [plæn] s Plan m; (intention) Vorhaben n; **according to p.** planmäßig;

what are your plans for this evening?
was haben Sie für heute abend vor?
|| *v* (*pret & pp* **planned**; *ger* **planning**) *tr* planen; (*one's time*) einteilen; **p. to** (*inf*) vorhaben zu (*inf*) || *intr*—**p. for** Pläne machen für; **p. on** rechnen mit

plane [plen] *s* (*airplane*) Flugzeug *n*, Maschine *f*; (*airfoil*) Tragfläche *f*; (*carp*) Hobel *m*; (*geom*) Ebene *f*; **on a high p.** (fig) auf e-m hohen Niveau || *tr* hobeln; **p. down** abhobeln

plane′ connec′tion *s* Fluganschluß *m*
plane′ geom′etry *s* Planimetrie *f*
planet [′plænɪt] *s* Planet *m*
planetari·um [‚plænɪ′terɪ-əm] *s* (**-a** [ə] & **-ums**) Planetarium *n*
planetary [′plænə‚terɪ] *adj* Planeten-
plane′ tick′et *s* Flugkarte *f*
plane′ tree′ *s* Platane *f*
plank [plæŋk] *s* Brett *n*, Planke *f*; (pol) Programmpunkt *m*
planned′ par′enthood *s* Familienplanung *f*
plant [plænt] *s* (*factory*) Anlage *f*; (*spy*) Spion -in *mf*; (bot) Pflanze *f* || *tr* (an)pflanzen; (*a field*) bepflanzen; (*a colony*) gründen; (*as a spy*) als Falle aufstellen; (*a bomb*) verstecken; **p. oneself** sich hinstellen
plantation [plæn′teʃən] *s* Plantage *f*
planter [′plæntər] *s* (*person who plants*; *plantation owner*) Pflanzer -in *mf*; (*decorative container*) Blumentrog *m*; (mach) Pflanzmaschine *f*
plasma [′plæzmə] *s* Plasma *n*
plaster [′plæstər] *s* Verputz *m*; (med) Pflaster *n* || *tr* verputzen; (*e.g., with posters*) bepflastern; **be plastered** (sl) besoffen sein
plas′terboard′ *s* Gipsdiele *f*
plas′ter cast′ *s* (med) Gipsverband *m*; (sculp) Gipsabguß *m*
plasterer [′plæstərər] *s* Stukkateur *m*
plas′tering *s* Verputz *m*
plas′ter of Par′is *s* Gips *m*
plastic [′plæstɪk] *adj* Plastik- || *s* Plastik *n*
plas′tic sur′gery *s* Plastik *f*
plas′tic wood′ *s* Holzpaste *f*
plate [plet] *s* (*dish*) Teller *m*; (*of metal*) Platte *f*; (*in a book*) Tafel *f*; (elec, phot, typ) Platte *f*; (electron) Plattenelektrode *f* || *tr* plattieren
plateau [plæ′to] *s* Plateau *n*
plate′ glass′ *s* Tafelglas *n*
platen [′plætən] *s* Schreibmaschinenwalze *f*
platform [′plæt‚fɔrm] *s* Plattform *f*; (*for a speaker*) Bühne *f*; (*for loading*) Rampe *f*; (pol) Programm *n*; (rr) Bahnsteig *m*
plat′form shoes′ *spl* Plateauschuhe *pl*
plat′ing *s* (*e.g., of gold*) Plattierung *f*; (*armor*) Panzerung *f*
platinum [′plætɪnəm] *s* Platin *n*
plat′inum blonde′ *s* Platinblondine *f*
platitude [′plætɪ‚t(j)ud] *s* Gemeinplatz *m*
Plato [′pleto] *s* Plato *m*

Platonic [plə′tɑnɪk] *adj* platonisch
platoon [plə′tun] *s* Zug *m*
platter [′plætər] *s* Platte *f*
plausible [′plɔzɪbəl] *adj* plausibel
play [ple] *s* Spiel *n*; (mach) Spielraum *m*; (sport) Spielzug *m*; (theat) Stück *n*; **in p.** im Spiel; **out of p.** aus dem Spiel || *tr* spielen; (*a card*) ausspielen; (*an opponent*) spielen gegen; **p. back** (*a tape, record*) abspielen; **p. down** bagatellisieren; **p. the horses** bei Pferderennen wetten || *intr* spielen; (*records, tapes*) abspielen; **p. about** (*the lips*) umspielen; **p. along** mitspielen; **p. around with** herumspielen mit; **p. for** (*stakes*) spielen um; (*a team*) spielen für; **p. into s.o.'s hands** j-m in die Hände spielen; **p. safe** auf Nummer Sicher gehen; **p. up to** schmeicheln (*dat*)
play′back′ *s* (*reproduction*) Wiedergabe *f*; (*device*) Abspielgerät *n*
play′boy′ *s* Playboy *m*
player [′ple-ər] *s* Spieler -in *mf*; (sport) Sportler -in *mf*; (theat) Schauspieler -in *mf*
playful [′plefəl] *adj* spielerisch
play′ground′ *s* Spielplatz *m*
play′house′ *s* Theater *n*; (*for children*) Spielhaus *n*
play′ing card′ *s* Spielkarte *f*
play′ing field′ *s* Spielfeld *n*
play′mate′ *s* Spielkamerad -in *mf*
play′-offs′ *spl* Vorrunde *f*
play′ on words′ *s* Wortspiel *n*
play′pen′ *s* Laufgitter *n*
play′room′ *s* Spielzimmer *n*
play′-school′ *s* Kindergarten *m*
play′thing′ *s* (& fig) Spielzeug *n*
playwright [′ple‚raɪt] *s* Schauspieldichter -in *mf*
plea [pli] *s* Bitte *f*; (jur) Plädoyer *n*
plead [plid] *v* (*pret & pp* **pleaded** & **pled** [plɛd]) *tr* (*ignorance*) vorschützen || *intr* plädieren; **p. guilty** sich schuldig bekennen; **p. not guilty** sich als nichtschuldig erklären; **p. with s.o.** j-n anflehen
pleasant [′plɛzənt] *adj* angenehm
pleasantry [′plɛzəntrɪ] *s* Heiterkeit *f*; (*remark*) Witz *m*
please [pliz] *tr* gefallen (*dat*); **be pleased to** (*inf*) sich freuen zu (*inf*); **be pleased with** sich freuen über (*acc*); **pleased to meet you!** sehr angenehm || *intr* gefallen; **as one pleases** nach Gefallen; **do as you p.** tun Sie, wie Sie wollen; **if you p.** wenn ich bitten darf; (iron) gefälligst; **p.!** bitte!
pleas′ing *adj* angenehm, gefällig
pleasure [′plɛʒər] *s* Vergnügen *n*
pleas′ure trip′ *s* Vergnügungsreise *f*
pleat [plit] *s* Plissee *n* || *tr* plissieren
pleat′ed skirt′ *s* Plisseerock *m*
plebeian [plɪ′bi-ən] *adj* plebejisch || *s* Plebejer -in *mf*
plect·rum [′plɛktrəm] *s* (**-rums** & **-ra** [rə]) Plektron *n*; (*for zither*) Schlagring *m*
pledge [plɛdʒ] *s* (*solemn promise*) Gelübde *n*; (*security for a payment*)

Pfand n; (fig) Unterpfand n || tr geloben; (money) zeichnen

plenary ['plinəri] adj Plenar-, Voll-

ple'nary indul'gence s vollkommener Ablaß m

ple'nary ses'sion s Plenum n

plenipotentiary [,plenɪpə'tenʃɪ ,ɛri] adj bevollmächtigt || s Bevollmächtigte mf

plentiful ['plentɪfəl] adj reichlich

plenty ['plenti] s Fülle f; **have p. of** Überfluß haben an (dat); **have p. to do** vollauf zu tun haben || adv (coll) reichlich

pleurisy ['plʊrɪsi] s Brustfellentzündung f

plexiglass ['pleksɪ ,glæs] s Plexiglas n

pliant ['plaɪ-ənt] adj biegsam; (fig) gefügig

pliers ['plaɪ-ərz] s & spl Zange f

plight [plaɪt] s Notlage f

plod [plad] v (pret & pp plodded; ger plodding) intr stapfen; **p. along** mühsam weitermachen

plop [plap] v (pret & pp plopped; ger plopping) tr plumpsen lassen || intr plumpsen || interj plumps!

plot [plat] s (conspiracy) Komplott n; (of a story) Handlung f; (of ground) Grundstück n || v (pret & pp plotted; ger plotting) tr (a course) abstecken; (intrigues) schmieden; (e.g., murder) planen || intr sich verschwören

plough [plaʊ] s, tr & intr var of plow

plow [plaʊ] s Pflug m || tr pflügen; **p. up** umpflügen; **p. under** unterpflügen || intr pflügen; **p. through the waves** durch die Wellen streichen

plow'man s (-men) Pflüger m

plow'share s Pflugschar f

pluck [plʌk] s (tug) Ruck m; (fig) Schneid m || tr (e.g., a chicken) rupfen; (flowers, fruit) pflücken; (eyebrows) auszupfen; (mus) zupfen || intr—**p. up** Mut fassen

plug [plʌg] s (for a sink) Pfropfen m; (of tobacco) Priem m; (old horse) alter Klepper m; (advertising) Befürwortung f; (aut) Zündkerze f; (elec) Stecker m || v (pret & pp plugged; ger plugging) tr (a hole) zustopfen; **p. in** an die Steckdose anschließen || intr—**p. away** (work hard) schuften; (study hard) pauken

plum [plʌm] s Pflaume f

plumage ['plumɪdʒ] s Gefieder n

plumb [plʌm] adj lotrecht || adv (coll) völlig || s Lot n; **out of p.** aus dem Lot || tr loten, sondieren

plumb' bob' s Lot n

plumber ['plʌmər] s Installateur m

plumb'ing s (plumbing work) Installateurarbeit f; (pipes) Rohrleitung f

plumb' line' s Lotschnur f

plume [plum] s Feder f; (on a helmet) Helmbusch m; **p. of smoke** Rauchfahne f || tr (adorn with plumes) mit Federn schmücken; **p. itself** sich putzen

plummet ['plʌmɪt] s Lot n || intr stürzen

plump [plʌmp] adj rundlich || tr plumpsen; **p. oneself down** sich schwerfällig hinwerfen

plum' tree' s Pflaumenbaum m

plunder ['plʌndər] s (act) Plünderung f; (booty) Beute f || tr & intr plündern

plunderer ['plʌndərər] s Plünderer m

plunge [plʌndʒ] s Sturz m || tr stürzen || intr (fall) stürzen; (throw oneself) sich stürzen

plunger ['plʌndʒər] s Saugglocke f

plunk [plʌŋk] adv (squarely) (coll) genau || tr (e.g., a guitar) zupfen; **p. down** klirrend auf den Tisch legen

pluperfect [,plu'pʌrfekt] s Vorvergangenheit f, Plusquamperfekt(um) n

plural ['plʊrəl] adj Plural- || s Mehrzahl f, Plural m

plurality [plʊ'rælɪti] s Mehrheit f; (pol) Stimmenmehrheit f

plus [plʌs] adj Plus-; (elec) positiv || s Plus n || prep plus (acc)

plush [plʌʃ] adj (coll) luxuriös

plus' sign' s Pluszeichen n

plutonium [plu'toni-əm] s Plutonium n

ply [plaɪ] s (of wood, etc.) Schicht f; (of yarn) Strähne f || v (pret & pp plied) tr (e.g., a needle) (eifrig) handhaben; (a trade) betreiben; (with questions) bestürmen; (a waterway) regelmäßig befahren || intr (between) verkehren (zwischen dat)

ply'wood' s Sperrholz n

pneumatic [n(j)u'mætɪk] adj pneumatisch

pneumat'ic drill' s Preßluftbohrer m

pneumonia [n(j)u'moni-ə] s Lungenentzündung f

poach [potʃ] tr (eggs) pochieren || intr wildern

poached' egg' s verlorenes Ei n

poacher ['potʃər] s Wilderer m

pock [pak] s Pocke f, Pustel f

pocket ['pakɪt] s (comb, flap, knife, money, watch) Tasche- || s Tasche f; (billiards) Loch n; (mil) Kessel m || tr in die Tasche stecken; (billiards) ins Loch spielen

pock'etbook' s Handtasche f; (book) Taschenbuch n

pock'et cal'culator s Taschenrechner m

pock'mark' s Pockennarbe f

pock'marked' adj pockennarbig

pod [pad] s Hülse f

podi-um ['podi-əm] s (-ums & -a [ə]) Podium n

poem ['po-ɪm] s Gedicht n

poet ['po-ɪt] s Dichter m, Poet m

poetaster ['po-ɪt ,æstər] s Dichterling m

poetess ['po-ɪtɪs] s Dichterin f

poetic [po'etɪk] adj dichterisch, poetisch || **poetics** s Poetik f

poetry ['po-ɪtri] s Dichtung f; **write p.** dichten, Gedichte schreiben

poignant ['pɔɪn(j)ənt] adj (touching) ergreifend; (pungent) scharf; (cutting) beißend

point [pɔɪnt] s (dot, score) Punkt m;

(tip) Spitze *f; (of a joke)* Pointe *f; (of a statement)* Hauptpunkt *m; (side of a character)* Seite *f; (purpose)* Sinn *m; (matter, subject)* Sache *f; (of a compass)* Kompaßstrich *m; (to show decimals)* Komma *n; (aut)* Zündkontakt *m; (geog)* Landspitze *f; (typ)* Punkt *m;* at this p. in diesem Augenblick; be on the p. of *(ger)* gerade im Begriff sein zu *(inf);* come to the p.! zur Sache!; get the p. verstehen; in p. of fact tatsächlich; make a p. of bestehen auf *(dat);* make it a p. to *(inf)* es sich *[dat]* zur Pflicht machen zu *(inf);* not to the p. nicht zur Sache gehörig; off the p. unzutreffend; on points *(sport)* nach Punkten; p. at issue strittiger Punkt *m;* p. of order! zur Tagesordnung!; p. of time Zeitpunkt *m;* score a p. *(fig)* e-n Punkt für sich buchen; that's beside the p. darum handelt es sich nicht; there's no p. to it es hat keinen Zweck; to the p. zutreffend; up to a certain p. bis zu e-m gewissen Grade ‖ *tr (e.g., a gun)* (at) richten *(auf acc);* p. out *(auf)*zeigen; p. s.th. out to s.o. j-n auf etw *(acc)* hinweisen; p. the finger at mit dem Finger zeigen auf *(acc)* ‖ *intr* mit dem Finger zeigen; p. to deuten auf *(acc); (fig)* hinweisen auf *(acc)*

point'-blank' *adj (refusal)* glatt; *(shot)* rasant, Kernschuß-; at p. range auf Kernschußweite ‖ *adv (at close range)* aus nächster Nähe; *(fig)* glatt; *(arti)* auf Kernschußweite

point'ed *adj* spitzig; *(remark)* anzüglich; *(gun)* gerichtet; *(arch, nose)* Spitz-

pointer ['pɔintər] *s (of a meter)* Zeiger *m; (stick)* Zeigestock *m; (advice)* Tip *m; (hunting dog)* Vorstehhund *m*

point'less ['pɔintlis] *adj* zwecklos

point' of hon'or *s* Ehrensache *f*

point' of law' *s* Rechtsfrage *f*

point' of view' *s* Gesichtspunkt *m*

poise [pɔiz] *s* sicheres Auftreten *n* ‖ *tr* im Gleichgewicht halten ‖ *intr* schweben

poison ['pɔizən] *s* Gift *n* ‖ *tr (& fig)* vergiften

poi'son gas' *s* Giftgas *n*

poi'son i'vy *s* Giftsumach *m*

poisonous ['pɔizənəs] *adj* giftig

poke [pok] *s* Stoß *m,* Knuff *m* ‖ *tr* anstoßen, knuffen; *(the fire)* schüren; *(head, nose)* stecken; p. fun at sich lustig machen über *(acc);* p. out *(an eye)* ausstechen; p. s.o. in the ribs j-m e-n Rippenstoß geben ‖ *intr* bummeln; p. around herumstochern; *(be slow)* herumbummeln; *(in another's business)* herumstöbern

poker ['pokər] *s* Schürhaken *m; (cards)* Poker *m*

pok'er face' *s* Pokergesicht *n*

poky ['poki] *adj* bummelig

Poland ['polənd] *s* Polen *n*

polar ['polər] *adj* Polar-

po'lar bear' *s* Eisbär *m*

polarity [po'læriti] *s* Polarität *f*

polarize ['polə ,raiz] *tr* polarisieren

pole [pol] *s (rod)* Stange *f; (for telephone lines, flags, etc.)* Mast *m; (astr, geog, phys)* Pol *m;* **Pole** Pole *m,* Polin *f* ‖ *tr (a raft, boat)* staken

pole'cat' *s* Iltis *m*

polemic(al) [pə'lemik(əl)] *adj* polemisch

polemics [pə'lemiks] *s* Polemik *f*

pole'star' *s* Polarstern *m*

pole'-vault' *intr* stabhochspringen

pole' vault'ing *s* Stabhochsprung *m*

police [pə'lis] *adj* polizeilich ‖ *s* Polizei *f* ‖ *tr* polizeilich überwachen; *(clean up)* (mil) säubern

police' es'cort *s* Polozeibedeckung *f*

police'man *s* (-men) Polizist *m*

police' of'ficer *s* Polizeibeamte *m,* Polizeibeamtin *f*

police' pre'cinct *s* Polizeirevier *n*

police' state' *s* Polizeistaat *m*

police' sta'tion *s* Polizeiwache *f*

police'wom'an *s* (-wom'en) Polizistin *f*

policy ['pɑlisi] *s* Politik *f; (ins)* Police *f*

polio ['pɔli ,o] *s* Polio *f*

polish ['pɑlif] *s (material; shine)* Politur *f; (for shoes)* Schuhcreme *f; (fig)* Schliff *m* ‖ *tr* polieren; *(fingernails)* lackieren; *(shoes, silver, etc.)* putzen; *(floors)* bohnern; *(fig)* abschleifen; p. off *(eat)* (sl) verdrücken; *(an opponent)* (sl) erledigen; *(work)* (sl) hinhauen ‖ *intr*—p. up on aufpolieren ‖ **Polish** ['pɔlif] *adj* polnisch ‖ *s* Polnisch *n*

polite [pə'lait] *adj* höflich

politeness [pə'laitnis] *s* Höflichkeit *f*

politic ['pɑlitik] *adj* diplomatisch

political [pə'litikəl] *adj* politisch

poli'tical econ'omy *s* Volkswirtschaft *f*

poli'tical sci'ence *s* Staatswissenschaften *pl*

politician [,pɑli'tiʃən] *s* Politiker –in *mf*

politics ['pɑlitiks] *s* Politik *f;* be in p. sich politisch betätigen; talk p. politisieren

polka ['po(l)kə] *s* Polka *f*

pol'ka-dot' *adj* getupft

poll [pol] *s (voting)* Abstimmung *f; (of public opinion)* Umfrage *f;* be defeated at the polls e-e Wahlniederlage erleiden; go to the polls zur Wahl gehen; polls *(voting place)* Wahllokal *n;* take a p. e-e Umfrage halten ‖ *tr* befragen

pollen ['pɑlən] *s* Pollen *m*

poll'ing booth' *s* Wahlzelle *f*

pollster ['polstər] *s* Meinungsforscher –in *mf*

poll' tax' *s* Kopfsteuer *f*

pollute [pə'lut] *tr* verunreinigen

pollution [pə'luʃən] *s* Verunreinigung *f*

polo ['polo] *s (sport)* Polo *n*

po'lo shirt' *s* Polohemd *n*

polygamist [pə'ligəmist] *s* Polygamist *m*

polygamy [pə'ligəmi] *s* Polygamie *f*

polyglot ['pɑli ,glɑt] *s* Polyglott *m*

polygon ['palɪ,gan] s Vieleck n
polyp ['palɪp] s Polyp m
polytheism ['palɪ'θi,ɪzəm] s Vielgötterei f, Polytheismus m
polytheistic [,palɪθiˈɪstɪk] adj polytheistisch
pomade [pəˈmed] s Pomade f
pomegranate ['pam,grænɪt] s Granatapfel m; (tree) Granatapfelbaum m
Pomerania [,pamə'renɪ,ə] s Pommern n
pom·mel ['pʌməl] s (of a sword) Degenkopf m; (of a saddle) Sattelknopf m ‖ v (pret & pp -mel[l]ed; ger -el[l]ing) tr mit der Faust schlagen
pomp [pamp] s Pomp m, Prunk m
pompous ['pampəs] adj hochtrabend
pon·cho ['pant͡ʃo] s (-chos) Poncho m
pond [pand] s Teich m
ponder ['pandər] tr erwägen; (words) abwägen ‖ intr (over) nachsinnen (über acc)
ponderous ['pandərəs] adj schwerfällig
pontiff ['pantɪf] s (eccl) Papst m; (hist) Pontifex m
pontifical [pan'tɪfɪkəl] adj pontifikal
pontoon [pan'tun] s Ponton m; (aer) Schwimmer m
pony ['poni] s (small horse; hair style) Pony n; (crib) Eselsbrücke f
poodle ['pudəl] s Pudel m
pool [pul] s (small pond) Tümpel m; (of blood) Lache f; (swimming pool) Schwimmbecken n; (in betting) Pool m; (game) Billiard n; (fin) Pool m ‖ tr zusammenlegen
pool'room' s Billardsalon m
pool' ta'ble s Billardtisch m
poop [pup] s Heck n ‖ tr (sl) erschöpfen; be pooped (out) erschöpft sein
poor [pur] adj arm; (e.g., in spelling) schwach; (soil, harvest) schlecht; (miserable) armselig; p. in arm m (dat)
poor' box' s Opferstock m
poor'house' s Armenhaus n
poorly ['purli] adv schlecht
pop [pap] adj (concert, singer, music) Pop- ‖ s Puff m, Knall m; (dad) Vati m; (soda) Brauselimonade f; (mus) Popmusik f ‖ v (pret & pp popped; ger popping) tr (corn) rösten; (cause to pop) knallen lassen; pop the question (coll) e-n Heiratsantrag machen ‖ intr (make a popping noise) knallen; (said of popcorn) aufplatzen; pop in (visit unexpectedly) (coll) hereinplatzen; pop off (sl) das Maul aufreißen; pop up (appear) (coll) auftauchen; (jump up) hochfahren
pop'corn' s Puffmais m
pope [pop] s Papst m
pop'eyed' adj glotzäugig
pop'gun' s Knallbüchse f
poplar ['paplər] s Pappel f
poppy ['papi] s Mohnblume f, Mohn m
pop'pycock' s (coll) Quatsch m
pop'pyseed' s Mohn m
popsicle ['pap,sɪkəl] s Eis n am Stiel
populace ['papjəlɪs] s Pöbel m

popular ['papjələr] adj populär; (e.g., music, expression) volkstümlich; p. with beliebt bei
popularity [,papjə'lærɪti] s Popularität f, Beliebtheit f
popularize ['papjələ,raɪz] tr popularisieren
populate ['papjə,let] tr bevölkern
population [,papjə'leʃən] s Bevölkerung f
popula'tion explo'sion s Bevölkerungsexplosion f
populous ['papjələs] adj volkreich
porcelain ['pɔrs(ə)lɪn] s Porzellan n
porch [pɔrt͡ʃ] s Vorbau m, Veranda f
porcupine ['pɔrkjə,paɪn] s Stachelschwein n
pore [por] s Pore f ‖ intr—p. over eifrig studieren
pork [pork] adj Schweine- ‖ s Schweinefleisch n
pork'chop' s Schweinekotelett n
pornography [pɔr'nagrəfi] s Pornographie f
porous ['porəs] adj porös
porphyry ['pɔrfɪri] s Porphyr m
porpoise ['pɔrpəs] s Tümmler m
porridge ['pɔrɪd͡ʒ] s Brei m
port [port] s Hafen m; (wine) Portwein m; (slit for shooting) Schießscharte f; (naut) Backbord m & n; to p. (naut) backbord
portable ['portəbəl] adj tragbar; (radio, television, typewriter) Koffer-
portal ['portəl] s Portal n
portend [pɔr'tend] tr vorbedeuten
portent ['portənt] s schlimmes Vorzeichen n, böses Omen n
portentous [pɔr'tentəs] adj unheildrohend
porter ['portər] s (in a hotel) Hausdiener m; (at a station) Gepäckträger m; (doorman) Portier m
portfoli·o [port'foli,o] s (-os) Aktenmappe f; (fin) Portefeuille n; without p. ohne Geschäftsbereich
port'hole' s (for shooting) Schießscharte f; (naut) Bullauge n
porti·co ['portɪ,ko] s (-coes & -cos) Säulenvorbau m, Portikus m
portion ['porʃən] s Anteil m; (serving) Portion f; (dowry) Heiratsgut n ‖ tr —p. out austeilen, einteilen
portly ['portli] adj wohlbeleibt
port' of call' s Anlaufhafen m
port' of en'try s Einfuhrhafen m
portrait ['portret] s Porträt n
portray [por'tre] tr porträtieren; (fig) beschreiben; (theat) darstellen
portrayal [por'tre·əl] s Porträtieren n; (fig) Beschreibung f; (theat) Darstellung f
port'side' s Backbord m & n
Portugal ['port͡ʃəgəl] s Portugal n
Portuguese ['port͡ʃə,giz] adj portugiesisch ‖ s Portugiese m, Portugiesin f; (language) Portugiesisch n
port' wine' s Portwein m
pose [poz] s Haltung f, Pose f ‖ tr (a question, problem) stellen ‖ intr posieren; p. as sich ausgeben als; p. for an artist e-m Künstler Modell ste-

hen; **p. for a picture** sich e—m Photographen stellen

posh [paʃ] *adj* (sl) großartig

position [pə'zi/ən] *s* Stellung *f*; (*situation, condition*) Lage *f*; (*job; place of defense*) Stellung *f*; (*point of view*) Standpunkt *m*; (aer, naut) Standort *m*; (astr, mil, naut) Position *f*; **be in a p. to** (*inf*) in der Lage sein zu (*inf*); **in p.** am rechten Platz; **p. wanted** (*as in an ad*) Stelle gesucht; **take a p. on** Stellung nehmen zu; **take one's p.** sich aufstellen

positive ['pazɪtɪv] *adj* (*reply, result, attitude*) positiv; (*answer*) zustimmend; (*sure*) sicher; (*offer*) fest; (elec, math, med, phot, phys) positiv || *s* (gram) Positiv *m*; (phot) Positiv *n*

posse ['pasi] *s* Polizeiaufgebot *n*

possess [pə'zes] *tr* besitzen; **be possessed by the devil** von dem Teufel besessen sein

possession [pə'ze/ən] *s* Besitz *m*; (*property*) Eigentum *n*; **be in p. of s.th.** etw besitzen; **take p. of s.th.** etw in Besitz nehmen

possessive [pə'zesɪv] *adj* eifersüchtig; (gram) besitzanzeigend, Besitz-

possibility [,pasɪ'bɪlɪtɪ] *s* Möglichkeit *f*

possible ['pasɪbəl] *adj* möglich; **make p.** ermöglichen

possibly ['pasɪblɪ] *adv* möglicherweise

possum ['pasəm] *s* Opossum *n*; **play p.** sich verstellen; (*play dead*) sich tot stellen

post [post] *s* (*pole*) Pfahl *m*; (*job; of a sentry*) Posten *m*; (*military camp*) Standort *m* || *tr* (*a notice*) anschlagen; (*a guard*) aufstellen; **p. bond** Kaution stellen; **p. no bills** Plakatankleben verboten

postage ['postɪdʒ] *s* Porto *n*

post'age due' *s* Nachporto *n*

post'age stamp' *s* Briefmarke *f*

postal ['postəl] *adj* Post-

post'al mon'ey or'der *s* Postanweisung *f*

post'card' *s* Ansichtskarte *f*

post'date' *tr* nachdatieren

post'ed *adj*—**keep s.o. p.** j—n auf dem laufenden halten

poster ['postər] *s* Plakat *n*

posterity [pas'terɪtɪ] *s* Nachkommenschaft *f*, Nachwelt *f*

postern ['postərn] *s* Hintertür *f*

post' exchange' *s* Marketenderei *f*

post'haste' *adv* schnellstens

posthumous ['past/uməs] *adj* posthum

post'man *s* (**-men**) Briefträger *m*

post'mark' *s* Poststempel *m* || *tr* abstempeln

post'mas'ter *s* Postmeister *m*

post'master gen'eral *s* Postminister *m*

post-mortem [,post'mortəm] *s* Obduktion *f*

post' of'fice *s* Post *f*, Postamt *n*

post'-office box' *s* Postschließfach *n*

post'paid' *adv* frankiert

postpone [post'pon] *tr* (**till, to**) aufschieben (auf *acc*)

postponement [post'ponmənt] *s* Aufschub *m*

post'script' *s* Nachschrift *f*

posture ['past/ər] *s* Haltung *f*

post'war' *adj* Nachkriegs—

posy ['pozi] *s* Sträußchen *n*

pot [pat] *s* Topf *m*; (*for coffee, tea*) Kanne *f*; (*in gambling*) Einsatz *m*; **go to pot** (sl) hops gehen; **pots and pans** Kochgeschirr *n*

potash ['pat,æʃ] *s* Pottasche *f*, Kali *n*

potassium [pə'tæsɪəm] *s* Kalium *n*

pota·to [pə'teto] *s* (**–toes**) Kartoffel *f*

pota'to chips' *spl* Kartoffelchips *pl*

potbellied ['pat,belid] *adj* dickbäuchig

pot'bel'ly *s* Spitzbauch *m*

potency ['potənsi] *s* Stärke *f*; (physiol) Potenz *f*

potent ['potənt] *adj* (*powerful*) mächtig; (*persuasive*) überzeugend; (*e.g., drugs*) wirksam; (physiol) potent

potentate ['potən,tet] *s* Potentat *m*

potential [pə'ten/əl] *adj* möglich; (phys) potentiell || *s* (& elec, math, phys) Potential *n*

pot'hold'er *s* Topflappen *m*

pot'hole' *s* Schlagloch *n*

potion ['po/ən] *s* Trank *m*

pot'luck' *s*—**take p.** mit dem vorliebnehmen, was es gerade gibt

pot' roast' *s* Schmorbraten *m*

pot'sherd' *s* Topfscherbe *f*

pot' shot' *s* müheloser Schuß *m*; **take a p.** at unfair bekritteln

pot'ted *adj* Topf-

potter ['patər] *s* Töpfer *m*

pot'ter's clay' *s* Töpferton *m*

pot'ter's wheel' *s* Töpferscheibe *f*

pottery ['patəri] *s* Tonwaren *pl*

potty ['pati] *s* (coll) Töpfchen *n*

pouch [paut/] *s* Beutel *m*

poultice ['poltis] *s* Breiumschlag *m*

poultry ['poltri] *s* Geflügel *n*

poul'try-man *s* (**-men**) Geflügelzüchter *m*; (*dealer*) Geflügelhändler *m*

pounce [pauns] *intr*—**p. on** sich stürzen auf (*acc*)

pound [paund] *s* Pfund *n*; (*for animals*) Pferch *m* || *tr* (zer)stampfen; (*meat*) klopfen; **p. the sidewalks** Pflaster treten || *intr* (*said of the heart*) klopfen; **p. on** (*e.g., a door*) hämmern an (*acc*)

–pound *suf* –pfündig

pound' ster'ling *s* Pfund *n* Sterling

pour [por] *tr* gießen; (*e.g., coffee*) einschenken; **p. away** wegschütten || *intr* (meteor) gießen; **p. out of** (*e.g., a theater*) strömen aus || *impers*—**it's pouring** es gießt

pout [paut] *s* Schmollen *n* || *intr* schmollen

pout'ing *adj* (*lips*) aufgeworfen || *s* Schmollen *n*

poverty ['pavərti] *s* Armut *f*

pov'erty-strick'en *adj* verarmt

POW ['pi'o'dʌbl,ju] *s* (**prisoner of war**) Kriegsgefangener *m*

powder ['paudər] *s* Pulver *n*; (*cosmetic*) Puder *m* || *tr* (*e.g., the face*) pudern; (*plants*) stäuben; (*a cake*) bestreuen || *intr* zu Pulver werden

pow'der box' s Puderdose f
pow'dered milk' s Milchpulver n
pow'dered sug'ar s Staubzucker m
pow'der keg' s Pulverfaß n
pow'der puff' s Puderquaste f
pow'der room' s Damentoilette f
powdery ['paʊdəri] adj pulverig
power ['paʊ-ər] s Macht f; (*personal control*) Gewalt f; (*electricity*) Strom m; (math) Potenz f; (opt) Vergrößerungskraft f; (phys) Leistung f; (pol) Macht f; **be in p.** an der Macht sein; **be in s.o.'s p.** in j-s Gewalt sein; **be within s.o.'s p.** in j-s Macht liegen; **come to p.** an die Macht gelangen; **have the p. to** (*inf*) vermögen zu (*inf*); **more p. to you!** viel Erfolg!; **the powers that be** die Obrigkeit f || tr antreiben
pow'er brake' s (aut) Servobremse f
pow'er dive' s (aer) Vollgassturzflug m
pow'er drill' s Elektrobohrer m
pow'er-driv'en adj mit Motorantrieb
pow'er fail'ure s Stromausfall m
powerful ['paʊ-ərfəl] adj mächtig; (opt) stark
pow'erhouse' s Kraftwerk n; (coll) Kraftprotz m
pow'erhun'gry adj herrschsüchtig
powerless ['paʊ-ərlɪs] adj machtlos
pow'er line' s Starkstromleitung f
pow'er mow'er s Motorrasenmäher m
pow'er of attor'ney s Vollmacht f
pow'er plant' s (powerhouse) Kraftwerk n; (aer, aut) Triebwerk n
pow'er shov'el s Löffelbagger m
pow'er sta'tion s Kraftwerk n
pow'er steer'ing s Servolenkung f
pow'er supply' s Stromversorgung f
practicable ['præktɪkəbəl] adj praktikabel, durchführbar
practical ['præktɪkəl] adj praktisch
prac'tical joke' s Streich m
practically ['præktɪkəli] adv praktisch; (almost) fast, so gut wie
prac'tical nurse' s praktisch ausgebildete Krankenschwester f
practice ['præktɪs] s (exercise) Übung f; (habit) Gewohnheit f; (of medicine, law) Praxis f; **in p.** (in training) in der Übung; (in reality) in der Praxis; **make it a p. to** (inf) es sich [dat] zur Gewohnheit machen zu (inf); **out of p.** aus der Übung || tr (a profession) tätig sein als; (patience, reading, dancing, etc.) sich üben in (dat); (music, gymnastics) treiben; (piano, etc.) üben || intr üben; (said of a doctor) praktizieren; **p. on** (e.g., the violin, piano, parallel bars) üben auf (dat)
prac'tice game' s Übungsspiel n
prac'tice teach'er s Studienreferendar –in mf
practitioner [præk'tɪʃənər] s Praktiker –in mf
pragmatic [præg'mætɪk] adj pragmatisch
pragmatism ['prægmə,tɪzəm] s Sachlichkeit f; (philos) Pragmatismus m
Prague [prɑg] s Prag n
prairie ['preri] s Steppe f, Prärie f

praise [prez] s Lob n || tr (for) loben (wegen); **p. to the skies** verhimmeln
praise'wor'thy adj lobenswert
prance [præns] intr tänzeln
prank [præŋk] s Schelmenstreich m
prate [pret] intr schwätzen
prattle ['prætəl] s Geplapper n || intr plappern, schwätzen
prawn [prɔn] s Garnele f
pray [pre] tr & intr beten
prayer [prer] s Gebet n; **say a p.** ein Gebet sprechen
prayer' book' s Gebetbuch n
preach [pritʃ] tr & intr predigen
preacher ['pritʃər] s Prediger m
preamble ['pri,æmbəl] s Präambel f
precarious [prɪ'kɛrɪ-əs] adj prekär
precaution [prɪ'kɔʃən] s Vorsichtsmaßnahme f; **as a p.** vorsichtshalber; **take precautions** Vorkehrungen treffen
precede [prɪ'sid] tr vorausgehen (dat) || intr vorangehen
precedence ['prɛsɪdəns] s Vorrang m; **take p. over** den Vorrang haben vor (dat)
precedent ['prɛsɪdənt] s Präzedenzfall m; **set a p.** e-n Präzedenzfall schaffen
preced'ing adj vorhergehend
precept ['prisɛpt] s Vorschrift f
precinct ['prisɪŋkt] s Bezirk m
precious ['prɛʃəs] adj (expensive) kostbar; (valuable) wertvoll; (excessively refined) geziert; (child) lieb || adv **p. few** (coll) herzlich wenige
pre'cious stone' s Edelstein m
precipice ['prɛsɪpɪs] s Abgrund m
precipitate [prɪ'sɪpɪ,tet] adj steil abfallend || s (chem) Niederschlag m || tr (hurl) (into) stürzen in (acc); (bring about) heraufbeschwören; (vapor) (chem) niederschlagen; (from a solution) (chem) ausfällen || intr (chem, meteor) sich niederschlagen
precipitation [prɪ,sɪpɪ'teʃən] s (meteor) Niederschlag m
precipitous [prɪ'sɪpɪtəs] adj jäh
precise [prɪ'saɪs] adj präzis, genau
precision [prɪ'sɪʒən] s Präzision f
preclude [prɪ'klud] tr ausschließen
precocious [prɪ'koʃəs] adj frühreif
preconceived [,prikən'sivd] adj vorgefaßt
predatory ['prɛdə,tori] adj Raub-
predecessor ['prɛdɪ,sɛsər] s Vorgänger –in mf
predestination [,pridɛstɪ'neʃən] s Prädestination f
predicament [prɪ'dɪkəmənt] s Mißliche Lage f
predicate ['prɛdɪkɪt] s (gram) Aussage f, Prädikat n || ['prɛdɪ,ket] tr (of) aussagen (über acc); (base) (on) gründen (auf acc)
predict [prɪ'dɪkt] tr voraussagen
prediction [prɪ'dɪkʃən] s Voraussage f
predispose [,pridɪs'poz] tr (to) im voraus geneigt machen (zu); (pathol) empfänglich machen (für)
predominant [prɪ'dɑmɪnənt] adj vorwiegend

preeminent [prɪ'emɪnənt] *adj* hervorragend

preempt [prɪ'empt] *tr* (*a program*) ersetzen; (*land*) durch Vorkaufsrecht erwerben

preen [prin] *tr* putzen

prefabricated [pri'fæbrɪ,ketɪd] *adj* Fertig-

preface ['prefɪs] *s* Vorwort *n*, Vorrede *f* || *tr* einleiten

prefer [prɪ'fʌr] *v* (*pret & pp* –ferred; *ger* –ferring) *tr* bevorzugen; (*charges*) vorbringen; **I p. to wait** ich warte lieber

preferable ['prefərəbəl] *adj* (**to**) vorzuziehen(d) (*dat*)

preferably ['prefərəbli] *adv* vorzugsweise

preferred' stock' *s* Vorzugsaktie *f*

prefix ['prifɪks] *s* Vorsilbe *f*, Präfix *n* || *tr* vorsetzen

pregnancy ['pregnənsɪ] *s* Schwangerschaft *f*; (*of animals*) Trächtigkeit *f*

pregnant ['pregnənt] *adj* schwanger; (*animals*) trächtig; (*fig*) inhaltsschwer

prehistoric [,prihɪs'tɔrɪk] *adj* vorgeschichtlich, prähistorisch

prejudice ['predʒədɪs] *s* Voreingenommenheit *f*; (*detriment*) Schaden *m* || *tr* beeinträchtigen; **p. s.o. against** j–n einnehmen gegen

pre'judiced *adj* voreingenommen

prejudicial [,predʒə'dɪʃəl] *adj* (**to**) schädlich (für)

prelate ['prelɪt] *s* Prälat *m*

preliminary [prɪ'lɪmɪ,nerɪ] *adj* einleitend, Vor– || *s* Vorbereitung *f*

prelude ['prel(j)ud] *s* (fig, mus, theat) Vorspiel *n*

premarital [pri'mærɪtəl] *adj* vorehelich

premature [,primə't(j)ur] *adj* verfrüht; **p. birth** Frühgeburt *f*

premeditated [pri'medɪ,tetɪd] *adj* vorbedacht; (*murder*) vorsätzlich

premier [prɪ'mɪr] *s* Premier *m*

premiere [prɪ'mɪr] *s* Erstaufführung *f*

premise ['premɪs] *s* Voraussetzung *f*; **on the premises** an Ort und Stelle; **the premises** das Lokal

premium ['primɪ·əm] *s* Prämie *f*; **at a p.** (*in demand*) sehr gesucht; (*at a high price*) über pari

premonition [,primə'nɪʃən] *s* Vorahnung *f*

preoccupation [pri,akjə'peʃən] *s* (**with**) Beschäftigtsein *n* (mit)

preoccupied [pri'akjə,paɪd] *adj* ausschließlich beschäftigt

preparation [,prepə're ʃən] *s* Vorbereitung *f*; (med) Präparat *n*

preparatory [prɪ'pærə,torɪ] *adj* vorbereitend; **p. to** vor (*dat*)

prepare [prɪ'per] *tr* vorbereiten; (*a meal*) zubereiten; (*a prescription*) anfertigen; (*a document*) abfassen

preparedness [prɪ'perɪdnɪs] *s* Bereitschaft *f*; (mil) Einsatzbereitschaft *f*

pre·pay [pri'pe] *v* (*pret & pp* –paid) *tr* im voraus bezahlen

preponderant [prɪ'pandərənt] *adj* überwiegend

preposition [,prepə'zɪʃən] *s* Präposition *f*, Verhältniswort *n*

prepossessing [,pripə'zesɪŋ] *adj* einnehmend

preposterous [prɪ'pastərəs] *adj* lächerlich

prep' school' [prep] *s* Vorbereitungsschule *f*

prerecorded [,prirɪ'kɔrdɪd] *adj* vorher aufgenommen

prerequisite [pri'rekwɪzɪt] *s* Voraussetzung *f*, Vorbedingung *f*

prerogative [prɪ'ragətɪv] *s* Vorrecht *n*

presage ['presɪdʒ] *s* Vorzeichen *n* || [prɪ'sedʒ] *tr* ein Vorzeichen sein für

Presbyterian [,prezbɪ'tɪrɪ·ən] *adj* presbyterianisch || *s* Presbyterianer –in *mf*

prescribe [prɪ'skraɪb] *tr* vorschreiben; (med) verordnen

prescription [prɪ'skrɪpʃən] *s* Vorschrift *f*; (med) Rezept *n*, Verordnung *f*

presence ['prezəns] *s* Anwesenheit *f*

pres'ence of mind' *s* Geistesgegenwart *f*

present ['prezənt] *adj* (at this place) anwesend; (*of the moment*) gegenwärtig || *s* (*gift*) Geschenk *n*; (present time or tense) Gegenwart *f*; **at p.** zur Zeit; **for the p.** vorläufig || [prɪ'zent] *tr* bieten; (*facts*) darstellen; (*introduce*) vorstellen; (theat) vorführen; **p. s.o. with s.th.** j–m etw verehren

presentable [prɪ'zentəbəl] *adj* presentabel

presentation [,prezən'teʃən] *s* Vorstellung *f*; (theat) Aufführung *f*

pres'ent-day' *adj* heutig, aktuell

presentiment [prɪ'zentɪmənt] *s* Ahnung *f*

presently ['prezəntlɪ] *adv* gegenwärtig; (*soon*) alsbald

preservation [,prezər'veʃən] *s* Erhaltung *f*; (from) Bewahrung *f* (vor *dat*)

preservative [prɪ'zɑrvətɪv] *s* Konservierungsmittel *n*

preserve [prɪ'zɑrv] *s* Revier *n*; **preserves** Konserven *pl* || *tr* konservieren; **p. from** schützen vor (*dat*)

preside [prɪ'zaɪd] *intr* (over) den Vorsitz führen (über *acc* or bei)

presidency ['prezɪdənsɪ] *s* Präsidentschaft *f*

president ['prezɪdənt] *s* Präsident –in *mf*; (*of a university*) Rektor –in *mf*; (*of a board*) Vorsitzende *mf*

presidential [,prezɪ'dentʃəl] *adj* Präsidenten–

press [pres] *adj* (agency, agent, conference, gallery, report, secretary) Presse– || *s* (wine press; printing press; newspapers) Presse *f*; **go to p.** in Druck gehen || *tr* drucken; (*a suit*) (auf)bügeln; (*a person*) bedrängen; (*fruit*) ausdrücken; **be pressed for** knapp sein an (*dat*); **p. s.o. to** (*inf*) j–n dringend bitten zu (*inf*); **p. the button** auf den Knopf drücken || *intr* (*said of time*) drängen; **p. for** drängen auf (*acc*); **p. forward** sich vorwärtsdrängen

press' box' *s* Pressekabine *f*

press' card' *s* Presseausweis *m*

press'ing *adj* dringend, dringlich

press' release' *s* Pressemitteilung *f*

pressure ['preʃər] *s* Druck *m; (of work)* Andrang *m; (aut)* Reifendruck *m;* **put p. on** unter Druck setzen || *tr* drängen

pres'sure cook'er *s* Schnellkochtopf *m*

pres'sure group' *s* Interessengruppe *f*

pressurize ['preʃə‚raɪz] *tr* druckfest machen

prestige [pres'tiʒ] *s* Prestige *n*

presumably [prɪ'z(j)uməbli] *adv* vermutlich

presume [prɪ'z(j)um] *tr* vermuten || *intr* vermuten; **p. on** pochen auf *(acc)*

presumption [prɪ'zʌmpʃən] *s* Vermutung *f; (presumptuousness)* Anmaßung *f*

presumptuous [prɪ'zʌmptʃʊ-əs] *adj* anmaßend

presuppose [‚prisə'poz] *tr* voraussetzen

pretend [prɪ'tend] *tr* vorgeben; **he pretended that he was a captain** er gab sich für e-n Hauptmann aus || *intr* so tun, als ob

pretender [prɪ'tendər] *s* Quaksalber *m;* **p. to the throne** Thronbewerber *m*

pretense [prɪ'tens], ['pritəns] *s* Schein *m;* **under false pretenses** unter Vorspiegelung falscher Tatsachen; **under the p. of** unter dem Vorwand *(genit)*

pretentious [prɪ'tenʃəs] *adj (person)* anmaßend; *(home)* protzig

pretext ['pritekst] *s* Vorwand *m*

pretty ['prɪti] *adj* hübsch || *adv* (coll) ziemlich

pretzel ['pretsəl] *s* Brezel *f*

prevail [prɪ'vel] *intr (predominate)* (vor)herrschen; *(triumph)* **(against)** sich behaupten *(gegen);* **p. on** überreden

prevail'ing *adj (fashion, view)* (vor)herrschend; *(situation)* obwaltend

prevalence ['prevələns] *s* Vorherrschen *n*

prevalent ['prevələnt] *adj* vorherrschend; **be p.** herrschen

prevaricate [prɪ'væri‚ket] *intr* Ausflüchte machen

prevent [prɪ'vent] *tr* verhindern; *(war, danger)* abwenden; **p. s.o. from** j-n hindern an *(dat);* **p. s.o. from** *(ger)* j-n daran hindern zu *(inf)*

prevention [prɪ'venʃən] *s* Verhütung *f*

preventive [prɪ'ventɪv] *adj* vorbeugend || *s* Schutzmittel *n*

preview ['pri‚vju] *s* Vorschau *f*

previous ['privi-əs] *adj* vorhergehend, vorig; Vor-, *e.g.,* **p. conviction** Vorstrafe *f;* **p. day** Vortag *m;* **p. record** Vorstrafenregister *n*

previously ['privi-əsli] *adv* vorher

prewar ['pri‚wɔr] *adj* Vorkriegs-

prey [pre] *s* Beute *f,* Raub *m; (fig)* Opfer *n;* **fall p. to** (& fig) zum Opfer fallen *(dat)* || *intr*—**p. on** erbeuten; *(exploit)* ausbeuten; **p. on s.o.'s mind** an j-s Gewissen nagen

price [praɪs] *s* Preis *m; (st. exch.)* Kurs *m;* **at any p.** um jeden Preis; **at the p. of** im Wert von || *tr* mit Preisen versehen; *(inquire about the price of)* nach dem Preis fragen *(genit)*

price' control' *s* Preiskontrolle *f*

price' fix'ing *s* Preisbindung *f*

price' freeze' *s* Preisstopp *m*

priceless ['praɪslɪs] *adj* unbezahlbar; *(coll)* sehr komisch

price' range' *s* Preislage *f*

price' rig'ging *s* Preistreiberei *f*

price' tag' *s* Preiszettel *m,* Preisschild *n*

price'-wage' spi'ral *s* Preis-Lohn-Spirale *f*

price' war' *s* Preiskrieg *m*

prick [prɪk] *s* (& fig) Stich *m* || *tr* stechen; **p. up** *(ears)* spitzen

prickly ['prɪkli] *adj* stachelig, Stech-

prick'ly heat' *s* Hitzepickel *pl*

pride [praɪd] *s* Stolz *m; (pej)* Hochmut *m;* **swallow one's p.** seinen Stolz in die Tasche stecken; **take p. in** stolz sein auf *(acc)* || *tr*—**p. oneself on** sich viel einbilden auf *(acc)*

priest [prist] *s* Priester *m*

priestess ['pristɪs] *s* Priesterin *f*

priest'hood' *s* Priestertum *n*

priestly ['pristli] *adj* priesterlich

prig [prɪg] *s* Tugendbold *m*

prim [prɪm] *adj* **(primmer; primmest)** spröde

primacy ['praɪməsi] *s* Primat *m* & *n*

primarily [praɪ'merɪli] *adv* vor allem

primary ['praɪ‚meri] *adj* primär, Haupt-; *(e.g., color, school)* Grund- || *s* (pol) Vorwahl *f*

primate ['praɪmet] *s* (zool) Primat *m*

prime [praɪm] *adj (chief)* Haupt-; *(best)* erstklassig || *s* Blüte *f; (math)* Primzahl *f;* **p. of life** Lenz *m* des Lebens || *tr (a pump)* ansaugen lassen; *(ammunition)* scharfmachen; *(a surface for painting)* grundieren; *(with information)* vorher informieren

prime' min'ister *s* Ministerpräsident *m; (in England)* Premierminister *m*

primer ['praɪmər] *s* Fibel *f* || ['praɪmər] *s (for painting)* Grundierfarbe *f; (of an explosive)* Zündsatz *m; (aut)* Einspritzpumpe *f*

prime' time' *s* schönste Zeit *f*

primeval [praɪ'mivəl] *adj* urweltlich, Ur-; **p. world** Urwelt *f*

primitive ['prɪmɪtɪv] *adj* primitiv || *s* Primitive *mf,* Urmensch *m*

primp [prɪmp] *tr* aufputzen || *intr* sich aufputzen, sich zieren

prim'rose' *s* Himmelschlüssel *m*

prince [prɪns] *s* Prinz *m,* Fürst *m*

Prince' Al'bert *s* Gehrock *m*

princely ['prɪnsli] *adj* prinzlich

princess ['prɪnsɪs] *s* Prinzessin *f,* Fürstin *f*

principal ['prɪnsɪpəl] *adj* Haupt- || *s (educ)* Schuldirektor -in *mf; (fin)* Kapitalbetrag *m,* Kapital *n*

principality [‚prɪnsɪ'pæliti] *s* Fürstentum *n*

principally ['prɪnsɪpəli] *adv* größten-teils

principle ['prɪnsɪpəl] *s* Grundsatz *m*, Prinzip *n;* **in p.** im Prinzip

print [prɪnt] *s* (*lettering; design on cloth*) Druck *m;* (*printed dress*) be-drucktes Kleid *n;* (phot) Abzug *m;* **in cold p.** schwarz auf weiß; **out of p.** vergriffen ‖ *tr* drucken; (*e.g., one's name*) in Druckschrift schrei-ben; (phot) kopieren; (tex) be-drucken

print'ed mat'ter *s* Drucksache *f*

printer ['prɪntər] *s* Drucker *m;* (phot) Kopiermaschine *f*

prin'ter's ink' *s* Druckerschwärze *f*

print'ing *s* Drucken *n;* (*of a book*) Buchdruck *m;* (*subsequent printing*) Abdruck *m;* (phot) Kopieren *n*, Ab-ziehen *n*

print'ing press' *s* Druckerpresse *f*

print' shop' *s* Druckerei *f*

prior ['praɪ·ər] *adj* vorherig; **p. to** vor (*dat*) ‖ *s* (eccl) Prior *m*

priority [praɪ'ɔrɪti] *s* Priorität *f*

prism ['prɪzəm] *s* Prisma *n*

prison ['prɪzən] *s* Gefängnis *n*

pris'on camp' *s* Gefangenenlager *n*

prisoner ['prɪz(ə)nər] *s* Gefangene *mf;* (*in a concentration camp*) Häft-ling *m;* **be taken p.** in Gefangenschaft geraten; **take p.** gefangennehmen

pris'oner of war' *s* Kriegsgefangene *mf*

prissy ['prɪsi] *adj* zimperlich

privacy ['praɪvəsi] *s* Zurückgezogen-heit *f;* **disturb s.o.'s p.** j-s Ruhe stören

private ['praɪvɪt] *adj* privat; (*per-sonal*) persönlich; **keep p.** geheim-halten ‖ *s* (mil) Gemeine *mf;* **in p.** privat(im); **privates** Geschlechtsteile *pl*

pri'vate cit'izen *s* Privatperson *f*

pri'vate eye' *s* (coll) Privatdetektiv *m*

pri'vate first' class' *s* Gefreite *mf*

privately ['praɪvɪtli] *adv* privat(im)

privet ['prɪvɪt] *s* Liguster *m*

privilege ['prɪvɪlɪdʒ] *s* Privileg *n*

privy ['prɪvi] *adj*—**p. to** eingeweiht in (*acc*) ‖ *s* Abtritt *m*

prize [praɪz] *s* Preis *m*, Prämie *f;* (nav) Prise *f* ‖ *tr* schätzen

prize' fight' *s* Preisboxkampf *m*

prize' fight'er *s* Berufsboxer *m*

prize' ring' *s* Boxring *m*

pro [pro] *s* (**pros**) (coll) Profi *m;* **the pros and the cons** das Für und Wider ‖ *prep* für (*acc*)

probability [,prɑbə'bɪlɪti] *s* Wahr-scheinlichkeit *f;* **in all p.** aller Wahr-scheinlichkeit nach

probable ['prɑbəbəl] *adj* wahrschein-lich

probate ['probet] *s* Testamentsbestäti-gung *f* ‖ *tr* bestätigen

pro'bate court' *s* Nachlaßgericht *n*

probation [pro'beʃən] *s* Probe *f;* (jur) Bewährungsfrist *f;* **on p.** auf Probe; (jur) mit Bewährung

proba'tion of'ficer *s* Bewährungshelfer –in *mf*

probe [prob] *s* (jur) Untersuchung *f;*

(mil) Sondierungsangriff *m;* (rok) Versuchsrakete *f;* (surg) Sonde *f* ‖ *tr* (*with the hands*) abtasten; (fig & surg) sondieren

problem ['prɑbləm] *s* Problem *n;* (math) Aufgabe *f*

prob'lem child' *s* Sorgenkind *n*

procedure [pro'sidʒər] *s* Verfahren *n*

proceed [pro'sid] *intr* (*go on*) fortfah-ren; (*act*) verfahren; **p. against** (jur) vorgehen gegen; **p. from** kommen von; **p. to** (*inf*) darangehen zu (*inf*)

proceed'ing *s* Vorgehen *n;* **proceedings** (*of a society*) Sitzungsberichte *pl;* (jur) Verfahren *n*

proceeds ['prosidz] *spl* Erlös *m*

process ['prɑsɛs] *s* Verfahren *n*, Pro-zeß *m;* **be in p.** im Gang sein; **in the p. dabei** ‖ *tr* (*raw materials*) ver-arbeiten; (*applications*) bearbeiten; (*persons*) abfertigen; (phot) ent-wickeln und vervielfältigen

procession [pro'sɛʃən] *s* Prozession *f*

proclaim [pro'klem] *tr* ankündigen; (*a law*) bekanntmachen; **p. (as) a holi-day** zum Feiertag erklären

proclamation [,prɑklə'meʃən] *s* Auf-ruf *m*, Proklamation *f*

procrastinate [pro'kræstɪ,net] *intr* zaudern

proctor ['prɑktər] *s* Aufsichtsführende *mf* ‖ *tr* beaufsichtigen

procure [pro'kjʊr] *tr* besorgen, ver-schaffen; (*said of a pimp*) verkup-peln

procurement [pro'kjʊrmənt] *s* Besor-gung *f*

procurer [pro'kjʊrər] *s* Kuppler *m*

prod [prɑd] *s* Stoß *m;* (stick) Stachel-stock *m* ‖ *v* (*pret & pp* **prodded**) *ger* **prodding**) *tr* stoßen; **prod s.o. into** (*ger*) j–n dazu anstacheln zu (*inf*)

prodigal ['prɑdɪgəl] *adj* verschwen-derisch

prod'igal son' *s* verlorener Sohn *m*

prodigious [pro'dɪdʒəs] *adj* großartig

prodigy ['prɑdɪdʒi] *s* Wunderzeichen *n;* (*talented child*) Wunderkind *n*

produce ['prɑd(j)us] *s* (*product*) Er-zeugnis *n;* (*amount produced*) Ertrag *m;* (*fruits and vegetables*) Boden-produkte *pl* ‖ [pro'd(j)us] *tr* pro-duzieren; (*manufacture*) herstellen; (*said of plants, trees*) hervorbringen; (*interest, profit*) abwerfen; (*proof*) beibringen; (*papers*) vorlegen; (cin) produzieren; (theat) inszenieren ‖ *intr* (bot) tragen; (econ) Gewinne abwerfen

pro'duce depart'ment *s* Obst– und Gemüseabteilung *f*

producer [pro'd(j)usər] *s* Hersteller *m;* (cin, theat) Produzent –in *mf*

product ['prɑdʌkt] *s* Erzeugnis *n*, Pro-dukt *n*

production [pro'dʌkʃən] *s* Erzeugung *f*, Produktion *f;* (fa, lit) Werk *n*

productive [pro'dʌktɪv] *adj* produktiv

profane [pro'fen] *adj* profan; **p. lan-guage** Fluchen *n* ‖ *tr* profanieren

profanity [pro'fænɪti] *s* Fluchen *n;* **profanities** Flüche *pl*

profess [pro'fes] *tr* gestehen

profession [pro'feʃən] *s* Beruf *m; (of faith)* Bekenntnis *n;* **by p.** von Beruf

professional [pro'feʃənəl] *adj* berufsmäßig, professionell || *s (expert)* Fachmann *m; (sport)* Profi *m*

profes'sional jea'lousy *s* Brotneid *m*

professor [pro'fesər] *s* Professor –in *mf*

profes'sorship' *s* Professur *f*

proffer ['prafər] *s* Angebot *n* || *tr* anbieten

proficient [pro'fiʃənt] *adj* tüchtig

profile ['profail] *s* Profil *n; (biographical sketch)* Kurzbiographie *f*

profit ['prafit] *s* Gewinn *m;* **show a p. e–n** Gewinn abwerfen || *tr* nutzen || *intr* **(by)** Nutzen ziehen aus

profitable ['prafitəbəl] *adj* einträglich

profiteer [,prafi'tir] *s* Wucherer *m,* Schieber *m* || *intr* wuchern, schieben

prof'it shar'ing *s* Gewinnbeteiligung *f*

profligate ['prafligit] *adj* verkommen; *(extravagant)* verschwenderisch || *s* verkommener Mensch *m; (spendthrift)* Verschwender –in *mf*

profound [pro'faund] *adj (knowledge)* gründlich; *(change)* tiefgreifend

profuse [prə'fjus] *adj* überreichlich

progeny ['pradʒəni] *s (& bot)* Nachkommenschaft *f; (of animals)* Junge *pl*

progno·sis [prag'nosis] *s* (–ses [siz]) Prognose *f*

prognosticate [prag'nasti,ket] *tr* voraussagen

pro·gram ['progræm] *s* Programm *n; (radio or television show)* Sendung *f* || *v (pret & pp* –**grammed;** *ger* –**gramming)** *tr* programmieren

progress ['pragres] *s* Fortschritt *m;* **be in progress** im Gang sein || [prə'gres] *intr (make progress)* fortschreiten; *(develop)* sich fortentwickeln

progressive [prə'gresɪv] *adj* fortschrittlich; *(party)* Fortschritts– || *s* Fortschrittler –in *mf*

prog'ress report' *s* Tätigkeitsbericht *m*

prohibit [pro'hibit] *tr* verbieten

prohibition [,proə'biʃən] *s* Verbot *n; (hist)* Prohibition *f*

prohibitive [pro'hibitiv] *adj (costs)* unertragbar; *(prices)* unerschwinglich

project ['pradʒekt] *s* Project *n,* Vorhaben *n* || [prə'dʒekt] *tr (light, film)* projizieren; *(plan)* vorhaben || *intr* vorspringen, vorragen

projectile [prə'dʒektil] *s (fired from a gun)* Projektil *n; (thrown object)* Wurfgeschoß *n*

projection [prə'dʒekʃən] *s (jutting out)* Vorsprung *m,* Vorbau *m; (cin)* Projektion *f*

projector [prə'dʒektər] *s* Projektor *m*

proletarian [,proli'teri·ən] *adj* proletarisch || *s* Proletarier –in *mf*

proletariat [,proli'teri·ət] *s* Proletariat *n*

proliferate [prə'lifə,ret] *intr* sich stark vermehren

prolific [prə'lifik] *adj* fruchtbar

prolix [pro'liks] *adj* weitschweifig

prologue ['prolɔg] *s* Prolog *m*

prolong [pro'lɔŋ] *tr* verlängern

promenade [,pramɪ'ned] *s* Promenade *f* || *intr* promenieren

promenade' deck' *s* Promenadendeck *n*

prominent ['pramɪnənt] *adj* hervorragend, prominent; *(chin)* vorstehend

promiscuity [,pramɪs'kju·ɪti] *s* Promiskuität *f*

promiscuous [pro'mɪskju·əs] *adj* unterschiedslos; *(sexually)* locker

promise ['pramɪs] *s* Versprechen *n* || *tr* versprechen

prom'ising *adj (thing)* aussichtsreich; *(person)* vielversprechend

prom'issory note' ['pramɪ,sori] *s* Eigenwechsel *m*

promontory ['pramən,tori] *s* Landspitze *f*

promote [prə'mot] *tr (in rank)* befördern; *(a cause)* fördern; *(a pupil)* versetzen; *(wares)* werben für

promoter [prə'motər] *s* Förderer –in *mf; (sport)* Veranstalter –in *mf*

promotion [prə'moʃən] *s (in rank)* Beförderung *f; (of a cause)* Förderung *f; (of a pupil)* Versetzung *f*

prompt [prampt] *adj* prompt || *tr* veranlassen; *(theat)* soufflieren *(dat)*

prompter ['pramptər] *s* Souffleur *m,* Souffleuse *f*

prompt'er's box' *s* Souffleurkasten *m*

promptness ['pramptnɪs] *s* Pünktlichkeit *f*

promulgate [pro'mʌlget] *tr* bekanntmachen

prone [pron] *adj*—**be p. to** neigen zu; **in the p. position** auf Anschlag liegend

prong [prɔŋ] *s (of a fork)* Zinke *f; (of a deer)* Sprosse *f*

pronoun ['pronaun] *s* Fürwort *n*

pronounce [prə'nauns] *tr (enunciate)* aussprechen; **p. sentence das** Strafausmaß festsetzen; **p. s.o.** *(e.g., guilty, insane, man and wife)* sich erklären für

pronouncement [prə'naunsmənt] *s (announcement)* Erklärung *f; (of a sentence)* (jur) Verkündung *f*

pronunciation [prə,nʌnsi'eʃən] *s* Aussprache *f*

proof [pruf] *adj*—**p. against** (fig) gefeit gegen; **90 p. 45** prozentig || *s* Beweis *m;* (phot) Probebild *n;* (typ) Korrekturbogen *m*

proof'read'er *s* Korrektor –in *mf*

prop [prap] *s* Stütze *f;* **props** (coll) Beine *pl;* (theat) Requisiten *pl* || *v (pret & pp* **propped;** *ger* **propping)** *tr* stützen; **p. oneself up** sich aufstemmen; **p. up** abstützen

propaganda [,prapə'gændə] *s* Propaganda *f*

propagate ['prapə,get] *tr* fortpflanzen; (fig) propagieren || *intr* sich fortpflanzen

pro·pel [prə'pel] *v (pret & pp* –**pelled;** *ger* –**pelling)** *tr* antreiben

propeller [prə'pelər] *s* (aer) Propeller *m;* (naut) Schraube *f*

propensity [prə'pensiti] *s* Neigung *f*

proper ['prɑpər] *adj* passend; (*way, time*) richtig; (*authority*) zuständig; (*strictly so-called*) selbst, e.g., **Germany p.** Deutschland selbst

properly ['prɑpərli] *adj* gehörig

prop'er name' *s* Eigenname *m*

property ['prɑpərti] *s* Eigentum *n*; (*land*) Grundstück *n*; (*quality*) Eigenschaft *f*

prop'erty dam'age *s* Sachschaden *m*

prop'erty tax' *s* Grundsteuer *f*

prophecy ['prɑfɪsi] *s* Prophezeiung *f*

prophe·sy ['prɑfɪ‚saɪ] *v* (*pret & pp -sied*) *tr* prophezeien

prophet ['prɑfɪt] *s* Prophet *m*

prophetess ['prɑfɪtɪs] *s* Prophetin *f*

prophylactic [‚prɑfɪ'læktɪk] *adj* prophylaktisch || *s* Prophylaktikum *n*; (*condom*) Präservativ *n*

propitiate [prə'pɪʃɪ‚et] *tr* versöhnen

propitious [prə'pɪʃəs] *adj* günstig

prop'jet' *s* Flugzeug *n* mit Turboprop

proportion [prə'pɔrʃən] *s* Verhältnis *n*; **in p. to** im Verhältnis zu; **out of p. to** in keinem Verhältnis zu; **proportions** Proportionen *pl* || *tr* bemessen; **well proportioned** gut proportioniert

proposal [prə'pozəl] *s* Vorschlag *m*; (*of marriage*) Heiratsantrag *m*

propose [prə'poz] *tr* vorschlagen; (*intend*) beabsichtigen; **p. a toast to** e-n Toast ausbringen auf (*acc*) || *intr* (**to**) e-n Heiratsantrag machen (*dat*)

proposition [‚prɑpə'zɪʃən] *s* Vorschlag *m*; (*log, math*) Lehrsatz *m* || *tr* ansprechen

propound [prə'paʊnd] *tr* vortragen

proprietor [prə'praɪ‚ətər] *s* Inhaber *m*

proprietress [prə'praɪ‚ətrɪs] *s* Inhaberin *f*

propriety [prə'praɪ‚əti] *s* Anstand *m*; **proprieties** Anstandsformen *pl*

propulsion [prə'pʌlʃən] *s* Antrieb *m*

prorate [pro'ret] *tr* anteilmäßig verteilen

prosaic [pro'ze‚ɪk] *adj* prosaisch

proscribe [pro'skraɪb] *tr* proskribieren

prose [proz] *adj* Prosa– || *s* Prosa *f*

prosecute ['prɑsɪ‚kjut] *tr* verfolgen

prosecutor ['prɑsɪ‚kjutər] *s* Ankläger –in *mf*

proselytize ['prɑsɪlə‚taɪz] *intr* Anhänger gewinnen

prose' writ'er *s* Prosaiker –in *mf*

prosody ['prɑsədi] *s* Silbenmessung *f*

prospect ['prɑspekt] *s* Aussicht *f*; (*person*) Interessent –in *mf*; **hold out the p. of s.th.** etw in Aussicht stellen || *intr* (**for**) schürfen (nach)

prospector ['prɑspektər] *s* Schürfer *m*

prospectus [prə'spektəs] *s* Prospekt *m*

prosper ['prɑspər] *intr* gedeihen

prosperity [prɑs'perɪti] *s* Wohlstand *m*

prosperous ['prɑspərəs] *adj* wohlhabend

prostitute ['prɑstɪ‚t(j)ut] *s* Prostituierte *f* || *tr* prostituieren

prostrate ['prɑstret] *adj* hingestreckt; (*exhausted*) erschöpft || *tr* niederwerfen; (*fig*) niederzwingen

prostration [prɑs'treʃən] *s* Niederwerfen *n*; (*abasement*) Demütigung *f*

protagonist [pro'tægənɪst] *s* Protagonist *m*, Hauptfigur *f*

protect [prə'tekt] *tr* (be)schützen; (*interests*) wahrnehmen; **p. from** schützen vor (*dat*)

protection [prə'tekʃən] *s* (**from**) Schutz *m* (vor *dat*)

protector [prə'tektər] *s* Beschützer *m*

protein ['protin] *s* Protein *n*

protest ['protest] *s* Protest *m* || [pro-'test] *tr & intr* protestieren

Protestant ['prɑtɪstənt] *adj* protestantisch || *s* Protestant –in *mf*

protocol ['protə‚kal] *s* Protokoll *n*

proton ['protan] *s* Proton *n*

protoplasm ['protə‚plæzəm] *s* Protoplasma *n*

prototype ['protə‚taɪp] *s* Prototyp *m*

protozo·an [‚protə'zo·ən] *s* (**-a** [ə]) Einzeller *m*

protract [pro'trækt] *tr* hinziehen

protrude [pro'trud] *intr* hervorstehen

proud [praʊd] *adj* (**of**) stolz (auf *acc*)

prove [pruv] *v* (*pret* **proved**; *pp* **proved & proven** ['pruvən]) *tr* beweisen; **p. a failure** sich nicht bewähren; **p. one's worth** sich bewähren || *intr*—**p. right** zutreffen; **p. to be** sich erweisen als

proverb ['prɑvərb] *s* Sprichwort *n*

proverbial [prə'vʌrbɪ·əl] *adj* sprichwörtlich

provide [prə'vaɪd] *tr* (*s.th.*) besorgen; **p. s.o. with s.th.** j–n mit etw versorgen || *intr*—**p. for** (*e.g., a family*) sorgen für; (*e.g., a special case*) vorsehen; (*the future*) voraussehen

provid'ed *adj* (**with**) versehen (mit) || *conj* vorausgesetzt, daß

Providence ['prɑvɪdəns] *s* Vorsehung *f*

providential [‚prɑvɪ'dentʃəl] *adj* von der Vorsehung beschlossen

provid'ing *conj* vorausgesetzt, daß

province ['prɑvɪns] *s* (*district*) Provinz *f*; (*special field*) Ressort *n*

provision [prə'vɪʒən] *s* (*providing*) Versorgung *f*; (*stipulation*) Bestimmung *f*; **make p. for** Vorsorge treffen für; **provisions** Lebensmittelvorräte *pl* || *tr* (mil) verpflegen

provisional [prə'vɪʒənəl] *adj* vorläufig

provi·so [prə'vaɪzo] *s* (**-sos & -soes**) Vorbehalt *m*

provocation [‚prɑvə'keʃən] *s* Provokation *f*

provocative [prə'vakətɪv] *adj* aufreizend

provoke [prə'vok] *tr* (*a person*) provozieren; (*e.g., laughter*) erregen

provok'ing *adj* ärgerlich

prow [praʊ] *s* Bug *m*

prowess ['prau·ɪs] *s* Tapferkeit *f*

prowl [praʊl] *intr* herumschleichen

prowl' car' *s* Streifenwagen *m*

prowler ['praʊlər] *s* mutmaßlicher Einbrecher *m*

proximity [prɑk'sɪmɪti] *s* Nähe *f*

proxy ['prɑksi] *s* Stellvertreter –in *mf*; **by p.** in Vertretung

prude [prud] *s* prüde Person *f*
prudence [′prudəns] *s* Klugheit *f*; (*caution*) Vorsicht *f*
prudent [′prudənt] *adj* klug; (*cautious*) umsichtig
prudish [′prudɪʃ] *adj* prüde
prune [prun] *s* Zwetschge *f* ‖ *tr* stuzen
Prussia [′prʌʃɪ·ə] *s* Preußen *n*
Prussian [′prʌʃən] *adj* preußisch ‖ *s* Preuße *m*, Preußin *f*
pry [praɪ] *v* (*pret & pp* pried) *tr—*pry open aufbrechen; **pry s.th. out of s.o.** etw aus j-m herauspressen ‖ *intr* herumschnüffeln; **pry into** seine Nase stecken in (*acc*)
P.S. [′pi′es] *s* (postscript) NS
psalm [sɑm] *s* Psalm *m*
pseudo— [′sudo] *adj* Pseudo—, falsch
pseudonym [′sudənɪm] *s* Deckname *m*
psyche [′saɪki] *s* Psyche *f*
psychiatrist [saɪ′kaɪ·ətrɪst] *s* Psychiater —*in* *mf*
psychiatry [saɪ′kaɪ·ətri] *s* Psychiatrie *f*
psychic [′saɪkɪk] *adj* psychisch ‖ *s* Medium *n*
psychoanalysis [ˌsaɪko·ə′nælɪsɪs] *s* Psychoanalyse *f*
psychoanalyze [ˌsaɪko′ænəˌlaɪz] *tr* psychoanalytisch behandeln
psychologic(al) [ˌsaɪko′lɑdʒɪk(əl)] *adj* psychologisch
psychologist [saɪ′kɑlədʒɪst] *s* Psychologe *m*, Psychologin *f*
psychology [saɪ′kɑlədʒi] *s* Psychologie *f*
psychopath [′saɪkəˌpæθ] *s* Psychopath —*in* *mf*
psycho·sis [saɪ′kosɪs] *s* (—ses [siz]) Psychose *f*
psychotic [saɪ′kɑtɪk] *adj* psychotisch ‖ *s* Psychosekranke *mf*
pto′main poi′soning [′tomen] *s* Fleischvergiftung *f*
pub [pʌb] *s* Kneipe *f*
puberty [′pjubərti] *s* Pubertät *f*
public [′pʌblɪk] *adj* öffentlich ‖ *s* Öffentlichkeit *f*, Publikum *n*
pub′lic address′ sys′tem *s* Lautsprecheranlage *f*
publication [ˌpʌblɪ′keʃən] *s* Veröffentlichung *f*
pub′lic domain′ *n—*in the p. d. gemeinfrei
publicity [pʌb′lɪsɪti] *s* Publizität *f*
publicize [′pʌblɪˌsaɪz] *tr* bekanntmachen
pub′lic opin′ion *s* öffentliche Meinung *f*
pub′lic-opin′ion poll′ *s* öffentliche Meinungsumfrage *f*
pub′lic pros′ecutor *s* Staatsanwalt *m*
pub′lic rela′tions *spl* Kontaktpflege *f*
pub′lic serv′ant *s* Staatsangestellte *mf*
pub′lic util′ity *s* öffentlicher Versorgungsbetrieb *m*
publish [′pʌblɪʃ] *tr* veröffentlichen
publisher [′pʌblɪʃər] *s* Verleger —*in* *mf*
pub′lishing house′ *s* Verlag *m*
puck [pʌk] *s* Puck *m*
pucker [′pʌkər] *tr* (*the lips*) spitzen ‖ *intr—*p. up den Mund spitzen
pudding [′pudɪŋ] *s* Pudding *m*

puddle [′pʌdəl] *s* Pfütze *f*, Lache *f*
pudgy [′pʌdʒi] *adj* dicklich
puerile [′pju·ərɪl] *adj* knabenhaft
puff [pʌf] *s* (*on a cigarette*) Zug *m*; (*of smoke*) Rauchwölkchen *n*; (*on sleeves*) Puff *m* ‖ *tr* (*e.g., a cigar*) paffen; **p. oneself up** sich aufblähen; **p. out** ausblasen ‖ *intr* keuchen; **p. on** (*a pipe, cigar*) paffen an (*dat*)
pugilist [′pjudʒɪlɪst] *s* Faustkämpfer *m*
pugnacious [pʌg′neʃəs] *adj* kampflustig
pug-nosed [′pʌgˌnozd] *adj* stupsnasig
puke [pjuk] *s* (sl) Kotze *f* ‖ *intr* (sl) kotzen
pull [pul] *s* Ruck *m*; (*influence*) Beziehungen *pl*; (*of gravity*) Anziehungskraft *f* ‖ *tr* ziehen; (*a muscle*) zerren; (*proof*) (typ) abziehen; **p. down** (*e.g., a shade*) herunterziehen; (*a building*) niederreißen; **p. off** (coll) zuwegebringen; **p. oneself together** sich zusammennehmen; **p. out** (*weeds*) herausreißen; **p. up** (*e.g., a chair*) heranrücken ‖ *intr* (on) ziehen (an *dat*); **p. back** sich zurückziehen; **p. in** (*arrive*) ankommen; **p. out** (*depart*) abfahren; **p. over to the side** an den Straßenrand heranfahren; **p. through** durchkommen; **p. up** (*e.g., in a car*) vorfahren
pullet [′pulɪt] *s* Hühnchen *n*
pulley [′puli] *s* Rolle *f*; (*pulley block*) Flaschenzug *m*
pull′o′ver *s* Pullover *m*
pulmonary [′pʌlməˌneri] *adj* Lungen—
pulp [pʌlp] *s* Brei *m*; (*to make paper*) Papierbrei *m*; **beat to a p.** windelweich schlagen
pulpit [′pulpɪt] *s* Kanzel *f*
pulsate [′pʌlset] *intr* pulsieren
pulsation [pʌl′seʃən] *s* Pulsieren *n*
pulse [pʌls] *s* Puls *m*; **take s.o.'s p.** j-m den Puls fühlen
pulverize [′pʌlvəˌraɪz] *tr* pulverisieren
pum′ice stone′ [′pʌmɪs] *s* Bimsstein *m*
pum·mel [′pʌməl] *v* (*pret & pp* —mel[l]ed; *ger* —mel[l]ing) *tr* mit der Faust schlagen
pump [pʌmp] *s* Pumpe *f*; (*shoe*) Pump *m* ‖ *tr* pumpen; (*for information*) ausfragen; **p. up** (*a tire*) aufpumpen
pump′han′dle *s* Pumpenschwengel *m*
pumpkin [′pʌmpkɪn] *s* Kürbis *m*
pun [pʌn] *s* Wortspiel *n* ‖ *v* (*pret & pp* punned; *ger* punning) *intr* ein Wortspiel machen
punch [pʌntʃ] *s* Faustschlag *m*; (*to make holes*) Locher *m*; (*drink*) Punsch *m* ‖ *tr* mit der Faust schlagen; (*a card*) lochen; (*a punch clock*) stechen
punch′ bowl′ *s* Punschschüssel *f*
punch′ card′ *s* Lochkarte *f*
punch′ clock′ *s* Kontrolluhr *f*
punch′-drunk′ *adj* von Faustschlägen betäubt
punch′ing bag′ *s* Punchingball *m*
punch′ line′ *s* Pointe *f*
punctilious [pʌŋk′tɪlɪ·əs] *adj* förmlich
punctual [′pʌŋktʃʊ·əl] *adj* pünktlich
punctuate [′pʌŋktʃʊˌet] *tr* interpunktieren

punctuation [ˌpʌŋktʃʊ'eʃən] s Interpunktion f
punctua'tion mark' s Satzzeichen n
puncture ['pʌŋktʃər] s Loch n || tr durchstechen; **p. a tire** e-e Reifenpanne haben
punc'ture-proof' adj pannensicher
pundit ['pʌndɪt] s Pandit m
pungent ['pʌndʒənt] adj beißend, scharf
punish ['pʌnɪʃ] tr (be)strafen
punishment ['pʌnɪʃmənt] s Strafe f, Bestrafung f; (educ) Strafarbeit f
punk [pʌŋk] adj (sl) mies; **I feel p.** mir ist mies || s (sl) Rocker m
punster ['pʌnstər] s Wortspielmacher m
puny ['pjunɪ] adj kümmerlich, winzig
pup [pʌp] s junger Hund m
pupil ['pjupəl] s Schüler –in mf; (of the eye) Pupille f
puppet ['pʌpɪt] s Marionette f
pup'pet gov'ernment s Marionettenregierung f
pup'pet show' s Marionettentheater n
puppy ['pʌpɪ] s Hündchen n
pup'py love' s Jugendliebe f
purchase ['pʌrtʃəs] s Kauf m; (leverage) Hebelwirkung f || tr kaufen
pur'chasing pow'er s Kaufkraft f
pure [pjʊr] adj (& fig) rein
purgative ['pʌrgətɪv] s Abfuhrmittel n
purgatory ['pʌrgəˌtorɪ] s Fegefeuer n
purge [pʌrdʒ] s (pol) Säuberungsaktion f || tr reinigen; (pol) säubern
puri·fy ['pjʊrɪˌfaɪ] v (pret & pp –fied) tr reinigen, läutern
puritan ['pjʊrɪtən] adj puritanisch || **Puritan** s Puritaner –in mf
purity ['pjʊrɪtɪ] s Reinheit f
purloin [pər'lɔɪn] tr entwenden
purple ['pʌrpəl] adj purpurn || s Purpur m
purport ['pʌrport] s Sinn m || [pər'port] tr vorgeben; (imply) besagen
purpose ['pʌrpəs] s Absicht f; (goal) Zweck m; **on p.** absichtlich; **to no p.** ohne Erfolg
purposely ['pʌrpəslɪ] adv absichtlich
purr [pʌr] s Schnurren n || intr schnurren
purse [pʌrs] s Beutel m; (handbag) Handtasche f || tr—**p. one's lips** den Mund spitzen
purse' strings' spl—**hold the p.** über das Geld verfügen
pursue [pər'sju] tr (a person; a plan, goal) verfolgen; (studies, profession) betreiben; (pleasures) suchen
pursuit [pər'sjut] s Verfolgung f; **in hot p.** hart auf den Fersen
pursuit' plane' s Jäger m
purvey [pər've] tr liefern, versorgen
pus [pʌs] s Eiter m
push [pʊʃ] s Schub m; (mil) Offensive f || tr (e.g., a cart) schieben; (jostle) stoßen; (a button) drücken auf (acc); **p. around** (coll) schlecht behandeln; **p. aside** beiseite schieben; (curtains) zurückschlagen; **p. one's way through** sich durchdrängen; **p. through** durchsetzen || intr drängen

push' but'ton s Druckknopf m
push' cart' s Verkaufskarren m
push'o'ver s (snap) (coll) Kinderspiel n; (sucker) Gimpel m; (easy opponent) leicht zu besiegender Gegner m
push'-up' s (gym) Liegestütz m
pushy ['pʊʃɪ] adj zudringlich
puss [pʊs] s (cat) Mieze f; (face) (sl) Fresse f
pussy ['pʌsɪ] adj eit(e)rig || ['pʊsɪ] s Mieze f
puss'y wil'low s Salweide f
put [pʊt] v (pret & pp put; ger putting) tr (stand) stellen; (lay) legen; (set) setzen; **feel put out** ungehalten sein; **put across** to beibringen (dat); **put aside** beiseite legen; **put down** (a load) abstellen; (a rebellion) niederschlagen; (in writing) aufschreiben; **put in** (e.g., a windowpane) einsetzen; (e.g., a good word) einlegen; (time) (on) verwenden (auf acc); **put off** (a person) hinhalten; (postpone) aufschieben; **put on** (clothing) anziehen; (a hat) aufsetzen; (a ring) anstecken; (an apron) umbinden; (the brakes) betätigen; (to cook) ansetzen; (a play) aufführen; **put on an act** sich in Szene setzen; **put oneself into** sich hineindenken in (acc); **put oneself out** sich [dat] Umstände machen; **put on its feet again** (com) auf die Beine stellen; **put s.o. on to s.th.** j-n auf etw [acc] bringen; **put out** (a fire) löschen; (lights) auslöschen; (throw out) herauswerfen; (a new book) herausbringen; **put out of action** kampfunfähig machen; **put over on s.o.** j-n übers Ohr hauen; **put through** durchsetzen; (a call) (telp) herstellen; **put (s.o.) through to** (telp) j-n verbinden mit; **put to good use** gut verwenden; **put up** (erect) errichten; (bail) stellen; (for the night) unterbringen; **put up a fight** sich zur Wehr setzen; **put up to** anstiften zu; **to put it mildly** gelinde gesagt || intr —**put on** sich verstellen; **put out to sea** (said of a ship) in See gehen; **put up with** sich abfinden mit
put'-on' adj vorgetäuscht || s (affectation) Affektiertheit f; (parody) Jux m
put-put ['pʌt'pʌt] s Tacktack n || intr —**p. along** knattern
putrid ['pjutrɪd] adj faul(ig)
putt [pʌt] tr & intr (golf) putten
putter ['pʌtər] s (golf) Putter m || intr—**p. around** herumwursteln
put·ty ['pʌtɪ] s Kitt m || v (pret & pp –tied) tr (ver)kitten
put'ty knife' s Spachtel m & f
put'-up job' s abgekartete Sache f
puzzle ['pʌzəl] s Rätsel n; (game) Geduldspiel n || tr verwirren; **be puzzled** verwirrt sein; **p. out** enträtseln || intr—**p. over** tüfteln an (dat)
puzzler ['pʌzlər] s Rätsel n
puz'zling adj rätselhaft
PW ['pi'dʌbəlˌju] s (prisoner of war) Kriegsgefangene mf

pygmy ['pɪgmi] s Pygmäe m, Pygmäin f

pylon ['paɪlən] s (entrance to Egyptian temple) Pylon m; (aer) Wendemarke f; (elec) Leitungsmast m

pyramid ['pɪrəmɪd] s Pyramide f

pyre [paɪr] s Scheiterhaufen m

Pyrenees ['pɪrɪ,niz] spl Pyrenäen pl

pyrotechnics [,paɪrə'tekniks] spl Feuerwerkskunst f, Pyrotechnik f

python ['paɪθən] s Pythonschlange f

pyx [pɪks] s (eccl) Pyxis f

Q

Q, q [kju] s siebzehnter Buchstabe des englischen Alphabets

quack [kwæk] s Quacksalber m, Kurpfuscher m ‖ intr schnattern

quadrangle ['kwad,ræŋgəl] s Viereck n; (inner yard) Innenhof m, Lichthof m

quadrant ['kwadrənt] s Quadrant m

quadratic [kwad'rætɪk] adj quadratisch

quadruped ['kwadrʊ,ped] s Vierfüßer m

quadruple [kwad'rupəl] adj vierfach ‖ s Vierfache n ‖ tr vervierfachen ‖ intr sich vervierfachen

quadruplets [kwad'ruplets] spl Vierlinge pl

quaff [kwaf] tr in langen Zügen trinken

quagmire ['kwæg,maɪr] s Morast m

quail [kwel] s Wachtel f ‖ intr verzagen

quaint [kwent] adj seltsam

quake [kwek] s Zittern n; (geol) Beben n ‖ intr zittern; (geol) beben

Quaker ['kwekər] s Quäker –in mf

qualification [,kwalɪfɪ'keʃən] s (for) Qualifikation f (für)

quali•fy ['kwalɪ,faɪ] v (pret & pp –fied) tr qualifizieren; (modify) einschränken ‖ intr sich qualifizieren

quality ['kwalɪti] s (characteristic) Eigenschaft f; (grade) Qualität f

qualm [kwam] s Bedenken n

quandary ['kwandəri] s Dilemma n

quantity ['kwantɪti] s Menge f, Quantität f; (math) Größe f; (pros) Silbenmaß n; buy in q. auf Vorrat kaufen

quan'tum the'ory ['kwantəm] s Quantentheorie f

quarantine ['kwɔrən,tin] s Quarantäne f ‖ tr unter Quarantäne stellen

quar•rel ['kwɔrəl] s Streit m; pick a q. Händel suchen ‖ v (pret & pp –rel[l]ed; ger –el[l]ing) intr (over) streiten (über acc or um)

quarrelsome ['kwɔrəlsəm] adj streitsüchtig, händelsüchtig

quar•ry ['kwɔri] s Steinbruch m; (hunt) Jagdbeute f ‖ v (pret & pp –ried) tr brechen

quart [kwɔrt] s Quart n

quarter ['kwɔrtər] s Viertel n; (of a city) Stadtviertel n; (of the moon) Mondviertel n; (of the sky) Himmelsrichtung f; (coin) Vierteldollar m; (econ) Quartal n; (sport) Viertelzeit f; a q. after one (ein) Viertel nach

eins; a q. of an hour e–e Viertelstunde f; a q. to eight dreiviertel acht, (ein) viertel vor acht; at close quarters im Nahkampf; from all quarters von überall; give no q. keinen Pardon geben; quarters (& mil) Unterkunft f, Quartier n ‖ tr (lodge) einquartieren; (divide into four, tear into quarters) vierteilen ‖ intr im Quartier liegen

quar'ter-deck' s Quarterdeck n

quar'terfi'nal s Zwischenrunde f

quar'ter-hour' s Viertelstunde f

quarterly ['kwɔrtərli] adj vierteljährig; (econ) Quartals– ‖ s Vierteljahresschrift f

quar'termas'ter s Quartiermeister m

Quar'termaster Corps' s Versorgungstruppen pl

quar'ter note' s (mus) Viertelnote f

quar'ter rest' s (mus) Viertelpause f

quartet [kwɔr'tet] s Quartett n

quartz [kwɔrts] s Quarz m

quash [kwaʃ] tr niederschlagen

quatrain ['kwatren] s Vierzeiler m

quaver ['kwevər] s Zittern n; (mus) Triller m ‖ intr zittern; (mus) trillern, tremolieren

queasy ['kwizi] adj übel

queen [kwin] s Königin f; (cards) Dame f

queen' bee' s Bienenkönigin f

queen' dow'ager s Königinwitwe f

queenly ['kwinli] adj königlich

queen' moth'er s Königinmutter f

queer [kwɪr] adj sonderbar; (homosexual) schwul ‖ s (homosexual) Schwule mf

queer' duck' s (coll) Unikum n

quell [kwel] tr unterdrücken

quench [kwentʃ] tr (thirst) löschen; (a fire) (aus)löschen

que•ry ['kwɪri] s Frage f ‖ v (pret & pp –ried) tr befragen; (cast doubt on) bezweifeln

quest [kwest] s Suche f; in q. of auf der Suche nach

question ['kwestʃən] s Frage f; ask (s.o.) a q. (j–m) e–e Frage stellen; be out of the q. außer Frage stehen; beyond q. außer Frage; call into q. in Frage stellen; call the q. (parl) um Abstimmung bitten; in q. betreffend; it is a q. of (ger) es handelt sich darum zu (inf); q. of time Zeitfrage f; that's an open q. darüber läßt sich streiten; there's no q. about it darüber besteht kein Zweifel ‖ tr be-

fragen; (said of the police) verhören; (cast doubt on) bezweifeln
questionable ['kwest/ənəbəl] adj fraglich, fragwürdig; (doubtful) zweifelhaft; (character) bedenklich
ques'tioning s Verhör n, Vernehmung f
ques'tion mark' s Fragezeichen n
questionnaire [ˌkwest/ə'ner] s Frage-
bogen m
queue [kju] s Schlange f || intr—q. up
sich anstellen
quibble ['kwɪbəl] s Deutelei f || intr
(about) deuteln (an dat)
quibbler ['kwɪblər] s Wortklauber m
quick [kwɪk] adj schnell, fix || s—cut
to the q. bis ins Mark treffen
quicken ['kwɪkən] tr beschleunigen ||
intr sich beschleunigen
quick'lime' s gebrannter ungelöschter
Kalk m
quick' lunch' s Schnellimbiß m
quick'sand' s Treibsand m
quick'sil'ver s Quecksilber n
quick'-tem'pered adj jähzornig
quick'-wit'ted adj scharfsinnig
quiet ['kwaɪ·ət] adj ruhig; (person)
schweigsam; (still) still; (street) un-
belebt; be q.! sei still!; keep q.
schweigen || s Stille f || tr beruhigen
|| intr—q. down sich beruhigen; (said
of excitement, etc.) sich legen
quill [kwɪl] s Feder f, Federkiel m;
(of a porcupine) Stachel m
quilt [kwɪlt] s Steppdecke f || tr step-
pen
quince [kwɪns] s Quitte f
quince' tree' s Quittenbaum m
quinine ['kwaɪnaɪn] s Chinin n
quintessence [kwɪn'tesəns] s Inbegriff
m
quintet [kwɪn'tet] s Quintett n
quintuplets [kwɪn'tʌplets] spl Fünf-
linge pl
quip [kwɪp] s witziger Seitenhieb m ||
v (pret & pp quipped; ger quipping)
tr witzig sagen || intr witzeln

quire [kwaɪr] s (bb) Lage f
quirk [kwʌrk] s Eigenart f; (subterfuge) Ausflucht f; (sudden change)
plötzliche Wendung f
quit [kwɪt] adj quitt; let's call it quits!
(coll) Strich drunter! || v (pret & pp
quit & quitted; ger quitting) tr aufgeben; (e.g., a gang) abspringen von;
q. it! hören Sie damit auf! || intr
aufhören; (at work) seine Stellung
aufgeben
quite [kwaɪt] adv recht, ganz; q. a disappointment e-e ausgesprochene Enttäuschung f; q. recently in jüngster
Zeit; q. the reverse genau das Gegenteil
quitter ['kwɪtər] s Schlappmacher m
quiver ['kwɪvər] s Zittern n; (to hold
arrows) Köcher m || intr zittern
quixotic [kwɪks'ɑtɪk] adj überspannt
quiz [kwɪz] s Prüfung f; (game) Quiz
n || v (pret & pp quizzed; ger quiz-
zing) tr ausfragen; q. s.o. on s.th.
j-n etw abfragen
quiz'mas'ter s Quizonkel m
quiz' show' s Quizshow f
quizzical ['kwɪzɪkəl] adj (puzzled)
verwirrt; (strange) seltsam; (mocking) spöttisch
quoit [kwɔɪt] s Wurfring m
quondam ['kwɑndæm] adj ehemalig
Quon'set hut' ['kwɑnsət] s Nissen-
hütte f
quorum ['kworəm] s beschlußfähige
Anzahl f
quota ['kwotə] s Quote f, Anteil m;
(work) Arbeitsleistung f
quotation [kwo'te/ən] s Zitat n; (price)
Notierung f
quota'tion marks' spl Anführungszei-
chen pl
quote [kwot] s Zitat n; (of prices)
Notierung f || tr zitieren; (prices)
notieren || interj—q. ... unquote Be-
ginn des Zitats! ... Ende des Zitats!
quotient ['kwo/ənt] s Quotient m

R

R, r [ɑr] s achtzehnter Buchstabe des
englischen Alphabets
rabbet ['ræbɪt] s Falz m || tr falzen
rabbi ['ræbaɪ] s Rabbiner m
rabbit ['ræbɪt] s Kaninchen n
rabble ['ræbəl] s Pöbel m
rab'ble-rous'er s Volksaufwiegler -in
mf
rabid ['ræbɪd] adj rabiat; (dog) toll-
wütig
rabies ['rebiz] s Tollwut f
raccoon [ræ'kun] s Waschbär m
race [res] s Rasse f; (contest) Wettren-
nen n; (fig) Wettlauf m || tr um die
Wette laufen mit; (in a car) um die
Wette fahren mit; (a horse) rennen
lassen; (an engine) hochjagen || intr

rennen; (on foot) um die Wette laufen; (in a car) um die Wette fahren
race' driv'er s Rennfahrer -in mf
race' horse' s Rennpferd n
racer ['resər] s (person) Wettfahrer
-in mf; (car) Rennwagen m; (in
speed skating) Schnelläufer -in mf
race' ri'ot s Rassenaufruhr m
race' track' s Rennbahn f
racial ['re/əl] adj rassisch, Rassen—
rac'ing s Rennsport m
racism ['resɪzəm] s Rassenhaß m
rack [ræk] s (shelf) Regal n, Ablage f;
(for clothes, bicycles, hats) Ständer
m; (for luggage) Gepäcknetz n; (for
fodder) Futterraufe f; (for torture)
Folter f; (toothed bar) Zahnstange f;

go to r. and ruin völlig zugrunde gehen; **put to the r.** auf die Folter spannen || *tr* (*with pain*) quälen; **r. one's brains** (**over**) sich [*dat*] den Kopf zerbrechen (über *acc*)

racket [ˈrækɪt] *s* (*noise*) Krach *m*; (*illegal business*) Schiebergeschäft *n*; (*tennis*) Rakett *n*

racketeer [ˌrækɪˈtɪər] *s* Schieber –in *mf*

racketeer'ing *s* Schiebertum *n*

rack/ rail/way *s* Zahnradbahn *f*

racy/ rail/way *adj* (*off-color*) schlüpfrig; (*vivacious, pungent*) rassig

radar [ˈreɪdər] *s* Radar *n*

ra'darscope' *s* Radarschirm *m*

radial [ˈreɪdɪəl] *adj* radial

radiance [ˈreɪdɪəns] *s* Strahlung *f*

radiant [ˈreɪdɪ-ənt] *adj* (*with*) strahlend (vor *dat*); (*phys*) Strahlungs-

radiate [ˈreɪdɪˌeɪt] *tr & intr* ausstrahlen

radiation [ˌreɪdɪˈeɪʃən] *s* Strahlung *f*

radia'tion belt' *s* Strahlungsgürtel *m*

radia'tion treat'ment *s* Bestrahlung *f*; **give r. treatment to** bestrahlen

radiator [ˈreɪdɪˌeɪtər] *s* Heizkörper *m*; (aut) Kühler *m*

ra'diator cap' *s* Kühlerverschluß *m*

radical [ˈrædɪkəl] *adj* radikal || *s* Radikale *f*

radically [ˈrædɪkəli] *adv* von Grund auf

radi-o [ˈreɪdɪˌo] *s* (**-os**) Radio *n*, Rundfunk *m*; **go on the r.** im Rundfunk sprechen || *tr* funken

ra'dioac'tive *adj* radioaktiv

ra'dio announc'er *s* Rundfunkansager –in *mf*

ra'dio bea'con *s* (aer) Funkfeuer *n*

ra'dio beam' *s* Funkleitstrahl *m*

ra'dio broad'cast *s* Rundfunksendung *f*

radiocar'bon dat'ing *s* Radiokarbonmethode *f*

ra'diofre'quency *s* Hochfrequenz *f*

radiogram [ˈreɪdɪˌoˌgræm] *s* Radiogramm *n*

radiologist [ˌreɪdɪˈɑlədʒɪst] *s* Röntgenologe *m*, Röntgenologin *f*

radiology [reɪdɪˈɑlədʒi] *s* Röntgenologie *f*

ra'dio net'work *s* Rundfunknetz *n*

ra'dio op'erator *s* Funker –in *mf*

radioscopy [ˌreɪdɪˈɑskəpi] *s* Durchleuchtung *f*

ra'dio set' *s* Radioapparat *m*

ra'dio sta'tion *s* Rundfunkstation *f*

radish [ˈrædɪʃ] *s* Radieschen *n*

radium [ˈreɪdɪəm] *s* Radium *n*

radi-us [ˈreɪdɪ-əs] *s* (**-i** [ˌaɪ] & **-uses**) Halbmesser *m*; (anat) Speiche *f*; **within a r. of** in e-m Umkreis von

raffish [ˈræfɪʃ] *adj* gemein, niedrig

raffle [ˈræfəl] *s* Tombola *f* || *tr*—**r. off** in e-r Tombola verlosen

raft [ræft] *s* Floß *n*; **a r. of** (coll) ein Haufen *m*

rafter [ˈræftər] *s* Dachsparren *m*; **rafters** Sparrenwerk *n*

rag [ræg] *s* Lumpen *m*; **chew the rag** (sl) quasseln

ragamuffin [ˈrægəˌmʌfɪn] *s* Lump *m*

rag' doll' *s* Stoffpuppe *f*

rage [redʒ] *s* Wut *f*; **all the r.** letzter Schrei *m*; **be the r.** die große Mode sein; **fly into a r.** in Wut geraten || *intr* wüten, toben

ragged [ˈrægɪd] *adj* zerlumpt, lumpig

rag'man *s* (**-men**) Lumpenhändler *m*

ragout [ræˈgu] *s* Ragout *n*

rag'weed' *s* Ambrosiapflanze *f*

raid [red] *s* Beutezug *m*; (*by police*) Razzia *f*; (mil) Überfall *m* || *tr* überfallen; **e-e** Razzia machen auf (*acc*)

raider [ˈredər] *s* (naut) Kaperkreuzer *m*; **raiders** (mil) Kommandotruppe *f*

rail [rel] *s* Geländerstange *f*; (naut) Reling *f*; (rr) Schiene *f*; **by r.** per Bahn ||—**r. at** beschimpfen

rail'head' *s* Schienenkopf *m*

rail'ing *s* Geländer *n*; (naut) Reling *f*

rail'road' *s* Eisenbahn *f* || *tr* (*a bill*) durchpeitschen

rail'road cross'ing *s* Bahnübergang *m*

rail'road embank'ment *s* Bahndamm *m*

rail'road sta'tion *s* Bahnhof *m*

rail'road tie' *s* Schwelle *f*

rail'way' *adj* Eisenbahn- || *s* Eisenbahn *f*

raiment [ˈremənt] *s* Kleidung *f*

rain [ren] *s* Regen *m*; **it looks like r. es** sieht nach Regen aus; **r. or shine** bei jedem Wetter || *tr*—**r. cats and dogs** Bindfäden regnen; **r. out** verregnen || *intr* regnen

rainbow [ˈrenˌbo] *s* Regenbogen *m*

rain'coat' *s* Regenmantel *m*

rain'drop' *s* Regentropfen *m*

rain'fall' *s* Regenfall *m*; (*amount of rain*) Regenmenge *f*

rain' gut'ter *s* Dachrinne *f*

rain' pipe' *s* Fallrohr *n*

rain'proof' *adj* regenfest, regendicht

rainy [ˈreni] *adj* regnerisch; (*e.g., day, weather*) Regen-; **save money for a r. day** sich [*dat*] e-n Notpfennig aufsparen

rain'y sea'son *s* Regenzeit *f*

raise [rez] *s* Lohnerhöhung *f*; (*in poker*) Steigerung *f* || *tr* (*lift*) heben, erheben; (*increase*) erhöhen, steigern; (*erect*) aufstellen; (*children*) großziehen; (*a family*) ernähren; (*grain, vegetables*) anbauen; (*animals*) züchten; (*dust*) aufwirbeln; (*money, troops*) aufbringen; (*blisters*) ziehen; (*a question*) aufwerfen; (*hopes*) erwecken; (*a laugh, smile*) hervorrufen; (*the ante*) steigern; (*a siege*) aufheben; (*from the dead*) auferwecken; **r. Cain** (**or hell**) Krach schlagen; **r. the arm** (*before striking*) mit dem Arm ausholen; **r. the price of** verteuern; **r. to a higher power** potenzieren || *intr* (*in poker*) höher wetten

raisin [ˈrezən] *s* Rosine *f*

rake [rek] *s* Rechen *m*; (*person*) Wüstling *m* || *tr* rechen; (*with gunfire*) bestreichen; **r. in** (*money*) kassieren; **r. together** (**or up**) zusammenrechen

rake'-off' *s* (coll) Gewinnanteil *m*

rakish [ˈrekɪʃ] *adj* (*dissolute*) liederlich; (*jaunty*) schmissig

ral·ly [ˈræli] *s* (*meeting*) Massenversammlung *f*; (*recovery*) Erholung *f*;

(mil) Umgruppierung *f* || *v* (*pret & pp* –lied) *tr* (wieder) sammeln || *intr* sich (wieder) sammeln; (*recover*) sich erholen

ram [ræm] *s* Schafbock *m* || *v* (*pret & pp* rammed; *ger* ramming) *tr* rammen; **ram s.th. down s.o.'s throat** j-m etw aufdrängen

ramble ['ræmbəl] *intr*—**r. about** herumwandern; **r. on** daherreden

ramification [ˌræmɪfɪ'keʃən] *s* Verzweigung *f*

ramp [ræmp] *s* Rampe *f*

rampage ['ræmpedʒ] *s* Toben *n*, Wüten *n;* **go on a r.** toben, wüten

rampant ['ræmpənt] *adj*—**be r.** grassieren

rampart ['ræmpart] *s* Wall *m*, Ringwall *m*

ram'rod' *s* Ladestock *m;* (*cleaning rod*) Reinigungsstock *m*

ram'shack'le *adj* baufällig

ranch [ræntʃ] *s* Ranch *f*

rancid ['rænsɪd] *adj* ranzig

random ['rændəm] *adj* zufällig, Zufalls–; **at r.** aufs Geratewohl

range [rendʒ] *s* (*row*) Reihe *f;* (*mountains*) Bergkette *f;* (*stove*) Herd *m;* (*for firing practice*) Schießplatz *m;* (*of a gun*) Schießweite *f;* (*distance*) Reichweite *f;* (*mus*) Umfang *m;* **at a r. of** in e-r Entfernung von; **at close r.** auf kurze Entfernung; **come within s.o.'s r.** j-m vor den Schuß kommen; **out of r.** außer Reichweite; (*in shooting*) außer Schußweite; **within r.** in Reichweite; (*in shooting*) in Schußweite || *tr* reihen || *intr*—**r. from ...** to sich bewegen zwischen (*dat*) ... und

range' find'er *s* Entfernungsmesser *m*

ranger ['rendʒər] *s* Förster *m;* **rangers** Stoßtruppen *pl*

rank [ræŋk] *adj* (*rancid*) ranzig; (*smelly*) stinkend; (*absolute*) kraß; (*excessive*) übermäßig; (*growth*) üppig || *s* Rang *m;* **according to r.** standesgemäß; **person of r.** Standesperson *f* || *tr* einreihen, rangieren; **be ranked as** gelten als || *intr* rangieren; **r. above** stehen über (*dat*); **r. among** zählen zu; **r. below** stehen unter (*dat*); **r. with** mitzählen zu

rank' and file' *s* die breite Masse

rank'ing of'ficer *s* Rangälteste *mf*

rankle ['ræŋkəl] *tr* nagen an (*dat*) || *intr* nagen

ransack ['rænsæk] *tr* durchstöbern

ransom ['rænsəm] *s* Lösegeld *n* || *tr* auslösen

rant [rænt] *intr* schwadronieren

rap [ræp] *s* (*on the door*) Klopfen *n;* (*blow*) Klaps *m;* **not give a rap for** husten auf (*acc*); **take the rap** den Kopf hinhalten; **there was a rap on the door** es klopfte an der Tür || *v* (*pret & pp* rapped; *ger* rapping) *tr* (*strike*) schlagen; (*criticize*) tadeln || *intr* (*talk freely*) offen reden; (*on*) klopfen (an *dat*)

rapacious [rə'peʃəs] *adj* raffgierig; (*animal*) raubgierig

rape [rep] *s* Vergewaltigung *f* || *tr* vergewaltigen

rapid ['ræpɪd] *adj* rapid(e); (*river*) reißend || **rapids** *spl* Stromschnelle *f*

rap'id-fire' *adj* Schnell–; (mil) Schnellfeuer–

rap'id trans'it *s* Nahschnellverkehr *m*

rapier ['repɪ.ər] *s* Rapier *n*

rapist ['repɪst] *s* sexueller Gewaltverbrecher *m*

rap'ses'sion *s* zwanglose Diskussion *f*

rapt [ræpt] *adj* (*attention*) gespannt; (*in thought*) vertieft

rapture ['ræptʃər] *s* Entzückung *f;* **go into raptures** in Entzücken geraten

rare [rer] *adj* selten; (culin) halbgar

rare' bird' *s* (fig) weißer Rabe *m*

rare•fy ['rerɪˌfaɪ] *v* (*pret & pp* –fied) *tr* verdünnen

rarely ['rerlɪ] *adv* selten

rarity ['rerɪtɪ] *s* Rarität *f*

rascal ['ræskəl] *s* Bengel *m*

rash [ræʃ] *adj* vorschnell, unbesonnen || *s* Ausschlag *m*

rasp [ræsp] *s* (*sound*) Kratzlaut *m;* (*tool*) Raspel *f* || *tr* raspeln

raspberry ['ræzˌberɪ] *s* Himbeere *f*

rat [ræt] *s* Ratte *f;* (*deserter*) (sl) Überläufer –in *mf;* (*informer*) (sl) Spitzel *m;* (*scoundrel*) (sl) Gauner *m;* **smell a rat** (coll) den Braten riechen || *intr*—**rat on** (sl) verpetzen

ratchet ['rætʃɪt] *s* (*wheel*) Sperrad *n;* (*pawl*) Sperrklinke *f*

rate [ret] *s* Satz *m;* (*for mail, freight*) Tarif *m;* **at any r.** auf jeden Fall; **at the r. of** (*a certain speed*) mit der Geschwindigkeit von; (*a certain price*) zum Preis von; **at the r. of a dozen per week** ein Dutzend pro Woche; **at this** (*or that*) **r.** bei diesem Tempo || *tr* bewerten || *intr* (coll) hochgeschätzt sein

rate' of exchange' *s* Kurs *m*

rate' of in'terest *s* Zinssatz *m*

rather ['ræðər] *adv* ziemlich; **I would r. wait** ich würde lieber warten; **r. ... than** lieber ... als || *interj* na obl

rati•fy ['rætɪˌfaɪ] *v* (*pret & pp* –fied) *tr* ratifizieren, bestätigen

rat'ing *s* Beurteilung *f;* (mach) Leistung *f;* (mil) Dienstgrad *m;* (sport) Bewertung *f*

ra•tio ['reʃ(ɪ)ˌo] *s* (–tios) Verhältnis *n*

ration ['ræʃən], ['reʃən] *s* Ration *f;* **rations** (mil) Verpflegung *f* || *tr* rationieren

ra'tion card' *s* Bezugsschein *m*

ra'tioning *s* Rationierung *f*

rational ['ræʃənəl] *adj* vernünftig

rationalize ['ræʃənəˌlaɪz] *tr & intr* rationalisieren

rat' poi'son *s* Rattengift *n*

rat' race' *s* (fig) Hetzjagd *f*

rattle ['rætəl] *s* Geklapper *n;* (*toy*) Klapper *f*, Schnarre *f* || *tr* (*confuse*) verwirren; **get s.o. rattled** j-n aus dem Konzept bringen; **r. off** herunterschnarren; **r. the dishes** mit dem Geschirr klappern || *intr* klappern; (*said of a machine gun*) knattern;

(*said of windows*) klirren; **r. on daherplappern**
rat'tlebrain' *s* Hohlkopf *m*
rat'tlesnake' *s* Klapperschlange *f*
rat'tletrap' *s* (coll) Kiste *f*, Karre *f*
rat'trap' *s* Rattenfalle *f*
raucous ['rɔkəs] *adj* heiser
ravage ['rævɪdʒ] *s* Verwüstung *f*, Verheerung *f* ‖ *tr* verwüsten, verheeren
rave [rev] *s* (coll) Modeschrei *m* ‖ *intr* irrereden; **r. about** schwärmen von
raven ['revən] *adj* (*black*) rabenschwarz ‖ *s* Kolkrabe *m*, Rabe *m*
ravenous ['rævənəs] *adj* rasend
ravine [rə'vin] *s* Bergschlucht *f*
rav'ing *adj* (coll) toll ‖ *adv*—**r. mad** tobsüchtig
ravish ['rævɪʃ] *tr* vergewaltigen
rav'ishing *adv* entzückend
raw [rɔ] *adj* roh; (*weather*) naßkalt; (*throat*) rauh; (*recruit*) unausgebildet; (*skin*) wundgerieben; (*leather*) ungegerbt; (*wool*) ungesponnen
raw'-boned' *adj* hager
raw' deal' *s* (sl) unfaire Behandlung *f*
raw'hide' *s* Rohhaut *f*
raw' mate'rial *s* Rohstoff *m*
ray [re] *s* Strahl *m;* (ichth) Rochen *m;* **ray of hope** Hoffnungsstrahl *m*
rayon ['re·ɑn] *adj* kunstseiden ‖ *s* Kunstseide *f*, Rayon *f*
raze [rez] *tr* abtragen; **r. to the ground** dem Erdboden gleichmachen
razor ['rezər] *s* Rasiermesser *n;* (*safety razor*) Rasierapparat *m*
ra'zor blade' *s* Rasierklinge *f*
razz [ræz] *tr* (sl) aufziehen
re [ri] *prep* betreffs (*genit*)
reach [rit∫] *s* Reichweite *f;* **beyond the r. of s.o.** für j—n unerreichbar; **out of r.** unerreichbar; **within easy r.** leicht zu erreichen; **within r.** in Reichweite ‖ *tr* (*a goal, person, city, advanced age, an understanding*) erreichen; (*a certain amount*) sich belaufen auf (*acc*); (*a compromise*) schließen; (*an agreement*) treffen; (*e.g., the ceiling*) heranreichen an (*acc*); **r. out** ausstrecken ‖ *intr* (*extend*) reichen, sich erstrecken; **r. for** greifen nach; **r. into one's pocket** in die Tasche greifen
react [rɪ'ækt] *intr* (**to**) reagieren (auf *acc*); **r. upon** zurückwirken auf (*acc*)
reaction [rɪ'æk/ən] *s* Reaktion *f*
reactionary [rɪ'æk/ən‚eri] *adj* reaktionär ‖ *s* Reaktionär —in *mf*
reac'tion time' *s* Reaktionszeit *f*
reactor [rɪ'æktər] *s* Reaktor *m*
read [rid] *v* (*pret & pp* **read** [red]) *tr* lesen; **r. a paper on** referieren über (*acc*); **r. off** verlesen; **r. over** durchlesen; **r. to** vorlesen (*dat*) ‖ *intr* lesen; (*said of a passage*) lauten; (*said of a thermometer*) zeigen; **r. up on** studieren
readable ['ridəbəl] *adj* lesbar
reader ['ridər] *s* (*person*) Leser —in *mf;* (*book*) Lesebuch *n*
readily ['redɪli] *adv* gern(e)
readiness ['redɪnɪs] *s* Bereitwilligkeit *f;* (*preparedness*) Bereitschaft *f*

read'ing *s* (*act*) Lesen *n;* (*material*) Lektüre *f;* (*version*) Lesart *f;* (eccl, parl) Lesung *f*
read'ing glass'es *spl* Lesebrille *f*
read'ing lamp' *s* Leselampe *f*
read'ing room' *s* Lesesaal *m*
readjustment [‚ri·ə'dʒʌstmənt] *s* Umstellung *f*
ready ['redi] *adj* (*done*) fertig; **be r.** (*stand in readiness*) in Bereitschaft stehen; **get r.** sich fertig (or bereit) machen; **get s.th. r.** etw fertigstellen; **r. for bereit zu; r. for take-off** startbereit; **r. for use** gebrauchsfertig; **r. to** (*inf*) bereit zu (*inf*) ‖ *v* (*pret & pp* —**ied**) *tr* fertigmachen
read'y cash' *s* flüssiges Geld *n*
read'y-made' *adj* von der Stange
read'y-made' clothes' *spl* Konfektion *f*
reaffirm [‚ri·ə'fʌrm] *tr* nochmals beteuern
real ['ri·əl] *adj* wirklich; (*genuine*) echt; (*friend*) wahr
re'al estate' *s* Immobilien *pl*
re'al-estate' a'gent *s* Immobilienmakler —in *mf*
re'al-estate tax' *s* Grundsteuer *f*
realist ['ri·əlɪst] *s* Realist —in *mf*
realistic [ri·ə'lɪstɪk] *adj* wirklichkeitsnah, realistisch
reality [ri'ælti] *s* Wirklichkeit *f;* **in r.** wirklich; **realities** (*facts*) Tatsachen *pl*
realize ['ri·ə‚laɪz] *tr* einsehen; (*a profit*) erzielen; (*a goal*) verwirklichen; (*a good*) realisieren
really ['ri·əli] *adv* wirklich; **not r.** eigentlich nicht
realm [relm] *s* Königreich *n;* (fig) Reich *n*, Gebiet *n;* **within the r. of possibility** im Rahmen des Möglichen
realtor ['ri·əltər] *s* Immobilienmakler —in *mf*
ream [rim] *s* Ries *n* ‖ *tr* ausbohren
reamer ['rimər] *s* Reibahle *f*
reap [rip] *tr* (*cut*) mähen; (& fig) ernten
reaper ['ripər] *s* Mäher —in *mf;* (mach) Mähmaschine *f*
reappear [‚ri·ə'pɪr] *intr* wiederauftauchen, wiedererscheinen
rearmament [ri'ɑrməmənt] *s* Wiederscheinen *n*
reappoint [‚ri·ə'pɔɪnt] *tr* wieder anstellen
rear [rɪr] *adj* hintere, rückwärtig ‖ *s* Hinterseite *f;* (*of an army*) Nachhut *f;* (sl) Hintern *m;* **bring up the r.** den Schluß bilden; (mil) den Zug beschließen; **from the r.** von hinten; **to the r.** nach hinten; **to the r., march!** kehrt, marsch! ‖ *tr* (*children*) aufziehen; (*animals*) züchten; (*a structure, one's head*) aufrichten ‖ *intr* sich bäumen
rear' ad'miral *s* Konteradmiral *m*
rear' ax'le *s* Hinterachse *f*
rear' end' *s* (sl) Hintern *m*
rear' guard' *s* (mil) Nachhut *f*
rear' gun'ner *s* Heckschütze *m*

rearm [ri'ɑrm] *tr* wieder aufrüsten

rearmament [ri'ɑrməmənt] *s* Wiederaufrüstung *f*

rearrange [ˌri·ə'rendʒ] *tr* umstellen

rear' seat' *s* Hintersitz *m*

rear'-view mir'ror *s* Rückspiegel *m*

rear'-wheel drive' *s* Hinterradantrieb *m*

rear' win'dow *s* (aut) Heckfenster *n*

reason ['rizən] *s* Vernunft *f*; (*cause*) Grund *m*; **by r. of** auf Grund (*genit*); **for this r.** aus diesem Grund; **listen to r.** sich belehren lassen; **not listen to r.** sich (*dat*) nichts sagen lassen; **not without good r.** nicht umsonst || *tr*—**r. out** durchdenken || *intr*—**r. with** vernünftig reden mit

reasonable ['rizənəbəl] *adj* (*person*) vernünftig; (*price*) solid; (*wares*) preiswert

reassemble [ˌri·ə'sembəl] *tr* (*people*) wieder versammeln; (mach) wieder zusammenbauen || *intr* sich wieder sammeln

reassert [ˌri·ə'sert] *tr* wieder behaupten

reassurance [ˌri·ə'ʃurəns] *s* Beruhigung *f*

reassure [ri·ə'ʃur] *tr* beruhigen

reawaken [ˌri·ə'wekən] *tr* wieder erwecken || *intr* wieder erwachen

rebate ['ribet] *s* Rabatt *m*

re·bel ['rebəl] *adj* Rebellen- || *s* Rebell –in *mf* || [rɪ'bɛl] *v* (*pret & pp* –**belled**; *ger* –**belling**) *intr* rebellieren

rebellion [rɪ'beljən] *s* Aufstand *m*, Rebellion *f*

rebellious [rɪ'beljəs] *adj* aufständisch

rebirth ['rib₃rθ] *s* Wiedergeburt *f*

rebore [ri'bor] *tr* nachbohren

rebound ['ri,baund] *s* Rückprall *m* || [ri'baund] *intr* zurückprallen

rebroad·cast [ri'brɔd,kæst] *s* Wiederholungssendung *f* || *v* (*pret & pp* –**cast** & –**casted**) *tr* nochmals übertragen

rebuff [rɪ'bʌf] *s* Zurückweisung *f* || *tr* schroff abweisen

re·build [ri'bɪld] *v* (*pret & pp* –**built**) *tr* wiederaufbauen; (mach) überholen; (*confidence*) wiederherstellen

rebuke [rɪ'bjuk] *s* Verweis *m* || *tr* verweisen

re·but [rɪ'bʌt] *v* (*pret & pp* –**butted**; *ger* –**butting**) *tr* widerlegen

rebuttal [rɪ'bʌtəl] *s* Widerlegung *f*

recall [rɪ'kɔl], ['rikəl] *s* (*recollection*) Erinnerungsvermögen *n*; (com) Zurücknahme *f*; (dipl, pol) Abberufung *f*; **beyond r.** unwiderruflich || [rɪ'kɔl] *tr* (*remember*) sich erinnern an (*dat*); (*an ambassador*) abberufen; (*workers*) zurückrufen; (mil) wiedereinberufen

recant [rɪ'kænt] *tr & intr* (öffentlich) widerrufen

re·cap ['ri,kæp] *s* Zusammenfassung *f* || *v* (*pret & pp* –**capped**; *ger* –**capping**) *tr* zusammenfassen; (*a tire*) runderneuern

recapitulate [ˌrikə'pɪtʃə,let] *tr* zusammenfassen

recapitulation [ˌrikə,pɪtʃə'leʃən] *s* Rekapitulation *f*, Zusammenfassung *f*

re·cast ['ri,kæst] *s* Umguß *m* || [ri'kæst] *v* (*pret & pp* –**cast**) *tr* umgießen; (*a sentence*) umarbeiten; (theat) neubesetzen

recede [rɪ'sid] *intr* zurückgehen; (*become more distant*) zurückweichen

reced'ing *adj* (*forehead, chin*) fliehend

receipt [rɪ'sit] *s* Quittung *f*; **acknowledge r. of** den Empfang bestätigen (*genit*); **receipts** Eingänge *pl* || *tr* quittieren

receive [rɪ'siv] *tr* bekommen, erhalten; (*a guest*) empfangen; (*pay*) beziehen; (rad) empfangen

receiver [rɪ'sivər] *s* Empfänger –in *mf*; (jur) Zwangsverwalter –in *mf*; (telp) Hörer *m*

receiv'ership' *s* Zwangsverwaltung *f*

recent ['risənt] *adj* neu, jung; **in r. years** in den letzten Jahren; **of r. date** neueren Datums

recently ['risəntli] *adv* kürzlich

receptacle [rɪ'septəkəl] *s* Behälter *m*; (elec) Steckdose *f*

reception [rɪ'sepʃən] *s* (& rad) Empfang *m*

recep'tion desk' *s* Empfang *m*

receptionist [rɪ'sepənɪst] *s* Empfangsdame *f*; (med) Sprechstundenhilfe *f*

receptive [rɪ'septɪv] *adj* (**to**) aufgeschlossen (für)

recess [rɪ'ses], ['rises] *s* (*alcove*) Nische *f*; (*cleft*) Einschnitt *m*; (*at school*) Pause *f*; (jur) Unterbrechung *f*; (parl) Ferien *pl* || [rɪ'ses] *tr* (*place in a recess*) versenken || *intr* (*until*) sich vertagen (auf *acc*)

recession [rɪ'seʃən] *s* Rezession *f*, Rückgang *m*

recharge [rɪ'tʃɑrdʒ] *tr* wieder aufladen

recipe ['resɪ,pi] *s* Rezept *n*

recipient [rɪ'sɪpɪ·ənt] *s* Empfänger –in *mf*

reciprocal [rɪ'sɪprəkəl] *adj* gegenseitig

reciprocate [rɪ'sɪprə,ket] *tr* sich erkenntlich zeigen für || *intr* sich erkenntlich zeigen

reciprocity [ˌresɪ'prɑsɪti] *s* Gegenseitigkeit *f*

recital [rɪ'saɪtəl] *s* Vortrag *m*

recite [rɪ'saɪt] *tr* vortragen

reckless ['reklɪs] *adj* (*careless of consequences*) unbekümmert; (*lacking caution*) leichtsinnig; (*negligent*) fahrlässig

reck'less driv'ing *s* rücksichtsloses Fahren *n*

reckon ['rekən] *tr* (*count*) rechnen; (*compute*) (coll) schätzen || *intr* rechnen; (coll) schätzen; **r. on** rechnen auf (*acc*); **r. with** (*deal with*) abrechnen mit; (*take into consideration*) rechnen mit

reck'oning *s* (*accounting*) Abrechnung *f*; (*computation*) Berechnung *f*; (aer, naut) Besteck *n*

reclaim [rɪ'klem] *tr* (*demand back*) zurückfordern; (*from wastes*) rückgewinnen; (*land*) urbar machen

reclamation [ˌreklə'meʃən] s (of land) Urbarmachung f

recline [rɪ'klaɪn] intr ruhen; **r. against** sich lehnen an (acc); **r. in** (a chair) sich zurücklehnen in (dat)

recluse ['reklus] s Einsiedler –in mf

recognition [ˌrekəg'nɪʃən] s Wiedererkennung f; (acknowledgement) Anerkennung f; **gain r.** zur Geltung kommen

recognizable [ˌrekəg'naɪzəbəl] adj erkennbar

recognize ['rekəg,naɪz] tr (by) erkennen (an dat); **r. as** anerkennen als

recoil ['rɪkɔɪl] s (of a rifle) Rückstoß m; (arti) Rücklauf m || [rɪ'kɔɪl] intr (in fear) zurückfahren; (from, e.g., a challenge) zurückschrecken vor (dat); (said of a rifle) zurückstoßen; (arti) zurücklaufen

recoilless [rɪ'kɔɪllɪs] adj rückstoßfrei

recollect [ˌrekə'lekt] tr sich erinnern an (acc)

recollection [ˌrekə'lekʃən] s Erinnerung f

recommend [ˌrekə'mend] tr empfehlen

recommendation [ˌrekəmən'deʃən] s Empfehlung f

recompense ['rekəm,pens] s (for) Vergütung f (für) || tr vergüten

reconcile ['rekən,saɪl] tr (with) versöhnen (mit); **become reconciled** sich versöhnen; **r. oneself to** sich abfinden mit

reconciliation [ˌrekən,sɪlɪ'eʃən] s Versöhnung f, Aussöhnung f

recondite ['rekən,daɪt] adj (deep) tiefgründig; (obscure) dunkel

recondition [ˌrikən'dɪʃən] tr wiederinstandsetzen

reconnaissance [rɪ'kanɪsəns] s Aufklärung f

reconnoiter [ˌrekə'nɔɪtər] tr erkunden || intr aufklären

reconquer [rɪ'kaŋkər] tr zurückerobern

reconquest [rɪ'kaŋkwest] s Zurückeroberung f

reconsider [ˌrikən'sɪdər] tr noch einmal erwägen

reconstruct [ˌrikən'strʌkt] tr (rebuild) wiederaufbauen; (make over) umbauen; (e.g., events of a case) rekonstruieren

record ['rekərd] adj Rekord– || s (highest achievement) Rekord m; (document) Akte f, Protokoll n; (documentary evidence) Aufzeichnung f; (mus) Schallplatte f; **have a criminal r.** vorbestraft sein; **keep a r. of** Buch führen über (acc); **make a r. of** zu Protokoll nehmen; **off the r.** inoffiziell; **on r.** bisher registriert; **set a r.** e–n Rekord aufstellen || [rɪ'kɔrd] tr (in writing) aufzeichnen; (officially) protokollieren; (on tape or disk) aufnehmen || intr Schallplatten aufnehmen

rec'ord chang'er s Plattenwechsler m

recorder [rɪ'kɔrdər] s Protokollführer –in mf; (device) Zähler m; (on tape or disk) Aufnahmegerät; (mus) Blockflöte f

rec'ord hold'er s Rekordler –in mf

record'ing adj aufzeichnend; (on tape or disk) Aufnahme– || s Aufzeichnung f; (on tape or disk) Tonaufnahme f

record'ing sec'retary s Protokollführer –in mf

rec'ord play'er s Plattenspieler m

recount ['rɪ,kaunt] s Nachzählung f || [rɪ'kaunt] tr (count again) nachzählen || [rɪ'kaunt] tr (relate) im einzelnen erzählen

recoup [rɪ'kup] tr (losses) wieder einbringen; (a fortune) wiedererlangen; (reimburse) entschädigen

recourse [rɪ'kors], ['rikors] s (to) Zuflucht f (zu); (jur) Regreß m; **have r. to** seine Zuflucht nehmen zu

recover [rɪ'kʌvər] tr (get back) wiedererlangen; (losses) wiedereinbringen; (e.g., a spent rocket) bergen; (one's balance) wiederfinden; (e.g., a chair) neu beziehen || intr (from) sich erholen (von)

recovery [rɪ'kʌvəri] s Wiedererlangung f, Rückgewinnung f; (of health) Genesung f; (of a rocket) Bergung f

recreation [ˌrekrɪ'eʃən] s Erholung f

recrea'tion room' s Unterhaltungsraum m

recruit [rɪ'krut] s Rekrut m || (& mil) rekrutieren; **be recruited from** sich rekrutieren aus

recruit'ing of'ficer s Werbeoffizier m

recruitment [rɪ'krutmənt] s Rekrutierung f; (mil) Rekrutenaushebung f

rectangle ['rek,tæŋgəl] s Rechteck n

rectangular [rek'tæŋgjələr] adj rechteckig

rectifier ['rektə,faɪ·ər] s Berichtiger m; (elec) Gleichrichter m

recti·fy ['rektɪ,faɪ] v (pret & pp –fied) tr berichtigen; (elec) gleichrichten

rector ['rektər] s Rektor m

rectory ['rektəri] s Pfarrhaus n

rec·tum ['rektəm] s (–ta [tə]) Mastdarm m

recumbent [rɪ'kʌmbənt] adj liegend

recuperate [rɪ'k(j)upə,ret] intr sich (wieder) erholen

re·cur [rɪ'kʌr] v (pret & pp –curred; ger –curring) intr wiederkehren

recurrence [rɪ'kʌrəns] s Wiederkehr f

red [red] adj (redder; reddest) rot || s Rot n, Röte f; **be in the red** in den Roten Zahlen stecken; **Red** (pol) Rote mf; **see red** wild werden

red' ant' s rote Waldameise f

red'bird' s Kardinal m

red'blood' adj lebensprühend

red'breast' s Rotkehlchen n

red' cab'bage s Rotkohl m

red' car'pet s (fig) roter Teppich m

red' cent' s—not give a r. for keinen roten Heller geben für

red'-cheeked' adj rotbäckig

Red' Cross', the s das Rote Kreuz

redden ['redən] tr röten, rot machen || intr erröten, rot werden

reddish ['redɪʃ] adj rötlich

redecorate [rɪ'dekə‚ret] *tr* neu dekorieren

redeem [rɪ'dim] *tr* zurückkaufen; (*a pawned article, promise*) einlösen; **r. oneself** seine Ehre wiederherstellen

redeemable [rɪ'diməbəl] *adj* (fin) ablösbar, kündbar

Redeemer [rɪ'dimər] *s* Erlöser *m*

redemption [rɪ'dempʃən] *s* Rückkauf *m*, Wiedereinlösung *f*; (relig) Erlösung *f*

red'-haired' *adj* rothaarig

red'-hand'ed *adj*—**catch s.o. r.** j–n auf frischer Tat ertappen

red'head' *s* Rotkopf *m*

red' her'ring *s* Bückling *m*; (fig) Ablenkungsmanöver *n*

red'-hot' *adj* glühend heiß, rotglühend

redirect [‚ridɪ'rekt] *tr* umdirigieren

rediscover [‚ridɪs'kʌvər] *tr* wiederentdecken

red'-let'ter day' *s* Glückstag *m*

red' light' *s* rotes Licht *n*

red'-light' dis'trict *s* Bordellviertel *n*

red' man' *s* Rothaut *f*

redness ['rednɪs] *s* Röte *f*

re•do [ri'du] *v* (*pret* —**did**; *pp* —**done**) *tr* neu machen; (*redecorate*) renovieren

redolent ['redələnt] *adj* (**with**) duftend (**nach**)

redoubt [rɪ'daut] *s* Redoute *f*

redound [rɪ'daund] *intr*—**r. to** gereichen zu

red' pep'per *s* spanischer Pfeffer *m*

redress [rɪ'dres] *s* Wiedergutmachung *f* ‖ *tr* wiedergutmachen

Red' Rid'inghood' *s* Rotkäppchen *n*

red'skin' *s* Rothaut *f*

red' tape' *s* Amtsschimmel *m*

reduce [rɪ'd(j)us] *tr* reduzieren, verringern; (*prices*) herabsetzen; (math) (ab)kürzen

reduction [rɪ'dʌkʃən] *s* Verminderung *f*; (*gradual reduction*) Abbau *m*; (*in prices*) Absetzung *f*; (*in weight*) Abnahme *f*

redundant [rɪ'dʌndənt] *adj* überflüssig

red' wine' *s* Rotwein *m*

red'wing' *s* Rotdrossel *f*

red'wood' *s* Rotholz *n*

reecho [ri'eko] *tr* wiederhallen lassen ‖ *intr* wiederhallen

reed [rid] *s* Schilf *n*; (*in mouthpiece*) Rohrblatt *n*; (*of metal*) Zunge *f*; (*pastoral pipe*) Hirtenflöte *f*

reedit [ri'edɪt] *tr* neu herausgeben

reeducate [ri'edʒu‚ket] *tr* umerziehen

reef [rif] *s* Riff *n*; (naut) Reff *n* ‖ *tr* (naut) reffen

reek [rik] *intr* (**of**) riechen (**nach**)

reel [ril] *s* (*sway*) Taumeln *n*; (*for cables*) Trommel *f*; (angl, cin) Spule *f*; (min, naut) Haspel *f* ‖ *tr* (angl, cin) spulen; (min, naut) haspeln; **r. in** (*a fish*) einholen; **r. off** abhaspeln; (fig) herunterrasseln ‖ *intr* taumeln

reelect [‚ri•ɪ'lekt] *tr* wiederwählen

reelection [‚ri•ɪ'lekʃən] *s* Wiederwahl *f*

reenlist [‚ri•en'lɪst] *tr* wieder anwerben ‖ *intr* sich weiterverpflichten

reenlistment [‚ri•en'lɪstmənt] *s* Weiterverpflichtung *f*

reentry [rɪ'entri] *s* Wiedereintritt *m*

reexamination [‚ri•eg‚zæmɪ'neʃən] *s* Nachprüfung *f*

re•fer [rɪ'fʌr] *v* (*pret* & *pp* —**ferred**; *ger* —**ferring**) *tr*—**r. s.o. to** j–n verweisen an (*acc*) ‖ *intr*—**r. to** hinweisen auf (*acc*); (*e.g., to an earlier correspondence*) sich beziehen auf (*acc*)

referee [‚refə'ri] *s* (box) Ringrichter *m*; (sport) Schiedsrichter *m* ‖ *tr* als Schiedsrichter fungieren bei ‖ *intr* als Schiedsrichter fungieren

reference ['refərəns] *s* (**to**) Hinweis *m* (auf *acc*); (*person or document*) Referenz *f*; **in r. to** in Bezug auf (*acc*); **make r. to** hinweisen auf (*acc*)

ref'erence lib'rary *s* Handbibliothek *f*

ref'erence work' *s* Nachschlagewerk *n*

referen•dum [‚refə'rendəm] *s* (—**da** [də]) Volksentscheid *m*

referral [rɪ'fʌrəl] *s* (**to**) Zuweisung *f* (an *acc*, auf *acc*); **by r.** auf Empfehlung

refill ['rifɪl] *s* Nachfüllung *f*; (*for a pencil, ball-point pen*) Ersatzmine *f* ‖ [rɪ'fɪl] *tr* nachfüllen

refine [rɪ'faɪn] *tr* (metal) läutern; (*oil, sugar*) raffinieren; (fig) verfeinern

refinement [rɪ'faɪnmənt] *s* Läuterung *f*; (*of oil, sugar*) Raffination *f*; (fig) Verfeinerung *f*

refinery [rɪ'faɪnəri] *s* Raffinerie *f*

reflect [rɪ'flekt] *tr* (& fig) widerspiegeln ‖ *intr* (*throw back rays*) reflektieren; (**on**) nachdenken (über *acc*); **r. on** (*comment on*) sich äußern über (*acc*); (*bring reproach on*) ein schlechtes Licht werfen auf (*acc*)

reflection [rɪ'flekʃən] *s* (*e.g., of light*) Reflexion *f*; (*reflected image*) Spiegelbild *n*; (*thought*) Überlegung *f*; **that's no r. on you** das färbt nicht auf Sie ab

reflector [rɪ'flektər] *s* Reflektor *m*

reflex ['rifleks] *s* Reflex *m*

reflexive [rɪ'fleksɪv] *adj* (gram) reflexiv ‖ *s* Reflexivform *f*

reforestation [‚rifɔrɪs'teʃən] *s* Aufforstung *f*

reform [rɪ'fɔrm] *s* Reform *f* ‖ *tr* reformieren, verbessern ‖ *intr* sich bessern

reformation [‚refər'meʃən] *s* Besserung *f*; **Reformation** Reformation *f*

reformatory [rɪ'fɔrmə‚tori] *s* Besserungsanstalt *f*

reformer [rɪ'fɔrmər] *s* Reformator –in *mf*

reform' school' *s* Besserungsanstalt *f*

refraction [rɪ'frækʃən] *s* Ablenkung *f*

refrain [rɪ'fren] *s* Kehrreim *m* ‖ *intr*—**r. from** sich enthalten (*genit*); **r. from** (*ger*) es unterlassen zu (*inf*)

refresh [rɪ'freʃ] *tr* erfrischen; (*the memory*) auffrischen

refresh'er course' [rɪ'freʃər] *s* Auffrischungskurs *m*

refresh'ing *adj* erfrischend

refreshment [rɪ'freʃmənt] s Erfrischung f

refresh'ment stand' s Erfrischungsstand m

refrigerant [rɪ'frɪdʒərənt] s Kühlmittel n

refrigerate [rɪ'frɪdʒə,ret] tr kühlen

refrigerator [rɪ'frɪdʒə,retər] s Kühlschrank m; (walk-in type) Kühlraum m

refrig'erator car' s (rr) Kühlwagen m

re·fuel [rɪ'fjul] v (pret & pp –fuel[l]ed; ger –fuel[l]ing) tr auftanken || intr tanken

refuge ['refjudʒ] s Zuflucht f; take r. in (sich) flüchten in (acc)

refugee [,refju'dʒi] s Flüchtling m

refugee' camp' s Flüchtlingslager n

refund ['rifʌnd] s Zurückzahlung f || [rɪ'fʌnd] tr (pay back) zurückzahlen || [ri'fʌnd] tr (fund again) neu fundieren

refurnish [rɪ'fʌrnɪʃ] tr neu möblieren

refusal [rɪ'fjuzəl] s Ablehnung f

refuse ['refjus] s Abfall m || [rɪ'fjuz] tr ablehnen; r. to (inf) sich weigern zu (inf)

refutation [,refju'teʃən] s Widerlegung f

refute [rɪ'fjut] tr widerlegen

regain [rɪ'gen] tr zurückgewinnen

regal ['rigəl] adj königlich

regale [rɪ'gel] tr (delight) ergötzen; (entertain) reichlich bewirten

regalia [rɪ'gelɪ·ə] spl Insignien pl

regard [rɪ'gɑrd] s (for) Rücksicht f (auf acc); best regards to herzlichster Gruß an (acc); have little r. for wenig achten; in every r. in jeder Hinsicht; in (or with) r. to in Hinsicht auf (acc); in this r. in dieser Hinsicht; without r. for ohne Rücksicht auf (acc) || tr betrachten; as regards in Bezug auf (acc)

regard'ing prep hinsichtlich (genit)

regardless [rɪ'gɑrdlɪs] adv (coll) ungeniert; r. of ungeachtet (genit)

regatta [rɪ'gætə] s Regatta f

regency ['ridʒənsɪ] s Regentschaft f

regenerate [rɪ'dʒenə,ret] tr regenerieren

regent ['ridʒənt] s Regent –in mf

regicide ['redʒɪ,saɪd] s (act) Königsmord m; (person) Königsmörder –in mf

regime [re'ʒim] s Regime n

regiment ['redʒɪmənt] s (mil) Regiment n || ['redʒɪ,ment] tr reglementieren

regimental [,redʒɪ'mentəl] adj Regiments—

region ['ridʒən] s Gegend f, Region f

regional ['ridʒənəl] adj regional

register ['redʒɪstər] s Register n, Verzeichnis n || tr registrieren; (students) immatrikulieren; (feelings) erkennen lassen || intr sich einschreiben lassen; (at a hotel) sich eintragen lassen

reg'istered let'ter s eingeschriebener Brief m

reg'istered nurse' s (staatlich) geprüfte Krankenschwester f

registrar ['redʒɪstrɑr] s Registrator –in mf

registration [,redʒɪs'treʃən] s (e.g., of firearms) Registrierung f; (for a course; at a hotel) Anmeldung f; (of a trademark) Eintragung f; (aut) Zulassung f; (educ) Einschreibung f

registra'tion blank' s Meldeformular n

registra'tion fee' s Anmeldegebühr f

registra'tion num'ber s Registriernummer f

regression [rɪ'greʃən] s Rückgang m

regret [rɪ'gret] s (over) Bedauern n (über acc) || v (pret & pp –regretted; ger regretting) tr bedauern; I r. to say es tut mir leid, sagen zu müssen

regrettable [rɪ'gretəbəl] adj bedauerlich

regroup [rɪ'grup] tr umgruppieren

regular ['regjələr] adj (usual) gewöhnlich; (pulse, breathing, features, intervals) regelmäßig; r. army stehendes Heer n; r. guy (coll) Pfundskerl m; r. officer Berufsoffizier –in mf

regularity [,regjə'lærɪtɪ] s Regelmäßigkeit f

regulate ['regjə,let] tr regeln

regulation [,regjə'leʃən] s Regelung f; (rule) Vorschrift f, Bestimmung f; against regulations vorschriftswidrig

regulator ['regjə,letər] s Regler m

rehabilitate [,rihə'bɪlɪ,tet] tr rehabilitieren

rehash [rɪ'hæʃ] tr (coll) aufwärmen

rehearsal [rɪ'hʌrsəl] s Probe f

rehearse [rɪ'hʌrs] tr & intr proben

rehire [rɪ'haɪr] tr wiedereinstellen

reign [ren] s Regierung f; (period of rule) Regierungszeit f || intr regieren; r. over herrschen über (acc)

reimburse [ri·ɪm'bʌrs] tr (costs) rückerstatten; r. s.o. for s.th. j–m etw vergüten

rein [ren] s Zügel m; give free r. to die Zügel schießen lassen (dat) || tr —r. in (a horse) parieren

reincarnation [,ri·ɪnkɑr'neʃən] s Reinkarnation f, Wiedergeburt f

rein'deer' s Rentier n

reinforce [,ri·ɪn'fors] tr verstärken

reinforced' concrete' s Stahlbeton m

reinforcement [,ri·ɪn'forsmənt] s Verstärkung f; reinforcements (mil) Verstärkungen pl

reinstate [,ri·ɪn'stet] tr (in) wiedereinsetzen (in acc)

reiterate [ri'ɪtə,ret] tr wiederholen

reject ['ridʒekt] s Ausschußware f || [rɪ'dʒekt] tr ablehnen, zurückweisen; (a request, appeal) abweisen

rejection [rɪ'dʒekʃən] s Ablehnung f; (of a request, appeal) Abweisung f

rejoice [rɪ'dʒɔɪs] intr frohlocken

rejoin [rɪ'dʒɔɪn] tr (answer) erwidern; (a group) sich wieder anschließen (dat)

rejoinder [rɪ'dʒɔɪndər] s Erwiderung f; (jur) Duplik f

rejuvenate [rɪ'dʒuvɪ,net] tr verjüngen

rekindle [rɪ'kɪndəl] tr wieder anzünden; (fig) wieder entzünden

relapse [rɪ'læps] s (& pathol) Rückfall

m ‖ *intr* (*into*) wieder verfallen (in *acc*)

relate [rɪˈlet] *tr* (*a story*) erzählen; (*connect*) verknüpfen; **r. s.th. to s.th.** etw auf etw [*acc*] beziehen ‖ *intr*—**r. to** in Beziehung stehen mit

relat'ed *adj* (*by blood*) verwandt; (*by marriage*) verschwägert; (*subjects*) benachbart

relation [rɪˈleʃən] *s* Beziehung *f*, Verhältnis *n*; (*relative*) Verwandte *mf*; **in r. to** in Bezug auf (*acc*); **relations** (*sex*) Verkehr *m*

rela'tionship *s* (*connection*) Beziehung *f*; (*kinship*) Verwandtschaft *f*

relative [ˈrelətɪv] *adj* relativ, verhältnismäßig; **r. to** bezüglich (*genit*) ‖ *s* Verwandte *mf*

rel'ative clause' *s* Relativsatz *m*

rel'ative pro'noun *s* Relativpronomen *n*

relativity [ˌreləˈtɪvɪti] *s* Relativität *f*

relax [rɪˈlæks] *tr* auflockern; (*muscles*) entspannen ‖ *intr* sich entspannen

relaxation [ˌrilækˈseʃən] *s* Entspannung *f*; **r. of tension** Entspannung *f*

relay [ˈrile] *s* Relais *n*; (*sport*) Staffel *f* ‖ [rɪˈle] *v* (*pret & pp* –**layed**) *tr* übermitteln; (*through relay stations*) übertragen

re'lay race' *s* Staffellauf *m*

re'lay team' *s* Staffel *f*

release [rɪˈlis] *s* (*from*) Entlassung *f* (aus); (*of bombs*) Abwurf *m*; (*of news*) Mitteilung *f* ‖ *tr* entlassen; (*a film, book*) freigeben; (*bombs*) abwerfen; (*energy*) freisetzen; (*brakes*) lösen; **r. the clutch** auskuppeln

relegate [ˈrelɪˌget] *tr* (*to*) verweisen (an *acc*); **r. to second position** auf den zweiten Platz verweisen

relent [rɪˈlent] *intr* (*let up*) nachlassen; (*yield*) sich erweichen lassen

relentless [rɪˈlentlɪs] *adj* (*tireless*) unermüdlich; (*unappeasable*) unerbittlich; (*never-ending*) unaufhörlich

relevant [ˈrelɪvənt] *adj* sachdienlich

reliable [rɪˈlaɪəbl] *adj* zuverlässig

reliance [rɪˈlaɪəns] *s* Vertrauen *n*

relic [ˈrelɪk] *s* Reliquie *f*; **r. of the past** Zeuge *m* der Vergangenheit

relief [rɪˈlif] *s* Erleichterung *f*; (*for the poor*) Armenunterstützung *f*; (*replacement*) Ablösung *f*; (*sculpture*) Relief *n*; **on r.** von Sozialhilfe lebend; **bring r.** Linderung schaffen; **go on r.** stempeln gehen

relief' map' *s* Reliefkarte *f*

relieve [rɪˈliv] *tr* erleichtern; (*from guard duty*) ablösen; **r. oneself** seine Notdurft verrichten

religion [rɪˈlɪdʒən] *s* Religion *f*

religious [rɪˈlɪdʒəs] *adj* religiös; (*order*) geistlich

relinquish [rɪˈlɪŋkwɪʃ] *tr* aufgeben; **r. the right to s.th. to s.o.** j–m das Recht auf etw [*acc*] überlassen

relish [ˈrelɪʃ] *s* (*for*) Genuß *m* (an *acc*); (*condiment*) Würze *f* ‖ *tr* genießen

reluctance [rɪˈlʌktəns] *s* Widerstreben *n*

reluctant [rɪˈlʌktənt] *adj* widerstrebend; **be r. to do s.th.** etw ungern tun

reluctantly [rɪˈlʌktəntli] *adv* ungern

re·ly [rɪˈlaɪ] *v* (*pret & pp* –**lied**) *intr*—**r. on** sich verlassen auf (*acc*)

remain [rɪˈmen] *s*—**remains** Überreste *pl*; (*corpse*) sterbliche Reste *pl* ‖ *intr* bleiben; (*at end of letter*) verbleiben; **r. behind** zurückbleiben; **r. seated** sitzenbleiben; **r. steady** (*said of prices*) sich behaupten

remainder [rɪˈmendər] *s* Restbestand *m*, Rest *m* ‖ *tr* verramschen

remark [rɪˈmɑrk] *s* Bemerkung *f* ‖ *tr* bemerken

remarkable [rɪˈmɑrkəbəl] *adj* markant, bemerkenswert

remar·ry [rɪˈmæri] *v* (*pret & pp* –**ried**) *tr* sich wiederverheiraten mit ‖ *intr* sich wiederverheiraten

reme·dy [ˈremɪdi] *s* (*for*) Heilmittel *n* (für); (*fig*) (*for*) Gegenmittel *n* (gegen) ‖ *v* (*pret & pp* –**died**) *tr* abhelfen (*dat*); (*damage, shortage*) abheben

remember [rɪˈmembər] *tr* sich erinnern an (*acc*); **r. me** to empfehlen Sie mich (*dat*) ‖ *intr* sich erinnern

remembrance [rɪˈmembrəns] *s* Erinnerung *f*; **in r. of** zum Andenken an (*acc*)

remind [rɪˈmaɪnd] *tr* (*of*) erinnern (an *acc*); **r. s.o. to** (*inf*) j–n mahnen zu (*inf*)

reminder [rɪˈmaɪndər] *s* (*note*) Zettel *m*; (*from a creditor*) Mahnung *f*

reminisce [ˌremɪˈnɪs] *intr* in Erinnerungen schwelgen

remiss [rɪˈmɪs] *adj* nachlässig

remission [rɪˈmɪʃən] *s* Nachlaß *m*

re·mit [rɪˈmɪt] *v* (*pret & pp* –**mitted**; *ger* –**mitting**) *tr* (*in cash*) übersenden; (*by check*) überweisen; (*forgive*) vergeben

remittance [rɪˈmɪtəns] *s* (*in cash*) Übersendung *f*; (*by check*) Überweisung *f*

remnant [ˈremnənt] *s* Rest *m*; (*of cloth*) Stoffrest *m*

remod·el [rɪˈmɑdəl] *v* (*pret & pp* –**el[l]ed**; *ger* –**el[l]ing**) *tr* umgestalten; (*a house*) umbauen

remonstrate [rɪˈmɑnstret] *intr* protestieren; **r. with s.o.** j–m Vorwürfe machen

remorse [rɪˈmɔrs] *s* Gewissensbisse *pl*

remorseful [rɪˈmɔrsfəl] *adj* reumütig

remote [rɪˈmot] *adj* fern; (*possibility*) vage; (*idea*) blaß; (*resemblance*) entfernt; (*secluded*) abgelegen

remote' control' *s* Fernsteuerung *f*; (*telv*) Fernbedienung *f*; **guide by r.** fernlenken

removable [rɪˈmuvəbəl] *adj* entfernbar

removal [rɪˈmuvəl] *s* Entfernung *f*; (*by truck*) Abfuhr *f*; (*from office*) Absetzung *f*

remove [rɪˈmuv] *tr* entfernen; (*clothes*) ablegen; (*one's hat*) abnehmen; (*e.g., dishes from the table*) abräumen; (*a stain*) entfernen; (*from office*) absetzen; (*furniture*) ausräumen

remuneration [rɪˌmjunəˈreʃən] *s* Vergütung *f*

renaissance [ˌrenəˈsɑns] *s* Renaissance *f*

rend [rend] *v* (*pret & pp* **rent** [rent]) *tr* (& *fig*) zerreißen

render [ˈrendər] *tr* (*give*) geben; (*a service*) leisten; (*honor*) erweisen; (*thanks*) abstatten; (*a verdict*) fällen; (*translate; play*, *e.g., on the piano*) wiedergeben; **r. harmless** unschädlich machen

rendez·vous [ˈrɑndəˌvu] *s* (**-vous** [ˌvuz]) Rendezvous *n*, Treffpunkt *m*; (*mil*) Sammelplatz *m* ‖ *v* (*pret & pp* **-voused** [ˌvud]; *ger* **-vousing** [ˌvu·ɪŋ]) *intr* sich treffen; (*mil*) sich versammeln

rendition [renˈdɪʃən] *s* Wiedergabe *f*

renegade [ˈreniˌged] *s* Renegat *–in mf*

renege [rɪˈnig] *s* Renonce *f* ‖ *intr* (*cards*) nicht bedienen; **r. on** nicht einhalten

renew [rɪˈn(j)u] *tr* erneuern; (*e.g., a passport*) verlängern lassen

renewable [rɪˈn(j)u-əbəl] *adj* erneuerbar

renewal [rɪˈn(j)u-əl] *s* Erneuerung *f*; (*e.g., of a passport*) Verlängerung *f*

renounce [rɪˈnaʊns] *tr* verzichten auf (*acc*)

renovate [ˈrenəˌvet] *tr* renovieren; (*fig*) erneuern

renovation [ˌrenəˈveʃən] *s* Renovierung *f*

renown [rɪˈnaʊn] *s* Ruhm *m*

renowned [rɪˈnaʊnd] *adj* (**for**) berühmt (**wegen**)

rent [rent] *adj* zerrissen ‖ *s* Miete *f*; (*tear*) Riß *m* ‖ *tr* mieten; **r. out** vermieten

rental [ˈrentəl] *s* Miete *f*

rent′al serv′ice *s* Verleih *m*

rent′ed car′ *s* Mietwagen *m*, Mietauto *n*

renter [ˈrentər] *s* Mieter *–in mf*

renunciation [rɪˌnʌnsɪˈeʃən] *s* (**of**) Verzicht *m* (auf *acc*)

reopen [riˈopən] *tr* wieder öffnen; (*a business*) wieder eröffnen; (*an argument; school year*) wieder beginnen ‖ *intr* (*said of a shop or business*) wieder geöffnet werden; (*said of a school year*) wieder beginnen

reopening [riˈopənɪŋ] *s* (*of a business*) Wiedereröffnung *f*; (*of school*) Wiederbeginn *m*; (*jur*) Wiederaufnahme *f*

reorder [riˈɔrdər] *tr* nachbestellen

reorganization [ˌri·ɔrgənɪˈzeʃən] *s* Reorganisation *f*, Neuordnung *f*

reorganize [riˈɔrgəˌnaɪz] *tr* reorganisieren; (*an administration*) umbilden

repack [riˈpæk] *tr* umpacken

repair [rɪˈper] *s* Ausbesserung *f*, Reparatur *f*; **in bad r.** in schlechtem Zustand; **keep in good r.** im Stande halten ‖ *tr* ausbessern, reparieren ‖ *intr* (**to**) sich begeben (nach, zu)

repair′ gang′ *s* Störungstrupp *m*

repair′ shop′ *s* Reparaturwerkstatt *f*

repaper [riˈpepər] *tr* neu tapezieren

reparation [ˌrepəˈreʃən] *s* Wiedergutmachung *f*; **reparations** Reparationen *pl*, Kriegsentschädigung *f*

repartee [ˌreparˈti] *s* schlagfertige Antwort *f*

repast [rɪˈpæst] *s* Mahl *n*

repatriate [riˈpetrɪˌet] *tr* repatriieren

re·pay [rɪˈpe] *v* (*pret & pp* **–paid**) *tr* (*e.g., a loan*) zurückzahlen; (*a person*) entschädigen; **r. a favor** e–n Gefallen erwidern

repayment [rɪˈpemənt] *s* Rückzahlung *f*; (*reprisal*) Vergeltung *f*

repeal [rɪˈpil] *s* Aufhebung *f* ‖ *tr* aufheben, außer Kraft setzen

repeat [rɪˈpit] *tr* wiederholen; (*a story, gossip*) weitererzählen; **r. s.th. after s.o.** j–m etw nachsagen

repeat′ed *adj* abermalig, mehrmalig

repeatedly [rɪˈpitɪdli] *adv* wiederholt

re·pel [rɪˈpel] *v* (*pret & pp* **–pelled**; *ger* **–pelling**) *tr* (*an enemy, an attack*) zurückschlagen; (*e.g., water*) abstoßen

repellent [rɪˈpelənt] *s* Bekämpfungsmittel *n*

repent [rɪˈpent] *tr* bereuen ‖ *intr* Reue empfinden; **r. of** bereuen

repentance [rɪˈpentəns] *s* Reue *f*

repentant [rɪˈpentənt] *adj* reuig

repercussion [ˌripərˈkʌʃən] *s* Rückwirkung *f*

repertory [ˈrepərˌtori] *s* Repertoire *n*

repetition [ˌrepɪˈtɪʃən] *s* Wiederholung *f*

replace [rɪˈples] *tr* (**with**) ersetzen (**durch**)

replaceable [rɪˈplesəbəl] *adj* ersetzbar

replacement [rɪˈplesmənt] *s* (*act*) Ersetzen *n*; (*substitute part*) Ersatz *m*; (*person*) Ersatzmann *m*

replay [ˈriple] *s* (sport) Wiederholungsspiel *n* ‖ [riˈple] *tr* nochmals spielen

replenish [rɪˈplenɪʃ] *tr* wieder auffüllen

replete [rɪˈplit] *adj* angefüllt

replica [ˈreplɪkə] *s* Replik *f*

re·ply [rɪˈplaɪ] *s* Erwiderung *f*; (*letter*) Antwortschreiben *n*; **in r. to your letter** in Beantwortung Ihres Schreibens ‖ *v* (*pret & pp* **–plied**) *tr & intr* erwidern

report [rɪˈport] *s* Bericht *m*; (*rumor*) Gerücht *n*; (*e.g., of a gun*) Knall *m* ‖ *tr* (*give an account of*) berichten; (*give notice of*) melden; **r. s.o. to the police** j–n bei der Polizei anzeigen ‖ *intr* (**to**) sich melden (bei); **r. in** sich anmelden

report′ card′ *s* Zeugnis *n*

reportedly [rɪˈportɪdli] *adv* angeblich

reporter [rɪˈportər] *s* Reporter *–in mf*

repose [rɪˈpoz] *s* Ruhe *f* ‖ *intr* ruhen

repository [rɪˈpɑzɪˌtori] *s* Verwahrungsort *m*; (*of information*) Fundgrube *f*

represent [ˌreprɪˈzent] *tr* vertreten; (*depict*) darstellen

representation [ˌreprɪzenˈteʃən] *s* Vertretung *f*; (*depiction*) Darstellung *f*

representative [ˌreprɪˈzentətɪv] *adj* (*function*) stellvertretend; (*government*) parlamentarisch; (*typical*) (**of**) typisch (für) || *s* Vertreter –in *mf*; (pol) Abgeordnete *mf*

repress [rɪ'pres] *tr* unterdrücken; (psychoanal) verdrängen

repression [rɪ'preʃən] *s* Unterdrückung *f*; (psychoanal) Verdrängung *f*

reprieve [rɪ'priːv] *s* Strafaufschub *m*; (fig) Gnadenfrist *f*, Atempause *f*

reprimand ['reprɪˌmænd] *s* Verweis *m*; **give s.o. a r.** j–m e–n Verweis erteilen || *tr* (for) zurechtweisen (wegen, für), rügen (wegen, für)

reprint ['riːprɪnt] *s* Nachdruck *m* || [riː'prɪnt] *tr* nachdrucken

reprisal [rɪ'praɪzəl] *s* Vergeltung *f*; **take reprisals against** or **on** Repressalien ergreifen gegen

reproach [rɪ'proʊtʃ] *s* Vorwurf *m* || *tr* (for) tadeln (wegen); **r. s.o. with s.th.** j–m etw vorwerfen

reproduce [ˌriprə'd(j)us] *tr* reproduzieren; (copies) vervielfältigen; (an experiment) wiederholen; (a play) neuaufführen; (a sound) wiedergeben; (a lost limb) regenerieren || *intr* sich fortpflanzen

reproduction [ˌriprə'dʌkʃən] *s* Reproduktion *f*; (making copies) Vervielfältigung *f*; (of sound) Wiedergabe *f*; (biol) Fortpflanzung *f*

reproductive [ˌriprə'dʌktɪv] *adj* Fortpflanzungs-

reproof [rɪ'pruf] *s* Rüge *f*

reprove [rɪ'pruv] *tr* rügen

reptile ['reptaɪl] *s* Kriechtier *n*

republic [rɪ'pʌblɪk] *s* Republik *f*

republican [rɪ'pʌblɪkən] *adj* republikanisch || *s* Republikaner –in *mf*

repudiate [rɪ'pjudɪˌet] *tr* (disown) verleugnen; (a charge) zurückweisen; (a debt) nicht anerkennen; (a treaty) für unverbindlich erklären; (a woman) verstoßen

repugnant [rɪ'pʌgnənt] *adj* widerwärtig

repulse [rɪ'pʌls] *s* (refusal) Zurückweisung *f*; (setback) Rückschlag *m* || *tr* zurückweisen; (mil) zurückschlagen

repulsive [rɪ'pʌlsɪv] *adj* abstoßend

reputable ['repjətəbəl] *adj* anständig

reputation [ˌrepjə'teʃən] *s* Ruf *m*, Ansehen *n*; **have the r. of being** im Rufe stehen zu sein

repute [rɪ'pjut] *s* (be held in high r.) hohes Ansehen genießen; **bring into bad r.** in üble Nachrede bringen; **of r. von Ruf** || *tr*—**she is reputed to be a beauty** sie soll e–e Schönheit sein

reputedly [rɪ'pjutɪdli] *adv* angeblich

request [rɪ'kwest] *s* Bitte *f*, Gesuch *n*; **at his r.** auf seine Bitte; **on r.** auf Wunsch || *tr* (a person) bitten; (a thing) bitten um, ersuchen

Requiem ['rekwɪˌem] *s* (Mass) Seelenmesse *f*; (chant, composition) Requiem *n*

require [rɪ'kwaɪr] *tr* erfordern; **if required** erforderlichenfalls

requirement [rɪ'kwaɪrmənt] *s* Anforderung *f*

requisite ['rekwɪzɪt] *adj* erforderlich ||

s Erfordernis *n*; (required article) Requisit *n*

requisition [ˌrekwɪ'zɪʃən] *s* Anforderung *f*; (mil) Requisition *f* || *tr* anfordern; (mil) beschlagnahmen

requital [rɪ'kwaɪtəl] *s* (retaliation) Vergeltung *f*; (for a kindness) Belohnung *f*

requite [rɪ'kwaɪt] *tr* vergelten; **r. s.o. for a favor** sich j–m für e–n Gefallen erkenntlich zeigen

re-read [ri'rid] *v* (pret & pp –read [red]) *tr* nachlesen

rerun ['riˌrʌn] *s* (cin) Reprise *f*

resale ['riˌsel] *s* Wiederverkauf *m*

rescind [rɪ'sɪnd] *tr* (an order) rückgängig machen; (a law) aufheben

rescue ['reskju] *s* Rettung *f*, Bergung *f* || *tr* retten, bergen

rescuer ['reskjuˌər] *s* Retter –in *mf*

research [rɪ'sʌrtʃ], ['risʌrtʃ] *s* Forschung *f*; **do r. on** Forschungen betreiben über (acc) || *intr* forschen

researcher ['risʌrtʃər] *s* Forscher –in *mf*

re-sell [ri'sel] *v* (pret & pp –sold) *tr* wiederverkaufen, weiterverkaufen

resemblance [rɪ'zembləns] *s* (to) Ähnlichkeit *f* (mit); **bear a close r. to s.o.** große Ähnlichkeit mit j–m haben

resemble [rɪ'zembəl] *tr* ähneln (dat)

resent [rɪ'zent] *tr*—**I r. your remark** Ihre Bemerkung paßt mir nicht

resentful [rɪ'zentfəl] *adj* grollend

resentment [rɪ'zentmənt] *s* Groll *m*; **feel r. toward** Groll hegen gegen

reservation [ˌrezər've(ə)n] *s* Vorbestellung *f*; (Indian land) Reservation *f*; **do you have a r.?** haben Sie vorbestellt?; **make reservations** vorbestellen

reserve [rɪ'zʌrv] *s* (discretion) Zurückhaltung *f*; (econ, mil) Reserve *f*; **without r.** rückhaltlos || *tr* (e.g., seats) reservieren, belegen; **r. judgment** mit seinem Urteil zurückhalten

reserved' *adj* (place) belegt; (person) zurückhaltend

reserve' officer *s* Reserveoffizier *m*

reservist [rɪ'zʌrvɪst] *s* Reservist –in *mf*

reservoir ['rezərˌvwar] *s* Staubecken *n*

re-set [ri'set] *v* (pret & pp –set; ger –setting) *tr* (a gem) neu fassen; (mach) nachstellen; (typ) neu setzen

resettle [ri'setəl] *tr* & *intr* umsiedeln

reshape [ri'ʃep] *tr* umformen

reshuffle [ri'ʃʌfəl] *tr* (cards) neu mischen; (pol) umgruppieren

reside [rɪ'zaɪd] *intr* wohnen

residence ['rezɪdəns] *s* Wohnsitz *m*; (for students) Studentenheim *n*

resident ['rezɪdənt] *adj* wohnhaft || *s* Einwohner –in *mf*

residential [ˌrezɪ'dentʃəl] *adj* Wohn-

residue ['rezɪˌd(j)u] *s* Rest *m*; (chem) Rückstand *m*

resign [rɪ'zaɪn] *tr* (an office) niederlegen; **r. oneself to** sich ergeben in (acc) || *intr* zurücktreten

resignation [ˌrezɪg'neʃən] *s* (from an office) Rücktritt *m*; (submissive *state*) Ergebung *f*; **hand in one's r.** sein Entlassungsgesuch einreichen

resilience [rɪˈzɪlɪ-əns] *s* Elastizität *f*; (fig) Spannkraft *f*

resilient [rɪˈzɪlɪ-ənt] *adj* elastisch; (fig) unverwüstlich

resin [ˈrezɪn] *s* Harz *m*

resist [rɪˈzɪst] *tr* widerstehen (*dat*) || *intr* Widerstand leisten

resistance [rɪˈzɪstəns] *s* (& elec) Widerstand *m*

resole [riˈsol] *tr* neu besohlen

resolute [ˈrezəˌlut] *adj* entschlossen

resolution [rezəˈluʃən] *s* (*resoluteness*) Entschlossenheit *f*; (parl) Beschluß *m*; **make good resolutions** gute Vorsätze fassen

resolve [rɪˈzɔlv] *s* Vorsatz *m* || *tr* auflösen; (*a question, problem*) lösen; **r. to** (*inf*) beschließen zu (*inf*) || *intr* **—r. into** sich auflösen in (*acc*); **r. upon s.th.** sich [*dat*] etw vornehmen

resonance [ˈrezənəns] *s* Resonanz *f*

resort [rɪˈzɔrt] *s* (*refuge*) Zuflucht *f*; (*for health*) Kurort *m*; (*for vacation*) Ferienort *m*, Sommerfrische *f*; **as a last r.** als letztes Mittel || *intr*—**r. to** greifen zu

resound [rɪˈzaund] *intr* widerhallen

resource [ˈrisors] *s* Mittel *n*; **resources** (fin) Geldmittel *pl*

resourceful [rɪˈsorsfəl] *adj* findig

respect [rɪˈspekt] *s* (*esteem*) Achtung *f*, Respekt *m*; (*reference*) Hinsicht *f*; **in every r.** in jeder Hinsicht; **pay one's respects to s.o.** j-m seine Aufwartung machen; **with r. to** mit Bezug auf (*acc*) || *tr* achten

respectable [rɪˈspektəbəl] *adj* achtbar; (*e.g., firm*) angesehen

respect′ed *adj* angesehen

respectful [rɪˈspektfəl] *adj* ehrerbietig

respectfully [rɪˈspektfəlɪ] *adv*—**r. yours** hochachtungsvoll, Ihr ... or Ihre ...

respective [rɪˈspektɪv] *adj* jeweilig

respectively [rɪˈspektɪvlɪ] *adv* beziehungsweise

respiration [ˌrespɪˈreʃən] *s* Atmung *f*

respirator [ˈrespɪˌretɔr] *s* Atemgerät *n*

respiratory [ˈrespɪrəˌtorɪ] *adj* Atmungs-

respite [ˈrespɪt] *s* (*pause*) Atempause *f*; (*reprieve*) Aufschub *m*; **without r.** ohne Unterlaß

resplendent [rɪˈsplendənt] *adj* glänzend

respond [rɪˈspand] *tr* antworten || *intr* (*reply*) (**to**) antworten (auf *acc*); (*react*) (**to**) ansprechen (auf *acc*)

response [rɪˈspans] *s* Antwort *f*; (*reaction*) Reaktion *f*; (fig) Widerhall *m*; **in r. to** als Antwort auf (*acc*)

responsibility [rɪˌspansɪˈbɪlɪtɪ] *s* Verantwortung *f*

responsible [rɪˈspansɪbəl] *adj* (*position*) verantwortlich; (*person*) verantwortungsbewußt; **be held r. for** verantwortlich gemacht werden für; **be r. for** (*be answerable for*) verantwortlich sein für; (*be to blame for*) schuld sein an (*dat*); (*be the cause of*) die Ursache sein (*genit*); (*be liable for*) haften für

responsive [rɪˈspansɪv] *adj*—**be r. to** ansprechen auf (*acc*)

rest [rest] *s* (*repose*) Ruhe *f*; (*from work*) Ruhepause *f*; (*e.g., from walking*) Rast *f*; (*remainder*) Rest *m*; (*support*) Stütze *f*; (mus) Pause *f*; **all the r.** (*in number*) alle andern; (*in quantity*) alles übrige; **be at r.** (*be calm*) beruhigt sein; (*be dead*) ruhen; (*not be in motion*) sich in Ruhelage befinden; **come to r.** stehenbleiben; **put one's mind to r.** sich beruhigen; **take a r.** sich ausruhen; **the r. of the boys** die übrigen (or andern) Jungen || *tr* ruhen lassen, ausruhen; (*support, e.g., one's elbow*) stützen || *intr* sich ausruhen; **r. on** lasten auf (*dat*); (*be based on*) beruhen auf (*dat*); **r. with** liegen bei

restaurant [ˈrestərant] *s* Restaurant *n*

restful [ˈrestfəl] *adj* ruhig

rest′ home′ *s* Erholungsheim *n*

rest′ing place′ *s* Ruheplatz *m*; **final r.** letzte Ruhestätte *f*

restitution [ˌrestɪˈt(j)uʃən] *s* Wiedergutmachung *f*; **make r.** Genugtuung leisten

restive [ˈrestɪv] *adj* (*restless*) unruhig; (*balky*) störrisch

restless [ˈrestlɪs] *adj* ruhelos

restock [riˈstak] *tr* wieder auffüllen; (*waters*) wieder mit Fischen besetzen

restoration [ˌrestəˈreʃən] *s* (*of a work of art or building*) Restaurierung *f*

restore [rɪˈstor] *tr* (*order*) wiederherstellen; (*a painting, building*) restaurieren; (*stolen goods*) zurückstatten; **r. to health** wiederherstellen

restrain [rɪˈstren] *tr* zurückhalten; (*feelings; a horse*) zügeln; (*e.g., trade*) einschränken; **r. s.o. from** (*ger*) j-n davon abhalten zu (*inf*)

restrain′ing or′der *s* Unterlassungsurteil *n*

restraint [rɪˈstrent] *s* Zurückhaltung *f*; (*force*) Zwang *m*

restrict [rɪˈstrɪkt] *tr* begrenzen; **r. to** beschränken auf (*acc*)

restrict′ed ar′ea *s* Sperrgebiet *n*

rest′ room′ *s* Abort *m*, Toilette *f*

result [rɪˈzʌlt] *s* Ergebnis *n*, Resultat *n*; (*consequence*) Folge *f*; **as a r. of** als Folge (*genit*); **without r.** ergebnislos || *intr*—**r. from** sich ergeben aus; **r. in** führen zu

result′ clause′ *s* Folgesatz *m*

resume [rɪˈzum] *tr* wieder aufnehmen; (*a journey*) fortsetzen

résumé [ˈrezuˌme] *s* Zusammenfassung *f*

resumption [rɪˈzʌmpʃən] *s* Wiederaufnahme *f*

resurface [riˈsʌrfɪs] *tr*—**r. the road with** die Straßendecke erneuern von || *intr* (naut & fig) wiederauftauchen

resurrect [ˌrezəˈrekt] *tr* (*the dead*) wieder zum Leben erwecken; (fig) wieder aufleben lassen

resurrection [ˌrezəˈrekʃən] *s* Auferstehung *f*

resuscitate [rɪˈsʌsɪˌtet] *tr* wiederbeleben

retail ['ritel] *adj* Kleinhandels– || *adv* im Kleinhandel || *tr* im Kleinhandel verkaufen || *intr*–**r. at two dollars** im Kleinverkauf zwei Dollar kosten

re'tail busi'ness *s* Kleinhandel *m*

retailer ['riteler] *s* Kleinhändler –in *mf*

retain [rɪ'ten] *tr* (zurück)behalten; **(a lawyer)** sich [*dat*] nehmen

retainer [rɪ'tenər] *s* (hist) Gefolgsmann *m;* (jur) Honorarvorschuß *m*

retain'ing wall' *s* Stützmauer *f*

retake ['ritek] *s* (cin) Neuaufnahme *f* || [ri'tek] *tr* **(a town)** zurückerobern; (cin) nochmals aufnehmen

retaliate [rɪ'tælɪ,et] *intr* **(against)** Vergeltung üben **(an** *dat***)**

retaliation [rɪ,tælɪ'e/ən] *s* Vergeltung *f*

retaliatory [rɪ'tælɪ·ə,tori] *adj* Vergeltungs–

retard [rɪ'tard] *tr* verzögern

retard'ed *adj* zurückgeblieben

retch [ret/] *intr* würgen

retch'ing *s* Würgen *n*

retell [ri'tel] *tr* wiedererzählen

retention [rɪ'ten/ən] *s* Beibehaltung *f*

re·think [ri'θɪŋk] *v* (*pret & pp* –thought) *tr* umdenken

reticence ['retɪsəns] *s* Verschwiegenheit *f*

reticent ['retɪsənt] *adj* verschwiegen

retina ['retɪnə] *s* Netzhaut *f*, Retina *f*

retinue ['retɪ,n(j)u] *s* Gefolge *n*

retire [rɪ'taɪr] *tr* pensionieren || *intr* **(from employment)** in den Ruhestand treten; **(withdraw)** sich zurückziehen; **(go to bed)** sich zur Ruhe begeben

retired' *adj* pensioniert

retirement [rɪ'taɪrmənt] *s* Ruhestand *m;* **go into r.** in den Ruhestand treten, sich pensionieren lassen

retire'ment pay' *s* Pension *f*

retire'ment plan' *s* Pensionsplan *m*

retir'ing *adj* zurückhaltend

retort [rɪ'tɔrt] *s* schlagfertige Erwiderung *f;* (chem) Retorte *f* || *tr & intr* erwidern

retouch [ri'tʌt/] *tr* retuschieren

retrace [ri'tres] *tr* zurückverfolgen

retract [rɪ'trækt] *tr* **(a statement)** widerrufen; **(claws; landing gear)** einziehen

retract'able land'ing gear' [rɪ'træktəbəl] *s* Verschwindfahrgestell *n*

retrain [ri'tren] *tr* umschulen

retread ['ri,tred] *s* (aut) runderneuerter Reifen *m* || *tr* runderneuern

retreat [rɪ'trit] *s* **(quiet place)** Ruhesitz *m;* (mil) Rückzug *m;* (rel) Exerzitien *pl;* **beat a hasty r.** eilig den Rückzug antreten || *intr* sich zurückziehen

retrench [ri'trent/] *tr* einschränken || *intr* sich einschränken

retribution [,retrɪ'bju/ən] *s* Vergeltung *f*

retrieval [rɪ'trivəl] *s* Wiedererlangung *f*

retrieve [rɪ'triv] *tr* wiedererlangen; **(a loss)** wettmachen; (hunt) apportieren

retriever [rɪ'trivər] *s* Apportierhund *m*

retroactive [,retro'æktɪv] *adj* **(from)** rückwirkend von ... an

retrogressive [,retrə'gresɪv] *adj* rückläufig

retrorocket ['retro,rakɪt] *s* Bremsrakete *f*

retrospect ['retrə,spekt] *s*–**in r.** rückblickend

re·try [ri'traɪ] *v* (*pret & pp* –tried) *tr* (jur) nochmals verhandeln

return [rɪ'tʌrn] *s* Rückkehr *f;* **(giving back)** Rückgabe *f;* **(the way back)** Rückweg *m;* **(tax form)** Steuererklärung *f;* **(profit)** Umsatz *m;* (tennis) Rückschlag *m;* **in r. dafür; in r. for** als Entgelt für; **returns (profits)** Ertrag *m;* **(of an election)** Ergebnisse *pl* || *tr* zurückgeben; **(send back)** zurücksenden; **(put back)** zurückstellen; **(thanks)** abstatten; **(a verdict)** fällen; **(a favor, love, gun fire)** erwidern; (tennis) zurückschlagen || *intr* zurückkehren; **r. to (e.g., a topic)** zurückkommen auf **(acc)**

return' address' *s* Rückadresse *f*

return' flight' *s* Rückflug *m*

return' match' *s* Revanchepartie *f*

return' tick'et *s* Rückfahrkarte *f;* (aer) Rückflugkarte *f*

reunification [ri,junɪfɪ'ke/ən] *s* (pol) Wiedervereinigung *f*

reunion [ri'junjən] *s* Treffen *n*

rev [rev] *v* (*pret & pp* **revved;** *ger* **revving**) *tr* (up) auf Touren bringen || *intr* auf Touren kommen

revamp [ri'væmp] *tr* umgestalten

reveal [rɪ'vil] *tr* offenbaren

reveille ['revəli] *s* Wecken *n*

rev·el ['revəl] *s* Gelage *n* || *v* (*pret & pp* –el[l]ed; *ger* –el[l]ing) *intr* ein Gelage halten; **r. in** (fig) schwelgen in **(dat)**

revelation [,revə'le/ən] *s* Offenbarung *f;* **Revelations** (Bib) Offenbarung *f*

reveler ['revələr] *s* Zecher –in *mf*

revelry ['revəlri] *s* Zechgelage *n*

revenge [rɪ'vendʒ] *s* Rache *f;* **take r. on s.o. for s.th.** sich an j–m für etw rächen || *tr* rächen

revengeful [rɪ'vendʒfəl] *adj* rachsüchtig

revenue ['revə,n(j)u] *s* **(yield)** Ertrag *m;* **(internal revenue)** Steueraufkommen *n*

rev'enue stamp' *s* Banderole *f*

reverberate [rɪ'vʌrbə,ret] *intr* widerhallen

revere [rɪ'vɪr] *tr* verehren

reverence ['revərəns] *s* **(respect given or received)** Ehrerbietung *f;* **(respect felt)** Ehrfurcht *f*

reverend ['revərənd] *adj* ehrwürdig; **the Reverend** ... Hochwürden ...

reverie ['revəri] *s* Träumerei *f;* **be lost in r.** in Träumen versunken sein

reversal [rɪ'vʌrsəl] *s* Umkehrung *f;* **(of opinion)** Umschwung *m*

reverse [rɪ'vʌrs] *adj* umgekehrt; **(side)** linke || *s* **(back side)** Rückseite *f;* **(opposite)** Gegenteil *n;* **(setback)** Rückschlag *m;* **(of a coin)** Revers *m;*

(aut) Rückwärtsgang m || tr umkehren, umdrehen; (a decision) umstoßen || intr sich rückwärts bewegen

reverse' side' s Rückseite f, Kehrseite f

reversible [rɪ'vʌrsɪbəl] adj (decision) umstoßbar; (material) zweiseitig; (chem, phys) umkehrbar; (mach) umsteuerbar

revert [rɪ'vʌrt] intr—r. to zurückkommen auf (acc); (jur) zurückfallen an (acc)

review [rɪ'vju] s (of) Überblick m (über acc); (of a lesson) Wiederholung f; (of a book) Besprechung f; (periodical) Rundschau m; (mil) Besichtigung f; pass in r. mustern || tr (a lesson) wiederholen; (a book) besprechen; (e.g., the events of the day) überblicken; (mil) besichtigen

reviewer [rɪ'vju-ər] s Besprecher –in mf

revile [rɪ'vaɪl] tr schmähen

revise [rɪ'vaɪz] tr (a book) umarbeiten; (one's opinion) revidieren

revised' edi'tion s verbesserte Auflage f

revision [rɪ'vɪʒən] s Neubearbeitung f

revival [rɪ'vaɪvəl] s Wiederbelebung f; (rel) Erweckung f; (theat) Reprise f

reviv'al meet'ing s Erweckungsversammlung f

revive [rɪ'vaɪv] tr wieder aufleben lassen; (memories) aufrühren; (a victim) wieder zu Bewußtsein bringen || intr wieder aufleben

revoke [rɪ'vok] tr widerrufen

revolt [rɪ'volt] s Aufstand m || tr abstoßen || intr revoltieren

revolt'ing adj abstoßend

revolution [,revə'luʃən] s Revolution f; (turn) Umdrehung f; **revolutions per minute** Drehzahl f

revolutionary [,revə'luʃə,neri] adj revolutionär || s Revolutionär –in mf

revolve [rɪ'valv] intr (around) sich drehen (um)

revolver [rɪ'valvər] s Revolver m

revolv'ing adj Dreh-

revue [rɪ'vju] s (theat) Revue f

revulsion [rɪ'vʌlʃən] s Abscheu m

reward [rɪ'wɔrd] s Belohnung f || tr belohnen

reward'ing adj lohnend

re-wind [rɪ'waɪnd] v (pret & pp –wound) (a tape, film) umspulen; (a clock) wieder aufziehen

rewire [rɪ'waɪr] tr Leitungen neu legen in (dat)

rework [rɪ'wʌrk] tr umarbeiten

re-write [rɪ'raɪt] v (pret –wrote; pp –written) tr umschreiben

rhapsody ['ræpsədi] s Rhapsodie f

rheostat ['ri-ə,stæt] s Rheostat m

rhetoric ['retərɪk] s Redekunst f

rhetorical [rɪ'tɔrɪkəl] adj rhetorisch

rheumatic [ru'mætɪk] adj rheumatisch

rheumatism ['ruma,tɪzəm] s Rheumatismus m

Rhine [raɪn] s Rhein m

Rhineland ['raɪn,lænd] s Rheinland n

rhine'stone' s Rheinkiesel m

rhinoceros [raɪ'nasərəs] s Nashorn n

rhubarb ['rubarb] s Rhabarber m; (sl) Krach m

rhyme [raɪm] s Reim m || tr & intr reimen

rhythm ['rɪðəm] s Rhythmus m

rhythmic(al) ['rɪðmɪk(əl)] adj rhythmisch

rib [rɪb] s Rippe f || v (pret & pp ribbed; ger ribbing) tr (coll) sich lustig machen über (acc)

ribald ['rɪbəld] adj zotig

ribbon ['rɪbən] s Band n; (decoration) Ordensband n; (for a typewriter) Farbband n

rice [raɪs] s Reis m

rich [rɪtʃ] adj reich; (voice) volltönend; (soil) fruchtbar; (funny) (coll) köstlich; **r. in** reich an (dat) || **riches** spl Reichtum m

rickets ['rɪkɪts] s Rachitis f

rickety ['rɪkɪti] adj (building) baufällig; (furniture) wackelig

rid [rɪd] v (pret & pp rid; ger ridding) tr (of) befreien (von); **get rid of** loswerden

riddance ['rɪdəns] s Befreiung f; **good r.!** den (or die or das) wäre ich glücklich los!

riddle ['rɪdəl] s Rätsel n

ride [raɪd] s Fahrt f; **give s.o. a r.** j–n im Auto mitnehmen; **take for a r.** (murder) entführen und umbringen; (dupe) hochnehmen || v (pret rode [rod]; pp ridden ['rɪdən]) tr (a bicycle) fahren; (a horse) reiten; (a train, bus) fahren mit; (harass) hetzen; **r. out** (a storm) gut überstehen || intr (e.g., in a car) fahren; (on a horse) reiten; **let s.th. r.** sich mit etw abfinden

rider ['raɪdər] s (on horseback) Reiter –in mf; (on a bicycle) Radfahrer –in mf; (in a vehicle) Fahrer –in mf; (to a document) Zusatzklausel f

ridge [rɪdʒ] s (of a hill; of the nose) Rücken m; (of a roof) Dachfirst m

ridge'pole' s Firstbalken m

ridicule ['rɪdɪ,kjul] s Spott m || tr verspotten

ridiculous [rɪ'dɪkjələs] adj lächerlich; **look r.** lächerlich wirken

rid'ing acad'emy s Reitschule f

rid'ing boot' s Reitstiefel m

rid'ing breech'es spl Reithose f

rid'ing hab'it s Reitkostüm n

rife [raɪf] adj häufig; **r. with** voll von

riffraff ['rɪf,ræf] s Gesindel n

rifle ['raɪfəl] s Gewehr n || tr ausplündern

rift [rɪft] s (& fig) Riß m

rig [rɪg] s (gear) Ausrüstung f; (horse and carriage) Gespann n; (truck) Laster m; (oil drill) Bohrturm m; (getup) (coll) Aufmachung f; (naut) Takelung f || v (pret & pp rigged; ger rigging) tr (auf)takeln; (prices, elections, accounts) manipulieren

rig'ging s Takelung f

right [raɪt] adj (side, glove, angle) recht; (just) gerecht; (correct) richtig; (moment) richtig; **do you have the r. time?** können Sie mir die genaue Uhrzeit sagen?; **be in one's r. mind** bei klarem Verstand sein; **it is all r.** es ist schon gut; **r.?** nicht wahr?; **that's r.!** eben!; **the r.** thing das Richtige; **you are r.** Sie haben recht || *adv* direkt; *(to the right)* rechts; **r. along** durchaus; **r. away** sofort, gleich; **r. behind the door** gleich hinter der Tür; **r. glad** (coll) recht froh; **r. here** gleich hier; **r. now** *(at the moment)* momentan; *(immediately)* sofort; **r. through** durch und durch || *s* Recht *n*; (box) Rechte *f*; **all rights reserved** alle Rechte vorbehalten; **by rights** von Rechts wegen; **in the r.** im Recht; **on the r.** rechts, zur Rechten || *tr* aufrichten; *(an error)* berichtigen; *(a wrong)* wiedergutmachen || *interj* stimmt!

righteous ['raɪtʃəs] *adj* gerecht, rechtschaffen; *(smug)* selbstgerecht

rightful ['raɪtfəl] *adj (owner)* rechtmäßig; *(claim, place)* berechtigt

right'-hand' *adj* zur Rechten; *(glove)* recht

right'-hand'ed *adj* rechtshändig

right'-hand'er *s* Rechtshänder –in *mf*

right'-hand man' *s* rechte Hand *f*

rightist ['raɪtɪst] *adj* rechtsstehend || *s* Rechtspolitiker –in *mf*

rightly ['raɪtli] *adv* richtig; *(rightfully)* rechtmäßig

right' of way' *s (in traffic)* Vorfahrtsrecht *n*; *(across another's land)* Grunddienstbarkeit *f*

right' wing' *s* rechter Flügel *m*

rigid ['rɪdʒɪd] *adj* steif, starr

rigmarole ['rɪgmə‚rol] *s (meaningless talk)* Geschwafel *n*; *(fuss)* Getue *n*

rigorous ['rɪgərəs] *adj* hart, streng

rile [raɪl] *tr* aufbringen

rill [rɪl] *s* Bächlein *n*

rim [rɪm] *s* Rand *m*; *(of eyeglasses)* Fassung *f*; *(of a wheel)* Felge *f*

rind [raɪnd] *s* Rinde *f*

ring [rɪŋ] *s (for the fingers; for boxing; of criminals or spies; of a circus; circle under the eyes)* Ring *m*; *(of a bell, voice, laughter)* Klang *m*; **give s.o. a r.** (telp) j–n anrufen; **run rings around s.o.** j–n in die Tasche stecken || *v (pret & pp ringed) tr* umringen; **r. in** einschließen || *v (pret rang* [ræŋ]*; pp rung* [rʌŋ]*) tr* läuten; **r. the bell** läuten, klingeln; **r. out** ausläuten; **r. up** anrufen || *intr* läuten, klingeln; **my ears are ringing** mir klingen die Ohren; **r. for s.o.** nach j–m klingeln; **r. out** laut schallen; **the bell is ringing** es läutet

ring'ing *adj* schallend || *s* Läuten *n*; *(in the ears)* Klingen *n*

ring'lead'er *s* Rädelsführer *m*

ring'mas'ter *s* Zirkusdirektor *m*

ring'side' *s* Ringplatz *m*

ring'worm' *s* Scherpilzflechte *f*

rink [rɪŋk] *s* Eisbahn *f*; *(for roller-skating)* Rollschuhbahn *f*

rinse [rɪns] *s* Spülen *n* || *tr* ausspülen

riot ['raɪət] *s* Aufruhr *m*; **r. of colors**

Farbengemisch *n*; **run r.** sich austoben; *(said of plants)* wuchern || *intr* sich zusammenrotten

ri'ot act' *s*—**read the r. to s.o.** j–m die Leviten lesen

rioter ['raɪ‚ətər] *s* Aufrührer –in *mf*

rip [rɪp] *s* Riß *m* || *v (pret & pp ripped) ger ripping) tr* (zer)reißen; **rip off** abreißen; *(the skin)* abziehen; *(cheat)* betrügen || *intr* reißen

rip' cord' *s* Reißlinie *f*

ripe [raɪp] *adj* reif

ripen ['raɪpən] *tr (& fig)* reifen lassen || *intr (& fig)* reifen

rip' off' *s* (sl) Wucher *m*

ripple ['rɪpəl] *s* leichte Welle *f* || *intr* leichte Wellen schlagen

rise [raɪz] *s* Aufsteigen *n*; *(in prices)* Steigerung *f*; *(of heavenly bodies)* Aufgang *m*; *(increase, e.g., in population)* Zunahme *f*; *(of e–r Reaktion veranlassen)* Erhebung *f*; **get a r. out of s.o.** j–n zu e–r Reaktion veranlassen; **give r. to** veranlassen || *v (pret rose* [roz]*; pp rose* ['rɪzən]*) intr (said of the sun, of a cake)* aufgehen; *(said of a river, prices, temperature, barometer)* steigen; *(said of a road)* ansteigen; *(get out of bed)* aufstehen; *(stand up)* sich erheben; *(from the dead)* auferstehen; *(said of anger)* hochsteigen; **r. to the occasion** sich der Lage gewachsen zeigen; **r. up from the ranks** von der Pike auf dienen

riser ['raɪzər] *s (of a staircase)* Futterbrett *n*; **early r.** Frühaufsteher –in *mf*; **late r.** Langschläfer –in *mf*

risk [rɪsk] *s* Risiko *n*; **run the r. of** *(ger)* Gefahr laufen zu *(inf)* || *tr* wagen, aufs Spiel setzen

risky ['rɪski] *adj* riskant, gewagt

risque [rɪs'ke] *adj* schlüpfrig

rite [raɪt] *s* Ritus *m*; **last rites** Sterbesakramente *pl*

ritual ['rɪtʃʊəl] *adj* rituell || *s* Ritual *n*

ri'val ['raɪvəl] *adj* rivalisierend || *s* Rivale *m*, Rivalin *f* || *v (pret & pp -val[l]ed) ger -val[l]ing) tr* rivalisieren, wetteifern mit

rivalry ['raɪvəlri] *s* Rivalität *f*

river ['rɪvər] *adj* Fluß– || *s* Fluß *m*

riv'er ba'sin *s* Flußgebiet *n*

riv'erfront' *s* Flußufer *n*

riv'erside' *adj* am Flußufer gelegen || *s* Flußufer *n*

rivet ['rɪvɪt] *s* Niet *m* || *tr* nieten

riv'et gun' *s* Nietmaschine *f*

riv'eting *s (act)* Vernieten *n*; *(connection)* Nietnaht *f*

rivulet ['rɪvjəlɪt] *s* Flüßchen *n*

R.N. ['ar'en] *s (registered nurse)* staatlich geprüfte Krankenschwester *f*

roach [rotʃ] *s (ent)* Schabe *f*; (ichth) Plötze *f*

road [rod] *s (& fig)* Weg *m*; **be (much) on the r.** (viel) auf Reisen sein; **go on the r.** auf Tour gehen; (theat) auf Tournee gehen

road'bed' *s* Bahnkörper *m*

road'block' *s* Straßensperre *f*

road′ hog′ s rücksichtsloser Autofahrer m

road′ house′ s Wirtshaus n, Rasthaus n

road′ map′ s Straßenkarte f, Autokarte f

road′side′ adj Straßen– || s Straßenrand m

road′side inn′ s Rasthaus n

road′sign′ s Wegweiser m

road′stead′ s Reede f

road′ test′ s (aut) Probefahrt f

road′way′ s Fahrweg m

roam [rom] tr durchstreifen || intr herumstreifen

roar [ror] s Gebrüll n; (of a waterfall, sea, wind) Brausen n; (of an engine) Dröhnen n; (laughter) schallendes Gelächter n || intr brüllen; (said of a waterfall, sea, wind) brausen; **r. at** anbrüllen; (e.g., a joke) schallend lachen über (acc); **r. by** vorbeibrausen; **r. with** brüllen vor (dat)

roast [rost] adj gebraten || s Braten m || tr (meat, fish) braten, rösten; (coffee, chestnuts) rösten; (a person) (coll) durch den Kakao ziehen || intr braten

roast′ beef′ s Roastbeef n

roaster [′rostər] s (appliance) Röster m, Röstapparat m; (fowl) Brathuhn n

roast′ pork′ s Schweinsbraten m

rob [rab] v (pret & pp robbed; ger robbing) tr (a thing) rauben; (a person) (of) berauben (genit)

robber [′rabər] s Räuber –in mf

robbery [′rabəri] s Raubüberfall m

robe [rob] s Robe f; (house robe) Hausrock m || tr feierlich ankleiden || intr sich feierlich ankleiden

robin [′rabɪn] s Rotkehlchen n

robot [′robat] s Roboter m

robust [ro′bʌst] adj robust

rock [rak] s (mus) Rock– || s Fels m; (one that is thrown) Stein m; (mus) Rockmusik f; **on the rocks** mit Eiswürfeln; (ruined) kaputt || tr schaukeln, wiegen; **r. the boat** (fig) die Sache ins Wanken bringen; **r. to sleep** in den Schlaf wiegen || intr schwanken, wanken; (said of a boat) schaukeln

rock′-bot′tom adj äußerst niedrig || s Tiefpunkt m

rock′ can′dy s Kandiszucker m

rock′ crys′tal s Bergkristall m

rocker [′rakər] s Schaukelstuhl m; **go off one's r.** (coll) den Verstand verlieren

rocket [′rakɪt] s Rakete f

rock′et launch′er s Raketenwerfer m

rocketry [′rakətri] s Raketentechnik f

rock′et ship′ s Rakentenflugkörper m

rock′ gar′den s Steingarten m

rock′ing chair′ s Schaukelstuhl m

rock′ing horse′ s Schaukelpferd n

rock-′n-roll [′rakən′rol] s Rock 'n Roll m

rock′ salt′ s Steinsalz n

rocky [′raki] adj felsig; (shaky) wacklig

rod [rad] s Stab m, Stange f; (whip)

Zuchtrute f; (of the retina; of a microorganism) Stäbchen n; (revolver) (sl) Schießeisen n; (angl) Angelrute f; (Bib) Reis n; (mach) Pleuelstange f; (surg) Absteckpfahl m

rodent [′rodənt] s Nagetier n

roe [ro] s (deer) Reh n; (ichth) Rogen m

rogue [rog] s Schuft m, Schurke m

rogues′/ gal′lery s Verbrecheralbum n

roguish [′rogɪʃ] adj schurkisch

role, rôle [rol] s Rolle f

roll [rol] s Rolle f; (bread) Brötchen n; (of thunder, of a ship) Rollen n; (of drums) Wirbel m; (of fat) Wulst m; **call the r.** die Namen verlesen; (mil) Appell halten || tr rollen; (cigarettes) drehen; (metals, roads) walzen; **r. over** überrollen; **r. up** zusammenrollen; (sleeves) zurückstreifen || intr sich wälzen; **be rolling in money** im Geld wühlen

roll′back′ s (com) Senkung f

roll′call′ s Namensverlesung f; (mil) Appell m

roll′er bear′ing s Rollenlager n

roll′er coast′er s Berg-und-Tal-Bahn f

roll′er skate′ s Rollschuh m

roll′er-skate′ intr rollschuhlaufen

roll′er tow′el s Rollhandtuch n

roll′ing mill′ s Walzwerk n

roll′ing pin′ s Nudelholz n, Teigrolle f

roll′ing stock′ s (rr) rollendes Material n

roly-poly [′roli′poli] adj dick und rund

roman [′romən] adj (typ) Antiqua–; **Roman** römisch || s (typ) Antiqua f; **Roman Römer** –in mf

Ro′man can′dle s Leuchtkugel f

Ro′man Cath′olic adj römisch-katholisch || s Katholik –in mf

romance [ro′mæns] adj (ling) romanisch || s Romanze f

Romanesque [,romə′nesk] adj romanisch || s das Romanische

Ro′man nose′ s Römernase f

Ro′man nu′meral s römische Ziffer f

romantic [ro′mæntɪk] adj romantisch

romanticism [ro′mæntɪ,sɪzəm] s Romantik f

romp [ramp] intr umhertollen

rompers [′rampərz] spl Spielanzug m

roof [ruf] s Dach n; (aut) Verdeck n; **raise the r.** (coll) Krach machen; **r. of the mouth** Gaumendach n

roofer [′rufər] s Dachdecker m

roof′ gar′den s Dachgarten m

roof′ tile′ s Dachziegel m

rook [ruk] s (chess) Turm m; (orn) Saatkrähe f || tr (coll) (out of) beschwindeln (um)

rookie [′ruki] s (coll) Neuling m

room [rum] s Zimmer n; (space) Raum m, Platz m; **make r.** Platz machen; **r. for complaint** Anlaß m zur Klage; **take up too much r.** zu viel Platz in Anspruch nehmen || intr wohnen

room′ and board′ s Kost und Quartier n

room′ clerk′ s Empfangschef m

roomer [′rumər] s Mieter –in mf

room'ing house' *s* Pension *f*

room'mate' *s* Zimmergenosse *m*

room' serv'ice *s* Bedienung *f* aufs Zimmer

roomy ['rumi] *adj* geräumig

roost [rust] *s* Hühnerstange *f*; **rule the r.** Hahn im Korb sein || *intr* auf der Stange sitzen

rooster ['rustər] *s* Hahn *m*

root [rut] *s* Wurzel *f*; **get to the r. of s.th.** etw [*dat*] auf den Grund gehen; **take r.** Wurzel schlagen; (fig) sich einbürgern || *tr*—**be rooted in** wurzeln in [*dat*]; **rooted to the spot** festgewurzelt; **r. out** ausrotten || *intr* —**r. about** wühlen; **r. for** zujubeln (*dat*)

rope [rop] *s* Strick *m*, Seil *n*; **know the ropes** alle Kniffe kennen || *tr* mit e–m Seil festbinden; (*a steer*) mit e–m Lasso einfangen; **r. in** (coll) einwickeln; **r. off** absperren

rosary ['rozəri] *s* Rosenkranz *m*

rose [roz] *adj* rosenrot || *s* Rose *f*

rose'bud' *s* Rosenknospe *f*

rose'bush' *s* Rosenstock *m*

rose'-col'ored *adj* rosenfarbig; (fig) rosa(rot)

rosemary ['roz,meri] *s* Rosmarin *m*

rosin ['razɪn] *s* Harz *n*; (*for violin bow*) Kolophonium *n*

roster ['rastər] *s* Namenliste *f*; (educ) Stundenplan *m*; (mil, naut) Dienstplan *m*

rostrum ['rastrəm] *s* Rednerbühne *f*

rosy ['rozi] *adj* (& fig) rosig

rot [rat] *s* Fäulnis *f*; (sl) Quatsch *m* || *v* (*pret* & *pp* **rotted**; *ger* **rotting**) *tr* faulen lassen || *intr* verfaulen

rotate ['rotet] *tr* rotieren lassen; (*tires*) auswechseln; (agr) wechseln || *intr* rotieren; (*take turns*) sich abwechseln

rotation [ro'teʃən] *s* Rotation *f*; **in r.** wechselweise; **r. of crops** Wechselwirtschaft *f*

rote [rot] *s*—**by r.** mechanisch

rotisserie [ro'tɪsəri] *s* Fleischbraterei *f*

rotten ['ratən] *adj* faul; (*trick*) niederträchtig; **feel r.** (sl) sich elend fühlen

rotund [ro'tʌnd] *adj* rundlich

rotunda [ro'tʌndə] *s* Rotunde *f*

rouge [ruʒ] *s* Rouge *n* || *tr* schminken

rough [rʌf] *adj* (hands, voice, person) rauh; (*piece of wood*) roh; (*work, guess, treatment*) grob; (*water, weather*) stürmisch; (*road*) uneben; **have it r.** viel durchmachen || *tr*—**r. in** roh entwerfen; (carp) grob bearbeiten; **r. it** primitiv leben; **r. up** grob behandeln

rough' draft' *s* Konzept *n*

roughen ['rʌfən] *tr* aufrauhen

rough'house' *s* Radau *m* || *intr* Radau machen

roughly ['rʌfli] *adv* grob; (*about*) etwa

rough'neck' *s* (coll) Rauhbein *n*

roulette [ru'let] *s* Roulett *n*

round [raund] *adj* rund || *s* Runde *f*; (*of applause*) Salve *f*; (*shot*) Schuß *m*; (*of drinks*) Lage *f*; (*of a sentinel*,

policeman, inspector, mailman) Rundgang *m*; **daily r.** Alltag *m* || *prep* um (*acc*) herum || *tr* (*make round*) runden; (*a corner*) herumgehen (or herumfahren) um (*acc*); **r. off** abrunden; (*finish*) vollenden; **r. up** (*animals*) zusammentreiben; (*persons*) zusammenbringen; (*criminals*) ausheben

round'house' *s* (rr) Lokomotivschuppen *m*

round'-shoul'dered *adj* mit runden Schultern

round' steak' *s* Kugel *f*

round'-ta'ble *adj* am runden Tisch

round' trip' *s* Hin-und Rückfahrt *f*; (aer) Hin- und Rückflug *m*

round'-trip' tick'et *s* Rückfahrkarte *f*

round'up' *s* (*of cattle*) Zusammentreiben *n*; (*of criminals*) Aushebung *f*

rouse [rauz] *tr* (from) aufwecken (aus)

rout [raut] *s* völlige Niederlage *f*; (mil) wilde Flucht *f*; **put to r.** in die Flucht schlagen || *tr* (mil) zersprengen

route [rut], [raut] *s* Route *f*, Weg *m* || *tr* leiten

routine [ru'tin] *adj* routinemäßig || *s* Routine *f*; **be r.** die Regel sein

rove [rov] *intr* umherwandern

row [rau] *s* Krach *m*; **raise a row** (coll) Krach machen || [ro] Reihe *f*; **in a row** hintereinander || *tr* rudern

rowboat ['ro,bot] *s* Ruderboot *n*

rowdy ['raudi] *adj* flegelhaft || *s* Flegel *m*

rower ['ro·ər] *s* Ruderer -in *mf*

rowing ['ro·ɪŋ] *s* Rudersport *m*

royal ['rɔɪ·əl] *adj* königlich

royalist ['rɔɪ·əlɪst] *adj* königstreu || *s* Königstreue *mf*

royalty ['rɔɪ·əlti] *s* (*royal status*) Königswürde *f*; (*personage*) fürstliche Persönlichkeit *f*; (*collectively*) fürstliche Persönlichkeiten *pl*; (*author's compensation*) Tantieme *f*; (*inventor's compensation*) Lizenzgebühr *f*

r.p.m. ['ar'pi'em] *spl* (**revolutions per minute**) Drehzahl *f*

R.S.V.P. *abbr* u.A.w.g. (**um Antwort wird gebeten**)

rub [rʌb] *s* Reiben *n*; **there's the rub** (coll) da sitzt der Haken || *v* (*pret* & *pp* **rubbed**; *ger* **rubbing**) *tr* reiben; **rub down** abreiben; **rub elbows with** verkehren mit; **rub in** einreiben; **rub it in** (sl) es (j–m) unter die Nase reiben; **rub out** ausradieren; (sl) umbringen; **rub s.o. the wrong way** j–m auf die Nerven gehen || *intr* reiben; **rub against** sich reiben an (*dat*); **rub off on** (fig) abfärben auf (*acc*)

rubber ['rʌbər] *adj* Gummi– || *s* Gummi *m* & *n*; (*cards*) Robber *m*; **rubbers** Gummischuhe *pl*

ru'ber band' *s* Gummiband *n*

rubberize ['rʌbə,raɪz] *tr* gummieren

rub'ber plant' *s* Kautschukpflanze *f*

rub'ber stamp' *s* Gummistempel *m*

rub'ber-stamp' *tr* abstempeln; (coll) automatisch genehmigen

rubbery ['rʌbəri] *adj* gummiartig

rub'bing al'cohol *s* Franzbranntwein *m*

rubbish ['rʌbɪʃ] s (trash) Abfall m; (nonsense) dummes Zeug n

rubble ['rʌbəl] s Schutt m; (used in masonry) Bruchstein m

rub'down' s Abreibung f

rubric ['rubrɪk] s Rubrik f

ruby ['rubi] adj rubinrot || s Rubin m

ruckus ['rʌkəs] s (coll) Krawall m

rudder ['rʌdər] s (aer) Seitenruder n; (naut) Steuerruder n

ruddy ['rʌdi] adj rosig

rude [rud] adj grob

rudeness ['rudnɪs] s Grobheit f

rudiments ['rudɪmənts] spl Grundlagen pl

rue [ru] tr bereuen

rueful ['rufəl] adj reuig; (pitiable) kläglich; (mournful) wehmütig

ruffian ['rʌfɪ-ən] s Raufbold m

ruffle ['rʌfəl] s Rüsche f; (in water) Kräuseln n; (of a drum) gedämpfter Trommelwirbel m || tr kräuseln; (feathers, hair) sträuben

rug [rʌg] s Teppich m

rugged ['rʌgɪd] adj (country) wild; (robust) kräftig; (life) hart

ruin ['ru·ɪn] s Ruine f; (undoing) Ruin m; **go to r.** zugrunde gehen; **lie in ruins** in Trümmern liegen; **ruins** (debris) Trümmer pl || tr ruinieren

rule [rul] s (reign) Herrschaft f; (regulation) Regel f; **as a r.** in der Regel; **become the r.** zur Regel werden || tr beherrschen; (paper) linieren; **r. out** ausschließen || intr (over) herrschen (über acc)

rule' of law' s Rechtsstaatlichkeit f

rule' of thumb' s Faustregel f; **by r.** über den Daumen gepeilt

ruler ['rulər] s Herrscher –in mf; (for measuring) Lineal n

rul'ing adj herrschend || s Regelung f

rum [rʌm] s Rum m

Rumania [ru'menɪ-ə] s Rumänien n

Rumanian [ru'menɪ-ən] adj rumänisch || s Rumäne m, Rumänin f; (language) Rumänisch n

rumble ['rʌmbəl] s (of thunder) Rollen n; (of a truck) Rumpeln n || intr rollen; rumpeln

ruminate ['rumɪ‚net] tr & intr wiederkäuen

rum'mage sale' s Ramschverkauf m

rumor ['rumər] s Gerücht n || tr—**it is rumored that** es geht das Gerücht, daß

rump [rʌmp] s (of an animal) Hinterteil m & n; (buttocks) Gesäß n

rumple ['rʌmpəl] tr (clothes) zerknittern; (hair) zerzausen

rump' steak' s Rumpsteak n

rumpus ['rʌmpəs] s (coll) Krach m; **raise a r.** (coll) Krach machen

rum'pus room' s Spielzimmer n

run [rʌn] s Lauf m; (in stockings) Laufmasche f; (fin) Run m; (theat) Laufzeit f; **be on the run** auf der Flucht sein; **in the long run** auf die Dauer; **run of bad luck** Pechsträhne f; **run of good luck** Glückssträhne f ||

v (pret **ran** [ræn]; pp **run**; ger **running**) tr (a machine) bedienen; (a business, household) führen; (a distance) laufen; (a blockade) brechen; (a cable) verlegen; **run a race** um die Wette laufen; **run down** (with a car) niederfahren; (clues) nachgehen (dat); (a citation) aufspüren; (through gossip) schlechtmachen; **run off** (typ) Abzüge machen von; **run over** (with a vehicle) überfahren; (rehearse) nochmal durchgehen; **run through** (with a sword) erstechen; **run up** (bills) auflaufen lassen; (prices) in die Höhe treiben; (a flag) hissen || intr laufen, rennen; (flow) fließen; (said of buses, etc.) verkehren; (said of the nose) laufen, e.g., **ihm läuft die Nase** his nose is running; (said of colors) auslaufen; (said of a meeting) dauern; (said of a lease) (for) gelten (auf acc); **run across** zufällig treffen; **run after** nachlaufen (dat); **run around** herumlaufen; **run around with** sich herumtreiben mit; **run away** weglaufen; (said of a spouse) durchgehen; **run down** (said of a clock) ablaufen; **run dry** austrocknen; **run for** kandidieren für; **run high**, e.g., **feelings ran high** die Gemüter waren erhitzt; **run in the family** in der Familie liegen; **run into** (e.g., a tree) fahren gegen; (e.g., trouble, debt) geraten in (acc); (e.g., a friend) unerwartet treffen; **run into the thousands** in die Tausende gehen; **run low** knapp werden; **run out** (said of liquids) ausgehen; (said of supplies, time) zu Ende gehen; **run out of** ausgehen, e.g., **they ran out of supplies** die Vorräte gingen ihnen aus; **run over** (said of a pot) überlaufen; **run up against** stoßen auf (acc); **run up to s.o.** j-m entgegenlaufen; **run wild** verwildern

run'-around' s—**give s.o. the r.** j-n von Pontius zu Pilatus schicken

run'away' adj flüchtig; (horse) durchgegangen || s Ausreißer m; (horse) Durchgänger m

run'down' s kurze Zusammenfassung f

run'-down' adj (condition) heruntergekommen; (clock) abgelaufen; (battery) entladen

rung [rʌŋ] s (of a ladder) Sprosse f; (of a chair) Querleiste f

run-in' s (coll) Zusammenstoß m

runner ['rʌnər] s Läufer –in mf; (of a sled or skate) Kufe f; (of a sliding door) Laufschiene f; (rug) Läufer m; (bot) Ausläufer m; (mil) Meldegänger m

run'ner-up' s (runners-up) Zweitbeste mf; (sport) Zweite mf

run'ning adj (water) fließend; (debts, expenses, sore) laufend || s Laufen n, Lauf m; **be in the r.** gut im Rennen liegen; **be out of the r.** (out of the race) aus dem Rennen ausgeschieden sein; (not among the front runners) keine Aussichten haben

run'ning board' s Trittbrett n
run'ning start' s fliegender Start m
run'off' s (sport) Entscheidungslauf m
run'off elec'tion s entscheidende Vor-
wahl f
run'-of-the-mill' adj Durchschnitts–
runt [rʌnt] s Dreikäsehoch m
run'way' s Startbahn f
rupture ['rʌptʃər] s Bruch m || tr (re-
lations) abbrechen; **be ruptured** e–n
Bruch (or Riß) bekommen; **r. one-
self** sich [dat] e–n Bruch zuziehen ||
intr platzen
rural ['rurəl] adj ländlich
ruse [ruz] s List f
rush [rʌʃ] adj dringend || s Eile f; (for)
Ansturm m (auf acc); (bot) Binse f;
be in a r. es eilig haben; **what's your
r.?** wozu die Eile? || tr (a person)
hetzen; (a defensive position) im
Sturm nehmen; (work) schnell erledigen; (goods) schleunigst schicken;
(e.g., to a hospital) schleunigst schaffen; **be rushed for time** sehr wenig
Zeit haben; **r. through** (a bill) durch-
peitschen; **r. up** (reinforcements)
schnell herbeischaffen || intr eilen,
sich stürzen; **r. at** zustürzen auf

(acc); **r. forward** vorstürmen; **r. into**
stürzen in (acc); **r. up** to zuschießen
auf (acc); **the blood rushed to his
head** ihm stieg das Blut in den Kopf
rush' hours' spl Hauptverkehrszeit f
rush' or'der s Eilauftrag m
russet ['rʌsɪt] adj rotbraun
Russia ['rʌʃə] s Rußland n
Russian ['rʌʃən] adj russisch || s Russe
m, Russin f; (language) Russisch n
rust [rʌst] s Rost m || tr rostig machen
|| intr (ver)rosten
rustic ['rʌstɪk] adj (rural) ländlich;
(countryish) bäuerlich || s Bauer m
rustle ['rʌsəl] s Rauschen n; (of silk)
Knistern n || tr rascheln mit; (cattle)
stehlen || intr rauschen; (said of silk)
knistern
rust'proof' adj rostfrei
rusty ['rʌsti] adj rostig; (fig) einge-
rostet
rut [rʌt] s Geleise n, Spur f; (fig) alter
Trott m
ruthless ['ruθlɪs] adj erbarmungslos
rye [raɪ] s (grain) Roggen m; (whiskey)
Roggenwhisky m
rye' bread' s Roggenbrot n
rye' grass' s Raigras n

S

S, s [es] s neunzehnter Buchstabe des
englischen Alphabets
Sabbath ['sæbəθ] s Sabbat m
sabbat'ical year' [sə'bætɪkəl] s ein-
jähriger Urlaub m (e–s Professors)
saber ['sebər] s Säbel m
sable ['sebəl] adj schwarz || s (fur)
Zobelpelz m; (zool) Zobel m
sabotage ['sæbə,tɑʒ] s Sabotage f || tr
sabotieren
saboteur [,sæbə'tʌr] s Saboteur –in
mf
saccharin ['sækərɪn] s Saccharin n
sachet [sæ'ʃe] s Duftkissen n
sack [sæk] s Sack m; (bed) (coll) Falle
f; **hit the s.** (coll) in die Falle gehen
|| tr einsacken; (dismiss) (coll) an
die Luft setzen; (mil) ausplündern
sack'cloth' s Sacktuch n; **in s. and ashes**
in Sack und Asche
sacrament ['sækrəmənt] s Sakrament n
sacramental [,sækrə'mentəl] adj sakra-
mental
sacred ['sekrəd] adj heilig; **s. to** ge-
weiht (dat)
sacrifice ['sækrɪ,faɪs] s Opfer n; **at a
s.** mit Verlust || tr opfern
sacrilege ['sækrɪlɪdʒ] s Sakrileg n
sacrilegious [,sækrɪ'lɪdʒəs] adj frevel-
haft, gotteslästerlich
sacristan ['sækrɪstən] s Sakristan m
sacristy ['sækrɪsti] s Sakristei f
sad [sæd] adj traurig; (plight) schlimm
sadden ['sædən] tr traurig machen
saddle ['sædəl] s Sattel m || tr satteln;
be saddled with auf dem Halse haben

sad'dlebag' s Satteltasche f
sadism ['sedɪzəm] s Sadismus m
sadistic [se'dɪstɪk] adj sadistisch
sadness ['sædnɪs] s Traurigkeit f
sad' sack' s (sl) Trauerkloß m
safe [sef] adj (from) sicher (vor dat);
(arrival) glücklich; **s. and sound** heil
und gesund; (said of a thing) unversehrt; **to be on the s. side** vorsichts-
halber || s Geldschrank m
safe'-con'duct s sicheres Geleit n
safe'-depos'it box' s Schließfach n
safe' dis'tance s Sicherheitsabstand m
safe'guard' s Schutz m || tr schützen
safe'keep'ing s sicherer Gewahrsam m
safety ['sefti] adj Sicherheits– || s
Sicherheit f
safe'ty belt' s Sicherheitsgurt m
safe'ty pin' s Sicherheitsnadel f
safe'ty ra'zor s Rasierapparat m
safe'ty valve' s Sicherheitsventil n
saffron ['sæfrən] adj safrangelb || s
Safran m
sag [sæg] s Senkung f || v (pret & pp
sagged; ger **sagging**) intr sich senken;
(said of a cable) durchhängen; (fig)
sinken
sagacious [sə'geʃəs] adj scharfsinnig
sage [sedʒ] adj weise, klug || s Weise
m; (plant) Salbei f
sage'brush' s Beifuß m
sail [sel] s Segel n; **set s. for** in See
stechen nach || tr (a boat) fahren;
(the sea) segeln über (acc) || intr
segeln; (depart) abfahren; **s. across**
übersegeln; **s. along the coast** an der

Küste entlangsegeln; **s. into** (coll)
herunterputzen
sail'boat' s Segelboot n
sail'cloth' s Segeltuch n
sail'ing s Segelfahrt f; (sport) Segel-
sport m; **it will be smooth s.** (fig) es
wird alles glattgehen
sail'ing ves'sel s Segelschiff n
sailor ['selər] s Matrose m
Saint [sent] s Heilige mf; **S. George**
der heilige Georg, Sankt Georg
Saint' Bernard' s (dog) Bernhardiner m
sake [sek] s—**for her s.** ihretwegen;
for his s. seinetwegen; **for my s.**
meinetwegen; **for our s.** unsertwegen;
for their s. ihretwegen; **for the s.** of
um (genit) willen; **for your s.** deinetwegen, Ihretwegen
salable ['seləbəl] adj verkäuflich
salacious [sə'leʃəs] adj (person) geil;
(writing, pictures) obszön
salad ['sæləd] s Salat m
sal'ad bowl' s Salatschüssel f
sal'ad dress'ing s Salatsoße f
sal'ad oil' s Salatöl n
salami [sə'lɑmi] s Salami f
salary ['sæləri] s Gehalt n
sale [sel] s Verkauf m; (special sale)
Ausverkauf m; **be up for s.** zum Kauf
stehen; **for s.** zu verkaufen; **sales**
(com) Absatz m, Umsatz m; **put up
for s.** zum Verkauf anbieten
sales'' clerk' s Verkäufer –in mf
sales'girl' s Ladenmädchen n
sales'la'dy s Verkäuferin f
sales'man s (–men) Verkäufer m
sales'man'ship s Verkaufstüchtigkeit f
sales' promo'tion s Verkaufsförderung
f
sales' slip' s Kassenzettel m, Bon m
sales' tax' s Umsatzsteuer f
saliva [sə'laɪvə] s Speichel m
sallow ['sælo] adj bläßlich
sal·ly ['sæli] s (side trip) Abstecher
m; (mil) Ausfall m ‖ v (pret & pp
–lied) intr (mil) ausfallen; **s. forth**
sich aufmachen
salmon ['sæmən] adj lachsfarben ‖ s
Lachs m
saloon [sə'lun] s Kneipe f; (naut) Salon m
salt [sɔlt] s Salz n ‖ tr salzen; **s. away**
(coll) auf die hohe Kante legen
salt'cel'lar s Salzfaß n
salt'ed meat' s Salzfleisch n
salt' mine' s Salzbergwerk n; **back to
the salt mines** zurück zur Tretmühle
salt'pe'ter s Salpeter m
salt' shak'er s Salzfaß n
salty ['sɔlti] adj salzig
salutary ['sæljə‚teri] adj heilsam
salute [sə'lut] s Salut m ‖ tr & intr
salutieren
salvage ['sælvɪdʒ] s (saving by ship)
Bergung n; (property saved by ship)
Bergungsgut n; (discarded material)
Altmaterial n ‖ tr bergen; (discarded
material) verwerten
salvation [sæl've/ən] s Heil n
Salva'tion Ar'my s Heilsarmee f
salve [sæv] s Salbe f ‖ tr (one's conscience) beschwichtigen

sal·vo ['sælvo] s (–vos & –voes) Salve
f
Samaritan [sə'mærɪtən] s Samariter –in
mf; **good S.** barmherziger Samariter
m
same [sem] adj—**at the s. time** gleichzeitig; **it's all the s. to me** es ist mir
ganz gleich; **just the s.** trotzdem;
thanks, s. to you! danke, gleichfalls!;
the s. derselbe
sameness ['semnɪs] s Eintönigkeit f
sample ['sæmpəl] s Muster n, Probe f
‖ tr (aus)probieren
sancti·fy ['sæŋktɪ‚faɪ] v (pret & pp
–fied) tr heiligen
sanctimonious [‚sæŋktɪ'moni·əs] adj
scheinheilig
sanction ['sæŋkʃən] s Sanktion f ‖ tr
sanktionieren
sanctity ['sæŋktɪti] s Heiligkeit f
sanctuary ['sæŋktʃʊ‚eri] s (shrine)
Heiligtum n; (of a church) Altarraum
m; (asylum) Asyl n
sand [sænd] s Sand m ‖ tr mit Sandpapier abschleifen; (a road, sidewalk)
mit Sand bestreuen
sandal ['sændəl] s Sandale f
san'dalwood' s Sandelholz n
sand'bag' s Sandsack m
sand'bank' s Sandbank f
sand' bar' s Sandbank f
sand'blast' tr sandstrahlen
sand'box' s Sandkasten m
sand' cas'tle s Strandburg f
sand' dune' s Sanddüne f
sand'glass' s Sanduhr f
sand'man s (–men) (fig) Sandmann m
sand'pa'per s Sandpapier n ‖ tr mit
Sandpapier abschleifen
sand'stone' s Sandstein m
sand'storm' s Sandsturm m
sandwich ['sændwɪtʃ] s belegtes Brot
n, Sandwich n ‖ tr (in between) ein-
zwängen (zwischen dat)
sandy ['sændi] adj sandig; (color)
sandfarben
sane [sen] adj geistig gesund; (e.g.,
advice) vernünftig
sanguine ['sæŋgwɪn] adj (about) zuver-
sichtlich (in Bezug auf acc)
sanitarium [‚sænɪ'teri·əm] s Heilan-
stalt f, Sanatorium n
sanitary ['sænɪ‚teri] adj sanitär
san'itary nap'kin s Damenbinde f
sanitation [‚sænɪ'teʃən] s Gesundheits-
wesen n; (in a building) sanitäre Einrichtungen pl
sanity ['sænɪti] s geistige Gesundheit f
Santa Claus ['sæntə‚klɔz] s der Weih-
nachtsmann m, der Nikolaus
sap [sæp] s Saft m; (coll) Schwachkopf
m ‖ v (pret & pp sapped; ger sap-
ping) tr (strength) erschöpfen
sapling ['sæplɪŋ] s junger Baum m
sapphire ['sæfaɪr] s Saphir m
Saracen ['særəsən] adj sarazenisch ‖
s Sarazene m, Sarazenin f
sarcasm ['sɑrkæzəm] s Sarkasmus m
sarcastic [sɑr'kæstɪk] adj sarkastisch
sarcophagus [sɑr'kɑfəgəs] s Sarkophag
m
sardine [sɑr'din] s Sardine f; **packed**

in like sardines zusammengedrängt wie die Heringe

Sardinia [sɑr'dɪnɪ·ə] s Sardinien n

Sardinian [sɑr'dɪnɪ·ən] adj sardinisch || s Sardinier –in mf; (language) Sardinisch n

sash [sæʃ] s Schärpe f; (of a window) Fensterrahmen m

sass [sæs] s (coll) Revolverschnauze f || tr (coll) (off) patzig antworten (dat)

sassy ['sæsi] adj (coll) patzig

Satan ['setən] s Satan m

satanic(al) [sə'tænɪk(əl)] adj satanisch

satchel ['sætʃəl] s Handtasche f

sate [set] tr übersättigen

satellite ['sætə,laɪt] s Satellit m

sat'ellite coun'try s Satellitenstaat m

satiate ['seʃɪ,et] tr sättigen

satin ['sætɪn] s Seidenatlas m

satire ['sætaɪr] s Satire f

satiric(al) [sə'tɪrɪk(əl)] adj satirisch

satirize ['sætɪ,raɪz] tr verspotten

satisfaction [,sætɪs'fækʃən] s Befriedigung f, Genugtuung f

satisfactory [,sætɪs'fæktəri] adj friedenstellend, genügend

satis·fy ['sætɪs,faɪ] v (pret & pp –fied) tr (desires, needs) befriedigen; (requirements) genügen (dat); (a person) zufriedenstellen; **be satisfied with** zufrieden sein mit || intr befriedigen

saturate ['sætʃə,ret] tr (& chem) sättigen, saturieren

satura'tion bomb'ing s Bombenteppich m

satura'tion point' s Sättigungspunkt m

Saturday ['sætər,de] s Samstag m; **on S.** am Samstag

sauce [sɔs] s Soße f; (coll) Frechheit f || tr mit Soße zubereiten; (season) würzen

sauce'pan' s Stielkasserolle f

saucer ['sɔsər] s Untertasse f

saucy ['sɔsi] adj (impertinent) frech; (amusingly flippant) keß; (trim) flott

sauerkraut ['saʊr,kraʊt] s Sauerkraut n

saunter ['sɔntər] s Schlendern n || intr schlendern

sausage ['sɔsɪdʒ] s Wurst f

saute [so'te] v (pret & pp sauteed) tr sautieren

savage ['sævɪdʒ] adj wild || s Wilde mf

savant ['sævənt] s Gelehrte m

save [sev] tr (rescue) retten; (money, fuel) sparen; (keep, preserve) aufheben; (trouble) ersparen; (time) gewinnen; (stamps) sammeln; **s. face** das Gesicht wahren; **s. from** bewahren vor (dat) || prep außer (dat)

sav'ing adj (grace) seligmachend; (quality) ausgleichend || s (of souls) Rettung f; (in) Ersparnis f (an dat); **savings** Ersparnisse pl

sav'ings account' s Sparkonto n

sav'ings bank' s Sparkasse f

sav'ings certi'ficate s Sparbon m

sav'ings depos'it s Spareinlage f

savior ['sevjər] s Retter –in mf; **Saviour** Heiland m

savor ['sevər] s Wohlgeschmack m || tr auskosten || intr—**s. of** (smell of) riechen nach; (taste of) schmecken nach

savory ['sevəri] adj wohschmeckend

saw [sɔ] s Säge f; (saying) Sprichwort n || tr sägen; **saw up** zersägen

saw'dust' s Sägespäne pl

saw'horse' s Sägebock m

saw'mill' s Sägemühle f

Saxon ['sæksən] adj sächsisch || s Sachse m, Sachsin f

Saxony ['sæksəni] s Sachsen n

saxophone ['sæksə,fon] s Saxophon n

say [se] s—**have a** (or no) **say in etw** (or nichts) zu sagen haben bei; **have one's say** (about) seine Meinung äußern (über acc) || v (pret & pp said [sed]) tr sagen; (Mass) lesen; (a prayer) sprechen; (one's prayers) verrichten; (said of a newspaper article, etc.) besagen; **it says in the papers** in der Zeitung steht; (let's) **say** sagen wir; **no sooner said than done** gesagt, getan; **say!** (to draw attention) sag mal!; (to elicit agreement) gelt!; **say s.th. behind s.o.'s back** j–m etw nachsagen; **she is said to be clever** sie soll klug sein; **that is not to say** das will nicht sagen; **that is to say** das heißt; **they say** man sagt; **to say nothing of** ganz zu schweigen von; **you don't say so!** tatsächlich!

say'ing s Sprichwort n; **as the s. goes** wie man zu sagen pflegt; **it goes without s.** das versteht sich von selbst

say'-so' s (assertion) Behauptung f; (order) Anweisung f; (final authority) letztes Wort n

scab [skæb] s Schorf m; (sl) Streikbrecher –in mf

scabbard ['skæbərd] s Schwertscheide f

scabby ['skæbi] adj schorfig

scads [skædz] spl (sl) e–e Menge f

scaffold ['skæfəld] s Gerüst n; (for executions) Schafott n

scaf'folding s Baugerüst n

scald [skɔld] tr verbrühen; (milk) aufkochen

scale [skel] s (on fish, reptiles) Schuppe f; (pan of a balance) Waagschale f; (of a thermometer, wages) Skala f; (mus) Tonleiter f; **on a grand s.** im großen Stil; **on a large** (or **small**) **s.** in großem (or kleinem) Maßstab; **s. 1:1000** Maßstab 1:1000; **scales** Waage f; **to s.** maßstabgerecht || tr erklettern; **s. down** maßstäblich verkleinern; (prices) herabsetzen

scallop ['skæləp] s Kammuschel f; (sew) Zacke f || tr auszacken; (culin) überbacken

scalp [skælp] s Kopfhaut f; (Indian trophy) Skalp m || tr skalpieren

scalpel ['skælpəl] s Skalpell n

scaly ['skeli] adj schuppig

scamp [skæmp] s Fratz m, Wildfang m

scamper ['skæmpər] intr herumtollen; **s. away** davonlaufen

scan [skæn] v (pret & pp scanned; ger

scanning) *tr (a page)* überfliegen; *(a verse)* skandieren; *(examine)* genau prüfen; *(radar, telv)* abtasten

scandal ['skændəl] *s* Skandal *m*

scandalize ['skændə,laiz] *tr* schockieren

scandalmonger ['skændəl,mʌŋgər] *s* Lästermaul *n*

scandalous ['skændələs] *adj* skandalös

scan'dal sheet' *s* Sensationsblatt *n*

Scandinavia [,skændɪ'nevɪ·ə] *s* Skandinavien *n*

Scandinavian [,skændɪ'nevɪ·ən] *adj* skandinavisch ‖ *s* Skandinavier –in *mf*; *(language)* Skandinavisch *n*

scansion ['skænʃən] *s* Skandieren *n*

scant [skænt] *adj* gering; **a s. two hours** knapp zwei Stunden

scantily ['skæntɪli] *adv*—**s. clad** leicht bekleidet

scanty ['skænti] *adj* kärglich, knapp

scapegoat ['skep,got] *s* Sündenbock *m*

scar [skɑr] *s* Narbe *f*; *(fig)* Makel *m* ‖ *v (pret & pp scarred; ger scarring)* *tr (e.g., a face)* entstellen; *(e.g., a tabletop)* verschrammen; *(fig)* beinträchtigen

scarce [skɛrs] *adj* knapp, rar; **make oneself s.** *(coll)* das Weite suchen

scarcely ['skɛrsli] *adv* kaum; **be s. able to** *(inf)* Not haben zu *(inf)*

scarcity ['skɛrsɪti] *s (of)* Knappheit *f (an dat)*, Mangel *m (an dat)*

scare [skɛr] *s* Schrecken *m*; **be scared** erschrecken; **be scared stiff** e-e Hundeangst haben; **give s.o. a s.** j–m e-n Schrecken einjagen ‖ *tr* erschrecken; **s. away** verscheuchen; **s. up** *(money)* auftreiben ‖ *intr* erschrecken

scare'crow' *s* Vogelscheuche *f*

scarf [skɑrf] *s (scarfs & scarves [skɑrvz])* Schal *m*

scarlet ['skɑrlɪt] *adj* scharlachrot ‖ *s* Scharlachrot *n*

scar'let fe'ver *s* Scharlach *m*

scarred *adj* narbig, schrammig

scary ['skɛri] *adj* schreckerregend

scat [skæt] *interj* weg!

scathing ['skeðɪŋ] *adj* vernichtend

scatter ['skætər] *tr* zerstreuen ‖ *intr* sich zerstreuen

scat'terbrain' *s* Wirrkopf *m*

scat'tered show'ers *spl* einzelne Schauer *pl*

scenari·o [sɪ'nɛrɪ·o] *s (–os)* Drehbuch *n*

scene [sin] *s* Szene *f*; **be on the s.** zur Stelle sein; **behind the scenes** hinter den Kulissen; **make a s.** e-e Szene machen; **s. of the crime** Tatort *m*

scenery ['sinəri] *s* Landschaft *f*; *(theat)* Bühnenausstattung *f*

scenic ['sinɪk] *adj* landschaftlich; *(theat)* szenisch

scent [sɛnt] *s* Duft *m*; *(of a dog)* Witterung *f*; *(hunt)* Spur *f*; **have a s.** duften ‖ *tr* wittern

scepter ['sɛptər] *s* Zepter *n*

sceptic ['skɛptɪk] *s* Skeptiker –in *mf*

scepticism ['skɛptɪ,sɪzəm] *s (doubt)* Skepsis *f*; *(doctrine)* Skeptizismus *m*

schedule ['skɛdjul] *s* Plan *m*; *(for work)* Arbeitsplan *m*; *(in travel)* Fahrplan *m*; *(at school)* Stundenplan *m*; *(appendix to a tax return)* Einkommensteuerformular *n*; *(table)* Einkommensteuertabelle *f*; **on s. fahrplanmäßig** ‖ *tr* ansetzen; **the plane is scheduled to arrive at six** nach dem Flugplan soll die Maschine um sechs Uhr ankommen

scheme [skim] *s (schematic)* Schema *n*; *(plan, program)* Plan *m*; *(intrigue)* Intrige *f* ‖ *tr* planen ‖ *intr* Ränke schmieden

schemer ['skimər] *s* Ränkeschmied *m*

schilling ['ʃɪlɪŋ] *s (Aust)* Schilling *m*

schism ['sɪzəm] *s (fig)* Spaltung *f*; *(eccl)* Schisma *n*

schizophrenia [,skɪtso'frini·ə] *s* Schizophrenie *f*, Bewußtseinsspaltung *f*

schizophrenic [,skɪtso'frɛnɪk] *adj* schizophren

schmaltzy ['ʃmɔltsi] *adj* schmalzig

scholar ['skɑlər] *s* Gelehrte *mf*

scholarly ['skɑlərli] *adj* gelehrt

schol'arship' *s* Gelehrsamkeit *f*; *(award)* Stipendium *n*

scholastic [skə'læstɪk] *adj* Schul–, Bildungs–; *(hist)* scholastisch

school [skul] *adj (book, house, master, room, teacher, yard, year)* Schul– ‖ *s* Schule *f*; *(of a university)* Fakultät *f*; *(of fish)* Schwarm *m*; **s. is over** die Schule ist aus ‖ *tr* schulen

school' age' *s* schulpflichtiges Alter *n*; **of s.** schulpflichtig

school'bag' *s* Schulranzen *m*

school' board' *s* Schulausschuß *m*

school'boy' *s* Schüler *m*

school'girl' *s* Schülerin *f*

school'ing *s (formal education)* Schulbildung *f*; *(training)* Schulung *f*

school'mate' *s* Mitschüler –in *mf*

schooner ['skunər] *s* Schoner *m*

sciatica [saɪ'ætɪkə] *s* Hüftschmerz *m*

science ['saɪ·əns] *s* Wissenschaft *f*; **the sciences** die Naturwissenschaften *pl*

sci'ence fic'tion *s* Science-fiction *f*

scientific [,saɪ·ən'tɪfɪk] *adj* wissenschaftlich

scientist ['saɪ·əntɪst] *s* Wissenschaftler –in *mf*

scimitar ['sɪmɪtər] *s* Türkensäbel *m*

scintillate ['sɪntɪ,let] *intr* funkeln

scion ['saɪ·ən] *s* Sprößling *m*; *(bot)* Pfropfreis *n*

scissors ['sɪzərz] *s & spl* Schere *f*; *(in wrestling)* Zangengriff *m*

scoff [skɔf] *s* Spott *m* ‖ *intr (at)* spotten *(über acc)*

scold [skold] *tr & intr* schelten

scold'ing *s* Schelte *f*; **get a s.** Schelte bekommen

sconce [skɑns] *s* Wandleuchter *m*

scoop [skup] *s (ladle)* Schöpfkelle *f*; *(for sugar, flour)* Schaufel *f*; *(amount scooped)* Schlag *m*; *(journ)* Knüller *m* ‖ *tr* schöpfen; **s. out** ausschaufeln; **s. up** scheffeln

scoot [skut] *intr (coll)* flitzen

scooter ['skutər] *s* Roller *m*

scope [skop] *s (extent)* Umfang *m*;

(*range*) Reichweite *f*; **give free s. to the imagination** der Phatasie freien Lauf lassen; **give s.o. free s.** j-m freie Hand geben; **within the s. of** im Rahmen (*genit*) or von

scorch [skɔrtʃ] *tr* versengen

scorched'-earth' pol'icy *s* Politik *f* der verbrannten Erde

scorch'ing *adj & adv* sengend

score [skor] *s* (*of a game*) Punktzahl *f*; (*final score*) Ergebnis *n*; (*notch*) Kerbe *f*; (*mus*) Partitur *f*; **a s. of** zwanzig; **have an old s. to settle with s.o.** mit j-m e-e alte Rechnung zu begleichen haben; **keep s.** die Punktzahl anschreiben; **know the s.** (coll) auf Draht sein; **on that s.** diesbezüglich; **what's the s.?** wie steht das Spiel? || *tr* (*points*) erzielen; (*goals*) schießen; (*notch*) einkerben; (*mus*) in Partitur setzen || *intr* e-n Punkt erzielen

score'board' *s* Anzeigetafel *f*

score'card' *s* Punktzettel *m*

score'keep'er *s* Anschreiber –in *mf*

score'sheet' *s* Spielberichtsbogen *m*

scorn [skɔrn] *s* Verachtung *f*; **laugh to s.** auslachen || *tr* verachten

scornful ['skɔrnfəl] *adj* verächtlich

scorpion ['skɔrpi·ən] *s* Skorpion *m*

Scot [skɑt] *s* Schotte *m*, Schottin *f*

Scotch [skɑtʃ] *adj* schottisch; (sl) geizig || *s* schottischer Whisky *m*; (*dialect*) Schottisch *n* || *tr* (*a rumor*) ausrotten; (*with a chock*) blockieren; (*render harmless*) unschädlich machen

Scotch'man *s* (–men) Schotte *m*

Scotch' pine' *s* gemeine Kiefer *f*

Scotch' tape' *s* (trademark) durchsichtiger Klebstreifen *m*

scot'-free' *adj* ungestraft

Scotland ['skɑtlənd] *s* Schottland *n*

Scottish ['skɑtɪʃ] *adj* schottisch; *s* (*dialect*) Schottisch *n*; **the S.** die Schotten *pl*

scoundrel ['skaundrəl] *s* Lump *m*

scour [skaur] *tr* scheuern; (*the city*) absuchen

scourge [skʌrdʒ] *s* Geißel *f* || *tr* geißeln

scout [skaut] *s* Pfadfinder *m*; (mil, sport) Kundschafter *m* || *tr* aufklären || *intr* kundschaften

scout'mas'ter *s* Pfadfinderführer *m*

scowl [skaul] *s* finsterer Blick *m* || *intr* finster blicken; **s. at** grollend ansehen

scram [skræm] *v* (*pret & pp* **scrammed;** *ger* **scramming**) *intr* (coll) abhauen

scramble ['skræmbəl] *s* (for) Balgerei *f* (um) || *tr* (*mix up*) durcheinandermischen; (*a message*) unverständlich machen; **s. eggs** Rührei machen || *intr* (*e.g., over rocks*) klettern; **s. for s.th.** um etw reißen; **s. to one's feet** sich aufrappeln

scram'bled eggs' *spl* Rührei *n*

scrap [skræp] *s* (*of metal*) Schrott *m*; (*of paper*) Fetzen *m*; (*of food*) Rest *m*; (*refuse*) Abfall *m*; (*quarrel*) (coll) Zank *m*; (*fight*) (coll) Rauferei *f* || *v* (*pret & pp* **scrapped;** *ger*

scrapping) *tr* ausrangieren || *intr* (*quarrel*) (coll) zanken; (*fight*) (coll) raufen

scrap'book' *s* Einklebebuch *n*

scrape [skrep] *s* Kratzer *m*; (coll) Patsche *f* || *tr* schaben; (*the skin*) abscheuern; **s. off** abschaben; **s. together** (or **up**) zusammenkratzen

scrap' heap' *s* Schrotthaufen *m*; (*refuse heap*) Abfallhaufen *m*

scrap' i'ron *s* Schrott *m*, Alteisen *n*

scrapper ['skræpər] *s* Zänker –in *mf*

scrappy ['skræpi] *adj* (*made of scraps*) zusammengestoppelt; (coll) rauflustig

scratch [skrætʃ] *s* Kratzer *m*, Schramme *f*; **start from s.** wieder ganz von vorne anfangen || *tr* kratzen; (sport) streichen; **s. open** aufkratzen; **s. out** (*a line*) ausstreichen; (*eyes*) aushacken; **s. the surface of** nur streifen || *intr* kratzen; (*scratch oneself*) sich kratzen

scratch' pad' *s* Notizblock *m*

scratch' pa'per *s* Schmierpapier *n*

scrawl [skrɔl] *s* Gekritzel *n* || *tr & intr* kritzeln

scrawny ['skrɔni] *adj* spindeldürr

scream [skrim] *s* Aufschrei *m*; **he's a s.!** er ist zum Schreien || *tr & intr* schreien

screech [skritʃ] *s* Kreischen *n* || *intr* (*said of tires, brakes*) kreischen; (*said of an owl*) schreien

screech' owl' *s* Kauz *m*

screen [skrin] *s* Wandschirm *m*; (*for a window*) Fliegengitter *n*; (*camouflage*) Tarnung *f*; (aer) (of) Abschirmung *f* (durch); (cin) Leinwand *f*; (nav) Geleitschutz *m*; (radar, telv) Leinwand *f* || *tr* (*sand, gravel, coal; applications*) durchsieben; (*applicants*) überprüfen; (*a porch, windows*) mit Fliegengittern versehen; (mil) verschleiern; **s. off** abschirmen

screen'play' *s* Filmdrama *n*; (*scenario*) Drehbuch *n*

screen' test' *s* Probeaufnahme *f*

screw [skru] *s* Schraube *f*; **he has a s. loose** (coll) bei ihm ist e-e Schraube locker || *tr* schrauben; (*cheat*) (sl) hereinlegen; (*vulg*) vögeln; **s. tight** festschrauben; **s. up** (*courage*) aufbringen; (*bungle*) (coll) verpfuschen

screw'ball' *adj* (coll) verrückt || *s* (coll) Wirrkopf *m*

screw'driv'er *s* Schraubenzieher *m*

screw'-on cap' *s* Schraubendeckel *m*

screwy ['skru-i] *adj* (sl) verrückt

scribble ['skrɪbəl] *s* Gekritzel *n* || *tr & intr* kritzeln

scribe [skraɪb] *s* Schreiber *m*; (Bib) Schriftgelehrte *m*

scrimmage ['skrɪmɪdʒ] *s* (fb) Übungsspiel *n*

scrimp [skrɪmp] *tr* knausern mit || *intr* (on) knausern (mit)

scrimpy ['skrɪmpi] *adj* knapp

script [skrɪpt] *s* (*handwriting*) Handschrift *f*; (cin) Drehbuch *n*; (rad) Textbuch *n*; (typ) Schreibschrift *f*

scriptural ['skrɪptʃərəl] *adj* biblisch; **s. passage** Bibelstelle *f*

Scripture ['skrɪptʃər] *s* die Heilige Schrift; *(Bible passage)* Bibelzitat *n*
script'writ'er *s* (cin) Drehbuchautor *m*
scrofula ['skrɔfjələ] *s* Skrofeln *pl*
scroll [skrol] *s* Schriftrolle *f*; (archit) Schnörkel *m*
scroll'work' *s* Schnörkelverzierung *f*
scro·tum ['skrotəm] *s* (-ta [tə] or -tums) Hodensack *m*
scrounge [skraundʒ] *tr* stibitzen ‖ *intr* —s. around for herumstöbern nach
scrub [skrʌb] *s* Schrubben *n*; *(shrubs)* Buschwerk *n*; (sport) Ersatzmann *m* ‖ *v* (*pret & pp* **scrubbed**; *ger* **scrubbing**) *tr* schrubben
scrub'bing brush' *s* Scheuerbürste *f*
scrub'wom'an *s* (-wom'en) Scheuerfrau *f*
scruff [skrʌf] *s*—s. of the neck Genick *n*
scruple ['skrupəl] *s* Skrupel *m*
scrupulous ['skrupjələs] *adj* skrupulös
scrutinize ['skrutɪ ˌnaɪz] *tr* genau prüfen; *(a person)* mustern
scrutiny ['skrutɪni] *s* genaue Prüfung *f*
scud [skʌd] *s* Wolkenfetzen *pl*
scuff [skʌf] *tr* *(a shoe, waxed floor)* abschürfen ‖ *intr* *(shuffle)* schlurfen
scuffle ['skʌfəl] *s* Rauferei *f* ‖ *intr* raufen
scuff' mark' *s* Schmutzfleck *m*
scull [skʌl] *s* (sport) Skull *m* ‖ *intr* (sport) skullen
scullery ['skʌləri] *s* Spülküche *f*
scul'lery maid' *s* Spülerin *f*
sculptor ['skʌlptər] *s* Bildhauer *m*
sculptress ['skʌlptrɪs] *s* Bildhauerin *f*
sculptural ['skʌlptʃərəl] *adj* bildhauerisch
sculpture ['skʌlptʃər] *s* *(art)* Bildhauerei *f*; *(work of art)* Skulptur *f* ‖ *tr* meißeln ‖ *intr* bildhauern
scum [skʌm] *s* (& fig) Abschaum *m*
scummy ['skʌmi] *adj* schaumig; (fig) niederträchtig
scurrilous ['skʌrɪləs] *adj* skurril
scur·ry ['skʌri] *v* (*pret & pp* -**ried**) *intr* huschen
scurvy ['skʌrvi] *adj* gemein ‖ *s* Skorbut *m*
scuttle ['skʌtəl] *s* (naut) Springluke *f* ‖ *tr* *(hopes, plans)* vernichten; (naut) selbst versenken
scut'tlebutt' *s* (coll) Latrinenparole *f*
scut'tling *s* Selbstversenkung *f*
scythe [saɪð] *s* Sense *f*
sea [si] *s* See *f*, Meer *n*; at sea auf See; go to sea zur See gehen; heavy seas hoher (or schwerer) Seegang *m*
sea'board' *s* Küstenstrich *m*
sea' breeze' *s* Seebrise *f*
sea'coast' *s* Seeküste *f*, Meeresküste *f*
seafarer ['si ˌferər] *s* Seefahrer *m*
seafaring ['si ˌferɪŋ] *s* Seefahrt *f*
sea'food' *s* Fischgerichte *pl*
sea'go'ing *adj* seetüchtig
sea' gull' *s* Seemöwe *f*, Möwe *f*
seal [sil] *s* Siegel *n*; (zool) Seehund *m* ‖ *tr* *(a document)* siegeln; *(a deal, s.o.'s fate)* besiegeln; *(against leakage)* verschließen, abdichten; **s. off** (mil) abriegeln; **s. up** abdichten

sea' legs' *spl*—get one's s. seefest werden
sea'lev'el *s* Meereshöhe *f*
seal'ing wax' *s* Siegellack *m*
seal'skin' *s* Seehundsfell *n*
seam [sim] *s* *(groove)* Fuge *f*; (geol) Lager *n*; (min) Flöz *n*; (sew) Naht *f*
sea'man *s* (-men) Seemann *m*; (nav) Matrose *m*
sea' mile' *s* Seemeile *f*
seamless ['simlɪs] *adj* nahtlos
sea' mon'ster *s* Meeresungeheuer *n*
seamstress ['simstrɪs] *s* Näherin *f*
seamy ['simi] *adj* verrufen; **s. side** (fig) Schattenseite *f*
séance ['se·ɑns] *s* Séance *f*
sea'plane' *s* Seeflugzeug *n*
sea'port' *s* Seehafen *m*
sea'port town' *s* Hafenstadt *f*
sea' pow'er *s* Seemacht *f*
sear [sɪr] *tr* versengen
search [sʌrtʃ] *s* Durchsuchung *f*; *(for a person)* **(for)** Fahndung *f* (nach); **in s. of** auf der Suche nach ‖ *tr* durchsuchen ‖ *intr* suchen; **s. for** suchen, fahnden nach
search'ing *adj* gründlich; *(glance)* forschend
search'light' *s* Scheinwerfer *m*
search' war'rant *s* Haussuchungsbefehl *m*
seascape ['si ˌskep] *s* Seegemälde *n*
sea' shell' *s* Muschel *f*
sea'shore' *s* Strand *m*
sea'shore resort' *s* Seebad *n*
sea'sick' *adj* seekrank
sea'sick'ness *s* Seekrankheit *f*
sea'side' *adj* Meeres-, See-
season ['sizən] *s* Jahreszeit *f*; *(appropriate period)* Saison *f*; **closed s.** (hunt) Schonzeit *f*; **dry s.** Trockenzeit *f*; **in and out of s.** jederzeit; **in s.** zur rechten Zeit; **out of s.** *(game)* außerhalb der Saison; *(fruits, vegetables)* nicht auf dem Markt; **peak s.** Hochsaison *f* ‖ *tr* *(food)* würzen; *(wine)* lagern; *(wood)* austrocknen lassen; *(tobacco)* reifen lassen; *(soldiers)* abhärten ‖ *intr* (e.g., *said of wine)* (ab)lagern
seasonal ['sizənəl] *adj* jahreszeitlich; *(caused by seasons)* saisonbedingt
sea'sonal work' *s* Saisonarbeit *f*
sea'soned *adj* erfahren; *(troops)* kampfgewohnt, fronterfahren
sea'soning *s* Würze *f*
sea'son's greet'ings *spl* Festgrüße *pl*
sea'son tick'et *s* Dauerkarte *f*
seat [sit] *s* Sitz *m*, Platz *m*; *(of trousers)* Gesäß *n*; **have a s.** Platz nehmen; **keep one's s.** sitzenbleiben ‖ *tr* *(a person)* e-n Platz anweisen *(dat)*; *(said of a room)* Sitzplätze bieten für; **be seated** sich hinsetzen
seat' belt' *s* (aer, aut) Sicherheitsgurt *m*; **fasten seat belts!** bitte anschnallen!
seat' cov'er *s* (aut) Auto-Schonbezug *m*
seat'ing capac'ity *s* **(for)** Sitzgelegenheit *f* (für); **have a s. of** fassen
seat' of gov'ernment *s* Regierungssitz *m*
sea'wall' *s* Strandmauer *f*

sea'way' s Seeweg m; *(heavy sea)* schwerer Seegang m
sea'weed' s Alge f, Seetang m
sea'wor'thy adj seetüchtig
secede [sɪ'sid] intr sich trennen
secession [sɪ'sɛ/ən] s Sezession f
seclude [sɪ'klud] tr abschließen
seclud'ed adj abgeschieden; *(life)* zurückgezogen; *(place)* abgelegen
seclusion [sɪ'kluʒən] s Zurückgezogenheit f, Abgeschiedenheit f
second ['sɛkənd] adj zweite; **be s. to none** niemandem nachstehen; **in the s. place** zweitens; **s. in command** stellvertretender Kommandeur m || s *(unit of time)* Sekunde f; *(moment)* Augenblick m; *(in boxing or duelling)* Sekundant m; **George the Second** Georg der Zweite; **the s.** *(of the month)* der zweite || pron zweite || tr unterstützen
secondary ['sɛkən,dɛri] adj sekundär, Neben– || s *(elec)* Sekundärwicklung f; *(fb)* Spieler pl in der zweiten Reihe
sec'ondary school' s Oberschule
sec'ondary-school teach'er s Oberlehrer –in mf
sec'ondary sourc'es spl Sekundärliteratur f
sec'ondary tar'get s Ausweichziel n
sec'ond best' s Zweitbeste mfn
sec'ond-best' adj zweitbeste; **come off s.** den kürzeren ziehen
sec'ond-class' adj zweitklassig; **s. ticket** Fahrkarte f zweiter Klasse
sec'ond cous'in s Cousin m (or Kusine f) zweiten Grades
sec'ond fid'dle s—**play s.** die zweite Geige spielen
sec'ond hand' s *(horol)* Sekundenzeiger m
sec'ondhand' adj *(car)* gebraucht *(information)* aus zweiter Hand; *(books)* antiquarisch
sec'ondhand book'store s Antiquariat n
sec'ondhand deal'er s Altwarenhändler –in mf
sec'ond lieuten'ant s Leutnant m
secondly ['sɛkəndli] adv zweitens
sec'ond mate' s (naut) zweiter Offizier m
sec'ond na'ture s zweite Natur f
sec'ond-rate' adj zweitklassig
sec'ond sight' s zweites Gesicht n
sec'ond thought' s—**have second thoughts** Bedenken hegen; **on s.** bei weiterem Nachdenken
sec'ond wind' s—**get one's s.** wieder zu Kräften kommen
secrecy ['sikrəsi] s Heimlichkeit f
secret ['sikrɪt] adj geheim || s Geheimnis n; **in s.** insgeheim; **keep no secrets from** keine Geheimnisse haben vor *(dat)*; **keep s.** geheimhalten; **make no s. of** kein Hehl machen aus
secretary ['sɛkrə,tɛri] s *(man, desk, bird)* Sekretär m; *(female)* Sekretärin f; *(in government)* Minister m
sec'retary-gen'eral s Generalsekretär m
sec'retary of com'merce s Handelsminister m

sec'retary of defense' s Verteidigungsminister m
sec'retary of la'bor s Arbeitsminister m
sec'retary of state' s Außenminister m
sec'retary of the inter'ior s Innenminister m
sec'retary of the treas'ury s Finanzminister m
se'cret bal'lot s geheime Abstimmung f
secrete [sɪ'krit] tr *(hide)* verstecken; *(physiol)* absondern, ausscheiden
secretive ['sikrɪtɪv] adj verschwiegen
se'cret police' s Geheimpolizei f
se'cret serv'ice s Geheimdienst m
sect [sɛkt] s Sekte f
sectarian [sɛk'tɛri·ən] adj sektiererisch; *(school)* Konfessions–
section ['sɛk/ən] s *(segment, part)* Teil m; *(of a newspaper, chapter)* Abschnitt m; *(of a city)* Viertel n; *(group)* Abteilung f; *(cross section; thin slice, e.g., of tissue)* Schnitt m; *(jur)* Paragraph m; *(mil)* Halbzug m; *(rr)* Strecke f; *(surg)* Sektion f; **tr—s. off** abteilen
sectional ['sɛk/ənəl] adj *(view)* Teil–; *(pride)* Lokal–
sec'tional fur'niture s Anbaumöbel n
sec'tion hand' s Schienenleger m
sector ['sɛktər] s Sektor m
secular ['sɛkjələr] adj weltlich || s Weltpriester m, Weltgeistlicher m
secularism ['sɛkjələ,rɪzəm] s Weltlichkeit f, Säkularismus m
secure [sɪ'kjʊr] adj sicher || tr *(make fast)* sichern; *(obtain)* sich *[dat]* beschaffen
security [sɪ'kjʊriti] s (& jur) Sicherheit f; **securities** Wertpapiere pl
sedan [sɪ'dæn] s Limousine f
sedan' chair' s Sänfte f
sedate [sɪ'det] adj gesetzt
sedation [sɪ'de/ən] s Beruhigung f
sedative ['sɛdətɪv] s Beruhigungsmittel n
sedentary ['sɛdən,tɛri] adj sitzend
sedge [sɛdʒ] s (bot) Segge f
sediment ['sɛdɪmənt] s Bodensatz m; *(geol)* Ablagerung f, Sediment n
sedition [sɪ'dɪ/ən] s Aufruhr m
seditious [sɪ'dɪ/əs] adj aufrührerisch
seduce [sɪ'd(j)us] tr verführen
seducer [sɪ'd(j)usər] s Verführer –in mf
seduction [sɪ'dʌk/ən] s Verführung f
seductive [sɪ'dʌktɪv] adj verführerisch
sedulous ['sɛdʒələs] adj emsig
see [si] s *(eccl)* (erz)bischöflicher Stuhl m || v *(pret saw* [sɔ]; *pp* **seen** [sin]) tr sehen; *(comprehend)* verstehen; *(realize)* einsehen; *(a doctor)* gehen zu; **see red** rasend werden; **see s.o. off** j–n an den Zug (ans Flugzeug) bringen; **see s.o. to the door** j–n zur Tür geleiten; **see s.th. through** etw durchstehen; **that remains to be seen** das wird man erst sehen || intr sehen; **see through** (fig) durchschauen; **see to** sich kümmern um; **see to it that** sich darum kümmern,

daß; **you see** (*parenthetical*) wissen Sie

seed [sid] *s* Samen *m*; (*collective & fig*) Saat *f*; (*in fruit*) Kern *m*; (*physiol*) Samen *m*; **go to s.** in Samen schießen; **seeds** (fig) Keim *m* || *tr* besäen

seed'bed' *s* Samenbeet *n*

seed'ed rye' bread' *s* Kümmelbrot *n*

seedless ['sidlɪs] *adj* kernlos

seedling ['sidlɪŋ] *s* Sämling *m*

seedy ['sidi] *adj* (*person*) heruntergekommen; (*thing*) schäbig

see'ing *s* Sehen *n* || *conj*—**s. that** in Anbetracht dessen, daß

See'ing Eye' dog' *s* Blindenhund *m*

seek [sik] *v* (*pret & pp* **sought** [sɔt]) *tr* suchen; **s. s.o.'s advice** j–s Rat erbitten; **s. to** (*inf*) versuchen zu (*inf*) || *intr*—**s. after** suchen nach

seem [sim] *intr* scheinen || *impers*—**it seems to me** es kommt mir vor

seemingly ['simɪnli] *adv* anscheinend

seemly ['simli] *adj* schicklich

seep [sip] *intr* sickern

seepage ['sipɪdʒ] *s* Durchsickern *n*

seer [sɪr] *s* Seher *m*

seeress ['sɪrɪs] *s* Seherin *f*

see'saw' *s* Schaukelbrett *n*, Wippe *f* || *intr* wippen; (fig) schwanken

seethe [sið] *intr* sieden; **s. with** (fig) sieden vor (*dat*)

segment ['segmənt] *s* Abschnitt *m*

segregate ['segrɪ‚get] *tr* trennen, absondern

segregation [‚segrɪ'geʃən] *s* Absonderung *f*; (*of races*) Rassentrennung *f*

seismograph ['saɪzmə‚græf] *s* Erdbebenmesser *m*, Seismograph *m*

seismology [saɪz'malədʒi] *s* Erdbebenkunde *f*, Seismologie *f*

seize [siz] *tr* anfassen; (*a criminal*) festnehmen; (*a town, fortress*) einnehmen; (*an opportunity*) ergreifen; (*power*) an sich reißen; (*confiscate*) beschlagnahmen

seizure ['siʒər] *s* Besitzergreifung *f*; (*confiscation*) Beschlagnahme *f*; (*pathol*) plötzlicher Anfall *m*

seldom ['seldəm] *adv* selten

select [sɪ'lɛkt] *adj* erlesen || *tr* auslesen, auswählen

select'ed *adj* ausgesucht

selection [sɪ'lɛkʃən] *s* Auswahl *f*

selective [sɪ'lɛktɪv] *adj* Auswahl–; (rad) trennscharf

selec'tive serv'ice *s* allgemeine Wehrpflicht *f*

self [self] *s* (*selves* [selvz]) Selbst *n*, Ich *n*; **be one's old s. again** wieder der alte sein; **his better s.** sein besseres Ich || *pron*—**payable to s.** auf Selbst ausgestellt

self'-addressed en'velope *s* mit Anschrift versehener Freiumschlag *m*

self'-assur'ance *s* Selbstbewußtsein *n*

self'-cen'tered *adj* ichbezogen

self'-conceit'ed *adj* eingebildet

self'-con'fident *adj* selbstsicher

self'-con'scious *adj* befangen

self'-control' *s* Selbstbeherrschung *f*

self'-decep'tion *s* Selbsttäuschung *f*

self'-defense' *s* Selbstverteidigung *f*; **in s.** aus Notwehr

self'-deni'al *s* Selbstverleugnung *f*

self'-destruc'tion *s* Selbstvernichtung *f*

self'-determina'tion *s* Selbstbestimmung *f*

self'-dis'cipline *s* Selbstzucht *f*

self'-ed'ucated per'son *s* Autodidakt –in *mf*

self'-employed' *adj* selbständig

self'-esteem' *s* Selbsteinschätzung *f*

self'-ev'ident *adj* selbstverständlich

self'-explan'ator'y *adj* keiner Erklärung bedürftig

self'-gov'ernment *s* Selbstverwaltung *f*

self'-impor'tant *adj* eingebildet

self'-indul'gence *s* Genußsucht *f*

self'-in'terest *s* Eigennutz *m*

selfish ['selfɪʃ] *adj* eigennützig

selfishness ['selfɪʃnɪs] *s* Eigennutz *m*

selfless ['selflɪs] *adj* selbstlos

self'-love' *s* Selbstliebe *f*

self'-made man' *s* Selfmademan *m*

self'-por'trait *s* Selbstbildnis *n*

self'-possessed' *adj* selbstbeherrscht

self'-praise' *s* Eigenlob *n*

self'-preserva'tion *s* Selbsterhaltung *f*

self'-reli'ant *adj* selbstsicher

self'-respect' *s* Selbstachtung *f*

self'-right'eous *adj* selbstgerecht

self'-sac'rifice *s* Selbstaufopferung *f*

self'-same' *adj* ebenderselbe

self'-sat'isfied *adj* selbstzufrieden

self'-seek'ing *adj* selbstsüchtig

self'-serv'ice *adj* mit Selbstbedienung || *s* Selbstbedienung *f*

self'-styled' *adj* von eigenen Gnaden

self'-suffi'cient *adj* selbstgenügsam

self'-support'ing *adj* finanziell unabhängig

self'-taught' *adj* autodidaktisch

self'-willed' *adj* eigenwillig

self'-wind'ing *adj* automatisch

sell [sel] *v* (*pret & pp* **sold** [sold]) *tr* verkaufen; (*at auction*) versteigern; (*wares*) führen; **be sold on** (coll) begeistert sein von; **s. dirt cheap** verramschen; **s. s.o. on s.th.** (coll) j–n zu etw überreden; **s. out** ausverkaufen; (*betray*) verraten; **s. short** (st. exch.) in blanko verkaufen || *intr* sich verkaufen; **s. for** verkauft werden für; **s. short** fixen

seller ['selər] *s* Verkäufer –in *mf*; **good s.** (com) Reißer *m*

Seltzer ['seltsər] *s* Selterswasser *n*

selvage ['selvɪdʒ] *s* (*of fabric*) Salleiste *f*; (*of a lock*) Eckplatte *f*

semantic [sɪ'mæntɪk] *adj* semantisch || **semantics** *s* Wortbedeutungslehre *f*

semaphore ['semə‚for] *s* Winkzeichen *n*; (rr) Semaphor *m* || *intr* winken

semblance ['sembləns] *s* Anschein *m*

semen ['simən] *s* Samen *m*

semicircle ['semɪ‚sʌrkəl] *s* Halbkreis *m*

semicolon ['semɪ‚kolən] *s* Strichpunkt *m*

semiconductor [‚semɪkən'dʌktər] *s* Halbleiter *m*

semiconscious [‚semɪ'kanʃəs] *adj* halbbewußt

semifinal [ˌsemiˈfaɪnəl] *adj* Halb-finale- ‖ *s* Halbfinale *n*, Vorschluß-runde *f*

seminar [ˈsemiˌnɑr] *s* Seminar *n*

seminarian [ˌsemiˈneri·ən] *s* Semina-rist *m*

seminary [ˈsemiˌneri] *s* Seminar *n*

semiprecious [ˌsemiˈpreʃəs] *adj* halb-edel

Semite [ˈsemaɪt] *s* Semit –in *mf*

Semitic [sɪˈmɪtɪk] *adj* semitisch

semitrailer [ˈsemiˌtrelər] *s* Schleppan-hänger *m*

senate [ˈsenɪt] *s* Senat *m*

senator [ˈsenətər] *s* Senator *m*

senatorial [ˌsenəˈtori·əl] *adj* (*of one senator*) senatorisch; (*of the senate*) Senats-

send [send] *v* (*pret & pp* sent [sent]) *tr* schicken, senden; (rad, telv) sen-den; **s. back** zurückschicken; **s. back word** zurücksagen lassen; **s. down** (box) niederschlagen; **s. forth** (leaves) treiben; **s. off** absenden; **s. on** (forward) weiterbefördern; **s. word that** benachrichtigen, daß ‖ *intr*—**s. for** (*e.g., free samples*) be-stellen; (*e.g., a doctor*) rufen lassen

sender [ˈsendər] *s* Absender –in *mf*; (telg) Geber –in *mf*

send'-off' *s* Abschiedsfeier *f*

senile [ˈsinaɪl] *adj* senil

senility [sɪˈnɪlɪti] *s* Senilität *f*

senior [ˈsinjər] *adj* (*in age*) älter; (*in rank*) ranghöher; (*class*) oberste; **Mr. John Smith Senior** Herr John Smith senior ‖ *s* Älteste *mf*; (*student*) Student –in *mf* im letzten Studienjahr

sen'ior cit'izen *s* bejahrter Mitbürger *m*

seniority [sinˈjɑrɪti] *s* Dienstalter *n*

sen'ior of'ficer *s* Vorgesetzte *mf*

sen'ior part'ner *s* geschäftsführender Partner *m*

sen'ior year' *s* letztes Studienjahr *n*

sensation [senˈseʃən] *s* (*feeling*) Ge-fühl *n*; (*cause of interest*) Sensation *f*

sensational [senˈseʃənəl] *adj* sensatio-nell

sensationalism [senˈseʃənəˌlɪzəm] *s* Sensationsgier *f*

sense [sens] *s* (*e.g., of sight; meaning*) Sinn *m*; (*feeling*) Gefühl *n*; (*com-mon sense*) Verstand *m*; **be out of one's senses** von Sinnen sein; **bring s.o. to his senses** j–n zur Vernunft bringen; **in a s.** in gewissem Sinne; **in the broadest s.** im weitesten Sinne; **make s.** Sinn haben; **there's no s. to it** da steckt kein Sinn drin ‖ *tr* spüren, fühlen

senseless [ˈsenslɪs] *adj* sinnlos; (*from a blow*) bewußtlos

sense' of direc'tion *s* Ortssinn *m*

sense' of du'ty *s* Pflichtgefühl *n*

sense' of guilt' *s* Schuldgefühl *n*

sense' of hear'ing *s* Gehör *n*

sense' of hon'or *s* Ehrgefühl *n*

sense' of hu'mor *s* Humor *m*

sense' of jus'tice *s* Gerechtigkeits-gefühl *n*

sense' of responsibil'ity *s* Verantwor-tungsbewußtsein *n*

sense' of sight' *s* Gesichtssinn *m*

sense' of smell' *s* Geruchssinn *m*

sense' of taste' *s* Geschmackssinn *m*

sense' of touch' *s* Tastsinn *m*

sense' or'gan *s* Sinnesorgan *n*

sensibility [ˌsensɪˈbrlɪti] *s* Empfind-lichkeit *f*

sensible [ˈsensɪbəl] *adj* vernünftig

sensitive [ˈsensɪtɪv] *adj* (**to**, *e.g., cold*) empfindlich (gegen); (*touchy*) über-empfindlich; **s. post** Vertrauensposten *m*; **very s.** überempfindlich

sensitize [ˈsensɪˌtaɪz] *tr* (phot) licht-empfindlich machen

sensory [ˈsensəri] *adj* Sinnes-

sen'sory depriva'tion *s* Reizentzug *m*

sensual [ˈsensʊ·əl] *adj* sinnlich

sensuality [ˌsensʊˈælɪti] *s* Sinnlichkeit *f*, Sinnenlust *f*

sensuous [ˈsensʊ·əs] *adj* sinnlich

sentence [ˈsentəns] *s* (gram) Satz *m*; (jur) Urteil *n*; **pronounce s.** das Ur-teil verkünden ‖ *tr* verurteilen

sentiment [ˈsentɪmənt] *s* Empfindung *f*

sentimental [ˌsentɪˈmentəl] *adj* senti-mental, rührselig

sentinel [ˈsentɪnəl] *s* Posten *m*; **stand s.** Wache stehen

sentry [ˈsentri] *s* Wachposten *m*

sen'try box' *s* Schilderhaus *n*

separable [ˈsepərəbəl] *adj* trennbar

separate [ˈsepərɪt] *adj* getrennt; **under s. cover** separat ‖ [ˈsepəˌret] *tr* trennen; (*segregate*) absondern; (*scatter*) zerstreuen; (*discharge*) ent-lassen; **s. into** teilen in (*acc*) ‖ *intr* sich trennen, sich scheiden

sep'arated *adj* (*couple*) getrennt

separation [ˌsepəˈreʃən] *s* Trennung *f*

September [sepˈtembər] *s* September *m*

sep'tic tank' [ˈseptɪk] *s* Kläranlage *f*

sepulcher [ˈsepəlkər] *s* Grabmal *n*

sequel [ˈsikwəl] *s* Fortsetzung *f*; (fig) Nachspiel *n*

sequence [ˈsikwəns] *s* Reihenfolge *f*

se'quence of tens'es *s* Zeitenfolge *f*

sequester [sɪˈkwestər] *tr* (*remove*) ent-fernen; (*separate*) absondern; (jur) sequestrieren

sequins [ˈsikwɪnz] *spl* Flitter *m*

ser-aph [ˈseraf] *s* (-aphs & -aphim [əfɪm]) Seraph *m*

Serb [sʌrb] *adj* serbisch ‖ *s* Serbe *m*, Serbin *f*

Serbia [ˈsʌrbɪ·ə] *s* Serbien *n*

serenade [ˌserəˈned] *s* Ständchen *n* ‖ *tr* ein Ständchen bringen (dat)

serene [sɪˈrin] *adj* heiter; (*sea*) ruhig

serenity [sɪˈrenɪti] *s* Heiterkeit *f*

serf [sʌrf] *s* Leibeigene *mf*

serfdom [ˈsʌrfdəm] *s* Leibeigenschaft *f*

serge [sʌrdʒ] *s* (tex) Serge *f*

sergeant [ˈsɑrdʒənt] *s* Feldwebel *m*

ser'geant-at-arms' *s* (sergeants-at-arms) Ordnungsbeamter *m*

ser'geant first' class' *s* Oberfeldwebel *m*

ser'geant ma'jor *s* (sergeant majors) Hauptfeldwebel *m*

serial ['sɪrɪ-əl] *s* Fortsetzungsroman *m*, Romanfolge *f*

serialize ['sɪrɪ-ə‚laɪz] *tr* in Fortsetzungen veröffentlichen

se'rial num'ber *s* laufende Nummer *f*; (*of a product*) Fabriknummer *f*

se·ries ['sɪrɪz] *s* (**-ries**) Serie *f*, Reihe *f*; **in s.** reihenweise; (elec) hintereinandergeschaltet

serious ['sɪrɪ-əs] *adj* ernst; (*mistake*) schwerwiegend; (*illness*) gefährlich

seriously ['sɪrɪ-əslɪ] *adv* ernstlich; **s. wounded** schwerverwundet; **take s. ernst** nehmen

seriousness ['sɪrɪ-əsnɪs] *s* Ernst *m*

sermon ['sʌrmən] *s* Predigt *f*

sermonize ['sʌrmə‚naɪz] *intr* e–e Moralpredigt halten

serpent ['sʌrpənt] *s* Schlange *f*

serrated ['seretɪd] *adj* sägeartig

se·rum ['sɪrəm] *s* (**-rums** & **–ra** [rə]) Serum *n*

servant ['sʌrvənt] *s* Diener –in *mf*; (*domestic*) Hausdiener –in *mf*

serv'ant girl' *s* Dienstmädchen *n*

serve [sʌrv] *s* (tennis) Aufschlag *m* ‖ *tr* (*a master, God*) dienen (*dat*); (*food*) servieren; (*a meal*) anrichten; (*guests*) bedienen; (*time in jail*) verbüßen; (*one's term in the service*) abdienen; (*the purpose*) erfüllen; (tennis) aufschlagen; **s. mass** (eccl) zur Messe dienen; **s. notice on s.o.** j–n vorladen; **s. up** (*food*) auftragen ‖ *intr* (& *mil*) dienen; (*at table*) servieren; **s. as** dienen als; **s. on a committe** e–m Ausschuß angehören

server ['sʌrvər] *s* (eccl) Ministrant *m*; (tennis) Aufschläger *m*

service ['sʌrvɪs] *s* (*diplomatic, secret, foreign, public, etc.*) Dienst *m*; (*in a restaurant*) Bedienung *f*; (*set of table utensils*) Besteck *n*; (*set of dishes*) Service *n*; (*assistance at a repair shop*) Service *m*; (*maintenance*) Wartung *f*; (*transportation*) Verkehr *m*; (*relig*) Gottesdienst *m*; (tennis) Aufschlag *m*; **at your s.** zu Ihren Diensten; **be in s.** (mach) in Betrieb sein; **be in the s.** (mil) beim Militär sein; **be of s.** behilflich sein; **do s.o. a s.** j–m e–n Dienst erweisen; **essential services** lebenswichtige Betriebe *pl*; **fit for active s.** kriegsverwendungsfähig; **see s.** Kriegsdienst tun; **the services** die Waffengattungen *pl* ‖ *tr* (mach) warten

serviceable ['sʌrvɪsəbəl] *adj* (*usable*) verwendungsfähig; (*helpful*) nützlich; (*durable*) haltbar

serv'ice club' *s* (mil) Soldatenklub *m*

serv'ice en'trance *s* Dienstboteneingang *m*

serv'ice·man' *s* (**–men'**) Monteur *m*; (*at a gas station*) Tankwart *m*; (mil) Soldat *m*

serv'ice rec'ord *s* Wehrpaß *m*

serv'ice sta'tion *s* Tankstelle *f*

serv'ice-station atten'dant *s* Tankwart *m*

serv'ice troops' *spl* Versorgungstruppen *pl*

servile ['sʌrvaɪl] *adj* kriecherisch

serv'ing *s* Portion *f*; (*e.g., of a subpoena*) Zustellung *f*

serv'ing cart' *s* Servierwagen *m*

servitude ['sʌrvɪ‚t(j)ud] *s* Knechtschaft *f*

ses'ame seed' ['sesəmɪ] *s* Sesamsamen *m*

session ['seʃən] *s* Sitzung *f*, Tagung *f*; (educ) Semester *n*; **be in session** tagen

set [set] *adj* (*price, time*) festgesetzt; (*rule*) festgelegt; (*speech*) wohlüberlegt; **be all set** fix und fertig sein; **be set in one's ways** festgefahren sein ‖ *s* (*group of things belonging together*) Satz *m*, Garnitur *f*; (*of chess or checkers*) Spiel *n*; (*clique*) Sippschaft *f*; (rad, telv) Apparat *m*; (*tennis*) Satz *m*; (theat) Bühnenbild *n*; **younger set** Nachwuchs *m* ‖ *v* (*pret* & *pp* **set**; *ger* **setting**) *tr* (*put*) setzen; (*stand*) stellen; (*lay*) legen; (*a clock, a trap*) stellen; (*the hair*) legen; (*a record*) aufstellen; (*an example*) geben; (*a time, price*) festsetzen; (*the table*) decken; (*jewels*) (ein)fassen; (*a camera*) einstellen; (surg) einrenken; (typ) setzen; **set ahead** (*a clock*) vorstellen; **set back** (*a clock*) nachstellen; (*a patient*) zurückwerfen; **set down** niedersetzen; **set down in writing** schriftlich niederlegen; **set foot in** (or on) betreten; **set forth** (*explain*) erklären; **set free** freilassen; **set in order** in Ordnung bringen; **set limits to** Schranken setzen (*dat*); **set off** (*a bomb*) sprengen lassen; **set** (*s.o.*) **over** (j–n) überordnen (*dat*); **set right** wieder in Ordnung bringen; **set store by** Gewicht beimessen (*dat*); **set straight** (on) aufklären (über *acc*); **set the meeting for two** die Versammlung auf zwei Uhr ansetzen; **set up** (*at the bar*) (coll) zu e–m Gläschen einladen; (mach) montieren; (typ) (ab)setzen; **set up housekeeping** Wirtschaft führen; **set up in business** etablieren ‖ *intr* (*said of cement*) abbinden; (astr) untergehen; **set about** (*ger*) darangehen zu (*inf*); **set in** einsetzen; **set out** (for) sich auf den Weg machen (nach); **set out on** (*a trip*) antreten; **set to work** sich an die Arbeit machen

set'back' *s* Rückschlag *m*, Schlappe *f*

set'screw' *s* Stellschraube *f*

settee [se'ti] *s* Polsterbank *f*

setter ['setər] *s* Vorstehhund *m*

set'ting *s* (*of the sun*) Niedergang *m*; (*of a story*) Ort *m* der Handlung; (*of a gem*) Fassung *f*; (theat) Bühnenbild *n*

settle ['setəl] *tr* (*conclude*) erledigen; (*decide*) entscheiden; (*an argument*) schlichten; (*a problem*) erledigen; (*an account*) begleichen; (*one's affairs*) in Ordnung bringen; (*a creditor's claim*) befriedigen; (*a lawsuit*) durch Vergleich beilegen; (*a region*) besiedeln; (*people*) ansiedeln || *intr* (*in a region*) sich niederlassen; (*said of a building*) sich senken; (*said of a ship*) absacken; (*said of dust*) sich legen; (*said of a liquid*) sich klären; (*said of suspended particles*) sich setzen; (*said of a cold*) (**in**) sich festsetzen (in *dat*); **s. down** (*in a chair*) sich niederlassen; (*calm down*) sich beruhigen; **s. down to** (*e.g., work*) sich machen an (*acc*); **s. for** sich einigen auf (*acc*); **s. on** sich entscheiden für; **s. up** (*fin*) die Verbindlichkeit vergleichen

settlement ['sɛtəlmənt] *s* (*colony*) Siedlung *f*; (*agreement*) Abkommen *n*; (*of an argument*) Beilegung *f*; (*of accounts*) Abrechnung *f*; (*of a debt*) Begleichung *f*; **reach a s.** e-n Vergleich schließen

settler ['sɛtlər] *s* Ansiedler –in *mf*

set'up' *s* Aufbau *m*, Anlage *f*

seven ['sɛvən] *adj & pron* sieben || *s* Sieben *f*

seventeen ['sɛvən'tin] *adj & pron* siebzehn || *s* Siebzehn *f*

seventeenth ['sɛvən'tinθ] *adj & pron* siebzehnte || *s* (*fraction*) Siebzehntel *n*; **the s.** (*in dates or a series*) der Siebzehnte

seventh ['sɛvənθ] *adj & pron* sieb(en)te || *s* (*fraction*) Sieb(en)tel *n*; **the s.** (*in dates or a series*) der Sieb(en)te

seventieth ['sɛvəntɪ·θ] *adj & pron* siebzigste || *s* (*fraction*) Siebzigstel *n*

seventy ['sɛvəntɪ] *adj & pron* siebzig || *s* Siebzig *f*; **the seventies** die siebziger Jahre

sev'enty-first' *adj & pron* einundsiebzigste

sev'enty-one' *adj* einundsiebzig

sever ['sɛvər] *tr* (ab)trennen; (*relations*) abbrechen

several ['sɛvərəl] *adj & indef pron* mehrere; **s. times** mehrmals

severance ['sɛvərəns] *s* Trennung *f*; (*of relations*) Abbruch *m*

sev'erance pay' *s* (& *mil*) Abfindungsentschädigung *f*

severe [sɪ'vɪr] *adj* (*judge, winter, cold*) streng; (*blow, sentence, winter*) hart; (*illness, test*) schwer; (*criticism*) scharf

severity [sɪ'vɛrɪtɪ] *s* Strenge *f*; Härte *f*; Schärfe *f*

sew [so] *v* (*pret* **sewed**; *pp* **sewed** & **sewn**) *tr* & *intr* nähen

sewage ['su·ɪdʒ] *s* Abwässer *pl*

sew'age-dispos'al plant' *s* Kläranlage *f*

sewer ['su·ər] *s* Kanal *m* || ['so·ər] *s* Näher –in *mf*

sewerage ['su·ərɪdʒ] *s* Kanalisation *f*

sew'er pipe' ['su·ər] *s* Abwasserleitung *f*

sew'ing *s* Näharbeit *f*

sew'ing bas'ket *s* Nähkasten *m*

sew'ing kit' *s* Nähzeug *n*

sew'ing machine' *s* Nähmaschine *f*

sex [sɛks] *adj* (*crime, education, harmone*) Sexual– || *s* Geschlecht *n*; (*intercourse*) Sex *m*

sex appeal' *s* Sex-Appeal *m*

sex' pot' *s* (coll) Sexbombe *f*

sextent ['sɛkstənt] *s* Sextant *m*

sexton ['sɛkstən] *s* Küster *m*

sexual ['sɛkʃʊ·əl] *adj* geschlechtlich, Geschlechts–, sexuell

sex'ual in'tercourse *s* Geschlechtsverkehr *m*

sexuality [sɛkʃʊ'ælɪtɪ] *s* Sexualität *f*

sexy ['sɛksɪ] *adj* sexy

shabbily ['ʃæbɪlɪ] *adv* schäbig; (*in treatment*) stiefmütterlich

shabby ['ʃæbɪ] *adj* schäbig

shack [ʃæk] *s* Bretterbude *f*

shackle ['ʃækəl] *s* (naut) Schäkel *m*; **shackles** Fesseln *pl* || *tr* fesseln

shad [ʃæd] *s* Shad *m*, Alse *f*

shade [ʃed] *s* Schatten *m*; (*for a window*) Rollo *n*; (*of a lamp*) Schirm *m*; (*hue*) Schattierung *f*; **throw into the s.** (fig) in den Schatten stellen || *tr* beschatten; (paint) schattieren

shad'ing *s* Schattierung *f*

shadow ['ʃædo] *s* Schatten *m* || *tr* (*a person*) beschatten

shad'ow box'ing *s* Schattenboxen *n*

shadowy ['ʃædo·ɪ] *adj* (*like a shadow*) schattenhaft; (*indistinct*) verschwommen; (*shady*) schattig

shady ['ʃedɪ] *adj* schattig; (coll) dunkel; **s. character** Dunkelmann *m*; **s. deal** Lumperei *f*; **s. side** (fig) Schattenseite *f*

shaft [ʃæft] *s* Schaft *m*; (*of an elevator*) Schacht *m*; (*handle*) Stiel *m*; (*of a wagon*) Deichsel *f*; (*of a column*) Säulenschaft *m*; (*of a transmission*) Welle *f*

shaggy ['ʃægɪ] *adj* zottig, struppig

shake [ʃek] *s* Schütteln *n*; **he's no great shakes** mit ihm ist nicht viel los || *v* (*pret* **shook** [ʃʊk]; *pp* **shaken**) *tr* schütteln; **s. a leg!** (coll) rühr dich ein bißchen; **s. before using** vor Gebrauch schütteln; **s. down** (sl) erpressen; **s. hands** sich [*dat*] die Hand geben; **s. hands with** s.o. j–m die Hand drücken; **s. off** (& fig) abschütteln; **s. one's head** mit dem Kopf schütteln; **s. out** (*a rug*) ausschütteln; **s. up** aufschütteln; (fig) aufrütteln || *intr* (**with**) zittern (vor *dat*), beben (vor *dat*)

shake'down' *s* (sl) Erpressung *f*

shake'down cruise' *s* Probefahrt *f*

shaker ['ʃekər] *s* (*for salt*) Streuer *m*; (*for cocktails*) Shaker *m*

shake'-up' *s* Umgruppierung *f*

shaky ['ʃekɪ] *adj* (& fig) wacklig

shale [ʃel] *s* Schiefer *m*

shale' oil' *s* Schieferöl *n*

shall [ʃæl] *v* (*pret* **should** [ʃʊd]) *aux* (*to express future tense*) werden, e.g., **I s. go** ich werde gehen; (*to express obligation*) sollen, e.g., **s. I stay?** soll ich bleiben?

shallow ['ʃælo] *adj* (*river, person*) seicht; (*water, bowl*) flach || **shallows** *spl* Untiefe *f*

sham [ʃæm] *adj* Schein– || *s* Schein *m* || *v* (*pret & pp* **shammed**; *ger* **shamming**) *tr* vortäuschen

sham′ bat′tle s Scheingefecht n

shambles [ˈʃæmbəlz] s Trümmerhaufen m

shame [ʃem] s Schande f; (feeling of shame) Scham f; **put s.o. to s.** (outdo s.o.) j-n in den Schatten stellen; **s. on you!** schäm dich!; **what a s.!** wie schade! ‖ tr beschämen

shame′faced′ adj verschämt

shameful [ˈʃemfəl] adj schändlich

shameless [ˈʃemlɪs] adj unverschämt

shampoo [ʃæmˈpu] s Shampoo n ‖ tr shampoonieren

shamrock [ˈʃæmrɑk] s Kleeblatt n

Shanghai [ʃæŋˈhaɪ] s Schanghai n ‖ **shanghai** [ˈʃæŋhaɪ] tr schanghaien

shank [ʃæŋk] s Unterschenkel m; (of an anchor, column, golf club) Schaft m; (cut of meat) Schenkel m

shanty [ˈʃæntɪ] s Bude f

shan′tytown′ s Bretterbudensiedlung f

shape [ʃep] s Form f, Gestalt f; **in bad s.** (coll) in schlechter Form; **in good s.** in gutem Zustand; **out of s.** aus der Form; **take s.** sich gestalten ‖ tr formen, gestalten ‖ intr—**s. up** (coll) sich zusammenfassen

shapeless [ˈʃeplɪs] adj formlos

shapely [ˈʃeplɪ] adj wohlgestaltet

share [ʃer] s Anteil m; (st. exch.) Aktie f; **do one's s.** das Seine tun ‖ tr teilen ‖ intr—**s. in** teilhaben an (dat)

share′hold′er s Aktionär –in mf

shark [ʃɑrk] s Hai m, Haifisch m

sharp [ʃɑrp] adj scharf; (pointed) spitzig; (keen) pfiffig ‖ adv pünktlich ‖ s (mus) Kreuz n

sharpen [ˈʃɑrpən] tr schärfen; (a pencil) spitzen

sharply [ˈʃɑrplɪ] adv scharf

sharp′shoot′er s Scharfschütze m

shatter [ˈʃætər] tr zersplittern; (the nerves) zerrütten; (dreams) zerstören ‖ intr zersplittern

shat′terproof′ adj splittersicher

shave [ʃev] s—**get a s.** sich rasieren lassen ‖ tr rasieren ‖ intr sich rasieren

shav′ing brush′ s Rasierpinsel m

shav′ing cream′ s Rasierkrem m

shav′ing mug′ s Rasiernapf m

shawl [ʃɔl] s Schal m

she [ʃi] s Weibchen n ‖ pers pron sie

sheaf [ʃif] s (sheaves [ʃivz]) Garbe f

shear [ʃɪr] s—**shears** Schere f ‖ v (pret sheared; pp sheared & shorn [ʃɔrn]) tr scheren; **s. off** abschneiden

sheath [ʃiθ] s Scheide f

sheathe [ʃið] tr in die Scheide stecken

shed [ʃed] s Schuppen m ‖ v (pret & pp shed; ger shedding) tr (leaves) abwerfen; (tears) vergießen; (hair, leaves) verlieren; (peace) verbreiten; **s. light on** (fig) Licht werfen auf (acc)

sheen [ʃin] s Glanz m

sheep [ʃip] s (sheep) Schaf n

sheep′dog′ s Schäferhund m

sheep′fold′ s Schafhürde f, Schafpferch m

sheepish [ˈʃipɪʃ] adj (embarrassed) verlegen; (timid) schüchtern

sheep′skin′ s Schaffell n; (coll) Diplom n

sheep′skin coat′ s Schafpelz m

sheer [ʃɪr] adj rein; (tex) durchsichtig; **by s. force** durch bloße Gewalt ‖ intr—**s. off** (naut) abscheren

sheet [ʃit] s (for the bed) Leintuch n; (of paper) Blatt n, Bogen m; (of metal) Blech n; (naut) Segelleine f; **come down in sheets** (fig) in Strömen regnen; **s. of ice** Glatteis n; **s. of flame** Feuermeer n

sheet′ i′ron s Eisenblech n

sheet′ mu′sic s Notenblatt n

she′-goat′ s Ziege f

sheik [ʃik] s Scheich m

shelf [ʃelf] s (shelves [ʃelvz]) Regal n; **put on the s.** (fig) auf die lange Bank schieben

shell [ʃel] s Schale f; (conch) Muschel f; (of a snail) Gehäuse n; (of a tortoise) Panzer m; (explosive) Granate f; (bullet) Patrone f ‖ tr (eggs) schälen; (nuts) aufknacken; (mil) beschießen; **s. out money** (coll) mit dem Geld herausrücken ‖ intr—**s. out** (coll) blechen

shel·lac [ʃəˈlæk] s Schellack m ‖ v (pret & pp -lacked; ger -lacking) tr mit Schellack streichen; (sl) verdreschen

shell′fish′ s Schalentier n

shell′ hole′ s Granattrichter m

shell′ shock′ s Bombenneurose f

shelter [ˈʃeltər] s Obdach n; (fig) Schutz m ‖ tr schützen

shelve [ʃelv] tr auf ein Regal stellen; (fig) auf die lange Bank schieben

shenanigans [ʃɪˈnænɪgənz] spl Possen pl

shepherd [ˈʃepərd] s Hirt m; (fig) Seelenhirt m ‖ tr hüten

shep′herd dog′ s Schäferhund m

shepherdess [ˈʃepərdɪs] s Hirtin f

sherbet [ˈʃɑrbət] s Speiseeis n

sheriff [ˈʃerɪf] s Sheriff m

sherry [ˈʃerɪ] s Sherry m

shield [ʃild] s Schild m; (fig) Schutz m; (rad) Röhrenabschirmung f ‖ tr (from) schützen (vor dat); (elec, mach) abschirmen

shift [ʃɪft] s (of worker, work) Schicht– ‖ s Schicht f; (change) Verschiebung f; (loose-fitting dress) Kittelkleid n ‖ tr (a meeting) verschieben; (the blame) (on) (ab)schieben (auf acc); **s. gears** umschalten ‖ intr (said of the wind) umspringen; **s. for oneself** sich allein durchschlagen; **s. into second gear** in den zweiten Gang umschalten

shift′ key′ s Umschalttaste f

shiftless [ˈʃɪftlɪs] adj träge

shifty [ˈʃɪftɪ] adj schlau, gerissen

shimmer [ˈʃɪmər] s Schimmer m ‖ intr schimmern, flimmern

shin [ʃɪn] s Schienbein n

shin′bone′ s Schienbein n

shine [ʃaɪn] s Schein m, Glanz m ‖ v (pret & pp shined) tr polieren; (shoes) wichsen ‖ v (pret & pp shone [ʃon]) intr scheinen; (said of the *eyes*) leuchten; (*be outstanding*) (*in*) glänzen (*in dat*)

shiner ['ʃaɪnər] s (sl) blaues Auge n

shingle ['ʃɪŋgl] s (*for a roof*) Schindel f; (*e.g., of a doctor*) Aushängeschild n ‖ tr mit Schindeln decken

shin'ing adj (*eyes*) leuchtend, strahlend; (*example*) glänzend

shiny ['ʃaɪni] adj blank, glänzend

ship [ʃɪp] s Schiff n ‖ v (pret & pp **shipped**; ger **shipping**) tr senden; s. **water** e-e Sturzsee bekommen ‖ intr—s. **out** absegeln

ship'board' s Bord m; **on s.** an Bord

ship'build'er s Schiffbauer m

ship'build'ing s Schiffbau m

shipment ['ʃɪpmənt] s Lieferung f

ship'ping s Absendung f, Verladung f; (*ships*) Schiffe pl

ship'ping clerk' s Expedient –in m/f

ship'ping depart'ment s Versandabteilung f

ship'shape' adj ordentlich

ship'wreck' s Schiffbruch m ‖ tr scheitern lassen; **be s.** schiffbrüchig sein ‖ intr Schiffbruch erleiden

ship'yard' s Werft f

shirk [ʃɜrk] tr sich drücken vor (dat) ‖ intr (from) sich drücken vor (dat)

shirt [ʃɜrt] s Hemd n; **keep your s. on!** (sl) regen Sie sich nicht auf!

shirt'col'lar s Hemdkragen m

shirt'sleeve' s Hemdsärmel m

shirttail' s Hemdschoß m

shit [ʃɪt] s (vulg) Scheiße f ‖ v (pret & pp **shit**) tr & intr (vulg) scheißen

shiver ['ʃɪvər] s Schauder m ‖ intr (at) schaudern (vor dat); (with) zittern (vor dat)

shoal [ʃol] s Untiefe f

shock [ʃɑk] s Schock m; (*of hair*) Schopf m; (agr) Schober m; (elec) Schlag m ‖ tr schockieren; (elec) e-n Schlag versetzen (dat)

shock' absorb'er [æb'sɔrbər] s Stoßdämpfer m

shock'ing adj schockierend

shock' troops' spl Stoßtruppen pl

shock' wave' s Stoßwelle f

shoddy ['ʃɑdi] adj schäbig

shoe [ʃu] s Schuh m ‖ v (pret & pp **shod** [ʃɑd]) tr beschlagen

shoe'horn' s Schuhlöffel m

shoe'lace' s Schuhband n, Schnürsenkel m

shoe'mak'er s Schuster m

shoe' pol'ish s Schuhwichse f

shoe'shine' s Schuhputzen n

shoe' store' s Schuhladen m

shoe' string' s Schuhband m; **on a s.** mit ein paar Groschen

shoe'tree' s Schuhspanner m

shoo [ʃu] tr (away) wegscheuchen ‖ interj sch!

shook-up ['ʃʊk'ʌp] adj (coll) verdattert

shoot [ʃut] s Schößling m ‖ v (pret & pp **shot** [ʃɑt]) tr (an)schießen, (ab)schießen; (*kill*) erschießen; (cin) drehen; (phot) aufnehmen; **s. down** (aer) abschießen; **s. the breeze** zwanglos plaudern; **s. up** (*e.g., a town*) zusammenschie-

ßen ‖ intr schießen; **s. at** schießen auf (acc); **s. by** vorbeisausen an (dat); **s. up** (*in growth*) aufschießen; (*said of flames*) emporschlagen; (*said of prices*) emporschnellen

shoot'ing s Schießerei f; (*execution*) Erschießung f; (*of a film*) Drehen n

shoot'ing gal'lery s Schießbude f

shoot'ing match' s Preisschießen n

shoot'ing star' s Sternschnuppe f

shoot'ing war' s heißer Krieg m

shop [ʃɑp] s Laden m, Geschäft n; **talk s.** fachsimpeln ‖ v (pret & pp **shopped**; ger **shopping**) intr einkaufen; **go shopping** einkaufen gehen; **s. around for** sich in einigen Läden umsehen nach

shop'girl' s Ladenmädchen n

shop'keep'er s Ladeninhaber –in m/f

shoplifter ['ʃɑp,lɪftər] s Ladendieb –in m/f

shop'lift'ing s Ladendiebstahl m

shopper ['ʃɑpər] s Einkäufer –in m/f

shop'ping s Einkaufen n; (*purchases*) Einkäufe pl

shop'ping bag' s Einkaufstasche f

shop'ping cen'ter s Einkaufcenter n

shop'ping dis'trict s Geschäftsviertel n

shop'ping spree' s Einkaufsorgie f

shop'talk' s Fachsimpelei f

shop'win'dow s Schaufenster n

shop'worn' adj (fig) abgerissen

shore [ʃor] s Küste f; (*beach*) Strand m; (*of a river*) Ufer n; **go to the s.** ans Meer fahren ‖ tr—s. up abstützen

shore' leave' s Landurlaub m

shore'line' s Küstenlinie f; (*of a river*) Uferlinie f

shore' patrol' s Küstenstreife f

short [ʃɔrt] adj kurz; (*person*) klein; (*loan*) kurzfristig; **a s. time ago** vor kurzem; **be s. of**, e.g., **I am s. of bread** das Brot geht mir aus; **be s. with s.o.** j-n kurz abfertigen; **cut s.** abbrechen; **fall s. of** zurückbleiben hinter (dat); **get the s. end** das Nachsehen haben; **I am three marks s.** es fehlen mir drei Mark; **in s.** kurzum; **s. of breath** außer Atem; **s. of cash** knapp bei Kasse ‖ s (cin) Kurzfilm m; (elec) Kurzschluß m ‖ tr (elec) kurzschließen

shortage ['ʃɔrtɪdʒ] s (of) Mangel m (an dat); (com) Minderbetrag m

short'cake' s Mürbekuchen m

short'-change' tr zu wenig Wechselgeld herausgeben (dat); (fig) betrügen

short' cir'cuit s Kurzschluß m

short'-cir'cuit tr kurzschließen

short'com'ing s Fehler m, Mangel m

short'cut' s Abkürzung f; **take a s.** den Weg abkürzen

shorten ['ʃɔrtən] tr abkürzen

short'ening s Abkürzung f; (culin) Backfett n

short'hand' adj stenographisch ‖ s Stenographie f; **in s.** stenographisch; **take down in s.** stenographieren

short-lived ['ʃɔrt'laɪvd] adj kurzlebig

shortly ['ʃɔrtli] adv in kurzem; **s. after** kurz nach

short′-or′der cook′ s Schnellimbißkoch m, Schnellimbißköchin f

short′-range′ adj Nah-, auf kurze Sicht

shorts [ʃɔrts] s (underwear) Unterhose f; (walking shorts) kurze Hose f; (sport) Sporthose f

short′-sight′ed adj kurzsichtig

short′ sto′ry s Novelle f

short′-tem′pered adj leicht aufbrausend

short′-term′ adj kurzfristig

short′wave′ adj Kurzwellen– ‖ s Kurzwelle f

short′wind′ed adj kurzatmig

shot [ʃat] adj (sl) kaputt; (drunk) (sl) besoffen; **my nerves are s.** ich bin mit meinen Nerven ganz herunter ‖ s Schuß m; (shooter) Schütze m; (pellets) Schrot m; (injection) Spritze f; (snapshot) Aufnahme f; (of liquor) Gläschen n; **be a good s.** gut schießen; **s. in the arm** (fig) Belebungsspritze f; **s. in the dark** Sprung m ins Ungewisse; **take a s. at e-n Schuß abgeben auf (acc); (fig) versuchen; **wild s.** Schuß m ins Blaue

shot′gun′ s Schrotflinte f

shot′gun wed′ding s Mußehe f

shot′-put′ s (sport) Kugelstoßen n

should [ʃʊd] aux (to express softened affirmation) **I s. like to know** ich möchte wissen; **I s. think so** das will ich meinen; (to express obligation) **how s. I know?** wie sollte ich das wissen?; **you shouldn't** put that Sie sollten das nicht tun; (in conditional clauses) **if it s. rain tomorrow** wenn es morgen regnen sollte

shoulder [′ʃoldər] s Schulter f, Achsel f; (of a road) Bankett n; **have broad shoulders** e–n breiten Rücken haben ‖ tr (a rifle) schultern; (responsibility) auf sich nehmen

shoul′der bag′ s Umhängetasche f

shoul′der blade′ s Schulterblatt n

shoul′der strap′ s (of underwear) Trägerband n; (mil) Schulterriemen m

shout [ʃaʊt] s Schrei m, Ruf m ‖ tr schreien, rufen; **s. down** (to) niederschreien ‖ intr schreien, rufen

shove [ʃʌv] s Stoß m; **give s.o. a s.** j–m e–n Stoß versetzen ‖ tr stoßen; (e.g., furniture) rücken; **s. around** (coll) herumschubsen; **s. forward** vorschieben ‖ intr drängeln; **s. off** (coll) abschieben; (naut) vom Land abstoßen

shov•el [′ʃʌvəl] s Schaufel f ‖ v (pret & pp –el[l]ed; ger –el[l]ing) tr schaufeln

show [ʃo] s (exhibition) Ausstellung f; (outer appearance) Schau f; (spectacle) Theater n; (cin, theat) Vorstellung f; **by s. of hands** durch Handzeichen; **make a s. of s.th.** mit etw Staat machen; **only for s.** nur zur Schau ‖ v (pret showed; pp show [ʃon] & showed) tr zeigen; (prove) beweisen, nachweisen; (said of evidence, tests) ergeben; (tickets, passport, papers) vorweisen; **s. around** (a person) herumführen; (a thing) herumzeigen ‖ intr zu sehen sein;

(said of a slip) vorgucken; **s. off** (with) großtun (mit); **s. up** er erscheinen

show′ busi′ness s Unterhaltungsindustrie f

show′case′ s Schaukasten m, Vitrine f

show′down′ s entscheidender Wendepunkt m; (e.g., in a western) Kraftprobe f; (cards) Aufdecken n der Karten

shower [′ʃaʊ·ər] s (rain) Schauer m; (bath) Dusche f; (shower room) Duschraum m; (of stones, arrows) Hagel m; (of bullets, sparks) Regen m; (for a bride) Party f zur Überreichung der Brautgeschenke; **take a s.** (sich) duschen ‖ tr (with gifts) überschütten ‖ intr duschen; (meteor) schauern

show′er bath′ s Dusche f, Brausebad n

show′ girl′ s Revuegirl n

show′ing s Zeigen n; (cin) Vorführung f

show′ing off′ s Großtuerei f

show′man s (–men) s Schauspieler m

show′-off′ s Protz m

show′piece′ s Schaustück n

show′room′ s Ausstellungsraum m

show′ win′dow s Schaufenster n

showy [′ʃo·i] adj prunkhaft

shrapnel [′ʃræpnəl] s Schrapnell n

shred [ʃred] s Fetzen m; (least bit) Spur f; **tear to shreds** in Fetzen reißen; (an argument) gründlich widerlegen ‖ v (pret & pp shredded & shred; ger shredding) tr zerfetzen; (paper) in Streifen schneiden; (culin) schnitzeln

shredder [′ʃredər] s (of paper) Reißwolf m; (culin) Schnitzelmaschine f

shrew [ʃru] s böse Sieben f

shrewd [ʃrud] adj schlau

shriek [ʃrik] s Gekreische n, gellender Schrei m ‖ intr kreischen

shrill [ʃrɪl] adj schrill

shrimp [ʃrɪmp] s Garnele f; (coll) Knirps m

shrine [ʃraɪn] s Heiligtum n

shrink [ʃrɪŋk] v (pret shrank [ʃræŋk] & shrunk [ʃrʌŋk]; pp shrunk & shrunken) tr einlaufen lassen ‖ intr schrumpfen; **s. back from** zurückschrecken vor (dat); **s. from** sich scheuen vor (dat); **s. up** einschrumpfen

shrinkage [′ʃrɪŋkɪdʒ] s Schrumpfung f

shriv•el [′ʃrɪvəl] s (pret & pp –el[l]ed; ger –el[l]ing) intr schrumpfen; **s. up** zusammenschrumpfen

shriv′eled adj schrumpelig

shroud [ʃraʊd] s Leichentuch n; (fig) Hülle f; (naut) Want f ‖ tr (in) einhüllen (in acc)

shrub [ʃrʌb] s Strauch m

shrubbery [′ʃrʌbəri] s Strauchwerk n

shrug [ʃrʌg] s Zucken n ‖ v (pret & pp shrugged; ger shrugging) tr zucken; **s. off** mit e–m Achselzucken abtun; **s. one's shoulders** mit den Achseln zucken ‖ intr mit den Achseln zucken

shuck [ʃʌk] tr enthülsen

shudder [′ʃʌdər] s Schau(d)er m ‖

intr (at) schau(d)ern (vor *dat*); s. at
the thought of s.th. bei dem Gedanken an etw [*acc*] zittern

shuffle [ˈʃʌfəl] *s* Schlurfen *n*; (cards) Mischen *n*; **get lost in the s.** (fig) unter den Tisch fallen || *tr (cards)* mischen; *(the feet)* schleifen; || mischen die Karten mischen; *(walk)* schlurfen; **s. along** latschen

shun [ʃʌn] *v (pret & pp* **shunned;** *ger* **shunning)** *tr (a person)* meiden; *(a thing)* **(ver)meiden**

shunt [ʃʌnt] *s* (elec) Nebenschluß *m* || *tr (shove aside)* beiseite schieben; *(across)* parallelschalten (zu); (rr) rangieren

shut [ʃʌt] *adj* zu || *(pret & pp* **shut;** *ger* **shutting)** *tr* schließen, zumachen; **be s. down** stilliegen; **s. down** stillegen; **s. off** absperren; **s. one's eyes to** hinwegsehen über (*acc*); **s. out** aussperren; **s. s.o. up** j–m den Mund stopfen || *intr* sich schließen; **s. up!** (coll) halt's Maul!

shutʹ**down**ʹ *s* Stillegung *f*

shutter [ˈʃʌtər] *s* Laden *m*; (phot) Verschluß *m*

shuttle [ˈʃʌtəl] *s* Schiffchen *n* || *intr* pendeln, hin– und herfahren

shutʹ**tle bus**ʹ *s* Pendelbus *m*

shutʹ**tlecock**ʹ *s* Federball *m*

shutʹ**tle serv**ʹ**ice** *s* Pendelverkehr *m*

shutʹ**tle train**ʹ *s* Pendelzug *m*

shy [ʃaɪ] *adj* **(shyer; shyest)** schüchtern; **be a dollar shy** *n* Dollar los sein || *intr (said of a horse)* stutzen; **shy at** zurückscheuen vor (*dat*); **shy away from** sich scheuen vor (*dat*)

shyness [ˈʃaɪnɪs] *s* Scheu *f*

shyster [ˈʃaɪstər] *s* Winkeladvokat *m*

Siameseʹ **twins**ʹ [ˌsaɪ·əˈmiz] *spl* Siamesische Zwillinge *pl*

Siberia [saɪˈbɪri·ə] *s* Sibirien *n*

Siberian [saɪˈbɪri·ən] *adj* sibirisch || *s* Sibirier –in *mf*

sibilant [ˈsɪbɪlənt] *s* Zischlaut *m*

siblings [ˈsɪblɪŋz] *spl* Geschwister *pl*

sibyl [ˈsɪbɪl] *s* Sibylle *f*

sic [sɪk] *adv* sic || *v (pret & pp* **sicked;** *ger* **sicking)** *tr*—**sic 'em!** (coll) faß!; **sic the dog on** s.o. den Hund auf j–n hetzen

Sicilian [sɪˈsɪljən] *adj* sizilianisch || *s* Sizilianer –in *mf*

Sicily [ˈsɪsɪli] *s* Sizilien *n*

sick [sɪk] *adj* krank; **be s. and tired of** s.th. etw gründlich satt haben; **be s. as a dog** sich hundeelend fühlen; **I am s. to my stomach** mir ist übel; **play s.** krankfeiern

sickʹ **bay**ʹ *s* Schiffslazarett *n*

sickʹ**bed**ʹ *s* Krankenbett *n*

sicken [ˈsɪkən] *tr* krank machen; *(disgust)* anekeln || *intr* krank werden

sickʹ**ening** *adj* (fig) ekelhaft

sickʹ **head**ʹ**ache** *s* Kopfschmerzen *pl* mit Übelkeit

sickle [ˈsɪkəl] *s* Sichel *f*

sickʹ **leave**ʹ *s* Krankenurlaub *m*

sickly [ˈsɪkli] *adj* kränklich; *(smile)* erzwungen

sickness [ˈsɪknɪs] *s* Krankheit *f*

sickʹ **room**ʹ *s* Krankenzimmer *n*

side [saɪd] *adj* Neben–, Seiten– || *s* Seite *f*; *(of a team, government)* Partei *f*; *(edge)* Rand *m*; **at my s.** mir zur Seite; **dark s.** Schattenseite *f*; **off sides** (sport) abseits; **on the father's s.** väterlicherseits; **on the s.** (coll) nebenbei; **this s. up** Vorsicht, nicht stürzen; **to be on the safe s.** um ganz sicher zu gehen || *intr*— **s. with** s.o. j–s Partei ergreifen

sideʹ **aisle**ʹ *s* Seitengang *m*; *(of a church)* Seitenschiff *n*

sideʹ **al**ʹ**tar** *s* Nebenaltar *m*

sideʹ**arm**ʹ *s* Seitengewehr *n*

sideʹ**board**ʹ *s* Anrichte *f*, Büffet *n*

sideʹ**burns**ʹ *spl* Koteletten *pl*

sideʹ **dish**ʹ *s* Nebengericht *n*

sideʹ **door**ʹ *s* Seitentür *f*

sideʹ **effect**ʹ *s* Nebenwirkung *f*

sideʹ **en**ʹ**trance** *s* Seiteneingang *m*

sideʹ **glance**ʹ *s* Seitenblick *m*

sideʹ **is**ʹ**sue** *s* Nebenfrage *f*

sideʹ **job**ʹ *s* Nebenverdienst *m*

sideʹ**kick**ʹ *s* (coll) Kumpel *m*

sideʹ**line**ʹ *s (occupation)* Nebenbeschäftigung *f*; (fb) Seitenlinie *f* || *tr* (coll) an der aktiven Teilnahme hindern

sideʹ **of ba**ʹ**con** *s* Speckseite *f*

sideʹ **road**ʹ *s* Seitenweg *m*

sideʹ**sad**ʹ**dle** *adv*—**ride s.** im Damensattel reiten

sideʹ **show**ʹ *s* Nebenvorstellung *f*; (fig) Episode *f*

sideʹ**split**ʹ**ting** *adj* zwerchfellerschütternd

sideʹ**-step**ʹ *v (pret & pp* **–stepped;** *ger* **–stepping)** *tr* ausweichen (*dat*)

sideʹ **street**ʹ *s* Seitenstraße *f*

sideʹ**stroke**ʹ *s* Seitenschwimmen *n*

sideʹ**track**ʹ *s* Seitengeleise *n* || *tr* (& fig) auf ein Seitengeleise schieben

sideʹ **trip**ʹ *s* Abstecher *m*

sideʹ **view**ʹ *s* Seitenansicht *f*

sideʹ**walk**ʹ *s* Bürgersteig *m*, Gehsteig *m*

sideward [ˈsaɪdwərd] *adj* nach der Seite gerichtet || *adv* seitwärts

sideʹ**ways**ʹ *adv* seitlich, seitwärts

sidʹ**ing** *s (of a house)* Verkleidung *f*; (rr) Nebengeleise *n*

sidle [ˈsaɪdəl] *intr*—**s. up to** s.o. sich heimlich an j–n heranmachen

siege [sidʒ] *s* Belagerung *f*; **lay s. to** belagern

siesta [siˈestə] *s* Mittagsruhe *f*

sieve [sɪv] *s* Sieb *n* || *tr* durchsieben

sift [sɪft] *tr* (durch)sieben; (fig) sichten; **s. out** aussieben

sigh [saɪ] *s* Seufzer *m*; **with a s.** seufzend || *intr* seufzen

sight [saɪt] *s* Anblick *m*; *(faculty)* Sehvermögen *n*; *(on a weapon)* Visier *n*; **at first s.** auf den ersten Blick; **at s.** sofort; **be a s.** (coll) unmöglich aussehen; **by s.** vom Sehen; **catch s. of** erblicken; **in s.** in Sicht; **lose s. of** aus den Augen verlieren; **out of s.** außer Sicht; **s. for sore eyes** Augentrost *m*; **sights** Sehenswürdigkeiten *pl*; **s. unseen** unbesehen; **within s.** in Sehweite || *tr* sichten sigh...

...seeing s Besichtigung f; **go s. sich** [dat] die Sehenswürdigkeiten ansehen

sight'seeing tour' s Rundfahrt f

sightseer ['saɪt,si·ər] s Tourist –in mf

sign [saɪn] s (signboard) Schild n; (symbol, omen, signal) Zeichen n; (symptom, indication) Kennzeichen n; (trace) Spur f; (math, mus) Vorzeichen n; **s. of life** Lebenszeichen n || tr unterschreiben; **s. away** aufgeben; **s. over (to)** überschreiben (auf acc) || intr unterschreiben; **s. for** zeichnen für; **s. in** sich eintragen; **s. off** (rad) die Sendung beenden; **s. out** sich austragen; **s. up** (mil) sich anwerben lassen; **s. up for** (e.g., courses, work) sich anmelden für

sig·nal ['sɪgnəl] adj auffallend || s (by gesture) Zeichen n, Wink m; (aut, rad, rr, telv) Signal n || v (pret & pp –nal[l]ed; ger –nal[l]ing) tr signalisieren; (a person) ein Zeichen geben (dat)

sig'nal corps' s Fernmeldetruppen pl

sig'nal·man s (–men) (nav) Signalgast m; (rr) Bahnwärter m

signatory ['sɪgnə,tori] s Unterzeichner –in mf

signature ['sɪgnət/ər] s Unterschrift f

sign'board' s Aushängeschild n

signer ['saɪnər] s Unterzeichner –in mf

sig'net ring' ['sɪgnɪt] s Siegelring m

significance [sɪg'nɪfɪkəns] s Bedeutung f

significant [sɪg'nɪfɪkənt] adj bedeutsam

signi·fy ['sɪgnɪ,faɪ] v (pret & pp –fied) bedeuten, bezeichnen

sign' lan'guage s Zeichensprache f

sign' of the cross' s Kreuzzeichen n; **make the s.** sich bekreuzigen

sign'post' s Wegweiser m

silence ['saɪləns] s Ruhe f, Stille f; (reticence) Schweigen n; **in s.** schweigend || tr zum Schweigen bringen; (a conscience) beschwichtigen

silent ['saɪlənt] adj silent (night, partner) still; (movies) stumm; (person) schweigend; **be s.** stillschweigen; **keep s.** schweigen

silhouette [,sɪlu'ɛt] s Schattenbild n, Silhouette f || tr silhouettieren

silicon ['sɪlɪkən] s Silizium n

silicone ['sɪlɪkon] s Silikon n

silk [sɪlk] adj seiden || s Seide f

silken ['sɪlkən] adj seiden

silk' hat' s Zylinder m

silk' mill' s Seidenfabrik f

silk' worm' s Seidenraupe f

silky ['sɪlki] adj seiden, seidenartig

sill [sɪl] s (of a window) Sims m & n; (of a door) Schwelle f

silliness ['sɪlɪnɪs] s Albernheit f

silly ['sɪli] adj albern, blöd(e)

si·lo ['saɪlo] s (–los) Getreidesilo m; (rok) Raketenbunker m, Silo m

silt [sɪlt] s Schlick m || intr—**s. up** verschlammen

silver ['sɪlvər] adj silbern || s Silber n; (for the table) Silberzeug n; (money) Silbergeld n

---

sil'verfish' s Silberfischchen n

sil'ver foil' s Silberfolie f

sil'ver lin'ing s (fig) Silberstreifen m

sil'ver plate' s Silbergeschirr n

sil'ver-plat'ed adj versilbert

sil'versmith' s Silberschmied m

sil'ver spoon' s—**be born with a s. in one's mouth** ein Sonntagskind sein

sil'verware' s Silbergeschirr n

silvery ['sɪlvəri] adj silbern

similar ['sɪmɪlər] adj (to) ähnlich (dat)

similarity [,sɪmɪ'lærɪti] s Ähnlichkeit f

simile ['sɪmɪli] s Gleichnis n

simmer ['sɪmər] tr leicht kochen lassen || intr brodeln; **s. down** (coll) sich abreagieren

simper ['sɪmpər] s selbstgefälliges Lächeln n || intr selbstgefällig lächeln

simple ['sɪmpəl] adj einfach; (truth) rein; (fact) bloß

sim'ple-mind'ed adj einfältig

simpleton ['sɪmpəltən] s Einfaltspinsel m

simpli·fy ['sɪmplɪ,faɪ] v (pret & pp –fied) tr vereinfachen

simply ['sɪmpli] adv einfach

simulate ['sɪmjə,let] tr (illness) simulieren; (e.g., a rocket flight) am Modell vorführen

sim'ulated adj unecht

simultaneous [,saɪməl'teni·əs] adj gleichzeitig, simultan

sin [sɪn] s Sünde f || v (pret & pp sinned; ger sinning) intr sündigen; **sin against** sich versündigen an (dat)

since [sɪns] adv seitdem, seither || prep seit (dat); **s. then** seither; **s. when** seit wann || conj (temporal) seit(dem); (causal) da

sincere [sɪn'sɪr] adj aufrichtig

sincerely [sɪn'sɪrli] adv aufrichtig, ehrlich; **Sincerely yours** Ihr ergebener, Ihre ergebene

sincerity [sɪn'serɪti] s Aufrichtigkeit f

sinecure ['saɪnɪ,kjur] s Sinekure f

sinew ['sɪnju] s Sehne f, Flechse f; (fig) Muskelkraft f

sinewy ['sɪnju·i] adj sehnig; (fig) kräftig, nervig

sinful ['sɪnfəl] adj sündhaft

sing [sɪŋ] v (pret sang [sæŋ] & sung [sʌŋ]; pp sung) tr & intr singen

singe [sɪndʒ] v (singeing) tr sengen; (the hair) versengen

singer ['sɪŋər] s Sänger –in mf

single ['sɪŋgəl] adj einzeln; (unmarried) ledig; **not a s. word** kein einziges Wort || tr—**s. out** herausgreifen

sin'gle bed' s Einzelbett n

sin'glebreast'ed adj einreihig

sin'gle file' s Gänsemarsch m

sin'gle-hand'ed adj einhändig

sin'gle-lane' adj einbahnig

sin'gle life' s Ledigenstand m

sin'gle-mind'ed adj zielstrebig

sin'gle room' s Einzelzimmer n

sin'gle-track' adj (& fig) eingleisig

sing'song' adj eintönig || s Singsang m

singular ['sɪŋgjələr] adj (outstanding) ausgezeichnet; (unique) einzig; (odd) seltsam || s (gram) Einzahl f

sinister ['sɪnɪstər] adj unheimlich

sink [sɪŋk] s (in the kitchen) Ausguß m; (in the bathroom) Waschbecken n || v (pret sank [sæŋk] & sunk [sʌŋk]; pp sunk) tr (a ship; a post) versenken; (money) investieren; (min) abteufen; **s. a well** e-n Brunnen bohren || intr sinken; (said of a building) sich senken; **he is sinking fast** seine Kräfte nehmen rapide ab; **s. in** (coll) einleuchten; **s. into** (an easychair) sich fallen lassen in (acc); (poverty) geraten in (acc); (unconsciousness) fallen in (acc)

sink'ing feel'ing s Beklommenheit f

sink'ing fund' s Schuldentilgungsfonds m

sinless ['sɪnlɪs] adj sünd(en)los

sinner ['sɪnər] s Sünder –in mf

sinuous ['sɪnjʊ-əs] adj gewunden

sinus ['saɪnəs] s Stirnhöhle f

sip [sɪp] s Schluck m || v (pret & pp sipped; ger sipping) tr schlürfen

siphon ['saɪfən] s Siphon m, Saugheber m || tr entleeren; **s. off** absaugen; (profits) abschöpfen

sir [sʌr] s Herr m; **yes sir!** jawohl!; **Dear Sir** Sehr geehrter Herr

sire [saɪr] s (& zool) Vater m || tr zeugen

siren ['saɪrən] s (& myth) Sirene f

sirloin ['sʌrlɔɪn] s Lendenbraten m

sissy ['sɪsi] s Schlappschwanz m

sister ['sɪstər] s Schwester f

sis'ter-in-law' s (sisters-in-law) Schwägerin f

sisterly ['sɪstərli] adj schwesterlich

sit [sɪt] v (pret & pp sat [sæt]; ger sitting) intr sitzen; **sit down** sich (hin)setzen; **sit for a painter** e-m Maler Modell stehen; **sit in on** (a meeting) dabeisein bei; **sit up and beg** Männchen machen

sit'down strike' s Sitzstreik m

site [saɪt] s (position, location) Lage f; (piece of ground) Gelände n

sit'ting s—at one s. auf e-n Sitz

sit'ting duck' s wehrloses Ziel n

sit'ting room' s Gemeinschaftsraum m

situated ['sɪt/u ,etɪd] adj gelegen; **be s. liegen**

situation [,sɪt/u'e/ən] s Lage f; **s. wanted** Stelle gesucht

six [sɪks] adj & pron sechs || s Sechs f

sixteen ['sɪks'tin] adj & pron sechzehn || s Sechzehn f

sixteenth ['sɪks'tinθ] adj & pron sechzehnte || s (fraction) Sechzehntel n; **the s.** (in dates or in series) der Sechzehnte

sixth [sɪksθ] adj & pron sechste || s (fraction) Sechstel n; **the s.** (in dates or in series) der Sechste

sixtieth ['sɪkstɪ-ɪθ] adj & pron sechzig || s (fraction) Sechzigstel n

sixty ['sɪksti] adj & pron sechzig || s Sechzig f; **the sixties** die sechziger Jahre

six'ty-four dol'lar ques'tion s Preisfrage f

sizable ['saɪzəbəl] adj beträchtlich

size [saɪz] s Größe f; (of a book, paper) Format n || tr grundieren; **s. up** einschätzen

sizzle ['sɪzəl] s Zischen n || intr zischen

skate [sket] s Schlittschuh m || intr Schlittschuh laufen

skat'ing rink' s Eisbahn f

skein [sken] s Strähne f

skeleton ['skelɪtən] s Gerippe n

skel'eton crew' s Minimalbelegschaft f

skel'eton key' s Dietrich m

skeptic ['skeptɪk] s Zweifler –in mf

skeptical ['skeptɪkəl] adj skeptisch

skepticism ['skeptɪ ,sɪzəm] s (doubt) Skepsis f; (philos) Skeptizismus m

sketch [sket/] s Skizze f; (theat) Sketch m || tr & intr skizzieren

sketch'book' s Skizzenbuch n

sketchy ['sket/i] adj skizzenhaft

skewer ['skju-ər] s Fleischspieß m

ski [ski] s Schi m || intr schilaufen

ski' boot' s Schistiefel m

skid [skɪd] s Rutschen n, Schleudern n; **go into a s.** ins Schleudern geraten || v (pret & pp skidded; ger skidding) intr rutschen, schleudern

skid' mark' s Bremsspur f

skid'proof' adj bremssicher

skid' row' [ro] s Elendsviertel n

skiff [skɪf] s Skiff n

ski'ing s Schilaufen n

ski' jack'et s Anorak m

ski' jump' s Schisprung m; (chute) Sprungschanze f

ski' jump'ing s Schispringen n

ski' lift' s Schilift m

skill [skɪl] s Fertigkeit f

skilled adj gelernt

skillet ['skɪlɪt] s Bratpfanne f

skillful ['skɪlfəl] adj geschickt

skim [skɪm] v (pret & pp skimmed; ger skimming) tr (milk) abrahmen; (a book) überfliegen; **s. off** abschöpfen || intr—s. over the water über das Wasser streichen; **s. through** (a book) flüchtig durchblättern

skim' milk' s entrahmte Milch f

skimp [skɪmp] intr (on) knausern (mit)

skimpy ['skɪmpi] adj (person) knauserig; (thing) knapp, dürftig

skin [skɪn] s Haut f; (fur) Fell n; (of fruit) Schale f; **by the s. of one's teeth** mit knapper Not; **get under s.o.'s s.** j-m auf die Nerven gehen || v (pret & pp skinned; ger skinning) tr (an animal) enthäuten; (a knee) aufschürfen; (fleece) das Fell über die Ohren ziehen (dat); (defeat) schlagen; **s. alive** zur Sau machen

skin'-deep' adj oberflächlich

skin' div'er s Schwimmtaucher –in mf

skin'flint' s Geizhals m

skin' graft' s Hautverpflanzung f

skinny ['skɪni] adj spindeldürr, mager

skin'tight' adj hauteng

skip [skɪp] s Sprung m || v (pret & pp skipped; ger skipping) tr (omit) auslassen; (a page) überblättern; **s. it!** Schwamm drüber!; **s. rope** Seil springen; **s. school** Schule schwänzen || intr springen; **s. out** abhauen

ski' pole' s Schistock m

skipper ['skɪpər] s Kapitän m
skirmish ['skɑrmɪʃ] s Scharmützel n || intr scharmützeln
skir'mish line' s (mil) Schützenlinie f
skirt [skɑrt] s Rock m || tr (border) umsäumen; (pass along) sich entlanglziehen (an dat)
ski' run' s Schipiste f
skit [skɪt] s Sket(s)ch m
skittish ['skɪtɪʃ] adj (lively) lebhaft; (horse) scheu
skull [skʌl] s Schädel m
skull' and cross'bones s Totenkopf m
skull'cap' s Käppchen n
skunk [skʌŋk] s Stinktier n; (sl) Saukerl m
sky [skaɪ] s Himmel m; out of the clear blue sky wie aus heiterem Himmel; praise to the skies über den grünen Klee loben
sky'-blue' adj himmelblau
sky'div'er s Fallschirmspringer –in mf
sky'div'ing s Fallschirmspringen n
sky'lark' s Feldlerche f
sky'light' s Dachluke f
sky'line' s Horizontlinie f; (of a city) Stadtsilhouette f
sky'rock'et s Rakete f || intr in die Höhe schießen
sky'scrap'er s Wolkenkratzer m
sky'writ'ing s Himmelsschrift f
slab [slæb] s Platte f, Tafel f
slack [slæk] adj schlaff; (period) flau || s Spielraum m; slacks Herrenhose f, Damenhose f || intr—s. off nachlassen
slacken ['slækən] tr (slow down) verlangsamen; (loosen) lockern || intr nachlassen
slack' pe'riod s Flaute f
slack' sea'son s Sauregurkenzeit f
slag [slæg] s Schlacke f
slag' pile' s Schlackenhalde f
slake [slek] tr (thirst, lime) löschen
slalom ['slɑləm] s Slalom m
slam [slæm] s Knall m; (cards) Schlemm m || v (pret & pp slammed; ger slamming) tr zuknallen; s. down hinknallen || intr knallen
slander ['slændər] s Verleumdung f || tr verleumden
slanderous ['slændərəs] adj verleumderisch
slang [slæŋ] s Slang m
slant [slænt] s Schräge f; (view) Einstellung f; (personal point of view) Tendenz f || tr abschrägen; (fig) färben
slap [slæp] s Klaps m; s. in the face Ohrfeige f || v (pret & pp slapped; ger slapping) tr schlagen; (s.o.'s face) ohrfeigen; s. together zusammenhauen
slap'stick' adj Radau– || s Radaukomödie f
slash [slæʃ] s Schnittwunde f || tr aufschlitzen; (prices) drastisch herabsetzen
slat [slæt] s Stab m
slate [slet] s Schiefer m; (to write on) Schiefertafel f; (of candidates) Vorschlagsliste f || tr (a roof) mit Schie-

fer decken; (schedule) planen; he is slated to speak er soll sprechen
slate' roof' s Schieferdach n
slattern ['slætərn] s (slovenly woman) Schlampe f; (slut) Dirne f
slaughter ['slɔtər] s Schlachten n; (massacre) Metzelei f || tr schlachten; (massacre) niedermetzeln
slaugh'terhouse' s Schlachthaus n
Slav [slɑv], [slæv] adj slawisch || s (person) Slawe m, Slawin f
slave [slev] s Sklave m, Sklavin f || intr (coll) schuften; s. at a job sich mit e–r Arbeit abquälen
slave' driv'er s (fig) Leuteschinder m
slaver ['slævər] s Geifer m
slavery ['slevəri] s Sklaverei f
slave' trade' s Sklavenhandel m
Slavic ['slɑvɪk], ['slævɪk] adj slawisch
slavish ['slevɪʃ] adj sklavisch
slay [sle] v (pret slew [slu]; pp slain [slen]) tr erschlagen
slayer ['sle-ər] s Totschläger –in mf
sled [sled] s Schlitten m || v (pret & pp sledded; ger sledding) intr Schlitten fahren
sledge [sledʒ] s Schlitten m
sledge' ham'mer s Vorschlaghammer m
sleek [slik] adj (hair) glatt; (cattle) fett || tr glätten
sleep [slip] s Schlaf m; get enough s. sich ausschlafen || v (pret & pp slept [slept]) tr (accommodate) Schlafgelegenheiten bieten für; s. off a hangover seinen Kater ausschlafen || intr schlafen; I didn't s. a wink ich habe kein Auge zugetan; s. like a log wie ein Murmeltier schlafen; s. with (a woman) schlafen mit
sleeper ['sliper] s Schläfer –in mf; (sleeping car) Schlafwagen m; (fig) überraschender Erfolg m
sleepiness ['slipinɪs] s Schläfrigkeit f
sleep'ing bag' s Schlafsack m
Sleep'ing Beau'ty s Dornröschen n
sleep'ing car' s Schlafwagen m
sleep'ing compart'ment s Schlafabteil n
sleep'ing pill' s Schlaftablette f
sleep'ing sick'ness s Schlafkrankheit f
sleepless ['sliplɪs] adj schlaflos
sleep'walk'er s Nachtwandler –in mf
sleepy ['slipi] adj schläfrig
sleep'yhead' s Schlafmütze f
sleet [slit] s Schneeregen m; (on the ground) Glatteis n || impers—it is sleeting es gibt Schneeregen, es graupelt
sleeve [sliv] s Ärmel m; (mach) Muffe f; have s.th. up one's s. etw im Schilde führen; roll up one's sleeves die Ärmel hochkrempeln
sleeveless ['slivlɪs] adj ärmellos
sleigh [sle] s Schlitten m
sleigh' bell' s Schlittenschelle f
sleigh' ride' s Schlittenfahrt f; go for a
sleight' of hand' [slaɪt] s Taschenspielertrick m
slender ['slɛndər] adj schlank; (means) gering
sleuth [sluθ] s Detektiv m
slice [slaɪs] s Scheibe f, Schnitte f;

(tennis) Schnittball *m* || *tr* aufschneiden

slicer ['slaɪsər] *s* Schneidemaschine *f*

slick [slɪk] *adj* glatt; (*talker*) raffiniert

slicker ['slɪkər] *s* Regenmantel *m*

slide [slaɪd] *s* (*slip*) Rutsch *m;* (*chute*) Rutschbahn *f;* (*of a microscope*) Objektträger *m;* (phot) Diapositiv *n* || *v* (*pret & pp* **slid** [slɪd]) *tr* schieben || *intr* rutschen; **let things s.** die Dinge laufen lassen

slide′ rule′ *s* Rechenschieber *m*

slide′ valve′ *s* Schieberventil *n*

slide′ view′er *s* Bildbetrachter *m*

slid′ing door′ *s* Schiebetür *f*

slid′ing scale′ *s* gleitende Skala *f*

slight [slaɪt] *adj* gering(fügig); (*illness*) leicht; (*petite*) zart || *tr* mißachten

slim [slɪm] *adj* schlank; (*chance*) gering || *intr*—**s. down** abnehmen

slime [slaɪm] *s* Schlamm *m;* (*e.g., of fish, snakes*) Schleim *m*

slimy ['slaɪmi] *adj* schleimig; (*muddy*) schlammig

sling [slɪŋ] *s* (*to hurl stones*) Schleuder *f;* (*for a broken arm*) Schlinge *f* || *v* (*pret & pp* **slung** [slʌŋ]) *tr* schleudern; **s. over the shoulders** umhängen

sling′shot′ *s* Schleuder *f*

slink [slɪŋk] *v* (*pret & pp* **slunk** [slʌŋk]) *intr* schleichen; **s. away** wegschleichen

slip [slɪp] *s* (*slide*) Ausrutschen *n;* (*cutting*) Ableger *m;* (*underwear*) Unterrock *m;* (*paper*) Zettel *m;* (*pillowcase*) Kissenbezug *m;* (*error*) Flüchtigkeitsfehler *m;* (*for ships*) Schlipp *m;* **give s.o. the s.** j—m entwischen; **s. of the pen** Schreibfehler *m;* **s. of the tongue** Sprechfehler *m* || *v* (*pret & pp* **slipped;** *ger* **slipping**) *tr*—**s. in** (*a remark*) einfließen lassen; (*poison*) heimlich schütten; **s. on** (*a glove*) überstreifen; (*a coat*) überziehen; (*a ring*) auf den Finger streifen; **s. s.o. money** j—m etw Geld zustecken; **s. s.o.'s mind** j—m entfallen || *intr* rutschen; (*e.g., out of or into a room*) schlüpfen; (*lose one's balance*) ausgleiten; **let s.** sich [*dat*] entgehen lassen; **s. by** verstreichen; **s. in** (*said of errors*) unterlaufen; **s. through one's fingers** durch die Finger gleiten; **s. out on s.o.** j—m entschlüpfen; **s. up (on)** danebenhauen (bei); **you are slipping** (coll) Sie lassen in der Leistung nach

slip′cov′er *s* Schonbezug *m*

slip′knot′ *s* Schleife *f*

slipper ['slɪpər] *s* Pantoffel *m*

slippery ['slɪpəri] *adj* glatt

slipshod ['slɪp‚ʃad] *adj* schlampig; **do s. work** schludern

slip′stream′ *s* Luftschraubenstrahl *m*

slip′-up′ *s* (coll) Flüchtigkeitsfehler *m*

slit [slɪt] *s* Schlitz *m* || *v* (*pret & pp* **slit;** *ger* **slitting**) *tr* schlitzen; **s. open** aufschlitzen

slit′-eyed′ *adj* schlitzäugig

slither ['slɪðər] *intr* gleiten

slit′ trench′ *s* (mil) Splittergraben *m*

sliver ['slɪvər] *s* Splitter *m*, Span *m*

slob [slab] *s* (sl) Schmutzfink *m*

slobber ['slabər] *s* Geifer *m* || *intr* geifern

sloe [slo] *s* (bot) Schlehe *f*

sloe′-eyed′ *adj* schlitzäugig

slog [slag] *v* (*pret & pp* **slogged;** *ger* **slogging**) *intr* stapfen

slogan ['slogən] *s* Schlagwort *n*

sloop [slup] *s* Schaluppe *f*

slop [slap] *s* Spülicht *n;* (*bad food*) (sl) Fraß *m* || *v* (*pret & pp* **slopped;** *ger* **slopping**) *tr* (*hogs*) füttern; (*spill*) verschütten

slope [slop] *s* Abhang *m;* (*of a road*) Gefälle *n;* (*of a roof*) Neigung *f* || *tr* abschrägen || *intr* sich neigen; (*said of a road*) abfallen

sloppy ['slapi] *adj* schlampig; (*weather*) matschig

slosh [slaʃ] *intr* schwappen

slot [slat] *s* Schlitz *m*

sloth [sloθ] *s* Faulheit *f*, Trägheit *f;* (zool) Faultier *n*

slothful ['sloθfəl] *adj* faul, träge

slot′ machine′ *s* Spielautomat *m*

slouch [slautʃ] *s* nachlässige Haltung *f;* (*person*) Schlappschwanz *m* || *intr* in schlechter Haltung sitzen; **s. along** latschen

slouch′ hat′ *s* Schlapphut *m*

slough [slau] *s* Sumpf *m* || [slʌf] *s* (*of a snake*) abgestreifte Haut *f;* (pathol) Schorf *m* || *tr* (& fig) abstreifen || *intr* (*said of a snake*) sich häuten

Slovak ['slovak], ['slovæk] *adj* slowakisch || *s* (*person*) Sklowake *m*, Slowakin *f;* (*language*) Slowakisch *n*

slovenly ['slʌvənli] *adj* schlampig

slow [slo] *adj* langsam; (*dawdling*) bummelig; (*mentally*) schwer von Begriff; (com) flau; **be s.** (horol) nachgehen || *adv* langsam || *tr*—**s. down** verlangsamen || *intr*—**s. down** (*in driving*) langsamer fahren; (*in working*) nachlassen; **s. down** (public sign) Schritt fahren

slow′down′ *s* Bummelstreik *m*

slow′ mo′tion *s* (cin) Zeitlupe *f;* **in s.** (cin) im Zeitlupentempo

slow′-mo′tion *adj* Zeitlupen—

slow′poke′ *s* (coll) langsamer Mensch *m*

slow′-wit′ted *adj* schwer von Begriff

slug [slʌg] *s* Rohling *m;* (*drink*) Zug *m* (zool) Wegschnecke *f* || *v* (*pret & pp* **slugged;** *ger* **slugging**) *tr* (coll) hart mit der Faust treffen

sluggard ['slʌgərd] *s* Faulpelz *m*

sluggish ['slʌgɪʃ] *adj* träge

sluice [slus] *s* Schleuse *f*

sluice′ gate′ *s* Schleusentor *n*

slum [slʌm] *s* Elendsviertel *n*

slumber ['slʌmbər] *s* Schlummer *m* || *intr* schlummern

slum′ dwell′ing *s* Elendsquartier *n*

slump [slʌmp] *s* (st. exch.) Baisse *f;* **s. in sales** Absatzstockung *f* || *intr* zusammensacken; (*said of prices*) stürzen

slur [slʌr] *s* (*insult*) Verleumdung *f;* (mus) Bindezeichen *n* || *v* (*pret & pp* **slurred;** *ger* **slurring**) *tr* (*words*)

verschleifen; (mus) binden; **s. over**
hinweggehen über (acc)

slurp [slʌrp] s Schlürfen n ‖ tr & intr
schlürfen

slush [slʌʃ] s Matsch m, Schneematsch
m

slush′ fund′ s Schmiergeld n

slushy [ˈslʌʃi] adj matschig

slut [slʌt] s Nutte f

sly [slaɪ] adj (slyer & slier; slyest &
sliest) schlau ‖ s—**on the sly** im Verborgenen

sly′ fox′ s Pfiffikus m

smack [smæk] s (blow) Klaps m;
(sound) Klatsch m; (kiss) Schmatz
m; **s. in the face** Backpfeife f ‖ tr
klapsen; **s. one′s lips** schmatzen ‖
intr—**s. of** riechen nach

small [smɔl] adj klein; (difference) gering; (comfort) schlecht; (petty)
kleinlich

small′ arms′ spl Handwaffen pl

small′ busi′ness s Kleinbetrieb m

small′ cap′ital s (typ) Kapitälchen n

small′ change′ s Kleingeld n

small′ fry′ s kleine Fische pl

small′ intes′tine s Dünndarm m

small′-mind′ed adj engstirnig

small′ of the back′ s Kreuz n

smallpox [ˈsmɔlˌpaks] s Pocken pl

small′ print′ s Kleindruck m

small′ talk′ s Geplauder n

small′-time′ adj klein

small′-town′ adj kleinstädtisch

smart [smart] adj (bright) klug; (neat,
trim) schick; (car) schneidig; (pej)
überklug ‖ s Schmerz m ‖ intr weh
tun; (burn) brennen

smart′ al′eck s [ˌælɪk] s Neunmalkluge
mf

smart′-look′ing adj schnittig

smart′ set′ s elegante Welt f

smash [smæʃ] s (hit) (coll) Bombe f;
(tennis) Schmetterschlag m ‖ tr zerschmettern; (e.g., a window) einschlagen; (sport) schmettern; **s. up**
zerknallen ‖ intr zerbrechen; **s. into**
krachen gegen

smash′ hit′ s (theat) Bombenerfolg m

smash′-up′ s (aut) Zusammenstoß m

smattering [ˈsmætərɪŋ] s (of) oberflächliche Kenntnis f (genit)

smear [smɪr] s Schmiere f; (smudge)
Schmutzfleck m; (vilification) Verun-
glimpfung f; (med) Abstrich m ‖ tr
(spread) schmieren; (make dirty) beschmieren; (vilify) verunglimpfen;
(trounce) vollständig fertigmachen

smear′ campaign′ s Verleumdungsfeld-
zug m

smell [smel] s Geruch m; (aroma) Duft
m; (sense) Geruchssinn m ‖ v (pret
& pp smelled & smelt [smelt]) tr
riechen; (danger, trouble) wittern ‖
intr (of) riechen (nach)

smell′ing salts′ pl Riechsalz n

smelly [ˈsmeli] adj übelriechend

smelt [smelt] s (fish) Stint m ‖ tr
schmelzen, verhütten

smile [smaɪl] s Lächeln n ‖ intr lächeln; **s. at** anlächeln; (clandestinely)
zulächeln (dat); **s. on** lächeln (dat)

smirk [smɪrk] s Grinsen n ‖ intr grinsen

smite [smaɪt] v (pret smote [smot];
pp smitten [ˈsmɪtən] & smit [smɪt])
tr schlagen; (said of a plague) befallen; **smitten with** hingerissen von

smith [smɪθ] s Schmied m

smithy [ˈsmɪθi] s Schmiede f

smock [smak] s Kittel m, Bluse f

smog [smag] s Smog m

smoke [smok] s Rauch m; (heavy
smoke) Qualm m; **go up in s.** (fig) in
Dunst und Rauch aufgehen ‖ tr rauchen; (meat) räuchern ‖ intr rauchen;
(said of a chimney) qualmen

smoke′ bomb′ s Rauchbombe f

smoked′ ham′ s Räucherschinken m

smoker [ˈsmokər] s Raucher –in mf;
(sl) obszöner Film m

smoke′ screen′ s Rauchvorhang m

smoke′stack′ s Schornstein m

smok′ing s Rauchen n; **no s.** (public
sign) Rauchen verboten

smok′ing car′ s Raucherwagen m

smok′ing jack′et s Hausjacke f

smoky [ˈsmoki] adj rauchig

smolder [ˈsmoldər] intr (& fig) schwelen

smooch [smutʃ] intr sich abknutschen

smooth [smuð] adj (surface; talker;
landing, operation) glatt; (wine) mild
‖ tr glätten; **s. away** (difficulties)
beseitigen; **s. out** glätten; **s. over** beschönigen

smooth′-faced′ adj glattwangig

smooth-shaven [ˈsmuðˈʃevən] adj glattrasiert

smooth′-talk′ing adj schönrednerisch

smoothy [ˈsmuði] s Schönredner –in mf

smother [ˈsmʌðər] tr ersticken; **s. with
kisses** abküssen

smudge [smʌdʒ] s Schmutzfleck m ‖ tr
beschmutzen ‖ intr schmutzig werden

smug [smʌg] adj (smugger; smuggest)
selbstgefällig

smuggle [ˈsmʌgəl] tr & intr schmuggeln

smuggler [ˈsmʌglər] s Schmuggler –in
mf

smug′gling s Schmuggel m

smut [smʌt] s Schmutz m

smutty [ˈsmʌti] adj schmutzig, obszön

snack [snæk] s Imbiß m

snack′ bar′ s Imbißstube f, Snack Bar f

snaffle [ˈsnæfəl] s Trense f

snag [snæg] s—**hit a s.** auf Schwierigkeiten stoßen ‖ v (pret & pp snagged;
ger snagging) tr hängenbleiben mit

snail [snel] s Schnecke f; **at a snail′s
pace** im Schneckentempo

snake [snek] s Schlange f ‖ intr sich
schlängeln

snake′bite′ s Schlangenbiß m

snake′ in the grass′ s heimtückischer
Mensch m

snap [snæp] s (sound) Knacks m; (on
clothes) Druckknopf m; (of a dog)
Biß m; (liveliness) Schwung m; (easy
work) Kinderspiel n ‖ v (pret & pp
snapped; ger snapping) tr (break)
zerreißen, entzweibrechen; (a picture) knipsen; **s. a whip** mit der

Peitsche knallen; **s. back** (*words*) hervorstoßen; (*the head*) zurückwerfen; **s. off** abbrechen; **s. one's fingers** mit den Fingern schnalzen; **s. s.o.'s head off** j–n zusammenstauchen; **s. up** gierig an sich reißen; (*buy up*) aufkaufen ‖ *intr* (*tear*) zerreißen; (*break*) entzweibrechen; **s. at** schnappen nach; (fig) anfahren; **s. out of it!** komm zu dir!; **s. shut** zuschnappen; **s. to it!** mach zu!

snap'drag'on *s* (bot) Löwenmaul *n*

snap' fas'tener *s* Druckknopf *m*

snap' judg'ment *s* vorschnelles Urteil *n*

snap'per soup' ['snæpər] *s* Schildkrötensuppe *f*

snappish ['snæpɪʃ] *adj* bissig

snappy ['snæpi] *adj* (*caustic*) bissig; (*lively*) energisch; **make it s.!** mach schnell!

snap'shot' *s* Schnappschuß *m*

snare [sner] *s* Schlinge *f* ‖ *tr* mit e-r Schlinge fangen; (fig) fangen

snare' drum' *s* Schnarrtrommel *f*

snarl [snɑrl] *s* (*tangle*) Verwicklung *f*; (*sound*) Knurren *n* ‖ *tr* verwickeln; **s. traffic** e–e Verkehrsstockung verursachen ‖ *intr* knurren

snatch [snætʃ] *s*—**in snatches** ruckweise; **snatches** (*of conversation*) Bruchstücke *pl* ‖ *tr* schnappen; **s. away from** entreißen (*dat*); **s. up** schnappen

snazzy ['snæzi] *adj* (sl) schmissig

sneak [snik] *s* Schleicher –in *mf* ‖ *tr* (*e.g., a drink*) heimlich trinken; **s. in** einschmuggeln ‖ *intr* schleichen; **s. away** sich davonschleichen; **s. in** sich einschleichen; **s. out** sich herausschleichen; **s. up on s.o.** an j–n heranschleichen

sneaker ['snikər] *s* Tennisschuh *m*

sneaky ['sniki] *adj* heimtückisch

sneer [snɪr] *s* Hohnlächeln *n* ‖ *intr* höhnisch grinsen; **s. at** spötteln über (*acc*)

sneeze [sniz] *s* Niesen *n* ‖ *tr*—**not to be sneezed at** nicht zu verachten ‖ *intr* niesen

snicker ['snɪkər] *s* Kichern *n* ‖ *intr* kichern

snide' remark' [snaɪd] *s* Anzüglichkeit *f*

sniff [snɪf] *s* Schnüffeln *n* ‖ *tr* (be)riechen; **s. out** ausschnüffeln ‖ *intr* (at) schnüffeln (an *dat*)

sniffle ['snɪfəl] *s* Geschnüffel *n*; **sniffles** Schnupfen *m* ‖ *intr* schniefen

snip [snɪp] *s* (*cut*) Einschnitt *m*; (*small piece snipped off*) Schnippel *m* ‖ *v* (*pret & pp* **snipped**; *ger* **snipping**) *tr & intr* schnippeln

snipe [snaɪp] *intr*—**s. at** aus dem Hinterhalt schießen auf (*acc*)

sniper ['snaɪpər] *s* Heckenschütze *m*

snippet ['snɪpɪt] *s* Schnippelchen *n*; (*small person*) Knirps *m*

snippy ['snɪpi] *adj* schroff, barsch

snitch [snɪtʃ] *tr* (coll) klauen ‖ *intr* (coll) petzen; **s. on** (coll) verpfeifen

sniv·el ['snɪvəl] *s* (*whining*) Gewimmer *n*; (*mucus*) Nasenschleim *m* ‖ *v*

(*pret & pp* **–el[l]ed**; *ger* **–el[l]ing**) *intr* (*whine*) wimmern; (*cry with sniffling*) schluchzen; (*have a runny nose*) e–e tropfende Nase haben

snob [snɑb] *s* Snob *m*

snob' appeal' *s* Snobappeal *m*

snobbery ['snɑbəri] *s* Snobismus *m*

snobbish ['snɑbɪʃ] *adj* snobistisch

snoop [snup] *s* (coll) Schnüffler –in *mf* ‖ *intr* (coll) schnüffeln

snoopy ['snupi] *adj* schnüffelnd

snoot [snut] *s* (sl) Rüssel *m*; **make a s.** e–e Schnute ziehen

snooty ['snuti] *adj* hochnäsig

snooze [snuz] *s* (coll) Nickerchen *n* ‖ *intr* (coll) ein Nickerchen machen

snore [snor] *s* Schnarchen *n* ‖ *intr* schnarchen

snort [snort] *s* Schnauben *n* ‖ *intr* wütend schnauben ‖ *intr* prusten; (*said of a horse*) schnauben; (*with laughter*) vor Lachen prusten

snot [snɑt] *s* (sl) Rotz *m*

snotty ['snɑti] *adj* (sl & fig) rotzig

snout [snaut] *s* Schnauze *f*, Rüssel *m*

snow [sno] *s* Schnee *m* ‖ *tr* (sl) einwickeln; **s. in** einschneien; **s. under** mit Schnee bedecken ‖ *impers*—**it is snowing** es schneit

snow'ball' *s* Schneeball *m* ‖ *intr* (fig) lawinenartig anwachsen

snow'bank' *s* Schneeverwehung *f*

snow'bird' *s* Schneefink *m*

snow' blind'ness *s* Schneeblindheit *f*

snow' blow'er *s* Schneefräse *f*

snow'bound' *adj* eingeschneit

snow'-capped' *adj* schneebedeckt

snow' chain' *s* (aut) Schneekette *f*

snow'-clad' *adj* verschneit

snow'drift' *s* Schneeverwehung *f*

snow'fall' *s* Schneefall *m*

snow'flake' *s* Schneeflocke *f*

snow' flur'ry *s* Schneegestöber *n*

snow' job'—**give s.o. a s.** (sl) j–n hereinlegen

snow'man' *s* (**-men**) Schneemann *m*

snow'mobile' *s* Motorschlitten *m*

snow'plow' *s* Schneepflug *m*

snow'shoe' *s* Schneeteller *m*

snow' shov'el *s* Schneeschaufel *f*

snow'storm' *s* Schneesturm *m*

snow' tire' *s* Winterreifen *m*

Snow' White' *s* Schneewittchen *n*

snow'-white' *adj* schneeweiß

snowy ['sno·i] *adj* schneeig

snub [snʌb] *s* verächtliche Behandlung *f* ‖ *v* (*pret & pp* **snubbed**; *ger* **snubbing**) *tr* (*ignore*) schneiden; (*treat contemptuously*) verächtlich behandeln

snubby ['snʌbi] *adj* (*nose*) etwas abgestumpft; (*person*) abweisend

snub'-nosed' *adj* stupsnasig

snuff [snʌf] *s* Schnupftabak *m*; (*of a candle*) Schnuppe *f*; **up to s.** (sl) auf Draht ‖ *tr*—**s. out** (*a candle*) auslöschen; (*suppress*) unterdrücken

snuff'box' *s* Schnupftabakdose *f*

snug [snʌg] *adj* (*snugger*; *snuggest*) behaglich; (*fit*) eng angeschmiegt; **s. as a bug in a rug** wie die Made im Speck

snuggle ['snʌgəl] *intr*—s. up (to) sich schmiegen (an *acc*)

so [so] *adv* (with adjectives or adverbs) so; (*thus*) so; (*for this reason*) daher; (*then*) also; **and so forth und so weiter; or so etwa**, e.g., **ten miles or so etwa zehn Meilen; so as to** (*inf*) um zu (*inf*); **so far bisher; so far as soviel; so far, so good soweit ganz gut; so I see! das seh' ich!; so long!** (*coll*) bis bald!; **so much soviel; so much the better um so besser; so that damit; so what?** na, und?

soak [sok] *s* Einweichen *n* ‖ *tr* einweichen; (*soak through and through*) durchnässen; (*overcharge*) (sl) schröpfen; **soaked to the skin bis auf die Haut durchnäßt** ‖ *intr* weichen

so'-and-so' *s* (-sos) Soundso *mf*

soap [sop] *s* Seife *f* ‖ *tr* einseifen

soap'box der'by *s* Seifenkistenrennen *n*

soap'box or'ator *s* Straßenredner –in *mf*

soap' bub'ble *s* Seifenblase *f*

soap' dish' *s* Seifenschale *f*

soap' flakes' *spl* Seifenflocken *pl*

soap' op'era *s* (rad) rührselige Hörspielreihe *f*; (telv) rührselige Fernsehspielreihe *f*

soap' pow'der *s* Seifenpulver *n*

soap'stone' *s* Seifenstein *m*

soap'suds' *spl* Seifenlauge *f*

soapy ['sopi] *adj* seifig; (*like soap*) seifenartig

soar [sor] *intr* schweben, (auf)steigen; (*prices*) steigen

sob [sab] *s* Schluchzen *n* ‖ *v* (*pret* & *pp* sobbed; *ger* sobbing) *intr* schluchzen

sober ['sobər] *adj* nüchtern ‖ *tr* (up) ernüchtern ‖ *intr*—s. up wieder nüchtern werden

sobriety [so'braɪəti] *s* Nüchternheit *f*

sob' sto'ry *s* Schmachtfetzen *m*

so'-called' *adj* sogenannt

soccer ['sakər] *s* Fußball *m*

soc'cer play'er *s* Fußballer *m*

sociable ['soʃəbəl] *adj* gesellig

social ['soʃəl] *adj* gesellschaftlich ‖ *s* geselliges Beisammensein *n*

so'cial climb'er *s* Streber –in *mf*

socialism ['soʃə,lɪzəm] *s* Sozialismus *m*

socialist ['soʃəlɪst] *s* Sozialist –in *mf*

socialistic [,soʃə'lɪstɪk] *adj* sozialistisch

socialize ['soʃə,laɪt] *s* Prominente *mf*

socialize ['soʃə,laɪz] *intr* (with) verkehren (mit)

so'cialized med'icine *s* staatliche Gesundheitspflege *f*

so'cial reg'ister *s* Register *n* der prominenten Mitglieder der oberen Gesellschaftsklasse

so'cial sci'ence *s* Sozialwissenschaft *f*

so'cial secu'rity *s* Sozialversicherung *f*

so'cial wel'fare *s* Sozialfürsorge *f*

so'cial work'er *s* Sozialfürsorger –in *mf*

society [sə'saɪəti] *s* Gesellschaft *f*; (*an organization*) Verein *m*

soci'ety col'umn *s* Gesellschaftsspalte *f*

soci'ety for the preven'tion of cru'elty to an'imals *s* Tierschutzverein *m*

sociological [,sosɪ-ə'ladʒɪkəl] *adj* sozialwissenschaftlich, soziologisch

sociologist [,sosɪ'alədʒɪst] *s* Soziologe *m*, Soziologin *f*

sociology [,sosɪ'alədʒi] *s* Soziologie *f*

sock [sak] *s* Socke *f*; (sl) Faustschlag *m* ‖ *tr*—s. it to him! gib's ihm!; **s.o.** j–m eine 'runterhauen

socket ['sakɪt] *s* (anat) Höhle *f*; (elec) Steckdose *f*; (mach) Muffe *f*

sock'et joint' *s* (anat) Kugelgelenk *n*

sock'et wrench' *s* Steckschlüssel *m*

sod [sad] *s* Rasenstück *n* ‖ *v* (*pret* & *pp* sodded; *ger* sodding) *tr* mit Rasen bedecken

soda ['sodə] *s* (*refreshment*) Limonade *f*; (*in mixed drinks*) Selterswasser *n*; (chem) Soda *f* & *n*

so'da crack'er *s* Keks *m*

so'da wa'ter *s* Sodawasser *n*

sodium ['sodɪ-əm] *s* Natrium *n*

sofa ['sofə] *s* Sofa *n*

soft [saft] *adj* (*not hard or tough*) weich; (*not loud*) leise; (*light, music*) sanft; (*sleep, breeze*) leicht; (*effeminate*) verweichlicht; (*muscles*) schlaff; **be s. on weich sein gegenüber** (*dat*)

soft'-boiled egg' *s* weichgekochtes Ei *n*

soft' coal' *s* Braunkohle *f*

soft' drink' *s* alkoholfreies Getränk *n*

soften ['safən] *tr* aufweichen; (*palliate*) lindern; (*water*) enthärten; **s. up** (mil) zermürben ‖ *intr* (& fig) weich werden

soft'-heart'ed *adj* weichherzig

soft' job' *s* Druckposten *m*

soft' land'ing *s* (rok) weiche Landung *f*

soft' pal'ate *s* Hintergaumen *m*

soft'-ped'al *v* (*pret* & *pp* -al[l]ed; *ger* -al[l]ing) *tr* zurückhaltender vorbringen

soft'-soap' *tr* (coll) schmeicheln (*dat*)

soggy ['sagi] *adj* (*soaked*) durchnäßt; (*ground*) sumpfig

soil [sɔɪl] *s* Boden *m* ‖ *tr* beschmutzen ‖ *intr* schmutzen

soil' pipe' *s* Abflußrohr *n*

sojourn ['sodʒərn] *s* Aufenthalt *m* ‖ *intr* sich vorübergehend aufhalten

solace ['salɪs] *s* Trost *m* ‖ *tr* trösten

solar ['solər] *adj* Sonnen-

so'lar plex'us ['pleksəs] *s* (anat) Sonnengeflecht *n*

solder ['sadər] *s* Lötmetall *n* ‖ *tr* löten

sol'dering i'ron *s* Lötkolben *m*

soldier ['soldʒər] *s* Soldat *m*

sole [sol] *adj* einzig, alleinig ‖ *s* (*of a shoe, foot*) Sohle *f*; (*fish*) Scholle *f* ‖ *tr* (be)sohlen

solely ['soli] *adv* einzig und allein

solemn ['saləm] *adj* feierlich; (*expression*) ernst

solemnity [sə'lemnɪti] *s* Feierlichkeit *f*

solicit [sə'lɪsɪt] *tr* (*beg for*) dringend bitten um; (*accost*) ansprechen; (*new members, customers*) werben

solicitor [sə'lɪsɪtər] *s* (com) Agent –in *mf*; (jur) Rechtsanwalt *m*

solicitous [sə'lɪsɪtəs] *adj* fürsorglich

solid ['salɪd] *adj* (*hard, firm, e.g., ice, ground*) fest; (*sturdy, e.g., person, furniture; firm, e.g., foundation, learning; financially sound*) solid(e); (*compact*) kompakt, massiv; (*durable*) dauerhaft; (*gold*) gediegen; (*meal, blow*) kräftig; (*hour*) ganz, geschlagen; (*of one color*) einfarbig; (*color*) getönt; (*of one mind*) einmütig; (*grounds, argument*) stichhaltig; (*row of houses*) geschlossen; (*clouds, fog*) dicht; (*geom*) Raum– || *s* (geom, phys) Körper *m*

solidarity [,salɪ'dærɪti] *s* Solidarität *f*, Verbundenheit *f*

sol'id food' *s* feste Nahrung *f*

sol'id ge'ometry *s* Stereometrie *f*

solidi·fy [sə'lɪdɪ,faɪ] *v* (*pret & pp* –fied) *tr* fest werden lassen; (fig) konsolidieren || *intr* fest werden

solidity [sə'lɪdɪti] *s* (*state*) Festigkeit *f*; (*soundness*) Solidität *f*

solidly ['salɪdli] *adv*—**be s. behind s.o.** sich mit j–m solidarisch erklären

sol'id-state' *adj* Transistor–

soliloquy [sə'lɪləkwi] *s* Selbstgespräch *n*

solitaire ['salɪ,ter] *s* Solitär *m*

solitary ['salɪ,teri] *adj* allein; (*life*) zurückgezogen; (*exception*) einzig; (*lonely*) einsam

sol'itary confine'ment *s* Einzelhaft *f*

solitude ['salɪ,t(j)ud] *s* Einsamkeit *f*; (*lonely spot*) abgelegener Ort *m*

so·lo ['solo] *adj & adv* solo || *s* (–los) Solo *n*

so'lo flight' *s* Soloflug *m*

soloist ['solo-ɪst] *s* Solist –in *mf*

so'lo part' *s* (mus) Solostimme *f*

solstice ['salstɪs] *s* Sonnenwende *f*

soluble ['saljəbəl] *adj* (fig) (auf)lösbar; (chem) löslich

solution [sə'luʃən] *s* Lösung *f*

solvable ['salvəbəl] *adj* (auf)lösbar

solve [salv] *tr* (auf)lösen

solvency ['salvənsi] *s* Zahlungsfähigkeit *f*

solvent ['salvənt] *adj* zahlungsfähig; (chem) (auf)lösend || *s* Lösungsmittel *n*

somber ['sambər] *adj* düster, trüb(e)

some [sʌm] *indef adj* (with singular nouns) etwas; (with plural nouns) manche; (sometimes not translated) e.g., **I am buying s. stockings** ich kaufe Strümpfe; (coll) toll, e.g., **s. girl!** tolles Mädchen!; **at s. time or other** irgendeinmal, irgendwann; **s. ... or other** irgendein; **s. other way** sonstwie || *adv* (with numerals) etwa, ungefähr || *indef pron* manche; (*part of*) ein Teil *m*; **s. of these people** einige Leute; **s. of us** manche von uns

some'bod'y *indef pron* jemand, irgendwer; **s. else** jemand anderer || *s*—**be a s.** etwas Besonderes sein

some'day' *adv* e–s Tages

some'how' *adv* irgendwie; (*for some reason or other*) aus irgendeinem Grunde

some'one' *indef pron* jemand, irgendwer; **s. else** jemand anderer; **s. else's** fremd, e.g., **s. else's property** fremdes Eigentum

some'place' *adv* irgendwo; (*direction*) irgendwohin

somersault ['sʌmər,solt] *s* Purzelbaum *m*; (gym) Überschlag *m*; **do a s.** e–n Purzelbaum schlagen || *intr* sich überschlagen

some'thing *indef pron* etwas; **he is s. of an expert** er ist e–e Art Experte; **s. else** etwas anderes; **s. or other** irgend etwas

some'time' *adv* einmal; **s. today** irgendwann heute

some'times' *adv* manchmal; **sometimes ... sometimes ...** mal ... mal ...

some'way', some'ways' *adv* irgendwie

some'what' *adv* etwas

some'where' *adv* irgendwo; (*direction*) irgendwohin; **from s. else** sonstwoher; **s. else** sonstwo

somnambulist [sam'næmbjəlɪst] *s* Nachtwandler –in *mf*

somnolent ['samnələnt] *adj* schläfrig

son [sʌn] *s* Sohn *m*

sonar ['sonar] *s* Sonar *n*

sonata [sə'natə] *s* Sonate *f*

song [sɔŋ] *s* Lied *n*; (*of birds*) Gesang *m*; **for a s.** (coll) um ein Spottgeld

Song' of Songs' *s* (Bib) Hoheliet *n*

sonic ['sanɪk] *adj* Schall–

son'ic boom' *s* Kopfwellenknall *m*

son'-in-law' *s* (sons-in-law) Schwiegersohn *m*

sonnet ['sanɪt] *s* Sonett *n*

sonny ['sʌni] *s* Söhnchen *n*, Kleiner *m*

Son' of Man', **the** *s* (Bib) der Menschensohn

sonorous [sə'norəs] *adj* sonor

soon [sun] *adv* bald; **as s. as** sobald; **as s. as possible** sobald wie möglich; **just as s.** (*expressing preference*) genauso gern(e); **no sooner said than done** gesagt, getan; **sooner** (*expressing time*) früher, eher; (*expressing preference*) lieber, eher; **sooner or later** aber kurz oder lang; **the sooner the better** je eher, je besser; **too s.** zu früh

soot [sut] *s* Ruß *m*

soothe [suð] *tr* beschwichtigen, beruhigen; **have a soothing effect on** beruhigend wirken auf (*acc*)

soothsayer ['suθ,se·ər] *s* Wahrsager *m*

sooty ['suti] *adj* rußig

sop [sap] *s* eingetunktes Stück *n* Brot; (*something given to pacify*) Beschwichtigungsmittel *n*; (*bribe*) Schmiergeld *n*; (*spineless person*) Waschlappen *m* || *v* (*pret & pp* sopped; *ger* sopping) *tr* (*dip*) eintunken; **sop up** aufsaugen

sophist ['safɪst] *s* Sophist –in *mf*

sophisticated [sə'fɪstɪ,ketɪd] *adj* (*person*) weltklug; (*way of life*) verfeinert; (*highly developed*) hochentwickelt

sophistication [sə,fɪstɪ'keʃən] *s* Weltklugheit *f*

sophistry ['safɪstri] *s* Sophisterei *f*

sophomore ['sɑfə‚mor] s Student –in mf im zweiten Studienjahr

sop'ping adj klatschnaß || adv—s. wet klatschnaß

sopran-o [sə'præno] adj Sopran- || s (-os) (uppermost voice) Sopran m; (soprano part) Sopranpartie f; (singer) Sopranist –in mf

sorcerer ['sɔrsərər] s Zauberer m

sorceress ['sɔrsərɪs] s Zauberin f

sorcery ['sɔrsəri] s Zauberei f

sordid ['sɔrdɪd] adj schmutzig; (improper) unlauter

sore [sor] adj wund; (sensitive) empfindlich; (coll) (at) bös (auf acc); be s. weh tun; s. spot (& fig) wunder Punkt m || s Wunde f

sore'head' s (coll) Verbitterte mf

sorely ['sorli] adv sehr

soreness ['sornɪs] s Empfindlichkeit f

sore' throat' s Halsweh n

sorority [sə'rɔrɪti] s Studentinnenvereinigung f

sorrel ['sɔrəl] adj fuchsrot || s Fuchs m; (bot) Sauerampfer m

sorrow ['sɔro] s Kummer m || intr (for or over) Kummer haben (um)

sorrowful ['sɔrəfəl] adj betrübt

sorry ['sɔri] adj traurig, betrübt; (appearance) armselig; I am s. es tut mir leid; I am (or feel) s. for him er tut mir leid

sort [sɔrt] s Art f, Sorte f; all sorts of alle möglichen; nothing of the s. nichts dergleichen; out of sorts unpäßlich; s. of (coll) (with adjectives) etwas; (with verbs) irgendwie; (with nouns) so 'n, e.g., I had a s. of feeling that ich hatte so 'ne Ahnung, daß; these sorts of derartige; what s. of was für ein || tr sortieren; s. out aussortieren; (fig) sichten

sortie ['sɔrti] s (from a fortress) Ausfall m; (aer) Einzeleinsatz m || intr e-n Ausfall machen

so'-so' adj & adv soso, leidlich

sot [sɑt] s Trunkenbold m

soul [sol] s (spiritual being; inhabitant) Seele f; not a s. (coll) keine Seele f; upon my s.! meiner Seele!

sound [saʊnd] adj Schall-, Ton-; (healthy) gesund; (valid) einwandfrei; (basis) tragfähig; (sleep) fest; (beating) (coll) tüchtig; (business) solid; (judgment) treffsicher || s Laut m, Ton m; (noise) Geräusch n; (of one's voice) Klang m; (narrow body of water) Sund m; (phys) Schall m; (surg) Sonde f || adv—be s. asleep fest schlafen || tr ertönen lassen; (med) sondieren; (naut) loten; s. s.o. out (coll) j-m auf den Zahn fühlen; s. the alarm Alarm schlagen; s. the all-clear entwarnen || intr (er)klingen, (er)tönen; (seem) klingen; (naut) loten; it sounds good to me es kommt mir gut vor; s. off (coll) sich laut beschweren

sound' bar'rier s Schallgrenze f, Schallmauer f

sound' effects' spl Klangeffekte pl

sound' film' s Tonfilm m

sound'ing s Lotung f; take soundings loten

sound'ing board' s (on an instrument) Resonanzboden m; (over an orchestra or speaker) Schallmuschel f; (board for damping sounds) Schalldämpfungsbrett n

soundly ['saʊndli] adv tüchtig

sound'proof' adj schalldicht || tr schalldicht machen

sound' stu'dio s (cin) Tonatelier n

sound' techni'cian s Tontechniker m

sound' track' s (cin) Tonstreifen m

sound' truck' s Lautsprecherwagen m

sound' wave' s Schallwelle f

soup [sup] s Suppe f; (thick fog) (coll) Waschküche f; in the s. (coll) in der Patsche || tr—s. up (aut) frisieren

soup' kitch'en s Volksküche f

soup'meat' s Suppenfleisch n

soup' plate' s Suppenteller m

soup'spoon' s Suppenlöffel m

sour [saʊr] adj (& fig) sauer || tr säuern; (fig) verbittern || intr säuern; (fig) versauern

source [sors] s Quelle f

source' lan'guage s Ausgangssprache f

source' mate'rial s Quellenmaterial n

sour' cher'ry s Weichsel f

sour' grapes' spl (fig) saure Trauben pl

sour' note' s (& fig) Mißklang m

sour'puss' s (sl) Sauertopf m

souse [saʊs] s (sl) Säufer –in mf

soused adj (sl) besoffen

south [saʊθ] adj Süd-, südlich || adv (direction) nach Süden; s. of südlich von || s Süd(en) m

South' Amer'ica s Südamerika n

south'east' adj Südost- || adv (direction) südöstlich; s. of südöstlich von || s Südost(en) m

south'east'ern adj südöstlich

southerly ['sʌðərli] adj südlich

southern ['sʌðərn] adj südlich

southerner ['sʌðərnər] s Südländer –in mf; (in the U.S.A.) Südstaatler –in mf

south'paw' adj (coll) linkshändig || s Linkshänder –in mf

South' Pole' s Südpol m

South' Seas' spl Südsee f

southward ['saʊθwərd] adv südwärts

south'west' adj Südwest- || adv (direction) südwestlich; s. of südwestlich von || s Südwest(en) m

south'west'ern adj südwestlich

souvenir [‚suvə'nɪr] s Andenken n

sovereign ['sɑvrɪn] adj souverän || s Souverän m, Landesfürst m

sov'ereign rights' spl Hoheitsrechte pl

sovereignty ['sɑvrɪnti] s Souveränität f

soviet ['sovi‚et] adj sowjetisch || s Sowjet m, the Soviets die Sowjets pl

So'viet Rus'sia s Sowjetrußland n

So'viet Un'ion s Sowjetunion f

sow [saʊ] s Sau f || [so] v (pret sowed; pp sowed & sown) tr & intr säen

soybean ['sɔɪ‚bin] s Sojabohne f

spa [spɑ] s Bad n, Badekurort m

space [spes] s Raum m; (between ob-

jects) Zwischenraum *m;* (typ) Spatium *n;* **take up** s. Platz einnehmen ‖ *tr* in Abständen anordnen; (typ) spationieren

space' age' *s* Weltraumzeitalter *n*

space' bar' *s* (typ) Leertaste *f*

space' cap'sule *s* (rok) Raumkapsel *f*

space'craft *s* Weltraumfahrzeug *n*

space' flight' *s* Raumflug *m*

space'man' *s* (**-men'**) Raumfahrer *m*

space' probe' *s* Sonde *f*

space'ship' *s* Raumschiff *n*

space' shot' *s* Weltraumabschuß *m*

space' shut'tle *s* Raumfähre *f*

space' suit' *s* Raumanzug *m*

space' trav'el *s* Raumfahrt *f*

spacious ['speʃəs] *adj* geräumig

spade [sped] *s* Spaten *m;* (cards) Pik *n;* **call a s. a s.** das Kind beim richtigen Namen nennen

spade'work' *s* (fig) Pionierarbeit *f*

spaghetti [spə'geti] *s* Spaghetti *pl*

Spain [spen] *s* Spanien *n*

span [spæn] *s* (& fig) Spanne *f;* (of a bridge) Joch *n;* **s. of time** Zeitspanne *f* ‖ *v* (pret & pp **spanned**) *ger* **spanning** tr (e.g., the waist) umspannen; (a river) überbrücken; (said of a bridge) überspannen

spangle ['spæŋgəl] *s* Flitter *m* ‖ *tr* mit Flitter besetzen

Spaniard ['spænjərd] *s* Spanier –in *mf*

spaniel ['spænjəl] *s* Wachtelhund *m*

Spanish ['spænɪʃ] *adj* spanisch ‖ *s* Spanisch *n;* **the S.** die Spanier

Span'ish-Amer'ican *adj* spanisch-amerikanisch ‖ *s* Amerikaner –in *mf* mit spanischer Muttersprache

Span'ish moss' *s* Moosbärte *pl*

spank [spæŋk] *tr* (ver)hauen

spank'ing *adj* (quick) flink; (breeze) frisch ‖ *adv*—**s. new** funkelnagelneu ‖ *s* Schläge *pl*

spar [spar] *s* (aer) Holm *m;* (mineral) Spat *m;* (naut) Spiere *f* ‖ *v* (pret & pp **sparred**; *ger* **sparring**) *intr* sparren

spare [sper] *adj* Ersatz–; (thin) mager; (time) frei; (leftover) übrig ‖ *s* (aut) Ersatzreifen *m* ‖ *tr* (a person) schonen; (time, money) erübrigen; (expense) scheuen; (do without) entbehren; **have to s.** übrig haben; **s. s.o. s.th.** j-m etw ersparen

spare' bed' *s* Gastbett *n*

spare' part' *s* Ersatzteil *n*

spare' rib' *s* Rippenspeer *m*

spare' time' *s* Freizeit *f*

spare'-time' *adj* nebenberuflich

spare' tire' *s* Ersatzreifen *m*

spar'ing *adj* sparsam; **be s. with** sparsam umgehen mit

spark [spark] *s* Funke(n) *m* ‖ *tr* (set off) auslösen; (stimulate) anregen ‖ *intr* Funken sprühen

spark' gap' *s* Funkenstrecke *f*

sparkle ['sparkəl] *s* Funkeln *n* ‖ *intr* funkeln; (said of wine) moussieren

spark' plug' *s* Zündkerze *f*

spar'ring part'ner *s* Übungspartner *m*

sparrow ['spæro] *s* Spatz *m,* Sperling *m*

spar'row hawk' *s* Sperber *m*

sparse [spars] *adj* spärlich

Spartan ['spartən] *adj* spartanisch ‖ *s* Spartaner –in *mf*

spasm ['spæzəm] *s* Krampf *m,* Zuckung *f*

spasmodic [spæz'madɪk] *adj* sprunghaft; (pathol) krampfartig

spastic ['spæstɪk] *adj* spastisch

spat [spæt] *s* (coll) Wortwechsel *m*

spatial ['speʃəl] *adj* räumlich

spatter ['spætər] *s* Spritzen *n;* (stain) Spritzfleck *m* ‖ *tr* verspritzen

spatula ['spætʃələ] *s* Spachtel *m & f*

spawn [spɔn] *s* Fischlaich *m* ‖ *tr* hervorbringen ‖ *intr* (said of fish) laichen

spay [spe] *tr* die Eierstöcke entfernen aus

speak [spik] *v* (pret **spoke** [spok]; pp **spoken**) *tr* sprechen; **one's mind** sich aussprechen ‖ *intr* (about) sprechen (über *acc,* von); **generally speaking** im allgemeinen; **so to s.** sozusagen; **speaking!** (telp) am Apparat!; **s.** to sprechen mit; (give a speech to) sprechen zu; **s. up** lauter sprechen; (say something) den Mund aufmachen; **s. up!** heraus mit der Sprache!; **s. up** for eintreten für

speak'-eas'y *s* Flüsterkneipe *f*

speaker ['spikər] *s* Sprecher –in *mf;* (before an audience) Redner –in *mf;* (parl) Sprecher –in *mf;* (rad) Lautsprecher *m*

spear [spɪr] *s* Speer *m* ‖ *tr* durchbohren; (a piece of meat) aufspießen; (fish) mit dem Speer fangen

spear'head' *s* Speerspitze *f;* (mil) Stoßkeil *m* ‖ *tr* an der Spitze stehen von

spear'mint' *s* Krauseminze *f*

special ['speʃəl] *adj* besonder, Sonder– ‖ *s* (rr) Sonderzug *m;* **today's s.** Stammgericht *n*

spe'cial deliv'ery *s* Eilzustellung *f;* (tab on envelope) Eilsendung *f*

spec'ial-deliv'ery let'ter *s* Eilbrief *m*

specialist ['speʃəlɪst] *s* Spezialist –in *mf*

specialization [ˌspeʃəlɪ'zeʃən] *s* Spezialisierung *f*

specialize ['speʃə‚laɪz] *intr* sich spezialisieren; **specialized knowledge** Fachkenntnisse *pl*

spe'cial of'fer *s* (com) Sonderangebot *n*

specialty ['speʃəlti] *s* Spezialität *f;* (special field) Spezialfach *n*

spe'cialty shop' *s* Spezialgeschäft *n*

specie ['spiʃi] *s*—**in s.** der Art nach

spe-cies ['spiʃiz] *s* (**-cies**) Gattung *f*

specific [spɪ'sɪfɪk] *adj* spezifisch

specification [ˌspesɪfɪ'keʃən] *s* Spezifizierung *f;* **specifications** (tech) technische Beschreibung *f*

specif'ic grav'ity *s* spezifisches Gewicht *n*

speci-fy ['spesɪ‚faɪ] *v* (pret & pp **-fied**) *tr* spezifizieren; (stipulate) bestimmen

specimen ['spesɪmən] *s* (example) Exemplar *n;* (test sample) Probe *f*

specious ['spiʃəs] *adj* Schein–

speck [spek] *s* Fleck *m; (in the distance)* Pünktchen *n;* **s. of dust** Stäubchen *n;* **s. of grease** Fettauge *n*

speckle ['spekəl] *s* Sprenkel *m* ‖ *tr* sprenkeln

spectacle ['spektəkəl] *s* Schauspiel *n,* Anblick *m;* **spectacles** Brille *f*

spec'tacle case' *s* Brillenfutteral *n*

spectacular [spek'tækjələr] *adj* sensationell ‖ *s (cin)* Monsterfilm *m*

spectator ['spekteɪtər] *s* Zuschauer –in *mf*

specter ['spetər] *s* Gespenst *n*

spec·trum ['spektrəm] *s (–tra* [trə]*)* Spektrum *n*

speculate ['spekjə‚let] *intr* spekulieren; **s.** in spekulieren in *(dat);* **s. on** Überlegungen anstellen über *(acc)*

speculation [‚spekjə'leʃən] *s* Spekulation *f*

speculative ['spekjələtɪv] *adj (com)* Spekulations–; *(philos)* spekulativ

speculator ['spekjə‚letər] *s* Spekulant –in *mf*

speech [spitʃ] *s* Sprache *f; (address)* Rede *f;* **give a s.** e–e Rede halten

speech' defect' *s* Sprachfehler *m*

speech' imped'iment *s* Sprachstörung *f*

speechless ['spitʃlɪs] *adj* sprachlos

speed [spid] *s* Geschwindigkeit *f; (gear)* Gang *m;* **at top s.** mit Höchstgeschwindigkeit; **pick up s.** auf Touren kommen ‖ *v (pret & pp* **speeded & sped** [sped]*) tr* beschleunigen; **s. up** forcieren; **s. it up** (coll) ein scharfes Tempo vorlegen ‖ *intr (aut)* rasen; *(above the speed limit)* (aut) zu schnell fahren

speed'boat' *s* Schnellboot *n*

speed'ing *s* (aut) Schnellfahren *n;* **be arrested for s.** wegen Überschreitung der Höchstgeschwindigkeit verhaftet werden; **no s.** *(public sign)* Schnellfahren verboten

speed' lim'it *s* Geschwindigkeitsgrenze *f*

speed' of light' *s* Lichtgeschwindigkeit *f*

speed' of sound' *s* Schallgeschwindigkeit *f*

speedometer [spi'dɑmɪtər] *s* Tachometer *n; (mileage indicator)* Meilenzähler *m,* Kilometerzähler *m*

speed' rec'ord *s* Geschwindigkeitsrekord *m*

speed' trap' *s* Autofalle *f*

speed'way' *s* (aut) Rennstrecke *f*

speedy ['spidi] *adj* schnell, schleunig; *(reply)* baldig

speed' zone' *s* Geschwindigkeitsbeschränkung *f*

spell [spel] *s (short period)* Zeitlang *f; (attack)* Anfall *m; (magical influence)* Bann *m;* **be under s.o.'s s.** in j–s Bann stehen; **cast a s.** bannen ‖ *v (pret & pp* **spelled & spelt** [spelt]*) tr* buchstabieren; *(in writing)* schreiben; **s. out** Buchstaben für Buchstaben lesen; *(fig)* auseinanderklamüsern; **s. trouble** Schwie-

rigkeiten bedeuten ‖ *intr* buchstabieren

spell'bind'er *s* faszinierender Redner *m*

spell'bound' *adj* gebannt

spell'ing *s* Schreibweise *f; (orthography)* Rechtschreibung *f*

spell'ing bee' *s* orthographischer Wettbewerb *m*

spelt [spelt] *s* Spelz *m*

spelunker [spɪ'lʌŋkər] *s* Höhlenforscher –in *mf*

spend [spend] *v (pret & pp* **spent** [spent]*) tr (money)* ausgeben; *(time)* verbringen; **s. the night** übernachten; **s. time and effort on** Zeit und Mühe verwenden auf *(acc)*

spend'thrift' *s* Verschwender –in *mf*

spent [spent] *adj (exhausted)* erschöpft; *(cartridge)* leergeschossen

sperm [spʌrm] *s* Sperma *n*

sperm' whale' *s* Pottwal *m*

spew [spju] *tr* erbrechen; *(fig)* ausspeien ‖ *intr* sich erbrechen; *(fig)* herausströmen

sphere [sfɪr] *s* Kugel *f,* Sphäre *f; (fig)* Bereich *m;* **s. of influence** Einflußsphäre *f*

spherical ['sferɪkəl] *adj* sphärisch, kugelförmig

sphinx [sfɪŋks] *s (sphinxes & sphinges* ['sfɪndʒiz]*)* Sphinx *f*

spice [spaɪs] *s* Gewürz *n,* Würze *f; (fig)* Würze *f* ‖ *tr* würzen

spick-and-span ['spɪkənd'spæn] *adj* blitzblank

spicy ['spaɪsi] *adj* würzig; *(fig)* pikant

spider ['spaɪdər] *s* Spinne *f*

spi'derweb' *s* Spinnengewebe *n*

spiffy ['spɪfi] *adj (sl)* fesch

spigot ['spɪgət] *s* Wasserhahn *m*

spike [spaɪk] *s (nail)* langer Nagel *m; (in volleyball)* Schmetterball *m; (bot)* Ähre *f; (rr)* Schwellenschraube *f; (sport)* Dorn *m* ‖ *tr (a drink)* e–n Schuß Alkohol tun in *(acc); (in volleyball)* schmettern

spill [spɪl] *s (spilling)* Vergießen *n; (stain)* Fleck *m,* Klecks *m; (fall)* Sturz *m;* **take a s.** stürzen ‖ *v (pret & pp* **spilled & spilt** [spɪlt]*) tr* verschütten; *(a rider)* abwerfen; **s. out** ausschütten; **s. the beans** (sl) alles ausplaudern ‖ *intr* überlaufen; **s. over into** (fig) übergreifen auf *(acc)*

spill'way' *s* Überlauf *m*

spin [spɪn] *s (rotation)* Umdrehung *f; (short ride)* kurze Fahrt *f; (aer)* Trudeln *n;* **go for a s.** e–e Spritztour machen; **go into a s.** (aer) ins Trudeln kommen ‖ *v (pret & pp* **spun** [spʌn]*; ger* **spinning**) *tr (rotate)* drehen; *(tex)* spinnen; **s. out** *(a story)* ausspinnen; **s. s.o. around** j–n im Kreise herumwirbeln ‖ *intr* kreiseln, sich drehen; *(tex)* spinnen; **my head is spinning** mir dreht sich alles im Kopf

spinach ['spɪnɪtʃ] *s* Spinat *m*

spi'nal col'umn ['spaɪnəl] *s* Wirbelsäule *f*

spi'nal cord' *s* Rückenmark *n*

spi′nal flu′id s Rückenmarksflüssigkeit f

spindle [′spɪndəl] s Spindel f

spin′-dry′ v (pret & pp –dried) tr schleudern

spin′-dry′er s Trockenschleuder m

spine [spaɪn] s Rückgrat n, Wirbelsäule f; (bb) Buchrücken m

spineless [′spaɪnlɪs] adj (& fig) rückgratlos

spinet [′spɪnɪt] s Spinett n

spinner [′spɪnər] s Spinner –in mf; (mach) Spinnmaschine f

spin′ning adj (rotating) sich drehend; (tex) Spinn– ‖ s (tex) Spinnen n

spin′ning wheel′ s Spinnrad n

spinster [′spɪnstər] s alte Jungfer f

spi′ral [′spaɪrəl] adj spiralig ‖ s Spirale f; **s. of rising prices and wages** Lohn-Preis-Spirale f ‖ v (pret & pp –ral[l]ed; ger –ral[l]ing) intr sich in die Höhe schrauben

spi′ral stair′case s Wendeltreppe f

spire [spaɪr] s Spitze f

spirit [′spɪrɪt] s Geist m; (enthusiasm) Schwung m; (ghost) Geist m; **in high spirits** in gehobener Stimmung; **in low spirits** in gedrückter Stimmung; **spirits** Spirituosen pl; **that's the right s.!** das ist die richtige Einstellung! ‖ tr—**s. away** wegzaubern

spir′ited adj lebhaft; (horse) feurig

spiritless [′spɪrɪtlɪs] adj schwunglos

spiritual [′spɪrɪtʃʊ·əl] adj (incorporeal) geistig; (of the soul) seelisch; (religious) geistlich ‖ s geistliches Negerlied n

spiritualism [′spɪrɪtʃʊ·ˌlɪzəm] s Spiritismus m

spiritualist [′spɪrɪtʃʊ·əlɪst] s Spiritist –in mf

spir′itual life′ s Seelenleben n

spit [spɪt] s Spucke f; (culin) Spieß m ‖ v (pret & pp spat [spæt] & spit; ger spitting) tr & intr spucken

spite [spaɪt] s Trotz m; **for s.** aus Trotz; **in s. of** trotz (genit) ‖ tr kränken; **he did it to s. me** er hat es mir zum Trotz getan

spiteful [′spaɪtfəl] adj gehässig

spit′fire′ s (coll) Sprühteufel m

spit′ting im′age s (coll) Ebenbild n

spittoon [spɪ′tun] s Spucknapf m

splash [splæʃ] s Platschen n; (noise of falling into water) Klatschen n; **make a s.** (coll) Aufsehen erregen ‖ tr (a person, etc.) bespritzen; (e.g., water) spritzen ‖ intr klatschen, patschen; **s. about** planschen; **s. down** (rok) wassern ‖ interj schwaps!, platsch!

splash′down′ s (rok) Wasserung f

splatter [′splætər] tr & intr kleckern

spleen [splin] s Milz f; (fig) schlechte Laune f; **vent one's s. on** seiner schlechten Laune Luft machen gegenüber (dat)

splendid [′splɛndɪd] adj prächtig, herrlich; (coll) großartig

splendor [′splɛndər] s Herrlichkeit f

splice [splaɪs] s Spleiß m ‖ tr (a rope) spleißen; (film) zusammenkleben

splint [splɪnt] s Schiene f; **put in splints** schienen

splinter [′splɪntər] s Splitter m ‖ tr (zer)splittern

splin′ter group′ s Splittergruppe f

split [splɪt] adj rissig ‖ s Riß m, Spalt m; (fig) Spaltung f; (gym) Spagat m ‖ v (pret & pp split; ger splitting) tr spalten; (pants) platzen; (profits, the difference) sich teilen in (acc); **s. hairs** Haarspalterei treiben; **s. one's sides laughing** vor Lachen platzen; **s. open** aufbrechen ‖ intr (into) sich spalten (in acc); **splitting headache** rasende Kopfschmerzen pl; **s. up** (said of a couple) sich trennen

split′ infin′itive s gespaltener Infinitiv m

split′-lev′el adj mit Zwischenstockwerk versehen

split′ person′ality s gespaltene Persönlichkeit f

split′ sec′ond s Sekundenbruchteil m

splotch [splatʃ] s Klecks m ‖ tr kleckern

splotchy [′splatʃi] adj fleckig

splurge [splʌrdʒ] s—**go on a s.** verschwenderischen Aufwand treiben ‖ tr verschwenden ‖ intr (on) verschwenderische Ausgaben machen (für)

splutter [′splʌtər] s Geplapper n ‖ tr (words) heraussprudeln; (besplatter) bespritzen ‖ intr plappern; (said, e.g., of grease) spritzen

spoil [spɔɪl] s—**spoils** Beute f ‖ v (pret & pp spoiled & spoilt [spɔɪlt]) tr (perishable goods; fun) verderben; (a child) verziehen, verwöhnen ‖ intr verderben, schlecht werden; **spoiling for a fight** zanksüchtig

spoilage [′spɔɪlɪdʒ] s Verderb m

spoil′sport′ s Spielverderber –in mf

spoils′ sys′tem s Futterkrippensystem n

spoke [spok] s Speiche f

spokes′man s (–men) Wortführer –in mf

sponge [spʌndʒ] s Schwamm m ‖ tr schnorren ‖ intr schnorren; **s. on** (coll) schmarotzen bei

sponge′ cake′ s Sandtorte f

sponger [′spʌndʒər] s Schmarotzer –in mf

sponge′ rub′ber s Schaumgummi m & n

spongy [′spʌndʒi] adj schwammig

sponsor [′spansər] s Förderer –in mf; (of a program) Sponsor m; (of an immigrant) Bürge m, Bürgin f; (at baptism or confirmation) Pate m, Patin f ‖ tr fördern; (a program) finanziell fördern

spontaneity [spantə′ni·ɪti] s Spontaneität f

spontaneous [span′teni·əs] adj spontan

sponta′neous combus′tion s Selbstverbrennung f

spontaneously [span′teni·əsli] adv von selbst, unaufgefordert

spoof [spuf] s (hoax) Jux m; (parody) (on) Parodie f (auf acc) || intr albern

spook [spuk] s (coll) Spuk m

spooky ['spuki] adj spukhaft

spool [spul] s Spule f, Rolle f

spoon [spun] s Löffel m; **wooden s.** Kochlöffel m || tr (out) löffeln

spoonerism ['spunə‚rɪzəm] s Schüttelreim m

spoon'-feed' v (pret & pp –fed) tr (fig) es leicht machen (dat)

spoonful ['spunful] s Löffel m

sporadic [spə'rædɪk] adj vereinzelt

spore [spor] s Spore f

sport [sport] adj Sport– || s Sport m; (biol) Spielart f; **a good s.** ein Pfundskerl m; **go in for sports** sporteln; **in s.** im Spaß; **make s. of** sich lustig machen über (acc); **play sports** Sport treiben; **poor s.** Spielverderber –in mf; **sports** Sport m; (sportscast) Sportbericht m || intr sich belustigen

sport'ing event' s Sportveranstaltung f

sport'ing goods' spl Sportwaren pl

sport' jac'ket s Sportjacke f

sports' car' s Sportwagen m

sports'cast' s Sportbericht m

sports'cast'er s Sportberichterstatter m

sports' fan' s Sportfreund –in mf

sport' shirt' s Sporthemd m

sports'man s (–men) Sportsmann m

sports'manlike' adj sportlich

sports'manship' s sportliches Verhalten n

sports' news' s Sportnachrichten pl

sports'wear' s Sportkleidung f

sports' world' s Sportwelt f

sports' writ'er s Sportjournalist –in mf

sporty ['sporti] adj auffallend

spot [spɑt] s (stain) Fleck(en) m; (place) Platz m, Ort m; (as on a leopard) Tüpfel m & n; **be on the s.** (be present) zur Stelle sein; (be in difficulty) in der Klemme sein; **hit the s.** gerade das Richtige sein; **on the s.** auf der Stelle; **put on the s.** in Verlegenheit bringen || v (pret & pp spotted; ger spotting) tr (stain) beflecken; (espy) erblicken; (points in betting) vorgeben

spot' announce'ment s Durchsage f

spot' cash' s ungebundene Barmittel pl

spot' check' s Stichprobe f

spot'-check' tr stichprobenweise prüfen

spotless ['spɑtlɪs] adj makellos

spot'light' s Scheinwerfer m; **in the s.** (fig) im Rampenlicht der Öffentlichkeit || tr (fig) in den Vordergrund stellen

spot' remov'er [rɪ‚muvər] s Fleckputzmittel n

spotty ['spɑti] adj fleckig; (uneven) ungleichmäßig

spot' weld'ing s Punktschweißung f

spouse [spaʊs] s Gatte m, Gattin f

spout [spaʊt] s (of a pot) Tülle f; (jet of water) Strahl m || tr (& fig) hervorsprudeln || intr spritzen; (coll) große Reden schwingen

sprain [spren] s Verstauchung f || tr verstauchen; **s. one's ankle** sich [dat] den Fuß vertreten

sprat [spræt] s (ichth) Sprotte f

sprawl [sprɔl] intr (out) alle viere von sich ausstrecken; (said of a city) sich weit ausbreiten

spray [spre] s (of ocean) Gischt m; (from a can) Spray n; (from a fountain) Sprühwasser n; **s. of flowers** Blütenzweig m || tr spritzen; (liquids) zerstäuben; (plants) besprühen

sprayer ['spre·ər] s Zerstäuber m; (for a garden) Gartenspritze f

spray' gun' s Spritzpistole f

spray' paint' s Spritzfarbe f

spread [spred] s (act of spreading) Ausbreitung f; (extent) Verbreitung f; (e.g., of a tree) Umfang m; (on bread) Aufstrich m; (bedspread) Bettdecke f; (large piece of land) weite Fläche f; (of a shot) Streubereich m & n; (sumptuous meal) Gelage n || v (pret & pp spread) tr (warmth, light, news, rumors) verbreiten; (mortar, glue) auftragen; (e.g., butter) aufstreichen; (the legs) spreizen; (manure) streuen; **s. oneself too thin** sich verzetteln; **s. out over a year** über ein Jahr verteilen || intr sich verbreiten; (said of margarine) sich aufstreichen lassen

spree [spri] s Bummel m; (carousal) Zechgelage n; **go on a buying s.** sich in e–e Kauforgie stürzen

sprig [sprɪg] s Zweiglein n

sprightly ['spraɪtli] adj lebhaft; (gait) federnd

spring [sprɪŋ] adj Frühlings– || s (of water) Quelle f; (season) Frühling m; (resilience) Sprungkraft f; (of metal) Feder f; (jump) Sprung m; **springs** (aut) Federung f || v (pret sprang [spræŋ] & sprung [sprʌŋ]; pp sprung [sprʌŋ]) tr (a trap) zuschnappen lassen; (a leak) bekommen; (a question) (on) plötzlich stellen (dat); (a surprise) (on) bereiten (dat); **s. the news on s.o.** j–n mit der Nachricht überraschen || intr springen; **s. back** zurückschnellen; **s. from** entspringen (dat); **s. up** aufspringen; (said of industry, towns) aus dem Boden schießen

spring'board' s (& fig) Sprungbrett n

spring' chic'ken s Hähnchen n; **she's no s.** (sl) sie ist nicht die Jüngste

spring' fe'ver s Frühlingsmüdigkeit f

spring'time' s Frühlingszeit f

spring' wa'ter s Quellwasser n

springy ['sprɪŋi] adj federnd

sprinkle ['sprɪŋkəl] s Spritzen n; (light rain) Sprühregen m || tr (water, streets, lawns, laundry) sprengen; (e.g., sugar) streuen || intr sprühen

sprinkler ['sprɪŋklər] s (truck) Sprengwagen m; (for the lawn) Rasensprenger m; (eccl) Sprengwedel m

sprin'kling s Sprengung f; **a s. of** (e.g., sugar) ein bißchen; (e.g., of people) ein paar

sprin′kling can′ s Gießkanne f
sprin′kling sys′tem s Feuerlöschanlage f
sprint [sprɪnt] s Sprint m || intr sprinten
sprinter ['sprɪntər] s Sprinter –in mf
sprite [spraɪt] s Kobold m, Elfe f
sprocket ['sprakɪt] s Zahnrad n
sprout [spraut] s Sproß m || intr sprießen
spruce [sprus] adj schmuck || s (bot) Fichte f || intr—s. up sich schmücken
spry [spraɪ] adj (spryer & sprier; spry-est & spriest) flink
spud [spʌd] s (for weeding) Jäthacke f; (potatoe) (coll) Kartoffel f
spume [spjum] s Schaum m
spun′ glass′ s Glasfaser f
spunk [spʌŋk] s (coll) Mumm m
spunky ['spʌŋki] adj (coll) feurig
spur [spʌr] s (on riding boot; on a rooster) Sporn m; (of a mountain) Ausläufer m; (fig) Ansporn m; (archit) Strebe f; (bot) Stachel m; (rr) Seitengleis n; **on the s. of the moment** der Eingebung des Augenblicks folgend || v (pret & pp spurred; ger spurring) tr die Sporen geben (dat); **s. on** anspornen
spurious ['spjurɪ-əs] adj unecht
spurn [spʌrn] tr verschmähen
spurt [spʌrt] s Ruck m; (sport) Spurt m; **in spurts** ruckweise || tr speien || intr herausspritzen; (sport) spurten
sputnick ['spʌtnɪk] s Sputnik m
sputter ['spʌtər] s Stottern n || tr umherspritzen; (words) hervorsprudeln || intr (said of a person, engine) stottern; (said of a candle, fire) flackern
sputum ['spjutəm] s Sputum n
spy [spaɪ] s Spion –in mf || v (pret & pp spied) tr—**spy out** ausspionieren || intr spionieren
spy′glass′ s Fernglas n
spy′ing s Spionage f
spy′ ring′ s Spionageorganization f
squabble ['skwabəl] s Zank m || intr zanken
squad [skwad] s (gym) Riege f; (mil) Gruppe f; (sport) Mannschaft f
squad′ car′ s Funkstreifenwagen m
squad′ lead′er s (mil) Gruppenführer m
squadron ['skwadrən] s (aer) Staffel f; (nav) Geschwader n
squalid ['skwalɪd] adj verkommen
squall [skwɔl] s Bö f
squander ['skwandər] tr verschwenden
square [skwer] adj quadratisch; (mile, meter, foot) Quadrat–; (fellow, meal) anständig; (even) quitt; **ten meters s. meters** zehn Meter im Quadrat; **ten s. meters** zehn Quadratmeter || s Quadrat n; (city block) Häuserblock m; (open area) Platz m; (of a checkerboard or chessboard) Feld n; (carp) Winkel m; (math) zweite Potenz f || tr quadrieren; (a number) ins Quadrat erheben; (accounts) abrechnen || intr—s. off in Kampfstellung gehen; **s. with** (agree with)

übereinstimmen mit; (be frank with) aufrichtig sein zu
square′ dance′ s Reigen m
square′ deal′ s reelles Geschäft n
square′ root′ s Quadratwurzel f
squash [skwaʃ] s (bot) Kürbis m || tr (a hat) zerdrücken; (a finger, grape) quetschen; (fig) unterdrücken || intr zerdrückt (or zerquetscht) werden
squashy ['skwaʃi] adj weich, matschig
squat [skwat] adj gedrungen, untersetzt || s Hocken f || v (pret & pp squatted; ger squatting) intr hocken; **s. down** sich (hin)hocken
squatter ['skwatər] s Ansiedler –in mf ohne Rechtstitel
squaw [skwɔ] s Indianerin f
squawk [skwɔk] s Geschrei n; (sl) Schimpferei f || intr schreien; (sl) schimpfen
squeak [skwik] s (of a door) Quietschen n; (of a mouse) Pfeifen n || intr quietschen; (said of a mouse) pfeifen
squeal [skwil] s Quieken n || intr (said of a pig) quieken; (said of a mouse) pfeifen; (sl) petzen; **s. for joy** vor Vergnügen quietschen; **s. on** (sl) (a pupil) verpetzen; (to the police) verpfeifen
squealer ['skwilər] s (sl) Petze f
squeamish ['skwimɪʃ] adj zimperlich
squeeze [skwiz] s Druck m; **s. of the hand** Händedruck m || tr drücken; (oranges) auspressen; **s. into** (e.g., a trunk) hineinquetschen; **s. out** auspressen; **s. together** zusammenpressen; (e.g., people) zusammenpferchen || intr—s. in sich eindrängen; **s. through** sich durchzwängen (durch)
squelch [skwelt/] s schlagfertige Antwort f || tr niederschmettern
squid [skwɪd] s Tintenfisch m
squill [skwɪl] s (bot) Meerzwiebel f; (zool) Heuschreckenkrebs m
squint [skwɪnt] s Schielen n || intr (look with eyes partly closed) blinzeln; (be cross-eyed) schielen; (look askance) (at) argwöhnisch blicken (auf acc)
squint′-eyed′ adj schielend
squire [skwaɪr] s (hist) Knappe m; (jur) Friedensrichter m
squirm [skwʌrm] intr (through) sich winden (durch); (be restless) zappeln; **s. out of** sich herauswinden aus
squirrel ['skwʌrəl] s Eichhörnchen n
squirt [skwʌrt] s Spritzer m; (boy) (coll) Stöpsel m || tr (ver)spritzen || intr spritzen; **s. out** herausspritzen
S′S′ troops′ ['es'es] spl Schutzstaffel f
stab [stæb] s Stich m; (wound) Stichwunde f; **make a s. at** (coll) probieren || v (pret & pp stabbed; ger stabbing) tr stechen; (kill) erstechen; (a pig) abstechen; **s. s.o. in the back** j–m in den Rücken fallen
stability [stə'bɪlɪti] s Stabilität f
stabilization [ˌstebɪlɪ'zeʃən] s (e.g., of prices) Stabilisierung f; (aer) Dämpfung f

stabilize ['steɪbɪ͵laɪz] *tr* stabilisieren
stabilizer ['steɪbɪ͵laɪzər] *s* (aer) Flosse *f*
stab' in the back' *s* Stoß *m* aus dem Hinterhalt
stable ['steɪbəl] *adj* stabil || *s* Stall *m* || *tr* unterbringen
sta'ble boy' *s* Stalljunge *m*
stack [stæk] *s* (*of papers, books*) Stapel *m*; (*of wheat*) Schober *m*; (*of a ship*) Schornstein *m*; (*of rifles*) Pyramide *f*; **stacks** (libr) Bücherregale *pl* || *tr* (*wood, wheat*) aufstapeln; (*rifles*) zusammensetzen; (*cards*) packen
stadi·um ['steɪdɪ·əm] *s* (-ums & -a [ə]) Stadion *n*
staff [stæf] *s* (*rod*) Stab *m*; (*personnel*) Personal *n*; (*of a newspaper*) Redaktion *f*; (mil) Stab *m*; (mus) Notensystem *n* || *tr* mit Personal besetzen
staff' of'ficer *s* Stabsoffizier *m*
staff' ser'geant *s* Feldwebel *m*
stag [stæg] *adj* Herren- || *adv*—**go s.** ohne Damenbegleitung sein || *s* Hirsch *m*
stage [steɪdʒ] *s* (*of a theater*) Bühne *f*; (*phase*) Stadium *n*; (*stretch*) Strecke *f*; (*of life*) Etappe *f*; (*of a rocket*) Stufe *f*; (*scene*) Szene *f*; **at this s.** in diesem Stadium; **by easy stages** etappenweise; **final stages** Endstadien *pl* || *tr* (*a play*) inszenieren; (*a comeback*) veranstalten
stage'coach' *s* Postkutsche *f*
stage'craft' *s* Bühnenkunst *f*
stage' direc'tion *s* Bühnenanweisung *f*
stage' door' *s* Bühneneingang *m*
stage' effect' *s* Bühnenwirkung *f*
stage' fright' *s* Lampenfieber *n*
stage' hand' *s* Bühnenarbeiter –in *mf*
stage' light'ing *s* Bühnenbeleuchtung *f*
stage' man'ager *s* Bühnenleiter –in *mf*
stage' play' *s* Bühnenstück *n*
stage' prop'erties *spl* Theaterrequisiten *pl*
stagestruck ['steɪdʒ͵strʌk] *adj* theaterbegeistert
stagger ['stægər] *s* Taumeln *n* || *tr* (*e.g., lunch hours*) staffeln; (& fig) erschüttern || *intr* taumeln
stag'gering *adj* taumelnd; (*blow, loss*) vernichtend; (*news*) erschütternd
stagnant ['stægnənt] *adj* (*water*) stillstehend; (*air*) schlecht; (fig) träge
stagnate ['stægnet] *intr* stagnieren
stag' par'ty *s* Herrenabend *m*
staid [sted] *adj* gesetzt
stain [sten] *s* Fleck *m*; (*paint*) Beize *f* || *tr* beflecken; (*wood*) beizen
stained'-glass win'dow *s* buntes Glasfenster *n*
stainless ['stenlɪs] *adj* rostfrei
stair [ster] *s* Stufe *f*; **stairs** Treppe *f*
stair'case' *s* Treppenhaus *n*
stair'way' *s* Treppenaufgang *m*
stair'well' *s* Treppenschacht *m*
stake [stek] *s* Pfahl *m*; (*bet*) Einsatz *m*; **be at s.** auf dem Spiel stehen; **die at the s.** auf dem Scheiterhaufen sterben; **play for high stakes** viel riskieren; **pull up stakes** (coll) ab-

hauen || *tr* (*plants*) mit e–m Pfahl stützen; **s. off** abstecken; **s. out a claim** (fig) e–e Forderung umreißen
stake'-out' *s* polizeiliche Überwachung *f*
stalactite [stə'læktaɪt] *s* Stalaktit *m*
stalagmite [stə'lægmaɪt] *s* Stalagmit *m*
stale [stel] *adj* (*baked goods*) altbacken; (*e.g., beer*) schal; (*air*) verbraucht; (*joke*) abgedroschen; **get s.** abstehen
stale'mate' *s* (fig) Sackgasse *f*; (chess) Patt *n* || *tr* (fig) in e–e Sackgasse treiben; (chess) patt setzen
stalk [stɔk] *s* (*of grain*) Halm *m*; (*of a plant*) Stiel *m* || *tr* beschleichen; **s. game** pirschen
stall [stɔl] *s* (*for animals*) Stall *m*; (*booth*) Bude *f*; (sl) Vorwand *m* || *tr* (*a motor*) abwürgen; (*a person*) aufhalten || *intr* ausweichen; (aut) absterben; **s. for time** Zeit zu gewinnen suchen
stallion ['stæljən] *s* Hengst *m*
stalwart ['stɔlwərt] *adj* stämmig; (*supporter*) treu
stamen ['stemən] *s* Staubfaden *m*
stamina ['stæmɪnə] *s* Ausdauer *f*
stammer ['stæmər] *s* Stammeln *n* || *tr* & *intr* stammeln
stammerer ['stæmərər] *s* Stammler –in *mf*
stamp [stæmp] *s* (*mark*) Gepräge *n*; (*device for stamping*) Stempel *m*; (*for postage*) Briefmarke *f* || *tr* (*e.g., a document*) stempeln; (*a letter*) freimachen; (*the earth*) stampfen; **s. one's foot** mit dem Fuß aufstampfen; **s. out** (*a fire*) austreten; (*a rebellion*) niederschlagen
stampede [stæm'pid] *s* panische Flucht *f* || *tr* in die Flucht jagen || *intr* in wilder Flucht davonrennen
stamped' en'velope *s* Freiumschlag *m*
stamp'ing grounds' *spl* Lieblingsplatz *m*
stamp' machine' *s* Briefmarkenautomat *m*
stamp' pad' *s* Stempelkissen *n*
stance [stæns] *s* Haltung *f*, Stellung *f*
stanch [stɔntʃ] *tr* stillen
stand [stænd] *s* (*booth*) Stand *m*; (*platform*) Tribüne *f*; (*e.g., for bicycles*) Ständer *m*; (*view, position*) Standpunkt *m*; (*piece of furniture*) Ständer *m*; **take a s.** (**on**) Stellung nehmen (zu); **take one's s.** (*e.g., near the door*) sich stellen; **s. of timber** Waldbestand *m*; **stands** (sport) Tribüne *f*; **take the s.** (jur) als Zeuge auftreten || *v* (*pret & pp* **stood** [stʊd]) *tr* (*put*) stellen; (*the cold, hardships*) aushalten; (*a person*) leiden; **s. a chance** e–e Chance haben; **s. guard** Posten stehen; **s. one's ground** sich behaupten; **s. s.o. up** j–n aufsitzen lassen; **s. the test** sich bewähren || *intr* stehen; (*have validity*) gelten; **she wants to know where she stands** sie will wissen, wie sie daran ist; **s. aside** auf die Seite treten; **s. at attention** stillstehen; **s.**

back zurückstehen; **s. behind** s.o.
(fig) hinter j–m stehen; **s. by** (in
readiness) in Bereitschaft stehen; (a
decision) bleiben bei; (e.g., for the
latest news) am Apparat bleiben; **s.
by** s.o. j–m beistehen; **s. firm** fest
bleiben; **s. for** (champion) eintreten
für; (tolerate) sich [dat] gefallen
lassen; (mean) bedeuten; **s. good for**
gutstehen für; **s. idle** stillstehen; **s.
on end** sich sträuben, e.g., my hair
stood on end mir sträubten sich die
Haare; **s. on one's head** kopfstehen;
s. out (project) abstehen; (be conspicuous) hervorstechen; **s. out
against** sich abzeichnen gegen; **s.
s.o. in good stead** j–m zugute kommen; **s. up** aufstehen; **s. up against**
aufkommen gegen; **s. up for** (a thing)
verfechten; (a person) die Stange
halten (dat); **s. up to** s.o. j–m die
Stirn bieten; **s. up under** aushalten
standard ['stændərd] adj Standard–,
Normal– || s Standard m; (banner)
Banner n
stand'ard-bear'er s Bannerträger m
stand'ard-gauge track' s Normalspur f
standardize ['stændər‚daɪz] tr normen
stand'ard of liv'ing s Lebensstandard
m
stand'ard time' s Normalzeit f
stand'-by' adj Reserve– || s—**on s.** in
Bereitschaft
standee [stæn'di] s Stehplatzinhaber m
–in mf
stand'in' s (coll) Ersatzmann m; (cin,
theat) Double n
stand'ing adj (army, water, rule) stehend; (committee) ständig; (jump)
aus dem Stand || s Stehen n; (social)
Stellung f; (of a team) Stand m; **in
good s.** treu; **of long s.** langjährig
stand'ing or'der s (com) Dauerauftrag
m
stand'ing room' s Stehplatz m; **s. only**
nur noch Stehplätze
stand'-off' s Unentschieden n
stand'-offish ['stænd'ɔfɪʃ] adj zurückhaltend
stand'out' s Blickfang m
stand'point' s Standpunkt m
stand'still' s Stillstand m; **come to a s.**
zum Stillstand kommen
stanza ['stænzə] s Strophe f
staple ['stepəl] adj Haupt–, Stapel– ||
s (food) Hauptnahrungsmittel n;
(product) Hauptprodukt n; (clip)
Heftklammer f || tr mit Draht heften
stapler ['steplər] s Heftmaschine f
star [star] adj Spitzen–; (astr) Stern–
|| s Stern m; (cin, rad, telv, theat)
Star m; **I saw stars** (fig) Sterne tan-
ten mir vor den Augen || v (pret &
pp **starred**) ger **starring** tr (cin, rad,
sport, telv, theat) als Star heraus-
stellen; (typ) mit Sternchen kenn-
zeichnen || intr Star sein
starboard ['starbərd] adj Steuerbord–
|| s Steuerbord n
starch [start∫] s Stärke f || tr stärken
starchy ['start∫i] adj stärkenhaltig
stare [ster] s starrer Blick m || tr—

s. down durch Anstarren aus der
Fassung bringen || intr starren; **s. at**
anstarren; **s. into** space ins Leere
blicken, ins Blaue starren
star'fish' s Seestern m
stargazer ['star‚gezər] s Sterngucker
–in mf
stark [stark] adj (landscape) kahl;
(sheer) völlig || adv völlig
stark'-na'ked adj splitter(faser)nackt
starlet ['starlət] s Sternchen n
star'light' s Sternenlicht n
starling ['starlɪŋ] s (orn) Star m
star'lit' adj sternhell
Star' of Da'vid s David(s)stern m
starry ['stari] adj gestirnt; (night)
sternklar; (sky) Stern–
star'ry-eyed' adj verträumt
Stars' and Stripes' spl Sternenbanner n
Star'-Spangled Ban'ner s Sternenbanner n
start [start] s Anfang m; (sudden
springing movement) plötzliches
Hochfahren n; (lead, advantage) Vorgabe f, Vorsprung m; (of a race)
Start m; **give** s.o. **a s.** j–m auf die
Beine helfen || tr anfangen; (a mo-
tor) anlassen; (a rumor) in die Welt
setzen; (a conversation) anknüpfen;
s. a fire ein Feuer anmachen; (said
of an arsonist) e–n Brand legen ||
intr anfangen; **s. in to** (inf) anfangen
zu (inf); **s. out** (begin) anfangen;
(start walking) losgehen; **s. out on**
(a trip) antreten; **to s. with** zunächst
start'ing gate' s Startmaschine f
start'ing gun' s Startpistole f; **at the s.**
beim Startschuß
start'ing point' s Ausgangspunkt m
startle ['startəl] tr erschrecken; **be
startled** zusammenfahren
starvation [star've∫ən] s Hunger m;
die of s. verhungern
starva'tion di'et s Hungerkur f
starva'tion wag'es spl Hungerlohn m
starve [starv] tr verhungern lassen;
s. out aushungern || intr hungern;
(coll) furchtbaren Hunger haben; **s.
to death** verhungern
state [stet] adj staatlich, Staats–; (as
opposed to federal) bundesstaatlich
|| s (condition) Zustand m; (govern-
ment) Staat m; (of the U.S.A.) Bun-
desstaat m || tr angeben; (a rule,
problem) aufstellen; **as stated above**
wie oben angegeben
State' Depart'ment s Außenministerium
n
stateless ['stetlɪs] adj staatenlos
stately ['stetli] adj stattlich
statement ['stetmənt] s Angabe f;
(from a bank) Abrechnung f; (jur)
Aussage f
state' of affairs' s Lage f
state' of emer'gency s Notstand m
state' of health' s Gesundheitszustand
m
state' of mind' s Geisteszustand m
state' of war' s Kriegszustand m
state'-owned' adj staatseigen; (in com-
munistic countries) volkseigen
state' police' s Staatspolizei f

state′room′ s (*in a palace*) Prunkzimmer n; (*on a ship*) Passagierkabine f

states′man s (**-men**) Staatsmann m

states′manlike′ adj staatsmännisch

states′manship′ s Staatskunst f

static [′stætɪk] adj statisch ǁ s (rad) Nebengeräusche pl

station [′steɪən] s (*social*) Stellung f; (*of a bus, rail line*) Bahnhof m; (mil) Standort m ǁ tr aufstellen; (mil) stationieren

stationary [′steɪə‚neri] adj stationär

sta′tion break′ s Werbepause f

stationer [′steɪənər] s Schreibwarenhändler –in mf

stationery [′steɪə‚neri] s Briefpapier n

sta′tionery store′ s Schreibwarenhandlung f

sta′tion house′ s Polizeiwache f

sta′tion identifica′tion s (rad) Pausenzeichen n

sta′tionmas′ter s Bahnhofsvorsteher m

sta′tions of the cross′ spl Kreuzweg m

sta′tion wag′on s Kombiwagen m

statistic [stə′tɪstɪk] s Angabe f; **statistics** (*science*) Statistik f ǁ spl (*data*) Statistik f

statistical [stə′tɪstɪkəl] adj statistisch

statistician [‚stætɪs′tɪ/ən] s Statistiker –in mf

statue [′stæt/ʊ] s Statue f

statuesque [‚stæt/ʊ′esk] adj statuenhaft

stature [′stæt/ər] s Gestalt f; (fig) Format n

status [′stetəs] s (*in society*) Stellung f; (e.g., *mental*) Stand m

sta′tus quo′ [kwo] s Status m quo

sta′tus sym′bol s Statussymbol n

statute [′stæt/ʊt] s Satzung f, Statut n

statutory [′stæt/ʊ‚tori] adj statutenmäßig

staunch [stɔnt/] adj unentwegt

stave [stev] s (*of a barrel*) Daube f; (*of a chair*) Steg m; (*of a ladder*) Sprosse f; (mus) Notensystem n ǁ tr—s. off abwenden

stay [ste] s (*visit*) Aufenthalt m; (prop) Stütze f; (*of execution*) Aufschub m ǁ intr bleiben; **have to s. in** (*after school*) nachsitzen müssen; **s. away** wegbleiben; **s. behind** zurückbleiben; (*in school*) sitzenbleiben

stay′-at-home′ s Stubenhocker –in mf

stead [sted] s Statt f; **in s.o.'s s. an j-s Statt**

stead′fast′ adj standhaft

stead·y [′stedi] adj fest, beständig; (*hands*) sicher; (*ladder*) fest; (*pace*) gleichmäßig; (*progress*) ständig; (*nerves*) stark; (*prices*) stabil; (*work*) regelmäßig; **s. customer** Stammkunde m, Stammkundin f; **s. now!** immer langsam! ǁ v (*pret & pp* **-ied**) tr festigen

steak [stek] s Beefsteak n

steal [stil] s—**it's a s.** (coll) das ist geschenkt ǁ v (*pret* **stole** [stol]; pp **stolen**) tr stehlen; (*a kiss*) rauben; **s. s.o.'s thunder** j–m den Wind aus den Segeln nehmen; **s. the show** den Vogel abschießen ǁ intr stehlen; **s.**

away wegstehlen; **s. up on s.o.** sich an j–n heranschleichen

stealth [stelθ] s—**by s.** heimlich

stealthy [′stelθi] adj verstohlen

steam [stim] s Dampf m; (*vapor*) Dunst m; (fig) Kraft f; **full s. ahead!** Volldampf voraus!; **let off s.** Dampf ablassen; (fig) sich [*dat*] Luft machen; **put on s.** (fig) Dampf dahinter machen ǁ tr dämpfen; (culin) dünsten; **s. up** beschlagen ǁ intr dampfen; (culin) dünsten; **s. up** sich beschlagen

steam′ bath′ s Dampfbad n

steam′boat′ s Dampfer m

steam′ en′gine s Dampfmaschine f

steamer [′stimar] s Dampfer m

steam′ heat′ s Dampfheizung f

steam′ i′ron s Dampfbügeleisen n

steam′ roll′er s (& fig) Dampfwalze f ǁ tr glattwalzen; (fig) niederwalzen

steam′ship′ s Dampfschiff n

steam′ship line′ s Dampfschiffahrtslinie f

steam′ shov′el s Dampflöffelbagger m

steamy [′stimi] adj dampfig, dunstig

steed [stid] s Streitroß n

steel [stil] adj stählern, Stahl– ǁ s Stahl m ǁ tr stählen; **s. oneself against s.th.** sich gegen etw wappnen

steel′ wool′ s Stahlwolle f

steel′works′ spl Stahlwerk n

steely [′stili] adj (fig) stählern

steelyard [′stiljərd] s Schnellwaage f

steep [stip] adj steil; (*prices*) happig ǁ tr (*immerse*) eintauchen; (*soak*) einweichen; **be steeped in** (e.g., *prejudice*) durchdrungen sein von; (*be expert in*) ein Kenner sein (genit); **s. oneself in** sich versenken in (acc)

steeple [′stipəl] s Kirchturm m

stee′plechase′ s Hindernisrennen n

steer [stɪr] s Stier m ǁ tr lenken, steuern; **s. a middle course** e–n Mittelweg einschlagen ǁ intr lenken, steuern; **s. clear of** vermeiden

steerage [′stɪrɪdʒ] s Zwischendeck n

steer′ing wheel′ s Steuerrad n

stellar [′stelər] adj (*role*) Star–; (*attraction*) Haupt–; (astr) Stern(en)–

stem [stem] s (*of a plant*) Halm m; (*of a word*; *of a tree*) Stamm m; (*of a leaf, fruit*; *of a glass*; *of a smoke pipe*) Stiel m; (*of a watch*) Aufziehwelle f; (naut) Steven m; **from s. to stern** von vorn bis achtern ǁ v (*pret & pp* **stemmed**; ger **stemming**) tr (*check*) hemmen; (*fruit*) entstielen; (*the flow*) (an)stauen; (*the blood*) stillen; (*in skiing*) stemmen ǁ intr—**s. from** (ab)stammen von

stench [stent/] s Gestank m

sten·cil [′stensɪl] s (*for printing*) Schablone f; (*for typing*) Matrize f ǁ v (*pret & pp* **-cil[l]ed**; ger **-cil[l]ing**) tr mittels Schablone aufmalen

stenographer [stə′nɑgrəfər] s Stenograph –in mf

stenography [stə′nɑgrəfi] s Stenographie f

step [step] s Schritt m; (*of a staircase*) Stufe f; (*footprint*) Fußtritt m;

(*measure*) Maßnahme *f;* **be out of s.** nicht Schritt halten; **in. s.** im Takt; **keep in s. with the times** mit der Zeit Schritt halten; **s. by s.** schrittweise; **watch your s.!** Vorsicht! || *v* (*pret & pp* stepped; *ger* stepping) *tr*—**s. down** (elec) heruntertransformieren; **s. off** abschreiten || *intr* schreiten, treten; **s. aside** beiseitetreten; **s. back** zurücktreten; **s. forward** vortreten; **s. on** betreten; **s. on it** (coll) sich beeilen; **s. on s.o.'s toes** (fig) j-m auf die Zehen treten; **s. out** hinausgehen; **s. out on** (*a marriage partner*) betrügen

step'broth'er *s* Stiefbruder *m*

step'child' *s* (**–chil'dren**) Stiefkind *n*

step'daugh'ter *s* Stieftochter *f*

step'fa'ther *s* Stiefvater *m*

step'lad'der *s* Stehleiter *f*

step'moth'er *s* Stiefmutter *f*

steppe [step] *s* Steppe *f*

step'ping stone' *s* Trittstein *m;* (fig) Sprungbrett *n*

step'sis'ter *s* Stiefschwester *f*

step'son' *s* Stiefsohn *m*

stere-o ['stɛrɪ‚o] *adj* Stereo– || *s* (**–os**) (*sound*) Stereoton *m*, Raumton *m;* (*reproduction*) Raumtonwiedergabe *f;* (*set*) Stereoapparat *m*

stereotyped ['stɛrɪ‚ə‚taɪpt] *adj* (& fig) stereotyp

sterile ['stɛrɪl] *adj* keimfrei

sterility [stɛ'rɪlɪtɪ] *s* Sterilität *f*

sterilize ['stɛrɪ‚laɪz] *tr* sterilisieren

sterling ['stʌrlɪŋ] *adj* (fig) gediegen || *s* (*currency*) Sterling *m;* (*sterling silver*) Sterlingsilber *n;* (*articles of sterling silver*) Sterlingsilberwaren *pl*

stern [stʌrn] *adj* streng; (*look*) finster || *s* (naut) Heck *n*

stethoscope ['stɛθə‚skop] *s* Stethoskop *n*

stevedore ['stivə‚dor] *s* Stauer *m*

stew [st(j)u] *s* Ragout *n*, Stew *n* || *tr & intr* dünsten; (& fig) schmoren

steward ['st(j)u‚ərd] *s* (aer, naut) Steward *m;* (*of an estate*) Gutsverwalter *m;* (*of a club*) Tafelmeister *m*

stewardess ['st(j)u‚ərdɪs] *s* (aer, naut) Stewardeß *f*

stewed' fruit' *s* Kompott *n*

stick [stɪk] *s* Stecken *m*, Stock *m;* (*for punishment*) Prügel *pl;* (*of candy or gum*) Stange *f;* **the sticks** (coll) die Provinz *f* || *tr* (*with a sharp point; into one's pocket*) stecken; (*paste*) (on) ankleben (an *acc*); **s. it out** durchhalten; **s. one's finger** sich in den Finger stechen; **s. out** herausstrecken; **s. up** (sl) überfallen und berauben || *intr* (*adhere*) kleben; (*be stuck, be tight*) klemmen; **nothing sticks in his mind** (coll) bei ihm bleibt nichts haften; **s. around** (coll) in der Nähe bleiben; **s. by** (coll) bleiben bei; **s. close to** sich heften an (*acc*); **s. out** (*said of ears*) abstehen; (*be visible*) herausstehen; **s. to** (fig) beharren auf (*dat*); **s. together** zusammenkleben; (fig) zusammenhalten; **s. up for** sich einsetzen für

sticker ['stɪkər] *s* Klebezettel *m*

stick'-in-the-mud' *s* (coll) Schlafmütze *f*

stickler ['stɪklər] *s* (for) Pedant *m* (in *dat*)

stick'pin' *s* Krawattennadel *f*

stick'-up' *s* (sl) Raubüberfall *m*

sticky ['stɪkɪ] *adj* klebrig; (*air*) schwül; (*ticklish*) heikel

stiff [stɪf] *adj* steif; (*difficult*) schwer; (*drink*) stark; (*opposition*) hartnäckig; (*sentence*) streng; (*bearing*) steif; (*price*) hoch; **s. as a board** stocksteif || *s* (*corpse*) Leiche *f;* **big s.** (sl) blöder Kerl *m*

stiffen ['stɪfən] *tr* versteifen || *intr* sich versteifen

stiffly ['stɪflɪ] *adv* gezwungen

stiff'-necked' *adj* mit steifem Hals; (fig) eigensinnig

stifle ['staɪfəl] *tr* (*a yawn*) unterdrücken; (*a person*) ersticken

stig-ma ['stɪgmə] *s* (**–mas** & **mata** [mətə]) Brandmal *n;* stigmata Wundmale *pl* Christi

stigmatize ['stɪgmə‚taɪz] *tr* brandmarken

stile [staɪl] *s* Stiege *f*

stilet-to [stɪ'lɛto] *s* (**–os**) Stilett *n*

still [stɪl] *adj* still, ruhig || *adv* (*up to this time, as yet, even*) noch; (*yet, nevertheless*) dennoch; **keep s.** stillbleiben || *s* (*stillness*) Stille *f;* (*for whiskey*) Brennapparat *m;* (cin) Einzelphotographie *f;* (phot) Standphoto *n* || *tr* stillen

still'born' *adj* totgeboren

still' life' *s* (**still lifes** & **still lives**) Stilleben *n*

stilt [stɪlt] *s* Stelze *f*

stilt'ed *adj* (*style*) geschraubt; (archit) auf Pfeilern ruhend

stimulant ['stɪmjələnt] *s* Reizmittel *n;* **act as a s.** anregend wirken

stimulate ['stɪmjə‚let] *tr* anregen

stimulation [‚stɪmjə'leʃən] *s* Anregung *f*

stimu-lus ['stɪmjələs] *s* (**–li** [‚laɪ]) (& fig) Reizmittel *n;* (fig) Ansporn *m*

sting [stɪŋ] *s* Biß *m*, Stich *m;* (*stinging organ*) Stachel *m* || *v* (*pret & pp* stung [stʌŋ]) *tr & intr* stechen

stingy ['stɪndʒɪ] *adj* geizig

stink [stɪŋk] *s* Gestank *m;* (sl) Krach *m* || *v* (*pret* stank [stæŋk]; stunk [stʌŋk]) *tr*—**s. up** verstänkern || *intr* stinken

stinker ['stɪŋkər] *s* (sl) Stinker *m*

stinky ['stɪŋkɪ] *adj* stinkend, stinkig

stint [stɪnt] *s* bestimmte Arbeit *f;* **without s.** freigebig || *tr* einschränken || *intr* (on) knausern (mit)

stipend ['staɪpənd] *s* (*salary*) Gehalt *n;* (*of a scholarship*) Zuwendung *f*

stipple ['stɪpəl] *tr* punktieren

stipulate ['stɪpjə‚let] *tr* bedingen; **as stipulated** wie vertraglich festgelegt

stipulation [‚stɪpjə'leʃən] *s* Bedingung *f*

stir [stʌr] *s* (*movement*) Bewegung *f;* (*unrest*) Unruhe *f;* (*commotion, ex-*

citement) Aufsehen *n;* **create quite a s.** großes Aufsehen erregen ‖ *v* (*pret & pp* stirred; *ger* stirring) *tr e.g.*, *with a spoon*) (um)rühren; (*said of a breeze*) bewegen; (*the fire*) schüren; **s. up** (*hatred*) entfachen; (*trouble*) stiften; (*people*) aufhetzen ‖ *intr* sich rühren

stir′ring *adj* erregend; (*times*) bewegt; (*speech*) mitreißend; (*song*) schwung-voll

stirrup [′stʌrəp] *s* Steigbügel *m*

stitch [stɪtʃ] *s* Stich *m;* (*in knitting*) Masche *f;* **stitches** (*surg*) Naht *f;* **s. in the side** Seitenstechen *n* ‖ *tr* heften; (*surg*) nähen

stock [stak] *s* (*supplies*) Lager *n;* (*of a gun*) Schaft *m;* (*lineage*) Zucht *f;* (*of paper*) Papierstoff *m;* (*culin*) Fond *m;* (st. exch.) Aktie *f;* **in s.** vorrätig, auf Lager; **not put much s. in** nicht viel Wert legen auf (*acc*); **out of s.** nicht (mehr) vorrätig; (*books*) vergriffen; **stocks** (hist) Stock *m;* **take s.** den Bestand auf-nehmen; **take s. of** (fig) in Betracht ziehen ‖ *tr* auf Lager halten; (*a stream*) (mit Fischen) besetzen; (*a farm*) ausstatten ‖ *intr*—**s. up** (**on**) sich eindecken (mit)

stockade [sta′ked] *s* Palisade *f;* (mil) Gefängnis *n*

stock′breed′er *s* Viehzüchter –in *mf*

stock′brok′er *s* Börsenmakler –in *mf*

stock′ car′ *s* (aut) Serienwagen *m;* (sport) als Rennwagen hergerichteter Personenkraftwagen *m*

stock′ com′pany *s* (com) Aktiengesell-schaft *f;* (theat) Repertoiregruppe *f*

stock′ div′idend *s* Aktiendividende *f*

stock′ exchange′ *s* Börse *f*

stock′hold′er *s* Aktionär –in *mf*

stock′ing *s* Strumpf *m*

stock′ in trade′ *s* Warenbestand *m;* (fig) Rüstzeug *n*

stock′pile′ *s* Vorrat *m* ‖ *tr* aufstapeln

stock′room′ *s* Lagerraum *m*

stocky [′staki] *adj* untersetzt

stock′yard′ *s* Viehhof *m*

stodgy [′stadʒi] *adj* gezwungen

stogy [′stogi] *s* (coll) Glimmstengel *m*

stoic [′sto·ɪk] *adj* stoisch ‖ *s* Stoiker *m*

stoke [stok] *tr* (*a fire*) schüren; (*a furnace*) heizen

stoker [′stokər] *s* Heizer *m*

stole [stol] *s* (*woman's fur piece*) Pelz-stola *f;* (eccl) Stola *f*

stolid [′stalɪd] *adj* unempfindlich

stomach [′stʌmək] *s* Magen *m;* (fig) (**for**) Lust *f* (zu) ‖ *tr* (*food*) ver-dauen; (fig) vertragen

stom′ach ache′ *s* Magenschmerzen *pl*

stone [ston] *adj* steinern *f;* s Stein *m;* (*of fruit*) Kern *m;* (pathol) Stein *m* ‖ *tr* steinigen; (*fruit*) entsteinen

stone′ age′ *s* Steinzeit *f*

stone′-broke′ *adj* (coll) völlig abge-brannt

stone′-deaf′ *adj* stocktaub

stone′ ma′son *s* Steinmetz *m*

stone′ quar′ry *s* Steinbruch *m*

stone′s′ throw′ *s* Katzensprung *m*

stony [′stoni] *adj* steinig

stooge [studʒ] *s* Lakai *m*

stool [stul] *s* Schemel *m;* (*e.g.*, *at a bar*) Hocker *m;* (*bowel movement*) Stuhl *m*

stool′ pi′geon *s* Polizeispitzel *m*

stoop [stup] *s* Beugung *f;* (*condition of the body*) gebeugte Körperhaltung *f;* (*porch*) kleine Verande *f* ‖ *intr* sich bücken; (*demean oneself*) sich erniedrigen

stoop′-shoul′dered *adj* gebeugt

stop [stap] *s* (*for a bus or streetcar*) Haltestelle *f;* (*layover*) Aufenthalt *m;* (*station*) Station *f;* (*of an organ*) Register *n;* (ling) Verschlußlaut *m;* **bring to a s.** zum Halten bringen; **come to a s.** anhalten; **put a s. to** ein Ende machen (*dat*) ‖ *v* (*pret & pp* stopped; *ger* stopping) *tr* (*an activity*) aufhören mit; (*ger*) auf-hören (zu *inf*); (*e.g.*, *a thief, car*) anhalten; (*bring to a stop with diffi-culty*) zum Halten bringen; (*delay, detain*) aufhalten; (*a leak*) stopfen; (*a check*) sperren; (*payment*) ein-stellen; (*the blood*) stillen; (*traffic*) lahmlegen; **s. down** (phot) abblen-den; **s. s.o. from** (ger) *j*-n davon-halten zu (*inf*) ‖ *intr* (*cease*) auf-hören; (*come to a stop; break down*) stehenbleiben; (*said of a person stopping for a short time or of a vehi-cle at an unscheduled stop*) anhalten; (*said of a vehicle at a scheduled stop*) halten; **s. at nothing** vor nichts zurückschrecken; **s. dead** plötzlich stehenbleiben; **s. in** vorbeikommen; **s. off** at e-n kurzen Halt machen bei

stop′gap′ *adj* Not-, Behelfs– ‖ *s* Notbe-helf *m*

stop′light′ *s* (*on a car*) Bremslicht *n;* (*traffic light*) Verkehrsampel *f*

stop′o′ver *s* Fahrtunterbrechung *f;* (aer) Zwischenlandung *f*

stoppage [′stapɪdʒ] *s* (*of a pipe*) Ver-stopfung *f;* (*of payment, of work*) Einstellung *f;* (pathol) Verstopfung *f*

stopper [′stapər] *s* Stöpsel *m;* (*made of cork*) Korken *m*

stop′ sign′ *s* Haltezeichen *n*

stop′watch′ *s* Stoppuhr *f*

storage [′storɪdʒ] *s* Lagerung *f*

stor′age bat′tery *s* Akkumulator *m*

stor′age charge′ *s* Lagergebühr *f*

stor′age room′ *s* Rumpelkammer *f;* (com) Lagerraum *m*

stor′age tank′ *s* Sammelbehälter *m*

store [stor] *s* (*small shop*) Laden *m;* (*large shop*) Geschäft *n;* (*supply*) Vorrat *m;* **be in s. for** bevorstehen (*dat*); **have in s. for** bereithalten für; **set great s. by** viel Wert legen auf (*acc*); **s. of knowledge** Wissenschatz *m* ‖ *tr* einlagern; (*in the attic*) auf den Speicher stellen; **s. up** auf-speichern

store′house′ *s* Lagerhaus *n;* (fig) Schatz *m,* Fundgrube *f*

store′keep′er *s* Ladeninhaber –in *mf*

store'room' s Lagerraum m, Vorrats-
raum m

stork [stɔrk] s Storch m

storm [stɔrm] s Sturm m; (thunderstorm) Gewitter n; (fig) Sturm m;
take by s. (& fig) im Sturm nehmen
|| tr (er)stürmen || intr stürmen

storm' cloud' s Gewitterwolke f

storm' door' s Doppeltür f

storm' warn'ing s Sturmwarnung f

storm' win'dow s Doppelfenster n

stormy ['stɔrmi] adj stürmisch

story ['stori] s Geschichte f; (floor)
Stock m, Stockwerk n; **that's another
s.** das ist e-e Sache für sich

sto'rybook' s Geschichtenbuch n

sto'rytell'er s Erzähler –in mf

stout [staut] adj beleibt; (heart) tapfer
|| s Starkbier n

stout'-heart'ed adj beherzt

stove [stov] s Ofen m, Küchenherd m

stove'pipe' s Ofenrohr n; (coll) Angst-
röhre f

stow [sto] tr stauen; **s. away** verstauen
|| intr—**s. away** als blinder Passagier
mitreisen

stowage ['sto·ɪdʒ] s Stauen n; (costs)
Staugebühr f

stow'away' s blinder Passagier m

straddle ['strædəl] tr mit gespreizten
Beinen sitzen auf (dat)

strafe [stref] tr im Tiefflug mit Bord-
waffen angreifen

straggle ['strægəl] intr abschweifen

straggler ['stræglər] s Nachzügler –in
mf; (mil) Versprengte m

straight [stret] adj gerade; (honest)
aufrecht; (candid) offen; (hair) glatt;
(story) wahr; (uninterrupted) ununterbrochen; (whiskey) unverdünnt
|| adv (directly) direkt; (without in-
terruption) ununterbrochen; **give it
to s.o. s.** j-m die ungeschminkte
Wahrheit sagen; **go s.** (fig) einen
geraden Weg gehen; **is my hat on s.?**
sitzt mein Hut richtig?; **make s. for**
zuhalten auf (acc); **set the record s.**
den Sachverhalt klarstellen; **s. ahead**
(immer) geradeaus; **s. as an arrow**
pfeilgerade; **s. from the horse's
mouth** (coll) aus erster Hand; **s.
home** schnurstracks nach Hause; **s.
off** ohne weiteres || s (cards) Buch n

straight'away' adv geradewegs, sofort
|| s (sport) Gerade f

straighten ['stretən] tr gerade machen;
(e.g., a tablecloth) glattziehen; **s. out**
(fig) wieder in Ordnung bringen; **s.
s.o.'s tie** j-m die Krawatte zurecht-
rücken; **s. up** (a room) aufräumen ||
intr gerade werden; **s. up** sich aufrichten

straight' face' s—**keep a s.** keine
Miene verziehen

straight'for'ward adj aufrichtig

straight' left' s (box) linke Gerade f

straight' man' s Stichwortgeber m

straight' ra'zor s Rasiermesser n

straight' right' s (box) rechte Gerade f

straight'way' adv auf der Stelle

strain [stren] s Belastung f; (of a muscle or tendon) Zerrung f; (task re-
quiring effort) (coll) Strapaze f;
(stock, family) Linie f; (trait) Erbei-
genschaft f; (bot) Art f; **without s.**
mühelos || tr (filter) durchseihen;
(the eyes, nerves) überanstrengen;
s. oneself (make a great effort) sich
überanstrengen; (in lifting) sich
überheben; **s. the truth** übertreiben
|| intr sich anstrengen; **s. after** sich
abmühen um; **s. at** ziehen an (dat),
zerren an (dat)

strained adj (smile) gezwungen; (relations) gespannt

strainer ['strenər] s Seiher m, Filter m

strait [stret] s Straße f; **financial straits**
finanzielle Schwierigkeiten pl; **straits**
Meerenge f

strait' jack'et s Zwangsjacke f

strait'-laced' adj sittenstreng

strand [strænd] s Strähne f; (beach)
Strand m; **s. of pearls** Perlenschnur
f || tr auf den Strand setzen; (fig)
stranden lassen; **be stranded** (fig) in
der Patsche sitzen; **get stranded** auflaufen; **leave s.o. stranded** j-n im
Stich lassen

strange [strendʒ] adj (quaint) sonderbar; (foreign) fremd; **s. character**
Sonderling m || adv—**s. to say** merk-
würdigerweise

stranger ['strendʒər] s Fremde mf

strangle ['stræŋgəl] tr erwürgen || intr
ersticken

stran'glehold' s Würgegriff m

strap [stræp] s Riemen m, Gurt m; (of
metal) Band n || v (pret & pp
strapped; ger strapping) tr (to) anschnallen (an acc); (a razor) abziehen

strap'ping adj stramm

stratagem ['strætədʒəm] s Kriegslist f

strategic(al) [strə'tidʒɪk(əl)] adj strategisch

strategist ['strætɪdʒɪst] s Stratege m

strategy ['strætɪdʒi] s Strategie f

stratification [ˌstrætɪfɪ'keʃən] s Schich-
tung f

strati·fy ['strætɪˌfaɪ] v (pret & pp
-fied) tr schichten || intr Schichten
bilden

stratosphere ['strætəˌsfɪr] s Strato-
sphäre f

stra·tum ['stretəm], ['strætəm] s (-ta
[tə] & -tums) Schicht f

straw [strɔ] adj (e.g., hat, man, mat)
Stroh– || s Stroh n; (single stalk; for
drinking) Strohhalm m; **that's the
last s.!** das schlägt dem Faß den
Boden aus!

straw'ber'ry s Erdbeere f

straw'berry blond' adj rotblond

straw' mat'tress s Strohsack m

straw' vote' s Probeabstimmung f

stray [stre] adj (e.g., bullet) verirrt;
(cat, dog) streunend; **s. shell** (mil)
Ausreißer m || s verirrtes Tier n ||
intr herumirren; (fig) abschweifen

streak [strik] s Streifen m; **like a s.**
wie der Blitz; **s. of bad luck** Pech-
strähne f; **s. of luck** Glückssträhne
f; **s. of light** Lichtstreifen m || tr
streifen || intr streifig werden; **s.
along** vorbeisausen

streaky ['striki] *adj* gestreift; (*uneven*) (coll) ungleich(mäßig)

stream [strim] *s* Fluß *m;* (*of people, cars, air, blood, lava*) Strom *m;* (*of words*) Schwall *m;* (*of tears*) Flut *f;* (*of a liquid*) Strahl *m* ‖ *intr* (aus)strömen

streamer ['strimər] *s* (*pennant*) Wimpel *m;* (*ribbon*) herabhängendes Band *n;* (*rolled crepe paper*) Papierschlange *f*

stream'line' *tr* in Stromlinienform bringen; (fig) reorganizieren

stream'lined' *adj* stromlinienförmig

street [strit] *s* Straße *f*

street'car' *s* Straßenbahn *f*

street' clean'er *s* Straßenkehrer –in *mf;* (*truck*) Straßenkehrmaschine *f*

street' fight' *s* Straßenschlacht *f*

street' light' *s* Straßenlaterne *f*

street' sign' *s* Straßenschild *n*

street' ven'dor *s* Straßenhändler –in *mf*

street'walk'er *s* Straßendirne *f*

strength [streŋθ] *s* Kraft *f;* (*strong point; potency of alcohol; moral or mental power*) Stärke *f;* (mil) Kopfstärke *f;* **bodily s.** Körperkraft *f;* **on the s. of** auf Grund (*genit*)

strengthen ['streŋθən] *tr* stärken; (fig) bestärken ‖ *intr* stärker werden

strenuous ['strenju-əs] *adj* anstrengend; **s. effort** Kraftanstrengung *f*

stress [stres] *s* (*emphasis, weight*) Nachdruck *m;* (*mental*) Belastung *f;* (mus, pros) Ton *m,* Betonung *f;* (phys) Beanspruchung *f,* Spannung *f* ‖ *tr* (& mus, pros) betonen

stress' ac'cent *s* Betonungsakzent *m*

stress' mark' *s* Betonungszeichen *n*

stretch [stretʃ] *s* (*of road*) Strecke *f;* (*of the limbs*) Strecken *n;* (*of water*) Fläche *f;* (*of a racetrack*) Gerade *f;* (*of years*) Zeitspanne *f;* **do a s.** (sl) brummen; **in one s.** in e-m Zug ‖ *tr* (*a rope*) spannen; (*one's neck*) rekken; (*shoes, gloves*) ausdehnen; (*wire*) ziehen; (*strings of an instrument*) straffziehen; **s. a point** es nicht allzu genau nehmen; **s. oneself** sich strecken; **s. one's legs** sich [*dat*] die Beine vertreten; **s. out** (e.g., *hands*) ausstrecken ‖ *intr* sich (aus)dehnen; (*said of a person*) sich strecken; **s. out on** sich ausstrecken auf (*dat*)

stretcher ['stretʃər] *s* Tragbahre *f*

stretch'erbear'er *s* Krankenträger *m*

strew [stru] *v* (*pret* **strewed;** *pp* **strewed & strewn**) *tr* (aus)streuen; **s. with** bestreuen mit

stricken ['strikən] *adj* (**with** e.g., *misfortune*) heimgesucht (von); (**with** e.g., *fear, grief*) ergriffen (von); (**with** a *disease*) befallen (von)

strict [strikt] *adj* streng; **in s. confidence** streng vertraulich

strictly ['striktli] *adv* streng; **s. speaking** genau genommen

stricture ['striktʃər] *s* (**on**) kritische Bemerkung *f* (über *acc*)

stride [straid] *s* Schritt *m;* **hit one's s.** auf Touren kommen; **make great**

strides große Fortschritte machen; **take in s.** ruhig hinnehmen ‖ *v* (*pret* **strode** [strod]; *pp* **stridden** ['stridən]) *intr* schreiten; **s. along** tüchtig ausschreiten

strident ['straidənt] *adj* schrill

strife [straif] *s* Streit *m,* Hader *m*

strike [straik] *s* (*work stoppage*) Streik *m;* (*blow*) Schlag *m;* (*discovery,* e.g., *of oil*) Fund *m;* (baseball) Fehlschlag *m;* **go on s.** in Streik treten ‖ *v* (*pret & pp* **struck** [strʌk]) *tr* (*a person, the hours, coins, strings of an instrument*) schlagen; (*a match*) anstreichen; (*a bargain*) schließen; (*a note*) greifen; (**go on strike against**) bestreiken; (*a tent*) abbrechen; (*oil*) stoßen auf (*acc*); (*run into*) auffahren auf (*acc*); (s.o. *blind, dumb*) machen; (s.o. *with fear*) erfüllen; (*a blow*) versetzen; (*a pose*) einnehmen; (*seem to s.o.*) erscheinen (*dat*); **s. it rich** auf e-e Goldader stoßen; **s. fear into s.o.** j-m e-n Schrecken einjagen; **s. up** (*a conversation, an acquaintance*) anknüpfen; (*a song*) anstimmen ‖ *intr* schlagen; (*said of a person or clock*) schlagen; (*said of workers*) streiken; (*said of lightning*) einschlagen; **s. home** Eindruck machen; **s. out** (& fig) fehlschlagen

strike'break'er *s* Streikbrecher –in *mf*

striker ['straikər] *s* Streikende *mf*

strik'ing *adj* auffallend; (*example*) treffend; (*workers*) streikend

strik'ing pow'er *s* Schlagkraft *f*

string [striŋ] *s* Bindfaden *m;* (*row, series*) Reihe *f;* (*of a bow*) Sehne *f;* (*of a musical instrument*) Saite *f;* **pull strings** (fig) der Drahtzieher sein; **s. of pearls** Perlenkette *f;* **strings** (mus) Streicher *pl;* **with no strings attached** ohne einschränkende Bedingungen ‖ *v* (*pret & pp* **strung** [strʌŋ]) *tr* (*pearls*) auf e-e Schnur (auf)reihen; (*a bow*) spannen; **s. along** hinhalten; **s. up** (coll) aufknüpfen

string' band' *s* Streichorchester *n*

string' bean' *s* grüne Bohne *f;* (*tall, thin person*) Bohnenstange *f*

stringed' in'strument *s* Saiteninstrument *n*

stringent ['strindʒənt] *adj* streng

string' quartet' *s* Streichquartett *n*

stringy ['striŋi] *adj* (*vegetables*) holzig; (*meat*) sehnig; (*hair*) zottelig

strip [strip] *s* Streifen *m* ‖ *v* (*pret & pp* **stripped;** *ger* **stripping**) *tr* (**off**) abziehen; (*clothes*) (**off**) abstreifen; (*a thread*) überdrehen; (*gears*) beschädigen; **s. down** abmontieren; **s. s.o. of office** j-n seines Amtes entkleiden ‖ *intr* sich ausziehen

stripe [straip] *s* Streifen *m;* (*elongated welt*) Striemen *m;* (mil) Tresse *f* ‖ *tr* streifen

strip' mine' *s* Tagebau *m*

stripper ['stripər] *s* Stripperin *f*

strip'tease' *s* Entkleidungsnummer *f*

stripteaser ['strip͵tizər] *s* Stripperin *f*

strive [straiv] *v* (*pret* **strove** [strov]);

pp **striven** ['strɪvən]) *intr* (for) streben (nach); **s. to** (*inf*) sich bemühen zu (*inf*)

stroke [strok] *s* Schlag *m;* (*caress with the hand*) Streicheln *n;* (*of a piston*) Hub *m;* (*of a pen, brush*) Strich *m;* (*of a sword*) Hieb *m;* (*in swimming*) Schwimmstoß *m;* (*of the leg*) Beinstoß *m;* (*of an oar*) Schlag *m;* (*pathol*) Schlaganfall *m;* **at a single s.** mit e–m Schlag; **at the s. of twelve** Schlag zwölf Uhr; **not do a s. of work** keinen Strich tun; **she'll have a s.** (coll) dann trifft sie der Schlag; **s. of genius** Genieblitz *m;* **s. of luck** Glücksfall *m;* **with a s. of the pen** mit e–m Federstrich ‖ *tr* streicheln

stroll [strol] *s* Spaziergang *m* ‖ *intr* spazieren

stroller ['strolər] *s* Spaziergänger –in *mf;* (*for a baby*) Kindersportwagen *m*

strong [strɔŋ] *adj* kräftig; (*firm*) fest; (*drink, smell, light, wind, feeling*) stark; (*glasses*) scharf; (*wine*) schwer; (*suspicion*) dringend; (*memory*) gut; (*candidate*) aussichtsreich; (*argument*) triftig

strong'-arm' *adj* (e.g., *methods*) Zwangs–

strong'box' *s* Geldschrank *m*

strong'hold' *s* Feste *f;* (fig) Hochburg *f*

strong' lan'guage *s* Kraftausdrücke *pl*

strongly ['strɔŋli] *adv* nachdrücklich; **feel s. about** sich sehr einsetzen für

strong'-mind'ed *adj* willensstark

strontium ['stranɪ·əm] *s* Strontium *n*

strop [strap] *s* Streichriemen *m* ‖ *v* (*pret & pp* **stropped;** *ger* **stropping**) *tr* abziehen

strophe ['strofi] *s* Strophe *f*

structural ['strʌktʃərəl] *adj* strukturell, Bau–

structure ['strʌktʃər] *s* Struktur *f;* (*building*) Bau *m*

struggle ['strʌgəl] *s* Kampf *m* ‖ *intr* (for) kämpfen (um); **s. against** ankämpfen gegen; **s. to one's feet** sich mit Mühe erheben

strum [strʌm] *v* (*pret & pp* **strummed;** *ger* **strumming**) *tr* klimpern auf (*dat*)

strumpet ['strʌmpɪt] *s* Dirne *f*

strut [strʌt] *s* (*brace*) Strebebalken *m;* (*haughty walk*) stolzer Gang *m* ‖ *v* (*pret & pp* **strutted;** *ger* **strutting**) *intr* stolzieren

strychnine ['strɪknaɪn] *s* Strychnin *n*

stub [stʌb] *s* (*of a checkbook*) Abschnitt *m;* (*of a ticket*) Kontrollabschnitt *m;* (*of a candle, cigarette*) Stummel *m* ‖ *v* (*pret & pp* **stubbed;** *ger* **stubbing**) *tr*—**s. one's toe** sich an der Zehe stoßen

stubble ['stʌbəl] *s* Stoppel *f;* (*facial hair*) Bartstoppeln *pl*

stubbly ['stʌbli] *adj* stopp(e)lig

stubborn ['stʌbərn] *adj* eigensinnig; (e.g., *resistance*) hartnäckig; (*hair*) widerspenstig

stubby ['stʌbi] *adj* kurz und dick; (*person*) untersetzt

stuc·co ['stʌko] *s* (**–coes & –cos**) Verputz *m* ‖ *tr* verputzen

stuc'co work' *s* Verputzarbeit *f*

stuck [stʌk] *adj*—**be s.** feststecken; (*said, e.g., of a lock*) klemmen; **be s. on** vernarrt sein in (*acc*); **get s.** steckenbleiben

stuck'-up' *adj* (coll) hochnäsig

stud [stʌd] *s* (*ornament*) Ziernagel *m;* (*horse*) Zuchthengst *m;* (archit) Wandpfosten *m* ‖ *v* (*pret & pp* **studded;** *ger* **studding**) *tr* mit Ziernägeln verzieren

stud' bolt' *s* Schraubenbolzen *m*

student ['st(j)udənt] *adj* Studenten– ‖ *s* (*in college*) Student –in *mf;* (*in grammar or high school*) Schüler –in *mf;* (*scholar*) Gelehrte *mf*

stu'dent bod'y *s* Studentenschaft *f*

stu'dent nurse' *s* Krankenpflegerin *f* in Ausbildung

stud' farm' *s* Gestüt *n*

stud'horse' *s* Zuchthengst *m*

stud'ied *adj* gesucht

studi·o ['st(j)udɪ‿o] *s* (**–os**) (fa, phot) Atelier *n;* (cin, fa, phot, telv) Studio *n*

studious ['st(j)udɪ·əs] *adj* fleißig

stud·y ['stʌdi] *s* Studium *n;* (*room*) Studierzimmer *n;* (paint) Studie *f* ‖ *v* (*pret & pp* **–ied**) *tr & intr* studieren

stuff [stʌf] *s* Stoff *m;* (coll) Kram *m;* **do your s.!** (coll) schieß los!; **know one's s.** (coll) sich auskennen ‖ *tr* (*animals*) ausstopfen; (*a cushion*) polstern; (e.g., *cotton in the ears*) sich [*dat*] stopfen; (culin) füllen; **s. oneself** sich vollstopfen

stuffed' shirt' *s* steifer, eingebildeter Mensch *m*

stuff'ing *s* Polstermaterial *n;* (culin) Fülle *f*

stuffy ['stʌfi] *adj* (*room*) stickig; (*nose*) verstopft; (*person*) steif

stumble ['stʌmbəl] *intr* stolpern; (*in reading*) holpern; **s. across** stoßen auf (*acc*)

stum'bling block' *s* Stein *m* des Anstoßes

stump [stʌmp] *s* (*of an arm, tree, cigarette, pencil*) Stummel *m* ‖ *tr* (*a cigarette*) ausdrücken; (*nonplus*) verblüffen; (*a district, state*) als Wahlredner bereisen

stump' speak'er *s* Wahlredner –in *mf*

stun [stʌn] *v* (*pret & pp* **stunned;** *ger* **stunning**) *tr* betäuben

stun'ning *adj* (coll) phantastisch

stunt [stʌnt] *s* Kunststück *n;* **do stunts** Kunststücke vorführen ‖ *tr* hemmen

stunt'ed *adj* verkümmert

stunt' fly'ing *s* Kunstflug *m*

stunt' man' *s* (**men'**) Sensationsdarsteller *m*

stupe·fy ['st(j)upɪ ‚faɪ] *v* (*pret & pp* **–fied**) *tr* verblüffen

stupendous [st(j)u'pɛndəs] *adj* erstaunlich

stupid ['st(j)upɪd] *adj* dumm, blöd

stupidity [st(j)u'pɪdɪti] *s* Dummheit *f*

stupor ['st(j)upər] *s* Stumpfsinn *m*

sturdy ['stʌrdi] *adj* (*person*) kräftig;

(thing) stabil; *(resolute)* standhaft; *(plant)* widerstandsfähig

sturgeon ['stɜːdʒən] *s* Stör *m*

stutter ['stʌtər] *s* Stottern *n* || *tr & intr* stottern

sty [staɪ] *s* Schweinestall *m*; *(pathol)* Gerstenkorn *n*

style [staɪl] *s* Stil *m*; *(manner)* Art *f*; *(fashion)* Mode *f*; *(cut of suit)* Schnitt *m*; **be in s.** in Mode sein; **go out of s.** veralten; **live in s.** auf großem Fuße leben || *tr (title)* betiteln; *(e.g., clothes)* gestalten; *(hair)* nach der Mode frisieren

stylish ['staɪlɪʃ] *adj* modisch; *(person)* modisch gekleidet

stylistic [staɪ'lɪstɪk] *adj* stilistisch

stymie ['staɪmi] *tr* vereiteln

styp'tic pen'cil ['stɪptɪk] *s* Alaunstift *m*

suave [swɑv] *adj* verbindlich

sub [sʌb] *s* *(naut)* U-boot *n*; *(sport)* Ersatzspieler –in *mf*

sub'chas'er *s* U-bootjäger *m*

sub'commit'tee *s* Unterausschuß *m*

subconscious [sʌb'kɑnʃəs] *adj* unterbewußt || *s* Unterbewußtsein *n*

sub'con'tinent *s* Subkontinent *m*

sub'con'tract *s* Nebenvertrag *m* || *tr* e–n Nebenvertrag abschließen über *(acc)*

sub'con'tractor *s* Unterlieferant –in *mf*

sub'divide', **sub'divide'** *tr* unterteilen || *intr* sich unterteilen

sub'divi'sion *s* *(act)* Unterteilung *f*; *(unit)* Unterabteilung *f*

subdue [səb'd(j)u] *tr (an enemy)* unterwerfen; *(one who is struggling)* überwältigen; *(light, sound)* dämpfen; *(feelings, impulses)* bändigen

sub'floor' *s* Blindboden *m*

sub'head' *s* Untertitel *m*

subject ['sʌbdʒɪkt] *adj* (to) untertan *(dat)*; **be s. to** *(e.g., approval, another country)* abhängig sein von; *(e.g., colds)* neigen zu; *(e.g., laws of nature, change)* unterworfen sein *(dat)*; **s. to change without notice** Änderungen vorbehalten || *s* Thema *n*; *(of a religion)* Untertan –in *mf*; *(educ)* Fach *n*; *(fa)* Vorwurf *m*; *(gram)* Satzgegenstand *m*, Subjekt *n*; *(libr)* Stichwort *n*; **change the s.** das Thema wechseln; **get off the s.** vom Thema abkommen || [səb'dʒɛkt] *tr (& fig)* unterwerfen *(dat)*

subjection [səb'dʒɛkʃən] *s* Unterwerfung *f*

subjective [səb'dʒɛktɪv] *adj* subjektiv; **s. case** Werfall *m*

sub'ject mat'ter *s* Inhalt *m*

subjugate ['sʌbdʒəˌget] *tr* unterjochen

subjunctive [səb'dʒʌŋktɪv] *adj* konjunktiv(isch) || *s* Konjunktiv *m*

sub'lease' *s* Untermiete *f* || **sub'lease'** *tr & intr (to s.o.)* untervermieten; *(from s.o.)* untermieten

sublet [səb'lɛt] *v (pret & pp* –let; *ger* –letting) *tr & intr (to s.o.)* untervermieten; *(from s.o.)* untermieten

sublimate ['sʌblɪmet] *s* *(chem)* Sublimat *m* || ['sʌblɪˌmet] *tr* sublimieren

sublime [sə'blaɪm] *adj* erhaben || *s* Erhabene *n*

submachine' gun' *s* Maschinenpistole *f*

sub'marine' *adj* U-boot– || *s* U-boot *n*

sub'marine' base' *s* U-bootstützpunkt *m*

submerge [səb'mʌrdʒ] *tr & intr* untertauchen; **ready to s.** tauchklar

submersion [səb'mʌrʒən] *s* Untertauchen *n*

submission [səb'mɪʃən] *s* (to) Unterwerfung *f* (unter *acc*); *(of a document)* Vorlage *f*; *(of a question)* Unterbreitung *f*

submissive [səb'mɪsɪv] *adj* unterwürfig

sub-mit [səb'mɪt] *v (pret & pp* –mitted; *ger* –mitting) *tr (a question)* unterbreiten; *(a document)* vorlegen; *(suggest)* der Ansicht sein || *intr (to)* sich unterwerfen *(dat)*

subordinate [səb'ɔrdɪnɪt] *adj (lower in rank)* untergeordnet; *(secondary)* Neben– || *s* Untergebene *mf* || [səb'ɔrdɪˌnet] *tr* (to) unterordnen *(dat)*

subor'dinate clause' *s* Nebensatz *m*

suborn [sə'bɔrn] *tr* verleiten; *(bribe)* bestechen

sub'plot' *s* Nebenhandlung *f*

subpoena [səb'pinə] *s* Vorladung *f* || *tr* (unter Strafandrohung) vorladen

subscribe [səb'skraɪb] *tr* unterschreiben; *(money)* zeichnen || *intr*—**s. to** *(a newspaper)* abonnieren; *(to a series of volumes)* subskribieren; *(an idea)* billigen

subscriber [səb'skraɪbər] *s* Abonnent –in *mf*

subscription [səb'skrɪpʃən] *s* (to) Abonnement *n* (auf *acc*); *(to a series of volumes)* Subskription *f* (auf *acc*); **take out a s. to** sich abonnieren auf *(acc)*

sub'sec'tion *s* Unterabteilung *f*

subsequent ['sʌbsɪkwənt] *adj* (nach)-folgend; **s. to** anschließend an *(acc)*

subsequently ['sʌbsɪkwəntli] *adv* anschließend

subservient [səb'sʌrvɪ-ənt] *adj* (to) unterwürfig (gegenüber *dat*)

subside [səb'saɪd] *intr* nachlassen; *(geol)* sich senken

subsidiary [səb'sɪdɪˌeri] *adj* Tochter– || *s* Tochtergesellschaft *f*

subsidize ['sʌbsɪˌdaɪz] *tr* subventionieren

subsidy ['sʌbsɪdi] *s* Subvention *f*

subsist [səb'sɪst] *intr (exist)* existieren; **s. on** leben von

subsistence [səb'sɪstəns] *s* *(existence)* Dasein *n*; *(livelihood)* Lebensunterhalt *m*; *(philos)* Subsistenz *f*

subsist'ence allow'ance *s* Unterhaltszuschuß *m*

sub'soil' *s* Untergrund *m*

subsonic [səb'sɑnɪk] *adj* Unterschall–

sub'spe'cies *s* Unterart *f*

substance ['sʌbstəns] *s* Substanz *f*, Stoff *m*; **in s.** im wesentlichen

substand'ard *adj* unter dem Niveau

substantial [səb'stænʃəl] *adj* *(sum, amount)* beträchtlich; *(difference)* wesentlich; (*meal*) kräftig; **be in s. agreement** im wesentlichen übereinstimmen

substantiate [səb'stænʃɪ‚et] *tr* begründen, nachweisen

substantive ['sʌbstəntɪv] *adj* wesentlich ‖ *s* (*gram*) Substantiv *m*

sub'sta'tion *s* Nebenstelle *f*; (*post-office*) Zweigpostamt *n*; (*elec*) Umspannwerk *n*

substitute ['sʌbstɪ‚t(j)ut] *s* (*person*) Stellvertreter –in *mf*; (*material*) Austauschstoff *m*; (*pej*) Ersatz *m*; (*sport*) Ersatzspieler –in *mf*; **act as a s. for** vertreten; **beware of substitutes** for Nachahmung wird gewarnt ‖ *tr*—**s. A for B** B durch A ersetzen ‖ *intr*— **s. for** einspringen für

sub'stitute teach'er *s* Aushilfslehrer –in *mf*

substitution [‚sʌbstɪ't(j)uʃən] *s* Einsetzung *f*; (*chem, math, ling*) Substitution *f*; (*sport*) Auswechseln *n*

sub'stra'tum *s* (**-ta** [tə] **& -tums**) Unterlage *f*; (*biol*) Nährboden *m*

sub'struc'ture *s* Unterbau *m*

subsume [sʌb'sjum] *tr* unterordnen

subterfuge ['sʌbtər‚fjudʒ] *s* Winkelzug *m*

subterranean [‚sʌbtə'renɪ·ən] *adj* unterirdisch

sub'ti'tle *s* Untertitel *m*

subtle ['sʌtəl] *adj* fein; (*poison*) schleichend; (*cunning*) raffiniert

subtlety ['sʌtəlti] *s* Feinheit *f*

subtract [səb'trækt] *tr* subtrahieren

subtraction [səb'trækʃən] *s* Subtraktion *f*

suburb ['sʌbɜrb] *s* Vorstadt *f*, Vorort *m*; **the suburbs** der Stadtrand

suburban [sʌ'bɜrbən] *adj* Vorstadt-

suburbanite [sə'bɜrbə‚naɪt] *s* Vorstadtbewohner –in *mf*

subvention [səb'venʃən] *s* Subvention *f*

subversion [səb'vʌrʒən] *s* Umsturz *m*

subversive [səb'vʌrsɪv] *adj* umstürzlerisch ‖ *s* Umstürzler –in *mf*

subver'sive activ'ity *s* Wühlarbeit *f*

subvert [səb'vʌrt] *tr* (*a government*) stürzen; (*the law*) umstoßen; (*corrupt*) (sittlich) verderben

sub'way' *s* U-Bahn *f*, Untergrundbahn *f*

succeed [sʌk'sid] *tr* folgen (*dat*) ‖ *intr* (*said of persons*) (**in**) Erfolg haben (**mit**); (*said of things*) gelingen; **I succeeded in** (*ger*) es gelang mir zu (*inf*); **not s.** mißglücken; **s. to the throne** die Thronfolge antreten

success [sʌk'ses] *s* Erfolg *m*; (*play, song, piece of merchandise*) Knüller *m*; **be a s.** Erfolg haben; **without s.** erfolglos

successful [sʌk'sesfəl] *adj* erfolgreich

succession [sʌk'seʃən] *s* Reihenfolge *f*; (*as heir*) Erbfolge *f*; **in s.** nacheinander; **s. to** (*e.g., an office, estate*) Übernahme *f* (*genit*)

successive [sʌk'sesɪv] *adj* aufeinanderfolgend

successor [sʌk'sesər] *s* Nachfolger –in

mf; **s. to the throne** Thronfolger –in *mf*

succor ['sʌkər] *s* Beistand *m* ‖ *tr* beistehen (*dat*)

succotash ['sʌkə‚tæʃ] *s* Gericht *n* aus Süßmais und grünen Bohnen

succulent ['sʌkjələnt] *adj* saftig

succumb [sə'kʌm] *intr* (**to**) erliegen (*dat*)

such [sʌtʃ] *adj* solch; **as s.** als solcher; **no s. thing** nichts dergleichen; **some s. thing** irgend so (et)was; **s. and s.** der und der; **s. as we** (etwa); **s. a long time** so lange; **s. as it is** wie es nun einmal ist

suck [sʌk] *s* Saugen *n*; (*licking*) Lutschen *n* ‖ *tr* saugen; **s. in** einsaugen; (*sl*) reinlegen ‖ *intr* saugen; **s. on** (*e.g., candy*) lutschen

sucker ['sʌkər] *s* (coll) Gimpel *m*; (*carp*) Karpfenfisch *m*; (bot) Wurzelschößling *m*; (zool) Saugröhre *f*

suckle ['sʌkəl] *tr* stillen; (*animals*) säugen

suck'ling *s* Säugling *m*

suck'ling pig' *s* Spanferkel *n*

suction ['sʌkʃən] *s* Saugen *n*, Sog *m*

suc'tion cup' *s* Saugnapf *m*

suc'tion pump' *s* Saugpumpe *f*

sudden ['sʌdən] *adj* plötzlich, jäh; **all of a s.** (ganz) plötzlich

suddenly ['sʌdənli] *adv* plötzlich

suds [sʌdz] *spl* Seifenschaum *m*

sudsy ['sʌdzi] *adj* schaumig

sue [s(j)u] *tr* (**for**) verklagen (auf *acc*) ‖ *intr* (**for**) klagen (auf *acc*)

suede [swed] *adj* Wildleder– ‖ *s* Wildleder *n*

suet ['s(j)u·ɪt] *s* Talg *m*

suffer ['sʌfər] *tr* erleiden; (*damage*) nehmen; (*put up with*) ertragen ‖ *intr* (**from**) leiden (an *dat*)

sufferance ['sʌfərəns] *s* stillschweigende Einwilligung *f*

suf'fering *s* Leiden *n*

suffice [sə'faɪs] *intr* ausreichen

sufficient [sə'fɪʃənt] *adj* (**for**) ausreichend (für)

suffix ['sʌfɪks] *s* Nachsilbe *f*

suffocate ['sʌfə‚ket] *tr* & *intr* ersticken

suffrage ['sʌfrɪdʒ] *s* Stimmrecht *n*

suffuse [sə'fjuz] *tr* übergießen

sugar ['ʃugər] *s* Zucker *m* ‖ *tr* zuckern

sug'ar beet' *s* Zuckerrübe *f*

sug'ar bowl' *s* Zuckerdose *f*

sug'ar cane' *s* Zuckerrohr *n*

sug'ar-coat' *tr* (& fig) überzuckern

sug'ar dad'dy *s* Geldonkel *m*

sug'ar ma'ple *s* Zuckerahorn *m*

sug'ar tongs' *spl* Zuckerzange *f*

sugary ['ʃugəri] *adj* zuckerig

suggest [səg'dʒest] *tr* vorschlagen; (*hint*) andeuten

suggestion [səg'dʒestʃən] *s* Vorschlag *m*

suggestive [səg'dʒestɪv] *adj* (*remark*) zweideutig; (*thought-provoking*) anregend; (*e.g., dress*) hauteng; **be s. of** erinnern an (*acc*)

suicidal [‚su·ɪ'saɪdəl] *adj* selbstmörderisch

suicide ['su·ɪ‚saɪd] *s* Selbstmord *m*;

(person) Selbstmörder –in *mf;* **commit s.** Selbstmord begehen

suit [sut] *s (men's)* Anzug *m; (women's)* Kostüm *n; (cards)* Farbe *f; (jur)* Prozeß *m;* **bring s. (against)** e–e Klage einbringen (gegen); **follow s.** Farbe bekennen; (fig) sich nach den anderen richten ∥ *tr (please)* passen *(dat); (correspond to)* entsprechen *(dat); (said, e.g., of colors, style)* gut passen *(dat);* **be suited for** sich eignen für; **s. s.th. to** etw anpassen *(dat);* **s. yourself!** wie Sie wollen!

suitable ['sutəbəl] *adj* **(to)** geeignet (für)

suit'case' *s* Handkoffer *m*

suit' coat' *s* Sakko *m & n*

suite [swit] *s (series of rooms)* Zimmerflucht *f; (set of furniture)* Zimmergarnitur *f;* (mus) Suite *f*

suitor ['sutər] *s* Freier *m*

sul'fa drug' *s* Sulfonamid *n*

sulfate ['sʌlfet] *s* Sulfat *n*

sulfide ['sʌlfaɪd] *s* Sulfid *n*

sulfur ['sʌlfər] *adj* Schwefel– ∥ *s* Schwefel *m* ∥ *tr* einschwefeln

sulfur'ic ac'id [sʌl'f(j)urɪk] *s* Schwefelsäure *f*

sul'fur mine' *s* Schwefelgrube *f*

sulk [sʌlk] *intr* trotzen

sulky ['sʌlki] *adj* trotzend, mürrisch ∥ *s (sport)* Traberwagen *m*

sulk'y race' *s* Trabrennen *n*

sullen ['sʌlən] *adj* mißmutig

sul·ly ['sʌli] *v (pret & pp –lied) tr* besudeln

sulphur ['sʌlfər] *var of* **sulfur**

sultan ['sʌltən] *s* Sultan *m*

sultry ['sʌltri] *adj* schwül

sum [sʌm] *s* Summe *f*, Betrag *m;* **in sum** kurz gesagt ∥ *v (pret & pp summed; ger summing)—***sum up** summieren; *(summarize)* zusammenfassen; *(make a quick estimate of)* kurz abschätzen

sumac, sumach ['ʃumæk] *s* Sumach *m*

summarize ['sʌmə‚raɪz] *tr* zusammenfassen

summary ['sʌməri] *adj* summarisch ∥ *s* Zusammenfassung *f*

sum'mary court'martial *s* summarisches Militärgericht *n*

summer ['sʌmər] *s* Sommer *m*

sum'mer cot'tage *s* Sommerwohnung *f*

sum'mer resort' *s* Sommerfrische *f*

sum'mer school' *s* Sommerkurs *m*

sum'mertime' *s* Sommerzeit *f*

summery ['sʌməri] *adj* sommerlich

summit ['sʌmɪt] *s (& fig)* Gipfel *m*

sum'mit con'ference *s* Gipfelkonferenz *f*

sum'mit talks' *spl* Gipfelgespräche *pl*

summon ['sʌmən] *tr (e.g., a doctor)* kommen lassen; *(a conference)* einberufen; *(jur)* vorladen; **s. up** *(courage, strength)* aufbieten

summons ['sʌmənz] *s (jur)* Vorladung *f*

sumptuous ['sʌmptʃ/ʊ·əs] *adj* üppig

sun [sʌn] *s* Sonne *f* ∥ *v (pret & pp sunned; ger sunning) tr* sonnen; **sun oneself** sich sonnen

sun' bath' *s* Sonnenbad *n*

sun'beam' *s* Sonnenstrahl *m*

sun'burn' *s* Sonnenbrand *m*

sun'burned' *adj* sonnverbrannt

sundae ['sʌnde] *s* Eisbecher *m* mit Sirup, Nüssen, Früchten und Schlagsahne

Sunday ['sʌnde] *adj* sonntäglich; **dressed in one's S. best** sonntäglich gekleidet ∥ *s* Sonntag *m;* **on S.** am Sonntag

Sun'day driv'er *s* Sonntagsfahrer –in *mf*

Sun'day school' *s* Sonntagsschule *f*

sunder ['sʌndər] *tr* trennen

sun'di'al *s* Sonnenuhr *f*

sun'down' *s* Sonnenuntergang *m*

sun'-drenched' *adj* sonnenüberflutet

sundries ['sʌndriz] *pl* Diverses *n*

sundry ['sʌndri] *adj* verschiedene

sun'fish' *s* Sonnenfisch *m*

sun'flow'er *s* Sonnenblume *f*

sun'glass'es *pl* Sonnenbrille *f*

sun' hel'met *s* Tropenhelm *m*

sunken ['sʌŋkən] *adj (ship)* gesunken; *(eyes; garden)* tiefliegend; *(treasure)* versunken; *(cheeks)* eingefallen; **s. rocks** blinde Klippe *f*

sun' lamp' *s* Höhensonne *f*

sun'light' *s* Sonnenlicht *n*

sunny ['sʌni] *adj* sonnig

sun'ny side' *s* Sonnenseite *f*

sun' par'lor *s* Glasveranda *f*

sun'rise' *s* Sonnenaufgang *m*

sun' roof' *s (aut)* Schiebedach *n*

sun'set' *s* Sonnenuntergang *m*

sun'shade' *s* Sonnenschirm *m; (awning)* Sonnendach *n;* (phot) Gegenlichtblende *f*

sun'shine' *s* Sonnenschein *m*

sun'spot' *s* Sonnenfleck *m*

sun'stroke' *s* Sonnenstich *m*

sun'tan' *s* Sonnenbräune *f*

sun'tanned' *adj* sonnengebräunt

sun' vis'or *s (aut)* Sonnenblende *f*

sup [sʌp] *v (pret & pp supped; ger supping) intr* zu Abend essen

super ['supər] *adj (oversized)* Super–; *(sl)* prima ∥ *s (theat)* Komparse *m*

su'perabun'dance *s (of)* Überfülle *f (an dat)*

su'perabun'dant *adj* überreichlich

superannuated [‚supər'ænju‚etɪd] *adj (person)* pensioniert; *(thing)* veraltet

superb [su'pɜrb] *adj* prachtvoll, herrlich

su'perbomb' *s* Superbombe *f*

su'perbomb'er *s* Riesenbomber *m*

supercilious [‚supər'sɪlɪ·əs] *adj* hochnäsig

superficial [‚supər'fɪʃəl] *adj* oberflächlich

superfluous [su'pʌrflu·əs] *adj* überflüssig

su'perhigh'way' *s* Autobahn *f*

su'perhu'man *adj* übermenschlich

su'perimpose' *tr* darüberlegen; *(elec, phys)* superlagern

su'perintend' *tr* die Aufsicht führen über *(acc),* beaufsichtigen

superintendent [‚supərɪn'tendənt] *s* Oberaufseher –in *mf; (in industry)*

Betriebsleiter –in *mf; (of a factory)* Werksleiter –in *mf; (of a building)* Hausverwalter –in *mf;* (educ) Schulinspektor –in *mf*

superior [sə'pɪrɪ.ər] *adj (physically)* höher; *(in rank)* übergeordnet; *(quality)* hervorragend; **s.** in überlegen an *(dat);* **s. to** überlegen *(dat)* ǁ *s* Vorgesetzte *mf*

supe'rior court' *s* Obergericht *n*

superiority [sə‚pɪrɪ'ɑrɪti] *s* **(in)** Überlegenheit *f (in dat, an dat);* (mil) Übermacht *f*

superlative [su'pʌrlətɪv] *adj* hervorragend; (gram) superlativisch, Superlativ– ǁ *s* (gram) Superlativ *m*

su'perman' *s* **(–men)** Übermensch *m*

su'permar'ket *s* Supermarkt *m*

su'pernat'ural *adj* übernatürlich ǁ *s* Übernatürliche *n*

supersede [‚supər'sid] *tr* ersetzen

su'persen'sitive *adj* überempfindlich

su'person'ic *adj* Überschall–

superstition [‚supər'stɪʃən] *s* Aberglaube *m; (superstitious idea)* abergläubische Vorstellung *f*

superstitious [‚supər'stɪʃəs] *adj* abergläubisch

su'perstruc'ture *s* Überbau *m; (of a bridge)* Oberbau *m; (of a building or ship)* Aufbauten *pl*

supervise ['supər‚vaɪz] *tr* beaufsichtigen

supervision [‚supər'vɪʒən] *s* Beaufsichtigung *f*

supervisor ['supər‚vaɪzər] *s* Vorgesetzte *mf*

su'pine posi'tion ['supaɪn] *s* Rückenlage *f*

supper ['sʌpər] *s* Abendessen *n;* **eat s.** zu Abend essen

sup'pertime' *s* Abendbrotzeit *f*

supplant [sə'plænt] *tr* ersetzen

supple ['sʌpəl] *adj* geschmeidig; *(mind)* beweglich

supplement ['sʌplɪmənt] *s (e.g., to a diet)* **(to)** Ergänzung *f (genit); (to a writing)* Anhang *m; (to a newspaper)* Beilage *f* ǁ ['sʌplɪ‚ment] *tr* ergänzen

supplementary [‚sʌplɪ'mentəri] *adj* ergänzend

suppliant ['sʌplɪ-ənt] *adj* flehend ǁ *s* Bittsteller –in *mf*

supplicant ['sʌplɪkənt] *s* Bittsteller –in *mf*

supplicate ['sʌplɪ‚ket] *tr* flehen

supplication [‚sʌplɪ'keʃən] *s* Flehen *n*

supplier [sə'plaɪ.ər] *s* Lieferant –in *mf*

sup-ply [sə'plaɪ] *s (supplying)* Versorgung *f; (stock)* **(of)** Vorrat *m* (an *dat);* (com) Angebot *n;* **supplies** Vorräte *pl; (e.g., office supplies, dental supplies)* Bedarfsartikel *pl; (mil)* Nachschub *m* ǁ *v (pret & pp* –plied) *tr* **(with)** versorgen (mit); *(deliver)* liefern; *(procure)* beschaffen; *(with a truck)* zuführen; *(equip)* **(with)** versehen (mit); *(a loss)* ausgleichen; *(missing words)* ergänzen; (mil) mit Nachschub versorgen

supply' and demand' *spl* Angebot *n* und Nachfrage *f*

supply' base' *s* Nachschubstützpunkt *m*

supply' line' *s* Versorgungsweg *m;* (mil) Nachschubweg *m*

support [sə'port] *adj* Hilfs– ǁ *s (prop, brace, stay; person)* Stütze *f; (of a family)* Unterhalt *m;* **in s. of** zur Unterstützung *(genit);* **without s.** *(unsubstantiated)* haltlos; *(unprovided)* unversorgt; **with the s. of** mit dem Beistand von ǁ *tr* stützen, tragen; *(back)* unterstützen; *(a family)* erhalten; *(a charge)* erhärten; *(a claim)* begründen

supporter [sə'portər] *s (of a family)* Ernährer –in *mf; (backer)* Förderer –in *mf;* (jockstrap) Suspensorium *n*

support'ing role' *s* Nebenrolle *f*

suppose [sə'poz] *tr* annehmen; **be supposed to** sollen; **I s. so** ich glaube schon; **it rains gesetzt den Fall (or angenommen), es regnet; s. we take a walk wie wäre es, wenn wir e-n Spaziergang machten?; what is that supposed to mean?** was soll das bedeuten? ǁ *intr* vermuten

supposed' *adj* mutmaßlich

supposedly [sə'pozɪdli] *adv* angeblich

supposition [‚sʌpə'zɪʃən] *s* Annahme *f*

suppository [sə'pazɪ‚tori] *s* Zäpfchen *n*

suppress [sə'pres] *tr* unterdrücken; *(news, scandal)* verheimlichen

suppression [sə'preʃən] *s* Unterdrückung *f; (of news, truth, scandal)* Verheimlichung *f*

suppurate ['sʌpjə‚ret] *intr* eitern

supremacy [sə'preməsi] *s* Oberherrschaft *f*

supreme [sə'prim] *adj* Ober–, höchste

supreme' author'ity *s* Obergewalt *f*

Supreme' Be'ing *s* höchstes Wesen *n*

supreme' command' *s* Oberkommando *n;* **have s.** den Oberbefehl führen

supreme' command'er *s* oberster Befehlshaber *m*

Supreme' Court' *s* Oberster Gerichtshof *m*

surcharge ['sʌr‚tʃɑrdʒ] *s* **(on)** Zuschlag *m* (zu)

sure [ʃur] *adj* sicher, gewiß; *(shot, cure)* unfehlbar; *(shot, footing, ground, way, proof)* sicher; **are you s. you won't come?** kommen Sie wirklich nicht?; **be s. of** sicher sein *(genit);* **be s. to** *(inf)* vergiß nicht zu *(inf);* **feel s. of oneself** s-r selbst sicher sein; **for s.** sicherlich; **she is s. to come** sie wird sicher(lich) kommen; **s. enough** wirklich; **to be s.** *(parenthetically)* zwar

sure'-foot'ed *adj* trittsicher

surely ['ʃurli] *adv* sicher(lich), gewiß

surety ['ʃur(ɪ)ti] *s* Bürgschaft *f;* **stand s. (for)** bürgen (für)

surf [sʌrf] *s* Brandung *f* ǁ *intr* wellenreiten

surface ['sʌrfɪs] *adj (superficial)* oberflächlich; *(apparent rather than real)*

Schein– ‖ s Oberfläche f; (of a road) Belag m; (aer) Tragfläche f; on the s. oberflächlich (betrachtet) ‖ tr (a road) mit e–m Belag versehen ‖ intr auftauchen

sur'face mail' s gewöhnliche Post f

sur'face-to-air' mis'sile s Boden-Luft-Rakete f

sur'face-to-sur'face mis'sile s Boden-Boden-Rakete f

surf'board' s Wellenreiterbrett n

surf'board'ing s Wellenreiten n

surfeit ['sʌrfɪt] s Übersättigung f ‖ tr übersättigen

surfer ['sʌrfər] s Wellenreiter –in mf

surf'ing s Wellenreiten n

surge [sʌrdʒ] s (forward rush of a wave or crowd) Wogen n; (swelling wave) Woge f; (swelling sea) Wogen n; (elec) Stromstoß m ‖ intr (said of waves or a crowd) wogen; (said of emotions, blood) (up) (auf)wallen

surgeon ['sʌrdʒən] s Chirurg –in mf

surgery ['sʌrdʒəri] s Chirurgie f; (room) Operationssaal m; undergo s. sich e–r Operation unterziehen

surgical ['sʌrdʒɪkəl] adj chirurgisch; (resulting from surgery) Operations-

surly ['sʌrli] adj bärbeißig

surmise [sər'maɪz] s Vermutung f ‖ tr & intr vermuten

surmount [sər'maunt] tr überwinden

surname ['sʌr,nem] s (family name) Zuname m; (epithet) Beiname m ‖ tr e–n Zunamen (or Beinamen) geben (dat)

surpass [sər'pæs] tr (in) übertreffen (an dat)

surplice ['sʌrplɪs] s Chorhemd n

surplus ['sʌrplʌs] adj überschüssig, Über– ‖ s (of) Überschuß m (an dat)

surprise [sər'praɪz] s Überraschungs– ‖ s Überraschung f; take by s. überraschen; to my (great) s. zu meiner (großen) Überraschung ‖ tr überraschen; be surprised at sich wundern über (acc); be surprised to see how staunen, wie; I am surprised that es wundert mich, daß

surpris'ing adj überraschend

surrealism [sə'ri·ə,lɪzəm] s Surrealismus m

surrender [sə'rendər] s (e.g., of a fortress) Übergabe f; (of an army or unit) Kapitulation f; (of rights) Aufgabe f; (of a prisoner) Auslieferung f ‖ tr übergeben; (rights) aufgeben; (a prisoner) ausliefern ‖ intr sich ergeben

surren'der val'ue s (ins) Rückkaufswert m

surreptitious [,sʌrep'tɪʃəs] adj heimlich; (glance) verstohlen

surround [sə'raund] tr umgeben; (said of a crowd, police) umringen; (mil) einschließen

surround'ing adj umliegend ‖ surroundings spl Umgebung f

surtax ['sʌr,tæks] s Steuerzuschlag m

surveillance [sər'vel(j)əns] s Überwachung f; keep under s. unter Polizeiaufsicht halten

survey ['sʌrve] s (of) Überblick m (über acc); (of opinions) Umfrage f; (of land) Vermessung f; (plan or description of the survey) Lageplan m ‖ [sʌr've] tr überblicken; (a person) mustern; (land) vermessen; (people for their opinion) befragen

sur'vey course' s Einführungskurs m

survey'ing s Landvermessung f

surveyor [sər've·ər] s Landmesser m

survival [sər'vaɪvəl] s Überleben n; (after death) Weiterleben n

surviv'al of the fit'test s Überleben n des Tüchtigsten

survive [sər'vaɪv] tr (a person) überleben; (a thing) überstehen; be survived by hinterlassen ‖ intr am Leben bleiben

surviv'ing adj überlebend

survivor [sər'vaɪvər] s Überlebende mf

susceptible [sə'septɪbəl] adj (impressionable) eindrucksfähig; be s. of zulassen; be s. to (disease, infection) anfällig sein für; (flattery) empfänglich sein für

suspect ['sʌspekt] adj verdächtig ‖ s Verdächtige mf ‖ [səs'pekt] tr in Verdacht haben; (surmise) vermuten; (have a hint of) ahnen; s. s.o. of j–n verdächtigen (genit)

suspend [səs'pend] tr (from a job, office) suspendieren; (payment, hostilities, proceedings, a game) einstellen; (a rule) zeitweilig aufheben; (a sentence) aussetzen; (a player) sperren; (from a club) zeitweilig ausschließen; (from) hängen (an dat)

suspenders [səs'pendərz] spl Hosenträger pl

suspense [səs'pens] s Spannung f; hang in s. in der Schwebe sein; keep in s. im ungewissen lassen

suspension [səs'penʃən] s Aufhängung f; (of a sentence) Aussetzung f; (of work) Einstellung f; (e.g., of telephone service) Sperrung f; (aut) Federung f; (chem) Suspension f; s. of driver's license Führerscheinentzug m

suspen'sion bridge' s Hängebrücke f

suspen'sion points' spl (indicating unfinished thoughts) Gedankenpunkte pl; (indicating omission) Auslassungspunkte pl

suspicion [səs'pɪʃən] s Verdacht m; above s. über jeden Verdacht erhaben; be under s. unter Verdacht stehen; on s. of murder unter Mordverdacht

suspicious [səs'pɪʃəs] adj (person) verdächtig; (e.g., glance) argwöhnisch; (character) zweifelhaft

sustain [səs'ten] tr aufrechterhalten; (a loss, defeat, injury) erleiden; (a family) ernähren; (an army) verpflegen; (a motion, an objection) stattgeben (dat); (a theory, position) erhärten; (a note) dehnen

sustenance ['sʌstɪnəns] s (nourishment) Nahrung f; (means of livelihood) Unterhalt m

swab [swɑb] s (med, surg) Tupfer m;

(*matter collected on a swab*) Abstrich *m;* (*naut*) Schwabber *m* ‖ *v* (*pret & pp* swabbed; *ger* swabbing) *tr* (*med, surg*) abtupfen; (*naut*) schrubben

Swabia ['swebɪ·ə] *s* Schwaben *n*

Swabian ['swebɪ·ən] *adj* schwäbisch ‖ *s* Schwabe *m*, Schwäbin *f;* (*dialect*) Schwäbisch *n*

swad'dling clothes' ['swɑdlɪŋ] *spl* Windeln *pl*

swagger ['swægər] *s* (*strut*) Stolzieren *n;* (*swaggering manner*) Prahlerei *f* ‖ *intr* stolzieren; (*show off*) prahlen

swain [swen] *s* (*lover*) Liebhaber *m;* (*country lad*) Bauernbursche *m*

swallow ['swɑlo] *s* Schluck *m;* (*orn*) Schwalbe *f* ‖ *tr* schlucken; (fig) hinunterschlucken ‖ *intr* schlucken; **s. the wrong way** sich verschlucken

swamp [swɑmp] *s* Sumpf *m*, Moor *n* ‖ *tr* überfluten; (*with work*) überhäufen

swamp'land' *s* Moorland *n*

swampy ['swɑmpi] *adj* sumpfig

swan [swɑn] *s* Schwan *m*

swan' dive' *s* Schwalbensprung *m*

swank [swæŋk], **swanky** ['swæŋki] *adj* (*luxurious*) schick; (*ostentatious*) protzig

swan's'-down' *s* Schwanendaunen *pl*

swan' song' *s* Schwanengesang *n*

swap [swɑp] *s* (coll) Tauschgeschäft *n* ‖ *v* (*pret & pp* swapped; *ger* swapping) *tr & intr* (coll) tauschen

swarm [swɑrm] *s* Schwarm *m;* (*of children*) Schar *f* ‖ *intr* schwärmen; **s. around** umschwärmen; **s. into** sich drängen in (*acc*); **s. with** (fig) wimmeln von

swarthy ['swɔrði] *adj* dunkelhäutig

swashbuckler ['swɑʃ͵bʌklər] *s* Eisenfresser *m*

swastika ['swɑstɪkə] *s* Hakenkreuz *n*

swat [swɑt] *s* Schlag *m* ‖ (*pret & pp* swatted; *ger* swatting) *tr* schlagen

swath [swɑθ] *s* Schwaden *m*

swathe [sweð] *tr* umwickeln, einwickeln

sway [swe] *s* Schwanken *n*, Schwingen *n;* (*domination*) Herrschaft *f* ‖ *tr* (*e.g., tree*) hin- und herbewegen; (*influence*) beeinflussen; (*cause to vacillate*) ins Wanken bringen ‖ *intr* schwanken

sway'-back' *s* Senkrücken *m*

swear [swer] *v* (*pret* swore [swor]; *pp* sworn [sworn]) *tr* schwören; **s. in** vereidigen; **s. s.o. to secrecy** j-n auf Geheimhaltung vereidigen ‖ *intr* schwören; (coll) fluchen; **s. at** schimpfen über (*acc*) *or* auf (*acc*); **s. by** schwören bei; **s. off** abschwören (*dat*); **s. on a stack of Bibles** Stein und Bein schwören; **s. to** (*a statement*) beschwören; **s. to it** darauf schwören

swear'ing-in' *s* Vereidigung *f*

swear'word' *s* Fluchwort *n*

sweat [swet] *s* Schweiß *m;* **break out in s.** in Schweiß geraten ‖ *v* (*pret & pp* sweat *or* sweated) *tr* (*blood*)

schwitzen; (*metal*) seigern; (*a horse*) in Schweiß bringen; **s. off** abschwitzen; **s. out** (sl) geduldig abwarten; **s. up** durchschwitzen ‖ *intr* schwitzen

sweater ['swetər] *s* Sweater *m*, Pullover *m*

sweat'er girl' *s* vollbusiges Mädchen *n*

sweat' shirt' *s* Trainingsbluse *f*

sweat' shop' *s* (sl) Knochenmühle *f*

sweaty ['sweti] *adj* verschwitzt; (*hand*) schweißig

Swede [swid] *s* Schwede *m*, Schwedin *f*

Swedish ['swidɪʃ] *adj* schwedisch ‖ *s* Schwedisch *n*

sweep [swip] *s* (*sweeper*) Kehrer –in *mf;* (*of the arm, scythe, weapon*) Schwung *m;* (*of an oar*) Schlag *m;* (*range*) Reichweite *f;* (*continuous stretch*) ausgedehnte Strecke *f;* **in one clean s.** mit e-m Schlag; **make a clean s. of it** reinen Tisch machen ‖ *v* (*pret & pp* swept [swept]) *tr* kehren, fegen; (*mines*) räumen; (*with machine-gun fire*) bestreichen; (*with a searchlight*) absuchen; **he swept her off her feet** er hat sie im Sturm erobert; **s. clean** reinemachen ‖ *intr* kehren, fegen

sweeper ['swipər] *s* Kehrer –in *mf;* (*carpet sweeper*) Teppichkehrer *m*

sweep'ing *adj* weitreichend ‖ **sweepings** *spl* Kehricht *m & n*

sweep'-sec'ond *s* Zentralsekundenzeiger *m*

sweep'stakes' *s & spl* Lotterie *f;* (sport) Toto *m & n*

sweet [swit] *adj* süß; (*person*) lieb; (*butter*) ungesalzen; **be s. on** scharf sein auf (*acc*) ‖ **sweets** *spl* Süßigkeiten *pl*

sweet'bread' *s* Bries *n*

sweet'bri'er *s* Heckenrose *f*

sweet' corn' *s* Zuckermais *m*

sweeten ['switən] *tr* süßen; (fig) versüßen ‖ *intr* süß(er) werden

sweet'heart' *s* Liebste *mf*, Schatz *m*

sweet'meats' *spl* Zuckerwerk *n*

sweetness ['switnɪs] *s* Süßigkeit *f*

sweet' pea' *s* Gartenwicke *f*

sweet' pep'per *s* grüner Paprika *m*

sweet' pota'to *s* Süßkartoffel *f*

sweet'-scent'ed *adj* wohlriechend

sweet' tooth' *s*—**have a s.** gern naschen

sweet' wil'liam *s* Fleischnelke *f*

swell [swel] *adj* (coll) prima ‖ *s* (*of the sea*) Wellengang *m;* (*of an organ*) Schweller *m* ‖ *v* (*pret* swelled; *pp* swelled & swollen ['swolən]) *tr* zum Schwellen bringen; (*the number*) vermehren; (*a musical tone*) anschwellen lassen ‖ *intr* anschwellen

swell'ing *s* Schwellung *f*

swelter ['sweltər] *intr* unter der Hitze leiden

swept'-back' *adj* (aer) keilförmig

swerve [swʌrv] *s* Abweichung *f* ‖ *tr* ablenken ‖ *intr* scharf abbiegen

swift [swɪft] *adj* geschwind, rasch

swig [swɪg] *s* (coll) kräftiger Schluck

m ‖ *v* (*pret & pp* **swigged; *ger* swigging**) *tr* in langen Zügen trinken

swill [swɪl] *s* Spülicht *n;* (*for swine*) Schweinefutter *n;* (*deep drink*) tüchtiger Schluck *m* ‖ *tr & intr* gierig trinken

swim [swɪm] *s* Schwimmen *n;* **take a s.** schwimmen ‖ *v* (*pret* **swam** [swæm]; *pp* **swum** [swʌm]; *ger* **swimming**) *tr* (*e.g., a lake*) durchschwimmen; (*cause to swim*) schwimmen lassen; (*challenge in swimming*) um die Wette schwimmen mit ‖ *intr* schwimmen; **my head is swimming** mir schwindelt der Kopf

swimmer ['swɪmər] *s* Schwimmer –in *mf*

swim′ming *adj* Schwimm– ‖ *s* Schwimmen *n;* (*sport*) Schwimmsport *m*

swim′ming pool′ *s* Schwimmbecken *n*

swim′ming suit′ *s* Badeanzug *m*

swim′ming trunks′ *spl* Badehose *f*

swindle ['swɪndəl] *s* Schwindel *m* ‖ *tr* gaunern; **s. s.th. out of** etw erschwindeln von

swindler ['swɪndlər] *s* Schwindler –in *mf*

swind′ling *s* Schwindelei *f*

swine [swaɪn] *s* Schwein *n*

swine′herd′ *s* Schweinehirt *m*

swing [swɪŋ] *s* (*for children*) Schaukel *f;* (*swinging movement*) Hin– und Herschwingen *n;* (*box*) Schwinger *m;* (*mus*) Swing *m;* **in full s.** in vollem Gang; **take a s. at s.o.** nach j–m schlagen ‖ *v* (*pret & pp* **swung** [swʌŋ]) *tr* schwingen; (*children on a swing*) schaukeln; (*an election*) entscheidend beeinflussen; **s.** (*e.g., a car*) **around** herumdrehen; **we'll s. it somehow** (coll) wir werden es schon schaffen ‖ *intr* pendeln; (*on a swing*) schaukeln; **s. around** sich umdrehen; **s. into action** in Schwung kommen; **things are swinging around here** (coll) hier geht es lustig zu

swing′ing door′ *s* Pendeltür *f*

swinish ['swaɪnɪʃ] *adj* schweinisch

swipe [swaɪp] *s* (coll) Hieb *m;* **take a s. at** (coll) schlagen nach ‖ *tr* (*hit with full force*) (coll) kräftig schlagen; (*steal*) (sl) mausen

swirl [swʌrl] *s* Wirbel *m* ‖ *tr* (*about*) herumwirbeln ‖ *intr* wirbeln; (*said of water*) Strudel bilden

swish [swɪʃ] *s* (*e.g., of a whip*) Sausen *n;* (*of a dress*) Rauschen *n* ‖ *tr* (*a whip*) sausen lassen; **s. its tail** mit dem Schwanz wedeln ‖ *intr* (*said of a whip*) sausen; (*said of a dress*) rauschen

Swiss [swɪs] *adj* schweizerisch ‖ *s* Schweizer –in *mf*

Swiss′ cheese′ *s* Schweizer Käse *m*

Swiss′ franc′ *s* Schweizerfranken *m*

Swiss′ Guard′ *s* Schweizergarde *f*

switch [swɪtʃ] *s* (*exchange*) Wechsel *m,* Umschwung *m;* (*stick*) Rute *f;* (elec) Schalter *m;* (rr) Weiche *f* ‖ *tr* wechseln; (*e.g., coats by mistake*) verwechseln; (rr) rangieren; **s. off** (elec, rad, telv) ausschalten; **s. on** (elec, rad, telv) einschalten ‖ *intr* Plätze wechseln

switch′-blade knife′ *s* feststellbares Messer *n*

switch′board′ *s* Schaltbrett *n,* Zentrale *f*

switch′board op′erator *s* Telephonist –in *mf*

switch′ box′ *s* Schaltkasten *m*

switch′man *s* (–men) (rr) Weichensteller *m*

switch′ tow′er *s* (rr) Blockstation *f*

switch′yard′ *s* Rangierbahnhof *m*

Switzerland ['swɪtsərlənd] *s* die Schweiz

swiv•el ['swɪvəl] *s* Drehlager *n* ‖ *v* (*pret & pp* **-el[l]ed; *ger* -el[l]ing**) *tr* herumdrehen ‖ *intr* sich drehen

swiv′el chair′ *s* Drehstuhl *m*

swiz′zle stick′ ['swɪzəl] *s* Rührstäbchen *n*

swollen ['swolən] *adj* (an)geschwollen; (*eyes*) verquollen

swoon [swun] *s* Ohnmacht *f* ‖ *intr* ohnmächtig werden

swoop [swup] *s* Herabstoßen *n;* **in one fell s.** mit e–m Schlag ‖ *intr*—**s. down** (**on**) herabstoßen (auf *acc*)

sword [sord] *s* Schwert *n;* **put to the s.** mit dem Schwert hinrichten

sword′ belt′ *s* Schwertgehenk *n*

sword′fish′ *s* Schwertfisch *m*

swords′man *s* (–men) Fechter *m*

sworn [sworn] *adj* (*statement*) eidlich; **s. enemy** Todfeind *m*

sycamore ['sɪkəmor] *s* Platane *f*

sycophant ['sɪkəfənt] *s* Sykophant *m*

syllabary ['sɪlə,beri] *s* Silbenschrift *f*

syllabification [sɪ,læbɪfɪ'keʃən] *s* Silbentrennung *f*

syllable ['sɪləbəl] *s* Silbe *f*

sylla•bus ['sɪləbəs] *s* (–bai [,baɪ] & –buses) Lehrplan *m*

syllogism ['sɪlə,dʒɪzəm] *s* Syllogismus *m*

sylvan ['sɪlvən] *adj* Wald–

symbol ['sɪmbəl] *s* Sinnbild *n,* Symbol *n*

symbolic(al) [sɪm'bɑlɪk(əl)] *adj* sinnbildlich, symbolisch

symbolism ['sɪmbə,lɪzəm] *s* Symbolik *f*

symbolize ['sɪmbə,laɪz] *tr* symbolisieren

symmetric(al) [sɪ'metrɪk(əl)] *adj* symmetrisch

symmetry ['sɪmɪtri] *s* Symmetrie *f*

sympathetic [,sɪmpə'θetɪk] *adj* mitfühlend; (physiol) sympathisch

sympathize ['sɪmpə,θaɪz] *intr*—**s. with** mitfühlen mit; (*be in accord with*) sympathisieren mit

sympathizer ['sɪmpə,θaɪzər] *s* Sympathisant –in *mf*

sympathy ['sɪmpəθi] *s* Mitleid *n;* **be in s. with** im Einverständnis sein mit; **offer one's sympathies to s.o.** j–m sein Beileid bezeigen

sym′pathy card′ *s* Beileidskarte *f*

sym′pathy strike′ *s* Sympathiestreik *m*

symphonic [sɪm'fɑnɪk] *adj* sinfonisch

symphony ['sɪmfəni] *s* Sinfonie *f*

symposi·um [sɪm'pozɪ-əm] s (–a [ə] & –ums) Symposion n

symptom ['sɪmptəm] s (of) Symptom n (für)

symptomatic [,sɪmtə'mætɪk] adj (of) symptomatisch (für)

synagogue ['sɪnə,gɔg] s Synagoge f

synchronize ['sɪŋkrə,naɪz] tr synchronisieren

synchronous ['sɪŋkrənəs] adj synchron; (elec) Synchron–

syncopate ['sɪŋkə,pet] tr synkopieren

syncopation [,sɪŋkə'peʃən] s Synkope f

syncope ['sɪŋkə,pi] s Synkope f

syndicate ['sɪndɪkɪt] s Interessengemeinschaft f, Syndikat n ‖ ['sɪndɪ,ket] tr zu e–m Syndikat zusammenschließen; (a column) in mehreren Zeitungen zugleich veröffentlichen ‖ intr ein Syndikat bilden

synod ['sɪnəd] s Synode f

synonym ['sɪnənɪm] s Synonym n

synonymous [sɪ'nɑnəməs] adj sinnverwandt; **s. with** gleichbedeutend mit

synop·sis [sɪ'nɑpsɪs] s (–ses [siz]) Zusammenfassung f

synoptic [sɪ'nɑptɪk] adj synoptisch

syntax ['sɪntæks] s Satzlehre f, Syntax f

synthe·sis ['sɪnθɪsɪs] s (–ses [,siz]) Synthese f

synthesize ['sɪnθɪ,saɪz] tr (& chem) zusammenfügen

synthetic [sɪn'θetɪk] adj künstlich, Kunst– ‖ s Kunststoff m

syphilis ['sɪfɪlɪs] s Syphilis f

Syria ['sɪrɪ-ə] s Syrien n

Syrian ['sɪrɪ-ən] adj syrisch ‖ s Syrer –in mf; (language) Syrisch n

syringe [sɪ'rɪndʒ] s Spritze f ‖ tr (inject) einspritzen; (wash) ausspritzen

syrup ['sɪrəp] s Sirup m

system ['sɪstəm] s System n; (bodily system) Organismus m

systematic(al) [,sɪstə'mætɪk(əl)] adj systematisch, planmäßig

systematize ['sɪstəmə,taɪz] tr systematisieren, systematisch ordnen

systole ['sɪstəli] s Systole f

T

T, t [ti] s zwanzigster Buchstabe des englischen Alphabets

tab [tæb] s (label) Etikett n; (on file cards) Karteireiter m; **keep tabs on** (coll) genau kontrollieren; **pick up the tab** (coll) die Zeche bezahlen ‖ v (pret & pp tabbed; ger tabbing) tr (designate) ernennen

tabby ['tæbi] s getigerte Katze f

tabernacle ['tæbər,nækəl] s Tabernakel n

table ['tebəl] s Tisch m; (list, chart) Tafel f, Tabelle f; (geol) Tafel f; **at t.** bei Tisch; **the tables have turned** das Blatt hat sich gewendet ‖ tr (parl) verschieben

tab·leau ['tæblo] s (–leaus & leaux [loz]) Tableau n

ta'blecloth' s Tischtuch n

ta'bleland' s Tafelland n

ta'ble man'ners spl Tischmanieren pl

ta'ble of con'tents s Inhaltsverzeichnis n

ta'ble salt' s Tafelsalz n

ta'ble set'ting s Gedeck n

ta'blespoon' s Eßlöffel m

tablespoonful ['tebəl,spun,ful] s Eßlöffel m

tablet ['tæblɪt] s (writing pad) Schreibblock m; (med) Tablette f

ta'ble talk' s Tischgespräch n

ta'ble ten'nis s Tischtennis n

ta'bletop' s Tischplatte f

ta'bleware' s Tafelgeschirr n

ta'ble wine' s Tafelwein m

tabloid ['tæblɔɪd] adj konzentriert ‖ s Bildzeitung f; (pej) Sensationsblatt n

taboo [tə'bu] adj tabu ‖ s Tabu n ‖ tr für Tabu erklären

tabular ['tæbjələr] adj tabellarisch

tabulate ['tæbjə,let] tr tabellarisieren

tabulator ['tæbjə,letər] s Tabelliermaschine f

tacit ['tæsɪt] adj stillschweigend

taciturn ['tæsɪtɜrn] adj schweigsam

tack [tæk] s (nail) Zwecke f, Stift m; (stitch) Heftstich m; (stickiness) Klebrigkeit f; (course of action) Kurs m; (gear for a riding horse) Reitgeschirr n; (course run obliquely to the wind) Schlag m; **be on the wrong t.** (fig) auf dem Holzweg sein ‖ tr (down) mit Zwecken befestigen; (sew) heften; **t. on (to)** anfügen (an acc) ‖ intr (fig & naut) lavieren

tackle ['tækəl] s (gear) Ausrüstung f; (for lifting) Flaschenzug m; (fb) Halbstürmer m; (naut) Takelwerk n ‖ tr (a problem) anpacken; (fb) packen

tacky ['tæki] adj klebrig; (gaudy) geschmacklos

tact [tækt] s Takt m, Feingefühl n

tactful ['tæktfəl] adj taktvoll

tactical ['tæktɪkəl] adj taktisch

tac'tical u'nit s Kampfeinheit f

tactician [tæk'tɪʃən] s Taktiker m

tactics ['tæktɪks] spl (& fig) Taktik f

tactless ['tæktlɪs] adj taktlos

tadpole ['tæd,pol] s Kaulquappe f

taffeta ['tæfɪtə] s Taft m

taffy ['tæfi] s Sahnebonbon n

tag [tæg] s (label) Etikett n; (loose end) loses Ende n; (on a shoestring) Stift m; (loop for hanging up a coat) Aufhänger m; (on a fish hook) Glitzerschmuck m; (game) Haschen n; **play tag** sich haschen; **tags** (aut)

Nummernschild *n* ‖ *v* (*pret & pp* tagged; *ger* tagging) *tr* (*mark with a tag*) mit e-m Etikett versehen; (*touch*) haschen; (*hit solidly*) heftig schlagen; (*give a traffic ticket to*) e-n Strafzettel geben (*dat*) ‖ *intr—tag after s.o.* sich an j-s Sohlen heften

tag' line' *s* (*e.g., of a play*) Schlußworte *pl*; (*favorite phrase*) stehende Redensart *f*

tail [tel] *s* Schwanz *m*; (*of a horse, comet*) Schweif *m*; (*of a shirt*) Schoß *m*; (*aer*) Heck *n*; **tails** ein Frack *m*; (*of a coin*) Rückseite *f*; **turn t.** ausreißen; **wag its t.** mit dem Schwanz wedeln ‖ *tr* (coll) beschatten ‖ *intr—t. after* nachlaufen (*dat*); **t. off** abflauen

tail' end' *s* (*e.g., of a conversation*) Schlußteil *n*; **come in at the t. end** als letzter durchs Ziel gehen

tail'gate' *s* (*of a station wagon*) Hecktür *f*; (*of a truck*) Ladeklappe *f* ‖ *intr* dicht hinter e-m anderen fahren

tail' gun'ner *s* (aer) Heckschütze *m*

tail'-heav'y *adj* schwanzlastig

tail'light' *s* (aer) Hecklicht *n*; (aut) Rücklicht *n*

tailor ['telər] *s* Schneider *m* ‖ *tr & intr* schneidern

tai'loring *s* Schneiderarbeit *f*

tai'lor-made suit' *s* Maßanzug *m*

tai'lor shop' *s* Schneiderei *f*

tail'piece' *s* (*appendage*) Anhang *m*; (*of a stringed instrument*) Saitenhalter *m*; (typ) Zierleiste *f*

tail' pipe' *s* (aut) Auspuffrohr *n*

tail'skid' *s* (aer) Sporn *m*

tail'spin' *s—go into a t.* abtrudeln

tail' wheel' *s* (aer) Spornrad *n*

tail'wind' *s* Rückenwind *m*

taint [tent] *s* Fleck *m*; (fig) Schandfleck *m* ‖ *tr* beflecken; (*food*) verderben

take [tek] *s* (*income*) (sl) Einnahmen *pl*; (*loot*) (sl) Beute *f*; (angl) Fang *m*; (cin) Szenenaufnahme *f*; **be on the t.** (sl) sich bestechen lassen ‖ *v* (*pret* **took** [tuk]; *pp* **taken**) *tr* nehmen; (*in a car*) mitnehmen; (*bring, carry*) bringen; (*subtract*) abziehen; (*require*) erfordern; (*insults, criticism*) hinnehmen; (*bear, stand*) ertragen; (*with a camera*) aufnehmen; (*food, pills*) einnehmen; (*s.o.'s temperature*) messen; (*courage*) schöpfen; (*a deep breath*) holen; (*precautions*) treffen; (*responsibility*) übernehmen; (*an oath, test*) ablegen; (*inventory*) aufnehmen; (*a walk, trip, examination, turn, notes*) machen; (*the consequences*) tragen; (*measures*) ergreifen; (*a certain amount of time to travel*) in Anspruch nehmen; (*a step*) tun; (*advice*) befolgen; (*a game*) gewinnen; (*e.g., third place*) belegen; (*a trick*) (cards) stechen; (gram) regieren; **be able to t. a lot** e-n breiten Rücken haben; **be taken in by s.o.** j-m auf den Leim gehen; **I'm not going to t. that**

das lasse ich nicht auf mir sitzen; **t. along** mitnehmen; **t. aside** beiseitenehmen; **t. at one's word** beim Wort nehmen; **t. away** wegschaffen; **t. away from** wegnehmen (*dat*); **t. back** zurücknehmen; **t.** (*e.g., s.o.'s hat*) **by mistake** verwechseln; **t. down** herunternehmen; (*in writing*) aufschreiben; (*dictation*) aufnehmen; (*minutes*) zu Protokoll nehmen; **t. in** (*money*) einnehmen; (*washing*) ins Haus nehmen; (*as guest*) beherbergen; (*deceive*) täuschen; (*encompass*) umfassen; (*observe*) beobachten; (*sightsee*) besichtigen; (*sew*) enger machen; **t. it out on s.o.** seinen Zorn an j-m auslassen; **t. it that** annehmen, daß; **taken** (*occupied*) besetzt; **t. off** (*subtract*) abziehen; (*clothes*) ausziehen; (*a coat*) ablegen; (*gloves*) abstreifen; (*a hat*) abnehmen; (*a tire, wheel*) abmontieren; (*e.g., a day from work*) sich [*dat*] freinehmen; **t.** (*e.g., wares*) **off s.o.'s hands** j-m abnehmen; **t. on** (*hire*) anstellen; (*passengers*) aufnehmen; **t. out** (*from a container*) herausnehmen; (*a spot*) entfernen; (*a girl*) ausführen; (*a mortgage, loan*) aufnehmen; (*ins*) abschließen; (libr) sich [*dat*] ausleihen; **t. over** übernehmen; **t. s.o. for** j-n halten für; **t. up** aufnehmen; (*absorb*) aufsaugen; (*a profession*) ergreifen; (*room, time*) wegnehmen; (*a collection*) veranstalten; (*a skirt*) kürzer machen; **t. upon oneself** auf sich; **t. up** (*a matter*) with besprechen mit ‖ *intr* (*said of an injection*) anschlagen; (*said of seedlings, skin transplants*) anwachsen; **how long does it t.?** wie lange dauert es?; **how long does it t. to** (*inf*)? wie lange braucht man, um zu (*inf*)?; **t. after** nachgeraten (*dat*); **t. off** (*depart*) (coll) abhauen; (*from work*) wegbleiben; (aer, rok) starten; (aut) abfahren; **t. over for s.o.** für j-n einspringen; **t. to** (*a person*) warm werden mit; (*an idea*) aufgreifen; **t. up with** sich abgeben mit

take'-home pay' *s* Nettolohn *m*

take'-off' *s* Karikatur *f*; (aer) Start *m*

take'-off ramp' *s* (*in skiing*) Schanzentisch *m*

take'o'ver *s* Übernahme *f*

tal'cum pow'der ['tælkəm] *s* Federweiß *n*

tale [tel] *s* Geschichte *f*; **tell tales out of school** aus der Schule plaudern

tale'bear'er *s* Zuträger –in *mf*

talent ['tælənt] *s* Talent *n*

tal'ented *adj* talentiert, begabt

talisman ['tælɪsmən] *s* Talisman *m*

talk [tɔk] *s* Gespräch *n*; (*gossip*) Geschwätz *n*; (*lecture*) Vortrag *m*; (*speech*) Rede *f*; **cause t.** von sich reden machen; **give a t. on** e-n Vortrag halten über (*acc*); **t. of the town** Stadtgespräch *n* ‖ *tr* (*business, politics, etc.*) sprechen über (*acc*); **t. down** zum Schweigen bringen; (aer) heruntersprechen; **t. one-**

self hoarse sich heiser reden; **t. one's way out of** sich herausreden aus; **t. over** besprechen; **t. sense** vernünftig reden; **t. s.o. into** (ger) j-n überreden zu (inf); **t. up** Reklame machen für || intr reden; (chat) schwätzen; **t. back** scharf erwidern; **t. big** große Töne reden; **t. dirty** Zoten reißen; **t. down to** herablassend reden zu; **talking of food** à propos Essen; **t. on** (a topic) e-n Vortrag halten über (acc); **t. to the walls** in den Wind reden

talkative ['tɔkətɪv] adj redselig

talker ['tɔkər] s Plauderer –in mf; **big t.** Schaumschläger m

talkie ['tɔki] s (cin) Sprechfilm m

talk'ing-to' s Denkzettel m

tall [tɔl] adj hoch; (person) hochgewachsen; **t. story** Mordsgeschichte f

tallow ['tælo] s Talg m

tal·ly ['tæli] s (reckoning) Rechnung f; (game score) Punktzahl f || v (pret & pp –lied) tr (up) berechnen || intr (with) übereinstimmen (mit)

tallyho [ˌtæli'ho] interj hallo!

tal'ly sheet' s Zählbogen m

talon ['tælən] s Klaue f

tambourine [ˌtæmbə'rin] s Tamburin n

tame [tem] adj zahm; (docile) gefügig; (dull) langweilig || tr zähmen; (e.g., lions) bändigen || intr–t. down (said of a person) gesetzter werden

tamp [tæmp] tr (a tobacco pipe) stopfen; (earth, cement) stampfen; (a drill hole) zustopfen

tamper ['tæmpər] s Stampfer m || intr –t. with sich einmischen in (acc); (machinery) herumbasteln an (dat); (documents) frisieren

tampon ['tæmpɑn] s Damenbinde f; (surg) Tampon m || tr (surg) tamponieren

tan [tæn] adj gelbbraun || s Sonnenbräunung f || v (pret & pp tanned; ger tanning) tr (the skin) bräunen; (leather) gerben || intr sich bräunen

tandem ['tændəm] adj & adv hintereinander (geordnet) || s Tandem n; **in t.** hintereinander

tang [tæŋ] s Herbheit f; (sound) Geklingel n

tangent ['tændʒənt] adj—**be t. to** tangieren || s Tangente f; **fly off on a t.** plötzlich vom Thema abschweifen

tangerine [ˌtændʒə'rin] s Mandarine f

tangible ['tændʒɪbəl] adj (& fig) greifbar

tangle ['tæŋgəl] s Verwicklung f; (twisted strands; confused jumble) Gewirr n; (conflict) Auseinandersetzung f || tr verwirren; **get tangled** sich verfilzen || intr sich verwirren; **t. with** sich in e-n Kampf einlassen mit

tango ['tæŋgo] s Tango m || intr Tango tanzen

tangy ['tæŋi] adj herb

tank [tæŋk] s Behälter m; (of a toilet) Spülkasten m; (mil) Panzer m

tank' attack' s Panzerangriff m

tank' car' s (rr) Kesselwagen m, Tankwagen m

tanker ['tæŋkər] s (truck) Tankwagen m; (ship) Tanker m; (plane) Tankflugzeug n

tank' trap' s Panzersperre f

tank' truck' s Tankwagen m

tanned adj gebräunt

tanner ['tænər] s Gerber –in mf

tannery ['tænəri] s Gerberei f

tantalize ['tæntəˌlaɪz] tr quälen

tantamount ['tæntəˌmaunt] adj—**be t. to** gleichkommen (dat)

tantrum ['tæntrəm] s Koller m; **throw a t.** e-n Koller kriegen

tap [tæp] s (light blow) Klaps m; (on a window or door) Klopfen n; (faucet) Wasserhahn m; (in a cask) Faßhahn m; (elec) Anzapfung f; (mach) Gewindebohrer m; (surg) Punktion f; **on tap** vom Faß; **play taps** (mil) den Zapfenstreich blasen || v (pret & pp tapped; ger tapping) tr (a cask, powerline, telephone) anzapfen; (fluids) abzapfen; (a person on the shoulder) antippen; (a hole) mit e-m Gewinde versehen; **tap one's foot** (to mark time) Takt treten; **tap s.o. for** (money) (coll) j-n anpumpen um; **tap s.o.'s spine** j-n punktieren; **tap the window** am Fenster klopfen || intr tippen

tap' dance' s Steptanz m

tap'-dance' intr steppen

tap' dan'cer s Stepper –in mf

tape [tep] s Band n; (electron) Tonband n; (friction tape) Isolierband n; (of paper) Papierstreifen m; (med) Klebstreifen m; (sport) Zielband n || tr (mit Band) umwickeln; (electron) auf Tonband aufnehmen

tape' meas'ure s Meßband n

taper ['tepər] s Wachsfaden m || tr zuspitzen || intr spitz zulaufen; **t. off** langsam abnehmen

tape' record'er s Tonbandgerät n

ta'pered adj kegelförmig, Keil-

tapestry ['tæpɪstri] s Wandteppich m

tape'worm' s Bandwurm m

tapioca [ˌtæpɪ'okə] s Tapioka f

tappet ['tæpɪt] s (mach) Stößel m

tap'room' s Ausschank m

tap'root' s Pfahlwurzel f

tap' wa'ter s Leitungswasser n

tap' wrench' s Gewindeschneidkluppe f

tar [tɑr] s Teer m || v (pret & pp tarred; ger tarring) tr teeren

tardy ['tɑrdi] adj säumig

target ['tɑrgɪt] s Ziel n; (on a firing range; of ridicule) Zielscheibe f

tar'get ar'ea s Zielraum m

tar'get date' s Zieltag m

tar'get lan'guage s Zielsprache f

tar'get prac'tice s Scheibenschießen n

tariff ['tærɪf] s Tarif m

tarnish ['tɑrnɪʃ] tr matt (or blind) machen; (fig) beflecken || intr matt (or blind) werden

tar' pa'per s Teerpappe f

tarpaulin ['tɑrpəlɪn] s Plane f

tar·ry ['tɑri] adj teerig || ['tæri] v

(*pret* & *pp* **-ried**) *intr* verweilen;
(*stay*) bleiben

tart [tɑrt] *adj* sauer; (*reply*) scharf ||
s Tortelett *n*

tartar ['tɑrtər] *s* (dent) Zahnstein *m*

tar'tar sauce' *s* pikante Soße *f*

task [tæsk] *s* Aufgabe *f*; **take to t.** zur
Rede stellen

task' force' *s* Sonderverband *m*

task'mas'ter *s* Zuchtmeister *m*

tassel ['tæsəl] *s* Quaste *f*; (*on corn*)
Narbenfäden *pl*

taste [test] *s* (& fig) Geschmack *m*;
develop a t. for Geschmack gewinnen an (*dat*); **have a bad t.** schlecht
|| *intr*—**t. like** (*or* **of**) schmecken
schmecken; **have bad t.** e-n schlechten Geschmack haben; **in bad t.** geschmacklos; **in good t.** geschmackvoll; **to t.** (culin) nach Gutdünken
|| *tr* schmecken; (*try out*) kosten;
(*e.g., the pepper in soup*) heraus-
schmecken; **t. blood** (fig) Blut lecken
nach

taste' bud' *s* Geschmacksknospe *f*

tasteful ['testfəl] *adj* geschmackvoll

tasteless ['testlɪs] *adj* (& fig) geschmacklos

tasty ['testi] *adj* schmackhaft

tatter ['tætər] *s* Lumpen *m* || *tr* zer-
fetzen

tat'tered *adj* zerlumpt

tattle ['tætəl] *intr* petzen

tattler ['tætlər] *s* Petze *f*

tat'fletale *s* Petze *f*

tattoo [tæ'tu] *s* Tätowierung *f* || *tr*
tätowieren

taunt [tɔnt] *s* Stichelei *f* || *tr* sticheln
gegen

taut [tɔt] *adj* straff, prall

tavern ['tævərn] *s* Schenke *f*

tawdry ['tɔdri] *adj* aufgedonnert

tawny ['tɔni] *adj* gelbbraun

tax [tæks] *s* Steuer *f* || *tr* besteuern;
(fig) beanspruchen; **tax s.o. with**
j-n rügen wegen

taxable ['tæksəbəl] *adj* steuerpflichtig

tax' assess'ment *s* Steuereinschätzung *f*

taxation [tæk'seʃən] *s* Besteuerung *f*

tax' brac'ket *s* Steuerklasse *f*

tax' collec'tor *s* Steuereinnehmer –in
mf

tax' cut' *s* Steuersenkung *f*

tax' eva'sion *s* Steuerhinterziehung *f*

tax' exemp'tion *s* steuerfreier Betrag *m*

tax-i ['tæksi] *s* Taxi *n*; **go by t.** mit
e-m Taxi fahren || *v* (*pret* & *pp*
-ied) *ger* **-iing** & **-ying**) *tr* (aer)
rollen lassen || *intr* mit e-m Taxi
fahren; (aer) rollen

tax'icab' *s* Taxi *n*

tax'i danc'er *s* Taxigirl *n*

taxidermist ['tæksɪ ˌdɑrmɪst] *s* Tier-
präparator –in *mf*

tax'i driv'er *s* Taxifahrer –in *mf*

tax'ime'ter *s* Taxameter *m*

tax'i stand' *s* Taxistand *m*

tax'pay'er *s* Steuerzahler –in *mf*

tax' rate' *s* Steuersatz *m*

tax' return' *s* Steuererklärung *f*

tea [ti] *s* Tee *m*

tea' bag' *s* Teebeutel *m*

tea' cart' *s* Teewagen *m*

teach [tit/] *v* (*pret* & *pp* **taught** [tɔt])
tr lehren; (*instruct*) unterrichten; **t.
school** an e-r Schule unterrichten;
t. s.o. manners j-m Manieren beibringen; **t. s.o. music** j-n in Musik
unterrichten; **t. s.o. (to play) tennis**
j-m das Tennisspielen beibringen ||
intr lehren, unterrichten

teacher ['tit/ər] *s* Lehrer –in *mf*

teach'er's pet' *s* Liebling *m* des Leh-
rers (or der Lehrerin)

teach'ing *s* Lehren *n*; (*profession*) Lehr-
beruf *m*

teach'ing aid' *s* Lehrmittel *n*

teach'ing staff' *s* Lehrkörper *m*

tea'cup' *s* Teetasse *f*

teak [tik] *s* Teakholz *n*

tea'ket'tle *s* Teekessel *m*

tea' leaves' *spl* Teesatz *m*

team [tim] *s* Team *n*; (*of draught animals*) Gespann *n*; (sport) Mannschaft
f || *tr* (*draft animals*) zusammen-
spannen || *intr*—**t. up with** sich ver-
einigen mit

team' cap'tain *s* Spielführer –in *mf*

team'mate' *s* Mannschaftskamerad –in
mf

teamster ['timstər] *s* Fuhrmann *m*;
(*trucker*) Lastwagenfahrer *m*

team'work' *s* Gemeinschaftsarbeit *f*;
(sport) Zusammenspiel *n*

tea'pot' *s* Teekanne *f*

tear [tɪr] *s* Träne *f*; **bring tears to the
eyes** Tränen in die Augen treiben;
burst into tears in Tränen ausbrechen
|| [ter] *s* Riß *m* || *v* (*pret* **tore** [tor];
pp **torn** [torn]) *tr* (zer)reißen; **t.
apart** (*meat*) zerreißen; (*a speech*)
zerpflücken; **t. away** wegreißen; **t.
down** (*a building*) abreißen; (mach)
zerlegen; (*a person*) sich [*dat*] das
Maul zerreißen über (*acc*); **t. off**
abreißen; **t. open** aufreißen; **t. oneself away** sich losreißen; **t. out** ausreißen; **t. up** (*a street*) aufreißen;
(*e.g., letter*) zerreißen || *intr* (zer)-
reißen; **t. along** (*at high speed*) da-
hinsausen

teardrop ['tɪr ˌdrɑp] *s* Träne *f*

tear' gas' [tɪr] *s* Tränengas *n*

tear-jerker ['tɪr ˌdʒʌrkər] *s* (sl)
Schnulze *f*

tea'room' *s* Teestube *f*

tease [tiz] *tr* necken; (*e.g., a dog*)
quälen; (*hair*) auflockern

teas'ing *s* Neckerei *f*

tea'spoon' *s* Teelöffel *m*

teaspoonful ['ti ˌspun ˌful] *s* Teelöffel
m

teat [tit] *s* Zitze *f*

technical ['teknɪkəl] *adj* technisch,
Fach–

tech'nical in'stitute *s* technische Hochschule *f*

technicality [ˌtekni'kælɪti] *s* technische Einzelheit *f*

tech'nical school' *s* Technikum *n*

tech'nical term' *s* Fachausdruck *m*

technician [tek'nɪ/ən] *s* Techniker –in
mf

technique [tek'nik] *s* Technik *f*

technocrat ['tɛknə‚kræt] s Technokrat m

technological [‚tɛknə'lɑdʒɪkəl] adj technologisch

technology [tɛk'nɑlɪdʒɪ] s Technologie f

ted'dy bear' ['tɛdɪ] s Teddybär m

tedious ['tidɪ‚əs] adj langweilig

tee [ti] s (mound) Abschlagplatz m; (wooden or plastic peg) Aufsatz m; **to a tee** aufs Haar || intr—**tee off** (sl) aufregen; **tee up** (golf) auf den Aufsatz stellen || intr—**tee off** (golf) abschlagen

teem [tim] intr (**with**) wimmeln (von)

teem'ing adj wimmelnd; (rain) strömend

teen-age ['tin‚edʒ] adj halbwüchsig

teen-ager ['tin‚edʒər] s Teenager m

teens [tinz] spl Jugendalter n (vom dreizehnten bis neunzehnten Lebensjahr); **in one's t.** in den Jugendjahren

teeny ['tini] adj (coll) winzig

tee' shot' s (golf) Abschlag m

teeter ['titər] s Schaukeln n || intr schaukeln

teethe [tið] intr zahnen

teeth'ing ring' s Beißring m

teetotaler [ti'totələr] s Abstinenzler m

tele·cast ['tɛlɪ‚kæst] s Fernsehsendung f || v (pret & pp -cast & -casted) tr im Fernsehen übertragen

telecommunications [‚tɛlɪkə‚mjunɪ'ke‚ʃəns] spl Fernmeldewesen n

telegram ['tɛlɪ‚græm] s Telegramm n

telegraph ['tɛlɪ‚græf] s Telegraph m || tr & intr telegraphieren

telegrapher [tɪ'lɛgrəfər] s Telegraphist –in mf

tel'egraph pole' s Telegraphenstange f

telemeter [tɪ'lɛmɪtər] s Telemeter n

telepathy [tɪ'lɛpəθɪ] s Telepathie f

telephone ['tɛlɪ‚fon] s Telephon n, Fernsprecher m; **be on the t.** am Apparat sein; **by t.** telephonisch; **speak on the t. with** telephonieren mit || tr & intr anrufen

tel'ephone booth' s Telephonzelle f

tel'ephone call' s Telephonanruf m

tel'ephone direc'tory s Teilnehmerverzeichnis n

tel'ephone exchange' s Telephonzentrale f

tel'ephone num'ber s Telephonnummer f

tel'ephone op'erator s Telephonist –in mf

tel'ephone receiv'er s Telephonhörer m

tel'ephoto lens' ['tɛlɪ‚foto] s Teleobjektiv n

telescope ['tɛlɪ‚skop] s Fernrohr n, Perspektiv n || tr ineinanderschieben; (fig) verkürzen || intr sich ineinanderschieben

telescopic [‚tɛlɪ'skɑpɪk] adj teleskopisch

telescop'ic sight' s Zielfernrohr n

Teletype ['tɛlɪ‚taɪp] s (trademark) Fernschreiber m || **teletype** tr durch Fernschreiber übermitteln || intr fernschreiben

tel'etype'writ'er s Fernschreiber m

televiewer ['tɛlɪ‚vju‚ər] s Fernsehteilnehmer –in mf

televise ['tɛlɪ‚vaɪz] tr im Fernsehen übertragen (or senden)

television ['tɛlɪ‚vɪʒən] adj Fernseh– || s Fernsehen n; **watch t.** fernsehen

tel'evision net'work s Fernsehnetz n

tel'evision screen' s Bildschirm m

tel'evision set' s Fernsehapparat m; **color t.** Farbfernsehapparat m

tel'evision show' s Fernschau f

telex ['tɛlɛks] s Fernschreiber m; (message) Telex n || tr fernschreiben

tell [tɛl] v (pret & pp told [told]) tr (the truth, a lie) sagen; (relate) erzählen; (a secret) anvertrauen; (let know) Bescheid sagen (dat); (inform) bestellen; (express) ausdrücken; (the reason) angeben; (distinguish) auseinanderhalten; **be able to t. time** die Uhr lesen können; **t. apart** auseinanderhalten; **t. me another!** (sl) das machst du mir nicht weis!; **t. s.o. off** j-n abkanzeln; **t. s.o. that** (assure s.o. that) j-m versichern, daß; **t. s.o. to** (inf) j-m sagen, daß er (inf) soll; **t. s.o. where to get off** (sl) j-m e-e Zigarre verpassen; **to t. the truth** ehrlich gesagt; **you can t. by looking at her that** man sieht es ihr an, daß || intr—**t. on t. me!** na, so was!; **t. on** (betray) verraten; (produce a marked effect on) sehr mitnehmen; **you're telling me!** wem sagst du das!

teller ['tɛlər] s (of a bank) Kassierer –in mf; (of votes) Zähler –in mf

tell'ing adj (blow) wirksam

tell'-tale' adj verräterisch

temper ['tɛmpər] s (anger) Zorn m; (of steel) Härtegrad m; **bad t.** großer Zorn m; **even t.** Gleichmut m; **lose one's t.** in Wut geraten || tr (with) mildern (durch); (steel) härten; (mus) temperieren

temperament ['tɛmpərəmənt] s Temperament n

temperamental [‚tɛmpərə'mɛntəl] adj launisch, temperamentvoll

temperance ['tɛmpərəns] s Mäßigkeit f

temperate ['tɛmpərɪt] adj mäßig; (climate) gemäßigt

Tem'perate Zone' s gemäßigte Zone f

temperature ['tɛmərət/ər] s Temperatur f

tempest ['tɛmpɪst] s Sturm m; **a t. in a teapot** ein Sturm im Wasserglas

tempestuous [tɛm'pɛst/ʊ‚əs] adj stürmisch

temple ['tɛmpəl] s Tempel m; (of glasses) Bügel m; (anat) Schläfe f

tem·po ['tɛmpo] s (-pos & -pi [pi]) Tempo n

temporal ['tɛmpərəl] adj zeitlich

temporary ['tɛmpə‚rerɪ] adj zeitweilig; (credit, solution) Zwischen–

temporize ['tɛmpə‚raɪz] intr Zeit zu gewinnen suchen

tempt [tɛmpt] tr versuchen; (said of things) reizen, locken

temptation [temp'teʃən] s Versuchung f

tempter ['temptər] s Versucher m

tempt'ing adj verlockend

temptress ['temptrɪs] s Versucherin f

ten [ten] adj & pron zehn ‖ s Zehn f

tenable ['tenəbəl] adj haltbar

tenacious [tɪ'neʃəs] adj (obstinate) nartnäckig; (memory) verläßlich

tenacity [tɪ'næsɪti] s Hartnäckigkeit f

tenant ['tenənt] s Mieter –in mf

ten'ant farm'er s Pächter –in mf

tend [tend] tr (flocks) hüten; (the sick) pflegen; (a machine) bedienen ‖ intr—t. to (attend to) sich kümmern um; (inf) dazu neigen zu (inf); t. toward(s) neigen zu

tendency ['tendənsi] s Tendenz f

tender ['tendər] adj zart ‖ s Angebot n; (nav, rr) Tender m ‖ tr anbieten

ten'derfoot' s Neuankömmling m; (boyscout) neu aufgenommener Pfadfinder m

ten'derheart'ed adj zartfühlend

ten'derloin' s Rindslendenstück n

tenderness ['tendərnɪs] s Zartheit f

tendon ['tendən] s Sehne f

tendril ['tendrɪl] s Ranke f

tenement ['tenɪmənt] s (dwelling) Wohnung f; (rented dwelling) Mietwohnung f

ten'ement house' s Mietskaserne f

tenet ['tenɪt] s Grundsatz m, Lehrsatz m

ten'fold' adj & adv zehnfach

tennis ['tenɪs] s Tennis n

ten'nis court' s Tennisplatz m

ten'nis rack'et s Tennisschläger m

tenor ['tenər] s (drift, meaning; singer; voice range) Tenor m

ten'pin' s Kegel m

tense [tens] adj gespannt, straff; **make t.** spannen ‖ s (gram) Tempus n, Zweitform f

tension ['tenʃən] s (& elec) Spannung f; (phys) Spannkraft f

tent [tent] s Zelt n

tentacle ['tentəkəl] s Fühler m; (bot) Tentakel m

tentative ['tentətɪv] adj vorläufig

tenth [tenθ] adj & pron zehnte ‖ s (fraction) Zehntel n; the t. (in dates and in series) der Zehnte

tent' pole' s Zeltstange f

tenuous ['tenju·əs] adj (thin) dünn; (rarefied) verdünnt; (insignificant) unbedeutend; (weak) schwach

tenure ['tenjər] s (possession) Besitz m; (educ) Anstellung f auf Lebenszeit; **t. of office** Amtsdauer f

tepid ['tepɪd] adj lauwarm

term [tʌrm] s (expression) Ausdruck m; (time period) Frist f; (of office) Amtszeit f; (jur) Sitzungsperiode f; (math) Glied n; (log) Begriff m; **be on good terms with** in guten Beziehungen stehen mit; **come to terms with** handelseinig werden mit; **in plain terms** unverblümt; **in terms of** im Sinne von; **in terms of praise** mit lobenden Worten; **on easy terms** zu günstigen Bedingungen; **on equal terms** auf gleichem Fuß; **on t.** (com) auf Zeit; **not be on speaking terms with** nicht sprechen mit; **tell s.o. in no uncertain terms** j–m gründlich die Meinung sagen; **terms** (of a contract, treaty, payment) Bedingungen pl ‖ tr bezeichnen

termagant ['tʌrməgənt] s Xanthippe f

terminal ['tʌrmɪnəl] adj End–; (disease) unheilbar ‖ s (aer) Flughafenempfangsgebäude n; (pole) (elec) Pol m; (rr) Kopfbahnhof m

terminate ['tʌrmɪˌnet] tr (end) beenden; (limit) begrenzen ‖ intr enden, endigen; (gram) (in) auslauten (auf acc)

termination [ˌtʌrmɪ'neʃən] s Beendigung f; (gram) Endung f

terminology [ˌtʌrmɪ'nɑlɪdʒi] s Terminologie f

terminus ['tʌrmɪnəs] s (end) Endpunkt m; (boundary) Grenze f; (rr) Endstation f

termite ['tʌrmaɪt] s Termite f

term' pa'per s Referat n

terrace ['terəs] s Terrasse f ‖ tr abstufen, terrassieren

terra cotta ['terə'kɑtə] s Terrakotta f

ter'ra-cot'ta adj Terrakotta–

terrain [te'ren] s Gelände n, Terrain n

terrestrial [tə'restrɪ·əl] adj irdisch

terrible ['terɪbəl] adj furchtbar

terribly ['terɪbli] adv (coll) furchtbar

terrier ['teri·ər] s Terrier m

terrific [tə'rɪfɪk] adj (frightful) fürchterlich; (intense) (coll) gewaltig; (splendid) (coll) prima

terri•fy ['terɪˌfaɪ] v (pret & pp –fied) tr Entsetzen einjagen (dat)

ter'rifying adj schrecklich

territorial [ˌterɪ'tori·əl] adj territorial; **t. waters** Hoheitsgewässer pl

territory ['terɪˌtori] s Gebiet n, Territorium n; (of a salesman) Absatzgebiet n; (pol) Hoheitsgebiet n; (sport) Spielhälfte f

terror ['terər] s Schrecken m; **in t. vor** Schrecken

terrorism ['terəˌrɪzəm] s Terrorismus m

terrorist ['terərɪst] s Terrorist –in mf

terrorize ['terəˌraɪz] tr terrorisieren

ter'ror-strick'en adj schreckerfüllt

ter'ry cloth' ['teri] s Frottee m & n

terse [tʌrs] adj knapp

tertiary ['tʌrʃɪˌeri] adj Tertiär–

test [test] s Probe f, Prüfung f; (criterion) Prüfstein m; (med) Probe f; **put to the t.** auf die Probe stellen ‖ tr (for) prüfen (auf acc); (chem) (for) analysieren (auf acc); **t. out** (coll) ausprobieren

testament ['testəmənt] s Testament n

testator [tes'tetər] s Erblasser –in mf

test' ban' s Atomstopp m

test' case' s Probefall m; (jur) Präzedenzfall m

test'flight' s Probeflug m

testicle ['testɪkəl] s Hoden m

testi•fy ['testɪˌfaɪ] v (pret & pp –fied)

intr (*against*) zeugen (gegen), aussagen (gegen); **t. to** bezeugen

estimonial [‚testɪˈmonɪ-əl] *adj* (*dinner*) Ehren– || *s* Anerkennungsschreiben *n*

estimony [ˈtestɪˌmoni] *s* Zeugnis *n*

est' pa'per *s* Prüfungsarbeit *f*

est' pi'lot *s* Versuchsflieger –in *mf*

est' tube' *s* Reagenzglas *n*

esty [ˈtesti] *adj* reizbar

etanus [ˈtetənəs] *s* Starrkrampf *m*

ether [ˈteðər] *s* Haltestrick *m*; **be at the end of one's t.** nicht mehr weiter wissen || *tr* anbinden

Teuton [ˈt(j)utən] *s* Teutone *m*, Teutonin *f*

Teutonic [t(j)uˈtɑnɪk] *adj* teutonisch

text [tekst] *s* Text *m*

text'book' *s* Lehrbuch *n*

textile [ˈtekstaɪl] *adj* Textil– || *s* Webstoff *m*; **textiles** Textilien *pl*

textual [ˈtekst/ʊ-əl] *adj* textlich

texture [ˈtekst/ər] *s* (*structure*) Gefüge *n*; (*of a fabric*) Gewebe *n*; (*of a play*) Aufbau *m*

Thai [taɪ] *adj* Thai– || *s* (*person*) Thai –in *mf*; (*language*) Thai *n*

Thailand [ˈtaɪlənd] *s* Thailand *n*

Thames [temz] *s* Themse *f*

than [ðæn] *conj* als; **t. ever** denn je

thank [θæŋk] *adj* (*offering*) Dank– || **thanks** *spl* Dank *m*; **give thanks to** danken (*dat*); **many thanks!** vielen Dank!; **return thanks** danksagen; **thanks a lot!** danke vielmals!; **thanks to her, I** ich verdanke es ihr, daß ich || **t danken** (*dat*); **t. God!** Gott sei Dank!; **t. goodness!** gottlob!; **t. you!** danke schön!; **t. you ever so much!** verbindlichsten Dank!; **you have only yourself to t. for that** das hast du dir nur selbst zu verdanken

thankful [ˈθæŋkfəl] *adj* dankbar

thankless [ˈθæŋklɪs] *adj* undankbar

Thanksgiv'ing Day' *s* Danksagungstag *m*

that [ðæt] *adj* jener, der; **t. one** der da, jener || *adv* (coll) so, derart || *rel pron* der, welcher; (*after indefinite pronouns*) was || *dem pron* das; **about t.** darüber; **after t.** danach; **and that's t.** und damit punktum!; **at t.** so, dabei; **by t.** dadurch; **for t.** dafür; **from t.** daraus; **in t.** darin, daran; **on t.** darauf, drauf; **t. is** das heißt; **that's out** das kommt nicht in Frage!; **t. will do!** das reicht! || *conj* daß

thatch [θæt/] *s* Dachstroh *n*

thatched' roof' *s* Strohdach *n*

thaw [θɔ] *s* Tauwetter *n* || *tr & intr* (auf)tauen

the [ðə], [ði] *def art* der, die, das || *adv*—**so much the better** um so besser; **the ... the** je ... desto, je ... um so

theater [ˈθi-ətər] *s* Theater *n*

the'atergo'er *s* Theaterbesucher –in *mf*

the'ater of war' *s* Kriegsschauplatz *m*

theatrical [θɪˈætrɪkəl] *adj* (& fig) theatralisch

thee [ði] *pers pron* dich; **to t.** dir

theft [θeft] *s* Diebstahl *m*

their [ðer] *poss adj* ihr

theirs [ðerz] *poss pron* ihrer

them [ðem] *pron* sie; **to t.** ihnen

theme [θim] *s* Thema *n*; (*essay*) Aufsatz *m*; (mus) Thema *n*

theme' song' *s* Kennmelodie *f*

themselves' *intens pron* selbst, selber || *reflex pron* sich

then [ðen] *adv* (*next; in that case*) dann; (*at that time*) damals; **by t.** bis dahin; **from t. on** von da an; **t. and there** auf der Stelle; **till t.** bis dahin; **what t.?** was dann?

thence [ðens] *adv* von da, von dort; (*from that fact*) daraus

thence'forth' *adv* von da an

theologian [‚θi-əˈlodʒən] *s* Theologe *m*, Theologin *f*

theological [‚θi-əˈlɑdʒɪkəl] *adj* theologisch

theology [θiˈɑlədʒi] *s* Theologie *f*

theorem [ˈθi-ərəm] *s* Lehrsatz *m*

theoretical [‚θi-əˈretɪkəl] *adj* theoretisch

theorist [ˈθi-ərɪst] *s* Theoretiker –in *mf*

theorize [ˈθi-əˌraɪz] *intr* theoretisieren

theory [ˈθi-əri] *s* Theorie *f*, Lehre *f*

the'ory of relativ'ity *s* Relativitätstheorie *f*

therapeutic [‚θerəˈpjutɪk] *adj* therapeutisch || **therapeutics** *s* Therapeutik *f*

therapy [ˈθerəpi] *s* Therapie *f*

there [ðer] *adv* (*position*) da; (*direction*) dahin; **down t.** da unten; **not be all t.** (coll) nicht ganz richtig sein; **over t.** da drüben; **t. are es gibt, es sind; t. is es gibt, es ist; t., t.!** sachte, sachte!; **up t.** da (or dort) oben

there'abouts' *adv* daherum; **ten people or t.** so ungefähr zehn Leute

there'af'ter *adv* danach

there'by' *adv* dadurch, damit

therefore [ˈðer ˌfor] *adv* deshalb, darum

there'in' *adv* darin

there'of' *adv* davon

there'to' *adv* dazu

there'upon' *adv* daraufhin, danach

there'with' *adv* damit

thermal [ˈθɑrməl] *adj* Thermal–, Wärme–

thermodynamic [‚θɑrmodaɪˈnæmɪk] *adj* thermodynamisch || **thermodynamics** *s* Thermodynamik *f*, Wärmelehre *f*

thermometer [θerˈmɑmɪtər] *s* Thermometer *n*

thermonuclear [‚θermoˈn(j)uklɪ-ər] *adj* thermonuklear

ther'mos bot'tle [ˈθɑrməs] *s* Thermosflasche *f*

thermostat [ˈθɑrmə ˌstæt] *s* Thermostat *m*

thesau·rus [θɪˈsɔrəs] *s* (**–ri** [raɪ]) Thesaurus *m*

these [ðiz] *dem adj & pron* diese

the·sis [ˈθisɪs] *s* (**–ses** [siz]) These *f*

they [ðe] *pers pron* sie; **t. say** man sagt

thick [θɪk] *adj* dick; (*dense*) dicht;

(*stupid*) stumpfsinnig; (*lips*) wulstig; (*intimate*) (coll) dick; **t. with dust** dick bedeckt mit Staub ‖ *adv*—**be in t. with** (coll dicke Beziehungen haben mit; **come t. and fast** Schlag auf Schlag gehen; **lay it on t.** (coll) dick auftragen ‖ *s*—**in the t. of** mitten in (*dat*); **through t. and thin** durch dick und dünn

thicken ['θɪkən] *tr* verdicken; (*make denser*) verdichten; (*a sauce*) eindicken ‖ *intr* sich verdicken; (*become denser*) sich verdichten; (*said of liquids*) sich verfestigen; (*said of a sauce*) eindicken; **the plot thickens** der Knoten schürzt sich

thicket ['θɪkɪt] *s* Dickicht *n*

thick'head' *s* (coll) Dickkopf *m*

thick'-head'ed *adj* (coll) dickköpfig

thickness ['θɪknɪs] *s* Dicke *f*

thick'-set' *adj* stämmig

thick'skinned' *adj* (coll) dickfellig

thief [θif] *s* (thieves [θivz]) Dieb –in *mf*

thieve [θiv] *intr* stehlen

thievery ['θivəri] *s* Dieberei *f*

thievish ['θivɪʃ] *adj* diebisch

thigh [θaɪ] *s* Schenkel *m*, Oberschenkel *m*

thighbone' *s* Oberschenkelknochen *m*

thimble ['θɪmbəl] *s* Fingerhut *m*

thin [θɪn] *adj* (thinner; thinnest) dünn; (*hair*) schütter; (*lean*) mager; (*excuse*) schwach; (*soup*) wäßrig ‖ *v* (*pret* & *pp* thinned; *ger* thinning) *tr* (*a liquid*) verdünnen; (*a forest*) lichten; **t. out** (*plants*) vereinzeln ‖ *intr* (*said of hair*) sich lichten; **t. out** (*said of a crowd*) sich verlaufen

thing [θɪŋ] *s* Ding *n*, Sache *f*; **among other things** unter anderem; **first t.** zu allerest; **how are things?** wie geht's?; **I'll do no such t.!** ich werde mich schön hüten; **of all things!** na sowas!; **the real t.** das Richtige; **things** (*the situation*) die Lage *f*; (*belongings*) Sachen *pl*

think [θɪŋk] *v* (*pret* & *pp* thought [θɔt]) *tr* denken; (*regard*) halten; (*believe*) glauben, denken; **he thinks he's clever** er hält sich für klug; **that's what you t.!** ja, denkste!; **t. better of it** sich e-s Besseren besinnen; **t. it best to** (*inf*) es für das Beste halten zu (*inf*); **t. little of** nicht viel halten von; **t. nothing of it!** es ist nicht der Rede wert!; **t. over** sich [*dat*] überlegen; **t. up** sich [*dat*] ausdenken; **what do you t. you're doing?** was soll das? ‖ *intr* denken; **be thinking of** (*ger*) beabsichtigen zu (*inf*); **do you t. so?** meinen Sie?; **t. about** (*call to consciousness*) denken an (*acc*); (*reflect on*) nachdenken über (*acc*); (*be concerned about*) bedacht sein auf (*acc*); **t. twice before** es sich [*dat*] zweimal überlegen, bevor

thinker ['θɪŋkər] *s* Denker –in *mf*

thin'-lipped' *adj* dünnlippig

thinner ['θɪnər] *s* Verdünnungsmittel *n*

third [θɪrd] *adj* & *pron* dritte ‖ *s* (*frac-*

tion) Drittel *n*; (mus) Terz *f*; **th third** (*in dates and in series*) de Dritte

third'-class' *adj* & *adv* dritter Klass

third' degree' *s*—**give s.o. the t.** j-e-m Folterverhör unterwerfen

third' par'ty *s* Dritter *m*, dritte Seite

third'-rate' *adj* drittrangig

thirst [θʌrst] *s* (for) Durst *m* (nach **t. for knowledge** Wissensdurst *m* **t. for power** Herrschsucht *f* ‖ *int* (for) dürsten (nach)

thirsty ['θʌrsti] *adj* durstig; **be t** Durst haben

thirteen ['θʌr'tin] *adj* & *pron* dreizeh ‖ *s* Dreizehn *f*

thirteenth ['θʌr'tinθ] *adj* & *pron* drei zehnte ‖ *s* (*fraction*) Dreizehntel *n* **the t.** (*in dates and in series*) de Dreizehnte

thirtieth ['θʌrtɪ-ɪθ] *adj* & *pron* drei ßigste ‖ *s* (*fraction*) Dreißigstel *n* **the t.** (*in dates and in series*) de Dreißigste

thirty ['θʌrti] *adj* & *pron* dreißig ‖ *s* Dreißig *f*; **the thirties** die dreißige Jahre

thir'ty-one' *adj* & *pron* einunddreißig

this [ðɪs] *dem adj* dieser; **t. afternoo** heute nachmittag; **t. evening** heut abend; **t. minute** augenblicklich; **t one** dieser ‖ *adv* (coll) so ‖ *den pron* dieser, der; **about t.** hierüber (*concerning this*) davon; **t. and tha** dies und jenes

thistle ['θɪsəl] *s* Distel *f*

thither ['θɪðər] *adv* dorthin, hinzu

thong [θɔŋ] *s* Riemen *m*; (*sandal* Sandale *f*

tho·rax ['θoræks] *s* (–raxes & –race [rə‚siz]) Brustkorb *m*

thorn [θɔrn] *s* Dorn *m*; **t. in the side** Dorn *m* im Fleisch

thorny ['θɔrni] *adj* dornig; (fig) heikle

thorough ['θʌro] *adj* gründlich; (coll. tüchtig

thor'oughbred' *adj* reinrassig ‖ *s* Voll blut *n*; (*horse*) Vollblutpferd *n*, Ras sepferd *n*

thor'oughfare' *s* Durchgang *m*; **no t** (*public sign*) Durchgang verboten

thor'oughgo'ing *adj* gründlich

thoroughly ['θʌroli] *adv* gründlich

those [ðoz] *dem adj* & *pron* jene, die da

thou [ðaʊ] *pers pron* du

though [ðo] *adv* immerhin ‖ *conj* ob wohl

thought [θɔt] *s* Gedanke(n) *m*; **be lost in t.** in Gedanken versunken sein; **give some t. to** sich [*dat*] Gedanke machen über (*acc*); **have second thoughts** sich [*dat*] eines Besseren besinnen; **on second t.** nach reiflicher Überlegung; **the mere t.** schon der Gedanke

thoughtful ['θɔtfəl] *adj* (*reflective*) nachdenklich; (*e.g., essay*) gedanken voll; (*considerate*) aufmerksam; (*gift* sinnig; **t. of** bedacht auf (*acc*)

thoughtless ['θɔtlɪs] *adj* gedankenlos

thought'-provok'ing *adj* anregend

thousand ['θauzənd] *adj & pron* tausend; **a t. times** tausendmal || *s* Tausend *f*; **by the t.** zu Tausenden

thousandth ['θauzəndθ] *adj & pron* tausendste || *s* (*fraction*) Tausendstel *n*

thrash [θræʃ] *tr* (& *fig*) dreschen; **t. out** (*debate*) gründlich erörtern || *intr* dreschen; **t. about** sich hin- und herwerfen

thrash'ing *s* Dreschen *n*; (*beating*) Dresche *f*

thread [θred] *s* Faden *m*; (*of a screw*) Gewinde *n*; (*of a story*) Faden *m*; **hang by a t.** an e-m Faden hängen || *tr* (*a needle*) einfädeln; (*pearls*) aufreihen; (*mach*) Gewinde schneiden in (*acc*)

thread'bare' *adj* fadenscheinig

threat [θret] *s* Drohung *f*

threaten ['θretən] *tr* drohen (*dat*), bedrohen; **t. so. with s.th.** j-m etw androhen || *intr* drohen

three [θri] *adj & pron* drei || *s* Drei *f*; **in threes** zu dritt

three' cheers' *spl* ein dreimaliges Hoch *n*

three'-dimen'sional *adj* dreidimensional

three'-en'gine *adj* dreimotorig

three'-piece' *adj* (*suit*) dreiteilig

three'-ply' *adj* dreischichtig

three'-point' land'ing *s* Dreipunktlandung *f*

threnody ['θrenədi] *s* Klagelied *n*

thresh [θreʃ] *tr* dreschen; **t. out** (*debate*) gründlich erörten || *intr* dreschen

thresh'ing floor' *s* Dreschtenne *f*

thresh'ing machine' *s* Dreschmaschine *f*

threshold ['θreʃold] *s* Türschwelle *f*; (*psychol*) Schwelle *f*

thrice [θrais] *adv* dreimal

thrift [θrift] *s* Sparsamkeit *f*

thrifty ['θrifti] *adj* sparsam

thrill [θril] *s* Nervenkitzel *m* || *tr* erregen, packen

thriller ['θrilər] *s* Thriller *m*

thrill'ing *adj* packend, spannend

thrive [θraiv] *v* (*pret* **thrived** & **throve** [θrov]; *pp* **thrived** & **thriven** ['θrivən]) *intr* gedeihen

throat [θrot] *s* Kehle *f*; **clear one's t.** sich räuspern; **cut one another's t.** (*fig*) sich gegenseitig kaputt machen; **cut one's own t.** (*fig*) sich [*dat*] sein eigenes Grab schaufeln; **jump down so.'s t.** j-m an die Gurgel fahren; **sore t.** Halsweh *n*

throb [θrab] *s* Schlagen *n*; (*of a motor*) Dröhnen *n* || *v* (*pret & pp* **throbbed**; *ger* **throbbing**) *intr* schlagen; (*said of a motor or head*) dröhnen

throes [θroz] *spl* Schmerzen *pl*; **be in the t. of death** im Todeskampf liegen

thrombosis [θram'bosis] *s* Thrombose *f*

throne [θron] *s* Thron *m*

throng [θrɔŋ] *s* Menschenmenge *f* || *tr* umdrängen; (*the streets*) sich drängen in (*acc*) || *intr* (*around*) sich drängen (um)

throttle ['θratəl] *s* Drossel(klappe) *f* || *tr* drosseln; (*a person*) erwürgen || *intr*—**t. back** (*aut*) das Gas zurücknehmen

through [θru] *adj* (*traffic, train*) Durchgangs–; (*street*) durchgehend; (*finished*) fertig; (*coll*) quitt || *adv*— **t. and t.** durch und durch || *prep* durch (*acc*)

throughout' *adv* durch und durch || *prep* hindurch (*acc*) (*postpositive*), e.g., **t. the summer** den ganzen Sommer hindurch; **t. the world** in der ganzen Welt

throw [θro] *s* Wurf *m*; (*scarf*) Überwurf *m* || *v* (*pret* **threw** [θru]; *pp* **thrown** [θron]) *tr* werfen; (*a rider*) abwerfen; (*sparks*) sprühen; (*a party, banquet*) geben; (*a game*) absichtlich verlieren; (*into confusion*) bringen; **t. away** wegwerfen; **t. down** niederwerfen; (*overturn*) umwerfen; **t. in** (*e.g., a few extras*) als Zugabe geben; **t. off** (*fig*) aus dem Gleichgewicht bringen; **t. out** hinauswerfen; (*a person*) vor die Tür setzen; (*the chest*) herausdrücken; **t. out of the game** vom Platz verweisen; **t. the book at so.** (*fig*) j-n zur Höchststrafe verurteilen; **t. up to so.** j-m vorwerfen || *intr* werfen; **t. up** sich erbrechen

throw'away' *adj* Einweg–

throw'back' *s* (to) Rückkehr *f* (zu)

throw' rug' *s* Vorleger *m*

thrum [θrʌm] *v* (*pret & pp* **thrummed;** *ger* **thrumming**) *intr* (on) mit den Fingern trommeln (auf *acc*)

thrush [θrʌʃ] *s* (orn) Drossel *f*

thrust [θrʌst] *s* (*shove*) Stoß *m*; (*stab*) Hieb *m*; (aer, archit, geol, rok) Schub *m*; (mil) Vorstoß *m* || *v* (*pret & pp* **thrust**) *tr* stoßen

thud [θʌd] *s* Bums *m* || *v* (*pret & pp* **thudded;** *ger* **thudding**) *tr & intr* bumsen || *interj* bums!

thug [θʌg] *s* Rocker *m*

thumb [θʌm] *s* Daumen *m*; **be all thumbs** zwei linke Hände haben; **be under so.'s t.** unter j-s Fuchtel stehen; **thumbs down!** pfui!; **thumbs up!** Kopf hoch! || *tr* (*a book*) abgreifen; **t. a ride** per Anhalter fahren; **t. one's nose at so.** j-m e-e lange Nase machen || *intr*—**t. through** durchblättern

thumb' in'dex *s* Daumenindex *m*

thumb'print' *s* Daumenabdruck *m*

thumb'screw' *s* Flügelschraube *f*

thumb'tack' *s* Reißnagel *m*

thump [θʌmp] *s* Bums *m* || *tr & intr* bumsen || *interj* bums!

thump'ing *adj* (coll) enorm

thunder ['θʌndər] *s* Donner *m* || *tr & intr* donnern

thun'derbolt' *s* Donnerkeil *m*

thun'derclap' *s* Donnerschlag *m*

thunderous ['θʌndərəs] *adj* donnernd

thun'dershow'er *s* Gewitterregen *m*

thun'derstorm' *s* Gewitter *n*

thunderstruck ['θʌndər‚strʌk] *adj* (fig) wie vom Schlag getroffen

Thursday ['θʌrzde] *s* Donnerstag *m*; **on T.** am Donnerstag

thus [ðʌs] *adv* so; (*consequently*) also;
t. far soweit

thwack [θwæk] *s* heftiger Schlag *m* ||
tr klatschen

thwart [θwɔrt] *adj* Quer– || *s* (naut)
Ruderbank *f* || *tr* (*plans*) durch-
kreuzen; (*a person*) in die Quere
kommen (*dat*)

thy [ðaɪ] *poss adj* dein

thyme [taɪm] *s* Thymian *m*

thy'roid gland' ['θaɪrɔɪd] *s* Schild-
drüse *f*

thyself [ðaɪ'sɛlf] *intens pron* selbst,
selber || *reflex pron* dich

tiara [taɪ'ɛrə] *s* Tiara *f*; (*lady's head-
dress*) Diadem *n*

tibia ['tɪbɪə] *s* Schienbein *n*

tic [tɪk] *s* (pathol) Tick *m*

tick [tɪk] *s* (*of a clock*) Ticken *n*;
(*mattress case*) Überzug *m*; (ent)
Zecke *f*; **on t.** (coll) auf Pump || *tr*—
be ticked off (*at*) (sl) verärgert sein
(über *acc*); **t. off** (*names*, *items*) ab-
haken; (*the minutes*) ticken || *intr*
ticken; **t. by vergehen

ticker ['tɪkər] *s* (*watch*) (sl) Uhr *f*,
Armbanduhr *f*; (*heart*) (sl) Herz *n*;
(st. exch.) Börsentelegraph *m*

tick'er tape' *s* Papierstreifen *m* (des
Börsentelegraphen)

tick'er-tape parade' *s* Konfettiregen-
parade *f*

ticket ['tɪkɪt] *s* Karte *f*; (*for travel*)
Fahrkarte *f*; (*by air*) Flugkarte *f*;
(*for admission*) Eintrittskarte *f*; (*in
a lottery*) Los *n*; (*for a traffic violation*) Strafzettel *m*; (pol) Wahlliste
f || *tr* etikettieren; (aut) mit e–m
Strafzettel versehen

tick'et a'gency *s* Vorverkaufsstelle *f*

tick'et a'gent *s* Fahrkartenverkäufer –in
mf

tick'et of'fice *s* Kartenverkaufsstelle *f*

tick'et win'dow *s* Schalter *m*

tick'ing *s* Ticken *n*

tickle ['tɪkəl] *s* Kitzel *m* || *tr* kitzeln
|| *intr* jucken

ticklish ['tɪklɪʃ] *adj* kitzlig; (*touchy*)
heikel

ticktock ['tɪk͵tak] *adv*—**go t.** ticktack
machen || *s* Ticken *n*

tid'al wave' ['taɪdəl] *s* Flutwelle *f*

tidbit ['tɪd͵bɪt] *s* Leckerbissen *m*

tiddlywinks ['tɪdlɪ͵wɪŋks] *s* Flohhüpf-
spiel *n*

tide [taɪd] *s* Gezeiten *pl*; **against the t.**
(fig) gegen den Strom; **the t. is com-
ing in** die Flut steigt; **the t. is going
out** die Flut fällt || *tr*—**t. s.o. over**
j–n über Wasser halten

tide'land' *s* Watt *n*

tide'wa'ter *s* Flutwasser *n*

tidings ['taɪdɪŋz] *spl* Botschaft *f*

ti·dy ['taɪdɪ] *adj* ordentlich; (*sum*)
hübsch || *v* (*pret & pp* –died) *tr* in
Ordnung bringen; **t. up** aufräumen
|| *intr*—**t. up** aufräumen

tie [taɪ] *adj* (sport) unentschieden ||
s (cord) Schnur *f*; (*ribbon*) Band *n*;
(*necktie*) Krawatte *f*; (*knot*) Schleife
f; (mus) Ligatur *f*; (parl) Stimmen-
gleichheit *f*; (rr) Schwelle *f*; (sport)

Unentschieden *n*; **end in a tie** punkt-
gleich enden; **ties** (*e.g.*, *of friend-
ship*) Bande *pl* || *v* (*pret & pp* tied;
ger tying) *tr* binden; **be tied up** (*said
of a person or telephone*) besetzt
sein; **get tied up** (*in traffic*) steckenbleiben; **my hands are tied** mir sind
die Hände gebunden; **tie in with**
verknüpfen mit; **tie oneself down**
sich festlegen; **tie to** festbinden an
(*dat*); **tie up** (*a wound*) verbinden;
(*traffic*) lahmlegen; (*money*) fest anlegen; (*production*) stillegen; (*the
telephone*) blockieren; (*a boat*) festmachen

tie'back' *s* Gardinenhalter *m*

tie'clasp' *s* Krawattenhalter *m*

tie'pin' *s* Krawattennadel *f*

tier [tɪr] *s* Reihe *f*; (theat) Rang *m*

tie'rod' *s* (aut) Zugstange *f*

tie'-up' *s* (*of traffic*) Stockung *f*

tiger ['taɪgər] *s* Tiger *m*

ti'ger shark' *s* Tigerhai *m*

tight [taɪt] *adj* (*firm*) fest; (*clothes*)
eng; (*taut*) straff; (*scarce*) knapp;
(*container*) dicht; (*drunk*) beschwipst; (*with money*) knaus(e)rig;
feel t. in the chest sich beengt fühlen
|| *adv* fest; **hold t.** festhalten; **sit t.**
sich nicht rühren; **pull t.** stramm-
ziehen || **tights** *spl* Trikot *m & n*

tighten ['taɪtən] *tr* (*a rope*) straff
spannen; (*a belt*) enger schnallen;
(*a jar lid*) festziehen; (*a screw*) anziehen; (*a spring*) spannen; (*a knot*)
zuziehen

tight'-fist'ed *adj* knaus(e)rig

tight'-fit'ting *adj* eng anliegend

tight'-lipped' *adj* verschlossen

tight'rope' *s* Drahtseil *n*; **walk a t.** auf
e–m festgespannten Drahtseil gehen

tight' spot' *s* (coll) Klemme *f*

tight' squeeze' *s* (coll) Zwickmühle *f*

tight'wad' *s* Geizkragen *m*

tigress ['taɪgrɪs] *s* Tigerin *f*

tile [taɪl] *s* (*for the floor or wall*)
Fliese *f*; (*for the roof*) Dachziegel
m; (*glazed tile*) Kachel *f* || *tr* (*a roof*)
mit Ziegeln decken; (*a floor*) mit
Fliesen auslegen; (*a bathroom*)
kacheln

tile' roof' *s* Ziegeldach *n*

till [tɪl] *s* Kasse *f* || *tr* ackern || *prep*
bis (*acc*); **t. now** bisher || *conj* bis

tiller ['tɪlər] *s* (naut) Pinne *f*

tilt [tɪlt] *s* Kippen *n*; **full t.** mit voller
Wucht || *tr* kippen; (*a bottle*, *the
head*) neigen; **t. back** (*e.g.*, *a chair*)
zurücklehnen; **t. over** umkippen ||
intr kippen; **t. over** umkippen

timber ['tɪmbər] *s* Holz *n*; (*for structural use*) Bauholz *n*; (*rafter*) Balken
m

tim'berland' *s* Waldland *n*

tim'ber line' *s* Baumgrenze *f*

timbre ['tɪmbər] *s* Klangfarbe *f*

time [taɪm] *s* Zeit *f*; (*limited period*)
Frist *f*; (*instance*) Mal *n*; (mus) Takt
m; **all the t.** ständig; **all this t.** die
ganze Zeit; **any number of times**
x-mal; **at no t.** nie; **at one t.** einst;
at some t. irgendwann; **at that t.**

damals; **at the present t.** derzeit; **at times** manchmal; **at what t.?** um wieviel Uhr?; **by this t.** nunmehr; **do t.** (sl) sitzen; **do you have the t.?** können Sie mir sagen, wie spät es ist?; **for a t.** e-e Zeitlang; **for the last t.** zum letzten Mal; **for the t. being** vorläufig; **give s.o. a hard t.** j–m das Leben schwer machen; **have a good t.** sich gut unterhalten; **have a hard t.** (ger) es schwer haben zu (inf); **in no t.** im Nu; **in t.** zur rechten Zeit; (in the course of time) mit der Zeit; **make good t.** Fortschritte machen; **on one's own t.** in der Freizeit; **on t.** pünktlich; (on schedule) fahrplanmäßig; (com) auf Raten; **several times** mehrmals; **take one's t.** sich [dat] Zeit lassen; **there's t. for that** das hat Zeit; **this t. tomorrow** morgen um diese Zeit; **t.!** (sport) Zeit!; **t. is up!** die Zeit ist um!; **t. of life** Lebensalter n; **times** Zeiten pl; (math) mal, e.g., **two times two** zwei mal zwei; **t. will tell the Zeit wird es lehren; what t. is it?** wieviel Uhr ist es? || tr (mit der Uhr) messen; **t. s.th. right** die richtige Zeit wählen für

time′ bomb′ s Zeitbombe f
time′ card′ s Stechkarte f
time′ clock′ s Stechuhr f
time′-consum′ing adj zeitraubend
time′ expo′sure s (phot) Zeitaufnahme f
time′ fuse′ s Zeitzünder m
time′-hon′ored adj altehrwürdig
time′keep′er s Zeitnehmer –in mf
time′-lag′ s Verzögerung f
timeless [′taɪmlɪs] adj zeitlos
time′ lim′it s Frist f; **set a t. on** befristen
timely [′taɪmli] adj zeitgerecht; (topic) aktuell
time′ pay′ment s Ratenzahlung f
time′piece′ s Uhr f
timer [′taɪmər] s (person) Zeitnehmer –in mf; (device) Schaltuhr f; (aut) Zündunterbrecher m; (phot) Zeitauslöser m
time′ sig′nal s Zeitzeichen n
time′ stud′y s Zeitstudien pl
time′ta′ble s Zeittabelle f; (aer) Flugplan m; (rr) Fahrplan m
time′work′ s Zeitlohnarbeit f
time′worn′ adj abgenutzt
time′ zone′ s Zeitzone f
timid [′tɪmɪd] adj ängstlich
tim′ing s genaue zeitliche Berechnung f; (aut) Zündeinstellung f
timorous [′tɪmərəs] adj furchtsam
tin [tɪn] adj Zinn– || s (element) Zinn n; (tin plate) Weißblech n
tin′ can′ s Blechdose f
tincture [′tɪŋktʃər] s Tinktur f
tinder [′tɪndər] s Zunder m
tin′derbox′ s (fig) Pulverfaß n
tin′ foil′ s Zinnfolie f
ting-a-ling [′tɪŋ‚lɪŋ] s Klingeling m
tinge [tɪndʒ] s (of color) Stich m; (fig) Spur f || v (pret tingeing & tinging) tr leicht färben

tingle [′tɪŋɡəl] s Kribbeln n, Prickeln n || intr kribbeln, prickeln
tinker [′tɪŋkər] s (bungler) Pfuscher m || intr basteln
tinkle [′tɪŋkəl] s Klingeln n || intr klingeln
tin′ mine′ s Zinnbergwerk n
tinsel [′tɪnsəl] s Lametta f; (fig) Flitterkram m
tin′smith′ s Klempner m
tin′ sol′dier s Zinnsoldat m
tint [tɪnt] s Farbton m || tr tönen, leicht färben
tint′ed glass′ s (aut) blendungsfreies Glas n
tiny [′taɪni] adj winzig
tip [tɪp] s Spitze f; (gratuity) Trinkgeld n; (hint) Tip m; **it's on the tip of my tongue** es schwebt mir auf der Zunge || v (pret & pp tipped; ger tipping) tr schief halten; (a waiter) ein Trinkgeld geben (dat); **tip off** e–n Tip geben (dat); **tip one's hat** auf den Hut tippen || intr—**tip over** umtippen
tip′-off′ s Tip m, rechtzeitiger Wink m
tipple [′tɪpəl] tr & intr süffeln
tippler [′tɪplər] s Säufer –in mf
tipster [′tɪpstər] s Wettberater m
tipsy [′tɪpsi] adj beschwipst
tip′toe′ s—**on t.** auf den Zehenspitzen || v (pret & pp –toed; ger –toeing) intr auf den Zehenspitzen gehen
tip′top′ adj tipptopp
tirade [′taɪred] s Tirade f
tire [taɪr] s Reifen m || tr ermüden; **t. out** strapazieren || intr ermüden
tired adj müde; **be t. of** (ger) es satt haben zu (inf); **be t. of coffee** den Kaffee satt haben; **t. out** abgespannt
tire′ gauge′ s Reifendruckmesser m
tireless [′taɪrlɪs] adj unermüdlich
tire′ pres′sure s Reifendruck m
tiresome [′taɪrsəm] adj (tiring) ermüdend; (boring) langweilig
tissue [′tɪʃju] s Gewebe n; (thin paper) Papiertaschentuch n; **t. of lies** Lügengewebe n
tis′sue pa′per s Seidenpapier n
tit [tɪt] s (sl) Brust f; **tit for tat** wie du mir, so ich dir
Titan [′taɪtən] s Titan(e) m
titanic [taɪ′tænɪk] adj titanisch
titanium [taɪ′teni‚əm] s Titan n
tithe [taɪð] s Kirchenzehnt m || tr (pay one tenth of) den Zehnten bezahlen von; (exact a tenth from) den Zehnten erheben von
Titian [′ti/ən] s tizianrot
titillate [′tɪtɪ‚let] tr & intr kitzeln, (angenehm) reizen
title [′taɪtəl] s Titel m; (to a property) Eigentumsrecht n; (claim) Rechtstitel m; (of a chapter) Überschrift f; (honor) Würde f; (aut) Kraftfahrzeugbrief m || tr titulieren
ti′tle bout′ s (box) Titelkampf m
ti′tled adj ad(e)lig
ti′tle deed′ s Eigentumsurkunde f
ti′tle hold′er s Titelverteidiger –in mf
ti′tle page′ s Titelblatt n
ti′tle role′ s Titelrolle f

titter ['tɪtər] s Gekicher n || intr kichern

titular ['tɪtʃələr] adj Titular-

to [tu], [tʊ] adv—to and fro hin und her || prep zu (dat); (a city, country, island) nach (dat); (as far as) bis (acc); (in order to) um ... zu (inf); (against, e.g., a wall) an (dat or acc); a quarter to eight viertel vor acht; how far is it to the town? wie weit ist es bis zur Stadt?; to a T haargenau

toad [tod] s Kröte f

toad'stool' s Giftpilz m

toad·y ['todi] s Schranze m & f || v (pret & pp –ied) intr (to) scharwenzeln (um)

to-and-fro ['tu‚ənd'fro] adj Hin- und Her- || adv hin und her

toast [tost] s (bread; salutation) Toast m; drink a t. to e–n Toast ausbringen auf (acc) || tr (bread) rösten

toaster ['tostər] s Toaster m

toast'mas'ter s Toastmeister m

tobac·co [tə'bæko] s (–cos) Tabak m

tobac'co pouch' s Tabaksbeutel m

toboggan [tə'bɑgən] s Rodel m & f || intr rodeln

tocsin ['tɑksɪn] s Alarmglocke f

today [tu'de] adv heute || s—from t. on von heute an; today's heutig

toddle ['tɑdəl] s Watscheln f || intr watscheln

toddler ['tɑdlər] s Kleinkind n

toddy ['tɑdi] s Toddy m

to-do [tə'du] s Getue n

toe [to] s Zehe f; be on one's toes auf Draht sein; step on s.o.'s toes j–m auf die Zehen treten || v (pret & pp toed; ger toeing) tr—toe the line nicht aus der Reihe tanzen

toe' dance' s Spitzentanz m

toe'-in' s (aut) Spur f

toe'nail' s Zehennagel m

together [tʊ'gɛðər] adv zusammen; t. with mitsamt (dat), samt (dat)

togetherness [tʊ'gɛðərnɪs] s Zusammengehörigkeit f

tog'gle switch' ['tɑgəl] s (elec) Kippschalter m

togs [tɑgz] spl Klamotten pl

toil [tɔɪl] s Mühe f; toils Schlingen pl || intr sich mühen

toilet ['tɔɪlɪt] s (room) Toilette f; (bathroom fixture) Klosett n

toi'let ar'ticle s Toilettenartikel m

toi'let bowl' s Klosettschüssel f

toi'let pa'per s Klosettpapier n

toi'let seat' s Toilettenring m

token ['tokən] adj (payment) symbolisch; (strike) Warn– || Zeichen n; (proof) Beweis m; by the same t. aus dem gleichen Grund; as (or in) t. of zum Beweis (genit)

tolerable ['tɑlərəbəl] adj erträglich

tolerably ['tɑlərəbli] adv leidlich

tolerance ['tɑlərəns] s Duldsamkeit f; (mach) Toleranz f

tolerant ['tɑlərənt] adj (of) duldsam (gegen), tolerant (gegen)

tolerate ['tɑlə‚ret] tr dulden

toleration [‚tɑlə're/ən] s Duldung f

toll [tol] adj (road) gebührenpflichtig || s Wegezoll m; (at a bridge) Brückenzoll m; (of bells) Läuten n; (number of victims) Zahl f der Opfer; (fig) Tribut m; (telp) Gebühr f für ein Ferngespräch; take a heavy t. of life viele Menschenleben kosten || tr & intr läuten

toll' booth' s Zahlkasse f

toll' bridge' s Zollbrücke f

toll' call' s Ferngespräch n

toll' collec'tor s Zolleinnehmer –in mf

toma·to [tə'meto] s (–toes) Tomate f

toma'to juice' s Tomatensaft f

tomb [tum] s Grab n, Grabmal n

tomboy ['tɑm‚bɔɪ] s Wildfang m

tomb'stone' s Grabstein m

tomcat ['tɑm‚kæt] s Kater m

tome [tom] s Band m

tomfoolery [tɑm'fuləri] s Albernheit f

Tom'my gun' ['tɑmi] s Maschinenpistole f

tom'myrot' s Blödsinn m

tomorrow [tu'mɔro] adv morgen; t. evening morgen abend; t. morning morgen früh; t. night morgen abend; t. noon morgen mittag || s morgen; tomorrow's morgig

tom-tom ['tɑm‚tɑm] s Hindutrommel f

ton [tʌn] s Tonne f

tone [ton] s Ton m; (of color) Farbton m; (phot) Tönung f || tr tönen; (phot) tönen; t. down dämpfen || intr milder werden

tone'-control knob' s (rad) Klangregler m

tongs [tɔŋz] spl Zange f

tongue [tʌŋ] s Zunge f; (language) Sprache f; (of a shoe) Zunge f; (of a buckle) Dorn m; (of a bell) Klöppel m; (of a wagon) Deichsel f; (carp) Feder f; hold one's t. den Mund halten

tongue'-tied' adj zungenlahm; (fig) sprachlos

tongue' twist'er s Zungenbrecher m

tonic ['tɑnɪk] adj tonisch || s (med) Tonikum n; (mus) Tonika f

tonight [tu'naɪt] adv heute nacht; (this evening) heute abend

tonnage ['tʌnɪdʒ] s Tonnage f

tonsil ['tɑnsɪl] s Mandel f

tonsilitis [‚tɑnsɪ'laɪtɪs] s Mandelentzündung f

tonsure ['tɑn/ər] s Tonsur f

too [tu] adv (also) auch; (excessively) zu; too bad! Schade!

tool [tul] s (& fig) Werkzeug n || tr (with tools) bearbeiten

tool'box' s Werkzeugkasten m

tool'mak'er s Werkzeugmacher m

tool' shed' s Geräteschuppen m

toot [tut] s (aut) Hupen n || tr (a trumpet) blasen; t. the horn (aut) hupen || intr (aut) hupen

tooth [tuθ] s (teeth [tiθ]) Zahn m; (of a rake) Zinke f; t. and nail mit aller Gewalt

tooth'ache' s Zahnschmerz m, Zahnweh n

tooth′brush′ s Zahnbürste f
tooth′ decay′ s Zahnfäule f
toothless ['tuθlɪs] adj zahnlos
tooth′paste′ s Zahnpaste f
tooth′pick′ s Zahnstocher m
tooth′ pow′der s Zahnpulver n
top [tɑp] adj oberste; (speed, price, form) Höchst–; (team) Spitzen–; (first-class) erstklassig ‖ s Spitze f; (of a mountain) Gipfel m; (of a tree) Wipfel m; (of a car) Verdeck n; (of a box) Deckel m; (of a garment) Oberteil m & n; (of a bottle) Verschluß m; (of an object) obere Seite f; (of the water) Oberfläche f; (of a turnip) Kraut n; (toy) Kreisel m; **at the top of one's voice** aus voller Kehle; **at the top of the page** oben auf der Seite; **be tops with s.o.** (coll) bei j–m ganz groß angeschrieben sein; **from top to bottom** von oben bis unten; **on top** (& fig) obenauf; **on top of** (position) auf (dat); (direction) auf (acc); **on top of that** obendrein ‖ v (pret & pp topped); **go topping** tr (a tree) kappen; (surpass) übertreffen; **that tops everything** das übersteigt alles; **top off** (a meal, an evening) abschließen; **to top it off** zu guter Letzt
topaz ['topæz] s Topas m
top′ brass′ s (mil) hohe Tiere pl
top′coat′ s Überzieher m
top′ dog′ s (coll) Erste mf
top′ ech′elon s Führungsspitze f
top′ hat′ s Zylinder m
top′-heav′y adj oberlastig
topic ['tɑpɪk] s Gegenstand m, Thema n
topical ['tɑpɪkəl] adj aktuell
top′ kick′ s (mil) Spieß m
topless ['tɑplɪs] adj Oben-ohne–
topmast ['tɑp ˌmest] s Toppmast m
top′most′ adj oberste
top′notch′ adj erstklassig
top′ of the head′ s Scheitel m
topography [tə'pɑgrəfi] s Topographie f
topple ['tɑpəl] tr & intr stürzen
topsail ['tɑpsəl] s Toppsegel n
top′-se′cret adj streng geheim
top′ ser′geant s Hauptfeldwebel m
top′side′ adv auf Deck ‖ s Oberseite f
top′soil′ s Mutterboden m
topsy-turvy ['tɑpsi'tʌrvi] adj drunter und drüber ‖ adv—**turn t.** durcheinanderbringen
torch [tɔrtʃ] s Fackel f; (Brit) Taschenlampe f; **carry the t. for** (coll) verknallt sein in (acc)
torch′bear′er s (& fig) Fackelträger m
torch′light′ s Fackelschein m
torch′light parade′ s Fackelzug m
torment ['tɔrment] s Qual f ‖ [tɔr'ment] tr quälen
tormentor [tɔr'mentər] s Quäler –in mf
torn [tɔrn] adj zerrissen, rissig
torna·do [tɔr'nedo] s (–does & –dos) Tornado m, Windhose f
torpe·do [tɔr'pido] s (–does) Torpedo m ‖ tr torpedieren

torpe′do boat′ s Torpedoboot n
torpe′do tube′ s Ausstoßrohr n
torpid ['tɔrpɪd] adj träge
torque [tɔrk] s Drehmoment n
torrent ['tɔrent] s Sturzbach m; (of words) Schwall m; **in torrents** stromweise
torrential [tə'rentʃəl] adj—**t. rain** Wolkenbruch m
torrid ['tɔrɪd] adj brennend
Tor′rid Zone′ s heiße Zone f
tor·so ['tɔrso] s (–sos) (of a statue) Torso m; (of a human body) Rumpf m
tortoise ['tɔrtəs] s Schildkröte f
tor′toise shell′ s Schildpatt n
torture ['tɔrtʃər] s Folter f, Qual f ‖ tr foltern, quälen
toss [tɔs] s Wurf m; (of the head) Zurückwerfen n; (of a ship) Schlingern n; (of a coin) Loswurf m ‖ tr (throw) werfen; (the head) zurückwerfen; (a ship) hin– und herwerfen; (a coin) hochwerfen; **t. off** (work) hinhauen; **t. s.o. for** mit j–m losen um ‖ intr (naut) schlingern; **t. for** e–e Münze hochwerfen um; **t. in bed** sich im Bett hin –und herwerfen
toss′up′ s Loswurf m; **it's a t. whether** es hängt ganz vom Zufall ab, ob
tot [tɑt] s Knirps m
to·tal ['totəl] adj Gesamt–, total ‖ s Gesamtsumme f ‖ v (pret & pp –tal[l]ed; ger –tal[l]ing) tr (add up) zusammenrechnen; (amount to) sich belaufen auf (acc); (sl) (Wagen) ganz kaputt machen
totalitarian [to ˌtælɪ'terɪ·ən] adj totalitär
tote [tot] tr schleppen
totem ['totəm] s Totem n
totter ['tɑtər] intr schwanken
touch [tʌtʃ] s Berührung f; (sense of touch) Tastsinn m; (e.g., of a fever) Anflug m; (trace, small bit) Spur f; (of a pianist) Anschlag m; **get in t. with** in Verbindung treten mit; **keep in t. with** in Verbindung bleiben mit; **put in t. with** in Verbindung setzen mit; **with sure t.** mit sicherer Hand ‖ tr berühren; (fig) rühren; **he's a little touched** (coll) er hat e–n kleinen Klaps; **t. bottom** anstoßen; **t. glasses** mit den Gläsern anstoßen; **t. off** auslösen; **t. s.o. for** (coll) j–n anpumpen um; **t. up** (with cosmetics) auffrischen; (paint, phot) retuschieren ‖ intr sich berühren; **t. down** (aer) aufsetzen; **t. on** (a topic) berühren; (e.g., arrogance) grenzen an (acc)
touch′ and go′ s—**be t.** auf der Kippe stehen
touch′ing adj rührend, herzergreifend
touch′stone′ s (fig) Prüfstein m
touch′-type′ intr blindschreiben
touchy ['tʌtʃi] adj (spot, person) empfindlich; (situation) heikel
tough [tʌf] adj (strong) derb; (meat) zäh; (life) mühselig; (difficult) schwierig ‖ s Gassenjunge m
toughen ['tʌfən] tr zäher machen; **t.**

up (through training) ertüchtigen ||
intr (up) zäher werden
tough' luck' s Pech n
tour [tur] s (of a country) Tour f; (of
a city) Rundfahrt f; (of a museum)
Führung f; (mus, theat) Tournee f;
go on t. auf Tournee gehen || tr be-
sichtigen; (a country) bereisen || intr
auf der Reise sein; (theat) auf Tour-
nee sein
tour' guide' s Reiseführer –in mf
tourism ['turɪzəm] s Touristik f
tournament ['turnəmənt] s Turnier n
tourney ['turnɪ] s Turnier n
tourniquet ['turnɪˌket] s Aderpresse f
tousle ['tauzəl] tr (zer)zausen
tow [to] s—**have in tow** im Schlepptau
haben; **take in tow** ins Schlepptau
nehmen || tr schleppen; **tow away**
abschleppen
toward(s) [tord(z)] prep (with respect
to) gegenüber (dat); (a goal, direction) auf (acc), zu; (shortly before)
gegen (acc); (for) für (acc); (facing)
zugewandt (dat)
tow'boat' s Schleppschiff n
tow-el ['tau-əl] s Handtuch n || v (pret
& pp –el[l]ed; ger –el[l]ing) tr mit
e–m Handtuch abtrocknen
tow'el rack' s Handtuchhalter m
tower ['tau-ər] s Turm m; **t. of strength**
starker Hort m || intr ragen; **t. over**
überragen
tow'ering adj hochragend; (rage) rasend
tow'ing serv'ice s Schleppdienst m
tow'line' s Schlepptau n
town [taun] adj städtisch, Stadt– || s
Stadt f; **in t.** in der Stadt; **out of t.**
verreist; **go to t. on** Feuer und
Flamme sein für
town' coun'cil s Stadtrat m
town' hall' s Rathaus n
town' house' s Stadthaus n
town'ship' s Gemeinde f
tow'rope' s Schlepptau n; (for a
glider) Startseil n
tow' truck' s Abschleppwagen m
toxic ['taksɪk] adj Gift–, toxisch || s
Giftstoff m
toy [tɔɪ] adj Spielzeug– || s Spielzeug
n; **toys** Spielsachen pl; (com) Spiel-
waren pl || intr spielen; **toy with**
(fig) herumspielen mit
toy' dog' s Schoßhund m
toy' shop' s Spielwarengeschäft n
toy' sol'dier s Spielzeugsoldat m
trace [tres] s Spur f; (of a harness)
Strang m; **without a t.** spurlos || tr
(a drawing) durchpausen; (lines)
nachziehen; (track) ausfindig machen; **t. (back) to** zurückführen auf
(acc)
tracer ['tresər] s Suchzettel m
trac'er bul'let s Leuchtspurgeschoß n
trac'ing pa'per s Pauspapier n
track [træk] s Spur f; (of a foot) Fuß-
spur f; (of a wheel) Radspur f;
(chain of a tank) Raupenkette f;
(parallel rails) Geleise n; (single rail)
Gleis n, Schiene f; (station platform)
Bahnsteig m; (path) Pfad m; (course

for running) Laufbahn f; (course for
motor and horse racing) Rennbahn f;
(running as a sport) Laufen n; **be off
the t.** (fig) auf dem Holzweg sein;
go off the t. (derail) entgleisen; **in
one's tracks** mitten auf dem Weg;
jump the t. aus den Schienen sprin-
gen || tr verfolgen; **t. down** (game,
a criminal) zur Strecke bringen; (a
rumor, reference) nachgehen (dat);
t. up (a rug) schmutzig treten
track'-and-field' adj Leichtathletik–
trackless ['træklɪs] adj pfadlos; (vehicle) schienenlos
track' meet' s Leichtathletikwettkampf
m
tract [trækt] s Strich m; (treatise)
Traktat m; **t. of land** Grundstück n
traction ['trækʃən] s (med) Ziehen n;
(of the road) Griffigkeit f
tractor ['træktər] s Traktor m; (of
a tractor-trailer) Zugmaschine f
trac'tor-trail'er s Sattelschlepper m mit
e–m Anhänger
trade [tred] s Handel m; (calling, job)
Gewerbe n; (exchange) Tausch m;
by t. von Beruf || tr (aus)tauschen;
t. in (e.g., a used car) in Zahlung
geben || intr Handel treiben
trade' agree'ment s Handelsabkommen
n
trade' bar'riers spl Handelsschranken
pl
trade'-in val'ue s Handelswert m
trade'mark' s Warenzeichen n
trade' name' s (of products) Handels-
bezeichnung f; (of a firm) Firmen-
name m
trader ['tredər] s Händler –in mf
trade' school' s Gewerbeschule f
trade' se'cret s Geschäftsgeheimnis n
trades'man s (–men) Handelsmann m
trade' un'ion s Gewerkschaft f
trade'wind' s Passatwind m
trad'ing post' s Handelsniederlassung f
trad'ing stamp' s Rabattmarke f
tradition [trə'dɪʃən] s Tradition f
traditional [trə'dɪʃənəl] adj herkömmlich, traditionell
traf-fic ['træfɪk] s Verkehr m; (trade)
(in) Handel m (in dat) || v (pret &
pp –ficked; ger –ficking) intr—**t. in**
handeln in (dat)
traf'fic ac'cident s Verkehrsunfall m
traf'fic cir'cle s Kreisverkehr m
traf'fic is'land s Verkehrsinsel f
traf'fic jam' s Verkehrsstockung f
traf'fic lane' s Fahrbahn f
traf'fic light' s Verkehrsampel f; **go
through a t.** bei Rot durchfahren
traf'fic sign' s Verkehrszeichen n
traf'fic tick'et s Strafzettel m
traf'fic viola'tion s Verkehrsdelikt n
tragedian [trə'dʒɪdɪ·ən] s Tragiker m
tragedy ['trædʒɪdɪ] s (& fig) Tragödie f
tragic ['trædʒɪk] adj tragisch
trail [trel] s (path) Fährte f; **be on
s.o.'s t.** j–m auf der Spur sein; **t. of
smoke** Rauchfahne f || tr (on foot)
nachgehen (dat); (in a vehicle) nach-
fahren (dat); (in a race) nachhinken
(dat) || intr (said of a robe) schleifen

trailer ['treilər] *s* Anhänger *m*; *(mobile home)* Wohnwagen *m*
trail'er camp' *s* Wohnwagenparkplatz *m*
train [tren] *s (of railway cars)* Zug *m*; *(of a dress)* Schleppe *f*; *(following)* Gefolge *n*; *(of events)* Folge *f*; **go by t.** mit dem Zug fahren; **t. of thought** Gedankengang *m* || *tr* ausbilden; *(for a particular job)* anlernen; *(the memory)* üben; *(plants)* am Spalier aufziehen; *(an animal)* dressieren; *(a gun)* *(on)* zielen (auf *acc*); *(sport)* trainieren || *intr* üben; *(sport)* trainieren
trained *adj* geschult, ausgebildet
trainee [tre'ni] *s* Anlernling *m*
trainer ['trenər] *s (of domestic animals)* Dresseur *m*, Dresseuse *f*; *(of wild animals)* Dompteur *m*, Dompteuse *f*; *(aer)* Schulflugzeug *n*; *(sport)* Sportwart –in *mf*
train'ing *s* Ausbildung *f*; *(of animals)* Dressur *f*; *(sport)* Training *n*
train'ing school' *s (vocational school)* Berufsschule *f*; *(reformatory)* Erziehungsanstalt *f*
trait [tret] *s* Charakterzug *m*
traitor ['tretər] *s* Verräter –in *mf*; *(of a country)* Hochverräter –in *mf*
trajectory [trə'dʒɛktəri] *s* Flugbahn *f*
tramp [træmp] *s* Landstreicher –in *mf*; *(loose woman)* Frauenzimmer *n* || *tr* trampeln; *(traverse on foot)* durchstreifen || *intr* vagabundieren; **t. on** herumtrampeln auf *(dat)*
trample ['træmpəl] *s* Getrampel *n* || *tr* trampeln; **t. to death** tottreten; **t. under foot** *(fig)* mit Füßen treten || *intr*—**t. on** herumtrampeln auf *(dat)*; *(fig)* mit Füßen treten
trampoline ['træmpə,lin] *s* Trampolin *n*
trance [træns] *s* Trance *f*
tranquil ['træŋkwil] *adj* ruhig
tranquilize ['træŋkwi,laiz] *tr* beruhigen
tranquilizer ['træŋkwi,laizər] *s* Beruhigungsmittel *n*
tranquillity [træn'kwiliti] *s* Ruhe *f*
transact [træn'zækt] *tr* abwickeln
transaction [træn'zækʃən] *s* Abwicklung *f*; **transactions** *(of a society)* Sitzungsbericht *m*
transatlantic [,trænsət'læntik] *adj* transatlantisch
transcend [træn'sɛnd] *tr* übersteigen
transcendental [,trænsɛn'dɛntəl] *adj* übersinnlich; *(philos)* transzendental
transcribe [træn'skraib] *tr (copy)* umschreiben; *(dictated or recorded material)* übertragen; *(mus)* transkribieren; *(phonet)* in Lautschrift wiedergeben; *(rad)* auf Band aufnehmen
transcript ['trænskript] *s* Transkript *n*
transcription [træn'skripʃən] *s* Umschrift *f*; *(mus)* Transkription *f*
transept ['trænsɛpt] *s* Querschiff *n*
trans·fer ['trænsfər] *s (of property)* Übertragung *f*; *(of money)* Überweisung *f*; *(of an employee)* Versetzung *f*; *(of a passenger)* Umsteigen *n*; *(ticket)* Umsteigefahrschein

m || [træns'fʌr], ['trænsfər] *v (pret & pp* **–ferred;** *ger* **–ferring)** *tr (property)* übertragen; *(money)* überweisen; *(to another account)* umbuchen; *(an employee)* versetzen || *intr (to)* versetzt werden (nach, zu); *(said of a passenger)* umsteigen
transfix [træns'fiks] *tr* durchbohren
transform [træns'fɔrm] *tr (a person)* verwandeln; *(into)* umwandeln (in *acc*); *(elec)* umspannen
transformer [træns'fɔrmər] *s* (elec) Stromwandler *m*, Transformator *m*
transfusion [træns'fjuʒən] *s* (med) Übertragung *f*, Transfusion *f*
transgress [træns'grɛs] *tr* überschreiten
transgression [træns'grɛʃən] *s* Vergehen *n*
transient ['trænʃənt] *adj* vorübergehend; *(fleeting)* flüchtig || *s* Durchreisende *mf*
transistor [træn'sistər] *adj* Transistor– || *s* Transistor *m*
transistorize [træn'sistə,raiz] *tr* transistorisieren
transit ['trænzit] *s* (astr) Durchgang *m*; (com) Transit *m*; **in t.** unterwegs
transition [træn'ziʃən] *s* Übergang *m*
transitional [træn'ziʃənəl] *adj* Übergangs–
transitive ['trænsitiv] *adj* transitiv
transitory ['trænsi,tori] *adj* vergänglich
translate [træns'let] *tr* übersetzen; **t. into action** in die Tat umsetzen
translation [træns'leʃən] *s* Übersetzung *f*
translator [træns'letər] *s* Übersetzer –in *mf*
transliterate [træns'litə,ret] *tr* transkribieren
translucent [træns'lusənt] *adj* durchscheinend, lichtdurchlässig
transmigration [,trænsmai'greʃən] *s*— **t. of the soul** Seelenwanderung *f*
transmission [træns'miʃən] *s (of a text)* Textüberlieferung *f*; *(of news, information)* Übermittlung *f*; *(aut)* Getriebe *n*; *(rad, telv)* Sendung *f*
trans·mit [træns'mit] *v (pret & pp* **–mitted;** *ger* **–mitting)** *tr (send forward)* übersenden; *(disease, power, light, heat)* übertragen; *(e.g., customs)* überliefern; *(by inheritance)* vererben; *(rad, telp, telv)* senden
transmitter [træns'mitər] *s* (rad, telg, telv) Sender *m*
transmutation [,trænsmu'teʃən] *s* Umwandlung *f*; *(biol)* Transmutation *f*; *(chem, phys)* Umwandlung *f*
transmute [træns'mjut] *tr* umwandeln
transoceanic [,trænzoʃi'ænik] *adj* überseeisch, Übersee–
transom ['trænsəm] *s (crosspiece)* Querbalken *m*; *(window over a door)* Oberlicht *n* mit Kreuzsprosse; *(of a boat)* Spiegel *m*
transparency [træns'pɛrənsi] *s* Durchsichtigkeit *f*, Transparenz *f*; *(phot)* Diapositiv *n*
transparent [træns'pɛrənt] *adj* durchsichtig, transparent

transpire [træns'paɪr] *intr* (*happen*) sich ereignen; (*leak out*) (fig) durchsickern

transplant ['træns͵plænt] *s* (bot, surg) Verpflanzung *f* ‖ [træns'plænt] *tr* (bot, surg) verpflanzen

transport ['trænspɔrt] *s* Beförderung *f*. Transport *m*; (nav) Truppentransporter *m* ‖ [træns'pɔrt] *tr* befördern

transportation [͵trænspɔr'teʃən] *s* Beförderung *f*; (*public transportation*) Verkehrsmittel *n*; **do you need t.?** brauchen Sie e-e Fahrgelegenheit?

trans'port plane' *s* Transportflugzeug *n*

transpose [træns'poz] *tr* umstellen; (math, mus) transponieren

trans·ship [træns'ʃɪp] *v* (*pret & pp* **–shipped;** *ger* **–shipping**) *tr* (com, naut) umladen

trap [træp] *s* (& fig) Falle *f*; (*snare*) Schlinge *f*; (*pit*) Fallgrube *f*; (*under a sink*) Geruchsverschluß *m*; (*mouth*) (sl) Klappe *f*; (chem) Abscheider *m*; (golf) Sandbunker *m*; **fall** (or **walk**) **into a t.** in die Falle gehen; **set a trap** e-e Falle stellen ‖ *v* (*pret & pp* **trapped;** *ger* **trapping**) *tr* mit e-r Falle fangen; (fig) erwischen; (mil) einfangen

trap' door' *s* Falltür *f*, Klapptür *f*; (theat) Versenkung *f*

trapeze [trə'piz] *s* Trapez *n*; (gym) Schwebereck *n*

trapezoid ['træpɪ͵zɔɪd] *s* Trapez *n*

trapper ['træpər] *s* Fallensteller *m*

trappings ['træpɪŋz] *spl* Staat *m*; (*caparison*) Staatsgeschirr *n*

trap'shoot'ing *s* Tontaubenschießen *n*

trash [træʃ] *s* Abfälle *pl*; (*junk*) Schund *m*; (*artistically inferior material*) Kitsch *m*; (*worthless people*) Gesindel *n*

trash' can' *s* Mülleimer *m*, Abfalleimer *m*

trashy ['træʃɪ] *adj* kitschig; (*literature*) Schund-

travail [trə'vel] *s* Plackerei *f*; (*labor of childbirth*) Wehen *pl*

trav·el ['trævəl] *s* Reisen *n*; (*trip*) Reise *f*; (*e.g., of a bullet, rocket*) Bewegung *f*; (*of moving parts*) Lauf *m*; **travels** Reiseerlebnisse *pl* ‖ *v* (*pret & pp* **–el[l]ed;** *ger* **–el[l]ing**) *tr* bereisen ‖ *intr* reisen; (*said of a vehicle or passenger*) fahren; (astr, aut, mach, phys) sich bewegen

trav'el a'gency *s* Reisebüro *n*

traveler ['trævələr] *s* Reisende *mf*

trav'eler's check' *s* Reisescheck *m*

trav'el fold'er *s* Reiseprospekt *m*

trav'eling bag' *s* Reisetasche *f*

trav'eling sales'man *s* (**–men**) Geschäftsreisende *m*

travelogue ['trævə͵lɔg] *s* Reisebericht *m*; (cin) Reisefilm *m*

traverse [trə'vʌrs] *tr* durchqueren ‖ *intr* (*said of a gun*) sich drehen

traves·ty ['trævɪstɪ] *s* Travestie *f* ‖ *v* (*pret & pp* **–tied**) *tr* travestieren

trawl [trɔl] *s* Schleppnetz *n* ‖ *tr* mit dem Schleppnetz fangen ‖ *intr* mit dem Schleppnetz fischen

trawler ['trɔlər] *s* Schleppnetzboot *n*

tray [tre] *s* Tablett *n*; (phot) Schale *f*

treacherous ['tretʃərəs] *adj* verräterisch; (*e.g., ice*) trügerisch

treachery ['tretʃərɪ] *s* Verrat *m*

tread [tred] *s* (*step*) Tritt *m*; (*imprint*) Spur *f*; (*on a tire*) Profil *n* ‖ *v* (*pret* **trod** [trad]; *pp* **trodden** ['tradən] & **trod**) *tr* betreten ‖ *intr* (**on**) treten (*auf acc*)

treadle ['tredəl] *s* Trittbrett *n*

tread'mill' *s* (& fig) Tretmühle *f*

treason ['trizən] *s* Verrat *m*

treasonable ['trizənəbəl] *adj* verräterisch

treasure ['treʒər] *s* Schatz *m* ‖ *tr* sehr schätzen

treasurer ['treʒərər] *s* Schatzmeister –in *mf*

treasury ['treʒərɪ] *s* Schatzkammer *f*; (*chest*) Tresor *m*; (*public treasury*) Staatsschatz *m*; **Treasury** Finanzministerium *n*

treat [trit] *s* Hochgenuß *m* ‖ *tr* behandeln; (*regard*) (as) betrachten (als); **t. oneself to s.th.** sich [*dat*] etw genehmigen; **t. s.o. to s.th** j–n bewirten mit

treatise ['tritɪs] *s* Abhandlung *f*

treatment ['tritmənt] *s* Behandlung *f*

treaty ['tritɪ] *s* Vertrag *m*

treble ['trebəl] *adj* (*threefold*) dreifach; (mus) Diskant– ‖ *s* Diskant *m*; (*voice*) Diskantstimme *f* ‖ *tr* verdreifachen ‖ *intr* sich verdreifachen

tre'ble clef' *s* Violinschlüssel *m*

tree [tri] *s* Baum *m*

treeless ['trilɪs] *adj* baumlos

tree'top' *s* Baumwipfel *m*

tree' trunk' *s* Baumstamm *m*

trellis ['trelɪs] *s* Spalier *n*; (*gazebo*) Gartenhäuschen *n*

tremble ['trembəl] *s* Zittern *n* ‖ *intr* zittern; (geol) beben; **t. all over am** ganzen Körper zittern

tremendous [trɪ'mendəs] *adj* ungeheuer

tremor ['tremər] *s* Zittern *n*; (geol) Beben *n*

trench [trentʃ] *s* Graben *m*; (mil) Schützengraben *m*

trenchant ['trentʃənt] *adj* schneidend; (*policy*) durchschlagend

trench' war'fare *s* Stellungskrieg *m*

trend [trend] *s* Richtung *f*, Trend *m*

trespass ['trespəs] *s* unbefugtes Betreten *n*; (*sin*) Sünde *f* ‖ *intr* unbefugt fremdes Eigentum betreten; **no trespassing** (*public sign*) Betreten verboten; **t. on** unbefugt betreten

trespasser ['trespəsər] *s* Unbefugte *mf*

tress [tres] *s* Flechte *f*

trestle ['tresəl] *s* Gestell *n*; (*of a bridge*) Brückenbock *m*

trial ['traɪəl] *s* (*attempt*) Versuch *m*; (*hardship*) Beschwernis *f*; (jur) Prozeß *m*; **a week's t.** e-e Woche Probezeit; **be on t. for** vor Gericht stehen wegen; **be brought up** (or **come up**) **for t.** zur Verhandlung kommen; **new t.** Wiederaufnahmeverfahren *n*; **on t.** (com) auf Probe; **put on t.** vor Gericht bringen

tri'al and er'ror s—by t. durch Ausprobieren

tri'al balloon' s Versuchsballon m

tri'al by ju'ry s Verhandlung f vor dem Schwurgericht

tri'al or'der s Probeauftrag m

tri'al run' s Probelauf m

triangle ['traɪˌæŋgəl] s Dreieck n

triangular [traɪˈæŋgjələr] adj dreieckig

tribe [traɪb] s Stamm m; (pej) Sippschaft f

tribunal [traɪˈbjunəl] s Tribunal n

tributary ['trɪbjəˌteri] adj zinspflichtig || s Nebenfluß m

tribute ['trɪbjut] s Tribut m, Zins m; **pay t. to** Anerkennung zollen (dat)

trice [traɪs] s—**in a t.** im Nu

trick [trɪk] s Trick m; (prank) Streich m; (technique) Kniff m; (artifice) Schlich m; (cards) Stich m; **be on to s.o.'s tricks** j-s Schliche kennen; **be up to one's old tricks** sein Unwesen treiben; **do the t.** die Sache schaffen; **play a dirty t. on s.o.** j-m e-n gemeinen Streich spielen || tr reinlegen; **t. s.o. into** (ger) j-n durch Kniffe dazu bringen zu (inf)

trickery ['trɪkəri] s Gaunerei f

trickle ['trɪkəl] s Tröpfeln n || intr tröpfeln, rieseln

trickster ['trɪkstər] s Gauner m

tricky ['trɪki] adj (wily) listig; (touchy) heikel; (difficult) verzwickt

trident ['traɪdənt] s Dreizack m

tried [traɪd] adj bewährt, probat

trifle ['traɪfəl] s Kleinigkeit f; **a t.** (e.g., too big) ein bißchen || tr—**t. away** vertändeln || intr tändeln

trif'ling adj geringfügig || s Tändelei f

trigger ['trɪgər] s Abzug m; **pull the t.** abdrücken || tr auslösen

trig'ger-hap'py adj schießwütig

trigonometry [ˌtrɪgəˈnɑmətri] s Trigonometrie f

trill [trɪl] s Triller m || tr & intr trillern

trillion ['trɪljən] s Billion f; (Brit) Trillion f

trilogy ['trɪlədʒi] s Trilogie f

trim [trɪm] adj (trimmer; trimmest) (figure) schick; (well-kept) gepflegt || s (e.g., of a hat) Zierleiste f; (naut) Trimm m; **be in t.** in Form sein || v (pret & pp trimmed; ger trimming) tr (clip) stutzen; (decorate) dekorieren; (a Christmas tree) schmücken; (beat) (coll) schlagen; (naut) trimmen

trim'ming s (e.g., of a dress) Besatz m; (of hedges) Stutzen n; **take a t.** (coll) e-e Niederlage erleiden; **trimmings** (decorations) Verzierungen pl; (food) Zutaten pl; (scraps) Abfälle pl; **with all the trimmings** (fig) mit allen Schikanen

trinity ['trɪnɪti] s Dreiheit f; **Trinity** Dreifaltigkeit f

trinket ['trɪŋkɪt] s Schmuckgegenstand m

tri·o ['tri·o] s (—os) (& mus) Trio n

trip [trɪp] s Reise f; (on drugs) Trip m; **go on** (or **take**) **a t.** e-e Reise machen || v (pret & pp tripped; ger tripping) tr ein Bein stellen (dat); **t. up** (fig) zu Fall bringen || intr stolpern

tripartite [traɪˈpɑrtaɪt] adj Dreiparteien–; (of three powers) Dreimächte–

tripe [traɪp] s Kutteln pl; (sl) Schund m

trip'ham'mer s Schmiedehammer m

triple ['trɪpəl] adj dreifach || s Dreifache n || tr verdreifachen

triplet ['trɪplɪt] s (offspring) Drilling m; (mus) Triole f

triplicate ['trɪplɪkɪt] adj dreifach || s—**in t.** in dreifacher Ausfertigung

tripod ['traɪpɑd] s Dreifuß m; (phot) Stativ n

triptych ['trɪptɪk] s Triptychon n

trite [traɪt] adj abgedroschen

triumph ['traɪˌəmf] s Triumph m || intr (over) triumphieren (über acc)

triumphal [traɪˈʌmfəl] adj Sieges–

triumphant [traɪˈʌmfənt] adj triumphierend

trivia ['trɪvɪə] spl Nichtigkeiten pl

trivial ['trɪvɪəl] adj trivial, alltäglich; (person) oberflächlich

triviality [ˌtrɪviˈælɪti] s Trivialität f, Nebensächlichkeit f

Trojan ['trodʒən] adj trojanisch || s Trojaner –in mf

troll [trol] s (myth) Troll m || tr & intr mit der Schleppangel fischen

trolley ['trɑli] s Straßenbahn f

trollop ['trɑləp] s (slovenly woman) Schlampe f; (prostitute) Dirne f

trombone ['trɑmbon] s Posaune f

troop [trup] s Trupp m; (mil) Truppe f

trooper ['truper] s Kavallerist m; **swear like a t.** fluchen wie ein Kutscher

troop'ship' s Truppentransporter m

trophy ['trofi] s Trophäe f; (sport) Pokal m

tropical ['trɑpɪkəl] adj Tropen–

tropics ['trɑpɪks] spl Tropen pl

trot [trɑt] s Trab m || v (pret & pp trotted; ger trotting) tr—**t. out** (coll) zur Schau stellen || intr traben

troubadour ['trubəˌdor] s Minnesänger m

trouble ['trʌbəl] s (inconvenience, bother) Mühe f; (difficulty) Schwierigkeit f; (physical distress) Leiden n; (civil disorder) Unruhe f; **ask for t.** das Schicksal herausfordern; **be in t.** in Schwierigkeiten sein; (be pregnant) schwanger sein; **cause s.o. a lot of t.** j-m viel zu schaffen machen; **get into t.** in Schwierigkeiten geraten; **go to a lot of t.** sich [dat] viel Mühe machen; **it was no t. at all!** gern geschehen!; **make t.** Geschichten machen; **take the t. to** (inf) sich der Mühe unterziehen zu (inf); **that's the t.** da liegt die Schwierigkeit; **what's the t.?** was ist los? || tr (worry) beunruhigen; (bother) belästigen; (disturb) stören; (said of ills) plagen

trou'blemak'er s Unruhestifter –in mf

troubleshooter ['trʌbəlˌʃutər] s Stö–

rungssucher –in *mf;* (*in disputes*) Friedensstifter –in *mf*

troublesome ['trʌbəlsəm] *adj* lästig

trough [trɔf] *s* Trog *m;* (*of a wave*) Wellental *n*

troupe [trup] *s* Truppe *f*

trousers ['trauzərz] *spl* Hose *f*

trous·seau [tru'so] *s* (–seaux & –seaus) Brautausstattung *f*

trout [traut] *s* Forelle *f*

trowel ['trau·əl] *s* Kelle *f*

truant ['tru·ənt] *adj* schwänzend ‖ *s—* **play t.** die Schule schwänzen

truce [trus] *s* Waffenruhe *f*

truck [trʌk] *s* Last(kraft)wagen *m;* (*for luggage*) Gepäckwagen *m* ‖ *tr* mit Lastkraftwagen befördern

truck'driv'er *s* Lastwagenfahrer *m*

trucker ['trʌkər] *s* (*driver*) Lastwagenfahrer *m;* (*owner of a trucking firm*) Fuhrunternehmer –in *mf*

truck' farm'ing *s* Gemüsebau *m*

truculent ['trʌkjələnt] *adj* gehässig

trudge [trʌdʒ] *intr* stapfen

true [tru] *adj* wahr; (*loyal*) (ge)treu; (*genuine*) echt; (*sign*) sicher; **come t.** sich verwirklichen; **prove t.** sich als wahr erweisen; **that's t.** das stimmt

truffle ['trʌfəl] *s* Trüffel *f*

truism ['tru·izəm] *s* Binsenwahrheit *f*

truly ['truli] *adv* wirklich; **Yours t.** Hochachtungsvoll

trump [trʌmp] *s* Trumpf *m* ‖ *tr* trumpfen; **t. up** erdichten ‖ *intr* trumpfen

trumpet ['trʌmpɪt] *s* Trompete *f* ‖ *intr* (*said of an elephant*) trompeten

truncheon ['trʌntʃən] *s* Gummiknüppel *m*

trunk [trʌŋk] *s* (*chest*) Koffer *m;* (*of a tree*) Stamm *m;* (*of a living body*) Rumpf *m;* (*of an elephant*) Rüssel *m;* (*aut*) Kofferraum *m;* **trunks** (sport) Sporthose *f*

trunk' line' *s* Fernverkehrsweg *m*

truss [trʌs] *s* (archit) Tragwerk *n;* (med) Bruchband *n* ‖ *tr* (archit) stützen; (*bind*) festbinden

trust [trʌst] *s* (*in*) Vertrauen *n* (auf *acc*); (com) Trust *m;* (jur) Treuhand *f* ‖ *tr* trauen (*dat*); (*hope*) hoffen ‖ *intr—***t.** in vertrauen auf (*acc*)

trust' com'pany *s* Treuhandgesellschaft *f*

trustee [trʌs'ti] *s* Aufsichtsrat *m;* (jur) Treuhänder –in *mf*

trustee'ship *s* Treuhandverwaltung *f*

trustful ['trʌstfəl] *adj* zutraulich

trust' fund' *s* Treuhandfonds *m*

trust'wor'thy *adj* vertrauenswürdig

trusty ['trʌsti] *adj* treu ‖ *s* Kalfaktor *m*

truth [truθ] *s* Wahrheit *f;* **in t.** wahrlich

truthful ['truθfəl] *adj* (*person*) ehrlich; (*e.g., account*) wahrheitsgemäß

try [traɪ] *s* Versuch *m* ‖ *v* (*pret & pp* **tried**) *tr* versuchen; (*one's patience*) auf e–e harte Probe stellen; (*a case*) verhandeln; **be tried for** vor Gericht kommen wegen; **try on** anprobieren; (*a hat*) aufprobieren; **try out** erproben; (*new food*) kosten; **try s.o. for**

gegen j–n verhandeln wegen ‖ *intr* versuchen

try'ing *adj* anstrengend

try'out' *s* (sport) Ausscheidungskampf *m*

T'-shirt' *s* T-Shirt *n*

tub [tʌb] *s* Wanne *f;* (*boat*) Kasten *m*

tubby ['tʌbi] *adj* (coll) kugelrund

tube [t(j)ub] *s* (*pipe*) Rohr *n*, Röhre *f;* (*e.g., of toothpaste*) Tube *f;* (*of rubber*) Schlauch *m;* (rad) Röhre *f*

tuber ['t(j)ubər] *s* (bot) Knolle *f*

tubercle ['t(j)ubərkəl] *s* Tuberkel *m*

tuberculosis [t(j)u‚bʌrkjə'losɪs] *s* Lungenschwindsucht *f*

tuck [tʌk] *s* (sew) Abnäher *m* ‖ *tr* (*into one's pocket, under a mattress*) stecken; (*under one's arm*) klemmen; (*into bed*) packen; **t. in** reinstecken; **t. up** (*trousers*) hochkrempeln; (*a skirt, dress*) hochschürzen

Tuesday ['t(j)uzde] *s* Dienstag *m;* **on T.** am Dienstag

tuft [tʌft] *s* Büschel *m* & *n* ‖ *tr* (*e.g., a mattress*) durchheften

tug [tʌg] *s* (*pull*) Zug *m;* (*boat*) Schlepper *m* ‖ *v* (*pret & pp* **tugged;** *ger* **tugging**) *tr* schleppen ‖ *intr* (at) zerren (an *dat*)

tug'boat' *s* Schleppdampfer *m*

tug' of war' *s* Tauziehen *n*

tuition [t(j)u'ɪʃən] *s* Schulgeld *n*

tulip ['t(j)ulɪp] *s* Tulpe *f*

tumble ['tʌmbəl] *s* (*fall*) Sturz *m;* (gym) Purzelbaum *m* ‖ *intr* (*fall*) stürzen; (gym) Saltos machen; **t. down the stairs** die Treppe herunterpurzeln

tum'ble-down' *adj* baufällig

tumbler ['tʌmblər] *s* (*glass*) Trinkglas *n;* (*of a lock*) Zuhaltung *f;* (*acrobat*) Akrobat –in *mf*

tumor ['t(j)umər] *s* Geschwulst *f*

tumult ['t(j)umʌlt] *s* Getümmel *n*

tuna ['tunə] *s* Thunfisch *m*

tune [t(j)un] *s* Melodie *f;* **be in t.** richtig gestimmt sein; **be out of t.** falsch singen; (*said of a piano*) verstimmt sein; **change one's t.** e–n anderen Ton anschlagen ‖ *tr* stimmen; **t. up** (aut) neu einstellen ‖ *intr—***t. in on** (rad) einstellen; **t. up** (*said of an orchestra*) stimmen

tungsten ['tʌŋstən] *s* Wolfram *n*

tunic ['t(j)unɪk] *s* Tunika *f*

tun'ing fork' *s* Stimmgabel *f*

tun·nel ['tʌnəl] *s* Tunnel *m;* (min) Stollen *m* ‖ *v* (*pret & pp* **-nel[l]ed;** *ger* **-nel[l]ing**) *intr* e–n Tunnel bohren

turban ['tʌrbən] *s* Turban *m*

turbid ['tʌrbɪd] *adj* trüb(e)

turbine ['tʌrbɪn] *s* Turbine *f*

turboprop ['tʌrbo‚prɑp] *s* Turboprop *m*

turbulence ['tʌrbjələns] *s* Turbulenz *f*

tureen [t(j)u'rin] *s* Terrine *f*

turf [tʌrf] *s* Rasendecke *f;* (*of a gang*) (sl) Gebiet *n;* **the t.** der Turf

Turk [tʌrk] *s* Türke *m*, Türkin *f*

turkey ['tʌrki] *s* Truthahn *m;* (*female*) Truthenne *f;* **Turkey** die Türkei

Turkish ['tɜrkɪʃ] *adj* türkisch ‖ *s* Türkisch *n*

Tur'kish tow'el *s* Frottiertuch *n*

turmoil ['tɜrmɔɪl] *s* Getümmel *n*

turn [tɜrn] *s* (*rotation*) Drehung *f*; (*change of direction or condition*) Wendung *f*; (*curve*) Kurve *f*; (*by a driver*) Abbiegen *n*; (*of a century*) Wende *f*; (*of a spool*) Windung *f*; **at every t.** bei jeder Gelegenheit; **good t.** Gunst *f*; **it's his t.** er ist dran; **out of t.** außer der Reihe; **take turns** sich abwechseln ‖ *tr* drehen; (*the page*) umblättern; (*one's head*) wenden; **t. down** (*refuse*) ablehnen; (*a radio*) leiser stellen; (*a bed*) aufdecken; (*a collar*) umschlagen; (*an appeal*) (*jur*) verwerfen; **t. in** (*an application, resignation*) einreichen; (*lost articles*) abgeben; (*a person*) anzeigen; **t. into** verwandeln in (*acc*); **t. loose** frei lassen; **t. off** (*light, gas*) abdrehen; (*rad, telv*) abstellen; **t. on** (*gas, light*) andrehen; (*excite*) (coll) in Erregung versetzen; (*rad, telv*) anstellen; **t. out** produzieren; (*pockets*) umkehren; (*eject*) vor die Tür setzen; **t. over** (*property*) abtreten; (*a business*) übertragen; (*e.g., weapons*) abliefern; **t. up** (*a card, sleeve*) aufschlagen ‖ *intr* (*rotate*) sich drehen; (*in some direction*) sich wenden; **it turned out that es** stellte sich heraus, daß; **t. against** (fig) sich wenden gegen; **t. around** sich herumdrehen; **t. back** umdrehen; **t. down** (*a street*) einbiegen in (*acc*); **t. in** (*go to bed*) zu Bett gehen; **t. into** werden zu; **t. out** ausfallen; **t. out for** sich einfinden zu; **t. out for the best** sich zum Guten wenden; **t. out in force** vollzählig erscheinen; **t. out to be** sich erweisen als; **t. over** (*tip over*) umkippen; (aut) anspringen; **t. to s.o. for help** sich an j-n um Hilfe wenden; **t. towards** sich wenden gegen; **t. up** auftauchen

turn'coat' *s* Überläufer -in *mf*

turn'ing point' *s* Wendepunkt *m*

turnip ['tɜrnɪp] *s* Steckrübe *f*

turn'out' *s* Beteiligung *f*

turn'o'ver *s* Umsatz *m*

turn'pike' *s* Autobahn *f*

turnstile ['tɜrn‚staɪl] *s* Drehkreuz *n*

turn'ta'ble *s* Plattenteller *m*; (rr) Drehscheibe *f*

turpentine ['tɜrpən‚taɪn] *s* Terpentin *n*

turpitude ['tɜrpɪ‚t(j)ud] *s* Verworfenheit *f*

turquoise ['tɜrk(w)ɔɪz] *adj* türkisfarben ‖ *s* Türkis *m*

turret ['tɜrɪt] *s* Turm *m*

turtle ['tɜrtəl] *s* Schildkröte *f*

tur'tledove' *s* Turteltaube *f*

tur'tleneck' *s* Rollkragen *m*

tusk [tʌsk] *s* (*of an elephant*) Stoßzahn *m*; (*of a boar*) Hauer *m*

tussle ['tʌsəl] *s* Rauferei *f* ‖ *intr* raufen

tutor ['t(j)utər] *s* Hauslehrer -in *mf*

tuxe·do [tʌk'sido] *s* (**-dos**) Smoking *m*

twang [twæŋ] *s* (*of a musical instrument*) Schwirren *n*; (*of the voice*) Näseln *n* ‖ *intr* schwirren; näseln

tweed [twid] *adj* aus Tweed ‖ *s* Tweed *m*

tweet [twit] *s* Gezwitscher *n* ‖ *intr* zwitschern

tweezers ['twizərz] *spl* Pinzette *f*

twelfth [twelfθ] *adj & pron* zwölfte ‖ *s* (*fraction*) Zwölftel *n*; **the t.** (*in dates or in series*) der Zwölfte

twelve [twelv] *adj & pron* zwölf ‖ *s* Zwölf *f*

twentieth ['twentɪ‚ɪθ] *adj & pron* zwanzigste ‖ *s* (*fraction*) Zwanzigstel *n*; **the t.** (*in dates or in series*) der Zwanzigste

twenty ['twenti] *adj & pron* zwanzig ‖ *s* Zwanzig *f*; **the twenties** die zwanziger Jahre

twen'ty-one' *adj & pron* einundzwanzig

twice [twaɪs] *adv* zweimal

twiddle ['twɪdəl] *tr* müßig herumdrehen; **t. one's thumbs** Daumen drehen

twig [twɪg] *s* Zweig *m*

twilight ['twaɪ‚laɪt] *adj* dämmerig ‖ *s* Abenddämmerung *f*

twin [twɪn] *adj* (*brother, sister*) Zwillings-; (*double*) Doppel- ‖ *s* Zwilling *m*

twine [twaɪn] *s* (*for a package*) Bindfaden *m*; (*sew*) Zwirn *m* ‖ *tr*—**t. around** winden um

twin'-en'gine *adj* zweimotorig

twinge [twɪndʒ] *s* stechender Schmerz *m*

twinkle ['twɪŋkəl] *s* Funkeln *n*; **in a t.** im Nu ‖ *intr* funkeln

twirl [twɜrl] *s* Wirbel *m* ‖ *tr* herumwirbeln ‖ *intr* wirbeln

twist [twɪst] *s* (*turn*) Drehung *f*; (*distortion*) Verdrehung *f*; (*strand*) Flechte *f*; (*bread roll*) Zopf *m*; (*dance*) Twist *m* ‖ *tr* (*revolve*) drehen; (*wind*) winden; (*an arm, words*) verdrehen; **t. one's ankle** sich [dat] den Knöchel vertreten ‖ *intr* sich drehen; (*wind*) sich winden

twister ['twɪstər] *s* (coll) Windhose *f*

twit [twɪt] *s* (sl) Depp *m* ‖ *v* (*pret & pp* **twitted**; *ger* **twitting**) *tr* verspotten; (*upbraid*) rügen

twitch [twɪtʃ] *s* Zucken *n* ‖ *intr* zucken

twitter ['twɪtər] *s* Zwitschern *n* ‖ *intr* zwitschern

two [tu] *adj & pron* zwei ‖ *s* Zwei *f*; **by twos** zu zweit; **in two** entzwei; **put two and two together** Schlußfolgerungen ziehen

two'-edged' *adj* zweischneidig

two'-faced' *adj* doppelzüngig

two' hun'dred *adj & pron* zweihundert

two'-piece' *adj* (*suit*) zweiteilig

twosome ['tusəm] *s* (*of lovers*) Liebespaar *n*; (golf) Einzelspiel *n*

two'-time' *tr* untreu sein (dat)

two'-tone' *adj* zweifarbig

two'-way traf'fic *s* Gegenverkehr *m*

tycoon [taɪ'kun] *s* Industriekapitän *m*

type [taɪp] *s* (*kind*) Art *f*; (*of person; of manufacture*) Typ *m*; (typ) Drucktype *f*, Letter *f* ‖ *tr & intr* tippen

type'face' s Schriftbild n
type'script' s Maschinenschrift f
type'set'ter s Schriftsetzer –in mf
type'write' v (pret –wrote; pp –written) tr & intr mit der Maschine schreiben
type'writ'er s Schreibmaschine f
type'writer rib'bon s Farbband n
ty'phoid fe'ver ['taifoid] s Typhus m
typhoon [tai'fun] s Taifun m
typical ['tipikəl] adj (of) typisch (für)
typi•fy ['tipi,fai] v (pret & pp –fied) tr (characterize) typisch sein für; (exemplify) ein typisches Beispiel sein für
typ'ing er'ror s Tippfehler m

typist ['taipist] s Maschinenschreiber –in mf
typographic(al) [,taipə'græfik(əl)] adj typographisch; (error) Druck-
typography [tai'pɑgrəfi] s (the skill) Buchdruckerkunst f; (the work) Buchdruck m
tyrannical [ti'rænikəl] adj tyrannisch
tyrannize ['tirə,naiz] tr tyrannisieren
tyranny ['tirəni] s Tyrannei f
tyrant ['tairənt] s Tyrann m
ty•ro ['tairo] s (-ros) Neuling m
Tyrol [ti'rol] s Tirol n
Tyrolean [ti'roli•ən] adj tirolerisch || s Tiroler –in mf

U

U, u [ju] s einundzwanzigster Buchstabe des englischen Alphabets
ubiquitous [ju'bikwitəs] adj allgegenwärtig
udder ['ʌdər] s Euter n
ugliness ['ʌglinis] s Häßlichkeit f
ugly ['ʌgli] adj häßlich
Ukraine [ju'kren] s Ukraine f
Ukrainian [ju'kreni•ən] adj ukrainisch || s (person) Ukrainer –in mf; (language) Ukrainisch n
ulcer ['ʌlsər] s Geschwür n
ulcerate ['ʌlsə,ret] intr eitern
ulte'rior mo'tive [ʌl'tiri•ər] s Hintergedanke m
ultimate ['ʌltimit] adj äußerste; (goal) höchst; (result) End- || s Letzte n
ultima•tum [,ʌlti'metəm] s (-tums & -ta [tə]) Ultimatum n
ul'trahigh fre'quency ['ʌltrə,hai] s Ultrahochfrequenz f
ultramodern [,ʌltrə'mɑdərn] adj ultramodern
ultraviolet [,ʌltrə'vai•əlit] adj ultraviolett || s Ultraviolett n
ultravi'olet lamp' s Höhensonne f
umbil'ical cord' [ʌm'bilikəl] adj Nabelschnur f
umbrage ['ʌmbridʒ] s—take u. at Anstoß nehmen an (dat)
umbrella [ʌm'brelə] s Regenschirm m; (aer) Abschirmung f
umlaut ['umlaut] s Umlaut m || tr umlauten
umpire ['ʌmpair] s Schiedsrichter –in mf || tr als Schiedsrichter leiten || intr Schiedsrichter sein
umpteen [ʌmp'tin] adj zig; u. times zigmal
UN ['ju'en] s (United Nations) UNO f
unable [ʌn'ebəl] adj unfähig
unabridged [,ʌnə'bridʒd] adj ungekürzt
unaccented [,ʌnæk'sentid] adj unbetont
unacceptable [,ʌnæk'septibəl] adj unannehmbar
unaccountable [,ʌnə'kauntəbəl] adj

nicht verantwortlich; (strange) seltsam
unaccounted-for [,ʌnə'kauntid,fɔr] adj unerklärt; (acct) nicht belegt
unaccustomed [,ʌnə'kʌstəmd] adj (to) nicht gewöhnt (an acc)
unaffected [,ʌnə'fektid] adj nicht affektiert; u. by unbeeinflusst von
unafraid [,ʌnə'fred] adj—be u. (of) sich nicht fürchten (vor dat)
unalterable [ʌn'ɔltərəbəl] adj unabänderlich
unanimity [,junə'nimiti] s Stimmeneinheit f
unanimous [ju'næniməs] adj (persons) einmütig; (vote) einstimmig
unannounced [,ʌnə'naunst] adj unangemeldet
unanswered [ʌn'ænsərd] adj (question) unbeantwortet; (claim, statement) unwiderlegt; (request) nicht erhört
unappreciative [,ʌnə'pri∫i•ətiv] adj (of) unempfänglich (für)
unapproachable [,ʌnə'prot∫əbəl] adj unzugänglich
unarmed [ʌn'ɑrmd] adj unbewaffnet
unasked [ʌn'æskt] adj (advice) unerbeten; (uninvited) ungeladen
unassailable [,ʌnə'seləbəl] adj unangreifbar
unassuming [,ʌnə's(j)umiŋ] adj nicht anmaßend
unattached [,ʌnə'tæt∫t] adj (to) nicht befestigt (an dat); (person) ungebunden; (mil) zur Verfügung stehend
unattainable [,ʌnə'tenəbəl] adj unerreichbar
unattended [,ʌnə'tendid] adj unbeaufsichtigt
unattractive [,ʌnə'træktiv] adj reizlos
unauthorized [ʌn'ɔθəraizd] adj unberechtigt
unavailable [,ʌnə'veləbəl] adj (person) unabkömmlich; (thing) nicht verfügbar
unavenged [,ʌnə'vendʒd] adj ungerächt
unavoidable [,ʌnə'vɔidəbəl] adj unvermeidlich

unaware [ˌʌnəˈwer] *adj* (**of**) nicht bewußt (*genit*)

unawares [ˌʌnəˈwerz] *adv* (*unexpectedly*) unversehens; (*unintentionally*) versehentlich; **catch u.** überraschen

unbalanced [ʌnˈbælənst] *adj* nicht im Gleichgewicht; (*fig*) unausgeglichen

un·bar [ʌnˈbɑr] *v* (*pret & pp* **–barred**; *ger* **–barring**) *tr* aufriegeln

unbearable [ʌnˈberəbəl] *adj* unerträglich

unbeaten [ʌnˈbitən] *adj* (& *fig*) ungeschlagen

unbecoming [ˌʌnbɪˈkʌmɪŋ] *adj* (*improper*) ungeziemend; (*clothing*) unkleidsam

unbelievable [ˌʌnbɪˈlivəbəl] *adj* unglaublich

unbeliever [ˌʌnbɪˈlivər] *s* Ungläubige *mf*

unbending [ʌnˈbendɪŋ] *adj* unbeugsam

unbiased [ʌnˈbaɪ·əst] *adj* unvoreingenommen

unbidden [ʌnˈbɪdən] *adj* ungebeten

un·bind [ʌnˈbaɪnd] *v* (*pret & pp* **–bound**) *tr* losbinden

unbleached [ʌnˈblitʃt] *adj* ungebleicht

unbolt [ʌnˈbolt] *tr* aufriegeln

unborn [ˈʌnbɔrn] *adj* ungeboren

unbosom [ʌnˈbuzəm] *tr*—**u. oneself to** sich offenbaren (*dat*)

unbowed [ʌnˈbaud] *adj* ungebeugt

unbreakable [ʌnˈbrekəbəl] *adj* unzerbrechlich

unbridled [ʌnˈbraɪdəld] *adj* ungezügelt

unbroken [ʌnˈbrokən] *adj* (*intact*) ungebrochen; (*line, series*) ununterbrochen; (*horse*) nicht zugeritten

unbuckle [ʌnˈbʌkəl] *tr* aufschnallen

unburden [ʌnˈbɑrdən] *tr* entlasten; **u. oneself** sein Herz ausschütten

unburied [ʌnˈberid] *adj* unbeerdigt

unbutton [ʌnˈbʌtən] *adj* aufknöpfen

uncalled-for [ʌnˈkɔldˌfɔr] *adj* unangebracht

uncanny [ʌnˈkæni] *adj* unheimlich

uncared-for [ʌnˈkerdˌfɔr] *adj* verwahrlost

unceasing [ʌnˈsisɪŋ] *adj* unaufhörlich

unceremonious [ˌʌnserɪˈmoni·əs] *adj* (*informal*) ungezwungen; (*rude*) unsanft

uncertain [ʌnˈsʌrtən] *adj* unsicher

uncertainty [ʌnˈsʌrtənti] *s* Unsicherheit *f*

unchain [ʌnˈtʃen] *tr* losketten; (*fig*) entfesseln

unchangeable [ʌnˈtʃendʒəbəl] *adj* unveränderlich

uncharacteristic [ˌʌnkærɪktəˈrɪstɪk] *adj* wesensfremd

uncharted [ʌnˈtʃɑrtɪd] *adj* auf keiner Karte verzeichnet

unchaste [ʌnˈtʃest] *adj* unkeusch

unchecked [ʌnˈtʃekt] *adj* ungehemmt

unchristian [ʌnˈkrɪstʃən] *adj* unchristlich

uncivilized [ʌnˈsɪvɪˌlaɪzd] *adj* unzivilisiert

unclad [ʌnˈklæd] *adj* unbekleidet

unclaimed [ʌnˈklemd] *adj* nicht abgeholt

unclasp [ʌnˈklæsp] *tr* loshaken; (*the arms, hands*) öffnen

unclassified [ʌnˈklæsɪˌfaɪd] *adj* nicht klassifiziert; (*not secret*) nicht geheim

uncle [ˈʌnkəl] *s* Onkel *m*

unclean [ʌnˈklin] *adj* unsauber; (*relig*) unrein

unclear [ʌnˈklɪr] *adj* unklar

un·clog [ʌnˈklɑg] *v* (*pret & pp* **–clogged**; *ger* **–clogging**) *tr* von e-m Hindernis befreien

uncombed [ʌnˈkomd] *adj* ungekämmt

uncomfortable [ʌnˈkʌmfərtəbəl] *adj* unbequem; **feel u.** sich nicht recht wohl fühlen

uncommitted [ˌʌnkəˈmɪtɪd] *adj* (*troops*) nicht eingesetzt; (*delegates, nations*) unentschieden

uncommon [ʌnˈkɑmən] *adj* ungewöhnlich; (*outstanding*) außergewöhnlich

uncomplaining [ˌʌnkəmˈplenɪŋ] *adj* klaglos

uncompromising [ʌnˈkɑmprəˌmaɪzɪŋ] *adj* unbeugsam

unconcealed [ˌʌnkənˈsild] *adj* unverholen

unconcerned [ˌʌnkənˈsʌrnd] *adj* (*about*) unbesorgt (um)

unconditional [ˌʌnkənˈdɪʃənəl] *adj* bedingungslos

unconfirmed [ˌʌnkənˈfɪrmd] *adj* unbestätigt, unverbürgt

unconquerable [ʌnˈkɑŋkərəbəl] *adj* unüberwindlich

unconquered [ʌnˈkɑŋkərd] *adj* unbezwungen

unconscious [ʌnˈkɑnʃəs] *adj* bewußtlos; (**of**) nicht bewußt (*genit*) ‖ *s*—**the u. das** Unbewußte

unconstitutional [ˌʌnkɑnstɪˈt(j)uʃənəl] *adj* verfassungswidrig

uncontested [ˌʌnkənˈtestɪd] *adj* unbestritten

uncontrollable [ˌʌnkənˈtroləbəl] *adj* unkontrollierbar; (*fig*) unbändig

unconventional [ˌʌnkənˈventʃənəl] *adj* unkonventionell

uncork [ʌnˈkɔrk] *tr* entkorken

uncouple [ʌnˈkʌpəl] *tr* abkoppeln

uncouth [ʌnˈkuθ] *adj* ungehobelt; (*appearance*) ungeschlacht

uncover [ʌnˈkʌvər] *tr* aufdecken

unctuous [ˈʌŋktʃu·əs] *adj* salbungsvoll

uncultivated [ʌnˈkʌltɪˌvetɪd] *adj* unbebaut

uncultured [ʌnˈkʌltʃərd] *adj* (*fig*) unkultiviert

uncut [ʌnˈkʌt] *adj* nicht abgeschnitten; (*gem*) ungeschliffen; (*grain*) ungemäht

undamaged [ʌnˈdæmɪdʒd] *adj* unbeschädigt, unversehrt

undaunted [ʌnˈdɔntɪd] *adj* unverzagt

undecided [ˌʌndɪˈsaɪdɪd] *adj* (*person*) unschlüssig; (*thing*) unentschieden

undefeated [ˌʌndɪˈfitɪd] *adj* unbesiegt

undefended [ˌʌndɪˈfendɪd] *adj* unverteidigt

undefiled [ˌʌndɪˈfaɪld] *adj* unbefleckt

undefined [ˌʌndɪˈfaɪnd] *adj* unklar

undeliverable [ˌʌndɪˈlɪvərəbəl] *adj* unbestellbar

undeniable [ˌʌndɪˈnaɪ·əbəl] *adj* unleugbar

under [ˈʌndər] *adj* Unter– ‖ *adv* unter–, e.g., **go u.** untergehen ‖ *prep* unter *(position)* (dat); *(direction)* unter *(acc)*

un'derage' *adj* unmündig

un'der·bid' *v (pret & pp* –bid; *ger* –bidding) *tr* unterbieten

un'derbrush' *s* Unterholz *n*

un'dercar'riage *s* Fahrgestell *n*

un'derclothes' *spl* Unterwäsche *f*

un'dercov'er *adj* Geheim–; **u. agent** Spitzel *m*

un'dercur'rent *s (& fig)* Unterströmung *f*

un'dercut' *v (pret & pp* –cut; *ger* –cutting) *tr* unterbieten

un'derdevel'oped *adj* unterentwickelt

un'derdog' *s (coll)* Unterlegene *mf*

un'derdone' *adj* nicht durchgebraten

un'deres'timate *tr* unterschätzen

un'derexpose' *tr (phot)* unterbelichten

un'dergar'ment *s* Unterkleidung *f*

un'der·go' *v (pret* –went; *pp* –gone) durchmachen; *(an operation)* sich unterziehen (dat)

un'dergrad'uate *s* Collegestudent –in *mf*

un'derground' *adj* unterirdisch; *(fig)* Untergrund–; *(water)* Grund–; *(min)* unter Tage ‖ **un'derground'** *s (secret movement)* Untergrundbewegung *f;* **go u.** untertauchen

un'dergrowth' *s* Buschholz *n*, Unterholz *n*

un'derhand' *adj (throw)* unter Schulterhöhe (ausgeführt)

un'derhand'ed *adj* hinterhältig

un'derline', un'derline' *tr* unterstreichen

underling [ˈʌndərlɪŋ] *s* Handlanger *m*

un'dermine' *tr (& fig)* untergraben

underneath [ˌʌndərˈniθ] *adj* Unter– ‖ *adv* unten ‖ *s* Unterseite *f* ‖ *prep (position)* unter (dat), unterhalb *(genit); (direction)* unter *(acc)*

un'dernour'ished *adj* unterernährt

un'dernour'ishment *s* Unterernährung *f*

un'derpad' *s (of a rug)* Unterlage *f*

un'derpaid' *adj* unterbezahlt

un'derpass' *s* Straßenunterführung *f*

un'der·pin' *v (pret & pp* –pinned; *ger* –pinning) *tr* untermauern

un'derplay' *tr* unterspielen

un'derpriv'ileged *adj* benachteiligt

un'derrate' *tr* unterschätzen

un'derscore' *tr (& fig)* unterstreichen

un'dersea' *adj* Unterwasser–

un'dersec'retar'y *s* Untersekretär –in *mf*

un'der·sell' *v (pret & pp* –sold; *ger* –selling) *tr (a person)* unterbieten; *(goods)* verschleudern

un'dershirt' *s* Unterhemd *n*

un'derside' *s* Unterseite *f*

un'dersigned' *adj* unterschrieben ‖ **un'der·signed'** *s* Unterzeichnete *mf*

un'der·stand' *v (pret & pp* –stood) *tr* verstehen; **it's understood that** es ist selbstverständlich, daß; **make oneself understood** sich verständlich machen

understandable [ˌʌndərˈstændəbəl] *adj* verständlich

understandably [ˌʌndərˈstændəbli] *adv* begreiflicherweise

un'derstand'ing *adj* verständnisvoll ‖ *s (of)* Verständnis *n* (für); *(between persons)* Einvernehmen *n; (agreement)* Übereinkommen *n;* **come to an u. with s.o.** sich mit j–m verständigen; **it is my u. that** wie ich verstehe

un'derstud'y *s* Ersatzmann *m; (cin, theat)* Ersatzschauspieler –in *mf*

un'der·take' *v (pret* –took; *pp* –taken) *tr* unternehmen

undertaker [ˈʌndər ˌtekər] *s* Leichenbestatter –in *mf*

un'dertak'ing *s* Unternehmen *n*

un'dertone' *s* leise Stimme *f; (fig)* Unterton *m*

un'dertow' *s* Sog *m*

un'derwa'ter *adj* Unterwasser–

un'derwear' *s* Unterwäsche *f*

un'derweight' *adj* untergewichtig

un'derworld' *s (of criminals)* Unterwelt *f; (myth)* Totenreich *n*

un'der·write', un'der·write' *v (pret* –wrote; *pp* –written) *tr* unterschreiben; *(ins)* versichern

un'derwrit'er *s* Unterzeichner –in *mf;* *(ins)* Versicherer –in *mf;* (st. exch.) Wertpapiermakler –in *mf;* **underwriters** Emissionsfirma *f*

undeserved [ˌʌndɪˈzɑrvd] *adj* unverdient

undeservedly [ˌʌndɪˈzɑrvɪdli] *adv* unverdientermaßen

undesirable [ˌʌndɪˈzaɪrəbəl] *adj* unerwünscht ‖ *s* Unerwünschte *mf*

undeveloped [ˌʌndɪˈveləpt] *adj* unentwickelt; *(land)* unerschlossen

undies [ˈʌndɪz] *spl (coll)* Unterwäsche *f*

undigested [ˌʌndɪˈdʒestɪd] *adj (& fig)* unverdaut

undignified [ʌnˈdɪgnɪ ˌfaɪd] *adj* würdelos

undiluted [ˌʌndɪˈlutɪd] *adj* unverdünnt

undiminished [ˌʌndɪˈmɪnɪ/t] *adj* unvermindert

undisciplined [ʌnˈdɪsəplɪnd] *adj* undiszipliniert, zuchtlos

undisputed [ˌʌndɪsˈpjutɪd] *adj* unbestritten, unangefochten

undisturbed [ˌʌndɪsˈtʌrbd] *adj* ungestört

undivided [ˌʌndɪˈvaɪdɪd] *adj* ungeteilt

un·do [ʌnˈdu] *v (pret* –did; *pp* –done) *tr (a knot)* aufschnüren; *(a deed)* ungeschehen machen

undo'ing *s* Ruin *m*

undone [ʌnˈdʌn] *adj (not done)* ungetan; *(ruined)* ruiniert; **come u.** sich lösen; **leave nothing u.** nichts unversucht lassen

undoubtedly [ʌnˈdautɪdli] *adv* zweifellos

undramatic [ˌʌndrəˈmætɪk] *adj* undramatisch

undress [ʌnˈdres] *s*—**in a state of u.** *(nude)* in unbekleidetem Zustand; *(in a negligee)* im Negligé ‖ *tr* ausziehen ‖ *intr* sich ausziehen

undrinkable [ʌn'drɪŋkəbəl] *adj* nicht trinkbar

undue [ʌn'd(j)u] *adj* (*inappropriate*) unangemessen; (*excessive*) übermäßig

undulate ['ʌndjə,let] *intr* wogen

undulating ['ʌndjə,letɪŋ] *adj* wellenförmig

unduly [ʌn'd(j)uli] *adv* übermäßig

undying [ʌn'daɪ-ɪŋ] *adj* unsterblich

un'earned in'come ['ʌnʌrnd] *s* Kapitalrente *f*

unearth [ʌn'ʌrθ] *tr* ausgraben; (fig) aufstöbern

unearthly [ʌn'ʌrθli] *adj* unirdisch; (*cry*) schauerlich; **at an u. hour** (*early*) in aller Herrgottsfrühe

uneasy [ʌn'izi] *adj* (*worried*) ängstlich; (*ill at ease*) unbehaglich

uneatable [ʌn'itəbəl] *adj* ungenießbar

uneconomic(al) [,ʌnekə'nɑmɪk(əl)] *adj* unwirtschaftlich

uneducated [ʌn'edjə,ketɪd] *adj* ungebildet

unemployed [,ʌnem'plɔɪd] *adj* arbeitslos || *s* Arbeitslose *mf*

unemployment [,ʌnem'plɔɪmənt] *s* Arbeitslosigkeit *f*

unemploy'ment compensa'tion *s* Arbeitslosenunterstützung *f*; **collect u.** (sl) Stempeln gehen

unencumbered [,ʌnən'kʌmbərd] *adj* unbelastet

unending [ʌn'endɪŋ] *adj* endlos

unequal [ʌn'ikwəl] *adj* ungleich; **u. to** nicht gewachsen (*dat*)

unequaled [ʌn'ikwəld] *adj* ohnegleichen

unequivocal [,ʌnə'kwɪvəkəl] *adj* eindeutig

unerring [ʌn'erɪŋ] *adj* unfehlbar

UNESCO [ju'nesko] *s* (**United Nations Educational, Scientific, and Cultural Organization**) UNESCO *f*

unessential [,ʌnə'senʃəl] *adj* unwesentlich

uneven [ʌn'ivən] *adj* (*not smooth*) uneben; (*unbalanced*) ungleich; (*not uniform*) ungleichmäßig; (*number*) ungerade

uneventful [,ʌnɪ'ventfəl] *adj* ereignislos

unexceptional [,ʌnek'sepʃənəl] *adj* nicht außergewöhnlich

unexpected [,ʌnek'spektɪd] *adj* unerwartet

unexplained [,ʌnek'splend] *adj* unerklärt

unexplored [,ʌnek'splord] *adj* unerforscht

unexposed [,ʌnek'spozd] *adj* (phot) unbelichtet

unfading [ʌn'fedɪŋ] *adj* unverwelklich

unfailing [ʌn'felɪŋ] *adj* unfehlbar

unfair [ʌn'fer] *adj* unfair; (*competition*) unlauter

unfaithful [ʌn'feθfəl] *adj* treulos

unfamiliar [,ʌnfə'mɪljər] *adj* unbekannt

unfasten [ʌn'fæsən] *tr* losbinden; (*e.g.*, *a seat belt*) aufschnallen

unfathomable [ʌn'fæðəməbəl] *adj* unergründlich

unfavorable [ʌn'fevərəbəl] *adj* ungünstig

unfeasible [ʌn'fizəbəl] *adj* unausführbar

unfeeling [ʌn'filɪŋ] *adj* unempfindlich

unfilled [ʌn'fɪld] *adj* ungefüllt; (*post*) unbesetzt

unfinished [ʌn'fɪnɪʃt] *adj* unfertig; (*business*) unerledigt

unfit [ʌn'fɪt] *adj* (**for**) ungeeignet (für); (*not qualified*) (**for**) untauglich (für); **u. for military service** wehrdienstuntauglich

unfold [ʌn'fold] *tr* (*a chair*) aufklappen; (*cloth, paper*) entfalten; (*ideas, plans*) offenbaren

unforeseeable [,ʌnfor'si-əbəl] *adj* unabsehbar

unforeseen [,ʌnfor'sin] *adj* unvorhergesehen

unforgettable [,ʌnfor'getəbəl] *adj* unvergeßlich

unfortunate [ʌn'fortʃənɪt] *adj* unglücklich

unfortunately [ʌn'fortʃənɪtli] *adv* leider

unfounded [ʌn'faʊndɪd] *adj* unbegründet

un-freeze [ʌn'friz] *v* (*pret* **–froze**; *pp* **–frozen**) *tr* auftauen; (*prices*) freigeben

unfriendly [ʌn'frendli] *adj* unfreundlich

unfruitful [ʌn'frutfəl] *adj* unfruchtbar

unfulfilled [,ʌnfəl'fɪld] *adj* unerfüllt

unfurl [ʌn'fʌrl] *tr* (*a flag*) entrollen; (*sails*) losmachen

unfurnished [ʌn'fʌrnɪʃt] *adj* unmöbliert

ungainly [ʌn'genli] *adj* plump

ungentlemanly [ʌn'dʒentəlmənli] *adj* unfein, unedel

ungodly [ʌn'gɑdli] *adj* (*hour*) ungehörig

ungracious [ʌn'greʃəs] *adj* ungnädig

ungrammatical [,ʌngrə'mætɪkəl] *adj* ungrammatisch

ungrateful [ʌn'gretfəl] *adj* undankbar

ungrudgingly [ʌn'grʌdʒɪŋli] *adv* gern

unguarded [ʌn'gardɪd] *adj* unbewacht; (*moment*) unbedacht

unguent ['ʌŋgwent] *s* Salbe *f*

unhandy [ʌn'hændi] *adj* unhandlich; (*person*) unbeholfen

unhappy [ʌn'hæpi] *adj* unglücklich

unharmed [ʌn'harmd] *adj* unversehrt

unharness [ʌn'harnɪs] *tr* abschirren

unhealthful [ʌn'helθfəl] *adj* ungesund

unhealthy [ʌn'helθi] *adj* ungesund

unheard-of [ʌn'hʌrd,ʌv] *adj* unerhört

unheated [ʌn'hitɪd] *adj* ungeheizt

unhesitating [ʌn'hezɪ,tetɪŋ] *adj* (*immediate*) unverzüglich; (*unswerving*) unbeirrbar; (*support*) bereitwillig

unhinge [ʌn'hɪndʒ] *tr* (fig) aus den Angeln heben

unhitch [ʌn'hɪtʃ] *tr* (*horses*) ausspannen; (*undo*) losmachen

unholy [ʌn'holi] *adj* unheilig

unhook [ʌn'hʊk] *tr* losmachen; (*a dress*) aufhaken; (*the receiver*) abnehmen

unhoped-for [ʌnˈhopt ˌfɔr] *adj* unverhofft

unhurt [ʌnˈhʌrt] *adj* unbeschädigt; *(person)* unversehrt

unicorn [ˈjunɪˌkɔrn] *s* Einhorn *n*

unification [ˌjunɪfɪˈkeʃən] *s* Vereinigung *f*

uniform [ˈjunɪˌfɔrm] *adj* gleichförmig || *s* Uniform *f*

uniformity [ˌjunɪˈfɔrmɪti] *s* Gleichförmigkeit *f*

uni-fy [ˈjunɪˌfaɪ] *v* (*pret & pp* –fied) *tr* vereinigen

unilateral [ˌjunɪˈlætərəl] *adj* einseitig

unimpaired [ˌʌnɪmˈperd] *adj* ungeschwächt

unimpeachable [ˌʌnɪmˈpitʃəbəl] *adj* unantastbar

unimportant [ˌʌnɪmˈpɔrtənt] *adj* unwichtig

uninflected [ˌʌnɪnˈflektɪd] *adj* (gram) unflektiert

uninhabited [ˌʌnɪnˈhæbɪtɪd] *adj* unbewohnt

uninspired [ˌʌnɪnˈspaɪrd] *adj* schwunglos

unintelligible [ˌʌnɪnˈtelɪdʒəbəl] *adj* unverständlich

unintentional [ˌʌnɪnˈtenʃənəl] *adj* unabsichtlich

uninterested [ʌnˈɪntəˌrestɪd] *adj* (in) uninteressiert (an *dat*)

uninteresting [ʌnˈɪntəˌrestɪŋ] *adj* uninteressant

uninterrupted [ˌʌnɪntəˈrʌptɪd] *adj* ununterbrochen

uninvited [ˌʌnɪnˈvaɪtɪd] *adj* ungeladen

union [ˈjunjən] *adj* Gewerkschafts– || *s* Vereinigung *f*; (*harmony*) Eintracht *f*; (*of workers*) Gewerkschaft *f*; (pol) Union *f*

unionize [ˈjunjəˌnaɪz] *tr* gewerkschaftlich organisieren || *intr* sich gewerkschaftlich organisieren

un'ion shop' *s* Betrieb *m*, der nur Gewerkschaftsmitglieder beschäftigt

unique [juˈnik] *adj* einzigartig

unison [ˈjunɪsən] *s* Einklang *m*

unit [ˈjunɪt] *s* (& mil) Einheit *f*

unite [juˈnaɪt] *tr* vereinigen; (chem) verbinden || *intr* sich vereinigen; (chem) sich verbinden

Unit'ed King'dom *s* Vereinigtes Königreich *n*

Unit'ed Na'tions *spl* Vereinte Nationen *pl*

Unit'ed States' *s* Vereinigte Staaten *pl*

unity [ˈjunɪti] *s* (*harmony*) Einigkeit *f*; (*e.g., of a nation*) Einheit *f*; (fa) Einheitlichkeit *f*

universal [ˌjunɪˈvʌrsəl] *adj* universal, allgemein || *s* Allgemeine *n*; (philos) Allgemeinbegriff *m*

u'niver'sal joint' *s* Kardangelenk *n*

u'niver'sal mil'itary train'ing *s* allgemeine Wehrpflicht *f*

universe [ˈjunɪˌvʌrs] *s* Universum *n*

university [ˌjunɪˈversɪti] *adj* Universitäts– || *s* Universität *f*

unjust [ʌnˈdʒʌst] *adj* ungerecht

unjustified [ʌnˈdʒʌstɪˌfaɪd] *adj* ungerechtfertigt

unjustly [ʌnˈdʒʌstli] *adv* zu Unrecht

unkempt [ʌnˈkempt] *adj* ungekämmt; (fig) verwahrlost

unkind [ʌnˈkaɪnd] *adj* unfreundlich

unknown [ʌnˈnon] *adj* unbekannt

un'known quan'tity *s* Unbekannte *f*

Un'known Sol'dier *s* Unbekannter Soldat *m*

unlatch [ʌnˈlætʃ] *tr* aufklinken

unlawful [ʌnˈlɔfəl] *adj* gesetzwidrig

unleash [ʌnˈliʃ] *tr* losbinden; (fig) entfesseln

unleavened [ʌnˈlevənd] *adj* ungesäuert

unless [ʌnˈles] *conj* wenn ... nicht

unlettered [ʌnˈletərd] *adj* ungebildet

unlicensed [ʌnˈlaɪsənst] *adj* unerlaubt

unlike [ʌnˈlaɪk] *adj* (*unequal*) ungleich; (*dissimilar*) unähnlich || *prep* im Gegensatz zu (*dat*); **be u. s.o.** anders als jemand sein

unlikely [ʌnˈlaɪkli] *adj* unwahrscheinlich

unlimited [ʌnˈlɪmɪtɪd] *adj* unbeschränkt

unlined [ʌnˈlaɪnd] *adj* (*clothes*) ungefüttert; (*paper*) unliniert; (*face*) faltenlos

unload [ʌnˈlod] *tr & intr* ausladen

unload'ing *s* Ausladen *n*; (naut) Löschen *n*

unlock [ʌnˈlɑk] *tr* aufsperren

unloose [ʌnˈlus] *tr* lösen

unloved [ʌnˈlʌvd] *adj* ungeliebt

unlucky [ʌnˈlʌki] *adj* unglücklich

un-make [ʌnˈmek] *v* (*pret & pp* –made) *tr* rückgängig machen; (*a bed*) abdecken

unmanageable [ʌnˈmænɪdʒəbəl] *adj* (*person, animal*) widerspenstig; (*thing*) unhandlich

unmanly [ʌnˈmænli] *adj* unmännlich

unmanned [ʌnˈmænd] *adj* (rok) unbemannt

unmannerly [ʌnˈmænərli] *adj* unmännlich

unmarketable [ʌnˈmɑrkɪtəbəl] *adj* nicht marktgängig

unmarriageable [ʌnˈmærɪdʒəbəl] *adj* nicht heiratsfähig

unmarried [ʌnˈmærɪd] *adj* unverheiratet

unmask [ʌnˈmæsk] *tr* (& fig) demaskieren || *intr* sich demaskieren

unmatched [ʌnˈmætʃt] *adj* (*not matched*) ungleichartig; (*unmatchable*) unvergleichlich

unmerciful [ʌnˈmʌrsɪfəl] *adj* unbarmherzig

unmesh [ʌnˈmeʃ] *tr* (mach) ausrücken

unmindful [ʌnˈmaɪndfəl] *adj* uneingedenk

unmistakable [ˌʌnmɪsˈtekəbəl] *adj* unmißverständlich

unmitigated [ʌnˈmɪtɪˌgetɪd] *adj* ungemildert; (*liar*) Erz–

unmixed [ʌnˈmɪkst] *adj* ungemischt

unmoor [ʌnˈmur] *tr* losmachen || *intr* sich losmachen

unmoved [ʌnˈmuvd] *adj* (fig) ungerührt

unmuzzle [ʌnˈmʌzəl] *tr* den Maulkorb abnehmen (*dat*)

unnatural [ʌn'nætʃərəl] *adj* unnatürlich; *(forced)* gezwungen

unnecessary [ʌn'nesə ˌseri] *adj* unnötig

unneeded [ʌn'nidɪd] *adj* nutzlos

unnerve [ʌn'nɜrv] *tr* entnerven

unnoticeable [ʌn'notɪsəbəl] *adj* unbemerkbar

unnoticed [ʌn'notɪst] *adj* unbemerkt

unobserved [ˌʌnəb'zɜrvd] *adj* unbeobachtet

unobtainable [ˌʌnəb'tenəbəl] *adj* nicht erhältlich

unobtrusive [ˌʌnəb'trusɪv] *adj* unaufdringlich

unoccupied [ʌn'ɑkjə ˌpaɪd] *adj (room, house)* leerstehend; *(seat)* unbesetzt; *(person)* unbeschäftigt

unofficial [ˌʌnə'fɪʃəl] *adj* inoffiziell

unopened [ʌn'opənd] *adj* ungeöffnet

unopposed [ˌʌnə'pozd] *adj (without opposition)* widerspruchslos; *(unresisted)* unbehindert

unorthodox [ʌn'ɔrθə ˌdɑks] *adj* unorthodox; (relig) nicht orthodox

unpack [ʌn'pæk] *tr* auspacken

unpalatable [ʌn'pælətəbəl] *adj* unschmackhaft; (fig) widerlich

unparalleled [ʌn'pærə ˌleld] *adj* unvergleichlich

unpardonable [ʌn'pɑrdənəbəl] *adj* unverzeihlich

unpatriotic [ˌʌnpetri'ɑtɪk] *adj* unpatriotisch

unpaved [ʌn'pevd] *adj* ungepflastert

unperceived [ˌʌnpər'sivd] *adj* unbemerkt

unpleasant [ʌn'plezənt] *adj* unangenehm; *(person)* unsympathisch

unpopular [ʌn'pɑpjələr] *adj* unbeliebt

unpopularity [ʌn ˌpɑpjə'lærɪti] *s* Unbeliebtheit *f*

unprecedented [ʌn'presɪ ˌdentɪd] *adj* unerhört; (jur) ohne Präzedenzfall

unpredictable [ˌʌnprɪ'dɪktəbəl] *adj* unberechenbar; *(weather)* wechselhaft

unprejudiced [ʌn'predʒədɪst] *adj* unvoreingenommen

unprepared [ˌʌnprɪ'perd] *adj* unvorbereitet

unpresentable [ˌʌnprɪ'zentəbəl] *adj* nicht präsentabel

unpretentious [ˌʌnprɪ'tenʃəs] *adj* anspruchslos

unprincipled [ʌn'prɪnsɪpəld] *adj* haltlos

unproductive [ˌʌnprə'dʌktɪv] *adj* unproduktiv; (of) unergiebig (an *dat*)

unprofessional [ˌʌnprə'feʃənəl] *adj (work)* unfachmännisch; *(conduct)* berufswidrig

unprofitable [ʌn'prɑfɪtəbəl] *adj (useless)* nutzlos; (fin) unrentabel

unpronounceable [ˌʌnprə'naunsəbəl] *adj* unaussprechlich

unprotected [ˌʌnprə'tektɪd] *adj (place)* ungeschützt; *(person)* unbeschützt

unpropitious [ˌʌnprə'pɪʃəs] *adj* ungünstig

unpublished [ʌn'pʌblɪʃt] *adj* unveröffentlicht

unpunished [ʌn'pʌnɪʃt] *adj* ungestraft

unqualified [ʌn'kwɑlə ˌfaɪd] *adj* unqualifiziert; *(full, complete)* unbedingt

unquenchable [ʌn'kwentʃəbəl] *adj* unstillbar

unquestionably [ʌn'kwestʃənəbli] *adv* fraglos, unbezweifelbar

unquestioning [ʌn'kwestʃənɪŋ] *adj (obedience)* bedingungslos

unquiet [ʌn'kwaɪ-ət] *adj* unruhig

unrav·el [ʌn'rævəl] *v (pret & pp el[l]ed; ger el[l]ing) tr (a knitted fabric)* auftrennen; (fig) entwirren ‖ *intr* sich fasern; (fig) sich entwirren

unreachable [ʌn'ritʃəbəl] *adj* unerreichbar

unreal [ʌn'ri·əl] *adj* unwirklich

unreality [ˌʌnri'ælɪti] *s* Unwirklichkeit *f*

unreasonable [ʌn'rizənəbəl] *adj* unvernünftig

unrecognizable [ʌn'rekəg ˌnaɪzəbəl] *adj* unerkennbar

unreel [ʌn'ril] *tr* abspulen

unrefined [ˌʌnrɪ'faɪnd] *adj* roh

unrelated [ˌʌnrɪ'letɪd] *adj (to)* ohne Beziehung (zu)

unrelenting [ˌʌnrɪ'lentɪŋ] *adj* unerbittlich

unreliable [ˌʌnrɪ'laɪ·əbəl] *adj* unzuverlässig; (fin) unsolid(e)

unremitting [ˌʌnrɪ'mɪtɪŋ] *adj* unablässig

unrepentant [ˌʌnrɪ'pentənt] *adj* unbußfertig

unrequited [ˌʌnrɪ'kwaɪtɪd] *adj* unerwidert

unreserved [ˌʌnrɪ'zɜrvd] *adj* vorbehaltlos

unresponsive [ˌʌnrɪ'spɑnsɪv] *adj (to)* unempfänglich (für)

unrest [ʌn'rest] *s* Unruhe *f*

unrestricted [ˌʌnrɪ'strɪktɪd] *adj* uneingeschränkt

unrewarded [ˌʌnrɪ'wɔrdɪd] *adj* unbelohnt

unrhymed [ʌn'raɪmd] *adj* ungereimt

un·rig [ʌn'rɪg] *v (pret & pp rigged; ger rigging) tr* abtakeln

unripe [ʌn'raɪp] *adj* unreif

unrivaled [ʌn'raɪvəld] *adj* unübertrefflich

unroll [ʌn'rol] *tr* aufrollen; *(e.g., a cable)* abrollen ‖ *intr* sich aufrollen; sich abrollen

unromantic [ˌʌnro'mæntɪk] *adj* unromantisch

unruffled [ʌn'rʌfəld] *adj* unerschüttert

unruly [ʌn'ruli] *adj* ungebärdig

unsaddle [ʌn'sædəl] *tr (a horse)* absatteln; *(a rider)* aus dem Sattel werfen

unsafe [ʌn'sef] *adj* unsicher

unsaid [ʌn'sed] *adj* ungesagt

unsalable [ʌn'seləbəl] *adj* unverkäuflich

unsanitary [ʌn'sænɪ ˌteri] *adj* unhygienisch

unsalted [ʌn'sɔltɪd] *adj* ungesalzen

unsatisfactory [ʌn ˌsætɪs'fæktəri] *adj* unbefriedigend

unsatisfied [ʌn'sætɪs ˌfaɪd] *adj* unbefriedigt

unsavory [ʌnˈsevəri] *adj* unschmack-haft; (fig) widerlich

unscathed [ʌnˈskeðd] *adj* unversehrt

unscientific [ˌʌnsaɪ-ənˈtɪfɪk] *adj* un-wissenschaftlich

unscramble [ʌnˈskræmbəl] *tr (a mes-sage)* entziffern; (fig) entflechten

unscrew [ʌnˈskru] *tr* aufschrauben

unscrupulous [ʌnˈskrupjələs] *adj* skru-pellos

unseal [ʌnˈsil] *tr* entsiegeln; *(eyes, lips)* öffnen

unseasonable [ʌnˈsizənəbl] *adj* unzei-tig; *(weather)* nicht der Jahreszeit entsprechend

unseasoned [ʌnˈsizənd] *adj* ungewürzt

unseat [ʌnˈsit] *tr (a rider)* aus dem Sattel heben; *(an official)* aus dem Posten verdrängen

unseemly [ʌnˈsimli] *adj* ungehörig

unseen [ʌnˈsin] *adj* ungesehen

unselfish [ʌnˈselfɪʃ] *adj* selbstlos

unsettle [ʌnˈsetəl] *tr* beunruhigen

unsettled [ʌnˈsetəld] *adj (matter, bill)* unerledigt; *(without a residence)* ohne festen Wohnsitz; *(restless)* un-ruhig; *(life)* unstet

unshackle [ʌnˈʃækəl] *tr* die Fesseln abnehmen *(dat)*

unshakable [ʌnˈʃekəbəl] *adj* unerschüt-terlich

unshapely [ʌnˈʃepli] *adj* mißgestaltet

unshaven [ʌnˈʃevən] *adj* unrasiert

unsheathe [ʌnˈʃið] *tr* aus der Scheide ziehen

unshod [ʌnˈʃad] *adj* unbeschuht

unsightly [ʌnˈsaɪtli] *adj* unansehnlich

unsinkable [ʌnˈsɪŋkəbəl] *adj* nicht ver-senkbar

unskilled [ʌnˈskɪld] *adj* ungelernt; **u. laborer** Hilfsarbeiter –in *mf*

unskillful [ʌnˈskɪlfəl] *adj* ungewandt

unsnarl [ʌnˈsnɑrl] *tr* entwirren

unsociable [ʌnˈsoʃəbəl] *adj* ungesellig

unsolicited [ˌʌnsoˈlɪsɪtɪd] *adj* unver-langt

unsold [ʌnˈsold] *adj* unverkauft

unsophisticated [ˌʌnsoˈfɪstɪˌketɪd] *adj* unverfälscht; *(naive)* arglos

unsound [ʌnˈsaund] *adj* ungesund; *(sleep)* unruhig; **of u. mind** geistes-krank

unspeakable [ʌnˈspikəbəl] *adj* unsag-bar

unspoiled [ʌnˈspɔɪld] *adj* unverdorben

unsportsmanlike [ʌnˈsportsmənˌlaɪk] *adj* unsportlich

unstable [ʌnˈstebəl] *adj* unbeständig; *(e.g., ladder)* wacklig; *(hand)* zittrig; *(market, walk)* schwankend; *(incon-stant)* unbeständig; (chem) unbestän-dig

unstinted [ʌnˈstɪntɪd] *adj* uneinge-schränkt

unstinting [ʌnˈstɪntɪŋ] *adj* freigebig

unstitch [ʌnˈstɪtʃ] *tr* auftrennen

unstressed [ʌnˈstrest] *adj* unbetont

unsuccessful [ˌʌnsəkˈsesfəl] *adj* er-folglos

unsuitable [ʌnˈsutəbəl] *adj* ungeeignet; *(inappropriate)* unangemessen

unsullied [ʌnˈsʌlid] *adj* unbefleckt

unsung [ʌnˈsʌŋ] *adj* unbesungen

unsuspected [ˌʌnsəsˈpektɪd] *adj* unver-dächtig; *(not known to exist)* un-geahnt

unsuspecting [ˌʌnsəsˈpektɪŋ] *adj* arglos

unswerving [ʌnˈswɜrvɪŋ] *adj* unentwegt

unsympathetic [ˌʌnsɪmpəˈθetɪk] *adj* teilnahmslos

unsystematic(al) [ˌʌnsɪstəˈmætɪk(əl)] *adj* unsystematisch

untactful [ʌnˈtæktfəl] *adj* taktlos

untalented [ʌnˈtæləntɪd] *adj* unbegabt

untamed [ʌnˈtemd] *adj* ungezähmt

untangle [ʌnˈtæŋɡəl] *tr (& fig)* ent-wirren

untenable [ʌnˈtenəbəl] *adj* unhaltbar

untested [ʌnˈtestɪd] *adj* ungeprüft

unthankful [ʌnˈθæŋkfəl] *adj* undank-bar

unthinking [ʌnˈθɪŋkɪŋ] *adj* gedanken-los

untidy [ʌnˈtaɪdi] *adj* unordentlich

un·tie [ʌnˈtaɪ] *v (pret & pp* –**tied**; *ger* –**tying**) *tr* aufbinden; *(a knot)* lösen; **my shoe is untied** mein Schuh ist auf-gegangen

until [ʌnˈtɪl] *prep* bis *(acc)*; **u. further notice** bis auf weiteres ‖ *conj* bis

untimely [ʌnˈtaɪmli] *adj* frühzeitig; *(at the wrong time)* unzeitgemäß

untiring [ʌnˈtaɪrɪŋ] *adj* unermüdlich

untold [ʌnˈtold] *adj (suffering)* unsäg-lich; *(countless)* zahllos

untouched [ʌnˈtʌtʃt] *adj* unangetastet; (fig) ungerührt

untoward [ʌnˈtord] *adj (unfavorable)* ungünstig; *(unruly)* widerspenstig

untrained [ʌnˈtrend] *adj* unausgebil-det; *(eye)* ungeschult; (sport) un-trainiert

untried [ʌnˈtraɪd] *adj (unattempted)* unversucht; *(untested)* unerprobt; *(case)* (jur) nicht verhandelt

untroubled [ʌnˈtrʌbəld] *adj (mind, times)* ruhig; *(peace)* ungestört

untrue [ʌnˈtru] *adj* unwahr; *(unfaith-ful)* un(ge)treu; *(not exact)* ungenau

untrustworthy [ʌnˈtrʌstˌwɜrði] *adj* un-glaubwürdig

untruth [ʌnˈtruθ] *s* Unwahrheit *f*

untruthful [ʌnˈtruθfəl] *adj (statement)* unwahr; *(person)* unaufrichtig

untwist [ʌnˈtwɪst] *tr* aufflechten ‖ *intr* aufgehen

unusable [ʌnˈjuzəbəl] *adj* nicht ver-wendbar; *(unconsumable)* unbenutz-bar

unusual [ʌnˈjuʒʊ-əl] *adj* ungewöhnlich

unutterable [ʌnˈʌtərəbəl] *adj* unaus-sprechlich

unvarnished [ʌnˈvɑrnɪʃt] *adj* nicht ge-firnißt; *(truth)* ungeschminkt

unveil [ʌnˈvel] *tr (a monument)* ent-hüllen; *(a face)* entschleiern

unventilated [ʌnˈventɪˌletɪd] *adj* un-gelüftet

unvoiced [ʌnˈvɔɪst] *adj* (ling) stimmlos

unwanted [ʌnˈwɑntɪd] *adj* uner-wünscht

unwarranted [ʌnˈwɑrəntɪd] *adj* unge-rechtfertigt

unwary [ʌnˈweri] *adj* unvorsichtig

unwavering [ʌn'weɪvərɪŋ] *adj* standhaft
unwelcome [ʌn'wɛlkəm] *adj* unwillkommen
unwell [ʌn'wɛl] *adj* unwohl
unwept [ʌn'wɛpt] *adj* unbeweint
unwholesome [ʌn'holsəm] *adj* schädlich; (& *fig*) unbekömmlich
unwieldy [ʌn'wildi] *adj* (*person*) schwerfällig; (*thing*) unhandlich
unwilling [ʌn'wɪlɪŋ] *adj* (*involuntary*) unfreiwillig; (*reluctant*) widerwillig; (*obstinate*) eigensinnig; **be u. to** (*inf*) nicht (*inf*) wollen
unwillingly [ʌn'wɪlɪŋli] *adv* ungern
un·wind [ʌn'waɪnd] *v* (*pret & pp* **–wound**) *tr* abwickeln || *intr* sich abwickeln; (*fig*) sich entspannen
unwise [ʌn'waɪz] *adj* unklug
unwished-for [ʌn'wɪʃt‚fɔr] *adj* unerwünscht
unwitting [ʌn'wɪtɪŋ] *adj* unwissentlich
unworkable [ʌn'wʌrkəbəl] *adj* (*plan*) unausführbar; (*material*) nicht zu bearbeiten(d)
unworldly [ʌn'wʌrldli] *adj* nicht weltlich; (*naive*) weltfremd
unworthy [ʌn'wʌrði] *adj* unwürdig
un·wrap [ʌn'ræp] *v* (*pret & pp* **–wrapped**; *ger* **–wrapping**) *tr* auspacken || *intr* aufgehen
unwrinkled [ʌn'rɪŋkəld] *adj* faltenlos
unwritten [ʌn'rɪtən] *adj* ungeschrieben; (*agreement*) mündlich
unyielding [ʌn'jildɪŋ] *adj* unnachgiebig
up [ʌp] *adj & adv* (*at a height*) oben; (*to a height*) hinauf; **be up** (*be out of bed; said of a shade*) aufsein; (*baseball*) am Schlag sein; **be up and around again** wieder auf dem Damm sein; **be up to** (*be ready for*) gewachsen sein (*dat*); (*e.g., mischief*) vorhaben; **from ten dollars and up** von zehn Dollar aufwärts; **it's up to you** es hängt von Ihnen ab; **prices are up** die Preise sind gestiegen; **up and down** (*back and forth*) auf und ab; (*from head to toe*) von oben bis unten; **up there** da oben; **up to** (*e.g., one hour*) bis zu; **up to the ears in debt** bis über die Ohren in Schulden || *v* (*pret & pp* **upped**; *ger* **upping**) *tr* erhöhen || *prep* (*acc*) hinauf (*postpositive*)
up-and-coming [‚ʌpən'kʌmɪŋ] *adj* (coll) unternehmungslustig
up-and-up [‚ʌpən'ʌp] *s*—**be on the u.** aufrichtig sein
upbraid *tr* Vorwürfe machen (*dat*)
upbringing [‚ʌp‚brɪŋɪŋ] *s* Erziehung *f*
update' *tr* aufs laufende bringen
up'draft' *s* Aufwind *m*
upend' *tr* hochkant stellen
up'grade' *s* Steigung *f*; **on the u.** (fig) im Aufsteigen || **up'grade'** *tr* (*reclassify*) höher einstufen; (*improve*) verbessern
upheaval [ʌp'hivəl] *s* Umbruch *m*
up'hill' *adj* ansteigend; (fig) mühsam; **u. struggle** harter Kampf *m* || *adv* bergauf
uphold' *v* (*pret & pp* **–held**) *tr* (*the law*) unterstützen; (*a verdict*) bestätigen

upholster [ʌp'holstər] *tr* (auf)polstern
upholsterer [ʌp'holstərər] *s* Polsterer –in *mf*
upholstery [ʌp'holstəri] *s* Polsterung *f*
up'keep' *s* Instandhaltung *f*; (*maintenance costs*) Instandhaltungskosten *pl*
upland [‚ʌplənd] *adj* Hochlands–, Berg– || **the uplands** *spl* das Hochland
up'lift' *s* (fig) Aufschwung *m*; **moral u.** moralischer Auftrieb *m* || **up'lift'** *tr* (fig) geistig (or moralisch) erheben
upon [ə'pɑn] *prep* (*position*) an (*dat*), auf (*dat*); (*direction*) an (*acc*), auf (*acc*); **u. my word!** auf mein Wort!
upper [‚ʌpər] *adj* obere, Ober– || **uppers** *spl* Oberleder *n*
up'per-case' *adj* in Großbuchstaben gedruckt (or geschrieben)
up'per class'es *spl* Oberschicht *f*
up'percut' *s* (box) Aufwärtshaken *m*
up'per deck' *s* Oberdeck *n*
up'per hand' *s* Oberhand *f*
up'per lip' *s* Oberlippe *f*
up'permost' *adj* oberste
uppish [‚ʌpɪʃ] *adj* (coll) hochnäsig
uppity [‚ʌpɪti] *adj* (coll) eingebildet
upraise' *tr* erheben
up'right' *adj* aufrecht; (fig) redlich || *s* (fb) Torpfosten *m*
up'ris'ing *s* Aufstand *m*
up'roar' *s* Aufruhr *m*
uproarious [ʌp'rorɪ‚əs] *adj* (*noisy*) lärmend; (*laughter*) schallend; (*applause*) tosend; (*very funny*) zwerchfellerschütternd
uproot' *tr* entwurzeln
ups' and downs' *spl* Auf und Ab *n*
upset' *adj* (*over*) verstimmt (über *acc*) || **up'set'** *s* unerwartete Niederlage *f* || **up'set'** *v* (*pret & pp* **–set**; *ger* **–setting**) *tr* (*throw over*) umwerfen; (*tip over*) umkippen; (*plans*) umstoßen; (*a person*) aufregen; (*the stomach*) verderben
up'shot' *s* Ergebnis *n*
up'side down' *adv* verkehrt; **turn u.** auf den Kopf stellen
up'stage' *adv* in den (or im) Hintergrund der Bühne || *tr* (coll) ausstechen
up'stairs' *adj* im oberen Stockwerk || *adv* (*position*) oben; (*direction*) nach oben || *s* oberes Stockwerk *n*
upstand'ing *adj* aufrecht; (*sincere*) aufrichtig
up'start' *s* Emporkömmling *m*
up'stream' *adj* weiter stromaufwärts gelegen || *adv* stromaufwärts
up'stroke' *s* Aufstrich *m*; (mach) Hub *m*
up'surge' *s* Aufwallung *f*
up'sweep' *s* Hochfrisur *f*
up'swing' *s* (fig) Aufschwung *m*
upsy-daisy [‚ʌpsi'dezi] *interj* hopsasa!
up-to-date [‚ʌptə'det] *adj* (*modern*) zeitgemäß; (*with latest information*) auf dem neuesten Stand
up'-to-the-min'ute news' [‚ʌptəðə'mɪnɪt] *s* Zeitfunk *m*
up'trend' *s* steigende Tendenz *f*

up'turn' s Aufschwung m
upturned' adj nach oben gebogen; **u. nose** Stupsnase f
upward ['ʌpwərd] adj nach oben gerichtet; (tendency) steigend ‖ adv aufwärts
U'ral Moun'tains ['jurəl] spl Ural m
uranium [ju'renı·əm] adj Uran– ‖ s Uran n
urban ['ʌrbən] adj städtisch, Stadt–
urbane [ʌr'ben] adj weltgewandt
urbanite ['ʌrbə͵naɪt] s Städter –in mf
urbanize ['ʌrbə͵naɪz] tr verstädtern
ur'ban renew'al s Altstadtsanierung f
urchin ['ʌrtʃɪn] s Bengel m
ure•thra [ju'riθrə] s (–thras & –thrae [θri]) Harnröhre f
urge [ʌrdʒ] s Drang m, Trieb m ‖ tr drängen; **u. on** antreiben
urgency ['ʌrdʒənsi] s Dringlichkeit f
urgent ['ʌrdʒənt] adj dringend
urinal ['jurɪnəl] s (in a toilet) Urinbecken n; (in a sick bed) Urinflasche f
urinary ['jurɪ͵neri] adj Harn–, Urin–
urinate ['jurɪ͵net] intr harnen
urine ['jurɪn] s Harn m, Urin m
urn [ʌrn] s Urne f; (for coffee) Kaffeemaschine f
urology [jɪ'rɑlədʒi] s Urologie f
us [ʌs] per pron uns
U.S.A. ['ju'es'e] s (United States of America) USA pl
usable ['juzəbəl] adj (consumable items) verwendbar; (non-consumable items) benutzbar
usage ['jusɪdʒ] s (using) Gebrauch m; (treatment) Behandlung f; (ling) Sprachgebrauch m; **rough u.** starke Beanspruchung f
use [jus] s (of consumable items) Verwendung f, Gebrauch m; (of non-consumable items) Benutzung f; (application) Anwendung f; (advantage) Nutzen m; (purpose) Zweck m; (consumption) Verbrauch m; **I have no use for him** ich habe nichts für ihn übrig; **in use** in Gebrauch; **it's no use** es nützt nichts; **make use of** ausnutzen; **of use** von Nutzen; **there's no use in** (ger) es hat keinen Zweck zu (inf) ‖ [juz] tr (ge)brauchen, verwenden; (non-consumable items) benutzen; (apply) anwenden; (e.g.,

troops) einsetzen; **use up** verbrauchen ‖ intr—**he used to live here er** wohnte früher hier
used [juzd] adj gebraucht; (car) gebraucht–; **be u. to** gewöhnt sein an (acc); **be u. to** (ger) gewöhnt sein zu (inf); **get s.o. u. to** j–n gewöhnen an (acc); **get u. to** sich gewöhnen an (acc)
useful ['jusfəl] adj nützlich
usefulness ['jusfəlnɪs] s Nützlichkeit f; (usability) Brauchbarkeit f
useless ['juslɪs] adj nutzlos; (not usable) unbrauchbar
user ['juzər] s (of gas, electric) Verbraucher –in mf; (e.g., of a book) Benutzer –in mf
usher ['ʌʃər] s Platzanweiser –in mf ‖ tr—**u. in** hereinführen; (a new era) einleiten
U.S.S.R. ['ju'es'es'ɑr] s (Union of Soviet Socialist Republics) UdSSR f
usual ['juʒu·əl] adj gewöhnlich; **as u.** wie gewöhnlich
usually ['juʒu·əli] adv gewöhnlich
usurp [ju'zʌrp] tr usurpieren
usurper [ju'zʌrpər] s Usurpator –in mf
usury ['juʒəri] s Wucher m
utensil [ju'tensɪl] s Gerät n; **utensils** Utensilien pl
uter•us ['jutərəs] s (–i [͵aɪ]) Gebärmutter f
utilitarian [͵jutɪlɪ'terɪ·ən] adj utilitaristisch, Nützlichkeits–
utility [ju'tɪlɪti] s (usefulness) Nützlichkeit f; (company) öffentlicher Versorgungsbetrieb m; **apartment with all utilities** Wohnung f mit allem Zubehör; **utilities** Gas, Wasser, Strom pl
utilize ['jutɪ͵laɪz] tr verwerten
utmost ['ʌt͵most] adj äußerste, höchste ‖ s—**do one's u.** sein Äußerstes tun; **to the u.** auf äußerste; **to the u. of one's power** nach besten Kräften
utopia [ju'topɪ·ə] s Utopie f
utopian [ju'topɪ·ən] adj utopisch
utter ['ʌtər] adj völlig, Erz– ‖ tr (a sigh) ausstoßen; (a sound) hervorbringen; (feelings) ausdrücken; (words) äußern
utterance ['ʌtərəns] s Äußerung f
utterly ['ʌtərli] adv ganz und gar, völlig

V

V, v [vi] s zweiundzwanzigster Buchstabe des englischen Alphabets
vacancy ['vekənsi] s (emptiness) Leere f; (unfilled job) freie Stelle f; **no v.** (public sign) kein freies Zimmer
vacant ['vekənt] adj frei; (stare) geistesabwesend; (lot) unbebaut
vacate [ve'ket] tr (a home) räumen; (a seat) freimachen ‖ intr ausziehen
vacation [ve'keʃən] s Urlaub m; (educ)

Ferien pl; **on v.** auf Urlaub ‖ intr Urlaub machen
vacationer [ve'keʃənər] s Urlauber –in mf
vaccinate ['væksɪ͵net] tr impfen
vaccination [͵væksɪ'neʃən] s Impfung f
vaccina'tion certi'ficate s Impfschein m
vaccine [væk'sin] s Impfstoff m

vacillate ['væsɪˌlet] *intr* schwanken

vacuous ['vækjuˑəs] *adj* nichtssagend

vacu·um ['vækjuˑəm] *s* (-ums & -a [ə]) Vakuum *n* ‖ *tr* & *intr* staubsaugen

vac'uum clean'er *s* Staubsauger *m*

vac'uum pump' *s* Absaugepumpe *f*

vac'uum tube' *s* Vakuumröhre *f*

vagabond ['vægəˌbɑnd] *s* Landstreicher –in *mf*

vagary ['vegərɪ] *s* Laune *f*

vagina [vəˈdʒaɪnə] *s* Scheide *f*

vagrancy ['vegrənsɪ] *s* Landstreicherei *f*

vagrant ['vegrənt] *adj* vagabundierend ‖ *s* Landstreicher –in *mf*

vague [veg] *adj* unbestimmt, vage

vain [ven] *adj* (proud) eitel; (pointless) vergeblich; **in v.** vergebens

vainglo'rious *adj* prahlerisch

valance ['væləns] *s* Quervolant *m*

vale [vel] *s* Tal *n*

valedictory [ˌvælɪˈdɪktərɪ] *s* Abschiedsrede *f*

valence ['veləns] *s* Wertigkeit *f*

valentine ['vælənˌtaɪn] *s* Valentinsgruß *m*

vale' of tears' *s* Jammertal *n*

valet ['vælɪt] *s* Kammerdiener *m*

valiant ['væljənt] *adj* tapfer

valid ['vælɪd] *adj* (law, ticket) gültig; (argument, objection) wohlbegründet; (e.g., contract) rechtsgültig; **be v.** gelten

validate ['vælɪˌdet] *tr* bestätigen

validation [ˌvælɪˈdeʃən] *s* Bestätigung *f*

validity [vəˈlɪdɪtɪ] *s* Gültigkeit *f*

valise [vəˈlis] *s* Reisetasche *f*

valley ['vælɪ] *s* Tal *n*

valor ['vælər] *s* Tapferkeit *f*

valorous ['vælərəs] *adj* tapfer

valuable ['væljuˑəbəl] *adj* wertvoll ‖ **valuables** *spl* Wertsachen *pl*

value ['vælju] *s* Wert *m* ‖ *tr* (at) schätzen (auf *acc*)

val'ue judg'ment *s* Werturteil *n*

valueless ['væljulɪs] *adj* wertlos

valve [vælv] *s* (anat, mach, zool) Klappe *f*; (mach, mus) Ventil *n*

vamp [væmp] *s* (coll) Vamp *m*

vampire ['væmpaɪr] *s* Vampir *m*

van [væn] *s* Möbelwagen *m*; (panel truck) Kastenwagen *m*; (fig) Avantgarde *f*; (mil) Vorhut *f*

vandal ['vændəl] *s* Vandale *m*; **Vandal** Vandale *m*

vandalism ['vændəˌlɪzəm] *s* Vandalismus *m*

vane [ven] *s* (of a windmill, fan, propeller) Flügel *m*; (in a turbine) Schaufel *f*

vanguard ['vænˌgɑrd] *s* (fig) Spitze *f*; (mil) Vorhut *f*

vanilla [vəˈnɪlə] *s* Vanille *f*

vanish ['vænɪʃ] *intr* (ver)schwinden; **v. into thin air** sich in blauen Dunst auflösen

van'ishing cream' *s* Tagescreme *f*

vanity ['vænɪtɪ] *s* (arrogance) Anmaßung *f*; (emptiness) Nichtigkeit *f*; (furniture) Frisiertisch *m*

van'ity case' *s* Kosmetikköfferchen *n*

vanquish ['væŋkwɪʃ] *tr* besiegen

van'tage point' ['væntɪdʒ] *s* (advantage) günstiger Ausgangspunkt *m*; (view) Aussichtspunkt *m*

vapid ['væpɪd] *adj* schal, fad(e)

vapor ['vepər] *s* Dampf *m*, Dunst *m*

vaporize ['vepəˌraɪz] *tr* & *intr* verdampfen

vaporizer ['vepəˌraɪzər] *s* Inhalationsapparat *m*

va'por trail' *s* Kondensstreifen *m*

variable ['verɪˑəbəl] *adj* veränderlich; (wind) aus wechselnden Richtungen ‖ *s* (math) Veränderliche *f*

variance ['verɪˑəns] *s* Veränderung *f*; (difference) Abweichung *f*; (argument) Streit *m*; **be at v. with** (a person) in Zwiespalt sein mit; (a thing) in Widerspruch stehen zu

variant ['verɪˑənt] *adj* abweichend ‖ *s* Variante *f*

variation [ˌverɪˈeʃən] *s* Veränderung *f*; (alg, biol, mus) Variation *f*

var'icose vein' ['verɪˌkos] *s* Krampfader *f*

varied ['verɪd] *adj* abwechslungsreich; (diverse) verschieden

variegated ['verɪˑəˌgetɪd] *adj* (diverse) verschieden; (in color) bunt

variety [vəˈraɪˑətɪ] *s* (choice) Auswahl *f*; (difference) Abweichung *f*; (sort) Art *f*; (biol) Spielart *f*; **for a v. of reasons** aus verschiedenen Gründen

vari'ety show' *s* Varietévorstellung *f*

various ['verɪˑəs] *adj* verschieden; (several) mehrere

varnish ['vɑrnɪʃ] *s* Firnis *m*, Lack *m* ‖ *tr* firnissen

varsity ['vɑrsɪtɪ] *adj* Auswahl– ‖ *s* Auswahlmannschaft *f*

var·y ['verɪ] *v* (pret & pp –ied) *tr* & *intr* abwechseln, variieren

vase [ves], [vez] *s* Vase *f*

vaseline ['væsəˌlin] *s* (trademark) Vaseline *f*

vassal ['væsəl] *s* Lehensmann *m*

vast [væst] *adj* riesig; (majority) überwiegend; **v. amount** Unmasse *f*

vastness ['væstnɪs] *s* Unermeßlichkeit *f*

vat [væt] *s* Bottich *m*

Vatican ['vætɪkən] *adj* vatikanisch; (city) Vatikan– ‖ *s* Vatikan *m*

Vat'ican Coun'cil *s* Vatikanisches Konzil *n*

vaudeville ['vodvɪl] *s* Varieté *n*

vaude'ville show' *s* Varietévorstellung *f*

vault [vɔlt] *s* (underground chamber) Gruft *f*; (of a bank) Tresor *m*; (archit) Gewölbe *n*; **v. of heaven** Himmelsgewölbe *n* ‖ *tr* überspringen

vaunt [vɔnt] *s* Prahlerei *f* ‖ *tr* sich rühmen (genit) ‖ *intr* sich rühmen

veal [vil] *s* Kalbfleisch *n*

veal' cut'let *s* Kalbskotelett *n*

veer [vɪr] *intr* drehen, wenden

vegetable ['vedʒɪtəbəl] *adj* pflanzlich; (garden, soup) Gemüse–; (kingdom, life, oil, dye) Pflanzen– ‖ *s* Gemüse *n*; **vegetables** Gemüse *n*

vegetarian [ˌvedʒɪ'terɪ·ən] *adj* vegetarisch || *s* Vegetarier –in *mf*

vegetate ['vedʒɪˌtet] *intr* vegetieren

vegetation [ˌvedʒɪ'teʃən] *s* Vegetation *f*

vehemence ['vi·ɪməns] *s* Heftigkeit *f*

vehement ['vi·ɪmənt] *adj* heftig

vehicle ['vi·ɪkəl] *s* Fahrzeug *n*

veil [vel] *s* Schleier *m* || *tr* (& fig) verschleiern

veiled *adj* verschleiert; (*threat*) verhüllt

vein [ven] *s* Vene *f*; (geol, min) Ader *f*

vellum ['veləm] *s* Velin *n*

velocity [vɪ'lasɪti] *s* Geschwindigkeit *f*

velvet ['velvɪt] *adj* Samt– || *s* Samt *m*

velveteen [ˌvelvɪ'tin] *s* Baumwollsamt *m*

velvety ['velvɪti] *adj* samtartig

vend [vend] *tr* verkaufen

vend'ing machine' *s* Automat *m*

vendor ['vendər] *s* Verkäufer –in *mf*

veneer [və'nɪr] *s* Furnier *n*; (fig) Tünche *f* || *tr* furnieren

venerable ['venərəbəl] *adj* ehrwürdig

venerate ['venəˌret] *tr* verehren

veneration [ˌvenə'reʃən] *s* Verehrung *f*

Venetian [vɪ'niʃən] *adj* venezianisch || *s* Venezianer –in *mf*

Vene'tian blind' *s* Fensterjalousie *f*

vengeance ['vendʒəns] *s* Rache *f*; take v. on sich rächen an (*dat*); with a v. mit Gewalt

vengeful ['vendʒfəl] *adj* rachsüchtig

venial ['vini·əl] *adj* (*sin*) läßlich

Venice ['venɪs] *s* Venedig *n*

venison ['venɪsən] *s* Wildbret *n*

venom ['venəm] *s* Gift *n*; (fig) Geifer *m*

venomous ['venəməs] *adj* giftig

vent [vent] *s* Öffnung *f*; give v. to Luft machen (*dat*) || *tr* auslassen

ventilate ['ventɪˌlet] *tr* ventilieren

ventilation [ˌventɪ'leʃən] *s* Ventilation *f*

ventilator ['ventɪˌletər] *s* Ventilator *m*

ventricle ['ventrɪkəl] *s* Ventrikel *m*

ventriloquist [ven'trɪləkwɪst] *s* Bauchredner –in *mf*

venture ['ventʃər] *s* Unternehmen *n* || *tr* wagen || *intr* (on) sich wagen (an *acc*); v. out sich hinauswagen; v. to (*inf*) sich vermessen zu (*inf*)

venturesome ['ventʃərsəm] *adj* (*person*) wagemutig; (*deed*) gewagt

venue ['venju] *s* zuständiger Gerichtsort *m*; change of v. Änderung *f* des Gerichtsstandes

Venus ['vinəs] *s* Venus *f*

veracity [vɪ'ræsɪti] *s* Wahrhaftigkeit *f*

veranda [və'rændə] *s* Veranda *f*

verb [vʌrb] *s* Verb *n*, Zeitwort *n*

verbal ['vʌrbəl] *adj* (*oral*) mündlich; (gram) verbal

verbatim [vər'betɪm] *adj* wortgetreu

verbiage ['vʌrbɪ·ɪdʒ] *s* Wortschwall *m*

verbose [vər'bos] *adj* weitschweifig

verdant ['vʌrdənt] *adj* grün

verdict ['vʌrdɪkt] *s* Urteilsspruch *m* (der Geschworenen); give a v. e–n Spruch fällen

verdigris ['vʌrdɪˌgris] *s* Grünspan *m*

verge [vʌrdʒ] *s* (fig) Rand *m*; on the v. of (*ger*) nahe daran zu (*inf*) || *intr*—v. on grenzen an (*acc*)

verifiable [ˌverɪ'faɪ·əbəl] *adj* nachprüfbar

verification [ˌverɪfɪ'keʃən] *s* Nachprüfung *f*

veri·fy ['verɪˌfaɪ] *v* (*pret & pp* **–fied**) *tr* nachprüfen

verily ['verɪli] *adv* (Bib) wahrlich

veritable ['verɪtəbəl] *adj* echt

vermilion [vər'mɪljən] *adj* zinnoberrot

vermin ['vʌrmɪn] *s* (*objectionable person*) Halunke *m*; v. *spl* Schädlinge *pl*; (*objectionable persons*) Gesindel *n*

vermouth [vər'muθ] *s* Wermut *m*

vernacular [vər'nækjələr] *adj* volkssprachlich || *s* Volkssprache *f*

ver'nal e'quinox ['vʌrnəl] *s* Frühlingstagundnachtgleiche *f*

versatile ['vʌrsətɪl] *adj* beweglich

verse [vʌrs] *s* (& Bib) Vers *m*; (stanza) Strophe *f*

versed [vʌrst] *adj* (in) bewandert in (*dat*)

versification [ˌvʌrsɪfɪ'keʃən] *s* (*metrical structure*) Versbau *m*; (*versifying*) Verskunst *f*; (*metrical version*) Versfassung *f*

versifier ['vʌrsɪˌfaɪ·ər] *s* Verseschmied *m*

version ['vʌrʒən] *s* Version *f*

ver·so ['vʌrso] *s* (**–sos**) (*of a coin*) Revers *m*; (typ) Verso *n*

versus ['vʌrsəs] *prep* gegen (*acc*)

verte·bra ['vʌrtɪbrə] *s* (**–brae** [ˌbri] & **–bras**) Rückenwirbel *m*, Wirbel *m*

vertebrate ['vʌrtɪˌbret] *s* Wirbeltier *n*

ver·tex ['vʌrteks] *s* (**–texes & –tices** [trˌsiz]) Scheitelpunkt *m*

vertical ['vʌrtɪkəl] *adj* senkrecht || *s* Vertikale *f*

ver'tical hold' *s* (telv) Vertikaleinstellung *f*

ver'tical take'off *s* Senkrechtstart *m*

vertigo ['vʌrtɪˌgo] *s* Schwindel *m*, Schwindelgefühl *n*

very ['veri] *adj*—that v. day an demselben Tag; the v. thought der bloße Gedanke; the v. truth die reine Wahrheit; the v. man genau der Mann || *adv* sehr; the v. best der allerbeste; the v. same ebenderselbe

vesicle ['vesɪkəl] *s* Bläschen *n*

vespers ['vespərz] *spl* Vesper *f*

vessel ['vesəl] *s* (ship) Schiff *n*; (container) Gefäß *n*

vest [vest] *s* Weste *f*; (for women) Leibchen *n* || *tr* (with) bekleiden (mit); be vested in zustehen (*dat*)

vest'ed in'terest *s* (for personal benefits) persönliches Interesse *n*; (jur) rechtmäßiges Interesse *n*

vestibule ['vestɪˌbjul] *s* Vestibül *n*

vestige ['vestɪdʒ] *s* Spur *f*

vestment ['vestmənt] *s* Gewand *n*

vest'-pock'et *adj* Westentaschen–

vestry ['vestri] *s* Sakristei *f*; (committee) Gemeindevertretung *f*

vetch [vetʃ] *s* Wicke *f*

veteran [ˈvetərən] s Veteran m; (sport) Senior m

veterinarian [ˌvetərɪˈnɛrɪ·ən] s Tierarzt m, Tierärztin f

veterinary [ˈvetərɪˌnɛri] adj (college) tierärztlich; **v. medicine** Tierheilkunde f

ve·to [ˈvito] s (-toes) Veto n || tr ein Veto einlegen gegen

vex [veks] tr ärgern

vexation [vekˈseʃən] s Ärger m

V′-forma′tion s (aer) Staffelkeil m

via [ˈvi·ə] prep über (acc)

viable [ˈvaɪ·əbəl] adj lebensfähig

viaduct [ˈvaɪ·əˌdʌkt] s Viadukt m

vial [ˈvaɪ·əl] s Phiole f

viands [ˈvaɪ·əndz] spl Lebensmittel pl

vibrate [ˈvaɪbret] intr vibrieren; **cause to v.** in Schwingung versetzen

vibration [vaɪˈbreʃən] s Schwingung f

vicar [ˈvɪkər] s Vikar m

vicarage [ˈvɪkərɪdʒ] s Pfarrhaus n

vicarious [vaɪˈkɛrɪ·əs] adj (pleasure) nachempfunden; (taking the place of another) stellvertretend; **v. experience** Ersatzbefriedigung f

vice [vaɪs] s Laster n

vice′-ad′miral s Vizeadmiral m

vice′-con′sul s Vizekonsul m

vice′-pres′ident s Vizepräsident –in mf

viceroy [ˈvaɪsrɔɪ] s Vizekönig m

vice′ squad′ s Sittenpolizei f

vice versa [ˈvaɪsəˈvʌrsə] adv umgekehrt

vicinity [vɪˈsɪnɪti] s Umgebung f; **in the v. of** in der Nähe (genit)

vicious [ˈvɪʃəs] adj (temper) bösartig; (dog) bissig; (person, gossip) heimtückisch

vi′cious cir′cle s Zirkelschluß m

vicissitudes [vɪˈsɪsɪˌtjudz] spl Wechselfälle pl

victim [ˈvɪktɪm] s Opfer n; (animal) Opfertier n; **fall v. to** zum Opfer fallen (dat)

victimize [ˈvɪktɪˌmaɪz] tr (make a victim of) benachteiligen; (dupe) hereinlegen

victor [ˈvɪktər] s Sieger –in mf

victorious [vɪkˈtorɪ·əs] adj siegreich

victory [ˈvɪktəri] adj Sieges– || s Sieg m; (myth) Siegesgöttin f; **flushed with v.** siegestrunken

victuals [ˈvɪtəlz] spl Viktualien pl

vid′eo sig′nal [ˈvɪdɪ·o] s Bildsignal n

vid′eo tape′ s Bildband n

vid′eo tape′ record′er s Bildbandgerät n

vid′eo tape′ record′ing s Bildbandaufnahme f

vie [vaɪ] v (pret & pp vied; ger vying) intr (with) wetteifern (mit)

Vienna [vɪˈɛnə] s Wien n

Vien·nese [ˌvi·əˈniz] adj wienerisch || s (-nese) Wiener –in mf

Vietnam [ˌvi·etˈnɑm] s Vietnam n

Vietnam·ese [vɪˌetnəˈmiz] adj vietnamesisch || s (-se) Vietnamese m, Vietnamesin f

view [vju] s Aussicht f; (opinion) Ansicht f; **come into v.** in Sicht kommen; **in my v.** meiner Ansicht nach; **in v. of** angesichts (genit); **with a v. to** (ger) in der Absicht zu (inf) || tr betrachten; (sights) besichtigen

viewer [ˈvju·ər] s Zuschauer –in mf

view′find′er s Bildsucher m

view′point′ s Standpunkt m

vigil [ˈvɪdʒɪl] s Nachtwache f; **keep v.** wachen

vigilance [ˈvɪdʒɪləns] s Wachsamkeit f

vigilant [ˈvɪdʒɪlənt] adj wachsam

vignette [vɪnˈjet] s Vignette f

vigor [ˈvɪgər] s (physical) Kraft f; (mental) Energie f; (intensity) Wucht f

vigorous [ˈvɪgərəs] adj (strong) kräftig; (act) energisch

vile [vaɪl] adj gemein; (coll) scheußlich

vileness [ˈvaɪlnɪs] s Gemeinheit f

vili·fy [ˈvɪlɪˌfaɪ] v (pret & pp –fied) tr verleumden

villa [ˈvɪlə] s Villa f

village [ˈvɪlɪdʒ] s Dorf n, Ort m

villager [ˈvɪlɪdʒər] s Dorfbewohner –in mf

villain [ˈvɪlən] s Bösewicht m, Schurke m

villainous [ˈvɪlənəs] adj schurkisch

villainy [ˈvɪləni] s Schurkerei f

vim [vɪm] s Mumm m

vindicate [ˈvɪndɪˌket] tr rechtfertigen

vindictive [vɪnˈdɪktɪv] adj rachsüchtig

vine [vaɪn] s Rebe f; (creeper) Ranke f

vinegar [ˈvɪnɪgər] s Essig m

vine′ grow′er [ˌgro·ər] s Winzer m

vineyard [ˈvɪnjərd] s Weinberg m

vintage [ˈvɪntɪdʒ] adj Qualitäts– || s Weinernte f

vin′tage year′ s Weinjahr n

vintner [ˈvɪntnər] s Weinbauer –in mf

vinyl [ˈvaɪnɪl] adj Vinyl–

viola [vaɪˈolə] s Bratsche f, Viola f

violate [ˈvaɪ·əˌlet] tr (a law) verletzen; (a promise) brechen; (the peace) stören; (a custom, shrine) entweihen; (a girl) vergewaltigen

violation [ˌvaɪ·əˈleʃən] s (of the law) Verletzung f; (of a shrine) Entweihung f; (of a girl) Vergewaltigung f

violence [ˈvaɪ·ələns] s Gewalt f

violent [ˈvaɪ·ələnt] adj (person) gewalttätig; (deed) gewaltsam; (anger, argument) heftig

violet [ˈvaɪ·əlɪt] adj violett || s Veilchen n

violin [ˌvaɪ·əˈlɪn] s Geige f

violinist [ˌvaɪ·əˈlɪnɪst] s Geiger –in mf

violoncel·lo [ˌvaɪ·ələnˈtʃɛlo] s (-los) Violoncello n

viper [ˈvaɪpər] s Natter f, Viper f

virgin [ˈvɜrdʒɪn] adj Jungfern–; (land) unberührt || s Jungfrau f

virginity [vərˈdʒɪnɪti] s Jungfräulichkeit f

virility [vɪˈrɪlɪti] s Zeugungskraft f

virology [vaɪˈrɑlədʒi] s Virusforschung f

virtual [ˈvʌrtʃʊ·əl] adj faktisch; (opt, tech) virtuell

virtue [ˈvʌrtʃu] s Tugend f; **by v. of** kraft (genit), vermöge (genit)

virtuosity [ˌvᴧrtʃuˈɑsɪti] s Virtuosität f

virtuo·so [ˌvᴧrtʃuˈoso] s (-sos & -si [si]) Virtuose m, Virtuosin f

virtuous [ˈvᴧrtʃu·əs] adj tugendhaft

virulence [ˈvɪrjələns] s Virulenz f

virulent [ˈvɪrjələnt] adj virulent

virus [ˈvaɪrəs] s Virus n

visa [ˈvizə] s Visum n

visage [ˈvɪzɪdʒ] s Antlitz n

viscera [ˈvɪsərə] s Eingeweide pl

viscosity [vɪsˈkɑsɪti] s Viskosität f

viscount [ˈvaɪkaunt] s Vicomte m

viscountess [ˈvaɪkauntɪs] s Vicomtesse f

viscous [ˈvɪskəs] adj zähflüssig

vise [vaɪs] s Schraubstock m

visibility [ˌvɪziˈbɪlɪti] s Sichtbarkeit f; (meteor) Sicht f

visible [ˈvɪzɪbəl] adj sichtbar

visibly [ˈvɪzɪbli] adv zusehends

vision [ˈvɪʒən] s (faculty) Sehvermögen n; (appearance) Vision f; of great v. von großem Weitblick

visionary [ˈvɪʒəˌneri] adj visionär || s Visionär –in mf

visit [ˈvɪzɪt] s Besuch m; (official) Visite f || tr besuchen; (a museum, town) besichtigen

visitation [ˌvɪziˈteʃən] s Visitation f; Visitation of our Lady Heimsuchung f Mariä

vis'iting hours' spl Besuchszeit f

vis'iting nurse' s Fürsorgerin f

visitor [ˈvɪzɪtər] s Besucher –in mf; have visitors Besuch haben

visor [ˈvaɪzər] s Schirm m; (on a helmet) Visier n

vista [ˈvɪstə] s (& fig) Ausblick m

Vistula [ˈvɪstʃʊlə] s Weichsel f

visual [ˈvɪʒu·əl] adj visuell

vis'ual aids' spl Anschauungsmaterial n

visualize [ˈvɪʒu·əˌlaɪz] tr sich [dat] vorstellen

vital [ˈvaɪtəl] adj (lebens)wichtig; (signs, functions) Lebens– || **vitals** spl edle Teile pl

vitality [vaɪˈtælɪti] s Lebenskraft f

vitalize [ˈvaɪtəˌlaɪz] tr beleben

vitamin [ˈvaɪtəmɪn] s Vitamin n

vi'tamin defi'ciency s Vitaminmangel m

vitiate [ˈvɪʃi·ˌet] tr verderben

vitreous [ˈvɪtri·əs] adj glasartig

vitriolic [ˌvɪtriˈɑlɪk] adj (fig) beißend; (chem) Vitriol–

vituperate [varˈt(j)upəˌret] tr schelten

vivacious [vɪˈveʃəs] adj lebhaft

vivid [ˈvɪvɪd] adj lebhaft

vivi·fy [ˈvɪvɪˌfaɪ] v (pret & pp –fied) tr beleben

vivisection [ˌvɪvɪˈsɛkʃən] s Vivisektion f

vixen [ˈvɪksən] s Füchsin f

viz. abbr nämlich

vizier [vɪˈzɪr] s Vezier m, Wesir m

vocabulary [voˈkæbjəˌleri] s (word range) Wortschatz m; (list) Wörterverzeichnis n

vocal [ˈvokəl] adj stimmlich, Stimm–; (outspoken) redselig

voc'al cord' s Stimmband n

vocalist [ˈvokəlɪst] s Sänger –in mf

vocalize [ˈvokəˌlaɪz] tr (phonet) vokalisieren || intr singen; (phonet) in e–n Vokal verwandelt werden

vocation [voˈkeʃən] s Beruf m; (relig) Berufung f

voca'tional guid'ance [voˈkeʃənəl] s Berufsberatung f

voca'tional school' s Berufsschule f

voca'tional train'ing s Berufsausbildung f

vocative [ˈvakətɪv] s Vokativ m

vociferous [voˈsɪfərəs] adj laut

vodka [ˈvadkə] s Wodka m

vogue [vog] s (herrschende) Mode f; be in v. Mode sein

voice [vɔɪs] s Stimme f; in a low v. mit leiser Stimme || tr äußern; (phonet) stimmhaft aussprechen

voiced adj (phonet) stimmhaft

voiceless [ˈvɔɪslɪs] adj stimmlos

void [vɔɪd] adj leer; (invalid) ungültig || s Leere f || tr für ungültig erklären; (the bowels) entleeren

volatile [ˈvalətɪl] adj (explosive) jähzornig; (changeable) unbeständig; (chem) flüchtig

volcanic [valˈkænɪk] adj vulkanisch

volca·no [valˈkeno] s (-noes & -nos) Vulkan m

volition [vəˈlɪʃən] s Wollen n; of one's own v. aus eigenem Antrieb

volley [ˈvali] s (of gunfire) Salve f; (of stones) Hagel m; (sport) Flugschlag m

vol'leyball' s Volleyball m

volt [volt] s Volt n

voltage [ˈvoltɪdʒ] s Spannung f

voluble [ˈvaljəbəl] adj redegewandt

volume [ˈvaljəm] s (book) Band m; (of a magazine series) Jahrgang m; (of sound) Lautstärke f; (amount) Ausmaß n; (of a container) Rauminhalt m; speak volumes Bände sprechen; v. of sales Umsatz m

vol'ume control' s Lautstärkeregler m

voluminous [vəˈluminəs] adj (writer) produktiv; (of great extent or size) umfangreich

voluntary [ˈvalənˌteri] adj freiwillig

volunteer [ˌvalənˈtɪr] adj Freiwilligen– || s Freiwillige mf || tr freiwillig anbieten || intr (for) sich freiwillig erbieten (für, zu)

voluptuary [vəˈlᴧptʃuˌeri] s Wollüstling m

voluptuous [vəˈlᴧptʃu·əs] adj wollüstig

vomit [ˈvamɪt] s Erbrechen n || tr (er)brechen; (smoke) ausstoßen; (fire) speien; (lava) auswerfen || intr sich erbrechen

voodoo [ˈvudu] adj Wudu– || s Wudu m

voracious [vəˈreʃəs] adj gefräßig

voracity [vəˈræsɪti] s Gefräßigkeit f

vor·tex [ˈvortɛks] s (-texes & -tices [tɪ‚siz]) (& fig) Wirbel m

votary [ˈvotəri] s Verehrer –in mf

vote [vot] s Stimme f; (act of voting) Abstimmung f; (right to vote) Stimmrecht n; put to a v. zur Abstimmung bringen || *tr (approve of, e.g., money)* (for) bewilligen (für); **v. down** niederstimmen || *intr* stimmen; **v. by acclamation** durch Zuruf stimmen; **v. for** wählen; **v. on** abstimmen über *(acc)*

vote′ get′ter [ˌgetər] *s* Wahllokomotive *f*

vote′ of con′fidence *s* Vertrauensvotum *n*

vote′ of no′ con′fidence *s* Mißvertrauensvotum *n*

voter [ˈvotər] *s* Wähler –in *mf*

vot′ing booth′ *s* Wahlzelle *f*

vot′ing machine′ *s* Stimmenzählapparat *m*

votive [ˈvotɪv] *adj* Votiv-, Weih-

vo′tive of′fering *s* Weihgabe *f*

vouch [vaut∫] *tr* bezeugen || *intr*—**v. for** bürgen für

voucher [ˈvaut∫ər] *s* Beleg *m*

vouchsafe′ *tr* gewähren

vow [vau] *s* Gelübde *n;* **take a vow of** geloben || *tr* geloben; *(revenge)* schwören; **vow to** *(inf)* sich *[dat]* geloben zu *(inf)*

vowel [ˈvau·əl] *s* Selbstlaut *m,* Vokal *m*

voyage [ˈvɔɪ·ɪdʒ] *s* Reise *f;* *(by sea)* Seereise *f* || *intr* reisen

voyager [ˈvɔɪ·ɪdʒər] *s* Reisende *mf;* *(by sea)* Seereisende *mf*

V′-shaped′ *adj* keilförmig

V′-sign′ *s* Siegeszeichen *n*

vulcanize [ˈvʌlkə ˌnaɪz] *tr* vulkanisieren

vulgar [ˈvʌlgər] *adj* vulgär

vulgarity [vʌlˈgærɪti] *s* Gemeinheit *f*

Vul′gar Lat′in *s* Vulgärlatein *n*

Vulgate [ˈvʌlget] *s* Vulgata *f*

vulnerable [ˈvʌlnərəbəl] *adj* verwundbar; *(position)* ungeschützt; *(fig)* angreifbar; **v. to** anfällig für

vulture [ˈvʌlt∫ər] *s* Geier *m*

W

W, w [ˈdʌbəl ˌju] *s* dreiundzwanzigster Buchstabe des englischen Alphabets

wad [wad] *s* *(of cotton)* Bausch *m;* *(of money)* Bündel *n;* *(of papers)* Stoß *m;* *(of tobacco)* Priem *m*

waddle [ˈwadəl] *s* Watscheln *n* || *intr* watscheln

wade [wed] *intr* waten; **w. into** *(fig)* anpacken; **w. through** *(fig)* sich mühsam durcharbeiten durch

wafer [ˈwefər] *s* Oblate *f*

waffle [ˈwafəl] *s* Waffel *f*

waf′fle i′ron *s* Waffeleisen *n*

waft [wæft] *s* [waft] *tr & intr* wehen

wag [wæg] *s* *(nod)* Nicken *n;* *(shake)* Schütteln *n;* *(of the tail)* Wedeln *n;* *(mischievous person)* Schalk *m* || *v* *(pret & pp* **wagged***; ger* **wagging***) tr (the tail)* wedeln mit; *(nod)* nicken mit; *(shake)* schütteln || *intr* (said of a tail) wedeln; *(said of tongues)* nicht still sein

wage [wedʒ] *adj* Lohn– || *s* Lohn *m;* **wages** Lohn *m* || *tr (war)* führen

wage′ cut′ *s* Lohnabbau *m*

wage′ freeze′ *s* Lohnstopp *m*

wager [ˈwedʒər] *s* Wette *f;* **lay a w.** e–e Wette eingehen || *tr & intr* wetten

waggish [ˈwægɪ∫] *adj* schalkhaft

wagon [ˈwægən] *s* Wagen *m*

wag′on load′ *s* Wagenladung *f*

waif [wef] *s* *(child)* verwahrlostes Kind *n;* *(animal)* verwahrlostes Tier *n*

wail [wel] *s* Wehklage *f* || *intr* (over) wehklagen (über *acc)*

wain·scot [ˈwenskət] *s* Täfelung *f* || *v* *(pret & pp* –scot[t]ed; *ger* –scot[t]ing*) tr* täfeln

waist [west] *s* Taille *f;* **strip to the w.** den Oberkörper freimachen

waist′-deep′ *adj* bis an die Hüften (reichend)

waist′line′ *s* Taille *f;* **watch one's w.** auf die schlanke Linie achten

wait [wet] *s* Warten *n;* **an hour's w.** e–e Stunde Wartezeit || *intr* warten; **that can w.** das hat Zeit; **w. for** *(a person)* warten auf *(acc)*; *(e.g., an answer)* abwarten; **w. on** bedienen; **w. up for** aufbleiben und warten auf *(acc)*

wait′-and-see′ pol′icy *s* Politik *f* des Abwartens

waiter [ˈwetər] *s* Kellner *m;* **w.!** Herr Ober!

wait′ing line′ *s* Schlange *f*

wait′ing list′ *s* Warteliste *f*

wait′ing room′ *s* Warteraum *m;* *(e.g., in a railroad station)* Wartesaal *m*

waitress [ˈwetrɪs] *s* Kellnerin *f*

waive [wev] *tr* verzichten auf *(acc)*

waiver [ˈwevər] *s* Verzicht *m*

wake [wek] *s (at a funeral)* Totenwache *f;* *(naut)* Kielwasser *n;* **in the w. of** im Gefolge *(genit)* || *v (pret* **waked** & **woke** [wok]; *pp* **waked***) tr* wecken; **w. up** aufwecken || *intr* erwachen; **w. up** aufwachen; **w. up to** *(fig)* bewußt werden *(genit)*

wakeful [ˈwekfəl] *adj* wachsam

waken [ˈwekən] *tr* (auf)wecken || *intr* erwachen

walk [wɔk] *s* Spaziergang *m;* *(gait)* Gang *m;* *(path)* Spazierweg *m;* **a five-minute w.** to fünf Minuten zu Fuß zu; **from all walks of life** aus allen Ständen; **go for a w.** spazierengehen; **take for a w.** spazierenführen || *tr (a dog)* spazierenführen; *(a person)* begleiten; *(a horse)* führen; *(the streets)* ablaufen || *intr* (zu Fuß) gehen, laufen; **w. off with** klauen; **w. out on** sitzenlassen; **w. up to** zugehen auf *(acc)*

walk′-away′ *s* (coll) leichter Sieg *m*

walker ['wɔkər] s Fußgänger –in *mf*

walkie-talkie ['wɔki'tɔki] s Sprechfunk-gerät *n*

walk'-in' *adj* (*closet*) begehbar

walk'ing pa'pers *spl* Laufpaß *m*

walk'ing shoes' *spl* Straßenschuhe *pl*

walk'ing stick' s Spazierstock *m*

walk'-on' s (theat) Statist –in *mf*

walk'out' s Ausstand *m*

walk'-o'ver s (sport) leichter Sieg *m*

walk'-up' s Mietwohnung *f* ohne Fahr-stuhl

wall [wɔl] s Mauer *f*; (*between rooms*) Wand *f* ‖ *tr*—**w. up** vermauern

wall' brack'et s Konsole *f*

wall' clock' s Wanduhr *f*

wallet ['wɑlɪt] s Brieftasche *f*

wall'flow'er s (coll) Wandblümchen *n*

wall' map' s Wandkarte *f*

wallop ['wɑləp] s Puff *m*; **have a w.** Schlagkraft haben ‖ *tr* verprügeln; (*defeat*) schlagen

wal'loping *adj* (sl) mordsgroß

wallow ['wɑlo] *intr* sich wälzen; **w. in** (fig) schwelgen in (*dat*)

wall'pa'per s Tapete *f* ‖ *tr* tapezieren

walnut ['wɔlnət] s Walnuß *f*; (*wood*) Walnußholz *n*; (*tree*) Walnußbaum *m*

walrus ['wɔlrəs] s Walroß *n*

waltz [wɔlts] s Walzer *m* ‖ *intr* Walzer tanzen

wan [wɑn] *adj* (**wanner**; **wannest**) bleich; (*smile*) schwach, matt

wand [wɑnd] s Stab *m*; (*in magic*) Zauberstab *m*

wander ['wɑndər] *intr* wandern; (*from a subject*) abschweifen

wanderer ['wɑndərər] s Wanderer –in *mf*

wan'derlust' s Wanderlust *f*

wane [wen] s—**be on the w.** abnehmen ‖ *intr* abnehmen

wangle ['wæŋgəl] *tr* sich [*dat*] er-schwindeln

want [wɑnt] s Bedürfnis *n*; **for w. of** mangels (*genit*) ‖ *tr* wollen; **wanted** (*sought, desired*) gesucht

want' ad' s Kleinanzeige *f*

want'ing *adj*—**be w. in** ermangeln (*genit*)

war [wɔr] s Krieg *m*; **at war** im Kriege; **go to war with** e-n Krieg beginnen gegen; **make war on** Krieg führen gegen ‖ *v* (*pret & pp* **warred**; *ger* **warring**) *intr* kämpfen

warble ['wɑrbəl] s Trillern *n* ‖ *intr* trillern

war' bond' s Kriegsanleihe *f*

war' cry' s Schlachtruf *m*

ward [wɔrd] s (*in a hospital*) Station *f*; (*of a city*) Bezirk *m*; (*person under protection*) Schützling *m*; (*person under guardianship*) Mündel *m*; (*guardianship*) Vormundschaft *f* ‖ *tr*—**w. off** abwehren

warden ['wɔrdən] s Gefängnisdirektor *m*

ward'robe' s Garderobe *f*

ward'room' s (nav) Offiziersmesse *f*

ware [wer] s Ware *f*

ware'house' s Lagerhaus *n*, Warenlager *n*

ware'house'man s (–men) Lagerist *m*

war'fare' s Kriegsführung *f*, Krieg *m*

war' foot'ing s Kriegsbereitschaft *f*

war'head' s Gefechtskopf *m*

war'-horse' s (coll) alter Kämpe *m*

war'like' *adj* kriegerisch

war' lord' s Kriegsherr *m*

warm [wɔrm] *adj* warm; (*friends*) in-tim ‖ *tr* wärmen; **w. up** aufwärmen ‖ *intr*—**w. up** warm werden; (sport) in Form kommen

warm'-blood'ed *adj* warmblütig

warm'front' s Warmfront *f*

warm'-heart'ed *adj* warmherzig

warmonger ['wɔr,mʌŋgər] s Kriegs-hetzer –in *mf*

warmth [wɔrmθ] s Wärme *f*

warm'-up' s (sport) Lockerungsübun-gen *pl*

warn [wɔrn] *tr* (**against**) warnen (vor *dat*)

warn'ing s Warnung *f*; **let this be a w. to you** lassen Sie sich das zur War-nung dienen

warn'ing shot' s Warnschuß *m*

war' of attri'tion s Zermürbungskrieg *m*

warp [wɔrp] s (*of a board*) Verziehen *n* ‖ *tr* (*wood*) verziehen; **w. s.o.'s mind** j–n verschroben machen ‖ *intr* sich verziehen

war'path' s Kriegspfad *m*

warped *adj* (*wood*) verzogen; (*mind, opinion*) verschroben

war'plane' s Kampfflugzeug *n*

warrant ['wɔrənt] s (*justification*) Rechtfertigung *f*; (*authorization*) Berechtigung *f*; **w. for arrest** Haft-befehl *m* ‖ *tr* (*justify*) rechtfertigen; (*guarantee*) garantieren

war'rant of'ficer s (mil) Stabsfeldwebel *m*; (nav) Deckoffizier *m*

warranty ['wɔrənti] s Gewährleistung *f*

war'ranty serv'ice s Kundendienst *m*

warren ['wɔrən] s Kaninchengehege *n*

war'ring *adj* kriegsführend

warrior ['wɔrɪ-ər] s Krieger *m*

Warsaw ['wɔrsɔ] s Warschau *n*

war'ship' s Kriegsschiff *n*

wart [wɔrt] s Warze *f*

war'time' *adj* Kriegs– ‖ s Kriegszeit *f*

war'-torn' *adj* vom Krieg verwüstet

wary ['weri] *adj* vorsichtig

war' zone' s Kriegsgebiet *n*

wash [wɑʃ] *adj* Wasch– ‖ s Wäsche *f*; (aer) Luftstrudel *m*; (paint) dünner Farbüberzug *m*; **do the w.** die Wäsche waschen ‖ *tr* waschen; (metal) schlämmen; (paint) tuschen; (phot) wässern; **w. ashore** anschwem-men; **w. away** wegspülen; **w. off** ab-waschen; **w. out** auswaschen; (a bridge) wegreißen; **w. up** aufwaschen ‖ *intr* waschen; **w. ashore** ans Land spülen

washable ['wɑʃəbəl] *adj* waschbar

wash'-and-wear' *adj* bügelfrei

wash'ba'sin s Waschbecken *n*

wash'bas'ket s Waschekorb *m*

wash'board' s Waschbrett *n*

wash'bowl' s Waschbecken *n*

wash'cloth' s Waschlappen *m*

wash'day' s Waschtag m

washed'-out' adj verwaschen; (tired) schlapp

washer ['wɔʃər] s Waschmaschine f; (of rubber) Dichtungsring m; (of metal) Unterlegscheibe f

washed'-up' adj (coll) erledigt

wash'er-wom'an s (-wom'en) Waschfrau f

wash'ing s Waschen n; (clothes) Wäsche f

wash'ing machine' s Waschmaschine f

wash'out' s Auswaschung f; (failure) Pleite f; (person who fails) Versager –in mf

wash'rag' s Waschlappen m

wash'room' s Waschraum m

wash'stand' s Waschtisch m

wash'tub' s Waschtrog m

wasp [wɑsp] s Wespe f

wasp' waist' s Wespentaille f

waste [west] adj (superfluous) überflüssig; (land) öde ‖ s (of material goods, time, energy) Verschwendung f; (waste material) Müll m; (wilderness) Wildnis f; go to w. vergeudet werden ‖ tr verschwenden, vergeuden ‖ intr—w. away verfallen

waste'bas'ket s Papierkorb m

wasteful ['westfəl] adj verschwenderisch

waste'land' s Ödland n

waste'pa'per s Makulatur f

waste'pipe' s Abflußrohr n

waste'pro'duct s Abfallprodukt n

wastrel ['westrəl] s Verschwender –in mf

watch [wɑtʃ] s Uhr f; (lookout) Wache f; be on the w. for acht haben auf (acc) ‖ tr (observe) beobachten; (guard) bewachen; (oversee) aufpassen auf (acc); w. how I do it passen Sie auf, wie ich es mache; w. your step! Vorsicht, Stufe! ‖ intr (keep guard) wachen; (observe) zuschauen; w. for abwarten; w. over überwachen; w. out! Vorsicht!; w. out for ausschauen nach; (some danger) sich hüten vor (dat); w. out for oneself sich vorsehen

watch'band' s Uhrarmband n

watch'case' s Uhrgehäuse n

watch' crys'tal s Uhrglas n

watch'dog' s Wachhund m

watch'dog commit'tee s Überwachungsausschuß m

watchful ['wɑtʃfəl] adj wachsam

watchfulness ['wɑtʃfəlnɪs] s Wachsamkeit f

watch'mak'er s Uhrmacher –in mf

watch'man s (-men) Wächter m

watch' pock'et s Uhrtasche f

watch' strap' s Uhrarmband n

watch'tow'er s Wachturm m

watch'word' s Kennwort n, Parole f

water ['wɔtər] s Wasser n; (body of water) Gewässer n; pass w. Wasser lassen ‖ tr (e.g., flowers) begießen; (fields) bewässern; (animals) tränken; (the garden, streets) sprengen; w. down (& fig) verwässern ‖ intr (said of the eyes) tränen; my mouth

waters das Wasser läuft mir im Mund zusammen

wa'ter boy' s Wasserträger m

wa'ter clos'et s Wasserklosett n

wa'tercol'or s (paint) Aquarellfarbe f; (painting) Aquarell n

wa'tercourse' s Wasserlauf m

wa'tercress' s Brunnenkresse f

wa'terfall' s Wasserfall m

wa'terfront' s Hafenviertel n

wa'ter heat'er s Warmwasserbereiter m

wa'tering can' s Wasserkanne f

wa'tering place' s (for cattle) Tränke f; (for tourists) Badeort m

wa'ter lev'el s Wasserstand m

wa'terlogged' adj vollgesogen

wa'ter main' s Wasserleitung f

wa'termark' s Wasserzeichen n

wa'ter mat'tress s Wasserbett n

wa'termel'on s Wassermelone f

wa'ter me'ter s Wasserzähler m

wa'ter pipe' s Wasserrohr n

wa'ter po'lo s Wasserball m

wa'ter pow'er s Wasserkraft f

wa'terproof' adj wasserdicht ‖ tr imprägnieren

wa'ter-repel'lent adj wasserabstoßend

wa'tershed' s Wasserscheide f

wa'ter-ski' intr wasserschifahren

wa'terspout' s (orifice) Wasserspeier m; (pipe) Ablaufrohr n

wa'ter supply' s Wasserversorgung f

wa'ter ta'ble s Grundwasserspiegel m

wa'ter tank' s Wasserbehälter m

wa'tertight' adj wasserdicht; (fig) eindeutig

wa'ter wag'on s—be on the w. Abstinenzler sein

wa'terway' s Wasserstraße f

wa'ter wheel' s (for raising water) Schöpfwerk n; (water-driven) Wasserrad n

wa'ter wings' spl Schwimmkissen n

wa'terworks' s Wasserwerk n

watery ['wɔtəri] adj wäss(e)rig

watt [wɑt] s Watt n

wattage ['wɑtɪdʒ] s Wattleistung f

wattles ['wɑtəlz] spl Flechtwerk s

watt'me'ter s Wattmeter m

wave [wev] s (fig, meteor, mil, phys, rad) Welle f; w. of the hand Wink m mit der Hand ‖ tr (a hat, flag) schwenken; (a hand, handkerchief) winken mit; (hair) wellen; w. one's hands about mit den Händen herumfuchteln; w. s.o. away j–n abwinken ‖ intr (said of a flag) wehen; (said of grain) wogen; (with the hand) winken; w. to zuwinken (dat)

wave'length' s Wellenlänge f

waver ['wevər] intr schwanken, wanken

wavy ['wevi] adj wellenförmig; w. line Wellenlinie f

wax [wæks] adj Wachs– ‖ s Wachs n ‖ tr (the floor) bohnern; (skis) wachsen ‖ intr werden; (said of the moon) zunehmen; wax and wane zu– und abnehmen

wax' muse'um s Wachsfigurenkabinett n

wax' pa'per s Wachspapier n

way [we] adv weit; **way ahead** weit

voraus || *s* Weg *m; (manner)* Art *f; (means)* Mittel *n; (condition)* Verfassung *f; (direction)* Richtung *f;* across the way gegenüber; a long way from weit weg von; a long way off weit weg; by the way übrigens; by way of über *(acc);* by way of comparison vergleichsweise; get s.th. out of the way etw aus dem Wege schaffen; get under way in Gang kommen; go all the way aufs Ganze gehen; go one's own way aus der Reihe tanzen; have a way with s.o. mit j-m umzugehen verstehen; have in the way of *(merchandise)* haben an *(dat);* have it both ways es sich *[dat]* aussuchen können; have one's own way seinen Willen durchsetzen; I'm on my way! ich komme schon!; in a way gewissermaßen; in no way keineswegs; in the way im Weg; in this way auf diese Weise; in what way in welcher Hinsicht; make one's way through the crowd sich *[dat]* e-n Weg durch die Menge bahnen; one way or another irgendwie; on the way unterwegs; on the way out *(fig)* im Begriff unmodern zu werden; see one's way clear bereit sein; that way auf diese Weise; *(in that direction)* in jener Richtung; the way it looks voraussichtlich; way back Rückweg *m;* way here Herweg *m;* way out Ausgang *m; (fig)* Ausweg *m;* way there Hinweg *m*

wayfarer ['we,fεrər] *s* Wanderer *m*

way'lay' *v (pret & pp –laid) tr* auflauern *(dat)*

way' of life' *s* Lebensweise *f*

way' of think'ing *s* Denkweise *s*

ways' and means' *spl* Mittel und Wege *pl*

way'side' *adj* an der Straße gelegen || *s* Wegrand *m;* fall by the w. dem Untergang anheimfallen

wayward ['weward] *adj* ungeraten

we [wi] *pers pron wir*

weak [wik] *adj* schwach

weaken ['wikən] *tr* (ab)schwächen || *intr* schwach werden

weakling ['wiklɪŋ] *s* Schwächling *m*

weak'-mind'ed *adj* willenlos

weakness ['wiknɪs] *s (& fig)* Schwäche *f*

weak' spot' *s* schwache Stelle *f*

weal [wil] *s* Strieme *f,* Striemen *m*

wealth [welθ] *s (of)* Reichtum *m (an dat)*

wealthy ['welθi] *adj* wohlhabend

wean [win] *tr (from)* entwöhnen *(genit)*

weapon ['wepən] *s* Waffe *f*

weaponry ['wepənri] *s* Bewaffnung *f*

wear [wer] *s (use)* Gebrauch *m; (durability)* Haltbarkeit *f; (clothing)* Kleidung *f; (wearing down)* Verschleiß *m* || *v (pret* wore *[wor]; pp* worn *[worn]) tr* tragen; w. down *(a heel)* abtreten; *(a person)* zermürben; w. out abnützen; *(tires)* abfahren; *(a person)* erschöpfen; w. the pants in the family die Hosen anhaben || *intr* sich tragen; w. off sich abtragen; w.

out sich abnützen; w. thin *(said of clothes)* fadenscheinig werden; *(said of patience)* zu Ende gehen

wearable ['werəbəl] *adj* tragbar

wear' and tear' [ter] *s* Verschleiß *m;* takes a lot of w. strapazierfähig sein

weariness ['wirinis] *s* Müdigkeit *f*

wearisome ['wirisəm] *adj* mühsam

wea·ry ['wiri] *adj* müde || *v (pret & pp* –ried) *tr* ermüden || *intr (of)* müde werden *(genit)*

weasel ['wizəl] *s* Wiesel *n* || *intr*—w. out of sich herauswinden aus

weather ['weðər] *s* Wetter *n;* be under the w. unpäßlich sein; w. permitting bei günstiger Witterung || *tr* dem Wetter aussetzen; *(the storm) (fig)* überstehen || *intr* verwittern

weath'erbeat'en *adj* verwittert

weath'er bu'reau *s* Wetterdienst *m*

weath'er condi'tions *spl* Wetterverhältnisse *pl*

weath'er fore'cast *s* Wettervoraussage *f*

weath'erman' *s (–men')* Wetteransager *m*

weath'er report' *s* Wetterbericht *m*

weath'erstrip'ping *s* Dichtungsstreifen *pl*

weath'er vane' *s (& fig)* Wetterfahne *f*

weave [wiv] *s* Webart *f* || *v (pret* wove *[wov] & weaved; pp* woven *['wovən]) tr* weben; *(a rug)* wirken; *(a basket)* flechten; *(a wreath)* winden; w. one's way through traffic sich durch den Verkehr schlängeln || *intr* weben

weaver ['wivər] *s* Weber –in *mf*

web [web] *s (of a spider)* Spinngewebe *n; (of ducks)* Schwimmhaut *f;* web of lies Lügengewebe *n*

web'-foot'ed *adj* schwimmfüßig

wed [wed] *v (pret & pp* wed *&* wedded; *ger* wedding) *tr & intr* heiraten

wed'ding *adj (cake, present, day, reception)* Hochzeits–; *(ring)* Trau– || *s* Hochzeit *f; (ceremony)* Trauung *f*

wedge [wedʒ] *s* Keil *m* || *tr*—w. in einkeilen

wed'lock' *s* Ehestand *m;* out of w. unehelich

Wednesday ['wenzde] *s* Mittwoch *m;* on W. am Mittwoch

wee [wi] *adj* winzig; a wee bit ein klein wenig

weed [wid] *s* Unkraut *n; (marijuana) (sl)* Marihuana *n; (cigarette) (sl)* Zigarette *f;* pull weeds jäten || *tr* jäten; w. out *(fig)* aussondern

weed' kill'er *s* Unkrautvertilgungsmittel *n*

week [wik] *s* Woche *f;* a w. from today heute in e-r Woche; a w. ago today heute vor acht Tagen; for weeks wochenlang

week'day' *s* Wochentag *m*

week'end' *s* Wochenende *n*

weekender ['wik,εndər] *s* Wochenendausflügler –in *mf*

weekly ['wikli] *adj* wöchentlich; *(wages)* Wochen– || *s* Wochenblatt *n*

weep [wip] *v (pret & pp* wept *[wept]) tr & intr* weinen weep'ing wil'low s Trauerweide f

weevil ['wivəl] s Rüsselkäfer m

weft [wɛft] s (tex) Schußfaden m

weigh [we] tr wiegen; (ponder) wägen; (anchor) lichten || intr wiegen; w. heavily on schwer lasten auf (dat)

weight [wet] s Gewicht n; (burden) Last f; (influence) Einfluß m; (importance) Bedeutung f; carry great w. sehr ins Gewicht fallen; lift weights Gewichte heben; pull one's w. das Seine tun; throw one's w. about sich breitmachen

weightless ['wetlɪs] adj schwerelos

weightlessness ['wetlɪsnɪs] s Schwerelosigkeit f

weighty ['weti] adj (& fig) gewichtig

weird [wɪrd] adj unheimlich

weir·do ['wɪrdo] s (-dos) (sl) Kauz m

welcome [wɛl] adj willkommen; (news) erfreulich; you're w.! bitte sehr!; you're w. to (inf) es steht Ihnen frei zu (inf) || s Empfang m, Willkomm m || tr empfangen; (an opportunity) mit Freude begrüßen || interj (to) willkommen! (in dat)

weld [wɛld] s Schweißnaht n || tr & intr schweißen

welder ['wɛldər] s Schweißer –in mf

weld'ing s Schweißung f, Schweißarbeit f

welfare ['wɛl,fɛr] s Wohlfahrt f

wel'fare work'er s Wohlfahrtspfleger –in mf

well [wɛl] adj gesund; all is w. alles ist in Ordnung; feel w. sich wohl fühlen || adv gut, wohl; as w. ebenso; as w. as so gut wie; (in addition to) sowohl ... als auch; he is doing w. es geht ihm gut; his company is doing w. seine Firma geht gut; leave w. enough alone es gut sein lassen; w. on in years schon bejahrt; w. on the way mitten auf dem Wege; (fig) auf dem besten Wege; w. over weit über || s Brunnen m; (hole) Bohrloch n; (source) Quelle f || intr— w. up hervorquellen || interj na!; (in surprise) nanu!

well'-behaved' adj artig

well'-be'ing s Wohlergehen n

well'born' adj aus guter Familie

wellbred ['wɛl'brɛd] adj wohlerzogen

well'-deserved' adj wohlverdient

well'-disposed' adj (toward) wohlgesinnt (dat)

well-done ['wɛl'dʌn] adj (culin) durchgebraten || interj gut gemacht!

well'-dressed' adj gut angezogen

well'-found'ed adj wohlbegründet

well'-groomed' adj gut gepflegt

well'-heeled' adj (coll) steinreich

well'-informed' adj wohlunterrichtet

well'-inten'tioned adj wohlmeinend

well-kept ['wɛl'kɛpt] adj gut gepflegt; (secret) gut gehütet

well'-known' adj wohlbekannt

well'-mean'ing adj wohlmeinend

well'-nigh' adv fast

well'-off' adj wohlhabend, vermögend

well'-preserved' adj gut erhalten

well-read ['wɛl'rɛd] adj belesen

well'-spent' adj (money) gut verwendet; (time) gut verbracht

well'spring' s Brunnquell m

well'-thought'-of' adj angesehen

well'-timed' adj wohl berechnet

well-to-do ['wɛltə'du] adj wohlhabend

well-wisher ['wɛl'wɪʃər] s Gratulant –in mf

well'-worn' adj (clothes) abgetragen; (phrase, subject) abgedroschen

Welsh [wɛlʃ] adj walisisch || s Walisisch n; the W. die Waliser pl || welsh intr—welsh on (a promise) brechen

Welsh' rab'bit or rare'bit ['rɛrbɪt] s geröstete Käseschnitte f

welt [wɛlt] s Striemen m

welter ['wɛltər] s Durcheinander n || intr sich wälzen

wel'terweight s Weltergewichtler m

we'lterweight divi'sion s Weltergewicht n

wench [wɛntʃ] s Dirne f, Weibsbild n

wend [wɛnd] tr—w. one's way seinen Weg nehmen

werewolf ['wɛr,wʌlf] s Werwolf m

west [wɛst] adj westlich || adv nach Westen || s Westen m

western ['wɛstərn] adj westlich || s (cin) Wildwestfilm m

West' Ger'many s Westdeutschland n

West' In'dies, the ['ɪndiz] spl Westindien n

Westphalia [,wɛst'feliə] s Westfalen n

westward ['wɛstwərd] adv westwärts

wet [wɛt] adj (wetter; wettest) naß; all wet (coll) auf dem Holzwege || v (pret & pp wet & wetted; ger wetting) tr naß machen

wet' blan'ket s (fig) Miesepeter m

wet' nurse' s Amme f

whack [wæk] s (coll) Klaps m || tr (coll) klapsen

whale [wɛl] s Wal(fisch) m; have a w. of a time sich großartig unterhalten

whaler ['wɛlər] s Walfänger m

wharf [wɔrf] s (wharves [wɔrvz]) Kaianlage f

what [wɑt] interr adj welcher, was für ein || interr pron was; so w.? na und?; w. about me? und was geschieht mit mir?; w. if was geschieht, wenn; w. is more außerdem; w. next? was noch?; w. of it? was ist da schon dabei?; what's new? was gibt es Neues? what's that to you? was geht Sie das an? || interj was für ein

whatev'er adj welch ... auch immer; no ... w. überhaupt kein || pron was auch immer; w. I have alles, was ich habe; w. you please was Sie wollen

what'not' s—and w. und was weiß ich noch (alles)

what's-his-name' s (coll) Dingsda m

wheal [wil] s Pustel f; (welt) Striemen m

wheat [wit] s Weizen m

wheedle ['hwidəl] tr—w. s.o. into (ger) j-n beschwatzen zu (inf); w. s.th. out of s.o. j-m etw abschwatzen

wheel [wil] s Rad n; **at the w.** (aut) am Steuer || tr fahren || intr sich drehen; **w. around** sich umdrehen

wheelbarrow ['wil‚bæro] s Schubkarre f

wheel'chair' s Krankenfahrstuhl m

wheeler-dealer ['wilər'dilər] s Drahtzieher –in mf

wheeze [wiz] s Schnaufen n || intr schnaufen

whelp [welp] s Welpe m || tr werfen

when [wen] adv wann || conj (once in the past) als; (whenever; at a future time) wenn

whence [wens] adv & conj woher

whenev'er conj wenn, wann immer

where [wer] adv & conj wo; (whereto) wohin; from w. woher

whereabouts ['werə‚bauts] adv wo ungefähr || s & spl Verbleib m

whereas' conj während, wohingegen

whereby' conj wodurch

where'fore adv & conj weshalb

wherefrom' adv woher

wherein' adv & conj worin

whereof' adv & conj wovon

whereto' adv wohin

where'upon' adv worauf, wonach

wherever [wer'evər] conj wo auch

wherewith' adv womit

wherewithal ['werwɪð‚ɔl] s Geldmittel pl

whet [wet] v (pret & pp whetted; ger whetting) tr wetzen, schleifen; (the appetite) anregen

whether [weðər] conj ob

whet'stone' s Wetzstein m, Schleifstein m

whew [hwju] interj hui!; uf!

which [wɪtʃ] interr adj welcher || interr pron welcher || rel pron der, welcher

whichev'er rel adj & rel pron welcher

whiff [wif] s Geruch m, Nasevoll f

while [waɪl] s Weile f || conj während || tr—w. away sich [dat] vertreiben

whim [wim] s Laune f, Grille f

whimper ['wimpər] s Wimmern n || tr & intr wimmern

whimsical ['wimzɪkəl] adj schrullig

whine [waɪn] s Wimmern n; (of a siren, engine, storm) Heulen n || intr wimmern; heulen

whin-ny ['wini] s Wiehern n || v (pret & pp –nied) intr wiehern

whip [wɪp] s Peitsche f || v (pret & pp whipped; ger whipping) tr peitschen; (egg whites) zu Schaum schlagen; (defeat) schlagen; **w. out** blitzschnell ziehen; **w. up** (a meal) hervorzaubern; (enthusiasm) erregen

whip'lash' s Peitschenhieb m; (fig) Peitschenhiebeffekt n

whipped' cream' s Schlagsahne f

whipper-snapper ['wɪpər‚snæpər] s Frechdachs m

whip'ping s Prügel pl

whip'ping boy' s Prügelknabe m

whip'ping post' s Schandpfahl m

whir [wʌr] s Schnurren n || v (pret & pp whirred; ger whirring) intr schnurren

whirl [wʌrl] s Wirbel m; **give s.th. a w.** (coll) etw ausprobieren || intr wirbeln || intr wirbeln; **my head is whirling** mir ist schwindlig

whirl'pool' s Strudel m, Wirbel m

whirl'wind' s Wirbelwind m

whirlybird ['wʌrli‚bʌrd] s (coll) Hubschrauber m

whisk [wɪsk] s Wedel m; (culin) Schneebesen m || tr wischen; **w. away** (fig) eilends mitnehmen; **w. off** wegfegen

whisk' broom' s Kleiderbesen m

whiskers ['wɪskərz] spl Bart m; (on the cheeks) Backenbart m; (of a cat) Barthaare pl

whiskey ['wɪski] s Whisky m

whisper ['wɪspər] s Flüsterton m || tr & intr flüstern

whistle ['wɪsəl] s (sound) Pfiff m; (device) Trillerpfeife f; **wet one's w.** sich [dat] die Nase begießen || tr pfeifen || intr pfeifen; (said of the wind, bullet) sausen; **w. for** (coll) vergeblich warten auf (acc)

whit [wɪt] s—**not care a w. about** sich keinen Deut kümmern um

white [waɪt] adj weiß; **w. as a sheet** kreidebleich || s Weiß n; (of the eye) Weiße f

white'caps' spl Schaumkronen pl

white'-col'lar work'er s Angestellte mf

white'fish' s Weißfisch m

white'-haired' adj weißhaarig

white'-hot' adj weißglühend

white' lie' s Notlüge f

white' meat' s weißes Fleisch n

whiten ['waɪtən] tr weiß machen || intr weiß werden

whiteness ['waɪtnɪs] s Weiße f

white' slav'ery s Mädchenhandel m

white' tie' s Frackschleife f; (formal) Frack m

white'wash' s Tünche f; (fig) Beschönigung f || tr tünchen; (fig) beschönigen

whither ['wɪðər] adv wohin

whitish ['waɪtɪʃ] adj weißlich

whittle ['wɪtəl] tr schnitzeln; **w. away** (or down) verringern || intr—**w. away at** herumschnitzeln an (dat); (fig) verringern

whiz(z) [wɪz] s Zischen n; (fig) Kanone f || v (pret & pp whizzed; ger whizzing) intr zischen; **w. by** flitzen

who [hu] interr pron wer; **who the devil** wer zum Teufel || rel pron der; **he who** wer

whoa [wo] interj halt!

whoev'er rel pron wer, wer auch immer

whole [hol] adj ganz || s Ganze n; **as a w. im** großen und ganzen

whole'-heart'ed adj ernsthaft

whole' note' s (mus) ganze Note f

whole' rest' s (mus) ganze Pause f

whole'sale' adj Massen–; (com) Großhandels– || adv en gros || s Großhandel m || tr en gros verkaufen || intr im großen handeln

wholesaler ['hol‚selər] s Großhändler –in mf

wholesome ['holsəm] *adj* gesund; (*food*) zuträglich

whole'-wheat' bread' *s* Vollkornbrot *n*

wholly ['holi] *adv* ganz, völlig

whom [hum] *interr pron* wen; **to w. wem** ‖ *rel pron* den, welchen; **to w. dem, welchem**

whomev'er *rel pron* wen auch immer; **to w. wem auch immer**

whoop [hup], [hwup] *s* Ausruf *m* ‖ *tr*—**w. it up** Radau machen

whoop'ing cough' *s* Keuchhusten *m*

whopper ['wapər] *s* Mordsding *n*; (*lie*) (coll) faustdicke Lüge *f*

whop'ping *adj* (coll) enorm, Riesen—

whore [hor] *s* Hure *f* ‖ *intr*—**w. around** huren

whose [huz] *interr pron* wessen ‖ *rel pron* dessen

why [war] *adv* warum; **that's why** deswegen; **why, there you are!** da sind Sie ja!; **why, yes!** aber ja! ‖ *s* Warum *n*; **the whys and the wherefores** das Warum und Weshalb

wick [wrk] *s* Docht *m*

wicked ['wrkid] *adj* (*evil*) böse; (*roguish*) boshaft; (*vicious*) bösartig; (*unpleasant*) ekelhaft; (*cold, pain, storm, wound*) (coll) schlimm; (*fantastic*) (coll) großartig

wicker ['wrkər] *adj* (*basket, chair*) Weiden— ‖ *s* (*wickerwork*) Flechtwerk *n*

wide [ward] *adj* breit; (*selection*) reich ‖ *adv* weit

wide'-an'gle lens' *s* Weitwinkelobjektiv *n*

wide'-awake' *adj* hellwach

wide'-eyed' *adj* mit weit aufgerissenen Augen; (*innocence*) naiv

widely ['wardli] *adv* weit

widen ['wardən] *tr* ausweiten, verbreiten ‖ *intr* sich ausweiten

wide'-o'pen *adj* weit geöffnet

wide' screen' *s* (cin) Breitleinwand *f*

wide'spread' *adj* weitverbreitet; (*damage*) weitgehend

widow ['wrdo] *s* Witwe *f*

widower ['wrdo-ər] *s* Witwer *m*

wid'owhood' *s* Witwenstand *m*

width [wrdθ] *s* Breite *f*; **in w. breit**

wield [wild] *tr* (*a weapon*) führen; (*power, influence*) ausüben

wife [warf] *s* (**wives** [warvz]) Frau *f*

wig [wrg] *s* Perücke *f*

wiggle ['wrgəl] *s* Wackeln *n* ‖ *tr* wackeln mit

wigwag ['wrg,wæg] *s* Winksignal *n*

wigwam ['wrgwam] *s* Wigwam *m* & *n*

wild [warld] *adj* wild; **w. about** scharf auf (*acc*); **go w.** verwildern; **grow w.** (*become neglected*) verwahrlosen; **make s.o. w.** (coll) j-n rasend machen ‖ *adv*—**grow w.** (*grow in the wild*) wild wachsen; **run w.** verwildern

wild' boar' *s* Wildschwein *n*

wild' card' *s* wilde Karte *f*

wild'cat' *s* Wildkatze *f*

wild'cat strike' *s* wilder Streik *m*

wilderness ['wrldərnıs] *s* Wildnis *f*

wild'fire' *s*—**like w. wie** Lauffeuer

wild' flow'er *s* Feldblume *f*

wild'-goose' chase' *s*—**go on a w.** sich [dat] vergeblich Mühe machen

wild'life' *s* Wild *n*

wild' oats' *spl*—**sow one's w.** sich [dat] die Hörner abstoßen

wile [warl] *s* List *f* ‖ *tr*—**w. away** sich [dat] vertreiben

will [wrl] *s* Wille(n) *m*; (jur) Testament *n*; **at w.** nach Belieben ‖ *tr* (*bequeath*) vermachen ‖ *v* (*pret & cond* **would** [wʊd]) *aux* werden

willful ['wrlfəl] *adj* absichtlich; (*stubborn*) eigensinnig

William ['wrljəm] *s* Wilhelm *m*

will'ing *adj* bereitwillig; **be w. to** (*inf*) bereit sein zu (*inf*)

willingly ['wrlıŋli] *adv* gern

willingness ['wrlıŋnıs] *s* Bereitwilligkeit *f*

will-o'-the-wisp' ['wrləðə'wɪsp] *s* (& fig) Irrlicht *n*

willow ['wrlo] *s* Weide *f*

willowy ['wrlo-i] *adj* biegsam

will' pow'er *s* Willenskraft *f*

willy-nilly ['wrli'nrli] *adv* wohl oder übel

wilt [wrlt] *tr* verwelken lassen ‖ *intr* verwelken

wilt'ed *adj* welk

wily ['warli] *adj* schlau, listig

wimple ['wrmpəl] *s* Kinntuch *n*

win [wrn] *s* Gewinn *m*; (sport) Sieg *m* ‖ *v* (*pret & pp* **won** [wʌn]; *ger* **winning**) *tr* gewinnen; **win over to one's side** auf seine Seite ziehen ‖ *intr* gewinnen, siegen

wince [wrns] *s* Zucken *n* ‖ *intr* zucken

winch [wrntʃ] *s* (*windlass*) Winde *f*; (*handle*) Kurbel *f*; (min, naut) Haspel *f* & *m*

wind [wrnd] *s* Wind *m*; **break w.** e-n Darmwind lassen; **get w. of** Wind bekommen von; **take the w. out of s.o.'s sails** j-m den Wind aus den Segeln nehmen; **there is s.th. in the w.** es liegt etw in der Luft ‖ [warnd] *v* (*pret & pp* **wound** [waʊnd]) *tr* wickeln, winden; (*a timepiece*) aufziehen; **w. up** aufwickeln; (*affairs*) abwickeln; (*a speech*) abschließen ‖ *intr* (*said of a river, road*) sich winden; **w. around** (*said of a plant*) sich ranken um

windbag ['wrnd,bæg] *s* (coll) Schaumschläger -in *mf*

windbreak ['wrnd,brek] *s* Windschutz *m*

windbreaker ['wrnd,brekər] *s* Windjacke *f*

winded ['wrndid] *adj* außer Atem, atemlos

windfall ['wrnd,fɔl] *s* (*fallen fruit*) Fallobst *n*; (fig) Glücksfall *m*

wind'ing road' ['warndrŋ] *s* Serpentinenstraße *f*; (*public sign*) kurvenreiche Straße *f*

wind'ing sheet' ['warndrŋ] *s* Leichentuch *n*

wind' in'strument [wrnd] *s* Blasinstrument *n*

windlass ['wrndləs] *s* Winde *f*

windmill ['wrnd,mıl] *s* Windmühle *f*

window ['wɪndo] s Fenster n; (of a ticket office) Schalter m; (for display) Schaufenster n

win'dow display' s Schaufensterauslage f

win'dow dress'er s Schaufensterdekorateur –in mf

win'dow dress'ing s Schaufensterdekoration f

win'dow en'velope s Fensterumschlag m

win'dow frame' s Fensterrahmen m

win'dowpane' s Fensterscheibe f

win'dow screen' s Fliegengitter n

win'dow shade' s Rollvorhang m, Rollo n

win'dow-shop' v (pret & pp –shopped; ger –shopping) intr e–n Schaufensterbummel machen

win'dow shut'ter s Fensterladen m

win'dow sill' s Fensterbrett n

windpipe ['wɪnd,paɪp] s Luftröhre f

windshield ['wɪnd,ʃild] s Windschutzscheibe f

wind'shield wash'er s Scheibenwäscher m

wind'shield wip'er s Scheibenwischer m

windsock ['wɪnd,sɑk] s Windsack m

windstorm ['wɪnd,stɔrm] s Sturm m

wind' tun'nel [wɪnd] s Windkanal m

wind-up ['waɪnd,ʌp] s (of affairs) Abwicklung f; (of a speech) Schluß m

windward ['wɪndwərd] adj (side) Wind– || adv windwärts || s Windseite f; turn to w. anluven

windy ['wɪndi] adj windig; (speech) weitschweifig; (person) redselig

wine [waɪn] s Wein m || tr mit Wein bewirten

wine' cel'lar s Weinkeller m

wine' glass' s Weinglas n

winegrower ['waɪn,gro·ər] s Weinbauer –in mf

wine' grow'ing s Weinbau m

wine' list' s Weinkarte f

wine' press' s Weinpresse f

winery ['waɪnəri] s Weinkellerei f

wine'skin' s Weinschlauch m

wing [wɪŋ] s (of a bird, building, party) Flügel m; (unit of three squadrons) Geschwader n; (theat) Kulisse f || tr (shoot) in den Flügel treffen; w. one's way dahinfliegen

wing' chair' s Ohrensessel m

wing' nut' s Flügelmutter f

wing'spread' s Spannweite f

wink [wɪŋk] s Augenwink m; quick as a w. im Nu || intr blinzeln; w. at zublinzeln (dat); (overlook) ein Auge zudrücken bei (dat)

winner ['wɪnər] s Gewinner –in mf, Sieger –in mf; (e.g., winning ticket) Treffer m

win'ning adj (e.g., smile) gewinnend; (sport) siegreich || winnings spl Gewinn m

winsome ['wɪnsəm] adj reizend

winter ['wɪntər] s Winter m || intr überwintern

winterize ['wɪntə,raɪz] tr winterfest machen

wintry ['wɪntri] adj winterlich; (fig) frostig

wipe [waɪp] tr wischen; w. clean abwischen; w. out auswischen; (e.g., a debt) tilgen; (destroy) vernichten; (fin) ruinieren; w. up aufwischen

wire [waɪr] s Draht m; (telg) Telegramm n; get in under the w. es gerade noch schaffen || tr mit Draht versehen; (a house) (elec) elektrische Leitungen legen in (dat); (a message) drahten; (a person) telegraphieren (dat)

wire' cut'ter s Drahtschere f

wire'draw' v (pret –drew; pp –drawn) tr drahtziehen

wire' entan'glement s Drahtverhau m

wire' gauge' s Drahtlehre f

wire'-haired' adj drahthaarig

wireless ['waɪrlɪs] adj drahtlos

wire' nail' s Drahtnagel m

Wire'pho'to s (–tos) (trademark) Bildtelegramm n

wire' record'er s Drahttonaufnahmegerät n

wire'tap' s Abhören n || v (pret & pp –tapped; ger –tapping) tr abhören

wir'ing s Leitungen pl; do the w. die elektrischen Leitungen legen

wiry ['waɪri] adj drahtig

wisdom ['wɪzdəm] s Weisheit f

wis'dom tooth' s Weisheitszahn m

wise [waɪz] adj (person, decision) klug; (impertinent) naseweis; be w. to sich [dat] klar werden über (acc); put s.o. w. to j–n einweihen in (acc) || s–in no w. keineswegs || intr–w. up endlich mal vernünftig werden

wise'a'cre s Neunmalkluge mf

wise'crack' s schnippische Bemerkung f

wise' guy' s (sl) Naseweis m

wisely ['waɪzli] adv wohlweislich

wish [wɪʃ] s Wunsch m || tr wünschen || intr–w. for sich [dat] wünschen

wish'bone' s Gabelbein n

wish'ful think'ing ['wɪʃfəl] s ein frommer Wunsch m

wishy-washy ['wɪʃi,wɑʃi] adj charakterlos; be w. ein Waschlappen sein

wisp [wɪsp] s (of hair) Strähne f

wistful ['wɪstfəl] adj versonnen

wit [wɪt] s Geist m; (person) geistreicher Mensch m; be at one's wit's end sich [dat] keinen Rat mehr wissen; keep one's wits about one e–n klaren Kopf behalten; live by one's wits sich durchschlagen

witch [wɪtʃ] s Hexe f

witch'craft' s Hexerei f

witch' doc'tor s Medizinmann m

witch' ha'zel s Zaubernuß f; (ointment) Präperat n aus Zaubernuß

witch' hunt' s Hexenjagd f

with [wɪð], [wɪθ] prep mit (dat); (at the house of) bei (dat); (because of) vor (dat), e.g., green w. envy grün vor Neid; (despite) trotz (genit); not be w. it nicht bei der Sache sein

with'draw' v (pret –drew; pp –drawn) tr zurückziehen; (money) abheben || intr sich zurückziehen

withdrawal [wɪð'drɔ:əl] *s* Zurückziehung *f*; (*retraction*) Zurücknahme *f*; (*from a bank*) Abhebung *f*; (*mil*) Rückzug *m*

withdraw'al slip' *s* Abhebungsformular *n*

wither ['wɪðər] *intr* verwelken

with·hold' *v* (*pret & pp –held*) *tr* (*pay*) einbehalten; (*information*) (*from*) vorenthalten (*dat*)

withhold'ing tax' *s* einbehaltene Steuer *f*

within' *adv* drin(nen); **from w.** von innen || *prep* (*time*) binnen (*dat*), innerhalb von (*dat*); (*place*) innerhalb (*genit*); **w. walking distance** in Gehweite

without' *adv* draußen || *prep* ohne (*acc*) **w.** (*ger*) ohne zu (*inf*), ohne daß; **w. reason** ohne allen Anlaß

with·stand' *v* (*pret & pp –stood*) *tr* widerstehen (*dat*)

witness ['wɪtnɪs] *s* Zeuge *m*, Zeugin *f*; (*evidence*) Zeugnis *n*; **bear w. to** Zeugnis ablegen von; **in w. whereof** zum Zeugnis dessen; **w. for the defense** Entlastungszeuge *m*; **w. for the prosecution** Belastungszeuge *m* || *tr* (*an event*) anwesend sein bei; (*an accident, crime, etc.*) Augenzeuge sein (*genit*); (*e.g., a contract, will*) als Zeuge unterschreiben

wit'ness stand' *s* Zeugenstand *m*

witticism ['wɪtɪ‚sɪzəm] *s* Witzelei *f*

wittingly ['wɪtɪŋli] *adv* wissentlich

witty ['wɪti] *adj* geistreich, witzig

wizard ['wɪzərd] *s* Hexenmeister *m*

wizardry ['wɪzərdri] *s* (& *fig*) Hexerei *f*

wizend ['wɪzənd] *adj* runzelig

wobble ['wɑbəl] *intr* wackeln

wobbly ['wɑbli] *adj* wackelig

woe [wo] *s* Weh *n* || *interj*—**woe is me!** weh mir!

woebegone ['wobɪ‚gɑn] *adj* jammervoll

woeful ['wofəl] *adj* jammervoll

wolf [wʊlf] *s* (*wolves* [wʊlvz]) Wolf *m*; (*coll*) Schürzenjäger *m*; **cry w.** blinden Alarm schlagen; **keep the w. from the door** sich über Wasser halten || *tr*—**w. down** verschlingen

wolf'pack' *s* Wolfsrudel *n*; (*nav*) U-bootrudel *n*

wolfram ['wʊlfrəm] *s* (*chem*) Wolfram *n*; (*mineral*) Wolframit *m*

woman ['wʊmən] *s* (*women* ['wɪmən]) Frau *f*

wom'an doc'tor *s* Ärztin *f*

wom'anhood' *s* Frauen *pl*; **reach w.** e-e Frau werden

womanish ['wʊmənɪʃ] *adj* weibisch

wom'ankind' *s* Frauen *pl*

womanly ['wʊmənli] *adj* fraulich

womb [wum] *s* Mutterleib *m*

wom'enfolk' *spl* Weibsvolk *n*

wom'en's dou'bles *spl* (tennis) Damendoppelspiel *n*

wom'en's sin'gles *spl* (tennis) Dameneinzelspiel *n*

wonder ['wʌndər] *s* Wunder *n* || *intr* (*be surprised*) sich wundern; (*ask*

oneself*) sich fragen; (*reflect*) überlegen; **wonder at** sich verwundern über (*acc*)

wonderful ['wʌndərfəl] *adj* wunderbar

won'derland' *s* Wunderland *n*

won'der work'er *s* Wundertäter –in *mf*

wont [wʌnt], [wont] *adj*—**be w. to** (*inf*) pflegen zu (*inf*) || *s* Gepflogenheit *f*

wont'ed *adj* gewöhnlich, üblich

woo [wu] *tr* den Hof machen (*dat*)

wood [wʊd] *s* Holz *n*; **out of the woods** (*fig*) über den Berg; **woods** Wald *m*

wood' al'cohol *s* Methylalkohol *m*

woodbine ['wʊd‚baɪn] *s* Geißblatt *n*; (*Virginia creeper*) wilder Wein *m*

wood' carv'ing *s* Holzschnitzerei *f*

wood'chuck' *s* Murmeltier *n*

wood'cock' *s* Holzschnepfe *f*

wood'cut' *s* (*block*) Holzplatte *f*; (*print*) Holzschnitt *m*

wood'cut'ter *s* Holzfäller *m*

wood'ed *adj* bewaldet

wooden ['wʊdən] *adj* (& *fig*) hölzern

wood' engrav'ing *s* Holzschnitt *m*

wood'en leg' *s* Stelzbein *n*

wood'en shoe' *s* Holzschuh *m*

woodland ['wʊdlənd] *adj* Wald– || *s* Waldland *n*

wood'man *s* (–*men*) Holzhauer *m*

woodpecker ['wʊd‚pɛkər] *s* Specht *m*

wood' pi'geon *s* Ringeltaube *f*

wood'pile' *s* Holzhaufen *m*

wood'pulp' *s* Holzfaserstoff *m*

wood' screw' *s* Holzschraube *f*

wood'shed' *s* Holzschuppen *m*

woods'man *s* (–*men*) Förster *m*; (*lumberman*) Holzhauer *m*

wood'winds' *spl* Holzblasinstrumente *pl*

wood'work' *s* Holzarbeit *f*; (*structure in wood*) Gebälk *n*

wood'work'er *s* Holzarbeiter –in *mf*

wood'worm' *s* (*ent*) Holzwurm *m*

woody ['wʊdi] *adj* waldig; (*woodlike*) holzig

wooer ['wu·ər] *s* Verehrer *m*

woof [wuf] *s* (*of a dog*) unterdrücktes Bellen *n*; (*tex*) Gewebe *n*

woofer ['wufər] *s* (*rad*) Tieftöner *m*

wool [wʊl] *adj* wollen || *s* Wolle *f*

woolen ['wʊlən] *adj* wollen, Woll– || **woolens** *spl* Wollwaren *pl*

woolly ['wʊli] *adj* wollig; (*e.g., thinking*) verschwommen

woozy ['wuzi] *adj* benebelt

word [wʌrd] *s* Wort *n*; **be as good as one's w.** zu seinem Wort stehen; **by w. of mouth** mündlich; **get w. from** Nachricht haben von; **give one's w.** sein Wort geben; **have a w. with** ein ernstes Wort sprechen mit; **have words** *e-n* Wortwechsel haben; **in a w.** mit *e-m* Wort; **in other words** mit anderen Worten; **in so many words** ausdrücklich; **leave w.** Bescheid hinterlassen; **not another w.!** kein Wort mehr!; **not a w. of truth in it** kein wahres Wort daran; **put in a good w. for s.o.** ein gutes Wort für *j-n* einlegen; **put into words** in

Worte kleiden; **put words in s.o.'s mouth** j-m Worte in den Mund legen; **send w. to s.o.** j-n benachrichtigen; **take s.o.'s w. for it** j-n beim Wort nehmen; **w. for w.** Wort für Wort || *tr* formulieren

word'-for-word' *adj* wörtlich

word'ing *s* Formulierung *f*

word' of hon'or *s* Ehrenwort *n*; **w.!** auf mein Wort!

word' or'der *s* Wortfolge *f*

wordy ['wʌrdi] *adj* wortreich

work [wʌrk] *s* Arbeit *f*; (*production, book*) Werk *n*; **be in the works** (coll) im Gang sein; **get to w.** sich an die Arbeit machen; (*travel to work*) zum Arbeitsplatz kommen; **give s.o. the works** (coll) j-n fertigmachen; **have one's w. cut out** zu tun haben; **it took a lot of w. to** (*inf*) es hat viel Arbeit gekostet zu (*inf*); **make short w. of** kurzen Prozeß machen mit; **out of w.** arbeitslos; **works** (horol) Uhrwerk *n* || *tr* (*a machine*) bedienen; (*a pedal*) treten; (*a mine*) abbauen; (*the soil*) bearbeiten; (*metal*) treiben; (*dough*) kneten; (*wonders*) wirken; **w. in** einarbeiten; **w. off** (*a debt*) abarbeiten; **w. oneself to death** sich totarbeiten; **w. one's way up** sich hocharbeiten; **w. out** (*a solution*) ausarbeiten; (*a problem*) lösen; **w. to death** abhetzen; **w. up an appetite** sich [*dat*] Appetit machen || *intr* arbeiten; (*function*) funktionieren; (*succeed*) klappen; **w. against** wirken gegen; **w. away at** losarbeiten auf (*acc*); **w. at** (*a trade*) ausüben; **w. both ways** für beide Fälle gelten; **w. loose** sich lockern; **w. on** (*a person*) bearbeiten; (*a patient, car*) arbeiten an (*dat*); **w. out** (sport) trainieren; **w. out well** gut ausgehen

workable ['wʌrkəbəl] *adj* brauchbar; (*plan*) durchführbar

work'bench' *s* Werkbank *f*

work'book' *s* Übungsheft *n*

work' camp' *s* Arbeitslager *n*

work'day' *s* Arbeitstag *m*

work' detail' *s* (mil) Arbeitskommando *n*

worked'-up' *adj* erregt; **get s.o. w.** j-n erregen; **get w.** sich erregen

worker ['wʌrkər] *s* Arbeiter –in *mf*

work' force' *s* Belegschaft *f*

work'horse' *s* Arbeitspferd *n*

work'ing day' *s* Arbeitstag *m*

work'ing girl' *s* Arbeiterin *f*

work'ing hours' *spl* Arbeitsstunden *pl*

work'ing-man' *s* (–men') Arbeiter *m*

work'ing or'der *s*—**in w.** betriebsfähig

work'ing-wom'an *s* (–wom'en) Arbeiterin *f*; (*professionally*) berufstätige Frau *f*

work'man *s* (–men) Arbeiter *m*

work'manship' *s* Ausführung *f*

work'men's compensa'tion insur'ance *s* Arbeiterunfallversicherung *f*

work' of art' *s* Kunstwerk *n*

work'out' *s* Training *n*

work' per'mit *s* Arbeitsgenehmigung *f*

work'room' *s* Arbeitszimmer *n*

work' sche'dule *s* Dienstplan *m*

work'shop' *s* Werkstatt *f*

work' stop'page *s* Arbeitseinstellung *f*

world [wʌrld] *s* Welt *f*; **a w. of** groß; **from all over the w.** aus aller Herren Ländern; **not for all the w.** nicht um die Welt; **see the w. in the** Welt herumkommen; **they are worlds apart** es liegen Welten zwischen den beiden; **think of** große Stücke halten auf (*acc*); **who (where) in the w.** wer (wo) in aller Welt

world' affairs' *spl* internationale Angelegenheiten *pl*

world'-fa'mous *adj* weltberühmt

worldly ['wʌrldli] *adj* (*goods, pleasures*) irdisch; (*person*) weltlich; (*wisdom*) Welt-

world'ly-wise' *adj* weltklug

world's' fair' *s* Weltausstellung *f*

world'-shak'ing *adj* weltbewegend

world'-wide' *adj* weltweit

worm [wʌrm] *s* Wurm *m* || *tr*—**w. one's way** sich schlängeln; **w. secrets out of s.o.** j-m die Würmer aus der Nase ziehen

worm-eaten ['wʌrm,itən] *adj* (& fig) wurmstichig

wormy ['wʌrmi] *adj* wurmig

worn [worn] *adj* (*clothes*) getragen; (*tires*) abgenutzt; (*wearied*) müde

worn'-out' *adj* (*clothes*) abgetragen; (*tires*) abgenutzt; (*exhausted*) erschöpft

worrisome ['wʌrisəm] *adj* (*causing worry*) beunruhigend; (*inclined to worry*) sorgenvoll

wor·ry ['wʌri] *s* Sorge *f*; (*source of worry*) Ärger *m* || *v* (*pret & pp* –ried) *tr* beunruhigen; **be worried** besorgt sein || *intr* (*about*) sich [*dat*] Sorgen machen (um); **don't w.!** keine Sorge!

worse [wʌrs] *comp adj* schlechter, schlimmer; **be w. off** schlimmer daran sein; **he's none the w. for it** es hat ihm nichts geschadet; **what's w.** was noch schlimmer ist

worsen ['wʌrsən] *tr* verschlimmern || *intr* sich verschlimmern

wor·ship ['wʌrʃip] *s* Anbetung *f*; (*services*) Gottesdienst *m* || *v* (*pret & pp* –ship[p]ed; *ger* –ship[p]ing) *tr* (& fig) anbeten || *intr* seine Andacht verrichten

worship(p)er ['wʌrʃipər] *s* Anbeter –in *mf*; (*in church*) Andächtige *mf*

worst [wʌrst] *super adj* schlimmste || *super adv* am schlimmsten || *s* Schlimmste *n*; **at the w.** schlimmstenfalls; **get the w. of** den kürzeren ziehen bei; **if w. comes to w.** wenn alle Stricke reißen; **the w. is yet to come** das dicke Ende kommt noch || *tr* schlagen

worsted ['wustid] *adj* Kammgarn-

worth [wʌrθ] *adj* wert; **it is w.** (*ger*) es lohnt sich zu (*inf*); **it is w. the trouble** es ist der Mühe wert; **ten dollars' w. of meat** für zehn Dollar Fleisch; **w. seeing** sehenswert || *s* Wert *m*

worthless ['wʌrθlɪs] *adj* wertlos; *(person)* nichtsnutzig
worth'while' *adj* lohnend
worthy ['wʌrði] *adj* würdig *(genit)*
would [wʊd] *aux* used to express 1) indirect statements, e.g., **he said he w. come** er sagte, er würde kommen; 2) the present conditional, e.g., **he w. do it if he could** er würde es tun, wenn er könnte; 3) past conditional, e.g., **he w. have paid, if he had had the money** er würde gezahlt haben, wenn er das Geld gehabt hätte; 4) habitual action in the past, e.g., **he w. always buy the morning paper** er kaufte immer das Morgenblatt; 5) polite requests, e.g., **w. you please pass me the butter?** würden Sie mir bitte die Butter reichen; 6) a wish, e.g., **w. that I had never seen it** wenn ich es nur nie gesehen hätte!; **w. rather** möchte lieber, e.g., **I w. rather go on foot** ich möchte lieber zu Fuß gehen
would'-be' *adj* angeblich, Möchtegern-
wound [wund] *s* Wunde *f* || *tr* verwunden
wound'ed *adj* verwundet || **the w.** *spl* die Verwundeten *pl*
wow [waʊ] *s* (coll) Bombenerfolg *m* || *tr* (coll) erstaunen || *interj* nanu!
wrack [ræk] *s*—**go to w. and ruin** untergehen, in Brüche gehen
wraith [reθ] *s* *(apparition)* Erscheinung *f*; *(spirit)* Geist *m*
wrangle ['ræŋgəl] *s* Streit *m* || *intr* streiten
wrap [ræp] *s* Überwurf *m* || *v* *(pret & pp* wrapped; *ger* wrapping) *tr* wikkeln; *(a package)* einpacken; **be wrapped up in** *(e.g., thoughts)* versunken sein in *(dat)*; **wrapped in darkness** in Dunkelheit gehüllt; **w. up** *(a deal)* abwickeln
wrapper ['ræpər] *s* Verpackung *f*; *(for mailing newspapers)* Streifband *n*
wrap'ping *s* Verpackung *f*
wrap'ping pa'per *s* Packpapier *n*
wrath [ræθ] *s* Zorn *m*, Wut *f*
wrathful ['ræθfəl] *adj* zornig, wütend
wreak [rik] *tr* *(vengeance)* üben; **w. havoc** schlimm hausen
wreath [riθ] *s* (wreaths [riðz]) Kranz *m*; **w. of smoke** Rauchfahne *f*
wreathe [rið] *tr* bekränzen, umwinden
wreck [rek] *s* *(of a car or train)* Unglück *n*; *(wrecked ship, car, person)* Wrack *n* || *tr* *(e.g., a car)* zertrümmern; *(a building)* in Trümmer legen; *(a marriage)* zerrütten; (fig) zum Scheitern bringen; **be wrecked** (fig & naut) scheitern
wreckage ['rekɪdʒ] *s* Wrackgut *n*; *(of an accident)* Trümmer *pl*
wrecker ['rekər] *s* Abschleppwagen *m*
wren [ren] *s* (orn) Zaunkönig *m*.
wrench [rentʃ] *s* *(tool)* Schraubenschlüssel *m*; *(of a muscle)* Verrenkung *f* || *tr* verrenken
wrest [rest] *tr* *(from)* entreißen *(dat)*
wrestle ['resəl] *tr* ringen mit || *intr* ringen

wrestler ['reslər] *s* Ringer *m*; *(professional wrestler)* Catcher *m*
wrestling ['reslɪŋ] *s* Ringen *n*; *(professional wrestling)* Catchen *n*
wres'tling match' *s* Ringkampf *m*
wretch [retʃ] *s* armer Kerl *m*; *(vile person)* Schuft *m*
wretched ['retʃɪd] *adj* elend; *(terrible)* scheußlich
wriggle ['rɪgəl] *s* Krümmung *f*; *(of a worm)* schlängelnde Bewegung *f* || *tr* hin- und herbewegen; **w. one's way** sich dahinschlängeln || *intr* sich winden
wring [rɪŋ] *v* *(pret & pp* wrung [rʌŋ]) *tr* *(the hands)* ringen; **w. out** *(the wash)* auswinden; **w. s.o.'s neck** j-m den Hals umdrehen
wringer ['rɪŋər] *s* Wringmaschine *f*
wrinkle ['rɪŋkəl] *s* Falte *f*; **new w.** (fig) neuer Kniff *m*; **take out the wrinkles** (fig) den letzten Schliff geben || *tr* falten, runzeln; *(paper, clothes)* zerknittern || *intr* Falten werfen
wrin'kle-proof' *adj* knitterfrei
wrinkly ['rɪŋkli] *adj* faltig, runzelig
wrist [rɪst] *s* Handgelenk *n*
wrist'band' *s* Armband *n*
wrist' watch' *s* Armbanduhr *f*
writ [rɪt] *s* gerichtlicher schriftlicher Befehl *m*
write [raɪt] *v* *(pret* wrote [rot]; *pp* written ['rɪtən]) *tr* schreiben; *(compose)* verfassen; **it is written** *(in the Bible)* es steht geschrieben; **it is written all over his face** es steht ihm im Gesicht geschrieben; **w. down** aufschreiben; **w. off** abschreiben; **w. out** ausschreiben; *(a check)* ausstellen || *intr* schreiben; **w. for information** Informationen anfordern
write'-off' *s* Abschreibung *f*
writer ['raɪtər] *s* Schreiber –in *mf*; *(author)* Schriftsteller –in *mf*
writ'er's cramp' *s* Schreibkrampf *m*
write'-up' *s* Pressebericht *m*
writhe [raɪð] *intr* *(in)* sich krümmen *(vor dat)*
writ'ing *s* Schreiben *n*; *(handwriting)* Schrift *f*; **in w.** schriftlich; **put in w.** niederschreiben
writ'ing desk' *s* Schreibtisch *m*
writ'ing pad' *s* Schreibblock *m*
writ'ing pa'per *s* Schreibpapier *n*; *(stationery)* Briefpapier *n*
written ['rɪtən] *adj* schriftlich; *(law)* geschrieben; *(language)* Schrift-
wrong [rɔŋ] *adj* *(incorrect)* falsch; *(unjust)* unrecht; **be w.** *(be incorrect)* nicht stimmen; *(be in error)* Unrecht haben; *(said of a situation)* nicht in Ordnung sein; **be w. with** fehlen *(dat)*; **sorry, w. number!** (telp) falsch verbunden! || *s* Unrecht *n*; **be in the w.** im Unrecht sein; **do w.** ein Unrecht begehen; **do w. to s.o.** j-m ein Unrecht zufügen; **get in w. with s.o.** es sich *(dat)* mit j-m verderben || *adv* falsch, unrecht; **go w.** *(morally)* auf Abwege geraten; *(in walking)* sich verirren; *(in reckoning)*

irregehen; (*in driving*) sich verfahren; (*said of plans*) schief gehen
wrongdoer ['rɔŋ,du·ər] *s* Missetäter –in *mf*

wrong'do'ing *s* Missetat *f*
wrought' i'ron [rɔt] *s* Schmiedeeisen *n*
wrought'-up' *adj* aufgebracht
wry [raɪ] *adj* schief

X

X, x [eks] *s* vierundzwanzigster Buchstabe des englischen Alphabets
xenophobia [,zenə'fobɪ·ə] *s* Fremdenhaß *m*
Xerox ['zɪrɑks] *s* (trademark) Xerographie *f* || **xerox** *tr* ablichten
Xer'ox-cop'y *s* Ablichtung *f*

Xmas ['krɪsməs] *adj* Weihnachts– || *s* Weihnachten *pl*
x'-ray' *adj* Röntgen– || *s* (picture) Röntgenbild *n;* **x-rays** Röntgenstrahlen *pl* || *tr* röntgen
x'-ray ther'apy *s* Röntgentherapie *f*
xylophone ['zaɪlə,fon] *s* Xylophon *n*

Y

Y, y [waɪ] *s* fünfundzwanzigster Buchstabe des englischen Alphabets
yacht [jɑt] *s* Jacht *f*
yacht' club' *s* Jachtklub *m*
yam [jæm] *s* Yamwurzel *f*
yank [jæŋk] *s* Ruck *m;* **Yank** Ami *m* || *tr*—**y. s.th. out of** reißen aus || *intr* —**y. on** heftig ziehen an (*dat*)
Yankee ['jæŋki] *s* Yankee *m*
yap [jæp] *s* (talk) (sl) Geschwätz *n;* (mouth) (sl) Maul *n;* (bark) Gekläff *n* || *v* (pret & pp **yapped**) ger **yapping**) *intr* (bark) kläffen; (talk) (sl) schwätzen
yard [jɑrd] *s* (measure) Yard *n;* (ground adjoining a building) Hof *m;* (naut) Rahe *f;* (rr) Rangierbahnhof *m*
yard'arm' *s* (naut) Nock *f* & *n*
yard' mas'ter *s* (rr) Rangiermeister *m*
yard'stick' *s* Yardmaß *n;* (fig) Maßstab *m*
yarn [jɑrn] *s* (thread; story) Garn *n;* **spin yarns** (fig) Garne spinnen
yaw [jɔ] *s* (aer, rok) Schwanken *n;* (naut) Gieren *n* || *intr* (aer, rok) schwanken; (naut) gieren
yawl [jɔl] *s* (naut) Jolle *f*
yawn [jɔn] *s* Gähnen *n* || *intr* gähnen; (said, e.g., of a gorge) klaffen
ye [ji] *pers pron* ihr
yea [je] *s* Jastimme *f* || *adv* ja
yeah [je] *adv* ja
year [jɪr] *s* Jahr *n;* **all y. round** das ganze Jahr hindurch; **a y. from to-day** heute übers Jahr; **for years** seit Jahren; jahrelang; **in years** seit Jahren; **y. in y. out** jahraus jahrein
year'book' *s* Jahrbuch *n*
yearling ['jɪrlɪŋ] *s* Jährling *m*
yearly ['jɪrli] *adj & adv* jährlich
yearn [jʌrn] *intr*—**y. for** sich sehnen nach; **y. to** (inf) sich danach sehnen zu (inf)
yearn'ing *s* Sehnsucht *f*

yeast [jist] *s* Hefe *f*
yell [jel] *s* Ruf *m*, Aufschrei *m;* (sport) Kampfruf *m* || *tr* (gellend) schreien; **y. one's lungs out** sich tot schreien || *intr* schreien; **y. at** anschreien
yellow ['jelo] *adj* gelb; (sl) feige || *s* Gelb *n* || *tr* gelb machen || *intr* vergilben
yellowish ['jelo·ɪʃ] *adj* gelblich
yel'lowjack'et *s* Wespe *f*
yel'low jour'nalism *s* Sensationspresse *f*
yel'low streak' *s* Zug *m* von Feigheit
yelp [jelp] *s* Gekläff *n* || *intr* kläffen
yen [jen] *s* (Japanese money) Yen *m;* (for) brennendes Verlangen *n* (nach)
yeo·man ['jomən] *s* (–men) (nav) Verwaltungsunteroffizier *m*
yeo'man's serv'ice *s* großer Dienst *m*
yes [jes] *adv* ja; **yes, Sir** jawohl || *s* Ja *n;* **say yes to** bejahen
yes' man' *s* Jasager *m*
yesterday ['jestər,de] *adv* gestern; **y. morning** gestern früh || *s* Gestern *n;* **yesterday's** gestrig
yet [jet] *adv* (still) noch; (however) doch; (already) schon; **and yet** trotzdem, dennoch; **as yet** schon; **not yet** noch nicht || *conj* aber
yew [ju] *s* Eibe *f*
Yiddish ['jɪdɪʃ] *adj* jiddisch || *s* Jiddisch *n*
yield [jild] *s* Ertrag *m* || *tr* (profit) einbringen; (interest) tragen; (crops) hervorbringen; (give up) überlassen || *intr* (to) nachgeben (dat)
yo·del ['jodəl] *s* Jodler *m* || *v* (pret & pp **–del[l]ed**; ger **–del[l]ing**) *intr* jodeln
yodeler ['jodələr] *s* Jodler –in *mf*
yogurt ['jogurt] *s* Yoghurt *m* & *n*
yoke [jok] *s* (part of harness; burden) Joch *n;* **pass under the y.** sich in ein Joch fügen; **y. of oxen** Ochsengespann *n* || *tr* ins Joch spannen

yokel ['jokəl] *s* Bauerntölpel *m*

yolk [jok] *s* Dotter *m & n*

yonder ['jɑndər] *adv* dort drüben

yore [jɔr] *s*—of y. vormals

you [ju] *pers pron* du; (*plural form*) ihr; (*polite form*) Sie; **to you** dir; (*plural form*) euch; (*polite form*) Ihnen; **you of all people!** ausgerechnet Sie! ‖ *indef pron* man

young [jʌŋ] *adj* (**younger** ['jʌŋgər]; **youngest** ['jʌŋgɪst]) jung; **y. for one's age** jugendlich für sein Alter ‖ *spl* (*of animals*) Jungen *pl*; **the y.** die Jungen, die Jugend; **with y.** (*pregnant*) trächtig

young' la'dy *s* Fräulein *n*

young' man' *s* junger Mann *m*; (*boyfriend*) Freund *m*

youngster ['jʌŋstər] *s* Jugendliche *mf*

your [jʊr] *poss adj* dein; (*plural form*) euer; (*polite form*) Ihr

yours [jʊrz] *poss pron* deiner; (*plural form*) euerer; (*polite form*) Ihrer; **y. truly** hochachtungsvoll

your·self [jʊr'sɛlf] *intens pron* (–**selves** ['sɛlvz]) selbst, selber ‖ *reflex pron* dich; (*plural form*) euch; (*polite form*) Sich; **to y.** dir; (*plural form*) Sich; **to yourselves** euch; (*polite form*) Sich

youth [juθ] *s* (**youths** [juθs], [juðz]) (*age*) Jugend *f*; (*person*) Jugendliche *mf*

youthful ['juθfəl] *adj* jugendlich

youth' hos'tel *s* Jugendherberge *f*

yowl [jaʊl] *s* Gejaule *n* ‖ *tr & intr* jaulen

Yugoslav ['jugo'slɑv] *adj* jugoslawisch ‖ *s* Jugoslawe *m*, Jugoslawin *f*

Yugoslavia ['jugo'slɑvɪ·ə] *s* Jugoslavien *n*

yule' log' [jul] *s* Weihnachtsscheit *n*

yule'tide' *s* Weihnachtszeit *f*

Z

Z, z [zi] *s* sechsundzwanzigster Buchstabe des englischen Alphabets

zany ['zeni] *adj* närrisch ‖ *s* Hanswurst *m*

zeal [zil] *s* Eifer *m*

zealot ['zɛlət] *s* Zelot –in *mf*

zealous ['zɛləs] *adj* eifrig

zebra ['zibrə] *s* Zebra *n*

zenith ['zinɪθ] *s* Scheitelpunkt *m*, Zenit *m*

zephyr ['zɛfər] *s* Zephir *m*

zeppelin ['zɛpəlɪn] *s* Zeppelin *m*

ze·ro ['ziro] *s* (–**ros** & –**roes**) Null *f* ‖ *tr*—z. **in a rifle** Visier e–s Gewehrs justieren ‖ *intr*—z. **in on** zielen auf (*acc*)

ze'ro hour' *s* Stunde *f* Null

zest [zɛst] *s* Würze *f*

Zeus [zus] *s* Zeus *m*

zig-zag ['zɪg,zæg] *adj* Zickzack– ‖ *adv* im Zickzack ‖ *s* Zickzack *m* ‖ (*pret & pp* –**zagged;** *ger* –**zagging**) *intr* im Zickzack fahren

zinc [zɪŋk] *s* Zink *n*

Zionism ['zaɪ·ə,nɪzəm] *s* Zionismus *m*

zip [zɪp] *s* (coll) Schmiß *m* ‖ *v* (*pret & pp* **zipped;** *ger* **zipping**) *tr* (*convey with speed*) mit Schwung befördern; (*fasten with a zipper*) mit e–m Reißverschluß schließen ‖ *intr* sausen; **zip by** vorbeisausen ‖ *interj* wuppdich!

zip' code' *s* Postleitzahl *f*

zipper ['zɪpər] *s* Reißverschluß *m*

zircon ['zʌrkɑn] *s* Zirkon *m*

zither ['zɪθər] *s* Zither *f*

zodiac ['zodɪ,æk] *s* Tierkreis *m*

zombie ['zɑmbi] *s* (sl) Depp *m*

zone [zon] *s* (& geol) Zone *f*; (*postal zone*) Postbezirk *m*; (mil) Bereich *m*

zoo [zu] *s* Zoo *m*, Tiergarten *m*

zoologic(al) [,zo·ə'lɑdʒɪk(əl)] *adj* zoologisch

zoologist [zo'ɑlədʒɪst] *s* Zoologe *m*, Zoologin *f*

zoology [zo'ɑlədʒi] *s* Zoologie *f*

zoom [zum] *s* lautes Summen *n*; (aer) Hochreißen *n* ‖ *intr* laut summen; **z. up** (aer) hochreißen

zoom' lens' *s* Gummilinse *f*

METRIC CONVERSIONS

Multiply:	By:	To Obtain:
acres	43,560	sq. ft.
	0.4047	hectares
	0.0015625	sq. mi.
ampere-hours	3600	coulombs
atmospheres	76.0	cm. of mercury
	33.90	ft. of water
	14.70	lbs./sq. in.
British thermal units	1054	joules
	777.5	ft.-lbs.
	252.0	gram calories
	0.0003927	horsepower-hrs.
	0.0002928	kilowatt-hrs.
B.T.U./hr.	0.2928	watts
B.T.U./min.	12.96	ft.-lbs./sec.
	0.02356	horsepower
bushels	3523.8	hectoliters
	2150.42	cu. ins.
	35.238	liters
°C + 17.78	1.8	°F
centimeters	0.3937	inches
cm-grams	980.1	cm.-dynes
chains	66	ft.
circumference	6.2832	radians
cubic centimeters	0.0610	cu. ins.
cu. feet	1728	cu. ins.
	62.43	lbs. of water
	7.481	gals. (liq.)
	0.0283	cu. m.
cu. ft./min.	62.43	lbs. water/min.
cu. ft./sec.	448.831	gals./min.
cu. inches	16.387	cu. cm.
	0.0005787	cu. ft.
cu. meters	264.2	gals. (liq.)
	35.3147	cu. ft.
	1.3079	cu. yds.
cu. yards	27	cu. ft.
	0.765	cu. m.
days	86,400	seconds
degrees/sec.	0.1667	revolutions/min.
°F − 32	0.5556	°C
faradays/sec.	96,500	amperes
feet	30.48	cm.
	0.3048	meters
	0.0001894	mi. (stat.)
	0.0001645	mi. (Brit. naut.)

Multiply:	By:	To Obtain:
ft. of water	62.43	lbs./sq. ft.
	0.4335	lbs./sq. in.
ft./min.	0.5080	cm./sec.
ft./sec.	0.6818	mi./hr.
	0.5921	knots
fluid ounces	29.573	milliliters
furlongs	660	feet
	0.125	mi.
gallons	231	cu. ins.
	8.345	lbs. of water
	8	pts.
	4	qts.
	3.785	liters
	0.003785	cu. m.
gals./min.	8.0208	cu. ft./hr.
grains	0.0648	grams
grams	980.1	dynes
	15.43	grains
	0.0353	oz. (avdp.)
	0.0022	lbs. (avdp.)
hectares	107,600	sq. ft.
	2.47	acres
hectoliters	2.838	bushels
horsepower	33,000	ft.-lbs./min.
	2545	B.T.U./hr.
	745.7	watts
	42.44	B.T.U./min.
	0.7457	kilowatts
inches	25.40	mm.
	2.540	cm.
	0.00001578	mi.
ins. of water	0.03613	lbs./sq. in.
kilograms	980,100	dynes
	2.2046	lbs. (avdp.)
kg. calories	3086	ft.-lbs.
	3.968	B.T.U.
kg. cal./min.	51.43	ft.-lbs./sec.
	0.06972	kilowatts
kilometers	3280.8	ft.
	0.621	mi.
km./hr.	0.621	mi./hr.
	0.5396	knots
kilowatts	737.6	ft.-lbs./sec.
	56.92	B.T.U./min.
	1.341	horsepower
kilowatt-hrs.	2,655,000	ft.-lbs.
	3415	B.T.U.
	1.341	horsepower-hrs.
knots	6080	ft./hr.
	1.151	stat. mi./hr.
	1	(Brit.) naut. mi./hr.
liters	61.02	cu. ins.
	2.113	pts. (liq.)
	1.057	qts. (liq.)
	0.264	gals. (liq.)
	1.816	pts. (dry)
	0.908	qts. (dry)
	0.1135	pecks
	0.0284	bushels

Multiply:	By:	To Obtain:
meters	39.37	inches
	3.2808	ft.
	1.0936	yds.
	0.0006215	mi. (stat.)
	0.0005396	mi. (Brit. naut.)
miles		
statute	5280	ft.
	1.609	km.
	0.8624	mi. (Brit. naut.)
nautical (Brit.)	6080	ft.
	1.151	mi. (stat.)
mi./hr.	1.467	ft./sec.
milligrams/liter	1	parts/million
milliliters	0.0338	fluid oz.
millimeters	0.03937	inches
ounces		
avoirdupois	28.349	grams
	0.9115	oz. (troy)
	0.0625	lbs. (avdp.)
troy	31.103	grams
	1.0971	oz. (avdp.)
pecks	8.8096	liters
pints		
liquid	473.2	cu. cm.
	28.875	cu. ins.
	0.473	liters
dry	0.550	liters
pounds		
avoirdupois	444,600	dynes
	453.6	grams
	32.17	poundals
	14.58	oz. (troy)
	1.21	lbs. (troy)
	0.4536	kg.
troy	0.373	kg.
lbs. (avdp.)/sq. in.	70.22	g./sq. cm.
	2.307	ft. of water
quarts		
liquid	57.75	cu. ins.
	32	fluid oz.
	2	pts.
	0.946	liters
dry	67.20	cu. ins.
	1.101	liters
quires	25	sheets
radians	3437.7	minutes
	57.296	degrees
reams	500	sheets
revolutions/min.	6	degrees/sec.
rods	16.5	ft.
	5.5	yds.
	5.029	meters
slugs	32.17	lbs. (mass)
square centimeters	0.155	sq. ins.
sq. feet	0.093	sq. m.
sq. inches	6.451	sq. cm.
sq. kilometers	247.1	acres
	0.3861	sq. mi.

Multiply:	By:	To Obtain:
sq. meters	10.76	sq. ft.
	1.1960	sq. yds.
sq. miles	27,878,400	sq. ft.
	640	acres
	2.5889	sq. km.
sq. yards	0.8361	sq. m.
tons		
long	2240	lbs. (avdp.)
	1.12	short tons
	1.0160	metric tons
metric	2204.6	lbs. (avdp.)
	1000	kg.
	1.1023	short tons
	0.9842	long tons
short	2000	lbs. (avdp.)
	0.9072	metric tons
	0.8929	long tons
watts	3.415	B.T.U./hr.
	0.001341	horsepower
yards	36	inches
	3	ft.
	0.9144	meters
	0.0005682	mi. (stat.)
	0.0004934	mi. (Brit. naut.)

LABELS AND ABBREVIATIONS

BEZEICHNUNGEN DER SACHGEBIETE UND ABKÜRZUNGEN

abbr abbreviation—Abkürzung
acc accusative—Akkusativ
(acct) accounting—Rechnungswesen
adj adjective—Adjektiv
(adm) administration—Verwaltung
adv adverb—Adverb
(aer) aeronautics—Luftfahrt
(agr) agriculture—Landwirtschaft
(alg) algebra—Algebra
(Am) American—amerikanisch
(anat) anatomy—Anatomie
(angl) angling—Angeln
(archeol) archeology—Archäologie
(archit) architecture—Architektur
(arith) arithmetic—Rechnen
art article—Artikel
(arti) artillery—Artillerie
(astr) astronomy—Astronomie
(atom. phys.) Atomic physics—Atomphysik
(Aust) Austrian—österreichisch
(aut) automobile—Automobile
aux auxiliary verb—Hilfsverb
(bact) bacteriology—Bakteriologie
(baseball) Baseball
(basketball) Korbball
(bb) bookbinding—Buchbinderei
(Bib) Biblical—biblisch
(billiards) Billard
(biochem) biochemistry—Biochemie
(biol) biology—Biologie
(bowling) Kegeln
(bot) botany—Botanik
(box) boxing—Boxen
(Brit) British—britisch
(cards) Kartenspiel
(carp) carpentry—Zimmerhandwerk
(checkers) Damespiel

(chem) chemistry—Chemie
(chess) Schachspiel
(cin) cinematography—Kinematographie
(coll) colloquial—umgangssprachlich
(com) commercial—Handels-
comb.fm. combining form—Wortbildungselement
comp comparative—Komparativ
conj conjunction—Konjunktion
(crew) Rudersport
(culin) culinary—kulinarisch
(data proc.) data processing—Datenverarbeitung
dem demonstrative—hinweisend
(dent) dentistry—Zahnheilkunde
(dial) dialectical—dialektisch
(dipl) diplomacy—Diplomatie
(eccl) ecclesiastical—kirchlich
(econ) economics—Wirtschaft
(educ) education—Schulwesen
e–e a(n)—eine
e.g. for example—zum Beispiel
(elec) electricity—Elektrizität
(electron) electronics—Elektronik
e–m to a(n)—einem
e–n a(n)—einen
(eng) engineering—Technik
(ent) entomology—Entomologie
e–r of a(n), to a(n)—einer
e–s of a(n)—eines
etw something—etwas
f feminine noun—Femininum
(fa) fine arts—schöne Künste
fem feminine—weiblich
(fencing) Fechtkunst
(fig) figurative—bildlich
(& fig) literal and figurative—buchstäblich und bildlich
(fin) finance—Finanzwesen
(fb) football, soccer—Fußball
fut future—Zukunft
genit genitive—Genitiv
(geog) geography, Geographie
(geol) geology—Geologie
(geom) geometry—Geometrie
ger gerund—Gerundium
(golf) Golf
(gram) grammar—Grammatik
(gym) gymnastics—Gymnastik
(heral) heraldry—Wappenkunde
(hist) history—Geschichte
(horol) horology—Zeitmessung
(hort) horticulture—Gartenbau
(hum) humorous—scherzhaft
(hunt) hunting—Jagdwesen
(ichth) ichthyology—Ichthyologie

imperf imperfect—Imperfekt
impers impersonal—unpersönlich
ind indicative—Indikativ
indecl indeclinable—undeklinierbar
indef indefinite—unbestimmt
(indust) industry—Industrie
inf infinitive—Infinitiv
(ins) insurance—Versicherungswesen
insep inseparable—untrennbar
intens intensive—verstärkend
interj interjection—Interjektion
interr interrogative—Frage-
intr intransitive—intransitiv
invar invariable—unveränderlich
(iron) ironical—ironisch
j-m to someone—jemandem
j-n someone—jemanden
(journ) journalism—Zeitungswesen
j-s someone's—jemand(e)s
(jur) jurisprudence—Rechtswissenschaft
(libr) library science—Bibliothekswissenschaft
(ling) linguistics—Linguistik
(lit) literary—literarisch
(log) logic—Logik
m masculine noun—Maskulinum
(mach) machinery—Maschinen
(mech) mechanics—Mechanik
(med) medicine—Medizin
(metal) metallurgy—Metallurgie
(meteor) meteorology—Meteorologie
mf masculine or feminine noun according to sex—Maskulinum
 oder Femininum je nach Geschlecht
(mil) military—Militär-
(min) mining—Bergwerkswesen
(mineral) mineralogy—Mineralogie
mod aux modal auxiliary—Modalverb
(mount) mountain climbing—Bergsteigerei
(mus) music—Musik
(myth) mythology—Mythologie
m & f masculine and feminine noun without regard to sex—
 Maskulinum oder Femininum ohne Rücksicht auf Geschlecht
(naut) nautical—nautisch
(nav) navy—Kriegsmarine
neut neuter—sächlich
(obs) obsolete—veraltet
(obstet) obstetrics—Geburtshilfe
(opt) optics—Optik
(orn) ornithology—Ornithologie
(paint) painting—Malerei
(parl) parliamentary—parlamentarisch
(pathol) pathology—Pathologie
(pej) pejorative—pejorativ
pers personal—Personal-

374

(pharm) pharmacy—Pharmazie
(philos) philosophy—Philosophie
(phonet) phonetics—Phonetik
(phot) photography—Photographie
(phys) physics—Physik
(physiol) physiology—Physiologie
pl plural—Plural
(poet) poetical—dichterisch
(pol) politics—Politik
poss possessive—besitzanzeigend
pp past participal—Partizip Perfekt
pref prefix—Präfix
prep preposition—Präposition
pres present—Gegenwart
pret preterit—Präteritum
pron pronoun—Pronomen
pros prosody—Prosodie
(Prot) Protestant—protestantisch
(psychol) psychology—Psychologie
(public sign) Hinweisschild
(rad) radio—Radio
(radar) Radar
recip reciprocal—wechselseitig
ref reflexive verb—Reflexivverb
reflex reflexive—reflexiv
rel relative—relativ
(relig) religion—Religion
(rhet) rhetoric—Rhetorik
(rok) rocketry—Raketen
(rr) railroad—Eisenbahn
s substantive—Substantiv
(sculp) sculpture—Bildhauerkunst
sep separable—trennbar
(sewing) Näherei
sg singular—Einzahl
(sl) slang—Slang
s.o. someone—jemand
s.o.'s someone's—jemand(e)s
spl substantive plural—pluralisches Substantiv
(sport) sports—Sports
(st. exch.) stock exchange—Börse
subj subjunctive—Konjunktiv
suf suffix—Suffix
super superlative—Superlativ
(surg) surgery—Chirurgie
(surv) surveying—Vermessungswesen
(tech) technical—Fachsprache
(telg) telegraphy—Telegraphie
(telp) telephone—Fernsprechwesen
(telv) television—Fernsehen
(tennis) Tennis
(tex) textiles—Textilien
(theat) theater—Theater

(theol) theology—Theologie
tr transitive—transitiv
(typ) typography—Typographie
usw. and so forth—und so weiter
v verb—Verb
var variant—Variante
(vet) veterinary medicine—Veterinärmedizin
(vulg) vulgar—vulgär
(zool) zoology—Zoologie